Current Law

Yearbook

2013

VOLUME ONE

Current Law

Yearbook

2013

Being a Comprehensive Statement of the Law of 2013

EDITOR
Claire Logan LLB

SWEET & MAXWELL EDITORIAL TEAM
Cases Department

SWEET & MAXWELL   THOMSON REUTERS

The Mode of Citation
of the Current Law Year Book is
[2013] C.L.Y.

The 2013 Year Book is published in two volumes.

A CIP catalogue record for this book is available from the British Library

Published in 2014 by Sweet & Maxwell, 100 Avenue Road, London NW3 3PF, part of Thomson Reuters (Professional) UK Limited (Registered in England & Wales, Company No 1679046. Registered Office and address for service: Aldgate House, 33 Aldgate High Street, London EC3N 1DL).

For further information on our products and services, visit:
www.sweetandmaxwell.co.uk

Printed and bound by CPI Group (UK) Ltd, Croydon, CR0 4YY.

ISBN 978-0-414-03174-6

No forests were destroyed to make this product; farmed timber was used and then replanted.

PREFACE

The *Current Law Year Book* 2013 supersedes the issues of *Current Law Monthly Digest* for 2013 and covers the law from January 1 to December 31 of that year.

Jurisdiction

The text of the *Current Law Year Book* 2013 is divided into three sections respectively: UK, England and Wales and EU, Northern Ireland and Scotland. The European material comprises cases appearing before the Court of First Instance and European Court of Justice, which are published in the reports series and newspapers, and a selection of books.

Cases

The *Current Law Year Book* includes digests of cases published in over 90 reports series, journals, *The Times* and *Independent* newspapers, transcripts and ex relatione contributions from barristers and solicitors. A number of reports concerning damages awards in personal injury cases in England and Wales appear under the subject heading PERSONAL INJURY and are collated in tabular form at the beginning of Volume 1.

The editors thank those barristers and solicitors who have submitted case reports, many of which demonstrate developments in county court litigation. Whilst all reasonable care is taken in the preparation of the digests, it is not possible to guarantee the accuracy of each digest, particularly those cases ex relatione which are not taken from an authorised judgment.

An alphabetical Table of Cases digested in the 2013 Year Book appears at the beginning of Volume 1. For more details please refer to the Current Law Case Citator series for the years 1947-76, 1977-1997, 1998-2001, 2002-2004, 2005, 2006, 2007, 2008, 2009, 2010, 2011, 2012 and 2013.

Legislation

All public and private Acts of Parliament published in 2013 are abstracted and indexed. All Statutory Instruments, Scottish Statutory Instruments and Statutory Rules of Northern Ireland are abstracted. Cumulative tables of Statutory Instruments, arranged alphabetically, numerically and by subject are published in Volume 1. Cumulative tables of Statutory Rules of Northern Ireland arranged alphabeticially, numerically and by subject are also published in Volume 1.

The Current Law Legislation Citator 2013 appears as a separate bound volume and form part of the series of bound volumes for the years 1989-1995, 1996-1999 and 2000-2001, 2002-2004, 2005, 2006, 2007, 2008, 2009, 2010, 2011, 2012 and 2013.

Books

The full title, reference and author of books of interest to the legal profession published in 2013 are arranged by subject heading. A separate list, arranged by author, is included in Volume 2.

Index

The subject matter index is closely associated with the Sweet and Maxwell Legal Taxonomy. The 30-year Index from 1947-76 may be found in the 1976 *Current Law Year Book*. The Scottish Index for the years 1972-86 may be found in the Scottish 1986 *Year Book*. Scottish material prior to 1972 can be found in the *Scottish Current Law Year Book Master Volumes*, published in 1956, 1961, 1966 and 1971.

March 2014

CONTENTS

VOLUME 1

THE LAW OF 2013 DIGESTED UNDER TITLES:
Note: (NI) denotes the Northern Ireland section and (S) denotes the Scottish section.

VOLUME 2

DIGEST HEADINGS IN USE

Accountancy
Administration of Justice
Administrative Law
Agency
Agriculture
Animals
Arbitration
Armed Forces
Arts and Culture
Aviation
Banking and Finance
Charities
Civil Evidence
Civil Procedure
Commercial Law
Company Law
Competition Law
Conflict of Laws
Constitutional Law
Construction Law
Consumer Law
Contracts
Criminal Evidence
Criminal Law
Criminal Procedure
Customs
Damages
Defamation
Dispute Resolution
Ecclesiastical Law
Economics
Education
Electoral Process
Employment
Energy
Environment
Environmental Health
Equity
European Union
Extradition
Family Law
Financial Regulation
Fisheries
Food
Forestry
Government Administration
Health
Health and Safety at Work
Heritable Property (Scotland)
Hospitality and Leisure
Housing
Human Rights
Immigration
Industry
Information Technology
Insolvency
Insurance
Intellectual Property
International Law
International Trade
Jurisprudence
Landlord and Tenant
Legal Advice and Funding
Legal Methodology
Legal Profession
Legal Services
Legal Systems
Legislation
Libraries
Licensing
Local Government
Media and Entertainment
Mental Health
Negligence
Nuisance
Partnerships
Penology and Criminology
Pensions
Personal Injury
Personal Property
Planning
Police
Postal Services
Professions
Public Procurement
Rates
Real Property
Restitution
Rights in Security (Scotland)
Road Traffic
Sale of Goods
Science
Sentencing
Shipping
Social Security
Social Welfare
Sport
Succession
Tax
Telecommunications
Torts
Transport
Trusts
Utilities
VAT
Water Law

TABLE OF CASES

QUANTUM OF DAMAGES
PERSONAL INJURIES OR DEATH

The table below is a cumulative guide to quantum of damages cases reported in *Current Law* in 2013. (FIA = Fatal injuries awards). * The stated ages below are, unless otherwise indicated, at the time of the accident not the time of trial.

Injury	*Age*	*Case*	*General Award, £*	*Reference*
Persistent vegetative state	46	*Gillett v Pogson*	175,000	2207
Cerebral palsy	7 (at award)	*G (A Child) v Poole Hospital NHS Foundation Trust*	260,000	2208
Cerebral palsy; Delay in diagnosis or treatment	0	*S (A Child) v Royal Bournemouth and Christchurch Hospitals NHS Trust*	230,000	2209
Brain damage: very severe	4	*S (A Child) v Peart*	180,000	2210
General psychiatric disorders; Head	8	*F (A Child) v P*	10,000	2211
	23	*Hodgson v Co-op Group Ltd*	10,000	2212
	3	*C (A Child) v Tesco Plc*	4,145	2213
	9	*L (A Child) v Reeve*	4,000	2214
	6	*G (A Child) v Bayes*	1,600	2215
	2	*F (A Child) v W W Realisation 1 Ltd (In Liquidation)*	1,500	2216
Head	5	*S (A Child) v John*	1,700	2217
	3	*K (A Child) v Ramoska*	1,200	2218
	1	*W (A Child) v Martin*	1,000	2219
Face; Nose	New-born, 4 (at award)	*B (A Child) v Taunton and Somerset NHS Trust*	3,000	2220
Teeth	11	*P (A Child) v Bath and North East Somerset Council*	9,500	2221
	10	*C (A Child) v Ramdoo*	1,400	2222
Lip; General psychiatric disorders	9	*T (A Child) v Brooker*	3,500	2223
Hair	31	*Jones v Mankoo*	4,800	2224
Hearing and speech; Ear	Between 31-41	*Dew v British Telecommunications Plc*	7,950	2225
	Between 23-46	*Aston v Cannon Industries*	6,700	2226
Neck: whiplash injury: no previous condition	10	*T (A Child) v Lazarov*	1,600	2227
	7	*J (A Child) v Ward*	1,600	2250
	10	*T (A Child) v Lazarov*	1,600	2227
	8	*N (A Child) v Louca*	1,400	2228
	11	*D (A Child) v Whayling*	1,350	2229
	12	*B (A Child) v Webster*	1,100	2230
Neck: whiplash injury: no previous condition; Knee	53	*Brereton v Stagecoach South Ltd*	5,000	2231
Neck: non-whiplash injuries	13	*R (A Child) v Haynes*	2,900	2232

Injury	*Age*	*Case*	*General Award, £*	*Reference*
Back and spine: no previous condition	57	*Bundy v Coe*	2,750	2233
	14	*Q (A Child) v Kayd*	2,100	2234
	11	*J (A Child) v Carlow*	2,000	2235
	9	*Y (A Child) v Desai*	1,750	2236
	8	*T (A Child) v Keys*	1,200	2237
Back and spine: making a previously asymptomatic condition symptomatic	40	*Morrison v Hanson Aggregates Ltd*	17,000	2238
Ribs and chest	81	*Buchan v Kender*	6,500	2239
Back and neck: whiplash injury: no previous condition	42	*Way v Roberts*	3,500	2240
	27	*Iqbal v Carew*	3,300	2241
	21	*Rutter v Wilson*	3,000	2242
	10	*E (A Child) v Fountain Holdings*	2,000	2243
	5	*M (A Child) v Metropolitan Police*	1,800	2244
	14	*J (A Child) v Atkinson*	1,650	2245
	11	*C (A Child) v Austin*	1,500	2246
	6	*C (A Child) v Stringer*	1,200	2247
	8	*E (A Child) v Sabre Insurance*	1,200	2248
Shoulder	New-born	*G (A Child) v Ipswich Hospital NHS Trust*	80,000	2249
	7	*J (A Child) v Ward*	1,600	2250
Wrist	45	*Hughes v Savills Plc*	7,000	2251
Finger	75	*Jowet v Windle*	3,350	2252
Sacrum, pelvis and hip	29	*EP v Bret*	50,000	2253
	81	*SB v London United Busways Ltd*	23,500	2254
	3 weeks	*J (A Child) v Ministry of Defence*	22,500	2255
Knee	50	*Allan v Warwick*	16,500	2256
Facial scarring	50	*Dawson v Greens Health & Beauty Ltd*	3,500	2257
	33	*Watson v Hall*	3,500	2258
Facial scarring; General psychiatric disorders	3	*L (A Child) v Wm Morrison Supermarkets Plc*	1,750	2259
Non-facial scarring; Neck: non-whiplash injuries	2 (at award)	*P (A Child) v Royal Berkshire NHS Foundation Trust*	11,500	2260
Non-facial scarring; Leg: less severe leg injuries	18	*Fray v Red Eye (Coventry) Ltd (t/a Kasbah Nightclub)*	5,750	2261
Burns; Non-facial scarring	9	*F (A Child) v Walters Leisure Ltd*	2,300	2262
Excretory organs: liver; Delay in diagnosis or treatment; Claims for death of wife	33	*N v South London Healthcare Trust*	100,000	2263
Reproductive organs: male	15	*T (A Child) v Epsom and St Helier University Hospitals NHS Trust*	10,000	2264
Minor injuries	2	*C (A Child) v Parvod*	1,300	2265
Claims for death of parent	Un-known	*DD v Tees Esk and Wear Valleys NHS Foundation Trust*	5,000	2266

ALPHABETICAL TABLE OF STATUTORY INSTRUMENTS 2013

The table below contains a list, in alphabetical order, of the Statutory Instruments digested by Current Law in 2013.

C.L.Y.

C.L.Y.

C.L.Y.

ALPHABETICAL TABLE OF STATUTORY INSTRUMENTS BY SUBJECT 2013

ACCOUNTANCY

ADMINISTRATION OF JUSTICE

ADMINISTRATIVE LAW

AGRICULTURE

ANIMALS

ARMED FORCES

AVIATION

BANKING AND FINANCE

CHARITIES

CONSUMER LAW

CRIMINAL EVIDENCE

CRIMINAL LAW

CRIMINAL PROCEDURE

CUSTOMS

DAMAGES

ECCLESIASTICAL LAW

ECONOMICS

EDUCATION

ELECTORAL PROCESS

EMPLOYMENT

ENERGY

EUROPEAN UNION

EXTRADITION

FAMILY LAW

FINANCIAL REGULATION

FISHERIES

FOOD

FORESTRY

GOVERNMENT ADMINISTRATION

HEALTH

HEALTH AND SAFETY AT WORK

HOSPITALITY AND LEISURE

HOUSING

HUMAN RIGHTS

IMMIGRATION

INDUSTRY

INSOLVENCY

INSURANCE

INTELLECTUAL PROPERTY

INTERNATIONAL LAW

INTERNATIONAL TRADE

LANDLORD AND TENANT

LEGAL ADVICE AND FUNDING

LEGAL PROFESSION

LEGISLATION

LICENSING

LOCAL GOVERNMENT

MEDIA AND ENTERTAINMENT

MENTAL HEALTH

PENOLOGY AND CRIMINOLOGY

PENSIONS

PERSONAL INJURY

PLANNING

POLICE

PROFESSIONS

PUBLIC PROCUREMENT

REAL PROPERTY

ROAD TRAFFIC

SHIPPING

SOCIAL SECURITY

SOCIAL WELFARE

SPORT

TAX

TELECOMMUNICATIONS

TRANSPORT

TRUSTS

UTILITIES

VAT

WATER LAW

NUMERICAL TABLE OF STATUTORY INSTRUMENTS 2013

2013	C.L.Y.
4	1401
5	3122
6 (C.1)	761
7 (S.1)	722
8	222
9	1930
10	528
13	3002
15	2015
18 (W.9)	1256
22	2495
23	85
24	516
38	1516
41	2858
50 (W.10)	2476
51 (W.11)	2510
52	123
53 (W.12)	2509
54	124
59	1485
61	3925
62 (W.13)	1975
63 (W.14)	1976
64	58
65	3158
67 (C.3)	3109
70	921
76	126
77 (C.4)	1939
86	180
87	167
88	153
89	137
90	174
92	1722
93	1911
94	150
95	151
99 (C.5)	933
103	2392
104	1927
105	2131
106	2030
107	2031
108	2032
109	80
110	2017
111 (W.16)	1978
112 (W.17)	1977
113 (C.6)	213
117	2274
123	1130
124	1412
125 (C.7)	1104
126	1109
132	1480
139	1087
147	2316
148	56
156	133

2013	C.L.Y.
157	2988
158	1754
160 (C.9)	1445
161	1351
162	196
163	205
164	811
165	210
175	1101
176	3695
177	1417
178 (c.10)	2920
189	2505
190	1089
192	518
198	3153
207	1511
215	2010
216 (W.28)	1988
217 (W.29)	1967
218	1447
219 (C.11)	925
220	1987
221	1983
225 (W.30)	2933
226	1613
227	1585
228	3146
232	3017
233	1386
234	3062
235	1411
236	1849
237	1859
238	63
239	1430
240	1502
241	2126
242	3548
243	2039
244	1853
245	819
246	24
247	2880
249	1572
250 (C.12)	12
251	1750
252	2867
253	2939
254	152
255	143
256	146
257	1404
258	2494
259	1465
260	1405
261	1413
262 (L.1)	254
263	193
264	1382
265	1910

2013	C.L.Y.
266	2861
267	221
271	3162
275	2155
276	2892
277	3250
278	961
280 (C.14)	3064
281	2371
282	1415
283	1024
284	498
287	3841
294	489
295	1472
296	1169
300	655
301	3183
317	1482
320	3307
335	1475
336	1402
339	3157
340	776
343	2297
348	2551
348	2852
349	1477
350	1466
351	1458
358 (C.16)	2921
359	2474
360 (W.42)	2482
361 (W.43)	2530
362	2499
363	1479
364	1421
365	1473
371 (W.44)	2034
372 (W.45)	2493
373	1418
374 (W.46)	859
375 (W.47)	862
376	2917
377	2901
378	2891
379	2873
380	2870
381	2853
382	2904
383	2899
384	2903
385	2909
386	2915
387	2865
388	2864
389	2844
390	1157
391	1469
392	169
395	461
398 (W.48)	73
406	147
406	179
407	3149
408	2013
409	2007
410	2144
411	2930
412	3215
413	2145
414 (W.50)	2824

2013	C.L.Y.
415	9
416	229
417	2987
418	1352
419	198
420	1805
421	1272
422	1931
423 (C.17)	214
424	148
425	2816
426	1095
427	2275
428	1656
429	1362
430	3238
431	1354
432	1961
433 (W.51)	881
434 (W.52)	834
435	1936
437 (W.53)	869
438 (W.54)	2489
447	1140
448	1501
449	1500
450 (C.18)	1725
451	1909
452	2033
453 (C.19)	1940
454	2859
455	2902
456	2876
457	1924
458	2860
459	2151
460	195
461	1416
462	1153
464	2999
465	5
466	1377
467	2003
468	2004
469	1422
470 (C.20)	2122
471	1922
472	200
473	898
474	1414
475	1468
476	1968
477 (L.2)	32
478	1357
479 (W.55)	1378
480	1915
481	1164
482	2521
483	1920
484	2149
485	2108
486	132
487	2152
488	55
489	3050
490	1391
491	268
492	2027
493	2990
494	87
495	2270
496	1360

2013	C.L.Y.
497	1456
498	2307
499	2957
500	1449
501	1980
502	1974
503	273
504	197
505	1126
506	2049
507	2943
508	1125
509	94
510	1495
511	1923
512	1926
513	3081
514	1144
515 (L.3)	252
516	2822
517	75
518	2948
519	3179
521	3090
522	2291
523	814
524	2913
525	1433
526	2820
527	2135
528	2136
529	2178
530 (L.4)	1206
531	1487
532	1409
533	3163
534	1938
535	1846
536	1771
537	51
538	1809
539	1816
540	122
541	818
542	820
543 (W.56)	1474
544 (W.57)	1419
545 (W.58)	1379
546	2875
547 (W.59)	54
548	804
549	817
552 (W.62)	2912
554	670
555	1358
556	1359
557	3003
558	2854
559	2855
560	827
561 (W.64)	1154
562 (W.65)	1141
569	1407
570 (W.66)	2008
573	2133
574	2910
575	828
585 (C.21)	2172
586	2283
587 (C.22)	3066
588 (W.67)	2011
589 (C.23)	135

2013	C.L.Y.
590	1981
591	2846
592 (C.24)	2383
593	1448
594	1471
595	1985
596	1984
597	2137
598	1361
599	2911
600	468
601	3187
602	1397
603	1086
604	2171
605	3089
606 (L.5)	53
608	683
609	781
610	134
611	271
612	1992
613	730
614	1921
615	684
616 (C.25)	719
617	1573
618	470
619	2856
620	3024
621	1912
622	2857
623	220
625	627
626	2894
627	2134
628	1925
629	2362
630	2872
631 (W.68)	2928
632	192
633 (W.69)	2932
634 (W.70)	2929
635	2363
636	202
637	212
638 (W.71)	1996
639 (W.72)	1998
640	3141
641	234
642	201
643	2024
644	191
645	1444
646	3136
647	1452
648	2298
649 (W.73)	1400
650	2905
651 (C.26)	215
653	2477
655	1353
657	3020
658	3106
659	3201
660	3186
661	3117
662	3007
663 (W.76)	2107
664 (W.77)	865
665	2879
666	2878

2013	C.L.Y.
667	2129
668 (C.27)	1260
669	1131
670	2200
671 (C.28)	1446
675	2485
676 (C.29)	3176
677	1528
678	1615
679	1484
680	1092
683 (W.81)	1467
684 (W.82)	2898
685 (C.30)	3161
686	4
687	49
688	920
689	1916
690	1507
694	1994
695	1979
701	3214
702 (C.31)	922
703	2163
704	2141
705 (C.32)	13
706	2105
707	2181
709	831
711	1420
713	3016
715	2914
716	2881
717	3435
721	189
722 (C.33)	1537
725	1995
728 (S.2)	3809
732	2391
733	1993
734 (L.6)	274
736 (W.88)	2139
737	2020
739	1721
744 (C.34)	3067
746	2882
747 (W.89)	527
748	1913
749	1574
750	2848
753	1908
754	1240
755 (W.90)	1145
756	867
757	873
758	868
759 (C.35)	3063
760	919
761	551
762	1611
763	948
764	2507
765 (W.91)	863
766	1143
767 (W.92)	3152
768	1117
772	1914
773 (C.36)	1320
783	546
784 (C.37)	117
785	1123
786	1851

2013	C.L.Y.
787	821
789 (L.7)	270
793	1614
794	916
795	1856
796	2847
797 (C.38)	2321
798	2317
801	682
803	2843
804	1373
805	2549
806	2543
807	2545
808	2546
809	2547
810	2548
811	2544
812	2539
813	2538
814	2537
815	1437
816	1112
817	636
818	2475
819	3249
821 (W.97)	76
822	3139
829	1105
831	128
832	155
834	184
835	163
836	170
837	165
838	1483
839	129
862	669
877	1857
888 (W.100)	84
889 (W.101)	77
898 (W.102)	1478
903	678
908	460
917	2041
918	182
919	159
920	840
921	127
922	144
930	3277
931	181
932	175
933	2320
934	2318
935	2319
938	238
968	1096
969 (C.39)	926
971	1142
973	1991
975 (C.40)	829
981	1521
982	2273
983 (C.41)	2922
984	2937
985	1202
986	20
992	2478
999	467
1000 (W.105)	875
1001	1137

2013	C.L.Y.
1011	1097
1013	3155
1026	1434
1030	3159
1031	1094
1033	1118
1034	1894
1036	31
1037	1132
1038	162
1040	164
1042 (C.44)	630
1046	1084
1047 (S.3)	3786
1048 (W.110)	1972
1049 (W.111)	1973
1050 (W.112)	2025
1051	173
1052	171
1096	1848
1097	1129
1098	1513
1099	1107
1100 (W.117)	942
1101	2325
1102	2341
1103 (C.46)	718
1104 (C.47)	698
1105	1085
1106	138
1107	145
1111	2167
1112 (W.118)	1443
1113	3075
1114	2991
1115	2806
1116	1850
1117	3123
1118	822
1119	1128
1120	1971
1123	2520
1124 (C.49)	2312
1125	231
1126	3049
1127 (C.50)	647
1128	3410
1129	1839
1130	176
1131	156
1133	3051
1138	1108
1139	2868
1140 (W.120)	872
1141 (W.121)	884
1142	2863
1144 (W.122)	888
1147	2535
1162	1356
1163	1399
1165	676
1168	1522
1169 (L.8)	27
1179	28
1180 (C.51)	2123
1185	30
1187	29
1188 (L.9)	45
1189	188
1190 (W.126)	938
1191 (W.127)	940
1192 (W.128)	937
1193	850
1194	2372
1195	1653
1196	2375
1197	1423
1198	2110
1199	25
1200	2374
1201	2522
1202 (W.129)	941
1203	1114
1204 (C.52)	847
1205	885
1215	154
1216	166
1217	178
1218	158
1221	837
1232	1106
1236 (C.53)	1384
1237	1063
1238	2295
1239	2288
1240	1388
1241 (W.133)	93
1242	846
1243	845
1244	547
1245	836
1250 (C.54)	2923
1253	3138
1254	3137
1255	866
1294	624
1302	632
1329	1110
1382	3129
1387	538
1388	199
1389	1103
1391	1609
1392	2142
1393	2132
1394	2946
1396 (W.135)	908
1397	539
1400	3004
1401	3019
1402	3243
1403	2271
1406	3104
1407 (L.10)	366
1408 (L.11)	367
1409 (L.12)	26
1410 (L.13)	272
1411	3118
1412 (L.14)	389
1413	2046
1414	2143
1417	139
1418	140
1420	1100
1431	2394
1437	3140
1441	1489
1442	2845
1443	1841
1444	1840
1445	1168
1446	1847
1447	1855
1448	826

2013	C.L.Y.
1455 (C.55)	78
1459	149
1460	1569
1466 (W.138)	2
1467	1520
1468 (W.139)	939
1469 (W.140)	1532
1471	1494
1472	1279
1473	2821
1474	1570
1477	83
1478	1655
1479	2299
1482 (C.58)	44
1483	1464
1487	841
1488	1111
1489 (C.59)	2826
1505	1519
1506	74
1507	1163
1508	2916
1509	2927
1510	2889
1512	1499
1513	830
1514	918
1516	131
1517	1236
1518 (C.61)	2176
1542	1587
1544	2907
1553	857
1554 (L.16)	720
1561 (W.142)	816
1562	672
1563	1426
1564	2130
1565	621
1566 (W.143)	1552
1567 (W.144)	2523
1568	2960
1569	2480
1570	1088
1571	277
1572	855
1573 (C.63)	1261
1575	552
1577 (W.145)	2140
1578	1959
1579	677
1582	3181
1583	1178
1590 (C.64)	1138
1598	611
1599	917
1600	1432
1601	1518
1605	1945
1609	2153
1617	1425
1618	3001
1624	815
1635	1946
1637	206
1644	2540
1648	1009
1652	2815
1653 (W.154)	1860
1655	2814
1656	2813
1658 (W.156)	81
1659 (W.157)	832
1662 (W.158)	91
1663 (W.159)	860
1665	943
1666	1496
1667	1497
1669	982
1671	1003
1672	466
1673 (W.162)	843
1674	10
1675	3247
1676	1150
1677	1134
1682 (C.67)	631
1683	1861
1686	1919
1693	260
1695	363
1698	1431
1700 (W.164)	88
1716	3018
1717	823
1718	1854
1719	1842
1721	2019
1722 (W.166)	1517
1723 (W.167)	1538
1724 (W.168)	861
1725 (C.69)	17
1727 (W.169)	842
1729 (W.170)	844
1733 (W.172)	858
1736	2850
1739	453
1740	3107
1741	3108
1742	2174
1745	1600
1746	662
1747 (W.173)	2483
1748	2050
1749	1624
1750	2502
1751	1982
1752	2296
1753	2498
1754	2150
1755 (C.71)	3069
1757	161
1758	1115
1759	893
1760	2109
1761	119
1762	2998
1764	235
1765	1350
1766 (C.72)	1018
1768	1368
1770	3119
1771	187
1772	2997
1773	186
1774	2442
1775 (C.73)	237
1776 (W.177)	2326
1777	47
1778	2370
1779	2369
1780	2382
1781	2513

2013	C.L.Y.
1782	1765
1783	2527
1785	2829
1787	2040
1788 (W.178)	2887
1792 (W.179)	852
1793 (W.180)	849
1794	168
1795	663
1796	1387
1797	185
1799 (W.181)	833
1800 (W.182)	894
1801	1275
1808	57
1810	3125
1811	3053
1813	609
1815 (C.76)	3068
1816	2368
1817 (C.77)	3070
1818	3025
1819	3076
1820	3103
1821	1146
1830 (W.184)	2941
1831	3052
1833	141
1840	2500
1843	3031
1844	2993
1846	3306
1848	177
1854	2043
1855	1491
1856	1481
1857	1149
1860 (C.79)	1237
1865	3145
1868	2300
1869 (C.80)	14
1873	1091
1875	1090
1876	1845
1877	1956
1878	46
1881	1355
1882	548
1883	2315
1885	157
1888	2817
1892	23
1893	22
1894	261
1896	3248
1897	3197
1906 (C.81)	68
1907	2897
1908	190
1916	805
1917	807
1918	809
1921	802
1922	808
1924	1755
1930	2508
1931	3156
1932	886
1933	3164
1940	876
1945	639
1947	469

2013	C.L.Y.
1948	1004
1949	949
1950	554
1956	950
1958	1396
1959	526
1960	2550
1961	605
1962	3022
1963 (C.82)	2114
1964	774
1965 (W.190)	854
1966 (C.83)	1658
1969 (W.191)	2541
1974 (L.19)	267
1977	1770
1979	1370
1980	2931
1981	464
1982 (W.192)	2484
1983 (W.193)	889
1984 (W.194)	1374
1985 (W.195)	1385
1986	1098
1987	1099
2005	465
2006 (W.197)	2825
2012	780
2013	1937
2013	2818
2014	2819
2020 (W.198)	1369
2021 (W.199)	2906
2025	2486
2029	835
2033	89
2036	1127
2042	3
2043 (C.86)	52
2049	871
2054	142
2060	2517
2061	2524
2062	2515
2063	929
2064	923
2067 (L.20)	50
2068	33
2069	34
2070	2886
2071	641
2086	1113
2090 (W.205)	848
2094	877
2100	2479
2104 (C.88)	1553
2111	1151
2112	1152
2114	2306
2115	2289
2124 (W.207)	878
2125	2166
2127 (W.208)	870
2135	1683
2136	2269
2137	2286
2139 (W.209)	544
2140	2329
2141	2328
2142	2330
2143 (C.89)	2313
2145	2287

2013	C.L.Y.
2146	2285
2147	2293
2148	2284
2153	2331
2155 (W.210)	851
2156 (W.211)	1986
2157	1408
2162	839
2172	2516
2173	2534
2174	3180
2181	2799
2184	2496
2190	2018
2191	39
2192	7
2193	8
2194	1476
2196	1375
2200 (C.90)	19
2201	2354
2202 (C.91)	2491
2203	2488
2210	1372
2212	1148
2213	980
2214	1457
2215	1990
2216	1015
2217	2038
2224	463
2227 (C.92)	506
2228	935
2230	879
2231	2900
2232	880
2235	1826
2236	1827
2237	1786
2241	3188
2242	3043
2243	2944
2244	3039
2247 (C.93)	2940
2249	2533
2258	648
2259	2156
2262	183
2265	1989
2268	497
2269	1451
2270	2945
2271 (C.94)	79
2272	2798
2273 (W.219)	2849
2274 (W.220)	2895
2275	2026
2276	1654
2277	927
2286	2014
2294	1262
2299	1235
2300	3059
2301	2871
2302 (L.2)	16
2306	3148
2314	3150
2318	1395
2321	130
2322	160
2325	1390
2326	1394

2013	C.L.Y.
2327	1403
2328	2128
2329	1512
2343	612
2349 (C.96)	1175
2352	1389
2354	1424
2356	2164
2375	1488
2376	1410
2378	1427
2380	2877
2384	1174
2388	1182
2389	2514
2396	2518
2397	2519
2398	2512
2408 (C.97)	2542
2410	1102
2421	172
2435	2294
2438 (W.235)	2029
2460 (C.98)	2120
2461 (C.99)	3177
2462	2111
2472 (C.100)	3065
2473	1093
2490	856
2493 (W.242)	1376
2494 (W.243)	2959
2496 (W.244)	3151
2501 (C.101)	118
2506 (W.245)	1136
2524	120
2525 (L.22)	727
2526	721
2527	114
2532	629
2533	1814
2534 (C.102)	2924
2535 (W.250)	887
2536	2908
2537	1438
2538	2851
2540	2888
2541	1571
2554	2377
2555	1470
2556	2127
2571	2992
2580	608
2584	2893
2585	136
2586	2180
2587	3160
2588	2161
2589	207
2591 (W.255)	1371
2592	2994
2593	1460
2594	2532
2595	3023
2596	824
2597	21
2598	1843
2599	1844
2600	2896
2601	1833
2602	1803
2603	116
2604	416

2013	C.L.Y.
2605	275
2606 (C.103)	2942
2607	72
2619	1133
2620	125
2621 (W.258)	529
2622 (C.105)	660
2646 (C.106)	2926
2655	883
2657 (C.107)	2925
2667	2481
2668	2958
2671	1459
2677	1450
2685	2381
2687	86
2688	891
2689	2866
2691	82
2696	1124
2701	462
2720	3061
2721	3060
2722	2869
2727 (W.262)	1498
2728	2828
2733	3021
2734	2165
2742	661
2770	2376
2774	754
2775	1381
2781	3029
2786	11
2787	115
2788	2385
2789 (C.110)	1324
2790	1917
2791	1933
2792	1934
2794	930
2795	914
2797	915
2799	2989
2803	1918
2804	1907
2814	1935
2815	2827
2818	2177
2819	204
2826	517
2828	2883
2830	701
2844	3154
2846 (C.114)	2919
2854	1135
2867	838
2871	825
2876	928
2877	1932
2880	224
2901 (W.206)	1203

ALPHABETICAL TABLE OF NORTHERN IRELAND STATUTORY RULES AND ORDERS

ALPHABETICAL TABLE OF NORTHERN IRELAND STATUTORY RULES AND ORDERS BY SUBJECT

ENVIRONMENT

FISHERIES

FOOD

FORESTRY

GOVERNMENT ADMINISTRATION

HEALTH

PERSONAL INJURY

PLANNING

POLICE

RATES

ROAD TRAFFIC

SENTENCING

SOCIAL SECURITY

SOCIAL WELFARE

TRANSPORT

WATER LAW

NORTHERN IRELAND

NUMERICAL TABLE OF STATUTORY RULES AND ORDERS 2013

2013	C.L.Y.
1	3336
4	3318
4	3326
5	3448
6	3449
7	3269
12	3314
15	3363
18	3256
19	3253
22	3379
23	3309
24	3322
25	3311
26	3312
28	3424
29	3273
30	3345
31 (C.1)	3348
32	3384
33 (C.2)	3333
34 (C.3)	3332
35	3398
36	3397
37	3304
38	3411
39	3340
40	3385
42	3349
43	3275
44	3276
45	3377
46	3378
47	3374
48	3361
49	3313
50	3439
54	3399
56	3362
57	3405
59	3356
60	3286
61	3380
62	3387
63	3433
65	3394
66	3343
67	3434
68	3279
69	3428
70	3441
71	3393
72	3388
73	3392
74	3357
75 (C.4)	3412
76	3270

2013	C.L.Y.
77	3296
78	3295
80	3415
82	3292
83 (C.5)	3402
84	3391
85	3390
86	3371
89	3300
90	3386
91	3403
92	3316
93	3317
94	3315
95	3396
96	3407
99	3418
102	3351
103	3268
104 (C.6)	3452
107	3301
108	3360
109	3350
114	3355
115	3446
116	3323
117	3274
118	3272
119	3335
120	3303
122	3267
125 (C.7)	3293
126 (C.8)	3290
127	3419
128	3302
131	3254
132	3257
137	3346
138 (C.9)	3347
139	3344
140	3255
141	3437
142	3262
143	3261
144	3266
145 (C.10)	3282
146	3280
147	3358
149	3367
150	3366
151	3453
160	3329
161	3330
162 (C.10)	3298
164	3370
165	3278
166	3287

2013	C.L.Y.
167	3427
170	3420
171	3263
172	3389
173	3319
174	3320
175	3284
178	3436
179	3375
180	3369
181	3308
182	3430
183	3373
189	3364
190	3431
191	3438
192 (C.12)	3299
196	3422
197	3421
198	3325
199	3368
201 (C.13)	3429
202	3258
203	3259
204	3359
205	3324
206	3264
207	3265
208	3321
209	3365
210	3408
211	3281
212	3338
213	3400
214	3372
215	3337
216 (C.14)	3310
217	3425
218	3450
219	3288
220	3339
221	3382
222	3383
223	3305
224	3445
225	3444
229	3341
236	3447
237	3451
238 (C.15)	3376
239	3260
241	3328
243	3381
244	3271
246	3440
247	3401
248	3327
249	3426
250	3432
251	3291
252	3294
253	3342
257	3423

ALPHABETICAL TABLE OF SCOTTISH STATUTORY INSTRUMENTS 2013

The table below contains a list, in alphabetical order, of the Scottish Statutory Instruments digested by Current Law in 2013.

ALPHABETICAL TABLE OF SCOTTISH STATUTORY INSTRUMENTS BY SUBJECT 2013

ADMINISTRATION OF JUSTICE

ADMINISTRATIVE LAW

AGRICULTURE

LEGAL PROFESSION

LEGISLATION

LIBRARIES

LICENSING

LOCAL GOVERNMENT

PENOLOGY AND CRIMINOLOGY

PENSIONS

PLANNING

POLICE

PUBLIC PROCUREMENT

ROAD TRAFFIC

NUMERICAL TABLE OF SCOTTISH STATUTORY INSTRUMENTS 2013

2013	C.L.Y.
1 (C.1)	3829
2	3477
3	3504
4	4019
5	3500
6	3641
8	3968
9	3489
14	4007
19 (C.2)	3801
20	3797
21	3503
22	3831
23	3459
24	3919
25	3910
26	3915
29	4030
31	3507
34	3850
35	3931
36	3853
37	3851
38 (C.3)	3784
39	3924
40	4011
41	4009
42	3930
43	3934
44	3852
45	3840
46	3996
47 (C.4)	3854
48	4001
49	4002
50	3874
51	3936
52	3755
53	3751
58	3907
59	3748
62	3926
63	3927
64	4005
65	4003
67	3963
68	3964
69	3959
70	3883
71	3889
72	3821
73	3933
74	3699
75	3667
76	3935
77	3509
78	3843
79	4029
80	3674
81	3455
82 (C.6)	3802

2013	C.L.Y.
83	3742
86	3932
89	3885
90	3796
92	3811
93	3962
94	3960
95	3957
96	3756
97	3844
98	3471
99	3469
100	3766
105	3912
106 (C.8)	3785
107	3849
108	4008
109	3758
110	4010
111	3454
112	3460
113	3848
114	4028
115	3675
116	3691
117	4027
120	3823
121	3845
122	3928
123	3702
124 (C.9)	3539
125	3929
127	3696
128	3881
129	3880
131	3544
135	3480
136 (C.10)	3485
137	4006
139	3481
141	4012
142	4000
143	3551
144	3808
146	3464
147	3462
148	3690
149	3714
150	3467
151	3505
152	3475
153	3479
154	3917
155	3920
156	3906
159 (C.11)	3752
160	4017
161	3825
162	3824
163 (C.12)	4033
168	3884

2013	C.L.Y.
169	3827
170	3828
172	3707
173	3506
174	3757
175	3669
177	3818
178	3597
179	3658
180	3659
181	3662
182	3664
183	3665
184	3886
185	3882
186	3887
187	3501
188	3775
189	3739
190 (C.13)	3472
191	3759
192	3747
193	3463
194	3465
195 (C.14)	3473
196	3623
198	3644
199	3830
200	3807
201	3604
202	3592
203	3461
204	3871
205	3872
210	3470
211	3466
212	3873
214 (C.15)	3595
215	3468
216	3603
217	3744
218	3839
219	3774
220	3753
221	3745
222	3700
225	3788
226	3958
228	4016
230	3997
236	3822
238	3736
239	3838
241	3585
247	3842
249 (C.16)	3738
250	3812
252 (C.17)	4031
253	3692
254 (C.18)	3999
256	3552
258	4021
259	4018
260 (C.19)	4020
261	3832
262	3816
264	3689
265	3491
266	3741
267	3666
268	3660
269	3661
270	3663
271 (C.21)	3815
276 (C.22)	3701
277	3916
278	3483
279	3490
280	3740
281 (C.23)	3672
282	3938
286	3694
288	3995
289	3763
290	4015
291	3474
292	3754
293	3458
294	3456
302	3476
303 (C.24)	3913
304	3693
305	3743
307	3704
308	3998
309	3499
310	3729
311	3967
312	3965
313	3966
314	3698
315	3697
317	3457
318	3789
319	3668

TABLE OF ABBREVIATIONS

Publishers name follows reports and journals.

(S&M = Sweet & Maxwell; ICLR = Incorporated Council of Law Reporting for England and Wales; LBC = Law Book Company of Australia; OUP = Oxford University Press; Kluwer = Kluwer Law International; Cass = Frank Cass & Co Ltd; CUP = Cambridge University Press; CLP = Central Law Publishing; TSO = The Stationery Office. LLP = Lloyd's of London Press Ltd.) All other names are in full.

A. & B. = Accounting & Business (*Association of Chartered Certified Accountants*)
A. & B.R. = Accounting and Business Research (*The Institute of Chartered Accountants in England & Wales*)
A. & O.P. & E.L.U. = Allen & Overy Pensions & Employment Law Update (*Allen & Overy*)
A. & S.L. = Air & Space Law (*Kluwer*)
A. and ADR Rev. = Arbitration and ADR Review (*First Law*)
A.A. & L. = Art Antiquity and Law (*Institute of Art and Law*)
A.B. = Advising Business (*XPL Publishing*)
A.B.T. Bull. = Association of Banking Teachers Bulletin (*Association of Banking Teachers Bulletin*)
A.C. = Law Reports Appeal Cases (*ICLR*)
A.C.D. = Administrative Court Digest (*S&M*)
A.C.L. Rev. = Asian Commercial Law Review (*S&M*)
A.D.R.L.J. = Arbitration and Dispute Resolution Law Journal (*Informa Publishing Group Ltd*)
A.D.R.L.N. = Arbitration & Dispute Resolution Law Newsletter (*Informa Publishing Group Ltd*)
A.E.L.N. = Alliance Environmental Law News (*Kluwer*)
A.F.I. = Asset Finance International (*Euromoney Institutional Investor Plc*)
A.I. & L. = Artificial Intelligence and Law (*Springer*)
A.I.A.J. = Asian International Arbitration Journal (*Kluwer*)
A.I.B. Review = Allied Irish Banks Review (*Allied Irish Banks Plc*)
A.I.I.J. = Australian Insurance Institute Journal (*Australian Insurance Institute*)
A.I.R. = Asia Insurance Review (*Ins Communications Pte Ltd*)
A.J.I.C.L. = African Journal of International and Comparative Law (*Edinburgh University Press Ltd*)
A.J.I.L. = Journal African De Droit International (*ISAL Publications*)
A.L.E.R. = American Law and Economic Review (*OUP*)
A.L.M. Brief. = Association of Lloyd's Members Briefing (*Association of Lloyd's Members*)
A.L.M. News = Association of Lloyd's Members News (*Association of Lloyd's Members*)
A.L.Q. = Arab Law Quarterly (*Brill Academic Publishers*)
A.P.J.E.L. = Asia Pacific Journal of Environmental Law (*Australian Centre for Environmental Law*)
A.P.J.H.R.L. = Asia-Pacific Journal on Human Rights and the Law (*Martinus Nijhoff Publishers*)
A.P.L.R. = Asia Pacific Law Review (*Butterworth Tolley Publishing*)
A.R.L.S.M.L. = Aegean Review of the Law of the Sea and Maritime Law (*Springer*)
A.S.L.R. = Aberdeen Student Law Review (*University of Aberdeen*)
A.W. EC News. = Alsop Wilkinson EC Newsletter (*Alsop Wilkinson*)
AIDA P.I.B. = AIDA Pollution Insurance Bulletin (*Dr Carl Martin Roos*)
ASA Bull. = ASA Bulletin (*Kluwer*)
AVMA M. & L.J. = Action for Victims of Medical Accidents Medical & Legal Journal (*Action for Victims of Medical Accidents Services Ltd*)
Accountancy = Accountancy (*Institute of Chartered Accountants in England and Wales*)
Accountancy Irl. = Accountancy Ireland (*Institute of Chartered Accountants in Ireland*)
Accountant = Accountant (*VRL Financial News*)
Acquisitions M. = Acquisitions Monthly (*Thomson Financial Services*)
Actuary = Actuary (*Institute of Actuaries*)
Ad. & Fos. = Adoption & Fostering (*Sage Publications Ltd*)
Ad. & Mar. L. & P. = Advertising & Marketing Law & Practice (*Cass*)
Ad. & Mar. L.L. = Advertising & Marketing Law Letter (*Informa Publishing Group Ltd*)
Admin. L.R. = Administrative Law Reports (*Butterworth Tolley Publishing*)
Adviser = Adviser (*National Association of Citizens Advice Bureaux*)
Agri. Law = Agricultural Law (*XPL Publishing*)
All E.R. = All England Law Reports (*Butterworth Tolley Publishing*)
All E.R. (EC) = All England Law Reports European Cases (*Butterworth Tolley Publishing*)
All E.R. Rev. = All England Law Reports Annual Review (*Butterworth Tolley Publishing*)
All. E.R. (Comm) = All England Law Reports (Commercial Cases) (*Butterworth Tolley Publishing*)
Amex. B.R. = Amex Bank Review (*American Express Bank Ltd*)
Amicus Curiae = Amicus Curiae (*Institute of Advanced Legal Studies*)
Anglo-Am. L.R. = Anglo-American Law Review (*Vathek Publishing*)
App. C.D. = Appeal Commissioners Decision (*First Law*)
App. Comp. & Comm. L. = Applied Computer & Communications Law (*Informa Publishing Group Ltd*)

Arb. L.M. = Arbitration Law Monthly (*Informa Publishing Group Ltd*)
Arbitration = Arbitration (*Chartered Institute of Arbitrators*)
Arbitration Int. = Arbitration International (*Kluwer*)
Arch. News = Archbold News (*S&M*)
Arch. Rev. = Archbold Review (*S&M*)
Arg. = Argumentation (*Springer*)
Ass. = Assurances (*Assurances Publications Ltd*)
Astin Bull. = Astin Bulletin (*Ceuterick S.A.*)
Aviation I.R. = Aviation Insurance Report (*Informa Publishing Group Ltd*)
Axiom = Axiom (*Hammicks*)

B. & C. Int. = Benefits & Compensation International (*Pension Publications Ltd*)
B. & F.T. = Banking & Financial Training (*Armstrong Information Ltd*)
B. & M.E.B.L. = Baker & McKenzie Employee Benefits Law (*Baker & McKenzie*)
B. & M.E.L. = Baker & McKenzie Employment Law (*Baker & McKenzie*)
B. & M.P.L. = Baker & McKenzie Pensions Law (*Baker & McKenzie*)
B. & M.P.L. & E.B. = Baker & McKenzie Pensions Law & Employee Benefits (*Baker & McKenzie*)
B. & W.A. = Bacon & Woodrow Analysis (*Bacon & Woodrow*)
B. & W.P. = Bacon & Woodrow Primer (*Bacon & Woodrow*)
B. Ire. = Banking Ireland (*Institute of Bankers in Ireland*)
B. News = Business News (*HM Customs and Excise*)
B.A.J. = British Actuarial Journal (*Institute of Actuaries*)
B.B. & F.L.R. = Butterworths Banking & Financial Law Review (*Butterworth Tolley Publishing*)
B.C.C. = British Company Cases (*S&M*)
B.C.L.C. = Butterworths Company Law Cases (*Butterworth Tolley Publishing*)
B.E.Q.B. = Bank of England Quarterly Bulletin (*Bank of England*)
B.F.I.T. = Bulletin For International Taxation (*IBFD Publications BV*)
B.H. Eur. Bus. Brief = Boodle Hatfield European Business Brief (*Boodle Hatfield*)
B.H.R.C. = Butterworths Human Rights Cases (*Butterworth Tolley Publishing*)
B.I.F.D. = Bulletin for International Fiscal Documentation (*IBFD Publications BV*)
B.I.L.A.J. = British Insurance Law Association Journal (*British Insurance Law Association*)
B.J.I.B. & F.L. = Butterworths Journal of International Banking & Financial Law (*Butterworth Tolley Publishing*)
B.L.E. = Business Law Europe (*Financial Times Finance*)
B.L.G.R. = Butterworths Local Government Reports (*Butterworth Tolley Publishing*)
B.L.R. = Building Law Reports (*Informa Publishing Group Ltd*)
B.M. & I.A. = Brokers' Monthly & Insurance Adviser (*LLP*)
B.M.C.R. = Butterworths Merger Control Review (*Butterworth Tolley Publishing*)
B.M.L.R. = Butterworths Medico-Legal Reports (*Butterworth Tolley Publishing*)
B.O.F. = Back Office Focus (*Informa Publishing Group Ltd*)
B.P.I.L.S. = Butterworths Personal Injury Litigation Service (*Butterworth Tolley Publishing*)
B.P.I.R. = Bankruptcy and Personal Insolvency Reports (*Jordan & Sons Ltd*)
B.P.L. = British Pension Lawyer (*Keith Wallace Publishers*)
B.S. = Balance Sheet (*Risk Publications*)
B.S. EU Bull. = Beachcroft Stanleys EU Bulletin (*Beachcroft Stanleys*)
B.S.L.R. = BIO-Science Law Review (*Lawtext Publishing Limited*)
B.T. = Banking Technology (*Banking Technology Ltd*)
B.T.C. = British Tax Cases (*Croner CCH Group Ltd*)
B.T.R. = British Tax Review (*S&M*)
B.V.C. = British Value Added Tax Reporter (*Croner CCH Group Ltd*)
B.W. = Banking World (*Headway, Home and Law Publishing Group Ltd*)
B.Y.B.I.L. = British Year Book of International Law (*OUP*)
BLG E.L.R. = Barlow Lyde & Gilbert Employment Law Review (*Barlow Lyde & Gilbert*)
BLG Ins. Law Q. = Barlow Lyde & Gilbert Insurance Law Quarterly (*Barlow Lyde & Gilbert*)
BLG P. & E.R.D. = Barlow Lyde & Gilbert Pollution & Environmental Risk Digest (*Barlow Lyde & Gilbert*)
Bank. L.R. = Banking Law Reports (*Informa Publishing Group Ltd*)
Bank. Law = Bankers' Law (*Guthrum House Ltd*)
Banker = Banker (*Financial Times Finance*)
Bankers Mag. = Bankers Magazine (*Warren, Gorham & Lamont*)
Bar Review = Bar Review (*S&M/Round Hall*)
Ben. File = Benefits File (*Wyatt Company (UK) Ltd*)
Bests Rev. L./H. = Best's Review Life/Health (*A.M. Best Co Inc*)
Bests Rev. P./C. = Best's Review Property/Casualty (*A.M. Best Co Inc*)
Bileta News. = Bileta Newsletter (*University of Warwick*)
Bracton L.J. = Bracton Law Journal (*Exeter University*)
Brit. J. Criminol. = British Journal of Criminology (*OUP*)
Broker = Broker (*LLP*)
Build. L.M. = Building Law Monthly (*Informa Publishing Group Ltd*)
Building = Building (*UBM*)
Bull. Med. E. = Bulletin of Medical Ethics (*Professional & Scientific Publications*)
Bus. Ins. = Business Insurance (*Crain Communications Inc.*)
Bus. L.B. = Business Law Bulletin (*Sweet & Maxwel/W. Green*)
Bus. L.I. = Business Law International (*International Bar Association*)
Bus. L.R. = Business Law Review (*Kluwer*)
Bus. Risk = Business Risk (*Informa Publishing Group Ltd*)
Bus. T.P. = Business Tax Planning (*S&M*)
Busy P. = Busy Practitioner (*Bloomsbury Publishing Plc*)
Buyer = Buyer (*Richard Lawson*)

C. & C.C. = Consumer & Commercial Contracts (*CLT Publishing*)
C. & E.E.B.L.B. = Central and East European Business Law Bulletin (*Butterworth Tolley Publishing*)
C. & E.L. = Construction & Engineering Law (*XPL Publishing*)
C. & F.L. = Credit and Finance Law (*Informa Publishing Group Ltd*)
C. & F.L.U. = Child & Family Law Update (*Law Society of Northern Ireland*)
C. Bank. = Central Banking (*Central Banking Publications Ltd*)
C. Mag. = Chambers Magazine (*Chambers & Partners Publishing*)
C. McK. Env. L.B. = CMS Cameron McKenna Environment Law Bulletin (*CMS Cameron McKenna & Co*)
C. Risk = Clinical Risk (*Sage Publications Ltd*)
C.A. = Certified Accountant (*Cork Publishing Ltd*)
C.A. Mag. = Chartered Accountant Magazine (*The Institute of Chartered Accountants of Scotland*)
C.B.Q. = Criminal Bar Quarterly (*Butterworths Tolley Publishing*)
C.B.S.I. Jour. = Chartered Building Societies Institute Journal (*Chartered Building Societies Institute Ltd*)
C.C. = Corporate Cover (*Corporate Cover Publications Ltd*)
C.C. Law = Current Criminal Law (*Sally Ramage*)
C.C.A. = Cargo Claims Analysis (*Turpin Distribution Serv Ltd*)
C.C.B. & E.B. = Clifford Chance Benefits and Employment Bulletin (*Clifford Chance*)
C.C.F. = Child Care Forum (*Child Care Forum Publishing Ltd*)
C.C.L. = Commercial Conflict of Laws (*Informa Publishing Group Ltd*)
C.C.L. Rep. = Community Care Law Reports (*Legal Action Group*)
C.C.L. Rev. = Carbon & Climate Law Review (*Lexxion Verlagsgesellschaft mbH*)
C.C.L.R. = Consumer Credit Law Reports (*S&M - published as part of the Encyclopaedia of Consumer Credit Law*)
C.C.M.L.R. = Clifford Chance Media Law Review (*Clifford Chance*)
C.C.N. = Civil Costs Newsletter (*Butterworth Tolley Publishing*)
C.C.R. = Chambers Client Report (*Chambers & Partners Publishing*)
C.D.F.N. = Clinical Disputes Forum Newsletter (*Clinical Disputes Forum*)
C.E. = Central European (*Euromoney Institutional Investor Plc*)
C.E.C. = European Community Cases (*S&M*)
C.E.L.J. = China-EU Law Journal (*Springer*)
C.F. = Corporate Finance (*Euromoney Institutional Investor Plc*)
C.F.I.L.R. = Company Financial and Insolvency Law Review (*Informa Publishing Group Ltd*)
C.F.L.Q. = Child and Family Law Quarterly (*Jordan & Sons Ltd*)
C.G. = Corporate Governance (*John Wiley & Sons Ltd*)
C.G.T.B. = Capital Gains Tax Brief (*Tax and Financial Publishing*)
C.H.R.L.D. = Commonwealth Human Rights Law Digest (*Interights*)
C.H.R.L.R. = Cyprus Human Rights Law Review (*Intersentia*)
C.I.C. Reps. = Captive Insurance Company Reports (*Risk Management Publications*)
C.I.C. Rev. = Captive Insurance Company Review (*Risk & Insurance Research Group Ltd*)
C.I.I. Jour. = Chartered Insurance Institute Journal (*Chartered Insurance Institute*)
C.I.L. = Contemporary Issues in Law (*Lawtext Publishing Limited*)
C.I.L.L. = Construction Industry Law Letter (*Informa Publishing Group Ltd*)
C.I.P.A.J. = Chartered Institute of Patent Agents Journal (*The Chartered Institute of Patent Agents*)
C.J. = Contract Journal (*Reed Business Information Ltd*)
C.J.I.C.L. = Cambridge Journal of International and Comparative Law (*University of Cambridge*)
C.J.I.L. = Chinese Journal of International Law (*OUP*)
C.J.Q. = Civil Justice Quarterly (*S&M*)
C.J.R.B. = Commercial Judicial Review Bulletin (*Chancery Law Publishing Ltd*)
C.L. & J. = Criminal Law & Justice Weekly (*Butterworth Tolley Publishing*)
C.L. & P. = Computer Law & Practice (*Butterworth Tolley Publishing*)
C.L. & P.R. = Charity Law and Practice Review (*Key Haven Publications Plc*)
C.L. & S.C. = Crime, Law and Social Change (*Springer*)
C.L. Int. = Competition Law International (*International Bar Association*)
C.L. Pract. = Commercial Law Practitioner (*S&M/Round Hall*)
C.L.B. = Commonwealth Law Bulletin (*Taylor & Francis Ltd*)
C.L.C. = Commercial Law Cases (*S&M*)
C.L.D. = Company Lawyer (*S&M*)
C.L.E. = Commercial Law of Europe (*S&M*)
C.L.E.A. Newsletter = Commonwealth Legal Education Association Newsletter (*Commonwealth Legal Education Association*)
C.L.H. = Comparative Legal History (*Hart Publishing Ltd*)
C.L.I. = Commodity Law International (*Business & Maritime Publications Ltd*)
C.L.J. = Cambridge Law Journal (*CUP*)
C.L.L. = Corporate Legal Letter (*Informa Publishing Group Ltd*)
C.L.L. Rev. = Commercial Liability Law Review (*Informa Publishing Group Ltd*)
C.L.M. = Company Law Monitor (*Informa Publishing Group Ltd*)
C.L.M.D. = Current Law Monthly Digest (*S&M/W. Green*)
C.L.N. = Construction Law Newsletter (*Informa Publishing Group Ltd*)
C.L.O.S. = Criminal Law Online Service (*First Law*)
C.L.P. = Current Legal Problems (*OUP*)
C.L.S. = Current Law Statutes (*S&M/W. Green*)
C.L.S. Rev. = Computer Law & Security Review (*Elsevier*)
C.L.S.R. = Computer Law & Security Report (*Elsevier Advanced Technology*)
C.L.W. = Current Law Week (*S&M*)
C.L.W.R. = Common Law World Review (*Portland Press Ltd*)
C.L.Y. = Current Law Year Book (*S&M*)

C.M. = Compliance Monitor (*Informa Publishing Group Ltd*)
C.M.I.R. = Continuous Mortality Investigation Reports (*The Alden Press*)
C.M.L. Rev. = Common Market Law Review (*Turpin Distribution Serv Ltd*)
C.M.L.J. = Capital Markets Law Journal (*OUP*)
C.M.L.N.U. = Council Mortgage Lenders News Update (*BSA CML Publications*)
C.M.L.R. = Common Market Law Reports (*S&M*)
C.M.L.R. (AR) = Common Markets Law Reports (*S&M*)
C.N. = Construction Newsletter (*Bloomsbury Publishing Plc*)
C.O.B. = Compliance Officer Bulletin (*S&M*)
C.O.D. = Crown Office Digest (*S&M*)
C.P. & P. = Civil Practice & Procedure (*First Law*)
C.P. Rep. = Civil Procedure Reports (*S&M*)
C.P. Rev. = Consumer Policy Review (*Consumers' Association Ltd*)
C.P.C.U. Jour. = Chartered Property and Casualty Underwriters Journal (*Society of Chartered Property and Law Casualty Underwriters*)
C.P.L.J. = Conveyancing and Property Law Journal (*S&M/Round Hall*)
C.P.L.R. = Civil Practice Law Reports (*XPL Publishing*)
C.P.N. = Civil Procedure News (*S&M*)
C.R. & I. = Corporate Rescue and Insolvency (*Butterworth Tolley Publishing*)
C.R.N.I. = Competition and Regulation in Network Industries (*Intersentia*)
C.S. = Corporate Solutions (*Financial Times Finance*)
C.S. Bull. = Credit Suisse Bulletin (*Credit Suisse*)
C.S.L.R. = Cambridge Student Law Review (*University of Cambridge*)
C.S.P. = Current Sentencing Practice (*S&M*)
C.S.R. = Company Secretary's Review (*Butterworth Tolley Publishing*)
C.S.R. & E.M. = Corporate Social Responsibility and Environmental Management (*John Wiley & Sons Ltd*)
C.S.W. = Chartered Surveyor Weekly (*Builder Group Ltd*)
C.T. & E.P.Q. = Capital Taxes and Estate Planning Quarterly (*S&M/Pearson Prof. Ltd*)
C.T. News & Reps. = Capital Taxes News & Reports (*S&M*)
C.T.C.J. = Cape Town Convention Journal (*Hart Publishing Ltd*)
C.T.L.R. = Computer and Telecommunications Law Review (*S&M/ESC Publishing*)
C.T.P. = Capital Tax Planning (*S&M*)
C.T.R. = Corporate Tax Review (*Key Haven Publications Plc*)
C.W. = Copyright World (*Informa Publishing Group Ltd*)
C.Y.E.L.S. = Cambridge Yearbook of European Legal Studies (*Hart Publishing Ltd*)
CJ Europe = Criminal Justice Europe (*OICJ Europe*)
CPD Papers = Criminal Law Week - CPD Extended Papers (*S&M*)
Cambrian L.R. = Cambrian Law Review (*University College of Wales*)
Can. Ins. = Canadian Insurance (*Stone & Cox Ltd*)
Can. J.L.I. = Canadian Journal of Life Insurance (*Canadian Journal of Life Insurance Publications Ltd*)
Cap. Tax. = Capital Taxes (*S&M*)
Ch. = Law Reports Chancery Division (*ICLR*)
Charities M. = Charities Management (*Mitre House Publishing Ltd*)
Charity F. = Charity Finance (*Civil Society Media Ltd*)
Chart. I. = Charter-Party International (*S&M*)
Childright = Childright (*Children's Legal Centre Ltd*)
Civ. Lit. = Civil Litigation (*XPL Publishing*)
Civ. P.B. = Civil Practice Bulletin (*S&M/W. Green*)
Clarity = Clarity (*Clarity International*)
Co. Acc. = Company Accountant (*Institute of Company Accountants*)
Co. L. Dig. = Company Law Digest (*Butterworth Tolley Publishing*)
Co. L.J. = Commercial Litigation Journal (*Legalease Ltd*)
Co. L.N. = Company Law Newsletter (*S&M*)
Com. Jud. J. = Commonwealth Judicial Journal (*Commonwealth Magistrates & Judges Association*)
Com. L.L. = Commonwealth Law Librarian (*Legal Library Services*)
Com. Lawyer = The Commonwealth Lawyer (*Commonwealth Lawyers' Association*)
Comm. Int. = Communications International (*EMAP Communications*)
Comm. L.J. = Commercial Law Journal (*Legalease Ltd*)
Comm. Law. = Commercial Lawyer (*Chambers and Partners Publishing*)
Comm. Leases = Commercial Leases (*Informa Publishing Group Ltd*)
Comm. Prop. = Commercial Property (*XPL Publishing*)
Comms. L. = Communications Law (*Bloomsbury Publishing Plc*)
Comp. L. Rev. = Competition Law Review (*Competition Law Scholars Forum*)
Comp. L.I. = Competition Law Insight (*Informa Publishing Group Ltd*)
Comp. L.J. = Competition Law Journal (*Jordan & Sons Ltd*)
Comp. L.M. = Competition Law Monitor (*Informa Publishing Group Ltd*)
Comp. Law E.C. = Competition Law in the European Communities (*Fairford Press Ltd*)
Comp. Law. = Company Lawyer (*S&M*)
Comps. & Law = Computers & Law (*Society for Computers and Law*)
Con. L.D. = Construction Law Digest (*John Wiley & Sons Ltd*)
Con. L.R. = Construction Law Reports (*Butterworth Tolley Publishing*)
Cons. & Mar. Law = Consumer and Marketing Law (*Informa Publishing Group Ltd*)
Cons. L. Today = Consumer Law Today (*Richard Lawson*)
Cons. L.I. = Construction Law International (*International Bar Association*)
Cons. Law = Construction Law (*Eclipse/Butterworth Tolley Publishing*)
Const. L.J. = Construction Law Journal (*S&M*)
Const. Ref. = Constitutional Reform (*Constitutional Reform Centre*)
Consum. L.J. = Consumer Law Journal (*CDC Publications*)

Consumer C. = Consumer Credit (*Consumer Credit Trade Association*)
Conv. = Conveyancer and Property Lawyer (*S&M*)
Converg. = Convergence (*International Bar Association*)
Corp. Brief. = Corporate Briefing (*Singlelaw*)
Corp. C. = Corporate Counsel (*Commercial Lawyer*)
Costs L.R. = Costs Law Reports (*XPL Publishing*)
Counsel = Counsel (*Butterworth Tolley Publishing*)
Cov. L.J. = Coventry Law Journal (*Coventry University*)
Cr. App. R. = Criminal Appeal Reports (*S&M*)
Cr. App. R. (S.) = Criminal Appeal Reports (Sentencing) (*S&M*)
Cr. L. & P. = Criminal Law and Philosophy (*Springer*)
Crim. L.B. = Criminal Law Bulletin (*S&M/W. Green*)
Crim. L.F. = Criminal Law Forum (*Springer*)
Crim. L.N. = Criminal Law News (*Sally Ramage*)
Crim. L.R. = Criminal Law Review (*S&M*)
Crim. Law. = Criminal Lawyer (*Bloomsbury Publishing Plc*)
Criminal Law Week = Criminal Law Week (*S&M*)
Criminologist = Criminologist (*Butterworth Tolley Publishing*)

D. & P. = Development & Planning (*Policy Journals*)
D.C.J. = Defense Counsel Journal (*International Association of Defense Counsels*)
D.D. & R.M. = Due Diligence & Risk Management (*XPL Publishing*)
D.E. & E.S.L.R. = Digital Evidence and Electronic Signature Law Review (*Pario Communications Ltd*)
D.E.J. = Digital Evidence Journal (*Pario Communications Ltd*)
D.F.I. = Derivatives & Financial Instruments (*IBFD Publications BV*)
D.H.B. & W. F. & T. News. = Denton Hall Burgin & Warren Film & Television Newsletter (*Denton Hall*)
D.H.E.L. = Denton Hall Energy Law (*Denton Hall*)
D.H.E.N. = Denton Hall Employment Newsletter (*Denton Hall*)
D.H.I.T. News. = Denton Hall Information Technology Newsletter (*Denton Hall*)
D.H.P.N. = Denton Hall Pensions Newsletter (*Denton Hall*)
D.H.T.I. News. = Denton Hall The Interface Newsletter (*Denton Hall*)
D.I. Bank. & F.N. = Denton International Banking & Finance Newsletter (*Denton Hall*)
D.I. Comp. & EC N. = Denton International Competition and EC Newsletter (*Denton Hall*)
D.I. F.T. News. = Denton International Film & Television Newsletter (*Denton International*)
D.I.C.S. = Denton International Creative Spark (*Denton International*)
D.L. = Daily List (*TSO*)
D.L.B. Bus. Brief = Dibb Lupton Broomhead Business Brief (*Dibb Lupton Broomhead*)
D.L.R. = Discrimination Law Reports (*CLT Publishing*)
D.N.Q. = Domain Names Quarterly (*Informa Publishing Group Ltd*)
D.P. & P.P. = Data Protection and Privacy Practice (*Pinsent Masons*)
D.P.I. = Data Protection Ireland (*Privacy & Data Protection*)
D.P.L. & P. = Data Protection Law & Policy (*Cecile Park Publishing Ltd*)
D.P.Q. = Data Protection Quarterly (*Pinsent Masons*)
D.R.I. = Dispute Resolution International (*International Bar Association*)
D.U.L.J. = Dublin University Law Journal (*S&M/Round Hall*)
DLi = DLi University College Galway Law Graduates Association Gazette (*Toevaro Investments Ltd*)
DNV. B.C.U. = DNV Bulk Carrier Update (*Fairplay Publications Ltd*)
Data Base Reps. = Data Base Reports (*Insurance Information Institute*)
De Voil I.T.I. = De Voil Indirect Tax Intelligence (*Butterworth Tolley Publishing*)
Denning L.J. = Denning Law Journal (*University of Buckingham*)

E-Law Review = E-Law Review (*S&M/W. Green*)
E. & L. = Education and the Law (*Taylor & Francis Ltd*)
E. & P. = International Journal of Evidence & Proof (*Vathek Publishing*)
E. & S.L.J. = Entertainment and Sports Law Journal (*Warwick*)
E. St. A.L. = European State Aid Law Quarterly (*Lexxion Verlagsgesellschaft mbH*)
E.A.F. = European Accounting Focus (*Informa Publishing Group Ltd*)
E.B. & F.L.J. = European Banking & Financial Law Journal (*Intersentia NV*)
E.B. Mag. = Environment Business Magazine (*Faversham House Group Ltd*)
E.B.J. = Employee Benefits Journal (*International Foundation of Employee Benefits Plans Inc*)
E.B.L. = Electronic Business Law (*Eclipse/Butterworth Tolley Publishing*)
E.B.L. Rev. = European Business Law Review (*Turpin Distribution Serv Ltd*)
E.B.L.R. = Electronic Business Law Reports (*Butterworth Tolley Publishing*)
E.B.M. = European Business Monitor (*Butterworth Tolley Publishing*)
E.B.O.R. = European Business Organization Law Review (*CUP*)
E.C. Law = European Company Law (*Kluwer*)
E.C.A. = Elderly Client Adviser (*Ark Publishing*)
E.C.C. = European Commercial Cases (*S&M*)
E.C.D.R. = European Copyright and Design Reports (*S&M*)
E.C.F.R. = European Company and Financial Law Review (*Walter de Gruyter GmbH & Co. KG*)
E.C.J. = Environmental Claims Journal (*Executive Enterprises Publications Co Inc*)
E.C.L. = European Corporate Lawyer (*Legalease Ltd*)
E.C.L. & P. = E-Commerce Law & Policy (*Cecile Park Publishing Ltd*)
E.C.L. Rep. = E-Commerce Law Reports (*Cecile Park Publishing Ltd*)
E.C.L. Rev. = Electronic Communications Law Review (*Kluwer*)

E.C.L. Review = European Constitutional Law Review (*CUP*)
E.C.L.R. = European Competition Law Review (*S&M/ESC Publishing*)
E.D.D. & R.M. = Environmental Due Diligence & Risk Management (*XPL Publishing*)
E.E.B.L. = East European Business Law (*Financial Times Finance*)
E.E.E.L.R. = European Energy and Environmental Law Review (*Kluwer*)
E.E.F.N. = Eastern European Forum Newsletter (*International Bar Association*)
E.E.I.R. = East European Insurance Report (*Financial Times Finance*)
E.E.J. = European Energy Journal (*Claeys & Casteels*)
E.E.L.R. = European Environmental Law Review (*Turpin Distribution Serv Ltd*)
E.F.A. Rev. = European Foreign Affairs Review (*Kluwer*)
E.F.F.L.R. = European Food and Feed Law Review (*Lexxion Verlagsgesellschaft mbH*)
E.F.P.L. & P. = E-Finance & Payments Law & Policy (*Cecile Park Publishing Ltd*)
E.F.S.L. = European Financial Services Law (*Kluwer*)
E.F.T.B. = Emmet and Farrand on Title Bulletin (*S&M*)
E.G. = Estates Gazette (*Estates Gazette Ltd*)
E.G.C.S. = Estates Gazette Case Summaries (*Estates Gazette Ltd*)
E.G.L.R. = Estates Gazette Law Reports (*Estates Gazette Ltd*)
E.H.L.R. = Environmental Health Law Reports (*S&M*)
E.H.R.L.R. = European Human Rights Law Review (*S&M*)
E.H.R.R. = European Human Rights Reports (*S&M*)
E.I.B. = Environment Information Bulletin (*Eclipse/Butterworth Tolley Publishing*)
E.I.M. = European Insurance Market (*Informa Publishing Group Ltd*)
E.I.P.R. = European Intellectual Property Review (*S&M/ESC Publishing*)
E.I.R.R. = European Industrial Relations Review (*Reed Business Information Ltd*)
E.I.S. = European Insurance Strategies (*Evandale Publishing Co Ltd*)
E.J.C. = European Journal of Criminology (*Sage Publications Ltd*)
E.J.C.L. = Electronic Journal of Comparative Law (*Electronic Journal of Comparative Law*)
E.J.E.L. & P. = European Journal for Education Law and Policy (*Kluwer*)
E.J.H.L. = European Journal of Health Law (*Martinus Nijhoff Publishers*)
E.J.I.L. = European Journal of International Law (*OUP*)
E.J.L. & E. = European Journal of Law & Economics (*Springer*)
E.J.L.E. = European Journal of Legal Education (*Taylor & Francis Ltd*)
E.J.L.R. = European Journal of Law Reform (*Boom Distributiecentrum BV*)
E.J.L.T. = European Journal of Law and Technology (*University of Warwick*)
E.J.M.L. = European Journal of Migration and Law (*Martinus Nijhoff Publishers*)
E.J.R.B. = Environmental Judicial Review Bulletin (*Chancery Law Publishing Ltd*)
E.J.R.R. = European Journal of Risk Regulation (*Lexxion Verlagsgesellschaft mbH*)
E.J.S.L. = European Journal of Social Law (*Ghent University*)
E.J.S.S. = European Journal of Social Security (*Intersentia NV*)
E.L. = Equitable Lawyer (*Gostick Hall Publications*)
E.L. & P.D. = European Life & Pensions Digest (*European Business Digest Ltd*)
E.L. Rev. = European Law Review (*S&M*)
E.L.A. Briefing = Employment Lawyers Association Briefing (*Employment Lawyers Association*)
E.L.B. = Environment Law Brief (*Informa Publishing Group Ltd*)
E.L.F. = Elder Law and Finance (*Jordan & Sons Ltd*)
E.L.G.L.B. = Encyclopedia of Local Government Law Bulletin (*S&M*)
E.L.J. = European Law Journal (*John Wiley & Sons Ltd*)
E.L.L.J. = European Labour Law Journal (*Intersentia NV*)
E.L.L.R. = Environmental Liability Law Review (*Koninklijke Vermande BV*)
E.L.M. = Environmental Law & Management (*Lawtext Publishing Limited*)
E.L.N. = Environmental Law Newsletter (*Butterworth Tolley Publishing*)
E.L.R. = Education Law Reports (*Jordan & Sons Ltd*)
E.L.R.I. = Employment Law Review - Ireland (*First Law*)
E.M. = European Mergers (*Informa Publishing Group Ltd*)
E.M.I. = Emerging Markets Investor (*Chiltern Magazine Services*)
E.M.L.R. = Entertainment and Media Law Reports (*S&M/ESC Publishing*)
E.N.P.R. = European National Patent Reports (*S&M*)
E.O.R. = Equal Opportunities Review (*Michael Rubenstein Publishing*)
E.O.R. Dig. = Equal Opportunities Review and Discrimination Case Law Digest (*Eclipse/Butterworth Tolley Publishing*)
E.P. & L. = Environmental Policy and Law (*IOS Press*)
E.P.E.F. = Economic Policy: A European Forum (*CUP*)
E.P.G. = Environmental Policy and Governance (*John Wiley & Sons Ltd*)
E.P.I.S. = EMIS Personal Injury Service (*XPL Publishing*)
E.P.L. = European Public Law (*Kluwer*)
E.P.L.I. = Education, Public Law and the Individual (*Education Law Association Ltd*)
E.P.L.P.B. = Encyclopedia of Planning Law and Practice Monthly Bulletin (*S&M*)
E.P.O.R. = European Patent Office Reports (*S&M*)
E.P.P.P.L.R. = European Public Private Partnership Law Review (*Lexxion Verlagsgesellschaft mbH*)
E.P.S. = EMIS Property Service (*XPL Publishing*)
E.R. & R.J. = Employee Responsibilities and Rights Journal (*Springer*)
E.R.C.L. = European Review of Contract Law (*Walter de Gruyter GmbH & Co. KG*)
E.R.P.L. = European Review of Private Law (*Kluwer*)
E.S.L.J. = E-Signature Law Journal (*Pario Communications Ltd*)
E.T. = Estates Times (*Morgan Grampian Plc*)

E.T.M.R. = European Trade Marks Reports (*S&M*)
E.U. News = European Union News (*S&M*)
E.W.C.B. = European Works Councils Bulletin (*Eclipse/Butterworth Tolley Publishing*)
EC C.P.N. = European Commission Competition Policy Newsletter (*Commission of The European Communities*)
EC E.M. = EC Energy Monthly (*Financial Times Finance*)
EC F.L.M. = EC Food Law Monthly (*Agra Europe (London) Ltd*)
EC P.R. = EC Packaging Report (*Agra Europe (London) Ltd*)
EC T.J. = EC Tax Journal (*Key Haven Publications Plc*)
EC T.R. = EC Tax Review (*Turpin Distribution Serv Ltd*)
EDI L.R. = Electronic Data Interchange Law Review (*Kluwer*)
EMIS E.L.S. = EMIS E-Law Service (*XPL Publishing*)
ENDS = ENDS Report (*Environmental Data Services Ltd*)
EPLC Brief = European Pharma Law Centre Brief (*European Pharma Law Centre Ltd*)
ERA Forum = ERA Forum (*Springer*)
EU Brief. Notes = EU Briefing Notes (*SJ Berwin & Co*)
EU Focus = EU Focus (*S&M*)
Eagle = Eagle (*Stratton Publishing Ltd*)
Ec. Aff. = Economic Affairs (*The Institute of Economic Affairs*)
Ec. Rev. = Economic Review (*Philip Allan Publishers Ltd*)
Ecc. L.J. = Ecclesiastical Law Journal (*CUP*)
Eco M. & A. = Eco-Management & Auditing (*John Wiley & Sons Ltd*)
Ed. C.R. = Education Case Reports (*S&M*)
Ed. L.M. = Education Law Monitor (*Informa Publishing Group Ltd*)
Ed. Law = Education Law Journal (*Jordan & Sons Ltd*)
Edin. L.R. = Edinburgh Law Review (*Edinburgh University Press Ltd*)
Eld. L.J. = Elder Law Journal (*Jordan & Sons Ltd*)
Emp. L. & L. = Employment Law & Litigation (*XPL Publishing*)
Emp. L. & L.U. = Employment Law and Litigation Updates (*XPL Publishing*)
Emp. L. Brief. = Employment Law Briefing (*S&M*)
Emp. L.B. = Employment Law Bulletin (*S&M/W. Green*)
Emp. L.J. = Employment Law Journal (*Legalease Ltd*)
Emp. L.N. = Employment Law Newsletter (*S&M*)
Emp. Law. = Employment Lawyer (*S&M*)
Emp. Lit. = Employment Litigation (*XPL Publishing*)
Employ. L. = Employer's Law (*Reed Business Information Ltd*)
Enc. C.S.P. = Encyclopedia of Current Sentencing Practice (*S&M*)
Enc. F.S.L. = Encyclopedia of Financial Services Law (*S&M*)
Enc. I.T.L. = Encyclopedia of Information Technology Law (*S&M*)
Enc. P.L. & P. = Encyclopedia of Planning Law & Practice (*S&M*)
Ent. L.R. = Entertainment Law Review (*S&M/ESC Publishing*)
Ent. Law = Entertainment Law (*Cass*)
Env. I.B. = Environment In Business (*Butterworth Tolley Publishing*)
Env. L. Rev. = Environmental Law Review (*Vathek Publishing*)
Env. L.B. = Environmental Law Bulletin (*S&M/W. Green*)
Env. L.M. = Environmental Law Monthly (*Informa Publishing Group Ltd*)
Env. L.N. = Environmental Law Newsletter (*SJ Berwin & Co*)
Env. L.R. = Environmental Law Reports (*S&M*)
Env. Law = Environmental Law (*UKELA*)
Env. Liability = Environmental Liability (*Lawtext Publishing Limited*)
Env. Man. = Environmental Manager (*Informa Publishing Group Ltd*)
Env. Risk = Environment Risk (*Euromoney Institutional Investor Plc*)
Eq. L.R. = Equality Law Reports (*Michael Rubenstein Publishing*)
Eu. C.L.R. = European Criminal Law Review (*Hart Publishing Ltd*)
Eu. L.F. = European Legal Forum (*IPR Verlag GmbH*)
Eu. L.R. = European Law Reports (*Hart Publishing Ltd*)
Eur. Access = European Access (*Chadwyck Healey Ltd*)
Eur. Counsel = European Counsel (*Legal & Commercial Publishing*)
Eur. J. Crime Cr. L. Cr. J. = European Journal of Crime, Criminal Law and Criminal Justice (*Martinus Nijhoff Publishers*)
Eurlegal = Eurlegal (*Incorporated Law Society of Ireland*)
Euro. C.J. = European Competition Journal (*Hart Publishing Ltd*)
Euro. C.L. = European Current Law (*S&M*)
Euro. Env. = European Environment (*John Wiley & Sons Ltd*)
Euro. L.B. = European Legal Business (*Legalease Ltd*)
Euro. L.M. = European Law Monitor (*Informa Publishing Group Ltd*)
Euro. Law. = European Lawyer (*Polyview Media Limited*)
Euro. News. = European Newsletter (*S&M*)
Euro. T.L. = European Transport Law (*Robert H Wijffels*)
Euro. T.S. = European Tax Service (*BNA International Inc*)
Euro. Tax. = European Taxation (*IBFD Publications BV*)
Euromoney = Euromoney (*Euromoney Institutional Investor Plc*)
Eurosafety = Eurosafety (*Butterworth Tolley Publishing*)
Exp. = Experiodica (*Swiss Reinsurance Company*)
Expert = Expert (*Bristish Academy of Experts*)

F. & C.L. = Finance & Credit Law (*Singlelaw*)
F. & D. = Finance & Development (*Finance & Development*)
F. & D.L.M. = Food & Drink Law Monthly (*Agra Europe*)
F. & D.L.R. = Futures & Derivatives Law Review (*Routledge-Cavendish*)

F.A. = Financial Adviser (*Financial Times Finance*)
F.C.R. = Family Court Reporter (*Butterworth Tolley Publishing*)
F.D. & D.I.B. = Food, Drinks & Drugs Industry Bulletin (*Informa Publishing Group Ltd*)
F.E. & P.I. = Freshfields Employment & Pensions Issues (*Freshfields*)
F.I. = Fraud Intelligence (*Informa Publishing Group Ltd*)
F.I.T.A.R. = Financial Instruments Tax & Accounting Review (*Informa Publishing Group Ltd*)
F.L.N. = Family Law Newsletter (*Butterworth Tolley Publishing*)
F.L.R. = Family Law Reports (*Jordan & Sons Ltd*)
F.L.T. = Family Law Today (*Informa Publishing Group Ltd*)
F.M. = Financial Management (*Chartered Institute Management Accountants*)
F.O.I. = Freedom of Information (*Privacy & Data Protection*)
F.P.B. = Four Pillars Bulletin (*Geneva Association*)
F.R. = Financial Regulator (*Central Banking Publications Ltd*)
F.R. & F.N. = Financial Reinsurance & Futures Newsletter (*Informa Publishing Group Ltd*)
F.R.B.N.Y.Q.R. = Federal Reserve Bank of New York Quarterly Review (*Federal Reserve Bank of New York*)
F.R.I. = Financial Regulation International (*Informa Publishing Group Ltd*)
F.R.N. = Financial Reinsurance Newsletter (*Informa Publishing Group Ltd*)
F.R.R. = Financial Regulation Report (*Informa Publishing Group Ltd*)
F.S. Bulletin = Financial Services Bulletin (*Informa Publishing Group Ltd*)
F.S.B. = Financial Services Brief (*S&M*)
F.S.L.J. = Financial Services Law Journal (*S&M/Round Hall*)
F.S.L.L. = Financial Services Law Letter (*Informa Publishing Group Ltd*)
F.S.R. = Fleet Street Reports (*S&M*)
F.T.I. = Financial Technology Insight (*Elsevier*)
Fairplay = Fairplay (*Fairplay Publications Ltd*)
Fam. = Law Reports Family Division (*ICLR*)
Fam. L.B. = Family Law Bulletin (*S&M/W. Green*)
Fam. L.J. = Family Law Journal (*Legalease Ltd*)
Fam. L.R. = Family Law Reports (Greens) (*S&M/W. Green*)
Fam. Law = Family Law (*Jordan & Sons Ltd*)
Fam. Law B. = Family Law Bulletin (*S&M*)
Fam. M. = Family Matters (*S&M*)
Fam. Med. = Family Mediation (*National Association of Family Mediation & Conciliation Services*)
Farm Law = Farm Law (*Agra Europe*)
Farm T. & F. = Farm Tax & Finance (*Tax and Financial Publishing*)
Farm T.B. = Farm Tax Brief (*Informa Publishing Group Ltd*)
Fem. L.S. = Feminist Legal Studies (*Springer*)
Fin. Con. = Finance Confidential (*Fleet Street Publications Ltd*)
Focus = Focus (*Zurich International (UK) Ltd*)
Food & Drugs I.B. = Food & Drugs Industry Bulletin (*Informa Publishing Group Ltd*)
Food L.M. = Food Law Monthly (*Agra Europe*)
Foresight = Foresight (*Risk & Insurance Research Group Ltd*)

G.A.R. = Global Arbitration Review (*Law Business Research Ltd*)
G.C. = Global Crime (*Taylor & Francis Ltd*)
G.C.L.R. = Global Competition Litigation Review (*S&M/ESC Publishing*)
G.C.R. = Global Competition Review (*Law Business Research Ltd*)
G.I.L.S.I. = Gazette Incorporated Law Society of Ireland (*The Law Society*)
G.L. & B. = Global Law & Business (*Global Law & Business Ltd*)
G.L.J. = Guernsey Law Journal (*Her Majesty's Greffier*)
G.L.S.I. = Gazette of the Law Society Ireland (*The Law Society*)
G.P.R.I.I.P. = Geneva Papers on Risk & Insurance Issues & Practice (*Geneva Association*)
G.P.R.I.T. = Geneva Papers on Risk & Insurance: Theory (*Geneva Association*)
G.R. = Global Reinsurance (*Southern Magazines Ltd*)
G.R.A. = Global Re Analysis (*Southern Magazines Ltd*)
G.T. & C.J. = Global Trade and Customs Journal (*Kluwer*)
G.T.B. = Global Telecoms Business (*Euromoney Institutional Investor Plc*)
G.W.D. = Greens Weekly Digest (*S&M/W. Green*)
Gen. Ins. = General Insurance (*Mitre House Publishing Ltd*)
Global Counsel = Global Counsel (*Legal & Commercial Publishing*)
Go. J.I.L. = Gottingen Journal of International Law (*Universitatsverlag Gottingen*)
Gov. = Governance (*Civil Society Media Ltd*)
Guide = Guide (*S&M*)

H. & S.B. = Health and Safety Bulletin (*Butterworth Tolley Publishing*)
H. & S.L. = Health & Safety Law (*XPL Publishing*)
H. & S.M. = Health & Safety Monitor (*Schofield Publishing*)
H. & S.R. = Health & Safety Review (*IRN Publishing*)
H. & S.W. = Health & Safety at Work (*Butterworth Tolley Publishing*)
H.A.L.L. = Health & Law Letter (*Business & Maritime Publications*)
H.C.L.M. = High Court Litigation Manual (*S&M*)
H.C.W.I.B. = House of Commons Weekly Information Bulletin (*TSO*)
H.J.R.L. = Hague Journal on the Rule of Law (*TMC Asser Press*)
H.K.L.J. = Hong Kong Law Journal (*Hong Kong Law Journal Ltd*)
H.L.J. = Hibernian Law Journal (*Law Society of Ireland*)
H.L.M. = Housing Law Monitor (*Informa Publishing Group Ltd*)
H.L.R. = Housing Law Reports (*S&M*)
H.P.L.R. = Housing & Property Law Review (*Arden Davies Publishing*)
H.R. = Human Rights (*Jordan & Sons Ltd*)
H.R. & I.L.D. = Human Rights & International Legal Discourse (*Intersentia*)
H.R. & UK P. = Human Rights & UK Practice (*XPL Publishing*)

H.R.A. = Human Rights Alerter (*S&M*)
H.R.C.D. = Human Rights Case Digest (*S&M*)
H.R.L. Rev. = Human Rights Law Review (*OUP*)
H.R.L.R. = Human Rights Law Reports (*S&M*)
H.R.R. = Human Rights Review (*Springer*)
H.R.U. = Human Rights Updater (*Butterworth Tolley Publishing*)
H.S. = Hazardous Substances (*Informa Publishing Group Ltd*)
H.S. Brief. = Herbert Smith Briefing (*Herbert Smith*)
H.S. at W. = Health & Safety at Work (*Bloomsbury Publishing Plc*)
H.S.I. = Halsbury's Statutory Instruments (*Legal Library Services Ltd*)
H.S.I.B. = Health & Safety Information Bulletin (*Butterworth Tolley Publishing*)
Haldane S.E.L.B. = Haldane Society Employment Law Bulletin (*Haldane Society of Socialist Lawyers*)
Halsbury S. = Halsbury's Statutes (*Legal Library Services Ltd*)
Health Law = Health Law for Healthcare Professionals (*Informa Publishing Group Ltd*)
Hert. L.J. = Hertfordshire Law Journal (*University of Hertfordshire*)
Hold. L.R. = Holdsworth Law Review (*University of Birmingham*)
Hous. L.R. = Greens Housing Law Reports (*S&M/W. Green*)
Howard Journal = Howard Journal of Criminal Justice (*John Wiley & Sons Ltd*)
Hull C.A. = Hull Claims Analysis (*S&M*)

I-A. J.I.C.J. = Ibero-American Journal of International Criminal Justice (*Hart Publishing Ltd*)
I. & C.T.L. = Information & Communications Technology Law (*Taylor & Francis Ltd*)
I. & N.L. & P. = Immigration & Nationality Law & Practice (*Butterworth Tolley Publishing*)
I. & P.E. = Investment & Pensions Europe (*IPE International Publishers Ltd*)
I. & R.I. = Insolvency and Restructuring International (*International Bar Association*)
I. & R.L.B. = Insurance & Reinsurance Law Briefing (*S&M*)
I. Bull. = Interights Bulletin (*Interights*)
I. Prop. = Intellectual Property (*CLT Publishing*)
I.A. & E.H.R.J. = Inter-American and European Human Rights Journal (*Intersentia*)
I.A.N.L. = Immigration, Asylum and Nationality Law (*Bloomsbury Publishing Plc*)
I.B.F.L. = International Banking and Financial Law (*S&M*)
I.B.L. = International Business Lawyer (*International Bar Association*)
I.B.L.J. = International Business Law Journal (*S&M*)
I.B.L.Q. = Irish Business Law Quarterly (*Clarus Press*)
I.B.N. = International Bar News (*International Bar Association*)
I.B.R. = Irish Banking Review (*Irish Bankers' Federation*)
I.C. = Investors Chronicle (*Investors Chronicle Publications Ltd*)
I.C. Lit. = International Commercial Litigation (*Euromoney Institutional Investor Plc*)
I.C.C.L.J. = International and Comparative Corporate Law Journal (*Institute of Advanced Legal Studies*)
I.C.C.L.R. = International Company and Commercial Law Review (*S&M/ESC Publishing*)
I.C.L. = International Corporate Law (*Euromoney Institutional Investor Plc*)
I.C.L. Rev. = International Construction Law Review (*Informa Publishing Group Ltd*)
I.C.L.B. = International Corporate Law Bulletin (*Kluwer*)
I.C.L.J. = Irish Criminal Law Journal (*S&M/Round Hall*)
I.C.L.M.D. = Irish Current Law Monthly Digest (*S&M/Round Hall*)
I.C.L.Q. = International & Comparative Law Quarterly (*CUP*)
I.C.L.S.A. = Irish Current Law Statutes Annotated (*S&M/Round Hall*)
I.C.R. = Industrial Cases Reports (*ICLR*)
I.D.P.L. = International Data Privacy Law (*OUP*)
I.E.L.J. = Irish Employment Law Journal (*S&M/Round Hall*)
I.E.L.R. = International Energy Law Review (*S&M*)
I.E.L.T.R. = International Energy Law & Taxation Review (*S&M*)
I.F.L. = International Family Law (*Jordan & Sons Ltd*)
I.F.L. Rev. = International Financial Law Review (*Euromoney Institutional Investor Plc*)
I.F.O.S.S.L.R. = International Free and Open Source Software Law Review (*Editorial Committee Board*)
I.H.L. = In-House Lawyer (*Legalease Ltd*)
I.H.P. = In-House Perspective (*International Bar Association*)
I.H.R.L.R. = Irish Human Rights Law Review (*Clarus Press*)
I.H.R.R. = International Human Rights Reports (*University of Nottingham, School of Law*)
I.I.E.L. = Immigration and International Employment Law (*Eclipse/Butterworth Tolley Publishing*)
I.I.I. = Insurance Industry International (*Lafferty Publications Ltd*)
I.I.L. Rev. = International Internet Law Review (*Euromoney Institutional Investor Plc*)
I.I.L.R. = Irish Insurance Law Review (*S&M/Round Hall*)
I.I.P.L.Q. = Irish Intellectual Property Law Quarterly (*First Law*)
I.I.P.R. = Irish Intellectual Property Review (*S&M/Round Hall*)
I.I.R. = International Insolvency Review (*John Wiley & Sons Ltd*)
I.I.U. = Insurance Issues Update (*Insurance Information Institute*)
I.J.B.L. = International Journal of Biosciences and the Law (*A B Academic Publishers*)
I.J.C.L. = International Journal of Constitutional Law (*OUP*)
I.J.C.L.E. = International Journal of Clinical Legal Education (*Northumbria Law Press*)
I.J.C.L.P. = International Journal of Communications Law and Policy (*Institute for Information, Telecommunications and Media Law*)
I.J.C.P. = International Journal of Cultural Property (*CUP*)
I.J.D.G. = International Journal of Disclosure and Governance (*Palgrave Macmillan*)
I.J.D.L. = International Journal of Discrimination and the Law (*Sage Publications Ltd*)
I.J.E.C.L. = International Journal of Estuarine and Coastal Law (*Kluwer*)

I.J.E.C.L. & P. = International Journal of Electronic Commerce Law & Practice (*XPL Publishing*)
I.J.E.L. = Irish Journal of European Law (*S&M/Round Hall*)
I.J.F.D.L. = International Journal of Franchising and Distribution Law (*Richmond Law & Tax Ltd*)
I.J.F.L. = Irish Journal of Family Law (*S&M/Round Hall*)
I.J.H.R. = International Journal of Human Rights (*Taylor & Francis Ltd*)
I.J.I.L. = International Journal of Insurance Law (*Informa Publishing Group Ltd*)
I.J.L. & I.T. = International Journal of Law & Information Technology (*OUP*)
I.J.L.B.E. = International Journal of Law in the Built Environment (*Emerald Group Publishing Limited*)
I.J.L.C.J. = International Journal of Law, Crime and Justice (*Elsevier*)
I.J.L.P. = International Journal of the Legal Profession (*Taylor & Francis Ltd*)
I.J.L.S. = Irish Journal of Legal Studies (*University College Cork*)
I.J.M.C.L. = International Journal of Marine & Coastal Law (*Martinus Nijhoff Publishers*)
I.J.N.L. = International Journal of Nuclear Law (*Inderscience Publishers*)
I.J.O.S.L. = International Journal Of Shipping Law (*Informa Publishing Group Ltd*)
I.J.P.L. = International Journal of Private Law (*Inderscience Publishers*)
I.J.P.L. & P. = International Journal of Public Law and Policy (*Inderscience Publishers*)
I.J.R.L. = International Journal of Refugee Law (*OUP*)
I.J.R.L. & P. = International Journal of Regulatory Law & Practice (*Henry Stewart Publications*)
I.J.S.L. = International Journal for the Semiotics of Law (*Springer*)
I.J.T. = Irish Journal of Taxation (*University of Ulster*)
I.J.T.J. = International Journal of Transitional Justice (*OUP*)
I.K. = Inside Knowledge (*Waterlow Legal & Regulatory*)
I.L. & P. = Insolvency Law & Practice (*Butterworth Tolley Publishing*)
I.L. & S. = Islamic Law and Society (*Brill Academic Publishers*)
I.L. Pr. = International Litigation Procedure (*S&M*)
I.L.D. = Immigration Law Digest (*Immigration Advisory Service*)
I.L.F.M. = International Law Firm Management (*Euromoney Institutional Investor Plc*)
I.L.J. = Industrial Law Journal (*OUP*)
I.L.P. = International Legal Practitioner (*International Bar Association*)
I.L.R.M. = Irish Law Reports Monthly (*S&M/Round Hall*)
I.L.T. = Irish Law Times (*S&M/Round Hall*)
I.M. & E. = Insurance: Mathematics & Economics (*Elsevier Science Publishers*)
I.M.L. = International Media Law (*S&M*)
I.N.L. = Internet Newsletter for Lawyers (*Delia Venables*)
I.N.L.R. = Immigration and Nationality Law Reports (*Jordan & Sons Ltd*)
I.O.L.R. = International Organizations Law Review (*Martinus Nijhoff Publishers*)
I.P. = International Peacekeeping (*Kluwer*)
I.P. & I.T. Law = Intellectual Property & Information Technology Law (*XPL Publishing*)
I.P. & I.T.L.U. = Intellectual Property & Information Technology Law Updates (*XPL Publishing*)
I.P. & T. = Intellectual Property and Technology (*Butterworth Tolley Publishing*)
I.P. Business = Intellectual Property Business (*OUP*)
I.P. Law. = Intellectual Property Lawyer (*S&M*)
I.P. News. = Intellectual Property Newsletter (*Informa Publishing Group Ltd*)
I.P.B. Rev. = Intellectual Property in Business Review (*Euromoney Institutional Investor Plc*)
I.P.B. Rev. Brief. = Intellectual Property in Business Briefing (*Euromoney Institutional Investor Plc*)
I.P.D. = Intellectual Property Decisions (*Informa Publishing Group Ltd*)
I.P.E.L.J. = Irish Planning and Environmental Law Journal (*S&M/Round Hall*)
I.P.L. = International Pension Lawyer (*International Association of Pension and Employee Benefits Lawyers*)
I.P.M. = Intellectual Property Magazine (*Informa Publishing Group Ltd*)
I.P.Q. = Intellectual Property Quarterly (*S&M*)
I.R.L.A. = Insurance & Reinsurance Law Alert (*Informa Publishing Group Ltd*)
I.R.L.B. = Industrial Relations Law Bulletin (*Reed Business Information Ltd*)
I.R.L.C.T. = International Review of Law Computers & Technology (*Taylor & Francis Ltd*)
I.R.L.I.B. = Industrial Relations Legal Information Bulletin (*Eclipse/Butterworth Tolley Publishing*)
I.R.L.N. = Insurance and Reinsurance Law Newsletter (*Informa Publishing Group Ltd*)
I.R.L.R. = Industrial Relations Law Reports (*Eclipse/Butterworth Tolley Publishing*)
I.R.N. = Industrial Relations News (*IRN Publishing*)
I.R.R.R. = Industrial Relations Review and Report (*Eclipse/Butterworth Tolley Publishing*)
I.R.S.R. = Insurance & Reinsurance Solvency Report (*Informa Publishing Group Ltd*)
I.R.T.B. = Inland Revenue Tax Bulletin (*Inland Revenue*)
I.R.T.L. = Irish Road Traffic Law (*First Law*)
I.R.V. = International Review of Victimology (*Sage Publications Ltd*)
I.S.B. = Insurance Systems Bulletin (*Chiltern Magazine Services*)
I.S.I. = Insurance Systems International (*Informa Publishing Group Ltd*)
I.S.L.J. = International Sports Law Journal (*Springer*)
I.S.L.R. = International Sports Law Review (*S&M*)
I.S.L.Rev. = Irish Student Law Review (*The Honourable Society of Kings' Inn*)
I.S.R. = International Securitisation Report (*IFA Publishing Ltd*)
I.T. & C.L.J. = Information Technology & Communications Law Journal (*Legalease Ltd*)
I.T. Rep. = International Tax Report (*Informa Publishing Group Ltd*)
I.T. Rev. = International Tax Review (*Euromoney Institutional Investor Plc*)
I.T.E.L.R. = International Trust and Estate Law Reports (*Bloomsbury Publishing Plc*)
I.T.I. = Information Technology in Insurance (*Informa Publishing Group Ltd*)

I.T.L. Rep. = International Tax Law Reports (*Butterworth Tolley Publishing*)
I.T.L.J. = International Travel Law Journal (*The Travel Law Centre*)
I.T.L.Q. = International Trade Law Quarterly (*Informa Publishing Group Ltd*)
I.T.L.R. = International Technology Law Review (*Euromoney Institutional Investor Plc*)
I.T.P.J. = International Transfer Pricing Journal (*IBFD Publications BV*)
I.V.M. = International VAT Monitor (*IBFD Publications BV*)
I.Y.L.C.T. = International Yearbook of Law, Computers & Technology (*Taylor & Francis Ltd*)
IALS Bull. = Institute of Advanced Legal Studies Bulletin (*Institute of Advanced Legal Studies*)
IBA Global Insight = IBA Global Insight (*International Bar Association*)
IBIS Rep. = International Benefits Information Service Report (*Charles D. Spencer & Associates, Inc.*)
IBIS Review = International Benefits Information Service Review (*Charles D. Spencer & Associates Inc*)
ICSID Rev. = ICSID Review (*OUP*)
IDS Brief = IDS Brief Employment Law & Practice (*S&M/IDS*)
IDS D.W. = IDS Diversity at Work (*S&M/IDS*)
IDS Emp. E. = IDS Employment Europe (*S&M/IDS*)
IDS Emp. L. Brief = IDS Employment Law Brief (*S&M/IDS*)
IDS Euro. R. = IDS European Report (*S&M/IDS*)
IDS HR Study = IDS HR Studies (*S&M/IDS*)
IDS P.B. = IDS Pensions Bulletin (*S&M/IDS*)
IDS P.L.R. = IDS Pensions Law Reports (*S&M/IDS*)
IDS P.S.B. = IDS Pensions Service Bulletin (*S&M/IDS*)
IFA Review = Independent Financial Adviser Review (*Mitre House Publishing Ltd*)
IIB Mag. = Institute of Insurance Brokers Magazine (*MSM International Ltd*)
IIC = International Review of Intellectual Property and Competition Law (*IPR Verlag GmbH*)
INSOL W. = INSOL World (*INSOL International*)
IP Scan = IP Scan (*Register.com, Corporate Services Division*)
IRS Emp. L.B. = IRS Employment Law Bulletin (*Reed Business Information Ltd*)
IRS Emp. Law = IRS Employment Law (*Reed Business Information Ltd*)
IRS Emp. Rev. = IRS Employment Review (*Reed Business Information Ltd*)
IRS Emp. Trends = IRS Employment Trends (*Butterworth Tolley Publishing*)
IRS Euro. Emp. Rev. = IRS European Employment Review (*Reed Business Information Ltd*)
ISBA L. & R.R. = ISBA Legislative & Regulatory Review (*The Incorporated Society of British Advertisers Ltd*)
IT & C.L.R. = IT & Communications Law Reports (*Legalease Ltd*)
IT & Comm. News. = Information Technology & Communications Newsletter (*Legalease Ltd*)
IT L.T. = IT Law Today (*Singlelaw*)
Imm. A.R. = Immigration Appeal Reports (*TSO*)
In Comp. = In Competition (*S&M*)
In-House L. = In-House Lawyer (*Legalease Ltd*)
Ind. L.R. = Independent Law Review (*Clarus Press*)
Ind. Sol. = Independent Solicitor (*British Legal Association*)
Ind. T.R. = Industrial Tribunal Reports (*TSO*)
Info. T.L.R. = Information Technology Law Reports (*Lawtext Publishing Limited*)
Ins. & Reins. Law Int. = Insurance & Reinsurance Law International (*Kluwer*)
Ins. Age = Insurance Age (*Maxwell Business Communications Ltd*)
Ins. Int. = Insurance International (*Mitre House Publishing Ltd*)
Ins. L. & C. = Insurance Law & Claims (*Mitre House Publishing Ltd*)
Ins. L. & P. = Insurance Law & Practice (*Butterworth Tolley Publishing*)
Ins. L.J. = Insurance Law Journal (*Butterworths Pty Ltd*)
Ins. L.M. = Insurance Law Monthly (*Informa Publishing Group Ltd*)
Insolv. B. = Insolvency Bulletin (*Informa Publishing Group Ltd*)
Insolv. Int. = Insolvency Intelligence (*S&M*)
Insolv. L. = Insolvency Lawyer (*S&M*)
Insolv. L. & P. = Insolvency Litigation & Practice (*CLT Publishing*)
Insolv. P. = Insolvency Practitioner (*Association of Business Recovery Professionals*)
Insolvency = Insolvency (*Griffin Multimedia*)
Int. A.L.R. = International Arbitration Law Review (*S&M*)
Int. Acc. = International Accountant (*Association of International Accountants*)
Int. Bank. L. = International Banking Law (*S&M*)
Int. Broker = International Broker (*Risk & Insurance Research Group Ltd*)
Int. C.L. Rev. = International Community Law Review (*Martinus Nijhoff Publishers*)
Int. C.L.R. = International Criminal Law Review (*Martinus Nijhoff Publishers*)
Int. C.R. = International Corporate Rescue (*Chase Cambria Co (Publishing) Ltd*)
Int. I.L.R. = International Insurance Law Review (*S&M/ESC Publishing*)
Int. I.R. = International Insurance Report (*Risk & Insurance Research Group Ltd*)
Int. J. Comp. L.L.I.R. = International Journal of Comparative Labour Law and Industrial Relations (*Kluwer*)
Int. J. Law & Fam. = International Journal of Law & the Family (*OUP*)
Int. J. Soc. L. = International Journal of the Sociology of Law (*Elsevier*)
Int. J.F.L. = International Journal of Franchising Law (*Claerhout Publishing Ltd*)
Int. J.I.P.M. = International Journal of Intellectual Property Management (*Inderscience Publishers*)
Int. J.L.C. = International Journal of Law in Context (*CUP*)
Int. J.L.M. = International Journal of Law and Management (*Emerald Group Publishing Limited*)
Int. J.L.P.F. = International Journal of Law, Policy and the Family (*OUP*)
Int. M.L. = International Maritime Law (*Lawtext Publishing Limited*)
Int. Rel. = International Relations (*Sage Publications Ltd*)
Int. Rev. Law & Econ. = International Review of Law & Economics (*Butterworth Tolley Publishing*)
Int. T.L.R. = International Trade Law & Regulation (*S&M/ESC Publishing*)
Intertax = Intertax (*Kluwer*)

Inv. Man. = Investment Management (*Mitre House Publishing Ltd*)
Ir. B.L. = Irish Business Law (*Inns Quay Publishing*)
Ir. L.R. = Irish Law Review (*Clarus Press*)
Ir. T.R. = Irish Tax Review (*Institute of Taxation in Ireland*)
Irish Jurist = Irish Jurist (*S&M/Round Hall*)

J. Civ. Lib. = Journal of Civil Liberties (*Northumbria Law Press*)
J. Com. Mar. St. = Journal of Common Market Studies (*John Wiley & Sons Ltd*)
J. Crim. L. = Journal of Criminal Law (*Vathek Publishing*)
J. En. & Nat. Res. L. = Journal of Energy & Natural Resources Law (*Turpin Distribution Serv Ltd*)
J. Env. L. = Journal of Environmental Law (*OUP*)
J. Int. Arb. = Journal of International Arbitration (*Kluwer*)
J. Int. P. = Journal of International Trust and Corporate Planning (*Jordan & Sons Ltd*)
J. Law & Soc. = Journal of Law and Society (*John Wiley & Sons Ltd*)
J. Leg. Hist. = Journal of Legal History (*Cass*)
J. Priv. Int. L. = Journal of Private International Law (*Hart Publishing Ltd*)
J. Prop. Fin. = Journal of Property Finance (*MCB University Press Ltd*)
J. Soc.Wel. & Fam. L. = Journal of Social Welfare and Family Law (*Taylor & Francis Ltd*)
J. Soc. Wel. L. = Journal of Social Welfare Law (*S&M*)
J.A.C.L. = Journal of Armed Conflict Law (*Nottingham University Press*)
J.A.L. = Journal of African Law (*CUP*)
J.A.M.N. = Journal of ADR, Mediation and Negotiation (*XPL Publishing*)
J.B.L. = Journal of Business Law (*S&M*)
J.B.R. = Journal of Banking Regulation (*Palgrave Macmillan*)
J.C. & S.L. = Journal of Conflict & Security Law (*OUP*)
J.C.C. Law = Journal of Commonwealth Criminal Law (*Association of Commonwealth Criminal Lawyers*)
J.C.C.L. = Journal of Community Care Law (*Arden Davies Publishing*)
J.C.L. = Journal of Child Law (*Butterworth Tolley Publishing*)
J.C.L. & E. = Journal of Competition Law & Economics (*OUP*)
J.C.L.L.E. = Journal of Commonwealth Law and Legal Education (*Taylor & Francis Ltd*)
J.C.L.P. = Journal of Competition Law & Policy (*OECD Publications Service (Databeuro Ltd)*)
J.C.L.S. = Journal of Corporate Law Studies (*Hart Publishing Ltd*)
J.C.P. = Journal of Consumer Policy (*Springer*)
J.C.P.P. = Journal of Civil Practice and Procedure (*S&M/Round Hall*)
J.E.C.L. & P. = Journal of Electronic Commerce Law & Practice (*Butterworth Tolley Publishing*)
J.E.C.L. & Pract. = Journal of European Competition Law & Practice (*OUP*)
J.E.E.P.L. = Journal for European Environmental & Planning Law (*Brill Academic Publishers*)
J.E.L.P. = Journal of Employment Law & Practice (*Butterworth Tolley Publishing*)
J.E.L.S. = Journal of Empirical Legal Studies (*John Wiley & Sons Ltd*)
J.E.P.P. = Journal of European Public Policy (*Taylor & Francis Ltd*)
J.E.R.L. = Journal of Energy & Natural Resources Law (*International Bar Association*)
J.F.C. = Journal of Financial Crime (*Emerald Group Publishing Limited*)
J.F.R. & C. = Journal of Financial Regulation and Compliance (*Emerald Group Publishing Limited*)
J.F.S.M. = Journal of Financial Services Marketing (*Henry Stewart Publications*)
J.G.L.R. = Jersey and Guernsey Law Review (*The Jersey and Guernsey Law Review Ltd*)
J.H.L. = Journal of Housing Law (*S&M*)
J.H.R.E. = Journal of Human Rights and the Environment (*Marston Book Services*)
J.I.A. = Journal of the Institute of Actuaries (*Institute of Actuaries*)
J.I.A.N.L. = Journal of Immigration Asylum and Nationality Law (*Bloomsbury Publishing Plc*)
J.I.B. Law = Journal of International Biotechnology Law (*Walter de Gruyter GmbH & Co. KG*)
J.I.B.L. = Journal of International Banking Law (*S&M/ESC Publishing*)
J.I.B.L.R. = Journal of International Banking Law and Regulation (*S&M/ESC Publishing*)
J.I.B.R. = Journal of International Banking Regulation (*Palgrave Macmillan*)
J.I.C.J. = Journal of International Criminal Justice (*OUP*)
J.I.C.L. = Journal of International Commercial Law (*Ashgate Publishing Ltd*)
J.I.C.L.T. = Journal of International Commercial Law and Technology (*International Association of IT Lawyers*)
J.I.C.M. = Journal of the Institute of Credit Management (*Institute of Credit Management*)
J.I.D.S. = Journal of International Dispute Settlement (*OUP*)
J.I.E.L. = Journal of International Economic Law (*OUP*)
J.I.F.D.L. = Journal of International Franchising & Distribution Law (*Butterworth Tolley Publishing*)
J.I.F.M. = Journal of International Financial Markets (*S&M*)
J.I.L. & C. = Journal of Islamic Law and Culture (*Taylor & Francis Ltd*)
J.I.L.T. = Journal of Information, Law & Technology (*CTI Law Technology Centre*)
J.I.M.F. = Journal of International Money and Finance (*Elsevier*)
J.I.M.L. = Journal of International Maritime Law (*Lawtext Publishing Limited*)
J.I.P.L.P. = Journal of Intellectual Property Law & Practice (*OUP*)
J.I.T.L. & P. = Journal of International Trade Law & Policy (*Emerald Group Publishing Limited*)
J.I.T.T.C.P. = Journal of International Tax, Trust and Corporate Planning (*Jordan & Sons Ltd*)
J.J. = Justice Journal (*Justice*)
J.L.A. = Journal of Legal Analysis (*OUP*)
J.L.E. & O. = Journal of Law, Economics & Organization (*OUP*)
J.L.G.L. = Journal of Local Government Law (*S&M*)
J.L.M &. E. = Journal of Law, Medicine & Ethics (*John Wiley & Sons Ltd*)
J.L.S. = Journal of Legislative Studies (*Taylor & Francis Ltd*)

J.L.S.S. = Journal of the Law Society of Scotland (*The Law Society of Scotland*)
J.M.C.B. = Journal of Money, Credit and Banking (*Ohio State University Press*)
J.M.H.L. = Journal of Mental Health Law (*Northumbria Law Press*)
J.M.L. = Journal of Media Law (*Hart Publishing Ltd*)
J.M.L. & P. = Journal of Media Law and Practice (*Butterworth Tolley Publishing*)
J.M.L.C. = Journal of Money Laundering Control (*Emerald Group Publishing Limited*)
J.N.I. = Journal of Network Industries (*Intersentia*)
J.O. & R. = Journal of Obligations and Remedies (*Northumbria Law Press*)
J.P. = Justice of the Peace & Local Government Law (*Butterworth Tolley Publishing*)
J.P.I. Law = Journal of Personal Injury Law (*S&M*)
J.P.I.L. = Journal of Personal Injury Litigation (*S&M*)
J.P.L. = Journal of Planning & Environment Law (*S&M*)
J.P.M. = Journal of Pensions Management (*Henry Stewart Publications*)
J.P.M. & M. = Journal of Pensions Management & Marketing (*Henry Stewart Publications*)
J.P.N. = Justice of the Peace & Local Government Law (*Butterworth Tolley Publishing*)
J.R. = Judicial Review (*Hart Publishing Ltd*)
J.R. & I. = Journal of Risk and Insurance (*American Risk & Insurance Association Inc*)
J.R.L.S. = Jerusalem Review of Legal Studies (*OUP*)
J.R.S. = Journal of Refugee Studies (*OUP*)
J.S.B.J. = Judicial Studies Board Journal (*OUP*)
J.S.F. = Journal of the Society of Fellows (*Chartered Insurance Institute*)
J.S.I.J. = Judicial Studies Instiutute Journal (*Judicial Studies Institute*)
J.S.S.L. = Journal of Social Security Law (*S&M*)
J.T.C.P. = Journal of International Trust & Corporate Planning (*Jordan & Sons Ltd*)
J.W.B.L. = Journal of Welfare Benefits Law (*Arden Davies Publishing*)
J.W.E.L. & B. = Journal of World Energy Law & Business (*OUP*)
J.W.I.P. = Journal of World Intellectual Property (*John Wiley & Sons Ltd*)
J.W.T. = Journal of World Trade (*Turpin Distribution Serv Ltd*)
J.W.T.L. = Journal of World Trade Law (*Werner Publishing Co Ltd*)
Jersey L.R. = Jersey Law Review (*The Jersey and Guernsey Law Review Ltd*)
Jour. G.M. = Journal of General Management (*Braybrooke Press Ltd*)
Jur. Rev. = Juridical Review (*S&M/W. Green*)
Juris. = Jurisprudence (*Hart Publishing Ltd*)

K.B. = Law Reports Kings Bench (*ICLR*)
K.C.L.J. = Kings College Law Journal (*Hart Publishing Ltd*)
K.H.R.P.L.R. = Kurdish Human Rights Project Legal Review (*Kurdish Human Rights Project*)
K.I.R. = Knights Industrial Reports (*Charles Knight Publishing*)
K.L.J. = King's Law Journal (*Hart Publishing Ltd*)
KIM Legal = Knowledge and Information Management (*Waterlow Legal & Regulatory*)
KM Legal = KM Legal (*Ark Publishing*)
Kemp & Kemp = Kemp & Kemp The Quantum of Damages (*S&M*)
Kemp News = Kemp News (*S&M*)
King's Counsel = King's Counsel (*King's College London*)
Kingston L.R. = Kingston Law Review (*Kingston Polytechnic*)

L & T.R. = Landlord and Tenant Reports (*S&M*)
L&P Comp. EC = Linklaters & Paines Competition EC (*Linklaters*)
L&P E. & B.L.N. = Linklaters & Paines Employment & Benefits Law Newsletter (*Linklaters*)
L&P E.C. Law = Linklaters & Paines European Community Law (*Linklaters*)
L&P F.S. News. = Linklaters & Paines Financial Services Newsfile (*Linklaters*)
L&P I.F. News. = Linklaters & Paines Investment Funds Newsfile (*Linklaters*)
L&P I.M. Rep. = Linklaters & Paines Internal Market Report (*Linklaters*)
L&P I.P.N. = Linklaters & Paines Intellectual Property News (*Linklaters*)
L&P P.L.N. = Linklaters & Paines Property Law Now (*Linklaters*)
L. & F.M.R. = Law & Financial Markets Review (*Hart Publishing Ltd*)
L. & H. = Law & Humanities (*Hart Publishing Ltd*)
L. & T. Review = Landlord & Tenant Review (*S&M*)
L. D'I. = Lettre D'Information (*Geneva Association*)
L. Ex. = Legal Executive (*ILEX Publishing & Advertising Services Ltd*)
L.A.L. = Local Authority Law (*S&M*)
L.B.E.B. = Lloyds Bank Economic Bulletin (*Lloyd's Bank Plc*)
L.B.R. = Law Business Review (*Butterworths Tolley Publishing*)
L.C. & A.I. = Law, Computers & Artificial Intelligence (*Taylor & Francis Ltd*)
L.C. News = Law Centres News (*Law Centres Federation*)
L.C.B. = Legal Compliance Bulletin (*Law Society Publishing*)
L.D. = Legal Director (*Legal Week Global Media*)
L.E. = Lawyers' Europe (*The Journal of the Law Society's European Group*)
L.F. = Litigation Funding (*Law Society Publishing*)
L.G. Rev. = Local Government Review (*Butterworth Tolley Publishing*)
L.G. Review = Local Government Review (*First Law*)
L.G. and L. = Local Government and Law (*Informa Publishing Group Ltd*)
L.G.C. = Local Government Chronicle (*Local Government Chronicle Ltd*)
L.G.C. Law & Admin. = Local Government Chronicle Law & Administration (*Local Government Chronicle Ltd*)
L.G.D. = Law, Social Justice & Global Development (*Electronic Law Journals*)
L.G.I. = Law Gazette International (*Law Society Services Ltd*)
L.G.L.R. = Local Government Law Reports (*S&M*)

L.G.R. = Local Government Reports (*Charles Knight Publishing*)
L.G.R. Rep. = Local Government Review Reports (*Barry Rose Law Periodicals*)
L.I.E.I. = Legal Issues of European Integration (*Turpin Distribution Serv Ltd*)
L.I.I. = Life Insurance International (*L.L.P Ltd*)
L.I.M. = Legal Information Management (*CUP*)
L.I.T. = Law, Innovation and Technology (*Hart Publishing Ltd*)
L.J.I.L. = Leiden Journal of International Law (*CUP*)
L.L.I.D. = Lloyd's List Insurance Day (*Informa Publishing Group Ltd*)
L.L.R. = London Law Review (*London Law Review*)
L.M.C.L.Q. = Lloyd's Maritime and Commercial Law Quarterly (*Informa Publishing Group Ltd*)
L.M.E.L.R. = Land Management and Environmental Law Report (*Chancery Law Publishing Ltd*)
L.M.L.N. = Lloyd's Maritime Law Newsletter (*Informa Publishing Group Ltd*)
L.M.N. = London Market Newsletter (*Informa Publishing Group Ltd*)
L.P. & R. = Law, Probability & Risk (*OUP*)
L.P.I.C.T. = Law & Practice of International Courts and Tribunals (*Martinus Nijhoff Publishers*)
L.Q.R. = Law Quarterly Review (*S&M*)
L.R. = Licensing Review (*Benedict Books*)
L.R. & I. = Liability Risk & Insurance (*Informa Publishing Group Ltd*)
L.R.L.R. = Lloyd's Reinsurance Law Reports (*LLP*)
L.S. = Legal Studies (*John Wiley & Sons Ltd*)
L.S. & P. = Law, Science and Policy (*A B Academic Publishers*)
L.S.G. = Law Society's Gazette (*The Law Society's Hall*)
L.T. = Legal Theory (*CUP*)
L.T.J. = Law Technology Journal (*CTI Law Technology Centre*)
L.W.D. EC News. = Lovell White Durrant EC Newsletter (*Lovell White Durrant*)
L.W.D. L.A.P. = Lovell White Durrant Legal Advice on Pensions (*Lovell White Durrant*)
Law = Law (*The Law*)
Law & Crit. = Law and Critique (*Springer*)
Law & Just. = Law & Justice (*Edmund Plowden Trust*)
Law & Phil. = Law & Philosophy (*Springer*)
Law & Pol. = Law & Policy (*John Wiley & Sons Ltd*)
Law & Tax R. = Law & Tax Review (*S&M*)
Law Lib. = Law Librarian (*S&M*)
Law Mag. = Law Magazine (*S&M*)
Law Teach. = Law Teacher (*Taylor & Francis Ltd*)
Law for Bus. = Law for Business (*Wallace Publishing Ltd*)
Law. in Eur. = Lawyers in Europe (*Lawyers in Europe Ltd*)
Lawyer = Lawyer (*Centaur Communications Group*)
Lawyer 2B = Lawyer 2B (*Centaur Communications Group*)
Leg. = Legisprudence (*Hart Publishing Ltd*)
Legal Action = Legal Action (*Legal Action Group*)
Legal Bus. = Legal Business (*Legalease Ltd*)
Legal Ethics = Legal Ethics (*Hart Publishing Ltd*)
Legal I.E.I. = Legal Issues of Economic Integration (*Kluwer*)
Legal IT = Legal IT (*Legal Week Global Media*)
Legal M. = Legal Marketing (*Ark Publishing*)
Legal T.J. = Legal Technology Journal (*Legalease Ltd*)
Legal Times = Legal Times (*Legalease Ltd*)
Legal Week = Legal Week (*Incisive Financial Publishing Ltd*)
Link AWS = Link Association of Women Solicitors (*Association of Women Solicitors*)
Lit. = Litigation (*Butterworth Tolley Publishing*)
Lit. L. = Litigation Letter (*Informa Publishing Group Ltd*)
Litigator = Litigator (*S&M*)
Liverpool L.R. = Liverpool Law Review (*Springer*)
Ll. Ins. Int. = Lloyd's Insurance International (*Lloyd's of London Press Inc*)
Ll. Log = Lloyds Log (*Informa Publishing Group Ltd*)
Ll. News. = Lloyd's of London Newsletter (*Informa Publishing Group Ltd*)
Lloyd's List = Lloyd's List (*Informa Publishing Group Ltd*)
Lloyd's Rep. = Lloyd's Law Reports (*Informa Publishing Group Ltd*)
Lloyd's Rep. Bank. = Lloyd's Law Reports Banking (*Informa Publishing Group Ltd*)
Lloyd's Rep. I.R. = Lloyd's Law Reports Insurance & Reinsurance (*Informa Publishing Group Ltd*)
Lloyd's Rep. Med. = Lloyd's Law Reports Medical (*Informa Publishing Group Ltd*)
Lloyd's Rep. P.N. = Lloyd's Law Reports Professional Negligence (*Informa Publishing Group Ltd*)

M. & A. Ins. Rep. = Marine & Aviation Insurance Report (*Informa Publishing Group Ltd*)
M. Advice = Money Advice (*Money Advice Association*)
M. Advocate = Maritime Advocate (*Merlin Legal Publishing*)
M. Bulletin = Mercer Bulletin European Newsletter (*William M Mercer Ltd*)
M. Direct = Mercer Direct European Communication Newsletter (*William M Mercer Ltd*)
M. EC News. = Mercer European Community Newsletter (*William M Mercer Ltd*)
M. Euro. News = Mercer European News (*William M Mercer Ltd*)
M. Man. = Money Management (*Financial Times Finance*)
M. Prospect = Mercer Prospect Eastern European Newsletter (*William M Mercer Ltd*)
M. Review = Mercer Review (*William M Mercer Ltd*)
M. Transatlantic = Mercer Transatlantic (*William M Mercer Ltd*)
M. Update = Mercer Update (*William M Mercer Ltd*)
M. World = Media World (*Informa Publishing Group Ltd*)
M.A. = Management Accounting (*Chartered Institute Management Accountants*)
M.A.L.Q.R. = Model Arbitration Law Quarterly Reports (*Simmonds & Hill Publishing Ltd*)
M.C.P. = Magistrates' Courts Practice (*XPL Publishing*)
M.D.U. Jour. = Medical Defence Union Journal (*The Medical Defence Union*)

M.E.C.L.R. = Middle East Commercial Law Review (*S&M/ESC Publishing*)
M.F.G. = Mortgage Finance Gazette (*Metropolis International Group Ltd*)
M.F.S. = Managing for Success (*Law Management Section/The Law Society*)
M.I.M. = Motor Insurance Market (*Informa Publishing Group Ltd*)
M.I.P. = Managing Intellectual Property (*Euromoney Institutional Investor Plc*)
M.J. = Municipal Journal (*Hemming Information Services*)
M.J.L.S. = Mountbatten Journal of Legal Studies (*Southampton Institute*)
M.L.B. = Manx Law Bulletin (*Attorney General's Chambers*)
M.L.J.I. = Medico-Legal Journal of Ireland (*S&M/Round Hall*)
M.L.N. = Media Lawyer Newsletter (*The Press Association*)
M.L.R. = Modern Law Review (*John Wiley & Sons Ltd*)
M.M. = Money Marketing (*Centaur Communications Group*)
M.P. = Managing Partner (*Wilmington Publishing and Information Ltd*)
M.R. = Media Review (*SJ Berwin & Co*)
M.R.D.B. = Monthly Report Deutsche Bundesbank (*Deutshe Bundesbank*)
M.R.I. = Maritime Risk International (*Informa Publishing Group Ltd*)
M.T. & F. = Matrimonial Tax & Finance (*Tax and Financial Publishing*)
M.W. = Money Week (*EMAP Communications*)
Maastricht J. = Maastricht Journal of European and Comparative Law (*Intersentia NV*)
Magistrate = Magistrate (*Magistrates Association*)
Man. L. = Managerial Law (*MCB University Press Ltd*)
Marine I.R. = Marine Insurance Report (*Informa Publishing Group Ltd*)
Masons C.L.R. = Masons Computer Law Reports (*Mason's Solicitor*)
McK. E.B.B. = McKenna Employment Benefits Bulletin (*McKenna & Co*)
McK. Env. L.B. = McKenna Environmental Law Bulletin (*Cameron McKenna & Co*)
McK. Euro. R. = McKenna European Review (*McKenna & Co*)
McK. Law Let. = McKenna Law Letter (*McKenna & Co*)
McK. P.B. = McKenna Pension Brief (*McKenna & Co*)
McK. P.L.B. = McKenna Pension Law Bulletin (*McKenna & Co*)
Med. L. Int. = Medical Law International (*Sage Publications Ltd*)
Med. L. Mon. = Medical Law Monitor (*Informa Publishing Group Ltd*)
Med. L. Rev. = Medical Law Review (*OUP*)
Med. L.R. = Medical Law Reports (*Informa Publishing Group Ltd*)
Med. Leg. J. = Medico-Legal Journal (*Sage Publications Ltd*)
Med. Lit. = Medical Litigation (*Medical Litigation Strategies*)
Med. Sci. Law = Medicine, Science & the Law (*The Royal Society of Medicine Press*)
Money L.B. = Money Laundering Bulletin (*Informa Publishing Group Ltd*)
Mortgage M. = Mortgage Monthly (*BSA CML Publication*)

N.E.G.R.I.E. = Newsletter of the European Group of Risk and Insurance Economists (*Geneva Association*)
N.I.C. & L.L.J. = Northern Ireland Conveyancing and Land Law Journal (*SLS Legal Publications (NI)*)
N.I.E.R. = National Institute of Economic Review (*The National Institute of Economic Review*)
N.I.L. Rev. = Netherlands International Law Review (*CUP*)
N.I.L.Q. = Northern Ireland Legal Quarterly (*School of Law*)
N.I.L.R. = Northern Ireland Law Reports (*Butterworth Tolley Publishing*)
N.J.I.L. = Nordic Journal of International Law (*Martinus Nijhoff Publishers*)
N.L.J. = New Law Journal (*Butterworths Tolley Publishing*)
N.L.T. = Northern Law Today (*Northern Law Today*)
N.N. EC News = Nabarro Nathanson EC News (*Nabarro Nathanson*)
N.N.P.D. = Nabarro Nathanson The Pension Dimension (*Nabarro Nathanson*)
N.N.R. = Nabarro Nathanson Resource (*Nabarro Nathanson*)
N.P.C. = New Property Cases (*New Property Cases Ltd*)
N.Q.H.R. = Netherlands Quarterly of Human Rights (*Intersentia NV*)
N.R. EC Init. = Norton Rose M5 Group EC Initiative (*Norton Rose M5 Group*)
N.R. EU Init. = Norton Rose M5 Group EU Initiative (*Norton Rose M5 Group*)
N.R.G.Q. = Netherlands Reinsurance Group Quarterly (*Nederlandse Reassurantie Groep nv*)
N.S.A.I.L. = Non-State Actors and International Law (*Martinus Nijhoff Publishers*)
N.W.B.Q.R. = National Westminster Bank Quarterly Review (*National Westminster Bank Plc*)
Natwest I.T.B. = National Westminster Bank International Trade Bulletin (*National Westminster Bank*)
Nott. L.J. = Nottingham Law Journal (*Nottingham Law School*)

O. & I.T. Rev. = Offshore & International Taxation Review (*Key Haven Publications Plc*)
O.D. and I.L. = Ocean Development and International Law (*Taylor & Francis Ltd*)
O.G.J.F.I. = Open Government: A Journal on Freedom of Information (*Liverpool John Moores University*)
O.G.L.T.R. = Oil & Gas Law & Taxation Review (*S&M/ESC Publishing*)
O.H.R. = Occupational Health Review (*Eclipse/Butterworth Tolley Publishing*)
O.J.L.R. = Oxford Journal of Law and Religion (*OUP*)
O.J.L.S. = Oxford Journal of Legal Studies (*OUP*)
O.L.S. = One Lime Street (*Informa Publishing Group Ltd*)
O.N. = Oftel News (*Oftel Update*)
O.P.L.R. = Occupational Pensions Law Reports (*Eclipse/Butterworth Tolley Publishing*)
O.R. & C. = OpRisk & Compliance (*Incisive Financial Publishing Ltd*)

O.R. & R. = OperationalRisk & Regulation (*Incisive Media Plc*)
O.S.S. Bull. = Office for the Supervision of Solicitors Bulletin (*The Law Society's Gazette*)
O.T.P.R. = OffshoreTax Planning Review (*Key Haven Publications Plc*)
O.T.R. = Offshore Tax Planning Review (*Key Haven Publications Plc*)
O.U.C.L.J. = Oxford University Commonwealth Law Journal (*Hart Publishing Ltd*)
Observer = OECD Observer (*Databeuro Ltd*)
Occ. Pen. = Occupational Pensions (*Eclipse/Butterworth Tolley Publishing*)
Offshore Red = Offshore Red (*ClearView Financial Media Ltd*)

P & I Int. = P & I International (*Informa Publishing Group Ltd*)
P. & C.R. = Property, Planning and Compensation Reports (*S&M*)
P. & D.P. = Privacy & Data Protection (*Privacy & Data Protection*)
P. & E.B. = Pensions & Employee Benefits (*Butterworth Tolley Publishing*)
P. & M.I.L.L. = Personal and Medical Injuries Law Letter (*Informa Publishing Group Ltd*)
P. & O.J. = Procurement and Outsourcing Journal (*Legalease Ltd*)
P. & P. = Practice and Procedure (*S&M/Round Hall*)
P. & S. = Punishment & Society (*Sage Publications Ltd*)
P. Injury = Personal Injury (EMIS) (*XPL Publishing*)
P. Int. = Portfolio International (*MSM International*)
P. Treas. = Public Treasurer (*Local Government Chronicle Ltd*)
P. Week = Property Week (*CMP Information Ltd*)
P.A. = Product Adviser (*Financial Times Finance*)
P.A.B.B. = Pay And Benefits Bulletin (*Butterworth Tolley Publishing*)
P.A.D. = Planning Appeal Decisions (*S&M*)
P.B. = Professional Broking (*Timothy Benn Publishing Ltd*)
P.C. & L. = Psychology, Crime & Law (*Taylor & Francis Ltd*)
P.C.A. = Private Client Adviser (*Wilmington Publishing and Information Ltd*)
P.C.B. = Private Client Business (*S&M*)
P.C.L.B. = Practitioners' Child Law Bulletin (*S&M*)
P.C.P. = Private Client Practitioner (*PAM Insight Ltd*)
P.C.R. = Proceeds of Crime Review (*John Edward Law*)
P.E.B.L. = Perspectives on European Business Law (*European Perspectives Publicatons Ltd*)
P.E.L.B. = Planning and Environmental Law Bulletin (*S&M*)
P.F. = Property Finance (*Informa Publishing Group Ltd*)
P.F. & D. = Property Finance & Development (*Informa Publishing Group Ltd*)
P.H.B. = Parliament House Book (*S&M/W. Green*)
P.I. = Personal Injury (Wiley) (*John Wiley & Sons Ltd*)
P.I. Comp. = Personal Injury Compensation (*Informa Publishing Group Ltd*)
P.I.B.U.L.J. = Personal Injury Brief Update Law Journal (*Law Brief Publishing Ltd*)
P.I.C. = Palmer's In Company (*S&M*)
P.I.J. = Planning Inspectorate Journal (*The Planning Inspectorate*)
P.I.L.J. = Personal Injury Law Journal (*Legalease Ltd*)
P.I.L.M.R. = Personal Injury Law and Medical Review (*Butterworth Tolley Publishing*)
P.I.N. = Personal Injury Newsletter (*Butterworth Tolley Publishing*)
P.I.P. = Property in Practice (*Property Section/The Law Society*)
P.I.Q.R. = Personal Injuries and Quantum Reports (*S&M*)
P.L. = Public Law (*S&M*)
P.L. & B.I.N. = Privacy Laws & Business International Newsletter (*Privacy Laws & Business*)
P.L. & B.U.K.N. = Privacy Laws & Business United Kingdom Newsletter (*Privacy Laws & Business*)
P.L. Today = Purchasing Law Today (*Richard Lawson*)
P.L.B. = Property Law Bulletin (S&M) (*S&M*)
P.L.C. = Practical Law Companies (*Practical Law Company Ltd*)
P.L.C.R. = Planning Law Case Reports (*S&M*)
P.L.I. = Product Liability International (*Informa Publishing Group Ltd*)
P.L.J. = Property Law Journal (*Legalease Ltd*)
P.L.N. = Property Law Newsletter (*Butterworth Tolley Publishing*)
P.L.R. = Estates Gazette Planning Law Reports (*Estates Gazette*)
P.L.T. = Professional Liability Today (*Informa Publishing Group Ltd*)
P.L.U. = Pensions Law Update (*Ellison Westhorp Publications*)
P.M. = Pensions Management (*Financial Times Finance*)
P.N. = Professional Negligence (*Bloomsbury Publishing Plc*)
P.N. & L. = Professional Negligence & Liability (*CLT Publishing*)
P.N.L.R. = Professional Negligence and Liability Reports (*S&M*)
P.P. = Professional Pensions (*MSM International Ltd*)
P.P. & D. = Practical Planning & Development (*CLT Publishing*)
P.P.L. = Practical Planning Law (*CLT Publishing*)
P.P.L.R. = Public Procurement Law Review (*S&M*)
P.P.M. = Professional Practice Management (*Informa Publishing Group Ltd*)
P.R. = Property Review (*Eclipse/Butterworth Tolley Publishing*)
P.S. = Pensions Systems (*Mitre House Publishing Ltd*)
P.S.E.L.J. = Public Sector Employment Law Journal (*Legalease Ltd*)
P.S.P. = Police Station Practice (*XPL Publishing*)
P.S.T. = Pension Scheme Trustee (*Informa Publishing Group Ltd*)
P.T. = Pensions Today (*Informa Publishing Group Ltd*)
P.T.P.R. = Personal Tax Planning Review (*Key Haven Publications Plc*)
P.V. = Property Valuer (*Irish Auctioneers & Valuers Institute*)
P.W. = Patent World (*Informa Publishing Group Ltd*)
PS = Private Client Section (*Private Client Section/The Law Society*)

Paisner C.U. = Paisner Company Update (*Paisner & Co*)
Paisner E.B. = Paisner European Bulletin (*Paisner & Co*)
Paisner E.U. = Paisner Environment Update (*Paisner & Co*)
Paisner I.P.B. = Paisner Intellectual Property Briefing (*Paisner & Co*)
Palmer's C.L. = Palmer's Company Law (*S&M*)
Parl. Aff. = Parliamentary Affairs (*OUP*)
Pay Mag. = Pay Magazine (*Wolters Kluwer (UK) Ltd*)
Pen. = Pensions (*Palgrave Macmillan*)
Pen. L.R. = Pensions Law Reports (*Incomes Data Services Ltd*)
Pen. Law. = Pension Lawyer (*Association of Penion Lawyers*)
Pen. Week = Pensions Week (*Financial Times Finance*)
Pen. World = Pensions World (*Butterworth Tolley Publishing*)
Pers. Today = Personnel Today (*Reed Business Information Ltd*)
Pharm. L.I. = Pharmaceutical Law Insight (*Informa Publishing Group Ltd*)
Pl. Sav. = Planned Savings (*EMAP Media Ltd*)
Pol. J. = Police Journal (*Vathek Publishing*)
Policing = Policing (*Police Review Publishing Co Ltd*)
Policing T. = Policing Today (*Police Review Publishing Co Ltd*)
Post Mag. = Post Magazine (*Incisive Media Plc*)
Pract. Today = Practice Today (*S&M*)
Pract. VAT = Practical VAT (*Butterworth Tolley Publishing*)
Press R. = Press Releases (*Centre Office of Information*)
Prison Serv. J. = Prison Service Journal (*Governor, H.M. Prison Leyhill*)
Probat. J. = Probation Journal (*Sage Publications Ltd*)
Prof. L. = Professional Lawyer (*Chancery Law Publishing Ltd*)
Progres = Progres (*Geneva Association*)
Prop. L.B. = Property Law Bulletin (W Green) (*S&M/W. Green*)
Prop. S. = Property Service (*XPL Publishing*)
Prospect = Prospect (*Life Insurance Association*)
Pub. Law Bull. = Public Law Bulletin (*Manchester Metropolitan University*)
Public F. = Public Finance (*FSF Limited*)

Q.A. = Quarterly Account (*Institute of Money Advisers*)
Q.B. = Law Reports Queen's Bench (*ICLR*)
Q.M.J.I.P. = Queen Mary Journal of Intellectual Property (*Marston Book Services*)
Q.R. = Quantum Reports (*S&M*)
Q.R.T.L. = Quarterly Review of Tort Law (*Clarus Press*)
Quantum = Quantum (*S&M*)

R. & B.C.P. = Renton & Brown's Criminal Procedure (*S&M/W. Green*)
R. & B.C.P.L. = Renton & Brown's Criminal Procedure Legislation (*S&M/W. Green*)
R. & B.S.O. = Renton & Brown's Statutory Offences (*S&M/W. Green*)
R.A. = Rating Appeals (*Rating Publishers Ltd*)
R.A.D.I.C. = African Journal of International and Comparative Law (*African Society of International and Comparative Law*)
R.A.L.Q. = Receivers, Administrators and Liquidators Quarterly (*Key Haven Publications Plc*)
R.E.C.I.E.L. = Review of European Community and International Environmental Law (*John Wiley & Sons Ltd*)
R.E.L.P. = Renewable Energy Law and Policy Review (*Lexxion Verlagsgesellschaft mbH*)
R.J. = Restorative Justice (*Hart Publishing Ltd*)
R.L.E.J.P. = Research in Law and Economics: A Journal of Policy (*Emerald Group Publishing Limited*)
R.L.R. = Restitution Law Review (*Marenex Productions*)
R.M.B. = Risk Management Bulletin (*Ark Publishing*)
R.M.H.L. = Review of Mental Health Law (*Arden Davies Publishing*)
R.M.R. = Reinsurance Market Report (*Informa Publishing Group Ltd*)
R.P.C. = Reports of Patent, Design and Trade Mark Cases (*S&M*)
R.P.R.M. = Research Programme on Risk Management (*Geneva Association*)
R.Q. = Reinsurance Quarterly (*Evandale Publishing Co Ltd*)
R.R.L.R. = Rent Review & Lease Renewal (*Informa Publishing Group Ltd*)
R.S.I. = Reinsurance Security Insider (*Evandale Publishing Co Ltd*)
R.T.I. = Road Traffic Indicator (*S&M*)
R.T.R. = Road Traffic Reports (*S&M*)
R.V.R. = Rating and Valuation Reporter (*Rating Publishers Ltd*)
R.W.B. = Rights Workers Bulletin (*NACAB*)
R.W.L.R. = Rights of Way Law Review (*Rights of Way Law Review*)
ROW Bulletin = Rights Of Women Bulletin (*Rights Of Women*)
Ratio Juris = Ratio Juris (*John Wiley & Sons Ltd*)
Re Re. = Re Report (*Evandale Publishing Co Ltd*)
Re. L.R. = Reinsurance Law Reports (*Informa Publishing Group Ltd*)
Reactions = Reactions (*Euromoney Institutional Investor Plc*)
Recovery = Recovery (*Association of Business Recovery Professionals*)
Regulator = Regulator & Professional Conduct Quarterly (*Butterworth Tolley Publishing*)
Reins. = Reinsurance (*Incisive Media Plc*)
Rep. B. = Reparation Bulletin (*S&M/W. Green*)
Rep. L.R. = Reparation Law Reports (*S&M/W. Green*)
Res Publica = Res Publica (*Springer*)
Res. B. = Home Office Research Bulletin (*Home Office Research & Statistics Department*)
Resolver = The Resolver (*Chartered Institute of Arbitrators*)
Rev. = The Review (*Resolution*)
Rev. C.E.E. Law = Review of Central and East European Law (*Martinus Nijhoff Publishers*)
Revenue = Revenue (*S&M*)
Review = Review (*Informa Publishing Group Ltd*)
Risk M.R. = Risk Management Reports (*Seawrack Press, Inc.*)
Risk Man. = Risk Management (*Risk Management Society Publishing Inc*)

Risk Update = Risk Update (*Informa Publishing Group Ltd*)
Road L. = Road Law (*Butterworth Tolley Publishing*)
Road L.R. = Road Law Reports (*Butterworth Tolley Publishing*)
Road Law = Road Law and Road Law Reports (*Butterworth Tolley Publishing*)

S. & C.L. = Sports and Character Licensing (*Informa Publishing Group Ltd*)
S. & L.J. = Sport and the Law Journal (*British Association for Sport and Law*)
S. & L.S. = Social & Legal Studies (*Sage Publications Ltd*)
S. & T.I. = Shipping & Transport International (*Guthrum House Ltd*)
S. & T.L.I. = Shipping & Transport Lawyer International (*Guthrum House Ltd*)
S. News = Sentencing News (*S&M*)
S.B. = Scottish Banker (*The Chartered Institute of Bankers in Scotland*)
S.B.T. & F. = Small Business Tax & Finance (*Cyan Publishing Services*)
S.C. = Session Cases (*S&M/W. Green*)
S.C.A.L. & P. = Scottish Constitutional and Administrative Law & Practice (*XPL Publishing*)
S.C.C.R. = Scottish Criminal Case Reports (*The Law Society of Scotland*)
S.C.L. = Scottish Criminal Law (*S&M/W. Green*)
S.C.L. Rev. = Scottish Construction Law Review (*S&M/W. Green*)
S.C.L.R. = Scottish Civil Law Reports (*The Law Society of Scotland*)
S.C.L.T. = Social Care Law Today (*Arden Davies Publishing*)
S.C.P. = Supreme Court Practice, The (*S&M*)
S.C.P. News = Supreme Court Practice News (*S&M*)
S.E.G.J. = Law Society Solicitors' European Group Journal (*Butterworth Tolley Publishing*)
S.F.L.L. = Scottish Family Law Legislation (*S&M/W. Green*)
S.H.E. & P.G. = Stephenson Harwood Employment and Pensions Group (*Stephenson Harwood*)
S.H.R.J. = Scottish Human Rights Journal (*S&M/W. Green*)
S.I. = Statutory Instruments (*TSO*)
S.I.R. = Space Insurance Report (*Informa Publishing Group Ltd*)
S.J. = Solicitors Journal (*Waterlow Legal & Regulatory*)
S.J.L.B. = Solicitors Journal LawBrief (*Waterlow Legal & Regulatory*)
S.L. & F. = Sports Law & Finance (*Informa Publishing Group Ltd*)
S.L. Rev. = Student Law Review (*Routledge-Cavendish*)
S.L.A. & P. = Sports Law Administration & Practice (*Ivy House Sports Law Publications Ltd*)
S.L.B. = Sports Law Bulletin (*Anglia Sports Law Research Centre*)
S.L.C.R. = Scottish Land Court Reports (*The Law Society of Scotland*)
S.L.G. = Scottish Law Gazette (*Scottish Law Agents Society*)
S.L.L.P. = Scottish Licensing Law and Practice (*Licensing Services Ltd*)
S.L.P.Q. = Scottish Law & Practice Quarterly (*Butterworth Tolley Publishing*)
S.L.T. = Scots Law Times (*S&M/W. Green*)
S.M.M. = Single Market Monitor (*Butterworth Tolley Publishing*)
S.P.C.L.R. = Scottish Private Client Law Review (*S&M/W. Green*)
S.P.E.L. = Scottish Planning and Environmental Law (*IDOX Information Solutions Ltd*)
S.P.L.P. = Scottish Planning Law & Practice (*IDOX Information Services*)
S.P.L.R. = Scottish Parliament Law Review (*S&M/W. Green*)
S.P.T.L. Reporter = Society of Public Teachers of Law Reporter (*OUP*)
S.S.L.R. = Southampton Student Law Review (*University of Southampton*)
S.T.C. = Simon's Tax Cases (*Butterworth Tolley Publishing*)
S.T.L. = Shipping and Trade Law (*Informa Publishing Group Ltd*)
S.W.T.I. = Simon's Weekly Tax Intelligence (*Butterworth Tolley Publishing*)
SCOLAG = SCOLAG (*Scottish Legal Action Group*)
SCRIPT-ed = SCRIPT-ed (*University of Edinburgh*)
STEP Journal = The STEP Journal (*Barker Brooks Media Ltd*)
Sigma = Sigma (*Swiss Reinsurance Company*)
Soc. L. = Socialist Lawyer (*Haldane Society of Socialist Lawyers*)
Sol. = Solutions (*Dispute Resolution Section/ The Law Society*)
Stat. L.R. = Statute Law Review (*OUP*)
Sudebnik = Sudebnik (*Wildy & Sons Ltd*)

T. & E.P. = Trust & Estates Practitioner (*Tru-Est Limited*)
T. & E.T.J. = Trusts and Estates Tax Journal (*Legalease Ltd*)
T. & T. = Trusts & Trustees (*OUP*)
T. Sol. = Today's Solicitor (*S&M*)
T.A.Q. = The Aviation Quarterly (*Informa Publishing Group Ltd*)
T.B. = Technical Bulletin (*Association of Business Recovery Professionals*)
T.B.S.P.I. = Technical Bulletin of the Society of Practitioners of Insolvency (*Association of Business Recovery Professionals*)
T.C. = Tax Cases (*TSO*)
T.C.L.R. = Technology and Construction Law Reports (*S&M*)
T.E.L. & P. = Tolley's Employment Law & Practice (*Butterworth Tolley Publishing*)
T.E.L. & T.J. = Trusts and Estates Law & Tax Journal (*Legalease Ltd*)
T.E.L.J. = Technology and Entertainment Law Journal (*S&M/Round Hall*)
T.E.L.L. = Tolley's Employment Law-Line (*Butterworth Tolley Publishing*)
T.F.A. = Transactions of the Faculty of Actuaries (*Faculty of Actuaries*)
T.I.A. = Troubled Insurer Alert (*Evandale Publishing Co Ltd*)
T.I.J.M.C.L. = The International Journal of Marine & Coastal Law (*Martinus Nijhoff Publishers*)
T.K.B.E.L.I.S. = Turner Kenneth Brown European Legal Information Service (*Turner Kenneth Brown*)
T.L. & P. = Trust Law & Practice (*Cass*)
T.L.J. = Travel Law Journal (*The Travel Law Centre*)

T.L.P. = Transport Law & Policy (*The Waterfront Partnership*)
T.L.T. = Telecoms Law Today (*Informa Publishing Group Ltd*)
T.M.I.F. = Tax Management International Forum (*BNA International Inc*)
T.N.I.B. = Tolley's National Insurance Brief (*Butterworth Tolley Publishing*)
T.O.C. = Transnational Organized Crime (*Cass*)
T.O.T.R. = Tolley's Overseas Tax Reporter (*Butterworth Tolley Publishing*)
T.P.A. & A. = Tolley's Practical Audit & Accounting (*Butterworth Tolley Publishing*)
T.P.H. = Towers Perrin Headlines (*Towers Perrin*)
T.P.I. e-commerce = Tax Planning International e-commerce (*BNA International Inc*)
T.P.I.A.P.F. = Tax Planning International Asia-Pacific Focus (*BNA International Inc*)
T.P.I.E.U.F. = Tax Planning International European Union Focus (*BNA International Inc*)
T.P.I.I.T. = Tax Planning International Indirect Taxes (*BNA International Inc*)
T.P.I.J. = Transfer Pricing International Journal (*BNA International Inc*)
T.P.I.R. = Tax Planning International Review (*BNA International Inc*)
T.P.I.T.P. = Tax Planning International Transfer Pricing (*BNA International Inc*)
T.P.I.U. = Towers Perrin International Update (*Towers Perrin*)
T.P.N. = Tolley's Practical NIC (*Butterworth Tolley Publishing*)
T.P.N.N. = Tolley's Practical NIC Newsletter (*Butterworth Tolley Publishing*)
T.P.N.S. = Tolley's Practical NIC Service (*Butterworth Tolley Publishing*)
T.P.T. = Tolley's Practical Tax (*Butterworth Tolley Publishing*)
T.P.T.N. = Tolley's Practical Tax Newsletter (*Butterworth Tolley Publishing*)
T.P.T.S. = Tolley's Practical Tax Service (*Butterworth Tolley Publishing*)
T.P.U. = Towers Perrin Update (*Towers Perrin*)
T.P.V. = Tolley's Practical VAT (*Butterworth Tolley Publishing*)
T.P.V.N. = Tolley's Practical VAT Newsletter (*Butterworth Tolley Publishing*)
T.P.V.S. = Tolley's Practical VAT Service (*Butterworth Tolley Publishing*)
T.Q.R. = Trust Quarterly Review (*Barker Brooks Media Ltd*)
T.T.I. = Tolley's Tax Investigation (*Butterworth Tolley Publishing*)
T.W. = Trademark World (*Informa Publishing Group Ltd*)
TACT Review = The Association of Corporate Trustees Review (*The Association of Corporate Trustees*)
Tax & Inv. = Tax and Investment (*Tax & Financial Publishing*)
Tax A. = Tax Adviser (*Butterworth Tolley Publishing*)
Tax B. = Tax Briefing (*Office of the Revenue Commissioners*)
Tax Bus. = Tax Business (*Legalease Ltd*)
Tax C. = Tax Commentary (*Incorporated Law Society of Ireland*)
Tax J. = Tax Journal (*Butterworth Tolley Publishing*)
Tax P.N. = Tax Practice Notes (*Incorporated Law Society of Ireland*)
Tax. = Taxation (*Butterworth Tolley Publishing*)
Tax. Int. = Taxation International (*Butterworth Tolley Publishing*)
Tax. P. = Taxation Practitioner (*The Chartered Institute of Taxation*)
Taxline = Taxline (*ICAEW*)
The Sentence = The Sentence (*Sentencing Guidelines Secretariat*)
Theo. Crim. = Theoretical Criminology (*Sage Publications Ltd*)
Tort & Ins. L.J. = Tort and Insurance Law Journal (*Tort and Insurance Practice Section*)
Tort. L.R. = Tort Law Review (*S&M/ESC Publishing*)
Tr. & Est. = Trusts & Estates (*Informa Publishing Group Ltd*)
Tr. L.R. = Trading Law Reports (*Butterworth Tolley Publishing*)
Tr. Law = Trading Law & Trading Law Reports (*Butterworth Tolley Publishing*)
Trad. L. = Trading Law (*Barry Rose Law Periodicals*)
Trans. L. & P. = Transport Law & Policy (*The Waterfront Partnership*)
Trans. L.T. = Transnational Legal Theory (*Hart Publishing Ltd*)
Trent L.J. = Trent Law Journal (*Nottingham Law School*)
Tribunals = Tribunals (*Judicial Studies Board*)
Tru. & E.L.J. = Trusts & Estates Law Journal (*Legalease Ltd*)
Tru. L.I. = Trust Law International (*Bloomsbury Publishing Plc*)
Trustee = Trustee (*MSM International Ltd*)

U.K. Ins. Broker = UK Insurance Broker (*Institute of Insurance Broker Publication Ltd*)
U.K.C.L.R. = UK Competition Law Reports (*Jordan & Sons Ltd*)
U.K.H.R.R. = United Kingdom Human Rights Reports (*Jordan & Sons Ltd*)
U.L.R. = Utilities Law Review (*Lawtext Publishing Limited*)
UCELNET = Universities and Colleges Education Law Network (*University of Stirling*)
UCL J.L. and J. = UCL Journal of Law and Jurisprudence (*University College London*)
UCL Juris. Rev. = UCL Jurisprudence Review (*University College London*)
UK Prac. Dir. = UK Practice Directions (*TSO*)
UK Pre. Pro. = UK Preaction Protocols (*TSO*)
Uniform L.R. = Uniform Law Review (*UNIDROIT*)

V. & D.R. = Value Added Tax and Duties Tribunals Reports (*TSO*)
V.A.T.T.R. = Value Added Tax Tribunal Reports (*TSO*)
VAT Dig. = VAT Digest (*Bloomsbury Publishing Plc*)
VAT Int. = VAT Intelligence (*Watchfield Publishing Ltd*)
VAT Plan. = VAT Planning (*Butterworth Tolley Publishing*)

W. Comp. = World Competition (*Turpin Distribution Serv Ltd*)
W.B. = Welfare Benefits (*XPL Publishing*)
W.C.R.R. = World Communications Regulation Report (*BNA International Inc*)

W.D.P.R. = World Data Protection Report (*BNA International Inc*)
W.E.C. & I.P.R. = World E-Commerce & IP Report (*BNA International Inc*)
W.F.S.B. = World Fire Statistics Bulletin (*Geneva Association*)
W.I. Rep. = World Insurance Report (*Financial Times Finance*)
W.I.C.R. = World Insurance Corporate Report (*Financial Times Finance*)
W.I.P.O.J. = WIPO Journal (*Sweet and Maxwell*)
W.I.P.R. = World Intellectual Property Report (*BNA International Inc*)
W.J.V. = World Journal of VAT/GST Law (*Hart Publishing Ltd*)
W.L. = Water Law (*Lawtext Publishing Limited*)
W.L.L.R. = World Licensing Law Report (*BNA International Inc*)
W.L.R. = Weekly Law Reports (*ICLR*)
W.L.T.B. = Woodfall Landlord & Tenant Bulletin (*S&M*)
W.M. = Wastes Management (*IWM Business Services Ltd*)
W.O.G.L.R. = World Online Gambling Law Report (*Cecile Park Publishing Ltd*)
W.P.G. = World Policy Guide (*Financial Times Finance*)
W.Q. = Watsons Quarterly (*R. Watson & Sons*)
W.R.T.L.B. = Wilkinson's Road Traffic Law Bulletin (*S&M*)
W.S.L. Rev. = Warwick Student Law Review (*University of Warwick*)
W.S.L.R. = World Sports Law Report (*Cecile Park Publishing Ltd*)
W.T.J. = World Tax Journal (*IBFD Publications BV*)
W.T.L.R. = Wills & Trusts Law Reports (*Legalease Ltd*)
W.T.R. = World Tax Report (*Financial Times Finance*)
Watsons E.C. = Watsons Euro Comment (*R. Watson & Sons*)
Watsons I.R. = Watsons Insurance Review (*R. Watson & Sons*)
Watsons P.N. = Watsons Pensions News (*R. Watson & Sons*)
Watsons R.R. = Watsons Remuneration Review (*R. Watson & Sons*)
Watsons W.R. = Watsons Worldwide Review (*R. Watson & Sons*)
Web J.C.L.I. = Web Journal of Current Legal Issues (*Web Journal of Current Legal Issues*)
Wel. & Fam. L. & P. = Welfare and Family: Law & Practice (*XPL Publishing*)
Welf. R. Bull. = Welfare Rights Bulletin (*Child Poverty Action Group Ltd*)
Woodfall = Woodfall: Landlord & Tenant (*S&M*)
World I.L.R. = World Internet Law Report (*BNA International Inc*)
World T.R. = World Trade Review (*CUP*)
Worldlaw Bus. = Worldlaw Business (*Euromoney Institutional Investor Plc*)
Writ = Writ (*Law Society of Northern Ireland*)

Y.C. & M.L. = Yearbook of Copyright & Media Law (*OUP*)
Y.E.L. = Yearbook of European Law (*OUP*)
Y.J. = Youth Justice (*Sage Publications Ltd*)
Y.L.C.T. = Yearbook of Law Computers & Technology (*Taylor & Francis Ltd*)
Y.M.E.L. = Yearbook of Media & Entertainment Law (*OUP*)
YSG Mag. = Young Solicitors Group Magazine (*Young Solicitors Group*)
Yb. Int'l Env. L. = Yearbook of International Environmental Law (*OUP*)

CURRENT LAW

YEAR BOOK 2013

UK, ENGLAND & WALES & EU

ACCOUNTANCY

1. **Disciplinary tribunals–Natural justice–Temporary absence of panel member with consent–Whether outside tribunal's powers and jurisdiction–Whether breach of natural justice waived**

The appellant chartered accountant (H) appealed against a decision ([2012] EWHC 1731 (QB)) refusing his application for judicial review of a decision by the respondent Institute in disciplinary proceedings. On the fourth day of the disciplinary hearing, during cross-examination of H, and with the agreement of the advocates acting for each party, one of the tribunal members left early. He read a transcript of what he had missed and returned for the final two days which were heard almost six weeks later. The tribunal found H guilty of unprofessional conduct. On H's judicial review application the judge held that by allowing a member to depart and then take part in the rest of the hearing there had been a breach of the rules of natural justice, but that the breach had been waived. H argued that (1) the tribunal had acted beyond its powers, and that could not be cured by agreement; (2) the breach of natural justice that "he who decides must hear" had been so grave that the tribunal had acted without jurisdiction, and acting without jurisdiction could not be consented to; (3) any consent had to be from H personally.

Held: Appeal dismissed. (1) It would be surprising if there were no power at all for a disciplinary tribunal to permit one member to depart and return if all parties agreed. That would introduce an undesirable degree of rigidity. The fact that express power was given under the respondent's bye-law 19 to carry on as a tribunal of a lesser number if one member was "unable to continue... to attend" did not preclude a member absenting himself and returning. When dealing with bye-laws and regulations of professional disciplinary bodies it could not be expected that every contingency would have been foreseen and provided for, *Virdi v Law Society* [2010] EWCA Civ 100, [2010] 1 W.L.R. 2840, [2010] C.L.Y. 2144 applied. The right question to ask of any procedure adopted should therefore be not whether it was permitted but whether it was prohibited. In the instant case, the procedure adopted was not prohibited (see paras 11-13 of judgment). (2) A decision reached in breach of the rules of natural justice was not a decision reached without jurisdiction. The most it could be was a breach of the tribunal's adjudicative jurisdiction, and there was no reason why such breach could not be agreed to or waived, *Carter v Ahsan* [2007] UKHL 51, [2008] 1 A.C. 696, [2008] C.L.Y. 379 considered. Further, if there was an agreement to the procedure adopted, it was preferable to say that there had been no breach of natural justice at all (paras 25-26, 30). (3) A tribunal was entitled, in the absence of evidence of pressure on the client or concealment of material facts, to rely on the agreement of a properly qualified advocate to any proposed procedural course without having to check that his client personally agreed with what the advocate had said. H's advocate had agreed to the proposed course, there had been an opportunity on the day for H to speak to his advocate before the hearing continued after the member's departure and there had been six weeks before the resumed hearing which gave every opportunity for second thoughts. It could not be accepted that H's consent had not been voluntary or had been uninformed (paras 33-34, 36).

R. (ON THE APPLICATION OF HILL) v INSTITUTE OF CHARTERED ACCOUNTANTS IN ENGLAND AND WALES, [2013] EWCA Civ 555, [2014] 1 W.L.R. 86, Longmore, L.J., CA (Civ Div).

2. **Public Audit (Wales) Act 2013 (anaw 3)–Commencement, Consequential Amendments, Transitional and Saving Provisions Wales Order–Wales**

THE PUBLIC AUDIT (WALES) ACT 2013 (COMMENCEMENT, CONSEQUENTIAL AMENDMENTS, TRANSITIONAL AND SAVING PROVISIONS) (WALES) ORDER 2013, SI 2013/SI 2013/1466 (W.138) (C.56); made under the Public Audit (Wales) Act 2013 s.35. Commencement details: bringing into force various provisions of the 2013 Act on July 4, 2013 and April 1, 2014.; .

This Order is made in consequence of the Public Audit (Wales) Act 2013, which makes provision reforming public audit arrangements in Wales.

ADMINISTRATION OF JUSTICE

3. **Administrative Justice and Tribunals Council–Consequential amendments–Dissolution**

THE PUBLIC BODIES (ABOLITION OF ADMINISTRATIVE JUSTICE AND TRIBUNALS COUNCIL) ORDER 2013, SI 2013/2042; made under the Public Bodies Act 2011 s.1, s.6, s.35. In force: August 19, 2013 except for Sch.1 para.41 (a) on August 20, 2013.; .

The purpose of this instrument is to abolish the Administrative Justice and Tribunals Council (AJTC). The Order abolishes the AJTC and the Schedule to the Order makes a number of consequential amendments and repeals to legislation which refer to the AJTC or its Committees.

4. **Aircraft–Arbitration–Shipbuilding–Tribunals**

THE PUBLIC BODIES (ABOLITION OF THE AIRCRAFT AND SHIPBUILDING INDUSTRIES ARBITRATION TRIBUNAL) ORDER 2013, SI 2013/686; made under the Public Bodies Act 2011 s.1, s.6, s.35. In force: March 22, 2013 except for Sch.1 para.10 on March 23, 2013.; .

This instrument abolishes the Aircraft and Shipbuilding Industries Arbitration Tribunal.

5. **Appeals–Council tax–Non-domestic rates–Valuation Tribunal for England**

THE VALUATION TRIBUNAL FOR ENGLAND (COUNCIL TAX AND RATING APPEALS) (PROCEDURE) (AMENDMENT) REGULATIONS 2013, SI 2013/465; made under the Local Government Finance Act 1988 s.143, Sch.11 para.A19, Sch.11 para.8, Sch.11 para.11. In force: April 1, 2013; .

These Regulations amend the Valuation Tribunal for England (Council Tax and Rating Appeals) (Procedure) Regulations 2009 and make certain changes in relation to how council tax appeals are treated.

6. Appeals–Findings of fact–Dispute between father and son over disposition of heritable properties–Approach of appellate court to findings of fact by first instance court

The appellant father (M) appealed against a decision of the Inner House ([2012] CSIH 23, 2012 G.W.D. 15-310) allowing an appeal by the respondents, his son (X) and his son's partner (Y), in respect of the disposition of one of two heritable properties. M had returned to Scotland from living in the United States and asked X, who was a property developer, to find him a suitable property. X identified one and M transferred the necessary funds to X to arrange the purchase. Unknown to M, X arranged for the title to be in his own name. M moved into the property. A year later, M gave X a cheque for £285,000. X and Y used most of the money to buy another property in their names. Later that year, M brought proceedings against X and Y seeking various remedies, including the conveyance of the properties to him. He claimed that X had acted without his authority in taking title to them. The Outer House concluded that X's evidence was unreliable and preferred M's evidence. It found that X had taken title to the first property without any instructions to do so, or any indication that M intended to gift it to him. That breach of trust was a consideration in its decision that M was also entitled to the second property. X's appeal was confined to the second property. The Inner House identified a number of aspects of the evidence which it considered undermined M's account, and concluded that the Outer House had been "plainly wrong" to find otherwise. It concluded that it was therefore entitled to reach its own decision and found that the £285,000 was a gift to X. The issue was whether there had been a failure by the Inner House to follow the proper approach of an appellate court to a decision on fact made by the court of first instance.

Held: Appeal allowed. The aspects of the evidence that the Inner House considered undermined M's account and supported X's had been expressly taken into account by the Outer House in reaching its conclusion regarding M's credibility. Even if it had not mentioned those aspects, it would be presumed to have taken the whole of the evidence into consideration, *Thomas v Thomas* [1947] A.C. 484, [1947-51] C.L.Y. 7496 and *Clarke v Edinburgh & District Tramways Co Ltd* 1919 S.C. (H.L.) 35 followed. Where the court was faced with a stark choice between irreconcilable accounts, the credibility of the parties' testimony was an issue of primary importance. The Outer House found that M was a credible witness on the central issue, notwithstanding a number of aspects of the evidence which could be regarded as detracting from his credibility. The weight of the evidence adverse to M's credibility had to be considered in the context of the evidence as a whole, and it was for the Outer House to determine his overall credibility. The Inner House had focused solely on those aspects of the evidence detracting from M's credibility, and there was no indication in its opinion that any weight had been given to the extent to which the Outer House's conclusion had been affected by the way in which the principal witnesses gave their evidence; a matter which the Inner House was unable to assess from the printed record. However, it was plain that that aspect of the evidence had an important bearing on the Outer House's assessment of credibility, and there was no evidence that the Inner House had considered the significance of the Outer House's assessment of M and X's character. Those character findings had an evident bearing on the likelihood of M having made a gift of the £285,000 and X having acted contrary to M's instructions. There was also no indication that the Inner House had considered the significance of the unchallenged finding that X had acted in breach of trust in relation to the purchase of the first property, a finding which evidently bore on the likelihood of his having done so again. Nowhere in its opinion did the Inner House subject X's evidence to the evaluation against other evidence that it had carried out in respect of M. With regard to the Inner House's criticism that the Outer House must have failed to appreciate the weight or bearing of the aspects of the evidence on which the Inner House had focused its attention, the Outer House had plainly taken that evidence into account and had nonetheless concluded that M was telling the truth about the central issue. In the overall circumstances, the Inner House had had no proper basis for concluding that the Outer House had erred, let alone that on a reconsideration of the whole evidence the opposite conclusion should be reached, *Piglowska v Piglowski* [1999] 1 W.L.R. 1360, [1999] C.L.Y. 2421 and *Housen v Nikolaisen* [2002] 2 S.C.R. 235 considered (see paras 26-33 of judgment).

McGRADDIE v McGRADDIE, [2013] UKSC 58, [2013] 1 W.L.R. 2477, Lord Neuberger (President), SC.

7. **Appointments–Judges–Judiciary**

THE JUDICIAL APPOINTMENTS REGULATIONS 2013, SI 2013/2192; made under the Constitutional Reform Act 2005 s.94, s.94C. In force: October 1, 2013; .

These Regulations make provision for the selection process applicable to the appointment of a variety of judicial office holders.

8. **Appointments–Justices of the Supreme Court–Supreme Court**

THE SUPREME COURT (JUDICIAL APPOINTMENTS) REGULATIONS 2013, SI 2013/2193; made under the Constitutional Reform Act 2005 s.27A. In force: October 1, 2013; .

These Regulations set out details of the selection process for the appointment of Supreme Court Justices, including the composition of selection commissions.

9. **Closure–County courts–Divorce–Wiltshire**

THE CIVIL COURTS (AMENDMENT) ORDER 2013, SI 2013/415; made under the County Courts Act 1984 s.2; the Matrimonial and Family Proceedings Act 1984 s.33; the Insolvency Act 1986 s.117, s.374; and the Companies Act 2006 s.1156. In force: March 25, 2013; .

This Order amends the Civil Courts Order 1983 (SI 1983/713). It provides for a new county court at Chippenham, named Chippenham and Trowbridge County Court which is to have divorce jurisdiction. Burton-on-Trent County Court and Trowbridge County Court are discontinued.

10. **Complaints–Coroners–Disciplinary procedures–Investigations**

THE JUDICIAL DISCIPLINE (PRESCRIBED PROCEDURES) REGULATIONS 2013, SI 2013/1674; made under the Coroners and Justice Act 2009 Sch.3 para.14; and the Constitutional Reform Act 2005 s.115, s.120, s.121. In force: October 1, 2013; .

These Regulations make provision for the investigation and determination of complaints of misconduct by a judicial office holder, a senior coroner, an area coroner, an assistant coroner or an office that has been designated by an order under the Constitutional Reform Act 2005 s.118.

11. **Contempt of court–Court of Appeal–Broadcasting–Video recordings**

THE COURT OF APPEAL (RECORDING AND BROADCASTING) ORDER 2013, SI 2013/2786; made under the Crime and Courts Act 2013 s.32. In force: October 30, 2013; .

This Order prescribes the conditions to be satisfied for the recording and broadcast of hearings in the Court of Appeal. Where the conditions are satisfied, s.41 of the Criminal Justice Act 1925 and s.9 of the Contempt of Court Act 1981 do not have effect. It also sets out the types of hearing that can be recorded, what part of the hearing can be recorded and who can record a hearing, and when the recording of a hearing can be broadcast and what content is permitted in a broadcast.

12. Coroners and Justice Act 2009 (c.25)–Commencement No.11 Order 2013

THE CORONERS AND JUSTICE ACT 2009 (COMMENCEMENT NO.11) ORDER 2013, SI 2013/SI 2013/250 (C.12); made under the Coroners and Justice Act 2009 s.176, s.182. Commencement details: bringing into force various provisions of the 2009 Act on February 12, 2013.; .

This Order brings into force provisions of the Coroners and Justice Act 2009. Article 2 commences the repeal of section 5(2) of the Coroners Act 1988. Section 5(2) of that Act permitted the coroner to hold an inquest only within that coroner's district. This repeal will remove the geographical restriction on where an inquest may take place.

13. Coroners and Justice Act 2009 (c.25)–Commencement No.12 Order

THE CORONERS AND JUSTICE ACT 2009 (COMMENCEMENT NO.12) ORDER 2013, SI 2013/SI 2013/705 (C.32); made under the Coroners and Justice Act 2009 s.182. Commencement details: bringing into force various provisions of the 2009 Act on April 22, 2013.; .

This Order brings into force the Coroners and Justice Act 2009 ss.117(4), (5), (6), (7) and (8) on April 22, 2013. These provisions amend the Police Reform Act 2002 s.51 so that local policing bodies must ensure that particular arrangements in relation to the visiting of terrorist detainees by independent custody visitors are in place.

14. Coroners and Justice Act 2009 (c.25) Commencement No.15, Consequential and Transitory Provisions Order

THE CORONERS AND JUSTICE ACT 2009 (COMMENCEMENT NO.15, CONSEQUENTIAL AND TRANSITORY PROVISIONS) ORDER 2013, SI 2013/SI 2013/1869 (C.80); made under the Coroners and Justice Act 2009 s.176, s.182. Commencement details: bringing into force various provisions of the 2009 Act on July 25, 2013.; .

This Order commences the majority of provisions relating to coroners in the Coroners and Justice Act 2009 and repeals most of the Coroners Act 1988.

15. Court of Appeal–Judicial decision-making–Power to review and alter custodial sentence imposed by Special Immigration Appeals Commission for contempt of court

[Administration of Justice Act 1960 (c.65) s.13; European Convention on Human Rights 1950 Art.3, Art.8.]

The appellant (B) appealed against the dismissal ([2011] EWCA Civ 828, (2011) 161 N.L.J. 1060) of his appeal against a sentence of four months' imprisonment imposed by the Special Immigration Appeals Commission (SIAC) for his deliberate refusal to comply with an order to reveal his true identity. B had unsuccessfully argued before the Court of Appeal (Civil Division) that committal to prison would violate his rights under the European Convention on Human Rights 1950 art.3 and art.8, and that the term of imprisonment was excessive. The court held that although SIAC had erred in its interpretation and rejection of expert medical reports, the appeal should be dismissed. The majority found the custodial sentence to be quite lenient. B's case was that the Court of Appeal had deferred to SIAC's selection of the appropriate sentence, wrongly determining that it was proper just because it was not manifestly excessive, and that it should have performed a fresh assessment of the proper penalty. The Court of Appeal refused permission to appeal but certified two questions, namely (i) whether it was correct to adopt the approach of the Court of Appeal (Criminal Division) and only allow an appeal where a sentence was manifestly excessive or whether the Administration of Justice Act 1960 s.13 gave it a broader discretion enabling it to remit a case where a first instance judgment regarding sentence was flawed and/or procedurally unfair; (ii) whether it had to remit a case where a first instance judgment regarding sentence imposed in a contempt case was flawed and/or procedurally unfair unless the same conclusion would have been reached absent the error.

Held: Appeal dismissed. (1) The first certified question did not require an answer because the Court of Appeal had concentrated exclusively on the propriety of the length of sentence in order to decide how long B should serve as punishment for his contempt. It did not follow that the sentence chosen by a lower court was inevitably wrong where an appellate court concluded that it had been made on a flawed basis. Affirming the original sentence did not necessarily entail endorsing the reasons on which it was based. However, where an appellate court held that a sentence had been imposed on the wrong basis, a *de novo* assessment had to occur. That did not necessarily mean remitting the case to the sentencing court. It was beyond argument that the Court of Appeal had performed a *de novo* assessment, because it had reached conclusions favourable to B in the process, and because its decision that committal to prison was appropriate had been reached on a completely different basis from that on which the SIAC had deemed committal appropriate. The Court of Appeal had been faced with a sentence chosen on an erroneous basis, but it was nevertheless a sentence designed to punish contempt which the SIAC had found to exist. The Court of Appeal had found that some term of imprisonment was required and had examined whether the term was suitable punishment. It would have been artificial to ignore the sentence already imposed by the SIAC (see paras 11-13, 15, 20-24 of judgment). (2) An appellate court only had to remit a case where a first instance judgment regarding sentence imposed in a contempt case was flawed and/or procedurally unfair if it considered that a fresh investigation of new facts was required and that it was desirable for the first instance court to undertake that investigation (para.24). (3) Committal was appropriate for a contempt of court where it could reasonably be expected to have a coercive effect and induce the contemnor to purge his contempt. It was also appropriate as a penal tool to punish contempt of a court order. Frequently both elements would underlie a committal order. The fact that the person subject to it already had substantial restrictions on his liberty was immaterial (para.14).

B (ALGERIA) v SECRETARY OF STATE FOR THE HOME DEPARTMENT, [2013] UKSC 4, [2013] 1 W.L.R. 435, Lord Neuberger (President), SC.

16. Courts–Fees–Judicial review–Tribunals

THE COURTS AND TRIBUNALS FEE REMISSIONS ORDER 2013, SI 2013/SI 2013/2302 (L.2); made under the Insolvency Act 1986 s.414, s.415; the Courts Act 2003 s.92; the Constitutional Reform Act 2005 s.52; the Mental Capacity Act 2005 s.54; and the Tribunals, Courts and Enforcement Act 2007 s.42. In force: October 7, 2013; .

This Order will introduce: a single fee remissions system to all court and tribunals subject to this instrument; and a new £215 Judicial Review oral renewal hearing fee.

17. Crime and Courts Act 2013 9 (c.22)–Commencement No.3 Order

THE CRIME AND COURTS ACT 2013 (COMMENCEMENT NO.3) ORDER 2013, SI 2013/SI 2013/1725 (C.69); made under the Crime and Courts Act 2013 s.61. Commencement details: bringing into force various provisions of the 2013 Act on July 15, 2013 and October 1, 2013.; .

This Order commences provisions of the Crime and Courts Act 2013 concerning matters including: judicial appointments; permission to appeal from the Upper Tribunal to the Court of Session; and the appointment and terms and conditions of the chief executive, officers and staff of the Supreme Court.

18. Crime and Courts Act 2013 (c.22)

This Act establishes, and makes provision about, the National Crime Agency; abolishes the Serious Organised Crime Agency and the National Policing Improvement Agency; makes provision about the judiciary and the structure, administration, proceedings and powers of courts and tribunals; makes provision about border control; and makes provision about drugs and driving.

This Act received Royal Assent on April 25, 2013.

19. Crime and Courts Act 2013 (c.22)–Commencement No.4 Order

THE CRIME AND COURTS ACT 2013 (COMMENCEMENT NO.4) ORDER 2013, SI 2013/SI 2013/2200 (C.90); made under the Crime and Courts Act 2013 s.61. Commencement details: bringing into force various provisions of the 2013 Act on September 4, 2013, October 1, 2013 and November 1, 2013.; .

This Order commences a number of provisions of the Crime and Courts Act 2013 September 4, 2013, October 1, 2013 and November 1, 2013. The provisions concern judicial appointments and the deployment of the judiciary.

20. Crown Office–Fees–Revocation

THE CROWN OFFICE FEES ORDER 2013, SI 2013/986; made under the Great Seal (Offices) Act 1874 s.9. In force: May 20, 2013; .

This Order revokes and replaces the Crown Office Fees Order 2008 (SI 2008/1977) and lists fees taken in the office of the Clerk of the Crown in Chancery that have been increased.

21. Department for Communities and Local Government–Lord President–Secretaries of State–Transfer of functions

THE TRANSFER OF FUNCTIONS (ELECTIONS AND REFERENDUMS) ORDER 2013, SI 2013/2597; made under the Ministers of the Crown Act 1975 s.1. In force: November 6, 2013; .

This Order makes provision for various functions of the Secretary of State for Communities and Local Government in relation to elections and referendums to be exercisable concurrently with the Lord President of the Council.

22. Employment Appeal Tribunal–Employment tribunals

THE EMPLOYMENT TRIBUNALS AND THE EMPLOYMENT APPEAL TRIBUNAL FEES ORDER 2013, SI 2013/1893; made under the Tribunals, Courts and Enforcement Act 2007 s.42, s.49. In force: July 29, 2013; .

The Added Tribunals (Employment Tribunals and the Employment Appeal Tribunal) Order 2013 (SI 2013/1892) provides for employment tribunals and the Employment Appeal Tribunal to be "added tribunals" to enable fees to be introduced. This Order stipulates the fees to be paid.

23. Employment tribunals–Employment Appeal Tribunal

THE ADDED TRIBUNALS (EMPLOYMENT TRIBUNALS AND EMPLOYMENT APPEAL TRIBUNAL) ORDER 2013, SI 2013/1892; made under the Tribunals, Courts and Enforcement Act 2007 s.42. In force: July 28, 2013; .

This Order provides for employment tribunals and the Employment Appeal Tribunal to be "added tribunals" to enable fees to be introduced.

24. Fees–Jurisdiction–Privy Council–Records

THE JUDICIAL COMMITTEE (APPELLATE JURISDICTION) RULES (AMENDMENT) ORDER 2013, SI 2013/246; made under the Judicial Committee Act 1833 s.24; the Judicial Committee Act 1844 s.1; the Veterinary Surgeons Act 1966 s.17; and the Brunei (Appeals) Act 1989 s.1. In force: April 1, 2013; .

This Order amends the rules which govern the practice and procedure for appeals to the Judicial Committee of the Privy Council, the Judicial Committee (Appellate Jurisdiction) Rules 2009. One of the main changes effected by this Order is to introduce a revised fee structure under which the amount of the fee depends upon the value of the appeal, that is, the sum of money sought to be recovered or the value of the land, property or relief which is the subject of the appeal. The amendment to Rule 7 introduces the requirement to provide a certificate of value.

25. Fees–Lands Chamber–Upper Tribunal

THE UPPER TRIBUNAL (LANDS CHAMBER) FEES (AMENDMENT) ORDER 2013, SI 2013/1199; made under the Tribunals, Courts and Enforcement Act 2007 s.42, s.49. In force: July 1, 2013; .

This Order provides that where a case has been transferred from the Property Chamber to the Upper Tribunal (Lands Chamber) the fee payable is the fee that would have applied in the Property Chamber.

26. Fees–Magistrates' courts

THE MAGISTRATES' COURTS FEES (AMENDMENT) ORDER 2013, SI 2013/SI 2013/1409 (L.12); made under the Courts Act 2003 s.92, s.108. In force: July 1, 2013; .

This Order amends the Magistrates' Courts Fees Order 2008 (SI 2008/1052). It increases certain fees that are payable in magistrates courts by the cumulative rate of inflation since those fees were last increased.

27. First-tier Tribunal–Lands Chamber

THE TRIBUNAL PROCEDURE (FIRST-TIER TRIBUNAL) (PROPERTY CHAMBER) RULES 2013, SI 2013/SI 2013/1169 (L.8); made under the Agriculture Act 1947 s.75; the Landlord and Tenant Act 1987 s.35; and the Tribunals, Courts and Enforcement Act 2007 s.9, s.22, s.29, Sch.5. In force: July 1, 2013; .

These Rules consolidate and reform the rules of procedure previously governing proceedings in several tribunals which are due to transfer in to the First-tier Tribunal and the new Property Chamber.

28. First-tier Tribunal–Lands Chamber–Leasehold valuation tribunals–Residential property tribunals

THE FIRST-TIER TRIBUNAL (PROPERTY CHAMBER) FEES ORDER 2013, SI 2013/1179; made under the Tribunals, Courts and Enforcement Act 2007 s.42, s.49. In force: July 1, 2013; .

The First-tier Tribunal (Property Chamber) Fees Order 2013 prescribes the fees payable by users of the Property Chamber of the First-tier Tribunal (the "Property Chamber"), which will include the transferred Residential Property and Leasehold Valuation Tribunals.

29. First-tier Tribunal–Lands Chamber–Tax and Chancery Chamber–Upper Tribunal

THE FIRST-TIER TRIBUNAL AND UPPER TRIBUNAL (CHAMBERS) (AMENDMENT) ORDER 2013, SI 2013/1187; made under the Tribunals, Courts and Enforcement Act 2007 s.7. In force: July 1, 2013; .

This Order creates the Property Chamber of the First-tier Tribunal and allocates functions to this new Chamber. It also adds to the functions of the Lands Chamber and the Tax and Chancery Chamber of the Upper Tribunal.

30. First-tier Tribunal–Qualifications–Upper Tribunal

THE QUALIFICATIONS FOR APPOINTMENT OF MEMBERS TO THE FIRST-TIER TRIBUNAL AND UPPER TRIBUNAL (AMENDMENT) ORDER 2013, SI 2013/1185;

made under the Tribunals, Courts and Enforcement Act 2007 Sch.2 para.2, Sch.3 para.2. In force: July 1, 2013; .

This Order enlarges the range of existing qualifications and experience that make a person who is not a judge of the tribunal eligible for appointment as a member of the First-tier Tribunal or Upper Tribunal.

31. First-tier Tribunal – Reorganisation – Upper Tribunal

THE TRANSFER OF TRIBUNAL FUNCTIONS ORDER 2013, SI 2013/1036; made under the Tribunals, Courts and Enforcement Act 2007 s.30, s.31, s.32, s.35, s.36, s.38, Sch.5 para.30. In force: July 1, 2013; .

This Order creates a two-tier tribunal structure; the First-tier Tribunal and the Upper Tribunal. The tribunals were established under the Tribunals, Courts and Enforcement Act 2007 s.3. This Order ensures that powers are provided under Pt.1 of the 2007 Act to enable existing tribunals to be transferred into the new structure. This Order gives effect to the transfers and comes into force on July 1, 2013.

32. First-tier Tribunal – Upper Tribunal

THE TRIBUNAL PROCEDURE (AMENDMENT) RULES 2013, SI 2013/SI 2013/477 (L.2); made under the Social Security Act 1998 s.20; and the Tribunals, Courts and Enforcement Act 2007 s.22, s.29, Sch.5. In force: in accordance with rule 1 (2).;

.

These rules make changes to most of the rules that apply in the First-tier Tribunal, and to the Upper Tribunal Rules 2008.

33. First-tier Tribunal Chambers – Judicial review – Upper Tribunal Chambers

THE FIRST-TIER TRIBUNAL AND UPPER TRIBUNAL (CHAMBERS) (AMENDMENT NO.2) ORDER 2013, SI 2013/2068; made under the Tribunals, Courts and Enforcement Act 2007 s.7. In force: November 1, 2013; .

This Order amends the First-tier Tribunal and Upper Tribunal (Chambers) Order 2010 (SI 2010/2655) in consequence of the making of a direction by the Lord Chief Justice which transfers into the unified tribunal structure certain immigration and asylum judicial reviews from the High Court in England and Wales.

34. Immigration and Asylum Chamber – Upper Tribunal – Judicial review – England and Wales

THE UPPER TRIBUNAL (IMMIGRATION AND ASYLUM CHAMBER) (JUDICIAL REVIEW) (ENGLAND AND WALES) FEES (AMENDMENT) ORDER 2013, SI 2013/2069; made under the Tribunals, Courts and Enforcement Act 2007 s.42. In force: November 1, 2013; .

This Order amends the Upper Tribunal (Immigration and Asylum Chamber) (Judicial Review) (England and Wales) Fees Order 2011 (SI 2011/2344 in consequence of the making of a direction by the Lord Chief Justice which transfers into the unified tribunal structure certain immigration and asylum judicial reviews from the High Court in England and Wales.

35. Inquests – Coroners – Scope of inquest into patient's death by overdose – Role of general practitioner – Finding of unlawful killing

[Coroners Rules 1984 (SI 1984/552) r.43.]

The appellant general practitioner (S) appealed against the Divisional Court's refusal to grant him permission to judicially review the conduct of an inquest into the death of his patient (D). In 2002 D took an overdose of the drug Heminevrin which had been prescribed by S. D had a history of heroin abuse and S had first prescribed him the drug in 1997. It was highly toxic if combined with alcohol. D had overdosed twice on the drug taken with alcohol and had previously attempted suicide by hanging. By 2002 the drug was licensed mainly for use in detoxification on a short-term basis in a hospital setting. In 2002, D's mother had asked for a prescription of the drug for D which S provided without checking his recent history or seeing him. Two days later D took all the tablets and died in hospital. In 2007 the coroner referred allegations of gross negligence against S to the General Medical Council. At the inquest in 2011, evidence was heard from experts on GP practice who believed that S's conduct fell sufficiently far below the standard of a reasonably competent doctor so as to amount to gross negligence. S's account changed and inconsistencies emerged. The jury returned a verdict of unlawful killing. S argued that the inquest became a criminal trial against him for manslaughter and submitted that the coroner (1) had strayed beyond the legitimate scope of the inquest by admitting evidence of events years after D's death and evidence of marginal relevance including medical records and a Primary Care Trust review of S's performance, had displayed bias towards him and allowed a disproportionate focus on his conduct and credibility; (2) should have allowed the jury to consider a verdict of suicide.

Held: Appeal dismissed. (1) S's role in D's death was crucial to the investigation. S had prescribed drugs which killed D and the circumstances in which he did so raised the real possibility there had been an unlawful killing. The relevance of establishing whether D's medical records were reliable, accurate and in S's possession at material times was obvious. The question of whether S was telling the truth about the circumstances in which he came to prescribe the fatal drug was central to the inquiry. The evidence of the PCT performance review was said to have been relevant to S's credibility and character, whilst it might not have been probative, its admission did not undermine the lawfulness of the proceedings. It was within the coroner's discretion to decide that the evidence of S's referral to the GMC was relevant to a possible report under the Coroners Rules 1984 r.43. It was not surprising given the circumstances of D's death that the coroner authorised a full investigation of his prescribing history and S's system of issuing repeat prescriptions to him. Evidence regarding the prescription of the drug to another patient was highly relevant to the jury's consideration of whether any causative breach of duty on S's part was so bad in all the circumstances as to amount to a criminal act or omission. That patient's medical records demonstrated that some of S's evidence was untrue and showed S's general attitude to prescribing potentially lethal drugs. The admission of the evidence complained of by S was within the legitimate scope of the inquiry and did relate directly or indirectly to the circumstances of D's death. The coroner had a broad discretion as to the nature and extent of the inquiry. There was no bias or appearance of bias by the coroner. It was S's conduct in prescribing the lethal drug to a patient in those circumstances and his prevarication before the jury which put him in the spotlight (see paras 24, 30-31, 34, 36, 39, 43-44, 48, 59 of judgment). (2) D had a history of self-harm and suicide attempts and had threatened to kill himself days before his death. However there was no direct evidence that D intended to end his life. His chaotic approach to drugs and alcohol raised the real possibility that he simply kept drinking and taking the tablets without any specific intent. On that basis the coroner decided the jury could not safely conclude, to the criminal standard of proof, that D had intended the consequences of his actions. That was a reasonable approach to take and there was no error of law. The jury's verdict indicated that they had no doubt that the prescription of a dangerous drug to a vulnerable patient was a material cause of D's death and there was no break in the chain of causation (paras 69-74).

R. (ON THE APPLICATION OF SREEDHARAN) v HM CORONER FOR THE COUNTY OF GREATER MANCHESTER, [2013] EWCA Civ 181, [2013] Med. L.R. 89, Lord Dyson (M.R.), CA (Civ Div).

36. Inquests–Right to life–Death of 14-year-old boy assessed by local authority as being "in need"–Whether Middleton-type inquest necessary

[Children Act 1989 (c.41) s.17, s.31; Coroners Act 1988 (c.13) s.8(3)(d); European Convention on Human Rights 1950 Art.2.]

The claimant local authority applied for judicial review of decisions made by a coroner at a pre-inquest hearing. The inquest concerned the death of a 14-year-old boy (E), who had died after drinking methadone. E had been known to the local authority's social services department for some nine months before his death. In that time he had presented as being troubled: shoplifting, abusing drink and drugs, associating with drug users, and occasionally sleeping rough. Moreover, his school had expressed concern about his being depressed and harming himself. Four months before his death, he was assessed as being "in need" within the meaning of the Children Act 1989 s.17, and after his death a serious case review produced an executive summary setting out a number of shortcomings on the part of the local authority. The coroner ruled that the European Convention on Human Rights 1950 art.2 was engaged, and he ordered that an art.2-compliant inquest of the type set out in *R. (on the application of Middleton) v HM Coroner for Western Somerset* [2004] UKHL 10, [2004] 2 A.C. 182, [2004] C.L.Y. 37 should be held. He also held that the inquest should take place with a jury. The local authority submitted that the coroner had (1) erred in holding that there should be a *Middleton* inquest; (2) failed to give sufficient reasons for his decision to hold such an inquest; (3) erred in deciding to hold the inquest with a jury.

Held: Application granted. (1) Article 2 recognised three possible obligations on the state: a general duty to protect the right to life; a second layer to that duty, known as the "operational" duty; and a procedural duty to investigate any arguable breaches of the general duty. The operational duty arose in the following circumstances: where there was an allegation that the state had violated its general duty, it had to be established that, at the time, the authorities knew or ought to have known of the existence of a real and immediate risk to the life of an identified individual, and that they had failed to take measures within the scope of their powers which, judged reasonably, might have been expected to avoid that risk. The test of "real and immediate risk to life" was a stringent one with a very high threshold. While there was no doubt that the instant case entered into the potential territory of operational duty, there was insufficient evidence of a real and immediate risk to life. In the months before his death, E had undoubtedly been vulnerable and at risk but, viewed objectively, that risk was not a risk to life. It was a risk of harm, and that was not to be equated, with the wisdom of hindsight, with a risk to life. There was no evidence to justify the coroner's view that there had been a real and immediate risk to E's life. In those circumstances there was no operational duty in place at the time of E's death. The local authority did not have parental responsibility for E, and he was not 'in care' in the sense that no proceedings had been commenced under s.31 of the Act. Although the local authority had some measure of responsibility for him because he was vulnerable and had been assessed as being "in need" for the purposes of s.17, it would not be proportionate to require a local authority to exercise sufficient control over all such children within its jurisdiction so that an operational duty was exercised in every case, *Osman v United Kingdom (23452/94)* [1999] 1 F.L.R. 193, [1998] C.L.Y. 3102 considered. Since no operational duty was in place, there could be no breach of any such duty, and there could therefore be no breach of the general duty. It followed that no procedural duty arose, and there was no burden on the state to hold a *Middleton* inquest, *Middleton* referred to (see paras 41, 43-44, 46-52 of judgment). (2) While the coroner's reasons could have been fuller, it was unlikely that his decision would have been quashed on that ground alone. Resolving difficult issues arising from art.2, particularly where the law was evolving, was not a straightforward process, and a lengthy ruling was not necessarily required. What was needed, essentially, was that the coroner should give sufficient reasons to enable the losing party to know why he had lost (paras 53, 56). (3) The coroner had been entitled to rely on the Coroners Act 1988 s.8(3)(d) and to conclude that the inquest should be held with a jury. That was a matter within his discretion, there was nothing to suggest that he had exercised it unreasonably, and his decision on that issue would stand (para. 59).

R. (ON THE APPLICATION OF KENT CC) v HM CORONER FOR KENT (NORTH-WEST DISTRICT), [2012] EWHC 2768 (Admin), (2013) 177 J.P. 82, Foskett, J., DC.

37. Inquests–Unlawful killing–Whether driving offences capable of justifying verdict of unlawful killing

[Coroners Act 1988 (c.13) s.16; Criminal Law Act 1977 (c.45); Coroners (Indictable Offences) Rules 1956 (SI 1956/1692); Coroners Rules 1984 (SI 1984/552) r.42, Sch.4.]

The claimant (W) applied for judicial review of a verdict of unlawful killing. While driving on a motorway in bad conditions, W's vehicle spun out of control and struck a stationary vehicle on the hard shoulder, killing a vehicle recovery technician who was working on it. W was not prosecuted because there was no evidence that the accident had been caused by her driving rather than by snow and ice on the carriageway. The coroner directed the jury that they could return a verdict of unlawful killing if they were sure that the offence of causing death by careless driving had been committed. His view was that such a verdict was suitable where a person had been unlawfully "killed" by another. The issue was whether evidence of the commission of the offence of causing death by careless driving was capable of justifying a verdict of unlawful killing at an inquest.

Held: Application granted. (1) There was no statutory definition of "unlawful killing". Historically, there had been a clear, fixed and long-standing scheme, provided for by the Coroners (Indictable Offences) Rules 1956, that murder, manslaughter and infanticide, and no other offences, constituted a separate category for the purposes of recording a verdict at an inquest with the consequence of the person responsible for the death being charged and committed for trial. That scheme did not survive into the Criminal Law Act 1977. However, the Coroners Rules 1984 Sch.4 introduced for the first time the concept of lawful or unlawful killing within the coroner's jurisdiction, the object being to provide a comprehensive list of verdicts and to standardise them over the whole country. It was clear from the phraseology of the Notes to the Rules that the expression "unlawful killing" was, at that time, intended to embrace only murder, manslaughter or infanticide. Rule 42 specified that verdicts were not to be framed in such a way as to appear to determine the question of liability (see paras 31-33, 39-48 of judgment). The coroner's view as to the logic of permitting a verdict of unlawful killing in the context of driving offences was linguistically sound, but ignored the essential purpose of an inquest, which was to ascertain the identity of the deceased and how, when and where he came by his death without seeking to apportion blame or determine liability, *R. v HM Coroner for South London, Ex p. Thompson* Times, May 15, 1982, [1982] C.L.Y. 461, *R. v HM Coroner for North Humberside and Scunthorpe, Ex p. Jamieson* [1995] Q.B. 1, [1994] C.L.Y. 631 and *R. (on the application of Middleton) v HM Coroner for Western Somerset* [2004] UKHL 10, [2004] 2 A.C. 182, [2004] C.L.Y. 37 applied. The main purpose of having a verdict of unlawful killing was to distinguish between cases where there had been some kind of accident and those where it would be an abuse of language to describe the circumstances of death as an accident. Murder, manslaughter and infanticide involved a criminal state of mind or negligence of the grossest kind. Causing death by dangerous, careless or inconsiderate driving, and the morally more serious offence of causing death by careless driving under the influence of alcohol or drugs were, applying the basic tenets of coroner law, not to be treated as "unlawful killing"; despite contributory factors, they were still accidents. That conclusion accorded with current views in Paul Matthews, *Jervis on Coroners*, 12th edn (London: Sweet & Maxwell 2011), which the court endorsed. There was nothing in the Coroners Act 1988 s.16 to undermine that conclusion (paras 60-77, 79-80). (2) In the instant case, the coroner had been wrong to direct the jury that the offence of careless driving was a possible basis for a verdict of unlawful killing. The verdict of accident was substituted (paras 82-84).

R. (ON THE APPLICATION OF WILKINSON) v HM CORONER FOR GREATER MANCHESTER SOUTH DISTRICT, [2012] EWHC 2755 (Admin), [2013] C.P. Rep. 5, Foskett, J., QBD (Admin).

38. Judges–Bias–Excessive intervention in trial–Fairness of trial

The appellant firm of solicitors (S) appealed against a recorder's order as to costs in a dispute between the firm and the respondent (H). S had employed H to assist in undertaking professional work for the firm. There were factual disputes as to whether H's employment had been brought to an end by summary dismissal or whether he had repudiated the agreement by walking out, and whether H had been negligent. The only other issues went to quantum. Following a four-day trial, the recorder found for H, and ordered S to pay H's summarily assessed costs. S was represented at trial by counsel (R), and evidence was given by the firm's principal (K). There were two grounds of appeal: one related to the recorder's finding on the issue of termination, and the other to complaints as to the recorder's bias, partiality and unequal treatment of the parties, including allegations that he interrupted and intervened excessively.

Held: Appeal dismissed. (1) The recorder was faced with inconsistencies in S's pleaded case, differences in the account given by K in the course of his evidence and a stark conflict of evidence between K and H. The points taken by S in support of its appeal on the issue of termination were little more than an attempt to re-argue a variety of points arising from the conflicting evidence of K and H (see paras 14, 17 of judgment). (2) Ordinary civil proceedings in the United Kingdom were adversarial not inquisitorial. The duty of the judge was to hear and determine the issues raised by the parties as set out in the pleadings. In pursuit of that fundamental objective, the judge was not required to sit in silence. Appropriate intervention while a witness was giving evidence, even while the witness was being cross-examined, was not merely permissible but might be vital, *Jones v National Coal Board* [1957] 2 Q.B. 55, [1957] C.L.Y. 2871 applied. However, there was a difficult and delicate balance to be held. The dangers of inappropriate intervention were particularly acute during cross-examination. *Jones* remained the classic statement of principle and was an illuminating illustration of where the line was properly to be drawn between appropriate and inappropriate intervention, not least because it stood in striking contrast to what the transcripts revealed in the instant case. There had been a significant amount of intervention by the recorder but it did not give rise to any proper ground of complaint. He had stayed well within the boundaries described in *Jones*. His interventions were justified, many of them because of the way in which R was conducting the case. The recorder did not at any time attempt to take over the examination or cross-examination of the witness, nor was there anything in the transcript which began to suggest that R was not able to put his case properly. Moreover, there was no substance in any of the complaints of bias and partiality. Stepping back from the detail and looking at everything in the round, it was quite apparent that both parties had had the fair trial to which every party was entitled. The recorder had behaved entirely properly (paras 22-23, 25-26, 29, 31, 44, 49, 52).

HADI JEMALDEEN v A-Z LAW SOLICITORS; *sub nom*. JEMALDEEN v A-Z LAW SOLICITORS, [2012] EWCA Civ 1431, [2013] C.P. Rep. 8, Moore-Bick, L.J., CA (Civ Div).

39. Judicial Appointments Commission

THE JUDICIAL APPOINTMENTS COMMISSION REGULATIONS 2013, SI 2013/2191; made under the Constitutional Reform Act 2005 Sch.12 para.1 (b), Sch.12

para.3B, Sch.12 para.3C, Sch.12 para.6A, Sch.12 para.11, Sch.12 para.13, Sch.12 para.14, Sch.12 para.17A. In force: September 4, 2013; .

These Regulations contain provisions providing for the composition of the Judicial Appointments Commission, the selection of commissioners (including the vice-chairman) and the tenure of commissioners.

40. Judicial decision-making–Religious groups–Court's jurisdiction to determine matters of religious doctrine and practice

The defendant trustees of a charitable trust (K) appealed against a refusal of their application to stay the proceedings issued against them by the claimant trustees (S). All parties were members of the Sikh community. The dispute concerned the trusteeship and governance of two gurdwaras, which operated under charitable trusts established under English law. Most of the parties were, or had been, trustees of one of them. The power to appoint trustees was originally vested in the First Holy Saint, who had been the founder of the gurdwaras in the 1980s. The dispute was whether the ninth claimant (X) became entitled to exercise that power following the death of the Second Holy Saint in 2002. S's case was that X was in the designated line of spiritual succession and that upon the death of the Second Holy Saint, he had been entitled to remove K as trustees and replace them with S. S sought, by their proceedings, to construe the trust deeds and determine the meaning of "successor". K's case was that the claim should be struck out as non-justiciable because the question whether X was the "successor" could not be answered by the legal process of construction alone; it turned on the truth of disputed tenets of religious faith and subjective beliefs, which was outside the recognised perimeter of judicial competence. The judge below had refused K's application for a permanent stay or a strike-out of the proceedings, and had granted S permission to amend its pleadings.

Held: Appeal allowed. The central issue in the proceedings, namely whether X was the "successor" of the First Holy Saint was non-justiciable, *Buttes Gas & Oil Co v Hammer (No.3)* [1982] A.C. 888, [1981] C.L.Y. 1473 considered and *General Assembly of Free Church of Scotland v Lord Overtoun* [1904] A.C. 515 explained. Although *Free Church* and the cases preceding it supported some of the propositions on justiciability advanced by S, *Free Church* was about the determination of civil property rights under trust law, not about deciding the truth of whether a particular person was a holy person and a spiritual leader equipped with fundamental powers affecting the internal governance of a body of believers. The courts would not decline to decide cases about civil rights merely because there was a religious element to them; however controversial and profound the religious aspects might be, they could not serve to exclude or limit the jurisdiction of the civil courts to determine civil rights. However, the instant case did not fall within that category because the court was being asked to pronounce on matters of religious doctrine and practice, which it could not do with any degree of confidence or credibility. It was not simply a question of the meaning of the word "successor", but whether X fitted that description. The evidence was bound to be in conflict and the court had no objective criteria by which to decide whose evidence was the more truthful. The issue of succession to holy sainthood could not be determined by analysing evidence, or by finding facts on a balance of probabilities, or by ascertaining the wishes of a voting majority. Therefore, the court was being asked to pronounce on a matter on which it could not speak and should not pretend to speak with authority (see paras 15, 20-21, 26, 63-74 of judgment).

KHAIRA v SHERGILL; *sub nom.* SHERGILL v KHAIRA, [2012] EWCA Civ 983, [2012] P.T.S.R. 1697, Mummery, L.J., CA (Civ Div).

41. Judicial decision-making–Right to be heard–Application to strike out claims refused on reading of papers

The appellant trustees (T) appealed against a judge's refusal to strike out parts of a claim by the respondent beneficiary (L). L had brought claims for an account, an inquiry and an order for payment against T, based on contentions that T had charged excessive rates, had acted in breach of trust, and had failed to properly manage the trust. T applied to strike out some of the allegations and claims on the basis that L had also brought claims in other jurisdictions, including Switzerland and Liechtenstein, relying on the grounds of issue estoppel and/or abuse of process. T had submitted written arguments. The judge stated at the start of the hearing that he considered T's applications to be unsustainable, and that he did not intend to force T's counsel to try and persuade him to the contrary as it would be a pointless exercise. The judge gave his judgment the next day and referred to the fact that, having read the papers, he was quite confident that however long was spent on T's applications he would not be in a position to reach a concluded view. T claimed that the judge's refusal to hear the strike-out applications had breached their fundamental common law right to present their case, and that the decision should be set aside and their applications remitted to be heard by another judge.

Held: Appeal allowed. (1) It was a fundamental feature of the English civil justice system that a party should be allowed to bring his application to court and make his case before a judge. That principle was subject to some exceptions and limitations which existed to ensure the proper administration of justice, including where a party was in contempt of court or subject to a civil restraint order. However, even in those circumstances, the court would ensure that a party was not prevented from making an application or submissions where it would be unjust to shut him out. Accordingly, where an application was brought to strike out the whole or part of a claim, the judge had a duty to consider the application properly. In particular the judge was bound to listen to oral argument in support of the application. If the judge had had time to read all the papers and to consider full written arguments from the parties, he might quite properly be able to dispose of the application more quickly. While it might often be unwise to do so, the judge could: (a) give his provisional view that the application should be rejected on one of the grounds raised by the respondent; (b) give the applicant a fair opportunity to disabuse him of that view through oral argument; (c) if unpersuaded, end the hearing by giving judgment for the respondent on the ground in question. What a judge could not properly do was to dismiss the application without giving the applicant a fair opportunity to make out his case. It was vital that justice was seen to be done, but it was also vital that justice was done. Any experienced judge would have had the experience of coming into court with a view as to the likely outcome of a hearing, only to find himself of a very different view once oral argument had been heard. It was an advocate's duty to stand up to a judge who was proposing to take an inappropriate course. However, where a judge made it clear that he was resolved on taking a certain course and that there was no prospect of the advocate being able to dissuade him, it was hard to see what the advocate could do other than to appeal the decision. That was the position in the instant case. The judge's decision was simply unsustainable. T's strike-out applications would be remitted to the Chancery Division to be heard by another judge (see paras 22-27, 43-44 of judgment). (2) (Obiter) The instant decision should not have the effect of deterring first-instance judges from being properly robust. There was nothing wrong with a judge who had formed a preliminary view on points at issue prior to coming into court expressing that view to the parties, provided that it was made clear that it was only a provisional view and that the parties would be given the opportunity to try to dissuade him from that view. Equally, if a judge was satisfied that a particular issue could be disposed of on the basis of one of several points raised, there was no reason why he could not tell the parties that he provisionally considered that he did not need to hear argument on the other points, again provided that the parties were given the opportunity to persuade him that he should decide one or more of those points. On procedural and case management issues, trial judges should be encouraged to be robust when dealing with procedural and case management issues (paras 40-42).

FREY v LABROUCHE; *sub nom.* LABROUCHE v FREY, [2012] EWCA Civ 881, [2012] 1 W.L.R. 3160, Lord Neuberger (M.R.), CA (Civ Div).

42. Judicial proceedings immunity–Forensic science–Negligence action arising from mistakes by Forensic Science Service in handling criminal evidence–Whether Forensic Science Service protected by judicial proceedings immunity

[Firearms Act 1968 (c.27) s.1(1); Human Rights Act 1998 (c.42); European Convention on Human Rights 1950 Art.8.]

The appellant (S) appealed against the striking out of his claim against the respondent (the FSS) for negligence and breach of the European Convention on Human Rights 1950 art.8. S had pleaded guilty to the strict liability offence of possession of live ammunition contrary to the Firearms Act 1968 s.1(1). During a search of his home, police officers had found a bullet which he claimed he had bought as an ornament, assuming it not to be live. Whether it was live could not be discerned from a visual examination, and it was sent to the FSS for analysis. The FSS confirmed that it was live. Some months later, it transpired that there had been a mix-up at the FSS. S's bullet, which was not live, had been confused with another bullet, which was. The mix-up had resulted in S's bullet being wrongly labelled as live. When the mix-up was discovered, the case was re-listed, S's plea was vacated and the charge was dismissed. He then began civil proceedings alleging that the FSS owed him a duty to operate proper systems to ensure that the continuity of exhibits was secure, and that it had failed in that duty. A year into the proceedings, the FSS disclosed documents which showed that the exhibit numbers on the two bullets had been altered while they were in its possession. There was no adequate explanation for the alteration, the fact of which had initially been concealed from S. Nevertheless, S's claim was struck out on the basis that the FSS was protected by judicial proceedings immunity; that it owed S no duty of care; and that it was not a public authority for the purposes of the Human Rights Act 1998. During the course of the instant appeal, S sought to amend his pleadings to allege deceit on the basis of the altered exhibit numbers. The issues were whether (i) the amendment should be permitted; (ii) the order striking out the negligence and human rights claims should be maintained.

Held: Appeal allowed. (1) S would be permitted to amend his pleadings to allege deceit. The evidence showed that somebody had altered the exhibit numbers on the bullets, had made no contemporaneous note as to why, and had later concealed the fact of the alteration. Indeed, the fact of the alteration had not been disclosed until a year after the proceedings had been begun. S should have applied to amend his pleadings as soon as he became aware of the alteration. However, the FSS had neither explained the alteration nor indicated whether those responsible for it were still available to give evidence. It appeared to be a grave state of affairs, and it could not be assumed that the absence of an explanation was due to S's delay in applying for the amendment (see paras 19-23 of judgment). (2) In striking out the negligence and human rights claims, the judge had concluded, on the basis of *Evans v London Hospital Medical College (University of London)* [1981] 1 W.L.R. 184, [1981] C.L.Y. 2184, that evidence relating to the collection, transmission and examination of exhibits was protected by judicial proceedings immunity. However, *Darker v Chief Constable of West Midlands* [2001] 1 A.C. 435, [2000] C.L.Y. 4543 established that there was no immunity covering the fabrication of evidence in circumstances where the fabrication was never intended to appear in any statement. The paradigm circumstance falling within the protection of judicial proceedings immunity was the giving of evidence by a witness in court, and that had been extended to the preparation of evidence with a view to it being adduced. The rationale for the immunity was the need to protect witnesses from the fear that they would be harassed by subsequent actions against them. It was designed to encourage freedom of communication in judicial proceedings and to prevent a collateral attack on any decision arising from allegedly false evidence. Given that S's amendment had been allowed, the rationale for conferring judicial proceedings immunity had gone. Witnesses for the FSS, if called, would have to explain and justify their handling of the exhibits. If the trial of S's action continued on the basis of the deceit allegation, it would not be wise to maintain the striking out of the negligence claim, *Evans* and *Darker* considered. Similarly, it would not be appropriate to uphold the judge's view that the FSS owed S no duty of care. It would be wrong to exclude the proposition that whoever interfered with the exhibit numbers owed a duty to the person to whom the bullet would wrongly be attributed as a result of his interference. The effect of the interference, whether it was designed to conceal the mix-up or not, was just the same as planting a live bullet in S's house. The course of justice appeared to have been perverted by the alteration of the exhibit numbers and the failure to disclose that that had happened, and any court would be reluctant to allow immunity to be deployed in such a way as to prevent that matter being litigated. Finally, while it was unlikely that the human rights claim would need resolution, it would be wrong to allow the question of whether the FSS was a public body to rest upon a summary decision (paras 24-33).

SMART v FORENSIC SCIENCE SERVICE LTD, [2013] EWCA Civ 783, [2013] P.N.L.R. 32, Moses, L.J., CA (Civ Div).

43. Jurisdiction–Court of Appeal–Appeals against refusal of Upper Tribunal to grant permission to seek judicial review

[Tribunals, Courts and Enforcement Act 2007 (c.15) s.13(5); Civil Procedure Rules 1998 (SI 1998/3132) r.52.13; Tribunal Procedure (Upper Tribunal) Rules 2008 (SI 2008/2698) r.44(4); CPR PD 52 (Appeals) 2000.]

The court was required to determine jurisdictional issues in relation to applications for permission to appeal against a refusal by the Upper Tribunal to grant permission to apply for judicial review. The applicant (N) had been refused asylum and removal directions had been issued by the respondent secretary of state. Permission to seek judicial review of the removal decision was refused. N submitted a fresh asylum claim and applied again for permission to seek judicial review of his removal. A stay of removal was granted. N's fresh claim was rejected but a further stay was granted and his judicial review permission application was transferred from the High Court to the Upper Tribunal. The tribunal refused permission. N applied to the Court of Appeal for permission to appeal and for a further stay. The issues were whether (i) an applicant who had been refused permission by the Upper Tribunal to seek judicial review could, or should, seek permission to appeal from the tribunal or from the Court of Appeal immediately after the decision; (ii) on an application to the Court of Appeal for permission to appeal, the court could grant permission to seek judicial review, or had to first grant permission to appeal and entertain and allow the appeal before granting permission to seek judicial review.

Held: Issues determined. (1) On the face of it, the effect of CPR PD 52, the Tribunals, Courts and Enforcement Act 2007 and the Tribunal Procedure (Upper Tribunal) Rules 2008 was clear and prescriptive in relation to seeking the Court of Appeal's permission to appeal against a refusal by the Upper Tribunal to grant permission to apply for judicial review. First, under s.13(5) of the 2007 Act, it was necessary to seek permission of the tribunal to appeal to the Court of Appeal before an application for permission to appeal could be made. Second, under r.44(4), it was not possible to seek permission from the tribunal to appeal the refusal until it had given its written reasons for refusing permission to apply for judicial review. Third, such written reasons would often be provided some time after the tribunal's refusal to grant permission to seek judicial review had been made and communicated. Although that conclusion was obviously inconvenient, and an applicant could be in "no-man's land" for some time, it was correct (see paras 18-22 of judgment). (2) Where the Administrative Court refused permission to apply for judicial review and an applicant applied to the Court of Appeal for permission to appeal against that refusal, the Court of Appeal did not have to go through the cumbersome process of granting permission to appeal, hearing and allowing the appeal, and then remitting the application for the Administrative Court to reconsider whether to grant judicial review. The CPR r.52.13(3) entitled the Court of Appeal to grant permission to seek judicial review and remit the application for determination on the merits. However, that provision only applied to appeals from the High Court, and no such procedure existed in relation to application for permission against a refusal by the Upper Tribunal. It would be desirable if r.52.13(3) could be amended to also apply to appeals from the Upper Tribunal as that would enable the Court of Appeal not just to grant permission to appeal, and where appropriate a stay, but to grant permission to seek judicial review. The concern of an applicant such as N would be that he could be removed during the period between the refusal by the tribunal and its decision regarding permission to appeal to the Court of Appeal. However, the Court of Appeal had jurisdiction to grant a stay to protect a person's right to appeal in those circumstances, *YD (Turkey) v Secretary of State for the Home Department* [2006] EWCA Civ 52, [2006] 1 W.L.R. 1646, [2006] C.L.Y. 2242 followed. That could lead to the court being swamped with stay applications. A solution would be for the rule-makers or Parliament to amend the 2008 Rules so that an applicant could apply for permission to appeal to the tribunal, combined with a stay application, as soon as his application was refused. No primary legislation would need to be amended. However, until the amendments to the 2008 Rules were made, a short-term "least bad" *modus vivendi* was required and, although any stay application had to be dealt with on its merits, the Court of Appeal should be very ready to grant such applications. First, there had to be a default position. Second, it would be unfair to an applicant if it was hard to obtain a stay. Third, the stay's purpose was to protect the court's jurisdiction. Fourth, the damage to the public interest would be less if a stay was wrongly granted and an applicant was not removed, than the damage to the applicant if a stay was wrongly refused and he was removed before he could successfully appeal the tribunal's refusal to permit him to seek judicial review. Fifth, it would always be open to the secretary of state to apply to discharge any stay. Sixth, in the instant case, the secretary of state had very properly accepted that a stay should be the default position in the current legislative framework (paras 23-39). (3) The stay in the instant case would be continued until it had been decided whether N's application for permission to appeal should be granted (para.40).

R. (ON THE APPLICATION OF NB (ALGERIA)) v SECRETARY OF STATE FOR THE HOME DEPARTMENT, [2012] EWCA Civ 1050, [2013] 1 W.L.R. 31, Lord Neuberger (M.R.), CA (Civ Div).

44. Justice and Security Act 2013 (c.18)–Commencement, Transitional and Saving Provisions Order

THE JUSTICE AND SECURITY ACT 2013 (COMMENCEMENT, TRANSITIONAL AND SAVING PROVISIONS) ORDER 2013, SI 2013/SI 2013/1482 (C.58); made under the Justice and Security Act 2013 s.19, s.20, Sch.3 para.4. Commencement details: bringing into force various provisions of the 2013 Act on June 25, 2013.; .

This Order brings into force on June 25 2013 those provisions of the Justice and Security Act 2013 which are not already in force. These include extending the existing closed material procedure under the Special Immigration Appeals Commission Act 1997.

45. Lands Chamber–Upper Tribunal

THE TRIBUNAL PROCEDURE (AMENDMENT NO.3) RULES 2013, SI 2013/SI 2013/1188 (L.9); made under the Tribunals, Courts and Enforcement Act 2007 s.22, s.29, Sch.5. In force: July 1, 2013; .

These Rules make changes to the Upper Tribunal (Lands Chamber) Rules 2010 (SI 2010/2600) that will allow cases and appeals from the new Property Chamber to be dealt with in the Upper Tribunal. They also make amendments relating to costs and to address some practical issues.

46. Local justice areas

THE LOCAL JUSTICE AREAS (NO.2) ORDER 2013, SI 2013/1878; made under the Courts Act 2003 s.8, s.108. In force: January 1, 2014 except for Sch.1 Pt.1 on August 30, 2013.; .

This order combines: the local justice areas (LJAs) of Mansfield and Worksop and Nottingham and Newark to create a single LJA called Nottinghamshire; the LJAs of Dudley and Halesowen, Sandwell, Walsall and Aldridge and Wolverhampton to create a single LJA called Black Country; the LJAs of Birmingham and Solihull to create a single LJA called Birmingham and Solihull; and the LJAs of Coventry District and Warwickshire to create an LJA called Coventry and Warwickshire.

47. Local justice areas–Reorganisation

THE LOCAL JUSTICE AREAS ORDER 2013, SI 2013/1777; made under the Courts Act 2003 s.8, s.108. In force: January 1, 2014 except for Sch.1 Part 1 on August 30, 2013.; .

This Order combines the Local Justice Areas (LJAs): of Ashby and Market Bosworth, Leicester, Market Harborough and Lutterworth and Loughborough, Melton, Belvoir and Rutland to create a single LJA called Leicestershire and Rutland LJA; South Cheshire and Macclesfield to create a single LJA called South and East Cheshire, and the LJAs of East Lincolnshire, South Lincolnshire and West Lincolnshire to create a single LJA called Lincolnshire.

48. Recusal–Bias–Appeal against trial judge's refusal to recuse himself following finding of contempt against defendant–Real possibility of bias–Waiver of right to make application

[Civil Procedure Rules 1998 (SI 1998/3132) r.1.3.]

The appellant (X) appealed against a judge's refusal ([2012] EWHC 3023 (Comm)) to recuse himself from trying actions brought against X by the respondent bank (J). The trial, which was expected to last three months, had been imminent when X made his application. The judge had had a long and extensive involvement with the case, and in *JSC BTA Bank v Ablyazov* [2012] EWHC 237 (Comm) had disbelieved X's evidence on oath and found him guilty of contempt of court for failing to disclose his assets in breach of a freezing order. X sought an order for the judge to recuse himself on the basis of bias. The judge found that a fair-minded observer would not conclude that there was a real possibility that he would be biased and that X had waived his right to apply for the recusal by not making such an application at an earlier stage in proceedings.

Held: Appeal dismissed. (1) Although the principles of apparent bias were well established, their application was wholly fact-sensitive. Although matters of mere convenience could not palliate the appearance of bias, and the application of the doctrine of apparent bias was not a matter of discretion, it was relevant to consider, through the eyes of the fair-minded and informed observer, that there was not only convenience but also justice to be found in the efficient conduct of civil claims with the help of the designated judge. A case for recusal could always arise where a judge had expressed himself in vituperative or intemperate terms. However, that had not been alleged in the instant case. One significant development was the issuing of committal applications in very large and strongly fought civil litigation. As in the instant case, such applications could become a substantial "trial within a trial". The critical consideration was that a judge who had to bear in mind his own findings and observations did so as part and parcel of his judicial assessment of the litigation before him; he was not "pre-judging" by reference to extraneous matters or predilections or preference. If he judged the matter before him fairly and judicially, the fair-minded and informed observer would not consider that there was any possibility of bias, *Davidson v Scottish Ministers (No.2)* [2004] UKHL 34, 2005 1 S.C. (H.L.) 7, [2004] C.L.Y. 4467 and *Secretary of State for the Home Department v AF* [2008] EWCA Civ 117, [2008] 1 W.L.R. 2528,

[2009] C.L.Y. 358 considered. The judge in the instant case had at all times been bringing his objective judgement to bear on the material and would continue to do so. Any other judge would have to do the same, on the same material, which would necessarily include the judge's own judgments. The overlap between the issues at the committal proceedings and at trial would be small. The judge had not considered at all the essential causes of action on which the bank had based its claims and any issues decided in the committal proceedings would only play a relatively small role at trial, *Morel v France (31430/96)* (2001) 33 E.H.R.R. 47, [2002] C.L.Y. 2408 and *Sengupta v Holmes* [2002] EWCA Civ 1104, Times, August 19, 2002, [2002] C.L.Y. 452 considered. With regard to the judge's expressed view that the credibility of X and his witnesses at the committal hearing was wanting, he would be in much the same position as any other judge who would be referred to that judgment and the instant court's judgment on the contempt of court question. It was also relevant that there was no suggestion of unfairness against the judge. Irrespective of waiver, the fair-minded and informed observer would consider that there was no real possibility of bias, *Locabail (UK) Ltd v Bayfield Properties Ltd (Leave to Appeal)* [2000] Q.B. 451, [1999] C.L.Y. 38 applied (see paras 65-76 of judgment). (2) The question was whether X's failure to request recusal earlier in the proceedings, while still participating, was consistent with his subsequent application. There had been participation, not mere silence, in proceedings before a judge who, on X's case, had conducted himself in such a way as to give rise to the appearance of bias, *Allied Marine Transport v Vale do Rio Doce Navegacao SA (The Leonidas D)* [1985] 1 W.L.R. 925, [1985] C.L.Y. 110 considered. Moreover, X was under a duty to speak, arising out of his duty to help the court to further the overriding objective under CPR r.1.3. It was contrary to that duty to allow the court and the other parties to waste time and resources in preparing for a trial which, if the judge had to be replaced, would have to be adjourned to an uncertain date. The instant court was entitled to infer that X knew of his right to object to the judge continuing as trial judge. X had given no explanation for the lateness of his application and the court was obliged to form its own view on the question of knowledge. The timing of X's application was a tactical decision, designed to derail the trial. His failure to object to the judge as trial judge at all times from the delivery of the contempt judgments was an unequivocal, informed and voluntary waiver of any right he had to do so, *Locabail* applied, *Millar (David Cameron) v Dickson* [2001] UKPC D 4, [2002] 1 W.L.R. 1615, [2001] C.L.Y. 6372 considered (paras 85-93).

JSC BTA BANK v ABLYAZOV, [2012] EWCA Civ 1551, [2013] 1 W.L.R. 1845, Sir Maurice Kay (VP CA Civ), CA (Civ Div).

49. Shipbuilding–Abolition of British Shipbuilders

THE PUBLIC BODIES (ABOLITION OF BRITISH SHIPBUILDERS) ORDER 2013, SI 2013/687; made under the Public Bodies Act 2011 s.1, s.6, s.23, s.24, s.35. In force: March 22, 2013 except for Sch.1 para.15 on March 23, 2013.; .

This instrument abolishes British Shipbuilders (BS) and its subsidiaries. This instrument also transfers the property, rights and liabilities of BS and its subsidiaries to the Secretary of State.

50. Social Entitlement Chamber–Upper Tribunal–War Pensions and Armed Forces Compensation Chamber–Judicial review

THE TRIBUNAL PROCEDURE (AMENDMENT NO.4) RULES 2013, SI 2013/SI 2013/2067 (L.20); made under the Tribunals, Courts and Enforcement Act 2007 s.22, Sch.5. In force: November 1, 2013; .

These Rules amend the Tribunal Procedure (Upper Tribunal) Rules 2008 (SI 2008/2698), the Tribunal Procedure (First-tier Tribunal) (Social Entitlement Chamber) Rules 2008 (SI 2008/2685) and the Tribunal Procedure (First-tier Tribunal) (War Pensions and Armed Forces Compensation Chamber) Rules 2008 (SI 2008/2686). The amendments to the Tribunal Procedure (Upper Tribunal) Rules 2008 (the "Upper Tribunal Rules") are, for the most part, a consequence of the making of a direction by the Lord Chief Justice which transfers into the unified tribunal structure certain immigration and asylum judicial reviews from the High Court in England and Wales.

51. Transfer of functions

THE TRANSFER OF FUNCTIONS (CHEQUERS AND DORNEYWOOD ESTATES) ORDER 2013, SI 2013/537; made under the Ministers of the Crown Act 1975 s.1. In force: April 17, 2013; .

This Order transfers to the Chancellor of the Duchy of Lancaster various functions conferred by legislation on the Lord Privy Seal, and transfers to the Chancellor of the Duchy of Lancaster various functions under the Dorneywood Thomson Endowment Trust Fund B which were originally conferred on the Minister of Works. This Order transfers property, rights and liabilities in connection with those functions. The Order makes supplemental provision and consequential amendments to primary legislation.

52. Tribunals, Courts and Enforcement Act 2007 (c.15)–Commencement No.10 Order

THE TRIBUNALS, COURTS AND ENFORCEMENT ACT 2007 (COMMENCEMENT NO.10) ORDER 2013, SI 2013/SI 2013/2043 (C.86); made under the Tribunals, Courts and Enforcement Act 2007 s.148. Commencement details: bringing into force various provisions of the 2007 Act on August 19, 2013.; .

This Order is the tenth commencement order under the Tribunals, Courts and Enforcement Act 2007 and brings into force the repeal of the Tribunals and Inquiries Act 1992 s.5 and s.8, which related to recommendations of the Council on Tribunals as to appointment of members of tribunals and procedural rules for tribunals.

53. Upper Tribunal–Tribunal procedures

THE TRIBUNAL PROCEDURE (AMENDMENT NO.2) RULES 2013, SI 2013/SI 2013/606 (L.5); made under the Tribunals, Courts and Enforcement Act 2007 s.22, Sch.5; and the Financial Services and Markets Act 2000 s.133. In force: April 1, 2013; .

These Rules amend the Tribunal Procedure (Upper Tribunal) Rules 2008 (SI 2008/2698) which apply in financial services cases in the Upper Tribunal, adding new definitions and amending others to reflect the fact that in future a person may be regulated by more than one regulator and in consequence more than one regulator may be a respondent in a case that is referred to the Tribunal.

54. Valuation Tribunal for Wales–Wales

THE VALUATION TRIBUNAL FOR WALES (WALES) (AMENDMENT) REGULATIONS 2013, SI 2013/SI 2013/547 (W.59); made under the Local Government Finance Act 1988 s.140, s.143, Sch.11 para.1, Sch.11 para.5, Sch.11 para.8. In force: April 1, 2013; .

These Regulations amend the Valuation Tribunal for Wales Regulations 2010 (SI 2010/713), which establish the Valuation Tribunal for Wales and make provision about its membership, administration and procedures. Among the amendments is the provision for the minimum and maximum number of members that may be appointed to the Tribunal.

ADMINISTRATIVE LAW

55. Accounts–Public authorities

THE GOVERNMENT RESOURCES AND ACCOUNTS ACT 2000 (ESTIMATES AND ACCOUNTS) ORDER 2013, SI 2013/488; made under the Government Resources and Accounts Act 2000 s.4A. In force: April 1, 2013; .

This Order designates specified central government bodies in relation to named government departments for the purpose of those departments' supply estimates and resource accounts. The designations have effect for the financial year that ends on March 31, 2014.

56. Accounts–Public authorities–Timetables

THE GOVERNMENT RESOURCES AND ACCOUNTS ACT 2000 (ALTERATION OF TIMETABLES FOR ACCOUNTS) ORDER 2013, SI 2013/148; made under the Government Resources and Accounts Act 2000 s.22. In force: January 30, 2013; .

This Order alters s.6(4) of the Government Resources and Accounts Act 2000 (the Act) in relation to the resource accounts prepared by the Department for Culture, Media and Sport (DCMS) for the financial year ending on March 31, 2012 and will require the Treasury to lay the Accounts as certified by the Comptroller and Auditor General (C&AG) and the C&AG's related report not later than February 25, 2013. Without alteration the date for laying under section 6(4) would be January 31, 2013.

57. Businesses–Disclosure–Individuals–Information

THE ENTERPRISE ACT 2002 (PART 9 RESTRICTIONS ON DISCLOSURE OF INFORMATION) (SPECIFICATION) ORDER 2013, SI 2013/1808; made under the Enterprise Act 2002 s.241. In force: August 16, 2013; .

The Enterprise Act 2002 Pt 9 (the 2002 Act) restricts the disclosure of "specified information" and permits disclosure of that information in particular circumstances. Information is defined as specified information by Part 9. This Order specifies The Green Deal Framework (Disclosure, Acknowledgment, Redress etc.) Regulations 2012 (the Framework Regulations) as subordinate legislation for the purposes of s. 241 of the 2002 Act. The effect of this instrument is that specified information which is otherwise restricted from being disclosed by Part 9 of the 2002 Act may, in accordance with that Part, be disclosed by public authorities to any other person for the purpose of facilitating the exercise by that person of any function conferred on them under or by virtue of the Framework Regulations.

58. Committees–Cultural objects–Dissolution–Transfer of functions

THE PUBLIC BODIES (ABOLITION OF THE RAILWAY HERITAGE COMMITTEE) ORDER 2013, SI 2013/64; made under the Public Bodies Act 2011 s.1, s.6, s.35. In force: in accordance with art.1.; .

This Order abolishes the Railway Heritage Committee and transfers to the Board of Trustees of the Science Museum the Committee's functions, under the Railway Heritage Act 1996, relating to the designation and disposal of historically significant railway records and artefacts.

59. Criminal injuries compensation–Extensions of time–Waiving two-year time limit for compensation claim–Need to consider actual circumstances of particular case

The appellant (H) appealed against a decision of the Upper Tribunal refusing to grant permission to apply for judicial review of the dismissal by the First-tier Tribunal of an appeal against a claims officer's decision not to waive the two-year time limit for bringing claims under the Criminal Injuries Compensation Scheme. When H was an infant his father had been stabbed to death in the street after an argument in a pub. His attacker was found guilty of manslaughter and sentenced to 18 months' imprisonment. After the attack, H's mother had a nervous breakdown and H and his sister were taken into care. Both children knew of their father's death from about the age of eight but were not told any of the details. Once H reached adulthood he tried to find out details of the circumstances of his father's death. He had little or no success until he discovered relevant documents in the National Archive. H then made a claim for compensation to the Criminal Injuries Compensation Authority under the Criminal Injuries Compensation Scheme on behalf of himself, his mother and his sister. That was 42 years after the death of his father. The authority's claims officer refused the claim. He refused to exercise the discretion under para.18 of the scheme terms to extend the two-year time limit for making claims. That was because the authority had asked the relevant police force for information in connection with the death and had been told that any relevant papers had been destroyed. The authority upheld that decision on review and H appealed. The First-tier Tribunal dismissed his appeal and the Upper Tribunal refused judicial review of that decision.

Held: Appeal allowed. (1) The judge in the First-tier Tribunal erred in law in his construction of para.18. He had first considered whether there were "particular circumstances", meaning "special circumstances", in H's case. That was a misreading of para.18, which permitted a claims officer to waive the time limit where by reason of the particular circumstances of the case it was reasonable and in the interests of justice to do so. The words "particular circumstances" simply meant the actual circumstances of the particular case. The task of the claims officer was to establish the actual circumstances of the particular case and then ask whether it was reasonable and in the interests of justice to waive the time limit given those circumstances. In performing that exercise, the claims officer had to consider all relevant factors, including the length of any delay, the reasons for it and the nature of the claim itself (see paras 41-42 of judgment). (2) It was arguable that the judge applying the correct test might reasonably have concluded that the time limit should be waived in the instant case. The period of delay was very long and H's approach in gathering all the information he could find before making a claim might have been mistaken. The delay might make the assessment of compensation more difficult. But nevertheless the First-tier Tribunal could reasonably come to the conclusion that the time limit should have been waived (para.43). (3) The court granted permission to apply for judicial review of the decision of the First-tier Tribunal in respect of all three applicants. The case for H's mother and sister was even stronger because they were suffering from mental health problems and could not be blamed for any delay. It was not appropriate for the appeal court to decide whether to grant judicial review. That matter was remitted to the Upper Tribunal to reconsider all the relevant factors to see whether or not it was in the interests of justice to waive the two-year time limit (paras 44-46).

HUTTON v FIRST-TIER TRIBUNAL (SOCIAL ENTITLEMENT CHAMBER), [2012] EWCA Civ 806, [2013] 1 W.L.R. 124, Arden, L.J., CA (Civ Div).

60. Data protection–Monetary penalty notices–Approach to appeals against notices under s.49 Data Protection Act 1998

[Data Protection Act 1998 (c.29) s.41A, s.49, s.51 (7), s.55A, Sch.1.]

The appellant NHS trust appealed against a decision of the respondent Information Commissioner to issue, under the Data Protection Act 1998 s.55A, a monetary penalty notice in the sum of £90,000 in respect of a breach of the data protection principles in Sch.1 to the Act. The trust regularly faxed highly sensitive patient data to a hospice; its relevant protocol required the hospice to be telephoned to ensure receipt of the fax. The trust's administrator sent the data to an additional fax number. She made the telephone check in respect of the first fax number but not the second. The second number was wrong; that emerged when the recipient informed the trust. The trust had sent the data on 45 occasions; it related to 59 vulnerable adults. The recipient said he had shredded the documents, but he could not be traced to verify that. The trust informed the commissioner, who imposed a monetary penalty on the basis that there had been a serious breach of the seventh principle, namely that appropriate organisational measures should be taken against the loss of data. In accordance with the guidance on monetary penalties, the commissioner offered a 20 per cent discount for early payment. He declined the trust's offer to pay the reduced amount without prejudice to its right to appeal. The tribunal considered (i) the appropriate approach for appeals under s.49; (ii) whether the commissioner had conducted an assessment within s.51 (7) but had then impermissibly taken into account matters discovered on that assessment when deciding to impose a monetary penalty, thus wrongly using the voluntary notification process; (iii) whether the commissioner had departed from his own policy in imposing a monetary policy; (iv) mitigating features, including the voluntary notification; (v) whether the commissioner had explained the principles for setting the amount of the penalty; (vi) restoration of the discount.

Held: Appeal dismissed. (1) If the tribunal should be disinclined to disturb the commissioner's conclusions unless there had been an error of public law or he had not had all material evidence before him, s.49(1) (b) would be redundant: public law illegality would fall within s.49(1) (a). Its jurisdiction was wider. It had power to allow the appeal and/or substitute such other notice or decision as could have been served. Where the tribunal was asked to consider the amount of a penalty, it could increase as well as decrease the amount. However, if it were inclined to increase the penalty where the commissioner had not asked for a higher figure, as a matter of procedural fairness it expected to give the data controller the opportunity to make representations before making a final decision (see paras 36-39 of judgment). (2) Section 41A, s.51 (7) and s.55A provided the commissioner with three different powers, each requiring its own investigation and assessment to be made. In the case of s.55A, the statutory guidance explained that the commissioner would undertake an investigation and would then consider whether, in the circumstances, it would be appropriate to issue a monetary penalty notice. That latter stage was clearly an assessment. The trust had failed to satisfactorily explain where s.55A could apply where there was voluntary notification. Accordingly, a voluntary notification of a serious breach of the principles did not preclude the commissioner from investigating the breach with a view to issuing a monetary penalty as well as taking other enforcement action (paras 86-92). (3) The commissioner had not departed from his policy. The policy had made clear that regulatory action could be taken where there was a need to provide reassurance to the public, and that that need was most likely to arise where the circumstances of the breach were already in the public domain. When the trust had informed patients of the breach, it had gone public. As the trust had been unable to contact the recipient, it could not confirm that they had been shredded, so the personal data could still come into the wrong hands (para.102). (4) The commissioner had considered all the factors under s.55A and all the circumstances of the contravention as required by the guidance. Little weight was to be given to the mitigating features relied on by the trust (paras 126, 142, 148). (5) Although the commissioner had not spelt out his methodology, he had explained his reasoning, which appeared to be consistent with the guidance. He had explained the aggravating and mitigating features used in the guidance to assess the amount of the penalty. The trust had been given the opportunity to make representations as to the appropriate amount (paras 136-140). (6) The purpose of the early payment discount appeared to be to encourage early payment and early resolution to the matter. There was no provision for a without prejudice payment. The commissioner's failure to accept the without prejudice offer outside the basis of the guidance was not an error of law or a wrong exercise of discretion. At most, the guidance was a quasi-judicial obligation on the commissioner to provide a discount on specific terms. He had done so in the instant case. The discount would not be restored (paras 153-156).

CENTRAL LONDON COMMUNITY HEALTHCARE NHS TRUST v INFORMATION COMMISSIONER (2013) 130 B.M.L.R. 135, Judge John Angel, FTT.

61. Freedom of information–Provision of information–Whether disclosure necessary for purposes of legitimate interests pursued by data controller–Meaning of "necessary" in Sch.2 para.6 Data Protection Act 1998

[Data Protection Act 1998 (c.29) Sch.2 para.6; Directive 95/46 on the processing of personal data and on the free movement of such data Art.7(e); European Convention on Human Rights 1950 Art.8(2); Freedom of Information (Scotland) Act 2002 (asp 13).]

The appellant local authority appealed against a decision ([2012] CSIH 30) upholding the respondent commissioner's direction that it should disclose certain information pursuant to the Freedom of Information (Scotland) Act 2002. A freelance journalist (F) had made a number of freedom of information requests of the local authority, wanting to know how many of its employees in a particular post were placed at particular points on its pay scales. He did not ask for the employees' names. His purpose was to discover whether the local authority's pay gradings favoured work traditionally done by men: he wrote a blog on equal pay and had connections with a solicitor representing equal pay claimants against the local authority. The local authority refused his request on the ground that compliance would contravene the Data Protection Act 1998. The commissioner held that the information should be disclosed. In so concluding, he considered Data Protection Act 1998 Sch.2 para.6 of the 1998 Act, asking himself whether F had a legitimate interest in obtaining the data; whether disclosure was necessary to achieve his legitimate aims, in other words whether it was proportionate as to means and fairly balanced as to ends; and, if it was, whether it would nevertheless cause unwarranted prejudice to the rights, freedoms or legitimate interests of the data subjects. He also considered correspondence from two Members of the Scottish Parliament supporting F's position, though he did not disclose that correspondence to the local authority. The Inner House upheld his decision. The issues were (i) the proper interpretation of Sch.2 para.6; (ii) whether the commissioner had breached the rules of natural justice in failing to disclose the MSPs' correspondence.

Held: Appeal dismissed. (1) Information was exempt from disclosure under the 2002 Act if it constituted personal data under the 1998 Act and disclosure would contravene any of the data protection principles set out in the latter. Those principles included the stipulation that data ought not to be processed unless at least one of the conditions in Sch.2 of the 1998 Act was met. Thus, the right to disclosure conferred by the 2002 Act did not trump the 1998 Act. Because the conditions in Sch.2 of the 1998 Act applied to any kind of operation performed on the data, any interpretation of them had to be capable of being applied to all the ways in which data might be processed. The word "necessary" appeared in five of the six conditions, and it would be surprising if it were to have different meanings in different conditions. Its interpretation had to be capable of applying to each of the conditions in which it was used. Under Sch.2 para.6, three questions were to be answered: whether a legitimate interest was being pursued by the data controller, the third party or the parties to whom the data was disclosed; whether the processing was necessary for the purposes of that interest; and whether the processing was unwarranted by reason of prejudice to the rights, freedoms or legitimate interests of the data subjects. Authority from the European Court of Justice showed that the word "necessary" required the existence of a pressing social need, and required the interference to be proportionate as to means and fairly balanced as to ends. The ECJ had not, however, supplied its own definition of the word, which had to be considered in relation to the processing to which it related. If that processing involved an interference with the data subjects' rights under the European Convention on Human Rights 1950 art.8, then Rechnungshof v Osterreichischer Rundfunk [2003] 3 CMLR 265 indicated that the proportionality requirements of art.8(2) had to be fulfilled, *Rechnungshof* considered. However, that was a case about Directive 95/46 art.7(e), where there was no express counterbalancing of the necessary processing against the rights and interests of the data subjects. In a case like the instant one, where that balance was built into Sch.2 para.6, it might not matter so much where the proportionality requirements were considered, as long as the overall result was compliant. Because F's request would not enable anybody to discover the identity of the data subjects, it was difficult to see how there was any interference with their art.8 rights. It was enough to apply Sch.2 para.6 on its own terms. Under EU law, "necessary" meant "reasonably" rather than "absolutely" or "strictly" necessary, and it was part of the proportionality test. A measure that interfered with a right protected by EU law had to be the least restrictive for the achievement of a legitimate aim. The commissioner had adopted a test that was probably more favourable to the local authority than was required, and he had been entitled to reach the conclusion he did (see paras 4-8, 18-28 of judgment). (2) The commissioner had not breached the rules of natural justice in not disclosing the MSPs' correspondence to the local authority. He had a duty to act fairly, and he had to seek the local authority's observations and give it notice of any new material that was adverse to its interests. However, not every communication passing between the commissioner and either the applicant or a third party had to be disclosed. In the instant case, the local authority had been aware of the principal issues, F's reasons for seeking the information, and the nature of his interest in it. The correspondence added nothing to the arguments (paras 29-33).

SOUTH LANARKSHIRE COUNCIL v SCOTTISH INFORMATION COMMISSIONER, [2013] UKSC 55, [2013] 1 W.L.R. 2421, Lady Hale, J.S.C., SC.

62. Freedom of information–Public disclosure of information–Research trial concerning efficacy of treatments for medical condition–Appropriateness of ordering disclosure of certain information before date of intended publication

[Freedom of Information Act 2000 (c.36) s.22.]

The appellant university (Q) appealed against a decision of the respondent Information Commissioner ordering the disclosure of certain withheld information concerning a controlled trial, run between 2005 and 2010 and costing roughly £5 million, to examine the efficacy and safety of the currently used main clinical interventions for the treatment of chronic fatigue syndrome/ myalgic encephalopathy. The information requested was a full set of the deterioration (or negative outcome) data for each of the three types of therapy that were used to treat the condition. The Commissioner concluded that, while the Freedom of Information Act 2000 s.22, which concerned information intended for future publication, was engaged, the public interest lay in disclosing the withheld information. The issues were (i) whether it was reasonable for the information to be withheld until the date of intended publication; (ii) whether the public interest in maintaining the s.22 exemption outweighed the public interest in disclosure.

Held: Appeal allowed. (1) Q had given evidence that it intended to publish the information in a peer-reviewed paper. The main paper had been published in 2011. Another primary paper was published in 2012 and three other papers would be published in 2013; they would include the requested data. Q had established that, for the purposes of s.22, it intended to publish the information at a future date. The timescale given was reasonable and, subject to consideration of the public interest, it was reasonable to withhold the information until the date of publication (see paras 13-14 of judgment). (2) Disclosure would not be in the public interest. The additional time sought by Q before publication was necessary to enable the proper analysis and scientific commentary to be prepared and then scrutinised through a process of internal review and then external peer review, both of which were in the public interest in order to ensure that scientific rigour was maintained and that maximum value was achieved from the public investment (para.33).

QUEEN MARY UNIVERSITY OF LONDON v INFORMATION COMMISSIONER (2013) 133 B.M.L.R. 210, Judge Fiona Henderson, FTT (GRC).

63. Investigations–Parliamentary Commissioner for Administration

THE PARLIAMENTARY COMMISSIONER ORDER 2013, SI 2013/238; made under the Parliamentary Commissioner Act 1967 s.4, s.5. In force: April 1, 2013; .

This Order amends the Parliamentary Commissioner Act 1967. Article 2 of this Order amends Schedule 2 to the Act (departments etc. subject to investigation). It adds the Regulatory Policy Committee to the list of departments and authorities which are subject to investigation by the Parliamentary Commissioner for Administration; it omits from that list those bodies referred to in article 2(b); and it amends those entries in the list referred to in article 2(c) and (d). Article 3 amends Schedule 3 to the Act (matters not subject to investigation) to exclude certain actions of the Secretary of State in connection with the occupational benefit schemes under the Naval, Military and Air Forces etc. (Disablement and Death) Service Pensions Order 2006 and the Armed Forces and Reserve Forces (Compensation Scheme) Order 2011.

64. Irrationality–National security–List compiled by United Nations Security Council of names of individuals associated with Al-Qaida–Legality of Foreign Secretary's decision to agree to list individual–Criteria for designation

The claimant (Y) applied for judicial review of a decision of the defendant secretary of state to agree to his name being placed on a list of individuals associated with Al-Qaida. In September 2005 Y's name was placed on a list of entities and individuals associated with Al-Qaida by a committee of the United Nations Security Council; the committee consisted of all the member states of the Security Council and the identity of the designating state was not disclosed. The Security Service assessment was that Y had been a leading member of the Egyptian Islamic Jihad (EIJ); he was involved in falsifying documentation for the EIJ, his views remained extreme and the potential remained for him to re-engage with the EIJ. A few years prior to the listing, an Egyptian military court found Y guilty of terrorist offences in his absence although Y maintained that the evidence had probably been obtained by torture. The United Kingdom government subsequently unsuccessfully sought Y's de-listing as although it stood by the 2005 assessment, its view was that Y would be unlikely to re-engage with the EIJ. Y submitted that (1) the court should determine for itself whether he met the criteria for designation rather than limiting itself to judging whether the Foreign Secretary's decision was lawful under the usual public law principles; (2) if he failed in his rationality challenge on the open material, there should be a further hearing to examine the closed material; (3) there was nothing in the documentation submitted to the Foreign Secretary to show that Y had met the criteria that there was a subsisting association between him and Al-Qaida; (4) his conviction by the Egyptian military court was based on evidence obtained by torture and other members of the committee should have been prevented from designating him on an improper basis; (5) the standard of proof applied by the Foreign Secretary, namely that the Foreign Secretary would have considered whether there were reasonable grounds for suspecting that Y met the criteria for designation, was too low.

Held: Application refused. (1) There was no proper basis in law for applying principles other than the usual public law principles in considering the legality of the Foreign Secretary's decision. Furthermore, a decision as to whether a person would meet the criteria for designation would involve an evaluation of intelligence material which the Foreign Secretary would be in a better position to make than a judge (see paras 56-57 of judgment). (2) The two-stage process advocated by Y would not be right as a matter of case management and, more fundamentally, as a matter of justice. Nevertheless, the fact that the court did not have the full picture was recognised as a reason for it giving particular respect to the minister's decision, *Secretary of State for the Home Department v Rehman* [2001] UKHL 47, [2003] 1 A.C. 153, [2001] C.L.Y. 3662 applied (paras 68-71). (3) There did not have to be evidence of current involvement in the acts identified as indicative of association in order for the Foreign Secretary to have rationally concluded that Y met the criteria of being associated with Al-Qaida at the relevant time. Absence of evidence of current active participation may or may not signify absence of association, depending on all the circumstances. The Security Service's assessment was that Y continued to hold extremist views and presented a continuing risk of participation in the activities of the EIJ (paras 80-81). (4) The evidence did not support Y's submission. It would not be right for the court to dictate to the Foreign Secretary that he had to instruct other member states as to what might be a permissible basis for the designation and had to prevent a designation unless he was satisfied that they were all proceeding on a basis which he considered to be proper (paras 87-90). (5) The relevant test to be applied as set out by the Ombudsperson in her report to the Security Council was "whether there was sufficient information to provide a reasonable and credible basis for the listing". The accompanying explanation referred to a test of "reasonable grounds to suspect or believe" involvement in or commission of terrorist acts or activities. It was therefore not unlawful for the Foreign Secretary to have applied the test which he had done at the relevant time (paras 93-95).

R. (ON THE APPLICATION OF YOUSSEF) v SECRETARY OF STATE FOR FOREIGN AND COMMONWEALTH AFFAIRS; *sub nom.* YOUSSEF v SECRETARY OF STATE FOR FOREIGN AND COMMONWEALTH AFFAIRS, [2012] EWHC 2091 (Admin), [2013] Q.B. 906, Toulson, L.J., QBD (Admin).

65. Ministers' powers and duties–Access to justice–Staff at secure training centres using unlawful restraint techniques on trainees–Whether secretary of state obliged to inform trainees of unlawful nature of techniques

[European Convention on Human Rights 1950 Art.3, Art.6, Art.8.]

The appellant (C) appealed against a judge's refusal ([2012] EWHC 8 (Admin)) to order the respondent secretary of state to provide information about the unlawful use of restraint techniques in secure training centres. The centres were operated by the interested parties under contract with the secretary of state. They accommodated young offenders, known as trainees. The judge concluded that the unlawful use of bodily restraint techniques on the trainees had been widespread, officers having used the techniques in the mistaken belief that they were entitled to do so in order to maintain good order and discipline. At the time, few of the trainees realised that the use of the techniques was unlawful. C, a children's charity, asserted that the secretary of state was obliged to inform those potentially affected by the unlawful restraint that they might have been so affected. C submitted that the secretary of state was responsible for the trainees' ignorance; that common law required him to give them information about the use of the restraint techniques so that they might have proper access to justice; and that even if he had no duty to provide that information in the name of access to justice, to decline to do so would be *Wednesbury* unreasonable. The intervener (E) submitted that the secretary of state's failure to provide the information breached the European Convention on Human Rights 1950 art.3, art.6 and art.8.

Held: Appeal dismissed. (1) In the majority of cases the trainees had accepted the restraint techniques as part of the centres' routines. The secretary of state was responsible for that in the sense that it had been brought about by the confused thinking within the secure training centre regime as to the scope of the power of restraint. However, C had not established that the secretary of state was responsible in the sense of having taken steps to prevent exposure of any concerns about the use of restraint for good order and discipline (see para.28 of judgment). (2) The common law recognised a right of access to the courts and to legal advice, and the right to communicate confidentially with a legal adviser. C's argument was that it also recognised a right to have notice of an executive decision before it could take legal effect. Despite C's protestations that it applied uniquely to the instant case, that amounted to an argument that, at least in some circumstances, a potential defendant to a civil suit had to declare himself as such. That could not be right. Such a duty could not apply to a private tortfeasor, could not be owed universally, and would be inimical to the requirement that justice should be even-handed. While the cases recognised the state's duty not to impede access to justice, that was as far as they went. Not even *R. (on the application of Anufrijeva) v Secretary of State for the Home Department* [2003] UKHL 36, [2004] 1 A.C. 604, [2003] C.L.Y. 2223 assisted C, the House of Lords there requiring that notice of the fact of a decision should be given before it could operate to the detriment of affected persons. C was seeking notice of the legal quality of acts done, not of facts or events, *Anufrijeva* distinguished. A positive duty on the state to provide a potential claimant with the legal elements of his case would be discordant with the adversarial system of justice. The right of access to the courts was to be understood as a duty on the state not to place obstacles in the way of access to justice. The secretary of state had not breached that duty in the instant case (paras 29-38). (3) The *Wednesbury* unreasonableness argument had to fail. It depended on the proposition that the right of access to justice required that the information be given, and that proposition had been rejected. Moreover, the material information was in the public domain and there had been systems in place whereby trainees could raise concerns and seek legal advice (paras 42-47). (4) None of the cases cited supported an interpretation of art.6 that would impose a duty of the kind contended for by C and E. Such a duty could not be owed only in the instant case, and there was no basis for extending it to a wider, but not universal, class of beneficiaries. Strasbourg would not have perpetrated such an unprincipled state of affairs. Similarly, E's arguments on art.3 and art.8 failed. An order for the provision of information was not an investigation for the purposes of art.3, and the cases cited in support of the art.8 arguments were all instances of failures by the state to provide factual information that should have been given to secure the effectiveness of the Convention right. There was nothing in the Strasbourg case law to support the duty contended for, and nothing to show that the United Nations Convention on the Rights of the Child had been used as an interpretive tool to fashion such a duty. For the instant court to do so would be contrary to the principle in *R. (on the application of Ullah) v Special Adjudicator* [2004] UKHL 26, [2004] 2 A.C. 323, [2004] C.L.Y. 2009 (paras 50-59). (5) (Per curiam) It was hoped that the *Ullah* principle might be revisited. There was much to be gained from the development of a municipal jurisprudence of Convention rights, and that the law of human rights should be seen to be a part of domestic law, *Ullah* considered. (para.64).

R. (ON THE APPLICATION OF CHILDREN'S RIGHTS ALLIANCE FOR ENGLAND) v SECRETARY OF STATE FOR JUSTICE; *sub nom.* CHILDREN'S RIGHTS ALLIANCE FOR ENGLAND v SECRETARY OF STATE FOR JUSTICE, [2013] EWCA Civ 34, [2013] 1 W.L.R. 3667, Laws, L.J., CA (Civ Div).

66. Ministers' powers and duties–Regulations–Claimant's assets frozen as result of EU sanctions–Challenge to decisions of UK government to propose and maintain listing–Whether claim necessarily involved impermissible ruling on validity of Community act

[Regulation 314/2004 on restrictive measures in respect of Zimbabwe.]

The court was required to determine preliminary issues in a claim by a Zimbabwean national (B) challenging the lawfulness of decisions of the defendant secretary of state proposing that he be listed under Regulation 314/2004, concerning sanctions on Zimbabwe, and later refusing to assist in procuring the removal of his name from the list. The Regulation froze funds and economic resources belonging to persons, entities and bodies listed in Annex III. B and companies owned and controlled by him were listed between January 2009 and February 2012. He brought an action in the Court of Justice of the European Communities against the Commission seeking the annulment of the Commission Regulation by which his name and his companies had been added to the list. His case was stayed pending the judgment in another case and was only reconsidered after his delisting. The ECJ then decided that his case no longer required adjudication, because he no longer had any interest in annulling the Regulation, but it awarded him his costs. In the meantime B had brought judicial review proceedings against the defendant secretary of state seeking declarations that the decisions to propose his inclusion in Annex III and subsequently to refuse to assist in procuring the removal of his name were unlawful. Permission to apply for judicial review was granted but the secretary of state contended that the claim was in substance a challenge to the validity of the Commission Regulations including or maintaining his name on the list and that permitting the claim to proceed would be contrary to the decision in *Firma Foto Frost v Hauptzollamt Lubeck-Ost (314/85)* [1987] E.C.R. 4199, [1989] C.L.Y. 1646 which held that a national court did not have the power to declare a Community act to be invalid. The parties agreed to the hearing of preliminary issues. The secretary of state contended that the claim should be dismissed because B was in substance asking the court to declare Community acts invalid; alternatively the proceeding should be stayed while an appeal was made and pursued against the ECJ's decision. B submitted that his claim would not inevitably require the court to rule any Community act invalid, that an appeal was not an alternative remedy and that comity did not require a stay.

Held: Preliminary issues determined in favour of claimant. (1) Permission to apply for judicial review having been granted, it would require a strong and clear case on jurisdiction to deprive B of the opportunity to pursue that remedy. The *Foto Frost* principle was quite narrowly defined; it did not prevent a national court ruling on domestic unlawfulness where that might also involve implied or express criticism of Community processes or acts, *Foto Frost* considered. Unless a ruling that a Community act was invalid was the inevitable precursor to success for B, the claim should continue (see paras 40, 43-45 of judgment). (2) The refusal to request the delisting of B and his companies was a decision taken by the secretary of state, not a Community institution. It was taken on whatever material he had, but the fact that he might have taken account of Community or Member State material did not make it inevitable that success for B would require a ruling that a Community act was invalid. The position in respect of the proposal to list was more difficult. The secretary of state had reached and promoted the view that B should be listed, but the listing process was a Community process from the outset in which the United Kingdom participated, rather than possessing a distinctively UK national stage or decision. The fact of engagement in a collective intergovernmental process, the lawfulness of which could not itself be challenged, did not inevitably rule out a challenge to the domestic decision, *A v HM Treasury* [2010] UKSC 2, [2010] 2 A.C. 534, [2010] C.L.Y. 2031 considered. In the circumstances the court had jurisdiction to continue with the claim. On the basis that the tests for lawfulness were materially the same as between the national and Community courts, it could not be said to be inevitable that a distinct UK decision could not be disentangled so that its lawfulness rather than the lawfulness of the Community act could be resolved. It was not easy to see how the UK government's act could be unlawful when the Community act was assumed to be lawful, but that would be a matter for argument when the facts were known about what the UK government actually did (paras 52-60). (3) The existence of an appeal against the ECJ decision did not provide an alternative remedy to B's action since it could not provide any remedy in respect of the unlawfulness alleged against the secretary of state. It was doubtful whether an appeal would be effective or convenient either, *Kay v Lambeth LBC* [2006] UKHL 10, [2006] 2 A.C. 465, [2006] C.L.Y. 2173 considered (paras 63-66). (4) Comity did not require the action to be stayed while an appeal was pursued or on any other basis (paras 67-71).

R. (ON THE APPLICATION OF BREDENKAMP) v SECRETARY OF STATE FOR FOREIGN AND COMMONWEALTH AFFAIRS, [2012] EWHC 3297 (Admin), [2013] 2 C.M.L.R. 10, Ouseley, J., QBD (Admin).

67. Ministers' powers and duties–Regulations–Discretionary powers–Obligation to draft and lay regulations before Parliament under Mental Health (Care and Treatment) (Scotland) Act 2003–Failure to draft regulations

[Mental Health (Care and Treatment) (Scotland) Act 2003 (asp 13) s.268(2), s.271, s.333.]

The appellant patient (P) appealed against the refusal ([2011] CSIH 19, 2012 S.C. 397, [2011] C.L.Y. 3964) of his application for judicial review of the respondent Ministers' failure to bring certain legislation into effect. P had been detained in a non-state hospital since 1995. He wished to be transferred to an open ward to improve his prospects of release. The Mental Health (Care and Treatment) (Scotland) Act 2003 s.268(2) stated that "qualifying patients" detained in a "qualifying hospital" could apply to the Mental Health Tribunal for Scotland for an order that they were being detained in conditions of excessive security and should be transferred to an alternative hospital. Section 268 of the Act was required by s.333 to come into effect by May 1, 2006. However it was not effective in the absence of regulations defining "qualifying patients" and "qualifying hospital". P was therefore prevented from making an application to the tribunal. He sought judicial review of the ministers' failure to draft and lay regulations before the Scottish Parliament but his claim was refused. P submitted that the intention of the Scottish Parliament was that all of the relevant provisions of the Act should be in effective operation by May 1, 2006, and the Ministers' failure to make the regulations was unlawful. The Ministers argued that there was no duty to make regulations because the Act had not conferred a class of persons with a right but merely permitted the identification of such persons by regulation.

Held: Appeal allowed. (1) There was a distinction between bringing an Act into force and giving full effect to an Act. Section 333 stated that the relevant provisions "shall come into force on 1st May 2006". That referred only to the bringing of the provisions into force as law, and not to their being brought into effective operation. However, that did not permit one to infer that Parliament did not intend the provisions to be brought into effective operation on the date when they came into force. On the contrary, it was ordinarily reasonable to infer that when it fixed a date when a provision was to come into force Parliament was not envisaging that the provision would technically have the force of law but in practice be a dead letter. Parliament would legislate only for the purpose of bringing about an effective result that would have practical consequences for the life of the community, *Nokes v Doncaster Amalgamated Collieries Ltd* [1940] A.C. 1014 considered. It was natural to infer that Parliament's intention was that once the allotted time had expired, the provision should be brought into effective operation as well as being given legal effect. Further, Parliament's decision to fix the time by which the provisions were to come into force ordinarily reflected the importance which it attached to the practical effect of the provision in question (see paras 31-37, 41 of judgment). (2) The fundamental flaw in the Ministers' argument was to assume that an obligation to exercise a discretionary power could only arise where the exercise of the power was necessary to make effective a legal right. That approach was too narrow, *Padfield v Minister of Agriculture, Fisheries and Food* [1968] A.C. 997, [1968] C.L.Y. 1667 applied and *Julius v Lord Bishop of Oxford* (1880) 5 App. Cas. 214 considered. Even where a statute conferred a discretionary power, a failure to exercise the power would be unlawful if it was contrary to Parliament's intention. That intention might be to create legal rights which could only be made effective if the power was exercised or it might be to bring about some other result which was similarly dependent upon the exercise of the power (paras 44-47). (3) It was a basic principle of administrative law that a discretionary power could not be used to frustrate the object of the Act which conferred it. Given that it was the intention of the Scottish Parliament that the relevant provisions should be in effective operation by May 1, 2006 at the latest, it followed that although Ministers had a discretion as to the manner in which they exercised their power to make the necessary regulations, they were under a duty to exercise that power no later than May 1, 2006. Their failure to make the necessary regulations by or since that date had thus thwarted the intention of the Scottish Parliament and was unlawful (paras 42-47).

M v SCOTTISH MINISTERS; *sub nom.* RM v SCOTTISH MINISTERS, [2012] UKSC 58, [2012] 1 W.L.R. 3386, Lord Hope, J.S.C. (Deputy President), SC.

68. Protection of Freedoms Act 2012 (c.9)–Commencement No.8 Order

THE PROTECTION OF FREEDOMS ACT 2012 (COMMENCEMENT NO.8) ORDER 2013, SI 2013/SI 2013/1906 (C.81); made under the Protection of Freedoms Act 2012 s.120. Commencement details: bringing into force various provisions of the July 31, 2013 and September 1, 2013.; .

This Order commences provisions of the Protection of Freedoms Act 2012 relating to: the power to charge fees in relation to release of datasets for re-use; the release and publication of datasets held by public authorities; the meaning of "publicly owned company" in the 2000 Act; and the powers of the Information Commissioner.

AGENCY

69. Agency agreements–Commercial agents–Consequences of breach of duty under reg.3 Commercial Agents (Council Directive) Regulations 1993–Principal's entitlement to terminate agency contract

[Commercial Agents (Council Directive) Regulations 1993 (SI 1993/3053) reg.3, reg.5(2).]

The appellant principal (C) appealed against a judgment in favour of the respondent agent (S) in its claim against C for summarily terminating its commercial agency contract. S had been the United Kingdom agent for the sale of C's footwear products. S's employees posted comments about C on a website. A link was sent to S's other employees and to third parties, including some of C's customers and distributors. The website was later taken down. S said that the comments were a joke about C's failure to respond to orders; C claimed that they disparaged the products which it had appointed S to sell and constituted a repudiation of the agency contract. The judge held that while S had breached the contract, the breach was insufficiently serious to be repudiatory. C argued that (1) the judge had erred in holding that breach of the duty under the Commercial Agents (Council Directive) Regulations 1993 reg.3 only entitled the principal to determine the agency contract if it was sufficiently serious: reg.3 should be read as a condition, any breach of which would entitle the principal to terminate the contract; alternatively, reg.3 created a statutory duty, the breach of which repudiated the contract; (2) S's breach of fiduciary duty automatically entitled C to terminate the contract; (3) S's conduct had in any event been sufficiently serious to be repudiatory.

Held: Appeal dismissed. (1) Regulation 3 was not expressed as, nor did it create, a condition of the contract the breach of which would automatically terminate the agency contract. It did no more than set out the relevant obligations of the agent. Nor did the Regulations spell out that, as a specific consequence of breach, the agency contract was, or could be, terminated. Regulation 5(2) made that implication impossible by expressly providing that the consequence of the breach of that Regulation was a matter for the law governing that contract (see paras 45-46, 62 of judgment). (2) The general principles of fiduciary law did not support C's submissions of automatic termination of the contract by breach of fiduciary duty. The fiduciary character of the contractual relationship was clearly relevant, but was subject to the qualification that not all duties owed within a fiduciary relationship were properly classed as fiduciary duties, and not all breaches of duty properly classed as fiduciary either automatically or necessarily repudiated the contract. Breaches of fiduciary duty were capable of other consequences and remedies, depending on the nature of the duty, the circumstances of the breach and the parties' intentions in relation to the contract. An analogy with employees' duties did not assist C: there were cases in which an isolated act of misconduct had not justified summary termination of the contract (paras 47-49). (3) The judge had addressed the correct question, namely how serious, in all the circumstances, S's conduct had been. The evidence had been sufficient to support the judge's assessment that the breach was not as serious as C had contended and that S's conduct had not justified summary termination. The website had not in terms disparaged C's goods but had referred to its inability to meet delivery obligations, a state of affairs that was well known. Its style had been obviously jokey and its circulation limited and temporary. There was no evidence of harm suffered by C. The disparagement of C had been a breach of contract but not a breach going to the root of the agency relationship. It was a one-off incident that had not involved bad faith on S's part, was not shown to have involved a real risk of harm to C by dissemination to the world at large, and had not evinced an intention to abandon the agency contract (paras 50-52).

CROCS EUROPE BV v ANDERSON (T/A SPECTRUM AGENCIES (A PARTNERSHIP)), [2012] EWCA Civ 1400, [2013] 1 Lloyd's Rep. 1, Mummery, L.J., CA (Civ Div).

70. Agents' powers and duties–Conflict of interest–Entitlement of agent to act for multiple principals with conflicting interests–Dangers of preliminary issues trials

[Commercial Agents (Council Directive) Regulations 1993 (SI 1993/3053) reg.18(c).]

The appellant (D), the principal under an agency contract, appealed against orders made following the hearing of preliminary issues ([2011] EWHC 2482 (QB), [2012] 1 All E.R. (Comm) 18, [2012] C.L.Y. 59) in proceedings commenced by the respondent agents (S and R). The parties had entered into an agency agreement to which the Commercial Agents (Council Directive) Regulations 1993 applied. D was a Thai manufacturer of leather furniture and S was a company which helped Asian furniture manufacturers to penetrate the United Kingdom market. The agreement came to an end consensually after around four years when R was created with the same personnel as S, and D's contract moved seamlessly to R. D ended the agency contract after about six months in reliance on common law. In the ensuing proceedings by R for compensation under the Regulations, nine issues were determined preliminary to trial. Some of the determinations led to argument that was resolved in a second judgment. D appealed against (i) a finding that S and R had been entitled to act for D's competitors; (ii) the judge's characterisation of the process by which R replaced S as D's agent as an "assignment"; (iii) orders that it should make an interim payment of £500,000 in respect of R's substantive claim and a payment on account of R's costs of the preliminary issues trial of £300,000.

Held: Appeal allowed in part. (1) As a general proposition, an agent could act for two principals with conflicting interests only where either both principals agreed, or where the agent fell within the "residential estate agents" category as described in *Kelly v Cooper* [1993] A.C. 205, [1993] C.L.Y. 72. Although D had known, and not objected to, S acting for two of its competitors, it had been led to believe that their products did not clash with its own and it could not therefore be said that D had given informed consent to a potential conflict of interest situation. The judge had been right to find that *Kelly* did not apply, since there were no grounds to do so, or to conclude that the normal non-compete principle should not apply. It followed, therefore, that S could not act for principals other than D in so far as their product ranges clashed. What was said in Bowstead & Reynolds On Agency, edited by Peter G Watts, 19th edn (London: Sweet & Maxwell, 2010) para.6-045, fn 294 about the prospect of extending the reasoning in *Kelly* to other agency cases being highly questionable, was supported by commentary commending the approach of the House of Lords in *Hilton v Barker Booth & Eastwood* [2005] UKHL 8, [2005] 1 W.L.R. 567, [2005] C.L.Y. 2881 *Kelly* and *Hilton* considered. It was not clear, owing to certain ambiguities, whether the instant findings were consistent with those of the judge below or not (see paras 22-27, 30, 34-36, 39-42, 47 of judgment). (2) When R was established, with effectively the same ownership and directors as S, the judge had found the agency agreement between S and D to have been replaced with an identical arrangement between R and D. He had, however, erred in finding that that was an assignment at common law. Contractual assignment was not an easy concept, and it was more consistent with common law to term the arrangement as a new agency agreement, impliedly on the same terms as the previous one. It was arguably a novation, although there was no need to reach a conclusion on that issue. However S's agency agreement came to be replicated between R and D, R could still be treated as S's successor by virtue of reg.18(c): the fact that common law treated the new agency as a new contract rather than an assignment was irrelevant to the commercial purpose of the Regulations. R therefore had the benefit of S's rights and claims under the Regulations, but any claims by D could be set off against them (paras 50-51, 54-56). (3) The judge had been wrong to order the interim payment because the question whether D had been justified in invoking common law to terminate the agreement with R had not yet been determined and the judge had misconstrued a significant authority. It could not be said that R would be the net winner once D's set-off had been assessed. The interim payment was set aside (paras 58-60, 64, 67-68). The costs order was set aside for essentially the same reasons (para.72) (4) (Obiter) The case represented a cautionary tale about the dangers of preliminary issues. Matters were so unclear that not even the instant court knew whether it was allowing or dismissing the instant appeal. Preliminary issues hearings were to be resisted where possible, but where they went ahead, it was vital that both the issues and the agreed facts or assumptions on which they were based were simply, clearly and precisely formulated, and that the issues were answered in a clear and precise way (paras 1, 74-79).

ROSSETTI MARKETING LTD v DIAMOND SOFA CO LTD, [2012] EWCA Civ 1021, [2013] 1 All E.R. (Comm) 308, Lord Neuberger (M.R.), CA (Civ Div).

71. Secret profits–Equitable remedies–Agent receiving secret commission from third party–Whether constructive trust existed in favour of principal on commission received by agent

The appellant investors (F) appealed against a decision ([2011] EWHC 2999 (Ch)) concerning the appropriate remedy against the respondent agent (C) for making a secret profit. While advising F in relation to their purchase of a hotel in Monte Carlo, C entered into an agreement with the sellers of the hotel under which C was to receive a fixed commission of EUR 10 million for securing a purchaser for the hotel. C failed to notify F of that agreement. C received the commission from the sellers when they sold the hotel to F for EUR 211.5 million. In *FHR European Ventures LLP v Mankarious* [2011] EWHC 2308 (Ch), [2012] 2 B.C.L.C. 39, [2012] C.L.Y. 57 the court found that the commission amounted to a secret profit. At a further hearing the court decided that F were entitled to an account in equity rather than to a proprietary remedy against C's commission. F submitted that they were entitled to a proprietary remedy because C's commission had been paid out of the sale proceeds which came from F. F also argued that C had a duty as their agent to negotiate the lowest price and, in accepting the commission, C had diverted from F the opportunity to acquire the hotel for a lower price.

Held: Appeal allowed. (1) There was no challenge to the basic principle that a fiduciary was not entitled to profit from a breach of his fiduciary duty. The issue was whether F's remedy against C was personal or proprietary and therefore whether F had acquired a proprietary interest in the commission paid to C. The argument was really about following and tracing (see paras 13-14, 61 of judgment). (2) *Sinclair Investments (UK) Ltd v Versailles Trade Finance Ltd (In Administration)* [2011] EWCA Civ 347, [2012] Ch. 453, [2011] C.L.Y. 3499 divided into three categories the situations in which a fiduciary obtained a benefit in breach of fiduciary duty. The first category was where the benefit was an asset belonging beneficially to the principal, most obviously where the fiduciary had gained the benefit by misappropriating the principal's property. The second category was where the benefit had been obtained by the fiduciary taking advantage of an opportunity which was properly that of the principal. The third category was all other cases. The court held in *Sinclair* that the situations in categories one and two gave rise to a constructive trust, but those in category three did not, *Sinclair* applied. The issues in the instant case arose out of the difficulty of ascertaining the borderline between categories two and three (para.83). (3) F's first argument was founded on the proposition that the monies paid to the seller never ceased to belong beneficially to F. However, when F paid the seller, it must have been the intention of both parties that in return for the hotel, the seller would acquire the beneficial title to the sale price, *Westdeutsche Landesbank Girozentrale v Islington LBC* [1996] A.C. 669, [1996] C.L.Y. 4149 considered. It could not be said that any part of the payment by F to the seller remained F's property (paras 30-33). (4) It was not necessary to isolate the opportunity to acquire an asset at a lower price from the opportunity to acquire an asset at all, *Cadogan Petroleum Plc v Tolly* [2011] EWHC 2286 (Ch), [2012] 1 P. & C.R. DG5 doubted. Nor was there any need to enquire whether F could be said to have a proprietary interest in that opportunity. The principle to be applied was whether the fiduciary's exploitation of the opportunity was such as to attract the application of the rule that the fiduciary would hold the profit on trust for the principal, *Bhullar v Bhullar* [2003] EWCA Civ 424, [2003] B.C.C. 711, [2003] C.L.Y. 520, *Tyrrell v Bank of London* 11 E.R. 934, *Whaley Bridge Calico Printing Co v Green* (1879) 5 Q.B.D. 109 and *Boardman v Phipps* [1967] 2 A.C. 46, [1966] C.L.Y. 11052 applied. C's commission was paid within five working days of the seller's receipt of the purchase money. It was plain that in reality F's money funded the commission paid to C. It was material that the seller was in fact prepared to receive a net sum of EUR 201.5 million from the sale, after paying C's EUR 10 million commission. That fact was not made known to F. Had it been, F might have deferred contracting to purchase the hotel until C's agreement with the seller had lapsed. Alternatively, C could have reduced their fee to F, thereby reducing the cost to them of purchasing the hotel. Those facts brought the instant case into category two rather than category three. C's agreement with the seller diverted from F the opportunity to purchase the hotel at a lower price. C therefore held the commission on constructive trust for F (paras 59, 69-73, 106-110). (5) The instant case threw into clear relief the considerable difficulties inherent in the *Sinclair* decision. There was a need for the Supreme Court to overhaul the entire area of constructive trusts in order to provide a coherent and logical legal framework (para.116).

FHR EUROPEAN VENTURES LLP v MANKARIOUS, [2013] EWCA Civ 17, [2014] Ch. 1, Sir Terence Etherton (Chancellor), CA (Civ Div).

AGRICULTURE

72. Agricultural holdings–Agricultural land–Income–England

THE AGRICULTURAL HOLDINGS (UNITS OF PRODUCTION) (ENGLAND) ORDER 2013, SI 2013/2607; made under the Agricultural Holdings Act 1986 Sch.6 para.4. In force: November 7, 2013; .

This Order sets out values for agricultural production, which are used in assessing the productive capacity of agricultural land and to determine whether it is a "commercial unit" of agricultural land. A "commercial unit" of agricultural land is defined in the Agricultural Holdings Act 1986 and means a unit of agricultural land which, if farmed under competent management, is capable of producing a net annual income which is not less than the sum of the average earnings of two full-time, male agricultural workers aged twenty or over.

73. Animal by-products–Wales

THE BOVINE SEMEN (WALES) (AMENDMENT) REGULATIONS 2013, SI 2013/ SI 2013/398 (W.48); made under the Animal Health and Welfare Act 1984 s.10. In force: March 18, 2013; .

These Regulations amend the Bovine Semen (Wales) Regulations 2008 (SI 2008/1040) to establish two regimes: one by which semen may be collected and processed for trade with other EU member States; and one by which semen may be collected for use in the UK.

74. Biocidal products–EU law

THE BIOCIDAL PRODUCTS AND CHEMICALS (APPOINTMENT OF AUTHORITIES AND ENFORCEMENT) REGULATIONS 2013, SI 2013/1506; made under the European Communities Act 1972 s.2, Sch.2 para.1A; and the Health and Safety at Work etc. Act 1974 s.15, s.82, Sch.3 para.1, Sch.3 para.2, Sch.3 para.4, Sch.3 para.6, Sch.3 para.13, Sch.3 para.15.. In force: in accordance with reg.2.; .

These Regulations provide for the appointment of competent authorities in relation to Regulation 528/2012 concerning the making available on the market and use of biocidal products.

75. Cattle–Identification

THE CATTLE IDENTIFICATION (AMENDMENT) REGULATIONS 2013, SI 2013/ 517; made under the European Communities Act 1972 s.2. In force: April 6, 2013; .

This amendment to the Cattle Identification Regulations 2007 expands the choice of official channels available to cattle keepers to use in order to comply with their existing duties to notify cattle births, movements and deaths to the British Cattle Movement Service (BCMS). It removes, also, a requirement for the Official Veterinarians of the Food Standards Agency or their representatives to collect cattle passports for all cattle slaughtered in slaughterhouses and return them to BCMS. These will now be returned by slaughterhouse operators, simplifying the process. The change will improve the efficiency of the cattle tracing system, making it cheaper and more accurate, and decreasing the costs to businesses of complying with legislation.

76. Cattle–Identification–Wales

THE CATTLE IDENTIFICATION (WALES) (AMENDMENT) REGULATIONS 2013, SI 2013/SI 2013/821 (W.97); made under the European Communities Act 1972 s.2. In force: May 1, 2013; .

These Regulations amend the Cattle Identification (Wales) Regulations 2007, by: clarifying the role of the competent authority in relation to unidentified animals; making provision to remove the need for the occupiers of slaughterhouses to enter certain details into the passports of animals they have slaughtered; and making provision to allow keepers to report animal movements by using the new automated telephony system as a method of notification and also to report animal deaths using electronic methods as well as paper.

77. Crops–Seeds–Wales

THE SEED MARKETING (WALES) (AMENDMENT) REGULATIONS 2013, SI 2013/SI 2013/889 (W.101); made under the Plant Varieties and Seeds Act 1964 s.16, s.35. In force: May 10, 2013; .

These Regulations amend the Seed Marketing (Wales) Regulations 2012 (SI 2012/245). One of the amendments allows Welsh Ministers to license exemptions for temporary experiments organised under any of the five European Directives on the marketing of, respectively, beet seed, cereal seed, fodder plant seed, seed of oil and fibre plants and vegetable seed.

78. Enterprise and Regulatory Reform Act 2013 (c.24)–Commencement No.1, Transitional Provisions and Savings Order

THE ENTERPRISE AND REGULATORY REFORM ACT 2013 (COMMENCEMENT NO.1, TRANSITIONAL PROVISIONS AND SAVINGS) ORDER 2013, SI 2013/SI 2013/1455 (C.55); made under the Enterprise and Regulatory Reform Act 2013 s.100, s.103. Commencement details: bringing into force various provisions of the 2013 Act on June 25, 2013 and October 1, 2013.; .

This Order commences certain provisions of the Enterprise and Regulatory Reform Act 2013 relating to the Agricultural Wages Board in England and Wales and related English Agricultural Wages Committees and Agricultural Dwelling-House Advisory Committees.

79. Enterprise and Regulatory Reform Act 2013 (c.24)–Commencement No.1, Transitional Provisions and Savings (Amendment) Order

THE ENTERPRISE AND REGULATORY REFORM ACT 2013 (COMMENCEMENT NO.1, TRANSITIONAL PROVISIONS AND SAVINGS) (AMENDMENT) ORDER 2013, SI 2013/SI 2013/2271 (C.94); made under the Enterprise and Regulatory Reform Act 2013 s.100, s.103. In force: September 7, 2013; .

This Order amends the Enterprise and Regulatory Reform Act 2013 (Commencement No.1, Transitional Provisions and Savings) Order 2013 (SI 2013/145) as regards provisions concerning agricultural wages.

80. European Agricultural Guarantee Fund–European Agricultural Guidance and Guarantee Fund–Hill farming

THE UPLANDS TRANSITIONAL PAYMENT REGULATIONS 2013, SI 2013/109; made under the European Communities Act 1972 s.2. In force: February 15, 2013; .

These Regulations specify the rates of the uplands transitional payment for 2013. They also lay down the conditions of entitlement to such payments.

81. Fees–Plant health–Wales

THE PLANT HEALTH (EXPORT CERTIFICATION) (WALES) (AMENDMENT) ORDER 2013, SI 2013/SI 2013/1658 (W.156); made under the Plant Health Act 1967 s.3, s.4A. In force: July 31, 2013; .

This Order, which comes into force on July 31, 2013, amends the Plant Health (Export Certification) (Wales) Order 2006 (SI 2006/1701) and provides for increases on the fees specified in the 2006 Order as follows: fees for services in respect of application for certificates by a range from 15 per cent to 130 per cent; and fees for pre-export services by 85 per cent.

82. Forestry–Plant health

THE PLANT HEALTH (FORESTRY) (AMENDMENT) (ENGLAND AND SCOTLAND) ORDER 2013, SI 2013/2691; made under the Plant Health Act 1967 s.2, s.3; and the European Communities Act 1972 Sch.2 para.1A. In force: November 11, 2013; .

This Order amends the Plant Health (Forestry) Order 2005, which contains measures to prevent the introduction and spread of harmful tree pests and diseases. It introduces emergency measures to strengthen the existing measures against certain fungal diseases.

83. Fruit–Infectious disease control–Plant health–Brazil

THE PLANT HEALTH (ENGLAND) (AMENDMENT) (NO.2) ORDER 2013, SI 2013/1477; made under the Plant Health Act 1967 s.2, s.3; and the European Communities Act 1972 Sch.2 para.1A. In force: July 15, 2013; .

This Order amends the Plant Health (England) Order 2005 to on temporary emergency measures in respect of certain citrus fruits originating in Brazil.

84. Infectious disease control–Plant diseases–Plant protection products–Wales

THE PLANT HEALTH (WALES) (AMENDMENT) ORDER 2013, SI 2013/SI 2013/888 (W.100); made under the Plant Health Act 1967 s.2, s.3. In force: May 10, 2013; .

This Order prohibits the landing in or the spread within Wales of certain plants intended for planting of Fraxinus L. which are infected with Chalara fraxinea, and confers powers on the Welsh Ministers to grant licences for trial or scientific purposes or for work on varietal selections in relation to certain plant pests.

85. Plant diseases–Plant health–England

THE PLANT HEALTH (ENGLAND) (AMENDMENT) ORDER 2013, SI 2013/23; made under the Plant Health Act 1967 s.2, s.3. In force: January 17, 2013; .

This Order amends the Plant Health (England) Order 2005 (SI 2005/2530), which contains measures to prevent the introduction and spread of harmful plant pests and diseases. It introduces a statutory notification scheme for imports of Platanus (Plane), Quercus (Oak), Castanea (Sweet chestnut) and Fraxinus (Ash), to strengthen measures already in place in relation to imports of trees.

86. Plant health

THE PLANT HEALTH (ENGLAND) (AMENDMENT) (NO.3) ORDER 2013, SI 2013/2687; made under the Plant Health Act 1967 s.2, s.3; and the European Communities Act 1972 Sch.2 para.1A. In force: November 11, 2013; .

This instrument amends the Plant Health (England) Order 2005 (SI 2005/2530), which contains measures to prevent the introduction and spread of harmful plant pests and diseases.

87. Plant health–Crops–Fees–England

THE PLANT HEALTH (FEES) (ENGLAND) REGULATIONS 2013, SI 2013/494; made under the Finance Act 1973 s.56. In force: April 6, 2013; .

These Regulations, which apply in England only, specify fees payable to the Secretary of State in the field of plant health. They revoke and replace the Plant Health Fees (England) Regulations 2012. They do not introduce any new types of fee which were not provided for in the 2012 Regulations.

88. Plant health–Wales

THE PLANT HEALTH (FEES) (WALES) REGULATIONS 2013, SI 2013/SI 2013/1700 (W.164); made under the Finance Act 1973 s.56. In force: August 2, 2013; .

These Regulations, which apply in relation to Wales, specify fees payable to the Welsh Ministers in the field of plant health. They revoke and replace the Plant Health (Fees) (Wales) Regulations 2012 (SI 2012/1493).

ANIMALS

89. Additives–Fees–Veterinary medicines

THE VETERINARY MEDICINES REGULATIONS 2013, SI 2013/2033; made under the European Communities Act 1972 s.2; and the Finance Act 1973 s.56. In force: October 1, 2013; .

These Regulations revoke and replace the controls and procedures concerning the authorisation, manufacture, supply and use of veterinary medicines in the UK to ensure that the legislation remains up to date. They include provisions on medicated feeds and feed additives and a revised fee structure.

90. Animal cruelty–Horses–Whether defendant knew or ought to have known his actions would cause unnecessary suffering–Lawfulness of seizure of horses–Lawfulness of prosecution costs order

[Animal Welfare Act 2006 (c.45) s.4(1), s.4, s.9(1), s.9, s.18(6), s.18(5); Protection of Animals Act 1911 (c.27) s.1 (1) (a); Criminal Procedure Rules 2012 (SI 2012/1726) r.76.2.]

The claimants (G1 and G2) applied for judicial review of the defendant Crown Court's refusal to state a case on legal issues in respect of convictions under the Animal Welfare Act 2006 s.4 and s.9, and of its decision on payment of prosecution costs. G1 had been a horse trader and G2 was his wife. Following oral certification from vets a large number of his horses were seized. G1 was convicted of nine offences under s.4 and two under s.9; G2 was convicted of two offences under s.9. G1 was sentenced to imprisonment and disqualified from dealing in, owning or trading equines, and could not apply for termination of disqualification for 10 years. G2 received a non-custodial sentence and a disqualification order. G1 was ordered to pay £400,000 and G2 £750 towards the prosecution costs. Both appealed to the Crown Court, and, following 34 days of evidence, it dismissed two of the charges under s.4 against G1 and G2's conviction. G1 and G2 were ordered to pay £200,000 each towards the prosecution's costs of the appeal. The Crown Court refused G1's request to state a case on points of law, and G2's request in respect of the costs order made against her. G1 and G2 applied for judicial review. A draft case stated was drawn up, which the High Court ordered to be used. The questions for the High Court were whether (i) "ought to have reasonably known" in s.4(1) (b) had been correctly interpreted as providing an objective basis upon which to determine whether a defendant had caused unnecessary suffering under s.4(1); (ii) "such steps as are reasonable in the all the circumstances" in s.9(1) had been correctly interpreted as providing an objective standard for determining whether a defendant had failed to ensure the needs of an animal were met as required by s.9; (iii) s.18(5) had been correctly interpreted and whether the seizures were lawful as certification had been oral and not written; (iv) the Crown Court had jurisdiction to hand down a deprivation order; (v) a conviction under s.9 was bad for duplicity if it was based upon the same facts as a conviction under s.4; (vi) the costs judgment was lawful.

Held: Applications granted in part. (1) The expression "knew or ought to have reasonably known" was a common expression and required no gloss. The judge rightly directed himself that the prosecution had to establish that the defendant knew or ought to have reasonably known that his act or failure would cause an animal to suffer and that the suffering was unnecessary. Further, the Protection of Animals Act 1911 s.1 (1) (a) was irrelevant to the construction of the 2006 Act; the language of the provision was significantly different. The explanatory notes, the departmental select committee's report and the government's response to that report made it clear that s.4(1) of the 2006 Act was intended to capture unnecessary suffering caused by negligence (see paras 24, 26, 28-29 of judgment). (2) The judge had been right to construe s.9(1) as setting a purely objective standard of care for which a person responsible for an animal was required to provide (para.31). (3) To fall within s.18(5) the certification had to be in writing. It did not follow, however, that the seizures in the instant case were unlawful. The officer who seized the animals acted lawfully under s.18(6). If that was wrong, there was no basis for holding that the court erred in its application of *R. v Sang (Leonard Anthony)* [1980] A.C. 402, [1979] C.L.Y. 448, Sang considered. The court was entitled to conclude that the probative value of the evidence justified its admission and that no significant prejudice was caused because the vets' assessment of the animals was not in writing (paras 38-39, 41). (4) The Crown Court had been entitled to activate the deprivation orders after the appeal (para.42). (5) The court should not in such circumstances convict for the less serious offence as the guilty conduct would have been subsumed within the conduct giving rise to the more serious offence. There was no complete duplication in the instant case and there was no reason to interfere with G1's conviction under s.9 (paras 44-45). (6) The Crown Court was entitled to reject the submission that costs should not be grossly disproportionate to the fine. It had to make a balanced decision in light of the Criminal Procedure Rules 2012 r.76.2. Given the number of animals involved, the long appeal and the parties' conduct, the Crown Court had been entitled to impose the costs order upon G1 that it had. Its approach had been consistent with the principle that the purpose of a costs order was to compensate the prosecutor, not to punish a defendant, *R. v Northallerton Magistrates Court, Ex p. Dove* [2000] 1 Cr. App. R. (S.) 136, [1999] C.L.Y. 985 applied (paras 65-66). (7) There was no rule based on principle or precedent which prevented a court from making a costs order payable solely from capital assets (para.68). (8) Given the length of the proceedings before the district judge, the Crown Court was entitled to conclude that it had insufficient information before it to interfere with the district judge's costs decision (para.72). (9) The court was wrong to hold G1 and G2 equally liable for the prosecution's costs of the appeal. It should have considered what the position would have been had G2 been tried alone, R v Ronson and Parnes (1992) 13 cr app r 153 considered. The matter would be remitted for determination of G2's costs (paras78-79).

R. (ON THE APPLICATION OF GRAY) v AYLESBURY CROWN COURT, [2013] EWHC 500 (Admin), [2013] 3 All E.R. 346, Toulson, L.J., QBD (Admin).

91. **Animal diseases–Animal health–Horses–Wales**

THE AFRICAN HORSE SICKNESS (WALES) REGULATIONS 2013, SI 2013/SI 2013/1662 (W.158); made under the European Communities Act 1972 s.2. In force: July 31, 2013; .

These Regulations implement in relation to Wales the provisions of Directive 92/35 laying down control rules and measures to combat African horse sickness.

92. **Animal diseases–Badgers–Bovine tuberculosis–Lawfulness of policy concerning grant of licences to implement badger-culling measures–Whether s.10(2)(a) Protection of Badgers Act 1992 geographically limited**

[Animal Health Act 1981 (c.22) s.21(2); Protection of Badgers Act 1992 (c.51) s.1(1), s.10(2)(a).]

The appellant badger trust (B) appealed against a decision ([2012] EWHC 1904 (Admin)) that the respondent secretary of state's policy on bovine tuberculosis, pursuant to which farmers and landowners could cull badgers, was lawful. The secretary of state's proposed policy involved issuing licences to farmers and landowners under the Protection of Badgers Act 1992 s.10(2)(a) so that they could cull badgers to reduce the incidence of bovine tuberculosis in cattle and prevent transmission of the disease. The judge rejected B's contention that s.10(2)(a) did not empower the secretary of state to do what she proposed in her policy because the s.10(2)(a) power could only be exercised for the purpose of preventing the spread of disease and not for preventing the transmission of disease and to reduce its incidence. Section 10(2)(a) explained that licences could be granted allowing someone to interfere with a badger sett within an area specified in the licence for the purpose of preventing the spread of disease. The Animal Health Act 1981 s.21(2) provided that a minister could order the destruction of wild animals in an area if it was necessary to reduce the incidence of disease in that area. B drew a contrast between the words "preventing the spread of disease" in s.10(2)(a) and "reduce the incidence of disease" in s.21(2) in support of its argument that s.10(2)(a) had a geographical context which meant that the secretary of state's policy was unlawful; it submitted that, on a true construction of s.10(2)(a), the powers under it were limited to preventing the spread of disease outside the area of licences, and therefore the secretary of state's policy proposing the issue of licences for the purpose listed under s.21(2), to reduce the incidence of disease, was unlawful.

Held: Appeal dismissed. (1) The 1981 and 1992 Acts contemplated alternative routes for tackling the problem of controlling disease in wildlife; the 1981 Act conferred compulsory powers of entry, whereas the 1992 Act operated by voluntary cooperation with landowners. The history of the relevant legislation did not aid B's argument that the powers under s.10(2)(a) should be limited to preventing the spread of disease outside the area of the licence. the word "spread" might, in some contexts, indicate the occupaion of or penetration into a greater geographic area, but in the context of disease it connoted, or might readily connote, an intensification or increase of the incidence of disease, whether or not over a greater area, and in particular might indicate, as it did naturally in the instant case, the spread of disease from one species to another: from badgers to cattle. Further, it made little sense if s.10(2)(a) contemplated the spread of disease outside the licence area but not within it. Accordingly, the judge had been correct to reject B's ground on s.10(2)(a) (see paras 18-19 of judgment). (2) (Per curiam) If the secretary of state made an order under s.21 (2) of the 1981 Act for the destruction of animals, anyone killing animals pursuant to that order would, on the face of it, commit an offence under s.1 (1) of the 1992 Act which said that a person was guilty of an offence if, except as permitted by or under that Act, he wilfully killed a badger. The court reflected that the wording of s.1 (1) might have impliedly repealed s.21 (2), but did not decide the point. It expressed the view that Parliament might need to review the issue of whether s.21 (2) had been impliedly repealed (para.21).

R. (ON THE APPLICATION OF BADGER TRUST) v SECRETARY OF STATE FOR THE ENVIRONMENT, FOOD AND RURAL AFFAIRS, [2012] EWCA Civ 1286, *The Times*, December 14, 2012, Laws, L.J., CA (Civ Div).

93. Animal health–Department for Environment Food and Rural Affairs–Fees–Wales

THE ANIMAL HEALTH (MISCELLANEOUS FEES) (WALES) REGULATIONS 2013, SI 2013/SI 2013/1241 (W.133); made under the European Communities Act 1972 s.2, Sch.2 para.1A; the Finance Act 1973 s.56; the Animal Health Act 1981 s.1; and the Animal Health and Welfare Act 1984 s.10. In force: June 24, 2013; .

These Regulations make provision for consolidation and increase of several fees payable to the Welsh Ministers in the field of animal health into one statutory instrument. The fees are collected by an executive agency of the Department for Environment, Food and Rural Affairs known as the Animal Health and Veterinary Laboratories Agency.

94. Animals–Fees–Scientific research

THE ANIMALS (SCIENTIFIC PROCEDURES) ACT 1986 (FEES) ORDER 2013, SI 2013/509; made under the Animals (Scientific Procedures) Act 1986 s.8. In force: April 1, 2013; .

This Order, which extends to England, Wales and Scotland, prescribes the fees payable by the holder of a licence issued under s.2C of the Animals (Scientific Procedures) Act 1986 which was inserted by the Animals (Scientific Procedures) Act 1986 Amendment Regulations 2012, which transposed Directive 2010/63. This Order does not increase the fees, but reflects the amended terminology in the enabling Act.

ARBITRATION

95. Arbitral tribunals–Disputing the court's jurisdiction–Challenge to jurisdiction of Grade and Feed Trade Association tribunal–Application under s.67 Arbitration Act 1996–Whether time started to run from date of first tier award or date of appeal board award

[Arbitration Act 1996 (c.23) s.67, s.70(3).]

The applicant (P) sought an extension of time within which to challenge the jurisdiction of an arbitration tribunal. The respondent (X) had entered into a contract to sell P a large amount of rice. A dispute arose between the parties. A Grain and Feed Trade Association (GAFTA) tribunal found that the contract between the parties had incorporated the GAFTA Arbitration Rules, and the tribunal had jurisdiction to hear the dispute. It ordered P to pay $6,250,000 to X, plus interest and costs. P appealed to the GAFTA appeal board, and made the instant application to protect its position. P submitted that the time for making an application under the Arbitration Act 1996 s.67 started to run from the date of an appeal award, but in the event that that was wrong, the court should grant an extension of time.

Held: Application granted. (1) The effect of the GAFTA 125 Rules r.8.1 (b) and r.10(1) was that a first tier award in which the tribunal determined that it had jurisdiction was "conclusive and binding" so far as the question of jurisdiction was concerned. The only way in which a determination that the tribunal had jurisdiction could be challenged was by way of application to the High Court under s.67 of the 1996 Act. The time limit for bringing such a challenge was "within 28 days of the date of the award" pursuant to s.70(3). The first tier award was the only relevant award for that purpose. It was clear from r.8.1 (b) that so far as the question of jurisdiction was concerned, there was no "available arbitral process of appeal or review" within the terms of s.70(3). Accordingly, P's appeal to the GAFTA appeal board did not prevent time starting to run under s.70(3), because the appeal did not raise any question of jurisdiction. P should therefore have made its application to the High Court to challenge jurisdiction within 28 days of the first tier award, regardless of its pending appeal on the substance of the award, but had failed to do so (see paras 14-19 of judgment). (2) It was appropriate to grant an extension of time to P given that the length of the delay was only eight days; there had been some uncertainty as to whether the time limit applied; P's failure to comply with it was explicable and fuelled by a desire to avoid unnecessary costs; and no real prejudice had been suffered by X, *Kalmneft v Glencore International AG* [2002] 1 All E.R. 76, [2001] C.L.Y. 337 applied (para.21).

PEC LTD v ASIA GOLDEN RICE LTD, [2012] EWHC 846 (Comm), [2013] 1 Lloyd's Rep. 82, Hamblen, J., QBD (Comm).

96. Arbitration agreements–Anti-suit injunctions–Application to continue without notice injunction preventing proceedings in India connected with company restructuring–Whether Indian proceedings contrary to arbitration agreement between parties

The claimant (C) applied for a without notice anti-suit injunction to be continued against the defendants (D1 and D2). D1 was C and D2's father and had founded a group of companies (S) in 1949. S manufactured razor blades and related products. C and D2 became involved in the business. D1 also owned a number of separate Indian companies (T), which either manufactured products for S or owned land or intellectual property rights used by S. In 2010 and 2011, two agreements, a subscription and shareholders' deed (SSD) and a supplemental deed (SD), were entered into by the parties to effect a restructuring which left C effectively in control of S. The restructuring provided for "restructuring acquisitions" through "RA agreements", which included arrangements whereby certain of the Indian companies would sell or transfer assets to a newly established company within S. In 2012, five sets of proceedings were instigated in India by T, seeking relief for alleged mismanagement. The respondents included C. The effect of the injunction obtained by C was to stop D1 and D2 from commencing or continuing any proceedings in India or elsewhere in respect of any dispute arising from or connected with S's restructuring. The undisputed jurisdictional basis for seeking an injunction was that the SSD was governed by English law. C claimed that the disputes in the Indian proceedings were within the scope of an arbitration agreement included in the SSD. D1 and D2 argued that the court could not be satisfied to the required "high degree of probability" that C was entitled to restrain the Indian proceedings, because those disputes were not clearly within the scope of the arbitration agreement. C contended that the Indian proceedings sought to undo the arrangements that had been made for providing sufficient working capital to the restructured business, and therefore constituted a breach of D1 and D2's contractual obligation to refer any such dispute to arbitration.

Held: Application refused. The SSD, in its original form and as amended and supplemented by the SD, created contractual relationships between the parties, and there was nothing in its language which made it clear that any disputes between them were intended to be excluded from arbitration, *Fiona Trust & Holding Corp v Privalov* [2007] UKHL 40, [2007] 4 All E.R. 951, [2007] C.L.Y. 792 followed (see paras 28-34 of judgment). The issue was whether there was a high degree of probability, the "threshold requirement", that the bringing and continuing of the Indian petitions was contrary to the agreement to arbitrate, *Aggeliki Charis Compania Maritima SA v Pagnan SpA (The Angelic Grace)* [1995] 1 Lloyd's Rep. 87 applied. The base question was whether the Indian proceedings would fall within the arbitration clause in the SSD if they were brought against C by D1 and D2. The extent of the arbitration agreement was strongly contested. The substantive complaints in the Indian proceedings concerned dealings other than completion of the RA agreements, and undertakings given by D1 and D2 to amend the petitions where necessary removed any real risk that they would lead to anything which would undo those agreements. The Indian claims did not on their face make any express reference to the SSD or SD. A bland assertion that something was agreed was not enough to show a high degree of probability that it was. What would normally be expected would be assertions, supported by evidence, about (a) whether the agreement was express or implied; (b) to the extent that it was express, whether that was oral or written; (c) to the extent that oral statements were relied on, by whom, to whom, when, where, in whose presence and the gist of the words relied on. The draft arbitration points of claim made no assertions of any of those things. C had not therefore shown to a high degree of probability that there was any express oral agreement to the effect that a particular Indian claim was answered by the disputed agreement and should be arbitrated. It followed that his case for an injunction in relation to such claims would only be made good if inferences derived from documents or events were so strong as to show to a high degree of probability that an implied agreement or understanding existed on relevant matters. They were not. It was impossible to construe the actions alleged in the Indian petitions in relation to the management of T as actions "provided for in or contemplated by" the restructuring of S. The threshold requirement was therefore not met as regards the base question whether the Indian claims had been shown to a high degree of probability to involve the determination of issues which fell within the arbitration agreement (paras 153-176).

MALHOTRA v MALHOTRA, [2012] EWHC 3020 (Comm), [2013] 2 All E.R. (Comm) 353, Walker, J., QBD (Comm).

97. Arbitration agreements–Anti-suit injunctions–Court's power to grant injunction where proceedings brought in forum outside Brussels/Lugano regime

[Arbitration Act 1996 (c.23); Senior Courts Act 1981 (c.54) s.37; Civil Procedure Rules 1998 (SI 1998/3132) r.62.2, r.62.5.]

The appellant company (U) appealed against a decision of the Court of Appeal ([2011] EWCA Civ 647, [2012] 1 W.L.R. 920, [2011] C.L.Y. 130) upholding a judge's decision to grant the respondent company (H) an anti-suit injunction under the Senior Courts Act 1981 s.37 preventing U from bringing proceedings in Kazakhstan. H was the current grantee and lessee of a concession entitling it to operate an energy-producing hydroelectric plant in Kazakhstan. U was the current owner and grantor of the concession. The concession agreement was governed by Kazakh law but contained a London arbitration clause. That clause provided that disputes should be settled by arbitration in accordance with the Rules of Conciliation and Arbitration of the International Chamber of Commerce, with the arbitration to be conducted in London. U brought proceedings against H in a Kazakh court, alleging that H had failed to supply information concerning concession assets pursuant to a request duly made under the concession agreement. H obtained an interim anti-suit injunction in the English Commercial Court and that injunction was later made final. The Kazakh courts rejected H's attempts to rely on the interim injunction. The issue was whether the English courts had the power to injunct the commencement or continuation of proceedings brought in a forum outside the Brussels/Lugano regime where an arbitration agreement existed.

Held: Appeal dismissed. (1) U had argued that the negative aspect of an arbitration agreement was enforceable only when an arbitration was on foot or proposed, but there was no support in the case law for that proposition. Both before and after the Arbitration Act 1996, the negative aspect was well recognised, and it was well established that the English courts would give effect to it, where necessary by injuncting foreign proceedings brought in breach of either an arbitration agreement or an exclusive choice-of-court clause. Further, such relief was treated as the counterpart of the statutory power to grant a stay of domestic proceedings to give effect to an arbitration agreement. A stay was not made conditional on arbitration being on foot, proposed or brought. If there was power under s.37 to injunct the commencement or continuation of foreign proceedings, no reason was evident why the exercise of that power should depend on such a condition. The power to grant an anti-suit injunction of the type made by the judge was not inconsistent with the 1996 Act. It was inconceivable that the Act intended or should be treated *sub silentio* as effectively abrogating the protection enjoyed under s.37 in respect of their negative rights under an arbitration agreement by those who stipulated for an arbitration with an English seat. In some cases where foreign proceedings were brought in breach of an arbitration clause or exclusive choice-of-court agreement, the appropriate course would be to leave it to the foreign court to recognise and enforce the parties' agreement on forum, but in this case the foreign court had refused to do so. There was therefore every reason for the English courts to intervene to protect H's prima facie right to enforce the negative aspect of its arbitration agreement with U. It followed that the judge had jurisdiction under s.37 to make the order that he did and that there was nothing wrong in principle with the exercise of his power to do so (see paras 22-23, 60-62 of judgment). (2) As to the service of H's claim on U, the CPR r.62.2 and r.62.5 were wide enough to embrace a claim under s.37 to restrain foreign proceedings in breach of the negative aspect of an arbitration agreement (paras 49-50).

AES UST-KAMENOGORSK HYDROPOWER PLANT LLP v UST-KAMENOGORSK HYDROPOWER PLANT JSC; *sub nom.* UST-KAMENOGORSK HYDROPOWER PLANT JSC v AES UST-KAMENOGORSK HYDROPOWER PLANT LLP, [2013] UKSC 35, [2013] 1 W.L.R. 1889, Lord Neuberger, J.S.C., SC.

98. Arbitration agreements–Choice of law–Determining governing law of arbitration agreement–Parties' express or implied choice

The applicant companies (U, X and B) applied to challenge two arbitration awards on the grounds that the arbitral tribunals did not have substantive jurisdiction. U was the Indian parent company of X and B. The arbitrations arose out of a joint venture into which U, X and B entered with the respondent company (C). X and C formed a new company and entered into a shareholders' agreement (SHA), governed by Indian law. B subscribed to parts of the SHA. U, B and C entered into a keepwell agreement, also governed by Indian law, under which U agreed to put B in funds so that it could make payments due under the SHA. The SHA and the keepwell agreement both contained arbitration agreements providing for arbitration in London. A dispute arose concerning the validity of certain notices served by X under the SHA, and whether C had validly exercised a put option. In two separate arbitrations, the tribunals determined that X had not been entitled to give the notices and that C had validly exercised the put option, and ordered B and U to pay what was due under the put option. U, X and B submitted that (1) the law applicable to the arbitration agreement in the SHA was Indian law; therefore, Indian law determined whether B was a party to it; (2) B had not agreed to be bound by the arbitration agreement in the SHA; (3) under Indian law, where an arbitration was brought against two respondents only one of whom was party to the arbitration agreement, the arbitration could not be maintained against either respondent. Therefore, because the first tribunal did not have jurisdiction over B, it did not have jurisdiction to decide the claims against X either; (4) the law governing the arbitration agreement in the keepwell agreement was Indian law. Under Indian law and on the proper construction of the keepwell agreement, the claims against U and B could be brought only after B's liability under the SHA had been adjudicated, if not admitted; the claims were therefore premature and beyond the second tribunal's jurisdiction; (5) as the first award was invalid, B had not been validly found to be liable under the SHA and so the second tribunal had no jurisdiction to make an award against B or U under the keepwell agreement.

Held: Application granted in part. (1) The lex causae of the SHA was, by the parties' express choice, the law of India, whereas the seat of the arbitration was, again by the parties' express choice, London, so the curial law of the arbitration was English law. In order to determine which law was applicable to the arbitration agreement, the court had to consider whether the parties had chosen, impliedly if not expressly, a law to govern the arbitration agreement, before going on to consider which system of law had the closest and most real connection with the arbitration agreement, *Sulamerica Cia Nacional de Seguros SA v Enesa Engenharia SA* [2012] EWCA Civ 638, [2013] 1 W.L.R. 102, [2012] C.L.Y. 104 followed and *C v D* [2007] EWCA Civ 1282, [2008] 1 All E.R. (Comm) 1001, [2008] C.L.Y. 564 considered. The fact that the parties had chosen English law as the lex fori did not amount to an implied choice of English law as the law applicable to the arbitration agreement. It was relevant that the arbitration agreement included a specific agreement not to seek interim relief in India under certain legislation. Where parties had expressly excluded specific statutory provisions of a law, the natural inference was that they understood and intended that otherwise the law would apply. The parties to the SHA were to be taken to have evinced an intention that the arbitration agreement in it be governed by Indian law. The governing law clause was, at the least, a strong pointer to their intention, and there was no contrary intention other than choice of a London seat for arbitrations (see paras 9-23 of judgment). (2) By signing a signature page to the SHA, B had agreed to be bound by certain specified clauses of it. The arbitration agreement was not among the clauses identified. B was not a party to the arbitration agreement on the basis of Indian law or English law (paras 25-36). (3) Because the first tribunal did not have jurisdiction over B, the whole matter before it was not arbitrable, *Sukanya Holdings (Pvt) Ltd v Jayesh Pandya*considered. The tribunal did not have substantive jurisdiction over the claim against X, and its award was of no effect (paras 37-46, 63). (4) The arbitration agreement in the keepwell agreement was governed by Indian law. The Indian cases referred to by X, B and U did not establish a general proposition that, unless a liability was admitted, a judicial or arbitral determination was required before proceedings could be brought to enforce an obligation such as that undertaken by U. Even if the court could be persuaded that the second tribunal should have concluded that no liability of U had accrued because there had been no valid finding that anything was due from B under the SHA, it could not accept that that went to the tribunal's substantive jurisdiction (paras 47-57). (5) The second tribunal needed to determine whether B was liable under the SHA in order to determine whether U was liable under the keepwell agreement, and so it had both the jurisdiction and the duty to do so (paras 58-63).

ARSANOVIA LTD v CRUZ CITY 1 MAURITIUS HOLDINGS; CRUZ CITY 1 MAURITIUS HOLDINGS v UNITECH LTD; CRUZ CITY 1 MAURITIUS HOLDINGS v ARSANOVIA LTD, [2012] EWHC 3702 (Comm), [2013] 2 All E.R. (Comm) 1, Andrew Smith, J., QBD (Comm).

99. Arbitration agreements–Jurisdiction–Guarantor claiming guarantees unenforceable under Chinese law–Guarantees providing for London arbitration–Separability of arbitration clauses

[Arbitration Act 1996 (c.23) s.7.]

The applicant Chinese guarantor (J) challenged partial arbitration awards declaring that the relevant tribunal had substantive jurisdiction over the dispute referred to it and granting anti-suit relief. Vessels had been chartered by the respondents to J's subsidiary (H). The respondents had commenced arbitrations against J under letters of guarantee given by it in respect of H's obligations under the charters, claiming that H had repudiated those obligations and that J was liable as guarantor. The guarantees provided for London arbitration. J's principal defence under the guarantees was that the parties knew that it was illegal under Chinese law for a Chinese legal person to give a guarantee to a foreign entity without having obtained the prior authorisation of the State Administration for Foreign Exchange, that the guarantees did not and could not have had such authorisation, and that the funds needed to meet any demand on the guarantees would inevitably have to have been transferred from China, in contravention of Chinese law. On that basis, J contended that the guarantees were unenforceable as a matter of English public policy. The awards declared that the relevant tribunal had substantive jurisdiction over the dispute that had been referred to it and granted anti-suit injunction relief restraining J from continuing proceedings it had commenced in China. The arbitrators concluded that, even on the assumption that the guarantees were unenforceable because they involved the commission in a foreign country of acts that were unlawful under local law, the provisions for London arbitration were enforceable.

Held: Applications refused. (1) An arbitration agreement was to be treated as a distinct and separable agreement from the contract of which it formed part. Mere unenforceability of the contract would not of itself result in the unenforceability of the arbitration agreement, *Fiona Trust & Holding Corp v Privalov* [2007] UKHL 40, [2007] 4 All E.R. 951, [2007] C.L.Y. 792 considered. The concept of separability had been codified in the Arbitration Act 1996 s.7. However, an arbitration agreement could be rendered void or unenforceable if it was directly impeached on grounds which related to the arbitration agreement itself and were not merely a consequence of the invalidity of the underlying contract (see paras 23-2 of judgment). (2) An English law contract would not be enforceable if the common intention of the parties was to perform in a foreign friendly country some act which was illegal under the law of that country, even though that was not a term of the contract, *Foster v Driscoll* [1929] 1 K.B. 470 and *Regazzoni v KC Sethia (1944) Ltd* [1958] A.C. 301, [1957] C.L.Y. 585 considered. In the context of an arbitration clause it was necessary to ask whether the policy of the rule that invalidated the main contract also entailed the invalidity of an arbitration agreement, *Harbour Assurance Co (UK) Ltd v Kansa General International Insurance Co Ltd* [1993] Q.B. 701, [1993] C.L.Y. 153 applied. The court was not directly concerned with any illegality that might arise under Chinese law. Foreign law illegality was relevant only insofar as it might give rise to a public policy defence as a matter of English law. If the assumed facts were proved in the arbitrations the illegality would be established and the guarantees would not be enforced. That would not be contrary to international comity or public policy. The policy and purpose of the rule which invalidated the guarantees did not strike down the arbitration provisions (paras 19, 40-41).

BEIJING JIANLONG HEAVY INDUSTRY GROUP v GOLDEN OCEAN GROUP LTD; BEIJING JIANLONG HEAVY INDUSTRY GROUP v SHIP FINANCE INTERNATIONAL LTD, [2013] EWHC 1063 (Comm), [2013] 2 All E.R. (Comm) 436, Judge Mackie, Q.C., QBD (Comm).

100. Arbitration claims–Service by alternative permitted method–Application to court to appoint arbitrator–Permission to serve arbitration claim form in Thailand–Alternative service permitted retrospectively

[Arbitration Act 1996 (c.23) s.1 (a); Civil Procedure Rules 1998 (SI 1998/3132) r.6.15.]

The applicant (B) applied for the court to make an order retrospectively permitting service by the means that had been employed. B and the respondent (D) had entered into an umbrella agreement and contracts for the supply of bitumen. The contracts all had London arbitration clauses apart from one which provided for Hong Kong arbitration. B claimed damages for allegedly unlawful use made by D of specifications which B had developed for two grades of bitumen. B's case was that the specifications were commercially confidential, in the nature of trade secrets, and that D had agreed to keep them secret. B alleged that D had made supplies to its competitors. B invited D to agree to the appointment of a single arbitrator. D declined to agree and B applied to the court for appointment of an arbitrator. It issued an arbitration claim form and obtained permission to serve it on D at its registered office in Thailand. The documents were served by registered mail and also delivered by hand and had been received by D. D said that that was not valid service under Thai law and that valid service of process such as the arbitration claim form, under Thai law, required service by an officer of the Thai court at D's registered office. There were no bilateral or other service conventions between the United Kingdom and Thailand and service of process through diplomatic channels resulting in service by Thai court officials would take around 12 months. B sought an order under CPR r.6.15 retrospectively validating the service in Thailand.

Held: Application granted. The rules for service in the CPR served an important purpose and should in general be strictly complied with. If alternative or retrospective service was easily granted, compliance with the rules would become optional. Retrospective service was exceptional and was permitted in special circumstances only. The fact that alternative means might be much quicker that the Hague Convention was relevant but not of itself usually sufficient to be exceptional. Retrospective service could be justified by facts special to the proceedings. There was no bilateral agreement for service between the countries and so no direct obligations were being overlooked if retrospective service was permitted. The English court was not presuming to try a dispute itself, which, on D's case, had not been served to the standards required by local law for a trial in Thailand. The court was not being asked to try a dispute at all. It was being asked to assist the progress of an international arbitration in London, the method chosen by the parties for resolving their contractual disputes. Under the Arbitration Act 1996 s.1 (a) the parties were committed to fair resolution of disputes by an impartial tribunal without unnecessary delay or expense. D had, in breach of s.16, failed to join in the appointment of an arbitrator. It was fully aware of the existence of the arbitration. It was relying on the formalities relating to the appointment of an arbitrator by the court which did not apply to the initiation of the arbitration process itself. It was knowingly causing unnecessary delay and expense in the arbitration process. Those considerations were facts relating to the proceedings which were crucial and made the case exceptional, *Cecil v Bayat* [2011] EWCA Civ 135, [2011] 1 W.L.R. 3086, [2011] C.L.Y. 385 applied. They were considerations beyond the mere advantage of obtaining a speedier process than compliance with the local process would produce. The court would therefore order retrospective service as permitted by r.6.15, but subject to conditions.

BITUMEX (HK) CO LTD v IRPC PUBLIC CO LTD, [2012] EWHC 1065 (Comm), [2012] 2 All E.R. (Comm) 1131, Judge Mackie, Q.C., QBD (Comm).

101. Arbitration clauses–Jurisdiction–Application to set aside arbitrator's award under s.67 Arbitration Act 1996–Incorporation of English arbitration clause

[Arbitration Act 1996 (c.23) s.57, s.67, s.70(2)(a), s.72, s.73.]

The claimant (C) applied, under the Arbitration Act 1996 s.67, to set aside an award whereby an English arbitrator, appointed on the application of the defendant (D), decided that he had jurisdiction to determine a dispute between the parties. On July 28, 2011, D and C had signed a contract order for D to supply a belt-assisted boric acid filter to C. It was agreed that detailed terms would be agreed later. Various details were then agreed on October 4. However, there was a dispute about whether any arbitration terms had been incorporated. D relied upon its standard conditions, under which its contracts were to be construed in accordance with British law and disputes submitted to English arbitration. C claimed that the governing agreement was a Limited Manufacturing Licence (LML), which was subject to Swiss law and provided for arbitration in Switzerland. C challenged the arbitrator's jurisdiction under s.72 of the Act and made its non-participatory status clear. However, the arbitrator fixed a final hearing to take place before C's s.72 application was listed and C therefore decided that it would have to participate in the hearing and challenge the award under s.67. It also filed a defence in the arbitration, under protest as to jurisdiction. The arbitrator held that there was a valid arbitration agreement, governed by English law, by virtue of D's standard conditions. D submitted that (1) C was not entitled to bring its s.67 application because it should have exhausted the process of review available under s.57 of the Act; it had accepted jurisdiction by bringing a counterclaim in the arbitration; the grounds on which the s.67 application were based were not before the arbitrator, as required by s.73, because they were based on "mistake"; (2) the governing arbitration clause was the English one in D's standard conditions.

Held: Application granted. (1) No arbitral processes of review or appeal were available to C following the arbitrator's award. C was not, therefore, prevented from bringing its s.67 application by s.70(2)(a) of the Act. There had been no room for an application under s.57. For the tribunal to exercise its power to correct an award under s.57(3), the mistake had to have arisen as a result of an accidental slip or omission; the slip rule could not be used to reconsider an award, *Al-Hadha Trading Co v Tradigrain SA* [2002] 2 Lloyd's Rep. 512, [2003] C.L.Y. 201 applied. The arbitrator's power to correct errors in the award did not extend to oversights or errors in production of evidence or argument, *Craske v Norfolk CC (No.1)* (1991) 62 P. & C.R. 434, [1991] C.L.Y. 454 applied. C's case was that the arbitrator came to the wrong decision on his jurisdiction based upon an incomplete and incorrect account of events. The arbitrator had not "omitted" anything from his award; the award was simply based on D's version of events, since C had not participated in the proceedings (see paras 19-24 of judgment). The counterclaim had only been brought in order to support C's asserted right of set-off, which was a defence to a claim. The counterclaim did not seek to invoke the arbitrator's jurisdiction any more than any other defence. C was not seeking to recover anything on the pleaded counterclaim and had not submitted to the arbitrator's jurisdiction (paras 25-26). At all times up to the issue of the award, C had not participated in the arbitration proceedings. For that reason, s.73 could have no application in relation to what occurred up to that time. C had made no challenge before the arbitrator on any grounds, so there could be no new grounds in its s.67 application. When C decided that it would have to participate in the arbitration, it immediately made clear that it was doing so without prejudice to its objection to the arbitrator's jurisdiction. It raised its detailed grounds of objection in its s.67 application and defence with due speed. In any event, the essential basis of C's objection to the arbitrator's jurisdiction had always been the same and C was not seeking to raise new grounds of objection. All of D's procedural objections to the s.67 application would be dismissed (paras 31-38). (2) The only document that was contractually agreed at the meeting of July 28 was the contract order which contained only the essential contract terms. It referred to D's standard conditions, but they were not provided with or attached to the contract order. Incorporation of such terms would have been contrary to the parties' agreement to hold over discussion of detailed terms. Detailed conditions were set out in the documents of October 4, which did not refer to the standard conditions. Even if they were incorporated, the English arbitration clause would not be incorporated under English law because the specifically agreed Swiss arbitration clause in the LML would prevail over the English arbitration clause (paras 79-83, 99-110, 113-114, 119-120). If the applicability of the LML arbitration clause fell to be determined as a matter of Swiss law, the same conclusion would be reached. Even if D intended that its standard conditions arbitration clause applied, it could not be assumed in good faith that C would share that view (paras 121-136).

ASES HAVACILIK SERVIS VE DESTEK HIZMETLERI AS v DELKOR UK LTD, [2012] EWHC 3518 (Comm), [2013] 1 Lloyd's Rep. 254, Hamblen, J., QBD (Comm).

102. Arbitration clauses–Jurisdiction–Buyer issuing proceedings despite arbitration clause in contract–Whether clause breached–Whether to grant injunctive and declaratory relief sought

The claimant (E) claimed injunctive and declaratory relief relating to proceedings which the defendant (M) had issued in Bangladesh. E had contracted for the sale of Brazilian raw cotton to M. The "Rules" provision in the contract provided that "All disputes" not settled amicably would be referred to arbitration under the International Cotton Association (ICA) rules. Clause 12 of the contract provided that "any dispute... shall be" settled according to the ICA rules, which themselves provided that "All disputes relating to the contract will be resolved through arbitration in accordance with the Bylaws of the International Cotton Association Limited." M failed to open a letter of credit as he was supposed to pursuant to the contract. Settlement was unsuccessful and E commenced arbitration proceedings. Rather than taking part in the arbitration, M issued proceedings in Bangladesh in January 2012. It sought a declaration that the contract was void, had no binding effect on M and/or that the contract was frustrated as it was impossible to set up a letter of credit. It also sought a permanent injunction preventing E from pursuing any claim in proceedings relating to the contract before the ICA or elsewhere. M also obtained an interim anti-suit injunction to restrain E from pursuing any claim regarding the contract. In June 2012, E filed an appeal in Bangladesh against the interim injunction and took no further steps in the arbitration in the light of that injunction. In January 2013, when no date was fixed for the appeal, E issued the instant proceedings, seeking an injunction prohibiting M from taking steps in the Bangladeshi proceedings or commencing further proceedings relating to the contract, and ordering M to discontinue those proceedings. It also sought declarations that M was obliged to arbitrate all disputes relating to the contract, was obliged to bring any challenge to the tribunal's substantive jurisdiction or to the validity of the arbitration agreement before the tribunal or the instant court, and that the Bangladeshi proceedings constituted a breach of the contract. The issues to be determined were whether (i) the Bangladeshi proceedings were in breach of the arbitration clause; (ii) if so, there were strong reasons not to grant the injunction; (iii) to grant the declaratory relief sought.

Held: Applications granted. (1) The starting point was the "Rules" provision in the contract. As a matter of the natural and ordinary meaning of the wide words used, the underlying dispute between the parties clearly came within the terms of the arbitration agreement. That provision was further bolstered by cl.12. Although within the Bangladeshi proceedings M contended that the underlying dispute did not fall within the scope of arbitration as the dispute was not a "technical or quality dispute", that was simply another way of referring to "all" disputes. Every dispute that was not a quality dispute was categorised as a technical one under the rules and by-laws of the ICA. Further, M's apparent contention within the Bangladeshi proceedings that the arbitration clause did not apply because the contract had been frustrated or was otherwise invalid, was wrong as a matter of English law. It was clear that the underlying dispute was subject to the arbitration agreement in the contract, and the commencement of the Bangladeshi proceedings amounted to a breach of contract (see paras 22-29 of judgment). (2) It was not a good reason in English law not to grant an injunction, to suggest that the arguments put forward by M in Bangladesh raised principles of Bangladeshi law and public policy where M had agreed that all disputes under the contract should be submitted to arbitration. Indeed, that might be said to be a factor in favour of granting an injunction. Further, any delay in E's instant application was explained by E having thought that its appeal of the interim injunction would lead to the matter being dealt with more efficiently in Bangladesh. H had not submitted to the jurisdiction in Bangladesh by filing its appeal: the basis of the appeal was that the injunction should never have been granted since the dispute was manifestly governed by the arbitration clause. Moreover, where a defendant was bound by such a clause, it was an egregious breach of contract for him not only to commence proceedings in a non-contractual jurisdiction but to obtain an injunction from that forum to prevent the claimant from vindicating his rights under the arbitration clause, *Sabah Shipyard (Pakistan) Ltd v Pakistan* [2002] EWCA Civ 1643, [2003] 2 Lloyd's Rep. 571, [2003] C.L.Y. 624 applied. Finally, it was appropriate to grant a mandatory, rather than a prohibitory, injunction because the case concerned a final order and therefore an established breach of contract, it involved an exclusive forum clause, the breach was particularly egregious, and the order was necessary because of the existing interim injunction. In the circumstances, there were no strong reasons not to grant an anti-suit injunction. On the contrary, there was every reason to grant it (paras 31-39). (3) The question of whether to grant the declarations was a matter of the court's discretion. There were good and sufficient reasons to do so. The declarations would assist both E, in enforcing any award ultimately obtained, and the Bangladeshi court, should M not obey the injunction (paras 41, 43).

ECOM AGROINDUSTRIAL CORP LTD v MOSHARAF COMPOSITE TEXTILE MILL LTD, [2013] EWHC 1276 (Comm), [2013] 2 All E.R. (Comm) 983, Hamblen, J., QBD (Comm).

103. Arbitration clauses–Stay of proceedings–Arbitration clause if insurer and insured failed to agree on amount of loss–Whether arbitration clause for purposes of Arbitration Act 1996

[Arbitration Act 1996 (c.23) s.9.]

The applicant insurance company (C) applied for the claim of the respondent insured (T) to be stayed for arbitration. T's claim against C arose out of losses caused in a fire at a property owned or occupied by T. The policy contained a clause which provided that if the parties failed to agree on the amount of loss, either party could make a written demand for each to select an independent appraiser; the independent appraiser would select an arbitrator within 15 days; if an arbitrator was not agreed on within that time, either party could request that the arbitrator be selected by the Association of British Insurers or the Financial Services Authority; the independent appraisers would then appraise the loss and submit any differences to the arbitrator; a decision in writing agreed to by the two appraisers or either appraiser and the arbitrator would be binding. The parties appointed their appraisers but agreed to delay appointment of an arbitrator. The dispute was about the rebuilding costs, including professional fees, and whether part of the structure could have been salvaged. T then terminated the engagement of its appraiser and issued court proceedings. C said that the proceedings should be stayed under the Arbitration Act 1996 s.9 or the inherent jurisdiction of the court. T contended that (1) the clause was not an arbitration clause within the meaning of the 1996 Act so that C was not entitled to a stay under s.9; (2) the dispute was not limited to the amount of the loss and so the clause did not apply; (3) it would be inappropriate for the court to stay the proceedings under its inherent jurisdiction since it was more convenient to have all the matters in issue resolved by the court, and the dispute resolution machinery under the clause had broken down or was inoperable.

Held: Applications granted. (1) However it was presented, the claim did not involve anything more than a dispute about the amount of the loss. There was no dispute that T was entitled to an indemnity. English law did not give an insured a separate and discrete entitlement to damages for an insurer's failure to pay, or to pay the correct amount, under a policy (see paras 34-43 of judgment). (2) The clause did not cease to be an arbitration clause simply because it provided that a decision in writing agreed by the two appraisers would be binding on the parties. That meant no more than that if the appraisers were agreed as to the amount of the loss, there was no dispute to put before the arbitrator. There was nothing objectionable in the parties being able to withdraw their dispute from the arbitral process at any time. Nor was there anything objectionable about the two appraisers putting forward their respective views to the arbitrator; that did not preclude the arbitrator from inviting evidence or submissions from the parties direct if he considered that fairness required it. However, the fact that the clause provided for a decision agreed to by either appraiser and the arbitrator to be binding meant that it was not an arbitration clause within the meaning of the Act. The Act envisaged the resolution of disputes by an impartial tribunal and implicit in that was that it was the arbitrator alone who was to make the decision and not the arbitrator in conjunction with someone else. Equally, the appraisers who had reached their conclusions on behalf of the parties could not thereafter act as independent arbitrators. A decision of the arbitrator with which neither of the appraisers was prepared to agree would be of no effect (paras 44-60). (3) There should be a stay under the inherent jurisdiction. The procedure under the clause had not broken down and become inoperable. T had unilaterally dispensed with the services of its appraiser and commenced proceedings because it was frustrated by the delay. It was for the party resisting the stay to demonstrate why the stay should not be granted, *DGT Steel & Cladding Ltd v Cubitt Building & Interiors Ltd* [2007] EWHC 1584 (TCC), [2008] Bus. L.R. 132, [2007] C.L.Y. 528 applied. The strongest factors were that the parties had begun the arbitration clause process without protest and had invested considerable sums in that process. There was no question of parallel proceedings in court concerning issues of liability and so the arbitrator could deal with all the matters in dispute. Case management considerations and fairness pointed in favour of allowing the process to continue, rather than abandoning it in favour of court proceedings (paras 62-72).

TURVILLE HEATH INC v CHARTIS INSURANCE UK LTD (FORMERLY AIG UK LTD), [2012] EWHC 3019 (TCC), [2012] 2 C.L.C. 818, Edwards-Stuart, J., QBD (TCC).

104. Arbitration notices–Contracts of carriage–Alleged contract of affreightment concluded by conduct–Whether arbitration duly commenced under contract–Validity of discharge port bills of lading

[Arbitration Act 1996 (c.23) s.14; Carriage of Goods by Sea Act 1992 (c.50) s.2(1).]

The claimants (F and M) sought to challenge certain parts of an arbitration award determining preliminary issues as to the jurisdiction of the tribunal. F and M were part of a group which produced, imported and distributed food products in the Russian Federation. M sourced bananas from Ecuador and shipped them to St Petersburg by weekly shipments on reefer vessels. The carrying vessels were chartered for M by F and were supplied by the first defendant (B). B was the disponent owner of a number of vessels and also acted as manager on behalf of various shipowners. The carrying vessels had been supplied pursuant to written contracts of affreightment (COAs) based on the Gencon form of voyage charter and incorporating the normal Gencon arbitration clause. The COAs were signed by B as owner and F as charterer. After the COAs came to an end B continued to supply weekly reefer vessels. Bills of lading were issued to the shipper at the loadport naming M as the consignee, but once the shipper had been paid under the sale contract those bills were surrendered and new bills were issued to M at the discharge port. The claimants had cargo damage claims in relation to 12 cargoes of bananas. F commenced arbitration against B and the relevant shipowners on the basis that it was the charterer under a COA with B, alternatively under individual charters on the terms of the COA. M commenced arbitration against the shipowners which had issued the bills of lading on the basis that it was the lawful holder of them. B accepted the jurisdiction of the tribunal with regard to the vessels of which it was disponent owner but not otherwise, and the shipowners accepted the jurisdiction of the tribunal under the charterparty arrangements but not under the bills of lading. The claimants challenged parts of the tribunal's award on preliminary issues relating to the effect of the chartering arrangements, the validity of the bills of lading and the effect of the claimants' letters purporting to commence arbitration.

Held: Preliminary issues determined. (1) B had concluded the earlier COAs not as agent but as principal (see paras 17-18 of judgment). During the period of the disputed shipments there was no signed COA but a contract on the COA terms came into existence as a result of performance by the parties, *Maple Leaf Macro Volatility Master Fund v Rouvroy* [2009] EWHC 257 (Comm), [2009] 2 All E.R. (Comm) 287, [2009] C.L.Y. 729. The proper approach was to look at the conduct of the parties overall and on that basis there was a COA by conduct, *Brogden v Metropolitan Railway Co* (1877) 2 App. Cas. 666 followed (paras 21-30). The answer to the preliminary issues relating to the chartering arrangements was therefore that there was a COA by conduct between B and F covering the disputed voyages; B contracted as principal and not as agent; the disputed voyages were performed on charterparty terms binding on B as owner under the COA (para.37). (2) The practice adopted in the instant case involving surrender, cancellation and reissue of bills of lading was not uncommon. The fact that the loadport bills were never intended to be negotiated but were always intended to be and were in fact surrendered and cancelled following receipt of payment for the goods did not mean that there was no contract of carriage. The loadport bills were replaced by the disport bills which were duly issued on behalf of the owners and thereby became valid bills binding on the owners and containing or evidencing the original contract of carriage. That was a matter of mechanics and convenience only and did not affect the existence of the underlying contract of carriage (paras 39-46). The answer to the bill of lading preliminary issue was that M never became the lawful holder of the loadport bills but it did become the lawful holder of the disport bills and therefore had transferred to and vested in it, pursuant to the Carriage of Goods by Sea Act 1992 s.2(1), all rights of suit under the contract of carriage as if M had been a party to that contract (paras 47-50). (3) The arbitration against B had been validly commenced under the COA. The Arbitration Act 1996 s.14 should be interpreted broadly and flexibly, and having regard to the substance of the matter, *Seabridge Shipping AB v AC Orssleff's Eftf's A/S* [2000] 1 All E.R. (Comm) 415, [2000] C.L.Y. 4728, *Atlanska Plovidba v Consignaciones Asturianas SA (The Lapad)* [2004] EWHC 1273 (Admlty), [2004] 2 Lloyd's Rep. 109, [2004] C.L.Y. 193 and *Bulk & Metal Transport (UK) LLP v Voc Bulk Ultra Handymax Pool LLC (The Voc Gallant)* [2009] EWHC 288 (Comm), [2009] 2 All E.R. (Comm) 377, [2009] C.L.Y. 171 applied. On that basis the letters commencing arbitration, although they did not mention the COA, made clear that the disputes that had been submitted to arbitration were the claims for damage to the cargoes of bananas that were carried on the disputed voyages, and that the claims were being made both under the contractual arrangements by which the vessels were chartered and also under the contracts contained in or evidenced by the bills of lading. Confusion had arisen because the bills of lading referred to dates of individual charterparties, but, as the defendants knew, there were no such charterparties (paras 59-65). In the circumstances an arbitration had been duly commenced despite the failure to refer to one of the vessels (paras 67-70). If M was an undisclosed principal it was a party to the arbitration under the COA (paras 72-76).

FINMOON LTD v BALTIC REEFERS MANAGEMENT LTD, [2012] EWHC 920 (Comm), [2012] 2 Lloyd's Rep. 388, Eder, J., QBD (Comm).

105. Arbitrators–Appointments–Jurisdiction to entertain appeal against decision appointing sole arbitrator

[Arbitration Act 1996 (c.23) s.15(3), s.18(3)(a), s.18(5).]

The applicant (X) applied for permission to appeal against an order providing for the appointment of a sole arbitrator in an arbitration between it and the respondents (J) under a letter of guarantee. The letter of guarantee contained an arbitration clause in the following terms: "Any dispute arising out of this LETTER OF GUARANTEE shall be submitted to arbitration held in London in accordance with English law, and the award given by the arbitrators shall be final and binding on both parties". J asserted that the clause provided for a sole arbitrator, whereas X argued that it provided for more than one arbitrator so that the tribunal should consist of three arbitrators. J applied to the Commercial Court for an order under the Arbitration Act 1996 s.18(3)(d) that a particular individual should be appointed as sole arbitrator; X resisted the application, arguing that the court should instead give directions under s.18(3)(a) for the appointment of a tribunal of three arbitrators. The judge found that s.15(3) applied (s.15(3) provided that if there was no agreement as to the number of arbitrators, the tribunal should consist of a sole arbitrator) and made an order appointing the individual mentioned. The judge also refused an application by X for leave to appeal to the Court of Appeal.

Held: Application refused. (1) The first issue was whether the instant court had jurisdiction to entertain the intended appeal. The answer was no. X's intended appeal was caught by the restriction on appeal provided by s.18(5) of the Act. Section 18(5) stated that the leave of the court (being the court of first instance) was required for any appeal "from a decision of the court under this section". Section 18(5) applied here, because the judge's decision had been made under s.18(3), even if his reasons (necessarily) encompassed s.15, *Virdee v Virdi* [2003] EWCA Civ 41 applied, *Cetelem SA v Roust Holdings Ltd* [2005] EWCA Civ 618, [2005] 1 W.L.R. 3555, [2005] C.L.Y. 325, *ASM Shipping Ltd of India v TTMI Ltd of England (Permission to Appeal)* [2006] EWCA Civ 1341, [2007] 1 Lloyd's Rep. 136, [2007] C.L.Y. 249 and *Sumukan Ltd v Commonwealth Secretariat* [2007] EWCA Civ 243, [2007] 3 All E.R. 342, [2007] C.L.Y. 233 considered (see para.28 of judgment). (2) In any event, the judge had plainly been correct in the conclusion to which he came. The court was content to proceed on the assumption that the parties contemplated more than one arbitrator. Even so, it was impossible to read into the arbitration clause an agreement "as to the number of arbitrators". Absent such an agreement, s.15(3) provided unambiguously for a default position of a single arbitrator (para.31).

ITOCHU CORP v JOHANN MK BLUMENTHAL GmbH & CO KG, [2012] EWCA Civ 996, [2013] 1 All E.R. (Comm) 504, Maurice Kay, L.J., CA (Civ Div).

106. Arbitrators' powers and duties–Additional awards–Challenge to arbitrator's decision to make additional award concerning interest

[Arbitration Act 1996 (c.23) s.57(3)(b), s.57.]

The claimant (C) sought a declaration that an additional arbitration award in favour of the defendant (T) was of no effect. The dispute between the parties arose out of the sale of a vessel by T to C under a memorandum of agreement (MOA) dated June 21, 2007. The first instalment of the purchase price, in the sum of US $7.7 million, was paid to T by C. In return, T provided C with a refund guarantee for the same sum. In 2009, C argued that T was in repudiatory breach of the MOA and made a demand under the refund guarantee. The sum of US $7.7 million, plus interest that had by that time accrued, was paid into an escrow account pending the resolution of arbitration proceedings that had been begun by T. In those proceedings, T claimed a declaration that C had not been entitled to make any demand under the refund guarantee. It also argued that C had committed repudiatory breaches of the MOA, which it had accepted. In relation to that claim, T sought a declaration that it was entitled to retain the US $7.7 million paid by C; alternatively, T claimed damages for loss of bargain, in the sum of US $6 million. C's case was that it was entitled to avoid the MOA on the grounds of fraudulent or negligent misrepresentation or to treat it as having been repudiated by T. The tribunal rejected both claims and held that C had committed repudiatory breaches of the MOA, which T had accepted. It rejected T's claim to retain the US $7.7 million purchase price, but granted its claim for damages in the sum of US $6 million, with interest thereon. It ordered that those sums, together with any costs later awarded to T, be paid from the escrow account but that C was entitled to claim any balance in the account in restitution. After the award was published, T made an application to the tribunal under the Arbitration Act 1996 s.57. It claimed that it, not C, was entitled to the accrued interest in the escrow account and that the first award should be corrected, or an additional award made, to reflect that. The tribunal granted the application, having concluded that the claim for accrued interest had been overlooked. C argued that T had not made a claim in the arbitration for the accrued interest, so that the tribunal had no power to make the additional award under s.57(3)(b); alternatively, if T did make a claim in the arbitration for the accrued interest, that had been dealt with in the first award, so that again the tribunal had no power to make the additional award under s.57(3)(b).

Held: Application refused. (1) Section 57(3)(b) covered claims "presented" to the tribunal. No particular formality was required. Provided that the claim was before the tribunal and would reasonably be expected to be determined, it did not matter how the claim had been placed before the tribunal. The claim for accrued interest had been "presented to the tribunal". The matter had been raised in T's particulars of claim. Further, in its closing submissions it had claimed a declaration that it was "entitled... to all sums in the escrow account". Both a literal and a purposive construction of the words "all sums" led to the same conclusion: the claim for accrued interest was included. Moreover, C's own case acknowledged that T had a claim in respect of the accrued interest if C's case on repudiation succeeded (see paras 22-24, 27, 33-34, 42 of judgment). (2) The claim for accrued interest had not been "dealt with" in the first award. T's claim for a declaration that it was entitled to retain the US $7.7 million failed, and any claim for accrued interest consequential on that claim accordingly also failed. However, T also had a claim for a declaration and for other relief in respect of C's wrongful demand under the refund guarantee for both the principal sum and the accrued interest and was claiming "all sums" in the escrow account. Further, the fact that T had a claim to some or all of the accrued interest even if its retention claim failed was recognised by C's submissions. That claim, and C's mirror-image claim, was not determined as a result of the dismissal of the retention claim. Who was entitled to the accrued interest, in what proportion and on what basis therefore remained a matter to be determined by the tribunal notwithstanding the dismissal of the retention claim. Moreover, the dispositive parts of the first award dealt with the "balance" of the escrow account in relation to the principal sum but not the accrued interest (paras 47-49).

CADOGAN MARITIME INC v TURNER SHIPPING INC, [2013] EWHC 138 (Comm), [2013] 1 Lloyd's Rep. 630, Hamblen, J., QBD (Comm).

107. Awards–Enforcement–Party challenging awards on grounds of jurisdiction and serious irregularity–Whether security for costs and order for payment into court appropriate

[Arbitration Act 1996 (c.23) s.67, s.68, s.70(7).]

The applicant (Y) applied for orders that the respondent (X) provide security for Y's costs in relation to X's challenges to an arbitration award made in Y's favour, and that X pay into court the sum awarded. The parties had entered into a contract of affreightment by which X agreed to ship and Y agreed to provide tonnage to carry six cargoes of coal for the years 2008 to 2012. X only completed the first shipments in 2008. Y referred the dispute to arbitration in London in accordance with the contractual provisions. The arbitrators confirmed their jurisdiction and found that X had breached the contract by refusing to ship anything during 2009, 2010 and 2012 and awarded Y damages and costs. X obtained orders from the Indian court in 2012 restraining Y from taking any steps to enforce the awards in India. Y obtained a freezing order and anti-suit injunction against X in Australia where X owned coal mines and subsidiary companies. A final award was made in England after Y obtained anti-anti-suit injunctions against X in relation to applications by X in India for orders restraining Y from pursuing the arbitration proceedings. X then sought to challenge the final award under the Arbitration Act 1996 s.67 and s.68. Y sought the order for security for costs in relation to those challenges.

Held: Application granted in part. (1) The relevant question was whether X had assets which were available for the purposes of execution, *Azov Shipping Co v Baltic Shipping Co (No.2)* [1999] 1 All E.R. (Comm.) 716, [1999] C.L.Y. 224 applied. X was a substantial concern in India with considerable assets in Australia. It had decided not to honour any of the arbitration awards made against it, some of which had remained outstanding for over a year. It was to be expected therefore that X would resist any enforcement attempts. X's major asset was a shareholding in a subsidiary company, and it was doubtful whether that was readily realisable. Whilst X could probably be made to pay eventually, it was unlikely to occur promptly, *Longstaff International Ltd v Baker & McKenzie* [2004] EWHC 1852 (Ch), [2004] 1 W.L.R. 2917, [2005] C.L.Y. 465 considered. X had not expressed a willingness to pay any costs ordered against it, or explained how such a liability could readily be enforced by Y. There was a risk that X's assets were not readily available to satisfy any adverse costs order. Therefore, the expense of complying with an order for security for costs was necessary to ensure the fair resolution of the dispute in relation to the final award. Without any security, there was a risk that any costs order in Y's favour could not be enforced without considerable delay and expense (see paras 12-15, 17-18 of judgment). (2) In relation to a payment into court under s.70(7) of the 1996 Act, X's challenge to the jurisdiction was both flimsy and lacking in substance. There was an ad hoc submission in relation to the 2011 shipments: by seeking an indemnity in relation to future losses under the contract, X had put the future shipments in issue. Moreover, when Y introduced its claim in relation to those shipments, X did not challenge the jurisdiction of the arbitral tribunal. The question of a breach in 2011 was debated and Y's claim was held to be premature. That evinced a clear ad hoc submission. Y could therefore satisfy the threshold requirement in relation to the s.67 challenge, *A v B (Arbitration: Security)* [2010] EWHC 3302 (Comm), [2011] 2 All E.R. (Comm) 935, [2011] C.L.Y. 136 followed. There was no such requirement in relation to the s.68 challenge. However, the jurisdiction conferred by s.70 could not be used to assist a party in enforcing an award and Y would be so assisted by an order that X make a payment into court. Such an order could only be justified if the existence of the s.67 and s.68 challenges to the award somehow prejudiced Y's ability to enforce the award, or diminished X's ability to honour it. Then it might be an appropriate means of removing that prejudice or of restoring X's ability to honour the award. X's conduct was not a legitimate reason for ordering a payment into court. X's challenges would delay Y's attempts to enforce the final order in Australia, but an order for payment into court was not required to end that delay. Meanwhile the Australian freezing order protected Y. An order for payment in was therefore wrong in principle (paras 19-25, 27, 32-35).

X v Y; Y v X, [2013] EWHC 1104 (Comm), [2013] 2 Lloyd's Rep. 230, Teare, J., QBD (Comm).

108. Awards–Enforcement–Receivership application made to enforce arbitration award–Foreign insolvency proceedings previously opened

[Regulation 1346/2000 on insolvency proceedings Art.1.]

The court was required to determine issues in proceedings to enforce an arbitration award. The defendant (G) was the time charterer of a vessel from its owner (K). G sub-chartered the vessel to the claimant (W) and W sub-sub-chartered the vessel back to G for the balance of the period of the sub-charter from G. K withdrew the vessel from the charter service in order to carry out repairs. G then cancelled the sub-sub-charter on the ground that the vessel was off-hire or reasonably estimated to be off-hire for 60 days, relying on a clause in the sub-sub-charter which permitted cancellation in that event. W commenced an arbitration against G claiming that the actual or estimated off-hire had been caused by G's failure to meet its maintenance obligations under the sub-charter.

G did not bring arbitration proceedings up the charter chain against K as it could have done in reliance on the identical maintenance obligations in the head charter. In fact G had agreed not to make any claim against K or the vessel's managers. The arbitrators made an award in favour of W. G told W that it intended to honour the award but a few days later successfully applied to the German court for the appointment of a preliminary liquidator. W obtained permission to enforce the award and serve the enforcement application out of the jurisdiction, and obtained a freezing injunction without notice. It also applied for the appointment of receivers to bring a claim by G against K. W then discovered that G had given up its rights against K and had gone into liquidation. W did not seek to continue the freezing order or pursue the receivership application. The issues were whether the receivership application should be struck out or only stayed; and who should pay the costs.

Held: Judgment accordingly. (1) The order of the German court appointing a preliminary liquidator was a judgment opening insolvency proceedings for the purposes of Regulation 1346/2000. On the expert evidence G could not dispose of its assets without the liquidator's consent; it was subject to his supervision for the purpose of securing and conserving its assets and could not incur liabilities without his consent; it could not collect its debts for itself and they were to be paid to the liquidator; it could not suffer execution to be levied against it; and it had to hand over its books and records. To that not inconsiderable extent it had lost control of its assets. There had been at least a partial divestment of the debtor company as required by art.1, *Eurofood IFSC Ltd, Re (C-341/04)* [2006] Ch. 508, [2007] C.L.Y. 2428 considered. The fact that the order might become ineffective if the filing was withdrawn or if the court so decided did not mean that there had been no opening of proceedings under the Regulation. Thus the order fell to be recognised by the English court, and in particular the prohibition of measures of enforcement. That meant that the application for a receiver was prohibited. It should simply be dismissed (see paras 59-75 of judgment). (2) G had confirmed to W that it had reserved its rights against K when it had agreed not to pursue them; it had also said that it would in time pay the award and then started insolvency proceedings four days later; it then did not inform W that it had done so. It was unlikely that the applications would have been brought by W, if G had kept W properly informed. G's conduct was not reasonable or consistent with the overriding objective of saving costs. The court should make a costs order to reflect the degree of success and the conduct of the parties. G should pay W its costs of the application contained in the arbitration claim form up to and including the date when W learned of the appointment of the liquidator. G should not be entitled to recover from W any of its costs incurred before the date on which it had served most of its evidence and applied for the enforcement application to be struck out, except for the costs of the report of its German law expert. Thereafter W should pay the costs of the report and 50 per cent of G's costs, if and to the extent that it was shown that G was liable for such costs (paras 83-94).

WESTWOOD SHIPPING LINES INC v UNIVERSAL SCHIFFAHRTSGESELLSCHAFT MBH; WESTWOOD SHIPPING LINES INC v GMB SCHIFFAHRTS GmbH, [2012] EWHC 1394 (Comm), [2013] 1 B.C.L.C. 370, Christopher Clarke, J., QBD (Comm).

109. Awards–Permission to appeal–Applicable procedure and criteria

[Arbitration Act 1996 (c.23) s.69, s.69(3) (c).]

The claimant construction company (M) applied for permission to appeal against an arbitrator's award in favour of the respondents (K). M had purchased land from K upon which a medical centre was to be built. The agreement provided that, following completion, K would lease back the land. A dispute arose as to whether M had performed the construction work promptly in accordance with due diligence and best endeavours clauses in the agreement. The arbitrator had found M to be in breach of the agreement and had made an award in K's favour. M sought to appeal on two issues, one relating to the arbitrator's interpretation of the due diligence and best endeavours clauses, and the other relating to his assessment of K's losses. In relation to those questions, it was common ground that the requirements of the Arbitration Act 1996 s.69(3)(a) and s.69(3)(b) were met. The issue was whether, and to what extent, the requirements in s.69(3)(c) and s.69(3)(d) were met.

Held: Permission refused. (1) The process whereby the court dealt with an application for permission to appeal was a summary one. The case of *CMA CGM SA v Beteiligungs KG MS Northern Pioneer Schiffahrtsgesellschaft mbH & Co* [2002] EWCA Civ 1878, [2003] 1 W.L.R. 1015, [2003] C.L.Y. 204 indicated that such applications were to be dealt with on paper so as to simplify the process and save court time; where they were dealt with orally, they were to be disposed of within half an hour or so, as had been the practice in the Commercial Court for some time. The guidelines in *Pioneer Shipping Ltd v BTP Tioxide Ltd (The Nema) (No.2)* [1982] A.C. 724, [1981] C.L.Y. 76, which were essentially a threshold test for the grant of permission in arbitration cases, had been replaced with the statutory criteria in s.69 of the Act, but *CMA* defined the way in which that criteria had to be satisfied on an application. It would not always be possible to dispense with a permission case within "half an hour or so". However, irrespective of the amount of time it took for the judge to read and understand the relevant material, the process of actually determining the application was to be a summary one, in which the applicant had to establish that it was "clear-cut" that the appropriate criteria, in the instant case s.69(3)(c)(i)(ii) and s.69(3)(d), were established. That was consistent with the guidelines in *The Nema*, *CMA* applied and *The Nema* considered (see paras 22-27 of judgment). (2) In the instant case, M's arguments on its two issues raised subtle and complex matters, and it could not establish, in relation to either issue, that it was clear-cut that the arbitrator's decision was open to serious doubt. Although the parties basically agreed that there was a public interest in the court considering the interrelation of "best endeavours" and "due diligence" clauses in construction agreements, the events in the instant case were highly unusual and fell within the definition of "one-off" events in *The Nema*. The first issue was not, therefore, a question of general public importance. It was not just and proper for the court to determine either issue, and permission to appeal against the arbitrator's decision was therefore refused (paras 30-32, 44, 48-49, 58-65).

MORRIS HOMES (WEST MIDLANDS) LTD v KEAY, [2013] EWHC 932 (TCC), [2013] B.L.R. 370, Judge David Grant, QBD (TCC).

110. Awards–Permission to appeal–Jurisdiction to grant permission to appeal

[Arbitration Act 1996 (c.23) s.69(8).]

The applicant owners (K) challenged a judge's refusal of permission to appeal from his own decision on a question of law arising from an arbitration award in favour of the charterers (B). The charterparty contained a continuing warranty that K would ensure that the vessel was covered by specific insurance throughout its currency. The limit of cover for hull and machinery was $16 million. The vessel suffered considerable damage and K tendered notice of abandonment to the underwriters, asserting that the vessel was a constructive total loss. K informed B that the cost of repairing the vessel was uneconomical so the charterparty was frustrated and the voyage could not be completed. It was common ground between the parties that the sound market value of the vessel was $5.75 million. An arbitrator determined that the probable cost of repairing the vessel was $9 million and the charterparty had been frustrated because the cost of repair exceeded the value of the vessel. B appealed on a point of law, namely the effect on the doctrine of frustration of the clause in a time charterparty which required K to maintain insurance at a stipulated level and whether it created an assumption of risk and responsibility on K to repair hull damage up to that figure. Permission was granted on the papers on the ground that it raised a question of general public importance. However, the appeal judge held that K had chosen to walk away from the charterparty when the underwriters had been prepared to repair and the contract had not been frustrated. K's application for permission to appeal was refused by the judge. K submitted that

(1) once the judge giving permission had decided that there was a question of law of general public importance, the appeal judge could not say in refusing permission to appeal that the case turned on the construction of the particular charterparty; (2) the arbitrator had made no finding that the underwriters were prepared to repair the ship and the judge had no business in holding that when refusing permission to appeal.

Held: Application refused. (1) The Arbitration Act 1996 s.69(8) prevented an appeal to the Court of Appeal unless the question was of general importance or for some other special reason and the relevant "court" in that sub-section was the High Court not the Court of Appeal, *Henry Boot Construction (UK) Ltd v Malmaison Hotel (Manchester) Ltd (Leave to Appeal)* [2001] Q.B. 388, [2000] C.L.Y. 218 and *Athletic Union of Constantinople (AEK) v National Basketball Association (Application to Strike Out)* [2002] EWCA Civ 830, [2002] 1 W.L.R. 2863, [2002] C.L.Y. 209 followed. Therefore, the Court of Appeal could not hear an application for permission to appeal from a refusal of a High Court judge to grant permission to appeal from his decision on a question of law arising from an award. Nevertheless, there was a residual jurisdiction to set aside a refusal of permission if it resulted from an unfair or improper process such that no decision had been made, *Aden Refinery Co Ltd v Ugland Management Co Ltd (The Ugland Obo One)* [1987] Q.B. 650, [1986] C.L.Y. 91, *CGU International Insurance Plc v AstraZeneca Insurance Co Ltd (Permission to Appeal)* [2006] EWCA Civ 1340, [2007] 1 All E.R. (Comm) 501, [2006] C.L.Y. 204 and *North Range Shipping Ltd v Seatrans Shipping Corp (The Western Triumph)* [2002] EWCA Civ 405, [2002] 1 W.L.R. 2397, [2002] C.L.Y. 208 followed. That was an extraordinarily high hurdle to surmount and neither counsel could point to a case in which that residual jurisdiction had been recognised (see para.15 of judgment). Permission had been granted on the papers and without the assistance of oral argument, whereas the appeal judge had enjoyed the benefit of oral argument and of time to reflect, during which he had prepared a powerful judgment. He was not bound by the permission decision as he knew far more about the case. The requirement that the question was of general importance did not presuppose an appeal. It was merely a jurisdictional requirement without which leave to appeal could not be given, so, even if there had been procedural unfairness, his further decision that there was no real prospect of success prevented the court from exercising the narrow residual jurisdiction. (2) K had walked away from the charterparty and the additional observation that the underwriters were amenable to repair of the ship was merely a pendant to that decision. In any event, that could justifiably be inferred from the award. The supervising judge of commercial matters determined that there was no jurisdiction in the Court of Appeal to grant permission to appeal to itself and it could only decide whether or not to set aside the original decision to refuse leave to appeal to the Court of Appeal. Were that to be done in the instant case, K would be free to re-apply to the Commercial Court for a fresh decision; however, that course was expressly refused. Permission was given for the decision to be reported and cited in other cases.

BUNGE SA v KYLA SHIPPING CO LTD; KYLA, THE; *sub nom.* KYLA SHIPPING CO LTD v BUNGE SA, [2013] EWCA Civ 734, [2013] 3 All E.R. 1006, Longmore, L.J., CA (Civ Div).

111. Awards–Serious irregularity–Alleged failure by tribunal to consider issue–Assumption of responsibility for losses on failure to complete joint venture agreement

[Arbitration Act 1996 (c.23) s.33, s.68(2)(d).]

The applicant (P) applied for an order that two paragraphs of an arbitration award, and the question of the scope of P's liability for the consequential losses of the respondent (D), be remitted to a tribunal for reconsideration. P, a petrochemical company, had failed to complete a joint venture formation agreement with D, another petrochemical company by paying US$7.5m for a 50 per cent interest in certain of D's assets. Resolving that dispute, the tribunal, in a partial award, concluded that P had been in breach by failing to complete the agreement by paying the required sum, and that D had established that it was entitled to damages for consequential losses. The instant application impugned D's entitlement to damages for losses it suffered when, after P failed to complete, D had to raise US$15b in order to complete the acquisition of another company. P contended that those losses were not within the reasonable contemplation of the parties, and that irrespective of what the parties had known of the risk of such losses, P had not assumed responsibility for them, given D's assurances that it had not been relying on the joint venture funds to complete the third party transaction. P maintained that the recoverability of losses in applications such as the instant one did not depend entirely or ultimately on reasonable foreseeability, but also on whether a party was reasonably regarded as having assumed responsibility for losses of that kind (the assumption of responsibility test). The issues were whether there was a serious irregularity under the Arbitration Act 1996 s.68(2)(d) in that the tribunal failed (i) to deal with the question of the assumption of responsibility, which caused, or would cause, P substantial injustice; (ii) to comply with its general duty under s.33, which caused, or would cause, P substantial injustice.

Held: Application refused. (1) The instant application was to be determined on the basis that P's position on the assumption of responsibility question was at least well arguable. The question of whether there had been a serious irregularity within s.68(2)(d) involved three considerations: whether the assumption of responsibility was an issue within the meaning of the subsection; if so, whether it was put to the tribunal, and whether the tribunal failed to deal with it. The assumption of responsibility question, as P identified and presented, was an issue within the meaning of s.68(2)(d). It was difficult to decide quite where the line demarking issues from arguments fell, but almost the whole of D's claim could have depended on how the question of the assumption of responsibility was resolved. That accorded with the natural meaning of "issue", and fairness demanded that it be dealt with by the tribunal, and not ignored or overlooked, assuming it was put to it. Further, as matters stood after the exchange of pre-hearing memorials, P had "put to" the tribunal the assumption of responsibility question; nothing P did thereafter withdrew or qualified the assumption of responsibility issue. The tribunal had dealt with the issue, albeit succinctly, in a single sentence which stated that P "should reasonably have been expected to be held liable for costs associated with its failure to close". P could not complain about the composite disposal of the issue as long as the issue had been dealt with, which it had, and the fact that the tribunal did not refer to the assurances on which it relied did not mean that it had failed to deal with the issue; much less did a failure to explain the weight given to particular considerations amount to a serious irregularity under s.68. However, if wrong on that conclusion and the tribunal could be said to have ignored the assumption of responsibility question, P would have been caused a substantial injustice. Even if the relevant sentence fell short of dealing with the issue in the sense that it was directed towards it, then no substantial injustice was or would be caused (see paras 10, 15, 21, 23, 25, 29-31, 33 of judgment). (2) P's complaint that the tribunal had failed to comply with its general duty under s.33 was rejected as the court could not infer that it had overlooked the evidence on which P relied, *Arduina Holdings BV v Celtic Resources Holdings Plc* [2006] EWHC 3155 (Comm) applied. Although it was true that the award did not refer to the evidence, the natural inference was that the tribunal considered it to be of lesser importance. Any other approach defied the proper approach to the court's appraisal of awards (paras 36-37).

PETROCHEMICAL INDUSTRIES CO (KSC) v DOW CHEMICAL CO, [2012] EWHC 2739 (Comm), [2012] 2 Lloyd's Rep. 691, Andrew Smith, J., QBD (Comm).

112. **Awards–Serious irregularity–Arbitration award determining rent payable by tenant of agricultural holding–Adequacy of arbitrator's reasons for award–Whether any failure in reason causing substantial injustice to landlord**

[Agricultural Holdings Act 1986 (c.5) s.48(3), s.53(7), s.53(6); Arbitration Act 1996 (c.23) s.52(4), s.68.]

The claimant landlord (C) sought an order setting aside an arbitration award determining the rent payable by the defendant tenant (S) for an agricultural holding. S had become a tenant under the succession provisions of the Agricultural Holdings Act 1986 s.53(7). C gave S notice under s.48(3) and s.53(6) of the 1986 Act requiring an arbitration as to the amount of the rent payable under S's tenancy. C contended that the rent properly payable was £46,000 per annum, and S contended for a rent of £28,500. Both parties served expert reports. The arbitrator found that all the experts were partisan. He determined that the rent properly payable was £34,800. Following the award, at the parties' request, the arbitrator gave further reasons. C applied under the Arbitration Act 1996 s.68 to have the award set aside in its entirety or remitted for reconsideration. C contended, inter alia, that, notwithstanding the further reasons, the arbitrator had failed sufficiently to explain why he had preferred the evidence of S's expert (H), who it submitted was unreliable, over C's expert. It argued that there were also inadequate reasons for the adjudicator's conclusions as to the productive capacity and related earning capacity of the holding, income from livestock, fixed costs, and the value of the farmhouse on the holding.

Held: Judgment for defendant. (1) A party challenging an arbitration award on the grounds of serious irregularity had to show that such irregularity had caused or would cause him substantial injustice, *Lesotho Highlands Development Authority v Impregilo SpA* [2005] UKHL 43, [2006] 1 A.C. 221, [2005] C.L.Y. 207 followed. Section 52(4) of the 1996 Act required an award to contain reasons which had not only to be intelligible, but also deal with the substantial points raised, *Poyser and Mills Arbitration, Re* [1964] 2 Q.B. 467, [1963] C.L.Y. 43 applied. Where there was a conflict of expert evidence before a court, a judge was entitled to prefer the evidence of one expert to the other but was under a duty to make his reasons for that plain, *English v Emery Reimbold & Strick Ltd* [2002] EWCA Civ 605, [2002] 1 W.L.R. 2409, [2002] C.L.Y. 301 followed. There was no reason why that duty should be fundamentally different for an adjudicator. A deficiency of reasons would amount to a serious irregularity causing an injustice within s.68(2) of the 1996 Act where it raised a substantial doubt as to whether the decision was based on relevant grounds and was otherwise free from any flaw in the decision-making process which would afford a ground for quashing the decision, *South Buckinghamshire DC v Porter (No.2)* [2004] UKHL 33, [2004] 1 W.L.R. 1953, [2004] C.L.Y. 3087 applied (see paras 35-36, 41, 43, 49-53 of judgment). (2) Had the issue over H's reliability been central to the arbitrator's decision, his preference for the evidence of S's experts would have been inadequately reasoned. However, with the exception of his evidence as to the value of the farmhouse, H's evidence had not affected the arbitration's outcome. The arbitrator had assessed the rental value of the holding by reference to the productive capacity and the related earning capacity of the holding and H had not given evidence on those points. Even if H's reliability was an essential issue, the failure to give reasons for that conclusion had not caused any substantial injustice to C (paras 60-61). (3) The arbitrator's reasoning in respect of productivity and related earning capacity, when read by a party who knew the issues and the relevant arguments, was just enough to tell the parties why he had reached the conclusions that he had in those respects. The arbitrator had not adequately explained his conclusion on income from livestock but his failure had not caused substantial injustice to C. The arbitrator's reasons in respect of his conclusions as to fixed costs were adequate (paras 65, 70, 72). (4) H was the only expert to have given evidence on the farmhouse's value but that issue was, overall, a minor one. Any failure in reasoning in that respect had caused no substantial prejudice to C. It could not be said that the decision left C in doubt as to whether the arbitrator had committed an error of law or whether the award would be open to challenge by reason of the assessment which the arbitrator had made of H; nor could it be said that the lack of reasoning adversely affected C's ability to assess its position in relation to future reviews of the rent payable (para.75).

COMPTON BEAUCHAMP ESTATES LTD v SPENCE, [2013] EWHC 1101 (Ch), [2013] 2 P. & C.R. 15, Morgan, J., Ch D.

113. Awards–Serious irregularity–Arbitrator awarding rescission of share purchase agreement–Whether arbitrator decided case on basis not advanced–Grounds for extending time for challenge

[Arbitration Act 1996 (c.23) s.33, s.67, s.68, s.70(3), s.73.]

The applicant (T) sought an anti-suit injunction restraining the respondents (R) from pursuing proceedings in Sharjah challenging the validity of an arbitration award and the respondents sought to set aside the award for lack of jurisdiction and serious irregularity and to set aside an order giving leave to enforce the award as a judgment. R were resident in Sharjah and owned a company (H) which held a lease of land in Sharjah with a permit to build and operate a cement plant. T became a joint venture partner and purchased 40 per cent of the shares in H under a share purchase agreement. The joint venture constructed the cement plant and it commenced operation. A dispute arose and T commenced arbitration under the share purchase agreement which provided for London arbitration under ICC rules. The arbitrator found that R were in breach of their representations, warranties or undertakings in the agreement and that T was entitled to rescission. She awarded T the amount that it had paid for its 40 per cent shareholding which was retransferred to R; she also awarded damages in the amount that T had contributed to H, and costs. T obtained permission to enforce the award as a judgment. R brought proceedings in Sharjah challenging the award. T sought an anti-suit injunction to restrain the Sharjah proceedings. R issued an arbitration claim form challenging the award for lack of jurisdiction and serious irregularity and seeking an extension of time within which to do so, and also applied to set aside the order giving permission to enforce the award as a judgment. R submitted that the arbitrator, in finding that T was entitled to rescind and that its shareholding should be retransferred to R, had decided the case on a basis that had not been advanced by T and which R had had no opportunity to address.

Held: Judgment accordingly. (1) The application to extend time was made almost 17 weeks after expiry of the 28-day period provided by the Arbitration Act 1996 s.70(3). That was a very substantial delay in the context of the statutory period. The overwhelming inference from the evidence was that a deliberate tactical decision was taken by R to challenge the award in Sharjah rather than in England and that that deliberate choice was maintained until it became apparent that the English proceedings initiated by T to enforce the award would be irresistible unless an application was made in England. It was a case of deliberate and tactical delay. The culpability for the delay was very high. T had not contributed to the delay by appearing content for the matter to be dealt with in Sharjah; its stance in the early stage of proceedings, consistent with the normal procedure, was neutral. An extension of time was refused because the application would in any event fail if time were extended. However, even if the challenge was a good one which would have succeeded, time would not have been extended in the light of the substantial delay which was a result of a deliberate choice for perceived tactical advantage (see paras 65-84 of judgment). (2) There was no serious irregularity within s.68. Section 33 required a party to be given a reasonable opportunity of addressing his opponent's case, but that did not mean that the tribunal was acting unfairly in deciding a case on a point to which the party raising it did not give any great emphasis, or which was not the subject matter of any great exposition. Provided the issue was raised, however briefly, the opposing party had an opportunity to address it at whatever length and in whatever detail he chose. An issue raised in written submissions did not have to be drawn attention to during any hearing, or mentioned or developed orally, in order for the other side to have a fair opportunity of dealing with it. The claim for rescission was advanced in T's statement of claim. The claim for rescission was an alternative form of relief but the grounds advanced for the primary relief were sufficient to support the alternative relief. They addressed the points which the parties were concerned to have decided, namely whether R were in breach of the agreements. Given that the claim for rescission and damages was raised as an issue, and that the amount sought was such sum as the arbitrator might determine, R had had the opportunity to address this aspect of the claim (paras 106-112). (3) If a serious irregularity had occurred, it had not given rise to substantial injustice (para.124). (4) R submitted that the arbitrator had no jurisdiction to consider the rescission claim because it was a new claim under the ICC rules, but R had lost the right to object under s.67, by virtue of s.73, since it had continued to take part in the arbitration without objection (para.126). (5) R's challenge to the award and the order giving leave to enforce it as a judgment failed (para.136). (6) T was entitled to an anti-suit injunction restraining R's pursuit of the Sharjah proceedings (paras 129-135).

TERNA BAHRAIN HOLDING CO WLL v AL SHAMSI; AL SHAMSI v TERNA BAHRAIN HOLDING CO WLL, [2012] EWHC 3283 (Comm), [2013] 1 All E.R. (Comm) 580, Popplewell, J., QBD (Comm).

ARMED FORCES

114. Alcohol testing–Criminal proceedings–Drug testing–Interpretation

THE ARMED FORCES (INTERPRETATION,TRANSLATION AND ALCOHOL AND DRUG TESTS) RULES 2013, SI 2013/2527; made under the Armed Forces Act 2006 s.112, s.151, s.153, s.163, s.288. In force: in accordance with rule 1; .

These Rules amend five Rules to give effect to the requirements of Directive 2010/64 on the right to interpretation and translation in criminal proceedings, insofar as those requirements apply to service disciplinary proceedings for the armed forces and those civilians who are subject to service discipline for certain purposes. The amendments also insert new rules for the use of specimens in proceedings for offences related to alcohol and drugs under the Armed Forces Act 2006 ss.20(1) (a), 20A and 42.

115. Alcohol testing–Samples–Service personnel

THE ARMED FORCES (ALCOHOL LIMITS FOR PRESCRIBED SAFETY-CRITICAL DUTIES) REGULATIONS 2013, SI 2013/2787; made under the Armed Forces Act 2006 s.20A, s.93F. In force: November 1, 2013; .

These Regulations prescribe the higher and lower limits for alcohol in breath, blood and urine for safety-critical duties in the armed forces.

116. Armed forces–Expiry–Extensions of time

THE ARMED FORCES ACT (CONTINUATION) ORDER 2013, SI 2013/2603; made under the Armed Forces Act 2006 s.382. In force: October 9, 2013; .

The instrument provides for the Armed Forces Act 2006 to expire at the end of November 2, 2014, instead of November 2, 2013.

117. Armed Forces Act 2011 (c.18)–Commencement No.3 Order

THE ARMED FORCES ACT 2011 (COMMENCEMENT NO.3) ORDER 2013, SI 2013/SI 2013/784 (C.37); made under the Armed Forces Act 2011 s.32. Commencement details: bringing into force various provisions of the 2011 Act on April 6, 2013.; .

This Order brings into force the Armed Forces Act 2011 s.25 on April 6, 2013.

118. **Armed Forces Act 2011 (c.18)–Commencement No.4 Order**

THE ARMED FORCES ACT 2011 (COMMENCEMENT NO.4) ORDER 2013, SI 2013/SI 2013/2501 (C.101); made under the Armed Forces Act 2011 s.32. Commencement details: bringing into force various provisions of the 2011 Act on November 1, 2013.; .

This Order brings into force certain provisions of the Armed Forces Act 2011 on November 1, 2013.

119. **Court Martial–Fines**

THE ARMED FORCES (FINANCIAL PENALTY ENFORCEMENT ORDERS) (AMENDMENT) REGULATIONS 2013, SI 2013/1761; made under the Armed Forces Act 2006 s.322. In force: November 1, 2013; .

The Armed Forces Act 2011 inserts new sections 269A and 269B in the Armed Forces Act 2006. Section 269A requires the Court Martial, when imposing a fine, to make an order fixing a term for which the person liable to pay the fine may be committed to prison if the fine is not paid. Section 269B enables the Court Martial, when making a service compensation order, to specify a maximum term for which the person liable to pay the compensation may be committed to prison if the compensation is not paid. These Regulations amend the Armed Forces (Financial Penalty Enforcement Orders) Regulations 2009 to give effect to an order made under section 269A or 269B in courts in the United Kingdom.

120. **Court Martial Appeal Court–Interpreters**

THE COURT MARTIAL APPEAL COURT (INTERPRETATION AND TRANSLATION) RULES 2013, SI 2013/2524; made under the Court Martial Appeals Act 1968 s.49. In force: October 27, 2013; .

Rule 16 of the Court Martial Appeal Court Rules 2009 provides for the appointment of interpreters for the purposes of proceedings to which those rules apply. These rules amend the 2009 Rules to implement requirements of Directive 2010/64 on the right to interpretation and translation in criminal proceedings, insofar as those requirements apply to the Court Martial Appeal Court.

121. **Service personnel–Right to life–United Kingdom jurisdiction under art.1 European Convention on Human Rights 1950–Application of jurisdiction to securing art.2 rights for service personnel serving outside country**

[European Convention on Human Rights 1950 Art.1, Art.2.]

The court had to determine whether claims brought against the Ministry of Defence by British service personnel injured, and by the families of personnel killed, while serving in Iraq should be struck out. The first group of claimants (S) were related to servicemen killed in an explosion beside their Land Rover. S alleged that the MoD had breached the European Convention on Human Rights 1950 art.2 by failing to take reasonable steps to protect the soldiers' lives from foreseeable risks, in relation to the procurement and deployment of appropriately armoured vehicles. The second set of claims concerned servicemen killed and injured in friendly fire between two tanks. The claimants (T) alleged that the MoD had breached its common law duty of care by failing to ensure that the tanks were properly equipped with devices which would have prevented the incident. The court had to determine (i) whether the United Kingdom's jurisdiction under art.1 of the Convention extended to securing the protection of art.2 to members of the armed forces serving outside its territory; (ii) if so, whether the art.2 claims should nevertheless be struck out; (iii) whether T's claims should be struck out under the doctrine of combat immunity; (iv) whether T's claims should be struck out on the basis that it would not be fair, just and reasonable to impose a duty of care to protect against such death or injury as had occurred.

Held: Judgment accordingly. (Lords Mance, Wilson and Carnwath JJ.S.C. dissenting in part) (1) Following *Al-Skeini v United Kingdom (55721/07)* (2011) 53 E.H.R.R. 18, [2011] C.L.Y. 1696, the view taken in *R. (on the application of*

Smith) v Oxfordshire Assistant Deputy Coroner [2010] UKSC 29, [2011] 1 A.C. 1, [2010] C.L.Y. 1737 that the state's armed forces abroad were not within its jurisdiction for the purposes of art.1 could no longer be maintained, *Al-Skeini* applied, *Smith* not followed. *Al-Skeini*'s statement that "whenever the state through its agents exercises control and authority over an individual, and thus jurisdiction" summarised the circumstances in which the state could be held to exercise jurisdiction extraterritorially. That resolved the inconsistency between *Issa v Turkey (31821/96)* (2005) 41 E.H.R.R. 27, [2005] C.L.Y. 2065 and *Bankovic v Belgium (Admissibility) (52207/99)* 11 B.H.R.C. 435, [2002] C.L.Y. 2535, on whether the relevant test was one of authority and control or was essentially territorial, in favour of *Issa*'s indication that the question was one of authority and control. *Bankovic* could no longer be regarded as authoritative, *Issa* applied, *Bankovic* considered. Further, *Al-Skeini* had departed from *Bankovic*'s indication that the package of rights in the Convention was indivisible and could not be tailored to the circumstances of the extraterritorial act in question. Such dividing and tailoring went with the principle that extraterritorial jurisdiction could exist whenever a state through its agents exercised authority and control over an individual. Further, both a state's agents and those whom they affected when exercising authority and control on the state's behalf were brought within the state's art.1 jurisdiction by the application of the same general principle, *Cyprus v Turkey (6780/74)* (1975) 2 D. & R. 125 considered. Accordingly, the UK's art.1 jurisdiction extended to securing the protection of art.2 to members of the armed forces serving outside its territory (see paras 45-55 of judgment). (2) The extent to which the application of the substantive obligation under art.2 could be held impossible or inappropriate would vary according to context. There was a fundamental difference between training manoeuvres in controlled conditions and active service where troops did not have complete control. Further, although procurement decisions were taken remote from the battlefield, they would not always be appropriate for review by the courts. The court had to avoid imposing unrealistic positive obligations on the state regarding planning and conducting military operations, but it had to give effect to obligations where it was reasonable to expect the protection of art.2, *Stoyanovi v Bulgaria (42980/04)*and *Giuliani v Italy (23458/02)* (2012) 54 E.H.R.R. 10 applied. The question required the exercise of judgement on the facts of each case. In T's cases, the circumstances in which the various decisions had been made had to be investigated before any breach of obligations could be determined. Those claims should not be struck out (paras 64-65, 76, 79-81). (3) The extension of combat immunity in *Multiple Claimants v Ministry of Defence* [2003] EWHC 1134 (QB), Times, May 29, 2003 to the planning and preparation of the operations in which injury was sustained was too loosely expressed, *Multiple Claimants* disapproved. S's claims were directed to things they said should have been done long before hostilities began. The doctrine of combat immunity should be narrowly construed: to apply it to S's claims would extend it further than it had previously been applied, *Bici v Ministry of Defence* [2004] EWHC 786 (QB), Times, June 11, 2004 approved. Nothing suggested that it extended that far (paras 89-96). (4) The question of whether S's claims fell within the exclusion from the imposition of a duty of care recognised in *Mulcahy v Ministry of Defence* [1996] Q.B. 732, [1996] C.L.Y. 5700, or any extension of it, could not be determined without hearing evidence, *Mulcahy* considered. Whether a duty should be held not to exist depended on the circumstances; the circumstances in which active operations were undertaken varied greatly (para.98).

SMITH v MINISTRY OF DEFENCE; ALLBUTT v MINISTRY OF DEFENCE; ELLIS v MINISTRY OF DEFENCE; REDPATH v MINISTRY OF DEFENCE; *sub nom.* MINISTRY OF DEFENCE v ELLIS; MINISTRY OF DEFENCE v ALLBUTT, [2013] UKSC 41, [2014] 1 A.C. 52, Lord Hope (Deputy President), SC.

122. Visiting forces

THE VISITING FORCES (DESIGNATION) ORDER 2013, SI 2013/540; made under the Visiting Forces Act 1952 s.1, s.15. In force: in accordance with art.2.; .

Section 9A of the Visiting Forces Act 1952 makes provision for the transfer to the Ministry of Defence of liability in certain claims against visiting forces. With the exception of Canada and Malta, to which s.9A already applies, it is necessary to designate North Atlantic Treaty Organisation (NATO) member countries and States which have accepted the invitation of NATO to take part in the Partnership for Peace as countries to which section 9A applies. This Order designates the countries to which section 9A is to apply.

AVIATION

123. Air Force–Air navigation–Public entertainments–Jet Formation Display Teams

THE AIR NAVIGATION (RESTRICTION OF FLYING) (JET FORMATION DISPLAY TEAMS) (RAF CRANWELL) REGULATIONS 2013, SI 2013/52; made under the Air Navigation Order 2009 (SI 2009/3015) art.161. In force: February 5, 2013; .

These Regulations impose restrictions on flying at Royal Air Force Cranwell during flying display rehearsals by the Red Arrows. The rehearsals are due to take place on a number of days during the period from February 5, 2013 to March 1, 2013.

124. Air navigation–Air Force–Public entertainments–Gloucestershire

THE AIR NAVIGATION (RESTRICTION OF FLYING) (CHELTENHAM FESTIVAL) REGULATIONS 2013, SI 2013/54; made under the Air Navigation Order 2009 (SI 2009/3015) s.161. In force: March 12, 2013; .

These Regulations impose restrictions on flying in airspace in the vicinity of Cheltenham, Gloucestershire, on the occasion of the Cheltenham Festival which is scheduled to take place there from March 12-15 2013. In view of the large numbers of helicopters operating from the temporary heliport at Cheltenham race course, the event organiser has requested measures to restrict flying in the vicinity of the race course. This has been agreed with the Civil Aviation Authority, Directorate of Airspace Policy (DAP) and the Department for Transport.

125. Air navigation–Air traffic control services–Civil Aviation Authority

THE SINGLE EUROPEAN SKY (NATIONAL SUPERVISORY AUTHORITY) REGULATIONS 2013, SI 2013/2620; made under the European Communities Act 1972 s.2. In force: December 12, 2013; .

These Regulations revoke and replace the Single European Sky (National Supervisory Authority) Regulations 2004 (SI 2004/1958) and the Single European Sky (Functions of the National Supervisory Authority) Regulations 2006 (SI 2006/3104) reflecting the updates introduced by Regulation 1070/2009 [2009] OJ L300/34.

126. Air navigation–Aviation safety–Northamptonshire

THE AIR NAVIGATION (RESTRICTION OF FLYING) (NORTHAMPTON SYWELL) REGULATIONS 2013, SI 2013/76; made under the Air Navigation Order 2009 (SI 2009/3015) art.161. In force: May 31, 2013; .

Theses Regulations restrict flying at the AeroExpo UK 2013 General Aviation Exhibition will take place at Northampton Sywell aerodrome, Northamptonshire, between May 31 and June 2, 2013 to the vicinity of Northampton Sywell aerodrome for reasons of flight safety.

127. Air navigation–Flying restrictions

THE AIR NAVIGATION (RESTRICTION OF FLYING) (FUNERAL OF BARONESS THATCHER) (AMENDMENT) REGULATIONS 2013, SI 2013/921; made under the Air Navigation Order 2009 (SI 2009/3015) art.161. In force: April 17, 2013; .

These Regulations amend the Air Navigation (Restriction of Flying) (Funeral of Baroness Thatcher) Regulations 2013 (SI 2013/878) to extend the duration of the flying restrictions imposed by those Regulations by one hour, as part of the overall security arrangements.

128. Air navigation–Flying restrictions

THE AIR NAVIGATION (RESTRICTION OF FLYING) (HER MAJESTY THE QUEEN'S BIRTHDAY FLYPAST) REGULATIONS 2013, SI 2013/831; made under the Air Navigation Order 2009 (SI 2009/3015) art.161. In force: June 11, 2013; .

These Regulations impose restrictions on flying by reason of the rehearsals for, and the flypast of, a large formation of aircraft to commemorate the birthday of Her Majesty The Queen that are scheduled to take place during the period June 11-15, 2013.

129. Air navigation–Flying restrictions

THE AIR NAVIGATION (RESTRICTION OF FLYING) (RNAS YEOVILTON) REGULATIONS 2013, SI 2013/839; made under the Air Navigation Order 2009 (SI 2009/3015) art.161. In force: July 12, 2013; .

These Regulations impose restrictions on flying in airspace in the vicinity of RNAS Yeovilton, Somerset for flying displays and associated rehearsals that are scheduled to take place there on July 12 and 13, 2013.

130. Air navigation–Flying restrictions–Dartford

THE AIR NAVIGATION (RESTRICTION OF FLYING) (DARTFORD) REGULATIONS 2013, SI 2013/2321; made under the Air Navigation Order 2009 (SI 2009/3015) art.161. In force: September 6, 2013 at 19.28 hrs.; .

These Regulations impose restrictions of an emergency nature on flying in the specified vicinity over Dartford.

131. Air navigation–Flying restrictions–Royal Air Force Leuchars

THE AIR NAVIGATION (RESTRICTION OF FLYING) (ROYAL AIR FORCE LEUCHARS) REGULATIONS 2013, SI 2013/1516; made under the Air Navigation Order 2009 (SI 2009/3015) art.161. In force: September 6, 2013; .

These Regulations impose restrictions on flying in airspace in the vicinity of Royal Air Force Leuchars, Fife on the occasion of the Battle of Britain Airshow and associated flying display practices to be held there on September 6th and 7th 2013.

132. Air service agreements–Aviation industry–Civil Aviation Authority–Fares

THE OPERATION OF AIR SERVICES IN THE COMMUNITY (PRICING ETC.) REGULATIONS 2013, SI 2013/486; made under the Tribunals, Courts and Enforcement Act 2007 Sch.7 para.24. In force: April 6, 2013; .

This instrument enables the effective implementation and enforcement of art.23 of Regulation 1008/2008 on common rules for the operation of air services in the Community (recast). It designates the Civil Aviation Authority and the Office of Fair Trading as enforcers for requirements on transparency and non-discrimination in the publication of air fares and air cargo rates, and establishes an enforcement regime.

133. Aircraft–Airspace–Flying restrictions–Shropshire

THE AIR NAVIGATION (RESTRICTION OF FLYING) (ROYAL AIR FORCE COSFORD) REGULATIONS 2013, SI 2013/156; made under the Air Navigation Order 2009 (SI 2009/3015) art.161. In force: June 7, 2013; .

These Regulations impose restrictions on flying in airspace in the vicinity of Royal Air Force Cosford, Shropshire during an air display for the general public that is scheduled to take place there between June 7th and June 9th 2013.

134. Aviation industry–Airports–Commencement

THE CIVIL AVIATION ACT 2012 (REGULATION OF OPERATORS OF DOMINANT AIRPORTS) (CONSEQUENTIAL AMENDMENTS) REGULATIONS 2013, SI 2013/610; made under the Civil Aviation Act 2012 s.108. In force: April 6, 2013 except for reg.3 and Sch.2 on April 1, 2014.; .

These Regulations implement legislative changes that arise from the commencement of provisions of the Civil Aviation Act 2012 that are concerned with the regulation of operators of dominant airports.

135. Civil Aviation Act 2012 (c.19)–Commencement No.1, Transitional, Transitory and Saving Provisions Order

THE CIVIL AVIATION ACT 2012 (COMMENCEMENT NO.1, TRANSITIONAL, TRANSITORY AND SAVING PROVISIONS) ORDER 2013, SI 2013/SI 2013/589 (C.23); made under the Civil Aviation Act 2012 s.110. Commencement details: bringing into force various provisions of the 2012 Act on April 6, 2013.; .

This is the first Commencement Order bringing into force provisions of the Civil Aviation Act 2012.

136. Flying restrictions

THE AIR NAVIGATION (RESTRICTION OF FLYING) (BRADFORD, WEST YORKSHIRE) REGULATIONS 2013, SI 2013/2585; made under the Air Navigation Order 2009 (SI 2009/3015) art.161. In force: October 12, 2013; .

These Regulations restrict flying in the vicinity of Bradford, West Yorkshire, as a result of a large gathering of people that is scheduled to take place there on October 12, 2013.

137. Flying restrictions

THE AIR NAVIGATION (RESTRICTION OF FLYING) (DUXFORD AERODROME) REGULATIONS 2013, SI 2013/89; made under the Air Navigation Order 2009 (SI 2009/3015) art.161. In force: May 26, 2013; .

These Regulations impose restrictions on flying in airspace in the vicinity of Duxford, Cambridgeshire, during flying displays that are scheduled to be held at the aerodrome there during various days in 2013.

138. Flying restrictions

THE AIR NAVIGATION (RESTRICTION OF FLYING) (DUXFORD AERODROME) (AMENDMENT NO.2) REGULATIONS 2013, SI 2013/1106; made under the Air Navigation Order 2009 (SI 2009/3015) art.161. In force: May 26, 2013; .

These Regulations amend the Air Navigation (Restriction of Flying) (Duxford Aerodrome) Regulations 2013 (SI 2013/89) to bring forward from 12:00 hours to 09:30 the commencement of the flying restrictions applicable under the principal Regulations in relation to the flying display at Duxford Aerodrome on September 8, 2013.

139. Flying restrictions

THE AIR NAVIGATION (RESTRICTION OF FLYING) (JET FORMATION DISPLAY TEAMS) (NO.2) (AMENDMENT) REGULATIONS 2013, SI 2013/1417; made under the Air Navigation Order 2009 (SI 2009/3015) art.161. In force: June 7, 2013; .

These Regulations restrict flying in the vicinity of places where jet formation display teams intend to give flying displays, by removing from the Schedule to those Regulations a display which was due to take place at Welshpool on June 8 2013 and adding additional displays scheduled to take place at Marham on July 4 and July 5 2013.

140. Flying restrictions

THE AIR NAVIGATION (RESTRICTION OF FLYING) (JET FORMATION DISPLAY TEAMS) (NO.3) REGULATIONS 2013, SI 2013/1418; made under the Air Navigation Order 2009 (SI 2009/3015) art.161. In force: August 9, 2013; .

These Regulations impose restrictions on flying in the locations and airspace specified in the Schedule during flying displays by the Royal Air Force Aerobatic Team, the Red Arrows and possibly other aerobatic display teams, which are due to take place during the period August 9 to September 17 2013.

141. Flying restrictions

THE AIR NAVIGATION (RESTRICTION OF FLYING) (JET FORMATION DISPLAY TEAMS) (NO.3) (AMENDMENT) REGULATIONS 2013, SI 2013/1833; made under the Air Navigation Order 2009 (SI 2009/3015) art.161. In force: July 12, 2013; .

These Regulations amend the Air Navigation (Restriction of Flying) (Jet Formation Display Teams) (No.3) Regulations 2013 (SI 2013/1418), which restrict flying in the vicinity of places where jet formation display teams intend to give flying displays.

142. Flying restrictions

THE AIR NAVIGATION (RESTRICTION OF FLYING) (JET FORMATION DISPLAY TEAMS) (NO.3) (AMENDMENT NO.2) REGULATIONS 2013, SI 2013/2054; made under the Air Navigation Order 2009 (SI 2009/3015) art.161. In force: August 9, 2013; .

These Regulations further amend the Air Navigation (Restriction of Flying) (Jet Formation Display Teams) (No.3) Regulations 2013 (SI 2013/1418), which restrict flying in the vicinity of places where jet formation display teams intend to give flying displays. They add further displays at Laverstoke on 25 August 2013 and at Duxford on 6-7 September 2013 and remove the display scheduled to take place at Carfest South on 25 August 2013.

143. Flying restrictions

THE AIR NAVIGATION (RESTRICTION OF FLYING) (JET FORMATION DISPLAY TEAMS) (RAF CRANWELL) (AMENDMENT) REGULATIONS 2013, SI 2013/255; made under the Air Navigation Order 2009 (SI 2009/3015) art.161. In force: February 5, 2013; .

These Regulations amend the Air Navigation (Restriction of Flying) (Jet Formation Display Teams) (RAF Cranwell) Regulations 2013 (SI 2013/52), by adding further days on which flying is restricted by reason of flying display rehearsals by the Red Arrows, namely February 18, 22, 25, and 28, 2013.

144. Flying restrictions

THE AIR NAVIGATION (RESTRICTION OF FLYING) (MORTLAKE) REGULATIONS 2013, SI 2013/922; made under the Air Navigation Order 2009 (SI 2009/3015) art.161. In force: April 17, 2013; .

These Regulations restrict flying in the vicinity of, Richmond, Greater London on the day of the cremation of BaronessThatcher, which is scheduled to take place at Mortlake Crematorium on April 17, 2013.

145. Flying restrictions

THE AIR NAVIGATION (RESTRICTION OF FLYING) (NORTHAMPTON SYWELL) (NO.2) REGULATIONS 2013, SI 2013/1107; made under the Air Navigation Order 2009 (SI 2009/3015) art.161. In force: August 30, 2013; .

These Regulations impose restrictions on flying in connection with the Light Aircraft Association Rally 2013 General Aviation Exhibition which will take place at Northampton Sywell aerodrome, Northamptonshire, between August 30, 2013 and September 1, 2013.

146. Flying restrictions

THE AIR NAVIGATION (RESTRICTION OF FLYING) (SILVERSTONE AND TURWESTON) REGULATIONS 2013, SI 2013/256; made under the Air Navigation Order 2009 (SI 2009/3015) art.161. In force: June 29, 2013; .

These Regulations impose restrictions on flying in airspace in the vicinity of Silverstone and Turweston Aerodromes on the occasion of the British Grand Prix international race car meeting that is scheduled to take place on June 29 and 30, 2013.

147. Flying restrictions

THE AIR NAVIGATION (RESTRICTION OF FLYING) (STATE OPENING OF PARLIAMENT) REGULATIONS 2013, SI 2013/406; made under the Air Navigation Order 2009 (SI 2009/3015) art.161. In force: May 8, 2013; .

These Regulations impose restrictions on flying during the State Opening of Parliament that is scheduled to take place on May 8, 2013.

148. Flying restrictions

THE AIR NAVIGATION (RESTRICTION OF FLYING) (TROOPING THE COLOUR) REGULATIONS 2013, SI 2013/424; made under theAir Navigation Order 2009 (SI 2009/3015) art.161. In force: June 15, 2013; .

These Regulations impose restrictions on flying during theTrooping of the Colour Ceremony on June 15, 2013.

149. Flying restrictions

THE AIR NAVIGATION (RESTRICTION OF FLYING) (TROOPING THE COLOUR) (AMENDMENT) REGULATIONS 2013, SI 2013/1459; made under the Air Navigation Order 2009 (SI 2009/3015) art.161. In force: June 15, 2013; .

These Regulations amend the Air Navigation (Restriction of Flying) (Trooping the Colour) Regulations 2013 to necessitate a change in the identity of the police officer from the Metropolitan Police Service who is able to grant authority to a pilot to depart from the flying restrictions set out in reg.3 of the principal Regulations. Thus, Chief Inspector Jonathan Schulten is replaced by Chief Inspector Aiden Gibson in reg.3 of those Regulations.

150. Flying restrictions

THE AIR NAVIGATION (RESTRICTION OF FLYING) (VAUXHALL BRIDGE) REGULATIONS 2013, SI 2013/94; made under the Air Navigation Order 2009 (SI 2009/3015) art.161. In force: January 16, 2013 at 09.00hrs.; .

These Regulations impose restrictions of an emergency nature on flying in the vicinity specified in the Schedule. They are intended to be of temporary duration and will be revoked as soon as the emergency in question has passed.

151. Flying restrictions

THE AIR NAVIGATION (RESTRICTION OF FLYING) (VAUXHALL BRIDGE) (REVOCATION) REGULATIONS 2013, SI 2013/95; made under the Air Navigation Order 2009 (SI 2009/3015) art.161. In force: January 16, 2012 at 18.00hrs.; .

These Regulations revoke the Air Navigation (Restriction of Flying) (Vauxhall Bridge) Regulations 2013(b).

152. Flying restrictions

THE AIR NAVIGATION (RESTRICTION OF FLYING) (WIMBLEDON) REGULATIONS 2013, SI 2013/254; made under the Air Navigation Order 2009 (SI 2009/3015) art.161. In force: June 24, 2013; .

These Regulations impose flying restrictions in vicinity of the Wimbledon tennis championships between June 24, 2013 and July 28, 2013.

153. Flying restrictions–Abingdon air and country show

THE AIR NAVIGATION (RESTRICTION OF FLYING) (ABINGDON AIR AND COUNTRY SHOW) REGULATIONS 2013, SI 2013/88; made under the Air Navigation Order 2009 (SI 2009/3015) art.161. In force: May 4, 2013; .

These Regulations restrict flying at the Abingdon Air and Country Show, Oxfordshire on May 4-5 2013 to the vicinity of Abingdon Aerodrome for reasons of public safety.

154. Flying restrictions–Air tattoo RAF Fairford

THE AIR NAVIGATION (RESTRICTION OF FLYING) (ROYAL INTERNATIONAL AIR TATTOO RAF FAIRFORD) (AMENDMENT) REGULATIONS 2013, SI 2013/1215; made under the Air Navigation Order 2009 (SI 2009/3015) art.161. In force: July 17, 2013; .

These Regulations amend the Air Navigation (Restriction of Flying) (Royal Air Tattoo RAF Fairford) Regulations 2013 by amending the height restriction in relation to the area mentioned in regulation 3(1) of those Regulations. The restriction now applies to all the airspace below Flight Level 85 within that area.

155. Flying restrictions–Balado

THE AIR NAVIGATION (RESTRICTION OF FLYING) (BALADO) REGULATIONS 2013, SI 2013/832; made under the Air Navigation Order 2009 (SI 2009/3015) art.161. In force: July 11, 2013; .

These Regulations impose restrictions on flying in airspace in the vicinity of Balado, Perth and Kinross, by reason of the T in the Park 2013 Music Festival that is scheduled to take place there from July 11-15, 2013.

156. Flying restrictions–Bournemouth

THE AIR NAVIGATION (RESTRICTION OF FLYING) (BOURNEMOUTH) REGULATIONS 2013, SI 2013/1131; made under the Air Navigation Order 2009 (SI 2009/3015) art.161. In force: August 29, 2013; .

These Regulations impose restrictions on flying in airspace in the vicinity of the seafront at Bournemouth, Dorset during the Bournemouth Air Festival which will take place between August 29 and September 1, 2013.

157. Flying restrictions–Bucklebury–Berkshire

THE AIR NAVIGATION (RESTRICTION OF FLYING) (BUCKLEBURY, BERKSHIRE) REGULATIONS 2013, SI 2013/1885; made under the Air Navigation Order 2009 (SI 2009/3015) art.161. In force: July 24, 2013; .

These Regulations restrict flying in the vicinity of Bucklebury, Berkshire, during the visit by the Duke and Duchess of Cambridge and their son that is scheduled to take place there from July 24, 2013.

158. Flying restrictions–Chandler's Cross

THE AIR NAVIGATION (RESTRICTION OF FLYING) (CHANDLER'S CROSS) REGULATIONS 2013, SI 2013/1218; made under the Air Navigation Order 2009 (SI 2009/3015) art.161. In force: June 5, 2013; .

These Regulations restrict flying in the vicinity of Chandler's Cross, Hertfordshire, during the Bilderberg Conference, which is scheduled to take place there from June 5-9, 2013.

159. Flying restrictions–Cholmondeley Castle

THE AIR NAVIGATION (RESTRICTION OF FLYING) (CHOLMONDELEY CASTLE) REGULATIONS 2013, SI 2013/919; made under the Air Navigation Order 2009 (SI 2009/3015) art.161. In force: June 14, 2013; .

These Regulations impose restrictions on flying in airspace in the vicinity of Cholmondeley Castle, Cheshire on the occasion of the Pageant of Power Air Show to be held there from June 14-16, 2013.

160. Flying restrictions–Dartford

THE AIR NAVIGATION (RESTRICTION OF FLYING) (DARTFORD) (REVOCATION) REGULATIONS 2013, SI 2013/2322; made under the Air Navigation Order 2009 (SI 2009/3015) art.161. In force: September 6, 2013 at 20.34 hrs.; .

These Regulations revoke the Air Navigation (Restriction of Flying) (Dartford) Regulations 2013.

161. Flying restrictions–Dawlish, Devon

THE AIR NAVIGATION (RESTRICTION OF FLYING) (DAWLISH) REGULATIONS 2013, SI 2013/1757; made under the Air Navigation Order 2009 (SI 2009/3015) art.161. In force: August 24, 2013; .

These Regulations impose restrictions on flying in airspace in the vicinity of Dawlish, Devon, on the occasion of an air show that will be held along the seafront and over the sea at Dawlish on August 24, 2013.

162. Flying restrictions–Dunsfold

THE AIR NAVIGATION (RESTRICTION OF FLYING) (DUNSFOLD) REGULATIONS 2013, SI 2013/1038; made under the Air Navigation Order 2009 (SI 2009/3015) art.161. In force: August 24, 2013; .

These Regulations impose restrictions on flying in airspace in the vicinity of Dunsfold, Surrey by reason of an air display that is scheduled to take place there on August 24 and 25, 2013.

163. Flying restrictions–Duxford Aerodrome

THE AIR NAVIGATION (RESTRICTION OF FLYING) (DUXFORD AERODROME) (AMENDMENT) REGULATIONS 2013, SI 2013/835; made under the Air Navigation Order 2009 (SI 2009/3015) art.161. In force: May 26, 2013; .

These Regulations amend the Air Navigation (Restriction of Flying) (Duxford Aerodrome) Regulations 2013 (SI 2013/89) (the principal Regulations). The amendment brings forward from 12:00 to 9:30 the commencement of the flying restrictions applicable under the principal Regulations in relation to the first day of flying displays at Duxford Aerodrome, namely on May 26, 2013.

164. Flying restrictions–Eastbourne

THE AIR NAVIGATION (RESTRICTION OF FLYING) (EASTBOURNE) REGULATIONS 2013, SI 2013/1040; made under the Air Navigation Order 2009 (SI 2009/3015) art.161. In force: August 15, 2013; .

These Regulations impose restrictions on flying in airspace in the vicinity of Eastbourne, East Sussex, on the occasion of an air show that will be held along the seafront and over the sea at Eastbourne during the period from August 15-18, 2013.

165. Flying restrictions–Folkstone

THE AIR NAVIGATION (RESTRICTION OF FLYING) (FOLKESTONE) REGULATIONS 2013, SI 2013/837; made under the Air Navigation Order 2009 (SI 2009/3015) art.161. In force: June 8, 2013; .

These Regulations impose restrictions on flying in airspace in the vicinity of Folkestone, Kent, on the occasion of an air show that will be held along the seafront and over the sea at Folkestone on June 8, 2013.

166. Flying restrictions–Folkstone

THE AIR NAVIGATION (RESTRICTION OF FLYING) (FOLKESTONE) (REVOCATION) REGULATIONS 2013, SI 2013/1216; made under the Air Navigation Order 2009 (SI 2009/3015) art.161. In force: May 24, 2013; .

These Regulations revoke the instrument which imposed restrictions on flying in airspace in the vicinity of Folkestone, Kent in connection with an air show that was to have been held there on June 8, 2013, as a result of the event in question having been cancelled.

167. Flying restrictions–Glastonbury Festival

THE AIR NAVIGATION (RESTRICTION OF FLYING) (GLASTONBURY FESTIVAL) REGULATIONS 2013, SI 2013/87; made under the Air Navigation Order 2009 (SI 2009/3015) art.161. In force: June 26, 2013; .

These Regulations apply flying restrictions to the Glastonbury Festival scheduled to take place from June 26, 2013 to July 1, 2013.

168. Flying restrictions–International Air Show

THE AIR NAVIGATION (RESTRICTION OF FLYING) (NORTHERN IRELAND INTERNATIONAL AIR SHOW) REGULATIONS 2013, SI 2013/1794; made under the Air Navigation Order 2009 (SI 2009/3015) art.161. In force: August 31, 2013; .

These Regulations impose restrictions on flying in airspace in the vicinity of Portrush, County Londonderry on the occasion of the Northern Ireland International Air Show to be held there on August 31 and September 1, 2013.

169. Flying restrictions–Jet formation display teams

THE AIR NAVIGATION (RESTRICTION OF FLYING) (JET FORMATION DISPLAY TEAMS) REGULATIONS 2013, SI 2013/392; made under the Air Navigation Order 2009 (SI 2009/3015) art.161. In force: February 28, 2013; .

These Regulations impose flying restrictions on jet formation display teams.

170. Flying restrictions–Jet Formation Display Teams

THE AIR NAVIGATION (RESTRICTION OF FLYING) (JET FORMATION DISPLAY TEAMS) (NO.2) REGULATIONS 2013, SI 2013/836; made under the Air Navigation Order 2009 (SI 2009/3015) art.161. In force: May 26, 2013; .

These Regulations impose restrictions on flying in the locations and airspace specified during flying displays by the Royal Air Force Aerobatic Team, the Red Arrows and possibly other jet formation aerobatic display teams, which are due to take place during the period May 26, 2013 to July 28, 2013.

171. Flying restrictions–Manston airport

THE AIR NAVIGATION (RESTRICTION OF FLYING) (MANSTON AIRPORT) REGULATIONS 2013, SI 2013/1052; made under the Air Navigation Order 2009 (SI 2009/3015) art.161. In force: June 22, 2013; .

These Regulations impose restrictions on flying in airspace in the vicinity of Manston Airport, Kent, on the occasion of an air show that will be held there on June 22, 2013.

172. Flying restrictions–Remembrance Sunday

THE AIR NAVIGATION (RESTRICTION OF FLYING) (REMEMBRANCE SUNDAY) REGULATIONS 2013, SI 2013/2421; made under the Air Navigation Order 2009 (SI 2009/3015) art.161. In force: November 10, 2013; .

These Regulations impose restrictions on flying in airspace specified in reg.3 by reason of the Remembrance Sunday Ceremony that is scheduled to take place at the Cenotaph, London, on November 10 2013 and are made pursuant to a request from the Metropolitan Police on the grounds of the security measures that will be in place for some of those persons present. This request has been agreed with the Department for Transport.

173. Flying restrictions–RNAS Culdrose

THE AIR NAVIGATION (RESTRICTION OF FLYING) (RNAS CULDROSE) REGULATIONS 2013, SI 2013/1051; made under the Air Navigation Order 2009 (SI 2009/3015) art.161. In force: July 24, 2013; .

These Regulations impose restrictions on flying in airspace in the vicinity of RNAS Culdrose, Cornwall for a flying display that is scheduled to take place there on July 24, 2013.

174. Flying restrictions–Royal Air Force Waddington

THE AIR NAVIGATION (RESTRICTION OF FLYING) (ROYAL AIR FORCE WADDINGTON) REGULATIONS 2013, SI 2013/90; made under the Air Navigation Order 2009 (SI 2009/3015) art.161. In force: January 10, 2013; .

These Regulations apply flying restrictions to the "Home Days" scheduled for July 6 and 7, 2013 at Royal Air Force Waddington, Lincolnshire.

175. Flying restrictions–Royal International Air Tattoo–RAF Fairford

THE AIR NAVIGATION (RESTRICTION OF FLYING) (ROYAL INTERNATIONAL AIR TATTOO RAF FAIRFORD) REGULATIONS 2013, SI 2013/932; made under the Air Navigation Order 2009 (SI 2009/3015) art.161. In force: July 17, 2013; .

These Regulations impose restrictions on flying in airspace in the vicinity of RAF Fairford, Gloucestershire during the arrival, rehearsals, displays and departure of aircraft participating in the Royal International Air Tattoo 2013 scheduled to take place between July 17 and July 22, 2013.

176. Flying restrictions–Shoreham-by-Sea

THE AIR NAVIGATION (RESTRICTION OF FLYING) (SHOREHAM-BY-SEA) REGULATIONS 2013, SI 2013/1130; made under the Air Navigation Order 2009 (SI 2009/3015) art.161. In force: August 31, 2013; .

These Regulations impose restrictions on flying in airspace in the vicinity of Shoreham-by-Sea, West Sussex, on the occasion of an air show that will be held on August 31, 2013 and September 1, 2013.

177. Flying restrictions–Shoreham-by-sea

THE AIR NAVIGATION (RESTRICTION OF FLYING) (SHOREHAM-BY-SEA) (AMENDMENT) REGULATIONS 2013, SI 2013/1848; made under the Air Navigation Order 2009 (SI 2009/3015) art.161. In force: August 31, 2013; .

These Regulations amend the Air Navigation (Restriction of Flying) (Shoreham-by-Sea) Regulations 2013 (SI 2013/1130) makes changes to the timing and upper limit of the flying restrictions applicable under the principal Regulations in relation to the Shoreham-by-Sea air show that will be held on August 31 and September 1, 2013.

178. Flying restrictions–Southport

THE AIR NAVIGATION (RESTRICTION OF FLYING) (SOUTHPORT) REGULATIONS 2013, SI 2013/1217; made under the Air Navigation Order 2009 (SI 2009/3015) art.161. In force: September 14, 2013; .

These Regulations impose restrictions on flying in airspace in the vicinity of Southport, Merseyside by reason of air displays that are scheduled to take place there on September 14-15, 2013.

179. Flying restrictions–State opening of Parliament

THE AIR NAVIGATION (RESTRICTION OF FLYING) (STATE OPENING OF PARLIAMENT) REGULATIONS 2013, SI 2013/406; made under the Air Navigation Order 2009 (SI 2009/3015) art.161. In force: May 8, 2013; .

These Regulations impose restrictions on flying in the airspace specified by reason of the State Opening of Parliament that is scheduled to take place May 8, 2013.

180. Flying restrictions–Stonehenge

THE AIR NAVIGATION (RESTRICTION OF FLYING) (STONEHENGE) REGULATIONS 2013, SI 2013/86; made under the Air Navigation Order 2009 (SI 2009/3015) art.161. In force: June 20, 2013; .

These Regulations restrict flying in the vicinity of Stonehenge, Wiltshire during the summer solstice period, in connection with which it is anticipated that a gathering of a large number of persons will be present there on June 20-21, 2013.

181. Flying restrictions–Sunderland

THE AIR NAVIGATION (RESTRICTION OF FLYING) (SUNDERLAND) REGULATIONS 2013, SI 2013/931; made under the Air Navigation Order 2009 (SI 2009/3015) art.161. In force: July 27, 2013; .

These Regulations impose restrictions on flying in airspace in the vicinity of Sunderland on the occasion of an Air Show that will be held from July 27-28, 2013.

182. Flying restrictions–Wales National Airshow

THE AIR NAVIGATION (RESTRICTION OF FLYING) (WALES NATIONAL AIRSHOW) REGULATIONS 2013, SI 2013/918; made under the Air Navigation Order 2009 (SI 2009/3015) art.161. In force: July 13, 2013; .

These Regulations impose restrictions on flying in airspace in the vicinity of Swansea Bay by reason of a flying display that is scheduled to take place along the seafront and over the sea on July13 and 14, 2013.

183. Flying restrictions–Wales Rally GB

THE AIR NAVIGATION (RESTRICTION OF FLYING) (WALES RALLY GB) REGULATIONS 2013, SI 2013/2262; made under the Air Navigation Order 2009 (SI 2009/3015) art.161. In force: November 14, 2013; .

These Regulations restrict flying in specified areas of Wales for reasons of public and flight safety during the Wales Rally GB 2013.

184. Flying restrictions–Weston Park

THE AIR NAVIGATION (RESTRICTION OF FLYING) (WESTON PARK) REGULATIONS 2013, SI 2013/834; made under the Air Navigation Order 2009 (SI 2009/3015) art.161. In force: August 16, 2013; .

These Regulations impose restrictions of flying in airspace in the vicinity of Weston Park, Staffordshire by reason of the V2013 Pop Concert that is scheduled to take place there from August 16-19, 2013.

BANKING AND FINANCE

185. Alternative Investment Market–Fund managers

THE ALTERNATIVE INVESTMENT FUND MANAGERS (AMENDMENT) REGULATIONS 2013, SI 2013/1797; made under the European Communities Act 1972 s.2; and the Financial Services and Markets Act 2000 Sch.3 para.13, Sch.3 para.22. In force: in accordance with reg.1.; .

These Regulations implement those provisions of Directive 2011/61 on Alternative Investment Fund Managers that must be transposed by July 22, 2013 but do not come into effect until a date to be specified by the European Commission in a delegated act.

186. Alternative Investment Market–Fund managers–Investment funds

THE ALTERNATIVE INVESTMENT FUND MANAGERS REGULATIONS 2013, SI 2013/1773; made under the European Communities Act 1972 s.2; the Financial Services and Markets Act 2000 s.183, s.188, s.213, s.214, s.224, s.262, s.349, s.428, Sch.3 para.13, Sch.3 para.14, Sch.3 para.17, Sch.3 para.22; and the Companies Act 2006 s.784, s.785. In force: July 22, 2013; .

These Regulations implement the majority of Directive 2011/61 on alternative investment fund managers. The Directive requires Member States to put in place a harmonised regulatory framework for funds currently not within the scope of European regulation.

187. Asian Development Bank–Payments

THE ASIAN DEVELOPMENT BANK (TENTH REPLENISHMENT OF THE ASIAN DEVELOPMENT FUND) ORDER 2013, SI 2013/1771; made under the International Development Act 2002 s.11. In force: July 11, 2013; .

This Order permits the Secretary of State for International Development, in her role as Governor for the UK at the Asian Development Bank, to make a payment of £200,000,000 towards the tenth replenishment of the Asian Development Fund.

188. Bank deposits–Bank of England

THE CASH RATIO DEPOSITS (VALUE BANDS AND RATIOS) ORDER 2013, SI 2013/1189; made under the Bank of England Act1998 Sch.2 para.5. In force: June 3, 2013; .

This Order changes the percentage of eligible liabilities that eligible financial institutions are required to deposit in a non-interest bearing account at the Bank of England under the cash ratio deposit (CRD) scheme. This Order changes: the CRD rate, which is the percentage of eligible liabilities that are required to be deposited at the Bank of England, from 0.11 per cent to 0.18 per cent; and the CRD threshold, which determines the minimum value of deposits that an institution must hold to be eligible for the scheme, from £500m to £600m.

189. Bank of England–Benchmarking–Interest rates

THE BANK OF ENGLAND (CALL NOTICE) (BENCHMARK RATE OF INTEREST) ORDER 2013, SI 2013/721; made under the Bank of England Act 1998 Sch.2 para.8. In force: June 3, 2013; .

This Order changes the benchmark rate of interest that eligible institutions are required to pay if they do not deposit the appropriate amount as specified by the bank of England in a call notice.

190. Bank of England–Central counterparties–Financial Conduct Authority–Over-the-counter market

THE FINANCIAL SERVICES AND MARKETS ACT 2000 (OVER THE COUNTER DERIVATIVES, CENTRAL COUNTERPARTIES AND TRADE REPOSITORIES) (NO.2) REGULATIONS 2013, SI 2013/1908; made under the European Communities Act 1972 s.2; the Companies Act 1989 s.155, s.186, s.187; and the Financial Services and Markets Act 2000 s.286, s.428. In force: in accordance with reg.1 (3).; .

These Regulations relates to the clearing of financial transactions through recognised clearing houses. They amend insolvency law to facilitate the segregation and transfer of indirect clients' assets and positions, and make minor amendments to the supervisory, investigatory and enforcement powers on Bank of England and the Financial Conduct Authority. They require recognised clearing houses to maintain recovery plans specifying the steps they will take if the continuity of their services is disrupted, and require recognised central counterparties to have rules to allocate losses if their solvency is threatened.

191. Bank of England–Financial Policy Committee

THE BANK OF ENGLAND ACT 1998 (MACRO-PRUDENTIAL MEASURES) ORDER 2013, SI 2013/644; made under the Bank of England Act 1998 s.9N. In force: April 1, 2013; .

The instrument sets out the measures (referred to as macro-prudential measures) which the Bank of England's Financial Policy Committee may direct the Prudential Regulation Authority or Financial Conduct Authority to implement.

192. Bank of England–Uncertificated securities

THE UNCERTIFICATED SECURITIES (AMENDMENT) REGULATIONS 2013, SI 2013/632; made under the Companies Act 2006 s.784, s.785, s.788, s.1292. In force: April 1, 2013; .

These Regulations transfer responsibility for the approval and regulation of operators of relevant systems from the Treasury to the Bank of England, and provide the Bank of England with new powers to require reports to be produced by skilled persons in respect of operators of relevant systems, and to appoint investigators for the purpose of making inquiries about operators of relevant systems in appropriate cases.

193. Banks–Building societies–Child trust funds

THE CHILD TRUST FUNDS (AMENDMENT) REGULATIONS 2013, SI 2013/263; made under the Child Trust Funds Act 2004 s.3, s.12, s.15, s.28. In force: March 16, 2013 except for reg.2(2) on April 6, 2013.; .

These Regulations amend the Child Trust Funds Regulations 2004 (SI 2004/1450) to increase the amount which can be paid into a Child Trust Fund (CTF) each year and remove the requirement on CTF providers to make fortnightly information returns to HM Revenue and Customs.

194. Banks–Financial restrictions proceedings–Application to set aside financial restrictions order–Justification for, and proportionality of, making order–Procedural requirement of opportunity for making prior representations

[Counter-Terrorism Act 2008 (c.28) Sch.7 Pt 3 para.13; European Convention on Human Rights 1950 Protocol 1 Art.1.]

The appellant Iranian bank (B) appealed against a decision ([2011] EWCA Civ 1, [2012] Q.B. 101, [2011] C.L.Y. 178) upholding measures taken by the respondent Treasury to restrict B's access to financial markets in the United Kingdom. The Treasury had imposed the restriction because B had been identified as having assisted Iran's nuclear weapons programme by providing banking and financial services to entities involved with them. The Treasury had made a direction under the Counter-Terrorism Act 2008 Sch.7 Pt 3 para.13 prohibiting all persons operating in the UK financial sector from having any commercial dealings with B or its UK subsidiaries. The direction was laid before Parliament in October 2009 and came into force three days later. B applied under s.63 of the Act to set the order aside. It relied on a substantive argument that the order was irrational and disproportionate, and that the Treasury had failed to give adequate reasons for making it and/or its reasons were vitiated by irrelevant considerations or mistakes of fact. It also relied on a procedural argument that the Treasury had failed to give it an opportunity to make representations before making the order, as required by common law and by the European Convention on Human Rights 1950 art.6 and protocol 1 art.1. The High Court and the Court of Appeal dismissed B's appeals under both heads.

Held: Appeal allowed. (1) (Lords Neuberger, Hope, Dyson and Reed dissenting) The essential question raised by B's substantive objections was whether the interruption of commercial dealings with B in the UK's financial markets bore some rational and proportionate relationship to the statutory purpose of hindering the pursuit by Iran of its weapons programmes. There were two serious difficulties about the conclusions of the courts below: first, they did not explain, let alone justify, the singling out of B, and second, their justification for the order was different to that advanced by ministers when the direction was laid before Parliament. The order had initially been explained as being attributable to specific concerns about B. However, both lower courts found that justification was not in any problem specific to B, but in a problem with Iranian banks generally. They considered the direction to be the only reasonably practicable means of ensuring that the facilities of an Iranian bank with international reach would not be used to facilitate Iran's weapons programme, yet the direction made no attempt to place restrictions on every Iranian bank, only on B. That was an arbitrary and irrational decision, as well as being a disproportionate measure. B's substantive challenge to the order was therefore made out (see paras 19-20, 24, 26-27 of judgment) (Per Lords Neuberger, Hope, Dyson and Reed) The Treasury had a wide margin of appreciation and sufficient grounds had been shown for making the direction only against B (paras 64-130, 132-133, 165-177, 197-201). (2) (Lords Hope, Reed and Carnwath dissenting) B ought to have received notice of the Treasury's intention to make the direction and to have been given an opportunity to make representations. Those were among the oldest principles of public law. The only ground on which it could be said that the Treasury had no duty to consult B in advance was that such a duty was statutorily excluded. It was not enough for the Treasury to argue that the statutory right of recourse to the courts provided by s.63 was enough to satisfy any duty of fairness; it was not implicit in s.63 that the right of recourse to the courts was the sole guarantee of fairness, nor was it implicit that what the common law would otherwise require to achieve fairness was excluded. The Treasury also failed in its argument that the direction was required to be made in subordinate legislation, which was not an area where the courts could imply a duty of fairness or prior consultation; the lawfulness of a statutory power to make delegated legislation was reviewable by the courts. A statutory instrument was an instrument of the minister, who was empowered by the enabling Act to make it. The fact that it required the approval of Parliament did not alter that. The focus of the court was therefore on his decision to make it, not on Parliament's decision to approve it. The Treasury's direction designating B was unlawful for want of prior notice or any procedure enabling it to be heard in advance. It was unnecessary to consider whether a duty of prior consultation arose by virtue of art.6 of the Convention (paras 28-29, 33-49). (Per Lords Hope, Reed and Carnwath) There was no provision in Sch.7 for a designated person to be given a hearing before the order was made and, although the absence of such a provision did not automatically mean that Parliament had not intended there to be any such entitlement, it was a pointer towards such an intention. It was not for the courts to re-write the scheme intended by Parliament (paras 55-63, 134-159).

BANK MELLAT v HM TREASURY, [2013] UKSC 39, [2013] 3 W.L.R. 179, Lord Neuberger, J.S.C., SC.

195. Building societies–Deferred shares–Tax

THE BUILDING SOCIETIES (CORE CAPITAL DEFERRED SHARES) REGULATIONS 2013, SI 2013/460; made under the Finance Act 2012 s.221. In force: March 1, 2013; .

These Regulations provide that where a building society issues deferred shares, or converts existing securities into deferred shares, (CCDS) that will form part of its core tier one capital those shares will be taxed as shares.

196. Central banks–International banks–Prohibition–Iran

THE FINANCIAL RESTRICTIONS (IRAN) (REVOCATION) ORDER 2013, SI 2013/162; made under the Counter-Terrorism Act 2008 Sch.7 para.14, Sch.7 para.16. In force: January 31, 2013; .

This Order prohibits all persons operating in the UK financial sector from entering into new transactions or business relationships with Iranian banks, their branches and subsidiaries, and the Central Bank of Iran, or continuing to participate in transactions or business relationships with them.

197. Central counterparties–Financial services–Over-the-counter market

THE FINANCIAL SERVICES AND MARKETS ACT 2000 (OVER THE COUNTER DERIVATIVES, CENTRAL COUNTERPARTIES AND TRADE REPOSITORIES) REGULATIONS 2013, SI 2013/504; made under the Companies Act 1989 s.158, s.174, s.185, s.186. In force: in accordance with reg.1 (2).; .

These Regulations implement certain Articles of Regulation 648/2012 on over-the-counter derivatives, central counterparties and trade reposit.

198. Central counterparties–Financial services–Over-the-counter market

THE FINANCIAL SERVICES AND MARKETS ACT 2000 (QUALIFYING EU PROVISIONS) ORDER 2013, SI 2013/419; made under the Financial Services and Markets Act 2000 s.1A, s.1L, s.2A, s.39, s.66, s.168, s.204A, s.239A, s.296, s.297, s.312E, s.380, s.382, s.384, Sch.1ZA para.23, Sch.1ZB para.31, Sch17A para.14, Sch17A para.26, Sch17A para.30, Sch17A para.36. In force: April 1, 2013; .

This Order identifies the directly applicable provisions of EU law which are specified as qualifying EU provisions and directly applicable EU provisions for the purposes of various provisions in the Financial Services and Markets Act 2000 (FSMA). The effect of the Order is to apply certain provisions of FSMA for purposes connected with specified EU provisions, especially those on enforcement. The EU law covered includes: the regulation on over the counter (OTC) derivatives, central counterparties and trade repositories (generally known as EMIR); any directly applicable regulation made under the Undertakings for Collective Investment in Transferable Securities (UCITS) directives; and the emission allowance auctioning regulation.

199. Collective investment schemes–Fund management–Investment management–Securities

THE COLLECTIVE INVESTMENT IN TRANSFERABLE SECURITIES (CONTRACTUAL SCHEME) REGULATIONS 2013, SI 2013/1388; made under the European Communities Act 1972 s.2. In force: June 6, 2013; .

These Regulations create a new fund vehicle for the UK investment management industry to make UK domiciled funds for collective investment in transferable securities more competitive.

200. Consequential amendments–Financial regulation–Financial services–Technical provisions

THE FINANCIAL SERVICES ACT 2012 (CONSEQUENTIAL AMENDMENTS AND TRANSITIONAL PROVISIONS) ORDER 2013, SI 2013/472; made under the Financial Services Act 2012 s.115, s.118, s.119. In force: April 1, 2013; .

This Order makes consequential amendments to subordinate legislation in connection with the Financial Services Act 2012 and provision made under the Act. The Order also makes transitional provision in connection with those amendments.

201. Consequential amendments–Financial services–Transitional provisions

THE FINANCIAL SERVICES ACT 2012 (CONSEQUENTIAL AMENDMENTS AND TRANSITIONAL PROVISIONS) (NO.2) ORDER 2013, SI 2013/642; made under the Financial Services Act 2012 s.115, s.118, s.119. In force: April 10, 2013; .

This instrument provides for various consequential and transitional arrangements in connection with the Financial Services Act 2012.

202. Consequential amendments–Financial Services Authority–Financial services

THE FINANCIAL SERVICES ACT 2012 (CONSEQUENTIAL AMENDMENTS) ORDER 2013, SI 2013/636; made under the Financial Services Act 2012 s.118. In force: April 1, 2013; .

This Order provides for consequential amendments of enactments in connection with the Financial Services Act 2012, giving effect to a provision for amendments of references to Financial Services Authority Instruments in various enactments and for amendments of references to provisions of the Financial Services and Markets Act 2000 which have been amended by the Financial Services Act 2012.

203. Corporate bonds–Resolutions–Legality of exit consent procedure in relation to corporate bonds–Coercion of minority

The claimant asset management company (C) sought a declaration as to the legality of a technique used by the issuers of corporate bonds known as exit consent. Exit consent occurred where the bond issuer wanted all the holders of a bond issue to exchange their bonds for replacement bonds on different terms. The holders were all invited to offer their bonds for exchange, but on terms that they were required vote at a bondholder's meeting for a resolution amending the terms of the existing bonds so as to damage or destroy the value of the right arising from them. That resolution was known as an exit consent. A holder who failed to offer his bonds for exchange and voted against the resolution or abstained took the risk, if the resolution was passed, that his bonds would be either devalued, or as in the instant case, be destroyed by being redeemed for a nominal consideration. C's challenge to the exit consent technique was based on an alleged abuse by the majority shareholders of their power to bind the minority, albeit at the invitation of the issuer. The terms of the bond issue to which the dispute related were contained in a trust deed. Following a noteholders' meeting and an exit consent resolution C had redeemed its EUR 17million worth of notes for a payment by the defendant bank (B) of EUR 170. C submitted that (1) the resolution constituted the conferral on B to expropriate the notes for no more than a nominal consideration and that it was ultra vires the power of the majority; (2) at the time of the noteholders' meeting all those noteholders who voted in support of the resolution held their notes beneficially, or for the account of, B and that those votes should be disregarded; (3) the resolution constituted an abuse of the power of the voting majority because it conferred no conceivable benefit or advantage on the noteholders as a class and it affected the notes of the minority who had not agreed to vote in favour of the resolution such that it was both oppressive and unfair.

Held: Judgment for claimant. (1) The resolution gave B an unqualified right to do away with the rights of the noteholders. Any attempt to justify the resolution otherwise than by reference to the power to sanction an abrogation of the rights of the noteholders would fall foul of *Mercantile Investment & General Trust Co v International Trust Co of Mexico* [1893] 1 Ch. 484 (Note), *Mercantile Investment* applied. Under the provisions of the trust deed, the noteholders must be taken to have assented to the exercise of a power in the majority to bind the minority to a cancellation of the principal payable on the notes and of the minimum interest payable thereon. That would be tantamount to forfeiture, confiscation or expropriation of the rights conferred by the notes, which conferred nothing of benefit on the noteholders other than repayment of principal and payment of interest. The power to abrogate was capable of extending to all the rights of noteholders as against B (see paras 50-55 of judgment). (2) At the date of the resolution the notes offered and accepted for exchange were held for B's benefit. Those notes were held under contracts for sale between the relevant majority noteholders and B and those contracts were specifically enforceable. The purpose of the contracts for the exchange of the notes was to terminate the market for the notes, and bring about a complete cancellation or redemption of the entire issue for the purposes of B's restructuring so as to meet conditions imposed by the Government for the provision of rescue funding at the expense of the taxpayer. It was clear that damages for breach of a contract would not be an adequate remedy for B. There was no reason why the court would deny to a noteholder an order that, for the purpose of completing the exchange contracts made in relation to the notes, B would issue the requisite new notes for that purpose, provided that it was within its corporate vires to comply with such specific performance (paras 56-68). (3) It could not be lawful for the majority to lend its aid to the coercion of a minority by voting for a resolution which expropriated the minority's rights under their bonds for a nominal consideration. The exit consent was a coercive threat which the issuer invited the majority to levy against the minority. Its only function was intimidation. That form of coercion was entirely at variance with the purposes for which majorities in a class were given power to bind minorities, and it was no answer for them to say that it was the issuer who had invited them to do so, *Azevedo v IMCOPA -Importacao, Exportaacao e Industria de Oleos Ltda* [2012] EWHC 1849 (Comm) and *Greenhalgh v Arderne Cinemas Ltd* [1951] Ch. 286, [1947-51] C.L.Y. 7818 considered (see paras 69-86).

ASSENAGON ASSET MANAGEMENT SA v IRISH BANK RESOLUTION CORP LTD (FORMERLY ANGLO IRISH BANK CORP LTD), [2012] EWHC 2090 (Ch), [2013] 1 All E.R. 495, Briggs, J., Ch D.

204. Corporation tax–Capital gains tax

THE UNAUTHORISED UNIT TRUSTS (TAX) REGULATIONS 2013, SI 2013/2819; made under the Finance Act 2013 s.217. In force: in accordance with re.1 (2) and (3); .

These Regulations make provision about the treatment of the trustees or unit holders of unauthorised unit trusts for the purposes of income tax, corporation tax and capital gains tax. They set out the requirements for an unauthorised unit trust to be approved as an exempt unauthorised unit trust; and make provision for the taxation of gains and income of exempt and non-exempt unauthorised unit trusts as well as the tax treatment of the unit holders and trustees of those trusts. These Regulations make provision for the treatment of certain types of investment or disposal made by exempt unauthorised unit trusts. They include provisions for consequential amendments to various enactments relating to the treatment of unauthorised unit trusts. These Regulations also contain transitional provisions.

205. Credit institutions–Financial institutions–Funds–Iran

THE IRAN (EUROPEAN UNION FINANCIAL SANCTIONS) (AMENDMENT) REGULATIONS 2013, SI 2013/163; made under the European Communities Act 1972 s.2. In force: January 31, 2013; .

These Regulations introduce a new prohibition on transfers of funds between EU credit and financial institutions and Iranian credit and financial institutions, subject to certain exemptions.

206. Credit rating agencies–Limitation periods

THE CREDIT RATING AGENCIES (CIVIL LIABILITY) REGULATIONS 2013, SI 2013/1637; made under the European Communities Act 1972 s.2. In force: July 25, 2013; .

These Regulations implement Regulation 1060/2009 art.35 on credit rating agencies by defining certain terms, providing for how certain terms will be interpreted and applied, applying a limitation period for claims under art.35a, and determining which courts have jurisdiction to hear a claim brought under art.35a.

207. Credit unions–Interest rates–Loans

THE CREDIT UNIONS (MAXIMUM INTEREST RATE ON LOANS) ORDER 2013, SI 2013/2589; made under the Credit Unions Act 1979 s.11. In force: April 1, 2014; .

This instrument increases the maximum interest a credit union may charge on a loan to 3 per cent per month.

208. Financial advice–Breach of statutory duty–Leveraged investments in structured notes–Alleged failure to take reasonable steps to explain risks–Causation of losses suffered

[Financial Services and Markets Act 2000 (c.8) s.150.]

The claimant (S) claimed that the two defendants (C and P) had advised her to enter into a series of leveraged transactions without taking reasonable steps to ensure that she understood the risks associated with the transactions in breach of their duty under the Financial Services and Markets Act 2000 s.150. S had received very substantial sums in a divorce settlement. She invested in a number of structured notes on the recommendation of C's employee (R). R left C and started his own business, P. S bought further notes through P. The notes were leveraged by loans from a bank (B) in the same group as C and were pledged as collateral together with cash deposits. Following the collapse of the financial markets the value of the notes that she had purchased with money borrowed from B fell significantly. B made a margin call and also changed its permitted loan-to-value ratio requiring greater collateral in respect of existing loans which resulted in an increased margin call which S did not meet. B sold the notes at their market value but the proceeds were insufficient to repay the loans. S sought to recover her losses on the basis that she would not have invested in the notes if it had been properly explained to her by C and P, as required by the Conduct of Business Rules, that B was entitled to call upon her to provide additional collateral in the shape of margin calls if the value of the notes dropped, and that if she did not provide such margin calls within the time stipulated by B, her notes could or would be sold with the consequent loss of some or all of her capital.

Held: Claim dismissed. (1) There was a conflict of evidence as to what R had said to S about leverage and its risks. On that issue R's evidence was to be preferred. S's case was based on a fiction that she was not told and did not understand the basics of loans, collateral, margin and margin call, despite leveraged trading in 23 of such notes through R, despite borrowing money elsewhere for investment, and despite signing numerous loan facility documents and pledges with various banks, some or all of which contained warnings of varying degrees of clarity. The terms of the documents were such that she would have been bound to ask when faced with something she did not understand. When money was borrowed, a borrower wanted to know the terms of the loan and of the security provided. R said he had explained those matters at the outset, and in the circumstances and by reference to the documents disclosed it was impossible for him not to have done so. S's evidence was not accepted, when set against that of R, the documents and the inherent probabilities (see paras 133-152 of judgment). (2) By the time of the purchase of the notes in issue, S had received many copies of term sheets, effect of leverage documents and other documents which cross-referred to the underlying concepts which she understood. On the documents alone, it appeared that sufficient explanation was given to her of the risks of leveraged investment in the notes and that C and P took reasonable steps under the Conduct of Business Rules to ensure that she understood the nature of the risks involved in her investments and that they were suitable for her in the light of her investment objectives, her knowledge and experience and her financial status. R also explained those matters orally to her. There was therefore no breach of statutory duty or any other duty in failing to explain the risks of the notes (paras 153-159). (3) If S had been told of the risks which she said she had not been, it would have had no impact on her desire to achieve higher returns and she would have invested in the notes in any event (paras 160-167). (4) Any failure on the part of C or P adequately to explain collateral, margin, margin calls and the consequences of failure to meet such a call was not the cause of S's losses. R had advised the sale of notes as the market fell, which S declined to do, and he advised her to put up margin in the shape of guarantees which she also failed to do. Her decision not to follow R's advice to sell notes and not to provide additional margin, when she was plainly in a position to do so, broke any chain of causation (para.210).

AL SULAIMAN v CREDIT SUISSE SECURITIES (EUROPE) LTD, [2013] EWHC 400 (Comm), [2013] 1 All E.R. (Comm) 1105, Cooke, J., QBD (Comm).

209. Financial advice–Breach of statutory duty–Losses incurred on purchase of structured notes–Claim for damages as result of breach of Conduct of Business Rules–Suitability tests under r.5.3.5 and r.7.9.3

The appellants (Z) appealed against a decision ([2011] EWHC 2422 (Comm), [2011] 2 C.L.C. 523, [2012] C.L.Y. 262) that the respondent bank (B) was not liable for financial losses suffered as a result of breaches of its statutory duty. Z were the widow and two daughters of an Egyptian businessman (X). X had died in 2010. He had invested in structured financial products, or notes, bought from B with the assistance of loans from an associate company of B's. The claim arose from the severe downturn in markets in 2008. B had issued a margin call which X was unable or unwilling to meet and he suffered substantial losses. Z claimed damages on the basis that the losses were caused by B's breach of its statutory duty. Under the Conduct of Business Rules, X was classified as a "private customer" to whom a full range of duties under the rules applied. Under r.5.3.5, B had to take reasonable steps to ensure that its investment advice was suitable for X, and under r.7.9.3, B had to assess X's financial standing, based on information disclosed by X, and take reasonable care to ensure that the arrangements for the loan, and its amount, were suitable for the type of transaction proposed. The judge found that B had not breached its duty in respect of the notes which were the subject of the instant appeal, and that the notes were suitable for X. Z's amended grounds of appeal claimed that the suitability tests under r.5.3.5 and r.7.9.3 were not the same; that the question under r.7.9.3 was the narrower issue of whether B had taken reasonable steps at the time of each transaction to ensure that the amount of leverage was suitable, based on the information it ought to have had available after a proper assessment of X's financial standing.

Held: Appeal dismissed. (1) The judge was correct in finding that the language of r.7.9.3, "lend... (or arrange for any other person to do so)", did not require any concept of B having control over the grant of financing facilities. On the contrary, the broad language of "arrange for any other person to do so" was used precisely to meet the type of situation in the instant case: namely, where the bank's customer obtained finance, for his investment business, within the same or an associated group. If it were otherwise, a group of companies could seek to avoid its conduct of business responsibilities by relying on the complexities of its group structure and internal arrangements. However, the judge had been wrong to focus exclusively on the overarching lending facility and to ignore the individual advances on each transaction. The hypothesis was that the rule was only concerned with overarching facility agreements and not with draw-downs to finance individual transactions. However, there was no reason in the wording of the rule, or in principle, practicalities or good sense, to limit the arrangements concerned to those of one kind or another. If that were so, difficult distinctions would arise as to whether the real loan was delivered on so-called "grant" or on draw-down. The facilities in the instant case were expressed in the most general terms, which was well-suited to arrangements which could be used for all kinds of transactions, at different times, on terms which would fluctuate as credit market conditions fluctuated. Those terms did not support the judge's assertion that the fact that the customer was required "to give his prior written consent to both the maximum amount of the loan or credit and the amount or basis of any interest or fees" showed that that would be done when the facility was granted, not when it was drawn on. Rule 7.9.3 was therefore engaged by the transactions (see paras 62-69 of judgment). (2) There were recorded assessments regarding X's financial standing, and any suggestion that the judge's findings supported a conclusion of any breach of r.7.9.3(1) was rejected. With regard to the matter of the process by which the obligation to take reasonable steps to ensure suitability under r.7.9.3(2) was facilitated, it was possible that the statutory requirements might mould their own solutions, so as to give greater weight to requirements of process. Nevertheless, what was aimed at was the provision of suitable advice, under r.5.3.5, or suitable lending arrangement, under r.7.9.3, for the client and his proposed investments and not merely suitable advice or lending arrangements in the abstract. The complex rules were an attempt to hold the balance between the parties fairly, giving weight both for the need to protect investors from ignorance or even from themselves, and for the need to permit ultimate autonomy to the properly informed investor to make and take responsibility for his own mistakes. Where it was ultimately to be found, giving all due weight to the statutory requirements, both of form and substance, that personal recommendations or lending arrangements were suitable, they could not be rendered unsuitable by some incidental and essentially immaterial failure of mere form (paras 70-84). (3) The tests raised by r.5.3.5 and r.7.9.3 were not the same. The r.7.9.3 test was narrower but, on the judge's approach, whereby he looked holistically at all aspects of the personal recommendations, including leverage, the test had been subsumed into the r.5.3.5 test he exercised. The judge did not therefore mismanage the suitability test, and Z were unable to pray in aid considerations of leverage or liquidity (paras 86-101).

ZAKI v CREDIT SUISSE (UK) LTD, [2013] EWCA Civ 14, [2013] 2 All E.R. (Comm) 1159, Sir Terence Etherton (Chancellor), CA (Civ Div).

210. Financial institutions–Recognised clearing houses–Recognised investment exchanges

THE FINANCIAL SERVICES AND MARKETS ACT 2000 (PRESCRIBED FINANCIAL INSTITUTIONS) ORDER 2013, SI 2013/165; made under the Financial Services and Markets Act 2000 s.192B, s.428, Sch.17A para.17. In force: April 1, 2013; .

This Order prescribes kinds of financial institution for the purposes of Pt.12A of the Financial Services and Markets Act 2000. The powers conferred by that Part may only be exercised in relation to parent undertakings of certain authorised persons, recognised investment exchanges or recognised clearing houses if the parent undertaking is a financial institution of a prescribed kind.

211. Financial markets–Fraud–Duties of Serious Fraud Office when presenting case for issue of search warrant

[Criminal Justice Act 1987 (c.38) s.2(4); Criminal Justice and Police Act 2001 (c.16) s.59.]

Two well-known businessmen (T) and the companies and trusts through which their businesses were carried on sought to set aside search warrants issued under the Criminal Justice Act 1987 s.2(4) at the Central Criminal Court, asserting that the warrants had been procured by misrepresentations and non-disclosure on the part of the Serious Fraud Office (SFO) in the written presentation made to the judge known as the Information and in the oral evidence of the case manager; challenges were also made to the manner in which the warrants were executed. Following the collapse, in October 2008, of what was then the largest Icelandic bank (K), the SFO had begun an investigation into what it considered to be irregular lending by K to T. It asserted, among other things, that there had been a deliberate, concerted and dishonest conspiracy between a number of senior executives of K and T to defraud and ultimately steal funds on a large scale from K. The SFO applied for the issue of search warrants. The judge acceded to the application, giving no reasons for his decision. The warrants were then executed at T's residences and at the business premises of the companies through which their businesses were carried on.

Held: Judgment accordingly. (1) T's allegations of misrepresentation and non-disclosure on the part of the SFO were made out. The SFO had a duty to ensure that what was put before the judge was clear and comprehensive, so that the judge could rely on it and form his judgment on the basis of a presentation in which he had complete trust and confidence as to its accuracy and completeness. Cases in the financial markets investigated by the SFO were likely to require the judge to be familiar with the commercial and market background. That background had to be set out in the written presentation to the judge. The transactions had then to be explained in a coherent and analytical manner. The allegations of reasonable suspicion had then to be set out. What was alleged had to be verified by persons expert in the market or accounting practices whose independent advice had been expressly sought. A record of that verification should be retained by the SFO. Not only had the case for reasonable suspicion to be put, but the matters that might undermine that case had to be enumerated. The skill and experience required to prepare a presentation of that kind could not be underestimated. The judge's duty was to be satisfied personally that what was presented met the statutory test of reasonable suspicion. It required careful consideration and rigorous and critical analysis by the judge. The judge had to give reasons; they would comprise a short summary of the detailed analytical process undertaken by him in his scrutiny of the material presented. None of that had been done in the instant case. The parties had provided suggestions as to what might be the best procedure for such applications in cases of serious fraud. For example, consideration needed to be given as to whether the practice of simply putting an Information without the underlying documents before the judge was the best practice for cases investigated by the SFO. Such issues should be addressed by a body such as the Criminal Procedure Rule Committee or an ad hoc body established for that purpose. These were difficult issues which required that level of review. It would be helpful if such a review might also raise with the Senior Presiding Judge the best way in which such cases should be listed before judges. The investigation and prosecution of serious fraud in the financial markets required proper resources, both human and financial; otherwise, incalculable damage would be done to the financial markets of London. It was quite clear that the SFO did not have such resources in the instant case (see paras 88-90, 293-294 of judgment). (2) Large quantities of privileged material had been seized during the search of T's business premises. The lawfulness of the SFO's actions would be determined at a later stage in the proceedings. However, it was appropriate to point out that the SFO's practice of using its own lawyers to assess claims for legal professional privilege during searches was misconceived; an independent lawyer should be present to assess such claims (paras 256, 264, 266-267). (3) After acknowledging that certain warrants should not have been issued, the SFO had issued "here and now" notices with a view to retaining some of the documents seized. That was unlawful: it should have returned the documents or used the statutory machinery in the Criminal Justice and Police Act 2001 s.59 (paras 274-281).

R. (ON THE APPLICATION OF RAWLINSON AND HUNTER TRUSTEES) v CENTRAL CRIMINAL COURT; R. (ON THE APPLICATION OF TCHENGUIZ) v DIRECTOR OF SERIOUS FRAUD OFFICE, [2012] EWHC 2254 (Admin), [2013] 1 W.L.R. 1634, Sir John Thomas (President), DC.

212. Financial services–Misleading statements

THE FINANCIAL SERVICES ACT 2012 (MISLEADING STATEMENTS AND IMPRESSIONS) ORDER 2013, SI 2013/637; made under the Financial Services Act 2012 s.93, s.115. In force: April 1, 2013; .

This Order specifies the relevant activities, investments and benchmarks, for the purposes of criminal offences in the Financial Services Act 2012 Pt 7.

213. Financial Services Act 2012 (c.21)–Commencement No.1 Order

THE FINANCIAL SERVICES ACT 2012 (COMMENCEMENT NO.1) ORDER 2013, SI 2013/SI 2013/113 (C.6); made under the Financial Services Act 2012 s.122. Commencement details: bringing into force various provisions of the 2012 Act on January 24, 2013 and Febraury 19, 2013.; .

This Order brings into force certain provisions of the Financial Services Act 2012. This is the first commencement order to be made under the Act.

214. Financial Services Act 2012 (c.21)–Commencement No.2 Order

THE FINANCIAL SERVICES ACT 2012 (COMMENCEMENT NO.2) ORDER 2013, SI 2013/SI 2013/423 (C.17); made under the Financial Services Act 2012 s.122. Commencement details: bringing into force various provisions of the 2012 Act on February 27, 2013 and April 1, 2013.; .

This Order brings into force certain provisions of the Financial Services Act 2012 into force. This is the second commencement order to be made under the Act.

215. Financial Services Act 2012 (c.21)–Commencement No.3 Order

THE FINANCIAL SERVICES ACT 2012 (COMMENCEMENT NO.3) ORDER 2013, SI 2013/SI 2013/651 (C.26); made under the Financial Services Act 2012 s.122. Commencement details: bringing into force various provisions of the 2012 Act on March 19, 2013.; .

This Order brings into force sections 17, 18 and 39 of the Financial Services Act 2012 on March 19 2013 for the purposes specified in this Order. This is the third commencement order to be made under the Act. This Order will have no effect on the costs of business and the voluntary sector independent of the provisions this Order brings into force. For that reason, no impact assessment has been produced for this instrument.

216. Financial spread betting–Illegal contracts–Claim for return of money provided for spread betting in reliance on inside information–Whether spread betting on Investor's gold Index constituted insider dealing–Availability of equitable relief including grant of locus poenitentiae

[Criminal Justice Act 1993 (c.36) s.52(3), s.52, s.59(4), s.59(2), Sch.2.]

The claimant (P) claimed for the recovery of funds from the defendant (M) on the basis of unjust enrichment or on the basis that M held them under a Quistclose trust or a resulting trust. M was a foreign exchange broker. He had offered P, and their mutual friend (G), an opportunity to use his spread-betting account to bet on the movement of Royal Bank of Scotland (RBS) shares. P had paid M more than £600,000 upon hearing that M had contacts within the bank who could supply advance information about a statement anticipated to be made by the Chancellor of the Exchequer about the Government's investment in the bank, which would affect the bank's share prices. The plan was that M would use P's money, along with his own, to bet on the Investor's Gold Index on movements in the quoted share price over a specified period using insider information. P's case was that M did not place the bets because the Government statement never materialised; that the money was supposed to be repaid, but that it was mistakenly paid to G instead. P was unable to recover it from G. P maintained that the money was recoverable from M as money paid for a consideration that had wholly failed, and/or that it was held by M on trust for P. M's case was that the money had been received for the purpose of general speculative trading in RBS shares. The issues were (i) whether the claim failed for illegality on the ground that insider dealing was a criminal offence under the Criminal Justice Act 1993; (ii) if so, whether there was any relief for P under equitable or trust principles. It was not in dispute that the advance information intended to form the basis of the bet fell within the definitions of "inside information" and "price affected securities" in s.52.

Held: Claim dismissed. (1) A spread bet with the Investor's Gold Index (IG Index) was a "contract for differences" as defined in Sch.2 of the Act and would therefore constitute a "security" for the purposes of s.52. Bets placed with a spread-betting company were not, themselves, dealings on a regulated market within the meaning of s.52(3), but the Act created an offence even if the dealing did not take place in a regulated market provided that there was "reliance" on a "professional intermediary". The counter-party on a contract for differences in the form of a spread bet would be IG Index, which was also a professional intermediary because it carried on a business of acquiring and/or disposing of such contracts. Whether a customer "relied" on IG Index when it entered into such a contract depended on whether the requirements for such reliance in s.59(4) and s.59(2) were met, which, in the instant case, they were. In the circumstances, the agreement or arrangement pleaded by P amounted to a criminal conspiracy (see paras 20-28, 30-31 of judgment). On the facts, there were strong reasons for concluding that the payments by P to M had not been for the purpose of general speculative trading in RBS shares, and P's account was to be preferred (para.32). (2) The court would refuse relief based on an agreement with an illegal object, but would, through the grant of *locus poenitentiae*, permit the recovery of money or property transferred under that agreement if the transferor voluntarily withdrew before the agreement had been performed. The analysis of failed consideration, or unjust enrichment, was inappropriate on the facts because the case concerned money paid by a principal to an agent for a specified purpose. Ordinarily, the agent would be obliged to account for it if the purpose was thwarted, without resort to any question of contractual consideration or its failure, *Kearley v Thomson* (1890) 24 Q.B.D. 742 and *Berg v Sadler and Moore* [1937] 2 K.B. 158 considered. Likewise, the Quistclose argument was also defeated because P had not paid the monies to M as a loan. The question was in what circumstances equity would refuse to enforce equitable rights which undoubtedly existed. The answer to that question depended on whether, in order to establish his equitable right, the claimant was obliged to rely on the illegal arrangement, *Tinsley v Milligan* [1994] 1 A.C. 340, [1993] C.L.Y. 1839 applied and *Harry Parker Ltd v Mason* [1940] 2 K.B. 590 followed (paras 35, 38-45). It was a question of fact whether the parties' understanding was that the monies passed to the agent were being held on trust. It would be difficult to conclude in favour of a trust unless the parties intended that the monies would be held separately from the agent's own monies and, in the instant case, there was no evidence of such an intention (para.46). The defence of *locus poenitentiae* was not, in modern times, tied to genuine repentance, but it acted as an incentive to a claimant to withdraw before the illegality was consummated. That rationale was missing where, as in the instant case, the purpose of the illegal contract was frustrated for reasons other than the claimant's actions *Bigos v Bousted* [1951] 1 All E.R. 92, [1947-51] C.L.Y. 1751 applied. P was therefore unable to recover the monies paid by him to M even if he were to establish all the matters alleged by him in his pleaded case (paras 47-50).

PATEL v MIRZA, [2013] EWHC 1892 (Ch), [2013] Lloyd's Rep. F.C. 525, David Donaldson Q.C., Ch D.

217. Futures exchanges–Duty of care–Forced close-out of hedge fund's trading portfolio following failure to respond to margin call–Broker's duties when exercising right of close-out

[Supply of Goods and Services Act 1982 (c.29) s.13.]

The claimant investment fund (E) claimed damages against the defendant investment bank (S) for breach of contract and negligence in the conduct of a forced close-out of its trading portfolio in October 2008. E's principal trading strategy was short selling of options. Once it had identified a trade that it wished to enter into, the trades were executed by its execution broker and passed to a clearing broker, who contracted with the clearing house. S was E's clearing broker between May and October 2008 pursuant to a formal mandate document. In order to manage the risks associated with trading in futures and options, cl.11 of the mandate required E to deposit cash margin payments with the clearing house in an amount, and at a time, specified by S. The clause stated that if E failed to provide sufficient margin in respect of a transaction, S was entitled to close-out any open contracts without reference to E. In early October 2008, there was unprecedented global volatility in the financial markets; the higher the level of market volatility, the greater the margin requirement. S asked for margin to cover its exposure, but E failed to pay and S therefore exercised its right to close-out E's portfolio. There was a significant drop in the markets overnight on October 9, 2008 and the dispute centred on precisely when the close-out took place, whether it should have been completed before or after October 9, and the manner in which it was conducted. E's case was that S had negligently delayed the close-out and conducted it incompetently, which had resulted in loss. S's defence was that it had a wide and unfettered discretion in relation to the conduct of the close-out and it had not breached its duty.

Held: Judgment for defendant. (1) On the evidence, S had not delayed in completing the close-out. It had taken control of E's portfolio on the morning of October 10, 2008, not around midday on October 9, as contended for by E. Limits had been imposed on E's trading on October 9, but they fell short of S taking over conduct of the trading. At close of business on October 9, E had still had massive open options positions on its portfolio and had been facing a potential loss of over EUR 50 million. That presented S with a major concern, since it had anticipated that the markets would fall significantly overnight. It was against that background that it decided to close-out E's positions early the next morning so as to protect it as far as possible from potential substantial losses (see paras 67, 72-77, 79-83, 85, 88-89, 96, 104 of judgment). (2) While S had had a duty to act rationally in its right to close-out E's portfolio, it did not owe a tortious duty of care, because to impose such a duty would involve expanding the law into a new context; the relationship between a clearing broker and an investment fund was not an appropriate relationship for a duty of care. Also, imposing such a duty would involve a new type of loss, namely loss of hypothetical investment opportunities, and that would, in turn, involve an expansion of the law of negligence beyond the normal heads of damage. Similarly, it was not appropriate to imply a term into the mandate that S would conduct the close-out using reasonable care and to a suitably professional standard. Such a term was not necessary to give business efficacy to the contract. Although the mandate was a contract for the supply of a service within the meaning of the Supply of Goods and Services Act 1982 s.13, the implied term referred to in that section only applied to the specific services that the mandate contemplated. Since S's right to close-out E's portfolio was not a service that S had agreed to carry out under the mandate, there was no basis on which to impose such an implied term, *Socimer International Bank Ltd (In Liquidation) v Standard Bank London Ltd (No.2)* [2008] EWCA Civ 116, [2008] Bus. L.R. 1304, [2008] C.L.Y. 669 and *Sucden Financial Ltd (formerly Sucden (UK) Ltd) v Fluxo-Cane Overseas Ltd* [2010] EWHC 2133 (Comm), [2010] 2 C.L.C. 216, [2011] C.L.Y. 188 applied, *ED&F Man Commodity Advisers Ltd v Fluxo-Cane Overseas Ltd* [2010] EWHC 212 (Comm) and *Marex Financial Ltd v Fluxo-Cane Overseas Ltd* [2010] EWHC 2690 (Comm) considered (paras 105, 109-135). (3) Each of three claims by E concerning breach of duty in specific aspects of the close-out was rejected (paras 136-184).

EUROPTION STRATEGIC FUND LTD v SKANDINAVISKA ENSKILDA BANKEN AB, [2012] EWHC 584 (Comm), [2013] 1 B.C.L.C. 125, Gloster, J., QBD (Comm).

218. Guarantees–Continuing guarantees–Guarantee given by company director to creditor for sums due by company–Whether guarantee was continuing or specific guarantee

The appellant (M) appealed against a decision ([2012] EWHC 2563 (Ch)) that he was liable to the respondent society (C) under the terms of a personal guarantee. C was an industrial and provident society which negotiated bulk purchasing agreements with suppliers for the benefit of its members. Its members were companies in the construction industry. M was a shareholder and joint director of a company (X) which was a member. X had a credit limit with C of £200,000 but appeared to be in financial difficulties. In 2002 C therefore asked M, and the other company director (B), to provide a written personal guarantee under which they jointly and severally guaranteed payment of "all sums which are now or may hereafter become owing" to C by X. In 2006 M resigned as a director and his shares were bought by B. C increased X's credit limit to £400,000 and then to £700,000. X continued to purchase supplies through C but became insolvent in 2008 owing C £330,000. C obtained part of that sum from its credit insurers and sought payment from B and M under the terms of the guarantee. M submitted that the guarantee had been given on the basis of the contract between X and C under which X had a credit limit of £200,000, which impliedly confined his liability to that limit. He argued that he had not consented to the increase in the credit limit and his liability under the guarantee was therefore discharged.

Held: Appeal dismissed. (1) The resolution of the instant proceedings turned upon the interpretation of the guarantee. If, upon its true interpretation, it was a guarantee of the due performance of obligations arising under a specific contract, that would be the limit of the guarantee obligations. If parties to that contract varied it in a way that was not insubstantial or incapable of prejudicing the guarantor, the rule in *Holme v Brunskill* (1878) 3 Q.B.D. 495 would apply and the guarantor would be released, because otherwise the variation would have exposed him to a liability to which he had never agreed, *Holme* considered. By way of contrast, a guarantee given in respect of obligations arising out of a contemplated course of dealing, rather than a specific contract, was treated differently. In those circumstances, provided the course of dealing remained within the scope of that contemplated by the guarantee, the details of the manner of dealing as between principal and creditor were of no concern to the guarantor; any variations in them would not affect the continuing nature of his liability. A typical example was a freestanding "all monies" guarantee in respect of present and future indebtedness commonly given by directors to banks in respect of their company's liabilities, *Wardens and Commonalty of the Mystery of Mercers of the City of London v New Hampshire Insurance Co Ltd* [1991] 1 W.L.R. 1173, [1991] C.L.Y. 1313 applied. Although the *Mystery of Mercers* case was reversed on the facts by the Court of Appeal, the statement of principle by

Phillips J. was not the subject of criticism, *Wardens and Commonalty of the Mystery of Mercers of the City of London v New Hampshire Insurance Co Ltd* [1992] 1 W.L.R. 792, [1992] C.L.Y. 3520 considered (see paras 31-33 of judgment). (2) M's submission was contrary to basic principles. His proposition was that a guarantee would be treated as in the "specific contract" class if, at the time it was given, the relationship between the principal and creditor was governed by a contract of which the guarantor knew the terms, so that the guarantee was regarded as given on the faith of that contract, and was confined to "seeing to" the principal's due performance of it. That proposition was wrong. A guarantee was merely a particular type of contract. The relevant question was the nature of the guarantee obligation that the guarantor had assumed. In interpreting the guarantee, it might well be appropriate to have regard to the commercial arrangements which were in place between the principal and the creditor at the time, as they formed part of the background against which the guarantee was given. But the proposition that the interpretation of the guarantee was conclusively dictated by knowledge that the guarantor might alone have had was inconsistent with the well-settled approach to the construction of written instruments, including guarantees, *Investors Compensation Scheme Ltd v West Bromwich Building Society (No.1)* [1998] 1 W.L.R. 896, [1997] C.L.Y. 2537 followed. M's guarantee was a freestanding "all monies" guarantee that was not linked to the credit limit to which X was then entitled. Its language pointed away from any such link (paras 38-41).

NATIONAL MERCHANT BUYING SOCIETY LTD v BELLAMY; *sub nom.* NATIONAL MERCHANT BUYING SOCIETY LTD v BELLAMY; MALLETT v NATIONAL MERCHANT BUYING SOCIETY LTD, [2013] EWCA Civ 452, [2013] 2 All E.R. (Comm) 674, Longmore, L.J., CA (Civ Div).

219. Guarantees–Termination–Defendants' request for consent for early termination of guarantees–Claimant's refusal to give consent unless fees received–Whether refusal commercially reasonable

The court was required to determine whether the claimant bank (B) had exercised its discretion in a commercially reasonable manner in refusing to consent to the early termination of three securitisations of loan portfolios entered into with the defendant banks (U). The securitisations had been embodied in three deeds of guarantee entered into in the wake of the financial crisis in 2008. The guarantees provided for B to receive quarterly payments and a fixed fee. Clause 12.1 (b) of the guarantees stated that where a regulatory change occurred in respect of U and provided that U had obtained prior consent from B, which was to be determined in a commercially reasonable manner, U could designate the next payment date as an optional early termination date. There were other grounds for early termination in respect of which it was agreed that B would be entitled to five years' fees. U sought early termination of the guarantees as a result of a change in their regulatory treatment, which adversely affected U's ability to obtain capital relief which the guarantees were designed to achieve. B stated that it would not consent unless it was paid the balance of five years' fees, which amounted to EUR 82 million. U declined to pay any sum and argued that B's insistence on five years' fees was not a commercially reasonable ground for declining consent. B contended that there had been a shared understanding that in the event of a regulatory change it could refuse consent unless or until it was paid five years' fees.

Held: Judgment for claimant. (1) B's determination of whether to consent to early termination for regulatory change under cl.12.1 (b) had to be commercially reasonable in the objective sense. It was not a question of whether B's decision was justified, but whether a reasonable commercial man in B's position might have reached such a decision. In determining what was commercially reasonable, B was entitled to take into account its own commercial interests. It was not obliged to conduct a balancing exercise between its interests and U's. B's commercial interests comprised its interest in earning profits from its fee income under the guarantees. B would be entitled to refuse consent to protect that income unless its nature or amount was so disproportionate to U's obligation to continue to pay it that a commercially reasonable man in B's position could have reached such a decision (see para.67 of judgment). (2) It was not open to B to seek to justify its refusal of consent on the basis that U had offered no payment of any kind. Its determination to refuse consent was based on its insistence on being paid at least five years' worth of fees. That was commercially reasonable as that was B's legitimate expectation when the guarantees were entered into; U expressly agreed to pay B a minimum of five years' fees if there was an optional early termination by U as a result of a rating event, which might have the same effect as a regulatory change; and B's expectation of a minimum of five years' fees was protected under the terms of the other early termination options (paras 68, 69, 71, 74-75). (3) U had not shared B's understanding and neither did they agree to it. It could not be said that U knew the assumption B was making nor that they did anything which conveyed acquiescence in that assumption. The estoppel argument failed on the facts (paras 91, 93, 96, 98-101). (4) B accepted that its primary interest in the guarantees was the fees that it would receive under them; B was also prepared to accept in principle that it might be compensated by way of damages for non-performance by U. However, whether an award of damages would fully compensate it for its losses depended on a number of factors that required further exploration. If it could be argued that B's position by way of damages was less favourable to it than continued performance of the guarantees, then B had a clear interest in continuing to insist on performance of the guarantees. Therefore, it could not be said that B had adopted an unreasonable approach in seeking to hold U to the performance of its contractual obligations, *White & Carter (Councils) Ltd v McGregor* [1962] A.C. 413, [1962] C.L.Y. 501 considered. The guarantees had not been terminated as a result of any unaccepted repudiatory breach by U, and declaratory relief was granted stating that B had validly refused its consent (paras 102, 106, 110-112).

BARCLAYS BANK PLC v UNICREDIT BANK AG (FORMERLY BAYERISCHE HYPO-UND VEREINSBANK AG), [2012] EWHC 3655 (Comm), [2013] 2 Lloyd's Rep. 1, Popplewell, J., QBD (Comm).

220. Individual savings accounts

THE INDIVIDUAL SAVINGS ACCOUNT (AMENDMENT NO.2) REGULATIONS 2013, SI 2013/623; made under the Taxation of Chargeable Gains Act 1992 s.151; and the Income Tax (Trading and Other Income) Act 2005 s.694, s.695, s.696, s.701. In force: April 5, 2013; .

This instrument secures that no tax disadvantage accrues to savers who withdrew and reinvested sums from their cash ISAs because of the fact that they were affected by the technical difficulties within Royal Bank of Scotland Group in 2012. It also removes the rule that ISA managers must send annual reminders to their investors at the start of a tax year about not subscribing to more than one ISA of the same type in that tax year and not exceeding the ISA subscription limits.

221. Individual savings accounts–Junior individual savings accounts

THE INDIVIDUAL SAVINGS ACCOUNT (AMENDMENT) REGULATIONS 2013, SI 2013/267; made under the Income Tax (Trading and Other Income) Act 2005 s.694; and the Taxation of Chargeable Gains Act 1992 s.151. In force: April 6, 2013; .

These Regulations amend the Individual Savings Account Regulations 1998 (SI 1998/1870) to increase the annual subscription limit for ISA and Junior ISA.

222. Individual savings accounts–National savings

THE NATIONAL SAVINGS BANK (AMENDMENT) REGULATIONS 2013, SI 2013/8; made under the National Savings Bank Act 1971 s.2, s.3, s.4, s.7, s.8. In force: February 22, 2013 except for reg.2(b), reg.3 on April 6, 2013.; .

These Regulations amend the National Savings Bank Regulations 1972 (SI 1972/764) and the National Savings Bank (Investment Deposits) (Limits) Order 1977 (SI 1977/1210). The primary purpose of these Regulations is to facilitate the closure of the two oldest varieties of individual savings account offered by the National Savings Bank. These closures form part of the modernisation programme currently being undertaken by National Savings and Investments.

223. Investment banks–Administration–Method of valuing customers' entitlement on bank's insolvency

The applicant administrators sought a direction from the court relating to the distributions to be made to clients of an insolvent investment bank (M). Investment firms were required to segregate money received from or held for their clients and hold it on trust for them. In certain circumstances, including the administration or liquidation of the firm, the money held for clients (client money) had to be distributed among the clients, pro rata according to their entitlements. The rules creating that obligation and governing the relevant arrangements were contained in chapters 7 and 7A (CASS 7 and 7A) of the Client Assets Sourcebook section of the Financial Services Authority Handbook. The value of a client's entitlement for distribution purposes was to be established as at the date when the obligation arose, the primary pooling event (PPE). The issue was whether in calculating a client's entitlement, at least in the context of administration or liquidation, the client's open positions on trades made with the firm were to be valued by reference to market value as at the PPE or by reference to the prices at which the trades were subsequently closed out, whether at the contractual settlement date or at an earlier date in accordance with applicable default provisions. Two respondents (X and S) were joined to the action to represent the clients of M who would gain from the adoption of one or other of the alternative valuation bases. X argued that valuation by reference to the market value as at the PPE was dictated by the terms of the relevant rules, while S argued that, just as it applied in the valuation of claims for the purposes of a distribution of a company's assets among its unsecured creditors in a liquidation or administration, the hindsight principle should be applied so that the return of client money was made on the basis of the prices at which open positions were later closed out.

Held: Judgment accordingly. The issue was governed by the proper construction and application of CASS 7 and 7A. The hindsight principle was used where an estimate was to be made of a claim as at a particular date, assessing the chances of the contingency occurring and the likely amount of any claim. However, CASS 7 and 7A required the quite different process of a notional valuation of open positions as at a particular date, in this case the PPE date. There was no indication in the CASS rules that the hindsight principle was to be applied. If it had been intended that open positions on the occurrence of a PPE should be valued for the purposes of a distribution by reference to actual close-out prices, CASS 7A, Annex 1 to CASS 7 and the definition of "client equity balance" would have been drafted very differently. They would first have drawn the distinction between valuation for daily reconciliation and valuation for distribution. Second, the hindsight principle would have been clearly expressed. Accordingly, the hindsight principle did not apply to the determination of claims to client money for the purposes of a distribution under CASS 7A, *Lehman Brothers International (Europe) (In Administration), Re* [2012] UKSC 6, [2012] 3 All E.R. 1, [2012] C.L.Y. 1786, *Lehman Brothers International (Europe) (In Administration), Re* [2009] EWHC 3228 (Ch), [2010] 2 B.C.L.C. 301 and *Global Trader Europe Ltd (In Liquidation), Re* [2009] EWHC 699 (Ch), [2009] Bus. L.R. 1327, [2010] C.L.Y. 1884 considered.

MF GLOBAL UK LTD (IN ADMINISTRATION), *Re; sub nom.* HEIS v ATTESTOR VALUE MASTER FUND LP, [2013] EWHC 92 (Ch), [2013] Bus. L.R. 1030, David Richards, J., Ch D (Companies Ct).

224. Investment banks–Financial assistance

THE ENTERPRISE AND REGULATORY REFORM (DESIGNATION OF THE UK GREEN INVESTMENT BANK) ORDER 2013, SI 2013/2880; made under the Enterprise and Regulatory Reform Act 2013. In force: November 7, 2013; .

This Order designates the UK Green Investment Bank for the purposes of the Enterprise and Regulatory Reform Act 2013 ss.3 to 6. Where the Bank is designated, s.3 of that Act limits the circumstances in which the Bank can alter its articles of association, section 4 makes provision for the Bank to receive financial assistance from the Secretary of State (with the consent of the Treasury) and ss.5 and 6 contain reporting and publication requirements relating to the Bank.

225. Loans–Payment protection insurance–Borrower sold payment protection insurance by lender–Whether intermediary failed to advise that payment protection insurance optional–Contemporaneous transcripts of telephone sales calls and documentation

[Financial Services and Markets Act 2000 (c.8) s.150.]

The claimants (G1 and G2) sought damages in respect of a payment protection insurance (PPI) policy sold to them by the defendant finance company (C). G1 and G2 took out the loan agreement with a financial services company (P) through a broker (T), as an intermediary, working at C. The loan was to be repaid over 25 years and the PPI was to last for five years. T had originally offered G1 and G2 a loan from a different provider, and sent the relevant paperwork, but that offer was withdrawn by the provider because of an unfavourable reference from G1's employer about his earnings. Despite that reference, an offer from P was available. At all times, T had followed a tightly-scripted process of fact-finding and recommendations that had been approved by C's regulator, the Financial Services Authority. G1 and G2 alleged that C had failed to advise them that PPI was optional and to take steps to communicate information about the policy in a way that was clear, fair and not misleading, and that C had failed to take reasonable steps to ensure that the policy was suitable for their demands and needs. C submitted that the allegations to the effect that PPI was a compulsory product, stood to be judged objectively in the light of the accurate and contemporaneous sales calls and the loan documentation, not the subjective rewriting of history by unreliable witnesses.

Held: Judgment for defendant. The Insurance Conduct of Business Rules were the relevant rules for the purposes of the instant claim, and breach of a rule gave a private person a right to claim damages under the Financial Services and Markets Act 2000 s.150 (see paras 11-12 of judgment). The court was fortunate to have the accurate and contemporaneous transcripts of the calls and the contemporaneous documentation and they cast grave doubts on the reliability of G1 and G2 as witnesses. Where the witness statements were at variance, the court chose the contemporaneous evidence over them. C pointed to a number of instances where it was demonstrably communicated to G1 and G2 that PPI was optional (paras 20-21). Accordingly, the court found that G1 and G2 were not truthful in either their witness statements or their evidence on oath in court. Their changes of position were classic examples of witnesses giving evidence on oath to suit their case, which had to be seismically shifted in the light of the decision in *Harrison v Black Horse Ltd* [2011] EWCA Civ 1128, [2012] E.C.C. 7, [2012] C.L.Y. 614, *Harrison* applied. The truth was to be found in the contemporaneous documents and the agreements they knowingly and knowledgeably signed up to after being carefully and informatively handled by the intermediaries. They had previous experience of PPI and they obtained the only PPI on offer that was suitable for their needs. The length of the term of PPI was amply discussed with the intermediary and they understood how it worked with rebates at the end of the period of cover and the option of taking out another period of coverage at the end of it should their personal circumstances have changed by then. It was only G1's income that needed protection, as it was his income that was servicing the loan. Their only concern was its added costs (paras 44-45).

GOODMAN v CENTRAL CAPITAL LTD, [2012] EWHC 8 (QB), [2012] C.T.L.C. 158, Judge Brown QC, QBD (Merc) (Birmingham).

226. Mortgages–Capitalisation–Repossession–Whether loan agreement regulated by Consumer Credit Act 1974–Meaning of "credit in the form of a cash loan" in art.4(1) Consumer Credit Act 2006 (Commencement No. 4 and Transitional Provisions) Order 2008

[Consumer Credit Act 1974 (c.39) s.82(2); Data Protection Act 1998 (c.29); Financial Services and Markets Act 2000 (c.8); Law of Property Act 1925 (c.20) s.136; Consumer Credit Act 2006 (Commencement No. 4 and Transitional Provisions) Order 2008 (SI 2008/831) Art.4(1), Art.4.]

The appellant mortgagors (H) applied for permission to appeal against a judgment that the respondent mortgagee bank could repossess the house in which H lived. The bank had made a loan to H under standard mortgage conditions and secured by way of a first charge over the property. H failed to maintain the payments and agreed to the bank's proposal to capitalise the arrears by adding them to the capital balance and increasing the payments. H fell further into arrears, but the bank refused their requests for further accommodation and brought possession proceedings. Judgment was given for the bank and H applied for permission to appeal. H submitted that since less than 40 per cent of the land involved was used or intended to be used as a dwelling, the original mortgage agreement and the later capitalisation were not regulated under the Financial Services and Markets Act 2000, which allowed the loan agreement to be subject to regulation by the Consumer Credit Act 1974 after the £25,000 limit was removed. H contended that, as a result, the capitalisation was a "modifying agreement" under s.82(2), for although the removal of the limit applied only to new agreements, and transitional provisions in the Consumer Credit Act 2006 (Commencement No. 4 and Transitional Provisions) Order 2008 stipulated that it did not apply to variations of existing agreements, there was an exception in art.4(1) of the Order if part of the variation was to provide "credit in the form of a cash loan", and H's capitalisation was such a loan. H argued that the 1974 Act was unenforceable against them because the bank had failed to comply with various requirements of the Act relating to the form of regulated credit agreements and the service of default notices. They submitted that they had discovered by means of the Data Protection Act 1998 that the bank's rights under the loan agreement had been assigned to a third party under a securitisation agreement, and that the discovery constituted the necessary express notice to them pursuant to the Law of Property Act 1925 s.136 so that the bank did not have title to sue in the instant action, although if the loan was not regulated by the 1974 Act, the bank's right to sue would not be affected.

Held: Permission granted in part, appeal dismissed. (1) The mere restructuring of an existing agreement by allowing more time to pay without making new funds available did not constitute a "cash loan" for the purpose of art.4(1). It constituted the giving of a form of financial accommodation, firstly, since that conclusion accorded with the natural meaning of the words and gave effect to the distinction between providing credit in the form of a cash loan, and other credit. H were saying that if the arrears were added to the capital amount outstanding that would necessarily be the making of a cash loan, but unless arrears were written off altogether, to allow further time to pay only meant that such arrears had to be added to the amount the borrower had to pay; the timing of the repayment obligations changed, but the overall effect was neutral. Secondly, it would be startling if a routine deferral of an instalment under an unregulated credit agreement, even if valid and enforceable when made, could cause the whole agreement to become unenforceable. That would be a trap to any such lender and could not have been intended. As there was no authority on the meaning of "credit in the form of a cash loan", the court was prepared to give permission to appeal on the capitalisation issue. However, no cash loan was provided, so the appeal was dismissed (see paras 29-34 of judgment). (2) Banks commonly assigned their rights under loan agreements while remaining entitled to receive payments and be the registered holders of legal charges. The loan agreement was not regulated under the 1974 Act, so permission to appeal on the issue was refused (paras 36, 44).

SANTANDER UK PLC v HARRISON, [2013] EWHC 199 (QB), [2013] Bus. L.R. 501, Males, J., QBD.

227. Mortgages–Completion–Solicitors' failure to discharge existing mortgage and obtain first legal charge over property–Whether breach of trust–Appropriate remedy

The appellant bank (B) appealed against a decision ([2012] EWHC 35 (Ch), [2012] P.N.L.R. 16, [2012] C.L.Y. 275) that the respondent firm of solicitors (M) had only acted in breach of trust to a limited extent in respect of a remortgage advance. M had acted for B and the borrowers (S) regarding an advance of £3.3 million. S's property was already subject to a £1.5 million mortgage in favour of another bank (K). B instructed M to pay the advance to discharge the existing mortgage and enable B's mortgage to be registered as a first legal charge. However, M paid approximately £1.2 million to K, which meant there was a £300,000 shortfall and B's mortgage was registered as a second charge. The rest of the advance was paid to S. S subsequently defaulted and were declared bankrupt. The judge determined as a preliminary issue that M had acted in breach of trust to the extent that it had released to S the additional sum required to pay the outstanding balance on K's mortgage, and awarded B equitable compensation in that sum. He rejected B's claim that it was entitled to equitable compensation of the full advance as the transaction had never completed. M denied committing a breach of trust, on the basis that it was a post-completion transaction.

Held: Appeal allowed in part. (1) A solicitor's failure properly to carry out some term of its retainer linked to a property transaction would not ordinarily expose them to any liability as a trustee. In a remortgage transaction of the instant kind, the solicitor was retained to enable the client to obtain the security stipulated as a term of the loan. A failure to take sufficient care entitled the lender to compensation for the loss occasioned by the lack of the appropriate security. However, the solicitor did not warrant that the transaction would be loss-free, and the lender would not be able to recover losses it would have suffered even with the benefit of the intended security. A breach of trust claim therefore had the potential to transform the measure of recovery available to the lender in such circumstances. The lender would, paradoxically, be in a better position as a result of the breach of duty. A solicitor who parted with client money before completion without authority committed a breach of trust. The issue of authority in the instant case largely turned on whether completion had occurred for the purposes of authorising release of the advance. The judge was wrong to treat the breach of trust as limited to that part of the advance which was paid to S instead of being used to discharge their liability to K. He failed to give proper effect to s.10.3 of the Council of Mortgage Lenders' Handbook. The effect of s.10.3 was that M had no authority to discharge the money, without B's express direction, except on completion of the relevant transaction. Completion required M to be in receipt of a solicitors' undertaking, or unconditional confirmation from K that the advance monies would be applied to redemption of its charge, before releasing the advance, *Lloyds TSB Bank Plc v Markandan & Uddin (A Firm)* [2012] EWCA Civ 65, [2012] 2 All E.R. 884, [2012] C.L.Y. 2757 and *Nationwide Building Society v Davisons Solicitors* [2012] EWCA Civ 1626, [2013] 3 Costs L.O. 464, [2013] 5 C.L. 232 applied. Had there been proper completion, a subsequent failure by M to pay sufficient monies to K to discharge the existing mortgage would not have been a breach of trust. If, on the other hand, completion had not taken place, then M had parted with trust monies without authority, regardless of the purpose for which they had been used. The difficulty with the judge's reasoning was that his finding had to be based on the premise that there had been completion in respect of the transaction generally, which meant that the trust imposed by s.10.3 would therefore be at an end (see paras 12-43 of judgment). (2) Equitable principles of compensation had the capacity to recognise what loss the beneficiary had actually suffered from the breach of trust, and to base the compensation recoverable on a proper causal connection between the breach and the eventual loss, *Target Holdings Ltd v Redferns* [1996] A.C. 421, [1995] C.L.Y. 2195 followed. B had enjoyed less security for its loan than if there had been no breach of trust. If M had obtained a proper redemption statement from K, coupled with an undertaking to apply the sum specified in satisfaction of the existing mortgage, the transaction would have proceeded to completion and B could have obtained a first legal mortgage over S's property. However, although that did not happen, B had obtained a valid mortgage from S which they were able to register as a second charge and use to recover part of its loan. It was not open to B to contend that, but for the breach of trust, it would have simply asked for its money back. The breach of trust comprised the unauthorised release, pre-completion, of the mortgage advance; not the failure by M to obtain a first charge. In calculating what loss had resulted from that breach, the court was required to take account of the beneficial effect of the security B was eventually able to obtain, *Target* followed (paras 44-50). (3) M were in breach of trust by releasing the advance monies, but the judge's calculation of equitable compensation was affirmed (para.51).

AIB GROUP (UK) PLC v MARK REDLER & CO SOLICITORS, [2013] EWCA Civ 45, [2013] P.N.L.R. 19, Arden, L.J., CA (Civ Div).

228. Mortgages–Suspended possession orders–Mortgagor's failure to demonstrate ability to repay within reasonable time–Omissions in financial and employment information provided

[Administration of Justice Act 1970 (c.31) s.36(1).]

The appellant mortgagor (J) appealed against the decision to dismiss her application to suspend a warrant for possession of her residential property obtained by the respondent mortgagee (P). J had obtained a mortgage from P in 2006. From 2008 she fell into arrears with her mortgage repayments and P commenced proceedings against her. J's income at that point was insufficient to meet the mortgage repayments. In 2011 a district judge gave judgment in favour of P for the total owing and granted a possession order in favour of P and a second mortgagee of the property (K). That warrant was suspended on an application by J on the basis that she would meet her monthly instalments and make a monthly repayment towards the accrued arrears. J failed to make payment in accordance with that order and in 2012 a further warrant was issued. A district judge refused to suspend that order and that refusal was upheld on appeal despite J's contentions that her financial and employment circumstances had improved due to an offer of partnership and new lodger agreements that were in place. The appeal judge concluded that the financial commitment was beyond her means. Permission to appeal was granted on the condition that J filed up-to-date information concerning her employment and finances. At the time of the instant appeal J's second mortgage and a buy-to-let mortgage were both in arrears which amounted to £10,000. The issue was whether in light of the further information before the appeal judge, he was right to refuse to suspend the warrant for the second time.

Held: Appeal dismissed. J had not provided any wage slips and the lodger agreements she had filed had either expired or were in conflict with a tenancy agreement that J also exhibited. Her explanation for that had not been remotely convincing. It was clear that under the Administration of Justice Act 1970 s.36(1) there was a jurisdictional gateway which allowed the court to exercise its discretion in cases where there was evidence to show that a mortgagor could repay the sums due within a reasonable period of time, *Zinda v Bank of Scotland Plc* [2011] EWCA Civ 95 applied. It was only if that gateway was open that the court had power to suspend a warrant. The mortgagor had to present frankly and fully to the court information about their income and expenditure. Assuming that the jurisdictional gateway was open in the instant case, both judges below decided to exercise their discretion against J. She had not demonstrated an ability to adhere to the terms of the original suspension order and there remained too much uncertainty and obvious omissions by her in the information that she had presented about her employment and finances. On her own account she had had the ability to make the repayments but had not done so. The judges had not considered irrelevant matters nor had they failed to take account of relevant factors in their decisions to refuse the suspension. Even on the up-to-date information, the court was not entitled to say that either of the judges had reached a decision which was plainly wrong. Other judges might have given J another chance to pay, however, the fact that the judges had not done so did not mean that their decisions were plainly wrong.

JAMEER v PARATUS AMc, [2012] EWCA Civ 1924, [2013] H.L.R. 18, Rix, L.J., CA (Civ Div).

229. National Savings Stock Register–Online services

THE NATIONAL SAVINGS STOCK REGISTER (AMENDMENT) REGULATIONS 2013, SI 2013/416; made under the National Debt Act 1972 s.3. In force: April 6, 2013; .

These Regulations amend the National Savings Stock Register Regulations 1976 (SI 1976/2012) to alter certain features of the variable interest stock offered by National Savings and Investments to modernise and make more cost-effective the administration of such stock and facilitate the introduction of a new computer system (which will enable online and telephone account management if required).

230. Private equity–Inter-creditor agreement–Power of security trustee to sell assets–Duties owed to subordinate lenders–Sale of assets to associated person

The claimant lender (S) sought a declaration that the restructure of a group of companies (X) was valid. X owed substantial sums of money to various lenders. The second defendant (J) had been appointed security trustee under an inter-creditor agreement (ICA). X ran into serious financial difficulties. J carried out a restructure of X on the instructions of the preferential lenders under the ICA, including S and the third and fourth parties. The first, third and fifth defendant subordinate lenders (M) did not consent to the restructuring, and their security was sold. Under the restructure X's business was transferred to the third and fourth parties, subject to the loans of the preferential lenders. M asserted that the restructure was effected without authority and was therefore void. In the alternative M claimed equitable compensation from J for breach of duty. The court was required to determine whether J had complied with its fiduciary duties and the duties it owed under cl.14 and cl.15 of the ICA. M submitted that J owed fiduciary duties to it. M also argued that where charged assets were sold to an associated party, J owed a special duty to obtain and follow expert advice as to the method of sale.

Held: Declaration granted in favour of claimant. (1) A person could be in a fiduciary position regarding a part of his activities and not regarding other parts. The suggestion that because J was a fiduciary in some respects it was a fiduciary in all respects was wrong. In the instant case the relevant duties were concerned with enforcement, and the ICA delineated the scope and nature of the duties. Under cl.14, J, as security trustee, was to enforce the security only at the request of the preferential lenders. They were given the right to control the timing and manner of enforcement, even though that could be detrimental to M, and J was obliged to follow their instructions. Clause 14.3 stated that J's only duty to M in relation to sale was that of mortgagee to mortgagor, which was not a fiduciary duty. J was therefore obliged to take reasonable care to obtain the true market value and/or the best price reasonably obtainable for the transaction security at the time of sale or disposal, and to exercise the power of sale bona fide and for its proper purpose (see paras 123, 130 of judgment). (2) Where the sale of a charged asset was to a connected, affiliated or associated person there was no absolute obligation for the mortgagee to take and act upon independent expert advice as to the steps which ought to be taken to make the sale a success, *Tse Kwong Lam v Wong Chit Sen* [1983] 1 W.L.R. 1349, [1983]

C.L.Y. 2484 considered. The authorities did not prescribe any particular procedure which a mortgagee should adopt in deciding the manner in which the charged asset should be sold, whether as to marketing, advertising or otherwise, *Silven Properties Ltd v Royal Bank of Scotland Plc* [2003] EWCA Civ 1409, [2004] 1 W.L.R. 997, [2004] C.L.Y. 3240 and *Michael v Miller* [2004] EWCA Civ 282, [2004] 2 E.G.L.R. 151, [2004] C.L.Y. 3259 considered. All that could be said was that the mortgagee had to take reasonable steps in the circumstances and those steps had to be looked at in the round, in practical commercial terms (paras 135-138, 144). (3) When X fell into financial difficulties, their advisers had carried out a limited marketing and sales process. It was carried out to a tight timetable in a holiday period, it had not had the benefit of the competitive tension which would have arisen if the process had progressed and it did not necessarily provide guidance as to what a proper market price might be several months later. J had relied upon that valuation as a guide to the appropriate price. However, that did not mean that J had breached its duty under cl.14 because: (a) there was no absolute obligation upon J to carry out a marketing and sale process; (b) despite the limited nature of the valuation process carried out on X's behalf, it was useful in that it pointed to a value which was well below the debt owed to the preferential lenders; (c) J had obtained an independent valuation, which, although only a desktop valuation, had been produced in co-operation with X's management and was based on X's projections; (d) a further sales and marketing process would have been wholly impracticable as well as potentially damaging. X's value could have become more depressed if the fact that it was in considerable financial difficulties became more widely known; (e) if the restructuring had not been agreed in time, X would have filed for insolvency; (f) even if J had carried out a full marketing and sale process, the overwhelming likelihood was that the price obtained would not have been higher than the liabilities owed to the preferential lenders. It followed that M had not suffered any loss, and there was no actionable breach of duty by J, *Newport Farm Ltd v Damesh Holdings Ltd* [2003] UKPC 54, Times, July 15, 2003, [2003] C.L.Y. 3584 applied (paras 139-141, 146-154, 202-205, 211-213). (4) J had not breached its obligations under cl.15.2 of the ICA concerning disposal of assets after enforcement action. M's debt had been "under water" and therefore had no value at the time of the restructure (paras 214-220).

SALTRI III LTD v MD MEZZANINE SA SICAR (T/A MEZZANINE FACILITY AGENT), [2012] EWHC 3025 (Comm), [2013] 1 All E.R. (Comm) 661, Eder, J., QBD (Comm).

231. Prospectuses–Securities–Securities markets–Trading

THE PROSPECTUS REGULATIONS 2013, SI 2013/1125; made under the European Communities Act 1972 s.2. In force: May 31, 2013; .

These draft Regulations amend the Financial Services and Markets Act 2000 to ensure complete transposition into domestic law of certain provisions of Directive 2010/73 on prospectuses published when securities are offered to the public or admitted to trading.

232. Supply and Appropriation (Anticipation and Adjustments) Act 2013 (28)

This Act authorises the use of resources for the years ending with March 31 2010, March 31 2011, March 31 2012, March 31 2013 and March 31 2014; authorises the issue of sums out of the Consolidated Fund for the years ending with March 31 2013 and March 31 2014; and appropriates the supply authorised by this Act for the years ending with March 31 2010, March 31 2011, 31 March 2012 and March 31 2013.

This Act received Royal Assent on March 26, 2013.

233. Supply and Appropriation (Main Estimates) Act 2013 (c.28)

This Act provides Parliamentary authority for funds requested by the Government. It is part of "supply procedure", which is how Parliament grants the Government's requests for resources.

This Act received Royal Assent on July 17, 2013.

CHARITIES

234. Charities–Churches–England and Wales

THE CHARITIES (INCORPORATED CHURCH BUILDING SOCIETY) (ENGLAND AND WALES) ORDER 2013, SI 2013/641; made under the Charities Act 2011 s.73, s.353. In force: March 27, 2013; .

This Order is made gives effect to the provisions contained in a Scheme settled by the Charity Commission for the administration of the Unincorporated Society for Promoting the Enlargement, Building and Repairing of Churches and Chapels. The purpose of the Scheme is to amend the existing trusts of the Charity and to simplify its administrative provisions.

235. Charities–Further education colleges–Regulation

THE CHARITIES ACT 2011 (PRINCIPAL REGULATORS OF EXEMPT CHARITIES) REGULATIONS 2013, SI 2013/1764; made under the Charities Act 2011 s.25, s.58, s.347. In force: September 1, 2013; .

These Regulations make provision for the regulation as charities of further education corporations in England and Wales and the governing body of Saint David's Catholic College, and any charities connected to them.

236. Charities–Non-domestic rates–Nature of applicable test under s.43(6)(a) Local Government Finance Act 1988

[Local Government Finance Act 1988 (c.41) s.43(6), s.43(6)(a).]

The court was required to consider by way of case stated the nature of the test for relief for charities from non-domestic rates in respect of commercial properties. A registered charity had taken leases of commercial premises in respect of which the owner would be otherwise liable to pay non-domestic rates. The leases were for a peppercorn rent and terminable on short notice. Under the leases, the landlord would pay a reverse premium to the charity, on the basis that as a charity, it could claim relief from the payment of non-domestic rates as an occupier of the relevant hereditament, which was "wholly or mainly used for charitable purposes" under the Local Government Finance Act 1988 s.43(6)(a). In that way the savings gained from the rate relief were shared between the charity and the landlord. In each of the leased premises, the charity arranged for the placement of a single or multiple transmitters, which took up minimal physical space, through which it provided free wireless internet access to those with access and within range. The provision of that service was charitable in nature. In two of the instant appeals, the charity appealed against the imposition of liability orders, while in the third appeal, the appellant local authority (C) appealed against the refusal of a liability order by a district judge. The issues were (i) the basis on which s.43(6)(a) ought to be interpreted; (ii) whether the district judge in C's appeal had erred in law.

Held: Judgment accordingly. (1) In the context of the relevant legislation and having regard to the language used in s.43(6), it was reasonable to infer that Parliament intended that the substantial mandatory exemption from rates for charities in occupation should depend on the charity actually making extensive use of the premises for charitable purposes, rather than leaving them mainly unused, *Kenya Aid Programme v Sheffield City Council* [2013] EWHC 54 (Admin), [2014] Q.B. 62, [2013] 6 C.L. 253 followed and *English Speaking Union Scottish Branches Educational Fund v Edinburgh City Council* [2009] CSOH 139, 2009 S.L.T. 1051, [2010] C.L.Y. 4486 applied. Moreover, the use of the word "wholly" in s.43(6) was not deprived of meaning under the extent of use interpretation; a building could fairly and properly be described as being wholly used for a particular purpose even though not every metre of floor space was in constant use; it could not therefore be concluded that the word "wholly" in the phrase "wholly or mainly used for charitable purposes" had no meaning or proper function if the extent of use interpretation of s.43(6) was adopted (see paras 34-35, 37 of judgment). (2) In C's appeal, the district judge had erred as it had not been properly open to him to question or set aside the wifi hereditament, and that on the proper and ordinary construction of the entry for the wifi hereditament in the local rating list, he should have held that it covered the entire wifi network installed and not just a single transmitter thereof. The district judge's treatment of 12 of the 13 transmitters as being part of the main hereditament amounted to a material error of law. There was also force in C's submission that the district judge had erred in saying that fairness dictated that the hereditament ought to be construed narrowly; fairness was not a sound basis for assuming that a narrow or a wide construction should be adopted. Rather, the magistrate's task was to construe the description of the hereditament in the list in an objective way that was neutral between the parties (paras 47, 50-52). (3) It was not open to challenge the validity of a hereditament in enforcement proceedings in the magistrates' court; a separate, dedicated avenue was available for that, by making a proposal for amendment of the list and pursuing an appeal to the Valuation Tribunal for England and the Upper Tribunal if necessary. Until challenged and changed by that avenue, the designation of a hereditament in the list was conclusive in law as to its meaning (paras 48-49).

PUBLIC SAFETY CHARITABLE TRUST v MILTON KEYNES COUNCIL; PUBLIC SAFETY CHARITABLE TRUST v SOUTH CAMBRIDGESHIRE DC; CHESHIRE WEST AND CHESTER BC v PUBLIC SAFETY CHARITABLE TRUST, [2013] EWHC 1237 (Admin), [2013] 2 E.G.L.R. 133, Sales, J., QBD (Admin).

237. Charities Act 2011 (c.25)–Commencement No.2 Order

THE CHARITIES ACT 2011 (COMMENCEMENT NO.2) ORDER 2013, SI 2013/SI 2013/1775 (C.73); made under the Charities Act 2011 Sch.1 para.29. Commencement details: bringing into force various provisions of the 2011 Act on September 1, 2013.; .

This Order brings into force certain provisions of the Charities Act 2011 for the purposes of specified exempt charities in the further education sector.

238. Community amateur sports clubs–Gift aid

THE SMALL CHARITABLE DONATIONS REGULATIONS 2013, SI 2013/938; made under the Small Charitable Donations Act 2012 s.11, s.12, s.13, s.17. In force: April 19, 2013; .

These Regulations contain the administrative framework for the Gift Aid Small Donations Scheme, which will allow charities and community amateur sports clubs to claim a gift aid style top-up payment on cash donations of £20 or less received in circumstances where it is difficult to collect donors' details, such as street collections.

239. Memorandums of association–Adoption agencies–Justification for religious charity's discriminatory practice–Non-provision of adoption services to same-sex couples–Failure to show weighty and convincing reasons for amendment

[Equality Act 2010 (c.15) s.193; European Convention on Human Rights 1950 Art.14.]

The appellant Roman Catholic charity (R) appealed against a dismissal of its appeal against the respondent Charity Commission's refusal to consent to an amendment of its memorandum of association. R had a practice of only providing adoption services to heterosexual couples. It received an inter-agency fee from local authorities for a successful placement and was supported in its work by funds raised through the church. The amendment to R's memorandum was necessitated by the enactment of the Equality Act 2010, which provided a limited exemption for charities under s.193 under which a person would not contravene the Act if benefits were restricted if that person acted in pursuance of a charitable instrument, and the restriction was a proportionate means of achieving a legitimate aim. The proposed amendment would explicitly state that R would only provide its adoption services to heterosexuals. The First-tier Tribunal concluded that although R had a legitimate aim, for the purposes of s.193, of seeking to place more children with adoptive families, the evidence did not support that that aim would be achieved by its proposed discrimination and that it was not objectively justified under s.193. R submitted that the discrimination was objectively justified because (1) it achieved the legitimate aim of placing more children with adoptive families; (2) if the amendment was permitted, R could potentially raise money through the church to enable it to offer its services without taking an inter-agency fee.

Held: Appeal dismissed. (1) The tribunal was right to conclude that R had not shown that there were weighty and convincing reasons why it should be permitted to change its memorandum of association in order to enable it to discriminate against homosexuals as proposed, *EB v France (43546/02)* [2008] 1 F.L.R. 850, [2008] C.L.Y. 1980, *Karner v Austria (40016/98)* [2003] 2 F.L.R. 623, [2004] C.L.Y. 1983 and *Kozak v Poland (13102/02)* (2010) 51 E.H.R.R. 16 applied. Although the extent of the benefits to children and the likelihood that such benefits might be achieved if R were allowed to discriminate were relevant considerations, the tribunal had been entitled to conclude that, for reasons associated with the inter-agency fee arrangements, the aim identified by R would not be achieved through its proposed discrimination, *P (A Child) (Adoption: Unmarried Couples), Re* [2008] UKHL 38, [2009] 1 A.C. 173, [2008] C.L.Y. 4303 and *Smith and Grady v United Kingdom* (1999) 27 E.H.R.R. CD42 considered. There was not a material probability that the number of children placed in adoptive care would be increased by R's work as children who might have potentially found adoptive parents through R's adoption service were likely to be placed elsewhere with suitable adoptive parents, by another voluntary adoption service (see paras 31, 54-55 of judgment). (2) The tribunal had considered the possibility of R potentially providing adoption services without the inter-agency fee but R's vague and speculative suggestion of offering free services could not begin to amount to weighty and convincing reasons which were sufficient to discharge the heavy onus on R to show that its proposed discrimination would be objectively justified under European Convention on Human Rights 1950 art.14 and s.193. Although some criticism could be made of the tribunal's reasoning and it had erred in some respects, its conclusion was correct in law (paras 57-58, 61-64).

CATHOLIC CARE (DIOCESE OF LEEDS) v CHARITY COMMISSION FOR ENGLAND AND WALES, [2012] UKUT 395 (TCC), [2013] 1 W.L.R. 2105, Sales, J., UT (Tax).

240. Objects clauses–Sexual orientation discrimination–Application to amend objects clause–Proposed exclusion of same-sex couples from adoption services

[Adoption and Children Act 2002 (c.38); Equality Act (Sexual Orientation) Regulations 2007 (SI 2007/1263) reg.18; European Convention on Human Rights 1950 Art.8, Art.14.]

The charity commission was required to determine whether a Catholic charity (C) should be permitted to amend its objects. C ran a voluntary adoption agency as part of its activities. It wished to amend its objects to limit its adoption services to heterosexual potential parents. It did not propose to discriminate on the grounds of sexual orientation in the provision of its other services. C stated that its overriding principles had to accord with Catholic tenets, including the principle that the model of family life was the Holy Family of Nazareth. Hiving off its adoption services would result in a loss of income from the Church. C considered that if permission to amend its objects was not granted, the adoption service would have to close. It suspended its adoption service pending the outcome of its application. The commission refused C's request, but that decision was overturned in *Catholic Care (Diocese of Leeds) v Charity Commission for England and Wales* [2010] EWHC 520 (Ch), [2010] 4 All E.R.1041, [2010] C.L.Y. 241, and C's application was remitted to the commission for re-determination. The commission wrote to all of the local authorities with whom C worked. They confirmed that the suspension of C's adoption services had not affected the number of children they had placed for adoption. C argued that the closure of its adoption service would result in fewer children being adopted. C also maintained that the discrimination would not prevent homosexual couples from adopting a child, as they could adopt through other agencies.

Held: Application refused. (1) The commission was a public authority and was required to act in a way which was compatible with the European Convention on Human Rights 1950. The right of same-sex couples to be considered as prospective parents in adoption, and not to suffer discrimination, fell within art.8 and art.14. Under the Equality Act (Sexual Orientation) Regulations 2007 reg.18, benefits could be provided only to persons of a particular sexual orientation if it was pursuant to a charitable instrument. That exception only applied where the provision of benefits to persons of a particular sexual orientation was a proportionate means of achieving a legitimate aim. Accordingly, the commission had to decide whether limiting the adoption service to prospective parents who were heterosexual was a proportionate means of achieving the legitimate aim of providing suitable adoptive parents for a significant number of children who would otherwise not be provided for (see paras 29, 31-34, 39-45 of judgment). (2) The commission appreciated that C provided a valuable, high-quality service on which much love and care had been bestowed, and that if it was withdrawn, it might have a negative impact which was difficult to quantify. However, the evidence did not show insufficient capacity within other adoption agencies to take up the demand for prospective parents if C closed its adoption service. That was especially so given that the number of placements made by C in a year was about 10. It was further supported by the local authorities who had all been able to place the children they had for adoption. It was possible that there might be occasions where a child had to wait longer for an adoption place than would otherwise be the case, but in the light of all of the information available the effect of C closing its adoption service was not a sufficiently weighty reason to justify the proposed discrimination (paras 54-60, 63, 66). (3) Whenever a court or adoption agency was coming to a decision relating to the adoption of a child the paramount consideration was the child's welfare. There might be cases where a same-sex couple would be the most appropriate match for a particular child. Accordingly, for a charity to exclude such couples from its adoption process would prima facie mean that the door was not being opened as widely as possible in the best interests of the child as required by the Adoption and Children Act 2002, *P (A Child) (Adoption: Unmarried Couples), Re* [2008] UKHL 38, [2009] 1 A.C. 173, [2008] C.L.Y. 4303 applied (paras 69-71). (4) C had asserted that gay and lesbian couples would not be disadvantaged by the proposed amendment to its objects. However, the availability of other routes to adoption for same-sex couples was not in itself appropriate justification for discrimination. Discrimination on the basis of sexual orientation was itself generally unacceptable to the community as well as to the individuals directly affected. Prohibition of such discrimination was a fundamental principle of human rights law, *Salgueiro da Silva Mouta v Portugal (33290/96)* [2001] 1 F.C.R. 653, [2001] C.L.Y. 2587, *EB v France (43546/02)* [2008] 1 F.L.R. 850, [2008] C.L.Y. 1980 and *R. (on the application of Carson) v Secretary of State for Work and Pensions* [2005] UKHL 37, [2006] 1 A.C. 173, [2005] C.L.Y. 3835 considered. Further, the fact that some donors would not fund C's work if it accepted same-sex couples as prospective parents did not justify the proposed discrimination because of the public nature of C's activities (paras 76, 92, 107).

(5) For all of those reasons the proposed amendment was not a proportionate means of achieving its legitimate aim.

CHARITY COMMISSION FOR ENGLAND AND WALES v CATHOLIC CARE (DIOCESE OF LEEDS) [2012] W.T.L.R. 1303, Charity Comm.

CIVIL EVIDENCE

241. Documents–Confidentiality–Claim for unlawful means conspiracy–Entitlement to rely on documents deployed in arbitration proceedings

The claimant shipping companies (W), which had brought an action claiming that various entities and individuals had been party to an unlawful means conspiracy to damage them, applied for permission to rely on documents deployed in arbitration proceedings between themselves and the first defendant German company (U). W were the time charterers of a vessel from U, U in turn having chartered the vessel from her head owners (K). Those charterparties were entered into at a time when W were using the vessel by way of a potential back-up for their trade. It transpired that they did not need her for that, so at a time when the market charterparty rates were very high they sub-chartered the vessel back to U. The market then dropped and U purported to terminate the sub-charter. W brought a claim against U for breach of the sub-charter and of the main charter between themselves and U. The matter was dealt with in a London arbitration. After the award was made, U went into liquidation in Germany. W wished to use the arbitration documents in support of a claim which they had issued in the Commercial Court. W alleged that certain entities and individuals had been party to an unlawful means conspiracy to damage them. W claimed that a backdated agreement had been prepared which purported to waive any rights that U had against K up the line, thereby precluding any claim under the head charter.

Held: Application granted. In *Michael Wilson & Partners Ltd v Emmott* [2008] EWCA Civ 184, [2008] 2 All E.R. (Comm) 193, [2008] C.L.Y. 166, the Court of Appeal set out four situations in respect of which the authorities had recognised that disclosure of arbitration documents would be permissible. The third was where disclosure was reasonably necessary for the protection of the legitimate interests of an arbitrating party. The fourth was where the interests of justice required disclosure. W had a very strong case for disclosure in both respects. They had a legitimate interest in pursuing the claim in unlawful means conspiracy, which, on the face of the pleading, was an arguable claim. It was a claim which they could not pursue properly, possibly not at all, unless they had access to the materials from the arbitration. Further, this was one of those cases in which the interests of justice clearly required disclosure, not just because otherwise W would be precluded from making what was otherwise an arguable claim, but also because the court should not allow the confidentiality of arbitration materials to stifle the ability to bring to light wrongdoing of one kind or another. It would therefore be appropriate to make the order sought. The documents in relation to which the order would be made comprised the written pleadings and submissions in the arbitration, all the disclosure in the arbitration, the witness statements, the experts' reports, the inter-solicitor correspondence, the correspondence with the tribunal, transcripts of the hearings, written opening and closing submissions, the award and the reasons, *Emmott* applied (see paras 13-15 of judgment).

WESTWOOD SHIPPING LINES INC v UNIVERSAL SCHIFFAHRTSGESELLSCHAFT MBH, [2012] EWHC 3837 (Comm), [2013] 1 Lloyd's Rep. 670, Flaux, J., QBD (Comm).

242. Expert evidence–Necessity–Case involving loss of chance–Court required to determine when matter would have been heard had referral been made–Whether expert evidence reasonably required

[Civil Procedure Rules 1998 (SI 1998/3132) r.35.1.]

The applicant (S) applied for permission to appeal against a case management decision in which he was refused permission to rely on an expert report. S had sought to rely on the report in the course of an action for professional negligence brought by him against the respondent (M). He claimed that M had not made a referral to the lands tribunal when it ought to have. His case centred on loss of chance, and the court was therefore required to determine the date on which the tribunal would have heard the case had a referral properly been made. S sought to adduce expert evidence about how long it would have taken to get to a final hearing before the tribunal, but the judge refused, holding that the question of when the case would have been heard was one of pure fact and was not a matter for expert evidence. He did, however, allow the factual material from the report to be put in a witness statement. S submitted that the judge was wrong to treat the matter as being a pure question of fact. He argued that the court would have to assess the length of time that a hypothetical case would have taken to come before the tribunal, and that evidence on that point amounted to opinion. He argued that the exercise carried out in the expert report was no different from that carried out by a valuer giving an opinion as to the correct valuation of a property.

Held: Application refused. The judge had taken the view that the issue was one on which the court could form a sound judgment on the basis of factual material alone, without the assistance of witnesses possessing special knowledge or experience. He concluded that, in terms of CPR r.35.1, expert evidence was not reasonably required to resolve the issue of when the case would have been heard, and that was a conclusion that was reasonably open to him. At the final hearing, the judge hearing the matter could extrapolate from the facts available and arrive at a sound judgment, on the balance of probabilities, as to the time it would have taken for a case to come to a hearing before the tribunal had it been referred when S said it should.

SPEAK v MYERSON, [2012] EWCA Civ 1723, [2013] R.V.R. 78, Richards, L.J., CA (Civ Div).

243. Judgments and orders–Mistake of fact–Judge's refusal to correct apparent typographical error–Effect of mistake on judge's consideration of other factual issues–Irregularity

The appellant (S) appealed against a decision of the High Court dismissing its action against the respondent (G), its former employee. G resigned his position as sales manager for S and took up employment with one of S's competitors (C). Several months before tendering his resignation, G printed out customer summaries containing information as to discounts given to customers. His explanation for printing those documents was that they were required to show the context of a dispute which had arisen concerning a credit limit given to one customer. S brought proceedings, alleging that G had acted in breach of contract by printing the documents and by passing customer contact details to C. The judge accepted G's evidence about the printouts as plausible and consistent with other contemporaneous evidence. The judgment was handed down without having previously been made available to counsel in draft. Paragraph 39 of the judgment stated that "The main documents relied upon were customer summaries. It is notable that such summaries do not show important discount information". The inclusion of the word not? was an error. In dismissing the action, the judge stated that S had not made out its case that G had used the discount information unlawfully. When the error was pointed out to the judge, she acknowledged it but declined to correct it as a typographical slip and refused permission to appeal on the ground that the inferences which S asked the court to draw could not be drawn from the facts found. S contended that the erroneous finding in para.39 meant that it had not had a fair trial of its case because there was a real doubt as to whether the judge appreciated the importance of the confidentiality factor which was central to its claim. S submitted that that error had coloured the judge's assessment of the evidence on other issues concerning G and C's actions.

Held: Appeal allowed. The court was faced with a choice between allowing the appeal and ordering a re-trial, or dismissing the appeal on the ground that the admittedly incorrect finding of fact did not make the judge's decision wrong, or constitute an irregularity that made it unjust. If a judgment contained what the judge acknowledged was an error when it was pointed out, the judgment should be corrected unless there was some very good reason for not doing so. A judgment should be an accurate record of the judge's findings and of the reasons for the decision. It should not normally be necessary for a party to bring an appeal to correct an error, if it turned out that the parties and the judge agreed that an error existed and that a correction should be made. Before the correction was made, the judge should give both sides an opportunity to make submissions on whether there was a valid objection to a proposed amendment of the judgment. In the instant case, it was impossible to accept that the likely explanation for the error was typographical only. Although that kind of mistake could easily happen, it was usually obvious and capable of being corrected by the omission of the word included in error. However, given the wording and immediate context of the key sentence in the instant case and the judge's decision not to amend the judgment, despite acknowledgement of the error, the court could not say with any confidence that the error was only a typographical one, when the judge herself would not say that it was. The error was on a material aspect of the case, namely the nature of the information in the customer summaries, which contained information which one would expect someone to print out if they were preparing to breach confidentiality. There was no point in remitting the matter to the judge for her to amplify her judgment, as she had already declined to do that when the error was pointed out. If the appeal were allowed on the ground of admitted error in the finding in para.39, the court would be acting on the basis of an assessment of the likely impact on the rest of the judgment resulting from an admitted error relating to a material, possibly fundamental, fact of the case. Given the admitted uncorrected error, it was unsafe to assume that it had no material impact on the judge s consideration of other factual issues in the case. It was possible that she had proceeded on a mistaken view of the contents of S's confidential customer documents. The appeal was therefore allowed on the ground that the decision below was either wrong or unjust as a result of an irregularity and the matter was remitted to the High Court for re-trial by a different judge (paras 8, 53-54, 60-64, 66).

SPACE AIRCONDITIONING PLC v GUY, [2012] EWCA Civ 1664, [2013] 1 W.L.R. 1293, Mummery, L.J., CA (Civ Div).

244. Legal professional privilege–Professional negligence–Professional negligence proceedings against solicitors operating as waiver of legal professional privilege–Whether privilege extended to counsel's advice

The applicant firm of solicitors (M), who were the defendants to a professional negligence action, sought a declaration that the respondent trustees in bankruptcy (X) of an individual (S) had waived legal professional privilege in relation to counsel's advice. It was alleged that M had acted negligently in failing to advise S properly on limitation issues. Both parties wished to refer to the advice of counsel in their pleadings. X submitted that privilege attaching to papers in counsel's possession but to which the clients and solicitors were not necessarily privy would remain privileged because counsel had not been sued.

Held: Application granted. Privilege would attach to confidential communications between solicitors, counsel and their clients. Once there had been a waiver in relation to those communications, any evidence as to those communications could be adduced, including evidence of anyone who was privy to the giving of the advice in question. The decision in *Paragon Finance Plc (formerly National Home Loans Corp) v Freshfields* [1999] 1 W.L.R. 1183, [1999] C.L.Y. 4024 did not cover that situation, as the new solicitors were not acting jointly with, or as agents of, the former solicitors, Paragon considered.

There was a new and separate retainer. As privilege had been waived in relation to counsel's advice, counsel could be asked about it, including before the trial itself, by any party to the proceedings and could give a witness statement to that party. The waiver would extend to the entirety of counsel's recall, working papers and notes, and not just to the parts of it that X had chosen to reveal by referring to counsel's advice in the pleadings. The waiver also extended to working papers and deliberations of counsel to which the solicitor may not have been directly privy. Those working papers, which must have been based upon or reflected the instructions received by counsel or legal advice given or to be given by him were equally subject to implied waiver because fairness required that by the bringing of the instant proceedings, M should be entitled to rely upon all evidence concerning relevant privileged communications (see paras 9-16 of judgment).

HELLARD v IRWIN MITCHELL, [2012] EWHC 2656 (Ch), [2012] B.P.I.R. 1132, Judge Purle Q.C., Ch D (Birmingham).

245. Litigation privilege–Contractor claiming documents produced with dominant purpose of contemplated litigation

The court was required to determine whether documents held by the defendant contractor (D) should be disclosed under its contract with the claimant (C). C was the body responsible for co-ordinating a city's public transport services and had engaged D to install and test a tram operating system. It issued Part 8 proceedings for specific performance of a contractual obligation to disclose certain documents, including documents relating to the involvement in the project of a firm of consultants (N). D resisted disclosing a report from N on the basis that it had been produced for the dominant purpose of contemplated litigation and was therefore covered by litigation privilege.

Held: Judgment for claimant. The onus of proof that documents were subject to litigation privilege was on the party asserting such privilege. It was not enough that there were two equal reasons why the documents had come into being, where one of them was in contemplation of litigation, because neither reason would then be a dominant one such as to justify a claim for litigation privilege. The exercise of determining whether that onus had been discharged rested with the judge, to be based on all the available information, *West London Pipeline & Storage Ltd v Total UK Ltd* [2008] EWHC 1729 (Comm), [2008] 2 C.L.C. 258, [2009] C.L.Y. 332 applied. On the evidence, D had not come near establishing that the dominant purpose of the report was contemplated litigation. There were omissions and discrepancies in the evidence filed on D's behalf. It did not appear that D's solicitors had been asked to verify the basis of the claim for privilege. There was no evidence from N and, extremely surprisingly, apparently no written instruction to it about the report which might reasonably have been expected if there was to be a departure from its previous retainer to something whose dominant purpose was contemplated litigation (see paras 9-12 of judgment).

TRANSPORT FOR GREATER MANCHESTER (FORMERLY GREATER MANCHESTER PASSENGER TRANSPORT EXECUTIVE) v THALES TRANSPORT & SECURITY LTD, [2013] EWHC 149 (TCC), [2013] B.L.R. 339, Akenhead, J., QBD (TCC).

246. Private hearings–Open justice–Respondents to unfair prejudice petition seeking private hearings to protect their reputation–Application of open justice principle to interlocutory proceedings

[Civil Procedure Rules 1998 (SI 1998/3132) r.39.2(3); European Convention on Human Rights 1950 Art.6, Art.8, Art.10.]

The appellants (G) appealed against a decision ([2013] EWHC 223 (Ch)) refusing their application that certain interlocutory hearings be held in private. The proceedings concerned competing unfair prejudice petitions about the same company. Each petition made serious allegations of misconduct. G, who were the company, two Saudi Arabian princes and a private adviser to one of the princes, had applied to have all the interlocutory hearings held in private under CPR r.39.2(3). The judge held that publicity would not defeat the object of any of the anticipated hearings, and that the importance of the principle of open justice was greater than the importance to be attached to G's reputations. G argued that (1) the judge had wrongly treated the open justice principle as inherently superior to, or meriting more weight than, competing rights under the European Convention on Human Rights 1950 art.8; (2) the judge did not apply the approach mandated by *Guardian News and Media Ltd, Re* [2010] UKSC 1, [2010] 2 A.C. 697, [2010] C.L.Y. 4 by failing to ask whether there was sufficient public interest in maintaining the open justice principle to justify the resulting curtailment of G's reputational rights under art.8; (3) the judge failed to carry out a balanced assessment of whether, and if so to what extent, the open justice principle and art.10 freedom of expression rights required the curtailment of G's art.8 rights, in particular their reputational rights; (4) the judge had failed to give due weight to G's art.6 fair trial rights in the sense that it was their case that the purpose in making allegations of egregious misconduct was abusive and designed to extort an unfair settlement or withdrawal; (5) the case should be seen as one in which G were seeking protection on an interim basis in circumstances where they were at risk of irremediable damage; (6) on a proper application of the correct approach, the only outcome was the grant of the protection sought.

Held: Appeal dismissed. (1) The judge had not accorded the open justice principle inherent superiority as a matter of law. In effect, he had said that, in general, and after consideration of the details of a particular case, the open justice principle prevailed. The competing rights did not exist within a presumptive legal hierarchy, but that did not mean that in given situations, for example open justice versus reputational damage, one would not generally trump the other, *S (A Child) (Identification: Restrictions on Publication), Re* [2004] UKHL 47, [2005] 1 A.C. 593, [2005] C.L.Y. 2121 considered. What was important was that a judge approached the balancing exercise in the correct way in the circumstances of the particular case (see para.25 of judgment). (2) Although the judge did not expressly set his consideration of the competing rights in the matrix of *Guardian News and Media*, he did refer to *Re S*. If a judge adhered to Lord Steyn's four propositions in *Re S* he would have also asked the question identified in *Guardian News and Media*, *Guardian News and Media* considered. The reference in Lord Steyn's second proposition to "an intense focus" on the comparative importance of the specific rights being claimed did not mean that every time a litigant relied on art.8 in support of an application for a private hearing there would have to be a protracted and expensive hearing to determine the issue; usually it could be determined very quickly (paras 26-27). (3) The judge had correctly applied the law to the instant case (para.29). (4) There had been nothing wrong in the judge's approach to the submission that the proceedings were being used to extort an unwarranted settlement. A person alleged to have committed serious misconduct would always be at significant risk of reputational damage. However, if the allegations were false he would obtain his vindication through the judicial process, if not as a result of an interlocutory application, then after a trial (paras 32-33). (4) There was no warrant for a general lowering of the bar for open justice in interlocutory hearings. Outside the area of statutory or other established exceptions, the open justice principle had universal application except where it was strictly necessary to depart from it in the interests of justice, whether at the interim or final stage. Sometimes a degree of protection was needed to avoid exposing a victim to the very detriment that his cause of action was designed to prevent, but to extend that to commercial cases in which misconduct was alleged would significantly erode the open justice principle and was not justified where adequate protection existed in the form of vindication of the innocent through the trial process itself (para.34). (6) The judge's conclusion had been inevitable (para.35).

FI CALL LTD, *Re*; *sub nom.* GLOBAL TORCH LTD v APEX GLOBAL MANAGEMENT LTD; APEX GLOBAL MANAGEMENT LTD v FI CALL LTD, [2013] EWCA Civ 819, [2013] 1 W.L.R. 2993, Maurice Kay, L.J., CA (Civ Div).

247. Public interest immunity–Disclosure–Possibility of ordering disclosure of material to parties within confidentiality ring–Need for consent by lawyers representing party outside confidentiality ring

The court had to determine whether information, in respect of which public interest immunity had been claimed, could be provided only to the lawyers representing the claimant (M) by means of a confidentiality ring.

Held: Judgment accordingly. The starting point was the fundamental principles of a right to a fair trial and the right to know the reasons for the outcome, *Al-Rawi v Security Service* [2011] UKSC 34, [2012] 1 A.C. 531, [2011] C.L.Y. 261 applied. The best way to achieve a fair trial was to ensure that a party had the fullest information of the allegations against him and the evidence in support. However, lawyers could consent to a restriction in respect of material disclosed to them, provided they were satisfied that they could do so without damaging their client's interests, *R. v G* [2004] EWCA Crim 1368, [2004] 1 W.L.R. 2932, [2004] C.L.Y. 872 and *R. v Davis (Michael George) (No.1)* [1993] 1 W.L.R. 613, [1994] C.L.Y. 878 considered. In the instant case, M's counsel would not see any documents in respect of which the claim to public interest immunity was upheld. The proposal for the confidentiality ring only entailed disclosure to counsel on a confidential basis once the court had seen the documents and heard argument as to where the balance between the public interest in non-disclosure and the public interest in the administration of justice lay. There was no question of pre-empting the ruling, *Somerville v Scottish Ministers* [2007] UKHL 44, [2007] 1 W.L.R. 2734, [2008] C.L.Y. 4963 considered. In ruling in favour of a confidentiality ring, a court was deciding that the public interest demanded not complete immunity, but rather that it could be protected by a more limited form of confidentiality. There was no principle in *Somerville* which precluded a confidentiality ring once the judge had had an opportunity to consider whether the public interest immunity claim could be upheld. The arrangement provided by means of a confidentiality ring appeared to be exactly what was suggested in *R. v Chief Constable of the West Midlands, Ex p. Wiley* [1995] 1 A.C. 274, [1996] C.L.Y. 876, *Wiley* considered. A confidentiality ring would not avoid all problems, but it would bring inequality of arms back to a point nearer equilibrium; although some evidence would be unavailable only to one party, his lawyers within the ring would know of it and could deploy it in their client's favour despite being unable to consult him as to the content of the material disclosed. They understood their client's needs better than a Special Advocate. In the instant case M was unlikely to have anything useful to add, because of the particular contents of the documents and as he was in prison in Afghanistan and there were no means of communicating with him, it was not clear how he could give any meaningful instructions anyway. A confidentiality ring could only exist where the client's legal team consented and was of the view that it would not damage their client's interests. Whilst the fact of M's lawyers consent to a confidentiality ring distinguished the instant case from *Al-Rawi*, that fact could not be dispositive. The secretary of state's objections, on the grounds that the ring would fail to maintain the confidentiality necessary to protect the public interest, were not matters of principle, but related to the circumstances of any particular case. There was no reason why the nature and description of that which had to be confined to the ring should not be carefully prescribed. If that was not possible, then that was a powerful argument against the use of a ring. The dangers of inadvertent disclosure in a judicial review case should not prevent disclosure to a ring. It was significant that confidentiality rings were used in competition cases without the suggestion of it being contrary to the fundamental principles inherent in a fair trial. There was no principle which prohibited a court from ordering that, whilst a claim for public interest immunity should not be upheld, the material should only be disclosed to those identified within a confidentiality ring on the terms specified in the parties' undertaking (see paras 7-8, 10, 14-15, 17, 20-22, 24-27 of judgment).

R. (ON THE APPLICATION OF MOHAMMED) v SECRETARY OF STATE FOR DEFENCE, [2012] EWHC 3454 (Admin), [2013] 2 All E.R. 897, Moses, L.J., QBD (Admin).

248. Specific disclosure–Foreign proceedings–Claim for damages arising out of illegal cartel–Application for specific disclosure against French companies–Effect of French law prohibiting foreign companies from seeking disclosure for purposes of foreign proceedings

[Regulation 1206/2001 on cooperation between the courts of the Member States in the taking of evidence in civil or commercial matters; Regulation 44/2001 on jurisdiction and the recognition and enforcement of judgments in civil and commercial matters Art.6(1).]

The applicant (N) applied for specific disclosure against the sixth, ninth, tenth and twenty-second respondents (F), all of whom were French companies. N claimed that it had suffered substantial losses because of overcharges resulting from an illegal cartel. Extensive disclosure had been given by the English respondents, namely those other than F. In the instant application, N sought the same level of disclosure from F as it had received from the other respondents. F resisted N's application on the basis of French law no.68-678, art.1 bis of which prohibited any person from requesting documents or information of an economic, commercial, industrial, financial or technical nature for the purposes of establishing evidence in view of foreign judicial proceedings. F argued that providing the disclosure sought by N would put them in breach of art.1 bis, which attracted criminal penalties, and therefore that disclosure should not be ordered. F also cross-applied for an order that the instant court make a request to the French court for the taking of evidence in accordance with Regulation 1206/2001. The expert for the sixth, ninth and twenty-second respondents produced two reports on the effect of art.1 bis. He stated that, although he did not know of any cases where French companies had been prosecuted for providing disclosure in breach of art.1 bis, it was possible that there had been such cases which had not been reported. He also explained that, as a law introducing a criminal penalty, art.1 bis would be strictly interpreted according to its unambiguous wording, and therefore that making the disclosure would constitute a violation.

Held: Application granted. (1) The court proceeded on the basis that production of the documents by F would infringe art.1 bis. The critical question was the likelihood of any prosecution being brought against F; on that issue, the respondents' expert's opinion was not at all persuasive. He failed to address the frequency with which French companies gave discovery in English proceedings, and his suggestion that there might have been other, unknown prosecutions was speculative. The context of the French statute was significant: art.1 bis had been introduced because of concern in France at what were seen as abusive discovery requests being made of French companies facing litigation, in particular in the United States. Even when French companies complied with regular US disclosure orders, it appeared that they were not prosecuted. Further, the nature and circumstances of the instant proceedings were important. Jurisdiction over F was exercised alongside the English respondents pursuant to Regulation 44/2001 art.6(1). Where jurisdiction over a company was exercised pursuant to an EU regulation to make it a defendant to proceedings in another Member State, for damages alleged to result from an established and serious violation of a fundamental provision of EU law, which proceedings served an objective of EU policy, it was virtually inconceivable that the public authorities of one Member State would in the exercise of their discretion institute criminal proceedings against that company for complying with the procedural rules of the courts of the Member State where the proceedings were brought. Again, that was not a point that the expert had directly considered (see paras 41-48 of judgment). (2) The existence of the 2006 Regulation did not mean that it was inappropriate to order F to provide disclosure. The 2006 Regulation was not basically concerned with the provision of disclosure between parties to litigation at all, *Masri v Consolidated Contractors International Co SAL* [2008] EWCA Civ 876, [2009] 2 W.L.R. 699, [2008] C.L.Y. 371 considered. Further, the relevant authorities did not support F's argument for use of the 2006 Regulation for the taking of evidence. It followed that it was appropriate to order F to provide specific disclosure and to refuse F's cross-application under the 2006 Regulation (paras 49-51, 58).

NATIONAL GRID ELECTRICITY TRANSMISSION PLC v ABB LTD, [2013] EWHC 822 (Ch), [2013] U.K.C.L.R. 177, Roth, J., Ch D.

CIVIL PROCEDURE

249. Abuse of process–Striking out–Previous decision by arbitral tribunal on same issue as that raised in instant action

The first and second defendants (S and C) applied for an order striking out the claim made by the claimant company (M). S was the managing director of and a major shareholder in C, a company with interests in Kazakhstan. M provided legal and business consultancy services; at the material time, the Part 20 defendant (E) was a director and employee of M. C had engaged M in relation to a transaction involving the purchase and on-sale of interests in certain oilfields in Kazakhstan to a listed company. Shortly before the transaction was concluded, certain shares were issued to the third defendant (X), a company in which E had an interest. It was M's case that the shares were issued to X for the benefit of E as his reward for his participation in and contribution to the transaction; that as E had been involved in the transaction as its agent and employee, the shares ought to have come to it; and that, wrongfully and in breach of his contractual and fiduciary duties, E had connived with S and C to divert the shares to himself (through X). S and C asserted, on the other hand, that the shares were issued to X for the sole benefit of S; that X was used as an offshore vehicle to receive the shares because the offshore trust structure which S had asked E to set up had not been completed in time; and that the shares were held by X on bare trust for S. The dispute had been the subject of an arbitration award, M having commenced arbitration proceedings against E pursuant to the arbitration clause in his contract of engagement. The arbitrators found in favour of E, holding that M had no claim to the shares and that they were held to S's order. S was not a party to the arbitration but he did give evidence in it. He also funded E's defence. In the instant action, M alleged that S and C had dishonestly assisted E in committing a breach of fiduciary duty. S and C argued, among other things, that (1) there was privity of estate between S and E such that M was estopped from making allegations against S which contradicted the findings of the arbitral tribunal; (2) it would be an abuse of the process of the court to permit M to challenge the findings of that tribunal.

Held: Judgment accordingly. (1) It was not disputed that estoppel *per rem judicatam* worked mutually so that a person could only take the benefit of an estoppel if he would have been prejudiced by the decision had it gone the other way. If the arbitrators had decided in favour of M, that decision would not have been binding on S, as he was not a party to the arbitration. Accordingly, M could not be estopped, as against S, from alleging that which the arbitrators had rejected (see para.44 of judgment). (2) As to the doctrine of abuse of process, the first question was whether it could apply where the previous decision was that of an arbitral tribunal. There was high authority for saying that it was unwise to limit to fixed categories the circumstances in which it was the court's duty to prevent its processes from being abused, *Hunter v Chief Constable of the West Midlands* [1982] A.C. 529, [1982] C.L.Y. 2382 and *Arthur JS Hall & Co v Simons* [2002] 1 A.C. 615, [2000] C.L.Y. 4269 considered. There could therefore be no rule that the court could have no such duty merely because the tribunal whose decision was under attack was an arbitral tribunal. However, it would probably be a rare case where an action in this court against a non-party to an arbitration could be said to be an abuse of process. Where a claimant had a claim against two or more persons and was obliged to bring one such claim in arbitration, the defeat of that claim in arbitration would not usually prevent the claimant from pursuing his claim against the other persons in litigation. Arbitrations were private and consensual and non-parties could not, in the absence of consent, be joined or be affected by the decisions of the arbitral tribunal. The second question was whether M's claims in this action amounted to a collateral attack on the findings of the tribunal and were an abuse of the process of the court. The burden of proof was on S, and the test was "exacting", *Calyon v Michailaidis* [2009] UKPC 34 considered. That was especially so where the decision under collateral attack was that of an arbitral tribunal. There was no doubt that the factual allegations being made in this action as to E's conduct mirrored exactly the failed allegations in the arbitration; there was therefore a collateral challenge to the findings of the arbitral tribunal. On the other hand, S had not been a party to the arbitration; this action was therefore the only means by which M could bring its claim against him. Had those been the only material circumstances, a finding of abuse of process would not have been justified. However, special circumstances were present which did justify such a finding: first, S had been a witness in the arbitration and was cross-examined; second, no doubt because of his interest in the outcome of the arbitration, he funded E's defence; third, the arbitral tribunal concluded that the shares were held to S's order; fourth, the tribunal intended and expected that the effect of its award would be that X would transfer those shares to S. Also relevant was the unfairness that would be caused to E by the putting to him of allegations a second time (paras 49-50, 56-57, 59-60, 62, 67-68).

MICHAEL WILSON & PARTNERS LTD v SINCLAIR, [2012] EWHC 2560 (Comm), [2013] 1 All E.R. (Comm) 476, Teare, J., QBD (Comm).

250. Addition of parties–Disputing the court's jurisdiction–Jurisdiction considerations under s.5(1) Regulation 44/2001 in claim involving Polish employee of Polish company–Usefulness of "legal relevance" test suggested in Swithenbank Foods Ltd v Bowers [2002] EWHC 2257 (QB)

[Regulation 44/2001 on jurisdiction and the recognition and enforcement of judgments in civil and commercial matters Art.6(1), Art.18, Art.20.]

The first appellant (J) and the second appellant (SP), a company controlled by J, appealed a judge's decision ([2012] EWHC 1155 (Ch), [2012] I.L.Pr. 40, [2012] C.L.Y. 308) granting permission for them to be added as defendants to the instant proceedings. The respondent companies (T) designed, manufactured and sold marine separators. The separators were manufactured in Poland and J was an employee of T in Poland. The second defendant (P) owned the first defendant English company (S) which procured and marketed spare parts for T's separators. P and J bribed an employee of T to supply T's drawings of various parts for the separators, which were copied and re-branded as S's drawings before being used to commission sub-contractors to manufacture the parts. Those parts were sold in competition with T. P and J then set up SP in Poland and J resigned from T. SP initially acted as S's sales agent in Poland, but T claimed that SP eventually took over part of S's business. T began the instant proceedings against P and S and subsequently sought to join J and SP as defendants, claiming breach of copyright and misuse of confidential information. J argued that as a former employee of T, the courts of Poland had exclusive jurisdiction over the claim against him pursuant to Regulation 44/2001 s.5(1).

Held: Appeal allowed. (1) It was not possible to accept that the "legal relevance" test under *Swithenbank Foods Ltd v Bowers* [2002] EWHC 2257 (QB), [2002] 2 All E.R. (Comm) 974, [2003] C.L.Y. 623 was an appropriate test for claims brought by an employer against an employee pursuant to s.5, *Swithenbank* overruled in part. It was not immediately obvious what the words "legally relevant" actually meant in that case. It appeared to suggest that it was a matter of pleading and whether the employer could frame a claim without relying on the contract of employment. If by that a distinction was being drawn between claims brought "under" the contract and those "arising out of" or "in connection with" the contract, that was a distinction which was impermissible, *Fiona Trust & Holding Corp v Privalov* [2007] UKHL 40, [2007] 4 All E.R. 951, [2007] C.L.Y. 792 followed. It was better not to depart from the actual words of art.18.1, but to ask "do the claims made against an employee relate to the individual's contract of employment?". That was a broad test and comparatively easy to apply. It might in many cases be helpful to ask whether the acts complained of by the employer constituted breaches of contract by the employee. If so, the claims were likely to "relate" to the employment contract. There were specific provisions in J's employment contract concerning misuse of confidential information and J also had an implied obligation of fidelity to T. Clearly, the instant allegations, if proved, amounted to breaches of J's employment contract. It could not be right that merely because the claims for misuse and breaches could also be framed in tort or delict that art.20.1 did not apply. To so hold would emasculate that provision. Even if, which was doubtful, s.5 contained rules of special jurisdiction which had to be strictly construed, art.20 did not require a strict construction since, in cases brought against an employee, it provided for the normal rule that a defendant had to be sued where he was domiciled. To the extent that cases had followed the first instance decision in the instant case, they should no longer be considered authoritative. J could only be sued in Poland and his joinder in England on the basis of art.6(1) could not be supported. That joinder had to be set aside (see paras 17-21, 23-33 of judgment). (2) It could not be expedient for proceedings against SP to be joined to what was effectively a dormant case against P when any proceedings against J had to take place in Poland. The risk of irreconcilable judgments would not be avoided because that risk existed once proceedings against J in Poland were begun. As much of the activity complained of took place in Poland, it did not make any difference that some might have taken place, or had consequences in England (paras 36-37).

ALFA LAVAL TUMBA AB v SEPARATOR SPARES INTERNATIONAL LTD, [2012] EWCA Civ 1569, [2013] 1 W.L.R. 1110, Sir Andrew Morritt (Chancellor), CA (Civ Div).

251. Adjournment–Competence–Missing-trader fraud case–Company's sole director suffering from depression–Ability to give instructions and evidence

The appellant commissioners appealed against a First-tier Tribunal judge's decision to adjourn the hearing of an appeal by the respondent (P) against their finding that P knew or should have known that its transactions were connected with the fraudulent evasion of VAT. P had applied for the hearing to be vacated because its sole director (W) was undergoing psychiatric treatment for depression and was medically unable to give instructions, to prepare for the trial and to attend the trial and give evidence. The judge considered a letter from W's psychiatrist and a report from an independent consultant psychiatrist and concluded that there was a real risk that W would be unfairly disadvantaged if the hearing of the appeal proceeded before he had recovered. The commissioners argued that the judge had not been entitled to conclude from the independent psychiatrist's report that there was real doubt that W would be able to give instructions and fully participate in the appeal proceedings without further medication and treatment.

Held: Appeal allowed. (1) The judge's conclusions on W's capacity to give instructions and evidence had been contrary to the evidence. The independent psychiatrist's firm and unqualified conclusion had been that W could give instructions relating to the hearing; he had also concluded that W suffered no substantial level of impairment and that any impairment could be mitigated during the hearing by frequent breaks in his evidence (see paras 30-33 of judgment). (2) In view of the independent psychiatrist's view that W could give instructions and also evidence if allowed to take frequent breaks and that there was no guarantee that he would be able to perform as well as he would wish if the hearing were to be postponed for a year, the Upper Tribunal would exercise its discretion in favour of not vacating the trial date (paras 43-44, 48-49).

REVENUE AND CUSTOMS COMMISSIONERS v PURPLE TELECOM LTD, [2013] UKUT 49 (TCC), [2013] S.T.C. 1276, Proudman, J., UT (Tax).

252. Admiralty Court–Commercial Court–Mercantile courts–Technology and Construction Court

THE CIVIL PROCEDURE (AMENDMENT NO.2) RULES 2013, SI 2013/SI 2013/515 (L.3); made under the Civil Procedure Act 1997 s.2. In force: April 1, 2013; .

These Rules make the following amendments to the Civil Procedure Rules 1998 (CPR): a substitution of rule 3.12(1), so that in addition to not applying to multi-track cases commenced on or after April 1, 2013 in the Admiralty and Commercial Courts, Section II of Part 3 of the CPR and Practice Direction 3E will also not apply to such multi-track cases commenced on or after April 1, 2013 in the Chancery Division as the Chancellor of the High Court may direct; and such multi-track cases commenced on or after April 1, 2013 in the Technology and Construction Court and the Mercantile Court as the President of the Queen's Bench Division may direct; and a substitution of rule 44.3, so that paragraphs (2)(a) and (5) of that rule will not apply to costs incurred in respect of work done before April 1, 2013, as well as not applying to cases commenced before that date.

253. Admissions–Withdrawal–Declaration in judicial review proceedings that Serious Fraud Office execution of search warrants unlawful on public law grounds–Effect of declaration on subsequent private law proceedings for trespass–Entitlement of SFO to withdraw pre-proceedings admission of liability

[Constables Protection Act 1750 (c.44) s.6; Civil Procedure Rules 1998 (SI 1998/3132) r.14.1(5).]

The applicant Serious Fraud Office (SFO), which was the defendant to a claim for damages by the respondent businessmen (R and V), applied to withdraw its admission, made prior to the issue of the instant proceedings, that it was liable to R and V in trespass. Following the collapse of a large Icelandic bank, the SFO had begun an investigation into a suspected dishonest conspiracy between senior executives to steal funds from the bank. It had applied for search warrants and executed them at the homes of R and V, who had subsequently been arrested and investigated. In prior related judicial review proceedings (*R. (on the application of Rawlinson and Hunter Trustees) v Central Criminal Court* [2012] EWHC 2254 (Admin), [2013] 1 W.L.R. 1634, [2013] 7 C.L. 35) it had been declared that the SFO's entries, searches and seizes were unlawful on public law grounds and that they should be quashed. The search warrants had been set aside and directions given for consequential claims. In preparation for the issue of the instant proceedings, R and V had served heads of claim and the SFO had admitted liability for trespass in its response. However, when the claims were issued, in which R and V sought damages of some £300 million, liability for trespass was denied, the SFO maintaining that it had only made the admission because it thought that liability in trespass followed automatically from the court's quashing of the warrants. The issues were (i) whether the order made in the judicial review proceedings precluded the SFO from disputing liability for trespass on the basis of estoppel per rem judicatem; (ii) if not, whether the SFO should be permitted to withdraw its admission of liability.

Held: Application granted. (1) It was permissible to claim private law damages as part of a judicial review claim which sought other public law relief. It was to be assumed for present purposes that the claims for damages by R and V included claims for private law damages for trespass, even though that was contrary to what they had told the court below. Based on that assumption, the SFO had failed to raise, in its detailed grounds for contesting the private law claims, the defences that it now wished to rely on, namely the Constables Protection Act 1750 s.6 and the defence of lawful justification under the principle in *Percy v Hall* [1997] Q.B. 924, [1996] C.L.Y. 5688. Looking simply at the order of the court below, the declaration of unlawfulness was limited to unlawfulness on public law grounds. That court had not intended to determine any private law claim for damages and the SFO was, therefore, not precluded from advancing cause of action estoppel or issue estoppel in relation to such claims. Looking at the issue in the context of the full history of the judicial review proceedings only served to reinforce that conclusion, *Percy, Olotu v Secretary of State for the Home Department* [1997] 1 W.L.R. 328, [1997] C.L.Y. 1299 and *R. v Governor of Brockhill Prison, Ex p. Evans (No.2)* [2001] 2 A.C. 19, [2000] C.L.Y. 5113 applied (see paras 11-12, 26-29, 32-3 of judgment). (2) The court had a discretion to allow the withdrawal of the SFO's admission under CPR r.14.1 (5). Although there was force in R's and V's objections, overall justice undoubtedly favoured withdrawal of the admission for the following reasons: (a) as it was agreed that the merits of the defences that the SFO now sought to raise should not be considered, it was to be assumed that they were at least arguable; (b) the amounts at stake were potentially significant; (c) there was no reason to suppose that the SFO's application had been made in anything other than good faith; (d) the overriding objective required the court to reach a decision that was correct in law, rather than on a foundation based upon an admission which might be incorrect as a matter of law; (e) there was no prejudice to R and V in being required to meet the defences on their merits, whereas there was considerable prejudice to the SFO if it was prevented from pursuing its defences (paras 56-60).

TCHENGUIZ v DIRECTOR OF THE SERIOUS FRAUD OFFICE; RAWLINSON AND HUNTER TRUSTEES SA v DIRECTOR OF THE SERIOUS FRAUD OFFICE, [2013] EWHC 1578 (QB), [2013] Lloyd's Rep. F.C. 535, Eder, J., QBD.

254. After the event insurance–Case management–Costs

THE CIVIL PROCEDURE (AMENDMENT) RULES 2013, SI 2013/SI 2013/262 (L.1); made under the Civil Procedure Act 1997 s.2; the Courts and Legal Services Act 1990 s.58AA; and the Legal Aid, Sentencing and Punishment of Offenders Act 2012 s.55. In force: April 1, 2013; .

These Regulations amend the Civil Procedure Rules 1998, inter alia to: strengthen the objective of the rules to enable to the costs to deal with cases "at proportionate cost" as well as justly; extend the court's case management powers in respect of costs; widen the scope of the rules on applications for relief from sanctions to provide the court with the power to deal with failure to conduct litigation at proportionate cost; and introduce rules for a new system of qualified one way costs shifting in personal injury cases, devised as an alternative to after the event insurance.

255. Allocation of jurisdiction–Civil proceedings–Issuing of writ in French court–Sending writ by fax to English authority responsible for service–Whether receipt of faxed writ sufficient to deem French court seised of proceedings

[Regulation 1393/2007; Regulation 44/2001 on jurisdiction and the recognition and enforcement of judgments in civil and commercial matters Art.30(2).]

The claimant (C) sought sums said to be owed by the defendants (D) pursuant to a loan agreement, overdraft facility and guarantees which were used to finance the refitting and maintenance of D1's yacht. On September 27, 2012, C had arrested D1's yacht in France on the basis that it had a maritime claim in relation to the loan and overdraft. On October 24, D issued a writ of summons before the French court claiming declarations of non-liability under the contracts, damages and an injunction preventing the sale of the yacht. On the same date, the French bailiffs sent the writ by fax to the French Process Section of the Royal Courts of Justice (FPS) which received the faxed documents that day. The same day, the bailiffs sent the writ by post to the FPS, which received the posted documents on October 30. Initially, the FPS issued an acknowledgement of receipt of the writ which stated the date of receipt as October 30. It subsequently issued a revised acknowledgement of receipt stating that the date of receipt was October 24. The revised acknowledgement was stamped and dated by the Senior Master who also annotated the original acknowledgment, "Permission to re-issue as the date of receipt was 24/10/12". Meanwhile, C issued the instant proceedings on October 26, 2012. The issue to be determined was whether the French court was the court first seised, which in turn required a determination of whether it was necessary for the FPS to have received the French writ by both fax and post prior to those documents being deemed received for the purpose of Regulation 44/2001 art.30(2).

Held: Preliminary issue determined. (1) In determining when the French writ was "received" by the FPS the court had to have regard to the meaning of "service" in Regulation 1393/2007. It also noted that, in the furtherance of the objectives of the 2007 Regulation, the European Commission had published a Manual Containing the Information Relating to the Receiving Agencies which stated in section III p.22 that "Documents will be transmitted by fax and post" (see paras 18, 22-23 of judgment). For a document to be deemed to have been received by the FPS, receipt by either fax or post sufficed. If the intention was to impose a double requirement of transmission by both fax and post one would expect that to be clearly set out. There was no good reason for requiring transmission by both means and a double receipt requirement might undermine certainty as there was a greater possibility for something to go wrong in the process. Faxes were generally both reliable and legible, they had the advantage of providing a timed receipt and many countries allowed receipt by that method. Further, allowing receipt by fax promoted the important aims of the 2007 Regulation of speed and efficiency. Moreover, the best evidence of the view and practice of the FPS was that reflected in the revised Acknowledgement of Receipt and the Senior Master's comments on the original acknowledgement (para.35). (2) The French court was the court first seised and a stay should be granted (para.36).

ARBUTHNOT LATHAM & CO LTD v M3 MARINE LTD, [2013] EWHC 1019 (Comm), [2014] 1 W.L.R. 190, Hamblen, J., QBD (Comm).

256. Anonymity–Children–Child claimant in personal injury claim–Appropriateness of anonymity order under s.39 Children and Young Persons Act 1933

[Children and Young Persons Act 1933 (c.12) s.39; Contempt of Court Act 1981 (c.49) s.4; Defamation Act 1996 (c.31) s.15(1); Civil Procedure Rules 1998 (SI 1998/3132) r.39.2(4).]

The applicant child (M) applied for an anonymity order under the Children and Young Persons Act 1933 s.39 in relation to personal injury proceedings that she had brought against the respondent trust.

Held: Application granted. (1) There was evidence before the court which demonstrated that it was necessary that there should be no reporting of M's name or of other means of identification to prevent the risk of her becoming the victim of those who might attempt to misuse the funds that she had been awarded as compensation. There was no sufficient general, public interest in publishing a report of the proceedings which identified M to justify the resulting curtailment of her and her family's rights to respect for their private and family life and the risk of defeating the purpose of the proceedings, namely to ensure that M received and kept the money necessary to compensate her for her injuries. Accordingly, it was appropriate to make an anonymity order. The court did not conclude on the scope of s.39, but decided that there was force in the argument that s.39 might not give it jurisdiction to prohibit the making of a report otherwise than in a newspaper or a sound or television broadcast. Therefore, if s.39 was not the basis of the jurisdiction for making the order, it was better not to use the wording derived from it in the order, but to follow the wording of CPR r.39.2(4) (see paras 13, 16, 18 of judgment). (2) (Per curiam) The court noted that Parliament had acknowledged in the Contempt of Court Act 1981 s.4 and the Defamation Act 1996 s.15(1) that identification in reports of proceedings otherwise than in newspapers required recognition. It expressed the view that s.39 of the 1933 Act might not have the implications or provide the protection that Parliament had originally intended, namely because it might only apply to reports in newspapers and not to reports in other mediums (paras 20, 24).

MXB v EAST SUSSEX HOSPITALS NHS TRUST, [2012] EWHC 3279 (QB), (2013) 177 J.P. 31, Tugendhat, J., QBD.

257. Anonymity–Open justice–Application for anonymity in relation to FSA disciplinary proceedings–Whether anonymisation or redaction of judgment in interests of justice

[Financial Services and Markets Act 2000 (c.8) s.67.]

The applicant (C) applied for an anonymity order in relation to disciplinary proceedings brought by the respondent FSA. The FSA had appealed against a decision quashing a decision notice given to C under the Financial Services and Markets Act 2000 s.67. The quashing decision had been conducted in private and the judgment was published in redacted and anonymised form to protect C's identity. The instant court declined to hear the FSA's appeal in private but an interim order was made prohibiting the identification of C until further notice. The FSA's appeal was upheld in *R. (on the application of C) v Financial Services Authority* [2013] EWCA Civ 677. C sought an order that the judgments be published in a redacted and anonymised form. C was seeking permission to appeal to the Supreme Court and relied on the statutory provisions which prohibited the FSA from disclosing the existence of an investigation, its progress or its outcome until it concluded, and then only if it resulted in some form of sanction. The FSA contended that the application raised important points of principle, in particular the principle of open justice. It argued that publication of the judgments in full was necessary to enable anyone who read them properly to understand the nature of, and the basis for, the court's decision.

Held: Application refused. The starting point was the principle of open justice, namely that proceedings were to be conducted and determined in public. One aspect of that principle was that judgments should be published in full without concealing the identity of the parties or others involved, whether by anonymisation or redaction. However, the principle was not absolute and had to give way to the requirements of justice and other countervailing public interest considerations. Anonymisation and redaction of judgments represented derogations from the principle of open justice which had to be justified, on the basis of cogent evidence, as strictly necessary to secure the proper administration of justice. In the instant case, the FSA was performing a disciplinary function. The proceedings would have been embarrassing for C if his identity had been made public and they might have caused some damage to his professional reputation, but he would not have been entitled to have his identity protected on those grounds if, for example, he had for some reason been facing criminal charges, which could have had a similar effect. Nor was there any positive evidence that he would suffer significant harm if the existence of the proceedings was disclosed at the instant stage. However, if he were to obtain permission to appeal to the Supreme Court and succeed in having the decision notice quashed, he would have lost the right to have his identity protected pending the outcome of the disciplinary proceedings. The question was whether it was necessary in the interests of justice to anonymise and redact the judgments in order to protect C's identity. It was not. The proposed redactions were extensive and went to the heart of the judgments. Complete anonymisation was proposed. Open justice required that the court's judgment should be published in full unless there were overriding grounds for not doing so. Although the FSA disciplinary proceedings were private, once C stepped outside those proceedings, whether by referring the matter to the Upper Tribunal or by making a claim for judicial review, he brought the matter into the public forum, and the principle of open justice applied. If one party invoked the assistance of the court, the court would not normally take steps to preserve the confidentiality of the proceedings or their subject matter. If anonymisation and redaction were necessary in the instant case in order to enable the court to grant effective relief, the position would be different. However, the primary object of the proceedings was not to protect C's privacy; it was to ensure that the procedure adopted by the FSA complied with the statutory requirements and to quash the existing decision notice to enable the FSA to reconsider the matter. In those circumstances, it was not strictly necessary in the interests of justice to publish the judgments in a form which would protect C's identification, *Pink*

Floyd Music Ltd v EMI Records Ltd [2010] EWCA Civ 1429, [2011] 1 W.L.R. 770, [2011] C.L.Y. 550 applied (see paras 5-10 of judgment).

R. (ON THE APPLICATION OF WILLFORD) v FINANCIAL SERVICES AUTHORITY, [2013] EWCA Civ 674, [2013] C.P. Rep. 43, Moore-Bick, L.J., CA (Civ Div).

258. Anti-suit injunctions–Jurisdiction clauses–Non-payment of bunkers–Shipowner seeking to restrain pursuit of action in Florida

The claimant shipowner (J) sought the continuation of an anti-suit injunction restraining the defendant (S) from pursuing proceedings in Florida and the Marshall Islands. J was a Bahamian corporation with a place of business in Florida. S was a company incorporated and registered in the British Virgin Islands. The dispute between S and J concerned the supply by S of two consignments of bunkers for J's vessel, the price of which had not been paid. J's case was that the price was payable by the company to which the vessel had been chartered at the time the bunkers were supplied. The contract for the supply of the bunkers incorporated S's standard terms and conditions, cl.19.1 of which read as follows: "Governing law: Save that the seller may take such action or actions as it shall in its absolute discretion consider necessary to enforce, safeguard or secure its rights hereunder in any court or tribunal or any state or country, the provisions hereof shall be governed by the law of England and the jurisdiction of the English courts". In October 2011, S began proceedings in Florida and the Marshall Islands. In February 2012, the action in the Marshall Islands was stayed. In May 2012, J and S agreed on a timetable for directions in connection with the action in Florida. In June 2012, J applied ex parte in the English court for an anti-suit injunction restraining S from pursuing proceedings abroad; its application was granted.

Held: Application refused. (1) The first issue was whether cl.19.1 of S's standard terms and conditions was an exclusive jurisdiction clause. The answer was no. The critical words were "enforce... its rights hereunder". The natural inference was that they had to be a reference to the enforcement of substantive contractual rights. Accordingly, cl.19 did not amount to a clause under which S had agreed not to take proceedings outside England to enforce the merits of any claim and in particular to enforce a claim to be paid the price of the bunkers in question. J had argued in the alternative that, if the clause was not an exclusive jurisdiction clause, it would nevertheless be vexatious or oppressive to allow the Florida and Marshall Islands proceedings to continue: first, there were reasons for the matter being litigated in England and England was, at least, a convenient forum for the resolution of the substantive dispute between the parties; second, S had sought in the Florida action to assert rights arising otherwise than under English law, which was impermissible by reason of the English law provision in the contract; third, S's actions were oppressive by virtue of its having commenced two sets of parallel proceedings, one in Florida and the other in the Marshall Islands. Those factors did not begin to meet the criteria necessary to support an anti-suit injunction in the absence of an exclusive jurisdiction clause. The English court could not be put forward as anything more than a convenient forum; it was not the natural forum. The fact that the Florida court might apply law other than English law was a matter for that court. It was well capable of applying English law if it be the proper law and of applying appropriate conflicts rules which were in accordance with international principles of comity. Nor was there any oppression in the fact that two actions were commenced, not least because, in any event, the Marshall Islands action had now been stayed. There were other good reasons for not granting an anti-suit injunction in any event. The first was delay. By October 2011, it was apparent that S was pursuing its claim on the merits in the Marshall Islands and in Florida; the time to make an application to the instant court for that course of conduct to be stopped was shortly thereafter. Further, it would be inequitable to prevent the continued pursuit of the Florida action, Florida being the forum in which both J and S had been envisaging for the last eight months that the substantive dispute would be resolved (see paras 15-25 of judgment). (2)

(Obiter) It was surprising how many spurious ex parte applications were made. On any ex parte application and in particular on an ex parte application for relief comprising an anti-suit injunction, it was incumbent on a party who had not given any or any sufficient notice to be in a position to persuade the judge of the appropriateness of that course, specifically by reference to the risk of irretrievable prejudice if the normal course was not taken under which the other party was entitled to be heard (para.29).

JEWEL OWNER LTD v SAGAAN DEVELOPMENTS TRADING LTD; MD GEMINI, THE, [2012] EWHC 2850 (Comm), [2012] 2 Lloyd's Rep. 672, Popplewell, J., QBD (Comm).

259. Anti-suit injunctions–Seat of arbitration–Determining seat of arbitration–Interim or conservatory measures before formation of arbitral tribunal–Ability to have recourse to local court

The claimant Zambian company (U) sought a final anti-suit injunction to restrain the defendant Zambian company (K) from pursuing proceedings in Zambia. K owned a large copper mine in Zambia. U operated the mine under a number of agreements. A common feature of the parties' various contracts was that they were governed by Zambian law and provided for LCIA arbitration in London. K terminated, or purported to terminate, a mining contract on the ground that U had failed to meet production targets. The contract provided that on termination U was to leave the site. U contended that given the size of operations and the nature of its mining equipment it needed a reasonable time to vacate and demobilise the operations. K then obtained from the Zambian court an ex parte interim mandatory injunction under Zambia's Arbitration Act compelling U to vacate the mine immediately and hand over certain identified equipment that had, in effect, been pledged by U to K as security for a guarantee given by U in K's favour. K asserted that its intention in bringing the proceedings was to protect its contractual rights and interests pending LCIA arbitration in London. U commenced an LCIA arbitration in London and then sought an anti-suit injunction restraining K from taking steps in the Zambian proceedings. U submitted that, if K genuinely required interim relief from a court for reasons of urgency, it was obliged to seek it from the English court, since the seat of the arbitration was England. K submitted that the seat of the arbitration was in Zambia and that in any event it was entitled to use the Zambian court to obtain interim remedies under art.25.3 of the LCIA rules.

Held: Judgment accordingly. (1) The contract did not use the word "seat". However, it provided that disputes were to be referred to LCIA arbitration in London and that the place of the arbitration would be England. It was plain that the parties thereby agreed that the seat of the arbitration should be England, *Shashoua v Sharma* [2009] EWHC 957 (Comm), [2009] 2 All E.R. (Comm) 477, [2009] C.L.Y. 625 considered. That conclusion was not affected by the provision conferring exclusive jurisdiction on the High Court of Zambia, which appeared in the part of the agreement dealing with governing law and jurisdiction and not that dealing with dispute resolution and arbitration (see paras 2-8 of judgment). (2) In principle, the natural court for the granting of interim injunctive relief was the court of the country of the seat of arbitration, especially where the curial law of the arbitration was that of the same country; but the power to grant interim relief was not confined to the court of the seat, *Econet Wireless Ltd v Vee Networks Ltd* [2006] EWHC 1568 (Comm), [2006] 2 All E.R. (Comm) 989, [2006] C.L.Y. 458 considered. In the instant case, the position was governed by the agreement between the parties providing for LCIA arbitration. Article 25.3 of the LCIA rules expressly stipulated that the power of the arbitral tribunal to order interim and conservatory measures was not to prejudice a party's right to apply to a state court before the formation of the tribunal; that implicitly recognised the party's right to do so. There was nothing in the parties' agreement inconsistent with the right to apply to the local court for interim measures. If U was right, then if it had wanted to apply for interim or protective measures, it would have had to apply to the English court. It was not clear that the English court could or would have made any order in a dispute between two Zambian companies concerning the operation of a copper mine in

Zambia. So far as judicial assistance by way of interim measures pending the appointment of the arbitrators was required, the natural forum for such proceedings was in Zambia, not in England. The Zambian proceedings were not in breach of the arbitration agreement between the parties and on that basis the injunction should be discharged (paras 63-73).

U&M MINING ZAMBIA LTD v KONKOLA COPPER MINES PLC, [2013] EWHC 260 (Comm), [2013] 2 Lloyd's Rep. 218, Blair, J., QBD (Comm).

260. Appeal notices–Employment Appeal Tribunal–Extensions of time

THE EMPLOYMENT APPEAL TRIBUNAL (AMENDMENT) RULES 2013, SI 2013/SI 1693; made under the Employment Tribunals Act 1996 s.30, s.34. In force: July 29, 2013; .

These Rules amend the Employment Appeal Tribunal Rules 1993 (SI 1993/2854) to remove a party's right to an extension of time to provide a fresh notice of appeal (or cross-appeal) where the judge or registrar has decided that the original notice or cross-appeal disclosed no reasonable grounds or amounted to an abuse of appeal tribunal process. It also removes a party's right to have the decision reviewed at a hearing where the notice or cross-appeal is considered to be totally without merit. These Rules also insert a new r.17A and amend r.26.

261. Bailiffs–Debt collection–Executive agencies–Landlords

THE TAKING CONTROL OF GOODS REGULATIONS 2013, SI 2013/1894; made under theTribunals, Courts and Enforcement Act 2007 s.73, s.77, s.81, s.90, Sch.12 para.3, Sch.12 para.7, Sch.12 para.8, Sch.12 para.13, Sch.12 para.14, Sch.12 para.15, Sch.12 para.19A, Sch.12 para.22, Sch.12 para.24, Sch.12 para.25, Sch.12 para.28 Sch.12 para.31, Sch.12 para.32, Sch.12 para.33, Sch.12 para.34, Sch.12 para.35, Sch.12 para.36, Sch.12 para.39, Sch.12 para.40, Sch.12 para.41, Sch.12 para.42, Sch.12 para.43, Sch.12 para.48, Sch.12 para.49, Sch.12 para.54, Sch.12 para.60. In force: April 6, 2014; .

These Regulations supplement theTribunals, Courts and Enforcement Act 2007 Pt 3 by making detailed provision for operation of the procedure which enforcement agents, who are acting under powers conferred by enactment, or under a warrant or writ of control or under instructions from a landlord of commercial premises who is owed rent arrears, must follow when taking control of goods and selling them to recover a sum of money.

262. Bias–Recusal–Apparent bias–Expert witness in breach of duty to court–Wasted costs orders

[Civil Procedure Rules 1998 (SI 1998/3132) Pt 35.]

The appellant solicitors (R) appealed against a judge's decision ([2012] EWHC 2782 (Ch)) refusing to recuse himself from hearing a stage one wasted costs order and making such an order against them in favour of the respondent, the defendant's solicitors. The claimant in the substantive proceedings had proffered an expert witness (J) on Ethiopian law. The judge had determined that J had failed to comply with his duty to assist the court and made trenchant criticisms of R for failing to prepare J adequately and for filing reports by J that did not comply with CPR Pt 35. R submitted that (1) the judge should have recused himself as he had made findings about them without hearing evidence, without warning, and they had had no opportunity to address him; (2) the stage one order should not have been made as the required prima facie strong case of improper, reckless, or negligent conduct had not been satisfied.

Held: Appeal allowed in part. (1) Normally the judge on a substantive application would deal with consequential issues as to costs, even if he had made adverse findings towards a party. However, the instant case was exceptional and showed apparent bias. The judge should have recused himself from hearing the wasted costs application because (a) his criticism of R, designed to ward off an application for a wasted costs order against J, was made in anticipation of an application that was never in fact made; (b) he had expressed his criticisms in absolute terms, failing to leave room for any explanation; and (c) the repetition of the criticisms and their severity made them extreme and unbalanced, *Freudiana Holdings Ltd, Re* Times, December 4, 1995, [1996] C.L.Y. 938 and *Porter v Magill* [2001] UKHL 67, [2002] 2 A.C. 357, [2002] C.L.Y. 3185 followed. The stage one cost order was set aside (see paras 58-64 of judgment). (2) R had admitted serious breaches of CPR Pt 35 and had also failed to invite the judge to disregard the passages in J's reports that went beyond his proper role as an expert witness. Consequently, R had failed to show that no judge could have concluded that a stage one order was appropriate.

MENGISTE v ENDOWMENT FUND FOR THE REHABILITATION OF TIGRAY; *sub nom.* TIGRAY v CHUBB; ENDOWMENT FUND FOR THE REHABILITATION OF TIGRAY v CHUBB, [2013] EWCA Civ 1003, [2014] C.P. Rep. 5, Arden, L.J., CA (Civ Div).

263. Case management–Electronic disclosure–Extension of time to comply with orders for electronic disclosure–Unless order in view of claimants' responsibility for failure

The claimants (P) sought an extension of time to comply with a disclosure order and permission to amend their damages claim against the defendants (H). P were claiming substantial damages for H's alleged negligence or incompetence. P had retained most and possibly all of H's electronic files. Eleven months ago, H had requested further information regarding P's particulars of claim and made proposals as to a way forward in relation to electronic disclosure by P. Eight months ago, P were ordered to respond to H's request for further information and to their disclosure proposals within two months. Four months ago, the court made a disclosure order, but at present, P had only disclosed a small part of the electronic documents ordered to be disclosed and had not disclosed any hard copy at all. Two months ago, the court made an unless order whereby those parts of P's amended particulars of claim and the further information would be struck out if they did not provide the required quantum information. That order was made in view of the fact that P had had nine months to answer the request for further information and even longer to properly quantify their money claims relating to the breaches of contract pleaded against H in the amended particulars of claim. P applied for an extension of time and permission to amend their quantum as set out in their consolidated further response to H's request for further information.

Held: Applications granted in part. (1) The problem with disclosure had very largely, if not entirely, been of P's own making: they did not commence the exercise for about six weeks after the disclosure order was made, and had made little or no effective preparation for the exercise before the order. In view of P's continuing and culpable failures to comply with their disclosure obligations under court orders on the court's timetable, an unless order would now be made allowing an extension. P would be required to disclose by list and provide for inspection their electronic documents and hard copy documents on a rolling basis within two weeks. If they had not complied with the order within three weeks, their claims and defences to H's counterclaims would be struck out and H would be at liberty to enter judgment in the full amount of the counterclaims (see paras 16-19 of judgment). (2) In accordance with the overriding objective, amendments should be permitted where that was just and proportionate. Amendments in general ought to be allowed so that the real dispute between the parties could be adjudicated upon, provided that any prejudice to the other party or parties caused by the amendments could be compensated for in costs, and the public interest in the efficient administration of justice was not significantly harmed. However, in the instant case, P would not be granted permission to amend for the following reasons: there was no good excuse for their application to have been made a mere six months before the trial when the proceedings had been going on almost three years in relation to one of the defendants and more than a year in relation to the other; P had chosen initially not to quantify their losses, although they were always said to be substantial; they failed to respond adequately or at all to H's request for further information on quantum in relation to investor losses; the only reasons that P found themselves in the position of having to make a late but substantial amendment were entirely of their own making; their disclosure was not yet even five per cent completed, so H would not see the bulk of the documents, let alone those relating to quantum, until four months before the trial; and there would be very real prejudice to H as an adjournment would mean that they would have serious and very costly litigation hanging over their heads for much longer than it should have done (paras 26, 39).

PHAESTOS LTD v HO; IKOS CIF LTD v GOVER, [2012] EWHC 1996 (TCC), 144 Con. L.R. 211, Akenhead, J., QBD (TCC).

264. Case management–Expert evidence–Claim for damages arising out of car engine failure–Appropriateness of disinstructing single joint expert–Relevance of expert evidence on critical issue of liability

The appellant (B) appealed against a judge's case management decision refusing him permission to call his own expert evidence and refusing to disinstruct a single joint expert. B had brought a claim for damages against the respondents following a serious, mechanical engine failure in his car. The critical issue between the parties was the cause of the engine failure. A single joint expert was instructed. B applied unsuccessfully for permission to call his own expert witness (S) and for the single joint expert to be disinstructed. S produced a report which doubted the single joint expert's technical expertise and reasoning. B submitted that the judge erred in (1) applying the wrong test when deciding whether the single joint expert should be disinstructed; (2) dismissing S's concerns regarding the technical inadequacy of the single joint expert's report and his alleged lack of expertise; (3) assessing the instant litigation as not being sufficiently "substantial" to justify dispensing with a single joint expert.

Held: Appeal allowed. (1) In contrast to *Kay v West Midlands Strategic Health Authority*, the expert evidence in the instant case went to an issue which was far from peripheral, namely the cause of the engine failure. It was fundamental to the resolution of the dispute between the parties and was technical. The judge allowed himself to become too focused on the "exceptionality" test attributed to the judge in *Kay*, namely whether or not the circumstances were so exceptional as to justify departing from the normal course of appointing a single joint expert, without making sufficient allowance for the fact that, unlike in *Kay*, the issue in question was not peripheral (see paras 18, 20 of judgment). (2) S's concerns about the single joint expert's expertise might be proved wrong on closer examination, but B's sense of grievance would be understandable if he had to go through a trial of the critical issue on liability while still being barred from having the relevant points properly investigated (paras 24, 27). (3) It was impossible to provide a bright line boundary between cases that were "substantial" and those which were not. In any event, whether or not litigation was substantial could not be determined solely by reference to the amount claimed. Issues raised in litigation might be important to the parties or the public generally for a variety of reasons other than financial considerations. The judge thought it appropriate to decide whether it was a "substantial" case, and having decided that it was not, he treated it as a significant factor in refusing B's application. Although it was a relevant factor, it should not have assumed such importance (paras 28-29). (4) The judge should have allowed S's evidence because it was technical and not peripheral. That was what the overriding objective required, whether the judge assessed the value of B's claim as substantial or not (para.29).

BULIC v HARWOODS, [2012] EWHC 3657 (QB), [2013] B.L.R. 89, Eady, J., QBD.

265. Case management–Extensions of time–14-day extension granted for filing of reply evidence owing to holiday absence of factual witness–Refusal of permission to adduce expert evidence on quantum

The applicant (D), the defendant to an action commenced by the respondent water company (X) applied for an extension of time within which to file evidence, and for permission to submit expert evidence addressing X's quantum calculations and the question of indexation. The tribunal had issued a timetable for the conduct of the claim, which required D to file reply evidence within 28 days of service of the re-amended defence. That date was August 17, 2012. D sought a 14-day extension on the ground that a factual witness on whose evidence D wished to rely was on holiday. X had no objection to the proposed extension.

Held: Application granted in part. (1) Taking into account the public holiday, which fell on August 27, there was little or no prejudice to X in granting D an extension of time for the filing of reply evidence until close of business on August 28, 2012. (2) Submission of the expert evidence proposed by D would be disproportionate at the instant stage of the litigation and would unnecessarily increase costs. D could address the tribunal by submission without the need for expert evidence.

ALBION WATER LTD v DWR CYMRU CYFYNGEDIG, [2012] CAT 23, [2012] Comp. A.R. 437, Vivien Rose, CAT.

266. Cause of action estoppel–Possession claims–Possession proceedings withdrawn by consent–Issue of second possession claim–Scope of principle of cause of action estoppel

[Civil Procedure Rules 1998 (SI 1998/3132) r.38.7; European Convention on Human Rights 1950 Art.6.]

The appellant (T) appealed against a decision upholding the refusal of her application to strike out possession proceedings, brought by the respondents (S), on the basis of cause of action estoppel. S had been appointed as receivers of a charge over a flat. When they sought to sell the property, they discovered that T was in occupation. S brought possession proceedings against her as a trespasser. Had the claim been a simple possession claim against a tenant, the claim form would have been different. By their claim, which alleged that T was occupying the flat without consent or the benefit of a licence, S simply sought possession and costs. Shortly before the hearing, T filed a defence asserting that she was a tenant under two tenancy agreements. S, taking the view that the tenancy agreements were not genuine, raised with T the possibility of withdrawing the proceedings in order to give themselves more time to inspect the documents. The proceedings were withdrawn by consent. That was a technical error, as the proceedings ought instead to have been discontinued under CPR r.38, since S had not wanted to stop any future claim, but had simply wanted time to investigate whether the tenancy agreements were genuine. They subsequently began fresh proceedings against T challenging her purported tenancy and claiming possession of the flat, charges for its use and occupation, and costs. T applied to strike out the claim on the grounds that it was barred by cause of action estoppel or as an abuse of process. The district judge considered that there was no abuse of process, since T's action had forced S to abandon the first action and it would be an injustice if the merits of the claim were not legally examined. On appeal, the judge found that the terms of the tenancies were strongly suggestive of fraud and that the public interest in investigating fraud outweighed other considerations. T contended that the consent order in the first action operated in the same way as a judgment, and established a cause of action estoppel. She submitted that the causes of action were the same, since in both S were asserting rights of possession and occupation over hers. T argued that that part of the decision in *Ako v Rothschild Asset Management Ltd* [2002] EWCA Civ 236, [2002] 2 All E.R. 693, [2002] C.L.Y. 1309, in which it was asserted that there was no inflexible rule that cause of action estoppel always arose after judgment by consent if it was clear that a party had intended to pursue a claim, was obiter and went too far in creating an exception to cause of action estoppel.

Held: Appeal dismissed. (1) In considering whether it would be an abuse of process to bring a second action after the first was agreed by consent, the parties' conduct in bringing the first action to an end was relevant, *Johnson v Gore Wood & Co (No.1)* [2002] 2 A.C. 1, [2001] C.L.Y. 410 considered. A broad merits-based approach was appropriate in determining whether the second action was fair. In the instant case, the basis for the consent order was S's intention to take further action if appropriate. It would be unconscionable to allow T to take advantage of the technical error in that the case was withdrawn rather than discontinued. Accordingly, if there was no cause of action estoppel, the second claim would not amount to an abuse of process (see paras 12, 14 of judgment). (2) Cause of action estoppel was grounded on the principle that there was a public interest in finality in litigation. Whilst cause of action estoppel was intended to prevent injustice, it was open to courts to recognise special circumstances in which the rigid application of estoppel might lead to injustice, *Carl Zeiss Stiftung v Rayner & Keeler Ltd* [1967] 1 A.C. 853, [1966] C.L.Y. 1665 and *Arnold v National Westminster Bank Plc (No.1)* [1991] 2 A.C. 93, [1991] C.L.Y. 1736 followed. The principle derived from *Ako*, that there were exceptions to the cause of action estoppel rule was not obiter, but an alternative ratio. Cause of action estoppel was created by judge-made law and judges had been careful not to apply too rigid a rule. The instant case was indistinguishable from *Ako* and the approach in that case would be adopted, *Ako* followed. The decision in *Zurich Insurance Co Plc v Hayward* [2011] EWCA Civ 641, [2011] C.P. Rep. 39, [2011] C.L.Y. 378, that estoppel was a strict rule and strictly confined, was not at odds with that approach, *Zurich Insurance Co Plc* considered. Moreover, the approach in *Ako* was given added force by the right to a fair and public hearing under the European Convention on Human Rights 1950 art.6. That right might be waived because of a friendly settlement, but the court had to look at the circumstances surrounding a consent order to see whether that was its nature. In the instant case, it was clear that S were not going to abandon their claims and T had known that (paras 16-21).

SPICER v TULI, [2012] EWCA Civ 845, [2012] 1 W.L.R. 3088, Lord Neuberger (M.R.), CA (Civ Div).

267. Chancery Division–Intellectual property claims–Patents County Court–Fixed costs

THE CIVIL PROCEDURE (AMENDMENT NO.7) RULES 2013, SI 2013/SI 2013/1974 (L.19); made under the Civil Procedure Act 1997 s.2. In force: October 1, 2013;

.

These Rules make amendments to the Civil Procedure Rules 1998 (SI 1998/3132) including amendments to Part 45 (fixed costs) and Part 63 (intellectual property claims) in consequence of the abolition of the Patents County Court and to give effect to its reconstitution as a specialist list of the Chancery Division, to be named the "Intellectual Property Enterprise Court".

268. Charging orders–Consumer credit agreements–Procurement thresholds

THE CHARGING ORDERS (ORDERS FOR SALE: FINANCIAL THRESHOLDS) REGULATIONS 2013, SI 2013/491; made under the Charging Orders Act 1979 s.3A. In force: April 6, 2013; .

These Regulations set a financial threshold for orders for sale to enforce a charge imposed by a charging order in cases where the charging order was made to secure the payment of money due under a judgment made for the purpose of enforcing payment of money owed under an agreement which is a regulated agreement under the Consumer Credit Act 1974, and the application to enforce is made on or after the date on which the Regulations come into force. The threshold is set at £1,000, so that if the amount of the judgment debt which remains unpaid at the date of the making of the application to enforce is less than £1,000, no order for sale may be made.

269. Charging orders–Costs orders–Application to discharge charging order–Effect of alleged breach of trust on status of costs debt–Whether debt outstanding following Danish arbitration award

The applicant (H) applied for a final charging order over his property to be discharged. H had employed the second respondent architectural firm (F), who was based in Denmark and owned by the first respondent architect (C), to act for it in relation to the development of a substantial domestic property in England. H had given C a power of attorney to enter into contracts on its behalf and authorise payments. H had provided C with money for that purpose which was held in Danish bank accounts. H's relationship with the respondents soured because it believed that their work was defective and that there were possible financial irregularities. In January 2007, H emailed C stating that all payments made on its behalf could only be made after its written authority had been obtained. H made a claim in the English courts against the respondents in respect of the work but the claim was stayed for arbitration to take place. In August 2007, without seeking H's authority, C authorised payment of DK606,000 from the Danish bank accounts for fees due to F. An English court subsequently ordered H to pay £45,000 to C and F in part payment of costs. The court made H the subject of a charging order after the costs were not paid. A Danish arbitrator subsequently issued a final award dismissing H's claims but a translated copy had not been before the court. The issue was whether the debt had been, or was to be considered to have been, discharged. H submitted that as C had acted in breach of trust by causing the payment to be made to F in August 2007, once authority to do so had been expressly withdrawn by H, it should be treated as if there was at least £45,000 still in the Danish bank accounts to meet the costs order.

Held: Application refused. There was no evidence from H that there was a pressing difficulty which required the charge to be lifted. H had made no payment to satisfy the costs order. The court faced two problems in respect of the alleged breaches of trust by C. Firstly, the applicable law relating to the bank accounts could be Danish law and it was unclear whether C's behaviour would be a breach of the Danish law relating to trusts, and, if so, what, if any, relief would be available. Secondly, even if English law applied, the remedy had to be determined and although damages could be an adequate remedy, it might be said that H had suffered no loss because the unauthorised payments were for sums which it owed F in any event. It was likely that, de facto, the Danish arbitrator had effectively dealt with the issue by determining that in effect F was entitled to the DK606,000 for its fees but that there was no need for an order or declaration about unlawful or improper withdrawals from the bank account because, as both parties accepted the award stated, H had suffered no economic loss as a result. H had not argued in the Danish courts that the arbitrator had wrongfully failed to deal with the issue about lawfulness or impropriety. For those reasons it would be wholly wrong to discharge the charging order (see paras 11, 14-16, 18 of judgment).

HEIFER INTERNATIONAL LTD v CHRISTIANSEN, [2013] EWHC 721 (TCC), [2013] B.L.R. 346, Akenhead, J., QBD (TCC).

270. Civil procedure–Court of Appeal–High Court–County courts

THE CIVIL PROCEDURE (AMENDMENT NO.3) RULES 2013, SI 2013/SI 2013/789 (L.7); made under the Civil Procedure Act 1997 s.2. In force: April 30, 2013; .

This instrument amends the Civil Procedure Rules 1998 (SI 1998/3132) rules of court that govern practice and procedure in the Civil Division of the Court of Appeal, the High Court and county courts. The amendments relate to a Government initiative.

271. Civil proceedings–Costs–Legal aid–Lord Chancellor

THE CIVIL LEGAL AID (COSTS) REGULATIONS 2013, SI 2013/611; made under the Legal Aid, Sentencing and Punishment of Offenders Act 2012 s.5, s.26. In force: April 1, 2013; .

The Civil Legal Aid (Costs) Regulations 2013 make provision about costs orders in civil proceedings in favour of or against a legally aided party and, in certain circumstances, against the Lord Chancellor.

272. Civil proceedings–Fees

THE CIVIL PROCEEDINGS FEES (AMENDMENT NO.2) ORDER 2013, SI 2013/SI 2013/1410 (L.13); made under the Insolvency Act 1986 s.414, s.415; and the Courts Act 2003 s.92, s.108. In force: July 1, 2013; .

This Order amends the Civil Proceedings Fees Order 2008 (SI 2008/1053), merging the fee payable on filing a request for detailed assessment of costs where the party filing the request is legally aided, funded by the Legal Services Commission or by the Lord Chancellor and no other party is ordered to pay the costs of the proceedings with the fee payable on an application for the court's approval of a certificate of costs payable from the Community Legal Service Fund or Lord Chancellor.

273. Civil proceedings–Legal aid–Statutory charge

THE CIVIL LEGAL AID (STATUTORY CHARGE) REGULATIONS 2013, SI 2013/503; made under the Legal Aid, Sentencing and Punishment of Offenders Act 2012 s.2, s.5, s.25, s.41. In force: April 1, 2013; .

These Regulations make provision about the statutory charge which arises over money and other property preserved or recovered by a legally aided party in civil proceedings and over costs payable to the legally aided party by another party to the proceedings.

274. Civil proceedings–Questionnaires

THE CIVIL PROCEEDINGS FEES (AMENDMENT) ORDER 2013, SI 2013/SI 2013/734 (L.6); made under the Courts Act 2003 s.92. In force: April 1, 2013; .

The Order amends the Civil Proceedings Fees Order 2008 (SI 2008/1053). The wording of fee 2.1 of Sch.1 of the civil order has been amended to reflect amendments to procedures made by the Civil Procedure (Amendment) Rules 2013 (SI 2013/262), which introduce a directions questionnaire in place of an allocation questionnaire.

275. Civil recovery proceedings–Investigations–Powers of seizure–Search warrants

THE PROCEEDS OF CRIME ACT 2002 (EXTERNAL INVESTIGATIONS) ORDER 2013, SI 2013/2605; made under the Proceeds of Crime Act 2002 s.445, s.459. In force: November 11, 2013; .

This Order makes provision to assist an external investigation (in a civil context) by obtaining orders and warrants from the High Court (or the sheriff or Court of Session in Scotland). It contains provisions which correspond (subject to modifications) to those concerning civil recovery investigations under the Proceeds of Crime Act 2002 Pt 8; namely production orders, search and seizure warrants, disclosure orders, customer information orders and account monitoring orders.

276. Civil recovery proceedings–Overseas assets–Effect of Supreme Court decision holding civil recovery not available for overseas assets on case already finally determined

[Proceeds of Crime Act 2002 (c.29) s.243, s.245A, s.245B, s.266, s.266(2), s.308(2); Civil Procedure Rules 1998 (SI 1998/3132) r.52.17.]

The appellant Serious Organised Crime Agency appealed against a decision to vary a property freezing order (PFO) that had been made against the respondent (O). O applied to reopen a refusal of permission to appeal against a civil recovery order (CRO). SOCA had concluded that O had obtained property through unlawful conduct. In 2008 it obtained, without notice, a PFO under the Proceeds of Crime Act 2002 s.245A. The trial of the issue was held in June 2011 before Kenneth Parker J, who reserved judgment. In October, the judge committed O for contempt for having disposed of property in breach of the PFO. In December he gave judgment in the substantive action. He granted a CRO under s.243 and s.266 in respect of property including property overseas, and ordered that the PFO should continue. O unsuccessfully sought permission to appeal against the CRO. In July 2012, the Supreme Court in *Serious Organised Crime Agency v Perry* [2012] UKSC 35, [2013] 1 A.C. 182, [2012] C.L.Y. 326 reversed the previous understanding of the law to hold that a CRO could only be made in respect of property within the jurisdiction. O applied to vary the PFO to exclude the overseas property. His Honour Judge Spencer granted that application, having regard to *Perry*. O sought to reopen the refusal of permission to appeal against the CRO, either on the basis that the CRO contained liberty to apply, or under CPR r.52.17; he also appealed against the order of committal as it had been based upon an unlawful extension of the court's jurisdiction. SOCA argued that Judge Spencer had wrongly varied the PFO.

Held: Appeals dismissed, application refused. (Mummery LJ dissenting regarding the variation of the PFO) (1) The CRO was a final order notwithstanding the liberty to apply. The order contained a final determination of status of the relevant property. The remaining parts of the order merely provided mechanisms to give effect to that final determination; it did not affect the finality of the decision. Accordingly, to reopen the issue, O had to bring his application within CPR r.52.17. The retrospective effect of a judicial decision was excluded from cases already finally determined, *Perry* considered. There was nothing exceptional about the instant case; if the fact of the common law taking a line which differed from earlier cases was exceptional, the finality of litigation would be undermined. Nor was the reopening of the decision necessary to remedy a real injustice: the CRO had been correctly made accordingly to the law as it was then understood. Accordingly, the CPR r.52.17 criteria had not been met. Further, no issue had been raised about the territorial reach of the order when permission to appeal was refused: it could not be necessary, for the avoidance of injustice, to reopen the refusal by reference to a point of law that could have been taken at the time. Accordingly, the CRO remained a binding order (see paras 28-29, 34-36 of judgment). (2) At the time the PFO had been made, it was justified in law and nobody had suggested the contrary. When the contempt was committed, and when the breach was dealt with, the order had remained valid. Only the subsequent change to the law had given rise to issues of jurisdiction, but that did not affect the legitimacy of the order when it was made or the gravamen of the breach (para.48). (3) The PFO was necessarily consequent upon the CRO: it was the intended mechanism for protecting the assets while the order was put into effect. Therefore, once it had been determined that the CRO remained in place, the consequential orders intended for the enforcement of that order should follow. That raised the question of the propriety of keeping property frozen when the Supreme Court had found that it fell outside the statute. Judge Spencer's analysis had ignored the order's continuing validity: he had simply imposed the Perry decision onto the consequential orders. However, under the statutory regime, it had not been possible to make a PFO in relation to the overseas, or indeed any, property, because s.266(2) provided that the CRO had to vest the recoverable property in the trustee for civil recovery. Under s.308(2), once the property vested in the trustee, it ceased to be recoverable. The answer to that conundrum was that once the PFO was made, it remained in force until set aside or revoked and so could remain in place after the CRO. Kenneth Parker J. had not made a PFO but had continued one. Once an application had been made to set aside the PFO, it was open to Judge Spencer to determine whether it was appropriate to provide additional protection in relation to property vested in the trustee. Bearing in mind s.245B, which mandated variation of a PFO if property ceased to be recoverable, his order in relation to that property had been justifiable. That did not free up the overseas properties: the CRO remained in place (paras 37-44, 50). (4) (Per Mummery LJ) *Perry* did not require the grant of a post-*Perry* application to vary a pre-*Perry* PFO. The ancillary character of the PFO was a major obstacle for O as long as the CRO continued. Prima facie, the PFO should continue without variation (paras 58-59).

SERIOUS ORGANISED CRIME AGENCY v O'DOCHERTY; *sub nom.* SERIOUS ORGANISED CRIME AGENCY v GIBBONS, [2013] EWCA Civ 518, [2013] C.P. Rep. 35, Mummery, L.J., CA (Civ Div).

277. Closed material–Disclosure–National security–Overriding objective

THE CIVIL PROCEDURE (AMENDMENT NO.5) RULES 2013, SI 2013/1571; made under the Justice and Security Act 2013 Sch.3 para.3. In force: June 28, 2013; .

These Rules amend the Civil Procedure Rules 1998 (SI 1998/3132) for the purpose of implementing the Justice and Security Act 2013 Pt 2.

278. Commencement of proceedings–Reserved legal activities–Laying of an information–Commencement of proceedings by director of company acting for reward–Acting as solicitor in breach of rules

[Copyright, Designs and Patents Act 1988 (c.48) s.297(1); Legal Services Act 2007 (c.29) s.1, s.12, s.127(1), Sch.2, Sch.2 para.4; Solicitors Act 1974 (c.47) s.20.]

The appellant company (M) appealed by way of case stated against an order dismissing the information that had been laid against the respondent licensees (L) alleging that they had dishonestly received a programme included in a broadcasting service from a place in the United Kingdom. M had brought a private prosecution, on behalf of the Football Association Premier League (F), alleging that L had showed a Premier League football match in their pub with intent to avoid payment of any charge applicable to the reception of that programme contrary to the Copyright, Designs and Patents Act 1988 s.297(1). M was a private limited company that traded for profit and that had been retained by F to investigate and prosecute infringements of F's intellectual property rights in relation to broadcasts of Premier League football matches. The information was laid against L by one of M's directors (H). L had received the broadcast that they showed from an Albanian satellite. Albania was not a member of the European Union. The issues before the court were (1) whether the laying of an information was the commencement of proceedings in the magistrates' court; and (2) whether there was a relevant restriction immediately before the appointed day.

Held: Appeal dismissed. (1) The laying of an information was the commencement of proceedings in the magistrates' court. What was tried by the magistrates was not the summons, or the description of an offence in a summons, but the information itself. It was the laying of the information that stopped time running and permitted the magistrates' court to try the information, and it was difficult to conclude that the information did not amount to the commencement of the proceedings, *R. v Manchester Stipendiary Magistrate, Ex p. Hill* [1983] 1 A.C. 328, [1982] C.L.Y. 1963 applied. The fact that an information might not lead to the issue of a summons was no objection to that conclusion. It followed that by laying the information against L, M was carrying on a reserved legal activity. The district judge was right to conclude that the laying of the information by H amounted to the commencement of proceedings and was therefore a conduct of litigation in accordance with the Legal Services Act 2007 Sch.2 and a "reserved legal activity" within the meaning of s.12 of that Act, *Murphy v Media Protection Services Ltd* [2012] EWHC 466 (Admin), [2012] 3 C.M.L.R. 2, [2012] C.L.Y. 1928 considered. (2) Prior to the 2007 Act there was no restriction on persons commencing and conducting a private prosecution and such activity was not a reserved legal activity. The regulatory objectives set out in s.1 of the 2007 Act and the duties owed to the court and to the defendant by the prosecutors, did not favour recognition of the right of unqualified and unregulated persons acting for reward to institute and to conduct private prosecutions. H had commenced proceedings in the magistrates' court. He did so not as a litigant acting on his own behalf but as a director of a company acting for reward for a client, namely F. He therefore acted as a solicitor within the meaning of and in breach of the Solicitors Act 1974 s.20. H was not an authorised litigator. It followed that M could not bring itself within Sch.2 para 4(2) of the 2007 Act. The reference in s.127(1) of the 2007 Act to the laying of an information must mean the lawful laying of an information. No information was laid lawfully against L and the prosecution was incompetent.

MEDIA PROTECTION SERVICES LTD v CRAWFORD, [2012] EWHC 2373 (Admin), [2013] 1 W.L.R. 1068, Stanley Burnton, L.J., DC.

279. Committal for contempt–Practice guidance issued

Held: Practice guidance issued. Practice guidance was issued to supplement *Practice Guidance (Sen Cts: Committal Proceedings: Open Court)* [2013] 1 W.L.R. 1316. The additional guidance provided, among other things, that a person who was not a party to the proceedings was not entitled as of right to a copy of the application notice relating to the committal application. The court could, however, authorise such a person to obtain a copy. Given the nature of committal proceedings, the court in every case where a committal application was made should, unless there were exceptional circumstances, direct that, upon payment of any appropriate charge that might be required, a copy of the application notice was to be made available to any person who requested it. If in an exceptional case the court decided that a copy of the application notice was not to be made available, the judge had to set out in writing the reasons for so deciding. It was also made clear that this guidance and the guidance to which it was supplemental applied to committal applications in family proceedings in the county court and the family proceedings court. It was also stated that, whenever a committal application in the Court of Protection or the Family Division or in family proceedings in the county court was being heard in public, the judge and the advocates should be robed.

PRACTICE GUIDANCE (FAM DIV: COMMITTAL PROCEEDINGS: OPEN COURT) [2013] 1 W.L.R. 1753, Sir James Munby (President, Fam), Fam Div.

280. Committal for contempt–Practice guidance issued

Held: Practice guidance issued. Practice guidance was issued on applications for committal for contempt of court. It was a fundamental principle of the administration of justice in England and Wales that such applications should be heard and decided in public, i.e. in open court. That principle applied as much to committal applications in the Court of Protection and in the Family Division as to committal applications in any other division of the High Court. The Court of Protection and, when the application arose out of proceedings relating to a child, the Family Division were vested with a discretionary power to hear a committal application in private. That discretion should be exercised only in exceptional cases where it was necessary in the interests of justice. The fact that the hearing of the committal application might involve the disclosure of material which ought not to be published did not of itself justify hearing the application in private if such publication could be restrained by an appropriate order. If, in an exceptional case, a committal application was heard in private and the court found that a person had committed a contempt of court, it had to state in public the name of that person, the nature of the contempt in respect of which the committal order or suspended committal order was being made, and the punishment imposed. Committal applications in the Court of Protection or the Family Division should at the outset be listed and heard in public. Whenever the court decided to exercise its discretion to sit in private, the judge should, before continuing the hearing in private, give a judgment in public setting out the reasons for doing so.

PRACTICE GUIDANCE (SEN CTS: COMMITTAL PROCEEDINGS: OPEN COURT); *sub nom.* PRACTICE GUIDANCE (SEN CTS: COMMITTAL FOR CONTEMPT OF COURT) [2013] 1 W.L.R. 1316, Lord Judge, L.C.J., Sen Cts.

281. Committal for contempt–Statements of truth–Application for permission under r.32.14 CPR–Whether directors had actual knowledge of insolvent company's financial position or reckless disregard for truth–Whether strong prima facie case

[Civil Procedure Rules 1998 (SI 1998/3132) r.32.14; CPR PD 18 (Further Information) 1999.]

The applicant company (S) sought permission to apply for committal for contempt under the CPR r.32.14 against the respondent directors (D) of a company in administration (B). S had engaged B as a sub-contractor. Following a payment dispute, B referred the matter to adjudication and was awarded over £20,000. S did not believe that the award represented the true state of the account between the parties and commenced arbitration proceedings. B issued enforcement proceedings seeking summary judgment on the adjudicator's award. S applied for a stay on the ground that B would be unable to repay the judgment sum, relying on evidence from an expert accountant (X) who considered that there was a significant risk of B becoming insolvent. D provided witness statements describing B as a solvent, profitable going concern. S's stay application was refused and B was awarded summary judgment. B subsequently went into administration. S obtained an arbitration award of just under £100,000. S claimed that there was a strong prima facie case that D had been aware that B would be unable to repay the judgment sum given what they had to have known about its true financial position. S contended that, although actual knowledge had been established, a reckless disregard for the truth was sufficient.

Held: Application refused. (1) It could be contempt of court for a witness to make a statement, supported by a recklessly made statement of truth, saying something which it could be proved beyond reasonable doubt that they consciously had no idea was true. That was supported by the wording of r.32.14, which did not introduce a new category of contempt, *Malgar Ltd v RE Leach (Engineering) Ltd* [2000] C.P. Rep. 39, [2000] C.L.Y. 383 applied, *Nield v Loveday* [2011] EWHC 2324 (Admin), [2011] 4 Costs L.O. 470, [2012] C.L.Y. 338 considered. Recklessness was a concept judges could address as they did in a criminal context. Logic also suggested that a person who represented as true something they consciously did not know was true was consciously misleading the court and that should be considered contemptuous. The correct approach was to consider whether there was a strong prima facie case, without straying into consideration of the merits of the case; whether the public interest required the committal proceedings to be brought; and whether such proceedings were proportionate and in accordance with the overriding objective, *Kirk v Walton* [2008] EWHC 1780 (QB), [2009] 1 All E.R. 257, [2009] C.L.Y. 403 applied. There was often a public interest in a given case to pursue people who appeared to have misled the court and where such conduct could have led to an interference with justice. However, optimism or even carelessness in the making of statements, particularly value judgement-type statements, would not be sufficient to establish that a party deliberately or recklessly made a misstatement. With regard to proportionality in the exercise of the court's discretion, it was not possible to give a blanket definition regarding the factors to be taken into account, as circumstances would vary widely. Regard could be had to the strength of the case, the sums involved, the likely court time and costs involved in the case, and the overriding objective. Statements of truth incorporated in witness statements or pleadings had to be regarded as important. People who signed them knowing they were untrue had to appreciate that they could face contempt proceedings and, possibly, independent criminal proceedings. The reliability of information about the solvency or viability of a company, deployed to secure a stay of execution of adjudication enforcement, was particularly important because, unlike a final judgment, which was binding, an enforced adjudication decision was only binding until final resolution of the underlying arbitration or litigation dispute. Compliance with CPR PD81 para.5.2 was also extremely important as contempt proceedings were in the nature of criminal proceedings, and the person against whom committal was sought was entitled to know what the charges were and broadly what the evidential basis was said to be (see paras 24-32 of judgment). (2) Although there had initially been non-compliance by S with para.5.2, that deficiency had been put right and D had been given sufficient time to deploy their evidence and arguments to challenge the application. However, although X's evidence just about established a prima facie case against B, it did not establish a strong case. X essentially concluded that D's evidence was incompatible with what they had known or should have known about B's finances. If the complaint was only that D "should have known", that was at best a complaint of carelessness on their part and not enough to found a charge of contempt. The court should be slow to infer a strong prima facie case when it could not be demonstrated that D had either actual knowledge or had acted recklessly in making their statements. It would be wholly disproportionate to proceed to a committal hearing. The original case only involved £24,000; the parties' joint costs were already £50,000 to £60,000. The public interest had to be weighed in what was at best a marginal case by the proportionality of the exercise. In cases such as the instant one, that was measured largely by reference to the cost and time likely to be involved. It was not in the public interest to allow S's application (paras 33-39).

BERRY PILING SYSTEMS LTD v SHEER PROJECTS LTD, [2013] EWHC 347 (TCC), [2013] B.L.R. 232, Akenhead, J., QBD (TCC).

282. Committal orders–Anti-social behaviour injunctions–Use of longer period to protect offender–Appropriate sentence length

The appellant (W) appealed against an order committing her to prison for 12 months for breaching two separate civil anti-social behaviour injunctions. W was a tenant of a flat owned by the respondent local authority. She was a recovering heroin addict and alcoholic with mental health problems, had a volatile relationship with a man (S) whose visits had caused nuisance to her neighbours, and had become pregnant. An interim order had been made, restraining W from admitting S to the communal parts of the flats and from causing nuisance to her neighbours. A power of arrest was attached to the order. The order was breached, W was arrested and a suspended committal order of two months' imprisonment was made. Another injunction with similar terms was later made. W breached that order and the local authority applied to commit her to prison. The judge passed a sentence of 12 months' imprisonment, comprising the activated two-month suspended sentence and an additional 10 months' imprisonment, to run consecutively. W argued that a sentence of 10 months' imprisonment for the latest breaches was manifestly excessive and that the judge failed to have sufficient regard to her attempt to wean herself from her drug addiction.

Held: Appeal allowed. The latest breaches were at a lower level of seriousness in the light of what had gone before. The proper approach was to ask what was the appropriate sentence for a second breach of the court's order while subject to a suspended order in respect of the first. In the case of criminal breaches of an anti-social behaviour order, the Sentencing Guidelines Council's guideline table did not apply to repeat offenders. W was wise to recognise that, for a second breach, a custodial order was inevitable. In a letter provided to the court, W had shown an insight into her own problems and a determination to improve her behaviour in the interests of herself and her unborn child. In the light of the information before the first judge and the instant court, a sentence of longer than three months' imprisonment was not appropriate. There was no sound reason why the suspended order should not be activated consecutively. The order for committal for 10 months would be quashed and replaced with a committal for three months, making five months in all. In imposing a much longer period, the judge was attempting to protect W and perhaps her unborn child from herself. However, deprivation of liberty was the most serious sanction available to the court and the appropriate period of custody was the least period which the seriousness of the offender's breaches could properly justify (see paras 22-27 of judgment)

WILLOUGHBY v SOLIHULL MBC, [2013] EWCA Civ 699, [2013] H.L.R. 36, Maurice Kay, L.J., CA (Civ Div).

283. Committal orders–Sentence length–Breaches of anti-social behaviour injunction by resident of shared accommodation for older people

The appellant (T) appealed against a sentence of four months' imprisonment imposed for breaches of an anti-social behaviour injunction. T was a tenant of a flat in shared accommodation for older people owned by the respondent (H). Complaints from other residents and members of staff about T's threatening and abusive behaviour led to H bringing possession proceedings against him. The district judge made an interim anti-social behaviour injunction with a power of arrest pending trial. T was arrested for alleged breaches of the injunction. The court adjourned the proceedings regarding those breaches and released T on bail pending trial. Two months later he was re-arrested for two further alleged breaches. The judge heard H's possession claim together with its application to commit T for breaches of the injunction. T denied all allegations of anti-social behaviour. The judge made a possession order and found that four breaches of the injunction were made out to the criminal standard. The first breach was entering the residents' lounge in the shared accommodation despite being banned, for which he was sentenced to two months' imprisonment; the second was on the same occasion refusing to leave and being drunk and swearing and shouting, for which he received four months; the third was swearing at an elderly resident, for which he received two months; and the fourth was swearing and uttering threatening words to a member of staff, for which he received four months. They were concurrent sentences.

Held: Appeal allowed. The Sentencing Guidelines Council's definitive guidelines in relation to breaches of anti-social behaviour orders were equally relevant to civil courts. The guidelines recommended different bands according to the gravity of the anti-social behaviour. T's overall sentence was towards the top end of the range for behaviour causing a lesser degree of harassment, alarm or distress, but most of the instances of behaviour were at the lower end of that category and some were in the lowest category. One aggravating feature was that the last two instances were committed while T was on bail. The two sentences each of four months were significantly outside the sentencing guidelines. Although often a first sentence for breach of an anti-social behaviour injunction would be suspended, in T's case there were grounds for immediate custody: it was not the first time he had caused trouble, and the court would have been aware that he was likely to cause further disturbance. Considered collectively, his breaches did pass the threshold for immediate custody. However, four months overall was excessive. He would receive a total of six weeks' imprisonment, comprising concurrent sentences of six weeks for the two breaches for which he had received four months, and two weeks for the two breaches for which he had received two months (see paras 5-7 of judgment).

AMICUS HORIZON LTD v THORLEY, [2012] EWCA Civ 817, [2012] H.L.R. 43, Lord Neuberger (M.R.), CA (Civ Div).

284. Control orders–Non-derogating control orders–Orders revoked by secretary of state–Power of court to order general stay of proceedings

[Prevention of Terrorism Act 2005 (c.2) s.3(12); Civil Procedure Rules 1998 (SI 1998/3132) Pt 76, r.76.21, r.76.31.]

The appellants (B and C) appealed against a decision ([2011] EWHC 1990 (Admin)) that the court had power to stay proceedings brought against them under the Prevention of Terrorism Act 2005 s.3. Non-derogating control orders had been imposed on B and C. Several weeks later C was arrested pursuant to an extradition request and remained in custody. B had voluntarily left the United Kingdom and gone to Pakistan. The secretary of state revoked the control orders as they had ceased to have any practical effect. A hearing concerning whether further disclosure should be given to B and C was adjourned part-heard. The court decided that it would be disproportionate to allow the proceedings to continue and therefore ordered a stay, despite B and C's objections. B and C submitted that the court had no power to stay control order proceedings.

Held: Appeal allowed. (1) Proceedings under s.3 of the 2005 Act were often time-consuming and expensive. Where a controlled person had left the jurisdiction, apparently for good, and the control order was revoked by the secretary of state, the value of pursuing a reference under s.3(2)(c) and s.3(10) with a view to deciding whether the decision to make the control order was flawed appeared, on first sight, to be highly questionable. However, when making a non-derogating control order the secretary of state was exercising an exceptionally invasive power over some of the fundamental freedoms of an individual. It would be unsurprising if the legislature considered that the executive should be given that draconian right only if its exercise was reviewed by the judiciary. There were also strong grounds for contending that it was appropriate, not merely for the benefit of the controlled person but also in the wider public interest, that the court had the opportunity to consider whether the order and its terms were justified in law. The provision in s.3(14), allowing for discontinuance of the proceedings if the controlled person so requested, was quite consistent with that analysis. It was quite appropriate that the specific desire of the controlled person for the judicial review to end should prevail over the more general public interest that such reviews take place as a matter of course (see paras 42-44, 46 of judgment). (2) If the instant proceedings were not control order proceedings, there would have been much to be said for the judge's approach and his order for a stay. However, the principal question was whether his order was permissible having regard to the provisions of the 2005 Act and the CPR Pt 76. The stay ordered by the judge was not intended, or framed, as an interlocutory order. It put an end to the proceedings without any finding as to whether the decision of the secretary of state to make the control order had been flawed. As such, it was not one of the orders permitted by s.3(12), s.3.(13) and s.3(14) of the 2005 Act. The court could not discontinue a hearing unless the controlled person requested such a course of action. That was consistent with the provisions of r.76.21 of the CPR, under which the types of proceedings listed (including those relating to non-derogating control orders) were to be "determined at a hearing". "Determined" meant "decided". Rule 76.31 also envisaged the court making a substantive determination. Nothing in Pt 76 supported the proposition that the court could order a permanent stay of proceedings in circumstances such as those in the instant case. It followed that the judge did not have the power to make the order staying the proceedings (paras 30-32, 34, 37-38).

SECRETARY OF STATE FOR THE HOME DEPARTMENT v CB; *sub nom.* CB v SECRETARY OF STATE FOR THE HOME DEPARTMENT, [2012] EWCA Civ 418, [2012] 1 W.L.R. 3259, Lord Neuberger (M.R.), CA (Civ Div).

285. Control orders–Terrorism prevention and investigation measures–Allegation of abuse of process–Whether usual rule on burden of proof should be modified

The court conducted statutory reviews of control orders made in respect of the respondents (C and F) and of terrorism prevention and investigation measures (TPIM) notices which had been served on them. The Security Service had assessed C and F as being linked to an extremist facilitation network. It was asserted, among other things, that they had received terrorist training in Somalia and that they had been involved in planning terrorist attacks. They had been detained by the Somaliland authorities for two months before being removed to the United Kingdom. It was their case that their arrest, detention and deportation were unlawful and that the Security Service had colluded with the Somaliland authorities in such unlawful acts. The issues were (i) whether the decisions of the applicant secretary of state to make control orders and TPIMs in respect of C and F were flawed in that she had no reasonable grounds for suspecting or believing (respectively) that they had been involved in terrorism-related activity; (ii) whether the secretary of state was reasonably entitled to conclude that it was and remained necessary, for purposes connected with protecting members of the public from a risk of terrorism, for control orders and TPIMs to be imposed on C and F; (iii) whether the secretary of state's decisions to impose and maintain certain obligations on F, such as an overnight residence measure and an association measure, were flawed; (iv) whether the control orders and TPIMs should be quashed as an abuse of process in the light of C and F's allegations that the Security Service had colluded with the Somaliland authorities in their arrest, detention and deportation; (v) whether, in deciding to make control orders and TPIMs, the secretary of state had wrongly disregarded C and F's allegations as to the events which had taken place in Somaliland; (vi) whether, as asserted by C and F, the secretary of state had failed to make full and frank disclosure when seeking permission to make the control orders and TPIMs.

Held: Judgment accordingly. (1) The secretary of state did have reasonable grounds for suspecting and believing that C and F had been involved in terrorism-related activity (see paras 38, 54 of judgment). (2) The secretary of state had been entitled to conclude that it was necessary to impose control orders and TPIMs on C and F (paras 44, 57). (3) It had not been established that the secretary of state's decisions to impose and maintain the relevant obligations on F were flawed (paras 63-75). (4) As to the abuse of process allegations, F had raised an issue as to the burden of proof. He argued that, because of the special procedure followed in these proceedings which denied respondents access to much of the relevant material, the court should depart from the rule that the burden of proof lay on the party alleging abuse of process. That could not be accepted. C and F were well aware of the case they wished to advance in relation to abuse of process. While the court would always be mindful of the limitations arising from the fact that certain relevant material could not be disclosed to respondents, it was not necessary to modify the well-established principles in relation to the burden of proof in abuse-of-process applications in order to maintain the essential fairness of the trial. The court would assume, for present purposes, that C and F's arrest, detention and deportation were not in accordance with Somaliland law. However, even when such considerations of illegality were brought into account, the high threshold which had to be crossed to render these proceedings an abuse of process had not been crossed. It was necessary, when considering whether the proceedings were an abuse of process, to evaluate the considerations of policy and justice in play: quite exceptional powers had been conferred on the secretary of state to act to protect members of the public from a particularly grave terrorist threat. The proceedings were an essential adjunct of those powers, intended to ensure by judicial supervision that those powers were exercised lawfully. There was an important public interest that control orders and TPIMs should be made where a particular risk made it necessary to do so, *R. v Horseferry Road Magistrates Court, Ex p. Bennett (No.1)* [1994] 1 A.C. 42, [1993] C.L.Y. 1867 and *R. v Mullen (Nicholas Robert) (No.2)* [2000] Q.B. 520, [1999] C.L.Y. 972 distinguished (paras 82, 85, 87, 134, 136). (5) The court was prepared to proceed on the basis that the secretary of state had not taken into account the events in Somaliland when making the control orders and the TPIMs. Those events were potentially relevant in two ways. First, the secretary of state was required to have regard to them when considering a question she had to address, namely whether the necessary applications to the court might be an abuse of process. Second, C and F's allegations were potentially relevant to the exercise of the discretion which applied when the secretary of state was considering whether to make the control orders and the TPIMs. As to the first matter, there had been no abuse of process. As to the second, the secretary of state would inevitably have exercised her discretion in precisely the same way had she taken account of the matters in question (paras 148, 151-153). (6) The obligation to give disclosure in the instant case was not limited to drawing the court's attention to all matters relevant to the statutory criteria but extended to require disclosure of matters which would be capable of founding an argument of abuse of process. Full disclosure had been given before the judge's grant of permission to impose the TPIMs, but the disclosure made before permission was given to make the control orders had been deficient. The principles applicable when non-disclosure occurred in without notice applications in criminal cases or private law civil cases had to be modified in cases such as this to permit the court to take account of the purpose of the legislation and the public interests which were in play. The relevant statutory powers were conferred on the secretary of state to enable her to act to protect the public from terrorism-related activity. In all the circumstances, which included the fact that the non-disclosure had not been deliberate, it would not be appropriate to quash the control orders by reason of such non-disclosure (paras 163, 168, 172, 174-176).

SECRETARY OF STATE FOR THE HOME DEPARTMENT v CC, [2012] EWHC 2837 (Admin), [2013] 1 W.L.R. 2171, Lloyd-Jones, L.J., QBD (Admin).

286. Cost protection–Appeals–Proceedings started in costs-free jurisdiction–Protection from costs in Court of Appeal

[Civil Procedure Rules 1998 (SI 1998/3132) r.52.3(7), r.52.9, r.52.9A; Transfer of Undertakings (Protection of Employment) Regulations 2006 (SI 2006/246) reg.7.]

The appellant college applied for reconsideration of an order imposing conditions on the grant of permission to appeal which gave costs protection to the respondent employees (H) in its appeal to the Court of Appeal against H's successful unfair dismissal claim. H were teachers at a prison. Their employment transferred to the college under the Transfer of Undertakings (Protection of Employment) Regulations 2006. Funding cuts caused financial difficulties for the college so it restructured staff and H were required to accept a salary reduction. They refused to sign their new contracts but were faced with the alternative of dismissal. They brought proceedings for unfair dismissal against the college which defended the claim under s.7(1)(b). The employment tribunal found in favour of H and ordered the college to re-engage them at their original salary. The college unsuccessfully appealed to the Employment Appeal Tribunal and was granted permission to appeal to the Court of Appeal. H feared their position if they were liable for costs so successfully applied for costs protection. H undertook not to seek their costs if they were successful. The college argued that CPR r.52.9 applied and there was no compelling reason for such an order. It contended that H could afford to risk the estimated £20,000 costs. H submitted that CPR r.52.3(7) gave the court an unfettered discretion to impose the conditions; they had succeeded twice where they were not at risk of costs so it was not just to litigate when they were at risk of costs in the Court of Appeal; they were both of modest means and could not risk the litigation; and the new rule CPR r.52.9A would come into force on April 1, 2013 which would offer the same protection.

Held: Application refused. (1) Many individuals litigated in no costs jurisdictions such as the employment tribunal and the EAT without representation, as H had. It was usually unjust to put them at risk of costs if they were dragged unwillingly to appeal. However it was not always desirable to make a costs protection order. There was no reason to disapply the normal costs-shifting rules if the appeal from the EAT involved a group of union-backed employees and a well-financed employer. In the past courts had had to do their best but a litigant could not rely on that, *Eweida v British Airways Plc* [2009] EWCA Civ 1025, [2010] C.P. Rep. 6, [2010] C.L.Y. 292 considered, *St Albans School for Girls Governors v Neary (Costs)* [2009] EWCA Civ 1214, [2010] 2 Costs L.R. 191, [2010] C.L.Y. 289 and *UNISON v Kelly* [2012] EWCA Civ 1148, [2012] I.R.L.R. 951, [2012] C.L.Y. 333 followed. The new rule CPR r.52.9A was intended to address the mischief that arose where a litigant moved from a no-costs jurisdiction to a costs-shifting jurisdiction. The court would be able to exclude or limit costs recovery in such a case. (2) The court could impose retrospective conditions under CPR r.52.9(1)(c) after leave to appeal had been granted if there was a compelling reason to do so. There were compelling reasons for making the order: (a) H had a claim which had been vindicated at two tribunal hearings; (b) they would not pursue their claim unless they were protected; (c) as teachers on modest salaries, they could not reasonably be expected to accept a risk of £20,000 costs; (d) if they lost, the court might be merciful on costs but they could not count on that; (e) they had undertaken not to seek their costs so the order achieved a level playing field; (f) it was accepted that the college was in financial difficulties but that did not put it in a similar situation to H for whom an order for costs would be a disaster; (g) setting aside the order would serve no useful purpose as H could make a fresh application under the new rule in two weeks which would be bound to succeed. It was a classic case in which the court would make such an order under the new rule. H was entitled to the costs protection order.

MANCHESTER COLLEGE v HAZEL, [2013] EWCA Civ 281, [2013] C.P. Rep. 28, Jackson, L.J., CA (Civ Div).

287. Costs–Administration orders–Dismissed applications–Whether discretion to award costs–Reconciling Sch.B1 para.13(1)(f) Insolvency Act 1986 with r.2.67 Insolvency Rules 1986

[Insolvency Act 1986 (c.45) Sch.B1 Pt 2 para.13; Insolvency Rules 1986 (SI 1986/1925) r.2.67, r.4.218.]

The court was required to determine the costs of a dismissed application by the applicant (R) for the appointment of an administrator for the respondent company (B). R had been a shareholder and company director of a restaurants business together with another party (X). The business became insolvent. R instructed accountants and they proposed a pre-pack administration with a sale to R. R was to buy the business for a sum plus extra monies to come from an earnout at one of the restaurants. A bank had a floating charge over the business. Two days before the administration hearing, X, who was a guarantor of the bank's debt, took an assignment of the charge and appointed administrators. That meant R could not pursue his own application for an appointment. However, R applied to be paid his costs of the administration application as an expense of the administration. The issues were (i) whether there was jurisdiction to order the costs of such an application to be costs in an out-of-court administration, even though an administration order had not been made; (ii) if so, what principle determined the level of priority given to those costs; (iii) whether, so far as jurisdiction allowed, discretion should be exercised in R's favour. R submitted that the ambit of the Insolvency Act 1986 schB1 para13(1)(f) was wide enough to give the court jurisdiction to make the order he sought, and that inferences and extensions from decided cases gave his case support. R argued that anomalies would arise if he was not found to be entitled to his costs and that the application was manifestly in the interests of B's creditors as a whole.

Held: Application granted. (1) The wording of para.13(1)(f) was indeed wide. That view had received support from the decided cases relied on by R, *SE Services Ltd, Re, Kayley Vending Ltd, Re* [2009] EWHC 904 (Ch), [2009] B.C.C. 578, [2009] C.L.Y. 2195, and *Johnson Machine and Tool Co Ltd, Re* [2010] EWHC 582 (Ch), [2010] B.C.C. 382, [2010] C.L.Y. 1842 considered. Further support could be found in *Irish Reel Productions Ltd v Capitol Films Ltd* [2010] EWHC 180 (Ch), [2010] Bus. L.R. 854, [2010] C.L.Y. 1838 concerning a winding-up petition, *Irish Reel* considered (see paras 16-25 of judgment). An important question was whether and for what purposes the Insolvency Rules 1986 r.2.67 was to be treated as a complete description of all the expenses in an administration. *SE Services* and *Johnson* held that it was. In *Toshoku Finance UK Plc (In Liquidation), Re* [2002] UKHL 6, [2002] 1 W.L.R. 671, [2002] C.L.Y. 2718 it was held that the winding-up equivalent in r.4.218 contained a complete enumeration of liquidation expenses, and the instant court would hold the same to apply to r.2.67; nevertheless, Lord Hoffman's view was that the completeness of r.4.218 did not exclude the application of the "liquidation expenses" rule that allowed certain expenses not strictly within that category to be treated as such where it was right to do so, *Toshoku* applied. A similar principle was applied to administrations in *Atlantic Computer Systems Plc, Re* [1992] Ch. 505, [1991] C.L.Y. 2127, albeit with a qualification regarding rigour, that the court could direct administrators to treat as proper expenses costs that were not strictly proper, *Atlantic* applied. That principle seemed to have been confirmed by the Court of Appeal, *Bloom v Pensions Regulator* [2011] EWCA Civ 1124, [2012] 1 All E.R. 1455, [2012] C.L.Y. 1791 applied. Therefore, despite r.2.67 being a complete code, there remained an avenue whereby other items could be considered "as if" they were expenses, Toshoku applied. Although the fruits of the discretion under para.13(1)(f) could not be an expense of the administration, they could be payable "as if" they were. The court could exercise a discretion in an analogous application (paras 26-31). (2) R's case fell within the court's discretion, and it was for R to justify such an order. The extent of benefit to the creditors rather than the management was relevant, *SE Services* and *Kayley* applied. R's proposals appeared to be in their interests, and what X's administrators had achieved was not sufficiently different to show otherwise. Further, those administrators risked not being able to do a deal at all, having lost R's deal. Without X's appointment, it was likely that R's application would have succeeded and he would have had his costs as an expense of the administration. The same result ought to follow as would have followed had R's application been acceded to, and it was difficult to avoid the conclusion that the creditors were not materially better off under the administration than under R's pre-pack. Considering the order of expenses within r.2.67 indicated in *Toshoku*, the costs should have the same level of priority as if an order been made on R's petition (paras 36-40).

BICKLAND LTD, *Re; sub nom.* ROHL v BICKLAND LTD, [2012] EWHC 706 (Ch), [2013] Bus. L.R. 361, Mann, J., Ch D.

288. Costs–Assessment–Cost management orders–Timing of application to revise or amend costs management order

[Civil Procedure Rules 1998 (SI 1998/3132) r.3.15(3), r.3.18(b).]

The court was required to determine costs following the dismissal of a claim by the claimant (E) for damages for breach of contract against the defendant (M). E had taken out after-the-event (ATE) insurance against the risk of having to pay M's costs. E notified M of both the funding and the limit of the cover. At a case management conference M was ordered to file and serve its costs budget in accordance with CPR PD 51G, the Costs Management in Mercantile Courts and Technology and Construction Courts -Pilot Scheme. Costs management orders were made approving the costs budget of both parties. At a pre-trial review the costs management orders were enlarged to cover the costs of daily transcripts at the forthcoming trial. That had the agreed effect of increasing M's approved costs budget to £268,488. Neither party applied before the trial to increase or revise the costs budget. A month before the trial M sent E and the court a revised costs budget, which doubled the previous estimate. E objected to the revised budget, but at the same time notified M of a much smaller increase in its own budget figure. In the run-up to the trial M's solicitors wrote a letter marked "without prejudice save as to costs" offering the sum of £150,000 in full and final settlement of E's claim, inclusive of costs. That offer was rejected by E, who instead indicated that it would accept £550,000 plus costs. The matter proceeded to trial as the parties were unable to reach an agreement. The total costs sought by M was £497,593. The issues were (i) whether M was entitled to costs on an indemnity basis; (ii) if so what was the relevance of the existing costs management orders; (iii) if not, so that the costs were assessed on the standard basis, whether M could recover more than £268,488 either by seeking to amend the costs budget after judgment, or by asserting good reasons to depart from the existing costs budget.

Held: Judgment accordingly. (1) Indemnity costs were not appropriate in the instant case. Although E had lost, the matters that it raised were plainly arguable. The case was not conducted in a disproportionate manner by E. M was entitled to its costs to be assessed on a standard basis and not an indemnity basis, *Euroption Strategic Fund Ltd v Skandinaviska Enskilda Banken AB* [2012] EWHC 749 (Comm) applied. The particular circumstances required for the indemnity basis had not been made out (see paras 17, 20, 22, 26 of judgment). (2) As the court had found that M was not entitled to costs on the indemnity basis, the relevance of the existing costs management order did not arise directly. Even if the court had been wrong and the costs should have been assessed on an indemnity basis, the costs management order and the approved budget costs would still be the starting point for any costs assessment (paras 27, 28-30, 67). (3) The finding that M was entitled to its costs to be assessed on a standard basis created a difficulty for M because, *prima facie*, the upper limit of its recoverable costs was £268,000, which was the subject of the modified costs management order. Whether regard was had to the pilot scheme or the new rules in the CPR, or guidance in *Henry v News Group Newspapers Ltd* [2013] EWCA Civ 19, [2013] 2 All E.R. 840, [2013] 7 C.L. 53, the result was the same; unless M could amend/revise upwards the costs management order or approved costs budget pursuant to CPR PD 51G para.6 (and now CPR r.3.15(3)) or persuade the court that there were good reasons to depart from it in accordance with para.8 (and now r.3.18(b)) then M's costs would be assessed by reference to the costs management order, *Henry* followed. Paragraph 6 allowed the court to approve or disapprove departures from the previous budget. If a defendant wanted the court to approve the significant changes to its costs budget, then it had to formally seek such approval. It was not enough simply to file the material at court. An application to revise or amend a costs management decision had to be made as soon as it became apparent that the original budget costs had been exceeded by more than a minimal amount. That application ought to be made before the trial, and there was nothing in para.6 which envisaged an application after the trial. E would be prejudiced if the claim was heard now. Even if the court was wrong to conclude that an application to amend the costs management order should not be entertained after judgment, at the very least M needed to demonstrate good reason why the application was made so late. M could not seek retrospectively to revise the budget under para.6 so as to all but double the original costs budget approved in the costs management order (paras 32-34, 36-38, 41-42, 44).

ELVANITE FULL CIRCLE LTD v AMEC EARTH & ENVIRONMENTAL (UK) LTD, [2013] EWHC 1643 (TCC), [2013] 4 All E.R. 765, Coulson, J., QBD (TCC).

289. Costs–Beddoe applications–Trustee's application for directions–Liability of trustee for costs

[Civil Procedure Rules 1998 (SI 1998/3132) r.48.4.]

The appellant executor (D) appealed against a decision that he was not entitled to take his costs of proceedings out of the estate of the deceased and that he pay the costs of the first respondent (W) out of his own assets. D was the executor of W's mother's estate. She died in 2005 and left her share of a company to her three sons in equal shares. W held the other share in the company. The company's articles of association did not contain a provision enabling D to require W to purchase the share from the estate so it was difficult for D to realise the bequeathed share. In 2007 W made a without prejudice offer of £125,000 to each of his brothers for their respective interests in the share but it was rejected. In 2008 D sought directions on how to deal with the share issue. The claim was brought under the principles in *Beddoe, Re* [1893] 1 Ch. 547. D made an offer to purchase the share and, following a hearing, a consent order was agreed. In 2011 W applied to have the date for the share's valuation determined. Judgment was given in favour of W and the share was valued at less than £6,000. The judge held that it was inappropriate for D to get his costs from the estate as he had not sent a pre-action protocol letter and he should have engaged with W's first offer. D submitted that the pursuit of proceedings had been reasonable and fully justified in that it had prompted W to make an offer that eventually led to the consent order.

Held: Appeal allowed. The normal rule on the costs of an application for directions was that, absent improper conduct, a trustee's costs would be paid out of the trust fund. The judge was wrong to approach the case as if it were costs in ordinary litigation. The court had to start from the special position of a trustee's application for directions, with the special rules and practice that apply to such proceedings. The judge erred because he overlooked the special nature of the *Beddoe* proceedings, *Beddoe* followed. CPR r.48.4 was relevant to the instant case as was the Costs Practice Direction para.50A.1 and 50A.2. When D applied for directions as to what he should do with regard to the share in the company, he was following the general guidance given consistently by cases and he could expect to be entitled to an indemnity for his costs of making the application out of the residuary estate unless he was found to have acted improperly in making the application. W's first offer had not been in satisfactory terms and a negotiated solution had not been reached. As regards the judge's criticism of D, there was no pre-action protocol which related to *Beddoe* applications so there was no default on his part and W had been given notice of the proceedings. Neither was the absence of a draft statement of case a legitimate criticism of D. The passage of time in D reacting to W's offer could not be regarded as improper conduct on D's part. The fact was that commencement of the proceedings led to W making a fresh offer which led without unreasonable delay to a compromise which resolved the problem. Nothing came near to satisfying the test for depriving a trustee of his indemnity for costs out of the fund. The judge's criticisms were not justified. His order was wrong in law and the result of an implicit misdirection. D was entitled to his costs of the *Beddoe* application from the estate (see paras 26, 28, 32-35, 37, 41, 43-46, 48, 52, 54 of judgment).

DAVIES v WATKINS, [2012] EWCA Civ 1570, [2013] C.P. Rep. 10, Thorpe, L.J., CA (Civ Div).

290. Costs–Conduct–Limited success of claims to recover insured and uninsured losses–Determination of costs–Relevant principles

[Civil Procedure Rules 1998 (SI 1998/3132) Pt 36, Pt 44, r.44.3.]

The court was required to determine the costs in two claims. The main action concerned a subrogated claim by the claimant company in liquidation and its directors (B) against the defendants (X) for insured losses arising from material damage to its premises and loss of profits caused by X's admitted negligence. The company's directors and its liquidator (V) brought a separate claim against X to recover uninsured losses. X had made an offer under CPR Pt 36 which was refused. They later made an offer under CPR Pt 44 which was open until May 30, 2012. It was not accepted. The parties made further Pt.36 offers to each other prior to trial, none of which were accepted. There were no further negotiations and the trial went ahead in June 2012. In the main claim, B recovered approximately 25 per cent of the sums claimed, and in the uninsured claim, V recovered just 3 per cent of the damages claimed. B sought their costs in full, V sought 50 per cent of their costs, and X claimed that their costs should be paid by B and V on an indemnity basis. The court was required to consider the relevance of offers under CPR Pt 36 and CPR Pt 44, the proper interpretation of "success" in CPR r.44.3, the parties' conduct before and during the litigation, the problems created by exaggeration of the claim and B and V's failure to provide proper information timeously.

Held: Costs determined. (1) In dealing with costs in cases like the instant one, the following principles applied: (a) in a commercial case, a successful party would usually be the one that recovered money from the other, *Multiplex Constructions (UK) Ltd v Cleveland Bridge UK Ltd* [2008] EWHC 2280 (TCC), 122 Con. L.R. 88, [2009] C.L.Y. 378 applied and *Gibbon v Manchester City Council* [2010] EWCA Civ 726, [2010] 1 W.L.R. 2081, [2010] C.L.Y. 387 followed; (b) the only certain way for a defendant to shift its potential costs liability was to make a Part 36 offer which it then bettered at trial, *Gibbon* and *Fox v Foundation Piling Ltd* [2011] EWCA Civ 790, [2011] C.P. Rep. 41, [2012] C.L.Y. 352 followed; (c) the pursuit of exaggerated claims might deprive the claimant of some or all of its costs, *Islam v Ali* [2003] EWCA Civ 612 followed and *Fulham Leisure Holdings Ltd v Nicholson Graham & Jones (Costs)* [2006] EWHC 2428 (Ch) applied, but it was usually only where the exaggeration was deliberate that the claimant would be ordered to pay the defendant's costs,

Painting v Oxford University [2005] EWCA Civ 161, [2005] 3 Costs L.R. 394, [2005] C.L.Y. 347 and *Ford v GKR Construction Ltd* [2000] 1 W.L.R. 1397, [1999] C.L.Y. 379 followed; (d) in general terms, for costs to be shifted as a result of conduct, so that the claimant who recovered something at trial still has to pay the defendant's costs, there needed to be more or less total failure on the issues that went to trial, *Hullock v East Riding of Yorkshire CC* [2009] EWCA Civ 1039 followed, or a failure to accept a Part 44 offer that would have put the claimant in a better position than going on, *Fulham Leisure* applied (see para.42 of judgment). (2) In the substantive claim, up until May 30, 2012, B were the successful parties for the purposes of CPR Pt 44.3(2) and the usual rule would be that X should pay their costs up to that date, subject to all questions of conduct under CPR r.44.3(4). Whilst B's claim was inflated, it was not dishonest or deliberately exaggerated, although it was not properly supported by the underlying material and B and their solicitors and experts had done little or nothing to address those deficiencies. It would, therefore, be manifestly unjust to allow B to recover all of their costs until May 30, 2012, but neither was it appropriate to order B to pay any part of X's costs up to that date. The right order was for X to pay 60 per cent of B's reasonable and proportionate costs up to May 30, 2012, excluding all costs in connection with the experts (paras 51, 54, 57, 61-63, 68). (3) The position changed when X bettered its Pt 44 offer, and B would be ordered to pay X's costs from May 30, 2012, making them liable for the entire costs of the trial. That outcome was justified because B's expert evidence was rejected and X had won on every substantive point (paras 69, 73-75). (4) V's separate claim for uninsured losses should have been run in the same action as the subrogated claim. The decision to pursue a second claim inevitably duplicated costs, and V had to pay for that luxury. It was, accordingly, appropriate to require V to pay 90 per cent of X's costs of the uninsured action (paras 15, 77, 82). (5) As the claims were not deliberately exaggerated, and because there was nothing else in the B and V's conduct which might be regarded as so out of the ordinary as to warrant an express statement of the court's disapproval, it was not appropriate to make an exceptional order for indemnity costs (para.84).

BRIT INNS LTD (IN LIQUIDATION) v BDW TRADING LTD (COSTS); *sub nom.* BARBER v BDW TRADING LTD (COSTS), [2012] EWHC 2489 (TCC), [2012] B.L.R. 531, Coulson, J., QBD (TCC).

291. Costs–Conduct–Relevance of defendant's decision to decline mediation

The court ruled on costs following the dismissal of the action brought by the claimant (C) against the defendant (E). C had claimed over $16 million for the breach and repudiation of an agreement between the parties for the exclusive distribution of satellite-tracking devices for aeroplanes or helicopters. E won on all the key issues. The trial began on July 2, 2012 and ended on July 17. On March 2, E's solicitors had attempted to initiate a settlement dialogue with C's solicitors but the latter said that they wanted to wait for the exchange of witness statements and possibly expert reports before any discussions could take place. E's solicitors made further unsuccessful attempts to enter into negotiations. On May 31, C's solicitors suggested mediation. E's solicitors declined, stating, among other things, that each side was now familiar with the other's case and that there was nothing to suggest that C would accept much less than $16 million. C argued that there should be a substantial reduction in E's costs to reflect its unwillingness to enter into mediation.

Held: Costs determined. There should be a costs order in E's favour whereby its costs, assessed on a standard basis, were to be paid by C. E had not acted unreasonably in not wishing to participate in mediation. First, there had been no willingness on C's part to engage even in a without-prejudice discussion until May 31, notwithstanding at least four attempts on E's part to initiate the same since early March. Second, it was clear from an offer to settle made by C in early June that it had a strong view that it was entitled to substantial compensation, and that was clear also to E. C gave every appearance that it was simply not interested in a nuisance payment, and there was no evidence that it would have been interested, even through the good offices of the mediator, in settling its claim at that level. Third, E was at all times prepared to engage in without-prejudice discussions with C, and there appeared to have been little or no good reason why that approach should not have been tried. Fourth, the suggestion of mediation had come at a late stage, when there were less than 20 working days before the trial. Without-prejudice discussions would have been quicker, cheaper and less intrusive into trial preparation than a mediation, which, even if it lasted only a day in itself, would have diverted solicitors and counsel by more than one day because they would have had to prepare for the mediation. Mediation would also have cost substantially more than without-prejudice discussions. Fifth, E had been entitled to take the view that it had a very strong case on liability, causation and quantum, *Halsey v Milton Keynes General NHS Trust* [2004] EWCA Civ 576, [2004] 1 W.L.R. 3002, [2004] C.L.Y. 291 applied (see para.8 of judgment).

ADS AEROSPACE LTD v EMS GLOBAL TRACKING LTD, [2012] EWHC 2904 (TCC), 145 Con. L.R. 29, Akenhead, J., QBD (TCC).

292. Costs–Costs assessments–Costs between the parties–Dispute over right of recovery by insurer against insured

[Road Traffic Act 1988 (c.52) s.151 (8); Civil Procedure Rules 1998 (SI 1998/3132) r.44.3.]

The court determined costs following its decision in conjoined appeals, [2012] EWCA Civ 1166, [2013] 1 W.L.R. 1776, [2013] 1 C.L. 194. The issue in the appeals was whether two insurers (C and E) had a right of recovery against the insured (W and X) after they were compensated for injuries in separate road traffic accidents in which they had been passengers of an uninsured driver. In C's case, in which the question of the compatibility of the Road Traffic Act 1988 s.151 (8) with European Directives and case law was raised as a preliminary issue, C sought its costs at all stages as it had won on the appeal from the trial of the preliminary issue (the first appeal). C claimed the costs of the instant appeal, the costs of the reference to the CJEU ordered by the instant court during the first appeal, the costs of the first appeal and the costs of the preliminary issue. W claimed that C should pay all its costs of the proceedings so far. X sought her costs for the trial, the reference to the CJEU and the appeal. E accepted that X had succeeded to a certain extent but submitted that her success was a qualified one such that E should be regarded as the successful party within CPR r.44.3. The secretary of state as intervener argued that its costs should be paid for by W and X.

Held: Costs determined. (1) The first question was which party, if any, was to be characterised as the successful party. The insurers had been successful before the Court of Appeal on the second round of the appeal, because it was accepted that their construction of s.151 (8) of the Act was to be preferred. Nevertheless there had to be an assessment of whether, in the circumstances of the two individual cases, the insurers were entitled to make any recovery from W or X (see para.8 of judgment). (2) In relation to the dispute between C and W, the order was as follows: (i) C would recover from W 50 per cent of its costs on the preliminary issue because although C was successful on the s.151 (8) point it had been wrong about the general relevance of European Directives and case law; (ii) C would pay 50 per cent of W's costs of the first appeal because it lost its primary argument that the obligation to meet a judgment could be separated from the insurer's right of recovery; (iii) C would pay 50 per cent of W's costs in the CJEU because C lost the argument that s.151 (8) was compatible with the Directives; (iv) W should pay 50 per cent of C's costs of the instant appeal because C's final stance was only adopted in March 2012 and ultimately C might not recover any sum from W under s.151 (8) (see para.9 of judgment). (3) In relation to the dispute between E and X the costs order made at trial should not be disturbed and the costs of the first appeal, the reference to the CJEU and the instant appeal should be the same as for C and W (para.10). (3) The secretary of state's intervention had been helpful but it was not the fault of either the claimants or the insurers that the legislation, in the form of s.151 (8), was not compatible with the European Directives. There should be no order as far as secretary of state's costs were concerned (para.13).

CHURCHILL INSURANCE CO LTD v FITZGERALD, [2012] EWCA Civ 1465, [2013] 3 Costs L.O. 424, Sir Maurice Kay (VP CA Civ), CA (Civ Div).

293. Costs–Costs between the parties–Claimant partially successful in claim–Defendant substantially successful in counterclaim–Appropriate order as to costs

The appellant (V) appealed against an order that it should pay two-thirds of the costs of the respondent (K). V had rented a property to K, which K rented to a third party. K paid for maintenance work on the property, and subsequently paid compensation to the third party who was unhappy that the air conditioning system was not working during his stay. V brought a claim for outstanding rent due from K, and K counterclaimed in the same amount for the repair work and the compensation that it had paid to the third party. A judge found that V had been in breach of contract in respect of the repair work and discounted an amount from the outstanding rent due from K. In deciding the issue of costs, the judge concluded that the trial had been "all about the counterclaim" and ordered that V pay two-thirds of K's costs.

Held: Appeal allowed. The judge had erred in principle and reached a decision that was plainly wrong. Although there were two separate contracts, there was one overall dispute. K could have paid the entirety of the outstanding rent due and sued for the remaining balance, but it made a tactical decision not to do that and it had to bear the risk of its decision. V had recovered a significant amount in its claim and the starting point was that V was the successful party, *Multiplex Constructions (UK) Ltd v Cleveland Bridge UK Ltd* [2008] EWHC 2220 (TCC), *Naseem (t/a SH Builders & Contractors) v Kang* [2011] EWCA Civ 737 and *Square Mile Partnership Ltd v Fitzmaurice McCall Ltd* [2006] EWCA Civ 1690, [2007] 2 B.C.L.C. 23, [2007] C.L.Y. 584 considered. The error of the judge was to categorise the case as having been "all about the counterclaim". The case was about whether K owed anything to V, and it was established that it had. In terms of a starting point, it was not realistic to describe K as the winner. In exercising its discretion afresh, the court had to respect the judge's view that most of the trial had been about the counterclaim, on which K had substantially succeeded. The court also had to respect the fact that V had succeeded overall, although only partially. Therefore it was appropriate that K bear its own costs and pay 25 per cent of V's costs (see paras 22-23, 25,27 of judgment).

VILLA AGENCIES SPF LTD v KESTREL TRAVEL CONSULTANCY LTD, [2012] EWCA Civ 219, [2012] 5 Costs L.R. 815, Maurice Kay, L.J., CA (Civ Div).

294. Costs–Costs between the parties–Dispute arising out of construction contract–Issues as to interest, time for payment and basis and amount of costs

[Late Payment of Commercial Debts (Interest) Act 1998 (c.20); Civil Procedure Rules 1998 (SI 1998/3132) Pt 36.]

Following its judgment in [2012] EWHC 1773 (TCC), [2012] B.L.R. 503, [2013] 1 C.L. 62 the court was required to determine a number of issues concerning costs and interest. The substantive judgment related to a successful claim by a building contractor (W) against a developer (M) arising out of delays in the completion of a building under a construction contract. The issues were as to (i) contractual and discretionary interest; (ii) the proper amount and basis for an award of costs; (iii) whether there should be an interim payment and whether M should be given time to pay.

Held: Judgment for claimant. (1) M would be required to pay £299,473 in contractual interest until March 26, 2010, together with a further £294,306 in discretionary interest. In its substantive judgment, the court had found that there was no claim for interest under the Late Payment of Commercial Debts (Interest) Act 1998 given that there was a substantive remedy under the contract between the parties. It was accepted, at least in relation to the first half of the claim, that it was appropriate to take a mid-point and calculate accordingly up to March 26, 2010 when proceedings had been issued. The rate was not in issue. In relation to the first half, the only issue was on interest relating to the static security. Although the static security claim concerned the period from February 2007 until August 2008, the particulars of claim erroneously put the start date at February 2008. That was not amended and, on the basis that a party should not recover what he did not claim, interest from February 2007 could not be claimed as contractual interest. However, it must have been obvious to M that the pleaded date was a mistake, and it was clear from the substantive judgment that W was entitled to the full sum claimed and had been wrongly kept out of its money for the longer period. On that basis, interest would be awarded on a discretionary basis (see paras 2-11 of judgment). (2) W would be allowed its costs on the standard basis up until its Pt 36 offer and on an indemnity basis thereafter. There could be little doubt that W had substantially succeeded on its claim. Both sides had made offers of settlement, but in October 2011 W had made a Pt 36 offer to settle at £1.85 million. M had been unwise not to accept that offer given that the final result approached £3 million. M had lost on virtually every issue, had pursued his defence and counterclaim almost as a vendetta against W, and had allowed some claims to be made which could not be supported. Moreover, his conduct at trial had been unimpressive. Although he was not dishonest as such, there were a number of important respects in which he had been careless with the truth. Finally, it was clear that he had not been prepared to compromise on any basis which would involve a substantive payment and costs to W (paras 12-25). (3) There would be an interim payment of costs in the sum of £1.9 million, just less than half of W's total costs. An application by M for further time to pay was rejected for lack of evidence (paras 26-28).

WALTER LILLY & CO LTD v MacKAY, [2012] EWHC 1972 (TCC), 143 Con. L.R. 79, Akenhead, J., QBD (TCC).

295. Costs–Costs between the parties–Late acceptance of Part 36 offer–No application of r.36.14 CPR where judgment not entered

[Civil Procedure Rules 1998 (SI 1998/3132) r.36.10, r.36.14, r.36.2(2)(c), r.36.3(1)(c)(i), r.36.10(5), r.36.10(4), r.36.11, r.36.11(5)(b), r.36.14(3)(b), r.44.3.]

The court had to consider whether the claimant (J) was entitled to have judgment entered for damages to be assessed in a personal injury claim brought on behalf of her late husband against the defendant (H). J's husband had died of mesothelioma. J brought her claim in June 2011. H denied liability. In April 2012, J made a Part 36 offer to settle the issue of liability 99 per cent in her favour. H did not accept the offer within the 21 days of service specified in CPR r.36.2(2)(c) and r.36.3(1)(c)(i). H made a without prejudice offer to apportion liability on an 80/20 basis in J's favour. J rejected that offer. A week later, H accepted J's 99 per cent offer. J sent a draft order confirming the terms of H's acceptance and stating that, pursuant to r.36.14(3)(b), H would pay J's costs on the issue of liability. H disputed the application of r.36.14 on the basis that judgment had not been entered. J contended that judgment should be entered for damages to be assessed on the basis that H pay 99 per cent of the value of the claim, and that the court was not precluded from entering judgment where a defendant denied liability for a considerable period and then sought to escape the costs consequences of r. 36.14.

Held: Judgment for defendant. If Part 36 was a self-contained code containing a highly structured and prescriptive set of rules, J was bound by the terms of that provision if she wished to take advantage of it, *Gibbon v Manchester City Council* [2010] EWCA Civ 726, [2010] 1 W.L.R. 2081, [2010] C.L.Y. 387 followed. As H had accepted J's part 36 offer outside the 21-day period specified in r.36.2(2)(c), but before its withdrawal, the applicable regime was r.36.10 and r. 36.11. Although r.36.10(5) appeared in principle to apply in the instant case, J was entitled to argue for a different order and was capable of succeeding. According to r.36.11(5)(b), a stay operating under that provision did not affect the power of the court to order costs. There was nothing in Part 36 which provided for judgment to be entered in the instant case, where the issue of liability had been compromised by the late acceptance of a Part 36 offer. H had not consented to judgment being entered. The appropriate order should follow r.36.10 and r.11. Accordingly, the issue of liability was stayed upon the terms of J's offer and the question of costs relating to that issue was postponed to be dealt with under r.36.10(4) and r.36.10(5) or under the general discretion under r.44.3 (see paras 12-14 of judgment).

JOLLY v HARSCO INFRASTRUCTURE SERVICES LTD, [2012] EWHC 3086 (QB), [2013] 1 Costs L.R. 115, Cranston, J., QBD.

296. Costs–Costs budgets–Proper approach on detailed assessment where costs budget approved

The applicant (M) sought permission to appeal against a costs management order made pursuant to the pilot scheme contained in Practice Direction 51G. The respondent (T) had brought an action for breach of contract against M. The parties prepared costs budgets in the prescribed form as required by the Practice Direction. T's budget was £129,176, while M's was £59,380. The judge approved the whole of M's budget but only part of T's. He did not approve T's budget for disclosure and preparation for trial but did approve the elements relating to witness statements and counsel's fees. M argued that the judge had adopted the wrong approach: when the court was asked to approve costs budgets, it should have regard to the principles that would be applied when costs were assessed on the standard basis, which involved, among other things, resolving any doubts in favour of the paying party; the judge failed to have regard to that principle and approved elements in T's budget despite having doubts about whether the figures were reasonable.

Held: Application granted. M's concern was that, on a detailed assessment, costs judges were likely to treat the approval of a budget, or any relevant part of it, as ipso facto establishing that the costs incurred in respect of the matter generally, or that particular element of it, were reasonable if they fell within the approved budget. In *Henry v News Group Newspapers Ltd* [2013] EWCA Civ 19, [2013] 2 All E.R. 840, [2013] 7 C.L. 53, it was said that an approved budget was not to be taken as a licence to conduct litigation in an unnecessarily expensive way. It could not be said therefore that costs judges should or would treat the court's approval of a budget as demonstrating, without further consideration, that the costs incurred by the receiving party were reasonable or proportionate simply because they fell within the scope of the approved budget. One of the main aims of costs budgeting was to control the parties' expenditure, and that would not be effective if judges did not apply the correct principles. It seemed that in the instant case the judge had proceeded on the basis that he would approve any figure for a particular element of the claim, provided it was not so unreasonable as to render it obviously excessive or "grossly disproportionate". It was arguable that he did not apply the correct principles and, as a result, approved an over-generous budget in respect of some elements of T's costs. Costs budgeting was still in its relative infancy, and it was important that the correct principles were established at an early stage. Permission to appeal should therefore be given. Given the way in which M had puts its argument, the court might wish to comment further on the proper approach to be taken by costs judges on a detailed assessment in a case in which the court had approved the receiving party's budget, *Henry* considered (see paras 8, 10-12 of judgment).

TROY FOODS v MANTON, [2013] EWCA Civ 615, [2013] 4 Costs L.R. 546, Moore-Bick, L.J., CA (Civ Div).

297. Costs–Counterclaims–Awards of costs to successful claimant and successful counterclaimant

[Civil Procedure Rules 1998 (SI 1998/3132) r.44.5.]

The appellant (C) appealed against an order for costs made following his construction dispute against the respondent building contractor (M). M had carried out works at C's property. Damp later appeared. A claim was brought in the name of C's property holdings company (P) alleging that had M satisfactorily carried out the work, the amount payable would have been £87,400, and since £90,600 had been paid, the return of an overpayment was claimed. It was also alleged that the roof works were defective and the cost of the remedial works was claimed. M denied the claims and counterclaimed for an unpaid balance due in respect of the works. The judge found that C, not P, had made the contract with M. He found that the overpayment claim failed and that M's counterclaim succeeded in the sum of £9,600. However, C's claim on the roofing issue succeeded in the sum of £22,300, meaning there was a net recovery by C. The judge ordered P to pay M's costs of its action and the counterclaim, ordered M to pay C the costs of his claim, and ordered C to pay M the costs of the counterclaim. He ordered a detailed assessment, issuing guidance to the costs judge as to how assessment should be conducted. C argued that the judge should have awarded him the costs of both the claim and the counterclaim.

Held: Appeal dismissed. Most judges would have simply awarded C a proportion of his costs; that was best practice, as reflected by CPR r.44.5(7). It would have been preferable had the judge adopted that course. On the other hand, the situation had been confused by P's failure to establish the primary case. The judge had had discretion to depart from the starting point that C was entitled to the costs of the action. He had thought that M's partial success had to be reflected and that the justice of the case was best served by making the order, combined with guidance to the costs judge as to the limited nature of M's envisaged recovery of his costs of the counterclaim. The judge had been uniquely well placed to make that assessment. The judge had plainly not intended that C should be deprived of almost all his costs, and, as he had observed that the roof was the major issue in the case, and that that issue had taken most of the time, that outcome was inconceivable, especially given the guidance to the costs judge. No proportionate recovery order could be safely substituted for the judge's order which would reliably carry through his assessment of the manner in which the relative levels of success and failure should be reflected in the costs. It would be a costly exercise to remit the matter for the judge to craft such an order, and that would set a bad precedent. No encouragement should be given to such appeals (see paras 26-28 of judgment).

CONNELL v MUTCH (T/A SOUTHEY BUILDING SERVICES), [2012] EWCA Civ 1589, [2013] C.P. Rep. 11, Mummery, L.J., CA (Civ Div).

298. Costs–Defamation claims–Claimant achieving vindication before service of claim form–Claim struck out as abuse of process

[Civil Procedure Rules 1998 (SI 1998/3132) r.44.12A.]

The court was required to determine costs after striking out a defamation claim brought by the claimant (C) against the defendant (W). The court had held that C had an arguable case that words it had alleged were slander and malicious falsehood had been published by W's employee and that they had been published to more than one publishee, but struck out the claim as an abuse of process because by the time it had served its claim form, it had already achieved all it could by way of vindicating its reputation. C had not alleged that any actual damage had been suffered by it but sought an injunction to restrain W from repeating the alleged defamatory words. W, while not admitting that its employee had said the words complained of, offered an undertaking not to repeat the words. W sought its costs of and incidental to the proceedings; C sought its costs up to the date of the claim form and no order for costs thereafter. C argued that (1) it would not be an abuse of process for a claimant to decline to settle a dispute, notwithstanding that he had been offered all he was entitled to by way of substantive relief, unless the offer included an acceptable offer in relation to costs; (2) the court would not have struck out the action at the instant stage had it pursued its damages claim; an order to pay all W's costs would penalise C for adopting the reasonable stance of not pursuing the claim.

Held: Costs determined. (1) The case did not come within CPR r.44.12A, because the parties had not reached agreement on any issues. Nor could C say that it had been offered all it was entitled to by way of substantive relief: that would have been so had W offered it an undertaking with which it was content, but the undertaking offered had not been acceptable to C. The CPR did not expressly address the situation where a claimant had good grounds for intimating a claim, but where there was no agreement between the parties, and where, before the claim form had been issued, it became clear that any factual basis which might originally have existed for the claim no longer existed. If no claim form was issued, then there was no litigation and so no costs of litigation, whatever costs might have been incurred in complying with a pre-action protocol. If a claim form was issued, the costs incurred in complying with a pre-action protocol could be recoverable as costs incidental to any subsequent proceedings, *McGlinn v Waltham Contractors Ltd* [2005] EWHC 1419 (TCC), [2005] 3 All E.R. 1126, [2006] C.L.Y. 402 applied. The CPR provided a strong incentive to parties to engage in pre-action communication, with the risk to those who did not do that that they might not recover their costs, even if they successfully brought an action. If C's contention were correct, there would be little advantage in the requirement in the pre-action protocols for parties to engage in pre-action communications (see paras 12-16, 20-23 of judgment). (2) Although the action would not have been struck out if C had made clear that it was pursuing a claim for damages, such a claim carried risks. The vindication represented by an award of damages was unlikely to be of value in such a case, and if C found no evidence on disclosure to support a claim for damages that would have been of value, the action would be liable to be struck out at that stage, with greater costs having been incurred. C's stance in not pursuing such a claim was consistent with it pursuing the course most in its interests. In the absence of a finding or admission of liability, or an undertaking in the terms sought by C, no order for costs could be made against W. C would be ordered to pay W's costs from service of the claim form. No order would be made for the costs up to service of the claim form. If C had not commenced the proceedings, W could not have sought an order for its costs for that period; the fact that C had commenced proceedings ought not to lead to the result that it became liable for such costs (paras 24-28).

CITATION PLC v ELLIS WHITTAM LTD, [2012] EWHC 764 (QB), [2012] 5 Costs L.R. 826, Tugendhat, J., QBD.

299. Costs–Detailed assessment–Change of solicitors–Proportionality of assessing costs of both sets of solicitors

The appellant (B) appealed against a detailed assessment decision arising from a claim in which the respondents (S) succeeded. In December 2002, S sought a declaratory judgment in relation to a boundary dispute. Following an abortive trial in February 2005, S terminated the retainer of their solicitors (X) and instructed new ones (Y). At trial, S were awarded costs subject to a detailed assessment and subject to any costs before March 13, 2005 being reduced by 20 per cent. S served bills of costs in relation to both X and Y. B made serious conduct allegations against X and Y and sought to have X's bill disallowed, contending that there had been a breach of the indemnity principle and that S had never been liable to pay any of X's costs. At a preliminary hearing before Deputy Master Williams, the allegations were rejected and the case was listed for detailed assessment. At the commencement of the detailed assessment hearing, B applied unsuccessfully for permission to appeal against the decision of Deputy Master Williams. Deputy Master Rogers assessed X and Y's original bills and held that the costs were proportionate. He also assessed Y's costs of the preliminary hearing and held that the indemnity principle issue had been determined at the preliminary hearing. B contended, among other things, that

Deputy Master Rogers had erred in finding that the bills were not disproportionate and in allowing the detailed assessment costs of both X and Y.

Held: Costs determined. (1) Deputy Master Rogers had interpreted the decision of the trial judge as meaning that the 20 per cent reduction in costs prior to March 13, 2005 was an assessment of the reduction in overall fees that was reasonable due to the change of representation. The trial judge had been in an excellent position to make the costs orders that she made, having heard all the evidence over several days, and her decision was about the principles to be applied to the costs bill as a whole. There was no error in the reasoning of Deputy Master Rogers in that regard (see para.29 of judgment). (2) It was clear that B had made very serious allegations against both X and Y and had taken every point they could before Deputy Master Williams to defeat the bills of costs submitted by both firms. Deputy Master Rogers had been justified in refusing to consider any matter in relation to the detailed assessment that amounted to the re-opening of an argument which had been considered by Deputy Master Williams. He had also been correct to approach the detailed assessment by applying the principles in *Lownds v Home Office* [2002] EWCA Civ 365, [2002] 1 W.L.R. 2450, [2002] C.L.Y. 333, so as to make a global assessment of the proportionality of the costs claimed and only to apply the tests of reasonableness and necessity if the costs were disproportionate. On that approach, he had been entitled to look at the bills and the complexity of the procedural and legal issues as a whole in making a decision on proportionality, *Lownds* followed. The decision he had reached was not so plainly wrong that it was outside the generous ambit of discretion entrusted to him, *Walbrook Trustees (Jersey) Ltd v Fattal* [2008] EWCA Civ 427 followed (paras 27, 30-32, 34). (3) It was clear from the approach taken by B before Deputy Master Williams and his attempts to re-open the same issues before Deputy Master Rogers that it was necessary for X to be separately represented at the detailed assessment. It was reasonable for X and Y to have taken the view that B would challenge everything they could in relation to X's bill. No representative appearing for Y would have been able to answer any such queries. There was therefore no basis on which to challenge Deputy Master Rogers' decision to allow two sets of costs for assessment. It followed that he had approached the detailed assessment in a correct and lawful manner and had reached a decision that he was entitled to reach (paras 36-37).

SHAH v BREED, [2013] EWHC 232 (QB), [2013] 2 Costs L.R. 359, Globe, J., QBD.

300. Costs–Detailed assessment–Hourly rates–London-based solicitors–Uplift on central London guideline hourly rates

[Civil Procedure Rules 1998 (SI 1998/3132) r.44.5(3), r.52.11.]

The appellant local authority appealed against decisions made by a costs judge on a detailed assessment of the respondents' costs. The respondents (R) were four young sisters who had brought a claim against the local authority concerning its alleged failure to protect them from sexual and physical abuse in the family home. There were complex issues concerning causation, and at the time the claims were brought the law on liability in such circumstances was unclear. The case was settled shortly before trial upon payment to R by the local authority of £155,000 in damages. R's solicitors were based in London. The judge found that it was appropriate for those solicitors to have been instructed. Using central London rates he allowed hourly rates of £335 for a partner, £255 for an associate, £180 for an assistant and £120 for a trainee or litigation assistant. The local authority submitted that the costs judge (1) had applied a subjective rather than objective test in determining the hourly rates; (2) was wrong to allow an uplift once he had determined that his starting point should be central London guideline hourly rates, as an uplift was already built into those rates.

Held: Appeal dismissed. (1) It was necessary to have in mind the test for an appellant court under CPR r.52.11. As the appeal was by way of review rather than rehearing, the court had to consider whether the costs judge had misdirected himself, erred in law, taken into account any irrelevant factors, failed to take into account relevant factors or whether his decision fell outside the range of reasonably possible solutions. In arriving at the hourly rates it was necessary to apply the test of whether they were proportionately and reasonably incurred, and proportionate and reasonable in amount. There was no doubt that the test was an objective one, as the costs judge reminded himself on a number of occasions in the course of his judgment. It was naturally appropriate to select the central London rates as the basis for consideration. The rates selected were on the high side but did not exceed the bounds of the reasonable options available to the judge in carrying out his task (see paras 2, 13-17 of judgment). (2) Guideline rates were not supposed to replace the experience and knowledge of those familiar with the local area and the field generally, *Higgs v Camden and Islington HA* [2003] EWHC 15 (QB), [2003] 2 Costs L.R. 211, [2003] C.L.Y. 329 applied. It was also important to have regard to the factors listed in r.44.5(3). The argument that once central London rates had been selected, a further uplift was inappropriate, could not be sustained. The factors listed in r.44.5(3) were just as relevant to London cases as to any other. It was true that when the rates were fixed some years ago a built-in uplift of 50 per cent was incorporated, but the judge was well aware of that and had explained that the appropriate uplift was in the region of 75 per cent. He therefore allowed an additional uplift over and above the built-in 50 per cent (paras 13, 18-19).

KMT (A CHILD) v KENT CC, [2012] EWHC 2088 (QB), [2012] 6 Costs L.R. 1039, Eady, J., QBD.

301. Costs–Detailed assessment–Service of redacted insurance certificate–Compliance with para.32.5(2)(c) CPR PD 47–Relief from sanctions

[Civil Procedure Rules 1998 (SI 1998/3132) r.3.9, r.3.9(1), r.44.3B(1)(e), r.47.6; CPR PD 47 (Procedure for Detailed Assessment of Costs and Default Provisions) 2000 para.32.5(2)(c).]

The appellant (L) appealed against decisions made in detailed costs assessment proceedings to disallow its claim for an after-the-event (ATE) insurance premium and to refuse relief from the sanction of disallowing that claim. In January 2010, L had issued proceedings against the respondent (Z) for breach of contract following the supply by Z to L of defective lights. Prior to issue, L had informed Z that its solicitors were acting under a conditional fee agreement and had ATE insurance. The claim settled six days before trial when Z agreed to pay L £120,000 plus costs. L served its bill of costs in April 2011, and claimed an ATE insurance premium of £60,375. In its points of dispute, Z stated that L had served no information in support of that premium contrary to CPR PD 47 para.32.5(2)(c). In November 2011, L served its points of reply and attached a redacted copy of the ATE insurance certificate with the prior stage premiums deleted and showing only the premium of £60,375 that was payable, and indeed paid, at the conclusion of the litigation. An unredacted copy of the insurance certificate was served on the court a week before the costs assessment hearing in December 2011. At that hearing, the master ruled that Z was entitled to see the prior stage premiums to ascertain the relevance and reasonableness of the premium paid, which he concluded was a global premium, and as such the redacted certificate did not comply with the requirement under para.32.5(2)(c) to serve details of the amount of the premium paid or payable. As a result he found that under the terms of CPR r.44.3B(1)(e) L could not recover the insurance premium. L immediately applied under CPR r.3.9 for relief from that sanction and the master refused that application.

Held: Appeal allowed. (1) The master had erred in concluding that para.32.5(2)(c) required an insurance certificate to disclose not only the premium paid but premiums that would have been payable had the proceedings concluded at an earlier stage. The mandatory requirement under the Practice Direction was that the insurance certificate showed the amount of the premium paid or payable. The two were alternatives. In the instant case, the obligation to pay the premium of £60,375 had crystallised and there was therefore no requirement that the disclosed certificate should show the premiums that would have been payable if the proceedings had concluded earlier. There was a distinction to be drawn between that mandatory requirement and evidence which might include amounts payable if proceedings had been concluded at earlier stages, which would enable the reasonableness of the claimed premium to be assessed. If necessary, Z could have made an application for disclosure of the unredacted insurance certificate (see paras 64-67 of judgment). (2) Although L had not breached para.32.5(2)(c) by providing the redacted rather than the unredacted insurance certificate, there was a clear breach of the requirement under CPR r.47.6 read with CPR PD 47 para.32.4 and para.32.5(2) to serve the insurance certificate with the bill of costs. The redacted insurance certificate was not served until six months later. The master's consideration of whether he should grant relief from the sanction of disallowing the insurance premium claim was based on two false premises. First, that there had been a breach of para.32.5(2)(c) by serving the insurance certificate in redacted form. Second, that a document complying with para.32.5(2) was supplied just before the hearing when the unredacted certificate was provided. On the basis of those two erroneous conclusions, the master's decision not to grant relief could not stand and was set aside (paras 69-70). (3) On any view. the certificate was served late. However, L had informed Z prior to issue that ATE insurance was in place and that the premium was to increase at stages that were specified. The amount of the premium was then included in the bill of costs. Accordingly, although it should have been given in a certificate, the substance of the required information had been given to Z. Once the redacted certificate had been served, there was nothing to prevent Z from asking for disclosure of the unredacted certificate and from obtaining evidence to challenge the reasonableness of the premium. If needed, Z could have applied for an adjournment to obtain such information and since the need for that would have been caused by L, it was highly likely that L would have had to bear the costs. The prejudice suffered by L if relief from sanctions was not granted, was that it would be unable to pursue its claim for the quite substantial insurance premium. Any prejudice to Z caused by the late service of the certificate could be reduced or eliminated by case management measures. Therefore, taking into account all relevant circumstances and having regard to the factors to be considered in CPR r.3.9(1), it was right that L should be granted relief from sanctions for failing to serve the insurance certificate on the due date.

LIGHT ON LINE LTD v ZUMTOBEL LIGHTING LTD, [2012] EWHC 3376 (QB), [2013] 1 Costs L.R. 129, Slade, J., QBD.

302. Costs–Detailed assessment–Statute bills of costs–Interim bills already paid

[Solicitors Act 1974 (c.47) s.70(4).]

The appellant solicitor (R) appealed against a master's decision that the respondent client (B) was entitled to a detailed assessment of his bills of costs. R, who had advised and acted for B under a general retainer, rendered a series of interim bills and a final bill, all of which B paid. Nearly 12 months after he paid the final bill, B made a Part 8 claim for detailed assessment of all of the bills. R argued that the retainer had given him a contractual entitlement to issue interim statute bills and since B's application had been made more than 12 months after he had paid those bills, the Solicitors Act 1974 s.70(4) prevented their being assessed. The master, however, found that the retainer letter, properly construed, did not provide for R to render interim statute bills since it allowed B to have them assessed at any time in the High Court. He considered that R's interim bills were therefore merely requests for payment on account which should be treated as a series of bills culminating in the final statute bill, and that all the bills were to be treated as one final statute bill. As a consequence, B's claim was within the 12-month time limit and detailed assessment could be granted if there were special circumstances. The master concluded that there were special circumstances as B had only paid the final bill under protest in order to obtain his papers and conclude negotiations in a negligence claim he had made, and it was the examination of those papers which led him to believe that the costs he had paid to R in relation to that negligence claim were not justified.

Held: Appeal dismissed. If a client paid a statute bill, which was a bill of costs complying with the requirements of the Act, the High Court would grant his application for it to be assessed as long as the application was within one month of its payment. If the application was more than one month but less than 12 months after the payment, the court would grant his application only in special circumstances. A solicitor was generally not entitled to any payment on account of his costs other than disbursements. However, a solicitor could contract with his client for the right to issue interim statute bills from time to time during the currency of the retainer. They were nevertheless final bills in respect of the work they covered, in that there could be no subsequent adjustment in the light of the outcome of the business. The master had been entitled to conclude that there was a plain conflict between the purported contractual right to have a bill assessed at any time and the complete inability of a true interim statute bill to meet that expectation. It followed that R had no contractual right to issue interim statute bills and his interim bills had to be regarded as mere requests for payment on account. The master had also been entitled to conclude that it was therefore permissible to treat them as a series culminating in the final statute bill, and all could properly be assessed as a single statute bill, *Chamberlain v Boodle & King* [1982] 1 W.L.R. 1443, [1982] C.L.Y. 3080 followed. The master had been right to find special circumstances in that B would not receive his papers unless he paid R's final bill; he needed the release of those papers to conclude his litigation and to substantiate his claim for costs; there was a mutual understanding that the reasonableness of R's costs could be measured by reference to the amount recovered in the negligence litigation; and, on the release of the papers, B was made aware that R could not justifiably recover a sum even close to the amount he had charged (see paras 13-15, 35, 37, 56-57, 66-67 of judgment).

BARI v ROSEN (T/A RA ROSEN & CO SOLICITORS), [2012] EWHC 1782 (QB), [2012] 5 Costs L.R. 851, Spencer, J., QBD.

303. Costs–Discontinuance–Claimant seeking disapplication of r.38.6(1) CPR–Relevance of defendant's failure to respond to pre-action correspondence

[Party Wall etc. Act 1996 (c.40); Civil Procedure Rules 1998 (SI 1998/3132) r.38.6.]

The appellants (N) appealed against a decision that they were liable for the costs of the respondent (E) following their discontinuance of their proceedings against him. E was the freehold owner of the adjoining premises to those owned by N. In January 2007, E began excavating close to the rear wall of N's premises. N sent four pre-action letters to E claiming that he had failed to serve a notice required under the Party Wall etc. Act 1996, and requesting access for their surveyor to inspect the foundations of their property. E did not respond. N issued the instant proceedings in January 2008 seeking injunctive relief to restrain E from carrying on further development pending the agreement of an award under the Act and to allow them access. N claimed that there was no planning permission for the work and that E refused their requests for their surveyor to have access. E served a defence in May 2008 disputing N's claims and arguing that the provisions of the Act did not apply and that his contractors had failed to carry out the work in accordance with his instructions. Subsequently, arrangements were made for N's surveyor to inspect. E also served a notice and paid an award under the Act, and paid a sum to N for minimal damage caused to the foundations. However, E claimed that they related to work carried out after the instant excavations. In 2012, N served notice of discontinuance, but applied for their costs on the basis of E's alleged obstructive and truculent behaviour throughout. The judge found that there was nothing in E's conduct overall such as to justify departing from CPR r.38.6(1) and that he could not determine the question of E's failure to respond to the pre-action correspondence in the absence of a hearing. The issue was whether the judge erred in his approach to the exercise of the court's discretion as to whether to depart from the default rule under r.38.6(1).

Held: Appeal allowed. The hurdle to displace r.38.6(1) was high. Because a claimant had got most of what he could reasonably hope to achieve from the proceedings did not justify him relying on the avoidance of a trial solely about costs as justifying a departure from r.38.6(1). Where there was to be no trial, it was not the function of a court considering costs to decide whether the claim would have succeeded, but it had to consider whether the unreasonableness of a defendant's conduct provided good reason for departing from r.38.6(1). The question of access to E's property by N's surveyors was a disputed factual matter and part of E's pleaded case. Which party would have succeeded on that point and the failure to serve a party wall notice prior to the works and the absence of a party wall award at that stage were matters that would have had to be determined at trial. With regard to E's failure to respond to the pre-action correspondence, he showed no willingness to set out his position, narrow the issues or discuss mediation or settlement. Therefore, the court could take into account non-compliance with the spirit of the pre-action protocol when making costs orders and a way to do so was to disapply the default rule in r.38.6(1). The judge referred to E's failure to respond, but erred in principle in concluding that consideration of the consequences of that failure involved pre-empting a hearing on the merits. Alternatively, in not taking into account E's failure, a matter which was a relevant consideration in the exercise of his discretion as to whether N had satisfied the burden of showing that r.38.6(1) should be disapplied, the judge was outside the generous margin of appreciation appellate courts accorded to judges in the exercise of their discretion. E's failure to respond was, given the reasonableness of N's perception of the danger to their wall and foundations, unreasonable conduct which justified disapplying r.38.6(1). It meant that N had little choice but to issue proceedings. They were entitled to protect their position and continue to seek to ascertain E's stance after issuing, *Teasdale v HSBC Bank Plc* [2011] EWCA Civ 354, [2012] 3 Costs L.O. 285, *Messih v McMillan Williams* [2010] EWCA Civ 844, [2010] C.P. Rep. 41, [2011] C.L.Y. 277, *Walker v Walker* [2005] EWCA Civ 247, [2006] 1 W.L.R. 2194, [2005] C.L.Y. 362 and *Teasdale v HSBC Bank Plc* [2010] EWHC 612 (QB), [2010] 4 All E.R. 630, [2010] C.L.Y. 299 applied. However, once the defence was served, had N considered it to be spurious, they could have sought to have it struck out or to seek summary judgment. They did not do either. Therefore, the appropriate order was for E to pay N's costs of the action to the date the defence was served and that there be no order for costs thereafter (see paras 30-32, 37, 40, 42-44, 46 of judgment).

NELSON'S YARD MANAGEMENT CO v EZIEFULA, [2013] EWCA Civ 235, [2013] C.P. Rep. 29, Arden, L.J., CA (Civ Div).

304. Costs–Fixed costs–Pre-action protocol for low-value personal injury claims–Offer made at end of Stage 2–Entitlement to Stage 3 costs

[CPR PD 8B (Pre-Action Protocol for low value personal injury claims in road traffic accidents) 1999 para.6.2.]

The court was required to determine costs in a personal injury claim where the fixed costs regime of the Pre-Action Protocol for Low Value Personal Injury Claims in Road Traffic Accidents applied. The claimant (B) sought damages for personal injuries and other losses against the defendant (M). The matter proceeded in accordance with the Protocol, through which M admitted liability. The parties were unable to reach an agreement as to the quantum of general damages as part of Stage 2 of the Protocol, and so in accordance with para.7.55, B prepared the Court Proceedings Pack and sent it to M's solicitors for approval. Under para.7.58, M was entitled to object to the Pack within five days for lack of compliance. In September 2011, at the end of the five-day period, M telephoned B's solicitors and made an offer of £3,200 in respect of general damages. The response of B's solicitor was that it would be prepared to accept the offer on payment of its Stage 3 costs. As M took the view that Stage 3 costs were not due under the Protocol, the conversation ended. Thereafter B issued Stage 3 proceedings. General damages were agreed prior to the hearing in the sum of £3,200. B contended that if no agreement had been reached as part of Stage 2 and the Court Proceedings Pack had been prepared, then B was entitled to its Stage 3 costs. B submitted that the purpose of Stage 3 costs was to cover in part expenses in preparing and filing the Pack and his solicitors would lose out financially if they had to prepare the Pack, but M could still agree settlement on receipt of the Pack and only pay Stage 2 costs. M argued that CPR PD 8B para.6.2 was clear in stating that the filing of the claim form and associated documents represented the start of Stage 3 for the purposes of fixed costs and B had acted unreasonably in insisting on payment of its Stage 3 fixed costs when that stage had not commenced.

Held: Judgment accordingly. It did appear that there was a lacuna in respect of the costs of B's solicitor. However, the judge was bound by the wording of CPR PD 8B and he did not have the discretion to allow B its costs; B's representatives should have realised that in September 2011 on reading the practice direction. Accordingly B had acted unreasonably in failing to accept M's offer and M was entitled to its Stage 3 fixed costs.

BRADLEY v MITCHELL, April 3, 2012, District Judge Griggs, CC (Plymouth). [*Ex rel.* Charlotte Robinson-Jones, Barrister, No.5 Chambers].

305. Costs–Fixed costs–Whether costs above fixed sum could be recovered–Meaning of "exceptional circumstances" in r.45.13 CPR–Minor's continued psychological symptoms revealed at hearing

[Civil Procedure Rules 1998 (SI 1998/3132) r.45.13.]

The applicant (C) renewed an application for permission to appeal against a district judge's refusal to allow a claim for costs exceeding the fixed recoverable amounts in a personal injury action. C was a minor who had been injured in a road traffic accident. Her physical injuries were not serious but she suffered nightmares after the accident. A settlement was proposed on the basis that she had recovered. However, during the hearing before the district judge she revealed that her psychological symptoms were continuing. The judge therefore refused to approve the settlement and adjourned for further medical evidence to be obtained. The case was subsequently settled for £10,000. C's counsel argued that the court should allow greater costs under the CPR r.45.13 because the circumstances were exceptional and, further, that because district judges across the country had reached different views as to the meaning of the words "exceptional circumstances" an important point of principle existed.

Held: Application refused. The words "exceptional circumstances" in r.45.13 spoke for themselves. The phrase could not possibly mean anything other than that, for reasons which made it appropriate to order the case to fall outside the fixed costs regime, exceptionally more money had to be expended on the case by way of costs than would otherwise have been necessary. In those circumstances it could not be argued that there was an important point of principle which required further review by the court.

COSTIN v MERRON, [2013] EWCA Civ 380, [2013] 3 Costs L.R. 391, Leveson, L.J., CA (Civ Div).

306. Costs–Funding arrangements–Road traffic claim–Whether reasonable for defendant driver and insurer to be represented separately

[Civil Procedure Rules 1998 (SI 1998/3132) r.3.1 (7).]

The second defendant insurer (D2) applied for an order revoking a direction that a detailed assessment of costs should be approached on the basis that it had been reasonable for the third and fourth defendants (D3 and D4) to a road traffic claim to be represented separately. The claimant (C) in the road traffic claim had been seriously injured in a collision when travelling as a passenger in a car driven by the first defendant (D1). D1 and D3, who was the driver of the other vehicle involved, blamed each other for the collision. D2 and D4 were D1 and D3's respective insurers and had obtained declarations from the court entitling them to avoid the policies. They were joined in the action as Article 75 insurers and as agents for the Motor Insurers' Bureau. D1 was found at trial to be wholly to blame for the accident and judgment was entered for C against D2. D3 and D4 had been separately represented at trial. D2 had raised the issue before trial, stating that, in view of D3 and D4's common interests, separate representation was inappropriate. D2 gave notice that it would raise objection to the disproportionate costs involved. D3 and D4 stated that D3 was potentially at personal risk given D4's Article 75 status and that each were entitled to their costs. Pre-trial correspondence between D3 and D4, disclosed in relation to the costs assessment, made it clear that D4 had agreed to indemnify D3 in respect of his legal costs and any damages incurred, dependent on D3 co-operating with the defence of the claim. The instant application was based on the ground that the information which gave rise to the direction, namely reference to a potential conflict of interest between D3 and D4, was inaccurate and did not properly reflect the funding arrangements between them.

Held: Application granted. (1) The natural interpretation to be placed on D3 and D4's submissions post-trial was that, because D4 had obtained a declaration from the court entitling it to avoid D3's insurance policy, D3 had not had the benefit of an indemnity from D4 protecting him from any award of damages. It had been recognised that the likelihood was that D4 had agreed to indemnify D3 in respect of his legal costs as, in the absence of such an arrangement, it was improbable that he would have been able to afford representation by leading counsel and a firm of city solicitors. However, the argument that it should have been obvious to D2 that D4 might also have entered into an indemnity arrangement in respect of damages, or that D2 should have sought disclosure of documents relating to any indemnity agreement, was not accepted, as there had been no reason to believe that any uncertainty existed. No reference had been made at trial to the fact that D3 was at personal risk if he failed to co-operate with his defence. If D2 had known or suspected that that was the case, it would not have agreed to the costs direction and should therefore be permitted to withdraw that agreement. Had the court been aware of the limited extent of D3's personal risk, it would have considered that he had been for all practical purposes in the same position as a motorist with a valid insurance policy who was a defendant in a road traffic claim. In the absence of some special feature, such a motorist would not be entitled to the costs of representation separate from his insurer. A divergence of interest between D3 and D4 could have arisen; however, there was no reason to believe that such a disagreement was more likely in the instant case than in any other claim involving a defendant motorist and their insurer. Had the court been aware of the true position, the issue of separate representation would have been left to the costs judge (see paras 37-40 of judgment). (2) The question was whether the court should exercise its power under CPR r.3.1 (7) to revoke the costs direction. D3 and D4 would not have argued so strenuously for the direction at the previous hearing if they had not considered that it would have a significant effect on the costs judge's decisions. The direction would require the judge to approach the task on the basis that it had in principle been reasonable for them to be represented separately throughout the proceedings. The outcome of an assessment on that basis might be very different from one conducted by a costs judge who approached the issue of separate representation unfettered. The costs direction had been made as a result of a misunderstanding regarding the funding position as between D3 and D4. There was no question of the court having been deliberately misled, but the direction would not have been given if the true position had been known. The interests of justice demanded that the direction should be revoked (paras 41-46).

ALI v ALI, [2013] EWHC 1233 (QB), [2013] 5 Costs L.O. 676, Swift, J., QBD.

307. Costs–Group litigation–Claimants overall winners–Failure to establish causative link for skin and bladder cancer–Whether appropriate to reduce claimants' costs

[Civil Procedure Rules 1998 (SI 1998/3132) r.44.3(5)(b), r.48.6A(2).]

The court was required to determine the issue of costs in Phurnacite Workers Group Litigation concerning claims for damages for industrial diseases and various types of cancer. Eight lead claimants alleged that they had suffered non-malignant respiratory disease (NMRD), namely chronic obstructive pulmonary disease (COPD) and chronic bronchitis (CB) and/or malignant disease, namely lung cancer, bladder cancer and skin cancer allegedly caused by exposure to dust and/or fumes in the course of their work. The claimants applied for interest on disbursements paid by their solicitors on the basis that they had agreed to pay interest at four per cent above the base rate under disbursement funding agreements. The claimants' application was deferred, and in the interim the defendants sought disclosure of the provisions in the conditional fee arrangements relating to the obligation to pay disbursements and other relevant documents which had been referred to in a witness statement prepared by the claimants' solicitors. The claimants submitted that overall they were the successful party and that although they had lost on certain issues, no reduction in their costs should be made. However, if any reduction was to be made, it should be a modest one. The defendants contended that success should be assessed on an issue-by-issue basis and the claimants' costs reduced accordingly. The defendants also contended that since the CFAs had been referred to in the witness statement, they were entitled to inspect them and since specific reliance had been placed on the provisions relating to disbursements, the claimants could not claim privilege for them.

Held: Judgment accordingly. Overall the claimants had been successful. There was no basis for reducing the claimants' entitlement to costs in relation to the issues of breach of statutory duty and exposure levels, causation of NMRD and lung cancer, and limitation. The defendants had wrongly focussed exclusively on the time spent on those issues at trial rather than looking at the outcome and course of those issues as a whole. The time spent on an issue at trial was not necessarily proportionate to the time spent on the issue as a whole. Whilst the defendants' expert evidence on breach of statutory duty and exposure levels had been preferred, the court had still required his calculations to be reworked. Although unsuccessful on causation of skin and bladder cancer, the claimants had acted reasonably within the meaning of CPR r.44.3(5)(b) in pursuing those issues. However, taking into account other relevant factors and the significance of the causation issues and the costs incurred in contesting them, it was right to reduce the claimants' entitlement to costs to reflect the defendants' success. The individual costs of the lead claims relating to the causation of bladder cancer were included in the common costs of the action under CPR r.48.6A(2), which were taken into account when assessing the reduction to the claimants' costs. In relation to the other lead claims, their failure, whether in whole or in part, would not result in a reduction to the claimants' costs as they had assisted the court in determining the issues of breach of duty and exposure levels, and provided guidance on the parameters by which the remainder of the claims should be resolved. Taking a broad brush approach, a 20 per cent reduction was appropriate (see paras 20, 53 -57, 60-64 of judgment). (2) The reference to the CFAs in the witness statement demonstrated that reliance had been placed on the provisions relating to the obligation to pay disbursements and, therefore, privilege in respect of those provisions had been waived. Accordingly, it was appropriate for the claimants to disclose the relevant CFAs, with inspection limited to the provisions of the CFAs relating to the obligation to pay disbursements and interest, and the specimen funding agreements annexed to the witness statement. There was no reason to believe that the claimants' solicitors had acted improperly and there had been no waiver or abrogation of the privilege that attached to correspondence between the claimants and their solicitors. There was no basis on which disclosure of that correspondence could be ordered. The precise nature and extent of the disbursements that were to be considered at the deferred hearing should be, as there had been uncertainty about them and it would be useful for the parties to know what was being considered (paras 74-76, 79, 81).

JONES v SECRETARY OF STATE FOR ENERGY AND CLIMATE CHANGE, [2012] EWHC 3647 (QB), [2013] 2 Costs L.R. 230, Swift, J., QBD.

308. Costs–Indemnity basis–Breach of warranty of authority to conduct litigation–Basis for personal indemnity costs orders–Costs order against personal representative of deceased estate

[Senior Courts Act 1981 (c.54); Civil Procedure Rules 1998 (SI 1998/3132) r.48.2.]

The applicant bank (B) applied for an order that the respondent (Q) be made personally liable, and liable as administrator of his deceased mother's estate, for the costs of an appeal on an indemnity basis and for an order for payment on account. The Court of Appeal had previously struck out an appeal that had been brought by Q, on the basis that he had deceived the court and B into believing that he acted as litigation friend for his deceased mother. The court also permitted B to add the costs of the appeal to security held over Q's property. However, B was unable to recover its costs out of that security. The issues were whether (i) Q could be made personally liable for costs on a basis analogous to solicitors who had been held personally liable for costs incurred where they had acted in conducting litigation without authority; (ii) it was just to exercise the court's discretion under the Senior Courts Act 1981 and CPR r.48.2 to make a personal costs order against Q.

Held: Costs determined. (1) There was no reason in principle why those considerations which applied to solicitors who act without authority should not apply to any person who conducted proceedings on behalf of another so as to represent that he had authority to do so: such a person was liable to pay damages for a breach of warranty of authority and was consequently personally liable to pay the opposing party's costs, *Yonge v Toynbee* [1910] 1 K.B. 215 applied. Q, who acted without authority in the instant proceedings, had no defence to B's claim for costs. He was personally liable for breach of warranty of authority, and the measure of damages was the amount of costs B incurred since Q ceased to conduct the litigation as his mother's litigation friend (see paras 7-9 of judgment). (2) The instant case was clearly a case where it was just for the court to exercise its statutory discretion to make a personal costs order against Q. Q had conducted the trial and obtained permission to appeal for his own personal benefit as a beneficiary of his mother's estate; he had deceived B into spending significant costs in the belief Q was entitled to conduct proceedings on his mother's behalf, and had been guilty of gross misconduct by making false representations in evidence and submissions that his mother was still alive, when he knew that she had died. Accordingly, as B's security was insufficient to discharge the costs it had incurred, B was awarded indemnity costs orders against Q personally and in his capacity as administrator of his mother's estate (paras 11-12, 15).

BANK OF SCOTLAND v QUTB (COSTS), [2012] EWCA Civ 1661, [2013] C.P. Rep. 14, Mummery, L.J., CA (Civ Div).

309. Costs–Indemnity basis–Continuation of claim doomed to failure–Appropriate costs order where extra submissions requested by court to assist in determination of unusual issue

The defendant broadcasting company (D) applied for indemnity costs against the claimant broadcasting company (X). X's action against D for trade mark infringement and passing off had been dismissed. D's counterclaim for invalidity of X's trade marks had also been dismissed. D's application for indemnity costs was on the basis that (i) X's case had been without merit and X had failed to see its inherent weaknesses; (ii) X had failed to respond to an early "drop hands" offer; (iii) the judgment indicated that the proceedings had had the collateral purpose of trying to coerce D into a negotiation; (iv) there had been late, piecemeal and enforced disclosure; and (v) there had been non-compliance with the relevant pre-action protocol. D also sought costs that it had incurred in relation to a Court of Appeal judgment, which had been pronounced in the months preceding the trial of the instant case and in respect of which the court had asked for submissions as to its impact.

Held: Costs determined. (1) The principles on which it was appropriate to order indemnity costs were contained in *Kiam v MGN Ltd (Costs)* [2002] EWCA Civ 66, [2002] 1 W.L.R. 2810, [2002] C.L.Y. 347 and *Excelsior Commercial & Industrial Holdings Ltd v Salisbury Hamer Aspden & Johnson (Costs)* [2002] EWCA Civ 879, [2002] C.P. Rep. 67, [2002] C.L.Y. 353, *Kiam* and *Excelsior* applied. Clearly there had to be something beyond what could be described as the litigation norm (see paras 5-7 of judgment). The key factor in the instant case was the inherent weakness of X's claim: it was hopeless, and there had been no realistic chance of achieving the outcome sought. Furthermore, X had known that, short of a miracle, its case was bound to fail. It had pursued the litigation even after its bluff had been called many times. Enormous costs had been incurred in what amounted to a crashing defeat. X should pay D's costs on a standard basis up until the date on which the period for accepting the drop hands offer expired, with payment on an indemnity basis after that (paras 14-16). (2) Regarding the Court of Appeal authority, it had been decided, after consideration of submissions, not to retrospectively apply it to the instant case. Giving the normal order of costs in the case would mean that X was effectively paying for the whole exercise even though it had maintained all along that application of that case to the litigation would be wrong. Although X considered itself to be the victor on that point, there was, in fact, no winner. Each party had simply been required to present written and oral submissions to assist the court in an unusual matter. The court itself had been the instigator of that. Neither side should have to bear the other's costs for that type of exercise. The proper order was therefore no order as to costs (paras 21-33).

A&E TELEVISION NETWORKS LLC v DISCOVERY COMMUNICATIONS EUROPE LTD, [2013] EWHC 276 (Pat), [2013] 3 Costs L.R. 381, Peter Smith, J., Ch D (Patents Ct).

310. Costs–Indemnity basis–Search warrants obtained by Serious Fraud Office set aside for misrepresentation–Conduct of Serious Fraud Office–Whether justifying costs on indemnity basis

Following its judgment in two joined cases ([2012] EWHC 2254 (Admin), [2013] 1 W.L.R. 1634, [2013] 7 C.L. 35), the court was required to deal with applications for costs to be paid on an indemnity basis. Both sets of proceedings had arisen out of an investigation launched by the Serious Fraud Office into the activities of two businessmen (VT and RT) and the companies through which they carried on their business. VT and RT alleged that search warrants executed by the SFO had been obtained by misrepresentations and non-disclosure, and had applied for them to be set aside. In the first action, the claimant was a company (RH), and VT was an interested party. In the second action, the claimant was RT. In its judgment of July 31, the court found the allegations of misrepresentation and non-disclosure proved, and quashed the search warrants. RH, RT and VT each claimed their costs on an indemnity basis. The SFO submitted that (1) in both actions it should pay costs on a standard basis; (2) in the first action, it should pay only one set of costs, either RH's or VT's, their interests having been the same.

Held: Applications granted. (1) There was no dispute as to the principles to be applied. While the court enjoyed a wide and generous discretion as to costs, it would only be appropriate to award costs on an indemnity basis where there had been some conduct or circumstance taking the case out of the norm. That meant that there had to be a significant level of unreasonableness or otherwise inappropriate conduct. In the instant case, the SFO's conduct had to be considered against the background of its duty to ensure that the information presented to the judge in support of an application for a search warrant contained accurate and comprehensive material that was the product of very careful and well-balanced investigation. The SFO had wholly failed to discharge that duty, in circumstances in which the claimants' reputations were bound to be seriously damaged by the very public issue and execution of the warrants. It was not helped by its argument that the judge would not have granted the warrants unless absolutely satisfied that it was the right thing to do. That fact only made the SFO's duty even more important. The SFO had made serious errors, but had not accepted that it had done so until a very late stage in the proceedings. Though it had made concessions during the July hearing, they were not sufficient to mitigate the effect of its errors. The case was an exceptional one by reason of the SFO's unacceptable approach to its duties of disclosure and its subsequent failure to appreciate its errors until a very late stage. In both actions, therefore, the SFO was to pay the claimants' costs on an indemnity basis (see paras 6, 9-15 of judgment). (2) In respect of the first action, VT had been an interested party. There had been no conflict of interest between it and RH, and the issues could have been covered by one legal team. However, RH was an international firm with a reputation completely independent of VT. VT had been a key suspect in a criminal investigation which had continued until after the July hearing, and he had been arrested in a great deal of publicity. That distinct interest, together with the complexity of the case, not only justified but also required, separate representation for RH and VT. In those circumstances it was right for a separate costs order to be made in favour of VT. VT's costs were also to be paid on an indemnity basis, key concessions not having been made by the SFO until the day before the hearing (paras 16-18, 20-21).

R. (ON THE APPLICATION OF RAWLINSON AND HUNTER TRUSTEES SA) v CENTRAL CRIMINAL COURT (COSTS); R. (ON THE APPLICATION OF TCHENGUIZ) v SERIOUS FRAUD OFFICE (COSTS), [2012] EWHC 3218 (Admin), [2013] 1 Costs L.R. 122, Sir John Thomas (President), DC.

311. Costs–Interim applications–Claims for misappropriation of family trust assets–Appropriate costs orders for interim applications

The claimants (C) sought their costs of various applications made in proceedings brought against the defendants (D) for alleged misappropriation of trust fund assets. C's substantive claims concerned a trust constituted by a settlement whereby certain assets had been settled on discretionary trusts for various beneficiaries. The main beneficiaries were the settlor's four children, which included C1, C2 and D1. There had been litigation between the family members for 10 years, mainly related to allegations about D1's behaviour as sole trustee. On C's application, he had been removed as trustee in 2012 and ordered to deliver up trust documents to the new trustees, C2 and C3. The second claim against D1 and D2, his partner, was in respect of alleged misappropriation of a trust asset, namely a property in Barbados. D1 was the sole director of a company (D3) incorporated in Barbados. C alleged that D1 had caused D3 to purchase the property and transfer it to D2 using trust fund money. C had obtained a world-wide freezing order against D and sought a continuation of that order and related orders. C also applied to amend their particulars of claim in relation to claim 2. D had not complied with orders for the provision of information and served a late defence, shortly before an application by C for judgment in default. D withdrew a strike out application and conceded C's injunction and leave to amend applications shortly before the hearing. C accepted that they should bear the parties' costs of the amendment application. The court was required to determine the appropriate order for the costs of C's injunction and default judgment applications, and of D's withdrawn strike out application. C submitted, referring to the decision in *Gorbunova v Berezovsky* [2013] EWHC 771 (Ch), that the appropriate approach was for the court to find the "battleground" on which the parties had engaged and to ask in relatively broad terms who was the winner and who was the loser. D agreed with that approach but argued that C's substantive claims had been fundamentally flawed and susceptible to being struck out, and that C had fallen short of their duty of full and frank disclosure such as to justify D being awarded their costs of the applications.

Held: Costs determined. (1) The general rule was that costs followed the event. To adopt the correct approach, the court had to ascertain at the outset, in a commercially sensible way, who was the successful party and give weight to that party's overall success, even if it meant departing from the general rule, *HLB Kidsons (A Firm) v Lloyd's Underwriters (Costs)* [2007] EWHC 2699 (Comm), [2008] 3 Costs L.R. 427, [2009] C.L.Y. 389 applied (see para.20 of judgment). (2) The pleadings in claim 2 were not so defective or confusing as to be likely to be struck out without further evidence being submitted by C. Even if the alleged defects had been present, it was most unlikely that the court would have refused to amend them on C's inevitable application to do so once the point had been raised. D had not identified any evidence that C had subsequently "put their house in order". It was unrealistic to suggest that the alleged difficulties were such as would have prevented the freezing injunction application from proceeding, or in some other way to have entitled D to a strike out or costs, other than any costs related to an amendment. The costs of the amendment were the appropriate recompense for any inconvenience or unfairness caused by the alleged defects. It was also not accepted that D1 had a genuine desire to submit to a properly arguable case on the injunctions. He did not even participate in the removal proceedings, at no stage had he offered undertakings in respect of the orders sought, and had only conceded the applications at the eleventh hour (paras 32-34). (3) There was nothing in the points raised by D regarding disclosure to support their claim for costs or to support their resistance to an order being made against them (paras 38-41). (4) Against the background of D's behaviour and the last-minute concessions, it was a bold submission to make that D should have their costs over and above those occasioned by the amendment to C's particulars of claim. The submission, and all D's arguments, would be rejected. It was clear that on the "battleground" in the instant case C were the clear winners and D could not resist the application of the general rule that C should have their costs, save those of the amendment, *Gorbunova* and *HLB Kidsons* applied (para.42).

FYFE v WATTS; WATTS v WATTS, [2013] EWHC 1374 (Ch), [2014] 1 Costs L.O. 1, Alison Foster Q.C., Ch D.

312. Costs–Issues–Overall winner failing on some issues–Whether court should make issues-based costs order–Appropriate amount of payment on account

The court was required to determine the issue of costs following its decision that a lender (C) had been entitled to cancel a loan agreement and to recover the sums it had advanced to the borrower (G). The dispute arose out of the development by G of a hotel and apartments on a site in central London. When G had had difficulties increasing its bank finance it had entered into a loan agreement with C. G claimed damages against C for failing to advance funding under the loan agreement. G said that the failure to lend any more money was in breach of contract, and that it starved the development of funding at a time of tight credit and thereby caused its failure. Its damages claim was valued at over £70 million. C's case was that it was not obliged to continue to lend because G was in default under the loan agreement. G's claims did not succeed. The judge held that C was entitled to succeed on its claim for the sums it advanced to G, and on its claim under a guarantee. C obtained judgment for EUR 65.9 million, subject to a deduction for sums received under a performance guarantee. G contended that it was appropriate for the court to take an issues-based approach to costs and that it should have its costs of three issues raised by C and on which G succeeded, namely G's ability to complete the development by the long stop date, material adverse change in the financial condition of the relevant companies, and the estoppel-like doctrine of Spanish law called actos propios; alternatively the court should award C a percentage only of its costs.

Held: Judgment accordingly. (1) A feature of C's case at trial was that it had two parts: the first concerning financial defaults, and the second concerning development defaults. It succeeded on both parts of its case, though not on every issue. For the purposes of costs the most significant point was that the three issues identified by G in respect of which C failed were not distinct, but were interwoven and interlinked with other issues in the case upon which it succeeded. That was particularly so as regards C's material adverse change case, and the same point about interlinking applied, albeit to a considerably lesser extent, in relation to the long stop date issue. The instant case was complex and it would be unrealistic to expect the costs judge to master the issues in sufficient detail to understand what costs were properly incurred in dealing with which issues, *English v Emery Reimbold & Strick Ltd* [2002] EWCA Civ 605, [2002] 1 W.L.R. 2409, [2002] C.L.Y. 301 considered. Where the relevant issues overlapped substantially, the authorities indicated that the court should hesitate before making an issues-based order. The order for costs sought by G could not readily be made by the costs judge and that alone was sufficient to rule it out (see paras 37-42 of judgment). (2) Although it was not practicable to make an issues-based order, the costs order should properly reflect C's failure to make good its case on the long stop date, and the material adverse change and actos propios issues. The question was as to the extent of the percentage reduction that should be ordered in respect of C's costs. A reduction of up to 80 per cent as advocated by G would bear no relation to the overall outcome of the case. C had in effect no option but to fight on a battleground of G's choosing. C was the overall winner. It had succeeded on both its claim and on G's claim, and in principle was entitled to recover its costs. However, there should be a substantial percentage deduction primarily to reflect G's success on the long stop date issue. Taking into account the other issues as well, a proper deduction was 25 per cent (paras 54-56). (3) C was entitled to an interim payment on account of 50 per cent of its likely costs recovery less the 25 per cent reduction, giving a figure of £4 million (paras 68-69).

GRUPO HOTELERO URVASCO SA v CAREY VALUE ADDED SL (FORMERLY LOSAN HOTELS WORLD VALUE ADDED I SL), [2013] EWHC 1732 (Comm), [2013] 5 Costs L.R. 669, Blair, J., QBD (Comm).

313. Costs–Legal costs insurance premiums–Recovery of cost of ATE insurance taken out during course of appeal proceedings–Meaning of "proceedings" within s.29 Access to Justice Act 1999

[Access to Justice Act 1999 (c.22) s.29; CPR PD 44 (General Rules about Costs) 2000 para.19.2.]

The court had to determine whether the cost of an after the event insurance (ATE) premium for cover purchased by the respondent (H) shortly before the appeal was recoverable in relation to the costs of the claim up to and including trial. H had succeeded at first instance but had not obtained ATE cover. The appellant (S) appealed, and H obtained ATE cover against the risk of liability for S's costs of the action up to trial and the costs of the appeal in the event that S's appeal succeeded. The premium was over £394,000, far in excess of the parties' costs of the appeal, and was not payable by H if S's appeal succeeded. It was only payable if a positive result was achieved for H. S's appeal was unsuccessful and H sought to recover the premium as part of its costs. The court was required to determine whether S could be ordered to pay that part of the ATE premium which related to the costs of the claim up to and including trial. It accepted that the premium relating to the costs of the appeal was recoverable. S submitted that the Access to Justice Act 1999 s.29 did not permit recovery of the premium relating to the costs of the trial because the cover had to be limited to the risk of incurring a liability in the proceedings in which the costs order was made, which, in the instant case, were the appeal proceedings not the trial at first instance.

Held: Issue determined in favour of appellant. (Patten L.J. dissenting) (1) It appeared that the words "in those proceedings" in s.29 required that the costs order had to be made in the same proceedings as those in which a costs liability might arise, the risk of incurring which had been insured against. The question was therefore whether a trial and an appeal from that trial were the same proceedings. It would be perfectly natural to think of an appeal as arising from, and being part of, the same proceedings as the trial from which the appeal was taken. However, it was clear that the trial and the appeal were treated as separate proceedings for the purposes of costs, *Masson Templier & Co v De Fries (Costs)* [1910] 1 K.B. 535 and *Wright v Bennett (No.1)* [1948] 1 K.B. 601, [1947-51] C.L.Y. 7615 considered. That distinction was recognised and written into the CPR. Further, it was plainly intended by the legislature that the 1999 Act should operate to improve access to justice for claimants with meritorious claims, but also operate fairly. For that purpose, rules of court were introduced to ensure that the potential liability for the ATE premium, amongst other things, should not bear unfairly on defendants who were not informed of the existence of such a funding arrangement, *Callery v Gray (No.1)* [2001] EWCA Civ 1117, [2001] 1 W.L.R. 2112, [2001] C.L.Y. 493, *Callery v Gray (No.2)* [2001] EWCA Civ 1246, [2001] 1 W.L.R. 2142, [2001] C.L.Y. 492 and *Callery v Gray (No.1)* [2002] UKHL 28, [2002] 1 W.L.R. 2000, [2002] C.L.Y. 360 considered. H had complied with its obligation to give S notification of the ATE premium in connection with the appeal, but CPR PD 44 para.19.2 did not expressly contemplate that an ATE arrangement in relation to the costs of trial would be entered into for the first time for the purposes of the appeal. The importance of fair notice being given to the other party of a potential liability in additional costs would be entirely undermined if the premium which the claimant sought to recover in the appeal could be recovered so far as it related to costs of trial: the defendant would have incurred all the costs of trial together with its potential, but retrospective, liability for the claimant's ATE premium in ignorance of what was coming when there was an appeal. When it learned of the ATE premium taken out in the appeal embracing cover for the costs of the trial it was too late to do anything. Such a situation was unfair and antithetical to the purpose of s.29.The word "proceedings" in s.29 should therefore be given its traditional meaning which distinguished between proceedings at trial and on appeal (see paras 41-45, 52-53, 63 of judgment). (2) The risk that the incidence of costs at trial might be changed by the costs order of the appeal court might be a new risk of the appeal, but the costs liability and costs order in question remained those of the trial. The risk insured against was a risk of incurring a liability in the trial proceedings, not in the appeal proceedings. It followed that the costs liability in respect of which H's premium had been taken out remained a costs liability in the trial proceedings, not in the appeal proceedings. The result was that the costs concerned were justifiable as neither costs of the appeal nor as costs of a trial which had already terminated. If it were otherwise, costs of trial would be increased retrospectively, to the prejudice of the opposing party (paras 58-59). (3) (Per Patten L.J.) The 1999 Act was designed to expand access to the courts via the use of CFAs and ATE insurance. It was unlikely that Parliament intended to lay down a rule that proceedings at first instance and those in the Court of Appeal should be treated as separate "proceedings" within the meaning of s.29 (paras 31-38).

HAWKSFORD TRUSTEES JERSEY LTD v STELLA GLOBAL UK LTD, [2012] EWCA Civ 987, [2012] 1 W.L.R. 3581, Rix, L.J., CA (Civ Div).

314. Costs–Legal representatives–Unreasonable conduct by solicitors in immigration case

[Civil Procedure Rules 1998 (SI 1998/3132) r.44.14.]

The court determined an application for an adjournment and liability for costs in connection with an application by the claimant national of Sierra Leone (G) for judicial review of the defendant secretary of state's decision to grant him only six months' discretionary leave to remain in the United Kingdom. G had originally been granted indefinite leave to remain, but following his conviction for wounding with intent, a deportation order was made against him. G's application for revocation of the order succeeded on appeal. The secretary of state subsequently granted him six months' discretionary leave to remain. G issued judicial review proceedings to challenge the lawfulness of that decision, asserting that the secretary of state should either have reinstated his indefinite leave or granted him three years' discretionary leave to remain. G was granted permission to apply for judicial review in September 2011. The judge granting permission gave a number of case management directions. They included directions about timescales for the filing and service of certain documents, including G's reply to the secretary of state's detailed grounds of defence, G's trial bundle and his skeleton argument. G was represented by a firm of solicitors (P). P failed to respond to a letter from the Treasury Solicitors dated January 20, 2012, which had suggested that it was appropriate for G to amend his grounds of review to reflect current case law. In March 2012, G's application was listed for a substantive hearing, scheduled for October 4, 2012. In August 2012, the Treasury Solicitors wrote to inform P that G had been granted discretionary leave to remain for three years and that his claim had therefore been rendered academic; confirmation was requested of whether G intended to pursue his claim. No response was received. On August 14, the secretary of state filed her detailed grounds of defence. Again there was no response from P or G. In September 2012, the Treasury Solicitors again wrote to P requesting confirmation of G's intentions and service of his skeleton argument, which was overdue. The Treasury Solicitors then wrote to the court on September 25, copying in P. They referred to the September 2011 court order and stated that G's skeleton argument had not been served, that P had not responded to previous requests for confirmation of G's intentions, and that the secretary of state was consequently not in a position to file and serve her skeleton argument in response. No skeleton argument had been served and no trial bundle prepared by G or P by the day of the hearing, and neither made an appearance. On the morning of the hearing, the court received a faxed letter from P, in which they wrote to withdraw from acting for G, stating that they did not have instructions to represent him at the hearing. While giving judgment, the court was handed a faxed letter from G, which stated that he had been unable to attend court because he had no legal representation, and that he sought an adjournment to enable him to appoint a legal aid solicitor.

Held: Application refused, liability for costs determined. (1) G and P had left the court entirely in the dark. The secretary of state, the Treasury Solicitors and their appointed counsel had had to continue to prepare the case on the assumption that G would or might appear. There had been a complete disregard by G and P of both the September 2011 directions and their duty to the court. It was remarkable that P had failed to have any contact with the Treasury Solicitors or the court in the nine months leading up to the instant hearing; that they had thought fit to ignore a series of sensible letters from the Treasury Solicitors; that they had thought fit to fax a letter at the eleventh hour withdrawing without any explanation for their conduct or apology; and that they might have thought that that was conduct fitting of a solicitor of the Supreme Court. It was not. P's failings had resulted in a great deal of wasted time and costs by the Treasury Solicitors and their counsel, the Administrative Court office and the present court. It was a paradigm case for the application of the CPR r.44.14; it was difficult to think of a more disgraceful dereliction of duty to the court. P had simply sat on their hands and done absolutely nothing except allow the fixture to remain in everybody's diaries and preparations to be made by Treasury Solicitors, their counsel and the court. In the circumstances, the costs of the Treasury Solicitors and their counsel incurred from January 20, 2012 up to and including the instant hearing were ordered to be paid personally by P on an indemnity basis, to be assessed if not agreed. The message should go out loud and clear that the court simply would not tolerate such lax behaviour by claimants' solicitors (see paras 21-24, 27-28, 50 of judgment). (2) G's application for an adjournment was refused and his claim was dismissed. Costs before January 20, 2012 were to be paid by him to the secretary of state on a standard basis, to be assessed if not agreed (paras 30-31, 36).

R. (ON THE APPLICATION OF GASSAMA) v SECRETARY OF STATE FOR THE HOME DEPARTMENT, [2012] EWHC 3049 (Admin), [2013] P.N.L.R.10, Haddon-Cave, J., QBD (Admin).

315. Costs–No order for costs–Appropriateness of depriving party of costs following successful applications–Whether correct to cap trustee in bankruptcy's reimbursements

[Access to Justice Act 1999 (c.22) s.11; Civil Procedure Rules 1998 (SI 1998/3132) Pt 44.]

The appellant husband and wife (H and W) appealed against a decision to make no order as to costs relating to two applications against the respondent trustees in bankruptcy (T) in insolvency proceedings relating to H. H and W had lived in a property that was registered in joint names. H was made bankrupt and T was appointed to administer H's estate, which included a second property solely owned by H. It was ordered that H would assist T in their sale of the second property, and that unless the expenses of the bankruptcy were paid to T within 120 days the first property would be sold. Although H had attempted to remortgage the second property to raise funds, that payment was not made within time and nor was the property put on the market. T was consequently granted a warrant of possession over the first property. H and W applied to vary the order to allow more time to give effect to it and applied to suspend the warrant of possession. Although that application was granted, no order as to costs was made but a cap on T's reimbursements from the estate was varied from 60 per cent to 30 per cent. At that time there was sufficient equity in the second property to discharge the costs of the insolvency and still leave a surplus in the estate. H and W submitted that (1) H should get his costs as he had been successful in the applications and T had acted disproportionately throughout; (2) it was contrary to the Access to Justice Act 1999 s.11 to make a costs order that awarded T any of their costs, which H contended were not properly incurred, out of the estate as that order had the effect of making H pay; (3) there had been no criticism of W by the court which justified her not getting her costs.

Held: Appeal allowed in part. (1) The starting point when considering costs was CPR Pt 44. H had been successful in his applications to amend the order and suspend the warrant of possession over the first property. The order had required H to do all that he could to assist in the sale of the second property. The court below had considered H's conduct to be dilatory. H had not wanted the sale to go through whilst he was making efforts to remortgage the property, however, he could have done more in the meantime to assist T. Having regard to all the evidence it was impossible to say that the courts below had been wrong in finding that the case was one where no order as to costs between H and T was appropriate (see para.28 of judgment). (2) The argument on s.11 that there should be a 100 per cent cap on T taking remuneration from the estate was rejected as it seemed perfectly clear that that section dealt with adverse costs orders and not a cap on reimbursements. That left the question of whether it was right to qualify what T could take by way of reimbursements out of the estate. A trustee in bankruptcy was not to be reimbursed only if his conduct had fallen below the standard of a reasonable insolvency practitioner acting reasonably. The courts below had plainly felt the need to qualify the right that T had to the costs that they had incurred in the two applications. The cap had been varied by the courts below but there had been room for a legitimate disagreement on that issue on the facts. The order reflected that T had in part acted reasonably and in part unreasonably. For that reason the appeal in respect of H was dismissed (paras 29-30, 32, 34). (3) W's position was, however, quite different. The judgment had not stated anywhere that W should have been deprived of the usual order for costs due to culpable conduct. In contrast it was said that she had been wholly successful and that there was no criticism of her. Having taken that view there appeared to be no basis for depriving W of an order for costs in her favour. The court below had considered it important that W had been legally aided and that it was therefore right to reduce the cap on what could be reimbursed out of the estate from 60 per cent to 30 per cent rather than to order her costs. That had been the wrong approach. W had the potential of a statutory charge being made over her property due to the legal aid that she had received. The correct order was for T to pay W's costs with the cap of 30 per cent applying in relation to both T's and W's costs (paras 35-36).

NUTTING v KHALIQ, [2012] EWCA Civ 1726, [2013] B.P.I.R. 340, Mummery, L.J., CA (Civ Div).

316. Costs–No order for costs–Winding-up petition arising from unpaid penalty issued to taxpayer–Dismissal of petition by agreement–Entitlement of registrar to make no order as to costs on basis of taxpayer's conduct

[Taxes Management Act 1970 (c.9); Civil Procedure Rules 1998 (SI 1998/3132) r.44.3(2).]

The appellant company (F) appealed against a decision dismissing its application for an order that the respondent commissioners pay F's costs, on an indemnity basis, of a winding-up petition dismissed by agreement. The commissioners had issued a penalty to F under the Taxes Management Act 1970. F indicated to the commissioners that it intended to appeal the penalty to the tax tribunal on the basis that it concerned tax already paid. In January 2010, the commissioners expressed the view that the penalty remained due and that if F did not appeal within 30 days, it would take the penalty to be settled and agreed. Three days later, they wrote again to confirm that the penalty remained due. In February 2010, F purported to have founded its appeal, but the tribunal had no record of receiving F's letter. In August 2010, the commissioners wrote to F requesting full details of all payments made. F did not respond, since it considered all tax had been paid. The commissioners wrote again in October 2010 with an application for payment of outstanding tax liabilities, and an indication that the penalty remained since they were unaware of any appeal to the tribunal. A further letter from the commissioners two weeks later made a further request for information as to payments made. F did not respond. In January 2011, the commissioners informed F that unless they received further information, they would serve a winding-up petition. The petition was served in March 2011. In June 2011, F appealed to the tax tribunal in relation to the penalty. The commissioners stated that they would seek the petition's dismissal if F demonstrated that the tax tribunal had received and listed the appeal, and if F provided evidence of alleged payment. In August 2011, the penalty was withdrawn, it being accepted by the commissioners that it was not a valid penalty since taxes were not due. The winding-up petition was dismissed by consent in November 2011 but the question of costs was adjourned. The registrar rejected F's claim to be awarded its costs of the petition and made no order as to costs, having found that F had acted unreasonably in failing to respond to many requests for information and that the commissioners had been driven to pursue the penalty and the winding-up petition as a result of F's conduct. F contended that the registrar had erred in finding that it had behaved unreasonably. It submitted that, having told the commissioners that the tax had been paid, it had no need to answer further correspondence because the commissioners could have discovered from their own records that they had already received the money. F argued further that the penalty was at all times under appeal and so demands for its payment were invalid. The commissioners contended that the registrar had been entitled to come to the conclusion he had where F had brought the winding-up petition upon itself as a result of its unreasonable behaviour in failing to respond to correspondence, and where the penalty remained due and owing until an appeal was mounted.

Held: Appeal dismissed. In deciding whether to disapply the general rule to award a successful party its costs under CPR r.44.3(2), the court could take accounts of parties' conduct before as well as during proceedings. The commissioners had made it clear to F that they did not know of and were not satisfied that payments had been made. F had been put on notice that unless it answered requests for information a winding-up petition would be issued. The parties had failed to communicate properly and the registrar had understood that and seen fault on both sides and, consequently, concluded that that conduct took the case out of the usual course so that it was inappropriate to award costs either way. In respect of the commissioners' pursuit of the penalty, F was the author of its own misfortune. It was fully on notice that the commissioners had thought the penalty was due and that F had was not pursuing an appeal. F had behaved unreasonably in failing to chase its application to the tribunal when it had to have been apparent that the tribunal had not received it in February 2010. Overall, the registrar's decision could not be faulted. He had looked at the matter in the round, and at the facts and detail, and exercised his discretion under CPR 44.3, and to have made no order for costs, in a way that should be upheld. There was fault on both sides and reason to deprive F of its costs.

FRANK SAUL (FASHIONS) LTD v REVENUE AND CUSTOMS COMMISSIONERS, [2012] EWHC 1603 (Ch), [2012] B.P.I.R. 985, Vos, J., Ch D.

317. Costs–Non-party costs–Conditional fee agreements–Solicitor failing to arrange ATE insurance–Conflict of interest between solicitor and client

[Senior Courts Act 1981 (c.54) s.51.]

The appellant employer (T) appealed against a decision (Heron v TNT (UK) Ltd) to dismiss its application for a non-party costs order against the respondent firm of solicitors (M). M's client (H) had brought a personal injury claim against T. H had entered into a conditional fee agreement (CFA) with M. M did not seek after the event (ATE) insurance for H; M confirmed to T the absence of insurance after it had inquired. T made Part 36 offers which H rejected. H, on advice from M and counsel, made offers which T rejected. Shortly before trial, M advised H that it would be unable to represent him at trial or instruct counsel unless it had monies on account to cover disbursements. An expert subsequently advised that much of the injury H had sustained in his accident would have occurred in any event. H, representing himself at trial, was awarded far less in damages than had been available in the Part 36 offers. He was ordered to pay T's costs. T applied for a non-party costs order against M under the Senior Courts Act 1981 s.51, alleging that M's failure to obtain ATE insurance had meant that there was an undeclared conflict of interest between M and H which had motivated M to continue with the case to ensure that H would not have a liability for T's costs. The judge found that the allegation that M had been aware of a conflict of interest had not been made out, and that there was no evidence to suggest conscious impropriety on M's part. T argued that the judge had made a factual error in finding that there had been no conflict of interest between M and H, and therefore in finding that M had not appreciated any such conflict.

Held: Appeal dismissed. (1) The judge had not rejected the allegation that there had been a conflict of interest. Had he reached that conclusion, he would have said so in terms. He had rejected the claim of conscious impropriety and it was not difficult to see why. If M had had its eye on the ball when T had asked about ATE, the position could have been rectified; an equally plausible inference was that M had mistakenly believed that there was some reason why ATE insurance had not been sought or obtained and failed to challenge that assumption. Although the court rejected M's submission that it would be wrong ever to make a finding of conscious impropriety when the relevant solicitor had not given evidence, the judge's rejection of the claim of conscious impropriety had been open to him on the evidence. On the facts as found by the judge, T's application had to be put on the basis that M's failure to obtain ATE insurance, and the subsequent failure to admit that to H, was itself sufficient not only to give rise to a breach of duty to him, but also to demonstrate that M had become a "real party" to the litigation, *Dymocks Franchise Systems (NSW) Pty Ltd v Todd (Costs)* [2004] UKPC 39, [2004] 1 W.L.R. 2807, [2004] C.L.Y. 328 considered. If that was so, every act of negligence by a solicitor in the conduct of litigation which meant that an opposing party incurred costs which might not otherwise have been incurred would be sufficient for a non-party costs order. The law did not go that far. A solicitor was entitled to act on a CFA for an impecunious client who he knew or suspected would not be able to pay costs if unsuccessful. As far as the other side was concerned, whether the solicitor had negligently failed to obtain ATE insurance did not impact on the costs they would incur unless it was demonstrably provable that the costs would not have been incurred, *Adris v Royal Bank of Scotland Plc* [2010] EWHC 941 (QB),

[2010] 4 Costs L.R. 598, [2010] C.L.Y. 316 considered. That was not the instant case (see paras 27-30, 36-37 of judgment). (2) A professional negligence claim brought by H was the appropriate forum to determine the extent to which M were liable to compensate H for any costs he would have to pay T. The summary procedure for a non-party costs order was not (para.38).

HERON v TNT (UK) LTD, [2013] EWCA Civ 469, [2013] 3 All E.R. 479, Leveson, L.J., CA (Civ Div).

318. Costs–Non-party costs–Solicitor acting under CFA and paying disbursements for impecunious client without ATE insurance–Whether solicitor controlling litigation–Liability to non-party costs order

The applicants applied for a non-party costs order and a wasted costs order against the solicitor who acted for the respondent company (T). The first applicant was a building contractor who was engaged by the second applicant to demolish part of a building as part of a road building project. T complained that R's work had created dust which had damaged machinery used by it in the other part of the building. T claimed for damage to the machinery and loss of production leading to loss of profit. The applicants raised issues as to whether T or another company was the occupier of the premises and owner of the machinery. T's solicitor (E) had agreed to act under a conditional fee agreement (CFA) knowing that T was impecunious and had no after the event (ATE) insurance. He was prepared to pay disbursements on T's behalf on the basis that he would be indemnified for that expenditure only if the claim succeeded. The court had decided as a preliminary issue that T had no cause of action in negligence or nuisance against the third or fourth applicants, which had commissioned the project; T was entitled to bring a claim in negligence and nuisance against the first and second applicants for any recoverable loss and damage proved to have been suffered, but the claims for loss of profits and wasted management time had no real prospect of success and were summarily dismissed, leaving only a modest claim for damage to machinery. Costs were awarded against T and its remaining claims were struck out when it failed to make interim payments on account of costs. The applicants submitted that E had controlled the litigation and had acted improperly, unreasonably or negligently, in particular in failing to undertake a sufficient investigation into T's title to sue; he had in substance funded the litigation as a business venture for his own financial benefit as well as that of his client and should be treated in the same way as any other commercial funder which could be made liable for the costs.

Held: Application refused. (1) The criticisms of E's conduct of the case had not been clearly established, even if they were relevant in the context of the non-party costs application. He had not deliberately or recklessly closed his eyes to the difficulties with a view simply to pushing the case forwards for his own financial interests. The outcome of the preliminary issue was not that the claim lacked merit in its entirety. There was no proper basis for suggesting that E "controlled" the litigation any differently from any solicitor conducting litigation for a client (see paras 23-26 of judgment). (2) There was no difference between the position of a solicitor acting under a CFA who had agreed to fund disbursements under the CFA and one who had not, since both arrangements were permitted and were regarded as meeting a recognised legitimate public policy aim. Nor did it make a difference that the solicitor knew that the client was impecunious and that there was no ATE policy in place; acting for clients who were impecunious did not take the solicitor outside his role as such and there was no obligation on a solicitor acting under a CFA to ensure that ATE insurance cover was in place when his client was impecunious. There had to be something beyond that combination of factors which would render it just to make a non-party costs order, such as some financial benefit to the solicitor over and above the benefit which he could expect to receive from the CFA, or some exercise of control of the litigation over and above that which would be expected from a solicitor acting on behalf of a client, or some combination of both, *Dymocks Franchise Systems (NSW) Pty Ltd v Todd (Costs)* [2004] UKPC 39, [2004] 1 W.L.R. 2807, [2004] C.L.Y. 328 considered, *Myatt v National*

Coal Board [2007] EWCA Civ 307, [2007] 1 W.L.R. 1559, [2007] C.L.Y. 428 followed and *Germany v Flatman* [2011] EWHC 2945 (QB), [2012] 2 Costs L.R. 271, [2012] C.L.Y. 2083 doubted. There was no basis for concluding that E took on the case in any capacity other than as a solicitor under a CFA who was willing to fund the disbursements. He did not take on the case or control the litigation for his own financial self-interest (paras 56-60, 63-68). (3) Normally it would be impermissible to seek a non-party costs order by reference to complaints that the solicitor had acted improperly, unreasonably or negligently in his capacity as solicitor; that was the province of wasted costs and the courts should be astute to keep the two applications separate (para.61). (4) Permission was refused for the first applicant to pursue a wasted costs application against E (paras 72-76).

TINSELTIME LTD v ROBERTS, [2012] EWHC 2628 (TCC), [2012] T.C.L.R. 9, Judge Stephen Davies, QBD (TCC).

319. Costs–Offer of amends–Rejection of offer to settle in defamation claim–Court award same amount as offer–Costs payable by claimant

[Defamation Act 1996 (c.31) s.2, s.4; Civil Procedure Rules 1998 (SI 1998/3132) Pt 36.]

The court was required to determine costs in an action brought by the claimant (C) against the defendant newspaper (M) for damages following the publication by M of a defamatory article about C in a newspaper. M published a full apology and made an offer of amends at an early stage. In December 2010 M made an offer of £50,000 together with payment of C's reasonable legal costs which was rejected. Various offers and negotiations followed with C stating that he would settle for £80,000 plus costs. M made a further offer of £50,000. In May 2011 M made a CPR Pt 36 offer of £75,000 plus costs which was rejected. Litigation began in June 2011. As the trial approached in September 2011 M made an offer of £50,000 plus legal costs. In December 2011 M suggested that the parties were agreed that £50,000 was the appropriate sum of damages and offered to pay C's legal costs up to December 2010 when the first offer expired. C rejected the offer. Following an appeal, C was awarded damages of £50,000. M contended that in the context of the Defamation Act 1996 s.2-s.4 an open offer of £50,000 was made in December 2010 which, at the end of the proceedings, C had failed to beat and so he should pay M's costs of the trial and the appeal from the day the offer was rejected on an indemnity basis.

Held: Costs determined. Long before the litigation began, M had made an appropriate apology and offer of amends in accordance with the Act. M had offered £50,000 with reasonable legal costs which was rejected. By the time the case came to hearing, both sides were agreed that £50,000 would represent a fair level of damages, an assessment which, but for its temporary withdrawal, had represented M's contention all along and which was available for acceptance in December 2010. The decision of the instant court confirmed what both sides had eventually agreed was the appropriate level of damages. By the date C had agreed that £50,0000 was appropriate the costs had escalated considerably. The objective of s.2-4 of the Act was vindication without litigation. If the court concluded that the offer of amends was adequate, it normally followed that any subsequent litigation was inappropriate and unnecessary. If, within the statutory procedure, a claimant chose, following an appropriate apology, to reject a clear and unequivocal offer of damages, and thus incurred additional legal expense and required the defendant to incur further expense, the burden of what proved to have been unnecessary legal expense would normally fall on the claimant who had caused it to be incurred. M was to pay C's costs on a standard basis up to December 2010; there would be no order as to costs to cover the temporary withdrawal of the offer between January and April 2011; C would pay M's costs after that date to include the costs of the trial and the appeal on a standard basis (see paras 12-14 of judgment).

KC v MGN LTD (COSTS), [2013] EWCA Civ 3, [2013] 2 Costs L.R. 269, Lord Judge, L.C.J., CA (Civ Div).

320. Costs–Part 36 offers–Defendants' offer not in compliance with Part 36

[Civil Procedure Rules 1998 (SI 1998/3132) Pt 36, r.36.14, r.44.3(4)(c), r.44.3.]

The appellants (F) appealed against a decision ([2011] EWHC 2807 (Ch), [2012] Bus. L.R. 891, [2012] 1 C.L. 33) that they should pay costs to the respondents (B) on the indemnity basis plus interest. B cross-appealed against the disallowance of 30 per cent of their costs. F had brought proceedings for a declaration that B's exercise of an option under a limited liability partnership agreement was not valid. Before the trial, B had made a settlement offer of £5.8 million. The offer was expressed to be open to a specified date. It was not a Part 36 offer. F rejected the offer. The court found that B's exercise of the option was valid and F was ordered to pay B approximately £7.8 million. B also succeeded in an unfair prejudice petition, but failed to establish a number of other allegations. F failed in their cross-petition for unfair prejudice. The judge ordered F to pay 70 per cent of B's costs on the standard basis up to the last date when they could have accepted B's offer. After that date, they were to pay B's costs on the indemnity basis. He justified his order on the basis that B's offer had been akin to a Part 36 offer. He also ordered F to pay interest on those costs at three per cent above base rate up to the offer's expiry date, thereafter at 10 per cent above base rate, rising to 40 per cent per annum, and then falling to 22 per cent, to reflect the borrowing rates paid by B on loans they had obtained to fund the litigation.

Held: Appeal allowed, cross-appeal dismissed. (1) The starting point was that B's offer was not a Part 36 offer. The judge's jurisdiction as to costs fell under the CPR r.44.3 and he had no jurisdiction to make a costs order under r.36.14. It was therefore difficult to see how the costs regime of Part 36, whether indirectly or by analogy, could properly be invoked. Rule 36.14 represented a departure from otherwise established costs practice and imposed deliberately swingeing costs sanctions on claimants who failed to beat a defendant's Part 36 offer. That was designed to encourage a sensible approach to offers and promote settlement. But there was no reason or justification to indirectly extend Part 36 beyond its expressed ambit. The general rule was that for an offer to be a Part 36 offer, it had to strictly comply with the requirements. It was not permissible to discount a number of failures to comply with the requirements of Part 36 as the merest technicality, *Huntley v Simmonds* [2009] EWHC 406 (QB) and *Fitzroy Robinson Ltd v Mentmore Towers Ltd* [2010] EWHC 98 (TCC) not applied. Since B's offer was not Part 36 compliant, either in substance or in form, the judge was wrong in principle to take as directly analogous the potential costs consequences of Part 36. There was no doubt that he was entitled under r.44.3(4)(c) to have regard to the offer in deciding what order to make. The difficulty was that the judge had not found that F's conduct in pursuing their case had been unreasonable, *Epsom College v Pierse Constructing Southern Ltd (In Liquidation) (formerly Biseley Construction Ltd) (Costs)* [2011] EWCA Civ 1449, [2012] T.C.L.R. 2, [2012] C.L.Y. 385 applied. The award of indemnity costs was therefore set aside (see paras 54-57, 61-68 of judgment). (2) The judge had selected a rate of three per cent interest above base rate for the period up to the expiry of B's offer. The higher rate for the subsequent period was made by reference to an analogy with Part 36. Since the position was not dictated by Part 36 in the instant case, there could be no justification for departing from the rate of three per cent above base rate. The court generally took a pragmatic approach. The rate set was often less than the successful party would have to pay as a borrower, but more than he would receive as a lender (paras 82-83, 88). (3) The judge had taken the view that B had suffered particularly high losses as a result of the litigation, in the form of interest charges on bridging loans taken out to fund the litigation. His award of interest at 40 per cent, and 22 per cent, could not stand because: (a) he had taken into account his award of indemnity costs before reaching his conclusions on interest; (b) there could be no justification for some kind of penal award of interest in the instant case; (c) although regard had to be had to the compensatory principle, reasonableness so far as the paying party was concerned was also relevant. F had been given no prior notification that B were borrowing at such rates. Further, the cost of funding litigation by way of bridging loans was not ordinarily recoverable as a cost of litigation, but the judge's approach came near to having that consequence. A rate of three per cent above base rate was therefore substituted for all other rates awarded by the judge (paras 94-100).

F&C ALTERNATIVE INVESTMENTS (HOLDINGS) LTD v BARTHELEMY (COSTS); F&C PARTNERS LLP, *Re*; *sub nom*. BARTHELEMY v F&C ALTERNATIVE INVESTMENTS (HOLDINGS) LTD, [2012] EWCA Civ 843, [2013] 1 W.L.R. 548, Arden, L.J., CA (Civ Div).

321. **Costs–Part 36 offers–Departing from normal costs rule–Insufficient weight given to particular facts of personal injury claim–Frontal lobe damage**

[Civil Procedure Rules 1998 (SI 1998/3132) Pt 36, r.36.10(5).]

The appellant (G) appealed against a decision (SG (A Child) v Hewitt (Costs)) requiring him to pay the costs of the respondent (H) from the date that he accepted H's CPR Pt 36 offer. G had been injured in a road traffic accident caused by H when he was six years old. He sustained a severe head injury with damage to the frontal lobes of the brain. Medical and other reports were obtained with a view to a claim for damages being made but the experts felt unable to predict what the impact of the brain injury would be until G matured. H made a pre-action Part 36 offer by way of full and final settlement. G accepted the offer after the date of its expiry. The court approved the settlement and costs were agreed. However each party contended that their costs incurred from the date that G accepted the Part 36 offer should be paid by the other party. H relied on the normal costs rule in CPR r.36.10(5) whereas G argued that because of the particular circumstances of his case, the court should depart from the normal costs rule. G submitted that it was unjust not to depart from the normal costs rule and that in declining to so find, the judge had given no weight, or insufficient weight, to the difficulties caused by the need to wait for him to go through puberty/adolescence. G argued that his situation was not the same as the situations in *Matthews v Metal Improvements Co Inc* [2007] EWCA Civ 215, [2007] C.P. Rep. 27, [2008] C.L.Y. 329 and that it could not be said that what happened was a change in circumstances or contingency inherent in litigation. G also claimed that H had made an offer when he had not yet reached an age where a firm enough prognosis for his condition could be given to enable his advisors to advise acceptance of the sum offered and that he had no choice but to wait and to incur costs in obtaining reports on his condition until the point was reached when a more reliable prediction could be made. H submitted that there were good policy reasons not to depart readily from the normal rule so as not to upset the clarity and balance of the Part 36 provisions.

Held: Appeal allowed. (1) Both parties were agreed that the approach of the court to an appeal such as the instant was encapsulated in *Summit Property Ltd v Pitmans (Costs)* [2001] EWCA Civ 2020, [2002] C.P.L.R. 97, [2003] C.L.Y. 374, *Summit* applied. G could not have reasonably accepted the offer when it was made and should not therefore have been at risk as to costs if he chose to wait. The judge came to the right conclusion in deciding that it would have been difficult for those advising G at the time of the Part 36 offer to have advised acceptance if there was a reasonable alternative strategy available, which there was. The judge adopted the principle in *Matthews* and found that the fact that any settlement would require the approval of the court was not of itself a relevant factor, *Matthews* considered. The nearest that he came thereafter to considering the question of approval was his acknowledgement that it would have been difficult to have prepared an advice for approval by the court and that G had acted reasonably throughout. More was required on the facts and the judge had erred in that approach (see paras 50-69 of judgment). (2) Other factors that were relevant were that the offer had been made before G had commenced proceedings at a time when the prognosis was uncertain, for a reason which was necessarily present when frontal lobe damage was caused to a child as was known to both parties throughout. The two stage process of the development of the consequences of G's particular injury, initial damage and damage developing as the brain evolved in puberty, and the resulting lack of safe prognosis did not fit easily under the ordinary contingency of litigation rubric.

In categorising the facts in that way the judge fell into error. It was material that the inherent uncertainty in prognosis would have resolved well before the limitation period expired by the passage of time so G would not need to commence proceedings before the position was clear. The offer was not rejected and H knew that further expert reports were being obtained as to G's development. The judge's conclusion did not give weight to the particular features of G's case. The consequence of omitting to give weight to matters that were in G's favour was that the normal rule dominated when it should not have done. It was unjust to make the normal costs order. The judge's order was set aside and an order substituted that G should have his costs throughout (paras 71-72).

SG (A CHILD) v HEWITT (COSTS), [2012] EWCA Civ 1053, [2013] 1 All E.R. 1118, Pill, L.J., CA (Civ Div).

322. Costs–Part 36 offers–Disclosure of existence of offer relating to instant proceedings and earlier related proceedings–Whether disclosure of terms of offer to court appropriate

[Civil Procedure Rules 1998 (SI 1998/3132) r.36.14.]

The court was required to determine issues relating to costs following patent infringement actions between the claimant airline (V) and the defendant airlines (J and X) and aircraft seat manufacturer (C). V had succeeded against C in relation to one of the patents, but the judgment did not provide it with an alternative route to damages; the alternative route was one of the purposes for which V had commenced the action. The route would have been "alternative" because V had obtained an enquiry as to damages in an earlier action against C. C had been given permission to appeal in the first action. That appeal would have been rendered moot had V recovered damages by the alternative route. V disclosed that it had made a Part 36 offer and that it related to both the first and the instant actions. The court considered (i) whether it should be shown V's offer; (ii) whether consideration of costs between V and C should be deferred until after C's appeal, on the basis that the overall winner of the disputes would then be clearer, which would affect the costs consequences under CPR r.36.14; (iii) X's costs from V; (iv) J's costs from V; (v) postponement of the application of the judgment interest rate to X's and J's costs.

Held: Judgment accordingly. (1) V had waived privilege in its offer by referring to one of the offer's terms. Parties could not pick and choose the terms of an otherwise privileged offer which they wished to bring to the court's attention. That made it difficult for a party to prevent the court from looking at an offer's terms where it wished to say that there was a relevant offer which also involved another set of proceedings, but it could not make that point without referring to the terms of the offer. However, that dilemma did not justify taking a different course. There was a very strong presumption that the court should be able to deal with all outstanding issues, including costs, at the end of a trial. The court should not decline to deal with costs at the end of the trial merely because of the possibility of a relevant offer. Unlike in a split trial, where it was inherently plausible that any offer would be inclusive of quantum and therefore relevant to costs, there was no such inherent plausibility where an offer concerned a separate action. A rigid rule that the court should not be told the terms of the offer would be open to abuse. One should be careful before obliging a party to waive privilege, but V could continue to rely on its privilege and deploy its offer at some later stage. If it wished to deploy its offer at the instant stage, in order to ask the court to deal with costs later, there was no injustice in requiring V to disclose its terms so the court could see whether the course suggested was justified (see paras 22-28). (2) The court considered whether there was a realistic prospect that a court would look at costs differently if they were being determined when V had succeeded in recovering damages exceeding the amount offered. In that case, V would have a realistic prospect of persuading the court that it had won and should have all its costs subject to deductions, unlike in the instant action, where the issue of who the winner was was less clear. The court might then consider that V had offered a solution to the litigation as a whole that was more advantageous to C than the ultimate result. The offer was not, therefore, unarguably irrelevant. Consideration of costs between V and C would be deferred (paras 35-36). (3) The figures suggested that X's costs were disproportionately high. Caution was needed in taking a percentage approach where one side's costs might be assessed down more severely than the other side's, *Research in Motion UK Ltd v Visto Corp* [2008] EWHC 819 (Pat), (2008) 31(5) I.P.D. 31033 applied. Instead, X would recover its costs subject to deduction of the sum it estimated to have incurred on an issue it had lost on. That ensured no recovery for that issue and left the remaining sums for scrutiny by the costs judge. V's conduct in not accepting X's offers to settle was not so unreasonable as to justify indemnity costs in X's favour. X was awarded an interim payment of 35 per cent of its costs (paras 39-46, 66-67). (4) J's costs seemed high given that it had not taken part in the action. An interim payment of 40 per cent of its costs was ordered. The fact that J's business was financed through loans with heavy interest rates did not qualify it for a higher than normal rate of interest on its costs; it was awarded interest at 1 per cent over the clearing bank base rate, *Tate & Lyle Industries Ltd v Greater London Council* [1982] 1 W.L.R. 149 applied (paras 68-72). (5) The judgment rate would apply to the interim payments from the judgment date. No postponement of application of the rate to the balance of J's costs was justified, but in respect of the balance of X's costs, application would be postponed for four months, *Standard Chartered Bank v Ceylon Petroleum Corp* [2011] EWHC 2094 (Comm), (2011) 108(33) L.S.G. 27 applied (paras 73-74).

VIRGIN ATLANTIC AIRWAYS LTD v JET AIRWAYS (INDIA) LTD; ZODIAC SEATS UK LTD v VIRGIN ATLANTIC AIRWAYS LTD; PREMIUM AIRCRAFT INTERIORS UK LTD v COMPTROLLER GENERAL OF PATENTS, [2012] EWHC 3318 (Pat), [2013] 1 W.L.R. 1005, Floyd, J., Ch D (Patents Ct).

323. Costs–Part 36 offers–Identifying successful party–Establishing whether offer amounting to valid Part 36 offer–Costs consequences

[Civil Procedure Rules 1998 (SI 1998/3132) Pt 36, r.36.2(2)(c), r.36.14(1), r.36.14(3), r.44.3.]

After delivering judgment in proceedings brought by the claimant (P) against the defendants (S), the court had to determine costs. In addition, S sought permission to appeal against the substantive decision. P had brought its claim in order to eliminate or reduce sums to which S claimed to be entitled from it. Though P was ordered to pay a certain sum to S, it was not the full amount claimed and was less than P had offered to pay in July 2011. P therefore claimed to be the successful party for the purposes of costs. However, S also claimed to be the successful parties, relying simply on the fact that P had been ordered to pay. The issues were (i) who was the successful party; (ii) whether it was appropriate to depart from the general principle that the successful party should be entitled to its costs; (iii) whether P's offer was a Pt 36 offer; (iv) if so, whether it would be unjust to order indemnity costs under CPR r.36.14(1); (v) whether there should be a payment on account; (vi) whether S should have permission to appeal.

Held: Judgment accordingly. (1) In the context of a money claim, S's approach had much to commend it. However, it risked being too simplistic in a claim for negative and declaratory relief in which the court was being asked to determine points of contractual construction. Although the claims were about money and one of the parties had been ordered to pay the other, that did not necessarily signify that the paying party had lost. The payee might have held out for a greater sum, and if his contractual interpretation proved incorrect it might not be realistic to depict him as the winner. A more nuanced approach was expressed in *Roache v News Group Newspapers Ltd* [1998] E.M.L.R. 161, [1992] C.L.Y. 3437, where it was said that the judge had to ask whether the claimant had won anything of value that he could not have won without fighting to the finish, or whether the defendant had substantially denied the claimant the prize which he had fought the action to win. In the instant case, P was, overall, the successful party, even though it had not succeeded on every point. The overall substance of the dispute, and what was truly in issue, was encapsulated in S's counterclaim, and S had lost on that. Moreover, it was not irrelevant that S, and not P, was seeking to appeal: S were demonstrably dissatisfied with the outcome, not having secured the prize they wanted, *Roache* and *AL Barnes Ltd v TimeTalk (UK) Ltd* [2003] EWCA Civ 402, [2003] B.L.R. 331, [2003] C.L.Y. 725 considered (see paras 7-14 of judgment). (2) Nevertheless, applying CPR r.44.3 and the principles in *Multiplex Constructions (UK) Ltd v Cleveland Bridge UK Ltd* [2008] EWHC 2280 (TCC), 122 Con. L.R. 88, [2009] C.L.Y. 378, P should only have 80 per cent of its costs up until its offer, *Multiplex* applied. S had had to advance a claim to meet an argument raised, but ultimately abandoned, by P, and they had succeeded on one of the three issues into which the dispute had been divided. Because that division had been done simply to facilitate orderly analysis, an issue-based approach to costs was not appropriate, but some allowance was necessary (paras 21-23, 25-26). (3) P's offer was a valid Pt 36 offer. Pt 36 was not confined to money claims, and the offer had been expressed to be Pt 36-compliant. S's objection was that it did not comply with r.36.2(2)(c) in that it failed to specify a period of not less than 21 days in which S would be liable for P's costs if the offer was accepted. Relying on *F&C Alternative Investments (Holdings) Ltd v Barthelemy (Costs)* [2012] EWCA Civ 843, [2013] 1 W.L.R. 548, it argued that Pt 36 was highly prescriptive and could not be applied by analogy. The relevant part of the offer read: "[P] will be liable for [S's] costs up to the date of notice of acceptance... if the offer is accepted within 21 days". *F&C* was distinguishable. There, the issue was whether a non-Pt 36 offer could have the same costs consequences as a Pt 36 offer. In the instant case, the issue was whether an offer could only comply with Pt 36 if it required the defendant to pay the claimant's costs, *F&C* distinguished. Pt 36 did not mandate that a claimant had to make the payment of costs a condition of his offer. Rather, it was to be read as requiring a claimant who sought his costs to specify a period of not less than 21 days within which the defendant was liable to pay them (paras 27-28, 44, 47, 50). (4) It would not be just to make an order for indemnity costs under r.36.14(3). S had argued that P's offer was, in substance, a defendant's offer, and a failure to beat such an offer did not occasion the costs consequences of r.36.14. It was not permissible to go behind the formal status of the parties, but the substance of the claim and which party was seeking to establish liability were relevant, and there was force in S's argument that P was in the position of a defendant. S was therefore to bear P's post-offer costs on the standard basis (paras 51, 54-62). (5) A £375,000 payment on account was appropriate (para.66). (6) S would have permission to appeal on the substantive issue (para.68).

PROCTER & GAMBLE CO v SVENSKA CELLULOSA AKTIEBOLAGET SCA, [2012] EWHC 2839 (Ch), [2013] 1 W.L.R. 1464, Hildyard, J, Ch D.

324. Costs–Part 36 offers–Offer close to sum awarded–Obligation to negotiate–"Near miss" rule

[Civil Procedure Rules 1998 (SI 1998/3132) r.44.2(2)(a), r.44.2(4)(c).]

The court had to consider the issue of costs arising out of a judgment awarding damages to the claimant landlord (H) in proceedings against the defendant tenant (S) for dilapidations on the termination of a lease. H had been awarded £900,000, which was limited to the value of the diminution of the reversion. Including the agreed cost of schedules, the total sum awarded was £1,058,768. S had made a Part 36 offer in the sum of £1 million. If interest was added to H's award up to the last date of acceptance of that offer, the sum awarded to H exceeded the Part 36 offer by only £3,637.

Held: Costs determined. (1) As H had only received a very small amount more than the sum offered, the court should not approach the CPR r.44.2(4)(c) on the basis that it could lead to an order that H should pay S's costs. To do so would be using the provisions of r.44.2(4)(c) to give a similar effect to a Part 36 offer and thereby introduce the same uncertainty into Part 36 offers which were near to but below the sum awarded, *Carver v BAA Plc* [2008] EWCA Civ 412, [2009] 1 W.L.R. 113, [2008] C.L.Y. 391 considered. While S should have offered a very small amount more and H should have reasonably accepted such an offer, the court should resist invitations to speculate whether offers to settle litigation which were not in fact made might or might not have been accepted, *Johnsey Estates (1990) Ltd v Secretary of State for the Environment, Transport and the Regions* [2001] EWCA Civ 535, [2001] L. & T.R. 32, [2002] C.L.Y. 374 followed. In reality, where a Part 36 offer was not sufficient to give rise to the automatic cost consequences of Part 36, an argument could always be made that if the parties had negotiated, the matter could have been resolved. However, most negotiations were conducted on a without-prejudice basis and were therefore not admissible in relation to costs. It was not desirable that the court should seek to attribute a particular consequence to a failure to negotiate when necessarily the court did not have the full information of any negotiations which did take place and both parties had sought costs protection under Part 36 by making offers. The principle expressed in *Multiplex Constructions (UK) Ltd v Cleveland Bridge UK Ltd* [2008] EWHC 2280 (TCC), 122 Con. L.R. 88, [2009] C.L.Y. 378, namely that a costs penalty might be appropriate where one party made a Part 36 offer which was nearly sufficient and the other party rejected that offer outright without any attempt to negotiate, no longer applied to Part 36 and should not be applied as a special "near miss" rule through r.44.2(4)(c), *Multiplex* not followed. It was doubtful that a "near miss" offer could generally add anything to what otherwise would be conduct in the form of an unreasonable refusal to negotiate. In any event, the instant case was not one in which the general principle in r.44.2(2)(a) should be departed from (see paras 26, 29-31, 34, 36-37 of judgment). (2) It was evident that S had not undertaken a proper pre-action process. Until proceedings were far advanced, it had not properly engaged in the detail of the schedule of dilapidations or in relation to the quantum of its case on diminution in value. Equally, at the time of S's Part 36 offer, the information it had provided to H made it difficult to assess S's case. The absence of information made it unrealistic to suggest that H was obliged to negotiate on receipt of the Part 36 offer. However, the fact that H recovered less than it claimed did not give rise to particular cost consequences. In relation to H's case on diminution, the sum awarded fell between the sums argued for by the parties. It could not be said that the conduct of either party in pursuing the case properly supported by its expert could be classed as unreasonable conduct. The fact that the court came to a figure closer to that put forward by S in relation to the schedule of dilapidations did not mean that H had exaggerated its claim. However, H had incurred additional costs by its approach to the carrying out of remedial works and had sought to rely on an intention to carry out the works to support its case when it did not have any clear intention to do so. Therefore, H did not intend to carry out the dilapidations for which it claimed, and that had to be reflected in costs (paras 48-49, 51-52, 54). (3) S's failure to undertake a proper pre-action process did not have a costs impact; if anything, it neutralised a number of points made by S in relation to the claims for dilapidations and diminution in value. In all the circumstances, it was appropriate to reduce the order for costs in favour of H accordingly. S would pay 80 per cent of H's costs (paras 65-66).

HAMMERSMATCH PROPERTIES (WELWYN) LTD v SAINT-GOBAIN CERAMICS & PLASTICS LTD, [2013] EWHC 2227 (TCC), [2013] B.L.R. 554, Ramsey, J., QBD (TCC).

325. Costs–Patents County Court–Determining successful defendant's costs–Stage to apply issue-based discount

[Civil Procedure Rules 1998 (SI 1998/3132) Pt 45, r.45.42(2); Directive 2004/48 on the enforcement of intellectual property rights Art.15; CPR PD 45 (Fixed Costs) 2000.]

The applicant company (P) applied for an order for dissemination of the judgment and its costs in infringement proceedings brought by the respondent company (B). The court had found that P's security net product did not infringe B's patent. Prior to that finding, B had been claiming for an order for dissemination of the judgment. During proceedings B and P had each incurred costs of just under

£200,000 and although P, the overall winner, had lost on four of its issues, those costs were subject to the scale limits of the Patents County Court (PCC) under CPR Pt 45. P submitted that (1) although Directive 2004/48 art.15 did not refer to an order for dissemination when the rights holder had lost the case, the court had jurisdiction to make such an order and, given the importance of the perception of P as a going concern in the market, it was right to do so; (2) the right approach to costs was to take the actual costs, apply the issue-based discount, summarily assess the costs and then apply the PCC scale limits. B contended that the omission from art.15 regarding an order for dissemination was deliberate due to the availability of other remedies to an accused infringer, including a declaration of non-infringement.

Held: Application for order for dissemination of judgment granted; Costs determined. (1) The particular market and circumstances of the case made an order for dissemination fair and appropriate. That would have applied whether P or B had won the case. If B had won, it would have asked for the same order but with the alternate outcome. It was not accepted that the availability of declaratory relief and the fact that a party could publicise a judgment itself justified applying a different standard to the making of orders for dissemination under the Directive depending on whether the rights holder had lost rather than won. In every case of exercising its discretion, the court had to consider those factors. However, a claimant who had included a claim for an order for dissemination could hardly complain if the court decided to make the converse order in favour of the defendant. It was fair and proportionate to make the order for dissemination sought by P (see paras 4, 10-13 of judgment). (2) Once the winner had been identified, the approach to costs involved deciding whether there were issues on which the winner should be deprived of its costs and whether there were issues which were suitably exceptional that the winner should actually pay the loser's costs of those issues, *MMI Research Ltd v Cellxion Ltd (Costs)* [2012] EWCA Civ 139, [2013] 3 Costs L.O. 387 applied. It was fair to find that 25 per cent of the costs were spent on issues that P had lost on. The court was not satisfied that all of those issues satisfied the higher standard that warranted P paying B's costs; only one issue had done which was worth about ten per cent of B's costs. Had the proceedings been in the High Court, a deduction of 35 per cent from P's costs would have been appropriate. The question was how to apply that discount in the PCC using the scale in CPR PD 45. The right approach was to start with the actual costs for a given stage of proceedings and summarily assess those costs on the normal basis. The result was the figure to apply the issue-based discount to. Once that discount was applied, the resulting figure could be compared to the scale and the lower figure of the two taken. Although CPR r.45.42(2) did not mention the scale costs it was sensible that the set off for the costs owed to B applied before the scale limits and cap on trial costs. That approach would not reduce the effect of costs as a disincentive to take bad points because a function of the PCC case management conference was to identify bad points, and, in most cases, the impact of the scale was not such that issue-based discounts would be completely drowned out. Accordingly, B was ordered to pay P £36,675.00 (paras 15, 18-20, 23-27).

BOS GmbH & CO KG v COBRA UK AUTOMOTIVE PRODUCTS DIVISION LTD (IN ADMINISTRATION) (COSTS), [2012] EWPCC 44, [2012] 6 Costs L.R. 1083, Judge Birss Q.C., PCC.

326. Costs–Permission to appeal–Respondent's costs of permission application–Respondent not normally entitled to costs–Whether case out of norm

[CPR PD 52C Appeals to the Court of Appeal 2010.]

The applicant (L) applied for its costs of resisting an application for permission to appeal which had been withdrawn by the respondent company (T). T had brought proceedings against L as a former employee for an injunction to restrain him from disclosing confidential information. An injunction had been granted without notice but at the hearing the judge discharged it and awarded indemnity costs against T. Two days after the judgment T applied for permission to appeal. It obtained a stay of execution to restrain publication of confidential information since otherwise, it was said, the appeal would be rendered nugatory. A single Lord Justice considering the application for permission adjourned the matter to a two-judge court and made an interim order on the basis that the stay would lapse if T did not pay £300,000 which the trial judge had ordered to be paid on account of L's costs. The Civil Appeals Office then wrote to L's solicitors informing them that the application for permission and an injunction would be heard in the Court of Appeal. T withdrew its application two days before it was due to be heard, by which time L had served a skeleton argument for the hearing.

Held: Application granted. CPR PD 52C para.20(1) provided that in most cases an application for permission to appeal would be determined without the need for the respondent to file submissions or attend a hearing. In such circumstances an order for costs would not normally be made in favour of a respondent who voluntarily made submissions or attended a hearing. However, by para.20(2) if the court directed the respondent to file submissions or attend a hearing, it would normally award costs to the respondent if permission was refused. When the application in the instant case remained a paper application it was a normal application under the rules. However, once the single Lord Justice adjourned it to a two-judge court and L received the letter from the Civil Appeals Office he was entitled to appear and be heard. The matter therefore fell within para.20(2). Furthermore, an application for permission did not normally act as a stay and therefore the application for a stay in an injunction case was also not normal. From that date L was entitled to its costs, with the exception of those relating to a prospective application for security, on the indemnity basis.

OJSC TNK-BP HOLDING v LAZURENKO, [2013] EWCA Civ 137, [2013] 4 Costs L.O. 552, Lewison, L.J., CA (Civ Div).

327. Costs–Persons lacking capacity–Proceedings regarding person's property–Charging costs to person's estate under general rule

[Court of Protection Rules 2007 (SI 2007/1744) r.156.]

The Court of Protection was required to determine costs following its decision that a property owned by a person lacking capacity (C) should not be sold or charged. C's deputy and two of her children (X) had considered that the property should be sold; her son (S), who was her carer and the beneficiary of her will, had vigorously opposed the sale. X and the deputy argued that their costs should be charged to C's estate in accordance with the general rule in the Court of Protection Rules 2007 r.156. S argued that the court should postpone a decision, saying that he, as beneficiary and executor of C's living will, instructed the court as a trustee that the property could not be charged with the costs.

Held: Costs determined. There was no basis for departure from the general rule. The overall conclusions as to C's capacity did not favour any party. Although a sale of the property had not been ordered, S's conduct of the proceedings, namely his use of his mother's case as a vehicle for his political views, his aggressive disrespect towards anyone with whom he disagreed, and his complete lack of regard for his mother and family's right to privacy, more than wiped out any weight that might be attached to that factor. X's and the deputy's conduct had been entirely reasonable and their costs would be charged to the estate. The court had ordered that the property could not be sold or charged "without an order of this court"; the instant orders regarding costs constituted an order within the meaning of that provision.

CLARKE, *Re* (COSTS), [2012] EWHC 2947 (COP), [2013] W.T.L.R. 59, Peter Jackson, J., CP.

328. Costs–Security for costs–Third parties–Impecunious husband pursuing appeal–Appropriateness of ordering wife to provide security for costs

[Civil Procedure Rules 1998 (SI 1998/3132) r.25.14(2)(b), r.25.14.]

The applicant university (K) applied for an order that the second respondent third party (S) give security for costs in a pending appeal brought by the first respondent

(C). C, who was S's husband, had sought damages and declaratory relief arising from K's failure to award him a degree. His claim was dismissed and he was granted permission to appeal against that decision. There was reason to believe that he was impecunious. His legal aid had been stopped after S was awarded a substantial lump sum as damages for a personal injury sustained at work. She also received a monthly disability pension. It was common ground that S had contributed substantially to C's legal costs since his legal aid was withdrawn. K argued that the court had jurisdiction to make an order for security for costs against a third party and that the requirements for making such an order under CPR r.25.14(2)(b) were met because the natural inference to be drawn from the fact that S had contributed to C's legal costs was that they had an agreement to share any proceeds of his claim. K submitted that that inference was supported and demonstrated by several references made by C and S in witness statements and documents to the effect that their matrimonial resources were treated by them as family assets available in common.

Held: Application refused. The court was prepared to assume that it had the power to make the order sought under CPR r.25.14 without formally deciding that point. The statutory precondition for the making of an order for security for costs against a third party under r.25.14(2)(b) was that the third party had to have contributed, or agreed to contribute, to a litigant's costs in return for a share of any money or property recovered in the proceedings. The court could not even remotely agree with K's assertion that the natural inference to be drawn from S's contributions was that a promise had been made to share in the proceeds of the claim. The natural inference was precisely the opposite: the contributions had been made by S because she was devoted to C and wished to support him in a matter that was important to him out of natural love and affection. S would have supported C even if there was no element of damages to his claim and only a declaration. The statutory condition made it clear that there had to be something quite different from natural love and affection. There was nothing like that here. References to spouses treating their assets as family assets came nowhere near to establishing an expectation of payment. The remedy applied for by K was misconceived (see paras 3, 7-10 of judgment).

CHILAB v KING'S COLLEGE LONDON, [2012] EWCA Civ 1178, [2013] 2 Costs L.R. 191, Hughes, L.J., CA (Civ Div).

329. Costs–Settlement–Settlement of claim for judicial review–No order for costs

[National Assistance Act 1948 (c.29) s.21; Civil Procedure Rules 1998 (SI 1998/3132) r.44.3.]

The appellants (N) appealed against a judge's refusal to award costs in their favour following the settlement of their claim for judicial review of the respondent local authority's refusal to provide them with accommodation and support under the National Assistance Act 1948 s.21. N were a married couple from Pakistan whose applications for asylum in the United Kingdom were refused. They had health problems and applied to the local authority to assess their needs in order to provide them with accommodation and support. The local authority did so and rejected their claims. N commenced judicial review proceedings against that decision and the local authority resisted the claim. N were granted interim relief by a judge so that the local authority would provide them with accommodation and support until the trial. The costs of that application were reserved. In February 2012, the Secretary of State for the Home Department granted N exceptional leave to remain. Accordingly N decided not to pursue their claim against the local authority. The judge, applying *R. (on the application of Bahta) v Secretary of State for the Home Department* [2011] EWCA Civ 895, [2011] C.P. Rep. 43, [2012] C.L.Y. 1733 and *Harripaul v Lewisham LBC* [2012] EWCA Civ 266, [2012] H.L.R. 24, [2012] C.L.Y. 344, ordered that there be no order for costs. N submitted that the judge failed (1) to give adequate reasons for his decision; and (2) to take into account relevant factors such as the conduct of the parties, the interim relief obtained and the strength of N's case and if he had done so he would have been bound to award costs to N.

Held: Appeal dismissed. (1) Six days after the judge's decision judgment was given in *M v Croydon LBC* [2012] EWCA Civ 595, [2012] 1 W.L.R. 2607, [2012] C.L.Y. 343 which became the governing authority on the question of costs following a settlement, *M* followed, *Bahta* and *Harripaul* considered. The judge reviewed the leading authorities at the time and concluded that it was not sufficiently clear who would have won if the matter had gone to trial. N's criticism that the judge had not given proper reasons was rejected (see paras 31-33, 37 of judgment). (2) N had achieved their ultimate objective because of the secretary of state's decision to grant exceptional leave to remain. The favourable intervention by a third party not involved in the litigation could not be a reason for ordering the local authority to pay N's costs. There was no basis on which the judge could have ordered the costs of the interim relief application to be paid by the local authority. N's success in applying for interim relief did not mean that they were successful in the action and was not a reason for awarding them the costs of the action. Nor was the fact that they had complied with the pre-action protocol. The local authority had been consistent in their position and their conduct had not been such as to attract an adverse costs order. It was not the function of the Court of Appeal on a costs appeal to give a substantive decision about litigation which never came to trial. On reading the material available to the judge, it was not surprising that he was uncertain who would have won if the action had gone to trial. His conclusion was not wrong or perverse and he made no error of law or principle in the exercise of his discretion under CPR r.44.3. The judge's costs order could not be faulted (paras 39-52).

R. (ON THE APPLICATION OF NAUREEN) v SALFORD CITY COUNCIL, [2012] EWCA Civ 1795, [2013] 2 Costs L.R. 257, Moore-Bick, L.J., CA (Civ Div).

330. Costs–Settlement–Test for assessing costs in favour of claimant following consent order

The appellant (E) appealed against a decision that there should be no order as to costs following a consent order in her favour. E had brought a claim against the respondent secretary of state seeking an order that she be provided with suitable accommodation in a self-contained ground floor flat, given her state of health and advanced pregnancy. That accommodation was eventually provided and a consent order was made. On the issue of costs, the judge found that the principal question was whether E would have obtained an order for the accommodation had the proceedings been fought to trial.

Held: Appeal allowed. The judge had applied the wrong test. He had used the test from *R. (on the application of Boxall) v Waltham Forest LBC* (2001) 4 C.C.L. Rep. 258, [2003] C.L.Y. 348 which was no longer applicable as it had been superseded by *M v Croydon LBC* [2012] EWCA Civ 595, [2012] 1 W.L.R. 2607, [2012] C.L.Y. 343, *Boxall* superseded, *Croydon* followed. The correct starting point for an award of costs in favour of a claimant when a claim had settled was whether E had achieved what she sought in her claim. If the judge had used the correct test he would not have made the order he did. E's letters before the issue of proceedings made clear what accommodation she was seeking and no acceptable offer was made until after the issue of proceedings. The proceedings would have been avoided if E had been given an assurance of self-contained ground floor accommodation being made available in the near future. Considering the matter afresh, the only just order was that the secretary of state pay E's costs, *Croydon* followed (see paras 3-7, 9 of judgment).

EMEZIE v SECRETARY OF STATE FOR THE HOME DEPARTMENT, [2013] EWCA Civ 733, [2013] 5 Costs L.R. 685, Elias, L.J., CA (Civ Div).

331. Costs–Solicitors–London solicitors instructed in personal injury claim–Reasonableness of instructing London firm

The appellant NHS trust appealed against a master's decision concerning the hourly rate which the solicitors for the respondent (R) were entitled to recover, and R cross-appealed. R worked as a radiographer but developed repetitive strain injury and was medically retired. She was a member of the Society of Radiographers. The society referred its personal injury work to London solicitors (H) on a fee paying basis, rather than instructing lawyers under a conditional fee agreement, on the basis that handling such claims required knowledge and experience of the working pattern of radiographers. However, the society advised R to consult the local branch of a well-known firm (T). T investigated R's claim against the trust as her employer. T concluded that R's case had no reasonable prospects of success and declined to take it further. The society agreed to fund a second opinion provided that R consulted H in London. She did so and H notified the trust that the claim would be pursued. H valued the claim at £140,000. However, it became apparent that R was medically unfit to litigate the case and it was settled for £8,000. The trust objected to R's bill of costs of £79,203 on the basis that it was disproportionate and there had been no need to instruct London solicitors. The master held that the costs were not disproportionate. He accepted that the case was a six-figure claim and merited a grade A fee earner, but not one in central London; to the extent that the case was out of the ordinary that could be addressed by increasing the hourly rate. He accordingly took a local rate of £215 and increased it by 30 per cent to £280.

Held: Judgment accordingly. (1) The question for the costs judge was whether it was reasonable for R to instruct London solicitors, taking into account the relevant factors, *Wraith v Sheffield Forgemasters Ltd* [1998] 1 W.L.R. 132, [1997] C.L.Y. 540 followed. The approach the appeal court should apply in deciding whether the costs judge was correct was whether the judge had taken into account all relevant considerations, not taken into account irrelevant considerations, and not reached an unreasonable decision on the facts, *Griffiths v Solutia UK Ltd* [2001] EWCA Civ 736, [2001] C.P. Rep. 92, [2001] C.L.Y. 523 followed. The master had erred in attributing T's decision to decline to take R's case further to unwillingness to act without a success fee under a conditional fee agreement. That was not a relevant consideration which the master could take into account, because the assessment of whether it was reasonable to instruct a London firm was to be made in the light of the circumstances at the time the decision was made, and at that time R and the society had only T's letter making clear that it believed the claim would not succeed on the merits. In all the circumstances it had been reasonable for R to instruct H (see paras 19-27 of judgment). (2) Since the cross-appeal succeeded, and since there had been no objection to H's rates if the decision to use them was reasonable, those were the rates which should apply. The outcome was no carte blanche for the instruction of central London solicitors in similar cases (para.30).

ROYAL DEVON AND EXETER NHS FOUNDATION TRUST v ACRES, [2013] EWHC 652 (QB), [2013] 3 Costs L.R. 406, Cranston, J., QBD.

332. Costs–Solicitors' remuneration–Payment of legal costs direct to client–Paying party on notice of solicitor's claim to fees

The appellant firm of solicitors (K) appealed against a decision that the second respondent secretary of state, having paid costs to the first respondent (C), bore no further liability for costs. C had instructed K in his judicial review claim against the secretary of state and had paid £1,500 on account of K's fees. The secretary of state settled C's claim and agreed to pay his costs. K submitted a bill for just under £9,500 and the secretary of state offered £6,000 in settlement of it. C then withdrew his instructions to K and accepted the secretary of state's offer asking for the money to be paid directly to him. K wrote to the Treasury Solicitor asking them not to part with any costs as they had a right to them. The Treasury Solicitor's draftsmen then made an improved offer of £7,125. They withdrew it when they realised that C had accepted £6,000. K brought judicial review proceedings to avoid C's £6,000 compromise, which were struck out. The Treasury Solicitor paid £6,000 to C who disappeared with it. K sought a declaration that the £6,000 compromise was not valid and either a charge or a lien on C's costs. The secretary of state successfully argued before the costs judge and an appeal to the High Court that, in the absence of collusion with C, she had no further liability for costs. K submitted that the Treasury Solicitor's knowledge of its unsatisfied interest in the recoverable costs was sufficient to impress the fund with a trust in its favour or otherwise to render payment to C ineffective to discharge the secretary of state's liability for costs.

Held: Appeal allowed in part. In principle it was unacceptable that a client could compromise his own solicitor's legitimate interests for any sum he chose, leaving the solicitor to sue him for money which he had since taken and spent. A paying party who was on notice that the receiving party's solicitor had a claim for fees upon part or all of the sum due paid the receiving party directly at his own risk. Collusion was not necessary. Collusion and notice were parallel routes to equitable interference with the disposal of damages and costs, *Ross v Buxton* (1889) 42 Ch. D. 190 approved, *Brunsdon v Allard* 121 E.R. 8 doubted. The court would intervene to protect a solicitor's claim on funds recovered or due to be recovered by a client or former client if the paying party was colluding with the client to cheat the solicitor of his fees; or the paying party was on notice that the other party's solicitor had a claim on the funds for outstanding fees. K should have applied in C's compromised proceedings against the secretary of state for the Treasury Solicitor to pay the costs into court to await allocation by the court. That would have relieved the secretary of state from making an invidious choice between solicitor and ex-client and have protected both K and C's interests in the costs fund. The compromise agreed by C for £6,000 was binding. The secretary of state was on clear notice not to pay C money which was K's. The payment could not stand as a good discharge of K's claim. The secretary of state should pay £4,500 to K (see paras 21-22, 27-28, 33-of judgment).

KHANS SOLICITORS v CHIFUNTWE, [2013] EWCA Civ 481, [2013] 4 All E.R. 367, Rix, L.J., CA (Civ Div).

333. Costs–Split trials–Costs of preliminary issues–Materiality of possible settlement offers–Consideration of Part 36 rules

[Civil Procedure Rules 1998 (SI 1998/3132) r.36.13, r.36.13(2), r.44.3(4).]

The court was required to consider costs issues following its decision on preliminary issues. The claimants (T) claimed against the defendant insurers (D) in respect of losses caused by employee theft. D raised various coverage and other issues which were decided as preliminary issues substantially in favour of T. T sought their costs of the preliminary issues to be assessed if not agreed and an order for an interim payment. It was not disputed that T were to be regarded as the successful parties in relation to the preliminary issues. D contended that the court should not make any order for costs until after determination of the further issues which were still outstanding, including certain further issues in relation to liability and also quantum, when the court would be able to decide who had succeeded or failed overall in the action, and to what extent, and also by comparison with any Part 36 or other relevant offers of settlement which the court could then consider; in any event, the court should order T to pay on an indemnity basis the costs wasted and thrown away by their failure until just before trial to admit that the risk was co-insured.

Held: Judgment accordingly. (1) There was no general rule that in the case of a split trial the court should ordinarily reserve the question of costs until the end of the case, *Weill v Mean Fiddler Holdings Ltd* [2003] EWCA Civ 1058 considered. In the instant case the fact that there had been a split trial should not make any difference. The preliminary issues were entirely discrete and it was always open to D, if they so wished, to concede those particular points. On the contrary, the preliminary issues had had to be determined in the course of a protracted trial. T had incurred substantial costs which they were in principle entitled to recover, subject to the question of possible settlement offers, even if they ultimately failed on other issues of liability or made no more than a nil recovery (see paras 5-7 of judgment). CPR r.36.13(2) prohibited the fact that a Part 36 offer had been made being communicated to the court "until the case has been decided". It did not appear to prohibit the fact that a Part 36 offer had not been made being communicated to the court. In the instant case the court had been told and should proceed on the basis that no Part 36 offer had been made specifically in relation to the preliminary issues. It remained ignorant as to whether any more general Part 36 offer had been made. It was unnecessary to decide whether "until the case has been decided" could refer to the conclusion of the first part of a split trial. There was an urgent need for r.36.13 to be reviewed and possibly reformulated in order to deal in particular with the question of split trials. The court would proceed on the assumption in favour of T that the prohibition applied in the instant case. However, although the court could not be informed that a Part 36 offer had been made, it could proceed on the basis that such an offer might have been made and might affect the court's discretion in relation to costs in respect of the preliminary issues. Such matters, although speculative, were relevant circumstances to which the court was bound to have regard under r.44.3(4), *Kew v Bettamix Ltd (formerly Tarmac Roadstone Southern Ltd)* [2006] EWCA Civ 1535, [2007] 4 Costs L.R. 527, [2007] C.L.Y. 475 considered. Justice demanded that in the particular circumstances the court should not make any immediate order for costs nor any order for an interim payment in favour of T. Notwithstanding the general desirability of dealing with costs of the preliminary issues at their conclusion, it would be unjust to make an order for costs in favour of T in ignorance of any offer that might have been made in circumstances where, if a Part 36 offer had in fact been made and the court were aware of such offer, it would make a different order. The costs of the preliminary issues were reserved but were to be paid by D to T, subject to any offers of settlement that might have been made (paras 11-28, 30). (2) T's case that the risk was not co-insured was hopeless. D were entitled to the costs in respect of the co-insurance issues on an indemnity basis, subject to any offer that might have been made (para.29-30).

TED BAKER PLC v AXA INSURANCE UK PLC, [2012] EWHC 1779 (Comm), [2012] 6 Costs L.R. 1023, Eder, J., QBD (Comm).

334. Costs–Split trials–Costs sought at conclusion of trial on liability–Meaning of "until the case has been decided" in r.36.13(2) CPR

[Civil Procedure Rules 1998 (SI 1998/3132) r.36.13(2).]

The claimant (B) sought an order for costs against the defendant (X) following a finding that the road accident in which he had been injured had been caused by X's negligence. There had been a split trial, with liability determined first. Damages were still to be decided. The issue was the meaning of the words "until the case has been decided" in the CPR r.36.13(2), which provided that the fact that a Part 36 offer had been made had not to be communicated to the trial judge until the case had been decided.

Held: Application refused. The words "until the case has been decided" had a clear meaning. It was clear that "the case" was used in the sense of "the action" or "the proceedings". The reference to "the case" could not be construed as referring to part of a case. If r.36.13(2) had been intended to refer to liability being decided as well as the case being decided, different wording would have been used. By reason of the rule, the court could not be told the position as to Part 36 offers, and because of that it could not deal with costs, *HSS Hire Services Group Plc v BMB Builders Merchants Ltd (Costs)* [2005] EWCA Civ 626, [2005] 1 W.L.R. 3158, [2005] C.L.Y. 816, *AB v CD* [2011] EWHC 602 (Ch) and *Ted Baker Plc v AXA Insurance UK Plc* [2012] EWHC 1779 (Comm), [2012] 6 Costs L.R. 1023 considered (see paras 12, 14 of judgment).

BEASLEY v ALEXANDER, [2012] EWHC 2715 (QB), [2013] 1 W.L.R. 762, Sir Raymond Jack, QBD.

335. Costs assessments–Conditional fee agreements–Apportionment of solicitors' costs between CFA clients and non-CFA clients–Base costs–Uplift on costs

[Courts and Legal Services Act 1990 (c.41) s.58A(6).]

The appellant villagers (V) appealed against an order made by the deputy adjudicator to HM Land Registry which assessed the costs payable by the respondent couple (B) to V. B cross-appealed against the decision to allow a success fee of 60 per cent on V's base costs as assessed. V and B had been involved in a dispute which related to the lordship of a manor, and whether it still existed. B were registered at the land registry as proprietors of the lordship. Disputes had arisen with the owners of various properties in the village when B purported to exercise rights deriving from the lordship to require V to cease obstructing pieces of land that B claimed were owned by them. Six villagers applied to the land registry to close the lordship and the fell title that went along with it. The deputy adjudicator closed the lordship but declined to order closure of the fell title on the basis that B had acquired that title in good faith. Under the costs order B were ordered to pay V's costs in full and 80 per cent of the other costs of the reference. V had jointly instructed solicitors who proposed a CFA. Only three of the six villagers were party to the CFA. The order for costs was in respect of the costs of all six villagers. V appealed on the basis that the adjudicator was wrong to apportion their solicitors' total costs for a specified period between those of them who were contractually liable to the solicitors, who acted for them all, and those who were not; the effect of that decision being to cut in half the recoverable amount for base costs.

Held: Appeal allowed in part, Cross-appeal dismissed. (1) All of the issues were common to all six of the villagers, or were issues that affected one or all of the three CFA villagers. None of the issues depended on the individual titles of any of the villagers and none of the non-CFA villagers advanced any arguments that were not relied on by the CFA villagers. It was irrelevant to the conduct and success of the action whether there was one or more named claimants. The adjudicator was wrong to make any apportionment of the villagers' costs. In so far as he thought he was required to do so in order to determine the amount for which the CFA clients were liable to the solicitor, that was wrong because he had already made findings that they were liable for the whole amount, from which it followed that there was no breach of the indemnity principle, *Baylis v Kelly* [1997] 2 Costs L.R. 54, [1997] C.L.Y. 579 considered. Insofar as he thought he was required to do so to give effect to the principle in *Ellingsen v Det Skandinaviske Compani* [1919] 2 K.B. 567, that was wrong for the same reasons, *Ellingsen* considered. The costs order was set aside insofar as it allowed only an apportioned part of the costs incurred (see paras 44-48 of judgment). (2) B's argument that nothing should be allowed in relation to the success fee because the costs order did not expressly order payment of additional liabilities was based on a false premise. It assumed that, but for Courts and Legal Services Act 1990 s.58A(6)), a success fee could not be recovered between parties and the receiving party would always have been limited to recovering the base costs assessed by the court to have been the reasonable charge by a solicitor to a client who had not entered into a CFA and so was liable to pay such costs irrespective of the outcome of the litigation. But the reason why success fees could not be recovered prior to 1990 was not because an agreement to pay anything over the normal base rate was by definition unreasonable but because the CFA could not be enforced at all, being deemed to be contrary to public policy. Once the CFA was made enforceable, that difficulty fell away. The adjudicator's decision was correct and the success fees were recoverable in so far as they were reasonable and proportionate (paras 52-62). (3) The adjudicator was right to recognise that the way in which success was defined in the CFA had to be taken into account. He was correct to evaluate the risks that the solicitor was running, taking no account of the one that he was not running. He was then required to make a broad overall assessment of the total risk borne by the solicitor and had done so. It was relevant that by the time the CFA came to be signed huge amounts of time had been spent by people with a direct interest on both sides in researching the historical and legal position. That was bound to affect the likelihood that new documents or arguments would come up. The assessment of an uplift of 60 per cent was within the reasonable range.

WALKER v BURTON; BURTON v WALKER, [2013] EWHC 811 (Ch), [2013] 3 Costs L.R. 469, Judge David Cooke, Ch D.

336. Costs between the parties–Costs orders–Financial circumstances of claimant–Ability to pay costs order–Costs order where no warning

The appellant employee (V) appealed against a decision of an employment tribunal that she should pay one-third of her opponents' costs following a claim brought against the respondent local authority and companies. V had brought claims of discrimination and harassment on grounds of race and/or disability and of detriments suffered as a whistleblower against the local authority, the previous employer from whom she had transferred and a number of colleagues. All of V's claims were dismissed by the tribunal and the respondents applied for costs which were assessed at one-third of their costs. All the respondents had common representation and claimed to have incurred costs amounting to £260,000 so that V's share after assessment would amount to around £60,000. The respondents had made a number of offers to settle. V submitted that: (1) no deposit order had been sought; (2) there had been no costs warning; (3) the order made was punitive rather than compensatory; (4) no account had been taken of the respondents' settlement offers; (5) the tribunal had been wrong to take the view that there was a realistic prospect that she might in future be able to meet the costs order.

Held: Appeal dismissed. (1) The respondents' failure to seek a deposit order, or otherwise to issue any costs warning asserting that the claims were hopeless, was not cogent evidence that those claims had in fact a reasonable chance of success (see paras 12-14 of judgment). (2) It was not the case that as a matter of law an award for costs could only be made where the party in question had been put on notice, by the making of a deposit order or otherwise, that she was at risk as to costs. The fact that V had not been put on notice was not a sufficient reason for withholding an order for costs which was otherwise justified (paras 18-19). (3) There was nothing to demonstrate that the tribunal was adopting a punitive approach (para.23). (4) The costs of defending a long claim against a persistent claimant could be such that it made more sense to pay a substantial sum by way of settlement than to pay the lawyers. The fact that an offer, even a substantial one, had been made to settle a claim did not necessarily render it unjust for the respondents to subsequently contend that the claim was misconceived (paras 14, 21). (5) The tribunal was not obliged as a matter of law to have regard to V's ability to pay but it had chosen to do so. If there was a realistic prospect that V might at some point in the future be able to afford to pay a substantial amount it was legitimate to make a costs order in that amount so that the respondents would be able to make some recovery if and when that occurred. There was no reason why the question of affordability had to be decided once and for all by reference to the party's means as at the moment the order fell to be made, *Arrowsmith v Nottingham Trent University* [2011] EWCA Civ 797, [2012] I.C.R. 159, [2012] C.L.Y. 1088 applied (paras 26-30).

VAUGHAN v LEWISHAM LBC [2013] I.R.L.R. 713, Underhill, J., EAT.

337. Costs between the parties–Costs orders–Rationale for no order for costs

The appellant Russian shipping company (J) appealed against a decision ([2011] EWHC 664 (Comm)) to grant no order for costs against the defendants (N) following the trial of its action against the dishonest conduct of former company officers which had been heard together with three other claims ([2010] EWHC 3199 (Comm)). J succeeded on two out of four of its claims against N but on an alternative basis of fraudulent diversion of commissions. The judge made no order for costs, acknowledging that was a major departure from the general rule but maintaining that it was justified because J had failed in its primary case, had been guilty of dishonest conduct before, and during the trial, and had already recovered part of its costs from its brokers, who had settled. J submitted that the judge had erred by confusing its claim with another (the Fiona) claim heard concurrently and that had led him to deprive a substantially successful claimant of the costs of its claims.

Held: Appeal dismissed. The judge had not erred in principle in making the order. He had correctly referred to CPR r.44.3(4) r.44.3(5) and directed himself appropriately (see paras 44-45 of judgment). The judgment dealt with the costs of all four claims and, though he had given examples of dishonest witness statements from the Fiona case, he had also summarised his damning indictment of the honesty of J's litigation manager and J's failures over disclosure. He had also clearly considered the dishonesty of N and the recovery of part of J's costs from its brokers (paras 48-52).

FIONA TRUST & HOLDING CORP v PRIVALOV; INTRIGUE SHIPPING INC v NIKITIN; NIKITIN v H CLARKSON & CO LTD; INTRIGUE SHIPPING INC v H CLARKSON & CO LTD; FIONA TRUST & HOLDING CORP v SKARGA, [2013] EWCA Civ 749, [2013] 5 Costs L.R. 689, Longmore, L.J., CA (Civ Div).

338. Costs between the parties–Part 36 offers–Consideration of Part 36 offers, including whether Part 36 offer required to contain details of offeror's costs

[Civil Procedure Rules 1998 (SI 1998/3132) r.36.2, r.36.8, r.36.10, r.36.14, r.36.14(1A).]

The court had to resolve a number of issues following the main judgment ([2013] EWHC 1500 (QB), [2013] B.T.C. 509, [2013] 11 C.L. 204) where the claimant (M) had been unsuccessful in its negligence claim against the first defendant (B1) and successful against the second defendant (B2). On September 21, 2012 M made a Part 36 offer of £1,024,000 to B2. The offer was not accepted and it expired. The trial ended in March 2013 but judgment was not handed down until June 5, 2013. M withdrew the offer on May 7. At trial, M was awarded £1,090,736 excluding interest. Under the judgment, M was also required to pay B2's costs of a Spanish tax claim by way of a set-off against any costs payable to M by B2. The issues included (i) what order should be made in relation to B1's costs; (ii) whether M was entitled to benefit from the provisions of CPR r.36.14(3); (iii) whether there should be a deduction from the costs awarded to M; (iv) what interim costs order payment should be made.

Held: Judgment accordingly. (1) The inclusion of B1 in the proceedings had led to some additional costs being incurred. Although those were not large sums, they could not be ignored. B1 was entitled to a costs order against M, but would have to decide if it was worthwhile having those costs assessed. M might want to consider making an offer (see paras 3-10 of judgment). (2) M had beaten the Part 36 offer. Under r.36.14(1A) the judgment was "better in money terms" than the offer made. It was not necessary to take account of sums payable by M to B1 or to B2 for the Spanish claim (paras 14-19). Under r.36.14, after the end of trial but before judgment had been handed down, there had been no need for M to withdraw the offer because it was no longer capable of acceptance without his consent, which would not have been forthcoming. The withdrawal therefore could not deprive M of the beneficial consequences of having made the offer in the first place (paras 20-23). The fact that M had not given details of his costs did not mean that he was not entitled to the normal consequences of r.36.10. The terms required for a valid Part 36 offer were set out in r.36.2, but it contained no requirement for details of the costs of the party making the offer having to be included in the offer or supplied. Further, the reference in r.36.14(4)(c) to the "information available to the parties" related to the information about the merits of the claim, not information as to what costs the maker of the offer had incurred at the date of the offer. In any event, a party accepting a Part 36 offer was protected against any liability for excessive costs incurred previously by r.36.10(2) and r.36.10(3). The absence of some information relating to the offeror's costs would not therefore mean that it would be "unjust" to make a Part 36 offer for the purposes of r.36.14(4). It was also important that the alleged deficiencies in the offer had not been the reason why B2 did not accept it. In addition, before a party was able to say that it would be unjust for a Part 36 offer to be made against it because of a failure to comply with an obligation to make information available, a party should have invoked r.36.8 to seek clarification of the offer (paras 24-35). The fact that there had been new developments in the case since the Part 36 offer was made was not a ground for saying that M was not entitled to an order under Part 36 either. There were continuously new developments in all cases, and in deciding whether to accept a Part 36 offer, a party had to assess what those developments would or could be. A Part 36 order would therefore be made in M's favour, entitling it to the relief set out in r.36.14(3) (paras 36-42). (3) There should be a reduction in the costs which M was entitled to claim as a result of his unsuccessful opposition to an application by B1 and B2 for permission to recall M for further cross-examination and as a result of his unnecessary cross-examination of a particular witness. In order to avoid an issue-based assessment, M would receive 95 per cent of his costs, *HLB Kidsons (A Firm) v Lloyd's Underwriters (Costs)* [2007] EWHC 2699 (Comm), [2008] 3 Costs L.R. 427, [2009] C.L.Y. 389 applied (paras 43-72). (4) Although M had sought an interim payment on account of costs of £2 million, there was a great discrepancy between M's costs and those of B2. M's costs also exceeded the value of the claim by 76 per cent, namely £3.8 million. That called for clear evidence justifying M's costs, which had not been provided. The appropriate figure for an interim award was £1.7 million because the court had not received all the information necessary to support an application for a larger award (paras 84-91).

MEHJOO v HARBEN BARKER (A FIRM), [2013] EWHC 1669 (QB), [2013] 5 Costs L.R. 645, Silber, J., QBD.

339. Costs between the parties–Professional negligence–Identity of successful party in professional negligence claim–Appropriate costs order–Whether interest payable

[Civil Procedure Rules 1998 (SI 1998/3132) r.44.3, r.44.3(2)(a).]

The court was required to determine costs in a professional negligence claim by the second claimant (P) against the first defendant solicitors firm (W). P had brought several allegations against W. She succeeded in relation to one of them, namely that W had acted negligently in failing to advise her to offer to buy a shareholder's shares before his removal as a shareholder. As a consequence of that failure, P had had to make payment in settlement of an unfair prejudice petition brought by the shareholder. P recovered £28,000 in damages. P had effectively only introduced the allegation on which she succeeded on the last day of the trial. The issues were (i) who was to be regarded as the successful party under CPR r.44.3(2)(a) for determining the appropriate costs order; (ii) whether interest should be payable on those costs.

Held: Costs determined. (1) In *Medway Primary Care Trust v Marcus* [2011] EWCA Civ 750, [2011] 5 Costs L.R. 808, [2011] C.L.Y. 300, the Court of Appeal was concerned with the question of who ought to be regarded in the substance as the successful party. In deciding that question, the court followed the decisions of *Roache v News Group Newspapers Ltd* [1998] E.M.L.R. 161, [1992] C.L.Y. 3437 and Oksuzoghu v Kay [1998] 2 All ER 631. Accordingly, since in *Fox v Foundation Piling Ltd* [2011] EWCA Civ 790, [2011] C.P. Rep. 41, [2012] C.L.Y. 352 the question of who was the successful party became common ground and did not have to be decided, it could not be taken as detracting from the consistent line of Court of Appeal authority on the correct approach to that question. In accordance with the principles in the *Roache* line of authorities, W had to be regarded in substance as the successful party, *Roache, Medway and Oksuzoghu* applied, *Fox* considered. The result of that analysis was that, in accordance with the general rule, W should receive its costs. However, there was some force in P's argument that W should have conceded the limited negligence which was subsequently found proved. In those circumstances, and in light of the considerations under CPR r.44.3, a 15 per cent reduction in the costs payable by P was appropriate (see paras 14-16, 24, 26-

27). (2) The £28,000 which P recovered depended upon a last minute amendment to her claim. On that basis, it was appropriate for P to obtain interest on her damages commencing at the midpoint in time between the date when payment became due, pursuant to her settlement with the shareholder, and the date upon which her amendment was allowed, *Claymore Services Ltd v Nautilus Properties Ltd* [2007] EWHC 805 (TCC), [2007] B.L.R. 452, [2008] C.L.Y. 608 applied (paras 30-31).

MAGICAL MARKING LTD v WARE AND KAY LLP, [2013] EWHC 636 (Ch), [2013] 4 Costs L.R. 535, Briggs, J., Ch D (Leeds).

340. Costs between the parties–Settlement–Construction dispute settled–Costs far exceeding value of claim and counterclaim–Liability for costs

[Civil Procedure Rules 1998 (SI 1998/3132) Pt 36, r.36.10(4).]

The court was required to determine liability for costs following the parties' settlement of the litigation between them. The claimant house builder (B) had engaged the defendant (S) to build a road. The works were completed 31.5 weeks later than had been agreed. Disputes over the delay were referred to adjudication. The adjudicator awarded S over £1 million, including £400,000 for prolongation costs. B paid the award but was dissatisfied with the decision and claimed against S for £527,000 made up of about £400,000 prolongation costs, increased costs and interest. B accepted liability for 12 of the 31.5 weeks of prolongation costs. S counterclaimed for prolongation costs of about £11,000 more than the adjudicator had allowed and for the return of a retention of £146,955 held by B. The parties' costs estimates far exceeded the value of their claims. S remedied most of the outstanding defects in respect of which B held the retention. S made a Part 36 offer to settle for £1. B did not accept it and disputed that it was compliant with CPR Pt 36. It then decided to release the retention to S. The parties made further offers. Just before the trial date they settled all claims and counterclaims on the basis that S paid B £146,953. B submitted that S should pay all its costs; that S's offer to settle for £1 was an offer to pay an amount equivalent to the retention, less £1, in respect of B's claim and it would be unfair if it was not responsible for B's costs. S submitted that it should recover all its costs because it was in effect the winner as it not only did not pay any net sum to B but was also £2 in credit; and that the result was at least as advantageous to it as its Part 36 offer.

Held: Costs determined. (1) The size of B's claim, realistically no more than about £350,000, was such that costs were always going to loom large. The combined latest costs estimates came to £1,336,932. If the court had been asked to make costs management orders, it would probably have imposed substantial reductions, but no doubt the parties would have argued that the case was very fact-heavy and that experts would have added substantially to the cost. That was relevant because both parties should have been proactively looking for ways to settle the case sooner rather than later and not making tactical manoeuvres (see para.32 of judgment). In approaching costs, the court could not decide issues that had arisen on the pleadings. Although the final settlement was made in effect without admission of liability, and doubtless commercial considerations and the narrowing of the debate between experts came into play, there was at the end of the litigation at least some recognition that it was appropriate for S to pay B £146,953. The court was entitled to draw inferences from those background facts that were unobjectionable and from the settlement itself. The implicit allowance within S's £1 offer of £146,954 for B's claim or the eventual settlement figure of £146,953 could not be considered simply a nuisance or commercial offer, commercially-minded though doubtless it was. It represented a proportion of 25 to 30 per cent of the claim and some acknowledgment that it had been overpaid for prolongation. It was necessary, to do justice to the parties, to proceed on the basis that there was a sum of money due to B which was virtually the same as the retention (paras 34-35). The complication was that B was itself entitled to seek to set off its own cross-claim for outstanding defects against the retention money. S was still putting right the actual or alleged defects after the start of the proceedings, so it was possible to infer that at least until that time much of the retention was not in commercial terms payable to S (para.36). (2) S should pay B its costs on the standard basis for the period in which the pre-action protocol process was started, the proceedings and counterclaim were issued, and most of the outstanding defects were remedied. For the period from when most of the defects had been remedied until B returned the retention to S, B should pay S's costs. Thereafter, each party should pay its own costs, to reflect the almost complete pointlessness of the litigation proceeding. Those findings were subject to the qualification that B should recover only 50 per cent of its costs, given that it had put a value on its claim far in excess of what it knew it could possibly achieve, *Multiplex Constructions (UK) Ltd v Cleveland Bridge UK Ltd* [2008] EWHC 2280 (TCC), 122 Con. L.R. 88, [2009] C.L.Y. 378 and *Brit Inns Ltd (In Liquidation) v BDW Trading Ltd (Costs)* [2012] EWHC 2489 (TCC), [2012] B.L.R. 531 considered (paras 38-49). (3) It was better and sensible for parties to settle earlier rather than later and, as importantly, if there were difficulties created by a Part 36 offer, it was sensible to agree that the court could be asked to resolve costs issues. It could be thought to be a lacuna of the CPR that there was no express provision for reference to the court by a party to permit it to accept the Part 36 offer during the relevant period of the offer but with the court being left to resolve costs issues; it could be said to be a lacuna because under CPR r.36.10(4), the court had the authority to make costs orders where a Pt 36 offer was accepted after expiry of the acceptance period. That might be explained by the fact that the offeree could make a "without prejudice save as to costs response" saying that it would accept what had been offered subject to the court deciding costs issues; ultimately, both offers could be considered by the court after the trial. That was something that the Rules Committee might want to consider (paras 50-51).

BELLWAY HOMES LTD v SEYMOUR (CIVIL ENGINEERING CONTRACTORS) LTD, [2013] EWHC 1890 (TCC), [2013] T.C.L.R. 8, Akenhead, J., QBD (TCC).

341. Costs between the parties–Unreasonable conduct–Refusal to agree terms of order directed at case management conference–Duty on solicitors and counsel to give effect to court orders

The applicant (J) applied for an order that the respondent (W) pay its costs unnecessarily incurred in attempting to agree a draft court order. W was the assignee of a mortgage lender. J was a firm of surveyors. W had sued J for allegedly negligent property valuations. At a case management conference the judge had proposed that issues about the validity of the assignment and negligence should be dealt with first, and that valuation issues should be heard separately. After considering the proposal and taking instructions both sides agreed to that course. The judge gave a judgment and asked W's counsel to prepare a draft order for agreement. The draft order sent to J did not reflect the judge's directions and there was correspondence attempting to reach agreement. J's solicitors sent their proposed draft order to the judge, who indicated that the order should be in that form. Despite that indication W's solicitors refused to agree its terms until very shortly before a further case management conference.

Held: Application granted. If a party was charged with drawing up an order it was the duty of its solicitors and counsel to produce a draft that fairly reflected what they thought that the judge had decided or directed. What W's solicitors had done was to produce an order that reflected the directions that they or their clients would have liked to have had, and not the directions that the court had ordered. That was wholly unacceptable: it was not just unreasonable, it was verging on the contumelious. Solicitors and counsel had to give effect to court orders; they were not to attempt to manipulate them to their own or their client's perceived advantage. There was no reason at all why J should have to pay the costs that were quite unnecessarily incurred as a result of W's manoeuvres. However, it would not be right for J to recover all of the costs incurred in dealing with the draft order, as some would have been incurred in any event (see paras 19, 21 of judgment).

WEBB RESOLUTIONS LTD v JV LTD (T/A SHEPHERD CHARTERED SURVEYORS), [2013] EWHC 509 (TCC), [2013] T.C.L.R. 6, Edwards-Stuart, J., QBD (TCC).

342. Costs budgets–Rectification–Revision of approved costs budget–Exclusion of after the event insurance premiums and success fees–Unusual circumstances

[Civil Procedure Rules 1998 (SI 1998/3132) r.3.9, r.3.12, r.3.18; CPR PD 51 (Transitional Arrangements) 1999.]

The applicants (M) applied under CPR r.3.9 for relief from sanctions and to revise or rectify an approved costs management order made with the respondent (D) to show that the approved budget excluded success fees and after the event insurance premiums received by M. M had entered into conditional fee agreements with their solicitors which provided for a success fee. M then obtained the benefit of after the event insurance. M gave notice to D of both the CFA and the ATE insurance. Court proceedings began initially under a pilot scheme and then under the relevant costs management provisions in CPR r.3.12 to CPR r.3.18 under which the court could approve, vary or disapprove any proposed revisions, having regard to any significant developments which had occurred since the date of the previous budget. Prior to the first hearing the parties exchanged costs budgets. M's costs budget was not in form HB, an omission which was the subject of adverse comment by the judge. However because the costs budget appeared to be in substantially the same form, the judge considered the budgets and made a costs management order. M's costs budget was approved in the sum of £82,500. D's solicitor pointed out that M's costs budget did not say that it excluded a success fee and the ATE insurance premium and that they would argue that M should not be permitted to recover any sum over and above the approved costs budget. D submitted that it would not be appropriate to revise or rectify the approved budget figure because the costs budget that had been provided originally was inadequate in making no reference to the success fee or the ATE insurance and that it was therefore flawed from the outset and if a change was necessary to cure a fundamental inadequacy in the approved budget that could not be a good reason for revision. It also argued that a mistake should not be capable of being remedied by an increase in the approved budget as if that were the cure for every mistake: costs management would become irrelevant or meaningless because all parties would seek to revise their approved budgets after the event on the basis that they had forgotten to include particular items originally.

Held: Application granted. (1) The situation that had arisen was not one to which r.3.9 obviously applied. There was no sanction as such from which M required relief. Detailed assessment was months, if not a year or more, away. There had been no failure of notification, and D had always known about the success fees and the ATE insurance premiums. Instead, what M wanted was akin to permission to revise an approved budget, or for it to be rectified, or at least clarified that the approved budget excluded the success fee and the ATE premiums, because these had been mistakenly omitted from the costs budget prepared. That made the instant situation at least similar to an application to revise the approved budget pursuant to CPR PD 51. (2) The amendments to the CPR coming into force on April 1, 2013, including the amendments to r.3.9(1) placed much more emphasis on the importance of complying with the orders of the court, rather than the previous lengthy shopping list of matters which the court was obliged to work through, *Henry v News Group Newspapers Ltd* [2013] EWCA Civ 19, [2013] 2 All E.R. 840, [2013] 7 C.L. 53 considered. There was clear authority that the changes meant that the courts would generally be less ready than before to grant relief from sanctions from procedural defaults, *Fred Perry (Holdings) Ltd v Brands Plaza Trading Ltd (t/a Brands Plaza)* [2012] EWCA Civ 224, [2012] 6 Costs L.R. 1007, [2012] C.L.Y. 484 applied. (3) In an ordinary case it would be extremely difficult to persuade a court that inadequacies or mistakes in preparation of a costs budget, which had been approved by a court, should be subsequently revised or rectified. However there were two factors that made the instant case very special. The first was that it was not a situation in which D could be said to have been misled or confused by the information provided by M and there had been no prejudice. The second and defining factor arose out of the wording of the costs budget forms themselves. Form HB, that M should have filled out, contained a number of tick boxes for specific items of cost which if ticked were thereby excluded from the costs budget and both success fees and ATE insurance premiums were listed as items that could be excluded. The reason why Form HB assumed that such items would be regularly excluded was that it was not always possible to identify their precise financial value at the time. Success fees and ATE insurance premiums were expressly dealt with differently in Form HB to the ordinary run of costs. The new costs budget form expressly excluded success fees and insurance premiums. Therefore the difficulty in which M found themselves arose out of the costs management pilot scheme and the particular court form which was used as part of that pilot. It was not appropriate to penalise a party to litigation because it failed to tick a box on a form, especially when that form had later been superseded so as not to include the box at all. In the particular and unusual facts of the instant case, it would be in accordance with the overriding objective if the approved costs budget was revised.

MURRAY v NEIL DOWLMAN ARCHITECTURE LTD, [2013] EWHC 872 (TCC), [2013] T.C.L.R. 5, Coulson, J., QBD (TCC).

343. Costs orders–Agreements–Defendant agreeing not to seek or enforce costs order from claimants under one-way costs-shifting agreement–Ability to set off earlier costs order against unenforceable costs

[Civil Procedure Rules 1998 (SI 1998/3132) r.44.3, r.44.12.]

The court was required to determine costs having granted the defendant (X) a declaration that the court lacked jurisdiction to hear personal injury claims brought by the claimants (V). If costs were awarded in accordance with the general rule in CPR r.44.3, V would be ordered to pay X's costs, since X was the successful party and V were unsuccessful. V contended that there should be no order for costs because of a contract made in correspondence between the parties on "one way costs shifting" whereby X had agreed not to seek any costs or any costs order against them, as a result of which V had cancelled after the event insurance cover. V argued that that was implicit from the expression "one way costs shifting" according to the Review of Civil Litigation costs: Final Report (the Jackson reforms), which had been published before the parties' exchanges, the glossary of which included the description of "one way costs shifting" as "A regime under which the defendant pays the claimant's costs if its claim is successful, but the claimant does not pay the defendant's costs if the claim is unsuccessful". X submitted that it was appropriate to make an order for costs limited to the amount of costs that it had previously been ordered to pay to V, namely 60 per cent of V's costs occasioned by applications for disclosure and information. Those costs had not been assessed and X had paid nothing on account of them.

Held: Costs determined. (1) The Jackson reforms did not present "A regime under which the defendant pays the claimant's costs if its claim is successful, but the claimant does not pay the defendant's costs if the claim is unsuccessful" as a definition of the expression "one way costs shifting" but as its "Meaning or description". Even if it was an exact definition, the earlier costs order would not be in accordance with the agreement since it was made before the claim or even the jurisdictional challenge had been decided, and it was made for only 60 per cent of V's costs. The parties' agreement on costs had been concluded only when V cancelled the ATE cover: before then, they had not contractually agreed to anything (see paras 9, 11 of judgment). (2) X was effectively seeking an order for costs to neutralise the earlier costs order, limited to the amount that it was then ordered to pay. It recognised that an order for any greater amount should not be made because it had agreed not to enforce it. The purpose of the agreement had been to provide V with protection equivalent to that which they would have obtained from ATE insurance. If the issue had to be determined as a matter of contractual construction, it would be concluded that by seeking to deploy an order for costs against the earlier costs order, X would be attempting to "enforce" a costs order against V within the meaning of the agreement. However, there was another route to the conclusion that no order for costs should be made since a judgment or order for payment of a sum could be set-off against another: that principle extended to orders for costs, *Reid v Cupper* [1915] 2 K.B. 147 followed. It was also reflected in CPR r.44.12. The court could order a set-off under its inherent jurisdiction to do what was fair. It would be unfair for X to set-off liability under an order that it had agreed should not be enforced against an enforceable order. Moreover, had V proceeded to an immediate assessment of their earlier costs, X's liability would probably have accrued and been paid before any decision about jurisdiction. In those circumstances, X could not properly have sought a costs order. It was not fair that V should be worse off because they sensibly did not rush to have their costs assessed with the risk of a series of separate costs assessments between the parties. It was, accordingly, appropriate to make no order for costs (paras 12-13, 15-18).

VAVA v ANGLO AMERICAN SOUTH AFRICA LTD, [2013] EWHC 2326 (QB), [2013] 5 Costs L.R. 805, Andrew Smith, J., QBD.

344. Costs orders–Applications without notice–Hearing following without-notice application–Whether court having jurisdiction to make final costs order

[Law of Property Act 1925 (c.20); Senior Courts Act 1981 (c.54) s.51; Civil Procedure Rules 1998 (SI 1998/3132) r.23.10, r.44.10(2)(c).]

The appellants (D) appealed against two orders made in the course of proceedings brought against them by the respondent receivers (C). D owned land subject to a legal charge in favour of a bank. The bank had appointed C under the Law of Property Act 1925 when it sought to enforce the charge. D denied that the appointment was valid. When C encountered serious difficulties in carrying out their functions, the bank applied for them to become court-appointed receivers. On June 29, 2013 the court made a receivership order and appointed C as joint receivers. It went on to make an order (the first order) upon C's without-notice application, declaring that D had no right to occupy the property or obstruct C's access to it. The order dealt with various other matters and provided that D should pay C's costs of the application to be summarily assessed. It concluded with the statement that any party to the application could apply to set aside or vary the order under CPR r.23.10. On July 5, the judge inserted into the order a more general liberty to apply than that afforded by r.23.10. On November 22, the same judge refused an application by D to set aside the costs order. He held that the liberty to apply did not give D a general ability to apply to vary or challenge the costs order, which had become final upon summary assessment, meaning that the proper route of challenge was an appeal. D appealed against both the costs order and the refusal to set it aside. D submitted that (1) the court had no jurisdiction to make a final order for costs on a without-notice application, or, if it had, it could not properly exercise its discretion to do so against somebody who had not been given notice of the hearing; (2) the judge had erred in holding that the right to apply under the liberty to apply provision had been lost by delay; (3) it was wrong to make a costs order against them when they disputed the bank's right to appoint C under the 1925 Act.

Held: Appeals dismissed. (1) The court had jurisdiction to make an order for costs on a without-notice application. Its power to make costs orders was conferred in general terms by the Senior Courts Act 1981 s.51, and the generality of that provision was at odds with D's contention as to the absence of jurisdiction in respect of without-notice applications. Furthermore, CPR r.44.10(2)(c) provided for a deemed order for costs to be made on a without-notice application, and that too was inconsistent with the proposition that no such order could be made. Finally, by virtue of r.23.10, the first order was subject to D's right to apply to have it set aside or varied. While it would rarely be appropriate for a judge to make an order for costs carrying a right to immediate payment on a without-notice application, it could be done (see paras 48-62 of judgment). (2) The judge had been right to hold that, even though there was no defined time limit on the liberty to apply, the court could take account of any unexplained delay by the affected party in making the application (paras 71-74). (3) The judge had been entitled to make the costs order, and he had been entitled to reject D's application to set it aside. There had been a significant, unexplained delay before D had made the application, and it had not been supported by evidence as to the merits of the dispute (paras 75-80). (4) (Obiter) Although C had not sought to argue that the costs order was not subject to the liberty to apply, either under r. 23.10 or under the general liberty inserted on July 5, the court would nevertheless comment. If the right to apply under r.23.10 applied to all aspects of an order made without notice to the party affected, there was no apparent reason why a general liberty to apply written into the order should not have the same wide scope. What lay beneath the judge's observation that the costs order was not subject to the general liberty to apply provision was his view that the right avenue of challenge was an appeal. That view was, however, incorrect. The assessment of the costs, if open to challenge at all, could only be challenged by way of an appeal. However, the party affected by the making of a costs order could apply to the court that made it to reconsider the merits at first instance, *Bank of Scotland v Pereira* [2011] EWCA Civ 241, [2011] 1 W.L.R. 2391, [2011] C.L.Y. 346 applied. The making of orders by way of substantive relief without notice to one party was exceptional. If such an order was made, the party affected should have the right to a first instance hearing at which it could present arguments that would have been relevant had the original hearing been on notice. In general, such a right was conferred by, and confined to, r.23.10. The court was not sure that it would recognise the existence of a free-standing right to apply, outside the scope of r.23.10 or any express provision made in the order (paras 63-70).

MacKAY v ASHWOOD ENTERPRISES LTD, [2013] EWCA Civ 959, [2013] 5 Costs L.R. 816, Lloyd, L.J., CA (Civ Div).

345. Costs orders–Costs between the parties–Costs of successful parties in litigation–Countervailing considerations to recovery

[Insolvency Act 1986 (c.45) s.281.]

The court was required to determine the appropriate costs orders between the claimants (C) and the first and third defendants (D1 and D3). C also sought an order for payment on account. C had brought a claim against D1, a former employee, alleging dishonest breaches of contractual obligations and of fiduciary duties, constituting fraudulent breaches of trust. C also brought a claim against the second defendant (D2), who was D1's wife, on the basis that she knowingly received bonus payments made to D1 from a joint account that D1 and D2 maintained. D3 was D1's trustee in bankruptcy who did not take any active part in the litigation. The litigation had initially proceeded alleging breach of contract and of fiduciary duties, but had widened to include allegations of fraud made in response to D1 raising a defence under the Insolvency Act 1986 s.281. Those allegations significantly extended the hearing. C had also alleged that D3 held monies received from the other defendants as constructive trustee in their favour. Following judgments on the trial of the issues, remedies, and interest on a sum of money D3 was found to be liable to C as a constructive trustee. C in the instant proceeding sought an order against D1 and D3 jointly and severally for 70 per cent of C's costs of the action to be assessed on the standard basis, if not agreed. The issues were (i) the quantum of costs recoverable by C against D1 and whether an order for payment on account of costs should be made; (ii) the quantum of costs recoverable by C against D3.

Held: Costs determined. (1) C's own costs of the action, after excluding the costs already the subject of orders, and the costs attributable to the constructive trust claim against D3, were to be reduced by 95 per cent. That was a just costs order in the circumstances as C had had no regard to any pre-action protocol; Cs' case against D1 and D2 included serious factual allegations unsupported by other than unreliable evidence; C's disclosure was woefully inadequate; C's trial bundle exceeded that which was pertinent to the real issues; C's case was riddled with flaws, and their approach to the litigation led to an express finding that winning was regarded by them as more important than the obligation to tell the truth. C's relatively deep pockets were also a relevant consideration. In exercising a discretion to order a payment on account of costs, it was necessary to have regard to whether the unsuccessful party wished to appeal; the parties' relative financial positions, and the overriding objective. In the instant case, D1 did intend to seek permission to appeal. He was also a discharged bankrupt, in contrast to C who were part of a substantial corporate group. In all of the circumstances, including avoiding the risk of D1 having to recover an overpayment from C, no order for a payment on account of costs was made (see paras 102-103, 105, 108, 110-111 of judgment). (2) In the light of the first judgment of the issues, it was difficult, if not impossible, to criticise D3 for not accepting at face value C1's assertion that D1 had no contractual entitlement to a bonus and for not accepting that C1 had a proprietary interest in the funds D1 passed to D2 which were then accepted by D3: it was not obvious, nor should it have been obvious, that that transaction was probably improper, *Sinclair Investments (UK) Ltd v Versailles Trade Finance Ltd (In Administration)* [2011] EWCA Civ 347, [2012] Ch. 453, [2011] C.L.Y. 3499 followed. The appropriate order for the costs of the action between C and D3 was no order as to costs (paras 133-134, 137).

TEMPLETON INSURANCE LTD v BRUNSWICK, [2012] EWHC 3319 (Ch), [2013] 3 Costs L.O. 429, Judge Simon Barker Q.C., Ch D.

346. Costs orders–Court-appointed receivers–Receivers appointed by court after defendant's death–Whether receivers entitled to indemnity out of estate for costs–Reasonableness of receiver's actions

The court was required to determine the appropriate costs orders on applications made by receivers appointed by the court over a deceased's estate. The deceased (B) had been a defendant to an action brought by a Russian airline (X) for fraud. He had left a will appointing five executors. Three of them renounced probate and the remaining executrices, his former partner (R1) and his daughter, failed to take out a grant of probate. X therefore obtained an order for the appointment of receivers over B's estate. The receivers sought documents from B's former solicitors (R3), including those relating to confidential settlement agreements with the fourth to seventh respondents (P), the other participants in X's litigation. R3 asserted a lien over the documents and raised the issue of privilege, asserting that privilege belonged to the estate and did not vest in the receivers. P's solicitors indicated that they would submit to an order for disclosure if it included a condition of confidentiality. The receivers sought further powers and orders against R3 for delivery-up of documents. The court ordered the application to be heard on notice, and R3 was joined as a respondent. R3, P and the receivers subsequently agreed to some disclosure, subject to a confidentiality agreement, and a consent order was made in those terms. R1, R3 and P submitted that their costs should be paid by the receivers. The receivers argued that they should be entitled to an indemnity, so that any costs orders against them, and their own costs, should be met from the assets of the estate.

Held: Costs determined. (1) A receiver appointed by the court was not an agent or trustee for the party at whose instance the appointment was made. He was an officer of the court whose duty was to act impartially in accordance with the court's directions in administering the property to which the receivership extended. He should be treated in the same way as litigants who were liquidators, trustees or personal representatives in an application made by them against a third party or outsider. The order appointing the receivers in the instant case provided that they were entitled to reasonable remuneration and reasonable costs properly incurred in the performance of their duties. That reflected the long-established position in relation to a receiver's right to be indemnified out of the relevant assets, *Boehm v Goodall* [1911] 1 Ch. 155

considered (see paras 24-25, 36-38 of judgment). (2) R3 had behaved properly throughout. R3 stated that it was willing to cooperate with the receivers, subject to the constraints it was under. The application was initiated by the receivers and R3 was a necessary respondent to it. R3 was a third party, not a representative of the estate, and it was being proceeded against because it was in possession of property of the estate over which it had its own independent rights. Further, R3 was legally obliged to assert the privilege of the estate. The orders that were made by consent respected that privilege, but the orders sought by the receivers would have overridden R3's rights and duties. Accordingly, the receivers should pay R3's costs of the application on the standard basis (paras 48-52). (3) P's solicitors had acted properly throughout and fully co-operated with the receivers' request for information. They offered to submit to an order requiring disclosure of the settlement agreement subject to a condition as to confidentiality. They made constructive suggestions as to how the matter could be handled and provided a draft confidentiality undertaking which proved to be acceptable to the receivers. P were third parties so far as the receivership was concerned and were caught up in the application and the various court hearings instigated by the receivers. The receivers should pay P's costs of the application on the standard basis (paras 59-61). (4) R1 was not a third party or an outsider. Substantial justice was done to all parties by directing that her costs should come out of the estate, making no direction that the receivers themselves should pay any part of those costs and giving appropriate weight to her criticism of the receivers when considering their application for an indemnity out of the estate (para.63). (5) If a receiver litigated and was unsuccessful, that did not necessarily mean that the costs of the litigation were not reasonable sums properly incurred. The receivers had found themselves in difficulties and considered that something needed to be done to enable progress to be made. However, some of their decisions were sufficiently unwise to justify a partial withholding of the right to indemnity. They had not sufficiently acknowledged the substance of the points made by R3. They had unwisely sought to obtain wide-ranging orders without making R3 a respondent to the application. Accordingly, one-third of the costs payable by the receivers to R3 were not indemnified out of the estate. Further, the receivers' own costs had increased as a result of their inappropriate handling of the application. They were therefore allowed to recover only 85 per cent of their own costs, in relation to the application, out of the estate. However, they were entitled to an indemnity in respect of the costs payable to P (paras 65-68).

WOOD (RECEIVER) v GORBUNOVA; *sub nom.* BEREZOVSKY (DECEASED), *Re*, [2013] EWHC 1935 (Ch), [2013] 5 Costs L.R. 713, Morgan, J., Ch D.

347. Costs orders–Indemnity basis–Unwillingness to accept offer to settle at requested figure–Indemnity costs from date of trial

The court gave directions on costs following a professional negligence claim between the claimant group of companies (C) and the defendant surveyors (D). C had sued D for professional negligence during the course of its surveying. C accepted that overall, having lost in the proceedings, they had to pay D's costs at least on a standard basis but D argued that it should be entitled to indemnity costs. Expert reports had been exchanged in the summer of 2012 and in October 2012 there were several Part 36 offers made between the parties. After various offers and counter-offers C offered to settle for £729,000 plus costs. That offer expired on a Monday afternoon, and D did not accept the offer by that time. A few days later D made an offer for settlement at exactly that level but C refused to accept that offer. On the first day of trial the judge adjourned the trial but before he did so he expressed doubts about some of the evidence of C's expert, which he thought led to concerns as to how C's claim could proceed.

Held: Costs determined. (1) C had an arguable case which raised relatively simple issues as to whether or not D had failed to exercise reasonable care and skill. At least up to September/October and possibly going into November 2012, whilst there had been some attempts to settle the case, matters had proceeded in the usual way to trial. If an appropriate Part 36 offer had been accepted there would have been no room for any costs basis other than a standard basis. However, after the trial date, a substantial amount of cost and effort was expended as the result of the putting forward of evidence from C's quantity surveyor, whose reasoning for that evidence did not appear anywhere in his exchanged reports. Up to that stage, it was a relatively standard professional negligence claim and C were putting forward a case which, if their evidence was believed and accepted, would have succeeded (see paras 4-5, 27-29 of judgment). (2) The parties should have considered seriously the impact of costs. It was not just the court which was bound by the overriding objective. Where effectively both parties were prepared to settle at exactly the same figure within a few days of each offer being put forward, for C to have withdrawn from settlement seemed unjustifiable. Nothing had happened between the time C's offer of £729,000 plus costs had expired and the timing of the offer made by D for settlement at exactly that level a few days later. An enormous amount of time and costs and court resource had been wasted thereafter as a result of C's unwillingness to accept the figure that they had been prepared to settle at only a few days earlier. That fact, coupled with the fact that the judge had expressed reservations about C's case, meant that there was no justification for going on with the case at that stage. The Monday following the hearing in front of the judge was an appropriate date for indemnity costs to start. D should have its costs on the standard basis until that date and indemnity costs thereafter (paras 31-35).

IGLOO REGENERATION (GENERAL PARTNER) LTD v POWELL WILLIAMS PARTNERSHIP (COSTS), [2013] EWHC 1859 (TCC), [2013] 5 Costs L.O. 746, Akenhead, J., QBD (TCC).

348. Costs orders–Part 36 offers–Claimant not accepting or bettering Part 36 offer–Judge approaching costs order on basis Part 36 offer not made

The appellant (W) appealed against a costs order in favour of the respondents (S). W had obtained judgment for damages in the sum of £16,965 plus interest following a finding that S had breached their fiduciary duty to him. However, he had been unsuccessful in his claim for an account of the profits made by S in consequence of breach of confidence. S had made a Part 36 offer; the last day for acceptance was October 13, 2010. W did not accept it, nor by the judgment obtained did he better it. Adopting a broad brush approach the judge determined that, without regard to the Part 36 offer, S would have been entitled to recover 90 per cent of their costs. Taking into account the Part 36 offer, by which S had offered an amount commensurate with that recovered by W, W was ordered to pay: (i) 90 per cent of S's costs down to and including October 13, 2010; (ii) all of their costs thereafter. W challenged limb (i). He submitted that the 10 per cent allowance could not fairly reflect his costs referable to the damages claim. The judge should have had specific regard to the fact that most of S's costs up to October 13 were likely to be attributable to their unsuccessful defences. The judge had erred in making an assessment as to what the fair order as to costs would have been if there had been no Part 36 offer, and then to ignore the consequences of that offer when making the order as to costs in relation to the period to October 13.

Held: Appeal dismissed. W's criticisms were unjustified. The order was a matter within the judge's discretion and the court would not review it unless he had erred in principle in arriving at it. The judge's approach was orthodox and rational. The consequence of W's rejection of the Part 36 offer was that the only costs in issue were those of the period to October 13. It was entirely appropriate for the judge to approach that issue by first asking himself what costs order would have been appropriate had no Part 36 offer been made. S had won on the account of profits issue and were the substantially successful parties, although their success was reduced by their unsuccessful resistance of the damages claim. The judge considered that the fair costs order to make, had there been no Part 36 offer, would have been to order W to pay 90 per cent of S's costs claim. That approach was, as conceded by W, unexceptionable. W's criticisms were comprehensively mistaken. First, the fact that W would have been entitled to his costs incurred in the relevant period had he accepted the Part 36 offer was irrelevant: he had not accepted it. Second, there was no reason why the application of the judge's 90 per cent approach to the costs of the relevant period was erroneous or unprincipled. Had no Part 36 offer been made, the judge would have ordered W to pay 90 per cent of S's costs. The logic of W's position was that apparently the judge's "unexceptionable" arrival at the 90 per cent figure required him to promptly jettison it and instead to focus on different periods of the history of the claim with a view to deciding what order to make in respect of such periods. That was an impossible argument. It could not stand with the acceptance of the correctness of the judge's arrival at the 90 per cent figure. W's sole objective had been to recover an account of profits. He was not remotely interested in recovering damages. It was with the aim of achieving that objective that he had been prepared to make the very considerable cost investment that he did. The judge had correctly assessed what the claim was about and made a costs order which involved no error of principle. Accordingly, there was no sound basis on which it could be challenged (see paras 14-17 of judgment).

WALSH v SHANAHAN, [2013] EWCA Civ 675, [2013] 5 Costs L.O. 738, Laws, L.J., CA (Civ Div).

349. Costs orders–Part 36 offers–Whether issue-based costs order should be made–Claimant successful overall but unsuccessful on some points

[Civil Procedure Rules 1998 (SI 1998/3132) Pt 44.]

The court was required to determine a number of issues concerning costs. The claimant (S) had brought proceedings against the defendants (B and D) for misrepresentation and breach of warranty regarding its purchase of shares in a company. S's misrepresentation claim failed, but the breach of warranty claim succeeded, and S was awarded £5.25 million in damages plus interest of approximately £1 million (see *Sycamore Bidco Ltd v Breslin* [2012] EWHC 3443 (Ch)). S had made two part 36 offers to settle the claim: one for £5.5 million including interest, and one for £4 million including interest. B and D rejected both offers. S beat the offers at trial. S had entered into a conditional fee agreement and its base costs were £3.9 million. Once the uplift was applied, S's costs were likely to exceed the damages. The court was required to determine: (i) whether some of S's costs should be disallowed to reflect the issues on which it failed; (ii) whether the normal consequences of beating a part 36 offer should apply; (iii) whether the start date for interest on costs should be postponed; (iv) whether there should be a stay of enforcement pending any appeal.

Held: Costs issues determined. (1) The matters on which S fought and lost were significant and costly enough to take the case out of the class of normal cases in which some issues were lost without reflecting that in costs, *Multiplex Constructions (UK) Ltd v Cleveland Bridge UK Ltd* [2008] EWHC 2280 (TCC), 122 Con. L.R. 88, [2009] C.L.Y. 378 applied. It was appropriate to make a cost deduction from the totality of S's costs to which it would otherwise be entitled. The biggest point on which S failed was the misrepresentation claim. S had sought damages under that head of £17 million. A significant part of the expert evidence was given over to the damages that would have been payable had the misrepresentation been established. A large amount of evidence was prepared and given, many hundreds of documents had to be disclosed and studied. The loss of that claim was significant enough to justify it being treated as a separate issue to be reflected in an issue-based costs order. The failure of the commission and rebate-related claims should also be treated as the source of an adjustment of the costs to which S would otherwise be entitled. The court was minded to make an issue-based costs order but was required by the CPR Pt 44 to consider making a proportionate order instead. Accordingly, applying a broad brush, the court ordered that S should receive 60 per cent of its costs (see paras 13-16, 19-22, 28 of judgment). (2) S had recovered more than its part 36 offer at trial. The offer was made to D and B to settle at £5.5 million. It was not apportioned between the defendants. D's liability in the action was only

£330,000. The consequences of part 36 should therefore not apply to him. The extra burdens imposed upon B in the form of the CFA uplift and interest on the judgment debt were not relevant to the question of the justice of applying the part 36 consequences. Both factors flowed from the normal costs and interest principles. The part 36 consequences were deliberately harsh in order to provide an incentive to reasonable behaviour. The cumulative burden was heavy, but since it was provided by the rules it could not be said to be unjust (paras 44-51, 64). (3) Interest on costs was to be paid at the same rate as that on the damages claim, subject to the higher rate of interest which flowed from the part 36 offer for the relevant period, *F&C Alternative Investments (Holdings) Ltd v Barthelemy (Costs)* [2012] EWCA Civ 843, [2013] 1 W.L.R. 548 followed. The court also exercised its discretion to postpone the interest at the Judgements Act rate for a period of four months (paras 70-72, 75-77). (4) S's financial state was such that there was a real risk that it would not be able to repay any substantial sums paid to it if B and D's appeal was successful. B and D had offered adequate and fair protection to S in the form of undertakings to deposit cash in an escrow account, and undertakings to prevent dissipation. The court therefore ordered a stay of enforcement pending appeal (paras 82-84). (5) Although D was only liable for £330,000, he had conducted himself as a joint defendant with B. They were both equally responsible for the costs having been incurred and the court declined to apportion costs between them (paras 38-41).

SYCAMORE BIDCO LTD v BRESLIN, [2013] EWHC 583 (Ch), [2013] 4 Costs L.O. 572, Mann, J., Ch D.

350. Court of Appeal–Jurisdiction–Refusal of permission to appeal under s.298(6) Town and Country Planning Act 1990–Jurisdiction of Court of Appeal under s.16(1) Senior Courts Act 1981

[Senior Courts Act 1981 (c.54) s.16(1); Town and Country Planning Act 1990 (c.8) s.174, s.289; European Convention on Human Rights 1950 Art.6.]

The applicant local authorities renewed their application for permission to appeal against enforcement notices that had been issued by the respondent secretary of state. The local authorities had been refused leave to appeal to the Court of Appeal which was required under the Town and Country Planning Act 1990 s.289(6) to challenge enforcement notices. The issue was whether the Court of Appeal had jurisdiction to hear the application for permission to appeal. The local authorities submitted that if the question of the court's jurisdiction was not answered by authority, the refusal of permission to appeal under s.289(6) contained an order of the High Court and reasons in the form of a judgment: accordingly, those reasons were both a "judgment" and an "order" of the High Court for the purposes of the Court of Appeal's jurisdiction to hear and determine appeals from any judgment or order of the High Court under the Senior Courts Act 1981 s.16(1).

Held: Application refused. A refusal of permission to appeal under s.289(6) of the 1990 Act did not fall within the jurisdiction of the Court of Appeal under s.16(1) of the 1981 Act: there was no further right of challenge to an enforcement notice where the High Court had decided that there was no arguable case and had accordingly refused permission to appeal, *Wendy Fair Markets Ltd v Secretary of State for the Environment* Times, March 1, 1995, [1995] C.L.Y. 4794 applied. The policy reasons underpinning s.289(6) were of no less force today than they were at the time of judgment in *Wendy Fair*. It was clear that Parliament had considered that the introduction of s.289(4A) did not prevent the bringing of unmeritorious appeals under s.289 and that the introduction of a further requirement for leave under s.289(6) was required. Furthermore, procedural amendments to Civil Procedure Rules did not lessen the need for the further filter for leave under s.289(6). The correctness of decisions that had followed *Wendy Fair* could not be questioned and the court was bound as the instant case did not fall within one of the exceptional categories in *Young v Bristol Aeroplane Co Ltd* [1944] K.B. 718, applied. Although there was authority in which the Court of Appeal had recognised that it had a residual discretion to set aside the refusal of permission to appeal and to that extent the principle in

Wendy Fair was tempered, and a distinction had been made between a challenge to the judicial decision-making process and the merits of a decision to refuse leave to appeal, far from casting doubt on the continued application of the principle in *Wendy Fair*, more recent decisions reflect its continued existence subject to a residual discretion which did not have any application in the instant case, *North Range Shipping Ltd v Seatrans Shipping Corp (The Western Triumph)* [2002] EWCA Civ 405, [2002] 1 W.L.R. 2397, [2002] C.L.Y. 208 and *CGU International Insurance Plc v AstraZeneca Insurance Co Ltd (Permission to Appeal)* [2006] EWCA Civ 1340, [2007] 1 All E.R. (Comm) 501, [2006] C.L.Y. 204 considered. The authorities the local authorities relied on emphasised a distinction between the High Court's powers of judicial review and statutory appeals and also emphasised the need for the decisions of lower courts and tribunals not to be immune from scrutiny by the higher courts, however, Parliament had chosen to provide for a statutory process to challenge enforcement notices on the grounds in s.174 of the 1990 Act, *R. (on the application of Cart) v Upper Tribunal* [2011] UKSC 28, [2012] 1 A.C. 663, [2011] C.L.Y. 48 considered. That did not mean that such decisions were immune from scrutiny by the higher courts, but that challenges by way of judicial review had been excluded. Furthermore, the possibility of appealing on a point of law with the court's leave under s.289(6) was sufficient to comply with the European Convention on Human Rights 1950 art.6, *Bryan v United Kingdom (A/335-A)* (1996) 21 E.H.R.R. 342, [1996] C.L.Y. 4707 and *R. (on the application of Holding & Barnes Plc) v Secretary of State for the Environment, Transport and the Regions* [2001] UKHL 23, [2003] 2 A.C. 295, [2001] C.L.Y. 4761 considered. Section 289 gave the High Court full jurisdiction to review the lawfulness of a planning inspector's decision on an appeal under s.174: there was sufficient judicial control to satisfy art.6. The filter of s.289(6) amply enabled the High Court to exercise full jurisdiction to ensure the court's resources were used in an effective way, and that time was not wasted on unarguable challenges.

WALSALL MBC v SECRETARY OF STATE FOR COMMUNITIES AND LOCAL GOVERNMENT; DARTFORD BC v SECRETARY OF STATE FOR COMMUNITIES AND LOCAL GOVERNMENT, [2013] EWCA Civ 370, [2013] J.P.L. 1183, Pill, L.J., CA (Civ Div).

351. Cross-undertakings–Freezing injunctions–Financial Services Authority obtaining freezing injunction–Requirement for cross-undertaking in respect of third party losses

[Financial Services and Markets Act 2000 (c.8) s.380(3); Senior Courts Act 1981 (c.54) s.37(1).]

The appellant bank (B) appealed against a decision ([2011] EWCA Civ 1158, [2012] Bus. L.R. 753, [2012] C.L.Y. 408) that the respondent Financial Services Authority was not required to give a cross-undertaking in respect of third party losses on its application for an interim freezing injunction against certain companies (S). The FSA believed that S were engaged in unlawful activity, and obtained without notice an injunction freezing S's assets under the Financial Services and Markets Act 2000 s.380(3) and/or the Senior Courts Act 1981 s.37(1). The FSA gave an undertaking in respect of costs incurred by third parties, but not in relation to losses incurred. B submitted that (1) *F Hoffmann La Roche & Co AG v Secretary of State for Trade and Industry* [1975] A.C. 295, [1974] C.L.Y. 3801, in which it was held that there was a usual or normal rule that a cross-undertaking would not be required from the Crown, was distinguishable because it concerned enforcement of an apparently valid executive order in relation to which the only defence was that the order was invalid. Subsequent authorities had read *Hoffmann La Roche* too broadly; (2) *Hoffmann La Roche* only related to the protection of defendants, whereas the instant case involved the protection of third persons who, unless the contrary was shown, had to be taken as having no involvement in the breach of the law alleged against the defendants; (3) no sensible distinction could exist between a cross-undertaking in respect of costs and a cross-undertaking in damages.

Held: Appeal dismissed. (1) There was a general distinction in *Hoffmann La Roche* and the subsequent line of authority between private litigation and public law enforcement action. In private litigation, a claimant acted in its own interests and had a choice whether to commit its assets and energies to doing so. If the claimant sought interim relief which might, if unjustified, cause loss or expense to the defendant, it was usually fair to require it to be ready to accept responsibility for that loss. Different considerations arose in relation to law enforcement action, where a public authority was seeking to enforce the law in the interests of the public generally, often in pursuance of a public duty to do so, and enjoyed only the resources which had been assigned to it for its functions. The risk that public authorities might be deterred from pursuing claims in the public interest, or might be burdened in the pursuit of such claims, had to be accepted as a material consideration. Authorities acting in the public interest could not be expected generally to back their legal actions with the public funds with which they were entrusted to undertake their functions. It was generally appropriate to adopt a starting point that public authority claims brought in the public interest required separate consideration, and that no cross-undertaking should be exacted as a matter of course, or without considering what was fair in the particular circumstances of the case, *Hoffmann La Roche* followed (see paras 20-33 of judgment). (2) The distinction that B suggested between cross-undertakings for the protection of defendants and those for the protection of third parties did not hold good. In both cases, it was loss caused by the grant of an injunction in circumstances where the person incurring the loss was essentially innocent that was covered by the cross-undertaking (para.34). (3) There was a pragmatic basis for a distinction between specific costs and general loss. The rationale of *Hoffmann La Roche*, namely that public authorities should be able to enforce the law without being inhibited by the fear of cross-claims and of exposing financially the resources allocated by the state for their functions, applied with particular force to any open-ended cross-undertaking in respect of third party loss. It did not apply in the same way to a cross-undertaking in respect of third party costs (para.35). (4) Where an authority like the FSA, acting in pursuance of a public duty, sought an interim injunction, there was no general rule that it should be required to give a cross-undertaking in damages in respect of losses incurred by third parties. There were no particular circumstances why the FSA should be required to do so in the instant case (paras 36-41).

FINANCIAL SERVICES AUTHORITY v SINALOA GOLD PLC; *sub nom.* FINANCIAL SERVICES AUTHORITY v BARCLAYS BANK PLC, [2013] UKSC 11, [2013] 2 A.C. 28, Lord Neuberger (President), SC.

352. Defamation claims–Costs budgets–Defamation Proceedings Costs Management Scheme–Successful claimant's costs exceeding court-approved costs budget–Whether good reason for departing from costs budget

[CPR PD 51D Defamation Proceedings Cost Management Scheme 2000 para.5.6.]

The appellant (H) appealed against a decision that there was no good reason in detailed assessment proceedings to depart from the court-approved costs budget. H was a senior social worker employed by a local authority. Following the death of a child known as "Baby P", H had been the victim of a sustained and vitriolic campaign by a newspaper published by the respondent (N). H brought defamation proceedings against N. N defended the case vigorously and amended its defence four times. Shortly before trial N settled the proceedings by making a substantial payment and a statement in open court and publishing an apology. It agreed to pay H's costs on the standard basis to be assessed if not agreed. The parties were unable to reach agreement on H's costs and she commenced detailed assessment proceedings. N objected to H's bill of costs on the grounds that it exceeded the costs budget approved by the master pursuant to the Defamation

Proceedings Costs Management Scheme in CPR PD 51D. The senior costs judge considered as a preliminary issue whether there was good reason under para.5.6 of the practice direction to depart from the costs budget. He held that, although it was strongly arguable that H's costs were both reasonable and proportionate, she had failed to comply with the mandatory requirements of the practice direction to keep N informed of the fact that her budget was being exceeded; it followed that the parties were no longer on an equal footing within para.1.3 and there was no good reason to depart from the approved budget under para.5.6.

Held: Appeal allowed. (1) The judge had misunderstood the reference in para.1.3 of the practice direction to the parties being on an equal footing and took too narrow a view of what could amount to good reason under para.5.6. The reference to the parties being on an equal footing was concerned with the unfair exploitation of superior resources rather than with the provision of information about how expenditure was progressing. Failure to exchange information about expenditure as required by para.5.5 did not of itself put the parties on an unequal footing within para.1.3. In the instant case neither party was financially embarrassed and there was no inequality of arms (see paras 17-20 of judgment). (2) Compliance with all the requirements of the practice direction was not essential before a party could ask the court to depart from the approved budget. It was no more than one factor which the court could take into account. In the instant case both parties exceeded their budgets to a significant extent and when the case was before the court it had failed to take the initiative by enquiring whether the parties' costs were within the approved budgets (para.21). (3) It was open to the costs judge to find that the essential objects of the scheme had not been frustrated. In those circumstances he was obliged to consider all the circumstances of the case, including the extent to which the parties and the court had exercised their respective responsibilities under the scheme, the way in which the proceedings had developed, the response of H's solicitors to the demands imposed by the way in which N's case had developed and N's agreement to pay H's costs as part of the compromise of the claim (para.24). (4) Unless the court departed from the budget H would not be able to recover the costs of the action. That alone would not be enough; if it were the scheme would be otiose, but it was an important factor to the extent that on examination the court was persuaded that the costs actually incurred were reasonable and proportionate to what was at stake in the litigation. H's failure to observe the requirements of the practice direction did not put N at a significant disadvantage and did not seem to have led to the incurring of costs that were unreasonable or disproportionate. It would be unreasonable and disproportionate to penalise H by refusing to depart from the budget simply because she had not complied with the practice direction. That was all the more so in the context of proceedings which were constantly changing. H was not alone in failing to comply with the practice direction. Taking those matters together there was good reason to depart from the approved costs budget (paras 25-26). (5) (Obiter) The Civil Procedure Rule Committee had decided to adopt the Jackson Report recommendation that the management of costs by the court should form an integral part of the ordinary procedure governing claims allocated to the multi-track. Those rules when implemented would impose greater responsibility on the court for costs management and on the parties for keeping budgets under review and laid greater emphasis on the importance of the approved or agreed budget as providing a prima facie limit on the amount of recoverable costs. Although the court would have the power to depart from the approved or agreed budget if it was satisfied that there was good reason to do so, where budgets were approved by the court and revised at regular intervals the receiving party was unlikely to persuade the court that costs incurred in excess of the budget were reasonable and proportionate to what was at stake (para.28).

HENRY v NEWS GROUP NEWSPAPERS LTD, [2013] EWCA Civ 19, [2013] 2 All E.R. 840, Moore-Bick, L.J., CA (Civ Div).

353. Derivative claims–Limited liability partnerships–Whether Companies Act 2006 abolishing multiple derivative actions–Standing of limited liability partnership to bring action–Appropriateness of granting permission to continue action

[Companies Act 2006 (c.46) Pt 11; Civil Procedure Rules 1998 (SI 1998/3132) Pt 19; CPR PD 19 (Addition and Substitution of Parties) 1999.]

The applicant (U) applied for permission to continue a derivative action against the second respondent (P). U and P were the only members in a limited liability partnership (LLP) carrying on a property development joint venture. The venture was carried on by way of single purpose vehicles. The first respondent (F) was incorporated as one of the vehicles used for the development of a particular location. P was one of only two directors in F. U claimed, as a member of the LLP owning all of F's shares, that, while remaining a director of F, P misappropriated a valuable business opportunity for F for his personal benefit, in breach of his fiduciary duty to F. The issues for the court were whether (i) the multiple derivative action was known to English common law before the Companies Act 2006 came into force, and if so whether it survived the coming into force of the Act; (ii) if so, whether it mattered that the corporate body which owned F's shares and which intended to bring the action was an LLP; (iii) if not, whether permission should be granted for U to continue the claim.

Held: Application granted. (1) The Act did not do away with the multiple derivative action. Before 2006, there was a common law procedural device, the derivative action, by which the court could permit a person with the closest sufficient interest to litigate on behalf of a company by seeking relief for the company in respect of a cause of action vested in it. In 2006, Parliament identified the main version of that device, namely where locus standi was accorded to the wronged company's members, labelled it a "derivative claim", and enacted a comprehensive statutory code in relation to it. As a matter of construction, Parliament did not expressly abolish the whole of the common law derivative action in relation to companies (see paras 44-46 of judgment). (2) Once it was recognised that the extension of locus standi beyond the immediate members of the wronged company was based upon the need to find a suitably interested claimant to pursue the claim when the company was disabled from doing so, the precise nature of the corporate body which owned the wronged company's shares was of no legal relevance, provided that it was itself in wrongdoer control and had at least some members who were interested in seeing the wrong done to the company put right. The locus standi given to the member of the intermediate entity was not an aspect of that person's rights as a member, but simply the consequence of the law's search for a suitably interested representative of the wronged company. It was irrelevant that the LLP's members had no recourse to a statutory derivative claim; that lacuna related to the remedies for wrongs done to the LLP rather than to the company that it owned (paras 50-52). (3) CPR Pt 19, and in particular CPR PD 19 para.1 (a) (i), made it clear that the permission regime applied to "derivative claims, whether under Pt 11 of the Act or otherwise". The circumstances of the instant case were such as to satisfy the relevant exception to the rule in *Foss v Harbottle* 67 E.R. 189 that the only person with locus standi to pursue a claim on behalf of a company was the company itself, *Foss* considered. The claim was for breach of fiduciary duty, and that was a species of "fraud" within the meaning of the common law rule, *Estmanco (Kilner House) Ltd v Greater London Council* [1982] 1 W.L.R. 2, [1982] C.L.Y. 330 considered. Further, it was clear that P's status, as an equal owner of the LLP and as one of the only two directors of F, meant that there was wrongdoer control: it was a form of negative control by which P could, by refusing to agree, ensure that F did not bring proceedings against him. A refusal of permission to continue the multiple derivative action would be less likely to focus the parties upon the negotiation of a just solution to their dispute. The best means of maximising the prospect that negotiations would succeed was to give permission to continue the multiple derivative action, and then to stay proceedings for negotiation (paras 53-54, 61-62).

FORT GILKICKER LTD, *Re; sub nom.* UNIVERSAL PROJECT MANAGEMENT SERVICES LTD v FORT GILKICKER LTD, [2013] EWHC 348 (Ch), [2013] Ch. 551, Briggs, J., Ch D (Companies Ct).

354. Derivative claims–Permission–Bringing proceedings in company's name–Availability of alternative route under shareholder agreement

[Civil Procedure Rules 1998 (SI 1998/3132) Pt 7.]

The applicant (B) applied for permission to commence derivative proceedings in the name of the second respondent company (C). B, and the first respondent (H), were the sole directors and equal shareholders of C. C had been incorporated in order to acquire a site for redevelopment from a company (E). The purchase price was payable in stages, and following the payment of a deposit and the first stage payment, a payment of £3.5m for VAT was payable by January 2012 with a further instalment of £20.35m due in November 2012. B personally guaranteed those payments. In late January 2012, H informed B that he had fallen into financial difficulties, and on H's representations that E had agreed to the deferral of C's January 2012 payment, and due to H's description of his need as urgent, B agreed to advance H £3.5m prior to the execution of loan documentation. B then discovered that E had not in fact agreed to any payment deferral and requested repayment of the loan. H failed to repay the debt. At the date of the instant hearing, B had personally made up a shortfall of £1.5m under a revised payment schedule with E, and indicated that he intended to provide further funds when the next payment fell due. H argued that B should have commenced proceedings under cl.11 of a shareholder agreement, and that H lacked any power to oppose that course. B submitted that a derivative action was appropriate as without H's participation in forming an effective quorum under the shareholder agreement, C could not take steps to allow it to secure funding for the litigation.

Held: Application refused. (1) It was clear that under the shareholder agreement B was expressly given "full authority" on behalf of C to litigate the claim against H. If C needed to borrow money in order to fund the litigation, on any sensible construction of cl.11, B had authority to do so and H was bound to "take all steps within [his] power" to assist. However, there was no evidence that C needed to borrow any money to fund the litigation. The question then became whether permission to commence a derivative action ought to be granted where B could have arranged for C to commence proceedings in its own right against H (see paras 24-25 of judgment). (2) Although there was no rule that a derivative action could only be endorsed where alleged wrongdoers remained in control, the potential for a company itself to commence proceedings was a relevant consideration in the exercise of a court's discretion; it was impossible to avoid the conclusion that the mechanism of instituting a claim under cl.11 of the shareholder agreement against H had simply been overlooked. If there were any doubt as to whether B could avail himself of the provisions of cl.11, then the application of a flexible approach could have justified a derivative claim, *Wishart, Petitioner* [2009] CSIH 65, 2010 S.C. 16, [2010] C.L.Y. 4009 considered. Similarly, if B had indicated an intention to proceed under cl.11 and H had objected, that might have justified a derivative claim. However, those features did not apply in the instant case. There was nothing in the point that H had not responded to B pointing out the availability of the procedure under cl.11; it was not for H to tell B how to bring the action he threatened. Nor was there any significance in H's failure to take the point in his initial response to service of proceedings. The first guiding principle that normally a company should be the only party entitled to enforce a cause of action belonging to it, and that a member should only be able to maintain proceedings in relation to alleged wrongs done to the company only in exceptional circumstances, meant that the appropriate course was to reconstitute the proceedings as a CPR Pt 7 claim,

Cinematic Finance Ltd v Ryder [2010] EWHC 3387 (Ch), [2012] B.C.C. 797 applied (paras 25, 29-30, 32).

BAMFORD v HARVEY, [2012] EWHC 2858 (Ch), [2013] Bus. L.R. 589, Roth, J., Ch D.

355. Derivative claims–Unfairly prejudicial conduct–Permission to continue derivative claim–Existing unfair prejudice petition

[Companies Act 2006 (c.46) s.172, s.994.]

The applicant director and shareholder (P) applied for permission to continue a derivative claim on behalf of the fourth respondent company (C) against the first and second respondents (F), who were also directors and shareholders of C. P and F each held 50 per cent of C's shares. P alleged that F had made substantial unauthorised withdrawals and payments from C's account, and brought proceedings against them for unfairly prejudicial conduct under the Companies Act 2006 s.994 in which he sought to recover those monies. P also sought an order for the sale of F's shares to him. The third respondent (R) was a company controlled by F which P alleged had received some of those monies. P contended that urgency was required because F had continued to wrongfully take C's money after the petition was issued, and submitted that it was expedient to permit a derivative claim, in which he could seek summary judgment, because that would take significantly less time than the six-day estimate for his existing unfair prejudice petition. F argued that all of the issues could be resolved, if appropriate by seeking a summary hearing of the petition, in the existing proceedings.

Held: Application granted. The instant case was different to *Stainer v Lee* [2010] EWHC 1539 (Ch), [2011] B.C.C. 134, [2011] C.L.Y. 416 and *Kiani v Cooper* [2010] EWHC 577 (Ch), [2010] B.C.C. 463, [2010] C.L.Y. 339 because P sought an order enabling him to acquire F's 50 per cent shareholding and had brought and pursued proceedings to achieve that end, and in his petition he sought precisely what was sought in the derivative action, namely an order requiring F and R to repay the sums wrongfully taken or an order authorising him to bring civil proceedings in C's name, *Stainer* and *Kiani* considered. The onus was therefore on P to show why he should be permitted to change his mind and bring a derivative claim in addition to his petition. Whilst it was not for the instant court to determine the merits of P's claim, F had not provided a convincing explanation in response to P's allegations, either in their defence to the petition or in their response to the instant application. There was no question as to P's bona fides and the fact that he was doing his best to recover the money he claimed had been taken as quickly as possible, and to stop further money from being taken. That was exactly what any director, seeking to promote the interests of his company, would do in accordance with s.172 of the Act. Without pre-judging its outcome, there were grounds for P making a summary judgment application which was unlikely to take as long as six days to hear. Further, there were additional claims not made in the petition, which would have had to be amended to raise them. In those circumstances, a derivative claim was the better way of proceeding and the court granted P's application (see paras 18-20, 24 of judgment).

PHILLIPS v FRYER [2013] B.C.C. 176, Nicholas Strauss Q.C., Ch D.

356. Devolution issues–Investigatory powers–Alleged breach of human rights by police–Supreme Court's jurisdiction to hear as devolution issue

[Scotland Act 1998 (c.46) s.44(1), Sch.6 Pt I para.1; European Convention on Human Rights 1950 Art.6, Art.8.]

The appellant (K) appealed against the refusal of a devolution minute he had raised while being prosecuted for money laundering. The prosecution had relied on evidence gained from covert police surveillance of K outside some flats. The police had not obtained authorisation for such surveillance. K moved a devolution minute claiming that the police had acted unlawfully, that his rights under the European Convention on Human Rights 1950 art.8 had been breached, and that the evidence was inadmissible. The sheriff refused the minute and K was convicted. K appealed against the sheriff's decision, arguing that *Gilchrist (Kenneth Alexander) v HM Advocate* 2005 1 J.C. 34, [2005] C.L.Y. 5086, which had bound the sheriff, was wrongly decided. The High Court of Justiciary refused leave to appeal, but the Appeal Court granted leave to appeal to the Supreme Court. K's statement of facts and issues for the instant appeal stated that the issues were whether the police's unauthorised observations had breached his art.8 rights, and if so whether the Lord Advocate's act of leading the surveillance evidence at trial had breached his art.8 and art.6 rights.

Held: Appeal dismissed. (1) The court considered whether it had jurisdiction to hear the appeal. The only one of the questions listed under the Scotland Act 1998 Sch.6 Pt I para.1 that was relevant was that in para.1 (d), namely whether the exercise of a function by a member of the Scottish Government was incompatible with a Convention right. That provision had to be read with s.44(1), which described the members of the Scottish Government. Although it was unlawful for the police to act incompatibly with Convention rights, they were not members of the Scottish Government, so whether they had acted incompatibly with Convention rights was not a devolution issue within para.1 (d). The devolution minute had referred to the acts of the police. K had sought to argue that *Gilchrist* was wrongly decided, but unlike in *Gilchrist* he had made no mention of whether the act of the Lord Advocate, who was a member of the Scottish Government, in leading the surveillance evidence would compromise K's rights. The terms of the devolution minute did not, therefore, appear to raise a devolution issue at all and the instant court did not have jurisdiction to determine it. K sought to remedy that by the second question in the statement of facts and issues. However, he had given no notice of intention to raise that issue in his devolution minute, so there had been no determination of it in the High Court of Justiciary, and the instant court did not have an original jurisdiction in such matters, *Follen (Gary) v HM Advocate* [2001] UKPC D 2, [2001] 1 W.L.R. 1668, [2001] C.L.Y. 6352 applied. The proper course might well have been to dismiss the instant appeal as incompetent; however, the court would hear argument on the second issue, because the Crown had not opposed K's motion for leave to appeal on that point, the Appeal Court had given leave, and what K really sought to do was enable *Gilchrist* to be re-examined (see paras 11-14 of judgment). (2) The starting point was whether there had been a breach of K's art.8 rights. Any breach of art.8 in the obtaining of the evidence was due to acts of the police, not the Lord Advocate; the Lord Advocate was, however, responsible for leading the evidence, *McGibbon (David) v HM Advocate* 2004 J.C. 60, [2004] C.L.Y. 4620 considered. The lawfulness of interference with private life had to be distinguished from the fairness of using evidence at trial. The way evidence was obtained could infringe art.8, but the leading of that evidence might not be incompatible with art.6. Nevertheless, it would be wrong to consider art.6 without examining the underlying art.8 issue, where the key to the whole argument lay. There was a zone of interaction with others, even in a public context, which could fall within the scope of private life, *PG v United Kingdom (44787/98)* (2008) 46 E.H.R.R. 51, [2001] C.L.Y. 3576 considered. However, measures effected in a public place would not, without more, be regarded as interfering with art.8 rights. A police officer encountering a person who had committed a crime in a public place and noting down his observations did not interfere with art.8 rights. The question was whether it made any difference that notes of the person's movements were kept by the police covertly over several hours as part of a planned operation. The answer to that was found by considering whether K had had a reasonable expectation of privacy when he was in public view. That was the basis for *Gilchrist*, *Gilchrist* considered. Nothing suggested that K could have had any such expectation. Accordingly, the actions of the police had not amounted to an infringement of art.8. Both the issues in the statement of facts would be answered in the negative (paras 15-22).

KINLOCH (JAMES) v HM ADVOCATE, [2012] UKSC 62, [2013] 2 A.C. 93, Lord Hope, J.S.C. (Deputy President), SC.

357. Directions–Tribunals–Circumstances in which appropriate to set aside tribunal directions under r.6(5) Tribunal Procedure (First-tier Tribunal) (Tax Chamber) Rules 2009

[Tribunals, Courts and Enforcement Act 2007 (c.15) Sch.1 Pt 4 para.14; Tribunal Procedure (First-tier Tribunal) (Tax Chamber) Rules 2009 (SI 2009/273) r.5(2), r.6(5).]

The applicant company (D) applied to have certain directions set aside and sought to have its application heard by a named judge. During the course of D's appeal against a decision concerning the respondent Revenue, a judge had directed that no evidence might be served in relation to dealings with or at a particular bank. A later judge set that direction aside and also made a direction permitting the Revenue to adduce and rely upon certain evidence. D now applied to have the later judge's directions set aside and the earlier direction reinstated. It also applied to set aside identical directions made by both judges that costs in respect of late evidence should be reserved until later. The issues were (i) whether the application should be heard by D's preferred judge; (ii) whether the later directions should be set aside; (iii) whether the costs directions should be set aside.

Held: Applications refused. (1) The tribunal was independent. It was axiomatic that neither party could choose the judge or panel which heard their case on any interim application. Under the Tribunals, Courts and Enforcement Act 2007 Sch.1 Pt 4 para.14, the allocation of a judge to a hearing was solely within the discretion of the president of the tribunal and was not something in respect of which it was proper for a party to make an application. Nor was it within the power of the tribunal judge to allow such an application. The power of a tribunal judge to make a direction was as set out in the Tribunal Procedure (First-tier Tribunal) (Tax Chamber) Rules 2009 r.5(2). That only permitted a direction in relation to the "conduct or disposal of proceedings". It was implicit that that referred to the conduct of proceedings by the parties. A judge was not given power to make directions to the tribunal. The power of a judge to make directions could not therefore include a direction determining the judge or panel to hear the proceedings (paras 6-9 of judgment). (2) The application to set aside the directions of the second judge was made under r.6(5) of the Rules. Legislation, including secondary legislation, had to be interpreted in such a way to avoid anomalous or absurd results. If any and every direction could be challenged merely by an application to set it aside, the tribunal and parties in any appeal could become ensnared in an endless game of ping pong, with one party challenging a direction it did not like unless and until it was set aside and the other party then challenging the setting aside of that direction. That would be an absurd and anomalous result, which Parliament could not have intended. The use of the word "may" in r.6(5) had to be interpreted, first, as leaving it open for a party to challenge a direction by another means and, secondly as not being a liberty which could be exercised in every case of challenge. Substantive decisions could only be set aside in certain cases and it seemed likely that Parliament intended that directions could be set aside in similar situations. The White Book stated that in respect of the High Court's power to "vary or revoke" any earlier order, that did not include a power to reverse itself simply because it had changed its mind: the court could not act as an appellate court from its own orders. A similar state of affairs existed in the instant tribunal. Parliament only intended r.6(5) to be used in limited circumstances, particularly where there had been a change of circumstances; an obvious error of law; procedural irregularity; or a party did not appear and was not represented at the directions hearing. A judge would only set aside a direction where it was in the interests of justice to do so. The above might not be an exclusive list of all the circumstances in which r.6(5) might be used, but additional circumstances in which it would be appropriate would be exceptional and would not include where a party considered that the original direction was wrong. The only proper course of action in such a case would be to appeal the direction (paras 14-23). In the instant case, D did not suggest that circumstances had changed, that there had been a procedural irregularity or that it had not appeared or been represented at the hearing. It applied to set aside the directions on the grounds that it considered them to be wrong. However, there had not been a clear, unarguable error of law, such that an appeal was bound to succeed. The later judge had been entitled to set aside the earlier direction because it was clear that there had been a change of circumstances and there was also an obvious error of law (paras 24-34). (3) The direction in relation to costs would not be set aside. Circumstances had not changed and it was not obviously wrong in law (paras 39-40).

DDR DISTRIBUTIONS LTD v REVENUE AND CUSTOMS COMMISSIONERS, [2012] UKFTT 443 (TC), [2012] S.F.T.D. 1249, Judge Barbara Mosedale, FTT (Tax).

358. Disclosure–Specific disclosure–Issues of jurisdiction in personal injuries claim–Lack of evidence to support contention company's central administration in England–Whether appropriate to order specific disclosure

[Civil Procedure Rules 1998 (SI 1998/3132) Pt 18, r.31.2; Regulation 44/2001 on jurisdiction and the recognition and enforcement of judgments in civil and commercial matters Art.60.]

The claimants (X) applied for specific disclosure and for further information from the defendant company (Y). X had claimed damages for personal injuries from Y, which was a company incorporated under the laws of South Africa. X commenced the proceedings in England on the basis that Y was in fact domiciled in England and was part of a multi-national group of companies and that a company (Z), which was incorporated in England, was the parent of Y. Y applied for declarations that the English courts did not have jurisdiction to hear the claims as it was domiciled in South Africa and not in England within the meaning of Regulation 44/2001 art.60. It was X's case that they had a good arguable case that Y's central administration and its principal place of business was in England and sought orders under CPR Pt 18 and r.31.2 in order to support that proposition.

Held: Application granted in part. (1) The location of the central administration of a company was not necessarily the same as the location of the principal place of business or of a company's registered office. The central administration of a company was where decisions were made and where the entrepreneurial management took place and was not simply where a company's board meetings and AGMs were held. Y was a separate company from Z and the fact that Y was a wholly-owned subsidiary did not mean that it had the same central administration as Z. However, on the evidence, X had an arguable case that the headquarters of Z, in England, was the place where management entrepreneurial decisions relating to Y's business were taken. If X relied solely on asserting that X's principal place of business was in England, on the material available, they could not establish they had an arguable case (see paras 42, 59-61 of judgment). (2) There was a striking absence of any direct and first-hand evidence to support X's contentions on jurisdiction. Y alone had access to the material relevant to determining where its managerial entrepreneurial decisions were taken. There was also a great disparity in the financial resources open to the parties. If no orders were granted there was a great risk that X would be unfairly disadvantaged when contesting the jurisdiction issue. It was appropriate to order disclosure of certain documents but to refuse to order Y to provide the information sought. A large number of the requests for information would be answered by the disclosed documents; there was a lot of duplication between the Pt.18 requests and the r.31.2 requests for specific disclosure. Further, it was possible, following disclosure, that the focus of X's claim might change making it premature and unnecessary to order the supply of further information at the instant stage of proceedings (paras 69, 72-74)

VAVA v ANGLO AMERICAN SOUTH AFRICA LTD; YOUNG v ANGLO AMERICAN SOUTH AFRICA LTD, [2012] EWHC 1969 (QB), [2012] 2 C.L.C. 684, Silber, J., QBD.

359. Disclosure and inspection–Public interest immunity–Public authority objecting to disclosure on public interest grounds–Application of Data Protection Act 1998 and CPR

[Data Protection Act 1998 (c.29) s.35; Civil Procedure Rules 1998 (SI 1998/3132) Pt 31; European Convention on Human Rights 1950 Art.6, Art.8.]

The appellant local authority appealed a judge's decision to allow disclosure of unredacted documents in proceedings brought by the respondent (D) for damages in respect of assaults alleged to have been committed by staff at a young people's centre for which the local authority was responsible. D had been a resident at the centre between 1980 and 1984. D's solicitors had written to the local authority intimating a claim and requesting sight of certain documents including the personnel files of members of staff against whom the allegations had been made. The letter referred to the Data Protection Act 1998, but a fee was not included and it more closely resembled a Pre-Action Protocol letter of claim. Some redacted documents were disclosed, but the local authority objected to disclosure of the personnel files. In the course of the instant proceedings, an order for redacted disclosure of those documents was made, although the application was erroneously approached on the basis that the governing regime was the 1998 Act. That order was successfully appealed and unredacted disclosure ordered.

Held: Appeal dismissed. It was misleading to refer to a duty to protect data as if it were a category of exemption from disclosure or inspection. The court was enabled and required under CPR Pt 31 to excuse disclosure or inspection on public interest grounds. In a case such as the instant one, it might be misleading to describe the issue as one of public interest immunity. The requisite balancing exercise, which depended upon the context of the particular litigation, was between a party's right to a fair trial at common law and pursuant to the European Convention on Human Rights 1950 art.6 and the rights of his opponent or a non-party to privacy or confidentiality which might most conveniently be protected by art.8. It was a distraction to start with the 1998 Act, as the Act itself acknowledged. A data controller was exempt under s.35 of the 1998 Act from the non-disclosure provisions where disclosure was required in the context of litigation. Effectively, the court was left to determine the issue by applying the appropriate balancing exercise under the CPR whereupon the court's decision impacted upon the operation of disclosure under the 1998 Act. Public interest immunity would arise in some contexts. However, it was wrong to treat all cases in which a public authority sought exemption from a disclosure or inspection obligation on public interest grounds as being a case of public interest immunity in the strict sense. In the instant case, the disputed documents were not social work records, but were not dissimilar in nature and should attract the same approach, *R (A Child) (Care: Disclosure: Nature of Proceedings), Re* [2002] 1 F.L.R. 755, [2002] C.L.Y. 1621 considered. The approach required that (a) obligations in relation to disclosure and inspection arose only when the "relevance" test was satisfied. Relevance could include "train of enquiry" points which were not merely fishing expeditions. That was a matter of fact, degree and proportionality; (b) if the relevance test was satisfied, then it was for the party in possession of the document, or who would be adversely affected by its disclosure or inspection, to assert exemption from disclosure or inspection; (c) any ensuing dispute fell to be determined ultimately by a balancing exercise, having regard to the fair trial rights of the party seeking disclosure or inspection and the privacy or confidentiality rights of the other party and any person whose right might require protection. Consideration of competing Convention rights would generally be involved; the denial of disclosure or inspection was limited to circumstances where such denial was strictly necessary; (d) in some cases the balance might need to be struck by a limited or restricted order which respected a protected interest by such things as redaction. Again, the limitation had to satisfy the test of strict necessity. The judge should not have been distracted by the 1998 Act as if it imposed additional requirements. However, ultimately his approach addressed relevance and concluded with the balancing of "the prejudice to the applying party of being deprived of information against the prejudice to the third party as a result of the disclosure". He applied a test of strict necessity, although on the basis that D had satisfied the test, whereas it had been for the local authority to establish that it was strictly necessary not to disclose. Notwithstanding those issues, his approach was substantially correct and his conclusion unassailable (see paras 21-24 of judgment).

DURHAM CC v D; *sub nom.* D v DURHAM CC, [2012] EWCA Civ 1654, [2013] 1 W.L.R. 2305, Maurice Kay, L.J. (VP, CA Civ), CA (Civ Div).

360. Disputing the court's jurisdiction–Default judgments–Connection between claims with separate defendants–Whether claims should be joined to avoid irreconcilable judgments

[Civil Procedure Rules 1998 (SI 1998/3132) r.13.1; Regulation 44/2001 on jurisdiction and the recognition and enforcement of judgments in civil and commercial matters.]

The appellant Latvian nationals (V), who were defendants in a fraud claim brought by the respondent Latvian company (L), appealed against a decision that the English courts had jurisdiction to entertain the whole of the claims against them under Council Regulation (EC) No 44/2001. V were former senior employees of L, who had been dismissed following claims of fraud and allegations of breach of fiduciary duty arising out of contracts between L and two other companies (M and R), who were also defendants in L's action. L's claim was that V conspired between themselves and with others to siphon funds from L under the cover of sham consultancy agreements, known as the media focus agreements. Default judgments had been entered against both M and R. Judgment in default was initially obtained against V but those judgments were set aside under CPR r.13.1. It was common ground that the burden was on L to demonstrate a good arguable case that the English courts had jurisdiction under Regulation 44/2001 which meant that it had to establish that its argument on the material available was much better than the argument against it. The issues were whether (i) it was material that L had obtained judgment in default against M; (ii) L had a good arguable case that M was party to the wider conspiracy alleged against V; (iii) the wider claim which L made against V was sufficiently connected with the claim against M to ground the English court with jurisdiction to hear it pursuant to art.6. V accepted that the media focus agreements were fraudulent schemes and that there was a good arguable case that V were parties to the fraud but submitted that L had not shown a good arguable case that M was a party to any conspiracy which went beyond the media focus agreements.

Held: Appeal dismissed. (1) It was not material that L had obtained judgment in default against M. European and domestic case law established that the relevant time for determining whether the court had jurisdiction under art.6 was the time at which the jurisdiction was invoked, which was the date of issue of the claim form. The fact that M did not respond to the proceedings and L obtained a judgment against it in default was immaterial. It would be absurd if the proper construction of the regulations required L to withhold from obtaining judgment against M solely for the court to retain its jurisdiction in relation to other defendants (see paras 30-34 of judgment). (2) There was a good arguable case that M had been party to a conspiracy of the scope alleged against V and that M and R had been parties to a fraudulent conspiracy with V, and not merely two distinct conspiracies. The evidence showed a prima facie case that V orchestrated the execution of the media focus agreements, using shell companies with nominee directors as vehicles for defrauding L (paras 35-37). (3) If that conclusion was wrong, the claim that L brought against V was sufficiently connected with the claim as against M for the court to have jurisdiction under art.6. On the hypothesis that L had failed to establish a good arguable case that M was party to a conspiracy that went beyond the media focus agreement, the connecting factors between R and M's respective services agreements were nevertheless strong. Those connecting factors made it expedient for the claims to be heard together to avoid the risk of irreconcilable judgments (paras 38-46).

LATMAR HOLDINGS CORP v MEDIA FOCUS LTD; *sub nom.* LINUZS v LATMAR HOLDINGS CORP, [2013] EWCA Civ 4, [2013] I.L.Pr. 19, Pill, L.J., CA (Civ Div).

361. Disputing the court's jurisdiction–Foreign property–Claim relating to Egyptian property–Jurisdiction of English court–Scope of exclusionary rule

[Regulation 44/2001 on jurisdiction and the recognition and enforcement of judgments in civil and commercial matters Art.22.]

The appellant Egyptian national (H) appealed against a decision ([2012] EWHC 1871 (Ch)) to dismiss his application challenging the English court's jurisdiction to hear a claim of unjust enrichment by the respondent (S). S, who was British, claimed to have advanced monies to H to purchase an Egyptian property. His case was that H was to hold the moneys pending completion and that they were repayable on demand before completion or if the transaction did not proceed. He claimed that H never transferred title to the property and commenced proceedings in England. H unsuccessfully challenged the English court's jurisdiction. The judge concluded that it was impossible to characterise the claim as relating to title to foreign land. He said that as the purchase was never completed and the property had been onward sold, S was not raising a claim as owner, and it was well-established that in personam claims were not covered by the exclusionary rule of jurisdiction. He stated that the English court could order specific performance of an agreement to sell foreign lands, and there was no distinction in principle between seeking completion by specific performance and seeking recovery of the purchase price of a property, the sale of which had not completed. He concluded that any judgment would have no effect on title, and would not involve the court adjudicating upon a disputed claim of title. The issue was whether the English court did not have jurisdiction to entertain the proceedings because, pursuant to the exclusionary rule first established in *British South Africa Co v Companhia de Mocambique* [1893] A.C. 602, it had no jurisdiction to entertain proceedings for the determination of the title to, or the right to possession of, immovable property situated outside England, except where the claim was based on a contract or equity between the parties. H submitted that the proceedings were principally concerned with ownership of immovable property in Egypt. He contended that the claim of unjust enrichment was merely an attempt to dress up a substantive claim involving the disputed title and/or trespass to the property. He placed emphasis on the judge's mistaken conclusion that it was common ground that there had been no completion.

Held: Appeal dismissed. (1) It was long established that before the exclusionary rule could apply, the proceedings had to raise directly the issue of title to foreign land, *British South Africa* followed and *St Pierre v South American Stores (Garth & Chaves) Ltd* [1936] 1 K.B. 382 considered. A similar rule had developed in EU law and was contained in Regulation 44/2001 art.22(1), which provided that in proceedings which had as their object rights in rem in immovable property or tenancies of immovable property, the courts of the Member State in which the property was situated would have exclusive jurisdiction regardless of domicile. The same rule applied under the Lugano Convention. The fact that proceedings involved a right in rem in immovable property or had some link with immovable property was not sufficient to bring the exclusionary rule into play. Thus an action for rescission of a contract of sale and for damages did not constitute proceedings which had as their object rights in rem in immovable property, *Gaillard v Chekili (C518/99)* [2001] E.C.R. I-2771, [2001] C.L.Y. 823 considered. Similarly, actions for damages based on infringements of rights in rem or on damage to property in which rights in rem existed did not fall within its scope, *Land Oberosterreich v CEZ as (C-343/04)* [2006] 2 All E.R. (Comm) 665, [2007] C.L.Y. 666 considered (see paras 14-15 of judgment). (2) If H pleaded by way of defence that there was completion under the contract, the court might have to decide whether that took place as an issue of contractual performance. However, that was not sufficient to bring the proceedings within the exclusionary rule because: (a) they were not proceedings for the determination of the title to or the right to possession of land situated outside England in the sense that that was the object of the proceedings; (b) any question of in whom title in the property was vested at any particular time would be purely incidental to the proceedings, which were principally concerned with questions of contractual performance and rights arising from alleged non-performance; (c) the court would not be required to adjudicate upon a current disputed claim of title, it being common ground that the title to the property was vested in a subsequent purchaser. Accordingly, there was no question of a judgment in the instant proceedings having any effect on title to land situated abroad. Any remedy which S might receive would be a personal remedy for the recovery of monies from H. There was no basis for H's suggestion that any determination by the English courts of whether the original transaction was completed might affect the validity of subsequent transactions in Egypt or the validity of the current owner's ownership. The instant case did not fall within the scope of the exclusionary rule, *British South Africa* followed. In any event, it fell within a long-established exception to the rule, which said that an English court might, as between parties before it, give an in personam judgment to enforce contractual or equitable rights in respect of immovable property situated in a foreign country, *Pattni v Ali* [2006] UKPC 51, [2007] 2 A.C. 85, [2007] C.L.Y. 448 considered (paras 17-19).

STEVENS v HAMED; HAMED v STEVENS, [2013] EWCA Civ 911, [2013] I.L.Pr. 37, Arden, L.J., CA (Civ Div).

362. Disputing the court's jurisdiction–Jurisdiction clauses–Fraudulent scheme involving companies entering into contracts containing English jurisdiction clauses–Piercing corporate veil–Whether company controller deemed to consent to English jurisdiction

[Regulation 44/2001 on jurisdiction and the recognition and enforcement of judgments in civil and commercial matters Art.23.]

The appellants (G) appealed against a decision ([2012] EWHC 1887 (Comm), [2012] 2 Lloyd's Rep. 365, [2012] C.L.Y. 473) that the English courts had no jurisdiction over their claim against the respondent (L). G claimed that a number of vessels had been chartered to offshore companies as part of a fraudulent scheme: the charters had been at less than the market rate, and the vessels had then been sub-chartered at the market rate, thereby transferring the difference to the offshore companies for the benefit of those who were said to control them including L. The charters were on the Shelltime 4 form containing exclusive English jurisdiction clauses. Relying on those clauses G sued the offshore companies in England and obtained judgment against them. G also sought to sue L in England on the basis that by piercing the corporate veil of the offshore companies he could be made a party to the charters and the jurisdiction clauses. The judge rejected that way of putting the case. He also held that L had not shown any willingness to consent to English jurisdiction for the purposes of Regulation 44/2001 art.23 if that could be done without L being party to the relevant contracts. G appealed on that issue. G submitted that the judge had erred in requiring L to show willingness to agree to the jurisdiction of the court; the jurisprudence of the European Court of Justice was that deemed consensus could be sufficient under art.23 irrespective of whether a defendant actually knew about the jurisdiction clause in question or intended to agree to it and although it was not possible to establish any actual consensus on the facts.

Held: Appeal dismissed. Whether a person against whom jurisdiction was asserted by virtue of an agreement within art.23 had consented to jurisdiction was an autonomous question of EU law, *Powell Duffryn Plc v Petereit (C-214/89)* [1992] E.C.R. I-1745, [1992] C.L.Y. 4826 applied (see para.42 of judgment). That agreement had to be clearly and precisely demonstrated as a matter of fact, *Estasis Salotti di Colzani Aimo e Gianmario Colzani v RUWA Polstereimaschinen GmbH (24/76)* [1976] E.C.R. 1831, [1977] C.L.Y. 1242 applied (para.43). Even if there was a good arguable case that L was a beneficial owner and controller of the offshore companies and that they were incorporated for the purpose of diverting profits from G, that did not lead automatically to the consequence that the corporate veil should be pierced, *VTB Capital Plc v Nutritek International Corp* [2013] UKSC 5, [2013] 2 A.C. 337 applied (paras 44-47). Consideration of the ECJ cases showed that "deemed consent" was only available where there had been a transfer of the contract or of all the rights and obligations for which it provided and that was not the position in the instant case, *Refcomp SpA v Axa Corporate Solutions Assurance SA (C-543/10)* [2013] 1 All E.R. (Comm) 1201 considered. The question whether to pierce the corporate veil appeared to be one of national rather than Community law. In the present state of English law, the court could only pierce the corporate veil when a person was under an existing legal obligation or liability or subject to an existing legal restriction which he deliberately evaded or whose enforcement he deliberately frustrated by interposing a company under his control, *Petrodel Resources Ltd v Prest* [2013] UKSC 34, [2013] 2 A.C. 415, [2013] 9 C.L. 193 applied (paras 64-65).

ANTONIO GRAMSCI SHIPPING CORP v RECOLETOS LTD; *sub nom.* ANTONIO GRAMSCI SHIPPING CORP v LEMBERGS, [2013] EWCA Civ 730, [2013] 4 All E.R. 157, Lloyd, L.J., CA (Civ Div).

363. Employers' liability–Fixed costs–Personal injury claims–Pre-action protocols

THE CIVIL PROCEDURE (AMENDMENT NO.6) RULES 2013, SI 2013/SI 1695; made under the Civil Procedure Act 1997 s.2. In force: July 31, 2013; .

These Rules make the following amendments to the Civil Procedure Rules 1998: r.14.1B (admissions made under the road traffic accidents protocol); r.27.14 (costs on the small claims track); Pt 36 (offers to settle); and Pt 45 (fixed costs), including the insertion of new section IIIA. These amendments concern the extension of the Pre-Action Protocol for Low Value Personal Injury Claims in Road Traffic Accidents (RTA protocol) to include claims up the value of £25,000, and to most employers' liability and public liability claims, via the introduction of the Pre-Action Protocol for Low Value Personal Injury (Employers' Liability and Public Liability) Claims.

364. Expedited hearings–Prejudice–Listings enquiries revealing no other litigant affected–Whether proper basis for granting order for expedition

The applicants (J) applied for an expedited trial of community trade mark infringement allegations they had made against the respondent (Z). J were members of a group of companies (M) that included some of the world's largest toy and game manufacturers. M owned the SCRABBLE brand in the European Union and the rest of the world, save for North America. It was the name of a well-known word board game that used square tiles with rounded edges, each bearing a centred letter and a numeral representing the letter's score in the bottom right-hand corner. M had developed several electronic versions, including "Scrabble Scramble", which had been successfully developed as an app for smart phones and similar devices. Z, the world's largest social gaming company and a leading developer of apps, had a range of Scramble games that it had developed. It launched a digital game for similar devices, called "Scramble with Friends". J alleged that Scramble with Friends infringed four United Kingdom registered trade marks: the word marks SCRAMBLE and SCRABBLE; the device mark SCRABBLE and a "tile" device mark. J also alleged that Scramble with Friends' get-up, unlike earlier Scramble-related games, was intended to give a similar overall impression to that used in Scrabble products, including the use of similarly-shaped tiles, the use of colours, and the use of a numeral on the tiles. J were also developing a new digital game under its SCRAMBLE mark to be launched in about eight months' time. It was foreseen that the trial would take place in one years' time. J submitted that its development of a new digital game was greatly prejudiced by Z's Scramble with Friends, that there was a risk of serious and unjustifiable damage to the Scrabble brand in J's digital version if it had to remain in competition with Z's game, and that a slot during court vacation that had opened up meant that no other litigant would be affected if expedition were ordered.

Held: Application refused. (1) An order for expedition could only be justified on the basis of real, objectively-viewed, urgency. It was only on the basis of such urgency that giving preference in the allocation of court time over other court users could be justified, *Daltel Europe Ltd (In Liquidation) v Makki (No.2)* [2004] EWHC 1631 (Ch) applied. The main factors in considering such an application were: the decision to expedite a hearing was discretionary; the court had to have regard to the wider responsibility it had to other litigants and not just the parties' position; it was always relevant to look at the parties' procedural history in which delay, although not conclusive, was a relevant factor; a respondent's attitude to expedition was comparatively unimportant unless it could show prejudice; and the threshold question, which was whether urgency was justified at all. Only once that urgency had been established was it necessary to consider which form of expedition would be the most appropriate, *Warner-Lambert Co LLC v Teva UK Ltd* [2011] EWHC 2018 (Ch), [2011] F.S.R. 44, [2011] C.L.Y. 1964 applied. Additionally, cogent reasons were required to give preference to one set of litigants over others. In the instant case, both J and Z were large players, each able to look after their own interests and meet any order for damages that might be ordered. A decision had been taken by Z to introduce its product with similarities to J's product, sailing as close to the wind as it could. There was an inevitable overlap where the parties' products would co-exist in the marketplace, and where J had not sought injunctive relief the sole question was the potential length of the damaging period. Although a speedy resolution was desirable from all points of view, there was no cogent justification for the matter to jump its place in the queue. Trade mark matters did not occupy a special position or enjoy a presumption in favour of expedition, and there was no reason to depart from general principles where the question was ultimately one of discretion exercised judicially with regard to the effect on both parties and the wider interests of litigants (see paras 18, 20, 22, 38-40 of judgment). (2) Although J had made enquiries with the listings officer as to whether any other matter would be affected if the instant matter were expedited and discovered that no other case would lose its hearing, an order for expedition ought not to be considered on such a narrow basis, *WL Gore & Associates GMBH v Geox Spa* [2008] EWCA Civ 622 considered and *Warner-Lambert* applied. Although prejudice to a particular litigant could not be identified, common sense suggested that someone would be disadvantaged where litigants were allowed to jump the queue (paras 26-28).

JW SPEAR & SONS LTD v ZYNGA INC, [2012] EWHC 1374 (Ch), [2013] F.S.R. 15, Henderson, J., Ch D.

365. Extensions of time–Disclosure–Effect of overriding objective amendment to include enforcement of compliance with orders–Appropriateness of unless order in conjoined actions

[Civil Procedure Rules 1998 (SI 1998/3132) r.1.1, r.3.1 (2) (a).]

The applicant liquidators (L) applied for an extension of time to comply with a disclosure order made by consent in conjoined proceedings concerning two companies (Atrium and Connor). In the Atrium proceedings, there had been four disclosure orders but the first and second respondents (X) were unhappy with the disclosure given and applied for an unless order for further disclosure. Pending the hearing L's solicitors embarked on a manual examination of over 300 boxes of documents. Shortly before the hearing L instructed new solicitors. By the consent order the parties agreed to allow a further six months for the disclosure exercise, and L were ordered to pay X's costs. After two months a decision was made to scan and upload the documents to an e-disclosure platform. Five days before the disclosure deadline, L applied for the disclosure order to be varied to allow a further three months for disclosure. The issues were whether (i) an extension of time should be granted; (ii) any extension should be made on "unless" terms; (iii) the disclosure order should be varied to provide for indemnity costs.

Held: Application granted. (1) The court had to exercise its discretion to extend time under CPR r.3.1 (2) (a) by having regard to the overriding objective in CPR r.1.1, which had been amended in April 2013 to include the enforcement of compliance with orders, *Robert v Momentum Services Ltd* [2003] EWCA Civ 299, [2003] 1 W.L.R. 1577, [2003] C.L.Y. 391 applied. The court would scrutinise an extension application more rigorously than it might have done before the amendment, and it had to firmly discourage any easy assumption that an extension of time would be granted if there would be no obvious prejudice to the other side. On the other hand, it was important not to encourage unreasonable opposition to extensions that were applied for in time and which involved no significant fresh prejudice. Although court orders were to be complied with even if made by consent, there might be some orders relating to specified stages in trial preparation, such as disclosure, where there might be so many imponderables when making the order that the date for compliance could not sensibly be regarded as written in stone. Everything would always depend on the circumstances. It would be unfortunate if the new emphasis on compliance with orders led to the rejection of reasonable requests for an extension in the hope that the court might be persuaded to refuse any extension at all. In the instant case an extension would be granted (see paras 51-54 of judgment). (2) The stage had been reached where it was appropriate to make an unless order in the Atrium proceedings because of the long and unsatisfactory history of disclosure, the deficiencies in L's attempts to comply with the disclosure order, and the increased emphasis which the court was now obliged to accord to compliance with court orders under the overriding objective. However, it would not be right to make an unless order in the Connor proceedings. There had been no previous disclosure order in the Connor proceedings and it was the first extension that had been sought. The parties had agreed that disclosure in the two proceedings should be combined, but it would be unfortunate if L's default in the Atrium proceedings were also to be visited on them in the Connor proceedings. Justice would be done if the sanction for non-compliance with the extension was confined to the Atrium proceedings (paras 64-65). (3) It would be wrong in principle to revisit the basis of assessment of the costs order. The work carried out by L's former solicitors was not valueless, and the deficiencies in L's conduct of disclosure had been reflected in the order that they pay the costs of X's disclosure application (paras 69-71).

ATRIUM TRAINING SERVICES LTD (IN LIQUIDATION), *Re*; CONNOR WILLIAMS LTD, *Re*; *sub nom.* SMAILES v McNALLY, [2013] EWHC 1562 (Ch), [2013] 5 Costs L.O. 707, Henderson, J., Ch D.

366. Family proceedings–Fees

THE FAMILY PROCEEDINGS FEES (AMENDMENT) ORDER 2013, SI 2013/SI 2013/1407 (L.10); made under the Courts Act 2003 s.92, s.108. In force: July 1, 2013; .

This Order amends the Family Proceedings Fees Order 2008 (SI 2008/1054). It increases certain fees that are payable in family proceedings in England and Wales in the Senior Courts and county courts by the cumulative rate of inflation since those fees were last increased.

367. Fees–Non-contentious probate proceedings

THE NON-CONTENTIOUS PROBATE FEES (AMENDMENT) ORDER 2013, SI 2013/SI 2013/1408 (L.11); made under the Courts Act 2003 s.92. In force: July 1, 2013; .

This Order amends the Non-Contentious Probate Fees Order 2004 (SI 2004/3120). It increases the fee for copies of any document which are made available on a computer disk or in other electronic form from £4 to £6 for each copy.

368. Fraud–Setting aside–Bank obtained summary judgment to recover advances–Setting aside judgment as obtained by fraud–Refusing anti-suit injunction on grounds of "unclean hands"

The appellant bank (R) appealed against a decision ([2012] EWHC 1278 (Comm), [2012] 2 C.L.C. 109, [2013] 2 C.L. 40) refusing to grant an anti-suit injunction to restrain proceedings in the United States, and the first to fourth respondents (H) cross-appealed against the dismissal of their claim to set aside a judgment in favour of R. H were part of a US group which had arranged a collateralised debt obligation (CDO) which involved the acquisition of a portfolio of loans and the issue of notes by a special purpose vehicle. R had financed the purchase of the loans. Because of the collapse of the financial markets the notes were never issued and the transaction never closed. In those circumstances the interim servicing deed entered into by the parties provided for the sale of the loans by R. R invited market participants to bid for the loans in an auction process, but purchased all the loans itself. It then sought to recover the shortfall from H and obtained summary judgment on liability. That decision was upheld on appeal. In the subsequent proceedings to determine the amount to be credited in H's favour as a result of the acquisition of the loans by R, it transpired that for accounting reasons R had decided to keep some of the loans and had transferred them from its trading book to its banking book before the auction process. H alleged that the auction process was accordingly a sham and that R was in breach of contract and its equitable duties as mortgagee. H claimed that if R had properly auctioned the loans there would have been no shortfall. The judge at the quantum hearing held that R had misconducted itself but that H owed a sum to R on the proper valuation of the loans. The respondents then commenced proceedings against R in Texas alleging fraud and R applied for an anti-suit injunction. H then claimed that the original judgment on liability should be set aside as having been obtained by fraud. The judge refused to set aside the liability judgment holding that concealment by R's employee (G) of the transfer of the loans before the auction had not been dishonest and that there would be no point in setting the judgment aside since the decision in the quantum judgment was correct and reflected the true position. He held that the Texan claims fell within an exclusive English jurisdiction clause but that R was not entitled to an anti-suit injunction because it had "unclean hands".

Held: Appeal dismissed, cross-appeal allowed. (1) There had been more than simple concealment of the transfer of the loans before the auction. The evidence and the findings of the judge overall led to the inevitable conclusion that at the time of the liability hearing and judgment G was continuing positively to mislead both H and the court as to what had happened in relation to the loans and was doing so consciously and deliberately. The acts of G were to be attributed to R, so there was a positive misstatement by R of the true position (see para.122 of judgment). The evidence and findings of the judge led to the conclusion that G's misstatement or concealment was dishonest (para.127). But for the deliberate and dishonest concealment there would have been no summary judgment on liability because R would not have applied for it (paras 134-139). The liability judgment had to be set aside as obtained by fraud. The fact that, subsequently, the judge was able to conduct the quantum trial on proper evidence was not relevant, *Odyssey Re (London) Ltd & anr v OIC Run-Off Ltd (formerly Orion Insurance Co plc)* applied (paras 141-142). It followed that the Court of Appeal judgment on liability and the quantum judgment had to be set aside (paras 144-145). (2) When G gave his evidence he had the status necessary to make his evidence that of R for the purposes of the "unclean hands" issue, *Odyssey Re (london) Ltd v Oic Run-off Ltd* applied (paras 155-157). The judge was entitled to conclude that there was a sufficient "immediate and necessary" relation between the misconduct of G and the claim by R for equitable relief in the form of an anti-suit injunction, such that R was to be denied it under the "unclean hands" doctrine. The judge had found that R, through G, had lied about central facts on which H founded the allegations that were made against R in the Texan proceedings; R, through G, had relied on that false evidence in the course of the English proceedings whose very object was to stop the Texan action; the misconduct could not be more immediately related to the equity that was sued for (paras 158-171).

ROYAL BANK OF SCOTLAND PLC v HIGHLAND FINANCIAL PARTNERS LP, [2013] EWCA Civ 328, [2013] 1 C.L.C. 596, Maurice Kay, L.J., CA (Civ Div).

369. Freezing injunctions–Assets–Loans used to fund legal and living expenses–Whether loans constituted assets–Whether exercise of borrowing rights disposal or dealing with asset

The court was required to determine whether the rights of the first defendant (X) under certain loan agreements were assets of his for the purposes of a freezing injunction. The claimant Kazakh bank (J) had obtained a freezing injunction against X and others. The order prevented X from removing assets from England or disposing of, dealing with or diminishing the value of his assets. There was an exception for X's individual ordinary living expenses and for legal advice and representation. Before spending any money on legal advice and representation X had to notify J where the money to be spent was to be taken from. X was party to four loan agreements with two companies. Each agreement provided for a £10 million facility available to X on favourable terms. Funds derived from the loans were used to pay X's legal expenses and living expenses. J contended that the loan agreements were shams. There was good reason to suppose that the lending companies were ultimately owned by X. On the assumption that the loan agreements were valid, J contended that X's rights under them were assets of his for the purposes of the freezing order and that any drawings could only lawfully be made after complying with the notice requirement. J argued that a right to borrow money from a lender under a loan facility was a chose in action and by directing the lender to pay money to a third party the borrower either disposed of or dealt with that chose in action; the definition of assets for the purposes of the order included "any asset which X had power, directly or indirectly, to dispose of, or deal with as if it were his own", and when the lender complied with X's instructions to pay his lawyers or anyone else it "held or controlled assets in accordance with his instructions" within the definition.

Held: Judgment accordingly. The freezing order was to be construed in the way in which it ought reasonably to be understood by a businessman to whom it was addressed in the light of the purpose which it was designed to serve. That purpose was to prevent X, against whom J might in the future secure a judgment, from disposing of his assets, otherwise than in the ordinary course of business, so as to frustrate any attempt by J to secure payment of its judgment by whatever process of execution might be open to it. In that context, the assets to which the freezing order referred were assets which would or could be of some value to J and against which it would be capable of securing execution. The standard form of freezing order, which precluded a disposal of or dealing with assets, prima facie caught dispositions which did not amount to dissipation, hence the ordinary course of business exception, and the terms of an order could relate to an asset which could not be seized in execution, *Iraqi Ministry of Defence v Arcepey Shipping Co SA* [1981] Q.B. 65, [1980] C.L.Y. 2157 considered. It was possible that the standard form covered the exercise of a right to borrow even though that would not, of itself, amount to dissipation, but the better view was that X's right to borrow was not to be regarded as an asset, and its exercise was not a disposal of or dealing with an asset, *Cantor Index Ltd v Lister* [2002] C.P. Rep. 25, [2002] C.L.Y. 471 and *Anglo Eastern Trust Ltd v Kermanshahchi (Costs) (No.1)* [2002] EWHC 1702 (Ch) applied (see paras 71-81 of judgment).

JSC BTA BANK v ABLYAZOV, [2012] EWHC 1819 (Comm), [2012] 2 All E.R. (Comm) 1243, Christopher Clarke, J., QBD (Comm).

370. Freezing injunctions–Jurisdiction–Imposition of freezing orders under s.25 Civil Jurisdiction and Judgments Act 1882

[Civil Jurisdiction and Judgments Act 1982 (c.27) s.25.]

The claimant Russian bank (J) applied for the continuation of a freezing order which had been made under the Civil Jurisdiction and Judgments Act 1982 s.25. J had made various substantial loans to a Russian group of companies (the SAHO group) and had started various proceedings in Russia to seek repayment. Each of the loans had been guaranteed by the first defendant (D1) who was chair of the SAHO group and appeared to control its business. D1 was resident in Russia. Proceedings had also been brought against D1 in Russia in respect of his guarantees. D1 was the beneficiary of two offshore trusts which owned the shareholding in the SAHO group. The trusts also owned the second and third defendants (D2 and D3), which were both limited liability partnerships in England and Wales. D2 and D3 had not provided full disclosure about the identity of their controlling parties. Ex parte orders had been made under s.25 of the Act in respect of all three defendants, with a view to preserving assets and interests within the United Kingdom against the event of enforcement of any Russian judgments in the jurisdiction. The issues were whether (i) the court had jurisdiction to serve an order under s.25 out of the jurisdiction; (ii) the order should be continued against D1; (iii) the order should be continued against D2 and D3.

Held: Application granted. (1) The statutory test expressly provided for the correct approach to applications for interim relief under s.25, namely that the court could grant the order but might refuse it within s.25(2). Although s.25(2) was an exorbitant jurisdiction, it was intended to assist foreign proceedings and foreign courts. The court would proceed with caution, but in the instant case the court was satisfied that it had jurisdiction, *Refco Inc v Eastern Trading Co* [1999] 1 Lloyd's Rep. 159, [1998] C.L.Y. 563 applied (see paras 26-29 of judgment). (2) There was a sufficiently arguable case that D1 had control over the trusts, and therefore owned D2 and D3 and/or that he could call for the assets from both trusts, not at the discretion of the trustee. Lack of available sanction was not a reason to refuse relief: there would be no need to enforce against a foreign defendant by way of committal for contempt in the event that an order enforcing foreign proceedings were made, because the court would be capable of appointing a receiver by way of equitable execution, *Tasarruf Mevduati Sigorta Fonu v Merrill Lynch Bank & Trust Co (Cayman) Ltd* [2011] UKPC 17, [2012] 1 W.L.R. 1721 applied. There was therefore jurisdiction and ground to make an order against D1 (paras 15-23, 30, 34-36). (3) The court could be satisfied that there was good reason to grant an order against parties, such as D2 and D3, against whom no cause of action was alleged if there was some other process of enforcement by which the claimant could obtain recourse to the assets held by those defendants. It was quite plain that, on the provisional findings of fact made, the appointment of an equitable receiver would fit the bill in that regard. It could enforce the rights of D1 in the shareholdings of D2 and D3. In that way, the shareholding could be realised, whether by its voluntary winding-up or otherwise, *Parbulk II A/S v PT Humpuss Intermoda Transportasi TBK (The Mahakam)* [2011] EWHC 3143 (Comm), [2012] 2 All E.R. (Comm) 513, [2012] C.L.Y. 426 applied, *Motorola Credit Corp v Uzan (No.6)* [2003] EWCA Civ 752, [2004] 1 W.L.R. 113, [2003] C.L.Y. 413 considered. It was not inexpedient to make an order (paras 39-42). (4) The question was whether, unless the freezing injunction was granted, assets which, on the face of the available evidence, were presently available to the defendants might be put beyond the reach of creditors. On the face of it, all or most of D1's assets or interests, including a substantial interest which he must have had in the SAHO group, had been sought to be locked away into trusts. D1 was in a position to deal with those assets. There was plainly a risk that those assets might be put beyond the reach of creditors and that must have been the intention. The very denial of any interest and the surprising lack of information provided caused grave concern if the position was as J submitted. There had also been material changes in the direct or indirect beneficial ownership of ten of the borrowing companies since the loans were made and guarantees given, at least some of them involving overseas companies. By the test applicable to domestic freezing orders there was a real risk of dissipation. Plainly, although the order against D1 had to be limited to assets in England and Wales, a worldwide order would have to be imposed against D2 and D3 (paras 43-47).

JOINT STOCK CO VTB BANK v SKURIKHIN, [2012] EWHC 3916 (Comm), [2013] 2 All E.R. (Comm) 418, Burton, J., QBD (Comm).

371. Freezing orders–Discharge–Companies seeking enforcement of judgment and obtaining without notice freezing order–Third party bank consequently suffering loss and seeking discharge–Matters not disclosed and/or unfairly presented on application

[State Immunity Act 1978 (c.33) s.13, s.14.]

The third party bank (B) applied to discharge a freezing order that had been granted to the applicant companies (T) against the respondent government (G). G and T had entered into an agreement to dig mines and construct an electricity generating plant in Laos. The agreement included an express waiver of immunity from execution by G. Disputes arose and G purported to terminate the agreement. The disputes were referred to arbitration and T were granted an award. T sought worldwide enforcement of the award. Meanwhile, G issued proceedings in Malaysia to set aside the award. The English High Court granted T's application for judgment on the award. The Malaysian court subsequently set aside the award. T then obtained the freezing order on a without notice basis which applied to G's assets in England and Wales up to almost US$74.5 million. The order said that it applied to any assets held in an account in which G had a beneficial interest, whether maintained in its own name or in B's name. The order also said that any bank where an account in B's name was maintained was ordered to restrain all activity in the account unless and until it obtained a sworn declaration from one of B's officers stating that G had no beneficial interest in the account. B's two London accounts were frozen. Over three working days later, following communications between T and B, its accounts were unfrozen. B claimed to have suffered losses of approximately US$4.5 million as a result. When the order was sought, T undertook to pay £100,000 into court. The issues were (i) the effect of the order on B; (ii) whether T had failed to disclose or unfairly presented certain matters when applying for the order; (iii) whether to order an inquiry into the losses allegedly suffered by B as a result of the order; (iv) whether to order fortification of T's undertaking in light of B's estimate of the loss it had suffered.

Held: Application refused. (1) No such freezing order should have been made against accounts in B's name because B's property enjoyed immunity from execution under the State Immunity Act 1978 s.13 and s.14. B had not consented to the order. Further, any order directed at execution against property in B's name would be permissible only if it could be said that B had no interests of a legal, equitable or contractual kind; it was difficult to see how that could be said of a bank account in B's name where B would at least have a contractual interest as the customer of the bank at which the account was held (see paras 19, 22-23 of judgment). (2) T's application for the order had been presented on the basis that B was a separate entity with separate judicial personality, and so it not was fair to say that T had not made that fact clear to the judge when making the application. However, T had inadequately explained the effect the order would have on B's property and how that effect was contrary to the immunity conferred by the Act. Further, it was fair to say that T had argued that G's waiver from immunity in the agreement was sufficient to remove immunity from B, without explaining how such waiver could be sufficient and without drawing attention to relevant authorities which supported the contrary position, *AIG Capital Partners Inc v Kazakhstan* [2005] EWHC 2239 (Comm), [2006] 1 W.L.R. 1420, [2006] C.L.Y. 2643 considered. Accordingly, breach of duty was made out. However, although those breaches were serious, it would not have been just to deprive T of the continuation of the freezing order as a result of them, *Brink's-MAT Ltd v Elcombe* [1988] 1 W.L.R. 1350, [1989] C.L.Y. 3030 followed. The breaches related solely to parts of the order from which T had deprived no benefit and which would not form part of the continued freezing order. The breaches had no logical relevance to the continuation of the freezing order in all its other respects against G, and they had not been deliberate. The presentation of T's application was muddled and inadequate but was not intended to mislead, and so to deprive T of an order against G which was ancillary to a judgment for over US$74 million by reason of such conduct would have been disproportionate (paras 29-30, 34-35, 38). (3) B was entitled to be compensated for the losses caused by the order, and the evidence was sufficient to show that an inquiry into the loss suffered was not clearly futile or disproportionate, *Yukong Line Ltd of Korea v Rendsburg Investments Corp of Liberia (The Rialto) (Injunctive Relief)* [2001] 2 Lloyd's Rep. 113, [2001] C.L.Y. 45 followed (para.41). (4) The court could not require a claimant to give an undertaking. When fortification of an undertaking was required, it was not imposed by an order of the court that it had to be given, *Commodity Ocean Transport Corp v Basford Unicorn Industries Ltd (The Mito)* [1987] 2 Lloyd's Rep. 197, [1987] C.L.Y. 3063 applied. Accordingly the court declined to order fortification (paras 45, 47).

THAI-LAO LIGNITE (THAILAND) CO LTD v LAOS; *sub nom.* THAI-LAO LIGNITE (THAILAND) CO LTD v LAO PEOPLE'S DEMOCRATIC REPUBLIC, [2013] EWHC 2466 (Comm), [2013] 2 All E.R. (Comm) 883, Popplewell, J., QBD (Comm).

372. Gang-related violence injunctions–Burden of proof–Whether ASBO more appropriate–No "closest fit" principle

[Crime and Disorder Act 1998 (c.37) s.1, s.1 (1); Housing Act 1996 (c.52) Pt V; Policing and Crime Act 2009 (c.26) Pt 4, s.34 (2); European Convention on Human Rights 1950 Art.8.]

The appellant (J) appealed against the grant of an injunction to restrain gang violence (IRGV) to the respondent local authority (B) which prevented him from entering a prescribed area or associating or gathering with named persons. There were two main urban street gangs in Birmingham and J was an influential member of one. J and about 30 others had congregated in the opposing gang's territory. J submitted that the judge had been wrong (1) to find that he had engaged in gang-related violence when he had not made threats or acted in any way to encourage violence or the threat of violence by others. J maintained that mens rea was necessary to invoke the Policing and Crime Act 2009 s.34(2) and he had not deliberately provoked violence; (2) to grant an IRGV when the alternative remedy of an ASBO was available and less disadvantageous to him; (3) in granting the IRGV, which infringed J's right to respect for private life contrary to the European Convention on Human Rights 1950 art.8.

Held: Appeal dismissed. (1) Although an IRGV was primarily directed to deliberate participation in, or encouragement of, gang-related violence, it was possible that it could apply even to inadvertent encouragement, but it was unnecessary to decide the point (see para.11 of judgment). (2) The standard of proof for an ASBO was higher than for an IRGV but the facts required were less serious. The two statutes were directed towards different social problems and although some gang activity could comprise anti-social behaviour, the Crime and Disorder Act 1998 s.1 (1) had not been enacted to deal specifically with gang culture but with all kinds of anti-social behaviour, whereas the Policing and Crime Act 2009 Pt 4 was Parliament's considered response to gang-related violence and the appropriate burden of proof, *Birmingham City Council v Shafi* [2008] EWCA Civ 1186, [2009] 1 W.L.R. 1961, [2009] C.L.Y. 2649 considered (para.13). (3) J's right to respect for private and family life was not absolute and interference with it could be justified if lawful and necessary to prevent crime and disorder and to safeguard the rights and freedoms of others (para.15). Although J was excluded from the area in which he had grown up and his mother lived, he could contact her elsewhere (para.17). In recent years Parliament had provided three different pre-emptive orders, an anti-social behaviour injunction (ASBI) under the Housing Act 1996 Pt V, an anti-social behaviour order (ASBO) under the Crime and Disorder Act 1998 s.1, and an IRGV under the Policing and Crime Act 2009 Pt 4. There were many situations in which more than one different pre-emptive order was available to a judge and there was no principle of "closest fit" to be derived from *Shafi* or from *R. (on the application of Samaroo) v Secretary of State for the Home Department* [2001] EWCA Civ 1139, [2001] U.K.H.R.R. 1150, [2001] C.L.Y. 3660, *Samaroo* considered and *Swindon BC v Redpath* [2009] EWCA Civ 943, [2010] 1 All E.R. 1003, [2010] C.L.Y. 1688 applied (paras 20-31).

BIRMINGHAM CITY COUNCIL v JAMES, [2013] EWCA Civ 552, [2014] 1 W.L.R. 23, Maurice Kay, L.J., CA (Civ Div).

373. Hearings–Pre-trial reviews–Guidance about conduct of pre-trial reviews in Technology and Construction Court

[Civil Procedure Rules 1998 (SI 1998/3132) r.31.8, r.35.12(3); CPR PD 31B (Disclosure of Electronic Documents) 2010.]

Following the hearing of a pre-trial review in the Technology and Construction Court in proceedings concerning a factory fire, the judge handed down guidance on various case management matters of wide application.

Held: Judgment accordingly. (1) The Technology and Construction Court Guide paras 6.5.5 and 14.2.2 stipulated that where an application was going to last more than a half day, or was a pre-trial review, the advocates for each party had to lodge skeleton arguments or notes with the court "by 4pm one clear working day before the PTR". Although judges understood that counsel were busy, those times were not there for the sake of it; they were designed to ensure that the judge had a proper opportunity to do all the necessary reading and preparation before the hearing. The time limits were not draconian and it was in everyone's interests that they be met. Compliance had deteriorated in recent years and was hampering judges' efforts to deal efficiently with full lists and long hearings. Continued non-compliance would be dealt with more harshly and was more likely to lead to adjournments and wasted costs orders (see paras 4-8 of judgment). (2) Parties to cases in the Technology and Construction Court tended to overload the pre-trial review with a wide variety of other applications. That frequently made it impossible to deal with everything at one hearing, and often meant that relief might be refused because of the need to keep a trial date. Many matters should be raised in applications independent of the pre-trial review, rather than the parties simply waiting to have a wide-ranging catch-up at the pre-trial review. (3) It was becoming common for expert witnesses to pay lip service to orders made under CPR r.35.12(3) that they should meet, and produce a joint statement before service of their individual reports. They often ignored the requirement for a joint statement or produced one which was of no help. That created the impression that some experts were not getting to grips with their cases until very late in the litigation and were not prepared to commit themselves to anything too early. That was not the correct approach (para.17). (4) Pursuant to CPR PD 31B, the court could order a search in relation to documents held electronically. It was implicit that such searches should be meaningful and effective. As a matter of principle, if an order to search for such documents could only be complied with if it was undertaken by a suitably qualified information technology consultant experienced in electronic disclosure, the court had jurisdiction, in accordance with its overriding objective, to make such an order. The cost had to be proportionate and ensuing costs orders might turn on whether or not the exercise led to a concrete result (paras 25-28). (5) In some claims, insurers often engaged their own independent assessors to investigate causation. Their contemporaneous notes and photographs were often the most reliable material in subsequent claims and their importance could not be underestimated. For the purposes of CPR r.31.8, such documents, while in the possession of the defendant's insurers, were in the "control" of the defendant and were therefore susceptible to an order for specific disclosure. If they could not be found, a statement would need to be produced identifying the nature of the searches undertaken and what had happened to the documents (paras 31, 36-37).

MUELLER EUROPE LTD v CENTRAL ROOFING (SOUTH WALES) LTD, [2012] EWHC 3417 (TCC), [2013] T.C.L.R. 2, Coulson, J., QBD (TCC).

374. Hearings in open court–Confidential information–Applications for privacy and anonymity orders–Whether orders justified

[Law of Property Act 1925 (c.20) s.149(3); Civil Procedure Rules 1998 (SI 1998/3132) r.31.22(2), r.39.2(3).]

The court was required to hear issues of privacy and anonymity in a rectification claim which the applicant (S) intended to bring. The claim concerned an instrument by which S and two other family members had purported to grant an interest in land. It was alleged that the instrument failed to create such an interest because of the operation of the Law of Property Act 1925 s.149(3). The instrument provided for rent to be payable, but it was alleged that this was in error, and the rectification claim sought to eliminate references to rent from the instrument, in order to make it effective to create the interest in the land. S feared there was a risk that the assets of another party to the claim (H), who was involved in other litigation, might become vulnerable if there was an adverse outcome to that litigation. Relying on CPR r.39.2(3)(a),(c),(d) and (f) and CPR PD 39A, S sought orders that (i) the rectification claim be heard in private; (ii) that the identity of the parties to and other persons named in the rectification claim be protected by an order for anonymity of those parties and persons and of the trusts and properties which were the subject of the rectification claim.

Held: Application refused. (1) In approaching any request by a party to litigation for the proceedings to be held in private or anonymised, the general rule was that, apart from certain narrowly defined exceptions, such as litigation about a secret process, the administration of justice had to be conducted in open court, *Scott v Scott* [1913] A.C. 417 applied, (see paras 7-9 of judgment). (2) Neither CPR 39.2(3) nor the Practice Direction gave any party to litigation a right to a hearing in private merely by establishing that his case fell within one of the classes identified. Many cases involved some confidential information which publicity could compromise. A mechanistic application of the rule could lead to a hearing in private wherever confidential information was involved. The court would have to form a view of the nature of the confidential information, its importance to the party, and the damage he would suffer by its disclosure before deciding whether it was necessary to hold a hearing in private. The court had a wide armoury of measures it could take to protect confidential information, even in the context of a trial in open court, including CPR r.31.22(2) and CPR r.5.4C(4) to (6) (paras 17-18). (3) It would not be right to make an order that the proposed claim be heard in private, as it would be wrong to fetter the court's discretion before the proceedings in the rectification claim had commenced. It would be for the trial judge to decide whether it was appropriate to impose any measures for the proper protection of the confidential information (para.29). (4) There was no adequate justification for an anonymity order and it was not necessary to protect the interests of any of the parties. The application for anonymity turned on the fear of the effects of publicity on H's litigation. It would not be right for the court to shield the rectification claim in that way, as to do so would open the door to applications for anonymity in any case where a party feared that the publicity would expose his family's financial arrangements to his creditors. The extension of the general rule in *Scott* was not supported by authority or justified in the instant case (para.30).

SHULDHAM, *Re*, [2012] EWHC 1420 (Ch), [2012] W.T.L.R. 1597, Floyd, J., Ch D.

375. Inherent jurisdiction–General civil restraint orders–Individuals using third parties to make totally without merit claims–Appropriate response of court to limit proceedings

[Insolvency Act 1986 (c.45) Sch.B1 para.75.]

The defendants (P) applied to strike out a claim brought by the first claimant (F) and the second and third claimant companies (C and X), in which F or his daughter were interested. P had been appointed as administrators of a company. They issued proceedings against C but later amended the proceedings so that over 96 per cent of their claim was abandoned. Judgment was entered against F. As a result, he became bankrupt and so any cause of action that he had became vested in his trustee. F brought proceedings against P alleging negligence on the basis that, by making the original claim and circulating their allegations widely, P had assumed a duty of care or entered into a special relationship with F, C and X giving rise to a duty of care; misfeasance pursuant to the Insolvency Act 1986 Sch.B1 para.75; malicious prosecution. At the date the action was commenced, C had been struck off but it was later restored. F's trustee was directed to assign to F his claims, although at the date of the instant hearing that had not yet occurred.

Held: Application granted. (1) The claim alleging a duty of care was really a complaint of malicious falsehood. It was not open to someone who might timeously have brought a malicious falsehood claim to say that the falsehood complained of gave rise to a special relationship or assumption of responsibility giving rise to a duty of care, so producing a longer limitation period. The idea that one claimant, by asserting a claim, came under or assumed a duty of care to the other party was unsound, *Kyrris v Oldham* [2003] EWCA Civ 1506, [2004] B.C.C. 111, [2004] C.L.Y. 2119 and *Peskin v Anderson* [2001] B.C.C. 874, [2001] C.L.Y. 724 considered. Insofar as the claims were based on any duty of care, there were no prospects of success and they should be struck out (see paras 7-10 of judgment). (2) As to the misfeasance claim, proceedings under Sch.B1 para.75 of the 1986 Act could only be brought by a shareholder or creditor. F was neither of those things and would not be even if the assignment took place. Any interest he might have had and indebtedness formerly due to him were vested in his trustee. The misfeasance claim also had no prospect of success (paras 13-15). (3) F had alleged that P's claims had been brought abusively, for an improper motive or an improper purpose. However, those proceedings were pursued to judgment, over an eight-day hearing, and the claim succeeded in substantial amounts. It was therefore difficult to see how the proceedings could be characterised as malicious or an abuse. The highest that the abuse of process claim could be put was that there was, in part, an illegitimate purpose, *JSC BTA Bank v Ablyazov* [2011] EWHC 1136 (Comm), [2011] 1 W.L.R. 2996, [2012] C.L.Y. 307 considered. However, the fact that there was ultimately a judgment wholly belied the assertion that the proceedings as a whole were improperly motivated or brought for an improper purpose (paras 23-24). (4) The proceedings were brought when F knew that the causes of action he wished to assert were vested in his trustee in bankruptcy and that he needed an assignment and so the court was bound to strike out F's claim on that ground also, *Pickthall v Hill Dickinson LLP* [2009] EWCA Civ 543, [2009] C.P. Rep. 40, [2009] C.L.Y. 340 followed. Further, when the proceedings were commenced, C had been struck off, had not then been restored and so did not exist. The proceedings were an abuse because F knew that it was an abuse of process for a claim form to be issued before restoration, *Pickthall* applied. The proceedings were totally without merit and should be struck out (paras 16-20, 28). (5) Previous applications issued by F were also totally without merit as was another claim he had issued against 20 defendants. The CPR requirements as against F for either an extended or a general civil restraint order were made out. The public interest required the making of a general civil restraint order against him. Where a third party was found to be controlled by an individual who had persistently made or issued totally without merit applications or claims, and that third party, still under the individual's control, was either making or issuing, or threatening to make or issue, such an application or claim, that was a special feature justifying the making of a civil restraint order in like terms against the third party, under the court's inherent jurisdiction. That was so even though the third party had not been associated with all the past applications or claims which justified the making of the order against the individual. It was therefore also appropriate to make a civil restraint order against C and X (paras 36, 41, 43, 46).

FABB v PETERS, [2013] EWHC 296 (Ch), [2013] B.P.I.R. 264, Judge Purle Q.C., Ch D.

376. Injunctions–Judicial review–Injunctive relief to halt construction of wind farm–Whether claim for injunctive relief ancillary to application for judicial review–Whether serious issue to be tried

[Wildlife and Countryside Act 1981 (c.69) s.1; Civil Procedure Rules 1998 (SI 1998/3132) Pt 7; Conservation of Habitats and Species Regulations 2010 (SI 2010/490) reg.41.]

The applicant (E) applied for injunctive relief against the respondent interested party (R) to prevent the continuation of its construction of a wind farm. The court also considered E's application for permission to apply for judicial review of the decision of the defendant (N) not to seek an injunction against R in its own right. E also sought a protective costs order against R and N. Following an inquiry, N had been granted planning permission to construct a 10-turbine wind farm, the inspector having found that on the basis of existing survey evidence there was unlikely to be any significant effect from the wind farm on either bats or birds in the area. Construction of the wind farm began in March 2012 and it was likely to become fully operational by spring 2013. E lived near the wind farm and was a member of a residents' association opposed to it. The basis of her application was the actual or threatened commission by R of offences under the Wildlife and Countryside Act 1981 s.1 and under the Conservation of Habitats and Species Regulations 2010 reg.41, by reason of the death of protected species of birds and bats as a result of collision with the turbine blades and/or disturbance due to the ongoing process of construction. It was common ground that it was necessary to determine whether there was a serious issue to be tried in the underlying merits of E's judicial review claim against N because her application for an injunction was simply ancillary to that claim. E submitted that it was inevitable that, by reason of the wind farm operating, R would commit the alleged offences. She argued that N had acted unlawfully in a judicial review sense because it could and should have sought an appropriate permanent injunction against R to prevent it committing those offences. N and R submitted that N was not really a defendant to the judicial review claim at all since the action was really a private law dispute between E and R, and what she was really doing was seeking both an interim and a permanent injunction against R on a quia timet basis to prevent it from committing criminal offences in the future.

Held: Applications refused. (1) N and R's characterisation of the true nature of E's claim was correct. If the injunction application was ancillary not to the main claim against N but rather to a separate claim for a permanent injunction against R it then faced two serious difficulties. First, it should never have been made within a judicial review claim but rather as a conventional claim under CPR Pt 7. Secondly, even if that procedural irregularity could be cured, E would have no locus to make such a claim: she could not seek an injunction to prevent the commission of criminal offences as a private citizen unless she could show that she had consequently suffered, or would suffer, some individual loss on a tortious basis, *Gouriet v Union of Post Office Workers* [1978] A.C. 435, [1977] C.L.Y. 690 followed. In those circumstances, there was no serious issue to be tried either in relation to the main judicial review claim or any free-standing claim against R. That was sufficient to dispose of the injunction application (see paras 35-36, 38 of judgment). (2) (Obiter) Even if there was a serious issue to be tried, the balance of convenience lay overwhelmingly in favour of R and against the grant of an injunction (para.72). (3) As a result of the court's findings on the merits of the main judicial review claim, E was refused permission to bring it (para.75). (4) It followed that the court refused to make any protective costs order in E's favour because her claim had no real prospect of success, *R. (on the application of Corner House Research) v Secretary of State for Trade and Industry* [2005] EWCA Civ 192, [2005] 1 W.L.R. 2600, [2005] C.L.Y. 354 followed (para.76).

EATON v NATURAL ENGLAND, [2012] EWHC 2401 (Admin), [2013] 1 C.M.L.R. 10, Judge Waksman Q.C., QBD (Admin).

377. **Injunctions–Newspapers–Application to reinstate claim against newspaper for damages and permanent injunction**

[Civil Procedure Rules 1998 (SI 1998/3132) r.3.9, r.15.5, r.15.5(1); European Convention on Human Rights 1950 Art.6, Art.8, Art.10.]

The claimant footballer (G) applied under CPR r.3.9 for relief from sanction against the striking out of his claim for damages against the first defendant newspaper (N). N had published a story about an alleged sexual relationship between G, who was married, and the second defendant (T). G was not named in the article. A non-disclosure injunction was granted restraining any further publication about the alleged relationship and G brought a claim for damages and a permanent injunction against N. An order was made requiring service of N's defence by May 18, 2011. G and N agreed a general stay regarding service of the defence; however, that information was not communicated to the court until five months later. That was a clear breach by both parties of r.15.5(1) and (2). A further order made in November 2011 required G to make an appointment to fix a further trial date by November 18. G did not make an appointment and the action was automatically struck out on that date. The effect of what had happened was not appreciated by either party until four weeks later, at which point G made the instant application. G had also brought proceedings against T but on February 1, 2012, a consent order provided that such proceedings be stayed, and G's anonymity was lifted. N did not learn of that development until 19 days later. G argued that the failure to fix an appointment had been an oversight by his solicitors. He further argued that the trial could commence on March 19, 2012 if relief were granted, and that therefore non-compliance with the order had had no practical effect. N argued that the continuance of the action would be an interference with its rights under the European Convention on Human Rights 1950 art.10 and those of third parties. It also argued that G's failure to inform it that anonymity had been lifted was a breach of an undertaking to give notice to third parties if that order ceased to have effect.

Held: Application refused. (1) Refusal to grant relief would not be a material interference with G's rights under the European Convention on Human Rights 1950 art.6 or art.8 because G could commence a new action against N. However, it was hard to see what serious interference with N's art.10 rights there could be if proceedings continued as it had stated that it did not have the means or intention to publish further information relating to a sexual relationship between G and T. However, it was necessary for a claimant to plead the matters he relied on when he alleged that the publisher of an anonymous article was to be held liable for the fact that it was understood to refer to the claimant. G had not done so. As presently pleaded, it could not be said that the claim for damages could give rise to any award, even if it could give rise to an award at all. The claim for an injunction to restrain publication of G's identity would have been futile and unreal given that his identity was in the public domain. There was no purpose to be served by granting relief under r.3.9 (see paras 68-73 of judgment). (2) The non-disclosure order had been made fully in accordance with the *Practice Guidance (HC: Interim Non-Disclosure Orders)* [2012] 1 W.L.R. 1003, [2012] C.L.Y. 436 and had been designed to achieve as quick a trial as practicable. The court had to be particularly alert for the need to have regard to the rights of third parties under art.10. The agreement between N and G to stay service of the defence had the effect of interfering with such rights, including by the continuation of the anonymity order. G and N's breach of r.15.5(1) and (2) was a serious and clearly intentional breach of the rules of the court for which they had failed to provide a good explanation. It was all the more serious in that it had not been disclosed on subsequent applications to the court to lift the anonymity order (paras 80-84). (3) It was plain that G had breached the undertaking he had given to take all reasonable steps to inform the relevant people that the anonymity order had ceased to have effect. The order had been lifted by the court and a public document named G in its title. It was difficult to see what further steps needed to be taken to demonstrate that anonymity no longer persisted (paras 87-88). (4) Claimants and defendants had to prosecute a claim for breach of confidence and privacy so as to ensure that the interference with art.10 rights of third parties was kept to as short a time as possible. The court should not grant extensions of time for service of statements of case, or any other step in the action, unless satisfied that the extension of the period during which there would be an interference with the art.10 rights of third parties was necessary and proportionate (para.111).

GIGGS v NEWS GROUP NEWSPAPERS LTD; *sub nom.* CTB v NEWS GROUP NEWSPAPERS LTD, [2012] EWHC 431 (QB), [2013] E.M.L.R. 5, Tugendhat, J., QBD.

378. Interest–Disbursements–Appropriate rate of pre-judgment interest on disbursements incurred in personal injury claim

The claimants (J) applied for an order that the defendants, namely the Secretary of State for Energy and Climate Change and Coal Products Ltd, should pay pre-judgment interest on disbursements incurred in what was known as the Phurnacite Workers Group Litigation. Each of the conditional fee agreements entered into by the lead claimants contained a provision that the claimant was liable for the payment of any disbursements incurred on his behalf, whether or not the claim was successful. The disbursements, which consisted mainly of payments for experts' and counsel's fees, amounted in total to more than £787,500. The disbursements were paid by J's solicitors (H) pursuant to an arrangement which was somewhat novel. H entered into a "credit agreement" with each of the lead claimants whereby H undertook to provide credit in such sums as were required from time to time to pay disbursements relating to that claimant's claim up to a maximum of £5,000 in return for payment of a credit charge. The charge for credit was agreed at 4 per cent above base rate. The credit agreement provided that, if the claim was successful, the credit charge would be paid by the claimant out of his damages, while, if the claim was unsuccessful, the credit would be paid under the terms of the claimant's policy with his after-the-event (ATE) insurance provider.

Held: Judgment accordingly. The determination of the rate of interest payable on disbursements was a matter for the exercise of the court's discretion, having regard to all the circumstances of the case and in particular the requirement to do justice as between the parties. The starting point was the fact that it was essential, if J's claims were to proceed, that the necessary disbursements should be paid as the case went along. It was quite clear that J would not have been in a position to fund the disbursements from their own pockets. The credit agreements provided a means by which they could obtain funding for their disbursements without being required to advance any monies themselves and without financial risk, as the agreements provided that, in the event of a claim failing, the disbursements would be paid by the ATE insurers. It was likely that the interest demanded by a third party for an unsecured loan in order to fund disbursements would have been significantly in excess of the 4 per cent above base rate agreed with H. Further, such loans would not have been contingent, as were the credit agreements. The court had no information about the likely terms of a disbursement funding agreement with a third party but it seemed highly unlikely to have been as advantageous to J as the credit agreements with H. The rate of interest agreed between H and J could not of itself be determinative of the rate which should be awarded; the credit charges specified in the credit agreements provide only prima facie evidence of the cost to J of obtaining the credit necessary to fund their disbursements, and that prima facie evidence would plainly be displaced by evidence that the charges were excessive. No direct evidence had been given about the likely cost to J of funding their disbursements by alternative means. There could be no doubt, however, that the cost of unsecured borrowing to a private individual would be considerably higher than would be paid by a large company litigating in the Commercial Court. The defendants had not argued that J would have been able to obtain the necessary funding at a more advantageous rate of interest than 4 per cent above base rate, let alone on a contingency basis. Nor had they argued that the rate of interest charged by H was excessive or unreasonable. H had fulfilled the role of a bank but on terms more advantageous to J than those which would have been offered by any bank. In the circumstances, the appropriate rate of interest on pre-judgment disbursements was 4 per cent above base rate (see paras 22-26 of judgment).

JONES v SECRETARY OF STATE FOR ENERGY AND CLIMATE CHANGE, [2013] EWHC 1023 (QB), [2013] 3 All E.R. 1014, Swift, J., QBD.

379. Interim injunctions–Abuse of process–Application to restrain defendants from harassment or defamation in their defence of employment tribunal proceedings

The applicant (V) applied for an interim injunction in libel and harassment against the respondents who opposed the application and applied for a stay of the action pending the hearing of V's claim in the employment tribunal. V had brought nine claims for discrimination, unlawful detriment following a protected disclosure, harassment, victimisation and unfair dismissal against the first respondent employer (L). The second to seventh respondents (R) were employees of L and the eighth respondent was an occupational health consultant who had interviewed her. In February 2012 the first three sets of proceedings brought by V were dismissed by the employment tribunal. V was ordered to pay a third of L's costs. The rest of her claim was due to be heard in September 2013. V brought the instant claim in February 2012 and L applied to stay the proceedings until the hearing had taken place in the employment tribunal. V then issued her application for an interim injunction to restrain L and R from harassing or publicly defaming her in their conduct and defence of the tribunal proceedings. L and R submitted that (1) the injunction application was ill-founded and was being made for a collateral and abusive purpose to interfere with the proper resolution of the issues between the parties; (2) the proper course was to let the tribunal proceedings take their course and for V's libel action to be stayed.

Held: Application refused. (1) The sole purpose of the injunction application was to prevent L and R from making statements which V anticipated would be defamatory of her when defending her claims before the tribunal. That would obviously interfere with the proper conduct of those proceedings and their just resolution. It was a clear abuse of the court's process. L and R intended to defend V's claim by relying on defences of justification, honest comment and qualified privilege and an interim injunction would not generally be granted in such circumstances, *Bonnard v Perryman* [1891] 2 Ch. 269 and *Greene v Associated Newspapers Ltd* [2004] EWCA Civ 1462, [2005] Q.B. 972, [2005] C.L.Y. 970 followed. It was not the sort of exceptionally rare case where the court should make a determination in advance of trial, particularly having regard to the background of the litigation and the inadequacy of V's pleaded case. There was no evidence that L and R had done anything or were likely to do anything in the tribunal proceedings which gave rise to a claim in harassment. Further, it was a defence that the conduct of which V complained was pursued in accordance with case management directions and orders made by the tribunal in accordance with its statutory powers. V had not demonstrated that she was likely to succeed in her claim of harassment at trial and an interim injunction was not granted (see paras 17-18, 22, 24-26, 31-33 of judgment). (2) The tribunal proceedings and V's claim in harassment and defamation centred on the same circumstances relating to her treatment as an employee. There were cogent considerations in favour of the tribunal proceedings being dealt with first: it was first seised of the matter and was the obvious place for the resolution of V's claims relating to her employment; the tribunal proceedings were well-advanced and time and resources had already been dedicated to them. It would not be just and proportionate for the High Court proceedings to be heard before the tribunal proceedings. A stay of the High Court proceedings was ordered (paras 38, 40-41, 43, 47).

VAUGHAN v LEWISHAM LBC, [2013] EWHC 795 (QB), [2013] I.R.L.R. 720, Sharp, J., QBD.

380. Interim injunctions–Conflict of interest–Shareholder and director in competition with company–Adequate record-keeping to establish damages–Appropriateness of granting interim injunction preventing competition

The appellant (W) appealed against a decision refusingf his application for an interim injunction. W and the first respondent (P) had been equal shareholders in a dental laboratory business, the second respondent (L). P had been the sole director of L. Without W's knowledge, P had formed a new dental laboratory business (X), with himself as the sole director and shareholder, which he operated from L's premises with L's employees. He sent a letter to L's customers and suppliers telling them that L's bank account was no longer in operation, asking that all invoices henceforth be made out to X, and providing X's bank details. After learning of X's existence, W, as a shareholder of L, filed a derivative action against P alleging breach of confidence and fiduciary duty. W applied for an interim injunction to prevent P from using or disclosing L's confidential information, soliciting or conducting business in competition with L, doing business with L's clients or employees, encouraging L's employees to leave, or otherwise acting in conflict with his interest as a shareholder and director of L. The application was refused on the ground that the balance of convenience lay in allowing P to continue doing business as X subject to his undertaking to keep adequate financial records so that W could establish damages.

Held: Appeal dismissed. An appellate's court function in dealing with the grant or refusal of an interim injunction was one of review only, and it might set aside a judge's exercise of discretion only on the ground that it was based on a misunderstanding of the law or of the evidence, *Hadmor Productions v Hamilton* [1983] 1 A.C. 191, [1982] C.L.Y. 3280 followed. That had not been demonstrated instant case, and the court was not, therefore, persuaded to exercise its own discretion by granting the injunction where the court below had not, *Hadmor Productions* followed. W had not suggested an error of law, and the judge had not erred in the way he balanced the factors. The judge had said that there would be adequate protection until trial by P's keeping records in accordance with the undertaking. There was a real risk that, if the injunction were granted, the parties would get the worst of both worlds: P and the employees would not return to L, but would also be prevented from carrying on the business of X, which was allegedly being carried on for the benefit of L. The injunction would inflict definite damage on X without any certainty of a benefit for L or W. The judge's solution, on the other hand, meant that there was some certainty that there would be adequate information available, if liability were established at trial, to work out the nature of damages. That was a solution which was more likely to be productive of justice than the grant of the injunction W sought (see paras 22, 27-29, 31).

WRIGHT v PYKE, [2012] EWCA Civ 931, [2013] B.C.C. 300, Mummery, L.J., CA (Civ Div).

381. Interim injunctions–Permission to appeal–Permission to appeal against finding that pharmaceutical patents invalid–Application to restrain marketing of generic products pending appeal–Principles governing grant of interim injunctions pending appeal where claimant losing at first instance

The appellant (N) appealed against the refusal to grant it an interim injunction pending its appeal against the decision that its patents were invalid. The patents for N's drug "Aclasta" concerned the intravenous use of zoledronic acid for the treatment of osteoporosis. N had an earlier patent and supplementary protection certificate (SPC) covering zoledronic acid itself. The SPC was due to expire on May 15, 2013. In 2011, the respondent (H) commenced revocation proceedings against the Aclasta patents, intending to market a generic zoledronic acid product. Trial was fixed for February 2013. In November 2012, H obtained a marketing authorisation for a generic zoledronic acid product. At N's request, H undertook not to sell any zoledronic acid product prior to the SPC's expiry. In December 2012, N wrote to H requesting it to confirm that if the patents were found valid, it would undertake not to launch its generic product in the United Kingdom after May 15, 2013. H indicated that it would review which products it might market in the future once it knew the outcome of the proceedings. The trial judge subsequently found the Aclasta patents invalid. N was granted permission to appeal. H told N of its intention to launch its product in the UK following expiry of the SPC on May 15. N commenced infringement proceedings and applied for an interim injunction. The judge considered that the case for an interim injunction pending trial would have been likely to have been made out, but that since the merits had been decided the overall balance was different. He found that, as the December 2012 letter indicated, the proceedings were conducted on the footing that they would be concluded before the SPC expired, and that N should have asked for the case to be scheduled sufficiently far in advance of May 15, 2013, to allow an appeal to take place before that date. He refused to grant an injunction, having concluded that, faced with an arguable appeal and a risk of inflicting significant uncompensatable harm on either side, the risk should be borne by N. N contended that the judge had been wrong to hold that the fact that the merits of the validity action had been decided affected the overall balance of convenience and to place weight on the December 2012 letter.

Held: Appeal allowed. (1) The principles applying to the grant of an interim injunction pending appeal where the claimant had lost at first instance were: (a) the court had to be satisfied that the appeal had a real prospect of success; (b) if the court was satisfied that it did, it would not usually be useful to attempt to form a view as to how strong the prospects of an appeal were, or to attempt to give weight to that view in assessing the balance of convenience; (c) it did not follow automatically from the fact that an interim injunction had or would have been granted pre-trial that an injunction pending appeal should be granted; the court had to assess all the relevant circumstances following judgment, including the period of time before any appeal was likely to be heard and the balance of hardship to each party if an injunction was refused or granted; (d) the grant of an injunction was not limited to the case where its refusal would render an appeal nugatory: such a case merely represented the extreme end of a spectrum of possible factual situations in which the injustice to one side was balanced against the injustice to the other; (e) as in the case of the stay of a permanent injunction which would otherwise be granted to a successful claimant, the court should endeavour to arrange matters so that the Court of Appeal was best able to do justice between the parties once the appeal had been heard (see para.41 of judgment). (2) N's appeal had a real prospect of success. The exercise of discretion should not be approached on the basis that the merits were clear in favour of one side or the other. The judge had wrongly decided against N merely because it could not satisfy some higher threshold on the merits. He had placed weight on the December 2012 letter as illustrating the fact that the trial was scheduled to take place before May 2013. However, until H had obtained a marketing authorisation in November 2012, there was no commercial urgency on N's part, and it was wrong in principle to require N to assume the burden of expediting the trial. The parties were aware that litigation was not finally concluded until all appeals were disposed of, *Polini v Gray (Interlocutory Injunction)* (1879) 12 Ch. D. 438 followed. That was particularly true in the pharmaceutical industry. Both grounds of appeal were made out, and it fell to the instant court to exercise the discretion afresh (paras 45, 47-52, 56). (3) In all the circumstances, it was appropriate to grant an injunction to restrain the sale of H's product pending the appeal (paras 61-65).

NOVARTIS AG v HOSPIRA UK LTD, [2013] EWCA Civ 583, [2013] C.P. Rep. 37, Lewison, L.J., CA (Civ Div).

382. Interim injunctions–Supply of goods–Whether refusal to supply pharmaceutical drug was abuse of dominant position

The applicant (C) applied for an interim injunction in relation to the supply to it by the respondent (R) of the patented drug Kaletra, which was a protease inhibitor used to treat HIV patients. R distributed the drug in the United Kingdom. C provided homecare services for NHS hospitals and was also a licensed drugs wholesaler. For about seven years C and R had had a contract by which R supplied Kaletra to C. C ordered increasing quantities of Kaletra, to the extent that R ran short of supplies, without revealing that it was making wholesale sales. When R discovered that C was selling the drug wholesale, it refused to supply C with more than it needed for its homecare contracts on the basis that that was the proper interpretation of their agreement. C's case was that R held a dominant market position and had abused it.

Held: Application refused. (1) C had not shown that it had a real prospect of proving that R had a dominant market position. R had adduced evidence to show that it was possible for patients to switch within the same category of protease inhibitors, and C had adduced no evidence to contradict that. There would be some patients who could not switch from Kaletra, but there was no evidence about what share of the market they represented. C had provided no evidence of its own patients. There was no doubt that patients for whom Kaletra was absolutely essential would be supplied; R was not refusing to supply them. The burden was on C to found an evidential case on dominance and it had not done so. That was sufficient to dismiss its application for an interim injunction. (2) A refusal to supply could equal abuse of dominant position. However, R was refusing to supply only in respect of the wholesale market. C had been disingenuous when R had repeatedly asked it to explain the sharp increase in demand and it had not mentioned its wholesaling business. There was no real prospect that C could show that R had been abusive. (3) C could show no loss in respect of its domestic business as there was no effective refusal in respect of that supply. It might suffer loss in respect of its wholesale business, but any loss would be purely financial and could be compensated accordingly.

CHEMISTREE HOMECARE LTD v ABBVIE LTD, [2013] EWHC 264 (Ch), [2013] U.K.C.L.R. 135, Roth, J., Ch D.

383. Interim payments–Group litigation orders–Franked investment income group litigation order–Ability of non-test claimant to apply for interim payment–Stay of proceedings save for test claims

[Finance Act 2007 (c.11) s.107; Limitation Act 1980 (c.58) s.32(1)(c); Civil Procedure Rules 1998 (SI 1998/3132) r.25.7(1)(c), r.25.7(1).]

The applicant taxpayers (G) applied for an interim payment and the respondent commissioners applied to amend the terms of the Franked Investment Income (FII) Group Litigation Order to prevent any individual claimant applying for an interim payment. After the European Court of Justice had held that the United Kingdom's advance corporation tax regime had infringed Community law, G had applied for an interim payment in respect of their claims for repayment of tax unlawfully levied. The commissioners had been ordered to make an interim payment of £4.4 million. The Court of Appeal then held that part of G's claim for repayment was statute barred because reliance on the extended limitation period under the Limitation Act 1980 s.32(1)(c) was prevented by the Finance Act 2007 s.107. As a consequence of that decision G made a voluntary repayment to the commissioners of approximately £2.9 million with compound interest. Thereafter the Supreme Court ruled that s.107 of the 2007 Act was incompatible with EU law so that the commissioners could not rely on s.107 as an answer to G's mistake claims which relied on the extended limitation period under s.32(1)(c). G accordingly sought to reinstate the original interim payment order and recover the £2.9 million plus interest which they had voluntarily repaid to the commissioners. The commissioners submitted that para.12 of the GLO, which stayed the claims enrolled in the GLO save for those proceeding as test claims, had the effect of preventing G's interim payment application since they were not test claimants; alternatively the terms of the GLO should be amended to make clear that it operated to prevent interim payment applications by non-test claimants.

Held: Judgment accordingly. (1) Nothing in CPR r.25.7(1) prevented a party to a GLO from making an application for an interim payment order. Very strong grounds would be needed to deprive a non-test claimant of the right to make an interim payment application if the necessary conditions in r.25.7(1)(c) were satisfied. If the stringent test in r.25.7(1)(c) was satisfied it would not be fair to deprive a non-test claimant of the opportunity to invoke the interim payment jurisdiction, which was of general application to claims of all kinds, merely because for good case management reasons the claimant had been enrolled in a GLO but had not been designated as a test claimant. It would be wrong to impose a blanket stay on such applications in the terms proposed by the commissioners. On the proper interpretation of para.12 the stay applied to any interim applications made by non-test claimants, including applications for interim payments; but the stay should be lifted by the court to the extent necessary to permit meritorious interim payment applications to be made and determined. Even if a stay had been ordered in respect of future interim payment applications, it would have been right to deal with G's application in view of the history of the matter (see paras 21-27 of judgment). (2) The interim payment application succeeded, subject to a reduction to reflect the uncertainty about G's claim to be able to carry forward certain tax credits. The court could not be satisfied that, if G's claim went to trial, they would obtain judgment for that part of their claim which depended on the carry forward of notional FII. On the other hand, G would be entitled to judgment for the remainder of their claim. Following the judgment of the Supreme Court and pending a further reference to the ECJ, the court could be satisfied that G's mistake claims would succeed at trial on the basis that they were protected by the EU principles of effectiveness and/or equivalence. On that basis, the commissioners would be unable to rely on change of position as a defence to the claims (paras 34-44).

GKN HOLDINGS PLC v REVENUE AND CUSTOMS COMMISSIONERS; *sub nom.* GKN HOLDINGS PLC v INLAND REVENUE COMMISSIONERS, [2013] EWHC 108 (Ch), [2013] B.T.C. 113, Henderson, J., Ch D.

384. Interim payments–Measure of damages–Rejection of broad-brush approach–Title to sue argument not giving rise to complete defence–Measure of loss to be applied in order to establish irreducible minimum

[Civil Procedure Rules 1998 (SI 1998/3132) Pt 25, r.25.7(1).]

The claimants (C) sought an interim payment of £15 million pursuant to the CPR r.25.7(1) from the defendant (D). A confectionary manufacturing unit owned and/or operated by C was destroyed by fire. It was established that C had failed to properly protect the unit against the risk of fire; however, a fire detection system designed and operated by D had failed to operate. Following a trial on liability, D was found to be liable but, as a result of C's contributory negligence, the value of the claim was to be reduced by 75 per cent. There was a residual issue concerned with C's title to sue, which the parties agreed to keep back from the liability trial. C valued the claim at £120 million, reduced to £30 million following deduction for contributory negligence; C then halved that amount to reflect the litigation risks. C submitted that the court could be satisfied that they would recover at least £15 million and that the measure of loss to be applied was the cost of reinstatement. D argued that each aspect of C's claim had to be considered and that the court could not be satisfied that there was any irreducible minimum to which they were entitled; on the basis of various events that had occurred since the fire, C did not have title to sue and thus had no remedy at all; and the proper measure of loss to be applied was diminution in value.

Held: Application granted. (1) Adopting a broad-brush approach would do no more than suggest that, in the round, C was likely to recover half their claim; that was the very approach which the court in *Revenue and Customs Commissioners v GKN Group* [2012] EWCA Civ 57, [2012] 1 W.L.R. 2375, [2012] C.L.Y. 437 held was incorrect. The court had to be satisfied that, on the material before it, C would actually succeed in its claim, *GKN Group* applied. That meant looking at the issues individually and deciding, in accordance with the approach in *Chiron Corp v Murex Diagnostics Ltd (No.13)* [1996] F.S.R. 578, [1996] C.L.Y. 4544, whether there was an irreducible amount due in any event. In order to do that, the court had to consider C's title to sue and the proper measure of loss to be applied, *Chiron* considered (see paras 13-14 of judgment). (2) On the basis of the material before the court, the title to sue arguments did not give rise to a complete defence to the claim. While there was some doubt as to which of the claimant entities might ultimately be able to recover, it did not seem that, for the purposes of the interim payment application, it mattered. It would be wrong in principle if an otherwise clear entitlement to an interim payment was frustrated because of an absence of clarity as to which claimant entity might be the ultimate beneficiary, in circumstances where there was no evidence that repayment, if necessary, might not be made (para.37). (3) As a result of being unable to reach a concluded view on the arguments concerned with the measure of loss, the irreducible minimum for the purposes of r.25 had to be the figures put forward by D by way of diminution of value. On the basis that the diminution in value case was at least arguable, it seemed that, for the purposes of an interim payment, and on D's own figures, the sum of £3.25 million would be inevitably due by way of an interim payment; that figure was the midpoint of D's valuation of the business at the time of the fire less 75 per cent. As to C's loss of profit, it was appropriate to adopt a broad-brush approach because, whatever the outcome, on the material C would recover at trial a substantial sum by way of loss of profit, albeit probably much less than they claimed. Even taking into account the 75 per cent reduction, that figure could not be put at less than £750,000. Accordingly, an irreducible minimum in the sum of £4 million would be recovered; therefore that was the sum to be paid on account by way of interim payment (paras 46-50). Even if it was wrong to conclude that D's diminution in value case was arguable and C's basis of quantification had been adopted, the amount of the interim payment would not have been significantly higher than the £4 million awarded (para.51).

TREBOR BASSETT HOLDINGS LTD v ADT FIRE & SECURITY PLC, [2012] EWHC 3365 (TCC), 145 Con. L.R. 147, Coulson, J., QBD (TCC).

385. Interim relief–Freezing injunctions–Lack of assets within jurisdiction–Expediency of worldwide asset freezing injunction and disclosure order–Real risk of dissipation

[Civil Jurisdiction and Judgments Act 1982 (c.27) s.25.]

The applicant bank (R) applied under the Civil Jurisdiction and Judgments Act 1982 s.25 for the continuation of domestic and worldwide freezing orders against the respondents (F), and for an order requiring F to disclose information as to the nature and location of their worldwide assets. F consisted of four companies, two of which were incorporated under the laws of the United Arab Emirates (UAE) and two under Liberian law. The directors and shareholders of F were mostly members of the same family resident outside the United Kingdom. Two further companies belonging to the F group were incorporated in the UK but were not defendants to the instant proceedings. R granted secured loans to F for the purchase of ships. The loan agreements were subject to English law and exclusive jurisdiction provisions. Those agreements provided for F to pay the earnings of the ships into English bank accounts, which had to be maintained at a minimum level of credit. F defaulted on the loans and failed to respond to R's inquiries as to the whereabouts of one of the ships. R issued proceedings against F in the UAE under the loan agreements. F sought to sell the ships to third parties. R obtained interim freezing orders in the English court. F remained unwilling to provide details of its assets or financial position.

Held: Application granted. (1) The correct approach to an application for interim relief under s.25 of the 1982 Act was, firstly, to consider if the facts would warrant the relief sought if the substantive proceedings had been brought in England; in particular, whether the claimant had a good arguable case and whether there was a real risk of dissipation; if so, secondly, to consider whether the fact that the court had no jurisdiction except s.25 made it "inexpedient" for the purposes of s.25(2) to grant the relief, *Refco Inc v Eastern Trading Co* [1999] 1 Lloyd's Rep. 159, [1998] C.L.Y. 563 followed (see para.36 of judgment). (2) It was common ground that R had a good arguable case against F. The only issue in that regard was whether the failure to pay was attributable to genuine financial inability or reluctance. F appeared to have taken deliberate steps to dispose of their assets or put them out of reach of their creditors, as demonstrated by the failure to pay the ships' earnings into the UK bank accounts, the lack of information given as to the whereabouts of one of the ships and F's refusal to provide financial information. There was a strong inference that F, given the geographical extent and nature of their business operations, were likely to have assets in jurisdictions other than England or the UAE. It was realistically conceded that the evidence demonstrated a real risk of dissipation (paras 38-40). (3) In the absence of any jurisdiction in the UAE to make orders such as those sought in the instant case, there was little danger of conflict between decisions or jurisdictions. The identification and location of assets, and any subsequent attachment orders made in the relevant jurisdictions where such assets might be found, would necessarily assist the enforcement of any judgments of the UAE courts. R was well within its contractual rights in bringing the substantive proceedings in the UAE. Although very careful consideration had to be given to the making of worldwide freezing orders, the necessary links with the jurisdiction of England and Wales were established on the evidence before the court. The loans had been raised from a UK bank and were subject to English law and English exclusive jurisdiction clauses. F had therefore become subject to contractual obligations, and had also acquired substantive rights, under English law. Likewise, the ships' operating accounts demonstrated a real link or connection with the jurisdiction, even in the absence of any funds in them. Although it was not legitimate to deem the assets of F's English subsidiaries as assets of F within the jurisdiction, the evidence nonetheless demonstrated that F held themselves out as having an operational presence in England. It was therefore clearly expedient and appropriate to grant a worldwide asset freezing injunction and disclosure orders against F in aid of the UAE proceedings under s.25, notwithstanding the absence of assets within the jurisdiction, *Credit Suisse Fides Trust SA v Cuoghi* [1998] Q.B. 818, [1997] C.L.Y. 893 and *Motorola Credit Corp v Uzan (No.6)* [2003] EWCA Civ 752, [2004] 1 W.L.R. 113, [2003] C.L.Y. 413 followed (paras 41-45, 47).

ROYAL BANK OF SCOTLAND PLC v FAL OIL CO LTD, [2012] EWHC 3628 (Comm), [2013] 1 Lloyd's Rep. 327, Gloster, J., QBD (Comm).

386. Joinder–Jurisdiction–Similar issues relating to incapacitated person's accommodation and treatment regime in Court of Protection and High Court–Difference of jurisdiction of each court–Whether joinder appropriate

[Court of Protection Rules 2007 (SI 2007/1744) r.73, r.75.]

The first and second applicants (C and G) applied to be joined in the instant proceedings. C was the brother of the first respondent (S) and G was a bus company whose bus had struck S, causing him severe brain and physical injuries. S, who was likely to need full-time care for the rest of his life, had issued High Court proceedings for damages against G, and was represented there by C as his litigation friend. Judgment had been entered against G but damages such as the cost of, amongst other things, C's care, accommodation, treatment and rehabilitation regime had not been quantified. In the instant proceedings, where the Official Solicitor was S's litigation friend, the issue was as to the sort of home in which S should be placed and with what rehabilitation regime. The parties and experts agreed that there should be modest, rather than intensive, rehabilitation. G's expert within the High Court proceedings agreed. However, C had obtained an expert opinion that S could well significantly benefit from intensive rehabilitation, and could improve sufficiently to ultimately be cared for in the community. C was anxious for the expert's reports to be formally in evidence within the Court of Protection proceedings. G sought the consolidation of both sets of proceedings, or, in the alternative, for the Court of Protection to crystallise a discrete issue as to S's accommodation, care and level of rehabilitation, and for G to be heard on that issue.

Held: Applications granted in part. (1) There was nothing controversial about C's application. Close family members were regularly joined in Court of Protection proceedings. C clearly cared for S and wanted to do his best for him. He came within the category of person who would be likely to be joined, and met the requirements of joinder in the Court of Protection Rules 2007. The court was not persuaded by suggestions that those instructing C were manipulating him to try to maximise S's High Court damages. The court approached C's application on the basis that he genuinely wished to place what might be a viable option before the court, to ensure the best possible outcome for S (see paras 23, 27 of judgment). (2) At first sight there was great attraction in the argument that there should be one hearing to decide where S should live and the level of rehabilitation. It would save costs, avoid duplication, and both the overriding objective and common sense required good reasons to decline a single hearing to resolve similar or connected issues. However, sometimes an attractive pragmatic approach had to yield for good reason to a more legalistic one. The key point was that the underlying issue in the two sets of proceedings, however similar, was not the same. The jurisdiction of the Court of Protection was as to best interests and that of the High Court was compensatory. The tests, of "best interests" as against "reasonable needs", however similar, were not the same. If the Court of Protection held that intensive rehabilitation was in S's best interests and those responsible for his next move could not arrange for that without securing the necessary resources, funding would be sought from G's insurers. If they refused, those responsible for furthering S's best interest would doubtless apply for a hearing within the High Court proceedings to decide the issue. Whilst that court would pay regard to the Court of Protection declaration, it would not be bound by it and would decide the issue according to the principles relating to the assessment of damages. G would not have been treated unfairly by its absence from the Court of Protection proceedings. It was not a situation where the party seeking joinder was bound to pay damages as a direct consequence of the outcome of the proceedings in which he asked to be joined. Further, if there were a single hearing, a High Court decision on quantum was not reviewable in the same way as in the Court of Protection where jurisdiction was ongoing. The applicable Court of Protection Rules, namely r.73 and r.75, ought to be considered together. The requirement in r.75 that the applicant for joinder had "sufficient interest" in the context of r.73 should be interpreted to mean "a sufficient interest in the proceedings" as distinct from some commercial interest of the applicant's own. The clear import of r.73 as to the joinder of a party if it was "desirable... for the purpose of dealing with the application" was that it would enable the court better to deal with the substantive application. Here, the substantive application of the level of S's rehabilitation regime would not be dealt with better with G's participation since the two sides of the issue were well evidenced. "Desirable" imported a judicial discretion in balancing the pros and cons of a particular joinder sought. The joinder of G was not proportionate, having regard to the alleged mischief that joinder was said to be necessary to prevent (paras 36-38, 40-43).

SK, *Re*, [2012] EWHC 1990 (COP), [2013] P.I.Q.R. P4, Bodey, J., CP.

387. Judgments and orders–Procedure–Judge constructing judgment almost entirely on basis of counsel's written submissions

The appellants (F and S) appealed against a decision giving judgment against them in an action begun by the respondent company (X). F and S were father and son. S opened three accounts with X, one being in F's name, to enable him to conduct contracts for differences, and he proceeded to operate those accounts over several months. Very substantial debts were run up on all three accounts and X issued proceedings for their recovery. It was F's case that S had no authority to set up and operate the account on his behalf. It was (eventually) common ground that his signature on a power of attorney purporting to grant such authority had been forged by S. X argued that F had nevertheless either given express authority to S to submit such a document or in any event given him express or implied authority to open and operate the account; alternatively, F had subsequently ratified his doing so. S's case was that one of the accounts was operated on behalf of a company and that he had no personal liability in respect of the accounts. Both F and S argued that X was in breach of various obligations under its own terms of business and/or the applicable industry rules, as a result of which any debts were unenforceable. The judge upheld X's claims in full and gave judgment against F and S. F and S argued that almost all of the judge's judgment was taken word-for-word from the closing submissions of X's counsel; that represented a serious procedural irregularity causing the decision to be unjust: for the judge to base his judgment to such an extent on counsel's submissions created the impression that he had abdicated his core judicial responsibility to think through for himself the issues which it was his job to decide; further, in following the course that he had, the judge failed to address their own case.

Held: Appeal dismissed. The judge's judgment did give the overall impression that it was derived almost entirely from counsel's closing submissions. It was thoroughly bad practice for the judge to construct his judgment in the way that he had, essentially for the reasons given by F and S. Appearances mattered. For the judge to rely as heavily as he had on counsel's written submissions did indeed risk giving the impression that he had not performed his task of considering both parties' cases independently and evenhandedly. A judge would often derive great assistance from counsel's written submissions, and there was nothing inherently wrong in his making extensive use of them, with proper acknowledgment, whether in setting out the facts or in analysing the issues or the applicable legal principles or indeed in the actual dispositive reasoning. But where that occurred, the judge should take care to make it clear that he had fully considered such contrary submissions as had been made and had brought his own independent judgment to bear. The more extensive the reliance on material supplied by only one party, the greater the risk that the judge would in fact fail to do justice to the other party's case and, in any event, that that would appear to have been the case. However, to say that the judgment was defective, even seriously so, was not necessarily to say that there had been an injustice which required the appeal to be allowed. Wrong though the way in which the judge constructed his judgment was, it could be seen from a careful examination that he did in fact bring an independent judgment to bear on the decisive issues in the case, and it was sufficiently clear why he decided those issues in the way that he had. Further, there was nothing in the submissions made on F and S's behalf in the court below which justified the conclusion that they ever had a real defence to X's claims (see paras 11, 16-17, 36-37 of judgment).

IG MARKETS LTD v CRINION; *sub nom.* CRINION v IG MARKETS LTD, [2013] EWCA Civ 587, [2013] C.P. Rep. 41, Longmore, L.J., CA (Civ Div).

388. Judgments and orders–Setting aside–Requirement of promptness under r.39.3(5)(a) CPR–Litigants in person

[Civil Procedure Rules 1998 (SI 1998/3132) r.1.1, r.39.3(3).]

The appellant company (W) and its chairman (T) appealed against a decision ([2012] EWHC 600 (QB)) setting aside a permanent injunction against the respondent (E). E had been engaged by W as a helicopter pilot and aviation consultant. The breakdown of the relationship resulted in a number of claims between them. Proceedings were compromised in July 2007 and E gave an undertaking not to repeat allegations he had made against W and T. Various proceedings instigated by E against W and T in 2009 were struck out as being totally without merit. W and T obtained an interim without notice injunction to enforce E's compliance with the undertaking. They then claimed damages and a permanent injunction in the same terms as the undertaking. E did not attend the trial, relying on a letter from his general practitioner indicating that he was unfit to attend court. The injunction was granted and a general civil restraint order imposed in March 2010. E was not served with a note of the outcome of the hearing at that time. In April 2010 and July 2011, he applied for permission to appeal against a striking out order from 2009 and, in July 2011, for an extension of time to appeal against the March 2010 decision. In March 2012, he successfully applied to set aside that decision. The judge referred to the 20-month period between E being aware of the judgment and making his application, but regarded it as a "special case on its facts" when finding the promptness requirement under CPR r.39.3(5)(a) satisfied. She concluded that E was under a significant disadvantage as a result of his health problems and the fact that he was acting in person. E submitted that the court should approach the issue of promptness with maximum flexibility, in line with the overriding objective under CPR r.1.1 of dealing with cases justly.

Held: Appeal allowed. (1) The following propositions could be derived from the authorities: (a) promptness was a mandatory requirement; (b) it required the applicant to act "with all reasonable celerity in the circumstances"; (c) only if the mandatory requirements were satisfied did the court have a discretion which, at that stage, was "somewhat narrow"; (d) the instant court had a reviewing, as opposed to a rehearing, function, and could only interfere if satisfied that the judge below was wrong, *Bank of Scotland v Pereira* [2011] EWCA Civ 241, [2011] 1 W.L.R. 2391, [2011] C.L.Y. 346 applied, *Regency Rolls Ltd v Carnall* and *Standard Bank Plc v Agrinvest International Inc* [2009] EWHC 1692 (Comm) considered (see paras 18-25 of judgment). (2) The flaw in the approach submitted by E was that it invested the judicial division with a degree of discretion which was contrary to the structure of r.39.3(3). The element of discretion came into play only after an applicant had satisfied the three positive requirements, including promptness. The judge's approach at that stage was essentially evaluative rather than discretionary. There could be facts and circumstances in relation to a litigant in person which might go to an assessment of promptness; however, they would only operate close to the margins. An opponent of a litigant in person was entitled to assume finality without expecting excessive indulgence to be extended to the litigant in person. The fact that a litigant in person did not really understand or appreciate the procedural courses open to them did not entitle them to extra indulgence. In the instant case, even if E's health problems were factored in, the evidence showed that he was active in the litigation between April and July 2010, and the fact that, if properly advised, he might have made a different application could not avail him. That would be to take sensitivity to the difficulties faced by a litigant in person too far. The judge had erred in regarding the case as "a special case on its facts". It could only be considered such if the allowance made for a litigant in person went too far. It had not been open to the judge to find the promptness requirement satisfied (paras 28-32). (3) Allowing the appeal would prevent E from obtaining judgment on the merits. However, promptness was a mandatory requirement under r.39.3(2) and, if an applicant was doomed to fail on that basis, he could nevertheless obtain an extension of time to apply for permission to appeal if he merited such an extension and the proposed appeal had a real prospect of success. Extension of time in that context was a discretionary matter, whereas promptness in the instant context was not (para.34).

TINKLER v ELLIOTT, [2012] EWCA Civ 1289, [2013] C.P. Rep. 4, Sir Maurice Kay (VP CA Civ), CA (Civ Div).

389. Judicial review–Procurement

THE CIVIL PROCEDURE (AMENDMENT NO.4) RULES 2013, SI 2013/SI 2013/1412 (L.14); made under the Civil Procedure Act 1997 s.2. In force: July 1, 2013; .

These Rules amend the Civil Procedure Rules 1998 (SI 1998/3132) to: shorten the time limit for bringing a judicial review to six weeks in certain planning cases and thirty days in certain procurement cases; and remove the right to a reconsideration at a hearing of the refusal of permission to bring judicial review (oral renewal) in cases where the application is certified as totally without merit by the judge considering the application on the papers.

390. Justice and Security Act 2013 (18)

This Act provides for oversight of the Security Service, the Secret Intelligence Service, the Government Communications Headquarters and other activities relating to intelligence or security matters; provides for closed material procedure in relation to certain civil proceedings; and prevents the making of certain court orders for the disclosure of sensitive information.

This Act received Royal Assent on April 25, 2013.

391. Limitation periods–Contingent liabilities–Professional negligence–Failure of solicitors to advise joint tenant that tenancy vulnerable to unilateral severance–Date of accrual of cause of action–Date and extent of knowledge

[Limitation Act 1980 (c.58) s.14, s.14A(8)(a).]

The court was required to determine as a preliminary issue whether the professional negligence action brought by the claimant (B) against the first defendant firm of solicitors (P) was statute-barred. P had acted for B and his then girlfriend (W) in the purchase of a property. The purchase completed in October 1996. B and W held the property as joint tenants but only W lived there. In May 2007, W served a notice of severance of the joint tenancy on B. In July 2007, B informed W that severance breached their agreement, made at the time of purchase, that upon the death of either of them the entire property would pass to the survivor. W died in January 2009 and B was left with only half the property. In March 2009, solicitors advised him of a potential negligence action against P. He began the instant proceedings in August 2010. His substantive case was that P had failed to give legal effect to his intentions and that they had failed to advise him that W could unilaterally sever the joint tenancy. The issues for the instant hearing were (i) whether B's cause of action accrued in October 1996, May 2007 or July 2007; (ii) whether, for requisite knowledge to be established, it had to be shown that B knew that P owed a duty to take precise instructions from him and to advise him of W's right to unilaterally sever the joint tenancy; (iii) when B had acquired actual knowledge for the purposes of the instant claim.

Held: Preliminary issue determined in favour of defendants. (1) The tort had been complete, at the latest, when the transfer of the property was executed in October 1996. There was clearly a measurable loss from the moment that B acquired the property because he had something quite different from what he alleged he should have had: he had a severable joint tenancy, which had a lower value than the unseverable one that he wanted and thought he had. It did not matter that the damages would have been difficult to assess in 1996, nor that many of the losses depended on future contingencies, *Law Society v Sephton & Co* [2006] UKHL 22, [2006] 2 A.C. 543, [2006] C.L.Y. 474 applied (see paras 60-61, 65 of judgment). (2) There was no need in law for B to know that P owed him a legal duty to advise him that the joint tenancy was unilaterally severable, *Hallam-Eames v Merrett Syndicates Ltd (No.1)* [1995] C.L.C. 173, [1995] C.L.Y. 3166 and *Fennon v Anthony Hodari & Co* [2001] Lloyd's Rep. P.N. 183, [2001] C.L.Y. 605 considered and *Haward v Fawcetts (A Firm)* [2006] UKHL 9, [2006] 1 W.L.R. 682, [2006] C.L.Y. 472 followed (paras 71-74, 100). Some of the speeches in *Haward* could be construed as saying something slightly different from *Hallam-Eames* and *Fennon*. However, the Lords in *Haward* had not overruled *Fennon* or expressly endorsed the criticisms of it and had therefore not displaced the test to be applied (paras 76-89). (3) The fact that B did not address his mind to the damage having been attributable to P's omission was not fatal to his actual knowledge under the Limitation Act 1980 s.14A(8)(a); he did not need to know that the acts or omissions involved negligence, only that they had occurred. Knowledge of the facts was crucial because the law under s.14A was structured so as to make it an objective test as to whether it was reasonable for a claimant to consider it sufficiently serious to sue, and that was in line with *Haward* and *Hallam-Eames* (paras 97-98, 100). On the facts, B had, by July 2007 at the latest, acquired actual knowledge of the material facts that he needed to know to make it sufficiently serious to bring proceedings. His claim against P was therefore statute-barred, the six-year limitation period having expired in October 2002 and the three-year period allowed by s.14A having expired in July 2010 (paras 101, 104, 110).

BOYCOTT v PERRINS GUY WILLIAMS, [2011] EWHC 2969 (Ch), [2012] P.N.L.R. 25, Vos, J., Ch D.

392. Limitation periods–Date from which limitation period ran–Acknowledgment of claim–Meaning of "debt or other liquidated pecuniary claim" in s.29(5) Limitation Act 1980–Whether solicitors' unassessed costs amounted to debt or liquidated claim

[Limitation Act 1980 (c.58) s.29(5); Solicitors Act 1974 (c.47) s.66.]

The appellant (B) appealed against a decision that it was liable to pay legal costs to the respondent solicitors (S). B had instructed S to act on its behalf in a matter concerning possession of a flat. S sent B a bill of costs for the work done. By a letter dated September 20, 2004 B objected to the level of fees. On September 8, 2010, S brought proceedings against B for unpaid fees and interest. B obtained summary judgment on the basis that the proceedings were out of time. On appeal, the judge found that B's letter amounted to an acknowledgment under the Limitation Act 1980 s.29(5), with the effect that the six-year limitation period started again from that date. The claim was therefore in time. The court was required to determine whether S's costs, billed but not yet fixed by assessment or agreement, were a "debt or other liquidated pecuniary claim" falling within the terms of s.29(5), and, if so, whether B's letter amounted to an acknowledgment of that claim.

Held: Appeal dismissed. (1) There had been no agreement as to the basis of the costs payable by B for the contentious business S was carrying out on its behalf. Accordingly, under the Solicitors Act 1974 s.66 S's entitlement was to an amount which, if B sought an assessment of the bill, would be determined by a costs judge having regard to the skill, labour and responsibility involved in the work done. A solicitor's claim for fees in such circumstances was a claim in debt, as opposed to damages, in the nature of a quantum meruit, but it was not quantified until it was either assessed by the court, agreed by the client, or was the subject of a judgment, *Turner & Co v O Palomo SA* [2000] 1 W.L.R. 37, [1999] C.L.Y. 416, *Thomas Watts & Co v Smith* [1998] 2 Costs L.R. 59, [2000] C.L.Y. 402 and *Coburn v Colledge* [1897] 1 Q.B. 702 considered (see paras 14, 19 of judgment). (2) The statutory phrase in s.29(5) was "debt or other liquidated pecuniary claim". There was some debate as to the width of the word "debt" in that context. In ordinary legal usage the word "liquidated" required the liability to be for an ascertained amount. However, an acknowledgment could arise at quite an early stage in the history of dealings between the parties about the claim. By the time the question came to be decided, six or more years would have run from the date when the cause of action accrued. In that context it would be understandable that the legislation should not require the same precision and certainty as it did for presentation of a bankruptcy petition, or for consideration of what a claimant was entitled to by way of summary judgment, *Truex v Toll* [2009] EWHC 396 (Ch), [2009] 1 W.L.R. 2121, [2009] C.L.Y. 2221 and *Lagos v Grunwaldt* [1910] 1 K.B. 41 considered. It would be understandable if matters occurring at that stage could be looked at in a more general way than was appropriate or necessary once one came to a judicial determination of rights, or, as in the case of bankruptcy, the assertion of remedies against the debtor. It was likely that the draftsman of the Limitation Act 1939, which preceded the 1980 Act, had in mind the then rule of court (RSC Ord.3 r.6) about specially endorsed writs and summary judgment, as considered in *Grunwaldt*. That rule, as interpreted and applied by the courts, showed that a "liquidated demand" was not treated as requiring that the amount of the liability should already have been ascertained. It therefore cast a different light on the use of the word "liquidated" in the 1939 Act, and would allow a solicitor's claim for professional fees to be regarded as within the provision. It followed that a quantum meruit claim was also classified for that purpose as a liquidated claim, *Amantilla v Telefusion* 9 Con. L.R. 139, [1988] C.L.Y. 2163 and *Byatt (t/a MBP Byatt & Co) v Nash*approved. It would have been odd if the effect of the 1939 Act was to narrow the range of claims which could be acknowledged. For those reasons, and despite the possible oddity of a quantum meruit claim being classified as a liquidated claim, a claim by solicitors for remuneration, even though not yet fixed by assessment, was within the phrase "debt or other liquidated pecuniary claim" in s.29(5)(a). It was not necessary to decide whether it qualified as a "debt" or "a liquidated pecuniary claim". Either way, it was within the statutory phrase (paras 25, 40-42, 46-48). (3) B's letter took issue with the amount claimed, but not with the principle that something was payable. The judge had therefore been correct to find that the claim had been acknowledged, and the proceedings were not barred by the lapse of time (para.53).

PHILLIPS & CO v BATH HOUSING CO-OPERATIVE LTD, [2012] EWCA Civ 1591, [2013] 1 W.L.R. 1479, Longmore, L.J., CA (Civ Div).

393. Limitation periods–Discretion–Delay in commencing court proceedings–Nature of burden on claimant seeking to rely on s.33 Limitation Act 1980

[Limitation Act 1980 (c.58) s.11, s.33.]

The appellant (S) appealed against a decision of a circuit judge that his personal injury claim against the respondents (H and W) was statute-barred, and against a refusal to exercise discretion under the Limitation Act 1980 s.33 to allow it to proceed. From 1981, S had worked for H and W as a gardener with responsibility for maintaining a large garden and forest. H died in 1989 and S remained employed by W until May 2000, when he took up employment elsewhere. By that time, he was suffering from hearing loss and tinnitus. In 2002, S was told by a nurse during an occupational health-check that he might be suffering from noise-induced industrial hearing loss. In April 2005 he consulted his general practitioner, who referred him to a specialist. S was reviewed by the specialist in June 2006. He retained a firm of solicitors in October 2006 and was advised in December of that year that he was eligible to bring a claim against H and W. A letter of claim was sent in July 2008 and proceedings were started in September 2009. A deputy district judge found, as a preliminary issue, that S's date of knowledge for the purposes of limitation was December 2006 and that his claim was therefore in time. The circuit judge allowed W's appeal, concluding that the claim was out of time because the date of knowledge was 2002, when S received advice from the nurse. He held that the burden on S under s.33 of the Act was particularly heavy and that it would not be appropriate to exercise discretion to allow the claim to proceed because there had been unreasonable delay without explanation; the equipment used by S at the relevant time was long gone; much of the complaint pre-dated H's death at a time when W had been less closely involved, and W, at the age of 88, did not have a fair opportunity to defend the claim. S submitted that (1) the proposition in *KR v Bryn Alyn Community (Holdings) Ltd (In Liquidation)* [2003] EWCA Civ 85, [2003] Q.B. 1441, [2003] C.L.Y. 432 that s.33 imposed a "heavy burden" on the claimant was no longer good law; (2) the instant court should re-exercise the discretion under s.33 and allow the action to proceed.

Held: Appeal dismissed. (1) There was a wealth of conflicting authority on the question of what test should be applied under s.33. It should not be necessary for judges in the county court to engage in textual analysis of a series of appellate decisions in order to discern whether a claimant relying on s.33 had a "burden" or a "heavy burden" to discharge. All that could properly be said about the general approach to the section was that the burden was on the claimant, because it was he who was seeking to be exempted from the normal consequences of failing to issue proceedings in time. It was not helpful to discuss in the abstract whether that burden was a heavy one or a light one. In *Horton v Sadler* [2006] UKHL 27, [2007] 1 A.C. 307, [2006] C.L.Y. 475 and *A v Hoare* [2008] UKHL 6, [2008] 1 A.C. 844, [2008] C.L.Y. 385, the House of Lords stressed that the court's discretion under s.33 was broad and unfettered. Those comments made it difficult to maintain that the claimant's burden was necessarily a heavy one; every case was fact-specific, *B v Ministry of Defence* [2010] EWCA Civ 1317, (2011) 117 B.M.L.R. 101, [2011] C.L.Y. 350 followed, *KR* not followed and *Davies v Secretary of State for Energy and Climate Change* [2012] EWCA Civ 1380, *Horton*, and *Hoare* considered. In the instant case the judge had applied the wrong test; he ought simply to have said that the burden was on S. However, given that he had been faced with an array of inconsistent dicta from superior courts, and had not had the benefit of hearing full argument on the issue, it was difficult to criticise him for applying the wrong test (see paras 37-40, 42, 46-49, 54, 56-58 of judgment). (2) A fresh consideration of the factors in s.33 supported a conclusion that it would not be appropriate to disapply s.11 of the Act and enable S's claim to proceed. The action had been commenced four years after the expiry of the limitation period with no explanation for the delay. That delay made it substantially more difficult for the parties to adduce relevant evidence. Both S and his legal advisers had progressed the claim in a leisurely manner. The prejudice to W far outweighed the prejudice to S (paras 61-69).

SAYERS v CHELWOOD (DECEASED); *sub nom.* SAYERS v HUNTERS, [2012] EWCA Civ 1715, [2013] 1 W.L.R. 1695, Arden, L.J., CA (Civ Div).

394. Litigants in person–Practice guidance clarifying whether term "litigant in person" or "self-represented litigant" should be adopted

The Master of the Rolls issued Practice Guidance to clarify the correct term to be used to refer to individuals who conducted legal proceedings on their own behalf. In November 2011, the Civil Justice Council had recommended that individuals who conducted legal proceedings on their own behalf, and had traditionally been referred to as litigants in person (LiPs), should in future be referred to as self-represented litigants (SRLs). Subsequently the term SRL had gained some currency, but LiP also continued to be used. The use of two terms to refer to the same thing was less than ideal. It was confusing both for individual litigants and the courts. The term LiP was used in statute; it was and would continue to be used by Government; and it was commonly understood and well known, both by the legal profession and individuals generally. The term SRL, however, was unclear in its scope as it could variously be understood to suggest that individuals were conducting the entirety of legal proceedings on their own behalf, that they were only conducting court advocacy on their own behalf, or that they had themselves obtained representation. In the light of those factors, the Master of the Rolls determined that the term SRL should not be adopted or used in future. The term 'litigant in person' should continue to be the sole term used to describe individuals who exercised their right to conduct legal proceedings on their own behalf. The Guidance applied to all proceedings in all criminal, civil and family courts.

PRACTICE GUIDANCE (SEN CTS: LITIGANTS IN PERSON: TERMINOLOGY); *sub nom.* PRACTICE GUIDANCE (SEN CTS: TERMINOLOGY FOR LITIGANTS IN PERSON) [2013] 1 W.L.R. 1318, Lord Dyson (M.R.), Sen Cts.

395. Mental capacity–Assessment–Assessment of mental capacity in absence of medical evidence–Finding of mental impairment

[Mental Capacity Act 2005 (c.9) s.2, s.3; Civil Procedure Rules 1998 (SI 1998/3132) Pt 21, r.21.3.]

The appellant accountancy firm (B) appealed against an order of a master staying cost assessment proceedings. B had been instructed by the respondent (M) to carry out work on her behalf. B commenced proceedings to claim its fees and M was ordered to pay an amount with interest and an additional amount on account of costs. The detailed assessment hearing began on July 17, 2012 and M appeared in person. On the second day of the hearing M became tearful and distressed and lay on the floor screaming. The master became concerned about M's capacity and sought the intervention of the Official Solicitor. M did not co-operate and refused to grant access to her medical files. The master made an unless order essentially debarring M from participating in the assessment process unless she provided consent to the release of her records to the Official Solicitor. At a further hearing the master concluded in the absence of formal medical evidence that M lacked capacity to conduct the costs litigation, that she suffered an impairment of or a disturbance in the functioning of her mind or brain for the purposes of the Mental Capacity Act 2005 s.2 and s.3 and was therefore a protected person for the purposes of CPR Pt 21. The master stayed the proceedings pursuant to CPR r.21.3 pending the appointment of a litigation friend to act for M. When making his decision the master was aware that M had continued to represent herself in other litigation. .

Held: Appeal allowed. The master had no evidence about M's mental capacity apart from his own impression following the events on July 18 where M had suffered a serious but brief loss of control. The master put more weight on the incident than was necessary. He should have taken account of M's ability to take part in other litigation where no question about her lack of capacity had arisen. Where medical evidence could not be obtained a court had to be cautious before concluding that a litigant was suffering from a disturbance of the mind. Such a finding had serious consequences for both parties. The proceedings should not have been stayed pending the appointment of a litigation friend for M.

BAKER TILLY v MAKAR, [2013] EWHC 759 (QB), [2013] 3 Costs L.R. 444, Sir Raymond Jack, QBD.

396. Non-party costs–Local authorities' powers and duties–Local authority's failure to comply with direction under s.37 Children Act 1989 causing wasted hearings–Appropriateness of making non-party costs order against local authority

[Children Act 1989 (c.41) s.8, s.37; Family Procedure Rules 2010 (SI 2010/2955) r.28.1.]

The applicant father (F) applied for a costs order against the respondent local authority, which had been a non-party in private proceedings under the Children Act 1989. F and the mother (M) of his six-year-old son (O) had separated. M applied for a residence order under s.8 of the Act and F cross-applied for residence and contact orders, thereby raising serious allegations about M's behaviour including that she had fabricated details of serious illnesses and medical conditions suffered by her and O. The district judge made an order under s.37 of the Act directing a report from the local authority. A final hearing for the parents' cross-applications was listed for December 2012. At that hearing, it became apparent from the social worker's oral evidence that in preparing her s.37 report, she had not considered the relevant guidance for social workers in dealing with fabricated illness, nor the guidance in *X (Children) (Care Proceedings: Costs), Re* [2011] 1 F.L.R. 1045, [2011] C.L.Y. 1324. The parties agreed that the hearing could not proceed effectively, and the case was transferred to the High Court for directions. A further s.37 report was directed and the costs of the aborted fact-finding hearing and the subsequent directions hearing were reserved. In commenting on the s.37 reports in the adjourned fact-finding judgment, the judge stated that the local authority's reports did not assist him, and that the assessment was predicated on an unclear factual foundation with internal confusions. At the hearing's conclusion, F applied for the local authority to pay his wasted costs of £10,311 arising from the December 2012 hearings. F contended that a costs order against a non-party was appropriate since the local authority's systemic and specific failures had fundamentally undermined the purported work for the s.37 enquiry, which led to the wasted court days in December 2012.

Held: Application granted. (1) The Family Procedure Rules 2010 r.28.1 gave the court a wide discretion to make any such order as to costs it thought just at any time. There was limited authority on how the court should exercise its wide discretion in family cases to make orders against non-parties, other than lawyers. The clear rule in non-family cases was that a non-party costs order would be exceptional; however, it was not necessary for a determination of the issue of exceptionality for there to be a finding that the conduct of the non-party was "improper", *Globe Equities Ltd v Globe Legal Services Ltd* [2000] C.P.L.R. 233, [1999] C.L.Y. 390 applied (see paras 35, 38-41 of judgment). (2) Local authorities' human and financial resources were currently more hard-pressed than ever, and minor failures could, in practice, be dealt with in ways which did not involve financial penalty. The failures in the instant case were, however, not minor: they were extensive and had a profound effect on the conduct of the proceedings. The local authority had failed fundamentally to investigate, address, or analyse the serious issues in the case raised by F's allegations when it prepared its s.37 report or prior to the December 2012 hearing. The inadequacy of the investigation and the report-writing could in some respects be ascribed to the social worker's inexperience; that was not a matter of criticism, because experience had to be acquired over time and through professional practice. However, the local authority's failure was systemic in that there was no training of social workers in the assessment or management of cases of the instant kind. The admitted failure to follow the relevant guidance was a serious failing; the court was entitled to expect a social work team to have acted in accordance with the guidance on factitious illness syndrome, *X (A Child), Re* [2006] EWHC 510 (Fam), [2006] 2 F.L.R. 701, [2006] C.L.Y. 1676 applied. The local authority's hard-pressed financial resources did not release it from its clear statutory responsibility to investigate in accordance with the provisions of s.37 in fulfilment of a specific court direction, *T (Care Proceedings: Costs: Serious Allegations Not Proved), Re* [2012] UKSC 36, [2012] 1 W.L.R. 2281, [2012] C.L.Y. 1340 followed. A local authority in a private law case in which a s.37 direction had been given was sufficiently closely connected with the litigation to justify a non-party costs order. The local authority's failings comfortably carried the instant case over the "exceptionality" threshold. The consequence of the local authority's failure to comply appropriately with the s.37 direction was the inevitable abandonment of the fact-finding hearing, the requirement for a further directions hearing, and the consequent delay (with its financial and emotional cost to the parties) in re-listing it (paras 51-53, 55, 58-60, 63). (3) F was entitled to his costs of the wasted hearings in December 2012 from the local authority. His schedule of costs was conservatively drawn and there was nothing within it which fell outwith the reasonable recoverable costs of the wasted hearings. The costs award was, accordingly, summarily assessed in the sum claimed (paras 64-65).

HB v PB, [2013] EWHC 1956 (Fam), [2013] P.T.S.R. 1579, Cobb, J., Fam Div.

397. Norwich Pharmacal orders–Foreign proceedings–Foreign criminal proceedings–Availability of Norwich Pharmacal relief

[Crime (International Co-operation) Act 2003 (c.32).]

The appellants (C) appealed against a Divisional Court decision ([2012] EWHC 1737 (Admin), [2013] 1 All E.R. 161, [2013] 6 C.L. 37) to refuse their application for a [1974] A.C. 133, [1973] C.L.Y. 2643 order against the respondent secretary of state for material for use in proceedings in Uganda. The secretary of state cross-appealed against the court's order to file a public interest immunity (PII) certificate notwithstanding that a closed material procedure order had already been made. C had been prosecuted in Uganda in relation to bombings there. They petitioned the Ugandan Constitutional Court claiming that their prosecution was an abuse of process and unconstitutional, alleging that they had been unlawfully rendered from Kenya to Uganda and had been tortured. They claimed that the secretary of state had material which would assist them in the Constitutional Court proceedings. Those proceedings were criminal proceedings within the meaning of the Crime (International Co-operation) Act 2003. For tactical reasons, C did not make an application for the material in the Ugandan court. The Divisional Court concluded that the 2003 Act regime precluded it from making a *Norwich Pharmacal* order. It also found that C's failure to demonstrate that the application was necessary or that the secretary of state had facilitated any wrongdoing meant that it should not grant relief. During proceedings, the court had made a closed material procedure order. However, after giving an open judgment, it ordered the secretary of state to file a PII certificate in relation to the withholding from publication of a summary of closed annexes to the judgment.

Held: Appeal dismissed, cross-appeal dismissed. (1) The *Norwich Pharmacal* jurisdiction could not penetrate an area fenced off by statute. The jurisdiction to order persons to provide evidence for use in foreign proceedings had always been exclusively statutory, *Westinghouse Electric Corp Uranium Contract Litigation MDL Docket 235 (No.2)* [1978] A.C. 547, [1978] C.L.Y. 1422 applied, *Norway's Application (Nos.1 and 2), Re* [1990] 1 A.C. 723, [1989] C.L.Y. 1692 and *Shlaimoun v Mining Technologies International Inc* [2011] EWHC 3278 (QB), [2012] 1 W.L.R. 1276, [2012] C.L.Y. 318 considered. There were differences between the *Norwich Pharmacal* remedy and the 2003 Act regime. That regime included discretion for the secretary of state, the confinement of requests to foreign courts and prosecuting authorities, and national security and Crown servant exceptions. None of those features was in the *Norwich Pharmacal* jurisprudence as a mandatory requirement. Those were substantial differences such that Parliament could not have intended the common law remedy to survive the introduction of the statutory scheme, *R. (on the application of Child Poverty Action Group) v Secretary of State for Work and Pensions* [2010] UKSC 54, [2011] 2 A.C. 15, [2011] C.L.Y. 3157 applied. That led to the conclusion that Parliament had not created a parallel procedure but an exclusive one in the area it had addressed. To relegate national security to the status of a material consideration to be weighed on a case-by-case basis on a *Norwich Pharmacal* application would subvert the statutory scheme. Where the scheme of the 2003 Act was in play, *Norwich Pharmacal* did not run, *Norwich Pharmacal* considered. C's appeal therefore failed (see paras 21-27 of judgment). (2) In dealing with the issue of necessity, the Divisional Court's approach had been based on a correct understanding of the law and it had reached the correct conclusion. Although C's decision not to seek disclosure in Uganda had been rational, it did not allow them to avoid the requirement of necessity. It had not been the only rational decision that could have been made on their behalf (paras 32, 35). (3) There would be cases where there was a real difference between involvement or participation in wrongdoing on the one hand and facilitation on the other. A person present and involved might be attempting to prevent the wrongful act rather than facilitating it, but might nevertheless come into possession of the material sought by the applicant. *Norwich Pharmacal* relief was not intended to be beyond his reach in such circumstances, *Ashworth Hospital Authority v MGN Ltd* [2002] UKHL 29, [2002] 1 W.L.R. 2033, [2002] C.L.Y. 3221 considered. In concluding that an applicant had to establish facilitation, the Divisional Court had erred (paras 38-40). (4) The Divisional Court had attached some importance to the fact that C had sought evidence rather than information. However, the distinction between the two was illusory; nothing turned on it (para.12). (5) The question whether there was a statutory prohibition against the grant of *Norwich Pharmacal* relief in relation to foreign proceedings had not been raised in *R. (on the application of Mohamed) v Secretary of State for Foreign and Commonwealth Affairs* [2010] EWCA Civ 65, [2011] Q.B. 218, [2010] C.L.Y. 370. That case could therefore not have opened a path to relief in the instant case if the statutory provisions closed it, *Mohamed* considered (para.2). (5) The insistence on a PII certificate had not been wrong. Neither as a matter of principle nor on a construction of the closed material procedure order had the Divisional Court been constrained to deal with all subsequent issues exclusively pursuant to the order. If the court rationally considered that, at the stage of judgment, the interests of open justice demanded a more exacting regime, there was no reason why it should not require a PII certificate. However, that was not to say that reversion to PII would always be necessary or justifiable (para.50).

R. (ON THE APPLICATION OF OMAR) v SECRETARY OF STATE FOR FOREIGN AND COMMONWEALTH AFFAIRS; R. (ON THE APPLICATION OF NJOROGE) v SECRETARY OF STATE FOR FOREIGN AND COMMONWEALTH AFFAIRS, [2013] EWCA Civ 118, [2014] Q.B. 112, Lord Judge, L.C.J., CA (Civ Div).

398. Norwich Pharmacal orders–Proportionality–Order requiring disclosure of personal data–Factors to be considered–Effect of consideration of art.8 Charter of Fundamental Rights of the European Union

[Charter of Fundamental Rights of the European Union Art.8.]

The appellant (V) appealed against a decision of the Court of Appeal ([2011] EWCA Civ 1585, [2012] 2 C.M.L.R. 3, [2012] C.L.Y. 450) upholding the granting of a *Norwich Pharmacal* order in favour of the respondent (R). R was the governing body for rugby union in England and issued tickets for matches played at the Twickenham stadium. Pursuant to its policy of developing the sport, it distributed tickets to certain approved bodies and placed restrictions on their onward sale. In particular, it stipulated that the resale of a ticket at more than face value would constitute a breach of contract. V operated a website on which tickets for various events, including rugby matches at Twickenham, were offered for sale. Sellers anonymously registered tickets for sale on the site and V received a percentage of the price paid. When R discovered that the site had been used to advertise thousands of Twickenham tickets at prices far in excess of their face value, it obtained a *Norwich Pharmacal* order requiring V to disclose the identities of those involved in the sale and purchase of the tickets. V appealed, arguing that the order was a disproportionate interference with the rights of potential wrongdoers under the Charter of Fundamental Rights of the European Union art.8. The Court of Appeal found that any such interference was proportionate in light of R's legitimate aim of obtaining redress for the arguable wrongs. V submitted that in assessing whether the order was proportionate, the court had to ask itself whether obtaining information about a particular person who had sold a ticket at more than face value would benefit R to an extent that outweighed that individual's right to have his personal data protected from disclosure.

Held: Appeal dismissed. (1) Many of the factors to be considered in the making of a *Norwich Pharmacal* order were also relevant to the question of whether such an order was proportionate under art.8 of the Charter. Although the Charter bound Member States only when they were implementing EU law, that phrase was to be interpreted broadly, and R accepted that in the instant case, the court making the order had been implementing EU law. When dealing with an application for disclosure of personal data, the court had to weigh the potential value to the party seeking disclosure against the interests of the data subject, *Productores de Musica de Espana (Promusicae) v Telefonica de Espana SAU (C-275/06)* [2008] All E.R. (EC) 809, [2008] C.L.Y. 2256 considered. However, V's argument went further, suggesting that the court had to assess only the potential benefit to R of obtaining information about particular individuals, and that it was not to consider the value of that information in its broader context. On that argument, the fact that obtaining the information might deter others from selling or buying overpriced tickets could not be taken into account. That approach was somewhat artificial, and it was unrealistic to disregard R's overall aim of discouraging people from selling tickets at prices in excess of their face value. There was nothing in *Promusicae* to support the restriction contended for by V, and nor did *Bonnier Audio AB v Perfect Communication Sweden AB (C-461/10)* [2012] 2 C.M.L.R. 42 support its argument, *Bonnier* considered. Clearly, the court had to consider the facts of each case, but that did not mean ignoring their possible impact on issues going beyond their significance to the individual whose data was sought. There was no reason to disregard the wider context. R's desire to prevent the sale of tickets at inflated prices was intimately connected to its *Norwich Pharmacal* application, and the ability to demonstrate that those selling or buying overpriced tickets could be detected was a legitimate aspiration justifying disclosure. While Arnold J had, in *Golden Eye (International) Ltd v Telefonica UK Ltd* [2012] EWHC 723 (Ch), [2013] E.M.L.R. 1, [2013] 2 C.L. 203, correctly stated the proper approach to proportionality, its application to the instant case did not, as V suggested, lead to the conclusion that the order should be refused. An "intense focus" on the rights claimed in individual cases did not mean that the individuals affected by the granting of the order would have been unfairly or oppressively treated. All that would be revealed was the identity of those who sold and bought tickets in breach of R's terms, *Goldeneye* considered. R's entirely worthy motive in seeking to maintain the price of tickets at a reasonable level was in the interests of everybody who wanted to watch international rugby matches, and the only possible outcome of the weighing exercise was the granting of the order sought. The Court of Appeal might, in the instant case, be said to have somewhat overstated the position when it suggested that it would "generally be proportionate" to make an order where there was arguable wrongdoing and no other means of identifying the wrongdoers. However, it had not expressed that to be a presumption in favour of the grant of an order. The particular circumstances affecting the individual whose personal data would be revealed would always call for close consideration and might, in some limited instances, displace the interests of the applicant even where there was no immediately feasible alternative way for him to obtain the information. In the instant case, though, the impact on the individuals could not possibly offset R's interests (see paras 18, 28, 32, 36-37, 40, 45-46 of judgment).

RUGBY FOOTBALL UNION v VIAGOGO LTD; *sub nom.* RUGBY FOOTBALL UNION v CONSOLIDATED INFORMATION SERVICES (FORMERLY VIAGOGO LTD), [2012] UKSC 55, [2012] 1 W.L.R. 3333, Lord Phillips, J.S.C., SC.

399. Oral hearings–Witness statements–Determination of dispute on written evidence only despite party's request to call witness–Need for trial conducted on oral evidence

The appellant companies (MW and TW) appealed against a decision that they had failed to pay the respondent (W) in full for his shareholding in MW and that as a result his shares had to be reinstated. In 2002, W had agreed to sell MW to one of his employees (T). W owned the entire share capital in MW and T agreed to pay the purchase price over a number of years from the profits expected to be earned by MW. W was to continue being actively involved in the management of MW as a consultant. To achieve that arrangement, a new company (TW) was incorporated, which purchased W's shares in MW. T and W each owned half the shares in TW and T became sole director of TW. T and W entered into a shareholders' agreement by which T undertook to ensure that TW paid W the money due to him out of the dividend payments TW received from MW. No consultancy agreement was entered into, but W worked almost full-time as a consultant until 2009 when T terminated his services. W claimed not to have been fully paid for his shares and that he was therefore entitled to their return. He also claimed that TW had sold MW as a going concern to a connected third party, in which T had a stake, for nominal consideration so as to frustrate W's claims. MW denied that any sums were outstanding and that there had been a sale at undervalue. MW's accountant (P), who was also TW's accountant, submitted a detailed witness statement to assist the understanding of the accounts, which were very complicated. P concluded that a schedule to his statement provided an accurate account of payments made to W, after taking into account his loans to MW, and therefore W had been paid in full for his shares. On various occasions, the judge and the parties considered whether the case could be determined on the basis of the written documents or whether an oral hearing was necessary. MW and TW indicated that they required an oral hearing at which P could give evidence, but W objected. Eventually the judge allowed each party one further opportunity to submit a document by way of explanation of their particular case. The judge stated that he agreed to dispense with a trial at the request of the parties and to determine the dispute on the documents lodged at court. He found, amongst other things, that a proportion of the share price remained unpaid and that the obligation on TW to return MW's shares had crystallised. MW and TW submitted that there was a procedural irregularity in that the judge reached a conclusion of fact which was contrary to the evidence of a witness who, despite the wishes of one of the parties, had not been heard by the court.

Held: Appeal allowed. It was apparent from his judgment that the judge relied heavily upon P's detailed witness statement, which he had found invaluable. He was a vital witness to resolving the several issues which the judge was able to identify. However, the judge did not find that W had been paid in full as P had concluded in his statement. It was clear that the judge did not accept the totality of P's evidence. Therefore, there was unfairness in the conduct of the case. MW and TW made it plain that they wanted P to give evidence to the court and did not agree to a trial on the documents only. The judge made findings against the evidence MW and TW wished to call. It was invaluable evidence for the court to consider and was obviously and clearly highly relevant and should not have been excluded. Therefore, although unfortunate because of the costs wasted and because the judge had tried hard to manage the case and keep it within proportionate bounds, the appeal had to be allowed. A trial had been conducted on oral evidence where matters were in dispute and the judge ought to have acceded to the request to hear the witnesses that MW and TW wished to call. The matter was to be remitted for re-hearing before a different judge (see paras 12, 28-31 of judgment).

WRIGHT v MICHAEL WRIGHT (SUPPLIES) LTD, [2013] EWCA Civ 234, [2013] C.P. Rep. 32, Hughes, L.J., CA (Civ Div).

400. Part 20 claims–Apportionment–Claimants sustaining personal injury from falling commercial sign–Apportionment of liability between defendants–Determination of Pt 20 CPR claims

[Civil Liability (Contribution) Act 1978 (c.47); Civil Procedure Rules 1998 (SI 1998/3132) Pt 20.]

The court was required to determine various CPR Pt 20 claims following the claimants' successful personal injury claim against the second respondent (R2). In 2005 R2 had contracted with the third respondent (R3) to carry out alteration works at its premises, including the fitting of an awning box and a new sign. In early 2007 R2 noticed that the awning box had moved, and it contacted the fourth respondent surveyors (R4). R4 visited the premises and supposedly identified the cause. R2's sign subsequently fell on the claimants when the structure supporting the awning box and sign failed. Judgment was entered on the claimants' claim against R2. The court was required to determine (i) R2's claim against R3 in contract and for a contribution under the Civil Liability (Contribution) Act 1978; (ii) R2's claim against R4 in negligence and for a contribution under the Act; (iii) R3's claim against R4 for a contribution under the Act. In relation to R2's contractual claim, R3 argued that there was a break in the chain of causation because R2 had realised that the awning box had moved, it was under a duty to investigate the structure supporting the box, and it should have known that the box and sign were hazardous.

Held: Judgment accordingly. (1) R2 did not know about any details or particulars of R3's breach of contract in carrying out the alteration works; all R2 knew was that the awning box had slipped and/or moved since. While R2 was generally concerned about the problems with the awning, at no material time did it know or appreciate that the situation was dangerous. As a result, R2 was unaware of the need to take remedial measures, *Borealis AB v Geogas Trading SA* [2010] EWHC 2789 (Comm), [2011] 1 Lloyd's Rep. 482, [2011] C.L.Y. 529 applied. R3's breach constituted a "category 1" breach, and therefore it was not open to it to argue that its liability fell to be diminished by any finding of contributory negligence on R2's part, *Barclays Bank Plc v Fairclough Building Ltd (No.1)* [1995] Q.B. 214, [1995] C.L.Y. 754 applied. As for R2's contribution claim, it was entitled to recover a 100 per cent contribution from R3 in respect of its liability to the claimants (see paras 62, 66, 70 of judgment). (2) The key evidence that R4 owed R2 a duty of care was found in R2's request that R4 attend the premises and investigate the matters that it had reported, the acceptance by R4 to do so, and R4's subsequent inspection. It would have been foreseeable to the ordinary, reasonably competent surveyor, had he failed to observe the problems with the supporting structure at the time of the visit to the premises, that a failure to do so could result in economic loss to R2. Further, there was sufficient proximity, and it was fair, just and reasonable to impose a duty on R4. R4's duty was limited to carrying out the inspection with reasonable care and skill, recording its findings appropriately, and thereafter advising R2 or recommending how the matter should be investigated or resolved. R4 had breached that duty. As to R2's contribution claim, R4 owed the claimants a similar limited duty of care. It had breached that duty, which caused the claimants loss and damage, and therefore R2 was entitled to a contribution from R4 (paras 72, 78-81, 84, 87, 97). (3) Since R3 and R4 would have been liable to the claimants, it was necessary to apportion liability between them. R3's failure was in being wholly responsible for causing the relevant danger when carrying out the works. R4's fault was in failing thereafter to observe problems at the inspection. The causative potency of R3's fault was at least twice that of R4. As for blameworthiness, R3 was in breach of a category 1 contractual obligation, whereas R4 was only in breach of a limited duty of care. In light of those factors, R3 was entitled to recover from R4 only 11 per cent of any sum it was liable to pay to R2 (paras 107, 109-111).

HARRISON v TECHNICAL SIGN CO LTD; *sub nom.* ACTIVE COMMERCIAL INTERIORS LTD v CLUTTONS LLP, [2012] EWHC 2887 (TCC), [2013] B.L.R. 244, Judge David Grant, QBD (TCC).

401. **Part 36 offers–Commencement of proceedings–Attempt to accept Part 36 offer after conclusion of trial on preliminary issue–Meaning of "the trial has started" in r.36.9(3)(d) CPR–Whether court's permission needed to accept offer**

[Civil Procedure Rules 1998 (SI 1998/3132) r.3.1, Pt 36, r.36.9, r.36.9(3)(d), Pt 45, r.45.15(6)(b).]

The appellant Ministry of Defence appealed against a decision that it needed the court's permission to accept a CPR Pt 36 offer made by the respondent (W) after the trial of a preliminary issue had concluded but when the case was not concluded as a whole. W was married to man who was employed by the MoD. During his employment W's husband had come into contact with asbestos fibres. W washed his work clothing and had been exposed to quantities of asbestos dust. W developed a medical condition related to her exposure to asbestos. The MoD admitted liability for W's injuries. W later made a CPR Pt 36 offer to accept a particular sum by way of immediate provisional damages, which said it would remain open until it was either accepted or withdrawn. The MoD rejected the offer and argued that W's claim was statute barred. Pursuant to CPR r.3.1, a trial was ordered to deal with the separate issue of limitation. At that trial judgment was given for W. The MoD then attempted to accept W's CPR Pt 36 offer. W responded asserting that the MoD required the court's permission under CPR r.36.9(3)(d) to accept the offer because the trial had started. The recorder decided that MoD could not accept the offer. The MoD submitted that "trial" in CPR r.36.9(3)(d) meant the trial or any part of it that was currently underway before the court, and during the period between the limitation trial and the judgment, it was not possible to accept a CPR Pt 36 offer without the court's permission. It argued, however, that the fact that the trial of the preliminary issue had concluded did not prevent it from accepting the CPR Pt 36 offer before the start of the assessment of damages, because where trials of separate issues had been ordered, CPR Pt 36 offers could not be accepted during each of those trials but could be in the time between those trials. W submitted that the "trial has started" in CPR r.36.9(3)(d) meant the start of the trial of the action or the first trial of an issue in the case, and that after that point, a CPR Pt 36 offer could not be accepted without the court's permission, even if several issues were to be tried separately over a period of time.

Held: Appeal dismissed. (1) *Gibbon v Manchester City Council* [2010] EWCA Civ 726, [2010] 1 W.L.R. 2081, [2010] C.L.Y. 387 was not authority for the proposition that a CPR Pt 36 offer had to be construed without regard to the CPR, *Gibbon* considered. CPR Pt 36 did not exist in a vacuum apart from the rest of the CPR. *Gibbon* did not prohibit interpreting words and phrases used in CPR Pt 36 by reference to similar phrases used elsewhere in the CPR. For example, CPR Pt 45 had been drafted to make explicit that in CPR Pt 45 "trial" meant a contested hearing as a whole, from start to finish. "Trial" therefore included the period of time between the trial being called on and the conclusion of the contested hearing. There was no similar provision in CPR r.36.9. Instead, it was drafted in such a way as to identify only a single starting point. That implied that once the trial commenced, or the start of the first contested issue, it must then continue to the end of the trial or contested issue (see paras 32, 34-35 of judgment). (2) The language of CPR r.36.9(3)(d) was specific. It was the start of the trial which was significant. The wording of CPR r.36.9(3)(d) necessarily implied with the use of the definite article "the" that a single event was identifiable. That could mean the start of the first contested hearing of an issue ordered to be tried. For CPR r.36.9 to be workable in practice, all parties and the court had to be able to readily identify the moment when the requirement to obtain the permission of the court applied (paras 37, 41). (3) The omission from CPR r.36.9 of any provision equivalent to that found in CPR r.45.15(6)(b) defining "trial" was significant. It could have easily contained an equivalent provision if it had been intended by those drafting the rules, and its omission supported W's interpretation (para.42). (4) The scheme of CPR Pt 36 was to encourage the amicable settlement of contentious actions as early as possible. It could not be right to allow a defendant to bank an early CPR Pt 36 offer by a claimant only to await the result of trial on a preliminary issue and then, depending on the result, either accept the offer or continue to reject it. In such a situation the only way a claimant could protect themselves would be to withdraw their offer, but that would have the consequence of depriving him of the benefits provided in CPR r.36.14. Such protection should be extended beyond the conclusion of a contested hearing. A defendant should not have the advantage of knowing a result before deciding whether to accept an offer (paras 43-45). (5) Accordingly, once the recorder started to hear the trial of the issue of limitation, CPR r.36.9(3)(d) took effect and the MoD could not accept the offer without first obtaining the court's permission (para.47).

WILSON v MINISTRY OF DEFENCE [2013] C.P. Rep. 33, Judge Iain Hughes QC, CC (Winchester).

402. Particulars of claim–Amendments–Late application for permission to amend–Addressing concerns over evidence through cross-examination at trial

The applicant company (F) made a late application for permission to re-amend particulars of claim and for the admission of two witness statements in data infringement proceedings. F had acted on behalf of professional football leagues in the United Kingdom to protect, market and commercialise their fixtures and match-related data. F had alleged in separate proceedings that the first respondent betting company (SJ) and the second respondent internet provider of live sports results (SR) had infringed the rights F held in a database containing football match data. The issue at the forthcoming trial was whether SJ and SR were liable as joint tortfeasors for the acts of SJ and another betting company and its customers. F sought permission to re-amend its particulars of claim by adding an allegation of a seeding exercise that had been recently undertaken, and for permission to admit two witness statements in relation to the seeding exercise. The seeding exercise concerned the seeding of information on F's datastream in relation to three football matches that had taken place in February 2012. SR had also issued an application seeking disclosure of materials related to F's seeding exercise. The trial was to take place in 11 days' time. The issues for determination included: (i) whether permission to amend should be allowed where F did not agree to waive privilege in documents surrounding the seeding exercise; (ii) the basis on which discretion should be exercised to permit late amendment; (iii) whether F's application should be refused on the ground that the seeding exercise was akin to an experiment and therefore of little or no probative value unless previously sanctioned by the court.

Held: Application granted. (1) Although the court was unable to force F to waive privilege, the court accepted that it could require that the amendment and evidence not be permitted unless F chose to waive privilege. However, that course was not appropriate as the seeding exercise was not a situation akin to, or closely akin to, an experiment in a patent action. In such a case, an experiment would be of little or no value unless its scientific basis was revealed, together with the steps taken in the lead up to the experiment and the results that had been expected. In the instant case, all the arguments that the respondents might want to adduce in response could be made without the knowledge of what F discussed in its decision to seed the matches in question. Those questions were clear and obvious, and involved observations such as the fact that the seeding exercise involved teams in lower divisions not in a promotion zone that were of lesser interest to the public and that the teams appeared to have been carefully chosen to make it more likely that F's data would have gone to the respondents' databases. All of those questions could be put to F in cross-examination at trial, and the respondents' position would not be improved by requiring that F reveal privileged information to show that they had been aware of those points at the relevant time. As it was perfectly obvious that F had been aware of those points, the suggestion that F be required to waive privilege as a condition of being granted permission to amend was misconceived (see paras 24-27 of judgment). (2) Although the question of the seeding exercise's probative value was a matter for the trial judge, it did seem to be of relevance as, as F submitted, the evidence went to the question of copying which was the primary issue in the case. However, while that indicated the evidence's potential probative value, it was not appropriate for the court, without full knowledge, to comment on how probative the evidence was (para.29). (3) Although it was true that the catalyst for the seeding exercise was the refusal of an earlier application for disclosure, there was no real reason why the seeding exercise could not have taken place earlier. However, the exercise had been undertaken late whether for good or bad. There was some force in F's argument in relation to questioning how the anticipated trial would be conducted without the evidence of the seeding exercise, and it was difficult to see how the evidence would be evaluated if it were not allowed in. The respondents could rest assured that they could raise their points at trial. Accordingly, it was preferable that the material be allowed in rather than have a trial on a basis that F would consider unsatisfactory (paras 31-34).

FOOTBALL DATACO LTD v STAN JAMES (ABINGDON) LTD; FOOTBALL DATACO LTD v SPORTRADAR GmbH, [2012] EWHC 747 (Ch), [2013] F.S.R. 2, Vos, J., Ch D.

403. Particulars of claim–Amendments–Whether amendment amounted to new cause of action–Whether amendment arose from same facts originally pleaded

[Limitation Act 1980 (c.58) s.35.]

The appellants (B and S) appealed against a decision allowing the respondent (C) to amend its particulars of claim. C owned a distribution centre. B had been contracted to design and build two large warehouses and an office block. B sub-contracted S to design and build the internal warehouse floors. Two years after completion of the works C issued a claim for breach of contract. C asserted that the internal concrete floors were defective as large cracks had appeared. C also alleged that the floors did not meet the required standards set out in the contract, they were below the required thickness in places and were suffering from movement and/or heave. The cost of repairing the defects was estimated to be £381,000. C later discovered that the steel fibre content of the concrete floors was substantially less than required and the floors were in danger of collapse. As a result, the floors would have to be replaced at a cost of £2.5 million. C sought to amend its claim accordingly. The judge allowed the amendment, concluding that it did not introduce a new cause of action. B and S submitted that the amendment introduced a new cause of action which was out of time. C argued that even if it amounted to a new cause of action, it was one which arose out of the same or substantially the same facts, and therefore fell within the terms of the Limitation Act 1980 s.35.

Held: Appeal allowed. (1) In determining what constituted a "new" cause of action, the court had to compare the essential factual elements in the cause of action already pleaded with the essential factual elements in the cause of action proposed, *Revenue and Customs Commissioners v Begum* [2010] EWHC 1799 (Ch), [2011] B.P.I.R. 59, [2011] C.L.Y. 361 and *Steamship Mutual Underwriting Association Ltd v Trollope & Colls (City) Ltd* 33 B.L.R. 77, [1986] C.L.Y. 2699 applied. The court agreed with the distillation of the principles in *Secretary of State for Transport v Pell Frischmann Consultants Ltd* [2006] EWHC 2909 (TCC), [2007] B.L.R. 46, [2007] C.L.Y. 492, namely that (a) where a claimant asserted breach of a duty which was not previously pleaded, that would usually amount to a new claim; (b) where a claimant alleged a different breach of a duty already pleaded, it was a question of fact and degree whether it constituted a new claim; (c) in the case of construction projects, where the claimant alleged breach of a previously pleaded duty causing damage to a different element of the building, that would generally amount to a new claim. Further, if the new breach did not arise out of the same or substantially the same facts as those already in issue on a claim previously made in the original action, it was likely to be a new cause of action, *Frischmann* applied. C's original allegation was of a group of relatively disparate defects in the floors, capable of disparate replacement and repair. What was now alleged was that the concrete of which the floors were constructed suffered from a systemic defect which resulted in its entire condemnation and replacement because of its inability to withstand the design load to which it had not yet been subjected. That allegation was an entirely new and different cause of action. It relied upon a specific facet of the contractual duty of which no breach had been asserted and upon facts and consequences wholly different in kind from those hitherto alleged or relied upon (see paras 20-27 of judgment). (2) The policy of s.35 was that if factual issues were in any event going to be litigated between the parties, they should be able to rely upon any cause of action which substantially arose from those facts. Therefore, a new cause of action could be permissible if it arose out of the same or substantially the same facts as were already in issue, *Lloyds Bank Plc v Rogers (No.1)* Times, March 24, 1997, [1997] C.L.Y. 687 applied. However, the judge had been correct to conclude that the allegation concerning the steel fibre content did not arise out of the same or substantially the same facts. Accordingly, the proposed amendment of the particulars of claim was disallowed (paras 28-30).

CO-OPERATIVE GROUP LTD v BIRSE DEVELOPMENTS LTD, [2013] EWCA Civ 474, [2013] B.L.R. 383, Longmore, L.J., CA (Civ Div).

404. Particulars of claim–Striking out–Claims of breach of contract and breach of statutory duty against company director–Whether expert opinion on negligence and breach of duty necessary

[Civil Procedure Rules 1998 (SI 1998/3132) r.16.4(1)(a).]

The defendant (D) applied for an order striking out the particulars of claim of the first claimant company (W). W and the second claimant (C) had worked together on a construction project. D, who was W's managing director, had been the project manager and had been responsible for all key areas of the operation. The project was a commercial disaster. W and C claimed damages from D, alleging that he had breached his statutory duties as a director and that he was in breach of contract in respect of his management of the project. A master ordered the parties to serve reports of experts in construction project management. D made his strike-out application, in relation only to the claim brought by W, following the service of the reports. D submitted that W's claim should be struck out because (1) the information in W's expert's report was insufficient to support a case of negligence or breach of duty; (2) it was so poorly particularised that he did not know the nature of the allegations against him.

Held: Application refused. (1) It was unnecessary for W's case to be supported by an expert's opinion on whether there had been negligence or breach of duty. The obligations upon D as employee and director were not necessarily coterminous with those which arose upon the assumption of professional responsibility by an independent contractor and therefore CPR r.16.4(1)(a) did not require the provision of an expert report as a necessary preliminary, *Pantelli Associates Ltd v Corporate City Developments Number Two Ltd* [2010] EWHC 3189 (TCC), [2011] P.N.L.R. 12, [2011] C.L.Y. 390 considered. The fact that a significant part of the complaint involved assertions that D had failed to exercise reasonable care and skill did not convert the claim into one of professional negligence. Whilst expert evidence might be required on aspects of the case, such as quantum, the claim could not be struck out simply because it was not supported by expert evidence on breach of possible professional standards. The master had required W to provide an expert report, probably because of his concerns as to the thinness of the particulars of claim, but his order did not amount to a declaration that, unless adequate expert evidence was deployed, those particulars would be struck out. Rather, it served as a warning that W needed to amplify and explain its case, not only as to liability but also as to causation and quantum (see paras 33-34 of judgment). (2) W's pleading was extremely thin and lacking in essential particulars, particularly regarding causation and loss. It pleaded no material facts linking the loss to the breaches. Consequently, D would have no idea what W's case was and it would be extremely difficult for him to prepare for trial on the point. Regarding quantification, it was not credible for W to say that the vestigial case pleaded was the best it could do prior to disclosure or the provision of further information. The question was whether the case as pleaded was so unreasonably vague, incoherent or embarrassing that it should be struck out. The pleading was not incoherent because one could understand what the words meant, although it was difficult to understand in the particular context of the case. However, it was embarrassing in that it did not set an appropriate agenda for trial. In the circumstances, it was appropriate to give W the opportunity to provide proper particulars and plead the material facts relied upon, because the master had not explained why he had ordered it to provide an expert report and because D could have said earlier that further information had to be pleaded. The master had not explained the consequences of the production of an inadequate expert report. On balance, it would have been unfair to strike out W's claim without giving it a final opportunity adequately to particularise it. Accordingly, D's strike-out application would be adjourned on terms that W provide full particulars of breach of duty, loss and causation, together with all material facts relied upon (paras 35-36, 39, 41, 44).

WHESSOE OIL AND GAS LTD v DALE, [2012] EWHC 1788 (TCC), [2012] P.N.L.R. 33, Akenhead, J., QBD (TCC).

405. Particulars of claim–Time limits–Failure to serve particulars of claim within time limit–Whether appropriate to grant permission to extend time for service–Relevant factors

[Civil Procedure Rules 1998 (SI 1998/3132) r.1.1, r.3.9, r.7.5(1).]

The applicant (V) applied for permission to extend time for service of its particulars of claim which was opposed by two of the respondents (M). V, a property development company, had purchased land with detailed planning permission for the erection of residential units with accompanying parking spaces. M were an estate agent and the firm for which he worked. It was alleged that shortly after the purchase, in February 2007, V became aware that the supporting posts for the underground car park would not support the building, which, argued V, ultimately meant that the value of the land was far less than it had paid for it. V issued a claim form in November 2012, but it was served on March 12, 2013, the last day permitted by CPR r.7.5(1). V's solicitors thought wrongly that they had a further 14 days in which to serve the particulars of claim. V made allegations that M had acted in bad faith in both the professional negligence pre-action protocol letter and the particulars of claim, although the allegations were worded differently in each. One allegation referred to "... a preparedness [by M] to act in breath of their duties". M opposed the instant application because a fresh action against them would be statute barred. M submitted that as a result of the amendments to the relief from sanctions in CPR r.3.9, and of the addition of a new sub-paragraph (f) to the overriding objective in CPR r.1.1, both effective from April 1, 2013, the court was required to take a less tolerant approach to failures to comply with time limits.

Held: Application refused. The factors to be considered under CPR r.3.9 prior to its amendment were fairly evenly balanced between V and M. Against V was the fact that there was no good reason for the failure to serve the particulars of claim in time: it was an oversight by its solicitors. However, M were aware of the claim, and a refusal to grant the application would shut out V's claim against M for good. All other things being equal, it would be difficult to see how it could be just and reasonable for a few days' delay in the service of the particulars of claim, particularly where the application for extension of time was made promptly, to result in V being prevented from pursuing a claim against M for all time. However, three factors were of particular importance. Firstly, there was V's wholly unexplained delay of over five years in instructing solicitors once it was aware of the problem with the supporting posts. Secondly, there was reason to believe that if, as it appeared, V had a strong case against M, it probably had an equally good or better case against some of the other defendants. Thus, the consequence of not allowing V to pursue a claim against M might well not result in any demonstrable prejudice. Thirdly, V was seeking to advance a claim for bad faith which was pleaded in particularly vague terms, which was a course that did not merit indulgence. When the circumstances were considered as a whole, particularly in the light of the stricter approach required towards those who failed to comply with rules following the changes to the CPR, the instant case was one where the court should refuse permission to extend time, *Fred Perry (Holdings) Ltd v Brands Plaza Trading Ltd (t/a Brands Plaza)* [2012] EWCA Civ 224, [2012] 6 Costs L.R. 1007, [2012] C.L.Y. 484, *Hashtroodi v Hancock* [2004] EWCA Civ 652, [2004] 1 W.L.R. 3206, [2004] C.L.Y. 284 and *Hoddinott v Persimmon Homes (Wessex) Ltd* [2007] EWCA Civ 1203, [2008] 1 W.L.R. 806, [2008] C.L.Y. 359 considered and *Totty v Snowden* [2001] EWCA Civ 1415, [2002] 1 W.L.R. 1384, [2001] C.L.Y. 654 applied.

VENULUM PROPERTY INVESTMENTS LTD v SPACE ARCHITECTURE LTD, [2013] EWHC 1242 (TCC), [2013] 4 Costs L.R. 596, Edwards-Stuart, J., QBD (TCC).

406. Payment into court–Overriding objective–Dispute regarding defects in development of luxury flat–Defendant's failure to comply with rules of court–Appropriateness of relief under r.3.1 and r.25.7 CPR

[Defective Premises Act 1972 (c.35); Civil Procedure Rules 1998 (SI 1998/3132) r.1.4, r.3.1 (5), r.3.1, r.25.6, r.25.7.]

The claimant (C) applied for a conditional order under the CPR r.3.1 requiring the defendant property developer (D) to make a payment into court. C had bought a luxury flat, developed by D, for £1.45 million. C claimed that she was unable to move into the flat because of excessive overheating of the flat. D initially denied responsibility for the problem but subsequently, following receipt of a surveyors report commissioned by C, initiated remedial works. C considered that the remedial work was incomplete and had not resolved the problem, and brought proceedings for breach of contract and breach of the Defective Premises Act 1972. She obtained injunctions requiring D to co-operate with her expert in attempting to resolve the issue. D denied liability. C issued the instant application, seeking a payment of £100,000 into court. D accepted liability for the substantive defects which led to the overheating, though there remained issues regarding whether the remedial works carried out represented a complete and reasonable solution to the problem. C was granted permission to amend her application to include an application for relief under the interim payments provisions in r.25.6 and r.25.7.

Held: Applications granted. (1) Rule 3.1 gave the court very wide powers of case management additional to, albeit that they might complement or supplement, other powers elsewhere in the rules or within the inherent jurisdiction. The powers were to secure the overriding objective. They were not as such given so as to punish a party, save in the context of r.3.1 (5) to secure the future smooth running of the case. Rule 1.4 required the court to further the overriding objective by actively managing cases. The overriding objective enabled the court "to deal with cases justly"; in practice, that involved the court seeking to secure that any given case was "dealt with expeditiously and fairly". Rule 3.1 empowered the court to order a party to provide security for costs, in addition to r.25. However, security for costs under r.3.1 should not be granted if it would stifle the other party in the pursuit of their claim or defence. Other relevant considerations were the respondent's conduct of the proceedings, including in particular compliance or otherwise with any applicable rule, practice direction or protocol, and the apparent strength of their case, be it claim or defence. Security for costs should generally only be ordered where a respondent party had regularly flouted proper court procedures, which inevitably inflated the costs of the proceedings, or otherwise was demonstrating a want of good faith, namely an unwillingness to litigate a genuine claim or defence as economically and expeditiously as reasonably possible in accordance with the overriding objective. The court should be slow to investigate the merits of a claim or defence, and it was only in clear cases that security might be ordered. There were no hard and fast rules. An order for payment in did not have to be classified as security for costs. An underlying consideration was the need for the court to exercise a degree of control over the future conduct of the litigation. However, r.3.1(3) was to be deployed to enable the court to grant relief on terms, and when the power was exercised the condition ought properly to be expressed as part of the order granting the specific relief to which it related, *Olatawura v Abiloye* [2002] EWCA Civ 998, [2003] 1 W.L.R. 275, [2002] C.L.Y. 386 and *Huscroft v P&O Ferries Ltd* [2010] EWCA Civ 1483, [2011] 1 W.L.R. 939, [2011] C.L.Y. 363 applied (see paras 22-25 of judgment). (2) Although there was strength in C's claims against D for the purposes of r.3.1, including D's concessions regarding acceptance of substantive liability for the defects, it was not an appropriate case for an order under r.3.1(3) because there was no continuing non-compliance or other order for the court to make to which a payment into court would be ancillary. However, it was appropriate to make an order requiring some money to be paid into court. D had failed to comply with the rules of court and the overriding objective, and had unequivocally accepted that it was liable for the basic defects in question. An order would be made pursuant to r.3.1(5) and r.25.7, essentially as in the instant case the one rule informed the other, for D to pay £30,000 into court. The case ought to be resolved by mediation or some other settlement process, and the relatively small payment into court would concentrate the minds of the parties in that respect. Such a payment should not stifle D's defence of the proceedings as there was no suggestion that it would give rise to any financial embarrassment or difficulty (paras 26-36).

LAZARI v LONDON AND NEWCASTLE (CAMDEN) LTD, [2013] EWHC 97 (TCC), [2013] C.P. Rep. 26, Akenhead, J., QBD (TCC).

407. Permission to appeal–Extensions of time–Permission to appeal against detailed assessment of costs–Delay in making application–Minimal amount in issue

[Civil Procedure Rules 1998 (SI 1998/3132) r.44.5(3).]

The applicant (N) sought an extension of time and permission to appeal against an order made on a detailed assessment of costs. N was a golf club and had brought a claim for subsidence damage to its club house caused by tree roots in the gardens of adjacent properties for which the respondent housing trust (D) was responsible. N's pleaded claim was for over £1.5 million. The claim went to mediation. The mediation agreement stated that the parties would share equally the mediator's fees, the costs of the room and any costs attributed to the mediator. The claim was eventually settled upon D agreeing to pay £850,000 in damages, remove the trees and pay N's reasonable costs. N's bill of costs amounted to over £1.2 million including a success fee. On a detailed assessment N's costs were reduced on the basis that they were disproportionate. The bill had included the costs of the mediation, but the costs master concluded that whilst costs of preparation and presentation to the mediator were allowed, the costs of participation, such as the mediator's fee and the room hire, were not allowed. N's application for permission to appeal was made six months out of time.

Held: Application refused. (1) The master had well in mind the correct legal approach and referred correctly to the factors he had to take into account under CPR r.44.5(3). He was not overly influenced by the settlement figure and he accepted that the case was one of complexity or difficulty in relation to expert evidence on causation and the history of the damage. He was, however, influenced by the almost complete lack of planning in respect of the work to be done and the costs. He also found that there were items in the bill which should not have been included. He was fully entitled to conclude that the costs were disproportionate, *Cox v MGN Ltd* [2006] EWHC 1235 (QB), [2006] 5 Costs L.R. 764, [2007] C.L.Y. 389 considered (see paras 9-10 of judgment). (2) The question of the mediation costs was an area where there was room for argument as the authorities did not provide a clear answer, *National Westminster*

Bank Plc v Feeney (Costs), *Lobster Group Ltd v Heidelberg Graphic Equipment Ltd* [2008] EWHC 413 (TCC), [2008] 2 All E.R. 1173, [2008] C.L.Y. 414 and *Roundstone Nurseries Ltd v Stephenson Holdings Ltd* [2009] EWHC 1431 (TCC), [2009] 5 Costs L.R. 787, [2010] C.L.Y. 399 considered. However, the master was probably entitled to reach the conclusion that he did. Further, the sum being argued about in respect of mediation costs was very small, on N's figures the amount of costs disallowed was only £3,315.90, and N faced an uphill task in justifying the very substantial delay in submitting the application for permission. Those matters were not consistent with the overriding objective. Consequently, permission to appeal was refused and N was ordered to pay D's costs of over £21,000 (paras 20-23).

NORTH OXFORD GOLF CLUB v A2 DOMINION HOMES LTD, [2013] EWHC 852 (QB), [2013] 3 Costs L.R. 509, Royce, J., QBD.

408. **Permission to appeal–Fresh evidence–Road traffic claims–Claimants provided with hire cars on credit hire rates–Unreliable and dishonest evidence of recoverable hire rate**

The appellants (D, S, V and M) sought permission to appeal out of time and to adduce fresh evidence in their road traffic accident claims. A company (AEL) provided claimants in road traffic accidents with hire cars on credit hire terms while their own cars were being repaired. It had provided such cars to the appellants. In each case, the court had accepted quasi-expert evidence from a company (AF) that the appropriate daily hire rate was less than the rate charged by AEL. The quantum of each claimant's car-hire claim had been determined on the basis of AF's evidence. After judgment, AEL produced evidence that AF's evidence was dishonest and unreliable. It sought to challenge the quantum of car-hire awards in D, S, V and M's cases. The issues were (i) whether S, V and M should have permission to adduce the fresh evidence; (ii) whether S and V should have an extension of time in which to seek permission to appeal: (iii) whether S and V should have permission to appeal; (iv) whether the appeals should be allowed; (v) what form any retrials should take.

Held: Applications granted. (1) The fresh evidence could be adduced. It was accepted that it was entirely credible, if not incontrovertible, and it went to show that AF's evidence was neither honest nor independent, and that the system by which it was produced was dishonest and unreliable. It could not have been adduced at trial. Had it been, the courts would probably have rejected AF's evidence. Thus, it would have had an important influence on the result of the cases. The *Ladd v Marshall* test was satisfied, and the reception of the evidence was consistent with the overriding objective of dealing with the cases justly. There was strong evidence that the judges had determined quantum on the basis of evidence produced by a dishonest system. It was in the interests of justice to allow evidence of that dishonest system to be adduced on appeal (see paras 78-84 of judgment). (2) It was in the interests of justice to extend time for seeking permission to appeal: it was in the interests of the administration of justice that AF's evidence should be examined on appeal; the fact that the applications could have been made earlier was not a major point against granting an extension of time; and there had been no culpable delay on the part of S and V, the position having changed as new material had been discovered (paras 85-95). (3) In S's case there was no opposition to an appeal on the judgment sum and an order that S repay part of an interim payment. S thus had to have permission to appeal on those issues, as well as in respect of costs. In V's case the only issue was the hire charge, and there were good prospects of success on appeal. Permission would therefore be granted (paras 96-97). (4) All four appeals would be allowed. The essence of allowing an appeal based on fresh evidence was that the evidence would probably have had an important, though not necessarily decisive, influence on the outcome of the case. In the instant cases, the fresh evidence had not been seriously challenged but had not been tested by cross-examination. It aimed to show that the judges had wrongly accepted AF's evidence as being honest and accurate when there were, in fact, serious irregularities. In each case, the appeals had to be allowed to the extent that the judge's decision on the recoverable hire rate had to be set aside (paras 98, 103-107). (5) In all four cases there had to be retrials limited to the issue of the recoverable hire rate. The evidence that could be adduced by either side would not, however, be restricted. The defendants' insurers had already paid the penalty for relying on AF's evidence, and it would be unfair and disproportionate to prevent them adducing at any retrial evidence of recoverable hire rates. All four retrials were to be reallocated to the multi-track. It would be sensible for them to be heard by the same judge, at the same time and under the same procedure (paras 108-110). (6) It was not possible to give general guidance in respect of other cases in which AEL had made similar applications. While there were general principles to be followed on such applications, each case depended on its own facts, and it did not necessarily follow that extensions of time would be granted, or fresh evidence admitted, in all cases. The court was not prepared to indicate the appropriate way to proceed in a case that had been settled after AF's evidence had been adduced. Nor would it give a general indication on reallocation, or state a general principle that no "AF-evidence" appeal should be allowed unless the appellant could show that the judge would have awarded an increased amount had the fresh evidence been before him. AEL's fresh evidence strongly supported the conclusion that AF's evidence was fabricated, misleading or unreliable because the systems on which it was based had been deliberately manipulated. It did not attempt to demonstrate what specific amount should have been awarded. The general rule was that it was for the respondent to demonstrate that the hire rate claimed was not reasonable (paras 112-113).

DICKINSON v TESCO PLC; SIMMONDS v STEWART ALEXANDER GROUP LTD; VERLEY v O'NEIL; MOONSAM v AXA CORPORATE SOLUTIONS ASSURANCES SA, [2013] EWCA Civ 36, [2013] C.P. Rep. 24, Moore-Bick, L.J., CA (Civ Div).

409. Permission to appeal–Oral hearings–Application for permission to appeal against refusal of permission to bring judicial review proceedings against Upper Tribunal decision–Right to renew application at oral hearing

[Civil Procedure Rules 1998 (SI 1998/3132) r.52.3(4), r.52.15(1A), r.54.7A(8).]

The applicant (P) applied for the Court of Appeal to overturn a decision of the Civil Appeals Office that he had no right to an oral hearing before a Court of Appeal judge because of the application of CPR r.52.15(1A). P had appealed to the First-tier Tribunal against a decision to refuse him entry clearance. The First-tier Tribunal dismissed his appeal. P's application for permission to appeal was refused on the papers by the Upper Tribunal. He applied for permission to apply for judicial review. A High Court judge refused that on the papers; another judge refused it when P renewed the application at an oral hearing. P applied for permission to appeal; a single judge of the Court of Appeal refused that application on the papers. P sought to renew his application, but the Civil Appeals Office informed him that he had no right to an oral hearing. P argued that (1) r.52.15(1A) had not excluded, in sufficiently clear terms, the right to renew an application given in r.52.3(4); that contrasted with r.54.7A(8), which explicitly ruled out a renewed oral hearing after refusal on the papers; (2) r.52.15(1A) did not apply because his judicial review claim had been issued before October 1, 2012, when the rule had come into force.

Held: Application refused. (1) If the right to renew to an oral hearing was retained by reference to r.52.3(4), then r.52.15(1A) was otiose. Rule 52.3 related to applications for permission to appeal from lower courts in general terms, whereas r.52.15 related specifically to judicial review appeals such as the instant case. Further, r.52.15(1A) related specifically to cases where permission to apply for judicial review of a decision of the Upper Tribunal had been refused by the High Court, such as the instant case. The specific rule should take precedence over the general rule. "Determined" could have various shades of meaning, depending on context. However, naturally read in the context of r.52.15(1A) and coupled with "without an oral hearing", it connoted finality in the process. The matter was to be determined without an oral hearing. That precluded there being a subsequent oral hearing on the point. Although no such specific provision as that in r.54.7A(8) was included, that rule dealt with a different situation, and total consistency in the drafting approach had not been mandated (see para.13 of judgment). (2) The general rule was that statutes were not to be read, in the absence of explicit wording, so as to remove or impair an existing substantive right; however, no such presumption applied with regard to procedural matters, one rationale for that being that a change in procedural provisions was expected to be for the general benefit of litigants, *Wilson v First County Trust Ltd (No.2)* [2003] UKHL 40, [2004] 1 A.C. 816, [2004] C.L.Y. 628 applied. The normal presumption was that procedural provisions applied to current as well as future proceedings. The amended rule in the instant case was a procedural provision. There was nothing to suggest that it should not apply to proceedings current on October 1, 2012 and there were no relevant transitional provisions. P had had no relevant vested right, and no injustice could result from r.52.15(1A) applying to current proceedings. A statement in *R. (on the application of Sharma) v Upper Tribunal* [2012] EWHC 3930 (Admin), relating to r.54.7A, that the abolition of the right of oral renewal would only affect claims lodged after October 1 had been obiter and had been made without the benefit of sustained argument. Moreover, r.54.7A was very different from r.52.15(1A); the observations in *Sharma* did not bear on the true meaning and effect of r.51.15(1A), *Sharma* considered. The court had no further jurisdiction to entertain the application for permission to appeal (paras 16-21).

R. (ON THE APPLICATION OF PAREKH) v UPPER TRIBUNAL (IMMIGRATION AND ASYLUM CHAMBER), [2013] EWCA Civ 679, [2013] C.P. Rep. 38, Hallett, L.J., CA (Civ Div).

410. Permission to appeal–References to European Court–Propriety of delaying reference until after appeal

The Upper Tribunal was required to determine whether to grant the applicant commissioners permission to appeal to the Court of Appeal against its decision or to make an immediate reference for a preliminary ruling by the European Court of Justice. The commissioners had refused VAT bad debt relief for two taxable persons (G and B). The First-tier Tribunal allowed G's appeal, while three preliminary issues had arisen in B's appeal. In *Revenue and Customs Commissioners v GMAC UK Plc* [2012] UKUT 279 (TCC), [2012] S.T.C. 2349, [2012] C.L.Y. 3381, the Upper Tribunal had had determined the preliminary issues in B's appeal and decided that it might be necessary to refer one of the issues in G's appeal to the ECJ.

Held: Judgment accordingly. (1) The Upper Tribunal was minded to grant the commissioners permission to appeal against its decision in the case involving B because, although it had been determining preliminary issues and was not acting as an appellate tribunal, the preliminary issues raised matters of general importance which would merit further consideration by the Court of Appeal. However, the commissioners would first need to formally apply for permission, setting out the grounds of appeal, within 14 days before the Upper Tribunal could give a formal decision (see paras 3-5 of judgment). (2) In the case involving G, whether or not the previous decision contained any determinations which were appealable, it would not be right to delay making the reference simply because the commissioners had a right to appeal against those determinations. A reference would ensure that a final answer was given as soon as possible, whereas if the commissioners appealed to the Court of Appeal first, that reference would be delayed by many months, although such an appeal could eliminate the need for a reference at all. However, the balance came down in favour of making an immediate reference (paras 12-18).

REVENUE AND CUSTOMS COMMISSIONERS v GMAC UK PLC; BRITISH TELECOMMUNICATIONS PLC v REVENUE AND CUSTOMS COMMISSIONERS; *sub nom.* GMAC UK PLC v REVENUE AND CUSTOMS COMMISSIONERS [2012] B.V.C. 1939, Warren, J., UT (Tax).

411. Permission to appeal–Renewed applications–Litigant entitled to hearing of renewed application–Litigant unable to attend with good reason–Consideration on papers

[CPR PD 52 (Appeals) 2000.]

The appellant (P) appealed against an order giving directions for the future conduct of her renewed application for permission to appeal against a finding that she pay legal fees to the respondent solicitors (R). R had obtained summary judgment against P for its fees in representing P in a disability discrimination claim brought against her former employers. P filed a notice raising nine grounds of appeal and requested that any appeal be determined on the papers by reason of her disability. P claimed that she could not afford legal representation and was unable to attend a hearing either in person or by video link or telephone as she suffered from chronic fatigue syndrome. She provided medical evidence in support. Permission to appeal was granted on three of the grounds and R's views were sought on P's request that her appeal be determined on the papers. R lodged strong objections, including that the medical evidence provided was not up to date and did not record P's current state of health. P then indicated her wish to renew her application for permission to appeal on the previously refused grounds, again requesting that that be dealt with on the papers. Directions were given that P could only make a renewed application for permission to appeal orally, by counsel if necessary. The judge directed that if such an application was made, P's request for the appeal to be dealt with on the papers would be heard at the same time, and if no such application was made, that request would be dealt following receipt of submissions. P submitted that the directions had the effect of denying her a fair hearing by reason of her disability and that the court should have given consideration to making reasonable adjustments to enable a disabled litigant to pursue her case properly.

Held: Appeal allowed. The judge's form of direction was too rigid in relation to the procedure he laid down for determining the renewed application for permission to appeal. The judge directed in effect that unless the application was made orally through counsel at a hearing, it was to be refused. That was evidently because he considered that an oral hearing was required by CPR PD 52 and that the only way an effective hearing could take place was if P was represented by counsel, since she had made clear her position that she could not attend in person. The judge also reasoned that no useful purpose would be served by requiring the same material to be considered by another judge on the papers. That conclusion was incorrect. Provided that an application was not one that was totally without merit, it would not necessarily be without useful purpose for a different judge to consider the application on the papers, including any further material that might have been lodged since the papers were first considered. In the situation under consideration, where a litigant was entitled to a hearing of a renewed application but for good reason was unable to attend the hearing, that seemed a proper course to adopt. It was true that a hearing was envisaged by the practice direction, but the court had power in an appropriate case to dispense with a hearing and to deal with the matter by way of a written decision, or to proceed with a hearing and to give judgment in open court in the absence of the applicant. In either case, after consideration of the papers the court could seek clarifications that were necessary for the purposes of reaching a decision. The directions should therefore be varied so as to allow for a determination of the renewed application on the papers before the court if P was unable to secure representation or to attend the hearing in person, and the application for the appeal to be dealt with on the papers should be determined at the same time as the renewed application to appeal. The matter could be dealt with in that way without the elaboration of additional medical evidence, but P might wish to submit such evidence in support of her application for the appeal itself to be dealt with on the papers, given R's strong resistance to dispensing with a hearing and its strongly expressed scepticism as to P's claim to be unfit to attend a hearing (see paras 19-21 of judgment).

ROYDS LLP v PINE, [2012] EWCA Civ 1734, [2013] 1 W.L.R. 717, Lord Dyson (M.R.), CA (Civ Div).

412. Possession orders–Right to respect for private and family life–Proportionality as defence against enforcement of possession order

[European Convention on Human Rights 1950 Art.8, Art.14.]

The appellant (L) appealed against the dismissal of her claim for judicial review of a decision to enforce an order for possession of residential premises occupied by the claimant and her family as their home. L's husband had been a soldier and he and his family lived in service accommodation. He resigned in 1989 after a court martial, and the respondent Ministry of Defence on compassionate grounds, continued to provide a home to L and the twin daughters of the marriage, one of whom had permanent, serious, mental health difficulties thought to be partly attributable to having suffered sexual abuse by her father. At the time of the instant case L was confined to a wheelchair with a permanent condition, and suffered from other health problems. The other daughter cared for them and for her son. From 1993 the MOD made attempts to recover possession of the premises, and in 2007 brought possession proceedings, which L resisted on the ground that her eviction would be an unjustified interference in her European Convention on Human Rights 1950 art.8 rights. The proceedings were transferred to the Administrative Court which concluded, as the law then stood, that art.8 rights could not be invoked as a defence to the right of a property owner, even a public authority, for possession and he made an order for possession and suggested that the MOD might permit the premises to be treated as temporary accommodation while the local authority found L permanent accommodation. L appealed unsuccessfully against the order and filed an application with the European Court alleging breach of art.8 and art.14. L was given an extra six months to identify suitable accommodation but failed. A ministerial submission was made recommending enforcement of the possession order on various grounds. After the possession order there was a change in the law whereby a court that was asked for an order for possession by a local authority had to have the power to assess proportionality and so to consider a defence based on alleged breach of art.8 rights. The main issue for the instant court was whether the decision to enforce the possession order constituted disproportionate interference with L's art.8 rights.

Held: Appeal dismissed. Any interference with an art.8 right had to be both lawful and a proportionate means to a legitimate end. The whole process of dispossession had to be subjected to a proportionality review, including the enforcement stage. Usually, such a review as part of a defence and conducted at the occupant's request, would be considered during possession proceedings, as they were meant to give a final determination of the claim. The court was not obliged to conduct a review of its own motion. Thus, in the absence of special circumstances, the owner could only seek a writ of possession after the occupant's art.8 rights had been exhausted, either because they were not invoked, or because they were raised as a defence and rejected. Generally, litigation of art.8 issues at the enforcement stage would be an abuse of process. However, there were exceptional cases such as L's where it would not be, because of a fundamental change in personal circumstances after a possession order, but before its enforcement. L had pursued her art.8 rights during the possession proceedings, but following *Kay v Lambeth LBC* [2006] UKHL 10, [2006] 2 A.C. 465, [2006] C.L.Y. 2173 and *Doherty v Birmingham City Council* [2008] UKHL 57, [2009] 1 A.C. 367, [2008] C.L.Y. 1978 as he then had to, the judge could not accept the defence, *Kay* and *Pinnock* not followed. Since then it had become recognised that there was a right to a proportionality review, *Manchester City Council v Pinnock* [2011] UKSC 6, [2011] 2 W.L.R. 220, [2011] C.L.Y. 2067 followed. There was no other occasion on which a review could be conducted in L's case than the instant proceeding. However, regarding a proportionality review at the enforcement stage, there was nothing in *Pinnock* or other authority that decided the question. The judge had been correct in the wholly exceptional circumstances of L's case to accede to her reqest to have a review of the requested eviction, even though it would be a very rare case where it was appropriate at the enforcement stage.

R. (ON THE APPLICATION OF JL) v SECRETARY OF STATE FOR DEFENCE, [2013] EWCA Civ 449, [2013] P.T.S.R. 1014, Arden, L.J., CA (Civ Div).

413. Private hearings–Witness protection–Open justice–Application for witnesses to give evidence in private–Risk of reprisals

[Civil Procedure Rules 1998 (SI 1998/3132) r.39.2; European Convention on Human Rights 1950 Art.2.]

The appellant (D) appealed against a judge's refusal of his application for witnesses to give evidence in private. The respondent (C) had brought a claim against D concerning an agreement for D to sell shares to him. D alleged that C was involved with an organised crime group. He claimed to be the victim of an extortion and protection racket perpetrated by C and the group. He applied under CPR r.39.2 for his witnesses to give their evidence in private to prevent reprisals against them. By that point, statements had been exchanged and C was already aware of the identity of the witnesses. D argued that it would infringe their right to life if such protection were refused, and that it was in the interests of justice for the order to be made. No evidence was adduced of any direct threats to the witnesses. The judge allowed certain witness protection measures to be put in place in respect of two witnesses. However, he refused the application in respect of 10 other witnesses. D submitted that the judge had attached insufficient weight to evidence that the criminal group was still active in Russia. He also argued that the judge was wrong to take into account the fact that the witnesses would give evidence if they were not protected, as they might change their minds as the trial approached.

Held: Appeal dismissed. (1) D had not demonstrated a real and immediate risk, objectively verified, to the lives of any of the witnesses in question. The judge had therefore been right to conclude that the European Convention on Human Rights 1950 art.2 would not be infringed if the application was refused (see paras 12-13 of judgment). (2) The judge's decision fell within the general area of case management. However, the question was not one of discretion; either an order was necessary or it was not. In deciding whether an order was necessary, the judge had to weigh different factors. The ultimate decision was one on which different people could come to different conclusions on the same facts without any of them being wrong, *AMM v HXW* [2010] EWHC 2457 (QB), (2010) 160 N.L.J. 1425 applied. It was therefore incumbent on D to satisfy the court that the judge was wrong, not merely that different inferences could have been drawn from the evidence (paras 15-18). (3) The weight to be given to particular factors was a matter for the judge. He had taken into account the evidence that the organisation was still active, but the real question was whether there was a risk of reprisals against the witnesses arising out of their evidence. Most of the events had taken place nearly 20 years ago, and the facts were in the public domain or had already been reported to the authorities. Since it was D's case that a derogation from the principle of open justice was necessary, it was for him to identify what parts of the evidence were new revelations. Further, the fact that the case had attracted considerable publicity in the United Kingdom and abroad was a powerful pointer towards the public interest in the conduct of the whole trial being public. Finally, D's argument that the witnesses might change their minds about giving evidence was speculation. The judge had made it clear that his decision was provisional and that changed circumstances might justify reconsideration of his order. The judge's balancing exercise had been conducted in accordance with the law and D had not shown it to be plainly wrong (paras 17, 19-22, 28).

DERIPASKA v CHERNEY, [2012] EWCA Civ 1235, [2013] C.P. Rep. 1, Maurice Kay, L.J., CA (Civ Div).

414. Procedural irregularity–Oral hearings–First-tier Tribunal's ruling to proceed on papers alone–Whether in interests of justice to set aside

[Tribunal Procedure (First-tier Tribunal) (General Regulatory Chamber) Rules 2009 (SI 2009/1976) r.32, r.41.]

The applicant (B) sought permission to appeal against the First-tier Tribunal's dismissal of his appeals against decisions of the first respondent commissioner (C) to uphold the refusals of the respondent NHS trusts (T) to supply him with information which he had requested or to confirm or deny whether they held that information. Alternatively, he sought the tribunal to set aside its earlier decision. B submitted that the tribunal should not have reached its decision without an oral hearing.

Held: Application refused. (1) Although the Tribunal Procedure (First-tier Tribunal) (General Regulatory Chamber) Rules 2009 r.32 mandated the tribunal to hold an oral hearing, if one party had not otherwise consented, the decision not to do so in the instant case had been made with specific reasons in an earlier ruling as to the appropriate mode of trial and B had not appealed against that ruling. Even if that ruling constituted a procedural irregularity or even if the manner in which the appeals were finally determined could be said to constitute such an irregularity, under r.41 the tribunal could only set aside its decision if in addition to the presence of any such irregularity, it also considered that it was in the interests of justice to do so. In the instant case, it would not be in the interests of justice to set the substantive decision aside. Nothing raised by B since promulgation of the decision in any way added to the contentions he had made prior to the full tribunal's consideration of the appeal. In any event, it was distinctly questionable that the ruling on the mode of trial was a procedural irregularity. Hence there were no grounds for setting aside the principal tribunal decision (see paras 20-22 of judgment). (2) As for the application seeking permission to appeal, no proper legal grounds of appeal had been articulated (para.24).

BOUSFIELD v INFORMATION COMMISSIONER (2012) 128 B.M.L.R. 184, Judge David Marks Q.C., FTT (GRC).

415. Property freezing orders–Exclusion–Applications for exclusion from property freezing order to pay legal expenses–Availability of unfrozen assets

[Proceeds of Crime Act 2002 (c.29) s.245A, s.245C; European Convention on Human Rights 1950 Art.6, Protocol 1 Art.1; Practice Direction Civil Recovery Proceedings 2003 para.7A.2; Practice Direction Civil Recovery Proceedings 2003 para.7A.3; Practice Direction Civil Recovery Proceedings 2003 para.7A.4.]

The appellant (X) appealed against a decision ([2013] EWHC 1480 (QB)) that a property freezing order (PFO) made against him under the Proceeds of Crime Act 2002 s.245A in proceedings brought against him by the respondent Serious Organised Crime Agency should not be varied under s.245C so as to permit him to apply some of the assets subject to the order in paying for his legal representation in the proceedings. The PFO required X to disclose all his assets by way of a witness statement verified by a statement of truth. SOCA later discovered a bank account that X had not disclosed, and was critical of his explanations for not having disclosed it. The judge considering the application for an exclusion from the PFO considered that X had to show that there were no other assets available to him to use for his legal expenses. Finding that X had withheld the existence of the account, the judge was satisfied that his statements could not be relied on and that he had failed to show that he had no other assets. The judge found that he did have other such assets and refused to make the exclusion sought.

Held: Appeal allowed. (1) It was for the applicant to persuade the court that it would be just to permit the expenditure out of assets affected by the PFO, having regard to all the circumstances, *Serious Fraud Office v X* [2005] EWCA Civ 1564 applied. If the court was able to be satisfied that the applicant had other available assets from which he could meet the costs, applying PD Civil Recovery Proceedings para.7A.4, it plainly would not make the order. That was not to say that there would be an exclusion if the court was not so satisfied. The Practice Direction did not give guidance in such cases. Paragraph 7A.2 did not mean that no exclusion could be made unless a statement as to assets fully compliant with para.7A.3 had been made: that would mean that if there was a defect in any statement of assets, even if it was one for which the statement's maker was not culpable, the exclusion would be liable to be set aside, whereas any such setting aside was a matter for the court depending on all the circumstances. If the evidence left the court with specific grounds for suspicion that the applicant had other available assets, it might well not be satisfied that he had discharged the burden on him. The more difficult position was where there were no specific grounds for suspicion, and where SOCA sought to rely on a previous instance of non-disclosure. The court considered whether such cases could proceed on the basis that there were other assets the applicant was concealing. Recovery orders backed up by PFOs were procedures by way of confiscation by the state, engaging the European Convention on Human Rights 1950 Protocol 1 art.1 as well as art.6: the requirement in s.245C(6) to have regard to the desirability of legal representation conformed with that. It was not right to transpose to proceedings under Pt 5 of the 2002 Act the principles applying in cases of freezing injunctions in civil proceedings: unlike in most such cases, PFOs could extend to every asset known to SOCA, leaving nothing from which the defendant could pay his lawyers. It was not for an applicant to prove positively the absence of available assets. If there was nothing to cast light on the probabilities one way or the other, the fact that the applicant had previously concealed assets was not sufficient to show that he was still concealing assets and thereby deprive him of the ability to use his own assets for legal representation, *SFO v X* applied, *R. (on the application of Director of the Assets Recovery Agency) v Gale* [2008] EWHC 1320 (Admin) and *Serious Organised Crime Agency v Azam* [2011] EWHC 1551 (Admin) approved and *Serious Organised Crime Agency v Szepietowski* [2009] EWHC 1560 (Ch), [2010] 1 W.L.R. 1316, [2009] C.L.Y. 433 considered (see paras 53-66 of judgment). (2) The judge had been entitled to hold that X's statements of truth and his statement that he had no unfrozen assets could not be relied upon. However, he had not been entitled to conclude that he could be satisfied that X had other assets which had not been discovered, nor had he had any basis for saying that there were substantial deposits sufficient to defray X's defence costs. There was therefore nothing to displace the desirability of X being represented. He had shown that an exclusion from the PFO would be just (paras 73, 77).

SERIOUS ORGANISED CRIME AGENCY v AZAM, [2013] EWCA Civ 970, [2013] 1 W.L.R. 3800, Lloyd, L.J., CA (Civ Div).

416. Property freezing orders–Recovery orders

THE PROCEEDS OF CRIME ACT 2002 (EXTERNAL REQUESTS AND ORDERS) (AMENDMENT) ORDER 2013, SI 2013/2604; made under the Proceeds of Crime Act 2002 s.444, s.459. In force: November 11, 2013; .

This Order sets out a framework for the UK to co-operate with overseas authorities in civil cases for the freezing of property in anticipation of a future external (recovery) order.

417. Relief–Striking out–Striking out personal injury claim for failure to file costs schedule–Appropriateness of granting relief from sanction–Appropriate approach to granting relief in accordance with r.3.9 CPR

[Civil Procedure Rules 1998 (SI 1998/3132) r.3.9.]

The appellant company (R) appealed against a decision to reverse a district judge's earlier decision to refuse to grant the respondent (B) relief from sanction. B had claimed damages against R after sustaining personal injury in a road traffic accident. R admitted liability and judgment was entered in B's favour with damages to be assessed. Despite correspondence between the parties, B failed to serve a costs schedule. R's solicitors wrote to the court complaining that B had not served a costs schedule, but did not copy that letter to B's solicitors. The court ordered, of its own motion and without giving notice to B, that unless B filed and served a costs schedule by a specific date, his claim would be struck out. The solicitor in charge of B's file, unaware of the unless order, was on holiday from the day after the unless order was made until its expiry. B's claim was struck out. B's application for relief from sanction, which was accompanied by a costs schedule, was refused by the district judge. B successfully appealed against that decision to a second judge, who concluded that the district judge had erred in his assessment of the factors under CPR r.3.9.

Held: Appeal dismissed. (1) Although some of the second judge's observations could be criticised, they did not undermine his conclusion. He was entitled to hold that the district judge had erred and therefore that he had to exercise his discretion afresh. He was right to say that the district judge had not properly balanced the various relevant factors when considering whether it was proportionate to refuse relief from sanction. He was correct in saying that the district judge had taken a mistaken view of the gravity of the delay in making the application for relief. The district judge focussed on B's defaults without considering whether they had had a significant effect on the progress of the action or had significantly prejudiced R. In particular, no reference was made to the fact that B served the costs schedule with his application for relief. Thus, although R had been prejudiced to some extent by the overall delay in receiving B's costs estimate, the delay after the expiry of the unless order was only eight days. Accordingly, the second judge was entitled to interfere with the district judge's decision for the reasons he gave. Even if the instant court had not considered that the second judge's criticisms of the district judge were satisfied, it would still have thought that he was entitled to exercise his discretion afresh because the district judge had been unaware of a highly relevant factor, namely that B's solicitors had not received a copy of the letter complaining about the failure to serve a costs schedule (see paras 44-47 of judgment). (2) Even though the second judge was entitled to interfere with the district judge's decision, his approach was not ideal. Where a judge on the first appeal concluded that the judge below had erred and that he must exercise his discretion afresh, the appellate judge should consider the various CPR r.3.9 factors for himself and explain his own assessment of the significance and weight of all the relevant circumstances. Since the second judge had not done that, it was unclear what he thought about certain factors and to what extent some of his observations influenced his decision. In those circumstances, the instant court considered the various CPR r.3.9 factors and extracted what it understood to be the second judge's attitude to them. Having considered those factors, there appeared to be sound reasons why relief should be granted, and no strong reason why it should be refused. Although there were several potential criticisms concerning the conduct of B's solicitors, they did not amount to the kind of conduct which justified striking out the action (paras 48-49, 61). (3) In addition to CPR r.3.9, it was germane to consider the circumstances in which the unless order came to be made because they were highly relevant to the exercise of the court's discretion on the grant of relief. Since B's solicitors did not receive a copy of the relevant letter, they were unaware that the court might make an order which could result in striking out the claim. Whilst the court had the power to make an order striking out an action of its own motion, it was far preferable for an application to be issued, particularly where there was a possibility of a "strike out unless" order, in which case notice of the application would be served on the opposing party. If a court regarded it as desirable to make an unless order without the issue of an application, it should be slow to make such an order without giving the party affected the opportunity to be heard (para.62). (4) Although the second judge had not made it clear that he had taken account of all the relevant circumstances, he had reached the right conclusion (para.63).

RYDER PLC v BEEVER, [2012] EWCA Civ 1737, [2013] 2 Costs L.O. 364, Etherton, L.J., CA (Civ Div).

418. Reporting restrictions–Prisoners' rights–Life prisoner challenging decision of Parole Board–Whether reporting restrictions order should be maintained

[European Convention on Human Rights 1950 Art.2, Art.3, Art.5, Art.8.]

Various media organisations sought the discharge of a reporting restrictions order made on the hearing of the application of the claimant prisoner (M) for judicial review of a decision of the Parole Board declining to recommend his transfer to open conditions. M had been convicted of the brutal murder of three infant children in 1973. Since then he had been subject to intermittent assaults and threats by fellow prisoners. Threats of violence or a risk of violence appeared to have been precipitated by press reports in 1994, 1996 and 2005. In 2007, he was transferred to a prison environment in which, in effect, the whole prison was a vulnerable prisoners unit (VPU). M argued that the reporting restrictions order should remain in place, having regard to his rights under the European Convention on Human Rights 1950 art.2, art.3, art.5 and art.8. In relation to arts 2 and 3, press reports had triggered attacks or threats of attacks on him. As to art.5, if he was, in consequence of the risk presented by disclosure of his details, to remain in the segregated conditions of a VPU, he would be unable to progress towards release. Under art.8, he had the right to respect for his "physical and psychological integrity".

Held: Application granted. (1) The most influential of M's Convention rights were those which arose under arts 2 and 3; the state would be required to act when there was a "real and immediate" risk, objectively verified, of death or serious injury, *Officer L, Re* [2007] UKHL 36, [2007] 1 W.L.R. 2135, [2007] C.L.Y. 544 considered. Hostility towards M was likely to be renewed following reports of the judicial review proceedings. However, there was at present no real and immediate risk to his life and safety, because he was serving his sentence in conditions in which his safety could be closely monitored. M's counsel had been wrong to argue that the court should consider the degree of risk inherent in disclosure on the assumption that M was and would remain within the general population of a category C prison. Experience had shown that interest in him waxed and waned depending on the prominence given to his offences and the profile of the prison population with whom he was serving his sentence. The instant decision by no means consigned him to a VPU for the rest of his sentence. As to art.5, regard should be had to the effect of disclosure on the exercise by M of his right of access to a court for a resolution of the lawfulness of his detention in closed or open conditions. However, there was at present no evidence of denial to him of the means to engage in offence-related work which would enhance his progression within the prison system. As to art.8, M's psychological health was not significantly at risk. Having regard to the parties' respective Convention rights, reports of the judicial review proceedings should be permitted, there being a strong public interest in favour of such reports. It had not been shown that the public interest should yield to M's Convention rights. The reporting restrictions order should therefore be discharged (see paras 50-54 of judgment). (2) Attention was required to the issue as to what, if any, notice should be given to media organisations of an application for a reporting restrictions order in the Administrative Court for the purpose of enabling any interested party to make representations if so advised (para.69).

R. (ON THE APPLICATION OF M) v PAROLE BOARD; *sub nom.* R. (ON THE APPLICATION OF McGREAVY) v PAROLE BOARD, [2013] EWHC 1360 (Admin), [2013] E.M.L.R. 23, Pitchford, L.J., DC.

419. Res judicata–Abuse of process–Application to strike out evidence as abuse of process–Privity of interest between parties in earlier proceedings–Whether allowing issue to be relitigated manifestly unfair or bringing administration of justice into disrepute

[Company Directors Disqualification Act 1986 (c.46) s.6.]

The applicant secretary of state applied to strike out part of the evidence of the respondent (P) in an application for P's disqualification as a director. P was the sole director of a company (R) whose VAT claims had been disallowed by the HMRC. On R's appeal against that decision, the VAT Tribunal held that P had known that R was participating in the fraudulent evasion of VAT. The secretary of state applied for P's disqualification as a director under the Company Directors Disqualification Act 1986 s.6 on the ground that he was unfit to be concerned in the management of a limited company because he had caused R to participate in transactions connected with the fraudulent evasion of VAT, which P had either known or should have known about, and had caused R wrongfully to claim a VAT refund of more than £2m. P admitted that R had fraudulently evaded VAT, but denied in affidavit evidence that he had known or ought to have known about R's participation in that fraud. The secretary of state sought to strike out that evidence. The secretary of state contended that that P was estopped per rem judicatam from denying that he had the requisite knowledge in relation to R's participation in VAT evasion because of the tribunal's contrary conclusion. Alternatively, it was submitted that P's denial was an abuse of process because it would be manifestly unfair for the secretary of state to be put to the substantial cost and delay of proving that allegation against P and/or that to permit the issue as to P's knowledge to be re-litigated would bring the administration of justice into disrepute. P argued that there could be no question of res judicata between him and the secretary of state due to the absence of the requisite privity of interest between them and the parties to the proceedings before the tribunal, namely HMRC and R.

Held: Application granted. (1) There would be no estoppel unless both parties to the second proceedings were either the same as, or in privity with, both parties to the earlier proceedings. The question whether one person was privy on another was highly fact-dependent, *Dadourian Group International Inc v Simms (Damages)* [2006] EWHC 2973 (Ch) applied. There had to be a sufficient degree of identification between the two to make it just to hold that the decision to which one was party should be binding in proceedings to which the other was party, and for privity with a party to the proceedings to take effect, it had to take effect whether that party had won or lost, *Gleeson v J Wippell & Co Ltd* [1977] 1 W.L.R. 510, [1977] C.L.Y. 2399 applied. P and R were clearly privies in the context of the proceedings before the tribunal. The question whether the secretary of state had the requisite privity of interest with the HMRC was more difficult. Both represented government departments charged with the protection and furtherance of the public interest, and both were ultimately funded by the taxpayer. However, despite the substantial overlap in interest between them in relation to the issue as to P's knowledge, it was not quite sufficient to make them privies since they were different arms of government pursuing different aspects of the public interest, and were motivated in particular cases by different policy and funding considerations when doing so. There was, therefore, no estoppel binding P as to his knowledge of the VAT fraud because of the absence of the requisite privity of interest between HMRC and the secretary of state in relation to that issue (see paras 9, 11-13, 17-18, 20-22 of judgment). (2) It did not follow from that conclusion that the relitigation of the issue as to P's knowledge was nonetheless not an abuse. R had gone into creditors' voluntary liquidation after the conclusion of the tribunal proceedings, and the HMRC had been unable to recoup its costs from R, despite the tribunal's order that it should. If P was to be permitted by a simple denial of the requisite knowledge to require the case to be proved against him a second time, hundreds of thousands of pounds of further costs, again funded by the taxpayer, would have to be incurred by the secretary of state, and there was no evidence that, if successful, a costs order would be practically enforceable against P. In those circumstances, it would be manifestly unfair to impose the cost of relitigating that issue on the secretary of state. Moreover, to permit the issue as to P's knowledge to be relitigated would indeed bring the administration of justice into disrepute, in the eyes of right-thinking people. Accordingly, those passages in P's evidence in which he denied that he had knowledge of the VAT fraud in which R had participated, to the extent found against him by the tribunal, were struck out as an abuse of process (paras 23-24, 27-28, 32).

SECRETARY OF STATE FOR BUSINESS, INNOVATION AND SKILLS v POTIWAL, [2012] EWHC 3723 (Ch), [2013] Lloyd's Rep. F.C. 124, Briggs, J., Ch D.

420. Risk of sexual harm orders–Standard of proof–Appropriate standard of proof under s.123(4) Sexual Offences Act 2003

[Sexual Offences Act 2003 (c.42) s.123(4), s.123(3).]

The appellant commissioner appealed by way of case stated against a decision of a magistrates' court that the standard of proof on an application for a risk of sexual harm order under the Sexual Offences Act 2003 s.123(4) was the criminal standard. In order to make a risk of sexual harm order, which prohibited a defendant from doing anything prescribed by the order, a magistrates' court had to be satisfied that the defendant had, on at least two occasions, done an act specified in s.123(3), and that the order was necessary to protect a child. A risk of sexual harm order was a civil order, breach of which was a criminal offence with a maximum sentence of five years' imprisonment. The issue was whether the correct standard of proof under s.123(4) was the criminal standard or the civil standard. The commissioner argued that by applying the criminal standard the court would be failing to provide an effective deterrent against sexual abuse, and would make risk of sexual harm orders unrealistically difficult to obtain, making them virtually redundant.

Held: Appeal dismissed. The Act was silent on the standard of proof under s.123(4) and there was no direct authority on the issue. The making of a risk of sexual harm order could have a significant impact on someone who might never have been convicted of a child sex offence. There were a range of cases where the proceedings were civil, but because of the serious potential consequences of an order the standard of proof should be the criminal standard, *B (Children) (Sexual Abuse: Standard of Proof), Re* [2008] UKHL 35, [2009] 1 A.C. 11, [2008] C.L.Y. 1501 applied, *D, Re* [2008] UKHL 33, [2008] 1 W.L.R. 1499, [2008] C.L.Y. 4142 and *R. (on the application of McCann) v Manchester Crown Court* [2002] UKHL 39, [2003] 1 A.C. 787, [2002] C.L.Y. 3 considered. The whole essence of the Act was to provide deterrence. A risk of sexual harm order was not a substitute for a punishment, it applied where the behaviour of an adult gave rise to a belief that there was a risk of harm to a child and intervention was required at an early stage to protect the child. The behaviour triggering an application for an order did not depend on there being a planned meeting between the adult and the child; where there had been a meeting, the police would wish to consider charging the adult with an offence. As the consequences of breaching an order were very serious, it was understandable that the standard of proof should be the same as for an offence; that would not make an application for an order redundant. If the standard were lower, it would lead to the defendant being subjected to restrictions and liable to serious consequences, which would not be the position if he were acquitted of an offence. The criminal standard of proof applied (see paras 5, 8, 16, 18-20 of judgment).

COMMISSIONER OF POLICE OF THE METROPOLIS v EBANKS, [2012] EWHC 2368 (Admin), (2012) 176 J.P. 751, Aikens, L.J., DC.

421. Security for costs–After the event insurance–Whether claimant's ATE insurance policy reliable source of funding–Likelihood of avoidance or cancellation of policy

[Civil Procedure Rules 1998 (SI 1998/3132) r.25.13.]

The applicant company (S) applied for security for costs against the respondent (G). G was a company incorporated in Jordan which undertook seismic exploration in the oil industry in the Middle East. S was a company incorporated in Panama which undertook similar work. They entered into an agreement to co-operate in bidding for a contract with BP to jointly undertake seismic work in Jordan. G brought proceedings against S for breach of contract, claiming that S had excluded it from the BP contract and relying on a number of alleged representations made about the BP contract. S sought security for costs in the sum of £500,000. G had the benefit of an After the Event (ATE) insurance policy to cover S's costs. S submitted that G would be unable to pay its costs, even with the benefit of the ATE policy, because the policy could be avoided by the insurer if the court found in S's favour in relation to alleged representations.

Held: Application refused. (1) The burden was on S to show that there was reason to believe that G would be unable to pay the costs. Unless the threshold conditions in CPR r.25.13 were satisfied, the jurisdiction to make an order for security for costs did not arise. If the jurisdiction arose, the court had discretion as to whether to order security (see paras 11-12 of judgment). (2) The ATE market was considerably more mature than at the date of the judgment in *Nasser v United Bank of Kuwait (Security for Costs)* [2001] EWCA Civ 556, [2002] 1

W.L.R. 1868, [2002] C.L.Y. 385. G's insurer was a reputable insurer in the market, and the funding of litigation by ATE policies had for many years been a central feature of the ability of parties to gain access to justice. In the absence of evidence to the contrary, the court's starting position should be that a properly drafted ATE policy, provided by a substantial and reputable insurer, was a reliable source of litigation funding, *Nasser* considered, *Michael Phillips Architects Ltd v Riklin* [2010] EWHC 834 (TCC), [2010] B.L.R. 569, [2010] C.L.Y. 411 applied. The question was not whether the assurance provided by an ATE policy was better security than cash, but whether there was reason to believe that the claimant would be unable to pay the defendant's costs despite the existence of the ATE policy. Depending on the terms of the policy, an ATE policy could suffice so that the court was not satisfied that there was reason to believe that the claimant would be unable to pay the defendant's costs. Subject to the existence of the ATE policy, there would be reason to believe that G would not be able to discharge an order for payment of S's costs. It was therefore necessary to form a view on the meaning of G's ATE policy, how readily it might be legitimately avoided, and the likelihood of circumstances arising which would enable the policy to be legitimately avoided (paras 13-15, 19-21). (3) The terms of G's policy were similar to the term at issue in *Riklin*. However, there was no material that raised anything more than a theoretical chance that insurers might seek to avoid the policy if the court found in S's favour on the representations. It was not S's case that the claim was fraudulent or a sham and there was a world of difference between a finding that an account was not true, in the sense of being incorrect, and a finding that an account was fraudulent, *Al-Koronky v Time Life Entertainment Group Ltd* [2006] EWCA Civ 1123, [2006] C.P. Rep. 47, [2006] C.L.Y. 501 considered. Unlike *Riklin*, if the insurer cancelled the policy it would remain liable to indemnify against defendant's costs which had been incurred before the date of cancellation, *Riklin* considered. Further, there was evidence of a clear and long-standing relationship between G's solicitors and the insurers which made it commercially much less likely that the insurers would seek to avoid on spurious or tenuous grounds, thereby jeopardising the relationship which had been built up over the years. The insurance contract conditions were not onerous and G had no commercial interest in breaching them. G was represented by very experienced legal representatives who were there to make plain to G its obligations under the policy if any doubt existed. There was no reason to believe that there was more than a theoretical risk of breach. On the facts of the instant case there was no reason to believe that the insurers would seek to avoid the policy or that G would be unable to pay an adverse order for S's costs. The application therefore failed to satisfy the threshold conditions (paras 24-32, 36-44).

GEOPHYSICAL SERVICE CENTRE CO v DOWELL SCHLUMBERGER (ME) INC, [2013] EWHC 147 (TCC), 147 Con. L.R. 240, Stuart Smith, J., QBD (TCC).

422. Security for costs–Appropriateness of ordering payment into court by shipowner in respect of arbitral award made in charterer's favour–Appropriateness of ordering provision of security for costs by shipowner in respect of charterer's claim challenging previous arbitral award

[Arbitration Act 1996 (c.23) s.68, s.70(6), s.70(7); Civil Procedure Rules 1998 (SI 1998/3132) r.25.13(2)(g).]

The applicant charterer (C) applied for orders that the respondent ship owner (M) make a payment into court and provide security for costs under the Arbitration Act 1996 s.70(7) and s.70(6) respectively. An arbitration tribunal had dismissed M's claim against C, which was based on misrepresentations relating to the charterparty, and had directed M to pay C's costs. M had applied under s.68 of the Act challenging the tribunal's award. C was later declared bankrupt. A second tribunal awarded M unpaid hire and associated debts for C's repudiatory breach of the charterparty, damages and its costs. M's overall costs in relation to both arbitrations had been assessed, but C's had not been. The issues were whether M should be ordered to (i) make a payment into court under s.70(7) in respect of costs payable under the award made in C's favour by the first tribunal; (ii) provide security for costs under s.70(6) in respect of its s.68 application.

Held: Application for payment into court refused, application for security for costs granted. (1) In the absence of a costs assessment, none of the sums which C claimed should be paid into court were "payable under" the first tribunal's award within the meaning of s.70(7). Therefore, the court had no jurisdiction to order a payment into court. Section 70(7) was predicated on there having been a specific sum of money ordered to be paid under the award which was appealed or challenged. Since C's costs had not been assessed, it was not appropriate to order M to pay a sum into court (see para.9 of judgment). (2) It was just to order M to provide security for C's costs in relation to the s.68 application. Further, the condition in CPR r.25.13(2)(g) was satisfied because there was evidence that M had taken steps in relation to its assets that would make it difficult to enforce an order for costs made against it. Against that background, it was necessary to decide whether the sums awarded by the second tribunal in M's favour constituted an equitable set-off in respect of a potential costs order in C's favour in the s.68 application. The existence of the monetary awards made against C by the second tribunal afforded no reason for not ordering M to provide security for C's costs in the s.68 application, whether as a matter of set-off or discretion. A costs order in C's favour in the s.68 application would be connected with M's cross-claims for the awards made by the second tribunal, because both arbitrations were brought under and in connection with the same charterparty. However, M's cross-claims would not be so closely connected to a costs order made in C's favour as to make it manifestly unjust to allow C to enforce a costs award, *Geldof Metaalconstructie NV v Simon Carves Ltd* [2010] EWCA Civ 667, [2010] 4 All E.R. 847, [2010] C.L.Y. 1241 applied. It was not right that M's success before the second tribunal should result in washing out the positive cash-flow consequences for C of costs orders in its favour arising out of M's failure in its earlier misrepresentation claim. Accordingly, it was appropriate to order M to provide security for C's costs in the s.68 application, and if it failed to do so within 21 days its s.68 application would be dismissed (paras 11, 14-16).

MOONDANCE MARITIME ENTERPRISES SA v CARBOFER MARITIME TRADING APS; MOONDANCE II, THE, [2012] EWHC 3618 (Comm), [2013] 1 Lloyd's Rep. 269, Field, J., QBD (Comm).

423. Security for costs–Impecuniosity–Order for impecunious defendant to give security for claimant's costs of counterclaim–Whether security for costs stifling counterclaim

[European Convention on Human Rights 1950 Art.6.]

The appellant company (X) appealed against a decision ordering it to give security for the costs of the respondent solicitors' firm (P) in relation to X's counterclaim. P had briefly advised X and acted for it in relation to claims which X wished to bring against third parties for the alleged infringement of its intellectual property rights. When X paid only a small part of the fees billed, P terminated X's retainer and brought proceedings seeking to recover the unpaid fees. X issued a counterclaim alleging that P should have, without delay, initiated proceedings on its behalf and obtained interim relief against the alleged infringing parties and that P had failed to give the right advice or take the appropriate action in that respect. X claimed to have suffered very heavy trading losses as a result, such that the sum counterclaimed would extinguish P's claim. P denied that it was negligent in any way and contended that the alleged shortcomings on its part had not caused any loss to X. The action did not progress and P incurred expenses which X was ordered to pay by way of three costs orders. The costs were not paid as X claimed it was wholly unable to do so. P subsequently sought an order that X should provide security for its costs of defending the counterclaim. The district judge considered that X had a low prospect of success on the counterclaim and was not satisfied that an order for security would stifle it or be otherwise oppressive. She concluded that it would be just to order security. The counterclaim was stayed pending the payment of security. X contended that, in the light of *BJ Crabtree (Insulation) v*

GPT Communications Systems 59 B.L.R. 43, [1993] C.L.Y. 3162, where effectively the same issues arose in both the claim and the counterclaim it would be wrong to order an impecunious defendant to pay security for costs. It submitted that it lacked any worthwhile assets and had no access to funds, and that the request for security should have been declined on the ground that it would stifle the counterclaim, and that an order for security for costs with which it could not comply infringed its right of access to the court under the European Convention on Human Rights 1950 art.6.

Held: Appeal allowed. There was no rule of thumb that when the trial of the counterclaim would raise the same issues as the trial of the claim, security for costs of the claim would not be ordered; in each case, the court had to consider whether it was just to make an order for security, *Crabtree* and *Hutchison Telephone (UK) v Ultimate Response* [1993] B.C.L.C. 307, [1993] C.L.Y. 3161 considered. Neither side had clearly shown that it had a very high degree of probability of success. The counterclaim raised many points both as to liability and quantum which might cause very serious difficulties for X in the pursuit of its claim. Conversely, in the absence of a much more detailed examination of the facts, it was not right to conclude that P had clearly demonstrated a very high degree of probability of success on liability in defending the counterclaim. Before refusing to order security on the ground that it would unfairly stifle a valid claim, the court had to be satisfied that, in all the circumstances, it was probable that the claim would be stifled, *Keary Developments Ltd v Tarmac Construction Ltd* [1995] 3 All E.R. 534, [1996] C.L.Y. 724 followed. X had done enough to prove that it did not have any funds of its own and it would not be able to obtain funding which would enable it to comply with the order for security for costs. It followed that the instant court disagreed with the district judge on the question of the counterclaim being stifled. Her decision that it was just to order security was therefore made on an incorrect basis as to the stifling point and the instant court had to reach its own conclusion on that issue. To require an unaffordable amount of security as a way of disciplining a wayward litigant was to transform security for costs into a means of striking out a claim without any of the ordinary safeguards, *Al-Koronky v Time Life Entertainment Group Ltd* [2006] EWCA Civ 1123, [2006] C.P. Rep. 47, [2006] C.L.Y. 501 followed. In all the circumstances, the order for security made by the district judge and any order for security for a substantial sum would stifle the counterclaim and an order which had that effect should not be made. Even taking the merits of the counterclaim into account, the court was unable to conclude that it was so weak that it would be just for it to be stifled. The order for security for costs was, accordingly, set aside (see paras 26, 34, 38, 47, 50-51, 62-63, 65).

PANNONE LLP v AARDVARK DIGITAL LTD, [2013] EWHC 686 (Ch), [2013] 4 Costs L.O. 607, Morgan, J., Ch D.

424. Security for costs–Maintenance of security pending determination of application for leave to appeal

The court was required to determine issues related to costs in an appeal by the appellant patentee (M) against a High Court decision that one of its patents should be revoked because it did not sufficiently disclose the invention. The respondent (O) had sought to have two of M's patents revoked on the grounds of obviousness and insufficiency. The High Court held that the first patent was neither obvious nor insufficient, but that the second patent, whilst not obvious, was insufficient. M's appeal was dismissed. Four issues arose in relation to costs: (i) the appropriate order in relation to the costs of O's notice and cross-appeal; (ii) whether the costs of the applications for maintenance of security which O had been ordered to pay should be expressed as a percentage deduction from O's costs of the appeal or be left to a detailed separate assessment; (iii) whether there should be a payment on account of O's costs of the appeal and, if so, how much; (iv) whether O's solicitors should be required to maintain the security for costs of £699,650 which they currently held pending the determination of any application by M for permission to appeal to the Supreme Court.

Held: Judgment accordingly. (1) O was entitled to the costs of its notice and cross-appeal because it had been the winner, having achieved its commercial aim on the appeal, whereas M's appeal against the judge's finding of insufficiency had failed. Furthermore, O had only intended to pursue its cross-appeal in relation to the obviousness of either patent in the event that it was unsuccessful in upholding the decision of the judge that the second patent was insufficient. Once the appeal against the judge's finding of insufficiency of the second patent was dismissed, the cross-appeal on obviousness in relation to both patents fell away (see paras 4-6 of judgment). (2) M's costs were to be assessed and set off against the costs it was required to pay, as the issues were self-contained and the costs were, on any basis, substantial. Moreover, there was a real issue as to whether the 7.5 per cent deduction suggested by O would properly compensate M (paras 8-9). (3) O was entitled to its costs, including the costs of the cross-appeal and respondent's notice. It was appropriate to order a payment on account of about half of O's estimate of its appeal costs, that was to say £100,000, upon O's undertaking to repay that sum if the order was varied on further appeal (para.11). (4) O would not be required to maintain the security, given that it had had the benefit of concurrent findings of the High Court and the Court of Appeal on the issue in relation to which M intended to seek permission to appeal to the Supreme Court. If the Supreme Court gave M permission to appeal and considered that security was appropriate, there was no reason to suppose O would not again provide security pursuant to the undertaking offered (para.15).

OMNIPHARM LTD v MERIAL (COSTS), [2013] EWCA Civ 10, [2013] 4 Costs L.O. 505, Richards, L.J., CA (Civ Div).

425. Service by alternative permitted method–Service out of jurisdiction–Service of claim form on party's lawyer in Lebanon–Good service

[Civil Procedure Rules 1998 (SI 1998/3132) r.6.15, r.6.37(5)(b); Hague Convention on the Service Abroad of Judicial and Extrajudicial Documents in Civil or Commercial Matters 1965.]

The appellants (X) appealed against a decision ([2011] EWCA Civ 1571, [2012] C.P. Rep.11, [2012] C.L.Y. 470) that their service of a claim form on the lawyer of the respondent (B) in Lebanon did not amount to good service. X had issued proceedings in England against B. They took no steps for three of the six months of the claim form's validity, then instructed counsel to settle particulars. They obtained permission to serve the proceedings outside the jurisdiction and an extension of the claim form's validity. X failed to effect service at an address in Lebanon believed to be B's home address, and instead effected service at the office of his Lebanese lawyer. X later applied for an order under CPR r.6.15 and/or r.6.37(5)(b) for an order that the steps they had taken amounted to good service. The judge granted that application; the Court of Appeal reversed that decision.

Held: Appeal allowed. (1) Whether there was good reason to order that delivery of documents amounted to good service was essentially a matter of fact. It was not appropriate to add a gloss to the test by saying that there would only be good reason in exceptional circumstances. In cases under r.6.15(2) not involving the Hague Convention on the Service Abroad of Judicial and Extrajudicial Documents in Civil or Commercial Matters 1965 or a bilateral service treaty, the court should simply ask whether, in all the circumstances, there was good reason to order that steps taken to bring the claim form to the defendant's attention constituted good service. The Convention did not apply in the instant case, nor was there a service treaty between the United Kingdom and Lebanon. An alternative service order therefore did not risk subverting the provisions of any such convention or treaty. The mere fact that the defendant had learned of the claim form could not constitute good reason to make an order under r.6.15(2). However, the wording of the rule showed that it was a critical factor. The most important purpose of service was to ensure that the contents of the document served were communicated to the defendant, *Olafsson v*

Gissurarson [2008] EWCA Civ 152, [2008] 1 W.L.R. 2016, [2008] C.L.Y. 419 applied. The judge had taken account of a series of factors. He had said that, most importantly, B had through his advisers been fully apprised of the nature of the claim being brought. He had had regard to the facts that service through diplomatic channels had proved impractical and that any further attempts would lead to unacceptable delay and expense. He had noted that B had been unwilling to co-operate with service by disclosing his address in Lebanon; although he had not been under a duty to disclose his address, his refusal to co-operate was highly relevant to deciding whether there was a good reason for making a r.6.15(2) order. B's submission that the judge had not had regard either to the delay between issue of the claim form and the time X instructed counsel to settle particulars or to the fact that the claim was time-barred was rejected. It seemed likely that he considered that, given X's difficulties in serving the claim form, the delay had made no difference; he had been entitled to do so. The critical points were that the documents had been delivered within the validity of the claim form and brought to B's attention and that service via diplomatic channels had proved impracticable. The judge had not made an error of principle (see paras 33-41 of judgment). (2) The Court of Appeal had not focused on the judge's reasoning. It had wrongly held that the judge had decided that there had been valid service under Lebanese law. It had also been wrong to state that a r.6.15(2) order would make an already exorbitant power still more exorbitant. Although service out of the jurisdiction had traditionally been regarded as the exercise of an exorbitant jurisdiction, such a description was no longer necessary; in any event, it had been accepted that it was proper to serve the claim form out of the jurisdiction. The Court of Appeal had also been wrong to say that a claimant seeking retrospective validation of alternative service abroad had to show that the method used was good service under local law, save where there were adequate safeguards. That would render r.6.15(1) and (2) otiose, and it was unclear what safeguards the court had in mind. The delay before issue of the claim form had been a significant part of the Court of Appeal's reasoning, but events before issue were not relevant. There was no legitimate basis on which to interfere with the judge's decision (paras 32, 42-54).

ABELA v BAADARANI, [2013] UKSC 44, [2013] 1 W.L.R. 2043, Lord Neuberger (President), SC.

426. Service out of jurisdiction–Claim forms–Service of unsealed copy of claim form out of jurisdiction–Validity of service–Whether sealed copy required

[Civil Procedure Rules 1998 (SI 1998/3132) Pt 6, r.6.40(3)(c), r.7.5.]

The appellant (B) appealed against a decision that he had been validly served in Monaco with proceedings issued by the respondent (W). W had purported to serve B with a claim form under the CPR r.6.40(3)(c), which stated that a claim form could be served by any method permitted by the law of the country in which it was to be served. W took steps to serve B in Monaco in accordance with a procedure permitted by local law. B was served with a copy of the claim form. B maintained that he had not been validly served with proceedings as he had not been served with an original sealed claim form, and therefore the English court had no jurisdiction to try the claim against him. A master held that the method of service was permitted by the law of Monaco, and concluded that B had been validly served. B submitted that it was immaterial that service was in accordance with the law of Monaco as there was a distinction between what was to be served, which was a matter for English law, and how it was served, which was a matter for the law of the country of service. B submitted that English law required service of a sealed copy of a claim form, and that an unsealed copy was insufficient.

Held: Appeal dismissed. (1) English law determined what was required to be served. The only explicit reference in subpart IV of Pt 6 to service of a copy of a document which the court had sealed was in relation to a Hague Convention case; therefore it might be inferred that there was no requirement for a claim form to have affixed to it the court seal in order to effect service under r.6.40(3)(c). In addition, CPR r.7.5 did not include an express reference to the court sealing a claim form. Further, PD 6A para 4.3 clearly provided that it was not always necessary to serve an original or "first generation" copy of the claim form. Therefore, all that was required by r.6.40(3)(c) was that the steps needed to bring a claim form to a person's attention could be taken by any method permitted by the law of the country in which those steps were taken, *Kuenyehia v International Hospitals Group Ltd* [2006] EWCA Civ 21, [2006] C.P. Rep. 34, [2006] C.L.Y. 347 considered. If those steps were successful in bringing the claim form to that person's attention, as in the instant case, there was no additional requirement that a particular hard copy of the claim form be used. For the purposes of the CPR, what constituted a claim form was a matter of substance. The reference to "claim form" was not a reference to a particular hard copy of a document (see paras 46-47, 50, 59, 61, 63 of judgment). (2) (Obiter) Parties proposing to serve a claim form would be well advised to continue to serve a copy of the claim form which bore a seal affixed by the court office. A claim form was an important document and there ought to be no room to doubt that the date on the form had been entered by the court (para.64).

WESTON v BATES, [2012] EWHC 590 (QB), [2013] 1 W.L.R. 189, Tugendhat, J., QBD.

427. Service out of jurisdiction–Declaratory orders–Claim for negative declarations and anti-suit injunction–Putative parties to bill of lading contracts–Putative law of contracts

[CPR PD 6B (Service out of the Jurisdiction) 2000 para.3.1 (6)(c).]

The applicant Jordanian company (R) challenged the jurisdiction of the court over proceedings brought by the respondent Singaporean company (N). The dispute concerned a shipment of palm oil and palm olein from Malaysia to Jordan, which was apparently delivered in poor condition and was rejected by R. R had bought the cargo from the shipper (P), a Malaysian company, which sub-chartered the vessel from N. The sub-charter was governed by English law and provided for arbitration in London. The bills of lading incorporated the terms of the sub-charter and further provided that, if a person other than the shipowner or demise charterer was judged to be a carrier or bailee of the shipment, that person would be entitled to all limitations of or exonerations from liability and/or defences provided by law or by the terms of the contract of carriage. R issued proceedings for damages in Jordan against P as seller and N as carrier under the bills. Under Jordanian law R's claims had a real prospect of success, including its claim that N was the carrier under the bills of lading contracts. N issued a claim in England for declarations that it was not liable to R because it was not party to the bills of lading contracts and not a bailee of the cargo, and for an anti-suit injunction and damages.

Held: Application refused. (1) N's claim for an injunction on the basis that pursuit of the Jordanian proceedings was vexatious and oppressive was not within the jurisdictional gateway in CPR PD 6B para.3.1 (6)(c) because it was not a claim made "in respect of" a contract governed by English law, *Alliance Bank JSC v Aquanta Corp* [2012] EWCA Civ 1588, [2013] 1 All E.R. (Comm) 819, [2013] 5 C.L. 44 applied. Nor did N have a reasonably arguable case that R's conduct was unconscionable, which was the usual requirement for such relief: the Jordanian proceedings were brought comfortably before the English proceedings, the claim in Jordan could not be regarded as hopeless and R had not submitted to the English court's jurisdiction, *Star Reefers Pool Inc v JFC Group Co Ltd* [2012] EWCA Civ 14, [2012] 2 All E.R. (Comm) 225, [2012] C.L.Y. 315 applied. There was no good arguable claim that R by its prosecution of the Jordanian proceedings sought to prevent N from availing itself of the exclusions and limitations of liability in the bills of lading. It followed that N should not be permitted to serve out of the jurisdiction a claim for an injunction or for damages (see paras 13-22 of judgment). (2) N had established that England was the proper place in which to bring the declaration claims on the basis that the lex causae was English law. The facts that under English conflict of laws rules the governing law of the dispute and of the putative contracts between N and R was English law, that the putative parties to the bills of lading contracts had chosen English law and that there were differences between English and Jordanian law relevant to the dispute, outweighed the countervailing considerations relied on by R, *VTB Capital Plc v Nutritek International Corp* [2013] UKSC 5, [2013] 2 A.C. 337, [2013] 4 C.L. 35 applied (paras 26-29). (3) The court would only exercise its discretion to allow service out of the jurisdiction of a claim for a negative declaration if satisfied that a solid practical benefit would ensue, *Citigroup Global Markets Ltd v Amatra Leveraged Feeder Holdings Ltd* [2012] EWHC 1331 (Comm), [2012] 2 C.L.C. 279 applied. A ruling on the question whether N was party to the bill of lading contracts would be of assistance to N in resisting enforcement outside Jordan. That was a real benefit potentially arising from a declaration (paras 31-36). (4) The parties to the putative contracts between R and N had evinced an intention that English law should govern them, and N had a sufficient case that that choice could not be vindicated without a declaration and potentially an ancillary anti-suit order, and so could not be vindicated without permission to serve its claims for declaratory relief on R in Jordan, *Akai Pty Ltd v People's Insurance Co Ltd* [1998] 1 Lloyd's Rep. 90, [1998] C.L.Y. 771 considered. N had a sufficient case to justify permission to serve out of the jurisdiction claims for declaratory relief (paras 37-39).

NAVIG8 PTE LTD v AL-RIYADH CO FOR VEGETABLE OIL INDUSTRY; LUCKY LADY,THE, [2013] EWHC 328 (Comm), [2013] 2 All E.R. (Comm) 145, Andrew Smith, J., QBD (Comm).

428. Service out of jurisdiction–Forum non conveniens–Claim by Kazakh bank alleging fraud and conspiracy–Permission to serve proceedings out of jurisdiction–Whether Kazakhstan or England appropriate forum

[CPR PD 6B (Service out of the Jurisdiction) 2000.]

The appellant Kazakhstan bank (C) appealed against a decision ([2011] EWHC 3281 (Comm), [2012] 1 Lloyd's Rep. 181, [2012] C.L.Y. 475) that it had failed to establish that the English court was the most appropriate forum for the resolution of its disputes with the defendants. The defendants cross-appealed against various aspects of the decision. C claimed to be the victim of a fraudulent conspiracy by the defendants. It believed the principal conspirator to be the sixth respondent (D6), who was the former chair of its board. The seventh and eight respondents (D7 and D8) were the brothers of D6 and they owned D9, a Kazakh holding company, which owned the majority of C. The other corporate defendants (D1 to D5) were beneficially owned by D6 and controlled by the three brothers. There were also personal defendants (D10 to D15). C's case was that it had been required to purchase American treasury notes, which were subsequently pledged to two Cypriot banks as security for loans made to D1-D4. It alleged that the money had been laundered to the other defendants. Loan agreements and guarantees between the Cypriot banks and the borrowers contained English jurisdiction clauses. C maintained that it had a subrogated claim to enforce the loan agreements against D1-4 and D6-8. Permission had been granted for C to serve the proceedings out of the jurisdiction. The issues were whether (i) C had a real prospect of success in its subrogated claims against D3 and D4; (ii) C had a cause of action in implied contract against D3 and D4; (iii) C's non-contractual claims could, for the purposes of the jurisdictional gateways in CPR PD 6B be regarded as claims made in respect of a contract; (4) a good arguable case existed for the resolution of the non-contractual claims under English law.

Held: Appeal dismissed. (1) There were grave reservations about the availability of subrogated rights; any rights that had arisen could not be exercised in C's name. Since D3 and D4 were insolvent, the concept of a subrogated claim was contrived, and constituted an artificial device to enable C to rely upon the exclusive jurisdiction clauses as pointing towards the English court being the appropriate forum, *VTB Capital Plc v Nutritek International Corp* [2012] EWCA Civ 808, [2012] 2 Lloyd's Rep. 313, [2012] C.L.Y. 474 applied. Although C had offered an undertaking not to pursue any claim against the Cypriot banks in respect of the guarantees, an undertaking would not assist it because it had no cause of action in its own name against D3 and D4. There was no basis on which service out of the jurisdiction ought to have been permitted against D3 and D4. Such a conclusion, in the context of the decision below concerning appropriate forum, deprived C of reliance as a matter of contractual entitlement upon the exclusive jurisdiction clauses in the agreements with the Cypriot banks, *Societe Generale de Paris v Dreyfus Bros* (1885) 29 Ch. D. 239 approved. It would be very rare for a court to permit a claimant to perfect or complete his cause of action by reliance upon an undertaking, let alone a conditional undertaking, and especially where the undertaking depended on the court assuming jurisdiction over different causes of action asserted against different overseas parties rather than those parties immediately affected by the defective cause of action in respect of which the undertaking had been given (see paras 39-40, 42-46 of judgment). (2) C sought to rely upon an implied indemnity as justifying the grant of permission to serve D3 and D4 out of the jurisdiction. A collateral contract, such as, in the instant case, an implied indemnity, would be governed by the same law as the substantive contract which generated it, at least where that contract contained an express choice of law, *Golden Ocean Group Ltd v Salgaocar Mining Industries Pvt Ltd* [2012] EWCA Civ 265, [2012] 1 W.L.R. 3674, [2012] C.L.Y. 3047 applied. There was nothing to displace the inference that the parties intended both contracts to be governed by the same system of law. Subject to proving that England was the correct forum, C would be permitted to serve D3 and D4 out of the jurisdiction with the claim in implied contract (paras 46, 54). (3) There was no basis upon which D1 and D2 could be served out of the jurisdiction in reliance on gateway 5. C had no subrogated claim against D3, so there was no issue which it was reasonable for the court to try. There was a potential reliance on gateway 6 in respect of the implied claims against D3 and D4, subject to appropriate forum and to the court's reservation that those defendants did not constitute anchor defendants for the purpose of the necessary or proper party gateway. Gateway 6 was unavailable for D6 to D9 (paras 60-73). Since there was no anchor defendant, the application of gateway 3 was academic, but the court expressed a view upon it in any event (paras 74-79). (4) The conclusion of the judge below concerning forum was unsurprising and ought not to be interfered with: the dispute had very little connection with the domestic jurisdiction in terms of the torts committed, the agreements made, the loss suffered and the domicile of the parties. The fact that some of the instruments used to further the fraud were expressly governed by English law was incidental to the real essence of the dispute, *VTB* applied (paras 83-120)

ALLIANCE BANK JSC v AQUANTA CORP, [2012] EWCA Civ 1588, [2013] 1 All E.R. (Comm) 819, Lloyd, L.J., CA (Civ Div).

429. Service out of jurisdiction–Interim injunctions–Claim arising out of charterparty–Permission to serve claim out of jurisdiction–Interim anti-arbitration injunction preventing arbitral proceedings abroad

The claimant (C) applied for permission to serve its claim on the defendant parent and subsidiary companies (D1 and D2) out of the jurisdiction, and for an interim anti-arbitration injunction to restrain D2 from pursuing arbitration proceedings in Singapore. An email had recorded the charter of a vessel from its owners to C and D1. The charter provided that any dispute would be referred to arbitration in London, and that it would be governed by English law. C subsequently claimed that D1 was the disponent owner of the vessel, and was thus liable in respect of overpaid hire charges and other sums. D2 counterclaimed on the basis that it, and not D1, was the disponent owner under the charterparty. C and D2 participated in several meetings, which culminated in the creation of an addendum to the charterparty signed by both of them. The addendum provided that the charterparty be amended ab initio so that all disputes arising under it would be determined by arbitration in Singapore. C then commenced arbitration proceedings in London against D1. D1 and D2 appointed the same firm of solicitors in Singapore, who denied the existence of any charterparty to which D1 was a party. The firm wrote to C to say that D2 had appointed an arbitrator in Singapore. D1 subsequently consented to an arbitral tribunal in London determining whether there was a contract, and so an arbitration agreement, to which it was a party. In the London arbitration, to which D2 was not a party, the arbitrator decided that C had contracted with D1, and that accordingly the London arbitral tribunal had jurisdiction to determine the substantive merits of the dispute pursuant to the arbitration agreement in the charterparty. The issues were whether (i) there was a serious issue to be tried that D2 had a privity of interest with D1 such that D2 was bound by the arbitration award; (ii) there was a serious issue to be tried that C was entitled to a declaration that D2 was not a party to the charterparty, and that C was not a party to an applicable agreement to submit the disputes to arbitration in Singapore; (iii) the court should exercise its discretion to grant an anti-arbitration injunction against D2.

Held: Applications granted. (1) It did not follow that because D1 and D2 were group companies, D2 had to be taken to have decided to sit back and let D1 fight its battle as to who was the single counterparty to the charter. D1 and D2 were conducting separate business under separate corporate entities, they were managed from different countries, and the constitution of their boards of directors was different. The mere fact that D1 was D2's parent company did not mean that they had an identity of interest in which of them owed a liability to C. However, the fact that the same firm of solicitors was instructed for D1 and D2, who denied that D1 was a party to the charter and asserted that D2 was, was sufficient to give rise to a triable issue that D1 and D2 had an identity of interest at that stage. Nevertheless, D2 was not a party to the proceedings, and did not consent to the London arbitration. D2 was not asked to participate in the process or to agree to abide by the outcome. C did not at that stage ask the court to decide the issue on a tripartite basis, or invite consent to a tripartite London arbitration. D2 could not reasonably be taken to have given up its contention that the issue should be resolved in the Singapore arbitration. It would have been unfair to hold D2 bound by the result of an arbitration in which it had no reasonable opportunity to participate. Accordingly, C's argument that D2 was privy to and bound by the arbitration award had no real prospect of success (see paras 34-36 of judgment). (2) C's arguments that it was entitled to a declaration and that it was not party to an applicable agreement to submit the disputes to Singapore arbitration had a real prospect of success. However, in order to grant permission to serve out of the jurisdiction, the court also had to be persuaded that the English court, and not the Singapore arbitral tribunal, was the appropriate forum to address the substantive issues. It was appropriate for the English court to decide the disputed arbitrality issue for itself. The most significant factor was the need to seek to minimise inconsistent judgments in England and Singapore. Further, there was a strong connection between the arbitrality issue and England, and in a dispute which raised questions as to the doctrine of mistake and implied conditions in that context, the English court was bound to be better placed to divine and apply the nuances of English law than a Singaporean arbitral tribunal, from whom there might be limited rights of appeal on what might be treated in that jurisdiction as a factual dispute. The instant case was not one where it was right to wait for the decision of the Singapore tribunal on the basis that if it decided the arbitrality issue against D2, the problem would fall away. Accordingly, it was appropriate to grant C permission to serve out of the jurisdiction (paras 37, 46, 61-63, 67). (3) The balance of convenience favoured granting the injunction to avoid unnecessary duplication and expense, and to put the Singapore arbitration on hold pending the determination of the jurisdiction issue by the English court (para.73).

GOLDEN OCEAN GROUP LTD v HUMPUSS INTERMODA TRANSPORTASI TBK LTD; BARITO, THE, [2013] EWHC 1240 (Comm), [2013] 2 All E.R. (Comm) 1025, Popplewell, J., QBD (Comm).

430. Service out of jurisdiction–Quantum meruit–Whether order to serve claim out of jurisdiction extended to quantum meruit claim–Meaning of "claims in respect of a contract"

[CPR PD 6B (Service out of the Jurisdiction) 2000 para.3.1.]

The court was required to determine whether an order for the claimant (S) to serve proceedings out of jurisdiction was confined to claims made in respect of a contract. The defendant member of the Saudi royal family (P) applied to vary the order so that it would not extend to a claim in restitution. S ran a consultancy business effecting commercial introductions, mainly for clients in Libya. S brought proceedings claiming a commission for services rendered in relation to the sale of an aircraft owned by P which was intended for Colonel Gaddafi's use. She relied on an oral agreement reached at a meeting in London with P's agent but also claimed, in the alternative, commission upon a quantum meruit basis. P denied that he was contractually bound to pay commission. At a hearing for permission to serve the claim out of jurisdiction, a master granted the order allowing service out as he decided that the first two "gateways" relating to "claims in respect of a contract" had been satisfied. The gateways at the relevant time were CPR 6.20 (5) (a) and (b), namely that the contract had been made within the jurisdiction and made through an agent. The master found that the claim did not fall within gateway 5(c) because he was doubtful whether the agreement was governed by English law. S maintained that (1) the order allowing service out of jurisdiction applied to the whole of the claim form and particulars of claim and it was not limited to the claim in respect of a contract; (2) S should be permitted to pursue the quantum meruit claim on the footing that it satisfied CPR PD 6B para.3.1 (16).

Held: Judgment accordingly. (1) An essential requirement of a claim if it came within gateway 5 was that a contract existed, albeit that it had to be established at trial. In obtaining the court's permission to serve out of jurisdiction, the claimant had to establish that he had a better argument than the defendant. Once, however, the assumption was made that there was no contract between the claimant and the defendant, which was the assumption upon which, as advanced by S, the quantum meruit claim proceeded, it was no longer possible to contend that the claim arose "in respect of a contract". It was irrelevant that it arose as an alternative to a claim which asserted a contract. It was not permissible to elide the two claims to bring the quantum meruit claim within the purview of the contract gateway. Accordingly, the permission to serve the proceedings out of jurisdiction on P was confined to those claims which were in respect of a contract. Those claims did not include the quantum meruit claim insofar as it was of the restitutionary (non-contractual) kind (see paras 53-54 of judgment). (2) The acts which gave rise to P's alleged liability took place almost entirely outside the jurisdiction and the few acts which could be identified as having occurred within the jurisdiction played no more than a minor part in the establishment of that liability. Accordingly, the restitutionary claim did not meet the requirements of gateway 16 and the permission sought was therefore declined (para.77). (3) P's application to vary the order was granted; the permission granted to S to serve the claim form on P out of jurisdiction did not extend to the claim in restitution. That declaration did not affect the quantum meruit claim insofar as it was contractual in nature (paras 82, 84).

SHARAB v PRINCE AL-WALEED BIN TALAL BIN ABDUL-AZIZ AL-SAUD, [2012] EWHC 1798 (Ch), [2012] 2 C.L.C. 612, Sir William Blackburne, Ch D.

431. Service out of jurisdiction–Setting aside–Application to set aside orders permitting service out of jurisdiction–Whether trust governed by English law–Appropriate forum for dispute

The applicant Guernsey company (S) applied to set aside orders granting permission to the respondents (X) to serve proceedings out of the jurisdiction. S had become a partner in a Scottish limited partnership by making an investment. S made the investment on X's behalf pursuant to investment agreements. Each agreement provided for S to invest the money "on behalf of" X, for S to manage

X's investment "as nominee", and for X to be bound by any decision that S made "as nominee on its behalf". A clause also provided that the agreements would be subject to and construed in accordance with the laws of England and Wales, and that any disputes would be subject to the jurisdiction of the English courts, to which both parties submitted. After making the investment, S executed a deed of trust in relation to each of X. The deed declared that S held a defined commitment in the partnership "as nominee and trustee" for X "pursuant to the terms" of the agreements. Disputes subsequently arose, and X asked S to transfer the partnership interest to another trustee. S applied to the Guernsey court for interpleader relief in respect of the funds it held on the ground that there were or might be at least two competing claims to those funds, namely by X and another (M). M later applied for S's winding-up. X issued a claim in the English court seeking an order appointing a new trustee of the partnership interest in S's place, an order giving the new trustee permission to take all necessary steps to obtain a vesting order in Scotland in relation to the partnership interest, and an order for an account to be taken of all sums due to them from S. X obtained permission to serve their claim on S out of the jurisdiction on the ground that the claim was to execute a trust governed by English law. S argued that (1) the trust was governed by Guernsey, not English, law; (2) the English court should stay X's claim on the basis that Guernsey was the more appropriate forum for the dispute; (3) service of the claim should be set aside because, when applying to serve out of the jurisdiction, X had failed to discharge their duty of disclosure.

Held: Application refused. (1) The investment agreements created a trust of the partnership interest, and by virtue of the governing law clause, that trust was governed by English law. By agreeing to receive money from X and to invest it "on behalf of" X by itself becoming a limited partner, and by agreeing to manage X's investment "as nominee for" X, S agreed to act as a trustee for X, and not as a mere agent. That analysis was supported by the terms of the deed of trust, whereby S expressly acknowledged that it held the partnership interest as nominee and trustee for X "pursuant to" and "pursuant to the terms of" the investment agreements. Accordingly, the terms of the investment agreements, including the governing law clause, were the terms of the trust, and therefore the trust was governed by English law (see paras 19-22 of judgment). (2) The Guernsey court was not the more appropriate forum. The parties had agreed that disputes would be subject to the jurisdiction of the English court, to which they had submitted. Further, the claim did not cover the same subject as the Guernsey interpleader proceedings: the subject of X's claim was whether S should be removed as trustee of the partnership, if so on what terms, and how much was due from S to X; by contrast, the subject of the Guernsey interpleader proceedings was whether certain funds in S's name belonged beneficially to X or M. In any event, the Guernsey proceedings had not passed beyond the stage of the initiating process and had been stayed. Accordingly, the English court was clearly the more appropriate forum for the trial of the claim. Even apart from the jurisdiction clause, the trust of the partnership interest was governed by English law, and so the English court, unlike the Guernsey court, could deal with the claim without the need for expert evidence (paras 25-27, 29-30) (3) As to X's disclosure obligation, there was no question of the English court having been misled or inadequately informed of the Guernsey interpleader proceedings or of M's application to wind-up S (para.34). (4) Accordingly, it was not appropriate to set aside service of the claim or to stay it (para.35).

ACKERMAN v SYNERGY CAPITAL LTD, [2013] EWHC 887 (Ch), [2013] I.L.Pr. 34, Kevin Prosser Q.C., Ch D.

432. Settlement–Penal notices–Settlement of litigation between husband and wife–Appropriateness of making settlement terms binding on third parties

The applicant (W) applied for an order confirming the terms of a settlement between her and the respondent husband (H). W had started divorce proceedings in Greece. H had subsequently issued an application for provisional measures in relation to their son. In the application notice, he made various allegations relating to disputes that had arisen between him and W. H had provided a redacted version of that notice to the media, which had resulted in the publication of a newspaper article about H and W's relationship and divorce. The Court of Appeal subsequently granted an interim injunction preventing H from publishing the redacted material or the application notice. In relation to the instant application, H consented to an order which included injunctions restraining him from disclosing or publishing the redacted information or other information concerning their son, their marriage and the personal relationship between him and W. He did not consent to the inclusion of a penal notice, which would have the effect of binding third parties who were not party to the litigation. W submitted that a penal notice should be included in the order because she could not safely proceed on the basis that third parties who had been notified of the terms of the settlement would be in contempt of court if they disclosed information of the kind specified.

Held: Application granted in part. W had not shown that an order expressly addressed to third parties was necessary or proportionate. No third party had disputed or was likely to dispute that the parties and their son had a reasonable expectation of privacy in respect of the relevant information. There was no evidence of a threat from any third party to publish, nor of a real risk that any third party might publish, information in respect of which the parties or their son had a reasonable expectation of privacy. The court confirmed the draft terms of the order, save for the inclusion of a penal notice making the terms expressly binding on third parties (see paras 27, 30 of judgment).

AMBROSIADOU v COWARD, [2013] EWHC 58 (QB), [2013] 2 F.C.R. 359, Tugendhat, J., QBD.

433. Statements of case–Summary judgments–Pleadings alleging fraud–Extent to which particularisation necessary

[Limitation Act 1980 (c.58) s.21 (3), s.28, s.32(1), s.38(2); Mental Capacity Act 2005 (c.9); Civil Procedure Rules 1998 (SI 1998/3132) r.16.4(1)(a); CPR PD 16 (Statements of Case) 1999.]

The claimants (M) applied for permission to amend their particulars of claim in an action against fourteen defendants. The first five defendants (W) applied for summary judgment on the claim against them. M were the former members of a child reggae band who had had a hit single entitled "Pass the Dutchie". The single was an arrangement of a song entitled "Pass the Kouchie", which was itself derivative of another piece of music. The claim arose out of an agreement made in 1984 dividing any royalties from the single between the owner of the copyright in "Pass the Kouchie" (P) and the owner of the copyright in the second piece of music. W, who were at the relevant time M's solicitors, had acted for P in the making of that agreement. They did not tell M about it. M claimed that their single was sufficiently original as to attract distinct copyright in the arrangement. In 2010 they brought a claim against W and others, alleging conflict of interest, fraudulent breach of trust, breach of fiduciary duty and misrepresentation. The issues were (i) to what extent an allegation of fraud had to be particularised, and whether the pleaded facts supported M's fraud plea; (ii) whether the limitation period could be disapplied or postponed under the Limitation Act 1980 s.21 or s.32(1); (iii) the effect on limitation of the fact that the fourth claimant had schizophrenia.

Held: Judgment accordingly. (1) The obligation imposed by CPR PD 16 to specifically set out any allegation of fraud had to be read together with CPR r.16.4(1)(a) and was to be interpreted as requiring more than a simple statement that fraud was alleged. It required the specific basis of the allegation, the facts relied upon, to be pleaded. The CPR had introduced no substantial change as regards a pleading of fraud, *Three Rivers DC v Bank of England (No.3) (Summary Judgment)* [2001] UKHL 16, [2003] 2 A.C. 1, [2001] C.L.Y. 5355 followed (see paras 45-46 of judgment). As particularised, M's allegation of fraud had no realistic prospect of success. It centred on an allegation that W had been dishonest in acting for P in the formation of the agreement when they must have known, as specialist music industry solicitors, that M had a distinct copyright in their arrangement of "Pass the Dutchie". However, the test for distinct copyright in an arrangement was a matter of fact and degree, and the mere fact that the defendant was a solicitor who specialised in the music industry was not a realistic basis for a finding of dishonesty (paras 52-53, 57, 60). (2) The claims against W were out of time. The causes of action had accrued in 1984 when the agreement had been executed, and the six-year period from when M had attained their majority had expired long before the issue of the claim form. In relation to the breach of trust claim, the trust was a Class 2 trust and fell within s.21 (3) of the Act so that the six-year limitation period applied. The fact that W were M's solicitors could not, of itself, make them trustees over all of M's assets, *Paragon Finance Plc v DB Thakerar & Co* [1999] 1 All E.R. 400, [1998] C.L.Y. 536 considered. While the claim for breach of fiduciary duty was conceptually distinct, the allegations simply mirrored those that would lie for breach of contract or negligence, and the six-year limitation period applied by analogy, *Cia de Seguros Imperio v Heath (REBX) Ltd (formerly CE Heath & Co (America) Ltd)* [2001] 1 W.L.R. 112, [2000] C.L.Y. 513 and *DEG-Deutsche Investitions und Entwicklungsgesellschaft mbH v Koshy (Account of Profits: Limitations)* [2003] EWCA Civ 1048, [2004] 1 B.C.L.C. 131, [2003] C.L.Y. 519 followed. The remaining claims were tort claims subject to the six-year limitation period. Section 32(1) did not apply to postpone the start of the limitation period since the facts showed that M had been aware of the agreement, and W's involvement, in 2002 (paras 62-63, 75-77, 81-82). (3) As at the date of the accrual of the causes of action, the fourth claimant was a minor. Ordinarily, limitation would start to run once he reached 18. However, s.28(1) of the Act was to be interpreted as meaning that so long as a person was under a disability, the limitation period should not start to run. Therefore, if a child was suffering from a mental illness on his 18th birthday, the limitation period would not start to run. Where s.28 was engaged on the grounds of mental incapacity, the applicable test was that determined by the law when the cause of action accrued, *Maga v Birmingham Roman Catholic Archdiocese Trustees* [2009] EWHC 780 (QB) not applied. The relevant test in the instant case was therefore the version of s.38(2) in force before the amendment introducing reference to mental incapacity within the meaning of the Mental Capacity Act 2005. It was clear that the fourth claimant could neither show that he was of unsound mind under that test, or that he lacked capacity under the new test. The limitation period would therefore not be disapplied (paras 87-88, 94, 96-97, 110). (4) W's application for summary judgment succeeded and M's application for permission to amend failed, except in so far as the amendments related to the 8th-12th and the 15th defendants (para.126).

SEATON v SEDDON, [2012] EWHC 735 (Ch), [2012] 1 W.L.R. 3636, Roth, J., Ch D.

434. Statements of claim–Amendments–Permission to amend claim to include claim for psychiatric injury–Whether event separate from unfair dismissal claim

The appellant (M) appealed against a decision ([2012] EWHC 3819 (QB)) dismissing her claim for damages for personal injury against her former employer the first respondent (C), a primary school, and the second respondent local authority. M was made redundant after 11 years of service as an administrative assistant with C. She would normally have worked until the end of term, but ten days before, the governors decided to deny her access to the school immediately. She had to clear her desk and hand over her keys, before being publicly escorted from the premises by a governor. M was humiliated by her treatment in front of teachers, children, and parents in a way that suggested that she had committed an act of gross misconduct. Her claims for damages for unfair dismissal in the employment tribunal and for defamation were compromised but she subsequently claimed damages for psychiatric injury in the High Court. In a letter and in its defence the local authority admitted liability, but disputed causation and quantum. Before trial, the local authority became aware of the decision in *Johnson v Unisys Ltd* [2001] UKHL 13, [2003] 1 A.C. 518, [2001] C.L.Y. 2253 and applied for permission to withdraw its admissions, and to strike out M's claim. The judge gave permission and struck out the claim as disclosing no cause of action. M appealed. M submitted that (1) the judge had been wrong to allow the local authority to withdraw its admissions because that was unnecessary and inappropriate merely to raise the *Johnson* point. It was also unconscionable because of its conduct in the employment tribunal; (2) had M known that she could not make a claim for personal injury, she would not have compromised her tribunal claim on the same terms; (3) the actions of the governor which had caused her injury were not integral to her dismissal, which had taken place later, and were outwith the *Johnson* exclusion and so M should be allowed to amend her claim to assert that her contract had ended later.

Held: Appeal allowed. (1) Given the proximity of the trial and the likely effect on cost and delay, there was some force in the argument that the local authority should not have been allowed to withdraw its admissions. However, the local authority had not contested the facts but only wished to remove any impediment to raising the *Johnson* point and it was unnecessary to consider the question, *Johnson* followed (see para.8 of judgment). (2) The tribunal had no jurisdiction to consider a personal injury claim, so the compromise agreement had excluded only a "potential" claim and had made no findings on whether M had a good cause of action, nor had it limited the arguments the local authority might raise in defence but had simply preserved her right to pursue a claim. Moreover, there was no evidence that the agreement rested on a common assumption that she had a good cause of action, so *Johnson v Gore Wood & Co (No.1)* [2002] 2 A.C. 1, [2001] C.L.Y. 410 did not support M's submission that it would be unconscionable for the local authority to raise the *Johnson* point, *Gore Wood* followed. It was pure speculation that M would have obtained a more generous settlement had the local authority raised the point at tribunal. In the absence of estoppel, the judge's decisions had been within his discretion and were not open to challenge (para.13). (3) Although injury to feelings or future employment prospects and damages for personal injury resulting from breach of the common law duty of care were not recoverable in an action for wrongful dismissal, a claim at common law before dismissal was available, *Addis v Gramophone Co Ltd* [1909] A.C. 488, *Johnson, Eastwood v Magnox Electric Plc* [2004] UKHL 35, [2005] 1 A.C. 503, [2004] C.L.Y. 1183 and *Edwards v Chesterfield Royal Hospital NHS Foundation Trust* [2011] UKSC 58, [2012] 2 A.C. 22, [2012] C.L.Y. 1167 followed. The judge had been wrong to stick rigidly to the pleadings and, as the point had been raised in argument, he should have allowed M to rely on it. M was granted permission to amend her claim to change the pleaded date of dismissal (paras 19-29).

MONK v CANN HALL PRIMARY SCHOOL, [2013] EWCA Civ 826, [2013] I.R.L.R. 732, Moore-Bick, L.J., CA (Civ Div).

435. Statutory appeals–Judicial review–Stay of proceedings–Simultaneous appeal and judicial review claim against Revenue decisions

The appellant taxpayer (D) appealed against a decision to stay his claim for judicial review of decisions made by the respondent commissioners pending determination of his statutory appeal against those decisions. The commissioners had issued a determination to D to the effect that he had been resident and ordinarily resident in the United Kingdom in a particular tax year, and issued a discovery assessment as to his tax liability accordingly. D challenged those decisions on the basis that he had left the UK to take up full-time employment abroad. The commissioners considered that he had left the UK too late for that tax year and that his employment was not full-time. D issued a statutory appeal in the First-tier Tribunal against the commissioners' decisions. He also began proceedings in the Upper Tribunal for judicial review of the decisions on the basis that the commissioners had failed properly to apply the relevant guidance in their booklet IR20. D sought to stay the statutory appeal pending determination of the judicial review claim, but the judge instead stayed the judicial review claim. D argued that the First-tier Tribunal's enquiry would be of no relevance to the determination of the judicial review claim: for that purpose, no further findings of fact were necessary as the commissioners had either reached a lawful decision by application of IR20 or they had not.

Held: Appeal dismissed. The judge had come to entirely the right conclusion. If that had not been the case, his decision would still have fallen well within the range of reasonable decision-making. He had correctly identified that there could be no hard and fast rule and that the appropriate course had inevitably to be determined on a case by case basis. D had taken too narrow a view of the ambit of the dispute. Although from his point of view obtaining an order quashing the decisions would be a valuable result, it would not, without more, resolve the issue of whether he had a further tax liability in respect of the relevant year. To bring himself within IR20, D required a finding that he had left the UK to work full-time abroad under a contract of employment and that his full-time employment had continued for at least a whole tax year. The Upper Tribunal exercising its judicial review jurisdiction might be able to determine that the commissioners had or had not properly applied IR20, but if it found that they had not properly applied it, the tribunal would be unable to substitute its own findings of fact which would enable D to bring himself within IR20. Such findings could be made only in the First-tier Tribunal. The judicial review claim could be dealt with much more quickly and cheaply than the statutory appeal, but resolution of the judicial review claim would not dispose of the dispute. If, however, D won his statutory appeal, that was likely to be conclusive of his status and of his liability. If he lost the appeal, he could proceed with the judicial review claim. If he then won that, a fresh determination would be made in the light of the First-tier Tribunal's findings of fact. It would be wrong to make a procedural decision on the basis that if the judicial review claim succeeded, a fresh determination would be to the same effect; the judge had not taken that approach. However, it seemed unrealistic to imagine that the commissioners would make a fresh determination in D's favour without there being the sort of forensic exercise which the statutory appeal would in any event involve. Proceeding first with the judicial review claim risked delay and the ultimately fruitless expenditure of costs. It would not always be the case that the statutory appeal preceded the judicial review claim: the position would be different where the judicial review claim required no resolution of disputed facts and had the potential to dispose of the underlying dispute, *R. (on the application of Lower Mill Estate Ltd) v Revenue and Customs Commissioners* [2008] EWHC 2409 (Admin), [2008] B.T.C. 5743, [2009] C.L.Y. 78 and *R. (on the application of Davies) v Revenue and Customs Commissioners* [2011] UKSC 47, [2011] 1 W.L.R. 2625, [2011] C.L.Y. 3419 considered (see paras 12-23 of judgment).

DANIEL v REVENUE AND CUSTOMS COMMISSIONERS, [2012] EWCA Civ 1741, [2013] S.T.C. 744, Rix, L.J., CA (Civ Div).

436. Stay of proceedings–Anti-competitive practices–Stay pending appeal to CJEU–Balancing factors

The claimant (W) claimed that intra-European Economic Area and intra-United Kingdom "interchange fees" charged by the defendants (M) restricted competition and applied for damages and declarations that the fees were void and unenforceable. Identical "follow-on" and "read-across" claims against M had subsequently been brought in 11 separate sets of proceedings by numerous other major high street retailers. M applied for an immediate stay of proceedings until the determination of their appeal in the Court of Justice of the European Union (CJEU), expected in 2014, against a Commission Decision that they had restricted competition. W and the fourth defendant (D4) applied for a case management conference (CMC) to be held. Since at least 1992, M had operated the Mastercard credit and Maestro debit schemes providing credit card services to both merchants and consumers, in which they charged an "interchange fee". The fee purported to cover losses from fraud, or from defaulting cardholders. After an investigation, the Commission had determined that cross-border default interchange fees restricted competition between banks by inflating the charges that acquiring banks charged merchants. M initially reduced the charges to zero but then re-introduced a smaller charge. M submitted that there was such a close relationship between the follow-on claim and the read-across claim that annulment of the Decision would determine all the claims and there should be an immediate stay to avoid the wasted time and expense of pleading a defence and preparing for a CMC. W contended that the claim would continue regardless of the outcome of M's appeal. D4 submitted that the issue of limitations should be resolved as a preliminary issue.

Held: Applications refused. It was common ground that the claims should not be determined before the CJEU's decision but that the court had jurisdiction to order that the action should proceed some way towards trial before it was stayed pending that decision, *Masterfoods Ltd (t/a Mars Ireland) v HB Ice Cream Ltd (C-344/98)* [2001] All E.R. (EC) 130, [2001] C.L.Y. 762 and *National Grid Electricity Transmission Plc v ABB Ltd* [2009] EWHC 1326 (Ch), [2009] U.K.C.L.R. 838, [2009] C.L.Y. 454 applied (see para.26 of judgment). In deciding whether to grant a stay pending an appeal to the CJEU, the court had a general discretion but had to avoid a decision running counter to the Commission, or the CJEU, and had to have regard to the overriding objective to deal with the claim justly, *National Grid* applied. On balance, the court was against an immediate stay and in favour of the action continuing to a CMC because the expense to which M would be put in pleading defences and preparing for a CMC was relatively modest, whereas the anti-competitive behaviour complained of had begun as long ago as 1992 and there was a pressing need for the litigation to progress. Furthermore, even if M's appeal were successful and the Commission Decision was annulled, there was a real chance that the intra-UK claim would continue, so that the risk of wasted expenditure for which M was not fully compensated in costs was not compelling. On the other hand, if an immediate stay were granted and the appeal to the CJEU was dismissed, W would certainly suffer the prejudice of a considerable delay in the determination of its claims, for which it might not be fully compensated by an award of interest (para.33). M was ordered to serve its defences within six weeks and a CMC listed at which the future progress of the proceedings would be considered by the court (para.34).

WM MORRISON SUPERMARKETS PLC v MASTERCARD INC, [2013] EWHC 1071 (Comm), [2013] U.K.C.L.R. 197, Field, J., QBD (Comm).

437. Stay of proceedings–Arbitration agreements–Partnership deed conferring rights of exclusion and indemnity on third parties–Claims against third parties–Whether third parties entitled to stay of proceedings for arbitration

[Arbitration Act 1996 (c.23) s.9; Contracts (Rights of Third Parties) Act 1999 (c.31) s.1 (6), s.8(2).]

The appellants (D) appealed against a decision ([2012] EWHC 1486 (Comm)) that they were not entitled to a stay of the proceedings against them by reason of an arbitration agreement. D were the managers of an investment structure, the underlying assets of which were businesses in Italy said to have a value of EUR 200 million. The investment structure was based around an English limited partnership, called the Blue Skye Fund, which had a general partner and three limited partners, including a company (S). S had assigned its interest in the Fund to the first respondent (F) as security for a loan. F brought claims against D as assignee of S, alleging that they and others had designed and implemented a dishonest scheme to reorganise the fund and its assets to diminish or eliminate the rights and interests of S and others and to take the control and benefit of the assets themselves. The claims were tort claims under English law and the law of Luxembourg. The defendants including D applied to stay the proceedings under the Arbitration Act 1996 s.9 on the basis of the arbitration clause in the partnership deed. D were not parties to the deed but relied on the Contracts (Rights of Third Parties) Act 1999 on the basis that they were given rights and benefits under the deed including exclusions from and indemnities in respect of liability to the partnership or the partners, including S. It was accepted that D's ability to enforce the indemnities was subject to the arbitration clause. The judge held that since D did not rely in their defence on the exclusion clause there was no dispute relating to the enforcement of a substantive term by them and s.8(1) of the 1999 Act did not result in their being treated as parties to the arbitration agreement. Further D's right to rely on the exclusion clause as against S fell outside the arbitration clause, because it was a contractual defence, as opposed to a contractual right of action which would be subject to arbitration by virtue of s.8(1). D submitted that by reason of s.8(1) they were to be treated as parties to the arbitration agreement as regards the dispute between themselves and S and F which potentially engaged the exclusion clause in the partnership deed; alternatively, they could rely on s.8(2) and exercise their right to rely on the arbitration agreement which was sufficiently widely drawn to encompass a dispute between S and a third party such as D arising out of or connected with the partnership deed.

Held: Appeal dismissed. (1) The distinction drawn by the judge between a right of action and a contractual defence could not be sustained in the light of the provisions of the 1999 Act. Section 1(6) and s.8(1)(a) in effect provided that the third party availing himself of the exclusion was the equivalent of enforcing a term in the contract. The Act contemplated that the right to take the benefit of a contractual exclusion might be subject to a term providing for the submission of disputes to arbitration. Whether it was so subject was a question of construction of the agreement (see para.28 of judgment). (2) As a matter of interpretation, D's submissions on s.8(1) could not be accepted. The result would be that the third party had not only had conferred on him a right or benefit, but had also had imposed on him a burden which he did not agree to undertake, namely a positive obligation to submit to arbitration a dispute concerning his entitlement to rely upon the exclusion clause. If the third party was to be treated as a party to the arbitration agreement, then the arbitrators appointed to determine whether he had a liability to the promisor to which the exclusion would be an answer would have jurisdiction conclusively to determine that that defence was unavailable, even if the third party did not wish to participate in the arbitration and would prefer to be sued in a different forum. That result was contrary to the principle that arbitration was a consensual process. Although the statutory language appeared to envisage that that result was possible, it would need very clear language to bring about the result that the right of a third party to avail himself of an exclusion clause in an agreement to which he was not party was in turn subject to an arbitration clause in the same agreement. There was no such clear language in the partnership deed (paras 29, 36). (3) D could not rely on s.8(2) because it only applied where the contract on its true construction gave to the third party a right to arbitrate, and the arbitration clause conferred that right only on the parties to the deed (para.31). (4) The availability of a stay had to be ruled on the basis of the materials placed before the court on the application to stay, which would not ordinarily include a defence. However, the judge was wrong to say that the availability of a stay depended on the nature of the claim and not on the nature of an "exclusion defence". If s.8(1) was to have any content at all, then having regard to the terms of s.9(3) of the 1996 Act it had to be possible for the court to impose a stay in favour of a third party on the basis of an intention to rely on a contractual defence which was subject to a term providing for the submission of disputes to arbitration (para.34).

FORTRESS VALUE RECOVERY FUND I LLC v BLUE SKYE SPECIAL OPPORTUNITIES FUND LP, [2013] EWCA Civ 367, [2013] 1 W.L.R. 3466, Pill, L.J., CA (Civ Div).

438. Stay of proceedings–Financial regulation–Claim for declarations of non-liability–Defendants referring financial dispute to mandatory US arbitration–Grounds for staying English proceedings

The defendants challenged the court's jurisdiction over some claims in the proceedings and applied for a stay of the proceedings. The claimant English company (C) was part of an international banking group. The defendants were two foreign companies (D1 and D2), which were the corporate vehicles of family trusts, and two individuals (D3 and D4) who were the settlors of those trusts and were resident in Saudi Arabia. D1 and D2 had entered into investment transactions with C which were subject to English law and jurisdiction. The investments had been lost. The defendants had brought arbitration proceedings against a United States company (X) in the same group as C claiming that the investments had been negotiated and structured with X and that C had been introduced into the transaction at the last moment. They alleged a pattern of gross misconduct by X and its employees and affiliates, for which X was liable, leading to loss of the investment. X was subject to the rules of the US regulator which mandated arbitration of a dispute between a customer and a member or associated person of a member arising from the business activities of the member or associated person. X had applied to the New York court for an order restraining pursuit of the arbitration on grounds that the defendants were not customers of X and no dispute arose from X's business activities. C brought English proceedings for declarations that neither it nor its affiliates were liable to the defendants, relying on provisions of the investment agreements which prevented the imposition of liability on C and its affiliates. They obtained permission to serve the proceedings out of the jurisdiction on the basis that the claims against D1 and D2 were in respect of contracts subject to English law and jurisdiction and that D3 and D4 were necessary or proper parties to those claims. The defendants applied to stay the proceedings on the ground that issues should be determined in the US arbitration, and challenged the jurisdiction of the English court in respect of C's claims for declarations of non-liability in favour of its affiliates ("the affiliate claims"). D4 contended that he was not a necessary or proper party to the proceedings.

Held: Applications granted. (1) There was no serious issue to be tried in respect of the affiliate claims against D1 and D2. The affiliate claims reflected no real and present dispute between C and D1 and D2 and it was not realistic to think that C would be affected in any significant way by their determination. It was not the most effective way of resolving the issues raised by the affiliate claims to allow C to claim declaratory relief. They would more effectively be resolved in the US arbitration if D1 and D2 were not restrained from pursuing it. If they were restrained, the issues would not need to be resolved unless they were to pursue claims in another forum; but in that case they were better resolved in a forum seised of the real issue, namely whether X was liable to the defendants. The affiliate claims served no useful purpose, and seemed to be inappropriate forum shopping, notwithstanding the jurisdiction agreements, because the jurisdiction agreements covered only disputes between C and D1 and D2, and in reality the disputes to which the affiliate claims were directed were between X and the defendants. Therefore the claims would be rejected under the principles applicable to declarations generally and to negative declarations where permission for service out was required, *Rolls-Royce Plc v Unite the Union* [2009] EWCA Civ 387, [2010] 1 W.L.R. 318, [2009] C.L.Y. 1162 and *New Hampshire Insurance Co Ltd v Philips Electronics North America Corp (No.1)* [1998] C.L.C. 1062, [1997] C.L.Y. 890 followed (see para.59 of judgment). (2) For similar reasons the court would decline to exercise exorbitant jurisdiction as a matter of discretion. Although the affiliate claims were within the letter of contractual jurisdictional gateways, because the relevant contracts were subject to English law and jurisdiction, they did not fall within their spirit. C had no significant purpose of its own in claiming the declarations. The real dispute was between the defendants and X, against which they had brought their claim in arbitration, and the English court should not trespass on the territory of the reference unless there was proper reason to do so (para.62). (3) The challenge of D3 and D4 to English jurisdiction in respect of the affiliate claims also succeeded (para.63). (4) D4's challenge to the jurisdiction succeeded in respect of C's non-affiliate claims as well, because D4 was not a necessary or proper party to the proceedings (paras 64-70). (5) The court had jurisdiction in rare and compelling circumstances to stay an action pending determination of foreign litigation or arbitration proceedings related to the action but between different parties, *Reichhold Norway ASA v Goldman Sachs International* [2000] 1 W.L.R. 173, [1999] C.L.Y. 546 followed. The duplication of proceedings and risk of inconsistent decisions did not in themselves amount to unusual and compelling circumstances justifying a stay, but what was unusual and compelling was that the foreign proceedings were brought under a regulatory regime to which C's affiliate was subject as a matter of US public policy. The English proceedings risked unwarranted interference with that regime. In the unusual circumstances the proceedings should be stayed pending resolution of the arbitration if the New York court allowed the defendants to pursue it (paras 73-82).

CITIGROUP GLOBAL MARKETS LTD v AMATRA LEVERAGED FEEDER HOLDINGS LTD, [2012] EWHC 1331 (Comm), [2012] 2 C.L.C. 279, Andrew Smith, J., QBD (Comm).

439. Stay of proceedings–Pending actions–Shipowner bringing tort claims against insurers in Greece–Whether same causes of action–Whether Greek court first seised

[Regulation 44/2001 on jurisdiction and the recognition and enforcement of judgments in civil and commercial matters Art.27, Art.28.]

The appellant insured shipowner (S) appealed against a decision granting summary judgment and declarations to the respondent insurers (D). S's vessel had become a total loss and S had sued D in respect of that loss in England pursuant to English law and jurisdiction clauses in the insurance policies. Liability was denied and vigorously contested. S alleged that D had bribed the bosun to give false evidence and had spread false and malicious rumours against S. The proceedings were settled for 100 per cent of the claim but without interest and costs and Tomlin orders were made by consent reflecting the settlements. S and associated persons later began proceedings in Greece against D and others claiming damages for late payment of the sum insured, whether deliberate or otherwise, and in respect of supposed misconduct by D in relation to the claim. D sought in the original proceedings and by way of new actions to enforce the settlement agreements in the Tomlin orders and the judge granted summary judgment for a declaration that the matters sought to be raised in Greece were part of the settlement of the claim and that S was bound to indemnify D against any costs incurred and any sums that might be adjudged against them in the Greek proceedings. S appealed and sought for the first time on appeal a stay of the English proceedings under Regulation 44/2001 art.27.

Held: Appeal allowed. (1) It was no bar to an application under art.27, or art.28, that a defendant had filed an acknowledgment of service and a defence (see para.26 of judgment). It was not too late for S to rely on art.27, even though it had disavowed any intention to rely on art.27 at first instance and the judge had refused a stay under art.28 and given judgment against it. The appeal court had a discretion to entertain a new point on appeal if the respondent had suffered no prejudice which could not be cured by costs, *Pittalis v Grant* [1989] Q.B. 605, [1989] C.L.Y. 2890 considered. If the proceedings involved the same cause of action and the same parties within art.27, the court second seised had to grant a stay of its own motion. Thus once the art.27 point came to the notice of the court, it had to consider it (paras 27-28). The fact that the judge had given a judgment on the merits did not prevent the application of art.27. It was not necessary that the judgment should first be set aside before any application for a stay was made. It was sufficient that permission to appeal had been given (para.30). (2) It was clear from the authorities that if a cause of action in one Member State was a "mirror image" of a cause of action in another Member State, the cause of action would be regarded as the same for the purposes of art.27. S had abandoned in Greece any claim for late payment under the policy. Its claim was that D were liable for the consequences of malicious statements in Greece intentionally made. The key assertion in England was that D were not liable because those non-contractual claims had been compromised by the settlement agreements. There was a considerable risk of inconsistent judgments if one of the sets of proceedings was not stayed and the rationale behind art.27 therefore favoured a stay if the Greek court was the court first seised. In so far as the English proceedings asserted non-liability by reason of the settlement agreements, there was an identity of issues and the respective causes of action were the same for the purposes of art.27. Various other claims in England were parasitic and dependent on the basic cause of action in England for a declaration of non-liability. The parties in the proceedings were in substance the same (paras 41, 44-45, 48-49, 51). (3) The English court was not first seised of the claims being pursued in Greece. Those were claims in tort or delict equivalent to defamation and malicious falsehood; those causes of action were different from the original claim to be indemnified under the policy. The rule that a litigant should bring forward all his claims at the same time and the fact that an English court might strike out as an abuse proceedings raising such claims did not make the English court the court first seised of the cause of action being pursued in Greece. Furthermore, to the extent that the Greek claimants apart from S had causes of action, the English court could not be first seised since S was the only claimant in the original English action. The English proceedings had to be stayed under art.27 because the parties and causes of action were essentially the same as those in Greece and the Greek court was first seised (paras 52-59). (4) The summary judgments granted by the judge had to be set aside (para.70).

STARLIGHT SHIPPING CO v ALLIANZ MARINE & AVIATION VERSICHERUNGS AG; ALEXANDROS T, THE; BRIT UW LTD v IMPERIAL MARINE CO; BRIT UW LTD v STARLIGHT SHIPPING CO, [2012] EWCA Civ 1714, [2013] 1 All E.R. (Comm) 1297, Longmore, L.J., CA (Civ Div).

440. Stay of proceedings–Time limits–Requirement to serve particulars of claim within 14 days of service of claim form–Effect of three-month stay of proceedings

[Civil Procedure Rules 1998 (SI 1998/3132) r.3.1, r.3.9.]

The defendant companies (H) applied for summary judgment or to strike out the claim brought against them by the claimants (U), U having failed to serve particulars of claim within 14 days of the service of the claim form. U applied for an extension of time within which to serve the particulars of claim. U had engaged H to provide design services in relation to the design of a road. The road was built between 1999 and 2001. The road soon showed signs of surface degradation. In October 2009, U wrote to H in accordance with the Pre-action Protocol for Construction and Engineering Disputes and asserted that H had failed to use all reasonable skill, care and diligence in carrying out the design work. In May 2010, U served the claim form. Before the 14-day period for serving the particulars of claim expired, U invited H to agree to a stay of proceedings in order to allow the protocol process to run its course. H agreed to a three-month stay, and a consent order was made. The parties subsequently agreed to three further stays. The final stay expired on June 23, 2011. Mediation never took place, and U eventually served their particulars of claim in September 2012. The particulars of claim introduced a new allegation, described as a "failure to supervise". U's primary case was that they did not require an extension of time to serve the particulars of claim. U argued that if particulars of claim had to be served within 14 days of service of the claim form, then if, within that period, the action was stayed for a period in excess of 14 days, it became impossible to serve the particulars of claim within the prescribed time; thus, the effect of the stay had to be to abrogate that time limit. H submitted that the effect of a stay was to suspend the proceedings until the stay was lifted or until it expired, whereupon they resumed automatically from where they left off; so the effect of a stay was simply to push back any outstanding time limits by an amount of time equivalent to the length of the stay.

Held: Applications granted in part. (1) CPR r.3.1 provided that the court could stay any proceedings or judgment either generally or until a specified date or event. If the court stayed proceedings generally, the stay remained in force until it was lifted, whereas if the court stayed proceedings until a specified date, the stay would automatically cease when that date was reached. That meant that the proceedings would start up again at the point where they left off when the stay was imposed. That approach avoided the "impossibility" problem raised by U, and had the sensible result that the proceedings could resume where they left off without any party having to go to the trouble and expense of making an application to the court. Accordingly, H's submissions on the point were to be preferred. The time for service of the particulars of claim had expired before the second stay was imposed by consent in September 2010. However, since the parties had plainly intended that the proceedings should be stayed from the date of the first consent order until the expiry of the fourth consent order on June 23, 2011, it would be unjust if H were permitted to take the point that the particulars of claim should have been served in August or September 2010. Further, by agreeing to the making of the subsequent consent orders, H had probably waived their right to take such a point (see paras 47-50 of judgment). (2) Between June 2011 and March 2012, the parties had continued to discuss the claim and to exchange information on a without prejudice basis. However, by March 2012, U no longer had any reasonable ground for not serving their particulars of claim and pursuing the litigation. It was open to H to complain about the failure to serve the particulars of claim between late April 2012 and September 12, 2012 (paras 55-61). (3) H had been prejudiced by the overall delay which had occurred since the conclusion of the design some 12 years previously. That prejudice consisted of the loss of documents, the unavailability of many witnesses and the inevitable impairment of individual memories. However, much of that prejudice arose within a few years of the completion of the project. If U were allowed to pursue a claim based solely on negligent design, the balancing exercise that the court had to carry out, having regard to the matters in CPR r.3.9, in the context of the history and circumstances of the proceedings, fell to be resolved in favour of allowing the claim to proceed, *Price v Price (t/a Poppyland Headware)* [2003] EWCA Civ 888, [2003] 3 All E.R. 911, [2003] C.L.Y. 392 and *Fred Perry (Holdings) Ltd v Brands Plaza Trading Ltd (t/a Brands Plaza)* [2012] EWCA Civ 224, [2012] 6 Costs L.R. 1007, [2012] C.L.Y. 484 applied. The parts of the particulars of claim raising the issues of failure to supervise would be disallowed (paras 102-112).

UK HIGHWAYS A55 LTD v HYDER CONSULTING (UK) LTD, [2012] EWHC 3505 (TCC), [2013] B.L.R. 95, Edwards-Stuart, J., QBD (TCC).

441. Striking out–Abuse of process–Whether claim for declaration as to employee's rights under pension scheme amounted to abuse of process

The fourth defendant (L) applied for an order striking out as an abuse of process the claim of the claimant companies (P) for a declaration that he was not entitled to an enhanced pension. In the alternative, he sought a prospective costs order. L had been an employee and a director of P. He claimed to be entitled to an enhanced pension under P's pension scheme of two-thirds of his final salary rather than the one-third argued for by P; in that respect, he relied on a letter sent to him by one of the scheme's trustees in 1991. A power existed under the relevant trust deed for the trustees to augment benefits; however, the employer had to consent to their doing so. P's case was that L was not entitled to an enhanced pension, because the trustees at the material time did not agree to exercise their powers and did not delegate their functions to the trustee who had written the 1991 letter; further, P did not consent to the power being exercised. In March 2012, L invoked the dispute-resolution procedure set up in respect of the scheme. A resolution could not be achieved and in July 2012 P issued the instant action. L argued that (1) P's claim amounted to an abuse of process, since they had issued proceedings with the improper motive of preventing him from complaining to the Pensions Ombudsman and without complying with the pre-action protocol; (2) a prospective costs order should be made because, among other things, the claim fell within category 2 of *Buckton (Costs), Re* [1907] 2 Ch. 406, being a claim by a beneficiary (which could have been made by the trustees) to have an instrument construed.

Held: Applications refused. (1) As to L's submission that the action had been commenced for an improper motive, it was not an abuse of process to issue proceedings if there was also a genuine right to be vindicated, *JSC BTA Bank v Ablyazov* [2011] EWHC 1136 (Comm), [2011] 1 W.L.R. 2996, [2012] C.L.Y. 307 applied. P clearly did have such a right. They were entitled to have decided by the courts the dispute which had arisen as to whether L was entitled to an enhanced pension. If he was so entitled, P would be required to contribute to the fund (estimates of how much the enhancement would cost were between £420,000 and £520,000). Given that P were aware that the dispute-resolution procedure was in progress when they issued proceedings, to do so without any further reference to L was not within the spirit of the protocol. However, by the time proceedings were issued, each party knew what the issues between them were in essence. In any event, a breach of the protocol would not justify striking out the claim (see paras 38-39, 51-52 of judgment). (2) It would not be appropriate to make a prospective costs order. L's claim was a personal claim brought by him for his benefit for an enhanced pension. His claim could not on any basis be regarded as a *Buckton* category 2 claim, there being no issues as to the construction of the trust deed, *Buckton* considered (paras 59-60).

PELL FRISCHMANN CONSULTANTS LTD v PRABHU, [2013] EWHC 2203 (Ch), [2014] I.C.R. 153, Penelope Reed QC, Ch D.

442. Striking out–Particulars of claim–Reorganisation of investment structure–Alleged dishonest scheme–Striking out parts of particulars of claim

[Insolvency Act 1986 (c.45) s.423; Civil Procedure Rules 1998 (SI 1998/3132) r.38.6; Regulation 1346/2000 on insolvency proceedings Art.4, Art.15; Regulation 44/2001 on jurisdiction and the recognition and enforcement of judgments in civil and commercial matters Art.27; Regulation 864/2007 Art.4(3).]

The applicants applied to strike out certain paragraphs of the amended particulars of claim, or for summary judgment, and resisted the permission sought by the respondents (F) to amend the particulars of claim. F were investors in certain Italian assets. As originally set up the investment structure was based around a fund, in the form of an English limited partnership, which held the shares in a Luxembourg company which held the Italian assets. The principal limited partner in the fund was a Luxembourg company (S) which held a 99.999 per cent interest in the fund. S was the joint venture vehicle by which F and others invested in the structure. F's case was that the applicants and others had implemented a dishonest scheme to reorganise the fund and its assets, diminishing or eliminating F's rights and interests in the assets and taking the control and benefit of the assets for themselves. F made claims against S for breach of a loan agreement and security assignment, and against the other defendants, including the applicants, in tort for conspiracy and unlawful interference and procuring breach of contract by S, and sought orders under the Insolvency Act 1986 s.423 to unwind the reorganisation. The applicants denied that the reorganisation was pursuant to a dishonest scheme. S had been declared bankrupt by the Luxembourg court which appointed an official receiver who concluded that there had been a fraudulent scheme of which S was a victim and brought Part 20 proceedings.

Held: Applications refused. (1) It was neither necessary nor appropriate to decide on a summary basis before trial whether the applicable law of any claim F had against the applicants in tort was the law of England or Luxembourg. There was no discernible benefit in terms of case management given that, if F established their case on the facts, the applicants would face a liability in tort irrespective of which system of law applied, since they had abandoned their assertion that the claims were unarguable as a matter of Luxembourg law and F had a real prospect of establishing that English law applied because the tortious acts and conduct were more closely connected with England for the purposes of Regulation 864/2007 art.4(3) (see paras 56-75 of judgment). (2) The first respondent pursued a number of contractual and non-contractual claims as assignee of S pursuant to cl.3 of the security assignment. The applicants argued that some of those claims fell outside the scope of that clause, but it was difficult to see the point of that objection since they would face the same claims from S in the Part 20 proceedings if they were right that they had not been assigned. In any event the respondents' construction of the clause was arguable (paras 83-88). (3) The applicants objected to proposed amendments to the particulars of claim, making contractual indemnity claims under the loan agreement and security assignment against S, contending that, by virtue of Regulation 1346/2000 art.4, the effect of the insolvency of S was a matter for the Luxembourg courts. However, by virtue of art.15 of the 2000 Regulation, the effect of the insolvency of S on the proposed indemnity claims was a matter for the English court applying English procedural law, *Syska v Vivendi Universal*

SA [2009] EWCA Civ 677, [2009] 2 All E.R. (Comm) 891, [2010] C.L.Y. 161 followed. The applicants' reliance on Regulation 44/2001 art.27 was misplaced, *FKI Engineering Ltd v Stribog Ltd* [2011] EWCA Civ 622, [2011] 1 W.L.R. 3264, [2011] C.L.Y. 392 considered (paras 89-100). (4) The respondents' pleading of their claim under s.423 was sustainable. The authorities gave a wide scope to that section and, if the respondents' allegations were made out, they were arguably entitled to bring a claim under s.423 on the basis that the scheme was a transaction which had the purpose of defeating a claim by S or the fund. The issue whether there was a sufficient connection with England to justify relief under s.423 was not a threshold question of jurisdiction but a matter which depended on all the circumstances of the case, *Jyske Bank (Gibraltar) Ltd v Spjeldnaes (No.2)* [2000] B.C.C. 16, [1998] C.L.Y. 529 considered (paras 104-118). (5) The applicants' costs of various claims that had been discontinued should be paid by F in the usual way under CPR r.38.6 (paras 119-123).

FORTRESS VALUE RECOVERY FUND I LLC v BLUE SKYE SPECIAL OPPORTUNITIES FUND LP; STEPSTONE ACQUISITION SARL (IN BANKRUPTCY) v CERCHIONE, [2013] EWHC 14 (Comm), [2013] 1 All E.R. (Comm) 973, Flaux, J., QBD (Comm).

443. Striking out–Relief–Failure to comply with costs order–Relief from automatic strike-out of claim–Effect of delayed compliance by one working day

[Civil Procedure Rules 1998 (SI 1998/3132) r.3.9.]

The applicant (T) applied for relief from the striking out of its claim against the respondents (H) for a failure to comply with a costs order. As a result of unsuccessfully opposing H's application to vary a freezing order, T was ordered to pay H's costs. That payment was not made on time. H made two further applications which were not successful and costs orders were made against them. Those orders were set off against the sum that T owed and it was ordered that unless the remainder was paid to H by a date set in the order, T's claim would be automatically struck out. T had given payment instructions to a bank the day before the date for compliance but the transfer did not occur due to an absence of H's IBAN number. H supplied the IBAN the following day, which was the date for complying with the order. Although at the instant hearing T provided a receipt showing that it had given payment instructions again on the date of compliance, H did not receive the transfer until the next working day. T submitted that (1) it had complied with the order as it had irrevocably instructed its bank to make a payment within the time for compliance; (2) if not, the court should grant relief from the striking out sanction in the circumstances.

Held: Application granted. (1) Giving instructions to a bank to make a payment could not be equated with the making of a bank transfer. T's contention was hopeless and if correct would have the consequence that if the bank never acted upon those instructions, and no payment was ever received by H, T would nonetheless have complied with the costs order. The position might have been different if the money had been dispatched by T's bank on the date for compliance but was not received by H until the following working day. However, there was no evidence to show that that was the case and therefore it had to be assumed that the transfer occurred on the next working day after the date for compliance. Accordingly, there was a clear failure to comply with the unless order and T's claim should be automatically struck out. (2) It was overwhelmingly clear that relief should be granted in the instant case. It would be wholly disproportionate for T to forfeit its entire claim without having it determined on the merits because of its failure to pay costs, which was a small sum compared to the substantial value of the claim, and in circumstances where the delay in payment was just one working day. Considering the requirements of CPR r.3.9: it was in the interests of justice that the claim was heard on its merits; the application for relief was made promptly, it was intimated immediately if not made immediately; and non-compliance with the order was not intentional, there was an attempt made to comply by giving payment instructions within time. However, T had not offered a good explanation for its non-compliance, particularly in respect of why payment instructions were left to the last minute, which meant incurring the risk that the order would not be complied with. Nevertheless, the fault on T's part was not as severe as a deliberate breach and its failure was strongly outweighed by the countervailing factors which militated for the granting of relief. T had delayed in complying with previous orders but that had not caused material prejudice to H and was not a matter that weighed in terms of whether to grant relief. Nor was the fact that T had delivered the trial bundles late, although that was more serious and did impact on when the trial could take place it did not justify refusing T the relief sought. H had lost some preparation time but in the interests of justice, it was overwhelmingly right to grant the relief sought and re-instate T's claim so that it could be determined on the merits.

TRAVEL & HOLIDAYS LLC v HAJJ CHARTER LTD, [2013] EWHC 1212 (QB), [2013] 5 Costs L.O. 657, Leggatt, J., QBD.

444. Striking out–Sufficiency of evidence–Prospect of success of deceit claim–Appropriateness of extended civil restraint order

The applicant (G) applied to strike out a claim for deceit brought by the respondent husband and wife (H and W) and an extended civil restraint order. H had been declared bankrupt in 2001 following protracted litigation concerning the dissolution of a firm of solicitors in which he had been a partner. H's trustee in bankruptcy had engaged G to sell the matrimonial home that had been owned equally by H and W. An independent valuation gave a figure between £900,000 and £1.25 million which H had criticised, contending that a value of £750,000 was more accurate. G stated that it had received 10 bids, the highest of which came from a firm whose director was a relative of a manager of G. That bid was increased twice, from £977,500 to £1 million. W, not wishing to leave the property, purchased H's share of the house based on the notional value of £1 million. H and W then brought numerous claims against the trustee and others connected with the bankruptcy and the acquisition of the home, including a claim against G and others for deceit. They were argued on the bases that: G had concocted the bids in order to inflate the price so as to be able to obtain a commission; it was unlikely that 10 people would have bid for the property; a similar property had been sold for only £810,000 at the material time; G had refused to provide an unredacted list of the bidders; an employee of G's had, in other proceedings, been found to have lied under oath; it was inconceivable that someone would bid such a high sum for a property without conducting local authority searches or pre-contract enquiries. H purported to have taken an assignment of W's claim for the consideration of £1. The applicant contended that: (1) the particulars of claim disclosed no reasonable grounds for bringing a claim as they did not fulfil each element of the cause of action; (2) H's assignment of W's claim was invalid; (3) an extended civil restraint order should be made against H and W.

Held: Application granted. (1) It was fatal to H's claim that he had admitted in his witness statement that there had been no reliance on the representations as he and his wife had suspected that the bids were concocted. In any event, H's case was inherently improbable. To have concocted ten bids would have been a very elaborate fraud involving numerous participants. There was no substantial evidence that the representations that had been made were either untrue or dishonestly so. (2) H's assignment of W's claim was invalid as he did not have a sufficient interest. He had candidly admitted that W did not want to be a part of the litigation. There was no special rule for husbands and wives, *Glegg v Bromley* [1912] 3 K.B. 474 applied. (3) It was appropriate to make an extended civil restraint order against both H and W. The claim had been totally without merit and H had persistently issued claims or made applications which were totally without merit. The central allegations had been considered twice previously where it had been held that there was insufficient evidence to make an inference of fraud. Whilst some further evidence had been adduced since then, it did not fundamentally change the complexion of the claim.

HURST v GLENTREE ESTATES LTD, [2012] EWHC 4024 (Ch), [2013] B.P.I.R. 331, Arnold, J., Ch D.

445. Substitution of parties–Defendants–Application of test in The Sardinia Sulcis [1991] 1 Lloyd's Rep. 201–Identification of intended party by reference to material legal description–Discretion to order substitution of parties

[Limitation Act 1980 (c.58) s.35(6)(b); Civil Procedure Rules 1998 (SI 1998/3132) r.19.5(3)(b).]

The appellant (X) appealed against a master's decision setting aside an order to substitute the respondent partnership (K), a firm of chartered accountants, as defendant to its claim in place of the limited liability partnership (LLP) which K had formed in May 2006. X lost ownership of intellectual property rights in the software it developed as a result of the striking off of the company to which they had been transferred on K's advice. In November 2010, X brought a claim against the LLP seeking damages for losses arising between 1999 and 2006 from alleged failures of K in the performance of its function as an auditor and in the provision of fiduciary or administrative services, which had resulted in the loss of rights. By the time the particulars of claim were prepared in April 2011, X had realised that they were suing the wrong defendant, given that the majority of the acts complained of took place before the formation of the LLP. X therefore obtained an order substituting K as defendant in place of the LLP. That order was set aside and, as X had no viable claim against the LLP, its whole claim was consequently struck out. Relying on the Limitation Act 1980 s.35(6)(a) and CPR r.19.5(3)(a), X contended that the name of the LLP had been given "in mistake" for K's name when the action was commenced. Alternatively, X relied on s.35(6)(b) of the Act and CPR r.19.5(3)(b) in arguing that it could not carry on the relevant claims unless K was substituted as defendant in the action.

Held: Appeal allowed. (1) In *Adelson v Associated Newspapers Ltd* [2007] EWCA Civ 701, [2008] 1 W.L.R. 585, [2007] C.L.Y. 534 it was decided that, in order to fall within CPR r.19.5(3)(a), the mistake had to be as to the name rather than as to the identity of the party, applying the generous test in *Owners of the Sardinia Sulcis v Owners of the Al Tawwab* [1991] 1 Lloyd's Rep. 201, [1991] C.L.Y. 3204 as to whether it was possible to identify the intended party "by reference to a description which was more or less specific to the particular case", *Adelson* and *Sardinia Sulcis* followed. In holding that that test still applied, the Court of Appeal could not have intended to suggest that it remained necessary to show that the mistake was not misleading or such as to cause any reasonable doubt as to the identity of the person intended to be sued. The only way in which the *Sardinia Sulcis* test was workable was to identify the relevant description of the intended party by reference to what description was material from a legal point of view to the claim made. In the instant case, the relevant description of the defendant was that of professional adviser, because it was that capacity which potentially gave rise to legal liability. If X was suing the LLP in the mistaken belief that it was the LLP which provided negligent services, not K, then the court had power to grant relief. However, if X knew that the services were provided by K but mistakenly believed that the LLP was legally liable for K's negligence, then there was no such power. On the evidence, the LLP had been named in the claim form in the mistaken belief that it had provided the professional services which were the subject of the claim. The mistake was therefore as to which body satisfied the description of auditor and provider of fiduciary services during the relevant period. It was not simply an error of law as to the legal liability of the LLP for K's prior negligence. The mistake therefore satisfied the *Sardinia Sulcis* test and the requirements of s.35(6)(a) of the Act and CPR r.19.5(3)(a). It followed that the court had power to order substitution of K for the LLP as defendant (see paras 29, 35, 43, 52, 56-57, 82-83, 85 of judgment). (2) The court had power to order substitution under s.35(6)(b) of the Act and CPR r.19.5(3)(b) if a claim made in the original action was not sustainable by or against the existing party, and the same claim would be carried on by or against the new party, *Parkinson Engineering Services Plc (In Liquidation) v Swan* [2009] EWCA Civ 1366, [2010] Bus. L.R. 857, [2010] C.L.Y. 1887 and *Irwin v Lynch* [2010] EWCA Civ 1153, [2011] 1 W.L.R. 1364, [2011] C.L.Y. 395 followed. In the instant case, however, the claims which X sought to carry on against K were not the same as those made against the LLP; the claims asserted against K after X had realised its mistake alleged that K, not the LLP, acted as auditor and provided the relevant services (paras 95-97). (3) The master had not been justified in refusing to make an order for substitution which was necessary to enable viable claims to be carried on and which caused no prejudice to the new party, namely K. The Master's order was therefore varied so as to substitute K as defendant in relation to claims which became time-barred between November 11, 2010 and April 11, 2011 (paras 112-114).

INSIGHT GROUP LTD v KINGSTON SMITH (A FIRM), [2012] EWHC 3644 (QB), [2013] 3 All E.R. 518, Leggatt, J., QBD.

446. Substitution of parties–Whether original party had to fall within r.19.2(4) CPR or whether r.19.2(2) and (3) could be used to achieve same result

[Civil Procedure Rules 1998 (SI 1998/3132) r.19.2, r.19.2(4).]

The Court of Appeal was required to determine an issue concerning the correct interpretation of CPR r.19.2. The local authority had caused proceedings to be brought against the tenant (T) for possession on the ground of rent arrears. The proceedings were brought in the name of Hounslow Homes (H), a limited company 100 per cent owned by the local authority. T asserted that H merely acted as managing agent and had no interest in the property and therefore no right to possession. H therefore applied for the local authority to be named as claimant in its place under the CPR r.19.2. The judge granted its application and T appealed. The Court of Appeal was required to determine whether r.19.2(4) was to be regarded as the only basis upon which one party could replace or be substituted for another, or whether a judge could use the combined effect of r.19.2(2) and r.19.2(3) to achieve such a result. The local authority conceded that it could not bring itself within the terms of r.19.2(4) because no interest or liability had passed to it from H.

Held: Appeal dismissed. Part.19.2 was not to be construed in a narrow way. To adopt a narrow construction would be to limit the substitution of one party for another in a way which would unduly restrict the court's powers in seeking to achieve the prompt, efficient and cost-effective resolution of disputes. To limit the power to substitute to circumstances where an interest or liability had passed from the existing party to the new party would be to read the whole of pt.19.2 in a way which would not do justice to a number of other situations where it would be clearly desirable to permit a change of party, *United Film Distribution Ltd v Chhabria* [2001] EWCA Civ 416, [2001] 2 All E.R. (Comm) 865, [2001] C.L.Y. 651 and *Coal Mining Contractors v Davies* [2006] EWCA Civ 1360, [2007] 1 W.L.R. 3232, [2007] C.L.Y. 451 considered. The language of pt.19.2 was permissive, and did not preclude consideration of the application under any other provision. The language of r.19.2(2) and (3) was apt to achieve in two steps what could be done in a single step in the particular circumstances set out in r.19.2(4).

HOUNSLOW LBC v CUMAR, [2012] EWCA Civ 1426, [2013] H.L.R. 17, Lord Dyson (M.R.), CA (Civ Div).

447. Summary assessment–Breach of fiduciary duty–Claimant suffering loss of business caused by defendants' attempts to poach its contracts–Court assessing damages and costs

The claimant companies (S) sought damages from the defendants (D) for their breach of contractual and fiduciary obligations. S was engaged in the supply of seating for major sports events worldwide. It was a very niche and lucrative area of business. D had attempted to poach S's customers and their activities had caused S to lose business. A search order and injunctive relief had been granted to S in February 2012. D had largely failed to participate in the ensuing litigation, apart from sending occasional emails to S. They did not attend the instant hearing, the purpose of which was to quantify S's loss.

Held: Judgment for claimants. (1) On the evidence, D's activities had caused S to lose a cast iron opportunity to receive substantial well-earned profits from two contracts. They indicated that they had also lost out on other events, but the problem and cost of investigating them to the standard necessary to prove their loss had been prohibitive, and made worse by D's lack of co-operation. S had fairly not pursued those matters when they would have been perfectly justified in doing so. The overall loss amounted to £4.4 million, which was the amount they were entitled to receive from D (see paras 6-7 of judgment). (2) S were to be commended for keeping their costs within the budget of £360,000 stipulated by the court during active case management. That figure was proportionate to the amount at stake in the proceedings and was to be paid by D within 14 days. D's conduct meant that indemnity costs would, in principle, have been applicable if S had exceeded the costs budget. D should have made a decision whether to participate in the proceedings or not. Dropping out of the litigation while occasionally sending emails to S made S's burden greater and involved the court in additional work. Had the costs budget been exceeded, the onus would have been upon D to show that the costs were unreasonable, which it would have been difficult for them to discharge (para.11)

SLICK SEATING SYSTEMS v ADAMS [2013] 4 Costs L.R. 576, Judge Simon Brown Q.C., QBD (Merc) (Birmingham).

448. Summary judgments–Intention to create legal relations–Application for summary judgment on claim for repudiatory breaches of sale contract–Whether real issue to be tried as to existence of legally binding contract–Admissibility of expert evidence on parties' objective intentions

The applicant (P) applied for summary judgment on its claim for repudiatory breaches of contract against the respondent (O). P had made what was described as a "firm offer" on June 14, 2012 to sell O a quantity of crude oil mix. Email correspondence ensued between the parties, culminating in a one-word email from O on June 20, 2012 which said "confirmed". P sent O a draft sale contract on that same day, which generated further email exchange. On June 27, 2012, P sent O a revised draft contract. Two days later O wrote to P to say that it was withdrawing from the negotiations. It did not open any letter of credit and did not accept the cargo. P notified O that it was accepting O's failures to open a letter of credit or to take delivery of the cargo as repudiatory breaches of contract. P applied for summary judgment on the basis that the alleged contract was formed on June 14, 2012, or alternatively on June 27, 2012 at the latest. An expert (T) gave evidence that O's confirmatory email would not have been understood by reasonable market participants in the oil trading industry to have created a binding contract.

Held: Application refused. The relevant question was whether the parties were agreed on all the terms that they objectively regarded as essential for the formation of legally binding relations on June 14, 2012, or at the latest by June 27, 2012, *RTS Flexible Systems Ltd v Molkerei Alois Muller GmbH & Co KG* [2010] UKSC 14, [2010] 1 W.L.R. 753, [2010] C.L.Y. 631 followed. While it was clear from the exchanges on June 14, 2012 that the parties understood that they had not agreed all of the contractual terms, that in itself did not demand the conclusion that the parties had not already concluded a legally binding contract. There were powerful, objectively ascertainable indications in the exchanges that a legally binding contract had been concluded by O's confirmatory email. Those indications were reinforced to a degree by the parties' conduct in the days after June 14, 2012. However, there were several indications in the exchanges between the parties after June 14, 2012 which suggested that O did not consider any legally binding contract to have been concluded. Whether two parties had entered into a legally binding contract depended in large part upon an objective evaluation of what was communicated between them by words and conduct, *RTS* and *Pagnan SpA v Feed Products Ltd* [1987] 2 Lloyd's Rep. 601, [1988] C.L.Y. 429 followed. T's evidence on that issue was properly admissible: the parties' objective intentions as expressed to each other could and should be judged against the relevant contextual background that they both knew and in which they were operating when communicating with each other. T's evidence would genuinely assist the trial judge in determining whether a binding contract was concluded on June 14, 2012, and the importance and significance of it meant that it should not be shut out in the instant application. P's case for summary judgment was not improved by reference to what had occurred between the parties between June 14, 2012 and June 27, 2012. There was a real issue to be tried as to whether a legally binding contract was concluded between the parties on June 14, 2012, and therefore it was not appropriate to grant P summary judgment (see paras 11, 21-22, 25, 29-30, 32, 35-36, 39 of judgment).

PROTON ENERGY GROUP SA v PUBLIC CO ORLEN LIETUVA, [2013] EWHC 334 (Comm), [2013] 1 C.L.C. 389, Gavin Kealey Q.C., QBD (Comm).

449. Third party costs orders–Oral evidence–Appropriateness of allowing cross-examination of witnesses in application for third party costs order

[Senior Courts Act 1981 (c.54) s.51.]

The court had to decide whether to allow the claimant company (C) to cross-examine eight witnesses who had signed witness statements on behalf of the defendants (K) in its application for a third party costs order against the fourth and fifth defendants under the Senior Courts Act 1981 s.51. The application arose from underlying litigation where judgment and a costs order had been granted in favour of C. There had not been a trial on liability because the claim had been settled and the issue of quantum had also been dealt with without a trial. The fourth and fifth defendants had been added as defendants so that C could seek a third party costs order against them. The third defendant had gone into liquidation and a liquidator had been appointed. Reports of the liquidator's investigations were available to the court and the liquidator had also made available to C a substantial quantity of documents which would otherwise be privileged. An order for specific disclosure of specified classes of documents had also been made. C sought to cross-examine the eight witnesses who had signed statements on behalf of K on the whole range of factual dispute which existed between the parties. If that were permitted, the trial was likely to take five days, rather than two. C submitted that because there had been no trial on the merits, the underlying facts of the litigation had never been the subject of investigation at a trial. It argued that the disputes of fact relevant to the s.51 hearing could only be dealt with justly if the witnesses whose witness statements were to be relied upon attended to give oral testimony and were cross-examined.

Held: Application refused. An applicant for an order under s.51 was not usually entitled to have a full trial with pleadings, disclosure, and cross-examination of witnesses on every matter of fact which was potentially material. The authorities had taken the line that, as a matter of policy, s.51 applications were to be kept within proper bounds. The court normally did the best it could in an attempt to be fair to both parties and achieve a just result. It had to be recognised that an attempt to do justice in that way would often fall short of the very high standards which were conventionally applied where there was a full trial preceded by pre-trial procedures, and involving cross-examination of witnesses. In the instant case, a number of matters were material. First, C had identified the allegations they wished to make. Second, C had had more extensive disclosure from the liquidator than would typically be given in such a case, including privileged documents. Third, the court had been persuaded to make an order for specific disclosure against the third and fourth defendants, and that disclosure had been given. Fourth, K had filed very considerable evidence explaining their particular involvement in the matters in dispute. Finally, C did not want to cross-examine one or a few witnesses on isolated matters central to their case. They wanted to cross-examine eight witnesses on every factual issue in dispute and the scope of the cross-examination would in many respects be exploratory. C did not have much direct evidence of their own serving to contradict the eight defence witnesses. In substance, C wished to have a full-blown trial in relation to the application. The court would be left to produce as just a result as was possible on the basis of the material already in play. There was no feature which turned the case from one appropriate for a summary disposal to one which exceptionally had to be regarded as requiring a full trial of the whole range of the disputed matters of fact, *Grecoair Inc v Tilling* [2009] EWHC 115 (QB) considered (see paras 41-45 of judgment).

CENTREHIGH LTD v AMEN, [2013] EWHC 625 (Ch), [2013] 4 Costs L.O. 556, Morgan, J., Ch D.

450. Tomlin orders–Interpretation–Agreement to award construction contracts–Nature of "award"

The claimant company (J) claimed against the defendant company (S) for a lump sum pursuant to a compromise agreement. The parties had comprised a commercial dispute by way of an agreement which recognised that S owed J money. S would pay a lump sum for part of the amount owed and would only be required to pay a second lump sum if it failed to fulfil its obligation to "award" J contracts for the provision of not less than 33,500 hours of J's services. If S failed to fulfil its obligation, it had to pay J a lump sum calculated by an hourly charge for any contract hours not awarded. S only awarded J one contract within the set time period for the agreement, which equated to 250 hours of work. At the instant hearing, J claimed a lump sum for the remaining contractual hours. The issues were whether (i) the word "award" in the agreement meant an offer of a contract by S to J; (ii) the agreement was unenforceable as it was no more than an agreement to agree.

Held: Judgment for claimant. (1) The word "award" meant the award of a concluded contract by S to J, not merely the making of an offer. The construction industry commonly referred to the awarding of a contract to mean the process in which an employer accepted a contractor's offer, or a main contractor accepted a sub-contractor's offer. That interpretation of "award" was entirely consistent with the dictionary definitions and denoted a binding agreement. By contrast, an "offer" happened much earlier in the process, before an acceptance of an offer was formalised by the award of a contract. The agreement would have been very different if all S had had to do was offer J any contracts, irrespective of J's availability, capability or suitability, knowing that it could quickly discharge its liability under the agreement without actually entering into any binding contracts with J. That would have been a much inferior agreement for J. The use of the word "award" was intended to short-circuit matters such as implied terms about the nature of the contracts S offered, as J could turn down any obviously unsuitable contract offers. On that interpretation, the hours in the agreement were only reduced when contacts were actually agreed by both parties and awarded to J. Beyond the implication of good faith to make the agreement work, there was no need to imply terms into the agreement to achieve mutuality. The obligations were plain and so were the consequences of not fulfilling them (see paras 11-14, 17, 19-20 of judgment). (2) The agreement was not incomplete, and therefore unenforceable, merely because it called for some further agreement between the parties, *Foley v Classique Coaches Ltd* [1934] 2 K.B. 1 applied. The parties had expressly agreed a mechanism for dealing with any dispute regarding the level of fees payable and what was to happen if further contracts were not awarded. The rest of the agreement operated as a framework for S and J to negotiate each separate contract. Even if that finding was wrong and the first part was unenforceable, that did not affect the enforceability of the lump sum fall-back which expressly provided for what was to happen if the contracts were not awarded. J was therefore entitled to the entire sum claimed (paras 24-25, 54).

JACOBS UK LTD v SKIDMORE OWINGS & MERRILL LLP, [2012] EWHC 3293 (TCC), [2013] B.L.R. 18, Coulson, J., QBD (TCC).

451. Transfer of proceedings–Registrars in bankruptcy–Registrar refusing to transfer application to annul bankruptcy to Family Division–Judge in ancillary relief proceedings ordering transfer–Whether judge had jurisdiction to order transfer

[Insolvency Act 1986 (c.45) s.375(2); Civil Procedure Rules 1998 (SI 1998/3132) r.3.1 (7), r.30.5; Insolvency Rules 1986 (SI 1986/1925) r.7.6A(3), r.7.15(3), r.7.51A.]

The appellant husband (H) and his trustees in bankruptcy (T) appealed against an order transferring an application by his wife (W) for the annulment of his bankruptcy to the Family Division to be heard together with her application for ancillary relief in divorce proceedings. H was made bankrupt on his own petition. He had worked for a company which went into administration and he claimed to have had serious cash flow difficulties for a number of years. He said that before the bankruptcy order was made he had exhausted an overdraft facility and any other sources of finance. He therefore had no income with which to pay his debts. The annulment application was important for W: unless she could set the bankruptcy order aside her application for ancillary relief was likely to be severely prejudiced. Her case was that many of H's alleged debts were in fact shams; the creditors were H's friends and family members who had fabricated liabilities in order to facilitate his bankruptcy. W applied for the annulment application to be transferred to the Family Division. The bankruptcy registrar dismissed the transfer application and sent the annulment application to be determined in the Chancery Division on a summary basis without cross-examination of witnesses. At a case management conference in the ancillary relief proceedings at which H, W and T were represented, the judge made an order for transfer pursuant to CPR r.3.1 (7) and varied the registrar's directions for the hearing.

Held: Appeals allowed. Under the Insolvency Rules 1986 r.7.6A(3) all High Court hearings in bankruptcy had to come before a registrar in the first instance. An appeal against an order made by the registrar lay to a High Court judge under the Insolvency Act 1986 s.375(2). The Insolvency Rules 1986 r.7.51A applied the provisions of the CPR to insolvency proceedings, except so far as inconsistent with the Insolvency Rules. Although the power to transfer proceedings between the divisions of the High Court under CPR r.30.5 was general, the power of a High Court judge of another division to transfer proceedings involving an estate in bankruptcy into that division of his own motion was limited under r.7.15(3) of the Insolvency Rules to proceedings brought to enforce a claim by or against the insolvent estate. An annulment application did not fall within that rule. Thus any application to transfer an annulment application had to be made to a registrar, as it was, or a judge of the Chancery Division. The judge purported to exercise the case management powers contained in CPR r.3.1 (7) to vary or revoke an order, which he described as unbounded. He was clearly wrong about that, since that power was ordinarily limited to cases where there had been a material change of circumstances or where the original order was based on misstated facts or material non-disclosure, *Tibbles v SIG Plc (t/a Asphaltic Roofing Supplies)* [2012] EWCA Civ 518, [2012] 1 W.L.R. 2591, [2012] C.L.Y. 443 followed. In most other cases the finality of the court's order had to be respected and the proper way of challenging the order was by appeal. The instant case was no exception. None of the grounds relied on before the judge constituted a change of circumstances or material non-disclosure. They were all criticisms of the merits of the decision. The proper forum for raising those points was on appeal to a judge of the Chancery Division. It had not been open to the judge under CPR r.3.1 (7) to transfer the annulment application to the Family Division and to vary the registrar's order (see paras 24-28 of judgment).

ARIF v ZAR, [2012] EWCA Civ 986, [2012] B.P.I.R. 948, Thorpe, L.J., CA (Civ Div).

452. Trials–Adjournment–Third application to adjourn trial–Incapacity of defendant–Factors to be balanced

[Civil Procedure Rules 1998 (SI 1998/3132) r.1.1 (2) (d); European Convention on Human Rights 1950 Art.6.]

The appellant (D) appealed against a judge's refusal to adjourn a trial. D had borrowed £200,000 from the respondent (Y) as part of a property transaction. D had relied upon a friend (M) to negotiate with Y on her behalf. She failed to repay the loan and Y issued proceedings against her. The trial was listed for May 2010 but was vacated when M died unexpectedly. D suffered a severe bereavement reaction. A new trial date was fixed for the period January to March 2011. However, D remained unwell and the trial was again vacated. D failed to comply with an unless order to serve her witness statement, and missed two further deadlines to file the statement. She was then debarred from relying upon witness evidence at trial. Her application to adjourn the third trial date was refused, and a litigation friend was appointed to act on her behalf. Medical evidence filed shortly before the trial indicated that she lacked capacity. An application for an adjournment on the day of the trial was also refused. D submitted that it was fundamentally unfair for the trial to continue given that she lacked capacity and was unable to attend the trial to give evidence or be cross-examined.

Held: Appeal dismissed. (1) It was clear from the authorities that: (a) the overriding objective required cases to be dealt with justly. CPR r.1.1 (2) (d) required the court to deal with cases "expeditiously and fairly". Fairness required the position of both sides to be considered, and was in accordance with the European Convention on Human Rights art.6; (b) fairness could only be determined by taking all relevant matters into account, and also by excluding irrelevant matters; (c) a number of fair outcomes might be possible. Therefore a balancing exercise had to be conducted in each case. It was only where the decision of the first instance judge was plainly wrong that the Court of Appeal would interfere; (d) unless the appeal court could identify that the judge had taken into account immaterial factors, omitted to take into account relevant factors, erred in principle or come to a decision that was impermissible, the decision at first instance had to prevail, *Tanfern Ltd v Cameron-MacDonald* [2000] 1 W.L.R. 1311, [2000] C.L.Y. 358 and *Berezovsky v Russian Television and Radio Broadcasting Co* [2010] EWCA Civ 1345 applied, *Albon (t/a NA Carriage Co) v Naza Motor Trading Sdn Bhd* [2007] EWHC 2613 (Ch), [2008] 1 W.L.R. 2380, [2008] C.L.Y. 436 considered (see paras 30-33 of judgment). (2) D's complaints failed for the following reasons: (a) the judge was fully entitled to reach the conclusion that the late arrival of the evidence of incapacity was not a sufficient factor to merit an adjournment. If there were difficulties, the evidence demonstrated that they stemmed primarily from a lack of proper preparation on behalf of D; (b) it was clear that the judge accepted that D lacked capacity for he permitted the litigation friend to conduct the case on her behalf. By offering D the opportunity to attend to give evidence he was doing no more than stating that she could attend if she was able; (c) no proper steps were taken by D's legal team to introduce such evidence as they had amassed from D. During certain periods D could and should have prepared a full witness statement. The judge was correct to criticise her for failing to comply with the numerous unless orders when she clearly had capacity during the time that the orders were made; (d) the judge had a balancing exercise to carry out and was entitled to take into account the fact that Y lived abroad and had flown to the United Kingdom especially for the hearing, which was the third time that the case had been listed; (e) it was obvious that oral agreements were a key part of D's case. However, the trial judge found that the major part of the negotiations had been carried out by M. Even though D was debarred from filing evidence it was most unlikely that she could have given material evidence in any event. In those circumstances it was within the permissible limits of an exercise of discretion to refuse an adjournment. The judge had balanced all relevant factors (paras 34-39).

DHILLON v ASIEDU, [2012] EWCA Civ 1020, [2012] C.P. Rep. 44, Arden, L.J., CA (Civ Div).

453. Tribunals, Courts and Enforcement Act 2007 (c.70)–Commencement No.9 Order

THE TRIBUNALS, COURTS AND ENFORCEMENT ACT 2007 (COMMENCEMENT NO.9) ORDER 2013, SI 2013/SI 1739; made under the Tribunals, Courts and Enforcement Act 2007 s.148. Commencement details: bringing into force various provisions of the 2007 Act on July 15, 2013; .

This Order brings into force for limited purposes a number of provisions in Pt 3 of the Tribunals, Courts and Enforcement Act 2007, which provides for the replacement of various powers of enforcement by way of execution and distraint by a procedure known as taking control of goods, and for the replacement of distress for rent by a power (to be known as commercial rent arrears recovery, or CRAR) to use the taking control of goods procedure.

454. Unless orders–Surrender–Order debarring defendant from defending claims in case of failure to surrender

[European Convention on Human Rights 1950 Art.6.]

The appellant (X) appealed against three decisions in litigation brought against him by the respondent Kazakh bank (J). J's claims alleged that X had defrauded it of almost $5 billion. The three judgments appealed against had respectively (i) found X guilty of contempt of court; (ii) sentenced him on each of three proven contempts to 22 months' imprisonment concurrently; (iii) made unless orders whereby X would be debarred from defending the claims against him, and his defences would be struck out, unless within a stated period he both surrendered to custody and made proper disclosure of all his assets and his dealings with them. The contempt of court involved non-disclosure of assets, lying during cross-examination, and dealing with assets. X failed to attend the handing down of the judgment committing him to prison for contempt, and absconded to avoid his sentence. X argued that (1) in concluding that he was in contempt of court, the judge had failed to apply the criminal standard of proof which he had set for himself and had made findings that he was not entitled to make. Furthermore, there were a number of pervasive flaws in his analysis; (2) the sentence of 22 months was too long, in circumstances where the maximum sentence was two years; (3) the judge lacked jurisdiction to make the surrender order. Furthermore, the European Convention on Human Rights 1950 art.6 gave him an express right to be heard, or a right to an adjudication on the merits, and the curtailment of that right inherent in the unless orders was absolutely wrong. The unless orders were not necessary, proportionate or justified.

Held: Appeals dismissed. (Toulson L.J. dissenting in part) (1) The judge had overwhelmingly used the language of the criminal standard, and he uniformly did so when reaching his conclusions on any essential plank of J's case. There was no doubt that the judge had applied the criminal standard of proof. X's complaints about the judge's analysis fell to be rejected. X was simply attempting to reargue the trial, down to the smallest details. There was no error shown in the judge's findings or reasoning (see paras 48-101 of judgment). (2) There was no justification for interference with the sentence imposed. Although there had not been a total failure of compliance with the orders imposed, X was of central importance within the litigation, and his contempts had been multiple, persistent and protracted, involving offences of non-disclosure, lying in cross-examination, and dealing with assets, and had been supported by the suborning of false testimony and the forging of documents. Furthermore, X had failed to attend the handing down of the committal judgment and had subsequently absconded to avoid his sentence. The sentence imposed was fully justified, *JSC BTA Bank v Solodchenko* [2011] EWCA Civ 1241, [2012] 1 W.L.R. 350, [2012] C.L.Y. 337 applied (paras 102-109). (3) X had failed to provide any authority for the proposition that a full hearing on the merits was required in circumstances where a litigant had forfeited his right to a full trial by his own conduct of the litigation. The court was not required to persevere to a full trial on the merits whatever the circumstances. It was clearly in order to deploy even the final sanction of striking out, where necessary and proportionate to protect the interests of justice. X had not been able to show that there had been any element of judicial unfairness in the way that any of the numerous hearings concerning him had been conducted. X had been granted the opportunity for trial, if he complied with the court's orders, but had chosen to forfeit the opportunities which had been given to him. It was impossible to submit that the court lacked jurisdiction to do what was just and convenient, and necessary, to protect its own orders and to give effect to the interests of justice, *AJ Bekhor & Co Ltd v Bilton* [1981] Q.B. 923, [1981] C.L.Y. 2159 applied. The order that X surrender to custody was not beyond the power of the court, nor was it particularly novel. The judge had been entitled to make the order, *CIBC Mellon Trust Co v Stolzenberg (Sanctions: Non-compliance)* [2004] EWCA Civ 827, Independent, July 2, 2004 and *Lexi Holdings plc v Luqman* [2007] EWCA Civ 1501 applied (paras 123-189). (4) (Per Toulson L.J.) The appeal against the order debarring X from defending the claims, unless he made proper disclosure of his assets and his dealings with them, should be dismissed. However, to debar X from defending if he failed to surrender was wrong in principle, and would be a form of additional punishment (paras 195-200).

JSC BTA BANK v ABLYAZOV, [2012] EWCA Civ 1411, [2013] 1 W.L.R. 1331, Sir Maurice Kay (VP CA Civ), CA (Civ Div).

455. Upper Tribunal–Permission to appeal–Permission to appeal refused under s.175(2) Commonhold and Leasehold Reform Act 2002–Whether right of appeal to Court of Appeal

[Commonhold and Leasehold Reform Act 2002 (c.15) s.175(2), s.175; Lands Tribunal Act 1949 (c.42) s.3(4); Tribunals, Courts and Enforcement Act 2007 (c.15) s.11, s.13(8), s.13(1), s.31 (2).]

The Court of Appeal was required to determine whether it had jurisdiction to consider an application for permission to appeal against a decision of the Upper Tribunal (Lands Chamber) or whether the challenge should be made by way of an application for permission to apply for judicial review in the Administrative Court. The Upper Tribunal (Lands Chamber) had refused an application of the applicant (W) under the Commonhold and Leasehold Reform Act 2002 s.175(2) for permission to appeal against a decision of the Leasehold Valuation Tribunal (LVT). It held that there was no right to appeal against the decision in the Court of Appeal but that it could be judicially reviewed if permission by the Administrative Court was granted. W disagreed and applied for permission to appeal to the Court Appeal but the Upper Tribunal refused his application. It held, applying *Lane v Esdaile* [1891] A.C. 210, that an appeal from an LVT lay under s.175(2) with permission to the Upper Tribunal and that *R. (on the application of Sinclair Gardens Investments (Kensington) Ltd) v Lands Tribunal* [2004] EWHC 1910 (Admin), [2004] 3 E.G.L.R. 15, [2005] C.L.Y. 2661 confirmed that the right of appeal to the Court of Appeal on a point of law under the Lands Tribunal Act 1949 s.3(4) did not apply to decisions of the Lands Tribunal refusing permission to appeal unders.175. It further held that an appeal lay under the Tribunals, Courts and Enforcement Act 2007 s.31(2) to the Court of Appeal from a decision of the Upper Tribunal other than an excluded decision under s.11 of the 2007 Act; that a decision under s.175 of the 2002 Act was not an excluded decision; the effect of the authorities on which *Sinclair* was based, particularly *Lane v Esdaile*, applied to a decision of the Upper Tribunal under s.175; and that there was no right of appeal to the Court of Appeal. W filed an appellant's notice seeking permission to appeal to the Court of Appeal and a claim seeking permission to apply for judicial review.

Held: Judgment accordingly. It was clear that there was no right of appeal against a refusal by the Lands Tribunal of permission to appeal against an LVT's decision, *R. (on the application of Sinclair Gardens Investments (Kensington) Ltd) v Lands Tribunal* [2004] EWHC 1910 (Admin), [2004] 3 E.G.L.R. 15, [2005] C.L.Y. 2661 applied. The Lands Tribunal's decision to refuse permission to appeal was not a decision for the purposes of s.3(4) of the 1949 Act which conferred a right of appeal to the Court of Appeal against the Lands Tribunal's decisions, *Lane v Esdaile* [1891] A.C. 210 applied. The position remained the same even though the Lands Tribunal was now the Upper Tribunal and the right of appeal was governed by s.13(1) of the 2007 Act. W was effectively seeking to overturn the decision in *Sinclair* by converting an express exclusion of a right to appeal against refusals of permission to appeal in s.11 of the 2007 Act into an express provision of a new right of appeal against refusals of permission in s.175 cases. That intention could not be imputed into s.13 of the 2007 Act. It was not necessary to include a decision to refuse permission to appeal under s.175(2) of the 2002 Act in the list of excluded decisions within s.13(8) of the 2007 Act because the position was governed by *Sinclair*, which made it clear that there was no right of appeal against such decisions, *Sinclair* applied and *R. (on the application of Cart) v Upper Tribunal* [2011] UKSC 28, [2012] 1 A.C. 663, [2011] C.L.Y. 48 followed. The practical and policy reasons advanced by W were not sufficient to oust the application of the *Lane v Esdaile* principle as applied in *Sinclair*. Protective applications within the two-month appropriate period still needed to be made irrespective of which court would decide the merits of a challenge to a decision of the Upper Tribunal under s.175(2). Accordingly, there was no right of appeal to the Court of Appeal against the relevant decision; it had to be challenged by way of an application for permission to apply for judicial review (see paras 18-22 of judgment).

WELLCOME TRUST LTD v 19-22 ONSLOW GARDENS FREEHOLD, [2012] EWCA Civ 1024, [2012] R.V.R. 342, Lloyd, L.J., CA (Civ Div).

456. Wasted costs orders–Adjournment–Unreasonable refusal to adjourn trial date

The applicant (L) applied for a wasted costs order against the respondent (S). S had brought a claim against L in relation to a family property partnership. Directions had been given in June 2012 for the preparation of a joint expert report by a forensic accountant. There was a delay of two months and, in an attempt to move matters forward, L suggested an expert which S found too expensive. An expert was instructed in December 2012 but he did not receive the papers until January 2013. His report was due on February 22, 2013 and the trial was scheduled for March 4, 2013. On February 8, 2013 L's solicitors wrote to S's solicitors commenting that there would be little time for reflection on his report before trial and suggesting the trial date be re-fixed. There was no reply so L wrote again on February 15 asking for S's consent to an adjournment. S consented on February 26. L submitted that S's refusal to consent to an adjournment by February 16 at the latest was unreasonable and had caused costs to be wasted because they were forced to prepare for trial. S submitted that the fact that L's counsel accepted the brief meant that they believed that it would be possible for the trial date to go ahead.

Held: Application granted. L's solicitors had to instruct counsel to prepare for the trial in case the trial did go ahead. S accepted that L had taken a reasonable position in requesting an adjournment and that, as of February 15, it was virtually impossible to prepare the case for March 4. S's refusal to consent earlier to L's request for an adjournment was unreasonable. S was ordered to pay L's wasted costs insofar as they were incurred because of S's refusal between February 16 and 26.

STREET v LARKINS, [2013] EWHC 1408 (Ch), [2013] 5 Costs L.O. 667, Jonathan Gaunt, Q.C., Ch D.

457. Wasted costs orders–Solicitors–Without notice applications–Solicitors' failure to act in co-operative and open way in care proceedings–Whether actions causative of costs incurred by other parties

[Senior Courts Act 1981 (c.54) s.51 (6); Family Procedure Rules 2010 (SI 2010/2955) Pt 25; CPR PD 52C Appeals to the Court of Appeal 2010.]

The applicant local authority applied for a wasted costs order against the respondent firm of solicitors (F). F represented the parents of a child in care proceedings brought by the local authority. In *A (A Child) (Permission to Appeal Fact-Finding Judgment), Re* [2012] EWCA Civ 1477, [2013] 1 F.L.R. 1187, [2013] 10 C.L. 151 the parents were refused permission to appeal against a decision of the trial judge not to re-open a fact-finding determination regarding injuries sustained by the child. The notice of appeal had been issued 30 days outside the three-week time limit. The initial without notice application had been adjourned for the parents to obtain a report from a medical expert (N). The local authority claimed that F's conduct in preparing for and pursuing the without notice permission application amounted to "improper, unreasonable or negligent" litigation conduct sufficient to trigger the instant court's jurisdiction under the Senior Courts Act 1981 s.51 (6) to award wasted costs. The local authority's application was founded on the basis that the permission application should have been withdrawn following receipt of N's report, and that the instant hearing would have been unnecessary but for the way in which F had conducted the proceedings. The local authority argued that F had failed in their duty to provide the court with full and frank disclosure of all relevant material, including the original fact-finding judgment and the expert medical evidence adduced at trial. It further argued that F had failed to properly disclose relevant information to the other parties, and had not complied with the Family Procedure Rules 2010 Pt 25 when instructing N.

Held: Application refused. (1) It had been incumbent on F to furnish the court with the core relevant material, including the judge's fact-finding judgment and the expert section in the bundle, *S (A Child) (Family Division: Without Notice Orders), Re* [2001] 1 W.L.R. 211, [2000] C.L.Y. 2508 applied. F's submission that the purpose of the without notice application was to seek direction on whether a full application to instruct an expert should be made was unsustainable. The general approach of the 2010 Rules had to, by extension, apply to appellate proceedings, *M (A Child), Re* [2012] EWCA Civ 165, [2012] 2 F.L.R. 121, [2012] C.L.Y. 1415 applied. The basic requirement of any litigant to be open with the court had to be applicable across the board. However, F's errors in that regard were not causative of any wasting of cost on the part of the local authority or the child (see paras 17-25 of judgment). F had been instructed for some 18 weeks prior to issuing the notice of appeal and any plea by them to the effect that they had "a limited time" to prepare the case was hard to sustain. However, no adverse consequence in terms of wasted costs flowed from that misstatement of the position, nor had it affected the court's decision to permit N's instruction (para.26). The court orders had made it plain that the court expected the other parties to be fully aware of and involved in the permission application, including having scrutiny of any material flowing from N's instruction. The privilege of instructing an expert in family proceedings came with the responsibility of transparency, proportionality and neutrality. CPR PD 52C para.16 required that, where the court had directed a respondent to attend an oral permission hearing, the appellant had to supply the respondent with a copy of the skeleton argument "and any documents to which the appellant intends to refer". F's failure to act in a co-operative and open way was a serious and gross failure, and betrayed an attitude which sought to maintain and capitalise on some perceived tactical forensic advantage gained by obtaining the court's leave to instruct an expert at a without notice hearing. Such an attitude could have no place in family proceedings (paras 29-32). F's failure to send relevant material to N when instructing him was a clear error of judgment, but no additional costs had been incurred by the other parties as a result (paras 33-34). The manner in which the permission application was pursued after receipt of N's report had removed any true validity, arose almost entirely from the wholly over-optimistic judgement of counsel, and not from any improper or unreasonable act or omission by F (paras 35-41). (2) Despite litigation conduct which on occasion fell woefully short of that which was required in mounting a without notice application for permission to appeal in a child case where the Court of Appeal had given permission to one party to instruct a new expert, none of the identified errors had been causative of costs being wasted by either of the opposing parties, *Ridehalgh v Horsefield* [1994] Ch. 205, [1994] C.L.Y. 3623 and *Harrison v Harrison* [2009] EWHC 428 (QB), [2009] 1 F.L.R. 1434, [2009] C.L.Y. 385 applied. In addition, to award the local authority the costs of the instant hearing, where it had failed to achieve the substantive order for wasted costs, would be wrong in principle (paras 42-43).

A (A CHILD) (WASTED COSTS ORDER), *Re*, [2013] EWCA Civ 43, [2013] 6 Costs L.R. 873, McFarlane, L.J., CA (Civ Div).

458. Wasted costs orders–Solicitors' powers and duties–Solicitors litigating on behalf of bankrupt without trustee in bankruptcy's consent–Whether order that solicitors pay defendant's wasted costs properly made

[Senior Courts Act 1981 (c.54) s.51 (6); Civil Procedure Rules 1998 (SI 1998/3132) Pt 23, r.48.7; CPR PD 48 (Costs -Special Cases) 2000 para.53.6.]

The appellant solicitors (T) appealed against a decision ordering them to pay the wasted costs of the defendant (M) in proceedings brought by their client (S). In June 2010, S had issued a claim against M seeking to recover a debt. S was declared bankrupt on June 29. S later instructed T to represent him. M's solicitors wrote to T enquiring about S's bankruptcy. T replied that they did not understand why a consent letter from S's trustee in bankruptcy was required. M applied to strike out the claim on the grounds that S had been made bankrupt. In March 2012, the judge ordered that the claim be struck out if the trustee did not consent to its continuation, and required T to provide a witness statement addressing S's current financial standing and their knowledge of it and whether there were any grounds why they should not be liable for wasted costs from June 29, 2010. S's trustee subsequently assigned the cause of action to S for £2,300 and thereafter had no interest in the claim, and so did not give his consent to the proceedings' continuation. S contended that the trustee's assignment should be treated as consent so that the action had not been struck out. M asked that T should pay his costs. The parties were directed to serve evidence in respect of that application. On November 30, 2012, the judge declared that the action had been struck out in accordance with the March 2012 order, and ordered T to pay M's costs incurred between June 29, 2010 and November 30, 2012, on the indemnity basis, having found that when accepting S's instructions T had known that he was bankrupt and had wrongly conducted litigation on his behalf without having ensured that there was consent. T contended that (1) M had made no proper application for a wasted costs order; (2) there was no causative link because S would have carried on the action himself even if they had not been instructed; (3) the court had not laid down a fair and proper procedure in dealing with the wasted costs order; (4) the order was unjust by reason of a procedural irregularity because no application had been made under CPR Pt 23; (5) the order did not comply with CPR r.48.7(4).

Held: Appeal dismissed. Under CPR r.48.7, where the court was considering making a wasted costs order under the Senior Courts Act 1981 s.51 (6), it was required to give the legal representative a reasonable opportunity to attend a hearing to give reasons why it should not make such an order. There was a strong prima facie case as from March 2012 that T had acted improperly, unreasonably and negligently. That met the first requirement for a wasted costs order under the CPR PD 48 para.53.6. T had known when accepting instruction from S that he was a bankrupt. Any competent solicitor had to know that a bankrupt's assets vested in a trustee, and that proceedings to enforce a claim would only be pursued with the trustee's consent. They had not understood the need for that consent, as made clear in their letter to M's solicitors. In the circumstances, it was unnecessary for M to have issued a Pt 23 application since the case against T on whether they had acted unreasonably and negligently had been made sufficiently clear. T had been given more than one reasonable opportunity to give reasons why a wasted costs order should not be made. The argument that if T had not been instructed S would nevertheless have pursued the claim in person was rejected as speculation. The claim was liable to be struck out because S had no interest in the cause of action. The order that T pay wasted costs had been properly made under CPR r.48.7(4)(b) (see paras 27, 44-45, 47-50).

THAMES CHAMBERS SOLICITORS v MIAH, [2013] EWHC 1245 (QB), [2013] 4 Costs L.R. 582, Tugendhat, J., QBD.

459. Witness statements–Extensions of time–Failure to comply with rules, directions and orders–Effect of r.1.1 (2)(f) CPR on courts' approach

[Civil Procedure Rules 1998 (SI 1998/3132) r.1.1 (2)(f).]

The court had to decide whether to extend time for the filing of witness statements in a claim which had been ongoing since April 2011. The claim had been commenced before the reforms to the CPR in April 2013, which included the addition of subparagraph (f) to r.1.1 (2). The district judge had made an order for the exchange of witness statements in October 2011, but that had not been complied with. A further order was made in November 2012 and various extensions were agreed, the most recent having expired three weeks before the instant hearing, without being complied with.

Held: Extension of time granted. Rule 1.1 (2)(f) required the court to pay close attention to the failure of parties to comply with rules, direction and orders. A failure to comply with a rule, direction or order was of itself a clear breach of the overriding objective and was likely to result in severe sanctions. The problem was all the more difficult in the instant case because the case had been listed with a trial estimate of five days, but if witness statements had been served, it would have become apparent much earlier that certain issues were no longer live and that the trial would be completed in a fraction of that time. As a result, a valuable national resource, namely court sitting days, would be wasted because of the parties' failure to comply with the judge's directions. Ultimately, however, the court was persuaded to extend the time for the filing of witness statements, only because the hearing was taking place a very short while after the amendment of the CPR and because the period that had elapsed since the final extension was relatively short. However, all parties and the wider litigation world had to be aware that all courts at all levels were now required to take a very much stricter view of the failure by parties to comply with directions, particularly where the failure to comply was likely to lead to a waste of the limited resources made available to those with cases to litigate. Time would be extended until the following day. Any party failing to comply with that order would be debarred from relying upon any evidence at trial (see paras 8-11 of judgment).

FONS HF v CORPORAL LTD, [2013] EWHC 1278 (Ch), [2013] 4 Costs L.O. 646, Judge Pelling Q.C., Ch D (Manchester).

COMMERCIAL LAW

460. Debts–Delay–Payments

THE LATE PAYMENT OF COMMERCIAL DEBTS (NO.2) REGULATIONS 2013, SI 2013/908; made under the European Communities Act 1972 s.2. In force: May 14, 2013; .

These Regulations implement Directive 2011/7 on combating late payment in commercial transactions.

461. Debts–Late payments

THE LATE PAYMENT OF COMMERCIAL DEBTS REGULATIONS 2013, SI 2013/395; made under the European Communities Act 1972 s.2. In force: March 16, 2013; .

These Regulations amend the provisions governing the late payment of commercial debts. They set limits on payment periods for commercial debts to a maximum of 60 days in most cases and 30 days for those incurred by public authorities, limit the amount of time for purchasers to verify the conformity of goods or services with the contract to 30 days in most cases and permit suppliers to recover their reasonable costs in recovering debts.

462. Electricity markets–Gas markets–Misleading advertising–OFGEM

THE BUSINESS PROTECTION FROM MISLEADING MARKETING (AMENDMENT) REGULATIONS 2013, SI 2013/2701; made under the European Communities Act 1972 s.2. In force: November 14, 2013; .

These Regulations amend the Business Protection from Misleading Marketing Regulations 2008.

COMPANY LAW

463. Accounts–Companies–Reports–Revocation

THE COMPANIES (REVISION OF DEFECTIVE ACCOUNTS AND REPORTS) (AMENDMENT) (NO.2) REGULATIONS 2013, SI 2013/2224; made under the Companies Act 2006 s.454. In force: October 1, 2013; .

This instrument revokes and replaces the Companies (Revision of Defective Accounts and Reports) (Amendment) Regulations 2013 (SI 2013/1971) before they comes into force on October 1, 2013.

464. Accounts–Directors' remuneration–Financial reporting

THE LARGE AND MEDIUM-SIZED COMPANIES AND GROUPS (ACCOUNTS AND REPORTS) (AMENDMENT) REGULATIONS 2013, SI 2013/1981; made under the Companies Act 2006 s.421, s.422A, s.1292. In force: October 1, 2013; .

The Enterprise and Regulatory Reform Act 2013 amended the Companies Act 2006 to provide that a quoted company be bound by the company's shareholder approved directors' remuneration policy in relation to payments to directors of remuneration or for loss of office, and further amended Pt of the 2006 Act to require that policy to be set out in a separate part of the company's directors' remuneration report. These Regulations revise the existing provisions which set out the content of the annual report on remuneration paid in the financial year and also set out for the first time the minimum requirements for the directors' remuneration policy in order to ensure that shareholders will have clear information on how directors will be paid in the future.

465. Accounts–Limited liability partnerships–Unlimited companies

THE COMPANIES AND PARTNERSHIPS (ACCOUNTS AND AUDIT) REGULATIONS 2013, SI 2013/2005; made under the Limited Liability Partnerships Act 2000 s.15; and the Companies Act 2006 s.409, s.468, s.484, s.1292. In force: September 1, 2013; .

This instrument amends the Companies Act 2006 Pt 15 (the 2006 Act) and the Partnerships (Accounts) Regulations 20082 (the 2008 Regulations). It corrects defects in the implementation of Directive 90/605. The principle effect of these regulations is to amend the scope of application of those provisions of the 2006 Act and 2008 Regulations that implement the Directive, to make sure that all the partnerships and unlimited companies covered by the Directive are also covered in the UK's implementation.

466. Annual accounts–Companies–Statutory auditors–Third countries

THE STATUTORY AUDITORS AND THIRD COUNTRY AUDITORS REGULATIONS 2013, SI 2013/1672; made under the European Communities Act 1972 s.2; and the Companies Act 2006 s.1239, s.1246, s.1292. In force: in accordance with reg.2 and reg.3.; .

These Regulations: amend that part of the Companies Act 2006 and the regulatory framework under that Act which implements EU law on relations between the countries of the European Economic Area and other countries on the regulation of auditors of listed multinational companies; implement a new Commission Decision issued under Directive 2006/43 art.47 (the Audit Directive) and make amendments necessary to facilitate the implementation by the Financial Reporting Council (FRC) of two more Decisions issued under art.46 of the Audit Directive; consolidates the provisions of the Statutory Auditors and Third Country Auditors Regulations 2007 (SI 2007/3494) Pt 5 on the registration of "third country auditors"; and makes other amendments to the framework in the Companies Act on the regulation of these auditors, completing a package of reforms to the FRC begun in 2012.

467. Buy-back agreements–Companies–Share purchases

THE COMPANIES ACT 2006 (AMENDMENT OF PART 18) REGULATIONS 2013, SI 2013/999; made under the Companies Act 2006 s.737. In force: April 30, 2013; .

This instrument includes amendments that make deregulatory changes to provisions of the Companies Act 2006 relating to the purchase by a company of its own shares (share buy backs), in particular the authorisation and financing of share buy backs and the holding of repurchased shares "in treasury".

468. Charges–Companies–Company registration–Corporate governance

THE COMPANIES ACT 2006 (AMENDMENT OF PART 25) REGULATIONS 2013, SI 2013/600; made under the Companies Act 2006 s.894, s.1292. In force: April 6, 2013; .

These Regulations repeal and replace the provisions of the Companies Act 2006 which provides a scheme for the registration of charges created by companies.

469. Companies–Forms–Limited liability partnerships

THE COMPANIES AND LIMITED LIABILITY PARTNERSHIPS (FORMS, ETC.) AMENDMENT REGULATIONS 2013, SI 2013/1947; made under the Companies Act 1985 s.6, s.10, s.12, s.30, s.43, s.49, s.51, s.53, s.54, s.88, s.117, s.169, s.169A, s.190, s.225, s.228, s.242, s.244, s.266, s.287, s.288, s.288A, s.318, s.325, s.353, s.363, s.364, s.391, s.652A, s.652D, s.691, s.692, s.694, s.701, s.702, s.703P, s.703Q, s.706, s.710B, s.744, Sch.9 para.6, Sch.13 para.27, Sch.21A para.1, Sch.21A para.4A, Sch.21A para.7, Sch.21A para.8, Sch.21A para.9; the Water Act 1989 s.185, Sch.25 para.71; the Companies Act 1989 s.144; the Welsh Language Act 1993 s.26; and the Companies Act 2006 s.1292, s.1296, s.1300. In force: October 1, 2013; .

These Regulations repeal a number of statutory instruments relating to the forms which companies and Limited Liability Partnerships are required to complete when returning information to Companies House.

470. Companies House–Limited liability partnerships

THE LIMITED LIABILITY PARTNERSHIPS (APPLICATION OF COMPANIES ACT 2006) (AMENDMENT) REGULATIONS 2013, SI 2013/618; made under the Limited Liability Partnerships Act 2000 s.15, s.17. In force: in accordance with reg.1 (2).; .

The Regulations amend the Limited Liability Partnerships (Application of Companies Act 2006) Regulations 2009 (SI 2009/1804) to apply, with modifications, the amended provisions of the Companies Act 2006 Pt 25. The provisions of the Companies Act 2006 Pt 26 (which relate to the scheme for registration at Companies House of charges created by companies) are amended by the Companies Act 2006 (Amendment of Part 25) Regulations 2013.

471. Corporate personality–De facto directors–Transfer of property to company to conceal true ownership–Piercing corporate veil–Transfer of property to liquidator

The liquidator for the claimant company (C) claimed for the transfer of a property from the first defendant company (D) to it. The property had been bought by a de facto director (T) of C, who had then transferred it to D. The liquidator, supported by the seventh defendant Revenue and Customs, submitted that T had set up D in order to conceal his assets and prevent their seizure for his involvement in tax evasion, and accordingly that D had no genuine corporate existence. On that basis, they argued that the liquidator was entitled to pierce the corporate veil and to require a transfer of the property from D to C.

Held: Judgment for claimant. In order to pierce the corporate veil, C was required to show that T had control of D and that D had been used as a device or facade to facilitate or conceal T's wrongdoing, *Trustor AB v Smallbone (No.2)* [2001] 1 W.L.R. 1177, [2001] C.L.Y. 705 applied. Those conditions were satisfied. D was clearly owned and controlled by T, and the purpose of transferring the property was to conceal T's ownership of it until his liabilities arising out of his fraudulent activities were resolved. Accordingly, T was the true owner of the property and a declaration was granted to that effect (see paras 22-24 of judgment).

ANGLO GERMAN BREWERIES LTD (IN LIQUIDATION) v CHELSEA CORP INC, [2012] EWHC 1481 (Ch), [2012] 2 B.C.L.C. 632, Nicholas Strauss Q.C., Ch D.

472. Corporate personality–Tortious claim brought against company and others–Appropriateness of piercing corporate veil to allow pursuit of contractual claim

The appellant bank (V) appealed against a decision ([2012] EWCA Civ 808, [2012] 2 Lloyd's Rep. 313, [2012] C.L.Y. 474) refusing it permission to effect service on the respondents (D1, D4 and others) out of the jurisdiction and refusing it permission to amend its particulars of claim. V had lent money to a Russian company (R) to fund R's acquisition of Russian companies from D1. The facility agreement provided for English law and jurisdiction. R defaulted. V alleged that it had been induced to enter into the agreement by D1's fraudulent misrepresentations, for which the other respondents were alleged to be jointly liable. D4 was an individual said to be the owner and controller of D1 and R. V's case was pleaded in deceit and unlawful means conspiracy. It applied to amend to add claims in contract on the basis that the court should pierce R's corporate veil so as to make the respondents liable as parties under the facility agreement. The High Court refused permission to amend, set aside permission to serve the proceedings on the defendants out of the jurisdiction, holding that V had not demonstrated that England was the appropriate forum, and discharged a freezing injunction obtained against D4, although the injunction was maintained pending V's appeals. The Court of Appeal upheld that decision. The Supreme Court was required to determine whether (i) the courts below had been justified in finding that England was not the appropriate forum; (ii) the court could ever pierce the corporate veil, or should in the instant case.

Held: Appeal dismissed. (Lords Clarke and Reed JJ.S.C. dissenting regarding forum) (1) The High Court had erred in its interpretation of the *Spiliada Maritime Corp v Cansulex Ltd (The Spiliada)* [1987] A.C. 460, [1987] C.L.Y. 3135 approach to determining the appropriate forum; however, its error had favoured V and did not affect its analysis, and it could not conceivably have come to any conclusion other than that V had failed to show that England was the appropriate forum, *Spiliada* considered. Although the High Court had wrongly concluded that Russian law governed the alleged torts, it had also considered the question on the basis that English law applied and correctly found that that would not be a strong factor in England's favour. The Court of

Appeal had itself erred in finding that Russian law governed the alleged torts, and failed to recognise the potential significance of the governing law. However, that factor had little potency in the instant case; had the court approached the issue on a correct basis, it would have made no difference to its conclusion. The High Court's analysis and exercise of its discretion could not be faulted in any substantial respect, and the instant court would not be justified in setting aside its discretion (paras 44-49, 54-55, 68-69). (2) It was unnecessary to resolve the issue of whether, unless any statute relied on in the particular case provided otherwise, the court could not pierce the corporate veil, because piercing the corporate veil could not succeed in the instant case in any event, and it was inappropriate to resolve the issue on an interlocutory appeal when it was unnecessary to do so (para.130). V's case involved an extension to the circumstances where it had traditionally been held that the corporate veil could be pierced: it would lead to the person controlling the company being held liable as if he had been a co-contracting party with the company to a contract where the company had been a party and he had not been. The principle had been subject to criticism, and strong justification would be required to extend it. In fact, there was an overwhelming case against such an extension. V had not suggested that any of the other contracting parties was not liable; there was no unfairness in a case such as the instant since the law provided redress against the controller of a company in a cause of action in misrepresentation. In any event, it would be wrong to treat D4 as a party to an agreement where none of the actual parties had intended that he should be and he had not conducted himself as if he was. Further, the facts V relied on to justify piercing the veil did not involve R being used as a facade concealing the true facts. If the veil was to be pierced, the person behind the company, rather than the company itself, had to be the relevant actor, *Antonio Gramsci Shipping Corp v Stepanovs* [2011] EWHC 333 (Comm), [2012] 1 All E.R. (Comm) 293, [2011] C.L.Y. 324 and *Alliance Bank JSC v Aquanta Corp* [2011] EWHC 3281 (Comm), [2012] 1 Lloyd's Rep. 181, [2012] C.L.Y. 475 doubted (paras 132-133, 137-148). (3) The worldwide freezing injunction against D4 would be discharged. The continuation of the injunction because of the appeals was highly unsatisfactory (paras 159-160). (4) It was disproportionate for parties to incur costs and spend many days on hearings concerning forum. Judges should invoke case management powers to ensure that applications were kept within proportionate bounds. If a defendant chose not to identify the nature of his case when challenging jurisdiction, the court could proceed on the basis that there was no more to the proceedings than would be involved in the claimant making out its case. Further, appellants should be discouraged from arguing the merits of an evaluative interlocutory decision (paras 81-94).

VTB CAPITAL PLC v NUTRITEK INTERNATIONAL CORP, [2013] UKSC 5, [2013] 2 A.C. 337, Lord Neuberger, J.S.C., SC.

473. Cross-border mergers–Approvals–Mergers by absorption of wholly-owned subsidiaries–Stage one requirements–Scope of court's task at stage one

[Companies (Cross-Border Mergers) Regulations 2007 (SI 2007/2974) reg.2, reg.6(2), reg.6, reg.7, reg.8, reg.10, reg.12, reg.16(1); Directive 2005/56 on cross-border mergers of limited liability companies.]

The applicant companies (L and G) applied for approval of pre-merger requirements for a cross-border merger between them under the Companies (Cross-Border Mergers) Regulations 2007 reg.6. L was a wholly-owned subsidiary of G, and although its head office, its employees and all its operations were in Germany it was an English company because when it was set up the requirements to do so for a limited liability company were much more onerous in Germany. G was a German holding company with no employees. The proposal was that G should acquire L, as "a merger by absorption of a wholly-owned subsidiary" under reg.2. L and G agreed draft terms and a directors' report was produced, with copies being sent to all L's employees, and a board resolution approved the merger. Copies of the report and the merger terms were available for inspection at L's registered office, and a notice was published in the London Gazette. The reg.6

application for a pre-merger certificate was issued, being the first of the two stages required by the Regulations that gave effect to Directive 2005/56]. The certificate was to be produced to the court in the country of the transferee company for approval of the merger. The Registrar had adjourned the case to the court because of issues arising, some of which had arisen in other cases, namely (i) whether to comply with the relevant provisions, particularly reg.7], reg.8], reg.10] and reg.12] the documents had to be accurate to a date falling within a given period leading up to the date of the hearing; (ii) where it appeared to the English court that the documents were so stale that there might have been material changes of circumstance; (iii) whether, in the light of the decision in *Diamond Resorts (Europe) Ltd, Re* [2012] EWHC 3576 (Ch), [2013] B.C.C. 275, [2013] 8 C.L. 52, the court should, before granting a pre-merger certificate, consider whether creditors would suffer material detriment such that the merger ought not to be approved, and if so, whether, on the evidence, the court might properly be satisfied that such creditors would not suffer.

Held: Application granted. (1) There was no specified or particular time limit for the various steps prescribed under reg.7, reg.8, reg.10 and reg.12, or for the preparation of an independent expert's report where applicable, but such documents could not be said to fulfil requirements no matter how stale they were. The six-month deadline for the production of the pre-merger certificate at stage two showed that the regulatory scheme could not be allowed to be very stale (see paras 19-20). (2) Where the requisite pre-merger documents were so old or where so much time had elapsed as to suggest material changes had occurred, the court would be entitled to view that as not constituting proper compliance. That did not involve a breach of legal certainty, but was simply applying a purposive construction to the requirements so that they could fulfil their intended role. That approach, though not applicable in the instant case, was supported by the provisions on the independent expert's report; it was a key point that the report was to give an opinion as to whether the methods to arrive at the share exchange ratio and values used were reasonable, and for that, the expert might need a fairly recent valuation of relevant companies (paras 21-22, 25). (3) *Diamond Resorts* dealt with reg.16(1) regarding approval at stage two, and the court found there was a discretion as to whether to approve the merger, which it had to consider exercising, and which involved a process of review over and above simply satisfying itself that the pre-merger steps had been undertaken, and a careful examination of whether the merger would cause stakeholders in the companies to suffer detriment. The wording of reg.16(1) was in contrast to reg.6(2) which only demanded fulfilment of the qualifying regulations. Therefore, *Diamond Resorts* did not apply when dealing with the stage one approval of the requirements, *Diamond Resorts*, distinguished. The task of the court at stage one was limited to ascertaining whether the regulatory requirements had been complied with, subject only to [DOCLINK DOC=AI0072974 TEXTeg.11] giving the court a discretion to order a meeting of creditors, and also, of members in the case of a merger by absorption of a wholly-owned subsidiary, as in the other two types of merger a meeting of members was mandatory under [DOCLINK DOC=AI0072974 TEXTeg.13] (paras 26-30). (4) The requirements under the Regulations had been satisfied in the instant case and it was appropriate to issue a reg.6 pre-merger certificate.

HOUSE-CLEAN LTD, *Re*; *sub nom.* HOUSE-CLEAN VERWALTUNGS GmbH, *Re*, [2013] EWHC 2337 (Ch), [2013] Bus. L.R. 1145, Roth, J., Ch D (Companies Ct).

474. Cross-border mergers–Discretionary powers–Pre-merger certification by foreign competent authority–English court scrutinising transaction–Scope of discretion in reg.16(1) Companies (Cross-Border Mergers) Regulations 2007

[Companies (Cross-Border Mergers) Regulations 2007 (SI 2007/2974) reg.16(1); Directive 2005/56 on cross-border mergers of limited liability companies.]

The applicant English resort company (D) applied jointly with 14 Spanish timeshare companies for approval of cross-border merger arrangements under the Companies (Cross-Border Mergers) Regulations 2007. D proposed to merge with the 14 Spanish companies. Once they were absorbed, D would assume their rights and liabilities, and their existence would be terminated following procedures under Spanish law. Under reg.16(1) the court had to consider whether to exercise its discretion to approve a merger. That exercise involved a review going beyond simply being satisfied that the pre-merger steps had been taken. D submitted that the court had to examine the proposed merger to see that it did not adversely affect any stakeholder in any of the merging companies, whether shareholder, employee or creditor, in any material way, and that there was no other good reason why approval should be refused.

Held: Application granted. D's submission had stated the correct test. To ensure proper review of stakeholder interests, the relevant foreign Member State had to nominate a competent authority to scrutinise the proposal, and Spain had exercised its discretion to nominate the Spanish Commercial Registry, which issued the certificates required by the Directive 2005/56 and the Regulations. According to its statutory accounts, D had been insolvent on a balance-sheet basis the year before and 13 of the 14 Spanish companies were solvent. A significant material detriment might be suffered by the creditors of those companies if the merger went ahead. The weight the court should accord to pre-merger certification given by a foreign competent authority under the Directive depended on the nature of the authority and the extent of any investigation it appeared to have made into the effects on stakeholders falling within its jurisdiction. It had not been confirmed that the Spanish Commercial Registry had the same status as a full court or that it had undertaken any substantive investigation into the merits of the merger from the stakeholders' point of view. Therefore, it was proper for the court to examine with care whether those stakeholders would suffer a material detriment such that the merger ought not to be approved. The object of the merger was to simplify the corporate structure of the group of companies to which D and the Spanish companies belonged, consolidating them operationally, with the view of enhancing synergy, simplifying procedures and administration, and reducing costs, which were entirely legitimate and proper objectives likely to be of benefit to all the companies. D's financial position had improved significantly in the current year as a result of capital injections, and the restated balance represented a fair and appropriate basis on which to make the assessment required under reg.16. Taking the companies as a whole, there would be an overall improvement if the merger were approved. On that basis there would not be a significant material detriment to the creditors of the Spanish companies or to the shareholders, employees or creditors of D. The merger was approved.

DIAMOND RESORTS (EUROPE) LTD, *Re*, [2012] EWHC 3576 (Ch), [2013] B.C.C. 275, Sales, J., Ch D (Companies Ct).

475. Directors–Appointments

[Senior Courts Act 1981 (c.54) s.37; Regulation 44/2001 on jurisdiction and the recognition and enforcement of judgments in civil and commercial matters Art.2(1), Art.22(2).]

The directors and a number of shareholders in a Cypriot company (U) applied for the appointment of a receiver to enable it to defend claims for damages in fraud proceedings brought by a bank (J). U was a party to the main proceedings (the "Chrysopa action") brought by J against an individual (MA) and several connected companies including U. Company law proceedings in Cyprus had determined the shareholding in U, whereupon the majority shareholders had appointed directors, who had in turn instructed solicitors (E) to defend the claim. There were ongoing proceedings in the Cypriot court in which MA and J challenged both the decision on shareholdings and the validity of the directors' appointments, in consequence of which, J had advised E that they might not have authority to act for U and were in danger of an action for damages for breach of warranty of authority. U submitted that unless the doubt was resolved, E would have to come off the record, leaving U without representation and at risk of substantial injustice. J contended that the application should be refused as the Cypriot court had exclusive jurisdiction. J referred to an identical application in the Cyprus court which had been abandoned a year before and claimed that the delay was fatal to the application.

Held: Application granted. The rules on jurisdiction in Regulation 44/2001 art.2(1) did not apply to the application as U was not seeking to "sue" J but was making an application in an action in which J was suing various parties, including U, in the English courts. The rules were engaged by the "Chrysopa action" in which J had sued several defendants including U and there was no dispute that the English court had jurisdiction in that action (see para.18 of judgment). Moreover the current application did not amount to "proceedings" for rights in rem for the purposes of art.22(2), because the relevant proceedings were those in the "Chrysopa action", in which there was no dispute either over the court's jurisdiction or over its power to appoint a receiver pursuant to the Senior Courts Act 1981 s.37 where it was just and convenient to do so. The application concerned the ability of one defendant to be represented at trial and, although it was made by persons not party to those proceedings, their standing to make the application had not been disputed (para.19). The court was not being asked to decide the identity of the shareholders, or whether the corporate directors had been validly appointed. Rather, the application was to appoint a receiver so that if the corporate directors had not been validly appointed, the receiver could confer authority on E to act. One of the purposes of the Regulation was to minimise the risk of irreconcilable judgments in different states, but there was no risk of conflict between the court and any decision which the Cypriot court might make (para.29). The similar application in Cyprus had been in respect of the Cypriot proceedings rather than for the limited purposes of the English claim, so, despite the delay, it was in the interests of justice that U be represented at trial.

JSC BTA BANK v ABLYAZOV, [2012] EWHC 2698 (Comm), [2012] I.L.Pr. 53, Teare, J., QBD (Comm).

476. Directors disqualification–Collective investment schemes–Individual acting as de facto or shadow director–Whether company operating unlawful collective investment scheme

[Company Directors Disqualification Act 1986 (c.46) s.6(3C), s.6, s.7(2A), s.22(5); Financial Services and Markets Act 2000 (c.8) s.235.]

The claimant secretary of state sought a disqualification order under the Company Directors Disqualification Act 1986 s.6 against the first defendant (C). A company (U) which had carried on business selling parcels of land to investors was investigated by the Financial Services Authority (FSA), who concluded that its operation of a collective investment scheme, which was a specified activity under the Financial Services and Markets Act 2000, without authorisation was unlawful. In 2008, U went into administration and then liquidation. The secretary of state issued proceedings against U's directors, but prior to trial five of the defendants agreed to give disqualification undertakings under s.7(2A) of the 1986 Act. The undertakings were accepted and the trial proceeded against C only. C disputed that he was or had acted as a director of U in the relevant period. The secretary of state accepted that C was not a de jure director, but contended that he was a de facto or shadow director, and that U had operated, to C's knowledge and at his ultimate direction, an unauthorised and prohibited collective investment scheme, and that C had caused U to make loans and pay dividends that were not in the interest of U and its customers.

Held: Judgment for claimant. (1) The purpose of a director's disqualification was to protect the public from unscrupulous corporate management. That objective would be frustrated if a person who was actually responsible for such management could escape disqualification by never formally being appointed a director. Section 6 of the 1986 Act extended to de facto directors, *Lo-Line Electric Motors Ltd, Re* [1988] Ch. 477, [1988] C.L.Y. 316 applied. A de facto director was so characterised by presuming to act as a director, being part of the corporate governing structure and directing the company's affairs in relation to the acts or conduct complained of. A shadow director was defined in s.22(5) of the 1986 Act, and s.6(3C) expressly provided that directors included shadow directors. A person could act as both a shadow and de facto director, *Secretary of State for Trade and Industry v Deverell* [2001] Ch. 340, [2000] C.L.Y. 658 followed. On the evidence, C was properly characterised as having acted as a de facto and a shadow director of U (see paras 24, 41-42, 44, 49 of judgment). (2) An unlawful collective investment scheme within the meaning of s.235 of the 2000 Act arose where an investment scheme's participants had no day-to-day control over the management of property, there was a pooling of the participants' contributions and the profits and income out of which payments were to be made to them, and the property was managed by or on behalf of the operator of the scheme, *Sky Land Consultants Plc, Re* [2010] EWHC 399 (Ch) applied. U's scheme and the manner in which it operated involved the collectivisation of plots of land with the objective of investment profit from the site, all managed by U. It therefore amounted to a collective investment scheme. C was well aware of the collectivised nature of what was offered and the FSA's concerns, but had sanctioned and encouraged U to proceed with it, acting in that regard as if he was U's managing or predominant director (paras 66-67, 124, 138). (3) On the evidence, C had procured U to make improper loans and dividends (para.168). (4) C's conduct constituted a sufficient departure from the standards to be expected of him to make him unfit to be concerned in the management of a company, and a disqualification order was therefore mandatory (paras 172, 175). (5) The appropriate period of disqualification in C's case was 12 years, *Sevenoaks Stationers (Retail) Ltd, Re* [1991] Ch. 164, [1991] C.L.Y. 401 followed (paras 176-181).

SECRETARY OF STATE FOR BUSINESS, INNOVATION AND SKILLS v CHOHAN; *sub nom.* UKLI LTD, *Re*, [2013] EWHC 680 (Ch), [2013] Lloyd's Rep. F.C. 351, Hildyard, J., Ch D (Companies Ct).

477. Directors disqualification–Misconduct–Failure to pay tax liabilities–Keeping Revenue and Customs fully informed–Extenuating circumstances

[Company Directors Disqualification Act 1986 (c.46) s.6.]

The appellant directors (C) appealed against disqualification orders made on the application of the respondent secretary of state under the Company Directors Disqualification Act 1986 s.6. C were directors of a company which supplied used printing machinery and sought to become the United Kingdom sales agent for overseas manufacturers of printing equipment. The company was 15 months in arrears with its payments to HM Revenue and Customs for PAYE and national insurance liabilities when it ceased trading, and the arrears amounted to £193,000. It went into liquidation six weeks later. The secretary of state applied for C's disqualification on grounds of unfitness. C's case was that, although they had not paid the tax liabilities as they fell due, they had kept the Revenue appropriately informed with sufficient accurate information with a view to agreeing to defer payment. The district judge held that they had discriminated against the Revenue by failing to pay their tax debts when from time to time they had money to do so, and failed to keep the Revenue fully informed of the company's position and prospects. He found that there were no exceptional extenuating circumstances. The judge upheld that decision. C submitted that the district judge had misdirected himself by introducing a test of exceptional circumstances when considering whether their misconduct led to a conclusion of unfitness; he had wrongly imposed a burden of proof on them to show that they had kept the Revenue fully informed; they were placed at a disadvantage because, through no fault of theirs, the company's files in relation to the Revenue were missing.

Held: Appeal dismissed. The task of the fact finder was to consider the evidence as a whole, including extenuating circumstances, and decide whether the director had fallen below the standards of probity and competence appropriate for persons fit to be directors of companies, *Grayan Building Services Ltd (In Liquidation), Re* [1995] Ch. 241, [1995] C.L.Y. 582 followed. The district judge did not depart from that test, but the use of the expression "exceptional circumstances" was better avoided, *Structural Concrete Ltd, Re* [2001] B.C.C. 578, [2000] C.L.Y. 664 considered. He had found misconduct in the treatment of the Revenue, and he had set against that the points in C's favour. He reached his conclusion on the evidence as a whole and was justified in finding that unfitness was established. The burden of proving misconduct was clearly on the secretary of state. If C sought to defeat the inference which arose from prolonged non-payment of tax and national insurance by demonstrating informed acceptance, or even forbearance, by the Revenue, it was for them to provide the evidence to do so. To that extent the onus of proving that the Revenue were kept appropriately informed was on C. The district judge took into account and assessed the disadvantages under which C were labouring. He also made substantial criticisms of the secretary of state's conduct in the litigation. Those considerations did not disentitle him, on the evidence, from making the findings he did, *Stakefields (Midlands) Ltd, Re* [2010] EWHC 2518 (Ch), [2011] Bus. L.R. 457, [2011] C.L.Y. 411 considered (see paras 46-63 of judgment).

CATHIE v SECRETARY OF STATE FOR BUSINESS, INNOVATION AND SKILLS, [2012] EWCA Civ 739, [2012] B.C.C. 813, Pill, L.J., CA (Civ Div).

478. Directors' powers and duties–Breach of fiduciary duty–Management of hedge funds–Whether fraud perpetrated by swap transactions and misrepresentations to investors

[Insolvency Act 1986 (c.45) s.423.]

The claimant company (W) and its liquidators (L) sought relief under the Insolvency Act 1986 against personnel involved in running W. The first defendant (D1), who was W's chief executive and managing director, had incorporated another company (X) to carry on business as a hedge fund, managed by W. He subsequently caused another hedge fund (M) to be incorporated, also managed by W. Within M's first month of trading, it lost over 19 per cent of its assets by value in exchange trading. D1 caused M to enter into two over-the-counter options on forward rate agreements with X, whereby M's loss was converted on paper into profit. Thereafter, D1 caused M to enter into further over-the-counter trades in forward rate agreements with X. M later entered into swap transactions with X and appeared to investors to be successful. Following difficult market conditions, M experienced a high volume of redemption requests, which it was unable to meet. Accountants discovered that M's asset valuation was over-inflated. M and W went into liquidation. W and L issued claims in fraud against D1 and the tenth defendant (D10), who was a senior and highly paid employee of W. The second defendant (D2), who was D1's wife and a director of W, was accused of negligently permitting the alleged fraud to happen. The same was alleged against the ninth defendant (D9), another director. There were also outstanding claims against the third to the seventh defendants (D3), who were the recipients of transfers made by D1. The claim against the eighth defendant, another recipient of funds, was settled. It fell to be determined whether a fraud had been perpetrated by the swaps and representations made to investors in M's offering memorandum and due diligence questionnaires, and whether the swaps were sham transactions or honest trades entered into as part of an honest trading strategy.

Held: Judgment for claimants in part. (1) On the evidence, the swaps had consistently been wrongly valued and there were serious flaws in the way the paperwork for the swaps had been dealt with. There were deficiencies in the swap tickets: they had been prepared in a "slapdash fashion". The trade confirmations for the swaps were also defective. The reason for the discrepancies might have been that in many instances the swap documentation was backdated, not just by a few days, but sometimes by several months. That was not standard industry practice. The backdating of the documents also gave rise to the inference that the trades were not genuine and that production of documentation after the event gave D1 the benefit of hindsight as to what swap positions would produce the best effect on M's reported profits. There was also some suggestion that signatures had been forged. Further, the offering memorandum contained a number of misrepresentations and the due diligence questionnaires contained several misleading statements. The actual risks were completely different from the picture presented. In all the circumstances, the swaps had never been intended to be enforceable instruments, but were simply used to manipulate figures to give the impression to investors that M was successful. The swaps were shams, *Snook v London and West Riding Investments Ltd* [1967] 2 Q.B. 786, [1967] C.L.Y. 1836 followed (see paras 106, 110, 112, 114, 116-117, 122-129, 139, 142-143 of judgment). (2) D1 was liable for breach of his fiduciary duties to W as a director and in the tort of deceit (para.147). (3) The test for D2's liability was whether she had done what a reasonable director of a hedge fund management company in her position, with her experience, actual knowledge and intelligence should have done, and whether she acquired a sufficient knowledge of W's business to discharge her duties. She did not meet that test (para.174). (4) D9 was in breach of his duties to W as director by failing to acquire sufficient knowledge and understanding of its business and failing to satisfy himself as to the details and propriety of the swaps. He was also liable in negligence for failing to act with reasonable care, skill and diligence and for negligently making false representations to investors (paras 182-183, 189). (5) D10 had been over-promoted and had accepted everything that D1 had told him as to trade customs, compensation, authorisation and the like. Although not fraudulent, D10 had plainly been negligent. It was an implied term of his contract with W that he would perform his duties with proper care. D10 was therefore not liable to W for dishonest assistance but liable in negligence (paras 207-210). (6) With one exception, relating to a single payment of £85,000, D1's transfer of assets to D3 were made out of moneys he held on constructive trust for W. Those payments were, accordingly, made in fraud of creditors under s.423 of the Act (para.243). (7) W and L had, accordingly, made out their claims with the exception of the claims in fraud against D10 and the claim in respect of the payment of £85,000 by D1 (para.246).

WEAVERING CAPITAL (UK) LTD (IN LIQUIDATION) v DABHIA; *sub nom.* WEAVERING CAPITAL (UK) LTD (IN LIQUIDATION) v PETERSON, [2012] EWHC 1480 (Ch), [2012] Lloyd's Rep. F.C. 561, Proudman, J., Ch D.

479. Directors' powers and duties–Breach of fiduciary duty–Preferences–Directors' duty to disclose misconduct–Application of Item Software (UK) Ltd v Fassihi [2004] EWCA Civ 1244, [2004] B.C.C. 994

[Companies Act 2006 (c.46) s.172, s.1157(1); Insolvency Act 1986 (c.45) s.239.]

The claimant company (G) sought relief against its former directors (M), the first and second defendants. It also sought relief from the third defendant company (Brocade), of which M were the sole directors, and from the fourth defendant (L). M owned several European clothing companies, which included G and Brocade. In 2004, M approached a family friend (B) for a loan. It was agreed in February 2005 that B would buy a £1 million shareholding in G and retain M as salaried directors. Over the years, B loaned M an additional £577,500. By May 2007, B had lost confidence in M and decided to close G's shops. Shortly before being suspended as directors, M sold G's stock to Brocade as a means of repaying themselves for a personal loan which was still outstanding. At the instant hearing, the court was required to make factual findings in order to determine the respective entitlements and liabilities of M and G. Those issues included M's use of their directors' loan account while directors of G, the effect of various commercial transactions and transfers between M's businesses, and whether relief pursuant to the Companies Act 2006 s.1157(1) should be ordered. The court was also required to determine issues concerning M's wrongdoing, namely (i) whether M's sale of G's stock to Brocade shortly before their removal as directors involved a breach of duty because they had acted to advance their own interests rather than those of G, and (ii) whether M's failure to disclose their wrongdoing to B as G's shareholder meant that G could recover remuneration paid to them.

Held: Judgment accordingly. After determining the factual issues on the basis that M were unreliable witnesses whose honesty was flawed and whose evidence was to be treated with great caution, the court went on to determine the issues concerning M's wrongdoing. (1) Whilst the interests of a company were normally identified with those of its members, creditors' interests were relevant if the company was in financial difficulties, *Liquidator of West Mercia Safetywear Ltd v Dodd* (1988) 4 B.C.C. 30, [1988] C.L.Y. 308, *Colin Gwyer & Associates Ltd v London Wharf (Limehouse) Ltd* [2002] EWHC 2748 (Ch), [2003] B.C.C. 885, [2003] C.L.Y. 521, *Knight v Frost* [1999] B.C.C. 819, [1999] C.L.Y. 628 and *Singer v Beckett* [2007] 2 B.C.L.C. 287, [2001] C.L.Y. 728 applied. In such a situation, the duty in the Companies Act 2006 s.172 applied similarly to the interests of creditors as a class. Advancing the interests of a particular creditor without believing the action to be in the interests of creditors as a class was a breach of that duty, even if, in the case of preferences, the conditions laid down in the Insolvency Act 1986 s.239 were not all met. A company seeking redress in respect of a "preference" outside s.239 needed to show that (a) it had suffered loss; (b) the director had profited; (c) the transaction was not binding on the company. The first two requirements could be problematic if the "preference" did not show on the company's balance sheet and if the company had not entered an insolvency regime. With regard to the third requirement, a company could disavow on ordinary agency principles a contract entered into by a director, but a better view was to consider the contract voidable where notice of it had been given to the company's members or creditors, in which case rescission might be a possible form of relief, *O'Sullivan v Management Agency and Music Ltd* [1985] Q.B. 428, [1984] C.L.Y. 388 considered. In the instant case, M had acted in breach of their duties as directors of G. The stock transaction had occurred when G was in financial difficulty and it had therefore been incumbent on M to have regard to G's creditors. They had pursued repayment of their own loan despite having been told that it was not acceptable to do so, and in the knowledge that B wanted them to resign as directors. As M were also directors of Brocade, the latter had had the requisite notice of the breach of duty, and the contract was therefore void (see paras 162-180 of judgment). (2) A director's duty of good faith potentially required him to disclose misconduct, *Item Software (UK) Ltd v Fassihi* [2004] EWCA Civ 1244, [2004] B.C.C. 994, [2005] C.L.Y. 524 applied. That decision made it clear that the duty of good faith focused on a fiduciary's subjective intentions. The question was not whether disclosure was in the interests of the shareholder, but what the director had thought was in the company's interests. On the facts and evidence, G had not made out its case on non-disclosure of wrongdoing to B (paras 181-207).

GHLM TRADING LTD v MAROO, [2012] EWHC 61 (Ch), [2012] 2 B.C.L.C. 369, Newey, J, Ch D.

480. Public companies–Re-registration–Standing of indirect investors to challenge re-registration

[Companies Act 2006 (c.46) s.98, Pt 9, s.145.]

The defendant companies (W and D) applied for summary judgment in respect of an application made by the three claimants (E) under the Companies Act 2006 s.98. D had been incorporated in England as a public company but it was managed and operated from Germany and its shares were only listed for trading on German exchanges. E claimed to be minority shareholders of D, holding between them some 6 per cent of its issued shares. In April 2011, D announced its intention to make a dividend distribution to shareholders. However, at the annual general meeting held in June 2011 the proposed dividend distribution was rejected by a majority of the shareholders. The majority votes were cast by W and by another company acting in concert. Shortly thereafter, W acquired from third parties or had transferred to it sufficient shares to be able to exercise more than 75 per cent of the votes, enough to secure the passing of a special resolution. In May 2012, the new board announced its intention to propose at the annual general meeting the cancellation of the listing of D's shares on all German exchanges and its re-registration as a private limited company. The intimation of such a proposal had a negative impact on the marketability of D's shares. E began proceedings alleging that their aggregate holding of D's shares gave them standing to apply under s.98 for the cancellation of the resolution for the re-registration of D as a private company. D's share register recorded only two registered shareholders, being an individual and a bank (B). B acted as the common depository agent of the issued shares in D, holding those shares on trust for the holders of accounts with an entity called Clearstream. Clearstream was the clearing and settlement division of Deutsche Borse, through which trades on the relevant exchange between Clearstream account-holders were transacted electronically. The Clearstream account-holders had to be banks or financial institutions. E were customers of those account-holders, being "end investors" in D. W argued that, for the purposes of s.98, E did not qualify as "holders" of not less than 5 per cent in aggregate of N's issued share capital and so lacked standing to make the application.

Held: Application granted. E did lack standing. The architecture of company law employed the concept of "member" or "shareholder" as a key element. A "shareholder" or "the holder of a share" was one (and only one) whose name was registered in the register of members. The 2006 Act proceeded entirely on that basis. When s.98 referred to "the holders of not less in the aggregate than 5% in nominal value of the company's issued share capital", the "holders" it was referring to were those who were registered as the members holding those shares, not the persons who owned the ultimate economic interest in shares registered in somebody else's name. The structure of the Act was such that where a right was directly enforceable by a non-member, specific provision was made. Such conclusions were supported by the Explanatory Notes to the Act and by commentators, none of whom had suggested that s.98 applied not to the holders of shares but to the holders of economic interests in them. Further, Pt 9 of the Act did not avail E: D's articles conferred no rights on the customers, such as E, of the account-holders. Section 145 of the Act represented a modest step for the protection of indirect investors but it did not confer rights enforceable against D by anyone other than the two registered shareholders. In the circumstances, E's claim had no real prospect of success. Such a reading of the Act deprived E as indirect investors of the sort of protection which those who formulated the 2006 Act thought ought to be extended to minority shareholders. That was not a particularly comfortable conclusion, but reaching any other conclusion would involve "an impermissible form of judicial legislation" (see paras 17-19, 22-26, 31 of judgment).

ECKERLE v WICKEDER WESTFALENSTAHL GmbH; *sub nom.* DNICK HOLDING PLC, *Re*, [2013] EWHC 68 (Ch), [2013] 3 W.L.R. 1316, Norris, J., Ch D.

481. Reflective losses–Debenture holders–Rule against reflective loss–Whether action by secured debenture holder offending rule

The appellants (L and C) appealed against a decision of a district judge striking out their claims on the basis that losses claimed offended the rule against reflective loss. The first appellant (L) operated a leisure resort, providing short-term lettings of holiday accommodation and timeshare lettings. The second appellant lender (C) provided funding to L under the terms of a debenture and legal mortgage. L's business failed, and C appointed the fourth respondent administrative receiver (K). C was dissatisfied with the way in which K conducted the receivership. Both C and L commenced separate proceedings, each claim mirroring the relief sought in the other, and each alleged various breaches of the receiver's duties. A district judge made an order that sought to consolidate the claims, and ordered that L's claim be the lead claim. K, and the third respondent solicitors' firm, successfully applied to strike out C's claim, a district judge holding that C's claims, as a secured debenture holder, offended against the reflective loss rule. The issues were (i) the nature of the primary duty owed by an administrative receiver; (ii) whether the no reflective loss rule extended to cover the claims of a secured creditor; (iii) whether rights to sums payable to L assigned to C meant that C had a vested cause of action that ought not be struck out.

Held: Appeal allowed. (1) The primary duty owed by an administrative receiver was to the appointing debenture holder and not to the company, *B Johnson & Co (Builders) Ltd, Re* [1955] Ch. 634, [1955] C.L.Y. 343 considered. None of the duties owed to a company could restrict the primary duty of a receiver to protect, and act in the best interests of, his appointor, even if that were to cause damage to the company. It followed that so long as a receiver acted in good faith it was unlikely that the duties he owed to a company would be wider in ambit than those he owed to a debenture holder [*Downsview Nominees Ltd v First City Corp Ltd* [1993] A.C. 295, [1993] C.L.Y. 2881 and *Medforth v Blake* [2000] Ch. 86, [1999] C.L.Y. 3286 considered. As an administrative receiver's primary duty was to bring about a situation in which the secured debt could be repaid, a receiver owed no duties whatsoever to a company's unsecured creditors (see paras 28-30, 32 of judgment). (2) Nothing required the extension of the no reflective loss rule to cover the position of a secured creditor; a secured creditor's position, such as C's position as debenture holder, was fundamentally distinct from that of a shareholder who sought to sue for loss primarily belonging to and suffered by a company as the primary loss in C's case belonged to C, the legal person to whom an administrative receiver's primary duties were owed, *Johnson* considered. Furthermore, issues of causation and policy considerations underpinning the no reflexive loss rule were absent in the instant case. Moreover, the court's need to be astute to ensure that a party who had suffered loss was not arbitrarily denied fair compensation mandated that C's claims not be struck out, Johnson applied. The positions of an unsecured creditor and a secured creditor were fundamentally different, *Gardner v Parker* [2004] EWCA Civ 781, [2005] B.C.C. 46, [2005] C.L.Y. 520 considered (paras 37-42, 44, 46). (3) Sums due to C under the assignment agreement meant that C had a cause of action in respect of those sums that vested solely in C. Those claims ought not be struck out (para.50).

INTERNATIONAL LEISURE LTD v FIRST NATIONAL TRUSTEE CO UK LTD, [2012] EWHC 1971 (Ch), [2013] Ch. 346, Edward Bartley Jones Q.C., Ch D.

482. Register of Companies–Restoration–Practice Note issued

[Companies Act 2006 (c.46) s.1029, s.1030; Insolvency Act 1986 (c.45) s.108; Third Parties (Rights against Insurers) Act 1930 (c.25).]

Held: Practice Note issued. A Practice Note was issued concerning applications under the Companies Act 2006 s.1029 for an order restoring the name of a company to the register. With effect from January 1, 2013 applications for orders of this type issued in the High Court in London would be given a return date three months from the date of issue. If the matter was not dealt with before or at the first hearing, the claimant would have to apply in writing or in person at the hearing for the application to be stood over to a later date, giving reasons why a further hearing was required. If an adjournment was granted, unless there was reason to the contrary, it would be for a further three months, when attendance might be required. Normally no further adjournment would be granted; if a further adjournment was required, there would need to be attendance at the hearing and sufficient cause established from the evidence in support to be filed not less than three days before that hearing. Where the requirements of the Registrar of Companies had been met and the Treasury Solicitor was able to approve the application before the date for the first hearing, a consent order could be filed for the court's approval without attendance. The documents which had to accompany the consent order were set out. They included a witness statement, which should include the following information: the reason why the claimant had the right to make the application; the circumstances in which and the reason(s) why the company's name had been struck off the register; the reason(s) for the application; any factors arising with regard to time limits in s.1030 of the Act; where the claimant was a director or member of the company, the financial position of the company at the time of its dissolution and (if different) its financial position at the time of its restoration; what was intended for the company and its assets and liabilities when it was restored; and any further matters relevant to the making of the application and to the future of the company if restored. Where the company was in liquidation at the date of dissolution and the liquidator had vacated office, unless the Third Parties (Rights against Insurers) Act 1930 was relied on for the purposes of the proposed application, the application for restoration should include an application for the appointment of a liquidator under the Insolvency Act 1986 s.108 and a letter from the proposed liquidator consenting to act. If the liquidator proposed was different from the liquidator who had vacated office, evidence would be required to explain why. The consent of the Registrar of Companies to the proposed appointment should not be sought.

PRACTICE NOTE (CH D: COMPANIES CT: CLAIMS FOR AN ORDER RESTORING THE NAME OF A COMPANY TO THE REGISTER) [2012] B.C.C. 880, Chief Registrar Baister, Ch D (Companies Ct).

483. Register of Companies–Restoration–Whether claim brought against dissolved company validated by subsequent restoration to register under s.1029 Companies Act 2006–Whether s.1032(1) having retrospective effect

[Companies Act 1948 (c.38); Companies Act 2006 (c.46) s.1029, s.1030, s.1032(2), s.1032(3); Companies Act 1985 (c.6) s.653; Civil Procedure Rules 1998 (SI 1998/3132) r.3.4(2)(b).]

The appellant company (P) appealed against the setting aside of an order striking out a personal injury claim brought against it by the respondent J, a former employee. P had been struck off the register of companies and dissolved in March 2009. In August 2009, J purportedly issued proceedings against P claiming damages for noise-induced hearing loss. In June 2010 he obtained an order under the Companies Act 2006 s.1029 restoring P to the register of companies. In obtaining that order he made no reference to the fact that he had already commenced proceedings against P. P did not, however, appeal against that order. Instead, it successfully applied to strike out J's personal injury claim as an abuse of process under CPR r.3.4(2)(b). The order striking out J's claim was subsequently set aside and P appealed, seeking its reinstatement. Its case was that because it had been dissolved when J issued his claim, that claim was a nullity and was not validated retrospectively by the s.1029 order. The central issue was whether an order made pursuant to s.1029 had the effect of retrospectively validating an action purportedly commenced against a company during the period of its dissolution. The answer depended on the meaning and effect of s.1032(1) of the Act.

Held: Appeal dismissed. The effect of s.1032(1) was retrospectively to validate an action purportedly commenced by, or against, a company during the period of its dissolution. In enacting the 2006 Act, Parliament had assimilated into a single procedure the two previously existing routes to the judicial restoration of a dissolved or struck-off company, and it had applied to the new procedure the principle to be found in s.1032(1) of the 2006 Act. In using precisely the same language in s.1032(1) as had previously appeared in the Companies Act 1985 s.653, Parliament was plainly seeking to carry forward, albeit in a wider context, the principle it had repeatedly used in successive Companies Acts for over a century. The pre-2006 jurisprudence was not only relevant, but was also determinative. The crucial decision was that of the Court of Appeal in *Tymans v Craven* [1952] 2 Q.B. 100, [1952] C.L.Y. 480, which elucidated and explained the meaning and effect of s.1032(1) in just the same way as it did the meaning and effect of Companies Act 1948 s.353, and thus s.653 of the 1985 Act. It mattered not that in *Tymans* the company was the claimant, whereas in the instant case it was the defendant; in each situation the purported proceedings were a nullity because one of the parties did not exist, *Tymans* applied (see paras 41-43, 49 of judgment). Moreover, the words "general effect" in s.1032(1) could not be read, as urged by P, as cutting down the otherwise unrestricted language of the subsection. The words signalled that the "general" provision in s.1032(1) was subject to what followed in s.1032(2) and s.1032(3). Nor was s.1032(1) to be read down by reference to s.1029 or s.1030. Those sections dealt only with the application for an order, and not with its effect. There were many different forensic routes to the making of an order, and the precise route taken in any particular case could not affect the meaning and effect of the order once it was made; that was spelled out by s.1032(1). The sweeping effect of s.1032(1) was illustrated by s.1032(3), which enabled the court to make directions "for placing the company and all other persons in the same position (as nearly as may be) as if the company had not been dissolved or struck off the register." That was a powerful and illuminating indication of the policy that Parliament had in mind. Finally, there was nothing in the point made by P that even if the effect of the order was retrospectively to validate the issue of the proceedings, it did not retrospectively validate their service. The effect of s.1032(1) was to retrospectively validate service (paras 44-48).

PEAKTONE LTD v JODDRELL; *sub nom.* JODDRELL v PEAKTONE LTD, [2012] EWCA Civ 1035, [2013] 1 W.L.R. 784, Etherton, L.J., CA (Civ Div).

484. Share valuation–Directions–Order requiring 50:50 shareholder to purchase other shareholder's shares following unfairly prejudicial conduct–Directions for ascertaining fair value of shares

[Companies Act 2006 (c.46) s.994; Senior Courts Act 1981 (c.54) s.35A.]

The appellant (M) appealed against a judge's directions for ascertaining the fair value of the shares in a property investment company (C) held by the respondent (X). M and X had effectively been 50:50 shareholders in C. X brought a petition for relief from unfair prejudice under the Companies Act 2006 s.994, and succeeded on the ground that M, as sole director, had procured C to transfer its entire portfolio of properties to him at an undervalue. The judge ordered M to purchase X's shares in C and made directions for ascertaining the fair value of those shares. He chose a valuation date which preceded the transfer of the properties and ordered that X should receive an award of "quasi-interest" on the price of his shares from that date, in order to compensate him for loss of the use of the money in the meantime. He awarded quasi-interest at the rate of 2 per cent over the Bank of England base rate from 2005 to 2008, and 3 per cent over from 2008 to 2012. He directed that the contingent liability for corporation tax payable on the disposal of the properties should be valued at the amount actually paid as tax by C on the disposal at an undervalue to M. He also decided that no deduction should be made for the costs of selling the properties, as such a deduction would have been a windfall for M. M submitted that (1) instead of directing a valuation of X's shares on a going concern business, the judge should have directed a valuation on a "break-up" basis, given his earlier finding that M should not have transferred the properties to himself without seeking X's agreement or putting C into liquidation; (2) in relation to corporation tax liability, the judge should have used a figure which was an estimate of the tax which would be payable if the properties were sold at valuation; (3) the rate for the award of quasi-interest was excessive.

Held: Appeal allowed in part. (1) There was no inflexible rule that only in a quasi-partnership case could the court order a valuation on a going concern basis. A valuation on a break-up basis would ignore the fact that M had acquired the assets, and would mean that M would receive the difference between the going concern value of C and its break-up value. He would therefore receive a windfall at the expense of X, *CVC/Opportunity Equity Partners Ltd v Demarco Almeida* [2002] UKPC 16, [2002] B.C.C. 684 considered (see paras 11-14 of judgment). (2) In valuing a contingent liability, the court should take into account events subsequent to the valuation date which shed light on its value, *Bwllfa and Merthyr Dare Steam Collieries (1891) Ltd v Pontypridd Waterworks Co* [1903] A.C. 426 followed. The judge had had that well-known principle in mind, and had been entitled on the facts of the case to rule that the actual corporation tax paid was a suitable deduction for the purpose of achieving fair value, *Shah v Shah* [2011] EWHC 1902 (Ch), [2012] W.T.L.R. 165, [2012] C.L.Y. 513 considered (paras 19-21). (3) The judge clearly saw the award of quasi-interest as an essential part of the relief granted. He had a discretion as to the rate to be awarded, and had to exercise caution so as not to overcompensate X. The rate he ultimately ordered was a rate often ordered under the Senior Courts Act 1981 s.35A. There was no error of law, nor any other basis for interfering with the judge's decision on the rates applicable to the award of quasi-interest (paras 31-36). (4) The judge should have ordered that there should be a deduction for the costs of selling the properties to reflect the fact that C could never have realised any value from the properties without paying those costs. The judge held that the appropriate rate for selling costs was 1.5 per cent. The liability for selling costs should be valued by applying the rate of 1.5 per cent to the actual sale proceeds on the sale to M. C had already disposed of the properties at an undervalue to M. C would never incur the costs of selling the properties at their agreed values, and any further disposal by M was uncertain. To make a deduction on the basis of the agreed values of the properties would confer a windfall on M (paras 25-26).

ANNACOTT HOLDINGS LTD, *Re; sub nom.* ATTWOOD v MAIDMENT, [2013] EWCA Civ 119, [2013] 2 B.C.L.C. 46, Arden, L.J., CA (Civ Div).

485. Unfairly prejudicial conduct–Directors' remuneration–Company director's excessive remuneration discoverable upon inspection of company accounts–Finding excessive remuneration not unfairly prejudicial to shareholder–Impermissible imposition of requirement for diligence on shareholders

[Companies Act 2006 (c.46) s.994.]

The appellant (M) appealed against a decision ([2011] EWHC 2186 (Ch)) dismissing his shareholder's petition for relief from unfairly prejudicial conduct by the respondent (Y). M owned 25 per cent of the share capital in a company (T) and the remainder was mostly held by Y, who was T's sole director. T had traded as an estate agency under the name "Oliver Jaques". When it entered creditors' voluntary liquidation, its business was carried on by a company (E) owned in part by Y. M issued an unfair prejudice petition under the Companies Act 2006 s.994 alleging that T's affairs had been conducted by Y in a manner which was unfairly prejudicial to him. M contended that Y had permitted E to trade as "Oliver Jaques" at a time when T had also been trading under that name without requiring any payment from E for its use, that Y had caused T to pay him excessive remuneration, and that when T was known to be proceeding towards insolvent liquidation, he had caused it to transfer its business and its goodwill in the name "Oliver Jaques" to E for only £5,000, which was paid to the liquidator in order to fund her putting T into liquidation. The judge found that Y's remuneration was excessive, but that since that had been clearly disclosed in T's accounts and had been unchallenged by M, it would not be proper to treat it as unfairly prejudicial to T's interests. The judge found that Y had also acted in breach of the duties he owed to T as a director by setting up E in order to open estate agencies trading under the "Oliver Jaques" name, but that because those offices were unprofitable, no loss was suffered by T as a result and that could not, therefore, constitute a ground of unfair prejudice. The judge also held that whilst E's acquisition of T's business name, trade connections and other assets was a matter of prejudice, given T's financial state M had suffered no relevant unfair prejudice for the purposes of s.994. He therefore dismissed M's petition. It fell to be determined whether the judge had been correct in law to rule that there had been no "unfair prejudice" for the purposes of s.994.

Held: Appeal allowed. (1) The judge's conclusion that Y's excessive remuneration was not unfairly prejudicial because M could have found the information about the excessive remuneration by inspecting T's accounts was wrong in principle since it involved a new restriction on the manner in which shareholders could enforce the liability of directors for wrongs to their company. The judge's approach meant that minority shareholders were at risk of losing their rights to enforce a director's liability to their company if they did not read their company's filed accounts. That imposed a requirement for diligence that had no basis in the statutory provisions or in principle or authority. M's appeal had to be allowed on the first ground (see paras 31-32 of judgment). (2) There was a real prospect that the claim based on excessive remuneration could lead to the grant of relief even though M did not adduce expert evidence as to how T's loss should be quantified at the liability trial. There were ample grounds on which the judge could have concluded that Y's remuneration was out of the norm for that particular company, and in that sense (if no other) that the remuneration was excessive. In the circumstances, it was just and convenient to remit the issue of the quantification of the element of Y's remuneration to a quantum hearing (paras 48-49). (3) By not negotiating a licence fee from E for use of the "Oliver Jaques" name, Y had failed to protect the interests of T as he was bound to do in order to discharge his duties as its director. The correct measure of loss for that prejudice was the amount that T would have received if Y and E had negotiated at arm's length for a licence for E to use T's trading name for the period 2005 to 2008 (para.53). (4) Y was clearly responsible in law for fixing the price of £5,000 for the eve of liquidation sale of T's assets, including its trading name, to E in his capacity as T's sole director, and he had not discharged his duties as a director in fixing it. Y had fixed it not by reference to T's best interests but by reference to the estimate of the sum that needed to be injected into T so that a meeting of creditors could be called and T put into voluntary liquidation. The question of the value of the claim arising out of that breach of duty would also be remitted to a further hearing (paras 56-57).

ANNACOTT HOLDINGS LTD, *Re; sub nom.* TOBIAN PROPERTIES LTD, RE; ATTWOOD v MAIDMENT; MAIDMENT v ATTWOOD, [2012] EWCA Civ 998, [2013] Bus. L.R. 753, Arden, L.J., CA (Civ Div).

486. Unfairly prejudicial conduct–Joint shareholders–Equal shareholder issuing petition alleging unfair prejudice–Fairness of continuing to prosecute petition despite refusal to accept offers to purchase shares

The applicants (K and S) applied for an order that the unfair prejudice petition brought by the respondent (H) be struck out as an abuse of process, or for summary judgment in their favour. S was a private company whose shares were registered in H's name. H held half the shares as nominee for one individual (M) and the other half as nominee for K. M and K each owned companies and in 2001 they incorporated S as a joint-venture company to provide their services together. K became a director of S and was to receive a salary, but it was agreed that he and M would operate S jointly and, as shareholders, each would receive dividends. In 2010 K informed M that since S had received little return business from M's company, S would no longer utilise its services, that S was unlikely to declare any dividends in the current or next financial year, and that it would be in S's best interests if M no longer remained a shareholder and that K was willing to purchase his shareholding. M was also to be excluded from any participation in S's management. M indicated his concern that K's threatened actions would unfairly prejudice M's interests as shareholder. The parties were unable to agree a price for M's shares in S and M raised the issue of appointing an accountant, agreed by both parties, to value S's assets and determine the share price. K informed M that, where an offer was made by the majority shareholder in the format set out in *O'Neill v Phillips* [1999] 1 W.L.R. 1092, [1999] C.L.Y. 634, in that there was an offer to purchase shares at a fair value which, if not agreed, should be determined by a competent expert, that would negate any claim for unfair prejudice and any petition M presented would be liable to be struck out or stayed with him suffering the costs consequences associated with that. Offers and counter-offers followed, expressed to be made in the *O'Neill* format, but there was no agreement and M, through H, issued his petition alleging unfair prejudice affecting his shareholding in S. K and S contended that M's refusal to accept K's offers to purchase his shares in S was unreasonable and that, consequently, the continued prosecution of the petition was either an abuse or was bound to fail, in accordance with the principles established in *O'Neill*.

Held: Application refused. The guidance in *O'Neill* did not have the status of legislation. The correspondence and argument between the parties in the instant case, and K's reference to an offer in the "*O'Neill* format" appeared to approach the matter as if what had to be considered was the extent to which the offer made complied with those guidelines, and that if a sufficient degree of compliance was achieved, K would inevitably be protected from any petition that M might issue. That was a cardinal error. The question for the court was always whether in all the circumstances of the case the applicant had satisfied the conditions required to have the petition struck out, or summary judgment in his favour given on it, in that it had been shown that the continued prosecution of the petition after the making of the offer amounted to an abuse of process, or was bound to fail. The issue was highly sensitive to the facts and circumstances of each case, and consideration of the nature and terms of any offer made could only ever be an intermediate step in the process. One obvious difference between the instant case and *O'Neill* was that M was not a minority shareholder but an equal 50 per cent shareholder, and in such cases it was by no means obvious which of two equal shareholders should sell to the other, *O'Neill* distinguished. The reasoning in *O'Neill* expressly concerned cases where there was a majority shareholder. In the case of equal shareholders, particularly if they were quasi partners as in the instant case, there was a clear potential for injustice if one of them was able to seize de facto control of the company and effectively force the other either to accept his offer to buy or be forever excluded from the participation that he bargained for and cut out from any remedy in respect of what would be a continuing breach of the quasi partnership arrangement originally made. The real question in the instant case was whether M had been offered a sale on terms that gave him all the advantages he could reasonably expect to achieve from the petition proceedings: if so, it would then be an abuse to continue those proceedings in the face of such an offer. In all the circumstances, the court could not be satisfied that that requirement had been met since M might well obtain an order which was more advantageous to him in material respects than the offers made (see paras 26-27, 35, 47 of judgment).

HARBORNE ROAD NOMINEES LTD v KARVASKI, [2011] EWHC 2214 (Ch), [2012] 2 B.C.L.C. 420, David Cooke, HHJ, Ch D (Birmingham).

COMPETITION LAW

487. Abuse of dominant position–Compensatory damages–Price for common carriage supply of water–Assessment of lost profit and lost chance of another customer–Appropriateness of exemplary damages

[Competition Act 1998 (c.41) s.47A.]

The claimant water company (C) claimed damages against the defendant water utility company (D) pursuant to the Competition Act 1998 s.47A. The tribunal had previously determined that the access price at which D was offering a common carriage service to carry water through its pipes from a pumping station to the premises of C's customer Shotton Paper was an abuse of its dominant position in the market. C submitted that (1) if D had not abused its position C would have accepted the offer of a reasonable price for common carriage and would have supplied water to Shotton Paper more profitably than it had done; (2) C would have won a contract with another customer, Corus; (3) D's conduct justified an award of exemplary damages.

Held: Damages assessed. (1) To calculate whether C had suffered any loss it was necessary to determine what C's costs of supply would have been, what income it would have received, and what part of any loss was attributable to D's infringement. There was a range of lawful access prices that D could have offered and the figure in the middle of that range should be taken, rather than an access price which was the highest it could lawfully have charged, *South Australia Asset Management Corp v York Montague Ltd* [1997] A.C. 191, [1996] C.L.Y. 4519 applied. The evidence was that C would have accepted a common carriage price, even one above what it thought was justifiable. Where a dominant undertaking offered an unlawfully abusive price, the loss caused by that price could continue until it withdrew it and offered a new price directly to the victim of the abuse. In the instant case damages would be awarded from the date that common carriage would have begun, being seven weeks after the offer in April 2001, to the date of the new price offer in November 2008 (see paras 71, 77, 169, 175 of judgment). (2) When assessing the loss of chance that C would have contracted with Corus it was necessary to draw a careful distinction between questions of causation and quantification, *Allied Maples Group Ltd v Simmons & Simmons* [1995] 1 W.L.R. 1602, [1996] C.L.Y. 4489 applied. The quantum was the relevant percentage of profit that would have been made if C had won the business. On the balance of probabilities, but for D's abusive conduct, C would have tendered for the Corus contract. It was foreseeable that, by offering an abusive access price and thereby preventing C from pursuing its business under a common carriage arrangement, C would be hampered in the development of its business. It was highly likely that C would have been awarded a contract to supply, but that could not be put as high as being a certainty or a near certainty, so it was appropriate to reduce damages for lost opportunity by one third, *Maden v Clifford Coppock & Carter* [2004] EWCA Civ 1037, [2005] 2 All E.R. 43, [2005] C.L.Y. 2880 applied. Simple interest was awarded at 2 per cent over base rate, *2 Travel Group Plc (In Liquidation) v Cardiff City Transport Services Ltd* [2012] CAT 19, [2012] Comp. A.R. 211, [2012] C.L.Y. 521 applied (see paras 191-192, 203-204, 219-220, 226). (3) (a) Exemplary damages should only be awarded in exceptional circumstances, *Broome v Cassell & Co Ltd (No.1)* [1972] A.C. 1027, [1972] C.L.Y. 2745 considered. Evidence was required that D knew that the way the price was calculated was unlawfully excessive or that it did not care whether it was excessive or not, *Rookes v Barnard (No.1)* [1964] A.C. 1129, [1964] C.L.Y. 3703 applied. Although D failed to cross-check its average pricing methodology and there were undoubtedly errors in the calculations, the evidence did not establish that that failure followed a deliberate decision by D to close its eyes to the likely result of such an exercise. Nor could it be concluded that the failures evidenced a decision taken in cynical disregard of C's rights, or that D was reckless as to the risk that the common carriage price might be unlawful. There was insufficient evidence to show that the access price was either clearly or probably unlawful, *2 Travel* applied (see paras 287-288, 309, 355); (b) there was no evidence that D had weighed the risks of going ahead with the access price against the likely downside in terms of future compensation payments to C, *Rookes* applied (see para.364); (c) accordingly, the claim for exemplary damages was dismissed (see para.366).

ALBION WATER LTD v DWR CYMRU CYFYNGEDIG, [2013] CAT 6, [2013] Comp. A.R. 200, Vivien Rose (Chairman), CAT.

488. Abuse of dominant position–Damages–Seeking damages for unlawful means conspiracy–Striking out of statement of case–Whether claim within scope of s.47A Competition Act 1998

[Competition Act 1998 (c.41) s.47A; Treaty on the Functioning of the European Union Art.101.]

The applicant companies (X) applied to strike out pleadings by the respondents (N) in a claim brought by N for damages for alleged losses arising from a cartel in which X had been involved. By a decision of the EU Commission (the decision) X was found to have been part of a cartel concerning the supply of copper plumbing tubes. N were purchasers of such tubes and pleaded their claim for damages on the basis of a breach of statutory duty under TFEU art.101. Further or alternate claims were pleaded in para.24(b) and para.24(c) of their claim form on the basis of unlawful means conspiracy, the unlawful means being the violation of TFEU art.101. The first to third applicants applied to strike out para.24(b) and the first and second applicants applied to strike out para.24(c) on the basis that such tortious conspiracy claims fell outside the statutory jurisdiction of the Competition Act 1998 s.47A. Section 47A applied to any claim for damages, or any other claim for a sum of money, which a person who had suffered loss or damage as a result of the infringement of a "relevant prohibition" might make in civil proceedings brought in any part of the United Kingdom. A relevant prohibition included the prohibition in art.101. The issue was whether the claims alleged in para.24(b) and para.24(c) fell within s.47A. X submitted that the basis of a claim under s.47A was the decision of the competition authority finding an infringement of the relevant prohibition; the question of liability in a s.47A claim was therefore determined by that decision, and for a claim to fall within the statutory jurisdiction, the issues had to be confined to causation and quantum.

Held: Application granted in part. (1) Although X's purpose in entering into the cartel was to promote their own economic interests, it was wholly unrealistic to regard that as divorced from the causation of loss to purchasers of copper plumbing tubes, even if the loss caused might not correspond to X's gain. That element of the tort of conspiracy could be established on the basis of the finding of infringement in the decision alone, *OBG Ltd v Allan* [2007] UKHL 21, [2008] 1 A.C. 1, [2007] C.L.Y. 4190 applied. The claim in para.24(b) fell within the scope of s.47A and should not be struck out (see paras 36, 38 of judgment). (2) The claim under para.24(c) was also for unlawful means conspiracy. However, it was significantly different from the claim under para.24(b). The alleged conspiracy was not the agreement comprising the cartel reached between addressees of the decision, but an antecedent agreement between the first and second applicants and others. That agreement was not the subject of the decision, nor could it amount to the infringement of a relevant prohibition since it was alleged to have been reached between companies in the same group (and thus part of the same economic entity for the purpose of competition law) and individuals. Although the unlawful means relied on was the entry into the cartel and it was the cartel which led to the damage, that could not alter the fact that the focus of that claim was very different from that of the infringement established by the decision. The claim alleged in para.24(C) did not fall within s.47A and should be struck out (paras 39, 40, 41).

WH NEWSON HOLDING LTD v IMI PLC, [2012] EWHC 3680 (Ch), [2013] Bus. L.R. 599, Roth, J., Ch D.

489. Anti-competitive practices–Dominant position

THE COMPETITION ACT 1998 (CONSEQUENTIAL PROVISIONS) ORDER 2013, SI 2013/294; made under the Competition Act 1998 s.75. In force: March 10, 2013;

.

The Competition Act 1998 (Commencement No.6) Order 2013 (SI 2013/284) brings into force on March 10, 2013 provisions of the Competition Act 1998 repealing the Restrictive Practices Court Act 1976. This Order makes consequential repeals and revocations.

490. Anti-competitive practices–Concerted practices–British cheese market–Supermarkets exchanging future pricing intentions via suppliers–Proving transmission of information and relevant state of mind

[Competition Act 1998 (c.41) s.2(1).]

The appellant supermarket (T) appealed against a decision of the Office of Fair Trading that T had participated in two separate concerted practices, referred to as the 2002 and 2003 cheese initiatives, which had as their object the restriction of competition in breach of the Chapter I prohibition in the Competition Act 1998 s.2(1). The background to the 2002 initiative was an attempt by a number of supermarkets and dairy processing companies to increase the price paid to dairy farmers for their raw milk by increasing the cost and retail prices of fresh liquid milk and other dairy products, including cheese. In 2003, one dairy processing company (M) sought to increase the cost prices it charged the supermarket chains for its cheeses in an effort to increase its profit margins. In both years, the cost price increases sought by the dairy processing companies were allegedly accompanied, or followed, by unlawful exchanges of the supermarkets' confidential future retail pricing information. The OFT found that a number of competing undertakings, including T, had indirectly exchanged their future retail pricing intentions in respect of British-produced cheddar and territorial cheeses, via their common suppliers. The transmissions of future pricing intentions from a supermarket to a supplier and from the supplier to another supermarket were referred to on the appeal as "strands". The other supermarkets and suppliers had admitted their involvement in the infringements of the Chapter I prohibition by entering into early resolution agreements with the OFT.

Held: Appeal allowed in part. (1) A retailer, a supplier and another retailer could properly be regarded as parties to a concerted practice, having as its object the restriction of competition, in circumstances where the first retailer disclosed to the supplier its future pricing intentions intending that the supplier would make use of that information to influence market conditions by passing that information to other retailers; the supplier passed that information to another retailer, which might be taken to know the circumstances in which the information was disclosed by the first retailer to the supplier; and the second retailer did use the information in determining its own future pricing intentions, *Argos Ltd v Office of Fair Trading* [2006] EWCA Civ 1318, [2006] U.K.C.L.R. 1135, [2007] C.L.Y. 621 followed (see paras 57-86 of judgment). (2) Entering into an early resolution agreement was a commercial decision but it nonetheless involved an admission of liability, *Crest Nicholson Plc v Office of Fair Trading* [2009] EWHC 1875 (Admin), [2009] U.K.C.L.R. 895, [2010] C.L.Y. 498 considered. However, the agreements even as regards the conduct and state of mind of the parties which entered into them had to be regarded as having little or no probative value in the context of an appeal by T. There were a number of factors that might lead an undertaking to take a commercial decision to admit liability for an infringement, which might be, at least in part, untrue or which the undertaking simply had not investigated (paras 101-111). (3) The tribunal would not draw adverse inferences from the OFT's decision not to call witnesses. The OFT had given a good reason for not calling witnesses, namely that the contemporaneous documents were sufficient evidence of the infringements, *Wiszniewski v Central Manchester HA* [1998] P.I.Q.R. P324, [1998] C.L.Y. 3961 applied (paras 129-136). (4) There was sufficient evidence to support the OFT's findings of infringement in respect of strands 2, 3 and 7 of the 2002 initiative (para.487). In respect of strand 2, a supermarket (S) had disclosed its future retail pricing intentions for cheese to M, intending and foreseeing that M would use that information to influence market conditions by passing it to other retailers, and M had passed it to T in circumstances where T could be taken to have known the circumstances in which the original disclosure was made (para.281). Strand 3 involved disclosure by T of its future retail pricing intentions for cheese to another supplier which passed that information on to S, both T and S having the relevant states of mind. That was an instance of T disclosing its future pricing intentions after it had already received those of S in strand 2, *Argos v OFT* considered (paras 303, 314). In strands 1 and 4 disclosure by T of future prices to the supplier had not been demonstrated (paras 220, 325). In strand 5 a supermarket had passed information to a supplier but it had not been shown, despite the existence of an early resolution agreement, that anyone at that supermarket intended or foresaw that the information would be passed to T and it was not appropriate to decide whether any lesser state of mind was sufficient for liability (paras 341-355). Strand 7 involved M disclosing T's future retail pricing intentions to S, both T and S having the relevant states of mind (para.371). In strand 6 the relevant state of mind of the recipient was not made out and in strands 8 and 9 transmission of the information was not proved (paras 358, 387, 397). (5) The OFT's finding that T had infringed the Chapter I prohibition by participating in the 2003 initiative was set aside in its entirety as against T. In the case of all five strands relied on by the OFT, although it had been shown that future retail price information had been conveyed to suppliers, it had not been shown that that was done with the relevant state of mind on the part of the supermarkets (paras 485-488).

TESCO STORES LTD v OFFICE OF FAIR TRADING, [2012] CAT 31, [2013] Comp. A.R. 23, Lord Carlile of Berriew Q.C., CAT.

491. Anti-competitive practices–Damages–Follow-on claims flowing from European Commission decisions–Finding of parent company's infringement of prohibition on anti-competitive practices–Entitlement to bring claim against subsidiary

[Competition Act 1998 (c.41) s.47A, s.47A(8); Treaty on the Functioning of the European Union Art.101 (1); Regulation 1/2003 Art.15.]

The appellants (E) appealed against a decision of the Competition Appeal Tribunal ([2011] CAT 4, [2011] Comp. A.R. 90, [2011] C.L.Y. 437) to strike out its follow-on claim, brought under the Competition Act 1998 s.47A, against the respondent (M). E had brought damages claims against a number of companies, including M and its parent company (C), following a European Commission decision that certain undertakings had participated in an infringement of the TFEU art.101 (1). C was one of the named infringers and addressees in the operative part of the Commission's decision. The recitals to the decision recorded that C was a parent company, and referred to cartel behaviour by its "UK subsidiary". M was a UK subsidiary of C but was not expressly named anywhere in the decision. The CAT found that it lacked jurisdiction to hear the claim against M as it had not been addressed by the Commission's decision. E argued that the Commission had made a finding that M had infringed competition law by virtue of the reference in the recitals to the UK subsidiary; doubt about that could be resolved by making a request to the Commission under Regulation 1/2003 art.15. E also argued that the undertaking which had infringed comprised M as well as its parent, C.

Held: Appeal dismissed. The appeal turned on the proper interpretation of the decision as cross-referred to in s.47A(6)(d) and (8). In EU law, "undertaking" was broader in scope than the English notion of a corporate entity, *Provimi Ltd v Aventis Animal Nutrition SA* [2003] EWHC 961 (Comm), [2003] 2 All E.R. (Comm) 683, [2003] C.L.Y. 625 applied. A parent company and its subsidiaries within the group could be treated as a single undertaking, *Manufacture Francaise des Pneumatiques Michelin v Commission of the European Communities (T-203/01)* [2003] E.C.R. II-4071, [2005] C.L.Y. 571 followed. However, the CAT had been correct in striking out the claim. Only the operative part of a decision was to be considered in determining the persons to whom a decision was addressed, *Adriatica di Navigazione SpA v Commission of the European Communities (T-61/99)* [2003] E.C.R. II-5349, [2006] C.L.Y. 592 followed. The operative part of the decision identified specifically by name those undertakings to which the decision was addressed, against which findings of infringements had been made and on which monetary claims in the CAT could be based. The decision was specifically addressed to the undertaking named as C, not the group of companies collectively, or to individual companies within the group. Even if M was regarded as part of the undertaking addressed as C, that still did not identify M as an infringing party so as to render it liable, as a separate entity, to E for infringement. M could not properly be made a defendant. The issue of liability had unambiguously been determined by the Commission in a way that imposed liability only on the undertaking named as C and not in a way that imposed liability on the separate company known as M. Had the Commission intended to impose such liability, it could and should have either named M as an addressee in the operative part of the decision or defined the addressee undertaking as including not only C but also all subsidiaries owned or controlled by it. The principle of legal certainty would be undermined if an entity which was not an addressee of a Commission decision could be made liable to proceedings in national courts based on that decision. The result was consistent with the principle of effectiveness, since remedies were available: it was only a matter of determining against which entities and in which jurisdictions the remedies were available. Further, art.15 of the

Regulation was not available or appropriate for asking which entities comprised the undertakings bound by the decision (see paras 72-84 of judgment).

EMERSON ELECTRIC CO v MERSEN UK PORTSLADE LTD (FORMERLY LE CARBONE (GREAT BRITAIN) LTD); *sub nom.* EMERSON ELECTRIC CO v MORGAN CRUCIBLE CO PLC, [2012] EWCA Civ 1559, [2013] Bus. L.R. 342, Mummery, L.J., CA (Civ Div).

492. Appeals–Extensions of time–Successful appeal against OFT decision by some addressees–Basis of OFT decision fundamentally undermined–Whether exceptional circumstances to extend time for other addressees

[Competition Appeal Tribunal Rules 2003 (SI 2003/1372) r.8.]

The applicants (S and G) applied for extensions of time to appeal against a decision of the respondent Office of Fair Trading (OFT). The decision was addressed to numerous parties and found that two manufacturers of tobacco products had agreed with various retailers, including S and G, to restrict retail prices charged for competing cigarette brands. S and G entered into early resolution agreements with the OFT which provided for a discount to the penalty levied if they did not appeal. S and G did not appeal, but six of the other addressees did. During that appeal the OFT accepted that the theory of harm that it had articulated could not be maintained and it sought to advance an alternative theory of harm (the refined case). The tribunal considered that the refined case ran contrary to what the OFT had previously submitted and that the decision had not included findings of infringement regarding the refined case. It therefore allowed the appeal and set aside the decision as against those that appealed, but it continued to bind the non-appealing addressees. The issue was whether there were exceptional circumstances under the Competition Appeal Tribunal Rules 2003 r.8(2) to extend S and G's time for appealing. S and G submitted that there were exceptional circumstances in that: (1) the decision was apt to mislead the reader such that they could not make an informed decision about whether to appeal; (2) it was contrary to the principle of legal certainty for the decision to be annulled in respect of the appellants in the earlier proceedings but to be allowed to stand in respect of S and G; (3) the OFT had acted outside its public law duties and powers in making a decision that was not supported by any adequate evidence; (4) the scale of the OFT's defeat in the tribunal was unprecedented; (5) the OFT had sought to persuade the tribunal to determine an unpleaded case as the primary decision-maker; (6) the OFT had indicated that it did not intent to proceed with any further investigation so the only proper course open to the OFT was to abandon its decision in its entirety as against all addressees; (7) the early resolution agreements contained an implied obligation on the OFT to defend the decision; (8) the early resolution agreements were not based on the refined case, which had never been put to them, and no decision was ever taken by the OFT on that basis; they never had the opportunity to appeal against a decision based on the OFT's refined case.

Held: Appeal allowed. (1) S and G had been in the same position as the other addressees. They had two-months in which to elect whether to appeal and chose not to. The fact that the decision may have been unclear and may have misled the parties did not alter that position. It was incumbent on each addressee of a decision to peruse it with care and to reach a view on whether to appeal. Provided an addressee was able to consider the decision in that way, its own decision whether to appeal would be an informed one, *RG Carter Ltd v Office of Fair Trading* [2011] CAT 25, [2011] Comp. A.R. 612, [2012] C.L.Y. 527612 considered (see paras 62-63, 65 of judgment). (2) There was nothing wrong or contrary to the principle of legal certainty in there being a risk of consequential civil proceedings being brought against some addressees but not others. That consequence was entirely in accordance with legal certainty as it tracked the fact that the decision was binding against some addressees but was quashed as against others (para.71). (3) By whichever route a decision of the OFT was challenged, it stood unless and until it was set aside by a court of competent jurisdiction (para.80). (4) The fact that a decision was successfully challenged in an appeal could not be described as an exceptional circumstance.

The fact that the successful challenge occurred in an unprecedented or unforeseeable manner could make no difference (para.86). (5) The OFT was entitled to seek to persuade the tribunal to exercise its powers (para.87). (6) The suggestion that where, in the course of an appeal, the OFT accepted that its theory of harm had to be corrected, amended or abandoned, that inevitably had an effect as regards non-appealing addressees ran contrary to the accepted nature of OFT decisions and EU jurisprudence, *Commission of the European Communities v AssiDoman Kraft Products AB (C-310/97 P)* [1999] All E.R. (EC) 737, [1999] C.L.Y. 2223 considered (para.90). (7) It was a hopeless contention that the OFT should be required to persist in defending the indefensible because it was under an implied obligation, owed only to those addressees of a decision that entered into early resolution agreements, to do so. There was a real danger in the OFT's public duties being fettered by contract (para.91). (8) S and G had entered into the early resolution agreements on a basis which had been fundamentally undermined: namely, on the basis of an entirely legitimate expectation that the OFT's decision was sufficiently robust, if appealed, to proceed to a determination on the merits. As events proved, the decision was not, and the OFT's case collapsed, on a point fundamental to the case not merely against the appellants, but also to the case that had been admitted by S and G in the early resolution agreements. That fact amounted to an exceptional circumstance so as to entitle S and G to revisit their decision not to appeal (para.93).

SOMERFIELD STORES LTD v OFFICE OF FAIR TRADING; GALLAHER GROUP LTD v OFFICE OF FAIR TRADING, [2013] CAT 5, [2013] Comp. A.R.165, Marcus Smith Q.C., CAT.

493. Cartels–Fines–Increase in basic amount of fine for recidivism–Right of defence–Extent of co-operation under Leniency Notice–European Union

[Treaty on the Functioning of the European Union Art.101.]

The applicant (X) applied for annulment of a decision of the respondent Commission finding X and its parent company (E) liable for participation in conduct infringing the EC Treaty art.81 (now TFEU art.101). By the contested decision, the Commission had imposed fines on a number of undertakings, including X and E, for participation in a cartel in the sodium chlorate sector. X was held to have participated in the cartel from May 17, 1995 until February 9, 2000. In calculating the fines, the Commission took as its basis the Guidelines on the Method of Setting Fines 2006. The basic amount of the fine imposed on X was increased by 90 per cent to take account of sanctions imposed on it in earlier decisions involving another undertaking (P). No attenuating circumstances were found to justify a reduction in the fine outside the scope of the Leniency Notice 2002. The Commission held that X, unlike some of the other participating undertakings, was not entitled to any reduction under the Leniency Notice because the information it had supplied did not constitute significant added value within the meaning of point 21 of the Leniency Notice. Accordingly, a fine of EUR 20,430,000 was imposed on X alone. X contended that the Commission had erred in (1) imposing an increase in the fine for recidivism, since it had taken the P decision into account for the purpose of establishing recidivism without mentioning that decision in the statement of objections; (2) refusing a reduction in the fine either within or outside the Leniency Notice.

Held: Application refused. (1) The Commission had indicated in its statement of objections that it intended to impose fines on the undertakings concerned, and that it would take into account any aggravating circumstances when doing so, such as those provided for at point 28 of the Guidelines, which expressly referred to repeated infringement. The Commission had also noted that certain of the undertakings concerned had already been the subject of decisions relating to a similar infringement, which referred specifically, in X's case, to the P decision. Accordingly, the Commission had not breached X's rights of defence when applying recidivism as an aggravating circumstance, notwithstanding its lack of any direct reference to the P decision in the statement of objections. Repeated infringement was an important factor which the Commission had to appraise, since the purpose of taking it into account was to induce undertakings which had demonstrated a tendency towards infringing the competition rules to change their conduct. In the instant case, the evidence showed that X had participated in cartels from 1961 to 1984 prior to the instant proceedings. Moreover, X had failed to demonstrate that the Commission had exceeded its discretion by increasing the basic amount of the fine by 90 per cent, or that such an increase was disproportionate or breached the principle of equal treatment, given X's strong tendency towards breaching the competition rules and the limited value of its co-operation in the instant case (see paras 57-63, 66, 71, 103-104 of judgment). (2) X was the second undertaking to have submitted an application under the Leniency Notice and the information which it supplied did not represent significant added value in the light of evidence already in the Commission's possession at the time of X's application. Moreover, the information supplied by X neither supported nor provided further details of the information already in the Commission's possession. Mere confirmation of existing evidence could not be regarded as having significant added value. Nor had X put forward any argument or evidence to establish that, without its co-operation, the Commission would not have been able to penalise the infringement found in the contested decision. Accordingly, X had failed to establish that the Commission had erred in not granting it a reduction of its fine on the basis of the fourth indent of point 29 of the Guidelines for co-operation outside the scope of the Leniency Notice (paras 139, 141, 143, 168, 171).

ARKEMA FRANCE v EUROPEAN COMMISSION (T-343/08) [2013] 4 C.M.L.R. 29, Judge Pelikanova (President), GC (2nd Chamber).

494. Cartels–Striking out–Tendering evidence–Arguable case established

[Competition Act 1998 (c.41) s.47A; Treaty Establishing the European Community (Nice version) Art.81; Treaty on the Functioning of the European Union Art.101; Regulation 1/2003 Art.16; Regulation 44/2001 on jurisdiction and the recognition and enforcement of judgments in civil and commercial matters Art.6(1).]

The first defendant (BPI) applied for summary judgment and to strike out a competition claim for breach of TFEU art.101 brought by the claimant companies (B). The second defendant (C), a Dutch subsidiary, applied to set aside service of the claim form outside the jurisdiction. B were two Irish companies which had purchased substantial quantities of plastic industrial bags from companies including BPI and C. B relied on a European Commission decision COMP/38354 of 30 November 2005 confirming that the defendants had participated in a cartel operating in the industrial bags sector in breach of art.81 EC (now TFEU art.101) in the German, French, Spanish, and Benelux markets. BPI submitted that the Commission Decision and the effect of Regulation 1/2003 art.16 precluded B from contending either that the anti-competitive conduct of the cartel had occurred not just in the continental markets to which the Decision related but also in the United Kingdom and Irish markets, or that the operation of the cartel in continental markets had affected competition in the the UK and Ireland. C contended that the English court was without jurisdiction.

Held: Applications refused. (1) A claim would not be struck out unless it was certain that it was bound to fail, *Richards (t/a Colin Richards & Co) v Hughes* [2004] EWCA Civ 266, [2004] P.N.L.R. 35, [2004] C.L.Y. 2725 applied, and the court should refrain from striking out unless an opportunity to amend the statement of case had been given (see para.29 of judgment). The court was more generous with the amendment of pleadings in a claim for damages against a member of a cartel because the allegations were largely within the exclusive knowledge of the defendants, *Nokia Corp v AU Optronics Corp* [2012] EWHC 731 (Ch), [2012] U.K.C.L.R. 245, [2012] C.L.Y. 454 considered and *Cooper Tire & Rubber Co Europe Ltd v Shell Chemicals UK Ltd* [2010] EWCA Civ 864, [2010] Bus. L.R. 1697, [2011] C.L.Y. 445 and *Toshiba Carrier UK Ltd v KME Yorkshire Ltd* [2012] EWCA Civ 1190 followed (para.30). In a follow-on claim under the Competition Act 1998 s.47A, the Competition Appeal Tribunal was bound by the decision of the regulator on the infringement and could not supplement or go beyond the regulator's findings. However, a "stand alone" claim was not so restricted and it was open to B to supplement the findings of the Commission with further evidence, *Enron Coal Services Ltd (In Liquidation) v English Welsh & Scottish Railway Ltd* [2011] EWCA Civ 2, [2011] U.K.C.L.R. 303, [2011] C.L.Y. 431 followed (paras 40-43). The Commission appeared not to have investigated the market in the UK or Ireland and neither the Decision nor the Regulation were engaged. It was open to B to seek to establish that a cartel had an anti-competitive effect in a neighbouring market without the cartel actually operating or having an agreement or concerted practice in that market. B's evidence of its own bidding process was sufficient to support an arguable case that cartel activity had adversely affected it (paras 72-74). (2) C's application fell with that of BPI so that jurisdiction was established under Regulation 44/2001 art.6(1) on the basis that BPI was an anchor defendant domiciled in England against whom there was a serious issue to be tried (para.92)

BORD NA MONA HORTICULTURE LTD v BRITISH POLYTHENE INDUSTRIES PLC, [2012] EWHC 3346 (Comm), [2013] U.K.C.L.R. 50, Flaux, J., QBD (Comm).

495. Commission Competition Decisions–Limitation periods–Claim for infringement of competition law–Meaning of "decision" in s.47A Competition Act 1998

[Competition Act 1998 (c.41) s.47A(8)(a); Competition Appeal Tribunal Rules 2003 (SI 2003/1372) r.40.]

The appellants (D) appealed against a decision ([2011] CAT 16, [2011] Comp. A.R. 569, [2012] 1 C.L. 50) striking out their claim for infringement of competition law against the respondent (M) on the ground that it had been brought out of time. The European Commission had imposed a fine on M and other companies (X) for participation in a cartel. X appealed, but M did not. D issued follow-on claims against M and X. In relation to X, it was accepted that the two-year limitation period for bringing such claims was deferred until after completion of the appeal process. M's case was that, since it had not appealed, the limitation period for a follow-on claim had expired. Its striking out application, brought under the Competition Appeal Tribunal Rules 2003 r.40, was successful on that basis. Determination of that application had involved the Competition Appeal Tribunal construing the word "decision" in the Competition Act 1998 s.47A(8)(a). It found that the word was not used in a wide sense to refer to the Commission's general finding of an infringement situation, but in a narrow sense to refer to the specific part of the dispositif section of the Commission Decision that made a finding of infringement by a particular undertaking, and that such a construction meant that D's claim was statute-barred. The issue in the instant appeal was whether the limitation period for making a follow-on claim against a non-appealing undertaking began to run from the expiration of the time limit for the non-appealing undertaking to appeal to the General Court, or from the expiration of the appeal process initiated by the other undertakings.

Held: Appeal allowed. It was not immediately obvious how the limitation provisions in s.47A were to be construed and applied. There was no binding authority and there were sensible arguments both ways. However, the two main factors determining the disputed construction of s.47A were the domestic procedural law context of the statutory provisions, and a careful reading of the detailed drafting of the critical subsections, namely s.47A(6)(d) and s.47A(8) (see paras 12,15, 98 of judgment). Section 47A dealt with purely domestic law enforcement matters, not with EU law; it related to private law claims in civil proceedings for the recovery of damages for the infringement of a right, not to the imposition of penalties to punish breaches of EU law. There was, however, a link between s.47A and EU law, because, in determining s.47A claims, the tribunal was bound by Commission Decisions containing findings of infringement of competition law. The purpose of the limitation period was therefore not to extinguish stale claims, but to enable the distribution of judicial business within the specialist tribunals. Section 47A laid down the limits of the tribunal's jurisdiction by providing for a detailed procedural regime; the wording of s.47A(6)(d) and s.47A(8) was critical. Both subsections referred to a decision that a relevant prohibition had been infringed, rather than to a decision that a particular party or addressee had infringed competition law. That was consistent with the approach to an appeal against infringement, which was an appeal against the basic decision that the relevant prohibition had been infringed; it was not an appeal against a decision addressed to a particular party. The addressing of an infringement decision to a particular undertaking was a secondary matter involving the allocation of responsibility consequential on a logically prior decision that the prohibition had been infringed and that an infringement situation existed. The tribunal had therefore erred in finding that "decision" in s.47A(8) referred to a specific part of the dispositif that made a decision as regards a particular addressee, and that it referred to a decision against a particular party. What "decision" actually referred to in that section, read with s.47A(6)(d) was a decision of the Commission that an infringement situation existed; the liability of particular parties did not feature in that decision. The appeal which had the effect of deferring the trigger date for limitation purposes was the appeal to the General Court against the decision that there had been an infringement, not against the addressing of that decision to the particular undertakings. That was consistent with the way in which the word "decision" was used in other parts of the 1998 Act. The tribunal's reasoning did not adequately reflect the different stages in the decision-making process. Accordingly, D's claim against M had not been brought out of time and could proceed along with the claims against X (paras 99-113, 115-116, 120).

DEUTSCHE BAHN AG v MORGAN CRUCIBLE CO PLC, [2012] EWCA Civ 1055, [2013] Bus. L.R. 125, Mummery, L.J., CA (Civ Div).

496. Commission Competition Decisions–Limitation periods–Claims under s.47A Competition Act 1998–Compliance with European legal principles of effectiveness and legal certainty

[Competition Act 1998 (c.41) s.47A; Competition Appeal Tribunal Rules 2003 (SI 2003/1372) r.31; Treaty Establishing the European Community (Nice version) Art.81.]

The appellant companies (X) appealed against a decision ([2010] EWCA Civ 1258, [2011] Bus. L.R. 428, [2011] C.L.Y. 453) that its claim for damages under the Competition Act 1998 s.47A and the Competition Appeal Tribunal Rules 2003 r.31 was time-barred and there was no power to extend time. Following an investigation into the operation of a cartel relating to the supply of vitamins for use in animal foodstuffs, the European Commission had held, in 2001, that the respondent companies (Y) had infringed the EC Treaty (Nice) art.81 and imposed fines accordingly. Y had until January 2002 to appeal against the Commission s decision. In the event, Y appealed against the fines but not the finding of infringement. That appeal concluded on March 15, 2006. X brought proceedings on March 13, 2008 under s.47A for losses resulting from that infringement on the understanding that, under s.47A and r.31, the two-year period to bring a claim started when all appeals had been concluded. The Court of Appeal held, in *BCL Old Co Ltd v BASF SE* [2009] EWCA Civ 434, [2009] Bus. L.R. 1516, [2009] C.L.Y. 572, that X's claim was time-barred because the time limit for bringing a claim under s.47A was only postponed where an infringement decision was being challenged, rather than the penalty imposed, and that it could proceed, if at all, only with an extension of time. X pursued an application to extend time. The Competition Appeal Tribunal assumed that it had power to grant an extension, but declined to do so on the merits. The Court of Appeal held that the Tribunal had no power to extend time under UK law and that European law did not override the UK time bar or require a power to extend to be treated as existing. The issue on appeal was whether the statutory limitation period failed to comply with European legal principles of effectiveness and legal certainty.

Held: Appeal dismissed. (1) National limitation periods were permissible under EU law but they should not operate so as to render virtually impossible or excessively difficult the exercise of EU law rights; whether or not they did so was a matter for the national courts to determine in light of the European principles of effectiveness and legal certainty, *Courage Ltd v Crehan (C-453/99)* [2002] Q.B. 507, [2001] C.L.Y. 783 and *Danske Slagterier v Germany (C-445/06)* [2009] E.C.R. I-2119 applied (see paras 11-12 of judgment). (2) EU law did not require that the interpretation or true effect of a statutory limitation period be clear beyond doubt. The true test was more flexible and did not impose a requirement for absolute clarity. Instead what was required was that national law must be sufficiently clear, precise and foreseeable as to enable individuals to ascertain their rights and obligations and exercise those rights without excessive difficulty, *European Commission v Ireland (C-456/08)* [2010] P.T.S.R. 1403 considered and *European Commission v France (C-512/08)* [2011] All E.R. (EC) 818 applied (paras 19-22). (3) In the instant case, there was no doubt that the commencement of the two-year limitation period for a claim for damages under s.47A and r.31 was sufficiently foreseeable and clear and did not make it excessively difficult for X to commence and pursue a claim in time. The statutory limitation period commenced following the expiry of the time within which Y could appeal against the Commission s infringement decision; it did not commence following the expiry of the time within which Y could appeal against the decision as to the level of the fine. The Competition Act used clear language throughout and repeatedly distinguished between infringement decisions on the one hand and penalty decisions on the other, making clear that only infringement decisions were of relevance in determining the date upon which a limitation period commenced. It was accepted that Y's appeal was only against the fine imposed upon it and not against infringement and there was no suggestion that X was misled into thinking otherwise. Given that Y did not appeal against the Commission s infringement decision it was sufficiently clear that the two-year limitation period started in January 2002 (paras 29-43). Further, the lack of any power to extend time for the commencement of claims for damages was also sufficiently foreseeable. It was plain from the language of the Rules that, in making them, the secretary of state had deliberately decided that there should be no such power (paras 41-43).

BCL OLD CO LTD v BASF SE (FORMERLY BASF AG); GRAMPIAN COUNTRY FOOD GROUP LTD v SANOFI-AVENTIS SA; *sub nom.* BCL OLD CO LTD v BASF PLC, [2012] UKSC 45, [2012] 1 W.L.R. 2922, Lord Phillips, J.S.C., SC.

497. Competition–Regulatory reform

THE ENTERPRISE AND REGULATORY REFORM ACT 2013 (COMPETITION AND MARKETS AUTHORITY) (CONSEQUENTIAL AMENDMENTS) ORDER 2013, SI 2013/2268; made under the Enterprise and Regulatory Reform Act 2013 s.99. In force: October 1, 2013; .

This Order makes an amendment which is consequential on the establishment of the Competition and Markets Authority on October 1, 2013.

498. Competition Act 1998 (c.41)–Commencement No.6 Order

THE COMPETITION ACT 1998 (COMMENCEMENT NO.6) ORDER 2013, SI 2013/284; made under the Competition Act 1998 s.76. In force: February 12, 2013; .

This Order brings into force on March 10, 2013 the provisions of the Competition Act 1998 which are not already in force. The provisions in question are section 1 (a), which provides for the Restrictive Practices Court Act 1976 to cease to have effect, and the provisions of section 74 and Part 1 of Schedule 14 which repeal that Act.

499. Competition Appeal Tribunal–Costs–Application to stay Competition Commission's investigation into airline's acquisition of minority share in rival–Competition Commission successful on all salient points–Costs of Competition Commission and successful intervener

[Enterprise Act 2002 (c.40) s.120.]

The Competition Appeal Tribunal was required to determine applications for costs arising out of an application brought by the applicant airline (R) against the respondent Competition Commission. R had challenged the Commission's decision to continue with an investigation into R's acquisition of a minority shareholding in the intervener rival airline (L). The CAT dismissed R's application and the Commission was successful on all substantive points. The Commission sought its costs of resisting R's application from R. L sought the costs of its intervention from R.

Held: Applications granted in part. (1) No order for costs was made in relation to L's application. There was no reason why the tribunal ought to depart from the general position that there should be no general expectation that a successful intervener would be entitled to its costs, *British Sky Broadcasting Group Plc v Competition Commission (Costs)* [2009] CAT 20, [2009] Comp. A.R. 247, [2010] C.L.Y. 473 applied. The Commission's and L's success could not be taken into account as a reason for diverging from the general position when that success was, of itself, a necessary part of the general position (see paras 2-3, 5 of judgment). (2) The Commission would recover the costs of its defence from R. In cases brought pursuant to the Enterprise Act 2002 s.120, the appropriate starting point was that a successful party would normally obtain a costs award in its favour. However, starting points were just that and all the relevant circumstances of each case had to be considered in order that each case was dealt with justly, *Merger Action Group v Secretary of State for Business, Enterprise and Regulatory Reform* [2009] CAT 19, [2009] Comp. A.R. 269, [2009] C.L.Y. 583 applied. Importantly, the Commission had been successful and was successful on all salient points. Furthermore, the fact that it could not be said that R had brought a public interest challenge, and was acting entirely in its own commercial interests, was a factor to be borne in mind in deciding whether the Commission, as an entirely successful public law defendant should have its costs (paras 11, 13, 15).

RYANAIR HOLDINGS PLC v COMPETITION COMMISSION, [2012] CAT 29, [2013] Comp. A.R. 18, Marcus Smith Q.C., CAT.

500. Competition Commission–Investigations–Competition Commission's investigation into airline's acquisition of minority share in rival–European Commission's investigation into airline's bid for entire share capital of rival–Competition Commission's ability to continue investigation

[Treaty on the Functioning of the European Union Art.101, Art.102; Regulation 139/2004 Art.21.]

The appellant airline (R) appealed against a decision of the Competition Appeal Tribunal ([2012] CAT 21, [2012] Comp. A.R. 439, [2013] 1 C.L. 56) to dismiss its application to quash or stay the first respondent Competition Commission's decision to continue its investigation into R's minority shareholding in the second respondent airline (L). After the investigation had begun, R announced its intention to make a public bid for the whole of L's share capital. The Competition Commission rejected R's submission that it should halt its investigation pending the European Commission's investigation into the public bid. R argued that *Ryanair Holdings Plc v Office of Fair Trading* [2012] EWCA Civ 643, [2013] Bus. L.R. 214, [2013] 5 C.L. 53 was binding authority that the duty of sincere co-operation required the suspension of the Competition Commission's investigation.

Held: Appeal dismissed. Whether and when the duty of sincere co-operation required a Member State to take or desist from taking any action, and precisely what was required to fulfil it, was highly fact-sensitive. Caution therefore had to be exercised in transferring the reasoning in one judicial decision about the requirements of the duty in that particular case to another case in which the court considered a quite different factual situation. Important statements about the principle were to be found in *Masterfoods Ltd (t/a Mars Ireland) v HB Ice Cream Ltd (C-344/98)* [2001] All E.R. (EC) 130, [2001] C.L.Y. 762 and *National Grid Electricity Transmission Plc v ABB Ltd* [2009] EWHC 1326 (Ch), [2009] U.K.C.L.R. 838, [2009] C.L.Y. 454, but those cases concerned the TFEU art.101 and art.102, where there were truly concurrent jurisdictions, *Masterfoods* and *National Grid* considered. The European Commission's jurisdiction on anti-competitive concentrations under Regulation 139/2004 and the Member States' jurisdiction under domestic merger legislation were not overlapping as they were mutually exclusive. If the European Commission's jurisdiction was engaged, it had exclusive jurisdiction; if not, then as between the European Commission and the Member State, the Member State's jurisdiction was necessarily exclusive. If the issue in the instant case was approached as a matter of first principles, there could be no doubt that a stay of the Competition Commission's investigation was neither necessary nor appropriate. The European Commission's jurisdiction did not extend to R's minority shareholding; whatever it decided, the United Kingdom had exclusive jurisdiction to consider the minority shareholding's competition implications. Article 21(3) of the Regulation had no application. Even if there was a theoretical possibility that the Competition Commission's decision on the minority shareholding could be relevant to that of the European Commission on the public bid, or vice versa, the European Commission's decision would be delivered first. In any event, even if the Competition Commission finished its investigation first, it could defer the implementation of any remedial action until the conclusion of the European Commission's investigation. That analysis was not rendered deficient because of the decision in *Ryanair*. The factual situation in *Ryanair* was materially different: in those proceedings, the parties had continued to invoke the European Commission's exclusive jurisdiction over the entire concentration, including the minority shareholding. The ratio of that case was that the duty of sincere co-operation arose because art.21 applied. Its references to "competing jurisdictions" referred, properly speaking, to cases where the Competition Commission wrongly assumed jurisdiction where it had no legal jurisdiction at all. That explained the statement in *Ryanair* that concurrent investigations would be mutually destructive: in context, that was saying that concurrent investigations in the UK and by the European Commission, when only one of them had jurisdiction, would be oppressive and mutually destructive. That was correct, but had nothing to do with the instant case, where only the UK had jurisdiction in respect of the minority shareholding, *Ryanair* considered. Accordingly, the Competition Commission's decision to continue its investigation was not a breach of the duty of sincere co-operation (see paras 55-67 of judgment).

RYANAIR HOLDINGS PLC v COMPETITION COMMISSION, [2012] EWCA Civ 1632, [2013] U.K.C.L.R. 100, Pill, L.J., CA (Civ Div).

501. Competition Commission–Investigations–Permission to appeal–Commission's investigation into airline's acquisition of minority share in rival–Commission's ability to continue investigation

The applicant airline (R) applied for permission to appeal against a decision of the tribunal refusing to quash or stay the respondent Commission's decision to continue an investigation into R's acquisition of a minority shareholding in a rival airline.

Held: Application refused. The proposed appeal had no real prospect of success. There was no principle of law requiring the Commission to cease its investigation and no other compelling reason for the matter to be considered by a higher court. However, the matter had a long history and it would be desirable for the Court of Appeal to be able to consider any application for permission as quickly as was consistent with justice. Given the extensive work already done by R in formulating its grounds of appeal, it was appropriate to direct it to renew its application to the Court of Appeal, if so advised, within seven days of the instant order.

RYANAIR HOLDINGS PLC v COMPETITION COMMISSION, [2012] CAT 22, [2012] Comp. A.R. 467, Marcus Smith Q.C., CAT.

502. Competition Commission–Market investigations–Distribution of newspapers and magazines–Office of Fair Trading's earlier decision not to refer market to Competition Commission–Later decision not to carry out short update review

[Enterprise Act 2002 (c.40) s.131, s.179(4), Sch.1 para.13.]

The applicants (X) sought a review under the Enterprise Act 2002 s.179(4) of a decision of the respondent (O) that it did not need to re-examine the market for the distribution of newspapers and magazines after its earlier decision not to make a market investigation reference to the Competition Commission. Under s.131, O could make a market investigation reference to the Commission if it had reasonable grounds for suspecting that any feature, or combination of features, of a market for goods or services prevented, restricted or distorted competition. Previously, O had found that there were certain features of the market for the distribution of newspapers and magazines which gave rise to a reasonable suspicion, but had decided in the exercise of its discretion not to make a reference. Now, under Sch.1 para.13, it had decided that, in light of its priorities, it did not need to conduct a short update review of the market. Its reasons were that there was evidence of: an overall improvement in in-store availability of newspapers and magazines, and significant investment by the publishers and wholesalers in systems aimed at ensuring that retailers could replenish their stocks easily and efficiently; retail outlet numbers having remained stable; the effective operation of the supply chains in distributing newspapers and magazines; and significant price competition between publishers of newspapers and magazines. However, X, two trade associations which represented independent retailers of newspapers and magazines, contended that the position in the market had worsened rather than improved since O's original decision and challenged each of O's reasons.

Held: Application refused. The tribunal's task was not to assess how well or badly the market for the distribution of newspapers and magazines was currently working; it was to consider whether, looking at O's new decision against the background of its original decision, O could reasonably have concluded on the basis of the evidence before it that it was not appropriate to carry out a short update review to see if the market should be referred to the Commission. O's conclusion that there had been an overall improvement in in-store availability was based on five items of evidence consisting of: availability data; survey data; improvements in retailers' ability to influence the supplies they received; significant investment in IT systems allowing sales-based replenishment; and funding by publishers and wholesalers of interest-free loans to enable retailers to improve their ability to manage the range of products sold. O had been entitled to rely on the availability data to infer that availability of newspapers and magazines was generally at a level which meant that it was unlikely that further investigation by it or the Commission would lead to a significant improvement for the benefit of consumers; the survey data fully justified O's inference that consumers were not suffering a significant detriment in the sense of being unable to read the magazine they wanted because they could not find it in the shops; and its inference from the last three items of evidence that retailers were achieving a greater degree of control over the deliveries they received could not be faulted. O's finding that retail outlet numbers had remained stable was based on evidence which it had not been wrong to accept and to rely on. Likewise, it had been entitled to conclude on the basis of the information before it that the operation of the supply chain did not inhibit the plurality of the media or raise other consumer issues. As regards its finding of significant price competition, O had recorded in its new decision that multiple retailers were able to impose financial penalties on wholesalers for poor service quality and that they had been able to push back on proposals from the wholesalers to increase the carriage service charge. Accordingly, it had been open to O to find that the likely consumer benefit did not justify it undertaking the short update review of the market. Its assessment of its priorities as regards the strategic significance of any update review was not flawed in any way (see paras 23, 27, 33-36, 39, 41, 46, 52 of judgment).

ASSOCIATION OF CONVENIENCE STORES v OFFICE OF FAIR TRADING, [2012] CAT 27, [2013] Comp. A.R. 1, Vivien Rose (Chairman), CAT.

503. Concerted practices–Penalties–Collusive tendering in construction industry–Appropriate level of penalty–Whether increase for purposes of deterrence justified

The appellant companies (X) appealed against a decision ([2011] CAT 7, 136 Con. L.R. 152, [2011] C.L.Y. 440) concerning the level of penalties imposed by the Office of Fair Trading (OFT). X and others had participated in collusive tendering practices in the construction industry which involved providing cover prices to other companies during tenders. The party awarding the contract was thereby deceived into believing that a competitive tendering process had taken place, as companies who did not wish to win the tender used the cover price. In some cases payments were made by one bidder to another, to compensate them for the costs involved in submitting a losing bid. When determining the appropriate penalty, the OFT decided that the starting point for simple cover pricing should be 5 per cent of turnover, and for infringements concerning payment to other bidders, 7 per cent of turnover. It did not make any adjustment for duration of the infringement and decided to impose up to three separate financial penalties for infringements. Due to the number of companies involved, the OFT also offered a 25 per cent discount to those which admitted their infringement under the fast-track scheme. X received two penalties at the starting rate of 5 per cent of relevant turnover. The resulting figure was then doubled for the purposes of deterrence, and a reduction of 5 per cent was applied to take account of its introduction of a compliance programme. X received a further 25 per cent reduction as part of the fast-track scheme. X's penalties were reduced on appeal by the Competition Appeal Tribunal. X submitted that the penalties were still far too high compared to the general level of penalties imposed on other undertakings for similar infringements, and the tribunal had failed to explain why the starting figure had been doubled.

Held: Appeal allowed in part. (1) The OFT guidance on penalties set out a five-step process, *Argos Ltd v Office of Fair Trading* [2006] EWCA Civ 1318, [2006] U.K.C.L.R. 1135, [2007] C.L.Y. 621 considered. Therefore, the correct approach to the assessment of a penalty was to proceed in stages beginning with an initial assessment for each infringement having regard to its seriousness. That was what the OFT and the tribunal had done in the instant case, and no criticism was made of the starting figure. When considering whether that figure should be increased in order to give effect to the policy objective of deterrence, two factors came into play. The first was whether the amount of the step one penalty would act as a sufficient deterrent for the particular undertaking on which it was imposed. The second was whether it would be sufficient to deter others operating in the same field by bringing home to them that such conduct was illegal and would be effectively punished (see paras 6-12, 58-64 of judgment). (2) It was troubling that the penalty for X was so out of line with the level of fines which the tribunal thought necessary to act as a deterrent in similar cases. X was fined 1.3 per cent of turnover, whereas four other companies were fined 0.37 per cent, 0.8 per cent, 0.19 per cent and 0.1 per cent. The step one penalty was 5 per cent of turnover in each case. The other relevant factors were common to all the cases. In terms of providing an effective deterrent for others, no differentiation between the various companies was necessary. Case-specific deterrence could differ, but there was nothing to indicate that X needed to be treated more harshly for that reason. In those circumstances, the overall level of penalty could not be justified. In a case where the tribunal had failed to give any real explanation for the uplift, it was permissible to take the general level of fines imposed at step three into account as a cross-check on whether something had gone wrong with the process. That approach was not dissimilar to the approach adopted in cases of disparity in criminal sentences, *R. v Coleman (George Romero)* [2007] EWCA Crim 2318 considered. X's penalty was therefore reduced from £324,000 to £202,000. However, a further ground of appeal concerning financial hardship was rejected (paras 65-71, 82).

GF TOMLINSON GROUP LTD v OFFICE OF FAIR TRADING; SOL CONSTRUCTION LTD v OFFICE OF FAIR TRADING; G&J SEDDON LTD v OFFICE OF FAIR TRADING; INTERCLASS HOLDINGS LTD v OFFICE OF FAIR TRADING; APOLLO PROPERTY SERVICES GROUP LTD v OFFICE OF FAIR TRADING; GALLIFORD TRY PLC v OFFICE OF FAIR TRADING, [2012] EWCA Civ 1056, [2012] U.K.C.L.R. 304, Sir Andrew Morritt (Chancellor), CA (Civ Div).

504. Costs–Interveners–Proceedings brought out of time–Intervener applying for its costs–Whether appropriate to depart from general practice to make no order for costs in respect of interveners

The applicant company (D) applied for the costs of its intervention in proceedings brought by the respondent company (J) against the Office of Fair Trading (OFT). The OFT had investigated the market for extended warranties on domestic electrical goods. D and other retailers offered the OFT undertakings in lieu of a reference to the competition commission. A term of the undertakings was the creation of a price comparison website. J had brought proceedings against the OFT (*John Lewis Plc v Office of Fair Trading* [2013] CAT 7, [2013] Comp. A.R. 301, [2013] 8 C.L. 64) after its refusal to allow J to place details of bundled warranties onto the price comparison website. D intervened in those proceedings and they were dismissed as they had been brought well out of time. D accepted that the general practice of the Competition Appeal Tribunal was to make no order for costs in respect of interveners. D submitted that it should be awarded its costs because: J's application had been hopeless; the proceedings should not have been brought as J should have been aware that they were out of time; it was in a different position to most interveners because it was a party to the undertakings in lieu; and, it had been inevitable and necessary for it to intervene in the proceedings.

Held: No order for costs made. The general position that an intervener's costs would not be the subject of any specific costs order was necessary to strike a balance between not discouraging legitimate interventions, and not unduly encouraging interventions that might have implications for the expeditious conduct of proceedings to the detriment of the main parties, *Ryanair Holdings Plc v Competition Commission* [2012] CAT 29, [2013] Comp. A.R. 18 and *British Sky Broadcasting Group Plc v Competition Commission (Costs)* [2009] CAT 20, [2009] Comp. A.R. 247, [2010] C.L.Y. 473 considered. There was no reason to depart from that position in the instant case. The fact that certain grounds of J's application were rejected as they were out of time did not entitle D to its costs. The circumstance was not any different from proceedings where a respondent, supported by an intervener, had prevailed in resisting a substantive challenge to a decision. That was not, by itself, a good enough reason to depart from the general position, *Ryanair* applied. To the extent that D considered that a time bar defence was open to the OFT, it was reasonable to have expected the OFT to prevail on that point without any assistance. D's status as a party to the undertakings in lieu accepted by the OFT did not mean that its position was different from other interveners with a strong commercial interest in the outcome of the proceedings, or that it should be awarded its costs. There was no suggestion that D would be exposed to important consequences in the event that J had prevailed, *Independent Media Support Ltd v Office of Communications* [2008] CAT 27, [2009] Comp. A.R. 1 considered. D's application for the costs of its intervention in the proceedings failed (see paras 5-10 of judgment).

JOHN LEWIS PLC v OFFICE OF FAIR TRADING, [2013] CAT 10, [2013] Comp. A.R. 315, Rose, J., CAT.

505. Enterprise and Regulatory Reform Act 2013 (24)

This Act makes provision about the UK Green Investment Bank; makes provision about employment law; establishes and make provision about the Competition and Markets Authority and to abolish the Competition Commission and the Office of Fair Trading; amends the Competition Act 1998 and the Enterprise Act 2002; makes provision for the reduction of legislative burdens; makes provision about copyright and rights in performances; and makes provision about payments to company directors.

This Act received Royal Assent on April 25, 2013.

506. Enterprise and Regulatory Reform Act 2013 (c.24)–Commencement No.3, Transitional Provisions and Savings Order

THE ENTERPRISE AND REGULATORY REFORM ACT 2013 (COMMENCEMENT NO.3, TRANSITIONAL PROVISIONS AND SAVINGS) ORDER 2013, SI 2013/SI 2013/2227 (C.92); made under the Enterprise and Regulatory Reform Act 2013 s.100, s.103, Sch.4 para.61. Commencement details: bringing into force various provisions of the 2013 Act on October 1, 2013.; .

This Order commences certain provisions of the Enterprise and Regulatory Reform Act 2013 on October 1, 2013, as regards the creation of the Competition and Markets Authority.

507. Merger control–Sincere co-operation–Pending appeal in General Court–Time period for reference by Office of Fair Trading to Competition Commission under s.22 Enterprise Act 2002

[Enterprise Act 2002 (c.40) s.22, s.122(4); Regulation 139/2004 Art.21.]

The appellant airline (R) appealed against a decision ([2011] CAT 23, [2011] Comp. A.R. 621, [2012] 1 C.L. 52) that a reference by the first respondent Office of Fair Trading to the Competition Commission under the Enterprise Act 2002 s.22 of a relevant merger situation could not have been made earlier than the expiry of the right to appeal from a decision of the General Court. In 2006 R, as a minority shareholder in the second respondent rival airline (L), announced its intention to bid for the outstanding shares. In June 2007 the European Commission prohibited R from taking control of L but, finding it lacked the necessary power, it refused L's request to require R to divest itself of its minority holding. In October 2007 the European Commission determined that it did not have power to open proceedings against R or take interim measures. R appealed against the prohibition decision. L appealed against the European Commission's opinion that it lacked power in relation to the minority holding. In July 2012 the General Court dismissed both appeals. After the time for appealing against those judgments expired in September 2010, the OFT considered whether to make a reference under s.22. R applied to the Competition Appeal Tribunal for a declaration that the time for such a reference had expired in October 2007, but the tribunal found in favour of the OFT on the basis that the duty of sincere co-operation under the EC Treaty art.10 required the United Kingdom merger control authorities to avoid potential conflicts with judgments of the General Court which risked infringement of Regulation 139/2004 art.21 (3). R submitted that (1) the jurisdiction of the European Commission in relation to R's proposed takeover of L terminated in October 2007 with the interim measures decision, so that art.21 ceased to apply; (2) the duty of sincere co-operation continued, but it did not preclude the OFT from making a s.22 reference of R's proposed takeover of L to the Competition Commission, as the risk of conflict did not arise at that stage; (3) Section 122(4) of the Act did not apply.

Held: Appeal dismissed. (1) R's first proposition was accepted for the purposes of the instant appeal (see paras 30-31 of judgment). (2) It was clear that the Regulation and the 2002 Act conferred extensive powers of investigation on, respectively, the European Commission, the OFT and the Competition Commission both before and after a notification or reference was made. Those bodies would be investigating the same events, and concurrent investigations in the UK and in Europe would be oppressive and mutually destructive. Therefore the duty of sincere co-operation went beyond avoiding inconsistent decisions, and extended to overlapping jurisdictions. If the appeals of either, or both, R or L had succeeded there would have been an immediate clash of jurisdictions and any steps taken by the OFT and the Competition Commission in the period the appeal was pending would have infringed art.21(3). The duty of sincere co-operation, which had existed at all material times, necessarily required the OFT to desist from making any reference during that period. Accordingly, as long as R's and L's appeals were pending, and after their conclusion, the time for any further appeal was still running, the duty of sincere co-operation applied. A risk of conflict did arise and the OFT was precluded from making a reference under s.22 until all appeals had been dismissed (paras 38, 40, 42). (3) Accordingly s.122(4) did apply and the decision of the tribunal was correct (paras 45, 45).

RYANAIR HOLDINGS PLC v OFFICE OF FAIR TRADING, [2012] EWCA Civ 643, [2013] Bus. L.R. 214, Sir Andrew Morritt (Chancellor), CA (Civ Div).

CONFLICT OF LAWS

508. Allocation of jurisdiction–Defendants–Suing in courts of place where one defendant domiciled–Ousting jurisdiction of court of domicile–Test of risk of irreconcilable judgments

[Lugano Convention on Jurisdiction and the Enforcement of Judgments in Civil and Commercial Matters 2007 Art.6(1).]

The applicants (S) applied to join the respondent Swiss individual (H) as a defendant under the Lugano Convention art.6(1) to an action arising out of a fraud involving the misappropriation of more than US$400 million. S were an energy company registered in England and its Cypriot and Russian subsidiaries. They brought proceedings against four defendants allegedly involved in the fraud: a Russian national who was a director and major shareholder of the first applicant; an English resident (C) who was that company's chief executive officer at the time of the fraud; a British Virgin Islands company owned by the first defendant and operated for him by H, which received directly $154.5 million of misappropriated funds; and a Cypriot company operated by H, which received $174 million of misappropriated funds. S had obtained judgment or settled the proceedings against the defendants apart from C. S claimed that H was liable to them in the tort of unlawful means conspiracy, as a co-conspirator with the other defendants, and also for dishonestly assisting the breaches of fiduciary duty perpetrated by the first defendant and C. H was originally not joined as a defendant to the claim, because he had offered to cooperate in S's recovery efforts on the basis that he had not personally benefited from the fraud and had minimal assets. S said that that had turned out not to be the case. S submitted that, under art.6(1), H, as one of a number of defendants, could be sued in England where one of the defendants, namely C, was domiciled, since the claims against them were so closely connected that it was expedient to hear and determine them together to avoid the risk of irreconcilable judgments resulting from separate proceedings. H submitted that the only reason why the action was being pursued against C was to bring H before the English court and that art.6(1) could not be used for the sole purpose of ousting the jurisdiction of the courts of H's domicile; if, as S had indicated, the case against C would not proceed unless H was joined, there could be no risk of irreconcilable judgments if he was not.

Held: Application granted. There was or should be no dispute about whether there was a serious issue to be tried or whether if the claims proceeded against C in England and H in Switzerland there would be a risk of conflicting judgments (see paras 12-13 of judgment). The case law of the European Court of Justice showed that art.6(1) could be used to bring a defendant within the court's jurisdiction even when in practice, as opposed to analysis of the nature of the claims, there could be no risk of irreconcilable judgments, *Reisch Montage AG v Kiesel Baumaschinen Handels GmbH (C-103/05)* [2006] E.C.R. I-6827, [2007] C.L.Y. 657 applied (para.18). The ECJ had repeated that art.6(1) could not be applied to allow an applicant to claim against a number of defendants with the sole object of ousting the courts of one defendant's domicile. That risk was, however, seen to be avoided by ensuring that the irreconcilability test was met. Once that test was satisfied, there was no further hurdle, *Freeport Plc v Arnoldsson (C-98/06)* [2008] Q.B. 634, [2008] C.L.Y. 558 applied (paras 19, 27). The language of art.6(1) suggested that it was primarily to the closeness of the connection that the court looked when carrying out its value judgment; questions such as whether a particular defendant would mount an active defence or whether the claim might be or had been allowed for a time to become dormant against a particular defendant did not go to the heart of the analysis, *Alfa Laval Tumba AB v Separator Spares International Ltd* [2012] EWHC 1155 (Ch), [2012] I.L.Pr. 40, [2012] C.L.Y. 308 considered (paras 28-29). However, the position might be different if the evidence clearly established that S were making a claim against C with the sole object of bringing a case against H. The court could refuse an application which otherwise met the requirements of art.6(1) if there was clear evidence of collusion or abuse (para.31). S insisted that there had been no collusion or other arrangement with C. S had disclosed what the contacts between them and C were about. If that disclosure was verified by witness statement the allegations of collusion and/or that S had no intention of pursuing C fell away. There was thus no factual basis for H to resist the application under art.6(1) (para.38).

SIBIR ENERGY LTD v TCHIGIRINSKI, [2012] EWHC 1844 (QB), [2012] 2 All E.R. (Comm) 1285, Judge Mackie, Q.C., QBD (Comm).

509. Allocation of jurisdiction–Disputing the court's jurisdiction–Demonstration of consent to agreement conferring jurisdiction

[Arbitration Act 1996 (c.23) s.9(4); Civil Procedure Rules 1998 (SI 1998/3132) r.6.36; Regulation 44/2001 on jurisdiction and the recognition and enforcement of judgments in civil and commercial matters Art.6; CPR PD 6B (Service out of the Jurisdiction) 2000 para.3.1(3); Lugano Convention on Jurisdiction and the Enforcement of Judgments in Civil and Commercial Matters 2007 Art.23.]

The appellant companies (C, H and F) appealed against a decision ([2012] EWHC 1610 (Ch), [2013] 1 Lloyd's Rep. 345, [2013] 6 C.L. 58) refusing to stay English proceedings or to decline jurisdiction, and the respondent (R) cross-appealed. R was a state-owned Russian airline. It claimed that a fraud had been perpetrated on it by two individuals, who had been served with proceedings in England where they were domiciled. Its case was that money had been siphoned off through a group of companies controlled by the individual defendants. The group included C, H and F, which were incorporated in Cyprus, Luxembourg and the British Virgin Islands, and a Swiss company (S). R had retained S as an advisor under an advisory mandate which provided for Swiss law and jurisdiction. R accepted that it had signed the mandate but argued that it was void for want of authority under Swiss law. R had then entered into credit agreements with S and then C, which provided for Swiss law and arbitration. R said that pursuant to those agreements payments due to R had been assigned and paid to the group companies for the benefit of the individual defendants. The group companies were said to be liable to compensate R for the payments under various articles of the Russian Civil Code. R served the companies out of the jurisdiction on the basis that they were necessary or proper parties to the claim against the individual defendants. They challenged the jurisdiction of the English court relying on the contractual provisions for Swiss jurisdiction and for arbitration. The judge held that S was entitled to rely on the Swiss jurisdiction clause in the advisory mandate so that the English court had no jurisdiction in respect of the claim against it; that there should be no stay of the proceedings against C under the Arbitration Act 1996 s.9 because the arbitration clause in the agreement between R and C was unenforceable as a matter of Swiss law; and that C, H and F remained necessary and proper parties to the proceedings.

Held: Appeals allowed in part. (1) Since S relied on the Swiss jurisdiction clause to displace the necessary and proper party basis of jurisdiction relied on by R, the burden lay on S to show that the Lugano Convention 2007 art.23 applied (see para.47 of judgment). The standard of proof was a good arguable case, *Bols Distilleries BV (t/a Bols Royal Distilleries) v Superior Yacht Services Ltd*

[2006] UKPC 45, [2007] 1 W.L.R. 12, [2007] C.L.Y. 349 considered (paras 48-50). Whether there was an agreement conferring jurisdiction for the purposes of art.23 was to be determined by autonomous Community law principles and not by the application of Swiss law as the putative applicable law. The trend of the case-law of the European Court of Justice was that it was sufficient to conclude for the purposes of art.23 that R's consent to the Swiss jurisdiction clause had been clearly demonstrated by the signing of the document, without the need to consider the attack on the validity of the advisory mandate under Swiss law, *Powell Duffryn Plc v Petereit (C-214/89)* [1992] E.C.R. I-1745, [1992] C.L.Y. 4826 and *Benincasa v Dentalkit Srl (C-269/95)* [1998] All E.R. (EC) 135, [1997] C.L.Y. 888 considered and *Deutsche Bank AG v Asia Pacific Broadband Wireless Communications Inc* [2008] EWCA Civ 1091, [2009] 2 All E.R. (Comm) 129, [2009] C.L.Y. 623 followed. The judge was right that S was entitled to rely on the Swiss jurisdiction clause under art.23. The English court had to decline jurisdiction in respect of the claims against S and R's appeal was dismissed (paras 51-68). (2) On the face of it there was an arbitration clause in the agreement between R and C. R failed to show that that arbitration agreement was null and void or inoperable under s.9(4) by virtue of the Swiss law doctrine of "double representation" because one of the individual defendants was acting on both sides of the transaction. That was not made out on the evidence. R also failed to show as a matter of Swiss law that that doctrine would affect the arbitration clause in the instant case as well as the credit agreement, or that R had suffered any prejudice in relation to the arbitration agreement (paras 86-89). The judge had been wrong to find that Swiss law had a doctrine of "abuse of right" which meant that the arbitration clause was null and void or inoperative, because to uphold it would cause the fragmentation of the dispute. It followed that C was entitled to a stay pursuant to s.9 and its appeal was allowed (paras 93-100). (3) In order to rely on the necessary and proper party head of jurisdiction under Regulation 44/2001 art.6 R did not have to show that there was a serious issue to be tried as against H; that would be inconsistent with the autonomous Community interpretation of art.6, *Unilever Plc v Chefaro Proprietaries Ltd (Discovery)* [1994] F.S.R. 135, [1995] C.L.Y. 4130 distinguished and *Freeport Plc v Arnoldsson (C-98/06)* [2008] Q.B. 634, [2008] C.L.Y. 558 applied (paras 101-109). R had shown a good arguable case that it could rely on art.6 as against H and its appeal was dismissed (paras 110-114). (4) R had shown a serious issue to be tried as against F under CPR r.6.36 and a good arguable case that F was a necessary and proper party within CPR PD 6B para.3.1 (3) and F's appeal was dismissed (paras 115-119).

AEROFLOT -RUSSIAN AIRLINES v BEREZOVSKY; *sub nom.* JOINT STOCK CO AEROFLOT RUSSIAN AIRLINES v BEREZOVSKY, [2013] EWCA Civ 784, [2013] 2 Lloyd's Rep. 242, Laws, L.J., CA (Civ Div).

510. Allocation of jurisdiction–Stay of proceedings–Application to stay proceedings under art.27(1) or art.28(1) Regulation 44/2001–Effect of party requesting stay refusing to consent to all claims being tried together

[Senior Courts Act 1981 (c.54) s.49(3); Regulation 44/2001 on jurisdiction and the recognition and enforcement of judgments in civil and commercial matters Art.27(1), Art.28(1), Art.28(3).]

The applicant (M) applied for a stay of the proceedings until judgment had been delivered in proceedings which it had brought against the respondent (T) in Spain. M and T were Spanish broadcasting companies. M had acquired the rights to broadcast the Formula One world championship for 2009-2013 in Spain. Under the same agreement, it sub-licensed the right to broadcast the championship in Spain to another broadcaster (S) and the right to broadcast it within Valencia to T. The agreement contained a clause by which M undertook not to grant various rights in the same territory to any other party, with certain exceptions. Under the agreement, the English court had exclusive jurisdiction to settle any disputes, save that if M was the plaintiff, the Spanish courts had exclusive jurisdiction, at M's election. If both parties agreed, the Spanish courts could have jurisdiction to settle any dispute. In September 2010, M commenced Spanish proceedings against T, claiming that T had not paid fees which were due. In February 2012, M terminated its agreement with S and granted a sub-licence to another company (N). T then terminated its agreement with M on the ground that the grant of a sub-licence to N was a repudiatory breach of the agreement. M disputed the validity of the termination. T sought to introduce the alleged repudiatory breach into the Spanish proceedings, but M denied that the issue was relevant to the dispute before the Spanish court and maintained that the English courts had exclusive jurisdiction over it. The Spanish court refused to admit the issue. The Spanish trial took place in June 2012, but the judge went missing before giving judgment. It therefore seemed likely that a re-trial would be necessary. T commenced the instant proceedings, seeking a declaration that M's actions amounted to a repudiatory breach of the contract and seeking damages for that breach. It offered to discontinue the English proceedings and commence them in Spain instead, but M refused to consent. M submitted that (1) the English proceedings should be stayed under Regulation 44/2001 art.27(1) because it was unclear what matters the Spanish court considered itself seised of until it gave judgment; (2) alternatively, the proceedings should be stayed under art.28(1) and the Senior Courts Act 1981 s.49(3) because it was unclear what matters the Spanish court considered itself seised of and there was a consequent risk of irreconcilable judgments.

Held: Application refused. (1) The Spanish and English proceedings involved different causes of action and different objects. The cause of action in the Spanish proceedings was T's alleged breach of the agreement in failing to pay fees when they fell due. The causes of action in the English proceedings were M's alleged repudiatory breach and T's claim that it had validly terminated the agreement on that ground. The facts and the rules of law relied on were both different. The object of the Spanish proceedings was recovery by M of the debts owed by T. The object of the English proceedings was to establish whether T had validly terminated the agreement and whether M had to pay T damages for breach of the agreement, The *Owners of Cargo Lately Laden on Board the Tatry v Owners of the Maciej Rataj (C-406/92)* [1999] Q.B. 515, [1995] C.L.Y. 704 and *Kolden Holdings Ltd v Rodette Commerce Ltd* [2008] EWCA Civ 10, [2008] 3 All E.R. 612, [2008] C.L.Y. 565 applied. Furthermore, there was no dispute that the Spanish court had exclusive jurisdiction over M's claim and the instant court had exclusive jurisdiction over T's claims. It followed that art.27(1) had no application (see paras 42-45, 49-56 of judgment). (2) It was not appropriate to grant a stay under art.28(1) or s.49(3). The Spanish and English proceedings were not "related" within the meaning of art.28(3). As a result of M's stance in refusing to consent to the English proceedings being commenced in Spain, there was no possibility of the two actions being heard and determined together. The risk of irreconcilable judgments was very slight. Even if there was a risk of irreconcilable judgments, that risk had been created by M's stance. It was not open to the party who had created a risk of irreconcilable judgments by refusing to agree to all claims being tried together to say that the other party's claim should be stayed as a result. Since it appeared likely that there would have to be a re-trial of the Spanish proceedings, the effect of granting a stay would be to delay the progress of the English proceedings for an unknown and potentially significant period even though the issue of the repudiatory breach could only be determined in the instant proceedings (paras 58-69).

TELEVISION AUTONOMICA VALENCIANA S.A. v IMAGINA CONTENIDOS AUDIOVISUALES S.L., [2013] EWHC 160 (Ch), [2013] I.L.Pr. 27, Arnold, J., Ch D.

511. Allocation of jurisdiction–Stay of proceedings–Debt claim brought in English courts–Effect of previous claim brought by debtor in French court

[Regulation 44/2001 on jurisdiction and the recognition and enforcement of judgments in civil and commercial matters Art.27, Art.28.]

The defendant French company (C) applied for a stay of an action brought by the claimant (L) in the United Kingdom. L had begun that action in June 2011. It sought the sum of $6 million, being the sum it claimed to be due under a settlement agreement entered into with C. Default notices relating to C's failure to pay instalments under the agreement had been served on C, the last one being dated March 11, 2010. In February 2010, C had begun debt-conciliation proceedings in France. Such proceedings constituted a judicial measure to assist debtors in financial difficulty. If a creditor did not wish to participate (L chose not to), the debtor could request a suspension of his debts. On March 30, 2010, the relevant tribunal ruled that C was entitled to a two-year suspension in respect of its obligations to L, that period being reduced on appeal to one year. C asserted that it had at least three potential defences to the claim that L had brought. The third relied on propositions of French domestic law and English private international law. The proposition of French law was that C had been under no obligation to pay at the time of the relevant default notice, given the French court's suspension of its payment obligations. The proposition of English private international law was that in the instant action the court would give effect to the French law proposition and would have to do so if the French court ruled that it was correct. C stated that proceedings were pending in France in which it had asked the French court to determine that the French law proposition was right. It maintained that, until that court decided the point or said that it would not decide it, the English action should be stayed. C argued that (1) the English court should stay the action in favour of the French court under Regulation 44/2001 art.27 as the two sets of proceedings involved the same cause of action between the same parties; (2) alternatively, the proceedings were "related actions" within the meaning of art.28.

Held: Application granted. (1) It was impossible to say that the two sets of proceedings involved the same facts and rules of law. The English action was concerned with the amount of the debt. The relevant rules of law were those concerning contractual agreements. The relevant rules of law in the French proceedings were those concerned with protection for businesses which were in difficulty. The argument based on art.27 therefore failed (see para.68 of judgment). (2) Article 28 was engaged where the two proceedings were so closely connected that it was expedient to hear and determine them together to avoid the risk of irreconcilable judgments resulting from separate proceedings. It was highly relevant that the English action could not be substantively determined in L's favour unless either the French law proposition was wrong or that proposition was right but as a matter of English private international law it did not assist C. In that regard, there was a substantial degree of connection. Pushing on with the English action ran a substantial risk of trespassing on the French proceedings with the consequent danger of irreconcilable judgments. A value judgment had to be made as to the expediency of hearing the two actions together in order to avoid the risk of inconsistent judgments. As to the French law proposition, that aim might be achieved if the French court concluded that it should be decided. Substantive consideration of the English action would be more advantageously dealt with after the French court had determined whether or not it would decide the French law proposition and, if it did, what the answer was and why, *Research in Motion UK Ltd v Visto Corp* [2008] EWCA Civ 153, [2008] 2 All E.R. (Comm) 560, [2008] C.L.Y. 566 applied (paras 70, 79-80).

LEHMAN BROTHERS BANKHAUS AG I INS v CMA CGM, [2013] EWHC 171 (Comm), [2013] 2 All E.R. (Comm) 557, Walker, J., QBD (Comm).

512. Allocation of jurisdiction–Stay of proceedings–Insolvency proceedings in Germany–Risk of irreconcilable judgments

The appellant (R) appealed against the dismissal of his application for an order that the High Court had no jurisdiction to try the claim brought by the respondent (G) and that the claim form and its service on R be set aside or stayed. G specialised in the provision of stock finance. By a facility agreement G agreed to extend funding to two German companies (H and HG), of which R was a director, which operated department stores in Germany. G agreed to lend up to a limit of EUR 55 million, but with the precise limit on the amounts to be advanced to them from time to time to be calculated by reference to the value of their inventories which were declared weekly in a form. R entered into a deed of warranty with G that he would procure that all inventory included in any schedule prepared by either H or HG would comprise unencumbered current assets of the company in question. Both the deed of warranty and the facility agreement contained provisions that they were governed by English law and that English courts had exclusive jurisdiction to settle any disputes. HG was placed into administration and the administrator brought a claim against G in Germany alleging that sums paid to G pursuant to the facility agreement out of the proceeds of sale of goods and used by G to reduce HG's overdraft with G wrongly prejudiced other creditors as H, and not HG, owned the relevant stock until the sale was made. G issued a claim form in England for EUR 28.5 million in respect of advances made by G to HG. G also claimed damages for breach of the deed of warranty in that the inventory forms were false as there was no inventory belonging to HG. The judge dismissed R's application for a stay of G's claim on the basis that the German proceedings were insolvency proceedings within Regulation (EC) No.1346/2000 and therefore Regulation (EC) No.44/2001 art.28 had no application and, in any event, the two proceedings were not related actions within art.28. R submitted that the proceedings were related and, if they both proceeded, there was a risk of irreconcilable judgments.

Held: Appeal dismissed. The judge had decided that, even if art.28 did apply where the proceedings before the court first seised were insolvency proceedings, the German proceedings and the instant proceedings were not related actions as defined by art.28(3). He further concluded that, even if they were related proceedings under art.28(3), he would not exercise his discretion in favour of a stay. He was entitled to reach those conclusions as, inter alia, the German court might rule against the administrator in the German proceedings without deciding the issue of ownership of stock or the accuracy of the inventory forms and G would then have the same substantial claim against H under the deed of warranty. In any event, a judgment of the German court on the inventory point would not be binding on an English court because the parties to the two sets of proceedings were different. It was also relevant that the deed of warranty on which G's claim was advanced expressly provided for English law and English jurisdiction. It was impossible to say that the judge was wrong to hold that the proceedings in Germany were not related as defined in art.28(3) or that he acted outside the bounds of a proper exercise of judicial discretion in holding that a stay should not be granted (see paras 18-25 of judgment).

RAHMAN v GMAC COMMERCIAL FINANCE LTD, [2012] EWCA Civ 1467, [2013] I.L.Pr. 5, Etherton, L.J., CA (Civ Div).

513. Choice of law–Agency agreements–Whether parties had made implied choice of English law

[Convention on the Law Applicable to Contractual Obligations 1980 Art.3, Art.4.]

The appellant (L) appealed against a decision ([2012] EWHC 1188 (QB), [2012] 2 Lloyd's Rep. 25, [2012] C.L.Y. 56) that his agency contract with the respondent company (S) was governed by Spanish law rather than by English law. L was a citizen of the Irish Republic. Some time between 1992 and 1994, he was employed as a salesman by a company (E) which had been incorporated in the United Kingdom to manufacture screening and crushing machinery. After completing his training, he was sent to E's distributor in Germany as an employed salesman, but that arrangement did not work out well. He was then sent to work in Spain, which from that point onwards was his main area of operation. In about 1994 or 1995, L's contractual status changed from that of an employee to that of a sales agent, although there was no formal agency agreement. S bought E's business in 2007. L, like other agents, was offered a contract of employment containing an English-law clause but negotiations did not lead to an agreement. In May 2008, S gave L notice terminating his agency with effect from June 1, 2009. L began the instant action, seeking compensation for the termination of his agency. His claim would be worth more if his contract was governed by English law than if it was governed by Spanish law. L argued before the judge that under the Rome Convention 1980 art.3 the parties had made an implied choice of English law. Article 3 provided that a contract would be governed by the law chosen by the parties and that the choice had to be "expressed or demonstrated with reasonable certainty by the terms of the contract or the circumstances of the case". The judge found that the requirements of art.3 had not been met, holding, among other things, that the agency agreement was informal and unwritten, no consideration having been given to the applicable law. The judge therefore applied art.4 of the Convention, which provided that, to the extent that the law applicable to the contract had not been chosen in accordance with art.3, the contract would be governed by the law of the country with which it was most closely connected.

Held: Appeal dismissed. The test of whether an implied choice of law had been established was objective. Evidence of the unspoken thoughts of the parties was inadmissible. The objective nature of the test meant that the party asserting an implied choice of law had to satisfy the court that, on an objective view, the parties must have taken it without saying that their contract should be governed by that law or that the contract taken as a whole pointed ineluctably to the conclusion that the parties intended it to be governed by that law. He had to satisfy the court that the only reasonable conclusion to be drawn from the circumstances was that the parties should be taken to have intended the putative law to apply. The judge had been right to conclude that L had not established an implied choice of English law as a matter of reasonable certainty. The evidence about the making of the agency agreement was vague. At the time it was made, L was living in Spain and Spain was to be the centre of his activities. On the sparse material before the judge, L had not established with reasonable certainty that it went without saying that the contract was intended to be governed by English law. The judge had been right to hold that it was not enough to establish that if a choice of law had been made, it would in all probability have been English law. The judge accepted that such a choice would have been in accordance with S's general wish for its contracts to be governed by English law, but L had to show that the nature and circumstances of the agency contract demonstrated an implied choice of English law, and the judge rightly recognised that there was a distinction between those two things (see paras 31, 33-34).

LAWLOR v SANDVIK MINING AND CONSTRUCTION MOBILE CRUSHERS AND SCREENS LTD, [2013] EWCA Civ 365, [2013] 2 Lloyd's Rep. 98, Lloyd, L.J., CA (Civ Div).

514. Choice of law–Variation–Entitlement of parties to contract to change governing law

[Regulation 593/2008 on the law applicable to contractual obligations (Rome I) Art.3.]

The defendants (H and S) applied for an order setting aside the claim form issued by the claimant bank (M) on the ground that the English court did not have jurisdiction to try M's claim. M was registered in Mauritius. H was a Mauritian-registered company. S, which was registered in India, was H's parent company. M sought to recover from H (as borrower) and S (as guarantor) money due under a Restated Facility Agreement (RFA), which replaced the Original Facility Agreement between the parties. The latter agreement provided that the governing law would be that of Mauritius. The RFA stipulated that English law would be the governing law. Clause 24.1 of the RFA provided as follows: (a) The courts of England have exclusive jurisdiction to settle any dispute arising out of or in connection with this Agreement... (b) The Parties agree that the courts of England are the most appropriate and the most convenient courts to settle Disputes and accordingly no Party will [argue] to the contrary (c) This Clause 24.1 is for the benefit of the Lender only. As a result the Lender shall not be prevented from taking proceedings related to a Dispute in any other courts in any jurisdiction...". H and S argued, among other things, that (1) under English rules of private international law, parties could not amend the governing law of their agreement; (2) cl.24.1 of the RFA was too one-sided to be compatible with fundamental principles regarding equal access to justice and should not be upheld under English law.

Held: Application refused. (1) There was nothing in the authorities to suggest that a prospective change of the proper law governing a contract was objectionable. It was difficult to identify any rationale or policy reason why such a change should be objectionable, especially given that the same result could be achieved by making a new agreement on amended terms rather than simply amending the terms. Indeed, the adoption in English law of Regulation 593/2008 art.3(2) was itself a powerful indicator that there was, at least now, no policy of English law which was opposed to the parties agreeing to change the governing law of their contract. On the contrary, there was a strong countervailing policy that they should be permitted to do so, which was to be found in the principle of contractual autonomy. One could imagine a variety of good commercial reasons why the parties might wish to change their governing law: there might be changes in the law first chosen which were unwelcome or they might only discover unwelcome aspects of that law after the contract was concluded. If commercial parties freely agreed to change their governing law, the court should strive to give effect to their bargain unless there were overwhelming policy objections. None applied in this context (see paras 29-30 of judgment). (2) H and S had argued that cl.24.1 (c) conferred a power on M to sue them in any court in the world, rather than those courts which would otherwise regard themselves under their own rules of private international law as having competent jurisdiction. That was an erroneous reading of the clause. Sub-paragraph (c) merely provided that sub-paragraph (a) would not prevent M from taking proceedings other than in England. It was not an agreement to confer jurisdiction on a foreign court where none would otherwise exist. It preserved M's right to sue in any court which would regard itself as of competent jurisdiction, notwithstanding what would otherwise have been the effect of cl.24.1 (a), which, if it had stood alone, would have required M to sue in England. H and S had also argued that c.24.1 was entirely one-sided because it conferred no rights on them to sue in any forum while subjecting them to any forum at the suit of M. That too was an erroneous reading of the clause. Clause 24.1 (c) referred to the lender taking proceedings. Clause 24.1 was for the benefit of M in the sense that H and S were obliged to sue in England but M was not. But that did not disapply cl.24.1 (a) to M completely. Where it was H or S which brought suit against M in England, cl.24.1 (a) was not disapplied by the operation of cl.24.1 (c). M was thereby agreeing to be sued in England subject to the liberty conferred by cl.24.1 (c). In those circumstances, M had agreed to be subjected to the exclusive jurisdiction of the English courts, subject to its right to bring claims abroad pursuant to cl.24.1 (c) (paras 37, 40).

MAURITIUS COMMERCIAL BANK LTD v HESTIA HOLDINGS LTD, [2013] EWHC 1328 (Comm), [2013] 2 All E.R. (Comm) 898, Popplewell, J., QBD (Comm).

515. Recognition of judgments–Winding-up proceedings–EEA credit institutions and insolvency measures–Cross-claims brought in insolvency proceedings in two EEA states–Whether claims extinguished in one state effective as set-off to claim brought in another

[Credit Institutions (Reorganisation and Winding up) Regulations 2004 (SI 2004/1045) reg.5, Pt 3, Pt 4, reg.28.]

The appellant winding-up board of an Icelandic company (L) appealed against a decision ([2011] CSIH 61, 2012 S.C. 209, [2012] C.L.Y. 4109) that the withdrawal of claims brought by the respondent administrators of a Scottish company (H) in L's winding-up proceedings in Iceland did not prevent the administrators from setting off those claims against one brought by L in H's administration in Scotland. L and H were credit institutions for the purposes of Directive 2001/24. H was a wholly-owned subsidiary of L, and both were in formal insolvency. A winding-up board had been appointed in respect of L, and joint administrators had been appointed in respect of H. L submitted a claim in H's administration in Scotland, and H submitted claims in L's winding up in Iceland. L's winding up board rejected three of H's claims, but accepted the fourth in a lesser amount. H's administrators rejected L's claim, applying the Scots law on the balancing of accounts in bankruptcy and finding that H's claims set off and extinguished L's claim. In November 2009, L's winding-up board appealed against that decision to the Scottish Court of Session, arguing that its rejection of H's claims was binding in the United Kingdom by reason of the Credit Institutions (Reorganisation and Winding up) Regulations 2004 reg.5. It argued that H thus had no claim against L to set off. In February 2010, H's administrators filed a notice of objection to the board's rejection of its claims, but asked that no steps be taken until the Court of Session had determined the appeal. The board referred the objection to the Icelandic court, which refused to stay it pending the determination of the board's appeal. In July 2010, the Lord Ordinary held that the board's rejection of H's claims should be given effect in the UK. H's administrators withdrew their claims in the Icelandic winding-up. The Court of Session then reversed the Lord Ordinary's decision. The issue was how cross-claims between two credit institutions were to be dealt with in insolvency proceedings in two different states in the European Economic Area. The question was whether Icelandic law governed the question of whether H's claims still subsisted for the purposes of a set-off in the Scottish proceedings, or whether they were to be regarded as having been extinguished because they could no longer be maintained in L's winding-up in Iceland.

Held: Appeal dismissed. The Regulations were designed to adopt the strict entity approach, based on the principle that the administrative or judicial authorities of the credit institution's home state were to be solely responsible for the opening of proceedings for its winding-up. In that context, there was nothing remarkable about reg.5. Even if an EEA credit institution had branches in the UK, the winding-up had to be conducted in its home state. An EEA insolvency measure in another EEA state had to have effect in the UK in relation to any of the credit institution's branches there as if it were part of the general law of insolvency of the UK. Thus, property or assets in Scotland were not to be disposed of in accordance with Scots law rules, and steps by a creditor to enforce claims against the credit institution had to be pursued solely in the Icelandic proceedings. Decisions taken in the Icelandic winding-up were to be given effect in Scotland so as to maintain the integrity of Iceland's exclusive jurisdiction. However, reg.5 was concerned only with an EEA insolvency measure in relation to a credit institution located in another EEA state. It applied to L's winding-up in Iceland, but not to H's administration in Scotland. Part 3 and Pt 4 of the Regulations applied to H, which was a UK credit institution. Their effect was that the general law of insolvency had effect in relation to UK credit institutions, subject to the provisions of Part 3. Such matters as the conditions under which set-off might be invoked and the rules governing the admission and ranking of claims were to be determined in accordance with the UK's general law of insolvency. Regulation 28 preserved the right of creditors to demand that their claims be set off against the claims of the affected credit institution, where set-off was permitted by the law applicable to the credit institution's claim. Issues of set-off were to be determined in the home EEA state, as the common law of Scotland required, according to the proper law of the contract. Regulation 5(1) was designed to give effect to the mandatory choice of the law of the credit institution's home state; it was not concerned with the effects of the mandatory choice of Scots law for H's administration in Scotland. Part 3 and Pt 4 of the Regulations, had nothing to do with the effect of the mandatory choice of Icelandic law for L's winding-up. The board's argument was therefore rejected: it failed to take account of the scheme of the Directive and the Regulations; it produced, arguably, an arbitrary and unprincipled outcome; and it gave universal priority to the process in which a decision happened to be made first. That would encourage forum shopping, and it was hard to believe that that was what the framers of the Directive intended. H's administrators could thus use their claims to set off L's claim in the Scottish administration (see paras 52-61 of judgment).

JOINT ADMINISTRATORS OF HERITABLE BANK PLC v WINDING UP BOARD OF LANDSBANKI ISLANDS HF; *sub nom.* HERITABLE BANK PLC v LANDSBANKI ISLANDS HF, [2013] UKSC 13, [2013] 1 W.L.R. 725, Lord Hope, J.S.C. (Deputy President), SC.

CONSTITUTIONAL LAW

516. Constitutional reform–House of Lords–Supreme Court

THE PROCEEDS OF CRIME ACT 2002 (APPEALS UNDER PART 2) (AMENDMENT) ORDER 2013, SI 2013/24; made under the Proceeds of Crime Act 2002 s.89, s.90, s.459. In force: February 8, 2013; .

This Order amends the Proceeds of Crime Act 2002 (Appeals Under Part 2) Order 2003. It contains provisions which correspond to those under the Proceeds of Crime Act 2002 (External Requests and Orders) Order 2005 (England and Wales) (Appeals Under Part 2) Order 2012 (SI 2012/138). SI 2012/138 makes provision corresponding to provisions in the Criminal Appeal Act 1968 with modifications for the purposes of an appeal to the Court of Appeal (and from there to the Supreme Court) introduced by the Proceeds of Crime Act 2002 (External Requests and Orders) Order 2005 art.47(3) and 48(2). The purpose of the amendments in this Order is to ensure consistency between appeals to the Court of Appeal and then on to the Supreme Court under the Proceeds of Crime Act 2002 Pt 2 and those which relate to external requests. It applies to appeals that are both.

517. Constitutional Reform and Governance Act 2010 (c.25)–Commencement No.8 and Saving Provision Order

THE CONSTITUTIONAL REFORM AND GOVERNANCE ACT 2010 (COMMENCEMENT NO.8 AND SAVING PROVISION) ORDER 2013, SI 2013/2826; made under the Constitutional Reform and Governance Act 2010 s.52. Commencement details: bringing into force various provisions of the 2010 Act on November 1, 2013; .

This Order brings into force provisions of the Constitutional Reform and Governance Act 2010 Sch.6 which make provision for the Independent Parliamentary Standards Authority to make a scheme, under the European Parliament (Pay and Pensions) Act 1979 s.4, with respect to pensions for certain Representatives to the European Parliament.

518. Legislative competence–Scottish Parliament–Social security

THE SCOTLAND ACT 1998 (MODIFICATION OF SCHEDULE 5) (NO.2) ORDER 2013, SI 2013/192; made under the Scotland Act 1998 s.30. In force: April 1, 2013;.

This Order modifies Sch.5 to the Scotland Act 1998 to provide an exception to the social security reservation therein. The exception gives the Scottish Parliament competence to legislate for financial or other assistance provided to or in respect of individuals for the purposes specified in the exception. Certain types of assistance which could otherwise fall within the exception are specifically excluded from the exception.

CONSTRUCTION LAW

519. Adjudication–Construction contracts–Application for summary judgment to enforce adjudicator's decision regarding liability under credit sub-contract–Cross-claim to set off liquidated damages

[Housing Grants, Construction and Regeneration Act 1996 (c.53).]

The claimant company (S) applied for summary judgment enforcing an adjudication decision against the defendant company (V). V had engaged S under a sub-contract for asbestos removal and demolition at a site. It was a credit sub-contract, in that S paid V a sum upfront for the site materials following demolition and V then paid S on a monthly basis for work done. The works were not completed by the agreed date and responsibility for the delay was disputed. There were no specific terms in the sub-contract setting out the final date for payment of sums due to S under the monthly valuations, or regarding when withholding notices were to be served. However, the ICE main contract terms were incorporated into the sub-contract, which meant that V had 28 days to pay S from the date of a valuation and any withholding notice had to be served not less than one day before the final date for payment. The sub-contract did provide for V to claim liquidated damages and to deduct, or set off, any amounts due to it against payments certified as due to S. S issued an adjudication claim. The adjudicator (X) decided that the ICE contract terms allowed S to claim for an extension of time and for additional loss and expense, which was to be paid within 14 days from the date of the decision, and that there had been no withholding notice from V in respect of any cross-claim for liquidated damages. V claimed that it was entitled to rely on a withholding notice served after X's decision.

Held: Judgment for claimant. V could not set off its claim for liquidated damages so as to defeat S's claim for summary judgment. First, as a matter of law the right to make such a set off had been generally excluded, because anything else would be contrary to the Housing Grants, Construction and Regeneration Act 1996 and the underlying purpose of construction adjudication. It would be contrary to the Act if the effect of an adjudicator's decision could be avoided altogether by the subsequent service of a withholding notice. It would allow the unsuccessful party a defence to the claim merely because the adjudicator had given that party time to pay the sum due, rather than ordering immediate payment. That would be counter-intuitive; it would mean that the unsuccessful party was taking undue advantage of the adjudicator's decision to allow them some time to pay, *Levolux AT Ltd v Ferson Contractors Ltd* [2003] EWCA Civ 11, [2003] 1 All E.R. (Comm) 385, [2003] C.L.Y. 667, *Balfour Beatty Construction v Serco Ltd* [2004] EWHC 3336 (TCC) and *William Verry Ltd v Camden LBC* [2006] EWHC 761 (TCC) applied. Second, X had not been giving some kind of declaratory relief as to how the payment mechanism under the sub-contract might operate. He was not providing a declaration as to what sum was payable under the contract or identifying a sum to "plug in" to the contract. He was deciding a one-off claim in a one-off way, *Shimizu Europe Ltd v LBJ Fabrications Ltd* [2003] EWHC 1229 (TCC), [2003] B.L.R. 381, [2003] C.L.Y. 645, *Conor Engineering Ltd v Constructions Industrielles de la Mediterranee (CNIM) SA* [2004] EWHC 899 (TCC), [2004] B.L.R. 212 and *R&C Electrical Engineers Ltd v Shaylor Construction Ltd* [2012] EWHC 1254

(TCC), [2012] B.L.R. 373, [2012] C.L.Y. 596 considered. Third, the sub-contract did not permit the intended withholding. There was nothing express or implied in the relevant clause which could allow an unsuccessful party to adjudication to override the effect of the adjudicator's decision, or to deprive the successful party of the sum otherwise due pursuant to that decision. The set-off provision was couched in very general terms and referred to certified payments, while the instant case involved a one-off payment ordered by X, *Ferson* considered. Fourth, it did not follow from X's decision that V were automatically entitled to liquidated damages for the shortfall period between the extended date for completion and the actual date of completion. A decision which extended the time for completion, but not for the whole period of delay, would not automatically entitle the employer to set off liquidated damages for the shortfall, *Avoncroft Construction Ltd v Sharba Homes (CN) Ltd* [2008] EWHC 933 (TCC), [2008] T.C.L.R. 7, [2009] C.L.Y. 657 considered. There had been no consideration by X of any mirror delay claim by V. Fifth, any other conclusion would be contrary to the clear words of X's decision that no sums could be properly payable by S by way of liquidated damages. To allow V a wholly contrary result would defeat that important element of the decision and would also be contrary to the general principles of adjudication enforcement, *VHE Construction Plc v RBSTB Trust Co Ltd* [2000] B.L.R. 187, [2000] C.L.Y. 806 and *Interserve Industrial Services Ltd v Cleveland Bridge UK Ltd* [2006] EWHC 741 (TCC) applied (see paras 19-27 of judgment).

SQUIBB GROUP LTD v VERTASE FLI LTD, [2012] EWHC 1958 (TCC), [2012] B.L.R. 408, Coulson, J., QBD (TCC).

520. Adjudication–Design and build contracts–Referral of single dispute to adjudication–Severability of erroneous part of decision from whole

The claimant (L) applied for summary judgment to enforce an adjudicator's decision that it was entitled to liquidated and ascertained damages. L had engaged the defendant contractor (R) to construct a food store and associated works. Under a design and build contract, the works were separated into three. The first two sections were to be completed by May 12, 2011 and the third by June 20, 2011. Clause 2.27 of the contract provided that, when practical completion of the works or of one of the sections had been achieved, L would issue a statement to that effect. The contract also provided that R would pay liquidated damages at the rate stated in the contract or at a lesser rate, or that L would deduct such damages from the payment due to R, for the period between the contractual completion date and the date of practical completion. On June 28, 2011, L certified what it described as "Part Practical Completion" of the works associated with section one as having taken place on June 27, 2011. On July 6, 2011, L certified that practical completion had been achieved in relation to the external works forming part of section two. In January 2012, L served a non-completion notice in relation to sections one and two stating that it had taken partial possession of part of the works on July 7, 2011 and claiming pro-rated liquidated damages from that date. The adjudicator found that practical completion had been achieved on March 26, 2012 in relation to section one and on March 30, 2012 in relation to section two, but that the certificates issued by L on June 28 and July 6 remained effective. L claimed: (i) £125,000 at the full contractual rate up to June 27, 2011 and July 6, 2011 respectively in relation to sections one and two; (ii) pro rata amounts from June 27, 2011 to March 26, 2012 in relation to section one, and from July 6, 2011 to March 30, 2012 in relation to section two. In a second decision, the adjudicator held that L was entitled to £125,000 in relation to the initial delays to sections one and two at the full contractual rate, and to a "lesser rate" until practical completion of those sections. It was common ground that the adjudicator lacked jurisdiction to find R liable for liquidated damages in the sum of £125,000, as in doing so he was answering a question that had not been put to him.

Held: Judgment accordingly. (1) The two items of liquidated damages that totalled £125,000 were clearly not part of or within the confines of the dispute. L's reasoning underpinning those claims had no bearing on the issues before the adjudicator. Accordingly, the rest of the decision could be severed from that part which related to the adjudicator's findings in excess of jurisdiction. The rationale underlying the principle that a decision could not be severed where only one dispute or difference had been referred was that, where a single dispute had been referred, it would generally be difficult to show that the reasoning in relation to the part of the decision which one of the parties sought to sever had no impact on the reasoning leading to the decision actually reached, or that the actual outcome would still have been the same. If that was the case, the part was not severable. However, where a single dispute was referred and additional questions were brought in, whether in oversight or error, there was no reason why any decision on those additional questions should not be severed provided that the reasoning giving rise to it did not form an integral part of the whole decision. Failing that, the entire decision would be unenforceable, *Cantillon Ltd v Urvasco Ltd* [2008] EWHC 282 (TCC), [2008] B.L.R. 250, [2008] C.L.Y. 606 and *Working Environments Ltd v Greencoat Construction Ltd* [2012] EWHC 1039 (TCC), [2012] B.L.R. 309, [2012] C.L.Y. 579 considered (see paras 57-61 of judgment). (2) In order for a breach of natural justice to invalidate a decision, it had to be sufficiently material or of significance to the decision so as to taint the decision as a whole, *Primus Build Ltd v Pompey Centre Ltd* [2009] EWHC 1487 (TCC), [2009] B.L.R. 437, [2010] C.L.Y. 557 and *Herbosch-Kiere Marine Contractors Ltd v Dover Harbour Board* [2012] EWHC 84 (TCC), [2012] B.L.R. 177, [2012] C.L.Y. 871 applied. Looking at it in the round, the central issue was whether or not there could be an entitlement to liquidated and ascertained damages following a so-called "Part Practical Completion" of a section. The adjudicator had erroneously decided that the position was in some way analogous to a case of partial possession. However, R had had every opportunity, which indeed it took, to put its case on the central issue. The real difficulty facing R was that the letter issued by L on June 28, 2011, referring to "Part Practical Completion", did not on the face of it describe a situation that fell within clause 2.27. However, it chose not to address that difficulty and to argue instead that there could be no entitlement to damages once a certificate of "Part Practical Completion" had been issued. There had therefore been no breach of natural justice (paras 71-73).

LIDL UK GmbH v RG CARTER COLCHESTER LTD; RG CARTER COLCHESTER LTD v LIDL UK GmbH, [2012] EWHC 3138 (TCC), 146 Con. L.R. 133, Edwards-Stuart, J., QBD (TCC).

521. Adjudication–Enforcement–Adjudicator's change of mind between first and second adjudication–Enforceability of second adjudication decision

[Housing Grants, Construction and Regeneration Act 1996 (c.53).]

The applicant contractor (V) sought summary judgment to enforce an adjudicator's decision that the respondent sub-contractor (S) should pay it liquidated damages. The sub-contract incorporated the ICE Design and Construct Conditions with amendments. It stated that S's work was to be completed in 18 weeks and that liquidated damages were payable thereafter at £15,000 per week. The sub-contract works were not completed until three months after the specified completion date. In a first adjudication, S argued that the delay was caused by matters for which V was responsible; it claimed a full extension of time and sought payment of consequential loss and damage in excess of £550,000. V contended that S was only entitled to an extension of one week and counter-claimed £180,000 in respect of liquidated damages for the delay. The adjudicator granted S a six-week extension and decided that V should pay S £167,501. He also found that V had not issued a withholding notice compliant with either the sub-contract or the Housing Grants, Construction and Regeneration Act 1996 and could not therefore withhold liquidated damages from the amount awarded to S. He then referred to S's argument that V did not have a right to claim liquidated damages under the sub-contract unless it had suffered an equivalent loss under its main contract with the employer. However, it was not clear whether that reference was part of his summary of S's arguments or part of his decision. In a second adjudication, the same adjudicator found that V did have a right under the sub-contract to be paid liquidated damages whether or not it had suffered a similar loss under the main contract. He ordered S to pay £184,813 to V. However, S refused to pay £105,000 of that sum, which had been in respect of liquidated damages, because the adjudicator had already decided that V was not entitled to liquidated damages as a result of the absence of equivalent loss under the main contract. The question therefore arose as to whether in the first adjudication the adjudicator had decided that V could not withhold liquidated damages solely because of the lack of notice or also because of the absence of equivalent loss under the main contract.

Held: Application refused. The wording of the second adjudication indicated that the adjudicator was saying that he was changing his view about one of the reasons that would absolve S from liability. That reason was that the absence of any equivalent loss demonstrated by V under the main contract would be fatal to its claim for liquidated damages. Accordingly, when the adjudicator referred in the first adjudication to that absence of any loss, he had been expressing his own view and not summarising a submission by S. His finding therefore in that adjudication that V had no entitlement to deduct liquidated damages was based on both the want of a withholding notice and the absence of any liability under the main contract. It followed that in the second adjudication he purported to change his mind about a finding made in his first decision. However, as, under the ICE Adjudication Procedure 2011 cl.6.6, that initial finding was final and binding on the parties until finally determined by litigation or arbitration, it had not been open to him to change it. The parties were bound by his decision in the first adjudication that the absence of any loss in respect of delay precluded V from claiming liquidated damages. That conclusion, until finally determined by litigation or arbitration, remained one with which the parties were bound to comply whether it was right or wrong, *Quietfield Ltd v Vascroft Contractors Ltd* [2006] EWCA Civ 1737, [2007] B.L.R. 67, [2007] C.L.Y. 723 applied. Therefore, V's application to enforce the second adjudication decision insofar as it related to the £105,000 failed (see paras 29, 35-36, 44, 50 of judgment).

VERTASE FLI LTD v SQUIBB GROUP LTD, [2012] EWHC 3194 (TCC), [2013] B.L.R. 352, Edwards-Stuart, J., QBD (TCC).

522. Adjudication–Jurisdiction–Referring more than one dispute to same adjudicator–Absence of referral notice–Sufficiency of other documents setting out statement of case

[Housing Grants, Construction and Regeneration Act 1996 (c.53) s.108(1).]

The applicant (W) applied for summary judgment against the respondent (N) to enforce two adjudication awards. N had employed W as a contractor under a contract in the ACA Standard Form of Contract for Project Partnering (PPC 2000), which provided that the parties should work together to achieve transparent and cooperative exchange of information in all matters relating to the project, that any party had the right to refer a dispute to adjudication by giving notice at any time, and that the adjudication would be conducted under the Construction Industry Council (CIC) Model Adjudication Procedure fifth edition. W had, on the same day, served two notices of intention to refer a dispute to adjudication. W then sent two letters to the adjudicator, each enclosing a referral document and a bundle of supporting documents. N raised a query about whether it and the adjudicator had received the referral documents within the required seven-day time limit, as it believed that W was relying on a referral served three months earlier. The adjudicator initially indicated that he had not received the referral documents, but later said that he had found them attached to the letter, and in his decision confirmed that they had been served on the correct date. He found in W's favour on both disputes. N argued that the awards should not be enforced because the adjudicator did not have jurisdiction as (1) the referral documents had not been properly served in accordance with r.14 of the CIC rules; (2) two disputes had been referred to the same adjudicator contrary to the Housing Grants, Construction and Regeneration Act 1996 s.108(1) and r.8 of the CIC rules.

Held: Application granted. (1) The adjudicator had expressly said that he had found the referral documents and there was no basis for challenging his statement. Further, he had incorporated a statement within his decision that the referral documents had been served on time, which was a finding of fact that was not open to challenge. Even if he had not received the referral documents on time, the covering letter and bundle had sufficiently set out W's statement of case. Rule 14 of the CIC did not prescribe a particular form by which a party had to set out its statement of case, nor did the list of matters to be included with the statement of case mean that if a particular document was not included, in technical breach of r.14, the adjudicator would not have jurisdiction. There was a distinction to be drawn between the fundamental obligation to refer a dispute to the adjudicator within seven days under r.14 and the other obligations relating to the details of the manner in which the matter was referred to the adjudicator, *Hart Investments Ltd v Fidler* [2006] EWHC 2857 (TCC), [2007] B.L.R. 30, [2007] C.L.Y. 433 applied (see paras 45-49 of judgment). The service of W's statement of case on N at the same time as it was sent to the adjudicator was not a matter which, if not complied with, could deprive the adjudicator of jurisdiction. In any event, the letter and bundle were a sufficient statement of W's case. That interpretation of r.14 was consistent with the general principle in r.1 that the object of adjudication was to reach a fair, rapid and inexpensive decision on a dispute and not one where technical breaches were to be taken to prevent such a decision. Further, the obligation in the project partnering contract to engage in the transparent and cooperative exchange of information extended to the adjudication clause. If N had complied with that obligation and queried whether the earlier referral document was really intended to be the referral for the instant dispute, N would have received the referral documents on time. N could not rely on its own breach of that obligation (paras 52-56). (2) There was nothing to prevent a party from giving two notices of adjudication, each relating only to a single dispute, and for each adjudication to be referred to the same adjudicator. On the contrary, the right to give notice of adjudication "at any time" under s.108(2) made it plain that there was no limit on the time when a party could commence one or more adjudications. The appointment of the same adjudicator was not objectionable as being contrary to the Act, the CIC rules or any requirement of the contract (paras 68-69, 71).

WILLMOTT DIXON HOUSING LTD (FORMERLY INSPACE PARTNERSHIP LTD) v NEWLON HOUSING TRUST, [2013] EWHC 798 (TCC), [2013] B.L.R. 325, Ramsey, J., QBD (TCC).

523. Adjudication–Jurisdiction–Two adjudications regarding similar issues–Propriety of second adjudicator having regard to first adjudicator's decision

The claimant contractor (X) sought the enforcement of an adjudicator's decision made in an adjudication that it had brought against the defendant (M). M had engaged X to carry out works at its site. The contract provided for "compensation events" which affected the contract price. M initially accepted that work to be carried out on the site's northern boundary was a compensation event and instructed X to proceed accordingly. Similar issues were identified on the southern boundary. M later withdrew its instructions and payment certifications in respect of the boundary works. X subsequently completed the works. A dispute arose as to X's entitlement to payment. The dispute in respect of the northern boundary work was referred to adjudication. The adjudicator found that M had not been entitled to withdraw its acceptance of a compensation event once the event had been implemented, and, holding that the northern boundary compensation event had been implemented, adjudicated in X's favour. M honoured that adjudication. X referred the southern boundary works dispute to adjudication. It argued that the second adjudicator was bound by the decision of the first. The adjudicator agreed that he would be bound if he found that the southern boundary works had been properly implemented as a compensation event, but found that it had not been properly implemented. He found that M had not been entitled to reverse its acceptance of the works as a compensation event. The adjudicator accepted the basis of calculating quantum that X advocated. Each party had prepared a figure on that basis, and the adjudicator chose to "split the difference" between the two to calculate the award. M did not honour that decision. M argued that (1) the second adjudicator had taken an erroneously restrictive view of his jurisdiction, and his decision was invalid for apparent bias, because the first adjudicator's decision had been put before him; (2) in splitting the difference, the adjudicator had decided the case on a basis that had not been argued by the parties; (3) the adjudicator had failed to consider part of its defence.

Held: Judgment for claimant. (1) There was nothing improper either in the first adjudicator's decision having been put before the second adjudicator or in the second adjudicator's having had regard to that decision. X had succeeded in the first adjudication on very similar issues. The first adjudicator's findings were germane and could have been persuasive. On any sensible reading of the second adjudicator's decision, it was clear that the adjudicator had not considered that he was bound by the earlier decision. He had made clear that he would only be bound if he found that the southern boundary work had been properly implemented as a compensation event; he had later found that it had not been properly implemented. It was clear from the rest of the decision that he had decided the issues on their own merits, not because he considered himself bound. The fact that the first adjudicator's decision had been put before him did not mean that the second adjudicator's decision was invalid for apparent bias. It would be a rare case in which the adjudicator's jurisdiction or conduct could be challenged in enforcement proceedings because he had looked at any material put forward by either party. The decision of a previous adjudicator did not obviously fall into such a rare case (see paras 31-35 of judgment). (2) There was no breach of natural justice in the second adjudicator's having split the difference. There had been a fundamental difference between the parties' approach to quantum; the adjudicator had adopted X's approach and had then had to choose between two figures, both of which had an evidential basis. He had not come up with a basis of assessment which the parties had not had opportunity to comment on, as the adjudicator in *Herbosch-Kiere Marine Contractors Ltd v Dover Harbour Board* [2012] EWHC 84 (TCC), [2012] B.L.R. 177, [2012] C.L.Y. 871 had wrongly done, *Herbosch* considered. The fact that the adjudicator had been persuaded that the proper answer lay between the two figures could not be considered to be a breach of natural justice (para.37). (3) It simply could not be said that the adjudicator had failed to consider the defence. It was not necessary for an adjudicator to address each and every point, piece of evidence or argument raised by each party unless, and then only to the extent that, it was necessary to resolve the dispute, *Pilon Ltd v Breyer Group Plc* [2010] EWHC 837 (TCC), [2010] B.L.R. 452, [2010] C.L.Y. 845 applied (para.39). (4) M had not lodged the contemporaneous documentation on which it wished to rely until shortly before the hearing, and after the date on which the court had required it to lodge evidence. Had X requested an adjournment, the court could either have refused M permission to rely on the documents or adjourned the hearing at its expense. Practitioners should be aware of the importance of complying with directions given in relation to adjudication enforcement proceedings (para.41).

ARCADIS UK LTD v MAY AND BAKER LTD (T/A SANOFI), [2013] EWHC 87 (TCC), [2013] B.L.R. 210, Akenhead, J., QBD (TCC).

524. Adjudication–Submission to jurisdiction–Unrepresented party seeking guidance from adjudicator and paying adjudicator's appointment fee–Extent of submission to jurisdiction

The applicant electrical contractor (C) applied for summary judgment on its claim to enforce an adjudication decision made against the respondent (J). J had engaged C to carry out electrical works. C, alleging that J failed to make adequate payments, served a notice of adjudication. J wrote an email to the adjudicator (L) explaining that it was not yet represented and requesting guidance on the adjudication procedures. J said that it had not received documents from C that it understood were required under the adjudication scheme and requested L's guidance as to extending the adjudication timetable to take account of that. Each party was required to contribute equally to L's appointment fee; J paid its part of the fee. After J obtained representation, it denied that L had jurisdiction. L, in a non-binding decision on jurisdiction, held that although there was no statutory jurisdiction, there was an ad hoc arbitration agreement arising out of the parties' payment of his fee. J stated that it would take no further part in the adjudication, and L made an award in C's favour. C accepted that there had been no express contractual right to adjudication and that it was arguable that there was no statutory right, but, relying on J's email and its payment of the fee, argued that J had submitted to L's jurisdiction in the full sense of the word, namely both in respect of the award itself and in respect of his jurisdiction to make the award, meaning that there was no defence to the enforcement of the award.

Held: Application refused. The court had to determine the meaning that would be conveyed to a reasonable adjudicator receiving J's email. The background knowledge available to the reasonable adjudicator included the facts that J had not received the relevant documents, was unrepresented, and was unfamiliar with the adjudication process. It was significant that L had not interpreted the email as a submission to jurisdiction in the full sense. Had there been a full submission his ruling on jurisdiction would have been binding; further, L had not referred to the email in his ruling. Although a representation did not have to be clear and unequivocal in every case to show submission, the email was at the opposite end of the spectrum. It contained no reference to the adjudicator's decision but was simply a request for guidance and for more time. It was impossible to interpret it as a submission to the adjudicator's jurisdiction in the full sense. Further, J's payment of the appointment fee did not amount to a submission in the full sense. At its highest, it was equivocal. J could have been liable for L's fee even if it contested jurisdiction, *Linnett v Halliwells LLP* [2009] EWHC 319 (TCC), [2009] 1 C.L.C. 157, [2009] C.L.Y. 991 applied. L's decision on jurisdiction based on an ad hoc agreement was wrong, *Thomas-Fredric's (Construction) Ltd v Wilson* [2003] EWCA Civ 1494, [2004] B.L.R. 23, [2004] C.L.Y. 591 followed (see paras 33-38 of judgment).

CLARK ELECTRICAL LTD v JMD DEVELOPMENTS (UK) LTD, [2012] EWHC 2627 (TCC), [2012] B.L.R. 546, Judge Behrens, QBD (TCC).

525. Adjudicators–Fees–Adjudicator found to have breached rules of natural justice–Entitlement to fees for unenforceable decision

[Housing Grants, Construction and Regeneration Act 1996 (c.53); Scheme for Construction Contracts (England and Wales) Regulations 1998 (SI 1998/649) Sch.1 Pt I para.8(4), Pt I para.9(2), Pt I para.11 (1).]

The appellant contractor (P) appealed against a decision ([2011] EWHC 2722 (TCC), [2012] 1 All E.R. (Comm) 381, [2012] C.L.Y. 584) that it was liable to pay the fees of an adjudicator (D) employed by the respondent company (S) even though his decision was unenforceable. Disputes had arisen between P and its sub-contractor in relation to three projects. They were referred to adjudication, with D appointed as adjudicator. The contracts and adjudications were all governed by the Housing Grants, Construction and Regeneration Act 1996 and the Scheme for Construction Contracts (England and Wales) Regulations 1998. D issued a decision, which failed to deal with P's principal defence. Although the court declared that the decision was unenforceable because the rules of natural justice had been breached, it held that D was still entitled to his fees because the bargained-for performance was not only the making of a decision, but included all the steps that had to be taken beforehand. P submitted that D was not entitled to any fee because he had failed to perform the service which he had been contracted to perform. S argued that D's functions were not limited to making a decision and that on the true construction of the contract, his entitlement to be paid accrued as and when the services were provided, not on the making of the decision.

Held: Appeal allowed. The question that arose was whether the contract was an entire contract such that the bargained-for consideration was an enforceable decision or a divisible contract for the performance of a series of ancillary and anterior functions culminating in the making of a decision. That was a question of construction of the contract, *Stocznia Gdanska SA v Latvian Shipping Co* [1998] 1 W.L.R. 574, [1998] C.L.Y. 861 and *Fibrosa Spolka Akcyjna v Fairbairn*

Lawson Combe Barbour Ltd [1943] A.C. 32 applied (see paras 17-19 of judgment). D was obliged to perform some ancillary and anterior functions, but the issue was whether he was entitled to be paid for them if they culminated in an unenforceable decision. The judge seemed to have regarded it as axiomatic that the performance of the preliminary steps amounted to partial performance of the bargain, but did not explain how he reached that decision and did not seem to have analysed the terms of engagement and the Scheme for Construction Contracts (the scheme) under the Regulations, which had to be read together. The only circumstances in which the adjudicator was entitled to remuneration where his appointment came to an end before he had made a decision were carefully defined in Sch.1 Pt I para.8(4), Sch.1 Pt I para.9(2) and Sch.1 Pt I para.11(1) of the Regulations. They showed clearly that it was not intended that D should be paid in every case where he did not perform all of his obligations. In the instant case, none of those circumstances existed. The contract did not contain any provision for payment of D's fees by reference to the completion of discrete parts of the engagement and there was no reference to instalment payments in the relevant parts of the 1996 Act or the scheme. The fact that the charges were to be calculated at an hourly rate and that D was permitted to demand interim payments did not indicate what the parties intended the position to be if he failed to produce an enforceable decision on the dispute which had been referred to him. D had no discrete entitlement to his fees and expenses for the ancillary and anterior functions that he performed, which had no discrete value to the parties. The bargained-for performance was an enforceable decision. The making of a decision which was unenforceable because it breached the rules of natural justice was a "default" or "misconduct" under Sch.1 Pt I para.11(2). It made no sense for the parties to agree that D was not entitled to be paid if his appointment was revoked for default or misconduct before he made his decision, but that he was entitled to full remuneration if the same default or misconduct first became manifest in the decision itself. There was nothing in the terms of engagement or the scheme which compelled the conclusion that that was the parties' intention (paras 22-24, 26-29, 31-34). The statutory provisions for adjudication reflected Parliament's intention to provide a scheme for a rough and ready temporary resolution of construction disputes, but that did not mean that courts would enforce decisions which adjudicators had no jurisdiction to make, or which breached the rules of natural justice. Rather than furthering the statutory policy of encouraging referral of disputes for temporary resolution by an adjudicator, such decisions caused parties to incur cost and suffer delay on a futile exercise (para.37).

SYSTECH INTERNATIONAL LTD v PC HARRINGTON CONTRACTORS LTD; *sub nom.* PC HARRINGTON CONTRACTORS LTD v SYSTECH INTERNATIONAL LTD, [2012] EWCA Civ 1371, [2013] 2 All E.R. 69, Lord Dyson (M.R.), CA (Civ Div).

526. Building regulations–Approved inspectors

THE BUILDING REGULATIONS &C. (AMENDMENT) (NO.2) REGULATIONS 2013, SI 2013/1959; made under the Building Act 1984 s.1, Sch.1 para.1, Sch.1 para.4, Sch.1 para.7, Sch.1 para.10, Sch.1 para.11. In force: in accordance with reg.1.; .

These Regulations amend the Building Regulations 2010 (SI 2010/2214), the Building (Approved Inspectors etc) Regulations 2010 (SI 2010/2215) and the Croydon Corporation Act 1960.

527. Building regulations–Certificates of completion–Wales

THE BUILDING REGULATIONS &C. (AMENDMENT) (WALES) REGULATIONS 2013, SI 2013/SI 2013/747 (W.89); made under the Building Act 1984 s.1, s.2A, s.8, s.16, s.17, s.34, s.47, s.49, s.51, Sch.1 para.1, Sch.1 para.2, Sch.1 para.4, Sch.1

para.4A, Sch.1 para.6, Sch.1 para.7, Sch.1 para.8, Sch.1 para.10. In force: in accordance with reg.1 (4).; .

These Regulations, amongst other things, introduce new provision regarding the giving by the local authority of completion certificates; transpose specified provisions of Directive 2010/31; add a further body that may register a person to issue a certificate of compliance with pressure testing requirements; and amend the list of bodies authorised under the self-certification scheme provided for by the Building Regulations.

528. Building regulations–Energy efficiency–England and Wales

THE ENERGY PERFORMANCE OF BUILDINGS (ENGLAND AND WALES) ETC. (AMENDMENT) REGULATIONS 2013, SI 2013/10; made under the Energy Act 2011 s.9, s.40, s.74. In force: January 27, 2013; .

These Regulations, which apply to England and Wales, amend the Building Regulations 2010 (SI 2010/2214) and the Energy Performance of Buildings (England and Wales) Regulations 2012 (SI 2012/3118) in connection with the green deal energy efficiency scheme created under the Energy Act 2011.

529. Building regulations–Wales

THE BUILDING (AMENDMENT NO.2) (WALES) REGULATIONS 2013, SI 2013/ SI 2013/2621 (W.258); made under the Building Act 1984 s.1, s.8, Sch.1 para.1, Sch.1 para.4, Sch.1 para.4A, Sch.1 para.7, Sch.1 para.8, Sch1. para.10. In force: November 14, 2013; .

These Regulations amend the Building Regulations 2010 (SI 2010/2214) adding bodies to the list of bodies in specified paragraphs to register persons authorised under the self-certification scheme provided for by regs 12 and 20 of the 2010 Regulations.

530. Commercial development–Freedom to provide services–Whether proposed agreement between local authority and owner of shopping centre in breach of art.56 TFEU

[Treaty on the Functioning of the European Union Art.56.]

The claimant (Q) sought a declaration that an agreement which the defendant local authority proposed to enter into with a third party (L) breached the freedom to provide services under TFEU art.56. There were two shopping centres in Hounslow town centre. Q owned one and L owned the other. The proposed agreement related to a site which was adjacent to the centre owned by L. Under it, the local authority, which was the freehold owner of the greater part of the site, agreed to enter into an agreement whereby it would grant L a long lease of the site. The local authority also agreed that, during a defined period, it would not enter into negotiations with any other party and would use its reasonable endeavours to agree detailed heads of terms. L issued a press release which referred to the proposal as offering "an excellent opportunity to deliver new shops, leisure facilities and public spaces that will help revitalise [the town centre] and create hundreds of new jobs for local people".

Held: Judgment for defendant. (1) This was not a case in which L was providing services of the type envisaged by art.56; this was no more than an agreement to agree the terms of a long lease of the site in question. The proposed agreement therefore fell outside art.56. There were additional reasons why art.56 did not apply. First, the proposed agreement did not contain any restriction being placed by the local authority on the provision of services. The local authority did not seek to restrict L's ability to contract with whom it liked, if and when it decided to develop the site, in order that the relevant services might be provided. Second, while the applicability of art.56 was not confined to specific types of contract, it was significant that the proposed agreement in this case was very different from any of the types of contract where art.56 had been found in the European cases to apply. Third, the matter was internal to the United Kingdom (see paras 41, 44, 57, 102-103 of judgment). (2) Had art.56

been applicable, the authorities required as a minimum a degree of advertising, sufficient to enable the market to be opened up to competition. That advertising had to allow undertakings in other Member States to access appropriate information so as to express an interest before the award of the contract. The absence of such an advertisement in this case meant that the local authority would not have complied with art.56. However, the circumstances of the case were such that, had art.56 been found to apply, it would not have been appropriate to grant the declaration sought; those circumstances included the hypothetical nature of the proceedings and the absence of any declared interest from an undertaking in another Member State (paras 78, 82, 95).

AG QUIDNET HOUNSLOW LLP v HOUNSLOW LBC, [2012] EWHC 2639 (TCC), [2013] P.T.S.R. 828, Coulson, J., QBD (TCC).

531. Construction contracts–Delay–Whether contractor responsible for delay in construction of house

The claimant contractor (W), which had been employed by the second defendant company (D) as the main contractor in respect of the construction of three adjoining high-quality houses in London, brought claims against D seeking various sums together with an extension of time until the date of practical completion of the relevant works. D was a purpose-designed vehicle for the acquisition of the land on which the houses were to be built. It was formed by three people, including the first defendant, who, together with his family, would reside in one of the houses. The instant litigation concerned that house. The contract between D and W was contained in a memorandum dated May 28, 2004; it stated that the conditions were to be those contained in the JCT Standard Form of Building Contract 1998 Edition Private Without Quantities, incorporating various specific amendments. W began work in the summer of 2004. The completion date was January 23, 2006. However, substantial delays occurred. Extensions of time were granted by D's architect pursuant to cl.25 of the contract until February 2007 but practical completion did not take place until July 2008. Among the issues were (i) which party was responsible for the delays that had occurred and whether W was entitled to the extension of time sought; (ii) how concurrent causes of delay, which arose where a period of delay was found to have been caused by two factors, should be dealt with; (iii) whether W was entitled to prolongation costs as a result of the delays and disruption which had occurred.

Held: Judgment for claimant. (1) W was entitled to an extension of time through to the date of practical completion in July 2008. Most of the actual or alleged major causes of delay involved design deficiencies but contractual responsibility for such deficiencies had not been imposed on W. While certain complaints relating to plasterwork and the lift in the property were W's responsibility, they had no impact on the overall delay (see para.459 of judgment). (2) The debate as to how concurrent causes of delay should be dealt with was only germane where at least one of the causes of delay was a "Relevant Event" under the contract and the other was not. Where there was an extension-of-time clause such as that agreed on in this case and where delay was caused by two or more effective causes, one of which entitled the contractor to an extension of time as being a Relevant Event, he would be entitled to a full extension of time. Part of the logic of this was that many of the Relevant Events would otherwise amount to acts of prevention and that it would be wrong in principle to construe cl.25 on the basis that the contractor should be denied a full extension of time in those circumstances. More importantly, there was a straight contractual interpretation of cl.25 which pointed very strongly in favour of the view that, provided that the Relevant Events could be shown to have delayed the works, the contractor would be entitled to an extension of time for the whole period of delay caused by the Relevant Events in question. There was nothing in the wording of cl.25 which expressly suggested that there was any sort of proviso to the effect that an extension should be reduced if the causation criterion was established. The fact that the architect had to award a "fair and reasonable" extension did not imply that there should be some apportionment in the case of concurrent delays. The test was primarily a causation one. In this case, the issue of concurrent delays did not arise, since the only occasions when there were concurrent causes of delay were occasions when such causes were the contractual risk of D (paras 366, 370, 459). (3) W's claim for prolongation costs had given rise to two issues. The first concerned the interpretation of cl.26.1.3 of the contract, which required the contractor to "submit to the Architect or to the Quantity Surveyor such details of... loss and/or expense as [were] reasonably necessary" for the ascertainment of such loss or expense. There was no need to construe that clause in a peculiarly strict way or in a way which was in some way penal as against the contractor, particularly bearing in mind that all the cl.26.2 grounds which gave rise to the loss and expense entitlements were the fault and risk of the employer. Further, it was legitimate to bear in mind that the architect and quantity surveyor were not strangers to the project when considering what needed to be provided to them, *Merton LBC v Stanley Hugh Leach Ltd* 32 B.L.R. 51, [1986] C.L.Y. 222 considered. The architect or quantity surveyor had to be put in a position where they could be satisfied that all or some of the loss and expense claimed was likely to be or had been incurred; they did not have to be "certain". W had provided the appropriate level of detail in the many applications which it had made for extensions of time under cl.25 and for losses and expenses under cl.26 (paras 462, 466-470). The second issue concerned D's argument that W's claim for prolongation costs amounted to an impermissible "global" claim, being a claim which identified numerous potential or actual causes of delay and/or disruption, a total cost on the job, a net payment from the employer and a claim for the balance between costs and payment which was attributed without more and by inference to the causes of delay and disruption relied on. However, what W had produced was not, on analysis, a global or "total cost" claim: it had sought to identify the specific additional or extended resources and to link them to the events on which it relied as having caused or given rise to its need for additional or extended resources. The court went to review the law on global claims (paras 474, 484, 486, 491). (4) Judgment in the sum of £2,330,666.26 would be given in W's favour. That included a sum for prolongation costs, a sum for delay-related loss of overhead and profit and a sum in relation to claims for delay and disruption which had been submitted by W's sub-contractors (paras 658-659).

WALTER LILLY & CO LTD v MacKAY, [2012] EWHC 1773 (TCC), [2012] B.L.R. 503, Akenhead, J., QBD (TCC).

532. Construction contracts–Guarantees–Guarantee for sums due under shipbuilding contract–Appeal against summary judgment on basis of material amendments to underlying contract–Interpretation of guarantee

The appellant guarantor (S) appealed against a decision granting summary judgment in respect of sums guaranteed to the respondent companies (R) under a construction contract. R cross-appealed against the decision to give S leave to defend at trial in respect of the greater amount due to R under a variation of the underlying contracts. S had guaranteed sums due on delivery of two drilling rigs to two of its subsidiary companies (B). After the guarantee had been made, the sums due on delivery were substantially increased by further agreement between R and B and the delivery dates delayed. R was late in delivering the rigs but sought to enforce the guarantee, and recover the greater sums due under the latest variation of the contracts. S argued that the guarantee had been discharged by the changes in B's obligations made without its consent and in any event did not cover the larger liability. R claimed that the guarantee expressly extended to such variations and was drafted so as to impose primary liability on S, and to therefore avoid doctrines designed to protect a secondary party such as a guarantor from being prejudiced by material changes to the underlying contract. The judge found that the post-guarantee amendments were within the purview of the guarantee and that the guarantee had not been discharged. He held that S was liable for at least the lesser sums due, but that the factual issues could not be resolved at summary judgment stage. R submitted that the language of section 2 of the guarantee, in particular "shall extend to any variation", constituted a positive consent to the additional obligations created by the post-guarantee amendments.

Held: Appeal allowed, cross-appeal dismissed. (1) It was more convenient to first consider R's cross-appeal as, if there was no defence to the proposition that the guarantee extended to the greater sums deferred under the post-guarantee contracts, that would be an end to the litigation. However, if the cross-appeal failed, S's appeal relating to the "purview" of the guarantee would have to be approached with caution to see whether there was some reason why that issue could still be treated as a pure question of law, irrespective of the guarantee's factual matrix, and could therefore be disposed of summarily. R's submission had to fail; the instant court could not properly reverse the judge's view that a trial was necessary. There was a powerful argument that the language of "extend to" had to be considered in the light of the section as a whole, which was primarily concerned with avoiding the possibility of "a legal or equitable defense or discharge", and with a stipulation that waiver or any variation or amendment "shall not alter or impair the liability of the Guarantor hereunder". In that context, it was reasonable to see that "shall extend to" meant no more than "shall survive". A question also arose regarding the nature of the "liability of the Guarantor hereunder". The cross-appeal would be dismissed. It followed that there would have to be a trial in which the true interpretation of the guarantee, and whether it extended to the post-delivery payments provided for by the post-guarantee amendments, would have to be considered in the light of its factual matrix (see paras 34-37 of judgment). (2) The issue on S's appeal was whether the provisions of the guarantee designed to avoid the consequences of the doctrine contained in *Holme v Brunskill* (1878) 3 Q.B.D. 495, whereby a material amendment might discharge a guarantee, extended to a variation of the contracts which lay outside "the purview" of the guarantee. The issue had to be closely aligned to the issue regarding the meaning of the guarantee which arose on R's cross-appeal. It was therefore only if the answer to the purview issue was one on which there could be no reasonable prospect of any uncertainty such as the guarantee's factual matrix might assist to resolve, that it would be proper or fair to give summary judgment in advance of trial. If it was a trial of R's claim, or even if the sole issue on the application for summary judgment was whether the guarantee had been discharged by the post-guarantee amendments having been made without S's consent, the instant court would strain to provide an answer on what were ultimately issues of law. However, that was not the situation. The various questions of construction which arose on both appeal and cross-appeal, or the closely allied question of the purview of the guarantee, would have to be considered as a whole, in the light of the evidence at trial. It was not a case where the issues of law which arose on the appeal were straightforward: each presented difficulties of analysis, and the jurisprudence was somewhat opaque, *Trade Indemnity Co Ltd v Workington Harbour and Dock Board (No.1)* [1937] A.C. 1 and *Holme* considered (paras 38-39, 64-65).

CIMC RAFFLES OFFSHORE (SINGAPORE) LTD v SCHAHIN HOLDING SA, [2013] EWCA Civ 644, [2013] 2 All E.R. (Comm) 760, Arden, L.J., CA (Civ Div).

533. Construction contracts–Repudiation–Delay in construction project–Entitlement to terminate on ground of repudiatory breach

The appellant construction company (T) appealed against a decision ([2012] EWHC 1820 (Ch), [2012] B.L.R. 387, [2013] 1 C.L. 63) that the respondent property company (H) had been entitled to terminate their contract on the ground that T's delay in carrying out works was a repudiatory breach of contract. In 2008 T and H had entered into an agreement for a lease. T was to develop four mixed-use blocks (A, B, C and D); H ultimately intended to take 999-year leases of commercial units in the blocks. The target date for completion of blocks C and D was July 2010; for A and B the date was February 2011. Work on C and D fell behind schedule but was completed by April 2011. Work on A and B was suspended because of funding difficulties. Unknown to H, work resumed on October 4, 2010. H purported to terminate the agreement on October 22. The judge found that there had been repudiation in that H would receive only two of the blocks and that continued building work on blocks A and B could interfere with H's efforts to market units in C and D. He found that repudiation had occurred by July 2010, on the basis that it would then have been clear that completion could not have taken place close to the target date. T argued that the judge had not (1) adequately analysed the benefit H had been intended to receive under the contract in order to decide whether the breaches of contract had deprived it of a substantial part of that benefit; (2) concentrated on the right date in assessing whether the breaches were repudiatory.

Held: Appeal allowed. (1) The starting point was considering the benefit the injured party was intended to obtain from performance of the contract. The judge had not given adequate weight to the ultimate objective of the contract, namely the 999-year leases for the four blocks. He had concentrated on the expected effects of the marketing period. The next thing to consider was the effect of the breach on the injured party. The judge had been impressed by the four blocks being envisaged as a single project and by the potential that sub-letting might be interfered with if H was compelled to take two blocks while building work continued on the remaining blocks. However, the contract had envisaged a staged handover and seven months' worth of such interference, so it overstated the case to say that the consequences of any gap between handover dates would be so serious as to amount to repudiatory breach. Moreover, it was not enough to say that a possible interference with marketing was of itself sufficient to satisfy the test. H accepted that the delay had not caused any actual loss; it was unusual that a breach that had caused no actual loss was repudiatory. If no actual loss had been caused by the breach, the future loss the injured party was seeking to avoid had to be considered. Had H delayed marketing of blocks C and D until construction of A and B had caught up, it would have incurred additional funding costs of the order of £100,000. Those costs were readily calculable, and H could have been compensated. Set against a purchase price exceeding £8 million, and against overall development costs exceeding £100 million, such loss was not of a scale sufficient to characterise it as repudiatory (see paras 51-57 of judgment). (2) In determining the relevant date, the judge had distinguished *Stocznia Gdanska SA v Latvian Shipping Co (Repudiation)* [2002] EWCA Civ 889, [2002] 2 All E.R. (Comm) 768, [2003] C.L.Y. 3933 on the basis that it dealt with anticipatory repudiatory breaches. However, the same test applied to actual breaches, *Hongkong Fir Shipping Co Ltd v Kawasaki Kisen Kaisha Ltd (The Hongkong Fir)* [1962] 2 Q.B. 26, [1962] C.L.Y. 2838 followed and *Stocznia Gdanska* applied. The judge had been wrong to differentiate the two. If a breach was remedied before the injured party purported to terminate, the fact of the remedy was an important factor to be taken into account. Likewise, if there was delay in performance of an ongoing obligation, it could be possible for the delay to be made up by faster performance. Accordingly, what fell to be considered was the position as at the date when the injured party purported to terminate the contract. The judge had applied the test to the wrong moment in time. H had not purported to terminate until October 22, 2010; by that time work on blocks A and B had restarted, meaning that it could no longer be said, as the judge had found, that the cessation of work was indeterminate. Bearing in mind the absence of actual loss, and the limited future loss, it was not possible to say, as at October 22, that the actual and reasonably foreseeable effects of T's breaches were such as to deprive H of a substantial part of the benefit of the contract (paras 63-69).

AMPURIUS NU HOMES HOLDINGS LTD v TELFORD HOMES (CREEKSIDE) LTD; *sub nom.* TELFORD HOMES (CREEKSIDE) LTD v AMPURIUS NU HOMES HOLDINGS LTD, [2013] EWCA Civ 577, [2013] 4 All E.R. 377, Longmore, L.J., CA (Civ Div).

534. Construction contracts–Residential property–Whether homeowner refurbishing property with view to renting or selling covered by residential exception in s.106 Housing Grants, Construction and Regeneration Act 1996–Meaning of "occupies, or intends to occupy, as his residence" in s.106

[Housing Grants, Construction and Regeneration Act 1996 (c.53) s.106.]

The applicant construction company (W) applied to enforce an adjudicator's award made against the respondent property owner (L). In February 2012, after protracted discussions and preparation of a number of quotes, the parties entered into a construction contract for the refurbishment of a house owned by L. The contract was in writing, but contained no express provisions regarding adjudication. Work began in February after L moved into a new property. W's case was that L had indicated an intention to let the property when the work was complete. When L failed to pay sums due, W referred the dispute to adjudication. L's case was that the adjudicator had no jurisdiction to decide the dispute because, L being a residential occupier, the exception in the Housing Grants, Construction and Regeneration Act 1996 s.106 applied. The adjudicator concluded that L was not a residential occupier and ordered him to pay the amount claimed within seven days. The issue was whether s.106 of the Act was applicable. The dispute turned on whether, at the time that the contract was made, it could be said that L occupied the property as his residence.

Held: Application granted. (1) The s.106 exception was limited; it was intended to protect ordinary householders not otherwise concerned with property or construction work from what had been, in 1996, a new and untried system of dispute resolution in circumstances where construction work was taking place to a property that they occupied, and intended to continue occupying, as their home. When considering the notion of "intention to occupy", the date of formation of the contract was important, but "occupation" was an ongoing process and could not be tested by reference to a single snapshot in time (see paras 10-11 of judgment). In the instant case, the evidence indicated that the contract had been formed on February 21. That was the date when agreement about the scope of the work and the price had been reached. The evidence indicated that, at that date, L had already moved out. Therefore, even if the "snapshot" test was the right approach, L would not satisfy it because he was not occupying the property at the time the contract was formed. The evidence was also quite clear and consistent that L intended to let the property on a commercial basis when the work was finished. That intention had been communicated to W before, after, and during the works, and L had acted in accordance with that intention at all times. Therefore, as a matter of common sense, s.106 did not apply because L was not intending to occupy the property. A person who moved out of a house in order to sell or rent it could not rely on the residential exception test merely because, at the time the refurbishment contract was agreed, he was still living in the house; such a person would fail both the intention and the occupation element of s.106, *Samuel Thomas Construction Ltd v Anon, Edenbooth Ltd v Cre8 Developments Ltd* [2008] EWHC 570 (TCC), [2008] C.I.L.L. 2592 and *Shaw v Massey Foundation & Pilings Ltd* [2009] EWHC 493 (TCC) considered (paras 6, 21, 24-40, 48, 57, 60). (2) The court commented that a more commercially sensible outcome would be for s.106 and other exceptions to statutory adjudication to be dispensed with so that all parties to a construction contract could enjoy the benefits of adjudication (para.61).

WESTFIELDS CONSTRUCTION LTD v LEWIS, [2013] EWHC 376 (TCC), [2013] 1 W.L.R. 3377, Coulson, J., QBD (TCC).

535. Construction contracts–Scheme for Construction Contracts–Adjudication provisions–Whether term could be implied allowing losing party to sue from date of payment of adjudication order

[Housing Grants, Construction and Regeneration Act 1996 (c.53) s.108(5); Limitation Act 1980 (c.58).]

The claimant (X) brought proceedings to overturn an adjudicator's decision and recover money it had paid to the defendant (H). In 2004 H had engaged X to carry out an asbestos survey. H alleged that X had failed to spot additional asbestos which had caused 17 weeks' delay to a building project. In 2009 H referred the dispute to adjudication. An adjudication decision was issued on July 28, 2009. It found that X was at fault and should pay H approximately £658,000, a lower sum than that put forward by H. X paid the award but issued proceedings on February 2, 2012 to overturn the adjudicator's decision. H maintained that the proceedings were time-barred by the Limitation Act 1980 and counterclaimed for the difference between the adjudicator's award and the sum that H had originally claimed was due. X relied on *Jim Ennis Construction Ltd v Premier Asphalt Ltd* [2009] EWHC 1906 (TCC), 125 Con. L.R. 141, [2010] C.L.Y. 555 and submitted that the contract with H contained an implied term that in the event of a dispute being referred to adjudication, and one party paying money in compliance with an adjudicator's decision, that party remained entitled to have the dispute finally determined by legal proceedings and to have the money repaid to it. X argued that its cause of action to recover the money therefore ran from the date of payment.

Held: Claim dismissed, counterclaim dismissed. (1) H and X's contract was a construction contract for the purposes of the Housing Grants, Construction and Regeneration Act 1996. As the parties had not made their own contractual provisions for adjudication, s.108(5) incorporated the adjudication provisions of the Scheme for Construction Contracts into the contract. Those provisions stated that a decision of an adjudicator was temporarily binding until the dispute was finally resolved, and that meanwhile the parties were to comply with the decision (see paras 26, 39 of judgment). (2) In deciding whether the term suggested by X could be implied into the contract the court took into account the following factors: (a) each party had a right to sue for a positive or negative declaration that X was or was not in breach of contract; (b) each party had a legally enforceable right to refer a dispute to adjudication; (c) the adjudicator's decision was binding until it was finally resolved by the court; (d) all defences, including limitation, would be open to the defending party in court and in adjudication; (e) the implication of X's suggested term would create a new cause of action from the date of payment which would have the effect of extending the period in which X could litigate the underlying dispute for an additional six years from the date of payment; (f) there was a possible undesirability in the losing party having to pursue a claim for a negative declaration within six years of performance under the contract to avoid the possibility of a limitation defence being raised against it; (g) there was a possible risk that if a party decided to wait until the outcome of an adjudication brought against it, it might not have time within the limitation period to seek a negative declaration after the decision was issued, and might not be able to recover a payment made pursuant to a decision which later turned out to be wrong; (h) the responding party in an adjudication could issue proceedings for a negative declaration once adjudication was threatened or started to protect its position; (i) there was a small risk that if a belated adjudication was started by a party whose claim was already barred by limitation, the adjudicator might reject the limitation defence with the result that there was no comeback for the losing party, unless it had instituted its claim for a negative declaration within the limitation period (paras 27, 41). (3) The implication of the term pleaded by X would not be reasonable, equitable or necessary to make the contract work, *Attorney General of Belize v Belize Telecom Ltd* [2009] UKPC 10, [2009] 1 W.L.R. 1988 and *BP Refinery (Westernport) Pty Ltd v Shire of Hastings* 180 C.L.R. 266 considered. X was seeking, in effect, to imply a term into the statutory wording of the Scheme. If one was to ask "does the Scheme as a statutory instrument, properly construed, mean that the losing party is to be given a new right to sue as from the date of payment of the adjudication decision for the recovery of sums paid", the answer would be in the negative. There was nothing to suggest that it had been Parliament's intention to incorporate such a term, *Jim Ennis* not followed. X could have brought a claim for a negative declaration at any time after performance of the contract in 2004. It did not have to wait until the adjudicator had issued his decision. There was no implied term and X's cause of action for a declaration that it was not in breach of contract was barred by limitation. It followed that H's counterclaim for the balance of its loss was also time-barred (paras 37, 45, 50).

ASPECT CONTRACTS (ASBESTOS) LTD v HIGGINS CONSTRUCTION PLC, [2013] EWHC 1322 (TCC), [2013] Bus. L.R. 1199, Akenhead, J., QBD (TCC).

536. Construction contracts–Target cost contracts–Interpretation–Unusual and badly-worded capping clause–Liability for costs payable above agreed cap

The court gave fuller reasons for its decision to refuse the applicant (X) permission to appeal against an award by a disputes review board which found that the costs of a project above an agreed capped level should only be paid to X by the respondent secretary of state where they were actual costs reasonably and properly incurred. The secretary of state had entered into a maximum price target cost contract with X for the design and construction of a nuclear submarine facility at a cost that had overrun by stages from an original maximum price of £89 million to £142.1 million at the date of the hearing. X expected a further overrun to £235.7 million. Under the contract, overrun costs were capped at £50 million, but it was not clear who was liable to pay them once the cap was reached. The question was whether the secretary of state was liable to pay anything above the cap, and if he was, whether the costs would be those contractually defined as actual costs reasonably and properly incurred, or whether he would be liable for all costs, howsoever incurred. A disputes review board decided by a majority that X was entitled to actual costs reasonably and properly incurred. The dissenting view was that all costs above the cap howsoever incurred were reimbursable to X.

Held: Application refused, fuller reasons given. The appropriate test was whether the majority view was obviously wrong. It was not only not wrong, it was not open to serious doubt, and was plainly right. It approached interpretation correctly in construing the capping clause by reference to other contractual terms, conclusively demonstrating that the entire pricing and payment regime depended on ascertaining actual costs that were to be measured against the target cost and the maximum price. In view of that regime it would be a curious result if actual costs were suddenly abandoned to make all costs recoverable by X, and it would render superfluous large parts of the capping clause and other clauses. The majority analysis showed that X's contrary view would give very unusual results, such as non-liability for its own breaches of contract and the consequent costs, which the secretary of state would have to pay, a state of affairs not even mentioned in the dissenting view. That situation would be highly unusual, and the contract would have to be as clear as possible that it was intended, but it had no such provisions. It would be commercially surprising for a contract depending throughout on ascertaining actual costs suddenly to change so that they became irrelevant, and all costs, however unreasonable and improperly incurred, became recoverable. The majority view showed that X's argument was at root a semantic one that meant arguing for different meanings for the same words depending on whether or not they had capital letters. In any case, "actual costs" was used interchangeably with "Actual Costs" (see paras 33-41 of judgment).

AMEC GROUP LTD v SECRETARY OF STATE FOR DEFENCE, [2013] EWHC 110 (TCC), 146 Con. L.R. 152, Coulson, J., QBD (TCC).

537. **Construction contracts–Termination–Early termination of contract–Contractor's entitlement to payment of specified sums under termination clause**

[Civil Procedure Rules 1998 (SI 1998/3132) Pt 8.]

The applicant contractor (T) applied to enforce an adjudication decision ordering the respondent housing association (S) to pay it a specified sum. S applied under CPR Pt 8 for declarations relating to the meaning of the underlying contract. S had engaged T to provide gas servicing and associated work programmes to S's housing stock. The contract was for four years. Clause 1.1 required that the parties "shall act reasonably and without delay". Under cl.13.3 each party "may terminate... at any time during the term". S terminated the contract early under cl.13.3. T sought payment from S in consequence of the termination. S did not respond and T referred three "issues" regarding its financial entitlements to adjudication. S challenged the adjudicator's jurisdiction on the basis that three distinct disputes had been referred when only a single dispute was permitted to be referred at any one time. The adjudicator considered that he had jurisdiction and issued a decision that T was entitled to payment of sums associated with the termination of appointment. The issues were whether (i) more than one dispute had been referred to the adjudicator and, if so, he nonetheless had jurisdiction; (ii) as a matter of construction cl.1.1 of the contract provided for any constraint, condition or qualification on either party's right to terminate under cl.13.3; (iii) there was an implied term of good faith.

Held: Application refused, Declaration granted. (1) Only one dispute had been referred to adjudication, albeit that it comprised three primary strands or issues. Both historically and on its face, the instant claim was one claim comprising three primary alleged financial entitlements which had been effectively challenged or at least not admitted prior to the initiation of adjudication. While it would have been theoretically possible for T to pursue the separate parts of its claim as separate claims, giving rise potentially to three disputes referable to adjudication, it had not. The adjudicator on any account had jurisdiction to resolve all the issues put before him, *Witney Town Council v Beam Construction (Cheltenham) Ltd* [2011] EWHC 2332 (TCC), [2011] B.L.R. 707, [2012] C.L.Y. 586 applied (see paras 19-21 of judgment). (2) The court needed to determine objectively what a reasonable person with all the background knowledge reasonably available to the parties at the time of the contract would have understood the parties to have meant, and to adopt the more, rather than less, commercial construction. It was necessary to consider not just what the words in cl.1.1 meant verbally but also what, from looking at the contract overall, they were intended to apply to. It was legitimate to consider whether they were intended to apply to the termination provisions at all. Clause 1.1 was primarily concerned with the assumption, deployment and performance of roles, expertise and responsibilities set out in the partnering documents, and the parties in doing so had to "work together and individually in the spirit of trust, fairness and mutual co-operation for the benefit of the term programme" and act reasonably and without delay in so doing. Properly construed, cl.1.1 did not require S to act reasonably as such in terminating under cl.13.3. Clause 13.1 made it clear that the four-year term was subject to cl.13. Clause 13 provided for automatic termination for bankruptcy and insolvency, termination for breach, and an unconditional and unqualified right to terminate. There was no doubt that if either party had applied their mind to it prior to signing the contract it was clear that such an unqualified right to either party existed; it was obvious to each that the other could terminate at any time, *Compass Group UK and Ireland Ltd (t/a Medirest) v Mid Essex Hospital Services NHS Trust* [2013] EWCA Civ 200, [2013] B.L.R. 265 considered (paras 32, 36-42). (3) There was not as such an implied term of good faith in the contract. S and T had gone as far as they wanted in expressing terms in cl.1.1 about how they were to work together in a spirit of "trust, fairness and mutual cooperation" and to act reasonably. An implied term of good faith could not circumscribe or restrict what they had expressly agreed in cl.13.3, which was effectively that either of them for any reason could terminate at any time before the four-year term was completed.

Each had voluntarily undertaken that risk when entering into the contract, even though each might have thought, hoped and assumed that the contract would run its full term. Had there been extreme and unusual facts, the law might well have provided T with some other remedy, *Attorney General of Belize v Belize Telecom Ltd* [2009] UKPC 10, [2009] 1 W.L.R. 1988 considered (para.51). (4) S was entitled to the declaration sought that, having exercised its right to terminate the contract under cl.13.3, T had no entitlement to receive monies and/or compensation in respect of overheads and profit which it would have recovered over the balance of the term following termination had the contract not been terminated. The adjudicator had erred in ordering S to pay T such monies (para.52).

TSG BUILDING SERVICES PLC v SOUTH ANGLIA HOUSING LTD, [2013] EWHC 1151 (TCC), [2013] B.L.R. 484, Akenhead, J., QBD (TCC).

538. Construction equipment–Construction materials

THE CONSTRUCTION PRODUCTS REGULATIONS 2013, SI 2013/1387; made under the European Communities Act 1972 s.2. In force: July 1, 2013; .

These Regulations make provision necessary for the operation in the UK of Regulation 305/2011 laying down harmonised conditions for the marketing of construction products.

539. Construction industry–Engineering Construction Industry Training Board–Engineering industry–Levies

THE INDUSTRIAL TRAINING LEVY (ENGINEERING CONSTRUCTION INDUSTRY TRAINING BOARD) ORDER 2013, SI 2013/1397; made under the Industrial Training Act 1982 s.11, s.12. In force: June 4, 2013; .

This Order will enable the Engineering Construction Industry Training Board to raise and impose a levy on employers in the engineering construction industry. This Order sets out the rate and exemptions from that levy.

540. Defective premises–Landlords' duties–Residential development–Scope of property developer's contractual responsibility for defects–Interpretation of contract terms

[Limitation Act 1980 (c.58) s.14A.]

The claimant leaseholders (H) sought damages against the first defendant property developer (O) for breach of sales agreements and repair covenants and against the second defendant property consultants (S) for negligence. O had developed a block of flats between 2001 and 2004. S were retained to carry out periodic inspections certifying, using architects' certificates, that the work had been constructed to a satisfactory standard. Under the sales agreements and leases, O agreed that the works would be completed to certain standards and that, as landlord, it would maintain, repair and renew the main structure of the building and common parts. Serious defects had emerged within the individual flats and common parts. It was claimed that O was in breach of its agreements with four of the claimants and its repairing covenant with all eight claimants. H also claimed that the certificates were enforceable warranties, that they constituted negligent misstatement and that S had breached its duty of care by failing to identify the defects. The court determined as a preliminary issue that the third defendant architect (E) and the fourth defendant were not liable. The main issues were the scope of (i) O's contractual responsibility; (ii) its repairing covenant; (iii) S's responsibility.

Held: Judgment for claimants. (1) The contract terms said to have been breached had to be analysed to determine when a cause of action could first be said to have arisen. It also needed to be determined whether there were potentially two causes of action which could arise in connection with one contractual term or in relation to the same facts but at different times, *Tameside MBC v Barlow Securities Group Services Ltd* [2001] EWCA Civ 1, [2001] B.L.R. 113, [2002] C.L.Y. 667 applied. Clause 3.1 of the agreements, which related to completion of the works, was expressed prospectively even though it had been clear to some of the claimants that sufficient work had been carried out to enable them to move in, though it could be mutually envisaged that there would be further works to be done. The primary obligation required "completion" of the premises "in a good and workmanlike manner and with suitable materials pursuant to any Planning Permissions", which suggested the emphasis was on completion. However, completion also meant that "the Premises shall be fit for occupation on completion" and "the Building will comply with all Planning Permissions and Building Regulations". Logic suggested that there were effectively two, or dual, obligations, and two stages in respect of which O could be sued. The purchaser could sue at any time when, having moved in, the flat was found to be badly built or of inadequate materials and a separate cause of action would arise when the building work had been completed and was found to be non-compliant with, say, the Building Regulations (see paras 102-108 of judgment). (2) It was first necessary to construe and interpret the "repairing" covenant in the appropriate context, *Quick v Taff Ely BC* [1986] Q.B. 809, [1985] C.L.Y. 1610 applied. O was in practice and in effect the developer of the building overall and of the particular premises. The scope and breadth of the repairing obligation was comprehensible in terms of having responsibility for the building overall. There was a real commercial and practical advantage to both landlord and tenant for there being a relatively broad repairing covenant. It enabled and obliged O to make good any design, workmanship or material deficiency within the building as a whole. The repairing covenant was therefore a wide obligation imposed on O, which obliged it to repair, renew or vary those parts of the building covered under the leases with H (paras 109-113). (3) The inspection certificates were issued by E on S's behalf knowing or believing that they would be relied on, and an actionable duty of care was therefore owed by S through E to H, *Hedley Byrne & Co Ltd v Heller & Partners Ltd* [1964] A.C. 465, [1963] C.L.Y. 2416 followed. The duty stemmed from a special relationship akin to a contract. Although engaged contractually by O, S were primarily engaged to do what was reasonably necessary to issue certificates to or for the benefit of the purchasers, and for the purchasers and their lenders to rely on them. The duty also extended to the performance of the services necessary to enable the certificates to be issued. The certificates could only be considered as a contractually enforceable warranty if supported by consideration. The courts had adopted a relatively flexible approach to what amounted to consideration, and the consideration to O amounted to valid consideration for the original purchasers under the sales agreements, *Wyvern Developments, Re* [1974] 1 W.L.R. 1097, [1974] C.L.Y. 357 applied. Those purchasers had also relied on the certificates such as to create a cause of action for negligent misstatement (paras 114-132). (4) With regard to limitation, proceedings had been issued by all the claimants except one (W) within six years of the date of issue of the certificates. W's claim in respect of breach of warranty was therefore prima facie barred. However, as she could not reasonably have known enough to enable her to bring an action for damages until well within the three-year period prior to the issue of proceedings, she was protected by the Limitation Act 1980 s.14A (paras 133-135, 231-233). (5) The court determined the appropriate remedial work costs in respect of the individual defects and the appropriate damages (paras 136-230, 234-264).

HUNT v OPTIMA (CAMBRIDGE) LTD, [2013] EWHC 681 (TCC), 148 Con. L.R. 27, Akenhead, J., QBD (TCC).

541. Lump sum contracts–Compensation events–Inherent risk in lump sum contracts–Commercial fairness–Arbitrator's analysis of relevant issues

[Arbitration Act 1996 (c.23) s.68.]

The claimant (X) challenged an arbitrator's award, pursuant to the Arbitration Act 1996 s.68, on the ground of "serious irregularity". X, a construction company, entered into a contract with the respondent secretary of state for the maintenance of an area of the highways network. The work included the remedying of minor defects in road surfaces, including potholes, for which X was to be paid a lump sum over the period of the contract. Clause 60.1 of the contract provided for certain "compensation events" which would entitle X to additional payment over and above what the contract otherwise allowed for. In that regard, cl.60.1 (11) referred to defects which were not evident and which, in terms of bullet point 4 of that provision, an experienced contractor "would have judged at the contract date to have such a small chance of being present that it would have been unreasonable for him to have allowed for it". A dispute arose between the parties when X claimed that the prevalence of potholes on the network was significantly greater than anticipated, and that it was therefore entitled to additional payment pursuant to the compensation event provisions. The matter was referred to arbitration. The arbitrator held that an excess volume of potholes beyond what it was reasonable to allow in the contract was not capable of constituting a defect in the physical condition of the area network under cl.60.1 (11). X contended that there had been a serious irregularity within the meaning of s.68 because the arbitrator had not decided the issue of whether each pothole over and above the number which should have been allowed for by X was a compensation event.

Held: Claim dismissed. (1) It was undisputed that potholes fell within the definition of "defects" for the purposes of the contract and were therefore capable of giving rise to a compensation event. However, there was nothing in the language of cl.60.1 (11) which expressly suggested that the number of defects was a key element in the compensation event equation, and there was no commercial logic or common sense in interpreting the clause in that way. The requirement set out at bullet point 4 of that provision made it extremely difficult to conclude that an excess number of potholes over and above a reasonable maximum number which could be considered to have been allowed for could form the basis for establishing the encountering of one or more potholes above that number as one or more compensation events. By providing for a lump sum, the nature of the contract was such that the parties took a collective risk that the defects to be addressed would be more or less in number and in terms of expense than the contract lump sums might allow for. There was nothing commercially unfair in such a risk (see paras 26, 29, 32-33 of judgment). (2) "Serious irregularity" within the meaning of s.68 did not mean in itself an error of fact or law on the part of the arbitrator and was not to be used as a ground for challenging the factual findings or legal reasoning of an arbitrator, *Petroships Pte Ltd of Singapore v Petec Trading & Investment Corp of Vietnam (The Petro Ranger)* [2001] 2 Lloyd's Rep. 348, [2001] C.L.Y. 340 considered. Where the court was asked to determine whether an arbitrator had failed to deal with all the issues put to him within the meaning of s.68(2)(d) of the Act, there was no requirement to carry out a hypercritical or excessively syntactical analysis of what the arbitrator had written. The court could only intervene under s.68 where an irregularity had caused substantial injustice. In the instant case, the arbitrator was not wrong in his overall reasoning or conclusion. Accordingly, there was no substantial injustice even if an irregularity was established. However, it was clear that the arbitrator had looked in some detail at the requirement under bullet point 4 of cl.60.1 (11) and had analysed whether the words used could sensibly relate to a foreseeable or allowable number of defects as being something upon which a claim could be based. Given that he had recognised the area of issue, analysed the wording, reviewed the commercial context and reached a decision, it was impossible to say that there had been any, let alone a serious, irregularity (paras 24, 36-39).

ATKINS LTD v SECRETARY OF STATE FOR TRANSPORT, [2013] EWHC 139 (TCC), [2013] B.L.R. 193, Akenhead, J., QBD (TCC).

542. Security–Performance bonds–Additional payments made to contractor by employer–Whether additional payments released bondsman's liability under performance bond

The appellant insurer (X) appealed against a decision ([2011] EWHC 2378 (TCC), [2011] B.L.R. 726, [2012] C.L.Y. 594) that it was liable to the respondent (H) under a bond securing the performance of a construction contract. H had engaged a construction company (S) to renovate a theatre. The works were estimated to cost £11 million. S and X executed a bond in H's favour for approximately £1.1 million to secure the performance of S's obligations under the construction contract. The construction work was delayed. S alleged that H had caused the delay because of the large number of instructions issued by H's architect. In a side agreement H agreed to pay S £1 million, in instalments, in respect of its claims for delay. H paid £750,000 under the side agreement. S went into administration prior to practical completion. H terminated the construction contract, engaged new contractors and claimed payment from X under the bond. The judge found that the side agreement was a separate, free-standing agreement, and X could not rely on the rule in *Holme v Brunskill* (1878) 3 Q.B.D. 495. He concluded that H's conduct in making the payments to S did not discharge X's liability under the bond. X submitted that the additional payments made by H to S had the effect of discharging X's liability under the bond. X also argued that even if it was still bound, H had lost the right to recover damages for failure to complete by terminating the contract under cl.27.

Held: Appeal dismissed. (1) The principles which were to be applied in the instant case were: (a) the rule in *Holme v Brunskill* only applied where parties to the contract guaranteed had varied the terms of that contract without the consent of the surety; (b) where the employer paid instalments of the agreed contract price before those instalments fell due under the terms of the original contract then, absent consent or an appropriate indulgence clause setting out what could be done without any need to consult the surety, those advance payments could result in discharging the liability of the surety. On the other hand, where the employer paid sums to the contractor under a separate agreement, rather than under the contract which the surety was guaranteeing, the liability of the surety was not discharged. The surety remained liable in respect of the original contract, but not in respect of the separate payments or loans which had been made; (c) a surety would not be released from liability by reason of contractual variations or advance payments if he had specifically consented to what was done, or there was an indulgency clause which covered what was done, *Calvert v London Dock Co* 48 E.R. 774, *General Steam Navigation Co v Rolt* 141 E.R. 572, and *Trade Indemnity Co Ltd v Workington Harbour and Dock Board (No.1)* [1937] A.C. 1 applied, *Holme* considered (see paras 78-79 of judgment). (2) H and S had not varied the construction contract and therefore the rule in *Holme v Brunskill* did not apply, *Holme* considered. The main issue was whether H's payment of £750,000 had the effect of discharging X from liability. S had intimated a substantial claim for loss caused by delay and disruption, and maintained that H was at fault because of the large number of instructions which the architect had issued. However, S had failed to substantiate those claims under the terms of the building contract. S therefore had no contractual entitlement to be paid in respect of loss. That left H with a dilemma as to whether it should stand on its contractual rights and leave S struggling with its financial problems or make additional payments in the hope that it would result in improved progress on the site. It chose the latter course. The effect of the side agreement was that H loaned £750,000 to S. If S subsequently substantiated its claimed loss, it could retain the money as payment or part-payment. If it failed to establish its loss, it would repay the money to H. The money was not part of the original contract sum. It did not discharge X from liability under the bond, but X was not liable in respect of the £750,000 (paras 83-92). (3) The construction contract was in the JCT standard form, 1998 edition, under which, in the event of the contractor's insolvency the employer had a choice whether or not to determine the contract. Clause 27.8 simply made it clear that the employer could exercise all of his rights under that clause and could also pursue his general remedies. H was therefore entitled to recover damages against X for delay, and for S's failure to complete (paras 93-103).

HACKNEY EMPIRE LTD v AVIVA INSURANCE UK LTD (FORMERLY T/A NORWICH UNION INSURANCE LTD); *sub nom.* AVIVA INSURANCE LTD v HACKNEY EMPIRE LTD, [2012] EWCA Civ 1716, [2013] 1 W.L.R. 3400, Sir John Thomas (President), CA (Civ Div).

543. Sub-contracts–Construction equipment–Termination of sub-contract by contractor–Ownership of sub-contractor's equipment under sub-contract

The claimant (X) sought a declaration against the defendant (S) as to the ownership of certain assets. X was engaged as the main contractor to construct a power plant. X employed S as sub-contractor to carry out mechanical and plant piping erection. Clause 54.2 of the sub-contract provided that all the sub-contractor's equipment when on the site was deemed to be the contractor's property. Clause 54.9 stated that goods supplied pursuant to the sub-contract would become the contractor's property when they were delivered to the site. In the event of termination of the sub-contract, clause 63.2 provided that the contractor could take possession of such equipment on the site which was reasonably required to complete the work. Clause 63.3 enabled the contractor to sell such equipment and use the proceeds to satisfy any debt if the sub-contract was terminated. S failed to perform its duties under the sub-contract and X terminated S's employment. S went into liquidation. X retained the equipment brought on site by S. The main works had been handed over to the client but the warranty period had not ended. X obtained summary judgment on its claim against S for £5.3 million and sought a declaration that all S's equipment on site was deemed to be X's property and that S was not allowed to remove it from the site. X submitted that the court on the summary judgment application had already decided the issue of ownership of the sub-contractor's equipment in its favour so that it was res judicata.

Held: Declaration granted in part. (1) The question of whether property had been transferred by a contract was one of construction and interpretation of the contract. Where the expression used was "deemed" to become property of one party to the contract, it was necessary to look at the other terms which cast light on the purpose, extent and duration of the requirement to see whether it was mutually intended that ownership was intended permanently to pass, *Cosslett (Contractors) Ltd, Re* [1998] Ch. 495, [1997] C.L.Y. 3057 applied. S had rightly conceded that, under clause 54.9, ownership of goods supplied by it on site pursuant to the sub-contract had passed to X. Clause 54.9 was clear and explained why commercially that was the case. However permanent ownership of S's equipment was not intended to be passed by clause 54.2 or any other provision. There was a marked difference between "deemed to be" the property of the contractor in clause 54.2 and "becoming" the property of the contractor in clause 54.9. The property was deemed to be the contractor's whilst on site but not before or after. There was no obvious commercial reason why it would be necessary to deem permanent ownership to be transferred to the contractor. Clause 63.2 only applied to the extent that such equipment was reasonably required to facilitate completion of the works. It was accepted that the clause 63.3 right might not have accrued yet to X; pending the completion of the warranty period (see paras 17-20 of judgment). (2) The issue of the ownership of S's equipment was not res judicata as there was no argument at the summary judgment application about the permanent or temporary nature of ownership set out in the deeming provision in clause 54.2 (para.21). (3) X clearly had contractual rights over S's equipment and S had no right to remove them. Given that there had been found to be a valid termination under clause 63, X had possessory rights over S's equipment until the work was completed at the end of the warranty period. X had rights to sell S's equipment under clause 63 if and when the procedure set out in clause 63.3 had been implemented. However, ultimate proprietary ownership of such equipment did not permanently transfer to X (paras 22-23).

ALSTOM POWER LTD v SOMI IMPIANTI SRL, [2012] EWHC 2644 (TCC), [2012] B.L.R. 585, Akenhead, J., QBD (TCC).

CONSUMER LAW

544. Aquaculture–Fishery products–Labelling

THE FISH LABELLING (WALES) REGULATIONS 2013, SI 2013/SI 2013/2139 (W.209); made under the European Communities Act1972 Sch.2 para.1A; and the Food SafetyAct 1990 s.6, s.16, s.17, s.26, s.48. In force: September 26, 2013; .

These Regulations enforce in Wales the consumer information requirements of European legislation on fishery and aquaculture products.

545. Cancellation–Cooling-off period–Meaning of reg.5(a) Cancellation of Contracts made in a Consumer's Home or Place of Work etc. Regulations 2008–Whether Regulations ultra vires

[Consumers, Estate Agents and Redress Act 2007 (c.17) s.59; European Communities Act 1972 (c.68) s.2(2); Cancellation of Contracts made in a Consumer's Home or Place of Work etc. Regulations 2008 (SI 2008/1816) reg.2(1), reg.5(a), reg.6(1)(d), reg.7(6), reg.10(1), Sch.3; Consumer Protection (Cancellation of Contracts Concluded away from Business Premises) Regulations 1987 (SI 1987/2117); Directive 85/577 to protect the consumer in respect of contracts negotiated away from business premises.]

The appellant (R) appealed against a county court decision that he was liable to pay a cancellation charge to the respondent (S), the proprietor of a removal firm, and that he had no right to recover the deposit which he had paid. R had asked S for a quote for undertaking a removal. S attended R's home and surveyed the contents. The two men orally agreed upon a price. When S returned to his office, he prepared a contract and emailed it to R along with a copy of his standard conditions, which included provision for a cancellation charge. S visited R's home again that evening in order to deliver some boxes. R signed the contract and paid a deposit. Two days later, having obtained a cheaper quote from another company, R telephoned S to cancel the agreement. S commenced proceedings against R in order to claim payment of the cancellation charge. R's defence and counterclaim denied any liability to S and sought recovery of the deposit. It was R's case that he had cancelled the agreement within the seven-day cooling-off period allowed by the Cancellation of Contracts made in a Consumer's Home or Place of Work etc. Regulations 2008, and he also asserted that the agreement was unenforceable under reg.7(6), as S had not given him notice of his right to cancel. The court held that the Regulations did not apply because the contract had been made in two separate visits to R's home, not a single visit as was required by reg.5(a). That decision was upheld on appeal. The issues were (i) the correct construction of reg.5(a); (ii) whether the 2008 Regulations were so wide in their effect as to be ultra vires; (iii) the financial consequences for R and S.

Held: Appeal allowed in part. (1) Regulation 5(a) applied if the consumer's home was the place where the contract was concluded, irrespective of whether there had been earlier negotiations between the parties at the consumer's home. The focus of reg.5(a) was upon the occasion when and the place where the consumer became legally committed. In the phrase "during a visit", the word "a" was simply the indefinite article. It was not limiting the contractual process to a single visit. If the offer was made in one visit and the acceptance occurred during a second visit, it would be bizarre if that took the contract outside reg.5(a). The removal agreement fell within the scope of reg.5(a). S had been under a duty, pursuant to reg.7(2), to give R written notice of his right to cancel. As he did not do so, the agreement was unenforceable against R. If such a notice had been given, R would have been entitled to cancel the agreement during the cancellation period (see paras 39-43 of judgment). (2) The 2008 Regulations were intended to give effect to Directive 85/577. When one looked at the mischief against which the directive was aimed, as set out in the preamble, it was far removed from the circumstances of the instant case. Neither the directive nor the Consumer Protection (Cancellation of Contracts Concluded away from Business Premises) Regulations 1987, which were replaced by the 2008 Regulations, applied if the trader visited the consumer's home at the express request of the consumer. However, the 2008 Regulations were wider in scope and, subject to certain exceptions set out in reg.6(1)(d), they applied even if the customer specifically requested the trader to come to his house in order to assess the services which he was to provide. The 2008 Regulations were made under the European Communities Act 1972 s.2(2) and the Consumers, Estate Agents and Redress Act 2007 s.59. Reading those two provisions together, there was no doubt that the 2008 Regulations had been made within the powers conferred by statute (paras 46-55). (3) As the agreement was unenforceable against R, S was not entitled to make any charge for cancellation. In relation to the counterclaim, since S did not serve any written notice under reg.7(2), there was no cancellation period as defined in reg.2(1). It followed that R was not entitled to cancel the contract under reg.7(1). The contract remained alive, but was unenforceable as against R. Regulation 10(1) did not apply, so R had no right to recover his deposit (paras 56-60). (4) (Per curiam) The decision in the instant case had been reached with regret. It was inappropriate for consumer protection regulations to apply in the circumstances of the case. Many removal firms were small businesses, and they necessarily visited customers at home in order to assess the proposed work. It must often happen that the remover and the customer entered into an agreement at the customer's home. Once the deal had been done, the remover had to incur costs in preparing for the move, and might also turn away other work during the relevant period. If the customer had seven days in which to cancel the contract, the remover was put in an impossible position. It was to be hoped that the Department for Business, Innovation and Skills would review the 2008 Regulations in the light of the instant case and consider whether any amendments were appropriate. It might be thought appropriate to include removal contracts in the list of "excepted contracts" in Sch.3 (para.58).

ROBERTSON v SWIFT; *sub nom.* SWIFT (T/A A SWIFT MOVE) v ROBINSON, [2012] EWCA Civ 1794, [2013] Bus. L.R. 479, Mummery, L.J., CA (Civ Div).

546. Citizens advice bureaux–Enforcement–Office of Fair Trading

THE PUBLIC BODIES (THE OFFICE OF FAIR TRADING TRANSFER OF CONSUMER ADVICE SCHEME FUNCTION AND MODIFICATION OF ENFORCEMENT FUNCTIONS) ORDER 2013, SI 2013/783; made under the Public Bodies Act 2011 s.5, s.6, s.35. In force: March 28, 2013; .

This Order transfers the power of the Office of Fair Trading to support a consumer advice scheme to the National Association of Citizens Advice Bureaux and the Scottish Association of Citizens Advice Bureaux, and makes modifications to the OFT's consumer enforcement functions.

547. Cleaning preparations–Consumer protection–Water pollution

THE DETERGENTS (AMENDMENT) REGULATIONS 2013, SI 2013/1244; made under the European Communities Act 1972 s.2. In force: June 30, 2013; .

These Regulations amend the Detergents Regulations 2010 (SI 2010/740) to enable the Government to enforce an EU-wide restriction on the sale of domestic laundry cleaning products containing phosphates.

548. Consumer credit–Financial Conduct Authority–Office of Fair Trading

THE FINANCIAL SERVICES ACT 2012 (CONSUMER CREDIT) ORDER 2013, SI 2013/1882; made under the Financial Services Act 2012 s.107, s.115. In force: in accordance with art.1.; .

This Order affects the transfer of consumer credit regulation from the Office of Fair Trading to the Financial Conduct Authority.

549. Consumer credit agreements–Bills of sale–Purchase of car under loan agreement with bill of sale as security–Bankruptcy of borrowers–Effect of finance company's proof in bankruptcy on entitlement to enforce security over car

[Bills of Sale Act (1878) Amendment Act 1882 (c.43) s.7; Consumer Credit Act 1974 (c.39) s.76, s.87, s.98; Insolvency Act 1986 (c.45) s.285(3).]

The appellant finance company (F) appealed against a declaration that a car had been discharged from a bill of sale executed in F's favour by the respondents (X and Y). F's counterclaim for delivery up of the car had been dismissed. X and Y had bought the car with finance provided by F under a loan agreement regulated by the Consumer Credit Act 1974. The loan was repayable in monthly instalments over four years and X and Y were jointly and severally liable. F could demand early repayment of the outstanding balance on stated events, including overdue payments and the bankruptcy of one or both of X and Y. Under the bill of sale giving F security over the car, F was entitled to take possession on similar specified events under the Bills of Sale Act (1878) Amendment Act 1882 s.7. X was made bankrupt. Y continued to make payments. F proved in X's bankruptcy for the total amount of its claim and received a dividend. X was discharged from bankruptcy, but Y was subsequently declared bankrupt. F served a default notice under s.87 of the 1974 Act. X and Y sought a declaration that the car was their property, on the basis that their contractual liability was discharged. F sought to enforce the bill of sale. The judge construed the bill of sale as making X and Y jointly, rather than jointly and severally, liable for the debt. He considered that it followed that the entire debt became due on X's bankruptcy and the loan agreement did not continue to bind Y. He held that F's failure to enforce its security following X's bankruptcy disentitled it from thereafter seeking to enforce it on the basis that the loan agreement continued to apply.

Held: Appeal allowed. The effect of X's bankruptcy was that F's contractual right to enforce repayment was replaced by a right to prove for the debt in the bankruptcy. X's estate was preserved for the benefit of the whole body of creditors, but the bankruptcy order did not affect the right of a secured creditor to enforce his security. F specified the security but did not put a value on it and the entire debt was admitted to proof. The consequence of the bankruptcy for X was that he was released from any personal claim against him by F, but F did not lose its right to enforce the security, *Household Mortgage Corp Plc v Whitehead* [2002] EWCA Civ 1657, [2003] 1 W.L.R. 1173, [2003] C.L.Y. 3582 applied. F was not therefore required to renounce its security as the price for being able to prove for the balance of the debt, or for having proved for the entire amount due. It did not exercise its right to enforce the security following X's bankruptcy while Y continued to meet the instalments. The judge's apparent reasoning that the satisfaction of X's contractual liability had released Y from any liability was a misconception. Although Y would have been discharged from liability if X had paid what was due, the effect of the Insolvency Act 1986 s.285(3) was to limit the creditor's right of recovery against the bankrupt debtor to proving in the bankruptcy. The bankrupt remained immune on discharge from further proceedings and was released from the debt. However, the debt continued against the joint debtor until extinguished by payment or release by the creditor. Nothing turned on that point in the instant case as Y's own bankruptcy protected her from any personal claim by F. However, the issue for the judge was not whether F could still pursue X or Y for the money, as obviously it could not, but whether their bankruptcy was the end of the matter. Y had not been obliged to continue to make the payments, but the arrangement which had continued de facto between Y and F was that, so long as the payments were kept up, F stayed its hand in relation to enforcement of the security. F should have proceeded by way of a s.98 notice under the 1974 Act, terminating the agreement on grounds other than a breach, which was a pre-requisite to enforcement of the creditor's right to enforce its security. However, as the term of the loan had expired by the date of the trial, F was entitled by then to recover possession of the car free from the statutory requirements to give notice under s.76 or s.98 of the 1974 Act. The only issue was whether F had retained the benefit of the security under the bill of sale and was entitled to enforce that security. Although there was much to be said for the judge's view that, following X and Y's discharge from bankruptcy, F could not base its contractual right to enforce the security on a failure to pay one or more of the instalments, the pleaded defence and counterclaim were wide enough to support F's reliance on the bankruptcy as an alternative basis for recovering the car, which had not been waived by subsequent events. The judge was wrong to conclude that F had lost its right to enforce the bill of sale based on X and Y's bankruptcy. F was entitled to ask the court to set aside the order and to make an order for delivery up of the car on the basis of one or other of the two bankruptcies (see paras 19-33 of judgment).

EVANS v FINANCE-U-LTD, [2013] EWCA Civ 869, [2014] R.T.R. 8, Mummery, L.J., CA (Civ Div).

550. Consumer credit agreements–Unfair relationships–Creditor's sale of payment protection insurance to debtor–Effect of creditor's non-disclosure of its commission

[Consumer Credit Act 1974 (c.39) s.140A.]

The appellant (B) appealed against a county court decision that it had created an unfair relationship with the respondent (C), contrary to the Consumer Credit Act 1974 s.140A. C had entered into a credit agreement with B, which then sold her a payment protection insurance policy to protect the repayments that she was to make to it. B did not disclose to her that it would be paid a commission of more than 40 per cent of the premium by the insurance company providing the cover. C maintained that she would not have purchased the insurance policy if she had known that the total cost was three times the cost of equivalent stand alone cover and that the commission element accounted for more than 40 per cent of the premium. The county court declared that the credit agreement and the payment protection insurance gave rise to an unfair relationship between a between creditor and a debtor, within the meaning of s.140A, as a result of B's withholding the facts about the commission, even though it had not been obliged to make such disclosure in law or by industry standards.

Held: Appeal allowed. The rule in the Financial Services Authority's Insurance Conduct of Business Rules that an insurance intermediary should, when asked, disclose its commission did not not apply in the instant case. C was not a commercial customer and there was no rule requiring B to disclose to its customers the existence or amount of commission earned by it from the insurer in the event that a customer took out a payment protection insurance contract in the context of a loan made by B to that customer. An unfair relationship did not arise where the only matter of complaint was the fact that the lender had acted in a manner that complied with the regulatory regime which had deliberately, and after proper consultation, decided not to impose any such requirement, *Harrison v Black Horse Ltd* [2011] EWCA Civ 1128, [2012] E.C.C. 7, [2012] C.L.Y. 614 applied. Where the sole matter of complaint was non-disclosure of the fact or extent of commission, and where the regulatory framework, at the time, had deliberately set its face against such a requirement in the instant kind of case, it would be anomalous to find that the relationship was unfair. B's decision not to disclose commission was one it had been free to take without breaking the rules and was a decision which could not be informed by any information as to whether a particular customer might wish to shop around if that information were disclosed. If a failure to disclose could, on its own, gave rise to an unfair relationship then B would always have to disclose the fact and extent of commission because it would not know whether a customer would wish to shop around if there were such disclosure. That would have undercut the regulatory regime which had been in force at the time and which had been deliberately drawn, for reasons which had then seemed proper to the FSA, not to require such disclosure in that type of business (see paras 10-13, 45-46, 50 of judgment).

CONLON v BLACK HORSE LTD [2012] C.T.L.C. 193, Wilkie, J., QBD.

551. Consumer protection–Domestic infringements–Surcharges

THE ENTERPRISE ACT 2002 (PART 8 DOMESTIC INFRINGEMENTS) ORDER 2013, SI 2013/761; made under the European Communities Act 1972 s.2; and the Enterprise Act 2002 s.211. In force: April 6, 2013; .

This Order adds the Consumer Rights (Payment Surcharges) Regulations 2012 to the list of consumer protection measures that may be enforced within the framework of the Enterprise Act 2002 Pt 8. The Order is laid in draft for approval by resolution of each House.

552. Consumer protection–Property misdescriptions

THE PROPERTY MISDESCRIPTIONS ACT 1991 (REPEAL) ORDER 2013, SI 2013/1575; made under the European Communities Act 1972 s.2. In force: October 1, 2013; .

This Order repeals the Property Misdescriptions Act 1991 and makes consequential amendments to other enactments.

553. Consumer protection–Warrants–Scope of powers under reg.21 and reg.22 Consumer Protection from Unfair Trading Regulations 2008

[Copyright, Designs and Patents Act 1988 (c.48) s.297A; Consumer Protection from Unfair Trading Regulations 2008 (SI 2008/1277) reg.21, reg.22, Sch.1 para.9; Directive 98/84 on the legal protection of services based on, or consisting of, conditional access.]

The claimants (V and C), being an individual and the company he owned, applied for orders quashing warrants issued by the first defendant magistrates' court at the request of the second defendant trading standards department. C's main business was described as "retailing and wholesaling satellite products", a product called a Spider HD box being a particularly successful product. Its activities were drawn to the attention of trading standards by a company (M) which had close connections with Football Association Premier League Limited (F) and BSkyB (B). In Albania, a company called Tring TV had (under licence from F) the exclusive rights to broadcast live Premier League matches. Tring TV had agreed with F that its broadcasting should be encrypted so that it could not be viewed outside Albania. Decoder cards were accordingly supplied in Albania by Tring TV on terms that they were authorised for use only in Albania and were for personal domestic use. M's complaint was that C was openly marketing and selling such Tring decoder cards for use in the United Kingdom, notwithstanding that they were permitted only to be sold and used in Albania; further, by being used in conjunction with Spider boxes, they were enabling purchasers, who also might not be using them simply for private domestic use, to view live in the UK relevant Premier League matches. In support of the application for the issue of warrants, trading standards asserted that the supply of the decoder cards within the UK was likely to constitute an offence under the Copyright, Designs and Patents Act 1988 s.297A as well as the banned practice of stating or otherwise creating the impression that a product could legally be sold when it could not, contrary to the Consumer Protection from Unfair Trading Regulations 2008 Sch.1 para.9. Warrants were issued enabling searches of V's home and C's business premises to be carried out; they gave the right to enter the identified premises under reg.22 of the 2008 Regulations and the power to inspect under reg.21.

Held: Judgment accordingly. (1) The warrants should be quashed by reason of material non-disclosure. In joined cases before the European Court of Justice, the Advocate General had given an opinion to the effect that an "illicit device", for the purposes of Directive 98/84, was to be construed as not covering foreign decoder devices used, in disregard of the broadcaster's will, outside the geographical area for which they were issued or in breach of a contractual limitation permitting their use only for private purposes. Specialist judges in the English courts, in directing a reference in the relevant cases, had also expressed preliminary views to that effect. Both M and F would have been aware of the Advocate General's and the judges' views. It was now established that the supplying of the decoder cards did not constitute an offence under s.297A of the 1988 Act, nor could it fairly be represented to the magistrates' court at the time that it was "likely" that it did, given the significant doubts which had been expressed by the Advocate General and the English courts. If criminality under s.297A was to be excluded, what was in dispute could be viewed in substance and commercial reality as a civil matter between F and/or B, on the one hand, and V and C, on the other. If that had been identified, it was difficult not to think that matters might well have taken a different course: the district judge may well have considered that some less draconian sanction than a warrant was appropriate, that the position should be left to be decided in civil proceedings and that the issue of interim relief should be considered by a specialist Chancery Division judge. There was often a need for speed and robustness in this context; further, prospective defendants often had no inclination or intention to abide by the law. But it should never be forgotten that the granting of a warrant was a most extreme and invasive kind of order, not to be granted without great caution and dependent on full and accurate disclosure by the applicant (see paras 24, 29, 34-35, 38 of judgment). (2) V and C had also challenged the lawfulness of the execution of the warrants, asserting that the 2008 Regulations conferred no power to search premises or to enter a private dwelling. Neither proposition could be accepted. The powers conferred by reg.21 and reg.22 plainly carried with them a power to search, as a matter of sensible construction. It was impossible to see how they could be effectively exercised if such a power was not available. Further, there was a power to enter a private dwelling. Regulation 22 referred to "premises" without qualification. To hold otherwise would entail depriving reg.22 of much of its evident purpose. It would also serve as a charter and encouragement to the unscrupulous to store incriminating items or documents in their private homes (paras 44, 48, 51).

R. (ON THE APPLICATION OF VUCITERNI) v BRENT MAGISTRATES' COURT, [2012] EWHC 2140 (Admin), (2012) 176 J.P. 705, Davis, L.J., DC.

554. Environmental protection–Fireworks–Health and safety at work

THE PYROTECHNIC ARTICLES (SAFETY) (AMENDMENT) REGULATIONS 2013, SI 2013/1950; made under the European Communities Act 1972 s.2. In force: August 30, 2013; .

These Regulations implement Directive 2013/29 on the harmonisation of the laws on the making available on the market of pyrotechnic articles.

555. Extended warranties–Time limits–Office of Fair Trading decision not to allow bundled extended warranties on price comparison website–Whether application for review out of time

[Enterprise Act 2002 (c.40) s.154, s.154(3), s.162, s.167(7), s.179; Competition Appeal Tribunal Rules 2003 (SI 2003/1372) r.8(2).]

The applicant company (J) applied for a review a decision of the respondent Office of Fair Trading refusing to allow J's offers of bundled extended warranties for domestic electrical goods to appear on a price comparison website. J had brought the application under the Enterprise Act 2002 s.179, where the time limit for such a review was two months from the date J was notified of the disputed decision. The decision related to the implementation of undertakings given by various retailers in lieu of a reference to the Competition Commission on June 27, 2012 of the market for extended warranties on domestic electrical goods. On August 8, 2012, J sent the OFT a letter setting out its objections in law to the OFT's position, and the OFT replied on 24 August. The issues were whether (i) the instant application was time-barred; (ii) the OFT had breached it duties under s.162 and s.167(7) in refusing to list J's extended warranties on the website was a breach of the undertakings in lieu; (iii) the OFT had unreasonably and unlawfully exercised its discretions under s.154; (iv) the OFT had misled customers and thus distorted trade in goods and services in breach of EU law.

Held: Application refused. (1) The decision of June 27 reflected the OFT's conclusion that bundled extended warranties would be referred to only in general terms and that the OFT's purpose was to create a website that would enable prices of standalone extended warranties to be compared. The correspondence made it abundantly clear that the OFT had explained to J what the website would say in relation to bundled extended warranties and that J could not reasonably claim not to have understood that. The OFT had decided the terms of the undertakings in lieu on June 27, on which date it formally accepted the undertakings from the retailers. J brought no application for review, not even when it received the reply of August 24, at a time when the two month period for bringing an application for review against the decision had still not expired. The need for legal finality and certainty was of overriding importance and respect for the deadline for commencing applications for review was crucial, *Fish Holdings Ltd v Office of Fair Trading* [2009] CAT 34, [2010] Comp. A.R. 169, [2010] C.L.Y. 478 and *British Sky Broadcasting Group Plc v Competition Commission* [2008] CAT 1, [2008] Comp. A.R. 1, [2008] C.L.Y. 536 applied. It was not a case of exceptional circumstances under the Competition Appeal Tribunal Rules 2003 r.8(2) such as would permit extending the time for bringing those claims (see paras 44, 48-52 of judgment). (2) The OFTs duties under s.162 and s.167(7) did not come into play. Although the undertakings in lieu contained a condition requiring establishment of the website, and that condition was taking some time to fulfil, that did not mean that it was not being complied with; rather, it appeared that the undertakings in lieu were being implemented in accordance with their terms (paras 54-55). (3) The decision taken on June 27 may or may not have fully been in accordance with s.154(3) but once taken could only be attacked by application to the tribunal within the prescribed time. That time expired on August 28, 2012 and the challenge was therefore time-barred (paras 56-58). (4) The complaint against the OFT was in reality a complaint against the terms of the decision and the terms of the undertakings in lieu rather than against its subsequent implementation with respect to the website. The OFT's actions in relation to the development of the website, within the limits set by the undertakings in lieu for bundled extended warranties, could not in themselves give rise any possible breach of EU law that was not already inherent in the decisions taken on June 27. Thus any application J made against that decision was time-barred (para. 60).

JOHN LEWIS PLC v OFFICE OF FAIR TRADING, [2013] CAT 7, [2013] Comp. A.R. 301, Vivien Rose (Chairman), CAT.

556. Groceries Code Adjudicator Act 2013 (19)

This Act sets up a Groceries Code Adjudicator with the role of enforcing the Groceries Code and encouraging compliance with it.

This Act received Royal Assent on April 25, 2013.

557. Regulated agreements–Restricted use credit agreements–Short-term loan agreement funding arrangement to obtain annulment of bankruptcy after paying creditors–Whether agreement regulated by Consumer Credit Act 1974

[Consumer Credit Act 1974 (c.39) s.11 (1) (c), s.11 (1), Pt V, s.87, s.127; Insolvency Act 1986 (c.45) s.285, s.286, s.360, s.382; Insolvency Rules 1986 (SI 1986/1925) r.12.3.]

The appellant husband and wife debtors (D) appealed against a determination of preliminary issues in favour of the respondent finance company (C). C and another company (P) were associated companies. They contacted bankrupt individuals offering to secure the annulment of their bankruptcy orders by advancing a sum on a short-term loan basis. That sum, together with substantial interest, fees and costs was secured on the bankrupt's property. P claimed that it could obtain annulments, ensuring that the bankrupts kept their homes. With D, the wife was bankrupt. She owned the home jointly with her husband. After instructing P to seek an annulment, D signed a facility letter from C informing them that C was willing to make a term loan of a sum estimated to be required to secure the annulment. Clause 2.1 of that letter provided that the loan was to be used for the purposes of refinancing the debt. The loan was to be repaid in full within three months of the drawdown. D also signed a third party legal charge over their home. C paid the sum to P who then paid D's creditors. The letter and the charge were held to D's order pending the annulment of the bankruptcy order when they were dated and the charge registered. D were unable to refinance their liabilities to C who brought the instant proceedings seeking payment of sums alleged to be due and to enforce the charge. C did not serve default notices required under the Consumer Credit Act 1974 s.87 in relation to regulated agreements. D claimed that the agreements, by which they were alleged to have incurred their liabilities to C, were regulated for the purposes of the Act and did not comply with the Act's requirements. The court determined as preliminary issues that C had loaned money to D under the terms of the facility letter and that the agreement was exempt under the Act and therefore enforceable. The issues were whether D were indebted to P or to C, and if the latter, then whether the agreement between it and D was regulated under the Act.

Held: Appeal allowed. In determining whether the agreement was a restricted use agreement within s.11 (1), the express definition of the loan in the instant case was meaningless and had to be disregarded. Clause 2.1 indicated agreement that the loan was to be used for a particular purpose only, that being to pay sums to P in connection with the annulment of the bankruptcy. Until the annulment order was made the facility letter and the legal charge were of no effect, being held to D's order. P had already paid D's creditors to secure the annulment, doing so at D's request and as a result D became liable to repay to P the sums it advanced. The documents provided to D led them to believe that P would pay off the creditors and together with the fact that P made those payments led to the conclusion that the sums were advanced by P and that D understood and agreed that it would do so. D was indebted to P in relation to those sums, certainly until the annulment order was made and the facility letter and the legal charge was delivered to C. The effect of the facility letter was to replace D's indebtedness to P with that owed to C. Therefore, the purpose of the agreement between D and C was to refinance D's indebtedness to P. The Insolvency Act 1986 s.285 was irrelevant, applying only to debts provable in D's bankruptcy. D's liability to P was incurred after the bankruptcy order and under s.382 of the 1986 Act and the Insolvency Rules 1986 r.12.3 it was not provable in the bankruptcy. Section 286 affected enforcement; it did not prevent a debt from coming into existence. P knew that D was an undischarged bankrupt, therefore s.360 was also irrelevant. On its true construction the purpose of the facility letter was to refinance D's indebtedness to P. The word "loan" used in the facility letter and the word "indebtedness" in s.11 (1) (c) of the 1974 Act were synonymous. It followed that the agreement between C and D fell within s.11 (1) (c). It was not an agreement within s.11 (1) (b), nor an exempt agreement; it was a regulated agreement and was unenforceable, as was the legal charge, owing to the failure to comply with the requirements under the 1974 Act. The judge failed to analyse correctly D's liabilities before the annulment order was made and on its being made. There was a loan at that point of time and it was refinanced under the agreement contained in the facility letter and the legal charges. Whether the agreement could be enforced in subsequent proceedings required service of a default notice and since it appeared that the agreement was not properly executed within the meaning of Part V of the 1974 Act that would require an enforcement order under s.127 (see paras 44-48, 50-52 of judgment).

CONSOLIDATED FINANCE LTD v COLLINS; CONSOLIDATED FINANCE LTD v BAILEY; CONSOLIDATED FINANCE LTD v ROTHOFF; CONSOLIDATED FINANCE LTD v TOYE, [2013] EWCA Civ 475, [2013] E.C.C. 21, Arden, L.J., CA (Civ Div).

558. Trading standards–Misleading advertising–Alleged misleading actions and misleading advertisements published by motor trading company–Liability of managing director

[Consumer Credit Act 1974 (c.39) s.169; Consumer Credit (Advertisements) Regulations 2004 (SI 2004/1484) reg.4, Sch.2; Consumer Protection from Unfair Trading Regulations 2008 (SI 2008/1277) reg.9, reg.15.]

The first appellant motor trading company and second appellant managing director (W) appealed by way of case stated against various convictions for trading standards offences. The company and W had received a series of summonses in respect of those alleged offences. One summons related solely to the company and alleged that it had acted misleadingly by representing to a purchaser that a vehicle was under warranty when it was not, contrary to the Consumer Protection from Unfair Trading Regulations 2008 reg.9. Other summonses relating to both the company and W alleged that they had acted in contravention of reg.9 by misleadingly stating on internet advertisements that finance available on its vehicles was interest-free, and that they had published credit advertisements without disclosing certain information required by the Consumer Credit (Advertisements) Regulations 2004 reg.4(1)(a) and Sch.2. W also faced allegations of personal liability on the basis that he had neglected his duty with regard to advertising contrary to reg.15 of the 2008 Regulations and the Consumer Credit Act 1974 s.169(2). The company and W were convicted on all counts. The judge found that the vehicle was not under warranty when the company represented that it was to the purchaser; that the interest-free statements were misleading so as to confuse the average consumer on how a car's purchase price was calculated; that there was a one-page advertisement, and information required by the 2004 Regulations had not been provided; that an inference could be drawn that W had a duty to review advertising and he had neglected that duty. The questions were whether (i) there was sufficient evidence before the judge to conclude that the vehicle was no longer under warranty when the company had so represented to the purchaser; (ii) the judge was right to accept that there was evidence to prove all elements of the offence relating to the interest-free advertisements; (iii) the judge was correct in his interpretation of reg.4(1)(a) and Sch.2 in finding that there was a one-page advertisement, and whether there was sufficient evidence to make such a finding; (iv) the judge was correct in his interpretation of the relevant case law, including *Huckerby v Elliott* [1970] 1 All E.R. 189, [1970] C.L.Y. 569, and whether there was evidence to support his finding in respect of W's duty and his neglect of it.

Held: Appeal allowed in part. (1) There was insufficient admissible evidence to sustain the judge's finding that the car was not under warranty when the company had represented that it was to the purchaser, and accordingly the company's conviction in that regard was quashed (see paras 26-27 of judgment). (2) The judge was entitled to conclude that the statements that finance available on the vehicles would be interest-free would have caused the average consumer to take a transactional decision that he would not have otherwise taken, and to think incorrectly that the costs normally borne by the purchaser would be borne by the seller. The advertisements were potentially misleading about how the price was calculated (paras 33-34). (3) The judge was entitled to find that there was a one-page advertisement. The purpose of the 2004 Regulations was to ensure that information was kept together and not to allow advertisements to draw in potential purchasers by highlighting favourable elements whilst concealing less favourable factors. If the company's webpage had shown pictures of various cars without any credit information that would have been acceptable, but it was unacceptable to be selective with the credit information advertised (paras 41-42). (4) It was necessary for W to show that there was no evidence on which the judge could properly convict. There was sufficient evidence for the judge to infer that W had responsibility for the drafting and presentation of advertisements. He gave reasons as to why it was an appropriate inference that, where the advertisements were central to the business and where W was treated as the boss, there would be such a duty on him. The judge was correct in his interpretation of the case law and there was sufficient evidence to find that W had a duty in relation to the advertisements and that he had neglected that duty, *Huckerby* considered (paras 48-51).

MOTOR DEPOT LTD v KINGSTON UPON HULL CITY COUNCIL, [2012] EWHC 3257 (Admin), (2013) 177 J.P. 41, Elias, L.J., DC.

559. Unfair commercial practices–Aggressive practices–Consumer informed of prize win–Lawfulness of cost incurred in claiming prize–European Union

[Directive 2005/29 on unfair business-to-consumer commercial practices in the internal market.]

The European Court of Justice was asked for a preliminary ruling on whether Directive 2005/29 Annex I para.31 prohibited the imposition of any cost on consumers who had been informed that they had won a prize. The appellants (P) in the main proceedings had informed consumers that they had won prizes and given the consumers the option of calling a premium rate telephone number, using a reverse SMS text messaging service or using the ordinary post to find out what prize they could claim. Less prominence was given to the postal method than to the premium rate telephone method, and there was evidence that most participating consumers responded by telephone or text, even though they were not told that the minimum time it would take them to obtain the information necessary to claim the most common award was a few seconds short of the maximum call duration or that from the cost per minute of £1.50, P took £1.21. In some cases, the consumer had to pay an additional cost stated to include delivery and insurance, part of which was used by the promoter to finance the cost of acquiring the item claimed. More than 99 per cent of those claiming a prize were entitled to receive the most common award, which was only worth about what they had to spend to receive it. The respondent regulator (O) brought proceedings before the High Court which found that P had been engaging in unfair commercial practices. P appealed and the Court of Appeal referred the question to the ECJ. P submitted that para.31 required the consumers to have been given a false impression, and so there was no unfair practice where they were sufficiently informed of the cost of claiming the prize.

Held: Preliminary ruling given. Annex I was a list of 31 paragraphs that described practices which were in all circumstances regarded as unfair. Paragraph 31 related to the creation of a false impression. According to that paragraph, a false impression was given where either there was no prize or the consumer incurred a cost in claiming the prize. A false impression was not an element of the unfair practice distinct from those two situations; rather those situations further explained what was a false impression. The second situation described in para.31 did not allow for any exception, meaning that it was evident that the consumer was not to bear the slightest cost, even if it was de minimis compared with the value of the prize or a cost which would not procure any advantage for the trader, such as the cost of a stamp. Given the absolute nature of the prohibition on imposing any cost, P's offer of a number of options could not eliminate the unfair character of the practice if any of the proposed options were to require the consumer to bear a cost (see paras 8, 26, 28, 30, 34 of judgment).

PURELY CREATIVE LTD v OFFICE OF FAIR TRADING (C-428/11) [2013] Bus. L.R. 985, Judge Rosas (President), ECJ (6th Chamber).

560. Unfair commercial practices–Misleading actions–Misrepresentations made by trader under building contract to one consumer–Meaning of "commercial practice" in reg.2(1) Consumer Protection from Unfair Trading Regulations 2008

[Consumer Protection from Unfair Trading Regulations 2008 (SI 2008/1277) reg.2(1), reg.9; Treaty on the Functioning of the European Union Art.114; Directive 2005/29 on unfair business-to-consumer commercial practices in the internal market.]

The defendant (S) was charged under the Consumer Protection from Unfair Trading Regulations 2008 reg.9 with three counts of engaging in a commercial practice which was a misleading action. S had been engaged by the claimant local authority to provide building works to a property. Following the termination of the contract, or while the contract was in the process of being terminated, S made representations that the works carried out had been passed by building control; they had not. S also claimed that the company's traders were all qualified; however, the gas fitter employed to carry out works at the property had not been approved or endorsed by the relevant body. S submitted that there was no case to answer on the basis that it did not fall within the definition of "commercial practice" under reg.2(1).

Held: Judgment for defendant. The Regulations were to be applied proportionately with a view to harmonisation with Directive 2005/29. The first question was whether the act or acts, having regard to all the circumstances, constituted a commercial practice. A commercial practice, as defined by reg.2(1), was any act directly connected with the promotion, sale or supply of a product to or from consumers. The reference to consumers in the plural was significant. The court took into account para.18 to the Preamble of the Directive and TFEU art.114 in reaching its decision. The commercial practice had to be "an outwardly facing aspect of the commercial strategy of the organisation", *Zentrale zur Bekampfung unlauteren Wettbewerbs eV v Plus Warenhandelsgesellschaft mbH (C-304/08)* [2011] 1 All E.R. (Comm) 658 considered. The evidence in the instant case concerned one consumer and one contract. There was no evidence of S'[s commercial practices or activities outside of his dealings with the local authority. There had not been established, and would not be established, on the evidence, a commercial practice as defined by reg.2(1) and therefore the case was bound to fail (see paras 8, 13, 20-22, 24-25 of judgment).

R. (ON THE APPLICATION OF TOWER HAMLETS LBC) v STEELE [2012] C.T.L.C. 109, Recorder Lowe Q.C., Crown Ct (Snaresbrook).

561. Unfair commercial practices–Misleading actions–Scope of term "commercial practice" in reg.5 Consumer Protection from Unfair Trading Regulations 2008

[Consumer Protection from Unfair Trading Regulations 2008 (SI 2008/1277) reg.3, reg.5, reg.8, reg.9, reg.12, Sch.1 para.12.]

The Crown appealed against a trial judge's ruling that the defendant company (X) had no case to answer in relation to four counts of engaging in an unfair commercial practice contrary to the Consumer Protection from Unfair Trading Regulations 2008. X sold domestic CCTV security systems, often by cold-calling. The prosecution arose after it sold a CCTV system and associated works to a 76-year-old customer (C) after two telephone calls and two visits. C was vulnerable by reason of his age and infirmity, and it was the Crown's case that his memory was poor and his vulnerabilities obvious. X's sales representative had told C that burglaries in his postcode area had risen by 46.2 per cent in the previous 12 months. That assertion was based on police statistics relating to a three-month period in C's ward area, which was wider than his postcode area. In fact, the burglary rate in C's postcode area had fallen over the previous 12 months. Although it was common ground that the system was installed in such a way that it was not fit for purpose, C had confirmed that he was happy with it before payment was taken. The indictment contained four counts of engaging in an unfair commercial practice. Count 1 charged breaches of reg.12 and Sch.1 para.12 on the basis that C had made materially inaccurate claims concerning the burglary risk. Count 3 charged breaches of reg.5 and reg.9 on the basis of false representations about the efficacy of the system. Counts 2 and 4 charged contraventions reg.3 and reg.8, alleging that X had knowingly or recklessly engaged in a commercial practice that contravened the requirements of professional diligence and was likely to materially distort the economic behaviour of the average consumer with regard to the products in question. On count 1, the judge found no evidence that the data relied upon by X was materially inaccurate. On count 3, he held that the Crown had to demonstrate a failure arising from a commercial practice rather than the actions of an individual installer. On counts 2 and 4 he found that although X's customer contact was lamentable, deplorable, dismissive and evidenced a breach of honest market practice and good faith, there was no evidence of knowledge or recklessness by at least one of X's controlling minds. The Crown argued that (1) there was clear material inaccuracy; (2) the phrase "commercial practice" in reg.5 and reg.9 covered both isolated acts and repeated behaviour; (3) the nature and extent of the failings by all those representatives of X who had had contact with C were consistent enough to give rise to the inference that X's controlling minds had not taken sufficient steps to ensure that its employees and contractors complied with its code of practice.

Held: Appeal allowed. (1) As to count 1, there was a clear case of material inaccuracy. It was clear that the data covered only three months and that the year-on-year burglary rate had fallen, not risen (see para.12 of judgment). (2) Count 3 turned on the proper construction of the phrase "commercial practice" in reg.5 and reg.9. Regulation 2 defined a "commercial practice" as "any act, omission, course of conduct, representation or commercial communication... by a trader which is directly connected with the promotion, sale or supply of a product to or from consumers, whether occurring before, during or after a commercial transaction...". Moreover, reg.2(2) talked about determining the effect of a commercial practice addressed to a consumer or consumers, singular or plural. It was clear that a commercial practice could, depending on the circumstances, cover both a single incident and a pattern of repeated behaviour; a course of conduct directly connected with the supply of a product after a commercial transaction could cover an implied representation as to fitness for purpose; and a "transactional decision" within the meaning of reg.5 was made when determining both whether to make payment and whether to exercise a contractual right. That interpretation did not place an undue burden on the company concerned: if a failure was the fault of a third party, no offence was committed as long as due diligence could be demonstrated (paras 17-27). (3) As to counts 2 and 4, there was clearly evidence from which a jury could reasonably infer that X was knowingly or recklessly operating a commercial practice in contravention of the requirements of professional diligence, likely to distort the economic behaviour of the average consumer in relation to the products in question. For example, X's directors had heard, but had found nothing wrong with, the conversations which the judge had described as lamentable, deplorable, dismissive and evidencing a breach of honest market practice and good faith. In the circumstances, a jury could infer that X's failure ran from top to bottom. It could not be a requirement that the evidence should relate to more than one customer, it would depend on the facts. The question was whether the depth of the evidence led to the inference that the way in which the company operated, through at least one of its controlling minds (whether identified or unidentified), demonstrated a reckless disregard for the requirements of professional diligence generally (paras 31-36).

R. v X LTD, [2013] EWCA Crim 818, [2014] 1 W.L.R. 591, Leveson, L.J., CA (Crim Div).

CONTRACTS

562. Aircraft–Leasing–Aircraft not in airworthy condition at time of delivery–Effect of contract terms

The appellant airline (O) appealed against a decision ([2012] EWHC 1070 (Comm), [2012] 2 C.L.C. 48, [2013] 2 C.L. 76) allowing the claim of the respondent lessor (L) for the payment of rent and maintenance reserves under an aircraft lease and for damages for loss of rent following termination of the lease. In May 2008, the parties had entered into a five-year lease of a Boeing 737. Clause 7.9 provided as follows: "Delivery by lessee to lessor of the certificate of acceptance will be conclusive proof as between lessor and lessee that lessee has examined and investigated the aircraft, that the aircraft and the aircraft documents are satisfactory to lessee and that lessee has irrevocably and unconditionally accepted the aircraft for lease hereunder without any reservations whatsoever (except for any discrepancies which may be noted in the certificate of acceptance)". O accepted delivery of the aircraft in August 2008, signing a "Certificate of Acceptance" in a form prescribed by the lease. Under the Certificate of Acceptance, O confirmed that, among other things, "the Lease Property complied in all respects with the condition required at delivery under Section 4.2 and Schedule 2 of the Agreement, except for the items... listed on the attached Annex 2" (para.2(e) of the certificate). Clause 4.2 of and Sch.2 to the lease required the aircraft to be in a condition for safe operation. The judge below found that, unbeknown to O or L, the aircraft was not in fact on delivery in the condition required by Sch.2 to the lease; it was not in an airworthy condition or in a condition for safe operation. It had to be grounded in September 2008 and was never operated by O from that time until it ceased trading in October 2009. It was not redelivered to L until November 2010. Giving judgment for L in respect of the sums claimed, the judge held that statements made by O in the Certificate of Acceptance gave rise to an estoppel by representation, on which L had reasonably relied to its detriment, in accepting redelivery from the previous lessee which precluded O from arguing that the aircraft was not on delivery in the contractually required condition.

Held: Appeal dismissed. The judge had come to the right conclusion but for the wrong reason. He had rejected L's contention that the contractual terms rendered the Certificate of Acceptance conclusive proof that the aircraft complied in all respects with the condition required at delivery; if cl.7.9 of the lease did not provide that delivery of the Certificate of Acceptance was conclusive proof of compliance of the aircraft and of the aircraft documents with the contractual requirements, it was not possible to regard the Certificate as nonetheless giving rise to an estoppel by representation to the same effect. The natural meaning of the relevant provisions was clear. There was no ambiguity about para.2(e) of the Certificate of Acceptance: O as lessee confirmed that the aircraft at delivery complied in all respects with the condition required under cl.4.2 and Sch.2, except for the items listed on Annex 2, which were of no relevance in this case. Clause 7.9 provided that delivery by the lessee to the lessor of a certificate in that form would be conclusive proof that the aircraft and the aircraft documents were satisfactory to the lessee. There was no difficulty in deciding what was meant by the aircraft being "satisfactory" to O. The contract provided only one yardstick by which O's satisfaction with the aircraft was to be measured, and that was compliance with the condition required by Sch.2, as spelt out by cl.4.2. When O as lessee confirmed that the condition of the aircraft at delivery complied in all respects with that required under Sch.2, it was confirming that the aircraft was satisfactory to it in the only sense in which it was entitled, or expected, to express its satisfaction. Other factors supported such a conclusion. For example, it was commonplace for parties in this market to contract on a basis which, at first sight, appeared to be intended to provide a structure whereby a lessee elected whether or not to accept an aircraft on lease and with it the risk of non-compliance with the required delivery condition becoming apparent later. Further, the parties would know that neither could be absolutely certain of an aircraft's condition at the point at which the lessee was called on to accept delivery and the ongoing risk. And the lease itself contained an extensive provision of facilities for inspection by O of the aircraft and its associated documents before it was required to elect whether to accept delivery (see paras 42-43, 45-47, 54 of judgment).

ACG ACQUISITION XX LLC v OLYMPIC AIRLINES SA (IN LIQUIDATION); *sub nom.* OLYMPIC AIRLINES SA (IN SPECIAL LIQUIDATION) v ACG ACQUISITION XX LLC, [2013] EWCA Civ 369, [2013] 1 Lloyd's Rep. 658, Rix, L.J., CA (Civ Div).

563. Arbitration clauses–Incorporation–Contract between English parties–One party part of enterprise based in Utah–Clause providing for arbitration in Utah–Onerous or unreasonable nature of clause

[Arbitration Act 1996 (c.23).]

The appellant (K) appealed against a district judge's decision that an earlier default judgment she had obtained against the respondent (N) should be stayed to allow arbitration between the parties. K had entered into a distribution agreement with N, an English company, which was part of an enterprise based in Utah (NE). At the foot of the agreement, it stated: "This will form your contract with NE". The agreement contained a dispute resolution clause providing for mediation in Utah, and if that failed, arbitration in the same place. K's default judgment was for breach of contract. N successfully applied for a stay for arbitration to take place. K submitted that the arbitration clause was unduly onerous and had not sufficiently been brought to her attention.

Held: Appeal dismissed. If a condition was particularly onerous or unusual, the party seeking to enforce it had to show that it had fairly been brought to the attention of the other party, *Parker v South Eastern Railway Co* (1877) 2 C.P.D. 416, *J Spurling Ltd v Bradshaw* [1956] 1 W.L.R. 461, [1956] C.L.Y. 525 and *Interfoto Picture Library Ltd v Stiletto Visual Programmes Ltd* [1989] Q.B. 433, [1988] C.L.Y. 430 applied. In the instant case, the arbitration clause had clearly been incorporated into the agreement and K was bound by it. Therefore, the only question was whether it was so unreasonable that it ought to have been brought to K's attention. The provisions of the Uniform Arbitration Act (Utah) were very similar to the Arbitration Act 1996 and stated clear and transparent rules governing the appointment and conduct of the arbitrator. Therefore, the arbitration procedures in Utah were clear, were set out and were fair. Accordingly, the clause was not so unreasonable or onerous that it should very specifically have been brought to K's attention. Neither was it unfair or unconscionable for K to be bound by it (see paras 37, 42, 55, 60 of judgment).

KAYE v NU SKIN UK LTD, [2012] EWHC 958 (QB), [2012] C.T.L.C. 69, Judge Denyer Q.C., QBD.

564. Breach of contract–Bankruptcy orders–Whether bankruptcy order consequence of breached contract–Appropriate costs order

The appellant (W) appealed against a judge's decision arising out of an action he had brought against the respondent company (E) for breach of contract, negligence and malicious prosecution of a bankruptcy petition. W and E had entered into a contract, the supply contract, for the supply of electricity by E to licensed premises of which W was the licensee. The contract was said to be subject to a condition precedent: payment for the supply of electricity depended upon W's occupation of the premises. W asserted that he had never occupied the premises, thus the condition precedent was never fulfilled. The parties entered into a further contract, the compromise contract, whereby E agreed, in consideration of W agreeing to transfer some money taken via a direct debit to settle other accounts, to refund W a sum and cancel the supply contract. Notwithstanding that agreement, E issued a statutory demand to recover sums due under the supply contract. That resulted in a bankruptcy order against W, which was subsequently annulled by consent with no order for costs. W brought a claim against E, seeking damages of £450,000, which included among other things the interest on the refund that had not been paid when intended and the costs of setting aside the bankruptcy order. The judge, dismissing all of W's claims save the claim for the refund, held that: the supply contract had never been effective as the condition precedent was not engaged; E's statutory demand and bankruptcy petition were in breach of the compromise contract; W suffered loss as a natural consequence of E's failure to pay the refund in breach of the compromise contract; the remaining losses claimed were not in the contemplation of the parties when the compromise contract was made; and the bankruptcy order was not a natural consequence of E's breach. W submitted that the judge had been wrong to find that the costs incurred in dealing with the bankruptcy order were too remote a consequence of E's breach of contract.

Held: Appeal dismissed. The difficulty W faced was that the judge had effectively found that W had brought the order for bankruptcy on himself. It was clear from the judge's findings that it was not said that the bankruptcy order was the natural consequence of E's breach. Although the judge characterised that finding in terms of remoteness, it could also be characterised as, and it was more appropriate to characterise it as, a finding of causation. Although E had breached the compromise contract in demanding money from W, it could not be said in law that that breach caused the making of the bankruptcy order, or the necessity for W to incur costs to set it aside. That was plain as E had been met with a wall of obfuscation when attempting to serve the bankruptcy petition on W; the normal consequence of a bankruptcy petition on an unfounded ground would be to resist it. The question of causation had been before the judge. Whilst expressed in terms of remoteness, the judge had actually found that the costs incurred as a result of the bankruptcy order were not caused by the breach of contract in making an unjustified demand for payment. That finding was one that was open to the judge (see paras 31-32, 40-41 of judgment).

WILLETT v ECONOMY POWER LTD, [2012] EWCA Civ 1164, [2012] B.P.I.R. 1298, Ward, L.J., CA (Civ Div).

565. Breach of contract–Breach of duty of care–Anti-mould chemical used on leather furniture–Negligent and wrongful advice given in respect of chemical's safety–Scope of liability in contract and tort

The claimants sought to recover from the defendant (L) the sums they had paid out in a group action to those who had suffered injury from using leather furniture bought from them. The claimants (C1, C2, C3 and C4) were household retailers who sold leather furniture to the public. L provided to its subscribers services including assistance, testing and advice on leather. From 2004 the claimants began importing their leather furniture from China. In 2007 large numbers of people complained of suffering injuries as a result of using that furniture. The injuries ranged from minor irritation to serious skin complaints and respiratory problems requiring hospital treatment. The claimants admitted liability in a group action brought against them and paid out approximately £17 million. They sought to recover that from L. C3, having sustained only modest losses, did not pursue its claim. C1, C2 and C4 maintained their claims in contract and tort. They contended that, in breach of contract and negligently, L had initially advised them that an anti-mould chemical dimethyl fumerate (DMF) contained in sachets attached to the furniture and in the packaging was safe and not harmful to human health or, alternatively, that L had failed over a prolonged period, including inspections in 2006 and 2007, to alert them to the fact that DMF was not safe. L contended that it had a contractual relationship with C1 alone but denied breach of contract. It further denied that it owed a duty of care at common law to anyone but C1, and denied any breach of that duty. L submitted that if the claimants had suffered loss, it was as a result of their failure to take steps to clarify DMF's safety.

Held: Judgment for first and second claimants. (1) C1 was the only party to have entered into a contract with L. L therefore owed C1 a contractual duty to perform its services with reasonable skill and care. The undoubted common law duty owed by L to C1 added nothing to that contractual duty (see paras 32, 35 of judgment). (2) Before a duty of care at common law might be imposed a party was entitled to know precisely to whom the duty was to be owed. Since there was no evidence that L was aware of C4's existence, no duty was owed by it to C4. C2's position was different. L knew that it was part of C1's company group and that C2 would receive and rely on the advice given to C1. L therefore owed a duty of care to C2, *Hedley Byrne & Co Ltd v Heller & Partners Ltd* [1964] A.C. 465, [1963] C.L.Y. 2416 followed. Even if that was not the case and the duty was a novel one, it arose as a result of the three-limbed test of foreseeability of damage, proximity, and what was fair, just and reasonable, *Caparo Industries Plc v Dickman* [1990] 2 A.C. 605, [1990] C.L.Y. 3266 considered. C2 had relied on L's advice, and L knew that (paras 41-42). (3) C1 had consulted L over the use and safety of DMF. In accepting its request for advice, L was under a duty to exercise reasonable care. L had informed C1 that DMF was used in food, which was an indicator of its safety. It had led C1 to believe that DMF was safe, or at least not unsafe, to use. L had, however, done no effective research. It was thereby in breach of its contractual and common law duty to C1 and in breach of its common law duty to C2 in respect of the initial advice (paras 85, 90, 95). (4) In the course of inspections and consequent preparation of reports for C1 in 2006 and 2007, L had failed to investigate the efficacy and safety of DMF. In consequence, the claimants had allowed the sachets containing DMF to be used on the leather furniture they sold. L's negligence had caused the damage which the claimants had suffered in having to compensate the group litigants (paras 113, 120). (5) There was no contributory negligence. C1 had made it plain to L what it needed to know and had clearly considered L to be the experts. It was not incumbent on C1 to check what had been done, and there was no requirement for it to have made further enquiries as to the adequacy of L's research and advice (para.96). (6) C1 had therefore proved breach of contract and breach of the common law duty of care and causation of loss in respect of L's advice and reports. C2 had proved breach of duty and causation. C3 and C4 had proved nothing (paras 122-123).

ARGOS LTD v LEATHER TRADE HOUSE LTD (FORMERLY BLC LEATHER TECHNOLOGY CENTRE LTD), [2012] EWHC 1348 (QB), [2012] E.C.C. 34, Thirlwall, J., QBD.

566. Breach of contract–Certainty–Contract leaving matters to be agreed–Whether unenforceable for uncertainty–Consideration of wider context and parties' intentions

The appellant (E) appealed against the setting aside ([2012] EWHC 1988 (Comm), [2013] 1 All E.R. (Comm) 1, [2013] 1 C.L. 67) of an arbitration award made in favour of the respondent (M). E had contracted to sell copper concentrates to M. Disputes arose as to the performance of the contract and were referred to arbitration. The arbitration was terminated by a settlement agreement which contained an arbitration clause and was expressly governed by English law. The agreement provided for three fresh contracts for the sale of copper concentrates. Only two were fully performed. A dispute arose as to the third, and M sought to have it enforced. E claimed that the contract was unenforceable because it left certain matters, including particular charges and the shipping schedule, to be agreed. The arbitrators found for E, holding that the contract left material terms as "agreements to agree", and that there was consequently no enforceable obligation to deliver the copper. In reaching that conclusion they construed the contract without regard to the settlement agreement. The judge concluded that no reasonable tribunal correctly applying the relevant principles could have reached such a conclusion. He declined to remit the matter, but instead varied the award in accordance with what he concluded to be the correct legal principles, and otherwise set it aside. He was, however, persuaded that another tribunal might take the view that the appropriate course was to remit the matter, and he granted permission to appeal generally.

Held: Appeal dismissed. The judge had been right to find as he did. The contract fell to be construed in the light of the fact that it was part of the settlement agreement. The overall transaction comprised the settlement of the original dispute, M's claim against E having been compromised on terms that the three new contracts were entered into. The contract was part of a wider agreement which the parties had been acting upon, E having derived the benefit of M abandoning its claim. It was an integral part of an overall deal pursuant to which both parties had derived benefits, and on which they had worked for a year. During that time there had been no suggestion that the contract fell into a different and unenforceable category of obligation, *Mamidoil-Jetoil Greek Petroleum Co SA v Okta Crude Oil Refinery AD (No.1)* [2001] EWCA Civ 406, [2001] 2 All E.R. (Comm) 193, [2001] C.L.Y. 956 and *Foley v Classique Coaches Ltd* [1934] 2 K.B. 1 applied. The language of both the contract and the settlement agreement showed beyond doubt that the parties had not intended that if they could not reach any agreement on the matters left to be agreed, there would be no obligation at all in respect of the contract. A term was to be implied that the charges and the shipping schedule were to be reasonable and were to be determined by arbitration in the event of any dispute. The arbitrators had failed to address the central question, which was what the parties had intended would happen in the event that the charges and shipping schedule were not agreed. Nor had they asked themselves whether the parties had supplied a machinery whereby any uncertainty could be resolved. Given the judge's view that no reasonable tribunal could have come to the conclusion reached by the arbitrators, there was no scope for remission; only one answer was possible. Nor should the judge have reached a less trenchant conclusion: the matter was one of construction of the contract and there were no matters of context that could have led him to a different conclusion (see paras 14-29 of judgment).

MRI TRADING AG v ERDENET MINING CORP LLC, [2013] EWCA Civ 156, [2013] 1 Lloyd's Rep. 638, Pill, L.J., CA (Civ Div).

567. Breach of contract–Diminution in value–Delayed performance–Foreseeability of diminution in value of property development as result of delay

The appellant consulting engineer (J) appealed against a finding (John Grimes Partnership Ltd v Gubbins) that it was liable to pay damages to the respondent developer (G) for the diminution in the market value of a development whose completion had been delayed by J's breach of contract. G had engaged J to design a road and drainage for a residential development and to obtain approval from the local authority for the road's design. J failed to complete the work by the date agreed. G eventually engaged another engineer, who completed the designs and obtained approval 15 months after the agreed date. J successfully claimed against G for unpaid fees, but the judge also allowed G's counterclaim, which included damages for the decline in value of the development during the period for which its completion had been delayed as a result of J's breach of contract in failing to complete its work on time. J submitted that the diminution in value loss had not been reasonably foreseeable.

Held: Appeal dismissed. If a type or kind of loss was, at the time of contract, reasonably foreseeable by the defendant as not unlikely to result from his breach, such a type or kind of loss was not too remote, *Koufos v C Czarnikow Ltd (The Heron II)* [1969] 1 A.C. 350, [1967] C.L.Y. 3623 followed. *Transfield Shipping Inc v Mercator Shipping Inc (The Achilleas)* [2008] UKHL 48, [2009] 1 A.C. 61, [2008] C.L.Y. 3443 had not effected a major change in the approach given in *The Heron II*, *The Achilleas* considered and *Siemens Building Technologies FE Ltd v Supershield Ltd* [2010] EWCA Civ 7, [2010] 2 All E.R. (Comm) 1185, [2010] C.L.Y. 626 followed. It was right to bear in mind that one was dealing with the law of contract, where the situation was governed by what the parties had agreed. If there was no express term dealing with what types of losses a party accepted potential liability for, the law in effect implied a term to determine the answer. Normally, an implied term accepted responsibility for the types of losses which could reasonably be foreseen at the time of contract to be not unlikely to result if the contract was broken. However, if there was evidence in a particular case that the nature of the contract and the commercial background, or other relevant special circumstances, rendered that implied assumption of responsibility inappropriate for a type of loss, the contract breaker escaped liability (see paras 17, 23-24 of judgment). The judge had considered whether losses arising from movement in the property market were reasonably foreseeable at the time of contract as a consequence of delay by J, and had concluded that they were. He had gone on to consider whether the case was unusual so as to take it outside the more common *Hadley v Baxendale* approach. He had expressly considered the commercial background of the contract and whether the standard approach would reflect the expectation or intention reasonably to be imputed to the parties. His approach to and summary of the legal principles could not be faulted. There had been no evidence before the judge to show that there was some general understanding or expectation in the property world that a party in J's position would not be taken to have assumed responsibility for losses arising from movement in the market where there had been delay in breach of contract. The fact that a loss was suffered because of a change in market values during the wrongful delay did not render the case out of the ordinary. Although it seemed that there were very few cases where a decline in the property market had been held to give rise to an actionable loss, nor were there cases deciding the other way. Further, J's argument that the scale of the loss might be disproportionate to the fee payable under the contract was unpersuasive. That situation was not infrequent. Moreover, any such contrast was merely a possible pointer towards a party not having undertaken a potential liability which was reasonably foreseeable; by itself it would not normally suffice to establish an absence of responsibility. The judge had been right to find that there was nothing to take the case out of the conventional approach to remoteness of damage in contract cases (paras 25-31).

JOHN GRIMES PARTNERSHIP LTD v GUBBINS, [2013] EWCA Civ 37, [2013] B.L.R. 126, Laws, L.J., CA (Civ Div).

568. Breach of contract–Penalty clauses–Share purchase agreement–Clause stipulating reduced price in event of default by vendor–Whether clauses amounted to penalty

The first claimant company (C) sought a declaration that the defendant (M) was in breach of a share-purchase agreement. M was the founder, an employee and a non-executive director of the second claimant company (T). C owned 12.6 per cent of the shares in T and had entered into a written agreement to buy a further 47.4 per cent from M, with put and call options in respect of the remaining 40 per cent. The agreement contained a number of restrictive covenants. Clause 11.2 imposed a series of restrictions preventing M from competing with T. Clause 5.1 provided that a "defaulting shareholder" would not be entitled to payment as agreed, with cl.5.6 providing that the purchaser could require a defaulting shareholder to sell his shares at "the defaulting shareholder option price". That was to be calculated by reference to the net asset value on the date the seller became a defaulting shareholder. C and T brought the instant proceedings when they discovered that M had been acting in breach of his fiduciary duties to T. C claimed that M's actions amounted to a breach of the agreement. It sought a declaration that M, as a defaulting shareholder, was not entitled to payment under the agreements but was obliged to sell his shares at the defaulting shareholder option price. It also sought specific performance of that obligation. M admitted breaching his fiduciary duty and settled T's claim. Accepting that he had no factual defence to C's claim, he raised arguments as to the legal effect of the agreement. M submitted that (1) cl.11.2 was an unreasonable restraint of trade; (2) cl.5.1 and cl.5.6 were unenforceable penalty clauses; (3) cl.5.6 obliged him to sell his shares only when the correct defaulting shareholder option price was tendered, and that because the date on which he became a defaulting shareholder had not been formally declared, the correct price could not yet be determined, and C had to serve a fresh notice.

Held: Application granted. (1) Clause 11.2 was not an unreasonable restraint of trade. While the onus was on C to establish the reasonableness of the restraints, it was not a heavy onus, the clause being a vendor-purchaser covenant. M did not criticise any particular aspect of the restrictions, and what they amounted to was simply an effective protection of the goodwill in T against competition by M. The clause had been fully negotiated on a level playing field between experienced lawyers and it was entirely reasonable for C, and the court, to conclude that any "competition breach" was material. C was entitled to protect itself from competition by M, who was an influential vendor who was continuing as a director of, and shareholder in, T. The deferred restraint was clear, certain and required, and its eight-and-a-half-year duration was tied to a relevant interest of C's and was not an unreasonable period of protection. In any event, there was no reported case in which an otherwise reasonable restriction had been held to be unreasonable on the basis of its duration (see paras 16-24 of judgment). (2) As to penalties, the following propositions arose from the authorities: the law on penalties applied to the transfer of property as well as to the payment of money and to clauses that could also be treated as forfeiture clauses; penalty clauses could not be enforced; and the court could not rewrite the contract. There was an equitable jurisdiction applicable in the case of penalties, which could be operated by not enforcing the penalty to such extent as was equitable, without rewriting the contract. In commercial contracts, the court should very rarely interfere so as to descry a penalty clause, *Firma C-Trade SA v Newcastle Protection and Indemnity Association (The Fanti)* [1989] 1 Lloyd's Rep. 239, [1989] C.L.Y. 3383 and *Jobson v Johnson* [1989] 1 W.L.R. 1026, [1988] C.L.Y. 353 considered (paras 33-41). M bore the burden of showing that cl.5.1 and cl.5.6 were penalty clauses. The court was not persuaded that cl.5.6 was a penalty clause. First, it served the commercial purpose of decoupling the parties on a speedy and conventional basis in the event of a breach. Second, part of its purpose was to adjust the consideration between them. Third, it related to a valuation of the last 20% of T's shares, which were supposed to carry substantial goodwill. Fourth, it related to the event of competition breach by M. Finally, it had been included after thorough negotiation and was not oppressive. Similarly, cl.5.1 was commercially justified, had been the subject of detailed negotiation, and was neither extravagant nor oppressive. The juxtaposition of substantial delayed payment for goodwill and a series of covenants intended to safeguard that goodwill was of particular significance (paras 33-53, 59-63). (3) There was nothing in cl.5.6 to support M's argument that C had to specify the correct defaulting shareholder option price in the notice. All that was required was a notice exercising the option. The agreement was a normal agreement for sale at a price to be calculated by a specified method. It was binding and certain (paras 64-67). (4) The court would therefore make the declaration sought and would order specific performance of M's obligations under cl.5.6, though the price could not be finally calculated until the date of default had been determined (para.68).

MAKDESSI v CAVENDISH SQUARE HOLDINGS BV, [2012] EWHC 3582 (Comm), [2013] 1 All E.R. (Comm) 787, Burton, J., QBD (Comm).

569. Breach of contract–Supply of services–Negligent design and installation of bespoke fire suppression system–Fitness for purpose–Whether chain of causation broken–Extent of contributory negligence

[Law Reform (Contributory Negligence) Act 1945 (c.28); Supply of Goods and Services Act 1982 (c.29) s.4(4).]

The claimant manufacturer (M) appealed against a decision ([2011] EWHC 1936 (TCC), [2011] B.L.R. 661, [2012] C.L.Y. 619) reducing the amount of damages that it was entitled to claim from the defendant (D), a supplier of fire suppression systems, following a finding that a fire at its premises had been caused by D's breach of contractual and tortious duties. D cross-appealed on the basis that its breach had not been fully causative of M's loss and damage. M manufactured popcorn and other confectionery. In the popcorn production area of the factory, corn was popped in pans of oil before being transported via an elevator to a hopper for packaging. The parties had contracted for the design and installation of an automatic "CO2 suppression" system in the elevator and hopper. The system was supposed to discharge CO2 into the hopper upon fire being detected, thereby extinguishing the fire. A fire broke out in the hopper, but no CO2 was discharged. M's operatives ejected a burning ball of popcorn, together with the hopper's entire load, and tried to stamp out the fire. The fire consequently spread and destroyed the whole factory. The judge below found that although D was liable to M for design and installation faults, M shared responsibility for the damage because it had been negligent in failing to segregate the production area from the rest of the building, failing to install sprinklers, and encouraging the spread of the fire by taking inappropriate action upon its discovery. The judge made a 75 per cent reduction in damages to reflect M's contribution. M's case on appeal was that the obligation on D to supply a system which met the desired specification and was fit for purpose was absolute, and the court therefore had no power under the Law Reform (Contributory Negligence) Act 1945 to reduce the ensuing damages because D's contractual duty extended beyond the tortious duty that it also owed. D's case was that even if M could establish that D had effectively guaranteed the efficacy of the system so as to provide absolute liability, it could not rely upon D's breach as causative of its losses because a similar fire one year earlier had broken the chain of causation. It also alleged that the panicked reaction of M's operatives to the fire had caused it to spread and had broken the chain of causation.

Held: Appeal dismissed, cross-appeal dismissed. (1) M had characterised its contract with D inappropriately. D could not be regarded as having supplied a system which could be equated with "goods", thereby attracting the express requirement that it be of good quality and reasonably fit for purpose. It had not supplied an off-the-shelf product, but had offered to undertake the design and supply of a bespoke, tailor-made, system. It was not possible to say, in the abstract, that the system was not of good quality, because it did not have any inherent characteristics which could be independently assessed, and because there were no purposes for which it was commonly supplied. The shortcomings in the system were matters of design, not matters concerning the inherent quality of the goods (see paras 45-48 of judgment). (2) It was inappropriate to read the system specification document as a guarantee of the system's success or as importing the result that a system failure would automatically amount to a breach of contractual obligation as to suitability. The context of the agreement had been fire suppression, not fire prevention. Very clear words would have been needed to create a situation where a designer and supplier of fire suppression systems had contracted to extinguish all fires, *Thake v Maurice* [1986] Q.B. 644, [1986] C.L.Y. 422 applied. M had not, for the purposes of the Supply of Goods and Services Act 1982 s.4(4), communicated to D a particular purpose for which the system was being acquired, nor had it sufficiently explained its process or its hazardous nature. The judge had been right to find that the obligation undertaken by D was merely to exercise reasonable skill and care in the design (paras 50, 52, 54, 57-58). (3) (Obiter) Had the point arisen, the occurrence of the earlier fire would not have been held to preclude M from recovering damages from D in relation to the instant fire. Whether or not knowledge alleged to have broken the chain of causation or to have given rise to a duty to mitigate could be attributed to M depended on the system of delegation and supervision that it had in place. The judge below had made no finding on the point because the issue had not been properly addressed in evidence, *Schering Agrochemicals Ltd v Resibel NV SA*considered (paras 61-69). (4) The judge had plainly found that D's breach was causative of M's loss and that the spread of the fire was, effectively, one seamless development without any intervening cause. The employees' reaction to the fire was entirely predictable and it was inappropriate and unnecessary to attempt to distinguish between the contribution of the initial burning ball of popcorn and that later ejected from the machine (paras 74-76).

TREBOR BASSETT HOLDINGS LTD v ADT FIRE & SECURITY PLC, [2012] EWCA Civ 1158, [2012] B.L.R. 441, Sir Andrew Morritt (Chancellor), CA (Civ Div).

570. Commercial contracts–Implied terms–Contract between NHS trust and catering company–Provision for deductions for performance failures–Whether contract terms conferred discretion on trust giving rise to implied term not to act in arbitrary, capricious or irrational manner

The appellant NHS trust appealed against a decision ([2012] EWHC 781 (QB), [2012] 2 All E.R. (Comm) 300, [2012] C.L.Y. 625) that it and the respondent catering company (C) had both been entitled to terminate a commercial contract on the basis of the other party's conduct. The trust and C had brought cross-claims for post-termination losses following termination of a seven-year contract for C to provide catering and cleaning services in two hospitals. The contract contained a mechanism whereby the trust could award "service failure points" from which it could calculate the appropriate payment deductions for C's performance failures.

The parties were obliged to "co-operate with each other in good faith". The trust identified a number of service failures and made payment deductions representing more than half the payment due for a six-month period. The trust accepted that it had awarded excessive service failure points and had made excessive deductions but the parties were unable to agree the correct figures. Both parties maintained that they had terminated the contract. The judge found that the trust had breached its obligation to co-operate in good faith and, in exercising what the judge found to be a discretionary power to make deductions, had breached an implied term that it would not act in an arbitrary, capricious or irrational manner. The judge further found that C had not terminated the contract for repudiatory breach. He held that neither party could succeed in its claims for post-termination losses. The trust contended that the judge had erred in finding that it had a discretion when awarding service failure points or making payment deductions, and that there could therefore be no such implied term.

Held: Appeal allowed. (1) There were precise rules under the contract for determining how many service failure points C had incurred and what deductions were due. That exercise did not involve discretion and there was only one right answer. If the parties were unable to agree, the issue could be resolved through the dispute resolution procedure provided for in the contract. Once the correct figures had been established, the trust had a discretion. It could "award" the service failure points to C and levy deductions against the monthly payments or it could choose not to. Against that background, the question had arisen as to whether there was an implied term that the trust would not act in an arbitrary, capricious or irrational manner. The trust was a public authority delivering a vital service to vulnerable members of the public and it rightly demanded high standards from those with whom it contracted. There could be circumstances in which it decided to award less than the full amount of service failure points, or to deduct less than it was entitled to from a monthly payment. However, it could not be criticised if it awarded the full number of points or made the full deduction. The discretion conferred permitted the trust to decide whether to exercise an absolute contractual right and there was no justification for implying a term that the trust would not act in an arbitrary, irrational or capricious manner. If it awarded more than the correct number of points or deducted more than the correct amount, that would be a breach of the express provisions of the clause. There was no need for any implied term to regulate the operation of the clause, and the judge's finding that the trust was in breach of the implied term could not stand (see paras 84-95 of judgment). (2) The trust's reading of the provision regarding the parties' obligations to co-operate in good faith was correct. The obligation was not a general one which qualified or reinforced all the parties' obligations in all situations where they interacted. It specifically focused on the two purposes stated: the efficient transmission of information and instructions, and enabling the trust to derive the full benefit of the contract. The obligation meant that the parties would work together, honestly endeavouring to achieve those stated purposes, *CPC Group Ltd v Qatari Diar Real Estate Investment Co* [2010] EWHC 1535 (Ch), [2010] C.I.L.L. 2908 considered. It was clear from the judge's findings that the parties did co-operate effectively on all matters concerning the delivery of services to the hospital patients. Information which was needed to pass between the parties to facilitate the delivery of services to patients was duly transmitted. The trust received the full benefit of the contract in the sense that the patients were given meals at the proper times and the wards were kept clean. The conclusion therefore was that, despite the breakdown of the relationship at management level, there had been no breach of the "good faith" provision on either side (paras 97-121). (3) The trust's breach of the contract in awarding an excessive number of service failure points did not amount to a material breach. C was not therefore entitled to terminate the contract, and its purported notice of termination was invalid (paras 122-128). (4) The trust was entitled to pursue its claim for financial relief on the basis that it had effectively terminated the contract and C's purported termination was invalid.

COMPASS GROUP UK AND IRELAND LTD (T/A MEDIREST) v MID ESSEX HOSPITAL SERVICES NHS TRUST; *sub nom.* MID ESSEX HOSPITAL SERVICES

NHS TRUST v COMPASS GROUP UK AND IRELAND LTD (T/A MEDIREST), [2013] EWCA Civ 200, [2013] B.L.R. 265, Jackson, L.J., CA (Civ Div).

571. Construction contracts–Formation of contract–Amended NEC3 form of contract–Whether contracting party named by mistake–Whether contract should be rectified

[Companies Act 2006 (c.46).]

The claimant (L) sought a declaration that it had entered into a contract with the second defendant company (D2) and that the contracting party remained liable to deliver a parent company guarantee, a performance bond and warranties. L had entered into an amended NEC3 form of contract for the construction of a new retail plateau for future construction of a supermarket. A tender form for the works had been completed naming the contractor as "Cuddy Group", which was a trading name of D2. L sent "Cuddy Group" a letter of intent and D2 commenced work on site. L's solicitors conducted an internet search and found the name of the first defendant (D1). That was a dormant company which had the same shareholders as D2 and common directors. The solicitors informed the supermarket operator (S), in respect of a warranty to be entered into between the contractor, L and S that the contractor would be D1. The warranty was executed naming D1 as the contractor. D2 continued to work on the site and presented invoices to L which were paid. The payments were made into D2's bank account. The NEC contract was eventually executed naming D1 as the contractor. The defendants' evidence was that they had understood that L and S had requested that D1 should be the contractor and that they were happy to go along with that in order to finalise the contract. Thereafter problems arose on the project and L purported to terminate for failure to remedy defects. D1 accepted that purported termination as a repudiatory breach. L began proceedings against D1 seeking a declaration that it was obliged to deliver a parent company guarantee, performance bond and deeds of warranty, which had never been provided under the contract. L subsequently contended that a mistake had been made in the identity of D1 as the contracting party and amended to plead that the contractor was or should be D2.

Held: Judgment accordingly. (1) L failed to show that it had entered into a contract with D2 at some stage before the execution of the contract documents. In accordance with what the standard form of agreement envisaged, a contract was to be entered into by the signature of both parties. Providing a copy of the contract documents for one party to sign did not amount to an offer which was accepted by that party signing. Rather the agreement signed by that party amounted to an offer which was accepted by the other party signing in its turn. Even if there had been a binding agreement earlier, it was subject to agreed variations and it was the form of contract which was signed and dated by both parties which became the contract which set out the terms finally agreed between the parties (see paras 51-56 of judgment). (2) L failed to show that, considering the admissible background evidence relating to the formation of the contract, it was plain that the parties intended the contractor to be D2 and that naming D1 as the contractor in the contractual documentation was a "misnomer" which could be corrected as a matter of construction. Having regard to the background or matrix, the reference to D1 on the face of the contract could not be characterised as a clear mistake, *Chartbrook Ltd v Persimmon Homes Ltd* [2009] UKHL 38, [2009] 1 A.C. 1101, [2009] C.L.Y. 722 applied. There was nothing to show that on an objective analysis of the position, taking into account matters known to both parties, the request for the contract to be in the name of D1 was a mistake. D1 was then in existence although dormant. At that stage the parties had signed the warranty which named D1. It was not possible to say that the parties intended to refer to D2 rather than D1, *Nittan (UK) v Solent Steel Fabrications* [1981] 1 Lloyd's Rep. 633, [1981] C.L.Y. 300 and *Dumford Trading AG v OAO Atlantrybflot* [2005] EWCA Civ 24, [2005] 1 Lloyd's Rep. 289, [2005] C.L.Y. 710 considered (paras 98-109). (3) In the absence of a common continuing intention, there had been no mutual mistake and therefore no question of rectification arose. There had been a mistake in identifying Cuddy Group as D1, leading to the warranty being given by D1. The objective observer would have concluded that it was the intention of the parties that the party acting as the contractor should change from Cuddy Group to D1 as requested, no matter who was then carrying out the works. There was therefore objectively no mistake since the previous common intention to enter into the contract with Cuddy Group had changed as a result of the request (paras 124-131). (4) L erroneously believed that D1 was the same as Cuddy Group, but the evidence came nowhere near to establishing that, in relation to the mistake, the defendants either had actual knowledge or wilfully shut their eyes to the obvious or wilfully and recklessly failed to make the enquiries which an honest and reasonable person would make, *Daventry DC v Daventry and District Housing Ltd* [2011] EWCA Civ 1153, [2012] 1 W.L.R. 1333, [2012] C.L.Y. 626 applied. Therefore rectification for unilateral mistake was unavailable (paras 139-147). (5) There was nothing in the evidence to indicate that there was a convention that, although the named contractor was D1, the contract was entered into by the party carrying out the works, namely D2. Both parties operated the contract as if the contractor was D2. However, in doing so, they did not adopt a convention that D1 was to be treated as D2. Therefore there was no estoppel by convention (para.162). (6) The obligation on the contractor to provide a parent company guarantee, the bond and warranties continued even after termination. That obligation was not part of the primary obligation to provide the works but was merely procedural and ancillary and survived termination or repudiation, *Yasuda Fire & Marine Insurance Co of Europe Ltd v Orion Marine Insurance Underwriting Agency Ltd* [1995] Q.B. 174, [1995] C.L.Y. 179 applied. Accordingly, at termination the contractor was under a continuing obligation to provide the documents that had been demanded and had failed to do so (paras 199-201). (7) D1 and D2 had directors and shareholders in common but D2 was not the parent of D1 as a matter of general law or under the Companies Act 2006. There was no obligation on D1 to provide a parent company guarantee from D2, nor was there any other party that could objectively be described as D1's parent (paras 223-228). (8) D1 was in breach of its obligation to provide a performance bond and warranties (para.241).

LIBERTY MERCIAN LTD v CUDDY CIVIL ENGINEERING LTD, [2013] EWHC 2688 (TCC), [2013] T.C.L.R. 9, Ramsey, J., QBD (TCC).

572. Contract documents–Signatures–Whether signatory principal or agent–Whether signature qualified by reference to trading company

The appellant engineering firm (F) appealed against a decision on a preliminary issue that the respondent (H) had employed them in person rather than as an agent for a limited company (C). H was the sole director and sole shareholder of C, which traded under the name "Moon Furniture" (M). H employed F by a contract partly made orally in a meeting and by telephone and partly by a letter written on M's headed notepaper and signed by H above the name of M. The contract was for the construction of a new showroom on sloping ground that required piled retaining walls. The walls proved inadequate and H claimed damages against F. There was a trial of a preliminary issue at which it was determined that the contract had been made with H personally and not with C. F submitted that the judge had erred and F had contracted on behalf of M, which was the trading arm of C.

Held: Appeal dismissed. The parol evidence rule prevented oral evidence from affecting the written contract terms (see para.46 of judgment). However, where the identity of a contracting party was unclear from a written contract, it was legitimate to consider what the parties had said to each other in the period leading up to the offer and acceptance and the correct approach was an objective one. The court would take into account facts known to both parties, but not their private thoughts, *Estor Ltd v Multifit (UK) Ltd* [2009] EWHC 2565 (TCC), [2010] C.I.L.L. 2800 applied (para.56). Further principles derived from the authorities as to the identity of a party referred to in a deed or contract were: (i) extrinsic evidence was admissible to assist the resolution of an identity issue; (ii) the court's approach was objective, not subjective. The question was what a reasonable person, furnished with the relevant information, would conclude and the private thoughts of the protagonists concerning who was contracting with whom were irrelevant and inadmissible; (iii) if the extrinsic evidence established that a party had been misdescribed in a document, the court could correct that error as a matter of construction without any need for formal rectification; (iv) in deciding whether a party had signed a document as principal or as agent, there was no automatic relaxation of the parol evidence rule. The person who signed was the contracting party unless (a) the document made clear that he signed as agent for a sufficiently identified principal, or company, or (b) extrinsic evidence established that both parties knew he was signing as agent or company officer, *Investors Compensation Scheme Ltd v West Bromwich Building Society (No.1)* [1998] 1 W.L.R. 896, [1997] C.L.Y. 2537 applied, *Shogun Finance Ltd v Hudson* [2003] UKHL 62, [2004] 1 A.C. 919, [2004] C.L.Y. 645 followed and *Badgerhill Properties Ltd v Cottrell* [1991] B.C.C. 463, [1992] C.L.Y. 378 considered (paras 47-57). In the instant case, H's signature at the foot of the letter made him a contracting party, unless he qualified his signature or otherwise made it plain that the contract did not bind him personally, which he did not. The mere reference to M, without any indication that this was the trading name of C or that C was a limited company, was not an effective qualification (paras 60-73).

HAMID (T/A HAMID PROPERTIES) v FRANCIS BRADSHAW PARTNERSHIP, [2013] EWCA Civ 470, [2013] B.L.R. 447, Rix, L.J., CA (Civ Div).

573. Contract terms–Debts–Non-payment of invoices for consultancy services–Construction of contract terms

[Late Payment of Commercial Debts (Interest) Act 1998 (c.20) s.5(4).]

The applicant IT services company (E) applied for summary judgment on its claim against the respondent government department (G) for unpaid invoices. E had entered into a contract in April 2009 with G to provide IT consultancy services. Clause 2.1 of the contract stated that G undertook to purchase a minimum of 500 days of consultancy from E per year based on project requirement and additional days would be required once the purchased days had been exhausted. The contract rate was for not less than £850 per day. The dispute related to E's unpaid invoices from May to October 2011 for £760,000 including VAT. G submitted that clause 2.1 meant that if G's project requirements did not need at least 500 days of consultancy services, there was no obligation on it to purchase a minimum of 500 days of consultancy services from E. E contended that (1) the contract meant that G were obliged to purchase a minimum of 500 days consultancy services each year; (2) the minimum of 500 days could be prorated to 250 days for the period April to September 2011; (3) the rate of £850 per day was payable in return for E making its services available up to any such minimum level whether or not G requested or made use of such services; and (4) VAT was to be added to the £850 per day rate

Held: Application granted in part. (1) G's construction of clause 2.1 deprived the word "minimum" of any meaning. The words "based on project requirement" were explanatory, they did not mean "subject to project requirements" so as to possibly reduce the obligation to nil (see para.14 of judgment). (2) E's construction was correct. The undertaking to purchase and pay for consultancy services on the basis of a minimum of 500 days per year meant that, in a half-year, a minimum of half the 500 days per year was required to be purchased and paid for. Given that the purpose of the contract was to ensure and pay for the availability of E's services, the suggestion that no sums fell to be paid in the first half of the year was uncommercial, *Antaios Compania Naviera SA v Salen Rederierna AB (The Antaios)* [1985] A.C. 191, [1984] C.L.Y. 96 followed (para.19). (3) It was plain on the evidence that E continued to keep its services available until the termination of the contract and it was entitled to do so, *White & Carter (Councils) Ltd v McGregor* [1962] A.C. 413, [1962] C.L.Y. 501 followed. The claim was in debt and was not for an unenforceable penalty. The clauses were commercially justifiable, did not amount to oppression, were negotiated and freely entered into between parties of comparable bargaining power and did not amount to a provision *in terrorem* (paras 22, 25, 33). (4) VAT was not payable on E's invoices in addition to the contract price. Clause 3.7 of the contract established that it was for E to account to the Revenue for VAT and not G, so that the £850 was inclusive of VAT (paras 27, 32). (5) The error in the invoices showing that VAT was payable did not disengage the Late Payment of Commercial Debts (Interest) Act 1998, *Ruttle Plant Hire Ltd v Secretary of State for the Environment, Food and Rural Affairs* [2009] EWCA Civ 97, [2010] 1 All E.R. (Comm) 444, [2009] C.L.Y. 473 followed. The invoices were valid but included an extra sum for VAT which was not due. There was no reduction to the interest under s.5(4) of the Act. Summary judgment was granted to E for the sum claimed excluding the VAT (paras.33, 36, 38-39).

E-NIK LTD v SECRETARY OF STATE FOR COMMUNITIES AND LOCAL GOVERNMENT, [2012] EWHC 3027 (Comm), [2013] 2 All E.R. (Comm) 868, Burton, J., QBD (Comm).

574. Contract terms–Interpretation–Hive down agreement–One party assuming liability for claims in respect of specified asset–Scope of assumption of liability

The appellant (M) appealed against a refusal ([2011] EWHC 3310 (Ch), [2012] 1 All E.R. (Comm) 592, [2012] 6 C.L. 426) to join the four respondents as defendants in an action brought by a company (C). The fourth respondent (R4) was a company which manufactured steel. It had entered into a contract for C to provide a hot strip mill at its premises. The mill remained C's property. R4 went into administration. The first, second and third respondents (X) were its administrators. They offered R4's assets for sale, including the mill. C sent them formal notification of its claim to ownership of the mill, but they hived down all of the assets into M, a wholly-owned subsidiary company. In cl.9.5 of the hive down agreement M agreed to be responsible for settling "any claim" made against it by C concerning the mill. M was then purchased by another company (L). C brought proceedings against M and L for conversion, inducing a breach of contract and unlawful means conspiracy. M accepted that cl.9.5 covered the conversion claim. It sought permission to join X and R4 as defendants, on the basis that it had prospective claims against them for a contribution in relation to C's inducement and conspiracy claims. M relied upon *Canada Steamship Lines Ltd v King, The* [1952] A.C. 192, [1952] C.L.Y. 610 and submitted that clear words would have to be used to include claims based upon intentional wrongdoing in the scope of cl.9.5.

Held: Appeal dismissed. (1) The *Canada Steamship* principles were not to be applied mechanistically and should be regarded as no more than guidelines, *HIH Casualty & General Insurance Ltd v Chase Manhattan Bank* [2003] UKHL 6, [2003] 1 All E.R. (Comm) 349, [2003] C.L.Y. 2461 applied. The court's function was always to interpret the particular contract in the context in which it was made, *Canada Steamship* applied. In the instant case the court's task was to approach the interpretation of cl.9.5 in light of the overall commercial purpose of the hive down agreement, and to determine whether it was "inherently improbable" that it was directed at releasing the respondents not just from liability to contribute to a claim in conversion, but also from liability to contribute to any other claim that C might bring against M in respect of the mill (see paras 35-36 of judgment). (2) The commercial purpose of the hive down agreement was obvious to all the parties. R4 had entered into administration and X were under a statutory duty to achieve the purpose of administration as quickly and efficiently as reasonably practicable. They resolved to perform that duty by selling R4's business and assets to M, their objective being to achieve a prompt realisation and distribution of proceeds to creditors. M's objective, as purchaser, was to acquire the business and assets with a view to exploiting them for its own commercial advantage. However, unlike most such cases, when X, R4 and M entered into the hive down agreement they all knew that C had asserted a claim to the ownership of the mill, and they were aware of the factual basis upon which C might assert its title. X were admittedly selling M an asset to which the title was possibly flawed, but M was nevertheless prepared to buy it, and, by cl.9.5 to assume responsibility for "settling any claim made against it" by C in respect of the mill. Therefore, if C made claims against M in respect of the mill, it could not realistically have been the parties' intention that M would then be entitled to claw back from X and R4 part of the price that it had agreed to pay for the mill, being a price it had agreed in full knowledge of the possible flaw in the mill's title, and of the risk of claims by C. Further, if the sale to M involved any wrongdoing, whether by conversion, inducing a breach of contract or conspiracy, the parties to the hive down agreement were all engaged in it together, and M should have realised that. The whole point of cl.9.5 was therefore to shift to M the entire risk and burden of any claim that C might make in respect of the mill. Its words extended to all the claims that C had in fact brought and the judge had been correct to refuse to join X and R4 as parties to the claims (paras 37-39, 41-42).

LICTOR ANSTALT v MIR STEEL UK LTD; *sub nom.* MIR STEEL UK LTD v MORRIS, [2012] EWCA Civ 1397, [2013] 2 All E.R. (Comm) 54, Mummery, L.J., CA (Civ Div).

575. Contract terms–Notice–Service–Contractual provision for delivery of notice personally or by recorded delivery post–Whether methods of service permissive or exclusive–Meaning of "delivered personally"

The appellant company (E) appealed against a decision that it was precluded from pursuing its claim against the respondent (H) for breach of warranties under an agreement for the sale of shares because it had failed to serve the claim on H within the period specified by the agreement. Under the agreement E, as the buyer, had to give written notice of any breach of warranty claim to H, as the seller, by the second anniversary of completion. Where notice had been given in respect of any claim, that claim would be deemed to have been irrevocably withdrawn and lapsed unless proceedings were issued and served on H not later than the expiry of the period of 12 months after the date of that notice. Under cl.13.2 any such notice "may be served by delivering it personally or by sending it by pre-paid recorded delivery post to each party". E decided that it had claims against H for breaches of warranty and arranged for notice of the claim to be served on him in two different ways. First, a process server delivered a notice to H's home address; he rang the bell but no one was at home; accordingly he left the notice in the front porch on a table, where it was found by H later that day. On the same day, a second notice was sent by recorded delivery. E's claim form was subsequently left in the letterbox at H's home by the process server. Clause 14.2 permitted service of the claim form to be effected, inter alia, by any manner permitted by cl.13.2. H's case was that the first notice was effectively served, because, although it was not served in accordance with cl.13.2, that clause did not set out an exclusive code; on that basis the claim form was served too late. Whether the claim was in time depended on the meaning of "delivering it personally" in cl.13.2 and whether the two methods of service in cl.13.2 were exclusive.

Held: Appeal dismissed. (Longmore LJ dissenting on the issue of exclusivity) (1) As the judge held, the words "deliver personally" meant that the notice had to be served on the person of the recipient and not that it had to be served by a personal deliverer, *Kenneth Allison Ltd (In Liquidation) v AE Limehouse & Co* [1992] 2 A.C. 105, [1992] C.L.Y. 3593 considered and *Bottin (International) Investments Ltd v Venson Group Plc* [2004] EWCA Civ 1368 followed (see paras 16-24 of judgment). (2) As the judge held, the methods of service in cl.13.2 were permissive rather than exclusive. The notion that it was intended to be permissive rather than exclusive received obvious support from the use of the word "may". The purpose of a provision such as cl.13.2, if it was not exclusive, was to shift any risk from the server to the intended recipient, *Blunden v Frogmore Investments Ltd* [2002] EWCA Civ 573, [2003] 2 P. & C.R. 6, [2002] C.L.Y. 3031. Clear words would normally be required before one could ascribe to the parties an intention that a recipient who actually received a notice in time should nonetheless be treated as not having received the notice at all. There was a strong commercial argument, as well as a strong argument based on the language of the agreement, for saying that the first notice was delivered when H saw it, *Yates Building Co Ltd v RJ Pulleyn & Sons (York) Ltd* (1975) 237 E.G. 183, [1975] C.L.Y. 388 considered. The fact that E delivered a second notice could not retrospectively cause the first notice not to have been validly delivered (paras 26-38). (3) The judge was right that the first notice and the claim form were not "delivered personally" within the meaning of cl.13.2, but the first notice was nonetheless validly served so that the claim form was served out of time (para.39).

ENER-G HOLDINGS PLC v HORMELL, [2012] EWCA Civ 1059, [2013] 1 All E.R. (Comm) 1162, Lord Neuberger (M.R.), CA (Civ Div).

576. Contract terms–Planning applications–Liability of planning advisory company for delayed submission of planning application–Operation of limitation clause in contract–Proper construction of "filing" of claims

The claimant landowner (E) claimed damages for breach of contract and/or negligence against the defendant advisory company (M) arising out of the timing and content of an application for planning permission. M counterclaimed for the cost of alleged additional work falling outside the remit of the contract. E had acquired industrial land to sell for development of a waste recycling site. In July 2007 it retained M, a specialist in planning matters concerning waste management, to apply for planning permission "within the next three to four months at latest". In fact the application was not made until April 2008. It was due to be processed by July 25. On July 15, E sacked M and made a fresh planning application using different consultants. Planning permission was granted in March 2009. E had since been unable to sell the site. Its case was that M was in breach of contract for failing to complete the planning application by November 2007; that the application, when eventually submitted, was deficient and would have been unsuccessful if it had not been withdrawn; and that if planning permission had been granted within the original timescale, E would have been able to sell the site in spring 2008 to a specified buyer. It sought damages for loss of profit of around £800,000. M's defence was that the planning application was unconnected to the sale negotiations, that its planning application would have resulted in the grant of permission, and that the site would never have sold for the price that E wanted.

Held: Judgment for defendant. (1) Whilst M was in breach of contract by failing to complete some aspects of the planning application by November 2007, those failures were not the cause of the delay in submitting the application. At best, it would have been liable in nominal damages to E, assessed in the sum of £5. Delay up to mid-December 2007 was attributable to uncertainty over the proposed site layout, which was entirely E's responsibility; later delay was attributable to E's decision to involve the prospective buyer in the planning process (see paras 56-58, 61, 64-70, 75, 84, 88, 99-104, 170-175, 226, 328 of judgment). (2) On a balance of probabilities, if the first planning application had not been abandoned, planning permission would have been granted. There was no recognised profession of planners, and no right or wrong way to make a planning application. A planner would generally only be liable for damage caused by advice which no reasonably well informed and competent planner would have given *Middle Level Commissioners v Atkins Ltd* [2012] EWHC 2884 (TCC), [2012] C.I.L.L. 3257, [2013] 4 C.L. 242 applied (paras 177-178, 193, 227-228, 234, 329). (3) (Obiter) Even if M had been in breach of contract, E's case on causation failed at every stage, most notably because relations with the prospective purchaser would have broken down for commercial reasons unconnected with the planning application. E had failed to prove its assertion that a decline in the property market from 2008 onwards was responsible for the failed sale. It would have needed to rely on evidence relating, not to general market conditions, but to market demand for the type of specialist site concerned (paras 232-264, 330). (4) (Obiter) Even if E's case had been upheld on causation, its case on quantum failed. It had not demonstrated any loss of profit (paras 265-281, 331). (5) (Obiter) Specific contractual provisions would, in any event, have operated as a bar to E's claim: cl.11 stipulated that any claim had to be "filed" within one year of substantial completion of the services. "Completion" in the instant case was the date when E terminated the retainer. The clause could not be construed as requiring E to issue proceedings within a year. Parties to a contract could vary the ordinary six-year limitation period, but the word "filed" was not apt to describe the commencement of court proceedings because the "filing" of claims was not a process recognised by the English courts, *Inframatrix Investments Ltd v Dean Construction Ltd* [2012] EWCA Civ 64, [2012] 2 All E.R. (Comm) 337, [2012] C.L.Y. 593 distinguished. The clause was, however, intended to provide a measure of certainty and could be construed as requiring a formal and particularised letter of claim within a year, which E had not provided. Clause 10 provided that M would not be responsible for any consequential, incidental or indirect damages. The loss of profit claim was probably too remote, but if not, any recovery would have been excluded by the operation of cl.10 (paras 27, 284-320, 332). (6) M's counterclaim was allowed in part. M was entitled to recover from E sums that were solely due to the involvement of the prospective buyer in the planning process (paras 327, 333).

ELVANITE FULL CIRCLE LTD v AMEC EARTH & ENVIRONMENTAL (UK) LTD, [2013] EWHC 1191 (TCC), 148 Con. L.R. 127, Coulson, J., QBD (TCC).

577. Contracts of hire–Indemnities–Allegedly defective lorry sold on expiry of period of hire–Whether hirer liable for sum paid to buyer in respect of defects

The appellant (W) appealed against a decision that he was liable to indemnify the respondent finance house (P) in respect of a payment which P had made to settle a claim relating to an allegedly defective lorry. W and P had entered into a lease agreement relating to the hire of the lorry by W. Clause 8 of the agreement enabled the lorry to be sold when the period of hire came to an end. It stated that P could at its discretion appoint W as its sale agent for that purpose on certain terms: in cl.8(b)(iii), it was said that "the vehicle must be sold for business use without the benefit of any warranty, representation or condition on our part"; in cl.8(b)(iv), it was said that "you must indemnify us against all losses, damage, costs, claims and expense arising out of the sale (including legal fees) on a full indemnity basis in connection with any proceedings against us brought by any purchaser". At the conclusion of the initial period of hire, W identified a buyer for the lorry, although the sale was executed between P and another finance house (F), which was facilitating the purchase for the ultimate use of the buyer identified by W. The buyer complained that the lorry lacked pulling power and issued proceedings against F. P was notified and made a payment towards the settlement of the buyer's claim. It then issued proceedings against W, seeking reimbursement of that contribution together with ancillary costs. The issue was whether W was obliged to indemnify P as P had asserted.

Held: Appeal allowed. Although the sale of the lorry had not been concluded, as cl.8 provided, by W acting as agent for P, both parties had conducted themselves as if it had been; they were therefore estopped from contending that cl.8 did not apply. It followed that P was able to rely on cl.8(b)(iv) as against W, but W was in turn entitled to rely on cl.8(b)(iii) as against P. The code in cl.8(b) governed the sale. It was a sale without warranty as to the lorry's condition and any payment made by P to the buyer could not, as a matter of law, have arisen out of such a sale. Accordingly, W was not liable under cl.8(b) (see paras 29-32 of judgment).

WAITE v PACCAR FINANCIAL PLC, [2012] EWCA Civ 901, [2012] C.T.L.C. 222, Sir Andrew Morritt (Chancellor), CA (Civ Div).

578. Deeds–Interpretation–Deed entitling charitable foundation to percentage of bank's pre-tax profit–Change in applicable accounting standards concerning calculation of profit–Correct construction of deed

[Companies Act 1985 (c.6).]

The appellant banking group (B) appealed against a decision ([2011] CSIH 87, 2012 S.C. 259, [2013] 1 C.L. 396) concerning the correct construction of a deed. In 1986 B had entered into a deed in favour of the respondent charitable foundation (F). The intention was for F to receive a small percentage of B's pre-tax profits. The deed was varied and replaced in 1997 and B covenanted to pay F the greater of a specified percentage of pre-tax profits and the sum of £38,920. Pre-tax profit and loss were defined as the group profit and group loss before taxation shown in the audited accounts. In 2008 B acquired a bank (H) which was in difficulties. As a result of new European legislation, B was required to enter a figure for the "gain on acquisition" in its group accounts. The figure represented the book value of H's assets, but it was unlikely that the assets would realise that value. B's accounts had shown a loss of £10 billion. When the "gain on acquisition" was taken into account, the figures showed a profit before tax of £1 billion. F claimed that it was therefore entitled to £3,543,333. B submitted that if its argument on construction failed, the court should apply the doctrine of equitable adjustment to exclude negative goodwill from the calculation of the group's profit before taxation.

Held: Appeal allowed. (1) To understand the deed it was necessary to place it in the legal and accounting context at the date when it was executed. When the original deed was made in 1986, and replaced in 1997, there were two fundamental legal and accounting principles deriving from the Companies Act 1985: first, that a profit and loss account was concerned with ordinary activities before taxation; second, that only profits realised at the balance sheet date could lawfully be included in the profit and loss account. The European Union's adoption of Regulation 1606/2002 led to the fundamental change that listed companies had to prepare their consolidated accounts in conformity with International Financial Reporting Standards (IFRS) rather than the 1985 Act. IFRS 3 para.34 required negative goodwill arising from a "bargain purchase" to be recognised in the profit and loss account as of the acquisition date even though the gain was unrealised. Neither party to the deed foresaw the potential impact of that change until after B's rescue of H (see paras 7-8, 15-17 of judgment). (2) The landscape, matrix and aim of the 1997 deed could not have been clearer. When made it could only have been aimed at realised profits and losses before taxation. The change in 2005 to introduce negative goodwill into the profit and loss account as a "gain on acquisition" did not appear in the individual company accounts, and could never attract taxation. In the light of the legal position in the 1980s and 1990s, the change was wholly outside the parties' original contemplation, and was something which they would not have accepted if they had foreseen it. It was not suggested that the change meant that the 1997 deed was frustrated. The question was therefore how its language best operated in the fundamentally changed and entirely unforeseen circumstances, in the light of the parties' original intentions. The answer was evident: it operated best by ignoring the unrealised gain on acquisition and treating the loss which existed apart from that as the relevant figure for the purposes of calculating the sum due to F. The proper approach was therefore to use the figures in the consolidated income statement which showed the group profit or loss before taxation in the sense intended by the deed. That meant realised profit or loss before taxation. It followed that the sum of £38,920 was payable to F under the deed, rather than £3,543,333 (paras 21-25, 28-30). (3) There was much to be said for giving effect to what, on ordinary principles of construction, the parties had agreed, *Bank of Credit and Commerce International SA (In Liquidation) v Ali (No.1)* [2001] UKHL 8, [2002] 1 A.C. 251, [2001] C.L.Y. 2228 considered. There was no need to strive to find a basis in equity for arriving at a different result. There was a place for such a result where the contract had become impossible to perform, or something essential to its performance had been totally or partially destroyed, *William Campbell Muir v John M'Intyre and Others* (1887) 14 R. 470 and *Sharp v Thomson* 1930 S.C. 1092 considered. However, it could hardly be said to be inequitable if the result of ordinary construction had been in F's favour. Therefore, the proposition that the court could equitably adjust a contract on the basis that its performance, while not frustrated, was no longer what was originally contemplated, was not part of Scots law. To hold otherwise would be to undermine the principle enshrined in the maxim pacta sunt servanda, which lay at the root of the whole law of contract (paras 44-47).

LLOYDS TSB FOUNDATION FOR SCOTLAND v LLOYDS BANKING GROUP PLC, [2013] UKSC 3, [2013] 1 W.L.R. 366, Lord Hope, J.S.C. (Deputy President), SC.

579. Default–Measure of damages–Default clause in Federation of Oils, Seeds and Fats Associations' Contract 201–Relevance of matters occurring after breach in calculating damages

The appellant seller (N) appealed against an arbitration award made by the Board of Appeal of the Federation of Oils, Seeds and Fats Associations (FOSFA) in favour of the respondent buyer (X). N had contracted to sell groundnut oil to X. The contract provided for shipment from Senegal and incorporated FOSFA Contract 201, which included prohibition and default clauses. On April 2, 2008, when the contract was still in force, there was in force in Senegal an export prohibition fulfilling the requirements of the prohibition clause. N notified X of the prohibition in accordance with the clause so as to extend the shipment period for 30 days. However, it made a further statement which purported to be a termination of the contract; that amounted to an anticipatory repudiation of the contract, which X accepted on the same day. The export prohibition was still in force on May 2, when the extension of the shipment period would have expired. N argued before the board that no loss had been suffered by X because but for N's breach of contract on April 2, the contract would in any event have ended without liability on N's part on May 2. The board rejected that argument and held that default damages were to be awarded at the difference between the contract price and the market price on April 2. N argued that the board should have taken account of matters occurring after the breach when assessing whether X had suffered a loss and was entitled to damages.

Held: Appeal allowed. If no remedy was conferred by law, clear words would be required to confer a contractual entitlement to such remedy, especially where the contractual term was a standard clause drafted and adopted by a trade body and the term was to confer a right of recovery in circumstances where no loss had in fact been suffered. Such a remedy was contrary to the compensatory principle governing the quantum of damages for breach of contract. That principle took precedence over considerations of certainty and finality, *Golden Strait Corp v Nippon Yusen Kubishika Kaisha (The Golden Victory)* [2007] UKHL 12, [2007] 2 A.C. 353, [2007] C.L.Y. 3816 applied. Accordingly, considerations of certainty and finality would not be sufficient to confer on X an entitlement at law to recover where no loss had occurred, so it would require clear words if the parties had wished to achieve the opposite result (see para.17 of judgment). The default clause's language was clear. Where a seller defaulted, the innocent buyer could go into the market to buy against the default. If he chose to do so, the clause imposed an obligation on the defaulting seller to reimburse the buyer for the difference between the repurchase price and the contract price. That obligation was tempered by the provisions that if the seller was dissatisfied with the buyer's repurchase price he could refer the matter to arbitration, wherein the damages would be limited to the differential with the market price if that was lower than the repurchase price actually obtained. To that extent the clause modified the common law position. It entitled the buyer to compensation irrespective of subsequent events and the effect they might have had on the contract had it remained in force. However, the buyer was not obliged to buy against the default, and if he chose not to, he was entitled to recover damages, if any, in arbitration. That would be the common law measure. That conferred no right to damages if no damage had been suffered. The clause thus struck a balance between the common law position and commercial considerations of certainty and finality (paras 19-23). The court was reluctant to differ from a trade tribunal on a question of interpretation of one of its standard clauses unless satisfied that it was wrong. Deference to the board's view in the instant case was tempered by the fact that it had not articulated any reasoning for its conclusions as to the wording of the clause or as to the commercial considerations. The award would be remitted to the board (paras 26, 36).

NOVASEN SA v ALIMENTA SA, [2013] EWHC 345 (Comm), [2013] 2 All E.R. (Comm) 162, Popplewell, J., QBD (Comm).

580. Disclosure–Documents–Documents disclosable under contract for installation and testing of tram system

The claimant (C), the body responsible for co-ordinating a city's public transport services, sought specific performance by the defendant contractor (D) to provide documents. C had engaged D to deliver, install and test a tram operating system. A clause of the contract required D to record for at least 12 years the performance of its contractual obligations. Under another clause, D was also obliged to submit to C or an auditor those records or any other information they might reasonably request which related to the records. Disputes arose over payments and delays, and D presented several substantial claims. C requested a number of documents and eventually issued Part 8 proceedings for specific performance. D agreed to disclose only some of the categories of documents requested. D submitted that upon a proper, narrow interpretation of the contract, (1) documents which related to the performance of its contractual obligations did not include cost records or documents; (2) C was only contractually entitled to request documents in order to audit information supplied to it or to verify D's compliance with its obligations under the agreement, but C's requests were for neither purpose.

Held: Judgment for claimant in part. (1) Documentation disclosable by D went beyond simply contemporaneous documents that recorded what it had done. Documentation relating to what it had done or not done pursuant to the contract was disclosable. Such documentation could include records of the cost of labour, materials, plant, sub-contractors, suppliers and the like because they related to the performance of the obligations. The fact that a cost had been incurred demonstrated that there had been an attempt to perform the obligations. It was not only the original contemporaneous records which had to be disclosed but also related information records or documents. Therefore, documents such as reports or internal audits, created after the events that had been recorded originally, which addressed previous events or matters otherwise earlier recorded, were linked to the supply of the deliverables or the performance or non-performance by D of its obligations under the contract. The request for documents or information had to be reasonable; if and to the extent that it was not, D did not have to comply with it. The request had only to be complied with if the purpose was either to enable C to vet or check information supplied to it under the contract or to enable it verify whether or not D had complied with its obligations. The fact that documents which were otherwise disclosable under the contract were confidential was immaterial and could not be used as an excuse to withhold disclosure, although, once disclosed, C was required to comply with the contractual clause relating to confidentiality (see para.26 of judgment). (2) Either C or D was responsible for all the delay and alleged extra cost or, more likely, there was an element of responsibility on each party. Either way, C had a very real interest in determining whether and to what extent it or D was responsible for what had happened. On either basis, C had a legitimate interest in determining the responsibility for the allegedly poor or satisfactory performance by D of its obligations under the contract. It was clear from the evidence that the purpose, at least broadly, of C's request for documents had been to audit, vet or check information supplied by D already to support its claim. It was perfectly legitimate for C to need to audit the information supplied and it could therefore see the information, records or documents relating to not only the original performance but also the performance of D's obligations under the clauses as to whether they had provided all requisite information, records or documents relating to the claims which had been made. That was not intrinsically unfair or non-commercial, particularly in the light of the fact that, as soon as a dispute arose on a given claim, D could be entitled to refer it to adjudication for a quick decision within 28 days. It was not unfair that D had to supply or make available documents which might help, undermine or hinder its claims (see paras 30, 32). (3) Specific performance would be ordered in respect of several categories of documents (paras 37-61).

TRANSPORT FOR GREATER MANCHESTER v THALES TRANSPORT & SECURITY LTD, [2012] EWHC 3717 (TCC), 146 Con. L.R. 194, Akenhead, J., QBD (TCC).

581. Distribution agreements–Breach of contract–Manufacture and sale of satellite tracking devices–Requirement to give 12 months' notice of intention to cease manufacture–Product including subsequent derivatives

The claimant (C) claimed damages against the defendant (E) for breach of contract. E made satellite tracking devices. It sold a device for land and marine services called the SAT-101. C worked with E to develop a version of the SAT-101 to work in aircraft. It was called the SAT-111. The parties entered into an exclusive distribution agreement by which E was to produce the SAT-111 and C was given exclusive worldwide distribution rights for a five-year term for the SAT-111 and any subsequent derivatives of it. The agreement provided for E to give C 12 months' notice of its intention to cease to manufacture the SAT-111. During the period of the agreement E developed a new land and marine device, the SAT-201, to replace the SAT-101. C were unable to sell a significant number of the SAT-111. The parties discussed a new aeronautical product to be called the SAT-221, but the parties then fell out and C issued proceedings. C claimed that the SAT-221 was a derivative product and that E had ceased manufacture of the SAT-111 and derivatives thereof without giving 12 months' notice to C. C claimed that E had repudiated the agreement and claimed damages for loss of the chance to sell the products. E denied that it had ceased to manufacture and denied that the SAT-221 was a derivative product.

Held: Claim dismissed. (1) E had not ceased to manufacture the SAT-111. The manufacture of the SAT-111 was largely sub-contracted out by E. The manufacturing process was done to order. E's obligation under the agreement was to react and respond to orders from C. There was no obligation to maintain stores of the SAT-111. At all material times E held sufficient quantities of the printed circuit board used in the SAT-101 and SAT-111. Although the boards were needed to service and support the SAT-101s, they would be made available for SAT-111s to the limited extent likely to be ordered or if substantial orders were made then it would be in E's interest to secure a replacement board. In any event, there was no realistic prospect of any significant quantity of SAT-111s actually being ordered by C. Only 17 units were ever ordered and even C was not expecting orders for more than one or two SAT-111s (see para.128 of judgment). (2) The SAT-221 was not, and to the extent that it was developed had not become, a "derivative" product within the meaning of the agreement and E never became obliged to manufacture and supply the SAT-221 at any stage. There was no obligation under the agreement on E to develop derivatives or produce the SAT-221. The parties developed a prototype but there was not variation of the agreement and no obligation on E to go ahead (paras 129-136). (3) There could be no estoppel because of the clear understanding between the parties that there was no commitment on either side to the SAT-221 project. The development of the prototype did not reflect any binding agreement or variation of the original agreement. The arrangement by which the prototype was produced was essentially subject to final agreement and to each party being satisfied from their own standpoint that it represented a commercially viable product. The representations on which C relied were not made out (para.147). (4) Since there was no breach there was no repudiation. In any event any repudiation was not accepted (paras 149-151).

ADS AEROSPACE LTD v EMS GLOBAL TRACKING LTD, [2012] EWHC 2310 (TCC), 145 Con. L.R. 29, Akenhead, J., QBD (TCC).

582. Economic duress–Anticipatory breach–Inducement to agree contract with increased prices for reduced quantity of goods–Concept of duress under Japanese law

[Civil Code (Japan) Art.96, Art.703, Art.709.]

The appellant English company (L) appealed against a decision ([2012] EWHC 2013 (QB)) dismissing its counterclaim alleging economic duress and giving judgment for the respondent Japanese hop supplier (S). S sold hops to domestic and international customers including L, who contracted for a certain amount at a fixed price. S told L that it was expecting a decrease in production as harvests were adversely affected by bad weather and pests. S proposed to supply 20 per cent less on condition of a substantial price increase. As L had made onward sale contracts which it could only fulfil by purchasing the hops from S or in the spot market at exorbitant prices, it maintained that it had only agreed to the revised contracts under duress. S supplied the goods under the revised contracts but L did not pay and instead counterclaimed for duress. The purchase orders did not contain any express choice of law clause. L submitted that the judge had erred by finding that the applicable law was Japanese and (1) by finding that L's claim to duress failed under the Civil Code 1896 (Japan) art.96 and art.703; (2) by finding the revised contracts had not preserved L's right to claim damages under art.709 for non-performance of the earlier contracts; in fact they did not waive L's right to damages, but entitled S to render alternative performance; (3) by finding that L's agreement to the revised 2007 contract had not been conditional upon compliance by S with the original 2008 contract; (4) by wrongly dismissing L's claim in misrepresentation in relation to the 2007 contract because S had provided insufficient evidence to prove that if the truth had emerged in the course of negotiations, it would have persisted in demanding a 20 per cent price reduction; (5) by dismissing L's claim for damages for failure to perform the original 2007 and 2008 contracts and wrongly concluding that Japanese law entailed no doctrine of anticipatory breach of contract.

Held: Appeal dismissed. It was usually the case in a commercial contract of sale that the law of the vendor's place of business governed the contract and the judge had been correct to find that the contracts were governed by Japanese law (see para.28 of judgment). (1) There was no concept of economic duress in Japanese law and the judge below had been right to reject the idea that a Japanese court would for the first time recognise economic pressure as amounting to duress. Furthermore, L had lost any right to rescind by its ratification of the subsequent contracts (paras 46-47, 49-52). (2) It was common ground that the right to receive goods under a contract of sale was a "right or legally protected interest" within the meaning of art.709. Although the experts were agreed that an essential element in the tort was "illegitimacy", whether misrepresentation could constitute a sufficiently grave illegitimacy had not been established (paras 53-63). (3) The argument that agreement to the revised terms for 2008 invested L with an entitlement to damages for non-performance of the 2007 agreement was absurd. Even if there had been such a condition, by agreeing to vary the 2008 contract the parties had to have agreed to dispense with the earlier condition (para.38). (4) The judge had correctly asked whether, if it had known what the true position was, L would nonetheless have agreed to the proposed terms. The answer to that was yes and the causal nexus was not made out so the claim in misrepresentation under art.709 had to fail (paras 40-41). (5) As a matter of construction of the revised 2007 and 2008 contracts it was plain that they released S from the obligation to perform the earlier contracts which they superseded. Even English law did not contemplate the award of damages for an unaccepted anticipatory repudiatory breach and L had agreed to terminate the earlier contracts, not repudiated them. Whether Japanese law recognised a concept of anticipatory breach was also beside the point as, even if it did, that was not what had occurred. S had obtained L's consent to replace the previous contracts relating to the 2007 crop before the time for delivery of that crop had arrived (para.36)

SAPPORO BREWERIES LTD v LUPOFRESH LTD; *sub nom.* LUPOFRESH LTD v SAPPORO BREWERIES LTD, [2013] EWCA Civ 948, [2014] 1 All E.R. (Comm) 484, Moses, L.J., CA (Civ Div).

583. Exclusion clauses–Interpretation–Clause excluding liability for loss of profits following contract termination

The appellant catering company (K) appealed against a decision which construed an exclusion of liability clause in favour of the respondent conference centre operator (M). By a written agreement, M appointed K the exclusive supplier of catering services at its venues for a five-year period. After three years, M purported to terminate the agreement. K responded by purporting to treat M's actions as a repudiatory breach of the agreement and to accept that as terminating the agreement. K claimed loss of profits that would have been earned during the remaining term of the agreement. M denied repudiation and argued that K's claim for loss of profits was precluded by clause 18.6 of the agreement which provided that M should "have no liability whatsoever in contract, tort (including negligence) or otherwise for any loss of goodwill, business, revenue or profits... suffered by the Contractor or any third party in relation to this Agreement". The judge determined as a preliminary issue that clause 18.6 excluded M's liability for K's loss of profits.

Held: Appeal allowed. If the judge's construction of clause 18.6 was adopted, the agreement would be effectively devoid of contractual content since there was no sanction for non-performance by M. It was inherently unlikely that the parties intended the clause to have that effect. The judge fell into error in thinking that the ascertainment of the meaning of apparently clear words was not itself a process of contractual construction. He failed to consider the words of the clause in their wider context. Clause 18.6 fell under the section of the agreement headed "Indemnity and Insurance". Although the agreement provided that the condition headings were for ease of reference and would not affect the construction of the agreement, that did not preclude close attention to the nature and content of the provisions following each heading. K provided M with an indemnity by means of clause 18.4 under that heading, and although it arose only on M's negligence, it was wide-ranging. Both its position and content showed that clause 18.6 was intended to be read with clause 18.4, to qualify the apparently wide ambit of that indemnity. Considering the content of that section of the agreement, a wide-ranging exclusion clause of general application would not have been expected there. However, it was not clear that clause 18.6 served only to qualify the extent of the indemnity under clause 18.4. It was not possible to read "no liability whatsoever in contract, or tort (including negligence) or otherwise" as simply restricting an indemnity which was only expressed to arise in the event of M's negligence. The key appeared to be that the provision excluded heads of loss suffered by M "or any third party" in relation to the agreement. In that context, the third party loss referred to in clause 18.6 could only be a loss suffered in consequence of negligent performance by M of its contractual obligation, express or implied. It was only such losses that would, if suffered by K, generate in M an obligation to indemnify. Such a loss presupposed defective performance of the contract, but not a refusal to perform it or be bound by it. M did not undertake to indemnify K against liability it incurred to third parties in consequence of its refusal to perform the contract. Had it been intended to exclude all liability for loss of profits in the event of any breach by M then there would have been no need to refer to third party losses as a separate category as they would have been excluded from the scope of the indemnity by the general words. To construe the provision consistently with business common sense, "in relation to this Agreement" meant "in relation to the performance of this Agreement" and therefore as not extending to losses suffered in consequence of a refusal to perform or be bound by the agreement. The instant construction was an attempt to give effect to the presumption that parties do not lightly abandon a remedy for breach of contract afforded them by the general law. The declaration at first instance would be substituted with a declaration that on the proper construction of clause 18.6, liability for K's loss of profits was not excluded, on the assumption that the liability asserted arose out of M's repudiatory refusal further to perform the contract (see paras 19, 22-28 of judgment).

KUDOS CATERING (UK) LTD v MANCHESTER CENTRAL CONVENTION COMPLEX LTD, [2013] EWCA Civ 38, [2013] 2 Lloyd's Rep. 270, Laws, L.J., CA (Civ Div).

584. Formation of contract–Groups of companies–International transport agreement entitling supplier to provide services through overseas agents–Summary judgment based on absence of contractual relationship between parties–Whether supplier acting as agent for signatory to contract

[Civil Procedure Rules 1998 (SI 1998/3132) Pt 24.]

The appellant bank (S) appealed against the grant ([2012] EWHC 574 (Comm)) of summary judgment in favour of the first respondent company (V), and against the setting aside of service of its claim form and particulars of claim against the second respondent company (H). In 2001 S had entered into an international transport agreement with V, which was part of a group of companies providing secure storage and transportation of valuables. The agreement incorporated the group's general trading conditions. It identified the group's United Kingdom company (V UK) as the sole contracting party, but entitled V to provide services through agents abroad. The group had subsidiary companies in various countries, including H, which operated in Hong Kong. In 2005, S started buying silver from Chinese refineries under a contract which provided for delivery to a security agent in Hong Kong. In 2009 and 2010, the silver was delivered to a vault operated by H. Warehouse receipts were issued to S. Some of the silver disappeared. An employee of H confessed to accepting bribes from the refineries to issue false receipts. S claimed a loss of $20 million in proceedings for breach of contract and breach of duty as bailees against V and H. Summary judgment was granted on the basis that the international transport contract between S and V was a framework agreement, which merely established the terms on which individual consignments would be handled as and when required under further instructions from S. In the absence of further instructions from S relating specifically to the silver in the missing consignments, the judge found that there was no claim against V. He held that H's services had been provided exclusively under contracts with the refineries, in which H was the principal in its own right. He accepted H's challenge to the English jurisdiction.

Held: Appeal allowed. (1) The judge had been right to view the international transport agreement as a framework agreement, but there was nothing in that agreement which prevented S from giving instructions to one of V's agents. On the evidence, S had regularly given instructions to H regarding the silver delivered to H's vault. Given that V UK was stated in the agreement to be the sole contracting party, and that V had retained an entitlement to provide services through its overseas agents, there was a real prospect of S establishing that V's associated companies were to be treated as its agents. The general trading conditions seemed to govern all business undertaken by the entire group, apart from activities performed entirely within Switzerland, to which separate conditions applied. If the subsidiary companies contracted on those terms, it was arguable that they all contracted as agents for V UK, rather than as principals. The judge below had been heavily influenced by the fact that H had entered into carriage agreements with individual refineries and invoiced the refineries rather than S. He thought that those agreements excluded the possibility that H was providing services to S, either on its own behalf or as agent for V UK. That was not necessarily the case; much depended on the terms on which S had agreed to buy the silver. It was also arguable that the warehouse receipts were capable of a wider construction than the judge had given them; in any event, they needed to be evaluated in the context of a full understanding of the relationships between the different parties. It was regrettable that S's evidence relating to its dealings with V and H was incomplete, but the position was not clear enough to support a finding that the claim had no prospects of success. The purpose of CPR Pt 24 was to enable the court to dispose summarily of cases that were fanciful, hopeless or bound to fail, not to conduct an abbreviated form of trial on the basis of incomplete evidence (see paras 17-24 of judgment). (2) It was to be emphasised that the purpose of skeleton arguments was to inform the court of the essential elements of the parties' submissions, thereby enabling an understanding of the issues and arguments; they were not intended to serve as vehicles for extended advocacy. A short, concise skeleton was more helpful to the court, and more likely to be persuasive, than a longer document that sought to develop every point. The court expected the requirements of CPR PD 52A para.5 and CPR PD 52C to be rigorously observed, failing which costs penalties might be imposed, *Khader v Aziz* [2010] EWCA Civ 716, [2010] 1 W.L.R. 2673, [2011] C.L.Y. 870 applied.

STANDARD BANK PLC v VIA MAT INTERNATIONAL LTD, [2013] EWCA Civ 490, [2013] 2 All E.R. (Comm) 1222, Moore-Bick, L.J., CA (Civ Div).

585. Formation of contract–Intention to create legal relations–Vendor of company wishing to invest in purchaser–Side letter to sale of company–Whether side letter enforceable contract

The appellant (B) appealed against a decision that a side letter was not legally enforceable. B was the major shareholder and chief executive of a company which operated a cable television and internet business in Bulgaria. The company was to be sold but B wanted to retain an investment in the business. It was agreed in principle that he would invest EUR 1.65 million and have a 10 per cent participation in the purchaser. Closing of the agreement for the sale of B's company was made conditional on execution of an investment agreement with B. However, the sale agreement further provided that that condition could be waived by written notice from either party. B was concerned about the ability of the purchaser to waive signing of the investment agreement as a condition precedent to closing of the sale agreement. The parties therefore executed the side letter, under which the purchaser agreed that, as soon as reasonably practicable after the signing of the sale agreement, it would offer B the opportunity to invest in the purchaser on terms to be agreed and to be set out in an investment agreement negotiated in good faith. Closing of the sale agreement took place and the parties waived the pre-condition of signing the investment agreement. There were negotiations for an investment agreement but they came to nothing. Eventually B brought proceedings against the respondent for alleged failure to honour the terms of the side letter. The judge held that the side letter was only an agreement to agree and was too uncertain to constitute a binding contract; it followed that the parties could not have intended to create legal relations. The side letter was, accordingly, unenforceable.

Held: Appeal dismissed. (1) The judge had been entitled to conclude that B had not been given an oral assurance, amounting to a collateral contract, that the side letter was a separate contract protecting his right to invest in the purchaser. The judge's finding of fact was not unreasonable or against the weight of the evidence (see paras 33-36 of judgment). (2) Contrary to the judge's conclusion, it was clear from the terms of the side letter itself that the parties intended to create legal relations. However, it did not follow that the side letter created a legally enforceable contract, *Dhanani v Crasnianski* [2011] EWHC 926 (Comm), [2011] 2 All E.R. (Comm) 799, [2012] C.L.Y. 636 considered (paras 37-38). (3) Any agreement between the parties was solely contained in the side letter, as the judge concluded. The terms of the side letter were no more than an agreement to agree. It was an agreement to offer B the opportunity to invest, and the terms of the investment agreement were not agreed but remained to be negotiated. Particular terms were set out, but they were not certain. The side letter was therefore unenforceable, *Walford v Miles* [1992] 2 A.C. 128, [1992] C.L.Y. 514 followed (paras 40-46). (4) Even if the side letter was more than an agreement to agree, it was not sufficiently certain to be an enforceable contract. The essential terms were not dealt with. Identifying the minimum sum of investment and the minimum amount of shares and shareholder debt was insufficient to create certainty as to the proposed relations between the parties (paras 48-52).

BARBUDEV v EUROCOM CABLE MANAGEMENT BULGARIA EOOD, [2012] EWCA Civ 548, [2012] 2 All E.R. (Comm) 963, Sir John Thomas (President), CA (Civ Div).

586. Formation of contract–Offer and acceptance–Parties negotiating purchase of secondhand equipment–Conclusion of binding contract–Damages for inability to buy equipment

[Sale of Goods Act 1979 (c.54) s.51 (3), s.51 (2).]

The claimant (S) sought damages from the respondent (L) for repudiation of contract. L had entered into three lease purchase agreements with a customer for equipment used in television and radio post-production, but subsequently the customer had gone into liquidation. S had expressed an interest in purchasing the equipment which included a digital film console. Although the lease referred to the console itself L had only provided finance for its software updates and there was an issue as to whether the parties were negotiating for the sale of the console or merely the updates. L then received an offer from elsewhere and emailed S on August 18, 2011, enquiring whether it wished to make a further offer. L's email referred to the assets under the agreements and sought a "FINAL" offer. On August 19 at 10.20 S emailed L with an offer "subject to contract" of £100,000. L immediately queried the condition and at 10.50 S emailed, "Our offer is not conditional but there will have to be a sale contract." L emailed back at 11.08, explaining that S would be notified after midday that day if it were successful and that the selling process would be conducted using their standard terms and conditions. L then emailed S at 15.08 confirming that S had been successful with its offer for "£100,000 plus VAT", and seeking a written order in which S confirmed acceptance of L's terms and conditions. The email also referred to new tenants having moved into the premises housing the equipment. L expressed concern about the equipment in those circumstances whilst L continued to seek an order confirming sale based on its terms and conditions. On August 24 L stated that as they had not been able to agree an unconditional sale, it would look elsewhere. S maintained that there was a concluded agreement on August 19. The issues were (i) whether the parties had concluded a contract on August 19, 2011 and, if so, what its terms were; (ii) whether the contract was void for uncertainty; (iii) how any damages should be calculated.

Held: Judgment for claimant. (1) L's August 18 email defined the basis on which S was being invited to bid, that the bid requested was unequivocally one which would cover all the equipment under the three agreements, and included the console, not just the upgrades. The reference to a final offer demonstrated that L was asking for an offer capable of a clean acceptance so as to give rise to an immediately binding contract (see para.31 of judgment). A binding contract was concluded on August 19, 2011. Once the qualification in the offer by S, that it was made "subject to contract", was removed, the offer was one capable of being accepted, notwithstanding that it contemplated the execution of a further, more formal, document. To conclude that the 10.50 email of August 19 meant that no binding contract would be concluded until the sale contract referred to was executed would mean that the two parts of the sentence in the email contradicted each other. The 11.08 email contemplated that S would be notified if its bid were successful which, should such notification occur, could only mean that its offer had been accepted, so as to give rise to a binding contract. The email then explained the process which L contemplated for the drawing up of a formal contract. To determine whether the 15.08 email constituted an acceptance of S's offer or was a counter offer stating the terms on which L would be prepared to contract, it had to be read as a whole against the background of the case, and to be given a meaning which made commercial sense. Adopting that approach, the email was a clean acceptance of S's offer to purchase the equipment which gave rise to a binding contract. There was nothing in the fact that the 15.08 email referred to S's offer of "£100,000 plus VAT"; it was not intended as a counter-offer, but was merely a statement that L had understood S's offer to be to purchase the equipment for £100,000 plus VAT, rather than for a VAT-inclusive price (paras 43, 46-47, 50, 54). (2) The contract was not void for uncertainty. In particular, its subject matter was certain regarding both the inclusion of the console, not merely the upgrades, and the rest of the equipment to be sold (para.73). (3) In assessing the quantum of damages, the Sale of Goods Act 1979 s.51(3) was not available. New equipment could not be regarded as being equivalent to "the goods in question", which were secondhand goods and, although the availability of equivalent secondhand goods would have constituted an available market, it would have taken three months to source a similar console, which fell short of constituting an available market within the meaning of s.51(3). Therefore, damages had to be measured by reference to s.51(2). That S did not purchase replacement equipment did not mean that it had suffered no loss. Damages should be assessed by reference to the cost of procuring the nearest equivalent goods which in the instant case meant by reference to the cost of replacement secondhand equipment. To award damages by reference to the cost of new equipment would leave S materially better off (paras 92, 96, 98-99, 101, 103).

AIR STUDIOS (LYNDHURST) LTD (T/A AIR ENTERTAINMENT GROUP) v LOMBARD NORTH CENTRAL PLC, [2012] EWHC 3162 (QB), [2013] 1 Lloyd's Rep. 63, Males, J., QBD.

587. Good faith–Implied terms–Importance of recognising doctrine of good faith and fair dealing in contractual relationships

The claimant (Y), a company incorporated in Singapore, claimed damages for breach of contract and misrepresentation against the defendant (D), an English company. D had contacted Y in January 2009 inviting negotiations for a distribution agreement, stating that it had "recently signed" a licence agreement relating to the products that it sought to distribute. In fact, D only obtained the licence in May 2009, around the same time as the distribution agreement with Y was signed. The agreement granted Y exclusive rights to distribute certain fragrances and toiletries in a number of specified territories. The contract period was 30 months. Y terminated the agreement after 15 months because of a catalogue of alleged breaches by D: failing to ship orders promptly; failing to comply with contractual obligations to make products available; refusing to supply certain products after Y had marketed them; undercutting agreed prices; attempting to claw-back certain distribution rights; and providing false information in the knowledge that Y would rely on it. As well as contractual damages, Y also sought damages for misrepresentation on the ground that it had been induced to enter into the agreement by D's assertion that it was licensed at a time when it was not. The court was required to make individual, fact-specific findings about each of the alleged breaches in order to determine whether any were repudiatory and thereby sufficient to justify Y's termination of the contract. The primary issue, however, was whether a duty of good faith was to be implied into the contract.

Held: Judgment for claimant. (1) English contract law did not, historically, recognise a general duty to perform contracts in good faith, *Interfoto Picture Library Ltd v Stiletto Visual Programmes Ltd* [1989] Q.B. 433, [1988] C.L.Y. 430 and *Walford v Miles* [1992] 2 A.C. 128, [1992] C.L.Y. 514 applied. However, good faith and fair dealing were infiltrating English law from Europe, and the principle had been gaining ground in other common law jurisdictions. There was strong authority that it was recognised in Scottish law, *Smith v Bank of Scotland* 1997 S.C. (H.L.) 111, [1997] C.L.Y. 6087 referred to. Under English law, a duty of good faith, although not implied into all commercial contracts by default, could be implied based on the presumed intention of the parties and the relevant background against which the contract was made, *Attorney General of Belize v Belize Telecom Ltd* [2009] UKPC 10, [2009] 1 W.L.R. 1988 and *Investors Compensation Scheme Ltd v West Bromwich Building Society (No.1)* [1998] 1 W.L.R. 896, [1997] C.L.Y. 2537 applied. Relevant background included not only facts known to the parties, but also shared values and norms of behaviour, often taken as read at the time of entering into a contract but without being spelled out in the actual document. Fidelity to the parties' bargain was one of many generally accepted standards of commercial dealing that were central to good faith; contracts could not expressly provide for every possible event, so their language had to be given a reasonable construction which promoted the values and purposes expressed or implicit in the contract, *Berkeley Community Villages Ltd v Pullen* [2007] EWHC 1330 (Ch), [2007] 3 E.G.L.R. 101, [2008] C.L.Y. 665 and *CPC Group Ltd v Qatari Diar Real Estate Investment Co* [2010] EWHC 1535 (Ch), [2010] C.I.L.L. 2908 applied. An expectation of honesty was a norm underlying almost all contractual relationships, *HIH Casualty & General Insurance Ltd v Chase Manhattan Bank* [2003] UKHL 6, [2003] 1 All E.R. (Comm) 349, [2003] C.L.Y. 2461 applied. Making a false statement with the intention of deceiving someone would be dishonest in any context, but conduct falling short of a lie, such as deliberately avoiding giving an answer, or being generally evasive, might also be dishonest. Traditionally, English law had drawn a sharp distinction between fiduciary relationships containing onerous disclosure obligations, and other contractual relationships where there was supposedly no duty of disclosure. That dichotomy was arguably too simplistic: contracts involving a longer term relationship and substantial commitment required a high degree of communication, cooperation and predictable performance based on mutual trust and confidence. They involved expectations of loyalty, which were not legislated for in the express terms of the contract, but were implicit in the parties' understanding, and were necessary to give business efficacy to the arrangements. Examples of such "relational contracts" included joint venture agreements, franchise agreements and long-term distributorship agreements. Although its requirements were sensitive to context, the test of good faith was objective: it depended, not on a party's perception of whether conduct was improper, but on whether the conduct would be regarded as commercially unacceptable by reasonable and honest people, *Royal Brunei Airlines Sdn Bhd v Tan* [1995] 2 A.C. 378, [1995] C.L.Y. 2193 applied. The traditional English hostility towards a doctrine of good faith in the performance of contracts was misplaced for a number of cogent reasons (see paras 120-154 of judgment). (2) D had committed two repudiatory breaches of the distribution agreement, either of which would have justified Y's termination (paras 173-174). (3) The court detailed its approach to Y's claim for loss of profits (paras 177-185) and wasted expenditure (186-192). (4) Y was entitled to recover the same loss as damages for misrepresentation, having been induced into the distribution agreement by false representations that D already had a licence. The fact that the licence was ultimately signed by the time of the distribution agreement did not make the statement any the less false (paras 16-17, 28, 193-219, 230).

YAM SENG PTE LTD v INTERNATIONAL TRADE CORP LTD, [2013] EWHC 111 (QB), [2013] 1 All E.R. (Comm) 1321, Leggatt, J., QBD.

588. Guarantees–Enforcement–Four guarantors giving guarantee to bank–Guarantee unsigned by one guarantor–Effect on liability of remaining guarantors

The appellant (H) appealed against a decision of a district judge refusing to set aside a statutory demand served on him by the respondent bank (D). The statutory demand was based on a guarantee under which H and, on the face of it, three other individuals had guaranteed the liabilities of a property-development company. One of H's co-sureties (L) had asserted that he had not signed the guarantee; in his case, the statutory demand served on him had been set aside. H argued that there was a triable issue as between him and D: it had been contemplated by D and all the guarantors that all four guarantors would be parties to the guarantee, so that the absence of L's signature meant that there was no contract in existence between the parties.

Held: Appeal dismissed. The terms of the guarantee were apt to exclude the principle established in *James Graham & Co (Timber) Ltd v Southgate-Sands* [1986] Q.B. 80, [1985] C.L.Y. 1590 to the effect that, unless all the guarantors signed the guarantee, there would be no contract. Clause 4(a)(iv) provided that neither the obligations of a guarantor nor the rights, powers and remedies conferred on D in respect of a guarantor would be "discharged impaired or otherwise affected by... [any] failure to take or fully to take any security contemplated by or otherwise agreed to be taken in respect of the Principal Debtor's obligations to [D]". The words "any security" should be construed as they stood and meant any security contemplated by, for example, the property-development company's obligations to D, including the security given by the guarantee itself. Clause 15 of the guarantee expressly said that the liability, where signed by more than one party, would be joint and several and that "every agreement and undertaking on their part should be construed accordingly". In cl.16(e), the expression "guarantor" meant and included therefore every person liable under the guarantee or any one or more of them. Accordingly, cl.4(a) was to be approached on the basis that it was a provision that applied to all four of the guarantors jointly and to each of them individually. A failure to take security from one of the signatories did not therefore discharge, impair or otherwise affect the obligations of the other signatories. In the circumstances, H remained liable to D even if it turned out that L had never signed the guarantee, *Southgate-Sands* distinguished and *Bank of Scotland v Henry Butcher & Co* [2003] EWCA Civ 67, [2003] 2 All E.R. (Comm) 557, [2003] C.L.Y. 3044 considered (see paras 31, 42-45, 49 of judgment).

HARVEY v DUNBAR ASSETS PLC, [2012] EWHC 2890 (Ch), [2013] B.P.I.R. 66, Judge Kaye Q.C., Ch D (Newcastle).

589. Hire purchase–Acceleration clauses–Date from which time ran–Proper interpretation of agreement

The appellant company (B) appealed against the decision that its claim had been issued outside of the primary limitation period. B and the respondent (H) had entered into a hire purchase agreement in relation to a vehicle owned by B. Under the agreement, H was required to make monthly instalments and a final balloon payment at the end of the agreement. B was entitled to claim monies from H when a notice of termination had been served on him or it had communicated acceptance of his repudiation of the agreement. In July and August 1999, H failed to make two payments. In a letter dated August 26, 1999, B stated that it accepted H's repudiation of the agreement and it gave notice of its termination. Under the agreement, the letter was considered served on August 28, 1999. H left the United Kingdom without settling the sum owed and nothing further was done by B until it made a claim issued on August 26, 2005 and on which default judgment was entered against H. H only became aware of the judgment on his return to the UK in 2011 when he successfully set aside default judgment on the ground that the claim had been issued outside of the primary limitation period. In reaching its decision, the judge had applied *Reeves v Butcher* [1891] 2 Q.B. 509 and held that time had run from when H failed to make the monthly instalment in July 1999.

Held: Appeal allowed. The judge had erred in his interpretation of *Reeves* and his interpretation of the contract in the instant case. In *Reeves*, the agreement had stated the monies would not be called in provided the borrower regularly paid the interest and that accelerated repayment of the loan applied 21 days after the borrower had defaulted on a payment when it became lawful for the creditor to demand payment of the principal sum and any interest that had accrued in respect thereof. In the instant case, B had no right to make a claim until a termination notice had been given or it had communicated acceptance of H's repudiation. It was only upon service of the notice of termination or acceptance of the repudiation that the sum under the agreement became due. Before that, the only sum B was able to claim was the outstanding instalments. The failure to pay an instalment did not by itself accelerate the obligation to pay the whole amount outstanding, *Reeves* and *Hemp v Garland* 114 E.R. 994 distinguished.

BMW FINANCIAL SERVICE (GB) LTD v HART, [2012] EWCA Civ 1959, [2013] 2 Lloyd's Rep. 313, Rix, L.J., CA (Civ Div).

590. Illegal contracts–Resulting trusts–Claim wrongly struck out without consideration of Tinsley v Milligan (1994) 1 A.C. 340

The appellant (O) appealed against a decision striking out his claim against the respondent (F). O had transferred a property he owned to F to be held on trust for him. He did that because he was at risk of becoming bankrupt and he was advised that such a transaction could put the asset out of reach of the trustee in bankruptcy. F sold the property and O claimed against him for the net proceeds of sale. His claim was struck out on the ground that it was based on a transaction to defraud creditors, which was an illegal contract on which a claim could not be founded. O's case on appeal was that F held the property on resulting trust.

Held: Appeal allowed. O's claim had been struck out on the basis of the law as stated by Lord Eldon in *Muckleston v Brown* 31 E.R. 934; the judge did not refer to *Tinsley v Milligan* [1994] 1 A.C. 340, [1993] C.L.Y. 1839, which was the law, *Tinsley v Milligan* followed. O's case was not sufficiently different from *Tinsley v Milligan*. If the claimant in that case could recover property, so too could O. A party to an illegality could recover property if he could establish his ownership without relying on that illegality (see paras 9-10, 16-17 of judgment).

ADEPEGBA-OGIDAN v FAGADE, [2012] EWHC1714 (Ch), [2012] B.P.I.R. 943, Judge Birss Q.C., Ch D.

591. Illegality–Performance–Party repudiating contract and alleging illegality of performance–Scope of principle of intended illegality of performance

The appellant supermarket operator (S) appealed against the rejection of its defence of illegality to an action for repudiatory breach of contract brought against it by the respondent (P). P and S had entered into a 15-month contract whereby P was to install and operate a monitoring and control system in a number of S's supermarket car parks. S allowed its customers a certain amount of free parking time, and levied a charge on overstayers. P's system read the registration numbers of vehicles using the car parks and recorded how long each was parked. P then sent overstayers a series of pro-forma letters demanding payment of the charge. Although the contract did not prescribe the form of those letters, they had been approved by S before the contract was made. P received no payment from S; rather, it was entitled to retain all the overstay charges collected. S terminated the contract after some six months, by which time the system had been installed in 17 of its car parks. P claimed damages for loss of revenue resulting from the early termination of the contract. S defended the claim on the ground of illegality, claiming that one of P's pro-forma letters was deceptive and used illegal means to induce overstayers to pay. It argued that even though the overstayers were liable to pay, the deception tainted the whole contract and public policy required that it should be held unenforceable as a whole. The judge rejected that defence. He found that the third letter contained serious and deliberate falsehoods, and he found that P was guilty of the tort of deceit in respect of it. However, he was not satisfied that P had had, at the time of the execution of the contract, a firm and settled intention to act in an unlawful manner. He found that insofar as there had been an agreement on the form of the third letter, that agreement was collateral to the main contract, which in itself was free from illegality.

Held: Appeal dismissed. S relied on the principle, expressed in *Colen v Cebrian (UK) Ltd* [2003] EWCA Civ 1676, [2004] I.C.R. 568, [2004] C.L.Y. 1202, that a contract would be unenforceable if, at the time of its formation, one of the parties had the intention of performing it in an unlawful manner. However, that principle could not be read as applying to any intended illegality of performance, however partial or peripheral. Moreover, in *Colen* the court was not considering a case such as the instant one, where the intention was limited to only a partial and minor mode of performance, and was itself qualified in that it could be changed at any time, and would have been changed had the illegality been pointed out. The law was not in a straitjacket: it was not the case that once it was shown that illegality of any sort was intended at the outset, unenforceability would follow automatically, *Colen* and *St John Shipping Corp v*

Joseph Rank Ltd [1957] 1 Q.B. 267, [1956] C.L.Y. 8303 considered. In considering the proper scope and application of the principle, a number of factors had to be considered: the object and intent of the party seeking to enforce the contract; the centrality and gravity of the illegality in the context of the contract and the claim; and the nature of the illegality. In the instant case, the contract was not all or nothing, legal or illegal, as regards its performance or its intended performance. Rather, it involved continuous performance over time, which was never intended to be carried out in a wholly illegal manner. On the contrary, its performance could be, had been intended to be, and in fact had been, carried out mainly lawfully. S's argument would lead to the disproportionate result that its wrongful repudiation of the contract left P with no remedy for a lost income that would have been wholly lawful. The judge had thus been right to reject S's illegality defence; P had had no fixed intention of acting unlawfully, and the illegality was incidental to only part of the performance of the contract and was far from central to it. Once S had become aware of the objectionable nature of the third letter, the proper course would have been for it to have drawn it to P's attention and to have honoured the contract on the provision that P perform it in a lawful manner. To allow S to repudiate would be to give it a windfall reward for its own previous illegality (see paras 30-32, 35, 37-40, 63-65, 69, 72, 75, 77-79).

PARKINGEYE LTD v SOMERFIELD STORES LTD, [2012] EWCA Civ 1338, [2013] Q.B. 840, Laws, L.J., CA (Civ Div).

592. Implied incorporation–Arbitration clauses–Arbitral tribunal deciding it had jursidiction because arbitration clause impliedly incorporated in agreement–Obviousness of parties' intention to include clause in agreement–Appropriateness of setting aside tribunal's award

The applicant (L) applied to set aside an arbitral tribunal's award made in favour of the respondent (C). L and C had entered into a ship repair fleet agreement. The agreement did not contain an express arbitration agreement, nor did it refer to L's general conditions of contract which included an arbitration clause. C claimed that L owed it rebates pursuant to their agreement. The tribunal's majority held that it had jurisdiction to entertain C's claim because the agreement incorporated L's general conditions, including the arbitration clause. It concluded that there was such a close relationship between the agreement and the general conditions, because the terms of the agreement amended, altered or superseded the conditions, that they had to be interpreted as one contract. It also held, applying the officious bystander test, that neither party could have anticipated that the arbitration clause would not apply to the agreement. The issue was whether the tribunal was correct to rule that the agreement incorporated the arbitration clause.

Held: Application granted. The relevant question was not whether it would have been reasonable for the parties to have agreed to incorporate the arbitration clause, but whether they must have intended to include it, *Trollope & Colls Ltd v North West Metropolitan Regional Hospital Board* [1973] 1 W.L.R. 601, [1973] C.L.Y. 270 followed. The instant case was not one of an informal contract following a succession of more formal contracts in which a set of terms had been incorporated, but involved a formal and detailed contractual document which did not even refer to the general conditions. Further, C did not seek incorporation of the general conditions as a whole, but only the arbitration clause. Those factors made it necessary to exercise greater caution than might otherwise have been appropriate before it was possible to conclude that the parties intended to incorporate into their agreement a clause to which they had not referred in the agreement itself. There was a fundamental difference between implying a term in circumstances where the parties regarded the application of the relevant contractual term as being obvious, and had not expressly mentioned it because it had been assumed and intended by both parties, and where the parties could not be regarded as having formed any intent about the matter. In the instant case, it was impossible to conclude that it was obvious that the parties intended that the arbitration clause was to apply to the agreement. Although there was a strong inter-relationship between the agreement and the general conditions, the closeness of the relationship did not make it obvious that the parties must have intended that the arbitration clause would be applicable to the agreement. Whilst there was at least the potential for some dispute between L and C as to the application of the terms of the agreement or their operation, it was not obvious that the potential for dispute would have been at the forefront of the parties' minds, and, objectively, it was possible that they simply did not address their minds to the potential for dispute. The language of the agreement was not consistent with an intention to incorporate any part of the conditions. The award was set aside, and a declaration was made to the effect that the tribunal did not have jurisdiction over C's claim (see paras 32, 39, 41, 44, 48-49, 53-54 of judgment).

LISNAVE ESTALEIROS NAVAIS SA v CHEMIKALIEN SEETRANSPORT GmbH, [2013] EWHC 338 (Comm), [2013] 2 Lloyd's Rep. 203, Colin Edelman Q.C., QBD (Comm).

593. **Implied terms–Purpose clauses–Whether purpose clause could be read into agreement to bring it within s.12(b) Consumer Credit Act 1974**

[Consumer Credit Act 1974 (c.39) s.11 (1) (b), s.12 (b); Consumer Credit (Exempt Agreements) Order 1989 (SI 1989/869) Art.3 (1) (a) (i).]

The appellant (C) appealed against a recorder's decision that its loan agreement with the respondents (D) was not an exempt agreement under the Consumer Credit (Exempt Agreements) Order 1989 art.3 (1) (a) (i). C, along with associated companies Bankruptcy Protection Fund (BPF) and Alpha Mortgage Brokers (AMB), restructured the debt of individual bankrupts who had owned property. On instructions from the bankrupt, BPF would annul the bankruptcy by arranging to pay off the creditors. Once the annulment was obtained C would provide the funds to pay off the creditors, and pay BPF's fees and solicitors' fees. The funds were a loan from C to the bankrupt secured by a second charge on the bankrupt's property, which the bankrupt was to repay in three months, during which time AMB would arrange a mortgage loan sufficient for the bankrupt to repay C. D entered into such an arrangement with C. The loan agreement contained a purpose clause stating, "The loan is to be used for purposes of refinancing the debt." No express term of the agreement set out the financing mechanism. C argued that there was an implied term in the agreement that its purpose was to finance a transaction between the debtor and a supplier other than the creditor, which would have brought the agreement within the ambit of the Consumer Credit Act 1974 s.11 (1) (b) and s.12 (b), making the agreement exempt under art.3 (1) (a) (i) of the 1989 Order.

Held: Appeal dismissed. If a term was not stated in an agreement, the usual presumption was that it was not intended to be there. Courts looked very critically at arguments that terms had to be implied into agreements that imposed additional obligations on the parties, *Attorney General of Belize v Belize Telecom Ltd* [2009] UKPC 10, [2009] 1 W.L.R. 1988 and *Stena Line Ltd v Merchant Navy Ratings Pension Fund Trustees Ltd* [2011] EWCA Civ 543, [2011] Pens. L.R. 223, [2011] C.L.Y. 2350 applied. The express purpose clause in the instant agreement was circular and meaningless because the debt and the loan were the same thing. In those circumstances it was difficult if not impossible to establish that there was any other purpose that had been agreed between the parties or that could be properly implied. Rather, the inference was that the express purpose clause had been the intended purpose, even though it turned out to be ineffective, and that no other purpose had been intended. A meaningless purpose clause could not provide support for another purpose such that the new purpose could be derived from it, even if they were in the same ballpark. Additionally, the agreement could have been performed in several ways; nothing in the agreement itself mandated that it be performed in the manner of the proposed implied term. Also, the proposed implied term lacked the necessary precision and detail to make it workable and determine its consequences. To imply a term the court had to know what it actually was, and the fact that it had been expressed in several ways in the instant court and below created doubt that it was a term that could be implied, *Belize* applied. Finally, a loan agreement could work perfectly well without a purpose clause.

Although the purpose clause in the instant case did not work, there was no reason that the agreement could not work without it. There was no need to create additional binding obligations on the parties as would be created by the proposed implied term. The only reason for having it was to bring the agreement within the meaning of s.12(b) of the 1974 Act so that the exemption could be applied (see paras 16, 35, 37, 38, 40, 41 of judgment).

CONSOLIDATED FINANCE LTD v McCLUSKEY, [2012] EWCA Civ 1325, [2012] C.T.L.C. 133, Laws, L.J., CA (Civ Div).

594. Indemnity clauses–Consent judgments–Purchaser's liability under asset purchase agreement for judgment against purchased company–Availability of estoppel

The appellant company in liquidation (R) appealed against two decisions ([2010] EWHC 3243 (TCC), [2011] 1 All E.R. (Comm) 951, [2011] 7 C.L. 86 and [2011] EWHC 1622 (TCC), [2011] P.N.L.R. 33, [2011] C.L.Y. 558) in favour of the respondent (P). A property development company (E) had engaged R to provide geotechnical engineering services in connection with the development of a shopping centre. R subsequently ceased to trade, and R and P entered into an asset purchase agreement, under which P assumed "responsibility for the satisfaction, fulfilment and discharge of all the outstanding liabilities and contracts of R's business" and indemnified R "against all proceedings, claims and demands" in respect of such liabilities. Ten years later, E claimed against R, alleging that R's advice in connection with the development was negligent and had led to buildings on the site suffering damage. R later went into creditors' voluntary liquidation, and P took over the defence of the claim. P consented to judgment being entered in favour of E against R for a total sum of around £8m. R's liquidators later claimed against P on the indemnities in respect of the consent judgment. In December 2010, the judge decided that any liability owed by R to E did not fall within the scope of the indemnity clause because such liability had not been reflected in R's accounts, and therefore R could not rely on the consent judgment to establish that its liability to E was actual, unless the circumstances leading to the judgment gave rise to an estoppel. In June 2011, a judge held that P was not estopped from denying that the consent judgment reflected the true state of affairs between R and E, and consequently that if E wanted to prove that R was liable to it, it had to prove its case. P argued that (1) the judge's construction of the asset purchase agreement was correct: unless liability was founded, then it did not fall within the indemnity clause; (2) regarding estoppel, it would not be unjust for E to prove its case, and it was only fair to take into account the fact that it had acted under a mistaken view as to its potential liability under the asset purchase agreement.

Held: Appeals allowed. (1) The court was not persuaded that the ordering of the wording in the indemnity clause had the effect that the judge had held that it did, namely because the reference to "liabilities" preceded the reference to "proceedings, claims and demands". The indemnity clause was capable of including settlements of claims. P had not only consented to the judgment in E's favour, but had also instructed R to submit to judgment being entered against it. It was unnecessary for R to rely on estoppel: it could simply say against P that it had liability to E under the judgment P caused it to enter. The underlying justification for that conclusion was that it should not be open to a party who caused judgment to be entered in the belief that it was in its financial interests to challenge the reasonableness of it when it later perceived its commercial interests differently (see paras 18, 22-23 of judgment). (2) P's motivation to prefer its interests over those of R's potential creditors was not a factor that should be taken into account in P's favour. On the contrary, it had to be remembered that once a company became insolvent, the shareholders' interests were secondary to the rights of the creditors. It did not matter that P acted under a mistaken view as to the effect of the asset purchase agreement; that was not a reason in itself to disapply the natural consequence of the choice it made (paras 25-26).

RUST CONSULTING LTD (IN LIQUIDATION) v PB LTD, [2012] EWCA Civ 1070, [2012] B.L.R. 427, Rix, L.J., CA (Civ Div).

595. Payments–Estoppel–Contractor seeking payment on basis not mentioned in contract–Employer applying to strike out claim–Nature of contractor's reliance on doctrine of estoppel

[Civil Procedure Rules 1998 (SI 1998/3132) r.3.4(2)(a).]

The appellant (S), a housing partnership, appealed against a refusal ([2013] EWHC 27 (TCC), [2013] B.L.R. 181, [2013] 7 C.L. 78) to strike out a claim issued against it by the respondent (M) for monies due. S and M had entered into a contract whereby M would repair and maintain S's properties. It was M's case that they had agreed that M would be paid on the basis of what were known as "Composite Rates", and that although the contract, as signed, did not permit payment on that basis, S had stated that there was no need to amend the contract to take account of it. In 2010, when M claimed payment for work done, S deducted £300,000 from the amount claimed on the basis that M had wrongly claimed payment on the basis of the Composite Rates. M began proceedings to recover the sum deducted. It relied on the principles of estoppel by convention and estoppel by representation, given that S had made payment on the Composite Rates for more than 13,000 jobs between July 2009 and January 2010. It also relied on misrepresentation in relation to S's assurance that the contract did not need amending. S's application under CPR r.3.4(2)(a) to strike out the claim was refused. The judge held that it would be wrong to second-guess the evidential strength of the case without the benefit of mutual disclosure and witness evidence, and that it was reasonably arguable that estoppel and misrepresentation might apply. S submitted that (1) the judge had wrongly confused the approach to an application under r.3.4.2(a) with that of an application for summary judgment; (2) M's claims were doomed to failure by the existence of an entire agreement clause; (3) M could not rely upon estoppel to illegitimately seek to create a cause of action where none existed, and to subvert the doctrine of consideration.

Held: Appeal dismissed. (1) The judge had applied the right test to the strike-out application and had been right to decide that the claim as pleaded satisfied the requisite test (see paras 11-13 of judgment). (2) It was realistically arguable that the "entire agreement" clause did not operate as a bar to M's claim, particularly if it could be established that there had been an understanding that no amendment was needed to the contract to revise the pricing structure, and that payment had been made on the Composite Rates basis previously. Also, an entire agreement clause did not operate as a bar to a claim in misrepresentation and, arguably, not to an estoppel argument, *AXA Sun Life Services Plc v Campbell Martin Ltd* [2011] EWCA Civ 133, [2012] Bus. L.R. 203, [2011] C.L.Y. 551 applied and *Springwell Navigation Corp v JP Morgan Chase Bank (formerly Chase Manhattan Bank)* [2010] EWCA Civ 1221, [2010] 2 C.L.C. 705, [2011] C.L.Y. 193 considered (paras 14-18). (3) It was to be assumed, for the purposes of the strike-out application, that S had paid M in accordance with the Composite Rates between July 2009 and January 2010. At trial, the onus would be on S to support its £300 deduction by way of legitimate set-off. It was not a question of M seeking to use estoppel as a sword, but of there needing to be a detailed factual analysis of how M had been paid, and the basis on which its services had been provided. Such an enquiry could only be conducted at trial; a strike-out application on the basis of uncertain, undetermined facts was not an appropriate arena for the resolution of conflict (paras 20-24)

MEARS LTD v SHORELINE HOUSING PARTNERSHIP LTD; *sub nom.* SHORELINE HOUSING PARTNERSHIP LTD v MEARS LTD, [2013] EWCA Civ 639, [2013] C.P. Rep. 39, McCombe, L.J., CA (Civ Div).

596. Sale of property–Retention money–Retention of part of purchase price–Interpretation of retention clause

The appellant building company (R) appealed against a decision and consequential order dismissing its claim for payment of sums retained from the sale price of a property owned and occupied by the respondents (C). R had been engaged by a company (F) to carry out building work on the property that F had acquired, which C agreed to buy. The agreement contained a number of special conditions. The local planning authority granted planning permission for the second floor of the property to be larger than that agreed during consultation. F and the local authority then agreed that the second floor would be the size agreed during consultation and that any alteration to it would be precluded by a s.106 agreement. To enable completion on the agreed date, despite outstanding matters on the snagging list that C had produced, R, F and C entered into three separate but related agreements. F and C entered into a supplemental agreement which provided that C should retain £35,000 of the purchase price. Clause 3.1.3 stated that the retention would be paid to F immediately upon the last of the following events: completion of the s.106 agreement; satisfactory completion of the works referred to in the agreement between R and C (the second agreement); and completion of the work by R. Clause 1.1 of the second agreement required R to complete the items on the snagging list. Completion occurred but C kept the retention, claiming that there had never been a s.106 agreement as the smaller second floor superseded the need for a s.106 agreement; and that not all of the snagging items had been remedied. C wrote to F asserting that the conditions in the supplemental agreement had not been met as no s.106 agreement had been reached, and that the supplemental and second agreements had been breached, and that damages would exceed the retention amount. R issued proceedings against F for outstanding payment. The matter was settled and F assigned its causes of action against C to R. R issued proceedings against C claiming the retention as due under the supplemental agreement or as damages for breach of it. The judge held that the preconditions in cl.3.1.3 had to be satisfied before the retention became payable and that they had not been satisfied. R submitted that on the correct interpretation of the supplemental agreement and in the event of non-fulfilment of any of the conditions within cl.3.1.3, C's remedy was a financial one, and that the retention was payable subject to an indemnity in respect of any loss and damage they had suffered. C contended that in the event that one or more of the events in cl.3.1.3 did not occur within a reasonable time or at all, no part of the retention would be payable to F.

Held: Appeal allowed. The interpretation that C attributed to the agreement would have led to an absurd result: they would be entitled to retain the retention and an indemnity and damages in respect of any breach, which would not be payable from the retention. That amounted to double recovery and deprived the retention of its real purpose. The parties' intention as to cl.3 of the supplemental agreement, although not fully stated, was clear. The purpose of the retention was to act as a security by ensuring that C had a sum available from which to indemnify themselves in respect of any loss or damage that they might suffer through a failure by F or R to address the outstanding items referred to in the supplemental agreement. C were obliged to give F a reasonable opportunity to fulfil its outstanding obligations and ensure that the events in cl 3.1.3 occurred. If F failed to meet its obligations, C were entitled to an indemnity in respect of any loss or damage suffered as a result. The balance of the retention would be payable to F as the outstanding part of the purchase price. While not expressly stated that was the understanding that any reasonable person would have of the agreement read against the relevant background as a whole. Therefore, the judge erred in how he construed the supplemental agreement. He should have found that R was entitled to the retention subject to a set off of any loss or damage suffered by C resulting from F and R's failure to perform their obligations (see paras 37-38, 40-41 of judgment).

RELICPRIDE BUILDING CO LTD v CORDARA, [2013] EWCA Civ 158, 147 Con. L.R. 92, Lord Dyson (M.R.), CA (Civ Div).

597. Standard terms–Incorporation–Contract for freight forwarding services–Whether incorporating BIFA standard terms and conditions–Applicability of anti-set-off clause to overpayments

The defendant (T) applied for summary judgment on its counterclaim in proceedings brought against it by the claimant (S). T was a freight forwarder which had entered into a contract with S for the supply of services. In January 2010 the parties had orally agreed that T would provide freight forwarding services subject to the provisions of a "service agreement". The service agreement was not a formal contract and it contained only a series of headings, without detail. The parties also agreed that T would draw up a document evidencing their contract, which it did in June 2010. That document expressly incorporated the standard trading conditions of the British International Freight Association (BIFA). The parties proceeded to do business, and between March 2010 and September 2011 T sent a number of invoices to S, all of which clearly set out the incorporation of the BIFA terms and conditions. A number of disputes arose between the parties. S challenged the amount of interest due under the invoices and issued debit notes on the basis of T's alleged failures in performance. In response, T exercised a lien over S's freight, whereupon S paid the charges due and began proceedings against T for the alleged performance failures. T counterclaimed for VAT paid on freight that had been redelivered to S. The central issue on the counterclaim was whether the BIFA terms and conditions were incorporated into the contract. That was significant because they contained an anti-set-off clause which would work to prevent S from withholding moneys due to T. S submitted that (1) an agreement had been concluded in January 2010 which did not incorporate the BIFA terms and conditions, and everything that happened after January was irrelevant; (2) even if the BIFA terms and conditions were incorporated, the anti-set-off clause did not bite because there had been a running account between the parties.

Held: Application granted. (1) The instant case was not one in which an invoice with new terms had followed a concluded contract effected by a clear offer and acceptance on standard terms. Rather, only the outline terms had been agreed in January 2010, with detailed terms and conditions following on by way of incorporation from a series of dealings on the basis of T's invoices. There had been an extensive course of dealings on the basis of the invoices and nothing to the contrary had ever been agreed. It would be obvious to anybody dealing with a freight forwarder that there would be standard terms and conditions applying above and beyond the matters agreed in January 2010. At no time before issuing the instant proceedings had S raised any issue about the incorporation of the BIFA terms and conditions and the services supplied, the invoices submitted and the payments made in the context thereof (see paras 13-14 of judgment). (2) While it was right that S had sometimes made payments without reference to the invoices, that was irrelevant. The reality was that at all times invoices had been rendered for services allegedly provided, and money had passed in only one direction, unless there had been an overpayment or a mischarging of some kind. The situation simply did not give rise to a running account, and there was no easy way for S to avoid the anti-set-off clause by that device. Furthermore, there was nothing to prevent the clause from applying to overpayments. Honest accounting errors resulting in overpayments by a customer were not intrinsically different from any other basis of liability, short of fraud. There were no allegations of fraud in the instant case and there was no material difference between an honest accounting error and a situation where, in the absence of fraud, something had gone wrong so that services were charged for but not provided. There was nothing in S's claim which made it one to which the anti-set-off clause could not apply. Finally, the anti-set-off clause was not unreasonable. While the burden was on T to show that it was reasonable, it was a common-form clause and there was nothing particularly onerous about it. It was a cash flow clause: the customer could bring a claim but had to pay upfront for services rendered, and that was exactly the sort of clause which was to be expected in the context of a freight forwarding agreement. Moreover, S had adduced no evidence to establish its unreasonableness. There was nothing about the clause that would offend against the Unfair Contract Terms Act 1977, *Rohlig (UK) Ltd v Rock Unique Ltd* [2011] EWCA Civ 18, [2011] 2 All E.R. (Comm) 1161, [2012] C.L.Y. 644 followed and *Stewart Gill Ltd v Horatio Myer and Co Ltd* [1992] Q.B. 600, [1992] C.L.Y. 510 considered (paras 20-21, 26-28). (3) It was clear that S had no realistic prospect of successfully defending the counterclaim, and in those circumstances T had to be entitled to summary judgment on it. That was not to say, however, that S was not in a position to pursue its claims for T's alleged failures in performance (paras 35-36).

SKNL (UK) LTD v TOLL GLOBAL FORWARDING, [2012] EWHC 4252 (Comm), [2013] 2 Lloyd's Rep. 115, Cooke, J., QBD (Comm).

598. Termination–Instalments–Entitlement of seller to instalments paid and due at termination–Application of penalty principle–Whether buyer entitled to relief against forfeiture

The claimant (C) claimed sums said to be due under a settlement agreement in respect of the sale of two gas stripping plants. The plants had been constructed by the defendant (G). G had agreed to sell them to C for use by its subsidiaries in the Ukraine. Disputes arose between the parties and proceedings were commenced. They were settled by an agreement which acknowledged that property in the plants was vested in C and provided for G to buy them back with a view to resale. The price of US$37.5 million was payable by instalments and property was not to pass until payment of the total price. If G failed to pay any instalment then C had the right under cl.22 of the agreement to terminate without prejudice to any accrued rights under the agreement or its right to claim damages for breach. G paid instalments totalling $7.5 million but did not pay further sums due. C gave notice of termination. It claimed to be entitled to retain the $7.5 million that had been paid at the date of termination, to recover the further instalments, totalling $20 million, which had accrued due and payable at the date of termination, and to claim damages for breach of contract. G maintained that C was obliged to make restitution of the $7.5 million and could not recover the further instalments; if C was entitled to those sums, G sought relief against forfeiture; C had suffered no loss and was entitled to nominal damages only, since the plants had a value of $40-48 million.

Held: Judgment for claimant. (1) As a matter of construction the agreement made it plain that C's accrued rights were to be unaffected by the exercise of the right of termination and that such accrued rights included the right to retain the amounts already paid and to recover the outstanding payments at the date of termination (see paras 18-21 of judgment). (2) Where the contract explicitly provided for the circumstances in which benefits would or would not be returned, as cl.22 did in the instant case, there was no room for the restitutionary claim on which G relied (para.27). (3) The essential purpose of a penalty provision was to deter breaches of contract and therefore the penalty principle applied only to provisions which took effect on breach and not to sums which became payable on events other than breach, *Export Credits Guarantee Department v Universal Oil Products Co* [1983] 1 W.L.R. 399, [1983] C.L.Y. 434 followed and *Workers Trust & Merchant Bank Ltd v Dojap Investments Ltd* [1993] A.C. 573, [1993] C.L.Y. 526 considered. Thus the penalty principle had no application to the obligation on G to pay the instalments which preceded and was quite independent of any breach (paras 32-35). (4) On the assumption that the court could order relief against forfeiture, it would not be right to order the return of the $7.5 million to G and to refuse to allow C to recover the further sum of US$20m in debt, pending sale of the plants. In the circumstances the court had to proceed on the basis that C was prima facie entitled to the sum of $27.5m, no buyer had yet been found for the plants and their present value was uncertain. The demands of justice would be fully satisfied by upholding C's rights to retain the sum paid of $7.5m and to recover the further sum of US$20m in debt and ordering that any further net sums that might be recovered by way of sale of the plants up to a maximum of $10m plus interest be paid to C with the balance, if any, paid into court or otherwise secured pending further order or agreement. C's claim for damages would be adjourned, with liberty to apply (paras 39-41).

CADOGAN PETROLEUM HOLDINGS LTD v GLOBAL PROCESS SYSTEMS LLC, [2013] EWHC 214 (Comm), [2013] 2 Lloyd's Rep. 26, Eder, J., QBD (Comm).

CRIMINAL EVIDENCE

599. Admissibility–Bad character–Admissibility of bad character evidence concerning witness–Possibility of trial within trial–Relevant factors when assessing probative value

[Criminal Justice Act 2003 (c.44) s.100(1)(b), s.101(3), s.109.]

The appellant police officer (D) appealed against his conviction for misconduct in public office and perverting the course of justice. D was a Commander in the Metropolitan police. He had arrested a man (W) for a public order offence after arguing with him outside a restaurant. There was a history of ill-feeling between the two men. W alleged that D had misused his power and arrested him when there was no cause to do so. D was tried for making false complaints and arresting W on spurious grounds. A fresh trial was ordered because evidence of W's bad character had not been put before the jury. In the second trial the jury was told that W had a conviction for fraud, he had lied on oath, had used false documents to obtain entry into the United Kingdom, and had hit a man in the face with a broken bottle during a fight in a nightclub. The judge refused to allow evidence to be adduced that W had raped his girlfriend and had slapped her around the face in a nightclub. D submitted that the excluded evidence provided substantive probative value in relation to the critical issue of W's credibility and his propensity to indulge in violence.

Held: Appeal dismissed. (1) The Criminal Justice Act 2003 s.101(3) prevented the admission of bad character evidence against a defendant if its admission would have "such an unfair effect on the fairness of the proceedings that it ought not to be admitted." In the context of the bad character of a non-defendant, there was no exclusionary discretion available to the judge, once he was satisfied that the pre-conditions to admissibility were met. When assessing the probative value of the bad character evidence for the purposes of s.100(1)(b) the judge was required by s.109 to assume that the allegations were true. The s.109 assumption provided the context in which the admissibility decision fell to be made but it was not determinative of the issue. The bare fact of an allegation, even if assumed to be true, was not necessarily conclusive of whether it constituted substantial probative evidence or evidence of substantial importance in the context of the case as a whole, *R. v Braithwaite (Stephen)* [2010] EWCA Crim 1082, [2010] 2 Cr. App. R. 18, [2011] C.L.Y. 578 applied. A trial concerning whether the defendant had committed a crime was liable to be derailed if the jury was required to decide whether a witness had committed a separate crime. Section 109 did not bind the jury, but they could not consider the alleged bad character evidence unless they were sure that it was true. That could lead to two trials being simultaneously in progress before the same jury: the trial of the defendant for the crime alleged by the prosecution, and the trial of the witness for the crime alleged by the defendant. Those matters were relevant considerations bearing on the assessment of the probative value of the evidence sought to be adduced, and its importance in the overall context of the case. When assessing the probative value of the evidence, the court should reflect upon whether the admission of the bad character evidence relating to the witness might make it difficult for the jury to understand the remainder of the evidence, and whether its understanding of the case as a whole might be diminished (see paras 31-38 of judgment). (2) The rape allegation had been bitterly contested by W. In the context of a trial in which W was alleged to have given D justifiable grounds for arresting him, and D was alleged to have none, it did not satisfy the pre-conditions for admissibility under s.100(1)(b). The allegation that W had slapped his girlfriend did satisfy those conditions. It was an incident of unpleasant violence in a public place. It was less serious than the incident already before the jury in connection with W's bad character, but it would have served to reinforce the contention that, when crossed, W was disposed to violence in public. The domestic nature of the incident did not reduce its probative value to the issues. However, even taken at its highest, the excluded evidence did not begin to undermine the powerful body of evidence, independent of W, such as the CCTV footage, which served to prove that D's guilty verdict was fully justified. D's conviction was safe (paras 40-42).

R. v DIZAEI (JAMSHID ALI), [2013] EWCA Crim 88, [2013] 1 W.L.R. 2257, Lord Judge, L.C.J., CA (Crim Div).

600. Admissibility–Hearsay evidence–Correct approach to admissibility of hearsay evidence in criminal trials

[Criminal Justice Act 2003 (c.44) s.114(2), s.114(1)(d), s.116(4)(c), s.116, s.124, s.125.]

In five conjoined criminal appeals, the court considered the correct approach to determining the admission of hearsay evidence in criminal trials.

Held: Appeals allowed in part. (1) The common law prohibition on the admission of hearsay evidence remained the default rule. The Criminal Justice Act 2003, although widening the categories of hearsay which might be admitted, did not elevate hearsay to the same level as first-hand evidence. *R. v Horncastle (Michael Christopher)* [2009] UKSC 14, [2010] 2 A.C. 373, [2010] C.L.Y. 658 was not to be construed as meaning that hearsay evidence had to be shown to be reliable or independently verified before it could be admitted or left to the jury. For the purposes of a Crown Court dealing with such cases on a day-to-day basis, five propositions deriving from *Horncastle* and subsequent case law were central: (a) the law was as stated in the Act, to which there was a six-step approach (see para.7 of judgment); (b) in case of conflict between *Horncastle* and *Al-Khawaja v United Kingdom (26766/05)* [2012] 2 Costs L.O. 139, [2012] C.L.Y. 657, a domestic court was obliged to follow the former; (c) although the importance of the hearsay evidence to the case was a vital consideration, there was no overarching rule that hearsay evidence which was "sole or decisive" was automatically inadmissible; (d) Crown Court judges generally needed to look no further than the Act and *Horncastle;* (e) neither the Act nor *Horncastle* permitted hearsay evidence to be automatically admissible as if it were first-hand evidence, *Horncastle* followed and *Al-Khawaja* considered (paras 2-8). (2) With regard to the statutory gateways permitting the admission of hearsay evidence, it was clear from s.116 of the Act that a reason for resorting to second-hand evidence had to be shown, for example, a witness's illness or death. Absence abroad would only suffice if it was not reasonably practicable to bring the witness to court in person or by video link. If a witness was lost, reasonably practicable steps must have been taken, not only to find him, but also to keep in touch with him before he disappeared. Where a witness was in fear of giving evidence, s.116(4)(c) required consideration of special measures. The observations of the instant court in *R. v Horncastle (Michael Christopher)* [2009] EWCA Crim 964, [2009] 4 All E.R. 183, [2009] C.L.Y. 761 paras 83-88 had also to be considered. Where a specific gateway for admission was passed, the court had then to consider the reliability of the evidence and the practicability of the jury testing its reliability, to which s.124 was critical (paras 9-18). Where a specific gateway was not passed, there was a general residual power to admit hearsay evidence under s.114(1)(d) subject to the non-exhaustive considerations in s.114(2). Even if hearsay evidence was prima facie admissible, it had not to be simply "nodded through"; it could still be ruled inadmissible under s.126 of the Act or under the Police and Criminal Evidence Act s.78 (paras 19-25). The evidence could also be stopped under s.125 of the 2003 Act, *R. v Ibrahim (Dahir)* [2012] EWCA Crim 837, [2012] 4 All E.R. 225, [2012] C.L.Y. 653 explained (paras 26-33). (3) In R's case, which concerned sexual offences committed by a teacher against a 13-year-old pupil who had died before the trial, statements from the deceased had been rightly admitted because they were strongly supported by other evidence and did not stand as bare, untestable allegations (paras 34-38). In D's case, where an elderly householder had died before D's trial for robbery and theft at his property was concluded, a video-recorded interview had been properly admitted (paras 39-43). In W's case, where he was charged with assault occasioning actual bodily harm and the complainant and two witnesses feared giving evidence at trial, it had been unfair to admit their statements because the fear gateway had not been established (paras 44-62). In C's case, the statement of a three-year-old victim of a sexual assault had been properly admitted even though there had been no assessment of her ability to be interviewed under Achieving Best Practice conditions. Her statement did not stand alone, and her very strong reaction to examination or enquiry was a powerful reason, at her age, not to trouble her further (paras 63-73). In B's case, a conviction of sexual activity by a psychiatric nurse with a person with a mental disorder was safe where the victim's statements were admitted under the s.116(2)(b) gateway to support other evidence (paras 74-81).

R. v RIAT (JASPAL); R. v DORAN (JAMES); R. v WILSON (MARTIN PAUL); R. v CLARE (WILLIAM HENRY); R. v BENNETT (JOHN), [2012] EWCA Crim 1509, [2013] 1 W.L.R. 2592, Hughes, L.J., CA (Crim Div).

601. Admissibility–Identification–Victim identifying attacker by nickname and address–Admissibility of information in police intelligence system supporting victim's evidence

[Criminal Justice Act 2003 (c.44) s.117, s.117(7); Police and Criminal Evidence Act 1984 (c.60) s.78.]

The appellant (G) appealed by way of case stated against a decision of a magistrates' court to admit certain evidence upon which it subsequently relied in identifying him as the perpetrator of an assault. The victim (V) had said that she knew G as her attacker because they had been brought up in the same area; she knew his first name; her parents lived or used to live in the same road as him; and he went by the street name "Nasty". The prosecution adduced evidence that a check had been conducted on a computer record of intelligence information received by officers of the Metropolitan Police in the course of their work. The check revealed that the street name "Nasty" was linked to G's name and the address that V had provided for him. The magistrates considered the Criminal Justice Act 2003 s.117 and concluded that the extract from the intelligence system was a business document and that its reliability was not doubtful. They admitted the information and relied on it to find that G was V's attacker. The issue was whether it was legitimate for them to have admitted the information as evidence. G challenged the admissibility of the information on the basis of s.117(2)(b). He argued that it could not be ascertained, without an identification of the person who had added the information to the intelligence system, that that person had or might reasonably be supposed to have had personal knowledge of the relevant matters, namely that G went by the street name Nasty and was linked to the relevant address. G contended that the absence of such an identification was fatal to the reliability of the information and the magistrates had erred in relying on it.

Held: Appeal dismissed. The importance of the information came from linking G not only with the name "Nasty" but also with a particular address. Those two features were linked and, coupled with V's physical identification matching G, there was powerful evidence that G was the individual known as "Nasty". Further, there was evidence that G had been arrested at the address given in the system, which indicated that the person who had supplied the information to the system had personal knowledge of that information. V had linked G to the name "Nasty" because she knew him by that name. Moreover, that name was linked to an address in the system which V had independently provided. The magistrates were entitled to conclude that the supplier of the information in the intelligence system had personal knowledge of the relevant matters. No separate point could be made that the information should have been excluded because it was unreliable under either s.117(7) or the Police and Criminal Evidence Act 1984 s.78. The information was contained in a business document and the magistrates had not erred in law in allowing it to be admitted and relying on it (see paras 12-18 of judgment).

GRAZETTE v DPP, [2012] EWHC 3863 (Admin), (2013) 177 J.P. 259, Moses, L.J., DC.

602. Admissibility–Previous convictions–Fatal injuries to victim–Previous conviction for grievous bodily harm–Admissibility at murder trial

[Civil Evidence Act 1968 (c.64); Offences against the Person Act 1861 (c.100) s.18; Police and Criminal Evidence Act 1984 (c.60) s.78.]

The appellants (C and H) appealed against their convictions for murder. In 2000, C had attacked the victim (V) with a screwdriver which penetrated his head, fractured his skull and caused a catastrophic brain injury. In 2002 he was convicted of an offence of wounding with intent to cause grievous bodily harm contrary to the Offences against the Person Act 1861 s.18, the jury having rejected his plea of self-defence. As a result of his injuries, V was fed through a tube. In 2009, V died following an operation to re-insert his tube. The post mortem concluded that his death was connected to the 2000 attack. At C's trial for V's murder, the judge ruled that his previous conviction in 2002 was admissible to prove the murder and rejected the submission that it should be excluded under the Police and Criminal Evidence Act 1984 s.78 as unfair. H had been convicted of a s.18 offence in 2008 and the victim died in 2009. He was convicted of murder in 2012 following a trial at which his previous conviction was adduced. H sought an extension of time to renew his application for leave to appeal against his 2008 conviction and leave to appeal against his murder conviction. C and H submitted that their previous convictions were irrelevant and inadmissible in reliance on *DPP v Humphrys (Bruce Edward)* [1977] A.C. 1, [1976] C.L.Y. 488. H argued that his 2008 conviction was unsafe as a possible s.20 verdict should have been left to the jury and, if his 2008 conviction was unsafe, it could not have been adduced at the 2012 trial.

Held: C's appeal dismissed, H's application refused. (1) The enactment of s.74 of the 1984 Act extended the provisions of the Civil Evidence Act 1968 to the criminal justice process but it did not revive the doctrine of issue estoppel, *Humphrys* considered. In circumstances such as in the instant case, the earlier conviction of the s.18 offence constituted admissible evidence to prove, following the death of the victim, that the defendant was guilty not merely of causing grievous bodily harm with intent, but of murder. The prosecution was not required to prove all the matters already proved to the criminal standard, and the defendant was not prevented or excluded from denying them. In relation to matters already proved against him, the burden shifted to him. There was an additional safeguard under s.78 of the 1984 Act which permitted the judge to exclude the evidence. Fairness went both ways: the exclusion of admissible evidence might be unfair to the prosecution. The evidence of earlier convictions could not be excluded on some nebulous sense of unfairness. The judge had been right not to exercise his s.78 jurisdiction (see paras 33, 35-37 of judgment). (2) H had had ample time to renew his application for leave to appeal against his 2008 conviction. He could still have done so after he was charged with murder but no attempt was made. The judge at the 2008 trial had been entitled not to leave the possibility of a s.20 offence to the jury and it had not led to injustice to H. In any event his substantive ground of appeal was without merit. His application for leave to appeal was refused (paras 22, 25).

R. v CLIFT (LEIGH GEORGE); R. v HARRISON (BRIAN LESLIE), [2012] EWCA Crim 2750, [2013] 1 W.L.R. 2093, Lord Judge, L.C.J., CA (Crim Div).

603. Adverse inferences–Vulnerable adults–Defendant with low IQ failing to give evidence at trial–Whether came within exception to drawing of adverse inferences–Consideration of wider circumstances

[Criminal Justice and Public Order Act 1994 (c.33) s.35(1)(b), s.35(2).]

The appellant (D) appealed against his conviction for murder and his sentence of detention with a minimum term of 14 years. D, aged 17, and two co-accused (C), aged over 18, had been part of a group who had become involved in a late-night dispute during which a man was assaulted and subsequently died. The Crown's case was that D and C were jointly liable for murder. D's primary defence was that he had been acting in self-defence. The judge directed the jury that it could draw an adverse inference from D's failure give evidence pursuant to the Criminal Justice and Public Order Act 1994 s.35(2). D had been diagnosed with Attention Deficit Hyperactivity Disorder, had an IQ of 68 and language levels of a seven-or eight-year-old. There were also reports from a specialist language therapist and a registered intermediary (B). In the light of the reports, the judge made the special measure of providing D with B's services during the trial. In making his adverse inference direction, the judge stated that he could take into account D's conduct before and after the offence, the fact that a physical or mental condition that might merely cause some difficulty in giving evidence was insufficient to satisfy the exception provided by s.35(1)(b) to the drawing of an adverse inference and that whilst such difficulties should be taken into account in assessing the weight of a defendant's evidence, they would not justify a comprehensive failure to give evidence. The judge observed that in the instant case the significance of asserting self-defence was "plain and obvious" even bearing in mind that the burden of proving it remained with the Crown. He also referred to the grant of an intermediary to assist D and that a fair-minded jury would take account of a witness' physical and learning difficulties in assessing the weight of his evidence. In relation to sentence, it was agreed that the appropriate starting point for D was 12 years and for C, 15 years. C received minimum terms of 16 years. D submitted that (1) given his intellect and condition the judge should not have permitted the jury to draw an adverse inference, and that the judge had wrongly relied on *R. v Ensor (Max Angus)* [2009] EWCA Crim 2519, [2010] 1 Cr. App. R. 18, [2011] C.L.Y. 600; (2) fresh evidence from two consultant clinical psychologists which provided material suggesting the use of an adverse inference was wrong ought to be admitted; (3) he did not participate meaningfully in the trial and *Practice Direction (Sen Cts: Criminal Proceedings: Further Directions)* [2007] 1 W.L.R. 1790 was not followed, so his trial was unfair; (4) there was no clear justification for increasing his minimum term by two years whilst only increasing C's by one year.

Held: Appeal against conviction dismissed, appeal against sentence allowed. (1) In deciding whether to give an adverse inference direction, it was recognised that the question for the judge was wide with a wide margin of appreciation. Section 35(1)(b) was not to be confined to cases where giving evidence would have an adverse effect on the health of a defendant, *R. v Tabbakh (Hassan)* [2009] EWCA Crim 464, (2009) 173 J.P. 201, [2009] C.L.Y. 935 followed, *R. v Cowan (Donald)* [1996] Q.B. 373, [1996] C.L.Y. 1511 applied, *R. v Friend (Billy-Joe) (Appeal against Conviction) (No. 2)* [2004] EWCA Crim 2661 and *R. (on the application of DPP) v Kavanagh* [2005] EWHC 820 (Admin), [2006] Crim. L.R. 370 considered. The judge's approach and assessment of the situation resulted in a decision to which he was entitled to come. He had been entitled to look beyond the expert material, and to consider D's subsequent behaviour, B's assistance and the approach of a fair-minded jury. He did not base himself on *Ensor*. His ruling was based on wider considerations which were appropriate, *Ensor* considered (see paras 45-54, 57 of judgment). (2) The proffered new evidence represented an amplification of materials which were before the court below. Although it pointed to a lower IQ figure for D, the figure remained within the general range figures provided at trial. The evidence did not afford a ground for allowing the appeal and it would not be in the interests of justice to receive the evidence (paras 73, 75). (3) Although it was accepted that no pre-trial meeting took place between judge, counsel and intermediary to assess the position and there was no adjustment to the normal court language used, the essential question was what effect the shortcomings had on the fairness of the trial. It was clear that D was able to give an account of the relevant events, to give instructions that he had acted in self-defence and that he understood in laymen's terms what the concept of joint enterprise involved. It was a relatively simple case, whose essentials D had grasped. It was clear that D's representatives were satisfied that he understood the situation, and B gave D positive assistance during the trial. Whilst the absence of a ground rules hearing before the trial and the failure to modify language at trial were regrettable they did not make the trial unfair. It was important that judges recognised that they had a responsibility in such cases to ensure that vulnerable defendants were actively participating in the proceedings. The court drew attention to the 2007 Practice Direction and "Raising the Bar", a report by the Advocacy Training Council (March 2011). (4) Whilst the 12-year starting point reflected D's age, when considering any increase, the judge should again have taken into account D's age and level of maturity. It was truly a joint enterprise and D should not have been singled out by a greater increase in the minimum term than C. D's minimum term was reduced to 13 years (paras 107-108).

R. v D, [2013] EWCA Crim 465, [2014] 1 W.L.R. 525, Treacy, L.J., CA (Crim Div).

604. Appeals against conviction–Fresh evidence–Admissibility of fresh evidence following post-trial retraction of allegations

[Criminal Appeal Act 1968 (c.19) s.23; Criminal Procedure Act 1865 (c.18).]

On a reference by the Criminal Cases Review Commission, the appellant father (F) appealed against a conviction for one count of assault by penetration of his 12-year-old daughter (J), and two counts of rape, committed when J was 13. J first made the allegations at the age of 14. A medical examination was neutral, it being accepted that J had engaged in other sexual activity. The trial had turned upon J's word against F's. The defence case had been that J was an attention-seeking liar. It was common ground that she had been sexually assaulted by a male relative at the age of 11, and it was suggested that she was unusually preoccupied with sex, and had "transferred" matters relating to that incident to her allegations against F. J's account contained discrepancies, which had been fully explored in cross-examination. Aspects of her behaviour had been revealed, including her acceptance that she had stolen from F, and that she had falsely accused her mother of being a drug dealer "to get at her". F had first appealed shortly after conviction on the basis that the judge should have allowed J to be cross-examined in relation to three incidents whereby it was said that she had made false or exaggerated complaints; two of sexual assault and one of physical abuse by a teacher. The appeal court had concluded that cross-examination ought to have been permitted regarding one of the sexual assault complaints which had allegedly occurred a few months after the offences committed by F, but that the conviction was nevertheless safe. At the instant appeal, F sought to rely on fresh evidence from three witnesses: his nephew, the daughter of his close friend, and a former school friend of J, all of whom could testify that J had made post-trial retractions of her allegations against him.

Held: Appeal dismissed. The purported fresh evidence was neither credible nor reliable and was therefore unacceptable. None of the witnesses was independent or objective: F's sister, who was the mother of the nephew, was at the forefront of the ongoing enquiries; J's former school friend had a plain reason to feel hostile to J, and had only produced her statement, a long time after the alleged retractions, because of pressure from F's father. The daughter of F's close friend hardly knew J and her evidence was inconsistent and implausible. It was a valid point that the proposed evidence needed to be looked at cumulatively, but in the instant circumstances, the accumulation of palpably unreliable and inconsistent evidence weakened rather than strengthened F's position. Importantly, the evidence of two of the witnesses had been available before the hearing of the first appeal. It had plainly been obtained with a view to advancing the appeal, but an informed decision had been made not to adduce it. Even if the evidence were credible and reliable, that, of itself, was a reason not to rule it admissible (see paras 20-26, 31-35 of judgment). (2) (Obiter) Allegations of post-trial retraction had to be treated with caution. The procedure followed in the instant case had been entirely appropriate: F had identified the witnesses he intended to call, and their evidence had been heard *de bene esse*. The decision in *R. v Conway (David Patrick)* (1980) 70 Cr. App. R. 4, [1980] C.L.Y. 498 was not to be regarded as binding authority on the procedure required to be adopted in applications or appeals based on evidence of alleged retractions or inconsistent statements. What constituted the best and fairest procedure had to be determined on a case-by-case basis. The reliance of the court in *Conway* on the Criminal Procedure Act 1865 was peculiar, since there was nothing in that Act which positively required a witness allegedly retracting his evidence after trial to "first" be called and cross-examined about the making of the alleged statements. That would reverse the usual approach and run counter to the Criminal Appeal Act 1968 s.23 in its current form. In the ordinary way, it was for an appellant first to adduce his evidence, which had to satisfy s.23 of the 1968 Act before it was formally received. If the witness alleged to have made the retraction was available, it would be sensible to obtain a statement at an early stage so that the actual existence of an issue could be identified. In any event, there should always be a directions hearing before the substantive hearing, *Conway* not followed and *R. v Johnston (Derek James)* [2003] EWCA Crim 312 applied (paras 48-58).

R. v SV, [2013] EWCA Crim 159, [2013] 1 Cr. App. R. 35, Davis, L.J., CA (Crim Div).

605. Codes of practice–Surveillance cameras

THE PROTECTION OF FREEDOMS ACT 2012 (CODE OF PRACTICE FOR SURVEILLANCE CAMERA SYSTEMS AND SPECIFICATION OF RELEVANT AUTHORITIES) ORDER 2013, SI 2013/1961; made under the Protection of Freedoms Act 2012 s.30, s.33. In force: August 12, 2013; .

The Order brings into force a code of practice (the Code) containing guidance about surveillance camera systems, which the Secretary of State is required to prepare, pursuant to the Protection of Freedoms Act 2012 s.29. The purpose of this Code is to set out guidance about the use of surveillance camera systems, and the use of images or information obtained by virtue of such systems.

606. Consent–Decisions to prosecute–Ejaculation within vagina despite agreement otherwise–Breach of consent constituting sexual offence–Judical review of refusal to prosecute

[Sexual Offences Act 2003 (c.42) s.1 (1), s.74.]

The claimant (F) applied for judicial review of a decision of the defendant Director of Public Prosecutions not to prosecute her former partner (X) for rape and/or sexual assault. F, a mother with one child, had entered into an Islamic marriage with (X) and claimed that afterwards their relationship was marred by his abusive dominance, including in sexual ways. F did not want another child and was unable for medical reasons to take contraceptive pills, and it had been clearly agreed between them that X would use a condom or withdraw. On one occasion during sexual intercourse without a condom X told F he would not withdraw and as a result F became pregnant. After their estrangement X texted F apologising "for raping you" and for degrading her "from the first day". F complained to the police of rape and sexual assault and X was arrested, but the DPP decided not to prosecute. F filed an application for judicial review against the DPP, who then reviewed the first decision and decided that, even if a jury were to believe the totality of F's evidence, there was still not enough evidence to establish a realistic prospect of conviction for any offence. F brought the instant application.

Held: Application granted. Within the statutory definition of rape in the Sexual Offences Act 2003 s.1 (1) ejaculation and pregnancy were irrelevant to proof of the offence. The reviewer of the DPP's first decision had not the advantage of the decision in *Assange v Sweden* [2011] EWHC 2849 (Admin), (2011) 108(44) L.S.G. 17 in which the complainant had consented to sexual intercourse only on the basis that Assange would use a condom and where the court held that if that were the basis of consent then there would be no consent if he did not use one, or removed or tore it, *Assange* applied. The incident that led to F's pregnancy could not be seen apart from the well-evidenced history, including X's own admissions, of his sexual dominance of F and her unenthusiastic acquiescence to his demands. The incident could reasonably be seen as one in which F consented to intercourse on the clear understanding that X would not ejaculate within her vagina and that she believed that he intended and agreed to withdraw before ejaculation. X allegedly knew that that was the only basis on which she consented, and there was evidence that despite that knowledge he intended that the occasion would culminate in ejaculation within her vagina. In short, there was evidence that he deliberately ignored the basis of her consent to penetration as a manifestation of his control over her. F had agreed to the penetration, provided, in the language of s.74, she agreed by choice. It had to be emphasised that the statutory definition of consent in s.74 applied equally to s.1 (1) (c) as it did to s.1 (1) (b). The evidence relating to "choice" and "freedom" to make any particular choice had to be approached in a broad commonsense way. If X had decided before penetration that he would act as he allegedly had done just because he deemed F to be subservient to his control, she was deprived of choice relating to the crucial feature on which her original consent to intercourse was based. Accordingly, her consent was negated. In law, the combination of circumstances fell within the statutory definition of rape (see paras 20-27 of judgment).

R. (ON THE APPLICATION OF F) v DPP, [2013] EWHC 945 (Admin), [2014] 2 W.L.R. 190, Lord Judge, L.C.J., DC.

607. Covert surveillance–Admissibility–Recordings of prisoners being transported to police station in prison van–Prisoners' incriminating admissions–Whether incriminating evidence admissible

[Police and Criminal Evidence Act 1984 (c.60) s.30(1A), s.78; Regulation of Investigatory Powers Act 2000 (c.23) s.28, s.48(1); European Convention on Human Rights 1950 Art.6(3), Art.6.]

The appellants (P1 and P2) appealed against convictions of aggravated burglary, false imprisonment, and possession of a firearm. The appellants and another man had dressed as policemen and forced their way into a family's home and tied them up. The husband (H) was threatened with a gun and a syringe, with what he was led to believe contained HIV-infected blood. After H had opened his safes, he was injected with the needle and the men threatened to kill him and his family if they reported the crime. The men made off with £37,000 and personal effects. Following a search of the appellants' home the police found syringes, a tracking device, a laptop, police equipment and H's watch. The police later searched a garage rented by P1 and found more police equipment, some of which contained P1 's DNA, a shotgun, syringes and a tracking device and phones that were used in the area in which the victims were attacked on the night of the attack. Whilst imprisoned for other offences, the appellants were arrested in connection with the aggravated burglary. They were transported to the police station in a prison van for interview on three separate occasions. They had the benefit of legal advice and gave "no comment" interviews. On each occasion covert surveillance took place while they were in the van, during which they made incriminating admissions. At trial the Crown relied on the surveillance, some identification evidence, the items recovered during the searches, cell site evidence and the laptop analysis, which showed searches for police equipment and H's address. P2 contended that the man from whom they had rented the garage admitted to committing the burglary, but would not name him for fear of reprisal. The appellants submitted that (1) the surveillance was intrusive as it had taken place in a private vehicle and therefore should have been authorised by the Chief Constable not a Detective Superintendent; (2) the surveillance should not have been authorised as it was neither necessary nor proportionate; (3) the first covert recording had been made before they had seen their solicitor, the disclosure made provoked discussion and therefore they were not give given adequate time or facilities to prepare their defence in breach of the European Convention on Human Rights 1950 art.6(3)(b); (4) the evidence should have been excluded under the Police and Criminal Evidence Act 1984 s.78.

Held: Appeal dismissed. (1) Taking the ordinary meaning, the police vehicle in which the recordings were made was a state-owned entity and was not being used for private purposes, but for state purposes. While there was force in the appellants' argument that a police cell in which a person slept like a prison cell were residential premises within the meaning of the Regulation of Investigatory Powers Act 2000 s.48(1) and as referred to in the Code of Practice para.2.16, the same reasoning could not be attributed to a police van. Nothing in the Code of Practice supported the appellants' contention and there was no reason why the ordinary meaning of the words in the 2000 Act should not apply. The Detective Superintendent was entitled to authorise direct surveillance under s.28 of the 2000 Act (see paras 28, 31-34 of judgment). (2) The judge heard evidence from the superintendent and was entitled to conclude that the superintendent believed that surveillance was necessary and that there were strong objective grounds for that belief given the severity of the attack, the fact that one of the attackers was still at large and that time was of the essence. Establishing who the attackers were was necessary. The judge was entitled to conclude that the Superintendent believed that the surveillance was proportionate and that it was in fact proportionate. The threat to the victims was real and it was not proportionate to wait for the examination of cell site and computer evidence (paras 37-39, 44). (3) Article 6(3) had not been infringed. There had been no breach of the confidentiality between an accused and his lawyer; the appellants must have known that they would be entitled to legal advice before interview. They had not been denied adequate time or facilities to prepare their defences; there had been plenty of time for discussion with their solicitor (para.48). (4) There was nothing in what the police did that called into question the integrity of the criminal justice system. The judge had rightly held that there had been no misrepresentation, entrapment or other conduct that could be characterised as misbehaviour; the police had simply afforded the appellants the opportunity to talk together. Further, there was nothing to suggest that what had been said was untrue, and the appellants had had an opportunity to test the other evidence and explain the van conversations. The judge was entitled to exercise the discretion under s.78 of PACE in the way that he did and was correct to do so. Even if there had been a breach of s.30(1A) of PACE, which there had not, the evidence was properly admitted and there were no grounds for exclusion under s.78 of PACE. (paras 58-60).

R. v PLUNKETT (DANIEL MICHAEL); *sub nom.* R. v PLUNKETT (JAMES GEORGE), [2013] EWCA Crim 261, [2013] 1 W.L.R. 3121, Sir John Thomas (President QBD), CA (Crim Div).

608. Databases–Fingerprints

THE PROTECTION OF FREEDOMS ACT 2012 (DESTRUCTION, RETENTION AND USE OF BIOMETRIC DATA) (TRANSITIONAL, TRANSITORY AND SAVING PROVISIONS) (AMENDMENT) ORDER 2013, SI 2013/2580; made under the Protection of Freedoms Act 2012 s.25. In force: October 31, 2013; .

This order allows DNA and fingerprints taken as part of the police "Operation Nutmeg", where police took material from those convicted of serious offences but not on the DNA database, to be retained on the database, even if the consent given is vitiated because it was not properly sought. It also allows individuals subject to Operation Nutmeg to have their DNA sample retaken, should the record be deleted for any reason.

609. DNA evidence–Destruction of evidence–Fingerprints

THE PROTECTION OF FREEDOMS ACT 2012 (DESTRUCTION, RETENTION AND USE OF BIOMETRIC DATA) (TRANSITIONAL, TRANSITORY AND SAVING PROVISIONS) ORDER 2013, SI 2013/1813; made under the Protection of Freedoms Act 2012 s.25. In force: October 31, 2013 except for art.3 on January 31, 2014.; .

This Order provides for the destruction or retention of DNA, fingerprints and other forensic material taken before commencement of the relevant sections of the Protection of Freedoms Act 2012.

610. DNA evidence–Expert evidence–Admission of expert DNA evidence–Evidence not based on statistical match probability

In three conjoined appeals against conviction, the court was required to consider the admissibility of expert DNA evidence. At each trial, the judge had admitted low-template DNA evidence against the defendant derived from a mixed sample to which at least two or three had contributed. In each case, 19 or 20 of the components of the defendant's DNA had been present in the mixture but the experts were unable to give a random match probability. In the first and third cases, although unable to give evidence using a hierarchy or sliding scale of expressions, the experts were able to say that finding all of a defendant's components in a mixed sample was "rare" or "somewhat unusual". In the second case, the expert evidence went solely to the question of whether the defendant was a possible contributor to the DNA and therefore could not be excluded. On appeal, the issue in the first and third cases was whether an evaluative opinion was admissible in the absence of statistical evidence or a hierarchy of support. In the second case the issue was whether the DNA evidence should have been admitted.

Held: Appeals allowed in part. (1) Providing the conclusions from the analysis of a mixed profile were supported by detailed evidence in the form of a report of the experience relied on and the particular features of the profile which made it possible to give an evaluative opinion, such an opinion was, in principle, admissible. That was so even though there was no statistical basis to provide a random match probability and the sliding scale could not be used. An expert was not bound to express an evaluative opinion by reference to the hierarchy; he could use other phrases. The applicable principle, when determining the issue of admissibility, was that the court must be satisfied that there was a sufficiently reliable scientific basis for the evidence to be admitted. The real significance of an expert's inability to use the hierarchy might be that it was indicative of the lack of proper basis on which to express an opinion. In the court's view it could be no more than that, *R. v Thomas (Ashley Kieron)* [2011] EWCA Crim 1295 applied (see paras 8-14 of judgment). There was a risk that a jury might attach a false or misleading significance to that evaluative opinion, bearing in mind the very substantial trust that could be placed on DNA evidence. That risk was no reason for excluding the evidence, but it had to be made clear to the jury that the evaluation had no statistical basis, that the opinion expressed was quite different from the usual DNA evidence based on statistical match probability and that it was no more than an opinion based upon the expert's experience which should then be explained. It should be stressed that, in contrast to the usual type of DNA evidence, it was of more limited assistance (paras 2-28). (2) In the first case, bearing in mind that all the components from the defendant's DNA were present in the mixed samples, and several were prominent, there was a sufficiently reliable scientific basis for an evaluative opinion to be given. Further the jury were properly and fully directed by the judge. The conviction was therefore safe. In the second case, the judge had been right to admit the DNA evidence. It was relevant and properly admitted and correctly summed up to the jury. Again the conviction was safe. In the third case, there was a sufficiently reliable scientific basis for the evidence to be given, but, for other reasons, the conviction was unsafe (paras 52-53, 60, 77-80, 104). (3) (Per curiam) It was now general practice to provide the jury with written materials explaining the basic science of DNA. The court hoped that, unless there were unusual circumstances, such material would be provided. The court saw great advantage in there being standardised material and hoped that the Forensic Science Regulator, in conjunction with the Royal Society and the Royal Statistical Society, could assist in providing such material in a format understandable by a jury and in a way that was not open to debate (para.29).

R. v DLUGOSZ (KUBA); R v PICKERING (MARK LEE); R v MDS, [2013] EWCA Crim 2, [2013] 1 Cr. App. R. 32, Sir John Thomas (President), CA (Crim Div).

611. Extradition proceedings–Video evidence–England and Wales

THE EVIDENCE THROUGH TELEVISION LINKS (ENGLAND AND WALES) ORDER 2013, SI 2013/1598; made under the Crime (International Co-operation) Act 2003 s.29. In force: July 22, 2013; .

This Order allows for evidence to be given through television link by witnesses who are outside the UK in extradition proceedings in England and Wales.

612. Fingerprints–Samples

THE PROTECTION OF FREEDOMS ACT 2012 (CONSEQUENTIAL AMENDMENTS) NO.3 ORDER 2013, SI 2013/2343; made under the Protection of Freedoms Act 2012 s.115. In force: October 31, 2013; .

The purpose of the instrument is to amend the Police and Criminal Evidence Act 1984 (Application to immigration officers and customs officials in England and Wales) Order 2013 (SI 2013/1542) to take into account relevant amendments to the Police and Criminal Evidence Act 1984 that have been made by the Protection of Freedoms Act 2012, as regards the destruction, retention and use of samples and fingerprints.

613. Identification–Police inquiries–Informal identification on Facebook–Failure by investigators to obtain materials about identification process–Jury properly directed to exercise caution

The appellants (L and M) appealed against convictions for robbery and attempted robbery having been initially identified by the victim (V) informally through Facebook. V had stopped his car at the side of the road in order to answer a mobile telephone call when his vehicle was approached by three men. One of the men opened V's car door, a second held a knife to his throat as his mobile telephone and money were taken, and the third opened the front passenger door and took a pizza that was on the seat. The next day, V and his sister looked through Facebook where V identified two of the men as L and M, having viewed their profiles. V reported the incident to the police a month later and made a statement detailing the procedure he had taken when identifying L and M. Police officers visited V and his sister and they went through the process together but no detailed record or statement was made of that meeting. L and M were subsequently arrested and formally identified. The third male was never identified. Before trial, a single photograph of L's Facebook profile page was provided to L and M, and requests were then made for photographs of the other Facebook pages that had been considered by V and his sister so that L and M could consider how their identifications might have been made. The requests went unanswered and no further material was provided. L and M both claimed that they did not remember what they had been doing on the night of the incident. M further asserted that he did not have a Facebook profile. The issues considered were whether: (i) the failure of the investigators to find or provide further photographs of what had been seen by V and his sister placed L and M at such a disadvantage that a fair trial was not possible; (ii) the summing up failed to address specific matters thus making it unsatisfactory and the convictions unsafe.

Held: Appeals dismissed. (1) It was clear that the main identification of L and M had occurred when V and his sister went through Facebook, and the absence of any documentation as to how that procedure was conducted put L and M at a clear disadvantage. It had not been suggested that where identification had occurred using Facebook and where that identification was unsatisfactory that it was impossible to proceed on a case based on identification. Such a submission would have been wholly untenable. However, it was clear that there should have been material before the jury that would have enabled them to assess in more detail the circumstances in which the identification had occurred. It was perfectly possible for the jury, properly directed, to consider the reliability of the identifications. It was entirely proper for the trial to have proceeded and the disadvantages L and M faced were able to be addressed during the course of the judge's summing up, *R. (on the application of Ebrahim) v Feltham Magistrates Court* [2001] EWHC Admin 130,

[2001] 1 W.L.R. 1293, [2001] C.L.Y. 1190 and *R. v Dobson (Malcolm Charles)* [2001] EWCA Crim 1606 considered. (2) When summing up, it had not been necessary to point out to the jury the danger that an identification was made as it had been prompted by V's sister as that was not an issue that had arisen on the facts. It was obvious that the jury had been made aware that some materials were not available, and it was clear that the jury were fully aware of the difficult position that L and M had been put in as a result. (3) V had been assessed as being an honest witness when he stated that he had looked at M's Facebook page and saw photographs. M had not taken steps to show that he did not have a Facebook page and the jury were entitled to take into account M's evidence in relation to that. (4) When giving a Turnbull direction, the judge had cautioned the jury more than once of the possibility of mistake and in doing so he had addressed any failing that had occurred in departing from the words commonly used in giving a Turnbull direction. (5) (Obiter) It was anticipated that identifications done in this way, through the use of Facebook, were likely to rise and it was therefore incumbent upon investigators to take steps to obtain, in as much detail as possible, evidence in relation to the initial identification.

R. v ALEXANDER (GORDON JOHN); R. v McGILL (DANIEL), [2012] EWCA Crim 2768, [2013] 1 Cr. App. R. 26, Sir John Thomas (President QBD), CA (Crim Div).

614. Identification–Police officers–Identification of offender by police officer from CCTV footage–Importance of compliance with Code of Practice for the Identification of Persons by Police Officers (Code D)

[Police and Criminal Evidence Act 1984 (c.60) s.78.]

The appellant young offender (D) appealed against his conviction for affray. A fight in a pub in the early hours had been caught on CCTV. The police had arrived when the violence was over and arrests were made at the scene after the officers had viewed the CCTV footage. The footage showed a young white man wearing a green top bearing the Adidas logo, who had been involved in the fighting, but who was not in the pub when the police arrived. Statements were provided by two people who knew D. They both identified various people on the CCTV footage but neither identified D as having been present. Four months after the incident, a police constable investigating the case asked a colleague, C, whether he remembered dealing with D in unrelated matters. When C replied that he did, the constable asked him to view the CCTV footage, which she believed had D on it. C viewed the footage three times and said that he was in no doubt that the man in the green top with the Adidas logo was D. He knew this because of a long-term police interest in D. It was not in dispute that the Code of Practice for the Identification of Persons by Police Officers (Code D) had not been applied. The trial judge refused D's application to exclude C's evidence under the Police and Criminal Evidence Act 1984 s.78. He described the breach of Code D as "flagrant" and "lamentable", but concluded that the footage was of a reasonable quality, that it was difficult for the police to achieve compliance with the Code, and that it did not prohibit the course of action which had been taken.

Held: Appeal allowed. C's evidence should have been excluded. Part of the reason why the relevant version of Code D had been introduced was because of concerns expressed by the instant court in earlier cases about the need for proper procedures and the dangers of not observing such procedures, *R. v Smith (Dean Martin)* [2008] EWCA Crim 1342, [2009] 1 Cr. App. R. 36, [2009] C.L.Y. 767 applied. There had been a wholesale breach of Code D, which would undoubtedly have created very significant difficulties for the defence in testing the validity of the position being articulated by the police; they could not test C's account that he watched the footage alone and no records had been made as to what features of the image triggered the recognition and other aspects of the recognition. It had been highly suggestive of the investigating constable to tell C that she believed D to feature in the CCTV footage rather than simply asking him to watch it and waiting to see if he recognised anybody. The judge's remark about it being difficult for the police to comply with Code D was difficult to understand. There had been very real prejudice to D, which outweighed such probative value as the recognition evidence might have had. The conviction was unsafe and was quashed (see paras 13, 22, 24-29 of judgment).

R. v D, [2012] EWCA Crim 2637, (2013) 177 J.P. 158, Davis, L.J., CA (Crim Div).

615. Murder–Diminished responsibility–Offender developing schizophrenia in prison–Whether evidence indicated early stages of schizophrenia at time of killing

The appellant (P) appealed against his conviction for murder on the grounds of diminished responsibility. P, aged 19 at the time, had met his co-accused (E) at college and had come under his influence. P believed that E was a paratrooper and, wishing to become a paratrooper himself, had undergone what he believed were initiative tests, culminating in the stabbing of an innocent passerby. At trial, P's defence that he was suffering from the early stages of schizophrenia was rejected. P subsequently developed schizophrenia in prison and was later transferred to a psychiatric hospital. The issue for determination was whether the evidence was such as to indicate that P was suffering from the early stages of schizophrenia at the time of the killing.

Held: Appeal allowed. (1) The evidence of development of the symptoms of schizophrenia after the killing cast light on P's condition at the time. Furthermore, there was ample evidence of the development of symptoms of the early stages of schizophrenia well before P went to college. P's illness made him vulnerable to the influence of E such that he was not able to take decisions for himself at the time of the killing. That evidence was not available at trial, was clearly capable of belief, and plainly established that P was not responsible for his actions at the relevant time, to the extent that he had established that his responsibility was diminished. (2) It was appropriate to make a hospital order and a restriction order in respect of P.

R. v PETROLINI (JAMIE), [2012] EWCA Crim 2055, [2012] M.H.L.R. 308, Moses, L.J., CA (Crim Div).

616. Video evidence–Editing–Agreement to edit out passage of witness's video evidence–Whether defendant unfairly prejudiced by decision to admit it during course of trial

The appellant (M) appealed against his convictions for five counts of sexual offences against two 12-year-old girls (W and K). W and K were friends of M's daughter (D) and regular visitors to his house. The convictions were for three offences of indecent exposure, one of incitement to engage in sexual activity and one of sexual assault of a child under 13. The defence and prosecution had agreed to edit out a passage in D's video interview when D indicated that W and K had told her about the second indecent exposure allegation when it happened, in April or May 2010. In cross-examination, the defence suggested that W and K had conspired to make up false allegations against M in June 2010, as a result of an argument with D. Towards the end of the prosecution case, the jury sent a note specifically asking whether D agreed that the second indecent assault had happened. The judge ruled that D should be recalled and the relevant part of the interview played. Because it was not possible to recall her that day, the prosecution case was concluded first. A previous conviction which M had for indecent assault was admitted, on the basis of the defence attack upon the character of the complainants, through the collusion allegation. The edited video passage was played the following morning and D was cross-examined. In summing up, the judge directed the jury about the limited value of that evidence. In doing so, he reminded the jury, almost word for word, of the additional passage from D's interview. M submitted that the introduction of the additional evidence, particularly at the end of the prosecution case, was unfair and prejudicial and undermined the whole thrust of his cross-examination of the complainants, to the effect that they had colluded in June 2010.

Held: Appeal allowed. It was of the greatest importance that an agreement reached between prosecution and defence about the editing of a video witness interview should be adhered to, unless there was very good reason to depart from it. Defence counsel had not behaved improperly or deviously in securing the agreed editing. Had the prosecution thought, when the offending line of cross-examination was pursued, that they had been unfairly taken by surprise, it would have been open to them to seek to adduce the edited passage in rebuttal. But for the jury's question, the prosecution would never have sought to introduce the edited passage. It was important to answer a jury's question truthfully and accurately wherever that could be done without unfair prejudice to the defendant or prosecution. However, it was important not to lose sight of the fact that the trial process was adversarial, not inquisitorial. An agreement as to the editing of the video interview of a witness was generally binding, but not absolute. Before overriding such an agreement, the judge had to be satisfied that there was good reason to do so and that the party who objected was not unfairly prejudiced by it (see paras 26-27, 29-30 of judgment). In the instant case, it was of crucial importance that the conduct of the defence case in cross-examining the complainants on collusion had not entitled the prosecution to revisit the agreement over editing. The prejudice suffered by M by reason of the late admission of the edited passage was not simply that it contradicted the suggestion that W and K had made up one of the allegations late in June. There was also prejudice in the fact that, relying on the agreement about editing, defence counsel had cross-examined the witnesses in a particular way. There was also crucial prejudice in the fact that by putting to the complainants that they had colluded to make false allegations, M had left himself vulnerable to cross-examination about his previous conviction. If the edited passage of D's interview had been in evidence from the outset, that specific line of cross-examination would probably not have been pursued and there was no certainty that the jury would have been permitted to hear about his previous conviction. On proper analysis, to allow the jury to hear the edited passage of D's interview had resulted in unfair prejudice to M. The jury should have been told instead that they had heard all the evidence from D which the parties regarded as relevant, and that they should not speculate as to what other evidence there might have been. The timing of the admission of the complaint evidence at the very end of the prosecution case, and so soon after the jury learnt of M's previous conviction, gave that evidence an undue prominence, reflected in the summing up. It could not be said that the convictions were safe (paras 33-35, 37-39).

R. v M, [2012] EWCA Crim 899, [2013] 1 Cr. App. R. 17, Pill, L.J., CA (Crim Div).

617. Witnesses–Competence–Profoundly deaf witness with learning difficulties–Effectiveness of competency hearing–Application of correct test

The appellant prosecution appealed against a Crown Court judge's ruling that the case against the respondent (F) would be dismissed because the complainant (H) was not a competent witness. F had been charged with the rape and sexual assault of H, who had learning difficulties and was profoundly deaf. The judge held a competency hearing and two registered intermediaries assessed H as being able to give evidence with special measures. However, the judge found that there were difficulties in asking H questions about body parts without partially suggesting the answer to her by way of leading questions, and that H had difficulty with abstract concepts such as time. The judge concluded that H was not competent to give evidence and made the terminating ruling. The Crown submitted that the competency hearing was flawed and the judge applied the wrong test.

Held: Appeal allowed. The hearing had not effectively explored H's ability to communicate. The exercise carried out was not a fair test of her competency. The shortcomings owed much to a lack of preparation and a lack of ability to respond flexibly to the difficulties which arose. Moreover, whilst the judge had set out the appropriate test, she had based her conclusion that H was not a competent witness firstly on the body parts issue. She had assumed that the interpreter would have to point to the body part in question, which would shed little or no light on H's true understanding of the matter. The judge had thereby substituted the issue of the interpreter's difficulties in communicating for the test of whether the witness could understand questions and give intelligible answers. The second limb of the judge's reasoning related to difficulty with concepts of time and other abstractions. In that respect the procedure adopted was an unsatisfactory way of testing H's understanding and ability to make herself understood. It did not represent a valid or thorough test, and so the judge's conclusion in that respect was undermined. The proceedings against F would be resumed (see paras 25-31, 38 of judgment).

R. v F; *sub nom.* R. v JRF, [2013] EWCA Crim 424, [2013] 1 W.L.R. 2143, Treacy, L.J., CA (Crim Div).

CRIMINAL LAW

618. Aggravated trespass–Demonstrators–Proof of distinct act other than trespass–Intention to intimidate

[Criminal Justice and Public Order Act 1994 (c.33) s.68(1).]

The appellants (B) appealed by way of case stated against a decision of a district judge convicting them of aggravated trespass under the Criminal Justice and Public Order Act 1994 s.68(1). B were 10 out of at least 130 people who had entered and stayed in a store in London for about two-and-a-half hours protesting as part of a group known as "UK Uncut" against tax avoidance. The protesters were shouting at high volume and chanting using megaphones. Some protesters were masked, many carried placards and handed out flyers, others hung banners, drums were beaten, horns sounded and bagpipes were played. Tents were erected and volleyball was played across the displays. Some goods were stolen, damaged or swept to the floor. Chants of "pay your taxes" were directed at some staff members and their photographs were taken. The management announced at 16.10 that the store was closing and asked those inside to leave the building. A number of UK Uncut protesters left at 16.19. Some of the customers continued as if the protest was not taking place, but others, as found by the district judge were "terrified, frightened, confused, angry, intimidated and tearful". Some staff and customers were unable to leave the store. The protesters were arrested at 18.30. In order to prove an offence of aggravated trespass under s.68(1) a trespass had to be proved, as well as a second act accompanied by the intention, by the second act, to intimidate, obstruct or disrupt. The charge against B was that having trespassed on land, B did an act, namely, they entered the premises in the company of others and demonstrated. The district judge found that the second alleged act, namely the act of demonstration, was proved and that they intended to intimidate. The judge used a dictionary and adopted the verb "cow" as a synonym for intimidate. The question for consideration was whether the court was right to conclude that B had committed the second act required by s.68(1) on a joint enterprise basis. B argued that the judge had erred in finding that their continued presence as part of the demonstration was a second or additional act.

Held: Appeal dismissed. The issue was whether occupation as a trespasser could amount to the second act required by s.68. It could not be said that continuing occupation on land on which a person had trespassed could not be a further distinct act from the initial trespass. Mass invasion and continuing occupation could constitute "doing" something on the land over and above trespassing on it, *Peppersharp v DPP* [2012] EWHC 474 (Admin), (2012) 176 J.P. 257, [2012] C.L.Y. 666 applied. From the terms of the charge, there was a clear allegation of an act over and above the act of trespass. The essential allegation was demonstrating, and the district judge clearly meant that the actual demonstration was a separate act from trespassing. In the light of those findings the next question was whether it had been open to the district judge to infer from the actions of the demonstrators that they intended to intimidate. The judge used the verb "cow" as a synonym for intimidate. It was highly dangerous to attempt to place an accurate definition on a word in common use. It was important not to diminish the force of the word intimidate. Although the district judge selected cow, it could not be said that he watered down the meaning of the word intimidate. It was necessary only to read his description of the chaotic scene inside the store to appreciate how intimidating the protest must have been to the staff and customers. There was ample evidence from which the district judge could infer that anyone who chose to remain in the store after it was closed had an intention to demonstrate and it was not unreasonable to infer that those who took part in it intended to intimidate. X were all guilty as principals. The conduct element of the offence was the trespass and mass demonstration, Each of them had committed a distinct act separate from the act of trespass. Therefore, it was wrong to consider the instant case on the basis that some of those taking part in the demonstration were perpetrators and or principals and others were merely accessories. Advancing the argument that if B were not guilty as principals they were guilty as accessories, led the judge into error. In the context of the invasion of a building by force, it made no difference to distinguish some of those participating by categorising some as principal offenders and others as accessories. It was better to ask whether B had been part of the demonstration and whether the demonstration was itself a distinct act from the trespass, and whether it could be inferred that those participating had one of the three intentions. The facts found by the judge justified the conclusion that B were guilty of aggravated trespass by virtue of their presence within the store over a period of nearly two-and-a-half hours as part of the demonstration. They were guilty because they had the intention to intimidate, and because they had committed the conduct element of that offence (see paras 14,16, 21-27, 35, 41 of judgment).

BAUER v DPP, [2013] EWHC 634 (Admin), [2013] 1 W.L.R. 3617, Moses, L.J., QBD (Admin).

619. Assisted suicide–Defences–Whether necessity potential defence to assisted suicide or euthanasia–Clarity of DPP's policy

[Human Rights Act 1998 (c.42); Suicide Act 1961 (c.60) s.2(1); European Convention on Human Rights 1950 Art.8.]

The appellants (M, N and L) appealed against a decision ([2012] EWHC 2381 (Admin), [2012] 3 F.C.R. 233, [2012] C.L.Y. 1517) concerning the illegality of assisted suicide and euthanasia. M, N and L suffered from catastrophic physical disabilities but their mental processes were unimpaired. They wished to die but were incapable of ending their own lives without the assistance of a third party or euthanasia carried out by the third party. It was likely that those who provided such assistance would be guilty of assisted suicide under the Suicide Act 1961 s.2(1), whilst those who carried out euthanasia would be guilty of murder. After the decision in *R. (on the application of Purdy) v DPP* [2009] UKHL 45, [2010] 1 A.C. 345, [2009] C.L.Y. 2046, the DPP had set out in a policy statement the factors to be taken into account when considering whether to prosecute assisted suicide cases. The court was required to determine whether (i) to grant a declaration, as sought by L, that necessity should be a defence to a charge of euthanasia and assisted suicide where certain conditions were met; (ii) the blanket legal prohibition on providing assistance to those wishing to die constituted a disproportionate interference with the European Convention on Human Rights 1950 art.8; (iii) the DPP should set out in greater detail, as sought by M, how he would exercise his discretion to initiate prosecution in cases of assisted suicide in order to make the law more accessible and foreseeable.

Held: First and second appellants' appeals dismissed, third appellant's appeal allowed in part. (Lord Judge dissenting on the issue of the DPP's policy) (1) The first issue could not be resolved in L's favour for the following reasons: (a) the sanctity of life was a fundamental principle of common law, reflected in the unqualified right to life found in art.2. There was no self-evident reason why it should give way to the values of autonomy or dignity, and there were cogent reasons why sensible people might think that it should not; (b) there was no right to commit suicide; s.1 of the 1961 Act merely conferred immunity from the criminal process for those who actually committed suicide. If there was no right to kill yourself, there could be no right to require the state to allow others to kill you or assist you to die; (c) it was not appropriate for the court to fashion a defence of necessity in such a complex and controversial field, it was a matter for Parliament, *Airedale NHS Trust v Bland* [1993] A.C. 789, [1993] C.L.Y. 2712 considered; (d) any defence provided to those who assisted someone to die would have to apply not merely to euthanasia but also to assisted suicide. That raised the question of how the courts could develop a defence to assisted suicide when Parliament had stated in unequivocal terms that it was a serious criminal offence carrying a maximum sentence of 14 years' imprisonment (see paras 55-56, 60, 64-66 of judgment). (2) The decision in *Pretty v United Kingdom (2346/02)* [2002] 2 F.L.R. 45, [2002] C.L.Y. 2528 made it clear that a blanket ban on assisted suicide was fully compatible with art.8(2) and was not disproportionate. The ECtHR's observations in para.76 of its judgment did not suggest otherwise. *Purdy* was not binding authority on that point as para.76 was not debated in that case. The instant court was bound by the authoritative ruling in *Pretty* but could not refuse to carry out the proportionality balancing exercise, even when the case fell within the margin of appreciation, *Purdy* considered, *Pretty* applied. The Human Rights Act 1998 created domestic rights enforceable in domestic courts, and the court was obliged to vindicate those rights and satisfy itself that any interference was proportionate as a matter of domestic law. However, it would be inappropriate for the courts to create domestic art.8(1) rights exceeding the protection afforded by the ECtHR in direct opposition to the will of Parliament as reflected in s.2 of the 1961 Act. Accordingly, there was no doubt that as a matter of domestic law the current blanket prohibitions were compatible with art.8. M had no right to require the DPP to desist from prosecuting a carer or doctor who helped him to die, and the DPP could not be required to identify a category of cases where a prosecution would not be initiated because to do so would infringe art.8 rights (paras 85-88, 105, 110-114). (3) The principles set out in the DPP's policy had to satisfy the requirements of accessibility and foreseeability, so that a person who was considering providing assistance to a victim to commit suicide was able to foresee, to a degree that was reasonable, the consequences of providing such assistance, *Sunday Times v United Kingdom (A/30)* (1979-80) 2 E.H.R.R. 245, [1980] C.L.Y. 1385 and *Hasan v Bulgaria (30985/96)* (2002) 34 E.H.R.R. 55, [2001] C.L.Y. 3486 considered. The DPP's policy was, in certain respects, not sufficiently clear to satisfy the requirements of art.8(2) in relation to healthcare professionals. The policy should give some indication of the weight that the DPP accorded to the fact that the helper was acting in his capacity as a healthcare professional and the victim was in his care, Gross v Switzerland and *Purdy* considered (paras 123, 140-145). (4) (Per Lord Judge) A family relationship was given no specific weight either way in the DPP's policy. The crucial question was the extent to which the suspect was motivated by compassion for the victim. The policy was sufficiently clear to enable M, or anyone who assisted him, to make an informed decision about the likelihood of prosecution (paras 167-172, 179-188).

R. (ON THE APPLICATION OF NICKLINSON) v MINISTRY OF JUSTICE; R. (ON THE APPLICATION OF LAMB) v MINISTRY OF JUSTICE; R. (ON THE APPLICATION OF AM) v DPP; *sub nom.* NICKLINSON v MINISTRY OF JUSTICE, [2013] EWCA Civ 961, [2014] 1 F.C.R. 316, Lord Judge, L.C.J., CA (Civ Div).

620. Benefits fraud–Tax credits–Meaning of "fraudulent activity" in s.35 Tax Credits Act 2002–Whether passive receipt of overpayments fell short of "fraudulent activity"

[Criminal Law Act 1977 (c.45) s.1 (1); Tax Credits Act 2002 (c.21) s.35.]

The appellants (N and H) appealed against their convictions for conspiracy to commit fraud under the Tax Credits Act 2002 s.35 and the Criminal Law Act 1977 s.1 (1). Both had been charged with being knowingly concerned in fraudulent activity by permitting payments of tax credits into their bank accounts to which they knew they were not entitled. At the centre of the operation was a tax credits employee who had manipulated the internal computer system in relation to 22 benefits claimants, falsifying their claims so as to inflate the benefits payments they received. H and N did not procure overpayment but merely signed review forms showing all the inflated benefits as confirmation that the details were correct, while knowing that they were not. N received some £12,000 in overpayments, and H £19,000. Although they had conceded a dishonest state of mind and had pleaded guilty to the offences, the court queried whether the legal representatives had analysed the law correctly and whether passive receipt of funds and a failure to report the matter could amount to "fraudulent activity" for the purposes of s.35 of the Act. The Crown argued that the offence was complete once the offender was knowingly concerned in a fraudulent act with a view to obtaining.

The approach was simple. Put neutrally, the Crown had to prove that H and N had behaved with a view to obtaining payments of tax credit. A strict reading of the section required proof of behaviour calculated to achieve, rather than behaviour calculated to capitalise upon what had already been achieved. The offence particulars alleged that H and N had "knowingly permitted" the payments, and that could not be dispositive of the issue. Permitting their accounts to be manipulated did not prove that either appellant had behaved so as to perpetrate the fraud. Their dishonesty was not in dispute and it would not have been difficult to plead a different count which would uncontroversially have caught the offending. However, the offences with which N and H had been charged were not made out and the convictions had to be quashed (see paras 21-23 of judgment).

R. v NOLAN (TRACEY); R. v HOWARD (ALISON), [2012] EWCA Crim 671, [2012] Lloyd's Rep. F.C. 498, Rafferty, L.J., CA (Crim Div).

621. Careless driving–Fixed penalty offences

THE FIXED PENALTY OFFENCES ORDER 2013, SI 2013/1565; made under the Road Traffic Offenders Act 1988 s.51. In force: June 28, 2013; .

The purpose of the Order is to make the offence under the Road Traffic Act 1988 s.3 (careless, and inconsiderate, driving) a fixed penalty offence.

622. Causing death by careless or inconsiderate driving–Causation–Driver having parked and alighted from vehicle when other vehicle collided with it–Whether no case to answer

[Road Traffic Act 1988 (c.52) s.2B.]

The appellant lorry driver (J) appealed against his conviction for causing death by careless driving, and the sentence of two years' imprisonment imposed for that offence. J had been making a delivery but had been unable to park in the driveway of the relevant premises, so he had parked his lorry on the road adjacent to the driveway, thus blocking most of that side of the road. The road was a single track carriageway, and there was a bend in the road near where J stopped. The conditions at the time were poor, with snow banked on the road verges and impaired visibility due to the sun being very low in the sky. J had been away from his lorry for ten minutes when another lorry approached from the same direction and collided with J's lorry. The driver (D) suffered catastrophic injuries and died at the scene. It was estimated that D's vehicle had been travelling at between 50-60mph at the time. At the close of the Crown's case, counsel for J submitted that there was no case to answer, given that D would have been aware of the hazard posed by the sun for several miles prior to the collision, and had been driving at a speed inappropriate for the conditions. He argued that all the relevant driving for the purposes of the offence had ended by the time of the impact and it therefore played no part in the fatality. J submitted that the judge had been wrong to reject the submission of no case to answer. He argued that it was one of those cases, like *R. v L* [2010] EWCA Crim 1249, [2011] R.T.R. 19, [2011] C.L.Y. 629, where the circumstances, rather than the accident itself, had been caused by the driving. He further submitted that, if the driving had not stopped at the relevant time, then there was a break in the causation and the resultant events were too remote. In relation to sentence, J argued that the judge had been wrong to place the offence into the highest category in the sentencing guidelines, namely "careless or inconsiderate driving falling not far short of dangerous driving".

Held: Appeal allowed in part. (1) It was no part of the statutory definition in the Road Traffic Act 1988 s.2B that the driving must be coterminous with the impact resulting in the death. The offence was "causing the death... by driving", not "causing the death while driving". It was not in dispute that J had been driving at least up to the point when he parked the lorry and alighted. It was not a requirement of s.2B or the relevant authorities that the Crown must show that J was still driving at the point of impact. The question was whether the driving played a part in causing the death, not simply in creating the occasion of the fatality, *R. v Skelton* [1995] Crim. L.R. 635 and *R. v L* considered. It had been for the jury in the instant case to decide whether the admitted driving was careless and whether it had caused the death, rather than merely the circumstances for the accident to occur. The judge had been correct to reject the submission of no case to answer and was correct in directing the jury in the manner he did (see paras 30-36 of judgment). (2) It was little short of dangerous driving to park a lorry on a bend in the road, with the sun so low in the sky and visibility so poor. The judge's conclusion that the offence fell towards the upper end of the range of seriousness could not be faulted. The only issue was whether appropriate allowance had been made for the fact that J was 62 with a virtually unblemished driving record, the fact that he had been driving for many years, and the other personal mitigation, including his remorse. In all the circumstances, the appropriate term was one of 15 months' imprisonment (paras 39-45).

R. v JENKINS (RAYMOND), [2012] EWCA Crim 2909, [2013] R.T.R. 21, McCombe, L.J., CA (Crim Div).

623. Causing sexual activity without consent–Irrebuttable presumptions–Defendant using false identities to make girlfriend perform sexual acts–Whether deception as to purpose triggered conclusive presumption under s.76 Sexual Offences Act 2003–Sufficiency of jury directions on "purpose"

[Sexual Offences Act 2003 (c.42) s.4, s.74, s.76.]

The appellant (B) appealed against his convictions for causing a person to engage in sexual activity without consent contrary to the Sexual Offences Act 2003 s.4. B had contacted his girlfriend (X) via a social networking site under a false name (G) and she sent topless photographs to him at his request. He later threatened her that if she did not engage in various sexual acts over the internet, he would send the topless pictures to her employers and publish them on the internet. She obeyed. X confided in B. He later told her that he had beaten and killed G. B then contacted X over the networking site under another false name (C) claiming to have known G and threatening to send the topless pictures to her employers if she did not carry out further sexual acts. X complied but later contacted the police who confirmed that G and C were both B. He was arrested. B admitted that he had assumed the false identities but said he believed that X was consenting to the sexual acts. He also denied that he would have carried out the threat. The judge, relying on *R. v Devonald (Stephen)* [2008] EWCA Crim 527, directed the jury that if they found that X had been deceived as to the true purpose of the sexual acts, then the conclusive presumption under s.76 of the Act applied, removing B's defence that he had a reasonable belief that X was consenting. B submitted that the judge had been wrong to apply *Devonald*, because in that case the true purpose was the complainant's humiliation rather than the defendant's sexual gratification. He contended that the judge's direction was wrong in law because X had never been asked at trial what she believed B's purpose was and presumably if she had been asked she would have said sexual gratification, in which case she had not been misled. Further, he argued that if the judge was satisfied that s.76 was triggered he should have directed the jury on the meaning of the word "purpose" and that the judge had failed to explain that deceit as to the consequences (that was whether B would have carried out his threat) and identity were not enough for the presumption to apply.

Held: Appeal allowed. There was no definition of "purpose" in the Act. It might not be straightforward to ascertain the purpose of a sexual act. Those engaging in a sexual act might have a number of reasons or objectives and each party might have a different objective or reason. The Act did not specify whose purpose was under consideration. There was, therefore, a great danger in attempting any definition of the word "purpose" and in defining it too widely as that could bring within the remit of s.76 situations never contemplated by Parliament. Where a statutory provision effectively removed from an accused his only line of defence to a serious criminal charge, it had to be strictly construed; thus, it would be a rare case in which s.76 should be applied, *R. v Jheeta (Harvinder Singh)* [2007] EWCA Crim 1699, [2008] 1 W.L.R. 2582, [2007] C.L.Y. 921 applied. If there was any conflict between the decisions in *Jheeta* and *Devonald, Jheeta* would be followed unhesitatingly, *Devonald* doubted. There had to be deception as to the nature or purpose of the sexual acts for the conclusive presumption to apply. X had been deceived in a cruel and despicable way but it was doubtful whether there was deception as to purpose so as to trigger the operation of s.76. Even if the definition of purpose was extended to include motivation, which was doubtful, X knew she was performing sexual acts for the camera, for the purpose of B's sexual gratification. It was incumbent on the judge to attempt an analysis of the word "purpose" if s.76 was to be put to the jury. Not only was there no analysis, but the jury were not informed that deception as to identity and consequence were not enough. Reliance on s.76 was misplaced; the prosecution needed to look no further than s.74 of the Act and its definition of consent, because if X had only complied because she was being blackmailed, the prosecution might argue forcefully that she did not agree by choice. However repellent B's behaviour was, he was entitled to a fair trial and his only line of defence had been taken away from him. Accordingly, his convictions were quashed and a retrial was ordered (see paras 19-26 of judgment).

R. v B, [2013] EWCA Crim 823, [2013] 2 Cr. App. R. 29, Hallett, L.J., CA (Crim Div).

624. Classification–Drugs–Temporary provisions

THE MISUSE OF DRUGS ACT 1971 (TEMPORARY CLASS DRUG) ORDER 2013, SI 2013/1294; made under the Misuse of Drugs Act 1971 s.2A, s.7A, s.31. In force: June 10, 2013; .

The Order subjects the following substances and products to temporary control under the Misuse of Drugs Act 1971.

625. Communications offences–Electronic communications–Alleged threat sent via Twitter–Actus reus for s.127(1) Communications Act 2003

[Communications Act 2003 (c.21) s.127(1)(a).]

The appellant (C) appealed by way of case stated against his conviction for sending by a public electronic communications network a message of a menacing character contrary to the Communications Act 2003 s.127(1)(a). C was registered under his own name on the social networking platform Twitter. He was due to fly on January 15, 2010 from Doncaster Robin Hood Airport to Belfast to meet another Twitter user. On January 6, having heard that the airport had closed, he posted the message "Crap! Robin Hood Airport is closed. You've got a week and a bit to get your shit together otherwise I am blowing the airport sky high!!" That could be seen by C's Twitter "followers". On January 11, the duty manager responsible for the airport's security saw C's "tweet" while searching for tweets referring to the airport. His manager considered the tweet a non-credible threat but referred it to airport police in accordance with standard practice. Airport police took no action but referred the matter to South Yorkshire Police, who arrested C on January 13. C asserted that the message was a joke. The

Crown Court found that the message was menacing. The Divisional Court considered the required actus reus and mens rea for the offence.

Held: Appeal allowed. (1) The tweet was a message sent by an electronic communications service for the purposes of s.127(1); accordingly, Twitter fell within its ambit (see para.25 of judgment). However, the offence could not be proved unless the message was of a "menacing character". C's submission that the message had to be credible as an immediate threat was not accepted: a message which could not or was unlikely to be implemented could nevertheless create a sense of apprehension in the person receiving it. However, unless it did so, it was difficult to see how it could be described as a message of a menacing character. Accordingly, if the person receiving the message, or who could reasonably be expected to receive it, would brush it aside as a joke or empty banter, it would be a contradiction to describe it as a message of menacing character. A message which did not create fear or apprehension in those to whom it was communicated, or who might reasonably be expected to see it, fell outside s.127(1)(a), for the simple reason that the message lacked menace. A message's precise terms, and any inferences to be drawn from those terms, had to be examined in the context in and the means by which the message was sent. It was clear that the message did not represent a threat. It had been posted on Twitter for widespread reading; although it purported to address those responsible for the airport, it had not been sent to the airport or anyone responsible for public security; the language and punctuation were inconsistent with the writer intending it to be taken as a serious warning; it was unusual for a terrorist threat to enable the person making it to be readily identified; and it was difficult to imagine a serious threat in which warning was given to a large number of followers in ample time for the threat to be reported and extinguished. It was relevant that none of those reading the message in the days after it appeared had thought anything of it: C's followers had not reported a threat and the authorities had acted with little urgency. The Crown Court had read too much into the observation in *DPP v Collins* [2006] UKHL 40, [2006] 1 W.L.R. 2223, [2006] C.L.Y. 832 that the sender's criminality could not depend on the receiver's reaction; that said no more than that a message proved by objective assessment to be menacing did not cease to be so just because the person who received it was not menaced, *Collins* considered. Respect had to be given to the court's finding of fact that the message was menacing, but the findings did not address the unbroken pattern of evidence to be derived from the responses of those reading the message. The court's decision that the tweet constituted a message of a menacing character had not been open to it (paras 29-34). (2) (Obiter) C's state of mind did not therefore arise for decision. However, there was no express provision in s.127(1)(a) for mens rea. It was therefore an offence of basic intent. It was not accepted that the sender of the message had to have intended to threaten the person to whom it was or was likely to be communicated, or that specific purpose was necessary, *Collins* considered. The mental element of the offence was satisfied if the offender had intended that the message should be of a menacing character, or if he had been aware at the time of sending the message that it might create fear or apprehension in any reasonable member of the public who saw it. If the offender had intended the message as a joke, it was unlikely that the required mens rea would be established (paras 35-38).

CHAMBERS v DPP, [2012] EWHC 2157 (Admin), [2013] 1 W.L.R. 1833, Lord Judge, L.C.J., DC.

626. Conspiracy to defraud–No case to answer–Safety of convictions for conspiracy to defraud and attempting to convert criminal property

The appellants (S and J) appealed against convictions for conspiracy to defraud and attempting to convert criminal property. S and J, who were husband and wife, had been accused of involvement in a series of fraudulent mortgage applications, as a result of which mortgage companies were induced to grant loans. Different individuals were involved in different fraud conspiracies. There were five separate trials to deal with the full array of offences, and the instant appeals arose out of the third trial. Count 14 had involved the sale of a property whose value was misrepresented. The prosecution case was that J and S had, together with other co-accused, conspired to defraud a mortgage lender by using a bogus purchaser. The prosecution alleged that J had been the vendor of the property and that S had been fully aware of her involvement in the fraud, in which she had received less than the property's market value. Count 15 concerned J's purchase of another property, which was transferred to her name for a reduced price, through an alleged fraudulent mortgage application. Count 16 concerned J and S's attempts to sell that second property. At trial, J had made a submission of no case to answer with respect to counts 14 and 15. The judge directed himself in accordance with the principles in *R. v Galbraith (George Charles)* [1981] 1 W.L.R. 1039, [1981] C.L.Y. 513 and observed that in the usual case the seller was not interested in how the buyer financed the purchase of property. He rejected J's submission, however, having concluded that it was enough for the case to go to the jury that S had some knowledge of what was involved. J contended that counts 14 and 15 ought not to have been left to the jury since there was no proper basis on which it could be inferred that she was party to any fraud. She submitted that it was not enough for the case to go to the jury that she had some knowledge of what was involved, and that it had to be shown that she had knowingly participated in the conspiracy. J argued that since the verdict on counts 14 and 15 were unsafe, so was that on count 16. S supported J's submissions but contended further that there were inconsistent verdicts arising out of the fact that he was acquitted on count 11, which concerned another conspiracy to defraud in respect of which a co-defendant had been convicted, but not counts 14 and 15.

Held: Appeals dismissed. (1) The only relevant issue was whether the jury could on the facts find J guilty of the offence for which she was charged, namely being party to a fraud on the building society. It was not necessary that a defendant in a conspiracy charge should know all the details of the scheme to which he attached himself, *R. v Griffiths (Douglas Anthony)* [1966] 1 Q.B. 589, [1965] C.L.Y. 750 applied. It was enough that there was a common criminal purpose, which in the instant case was to deceive the lender. There was evidence from which a reasonable jury could infer that J was guilty of conspiracy to defraud; she had to have known that she had received less than the ostensible price for the first property. The essential question was whether J was an innocent party duped by another or whether she had known much more than she claimed and was involved in the two conspiracies. The judge was entitled to conclude that that was a question for the jury to decide, and there was sufficient evidence on which the jury properly directed could have found her guilty. Moreover, counts 14 and 15 did not necessarily stand or fall together. The latter did not involve a bogus purchaser and there might well have been a case to answer with respect to that count even if there was no case to answer with respect to count 14. However, once the court was satisfied that there was a case on count 14, then there was inevitably a case to answer on count 15, as both S and J had realistically accepted. It followed that the verdict on count 16, the money laundering transaction, was also safe (see paras 32-33, 37, 39-41 of judgment). (2) Whilst it might be a surprising outcome that S was acquitted of having been a party to the count 11 conspiracy and yet was a party to the count 14 conspiracy, that did not begin to meet the rigorous test necessary to establish that there were inconsistent verdicts. They were not logically inconsistent. The nature of the two conspiracies was different, the parties were different, and the evidence for each was different. A jury properly following the direction to be sure before convicting could properly convict on one count without doing so on the other (para.43).

R. v CLARK (STEPHEN), [2012] EWCA Crim 1220, [2012] Lloyd's Rep. F.C. 606, Elias, L.J., CA (Crim Div).

627. Controlled drugs–Misuse of drugs–England, Wales and Scotland

THE MISUSE OF DRUGS (AMENDMENT NO.2) (ENGLAND, WALES AND SCOTLAND) REGULATIONS 2013, SI 2013/625; made under the Misuse of Drugs Act 1971 s.7, s.10, s.22, s.31. In force: April 10, 2013; .

These Regulations place Sativex, a cannabis-based medicine, in the Misuse of Drugs Regulations 2001 Sch.4 Pt 1.

628. Corporate liability–Mens rea–Whether senior employee fixing employer company with intent to deceive for prosecution under s.38 Goods Vehicles (Licensing of Operators) Act 1995

[Goods Vehicles (Licensing of Operators) Act 1995 (c.23) s.38.]

The appellant agency (V) appealed by way of case stated against a decision of the magistrates' court to dismiss its case against the respondent company (C) in respect of an alleged offence of allowing a sub-contractor to use an operator's licence under the Goods Vehicles (Licensing of Operators) Act 1995 s.38. A heavy goods vehicle registered to C had been stopped on a random vehicle check by V. The driver was a sub-contractor who was not entitled to drive the vehicle under the relevant operator's licence. The magistrates concluded that: an offence under s.38 was not an absolute offence; V bore the burden of showing that there was sufficient evidence to infer that C could have formed the necessary intent to deceive under s.38; there was insufficient evidence to infer that C's plant and asset manager (H), who was responsible for the administration of matters concerning operators' licences, was equal to a director or was one of the people who constituted C's "brains"; there was insufficient evidence to show that any of C's directors or office-holders, who did form the "brains" of C, had decided to allow the driver to use the licence; C could not have formed the necessary intention to deceive without knowledge of the facts constituting the offence. V submitted that the facts were sufficient to show that H was in charge of the area of C's business concerning operators' licences, and that although he was not a shadow director the facts were such that he formed part of C's "brains" and could therefore fix C with the requisite intention for the purposes of a prosecution under s.38.

Held: Appeal dismissed. A line of authorities had held that there needed to be evidence that those with real authority in a company had knowledge of the facts constituting an offence in order to fix a company with the requisite mens rea, *Hill and Sons (Botley and Denmead) Ltd v Hampshire Chief Constable* [1972] R.T.R. 29, [1972] C.L.Y. 2979, *Ross Hillman Ltd v Bond* [1974] Q.B. 435, [1974] C.L.Y. 3246 and *P Lowery & Sons Ltd v Wark* [1975] R.T.R. 45, [1975] C.L.Y. 2911 applied. Even where there had been a delegation of a significant area of business operation to a senior employee, as in the instant case, there was still a requirement that those with general authority within the company had knowledge of the facts constituting the offence so as to fix the company with the requisite intention; that was especially the case where prosecution for the offence required an intention to deceive. An offence under s.38 was not one of strict liability. The magistrates had not erred in finding that H did not fall within the class of persons who could properly be held to be within C's "brains" such that he could have committed an offence in C's name. The magistrates were entitled to find that there was no evidence from which a reasonable tribunal could infer that one of C's company officers had knowledge of the offence at the time that it was committed such that C could have formed the necessary intent to deceive (see paras 11, 16, 19, 29-30 of judgment).

VEHICLE OPERATOR SERVICES AGENCY v FM CONWAY LTD, [2012] EWHC 2930 (Admin), [2013] R.T.R. 17, Irwin, J., QBD (Admin).

629. Court security officers–Knives–Retention–Seized property

THE RETENTION OF KNIVES (SUPREME COURT) REGULATIONS 2013, SI 2013/2532; made under the Constitutional Reform Act 2005 s.51D. In force: November 1, 2013; .

These Regulations set out the process to be followed by the Supreme Court security officers when seizing knives from persons entering the Supreme Court.

630. Crime and Courts Act 2013 (c.22)–Commencement No.1 and Transitional and Saving Provision) Order

THE CRIME AND COURTS ACT 2013 (COMMENCEMENT NO.1 AND TRANSITIONAL AND SAVING PROVISION) ORDER 2013, SI 2013/SI 2013/1042 (C.44); made under the Crime and Courts Act 2013 s.60, s.61. Commencement details: bringing into force various provisions of the 2013 Act on May 8, 2013, May 27, 2013 and June 25, 2013.; .

This Order brings into force on May 8, 2013 the specified order making powers, the interpretation provisions in the Crime and Courts Act 2013 Pt.1 s.51. Section 51 makes some technical amendments to the immigration appeals provisions in the Nationality, Immigration and Asylum Act 2002 and the Immigration, Asylum and Nationality Act 2006 s.47 to facilitate combined appeals.

631. Crime and Courts Act 2013 (c.22)–Commencement No.2 and Saving Provision Order

THE CRIME AND COURTS ACT 2013 (COMMENCEMENT NO.2 AND SAVING PROVISION) ORDER 2013, SI 2013/SI 2013/1682 (C.67); made under the Crime and Courts Act 2013 s.60, s.61. Commencement details: bringing into force various provisions of the 2013 Act on July 29, 2013 and October 7, 2013.; .

This Order brings into force: on July 29, 2013, parts of the Crime and Courts Act 2013 (the Act) which deal with extradition and, human rights issues and devolution issues in Scotland; and, on October 7, 2013, part of the Act abolishing the Serious Organised Crime Agency and the National Policing Improvement Agency and establishing the National Crime Agency.

632. Dangerous dogs–Fees–England and Wales

THE DANGEROUS DOGS (FEES) (ENGLAND AND WALES) ORDER 2013, SI 2013/1302; made under the Dangerous Dogs (Amendment) Act 1997 s.4. In force: July 1, 2013; .

This Order increases the fee payable to the Index of Exempted Dogs for placing a dog on the Index that is exempt from the general prohibition on certain types of dogs.

633. Defences–Automatism–Insanity–Voluntary intoxication

The first appellant (C) appealed against his conviction and sentence for attempted murder, the second appellant (M) appealed against his conviction for wounding with intent, and the third appellant (H) appealed against his conviction for aggravated arson. C was 17 when one night he got up, entered his neighbour's house and repeatedly stabbed his neighbour's partner. C was a heavy cannabis user and had smoked a lot that evening. C had no history of violence. He did not deny responsibility for the injuries, but asserted that he had "blacked out" and had no memory of the attack, and had no idea why he did it. The psychiatric evidence was that C had no underlying mental illness or personality disorder, but that there was a real possibility that he committed the attack during a brief psychotic episode triggered by cannabis. The trial judge ruled that C's case was one of voluntary intoxication, not insanity, and he refused to leave to the jury the issues of insanity and automatism, so the issue for the jury was whether C had formed the intention to kill. It decided that he had. M suffered from severe tinnitus. He took a prescription tranquiliser, temazepam, to help him sleep, but also resorted to drinking alcohol, despite the warning that with temazepam he should not. At about 4am one night, after drinking a lot, he went to an off-licence to buy more alcohol. He became aggressive and fought with another customer before leaving. He returned armed with a kitchen knife and stabbed one of the shop assistants in the arm while they fled. M could not remember any of those events. An expert in the action of drugs on the brain gave evidence that temazepam combined with alcohol could reduce social restraint and lead to disinhibited behaviour. The trial judge rejected M's submission that he had no choice but to take alcohol to alleviate the symptoms of tinnitus and ruled that his intoxication was voluntary; he also ruled that there was no evidence that M was suffering from automatism. The jury found that M had intended to cause grievous bodily harm. H had started a fire in his own house, and was charged with doing so being reckless as to whether the lives of others, namely his neighbours, would be endangered. He took medication for clinical depression, and he had a pattern of drinking heavily only during periods of leave from work. The cessation of those bouts had led to episodes of alcohol psychosis or alcohol-induced hallucinosis. At the time of the fire he was suffering such an episode; he was seen acting strangely, but he removed important documents from his house before starting the fire. He accepted that he had deliberately started the fire and that he knew it was wrong but said he had given no thought to the risk to others. In light of the judge's ruling that the jury had to consider H's recklessness as if he had not been drinking, he pleaded guilty. C submitted that (1) his was not a case of intoxication but rather had passed to a recognised condition of mental illness, namely a psychotic episode, no matter how transient, and therefore the judge should have left the issues of insanity and automatism to the jury. M submitted that (2) the judge had been wrong to withdraw automatism from the jury. The Crown submitted in H's case that his mental illness was brought on by his past voluntary drinking and therefore should be treated in the same way as if he were drunk.

Held: Judgment accordingly. (1) The law had long recognised the distinction C identified between intoxication and a disease of the mind induced by intoxicants. Further, temporary insanity was as much insanity as that which was long-lasting or permanent, *DPP v Beard* [1920] A.C. 479 followed. The possible state of mind in which C stabbed the victim could properly be called a mental abnormality. To speak of a psychotic episode was to speak of a temporary abnormality of the brain or mind and thus of a defect of reason for the purposes of the *M'Naghten* rules, *R. v McNaughten* 8 E.R. 718 considered. However, whether there was a "disease of the mind" for the purpose of the *M'Naghten* rules had to be a question of law, not of medical usage. Insanity called for a special verdict of acquittal, while voluntary intoxication was generally no defence at all but might be relevant to whether the defendant formed a specific intention, if the offence in question required such, *DPP v Majewski* [1977] A.C. 443, [1976] C.L.Y. 487 considered. Regardless of precisely where the line fell between insanity and voluntary intoxication, C's case fell comfortably on the voluntary intoxication side. In order to engage the law of insanity, it was not enough that there was an effect on the mind; there also had to be a disease of the mind. Direct, acute effects on the mind of intoxicants, voluntarily taken, were not so classified, *R. v Davis* (1881) 14 Cox C.C. 563 followed, *R. v Quick (William George)* [1973] Q.B. 910, [1973] C.L.Y. 558 applied. C's argument amounted to treating every defect of reason as a disease of the mind, but that was not the law (see paras 15-21 of judgment). Automatism could be expressed as complete destruction of voluntary control, *Watmore v Jenkins* [1962] 2 Q.B. 572, [1962] C.L.Y. 2657, *Attorney General's Reference (No.2 of 1992), Re* [1994] Q.B. 91, [1994] C.L.Y. 3944 applied. The psychiatric evidence about C was of voluntary, if irrational, action, which would preclude a defence of automatism. Further, that defence was not available to a defendant who had induced an acute state of involuntary behaviour by his own fault, *Quick* applied. In addition, the trial judge had been right to hold that the possibility of automatism ran with the question of whether C had intended to kill so a separate direction about automatism was unnecessary. That would not have been so if there had been an alternative charge which was not of specific intent. The guilty verdict had involved a clear finding that despite his state of mind C intended to kill and thus he had acted voluntarily. However, it was not safe to say that in every case in which automatism was a possible and legitimate conclusion it should be removed from the jury if they had a decision to make about specific intent (paras 22-25). C's sentence was reduced from 18 to 15 years (paras 28-29). (2) The expert's evidence was about disinhibited behaviour rather than behaviour over which M had no voluntary control. Disinhibition was exactly not automatism. Moreover, video footage of the incident made clear that M's behaviour was voluntary and automatism was simply not in question. Even if M had been in a state of automatism, that defence would have very likely failed on the grounds that he had induced it through voluntarily drinking himself into a state of intoxication. To the extent that his intoxication was worsened by the combination of the drug with alcohol, he was well aware of the dangers. His distress about his tinnitus would not alter that (paras 46-47). (3) H's condition was caused by past voluntary intoxication, but he was not in any sense intoxicated at the time of the offence. He had stopped drinking five or six days earlier. As in *Davis*, H was not suffering from a direct or acute reaction to the voluntary taking of intoxicants. His condition was one of mental disorder with psychotic symptoms including the hearing of voices and hallucinations, complicated by clinical depression. He was entitled to have tried the question of whether he was actually aware of the risk that he created for his neighbours. His conviction was quashed. The Crown's argument would represent a significant extension to *Majewski* and the similar principle in *Quick*, *Majewski* and *Quick* considered. (4) C's appeal against conviction was dismissed and his appeal against sentence was allowed. M's appeal against conviction was dismissed. H's appeal against conviction was allowed.

R. v C; R. v McGHEE (COLIN); R. v HARRIS (DARREN), [2013] EWCA Crim 223, [2013] M.H.L.R. 171, Hughes, L.J., CA (Crim Div).

634. Diminished responsibility–Reverse burden–Compatibility of reverse burden with presumption of innocence

[Homicide Act 1957 (c.11) s.2(2); European Convention on Human Rights 1950 Art.6(2).]

The appellant (F) appealed against his conviction for murder. F had been serving a sentence of life imprisonment for murder when he killed another prisoner. In convicting F of murder, the jury rejected his partial defence of diminished responsibility. F argued that he should not have borne the burden of proving, even on the balance of probabilities, that he had been in a state of diminished responsibility at the time of the killing; the statutory rule in the Homicide Act 1957 s.2(2) to that effect was incompatible with the presumption of innocence in the European Convention on Human Rights 1950 art.6(2) and should be read down as imposing only an evidential burden, so that, once diminished responsibility was raised by some evidence, it should be for the Crown to disprove it and to the ordinary criminal standard.

Held: Appeal dismissed. In *R. v Lambert (Steven)* [2002] Q.B. 1112, [2000] C.L.Y. 3229, the Court of Appeal addressed directly the argument that s.2(2) contravened art.6(2) and held that it was "self evident" that it did not. That decision was binding. Nevertheless, in deference to the detailed argument mounted by F, the principle involved would be addressed. Two successive questions arose. The first was whether s.2(2) impinged at all on the presumption of innocence in art.6(2). If it did, the second was whether it was a proportionate and thus justified modification of the presumption, in accordance with the decision of the European Court of Human Rights in *Salabiaku v France (A/141-A)* (1991) 13 E.H.R.R. 379. Given that s.2(2) did not require the defendant to disprove an element of the offence but to establish an exception or excuse, the better view was that s.2(2) did not impinge on the presumption of innocence at all. In any event, s.2(2) was a justified modification of the presumption. Diminished responsibility depended on the inner workings of the defendant's mind at the time of the offence. It would be a practical impossibility in many cases for the Crown to disprove (beyond reasonable doubt) an assertion that he was suffering from diminished responsibility. Of course, if there was a bare assertion, or one supported only by poor evidence, it would be open to the Crown to invite the jury to reject it, but if the onus lay on the Crown to disprove the condition beyond reasonable doubt, that would not be enough. The Crown would have to adduce evidence of the absence of abnormality in the defendant's mental state. But the defendant was under no obligation to submit to a medical examination and might well refuse. If he did formally submit, he might fail to co-operate. He might refuse, lawfully, to make available past medical or other records which were necessary to a report on his condition. That was a simple but fundamental reason why the reverse onus was essential to the working of the law of diminished responsibility. The reverse onus was consistent with the law generally maintained in jurisdictions which knew the concept of diminished responsibility as a specific and partial defence to murder. It had been upheld for sound reason in accordance with the *Salabiaku* test in the courts of England, Scotland, Northern Ireland and Strasbourg, and it had been retained by Parliament after a comprehensive review. The alternative argued for was neither workable nor required by principle given the purpose of the partial defence as a moderation of a mandatory sentence. Provocation and self-defence, which F had suggested were analogous, were not. For all those reasons, even if *Lambert* was not binding, it could not be said that the reverse onus was an unwarranted infringement of art.6(2), *Lambert* and *Salabiaku* applied (see paras 18, 21-22, 28, 31-32, 35, 44 of judgment).

R. v FOYE (LEE ROBERT), [2013] EWCA Crim 475, (2013) 177 J.P. 449, Lord Hughes of Ombersley, CA (Crim Div).

635. Dissemination of terrorist publications–Admissibility–Dissemination by distribution of terrorist publications–Whether material capable of encouraging terrorism–Admissibility of evidence of possession by named terrorists of similar or identical material

[Terrorism Act 2006 (c.11) s.2(3), s.2; Terrorism Act 2000 (c.11) s.58.]

The appellant (F) appealed against his conviction on seven counts of dissemination, by distribution, of a "terrorist publication" contrary to the Terrorism Act 2006 s.2(1) (a) and s.2(2). F had been the manager of an Islamic bookshop. He was charged with a number of offences under s.2 of the 2006 Act and possessing information likely to be useful to a person committing or preparing an act of terrorism contrary to the Terrorism Act 2000 s.58. The indicted material included books, articles, videos and DVDs which, the prosecution contended, supported the case for militant Islam. The prosecution case was that each of the publications indicted amounted to a terrorist publication within the meaning of s.2(3) of the 2006 Act in that it was likely to be understood by at least some of the persons to whom it was available as a direct or indirect encouragement to commit acts of terrorism. F's defence was that upon a proper reading or viewing the published materials did not encourage acts of terrorism but placed into the market for interested readers and viewers material whose content was and encouraged only intelligent discussion of religious and political theory. F elected not to give evidence. It followed that the requirements of s.2 of the 2006 Act were to be judged by the jury solely upon a consideration of the indicted material assisted, to the extent they considered appropriate, by expert evidence. For that purpose, the judge permitted the prosecution to adduce in evidence the possession by named terrorist offenders of material similar or identical to that disseminated by F. The prosecution stated that, as at that date, the indicted material was found in 26 per cent of police terrorist investigations, and posed the question "Is it probable that the publication you are considering would be understood by a significant number of its readers as directly or indirectly encouraging terrorism? If the statistics are anything to go by, as well as the actual attribution of indicted publications in the most serious terrorist cases we have listed are anything to go by, the answer to that question is a resounding yes". The judge directed the jury to give that evidence the weight they felt it deserved. F was found guilty of seven counts under s.2 of the 2006 Act and four offences under the 2000 Act. He appealed in respect of the 2006 Act offences. F contended that his convictions were unsafe since the evidence of possession by known terrorists of the indicted material was inadmissible and prejudicial to his case.

Held: Appeal allowed. Consideration of the composition of the readership of a publication for the purpose of judging the publication's likely effect upon them was a quite separate and different exercise from consideration of evidence that people who had read it were in fact encouraged to commit terrorist offences. The danger in the instant case was the elision of those two issues. The evidence of possession of the material by known terrorists was admissible, if at all, for the extremely limited purpose of demonstrating that the readership of the indicted publications included those who were prepared to commit terrorist acts.

However, if the evidence was admitted for that purpose, it was relevant only to the question whether such people were likely to regard the contents of the publication as encouragement to commit terrorist acts. It was not admissible to prove the fact that people had been so encouraged. There was manifest danger inherent in admitting the evidence even for that extremely limited purpose. The danger was that the jury would condemn the publication purely by reason of its association with known terrorists. The temptation conclude that terrorists would not be in possession of a publication unless it encouraged them to commit acts of terrorism was a powerful one, but such a conclusion would be speculative, unfair and prejudicial. The prosecution's question to the jury revealed, graphically, the danger of elision of the two questions (a) whether some of the readership had understood the publication to be an encouragement to commit terrorist acts; and (b) whether the publications encouraged terrorists to commit the terrorist acts. The statistic, 26 per cent, added another prejudicial dimension and had no substantial probative value within the meaning of s.2(3) in showing either that those who possessed the relevant material were likely to be terrorists or that the relevant material was likely to encourage the commission of terrorist acts. The contested evidence was not admissible save for the narrowest of purposes; if it was to be admitted at all, the terms of the admission should have been strictly confined and expressed in uncontentious terms along with a firm health warning as to its limitations. The judge had clearly intended to provide the jury with suitable directions which headed off the risk of unfair prejudice. However, in the result the jury was told only that the evidence was relevant to the issue whether the publication was "a terrorist publication" and that they should judge the merits of the competing submissions on that issue. The convictions on the seven counts under s.2 of the 2006 were, accordingly, unsafe and were quashed (see paras 44, 46-48, 58 of judgment).

R. v FARAZ (AHMED RAZA), [2012] EWCA Crim 2820, [2013] 1 W.L.R. 2615, Pitchford, L.J., CA (Crim Div).

636. Electronic commerce–Trafficking in human beings

THE ELECTRONIC COMMERCE DIRECTIVE (TRAFFICKING PEOPLE FOR EXPLOITATION) REGULATIONS 2013, SI 2013/817; made under the European Communities Act 1972 s.2. In force: April 10, 2013; .

These Regulations implement the E-Commerce Directive in so far as it applies to human trafficking offences in England and Wales.

637. Entering into money laundering arrangements–Interpretation–Arrangement to meet trader in stolen cars to buy one–No sale took place–Whether contrary to s.328(1) Proceeds of Crime Act 2002

[Proceeds of Crime Act 2002 (c.29) s.328(1).]

The appellant (D) appealed by way of case stated against a conviction for an offence under the Proceeds of Crime Act 2002 s.328(1), namely of entering into an arrangement which he knew or suspected facilitated the acquisition of criminal property, in the instant case a stolen car, by or on behalf of another person. D's case was that a car trader, whom he knew to be someone who had been involved with missing and stolen cars, had offered to sell him the car for £800. D asked the trader for time to raise the money, and he raised around £500. D and the trader agreed to meet for a second time. The sale to D never took place. The magistrates found that D had agreed to meet the trader for a second time in order to buy the car, albeit at a reduced price, and in doing so had entered into an arrangement within the meaning of s.328(1). The Crown submitted that the arrangement which the court found, between the trader and D to meet for a second time with a view to a sale, was one which facilitated the future acquisition of the car by or on behalf of another, namely an unidentified future purchaser of the car.

Held: Appeal allowed. The Crown's submission was a strained interpretation of s.328(1). It would suggest that every case of handling stolen goods with a view to resale also constituted an offence under s.328(1). The court gave the example of a man who bought a stolen watch from a trader with a view to selling it on at a profit: such a person was undoubtedly guilty of handling stolen goods if he knew or suspected that the watch was stolen, and if the watch was stolen on those facts the purchaser had entered into an arrangement which he knew or suspected would facilitate, in the future, the acquisition of criminal property by or on behalf of another. On the Crown's submission, both individuals would have committed an offence at the moment that those individuals arranged to meet with a view to the watch being sold. That gave s.328(1) far too wide a construction. In the instant case, the arrangement was not even a contract of sale, but was an arrangement to meet with a view to negotiating the price of the car. If the price had been negotiated and the car was handed over, that would have facilitated the future acquisition of the car by another. However, s.328(1) said that the arrangement had to be one that "facilitates", not one that "will facilitate". Section 328(1) therefore envisaged a snapshot being taken at the moment of the arrangement so that one could say, in the present tense, that it "facilitates" the acquisition of criminal property by or on behalf of another person, and therefore that other person had to be identified or identifiable. In the instant case, D's acts were too preparatory for that to have occurred, and therefore the conclusion of law on the findings of fact had been incorrectly reached and D's conviction had to be quashed (see paras 7-11 of judgment).

DARE v CROWN PROSECUTION SERVICE, [2012] EWHC 2074 (Admin), (2013) 177 J.P. 37, Bean, J., QBD (Admin).

638. Failure to secure school attendance–Lesser offences–Mother unable to control child–Whether unavoidable cause prevented school attendance–Test for convicting of lesser offence

[Education Act 1996 (c.56) s.444(1), s.444(3)(b).]

The appellant local authority appealed by way of case stated against a decision of a magistrates' court to dismiss an information preferred against the respondent (C) for failing to secure the attendance at school of her 15-year-old daughter (D). C had been subjected to domestic violence by D's father and had separated from him when D was very young and had been rehoused out of London. D had gone missing and C then discovered that D had traced her father and had made contact with him and his family and had gone to stay with them. Although C took D to school, D did not stay there. Instead she travelled to London and visited or stayed with her father's family. C had been found guilty in her absence of an offence under the Education Act 1996 s.444(1) in respect of D and a younger sibling. The local authority then brought a further prosecution against C in respect of D for the aggravated offence under s.444(1A) alleging that C knew that D was failing to attend school and failed without reasonable justification to cause her to do so. C's defence was that she could not control D who had regularly misled her; C had mental health issues which had caused her not to attend meetings arranged to discuss D's non-attendance; at the relevant time D was only intermittently at home and spent more than half of the time in London with the father's family. The magistrates' court found that D's chaotic lifestyle was an unavoidable cause of her non-attendance within s.444(3)(b) and that C had a reasonable justification in all the circumstances within s.444(1A). The questions for the opinion of the High Court were whether (i) the magistrates' court was wrong in law to find that D's chaotic lifestyle amount to an unavoidable cause preventing her from attending school; (ii) it was wrong to find that C had not failed to cause D to attend school regularly; (iii) it should have convicted C.

Held: Appeal allowed. (1) Unfortunately the relevant decided cases had not been put before the magistrates' court. They showed that "unavoidable cause" had been strictly construed. Something in the nature of an emergency was required, which actually prevented attendance, *Jenkins v Howells* [1949] 2 K.B. 218, [1947-51] C.L.Y. 3343 applied. A deliberate decision by the child to remove herself from school was not an unavoidable cause, and the reasonableness of the actions of a mother who claimed not to be able to control the child was irrelevant, *Bath and North East Somerset DC v Warman* [1999]

Ed. C.R. 517, [1999] C.L.Y. 1832 applied. Where a child had behavioural difficulties and the mother had done all she could, there was no unavoidable cause because there was no emergency, *Islington LBC v D* [2011] EWHC 990 (Admin) applied. The magistrates' court had erred in concluding that D's chaotic lifestyle was an unavoidable cause preventing her from attending school within s.444(3). Even if C had a reasonable justification within s.444(1A) for failing to cause D to attend school, there was no unavoidable cause. (2) Even if C had a reasonable justification within s.444(1A) for failing to cause D to attend school, so that the aggravated offence was not made out, there was no defence to the lesser offence under s.444(1). The test for returning an alternative verdict was whether such a verdict would be in the interests of justice, *S LBC v S* [2004] EWHC 2876 (Admin), [2005] E.L.R. 276, [2005] C.L.Y. 792 applied. (3) There was good reason in the instant case for remitting the case to the magistrates' court with a direction to convict because that would tend to encourage the attendance of D's younger sibling.

WEST SUSSEX CC v C, [2013] EWHC 1757 (Admin), (2013) 177 J.P. 567, Hallett, L.J., DC.

639. Firearms certificates–Shotguns

THE FIREARMS (AMENDMENT) RULES 2013, SI 2013/1945; made under the Firearms Act 1968 s.26A, s.26B, s.53. In force: December 1, 2013; .

These Rules replace the existing two application forms for a firearm certificate and a shotgun certificate with one new single application form that applies for the purposes of both applications.

640. Fraud–Fraud by false representation–Essential elements of offence–Causative link required between false representation and loss

[Fraud Act 2006 (c.35) s.2.]

The appellant (G) appealed against her conviction for fraud by false representation. G and her stepson (S) were directors of a property development company. It was alleged that they had allowed G's husband (H) to run the company, even though he was the subject of a director's disqualification order. They had attended a bank in order to open a bank account in the company's name. During the meeting H dishonestly informed the bank that savings and assets were available to fund property development. G then signed a form confirming the truth of the information they had provided. After the account was opened, the company acquired computers and office equipment by issuing post-dated cheques to the supplier. The company subsequently stopped the cheques, causing a loss to the supplier of approximately £130,000. G, S and H were charged with various offences. G was convicted of fraud in relation to the dishonest representations made to the bank. However, it was not suggested that she was party to the fraudulent scheme to acquire the computer equipment. G submitted that the recorder had not identified a particular gain or loss which would result from the false representation or the opening of the bank account.

Held: Appeal allowed. An intention to make a gain, or to cause loss to another or expose another to risk of loss, was not of itself enough to meet the requirements of the Fraud Act 2006 s.2. In order to commit fraud by representation, a defendant had to make a false representation as defined in s.2(2) to s.2(5); do so dishonestly; and intend to make a gain or cause loss by making the representation. The jury therefore had to be sure that the defendant intended to make a gain or cause a loss by making the false representation. It was a matter for the jury on the facts of each case whether the causative link between the intention and the making of the false representation was established. In G's case, the need to be sure of that causative link was not properly addressed at the end of the prosecution case or in the summing-up. The recorder had misdirected the jury. G's conviction was therefore unsafe and was quashed (see paras 29-31 of judgment).

R. v GILBERT (STEPHANIE RAE), [2012] EWCA Crim 2392, [2013] Lloyd's Rep. F.C. 109, Lord Judge, L.C.J., CA (Crim Div).

641. Freezing of funds–International criminal law–Libya

THE LIBYA (ASSET-FREEZING) (AMENDMENT) REGULATIONS 2013, SI 2013/2071; made under the European Communities Act 1972 s.2. In force: September 13, 2013; .

These Regulations amend the Libya (Asset-Freezing) Regulations 2011 (the 2011 Regulations) which provide for enforcement of, and penalties for breaches, of EU financial sanctions in relation to Libya imposed by Regulation 204/2011 concerning restrictive measures in view of the situation in Libya. These Regulations implement Regulation 488/2013 (the amending Regulation). So far as is relevant, the amending Regulation amends an existing exemption to the asset freezing provisions in the first Council Regulation to permit the crediting of funds to frozen accounts when payments are due under judicial, administrative or arbitral liens, judgments or decisions as referred to in arts 8(1) and (2) of the first Council Regulation.

642. Harassment–Defences–Defence of prevention or detection of crime–Test to be applied when considering alleged harasser's purpose

[Protection from Harassment Act 1997 (c.40) s.1 (3) (a).]

The appellant (W) appealed against a decision ([2011] EWCA Civ 1541, [2012] 1 W.L.R. 1510, [2012] C.L.Y. 707) that he was not entitled to rely on the Protection from Harassment Act 1997 s.1 (3) (a) as a defence to allegations of harassment made against him by the respondent (H). The course of conduct on which H had relied began in late 2003, when W embarked on a personal vendetta against him. W had alleged that H's management of his companies, mainly in the accounting year 2002-3, was characterised by fraud, embezzlement and tax evasion. Over the years, W sent numerous letters to the Official Receiver, the police, the Department of Trade and Industry and other public bodies. The judge at first instance found as follows: at the outset of the campaign, there was a reasonable basis for W's suspicions; the crucial evidence was that of H's companies' bank statements; in June 2007, once it became clear that the Official Receiver had examined that material and that it did not support W's case, his persistence ceased to be reasonable. The issue was whether W was entitled to rely, in respect of his conduct after June 2007, on s.1 (3) (a), which exempted liability for a course of conduct "pursued for the purpose of preventing or detecting crime". To answer that question, it was necessary to determine the test that had to be applied when considering the alleged harasser's purpose.

Held: Appeal dismissed. (Lord Reed dissenting) (1) In the context of s.1 (3) (a), purpose was a subjective state of mind, but a wholly subjective test was problematic. The necessary control mechanism was to be found in the concept of rationality. Rationality was not the same as reasonableness. Reasonableness was an external, objective standard applied to the outcome of a person's thoughts or intentions; the question was whether a notional hypothetically reasonable person in his position would have engaged in the relevant conduct for the purpose of preventing or detecting crime. A test of rationality, by comparison, applied a minimum objective standard to the relevant person's mental processes. It imported a requirement of good faith, a requirement that there should be some logical connection between the evidence and the ostensible reasons for the decision, and an absence of arbitrariness, of capriciousness or of reasoning so outrageous in its defiance of logic as to be perverse. The judge's findings of primary fact, fairly read, meant that after June 2007 W's vendetta against H was more than objectively unreasonable. It was irrational, so that he was unable to rely on s.1 (3) (a) (see paras 12, 14, 16 of judgment). (2) It was unnecessary to decide whether the purpose specified in s.1 (3) (a) had to be the sole purpose of the alleged harasser. However, it was appropriate to point out that a person's purposes were almost always to some extent mixed and that the ordinary principle was that the relevant purpose was the dominant one (para.17). (3) (Per Lord Reed) Parliament could not have intended to impose a requirement that the pursuit of the course of conduct should have been rational. First, Parliament did not say so. Second, s.1 (3) (a) and the similarly worded provisions elsewhere in the Act provided defences to criminal as well as civil liability; it was trite that a statute was not normally to be construed as extending criminal liability beyond the limits which Parliament itself made clear in its enactment. Third, it could not be inferred that criminal liability was intended to turn on the subtle distinction between what was unreasonable and what was irrational (paras 25-28).

HAYES v WILLOUGHBY, [2013] UKSC 17, [2013] 1 W.L.R. 935, Lord Neuberger (President), SC.

643. Ill treatment–Persons lacking capacity–Wilful neglect–Whether conduct of carer amounted to wilful neglect

[Mental Capacity Act 2005 (c.9) s.2, s.3, s.44.]

The appellant (N) appealed against her conviction for neglect of a person who lacked capacity, contrary to the Mental Capacity Act 2005 s.44. N was a trained mental health nurse with a general nursing qualification. She ran a care home. The victim (G) was an elderly woman who had significant learning difficulties. G was resident in N's care home until it closed and then went to live at a property owned by N, where she was cared for by N. The police attended the premises whilst N was on holiday, as G had left the premises after a row with one of her replacement carers. The prosecution relied on a course of conduct allegedly constituting neglect including inattention to G's personal hygiene and failing to maintain her rooms in a clean condition or replace dirty bed linen. It extended to failing to administer medication correctly and at the right time, or to provide food and a balanced diet or to make sure that G's personal habits did not create problems with food hygiene. N maintained that G would sometimes refuse to accept her help, and she felt in those circumstances it was wrong to override G's wishes. N submitted that the Act was complex, and in the context of the criminal offence created by s.44, uncertain in its ambit. N argued that G was presumed to have capacity to make her own decisions, whether they were wise or not; if her wishes were not followed then, even if she lacked capacity generally, they should be disregarded in as limited a way as possible so as not to interfere with her freedom of choice.

Held: Appeal allowed. The Act recognised that it was the basic right of any adult to be free to take and implement decisions affecting his own life and living, and that a person who lacked mental capacity should not be deprived of that right unless absolutely necessary in his best interests, *S (Protected Person), Re* [2010] 1 W.L.R. 1082, [2009] C.L.Y. 2719 applied. Lack of capacity in s.44 was defined by reference to s.2 which identified people who lacked capacity for the purposes of the Act, and that definition was supplemented in s.3 which provided a series of tests that identified the circumstances in which an individual was to be found unable to make decisions for himself. The purpose of s.44 was clear; those in need of care were entitled to protection against ill-treatment or wilful neglect. The question whether they had been wilfully neglected had to be examined in the context of the statutory provisions which provided that, to the greatest extent possible, their autonomy would be respected. Those in care who still enjoyed some level of capacity for making their own decisions were entitled to be protected from wilful neglect which impacted on the areas of their lives over which they lacked capacity. However, s.44 did not create an absolute offence. Therefore, actions or omissions, or a combination of both, which reflected or were believed to reflect the protected autonomy of the individual needing care did not constitute wilful neglect. Within those clear principles, the issue in an individual prosecution was fact-specific. It was only after examining the elements of the offence in its overall statutory context that it emerged that, notwithstanding the care taken by the judge in his summing up, there was one significant respect in which the jury was misdirected. The judge explained the autonomy principle and in that context he directed the jury that if G was or may have been motivated by that consideration, then any neglect which was proved would not necessarily have been proved to be wilful. If the jury concluded that G may have been motivated by the wish or sense of obligation to respect G's autonomy any area of apparent neglect so motivated would not be wilful for the purposes of the offence. It followed that there was a misdirection which undermined the safety of the conviction (see paras 13, 18-19 of judgment).

R. v NURSING (LIGAYA), [2012] EWCA Crim 2521, [2013] 1 W.L.R. 1031, Lord Judge, L.C.J., CA (Crim Div).

644. Interception of communications–Mobile telephones–Interception of voicemail messages–Meaning of "in the course of its transmission" in s.1(1) Regulation of Investigatory Powers Act 2000–Extension to cover messages already accessed by recipient

[Criminal Law Act 1977 (c.45); Regulation of Investigatory Powers Act 2000 (c.23) s.1(1), s.2(7); Directive 2002/58 on the processing of personal data and the protection of privacy in the electronic communications sector; Directive 97/66 on the processing of personal data and the protection of privacy in the telecommunications sector.]

The appellants (W) appealed against a ruling made during a preparatory hearing that the interception of previously read voicemails was an offence under the Regulation of Investigatory Powers Act 2000 s.1(1). W had all worked as editors and journalists. They were charged with conspiring unlawfully to intercept communications in the course of their transmission without lawful authority contrary to the Criminal Law Act 1977 and s.1(1) of the 2000 Act. The relevant conduct, or "hacking", involved the remote accessing of a voicemail box by dialling, from another telephone, the telephone number relating to it and bypassing any security feature, so as to be able to listen to the message contents, without the knowledge or consent of the subscriber, at a time when the recorded message was stored there, not yet having been deleted. The court held that s.2(7) of the 2000 Act extended the concept of transmission to include the period when the transmission system stored the communication in such a manner that enabled the intended recipient to have access to it, whether or not it had previously been received or accessed by the intended recipient. The issue was whether, on the proper construction of s.2(7), the period of storage referred to came to an end on first access or collection by the intended recipient or whether it continued beyond such first access for so long as the system was used to store the communication in a manner which enabled the recipient to have subsequent or even repeated access to it. W submitted that (1) the references in the 2000 Act to "in the course of transmission" in the context of the use of a telephone system should be understood as meaning that the transmission ended when the signal delivered to the handset was converted back into soundwaves or the call was terminated; (2) the extension of the course of transmission contemplated by s.2(7) was limited to covering the transient storage of electronic communications before receipt.

Held: Appeal dismissed. (1) The words of s.2(7) in their natural meaning were entirely apt to cover a situation such as that under consideration, where a message having been initially received by the intended recipient was stored in the communication system where the intended recipient might thereafter have access to it by playing back the message. In that regard it was significant that the intended recipient could not gain access to the voicemail message without resort to the telecommunication system, but was totally dependent on the system. In those circumstances, there was no good reason why the first receipt of the communication should be considered as bringing the transmission to an end, nor was there any support for that within the statutory language. It was readily apparent from the plain words that it was the intention of Parliament that s.2(7) should extend the course of transmission to include that situation (see para.27 of judgment). (2) In interpreting the Act the court was required to do so, as far as possible, so as to achieve the results pursued by Directive 97/66 and Directive 2002/58 concerning the processing of personal data and the protection of privacy in the telecommunications sector. It was common ground between the parties in the hearing below that Parliament, in enacting s.2(7), had gone beyond the duty in EU law to implement the Directives and had afforded protection to communications in circumstances beyond those required by the

Directives. However, that greater protection afforded by s.2(7) was not prohibited by EU law (paras 36, 39).

R. v COULSON (ANDREW); *sub nom.* R. v KUTTNER (STUART); R. v WEATHERUP (JAMES); R. v EDMONDSON (IAN), [2013] EWCA Crim 1026, [2013] 4 All E.R. 999, Lord Judge, L.C.J., CA (Crim Div).

645. Intimidation of witnesses–Actus reus–Offender sending Facebook messages to victim–Victim not intimidated by messages–Whether intimidation necessary for conviction–Young offenders

[Criminal Justice and Public Order Act 1994 (c.33) s.51 (1), s.51 (4).]

The appellant (Z) appealed against his conviction for witness intimidation. Z had been charged with witness intimidation after sending two Facebook messages to the victim (V) asking her to drop charges against him and others for false imprisonment, assault and theft. V's evidence at trial was that Z's messages were read to her, but that she was very sleepy and could not recall how she felt upon learning of their contents. In reliance on *R. v Patrascu (Andrew)* [2004] EWCA Crim 2417, [2005] 1 W.L.R. 3344, [2004] C.L.Y. 752, the judge directed the jury that if they were satisfied that Z had done an act which sought to deter V from assisting the criminal investigation, it was not necessary for the Crown to prove that V was not in fact put in fear. The jury found Z guilty and he was sentenced to a 12-month youth rehabilitation order. The issue was whether it was necessary for the Crown to prove that V had actually been intimidated under the Criminal Justice and Public Order Act 1994 s.51 (1). Z submitted that the judge had (1) misdirected the jury because the Crown had to prove that V was in fact intimidated; (2) wrongly interrupted the closing speech made on his behalf to the jury.

Held: Appeal allowed. (1) The first ingredient of the offence of witness intimidation under s.51 (1) was that the defendant did an act which intimidated another person. Although, as s.51 (4) made clear, the other person did not have to be put in fear of physical violence, it was difficult to see, on the ordinary and natural language of s.51 (1), why the Crown was not required to prove that the other person was actually intimidated. On its ordinary and natural meaning, s.51 (1) required the Crown to prove that the victim whom the defendant intended to intimidate was in fact intimidated. That was because the Act made it clear that the act of intimidation was part of the actus reus of the offence, and therefore had to be proved. Accordingly, the observation in *Patrascu* that the offence could be committed without the victim being intimidated was not correct, *Patrascu* not followed. If the victim was not in fact intimidated, but the other ingredients of the offence were proved, then the defendant might well be guilty of an attempt. That was the position in the instant case. It was clear from the jury's verdict that they must have been sure that Z did an act intending to intimidate V with the necessary belief and further intention. In the circumstances, although Z might not in fact have intimidated V, the jury must have been satisfied of the alternative offence of an attempt to intimidate. It followed that, although the conviction for witness intimidation had to be quashed as the judge was wrong in his ruling and in his direction to the jury, a conviction for attempted witness intimidation had to be imposed in substitution. Z's original sentence was not quashed as it reflected the gravity of the substituted offence (see paras 13, 16-18, 27 of judgment). (2) The judge was wrong to interrupt V's counsel as he had, but the contention that the intervention had had any material effect on the fairness of the trial or the safety of the conviction was without any merit (paras 25-26).

R. v N; *sub nom.* R. v ZN, [2013] EWCA Crim 989, [2013] 1 W.L.R. 3900, Sir John Thomas (President), CA (Crim Div).

646. Involuntary manslaughter–Foreseeability–Whether defendant's act subjected victim to risk of some harm–Reasonable bystander

[Criminal Justice Act 2003 (c.44) s.58.]

The Crown appealed under the Criminal Justice Act 2003 s.58 against a Crown Court ruling that it would not be open to a jury to convict the respondents (J and S) of manslaughter. J and S had been charged with involuntary manslaughter and affray. The deceased (D), who was 40 and apparently fit, had worked as a nightclub doorman. Unbeknownst to anybody, he had a renal artery aneurysm. He died after becoming involved in an altercation with J and S in the course of his employment. J and S had begun a fight with D and other doormen on an elevated fire escape. The incident lasted for about two minutes and there was no evidence that D had thrown any punches or that he had been pushed or struck. What was clear was that he had quickly descended the fire escape and had died shortly after climbing back up, the aneurysm having ruptured. The Crown's case was that the rupture was caused by a sudden surge in D's blood pressure resulting from release of adrenalin into his bloodstream during the incident. Pursuant to *R. v Carey (Claire Anne)* [2006] EWCA Crim 17, [2006] Crim. L.R. 842, the trial judge directed himself that, to convict, the jury would have to be satisfied that J and S had committed an unlawful act; that the act was recognisably dangerous in relation to the characteristics of D apparent to them at the time; that it had caused or significantly contributed to his death; and that D had died as a result of the sort of physical harm that any reasonable and sober person would inevitably realise the act risked causing. He found that a jury could not be sure that a sober and reasonable bystander, having the knowledge that J and S did at the time, would inevitably realise that there was a risk that D would suffer an increase in blood pressure leading to an aneurysm rupture as a result of anything that occurred that night. For the purposes of the appeal it was accepted that the argument should be approached on the basis that J and S were involved in an affray in which the doormen were not the aggressors and which was a substantial cause of D's death. The issue was whether the judge had been right to hold that *Carey* required that the jury be satisfied that the victim died as a result of the sort of physical harm that any reasonable and sober person would inevitably realise the act in question risked causing.

Held: Appeal allowed. Unless it was appreciated that the level of danger required for the offence of involuntary manslaughter was not high, the reference to "dangerous" as part of the definition of involuntary manslaughter was liable to mislead. A reasonable and sober bystander did not have to recognise a risk of serious or potentially lethal harm. He would simply need to recognise that the act in question exposed the victim to a risk of "some harm", *R. v Church (Cyril David)* [1966] 1 Q.B. 59, [1965] C.L.Y. 848 followed. For the purposes of involuntary manslaughter, an affray could constitute an unlawful and dangerous act whether it took the form of fear created, or direct violence suffered, during the course of the incident. J and S accepted that the judge misdirected himself in requiring that the jury be satisfied that a reasonable and sober person would realise that there was a risk that the unlawful act would cause the sort of physical harm from which D in fact died. Such a requirement put an unjustified gloss on the ingredients of the offence. A requirement that the bystander had to appreciate the type of injury that might occur undermined the "some" harm principle in *Church*, and was not supported by *Carey* or *R. v Dawson (Brian)* (1985) 81 Cr. App. R. 150, [1985] C.L.Y. 628, *Carey* and *Dawson* considered. Since the decisions in *Church* and *DPP v Newbury (Neil)* [1977] A.C. 500, [1976] C.L.Y. 496, there was no requirement that the defendant should foresee any specific harm, or that the bystander should recognise the precise sort of harm that ensued, *Newbury* considered. What mattered was whether a reasonable and sober bystander would recognise that the defendant's act inevitably subjected the deceased to the risk of some harm. The decision in the instant case was confined to its facts: an affray in which D was personally involved, rather than an individual happening across a fight without becoming involved. Whether a reasonable and sober bystander would inevitably recognise a risk of physical harm in the form of shock would have to be resolved as a question of fact. There was, however, evidence from which a properly directed jury could conclude that a sober and reasonable bystander would readily have recognised that D was at risk of harm, and that the fatal injury was incurred during the incident or in its immediate aftermath while he was still subject to its effects (see paras 12-23 of judgment).

R. v M; *sub nom.* R. v JM; R. v SM, [2012] EWCA Crim 2293, [2013] 1 W.L.R. 1083, Lord Judge, L.C.J., CA (Crim Div).

647. Legal Aid, Sentencing and Punishment of Offenders Act 2012 (c.10)–Commencement No.8 Order

THE LEGAL AID, SENTENCING AND PUNISHMENT OF OFFENDERS ACT 2012 (COMMENCEMENT NO.8) ORDER 2013, SI 2013/SI 2013/1127 (C.50); made under the Legal Aid, Sentencing and Punishment of Offenders Act 2012 s.151. Commencement details: bringing into force various provisions of the 2012 Act on May 14, 2013.; .

This Order brings into force the Legal Aid, Sentencing and Punishment of Offenders Act 2012 s.148, which amends the Criminal Justice and Immigration Act 2008 s.76 as regards the law concerning self-defence and related defences.

648. Licences–Local authorities' powers and duties–Offences–Scrap metal dealing

THE SCRAP METAL DEALERS ACT 2013 (PRESCRIBED RELEVANT OFFENCES AND RELEVANT ENFORCEMENT ACTION) REGULATIONS 2013, SI 2013/2258; made under the Scrap Metal Dealers Act 2013 s.3, s.20. In force: October 1, 2013; .

A local authority must not issue or renew a scrap metal dealer's licence unless it is satisfied that the applicant is a suitable person to carry on business as a scrap metal dealer. In determining whether the applicant is a suitable person, a local authority may have regard to whether the applicant or scrap metal site manager has been convicted of a relevant offence or has been the subject of any relevant enforcement action. These Regulations prescribe what constitutes a relevant offence or relevant enforcement action for the purposes of a local authority's decision on suitability.

649. Misconduct in public office–Nurses–Whether nurses working in prison held public office

The appellants appealed against their convictions for misconduct in public office. They were all nurses who worked at a high security prison. The case against them was that the first appellant (A1) had for several months had a sexual relationship with an inmate (M), that she had failed to report M's possession of a mobile phone and had facilitated his use of the phone by buying credit for it; that the second and third appellants had failed to report, and had deliberately covered up, their knowledge of A1's relationship with M and failed to report his possession of the phone; and the second appellant had also bought credit for it. The appellants' principal defence was that they did not hold public office, each acting solely as a nurse albeit in a prison environment with a different title. The factual evidence was broadly agreed, save that A1 contended that her sexual relations with M had not been consensual. The issues for the jury were whether the appellants held public office, whether each of them had wilfully misconducted herself in the performance of her public duties, and whether the conduct of each in turn was such as to be deserving of criminal condemnation and sanction. All issues were decided adversely to the appellants and they were convicted. The only issue on appeal was whether the appellants held public office, and furthermore whether that was an issue of fact for the jury or, given that the facts which formed the basis for any finding were not in issue, a question of law for the judge. The appellants submitted that the judge had approached the issue of "public office" too widely in light of recent authorities. They further submitted that they were no different from nurses employed by the NHS, and their possession of keys or other accoutrements that flowed from their employment in a high security prison did nothing to evidence the requisite degree of trust or authority required before a criminal sanction could be applied to any misconduct arising from their position as nurses.

Held: Appeals dismissed. (1) Nothing in the authorities justified the conclusion that the "strict confinement" should be to the position held by whomsoever was carrying out the duty; rather, it should be addressed to the nature of the duty undertaken and, in particular, whether it was a public duty in the sense that it represented the fulfilment of one of the responsibilities of government such that the public had a significant interest in its discharge extending beyond an interest in anyone who might be directly affected by a serious failure in the performance of the duty, *Attorney General's Reference (No.3 of 2003), Re* [2004] EWCA Crim 868, [2005] Q.B. 73, [2004] C.L.Y. 753, *R. v Bembridge* 99 E.R. 679 and *R. v Belton (Alice Tara)* [2010] EWCA Crim 2857, [2011] Q.B. 934, [2011] C.L.Y. 668 considered. The language used to define "public officer" in *R. v Bowden (Terence)* [1996] 1 W.L.R. 98, [1995] C.L.Y. 165 was undeniably wide and was binding on the instant court, *Bowden* applied, (see paras 23-34 of judgment). (2) The responsibilities of a nurse, whether trained as a prison officer or not, in a prison setting were not only for the welfare of the prisoners; they were also responsible to the public for, so far as it was within their power to do so, the proper, safe and secure running of the prison in which they worked. The duties described in the uncontested trial evidence more than amply fulfilled the requirement of a public office; the judges in the instant case were correct. In the prison system there was no distinction between those who held a public office and those who were in private employment who did similar work. Whether the prison was run directly by the state or indirectly through a private company paid by the state did not alter the public nature of the duties of those undertaking the work: the responsibilities to the public were identical. Furthermore, the decisions as to whether the appellants were public officers were decisions of law. If there had been an issue as to the facts (either of the relationship or the duties), the decision as to the facts would have been for the jury. The existence or otherwise of a public office was for the judge. The judge's decision in the instant case to leave the question to the jury was overly favourable to the appellants (paras 36-38).

R. v COSFORD (KAREN); R. v FALLOON (CAROLYN); R. v FLYNN (JACQUELINE), [2013] EWCA Crim 466, [2014] Q.B. 81, Leveson, L.J., CA (Crim Div).

650. Misleading omissions–Vehicle registration–Pre-registration of cars to third-party company to obtain discount for fleet cars–Subsequent sale to consumer–Failure to alert consumer of risk of prosecution and prejudice to insurance claims

[Vehicle Excise and Registration Act 1994 (c.22) s.43C; Consumer Protection from Unfair Trading Regulations 2008 (SI 2008/1277) reg.10.]

The defendant (D) was charged under the Consumer Protection from Unfair Trading Regulations 2008 reg.10 with an offence of making a misleading omission by failing to mention to its customers that they were at risk of prosecution under the Vehicle Excise and Registration Act 1994 s.43C or that their potential claims on a motor insurance policy could be prejudiced. D bought cars from manufacturers and registered them in the name of a third-party company, thereby qualifying for the manufacturers' discounts for fleet cars. D would then sell the cars to its customers, who would not become the registered keeper for a period of months. The prosecution argued that the purchaser was consequently put at risk of being prosecuted for an offence of using an incorrectly registered vehicle under the 1994 Act during the time that the vehicle was registered to the third-party company, which had no interest in the vehicle and did not exercise any control over it. D argued that the purchaser was not the person registered and so should not be regarded as the keeper for the purposes of s.43C.

Held: Judgment accordingly. (1) Whether someone was keeping a vehicle was a question of fact and degree. It was a question of overall control. In the instant case, the registered keeper had no control over the vehicle and no interest in it. It followed that the purchaser was not only the legal owner of the vehicle but also the keeper of it. Therefore, there was a risk that the purchaser of a pre-registered vehicle could be prosecuted. That fact was omitted from the literature used by D. Accordingly, it would be open to the jury to conclude that offences had been committed under reg.10 (see paras 10-12 of judgment). (2) D, having then pleaded guilty, would be ordered to pay a fine of £500 and £3,000 towards the prosecution costs. That penalty should not serve as a benchmark for similar offences in the future: the industry as a whole had hitherto regarded the practice as legitimate, but from now on ought to know that consumers should be alerted to the consequences of purchasing a pre-registered car (paras 18-21).

R. v DERBY CAR AND VAN CONTRACTS LTD; *sub nom.* HOUSE OF CARS v DERBY CAR AND VAN CONTRACTS LTD [2012] C.T.L.C. 62, Judge Burgess, Crown Ct (Derby).

651. Murder–Loss of control–Qualifying trigger–Application of loss of control defence in context of violence offered to or feared by defendants

[Coroners and Justice Act 2009 (c.25) s.54(1)(a), s.55(6)(c), s.55(6)(a).]

The court was required to determine three appeals against convictions for murder concerning the loss of control defence in the Coroners and Justice Act 2009 s.54 and s.55. The first appellant (D) had fatally stabbed his victim after an altercation when he found him asleep on a sofa with his wife. The judge decided that D did not qualify for the defence of loss of self-control because he had incited the violence offered to him by the victim, so that no qualifying trigger was available to him under s.55. The second appellant (H) had fatally stabbed his victim after an argument with her and the break-up of their relationship. The judge decided that the defence of loss of self-control should not be left to the jury because there was insufficient evidence to raise that as an issue. The third appellant (B) had known his victim as both were in a relationship with a prostitute (K). B had entered the victim's home intending to burgle him, and then beaten him to death. His raised the defence of loss of control, claiming to have used force on his victim because he was in fear of serious violence from him and because he had made hurtful remarks about K which were immensely provocative to him. The court had to determine the application of s.54 and s.55 to the issues raised in the appeals, in particular in the context of violence offered to or feared by a defendant.

Held: Appeals dismissed. (1) Sections 54 and 55 replaced the former provocation defence. When a person killed or was party to the killing of another person he was to be convicted not of murder but manslaughter if each of three distinct ingredients which comprised the defence were present. Section 54(1)(a) required the killing to result from a loss of self-control, s.54(1)(b) required that there be a qualifying trigger, and s.54(1)(c) required that a person of the defendant's age and sex with a normal degree of tolerance and self-restraint might, in the circumstances, have acted in the same way. Section 55 elaborated the qualifying triggers. Under s.55(6)(c) sexual infidelity was to be disregarded, *R. v Clinton (Jon-Jacques)* [2012] EWCA Crim 2, [2013] Q.B. 1, [2012] C.L.Y. 714 considered. Under s.55(6)(a), if the loss of self-control was attributable to a defendant's fear of serious violence from the victim against him or some other identified person, the qualifying trigger might be present. A further qualifying trigger applied under s.55(6)(b) if the loss of self-control was attributed to things said or done, which constituted circumstances of an extremely grave character, and caused the defendant to have a justifiable sense of being seriously wronged. Neither qualifying trigger in s.55(6)(a) and s.55(6)(b) was available to a defendant who had deliberately sought to provide himself with an excuse to use violence by inciting, or encouraging or manufacturing a situation for that purpose. The decision in *R. v Johnson (Christopher Richard)* [1989] 1 W.L.R. 740, [1989] C.L.Y. 859, in which the court had rejected the submission that the mere fact that a defendant caused a reaction in others, which led him to lose his self-control, should result in the issue of provocation being outside a jury's consideration, had been decided in the context of the former provocation defence and no longer fully reflected the appropriate principle, *Johnson* disapproved. Provided the statutory conditions were met, loss of control should be left to the jury. However, the circumstances had to be extremely grave and the defendant's sense of being seriously wronged by them had to be justifiable. Those matters required objective assessment by the judge at the end of the evidence and, if the defence was permitted to stand, by the jury considering their verdict. Were it to be otherwise, it would mean that a qualifying trigger would be present if the defendant gave an account to the effect that the circumstances were extremely grave to him and caused him to have what he believed was a justifiable sense that he had been seriously wronged (see paras 48, 54-59, 61 of judgment). (2) In D's case, the judge's decision that the loss of control should not be left to the jury was fully justified. There was no sufficient evidence that D ever lost his self-control (para.64). (3) In H's case, the victim's death was a direct consequence of H's response to the breakdown of their relationship. There was no evidence to suggest that H had had any justifiable sense of being seriously wronged or that the fatal injuries were inflicted by him in consequence of loss of control (para.65). (4) B's victim had been entitled to say and do anything reasonable, including the use of force, to eject B, as a burglar, from his home and it would be absurd if his understandable response provided B with the remotest beginnings of a basis for suggesting that he had any justifiable sense of being wronged, let alone seriously wronged. One essential ingredient of the defence was, therefore, entirely absent (paras 66-67).

R. v DAWES (CARLOS); R. v BOWYER (BARRY FRANCIS); R. v HATTER (MARK JOHN), [2013] EWCA Crim 322, [2013] 3 All E.R. 308, Lord Judge L.C.J, CA (Crim Div).

652. Murder–Loss of control–Voluntary drunkenness–Circumstances for consideration under s.54(1)(c) Coroners and Justice Act 2009

[Coroners and Justice Act 2009 (c.25) s.54(1)(c), s.54(1)(a).]

The appellant (X) appealed against his conviction for murder. X had stabbed the victim (V) in the chest, penetrating his heart and lung. X and V lived in the same house and often used to drink together. Both were intoxicated at the time of the attack. X gave evidence to the effect that V had been aggressive and physically abusive towards him, and he had swung out at him with a knife because he was frightened. He claimed that he had not deliberately chosen to stab V in the chest, but that V had made him so angry that he could not control himself. In addressing the loss of control defence, the judge directed the jury to consider whether they were sure that a person of X's sex and age with a normal degree of tolerance and self-restraint and in the same circumstances, but unaffected by alcohol, would not have reacted in the same or similar way. X argued that, assuming the provisions of the Coroners and Justice Act 2009 s.54(1)(a) and s.54(1)(b) were engaged, the fact that he was drunk at the material time was one of his "circumstances" that had to be considered in accordance with s.54(1)(c): he should not be precluded from advancing the partial defence of loss of control simply because, entirely coincidentally, he happened to be intoxicated. The Crown argued that, in the absence of any express provision to the effect contended for by X, the court should proceed on the basis that the law was unchanged; furthermore, the issue of self-induced intoxication had already been considered by the instant court in the context of newly enacted provisions relating to diminished responsibility in *R. v Dowds (Stephen Andrew)* [2012] EWCA Crim 281, [2012] 1 W.L.R. 2576, [2012] C.L.Y. 695, and in that context, the defence could not be founded on voluntary intoxication, even if acute.

Held: Appeal dismissed. (1) The judge had been right to direct the jury as he did. It had long been understood that the consumption of alcohol or drugs might diminish the ability of an individual to control or restrain himself, so that a person affected by drink or drugs might behave in a way in which he would not have behaved when sober or drug-free. Although it might sometimes impact on the question whether the constituent elements of a crime, in particular in relation to the required intent, had been proved, self-induced intoxication did not provide a defence to a criminal charge. X's submission proceeded on the basis that in the absence of any express statutory provision, in the context of "loss of control", a new approach to the issue of voluntary drunkenness was required. That proposition could not be accepted. There was nothing in the loss of control defence to suggest that Parliament intended somehow that the normal rules which applied to voluntary intoxication should not apply. If that had been Parliament's intention, it would have been spelled out in unequivocal language. Moreover, in the light of the compelling reasoning of the court in *Dowds* in the context of diminished responsibility, it was inconceivable that different criteria should govern the approach to the issue of voluntary drunkenness depending on whether the partial defence under consideration was diminished responsibility or loss of control, *Dowds* applied. In some cases, both defences would be canvassed before the jury, and the potential for uncertainty and confusion which would follow the necessarily very different directions on the issue of intoxication depending on which partial defence was under consideration did not bear contemplation (see paras 22-24, 26 of judgment). (2) That conclusion did not mean that a defendant who had been drinking was deprived of any possible loss of control defence. It simply meant that the loss of control defence had to be approached without reference to the defendant's voluntary intoxication. If a sober person in the defendant's circumstances, with normal levels of tolerance and self-restraint, might have behaved in the same way as the defendant confronted by the relevant qualifying trigger, the defendant would not be deprived of the loss of control defence just because he was not sober. Different considerations would arise if a defendant had a severe problem with alcohol or drugs and was mercilessly taunted about the condition, to the extent that it constituted a qualifying trigger: the alcohol or drug problem would then form part of the circumstances for consideration (para.25).

R. v ASMELASH (DAWIT), [2013] EWCA Crim 157, [2014] Q.B. 103, Lord Judge, L.C.J., CA (Crim Div).

653. Murder–Sufficiency of evidence–Application of "lurking doubt" principle in R. v Cooper (Sean) [1969] 1 Q.B. 267

The appellant (P) appealed against his conviction for murder. The victim (V), a married female, had been walking her dogs shortly after midnight. Naked from the waist down, she had been thrown into the river with her hands tied behind her back, where she had drowned. There were two suspects: her husband (S), and P. S was tried first, the case against him being based on circumstantial evidence concerning motive and opportunity. V had started a sexual relationship with another man, professing commitment to each man while continuing to see the other. S had been aware of her duplicity and had been heard to say that he would kill her if she continued to be disloyal. The day before the murder, he had learned of a further infidelity. He was acquitted because three aspects of the evidence undermined the case against him: two blood stains matched P's DNA; a man matching P's description was sighted in the area shortly before the murder; and S had powerful alibi evidence. P was therefore tried. There was no evidence identifying him as the man who had been sighted and he maintained that the blood stains were the result of an incident three weeks earlier when V's dog had bitten his finger. He alleged that the killer was S, which resulted in S's re-prosecution. The jury was nevertheless sure that P was the killer and convicted him. P appealed when new evidence incriminating S came to light. A fresh trial was ordered at which P's evidence was considered implausible and his conviction was upheld. P submitted that the court should apply the "lurking doubt" principle first identified in *R. v Cooper (Sean)* [1969] 1 Q.B. 267, [1969] C.L.Y. 818 because it was inconceivable that the jury could have excluded S as the murderer, and because his own explanation for the presence of his blood on V's clothes could not safely have been rejected.

Held: Appeal dismissed. (1) As a matter of principle, the constitutional primacy and public responsibility for a verdict rested with the jury and it was not open to a court to set aside a verdict on the basis of some collective, subjective, judicial hunch that the conviction was, or might be, unsafe. The application of the "lurking doubt" concept required an inexorable conclusion, reached through a reasoned analysis of the evidence, or the trial process, or both, that the conviction was unsafe. A conviction would be quashed on that ground only in the most exceptional circumstances (see para.14 of judgment). (2) There was no basis for concluding that P's conviction should be quashed by the application of the "lurking doubt" principle in *Cooper*. The prosecution case was that the blood had been deposited on V's jeans and underwear during their removal by the killer. Before the jury could agree with that conclusion, it had first to be sure that P's explanation for the presence of the blood was untrue, and second that there was no reasonable possibility of V having been killed by S or anybody else. The evidence and the submissions had both been analysed in considerable detail in the summing up. S had been acquitted, and in both of P's trials, every effort to demonstrate the possibility of him being the killer had failed, *Cooper* considered (paras 37, 41).

R. v POPE (JOHN RANDALL), [2012] EWCA Crim 2241, [2013] 1 Cr. App. R. 14, Lord Judge, L.C.J., CA (Crim Div).

654. Perverting the course of justice–Restraint orders–Breach of restraint order made under Proceeds of Crime Act 2002–Whether breach capable of amounting in itself to offence of perverting course of justice

[Criminal Justice Act 1988 (c.33) s.77; Proceeds of Crime Act 2002 (c.29); European Convention on Human Rights 1950 Art.7.]

The appellant (K) appealed against his conviction for conspiracy to pervert the course of justice based on a breach of a restraint order. A company director (S), whose company (M) operated a large scale tax fraud, had been restrained by an order made under the Proceeds of Crime Act 2002 (POCA) from disposing of his own or the company's assets. The restraint order made no allowance for using the restrained funds to pay legal fees, and that prohibition could not be lawfully circumvented by borrowing money, as to do so would simply be using M's own funds indirectly to fund expenses. K managed a company which offered finance to other possibly insolvent businesses. S approached K and obtained a loan to pay his legal fees. S subsequently told K that he was subject to a restraint order and that his solicitors would accept money only if it was a gift and not a loan. K agreed to tell the solicitors that the funds to be transferred to them were a gift. S's solicitors accepted the money on that basis. Repayments on K's loan to S were effectively made using M's restrained funds. K was charged with conspiracy to pervert the course of justice by dishonestly removing or attempting to remove from the court's control assets which should have remained restrained and available for confiscation. The defence submitted that there was no case to answer since a breach of a restraint order made under POCA, involving no illegality beyond the breach of the order itself, should be punished by way of contempt proceedings alone rather than by a prosecution for perverting the course of justice. K relied on the unreported decision of *R. v Ludlam*. The judge ruled that *Ludlam* was specifically limited to the regime for High Court restraint orders under the Criminal Justice Act 1988 s.77, rather than POCA restraint orders, so that the observations in that case, to the effect that the same regime should not apply under POCA, were obiter. Following that ruling, K pleaded guilty. The issue was whether a breach of a restraint order made under POCA was capable, without further illegality beyond the breach of the order itself, of constituting the offence of perverting the course of justice. K contended that to justify prosecution for perverting the course of justice, there needed to be some free-standing criminality apart from the breach of the restraint order simpliciter.

Held: Appeal dismissed. (1) A variety of conduct was capable of constituting the offence of perverting the course of justice. The fact of overlap with other offences, including contempt of court, did not of itself mean that the offence of perverting the course of justice would not have been committed, *R. v Clark (Mark Grosvenor)* [2003] EWCA Crim 991, [2003] 2 Cr. App. R. 23 applied. Caution was, however, required in extending the ambit of that offence, *R. v Selvage (Pauline Ann)* [1982] Q.B. 372, [1981] C.L.Y. 502 considered. *Ludlam* was plainly distinguishable since its reasoning was focused on the 1988 Act, *Ludlam* considered. In any event, the instant court disagreed with it insofar as it suggested a limitation on the offence of perverting the course of justice, in the context of breaches of restraint orders, to acts which constituted independent criminal offences. Under POCA, where restraint orders were granted and enforced in the Crown Court, there was no need to guard against the circumventing of the High Court's enforcement jurisdiction contained in the 1988 Act. The express provisions in a restraint order (under whatever regime) warning of the sanction of contempt of court for breach of the order did not preclude the pursuit of other criminal proceedings. It was fanciful to suppose that a person contemplating disobedience to a restraint order acted on the basis that he would only be punished for contempt of court, whereas he would have desisted had he but realised that he might by so doing commit some further offence (see paras 28-32, 35 of judgment). (2) The state of the law concerning the offence of perverting the course of justice could, accordingly, be summarised as follows: (a) there was no closed list of acts which might give rise to the offence; (b) that said, any expansion of the offence should only take place incrementally and with caution, reflecting both principles of common law reasoning and the requirements of the European Convention on Human Rights 1950 art.7; (c) so far as the offence generally was concerned, neither authority nor principle supported confining the requisite acts to those giving rise to some other independent criminal wrongdoing; (d) if there was no such limitation generally, then there was no basis for importing such a restriction, as a matter of law, into the elements of the offence where it arose in the context of a breach of a restraint order. A breach of a restraint order made under POCA was therefore capable, without any more illegality beyond the breach of the order itself, of constituting the offence of perverting the course of justice (paras 35, 39, 41).

R. v KENNY (MARK), [2013] EWCA Crim 1, [2013] Q.B. 896, Gross, L.J., CA (Crim Div).

655. Police stations–Sexual offences

THE SEXUAL OFFENCES ACT 2003 (PRESCRIBED POLICE STATIONS) REGULATIONS 2013, SI 2013/300; made under the Sexual Offences Act 2003 s.87. In force: March 12, 2013; .

These Regulations revoke and replace the Sexual Offences Act 2003 (Prescribed Police Stations) Regulations 2011.

656. Possession of false identity documents–Defences–Defendant pleading guilty to possessing identity document with improper intention–Lawyers' failure to advise defendant of potential defence based on refugee status–Likelihood of defence succeeding given rejection of asylum claim

[Identity Documents Act 2010 (c.40) s.4(2), s.4(1); Immigration and Asylum Act 1999 (c.33) s.31.]

The appellant (S) appealed against his conviction for possession of an identity document with improper intention. S claimed to have fled Iran in fear of his life, having been attacked by the morality police for expressing anti-government sentiments. He travelled through Turkey, Tanzania and Zambia before entering the United Kingdom in 2012. He did not claim asylum in the UK, and it was his case that his agent had told him that he could only claim asylum in Canada. When S attempted to leave the UK for Canada five days later, he was arrested at the airport in possession of a false French passport. S then claimed asylum for the first time. In his police interview, S was represented by a solicitor who put forward a prepared statement in which S admitted the circumstances of his flight from Iran. He said that he had not claimed asylum on his initial arrival in the UK as he did not know what to do and had been told to follow the agent's instructions. S subsequently pleaded guilty to possession of an identity document with improper intention contrary to the Identity Documents Act 2010 s.4(1) and s.4(2). He was sentenced to 12 months' imprisonment and a deportation order was made. The Secretary of State for the Home Department rejected his asylum claim. S's appeal against that decision and the deportation order was dismissed by the First-tier Tribunal, which rejected S's account of his recent ill-treatment in Iran and found that he could reasonably have claimed asylum, if he needed to, in

Turkey. S contended that he had pleaded guilty to the charge on the advice of his solicitor and counsel, who had failed to advise him of any potential defence that he might have had under the Immigration and Asylum Act 1999 s.31, despite his having had a reasonable prospect of successfully relying upon such a defence. The Crown submitted that the s.31 defence could not have succeeded since S had failed to discharge the evidential burden of showing that he was a refugee. It asserted that once the secretary of state had refused to grant an asylum claim, the situation was different from that in which a defendant appeared before a criminal court in the absence of such a decision.

Held: Appeal dismissed. (1) It was open to anyone charged with an offence under s.4 of the 2010 Act to raise an issue that he was entitled to the protection of s.31, *R. v Makuwa (Liliane)* [2006] EWCA Crim 175, [2006] 1 W.L.R. 2755, [2006] C.L.Y. 804 applied. A guilty plea tendered where a possible line of defence had been overlooked might be one which the court would be prepared to set aside on appeal if the conviction was consequently regarded as unsafe, *R. v Boal (Francis Steven)* [1992] Q.B. 591, [1992] C.L.Y. 2217 applied. That was, however, not conclusive of S's appeal; it remained for the court to consider whether, had S availed himself of the s.31 defence, there were good prospects of it succeeding. The court would only intervene where it believed that the defence, if run, would quite probably have succeeded, so that a clear injustice had been done, *Boal* applied, *R. v AM* [2010] EWCA Crim 2400, [2011] 1 Cr. App. R. 35, [2011] C.L.Y. 681 and *R. v Dast Jerdi (Bakhshi Ali)* [2011] EWCA Crim 365 considered (see paras 13, 21-24 of judgment). (2) S had failed on the refugee question before the tribunal, even though the tribunal was applying a standard below the balance of probabilities. S's failure to satisfy that relatively low threshold showed the instant court that he was unlikely to be able to satisfy the evidential burden of showing that he was a refugee, as s.31 required. and that, in any event, the Crown would have strong prospects of disproving it. If that were so the s.31 defence would fail. To go behind a guilty plea was an exceptional step and S had failed to satisfy the instant court that he would meet the test in relation to refugee status were the matter to be retried. Accordingly, the circumstances for regarding S's conviction as unsafe after his plea of guilty were not established (paras 45, 47, 52).

R. v SADIGHPOUR (ALI REZA), [2012] EWCA Crim 2669, [2013] 1 W.L.R. 2725, Treacy, L.J., CA (Crim Div).

657. Possession of false identity documents–Defences–Refugees–Defence under s.31 Immigration and Asylum Act 1999–Membership of particular social group in art.1A Convention relating to the Status of Refugees 1951 (United Nations)

[Identity Documents Act 2010 (c.40) s.4(1)(a); Immigration and Asylum Act 1999 (c.33) s.31; Convention relating to the Status of Refugees 1951 Art.1A.]

The appellant (E) appealed against his conviction for possession of a false identity document contrary to the Identity Documents Act 2010 s.4(1)(a). E was a Jamaican national. He had lived in the United Kingdom but had been deported to Jamaica in 2009. He returned to the UK using a forged British passport and a false name. He later admitted his real identity to immigration officers. E subsequently claimed asylum on the basis that in Jamaica he had been targeted by a criminal gang. He admitted the facts of knowingly using a false passport but asserted that he had a defence under the Immigration and Asylum Act 1999 s.31, on the ground that he was a refugee within the Convention relating to the Status of Refugees 1951 (United Nations) art.1A, being a member of a particular social group, namely either a group of migrants of Jamaican origin returning to Jamaica having been resident in the United States, Canada or the UK, or people who had been removed or deported from the US, Canada or UK back to Jamaica. E argued that the judge had (1) wrongly directed the jury that he had no defence under s.31 of the 1999 Act on the basis that there was nothing to support his argument that he was part of a particular social group under art.1A of the Convention; (2) misdirected the jury on the burden and standard of proof regarding whether he was a refugee.

Held: Appeal dismissed. (1) There was no basis in logic or the evidence for saying that either collection of individuals was a particular social group within art.1A(2). The evidence had demonstrated that wealthy people were targeted by gangs in Jamaica. There was no evidence that returnees to Jamaica as a group, or persons deported to Jamaica as a subgroup, were specifically targeted by gangs. Neither group had any of the essential characteristics of a particular social group, *Islam v Secretary of State for the Home Department* [1999] 2 A.C. 629, [1999] C.L.Y. 3172 applied. E was not a wealthy person and had not been targeted for his wealth. The fact, if established, that E had been bullied by criminals and not protected by the police did not and could not make him a refugee. There had been no possible basis for classifying him as a refugee; the judge had rightly directed the jury that the s.31 defence could not succeed. Although in a conventional asylum claim, the primary decision was taken by the secretary of state, in the instant litigation the question of whether E was a refugee was one element of the defence he had wished to advance. The Crown Court had had to address the issue. It could not have been assumed without inquiry or evidence that E was a refugee simply because he had made an asylum claim (see paras 28-32 of judgment). (2) E had had to establish the matters set out in s.31(1)(a), (b) and (c) on the balance of probabilities. On the other hand, once the issue of whether E was a refugee had been raised by the defence, the burden was on the prosecution to prove, to the criminal standard, that he was not a refugee. The judge in his summing up had been in a difficult position. The ingredients of the offence had all been admitted, and he had ruled that the only suggested defence was not open to E on the evidence. Nevertheless, it had not been permissible for him to direct the jury to return a guilty verdict. In the circumstances the judge had delivered an entirely sensible summing up explaining what the issues in the case were and explaining why, as a matter of law, the s.31 defence could not succeed (paras 36-37).

R. v EVANS (FABIAN), [2013] EWCA Crim 125, [2013] 1 Cr. App. R. 34, Jackson, L.J., CA (Crim Div).

658. Possession of firearms–Burden of proof–Accused's knowledge that firearm was convertible–Type of burden imposed by s.1(5) Firearms Act 1982–Whether burden encroached on right to presumption of innocence

[Firearms Act 1982 (c.31) s.1(5), s.1; Firearms Act 1968 (c.27) s.5(1)(a); European Convention on Human Rights 1950 Art.6(2).]

The appellant (W) appealed against his conviction for possession of a prohibited weapon contrary to the Firearms Act 1968 s.5(1)(a). The weapon was a "Blow Crazy" imitation 9mm calibre gun, which was capable of firing blanks and was alleged by the prosecution to have been convertible into a firearm within the provisions of the Firearms Act 1982 s.1. The prosecution case was that W knew or suspected that it was convertible into a firearm. The trial judge ruled that s.1(5) gave rise to a persuasive burden on W and directed the jury that it was for W to establish, on the balance of probabilities, that he did not know, or have reason to suspect, that the firearm was readily convertible. The issues on appeal were (i) whether, properly construed, s.1(5) of the 1982 Act imposed an evidential or persuasive burden on an accused charged with an offence of possession of a readily convertible imitation firearm; (ii) if the latter, whether that burden involved an encroachment on the presumption of innocence in the European Convention on Human Rights 1950 art.6(2) and if it did, whether such an encroachment was justified as a necessary and proportionate derogation from the presumption of innocence.

Held: Appeal dismissed. (1) The mere fact that other firearms legislation imposed only an evidential burden did not signify that Parliament had intended the evidential burden to be the only kind of burden imposed on an accused in the context of firearms. As a matter of ordinary interpretation, s.1(5) imposed a reverse legal burden on an accused. Once the prosecution had proved to the criminal standard that the accused "has with him" in a public place such a firearm, the legal (persuasive) burden would then be on the accused to show lawful authority or reasonable excuse (see paras 26-27 of judgment). (2) The ostensible reverse legal burden created by s.1(5) of the 1982 Act did impact on an accused's rights under art.6(2) of the Convention. A reverse burden was not, of itself, an unjustified infringement. Legal authorities on the matter were not united. The case of *Sheldrake v DPP* [2004] UKHL 43, [2005] 1 A.C. 264, [2004] C.L.Y. 707 was binding authority for the proposition that the earlier decisions of *R. v Lambert (Steven)* [2001] UKHL 37, [2002] 2 A.C. 545, [2001] C.L.Y. 3504 and *R. v Johnstone (Robert Alexander)* [2003] UKHL 28, [2003] 1 W.L.R. 1736, [2003] C.L.Y. 2644 were to be read together because their differences in emphasis were attributable to the difference in their subject matter. It followed that whether a provision giving rise to a reverse burden was justified as proportionate would depend on its statutory context and circumstances, *Sheldrake* applied, *Lambert* and *Johnstone* considered (paras 28-36). In the instant case, there were compelling reasons for concluding that s.1(5) imposed a legal burden: firearms offences were a very serious problem. Where firearms were potentially lethal, as in the case of a readily convertible imitation, the need for protection of the public was obvious, hence the number of strict liability offences, *R. v Bradish (Liam Christopher)* [1990] 1 Q.B. 981, [1990] C.L.Y. 2339 applied. The legislative focus was on the nature of the item possessed rather than the accused's knowledge; s.1 of the 1982 Act therefore had to be read in the context of s.1 and s.5 of the 1968 Act. Where a defence of lack of knowledge was nevertheless available as an exception to the strict liability approach, as was the case in s.1(5) of the 1982 Act, it was justified and proportionate that the legal burden of such a defence should pass to the accused. It would be a real deterrent to prosecution if the burden of proof fell on the Crown (paras 40-44).

R. v WILLIAMS (ORETTE), [2012] EWCA Crim 2162, [2013] 1 W.L.R. 1200, Davis, L.J., CA (Crim Div).

659. Prevention of Social Housing Fraud Act 2013 (3)

This Act creates offences and makes other provision relating to sub-letting and parting with possession of social housing.

This Act received Royal Assent on January 31, 2013.

660. Prevention of Social Housing Fraud Act 2013 (c.3)–(Commencement) Order–England

THE PREVENTION OF SOCIAL HOUSING FRAUD ACT 2013 (COMMENCEMENT) (ENGLAND) ORDER 2013, SI 2013/SI 2013/2622 (C.105); made under the Prevention of Social Housing Fraud Act 2013 s.12. Commencement details: bringing into force various provisions of the 2013 Act on October 15, 2013.; .

This Order brings into force, in England, the Prevention of Social Housing Fraud Act 2013. The Act (apart from s.12, which came into force on Royal Assent) comes into force on the day after the day on which this Order is made.

661. Proscribed organisations–Pakistan

THE PROSCRIBED ORGANISATIONS (NAME CHANGES) (NO.2) ORDER 2013, SI 2013/2742; made under the Terrorism Act 2000 s.3. In force: ; .

This Order enables the Secretary of State to exercise the power to specify that Ahle Sunnat wal Jamaat is to be treated as another name for the proscribed organisation listed in Sch.2 of the Terrorism Act 2006 as Lashkar-e Jhangvi and Sipah-e Sahaba Pakistan.

662. Proscribed organisations–Terrorism

THE TERRORISM ACT 2000 (PROSCRIBED ORGANISATIONS) (AMENDMENT) ORDER 2013, SI 2013/1746; made under the Terrorism Act 2000 s.3. In force: July 12, 2013; .

This Order adds "Jama'atu Ahli Sunna Lidda Awati Wal Jihad (Boko Haram)" and "Minbar Ansar Deen (Ansar Al Sharia UK)" to the list of proscribed organisations in Sch.2 of the Terrorism Act 2000.

663. Proscribed organisations–Terrorists

THE PROSCRIBED ORGANISATIONS (NAME CHANGES) ORDER 2013, SI 2013/1795; made under the Terrorism Act 2000 s.3. In force: July 19, 2013; .

This instrument exercises the power to specify other names for an organisation that is already proscribed in the Terrorism Act 2000 Sch.2 as "Al Qa'ida". The alternative names are: "al-Nusrah Front" and "Jabhat al-Nusrah li-ahl al Sham".

664. Rape–Consent–Reasonableness of belief in consent to sexual intercourse–Effect of defendant's mental illness–Delusional belief in consent

[Sexual Offences Act 2003 (c.42).]

The appellant (B) appealed against his convictions for rape and common assault of his partner (V), and criminal damage to her house. The common assault counts related to a incident when B spat in V's face because he had objected to her speaking to a male neighbour, and an incident when he made her eat a bowl of peas and dried leaves, which he said would make her feel better. Shortly afterwards, on two occasions, B had insisted on having sexual intercourse with V. V said that she had objected, but had submitted in the face of B's insistence. The criminal damage count concerned B having dismantled the front step to V's house, which B said she had consented to. There was expert medical evidence that B had been suffering from a mental disorder, probably paranoid schizophrenia, at the time of the offences, but that he had had the capacity to know what he was doing and that it was wrong. The expert said that the acts of intercourse might have been motivated by B's delusional beliefs that he had sexual healing powers, but that any such delusions did not extend to a belief that V had consented. On the rape counts, the judge directed the jury that they should ignore B's mental illness when asking whether any belief that he might have had in V's consent had been reasonable. Regarding common assault, the judge declined B's request to direct the jury that if his motive or intention was to benefit V there would be no common assault because there would have been hostility. On the criminal damage count, the judge directed that if B honestly believed that V would have given him permission, that would be sufficient to give him lawful excuse. B argued that, on the rape counts, the judge ought to have directed the jury simply that his mental illness was a factor that they should consider when deciding whether any belief in consent was reasonable, and that B might not have understood that V was frightened and had thought that her submission to intercourse had been consent.

Held: Appeal dismissed. (1) Given the immediately prior incident of forced feeding, as well as V's evidence of the acts of intercourse, there was clearly a proper basis for the jury's finding that V had not consented to sexual intercourse. In the face of the expert evidence that B's illness did not affect his ability to understand whether V was saying no to intercourse, and in the absence of any account from B suggesting misunderstanding, B's submission that he might have thought that V's submission to intercourse was consent could only be mere speculation. For those reasons B's rape convictions could not be considered unsafe. If that were wrong, and B's delusional beliefs could have led him to believe that V had consented when she had not, such delusional beliefs could not render reasonable a belief that V was consenting when she was not. The Sexual Offences Act 2003 did not ask whether it was reasonable for a defendant to suffer from the mental condition that he did, it asked whether the belief in consent was a reasonable one. The Act deliberately did not make a genuine belief in consent enough. Unless the state of mind amounted to insanity in law, beliefs in consent arising from conditions such as delusional psychotic illness or personality disorders had to be judged by objective standards of reasonableness and not by taking into account a mental disorder that induced a belief which could not reasonably arise without it. It did not follow that there would be no cases in which the personality or abilities of the defendant might be relevant to whether his positive belief in consent was reasonable, but that was for determination on specific facts. The jury was entitled to know how it should approach the issue of reasonableness, and the general approach ought to be the same in similar cases. The judge had been correct to give the direction he had (see paras 22, 34-36, 39, 40 of judgment). (2) On the common assault count, the judge had been right to decline to direct the jury as B requested. In the absence of a belief that the assault was necessary to save the life of the assaulted person, or to avoid attack by a third party, a wish to do good did not generally justify an assault (para.44). (3) The direction regarding criminal damage was plainly sufficient (para.48).

R. v B (MA), [2013] EWCA Crim 3, [2013] 1 Cr. App. R. 36, Hughes, L.J., CA (Crim Div).

665. Road traffic offences–Causing death by unlicensed disqualified or uninsured driving–Fault–Whether offence satisfied by defendant's presence on road at wheel or whether fault in manner of driving required

[Road Traffic Act 1988 (c.52) s.3ZB.]

The appellant (H) appealed against a decision ([2011] EWCA Crim 1508, [2011] 4 All E.R. 761) that, by virtue of the Road Traffic Act 1988 s.3ZB, he was criminally responsible for the death of a driver (D) who had crashed into him while under the influence of heroin, even though H's own driving had been completely faultless. D had been driving erratically for some time, narrowly missing colliding with other vehicles. He rounded a bend on the wrong side of the road and crashed into H's vehicle. H tried to avoid the collision by steering to his left, but D took no avoiding action. It was accepted that H's driving had been faultless and that, on a common sense view, D was entirely responsible for his own death. H was, however, uninsured at the time, and driving under a provisional licence. Instead of being prosecuted for those offences, he was charged with causing D's death under s.3ZB. The trial judge accepted that H had not caused D's death, but the Court of Appeal, considering itself bound by *R. v Williams (Jason John)* [2010] EWCA Crim 2552, [2011] 1 W.L.R. 588, [2011] C.L.Y. 2720, ruled that he had caused the death because the offence did not require that there be anything wrong with the defendant's driving. The issue for determination was whether a driver caught by s.3ZB caused the death whenever he was on the road at the wheel and a fatal accident involving his vehicle occurred, or whether he only caused it if he did, or omitted to do, something connected to the control of his vehicle which was open to proper criticism and contributed in some more than minimal way to the death. The Crown maintained that the words of the section were sufficiently clear to establish that the former was Parliament's intention and that driving on the road without any right to be there was sufficient "fault" to justify the offence. H argued in favour of the application of principles of causation.

Held: Appeal allowed. Parliament might have intended to create an aggravated form of the offence of having no insurance or driving without a licence, but that raised the question whether the intention had been to attach criminal responsibility for a death to those whose driving had nothing to do with the death beyond being available on the road to be struck. The Crown's argument, when pressed to its logical limit, became unworkable, and represented double strict liability. Although a government consultation document produced in 2005 indicated that taking a vehicle on the road when disqualified was as negligent as sub-standard driving, it was clear that however culpable it might be to drive when uninsured, unlicensed, or disqualified, if the driving was of an acceptable standard, it could not be called negligent. Parliament could have legislated in terms which left it beyond doubt that a driver within s.3ZB was made guilty of causing death whenever a car that he was driving was involved in a fatal accident, but it had not adopted such language; instead it had used the expression "causes... death... by driving", which imported a concept of causation. There was a well-recognised distinction between conduct setting the stage for an occurrence and conduct which was instrumental in bringing about the occurrence, *Galoo Ltd v Bright Grahame Murray* [1994] 1 W.L.R. 1360, [1995] C.L.Y. 3691 considered. The driving in both the instant case and in *Williams* fell within the latter category, but the question still remained whether it was a legally effective cause of the deaths. By the test of common sense, H had created the opportunity for his car to be run into by D, but it was a matter of the merest chance that H's car was what D hit. He might just as easily have hit a tree, which would have been a similar intervening event, yet it would not be said that the death had been caused by the planting of the tree. To label a person a criminal killer was of the greatest gravity. Parliament could legislate for harsh penalties, but it was not to be assumed to have done so unless such an interpretation of the statute was compelled. The rule of construction applicable to penal legislation was somewhat analogous to the principle of legality, *R. v Secretary of State for the Home Department, Ex p. Simms* [2000] 2 A.C. 115, [1999] C.L.Y. 4105 applied. In the instant situation, Parliament had chosen not to adopt unequivocal language and, therefore, an intention to create the meaning contended for by the Crown could not be attributed to it. A defendant charged with an offence under s.3ZB had to be shown to have done something, or omitted to do something, by way of driving his vehicle so as to contribute in a more than minimal way to the death, *Williams* disapproved. It was impossible to pinpoint what type of "additional feature" of a defendant's driving might be required; the issue was further complicated by the possibility of the defendant making a "wrong movement" in the agony of the moment, or coming across an unexpected natural hazard. To draw fine distinctions or to attempt to foresee every possible scenario would make the law confusing, incoherent and unmanageable. Juries were to be directed that there had to be something open to proper criticism in the defendant's driving which contributed in some more than minimal way to the death (see paras 16-20, 23-33 of judgment)

R. v HUGHES (MICHAEL), [2013] UKSC 56, [2013] 1 W.L.R. 2461, Lord Neuberger (President), SC.

666. Robbery–Use of force–Snatching cigarette from victim's hand–Whether use of force within s.8 Theft Act 1968

[Larceny Act 1916 (c.50); Theft Act 1968 (c.60) s.8.]

The appellants (P) appealed by way of case stated against their convictions for robbery of the victim (G). G claimed that she had been walking along the road when she became aware of three young people, P, who asked her for a cigarette. She genuinely thought that P wanted a cigarette and she said she did not have a spare one. No violence was threatened at that time. Immediately after, one of them snatched a lit cigarette from her hand and passed it between the others. The prosecution case was that the snatching of the cigarette alone amounted to the use of force and did so whether or not there was any direct contact between G's hand and any of P's. The magistrates found that one of P had snatched a cigarette from G's hand; the snatch amounted to the use of force by P; the force was used to steal the cigarette; and there was a pre-arranged plan between P to rob G. The question for the court was whether the magistrates were correct to refuse a submission of no case to answer in respect of the allegation of robbery on the basis that the act of snatching the cigarette from G's hand, in the circumstances described, was sufficient to constitute "force" for the purposes of the Theft Act 1968 s.8. P submitted that the snatching of the cigarette could not reasonably be deemed to constitute the use of force as it did not involve direct physical contact between them and G.

Held: Appeal allowed. The appeal raised a narrow and far from straightforward point. Before the enactment of the 1968 Act, and under the old law in the Larceny Act 1916, the answer to the question posed would have to have been answered negatively, as the old law required greater force than the mere taking of an item to constitute the offence of robbery. Section 8 required the use of force on a person or putting any person in fear of being subjected to force. Although the old distinctions under the 1916 Act had gone, there remained a basic requirement for the commission of the offence of theft that force was used on a person, *R. v Dawson (Anthony Mark)* (1977) 64 Cr. App. R. 170, [1979] C.L.Y. 545 and *R. v Clouden* [1987] Crim. L.R. 56, [1987] C.L.Y. 823 considered. There was on the facts found by the magistrates no physical contact between the hands of P and G. Borderline questions such as what amounted to the use of force where the force used was minimal was a matter for the first instance court and not for the appeal court. However, the magistrates had not found that P had used force on G; it found that the cigarette was snatched without necessarily any contact with G and that that amounted to the use of force by P to steal the cigarette. Those findings did not amount to a finding that force was used on G, unless the mere removal of the cigarette from her fingers amounted to the use of force. The instant case was similar to pick-pocketing where there was no direct physical contact between a thief and a victim. It could not be said that the minimal use of force to remove the cigarette between the fingers of a person sufficed to amount to the use of force on that person. It could not cause any pain unless the person resisted strongly, in which case direct physical contact would be expected between the thief and the victim. The unexpected removal of the cigarette between the fingers of a person was no more the use of force than the removal of an item from a pocket. The offence committed by P was properly categorised as simple theft. Their convictions for robbery would be quashed and substituted by convictions for theft (see paras 1, 5-6, 8-10, 13-16 of judgment).

P v DPP; *sub nom.* DPP v RP, [2012] EWHC 1657 (Admin), [2013] 1 W.L.R. 2337, Mitting, J., QBD (Admin).

667. Sexual offences–Consent–Whether deception as to gender could vitiate consent to sexual activity–Young offenders

The appellant (X) appealed against her conviction on six counts of assault by penetration and against a sentence of three years' detention. X, when she was 13, had met another girl (Y), who was a year younger, on a social networking website. X claimed to be a boy. The relationship developed over the next three-and-a-half years; Y considered X to be her boyfriend. X, dressed as a boy, visited Y on four occasions when X was aged 17 and Y 16. On those visits, there were numerous occasions of oral and digital penetration of Y. Y subsequently discovered that X was a girl. X was prosecuted. Following a conference with counsel, she pleaded guilty. She was of previous good character. A pre-sentence report described a history of self-harm and confusion surrounding her gender identity and sexuality. The sentencing judge held that X's deception was an abuse of trust. He took a starting point of nine years' detention, reduced that by a third to reflect her guilty plea, and then by half to reach the custodial sentence. X argued that (1) she could not have been convicted at a trial, because the elements of the offence had not been made out: deception as to gender could not vitiate consent, being deception as to a quality or attribute, as discussed in relation to HIV status in *R. v B* [2006] EWCA Crim 2945, [2007] 1 W.L.R. 1567, [2007] C.L.Y. 920; in contrast, in *Assange v Sweden* [2011] EWHC 2849 (Admin), (2011) 108(44) L.S.G. 17, regarding deception as to the use of a condom, and *R. (on the application of F) v DPP* [2013] EWHC 945 (Admin), [2014] 2 W.L.R. 190, [2013] 10 C.L. 69, regarding deception as to whether ejaculation would take place outside the vagina, the deceptions found to vitiate consent concerned features of the act itself; (2) her legal advisers had failed to advise her properly before her decision to plead guilty; (3) the judge had been wrong to sentence her on the basis that there had been a breach of trust.

Held: Appeal against conviction dismissed, appeal against sentence allowed. (1) X's analysis was rejected. *R. v B* had not said that HIV status could not vitiate consent if, for example, the complainant had been positively assured that the defendant was not HIV positive: it had left the issue open, *R. v B* considered. The argument that in *Assange* and *F v DPP* the deceptions related to the features of the act was not sustainable: the wearing of a condom and ejaculation were irrelevant to the definition of rape and were not "features" of the offence.

In those cases, it had been alleged that the victim had consented on the basis of a premise that, at the time of the consent, was false, *Assange* and *F v DPP* considered. Some deceptions, for example in relation to wealth, would obviously not be sufficient to vitiate consent: the issue had to be approached in a common sense way, *F v DPP* applied. Thus, although in a physical sense the acts of assault by penetration were the same whether perpetrated by a male or a female, the sexual nature of the acts was, on any common sense view, different where the complainant was deliberately deceived by a defendant into believing that the latter was male. Assuming the facts to be proved as alleged, Y had chosen to have sexual encounters with a boy and her preference had been removed by X's deception. Depending on the circumstances, deception as to gender could vitiate consent. Accordingly, X's pleas were not vitiated by a fundamental mistake of law or fact (see paras 24-27 of judgment). (2) X's conference with counsel would have been a fraught occasion for her. It would not have been emotional for her barrister. The court accepted his account that he had properly advised X as to the law: it was clear from the defence statement that he had understood the ingredients of the offence and there was no reason for him not to have made them clear. Although there were equivocations in Y's statement that would have been available for cross-examination at a trial, that did not demonstrate that the case would have failed on evidential grounds. The criticism of X's legal advisers was not made out: there was no basis for concluding that the defence would have succeeded so that a clear injustice had been done, *R. v Boal (Francis Steven)* [1992] Q.B. 591, [1992] C.L.Y. 2217 applied (paras 45-46). (3) The circumstances of two teenagers of similar age did not fall within the definition of positions of trust, *R. v ZBT* [2012] EWCA Crim 1727, [2013] 1 Cr. App. R. (S.) 85 applied. In the absence of abuse of trust, the relevant starting point was two years' imprisonment with a range of one to four years. Further, the context and the personal circumstances demonstrated features of mitigation to which the court was bound to have regard. X had served three months of the custodial sentence. Although the length of the deception and the degree of harm caused to Y fully justified the conclusion that the custody threshold had been exceeded, in the circumstances justice could be served by a sentence of nine months' detention suspended for two years, together with a supervision order of two years (paras 50-52).

R. v McNALLY (JUSTINE), [2013] EWCA Crim 1051, [2014] 2 W.L.R. 200, Leveson, L.J., CA (Crim Div).

668. Terrorist offences–Terrorist financing–Freezing orders–Application of art.6 European Convention on Human Rights 1950 to appeals under s.26 Terrorist Asset-Freezing etc. Act 2010

[Counter-Terrorism Act 2008 (c.28) s.66, s.67(6), s.68; Terrorism Prevention and Investigation Measures Act 2011 (c.23); Terrorist Asset-Freezing etc. Act 2010 (c.38) s.2(1), s.26; Civil Procedure Rules 1998 (SI 1998/3132) Pt 79; European Convention on Human Rights 1950 Art.6.]

The appellant British citizen (M) appealed under the Terrorist Asset-Freezing etc. Act 2010 s.26 against two final designations imposed by the respondent Treasury under s.2(1) of the Act. The Treasury believed that M was involved in terrorism and that financial sanctions were necessary to protect the public. An asset-freezing order was made, which required his state benefits to be paid to his wife, except for a weekly sum of £10 in cash, which was returned to him. His bank accounts were frozen. M denied being involved in terrorism and said that he was unable to answer the allegations without knowing why he had been designated. Since it was inevitable that designations would be triggered by material that was not disclosable on the ground of public interest, the court was required to determine, as a preliminary issue, the effect of common law on the Treasury's disclosure obligations, and whether the European Convention on Human Rights 1950 art.6 was applicable to appeals under the Act. M submitted that the regime relating to designations under the 2010 Act was identical to the regime under the Terrorism Prevention and Investigation Measures Act 2011, and that the court was therefore bound by the principles relating to disclosure in *Secretary of State for the Home*

Department v MB [2007] UKHL 46, [2008] 1 A.C. 440, [2007] C.L.Y. 2171 and *Secretary of State for the Home Department v F* [2009] UKHL 28, [2010] 2 A.C. 269, [2009] C.L.Y. 428 where the applicability of art.6 was recognised.

Held: Appeal allowed. (1) It seemed inevitable that art.6 of the Convention would apply to the regime under the 2010 Act. The latter Act applied the Counter-Terrorism Act 2008 s.66 to s.68. Section 67 of the 2008 Act dealt specifically with rules about disclosure and stipulated that neither the section, nor the rules made under it, such rules being contained in CPR Pt 79, required the court to act inconsistently with art.6. An "irreducible minimum" of disclosure to enable a fair hearing had to be made, *Bank Mellat v HM Treasury* [2010] EWCA Civ 483, [2012] Q.B. 91, [2010] C.L.Y. 348 applied. In *R. (on the application of Khaled) v Secretary of State for Foreign and Commonwealth Affairs* [2011] EWCA Civ 350, [2012] Q.B. 477, [2011] C.L.Y. 1689, Sedley LJ seemed to have excluded art.6 in freezing orders generally. That reasoning, being obiter, was not binding on the instant court. In any event, it was plainly wrong because it was contrary to *Bank Mellat* and *F*, *F* applied and *Khaled* and *MB* considered (see paras 10-21 of judgment). A further reason for believing that art.6 was applicable was the content of the explanatory notes accompanying early drafts of the 2008 Act. They were a legitimate aid to construction. If art.6 was not applicable, then s.67(6) of the 2008 Act would be meaningless, *R. (on the application of Bhutta) v HM Treasury* [2011] EWHC 1789 (Admin), [2011] A.C.D. 106 disapproved on the basis that that court had not had the benefit of being referred to the explanatory notes (paras 22-26). (2) It was not necessary to consider whether common law would provide the same safeguards as art.6, although it looked as though common law was excluded by the 2010 Act (paras 27-28). (3) The extent of disclosure required to produce a fair hearing would depend on the facts of individual cases. The "irreducible minimum" was not particularly helpful, since that was also fact-specific; the minimum was whatever was needed to enable the designated person to give effective instructions to his special advocate. There was no real difference between the effect of measures taken under the 2011 Act and asset freezing orders under the 2010 Act: both involved interference with fundamental rights. The latter might be considered less severe since they did not interfere with liberty, but that would have a very limited effect on disclosure requirements, because disclosure still had to be such as to produce a fair hearing, *Tariq v Home Office* [2011] UKSC 35, [2012] 1 A.C. 452, [2011] C.L.Y. 1082 applied (paras 31, 33-36).

MASTAFA v HM TREASURY, [2012] EWHC 3578 (Admin), [2013] 1 W.L.R. 1621, Collins, J., QBD (Admin).

669. Trafficking for sexual exploitation

THE PROTECTION OF FREEDOMS ACT 2012 (CONSEQUENTIAL AMENDMENTS) ORDER 2013, SI 2013/862; made under the Protection of Freedoms Act 2012 s.115. In force: May 13, 2013; .

This Order introduces references to the newly created trafficking offence in the Sexual Offences Act 2003 s.59A in the Criminal Justice Act 1988 (Review of Sentencing) Order 2006, the Armed Forces (Review of Court Martial Sentence) Order 2009 and the Criminal Legal Aid (Remuneration) Regulations 2013.

670. Trafficking in human beings

THE TRAFFICKING PEOPLE FOR EXPLOITATION REGULATIONS 2013, SI 2013/554; made under the European Communities Act 1972 s.2. In force: April 6, 2013; .

These Regulations are made as part of the implementation in England and Wales of Directive 2011/36 on preventing and combating trafficking in human beings and protecting its victims.

671. Trafficking in human beings–Victims–Criminal activity under compulsion–Culpability of perpetrators–Guidance on court's approach after start of proceedings

[Directive 2011/36 on trafficking in human beings Art.8.]

The court was required to consider four separate appeals involving offenders who, at different stages after conviction, had been found to be victims of trafficking in human beings and to have been coerced into committing the offences. The second to fourth appellants had been found to have been trafficked from Vietnam. The second and fourth were sentenced to imprisonment for eight months and two years respectively for offences concerning the cultivation of cannabis, and the third to a detention and training order for 12 months. They had also later been found to have been under 18 years old when sentenced. The first appellant was a woman in her mid-thirties who had been sentenced to imprisonment for six months for possession of a false identity document. She had been given it when she was trafficked for the purposes of prostitution. It was not until after her imprisonment that it became clear that she had pleaded guilty because of a warning by her solicitor that if the police thought her account was false the charges would be more serious.

Held: Appeals allowed. (1) The instant appeals had given rise to broader issues, and guidance was given to courts about how the interests of those who were or might be victims of human trafficking and who became enmeshed in criminal activities in consequence, in particular child victims, should be approached after proceedings had begun. The court examined some of its decisions in the light of Directive 2011/36, *R. v LM* [2010] EWCA Crim 2327, [2011] 1 Cr. App. R. 12, [2011] C.L.Y. 635 and *R. v N* [2012] EWCA Crim 189, [2013] Q.B. 379, [2012] C.L.Y. 725 applied. Provision was made under art.8 for the non-prosecution or non-application of penalties to victims who had offended under compulsion as a result of trafficking. The principles applicable were not complicated and the assertion that every vulnerable victim of exploitation would be protected by the criminal law was repeated in various decided cases. However, it had not and could not have been argued that if and when such victims became involved in criminal activities they should be given some kind of immunity from prosecution just because of that, nor that a substantive defence was available to them for that reason alone. It was clearly established that the issue of prosecution and any subsequent proceedings required an approach of the greatest sensitivity. The reasoning was that the culpability of the victims might be significantly diminished, and sometimes effectively extinguished, not merely because of age, but because no realistic alternative was available to them but to comply with those controlling them. Where victims were under 18 years old their best interests were the primary, though not sole, consideration. Victims were not safeguarded from prosecution for offences unconnected with the trafficking, though it might constitute substantial mitigation. A level of protection was required and it was provided by the exercise of the abuse of process jurisdiction. Where a court considered issues relevant to age, trafficking and exploitation, the prosecution would be stayed if the court disagreed with the decision to prosecute. Fears that the exercise of the jurisdiction to stay would be inadequate were groundless. Where the relevant issues had reached the magistrates' court or Crown Court, they had to be resolved by the exercise of the jurisdiction to stay a prosecution, even after the Directive became effective, *LM* and *N* applied. Whether a potential defendant had been a victim of trafficking, and the extent to which he possessed ability to resist criminal involvement were fact-specific questions. The issue of age and the possibility of trafficking had to be considered from the moment of arrest. The court set out the circumstances commonly met with in the instant type of situation and gave guidance on the appropriate action to take in each. A list of numerous relevant materials were annexed to the instant judgment (see paras 10, 12-14, 17-33 of judgment). (2) If the facts of the second to fourth appellants' ages and their having been trafficked had been known when the decisions to prosecute were made, they would not have been prosecuted, and if they had been prosecuted an abuse of process argument would have been likely to succeed on the basis of the information later available. The same result would have been reached in the case of the first appellant (paras 45, 54-55, 67, 74).

R. v L; R. vT; R. vTHN; R. v HVN, [2013] EWCA Crim 991, [2014] 1 All E.R. 113, Lord Judge, L.C.J., CA (Crim Div).

672. Trespass on designated sites

THE SERIOUS ORGANISED CRIME AND POLICE ACT 2005 (DESIGNATED SITES UNDER SECTION 128) (AMENDMENT) ORDER 2013, SI 2013/1562; made under the Serious Organised Crime and Police Act 2005 s.128. In force: July 21, 2013 except for art.4 on October 3, 2013.; .

This Order designates one site under the Serious Organised Crime and Police Act 2005 s.128, under which a person commits an offence if he enters, or is on, any designated site in England or Wales as a trespasser.

673. Unlawful act manslaughter–Interference with vehicles–Proper construction of s.22A(1)(b) Road Traffic Act 1988

[Road Traffic Act 1988 (c.52) s.22A(1)(b).]

The appellant (M) appealed against her conviction for the manslaughter of her husband (D). Driving home from a night out, M and D had quarrelled. D was driving and M was in the front passenger seat. During the row, and without warning, M pulled on the handbrake, causing the car to spin across the road into a head-on collision with another vehicle. D died at the scene. M was convicted on the basis that it was unlawful act manslaughter, the alleged unlawful act being the endangering of road users contrary to the Road Traffic Act 1988 s.22A(1)(b). The trial judge held that pulling on the handbrake while the car was being driven could fall within the meaning of "interferes with a motor vehicle" in s.22A(1)(b) without straining the ordinary meaning of the words. M argued that in order for conduct to be covered by s.22A(1)(b), it must have occurred prior to the driving, must have been external to the vehicle, and must have amounted to something which changed the physical state of the vehicle. She maintained that the section did not cover conduct which merely interfered with the manner of driving.

Held: Appeal dismissed. (1) Section 22A(1) had been enacted to give effect to a need identified in a White Paper to create a new criminal offence of intentionally obstructing a road or interfering with traffic regulation devices. It was necessary to look at the Criminal Law Revision Committee's Report, to which the White Paper referred, for a fuller understanding of the purpose of the offence. In that report, the Committee had broadened certain offences relating to obstruction of railways: instead of requiring an intention to endanger the safety of users, it had indicated that the offences were made out if the act complained of was intentional and the defendant was negligent as to causing personal injury or damage to property. Furthermore, the Committee extended that principle to other forms of transport, including the deliberate obstruction of a highway. The effect of the Committee's recommendations was to create an offence of negligence, but one which required the act itself to have been deliberate and obviously dangerous to any reasonable person. There was no discernible reason why Parliament should have wanted to criminalise dangerous interference with a car before it was driven, but not interference while it was in the process of being driven. The language of the section did not impose such a limitation and its insertion would create an obvious anomaly. Nor was there any suggestion that the conduct had to be in some way external to the vehicle itself. Mere distraction of a motorist would not be an interference with the vehicle, but the braking system was a mechanical part of the car and interference with it was, in the ordinary and natural sense of the words, an interference with the vehicle (see paras 7-13 of judgment). (2) (Obiter) The offence of unlawful act manslaughter was capable of being committed by a negligent act. There would be possible ground for concern if a case involving an essentially negligent act was prosecuted as a form of unlawful act manslaughter. It might have been less complicated in the instant case for the prosecution to have relied on gross negligence manslaughter, but if that had been the case, a guilty verdict would still have been inevitable (para.14).

R. v MEEKING (CAROLINE), [2012] EWCA Crim 641, [2012] 1 W.L.R. 3349, Toulson, L.J., CA (Crim Div).

CRIMINAL PROCEDURE

674. Abuse of process–Autrefois acquit–No evidence offered on common assault charge in magistrates' court–Indictment for assault occasioning actual bodily harm stayed in Crown Court on basis of plea of autrefois acquit–Scope of autrefois acquit

[Criminal Justice Act 1988 (c.33) s.39, s.40; Magistrates' Courts Act 1980 (c.43) s.27.]

The Crown appealed against a Crown Court's decision to stay an indictment charging the respondent (J) with assault occasioning actual bodily harm (ABH) on the basis of a plea of autrefois acquit. J had pleaded not guilty to common assault in the magistrates' court. The Crown added a charge of ABH. J indicated a not guilty plea to that charge, the magistrates declined jurisdiction and adjourned the case for committal to the Crown Court. The Crown then offered no evidence on the common assault charge, which was dismissed by the magistrates' court. In the Crown Court, J argued that the dismissal gave rise to a plea of autrefois acquit, referring to the decision in *R. v FG (Autrefois Acquit)* [2001] EWCA Crim 1215, [2001] 1 W.L.R. 1727, [2001] C.L.Y. 1061. The judge considered that *R v FG* was indistinguishable and stayed the indictment. The issues to be determined were: (i) the scope of the decision in *Connelly v DPP* [1964] A.C. 1254, [1964] C.L.Y. 768, namely whether the plea of autrefois should be narrowly confined to cases where the offences were the same in fact or law, or was also applicable where the offences were substantially the same; (ii) whether J had been in peril given (a) that he had not objected to the common assault charge being dismissed and; (b) the stage at which the charge was dismissed; (iii) whether the court was bound by *R v FG*.

Held: Appeal allowed. (1) The scope of autrefois was narrow and the offence, as well as the facts, had to be the same for the plea of autrefois to be applicable, *Connelly* explained, *R. v Beedie (Thomas Sim)* [1998] Q.B. 356, [1997] C.L.Y. 1317 and *R. v JB* [2013] EWCA Crim 356 applied. The instant case provided a compelling illustration of the need to confine the plea of autrefois to a narrow basis as, if not so confined, a technical error would result in injustice. Although it could be said that it was incumbent on the Crown to avoid such errors, such a hope had never been reflected in experience. In any case where the narrow application of the principle would result in unfairness or injustice to a defendant amounting to oppression, the remedy lay in the power of the court to stay the proceedings, *R. (on the prosecution of Thompson) v Walker* 174 E.R. 345 and *R. v Elrington* 121 E.R. 870 considered. It could not be submitted that the Crown's conduct in seeking to have J tried on a greater charge when he had technically been acquitted on the lesser charge was in any way unfair or unjust, let alone abusive or oppressive (see paras 23-30 of judgment). (2) (a) When all that was being done was the reorganisation by the Crown of its case and no objection had been taken by the defence, it could not be said that J was in peril in such circumstances, *Haynes v Davis* [1915] 1 K.B. 332, *R. v Dabhade (Nitin Jayat)* [1993] Q.B. 329, [1993] C.L.Y. 700 and *R. v Brookes* [1995] Crim. L.R. 630 applied, *Connelly* considered. He was not at risk of conviction of the offence which was not to be pursued. Even though the magistrates' court record stated that there had been an acquittal on the common assault charge, that did not mean that J was in peril at the time. He plainly was not, and the formality of the court record should make no difference to the reality (paras 36-43); (b) there was no doubt that a defendant was in peril in the Crown Court when put in the charge of the jury, but the position in the magistrates' court was less clear. At the stage when no evidence was offered in the magistrates' court, J had also been charged with ABH and the court had adjourned the case for committal to the Crown Court. No objection had been taken to that course by the defence. J was not therefore in peril when the Crown offered no evidence, as a stage in the proceedings when he could be in peril had not yet been reached, *Haynes* and *Connelly* considered (paras 44-51). (3) The offences in *R v FG* were not the same in law, as they had to be if the plea of autrefois was to be available. If the decisions in *Connelly* and *Beedie* had been drawn to the attention of the court in *R v FG*, the decision would have been different, *Connelly* and *Beedie* considered. Had the court in that case considered whether the defendant was in peril either because the Crown was reorganising its case without defence objection or because of the stage of the proceedings when the decision to offer no evidence was made, it would also not have concluded as it had, *Haynes*, *Dabhade* and *Brookes* applied. Also, the court in *R v FG* had relied on the Magistrates' Courts Act 1980 s.27, whereas in the instant appeal s.27 had no application, as common assault was not an offence triable either way. It was a summary offence to which the Criminal Justice Act 1988 s.40 applied: common assault could be included on the indictment but, under s.39, it remained a summary offence. There was no equivalent to s.27, which equated the dismissal of a summary only offence to an acquittal on indictment. The instant court was not bound by *R v FG*, *R v FG* distinguished, *Connelly* followed (paras 52-58).

R. v J; *sub nom.* R. v JFJ, [2013] EWCA Crim 569, [2013] 2 Cr. App. R. 10, Sir John Thomas (President QBD), CA (Crim Div).

675. Alternative verdicts–Common assault–Indictment charging only assault by battery–Whether common assault could be left to jury as alternative

[Criminal Appeal Act 1968 (c.19) s.3; Criminal Justice Act 1988 (c.33) s.39; Criminal Law Act 1967 (c.58) s.6(3).]

The appellant (N) appealed against his conviction for common assault. The Crown's case was that N, a serving prisoner, had punched a prison officer (V) during a body search. N was indicted on a charge of assault by beating, contrary to the Criminal Justice Act 1988 s.39. His defence was twofold: first, that although he had thrown a punch, it had not landed; and second, that in any event it had not been unlawful for him to throw the punch in the light of the way the search was being conducted. Although V's evidence was that the punch had landed, none of the other witnesses could be sure that it had. Because the infliction of violence was a necessary ingredient of assault by battery, the Crown sought, shortly before the close of its case, to amend the indictment by adding a count of common assault, in which the infliction of violence was not a necessary ingredient. The judge refused to allow the amendment. N elected not to adduce any evidence, relying solely on his first line of defence that his punch had not landed. At the close of N's case, the judge decided to leave common assault to the jury as an alternative, pursuant to the Criminal Law Act 1967 s.6(3). The jury acquitted N of assault by beating, but convicted him of common assault. The issues were whether (i) common assault could be left as an alternative to an offence of assault by beating without it having been included in the indictment; (ii) the court should exercise its discretion under the Criminal Appeal Act 1968 s.3 to replace N's conviction for common assault with a conviction for attempted battery.

Held: Appeal allowed. (1) Section 6(3) of the 1967 Act provided that a defendant could be convicted of an alternative offence not charged on the indictment as long as the allegations in the indictment amounted to, or included the ingredients of, the alternative offence. A defendant was guilty of common assault when he did something physical which caused the victim to apprehend that he was about to be struck. Such an apprehension was not, however, required for assault by beating. Thus, an allegation of assault by beating did not amount to or include an allegation of common assault. It was therefore not open to the jury to convict the appellant of common assault by virtue of s.6(3). Nor did s.6(3A) of the 1967 Act permit a jury to convict of common assault as an alternative to assault by beating where common assault had not been included in the indictment (see paras 7-9 of judgment). (2) The power to substitute a conviction for an alternative offence under s.3 of the 1968 Act was discretionary and was to be exercised in the light of what would be just in all the circumstances. It would not be just to exercise it in N's case. The state of the evidence at the close of the Crown's case had caused him to make the tactical decision not to pursue his defence that he had not acted unlawfully in throwing the punch, and had been a factor in his decision not to give evidence. His choices might have been different had the judge not initially refused to add a count of common assault to the indictment as an alternative, and had he known that he was liable to be convicted of common assault even if the punch had not landed. Had he given evidence he might have been acquitted on the alternative charge of common assault and, had that happened, the opportunity for the instant court to substitute a verdict of guilty of attempted battery would not have arisen (paras 10-16).

R. v NELSON (GARY), [2013] EWCA Crim 30, [2013] 1 W.L.R. 2861, Rafferty, L.J. DBE, CA (Crim Div).

676. Anti-social behaviour–Penalty notices for disorder

THE PENALTIES FOR DISORDERLY BEHAVIOUR (AMOUNT OF PENALTY) (AMENDMENT) ORDER 2013, SI 2013/1165; made under the Criminal Justice and Police Act 2001 s.3. In force: July 1, 2013; .

This Order amends the Penalties for Disorderly Behaviour (Amount of Penalty) Order 2002 (SI 2002/1837) and increases the value of both lower and higher-tier Penalty Notices for Disorder, from £50 and £80 to £60 and £90 respectively.

677. Anti-social behaviour–Penalty notices for disorder

THE PENALTIES FOR DISORDERLY BEHAVIOUR (AMOUNT OF PENALTY) (AMENDMENT) (NO.2) ORDER 2013, SI 2013/1579; made under the Criminal Justice and Police Act 2001 s.3, s.10A. In force: July 1, 2013; .

This Order increases the value of both lower and higher-tier penalty notices for disorder by £10 from £50 and £80 to £60 and £90 respectively, in relation to an offence alleged to have been committed on or after July 1, 2013.

678. Antisocial behaviour–Penalty notices for disorder–Police powers and duties

THE LEGAL AID, SENTENCING AND PUNISHMENT OF OFFENDERS ACT 2012 (CONSEQUENTIAL AMENDMENTS) REGULATIONS 2013, SI 2013/903; made under the Legal Aid, Sentencing and Punishment of Offenders Act 2012 s.149. In force: May 20, 2013; .

These Regulations make consequential amendment to reflect the changes to penalty notices for disorderly behaviour (PND) in the Criminal Justice and Police Act 2001, as made by the Legal Aid Sentencing and Punishment of Offenders Act 2012. The changes: provide that a penalty notice can no longer be given to a person under the age of 18; remove the requirement that a constable who gives a PND to a person other than at a police station must be in uniform; remove the requirement that a constable in a police station may not give a PND unless they are an "authorised constable"; and permit a constable to give a penalty notice with an educational option, if an education course scheme is established in the chief officer's area.

679. Bail conditions–Sureties–Risk of reoffending–Provision of surety to support condition against reoffending–Scheme of Bail Act 1976

[Bail Act 1976 (c.63) s.3(6), s.3(7), s.8, s.9.]

The claimant (S) applied for judicial review of a decision of a Crown Court judge refusing to grant conditional bail. S was facing trial on indictment on charges of fraud. He enjoyed conditional bail in relation to that matter. He was then further charged with fraudulent trading. The magistrates' court refused bail in relation to that matter on the ground that there were substantial grounds to believe that he would commit further offences. A further application for bail was refused by the Crown Court for the same reason. The judge indicated that a further application would be considered if it could be established that an available surety, namely S's brother, could lawfully be put under an obligation to ensure compliance with a condition of bail designed to prevent reoffending, namely that S would not engage in any commercial activity. A bail application was made and refused, the judge not being satisfied that a surety could lawfully be taken to ensure compliance with a condition designed to prevent further offending. S submitted that the provisions of the Bail Act 1976 and in particular s.3(6) were permissive and did not prevent a surety being taken for the purpose of supporting a condition against engaging in commercial activity.

Held: Claim dismissed. Every reference in the Act to a surety was qualified by the words "to secure his surrender to custody" or impliedly subject to such a qualification. Section 8, which dealt with the position where a person was granted bail in criminal proceedings on condition that he provided one or more surety or sureties for the purpose of securing that he surrendered to custody, contained a scheme for the court to assess the suitability of sureties for that purpose. If S's submissions were correct there would be a power to take a surety but no criteria for assessing suitability unless the provision were read across and it could not be supposed that Parliament intended any gap to be filled in that way. Similar considerations applied in relation to s.9, which created an offence of agreeing to indemnify a person against a liability incurred as a surety to secure the surrender to custody of a person. There would be no equivalent provision in relation to indemnifying a surety given not in relation to surrender but observance of some other condition of bail. That would produce an incoherent and inconsistent scheme. The statutory scheme therefore strongly suggested that a surety could be provided only in relation to surrender to custody and not the performance of any other condition. It appeared that as a matter of policy Parliament had determined that where a defendant was at risk of reoffending removal of that risk could not safely be assured by the surety of a third party who could not be assumed to have sufficient control over the defendant to prevent further offending. That was confirmed by s.3(7) under which exceptionally a parent or guardian could stand surety for the good behaviour of a child under 17 but could not be bound in a sum of more than £50 to secure compliance with any requirement. That provision negated the existence of any residual power to take a surety for good behaviour in other cases. Parliament intended the Act to be a comprehensive code and if there was no power under the Act for provision of a surety except in the cases expressly identified in s.3 there was no power so to provide outside the Act. It was inappropriate and inconsistent with the legislative intention to have a stop-gap power to fill a non-existent lacuna.

R. (ON THE APPLICATION OF SHEA) v WINCHESTER CROWN COURT; *sub nom.* SHEA v WINCHESTER CROWN COURT, [2013] EWHC 1050 (Admin), [2013] Lloyd's Rep. F.C. 346, Pitchford, L.J., DC.

680. Burglary–Houses–Offender disputing that burgled property was domestic dwelling–Proper procedural process for determining status of premises

[Powers of Criminal Courts (Sentencing) Act 2000 (c.6) s.111.]

The appellant (F) appealed against a sentence of 29 months' imprisonment imposed following his plea of guilty to burglary of a dwelling house. One afternoon, F had broken into a house which was being refurbished and stolen a mobile phone from a builder who was working there. In interview, he said that the property was not a dwelling, but a building site. He pleaded guilty to the charge of domestic burglary, but the case was adjourned pending a Newton hearing as to whether the property was a house. The judge decided that it was. F already had convictions for two domestic burglaries and, under the Powers of Criminal Courts (Sentencing) Act 2000 s.111, he was liable to be sentenced to a minimum term of three years' custody with credit for his guilty plea limited to 20 per cent. F submitted that the instant burglary did not qualify for inclusion within s.111 because it lacked many of the harmful features of a normal domestic burglary and because the phone had been left accessible and its taking had been opportunistic. He also pointed out that, at the time of the first qualifying offence, he had just turned 16 years of age, and in both of the qualifying burglaries, he had entered with intent, but without taking any property.

Held: Appeal allowed in part. (1) Although the third burglary was not a trivial offence and the theft of the phone serious, it was unjust to impose a three-year minimum term. The appropriate starting point was one of two years' imprisonment. As the statutory minimum period was not being applied, the restriction on credit for the guilty plea was also not applicable. However, F had been caught red-handed, so the appropriate discount for his plea was 25 per cent. The original sentence was quashed and a sentence of 18 months' imprisonment substituted (see paras 12-13 of judgment). (2) It was wrong to have held a Newton hearing into whether the property was a dwelling. If it was not admitted that the burglary was of a dwelling, that fact should have been determined by a jury and F should have entered a not guilty plea. There would then have been two alternative counts on the indictment, one of which averred that the property was a dwelling, and one of which did not. Since F pleaded guilty to burglary of a dwelling, that is what he had to be sentenced for. The Newton hearing concluded that the property was a dwelling, but any other finding would have contradicted the entered plea, which is why a Newton hearing was not the appropriate way to resolve the issue (paras 4-5).

R. v FLACK (PERRY), [2013] EWCA Crim 115, [2013] 2 Cr. App. R. (S.) 56, Treacy, L.J., CA (Crim Div).

681. Citizen's arrest–Police officers–Off-duty police officer arresting individual for criminal damage–Failure to use word "arrest"–Lawfulness of arrest

[Police and Criminal Evidence Act 1984 (c.60) s.24, s.28; Criminal Procedure Rules 2011 (SI 2011/1709) r.64.5.]

The appellant (M) appealed by way of case stated on the question of whether there was sufficient evidence for the judge to find that a plain-clothed police officer (X) had lawfully arrested M's friend (JC) whom M had tried to free by assaulting X. X had been off duty and out jogging when he saw JC smash a car window. X called out to JC to stop upon which JC entered another car. X pulled JC from the car, told him that he was a police officer and that he had seen him smash the car window. X notified a bystander that he was a police officer and asked him to call the police as JC had smashed a window. JC tried to resist and X repeatedly told bystanders that he was a police officer and to call the police. M approached JC and X, and X explained that he was an off-duty police officer and therefore did not have his identification on him but that he had seen JC smash a car window. M tried to help JC escape and X repeatedly told both of them that he was a police officer and why he needed help. At trial X stated that he had not used the word "arrest" when dealing with JC, but had made it clear that JC was being detained so that he could be held to account for smashing the window. M was convicted of assault and the judge found that he did not believe he was trying to free JC from a racist attack. He further found that, although X had not used the word "arrest", he had made it clear to JC that he was detaining him, that X was entitled to arrest JC under the Police and Criminal Evidence Act 1984 s.24 and that the arrest was lawful as the requirements of s.28 had been fulfilled in that X had seen JC smash the window, it was clear from X's words and by his holding onto JC that JC was not free to leave, by calling out for police help X was ensuring JC could not escape before a uniformed officer took him to the station, X had made it clear that he was an officer and that JC was being arrested for criminal damage which he knew and understood. The issue was whether there was sufficient evidence for the judge to find that X had made clear by the use of appropriate language to JC that he was under arrest.

Held: Appeal dismissed. X had not used the words, "I am arresting you". However, the tenor of his evidence was that he was detaining JC and that he had made it clear that he was doing so because he had broken a car window. There was sufficient evidence for the judge to find that it had been made clear to JC that he was under arrest for criminal damage (see para.25 of judgment). (2) When stating cases for the Divisional Court, those requesting that a case be stated should make it clear what the issue was and those drafting it should comply with the requirements of the Criminal Procedure Rules 2011 r.64.5 (paras 3-6).

ADLER v CROWN PROSECUTION SERVICE, [2013] EWHC 1968 (Admin), (2013) 177 J.P. 558, Sir John Thomas (President QBD), QBD (Admin).

682. Codes of practice–Conditional cautions

THE CRIMINAL JUSTICE ACT 2003 (CONDITIONAL CAUTIONS: CODE OF PRACTICE) ORDER 2013, SI 2013/801; made under the Criminal Justice Act 2003 s.25. In force: April 7, 2013; .

This Order brings into force a revised code of practice in relation to conditional cautions.

683. Codes of practice–Youth conditional cautions

THE CRIME AND DISORDER ACT 1998 (YOUTH CONDITIONAL CAUTIONS: FINANCIAL PENALTIES) ORDER 2013, SI 2013/608; made under the Crime and Disorder Act 1998 s.66C. In force: April 8, 2013; .

This Order brings into force a revised code of practice in relation to youth conditional cautions.

684. Conditional cautions–Fines–Offences

THE CRIMINAL JUSTICE ACT 2003 (CONDITIONAL CAUTIONS: FINANCIAL PENALTIES) ORDER 2013, SI 2013/615; made under the Criminal Justice Act 2003 s.23A. In force: April 8, 2013; .

The Order sets out the descriptions of offences for which a financial penalty condition may be attached, under the Criminal Justice Act 2003 s.23A to a conditional caution given under s.22 of that Act.

685. Confiscation orders–Benefit from criminal conduct–Appellant pleading guilty to corruption in relation to securing of contracts for his company–Whether judge justified in piercing corporate veil when assessing benefit

[Proceeds of Crime Act 2002 (c.29) s.76(4).]

The appellant (S) appealed against a confiscation order in the sum of £1.9 million. S had pleaded guilty to corruption and to fraud by false representation. He was the managing director and sole shareholder of a company which installed and maintained air-conditioning units and undertook electrical engineering work. He entered into a corrupt relationship with a manager employed by Network Rail: in return for gifts and hospitality, the latter arranged for the award of a number of high-value contracts to S's company. £197,683.12 was agreed to be the gross value of the profit earned by the company, after deducting the costs of production, but before any taxation, together with interest. The figure in which the confiscation order was made represented the total sum paid to the company by Network Rail. S argued that (1) the judge had wrongly lifted the corporate veil in assessing his benefit: the judge should have found that his benefit was represented by a proportion of his salary and benefits from his employment with the company in relation to the company's trading with Network Rail compared with the total trading of the company during the relevant period; (2) in any event, the confiscation order was disproportionate.

Held: Appeal allowed in part. (1) The judge had been correct to rule that the corporate veil should be lifted when assessing S's benefit. The matter fell within the concealment principle identified in *Petrodel Resources Ltd v Prest* [2013] UKSC 34, [2013] 2 A.C. 415, [2013] 9 C.L. 193. In the circumstances of the case, where S was the sole controller of the company, and where there was a very close inter-relationship between his corrupt actions and steps taken by the company in advancing those corrupt acts and intentions, the reality was that the activities of both S and the company were so interlinked as to be indivisible. Both entities were acting together in the corruption. Accordingly, insofar as the company was involved, what it did served to hide what S was doing, *Prest* applied and *R. v Seager (Mornington Stafford)* [2009] EWCA Crim 1303, [2010] 1 W.L.R. 815, [2009] C.L.Y. 834 considered (see paras 40-41 of judgment). (2) The Proceeds of Crime Act 2002 s.76(4) was apt to capture the whole of the invoices paid (about £1.9 million) as benefit obtained as a result of or in connection with the admitted criminal conduct. However, the confiscation order in the sum stipulated was disproportionate, *R. v Waya (Terry)* [2012] UKSC 51, [2013] 1 A.C. 294 applied. A proportionate order would be one which took account the profit gained under the relevant contracts together with the value of the pecuniary advantage gained by obtaining a market share, excluding competitors and saving on the costs of preparing proper tenders. Unfortunately, the value of that pecuniary advantage had not been assessed. The amount of the order would therefore be reduced to the profit figure of £197,683.12. In cases of this nature in the future, it was to be hoped that prosecutors would be alert to this aspect of the case, so that the real benefit or pecuniary advantage derived by the wrongdoer could be identified (paras 45, 57-58, 60).

R. v SALE (PETER JOHN), [2013] EWCA Crim 1306, [2014] 1 W.L.R. 663, Treacy, L.J., CA (Crim Div).

686. Confiscation orders–Benefit from criminal conduct–Hidden assets–Judge's assessment that realisable assets same as benefit from criminal conduct

[Proceeds of Crime Act 2002 (c.29) s.7(2).]

The husband and wife appellants (L1 and L2) appealed against confiscation orders imposed following their pleas of guilty to money laundering and L1's plea of guilty to conspiracy to rob. L1 had been part of a conspiracy to rob trailer loads of chocolate, and both L1 and L2 had admitted an offence of money laundering that constituted using some of the proceeds of L1's crimes towards a deposit on a house. The house was then purchased with the aid of a mortgage. L2 ran a corner shop, the bookkeeping and accounts for which were chaotic. She called evidence from an accountant who had reconstructed the profit figures. He suggested that the shop income had been deliberately understated for tax purposes. His reconstructed figures showed £211,000 more profit than the original accounts. There was evidence that the shop had been used in the past to launder goods stolen by L1. Both appellants were found to be living substantially on the proceeds of crime. Accordingly, in calculating their confiscation orders, the assessment of the benefit sums extended to benefit that resulted from general criminal conduct, not just the offences of which they were convicted. L1 and L2 argued that (1) the mortgage advance should not have been included in the benefit assessments; (2) the judge had erred in completely ignoring the accountants' evidence, which would have rebutted the assumption of criminal origin in relation to unexplained credits in L2's accounts; (3) the judge had illegitimately moved directly from rejecting their cases to concluding that not only were there hidden assets, but those assets must be in the sum of the whole benefit figures.

Held: Appeals allowed in part. (1) The mortgage advance, although obtained by L2 fraudulently overstating her income to a considerable extent, should not have been included in the benefit figures as L1 and L2 had never obtained the loan for themselves because it was paid directly to the vendor of the house. They therefore had no proprietary interest in it, *R. v Waya (Terry)* [2012] UKSC 51, [2013] 1 A.C. 294, [2013] 2 C.L. 90 followed. Consequently, the benefit figure in each case was reduced accordingly (see para.9 of judgment). (2) In determining the shop income of L2 and its impact, if any, on the calculation of her benefit figure, the judge had not completely ignored the accountants' evidence. The reconstructed accounts depended on honest and regular trading, and the judge had been entitled to conclude that no one knew how the business had been run: there was no reason to know it had been run essentially regularly; further, the till rolls had been destroyed. It had been clearly open to the judge to conclude that L2 was well aware of L1's criminal source of income and was willing to use the obvious route of the shop to help realise it. She had been deliberately untruthful on a number of topics and had failed to make any attempt to account for the money that passed through her hands. She had not been able to show on the balance of probabilities both that she had an additional legitimate income from the shop and that it accounted for the unexplained credits to her accounts (paras 11, 15-17). (3) Under the Proceeds of Crime Act 2002 s.7(2), the burden was on L1 and L2 to show that their available amounts were less than their benefit figures, *R. v McIntosh (Leroy Samuel)* [2011] EWCA Crim 1501, [2011] 4 All E.R. 917, [2012] C.L.Y. 681 and *R. v Ahmad (Shakeel)* [2012] EWCA Crim 391, [2012] 1 W.L.R. 2335, [2012] C.L.Y. 758 followed. The judge had not moved directly from disbelieving them to finding that their hidden assets were necessarily the same sums as their benefits. He had looked at the whole evidence, which had shown that L1 had made frequent expenditures in cash for which the source remained wholly unknown, including some that were made after a restraining order had been made over his assets generally. L2 had withdrawn nearly £10,000 from her account immediately after her arrest, which gave grounds for believing she had taken steps to hide her money. She had said nothing at all to account for the profit on the sale of her previous home. The very fact that she was bent on helping L1 realise his criminal assets meant that she was likely to have hidden assets; past history demonstrated at least two examples of assets being put into her name for convenience. The judge had been entitled to find that there was no conclusion available other than that there must be hidden assets and no indication at all that provided any basis for holding that they were less than the benefit sums (paras 22, 24-26).

R. v LEE (PAUL); R. v MARTIN-LEE (SHARON), [2013] EWCA Crim 657, [2013] Lloyd's Rep. F.C. 453, Hughes, L.J., CA (Crim Div).

687. Confiscation orders–Benefit from criminal conduct–Inadequate evidence that assets no longer under offender's control–Admissibility of fresh evidence to explain inadequate evidence

The appellant (D) appealed against the amount of a confiscation order. D had pleaded guilty to being concerned in a money laundering arrangement, and to possessing criminal property, namely cash held in a safe deposit box. At the confiscation hearing, the judge found D's benefit from his criminal conduct to have been over £1.25 million, and that the available amount was just over £326,000, which included hidden assets of £141,000. After hearing evidence from D, he rejected his claim that some of the hidden assets had passed out of his control, either to others engaged in the fraud, or as gifts to his girlfriend. On appeal D sought to admit a fresh affidavit in which he sought to explain why his earlier evidence about the hidden assets had been lacking. The Crown agreed that there had been an element of double counting and that the benefit figure should be reduced.

Held: Appeal allowed in part. Despite questioning from his counsel at the confiscation hearing, D had given no positive evidence as to how much of the hidden assets had been disposed of as he alleged. In view of the quality of the evidence, the judge could not have reached a different conclusion. His determination was neither unjust nor disproportionate. There was no rational basis on which to admit a witness's fresh evidence for the purposes of trying to explain inadequacies in his earlier evidence. The appeal was dismissed, save to the extent that the benefit figure would be reduced in accordance with the Crown's concession (see paras 19, 21, 23 of judgment).

R. v DRUCE (LAWRENCE), [2013] EWCA Crim 40, [2013] Lloyd's Rep. F.C. 220, Davis, L.J., CA (Crim Div).

688. Confiscation orders–Benefit from criminal conduct–Offence of owning rented property without a licence–Availability of confiscation proceedings–Whether receipt of rent for unlicensed property amounting to benefit from criminal conduct

[Housing Act 2004 (c.34) s.80, s.95(1), s.96(3); Proceeds of Crime Act 2002 (c.29) s.70, s.76.]

The appellant company (S) appealed against the imposition of a confiscation order following its conviction for being the owner of a rented property without a licence. The Housing Act 2004 s.80 made provision for the introduction by local authorities of selective licensing of rented residential property in the private sector. S was the owner and landlord of a property in an area which was designated a selective licensing area by the respondent local authority. The local authority wrote to S informing it of the need for a license. S did not obtain a license and was prosecuted by the local authority. S was found guilty, after a trial in its absence in the Magistrates' Court, of being the owner of a rented property without a licence contrary to s.95(1) of the 2004 Act. S was committed to the Crown Court for sentence under the Proceeds of Crime Act 2002 s.70. The recorder subsequently fined S and ordered it to pay prosecution costs, and made a confiscation order under the 2002 Act in the sum of £6,450, having found that S had benefited from criminal conduct in the amount of the rent received whilst the property was unlicensed. It fell to be determined whether confiscation proceedings were available in the context of an offence under s.95(1) of the 2004 Act.

Held: Appeal allowed. Section 95(1) of the 2004 Act involved a "regulatory offence", rather than a case of obtaining property by dishonest means. Whether a regulatory offence could, when committed, give rise to the availability of a confiscation order would depend on the terms of the statute or regulations creating the offence, read with the terms of the 2002 Act and set in the context of the facts of the case. It was common ground that the instant case was not one of general criminal conduct. There were, ordinarily, three questions for the court in deciding whether to make a confiscation order: (a) whether the defendant benefited from the relevant criminal conduct; (b) if so, what the value of that benefit was; (c) what sum was recoverable from the defendant, *R. v May (Raymond George)* [2008] UKHL 28, [2008] 1 A.C. 1028, [2008] C.L.Y. 776 followed. The focus was, therefore, on the benefit obtained. Section 95(1) taken on its own confined the offence to that of having control of or managing a house which was required to be licensed but was not so licensed. The 2004 Act had, however, to be read as a whole. Under s.96(3), no rule of law relating to validity or enforceability of contracts in circumstances of illegality affected the validity or enforceability of the provisions of a tenancy or licence requiring payment of rent. It followed that the right to recover rent remained enforceable, notwithstanding that a landlord had no licence for the house in question. That was inconsistent with the notion that the landlord was unlawfully obtaining rent as a result of or in connection with his breach of s.95(1). It seemed extraordinary to attribute to Parliament an intention that a landlord of an unlicensed house might lawfully seek to recover in civil proceedings rent due under the tenancy whilst at the same time making it a criminal offence actually to receive such rent so recovered. That was not a tenable proposition. There had to be a causal connection between the criminal conduct and the benefit received from it, *R. v Nelson (John Stanley)* [2009] EWCA Crim 1573, [2010] Q.B. 678, [2009] C.L.Y. 848 applied. In the instant case, S had continued to receive rent not because of the s.95(1) offence but in spite of it. There was no sufficient causal connection; the continued receipt of the rent was not the product of S's crime. To impose a confiscation order would in substance be in the nature of a fine, and the provisions of s.76 of the 2002 Act read with the provisions of the 2004 Act did not permit it. By the continued receipt of rent S had not "obtained" property "as a result of or in connection with" the criminal conduct. The confiscation order was not, therefore, available and would be quashed (see paras 30-32, 35-37, 39, 43, 45 of judgment).

SUMAL & SONS (PROPERTIES) LTD v NEWHAM LBC; *sub nom.* R. v SUMAL & SONS (PROPERTIES) LTD, [2012] EWCA Crim 1840, [2013] 1 W.L.R. 2078, Davis, L.J., CA (Crim Div).

689. Confiscation orders–Benefit from criminal conduct–Valuation–Offender obtaining mortgage by deception–Property purchased partly from untainted funds–Increased value of property at confiscation proceedings–Correct approach to determination of benefit

[Proceeds of Crime Act 2002 (c.29) s.10(6)(b), s.10, s.79(3), s.80(3), s.84(2)(b); European Convention on Human Rights 1950 Protocol 1 Art.1.]

The appellant (W) appealed against a decision ([[2010] EWCA Crim 412, [2011] 1 Cr. App. R. (S.) 4, [2011] C.L.Y. 724) reducing a confiscation order made under the Proceeds of Crime Act 2002 (POCA). W obtained a 60 per cent mortgage to buy a flat by making false statements about his employment and earnings. He later remortgaged and redeemed the first mortgage. W was convicted of obtaining money transfers by deception on the first mortgage but acquitted of doing so on the second. A confiscation order of £1.54 million was imposed. On appeal, the order was reduced to £1,110,000, calculated as 60 per cent of the market value of the flat. The issue was whether the rules for the calculation of the financial benefit of crime contravened W's human rights. The Crown submitted that the confiscation order should be £465,000, the value of the mortgage that W had fraudulently obtained. W submitted that s.79(3) meant that the valuation of property which had been stolen or obtained by deception had to take into account the interest of the lender, reducing the value to nil.

Held: Appeal allowed. (Lords Phillips and Reid dissenting in part) Although POCA had removed all discretion from the Crown Court, the European Convention on Human Rights 1950 Protocol 1 art.1 required that the deprivation of property as a penalty had to be proportionate to the legitimate aim, which was to remove from criminals the pecuniary proceeds of their crime, the deterrent effect being secondary. A judge had to refuse to make a disproportionate confiscation order but this was not a reincarnation of a general judicial discretion (see paras 19-24 of judgment). There was a significant difference between those cases involving a criminal lifestyle and those which did not. In the former, the statutory assumptions under s.10 were qualified by s.10(6)(a) and s.10(6)(b), and could only be applied if there was no serious injustice and they were, therefore, proportionate. It was clear that a confiscation order for more than the net proceeds of crime was proportionate, *R. v May (Raymond George)* [2008] UKHL 28, [2008] 1 A.C. 1028, [2008] C.L.Y. 776 applied. Even if the proceeds had been spent, a confiscation order up to the value of the proceeds would follow against legitimately acquired assets (paras 26-27). Where a defendant had restored the proceeds of crime, it would be disproportionate to make a confiscation order as it would not satisfy the statutory purpose and would be an additional financial penalty. Instead, any additional penalty should be made openly by way of fine or imprisonment, *R. v Morgan (John)* [2008] EWCA Crim 1323, [2008] 4 All E.R. 890, [2009] C.L.Y. 853 and *R. v Wilkes (Gary John)* [2003] EWCA Crim 848, [2003] 2 Cr. App. R. (S.) 105, [2003] C.L.Y. 3658 approved. To the extent that *Crown Prosecution Service (Nottinghamshire) v Rose* [2008] EWCA Crim 239, [2008] 1 W.L.R. 2113, [2008] C.L.Y. 777 held that the recovery and restoration intact of the stolen property was irrelevant to the making of a confiscation order it should not be followed, *Rose* disapproved (paras 28-32). Here, money had been lent because of fraud but had been repaid in full and had been fully secured. W had benefitted from the increase in the property's value and a proportionate confiscation order would reflect the benefit he had gained by the increase in value attributable to the loan (para.35). However, on the well-established principle that the mortgage advance remained in the beneficial ownership of the lender until completion, when it passed directly to the vendor, W had only acquired an equity of redemption corresponding in value to his untainted down-payment of £310,000. To conclude that W had obtained £465,000 was a legally inaccurate account of the transaction, because the loan sum never came into his possession. All he obtained was a chose in action with no market value, *Target Holdings Ltd v Redferns* [1996] A.C. 421, [1995] C.L.Y. 2195 and *R. v Preddy (John Crawford)* [1996] A.C. 815, [1996] C.L.Y. 1530 applied, *Lloyds TSB Bank Plc v Markandan & Uddin (A Firm)* [2012] EWCA Civ 65, [2012] 2 All E.R. 884, [2012] C.L.Y. 2757 approved (paras 51-53). Under s.80(3) once property had been obtained criminally, it remained as a benefit whether or not it was retained, although it was an alternative and not an additional benefit, *R. v Pattison (Leslie)* [2007] EWCA Crim 1536, [2008] 1 Cr. App. R. (S.) 51, [2008] C.L.Y. 3270 approved (paras 55-60). It was clear that W no longer had the original chose in action and that it had been replaced by some interest in the property but it was difficult to value. Section 84(2)(b) meant that a limited interest in an item of property was itself property which counted as benefit. Similarly, s.84(2)(a) meant that a person who held an interest in property held property for the purposes of POCA. It followed that W held a limited interest in the flat (para.64). Under s.79(3) the value of W's limited interest was to be taken in calculating his benefit, both at the benefit calculation and at the assessment of realisable property stages, *Rose* approved (para.65). The value of W's chose in action was 60 per cent of the open market value of the property from time to time less the whole of the mortgage liability, *R. v Moulden (Leslie James)* [2004] EWCA Crim 2715, [2005] 1 Cr. App. R. (S.) 121, [2005] C.L.Y. 3593 not applied as here the mortgage was a fixed sum, whereas the defendant in *Moulden* had converted his money into the whole equity in a house (para.73). A confiscation order in the sum of £392,400 was substituted.

R. v WAYA (TERRY); *sub nom.* R. v WAYA SOLICITORS, [2012] UKSC 51, [2013] 1 A.C. 294, Lord Phillips, J.S.C., SC.

690. Confiscation orders–Benefit from criminal conduct–Whether beneficiary under fraudulent will obtained property prior to administration of estate–Proportionality of confiscation order where no additional benefit to offender as property restored–Meaning of "obtains property" pursuant to s.76(4) Proceeds of Crime Act 2002

[Proceeds of Crime Act 2002 (c.29) s.6(5), s.76(4); European Convention on Human Rights 1950 Protocol 1 Art.1.]

The appellant (H) appealed against a confiscation order following a plea of guilty to an offence of fraud. H's father had made a will effectively leaving his estate to H and his nephew (S). A later will emerged after his death which had been drawn up on an "over-the-counter" will form appointing H as the sole executor and leaving the whole of the residuary estate to her. Probate was granted to H as executor of the estate and S alerted the police that the second will was a forgery. H was arrested and a restraint order was made. At that time solicitors instructed by H had begun the process of administration of the estate, but it was incomplete and no distribution of monies had been made nor had H given instructions for distribution or made requests for monies. H was charged with being party to the forgery and knowingly swearing an affidavit instructing solicitors to obtain probate of what she knew to be a forged will. The Crown sought a confiscation order amounting to 50 per cent of the value of the estate which represented S's share under the genuine will and which the Crown said H had obtained by her dishonesty. H submitted that (1) she had not benefitted from her criminal conduct under the Proceeds of Crime Act 2002 s.6(4)(c) within the terms of "benefit" as defined in s.76(4) as she had not obtained property, because although H intended to become the sole recipient of the value of the settled estate she had not "got her hands on it"; (2) the confiscation order was disproportionate as H obtained no additional benefit by reason of the forged will and following the discovery of the forgery, S had received the inheritance to which he was entitled.

Held: Appeal allowed. (1) The word "obtained" under s.76(4) was not defined in the Act but a person ordinarily obtained property if in law he owned it, whether solely or jointly, which would connote a power of disposition or control, *R. v May (Raymond George)* [2008] UKHL 28, [2008] 1 A.C. 1028,

[2008] C.L.Y. 776 followed. On the grant of probate, if not before, H as executrix had acquired a power of disposition and control over the property comprised in the estate. By virtue of the grant of probate H's position as sole executrix and beneficiary was conclusively established against the world until such time as probate was revoked. She had obtained full legal and beneficial title to the estate. The solicitors were acting to her instructions and had to comply with them provided they were not unlawful. An offender need not have enjoyed the benefit of the property obtained, *R. v Smith (David Cadman)* [2001] UKHL 68, [2002] 1 W.L.R. 54, [2002] C.L.Y. 3898 and *R. v Wilkes (Gary John)* [2003] EWCA Crim 848, [2003] 2 Cr. App. R. (S.) 105, [2003] C.L.Y. 3658 applied. In those circumstances the submission that H should not be regarded as having obtained property under the Act because she had not "got her hands on it" was misdirected. Such an approach did not follow the language of the Act, nor did it apply the test indicated in *May.* In support of the conclusion that H had a sufficient degree of control over the estate assets, it was significant that as sole beneficiary H could, during the course of administration, have sold or assigned her interest in the estate as a contingent beneficial interest under a will was a "thing in action" or "other tangible property" capable of being assigned for consideration before the contingency occurred, *Maye, Re* [2008] UKHL 9, [2008] 1 W.L.R. 315, [2008] C.L.Y. 4167 and *R. v Walbrook (Martin)* (1994) 15 Cr. App. R. (S.) 783, [1995] C.L.Y. 1355 considered (see paras 13-14, 18-20, 22-23 of judgment). (2) The purpose of confiscation proceedings was to recover the financial benefit that an offender had obtained from his criminal conduct. In the instant case the Crown identified the benefit as the sum represented by S's share of the estate. Section 6(5) had to be read subject to the requirement of proportionality, so that a judge making a confiscation order should not make one in a sum which was disproportionate to the aim of removing from criminals the pecuniary proceeds of their crimes. Where property obtained by a criminal had been restored or was ready to be restored in full to a victim of a crime in circumstances where there was no additional benefit to the offender, a confiscation order would be disproportionate and a breach of the European Convention on Human Rights 1950 Protocol 1 art.1, *R. v Waya (Terry)* [2012] UKSC 51, [2013] 1 A.C. 294, [2013] 2 C.L. 90 followed. An order which required the offender to pay the same sum again would amount to a further pecuniary penalty, rather than achieving the legislative objective of removing from a defendant his proceeds of crime. That would in effect amount to double recovery and would be disproportionate. The making of the confiscation order in the instant case offended Protocol 1 art.1 as being disproportionate (paras 29-30, 32).

R. v HURSTHOUSE (SUSAN ANN), [2013] EWCA Crim 517, [2013] W.T.L.R. 887, Treacy, L.J., CA (Crim Div).

691. Confiscation orders–Compensation orders–Possibility of double-counting–Whether confiscation order which included sums due under compensation order was proportionate

[Powers of Criminal Courts (Sentencing) Act 2000 (c.6) s.130; Proceeds of Crime Act 2002 (c.29) s.13; European Convention on Human Rights 1950 Protocol 1 Art.1.]

The appellant (J) appealed against a confiscation order made after his conviction for money laundering offences. J had been involved in a fraud upon a bank. Due to the nature of his offence, the lifestyle provisions of the Proceeds of Crime Act 2002 applied. His benefit from criminal conduct was approximately £174,000 which was made up of the sum obtained through the fraud and other assets for which he was unable to show a legitimate origin. A confiscation order was made in that sum. A compensation order of approximately £64,000 was also made to reflect the loss to the bank. J submitted that the confiscation order was disproportionate and infringed the European Convention on Human Rights 1950 Protocol 1 art.1 because the inclusion of the £64,000 amounted to double-counting.

Held: Judgment accordingly. (1) A confiscation order under the 2002 Act was designed to remove from the defendant the fruits of crime. A compensation order under the Powers of Criminal Courts (Sentencing) Act 2000 s.130 was designed as a summary method of ordering the defendant to repay the loser. Under s.13 of the 2002 Act there was no mandatory duty to take the confiscation order into account when deciding on a compensation order. A compensation order was treated for the purposes of enforcement as if it had been made by the magistrates. However, the magistrates' methods of enforcement were limited by the availability of assets since there could clearly be no distraint or other civil enforcement action unless there were identifiable assets. Further, if an order for commitment in default was made, the effect was to bring to an end the obligation to pay the compensation order. The enforcement provisions meant that the making of a compensation order was not the equivalent of payment or restoration to the loser and it remained uncertain whether any such restoration would be made (see paras 12-13, 16-19 of judgment). (2) The Crown Court had a duty to avoid making a confiscation order which infringed art.1 because it was disproportionate, *R. v Waya (Terry)* [2012] UKSC 51, [2013] 1 A.C. 294, [2013] 2 C.L. 90 followed. It would generally be disproportionate if it required the defendant to pay, for a second time, money which he had already fully restored to the loser. If there was no additional benefit beyond that sum, any confiscation order was likely to be disproportionate. If there was an additional benefit, an order which double-counted the sum which had been repaid was likely, to that extent, to be disproportionate, and an order for the lesser sum excluding the double-counting should generally be the right order. However, the mere fact that a compensation order was made for an outstanding sum due to the loser, and thus that the money might be restored, was not enough to render disproportionate a confiscation order which included that sum. What would bring disproportion was the certainty of double payment. Accordingly, the mere making of a compensation order did not mean that the confiscation order had to be reduced by that amount, nor did it mean that the compensation order was irrelevant to the confiscation order (paras 8-9, 21-22). (3) It would be convenient if the 2002 Act provided for the power to make a confiscation order in the full sum and coupled it with an order that compensation in the relevant sum was paid to the loser out of it. However, that power was only available in the limited circumstances described in s.13, namely where a defendant had insufficient means to meet the confiscation order and the compensation order. Nevertheless, the same outcome could be achieved by the following route: (a) if the defendant was in control of his assets he should be able to make repayment in the knowledge that once he proved he had done so, credit would be given for it against a confiscation order. Repayment through solicitors on notice to the Crown should be sufficient; (b) if repayment had not been made before the confiscation hearing, proof that his solicitors were in funds and willing to give an undertaking to repay on his behalf was likely to suffice; (c) where the defendant was not in control of his assets similar principles should apply. If the assets were in the hands of the Crown, he could request repayment. If the assets were subject to a restraint order, he could apply for a variation of it for the purpose of repayment; (d) in very few cases there might be occasion for a brief adjournment of a confiscation hearing for immediate arrangements for payment to be made but the court should not entertain a defendant's well-meaning intentions not backed by assurance of repayment (para.23). (4) If, within 28 days of the instant judgment, J repaid £64,086.76 to the bank, together with interest, his appeal would be allowed to the extent of reducing the confiscation order by that sum. If he did not, the appeal would be dismissed (para.27). (5) An extension of time in which to appeal would not generally be granted simply because the law had changed, *R. v Cottrell (Steven)* [2007] EWCA Crim 2016, [2007] 1 W.L.R. 3262, [2007] C.L.Y. 970 considered. It would be granted only if substantial injustice would otherwise be done to the defendant and the mere fact of change of law did not ordinarily create such injustice. Defendants should not be encouraged to think that the effect of *Waya* was that confiscation orders could be re-opened (paras 29-30).

R. v JAWAD (MOHID), [2013] EWCA Crim 644, [2013] 1 W.L.R. 3861, Hughes, L.J., CA (Crim Div).

692. Confiscation orders–Drug trafficking–Conspiracy to fraudulently evade prohibition on importation of heroin–No finding that defendant had incurred expenditure in connection with conspiracy–Appropriateness of judge's inclusion of expenditure in recoverable amount in confiscation order

[Proceeds of Crime Act 2002 (c.29) s.10(4).]

The appellant (M) appealed against the imposition of a confiscation order for the sum of £240,917.61. M had been involved, along with a number of co-conspirators, in the importation of heroin. The drugs were smuggled in a consignment of rugs from Kabul to Birmingham airport, and were intended to be transported to premises in Leicester. The drugs were apprehended by customs officers at the airport and a dummy consignment was sent to Leicester where M and other co-conspirators were. The consignment was loaded into a car, which M followed for a while. The car was abandoned when the conspirators realised that they were under surveillance. M went to ground for two years, and in the meantime his co-conspirators were convicted and sentenced. M accepted that he had played a significant role in the conspiracy and was sentenced on that basis. Confiscation proceedings were issued. M accepted the prosecution's valuation of the drugs but argued that the benefit figure should reflect the valuation of the drugs, which should be apportioned between the co-conspirators to reflect their respective roles. The judge after hearing evidence from M concluded that he was neither reliable nor credible and held that M's benefit was £240,917.61, which comprised the value of the drugs, the expenditure during the course of the conspiracy, and the subsistence over the six years that M conceded he had been living a criminal lifestyle. The judge further held, referring to the assumption in the Proceeds of Crime Act 2002 s.10(4), that M had played a leading role and as such could not complain when held to account for the moneys expended, and that the recoverable amount was to be the same as the benefit amount as M had failed to provide evidence of assets or legitimate earnings being less than the benefit amount. M submitted that the judge erred in (1) applying the value of the drugs seized and expenses incurred in calculating his benefit; (2) ruling that he had no choice but to make a confiscation order in the sum of the benefit, having rejected his account of his current assets.

Held: Appeal allowed in part. (1) On the evidence, the judge was entitled to make the finding that he had about M's role and that he had joint ownership of the drugs. The judge had sentenced M on the basis of his role and his approach in the confiscation proceedings was consistent with that. The judge was entitled to take into account the familial and social relationships between M and the co-conspirators, of which he was at the hub. The judge erred in his treatment of M when addressing the expenditure incurred in the conspiracy. Joint liability of members during a conspiracy did not assist with identifying which member might have incurred expenditure in the course of its operation, nor did s.10(4). Evidence was needed about the identity of the particular member who incurred the expenditure. Section 10(4) did not mean that, unless he could prove otherwise, each conspirator was treated as having incurred all the expenditure. It might be that in particular circumstances the court could draw inferences that a particular member of a conspiracy had incurred expense. However, without a finding that the conspirator in question spent something, s.10(4) was not triggered. No finding had been made about M's expenditure on the carpet, import duty or vehicle hire, and so it was wrong to attribute those expenses to him. Accordingly, the expenses, namely £3,756.01, were deducted from the recoverable amount (see paras 21-22, 25-26, 32 of judgment). (2) The burden was on M to show that the amount he had available was less than the benefit amount. He had failed to engage with the confiscation process. The judge rejected M's evidence, finding that he had failed to discharge his burden, which was neither disproportionate nor unjust. A defendant who was found to be untruthful or who had failed to give truthful disclosure would find it difficult to discharge the burden imposed upon him, *R. v McIntosh (Leroy Samuel)* [2011] EWCA Crim 1501, [2011] 4 All E.R. 917, [2012] C.L.Y. 681 applied (para.31).

R. v MAHMOOD (SHAUKAT), [2013] EWCA Crim 325, [2013] 1 W.L.R. 3146, Hughes, L.J., CA (Crim Div).

693. Confiscation orders–Enforcement–Real property obtained from criminal conduct–Property registered in name of third party–Appointment of enforcement receiver–Establishing beneficial ownership

[Drug Trafficking Act 1994 (c.37) s.29(8), s.29, s.31(4).]

The applicant (CPS) applied under the Drug Trafficking Act 1994 s.29 for the appointment of an enforcement receiver to enforce an unsatisfied confiscation order made against the respondent (M). M had pleaded guilty to the supply of a controlled drug. A confiscation order was made against him for £2 million to be paid by a certain date with seven years' imprisonment in the event of default. The judge found, contrary to M's contentions, that he was the beneficial owner of a particular property, even though the registered owner was the interested party (L). The property had been bought at auction by a named buyer (W) who had paid the deposit which was said to have been repaid by L as well as the completion monies. Since L was claiming jobseekers allowance the source from which L was able to make such payments and to fund subsequent substantial renovations of the property was doubted. L objected to the appointment of a receiver and maintained that M had no interest in the property. The CPS submitted that the registering of the property in L's name was a sham to hide the true position, namely that M's money was used to purchase the property and that it was no more than a money laundering device to hide M's interest and that it was likely that the original intention was for W to act as M's nominee in the purchase but that L was then substituted for W.

Held: Application granted. The pre-conditions for the making of an order under s.29(1) were satisfied: a confiscation order had been made and not satisfied and was not subject to appeal. The 1994 Act expressly catered for the possibility that innocent third parties would be caught in the cross-fire between prosecutor and defendant and gave third parties the opportunity at the enforcement stage to make representations to the court in respect of their interests and to allow them to retain property which did not represent the proceeds of the defendant's crime or a gift (see s.29(8) and s.31(4). The CPS conceded that subject to the operation of the gift provisions of the 1994 Act, as a matter of ordinary principle there was a presumption that as the registered owner of the property, L owned the beneficial interest in the property and the onus was on it to establish on the balance of probabilities that the contrary was the case, *Stack v Dowden* [2007] UKHL 17, [2007] 2 A.C. 432, [2007] C.L.Y. 3367 applied. The inference was properly to be drawn from the circumstantial evidence that on the balance of probabilities the registering of the property in L's name was a sham, M's money funded the purchase, and M was the true beneficial owner. It was likely that the original intention had been that W would act as M's nominee in the purchase of the property but W was substituted by L (see paras 5, 7-8, 29, 72 of judgment).

LISCOTT v CROWN PROSECUTION SERVICE, [2013] EWHC 501 (Admin), [2013] Lloyd's Rep. F.C. 262, King, J., QBD (Admin).

694. Confiscation orders–Investigations–Disclosure orders and search warrants made after confiscation order–Powers only exercisable for purpose of confiscation investigation–Whether orders made for improper purpose

[Criminal Justice Act 1988 (c.33); Proceeds of Crime Act 2002 (c.29) Pt 8, s.341, s.352, s.357.]

The applicants applied to challenge the issue of disclosure orders and search warrants under the Proceeds of Crime Act 2002 Pt 8. The claimants were the wife, girlfriend and son of a person (M) who had been convicted of conspiracy to cheat in 2001, and against whom a confiscation order had been made in 2002 in the sum of £3,264,277 with six years' imprisonment in default under the Criminal Justice Act 1988. The default sentence was activated in 2010. The judge at the defendant Central Criminal Court then issued disclosure orders under s.357 of the 2002 Act, which were the precursor to disclosure notices requiring attendance at interviews and production of documents by the claimants, and search warrants under s.352 of the 2002 Act in respect of the girlfriend's flat and car. The claimants submitted that (1) the judge had no jurisdiction to issue the search warrants or disclosure orders because those powers could only be exercised for the purpose of a "confiscation investigation" as defined in s.341 of the 2002 Act, and once the confiscation order had been made in 2002 the confiscation investigation had ceased; (2) the powers were not being used to investigate the location of M's benefit from his conduct but for the improper purpose of seeking to enforce realisation of the realisable amount; (3) the warrants were defective on their face because they were not self-contained and did not identify material which could be seized and retained.

Held: Applications refused. (1) Search warrants and disclosure orders could only be made for the purposes of a confiscation investigation and a confiscation investigation was limited to identification of the existence, quantification and location of benefit and not of realisable amount. However, there was nothing in the language, structure or purpose of the 1988 Act or in Part 8 of the 2002 Act to confine an investigation into the whereabouts of a person's benefit to the period up to the making of the confiscation order. It followed that the judge had jurisdiction to make the orders in the instant case (see paras 17-19 of judgment). (2) The issue of the disclosure order and the warrant would only be lawful if the true and dominant purpose was to find out the location of M's benefit, *R. v Southwark Crown Court, Ex p. Bowles* [1998] A.C. 641, [1998] C.L.Y. 893 followed. The 2002 Act required there to be reasonable grounds for believing that the information which might be provided and the material which might be found were likely to be of substantial value to the investigation. M had never disclosed the whereabouts of the sum of over £3 million which he obtained as a result of his fraud on the Revenue. In the light of the fact that nothing else had revealed the whereabouts of the benefit, the judge was entitled to reach the conclusion that there were reasonable grounds for believing that material on his girlfriend's premises and in her vehicle was likely to be of substantial value to the investigation for the purposes for which the search warrant was sought. Similar considerations applied to the disclosure orders since the claimants were those closest to M and their relationship to him provided the most obvious justification for believing they would have information relevant to the means by which M might seek to obtain access to the benefit he had hitherto successfully concealed. The true purpose of the disclosure orders and the search warrants was to obtain information as to the whereabouts of M's benefit, and information obtained as a result of those orders and the warrants was likely to be of substantial value to that investigation (paras 21-29). (3) The warrants were drafted with sufficient precision, *R. (on the application of Energy Financing Team Ltd) v Bow Street Magistrates Court* [2005] EWHC 1626 (Admin), [2006] 1 W.L.R. 1316, [2005] C.L.Y. 930 applied. It would, however, have been preferable if they had identified the purpose as relating to the whereabouts of M's benefit from his criminal conduct (paras 31-33).

R. (ON THE APPLICATION OF HORNE) v CENTRAL CRIMINAL COURT, [2012] EWHC 1350 (Admin), [2012] 1 W.L.R. 3152, Moses, L.J., QBD (Admin).

695. Confiscation orders–Realisable property–Assets jointly owned by co-defendants–Extent to which available to each for purposes of determining realisable assets for confiscation order

[Criminal Justice Act 1988 (c.33); Drug Trafficking Act 1994 (c.37); Proceeds of Crime Act 2002 (c.29).]

The appellants (G and W) appealed against confiscation orders made under the Criminal Justice Act 1988 following their convictions for investment fraud. For the purposes of the confiscation orders, the benefit to each appellant was agreed to be £60.75 million. However, by the time of the confiscation hearings, there were few assets which could be identified with a view to seizure. The judge found that G had over £1.7 million-worth of assets available to him individually, and that W had around £185,000. He also found that they had joint assets of around £971,000. Considering that he was bound to do so by the decision in *R. v May (Raymond George)* [2008] UKHL 28, [2008] 1 A.C. 1028, [2008] C.L.Y. 776, he treated the whole of that sum as being available to each individually. The issue was whether he had been right to do so.

Held: Appeals allowed. (1) The judge had been wrong to treat the jointly-held assets as being wholly available to both G and W. In making a confiscation order, the court had to take four steps. First, it had to ask whether the defendant had benefited from his crime; second, it had to determine the amount of any benefit; third, it had to ascertain the assets available for realisation; and finally, it had to make an order for the amount of the benefit, or the amount available if that was smaller. In *May*, the House of Lords had dealt with the position where two or more defendants had jointly obtained property by their crime. Since property obtained was benefit, it followed that the benefit to each was the whole of the sum jointly obtained. That analysis, however, related only to the second of the four steps, ascertaining the benefit to the defendants, and the key to *May* was understanding that the questions under the second and third steps were distinct and that the answers were not to be elided. When it came to the third step, ascertaining the available assets, the court was not to make an order that it was beyond a defendant's means to pay. A partial interest was to not be treated as if it were a 100 per cent interest. A jointly-owned asset was part-owned by each of the owners, and at step three the court had to determine the extent of each owner's beneficial interest, *May* and *R. v Buckman (Andrew)* [1997] 1 Cr. App. R. (S.) 325, [1997] C.L.Y. 1468 followed, *R. v Chrastny (Charlotte Barbara) (No.2)* [1991] 1 W.L.R. 1385, [1992] C.L.Y. 1258 considered. G and W had not failed to show that their joint assets were available only as to half each. While one co-owner could, as against a third party, control the whole of the property, what he could do with the proceeds depended on his beneficial interest. If he was something less than the sole beneficial owner, then he could not treat the proceeds as being all his. That was the position whether the other co-owner was also a defendant or whether he was a third party unconnected to the crime. There could be real difficulties in determining the proprietary position when the deliberately obscured activities of criminals were concerned, but the judge simply had to make such findings as he could. In a case such as the instant one it was clear that on the balance of probabilities the beneficial interests of the two defendants were the same: the starting point in a case of co-ownership was that the beneficial interests were, prima facie, equal. There was nothing to displace that starting point in the instant case. If all of the jointly-held assets were treated as being wholly available to both G and W then the result would be orders which, by definition, required one or other defendant to pay what he did not have. It could not possibly be the law that a judge was required to make two confiscation orders on the basis that if one was satisfied, the other, which thus became impossible of obedience, would then require an application for a certificate of inadequacy or for a variation in order to cure a defect that was always apparent. The confiscation orders would be quashed and would be replaced that orders that did not contain any double counting of the available assets (see paras 3, 17-18, 22-24, 28-29, 31, 35-42 of judgment). (2) Although the order in the instant case had been made under the 1988 Act, the principles applied equally to cases arising under the Drug Trafficking Act 1994 and the Proceeds of Crime Act 2002 (para.2).

R. v GANGAR (SHINDER SINGH); R. v WHITE (ALAN), [2012] EWCA Crim 1378, [2013] 1 W.L.R. 147, Hughes, L.J., CA (Crim Div).

696. Confiscation orders–Realisable property–Valuation of tainted gifts–Whether recoverability of gift relevant factor in valuation

[Proceeds of Crime Act 2002 (c.29) s.9(1)(b), s.9(1)(a), s.77, s.79, s.81.]

The appellant (S) appealed against a confiscation order imposed following her pleas of guilty to three counts of dishonestly making false statements with a view to obtaining benefit. In February 2003, S had applied to the local authority for housing and council tax benefits, representing that she had no savings. In fact, she had savings of £1,500. She repeated that misrepresentation in 2004 and 2006, when she had over £24,000 in savings. She obtained more than £23,000 in benefits when she was entitled to none at all. Between 2010 and 2011 she repaid around £11,000. There was no dispute that the recoverable amount was just over £12,000, but S claimed that the amount available to her was much less than that. She claimed that by the time of the hearing she had no available assets, having spent the benefits she obtained on living expenses and in paying off debts. She also claimed that she had gifted sums totalling £8,394.99 to members of her family. It was common ground that any gifts made after May 2006 were tainted gifts within the meaning of the Proceeds of Crime Act 2002 s.77. However, S claimed that she had no prospect of recovering them and that they should therefore be treated as having no value. She argued that any confiscation order should be in a nominal amount. The judge disagreed. He accepted that S had no savings and no hidden assets. He made no specific finding about the gifts other than to say that while S had not made any real attempt to recover them, her family members had limited resources and could not easily repay her or return goods that they had bought. He made a confiscation order in the sum of £8,394.99 to be paid within six months, with four months' imprisonment in default of payment.

Held: Appeal dismissed. The appeal centred on the circumstances in which a tainted gift was to be regarded as having no value for the purposes of determining the recoverable amount under s.9(1)(b) of the Act. In the case of *R. v Najafpour (Ahmed)* [2009] EWCA Crim 2723, [2010] 2 Cr. App. R. (S.) 38, [2010] C.L.Y. 733, the Court of Appeal held that in calculating an offender's "free property" for the purposes of s.9(1)(a), debts that it would be impossible for him to recover were to be treated as available assets that had no value. While that decision dealt with the valuation of free property within the meaning of s.9(1)(a), it did not deal with the valuation of tainted gifts within the meaning of s.9(1)(b). Moreover, it was important to note that the judge in the instant case did not find that the sums gifted by S could not be recovered. His reading of s.9(1)(b) was unaffected by what was said in *Najafpour*, and he had taken the view that once a gift had been characterised as a tainted gift, there was no need for any investigation into its recoverability. That was the right approach for two reasons. First, s.81 of the Act provided a specific statutory regime governing the valuation of tainted gifts, and there was nothing in that section linking the value of the gift to its recoverability. There was no equivalent provision relating to the valuation of free property, and the basic rule in s.79 about valuing property focused only on market value and did not address the value of a debt that might be difficult or impossible to recover. That was why the court in *Najafpour* had been able to decide for itself whether the recoverability of such a debt was relevant to its valuation, *Najafpour* considered. Second, the whole point of including assets given away by the offender when assessing the available amount was to prevent the offender dissipating his assets by giving them away. If he could say that they were of no value because he could not get them back, that would defeat the object of s.9(1)(b). Since the recipient of a gift could not be sued for its return, there might be many occasions when gifts could not be recovered. Parliament could not have intended that such gifts were not to be included in the calculation of an offender's available assets (see paras 8-14 of judgment).

R. v SMITH (KIM), [2013] EWCA Crim 502, [2013] 2 Cr. App. R. (S.) 77, Laws, L.J., CA (Crim Div).

697. Convictions–Public order offences–Public order offence and racially aggravated version charged as alternatives–Whether magistrates could properly convict of both offences

[Crime and Disorder Act 1998 (c.37) s.31(1)(a); Public Order Act 1986 (c.64) s.4.]

The claimant (D) applied for judicial review of a decision of the defendant magistrates' court convicting him of two offences arising out of the same facts. D had visited a nightclub with friends. Afterwards his friends had got into a taxi and D tried to join them while smoking a cigarette. The taxi driver asked D to put out his cigarette. D refused to do so or to get out. An argument followed in which D swore and racially abused the taxi driver. D was charged with an offence under the Public Order Act 1986 s.4 and also with a racially aggravated version of the offence under the Crime and Disorder Act 1998 s.31 (1) (a). Before trial D offered to plead guilty to the s.4 offence but that was rejected by the Crown. He was found guilty by the magistrates of the racially aggravated offence but convicted of both offences. D submitted before the magistrates that it was unfair to record two convictions arising out of one set of facts where the elements of one offence were completely subsumed by the other. D submitted that (1) the magistrates had wrongly fettered their own discretion by applying an irrational and inflexible policy to convict of the aggravated and simple forms of the offence; (2) it was wrong in principle to convict a person of both the simple and racially aggravated forms of an offence.

Held: Application granted. (1) There was an insufficient evidential basis on which to conclude that the magistrates fettered their own discretion by applying a rigid policy. (2) Recording two convictions in the circumstances was wrong in principle. The two charges were laid as alternatives. The case of *DPP v Gane* (1991) 155 J.P. 846, [1992] C.L.Y. 926, approved in *R. (on the application of Crown Prosecution Service) v Blaydon Youth Court* [2004] EWHC 2296 (Admin), (2004) 168 J.P. 638, [2005] C.L.Y. 905, supported the proposition that the magistrates could convict of both offences; but the Divisional Court, sitting in its supervisory jurisdiction, was not bound by and could depart from its own previous decision, *R. v HM Coroner for Greater Manchester, Ex p. Tal* [1985] Q.B. 67, [1984] C.L.Y. 447 applied and *Gane* and *Blaydon* not applied. For D to be convicted twice for a single wrong was unfair and disproportionate. It was not a case of being punished or tried twice. A person's criminal record should record what he had done, no more and no less. The two offences were charged as alternatives but had been treated as cumulative. That infringed a basic principle of English justice. In such a case the magistrates should adjourn the lesser charge at the end of the trial but before conviction, so that if an appeal succeeded against conviction on the greater charge, the lesser charge could subsequently be dealt with. If that caused any practical difficulty, it could not override the principle that a person should be convicted only once for one wrong. Therefore the conviction on the lesser charge was quashed.

R. (ON THE APPLICATION OF DYER) v WATFORD MAGISTRATES' COURT, [2013] EWHC 547 (admin), (2013) 177 J.P. 265, Laws, L.J., DC.

698. Coroners and Justice Act 2009 (c.25)–Commencement No.13 Order

THE CORONERS AND JUSTICE ACT 2009 (COMMENCEMENT NO.13) ORDER 2013, SI 2013/SI 2013/1104 (C.47); made under the Coroners and Justice Act 2009 s.182. Commencement details: bringing into force various provisions of the 2009 Act on May 28, 2013.; .

This Order brings into force, on May 28, 2013, paragraphs of the Coroners and Justice Act 2009 concerning the requirement that, in the course of criminal proceedings against a person, previous convictions in other EU Member States are taken into account to the same extent as previous convictions in domestic courts.

699. Costs–Barristers' fees–Defendant absconding before trial–Defence barrister's entitlement to basic graduated fee for cracked trial

[Criminal Defence Service (Funding) Order 2007 (SI 2007/1174) Art.5(1), Sch.1 Pt 1 para.1.]

The appellant barrister (P) appealed against the respondent Legal Services Commission's refusal to pay him a basic graduated fee because the case to which it related had not concluded. P had represented a defendant charged with conspiracy to commit fraud by false representation who pleaded not guilty at a plea and case management hearing but was uncontactable thereafter and did not attend his trial. P submitted a graduated fee claim for payment on the basis of a cracked trial. The Commission refused payment because the case was yet to be concluded, the bench warrant still being outstanding.

Held: Appeal allowed. Although the Commission's litigator fee scheme guidance stated that as long as a bench warrant remained outstanding no fee could be paid, that guidance had no judicial effect and if it were followed, then in circumstances such as the instant case counsel would never be paid. The defendant had pleaded not guilty but the case had not proceeded to trial, and so, in accordance with the Criminal Defence Service (Funding) Order 2007 art.5(1) and Sch.1 para.1, P was entitled to a basic fee for a cracked trial, *R. v Al-Goni (Costs)* [2009] 2 Costs L.R. 356, [2010] C.L.Y. 750 applied (see paras 8, 14-16 of judgment).

R. v AJUFO (COSTS) [2013] 2 Costs L.R. 369, Costs Judge Simons, Sen Cts Costs Office.

700. Costs–Barristers' fees–Revision of trial material on appeal–Complex evidence

The court determined costs following an appeal by the appellant barristers (R and B) against decisions made by the determining officer following the redetermination of their fees for work undertaken on behalf of the respondent (D) in the Court of Appeal. R and B had represented D, who had been convicted of the murder of his young daughter, both during his trial and on appeal. R had sought £35,000 on the brief, plus £5,000 for grounds of application for leave to appeal, £3,000 for perfected grounds of appeal, £2000 for the skeleton argument together with a further £1,500 for three consultations. In addition R claimed £4,000 for refreshers, a further £250 for listening to tapes of summing up and £3,000 for a skeleton argument for leave to appeal to the Supreme Court. On determination he was allowed £18,700. The figures for B were £18,916.96 claimed and £9,350 allowed. It followed that the determining officer reduced R's claim by approximately 65 per cent and B's claim by approximately 50 per cent. The determining officer took account of the fact that in support of the fees claimed, R had logged 164 hours preparation and B had logged 87.5 hours, all of which had been undertaken after the single judge had granted leave to appeal. There had also been two family court proceedings, and the determining officer took account of submissions that the issues were exceptionally complex and difficult. R submitted that there was no dispute that the hours of preparation by both he and B had been undertaken and that the lapse of time between the perfected grounds of appeal and the appeal itself was a period of nine months so that they could not reasonably be expected to remember the details of what had to be advanced before the Court of Appeal without considerable and lengthy revision and updating.

Held: Costs determined. The allowance fell far short of providing counsel with reasonable remuneration. The three conferences and consultations were accepted, accounting for £1,500 and a claim of £2,000 for the skeleton argument was reasonable. £25,000 was allowed for the brief, which was reduced because the hours were incorrectly stated on the fee note by 10 hours and because the hours were high given the level of the material, albeit giving weight to the fact that new papers were being served which required consideration. A total of £1,500 was allowed for the refreshers, plus the summing up tapes at £750 and a further £2,000 for the skeleton argument, making a total of £40,750. Given that R had already been given £18,700 the appeal therefore succeeded to the extent that he should be paid a further £22,050. B should receive a brief fee of £12,500 being 50 per cent of his leader's fee, plus refreshers of £700, together with £500 for advice in conference and in writing and £1,416.70 for the grounds, totalling £15,116.70. Following redetermination, B was paid £9,350 and his appeal succeeded to the extent that he would receive a further £5,766.7 plus VAT.

R. v AKINRELE (COSTS) [2013] 4 Costs L.R. 637, Costs Judge Campbell, Sen Cts Costs Office.

701. Costs–Criminal proceedings

THE COSTS IN CRIMINAL CASES (GENERAL) (AMENDMENT) (NO.2) REGULATIONS 2013, SI 2013/SI 2830; made under the Prosecution of Offences Act 1985 s.20, s.29. In force: January 27, 2014; .

These Regulations make amendments to the Costs in Criminal Cases (General) Regulations 1986 (SI 1986/1335), which make provision for the determination of costs that are to be paid out of central funds pursuant to a defence costs order made under the Prosecution of Offences Act 1985 Pt 2. The amendments are made in consequence of the introduction of a financial eligibility threshold for legal aid in Crown Court proceedings, and set out the rates at which payments out of central funds in respect of costs properly incurred in such proceedings are to be calculated.

702. Costs–Defence costs–Jurisdiction–Crown Court's refusal of defendant's application for payment of defence costs out of central funds–Jurisdiction of Divisional Court to review refusal–Whether refusal constituting decision relating to trial on indictment under s.28(3) Senior Courts Act 1981

[Prosecution of Offences Act 1985 (c.23) s.16; Senior Courts Act 1981 (c.54) s.28(3), s.29(3).]

The appellant (H) appealed against a refusal of an application for his defence costs to be paid out of central funds. H and his co-accused twin brother had attended the respondent Crown Court to stand trial for offences relating to fraudulent trading. H's brother pleaded guilty to two of those offences, and on that basis the prosecution accepted H's not guilty pleas and offered no evidence against him. H applied unsuccessfully under the Prosecution of Offences Act 1985 s.16 for his defence costs to be paid out of central funds; the Court refused on the basis that he had brought the prosecution on himself. The issue was whether the instant court had jurisdiction to review the Crown Court's decision to refuse H's application. H relied on *R. v Wood Green Crown Court, Ex p. DPP* [1993] 1 W.L.R. 723, [1993] C.L.Y. 10 as authority for the proposition that the instant court did have such jurisdiction.

Held: Appeal dismissed. The High Court's power to review Crown Court decisions was limited by the Senior Courts Act 1981 s.28(3), which said that it could not review decisions relating to trial on indictment. The court in *Smalley, Re* [1985] A.C. 622, [1985] C.L.Y. 555 had ruled that the term "trial on indictment" included trials in which a defendant pleaded guilty; on that basis, it was difficult to see why the situation in the instant case, where the prosecution had decided to bring no evidence against H, would not also constitute a trial on indictment for the purposes of s.28(3), *Smalley* considered. The *Wood Green* that H on was no longer good law. Though the case of *R. v Harrow Crown Court, Ex p. Perkins* (1998) 162 J.P. 527, [1998] C.L.Y. 96 concerned the High Court's powers of review on a judicial review under s.29(3) of the 1981 Act rather than on an appeal by way of case stated under s.28(3), H's instant appeal was undermined by the reasoning in that case which said that a "trial on indictment" included the situation, such as in the instant case, where a defendant had pleaded not guilty and was subsequently acquitted by the judge, *Wood Green doubted, Harrow applied*. Accordingly, the instant court had no jurisdiction to entertain the appeal because the refusal of H's application was so intimately bound up in the trial process that it had to be treated as an integral part of it for the purposes of s.28(3), *Sampson, Re* [1987] 1 W.L.R. 194, [1987] C.L.Y. 2282 and *Ashton, Re* [1994] 1 A.C. 9, [1993] C.L.Y. 15 considered.

HUNTER v NEWCASTLE CROWN COURT, [2013] EWHC 191 (Admin), [2014] Q.B. 94, Leveson, L.J., DC.

703. Costs–Defence costs–Non-disclosure of material–Jurisdiction to re-open decision to make defendant's costs order

[Prosecution of Offences Act 1985 (c.23) s.16(6).]

The court was required to determine various issues following the making of a defendant's costs order in favour of the defendant (P). The order was made following P's successful appeal against conviction. P submitted a bill of costs for £3,487,953.12, including a sum of £2,373,205.76 claimed as profit costs for work done in the Crown Court. P's solicitors (X) certified the bill to be accurate and complete. Following a request by the determining officer for further documents it transpired that P and X had, in 2007, agreed that P's liability for profit costs in the Crown Court would be capped at £275,000. The documents also revealed that the cap had purportedly been lifted in 2009 by an oral agreement which increased the fees retrospectively. P argued that the court had no jurisdiction to re-open the decision to make a defendant's costs order and issues such as the validity of the cap were matters for the determining officer.

Held: Judgment accordingly. If the court had known about the cap, its purported removal and the retrospective increase in fees it would have been required, under the Prosecution of Offences Act 1985 s.16(6), to either determine the issue as to whether P had properly incurred the fees sought rather than the £275,000 he had previously agreed in 2007 or direct the determining officer to consider it. The court had jurisdiction to reconsider the application for a defendant's costs order as X had failed to make a disclosure in an ex parte hearing of information solely within their knowledge, *R. v Patel (Siraj)* [2009] EWCA Crim 1133 considered. However, in the instant case it was appropriate to let the assessment take its course. If it was concluded that prima facie there was a deliberate deception the determining authority could refer the matter to the appropriate authorities.

R. v PATEL (HITENDRA) (COSTS); *sub nom.* PATEL, *Re*, [2012] EWCA Crim 1508, [2012] 5 Costs L.R. 873, Hooper, L.J., CA (Crim Div).

704. Costs–Defendants' costs orders–Judicial comment–Whether defendant's costs order should be restricted to legal aid rates–Determining officer's authority

[Prosecution of Offences Act 1985 (c.23) s.16, s.16(7); Criminal Procedure Rules 2011 (SI 2011/1709) Pt 76.]

The Senior Courts Costs Office was required to consider whether a determining officer had been correct to limit a defendant's costs order to the costs the defendant (S) would have recovered if in receipt of legal aid. S had been charged with common assault, criminal damages and possession of a bladed article. He was acquitted of all charges after a two-day trial. The recorder took the view that S could have applied for legal aid but chose not to do so because he would have had to pay a contribution. Accordingly, the public purse should not be obliged to pay more than would have been necessary had legal aid been in place. He therefore made a defendant's costs order "limited to the amount [S] would have recovered had he been in receipt of legal aid". The determining officer stated that he could not question the recorder's order. S's costs were claimed at approximately £22,000 but the determining officer only allowed £4,885. That sum was increased slightly on redetermination.

Held: Appeal allowed. (1) It was no longer possible for a defendant who had funded his defence costs privately to obtain a defendant's costs order. However, the order in S's favour was made before October 1, 2012 and was subject to the Prosecution of Offences Act 1985 s.16 and the Criminal Procedure Rules 2011 Pt 76. It followed that when the application was made for a defendant's costs order it was open to the judge to: (a) refuse the application; (b) exercise his discretion under s.16(7) by assessing the amount which was just and reasonable for the Crown to pay; (c) specify under s.16(9) the amount of costs to be paid where the recipient agreed to the amount, in the absence of which there would be a determination of costs in accordance with the rules (see paras 3, 7 of judgment). (2) The determining officer had fallen into error in asking whether he had authority to disregard the judge's order. There was a distinction to be drawn between changing the order, for example by directing that the defendant should pay the Crown's costs in place of an order that the Crown should pay the defendant's costs, and taking into account comments, remarks or observations made by the court on granting a costs order. The determining officer was not bound by such comments or observations. The recorder had not identified a circumstance which made it inappropriate for S to recover the full amount of expenses, *Galandauer v Snaresbrook Crown Court* [2006] EWHC 1633 (Admin), [2007] 2 Costs L.R. 205, [2006] C.L.Y. 922 applied. If it was the court's intention to engage s.16(7), the court was required to assess what amount, in its opinion, would be just and reasonable. No such assessment was made by the recorder. If, on the other hand, the court was exercising its power to quantify the amount reasonably sufficient to compensate S the power to do so would only have arisen under s.16(9)(a), and the person in whose favour the order was made had to agree the amount. S had not agreed any amount nor were figures discussed before the recorder. The determining officer was therefore not fettered by legal aid rates and the rates claimed by S were reasonable to compensate him in accordance with r.76.2 (see paras 11-15).

R. v SMITH (IAN) (COSTS) [2013] 3 Costs L.R. 516, Costs Judge Campbell, Sen Cts Costs Office.

705. Costs–Graduated fees–Defendant's representation order discharged–Whether advocacy fees payable for standard appearances when no basic fee payable

[Criminal Defence Service (Funding) Order 2007 (SI 2007/1174) Sch.1 Pt 4 para.9(2), Pt 4 para.9(1).]

The Senior Courts Costs Office was required to determine whether a claim for fees made by the appellant advocate (K) to the Legal Services Commission should be granted. K had represented a defendant at a non-effective plea and case management hearing and at two mention hearings. The defendant had the benefit of a representation order but subsequently applied to discharge it as he wished to instruct different solicitors on a private basis. K's claim for £416.40 in respect of advocate fees was rejected on the basis that standard appearances did not attract payment. K submitted that *R. v Metcalf (Costs)* [2010] 4 Costs L.R. 646, [2010] C.L.Y. 747 applied and it could not have been the intention of the Graduated Fee Scheme for counsel to attend court with the benefit of a representation order for no payment.

Held: Appeal allowed. The point made in *Metcalf* was that the Graduated Fee Scheme Guidance was not a source of law, *Metcalf* considered. Whether a fee was payable was dependent upon the terms of the Criminal Defence Service (Funding) Order 2007. Standard appearances were included in the basic fee under Sch.1 Pt 4 para.9(1), but in the instant case Sch.1 Pt 4 para.9(2) applied. That paragraph was a wide-ranging provision that dealt with situations where there was more than one plea and case management hearing, or more than four standard appearances, as well as the situation in the instant case where no basic fee was payable. K was clearly a "substitute advocate" within para.9(2). It could not have been intended that counsel should not be paid in situations such as in the instant case. The Legal Services Commission was directed to process K's fee forthwith.

R. v MUOKA (COSTS) [2013] 3 Costs L.R. 523, Costs Judge Simons, Sen Cts Costs Office.

706. Costs–Graduated fees–Gap of more than one working day between hearings–Absence of retrial order–Right to claim retrial fee

[Criminal Defence Service (Funding) Order 2007 (SI 2007/1174) Sch.1 Pt 1 para.2.]

The appellant counsel (D) appealed against a decision of the respondent Legal Services Commission not to pay a fee for a retrial under the Criminal Defence Service (Funding) Order 2007 Sch.1 Pt 1 para.2. The trial, which began on a Monday, was halted on Thursday of the same week when the jury discharged. The trial was listed to restart the following Monday, and a new jury was sworn in on the Tuesday. The Commission refused the retrial fee on the basis that there had only been one trial which commenced on the first Monday, and that, despite the advocates' graduated fee scheme guidance, a gap of more than one working day did not prevent the conclusion that there had only been one trial.

Held: Appeal dismissed. There had not been a trial and a retrial. There would not be a new trial if it was part of the same procedural and temporal matrix as the first trial, *R. v Seivwright (Costs)* [2011] 2 Costs L.R. 327, [2011] C.L.Y. 754 applied. Accordingly, no fee for a retrial was due because the judge had not ordered a retrial, and the trial which began on the second Monday was all part of the same process that had started on the first Monday. The Commission had been correct to pay a graduated fee under the 2007 Order (see paras 12, 14 of judgment).

R. v NETTLETON (COSTS) [2013] 1 Costs L.R. 186, Costs Judge Gordon-Saker, Sen Cts Costs Office.

707. Costs–Litigators' fees–Starting point of time limit for submitting claim if confiscation order applied for after end of trial

[Criminal Defence Service (Funding) Order 2007 (SI 2007/1174) Art.6(3), Art.32(1), Art.32(2).]

The appellant firm of solicitors (C) appealed against the respondent Legal Services Commission's refusal to pay a litigator graduated fee because it had not submitted the claim within three months of the final trial date. After the defendant whom C had represented was sentenced, the Crown's application for a confiscation order was listed to be heard four months later. However, the Crown Prosecution Service decided not to proceed with the application and that decision was communicated to C a few days before the hearing. C submitted its claim for a graduated fee, but the Commission declined to determine the claim on the ground that it was out of time as the bill was independent of any proceedings under the Proceeds of Crime Act 2002. C submitted that (1) the claim had not been out of time as the proceedings did not conclude, for the purposes of the Criminal Defence Service (Funding) Order 2007 art.6(3), until the Crown's application for a confiscation order was determined; (2) if it was out of time, there was, within the meaning of art.32(1), a good reason for the failure and, within the meaning of art.32(2), exceptional circumstances.

Held: Appeal allowed. (1) Under art.6(3), a claim by a litigator for fees in respect of work done under the representation order had to be submitted within three months of the conclusion of the proceedings to which it related. The work done under the representation order included the confiscation proceedings, for which no separate representation order would be granted. The proceedings to which the representation order related therefore comprised the magistrates' court proceedings, any proceedings in the Crown Court including any re-trial or application under the 2002 Act, and advice and assistance regarding an appeal. The proper construction of art.6(3) was that claims had to be made within three months of the conclusion of the last proceedings funded under the representation order. On that basis, C's claim was not out of time, *R. v Dumbaya (Costs)* [2012] 5 Costs L.R. 976, [2013] 2 C.L. 91 and *R. v Hart-Badger (Costs)* [2013] 1 Costs L.R. 181 applied (see paras 17, 19 of judgment). (2) In any event, time for submitting the claim should be extended because there was a good reason for the failure, namely uncertainty as to when proceedings concluded for the purposes of art.6(3). Furthermore, as there were exceptional circumstances it would be a disproportionate sanction to disallow the whole fee, given the uncertainty and given that the claim was made while C was still conducting work under the representation order. It was not an appropriate case to impose a penalty (para.21).

R. v TAYLOR (COSTS) [2013] 2 Costs L.R. 374, Costs Judge Gordon-Saker, Sen Cts Costs Office.

708. Costs–Litigators' fees–Time limit for lodging fees claim–Conclusion of proceedings

[Criminal Defence Service (Funding) Order 2007 (SI 2007/1174) Art.6(3).]

The appellant solicitors (W) appealed against a refusal by the respondent Legal Services Commission to pay the fee it had claimed under the Litigators' Graduated Fee Scheme for work it had undertaken on behalf of a Crown Court defendant. W had requested payment of its graduated fee nearly four months after the end of the trial. The Commission refused the claim because it had been submitted outside of the three-month time limit contained in the Criminal Defence Service (Funding) Order 2007 art.6(3).

Held: Appeal allowed. Pursuant to art.6(3), a litigator under the scheme had to lodge any claim for payment within three months of the conclusion of the proceedings. There was, however, no definition of "conclusion of the proceedings" in the Order. The Commission had taken the conclusion of the proceedings to be the final trial date, but that was a factual error because, within the ambit of the representation order, proceedings had not concluded then: the litigator had undertaken further work with a view to an appeal, on which it had sought the advice of counsel (see paras 14-15 of judgment).

R. v DUMBAYA (COSTS) [2012] 5 Costs L.R. 976, Costs Judge Campbell, Sen Cts Costs Office.

709. Costs–Litigators' fees–Time limit for lodging fees claim–Exceptional circumstances justifying extension of time

[Criminal Defence Service (Funding) Order 2007 (SI 2007/1174) Art.6(3), Art.32(1), Art.32(2).]

The appellant solicitors (R) appealed against a refusal by the respondent Legal Services Commission to pay the fees it had claimed under the Litigators' Graduated Fee Scheme for work undertaken on behalf of four Crown Court defendants. The Commission had refused payment because R had failed to comply with the three-month time limit contained in the Criminal Defence Service (Funding) Order 2007 art.6(3) for requesting payment of its graduated fees.

Held: Appeal allowed in part. (1) The time limit could be extended under art.32(1) for good reason or under art.32(2) where there were exceptional circumstances (see para.3 of judgment). (2) Although R's claim in regard to the third trial had been five months after the final hearing date which it had stated on its claim form, that date had been when the defendant had been convicted. However, he had not been sentenced until four months later, so the claim had only been submitted one month after the conclusion of the proceedings and therefore would have been in time. R had simply been mistaken about the date on which the case finished: it had inserted the date of conviction instead of the date of sentence. That was not a situation in which the solicitors had failed to comply with the time limit through, for example, ignorance, neglect, oversight or general sloppiness. Therefore, there had been good reason for the delay and the time limit should be extended. However, there should also be a penalty of 10 per cent of the graduated fee under art.32(2) to recompense the Commission for the additional work it would be put to in re-processing the claim (paras 27-29). (3) In principle, the length of the delay and the amount of money involved were capable of being exceptional circumstances. However, each case turned on its own facts and had to be looked at on an individual basis; it was not possible to deal with such appeals by stipulating that a certain degree of lateness might not attract any penalty, but that a greater degree would do so, depending on the sum in question and the size of the litigator firm. In view of the fact that R's claim in regard to the first trial had been more than six months late and the amount involved had been £668, total disallowance had not been a disproportionate penalty. Likewise, in view of the fact that R's claim in regard to the second trial had been more than five months late and the amount involved had been £4,059, total disallowance did not amount to an exceptional circumstance. However, the delay after the fourth trial had been just over a month and the sum involved was £2,709, so total disallowance was a disproportionate penalty amounting to an exceptional circumstance. The graduated fee should be allowed, subject to a penalty of 20 per cent (paras 44-46).

R v GRIGOROPOLOU (COSTS) [2012] 5 Costs L.R. 982, Costs Judge Campbell, Sen Cts Costs Office.

710. Costs–Litigators' fees–Time limit for submission of fee claims after retrials

[Criminal Defence Service (Funding) Order 2007 (SI 2007/1174) Art.6(3).]

The appellant solicitors (W) appealed against a decision of the Legal Services Commission (LSC) refusing to pay part of the costs which they had incurred in representing a young offender (H) who had been charged with robbery. The magistrates' court had sent the case to the Crown Court because of its seriousness. The trial began on November 14, 2011 but the judge discharged the jury on the fourth day after a question about bad character was put to one of H's co-defendants, contrary to an earlier ruling. The trial resumed on January 9, 2012. At its conclusion five days later, H was acquitted. Separate bills for the November and January trials were sent to the LSC on March 9, 2012, but the LSC refused to pay the bill for the November trial on the ground that the fee claim had been submitted outside the relevant three-month time limit. The Criminal Defence Service (Funding) Order 2007 art.6(3) provided that "a claim by a litigator for fees in respect of work done under a representation order must not be entertained unless he [submitted] it within three months of the conclusion of the proceedings to which it [related]".

Held: Appeal allowed. On a proper reading of art.6(3), which had to be given its ordinary English meaning, the time limit ran from the conclusion of the proceedings to which the claim related. The proceedings in this case were, as was made clear in the representation order, the proceedings in the magistrates' court and in the Crown Court in relation to the robbery. The proceedings were concluded when the retrial in January concluded. Accordingly, both of W's fee claims had been lodged within the required time limit (see para.16 of judgment).

R. v HART-BADGER (COSTS) [2013] 1 Costs L.R. 181, Senior Costs Judge Hurst, Sen Cts Costs Office.

711. Costs–Litigators' fees–Transfer of solicitors responsible for cases to new firm–Applicability of Criminal Defence Service (Funding) (Amendment) Order 2009

[Criminal Defence Service (Funding) (Amendment) Order 2007 (SI 2007/3552); Criminal Defence Service (Funding) (Amendment) Order 2009 (SI 2009/1843); Criminal Defence Service (Funding) Order 2007 (SI 2007/1174) Art.26, Sch.2 Pt 2 para.10(2B), Sch.2 Pt 2 para.10(2)(a).]

The appellant solicitors (D) appealed against a decision of the respondent Legal Services Commission to recoup £73,215 under the Criminal Defence Service (Funding) Order 2007 art.26 from payments made to D under the Litigators' Graduated Fee Scheme. D had been the original solicitors acting for defendants in 14 cases in the Crown Court, but the solicitor (S) with responsibility for those cases moved to another firm of solicitors (E). D claimed for work prior to the transfer of legal aid to E. However, the Commission decided that, as S had been the litigator named on the representation orders, there had been no transfer to a new litigator and D could not claim transfer fees. Therefore, only one fee was payable in each case and was payable to E. It was a matter for E and D to divide the fee appropriately in each case.

Held: Appeal allowed. The 2007 Order had been amended by the Criminal Defence Service (Funding) (Amendment) Order 2007 by the introduction of Sch.2 para.10(2)(a), which included the notion of a transfer payment in certain circumstances. A further amendment to the 2007 Order made by the Criminal Defence Service (Funding) (Amendment) Order 2009 inserted Sch.2 para.10(2B), pursuant to which a case was not transferred to a new litigator where a firm of solicitors was named as litigator in the representation order and the solicitor with responsibility for the case moved to another firm. Although the Commission had applied that provision, it had not come into force at the time the representation orders had been granted. Having exercised its powers to recoup by reference to a statutory instrument which stated in terms that it did not apply to representation orders made before August 3, 2009, the Commission had fallen into error (see paras 8, 12 of judgment).

R. v RICHARDS (COSTS) [2012] 5 Costs L.R. 998, Costs Judge Campbell, Sen Cts Costs Office.

712. Costs–Non-parties–Costs order made against Crown Prosecution Service and in favour of defence counsel–Power to make costs order

[Prosecution of Offences Act 1985 (c.23) s.19(1), s.19A; Senior Courts Act 1981 (c.54) s.29(3); Costs in Criminal Cases (General) Regulations 1986 (SI 1986/1335) reg.3.]

The claimant Crown Prosecution Service (CPS) applied for judicial review of a decision of a Crown Court judge to make a costs order against it and in favour of counsel acting for the defence. The judge had made the order when a plea and case management hearing had to be adjourned because the CPS had not prepared adequately. The judge ordered the CPS to pay the defendant's counsel £100 plus VAT on the basis that she would not be able to be remunerated under the Graduated Fee Scheme for the second plea and case management hearing, which was only necessary because of the CPS's failings. The judge purported to make the order under the Costs in Criminal Cases (General) Regulations 1986 reg.3 and the Prosecution of Offences Act 1985 s.19(1). The issue was whether the judge had the power under the 1985 Act or the Regulations to make such an order. The CPS submitted that the judge had erred in law and acted without jurisdiction when making the order, and that such an order could only be made against a party to criminal proceedings.

Held: Application granted. The circumstances of the instant case did not fall within the exclusion in the Senior Courts Act 1981 s.29(3), and therefore the court had jurisdiction to entertain the CPS's application. Defence counsel was not a party to criminal proceedings. On the ordinary and natural meaning of "party", the parties in criminal proceedings were the Crown and the defendant. That conclusion was supported by s.19A of the 1985 Act which drew a distinction between parties and their representatives. The judge took the view that "party" had to be construed to include anyone who had a sufficient interest to make him a party, including counsel, but it was not open to him to construe the legislation in such a way. It followed that the costs order had to be quashed. The court endorsed the arguments of the intervening Bar Council that issues had been raised by the instant case that would need to be reviewed by the Legal Services Commission and the Ministry of Justice (see paras 11-17, 19-24, 25-28 of judgment).

R. (ON THE APPLICATION OF CPS) v BOLTON CROWN COURT, [2012] EWHC 3570 (Admin), [2013] 1 W.L.R. 1880, Richards, L.J., DC.

713. Costs–Prosecution costs–Environmental offences–Company chairman convicted of depositing contaminated silt without licence–Fine and costs order imposed–Proportionality of costs order

[Food and Environment Protection Act 1985 (c.48) s.5(a), s.9(1)(a), s.21(6).]

The applicant (F) applied for leave to appeal against his conviction for depositing substances or articles within United Kingdom waters without a licence contrary to the Food and Environment Protection Act 1985 s.5(a), s.9(1)(a) and s.21(6). Alternatively, he sought permission to appeal against a fine of £25,000 and an order that he pay prosecution costs of £44,159. F was the chairman of a waste management company (O) which had been contracted by the owner of Falmouth harbour (P) to dredge a section of the harbour in readiness for the construction of a marina. The work involved removing silt from one part of the harbour and depositing it a few yards away, without breaking the water's surface. P was aware that the silt was contaminated with toxins, and F knew, at an early stage, that the work could involve contaminated silt. However, neither P nor F applied for a licence to carry out the work. P pleaded guilty to carrying out the work without a licence and O pleaded guilty to depositing contaminated silt. At F's trial, O's conviction was admitted into evidence. The judge directed the jury that the issues were, firstly, whether O had deposited contaminated silt without a licence, and secondly, whether it had done so with F's consent or connivance or as a result of his neglect. He directed them that the word "deposit" was to be given its ordinary dictionary meaning. When sentencing, he took into account the fact that F had considerable experience in the hazardous waste industry and had turned a blind eye while O deposited the contaminated silt. He set the fine on the basis that F had fallen on hard times and had limited assets. F submitted that (1) the judge had wrongly directed the jury as to the meaning of the word "deposit", and as to the relevance and effect of O's conviction, and had wrongly directed them that F bore the burden of proving that there had been no "depositing"; (2) the combination of the fine and the costs amounted to an unreasonable and disproportionate financial penalty.

Held: Application to appeal against conviction refused; Appeal against sentence allowed in part. (1) In the light of the way the trial had been conducted, the judge had directed the jury appropriately on the issues of how they should approach O's conviction and whether there had been any depositing. While his direction on the burden of proof could have been better phrased, his directions were, overall, clear and careful. He expressly directed the jury that the Crown had to prove that there had been a deposit; defined the word "deposit" in the only way he could; and highlighted the issue of whatever O had done as being an important issue between F and the Crown. He understood the central issue to be F's state of mind, and that was understandable given the way the case had been conducted. F was critical of the fact that the judge had not directed the jury specifically about "redistribution" or "maintenance" of the harbour. While he acknowledged that the judge had referred in passing to "redistribution", he felt that that should have come earlier in the summing-up and should not have been divorced from the direction on the meaning of "deposit". That criticism was, however, rejected. The case had never truly been about redistribution or maintenance of the harbour. It was about the movement and deposit of silt during the construction of a new marina. There was no need for any elaboration of the word "deposit". The case was not one in which any of the exemptions applied. There was overwhelming evidence that the silt had been deposited, and F's defence was simply that if anyone was responsible for that deposit, then it was not him (see paras 24-28 of judgment). (2) While no long-term harm had been caused by the dredging, the point of the legislation was to prevent pollution. The potential for harm was considerable, and the dangers of the accumulation of toxins in the food chain were obvious. The financial penalties imposed upon those responsible for projects that might put the environment at risk were meant to act as both punishment and deterrent. Individuals and company boards had to think very carefully before they acted. F had not done so. Rather, he had turned a blind eye to the risk in order to secure what was, for his company, a large contract. Even accepting F's poor financial situation, his previous good character and his comparatively limited culpability, the fine was, of itself, not excessive. The question of costs was a matter for the trial judge's discretion. However, it was not clear that the judge had been provided with sufficient information upon which he could properly exercise that discretion. Accordingly, the question of costs was to be dealt with afresh. Taking a broad and proportionate approach, an order that F should pay costs of £25,000 was appropriate and proportionate. The application for permission to appeal against sentence would be granted only to that extent, and the original costs order would be quashed and replaced with one for the payment of £25,000 (paras 37-42).

R. v FRAMPTON (PETER JAMES), [2012] EWCA Crim 2697, [2013] Env. L.R. 18, Hallett, L.J., CA (Crim Div).

714. Costs–Wasted costs orders–Solicitor advocate's failure to appear at Crown Court at listed time on listed day–Failure to instruct alternative barrister already at court

[Costs in Criminal Cases (General) Regulations 1986 (SI 1986/1335).]

The appellant firm of solicitors (H) appealed against a wasted costs order. H employed a solicitor advocate (B) who had appeared at Derby Crown Court to represent a client (C) who was charged with possession of a Class B drug. C pleaded guilty and the matter was listed for sentence in that court on a later day and at a time when B was due to be in a Crown Court in Manchester for the sentencing of another client. B attempted to list C's case in the afternoon and to list the other case for an early time in the morning, in order that she could cover both cases. In the event, B's first case was not called early in the morning, and at just after midday it became clear that there was no realistic hope of B arriving in Derby in time for C's hearing. At that point H informed the listing officer in Derby and the matter was adjourned and the wasted costs order made. H submitted that B had acted properly at all times, save that she had made a mistake in failing to enquire of the other barristers at Derby Crown Court whether they were available to receive instructions to deal with the sentencing at short notice.

Held: Appeal dismissed. The wasted costs order was properly made. It did not automatically follow that because an advocate failed to appear at court at the listed time on the listed day that a wasted costs order would follow. The making of the wasted costs order would depend on the test provided by the Costs in Criminal Cases (General) Regulations 1986. No advocate should accept instructions in two cases on the same day in geographically distant Crown Courts when there was a real risk that a hold-up at the first court might result in wasted costs being incurred in the second. An advocate's first duty was to the court, and that duty was not fulfilled by clinging to a brief in the hope that both commitments could be fulfilled (see paras 9-10 of judgment). At the point when B realised that she could not fulfil both commitments she should have fulfilled her duty to the court by instructing a barrister who was already at Derby Crown Court. Such a barrister did not need the file: it was a guilty plea to simple possession of cannabis. The decision to cling to the brief was plainly negligent (para.11).

R. v HENRYS SOLICITORS, [2012] EWCA Crim 1480, [2012] 6 Costs L.O. 858, Pitchford, L.J., CA (Crim Div).

715. Costs orders–Third party costs orders–Misconduct–Failure to provide interpreter for hearing–Whether failure constituted serious misconduct

[Prosecution of Offences Act 1985 (c.23) s.19B; Costs in Criminal Cases (General) Regulations 1986 (SI 1986/1335) reg.3.]

The appellant (C) appealed against an order under the Prosecution of Offences Act 1985 s.19B requiring it to pay the costs thrown away by the prosecution in respect of a sentencing hearing that was adjourned because of the non-attendance of an interpreter. C provided language services to the Ministry of Justice and other bodies including HM Courts and Tribunals Service. C had received a booking for an interpreter for a sentencing hearing. The day before the hearing the courts service telephoned C to arrange for the interpreter to attend at 9.45am instead of the original time of 10.30am. Due to an internal error C did not tell the interpreter of the change. In the absence of the interpreter, the hearing was adjourned. The judge decided that C had been negligent and that such negligence constituted serious misconduct. He applied his discretion under the Costs in Criminal Cases (General) Regulations 1986 reg.3(f) and ordered C to pay half of prosecution counsel's fee for the adjourned hearing. C, exercising its rights under reg.3(h) and the Consolidated Practice Direction, appealed, contending that the judge had been wrong in finding that there had been serious misconduct.

Held: Appeal allowed. (1) The provision of an interpreter for a witness or a defendant in a criminal case was an integral part of the State's obligations to provide a fair and just system of criminal justice. If a private company took on the discharge of such an obligation, it assumed the responsibility to do so in accordance with the terms it had agreed. In order to determine whether there had been misconduct it was necessary to know the nature of C's contractual obligations. C was bound to provide 24 hours a day, 365 days a year an interpreter or translator of the appropriate agreed standard for each individual assignment; its obligations extended to much more than a booking facility. The provision of an interpreter where either a witness or a defendant did not speak English was essential: without one, a case could not proceed. It was inconceivable that the Ministry of Justice would have entered into a contract where the obligation on C was framed in any terms other than an absolute obligation. The provision in the agreement for a financial adjustment if C did not fulfil 98 per cent of bookings did not affect its obligation to provide interpreters on each occasion. C's conduct was to be considered in the light of the responsibility to discharge the State's obligation to provide an interpreter in criminal proceedings; a simple failure by the interpreter to attend was a failure for which C was responsible (see paras 13-15, 18-30 of judgment). (2) A single failure of the kind that occurred in the instant case could not, viewed in isolation, amount to serious misconduct. There was no evidence that the failure was anything other than an isolated failure. There was no evidence of a number of other previous failures by the interpreter in question or failures in C's system. However, a case of serious misconduct might arise if there was evidence that the non-attendance occurred where there had been a failure to remedy a defect in administrative systems which had caused non-attendance in the past. Equally, the failure of a particular interpreter to attend where there was evidence that there had been similar failures in the past might constitute serious misconduct for which C would be responsible. In any future case it would be open to a court to ask C to attend, to provide an explanation for an interpreter's non-attendance and, if appropriate, to provide the necessary disclosure of any system failures or previous failures by that interpreter. A court should not generally consider making an order under s.19B without clear evidence of serious misconduct unless there were unusual circumstances to justify such an order (paras 38-43).

R. v APPLIED LANGUAGE SOLUTIONS LTD (NOW CAPITA TRANSLATION AND INTERPRETING LTD); *sub nom.* APPLIED LANGUAGE SOLUTIONS LTD, *Re*, [2013] EWCA Crim 326, [2013] 1 W.L.R. 3820, Sir John Thomas (President QBD), CA (Crim Div).

716. Courts' powers and duties–Mode of trial–Alleged misleading commercial practice–Wrongful application of fraud sentencing guidelines–Effect on mode of trial

[Consumer Protection from Unfair Trading Regulations 2008 (SI 2008/1277) reg.9, reg.11.]

The appellant (P) appealed by way of case stated against a decision of the magistrates' court to commit him to the Crown Court for trial in respect of a prosecution brought by the respondent local authority. P had been charged with offences contrary to the Consumer Protection from Unfair Trading Regulations 2008 reg.9 and reg.11. The local authority alleged that P had led a consumer to believe that £6,000 worth of unnecessary building work to her property was required, and demanded payment. The offences were triable either way, but it was argued that the matter was suitable for summary trial. The magistrates agreed but their legal advisor stated that he had failed to advise them that the only penalty that they could impose following the summary trial was a maximum fine of £5,000. The magistrates reconsidered the matter and, on their legal advisor's advice, applied the fraud sentencing guidelines to determine the mode of trial, as there were no sentencing guidelines available for offences under the Regulations, and they believed the fraud guidelines to be analogous. The magistrates referred to confidence fraud, believing it to be similar to the instant offences, and adopted its six-week starting point for financial gain exceeding £10,000. They halved the starting point to three weeks as the alleged financial gain had been £6,000, and concluded that committal proceedings were necessary, as they did not have jurisdiction to hear the matter. The questions for the court were whether (i) absent specific sentencing guidelines, the magistrates had been wrong in law to consider starting points and ranges for offences that were of a similar level of seriousness to inform the decision as to their jurisdiction; (ii) it was an unreasonable exercise of their discretion to find that the most similar sentencing guideline was that pertaining to confidence fraud; (iii) it was unreasonable to conclude that, on conviction after trial, P would be highly likely to receive a custodial sentence.

Held: Appeal allowed. (1) The difficulty with the magistrates' adoption of the fraud sentencing guidelines to assist with their determination of the mode of trial was that the offences with which P had been charged did not involve allegations of dishonesty, whereas fraud offences did. Therefore, it was not appropriate to refer to sentencing guidelines of offences that had dishonesty as the basis of the offence, *R. v Stone (Rodney)* [2012] EWCA Crim 186 applied. In principle, the question posed would be answered affirmatively. However, the words "similar level of seriousness" were only relevant if the guidelines adopted were analogous and of a similar level of seriousness. The mistake that had been made here was basing the instant offences, which did not contain allegations of dishonesty, upon offences of dishonesty. (2) The exercise of the magistrates' discretion had been wrongful. (3) The magistrates had applied the wrong test. It was not a question of whether P was "highly likely" to receive a custodial sentence, it was a question of whether the custody threshold had been passed. Looking at the circumstances of the offence as known, it was a case where the magistrates would be justified in saying that a court might well form the view that a custodial or community sentence rather than a fine, or a fine in excess of what they could impose, would be appropriate. However, the magistrates had erred in that they were driven by the wrongful consideration of the fraud sentencing guidelines and had applied the wrong test. Accordingly, the case was remitted.

PRICE v CHESHIRE EAST BC, [2012] EWHC 2927 (Admin), [2013] 1 W.L.R. 1232, Collins, J., QBD (Admin).

717. Criminal appeals–Guilty pleas–Quashing of conviction entered after guilty plea–Extent of Court of Appeal's power to substitute conviction for alternative offence

[Criminal Appeal Act 1968 (c.19) s.3A(1)(b), s.3A, s.7(2).]

The appellant (L) appealed against her conviction for possessing a prohibited weapon. As part of a streamlined process and after very limited disclosure, L had pleaded guilty to possessing a prohibited weapon. In doing so, she had pleaded guilty to an offence that she had not committed. The undisputed position was that the shotgun she admitted to possessing was not in fact a prohibited weapon, though it was one for which a firearm certificate was required. On that basis, the Crown did not resist the quashing of her conviction. However, its position was that the court should, in the exercise of its powers under the Criminal Appeal Act 1968 s.3A, substitute a conviction for possessing a firearm without a certificate. The Crown submitted that the words "the indictment" in s.3A were to be construed as meaning "the indictment in a potentially amended form".

Held: Appeal allowed. (1) The substitution contended for did not satisfy the statutory requirements. Before a conviction for another offence could be substituted, s.3A(1)(b) required that the defendant could, on the indictment, have been found guilty of that other offence. In L's case, the indictment charged only the offence of possessing a prohibited weapon and did not allege the absence of a firearm certificate. Thus, on that indictment, L could not have been found guilty of possessing a firearm without a certificate. Nor could it be said that her plea of guilty to possessing a prohibited weapon was an admission of facts proving her guilty of possessing a firearm without a certificate, as required by s.3A(1)(c). The existence of a firearm certificate was irrelevant to the offence on the indictment. Furthermore, no valid distinction could be drawn between cases where a conviction had to be quashed because it was for an offence which had been repealed, and those where the conviction had to be quashed because the indicted offence had not, in fact, been committed. The test was simply whether the defendant could, on the indictment to which she had pleaded, have been convicted of the alternative offence. In L's case, the answer was no. The argument that the words "the indictment" in s.3A should be construed as meaning "the indictment in a potentially amended form" was not sustainable. It was inconsistent with the approach taken in *R. v Graham (Hemamali Krishna)* [1997] 1 Cr. App. R. 302, [1996] C.L.Y. 1532, and it had to be remembered that the ability to substitute a conviction was a limited exception to the fundamental rule that a defendant could only be convicted on his own plea or as a result of proof before a jury, *Graham* considered. Thus, s.3A had to be construed strictly and its operation had to be confined to cases where the originally tendered guilty plea inevitably involved an admission to the alternative offence. Any other approach involved the Court of Appeal evaluating whether there might be a defence, and that was not permissible. L's conviction could not stand and substitution was not possible (see paras 5-9 of judgment). (2) The only offence that could be remitted for retrial was that of possessing a prohibited weapon. However, since there could be no conviction in relation to that offence, a retrial would be inappropriate, even though the indictment could be amended before the retrial to include the lesser offence. The Court of Appeal could not circumvent the requirements of the s.7(2) of the Act by ordering a retrial on a count where it was clear that there could not be a conviction (paras 9-10).

R. v LAWRENCE (NYIRA), [2013] EWCA Crim 1054, [2014] 1 W.L.R. 106, Hallett, L.J., CA (Crim Div).

718. Criminal Justice Act 2003 (c.44)–Commencement No.31 and Saving Provisions Order

THE CRIMINAL JUSTICE ACT 2003 (COMMENCEMENT NO.31 AND SAVING PROVISIONS) ORDER 2013, SI 2013/SI 2013/1103 (C.46); made under the Criminal Justice Act 2003 s.330, s.336. Commencement details: bringing into force various provisions of the 2003 Act on May 28, 2013.; .

This Order brings into force provisions of the Criminal Justice Act 2003 that will: amend the provisions by which a magistrates' court decides on the mode of trial for adults charged with an offence which is triable either on indictment or summarily (either way offences); modify the provisions by which children and young persons are ordinarily tried summarily for an offence which is triable on indictment, subject to certain exceptions; and introduce provisions by which children and young persons may indicate intention as to plea in certain cases.

719. Criminal Justice and Immigration Act 2008 (c.4)–Commencement No.15 Order

THE CRIMINAL JUSTICE AND IMMIGRATION ACT 2008 (COMMENCEMENT NO.15) ORDER 2013, SI 2013/SI 2013/616 (C.25); made under the Criminal Justice and Immigration Act 2008 s.153, Sch.9 para.3. Commencement details: bringing into force various provisions of the 2008 Act on April 8, 2013.; .

This Order brings the Criminal Justice and Immigration Act 2008 Sch.9 para.3 fully into force. The effect of this is to enable the giving of youth conditional cautions to a person aged 10 or over but under 18.

720. Criminal procedure–Rules

THE CRIMINAL PROCEDURE RULES 2013, SI 2013/SI 2013/1554 (L.16); made under the Criminal Law Act 1977 s.48; the Bail Act 1976 s.5B; the Senior Courts Act 1981 s.52, s.73, s.74, s.87; the Police and Criminal Evidence Act 1984 s.81; the Criminal Procedure and Investigations Act 1996 s.19, s.20; the Terrorism Act 2000 Sch.5 para.10, Sch.6 para.4, Sch.6A para.5; the Powers of Criminal Courts (Sentencing) Act 2000 s.155; the Proceeds of Crime Act 2002 s.91, s.351, s.362, s.369, s.375; the Criminal Justice Act 2003 s.132, s.174; and the Courts Act 2003 s.69, s.72. In force: October 7, 2013; .

These Rules consolidate the Criminal Procedure Rules 2012 SI 2012/1726, with the amendments made by SI 2012/3089. The new Rules incorporate the amendments which: require the defendant to give notice of the identity of the intended defence trial advocate; and clarify the nature of the obligations imposed.

721. Criminal proceedings–Costs

THE COSTS IN CRIMINAL CASES (GENERAL) (AMENDMENT) REGULATIONS 2013, SI 2013/2526; made under the Prosecution of Offences Act 1985 s.19. In force: October 27, 2013; .

These Regulations amend the Costs in Criminal Cases (General) Regulations 1986 (SI 1986/1335) reg.14(2) and reg.15 in consequence of the abolition of committals for trial. They also amend reg.16, in order to allow an intermediary who is required to assist a defendant in criminal proceedings to receive payment from central funds. This latter amendment is made to give effect, in part, to the requirements of Directive 2010/64 on the right to interpretation and translation in criminal proceedings.

722. Criminal proceedings–Devolution–Permission to appeal–Supreme Court

THE SCOTLAND ACT 2012 (TRANSITIONAL AND CONSEQUENTIAL PROVISIONS) ORDER 2013, SI 2013/SI 2013/7 (S.1); made under the Scotland Act 2012 s.42. In force: April 22, 2013; .

This Order introduces a new system of "compatibility issues" in criminal proceedings in Scotland. It also makes provision for time limits for seeking permission to appeal to the Supreme Court against a determination of a devolution issue in Scottish criminal proceedings.

723. Decisions to prosecute–Reviews–Implementation of new process for reviewing CPS decisions not to prosecute–Consequences on subsequent judicial review applications

The claimants (L and P) renewed their applications for judicial review of decisions of the CPS not to prosecute. In both cases, after the commencement of judicial review, senior prosecutors had reviewed the decision not to prosecute. In L's case a detailed review concluded that there was no evidence to sustain two of the allegations made. In respect of a further two allegations, there was sufficient evidence but there was no public interest in bringing the case. In P's case a less detailed review concluded, similarly, that there was no evidence to sustain the allegations.

Held: Applications refused. (1) A challenge could be brought against a CPS decision on the following narrow grounds: (a) there had been some unlawful policy; (b) the Director of Public Prosecutions had failed to act in accordance with his own set policy; or (c) the decision was perverse, *R. v DPP, Ex p. Chaudhary* [1995] 1 Cr. App. R. 136, [1995] C.L.Y. 29 applied. Successful applications would be rare for the good and sound constitutional reason that decisions to prosecute were entrusted to the prosecuting authorities. It was important that the constitutional position of the CPS as an independent decision maker was respected and recognised. As a result of the decision in *R. v Killick (Christopher)* [2011] EWCA Crim 1608, [2012] 1 Cr. App. R. 10, [2012] C.L.Y. 742, the CPS considered new processes for reviewing decisions of prosecutors not to proceed, *Killick* considered. The instant cases served to illustrate the way in which the new process would work: a senior prosecutor would review the decision not to prosecute. It would be for the CPS to determine the type of review that was made. Some cases would call for very detailed review; others could be dealt with in short order. It was important to the future conduct of such cases to recognise that the CPS had that procedure in place. It was highly likely that where a review had taken place, and the review could be seen to be careful and thorough, judicial review proceedings would be more difficult to advance. The CPS would have independently reconsidered the position and, unless it could be shown that it was within one of the three categories established in *Chaudhury*, it would be more difficult to show that the decision was one that could be successfully challenged. In the light of the new procedure, the following was to be noted. First, judicial review proceedings should not be brought until the CPS had had an opportunity to conduct a further review under its victim right of review procedure. In the ordinary case, if a challenge was brought before that right of review had been taken up, it should not be entertained by the court. Second, if there had been a review in accordance with that procedure then the prospect of success would be very small. In cases where the right of review was not taken up, the CPS was to set out its position in its acknowledgment of service: it could either offer a review or consider that what it had done so far was sufficient. In those circumstances the court would either adjourn the matter pending review or, if the CPS did not wish to conduct a review, the judge would make his decision on the basis of the papers. If a review took place after the launch of judicial review proceedings then, if the applicant was content, that would be the end of the matter. If he was not content, the parties had to apply to the judge for appropriate directions. Those would include an amendment to the original application to ensure that the challenge to the further review was properly before the court; new grounds were to be served indicating why it was said that the review failed in one of the three respects above; directions for the CPS to respond. All of those had to be done before the judge would consider permission. In cases where a challenge was inappropriately brought, there was no reason why the CPS should not be entitled to seek costs from a person who was unsuccessful in his challenge. Such cases consumed considerable resources and it could not be right that people could have a "free ride" in the court in the light of what the CPS had done (see paras 3-4, 6-15, 18 of judgment). (2) There was nothing on the evidence to suggest that the review decisions in either case were wrong. The manner in which they had been looked at was satisfactory and their conclusions were proper and proportionate (paras 44-45, 66).

L v DPP; PRATT v CROWN PROSECUTION SERVICE (NORTHUMBRIA), [2013] EWHC 1752 (Admin), (2013) 177 J.P. 502, Sir John Thomas (President QBD), QBD (Admin).

724. Defence case–Withdrawal–Judge's withdrawal of defence prior to trial–Existence of reasonable excuse defence–Entering UK without passport

[Asylum and Immigration (Treatment of Claimants, etc.) Act 2004 (c.19) s.2(1), s.2(7).]

The appellant (X) appealed against a conviction for entering into the United Kingdom without a passport contrary to the Asylum and Immigration (Treatment of Claimants, etc.) Act 2004 s.2(1). X had fled Eritrea due to onerous and excessive military service, and came to the UK via Sudan. He travelled to Sudan with a valid Eritrean passport, paid an agent for his flight to the UK and handed over his passport as the agent asked for it. The agent gave X a different passport to use when boarding and checking in, but he did not retain it. X was interviewed upon arrival and explained that he had used the passport the agent had given him to board and check in. No further questions were asked about the whereabouts of the false passport. An expert report was prepared which concluded that agents, like the one that X had used, were usually connected to criminal organisations and that X's claim that he had little or no say in the handling of the passport was consistent with agents' behaviour. The prosecution applied, prior to trial, for a ruling that X had no defence. X's defence was that he had a reasonable excuse under s.2(4)(c) for not being in possession of a passport on his arrival. The judge granted the application on the basis that X's failure to bring the false passport with him or retain his Eritrean passport due to the agent s instructions did not constitute a reasonable cause under s.2(7)(b)(iii) and therefore he had no defence under s.2(4)(c).

Held: Appeal allowed. (1) The judge was wrong to rule that there was no defence to the charge before the case had even begun. Defence counsel could ask a judge for an indication at the outset of a trial to rule as to whether on certain facts a particular defence would be open to a defendant, or to indicate how the judge would propose to direct the jury in relation to that issue, with a view to a giving defendant advice about his plea. However, that had not happened in the instant case, and thus the proper time for the judge to have considered how to direct the jury on a defence under s.2(4)(c) would have been after the evidence had been given (see para.14 of judgment). (2) If the evidence had been foreshadowed in the material before the court it would have been wrong in principle for the judge to rule as matter of law that X had no available defence. The question of whether the evidence was sufficient to persuade the jury that X had a reasonable excuse for not holding his Eritrean passport would have been a matter for the jury to decide. Even if the judge had been satisfied that no reasonable jury could have resolved the issue in X's favour, he would still have been wrong to withdraw the defence from the jury. What might constitute a "reasonable excuse" was qualified by s.2(7), but it was for the jury to apply those qualifications, where relevant, to the facts as they found them. The prosecution's reliance on a statement in *R. v Clancy (Louise)* [2012] EWCA Crim 8, [2012] 1 W.L.R. 2536, [2012] C.L.Y. 799 to suggest that a judge could properly rule that facts were incapable of constituting a good reason if a finding that good reason existed would be perverse had to be treated as per incuriam, as it was contrary to *R. v Wang (Cheong)* [2005] UKHL 9, [2005] 1 W.L.R. 661, [2005] C.L.Y. 902, which was not cited in Clancy, Clancy considered and Wang applied. A court could only rule that a defendant's explanation was incapable of amounting to a good reason or reasonable excuse if it could be properly said, on the true construction of the Act, that it would be inconsistent with the essential nature and purpose of the offence for the defendant's explanation to be capable of amounting of to a defence, *R. v Kelleher (Paul)* [2003] EWCA Crim 3525, (2003) 147 S.J.L.B. 1395 applied. It would not have been contrary to the manifest purpose of the Act for X's explanation to be regarded by the jury as a reasonable excuse (paras 15, 16, 22). (3) There would have been no perversity in a jury concluding on the evidence that a defence under s.2(4)(c) was made out. A jury might well have concluded that it was reasonable to have expected X to hand over his passport to the agent when asked, given the expert evidence on the matter. The prosecution's submission that a defence would only be available to X if he could also establish that he had a reasonable excuse for not producing the false passport was wrong. Section 2(4)(c) contained no such qualification; it applied where an immigrant had a reasonable excuse for not possessing an immigration document, *Thet v DPP* [2006] EWHC 2701 (Admin), [2007] 1 W.L.R. 2022, [2007] C.L.Y. 2323 applied. It was unrelated to a false document on which an immigrant might have travelled. Non-production of a false immigration document would not vitiate a defence available under s.2(4)(c) (paras 23-24).

R. v ASMERON (ROBEL GIDE), [2013] EWCA Crim 435, [2013] 1 W.L.R. 3457, Toulson, L.J., CA (Crim Div).

725. Defendants' costs orders–Taxation of costs–Hourly fees–Reduction to solicitors' hourly rates

[Costs in Criminal Cases (General) Regulations 1986 (SI 1986/1335) reg.7, reg.7(5).]

The claimant (W) applied for judicial review of the taxation of his costs following the grant of a defendants' costs order when criminal proceedings against him in the magistrates' court were stayed. W submitted a claim for costs of just over £200,000 to the defendant national taxing team (T). W's solicitors had been privately instructed at a rate of between £250 and £275 per hour, and a 50 per cent uplift had been applied. T made an initial assessment of just over £110,000, having refused some expenses and having reduced the hourly rates to between £203 and £217. Following further correspondence, T allowed some of the expenses but continued to contest the hourly rates on the ground that they were unreasonable. W applied for judicial review of that decision. W adduced witness statements from two local firms which detailed the hourly rates of their partners to be between £220 and £250. W submitted that the amount assessed was Wednesbury unreasonable as it did not reasonably compensate him for expenses incurred and that the hourly rates claimed were comparable to other local firms. T contended that it was entitled to make the assessment that it did and that W's evidence did not substantiate his claim.

Held: Application refused. (1) It was important to bear in mind that the regime set out in the Costs in Criminal Cases (General) Regulations 1986 reg.7 provided that when considering a claim in relation to fees it was necessary first to consider the work that had actually and reasonably been done; and that reg.7(5) provided that the appropriate authority assessing the application should allow such a sum as was reasonably sufficient to compensate an applicant for costs properly incurred by him in the proceedings. That did not require an indemnity to be given by the taxing authority for the costs actually incurred and all that was necessary was for it to give weight to what was reasonably sufficient to compensate the applicant. The evidence W had supplied had not assisted his argument that T acted unreasonably in reducing his solicitors' hourly rates to under £250. That evidence fell short of the clear, cogent and convincing evidence that must have been envisaged when permission was granted. In the circumstances, T's taxation of W's costs was not unreasonable (see paras 16-19, 21, 23 of judgment). (2) (Obiter) In a taxation decision of this sort, it was not necessary for the taxing authority to deal with every point that was raised as might be expected in a judgment that might be given by a professional judge. All that was necessary was for the recipient of the decision to know what had been accepted and what had been objected to (para.26).

WATSON v HM COURTS AND TRIBUNALS SERVICE NATIONAL TAXING TEAM; *sub nom.* WATSON v HMCTS NATIONAL TAXING TEAM, [2012] EWHC 2865 (Admin), [2012] 6 Costs L.R. 1129, Laws, L.J., DC.

726. Drug trafficking–Proceeds of crime–Certificate certifying proceeds of drug trafficking–Effect of certification on others subsequently charged with laundering proceeds in excess of certified value–Permissibilty of revoking direction for preparatory hearing under s.29 Criminal Procedure and Investigations Act 1996

[Criminal Procedure and Investigations Act 1996 (c.25) s.29, s.31(3)(b); Drug Trafficking Act 1994 (c.37) s.5(2).]

The appellants (Y and Z) appealed against a ruling made at what was said to have been a preliminary hearing under the Criminal Procedure and Investigations Act 1996 s.29. An individual (X) had been convicted of participating in a conspiracy to import and supply drugs. The Crown commenced proceedings under the Drug Trafficking Act 1994 for a confiscation order, and in the course of those proceedings the court issued a certificate under s.5(2) certifying that the value of X's proceeds of drug trafficking was £100,000. A drug trafficking order in the sum of £100,000 was made against X and assets were seized. Y and Z were subsequently charged with laundering proceeds which X had derived from the conspiracy. At the hearing before the judge, Y and Z argued that the continuation of the proceedings would be an abuse of process. The judge confirmed that the hearing would be a preparatory hearing under s.29 of the 1996 Act. In his ruling he found against Y and Z and revoked the direction that he had made for a preparatory hearing. The issues were whether (i) the hearing was a preparatory hearing under s.29, and if so whether the judge was entitled to revoke the order he had made; (ii) the certificate had effect against anyone other than X. Y and Z argued that the certification was against the whole world and the Crown could not go behind it; the amount certified had been satisfied by the realisation of X's seized assets; it was not therefore permissible for the Crown to contend that any further sums were obtained by X from that conspiracy; they could therefore not be guilty of money laundering any additional proceeds allegedly derived from the conspiracy.

Held: Appeal dismissed. (1) It was common ground and was clear from the ruling that the judge had ordered the hearing to continue as a preparatory hearing. The conditions in s.29 were satisfied as he was being asked, under s.31(3)(b), to determine a question of law. In those circumstances, the question arose as to whether he had the power to revoke the order he had made. It was not permissible to declare retrospectively, after the relevant ruling had been given, that a pre-trial hearing had been a preparatory hearing for the purposes of s.29, *R. v C* [2010] EWCA Crim 2578, [2011] 3 All E.R. 509, [2011] C.L.Y. 581 considered. Similarly, it was not permissible, once a decision had been made to hold a preparatory hearing, for the judge in the course of his judgment to revoke that decision. The 1996 Act contained no such power and it was wrong in principle to allow a judge to take that course (see paras 12-15 of judgment). (2) There was nothing in the language of the 1994 Act which suggested that the certificate had effect against anyone other than the person in respect of whom it was made. Although that person could not after the lapse of six years have the value of the proceeds of drug trafficking re-assessed against him, there was no reason why Parliament would have intended that a person who held any proceeds of that drug trafficking should not be subjected to a criminal prosecution in respect of proceeds that were greater than the amount certified. The legislation was designed to impose a punitive regime on all who participated in drug trafficking or assisted in the laundering of proceeds. Parliament could not have intended that if years later it was discovered that an associate was knowingly dealing with what could be proved to be proceeds of the drug trafficking in excess of the amount certified, such a person could rely on the certificate given in the proceedings to which he was not a party. Further, there was nothing in the facts of the case that meant that Y and Z could rely on the certification to show that it was unfair for the Crown to proceed against them in respect of any sums that allegedly derived from the conspiracy (paras 25-26, 28-29).

R. v Y; R. v ZSB; *sub nom.* R. v YDG, [2012] EWCA Crim 2437, [2013] 1 W.L.R. 2014, Sir John Thomas (President QBD), CA (Crim Div).

727. Duty to make records–Interpretation–Rules–Translations

THE CRIMINAL PROCEDURE (AMENDMENT) RULES 2013, SI 2013/SI 2013/2525 (L.22); made under the Courts Act 2003 s.69. In force: October 27, 2013; .

These Rules amend rule 3.8 (Case preparation and progression) and rule 5.4 (Duty to make records) of the Criminal Procedure Rules 2013 (SI 2013/1554) in order to codify the procedure supplementing a defendant's common law right to interpretation and translation, where needed for a fair trial; and to give effect, in part, to the requirements of Directive 2010/64 on the right to interpretation and translation in criminal proceedings.

728. Enforcement receivers–Costs–Receiver appointed under Drug Trafficking Act 1994–Receiver's entitlement to claim litigation costs against third parties

[Drug Trafficking Act 1994 (c.37); Proceeds of Crime Act 2002 (c.29); Civil Procedure Rules 1998 (SI 1998/3132) r.48.6, r.69.7, r.69.7(4).]

The applicant enforcement receiver applied for an order that the respondents (S) pay his costs of applications for a declaration as to the beneficial interests in a property and for possession of the property. The receiver had been appointed under the Drug Trafficking Act 1994. The court granted his application for a declaration that the subject of the receivership held a 50 per cent share in the property while S held the other 50 per cent, and granted the possession application. S's argument was found to lack credibility, and they were found to have been deliberately obstructive to the receiver. S argued that the court did not have jurisdiction to order them to pay the costs of the receiver's own remuneration for bringing the applications. The receiver argued that the costs were litigation costs and were recoverable either under CPR r.69.7, whereby S as third parties would be responsible for the receiver's costs connected with the proceedings, or under CPR r.48.6, whereby S would be responsible for the receiver's costs incurred by him as a litigant in person.

Held: Application granted. (1) The reasoning in *Serious Organised Crime Agency v Gale* [2011] UKSC 49, [2011] 1 W.L.R. 2760, [2012] C.L.Y. 329

applied in the instant case, notwithstanding the differences in the statutory schemes between the Proceeds of Crime Act 2002, under which *Gale* had been decided, and the 1994 Act, *Gale* applied. Accordingly, the court had jurisdiction in an appropriate case to order a third party to pay a receiver's claim for litigation costs, notwithstanding that those costs might include the receiver's own remuneration. Were the position otherwise, the public purse would be at risk of underwriting third party litigation in receivership cases, notwithstanding that the litigation had been brought about by the unreasonable stance of a third party. The receiver's claim was a genuine claim for litigation costs and would be recoverable as costs of the proceedings if the work had been done by a solicitor. Such costs were in principle recoverable (see paras 17-19 of judgment). (2) An order for costs would be made against S under CPR r.69.7(4). The receiver's costs had been caused by S's stance, and at all material times the receiver had acted reasonably in the litigation. Such of the receiver's costs as were not recovered from S would be costs in the receivership (paras 20, 25). (3) It was not necessary to consider whether the receiver should be able to recover costs as a litigant in person, but the court would have been inclined to grant costs on that basis (para.22).

SINCLAIR v DHILLON, [2012] EWHC 3517 (Admin), [2013] Lloyd's Rep. F.C. 224, Haddon-Cave, J., QBD (Admin).

729. Fines–Enforcement–Proportionality of order for repayment of outstanding fines–Repayment of over £2,500 in fines at £5 a week–Adequacy of fine enforcement system in London

The claimant (P) applied for judicial review of the defendant magistrates' decision that he should repay outstanding fines at a rate of £5 a week. Fines imposed for offences committed in London were recorded on four databases run by the London Collection and Compliance Centre. P had completed a statement of means form. At the hearing before the magistrates, he answered questions put to him by a legal advisor about his means and why he had not paid the outstanding fines. The magistrates ordered him to pay outstanding fines totalling £950, which were owing on the North East London database, at a rate of £5 a week; they made that order without realising that he owed a further £1660.65 in outstanding fines on the South East and South West London databases. A collection order was subsequently issued requiring P to pay all of the outstanding fines at a rate of £5 a week.

Held: Application granted. (1) The general rule was that the period over which a fine should be paid had to be proportionate to the size of the fine; a large fine payable over a long period by small instalments was not desirable. The court had ordered P to pay the outstanding £950 at a rate of £5 a week; that would have taken him over three-and-a-half years to repay, which was too long a period. However, the other outstanding fines meant that £2610.65 was in fact outstanding at the time of the hearing, which would have taken P just over 10 years to repay at a rate of £5 a week. It was appropriate to quash the magistrates decision: if £5 a week was all that P could pay, they had imposed payment of an amount over a period which was disproportionate. The matter was remitted for reconsideration by the magistrates on the basis of the position at the date of the hearing, where a detailed enquiry into P's means would be required. If the amount outstanding and P's means both remained the same, the magistrates would have to consider whether to utilise the alternative means of enforcement, or consider remission of the fines or discharge or reduction of the amounts for costs (see paras 28, 30-31, 40-41 of judgment). (2) (Per curiam) There was no basis for concluding that the procedure followed by the legal advisor in the instant case was inappropriate or breached the requirements of the Consolidated Criminal Practice Direction. Neither the legal advisor nor the court staff could be blamed for being unable to ascertain the outstanding fines on the other London databases: they were operating a system which was outdated, in circumstances where there were insufficient resources for them to be able to remedy the serious deficiencies of the system by undertaking the investigative work that was necessary. The instant court stressed that, before imposing a fine at an enforcement hearing, the courts needed to enquire closely as to whether there were any other outstanding fines, and make clear the serious consequences to the defaulter in not providing accurate information. The court expressed the view that the means form that had been provided to P did not make it sufficiently clear that the amount in respect of which enforcement was sought was the total outstanding amount from all courts; it urged that the magistrates' clerks might wish to reconsider whether the means form required revision (paras 23, 38-39).

R. (ON THE APPLICATION OF PURNELL) v SOUTH WESTERN MAGISTRATES' COURT, [2013] EWHC 64 (Admin), (2013) 177 J.P. 201, Sir John Thomas (President), QBD (Admin).

730. Fines–Youth conditional cautions

THE CRIME AND DISORDER ACT 1998 (YOUTH CONDITIONAL CAUTIONS: CODE OF PRACTICE) ORDER 2013, SI 2013/613; made under the Crime and Disorder Act 1998 s.66G. In force: April 8, 2013; .

This Order sets out the descriptions of offences, for which a financial penalty condition may be attached, under the Crime and Disorder Act 1998 s.66C, to a youth conditional caution given under s.66A of that Act.

731. Fitness to plead–Learning disabled persons–Admission of police interview containing offender's confession–Fitness for interview

The appellant (B) appealed against a conviction for sexually assaulting a child under 13 years of age. B, who had learning difficulties, had been at a caravan park with his care workers. It was the complainant's case that after emerging from a shop on site, B had taken her behind some bins, pulled her pants down and touched her vagina twice. B's care worker gave evidence concerning the timing that B left the camp to visit the shop, which conflicted with the complainant's evidence. A police interview was conducted and B was accompanied by an experienced social care worker and a solicitor, prior to which an assessment had been done confirming B's fitness for interview. The police officer explained the caution to B in simple terms and B said that he understood it. The officer also explained the allegations to B and he admitted them. At trial an application to exclude the interview was rejected, the judge ruling that B's rights and the caution had been thoroughly explained to him, B had indicated his understanding and therefore was fit to be interviewed. The judge then went on to consider the question of B's fitness to plead, and, on the basis of expert evidence from two psychiatrists stating that B failed the *Pritchard* criteria and had significant learning difficulties, ruled that he was unfit to plead. The psychiatrists also gave evidence that B's condition was the same at the time of interview.

Held: Appeal allowed. (1) It was difficult to see how a judge who had accepted that B was unfit to plead could then say that B was capable of understanding the right to a caution, the caution itself and the significance of a police interview. There might be cases where a person's condition could change; however, that was not the case here. It was impossible to see how the judge could have admitted the interview in light of B's unfitness to plead. Accordingly, the conviction was set aside and an acquittal directed (see paras 13-14 of judgment). (2) (Per curiam) It was in the public interest to ensure that where a court did proceed to see if a defendant had committed the act with which they were charged that time was taken to ensure that matters were handled justly and fairly. Before the trial in the instant case, DNA evidence had been obtained and served the first day of trial and the court was told that it would be disputed. However, rather than adjourn, the judge proceeded with matters. Such cases required careful case management. Judges needed to be directed to the relevant passages of *Archbold: Criminal Pleading, Evidence and Practice,* edited by James Richardson, QC (London: Sweet & Maxwell, 2011) or *Blackstones Criminal Practice,* Anthony Hooper, David C. Ormerod, Peter Murphy, Brian Leveson, John Phillips, Duncan Atkinson -(Oxford University Press 2011), and care had to be taken to ensure that a defendant's rights and the public interest were taken into account, *R. v Norman (Leslie)* [2008] EWCA Crim 1810, [2009] 1 Cr. App. R. 13, [2009] C.L.Y. 909 applied. Whilst the Court of Appeal was sympathetic towards the judge, time should have been taken to assess the DNA evidence to see if there was a better way to proceed, especially since an acquittal had now been directed. If the Court of Appeal had the power to order a retrial, it would have done. It was time for Parliament to remedy that error in the law (paras 15-19).

R. v B, [2012] EWCA Crim 1799, [2012] M.H.L.R. 310, Sir John Thomas (President), CA (Crim Div).

732. Forfeiture–Conversion–Offences committed by drivers of lorries–Orders of depravation made over lorries–Owner's right to bring civil proceedings for conversion

[Police (Property) Act 1897 (c.30) s.1(1); Powers of Criminal Courts (Sentencing) Act 2000 (c.6) s.143(5), s.144(1)(b), s.144.]

The court was required to determine whether the appellant (O), a haulage company incorporated in the Republic of Ireland, could recover vehicles seized by the respondent police officers over which an order of deprivation had been made. O employed drivers to carry loads from Europe to Ireland. On four occasions, O's drivers were stopped by the police for various offences culminating with orders for forfeiture of their lorries being made under the Powers of Criminal Courts (Sentencing) Act 2000 s.143. On appeal to the Crown court the deprivation orders were upheld and O was not permitted to make representations as it was not a party. O applied for delivery of the lorries under the Police (Property) Act 1897 s.1(1) and contended that it would be disproportionate to refuse their return. The magistrates held that O had known what its drivers were doing but accepted that the loss of the vehicles was very substantial. It stated questions for the opinion of High Court as to the effect of s.144 of the 2000 Act. The CPS were joined as an interested party and submitted that an order under s.143 of the 2000 Act operated only to deprive the offender of his rights in the property and O would be entitled to bring a claim in the civil court to which the police would not have a defence. O issued proceedings for conversion and the two matters were conjoined. The police contended that O did not have a cause of action against them either in conversion or any other claim and that its only remedy was to apply in the magistrates' court under s.144

Held: Judgment accordingly. (1) A claimant did not have to proceed under the 1897 Act where property was in the possession of the police pursuant to their powers of seizure, *Raymond Lyons & Co Ltd v Commissioner of Police of the Metropolis* [1975] Q.B. 321, [1975] C.L.Y. 2574, *R. v Chester Justices, Ex p. Smith (Kenneth)* (1978) 67 Cr. App. R. 133, [1978] C.L.Y. 615, *R. v Troth (Jack)* (1980) 71 Cr. App. R. 1, [1980] C.L.Y. 574, *Jackson v Chief Constable of the West Midlands* [1994] C.O.D. 104, [1995] C.L.Y. 1174, *Webb v Chief Constable of Merseyside* [2000] Q.B. 427, [2000] C.L.Y. 4546, *Gough v Chief Constable of the West Midlands* [2004] EWCA Civ 206, [2004] Po. L.R. 164, [2004] C.L.Y. 3846 and *R. v Kearney (Kieran Andrew)* [2011] EWCA Crim 826, [2011] 2 Cr. App. R. (S.) 106, [2011] C.L.Y. 2840 considered. Section 1 of the 1897 Act only gave magistrates jurisdiction to deal with property in the possession of the police in connection with the investigation of an offence. The possession of property by the police under s.143 of the 2000 Act was by virtue of court orders. If the magistrates were to have jurisdiction then it was necessary to give them power to deal with such a case. Section 144 of the 2000 Act did not provide an exclusive remedy, it merely conferred an additional jurisdiction so that simple cases could be dealt with simply. If s.144 had been intended to be the exclusive remedy, it would have contained provisions corresponding to those in s.143(5) of the 2000 Act entitling the court to take account of matters such as the effect on the offender and the value of the property. It would also have been necessary to repeal s.1(1) of the 1897 Act. It would be contrary to fundamental principles for an owner to be deprived of any of his rights in proceedings to which he was not a party. O had the full rights of the true owner including a right to possession. The s.143 orders gave the police no defence to that right unless there was a public policy defence, which, in the instant case, there was not. Accordingly, delivery of the lorries to O was ordered (see paras 19, 25-28 of judgment). (2) (Obiter) It would not be proportionate for a court to have no power to consider the value of the property, the degree of culpability of the owner and the financial effect on the owner of the deprivation of his goods, Air Canada v UK [1995] ECHR 18465/91 and *Lindsay v Customs and Excise Commissioners* [2002] EWCA Civ 267, [2002] 1 W.L.R. 1766, [2002] C.L.Y. 921 considered. The words "or deprivation would be disproportionate" should be read into s.144(1)(b) to prevent the rights of the owner of the goods from being violated (paras 36-37).

O'LEARY INTERNATIONAL LTD v CHIEF CONSTABLE OF NORTH WALES, [2012] EWHC1516 (Admin), (2012) 176 J.P. 514, Sir John Thomas (President), DC.

733. Forfeiture–Costs–Reasonableness of costs order made against police in forfeiture proceedings

[Magistrates' Courts Act 1980 (c.43) s.64(1); Proceeds of Crime Act 2002 (c.29).]

The applicant chief constable applied for an extension of time within which to file an appeal notice. The police had applied to the magistrates for the forfeiture of cash in the sum of £3,400 which had been seized from the respondent (T) and detained by the police under the Proceeds of Crime Act 2002. The banknotes were analysed and some of them disclosed the presence of cocaine. In 2010, T had been convicted of being concerned in the production of cannabis and in 2011 he was sentenced to eight years' imprisonment for possessing cocaine with intent to supply. In support of their forfeiture application, the police relied both on T's drug offending and on "unlawful activities" which were said to be "not provable to a criminal standard"; that was a reference to an offence of blackmail of which T had been acquitted. T instructed solicitors and leading counsel, who had represented him at his trial for blackmail, to represent him in the forfeiture proceedings. The magistrates found that it was not proved on a balance of probabilities that the detained cash was the proceeds of criminal conduct or that it was intended for use in criminal conduct. They ordered the police to pay part (over £25,000) of T's costs, having concluded that they had acted unreasonably in relying on the blackmail charge. In their case stated, the magistrates asked whether their award of costs was wrong in law. The case was served on the parties on June 6, 2012.

Held: Application refused. An appellant's notice had to be filed within 10 days after receipt of the stated case but the chief constable had not filed his appeal notice until September 21, 2012. Further, the skeleton argument, which should have accompanied the appeal notice, was not served until October 3. It was contrary to the requirement of good administration that solicitors acting for the chief constable should be permitted to escape the consequences of their own incompetence at T's expense, particularly when the issue at stake was not the liberty of the subject or a conviction but an order for costs following the successful resistance of an application made by the chief constable. It was appropriate to reach a provisional view on the merits. It was clear from the reasons given by the magistrates that they concluded that T had been put to unnecessary expense by the decision to advance two forms of criminal conduct as a basis for a finding that the cash was recoverable property when only one was reasonably arguable. They concluded that, as a result of the unjustifiable advancement of the alleged blackmail as a foundation for a conclusion that the cash was recoverable property, it was necessary for leading counsel who represented T at trial to attend the forfeiture hearing. That was a sustainable finding. The magistrates were entitled to conclude that it was "just and reasonable" under the Magistrates' Courts Act 1980 s.64(1) to make an award of costs. The application for an extension of time would therefore be refused (see paras 17-20, 22 of judgment).

CHIEF CONSTABLE OF SUSSEX v TAYLOR, [2013] EWHC1616 (Admin), [2013] 5 Costs L.O. 692, Pitchford, L.J., QBD (Admin).

734. **Forfeiture orders–Benefits–Failure to declare cash to Department of Work and Pensions–Whether undeclared cash intended for use in unlawful conduct**

[Proceeds of Crime Act 2002 (c.29) s.298(2), s.298(2)(b).]

The appellant (B) appealed by way of case stated against a decision of the respondent magistrates' court ordering the forfeiture of cash under the Proceeds of Crime Act 2002 s.298(2). An application for forfeiture under s.298(2) was made in respect of £7,150 found in B's handbag. B had not placed the cash in her bank account as she knew it would affect her entitlement to benefits, as an amount in excess of £6,000 reduced one's entitlement. The magistrates ordering the forfeiture of the cash held that B had no existing or future intention of declaring the cash to the Department of Work and Pensions and that it was intended for use in unlawful conduct. The question for the High Court was whether in the circumstances the cash could be said to be intended for use in unlawful conduct for the purposes of s.298(2). The respondent contended that the words "connection with" should be read into s.298(2)(b) after the word "in" and before "unlawful conduct" as B's interpretation limited the provision's effect.

Held: Appeal allowed. B's admissions in the course of evidence showed that she intended to keep the £7,150 in cash and that she would not have declared its existence. Her failure to declare more than £6,000 involved unlawful conduct as she intended to deceive the DWP. That gave rise to more than one criminal offence and there was no doubt that B intended to engage in that unlawful conduct. However, the question was whether the cash was intended for use in that intended unlawful conduct. The fact that the relevant part of the Act provided for summary forfeiture of lawfully obtained property was draconian. Therefore, if there was any doubt or ambiguity about the wording the the relevant part of the Act, it had to be construed narrowly. The word "use" in s.298(2)(b) was a noun, and when used in conjunction with "cash", it was the application of the cash that had to be used for some purpose, namely unlawful conduct. B had not intended to apply the cash to deceive. Her unlawful conduct was in concealing its existence; that would have occurred whether or not B physically had the cash or placed it into a bank account. The unlawful conduct intended was to conceal the fact that she had more than £6,000; however, that did not mean that she had the intention to use the money for unlawful conduct. The situation was quite the opposite because B had no intention of using the money at all (see paras 15-18 of judgment).

BEGUM v WEST MIDLANDS POLICE; *sub nom.* BEGUM v CHIEF CONSTABLE OF WEST MIDLANDS, [2012] EWHC 2304 (Admin), [2013] 1 W.L.R. 3595, Aikens L.J., DC.

735. **Indictments–Mistake–Failure of burglary indictment to identify building as dwelling–Court's power to vacate pleas without application by defendant**

[Theft Act 1968 (c.60) s.9(1)(a).]

The appellants (H and L) applied for leave to appeal against their convictions for burglary of a dwelling. L applied for leave to appeal against his sentence of 10 months' imprisonment. H and L had entered pleas of guilty to an indictment charging them with an offence under the Theft Act 1968 s.9(1)(a). All concerned were aware that the building concerned was a dwelling, but the indictment did not specify that. When the error came to light, the judge granted permission to amend the indictment and ruled that the pleas should be vacated. H and L were then re-arraigned on the amended indictment and both pleaded guilty. L had 47 previous offences including a number of thefts and similar offences. In sentencing him, the judge found that the offence was a Category 2 burglary and, referring to his record, took a starting point of 15 months before giving full credit for the plea. H and L accepted that the judge had the power to allow the amendment to the indictment but submitted that the convictions were unsafe because the court did not have jurisdiction to vacate the guilty pleas without an application by a defendant. L submitted that the offence should have been assessed as a Category 3 burglary.

Held: Applications refused. (1) The court had to have the power to vacate the guilty pleas in the absence of an application by H and L or on their behalf. In any event, the judge could have dealt with the case by offering H and L an opportunity to vacate their pleas but allowing their pleas to stand as pleas to the amended indictment if they did not wish to vacate them. In substance, that was exactly the position that was reached by the alternative route adopted in the instant case, namely vacating the pleas and allowing H and L to enter fresh pleas, *R. v W*considered. H and L unequivocally accepted their guilt of the offence particularised in the amended indictment and there was nothing to cast the remotest doubt on the safety of their convictions (see paras 11-13 of judgment). (2) The judge was entitled to treat the offence as a Category 2 burglary. Taking everything into account, particularly L's antecedents, the starting point and sentence after full credit for the plea were not arguably excessive (para.17).

R. v LOVE (JAE JODIE); R. v HYDE (LEE), [2013] EWCA Crim 257, [2013] 1 W.L.R. 1987, Richards, L.J., CA (Crim Div).

736. Indictments–Summary offences–Offence under s.4(1) Public Order Act 1986 improperly added to indictment

[Criminal Justice Act 1988 (c.33) s.40; Criminal Law Act 1967 (c.58) s.6(1); Offences against the Person Act 1861 (c.100) s.16; Public Order Act 1986 (c.64) s.3(1), s.4(1), s.7(3).]

The appellant (S) appealed against his conviction and sentence for an offence under the Public Order Act 1986 s.4(1) of using threatening words or behaviour. S had approached the victim (V) at a train station and shouted insults at her at close range. He then boarded her train. She was a barrister who had represented him in proceedings in which he had lost the custody of his son. Her evidence was that S threatened to kill her. He was arrested. During interview he admitted that he had been intimidating and aggressive towards V but denied threatening her. He was charged with threatening to kill under the Offences against the Person Act 1861 s.16 (count 1). He was committed for trial at the Crown Court. Shortly before trial the prosecution amended the indictment by adding as an alternative to the s.16 count a count of affray contrary to s.3(1) of the 1986 Act (count 2). The trial judge allowed the prosecution further to amend the indictment to include a charge under s.4(1) of the 1986 Act (count 3). S pleaded guilty to that count. The prosecution proceeded on count 1 only and nothing was said regarding count 2. S was found not guilty on count 1, and the judge sentenced him to four months' imprisonment for the s.4 offence under count 3. S submitted that his conviction and sentence were unlawful as an offence under s.4 of the 1986 Act was a summary offence which could not be added to an indictment under the Criminal Justice Act 1988 s.40; therefore count 3 had been added to the indictment improperly and without jurisdiction.

Held: Appeal dismissed. (1) It was not in issue that the s.4 offence was not properly added to the indictment. Section 40(3) of the 1988 Act listed the summary offences that could be added to an indictment in the Crown Court and s.4 of the 1986 Act was not included. Therefore, if counts 1 and 3 had stood alone, count 3 would have been a nullity, *R. v Callaghan (Terence Alan)* (1992) 94 Cr. App. R. 226, [1993] C.L.Y. 832 considered. S should not have been asked to give a plea in relation to count 3. He should have been asked to plead again in relation to count 2, at which point he could have pleaded not guilty to count 2 but guilty to count 3, *R. v Livesey (Mark Ivan)* [2006] EWCA Crim 3344, [2007] 1 Cr. App. R. 35, [2007] C.L.Y. 1004 considered. The issue was whether the error was merely a procedural failure or was an excess of jurisdiction which rendered S's plea invalid and his sentence a nullity, *R. v Clarke (Ronald Augustus)* [2008] UKHL 8, [2008] 1 W.L.R. 338, [2008] C.L.Y. 829 considered. The court had to proceed from the understanding that by s.7(3) of the 1986 Act S could plead guilty to the s.4 offence while pleading not guilty to affray in count 2. S gave his plea in answer to count 3, which was invalid, rather than in answer to count 2. However, no prejudice was suffered as he was pleading guilty to the lesser offence. The question was whether Parliament intended that the plea of guilty under the Criminal Law Act 1967 s.6(1) should be treated as a nullity merely because it was taken in answer to a question about count 3, which had been improperly added to the indictment, rather than about count 2, *R. v Clarke, R. v Ashton (John)* [2006] EWCA Crim 794, [2007] 1 W.L.R. 181, [2006] C.L.Y. 950, *R. v Soneji (Kamlesh Kumar)* [2005] UKHL 49, [2006] 1 A.C. 340, [2005] C.L.Y. 842 and *R. v Jackson (Andrew David)* [1997] 2 Cr. App. R. 497, [1997] C.L.Y. 1319 considered. Parliament could not have so intended. S had wished to plead guilty, and thought he was pleading guilty, to the alternative count to affray. The overriding question was the fairness of proceedings; no unfair prejudice had arisen. There was no misunderstanding; any problem was as to form not substance. Count 3 was improperly added and S's plea should be treated as a plea in relation to count 2. The judge retained the power to sentence because count 3 was an alternative offence and S's conviction for it was lawful. (2) S's sentence was not manifestly excessive. The nature of his offence put it in the most serious category of such offences. His victim was a lone woman with whom his only previous contact was in a professional capacity. The offence took place in public, and she was left terrified by the experience. It was accepted that he had a loving relationship with his son and had some responsibility for him. However, he had previous convictions for robbery, for which he had been sentenced to 12 years' imprisonment, and for two assaults including one against a heavily pregnant woman.

R. v SMITH (JOSEPH ALEXANDER), [2013] EWCA Crim 11, [2013] 2 Cr. App. R. 5, Pitchford L.J., CA (Crim Div).

737. International co-operation–Letters of request–Letter of request by public prosecutor of Milan–Prosecutor acting outside scope of his authority–Secretary of state's decision to refer request unlawful

[Crime (International Co-operation) Act 2003 (c.32) s.13(2)(a), s.13(2), s.15(2); Criminal Justice Act 1987 (c.38) s.2.]

The claimant banks (B) applied for judicial review of a decision of the first respondent secretary of state not to withdraw a referral to the second respondent Serious Fraud Office under the Crime (International Co-operation) Act 2003 s.15(2) of a letter of request from the interested party, the public prosecutor of Milan, for assistance in obtaining evidence. The prosecutor sought assistance in respect of ongoing criminal proceedings brought against B in Italy that arose out of swap transactions agreed between B and the city of Milan. At the date of the letter of request 24 hearings had taken place in the proceedings. The request was made pursuant to the Council of Europe Convention on Mutual Assistance in Criminal Matters 1959 and sought evidence situated in the United Kingdom for the purpose of establishing various elements of the alleged offences. The secretary of state referred the request to the SFO and the SFO issued notices under the Criminal Justice Act 1987 s.2 to B. B invited the secretary of state and the SFO not to act on the request on the basis that the prosecutor lacked authority to issue the requests as the proceedings were at the main trial stage, and whilst the judge could have authorised the request the prosecutor had issued it without reference to the judge. Expert evidence on Italian law was served on the secretary of state and the SFO both by B and by the prosecutor. B contended that the secretary of state (1) had no jurisdiction to act upon the request as the prosecutor lacked authority under Italian law to issue the request and the pre-condition under s.13(2) of the 2003 Act was not met; (2) had erred as a matter of discretion in not withdrawing the referral to the SFO as the prosecutor lacked authority because as a matter of Italian law the request was not a mere request for the voluntary production of documents but was coercive.

Held: Application granted. (1) For the purpose of s.13(2)(a) of the 2003 Act an entity either was or was not a "prosecuting authority". If it was, it did not cease to be a prosecuting authority because of a challenge to its competence in issuing any particular request for assistance. Accordingly, even if the prosecutor lacked authority under Italian law to issue the request, the pre-condition in s.13(2) was met regardless, *R. (on the application of Abacha) v Secretary of State for the Home Department (No.2)* [2001] EWHC Admin 787 considered (see paras 51, 56 of judgment). (2) The prosecutor's authority to issue the request at the stage of proceedings which he did could only be justified if his actions in doing so fell within the Italian Code of Criminal Procedure art.430. Article 430 of the Code allowed the prosecutor to undertake supplementary investigations unless the participation of the accused or his counsel was required. It was clear from the expert evidence that there was a stark distinction under Italian law between a request to exhibit documents substantially based on the hope that the defendant would cooperate and a coercive action including a request backed subordinately or as an alternative by a coercive action. The terms of the request could not be characterised as no more than a request for voluntary production of the documents sought. It included a request for interviews and for any requisite court order to enable the provision of the requested assistance. Accordingly, the request was outside the scope of the prosecutor's authority and was unlawful under Italian law. Had the request been scrutinised by the secretary of state with reference to the expert evidence provided for the prosecutor she would have seen that it was obviously unlawful. As a result, the decisions of the secretary of state and of the SFO to issue notices could not stand (paras 64-67) (3) (Obiter) Nothing in the instant judgment should encourage others to inundate the secretary of state with opinions on foreign law with a view to, or with the effect of, delaying the process. In the majority of cases there would be no point in doing so as the secretary of state's task did not extend to entering into or resolving issues of foreign law (para.72).

JP MORGAN CHASE BANK NATIONAL ASSOCIATION v DIRECTOR OF THE SERIOUS FRAUD OFFICE, [2012] EWHC 1674 (Admin), [2012] Lloyd's Rep. F.C. 655, Gross, L.J., QBD (Admin).

738. Judicial indications–Goodyear indications–Defendant's freedom of choice in respect of plea–Effect of judge advocate's uninvited sentence indication

[Firearms Act 1968 (c.27) s.5(1)(c), s.5(1)(aba).]

The appellant army sergeant (N) appealed against his convictions by the military court for offences of possessing a prohibited firearm contrary to the Firearms Act 1968 s.5(1)(aba), and possessing ammunition contrary to s.5(1)(c) of the Act. As a result of information received about N's housemate (X), the civilian police searched N's rented accommodation. They found a working pistol and ammunition in N's room. At his hearing before a military court, N's counsel (W) requested more time to hold conference with N. At that point an exchange took place between the judge advocate and the prosecution about the statutory minimum term of five years' imprisonment which was attached to the firearm offence. The judge advocate referred to X, who had also been charged but had pleaded guilty and had received two years' military detention on the basis of exceptional circumstances. In the course of that discussion, without any invitation by W, the judge advocate indicated that if N fought the charges he would be looking at a sentence of, or close to, the minimum statutory term of five years' imprisonment in a civilian prison whereas if he pleaded guilty he would receive no more than two years' detention, if not less, with the added advantage of serving his sentence in a military prison with the possibility of continuing his military service at the end. W conveyed that indication to N who decided to plead guilty.

Held: Appeal allowed. (1) It was axiomatic that a defendant charged with a criminal offence was personally responsible for his plea and that he had to be free to choose whether to plead guilty or not guilty, *R. v Turner (Frank Richard) (No.1)* [1970] 2 Q.B. 321, [1970] C.L.Y. 479 and *R. v Goodyear (Karl)* [2005] EWCA Crim 888, [2005] 1 W.L.R. 2532, [2005] C.L.Y. 893 applied. That principle applied whether or not an advocate or judge thought the case was weak or apparently unanswerable. That principle did not mean that a defendant had to be free from the circumstantial pressure which was inevitable in the making of that choice, and considering a sentence of imprisonment was often possible. An advocate had a duty to point out the possible advantages of tendering a guilty plea through forthright and realistic advice even if a defendant had indicated an intention to plead not guilty. That necessary forensic pressure did not deprive a defendant of his choice. In contrast to the obligation on an advocate to offer advice, a judge had to remain outside that confidential process. (2) The cases of *Turner* and *Goodyear* identified a specific exception to that rule where a judge was permitted to give a sentence indication to a defendant following a request from the defence. It was not inappropriate judicial pressure for a judge to respond to such a request. However, a judge could only go so far as to remind the defence of their entitlement to make such a request. Where no request was forthcoming it was wholly inappropriate for a judge to insist on giving an indication anyway. (3) One further exception enabled a judge to use his own initiative to give an indication that the type of sentence would remain the same regardless of whether a defendant pleaded guilty or not guilty. That allowed a defendant to make up his mind without the extraneous pressure of the impact that his decision could have on sentence. However, a judge was not permitted to give an uninvited indication that a long sentence was inevitable if a defendant fought the charge but would be relatively short if he pleaded guilty. (4) In the instant case, the question was not whether the judge advocate had contravened the principles governing sentence indications but was whether the consequential effect of his uninvited indication was to create inappropriate pressure on N that narrowed his freedom of choice. The judge advocate's uninvited indication had inappropriately narrowed N's freedom of choice. His guilty plea was set aside and the convictions were quashed.

R. v NIGHTINGALE (DANNY HAROLD), [2013] EWCA Crim 405, [2013] 2 Cr. App. R. 7, Lord Chief Justice, CA (Crim Div).

739. Juries–Irregularities–Practice Direction issued

Held: Practice Direction issued. A Practice Direction was issued on the subject of jury irregularities. The Practice Direction set out the action to be taken both where the irregularity came to light during the course of the trial and where it came to light after the jury's verdict had been returned. As to the former situation, any irregularity should be drawn to the attention of the trial judge in the absence of the jury as soon as it became known. The judge should consider whether the juror concerned should be isolated from the rest of the jury. He or she should consult the advocates and invite submissions. The judge should also try to establish the basic facts of what had occurred. The options open to the judge where an irregularity was raised were set out. The Practice Direction also detailed how contempt by a juror should be dealt with. It was made clear that the trial judge had no jurisdiction in relation to inquiries about jury irregularities that came to light after the end of the trial. If information about an irregularity came to light during an adjournment after the verdict but before sentence, the trial judge should be considered functus officio in relation to the jury matter; he or she should inform the Registrar of Criminal Appeals about the information and, unless there was a good reason not to do so, should proceed to sentence. If the prosecution became aware of an irregularity which might form a basis for an appeal, they should notify the defence.

PRACTICE DIRECTION (QBD: CROWN COURT: JURY IRREGULARITIES) [2013] 1 W.L.R. 486, Sir John Thomas (President), QBD.

740. Juries–Jury selection–Breach of balloting requirement–Objection raised by Crown at time–Defence unable to rely on Crown's objection when appealing against conviction–Effect of s.18 Juries Act 1974

[Juries Act 1974 (c.23) s.11 (1), s.18.]

The appellant (M) appealed against his conviction for rape and administering chloroform. The jury had been randomly selected from a panel of 15 potential jurors. Shortly after the start of M's trial, it became apparent that one of the jurors did not understand enough English to participate effectively. The judge discharged the entire jury and proposed to re-swear 11 of the jurors and select a further juror from the remaining three on the panel. Counsel for the Crown urged the judge instead to select the jurors randomly from all 14 remaining jurors. The judge refused, re-swore 11 of the original jurors and selected a further juror from the panel. M's counsel made no objections to the judge's course of action.

Held: Appeal dismissed. (1) In almost identical circumstances the court found in *R. v Mulkerrins* that the judge had failed to comply with the Juries Act 1974 s.11 (1), and the balloting requirement had been breached. The ballot which took place before the original jury were sworn was irrelevant because that jury had been discharged. That decision was binding, *Mulkerrins* followed. Therefore, in accordance with s.18, if objection to the irregularity was taken at the time or as soon as practicable after it occurred, the verdict could not stand (see paras 11-12 of judgment). (2) Section 18(2) was clearly intended to avoid difficulties arising during the process of jury selection constituting the basis for an appeal in the event of conviction. That was why any possible irregularities had to be raised at the trial or as soon as practicable. The court was prepared to treat the points raised by counsel for the Crown as an objection. However, given the context in which the issues were addressed in s.18(1), and the purpose of s.18(2), it seemed clear that counsel for the appellant could not rely on objections raised by the Crown unless he had expressly adopted them. He could not simply take a neutral stance as to a possible irregularity and then rely on it after conviction as a basis for circumventing the prohibition in s.18(2). Accordingly, M's appeal against conviction was dismissed (paras 13-14). (3) When a case ran into trouble just after it had started, it was undesirable to continue with 11 jurors rather than starting again with a full complement of 12. At the same time, it was not in anyone's interests for a trial which had just started to be postponed to enable a new jury panel to be convened. The court did not expect purely technical objections to be raised if, as in the instant case, the reality was that the jurors were a random group of individuals who had formed part of the jury panel and whose irregular selection as jurors for the second trial followed an entirely regular selection process for the purposes of the first trial (para.15).

R. v M; *sub nom.* R. v AM, [2012] EWCA Crim 2056, [2013] 1 W.L.R. 958, Lord Judge, L.C.J., CA (Crim Div).

741. Jury directions–Child sex offences–Judge allowing parts of complainant's statement to be read–Directing jury as to likelihood of competent solicitor advising client to remain silent in interview–Whether impugning fairness of trial

[Criminal Justice Act 2003 (c.44) s.114.]

The appellant (T) appealed against his conviction on two counts of indecency with a child, two of indecent assault, and six of sexual activity with a child. The Crown's case was that T had engaged in sexual activity with two under-age girls (L and E). T accepted that he had had sex with the girls, but his case at trial was that they had consented and had been of age at the time. The only issues were therefore when the sexual activity had taken place and how old the girls had been. L, who was 22 years old at the time of the trial, had difficulty articulating her evidence. The judge therefore allowed the undisputed parts of her witness statement to be read to her and for her to adopt them. In his summing up, he told the jury that there was no evidence of "cross-contamination" in L and E's evidence, and told them that they could draw adverse inferences from the similarities between the two cases. He also told them that they could draw adverse inferences from the fact that T had given a "no comment" interview to the police, allegedly on his solicitor's advice. He said "if the solicitor was competent he would have advised of the risk of going 'no comment'...". T submitted that the judge had erred in (1) his treatment of L's evidence; (2) the direction he gave on the cross-contamination issue; (3) failing to sum up discrepancies in L and E's evidence as to dates and events; (4) his direction on the adverse inferences to be drawn from the police interview.

Held: Appeal dismissed. (1) The way in which the judge dealt with L's evidence legitimately enabled the best evidence to be given, while at the same time protecting T's interests. The judge could have permitted leading questions on the undisputed matters or he could have permitted the admission of L's statement under the Criminal Justice Act 2003 s.114. Instead, the procedure he adopted was a sensible adaptation of the court's processes and caused no prejudice to T. Indeed, it reduced the risk of any unfair prejudice to him. T's first ground of appeal therefore failed (see para.19 of judgment). (2) There was no evidence of any direct communication between L and E, and nor had any suggestion of cross-contamination been put to either. Moreover, the judge had told the jury that if there was any possibility of one complainant putting ideas into the other's head, then they were to ignore any conclusions that they might otherwise have drawn from the apparent similarities between the two cases. There was no evidence to suggest contamination as between the two cases, and what the judge said in his summing-up was entirely accurate (paras 21-22). (3) The summing up clearly identified the issues for the jury and narrated T's account in careful detail. There was no need for it to deal with each and every timing or date (paras 23-14). (4) T accepted in clear terms that the decision to give a "no comment" interview was ultimately his, and not that of his solicitor. Thus, the fairness of the trial was in no way impugned by the judge's observation about what a competent solicitor might have advised. Nonetheless, it might have been better for him to have avoided any comment on what the solicitor might have been expected to advise. Such comments could serve to undermine the inviolable principle of lawyer-client confidentiality (para.27).

R. v TURNER (SIMON PAUL), [2012] EWCA Crim 1786, [2013] 1 Cr. App. R. 25, Lord Judge, L.C.J., CA (Crim Div).

742. Jury directions–Defences–Taxi driver acting to prevent fare evasion–Adequacy of jury direction on available defences–Failure to focus jury on driver's honest belief

[Criminal Law Act 1967 (c.58) s.3(1), s.3.]

The appellant taxi driver (M) appealed against his conviction for dangerous driving. M had driven four passengers to an agreed destination. When the taxi stopped three passengers (P) alighted and quickly walked away. M, not realising that one passenger remained in the taxi, drove his taxi onto the pavement in order to stop what he thought was a fare evasion, and caused one passenger (P1) to fall and break his ankle. M's defence was that he had reasonably driven onto the pavement to prevent P from making off without payment and/or to assist in their lawful arrest. The trial judge ruled that only the latter limb of the general defence in the Criminal Law Act 1967 s.3(1), effecting or assisting in the lawful arrest of offenders, could be left to the jury as M could not have been preventing a crime under the first limb of s.3(1) because the offence of making off was made out at the point at which P had alighted from the taxi. He gave a jury direction to that effect. M submitted that the jury should have been left to decide whether he genuinely believed, however unreasonably, that P were in the act of making off without payment, and, if so, whether the degree of force used was reasonable with reference to that belief.

Held: Appeal allowed. If, under the Criminal Law Act 1967 s.3, honest belief provided a defence to the use of force in the prevention of crime, such as to prevent an unlawful attack on another, it equally provided a defence to a person claiming to have used reasonable force to prevent the commission of a crime other than a crime of violence against another. Accordingly, if M had honestly believed that the men were making off without payment, he was entitled to use reasonable force in order to prevent the commission of that offence. The jury would then be required to consider whether driving onto the pavement was the reasonable exercise of the use of force. The difficulty in the judge's direction was that it required the jury to consider whether M had reasonable grounds to believe that it was necessary to arrest P1 to prevent him making off. The jury would never get to the question of the use of reasonable force if they concluded that he did not have reasonable grounds. In his direction the judge had not dealt with the possibility that the jury could conclude that M was acting to prevent crime because he had concluded that, as a matter of law, once P had moved away from the taxi, they had "made off". He had failed to ensure that the jury focussed on what M honestly believed the facts to be before proceeding to decide whether he had reasonable grounds for suspecting that an offence was being committed, and whether the force used was reasonable. There was an error of law in the direction given to the jury and the conviction was unsafe (see paras 19-22, 24 of judgment).

R. v MORRIS (DARYL HOWARD), [2013] EWCA Crim 436, [2014] 1 W.L.R. 16, Leveson, L.J., CA (Crim Div).

743. Jury directions–Joint enterprise–Robbery using imitation firearm–Sufficiency of evidence to infer knowledge, and therefore possession, of firearm of member of joint enterprise

The appellant (X) appealed against his conviction for possession of an imitation firearm at the time of committing an offence. X had also been convicted of two offences of robbery and appealed against the total sentence imposed of 11 years' imprisonment. The applicant (Y) renewed his application for permission to appeal against a sentence of four-and-a-half years' imprisonment imposed following his conviction for robbery. A robbery had been committed at a mobile telephone shop. The shop manager thought that a gun had been held to the back of his head. There was no direct evidence that X had been one of the men who entered the shop, but the Crown's case was that he was party to a joint enterprise. He was linked to a car used in the robbery and in a subsequent robbery of a security van. There was also cell site phone evidence which placed him in the vicinity of the shop. No weapons or items connected with criminal activity were found at his home or business address. His case was that he had only provided the car and was unaware that any weapon would be used. The judge directed the jury regarding joint enterprise and referred to the need for knowledge on X's part that one of the robbers was carrying an imitation firearm. The issue was whether there was evidence from which the jury could properly infer that X had known that an imitation firearm was being carried and, if so, whether the judge had given the jury sufficient help in identifying that evidence. Y was convicted of participation in the robbery of the shop, but it was accepted that he had not been present at the time of the robbery and he was not charged with possession of the imitation firearm. Another co-defendant was sentenced to five years' detention for robbery and possession of an imitation firearm. Y submitted that the judge had adopted too high a starting point given his limited involvement, and that there was objectionable disparity between his sentence and those passed on his co-defendants.

Held: Appeals allowed, application refused. (1) The evidence relied on by the Crown, X's ownership of the car and the cell site analysis, was adequate to establish a significant role in the preparatory stage of the robbery. However, it did not amount to a firm basis for inferring that he knew that an imitation firearm was being carried. It needed to be stressed that, even if X had provided the car knowing that a robbery was to be committed and that some sort of weapon "might" be carried, that would be an insufficient basis for a conviction on possession of the firearm. Where knowledge and proof of joint possession depended on the drawing of an inference, as in the instant case, it was incumbent on a judge in summing up to identify the evidence of primary fact on the basis of which, if it was accepted, a jury might infer knowledge and thus possession. The judge had failed to do that and it was not possible to ascertain how the jury might have reached its decision. That position, coupled with the Crown's, and the instant court's, inability to identify a clear and firm basis for the inference of knowledge that an imitation firearm was being carried, led to the conclusion that the conviction in relation to possession of the imitation firearm was unsafe. In the particular circumstances of the case, proof of a significant preparatory role and of travel to the vicinity of the robbery did not provide an adequate basis for inferring that X had known that an imitation firearm was being carried (see paras 17-18 of judgment). (2) Although no separate penalty had been imposed in relation to possession of the imitation firearm, the judge treated it as an aggravating feature of the robbery. However, that made little difference. It was clearly a robbery in which it was reasonable to infer that at least the threat of serious violence was a feature. Against that background, a reduction in sentence of one year in respect of the first robbery was appropriate. The total sentence would therefore be reduced to one of 10 years' imprisonment (para.19).

(3) The most important factor in determining the proper length of Y's sentence was the nature and extent of his involvement. The judge, who had presided over the trial, was particularly well placed to decide such questions, and had obviously considered that Y's role was of sufficient importance, and the aggravating features of the offence of such significance, that a sentence higher than the four-year starting point for a level 2 offence was appropriate. There were also no real grounds for saying that there was objectionable disparity between the sentences imposed (paras 25-27).

R. v ABBAS (ISMAIL); R. v ASAFU-ADJAYE (PATRICK), [2012] EWCA Crim 2517, [2013] 1 Cr. App. R. 18, Moore-Bick, L.J., CA (Crim Div).

744. Miscarriage of justice–Compensation–Entitlement to compensation for conviction later set aside–Test to establish whether claim within category 2 in R. (on the application of Adams) v Secretary of State for Justice [2011] UKSC 18, [2012] 1 A.C. 48

[Criminal Justice Act 1988 (c.33) s.133; European Convention on Human Rights 1950 Art.6.]

The claimants (X, L, G, D and T) applied for judicial review of the defendant secretary of state's refusal to grant compensation under the Criminal Justice Act 1988 s.133 in respect of convictions which had subsequently been set aside. The claimants' applications had been refused before the Supreme Court's decision in *R. (on the application of Adams) v Secretary of State for Justice* [2011] UKSC 18, [2012] 1 A.C. 48, [2011] C.L.Y. 794 had broadened the band of persons who qualified for compensation. The claimants claimed to qualify for compensation by falling within "category 2" identified in *Adams*, namely where there was fresh evidence which, had it been available at trial, would have meant that no jury could properly have convicted. The secretary of state refused some of the claimants' renewed applications, and refused to reconsider the applications of others.

Held: Applications granted in part. (1) The differences in the preferred formulations of the test to establish whether a case was within category 2 given by the justices in *Adams* did not reflect a difference in substance. The formulation of the test had to be practicable and refer to the English criminal justice system. A useful formulation was "has the claimant established, beyond reasonable doubt, that no reasonable jury or magistrates properly directed as to the law could convict on the evidence now to be considered?", *Adams* considered (see paras 38-41 of judgment). The conclusions of the Court of Appeal (Criminal Division) would carry the greatest weight, but that court focused on the safety of a conviction rather than whether an appellant was innocent. Whether a retrial had been ordered could be relevant, but might not be conclusive. It would not be proper for the secretary of state to take a different view of a case from that of the Court of Appeal, save where the evidence had evolved after the appeal. A statement from the court that, given the state of the evidence, the case should have been withdrawn from the jury, could be particularly significant (paras 42-44). The secretary of state was not entitled to disregard "technical" rules of evidence. Nor could he dismiss judges' rulings. In the absence of a change in the evidence coming later than a judicial ruling, the secretary of state could only differ from such a ruling in the rarest circumstances and on a fully reasoned basis (paras 45-47). Where a retrial took place, save in the most exceptional circumstances, a claimant would be unable to establish a compensation claim, *Adams* followed. However, it might be possible for a defendant acquitted on a retrial to make a claim; the particular circumstances of each case had to be considered (paras 48-49). In view of the public interest in promptness, in general, only where a decision had been made within three months of the *Adams* decision would the secretary of state be required to reconsider an application in the light of *Adams* (para.50). (2) Under statute and common law, the court's role was not to itself determine whether the statutory test had been met. Parliament had given the secretary of state the function of determining whether the test had been met. That was an exercise of judgement. Adams had not adopted such a substitutionary approach, Adams considered (paras 56-64). It was doubtful whether the European Convention on Human Rights 1950 art.6 was engaged. If it was engaged, in general, an administrative decision together with access to the court would satisfy the requirement of an independent tribunal if the court had full jurisdiction over the decision. Full jurisdiction did not necessarily mean jurisdiction to re-examine the case's merits, *Begum v Tower Hamlets LBC* [2003] UKHL 5, [2003] 2 A.C. 430, [2003] C.L.Y. 55 applied (paras 65-72). (3) X's claim failed. The secretary of state had had the correct test in mind, and had been entitled to say that X had not established to the necessary degree of confidence that no jury could properly have convicted on the evidence: although it would have been a weak case advanced by the Crown, and there would have been a high chance of acquittal, it might have been open to the jury properly to convict (para.100). (4) The secretary of state's refusal to reconsider D's claim had been fully justified, as the time limit for judicial review of the original decision had expired. The claim failed. However, the secretary of state's approach was subject to valid criticism (paras 128-139). (5) G had been retried. The trial judge had not been wrong to leave the case against him to the jury; a reasonable jury, properly directed, could have convicted. G's claim failed (para.159). (6) Effectively the only evidence against L had been his confessions to several prosecution witnesses. Psychological evidence obtained after his conviction showed that he had personality disorders and a pathological need for attention; his conviction had then been quashed. Once all expert evidence agreed that L's confessions had been unreliable, no jury could properly have convicted on the basis of his admissions. His claim succeeded (paras 184-187). (7) T's claim failed on grounds of time (para.212).

R. (ON THE APPLICATION OF ALI) v SECRETARY OF STATE FOR JUSTICE; R. (ON THE APPLICATION OF LAWLESS) v SECRETARY OF STATE FOR JUSTICE; R. (ON THE APPLICATION OF GEORGE) v SECRETARY OF STATE FOR JUSTICE; R. (ON THE APPLICATION OF DENNIS) v SECRETARY OF STATE FOR JUSTICE; R. (ON THE APPLICATION OF TUNBRIDGE) v SECRETARY OF STATE FOR JUSTICE, [2013] EWHC 72 (Admin), [2013] 1 W.L.R. 3536, Beatson, L.J., DC.

745. Mode of trial–Plea and case management hearings–Whether Crown Court complied with Sch.3 para.7 Crime and Disorder Act 1998

[Crime and Disorder Act 1998 (c.37) s.51, Sch.3, Sch.3 para.7; Prison Act 1952 (c.52) s.40.]

The appellant (G) appealed against a conviction for possession of controlled drugs with intent to supply. G had been convicted and sentenced for an offence of possession of a Class A drug with intent to supply. At the beginning of his sentence he smuggled a substantial quantity of different drugs into prison. G was charged with an offence contrary to the Prison Act 1952 s.40(1)(b), which was an indictable offence, and sent for trial to the Crown Court on that charge pursuant to the Crime and Disorder Act 1998 s.51. The indictment that was signed at the plea and case management hearing contained no indictable-only offences, only three counts of possession with intent to supply and three counts of simple possession. G pleaded guilty to the possession counts and was convicted of possession with intent to supply. G submitted that the trial was a nullity as when he was sent to the Crown Court for trial on the Prison Act offence, no indictable-only offence was included in the signed indictment. G contended that the procedure to determine the mode of trial at the plea and case management hearing as required by Sch.3 para.7 was not followed.

Held: Appeal dismissed. The court had to ask itself whether there had been non-compliance with Sch.3 para.7, and if there had been, it then had to ask whether Parliament intended the consequence of any non-compliance to render any subsequent proceedings a nullity. Following G's guilty pleas to the lesser offences, the case was bound to remain in the Crown Court, which ended the possibility of a summary trial and had the same effect as the presence of an indictable only offence on the indictment. Non-compliance with the objective of Sch.3 para.7 was not established. Even assuming that was incorrect, it was the responsibility of the court, and not the defendant or prosecution, to consider whether counts in an indictment were more suitable for summary trial or trial by indictment. A defendant did however enjoy a right to be heard when that issue was being addressed. Proceeding on the basis that summary trial was available to G, and therefore that its suitability should have been considered by the Crown Court, it was a failure of process for the court not to seek representations from G or the prosecution on the issue. Had the omission been a deliberate attempt to circumvent sch.3 and deprive G of a summary trial, which it was not, it might have been an abuse of process. The omission of that procedural step did not vitiate the indictment or the subsequent proceedings. In any event, G could have remedied it by making an application to that effect. Had Parliament intended that depriving a defendant, who was sent to trial under s.51, of the opportunity to elect for summary trial for either way offences included in an indictment, it would have left the choice of summary trial entirely to a defendant by vesting in him an unequivocal right. It did not do so and it was clearly not Parliament's intention for the consequence of non-compliance to be that subsequent Crown Court proceedings were rendered null (see paras 19, 21, 23, 24 of judgment).

R. v GUL (HAMESH), [2012] EWCA Crim 1761, [2013] 1 W.L.R. 1136, Lord Judge, L.C.J., CA (Crim Div).

746. Notices–Demonstrations–Imposition of conditions on route of demonstration–Breach of conditions

[Public Order Act 1986 (c.64) s.12.]

The appellants (V) appealed by way of case stated against a decision of a district judge convicting them of breaching conditions imposed under the Public Order Act 1986 s.12. Following a meeting between the organisers of a protest march on education cuts and the metropolitan police, conditions were imposed under s.12 designating the route the march should take. A police cordon was placed along the route at the junction between a particular street and Trafalgar Square. At that junction V and other participants in the march discussed with the police their wish to go through the cordon to Trafalgar Square and they were advised to remain within the confines of the march. A police officer (W) noticed that marchers were becoming agitated and therefore let a group including V through the cordon after informing them that they would be arrested if they breached the conditions. The district judge found that V and other members took part in the march but intended to leave at Trafalgar Square so that they could join an encampment in protest of capitalism; the police cordon was not designated to prevent anyone from leaving the march and participants could be allowed to leave at the discretion of an individual police officer; the s.12 notice was valid and V were in breach of the conditions imposed in respect of the march. The questions posed were whether the district judge was right to conclude that (i) the s.12 notice was valid; (ii) V was guilty when W accepted that he had permitted them to pass through the cordon; (iii) whether E s conduct amounted to a criminal offence under s.12(5). V submitted that (1) the notice was not valid as it was vague and inconsistent; (2) when V left the route with the intention of joining the encampment the s.12 conditions no longer applied to them.

Held: Appeal dismissed. (1) There was nothing misleading, vague or inconsistent in the wording of the notice. (2) W had no power to waive the s.12 conditions but he was entitled to let participants leave if they wished. V were entitled to leave the procession but were not entitled to do so while they remained part of it. The district judge was entitled to find that V were still taking part in the procession to which the s.12 notice applied when they left the route on the way to the encampment at Trafalgar Square. (3) The answers to the questions posed in the case stated were yes.

JUKES v DPP; VAN EK v DPP; *sub nom.* VAN EL v DPP, [2013] EWHC 195 (Admin), (2013) 177 J.P. 212, Moses, L.J., DC.

747. Practice Directions–Criminal proceedings–Practice Direction replacing Practice Direction (CA (Crim Div): Criminal Proceedings: Consolidation) [2002] 1 W.L.R. 2870 with exceptions

The Lord Chief Justice made a Practice Direction replacing *Practice Direction (CA (Crim Div): Criminal Proceedings: Consolidation)* [2002] 1 W.L.R. 2870, [2002] C.L.Y. 899, as amended, which was revoked, with the exception of sections III.21, IV.31, IV.32, IV.33, IV.38 and IV.41.9. The Practice Directions, Practice Notes and Practice Statements listed in Annexes A and B of the 2002 consolidation were also revoked. Annexes D, E and F remained in force, *Practice Direction (CA (Crim Div): Criminal Proceedings: Consolidation)* superseded in part. The Practice Direction would be known as the Criminal Practice Directions. They took effect from October 7, 2013 and applied to all cases in all the criminal courts of England and Wales from that date. Amongst other things, the Criminal Practice Directions gave guidance on the following: case management; forms and court records; investigation orders and warrants; allocation and sending for trial; initial details of the prosecution case; the indictment; reporting, etc. restrictions; bail and custody time limits; disclosure; witness statements; witness summonses, warrants and orders; measures to assist a witness or defendant to give evidence; evidence of bad character; trial and sentence in a magistrates' court; trial on indictment; sentencing; contempt of court; appeal to the Crown Court; appeal to the Court of Appeal about conviction or sentence; requests to the European Court for a preliminary ruling; costs; court dress; modes of address and titles of judges and magistrates; availability of judgments given in the Court of Appeal and the High Court; citation of authority and provision of copies of judgments to the court; preparation of judgments: neutral citation and the citation of Hansard.

PRACTICE DIRECTION (CA (CRIM DIV): CRIMINAL PROCEEDINGS: GENERAL MATTERS); *sub nom.* PRACTICE DIRECTION (CRIMINAL PROCEEDINGS) (SEN CTS), [2013] EWCA Crim 1631, [2013] 1 W.L.R. 3164, Sir John Thomas, L.C.J., CA (Crim Div).

748. Private prosecutions–Discontinuance–Private prosecutions with no reasonable prospect of conviction–Lawfulness of policy of Director of Public Prosecutions

[Prosecution of Offences Act 1985 (c.23) s.6(1).]

The appellant (G) appealed against the dismissal of his application for judicial review ([2011] EWHC 472 (Admin), [2012] 1 W.L.R. 254, [2011] C.L.Y. 802) of a decision of the respondent CPS to take over and discontinue private prosecutions brought by him. G had brought the prosecutions against various persons for common assault. The CPS conducted a full review of the evidence and concluded that there was insufficient evidence to provide a realistic prospect of conviction against any of the accused. The Director of Public Prosecutions, acting by the CPS, then informed G that it intended to take over and discontinue the private prosecutions pursuant to his current policy, instigated in 2009, which provided that a private prosecution should be taken over and stopped unless the prosecution was more likely than not to result in a conviction. Prior to 2009, the DPP's policy in respect of private prosecutions was to ask whether there was clearly no case for the defendant to answer. If such was his conclusion, he took over the prosecution and discontinued it; otherwise, subject to the application of further criteria, he declined to take it over. The issue was whether the application of the DPP's current policy towards intervention and discontinuance frustrated the policy and objects underpinning the right to maintain a private prosecution in the Prosecution of Offences Act 1985 s.6(1).

Held: Appeal dismissed. (Lord Mance and Lady Hale dissenting) (1) Assertions and debate about the continuing constitutional importance of the right of private prosecutions made little contribution to the answer to the very focused question on appeal. By s.6(1) of the Act, Parliament chose, albeit in qualified terms, to reaffirm the right of private prosecution. Section 6(2) gave the DPP discretion to take over the conduct of any private prosecution. By reaffirming the right under s.6(1), Parliament could not have intended that the DPP should decline to exercise his discretion so as to intervene and discontinue a prosecution even if it lacked a reasonable prospect of success. In focusing, as the current policy of the DPP did, on the likely prospect of a private prosecution resulting in a conviction, the DPP posed to himself a much more relevant question than the "no case to answer" test. Further, private prosecutions were frequently instituted and the great majority survived the DPP's current tests and policy for intervention and discontinuance. Four additional reasons helped justify the DPP's current policy; (a) under s.6(2), Parliament did not choose expressly to confine the discretion it conferred upon the DPP to take over the conduct of a private prosecution; (b) the main object behind the 1985 Act, reflected in the report of the Royal Commission on Criminal Procedure in 1981, was to establish a nationwide CPS and to achieve consistent standards in instituting and conducting prosecutions. Where it fell to the DPP to prosecute, the report approved him applying the test "whether or not there was a reasonable prospect of conviction" and further it recommended that that test should be extended to all prosecutions; (c) a prosecution which lacked a reasonable prospect of success drew inappropriately upon the resources of the court; (d) a defendant would have a legitimate grievance about being subjected to private prosecution when, by the application of lawful criteria as to the strength of the evidence against him, there would be no public prosecution. Furthermore, the DPP acted unlawfully if he adopted too rigid an approach in applying his policy towards interventions with a view to discontinuance, which would be amenable to judicial review (see paras 30-37 of judgment). (2) (Per Lord Neuberger) The 1985 Act and the DPP's current policy left untouched the right of an individual to initiate a private prosecution and those meeting the evidential test and whose prosecution would not be contrary to public interest would be permitted to proceed save where there was a particular need for the DPP to take over. Whilst the courts should be mindful of cutting down individuals' right of access to the courts, the right to conduct a private prosecution had always been subject to being curtailed by the power of the Attorney General to stop the prosecution through issuing a nolle prosequi. (3) (Per Lord Mance) The scope of the right to institute, and pursue, a private prosecution preserved by s.6(1) could not have been intended to be emasculated in the manner indicated in the DPP's current policy. The Act must be construed in the light of the long-standing constitutional significance attaching to the right of private prosecution. The discretion conferred by the general words of s.6(2) must have been conferred to promote the policy and objects of the Act and those could not have been intended to undermine the right of private prosecution in the manner which the DPP s current policy would do, *R. v DPP, Ex p. Duckenfield* [2000] 1 W.L.R. 55, [1999] C.L.Y. 1043 considered (para. 113).

R. (ON THE APPLICATION OF GUJRA) v CROWN PROSECUTION SERVICE, [2012] UKSC 52, [2013] 1 A.C. 484, Lord Neuberger (President), SC.

749. Proceeds of crime–Benefit from criminal conduct–Assessment of benefit–Effect of R v Waya [2012] UKSC 51 on previous authorities

[Proceeds of Crime Act 2002 (c.29) s.10; European Convention on Human Rights 1950 Protocol 1 Art.1.]

The appellant (H) appealed against a confiscation order imposed following his conviction for arson and his guilty pleas to handling stolen goods. H owned a plant hire and contracting company (J), which had regularly acquired and sold stolen plant. The police recovered 39 such items from J's premises. The value when stolen was £314,700; when recovered, £159,800. H had set fire to several items, which related to the arson convictions. J had possessed other items of stolen plant during the relevant period. The judge found that H had benefited by £314,700. He assessed the revenue derived from the stolen plant as 38 per cent of J's total revenue, £1,960,754.40, and H's benefit from criminal conduct as that figure plus the £314,700, a total of £2,275,454.40. He made a confiscation order in that sum. H submitted that the judge had erred in (1) not deducting the VAT received from J's turnover figure; (2) failing to give him credit, in the amount of

£159,800, for the fact that stolen items had been restored to their owners; (3) his basis of assessment; (4) imposing a 10-year term of imprisonment in default.

Held: Appeal allowed in part. (1) The court considered the status of authorities decided prior to *R. v Waya (Terry)* [2012] UKSC 51, [2013] 1 A.C. 294, [2013] 2 C.L. 90 and concluded that: (a) *R. v Smith (David Cadman)* [2001] UKHL 68, [2002] 1 W.L.R. 54, [2002] C.L.Y. 3898 and *R. v May (Raymond George)* [2008] UKHL 28, [2008] 1 A.C. 1028, [2008] C.L.Y. 776 remained good law, as they had been expressly approved by the Supreme Court; (b) *R. v Singh (Jhalman)* [2008] EWCA Crim 243, [2008] 2 Cr. App. R. (S.) 69, [2008] C.L.Y. 780 was correctly decided; (c) *R. v Morgan (John)* [2008] EWCA Crim 1323, [2008] 4 All E.R. 890, [2009] C.L.Y. 853 was approved by the Supreme Court, but only remained good law because the defendant had failed to make full restoration, or indicate any willingness to do so, by the date of hearing; (d) *R. v Xu (David Kai)* [2008] EWCA Crim 2372 was consistent with *Waya*; (e) *R. (on the application of BERR) v Lowe* [2009] EWCA Crim 194, [2009] 2 Cr. App. R. (S.) 81, [2009] C.L.Y. 829 was probably no longer good law, as it involved full restoration of the property; (f) *R. v Del Basso (Luigi)* [2010] EWCA Crim 1119, [2011] 1 Cr. App. R. (S.) 41, [2011] C.L.Y. 723 was a "criminal lifestyle" case where the statutory assumptions under the Proceeds of Crime Act 2002 s.10 applied. Although *Waya* suggested that *Del Basso* was correctly decided, the decision seemed excessively harsh and might arguably be characterised as disproportionate; (g) *R. v James (Michael)* [2011] EWCA Crim 2991, [2012] 1 W.L.R. 2641, [2012] C.L.Y. 755 and *R. v Ahmad (Shakeel)* [2012] EWCA Crim 391, [2012] 1 W.L.R. 2335, [2012] C.L.Y. 758 were consistent with *Waya, Waya* followed (see paras 38-65 of judgment). (2) The monies received by J for hiring out, or performing work using, stolen plant constituted property obtained from criminal conduct. J had expended those monies in a variety of ways, including VAT payments, and did not hold the monies on trust for the intended payee. It was repugnant and contrary to the principles stated in *May* and *Waya* to carry out an accounting exercise in respect of those monies. J had expended three-quarters of the VAT it collected on purchasing goods and services, thereby using the proceeds of criminal conduct, and it would be wrong in principle for H to be given credit in respect of the VAT element, *Del Basso*, *Smith*, *May* and *Waya* applied, *James* and *Ahmad* distinguished (paras 76-82). (3) In cases of total restoration of property, the property originally obtained should not be treated as "benefit", *Waya* considered, *Baden Lowe* doubted. However, the instant case was one of partial restoration, of chattels, not real property, which depreciated rather than increased in value between acquisition and restoration. If a defendant obtained chattels as a result of his criminal conduct and used them for a substantial period, thereby materially reducing their value, and the chattels were ultimately restored to their true owners, the court assessing the defendant's benefit should not give credit for the residual value of those chattels. The court had to focus on the property that the defendant originally obtained. There was nothing in the wording of the 2002 Act or the European Convention on Human Rights 1950 Protocol 1 art.1 which required the court to deduct the residual value. A confiscation order based on the original value of the property would not be disproportionate, *Waya* and *Morgan* applied (paras 86-94). (4) The judge had been generous to H in his method of assessment. Some 42 per cent of the plant at H's premises was stolen property and the judge would have been entitled to hold that that percentage of H's receipts comprised property obtained from criminal conduct, *Xu* applied. There was no reason to believe that all the plant sold by J was legitimate. It was H's practice to falsify documents when advantageous to do so and the judge was entitled to treat the proceeds of plant sales as part of J's, and therefore H's, total receipts. The basis of assessment adopted by the judge was a proper one, *Singh* applied (paras 96-103). (5) The purpose of a term in default was to secure compliance with the confiscation order, not additional punishment. Eight years was the proper term in default in the instant case, and H's appeal would be allowed to that extent (paras 104-108).

R. v HARVEY (JACK FREDERICK), [2013] EWCA Crim 1104, [2014] 1 W.L.R. 124, Jackson, L.J., CA (Crim Div).

750. Proceeds of crime–Forfeiture–Forfeiture of money paid for purchase of aircraft–Interpretation of "executed consideration" under s.314(4) Proceeds of Crime Act 2002–Compliance of forfeiture order with Protocol 1 art.1 European Convention on Human Rights 1950

[Proceeds of Crime Act 2002 (c.29) Pt 5, s.298, s.308, s.308(1)(b), s.314(4); European Convention on Human Rights 1950 Protocol 1 Art.1.]

The appellant company and its sole director (E and B) appealed by way of case stated against a district judge's decision ordering the forfeiture of money pursuant to the Proceeds of Crime Act 2002 s.298. E had agreed to sell three aircraft to a purchaser. Under para.2 of the sale agreement, the purchaser agreed to pay E $700,000, and E agreed to supply and pay for three ferry permits. Under para.3, E agreed to have performed an inspection of the airworthiness of the aircraft, and to deliver possession of the aircraft together with a bill of sale. B received around $675,000 from the purchaser. E paid for the inspection of the aircraft and bought the ferry permits, but did not transfer the aircraft to the purchaser together with a bill of sale and the ferry permits. $310,000, representing the unspent balance of the $675,000 paid to B, was seized from B's address on the suspicion that it represented the proceeds of Class A drug trafficking. A forfeiture order was made in respect of it. The appellants argued before the district judge that, notwithstanding E's failure to deliver the aircraft together with a bill of sale and the ferry permits, the purchaser's payment of all but $25,000, E's payment of the inspection, and its purchase of the ferry permits amounted to "executed consideration" under s.314(4) of the Act, and therefore the money was not recoverable under s.308 of the Act. The district judge concluded that E's conduct in preparing the aircraft for transfer amounted to no more than the taking of steps towards the satisfaction by it of the contract terms, and therefore that it was unexecuted consideration under s.314(4) of the Act. The issues were whether (i) the money seized constituted "executed consideration" under s.314(4) so that it was not recoverable under s.308; (ii) the forfeiture order was incompatible with the appellants' rights under the European Convention on Human Rights 1950 Protocol 1 art.1.

Held: Appeal dismissed. (1) As a matter of construction of the sale agreement, the provisions under paras 2 and 3 were conditions precedent. It followed that the steps to be taken by E under those paragraphs amounted to no more than preparation of the aircraft for transfer, and so formed no part of the consideration. The mutual promises were the payment of the purchase price by the purchaser and the delivery of the aircraft, together with the ferry permits, by E; as the purchase price had not been paid in full and the aircraft were undelivered when the money was seized, the consideration remained unexecuted. Further, s.314(4) could not be construed so that "executed consideration" included the performance of some and not necessarily all of the promises. The wording of s.314(4) was very clear and meant that a person was only to be treated as having obtained property for value when all of the contractual promises had been performed. It followed that consideration could not be regarded as divisible. Accordingly, the consideration promised by B on E's behalf was indivisible for the purposes of s.314(4), and so would only have become executed once all the promises were performed. It followed that the consideration remained executory or unexecuted under s.314(4), that B had not obtained the recoverable property for value, and therefore that the property had not ceased to be recoverable for the purposes of s.308(1)(b) of the Act (see paras 25-26, 29, 36 of judgment). (2) There was nothing arbitrary about Pt 5 of the Act. It addressed the legitimate aim of the removal from circulation of criminal property, the intended consequential inhibition on the laundering of criminal monies, and the commission of crimes producing such monies. It struck a fair balance between the general interest that the proceeds of Class A drug trafficking should be forfeited, and the interests of the appellants, who had not been deprived of their consideration. The appellants had every opportunity throughout the proceedings to challenge the measures. Accordingly, the forfeiture order was not incompatible with their Convention rights (paras 34-35).

EXECUTIVE JET SUPPORT LTD v SERIOUS ORGANISED CRIME AGENCY, [2012] EWHC 2737 (QB), [2013] 1 W.L.R. 1433, Griffith Williams, J., QBD.

751. Proceeds of crime–Tainted gifts–Disposal of interest in aircraft–Commercial sense of disposal

[Criminal Justice Act 1988 (c.33) s.74(12), s.74(10); Proceeds of Crime Act 2002 (c.29).]

The appellant (B) appealed against a decision ([2011] EWHC 1950 (Admin), [2011] Lloyd's Rep. F.C. 445, [2011] C.L.Y. 803) that he should pay the respondent Revenue £268,039 on the basis that he had received a tainted gift. B had entered into a hire purchase agreement for an aircraft. He and his co-owner (J) made an agreement in December 2001. Under the agreement, J paid the hire purchase company $637,462 for a 50 per cent share in the aircraft. J had been arrested in connection with carousel fraud in April 2001. In December 2003, he made an agreement with B under which he made no further payments or received further benefits in relation to the aircraft. J was subsequently convicted of carousel fraud offences. The Revenue sought to recover sums from J under the Criminal Justice Act 1988, alleging that the disposal of J's share in the aircraft to B was a gift within s.74(10) and (12). The judge, finding that the December 2003 agreement made no commercial sense, agreed that in valuing J's interest in December 2003, the $637,462 he had paid should be credited back to him, resulting in the £268,039 valuation.

Held: Appeal allowed. (1) There was no justification for adding the $637,462 back in. J had been charged with serious offences and his appetite to use the aircraft diminished. His circumstances had changed substantially by December 2003 and his use of the aircraft declined. He had then owed B money for his share of the engine overhaul cost and been heavily in arrears in meeting his obligation to meet the expenses of aircraft ownership. He remained liable for half the sum outstanding on the mortgage and half the future expenses, which were likely to be substantial. For reasons beyond his control, he was unable to make much of the right to use the aircraft. Accordingly, it was not the case that the agreement J made in December 2003 made no commercial sense. It relieved J of substantial liabilities. There was therefore no tainted gift (see paras 26-29 of judgment). (2) There had been a lack of clear definition of the issues in the case. When civil claims were made under the Proceeds of Crime Act 2002 and its predecessors, it was vitally important that the issues were clearly defined. In more complicated cases, it would be better for the Revenue to set out its case in points of claim and for the defendant to respond in points of defence. In such cases it might then be appropriate for a list of issues to be drawn up in the way it was done in the Commercial Court. That was something that should be considered by the Rules Committee (para.30).

REVENUE AND CUSTOMS PROSECUTIONS OFFICE v JOHNSON; *sub nom.* BACKHOUSE v REVENUE AND CUSTOMS PROSECUTION OFFICE, [2012] EWCA Civ 1000, [2013] Lloyd's Rep. F.C. 1, Pill, L.J., CA (Civ Div).

752. Prosecution case–Closing speeches–Unrepresented defendant–Closing speech made by prosecution contrary to convention–Safety of conviction

[Criminal Procedure Act 1865 (c.18) s.2.]

The appellant (P) appealed against his conviction on two counts of fraud. P had hired cars using false names and particulars, and had been unanimously convicted by the jury on both counts. He had been legally represented at the start of the trial but dismissed his legal representatives at an early stage and was refused permission to seek new representation. He was therefore unrepresented for most of the trial. At the conclusion of the evidence, prosecuting counsel made a closing speech. P submitted that the standard convention did not normally permit a closing prosecution speech where a defendant was unrepresented.

Held: Appeal dismissed. Prosecuting counsel's right to make a closing speech arose from the Criminal Procedure Act 1865 s.2. There was a well-established rule whereby no such speech would be made where the defendant was unrepresented, and whereby a conviction would need to be quashed where that convention was breached, *R. v Mondon (Dorothy Rose)* (1968) 52 Cr. App. R. 695, [1969] C.L.Y. 810 considered. More recent authorities were conflicting as to whether, in the light of procedural and evidential changes, it was improper for prosecuting counsel to make a closing speech in such circumstances, *R. v Stovell (John)* [2006] EWCA Crim 27, [2006] Crim. L.R. 760, *R. v Rabani (Khalid)* [2008] EWCA Crim 2030 and *R. v Williams (James)* [2011] EWCA Crim 1739, [2012] R.T.R. 18, [2012] C.L.Y. 2813 considered. However, trial judges and counsel had a high responsibility to guard against breaching the convention. The starting point was that it was improper for a final speech to have been made and the question was whether, in spite of such a breach, P's conviction was safe, *Rabani* and *Williams* applied. The evidence against him was overwhelming and his account was wholly incredible. There was substantial direct and circumstantial evidence supporting the prosecution case, including the fact that P had previous convictions for similar offences. In the circumstances, notwithstanding that prosecution counsel should not have given a closing speech, P's conviction was entirely safe.

R. v PAUL (CHARLES TEMITOPE), [2013] EWCA Crim 978, [2013] 2 Cr. App. R. 26, Laws, L.J., CA (Crim Div).

753. Prosecutors' powers and duties–Gangmasters–Prosecution of offences under s.13 Gangmasters (Licensing) Act 2004–Application of prosecutorial policy

[Gangmasters (Licensing) Act 2004 (c.11) s.13(1).]

The appellant (M), a dairy farming business, appealed by way of case stated against the dismissal of its application to stay a prosecution brought against it by the Gangmasters Licensing Authority. The Authority, which licensed agencies who provided workers for the agricultural industry, alleged that M had committed the strict liability offence, under the Gangmasters (Licensing) Act 2004 s.13(1), of entering into an agreement under which an unlicensed gangmaster had supplied it with a herdsman. M had paid a monthly fee to the gangmaster, who had in turn paid the herdsman's wages, albeit below the applicable minimum wage. M argued that its prosecution was an abuse of process, having been brought in breach of the Authority's "Dairy Policy", which set out the factors to be taken into account in determining whether a case should be prosecuted. M's argument was that in order to come within the policy, it had not only to enter into an agreement with an unlicensed gangmaster, but had also to contribute to the exploitation of the worker. It also argued that the Authority's practice of using as a criterion for prosecution the employment of the supplied labourer for a minimum of 12 months, was arbitrary and outside the policy. The district judge found that there was no abuse of process. He took the view that his power to stay should be exercised sparingly, and only where there was a clear breach of a settled prosecution policy. He rejected M's submissions, finding that the application of a 12-month minimum period was a matter of the practical application of the policy and did not take the case outside it. The issues were (i) whether there had been a breach of the policy; (ii) if so, whether the district judge should have ordered a stay.

Held: Appeal dismissed. (1) Because the policy was not well drafted and did not follow the usual form of guidance given by the Crown Prosecution Service for prosecutions, it was not easy to give it a sensible and reasonable interpretation. It used the words "because [the farming business's] actions contributed to the exploitation of the worker", and they had been chosen because the Authority sought to prosecute those who facilitated, and those who were believed to be complicit in, such practices. The Authority also referred to prosecution of "those involved in the exploitation". As the s.13(1) offence was one of strict liability with the defence of due diligence, it made no sense to interpret those phrases as requiring knowledge. The policy was intended to provide for the prosecution of those whose use of the supplied labour made the exploitation greater, either by reason of the length of the employment or the number of people employed. It followed that the adoption of a minimum 12-month employment period was a permissible interpretation of the policy. There had been no breach and the district judge had been right to refuse to stay the prosecution (see paras 17-21 of judgment). (2) Even if there had been a breach, a stay would not have been appropriate. M quite properly accepted that a failure to follow and apply the policy would not of itself justify a stay, *R. v A* [2012] EWCA Crim 434, [2012] 2 Cr. App. R. 8, [2012] C.L.Y. 721 considered. Misconduct or oppression of the type explained in *R. v Horseferry Road Magistrates Court, Ex p. Bennett (No.1)* [1994] 1 A.C. 42, [1993] C.L.Y. 1867 had also to be shown, *Bennett* considered. That requirement was the same whether the challenge was by way of an application for a stay for abuse of process or by judicial review, *R. (on the application of E) v DPP* [2011] EWHC 1465 (Admin), [2012] 1 Cr. App. R. 6, [2012] C.L.Y. 783 considered. The policy had been drafted by the executive management board of an agency of the executive government, and not by an independent prosecutor. It would be highly undesirable for there to be a different standard of review in abuse of process applications depending on whether the setting of a policy or the control of a prosecution lay in the hands of an independent prosecutor such as the Director of Public Prosecutions, or in the hands of an emanation of the executive government. Nevertheless, there had to be a powerful argument that a court should apply a more stringent standard to prosecution policy devised and implemented by the executive. In the instant case the prosecutorial function had been transferred to the CPS and therefore no different test was applicable. Had there been breach of the policy in the instant case, the court would not have considered that the decision to prosecute was oppressive, the Authority having conscientiously tried to apply the policy and its decision having been adopted by the CPS. However, since many prosecutors were developing policies, and satellite litigation challenging decisions was unwelcome, it was of some importance that the principles in *Bennett* could be applied to all prosecutorial decisions. For that and other constitutional reasons, there should be clear arrangements which ensured that decisions on prosecution policy and the decision to prosecute were made by persons who could exercise their judgment entirely independently of the executive government or executive agency (paras 22-32).

MOSS & SON LTD v CROWN PROSECUTION SERVICE, [2012] EWHC 3658 (Admin), (2013) 177 J.P. 221, Sir John Thomas (President), DC.

754. Qualifying offences–Police powers and duties–Non-intimate samples

THE POLICE AND CRIMINAL EVIDENCE ACT 1984 (AMENDMENT: QUALIFYING OFFENCES) ORDER 2013, SI 2013/2774; made under the Police and Criminal Evidence Act 1984 s.65A. In force: November 11, 2013; .

This Order adds various offences to the list of "qualifying offences" in s.65A of the Police and Criminal Evidence Act 1984. Under Pt.5 of the Act, designation of an offence as a "qualifying offence" has implications for the circumstances in which a constable can require a person convicted of the offence to attend at a police station for the purpose of taking his fingerprints or a non-intimate sample, and has implications for the period for which such a person's fingerprints or sample can be retained.

755. Rape of child under 13–Fitness to plead–Expert evidence that offender not fit to plead–Appointment of intermediary–Whether continuation of trial appropriate

[Powers of Criminal Courts (Sentencing) Act 2000 (c.6) s.11; Sexual Offences Act 2003 (c.42) s.5.]

The appellant young offender (G) appealed by way of case stated against his conviction for intentionally penetrating the mouth of a boy under 13 contrary to the

Sexual Offences Act 2003 s.5. G was 15 years old. It was submitted at the start of the proceedings that he was unfit to plead, to take part in the trial and to instruct his defence team. An expert consultant forensic psychologist (C) on G's behalf and an expert on behalf of the prosecution prepared reports. C stated that G was not fit to engage in the trial process; the prosecution's expert disagreed. The judge declined to stay the proceedings and appointed an intermediary. The judge found that G was fit to take part in the trial and found the charge proved. The questions for the High Court were whether (i) the judge was bound by C's opinion or whether he could make his own decision based on the evidence; (ii) the judge was bound to conduct an enquiry as envisaged by *R. (on the application of P (A Juvenile)) v Barking Youth Court* [2002] EWHC 734 (Admin), [2002] 2 Cr. App. R. 19. G submitted that the judge (1) had no regard to the procedure to be followed; (2) erred in stating that there was no procedure for fitness to plead in the magistrates' court; (3) erred in not conducting an enquiry into the facts of which he was charged without finding guilt; (4) disregarded evidence of G's capacity; (5) failed to give adequate reasons for his conclusion.

Held: Appeal dismissed. (1) It was clear that the judge had followed the procedure in *Crown Prosecution Service v P* [2007] EWHC 946 (Admin), [2008] 1 W.L.R. 1005, [2007] C.L.Y. 1023, CPS v P considered. (2) The judge was correct that there was no equivalent procedure to that in the Crown Court to deal with fitness to plead. However, youth courts had two tools to deal with fitness to plead: an application for a stay and proceedings to make findings of fact rather than convicting, where appropriate. The judge had been aware of those two alternatives as they were referred to in the guidance laid down in *CPS v P*. (3) The discretion as to whether to proceed to making a finding of guilt depended on the court's assessment and whether it was necessary in the circumstances, CPS v P considered. (4) There was no evidential basis for the judge to accept the submission that G could not follow the trial, take part in the trial or give meaningful instructions to his defence team. The judge had observed G and the intermediary and ensured the intermediary's advice was complied with. (5) Reading the case stated as a whole, the judge had clearly had in mind the relevant evidence and principles to apply in reaching his decision. Further, G had never submitted that the court should embark on a course which would not involve conviction. On the evidence available, that was not a realistic course for the judge to take, especially given the absence of submissions. No procedural irregularities were present, the judge had followed the relevant guidance, and G was tried on the basis of fair evidence and was able to instruct adequately his representatives. The judge had been entitled to exercise his discretion under the Powers of Criminal Courts (Sentencing) Act 2000 s.11 and the 1983 Act having regard to all of the evidence and not just C's evidence. Having found that G knew his acts were wrong, the judge was entitled to make a finding of guilt.

G v DPP, [2012] EWHC 3174 (Admin), [2013] M.H.L.R. 143, Pitchford, L.J., DC.

756. Receivership orders–Remuneration–Court-appointed receivers–Recovery of receiver's costs from receivership assets–Entitlement to recover costs incurred after discharge of receivership

[Criminal Justice Act 1988 (c.33); Civil Procedure Rules 1998 (SI 1998/3132) Pt 69, r.69.7, r.69.11.]

The second and third appellants (X), being individuals or trusts connected with the first appellant solicitor (G), appealed against decisions [2010] EWHC 3619 (Admin) and ([2012] EWHC 2015 (Admin)) that the respondent receiver (R) was entitled to recover remuneration, disbursements and expenses from G for work done after the discharge of a receivership order relating to G. The court had appointed R under the Criminal Justice Act 1988 to act as receiver and manager of G's assets. The order provided that the costs of the receivership would be paid out of the receivership assets. The receivership was complex and acrimonious. G's appeal against conviction was dismissed and his application to discharge R refused. However, in March 2006, a confiscation order imposed against him was set aside, which prompted a successful without-notice application to discharge the receivership order. Despite discharge, the disputes between R, G and X continued. In September 2007, G applied for the detailed assessment of R's costs. By then, R had secured a lien for his charges over the receivership assets. It was decided, as confirmed in *Sinclair v Glatt* [2009] EWCA Civ 176, [2009] 1 W.L.R. 1845, [2009] C.L.Y. 927, that the lien extended to assets legally vested in G but beneficially owned by X. R applied for permission to realise assets to meet his remuneration, costs and interest for the period up to November 2010. In December 2010, it was held that R was entitled to be paid a substantial sum and a detailed assessment was ordered. In June 2012, the judge clarified that his December 2010 order extended to R's post-discharge remuneration and fees. The issues on the instant appeal were (i) whether the December 2010 order, as affirmed by the June 2012 order, permitted R to recover post-discharge costs; (ii) if so, whether it was too late for X to argue that the court had had no power to make such an order; (iii) whether the court had had power to make the December 2010 order.

Held: Appeal dismissed. (1) The orders made in December 2010 and June 2012 were clear that R could claim costs "up to and including 19 November 2010". That necessarily included post-discharge remuneration (see paras 19-22 of judgment). (2) It would be unjust to permit X to argue that the court had had no jurisdiction to make the December 2010 and June 2012 orders. R had undertaken work and acted on the footing of those orders, and would suffer significant detriment if the point were to be argued and established. Furthermore, X had been live to the issue in November 2010 but had not pursued it (paras 26-32). (3) The court had had jurisdiction to make the December 2010 order. The starting point was that the receivership order, although silent specifically as to post-discharge costs, sanctioned the payment of costs to R. Receivers appointed under the 1988 Act were officers of the court and subject to its supervision and to common law generally. It was an established common law principle that they were ordinarily entitled to be indemnified from the assets of the receivership estate. Importantly, the right to an indemnity was not extinguished by discharge of the receivership order; the lien could continue to exist for that purpose after discharge, *Mellor v Mellor* [1992] 1 W.L.R. 517, [1992] C.L.Y. 408 applied and *Crown Prosecution Service v Eastenders Group* [2012] EWCA Crim 2436, [2013] 1 W.L.R. 1494 considered. In *Glatt v Sinclair* [2010] EWHC 3082 (Admin), [2011] Lloyd's Rep. F.C. 140, [2011] C.L.Y. 370, Parker J had taken the correct approach, in principle, when he indicated that the receiver, post-discharge, continued to be a court officer, *Glatt* approved. After discharge, the receiver still had functions to perform in order to conclude the administration of the receivership, as was confirmed by CPR r.69.11, which was not to be construed as exhaustive. Such matters could be time-consuming and/or expensive. There was no principled basis for denying a receiver a right to claim remuneration in respect of them, and neither common law nor CPR Pt 69 called for that. The fact that r.69.7 made a receiver's remuneration subject to court approval provided protection to the person whose assets had been subject to receivership, but also indicated that the court retained a supervisory jurisdiction over a receiver, after discharge, in matters relating to the conclusion of the receivership, the transfer of assets and any enforcement of the lien, *Boehm v Goodall* [1911] 1 Ch. 155 applied (paras 32-50).

GLATT v SINCLAIR, [2013] EWCA Civ 241, [2013] 1 W.L.R. 3602, Maurice Kay, L.J., CA (Civ Div).

757. Reporting restrictions–Sexual offences–Anonymity of victim–No jurisdiction to prohibit publication of defendant's name–Freedom of press

[Contempt of Court Act 1981 (c.49) s.4(2); Sexual Offences (Amendment) Act 1992 (c.34) s.1 (2), s.1.]

The appellant (P) appealed against orders made by the respondent Crown Court aimed at restricting publication of the name of a defendant (D) convicted of sexual offences. D had been convicted of rape after a trial in open court and the case had been listed under his full name. At the sentencing hearing, counsel for the prosecution had sought to draw the judge's attention to concerns which would arise if D's name were published. Plainly thinking that counsel sought an order to impose a prohibition on the publication of D's name, the judge made an order under the Contempt of Court Act 1981 s.4(2) imposing an indefinite prohibition on the publication of anything relating to D's name which could lead to the identification of the complainant and thus have serious consequences for the course of justice. However, a press representative persuaded the judge that s.4(2) did not apply. The judge remained concerned about the consequences for the complainant's health and wellbeing if the identification of D led to her identification. Having weighed the freedom of the press against the complainant's interests, he made an order under the Sexual Offences (Amendment) Act 1992 s.1(2), which superseded the s.4(2) order. P submitted that the judge had no power to make any order anonymising D; since Parliament had rejected the reintroduction of anonymity for defendants in cases involving sexual offences, it was not open to the court to achieve the same result by way of injunction. The Crown submitted that, although the 1992 Act conferred automatic anonymity on victims of sexual crime, it was appropriate for the court to give guidance and directions as to the proper ambit of what could be reported.

Held: Appeal allowed. (1) The purpose of orders under s.4(2) of the 1981 Act was to avoid a substantial risk of prejudice either to the proceedings in which the order was made, or in subsequent proceedings such as a retrial involving the same defendants or witnesses. Essentially, s.4(2) was aimed at postponement of publication rather than a permanent ban. An order under s.4(2) should be made only when necessary and as a last resort. D had been tried, convicted and sentenced in public without any order restricting publication of his identity, and there were no pending proceedings which might be prejudiced by the publication of his name. The judge had therefore been correct to recognise that s.4(2) was inapt for the making of the initial order (see para.13 of judgment). (2) The 1992 Act did not confer any express power on the court to make an order restricting publication of a defendant's name in order to protect or enforce a complainant's right to anonymity. The absence of such an express power was telling. Moreover, since complainants enjoyed the protection provided by s.1 of the 1992 Act, there was no need, on the face of it, for any such power. Further, the absence of a judicial power to restrict publication provided a clear demarcation of responsibility which indicated that publication decisions were left to editors and reporters, *R. v B* [2006] EWCA Crim 2692, [2007] E.M.L.R. 5, [2007] C.L.Y. 1018 followed. Any contravention of s.1 involved the commission of a criminal offence. In view of the extremely high importance attached to the ability of the media to report criminal trials, the court's jurisdiction to grant anonymity to a defendant was not to be lightly inferred, *R. (on the application of Trinity Mirror Plc) v Croydon Crown Court* [2008] EWCA Crim 50, [2008] Q.B. 770, [2008] C.L.Y. 14 followed. The instant case was not one in which the identification of D would imperil his life or safety or that of his family, therefore an anonymity order was not justified on that basis, *Guardian News and Media Ltd, Re* [2010] UKSC 1, [2010] 2 A.C. 697, [2010] C.L.Y. 4 followed. Accordingly, the court lacked the jurisdiction to make either of the orders it had made. However, the judge was in charge of the court and he was entitled to express concerns as to the possible consequences of publication, and indeed to engage in a discussion with press representatives present in court about those issues. It was right to anticipate that a responsible editor would carefully consider before deciding what should be published (paras 15-21).

R. (ON THE APPLICATION OF PRESS ASSOCIATION) v CAMBRIDGE CROWN COURT; *sub nom.* PRESS ASSOCIATION, *Re,* [2012] EWCA Crim 2434, [2013] 1 W.L.R. 1979, Lord Judge, L.C.J., CA (Crim Div).

758. Reporting restrictions–Witness protection–Witness and her children–Publication of photographs or film prohibited–Freedom of expression

[Contempt of Court Act 1981 (c.49) s.4(2); Youth Justice and Criminal Evidence Act 1999 (c.23) s.46(9), s.46(6).]

The appellant media organisations (N) appealed against a reporting restriction order made for witness protection in a criminal trial. During the notorious criminal trial of a father (P) accused of causing the death of his six children in a fire, his girlfriend (W) was a key witness. Before the tragedy, W and her children had been extensively filmed on television and photographed in newspapers. At the trial W was fearful of P and his friends and, having changed her appearance and their surnames, was allowed to give evidence from behind screens under special measures. The judge made an order under the Contempt of Court Act 1981 s.4(2) prohibiting and postponing publication of any photographs of W, or her children. The following day she revoked that order and replaced it with a similar one made under the Youth Justice and Criminal Evidence Act 1999 s.46 with N given liberty to apply. N postponed any application for revocation until after W had given evidence. N had argued that the s.46 order had been made without jurisdiction and should be revoked under s.46(10). The judge dismissed the application, concluding that publication would have a damaging effect on W and her children. N appealed. N submitted that despite its narrow ambit the order was not covered under s.46(6) because (1) the protection of the children of an adult witness had not been in contention and such issues were better addressed in the family courts; and (2) W had already been fully identified in publications, television programmes, and on the internet as the mother of P's children and her name was common knowledge.

Held: Appeal dismissed. (1) In relation to the identification of children, separately from their parent, the Family Division was normally the appropriate venue. Nevertheless, the criminal courts had to control their own processes and the protection of the family court was not sufficient to deprive the Crown Court of jurisdiction under s.46. Publication of photographs of W's children would have been likely to lead to identification of W, which would have affected the quality of her evidence at trial (see para.29 of judgment). (2) N's submissions restricted s.46 to those cases where the witness was anonymous. However, the identity of the overwhelming majority of witnesses was known, so limiting the application of s.46 in that way was pointless, particularly as different special measures under another statutory scheme were available for anonymous witnesses. That conclusion was reinforced by analysis of the wide-ranging "excepting" direction in s.46(9) which showed that a reporting restriction could be much wider than the mere naming of the witness and could impose restrictions considered unreasonable from a public interest point of view. Section 46(9) also reaffirmed that even when made appropriately, a reporting restriction should be no wider than necessary (para.31).

R. v ITN NEWS; *sub nom.* ITN NEWS LTD, *Re*, [2013] EWCA Crim 773, [2014] 1 W.L.R. 199, Lord Judge, L.C.J., CA (Crim Div).

759. Restraint orders–Receivers–Quashing of restraint order–Whether receiver entitled to recover remuneration from assets covered by order

[Human Rights Act 1998 (c.42) s.3(1); Proceeds of Crime Act 2002 (c.29) s.41, s.48; European Convention on Human Rights 1950 Protocol 1 Art.1.]

The CPS appealed against a decision declining to make an order in favour of the second respondent receiver (B) for payment of his remuneration and expenses from the assets of the first respondent group of companies (E). The CPS also challenged the judge's decision that it should pay such remuneration and expenses. On December 6, 2010, the CPS had applied for restraint orders under the Proceeds of Crime Act 2002 s.41 against two persons (W and H) suspected of a fraud involving the evasion of duty on alcohol and tobacco. The orders restrained W and H from dealing with their assets generally and with the assets of most of the companies within E. The order also appointed B as receiver over E's assets. An appeal was brought against that order. In February 2011, the Court of Appeal held that it was "implicit" in the December order that E's assets were realisable property held by W and H. It held, however, that E's assets were not in fact such property, and it quashed the receivership and restraint orders. It considered that, as at December 6, 2010, there may have been "some force" in the allegation that the proceeds of fraud had been laundered through E but that, by December 23, when an application was made to set aside the order, substantial evidence had been filed tending to show that 95 per cent of E's business was or might well have been legitimate. The issue as to payment of B's remuneration and expenses then arose. The judge held that requiring E to bear them would breach its rights under the European Convention on Human Rights 1950 Protocol 1 art.1. He therefore held that the CPS should bear them.

Held: Appeal allowed in part. (Laws L.J. dissenting on the first issue) (1) The judge had been right to hold that requiring E to bear B's remuneration and expenses would give rise to a breach of Protocol 1 art.1. The critical question under that article was whether payment of B's remuneration and expenses out of the credit balances in E's bank accounts would be "subject to the conditions provided for by law". The law did not permit the making of a restraint order under s.41 of the 2002 Act or the appointment of a receiver under s.48 over property when there was no reasonable cause to believe that the offender had benefited from criminal conduct and when there was not a good arguable case that he had an interest in the property. As to the first condition, the Court of Appeal had concluded that the critical question was whether the CPS had shown that there was reasonable cause to believe that consignments of dutiable goods had been fraudulently diverted into the United Kingdom. It concluded that, on the material presented to the court on December 6, 2010, there was no reasonable cause to believe that they had been. As to the second condition, the Court of Appeal concluded that, as at December 6, there may have been some force in the CPS's case that the companies within E were "the wholesale and retail arm" of an organised criminal group operated by W and H but that, by December 23, there was insufficient material for the judge to decide that there was reasonable cause to believe that the companies were a front for a diversion fraud committed by W and H or that the latter were sheltering behind the facade of the companies to hide their frauds or the proceeds thereof. In a superficial sense, deprivation of E's property to pay B's remuneration and expenses was authorised by law: it was a settled principle of receivership law in civil proceedings that a receiver was entitled to be paid his remuneration and expenses out of the assets he was appointed to receive and manage. That proposition was, however, subject to an important caveat: the conditions on which a restraint order might be made and a receiver appointed had first to be satisfied. If they were not, there would be no lawful basis for the appointment of a receiver in respect of property belonging to an alleged offender, still less belonging to a third person. It had to be to the underlying lawfulness of the receiver's appointment that a court should look to determine, for the purpose of Protocol 1 art.1, whether he could, at the state's behest, deprive the true owner of the property in respect of which he was appointed of all or part of it, to satisfy his remuneration and expenses (see paras 77-82 of judgment). (2) The judge had, however, been wrong to require the CPS to meet B's remuneration and expenses. No express provision of the 2002 Act gave the court such a power, and the judge had been wrong to hold that the Human Rights Act 1998 s.3(1) could be used to construe the Act as providing such a power. That would conflict with the principle that a receivership order was good until set aside (paras 69-71).

CROWN PROSECUTION SERVICE v EASTENDERS GROUP; *sub nom.* EASTENDERS CASH & CARRY PLC v CROWN PROSECUTION SERVICE; BARNES v EASTENDERS CASH & CARRY PLC, [2012] EWCA Crim 2436, [2013] 1 W.L.R. 1494, Laws, L.J., CA (Crim Div).

760. Right to fair trial–Reasonable time–Murder–Date of charge for purposes of right to fair trial within reasonable time under art.6(1) European Convention on Human Rights 1950–Apparent bias–Right to independent and impartial tribunal

[European Convention on Human Rights 1950 Art.6(3).]

The court was required to determine issues in relation to the right of the appellants (L and N) to a fair trial within a reasonable time and before an independent and impartial tribunal. L and N had been convicted of sexual offences against children in June 1998 and imprisoned. On September 17, 1998, they were produced from custody at a police station and questioned on suspicion of conspiracy to murder. They were not arrested or charged. They were released from their respective custodial sentences in 2002 and 2003 but were subsequently imprisoned for breach of their sex offender notification requirements. On April 5, 2005, they were charged with murder. The indictment also included charges for further sexual offences against children, which were ordered to be tried separately. The sexual offences were tried first. L was convicted of three offences, N of two. When adjourning sentencing for those offences, the judge referred to L and N as "evil, determined, manipulative and predatory paedophiles of the worst sort". The same judge subsequently presided over the murder trial. The issues were whether (i) for the purposes of their right to a fair trial within a reasonable time under the European Convention on Human Rights 1950 art.6(1), L and N were "charged" on September 17, 1998 or April 5, 2005; (ii) whether the comments and conduct of the trial judge were such as to breach L and N's right to a fair trial by an independent and impartial tribunal under art.6(1) and, if so, whether the decision to proceed with the trial was incompatible with their rights under art.6(1).

Held: Issues determined, appeals remitted. (1) L and N were plainly entitled to the protection of art.6(1), read together with art.6(3), when they were interviewed. The date from which reasonable time began to run was therefore the subject of a separate guarantee from the guarantee that a trial would be fair, and had to be approached separately, *Ambrose v Harris* [2011] UKSC 43, [2011] 1 W.L.R. 2435, [2011] C.L.Y. 1674, *Salduz v Turkey (36391/02)* (2009) 49 E.H.R.R. 19, [2009] C.L.Y. 2017 and *Cadder (Peter) v HM Advocate* [2010] UKSC 43, [2010] 1 W.L.R. 2601, [2010] C.L.Y. 1733 considered. However, it was not enough that they were being questioned in circumstances that might have affected their right to a fair trial. The question was whether they were charged on that date, or whether they had been officially notified that they would be prosecuted or alerted to the likelihood of criminal proceedings against them, *Eckle v Germany (A/51)* (1983) 5 E.H.R.R. 1 and *Attorney General's Reference (No.2 of 2001), Re* [2003] UKHL 68, [2004] 2 A.C. 72, [2004] C.L.Y. 884 considered. They had not been formally "charged" at any stage of their interviews. They had both asked the police whether they were going to be charged and received indications to the contrary, but the fact that the question was asked was revealing. L and N had been through the process before and knew what to expect. It had to have been obvious to them that the reason they were not being charged was that the police did not have enough evidence at that stage. All the indications during the prolonged questioning to which they were subjected were that that was the position. The police had not yet established that the victim was dead; her body had not been found. They were not in a position to charge until April 5, 2005, and that was the date the reasonable time began (see paras 35-39 of judgment). (2) When the judge made his remarks, he was addressing L and N in the performance of his judicial function. The fair-minded and informed observer would appreciate that he was a professional judge who had taken the judicial oath and had years of relevant training and experience. They would understand the context in which the remarks were made. They were made in open court while he was performing his duty as a judge at the trial. The informed observer would also appreciate that when the judge was presiding over the second trial he would be doing so in the performance of his duty and that, while the facts were a matter for the jury, the judge had functions to perform which required him to be impartial. It would only be if the judge expressed outspoken opinions that were entirely gratuitous regarding L and N's character, and only if he made them at a time when it was plainly outside the scope of the proper performance of his duties in conducting the trial, that his ability to perform those duties with an objective judicial mind would be doubted. The context indicated that that was not the position in the instant case. L and N had been entitled to be given some indication of likely sentence and the judge's comments were directly relevant to that issue. L and N and their legal representatives were present when the remarks were made and no objection was made then or at the start of the murder trial to the fact that the same judge was presiding. There was no basis for the suggestion the judge was apparently biased, *Porter v Magill* [2001] UKHL 67, [2002] 2 A.C. 357, [2002] C.L.Y. 3185 applied. It followed that it was not incompatible with L and N's right to a fair trial to have proceeded with their trial on the murder charges before the same judge (paras 53-57).

O'NEILL (CHARLES BERNARD) v HM ADVOCATE; LAUCHLAN (WILLIAM HUGH) v HM ADVOCATE, [2013] UKSC 36, [2013] 1 W.L.R. 1992, Lord Hope, J.S.C. (Deputy President), SC.

761. Scotland Act 2012 (c.11)–Commencement No.3 Order

THE SCOTLAND ACT 2012 (COMMENCEMENT NO.3) ORDER 2013, SI 2013/ SI 2013/6 (C.1); made under the Scotland Act 2012 s.44. Commencement details: bringing into force various provisions of the 2012 Act on April 22, 2013.; .

The Commencement Order makes provision in relation to EU law issues and European Convention on Human Rights issues raised in Scottish criminal proceedings. These provisions include provision for a right of appeal to the Supreme Court in relation to such issues.

762. Search warrants–Conspiracy to defraud–Lawfulness of warrant–Failure to identify articles sought as far as practicable

[Police and Criminal Evidence Act 1984 (c.60) s.8(2), s.15(6)(a), s.15(6)(b), s.78; Civil Procedure Rules 1998 (SI 1998/3132) r.54.5(1).]

The claimant company director (N) applied for judicial review of the lawfulness of a search warrant issued by the second defendant magistrates' court to the first defendant commissioners. N was the sole director of an animation film production company (F), which had claimed substantial repayments of VAT in 2009 which were repaid in part. In 2010, F claimed Film Tax Relief (FTR) on production costs of £2.6 million but no film was ever released. The commissioners investigated after attempts to make contact with F's alleged suppliers in order to verify the claims failed. N was found to be a director of eight other companies which had received approximately £1.7 million in VAT and FTR repayments over a two year period. The commissioners regarded it as suspicious that N had not submitted a self-assessment tax return since 2005, given his directorships in companies with a substantial turnover, and suspected that N and his companies were involved in a conspiracy to cheat the Revenue. They obtained and executed a search warrant on N's London address which provided that all business records, accounts, electronic storage equipment and all items believed to be of evidential value could be searched for and seized. The evidence obtained was subsequently served in the prosecution of N for the offence of conspiracy to cheat the Revenue. N issued his claim for judicial review the day before the time limit expired under CPR r.54.5(1), some ten weeks after the information that had supported the warrant application had been disclosed to him. N submitted, in reliance on *R. (on the application of Energy Financing Team Ltd) v Bow Street Magistrates Court* [2005] EWHC 1626 (Admin), [2006] 1 W.L.R. 1316, [2005] C.L.Y. 930, that the warrant was invalid and unlawful in failing to comply with the Police and Criminal Evidence Act 1984 s.15(6)(b) as it was drawn so widely that no-one would have known what items fell within its scope other than all items found at the stated address. The commissioners contended that N's claim should be dismissed as it was not made promptly, and that, pursuant to *R. v Chief Constable of Warwickshire, Ex p. F* [1999] 1 W.L.R. 564, [1999] C.L.Y. 901, warrants which did not identify the stated offence were nevertheless valid where the offence had been identified in the information put before the issuing magistrate.

Held: Application granted. (1) Although the claim was not brought promptly, that did not automatically bar the claim for review. The exercise of the court's discretion to permit review was governed by the substantive merits of the claim, including the subject matter and whether prejudice had resulted from the delay. The subject matter of the claim was N's liberty and the intrusion into his home. There had been no prejudice to the commissioners as their investigation and subsequent prosecution had proceeded unhindered. Accordingly, the claim, which had merit, was permitted to proceed (see para.12 of judgment). (2) In *Chief Constable of Warwickshire*, the court had not analysed whether s.15(6)(b) had been complied with but considered s.8(2) of the Act, and no subsequent case had been identified that followed that part of the judgment, *Chief Constable of Warwickshire* considered. In contrast, *Energy Financing Team* had been followed, *Energy Financing* applied, *Gittins v Central Criminal Court* [2011] EWHC 131 (Admin), [2011] Lloyd's Rep. F.C. 219, [2011] C.L.Y. 816 and *R. (on the application of Power-Hynes) v Norwich Magistrates' Court* [2009] EWHC 1512 (Admin), (2009) 173 J.P. 573, [2010] C.L.Y. 788 considered. The issue was not whether a warrant fulfilled the purposes of s.8, but whether its terms complied with s.15(6)(a) and s.15(6)(b); it was intended that the requirements of s.15 should be "safeguards", *Power-Hynes* applied. The present warrant did not comply with s.15(6)(b) as it failed to specify in respect of what business or investigation the articles were sought. The requirements imposed by s.15 were independent of those under s.8. Section 15(6) did not cover the grounds on which the warrant should be issued as s.8 did but was concerned with the contents of the warrant which identified that material an officer was entitled to seek under s.8(2). The present warrant came nowhere near identifying the articles sought as far as practicable. It would have been a simple matter to specify the true scope of the material sought. The warrant was, in important respects, unlimited in its scope and did not identify the articles which the information revealed were being sought (paras 19-21, 25, 27-29). (3) The instant court was not the appropriate forum to decide whether the evidence obtained on the warrant was admissible in the prosecution against N; that was for the Crown Court under s.78 of the Act. The warrant was therefore declared unlawful and quashed, but no further relief was ordered (para.38).

R. (ON THE APPLICATION OF ANAND) v REVENUE AND CUSTOMS COMMISSIONERS, [2012] EWHC 2989 (Admin), [2013] C.P. Rep. 2, Pitchford, L.J., DC.

763. Search warrants–Identification–Warrant referring to "suspects" rather than naming individuals–Requirements of s.15(6) Police and Criminal Evidence Act 1984

[Criminal Justice and Police Act 2001 (c.16) s.59(5); Police and Criminal Evidence Act 1984 (c.60) s.15(6), s.15, Sch.1; European Convention on Human Rights 1950 Art.6.]

The claimant Dutch nationals (P) applied to challenge the validity of a search warrant granted by the defendant Crown Court to the first interested party police force and consequent orders made under the Criminal Justice and Police Act 2001 s.59. P were suspected of tax fraud and money laundering. The Dutch court requested a police search of P's residence, which was in the United Kingdom. The search warrant was granted under the Police and Criminal Evidence Act 1984 Sch.1, and was to allow entry into the premises to search for listed material. The text of the warrant referred to "the suspects". The warrant was executed and material was seized. The police obtained without notice orders under s.59 of the 2001 Act authorising them to retain computer images and material relating to companies owned, controlled or utilised by the claimants. P sought the return of the seized material. They submitted that (1) the material placed before the judge did not meet the conditions prescribed by Sch.1 of the 1984 Act and accordingly the grant of the warrant was unlawful; (2) the phrase "the suspects" was too vague to satisfy s15(6)(b) of the 1984 Act, which required the warrant to identify as far as practicable the articles or persons to be sought.

Held: Application granted. (1) The request for the warrant asserted either explicitly or by inference that the relevant offences had been committed, and that the material sought was likely to be of substantial value to the investigation and was likely to constitute relevant evidence. Accordingly there were reasonable grounds for the judge to believe that the conditions in Sch.1 were satisfied (see para.50 of judgment). (2) Section 15(6) of the 1984 Act addressed not the process of the application but the warrant itself, which was the only document that could make lawful an otherwise unlawful act; accordingly, the warrant had to be judged by reference exclusively to its own terms and not to any other material source. The descriptions of the categories of material did not satisfy s.15(6) even when taking the warrant as a whole. They would have done had the warrant at any point identified the suspects but it did not, *R. v Chief Constable of Warwickshire, Ex p. F* [1999] 1 W.L.R. 564, [1999] C.L.Y. 901 not followed, *R. (on the application of Energy Financing Team Ltd) v Bow Street Magistrates Court* [2005] EWHC 1626 (Admin), [2006] 1 W.L.R. 1316, [2005] C.L.Y. 930 applied, *Burgin v Commissioner of Police of the Metropolis* [2011] EWHC 1835 (Admin), [2011] Lloyd's Rep. F.C. 495, [2011] C.L.Y. 815 considered. Accordingly, the search warrant did not comply with s.15(6) and was unlawful (paras 57, 64-67). (3) As the orders made under s.59 of the 2001 Act were dependent on there having been a valid search warrant, those orders had to be quashed. Further, they would be liable to be quashed in any event because the police should have applied for them on notice. Although there was no express provision in the Crown Court Rules 1982 r.39 requiring an applicant under s.59(5) of the 2001 Act with possession of such seized property to give notice to any other person who had a relevant interest in the property, notice should have been given either under a common law duty to act fairly or by virtue of the European Convention on Human Rights 1950 art.6 (paras 68, 82-84). (4) Despite the quashing of the warrant, it would be open to the police to apply under s.59(5) to retain the property on the basis that s.59(7) applied, namely that if the property were returned it would immediately become appropriate to apply for a warrant under which it would be lawful to seize it. Therefore the orders were quashed and the police ordered to return within 14 days all property seized pursuant to the warrant and currently in their possession, unless they applied under s.59(5) for its retention. In respect of the materials passed on to the Dutch authorities it was sufficient for the police to inform them that the warrant and s.59 orders had been quashed and to use their best endeavours to persuade them to return the materials (paras 86-89). (5) (Per Sir John Thomas, PQBD) The 1982 Rules did not make it sufficiently clear that, except where an urgent without notice application was required, applications under s.59 had to be inter partes and therefore those with a relevant interest in the documents should be served. The Criminal Procedure Rule Committee was invited to consider the Rules in the light of the instant case (para.4 of judgment of Sir John Thomas).

R. (ON THE APPLICATION OF VAN DER PIJL) v KINGSTON CROWN COURT; *sub nom.* VAN DER PIJL v KINGSTON CROWN COURT, [2012] EWHC 3745 (Admin), [2013] 1 W.L.R. 2706, Sir John Thomas (President), DC.

764. Search warrants–Private prosecutions–Application to magistrates for warrants–Police failure to disclose that private company would prosecute any charges

[Police and Criminal Evidence Act 1984 (c.60) s.8, s.15, s.16, s.78.]

The first appellant (Z) appealed against his conviction for conspiracy to defraud and the second appellant (P) appealed against his sentence of six years' imprisonment imposed for conspiracy to defraud. Z was the director of a company which sold set top boxes which allowed the user to unscramble channels without authority or payment of a fee and thus view free of charge all television channels broadcast by Virgin Media Ltd (V). The set top boxes were sold blank and software enabling them to obtain the television channels was either emailed to wholesalers or posted on the internet for users to download. The prosecution case was that Z was the company's founder and prime mover and that P was the technical expert, and that through the company's actions V had been defrauded of millions of pounds in lost revenue. V covertly observed the company's activity and informed the police that it intended to prosecute, and sought assistance for arrest and search. A police officer applied on oath to the magistrates for warrants. He and a senior representative of V gave evidence, but the magistrates were not told that it was anticipated that V would prosecute. The warrants were executed. The trial judge rejected a submission that he should stay the prosecution as an abuse of process, holding that the police had no legal obligation to declare explicitly that V was the likely prosecutor. Z and P were convicted. Z was sentenced to eight years' imprisonment. Z submitted that the trial judge erred in finding that the identity of the likely prosecutor was not a matter which the applicant for a warrant was required to explain to the magistrates. P submitted that his sentence was manifestly excessive as it failed to reflect his lesser role in the conspiracy.

Held: First appellant's appeal against conviction dismissed, second appellant's appeal against sentence allowed. (1) It was plain that a constable making an application for a warrant had a duty of full disclosure of relevant matters, *Stanford International Bank Ltd (In Receivership), Re* [2010] EWCA Civ 137, [2011] Ch. 33, [2010] C.L.Y. 1873 applied. It was equally apparent that the Police and Criminal Evidence Act 1984 s.8, s.15 and s.16 did not require that any potential prosecutor be identified. The instant court did not understand why the police had felt that it was acceptable, during a without notice application with its duty of full disclosure, to keep from the magistrates that a private prosecution was expected. The obligation on an applicant for a warrant was the same as that imposed on any person making a without notice application to a court, namely one of full and frank disclosure, *Stanford International Bank* applied. The obligation was not necessarily fulfilled merely by an information demonstrating that the bare statutory minima for the grant of the warrant were met. The disclosure had to be as full and frank as the circumstances of each case required. The magistrates, once informed, might have probed the reason for the Crown not bringing the case, and taken an interest in why the police thought it was appropriate to help a large commercial entity in that fashion at that stage. After all, there was oral evidence from a senior representative of V, the intended prosecutor, and yet he had stopped short of explaining an uncomplicated and uncontroversial fact. It would have done no harm to explain it to the magistrates. Nevertheless, it would not have been surprising if the warrants had been granted in any event after full and frank disclosure, especially as bad faith was not made out. Z had not demonstrated that the magistrates would have refused the applications had they known that V would prosecute, *R. (on the application of Rawlinson and Hunter Trustees) v Central Criminal Court* [2012] EWHC 2254 (Admin), [2013] 1 W.L.R. 1634, [2013] 7 C.L. 35 considered. Given the conclusion that no harm would have been done by such disclosure, and that the warrants would have been granted, it could not be said that they would have been quashed as a result of material non-disclosure. Further, an application under s.78 of the Act would have failed: the discretion available to a judge was so wide that a decision not to exclude the evidence would have been very difficult to challenge successfully (see paras 15, 32-35 of judgment). (2) The judge did not fall into error in his description of P's role in the conspiracy, but on the information made available by the subsequent confiscation proceedings, which showed that Z had profited to a much greater extent than P, it was clear that the difference in role between them was greater than was reflected in the two years' difference in sentence. P's sentence was reduced from six to four years' imprisonment (paras 37-49).

R. v ZINGA (MUNAF AHMED); R. v PILLAI (MUKUNDAN), [2012] EWCA Crim 2357, [2013] Lloyd's Rep. F.C. 102, Rafferty, L.J., CA (Crim Div).

765. Summing up–Specimen charges–Indecent assault on children–Adequacy of summing up

The appellant (H) appealed against his conviction for two counts of indecent assault on two children. H had been a family friend of the complainants, who were sisters. The offences were said to have occurred when the families were visiting each other. The girls were between the ages of 6 and 9 and 9 and 12 respectively at the time of the alleged offences. The alleged incidents had taken place 15 to 30 years previously. Both of the counts for which he was convicted were specimen counts. H was acquitted of two further counts and the jury was unable to reach a verdict on three remaining counts. H gave full answers at interview but did not give evidence at the trial. H submitted that his convictions were unsafe as (1) the summing up in respect of his failure to give evidence was confusing; and (2) the summing up was misleading with regard to specimen counts.

Held: Appeal allowed. (1) H's complaint about the summing up was that it would have misled the jury into believing that it was being encouraged to consider H's failure to give evidence before concluding that he had a proper case to answer, thereby failing to apply the fourth principle in *R. v Cowan (Donald)* [1996] Q.B. 373, [1996] C.L.Y. 1511, namely that the jury had to be satisfied that the prosecution had established a case to answer before drawing any inferences from silence, *Cowan* applied. Reading the summing up in isolation H might have had a sustainable point, but read as a whole, the jury would not have been confused (see paras 9-12 of judgment). (2) In most cases where a specimen count was relied on, it was enough for the judge to tell the jury, as the judge did in the instant case, that it could convict if it was sure that the offence had been committed at least once. Where the complainant could not particularise any specific incident and merely alleged a pattern of similar conduct, the question for the jury was whether it was sure that the complainant's account was reliable. The critical question was whether the evidence before the jury was such that there was a realistic possibility that a reasonable jury could have reached its verdict in respect of a specimen count by focussing on different occasions. If so the summing up would be defective and the convictions would be unsafe without a direction that the jury had to be sure with respect to the same occasion. In answering that question in the instant case, it had to be noted that H had not given evidence and did not raise with the judge the need to distinguish between particular incidents or occasions. Nevertheless, the nature of the incidents was such that the jury could on the evidence have been satisfied about the course of conduct but not the specific occasion or vice-versa. Moreover, the fact that the jury found H not guilty of other specimen counts suggested that it must have had some doubts about the reliability of the complainants. It could not be said in those circumstances that the verdicts were safe (paras 23, 28-29).

R. v HOBSON (ANDREW CRAIG), [2013] EWCA Crim 819, [2013] 1 W.L.R. 3733, Elias, L.J., CA (Crim Div).

766. Verdicts–Inconsistent verdicts–Misleading actions–Whether appellant's conviction on one charge inconsistent with acquittal on others

[Consumer Protection from Unfair Trading Regulations 2008 (SI 2008/1277) reg.9.]

The appellant company (U), which provided parking-management facilities, appealed against its conviction for engaging in a commercial practice which was misleading, contrary to the Consumer Protection from Unfair Trading Regulations 2008 reg.9. The prosecution case was that U had sent out three documents to consumers which appeared as if they came from a public body and gave the impression that the addressee had broken a criminal traffic law, making him or her more likely to pay the money demanded than would otherwise have been the case. The first document was headed "Charge Certificate" and had the sub-heading "Civil Traffic Enforcement Notice". The second was headed "Civil Traffic Enforcement Notice, Charge Certificate, Final Reminder". The third was a letter sent to an individual who had received a parking ticket informing her that her appeal against the giving of the ticket had been unsuccessful. The documents were the subject of separate counts. U was acquitted in respect of the first and second documents but convicted in respect of the third.

Held: Appeal allowed. There was an unexplained inconsistency in the verdicts. No jury could reasonably conclude that the first two documents were not likely to deceive a consumer in the manner alleged but nevertheless come to the conclusion that the third document was likely to do so. It was quite clear that, of the three documents, the least potentially deceptive was the third. As to the statutory defence of taking all reasonable precautions to avoid committing the offence, U had asserted that it had done everything it reasonably could by sending the documents to be examined by the British Parking Association. However, no distinction had been made in that respect between the three documents, either when U's managing director was interviewed or when the judge gave his summing-up. There was therefore no possible evidential basis on which the jury could have been satisfied that U had done everything it could to avoid committing the offence in relation to the first two documents but not in relation to the third. U's conviction would therefore be quashed (see paras 17-21 of judgment).

R. v UK PARKING CONTROL LTD, [2012] EWCA Crim 1560, (2012) 176 J.P. 648, Moses, L.J., CA (Crim Div).

767. Verdicts–Magistrates' courts–Magistrates reversed guilty verdict after announcing it–Existence of power to do so

[Magistrates' Courts Act 1980 (c.43) s.142; Road Traffic Act 1988 (c.52) s.7(6).]

The appellant DPP appealed by way of case stated against a decision of a magistrates' court to reverse its own guilty verdict against the respondent (C) following his prosecution for failing to provide a specimen contrary to the Road Traffic Act 1988 s.7(6). C was seen by police officers driving in a car park. They approached him and thought he smelled of alcohol. They gave him five opportunities to provide a breath specimen: in the first three he sucked rather than blew, and in the final two he blew insufficiently for the test to be effective. He was arrested and taken to the police station. He failed to answer various questions asked of him in accordance with procedure Form MG DD/A, but when asked if he had used a mouth spray in the last 20 minutes he said that he had. That meant the police had to wait a further 20 minutes before trying to obtain a specimen. He was charged with failing without reasonable excuse to provide a specimen contrary to s.7(6). The magistrates found that C had been untruthful in relation to the mouth spray and found him guilty. Directly afterwards, counsel for C asked the court whether it should have made a finding regarding the fact that the police had not asked C whether he had brought anything up from his stomach, which was a further question on the form. The magistrates retired without stating a reason for doing so and without inviting any submission from the prosecution. When they returned they substituted a verdict of not guilty, relying on *Howard v Hallett* [1984] R.T.R. 353, [1985] C.L.Y. 2992. The questions posed for the consideration of the High Court were: (i) whether the magistrates were wrong to reconsider their verdict once they had announced it; (ii) if they were not wrong to reconsider the verdict, whether they were wrong to find C not guilty, given their findings that there was no lawful requirement to provide a specimen because of procedural irregularity.

Held: Appeal allowed. (1) It was very clear from the case stated why the magistrates reversed their verdict to not guilty. They found that the police officer had not asked C if he had brought up anything from his stomach in the previous 20 minutes, and they considered that *Howard v Hallett* required strict adherence to the procedure in order to convict under s.7(6). But for their belief that they were bound by *Howard v Hallett* they would have found C guilty. The procedure form followed by the police was useful but was of no statutory effect, *DPP v Coulter* [2005] EWHC 1533 (Admin) applied. Compliance by police officers with the form could only affect the reliability of a specimen provided; in C's case there was a failure to provide a specimen at all. The magistrates were completely wrong to find *Howard v Hallett* relevant and it was unfortunate that counsel for C had raised it, *Howard v Hallett* distinguished. The answer to the second question was yes and the not guilty plea had to be quashed. (2) The answer to the first question was also yes: the magistrates were wrong to reconsider their verdict once they had pronounced it. Magistrates' courts were creatures of statute so their powers were limited to those of the statutory scheme. They had no inherent powers. The only possible power under which a magistrates' court could revisit its decision was in the Magistrates' Courts Act 1980 s.142, but the purpose and scope of that provision was limited. It was intended to rectify a small or simple mistake, like the slip rule. The magistrates could not use it to change their verdict of guilty to not guilty, *R. v Croydon Youth Court, Ex p. DPP* [1997] 2 Cr. App. R. 411, [1998] C.L.Y. 1069 applied, *R. (on the application of Aitchison) v Sheffield Crown Court* [2012] EWHC 2844 (Admin), [2013] A.C.D. 7 considered. The right procedure would be an appeal to the Crown Court or the Divisional Court. The magistrates' reconsideration of the case on its merits was wrong, as was their failure to give the prosecution an opportunity to reply to C's point made after the verdict. That procedural irregularity compounded the mistake. (3) A retrial was unnecessary: the magistrates had found C guilty, and only changed their minds because they wrongly considered themselves to be bound by *Howard v Hallett*. Quashing the not guilty verdict left the guilty verdict in place.

DPP v CHAJED, [2013] EWHC188 (Admin), [2013] 2 Cr. App. R. 6, Laws, L.J., DC.

768. Voluntary bills of indictment–Conspiracy to defraud–Whether statutory provision under which allegation might be charged

[Copyright, Designs and Patents Act1988 (c.48) s.297; Criminal LawAct1977 (c.45) s.3.]

The Crown applied to prefer a voluntary bill of indictment on charges of conspiracy to defraud at common law and money laundering offences after a magistrate dismissed charges in relation to those offences brought against the respondents (D). The Crown had alleged that the first respondent (M), in conjunction with two of his companies, facilitated the illegal downloading of premier league football matches streamed over the internet from abroad for the payment of a £10 fee. D were charged with conspiracy to defraud at common law and money laundering charges, which were parasitic on the common law conspiracy charge. In D's application to dismiss the charges, the magistrate had concluded that it was wrong in principle to allow an allegation of conspiracy to defraud at common law to be maintained where there was at least one statutory offence which might have been charged, but had not been, in relation to which D may have had a defence. The Crown contended that it wished to prefer a voluntary bill alleging common law conspiracy rather than a charge under the Copyright, Designs and Patents Act 1988 s.297, as the six-month maximum sentence available under the latter was insufficient in light of M's offending.

Held: Application refused. A decision of a magistrate should be treated with the greatest respect, and exceptional circumstances were required to warrant a prosecution, *Brooks (Lloyd) v DPP* [1994] 1 A.C. 568, [1994] C.L.Y. 939 applied. Where a charge of common law conspiracy had been brought under a voluntary bill of indictment, the court had intially to look at whether there was a relevant statutory offence and if so, how and why the Crown had chosen not to prefer conspiracy charges in relation to that offence, and whether it was proper in all the circumstances to allow the common law allegation of conspiracy to be maintained. Section 297 caught precisely the criminal conduct alleged against M: the provision of a means to get around encryption for a fee amounted to a conspiracy to breach s.297 and M's conduct ought to have been charged as such. It was also wrong to allow the Crown to ignore the procedural safeguards in the Criminal Law Act 1977 s.3. Furthermore, to allow the Crown to prefer the voluntary bill deprived M the protection of being charged with an offence that was summary only, *R. v Rimmington (Anthony)* [2005] UKHL 63, [2006] 1 A.C. 459, [2006] C.L.Y. 873 applied. As the money laundering charges were parasitic, they fell away with the conclusion that there was no good reason to prefer the voluntary bill (see paras 5, 17, 21-23, 28 of judgment).

R. v DADY (MARC); *sub nom.* REDCAR AND CLEVELAND BC v DADY, [2013] EWHC 475 (QB), [2013] Lloyd's Rep. F.C. 300, Coulson, J., QBD.

769. Voluntary bills of indictment–Judicial decision-making–Need for exceptional circumstances to justify grant

The applicant Director of Public Prosecutions applied for leave to prefer a voluntary bill of indictment against the respondent (Z). Z and three co-defendants had been committed for trial on a charge of grievous bodily harm. A month before trial, Z successfully applied for the charge against him to be dismissed on the ground that there was no evidence of joint enterprise. The judge found that the two co-defendants who had attacked the victim had been on a "frolic of their own". He rejected the prosecution's submission, in reliance on *R. v A* [2010] EWCA Crim 1622, [2011] Q.B. 841, [2011] C.L.Y. 676, that a defendant who set out with others to commit a specific crime, would be guilty of whatever different crime was actually committed so long as he foresaw that his co-accused might commit that offence. The judge found that *R v A* was of no assistance because the defendant group in the instant case had split up, two chasing one victim and two another. On appeal, the prosecution repeated its submissions regarding the effect of *R v A*.

Held: Application refused. It was clear from various authorities and from *Practice Direction (CA (Crim Div): Criminal Proceedings: Consolidation)* [2002] 1 W.L.R. 2870, [2002] C.L.Y. 899 that a High Court judge should be cautious about granting leave to prefer a voluntary bill, especially where the "normal procedure", as referred to in the practice direction, involved a successful application to dismiss a case sent to the Crown Court, *R. v Davenport (Christine)* [2005] EWHC 2828 (QB) and *R. v McGuiness (Danny)* [2007] EWHC 1772 (QB) referred to. Such an order might be justified where, for example, the judge dismissing the charge had overlooked a statutory provision or relevant authority, or otherwise erred in law; or if the prosecution had new evidence which significantly affected the case, or if the decision to dismiss lacked a rational foundation. The circumstances had to be exceptional. In the instant case there was no evidence of exceptional circumstances and it was therefore inappropriate to grant leave (see paras 21-28 of judgment).

R. v ARFAN (MOHAMMED), [2012] EWHC 2450 (QB), (2012) 176 J.P. 682, Nicol, J., QBD.

770. Warrants–Misleading advertising–Entry of premises to search for evidence likely to disclose offences under Business Protection from Misleading Marketing Regulations 2008–Validity of warrant issued

[Police and Criminal Evidence Act 1984 (c.60) s.15(2A), s.15(2); Business Protection from Misleading Marketing Regulations 2008 (SI 2008/1276) reg.23(1), reg.24.]

The claimant (X) applied for judicial review of the first defendant magistrates' court's decision to grant, at the request of the second defendant local authority, a warrant authorising the entry and search of his premises by the local authority's trading standards officers and the seizure of various records, computers and other items. The local authority had received complaints that a number of associated companies (W) were operating a scam amounting to offences under the Business Protection from Misleading Marketing Regulations 2008. Following investigation, trading standards officers found evidence that X was involved in W's management and they applied for warrants to enter X's premises pursuant to reg.24. A magistrate granted a warrant authorising enforcement officers to enter and search the premises for business documentation relating to W, computer hardware and software used to produce that documentation, and other peripheral equipment, such as mobile phones. The warrant stated that there were reasonable grounds for believing that there were on X's premises items which an enforcement officer had power to inspect under reg.23(1) and that their inspection may disclose evidence of a breach of the Regulations, and that giving notice of an intention to apply for a warrant would defeat the object of entry. The warrant was executed and various records, computers and other items were seized. By his judicial review claim, X sought an order quashing the warrant, a declaration that the entry, search and seizure had been unlawful, an order for the return of the items seized, and damages. X contended, inter alia, that the warrant was defective because (1) properly construed, reg.24 did not allow premises that were used only as a dwelling to be searched; (2) the warrant was obtained on the basis of material non-disclosure in that the officers had failed to disclose their belief that the premises were being used for a non-dwelling purpose; (3) reg.24 required the magistrate considering the application to be satisfied from the content of the information alone that the conditions or grounds required to be satisfied by reg.24(1)(a) and reg.24(1)(b) were indeed satisfied; (4) on all of the material before the magistrate, he could not have been satisfied that those conditions were met; (5) the magistrate appeared to have misdirected himself as to the correct legal test as he was required to be satisfied that inspection of the specified items "is likely" to disclose evidence of breach of the Regulations, whereas the warrant stated that they "may" disclose such evidence; (6) it did not state which of conditions C, D or E in reg.24 had been met.

Held: Application refused. (1) Regulation 24 permitted entry of any premises, including dwellings, in different specified circumstances, *R. (on the application of Vuciterni) v Brent Magistrates' Court* [2012] EWHC 2140 (Admin), (2012) 176 J.P. 705, [2013] 2 C.L. 73 applied (see paras 27, 38 of judgment). (2) The power of entry and search under reg.23 did not arise if the enforcing authority had a reasonable belief that premises were being used for a non-dwelling purpose: it arose only if the premises were in fact "premises other than premises used only as a dwelling". Not disclosing that there were grounds for believing that premises were being used for non-residential purposes was not a material non-disclosure (para.41). (3) The Police and Criminal Evidence Act 1984 s.15(2) and s.15(2A) set out what an applicant had to state when making any application for a warrant, including an application under reg.24. Those provisions required a sworn statement, but did not require the information to include all of the facts and/or evidence upon which an applicant relied; nor did they require the magistrate to restrict his consideration of whether the relevant statutory requirements were met to the content of the information, *R. (on the application of Redknapp) v Commissioner of the City of London Police* [2008] EWHC 1177 (Admin), [2009] 1 W.L.R. 2091, [2008] C.L.Y. 864 and *R. (on the application of Dulai) v Chelmsford Magistrates' Court* [2012] EWHC 1055 (Admin), [2013] 1 W.L.R. 220, [2012] C.L.Y. 825 considered (paras 53-54). (4) The magistrate did have sufficient material before him, in sworn form, to be satisfied that the relevant statutory conditions were met (para.62). (5) Despite the wording of the warrant that inspection of the items may disclose breaches of the Regulation, the magistrate had, in fact, applied the correct statutory test and considered the application on the basis that the evidence was likely to disclose breaches of the Regulation (paras 69-71). (6) On the evidence, it was clear that the application for the warrant had been made on condition D in reg.24, and that the magistrate was satisfied that condition D had been met (para.75). (7) In issuing the warrant, the magistrate had performed his judicial function with a proper approach and diligence. The warrant was valid, and the search that was performed under it was therefore properly authorised and lawful (paras 76, 79).

R. (ON THE APPLICATION OF AHMED) v YORK MAGISTRATES' COURT, [2012] EWHC 3636 (Admin), (2013) 177 J.P. 233, Hickinbottom, J., QBD (Admin).

771. Wasted costs orders–Disclosure–Solicitors' failure to disclose details of potential alibi witnesses

[Criminal Procedure and Investigations Act 1996 (c.25) s.6A(2)(a).]

The appellant firm of solicitors (J) appealed against a wasted costs order made against them in respect of criminal proceedings against their client (X). X had been charged with violent disorder. He claimed to have been at home at the relevant time and informed J of three potential alibi witnesses. Counsel advised that the names and addresses of the potential witnesses should not be disclosed until they had provided J with a signed witness statement. J accepted that advice and did not inform the prosecution of the witnesses' existence. None of the witnesses gave a proof of evidence until the day before trial, when X's father gave a statement in support of X's alibi. The father gave evidence at trial. A delay was caused because the prosecution called rebuttal evidence which showed that his evidence was false. However, X was acquitted. The judge considered that J had deliberately breached the requirement in the Criminal Procedure and Investigations Act 1996 s.6A(2)(a) to give notice of the particulars of alibi, that that had been improper and unreasonable and that it had caused wasted costs.

Held: Appeal allowed. (1) The obligation on the defence under s.6A(2)(a) was important to the prosecution since it prevented "ambush" alibi defences. Further, full disclosure of the details of a truthful alibi could be an important safeguard to the defence because a timely investigation could lead to the prosecution being discontinued. Although it might be prudent for those drafting defence statements to have a signed proof of evidence from an alibi witness before drafting a defence statement, in many cases that would be impracticable, for example if the witnesses were reluctant. The statutory obligation to give the details was triggered by the defendant's belief that the witness could give evidence in support of the alibi. It was not necessary that the witness could give such evidence let alone that he was willing to do so. Nor was the defendant's belief in the witness' ability to give evidence dependent on the witness giving a proof of evidence. Any practice of advising that the details of alibi witnesses should not be disclosed until they had provided signed proofs of evidence was wrong. X had instructed J that his alibi could be confirmed by three potential witnesses; although he could give their names and addresses, he had apparently been unable to say which would actually come to court. Counsel had no doubt realised that that did not comply with the Act's requirements, but that did not justify omitting all reference to the potential witnesses. If X would not be more specific, counsel should have identified those members of the family who were in the house at the relevant time, for those were the persons who X had believed would be able to support his claim to have been there himself. Although the father had not come forward until the day before trial, X had known long before then that he was able to give evidence in support of his alibi. Justice was not served by concealing this until he gave a proof of evidence. Accordingly, there had been a breach of s.6A(2)(a) (see paras 32-38 of judgment). (2) Although they had fallen into error, it could not be said that J had acted in a way in which no reasonably competent solicitor could have acted, *Ridehalgh v Horsefield* [1994] Ch. 205, [1994] C.L.Y. 3623 applied. Their conduct had been neither improper nor unreasonable. J had been entitled to take into account views of experienced counsel, and the view taken by counsel had been quite widely held. However, the requirements of s.6A had now been properly explained, so no one could reasonably make that mistake again (paras 38-40). (3) On the facts, it was not clear that the breach had caused costs to be wasted, or that the delay in the trial had been caused by the father's late appearance. There was a further difficulty in that the judge had failed to specify the amount of the wasted costs order (paras 41-44). (4) The power to make a wasted costs order should be reserved for the clearest cases, otherwise more time, effort and cost went into making and challenging the order than had allegedly been wasted in the first place (para.46).

JOSEPH HILL & CO SOLICITORS, *Re*; *sub nom.* R. v X (WASTED COSTS ORDER), *Re*, [2013] EWCA Crim 775, [2014] 1 W.L.R. 786, Leveson, L.J., CA (Crim Div).

772. Youth courts–Committal for sentence–Child sex offences committed by 11-year-old–Jurisdiction initially accepted by youth court–Lawfulness of subsequent committal to Crown Court for sentence under s.3C Powers of Criminal Courts (Sentencing) Act 2000–Young Offenders

[Criminal Justice Act 2003 (c.44) Pt 12 s.226(3), s.228(2); Magistrates' Courts Act 1980 (c.43) s.24(1); Powers of Criminal Courts (Sentencing) Act 2000 (c.6) s.3C, s.91; Sexual Offences Act 2003 (c.42) s.5, s.7.]

The claimant (W) applied for judicial review of a decision by a district judge sitting in the defendant youth court to commit him to the Crown Court for sentence under the Powers of Criminal Courts (Sentencing) Act 2000 s.3C. W was 11 years old and had pleaded guilty to rape and sexual assault of a six-year-old girl. Prior to W entering any pleas, the district judge had accepted jurisdiction and adjourned the case for trial. However, following W's guilty pleas, having considered reports from the Youth Justice Service (YJS) and the Barnardo's TAITH service regarding W's background and risk of reoffending, the district judge found that W posed a significant risk of serious harm to the public from further specified offences and committed him for sentence. W claimed that, in the circumstances, the district judge had no power to commit him under s.3C. The Magistrates' Courts Act 1980 s.24(1) created a statutory presumption that a defendant under the age of 18 would be dealt with in the youth court. There were exceptions to that general rule, including where the defendant was charged with an offence to which s.91 of the 2000 Act applied, which included the instant offences under the Sexual Offences Act 2003 s.5 and s.7, or where the dangerousness criteria for the imposition of an indeterminate or extended sentence under the Criminal Justice Act 2003 Pt 12 s.226(3) or s.228(2) were satisfied.

Held: Application granted. If the youth court was to decline jurisdiction because a sentence under s.91 was appropriate or the dangerousness criteria were met, it should do so at the preliminary stage. However, under s.3C, the youth court had a residual power in very exceptional circumstances to commit to the Crown Court for sentence notwithstanding the original acceptance of jurisdiction. The issue was whether that power had been exercised properly. Offences contrary to s.5 and s.7 were serious specified offences for the purposes of s.226 and s.228. The statutory question was whether there was a significant risk to members of the public of serious harm occasioned by the commission of further specified offences by an offender. In view of the further information before the judge, he was entitled to be concerned about the risk presented by W. The question was whether it had been reasonably open to him to find that the statutory criteria for an indeterminate or extended sentence had been met. There were prominent features in the case. It was the first time W had exhibited sexually abnormal behaviour for three-and-a-half years; he was immature for his age, having a development age of approximately eight; he had been exposed to experiences which had generated learned behaviour, and for six months while in the care of his grandparents had not exhibited such behaviour; he had settled into a new school and had been open and co-operative with the YJS. Alarming though the offending was, it was unlikely that the Crown Court would conclude that W presented a significant risk of serious harm provided that the risk was contained by intervention and supervision. An important consideration for the district judge had been whether, to justify a sentence under s.226 or s.228, the facts of the case required a determinative sentence of four years' detention or more after a guilty plea. However, it did not appear from the judge's note to the court that that had been a significant consideration in his analysis of the statutory criteria. It was clear from the reports that W had limited culpability for his serious misbehaviour. Having concluded in the preliminary stages that a sentence of more than two years' detention after a trial was not appropriate, it did not seem that the further information before the judge changed the assessment of seriousness and risk so as to attract a sentence of four years' detention. An indeterminate or extended sentence could not properly be imposed on the information before him. Without minimising the seriousness of W's conduct, prevention was the dominant consideration. There was no suggestion in the reports that intervention was likely to be unsuccessful or difficult; on the contrary, W had shown every sign that he was susceptible to positive influence, *R. v Lang (Stephen Howard)* [2005] EWCA Crim 2864, [2006] 1 W.L.R. 2509, [2006] C.L.Y. 3836 considered. It had not therefore been reasonably open to the district judge to exercise his power under s.3C. The committal would be quashed and the youth court directed to proceed to sentence (see paras 9, 18-19, 21-22, 35, 38-43 of judgment).

R. (ON THE APPLICATION OF W) v CAERNARFON YOUTH COURT, [2013] EWHC 1466 (Admin), (2013) 177 J.P. 534, Pitchford, L.J., QBD (Admin).

CUSTOMS

773. Air passenger duty–Exemptions–Whether airline entitled to benefit from connected flights exemption–Interpretation of Finance Act 1994, Air Passenger Duty Regulations 1994 and Air Passenger Duty (Connected Flights) Order 1994–Whether airline treated less favourably than competitors

[Finance Act 1994 (c.9) s.30; Air Passenger Duty (Connected Flights) Order 1994 (SI 1994/1821) Sch.1 para.1; Air Passenger Duty Regulations 1994 (SI 1994/1738).]

The appellant airline (R) appealed against the respondent commissioners' decision that it was not entitled to benefit from the "connected flights exemption" under the Finance Act 1994 s.30 in respect of air passenger duty (APD). R also sought judicial review of the decision on the basis that it had been treated less favourably than comparable airlines. The relevant period was from September 16, 2007 to May 31, 2011. APD was a self-assessed excise duty payable by commercial aircraft operators in respect of each passenger travelling on a flight departing from a United Kingdom airport, save for those flights which came within the exemption. R had accounted for APD during the relevant period as it had, mistakenly it claimed, believed that it was not entitled to the exemption. It claimed a refund of over £10 million. The Revenue considered that R had not satisfied the necessary conditions during the period in question. The issues for determination in respect of the appeal, referred by the First-tier Tribunal, were: (i) the proper construction of the requirements set out in the applicable provisions of the 1994 Act, the Air Passenger Duty Regulations 1994 and the Air Passenger Duty (Connected Flights) Order 1994; (ii) whether R was entitled to claim an exemption in accordance with the proper construction of those provisions. R's judicial review claim was based on the Revenue's obligation to act fairly and to publish appropriate guidance and be open and forthcoming. The Revenue argued that it had treated R the same way as other airlines and that its published guidance was appropriate and complete, and readily available to R.

Held: Appeal dismissed, application refused. (1) The construction issue had to be broken down into two stages. First, it was necessary to ascertain whether it was Parliament's intention that two distinct conditions imposed under the 1994 Order, the temporal condition, which related to the interval between the arrival of flight A and the departure of flight B, and the ticketing condition, that two or more flights made up a single journey, had to each be satisfied and as free-standing conditions, or whether the aim was to ensure that the temporal condition was satisfied and the ticketing condition was no more than the means by which the airline was obliged to demonstrate that satisfaction. Second, it had to be determined how the wording used in the legislation was to be applied to electronic tickets, as almost all airlines, including R, required passengers to make "e-bookings". Section 30(8) of the 1994 Act made it clear that there had to be strict compliance with the order contemplated by that subsection if successive flights were to be treated as connected. Schedule 1 para.1 Note (5)(b) of the Order stated, without qualification, that flights were not connected where the tickets were not "conjunction tickets" within Note (6). The stipulation of conjunction tickets was consistent only with the conclusion that the ticketing condition amounted to a free-standing requirement. The two conditions were therefore discrete and had to both be met if the exemption was to apply. The purpose of the ticketing condition was to prescribe the method by which it was to be demonstrated that the flights said to be connected made up a single journey. Properly construed, the relevant legislative provisions stipulated that flights were connected for the purposes of the exemption only if: (a) the interval between the flights satisfied the relevant temporal condition and; (b) the customer had, or could readily access, a ticket or tickets, or their electronic equivalents, which provided all of the prescribed particulars of each flight sufficient to show, by their referring to each other or by means of a shared passenger name reference (PNR), or in a similar manner, that together they constituted a single journey (see paras 108, 126-134 of judgment). (2) Once it was accepted that conjunction tickets performed a function which was more than that of merely demonstrating satisfaction of the temporal condition, it became obvious that R had not met the terms of the 1994 Order during the relevant period, as the electronic substitutes for tickets it provided to passengers did not, and could not, satisfy the ticketing condition. Those parts of the statutory appeal before the instant tribunal were therefore determined in favour of the Revenue (paras 135-136). (3) R had not established that any other airline had been permitted to benefit from the exemption. No airline which had abandoned the use of paper tickets could comply with the ticketing condition, construed literally. However, in seeking a proxy for conjunction tickets so that the 1994 Order might be related to the world of electronic tickets, the Revenue were looking for a connection between flights, beyond the temporal, which could be shown by the fact that the flights shared a PNR, had been booked together in a single visit to the airline's website, could be readily displayed on a computer screen or on paper as the components of a single journey, or by some combination of those features. The two comparator airlines had systems which were able to meet those requirements. The difficulty R faced was that during the relevant period its systems did not make those things possible, and there was no evidence that any other airline whose systems lacked those features had been permitted to benefit from the exemption (paras 165-169).

RYANAIR LTD v REVENUE AND CUSTOMS COMMISSIONERS, [2013] UKUT 176 (TCC), [2013] S.T.C. 1360, Warren, J., UT (Tax).

774. Common foreign and security policy–Export controls–Sanctions–Myanmar

THE EXPORT CONTROL (BURMA SANCTIONS) ORDER 2013, SI 2013/1964; made under the European Communities Act 1972 s.2; and the Export Control Act 2002 s.1, s.2, s.3, s.4, s.5, s.7. In force: August 28, 2013; .

This Order makes provision relating to the enforcement of the trade sanctions against Burma which remain following the repeal and replacement of Regulation 194/2008 by Regulation 401/2013 concerning restrictive measures in respect of Myanmar/Burma.

775. Customs duty–Electronic products–Classification of high-speed camera products–Whether digital cameras or video camera recorders

The appellant commissioners appealed against a decision of the First-tier Tribunal that camera products imported into the European Union by the respondent company (P) should be classified for customs duty purposes as digital cameras rather than video camera recorders. P imported specialist high-speed camera products. The Combined Nomenclature classification code 8525 8091 applied to "video camera recorders". Such products attracted duty of 4.9 per cent, whereas "digital cameras" fell within code 8525 8030 and were free of duty. The commissioners had refused P's claim for repayment of customs duty paid on the importation of the products between 2004 and 2006, and had issued a decision classifying the products as video camera recorders. The tribunal reversed those decisions, finding that in both their properties and their use, the products in question accorded with the definition of a "digital camera", namely a camera which captured and recorded in digital format still photographic images. It held that the products were not designed to capture images of a given event for subsequent viewing as a video sequence. The tribunal made ancillary orders directing repayment of the customs duty already paid by P. The commissioners submitted that the object of both digital cameras and video camera recorders was simply to record images. They argued that recording a series of images to be seen in a moving characteristic, frame by frame, was applicable to video camera recorders, and that exercise was the same as with high-speed cameras.

Held: Appeal allowed in part. (1) The commissioners' appeal against the tribunal's decision ordering repayment of the customs duty already paid by P was allowed. The tribunal had had no power to make the order (see paras 4, 42 of judgment). (2) Both digital cameras and video camera recorders operated in the same way: they took a series of still pictures. However, it was not sufficient to assert that the purpose of all cameras was simply to record images. If that were the sole purpose, all three types of camera under debate would have to be considered as being identical. There had to be more for there to be a meaningful difference in classification between digital cameras and video camera recorders. The answer lay in ascertaining the purpose of the relevant device. The main purpose of a digital camera was to take single still photographs. A video camera recorder took a series of still photographs, but then played them back at a speed which was designed to give the impression that a continuous picture was created. The primary purpose of a video camera recorder was to present the series of still photographs as a moving image. In the case of high-speed cameras, the primary purpose was to view the series of still photographs individually in a sequence, in order to conduct a detailed examination of the event captured in the pictures. If one were to view the series of still pictures taken by a high-speed camera in a moving sequence, it would only take a fraction of a second, and it would not be possible to conduct any sort of meaningful analysis of the images. The tribunal's decision, as a matter of law, was impeccable. It had considered all the relevant arguments, and had come to the correct decision that high-speed cameras were to be classified as digital cameras (paras 29-38).

PHOTRON EUROPE LTD v REVENUE AND CUSTOMS COMMISSIONERS; *sub nom.* REVENUE AND CUSTOMS COMMISSIONERS v PHOTRON EUROPE LTD, [2012] UKUT 275 (TCC), [2012] S.T.C. 2475, Peter Smith, J., UT (Tax).

776. EU law–Export controls–Sanctions–Iran

THE EXPORT CONTROL (IRAN SANCTIONS) (AMENDMENT) ORDER 2013, SI 2013/340; made under the Export Control Act 2002 s.1, s.2, s.3, s.4, s.5, s.7; and the European Communities Act 1972 s.2. In force: March 12, 2013; .

This Order makes provision for the enforcement of new trade sanctions against Iran specified in Regulation 1263/2012, which amends Regulation 267/2012 concerning restrictive measures against Iran. It does so by amending the Export Control (Iran Sanctions) Order 2012 (SI 2012/1243), which makes provision for the enforcement of most of the current trade restrictions against Iran. The new measures include prohibitions on trade, technical assistance, financing, financial assistance or brokering on key naval equipment and technology, software for integrating industrial processes, graphite and certain specified raw or semi-finished metals and a ban on the trade of natural gas originating in Iran.

777. Excise duty–Exemptions–Cooking liquors–No excise duty in manufacturing Member State–Whether excise duty properly chargeable in UK–Reasonableness of refusal to restore seized goods

[Directive 92/83 on the harmonization of the structures of excise duties on alcohol and alcoholic beverages Art.20, Art.27(1)(f).]

The appellant (R) appealed against the respondent commissioners' refusal to restore a consignment of cooking liquors. The goods, wine, port and cognac to which salt and pepper had been added, were manufactured in France, whose government had treated them as being outside the scope of excise duty under Directive 92/83 art.20. The commissioners had seized the goods on the grounds that the United Kingdom excise duty for alcohol had not been paid.

They refused restoration because R was not involved in the production or manufacture of foodstuffs and was therefore ineligible to apply for exemption; it was a significant quantity which might damage UK trade, and R had imported those types of excise goods previously without contacting Customs to establish the correct position. On R's appeal, the Court of Justice of the European Union ruled, in a preliminary reference, that: (a) the cooking liquors had been correctly characterised as ethyl alcohol and were within the excise duty regime; (b) an exemption from excise duty in one Member State had to be recognised in another Member State unless there was concrete, objective and verifiable evidence that the exemption was contrary to the Directive; (c) a Member State might give effect to the exemption from excise duty under art.27(1)(f) by means of a refund of excise duty paid, depending on how the products in question were used. The issues were whether (i) the UK had to recognise the French treatment of the cooking liquors; (ii) the UK could properly require the payment of excise duty; (iii) the commissioners could reasonably have arrived at their decision to refuse restoration.

Held: Appeal allowed. (1) On the basis that the CJEU had declared the meaning of art.20 as it had always been, the commissioners had discharged the burden of showing that France's application of the Directive was incorrect. Therefore, the UK was not bound to treat the cooking liquors as outside the scope of the Directive, *Repertoire Culinaire Ltd v Revenue and Customs Commissioners (C-163/09)* [2011] S.T.C. 465, [2011] C.L.Y. 835 applied (see paras 94-95 of judgment). (2) The requirement to pay duty before it could be refunded on proof of a qualifying use of the products concerned was not a condition that had to be complied with for the exemption to apply. It was a direct consequence of the explicit link in art.27(1)(f) between the exemption and the use of the products to be exempted. Once a use within that article was shown, the duty had to be refunded. It did not prejudice the unconditional nature of the exemption, because once the use was shown the benefit of the exemption accrued unconditionally. Excise duty was therefore properly payable on the cooking liquors (paras 100, 102). (3) The decision to refuse restoration without expressly informing R of the procedure it should follow, namely to pay the excise duty and seek a refund once appropriate proof of use in the manufacture of foodstuffs could be demonstrated, caused the decision to be fundamentally flawed. The CJEU had stated that non-involvement in the production or manufacture of foodstuffs was an impermissible condition for qualification for the exemption, so reliance on it had therefore been irrational. Further, in all probability all cooking liquors taken into stock by R were eventually used in the manufacture of foodstuffs giving rise to qualification for the exemption. It was intrinsically unjust to refuse restoration thereby rendering impossible the eventual use of them which would qualify for a refund of any excise duty paid. There was no rational expectation that R's imports would damage legitimate trade, because the overwhelming practical likelihood was that they would be used in the legitimate manufacture of foodstuffs and so no net excise duty would be capable of being levied, once entitlement to refunds was taken into account. It was also more likely than not that R bona fide believed that the cooking liquors could legally be imported without payment of excise duty. The decision to refuse restoration could not reasonably have been arrived at and the commissioners were directed to review it (paras 113-114).

REPERTOIRE CULINAIRE LTD v REVENUE AND CUSTOMS COMMISSIONERS, [2013] UKFTT 278 (TC), [2013] S.F.T.D. 1071, Judge John Walters Q.C., FTT (Tax).

778. Excise duty–Policies–Commissioners' policy on drawback of duty paid–Changes to former practices–Verification in regard to duty-paid condition

[Finance Act 1994 (c.9) s.16; European Convention on Human Rights 1950 Protocol 1 Art.1.]

The appellant commissioners appealed against a decision of the First-tier Tribunal ([2011] UKFTT 635 (TC)) finding in favour of the respondent company (E) in its appeal against refusal of drawback of excise duty claims. The commissioners' review decisions had wholly rejected 63, and partly rejected five of E's claims for drawback of excise duty totalling over £1.2 million on beer that has been warehoused for export. The rejection was on the basis that E had not provided original evidence of United Kingdom duty payment, or other evidence that showed that the goods were UK duty-paid. The tribunal held that, as the commissioners had changed their former policy of "relaxed evidential requirements" when vetting claims to a more rigid policy retrospectively and without notice, they had violated European Union and human rights law. The commissioners appealed. The issues were whether the tribunal had been wrong to (i) conclude that they had applied new requirements to E's drawback claims; (ii) hold that it had jurisdiction to consider whether they had contravened EU law principles; (iii) hold that they had contravened EU principles; (iv) hold that they had breached the European Convention on Human Rights 1950 Protocol 1 art.1; (v) order the payment of E's drawback claims.

Held: Appeal allowed. (1) It was clear from the tribunal's decision read fairly as a whole that it did not find that the commissioners had a policy or practice of only denying drawback if a claimant failed to provide limited invoice information, or was otherwise shown to be acting fraudulently; if that had been so then the policy would have been denying the commissioners' right to undertake extended verification to ensure that the duty-paid condition had been satisfied in regard to a claim. It found that the condition regarding payment of duty required not only an invoice showing that it was paid, but also due diligence as to credibility of supplier and a realistic purchase price. There was a statutory requirement that a trader should show that the duty-paid condition was satisfied. The tribunal had been wrong to hold that the commissioners had applied new requirements to E and that its existing policy had needed to be altered or withdrawn to allow it to undertake its extended verification of E's drawback claims (see paras 76, 78, 80, 86 of judgment). (2) In that light the jurisdiction issue lost its significance, but in fact the tribunal had no jurisdiction to review and provide remedies for any conduct of the commissioners in withdrawing policies (paras 90-99). (3) The tribunal erred in finding that there had been breaches of EU law, as the commissioners had always been entitled to undertake verification in regard to the duty paid condition (paras 100-101). (4) For the same reasons the tribunal was wrong to hold that the commissioners had breached E's rights under Protocol 1 art.1 (para.102). (5) Having decided that the decision by the commissioners not to repay the duty was correct as a matter of law because the required conditions had not been satisfied, it was not open to the tribunal, governed as it was by the Finance Act 1994 s.16, to review the commissioners' conduct in relation to its policies or practices (para.105).

EUROPLUS TRADING LTD v REVENUE AND CUSTOMS COMMISSIONERS; *sub nom.* REVENUE AND CUSTOMS COMMISSIONERS v EUROPLUS TRADING LTD, [2013] UKUT 108 (TCC), [2013] S.T.C. 1210, Vos, J., UT (Tax).

779. Excise duty–Reasons–First-tier Tribunal making material error of law–Factual conclusion not properly reasoned

[Excise Duty Points (Duty Suspended Movements of Excise Goods) Regulations 2001 (SI 2001/3022) reg.3, reg.4, reg.7(1).]

The appellant commissioners appealed against a decision of the First-tier Tribunal ([2011] UKFTT 211 (TC)) overturning an assessment to excise duty made in respect of the respondent haulier (S) under the Excise Duty Points (Duty Suspended Movements of Excise Goods) Regulations 2001 reg.7(1). S had transported, and guaranteed the movement of, 65 consignments of spirits from duty warehouses in the United Kingdom to continental Europe. The commissioners formed the view that none of the consignments had reached their destinations. They asserted that S was liable for duty in the UK on the basis that an excise duty point had arisen under reg.3 or reg.4 of the Regulations because the goods had either never left the UK or it was impossible to ascertain where they had gone. S asserted that the goods had reached their destinations and that duty was payable only in the countries of destination. The only issue of fact for the tribunal was whether the goods had been delivered to their destinations. The evidence of S's drivers was that some of the consignments had been delivered. There was no direct evidence in relation to the remainder. The commissioners' case was that it was impossible for the drivers to have made some of the journeys they claimed to have made. Because S was strictly liable under reg.7(1), the tribunal did not have to determine precisely what had happened to the consignments or make any finding as to S's honesty. On that basis, the commissioners did not plead, or put to the witnesses, allegations of dishonesty. The tribunal found that all the consignments but one had arrived at their destinations.

Held: Appeal allowed in part. (1) The commissioners had not established that there had been any error in the tribunal's approach to the question of dishonesty. The tribunal had not said that, in the absence of any pleading or allegation of dishonesty, it had to treat S as being honest. It had not ruled out the possibility of concluding that S's drivers might have been involved in a conspiracy, but it had accepted their uncontradicted evidence and was satisfied that they had not diverted their loads. Moreover, it had concluded that there was no evidence to support an allegation that S had been involved in a criminal conspiracy. It had not regarded itself as being precluded from making a finding of dishonesty simply because the commissioners had made no specific allegation. It had regarded an allegation of dishonesty as being implicit in the commissioners' case, and had simply preferred S's evidence on the matter (see paras 22-30 of judgment). (2) The tribunal had correctly set out the position as to the burden of proof and had not treated the commissioners as either bearing the burden or having to show that S's scenario was improbable. Nor had it failed to consider the possibility that the position was unclear and that S had failed to prove its case on a balance of probabilities. The evidence of S's drivers was not inherently improbable and the tribunal had been entitled to accept it. It tipped the balance so that there was no uncertainty. Moreover, the tribunal had been entitled to draw inferences from that evidence so as to reach conclusions about the consignments for which there was no direct evidence of delivery, and its conclusions could not be challenged, *Rhesa Shipping Co SA v Edmunds (The Popi M)* [1985] 1 W.L.R. 948, [1985] C.L.Y. 3207 considered (paras 35, 38-46). (3) So far as the allegedly impossible journeys were concerned, there were apparent inconsistencies between the drivers' evidence and the evidence of the journey timings. The resolution of those inconsistencies was critical to the tribunal's conclusion. If the journeys were indeed impossible, the tribunal could not properly have concluded that they had been made. Further, evidence that a claimed journey was impossible would call into question the driver's truthfulness about other journeys. If one driver's evidence was found to be unreliable, that would cast doubt on other drivers' evidence of similar journeys. The tribunal had found that one of the claimed journeys was impossible, but it had not considered that that cast any doubt on the drivers' evidence in relation to other journeys. It found the other journeys to have been possible. Neither of those decisions was properly reasoned, and that was an error of law that was material to the tribunal's factual conclusion. On that basis, the commissioners' appeal would be allowed. The tribunal's decision would be set aside and the case remitted to a differently constituted tribunal to determine afresh the issue of the allegedly impossible journeys and to consider what effect its conclusion had on the evidence in relation to the other consignments (paras 55, 63-79, 83, 93). (4) The commissioners' remaining criticisms of the tribunal's decision fell foul of the guidance in *Georgiou (t/a Marios Chippery) v Customs and Excise Commissioners* [1996] S.T.C. 463, [1996] C.L.Y. 5905 and were not made out, *Georgiou* applied (paras 94-99),

SDM EUROPEAN TRANSPORT LTD v REVENUE AND CUSTOMS COMMISSIONERS; *sub nom.* REVENUE AND CUSTOMS COMMISSIONERS v SDM EUROPEAN TRANSPORT LTD, [2013] UKUT 251 (TCC), [2013] S.T.C. 2052, Judge Greg Sinfield, UT (Tax).

780. Export controls–Syria

THE EXPORT CONTROL (SYRIA SANCTIONS) ORDER 2013, SI 2013/2012; made under the European Communities Act 1972 s.2, Sch.2 para.1A; and the Export Control Act 2002 s.1, s.2, s.3, s.4, s.5, s.7. In force: September 6, 2013; .

This Order: makes provision relating to the enforcement of all existing trade sanctions against Syria set out in Regulation 36/2012; and creates national prohibitions on the export, transfer or the provision of brokering services to Syria or to Syrian persons in relation to certain equipment which might be used for internal repression as listed in Sch.2 to the Order.

DAMAGES

781. Conditional fee agreements–Legal aid–Legal services

THE DAMAGES-BASED AGREEMENTS REGULATIONS 2013, SI 2013/609; made under the Courts and Legal Services Act 1990 s.58AA, s.120. In force: April 1, 2013; .

These Regulations prescribe the requirements with which a damages-based agreement must comply in order to be enforceable under s.58AA of the Courts and Legal Services Act 1990.

782. General damages–10 per cent increase in general damages–Increase to apply to civil claims from April 1, 2013–Exception for some claimants funded through conditional fee agreements

[Legal Aid, Sentencing and Punishment of Offenders Act 2012 (c.10) s.44(6), s.44, s.46.]

The court was asked to reconsider aspects of a decision ([2012] EWCA Civ 1039, [2013] 1 W.L.R. 1239, [2012] C.L.Y. 852) to increase general damages in tort cases by 10 per cent. The court had decided that the level of damages for pain, suffering and loss of amenity in respect of personal injury and all other torts would rise by 10 per cent. The increase was to apply to all cases in which judgment was given after April 1, 2013 and was intended to give effect to a package of reforms recommended by Sir Rupert Jackson in his Final Report on Civil Litigation Costs (the report). The Association of British Insurers (ABI) submitted that the increase in damages should only apply to cases where the claimant's funding arrangements had been agreed after April 1, 2013, otherwise claimants who had entered into conditional fee agreements (CFAs) before that date would receive both the increased damages and the success fee.

Held: Judgment accordingly. (1) It was necessary to consider why the recommendation for the increase in damages had been made. One of the major proposals of the report was that, as was subsequently reflected in the Legal Aid, Sentencing and Punishment of Offenders Act 2012 s.44 and s.46, a successful claimant suing with the benefit of a CFA should no longer be able to recover the success fee from the defendant. The increase was recommended as a measure to assist such claimants in meeting success fees which they would have to pay out of damages. The report went on to say that whilst the increase might appear to be a windfall for claimants who were not on CFAs, the level of general damages was not high, so it would be an opportune moment to raise the level of damages generally. It was clear that the Ministry of Justice also regarded the proposed increase as a quid pro quo for depriving successful CFA claimants of the ability to recover success fees from the defendant, and that Sir Rupert Jackson intended his proposals to be accepted or rejected as a package (see paras 20-28 of judgment). (2) The ABI had argued that it was wrong to permit CFA claimants who were entitled to recover their success fee by virtue of s.44(6) to benefit from the increase in damages. It was hard to challenge that contention. The ABI further argued that the "misalignment" could easily be met by adding a qualification to the court's earlier decision, namely that it would not apply to claimants who had entered into a CFA before April 1, 2013. Such an amendment appeared to be simple and to dispose of the misalignment. However, rather than excluding from the increase those claimants who entered into CFAs before April 1, 2013 the court decided to exclude those claimants who fell within the ambit of s.44(6). That meant that there would be a guaranteed identity between those successful claimants who were statutorily entitled to recover their success fees and those who were disentitled from enjoying the 10 per cent increase in general damages. In addition, if there was any risk of satellite litigation, it would be limited to the formulation set out in s.44(6) (paras 31-32, 40). (3) It would be inconsistent and unfair to limit the 10 per cent increase to claims in tort. The court therefore declared that "with effect from April 1, 2013 the proper level of general damages in all civil claims for (i) pain and suffering; (ii) loss of amenity; (iii) physical inconvenience and discomfort; (iv) social discredit; (v) mental distress; or (vi) loss of society of relatives, will be 10 per cent higher than previously, unless the claimant falls within s.44(6) of the 2012 Act. It therefore follows that, if the action now under appeal had been the subject of a judgment after April 1, 2013, then (unless the claimant had entered into a CFA before that date) the proper award of general damages would be 10 per cent higher than that agreed in this case, namely £22,000 rather than £20,000" (see paras 46, 50).

SIMMONS v CASTLE, [2012] EWCA Civ 1288, [2013] 1 W.L.R. 1239, Lord Judge, L.C.J., CA (Civ Div).

783. General damages–Cross-undertakings–Claim for damages arising out of cross-undertaking given in support of freezing order–Basis on which general damages assessed

The court was required to conduct an inquiry concerning a claim by the defendants (D) for damages arising out of a cross-undertaking in standard form given to the court on behalf of the first claimant (F) in respect of a freezing order. F was a company that had operated a bonded warehouse. D were its directors. The Revenue alleged that F had been involved in the evasion of excise duty and raised assessments of £5.965 million. When F did not pay, it was wound up and a liquidator appointed. The liquidator brought an action against D, claiming negligence and complicity in F's fraudulent activity (*Abbey Forwarding Ltd (In Liquidation) v Hone* [2010] EWHC 2029 (Ch)). The freezing order, which restrained D from dealing with F's assets, was obtained in support of that claim. It was discharged when the claim was dismissed. D sought general and aggravated damages together with compensation for losses arising under a number of heads, including loss of potential profits from business opportunities. Although F did not appear, the Revenue adopted its defence.

Held: Judgment for defendants in part. (1) A cross-undertaking did not create a cause of action in favour of the defendant against whom the injunction was made. Rather, it entitled him to apply for compensation. In assessing that compensation, the court had to proceed as if the cross-undertaking was a contract between the claimant and defendant whereby the claimant would not prevent the defendant from doing that which he was restrained from doing by the terms of the injunction, *F Hoffmann La Roche & Co AG v Secretary of State for Trade and Industry (Discovery)* Times, April 19, 1975, [1975] C.L.Y. 2612 followed. As to causation, remoteness and mitigation, the principles applicable to claims for damages for breach of contract were incorporated by analogy, but that did not necessarily mean that all the rules relating to such claims had to be adopted. The onus was on D to prove that their claimed losses would not have occurred but for the existence of the freezing order. They had to identify the loss caused by the injunction, as opposed to that caused by the underlying litigation. The loss had to be reasonably foreseeable within the terms of *Hadley v Baxendale* 156 E.R. 145, and an injunctor would only be liable for such damage as he could reasonably foresee would be caused by the injunction, either from general knowledge of the circumstances or from his knowledge of the particular circumstances. That left out of account losses resulting from events developing after the injunction had been granted: ordinary contractual principles suggested that such losses would not be recoverable. In the context of cross-undertakings, however, such an approach would be unduly narrow. For that reason, the Revenue accepted that losses caused by the injunction would be recoverable, even though they were not foreseeable when the injunction was granted, provided that express notice of the post-injunction special circumstances had been given prior to the loss being suffered in sufficient time for the parties to agree the terms of an appropriate variation. Without such notice, compensation would not be recoverable in respect of those losses. The court was not persuaded by H's argument that loss should be recoverable applying the principles relevant to awards of compensation for breach of fiduciary duty. It was not appropriate to depart from the conventional approach in *Hoffman La Roche*; *Lilly Icos LLC v 8PM Chemists Ltd* [2009] EWHC 1905 (Ch), [2010] F.S.R. 4, [2010] C.L.Y. 2000, *R. v Medicines Control Agency, Ex p. Smith & Nephew Pharmaceuticals Ltd* [1999] R.P.C. 705, [1999] C.L.Y. 440 and *Les Laboratoires Servier v Apotex Inc* [2008] EWHC 2347 (Ch), [2009] F.S.R. 3, [2009] C.L.Y. 2312 and *Apex Frozen Foods Ltd (In Liquidation) v Ali* [2007] EWHC 469 (Ch), [2007] 6 Costs L.R. 818, [2008] C.L.Y. 338 considered (see paras 21-50 of judgment). In respect of the specific heads of loss, the majority of H's claims failed on foreseeability and remoteness (paras 63, 69, 78, 81, 87, 93, 95, 102, 110, 112). (2) General damages for breach of contract were generally not recoverable in respect of injury to reputation, feelings or mental distress, except where the object of the contract was to provide pleasure, relaxation, peace of mind or freedom from molestation, *Johnson v Gore Wood & Co (No.1)* [2002] 2 A.C. 1, [2001] C.L.Y. 410 and *Watts v Morrow* [1991] 1 W.L.R. 1421, [1992] C.L.Y. 1548 followed. In such cases, damages would be payable if the fruit of the contract was not provided, or if the contrary result was procured instead. It was difficult to see how preventing an individual from dealing with his assets was anything other than molestation, or why the "contrary result" was not the consequence of a wrongly made order preventing such activity. In principle, there was no general bar to the award of general damages for emotional distress, though whether such an award would be made was fact-sensitive, *Al-Rawas v Pegasus Energy Ltd* [2008] EWHC 617 (QB), [2009] 1 All E.R. 346, [2009] C.L.Y. 467 considered. In many cases where injunctions were wrongly granted, no question of general damages, much less damages for emotional distress, would arise. However, it was most likely to do so where the court was concerned with search and seizure and freezing orders where the defendants were individuals. There was no principle that damages for emotional distress were inappropriate in commercial cases (paras 113-121). (3) There was no reason why aggravated damages should not be awarded in an appropriate case, but whether such damages ought to be awarded was likely to be acutely fact-sensitive (para.122).

ABBEY FORWARDING LTD (IN LIQUIDATION) v HONE, [2012] EWHC 3525 (Ch), [2013] Ch. 455, Judge Pelling Q.C., Ch D.

784. Liquidated damages–Breach of contract–Liquidated damages for repudiatory breach of contract–Whether claim crystallised before adjudication–Appropriateness of severing claim

The court was required to determine issues arising out of an adjudication between the claimant contractor (B) and the defendant sub-contractor (U). B had entered into a sub-contract with U whereby U agreed to install carpets at a department store. The contract provided that, if U completed the work after a designated completion date, it would be liable to pay liquidated and ascertained damages at prescribed rates. U later withdrew from the contract. B subsequently advanced a schedule of costs that it alleged had been incurred as a result of U's repudiatory breach of contract. At approximately 17:00 before a four-day weekend, B emailed U to claim liquidated damages in the sum of £20,000 per week from the day after the designated completion date until the date of that email, and continuing thereafter until other contractors had completed the contracted work. On the first working day after that email, B issued a notice of adjudication; it asked the adjudicator to decide that damages were payable in respect of its increased costs for completing the work, and to decide that U owed it £36,000 in liquidated damages. B explained that it claimed £36,000 in liquidated damages on the basis of the date that other contractors had completed the work. The adjudicator awarded B for both its alleged losses and for its liquidated damages. The issues were whether (i) the adjudicator had jurisdiction to decide B's claim for liquidated damages, or whether that claim had not crystallised before adjudication commenced; (ii) whether the adjudicator's decision could be severed so that B's claim for the increased costs of completing the work could be enforced if he did not have jurisdiction in respect of the liquidated damages claim.

Held: Judgment accordingly. (1) The reality was that the claim for liquidated damages pursued in adjudication was not the same claim as that intimated in the email. The adjudication claim was predicated on the work having already been completed by other contractors, whilst the email was predicated upon completion of work not having occurred. The adjudication claim turned out to be for £36,000, whereas the claim in the email was for nearly five times as much and continuing at the rate of £20,000 per week. Further, in the circumstances, the gap of five days between B advancing the claim in the email and the notice of adjudication was insufficient to give rise to an inference that, whatever the email meant, it was disputed. The email was sent knowingly by B after close of business immediately before a four-day weekend; B had to be taken by inference to have known that U would have had no opportunity to consider it or respond to it in working hours before the next working day, which was when the notice of adjudication was issued. Accordingly, the liquidated damages claim had not crystallised and the adjudicator had no jurisdiction in relation it (see paras 25, 27-28, 31 of judgment). (2) The instant case was one where severance could take place and where the adjudicator's decision in relation to that for which he did have jurisdiction, namely B's claim for the increased costs of completing the work, should be enforced (para.32).

BECK INTERIORS LTD v UK FLOORING CONTRACTORS LTD, [2012] EWHC 1808 (TCC), [2012] B.L.R. 417, Akenhead, J., QBD (TCC).

785. Measure of damages–Expert evidence–Claim in England for accident in France–Form of expert evidence–Whether by reference to law of forum or applicable law

[Civil Procedure Rules 1998 (SI 1998/3132) Pt 35; Regulation 864/2007 Art.1, Art.15.]

The court was required to determine an issue which arose during the course of case management before a master who was assessing damages in a negligence claim brought by the claimant (W) against the defendant insurance company (M). W, who was English, had had an accident whilst on holiday in France involving a car which was being driven by a man who was insured by M in France. W was seriously injured and upon his return to England issued a claim form naming M as defendant. Liability was accepted and judgment was entered for W and for damages to be assessed. During the course of a case management hearing W applied for permission to call a number of experts, as was customary in such English litigation. The master ordered the trial of whether the issue of which expert evidence the court should consider fell to be determined (i) by reference to the law of the forum (English law) on the basis that it was an issue of "evidence and procedure" within Regulation 864/2007 art.1.3 (Rome II) or (ii) by reference to the applicable law (French law) on the basis that that was an issue falling within art.15. M submitted that the "law" within the meaning of art.15(c) included the practices, conventions and guidelines regularly used by judges in assessing damages in the courts of the state whose laws was the applicable law. The only way in which the legislative purposes of Rome II would be achieved was by rejecting the English panolpy of experts and permitting only a single expert of the kind customarily appointed by French courts, so as to arrive at a figure that would actually be awarded in France. M argued that any other interpretation would give undue weight to the law of a claimant's domicile.

Held: Preliminary issue determined. There was no dispute between the parties that CPR Pt 35 applied, on the footing that the rules as to expert evidence it contained were plainly matters of procedure. Rule 35 did not provide for the court to give permission to a single expert to convey to the opinions of other experts whom he had consulted on matters which were not within his expertise. There was no evidence before the court as to what level of damages would be awarded by a French court if the French court were seised of the case. Without such evidence there were no means by which the instant court could endeavour to reflect the level of damages. The instant court was not required to put itself in the position of a French court and decide the case as that court would have, or to adopt new procedures. It was clear that the questions of what expert evidence the court should order and in particular whether or not there should be one or more experts pursuant to r.35 fell to be determined by reference to the law of the forum (English law), on the basis that that was an issue of "evidence and procedure" within art.1.3, Dicey, Morris & Collins; *The Conflict of Laws, 15th Edition, (*Sweet & Maxwell, 2012*)* paras 7-022, 7-050, 34-036, 34-056 and Andrew Dickinson; *The Rome II Regulations: The Law Applicable to Non-contractual Obligations (Oxford 2008),* paras 3.39, 14.19, 14.34, 14.61 considered, (see paras 20-22, 43-45 of judgment).

WALL v MUTUELLE DE POITIERS ASSURANCES, [2013] EWHC 53 (QB), [2013] 1 W.L.R. 3890, Tugendhat, J., QBD.

786. Measure of damages–Injury to feelings–Lifting wheelchair user into restaurant against his wishes–Failure to offer ramp for access–Attitude of restaurant owner to proceedings

[Equality Act 2010 (c.15) s.29.]

The court was required to assess the damages payable to the claimant customer (H) under the Equality Act 2010 s.29 following judgment against the defendant restaurant owner (K) for his failure to make reasonable adjustments in the provision of access to his restaurant. H was a wheelchair user and had also developed spondylosis and stomach cancer. He had a strong sense of independence and let no one but his wife (W) touch his wheelchair, but seldom went out any longer. H and W went to K's restaurant for an anniversary meal, having telephoned in advance to ensure there was wheelchair access. H was assured that there was. There was a step up into the restaurant and the manager insisted on helping H by lifting the wheelchair, with another member of staff and W. H protested as he understood there was a portable ramp available. He found the experience undignified and embarrassing. H and W were so distressed by what happened that they did not stay to eat. H subsequently wrote several letters to the restaurant, primarily seeking to ensure that a ramp was provided for disabled customers in future. His only reply was a telephone call from a representative of the restaurant saying that he accepted that the service had been unacceptable. In a later telephone call the restaurant's representative suggested that the incident had not happened. H felt angry, insulted and frustrated at the incident and his subsequent treatment, in particular by (i) the restaurant's failure to engage in dialogue with a view to making good what had happened, especially by the provision of a ramp; (ii) K's description of him in the defence as a "racist and a conman"; (iii) the suggestion that the incident never took place.

Held: Damages assessed. (1) In assessing the appropriate level of damages for the unlawful discrimination suffered by H, the court had regard to the JSB Guidelines, Ch.4, Psychiatric and Psychological Damage, but bore in mind that H had not suffered psychiatric injury in the sense meant by the Guidelines so that that band was not strictly applicable. It further took into account the fact that H was still "consumed" by what had happened, a year after the incident. The instant case came within the lowest of the three broad bands of compensation established for injury to feelings by *Vento v Chief Constable of West Yorkshire* [2002] EWCA Civ 1871, [2003] I.C.R. 318, [2003] C.L.Y. 1306. It was envisaged that awards in that band would be between £500 to £6,000, for situations such as where the act of discrimination was "an isolated or one off occurrence", *Vento* followed and *Da'Bell v National Society for the Prevention of Cruelty to Children (NSPCC)* [2010] I.R.L.R. 19, [2010] C.L.Y. 1042 applied. The court balanced the depth of H's reaction with the general policy as to damages in other cases. On the facts, the appropriate award was £3,000, *Vento,*

Da'Bell, Royal Bank of Scotland Group Plc v Allen [2009] EWCA Civ 1213, (2010) 112 B.M.L.R. 30, [2010] C.L.Y. 1719, *Milner v Carnival Plc (t/a Cunard)* [2010] EWCA Civ 389, [2010] 3 All E.R. 701, [2010] C.L.Y. 829, *Ross v Ryanair Ltd* [2004] EWCA Civ 1751, [2005] 1 W.L.R. 2447, [2005] C.L.Y. 249, *Martins v Choudhary* [2007] EWCA Civ 1379, [2008] 1 W.L.R. 617, [2008] C.L.Y. 891, Langden v Webster and Shaban v Wharfe considered. (2) The sum of £500 was added by way of aggravated damages for the insulting and abusive way in which K responded to the claim and failed to engage with H or his representatives in relation to the incident.

HOSEGOOD v KHALID (T/A SALT & PEPPER VILLAGE) [2012] Eq. L.R. 1114, Deputy District Judge Whybrow, CC (Scunthorpe).

787. Measure of damages–Valuation–Negligent valuation of shopping centre–Assessment of loss–Judge not confined to experts' figures on quantum

The appellant firm of surveyors (D) appealed against a judgment ([2011] EWHC 2336 (Comm), 139 Con. L.R. 125, [2012] C.L.Y. 2305 awarding damages against it for the negligent valuation of a shopping centre. The first respondent (C) was a trustee of the second respondent (M), a property investment company. C and M retained D to advise them in relation to the acquisition of the shopping centre. C acquired the lease of the centre for £62.85 million as trustee of the investment vehicle through which individual investors invested on the basis of information provided by M. Before the acquisition, D prepared a valuation report giving the open market value of the development as £48.15 million, or £62.85 million with the benefit of enterprise zone allowances. The development was not a commercial success. C brought proceedings, arguing that D had given negligent advice overstating the commercial value and prospects of the centre. A key element of its case was that D had negligently failed to prepare an assessment of the development's likely ability to attract consumer spending (a CACI report). It was held at first instance that the correct market value at the relevant time would have been £44.8 million with the benefit of the enterprise zone allowance, as contrasted with D's figure of £62.85 million. That conclusion was reached on the judge's finding that a CACI report was an essential component of a competent valuation, and on his acceptance of evidence given by an expert (B) that a ground floor rental figure of £19 psf was realistic. The difference between the two valuation figures, namely £18.05 million, was awarded by way of damages. D contended that (1) B's evidence was based entirely on the evidence of another expert (P), which the judge had rejected; accordingly, there was no proper basis for the judge's conclusion as to the correct valuation which would have been given by a competent valuer, and therefore no established loss; (2) the judge had erred in failing to require C to give credit for the tax benefits received by investors as a result of the purchase of the shopping centre.

Held: Appeal allowed in part. (Lloyd LJ. dissenting on the issue of whether loss had been established) (1) It was for the judge to decide whether B's support for the £19 psf figure was to be relied upon and he had made that decision in C's favour. He had concluded that B was an impressive witness, while remarking upon the need to approach his evidence with caution. B's evidence had not been damaged by D's demolition of P's evidence to such an extent that no foundation remained upon which the judge could reasonably and rationally base his conclusion. While a judge had to have a reasoned or rational basis for a decision, he was not confined to the figures contended for by the experts. Indeed, the figure arrived at by a judge in a valuation case might well lie somewhere in between two figures proposed by opposing experts. Moreover, having regard to the nature of quantum disputes, a judge would often find himself having to do the best he could. It was not to be expected that pinpoint accuracy might be achieved in valuation matters. In order to establish negligence, it had to be shown both that the valuer failed to exercise reasonable skill and care and that the result was outside the permissible range or bracket. Depending on the property in question, margins of error might be of some degree of magnitude. There was no error in the judge's analysis or in his application of the relevant principles in the instant case. Given the inherent imprecision in the nature of any valuation exercise, there would have to be cogent reasons for interfering with the judge's conclusion. The judge had been entitled to conclude that D was negligent in failing to obtain a CACI report before undertaking the valuation (see paras 41, 43 of judgment). (2) It was necessary to look at the market value of the whole transaction in order to assess the loss actually suffered, *Ford v White & Co* [1964] 1 W.L.R. 885, [1964] C.L.Y. 3470 considered. On that approach, it would be unreal to ignore the entitlement of the investors to tax credits which in practical terms reduced the purchase price. Since tax considerations were part and parcel of the scheme in the instant case, they were relevant in calculating damages, *British Transport Commission v Gourley* [1956] A.C. 185, [1955] C.L.Y. 724 followed. The correct approach was to deduct tax relief from both the £62.85 million and £44.8 million figures, which reduced the sum awarded in damages to £11,861,738. That measure was fair and realistic, as it involved both sides of the equation and best reflected the actual losses suffered by investors. The appeal was therefore allowed to that extent (paras 55-56, 58-59, 61, 68).

CAPITA ALTERNATIVE FUND SERVICES (GUERNSEY LTD) (FORMERLY ROYAL & SUNALLIANCE TRUST (CHANNEL ISLANDS) LTD) v DRIVERS JONAS (A FIRM), [2012] EWCA Civ 1417, [2013] 1 E.G.L.R. 119, Lloyd, L.J., CA (Civ Div).

788. Reinstatement–Measure of damages–Restaurant business making insurance claim following damage caused by negligence of third party–Insurer seeking to recover sums paid on claim–Reasonableness of sums claimed

The claimants (B, V and L) claimed damages for losses arising from flooding of their restaurant caused by the admitted negligence of the defendant construction company (X). B was a company in liquidation; V and L were its directors. B had engaged X to demolish a public house that it had operated and to construct a new building in its place, comprising a ground-floor bar and a basement restaurant. When X completed the shell of the basement and ground floor, B took charge of the fitting-out works, which were largely completed by December 10, 2006. There was some dispute about the cost of those works, but the available, and possibly incomplete, documentation put it at around £279,229. On December 11, the basement was flooded as a result of the negligence of Thames Water, which paid B just over £255,000 in compensation. Some remedial work was carried out, but in January 2007 the basement flooded again. On that occasion, the flooding was the result of X's negligence. X did not dispute liability. B re-fitted the basement and the restaurant opened for business in mid-October 2007. Until December the restaurant was quite successful, but in the first half of 2008 its takings began to decline. There were problems with foul smells which, in mid-2008, were traced to a soil vent pipe which one of X's contractors had punctured. In June 2008, B closed the restaurant. It made an insurance claim of just under £400,000 for the material damage caused by the flood, and also claimed loss of profits. Its insurers paid £355,070 for the material damage, plus £240,905 for loss of profits. The central claim before the court was a subrogated claim, by which B's insurers sought to recover from X the monies it had paid to B. The issue was whether the sums claimed were reasonable.

Held: Damages assessed. (1) A claimant in B's position was entitled to recover the reasonable costs of reinstatement. Where the reinstatement works were complete by the time of trial, the actual cost of the works would almost always be the starting point in assessing what was reasonable. If a sum had been assessed as reasonable by an experienced loss adjuster, it would ordinarily take good evidence to demonstrate that it was not in fact reasonable. However, everything turned on the facts of the case. In respect of the second fit-out, B's claim was grossly exaggerated and had not been properly investigated by the insurer. There was no schedule of works and no record of the work carried out, and it was therefore impossible to say with certainty what had, and had not, been done. The invoices were inadequate, unreliable and impossible to analyse retrospectively: they failed to identify what work was the subject of the claim, did not identify the instructions pursuant to which the work had been carried out, and contained nothing to indicate to the way in which the sums claimed might be assessed. Moreover, the experts agreed that many of the invoices did not relate to remedial works properly undertaken. There was no evidence as to how payment for the work had been assessed, there had been no checks that work invoiced for had actually been done, and there was no proper record of invoices having been paid. The experts agreed that the £400,000 claimed by B was at least £100,000 too much, but alarm bells should have been ringing for the insurer much sooner. The cost of the original fit-out works for two floors was, on the balance of probabilities, less than £300,000. On that basis alone, the £400,000 claimed for the basement should have looked much too high. There was no evidence to justify the sizeable nature of the discrepancies, the loss adjuster had not consulted a quantity surveyor, and there had been no forensic investigation of the claim. Both the claim and its adjustment were fundamentally flawed. The proper quantum of the subrogated claims for material damage was £136,688.89 (see paras 13, 23, 29-32, 45, 48-56, 58, 61-62, 65, 71-72, 76-77, 92, 188-189, 296 of judgment). (2) B's claim for £240,905 loss of profits assumed that the restaurant would have been profitable immediately. Since the restaurant was a new business, that assumption was inappropriate. The claim appeared to calculate a loss of profit caused by both the first and the second floods, with an arbitrary reduction for the first flood. That approach was not legitimate, giving rise to the risk that X was being made liable for matters that were not its responsibility. Finally, the figures underpinning the claim did not come from the restaurant's own trading figures, but were instead extrapolated from those of a comparator. The actual figures were not even used for the purposes of comparison, which was surprising and erroneous. The experts agreed that where actual profit and loss figures were available, they ought to form the starting point for any calculation for loss of profit, unless there were good reasons for disregarding them. None of the reasons given by B justified disregarding its actual profits. On B's actual profit and loss figures, the appropriate quantum of the loss of profits claim was £20,779 (paras 190-191, 194-195, 200-203, 206, 229 297).

BRIT INNS LTD (IN LIQUIDATION) v BDW TRADING LTD; BARBER v BDW TRADING LTD, [2012] EWHC 2143 (TCC), 145 Con. L.R. 181, Coulson, J., QBD (TCC).

DEFAMATION

789. Defamation–Norwich Pharmacal orders–Order to reveal identities of makers of alleged defamatory statements–Application of defence of qualified privilege

The applicant (N) applied for a Norwich Pharmacal order against the first respondent (H). N was a consultant orthopaedic and spinal surgeon at a hospital in London. H was the chair of a research ethics committee (REC). N had carried out operations on children using a new magnetic growth rod which had received a CE mark in Germany, which meant that N had the right to implant them in patients so long as he did not do so as part of a patient study. N's application to the REC for permission to carry out a patient study into the use of magnetic growth rods was rejected. H was informed by some clinicians at the hospital about their concerns as to N's use of magnetic rods. N's case was that he had been defamed by the clinicians who had communicated with H, resulting in a letter being written by the director (W) of the National Research Ethics Service to the joint medical directors of the hospital trust. N alleged that the statement in the letter that there was a belief that N's "study was progressing and further that it was resulting in poor clinical outcomes for children" was defamatory and meant that he was carrying out an unapproved research study causing harm to children. N sought a *Norwich Pharmacal* order to find out the identity of the clinicians who had spoken to H so that he could bring proceedings against them for defamation.

Held: Application refused. There were two components to the statement in W's letter. The first was that N was carrying out an unapproved study. The court accepted that a statement that the study was progressing would arguably be defamatory of N, albeit subject to a defence of qualified privilege. The suggestion, if true, was rightly regarded by W as a very serious matter in circumstances where permission to carry out such a study had been expressly refused on ethical grounds. However, it was apparent from the facts that no such statement was made to H. She was merely told that N was using magnetic rods on his patients. It was H's own conclusion, from that information, that N was going ahead with the study for which ethics permission had been refused, but nobody actually said that to her. There was therefore no possibility of a successful action for defamation against those clinicians who spoke to H based on a statement to the effect that N was going ahead with his study. The second component of the sentence in W's letter was the reference to poor clinical outcomes for the children treated with magnetic rods. It was doubtful whether that statement could on its own be defamatory of N. Even assuming that what was said was defamatory, the defence of qualified privilege applied and there was no arguable case of malice. N's application for Norwich Pharmacal relief failed at the first hurdle, *Adam v Ward* [1917] A.C. 309 and *Horrocks v Lowe* [1975] A.C. 135, [1974] C.L.Y. 2144 applied (see paras 38-48 of judgment).

NOORDEEN v HILL, [2012] EWHC 2847 (QB), (2013) 129 B.M.L.R. 79, Males, J., QBD.

790. Defamation Act 2013 (26)

This Act amends the law of defamation.

This Act received Royal Assent on April 25, 2013.

791. Libel–Absolute privilege–Witness statements subject to absolute privilege–Subject matter of proceedings

The appellant solicitor-advocate (X) appealed against a decision dismissing his claim for libel against the respondent firm of solicitors (M). X had been employed as a solicitor by M before setting up his own practice. X subsequently acted against M in litigation brought by one of M's former clients (B), for whom he had also acted whilst employed by M. M wrote X several letters, which were also copied to the court, raising issues of X's professional misconduct in representing B, and X issued a harassment claim. X also brought a claim in libel complaining of 21 allegedly defamatory publications by M, which he alleged wrongly questioned his professional competence and conduct. However the libel claim was issued outside the limitation period for all but the last two publications (document 20 and document 21). Document 20 repeated some of the allegations against X which had been the subject of the harassment proceedings including that he was conducting a personal vendetta against M and that he was under investigation by the Solicitors Regulation Authority. Document 21 alleged that X had deliberately given a wrong address for service. The trial judge held that the first 19 publications were statute barred and that all 21 publications were covered by absolute privilege. X was granted permission to appeal on the issue of absolute privilege only. X submitted that the trial judge misstated and therefore misapplied the *Smeaton v Butcher (No.1)* [2000] E.M.L.R. 985, [2000] C.L.Y. 333 principles when he found that the documents had no reference at all to the proceedings and that the correct principle was "no reference at all to the subject matter of the proceedings".

Held: Appeal dismissed. (1) The test for absolute privilege was not one of relevance, but reference, to the proceedings in question, *Smeaton* and *Munster v Lamb* (1883) 11 Q.B.D. 588 applied. It was not enough for the defamatory language to be irrelevant to the matter in hand for it to fall outside the privilege, it had to have no reference at all to the subject-matter of the proceedings. The rule of absolute privilege as it affected witnesses was extended to cover statements made by potential witnesses in preparing for a trial, *Watson v McEwan* [1905] A.C. 480 applied. What was said by a witness outside his status or character as a witness would not be covered by the privilege. Document 20 was a witness statement and therefore prima facie within the ambit of the principles of absolute privilege. The burden of document 20 was to address the complaint of the paying party, M, that X, who was the receiving party's solicitor, had a conflict of interest which was relevant to the assessment of costs. However weak the relevance asserted, it was difficult to say that the document as a whole had no reference to the subject-matter of the costs proceedings in play. It plainly did (see paras 29-31, 46-50 of judgment). (2) Although the complaint in document 21 might indeed be defamatory, there could be no possible argument that it had no reference to the proceedings. The facts were disputed but that was not the point. The document as a whole plainly addressed the application to set aside a default costs certificate and the complaint about X's address for service, although in one sense an unnecessary insult, if untrue, was relevant and referred to the ongoing proceedings (paras 51-53).

IQBAL v MANSOOR; *sub nom.* IQBAL v DEAN MANSON SOLICITORS, [2013] EWCA Civ 149, [2013] C.P. Rep. 27, Sir Terence Etherton (Chancellor), CA (Civ Div).

792. Libel–Abuse of process–Internet blogs criticising university–Ability of university to bring libel action–Appropriateness of striking out as abuse of process

The appellant (D) appealed against a district judge's decision that the respondent university's libel action should not be struck out. D had published internet blogs criticising the university, in particular the conduct of its Vice Chancellor and Deputy Vice Chancellor (X). The university brought a libel action against him. D applied to strike out the claim but the judge refused, deciding that the university could bring the claim and that it had a reasonable prospect of successfully establishing that there had been a real and substantial tort. The issues were whether (i) the university could sue D for libel; (ii) the proceedings should be struck out as an abuse of process because there was no real or substantial tort.

Held: Appeal allowed. (1) Whilst universities received large sums of public money and had to comply with various statutory provisions, that did not equate them with central or local government who were prevented from suing for libel, *Derbyshire CC v Times Newspapers Ltd* [1993] A.C. 534, [1993] C.L.Y. 2581 distinguished and Hong Kong Polytechnic University v Next Magazine Publishing Ltd [1997] 7 HKPLR 286 applied. If it was decided that universities should not have the right to sue for libel as a matter of public policy, that could only be implemented by the legislature, or perhaps the Supreme Court. Accordingly, the university could sue D for libel (see paras 4-5 of judgment). (2) The university was undoubtedly referred to in various contexts. However, a persistent theme was the focus upon X. Any adverse comments about the university were, in context, incidental to the attacks made upon them. Whilst it was true that the fact that the libellous allegations reflected upon individual staff members did not mean that the university itself could not also be defamed by the same words, it was wholly unreal and an abuse of the court's process for the proceedings to continue on the basis that the only claimant was the university, when the conduct to be examined in any plea of justification or fair comment would be X's. There was no real and substantial tort, so far as the university was concerned, and it was not right that the proceedings should be allowed to continue purely so that the university could obtain an injunction to stifle criticism of X, *Jameel v Dow Jones & Co Inc* [2005] EWCA Civ 75, [2005] Q.B. 946, [2005] C.L.Y. 974 applied. The litigation was not worth pursuing if its sole objective was to protect the reputation of the university, any damage to which was purely incidental, or to obtain an injunction to prevent bloggers criticising X, since they were not parties, *Cammish v Hughes* [2012] EWCA Civ 1655, [2013] E.M.L.R. 13 applied. The action was struck out (paras 10-11, 23-24).

DUKE v UNIVERSITY OF SALFORD, [2013] EWHC 196 (QB), [2013] E.L.R. 259, Eady, J., QBD.

793. Libel–Blogs–Whether internet platform provider regarded as publisher–Failure to remove information after complaint–Inference of responsibility for continued publication

[Defamation Act 1996 (c.31) s.1.]

The appellant (T) appealed against a decision ([2012] EWHC 449 (QB), [2012] E.M.L.R. 24, [2012] C.L.Y. 870) to decline jurisdiction in his claim against the respondent corporation (G) and to set aside an order for service of proceedings on G out of the jurisdiction. G had a platform that allowed any internet user to create an independent blog. T complained to G that one of the blogs contained defamatory comments about him. The complaint reached G two months after the comments had been posted. Approximately one month later G passed the complaint to the blogger with a request to remove the comments, which he did three days later. T issued a libel claim against G. G successfully appealed against the grant of permission to serve proceedings on it out of the jurisdiction. The judge found that three of the comments complained of were arguably defamatory, but that on common law principles G had not published them. He held that, if G had been a publisher, the three conditions for a defence under the Defamation Act 1996 s.1 were satisfied as G did not itself issue material to the public, had taken reasonable care in relation to T's complaint and had not known, or had reason to believe, that it had done anything to cause or contribute to the publication. The judge also held that the period between notification of the complaint and removal of the comments was so short that any liability was so trivial that maintenance of the proceedings was not justified. The issues were whether (i) there was an arguable case that G was a publisher of the comments; (ii) if it was a publisher, it would have an unassailable defence under s.1 of the Act; (iii) any potential liability was so trivial as not to justify the maintenance of the proceedings.

Held: Appeal dismissed. (1) The judge had been wrong to regard G's role as purely passive and to attach the significance he did to the absence of any positive steps by G in relation to continued publication of the comments. G facilitated publication of the blogs, but its involvement was not such as to make it a primary publisher. It was doubtful that, prior to notification of the complaint, G could be considered to be a secondary publisher, facilitating publication in a manner analogous to a distributor, because it could not be said to have known, or ought reasonably to have known, of the comments. However, after notification additional considerations arose. The provision of a platform for the blogs was equivalent to the provision of a notice board. G provided tools to enable the blogger to design the layout of his part of the notice board, made the notice board available on terms of its own choice and could readily remove or block access to any notice that did not comply with those terms. In those circumstances, if G allowed defamatory material to remain after it had been notified, it might be inferred to have associated itself with, or to have made itself responsible for, the continued presence of the material and thereby to have become a publisher of the material, *Byrne v Deane* [1937] 1 K.B. 818 applied. Such an inference could not properly be drawn until G had had a reasonable time within which to remove the comments. It was open to argument that the time taken to respond was sufficiently long to leave room for an inference adverse to G on *Byrne* principles. Accordingly, there was an arguable case that G was a publisher of the comments (see paras 24-27, 33-35 of judgment). (2) There was no reason to disagree with the judge's conclusion on the satisfaction of the conditions in s.(1)(a) and (b), but the considerations leading to a conclusion that G arguably had become a publisher under the principles in *Byrne* also led to the conclusion that following notification it knew or had reason to believe that what it did caused or contributed to continued publication and that the condition in s.1(c) was not satisfied (para.44). (3) It was highly improbable that any significant number of readers would have accessed the comments after

G was notified and prior to removal. The judge was right to consider that any damage to T's reputation during that period would have been trivial (para.50).

TAMIZ v GOOGLE INC, [2013] EWCA Civ 68, [2013] 1 W.L.R. 2151, Lord Dyson (M.R.), CA (Civ Div).

794. Libel–Compensation–Approach to assessment of compensation–Analytical approach giving breakdown of award

In joined cases arising out of libel proceedings, the appellants (M and MGN) appealed against awards of compensation made in favour of the respondents (C and K). C was a well-known international cricketer; M was the ex-chairman of the Indian Premier League. M published a message on Twitter which referred to C being involved in match-fixing. An article repeating the allegation was subsequently published on a cricketing website, whereupon C sued for libel. C reached settlement with the cricketing website but M took the case to trial on a plea of justification. The judge awarded C £15,000 to reflect one aspect of aggravation, namely the conduct of M's former counsel during the trial. The total sum awarded was £90,000. In the other case, MGN was sued for libel by K, who was the father of the child known in the media as "Baby P". MGN published a newspaper article about Baby P's mother, which stated that K was a sex offender who had been convicted of raping a 14-year-old girl. The statements were completely untrue. MGN apologised promptly and made an unqualified offer of amends. The judge assessed compensation after the parties failed to agree on an appropriate figure. He identified a starting point of £150,000 and reduced it by 50 per cent to take account of all the mitigating factors. M argued that the sum awarded to C was disproportionate and excessive in the light of the relatively narrow scope of the original publication. He further submitted that there was a reduced need for an element of vindication in an award once a reasoned judgment vindicating the claimant had been promulgated at the conclusion of a trial. He also argued that the judge should have adopted a more analytical reasoning process, similar to that in *Vento v Chief Constable of West Yorkshire* [2002] EWCA Civ 1871, [2003] I.C.R. 318, [2003] C.L.Y. 1306, and should have given a more detailed breakdown of the award. MGN argued that the judge had not given sufficient consideration to the fact that K was anonymous throughout the currency of the libel.

Held: Appeals allowed in part. (1) Although only a small number of people would have read M's original message on Twitter, as a consequence of modern technology and communication systems, allegations such as the ones concerning C had the capacity to "percolate" more widely and more quickly than ever before. The "percolation" phenomenon was a legitimate factor to be taken into account in the assessment of damages, *Slipper v BBC* [1991] 1 Q.B. 283, [1991] C.L.Y. 2328 and *Ley v Hamilton* (1935) 153 L.T. 384 considered (see paras 26-27 of judgment). (2) The principle which M sought to argue for, namely that damages should always be less following a trial by a judge alone than after the verdict of a jury, on the basis that the judge would provide a reasoned judgment which, if favourable to the claimant, would vindicate him, could not be accepted, *Associated Newspapers Ltd v Dingle* [1964] A.C. 371, [1962] C.L.Y. 1741 and *Purnell v BusinessF1 Magazine Ltd* [2007] EWCA Civ 744, [2008] 1 W.L.R. 1, [2008] C.L.Y. 900 considered. Most lay observers would be unlikely to read a detailed judgment and would be more interested to find out what sum the court, whether judge or jury, had awarded the claimant. Given the wholesale attack on C's reputation in the course of the trial, it was safe to assume that such a person would only be convinced by an award of some magnitude (paras 30-31). (3) In *Vento* the court identified three broad bands of compensation for injury to feelings in the context of sex and race discrimination in the employment field. The process of determining compensation in defamation cases was well established, and was multi-layered, in the vast majority of cases going well beyond the assessment of compensation for injury to feelings arising in discrimination cases. Adopting a comparatively analytical approach in libel cases would give rise to practical difficulties. The combination of circumstances and the different features which fell for consideration in libel claims varied enormously, and did not lend themselves to straightforward categorisation, *Vento* considered (paras 35-38). (4) The sum awarded to C was proportionate to the seriousness of the allegation and its direct impact on C, and would serve to vindicate his reputation (para.41). (5) The judge, in assessing K's compensation, had attached too much importance to the large circulation and readership figures for MGN's newspaper. The very limited nature and extent of publication as it might have impacted on K's reputation, given that he was and remained anonymous, was not given sufficient focus. The appropriate starting point was £100,000, which would be reduced by 50 per cent to allow for the offer of amends procedure adopted by MGN, resulting in an award of £50,000 (paras 47-50).

CAIRNS v MODI; KC v MGN LTD; *sub nom.* C v MGN LTD, [2012] EWCA Civ 1382, [2013] 1 W.L.R. 1015, Lord Judge, L.C.J., CA (Civ Div).

795. Libel–Defamatory meaning–Documents sent anonymously–Whether words complained of capable of bearing defamatory meaning–Real and substantial tort remaining

The appellant (H) appealed against a judge's refusal to order the dismissal of defamation proceedings brought by the respondent (C) without a trial. H owned companies that sought planning permission for the construction of two power plants in South Wales. C, a businessman and a resident of South Wales, was the chairman of a local action group opposed to that application. A bundle of documents sent anonymously to a number of recipients, contained a handwritten message which read ".... Mr Cammish dissolved 15 companies = not able to run them..". The precise number of recipients of the bundle was unclear, but it was known to have been sent to six, who included the chair of a local residents' group and two planning inspectors. The statement caused distress and inconvenience to C. H was forced to admit authorship in his defence, but did not do so before the service of his defence. H denied that the publication was defamatory, and asserted that the words meant no more than that C was unsuitable to be a leader of an action group. Both parties asked the judge to determine the meaning of the statement, not just the meaning that it was capable of bearing. The judge found that the meaning included the assertion that C was seriously incompetent in business, and he declined to strike out the claim. H submitted that the words were comment which was based on accurate facts, and he was simply expressing a view based on data obtained from Companies House which was included in the bundle of documents.

Held: Appeal allowed. It was unreasonable to infer from the fact that C was a former director of dissolved companies that he was unfit to run them. The fact that a company was dissolved did not mean that its demise was the result of misconduct or mismanagement by the directors or any one of them. C had provided an explanation for the number of dissolved companies in a witness statement and that had not been challenged by H (see paras 12-14 of judgment). The determination of meaning did not depend solely on the documents, but on an evaluation of the words in their context. In the circumstances, the Court of Appeal would not depart from the judge's assessment of the meaning, unless it was clear that some other meaning applied. The fact that the bundle was sent anonymously indicated that the sender wanted the reader to draw from the fact that the companies had been dissolved an adverse inference about C's leadership role in the action group from his business experience. To accept that the criticism of C's ability was limited to the companies that he had dissolved would have deprived the words of all meaning in the context of their use, and the words could not be so limited. Accordingly, the instant court agreed with the judge's assessment of the meaning of the words, *Jeynes v News Magazines Ltd* [2008] EWCA Civ 130 applied (paras 31-32, 34). The words were defamatory, since the imputation was that C was a seriously incompetent businessman and the words denigrated or tended to denigrate him in the way of his business. The words complained of reached the requisite threshold of seriousness: they were capable of affecting C's livelihood. Reputation was important to a businessman as he needed to persuade others to trust that he would completely perform commitments entered into in the course of business. The words were clearly comment and were H's view as to what could be deduced from the Companies House search. It was clear from the judge's meaning that the words, involving as they did a conclusion as to serious incompetence, entailed not facts but a value judgment (paras 35, 37, 40-41, 45). On the question of whether the proceedings should continue, the test was whether there remained a real and substantial tort within the jurisdiction, *Jameel v Dow Jones & Co Inc* [2005] EWCA Civ 75, [2005] Q.B. 946, [2005] C.L.Y. 974 applied. Accordingly, since it had been established that the dissolution of the companies had nothing to do with C's business abilities, there was now no real and substantial tort to be tried. However, the instant court was of the view that an order for dismissal on its own did not reflect the seriousness of what had happened, and it made an order for the payment of costs as a condition of the summary dismissal of the proceedings, as a further protection and vindication to C, who had been fully justified in bringing the proceedings. H was ordered to pay C's costs of and incidental to the proceedings down to and including the date of service of the defence (paras 52, 61-64).

CAMMISH v HUGHES, [2012] EWCA Civ 1655, [2013] E.M.L.R. 13, Arden, L.J., CA (Civ Div).

796. Libel–Honest comment–MPs' expenses scandal–Whether statements in publications fact or comment

The appellants (L) were a Member of Parliament and his campaign agent. They appealed against a decision ([2011] EWHC 3197 (QB)) that they were guilty of libel against the respondent former MP (W). W had lost his seat to L in 2010, following a period when it had been widely reported in the national press that large numbers of MPs had made unlawful expenses claims, breached the parliamentary rules, or made claims which, although within the rules, were essentially improper. During the run-up to the general election, L had distributed two pieces of campaign literature, the first containing a general reference to "the MPs' expenses scandal" and the second referring to "the scandal of MPs abusing their expenses". The first publication referred to W's own "scandalous expenses claims" and both criticised his claim of £70,000 for a home which was 60 miles away from his constituents, and his claim for re-decorating his garage. L relied on the defence of honest comment, on the basis that the "scandal" referred to was confined to the criticism that W had claimed £70,000 for a home that was 60 miles from his constituency, not that his claims constituted a breach of any rules. The judge indicated that it was difficult to follow how a reasonable reader in the circumstances specified in *Jeynes v News Magazines Ltd* [2008] EWCA Civ 130 could be expected to understand the "scandal" in question to be confined to the mere fact that W made a claim in respect of a mortgage and decoration. He found that the scandal referred to in each publication would reasonably be understood as meaning, and did mean, that W was himself guilty of abuse of the parliamentary rules for his own financial advantage and that those were plainly statements of fact. L submitted that the "scandal" comments were clear expressions of opinion, based on non-defamatory facts and that the references to "the MPs' expenses scandal" and "the scandal of MPs abusing their expenses" were comments about the system as a whole, not about W. They argued that there had been no suggestion that W's expenses claims were unlawful, in breach of the rules, or otherwise improper.

Held: Appeal allowed. (Richards L.J. dissenting) Caution had to be exercised in disturbing findings of fact by judges at first instance in defamation cases. However, the meaning of the words complained of was quite simple: "[W] has claimed nearly £70,000 from the taxpayer for a family home that is 60 miles from Eastbourne (fact). That is a scandal (comment)". There was no statement, express or implied, to be identified in the publications to the effect that W had either broken the law or the parliamentary rules, or had been required to repay sums previously claimed. The reasonable reader would be well aware that there had been a significant criticism of the system of parliamentary expenses and that some MPs might have broken the law or the parliamentary rules, or might merely have made substantial claims strictly within the rules of the criticised system. However, all that had been stated was what W had claimed and the writers' view that that was "a scandal" or "scandalous". The conduct upon which comment was advanced had been clearly identified, *Joseph v Spiller* [2010] UKSC 53, [2011] 1 A.C. 852, [2011] C.L.Y. 865 applied, *Myerson v Smith's Weekly Publishing Co Ltd*considered. The judge had mischaracterised the matter: there was no allegation of scandal beyond the stated facts and the fact that there was thought to be a wider "scandal" did not alter that position. Those who thought that some claims to expenses, even within the law and the rules, were "scandalous" would not have strayed beyond comment if they identified the precise claims made and said that, in their view, they were scandalous. Deciding the matter in accordance with common sense and first impression, the matters complained of were comment, *Jeynes* and *Slim v Daily Telegraph* [1968] 2 Q.B. 157, [1968] C.L.Y. 2231 applied (see paras 50-61 of judgment).

WATERSON v LLOYD, [2013] EWCA Civ 136, [2013] E.M.L.R. 17, Laws, L.J., CA (Civ Div).

797. Libel–Justification–Inaccurate specific allegations

The appellant financier (R) appealed against a judgment ([2012] EWHC 177 (QB)) upholding the justification defence of the defendant newspaper (N) to R's claim for damages for libel. N had published a story about a trip to Russia undertaken by R and his friend (M), the European Union Trade Commissioner. N had alleged that R had brought M's reputation into disrepute by securing M's attendance at a dinner with a Russian oligarch (D) who controlled a Russian aluminium producing company, in which R had shares. In fact M had not attended the dinner. After the dinner, D had flown R and M to visit aluminium smelters in Siberia. Despite the facts of M's attendance at the dinner being inaccurate, the judge below had upheld a defence of justification on the basis of the trip to Siberia, during which it was alleged to be likely that M may have inappropriately discussed EU aluminium tariffs with D. R contended that the judge's second meaning, which was a general charge that R had sought to impress D with his friendship with M, had no sting when compared to the first charge in relation to the dinner, which it was common ground had been based on inaccurate facts.

Held: Appeal dismissed. (Sir David Eady dissenting over the need for a fifth principle). Where a general charge was employed to justify a specific allegation not justifiable on its own, a "common sting" was required, *Warren v Random House Group Ltd* [2008] EWCA Civ 834, [2009] Q.B. 600, [2009] C.L.Y. 984 applied, *Turcu v News Group Newspapers Ltd* [2005] EWHC 799 (QB) considered and *Grobbelaar v News Group Newspapers Ltd* [2002] UKHL 40, [2002] 1 W.L.R. 3024, [2002] C.L.Y. 958 followed (see paras 18-19 of judgment). It was also common ground that if the sting of the examples used to justify a general charge was less sharp than the unproved specific charge, then the justification would fail, *Berezovsky v Forbes Inc (No.2)* [2001] EWCA Civ 1251, [2001] E.M.L.R. 45, [2001] C.L.Y. 1824 applied (para.23). The authorities established a series of interlocking principles: (a) a justification defence would run if the defendant showed that the allegation was substantially true; as a general rule that was limited by (b); (b) a libel could not be justified by proof of obliquity on the claimant's part which was unconnected with the accusation complained of; (c) however, a defendant was entitled to justify a common sting derived from parts of a publication taken as a whole, provided there was a common sting; (d) an instance of (c) arose where a general charge was justified by proved examples, even where the published example was unproved; (e) but in such a case the sting of the proved instances had to be as sharp as the published, unproved libel, so that the claimant had no more reputation to lose (para.24). Those interlocking principles had to be understood in the context of the place of defamation in common law, not as a right of property, but as a balance between free speech and public interest as against private rights (paras 25-26). In the instant case, the judge had correctly pitched the sting of the "dinner" allegation and had correctly decided that the publication contained a general defamatory allegation that R was prepared to use his friendship with M to impress D and should have foreseen the effect on M's reputation (paras 35-36). That general charge had no less a sting than the "dinner" allegation and the justification defence was upheld (paras 50-51).

ROTHSCHILD v ASSOCIATED NEWSPAPERS LTD, [2013] EWCA Civ 197, [2013] E.M.L.R. 18, Laws, L.J., CA (Civ Div).

798. Libel–Qualified privilege–Claim for libel concerning wording of employment reference–Public interest in NHS employers being able to exchange honest references

[Human Rights Act 1998 (c.42) s.6; European Convention on Human Rights 1950 Art.8.]

The claimant (T) brought a claim of defamation against the defendant employer (R) concerning the wording of a reference. T had worked for R. He had received an offer of employment from another NHS trust which was conditional upon satisfactory references. His manager provided a reference to the prospective employer. In response to the question "would you re-engage the applicant", he had stated "No. During his time with us [T] was under investigation following allegations of aggressive behaviour. He resigned during the investigation process and therefore no formal action was taken". He also stated that the allegations had involved several different members of staff. T's manager subsequently told the prospective employer that he had been misinformed, as T had not resigned during the process but had been given a first formal warning. He further stated that he wished to amend his reference to leave that section of the questionnaire blank. T claimed that his manager knew that the statement was inaccurate, or had acted recklessly or negligently in failing to ascertain the true position. R submitted that the publication was covered by qualified privilege.

Held: Judgment for defendant. (1) In deciding what meaning a reader would attribute to the words complained of, the hypothetical readers in T's case were persons holding positions within the NHS with responsibility for employing professional people. They would not engage in speculation, and would not have understood the words complained of to impute any criminal misconduct. They would understand the words to mean that there had been more than one credible allegation that T had exhibited aggressive behaviour towards several different members of staff, that a formal investigation process had been commenced, and that formal action of some kind would or might have been appropriate, *Jeynes v News Magazines Ltd* [2008] EWCA Civ 130 applied. The formal warning had related to two incidents concerning two members of staff. Six further complaints had been made about T during his employment with R (see paras 11-12, 16, 23-24 of judgment). (2) As a public body R was under duties imposed by the Human Rights Act 1998 s.6. In the absence of malice or bad faith, a finding of a breach of a public law duty could be based only on the statement that T resigned "during the process", being an innocent mistake. However, that mistake had been rectified by the manager within a few days. Further, there was a strong public interest in employers, such as NHS bodies, being able to ask for and receive honest employment references. A public authority was not required in every case to prove that domestic law met the requirements of the European Convention on Human Rights 1950 art.8. The courts should in the first instance proceed on the assumption that domestic law struck a fair balance and was compatible with the requirements of art.8. Accordingly, the defence of qualified privilege was made out (paras 18, 20, 27-28). (3) There was no suggestion that T's manager had any motive for wishing to harm T. Further, T had produced no evidence that the manager knew the true position relating to the complaints mentioned in the reference. The case in malice was without foundation (paras 29-32).

THOUR v ROYAL FREE HAMPSTEAD NHS TRUST, [2012] EWHC 1473 (QB), (2012) 128 B.M.L.R. 137, Tugendhat, J., QBD.

799. Libel–Qualified privilege–Reportage–Fair and accurate extracts of particulars of claim–Failure to mention existence of defence

[Defamation Act 1996 (c.31) s.15(1), s.15(3), Sch.1 para.5, Sch.1 para.10.]

The court was required to determine preliminary issues concerning privilege and malice in a claim for defamation. The claimant banker (C) brought a claim against the defendant newspaper owner (D) concerning two newspaper articles. D had written the first article after obtaining a copy of particulars of claim issued in the High Court. The claim concerned an alleged dishonest business deal in which C was named as a defendant. D did not report that C disputed the claim, nor did it report the contents of C's defence, which had been filed five weeks before D's article was published. The article stated that C had "declined to comment", but C maintained he had not been asked for a comment. D relied on qualified privilege and common law privilege. The second article asserted that C had been "intimately involved" in "Britain's biggest mortgage fraud". Those comments had been made during a sentencing hearing by counsel for an offender convicted of fraud, but the judge had rebuked counsel, stating that he could not determine the complicity of others. The judge's comments had not been reported by D. D claimed absolute privilege on the basis that it was a report which was contemporaneous with legal proceedings. C claimed that both publications had been motivated by malice. The court was required to determine whether the defence of absolute or qualified privilege could succeed and whether the claim of malice was properly made.

Held: Preliminary issues determined in favour of claimant. (1) The qualified privilege available under the Defamation Act 1996 Sch.1 para.10 was subject to the claimant having been given an opportunity to contradict or explain the document. However, C had not had any opportunity to make a comment upon the first article before it was published. D could therefore only rely upon the qualified privilege available under Sch.1 para.5. Accordingly, the issues were whether the words complained of were an extract from the particulars of claim, whether they were a fair and accurate extract, and whether the publication concerned a matter which was of public concern and for the public benefit. An "extract" did not have to be word-for-word. To interpret "extract" in the wider sense of a summary or outline was likely to reflect the intention of Parliament. The words complained of were therefore an extract. What was fair and accurate was to be judged by comparing the words complained of with the document from which they came. Where the complaint was of unfairness arising out of the omission of information extraneous to that document, that issue was to be decided under s.15(3) or s.15(1). The words complained of, other than the extraneous matters added by D, were a fair and accurate extract from the particulars of claim, which was a document required by law to be available to public inspection. However, the fact that C was disputing the claim would have been known to any non-party who applied to the court for a copy of the particulars of claim, for otherwise the court could not supply it. It was also implicit in C having filed an acknowledgement of service. The instant case was therefore unlike the situation in *Tsikata v Newspaper Publishing Plc* [1997] 1 All E.R. 655, [1996] C.L.Y. 5662, *Tsikata* distinguished. As a general rule, it would not be for the public benefit to publish defamatory allegations made in a claim form without at the same time publishing the fact that the defendant denied or disputed the allegations. D had not only omitted to publish the fact that C disputed the allegations, but had also misleadingly stated that he had declined to comment. There was no public interest in the publication of that false information. The defences of statutory privilege and common law privilege therefore failed (see paras 22, 43-49, 68, 76, 99-103, 112-114 of judgment). (2) The part of the second article which related to the comments made in the sentencing hearing was not a fair and accurate report of those proceedings. The judge had stated very clearly that C had not lent any money in connection with the fraud. The omission of the judge's comments seriously unbalanced the report, to the extent that D could not rely upon the privilege, whether absolute or qualified (paras 169-172). (3) The question of malice did not arise in relation to qualified privilege. However, if the above conclusions were incorrect, the plea of malice would succeed in relation to the first article from the date when D became aware that a defence had been filed but had taken no steps to change the contents of the online article. The second article was unfair to C as it omitted to attribute to the judge the statement that C had not lent any money. The plea of malice would therefore also succeed in relation to that article (paras 231-234, 252). The judge also commented upon the law applicable to pleas of malice in circumstances where a publisher was relying upon the statutory defence of qualified privilege (paras 191-213).

QADIR v ASSOCIATED NEWSPAPERS LTD, [2012] EWHC 2606 (QB), [2013] E.M.L.R. 15, Tugendhat, J., QBD.

800. Misuse of private information–Breach of confidence–Letter of claim making unfounded allegations of hacking and threatening police involvement–Whether abuse of process

The claimant (P) sought damages for breach of confidence, or misuse of private information in relation to the publication of a number of emails by the defendants, a journalist (G) and a newspaper group (N). P was a consultant who helped companies with their business affairs. A well-known public figure (S) had been appointed chair of the London Organising Committee of the Olympic Games (LOCOG). P had helped S to set up a company (C) aiming to exploit S's intellectual property and image rights. In 2007, G obtained certain emails written by P to C's directors and used them to write a newspaper article alleging that C was unable to pay its debts, particularly to its auditors, and that it was threatened with legal action after defaulting on its statutory obligations to file annual accounts. The article pointed out that some of the emails were copied to S's personal assistant at LOCOG, suggesting that she had also acted for C. S claimed that C was a totally separate entity, created to ring fence his private interests from his public duties. A letter from S's solicitors claimed that P was a paid consultant and minority shareholder in C, who played no part in its management. In fact, P was not a shareholder in C, and had played an important part in its management, such as by corresponding on its behalf with solicitors and investors. As well as asserting breach of confidence and misuse of private information, P's letter of claim alleged that G and N were guilty of criminal offences relating to email hacking. The hacking allegation had now been withdrawn. The issues were whether (i) P had title to bring the claim; (ii) publication was justifiable in the public interest; (iii) the claim was an abuse of the process of the court.

Held: Claim dismissed. (1) P had no contractual or other legal relationship with G and N. With one exception, the emails all contained information relating to C. None of that information was personal to P. In sending and receiving the emails, P had not been acting, or purporting to act, as principal, but as consultant. G and N could not owe P any duty or obligation of confidence, the breach of which would give rise to substantial damages. P had no reasonable expectation of privacy in relation to any information which was not personal to him. The use of particular language might, in certain circumstances, give rise to a reasonable expectation of privacy, but not in the instant case. A request not to circulate an email could not, of itself, give P a title to sue that he would not otherwise have. Even the email which was confidential and personal to P was not so clearly private or confidential that it could be said that it was a breach of confidence or misuse of private information for G to obtain and read it. For those reasons, P's claims in confidentiality and misuse of private information failed (see paras 52-62 of judgment). (2) In case the findings about title to sue were wrong, the issue of public interest would be considered. The letter from S's solicitors could not be described as candid about P's role in C and publication of the article was therefore, in the public interest. C's financial situation was, on any view, a very serious one. There could be no doubt that the inability of C to pay its professional advisers, and other debts as they fell due, and the failure to file accounts when they were due, were both matters which could seriously put into question S's ability to carry out his role for LOCOG. When a person such as S assumed a role of national importance, which required a clear separation from his private business interests, the public had an interest in knowing to whom he had entrusted matters relating to his private business interests. S's decision to entrust matters to P called into question his private and professional judgement. On those grounds, G and N also ought to succeed on their public interest defence (paras 80-81, 84-107). (3) It was troubling that P had repeatedly alleged that G and N had committed serious criminal offences, without evidence. The fact that he never reported the matter to the police supported the inference that he made the threats for the purpose of obtaining a settlement on terms which he did not expect to achieve on the merits of his claim. That was an attempt at extortion and an abuse of the process of the court (paras 143-159). P never had a realistic prospect of obtaining substantial damages for breach of any duty of confidentiality owed to him, or for misuse of private information. The claim was an abuse of process and its costs were disproportionate to the benefit that could have accrued to P if he had succeeded, *Jameel v Dow Jones & Co Inc* [2005] EWCA Civ 75, [2005] Q.B. 946, [2005] C.L.Y. 974 followed (paras 177-184).

ABBEY v GILLIGAN, [2012] EWHC 3217 (QB), [2013] E.M.L.R. 12, Tugendhat, J., QBD.

DISPUTE RESOLUTION

801. Alternative dispute resolution–Certainty–Contractual provision setting out requirements for conciliation of disputes prior to arbitration–Test for determining whether provision sufficiently clear and certain to have binding effect

[Arbitration Act 1996 (c.23) s.67.]

The claimants (X), minority partners in a partnership governed by Hong Kong law, made a claim under the Arbitration Act 1996 s.67 to set aside the final award of an arbitral tribunal. X's partnership had been expelled from an accountancy and audit network, of which the first defendant (G) was the umbrella organisation. Membership of the network was governed by a master agreement, which was subject to English law. The agreement specified a three-step process for resolving issues arising from expulsion of a firm from the group. The relevant clause stipulated that disputes were to be referred to arbitration. After expulsion, the partnership instigated arbitration proceedings in Hong Kong. The majority partners (Z) subsequently purported to settle the dispute and agreed to a discontinuation of the arbitration. X contested their application to do so, alleging that the tribunal had no jurisdiction to determine the issue because the steps outlined in the master agreement had not been followed. The tribunal held that it did have jurisdiction because the steps in the agreement were not sufficiently precise or certain to be contractually binding; alternatively that they had not been intended to prevent a reference to arbitration. It made a final order terminating the arbitration and ordering X to pay G's costs. X submitted that the steps in the agreement were conditions precedent before an arbitral reference could be made.

Held: Claim dismissed. (1) Provisions for conciliation of disputes prior to arbitration had historically created tension between the desire to give effect to what the parties agreed, and the difficulty in giving what they had agreed objective and legally controllable substance. Agreements to agree, and agreements to negotiate in good faith, would generally be unenforceable because faith was too open-ended a concept to provide sufficient definition or clarity. However, especially where the relevant provision was part of an otherwise legally enforceable contract, the court would strain to find a construction which gave a conciliation provision effect: it might imply criteria to enable it to determine what process to follow, and when; and how, without the need for a further agreement, to treat the process as successful, exhausted, or properly terminated. The court would be especially ready to imply criteria for agreeing a fair and reasonable price. It would consider each case on its own terms rather than ticking off minimum ingredients for validity. The test was not whether there was valid provision for a recognised process of mediation, but whether obligations imposed were sufficiently clear and certain to be given legal effect. In the context of an obligation to attempt to resolve a dispute before referring it to arbitration, the test was whether the provision provided, without the need for further agreement: (a) a sufficiently certain and unequivocal commitment to commence a process; (b) a means of discerning the steps each party was required to take to start the process; (c) sufficient clarity and definition to enable the court to make an objective determination of the minimum participatory requirements for each party; (d) an indication of how the process would be exhausted or properly terminable without breach, *Sulamerica Cia Nacional de Seguros SA v Enesa Engenharia SA* [2012] EWCA Civ 638, [2013] 1 W.L.R. 102, [2012] C.L.Y. 104 applied, *Cable & Wireless Plc v IBM United Kingdom Ltd* [2002] EWHC 2059 (Comm), [2002] 2 All E.R. (Comm) 1041, [2003] C.L.Y. 965 explained and *Petromec Inc v Petroleo Brasileiro SA Petrobras (No.3)* [2005] EWCA Civ 891, [2006] 1 Lloyd's Rep. 121, [2006] C.L.Y. 757 considered (see paras 47-61, 71 of judgment). (2) The relevant provisions of the agreement were too equivocal and nebulous in communicating the parties' respective obligations to be given legal effect as an enforceable condition precedent to arbitration. The omission to give any guidance as to the quality or nature of the attempts to be made to resolve a dispute rendered the court unable to determine or direct compliance with the agreement. The tribunal's conclusion regarding the true effect of the provision was correct (paras 72, 76-79, 82).

WAH v GRANT THORNTON INTERNATIONAL LTD; *sub nom.* WAH (ALSO KNOWN AS TANG) v GRANT THORNTON INTERNATIONAL LTD, [2012] EWHC 3198 (Ch), [2013] 1 All E.R. (Comm) 1226, Hildyard, J, Ch D.

ECCLESIASTICAL LAW

802. Appeals–Complaints–Disciplinary procedures–Ministers of religion

THE CLERGY DISCIPLINE APPEAL (AMENDMENT) RULES 2013, SI 2013/1921; made under the Care of Churches and Ecclesiastical Jurisdiction Measure 1991 (1991 1) s.26. In force: in accordance with rule 20.; .

These rules are made pursuant to the Care of Churches and Ecclesiastical Jurisdiction Measure 1991 s.26 as amended by the Clergy Discipline Measure 2003 s.45. The rules amend the Clergy Discipline Appeal Rules (SI 2005/3201).

803. Burials and cremation–Exhumation–Husband's death in road accident–Widow moved to new area–Exhumation of remains to reinter them in family grave in new area

The petitioner (P) sought a faculty for the exhumation of the remains of her husband (D) and their reinterment. D had died suddenly in a road accident. P suffered a breakdown as a result, so her parents arranged D's funeral. His remains were buried in consecrated ground in the nearest available cemetery to where P and D had lived. It had been D's wish to move to another area with P and their two small children, and at the time of his death they had been looking for a house there. Subsequently P and the children moved to that area and she had a permanent job there. She wished D's remains to be moved to a cemetery where already one of her uncles was buried and another would be interred when he died. Another uncle and aunt owned the grave adjacent to that one. P and her parents had reserved two adjacent plots there. They had also bought a bench in that cemetery for the purposes of thought and reflection. All of D's close relatives supported the petition. P's view was that if she had been able to make decisions for herself after D died she would have arranged for his remains to be cremated and stored so that she could have deferred a decision about their ultimate destination.

Held: Petition granted. Permission to exhume human remains from consecrated ground was to be granted only in exceptional circumstances. "Exceptional" meant a case which formed an exception and imparted no additional test that a set of circumstances had to meet, *Blagdon Cemetery, Re* [2002] Fam. 299 followed. Generally, the creation or consolidation of a family grave was not of itself a sufficient reason justifying exhumation and a departure from the norm of permanence of Christian burial, *Blagdon* considered. However, where there were reasons why remains were not interred in the family grave in the first place or why a family grave was not established at the time of burial and/or other factors justified a departure from the norm of permanence, the fact that exhumation was to a family grave was an additional factor in its favour, being economical in the use of grave space and expressive of family unity. In the instant case there were reasons why a family grave had not been established earlier, namely that D had died suddenly and unnaturally without expressing any view about where he wanted to be buried, there was a link between him and the community in which he was buried but before his death he and his family had been hoping to move somewhere else, and moving the remains would facilitate the establishment of a family grave. Those matters, together with the benefits arising from the creation of a family grave, were sufficient to justify exhumation. Although tragedy could not of itself justify granting a petition, where an important part of the justification for permitting exhumation flowed from the circumstances arising following personal tragedy the court might more readily be satisfied that permission should be given in order not to add to pain that had already been endured. Such sympathetic treatment of cases involving personal tragedy did not need to be regarded as undermining the norm of the permanence of Christian burial (see paras 8-11, 43-58 of judgment).

PETERS' PETITION, *Re; sub nom.* PLUMSTEAD CEMETERY, GREENWICH, *Re* [2013] P.T.S.R. 420, Chancellor Petchey, Cons Ct (Southwark).

804. Church of England–Dioceses–Endowments–Primary schools

THE DIOCESE OF LINCOLN (EDUCATIONAL ENDOWMENTS) (WINTERTON CHURCH OF ENGLAND VOLUNTARY CONTROLLED PRIMARY SCHOOL) ORDER 2013, SI 2013/548; made under the Education Act 1996 s.554, s.556. In force: March 25, 2013; .

This Order appoints the Lincoln Diocesan Trust and Board of Finance Limited as trustee of the proceeds of sale of the former premises and teachers' house of the former Winterton Church of England Voluntary Controlled Primary School and makes new provision as to the use of the endowment of that foundation. It creates a separate foundation for the purpose of providing religious education in accordance with the doctrines of the Church of England within the Parish of Winterton.

805. Churches–Faculty jurisdiction

THE FACULTY JURISDICTION RULES 2013, SI 2013/1916; made under the Care of Churches and Ecclesiastical Jurisdiction Measure 1991 (1991 1) s.26. In force: January 1, 2014; .

These Rules are made under the Care of Churches and Ecclesiastical Jurisdiction Measure 1991 s.26. They regulate the procedure and practice of consistory courts in relation to the exercise of the faculty jurisdiction and the jurisdiction to issue injunctions and make restoration orders. They replace the Faculty Jurisdiction (Injunctions and Restoration Orders) Rules 1992 (SI 1992/2884), the Faculty Jurisdiction Rules 2000 (SI 2000/2047) and the Faculty Jurisdiction (Care of Places of Worship) Rules 2000 (SI 2000/2048).

806. Churches–Listed buildings–Relocation of chancel screen to another part of grade I listed church–Whether adverse effect justified–Guidelines for consideration of justification in relation to ecclesiastical buildings

[Planning (Listed Buildings and Conservation Areas) Act 1990 (c.9) s.7, s.16(2).]

The appellant vicar (V) appealed against a chancellor's refusal to grant a faculty for the removal of the chancel screen in his church and its relocation to a chapel within the church. The church was a grade I listed building, dating back to the 12th century. Many alterations had taken place over the centuries, including, in the 1890s, some designed by John Oldrid Scott. These included the provision of a new chancel screen, designed to separate the chancel from the nave. V's statement of needs listed three reasons for the proposed removal of the screen: (i) to remove its "Temple" symbolism; (ii) to create a feeling of unity and peace from opening the chancel to the nave; (iii) to provide space for the music group who were singing almost out of sight. The chancellor's approach to considering the effect of moving the screen on the character of the building was governed by the questions set out in *St Helen's, Bishopsgate, Re*. The second question required the consideration of "adverse" effects on the character of the church and the chancellor defined such an effect as "one that alters or affects, in a material way, the appearance or form and layout of the listed building". He concluded that to move it would be "adverse". V's main submissions were that the chancellor (1) erred in giving insufficient weight to the possibility of the screen's reinstatement; (2) did not assess whether the church's character as a building of special architectural and historic interest would be "adversely" affected.

Held: Appeal allowed. (1) The chancellor should have taken into account reinstatement or the ease with which it would be achievable (see para.51 of judgment). (2) In defining an "adverse" effect as he did the chancellor asked a materially different question from that which arose under the Planning (Listed Buildings and Conservation Areas) Act 1990 s.7. The focus should have been on whether there was an adverse effect on the character of the church as a building of special architectural and historic interest. Further, the chancellor failed first to identify what was the special architectural character and historic interest of the church as a whole and then to consider whether there would be an overall adverse effect by reason of the proposed change (para.52). (3) The judgment would be set aside, and the court considered it appropriate to substitute its own determination for that of the chancellor (paras 53-54). (4) Following analysis of the effect on the character of the listed building, the court concluded that the chancel screen impacted adversely on the overall character of the architecture; the Scott alterations were a valuable lesson in late Victorian architectural and ecclesiastical history; and the screen's relocation was likely to benefit the church's architecture as a whole. Therefore, looking at the question as a whole, there would be a loss to the character of the building as one of special architectural and historic interest (paras 55, 59-60). Any adverse effect on a listed building required justification. There was a genuine pastoral case for removing the screen because it was regarded as a hindrance not merely to worship but especially to mission. Its removal would create a feeling of unity and space and the chancel/nave combination would become a 'more glorious "whole"'. Those were matters to which the chancellor, wrongly, gave little credence. Those matters, together with the relocation of the musicians and singers on to a central dais, constituted public benefits and a clear and convincing justification for the proposal. When V's case was approached cumulatively, and proper account was taken of the ambitions of the congregation, V had established the existence of a genuine pastoral need for the alteration under all three heads of their statement of needs. Whilst *Bishopsgate* required consideration of "necessity" for the purpose of justification, there was no such test in secular law and no justification for applying a stricter test to ecclesiastical buildings. The court considered that chancellors should be freed from the constraints of *Bishopsgate* and suggested new guidelines: (a) consideration of whether proposals would result in harm to the significance of the church as a building of special architectural or historic interest; (b) if they would not, the ordinary rebuttable presumption in favour of leaving things as they stood applied; (c) if they would, the court should consider the seriousness of the harm, how clear and convincing any justification was and whether any resulting public benefit would outweigh the harm, *Bishopsgate* considered (paras 75-79, 81, 84, 86-87). Since the building was a grade I listed building, the court had to consider the desirability of preserving either it, or its features or its historic interest, under s.16(2) of the Act, for which there was a strong burden of proof on V. Whilst noting that substantial harm to grade I listed buildings should only be permitted very exceptionally, since the court found the harm not to be serious or substantial, the burden on V was more easily discharged. That was especially so in the instant case, where the court afforded considerable weight to relocation and reversibility, which it considered appropriate to consider at the final stage of its evaluation (paras 90, 93-94).

ST ALKMUND, DUFFIELD, *Re* [2013] Fam. 158, George Q.C. (Dean of Arches), Arches Ct.

807. Complaints–Disciplinary procedures–Ministers of religion–Misconduct

THE CLERGY DISCIPLINE (AMENDMENT) RULES 2013, SI 2013/1917; made under the Care of Churches and Ecclesiastical Jurisdiction Measure 1991 (1991 1) s.26. In force: in accordance with rule 37(2).; .

These rules are made pursuant to the Care of Churches and Ecclesiastical Jurisdiction Measure 1991 s.26 as amended by the Clergy Discipline Measure 2003 s.45. The rules amend the Clergy Discipline Rules (SI 2005/2022) which provide a code of procedure for the determination under the Clergy Discipline Measure of formal complaints alleging misconduct against a clerk in Holy Orders other than in relation to matters involving doctrine, ritual or ceremonial, and for the imposition of penalties following certain findings or orders of secular bodies.

808. Diocesan Boards–Ecclesiastical judges–Fees–Law Officers

THE ECCLESIASTICAL JUDGES, LEGAL OFFICERS AND OTHERS (FEES) ORDER 2013, SI 2013/1922; made under the Ecclesiastical Fees Measure 1986 s.6. In force: January 1, 2013; .

This Order increases the fees fixed by Table I of the Ecclesiastical Judges, Legal Officers and Others (Fees) Order 2012 (SI 2012/1846) in relation to faculty proceedings.

809. Diocesan Boards–Fees–Law Officers

THE LEGAL OFFICERS (ANNUAL FEES) ORDER 2013, SI 2013/1918; made under the Ecclesiastical Fees Measure 1986 s.5. In force: January 1, 2014; .

This Order applies an increase of 1.75 per cent (a weighted inflationary formula of 25 per cent RPI and 75 per cent AWE (3.1 per cent and 1.3 per cent respectively in 2012)) to the total of the annual fees for diocesan registrars fixed by the Legal Officers (Annual Fees) Order 2012 (SI 2012/1847).

810. Exhumation–Presumptions–Grant of licence to exhume and reinter venerated priest–Existence of presumption against exhumation–Whether grant of licence reasonable and proportionate

[Burial Act 1857 (c.81) s.25; European Convention on Human Rights 1950 Art.8, Art.9.]

The appellant (R) appealed against a decision ([2011] EWHC 3078 (Admin), [2012] A.C.D. 27) refusing her application for judicial review of the respondent secretary of state's decision to grant a licence for the exhumation and reinterment of the remains of a venerated Polish priest, Father Jarzebowski (J). J had belonged to the Marian Fathers religious order and achieved almost saint-like status among many in the Polish Roman Catholic community in the United Kingdom. After his death in 1964, he had been buried in a churchyard located within the grounds of a property owned by the Marian Fathers. In 2008, the

Marian Fathers decided to sell the property and it was deconsecrated. Thereafter, they applied to the secretary of state under the Burial Act 1857 s.25 for a licence to disinter J's remains and reinter them in a cemetery two miles away. The application was supported by the Provincial Superior of the Polish Province of the Marian Fathers, the Superior General of the Congregation of Marian Fathers in Rome and the local bishop. R, who was J's closest living relative although she had never met him, opposed the application, as did many members of the Polish Roman Catholic community. The secretary of state granted the licence on the basis that (i) in s.25 applications, the wishes of the deceased's next of kin were regarded as important, and for religious orders the head of the relevant order was generally regarded as the next of kin; (ii) J's reinterment would reunite him with the remains of his former brothers with whom he had lived and worked; (iii) if J remained at the property, there would be a problem for those who wished to visit his grave, whereas the removal of his remains would make access to his grave easier. R's challenge to that decision by way of judicial review was refused. R contended that the faculty to exhume ought not to be given on demand and that there was a general presumption of permanence arising from the initial act of interment. She submitted that the secretary of state's decision to grant a licence was unreasonable since it was made in reliance on people's desire to visit J's grave although nobody had written to support the proposal on that basis, and that if there had been a genuine desire to reunite J's remains with his brothers, the application for a licence could and would have been made years before. R also argued that her rights under the European Convention on Human Rights 1950 art.8, as J's next of kin, were engaged, as were the art.9 rights of all the objectors who felt strongly that J's remains should stay where they were, and that the grant of a licence was disproportionate.

Held: Appeal dismissed. (1) The secretary of state appeared to regard the wish of the next of kin to reinter remains elsewhere as a sufficient reason to grant a s.25 licence. It was for the secretary of state to decide on what grounds and in what circumstances to grant a licence and, apart from an obligation to act rationally, and otherwise in accordance with the general law (including in relation to human rights), there should be no operative presumption or fetter. The general presumption of permanence adopted by consistory courts was based on the theology of burial, *Blagdon Cemetery, Re* [2002] Fam. 299 considered. Whilst that theology was highly relevant to the faculty jurisdiction, it was plainly irrelevant to the exercise of the secular power in s.25 (see paras 29, 31, 33 of judgment). (2) In relation to the wish to visit J's grave, there might have been plenty of people who were happy for the Provincial Superior, the Superior General and the local bishop to speak for them, and it was not clear whether the objectors appreciated that they might not be able to visit J's grave if the licence was not granted. Moreover, it appeared likely that J would be beatified, which would mean that it was not just members of the Polish Roman Catholic community who would want to pay their respects to J's grave (para.35). (3) There was nothing in the argument that it was wrong to take into account as a significant reason the benefit of reinterring J next to his brothers on the ground that it had not been pursued earlier. Until the application for a licence had been made, it was not open to the secretary of state to consider moving J's remains to the cemetery. It was likely that the sale of the Marian Fathers' property had precipitated a wish to move J's remains and the consequent benefit of reuniting him with his brothers might have been appreciated as a benefit for the first time (paras 37-38). (4) It was difficult to see how R's art.8 rights were engaged; she had never met R and was a distant relative. It was also hard to fit the concerns of R and the objectors into the wording of art.9. The exhumation of J's remains might offend their religious feelings, but it would not affect their right to hold or manifest their religious beliefs. Even if art.8 and art.9 were engaged, given the careful balancing exercise carried out by the secretary of state and his reasons for granting the licence, the decision was proportionate (paras 39-40, 42-43).

R. (ON THE APPLICATION OF RUDEWICZ) v MINISTRY OF JUSTICE, [2012] EWCA Civ 499, [2013] Q.B. 410, Lord Neuberger (M.R.), CA (Civ Div).

ECONOMICS

811. Belarus–Designated persons–Economic resources–Freezing of funds

THE BELARUS (ASSET-FREEZING) REGULATIONS 2013, SI 2013/164; made under the European Communities Act 1972 s.2, Sch.2 para.1A. In force: February 21, 2013; .

These Regulations make provision relating to the enforcement of Regulation 765/2006 of May 18 2006 concerning restrictive measures in respect of Belarus. The measures include the freezing of funds and economic resources of designated persons and ensuring that funds and economic resources are not made available to them or for their benefit.

EDUCATION

812. Academies–Local authorities' liabilities–Disability discrimination claims–Conversion of maintained school into academy–Transfer of liabilities to local authority

[Academies Act 2010 (c.32) s.6(2); Disability Discrimination Act 1995 (c.50) s.28I(4)(a); Education Act 2002 (c.32) Sch.1 para.5, Sch.1 para.5(1); Equality Act 2010 (c.15) Sch.17.]

In two claims heard together the Upper Tribunal was required to determine as a preliminary issue the effect of a change in the respondent schools' status upon claims against them for disability discrimination. A parent had brought a claim of disability discrimination against the first maintained school concerning its treatment of her daughter. Her claim was dismissed and she appealed. By that time the school had become an academy, and the school argued that the governing body against whom the claim had been brought no longer existed. The second claim concerned alleged disability discrimination after the second school's refusal to allow a pupil to attend a skiing trip. Before the final hearing the school had converted into an academy. The First-tier Tribunal struck out the proceedings against the governing body and added the local authority as a respondent. The local authority indicated that it was likely to concede the claim as it had previously advised the school against excluding the pupil from the trip. The schools submitted that the governing body of each of the maintained schools was dissolved upon the school being converted into an academy, either by implication or under the Education Act 2002 Sch.1 para.5(1), and the liabilities of the governing body therefore passed to the local authority.

Held: Preliminary issue determined. (1) Nothing in the Academies Act 2010 expressly said what happened to the governing body of a maintained school upon conversion to an academy. It did not convert into the governing body of the academy. Schedule 1 para.5(1) of the 2002 Act applied only where a school was "discontinued". Schedule 1 para.5(2)(iv) implied that for the purposes of para.5(1) a maintained school was to be treated as discontinued when it ceased to be maintained by virtue of s.6(2) of the 2010 Act, even though that would not otherwise be the case. The liabilities therefore transferred to the local authority (see paras 8, 12 of judgment). (2) Some remedies available under the Disability Discrimination Act 1995 s.28I(4)(a) and the Equality Act 2010 Sch.17, such as an order for an apology, would be inappropriate where the governing body of a maintained school had ceased to exist and its liabilities had transferred to the local authority. However, the vindication of a claimant was not the only, or even the main, purpose of the legislation. The right of appeal to the First-tier Tribunal was intended to be a means of improving practice in schools with a view to eliminating disability discrimination against all pupils. It was not necessary for the tribunal to have power to make orders against an academy in order to achieve that broader aim. The secretary of state had a role through the enforcement of obligations under funding agreements. Further, an obligation to take appropriate action could be imposed by a declaration made in proceedings in which the responsible body had been a respondent or had otherwise had an opportunity to take part. However, if an opportunity was offered but declined, the academy could not complain if adverse findings were relied upon by the secretary of state in exercising his statutory or contractual powers, or by parents bringing judicial review proceedings (paras 20-25, 30, 34). (3) Where a local authority was substituted as a respondent there was no reason why the responsible body of the academy should not be added as a second respondent if it consented. Alternatively, it could co-operate with a local authority in the conduct of the case. In such cases there would be no need to add the academy as a second respondent. However, walking away from the case was not a responsible option, given that the purpose of the legislation was to enable the tribunal to examine whether the approach of a school needed to be modified (para.33). (4) In the first claim the academy was already conducting the case on the local authority's behalf and there was no need for the academy to be added as an additional respondent. The local authority was formally substituted as the respondent in place of the governing body of the discontinued maintained school (para.36.) (5) In the second case, the tribunal had not erred in making it plain that the liability had passed to the local authority. However, that did not mean that the academy could not remain a party, and it might be in its interests, or the public interest, for it to do so (para.37).

ML v TONBRIDGE GRAMMAR SCHOOL; SB v WEST BRIDGFORD ACADEMY, [2012] UKUT 283 (AAC), [2012] E.L.R. 508, Judge Rowland, UT (AAC).

813. Academies–Parental wishes–Decision to convert after consultation revealed majority of parents against–Requirements of consultation under s.5 Academies Act 2010

[Academies Act 2010 (c.32) s.1 (1), s.4(1) (b), s.5, s.9; Education Act1996 (c.56) s.9.]

The claimant (M) applied for permission to seek judicial review of the defendant secretary of state's decision that a primary school should become an academy school. Ofsted had twice judged the school as requiring special measures. The secretary of state made an academy order under the Academies Act 2010 s.4(1)(b) and appointed an interim executive board to replace the existing governing body. The board consulted and found that the vast majority of parents wanted the school to remain a local authority maintained school. Nevertheless, the secretary of state decided the school would become an academy school. M submitted that (1) as the consulting party under s.5, the board had been required to decide whether the school should be converted into an academy; (2) the consultation process was flawed as it had not allowed the parents the opportunity to work with the board and the local authority to prepare an alternative for the management and governance of the school as a community maintained school; (3) the secretary of state had failed to comply with the Education Act 1996 s.9, which provided that pupils were to be educated in accordance with their parents' wishes; (4) the secretary of state should have compared how the school would perform as an academy with how it would perform if a normally constituted governing body were restored.

Held: Application refused. (1) The core concept of consultation was eliciting the views of persons who were likely to be affected by a contemplated course of action. Neither in logic, nor in practice, did the person who carried out a consultation in that core sense also need to be a decision-maker or even a person who expressed his own view on the merits of any contemplated course of action, *R. (on the application of Wainwright) v Richmond upon Thames LBC* [2001] EWCA Civ 2062, Times, January 16, 2002, [2002] C.L.Y. 2260 considered. There was simply nothing in s.5 that permitted, let alone obliged, the governing body to take a decision on whether conversion should take place. On the contrary, the only relevant decision-maker was the secretary of state, who, by s.1 (1), could enter into academy arrangements with any person. Indeed, if a governing body were to purport to decide on the relevant question of conversion into an academy, its decision would lack the typical quality of a public law decision, namely an act having binding effect on the person to whom the decision was directed. Its purported decision could therefore be no more than an expression of a view or a recommendation. It was simply not arguable that on the proper interpretation of s.5, the secretary of state was not permitted to take the challenged decision unless and until the school's governing body had taken a decision, expressed a view or made a recommendation that the school be converted into an academy (see paras 52, 54, 56 of judgment). (2) Consultation was not negotiation, it was a process within which a decision-maker at a formative stage in the decision-making process invited representations on one or more possible courses of action, *R. (on the application of Medway Council) v Secretary of State for Transport, Local Government and the Regions* [2002] EWHC 2516 (Admin), [2003] J.P.L. 583, [2003] C.L.Y. 3363 applied. The board was under no obligation to engage with the parents to assist them in constructing an alternative to conversion into an academy, and any failure to do so could not render the process of consultation unfair. As a general rule, it was for those who were being consulted to come forward with any counter-proposals to the course of action under contemplation. Thus the alleged unfairness of the consultation process was not arguable (paras 58, 61, 63, 66). (3) Section 9 stated, in terms, that the secretary of state had to have regard to the general principle that pupils were to be educated in accordance with their parents' wishes. He was not obliged, having had regard to that principle, to ensure that pupils were educated in accordance with the wishes of their parents, particularly if there were relevant countervailing considerations, including the imperative expressly mentioned of providing efficient instruction. The secretary of state had recognised that the majority of those who responded to the consultation preferred the school to remain maintained by the local authority. However, he was not bound to accept that majority view. He was entitled, and indeed obliged, to consider whether it would be in the best interests of the pupils, specifically in terms of efficient instruction, for that preference to be respected. In the decision letter he set out in detail why he had concluded that conversion to an academy would further the best interests of the pupils and why maintenance of the school by the local authority would not further those interests. Parliament had entrusted the decision to him and his conclusion could only be challenged if it had no rational basis. It could not be argued that he had failed to have regard to the relevant principle under s.9 (paras 69-72). (4) In the light of the school's egregious past failures over a very substantial period, the secretary of state was not convinced that the future would be materially different. The court would interfere with such an assessment only if it had no rational basis. Plainly, the secretary of state had a rational basis for his decision (para.78).

R. (ON THE APPLICATION OF MOYSE) v SECRETARY OF STATE FOR EDUCATION, [2012] EWHC 2758 (Admin), [2012] E.L.R. 551, Kenneth Parker, J, QBD (Admin).

814. Adoption agencies–Boarding schools–Chief Inspector of Education Children's Services and Skills–Fees

HER MAJESTY'S CHIEF INSPECTOR OF EDUCATION, CHILDREN'S SERVICES AND SKILLS (FEES AND FREQUENCY OF INSPECTIONS) (CHILDREN'S HOMES ETC.) (AMENDMENT) REGULATIONS 2013, SI 2013/523; made under the Children Act 1989 s.87D, s.104; the Care Standards Act 2000 s.16, s.31, s.118; and the Education and Inspections Act 2006 s.147, s.155. In force: April 1, 2013; .

These Regulations amend Parts 4 (annual fees) and 5 (frequency of inspections) of Her Majesty's Chief Inspector of Education, Children's Services and Skills (Fees and Frequency of Inspections) (Children's Homes etc.) Regulations 2007 (SI 2007/694). These Regulations amend the annual fees that are paid under the Care Standards Act 2000, the Education and Inspections Act 2006 and the Children Act 1989 to Her Majesty's Chief Inspector of Education, Children's Services and Skills in respect of voluntary adoption agencies, adoption support agencies, children's homes, residential family centres, boarding schools, residential colleges, residential special schools and in respect of local authority fostering and adoption functions.

815. Allowances–Pupil referral units–School governors–England

THE SCHOOL GOVERNANCE (ROLES, PROCEDURES AND ALLOWANCES) (ENGLAND) REGULATIONS 2013, SI 2013/1624; made under the Education Act 1996 s.519, s.569, Sch.1 para.3, Sch.1 para.15; and the Education Act 2002 s.19, s.21, s.23, s.24, s.34, s.210. In force: September 1, 2013; .

These Regulations make provision for the core functions and procedures of governing bodies of maintained schools in England, and for the payment of allowances for out-of-pocket expenses that are incurred by school governors in connection with their duties as governors from September 1, 2013. They also amend the Education (Pupil Referral Units) (Management Committees etc) (England) Regulations 2007 (SI 2007/2978) and the School Governance (Federations) (England) Regulations 2012 (SI 2012/1035) to apply these Regulations to the management committees of pupil referral units and governing bodies of federations.

816. Annual reports–School governors–Wales

THE SCHOOL GOVERNORS' ANNUAL REPORTS (WALES) (AMENDMENT) REGULATIONS 2013, SI 2013/SI 2013/1561 (W.142); made under the Education Act 2002 s.30, s.210. In force: July 18, 2013; .

These Regulations make a number of changes to the School Governors' Annual Reports (Wales) Regulations 2011 (SI 2011/1939) as a consequence of the School Standards and Organisation (Wales) Act 2013 s.94 coming into force on May 4, 2013.

817. Appointments–Church of England–Dioceses–Trustees

THE DIOCESE OF LINCOLN (EDUCATIONAL ENDOWMENTS) (RIPPINGALE CHURCH OF ENGLAND SCHOOL) ORDER 2013, SI 2013/549; made under the Education Act 1996 s.554, s.556. In force: March 25, 2013; .

This Order appoints the Lincoln Diocesan Trust and Board of Finance Limited as trustee of the foundation known as Rippingale Church of England School and makes new provision as to the use of the endowment of that foundation.

818. Appointments–Education–Training–Wales

THE EDUCATION (INSPECTORS OF EDUCATION AND TRAINING IN WALES) ORDER 2013, SI 2013/541; made under the Education Act 2005 s.1a. In force: March 14, 2013; .

This Order appoints the persons named in the Schedule Her Majesty's Inspectors of Education and Training in Wales.

819. Appointments–Inspectors of Education Children's Services and Skills

THE INSPECTORS OF EDUCATION, CHILDREN'S SERVICES AND SKILLS ORDER 2013, SI 2013/245; made under the Education and Inspections Act 2006 s.114. In force: February 13, 2013; .

This Order appoints the persons named in the Schedule as Her Majesty's Inspectors of Education, Children's Services and Skills.

820. Appointments–Inspectors of Education Children's Services and Skills

THE INSPECTORS OF EDUCATION, CHILDREN'S SERVICES AND SKILLS (NO.2) ORDER 2013, SI 2013/542; made under the Education and Inspections Act 2006 s.114. In force: March 14, 2013; .

This Order appoints the persons named in the Schedule as Her Majesty's Inspectors of Education, Children's Services and Skills.

821. **Appointments–Inspectors of Education Children's Services and Skills**

THE INSPECTORS OF EDUCATION, CHILDREN'S SERVICES AND SKILLS (NO.3) ORDER 2013, SI 2013/787; made under the Education and Inspections Act 2006 s.114. In force: April 10, 2013; .

This Order appoints specified persons as HM Inspectors of Education, Children's Services and Skills.

822. **Appointments–Inspectors of Education Children's Services and Skills**

THE INSPECTORS OF EDUCATION, CHILDREN'S SERVICES AND SKILLS (NO.4) ORDER 2013, SI 2013/1118; made under the Education and Inspections Act 2006 s.114. In force: May 16, 2013; .

This Order appoints the persons named in the Schedule as Her Majesty's Inspectors of Education, Children's Services and Skills.

823. **Appointments–Inspectors of Education Children's Services and Skills**

THE INSPECTORS OF EDUCATION, CHILDREN'S SERVICES AND SKILLS (NO.6) ORDER 2013, SI 2013/1717; made under the Education and Inspections Act 2006 s.114. In force: July 11, 2013; .

This Order appoints the persons named in the Schedule as Her Majesty's Inspectors of Education, Children's Services and Skills.

824. **Appointments–Inspectors of Education Children's Services and Skills**

THE INSPECTORS OF EDUCATION, CHILDREN'S SERVICES AND SKILLS (NO.7) ORDER 2013, SI 2013/2596; made under the Education and Inspections Act 2006 s.114. In force: October 10, 2013; .

This Order appoints the persons named in the Schedule as Her Majesty's Inspectors of Education, Children's Services and Skills.

825. **Appointments–Inspectors of Education Children's Services and Skills**

THE INSPECTORS OF EDUCATION, CHILDREN'S SERVICES AND SKILLS (NO.8) ORDER 2013, SI 2013/2871; made under the Education and Inspections Act 2006 s.114. In force: November 7, 2013; .

This Order appoints the persons named in the Schedule as Her Majesty's Inspectors of Education, Children's Services and Skills.

826. **Appointments–Inspectors of Education Children's Services and Skills–School inspectors**

THE INSPECTORS OF EDUCATION, CHILDREN'S SERVICES AND SKILLS (NO.5) ORDER 2013, SI 2013/1448; made under the Education and Inspections Act 2006 s.114. In force: June 14, 2013; .

This Order appoints the persons named in the Schedule as Her Majesty's Inspectors of Education, Children's Services and Skills.

827. **Apprenticeships–Disabilities**

THE APPRENTICESHIPS (THE APPRENTICESHIP OFFER) (PRESCRIBED PERSONS) REGULATIONS 2013, SI 2013/560; made under the Apprenticeships, Skills, Children and Learning Act 2009 s.83A, s.262. In force: April 6, 2013; .

These Regulations prescribe a further category of persons for the purposes of the apprenticeship offer, namely persons who have a disability within the meaning of s.6(1) of the Equality Act 2010, that is a physical or mental impairment where such impairment has a substantial and long-term adverse effect on their ability to carry out normal day-to-day activities.

828. Apprenticeships–Standards–England

THE APPRENTICESHIPS (MODIFICATIONS TO THE SPECIFICATION OF APPRENTICESHIP STANDARDS FOR ENGLAND) ORDER 2013, SI 2013/575; made under the Apprenticeships, Skills, Children and Learning Act 2009 s.25. In force: April 6, 2013; .

This Order brings the modified specification of apprenticeship standards for England into effect under the Apprenticeships, Skills, Children and Learning Act 2009.

829. Apprenticeships, Skills, Children and Learning Act 2009 (c.22)–Commencement No.6 Order

THE APPRENTICESHIPS, SKILLS, CHILDREN AND LEARNING ACT 2009 (COMMENCEMENT NO.6) ORDER 2013, SI 2013/SI 2013/975 (C.40); made under the Apprenticeships, Skills, Children and Learning Act 2009 s.269. Commencement details: bringing into force various provisions of the 2009 Act on May 31, 2013.; .

This Order brings into force on May 31, 2013 provisions of the Apprenticeships, Skills, Children and Learning Act 2009 that: require Office of Qualifications and Examinations Regulation to set and publish criteria which a recognised body must apply when determining whether a qualification is relevant for the purposes of the 2008 Act and, if so, the number of hours of guided learning that should be assigned to a form of the qualification; and provide that a recognised body may only award a particular form of a qualification if conditions are met.

830. Assessment–National Curriculum–England

THE EDUCATION (NATIONAL CURRICULUM) (KEY STAGES 1 AND 2 ASSESSMENT ARRANGEMENTS) (ENGLAND) (AMENDMENT) ORDER 2013, SI 2013/1513; made under the Education Act 2002 s.87. In force: June 20, 2013; .

This Order amends the Education (National Curriculum) (Key Stage 2 Assessment Arrangements) (England) Order 2003.

831. Careers education–Pupils–Schools

THE CAREERS GUIDANCE IN SCHOOLS REGULATIONS 2013, SI 2013/709; made under the Education Act 1997 s.46, s.54. In force: September 1, 2013; .

These Regulations extend the relevant phase during which a pupil must be provided with independent careers guidance under the Education Act 1997.

832. Codes of practice–School admissions

THE SCHOOL ADMISSIONS CODE (APPOINTED DAY) (WALES) ORDER 2013, SI 2013/SI 2013/1659 (W.157); made under the School Standards and Framework Act 1998 s.85. In force: July 8, 2013; .

This Order appoints July 8, 2013 as the day on which the School Admissions Code issued under the School Standards and Framework Act 1998 ss.84 and 85 by the Welsh Ministers, comes into force.

833. Codes of practice–Schools–Wales

THE SCHOOL ORGANISATION CODE (APPOINTED DAY) (WALES) ORDER 2013, SI 2013/SI 2013/1799 (W.181); made under the School Standards and Organisation (Wales) Act 2013 s.39. In force: October 1, 2013; .

This Order appoints October 1, 2013 as the day on which the School Organisation Code issued under the School Standards and Organisation (Wales) Act 2013 ss.38 and 39, comes into force.

834. Curriculum–Wales

THE NATIONAL CURRICULUM (EDUCATIONAL PROGRAMMES FOR THE FOUNDATION PHASE AND PROGRAMMES OF STUDY FOR THE SECOND AND THIRD KEY STAGES) (WALES) ORDER 2013, SI 2013/SI 2013/434 (W.52); made under the Education Act 2002 s.108, s.210. In force: September 1, 2013; .

This Order gives legal effect to additional educational programmes for the language, literacy and communication skills and mathematical development areas of learning in the foundation phase. It also gives legal effect to the additional programmes of study in English, Welsh and mathematics in the second and third key stages.

835. Denominational schools–Designation–Federated schools–England

THE DESIGNATION OF SCHOOLS HAVING A RELIGIOUS CHARACTER (ENGLAND) ORDER 2013, SI 2013/2029; made under the School Standards and Framework Act 1998 s.69. In force: August 15, 2013; .

This Order designates the voluntary or foundation schools named in the Order as having a religious character in accordance with the Schools Standards and Framework Act 1998 s.69 and s.69.

836. Denominational schools–Endowments–Foundation schools–Religious education

THE DIOCESE OF LICHFIELD (EDUCATIONAL ENDOWMENTS) (HOLY TRINITY CHURCH OF ENGLAND SCHOOL) ORDER 2013, SI 2013/1245; made under the Reverter of Sites Act 1987 s.5; and the Education Act 1996 s.554, s.556. In force: June 17, 2013; .

This Order appoints the Lichfield Diocesan Board of Education as trustee of the foundation known as Holy Trinity Church of England School and makes new provision as to the use of the endowment of that foundation.

837. Denominational schools–Endowments–Foundation schools–Religious education

THE DIOCESE OF LICHFIELD (EDUCATIONAL ENDOWMENTS) (ST JOHN'S CHURCH OF ENGLAND SCHOOL) ORDER 2013, SI 2013/1221; made under the Education Act 1996 s.554, s.556. In force: June 14, 2013; .

This Order appoints the Lichfield Diocesan Board of Education as trustee of the foundation known as St John's Church of England School and makes new provision as to the use of the endowment of that foundation. It creates a separate foundation for the purpose of providing religious education in accordance with the doctrines of the Church of England in the Parish of Cheddleton.

838. Denominational schools–Independent schools

THE DESIGNATION OF SCHOOLS HAVING A RELIGIOUS CHARACTER (INDEPENDENT SCHOOLS) (ENGLAND) (NO. 2) ORDER 2013, SI 2013/2867; made under the School Standards and Framework Act 1998 s.69. In force: November 5, 2013; .

This Order designates specified independent schools as having a religious character and revokes The Designation of Schools Having a Religious Character (Independent Schools) (England) (No. 2) Order 2003 in relation to St Antony's school in Leweston.

839. Denominational schools–Independent schools–England

THE DESIGNATION OF SCHOOLS HAVING A RELIGIOUS CHARACTER (INDEPENDENT SCHOOLS) (ENGLAND) ORDER 2013, SI 2013/2162; made under the School Standards and Framework Act 1998 s.69. In force: August 30, 2013; .

This Order designates the independent schools listed in Sch.1 as having a religious character and revokes the instruments listed in Sch.2 to the extent set out in that Schedule. The revocations relate to schools which will no longer be designated with a religious character.

840. Dioceses–Endowed schools–Endowments–Foundations

THE DIOCESE OF YORK (EDUCATIONAL ENDOWMENTS) (ELLERTON PRIORY CHURCH OF ENGLAND SCHOOL) ORDER 2013, SI 2013/920; made under the Education Act 1996 s.554, s.556. In force: May 9, 2013; .

This Order appoints the York Diocesan Board of Education as trustee of the foundation known as Ellerton Priory Church of England School and makes new provision as to the use of the endowment of that foundation. It authorises the sale of specified land belonging to the foundation, and creates a separate foundation for the purpose of providing religious education in accordance with the doctrines of the Church of England within the Parish of Ellerton and Aughton.

841. Disapplication–National Curriculum–Schools–England

THE NATIONAL CURRICULUM (EXCEPTIONS FOR FIRST, SECOND, THIRD AND FOURTH KEY STAGES) (ENGLAND) REGULATIONS 2013, SI 2013/1487; made under the Education Act 2002 s.91. In force: September 1, 2013; .

These Regulations make provision for the National Curriculum for England to be disapplied, with exceptions, for all key stages for the school year 2013 to 2014.

842. Dissolution–Further Education Corporations–Transfer of assets–Wales

THE COLEG POWYS FURTHER EDUCATION CORPORATION (DISSOLUTION) ORDER 2013, SI 2013/SI 2013/1727 (W.169); made under the Further and Higher Education Act 1992 s.27C. In force: August 1, 2013; .

This Order dissolves the further education corporation established to conduct Coleg Powys with effect from August 1, 2013. It provides for the transfer of the property, rights and liabilities of Coleg Powys Further Education Corporation to Neath Port Talbot College Further Education Corporation. The Order also secures the employment rights of persons employed by Coleg Powys Further Education Corporation.

843. Dissolution–Further Education Corporations–Transfer of assets–Wales

THE YALE SIXTH FORM COLLEGE FURTHER EDUCATION CORPORATION AND DEESIDE COLLEGE FURTHER EDUCATION CORPORATION (DISSOLUTION) ORDER 2013, SI 2013/SI 2013/1673 (W.162); made under the Further and Higher Education Act 1992 s.27C. In force: August 1, 2013; .

This Order dissolves the further education corporations established to conduct Yale Sixth Form College and Deeside College with effect from August 1, 2013. It provides for the transfer of the property, rights and liabilities of each corporation to Coleg Cambria Further Education Corporation and secures the employment rights of the employees of the dissolved corporations.

844. Dissolution–Higher Education Corporations–Transfer of functions–Wales

THE SWANSEA METROPOLITAN UNIVERSITY HIGHER EDUCATION CORPORATION (DISSOLUTION) ORDER 2013, SI 2013/SI 2013/1729 (W.170); made under the Education Reform Act 1988 s.128. In force: August 1, 2013; .

This Order dissolves the higher education corporation established to conduct Swansea Metropolitan University, and provides for all property, rights and liabilities to which Swansea Metropolitan University was entitled or subject to immediately before its dissolution to be transferred to the University of Wales Trinity Saint David.

845. Education–Full-time employment–Training–Voluntary work

THE DUTY TO PARTICIPATE IN EDUCATION OR TRAINING (ALTERNATIVE WAYS OF WORKING) REGULATIONS 2013, SI 2013/1243; made under the Education and Skills Act 2008 s.5. In force: June 28, 2013; .

Under the Education and Skills Act 2008 there are three ways in which a person might participate in education and training: appropriate full-time education; a contract of apprenticeship; part-time education or training alongside full-time occupation. These Regulations prescribe ways of working (other than under a contract of employment) which could be considered as a full-time occupation for the purposes of the Education and Skills Act 2008 s.5: self-employment; working otherwise than for reward (for example, voluntary work); or as the holder of an office.

846. Education–Qualifications–Training

THE APPRENTICESHIPS, SKILLS, CHILDREN AND LEARNING ACT 2009 (CONSEQUENTIAL AMENDMENTS TO PART 1 OF THE EDUCATION AND SKILLS ACT 2008) ORDER 2013, SI 2013/1242; made under the Apprenticeships, Skills, Children and Learning Act 2009 s.265. In force: May 24, 2013; .

This Order is made under the Apprenticeships, Skills, Children and Learning Act 2009 and makes amendments to the Education and Skills Act 2008 Pt 1 in consequence of the provisions made by Pt 7 of the 2009 Act. Part 1 of the 2008 Act applies to persons in England who have ceased to be of compulsory school age but who are under the age of 18 and who have not attained a Level 3 qualification (within the meaning of section 3 of the 2008 Act). Section 2 of that Act requires them to participate in education or training.

847. Education and Skills Act 2008 (c.25)–Commencement No.9 and Transitory Provision Order

THE EDUCATION AND SKILLS ACT 2008 (COMMENCEMENT NO.9 AND TRANSITORY PROVISION) ORDER 2013, SI 2013/SI 2013/1204 (C.52); made under the Education and Skills Act 2008 s.173. Commencement details: bringing into force various provisions of the 2008 Act on June 28, 2013 and June 26, 2015.; .

This Order brings into force on June 28, 2013 a number of provisions of the Education and Skills Act 2008, including creating a duty to participate in education and setting out the definition of a Level 3 qualification.

848. Education (Wales) Measure 2011 (nawm 7)–Commencement No.2 Order

THE EDUCATION (WALES) MEASURE 2011 (COMMENCEMENT NO.2) ORDER 2013, SI 2013/SI 2013/2090 (W.205) (C.87); made under the Education (Wales) measure 2011 s.32. Commencement details: bringing into force various provisions of the 2011 Measure on September 19, 2013.; .

The Order brings the Education (Wales) Measure 2011 Pt 2 Ch.2, which makes provision about training for governors and clerks and the provision of a clerk to a school governing body, into force on September 19, 2013.

849. Educational institutions–Local curriculum–Pupils–Wales

THE OPERATION OF THE LOCAL CURRICULUM (WALES) REGULATIONS 2013, SI 2013/SI 2013/1793 (W.180); made under the Learning and Skills (Wales) Measure 2009 s.46, s.38. In force: September 1, 2013; .

These Regulations set out how various provisions of education related legislation are applied in relation to pupils and students following courses of study for the purpose of the local curriculum provided at a school or institution other than their own.

850. Educational policy–Information–Pupils–England

THE EDUCATION (INDIVIDUAL PUPIL INFORMATION) (PRESCRIBED PERSONS) (ENGLAND) (AMENDMENT) REGULATIONS 2013, SI 2013/1193; made under the Education Act 1996 s.537A. In force: June 28, 2013; .

These Regulations make amendments to reg.3 of the Education (Individual Pupil Information) (Prescribed Persons) (England) Regulations 2009 and come into force on June 28, 2013.

851. Endowments–Foundation schools–Statutory trusts–Wales

THE DIOCESE OF SWANSEA AND BRECON (EDUCATION ENDOWMENTS) (LLANFIHANGEL NANT BRAN) (WALES) ORDER 2013, SI 2013/SI 2013/2155 (W.210); made under the Reverter of Sites Act 1987 s.5; and the Education Act 1996 s.554, s.556. In force: October 1, 2013; .

This Order appoints Swansea and Brecon Diocesan Trust as trustee of the endowment of the educational foundation known as the Llanfihangel Nant Bran (more recently known as Llanfihangel Nant Bran Village Hall) School Foundation and makes new provision as to the use of that endowment. It authorises the sale of the school. It makes new provision for the trustee to hold the assets representing the endowment on the uniform statutory trusts as set out in the Schedule for the benefit of the Church in Wales voluntary and foundation schools in the Diocese.

852. European Union–Third country nationals–University fees–Wales

THE EDUCATION (STUDENT FEES, AWARDS, QUALIFYING COURSES AND PERSONS) (WALES) REGULATIONS 2013, SI 2013/SI 2013/1792 (W.179); made under the Education (Fees and Awards) Act 1983 s.1, s.2. In force: September 1, 2013; .

These Regulations remove the requirement for non-EU family members of EU nationals to have been ordinarily resident in the EEA for the three years immediately preceding the start of their course.

853. Examinations–Fairness–2012 GCSE English examinations–Whether marking process tainted by conspicuous unfairness

[Equality Act 2010 (c.15) s.149.]

The claimants (C) applied for judicial review of decisions of the defendants (Q, E and OFQUAL) concerning the award of GCSE English qualifications in August 2012. C were a number of local authorities, schools, teachers and students. Q and E were two of the four organisations awarding GCSE qualifications in the United Kingdom. New GCSE English examinations had been introduced in 2010, and the qualifications were first awarded in August 2012. OFQUAL required the awarding organisations to mark the new exam using a "comparable outcomes" approach, so that a student would get the same grade as he would have had he taken the old exam. The new courses were modular, comprising controlled assessments and an exam which could be submitted or taken at two assessment points each year: January and June. At each point, the awarding organisations marked the material submitted, and determined and published the "grade boundaries". C's complaint centred on the boundary between the C and D grades. They complained that too rigorous a standard had been adopted in June 2012, so that the January 2012 candidates were graded more leniently than were the June candidates. That meant that many students who, on the basis of the January grade boundary, had reasonably expected to attain a C grade, failed to do so. They argued that that amounted to conspicuous unfairness, compounded by two factors. The first was their legitimate expectation, created by an alleged assurance by the awarding organisations and OFQUAL, that the grade boundaries would be the same from one assessment point to the next. The second was that Q and E had given excessive weight to an OFQUAL direction that they should fix the June grade boundary so that the number of students exceeding it did not exceed the predicted number by more than one per cent (the "tolerance limit"). They sought either to have the June papers assessed in accordance with the January boundaries, or to have the June results declared invalid.

Held: Applications refused. (1) OFQUAL's guidance had not improperly fettered Q and E's discretion. It merely expressed the proper concern that they should only depart from the tolerance limit where there was sufficient justification. That was legitimate in order to ensure broad consistency in standards year on year. Q and E had neither treated the reported tolerance as an inflexible principle nor applied it slavishly (see para.90 of judgment). (2) The assurance relied on was not sufficiently unequivocal to create any legitimate expectation that the grade boundaries would not change from one assessment point to the next, *R. (on the application of Niazi) v Secretary of State for the Home Department* [2008] EWCA Civ 755, Times, July 21, 2008, [2008] C.L.Y. 70 applied. Moreover, the public documents were inconsistent with any such assurance. Even if there had been a sufficient assurance, the public interest would justify any failure to give effect to it (paras 93-104). (3) In order for there to be conspicuous unfairness, the decision had to be immoral or illogical or attract similar opprobrium. Conspicuous unfairness was to be treated a particular form of irrationality. While it was for the court to decide whether there had been an abuse of power, its role was supervisory and it did not have a wide discretion to substitute its own view of the merits, *R. v Inland Revenue Commissioners, Ex p. Unilever Plc* [1996] S.T.C. 681 applied. C's case came nowhere near establishing conspicuous unfairness. Q and E had used essentially the same process to fix the grade boundaries in both January and June, although fuller information had been available in June, allowing for a more reliable assessment. The June examiners made assessments that they thought fairly reflected the standard of the scripts and they had had no option other than to apply the standards they did, notwithstanding that they departed from the January standards. While OFQUAL could have permitted a loosening of the tolerance limits to give priority to fairness within the year, that would have been at the expense of fairness between the years. Whichever way it chose to resolve the problem, there was going to be an element of unfairness. The solution it chose was not unfair. It had become clear that the January cohort had been treated too leniently, and OFQUAL had to bear in mind that if the more lenient standard was applied in June, there would be a significant dilution of standards. Maintaining the currency of the qualification was a legitimate justification, in the public interest, for its decision, *R. (on the application of O'Brien) v Independent Assessor* [2007] UKHL 10, [2007] 2 A.C. 312, [2007] C.L.Y. 1003 and *R. (on the application of Tate & Lyle Industries Ltd) v Secretary of State for Energy and Climate Change* [2011] EWCA Civ 664, [2011] A.C.D. 92 applied (paras 115-129, 149-156). (4) Q and E's decisions had a sufficient public element to make them amenable to judicial review. Although the point was not argued, a complaint to OFQUAL, rather than judicial review, would not have been a realistic route. There was no realistic possibility that it would have provided the remedy sought, and a speedy resolution was important (paras 139-141). (5) The public sector equality duty under the Equality Act 2010 s.149 was irrelevant in the assessment of students' performance. It was not necessary to conduct an equality assessment in relation to the imposition of the tolerance limits, and it was legitimate to apply the comparable standards principle without regard to the duty. Q, E and OFQUAL had justifiably considered that it would be wrong to manipulate boundaries to favour groups with particular protected characteristics (paras 142-148).

R. (ON THE APPLICATION OF LEWISHAM LBC) v ASSESSMENT AND QUALIFICATIONS ALLIANCE (AQA), [2013] EWHC 211 (Admin), [2013] E.L.R. 281, Elias, L.J., QBD (Admin).

854. Funding–Higher education–Universities–Wales

THE EDUCATION (STUDENT SUPPORT AND EUROPEAN INSTITUTIONS) (WALES) REGULATIONS 2013, SI 2013/SI 2013/1965 (W.190); made under

theTeaching and Higher Education Act1998 s.22, s.42. In force: August 30, 2013; .
These Regulations provide for financial support for students who are ordinarily resident in Wales and undertaking postgraduate courses at the graduate school for international relations established by John Hopkins University of Bologna and at the College of Europe.

855. Funding–Higher Education Funding Councils–England

THE EDUCATION (DESIGNATED INSTITUTIONS) (ENGLAND) ORDER 2013, SI 2013/1572; made under the Education Reform Act 1988 s.129. In force: July 19, 2013; .
This Order designates The Liverpool School of Tropical Medicine as eligible to receive support from funds administered by the Higher Education Funding Council for England.

856. Funding–Higher Education Funding Councils–England

THE EDUCATION (DESIGNATED INSTITUTIONS) (ENGLAND) (NO.2) ORDER 2013, SI 2013/2490; made under the Education Reform Act 1988 s.129. In force: November 1, 2013; .
This Order designates the National Film and Television School as eligible to receive funding administered by the Higher Education Funding Council for England.

857. Funding–School admissions–Lawrence Sheriff School

THE LAWRENCE SHERIFF SCHOOL (PUPIL PREMIUM ADMISSIONS PRIORITY) ORDER 2013, SI 2013/1553; made under the Education Act 2002 s.2, s.210. In force: July 18, 2013; .
This Order relaxes the application of the School Admissions Code 2012 as it applies to admissions to Lawrence Sheriff School to allow it to give admissions priority to children attracting Pupil Premium Funding. The Order will allow the School to seek to vary its admission arrangements to allow for this in time for admissions in September 2014.

858. Funding Agency for Schools–Wales

THE HIGHER EDUCATION FUNDING COUNCIL FOR WALES (SUPPLEMENTARY FUNCTIONS) ORDER 2013, SI 2013/SI 2013/1733 (W.172); made under the Further and Higher Education Act 1992 s.69, s.89. In force: August 31, 2013; .
This Order confers supplementary functions on the Higher Education Funding Council for Wales.

859. Further education–Further education colleges–Wales

THE COLEG CAMBRIA (INCORPORATION) ORDER 2013, SI 2013/SI 2013/374 (W.46); made under the Further and Higher Education Act 1992 s.16, s.17. In force: March 26, 2013; .
This Order establishes a further education corporation called "Coleg Cambria" under section 16(1)(a) of the Further and Higher Education Act 1992 (the Act) for the purpose of conducting the educational institution of the same name. The Order also provides for the appointment of August 1, 2013 as the operative date for the purposes of Part 1 of the Act, being the date from which Coleg Cambria is to conduct the educational institution of the same name.

860. Further education colleges–Wales

THE COLEG SIR GAR FURTHER EDUCATION CORPORATION (DISSOLUTION) AND COLEG SIR GAR (DESIGNATED INSTITUTIONS IN FURTHER EDUCATION)

ORDER 2013, SI 2013/SI 2013/1663 (W.159); made under the Further and Higher Education Act 1992 s.27C. In force: August 1, 2013; .

This Order dissolves the further education corporation established to conduct Coleg Sir Gar with effect from August 1, 2013. It also designates Coleg Sir Gar (Coleg Sir Gar), a new college conducted by a registered company limited by guarantee, for the purposes of the Further and Higher Education Act 1992 s.28.

861. Further Education Corporations–Transfer of assets–Ystrad Mynach College Further Education Corporation–Wales

THE YSTRAD MYNACH COLLEGE FURTHER EDUCATION CORPORATION (DISSOLUTION) ORDER 2013, SI 2013/SI 2013/1724 (W.168); made under the Further and Higher Education Act 1992 s.27C. In force: August 1, 2013; .

This Order dissolves the further education corporation established to conduct Ystrad Mynach College with effect from August 1, 2013. It provides for the transfer of the property, rights and liabilities of Ystrad Mynach College Further Education Corporation to Coleg Morgannwg Further Education Corporation. The Order also secures the employment rights of persons employed by Ystrad Mynach College Further Education Corporation.

862. Further Education Corporations–Wales

THE COLEG CAMBRIA FURTHER EDUCATION CORPORATION (GOVERNMENT) REGULATIONS 2013, SI 2013/SI 2013/375 (W.47); made under the Further and Higher Education Act 1992 s.20, s.21, Sch.4 para.1, Sch.4 para.13, Sch.4 para.14, Sch.4 para.15, Sch.4 para.16, Sch.4 para.17, Sch.4 para.18, Sch.4 para.19, Sch.4 para.20, Sch.4 para.21, Sch.4 para.22, Sch.4 para.23, Sch.4 para.24, Sch.4 para.25. In force: March 26, 2013; .

These Regulations prescribe the Instrument of Government and Articles of Government for Coleg Cambria Further Education Corporation. The Instrument of Government and Articles of Government provide for the constitution and conduct of Coleg Cambria Further Education Corporation.

863. Graduates–Student grants–Wales

THE EDUCATION (EUROPEAN INSTITUTIONS) AND STUDENT SUPPORT (WALES) REGULATIONS 2013, SI 2013/SI 2013/765 (W.91); made under the Teaching and Higher Education Act 1998 s.22, s.42, s.43. In force: April 23, 2013; .

These Regulations provide for financial support for eligible students ordinarily resident in Wales undertaking postgraduate courses at the graduate school for international relations established by Johns Hopkins University at Bologna (known as the Bologna Center) and the College of Europe.

864. Higher education–Student loans–Eligibility of foreign nationals with discretionary leave to remain–Right to education–Justification for discriminatory measures

[Education (Student Support) Regulations 2011 (SI 2011/1986); European Convention on Human Rights 1950 Art.14, Protocol 1 Art.2.]

The claimants (K), two Ethiopian nationals, applied for judicial review of a decision of the defendant secretary of state that they were ineligible for student loans. K had been brought to the United Kingdom as children by their father, who had then abandoned them. The local authority assumed parental responsibility for them and they had discretionary leave to remain until November 30, 2014. K completed their school education and both were offered university places which were due to start in 2012. Having secured the places, K discovered that they were ineligible for student loans to finance their tuition fees. The secretary of state refused to treat them as if they were settled in the UK for loan purposes. The basis of K's case was the proposition that, although they did not have indefinite leave to remain, there was no realistic prospect of their being removed from the UK because they would have been resident in the UK for 10 years by the time their discretionary leave to remain expired. K argued that (1) the failure to provide them with student loans violated their right to education under the European Convention on Human Rights 1950 Protocol 1 art.2; (2) denial of student loans on the ground of their immigration status amounted to unlawful discrimination contrary to art.14 in conjunction with Protocol 1 art.2.

Held: Applications refused. (1) There had been very few cases in which alleged violations of Protocol 1 art.2 had been considered. None of them supported the proposition that the state was under a positive obligation to provide financial support to students in higher education as part of its obligations under that provision. Although the European Court of Human Rights had observed in *Sahin v Turkey (44774/98)* (2007) 44 E.H.R.R. 5, [2006] C.L.Y. 2103 that the Convention was a living instrument in need of interpretation in the light of present-day conditions and might be interpreted in the light of other international instruments dealing with education, to conclude that it had the reach for which K argued was to run ahead of that court's jurisprudence in a way which was impermissible, *Sahin* considered (see paras 24-26 of judgment). (2) Although Scott Baker L.J. had said in *R. (on the application of Douglas) v North Tyneside MBC* [2003] EWCA Civ 1847, [2004] 1 W.L.R. 2363, [2004] C.L.Y. 979 that art.14 did not, as a matter of course, stretch to the funding of higher education, that did not provide a hard-edged rule that university funding arrangements for individual students were necessarily outside the reach of art.14. The facts of *Douglas* were very specific and appeared to have influenced the conclusion in that case, in particular that the absence of the loan made no difference to the claimant's ability to complete the course, *Douglas* distinguished. The instant case was concerned with the argument that funding arrangements under the Education (Student Support) Regulations 2011 were designed to discriminate against foreign nationals who did not have indefinite leave to remain, were not refugees and did not have humanitarian protection. Despite differences between K's immigration status and the position of those granted asylum or humanitarian protection who were entitled to receive student loans under the 2011 Regulations, they were all in an analogous situation as far as tertiary education was concerned. Nobody could have access to university education without funding to discharge the fees. State support for the discharge of fees by way of loans was, for a large number of people, the only way of paying them. It was therefore an important feature in providing practical and effective access to university education. It followed that the current arrangements relating to funding were not too remote from the right guaranteed by Protocol 1 art.2 to fall outside its ambit and therefore to be considered by reference to art.14 (paras 28-28, 31, 33). (3) The European Court of Human Rights had recognised a wide margin of appreciation allowed to the state in relation to the application of Protocol 1 art.2 to education funding, *Ponomaryov v Bulgaria (5335/05)* [2011] Eq. L.R. 883 considered. The issue of whether a measure was justified depended on whether it was manifestly without reasonable foundation. In the instant case, even if the absence of loans denied K the opportunity to go to university, the alleged discriminatory measures were justified for the purposes of art.14 in the interests of husbanding scarce resources and using the available money on those who were entitled to remain to benefit the economy. As it was likely that K would in any event be granted indefinite leave to remain in due course, the impact of the impugned measures was at most to delay the immediate opportunity to begin a university course (paras 35, 37, 45, 47).

R. (ON THE APPLICATION OF KEBEDE) v SECRETARY OF STATE FOR BUSINESS, INNOVATION AND SKILLS; *sub nom.* KEDEBE v SECRETARY OF STATE FOR BUSINESS, INNOVATION AND SKILLS, [2013] EWHC 2396 (Admin), [2014] P.T.S.R. 92, Burnett, J., QBD (Admin).

865. Higher Education Corporations–Universities–Newport–Wales

THE UNIVERSITY OF WALES, NEWPORT HIGHER EDUCATION CORPORATION (DISSOLUTION) ORDER 2013, SI 2013/SI 2013/664 (W.77); made under the Education Reform Act 1988 s.128. In force: April 11, 2013; .

This Order dissolves the higher education corporation established to conduct the University of Wales, Newport.

866. Information–Local authorities' powers and duties–Primary education–England

THE INFORMATION AS TO PROVISION OF EDUCATION (ENGLAND) (AMENDMENT) REGULATIONS 2013, SI 2013/1255; made under the Education Act 1996 s.29, s.569. In force: July 1, 2013; .

These Regulations amend the Information as to Provision of Education (England) Regulations 2008 (SI 2008/4), which prescribe the information that local authorities have each year to provide to the Secretary of State in relation to the provision of primary and secondary education in their area. They extend the requirement to information about school places added to localised areas, and the funding used to provide them.

867. Leave of absence–Maintained schools–Registration–England

THE EDUCATION (PUPIL REGISTRATION) (ENGLAND) (AMENDMENT) REGULATIONS 2013, SI 2013/756; made under the Education Act 1996 s.434, s.551, s.569. In force: September 1, 2013; .

These Regulations amend the Education (Pupil Registration) (England) Regulations 2006 (SI 2006/1751). The changes prohibit the proprietor of a maintained school granting leave of absence to a pupil except where an application has been made in advance and the proprietor and the proprietor considers that there are exceptional circumstances relating to the application.

868. Literacy–Maintained schools–Numeracy–England

THE SCHOOL INFORMATION (ENGLAND) (AMENDMENT) REGULATIONS 2013, SI 2013/758; made under the Education Act 1996 s.537, s.569. In force: September 1, 2013; .

These Regulations amend the School Information (England) Regulations 2008 (SI 2008/3093). From September 1, 2013 they impose an additional requirement on maintained schools to publish specified details relating to the Year 7 literacy and numeracy catch-up premium grant on a website.

869. Literacy–Numeracy–Testing–Wales

THE NATIONAL CURRICULUM (AMENDMENTS RELATING TO EDUCATIONAL PROGRAMMES FOR THE FOUNDATION PHASE AND PROGRAMMES OF STUDY FOR THE SECOND AND THIRD KEY STAGES) (WALES) REGULATIONS 2013, SI 2013/SI 2013/437 (W.53); made under the Education Act 1996 s.29, s.408, s.537, s.537A, s.569; and the Education Act 2002 s.30. In force: May 1, 2013 except for reg.3(5) on September 1, 2013.; .

These Regulations amend a number of regulations as a consequence of the assessment arrangements specified by the Welsh Ministers in the Education (National Curriculum) (Assessment Arrangements for Reading and Numeracy) (Wales) Order 2013. The Assessment Order specifies the assessment arrangements for testing literacy and numeracy in the national curriculum for Wales. The Regulations come into force on May 1, 2013 except for regulation 3(5) which comes into force on September 1, 2013.

870. Local authorities' powers and duties–Maintained schools–School governors–Wales

THE GOVERNMENT OF MAINTAINED SCHOOLS (CLERK TO A GOVERNING BODY) (WALES) REGULATIONS 2013, SI 2013/SI 2013/2127 (W.208); made under the School Standards and Framework Act 1998 Sch.1A para.19; the Education Act 2002 s.23, s.210; and the Education (Wales) Measure 2011 s.23, s.24, s.32. In force: September 20, 2013; .

These Regulations set out within how many weeks a local authority must provide the governing body of a maintained school with a suitable clerk. They also set out the training requirements for the clerk to a governing body at maintained schools in Wales. The required content of the training is set out in a document published by the Welsh Ministers.

871. Local authorities' powers and duties–School admissions–England

THE INFORMATION AS TO PROVISION OF EDUCATION (ENGLAND) (AMENDMENT) (NO.2) REGULATIONS 2013, SI 2013/2049; made under the Education Act 1996 s.29, s.569. In force: January 1, 2014; .

These Regulations amend the Information as to Provision of Education (England) Regulations 2008 (SI 2008/4) to extend the requirement for each local authority in England to provide the Secretary of State with information about secondary school admissions (details of the applications they have received, the preferences expressed in those applications and the offers made in respect of children living in the authority's area) to include information about admissions to primary schools. They will also require each local authority to provide that information in respect of each individual child rather than the total number of applications received, preferences expressed and offers made.

872. Local authorities' powers and duties–School admissions–School performance–Wales

THE SCHOOL ADMISSIONS (VARIATIONOF ADMISSION ARRANGEMENTS) (WALES) REGULATIONS 2013, SI 2013/SI 2013/1140 (W.120); made under the School Standards and Framework Act 1998 s.89, s.138A. In force: July 8, 2013; .

These Regulations prescribe the circumstances in which an admission authority may vary the admission arrangements they have determined for a particular school year (in addition to the circumstances set out in s.89 of the School Standards and Framework Act 1998.

873. Local education authorities–School attendance–Truancy–England

THE EDUCATION (PENALTY NOTICES) (ENGLAND) (AMENDMENT) REGULATIONS 2013, SI 2013/757; made under the Education Act 1996 s.444B, s.569; and the Education and Inspections Act 2006 s.106, s.181. In force: September 1, 2013; .

These Regulations amend the Education (Penalty Notices) (England) Regulations 2007 (SI 2007/1867) to shorten the period in which the penalty notice must be paid to the local education authority.

874. Local education authorities' powers and duties–Voluntary aided schools

[Education Act 1996 (c.56) s.13, s.14; Education and Inspections Act 2006 (c.40) Pt 2, s.6A, s.7, s.10, s.11 (1A), s.11, Sch.2 Pt 2 para.8.]

The claimants (C) applied for judicial review of decisions of the defendant local authority to approve proposals put forward by the first interested party, the Roman Catholic Diocese of Westminster, to establish voluntary aided Catholic primary and secondary schools and to lease land to the Diocese to provide premises for those schools. The first claimant was a charity working on behalf of non-religious people, the second was an association of local residents which campaigned to seek to ensure that any new state schools in the borough operated open admissions policies. There were six Catholic primary schools in the borough but no Catholic secondary school; many Catholic children travelled out of the borough to attend Catholic schools. The local authority's report of its public consultation on the use of the site and on the Diocese's proposals noted that it had received many comments that the borough needed a Catholic secondary school. The council accepted its officers' report which noted that there was no current need for more secondary schools in the borough that would engage the operation of the Education and Inspections Act 2006 s.6A and it recommended the use of the site for the two schools proposed by the Diocese under s.11 (1A) of the Act. As voluntary aided schools, the new schools would give priority to the admission of Catholic children. C submitted that the local authority had identified a need for there to be two new schools in its area and therefore was under a duty under s.6A to invite proposals for the establishment of an academy, with the effect that it was not entitled to proceed to consider and approve the Catholic schools. C further submitted that factors relevant to the sufficient provision of education, diversity of provision and fostering of parental choice under the Education Act 1996 s.13 and s.14 were also relevant to the assessment by a local authority whether there was a need under s.6A of the 2006 Act to establish a new school.

Held: Application refused. (1) The local authority had made clear its provisional view in the consultation paper, subject to the outcome, that there was not a current need for a new state school in the area and its provisional view that introduction of the Catholic schools proposed by the Diocese would be beneficial, in that they would increase diversity of school provision, improve parental choice and help meet parental wishes for places at Catholic schools in-borough rather than having to send children out of the borough. The document's discussion of the issue was not a statement that there was a need for such a school (see para.47 of judgment). Nothing in the consultation paper or the associated questionnaire sent to the public constituted evidence that the local authority thought there was a need, in the s.6A sense, to establish a new school in the area or was liable to mislead the public into thinking that the local authority thought there was such a need (paras 53-54). (2) Factors under ss.13 and 14 of the 1996 Act could be relevant under s.6A, but it did not follow that whenever a local authority considered that it might be beneficial for there to be a new school it had to be taken to think that there was a need under s.6A to establish a new school. If it were otherwise, there would be no practical scope for the operation of s.7, which gave a local authority the power to invite proposals for the establishment of new schools, a power that existed alongside the obligation in s.6A and was not swallowed up by it. Further, the scheme of Pt 2 of the 2006 Act reinforced that view. If a local authority thought there was a need to establish a new school, the obligation under s.6A to seek proposals for the establishment of an academy was triggered. But the Act contemplated that it could act to foster or approve proposals for establishment of a new school in other circumstances, where in a wider and more general sense it thought it might be beneficial to do so. Where a proposal was made under s.10 or s.11 of the 2006 Act to establish a new school, Sch.2 Pt 2 para.8 required the local authority to consider whether the proposal should be approved. The test governing approval of such a proposal was not so narrow as to turn on a question of need; again, s.6A did not swallow up those provisions. It would be a matter of fact and degree for the local authority whether factors relevant under ss.13 and 14 of the 1996 Act were of such weight and so pressing that they led to the conclusion that there was a need to establish a new school under s.6A. A local authority was entitled to take a practical approach (paras 63-68). (3) The local authority had acted lawfully in making its assessment that it did not think that a new school was needed and hence that no duty under s.6A had arisen, but rather that it was merely desirable that the Diocese's proposals should be approved and the site made available for their implementation (paras 70-71). (4) Where a proposal to establish a new school had been published under s.11 (1A), as in the instant case, the local authority remained obliged under the Act to consider that proposal on its merits. Parliament did not intend s.6A to operate to disapply that obligation (paras 74-78).

R. (ON THE APPLICATION OF BRITISH HUMANIST ASSOCIATION) v RICHMOND UPON THAMES LBC; *sub nom.* BRITISH HUMANIST

ASSOCIATION v RICHMOND UPON THAMES LBC, [2012] EWHC 3622 (Admin), [2013] 2 All E.R. 146, Sales, J., QBD (Admin).

875. Maintained schools–Ministers' powers and duties–Local authorities' powers and duties

THE SCHOOL STANDARDS AND ORGANISATION (WALES) ACT 2013 (COMMENCEMENT NO.1) ORDER 2013, SI 2013/SI 2013/1000 (W.105) (C.42); made under the School Standards and Organisation (Wales) Act 2013 s.100. Commencement details: bringing into force various provisions of the 2013 Act on April 26, 2013 and May 4, 2013.; .

This is the first commencement order made by the Welsh Ministers under the School Standards and Organisation (Wales) Act 2013 (the 2013 Act). The Order brings ss.38, 39, 97 and 98 of the 2013 Act into force on April 26, 2013 insofar as they allow for the laying and making of a draft school organisation code.

876. Maintained schools–Misconduct–Teachers–England

THE SCHOOL STAFFING (ENGLAND) (AMENDMENT) REGULATIONS 2013, SI 2013/1940; made under the Education Act 2002 s.35, s.36, s.210. In force: September 1, 2013; .

These Regulations amend the School Staffing (England) Regulations 2009 (SI 2009/2680) so that the checks that maintained schools are required to carry out on new staff reflect recent changes to the regulation of teacher misconduct.

877. Maintained schools–Personal data–Pupil referral units–England

THE EDUCATION (INFORMATION ABOUT INDIVIDUAL PUPILS) (ENGLAND) REGULATIONS 2013, SI 2013/2094; made under the Education Act 1996 s.537A, s.569. In force: January 1, 2014; .

These Regulations consolidate the Education (Information About Individual Pupils) (England) Regulations 2006 (the 2006 Regulation) and make certain additions and modifications. The Regulations set out the individual pupil data items to be collected from schools in the School and Pupil Referral Unit Census and contain two new data items to be collected from 2014 onwards. Some drafting and structural changes have been made and three data items that are no longer collected have been removed.

878. Maintained schools–School governors–Training–Wales

THE GOVERNMENT OF MAINTAINED SCHOOLS (TRAINING REQUIREMENTS FOR GOVERNORS) (WALES) REGULATIONS 2013, SI 2013/SI 2013/2124 (W.207); made under the School Standards and Framework Act 1998 Sch.1A para.19; the Education Act 2002 s.19, s.23, s.210; and the Education (Wales) Measure 2011 s.22, s.32. In force: September 20, 2013; .

These Regulations set out the training requirements for governors at maintained schools in Wales. The required content of the training is set out in documents published by the Welsh Ministers.

879. Modern languages–National Curriculum

THE EDUCATION (NATIONAL CURRICULUM) (LANGUAGES) (ENGLAND) ORDER 2013, SI 2013/2230; made under the Education Act 2002 s.84, s.210. In force: September 1, 2013; .

This instrument provides for the languages that maintained schools can teach to pupils in relation to the foundation subject of a foreign language in respect of the second key stage, and to the subject of a modern foreign language in respect of the third key stage.

880. National Curriculum–Attainment targets–England

THE EDUCATION (NATIONAL CURRICULUM) (ATTAINMENT TARGETS AND PROGRAMMES OF STUDY) (ENGLAND) ORDER 2013, SI 2013/2232; made under the Education Act 2002 s.87, s.210. In force: September 1, 2013; .

This instrument revokes the Orders which give effect to the current attainment targets and programmes of study for individual core and other foundation subjects and in its place gives effect to a Framework Document which contains all the new attainment targets and programmes of study for core and other foundation subjects at each key stage which first take effect in the school year 2014/15, subject to certain exceptions.

881. National Curriculum–Wales

THE EDUCATION (NATIONAL CURRICULUM) (ASSESSMENT ARRANGEMENTS FOR READING AND NUMERACY) (WALES) ORDER 2013, SI 2013/SI 2013/433 (W.51); made under the Education Act 2002 s.108, s.210. In force: May 1, 2013; .

The Education Act 2002 s.108 provides a power for the Welsh Ministers to prescribe by way of an Order assessment arrangements of the National Curriculum. This Order gives legal effect to the assessment arrangements for reading and numeracy for pupils who attend schools maintained by a local authority (other than any established in a hospital) in Wales.

882. Office of the Independent Adjudicator for Higher Education–Examinations–Judicial review of OIA decisions–Advance disclosure of assessment criteria to students–Conflation with marking scheme

The claimant (B) applied for judicial review of an adjudication by the defendant OIA rejecting his complaint about an examination process at the London School of Economics (LSE). B had enrolled on the MRes/PhD Economics Track 1 programme at the LSE but had failed one of the courses twice. As a consequence, he was unable to complete the MRes and progress to the PhD. B complained to the LSE that the marking scheme of the examination in question was not communicated to class teachers, so that they were unable to prepare their students appropriately. That complaint was rejected, as was an internal appeal. B then lodged his complaint with the OIA, complaining that the LSE's failure to disclose to students the assessment criteria for the final examinations was in breach of para.6.1 of the LSE's internal instructions for examiners, according to which each department was to produce and publish assessment criteria in line with the school requirements. The Deputy Adjudicator found that the non-disclosure of the marking schemes to students was a conscious decision by the LSE to encourage students to prepare themselves to do the best they could, instead of targeting parts of the questions, and that it was free to make such a decision. The issues were (i) whether the Deputy Adjudicator erred when she interpreted para.6.1 as not dictating that the assessment criteria or marking schemes were to be disclosed to students in advance of examination; (ii) whether the LSE was in breach of its own instructions and rules by not publishing its assessment criteria for the examination in question in a form that was available to B as a student in advance of his taking that examination.

Held: Application refused. The marking scheme for the examination in question basically set out suggested answers to the questions. No model answer was given because there was no unique right answer. It was clear that, when making her ruling, the Deputy Adjudicator had assumed that a marking scheme and assessment criteria were synonymous. However, based on examples presented to the court, "assessment criteria" were merely verbal indicators of the standards needed for a student to achieve certain grades. They did not involve elements of description of the syllabus or information about the scope and subject matter of the course, and were therefore irrelevant. Paragraph 6.1 (b) did require the LSE to publish assessment criteria for examinations to students across the board, as part of the requirement of transparency, and the Deputy Adjudicator had erred in reaching the contrary conclusion. However, there was no suggestion that marking schemes should be published to students before an examination. Had the Deputy Adjudicator drawn a clear distinction between assessment criteria and marking schemes, she would have concluded that publication of the assessment criteria would have made no difference whatsoever to B's performance. Accordingly, his complaint would still have been dismissed. Although the OIA was amenable to judicial review, the court would generally be very slow to interfere with its decisions. However, where an inferior tribunal had made an error of fact, relief by way of judicial review would only be granted if the error was material. In the instant case, the error was not material. Instead, it arose from confusion as to what assessment criteria actually comprised and its conflation with a marking scheme, publication of which most definitely could not be made to students (see paras 7-8, 13, 18-22 of judgment).

BURGER v OFFICE OF THE INDEPENDENT ADJUDICATOR FOR HIGHER EDUCATION, [2013] EWHC 172 (Admin), [2013] E.L.R. 331, Mostyn, J., QBD (Admin).

883. Primary schools–Rural areas–School inspections

THE DESIGNATION OF RURAL PRIMARY SCHOOLS (ENGLAND) ORDER 2013, SI 2013/2655; made under the Education and Inspections Act 2006 s.15. In force: October 15, 2013; .

This Order designates those primary schools in England which are rural primary schools for the purpose of the Education and Inspections Act 2006 s.15.

884. Primary schools–School performance–Wales

THE SCHOOL ADMISSIONS (INFANT CLASS SIZES) (WALES) REGULATIONS 2013, SI 2013/SI 2013/1141 (W.121); made under the School Standards and Framework Act 1998 s.1, s.138. In force: July 8, 2013; .

These Regulations impose, for the purpose of s.1 of the School Standards and Framework Act 1998, a limit on class sizes for infant classes at maintained schools in Wales. They revoke and replace the Education (Infant Class Sizes) (Wales) Regulations 1998 and the Education (Infant Class Sizes) (Wales) (Amendment) Regulations 2009 (reg.3), adding new categories to the excepted pupils and changing the circumstances in which pupils cease to be excepted.

885. Qualifications–Training–Young persons

THE DUTY TO PARTICIPATE IN EDUCATION OR TRAINING (MISCELLANEOUS PROVISIONS) REGULATIONS 2013, SI 2013/1205; made under the Education and Skills Act 2008 s.3, s.4, s.5, s.7, s.8, s.62. In force: June 28, 2013; .

These Regulations are made under Pt.1 of the Education and Skills Act 2008 and make provision in relation to the duty on young people to participate in education or training until the age of 18, or until attaining a level 3 qualification if earlier.

886. Remuneration–Teachers

THE SCHOOL TEACHERS' PAY AND CONDITIONS ORDER 2013, SI 2013/1932; made under the Education Act 2002 s.122, s.123, s.124. In force: September 1, 2013; .

This Order makes provision for the remuneration and conditions of employment of school teachers to be determined by reference to the provisions set out in the "School Teachers' Pay and Conditions Document 2013 and Guidance on School Teachers' Pay and Conditions".

887. School admissions–Local education authorities appeals

THE EDUCATION (ADMISSION APPEALS ARRANGEMENTS) (WALES) (AMENDMENT) REGULATIONS 2013, SI 2013/SI 2013/2535 (W.250); made under the School Standards and Framework Act 1998 s.94, s.95, s.138. In force: January 1, 2014; .

These Regulations amend the Education (Admission Appeals Arrangements) (Wales) Regulations 2005 (SI 2005/1398) to provide that, when a child is refused a place at school on the basis that to admit the child would breach the statutory limit on infant class size unless a relevant measure were taken to avoid that breach, panels may only uphold the appeal on certain limited grounds.

888. School admissions–School performance–Wales

THE SCHOOL ADMISSIONS (COMMON OFFER DATE) (WALES) REGULATIONS 2013, SI 2013/SI 2013/1144 (W.122); made under the School Standards and Framework Act 1998 s.89B, s.138A. In force: July 8, 2013; .

These Regulations are made under s.89B and 138A of the School Standards and Framework Act 1998. They come into force on July 8 2013 and apply in relation to admission to secondary schools for the academic year 2015/2016 and in relation to admission to primary schools for the academic year 2018/2019 and subsequent academic years.

889. School attendance–Truancy–Parental responsibility–Wales

THE EDUCATION (PENALTY NOTICES) (WALES) REGULATIONS 2013, SI 2013/SI 2013/1983 (W.193); made under the Education Act 1996 s.444A, s.444B, s.569. In force: September 2, 2013; .

These Regulations prescribe the necessary details for the operation of the penalty notice scheme under the Education Act 1996 s.44A.

890. School exclusions–Disability discrimination–Propriety of First-tier Tribunal's approach to lawfulness of disabled pupil's exclusion

[Equality Act 2010 (c.15) s.85; Equality Act 2010 (Disability) Regulations 2010 (SI 2010/2128) reg.4.]

The appellant parents (P) appealed against a ruling of the First-tier Tribunal that the decision of the respondent governing body to permanently exclude their son (S) from the primary school he was attending did not contravene the Equality Act 2010 s.85. S had been diagnosed as having Asperger's syndrome and as being likely to be suffering also from attention deficit hyperactivity disorder. He was prone to aggressive and unpredictable behaviour. He was excluded following an incident in which he kicked a teaching assistant several times. The governing body gave the following reasons for upholding his exclusion: the school had put in place all recommended strategies to include and support him; there had been serious and ongoing breaches of the school's behaviour policy which had increased in severity; and the safety and welfare of pupils and staff in the school community had been compromised. P appealed to the tribunal, which held that it should take into account all facts leading to the decision to exclude. It found that the records showed a clear tendency to physical abuse on S's part during his stay at the school. It concluded that his claim failed since, by virtue of the Equality Act 2010 (Disability) Regulations 2010 reg.4, "a tendency to physical... abuse of other persons" was not to be treated as an impairment for the purposes of the 2010 Act.

Held: Appeal allowed. (1) The tribunal had erred by concentrating on the events at the time of S's exclusion and by failing properly to identify the reasons why he was permanently excluded. It had also erred by failing to consider the issue of reasonable adjustments. If the tribunal had followed through from the written decision of the governing body, it would have had to address that body's contention that the school had put in place all recommended strategies to include and support S. The case would be remitted to the tribunal (see paras 64, 71-72 of judgment). (2) The tribunal had not erred when interpreting and applying the exclusion in reg.4 of the 2010 Regulations. The phrase "physical abuse" had to be read as a whole. The language had not been chosen to import any formal or specific meaning. The phrase was to be applied under the Act to everyone who might be involved in alleged discrimination and was not specific to children or to education. "Physical abuse" should therefore be construed as ordinary words. S's actions could properly be described as showing a tendency to physical abuse, *Governors of X Endowed Primary School v Special Educational Needs and Disability Tribunal* [2009] EWHC 1842 (Admin), [2009] I.R.L.R. 1007, [2010] C.L.Y. 973 followed (paras 70, 73).

P v GOVERNING BODY OF A PRIMARY SCHOOL, [2013] UKUT 154 (AAC), [2013] Eq. L.R. 666, David Williams, UT (AAC).

891. School governors–School governors' powers and duties

THE SCHOOL GOVERNANCE (ROLES, PROCEDURES AND ALLOWANCES) (ENGLAND) (AMENDMENT) REGULATIONS 2013, SI 2013/2688; made under the Education Act 2002 s.19, s.210. In force: November 14, 2013; .

This instrument amends the School Governance (Roles, Procedures and Allowances) (England) Regulations 2013 (SI 2013/1624) which came into force on September 1, 2013. The purpose is to: insert a requirement, omitted from the 2013 Regulations in error, that papers must, subject to specific exceptions, be circulated in advance of meetings both of governing bodies and of committees of governing bodies of maintained schools; clarify that the power the governing body has to approve alternative arrangements for governors to participate or vote in meetings of the governing body, extends to meetings of committees of the governing body.

892. School governors–Suspension–Allegation of failure to comply with reg.14 School Governance (Procedures) (England) Regulations 2003

[Education Act 1996 (c.56) s.497; School Governance (Procedures) (England) Regulations 2003 (SI 2003/1377) reg.14(5), reg.14(2).]

The claimant (M) applied for judicial review of a decision of the first defendant governing body, made on October 5, 2011, to suspend him from attending governors' meetings for a period of six months. He also sought judicial review of a decision of the second defendant secretary of state not to make a direction under the Education Act 1996 s.497. M had been a teacher at the relevant school and an elected staff governor. He was suspended from his position as a governor on several occasions and dismissed from his employment as a teacher in March 2012, although unfair-dismissal proceedings were currently pending before the employment tribunal. As to his suspension on October 5, 2011, which had been sought on the basis that he was subject to disciplinary proceedings in relation to his employment, M had claimed that a number of the governors present at the relevant meeting had conflicts of interest. The chairman dealt with the matter by inviting each governor to consider whether he or she had a conflict of interest and/or whether there was any reasonable doubt about his or her ability to act impartially, in which case he or she should withdraw from the vote. No governor did withdraw, and 11 out of the 12 present voted in favour of M's suspension. The School Governance (Procedures) (England) Regulations 2003 reg.14(2) provided that where there might be a conflict between the interests of a relevant person and the interests of the governing body or where there was reasonable doubt about a relevant person's ability to act impartially in relation to any matter, that person, if present at the relevant meeting, should disclose his interest, withdraw from the meeting and not vote on the matter in question. Regulation 14(5) provided that where there was any dispute as to whether a relevant person was required to withdraw from a meeting and not vote, that question should be determined by the other governors present at the meeting. In February 2012, the secretary of state declined to make a direction to the governors under s.497 of the 1996 Act, having concluded that it would not be expedient to do so: although there had been a "procedural anomaly" regarding the conflict-of-interest issue at the meeting of October 5, the disciplinary hearing regarding M's suspension as a teacher was due to conclude shortly. M argued that (1) the decision of October 5, 2011 was of no effect, because there had been a failure to comply with reg.14(2) and reg.14(5) of the 2003 Regulations; (2) the secretary of state had acted unreasonably in the public-law sense by not making a direction to the governors under s.497 of the 1996 Act.

Held: Application refused. (1) It was difficult to see what could be a more fundamental disregard of the procedure in reg.14. That regulation concerned restrictions on persons taking part in proceedings. There had been no restriction on any person taking part in the proceedings on October 5 other than asking the individual to consider whether he or she had a conflict of interest. However, it would not be appropriate to make a declaration concerning such non-compliance, as the secretary of state had made it clear that there had been procedural defects in respect of M's suspension on October 5 and earlier suspensions. Given the background, it was for the local authority to consider whether the way it had handled the consequences of that, either in respect of this school's board of governors or in respect of that of any other school in its area, where similar issues had arisen, was adequate (see paras 79, 83-85 of judgment). (2) It had not been irrational for the secretary of state to conclude that M's suspension was not going to have effect for much longer and that his status as a governor was linked to his employment dispute and the outcome of it. It might be that he would be vindicated in the appropriate employment context; however, on the facts as they stood at the time the secretary of state made his decision, it was not possible to say that he had acted irrationally (para.90).

R. (ON THE APPLICATION OF McCORMACK) v ST EDMUND CAMPION CATHOLIC SCHOOL GOVERNING BODY, [2012] EWHC 3928 (Admin), [2013] E.L.R. 169, Beatson, J., QBD (Admin).

893. School performance–England

THE EDUCATION (SCHOOL PERFORMANCE INFORMATION) (ENGLAND) (AMENDMENT) REGULATIONS 2013, SI 2013/1759; made under the Education Act 1996 s.537A, s.569. In force: September 1, 2013; .

These Regulations amend the Education (School Performance Information) (England) Regulations 2007 (SI 2007/2324) to omit the reference to the Phonics Document.

894. School Standards and Organisation Act 2013 (anaw 1)–Commencement No.2, Savings and Transitional Provisions Order–Wales

THE SCHOOL STANDARDS AND ORGANISATION (WALES) ACT 2013 (COMMENCEMENT NO.2, SAVINGS AND TRANSITIONAL PROVISIONS) ORDER 2013, SI 2013/SI 2013/1800 (W.182) (C.74); made under the School Standards and Organisation (Wales) Act 2013 s.100. Commencement details: bringing into force various provisions of the 2013 Act on July 19, 2013 and October 1, 2013.; .

This Order commences the School Standards and Organisation (Wales) Act 2013 ss.38 and 39 in so far as those sections are not already in force on July 19, 2013.

895. School Standards and Organisation (Wales) Act 2013 ()

This Act reforms the powers of local authorities and the Welsh Ministers to intervene in the conduct of schools maintained by local authorities that are causing concern; reforms the powers of the Welsh Ministers to intervene in the exercise of education functions by local authorities; provides for school improvement guidance; reforms the statutory arrangements for the organisation of maintained schools; provides for Welsh in education strategic plans; and makes miscellaneous provision in relation to maintained schools.

This Act received Royal Assent on March 4, 2013.

896. School Standards and Organisation (Wales) Act 2013 ()

This Act reforms the powers of local authorities and the Welsh Ministers to intervene in the conduct of schools maintained by local authorities that are causing concern; reforms the powers of the Welsh Ministers to intervene in the exercise of education functions by local authorities; provides for school improvement guidance; reforms the statutory arrangements for the organisation of maintained schools; provides for Welsh in education strategic plans; makes miscellaneous provision in relation to maintained schools.

This Act received Royal Assent on March 4, 2013.

897. School transport–Local authorities' powers and duties–Extent of local authority's transport obligations–Lawfulness of imposing designated pick-up points on parents–Meaning of "suitable home to school travel arrangements" in s.508B(1) Education Act 1986

[Education Act 1996 (c.56) s.497, s.508B, s.508B(3).]

The claimant children (C) applied for judicial review of the defendant local authority's approach to its obligations under the Education Act 1996 s.508B to make travel arrangements for eligible children to get between home and school. C were eligible children with special needs under the Act. The local authority proposed to provide transport from a pick-up point rather than C's homes with the practical effect that C's parents (P) would have to accompany them from home to the pick-up point. C claimed that the local authority was obliged to make door-to-door travel arrangements for them to and from school. The local authority agreed to provide door-to-door transportation to C until the end of the school year, but reserved the future right to impose a pick-up point arrangement if it considered that P were acting unreasonably in refusing to agree to it. The issue was whether s.508B permitted a local authority to insist on transport from a pick-up point other than the home. The local authority submitted that (1) the availability of complaint to the secretary of state under s.497 of the Act was an appropriate alternative remedy to judicial review which C ought to have pursued; (2) under s.508B it could, in an appropriate case, arrange for transport to be provided from a pick-up point some reasonable distance from a child's home.

Held: Application refused. (1) As the secretary of state had already taken a view that the points of law raised should be answered adversely to C, the court would not treat the s.497 procedure as a satisfactory alternative procedure that precluded its own consideration of the case. Secondly, the issues raised were pure issues of law and statutory interpretation and it was the court, and not the secretary of state, which had primary responsibility for giving authoritative rulings on such issues. Thirdly, the issues were of general significance for a potentially wide range of cases and therefore judicial review was likely to be a more efficient way to resolve the issues so as to provide authoritative guidance for that range of cases (see paras 10-13 of judgment). (2) The concept of "suitable home to school travel arrangements" in s.508B(1) was to be interpreted in the light of the s.508B(3) definition. That definition did not state that travel arrangements had to cover the whole journey from home to school; they only had to be arrangements "relating to" travel in both directions between home and school. The drafter could have used a phrase other than "relating to" to indicate that relevant travel arrangements had to cover the entirety of the journey rather than just part of it. Therefore, to comply with s.508B(1) the local authority had to make travel arrangements that related to travel between home and school, which covered the whole or part of that journey, and had to be satisfied that those arrangements were "suitable" for the purpose of facilitating the child's attendance at school. "Suitable" was not limited to the mode of transportation but included the extent of the travel arrangements to be provided and whether it was reasonable to expect a parent to get their child to a proposed pick-up point. It followed that it was potentially lawful for a local authority to arrange for an eligible child to be transported to school via a pick-up point at a reasonable distance from the child's home, if it considered that such home to school travel arrangements were "suitable". Consequently, a local authority was not in every case obliged to arrange transport for an eligible child direct from the child's home to their school and was permitted, in an appropriate case, to designate pick-up points other than the child's home which were imposed rather than consented to by the child's parents (paras 15-18, 20-21, 24-26).

R. (ON THE APPLICATION OF M) v HOUNSLOW LBC, [2013] EWHC 579 (Admin), [2013] P.T.S.R. 942, Sales, J., QBD (Admin).

898. Schools–School year regulations

THE WEST EARLHAM INFANT SCHOOL AND WEST EARLHAM JUNIOR SCHOOL (SCHOOL DAY AND SCHOOL YEAR REGULATIONS) ORDER 2013, SI 2013/473; made under the Education Act 2002 s.2. In force: April 8, 2013; .

This Oder provides for the number of school sessions required at West Earlham Infant School and West Earlham Junior School to be reduced from 380 to 378 in the 2012-2013 school year.

899. Special educational needs–Disability discrimination–Student with dyslexia and depression scheduled to take four exams in one day–School failing to apply for rescheduling

[Disability Discrimination Act 1995 (c.50).]

The appellant mother (M) appealed against a decision of the First-tier Tribunal dismissing her claim of disability discrimination against the school attended by her daughter (V). V was academically gifted but suffered from mild dyslexia. She studied for an International Baccalaureate (IB) Diploma but struggled with the workload and showed symptoms of anxiety and depression. The timetable for her examinations in May 2009 resulted in a schedule of four exams on May 18. M sought extra time for those exams and a rescheduling so that one could take place on May 19. The school's IB coordinator (C) asked for additional time for the May 18 exams, which was granted. She did not request rescheduling but did secure "special consideration" for V, meaning all her exams would be graded with appropriate adjustments made for her depressive illness. M argued that the school had not taken reasonable steps to ensure that V was not placed under additional stress and pressure by failing to apply for rescheduling in the mistaken belief that it would be unsuccessful. M had telephoned the International Baccalaureate Organisation (IBO) who told her that it would have considered, and was likely to have granted, such a request. The tribunal accepted C's evidence that it was highly unusual for a student to achieve simultaneously additional time and special consideration. It concluded that V had already been put in a favourable position and it was highly improbable that rescheduling would have been granted as it would have created for her an unfair or disproportionate advantage over other candidates. M contended that the tribunal's finding was flawed in that (1) it had not explained its reasons for rejecting the statement M had obtained from the IBO; (2) the IBO would have been obliged by the Disability Discrimination Act 1995 to consider rescheduling, so C should at least have made the request.

Held: Appeal dismissed. (1) It was not plausible that the tribunal had overlooked the evidence of M's telephone call to the IBO, nor had it failed to adequately explain why it did not accept that it was accurate that the IBO would have been likely to agree to rescheduling. It was entitled to prefer to rely on the experience of C, particularly against the background of written guidance published by the IBO, and there was no direct evidence from the IBO that contradicted C's view (see para.17 of judgment). (2) The IBO might have been obliged by the Act to consider rescheduling but it did not follow that it would have been bound to agree to it or that C was bound to ask it to do so. There were two bases on which the IBO could properly have decided not to reschedule. First, rescheduling would have given V an advantage in comparison with other candidates and the more equitable approach would be to give her special consideration in the marking to ensure a level playing field. Although that was pre-eminently a matter for the IBO, C was not obliged to ask for rescheduling if the application was bound to fail on that ground. Second, rescheduling might have removed the disadvantage of four exams on one day but it would have given rise to an equivalent or worse disadvantage in that V would have been required to spend the night before the rescheduled exam away from home with a member of staff. That was something on which C was better placed to form a view and she was not required to ask for rescheduling if it was not in V's best interests and the IBO ought, on an objective view, to reject the application, even if there was a possibility it might not. C was not a mere advocate for M, and the IBO was entitled to expect her to exercise a degree of professional judgment before making an application, particularly as it might be appropriate to consider a package of adjustments, *Burke v College of Law* [2012] EWCA Civ 37, [2012] Eq. L.R. 279, [2012] C.L.Y. 926 considered. C should have applied if she considered there was a good case to be made regardless of the chance of success but she was not required to make a clearly bad application. She was right in her view that the application was bound to fail; the worst that could be said of the school was that it might not have explained as early as it could have done the reasons for the concessions sought (paras 18-20, 23).

ML v KENT CC, [2013] UKUT 125 (AAC), [2013] E.L.R. 364, Judge Rowland, UT (AAC).

900. Special educational needs–Learning difficulties–Appropriate school–Adequacy of tribunal's reasons

[Education (Special Educational Needs) (England) (Consolidation) Regulations 2001 (SI 2001/3455) reg.19.]

The appellant child (N) appealed against a decision refusing both her choice of named primary school and that of the respondent local authority (E). N attended a primary school under a statement of special educational needs. Her behaviour was such that she was excluded and subsequently refused to attend school. A final statement followed a diagnosis of autistic spectrum disorder and sensory processing and social communication difficulties. The tribunal found that neither party's proposed school was appropriate and amended the statement to show a different named primary day special school. N submitted that the tribunal had failed (1) to consider her secondary education; (2) to give an adequate decision given the available evidence.

Held: Judgment accordingly. (1) Although the hearing had taken place prior to the time for amendment of the statement to add the secondary school required by the Education (Special Educational Needs) (England) (Consolidation) Regulations 2001 reg.19, the tribunal should not have restricted its decision solely to N's primary education without providing reasons. It had clearly taken into account that both the original proposed schools had been "through schools" for the purposes of costs and also N's secondary education had clearly been in issue, *Wilkin v Goldthorpe* [1998] E.L.R. 345, [1998] C.L.Y. 1980 followed (see paras 31-34 of judgment). (2) Despite N's strong criticism of the lack of evidence and of the tribunal's failure to adopt an inquisitorial role, it was clear that the tribunal had acted correctly as an expert body in considering all the evidence and submissions and had acted inquisitorially, *W v Gloucestershire CC* [2001] EWHC Admin 481, Times, August 20, 2001, [2001] C.L.Y. 2028 applied (paras 38-40). The tribunal had not erred in law but its decision fell short of the full decision it should have taken. Instead of setting it aside, the instant decision was to be drawn to the attention of the judge in a separate pending appeal to ensure that any unresolved issues were fully before the First-tier Tribunal. In view of the fact that N had recently been taken into care and was now resident outside the local authority area, any rehearing of the appeal was likely to be entirely superfluous.

OR v EALING LBC, [2012] UKUT 211 (AAC), [2012] E.L.R. 436, Judge David Williams, UT (AAC).

901. Special educational needs–Schools–Propriety of tribunal's approach when naming type of school for severely disabled child

[Education Act 1996 (c.56) s.316(3)(b).]

The appellant local education authority (H) appealed against a decision of the First-tier Tribunal naming a particular type of school in the statement of special educational needs of an 11-year-old boy (F). F, who lived in the Harrow area, had a very rare form of muscular dystrophy and suffered from severe disabilities; among other things, he had sight in only one eye and no expressive language. His mother wanted him to be educated in a mainstream school, whereas H wanted to place him in a particular maintained day special school for students with complex/severe learning difficulties. The tribunal considered the option of placing him at a mainstream school in the Harrow area but rejected the idea, as F would be alone with adults there. It went on to specify a type of school in F's statement, being a maintained mainstream secondary school outside the Harrow area which had appropriate facilities, expertise and access to extensive therapy, and where F would be educated with other pupils with severe and complex disabilities.

Held: Appeal allowed. The tribunal's decision would be set aside. In considering whether the provision of education for F in a mainstream school would be incompatible with the provision of efficient education of other children in each of H's own schools, it was necessary to consider not only the effect on the other children presently in each of those schools and the reasonable steps that might be taken in that regard, but also the position of the notional additional children who would have to be introduced there to enable F's special needs to be met, as one of the provisions that had to be made for him was to ensure that he was educated with other similarly disabled children. The tribunal had erred in law in its approach to the question of what mainstream schools could be considered. At least in the absence of the clear availability of a suitable place at a mainstream school outside H's area, the tribunal, in considering the effect on other children, could only consider mainstream schools within H's area. It would have to consider the effect not only on the children already at those schools but also on the other children with severe and complex disabilities, who would, if legally possible, have to be brought in from other schools to enable F to be educated with them. If their inclusion with F at, for them, a new mainstream school would be incompatible with the provision of efficient education for them, that would be a basis on which H could rely on the Education Act 1996 s.316(3)(b). The tribunal attempted to resolve that difficulty by relying on its own knowledge that "there [were] mainstream schools where [F] would not receive his education in isolation". In that respect, it should not, at least on the evidence before it, and possibly at all, have had regard to schools outside H's area. It was also unclear whether any of those unnamed schools could make a place available for F at that time, and it would not appear that any of them was within reasonable travelling distance of F's home. Moreover, the tribunal had breached the rule that it ought not to rely on its own knowledge without giving the parties an opportunity to comment. In relying on its own factual knowledge, the tribunal overlooked the possibility that there could be issues as to the appropriateness of the schools that they had in mind and, if any were suitable, as to the availability of a place at one of them for F. It was plain that representations could also have been made as to whether H could be compelled to prove that the exception to the basic rule in s.316(3)(b) extended to other schools outside its area, and as to the potential impossibility of its being able to find a place for F there (see paras 29-31, 35, 38 of judgment).

HARROW LBC v AM, [2013] UKUT 157 (AAC), [2013] E.L.R. 351, Judge Michael Mark, UT (AAC).

902. Special educational needs–Special schools–Whether local authority entitled to refuse mother's request for disabled son to attend particular special school–Interpretation of duty under s.9 Education Act 1996 to have regard to parental preference–Application of s.9 to duty under Sch.27 para.8 of Act to accept parent's choice of school in statement of special educational needs

[Education Act 1996 (c.56) s.9, s.10, s.29, Sch.27, Sch.27 para.8, Sch.27 para.8(2).]

The appellant mother appealed against the First-tier Tribunal's decision to uphold the respondent's refusal of her request to allow her disabled son to attend a particular special school. The mother's request was refused on the ground that it would be incompatible with the efficient use of resources. It had been calculated that transporting her son to the school would cost the local authority an additional £26,000 annually. The issues were (i) the interpretation of the Education Act 1996 s.9, which provided that the secretary of state and local authorities, in exercising or performing all their respective powers and duties under the Education Acts, should have regard to the general principle that pupils were to be educated in accordance with their parents' wishes, insofar as that was compatible with the provision of efficient instruction and training and the avoidance of unreasonable public expenditure; (ii) the application of s.9 to a local authority's duty under Sch.27 para.8 to accept a parent's choice of school in a statement of special educational needs.

Held: Appeal dismissed. (1) Section 9 only applied when the secretary of state or local authority was performing a duty; it presupposed that duty and was irrelevant to whether a duty existed. It was not the source of an independent duty, but only applied in the course of powers and duties that otherwise arose under the Education Acts. That had two consequences: (a) it was always necessary to identify the power or duty in operation, and (b) s.9 had to be applied within that power or duty. The s.9 duty only required regard to be had to the principle that children should be educated in accordance with their parents' wishes; it did not provide that children were to be so educated. The s.9 duty was qualified: it only applied insofar as it was consistent with the provision of efficient instruction and training and the avoidance of unreasonable public expenditure. It was expressed to apply to all the powers and duties under the Acts, and it was natural in that context that the qualifications were global. The focus in the qualifications was on the overall impact of decisions on efficiency of provision and reasonableness of public expenditure. However, despite what s.9 said, it could not apply to every power and duty under the Acts. For example, it could operate within the secretary of state's duty under s.10 to promote education by requiring the secretary of state to take account of the principle of parental preference, but there was no scope for it to operate within the duty of the local authority under s.29 to make reports and returns as required by the secretary of state. The s.9 duty was not defined by the scope of the qualifications: it was to have regard to the principle, but other relevant factors had to be taken into account as well. There was still scope to take account of factors unique to the particular child or local authority, *CM v Bexley LBC* [2011] UKUT 215 (AAC), [2011] E.L.R. 413, [2011] C.L.Y. 986 applied (see paras 12-13, 15-20 of judgment). (2) Both Sch.27 and s.9 dealt with parents' preferences for a particular school, but there were differences between them: (a) s.9 applied to all powers and duties, whereas Sch.27 para.8 only applied to the choice of school; (b) the duty under s.9 was only to have regard to the principle of parental preference, whereas Sch.27 para.8 imposed a duty to accept the parents' choice; (c) the qualifications in s.9, as a provision that had to apply throughout the Education Acts, were stated very generally, whereas the qualifications in Sch.27 para.8, as a provision that had to apply to the circumstances of a specific case and an individual child, were stated more specifically; (d) s.9 was qualified by reference to the avoidance of unreasonable public expenditure, whereas Sch.27 para.8 was qualified by reference to the efficient use of resources: accordingly, s.9 covered all public expenditure, whereas Sch.27 para.8 was limited to resources of the home authority, *O v*

Lewisham LBC [2007] EWHC 2130 (Admin), [2008] B.L.G.R. 765, [2008] C.L.Y. 1083 and *B v Harrow LBC (No.1)* [2000] 1 W.L.R. 223, [2000] C.L.Y. 1946 considered. The duty, once it arose under Sch.27 para.8, was to name the parents' preferred school in the child's statement. The performance was merely adding the name to the statement. There was no scope for applying s.9 in the naming of a school in a statement or in the resulting performance of arranging for the child to attend that school. The nature of the duty and the performance involved in it did not allow other considerations to be taken into account. It followed that s.9 had no application to the duty under Sch.27 para.8 (paras 25-26). (3) On that basis, s.9 was irrelevant to the instant case. The tribunal had to decide if the qualifications set out in Sch.27 para.8(2) applied. If either or both applied, the local authority was not under a duty to name the mother's preferred school. If neither applied, it was under that duty. The tribunal decided that Sch.27 para.8(2)(b) applied because of the considerable additional expense for the local authority. On the evidence, it was entitled so to find. It was not obliged, or indeed permitted, to consider s.9 (para.31).

SM v HACKNEY LEARNING TRUST, [2013] UKUT 78 (AAC), [2013] E.L.R. 321, Judge Edward Jacobs, UT (AAC).

903. Special educational needs–Statements–Adequacy of tribunal's reasons for naming particular school

[Education Act 1996 (c.56) s.9.]

The appellant mother (M) appealed against a decision of the First-tier Tribunal to name the school proposed by the respondent local authority in the statement of special educational needs of her 14-year-old daughter (K). M wanted an independent school (school M) to be named, whereas the local authority preferred a maintained school (school B). The tribunal concluded that school M was not a "better alternative" for several reasons: (i) K did not require dyslexia specialist teachers in all subjects; she did require specialist subject teachers and that was reflected in Pt 3 of her statement; (ii) school M offered a limited range of peers for K; (iii) school M had limited flexibility to respond to issues raised by K that affected her ability to attend school; (iv) school M was a considerable distance from K's home.

Held: Appeal dismissed. As to M's views, the tribunal was required to apply the Education Act 1996 s.9. Nowhere in its decision did it set out s.9 in terms or even refer to it. Further, in saying that it did not consider that school M offered "a better alternative", it was, at first glance, applying the wrong test. Section 9 did not require the parent to show that his or her preference was for a "better alternative"; rather, the principle to which the local authority and, on appeal, the tribunal had to have regard was that pupils were to be educated in accordance with the wishes of their parents unless one or other of the qualifications created by the section was made out, namely incompatibility with the provision of efficient instruction and training or the avoidance of unreasonable public expenditure. However, items (i), (ii) and (iii) of the tribunal's decision were all to be found in the local authority's submission as to why a placement at school M would not be compatible with the provision of efficient instruction and training for the purposes of s.9. The tribunal's decision was accepting the authority's submission on the s.9 point because of the tribunal's adoption of the points made by the authority and the context in which the authority made them. M had argued that one should not have to go behind the tribunal's decision to other documents to reach a true understanding of what was meant by the reasons. In the context of a decision of the First-tier Tribunal in this jurisdiction, that was not necessarily so. This was not a case where the tribunal's reasons were likely to have an extensive readership beyond the immediate parties. It was the statement of special educational needs, rather than the statement of reasons, to which people without knowledge of the litigation were most likely to have occasion to refer. The standard of reasons required was reviewed by the Court of Appeal in *H v East Sussex CC* [2009] EWCA Civ 249, [2009] E.L.R. 161, [2009] C.L.Y. 1121, from which it was clear that the reasons had to tell the parties why they had won or lost and enable the Upper Tribunal or other appellate body to see whether there had been an error of law. The parties would be fully familiar with what had gone on previously. With that knowledge, it would be clear to them what the tribunal's position was. So far as appellate bodies were concerned, it was not uncommon for the Upper Tribunal to have to refer to other key documents, such as a party's notice of appeal to the First-tier Tribunal (or equivalent document), to assess whether a statement of reasons was adequate. In this case, it had been possible to see the context without undue difficulty. M had also suggested that it was not desirable that a specialist tribunal should leave in doubt what principle of law it was applying. When the tribunal's decision was read in its context, there was no real doubt. The decision could undoubtedly have put the point more clearly but, read in its context, it was clear despite its at times infelicitous wording that the tribunal did apply s.9 to the case, and it sufficiently explained its position to the parties, with their knowledge of what had gone before, and to the Upper Tribunal, *H v East Sussex* applied (see paras 6-10 of judgment).

SG v SOMERSET CC, [2012] UKUT 353 (AAC), [2013] E.L.R. 73, Judge Ward, UT (AAC).

904. Special educational needs–Statements–Child with ADHD and dyslexia–Local authority's decision that no statement of special needs required–Tribunal's finding that additional support in school not needed

The appellant parents (P) appealed against a decision of the First-tier Tribunal that the respondent local authority had been correct in refusing to make a statement of special educational needs in respect of their son (R). R was a pupil at an independent day school. P was of the view that a statement was needed because he had ADHD, dyslexia and expressive language and semantic difficulties that could not be met at school. The head teacher of R's current school reported that R exhibited classic symptoms of ADHD, lack of self-control, impulsiveness and distractibility, but that his disruption was managed by very small classes and by 1:1 mentoring. The local authority conducted a statutory assessment of his needs, and on the basis of that assessment it concluded that R did not require a statement and his special educational needs could be met from provision generally available to mainstream schools. P appealed the local authority's decision. The tribunal found that the key area of concern was R's behaviour, emotional and social development. It concluded that R did not need support which was additional to or different from provision currently available at a mainstream school, that what was needed were low-level strategies such as those employed on a daily basis at his current school, and there was no need for the local authority to determine special educational provision for R.

Held: Appeal allowed. While the tribunal did not have to give a decision that was a product of refined legal draftsmanship, the decision did have to contain an outline of the story which had given rise to the complaint, a summary of the tribunal's basic factual conclusions and a statement of the reasons which had led them to reach the conclusion which they did on those basic facts, *H v East Sussex CC* [2009] EWCA Civ 249, [2009] E.L.R. 161, [2009] C.L.Y. 1121 and *Meek v Birmingham DC* [1987] I.R.L.R. 250, [1987] C.L.Y. 1399 applied. A real issue before the tribunal was whether the sort of attention R was getting at his current school was the reason that his current problems were so limited and whether the transfer to a mainstream school without the small classes and possibly without the same mentoring would give rise to greater problems which would need to be addressed by increased resources beyond the school's ordinary resources. There was no doubt that R's ADHD did give rise to special educational needs, but the tribunal needed to make findings as to the extent of those needs and the provision for them in the context of a mainstream school, *NC v Leicestershire CC* [2012] UKUT 85 (AAC), [2012] E.L.R. 365, [2012] C.L.Y. 995 applied. There appeared to be no adequate explanation by the tribunal as to why it had rejected expert evidence that R needed consistent teaching in small classes with a high ratio of staff to pupils. While it was open to the tribunal to reject that evidence, or to find that despite that evidence no statement was needed, it did need to give its reasons. The tribunal's reasoning was defective and as a result its decision was in error of law and had to be set aside. The case was remitted for rehearing before a new tribunal (see paras 17-18, 21, 23-25 of judgment).

JS v WORCESTERSHIRE CC, [2012] UKUT 451 (AAC), [2013] E.L.R. 138, Judge Michael Mark, UT (AAC).

905. Special educational needs–Statements–Local authority decision to cease maintaining statement–First-tier Tribunal's failure to address criteria for cessation–Tribunal's jurisdiction

[Education Act 1996 (c.56) s.313, Sch.27 para.11; Tribunals, Courts and Enforcement Act 2007 (c.15) s.3(1).]

The appellant local authority appealed against a decision of the First-tier Tribunal that it had not followed the correct procedure when it decided to cease to maintain a statement for a 17-year-old boy (W). W had had a statement from the age of 10 years. The local authority decided that it would no longer maintain his statement on the ground that his needs could be met by a college at which he had been offered a place. His parents wanted the statement to be maintained and the tribunal allowed their appeal. The local authority submitted that the tribunal had not had regard to the provision that could be made for W at the college.

Held: Decision set aside and case remitted to tribunal for re-hearing by different panel. The local authority had to have regard to the provisions of the Special Educational Needs Code of Practice for England issued under the Education Act 1996 s.313, which provided that statements should be maintained only when necessary, and that a decision to cease to maintain one required careful consideration of all the circumstances by the local authority after close consultation with parents. The provisions required consideration of whether, notwithstanding the achievement of some or of all the statement objectives, the child's progress would be halted or reversed if the statement's special provision, or a modified version of it, were not made. The tribunal had not addressed itself to those substantive issues, but to how the local authority had made its decision. The tribunal was a statutory one constituted under the Tribunals, Courts and Enforcement Act 2007 s.3(1) and its jurisdiction in the instant case was conferred by Sch.27 para.11 of the Act. Its task was not to undertake a review of the decision-making process, but to consider whether the local authority's decision to cease to maintain W's statement was correct in fact and law. It had only two options: to dismiss the appeal or to order the statement to continue as it stood or with amendments. The local authority was not an independent decision-maker on the issue of whether to maintain a statement. The tribunal had not dealt with the statutory issue before it, but had concerned itself exclusively with the process followed by the local authority. It had erred in not taking account of the provision that the college could make for W (see paras 3-5, 17-20, 22-23, 26-27 of judgment).

CW v HERTFORDSHIRE CC, [2013] UKUT 90 (AAC), [2013] E.L.R. 423, Edward Jacobs, UT (AAC).

906. Special educational needs–Statements–Setting aside–Misunderstanding over named school–Validity of procedure for setting aside consent order

[Education Act 1996 (c.56) s.316(4), s.316, s.316A, Sch.27 para.3; Tribunals, Courts and Enforcement Act 2007 (c.15) s.9(10); Tribunal Procedure (First-tier Tribunal) (Health, Education and Social Care Chamber) Rules 2008 (SI 2008/2699) r.29, r.30, Pt 5, r.45(1), r.47, r.48.]

The applicant parents (P) of a child with special educational needs applied for judicial review of a decision to set aside and reopen a consent order agreed between them and the local education authority (L). P and L had agreed a consent order ostensibly naming in the statement P's choice of an "independent mainstream school with specialist classes" (E). Consent appeared to have been based on a misunderstanding between the parties and the judge and L had subsequently successfully applied ex parte to set aside the consent order on the basis that the Education Act 1996 s.316 excluded independent schools from the definition of "mainstream schools" and the tribunal's interpretation of s.316 therefore contained a procedural irregularity. P submitted that (1) there was no statutory power to reopen the consent order because a consent order was not a decision for the purposes of the Tribunal Procedure (First-tier Tribunal) (Health, Education and Social Care Chamber) Rules 2008 Pt 5. P argued that unlike decisions, no hearing or written reasons were required for consent orders; (2) if there was power to reopen the consent order, then the judge had erred in concluding that grounds existed; (3) an unfair procedure had been followed.

Held: Application granted. (1) The reason that neither a hearing nor written reasons were required for a consent order was that, given its consensual nature, they were superfluous. The term "decision" in s.316 was to be interpreted widely and was not confined to interlocutory decisions, *LS v Lambeth LBC* [2010] UKUT 461 (AAC) applied. Although there was a distinction between the terminology in r.29 for consent orders and r.30 for decisions, it was not appropriate to place any weight on that, when all other considerations pointed the opposite way (see para.30 of judgment). (2) It was common ground that E was not a "mainstream school" as defined by s.316(4) for the purposes of s.316 and s.316A. There had been some discussion of s.316 in the hearing, but there had been no ruling that E was a "mainstream school" and so could be named (para.34). Just prior to the hearing, L had changed its position from naming a maintained mainstream school, to naming a special school, so a discussion about s.316 had been relevant, but not to support P's choice of school, *R. (on the application of MH) v Special Educational Needs and Disability Tribunal* [2004] EWCA Civ 770, [2004] B.L.G.R. 844, [2004] C.L.Y. 1079 distinguished as being concerned with the priority between Sch.27 para.3 of the 1996 Act and s.316. The tribunal had not erred (para.42). (3) The decision to set aside had been taken under r.45(1) on the basis of procedural irregularity. However, the First-tier Tribunal could only review an application for permission under either r.47 or r.48. The tribunal had therefore erred by drafting the decision as a second review, which would have been prohibited by the Tribunals, Courts and Enforcement Act 2007 s.9(10), rather than as a set aside under r.45(1), under which only procedural irregularities, and not substantive matters, could be considered.

R. (ON THE APPLICATION OF LR) v FIRST-TIER TRIBUNAL, [2012] UKUT 213 (AAC), [2012] E.L.R. 456, Judge Ward, UT (AAC).

907. Special schools–Disability discrimination–Autistic female pupil excluded following sexual encounters–Whether school guilty of discrimination

[Equality Act 2010 (c.15) s.13, s.15, s.85.]

The parents of a 15-year-old girl (C) brought a claim alleging that the respondent school (S) had discriminated against her contrary to the Equality Act 2010 s.85. C's statement of special educational needs described her as having autistic spectrum disorder, attention deficit hyperactivity disorder and severe mood swings. It was said that she was vulnerable in social situations with peers, that she could fail to understand their intentions, that she was easily led and that she could engage in inappropriate behaviour. S was a residential special school which claimed to have an international reputation for educating children with a range of difficulties. During C's second term at S, which began in January 2011, information about her sexualised behaviour and inappropriate sexual encounters with boys at S came to the attention of members of staff. It was noted that C had expressed thoughts of suicide. During June 2011, she saw S's GP and was found to have a vaginal tear following a sexual encounter with a boy. S adopted the view that the encounter was "fully consensual" and that "there was no reason for concern". The matter was not reported to social services, the police or C's parents. The sexual encounters continued. In October 2011, S's head teacher wrote to C's parents requiring her withdrawal from S. It was stated, among other things, that, in the light of the incidents that had occurred, her best interests would be served by her being placed in another school. C's parents argued that S had failed to make a series of reasonable adjustments to its criteria, provisions or practices. They also argued that the decision to require them to withdraw C from S amounted to direct discrimination under s.13 of the Act or unfavourable treatment because of something arising in consequence of C's disability under s.15.

Held: Judgment for claimants. The evidence revealed that C was disabled within the meaning of the 2010 Act. Further, S knew that that was so. It also knew or should have known that she was sexually and emotionally vulnerable: there had been a series of warning signals. S had made no reasonable adjustments to its practices. The following were among the adjustments that were called for. S should have obtained and shared all available internal and external information with a view to assessing C's needs, including in relation to sexual exploitation. Formal risk assessments should have taken place in relation to each incident of concern relating to sexual conduct or mental health. Communications with C in relation to her understanding of appropriate behaviour should have been carried out by those trained in communicating with children with C's known difficulties. C should also have been appropriately counselled after each incident. The complaints under s.13 and s.15 were also made out. S's response to the circumstances that had arisen, namely of requiring C's parents to withdraw her, was wholly disproportionate to the actual situation, which was that it was responsible for the failure to provide C with adequate protection. She was excluded by reason of her being abused; the abuse arose in consequence of her vulnerability, and that vulnerability was a clear aspect of her disability. S had not attempted to understand her vulnerability or to establish ways of supporting and safeguarding her short of exclusion.

PARENTS OF C v STANBRIDGE EARLS SCHOOL [2013] Eq. L.R. 304, Judge H Brayne, FTT.

908. Student loans–Wales

THE CANCELLATION OF STUDENT LOANS FOR LIVING COSTS LIABILITY (WALES) REGULATIONS 2013, SI 2013/SI 2013/1396 (W.135); made under theTeaching and Higher Education Act 1998 s.22, s.42. In force: August 1, 2013; .

These Regulations govern the student loan liability of students who receive loans for living costs from theWelsh Ministers in respect of the academic year 2013/2014.

909. Students–Plagiarism–Refusal of degree–Entitlement of student to relief

The claimant student (E) applied for permission to judicially review a decision of the defendant university (U) that he was to be sent down without a degree. E had been educated in law at a Nigerian university and had applied to U to take a Masters degree in law. He had twice been found guilty of cheating by plagiarism but was given a last chance to redeem himself by passing an examination. E failed and was rusticated and refused a degree.

Held: Permission refused. The decision to fail E was an academic one, which could only be appealed to the relevant body or to the Adjudicator for Higher Education, over which the court had no jurisdiction, *Moroney v Anglo-European College of Chiropractice* [2008] EWHC 2633 (QB), [2009] E.L.R. 111, [2009] C.L.Y. 1056, *Clark v University of Lincolnshire and Humberside* [2000] 1 W.L.R. 1988, [2000] C.L.Y. 2001, and *S v Chapman* [2008] EWCA Civ 800, [2008] E.L.R. 603, [2008] C.L.Y. 1084 considered. Additionally, E had not availed himself of the alternative remedy; therefore the decision was not amenable to judicial review. U had acted with conspicuous fairness and leniency throughout, and the points raised by E were unarguable (see paras 1.20-1.28 of judgment).

R. (ON THE APPLICATION OF ECHENDU) v SCHOOL OF LAW, UNIVERSITY OF LEEDS, [2012] EWHC 2080 (Admin), [2012] E.L.R. 449, Judge Jeremy Richardson Q.C., QBD (Admin).

910. Universities–Disability discrimination–Proper forum for complaint by disabled medical practitioner concerning access to postgraduate training programme

[Equality Act 2010 (c.15) s.56(5).]

The defendants, namely the Governing Body of the University of London and the London Deanery, sought a declaration that the court did not have jurisdiction to hear the claim brought against them by the claimant (G). G was a registered medical practitioner. He had cancer and was disabled within the meaning of the Equality Act 2010. He sought enrolment on a three-year postgraduate medical training programme called the ACCS, which was aimed at doctors wishing to specialise in acute medicine, emergency medicine or anaesthetics. If successful in an application for ACCS training, the doctor would be employed by the NHS trust at which his training took place. The first two years of the programme involved generic training, with usually six months being spent in each of acute medicine, emergency medicine, anaesthetics and intensive care. In the final year, the doctor would undertake a speciality-specific year. The recruitment process was carried out by the London Deanery, using a scoring framework set by another Deanery. The London Deanery was a joint arrangement between the University of London and the North London Strategic Health Authority; it existed pursuant to a memorandum of agreement whose purpose was to "specify the arrangements under which the London Department of Postgraduate Medical and Dental Education... [would] be managed". G alleged that there had been a failure to make reasonable adjustments for his condition in that he had been refused access to less than full-time training under the ACCS. The issues were (i) whether the ACCS afforded "vocational training", in which case G's complaint would prima facie fall within the exclusive jurisdiction of the employment tribunal; (ii) if so, whether the ACCS was "training or guidance to which the governing body of the institution [had] power to afford access" for the purposes of s.56(5) of the 2010 Act, in which case the court would have jurisdiction.

Held: Declaration granted in favour of defendants. (1) It was difficult to see how the ACCS could be anything other than vocational training (see para.35 of judgment). (2) The memorandum of agreement did not allow for the university to interfere in any way with the admissions process to the ACCS administered by the London Deanery, and it could not be said that the university's governing body ultimately had the power to afford access to the training and guidance provided on the ACCS. Section 56(5) therefore had no application to the case (para.42).

GARRARD v UNIVERSITY OF LONDON [2013] Eq. L.R. 746, Judge Birtles, CC (Central London).

911. Universities–Examinations–Entitlement to masters degree–Applicable regulations–Whether breach of regulations by university

The appellant postgraduate student (C) appealed against the dismissal of his claim against the respondent university (K) that he had been entitled to the award of an MSc. C, an Iraqi national, had obtained a first medical degree in Baghdad in 1981. He sought asylum in the United Kingdom in 1995 and obtained full British nationality in 2004. He was working as an honorary specialist radiology registrar at a hospital and was advised to obtain a masters degree in nuclear medicine to obtain a paid post. He enrolled for a two-year part-time course in 1999. In June 2001 he undertook two written examinations, submitted coursework and a dissertation, and had a general oral examination. The assessment was also supposed to include an oral examination specific to his dissertation. The pass mark for each element was 50 per cent. C was failed, having received 47 per cent for his dissertation and 42 per cent for his general oral examination. On appeal, he was offered the opportunity of re-submitting his dissertation and being orally examined on it, as a first attempt and not a re-take. He declined that opportunity, on the basis that his overall mark entitled him to the award of the degree. He brought proceedings based on an alleged failure by K to correctly identify, interpret and apply the relevant regulations. The judge found that K's 1999/2000 programme regulations were applicable, and that K had not breached them. C contended that the applicable marking scheme was not the 1999/2000 or 2000/01 programme regulations but a document related to a new programme of study (PIF(C)), under which he was entitled to the award of an MSc. Alternatively, he argued that, as enrolment was annual, the applicable regulations were either the 2000/01 programme regulations or the postgraduate academic regulations 1999/2000.

Held: Appeal dismissed. (1) The examination and assessment of degree candidates was governed by a hierarchy of regulations. The overarching regulations in the instant case were K's general academic regulations which, for the academic year 1999/2000, provided that the conditions governing eligibility for an award were given in the general regulations for examinations and in individual programme regulations. The individual programme regulations had to specify which course had to be passed before a student was eligible for an award. There were also separate academic regulations for postgraduate students, which had to be read in conjunction with the individual programme regulations, the general regulations for examinations and the general academic regulations. The general regulations for examinations provided that a student had to have successfully completed all parts of the examination prescribed for the award. The postgraduate regulations referred to a core marking scheme for masters degrees, effective from 2000/01. The marking schemes and regulations for individual masters degree programmes were published as an appendix, the programme regulations. The 1999/2000 programme regulations provided that the pass mark for each element was 50 per cent, and that students had to achieve a pass in each module. The judge was fully justified, and right on the evidence, in rejecting document PIF(C) as the applicable marking scheme. Once the programme regulations, printed as an annexe to the postgraduate academic regulations, were seen, it was clear that PIF(C) was not applicable, although it might have been used as a basis on which individual programme regulations were drafted. It was an internal form, not part of the regulations (see paras 9-44 of judgment). (2) With regard to whether K had breached the regulations, the judge concluded that the decision requiring C to retake the general oral examination was consistent with the programme regulations. C's argument that an overall pass was sufficient was not accepted. The relevant terms of the regulations provided for a pass mark of 50 per cent in each element, and provided that a student who failed any element would be permitted one further attempt. Neither of those provisions made sense if a student was not required to pass each element. The core marking scheme was stated to apply from the start of the 2000/01 academic year. It did not therefore apply to full-time students on the 1999/2000 course, and it was difficult to see how it could apply to part-time students enrolled in 1999/2000, even though they would be taking their examinations in 2000/01. Even if the scheme did apply to those part-time students, it did not affect the proper interpretation of the programme regulations. The fact that it conflicted with them suggested that it was either not intended to apply or that it laid down minimum, not maximum, standards, leaving K free to impose higher standards for particular courses (paras 45-53).

CHILAB v KING'S COLLEGE LONDON, [2013] EWCA Civ 147, [2013] E.L.R. 339, Ward, L.J., CA (Civ Div).

912. Universities–Fairness–Student withdrawing from course of study–Request to resume studies following withdrawal–Reasonableness of university decision to close student's records

The claimant (M) applied for judicial review of a decision of the defendant university to formally close his records following his request to withdraw from a course of study. M had enrolled on a degree course in medicine and after completing a year of study had asked to withdraw formally from the course. The university invited him to a meeting with his course tutor to discuss his decision and the registry was informed of his decision to withdraw. Prior to the meeting, M changed his mind and asked if his decision could be reversed. However, at the meeting, M stated that he wished to withdraw from the course and he confirmed this in an email. The university wrote to him recording his final decision to withdraw from the course. M was not asked to complete a notification of withdrawal form as the course tutor was not aware of the form. M subsequently wrote to the university stating that his withdrawal from the course was a mistake and that he wished to resume his studies. The university stated that the matter was closed and that it was too late to reopen his record and M would have to reapply to the admissions office. After unsuccessfully invoking a grievance procedure, M complained to the Office of the Independent Adjudicator for Higher Education (OIA) and although the OIA was critical of the university not requiring M to complete the withdrawal form, it was satisfied that M's complaints were unjustified. M submitted that the university's actions were illegal and procedurally unfair and that the failure to complete a notification of withdrawal form rendered his withdrawal a nullity. The university submitted that any illegality or unfairness in its treatment towards M was cured by the OIA's decision.

Held: Application refused. (1) Although a decision of the OIA was not binding upon the court or determinative of the claim, the court would be slow to interfere with its decision, *R. (on the application of Maxwell) v Office of the Independent Adjudicator* [2011] EWCA Civ 1236, [2012] P.T.S.R. 884, [2012] C.L.Y. 968 applied (see paras 33-34 of judgment). (2) There was no doubt that M's decision to withdraw, which was repeated in writing, was unequivocal. The failure to complete the notification of withdrawal form did not nullify the withdrawal (para.39). (3) M had not been treated unfairly by the university. There was nothing unreasonable or irrational about the course tutor's decision to accept M's withdrawal. Furthermore, the conclusion reached by the grievance panel was one that was open to them on the basis of the information provided to them (para.50, 62).

MATIN v UNIVERSITY COLLEGE LONDON, [2012] EWHC 2474 (Admin), [2012] E.L.R. 487, Wyn Williams, J., QBD (Admin).

913. Universities–Qualifications–Student awarded lower level masters award instead of doctorate–University's non-compliance with own code of practice–Power of court to replace masters award with doctorate

The claimant (K) applied for judicial review of the defendant university's decision not to award him a doctorate in education. K was enrolled on a research degree with a view to obtaining a doctorate on successful completion of a thesis. When K submitted his thesis, it was assessed as insufficient for a doctorate award, but he was given the opportunity to revise and re-submit it and to attend a viva voce, namely an oral examination. Following the viva voce, the examiners changed their recommendation, finding that K's work met the standard of an award of a lower level than a doctorate. The change in recommendation prevented K from re-submitting his thesis for assessment. K submitted a complaint relying on procedural irregularities in the conduct of the assessment, particularly the university's non-compliance with its own code of practice in relation to the appointment of his supervisors and the examiners, and he referred to the extenuating circumstances of his domestic problems. His complaint was not upheld on the ground that any alleged irregularities should have been raised before the submission of his thesis.

Held: Application refused. (1) K's claim was misconceived. It was not open to the court to undertake an evaluation of K's pre-examination work and progress in order to determine whether they were of such a quality that the independent examiners must have departed from an acceptable norm and acted unreasonably. Were it to do so, it would be using its valuable resources to substitute academic, pastoral or religious decisions with its own probably ill-informed, if not hastily formed, judgment, *Clark v University of Lincolnshire and Humberside* [2000] 1 W.L.R. 1988, [2000] C.L.Y. 2001 applied. The fact that K had failed to satisfy the examiners on the viva voce did not give rise to a contractual breach by the university vicariously through his supervisor. When revising their initial views, the examiners had clearly relied on K's answers at the viva voce and they were entitled to come to the conclusion that they had (see paras 45, 47, 49 of judgment). (2) The university's code of practice was guidance without compulsory force. The university had informed K when his supervisors were changed and when external examiners were appointed; there was no requirement in the code of practice for K to approve those decisions, or for there to be a consultation process. His subsequent complaint about one of the examiners was one of form rather than substance and was borne out of frustration and disappointment. K had chosen not to avail himself of any special concessions and there was no provision for acknowledging extenuating circumstances retrospectively in relation to his performance at the viva voce. As for the grievance process, there were inbuilt safeguards that had allowed K to present his case, and there was no intrinsic unfairness (paras 54-56, 58, 60, 62-65). (3) Recourse to the Office of the Independent Adjudicator was an entirely appropriate alternative remedy. The university was obliged to adopt any recommendations that it might make, and if it failed to do so and adhered to its original decision, K would then have a solid case for judicial review (para.71).

R. (ON THE APPLICATION OF KWAO) v UNIVERSITY OF KEELE; *sub nom.* KWAO v UNIVERSITY OF KEELE, [2013] EWHC 56 (Admin), [2013] E.L.R. 266, Judge Graham Wood Q.C., QBD (Admin).

ELECTORAL PROCESS

914. Boundaries–Local elections–London

THE HACKNEY (ELECTORAL CHANGES) ORDER 2013, SI 2013/2795; made under the Local Democracy, Economic Development and Construction Act 2009 s.59. In force: in accordance with reg.1.; .

The Order provides for new borough electoral wards and numbers of borough councillors for the London Borough of Hackney at the borough elections in 2014.

915. Boundaries–Local elections–Nottinghamshire

THE RUSHCLIFFE (ELECTORAL CHANGES) ORDER 2013, SI 2013/2797; made under the Local Democracy, Economic Development and Construction Act 2009 s.59. In force: in accordance with reg.1.; .

The Order provides for new borough wards and numbers of borough councillors for Rushcliffe Borough Council at the borough elections in 2015 and thereafter. The Order also provides for new parish wards and numbers of parish councillors at the parish elections in 2015 and thereafter wherever this is necessary because a parish is to be split between new district wards.

916. Canvassing–Postponement–Registration

THE ELECTORAL REGISTRATION (POSTPONEMENT OF 2013 ANNUAL CANVASS) ORDER 2013, SI 2013/794; made under the Electoral Registration and Administration Act 2013 s.11, s.25, Sch.5 para.9. In force: March 27, 2013; .

This Order postpones the annual canvass for 2013 to be conducted under the Representation of the People Act 1983 s.10, as part of the transitional arrangements for the implementation of individual electoral registration under the Electoral Registration and Administration Act 2013.

917. Elections–Absent voting

THE ELECTIONS (FRESH SIGNATURES FOR ABSENT VOTERS) REGULATIONS 2013, SI 2013/1599; made under the Representation of the People Act 1983 s.201; the Representation of the People Act 2000 Sch.4 para.7B; and the European Parliamentary Elections Act 2002 s.7. In force: June 21, 2013; .

These Regulations modify (for a limited period) the Representation of the People (England and Wales) Regulations 2001 (SI 2001/341), the Representation of the

People (Scotland) Regulations 2001 (SI 2001/497) and the European Parliamentary Elections Regulations 2004 (SI 2004/293) in line with the transitional arrangements for the implementation of individual electoral registration under the Electoral Registration and Administration Act 2013. They modify the provisions relating to the mandatory signature refresh for absent voters so that the absent voters who would otherwise be requested to provide a new example of their signature in January 2014 (and, in Scotland, in January 2015) will instead be requested to do so between August 1 and 19, 2013.

918. Elections–Electoral process–Electoral register–National Assembly for Wales

THE NATIONAL ASSEMBLY FOR WALES (REPRESENTATION OF THE PEOPLE) (FRESH SIGNATURES FOR ABSENT VOTERS) ORDER 2013, SI 2013/1514; made under the Government of Wales Act 2006 s.13. In force: June 20, 2013; .

This Order modifies (for a limited period) the National Assembly for Wales (Representation of the People) Order 2007 in line with the transitional arrangements for the implementation of individual electoral registration under the Electoral Registration and Administration Act 2013.

919. Elections–Electoral register–Electoral registration officers

THE ELECTORAL REGISTRATION (DISCLOSURE OF ELECTORAL REGISTERS) REGULATIONS 2013, SI 2013/760; made under the Representation of the People Act 1983 s.53, Sch.2 para.1A, Sch.2 para.13. In force: March 27, 2013; .

These Regulations require registration officers in Great Britain to disclose the electoral registers and any related information maintained by them and authorise the comparison of that information against data held by the Secretary of State for Work and Pensions in order to assist registration officers in Great Britain for the purposes set out in the Representation of the People Act 1983, as amended by the Electoral Registration and Administration Act 2013.

920. Elections–Expenses

THE REPRESENTATION OF THE PEOPLE (ELECTION EXPENSES EXCLUSION) ORDER 2013, SI 2013/688; made under the Representation of the People Act 1983 Sch.4A para.15. In force: March 22, 2013; .

This Order amends the Representation of the People Act 1983 to exclude grant awards made by the Access to Elected Office Fund from the definition of election expenses.

921. Electoral process–Local elections–Local government

THE TONBRIDGE AND MALLING (ELECTORAL CHANGES) ORDER 2013, SI 2013/70; made under the Local Democracy, Economic Development and Construction Act 2009 s.58. In force: in accordance with art.1 (2).; .

This Order makes changes to electoral arrangements for the district of Tonbridge and Malling following recommendations made by the Local Government Boundary Commission for England. The electoral changes apply in respect of local government elections to be held on and after the ordinary day of election of councillors in 2015.

922. Electoral process–Registration

THE ELECTORAL REGISTRATION AND ADMINISTRATION ACT 2013 (COMMENCEMENT NO.2) ORDER 2013, SI 2013/SI 2013/702 (C.31); made under the Electoral Registration and Administration Act 2013 s.25, s.27. Commencement details: bringing into force various provisions of the 2013 Act on March 25, 2013 and April 2, 2013.; .

This Order brings into force provisions of the Electoral Registration and Administration Act 2013.

923. Electoral regions–European Parliament–Political parties–Returning officers

THE EUROPEAN PARLIAMENTARY ELECTIONS (RETURNING OFFICERS) ORDER 2013, SI 2013/2064; made under the European Parliamentary Elections Act 2002 s.6. In force: August 20, 2013; .

This Order revokes and replaces the European Parliamentary Elections (Returning Officers) Order 2008 (SI 2008/1914).

924. Electoral Registration and Administration Act 2013 (6)

This Act makes provision about the registration of electors and the administration and conduct of elections.

This Act received Royal Assent on January 31, 2013.

925. Electoral Registration and Administration Act 2013 (c.6)–Commencement No.1 Order

THE ELECTORAL REGISTRATION AND ADMINISTRATION ACT 2013 (COMMENCEMENT NO.1) ORDER 2013, SI 2013/SI 2013/219 (C.11); made under the Electoral Registration and Administration Act 2013 s.25, s.27. Commencement details: bringing into force various provisions of the 2013 Act on February 5, 2013.; .

This Commencement Order brings into force, on the day after the day on which it is made, provisions enabling regulations to be made about the disclosure of information for the purposes of electoral registration (Schedule 2) and provisions relating to the postponement of the annual canvass for 2013 to early 2014.

926. Electoral Registration and Administration Act 2013 (c.6)–Commencement No.3 Order

THE ELECTORAL REGISTRATION AND ADMINISTRATION ACT 2013 (COMMENCEMENT NO.3) ORDER 2013, SI 2013/SI 2013/969 (C.39); made under the Electoral Registration and Administration Act 2013 s.25, s.27. In force: bringing into order various provisions of the 2013 Act on April 23, 2013.; .

This Order brings into force, on April 26, 2013, the Electoral Registration and Administration Act 2013 s.6, which provides for the first review of parliamentary constituencies by the Boundary Commissions to be completed between September 1, 2018 and September 30, 2018 instead of by October 1, 2013.

927. European Parliamentary elections–Local elections

THE LOCAL ELECTIONS (ORDINARY DAY OF ELECTIONS IN 2014) ORDER 2013, SI 2013/2277; made under the Representation of the People Act 1983 s.37A. In force: September 7, 2013; .

This Order moves the ordinary day of election to county, district, London Borough and parish councils in England in 2014 to the same day as the date of the poll at the European Parliamentary election, and makes incidental, supplementary and consequential provision as a consequence of that change.

928. European Parliamentary elections–Right to vote

THE EUROPEAN PARLIAMENTARY ELECTIONS (AMENDMENT) REGULATIONS 2013, SI 2013/2876; made under the European Communities Act 1972 s.2; the European Parliamentary Elections Act 2002 s.2, s.6, s.7; and the European Parliament (Representation) Act 2003 s.17, s.18. In force: January 1, 2014; .

These Regulations make miscellaneous changes to the law governing European Parliamentary elections. In part these changes are made to transpose Directive 2013/1 of December 20 2012, which makes amendments to Directive of December 6, 1993 (laying down detailed arrangements for the exercise of the right to vote and stand as a candidate in elections to the European Parliament for citizens of the Union residing in a Member State of which they are not nationals).

929. General elections–Members of the European Parliament–Gibraltar

THE EUROPEAN PARLIAMENTARY ELECTIONS (APPOINTED DAY OF POLL) ORDER 2013, SI 2013/2063; made under the European Parliamentary Elections Act 2002 s.4. In force: September 2, 2013; .

The Order appoints May 22, 2014 as the day of the poll for the next general election of Members of the European Parliament in the UK and Gibraltar.

930. Local elections–Boundaries–West Sussex

THE ARUN (ELECTORAL CHANGES) ORDER 2013, SI 2013/2794; made under the Local Democracy, Economic Development and Construction Act 2009 s.59. In force: in accordance with reg.1.; .

The Order provides for new district wards and numbers of district councillors for the district of Arun at the district elections in 2015 and thereafter. The Order also provides for new parish wards and numbers of parish councillors at the parish elections in 2015 and thereafter wherever this is necessary because a parish is to be split between new district wards.

931. Local Government (Democracy) (Wales) Act 2012 ()

This Act makes provision about the constitution and functions of the Local Democracy and Boundary Commission for Wales; and makes various provisions relating to local government.

This Act received Royal Assent on July 30, 2013.

932. Overseas electors–Registration–Loss of right to register as overseas elector after 15 years' residence overseas–Effect on freedom of movement

[Representation of the People Act 1985 (c.50); Treaty on the Functioning of the European Union Art.21.]

The appellant (P) appealed against a decision ([2011] EWHC 3174 (Admin), [2012] 2 W.L.R. 1134, [2012] C.L.Y. 1030) dismissing his claim for judicial review of the refusal of his application to be registered as an overseas elector in United Kingdom parliamentary elections. P, whose name last appeared in the register of electors in a UK local authority in 1992, had lived in Spain since 1995. He retained his British passport. In 2009 P made his application to the local authority, which rejected it on the basis that P's entry on the register had not been in force during the period of 15 years immediately prior to his application, as required by the Representation of the People Act 1985 s.1 (3) (c). P challenged that refusal on the grounds that it was an unjustified and discriminatory restriction on the exercise of the right to move and reside freely within the European Union, contrary to the TFEU art.21, and that the UK courts had to either interpret s.1 (3) (c) in conformity with EU law or disapply it. The High Court held, among other things, that the 15-year rule was too indirect and uncertain to constitute a restriction on the right to free movement. P contended that the High Court had applied the wrong test to identify a restriction of a fundamental EU right; it ought to have concluded that the right to free movement was restricted if the national legislation at issue was capable of restricting that right or was liable to deter the exercise of it by disadvantaging certain nationals on the sole ground that they had exercised that right.

Held: Appeal dismissed. (1) It was undisputed that the conferral of the right to vote upon overseas residents was a matter of national sovereignty. Although there was no express mention in the TFEU of the right to vote in national elections, it did not follow from the fact that the right to vote in such elections was outside the ambit of the TFEU that Member States could lay down in their electoral law conditions which might have an impact on the exercise of fundamental rights under that treaty. The exercise of competence by the

Member States was subject to the applicable provisions of EU law, particularly those conferring fundamental rights. If the conditions for the parliamentary franchise laid down in the 1985 Act restricted the exercise of the right of free movement and residence, the national courts were bound to address the question whether those conditions were objectively justified (see paras 66, 68, 70-72 of judgment). (2) The High Court had been right to consider the potential effect of the 15-year rule on free movement in practice; it was not an express restriction on that freedom, nor was it a rule which, by its very nature, resulted in such a restriction. P had not adduced sufficient evidence to contradict the conclusion of the High Court that any interference with the right of free movement was too indirect and uncertain to require justification in the instant case. The 15-year rule would not discourage someone who had been resident overseas for almost 15 years from staying abroad in another Member State. Not every disadvantage of non-residence in the UK was a restriction on or deterrent to free movement. Moreover, as disenfranchisement was only triggered after the passing of 15 years' residence overseas, it was necessary to take a long term view when considering whether the cessation of eligibility as an overseas voter after that length of time could deter free movement. Disenfranchisement by reason of 15 years' non-residence in the UK was both qualitatively and quantitatively different from the more direct, certain and immediate obstacles and barriers to basic day-to-day living that were set up by social benefits rules requiring the claimant to be present in the UK for a relatively short period before the date of claiming the benefit. Thus, the national rule in the instant case did not create a restriction that had to be objectively justified under EU law (paras 75-81). (3) (Obiter) If justification of the 15-year rule had been required, cases heard in the European Court of Human Rights upholding residence rules in the electoral context would have been highly material to the court's assessment (paras 85-87).

R. (ON THE APPLICATION OF PRESTON) v WANDSWORTH LBC; *sub nom.* R. (ON THE APPLICATION OF PRESTON) v LORD PRESIDENT OF THE COUNCIL, [2012] EWCA Civ 1378, [2013] Q.B. 687, Mummery, L.J., CA (Civ Div).

933. Political Parties and Elections Act 2009 (c.12)–Commencement No.6 Order

THE POLITICAL PARTIES AND ELECTIONS ACT 2009 (COMMENCEMENT NO.6) ORDER 2013, SI 2013/SI 2013/99 (C.5); made under the Political Parties and Elections Act 2009 s.43. Commencement details: bringing into force various provisions of the 2009 Act on January 22, 2013 and January 1, 2014.; .

This Order brings s.27 of the Political Parties and Elections Act 2009, and brings s.27 into force on January 1, 2014. It also provides that the Greater London Authority returning officer is eligible to be designated by the Secretary of State as a returning officer for European Parliamentary elections, and that the local returning officers for European Parliamentary elections will be local authority returning officers, rather than returning officers for UK parliamentary elections.

EMPLOYMENT

934. Age discrimination–Redundancy payments–Older employees receiving larger payment under voluntary redundancy scheme

The appellant (L) appealed against a decision of an employment tribunal dismissing her claim of direct age discrimination against the respondent government department (the DWP). L had applied for voluntary redundancy under the Civil Service Compensation Scheme. Under the scheme, as a 26-year-old leaver with almost eight years' service, she was entitled to a payment of £10,849.04. However, had she been over 35, she would have received a further sum of £17,690.58. It was that disparity which caused her to lodge her complaint of direct age discrimination. The tribunal found that there were material differences between L's age group (those under 35) and the comparator group (those over 35) and that the two groups were not truly comparable. The tribunal also concluded that, if the two groups were truly comparable, the DWP had objectively justified the less favourable treatment of L.

Held: Appeal dismissed. (1) The question on the comparator issue was whether the difference between L and the comparator group, namely age, was material for the purpose in hand. On that approach, no error of law had been made out in relation to the tribunal's finding as to material differences. That finding was evidence-based, showing that the purpose of the different payments was to reflect the comparative difficulty of loss of employment suffered by the older workers (finding another job and family financial commitments) when compared with those in the younger age group (see paras 10-11 of judgment). (2) The finding on the comparator issue effectively disposed of the appeal. However, the tribunal had been entitled to find that the DWP had objectively justified the less favourable treatment of L (paras 13-15).

LOCKWOOD v DEPARTMENT OF WORK AND PENSIONS [2013] Eq. L.R. 206, Judge Peter Clark, EAT.

935. Agricultural workers–Working time–England

THE WORKING TIME (AMENDMENT) (ENGLAND) REGULATIONS 2013, SI 2013/2228; made under the European Communities Act 1972 s.2. In force: October 1, 2013; .

This instrument aligns the position for workers employed in agriculture in England with the position for workers in most other sectors under the Working Time Regulations 1998 (SI 1998/1833).

936. Annual leave–Pay reference periods–Inclusion of supplementary payments in calculation of paid annual leave–Effect of preliminary ruling by European Court of Justice on meaning of "paid annual leave"

[Civil Aviation (Working Time) Regulations 2004 (SI 2004/756) reg.4, reg.7; Directive 2000/79 on the European Agreement on the Organisation of Working Time of Mobile Workers in Civil Aviation concluded by the Association of European Airlines (AEA), the European Transport Workers' Federation (ETF), the European Cockpit Association (ECA), the ERA (ERA) and the IACA; Directive 2003/88 on certain aspects of the organisation of working time Art.7.]

The court had to consider the effect of a preliminary ruling given by the European Court of Justice on an appeal concerning the interpretation of "paid annual leave" in the Civil Aviation (Working Time) Regulations 2004 reg.4. The appellant (W) was a pilot employed by the respondent airline company (BA). According to their terms of employment, pilots received a fixed annual sum by way of remuneration plus a Flying Pay Supplement (FPS) and a Time Away from Base allowance (TAFB). The purpose of the TAFB was to replace meal allowances and other sundry expenses. The FPS and the TAFB varied according to the time spent flying. Pilots were required to take paid annual leave under the Regulations, which implemented Directive 2000/79 (the Aviation Directive). The payment to be made in respect of annual leave was based on the fixed annual sum only and did not take account of the two supplementary payments. Before an employment tribunal, W established that she was entitled to FPS and TAFB as well as the fixed annual sum as part of her paid annual leave. That decision was upheld by the Employment Appeal Tribunal but the Court of Appeal found in favour of BA. W appealed to the Supreme Court, which referred questions to the European Court of Justice on the nature and assessment of the concept of "paid annual leave" under EU law. The ECJ ruled that, under Directive 2003/88(the Working Time Directive) art.7 and clause 3 of the European Agreement annexed to the Aviation Directive, a pilot was entitled, during his annual leave, not only to his basic salary, but also to (i) all the components intrinsically linked to the performance of his employment contract which were included in his remuneration; and (ii) all the elements relating to his personal and professional status as an airline pilot. It was for the national court to assess into which of those categories any payment fell, based on "an average over a reference period" which was "judged to be representative".

Held: Judgment accordingly. (1) On a natural reading of the ECJ's ruling, an assessment to be carried out on the basis of an average over a representative reference period was something that the court could and would judge for itself. The ECJ's reasoning indicated that it contemplated an average over a reference period judged to be representative of "normal" working and remuneration, rather than a calculation based on what the employee might have earned during the holiday period had he been working then. The ECJ had not expressly addressed the question of how far a standard period, applicable to a range of employees, might be adopted in arriving at a reference period (see paras 13-14 of judgment). (2) The principles behind art.7 of the Working Time Directive and clause 3 of the European Agreement, as explained by the ECJ, had to be applied to the same wording used in reg.4 of the Regulations. In the absence of any other means of ascertaining a representative reference period, the choice of a reference period was one for BA to make in the first instance, within the parameters of what could reasonably be "judged to be representative". Failing such a choice, BA could not complain if a court or tribunal took its own view of what best represented a representative period in the case of an individual employee. It would be surprising if domestic courts or tribunals were to conclude that they could not give effect to a domestic provision using identical language to the Aviation Directive in the way which, according to the ECJ, was envisaged by the language of the Directive (paras 20-21). (3) There was no basis on which to interpret reg.18 of the Regulations as precluding a conclusion that, in the absence of a choice by BA, a tribunal could make its own assessment of an average over a representative reference period. Even though the Regulations did not expressly address complaints relating to the payment of annual leave, they had to be read as far as possible in such a way as to give effect to the Aviation Directive as interpreted by the ECJ. On that approach, reg.18(1) did permit complaint to a court in relation to the exercise of rights under art.4 and there was provision for compensation under reg.18(4) (paras 23, 25). (4) In relation to the proportion of TAFB to be included in paid annual leave, it did not appear from the ECJ's ruling that the reasonableness of such payments had to be evaluated precisely. The task of the tribunal was therefore to consider whether there was a genuine intention that those payments were meant exclusively to cover costs (para.31). (5) The matter was remitted to the employment tribunal for further consideration of the appropriate payments to be made to W in respect of the periods of paid annual leave in issue (paras 27, 32).

BRITISH AIRWAYS PLC v WILLIAMS, [2012] UKSC 43, [2013] 1 All E.R. 443, Lord Hope, J.S.C. (Deputy President), SC.

937. Apprentices–Apprenticeships–Standards–Wales

THE APPRENTICESHIPS (SPECIFICATION OF APPRENTICESHIP STANDARDS FOR WALES) ORDER 2013, SI 2013/SI 2013/1192 (W.128); made under the Apprenticeships, Skills, Children and Learning Act 2009 s.28. In force: June 23, 2013; .

This Order, made under s.28 of the Apprenticeships, Skills, Children and Learning Act 2009, brings the specification of apprenticeship standards for Wales into effect.

938. Apprentices–Apprenticeships–Training–Wales

THE APPRENTICESHIPS (ISSUE OF APPRENTICESHIP CERTIFICATES) (WALES) REGULATIONS 2013, SI 2013/SI 2013/1190 (W.126); made under the Apprenticeships, Skills, Children and Learning Act 2009 s.7, s.8, s.9. In force: June 23, 2013; .

These Regulations relate to the issue of the apprenticeship certificates under ss.7 and 8 of the Apprenticeships, Skills, Children and Learning Act 2009. They form part of the implementation of the statutory apprenticeships programme in Pt.1 of the Act.

939. Apprenticeships–Certificates–Wales

THE APPRENTICESHIPS (ALTERNATIVE WELSH COMPLETION CONDITIONS) REGULATIONS 2013, SI 2013/SI 2013/1468 (W.139); made under the Apprenticeships, Skills, Children and Learning Act 2009 s.2, s.262. In force: June 23, 2013; .

These Regulations make provision for circumstances where a person has not entered into an apprenticeship agreement but is working under alternative working arrangements, by specifying the alternative Welsh completion conditions which will entitle them to receive an apprenticeship certificate. They apply in cases where a person works as a self employed person; and where a person has been dismissed by reason of redundancy, so that that person can complete the apprenticeship within six months of the date of the redundancy.

940. Apprenticeships–Local Learning and Skills Councils–Wales

THE APPRENTICESHIPS (DESIGNATION OF WELSH CERTIFYING AUTHORITY) ORDER 2013, SI 2013/SI 2013/1191 (W.127); made under the Apprenticeships, Skills, Children and Learning Act 2009 s.262. In force: June 23, 2013; .

This Order, made under s.10 of the Apprenticeships, Skills, Children and Learning Act 2009, designates the Alliance of Sector Skills Councils as the "Welsh certifying authority" to issue apprenticeship certificates generally.

941. Apprenticeships–Qualifications–Vocational training–Wales

THE APPRENTICESHIPS (TRANSITIONAL PROVISION FOR EXISTING VOCATIONAL SPECIFICATIONS) (WALES) ORDER 2013, SI 2013/SI 2013/1202 (W.129); made under the Apprenticeships, Skills, Children and Learning Act 2009 s.22. In force: June 22, 2013; .

This Order specifies the existing vocational specifications which are to be treated as if they were apprenticeship frameworks issued under s.19 of the Apprenticeships, Skills, Children and Learning Act 2009. The existing vocational specifications are to be treated as being issued on June 23, 2013, and are to be treated as being withdrawn on June 28 2013. The Schedule to the Order specifies, for each of the existing vocational specifications, the qualification that is to be treated as the competencies qualification, and the level and apprenticeship sector that is to be treated as being stated in the deemed framework.

942. Apprenticeships, Skills, Children and Learning Act 2009 (c.22)–Commencement No.4 Order–Wales

THE APPRENTICESHIPS, SKILLS, CHILDREN AND LEARNING ACT 2009 (COMMENCEMENT NO.4) (WALES) ORDER 2013, SI 2013/SI 2013/1100 (W.117) (C.45); made under the Apprenticeships, Skills, Children and Learning Act 2009 s.269. Commencement details: bringing into force various provisions of the 2009 Act on May 10, 2013.; .

This Order is the fourth Commencement Order made by the Welsh Ministers under the Apprenticeships, Skills, Children and Learning Act 2009, and commences provisions concerning: the circumstances in which a person completes a Welsh apprenticeship; the issue of apprenticeship certificates; and apprenticeship frameworks.

943. Codes of practice–Employment–Settlements

THE EMPLOYMENT CODE OF PRACTICE (SETTLEMENT AGREEMENTS) ORDER 2013, SI 2013/1665; made under the Trade Union and Labour Relations (Consolidation) Act 1992 s.200. In force: July 29, 2013; .

This Order appoints July 29, 2013 as the day on which the code of practice on settlement agreements will come into effect. The code of practice is being issued by the Advisory, Conciliation and Arbitration Service under the Trade Union and Labour Relations (Consolidation) Act 1992 s.199.

944. Collective agreements–Pay rises–Construction of pay rise provision containing two figures–Whether void for uncertainty–Whether giving employer choice of which figure

The appellant employees (E) appealed against a decision ([2012] I.R.L.R. 888, [2012] C.L.Y. 1049) that a collective pay agreement with the respondent employer (L) enabled L to choose from two alternative pay increases. L had made the agreement with E's trade union for the years 2007 to 2009, and it was incorporated into E's employment contracts. It provided for set pay increases for 2007 and 2008, and for 2009 it provided that pay would be increased by 2.5 per cent or by the NJC Local Government Services settlement plus 1 per cent. In 2009 L took the view that it was not obliged to implement an increase of 2.5 per cent. E began proceedings claiming unlawful deductions from wages. The employment tribunal held that no contractual rights accrued in 2009 because the agreement left it open as to which of two alternatives would apply. On E's appeal, the Employment Appeal Tribunal held that the provision gave L a choice of two alternative pay increases, and that the existence of choice did not render the agreement unenforceable for uncertainty. The issues were (i) whether the provision gave rise to legally enforceable rights for 2009; (ii) the provision's construction.

Held: Appeal allowed. (1) The provision was not an agreement to agree, but was an agreement for a rate of pay to be determined in accordance with the agreed terms. If the provision did give L a choice, that would not have rendered it unenforceable. If the provision was not void for uncertainty, but was susceptible to meaningful construction, it was no less apt for incorporation into E's employment contracts than were the provisions for 2007 and 2008. That was implicit in the objective of a three-year deal (see paras 9-12 of judgment). (2) It was necessary to consider what the agreement conveyed to a reasonable person having all the background knowledge that would have reasonably been available to the parties, *Adams v British Airways Plc* [1996] I.R.L.R. 574, [1996] C.L.Y. 2527 and *Investors Compensation Scheme Ltd v West Bromwich Building Society (No.1)* [1998] 1 W.L.R. 896, [1997] C.L.Y. 2537 applied. It was clear that the parties to the agreement and to the employment contracts had as their central purpose a three-year pay deal. Whereas the provisions for 2007 and 2008 were simple, the provision for 2009 was more complicated. The construction of it adopted by the EAT was wholly improbable. The idea that a union would agree to a three-year pay deal in which the third year was covered by two alternatives, and that L should have the unfettered right to choose between them, was fanciful. The omission to use the words "whichever is the greater", or "whichever is the lesser", in the provision was not significant. Looking at the matter objectively, the provision meant that there would be an increase of 2.5 per cent or NJC plus 1 per cent whichever was the greater; no other meaning made, or would have made, sense (paras 22-23, 25).

ANDERSON v LONDON FIRE AND EMERGENCY PLANNING AUTHORITY, [2013] EWCA Civ 321, [2013] I.R.L.R. 459, Maurice Kay, L.J., CA (Civ Div).

945. Collective bargaining–Trade union recognition–Pilots employed throughout Europe by company–Jurisdiction of Central Arbitration Committee–Strength of workers' connection with Great Britain

[Trade Union and Labour Relations (Consolidation) Act 1992 (c.52) s.94(1), s.285, Sch.A1, Sch.A1 Pt I para.3(3), Sch.A1 Pt I para.3(4); European Convention on Human Rights 1950 Art.11.]

The claimant airline company (N) applied for judicial review of a decision by the defendant CAC that there were no territorial restrictions relevant to an application by the interested party trade union (U) for collective bargaining recognition. N operated a fleet of business jets in Europe with no fixed routes or schedules. Flights could start from anywhere in Europe and pilots employed by N could choose their own "gateway" airport to start and end assignments from. U applied to the CAC to be recognised for collective bargaining by N under the Trade Union and Labour Relations (Consolidation) Act 1992 Sch.A1 in respect of a bargaining unit comprising all the pilots employed by N. N stated that only 159 of its 779 pilots had a gateway in Great Britain, and that only approximately 21 per cent of flight departures were from the UK. It argued that there were no workers in the proposed bargaining unit in respect of whom the statutory system of union recognition could apply because of the limits on the territorial extent of Sch.A1. The CAC noted that, although N's operational base was in Portugal, it was registered in Great Britain and the contract between the workers and N was governed by English law. It referred to the approach adopted in *Ravat v Halliburton Manufacturing & Services Ltd* [2012] UKSC 1, [2012] 2 All E.R. 905, [2012] C.L.Y. 1176 and concluded that the connection of the workers with Great Britain was sufficiently strong for U to be able to seek recognition. N contended that the CAC had failed to apply the "stronger connection" test set out in *Ravat*.

Held: Application refused. (1) When considering the territorial jurisdiction of employment tribunals in cases concerned with individual employment rights, the starting point was that the employment had to have had a "stronger connection with Great Britain than with the foreign country where the employee works". However, the test to be applied was whether section 94(1) of the 1992 Act applied to that particular employment and whether the connection between the circumstances of the employment and Great Britain, and with British employment law, was sufficiently strong for the employee to have a claim for unfair dismissal in Great Britain, *Ravat* applied. That test had been correctly identified and applied to the facts of the instant case by the CAC. The CAC had not therefore erred in failing to adopt the "stronger connection" test. Even if, contrary to that view, that was the correct test to apply, the conclusion in the instant case would not be any different. Having regard to the factors identified by the CAC in connecting N and U to Great Britain, the mere fact that the administration of the employment relationship and the operating company were based in Portugal could not properly lead to the conclusion that a stronger relationship existed with Portugal than with Great Britain (see paras 27-29 of judgment). It was not appropriate to take into account characteristics of individual employees when considering whether U had collective bargaining rights. At that stage the focus was on workers as a group and the appropriate time to take into account individual characteristics was when considering those workers who should form the bargaining unit, *R. (on the application of BBC) v Central Arbitration Committee* [2003] EWHC 1375 (Admin), [2003] I.C.R. 1542, [2003] C.L.Y. 1322 applied (paras 30-31). The CAC had correctly identified the most important factors. In the absence of agreement between the parties as to matters that should be the subject of collective bargaining, under Sch.A1 Pt I para.3(3) and para.3(4) collective bargaining was limited to negotiations relating to pay, hours and holidays. As noted by the CAC, the contract between each worker in the proposed unit and N included terms relating to pay, hours and holidays, was governed by English law and was subject to the exclusive jurisdiction of the English courts. It was clear that the CAC considered those factors showed a sufficiently strong connection with Great Britain for recognition purposes (paras 36-37). (2) The conclusion reached by the CAC in relation to the territorial scope of Sch.A1 was not contrary to the intention of Parliament. Section 285 expressly provided for territorial limitations in respect of certain provisions of the Act, but Sch.A1 was not so limited (paras 38-40). (3) Schedule A1 had to be construed so as to give proper effect to the essential European Convention on Human Rights 1950 art.11 "right to bargain collectively with the employer". However, it was neither necessary nor appropriate to reconsider that right in detail in the instant case. The connection of workers within the proposed bargaining unit with Great Britain was sufficiently strong for U to be able to seek recognition to conduct collective bargaining on their behalf. N did not suggest that its employees should exercise such rights in any other European Union state, and the reality was that if U could not bargain collectively with N in Great Britain, it would not be able to exercise its art.11 right.

U's construction of Sch.A1 gave effect to art.11 whereas N's construction did not (paras 41-42).

NETJETS MANAGEMENT LTD v CENTRAL ARBITRATION COMMITTEE, [2012] EWHC 2685 (Admin), [2013] 1 All E.R. 288, Supperstone, J., QBD (Admin).

946. Collective redundancies–Jurisdiction–Court's jurisdiction to answer question affecting civilian staff at military base–European Union

[Directive 98/59 on collective redundancies Art.1.]

The court was asked to give a preliminary ruling on the interpretation of Directive 98/59. The applicant in the main proceedings was a British national who had been made redundant from her position as a civilian employee at an American military base in the United Kingdom. She brought proceedings against the United States before an employment tribunal, arguing that the employer had failed to consult staff representatives. The proceedings reached the Court of Appeal, which referred to the instant court a question concerning the time at which the employer's obligation to consult about collective redundancies under Directive 98/59 arose.

Held: Judgment accordingly. In order to rule on the question whether a dismissal, such as that at issue in the main proceedings, terminating an established employment relationship between a national of a Member State and a non-Member State, following the closure of a military base belonging to the latter and located on the territory of that Member State, fell within the scope of Directive 98/59, it was in the first instance necessary to interpret the wording of art.1 (2) (b) of the Directive. By virtue of that provision, which provided an exclusion from the scope of the Directive, the latter did not apply to workers employed by public administrative bodies or by establishments governed by public law (or, in Member States where that concept was unknown, by equivalent bodies). Given that armed forces fell within the public administration or equivalent body, it was clear from the wording of art.1 (2) (b) that the civilian staff of a military base were covered by the exclusion laid down by that provision. Further, Directive 98/59 formed part of the legislation concerning the internal market. While the size and functioning of the armed forces did have an influence on the employment situation in a given Member State, considerations concerning the internal market or competition between undertakings did not apply to them. As the court had already held, activities which, like national defence, fell within the exercise of public powers were in principle excluded from classification as economic activity. The EFTA Surveillance Authority had argued that it was possible to read art.1 (2) as referring only to public administrations of Member States and not to those of non-Member States, but the wording of that provision did not in any way lay down such a distinction between Member States and non-Member States. Therefore, it had to be held that, by virtue of the exclusion laid down by art.1 (2) (b), the dismissal of staff of a military base did not, in any event, fall within the scope of the Directive, irrespective of whether or not it was a military base belonging to a non-Member State. In those circumstances, it was not necessary specifically to take into account the fact that, in this case, it was a military base belonging to a non-Member State, that question having implications in international law. In the circumstances, the court did not have jurisdiction to reply to the question raised (see paras 32-34, 40-43, 57 of judgment).

UNITED STATES v NOLAN (C-583/10) [2013] 1 C.M.L.R. 32, Judge Silva de Lapuerta (President), ECJ (3rd Chamber).

947. Collective redundancies–Protective awards–Grant of protective award restricted to establishments employing more than 20–Meaning of "at one establishment" in s.188 Trade Union and Labour Relations (Consolidation) Act 1992–Objective of Directive 98/59

[Trade Union and Labour Relations (Consolidation) Act 1992 (c.52) s.188; Directive 98/59 on collective redundancies Art.1.]

The appellant (U), a trade union for shopworkers, appealed against a decision of an employment tribunal to limit protective awards to workplaces where 20 or more redundancies were made. The respondent (E) was a chain of 90 stores. When the business went into administration, U succeeded in obtaining protective awards for failure to consult it in advance of making redundancies. However, those employees who had been employed at locations with fewer than 20 employees received no award. The issue was whether the Trade Union and Labour Relations (Consolidation) Act 1992 s.188, which was introduced to transpose Directive 98/59, could be construed so as to require the court to delete the words "at one establishment", or to add the words "at one or more establishments", thereby allowing protective awards to be made to employees whose employer was to dismiss 20 employees as redundant in 90 days. U contended that s.188 of the 1992 Act should be interpreted as requiring the employer to consult where it proposed to dismiss as redundant 20 or more employees at one or more establishments; and/or at one establishment, broadly interpreted in accordance with the Directive to mean the whole of the retail business, rather than each of its individual store; and/or deleting the words "at one establishment" from s.188.

Held: Appeal allowed. (1) There was no requirement in the Directive for the words "at one establishment" to be introduced into the 1992 Act. Those words did not come from the Directive and had not been the subject of any consultation or parliamentary debate. Article 1 (1) (a) (ii) of the Directive imposed no site-based restriction on the number of employees made redundant and did not define the term "establishment". The consultation papers and the explanatory notes to the Transfer of Undertakings (Protection of Employment) Regulations showed that the "one establishment" limitation was not regarded as fundamental to the policy of the legislation: the term was never mentioned. The principle in *Marleasing SA v La Comercial Internacional de Alimentacion SA (C-106/89)* [1990] E.C.R. I-4135 permitted words to be added or removed when interpreting national law in accordance with EU law, *Marleasing* applied. The court was therefore entitled to construe s.188 so that it complied with the obligation under the Directive, *Ghaidan v Godin-Mendoza* [2004] UKHL 30, [2004] 2 A.C. 557, [2004] C.L.Y. 2538 followed. The only way to deliver the core objective of protection of the dismissed workers in the instant case was to construe "establishment" as meaning the retail business of the employer. That was a fact-sensitive approach which might not be the same in every case but was consistent with the core objective. Accordingly, the words "at one establishment" were to be deleted from s.188 as a matter of construction pursuant to the court's obligation to apply the purpose of the Directive (see paras 27, 49-50, 52-53 of judgment). (2) (Obiter) It was at least arguable that the Directive had direct effect relating to emanations of the state, so that U was entitled to a remedy against the Secretary of State in the instant case (paras 61-62).

$AW v ETHEL AUSTIN LTD (IN ADMINISTRATION); $AW v UNITE THE UNION; *sub nom.* $AW v WW REALISATION I LTD [2014] 1 C.M.L.R. 23, Judge McMullen Q.C., EAT.

948. Collective redundancies–Trade unions

THE TRADE UNION AND LABOUR RELATIONS (CONSOLIDATION) ACT 1992 (AMENDMENT) ORDER 2013, SI 2013/763; made under the Trade Union and Labour Relations (Consolidation) Act 1992 s.197, s.286. In force: April 6, 2013; .

This Order amends provisions relating to collective redundancies in the Trade Union and Labour Relations (Consolidation) Act 1992 (the 1992 Act). In cases where an employer proposes to dismiss 100 or more employees as redundant within a period of 90 days or less, the Order reduces the minimum period of time which must elapse before the first dismissal can take effect from 90 to 45 days. The Order also excludes the expiry of fixed term contracts from the provisions dealing with collective redundancies in the 1992 Act.

949. Compensatory awards–Unfair dismissal

THE UNFAIR DISMISSAL (VARIATION OF THE LIMIT OF COMPENSATORY AWARD) ORDER 2013, SI 2013/1949; made under the Enterprise and Regulatory Reform Act 2013 s.15. In force: July 29, 2013; .

This Order introduces an additional cap on the compensatory award for unfair dismissal claims. This cap is based on 12 months of an individual's pay and would exist alongside the current overall cap. The applicable cap in an individual case would be the lower of the two.

950. Compromise agreements–Contracts–Regulatory reform

THE ENTERPRISE AND REGULATORY REFORM ACT 2013 (CONSEQUENTIAL AMENDMENTS) (EMPLOYMENT) ORDER 2013, SI 2013/1956; made under the Enterprise and Regulatory Reform Act 2013 s.99. In force: August 30, 2013; .

This Order amends various pieces of secondary legislation to reflect the renaming of "compromise agreements" and "compromise contracts" as "settlement agreements" and "settlement contracts" by the Enterprise and Regulatory Reform Act 2013 s.23.

951. Constructive dismissal–Disability discrimination–Disciplinary procedures–Employee with personality disorder suspended for more than one year before resigning

[Disability Discrimination Act 1995 (c.50) s.4A(1), s.4A.]

The appellant employer (C) appealed against an employment tribunal's decision that it had discriminated against the respondent employee (M) on grounds of disability, and that it had constructively dismissed him. M had borderline personality disorder. C suspended M for breaching its trade-in policy for personal gain. Following a disciplinary hearing, M was found guilty of gross misconduct, his suspension was maintained due to his bankruptcy, and he was demoted. He appealed against the decision unsuccessfully. He commenced claims for unpaid wages and disability discrimination. He later resigned after 12 months of suspension and claimed constructive dismissal. The tribunal found that M had been (i) discriminated against on the ground of disability by C's failure to pay him correctly during his suspension; (ii) discriminated against by C's failure to end his suspension; (iii) constructively dismissed.

Held: Appeal allowed in part. (1) The tribunal effectively found that C's lack of competence or understanding in preparing M's wage slip was capable of being a "practice" under the Disability Discrimination Act 1995 s.4A, and that C should have taken the reasonable step of not delaying payment to M of the correct amount. However, a lack of competence in relation to a particular transaction could not, as a matter of proper construction of s.4A, amount to a "practice" applied by C any more than it could amount to a "provision" or "criterion". The obligation created by s.4A was to take reasonable steps. Taking care when making payments could not be properly described as taking a step or steps for the purposes of s.4A(1). Accordingly, the tribunal's finding that M was discriminated against by C's failure to pay him the correct amount could not stand (see para.19 of judgment). (2) The tribunal clearly regarded the length of M's suspension as wholly excessive and largely being C's fault. However, its finding that C had acted incompetently was misconceived. Incompetence, a woeful lack of application, or a failure of C to stick to its own time limits regarding suspension, could not be properly characterised as a "provision, criterion or practice" applied by it. Further, avoiding delay in the disciplinary process could not be characterised as the taking of steps. The tribunal's finding that M had been discriminated against by C's failure to end his suspension could not stand (para.21). (3) In light of its findings, it was open to the tribunal to say that there had been a repudiatory breach of contract. There was plenty of behaviour on which it was open to the tribunal to find that, when put together, there had been a breach of the term of trust and confidence. On all the findings made leading to the conclusion that M had been constructively dismissed, it was patently obvious that that constructive dismissal was unfair. Accordingly, C's appeal in respect of M's constructive dismissal failed (paras 23, 26, 30).

CARPHONE WAREHOUSE LTD v MARTIN [2013] Eq. L.R. 481, Judge Shanks, EAT.

952. Continuity of employment–Arrangement to preserve continuity–Meaning of "arrangement" in s.212(3)(c) Employment Rights Act 1996–Whether arrangement could be retrospective

[Employment Rights Act 1996 (c.18) s.212(3)(c), s.212(3)(b), s.230.]

The appellant employee (W) appealed against a decision that he did not have the requisite continuity of employment to bring a claim for unfair dismissal against the respondent (D). W had worked at D's Sheffield store for over a year. The store closed down on Tuesday February 23, 2010, and his working week ended on Saturday February 27, 2010. During the following week D offered him work at another store. He began work at a different store on Monday March 8, 2010. He resigned from that post approximately nine months later and brought a claim for unfair dismissal. The employment judge concluded that W could not rely on the Employment Rights Act 1996 s.212(3)(b) or (c) to preserve his continuity of employment; he had two separate periods of employment, the second of which was insufficient in length for a claim of unfair dismissal. W submitted that (1) he should be regarded as subject to a contract of employment during the week after the termination of his contract at Sheffield; (2) if not, his absence from work was on account of a temporary cessation of work; (3) if not, an arrangement was reached after the event that his absence should not break continuity of employment.

Held: Appeal allowed. (1) W's first submission begged the question of whether there was a contract of employment at some stage during the week of Sunday February 28, 2010, before he commenced work at the new store the following week. It was wholly unrealistic to suppose that W had not accepted the offer of work until his first day at the new store. Therefore, on acceptance of the job offer there was plainly a contract either "for employment" or "of employment". Section 230 envisaged the possibility that the contract of employment, and employment under it, were two separate things. The apparent approach of the draftsman of s.230, the principle adopted by the majority in *Gunton v Richmond upon Thames LBC* [1981] Ch. 448, [1980] C.L.Y. 895, and the reasoning in *Sarker v South Tees Acute Hospitals NHS Trust* [1997] I.C.R. 673, [1997] C.L.Y. 2203 all coincided: once a contract such as that in the instant case was made, it was one "of employment". Though not requiring performance of actual work until the week beginning March 8, 2010, it governed relations between W and D from its inception, *Sarker* and *Gunton* applied, *Hochster v De La Tour* 118 E.R. 922 considered. Accordingly, the week in which the contract of employment was made was a week which counted under s.212(1) and W's continuity of employment had not been broken (see paras 16-19, 22-26 of judgment). That conclusion was sufficient to dispose of W's appeal, but in case the Employment Appeal Tribunal was in error, W's other grounds were also considered. (2) Computation of W's period of continuous employment could not fairly be affected by the question of whether the employer was closing down a business or some department of it. Under the 1996 Act it was a pure question of fact whether the employer had work available for the employee to do personally during the week in question. The position of other employees and the reason for a cessation of work were irrelevant. Given that there was no contract of employment governing W's relations with his employer during the week beginning March 1, any work subsequently taken up by him for D would be under a fresh contract. There was no reason why it should not be in another department or location, provided it was for the same employer, *Fitzgerald v Hall Russell & Co Ltd* [1970] A.C. 984, [1969] C.L.Y. 1277 and *Wood v York City*

Council [1978] I.C.R. 840, [1978] C.L.Y. 908 followed. The judge should therefore have assessed whether the cessation of work was temporary, viewed in hindsight, comparing the length of absence from work with the period of work which came before and after it. She had not considered that factual question. Had she done so, on the facts, the only conclusion she could properly have reached was that the cessation of work was temporary (paras 30-35). (3) Continuity of employment was a statutory concept. Whether an arrangement could be reached retrospectively to preserve it had to be determined as a matter of statutory construction. Section 212(3)(c) stated that a week would count towards continuity if the employee "is absent from work in circumstances such that, by arrangement or custom, he is regarded as continuing in the employment of his employer for any purpose". The section was expressed in the present tense, which suggested that the relevant employment was current or prospective, but not retrospective. The circumstances referred to in the section were those which were present at the time of absence or preceded it. All those who had considered the construction of the statutory words took the same view, save only HHJ McMullen QC in *London Probation Board v Kirkpatrick* [2005] I.C.R. 965, [2005] C.L.Y. 1324. The proper approach was that of *Murphy v A Birrell & Sons Ltd* [1978] I.R.L.R. 458, [1978] C.L.Y. 1008, *Morris v Walsh Western UK Ltd* [1997] I.R.L.R. 562, [1998] C.L.Y. 2231 and *Joseph Ltd v Heath*. Tribunals should not follow *Kirkpatrick*. "Arrangements" in s.212 would not bridge the gap in continuity of employment unless the arrangement was in existence before, or arose contemporaneously with, the relevant weeks of absence from work during which there was no contract of employment, *Murphy, Morris* and *Joseph* applied, *Kirkpatrick* not followed (paras 47-54).

WELTON v DELUXE RETAIL LTD (T/A MADHOUSE (IN ADMINISTRATION)) [2013] I.C.R. 428, Langstaff, J. (President), EAT.

953. Contracts of employment–Bonus payments–Oral promise in "town hall" meeting to pay staff bonuses–Whether giving rise to contractual obligation–Validity of purported reduction in amount of bonuses

The appellants (D and C) appealed against a decision ([2012] EWHC 1189 (QB), [2012] I.R.L.R. 553, [2012] C.L.Y. 1053) that D had wrongfully denied the respondents, its employees and former employees, their contractual entitlement to certain discretionary bonuses. D was an investment bank in Dresdner Bank group (DB). On August 18, 2008, shortly before a takeover by C, D announced to its employees in a "town hall" meeting broadcast over the company intranet that DB's board had approved a "guaranteed" minimum bonus pool, which would be allocated to individuals on a discretionary basis according to individual performance "in the usual way". The aim was to retain employees at a time of speculation about DB's future. In December 2008, a letter to each employee confirmed that a discretionary bonus for 2008 had been provisionally awarded at a specified sum, subject to a "material adverse change clause" (MAC clause). On the same day, employees were reassured at a further town hall meeting that the MAC clause was unlikely to be invoked. In January 2009, after the acquisition of DB by C, the MAC clause was invoked and D's employees were told that their bonus awards would be cut by 90 per cent. The issues were (i) whether the August 18 announcement created an obligation to pay the bonus sums claimed; (ii) whether the introduction of the MAC clause was a breach of the implied duty of mutual trust and confidence. The first question involved consideration of three sub-issues: first, whether the announcement was an exercise of D's power to unilaterally vary its employees' terms and conditions under cl.1.4 of the employee handbook, which allowed such variation if the changes were made by a member of the human resources department and notified in writing, and also provided that a change affecting a group of people could be notified by "display" on the company intranet; second, whether the announcement was intended to be legally binding so as to be capable of having contractual effect; third, whether the employees had been obliged to communicate acceptance of the bonus offer. The judge found that D's communications amounted to a variation under cl.1.4 and were intended to be legally binding, and that the introduction of the MAC clause was a breach of the implied duty of mutual trust and confidence.

Held: Appeal dismissed. (1) (a) The variation had been effected in accordance with cl.1.4. D's communications had been made with the approval of the board of the remuneration committee. Since the HR director was a member of that board, no further endorsement by HR was necessary. Moreover, there was no reason why compliance could not be achieved by two documents. A change affecting a group of people did not need to be in writing, but needed only to be displayed on the company intranet. The August 18 announcement could be said to have been "displayed" on D's intranet by reason of its having been broadcast, even if the broadcast could not be viewed after the event (see paras 52-54 of judgment); (b) there was overwhelming evidence that D had intended its promise to be legally binding. Where a term was being introduced into a pre-existing contractual relationship, there was a very strong presumption that it was intended to be legally binding, and the onus was on the party asserting that there was no intention to create legal relations to establish that fact. The natural inference was that any promises made to staff relating to the terms of their employment would take effect in the same way as other contractual terms. That was supported by a number of matters: D's chief executive officer had made the promise, which implied that it must have been approved at the highest level; it was part of a vitally important staff retention strategy to prevent the potential collapse of the investment banking division; the nature of the promise assured staff that the fund was guaranteed come what may; and it was related to pay, the most fundamental obligation under the employment contract (paras 80-81, 89, 96); (c) D's employees were under no obligation to communicate acceptance of the bonus offer. D had plainly dispensed with the need for any response: it had made a promise without any disadvantage to its employees, and nobody hearing the announcement would expect that an employee could only benefit if he positively accepted the offer. That would have had the bizarre result that even if only a minority of the relevant employees accepted the offer, D would have had to pay them the whole of the bonus pool. Even if there was no unilateral change pursuant to cl.1.4, there was a binding contractual obligation to pay bonus payments in the usual way, at least to the limits of the guaranteed fund (paras 97-100). (2) The introduction of the MAC clause was a breach of the implied duty of mutual trust and confidence. The judge had been entitled to find that the MAC clause had been introduced as a result of pressure from C, which had been concerned about the public's negative perception of large bonus payments. He had objectively analysed the question of whether trust and confidence had been undermined and there was ample evidence to support his conclusion that it had (paras 130-140).

ATTRILL v DRESDNER KLEINWORT LTD; *sub nom.* DRESDNER KLEINWORT LTD v ATTRILL, [2013] EWCA Civ 394, [2013] 3 All E.R. 607, Maurice Kay, L.J. (VP, CA Civ), CA (Civ Div).

954. Contracts of employment–Breach of contract–Employee making comments on Facebook opposing gay marriages in church–Whether breach of contract established

The claimant employee (S) sought damages for breach of contract from the defendant employer (T). S had worked in a managerial position for T, a private housing trust. He was a practising Christian and occasional lay preacher. He was subject to disciplinary proceedings after commenting on his Facebook wall page, in response to a news item that gay church marriages were set to be approved, that this was "an equality too far" and after stating, in response to a Facebook enquiry from a work colleague, that the bible specified that marriage was for men and women and that the state should not impose its rules on places of faith and conscience. The disciplinary proceedings resulted in a finding of gross misconduct, S's demotion and a reduction in pay. The issue was whether S's Facebook postings amounted to a breach of T's Code of Conduct and/or its Equal Opportunities Policy. T argued that (1) the postings were activities which might bring it into disrepute, contrary to the Code of Conduct; (2) by his postings, S was promoting his religious views, contrary to that part of the Code of Conduct which dealt with relationships with customers, members of the public and colleagues; (3) S was failing to treat fellow employees with dignity and respect, including being non-judgmental in approach, and was engaging in conduct which might make another person feel uncomfortable, embarrassed or upset, contrary to the Equal Opportunities Policy and the Code of Conduct.

Held: Judgment for claimant. (1) S's postings about gay marriage in church were not such as did, or even could, bring T into disrepute. No reasonable reader of his Facebook wall page could rationally conclude that his two postings were made in any relevant sense on T's behalf. Having regard to the entries on S's wall for the period in question as a whole, it was obvious, and would be obvious even to a casual reader, that he used Facebook for personal and social rather than work-related purposes. His moderate expression of his particular views about gay marriage in church, on his personal Facebook wall at a weekend, could not sensibly lead any reasonable reader to think the worst of T for having employed him as a manager (see paras 57, 59, 63-64 of judgment). (2) The right of individuals to freedom of expression and freedom of belief, taken together, meant that they were in general entitled to promote their religious or political beliefs, as long as they did so lawfully. Of course, an employer could legitimately restrict or prohibit such activities at work, or in a work-related context, but it would be prima facie surprising to find that an employer had, by the incorporation of a code of conduct into the employee's contract, extended that prohibition to his personal or social life. S's Facebook wall was inherently non-work related, and his Facebook was an aspect of his social life outside work. The prohibition on the promotion of political and religious views in the Code of Conduct did not, as a matter of interpretation and application, extend to S's Facebook wall. In any event, the postings did not amount to "promotion" (paras 66, 75, 79). (3) To construe the provisions in the Code of Conduct and Equal Opportunities Policy which required employees to treat colleagues with dignity and respect and to refrain from conduct which might make others feel uncomfortable, embarrassed or upset as applying to every situation outside work where an employee came into contact with one or more work colleagues would be to impose a fetter on his freedom of speech in circumstances beyond those to which a reasonable reader of the Code and Policy would think they applied. On any view, their main application was to circumstances where the employee was working for T. S's use of his Facebook involved his work colleagues only to the extent that they sought his views by becoming his Facebook friends, and that did not detract to any significant extent from the essentially personal and social nature of his use of it as a medium for communication. In any event, his postings were not, viewed objectively, judgmental, disrespectful or liable to cause upset or offence (paras 82, 84). (4) In the circumstances, T did not have a right to demote S by reason of his Facebook postings and that demotion constituted a breach of contract. It also amounted to a wrongful dismissal. Given that T would have acted as it had but upon 12 weeks' notice, the correct measure of damages was the very small difference between S's contractual salary and the amount actually paid to him during the 12 weeks following the assumption of his new role. The injustice he had suffered, although very real, was unfortunately something which the court was unable to alleviate by an award of substantial damages (paras 86, 94, 104-106).

SMITH v TRAFFORD HOUSING TRUST, [2012] EWHC 3221 (Ch), [2013] I.R.L.R. 86, Briggs, J., Ch D (Manchester).

955. Contracts of employment–Death benefits–Suicide–Death of seaman lost at sea–Employer's decision about cause of death–Duty of decision-maker to give himself legal direction

The appellants (BP) appealed against a decision ([2012] EWHC 1423 (Comm), [2012] I.C.R. D39) that they were liable in contract for the death of the claimant's husband (B), who had been employed by BP as the chief engineer on board one of their vessels. While at sea B had disappeared from the vessel. BP's investigation concluded that suicide by jumping overboard was the most likely cause of B's death. The decision-maker at BP (S) decided therefore that B's actions amounted to wilful act or default, and therefore under the terms of his employment contract death in service benefits were not payable. The judge held that, although the contract provided that it was enough that in BP's opinion B's death resulted from his wilful act or default, that opinion had to be reasonably formed and S had to have been properly directed in law. He held that that it was unlikely that S had applied the correct legal test, and he then applied the test in *R. v HM Coroner for West London, Ex p. Gray* [1988] Q.B. 467, [1987] C.L.Y. 534 to find that the conclusions of BP's investigation team were not sufficiently cogent evidence commensurate with or proportionate to the seriousness of a finding of suicide. He also found that BP's opinion was unreasonable in that the investigation had failed to take into account the real possibility that B went out on deck in the night to check the weather for work reasons and accidentally fell overboard. BP submitted that the judge had been wrong to hold that (1) S had misdirected himself by failing to have regard to the requirement that there had to be cogent evidence commensurate or proportionate to the seriousness of a finding of suicide; (2) he had failed to take into account the fact that B had had good reason to be on deck to check the weather and that accordingly there was a possibility that he could have fallen overboard accidentally. The respondent submitted that the judge was right for the reasons he gave and there were other reasons why BP's decision was unreasonable because of their reliance on various factual details surrounding B's disappearance.

Held: Appeal allowed. (1) If a death benefit was not payable if in the employer's opinion the death resulted from the employee's wilful act or default, that opinion had to be formed honestly and on reasonable grounds. The judge had said that the lay body, namely BP, had to "act fairly and be properly directed in law". No doubt if a lay body misdirected itself in law the resulting decision could well be unreasonable, but it was rather different to say that the lay body had to be properly directed in law if that envisaged that the lay body had to give itself a legal direction. The whole point of a lay body was that it was not encumbered by lawyers. It could not be the law that a non-lawyer such as S should have given himself directions before forming his opinion that B probably committed suicide, *CVG Siderurgicia del Orinoco SA v London Steamship Owners Mutual Insurance Association Ltd (The Vainqueur Jose)* [1979] 1 Lloyd's Rep. 557, [1979] C.L.Y. 2473 considered (see paras 13-14 of judgment). The opinion of BP's investigation team was not formed by reference to the death benefit clause of B's contract but rather to see whether lessons could be learned. Any question of the application of the standard of proof was entirely academic for that purpose but it was clear that their conclusion was based on the probabilities of the case. S was naturally influenced by the findings of the investigation. Naturally enough also he did not give himself any direction of law as to how he should approach the evidence received by and the findings made by the investigation team. As the judge had said, it was unlikely that S directed himself that "there should be cogent evidence commensurate with or proportionate to the seriousness of a finding of suicide", *Ex p. Gray* considered. It was not right to say that he should have so directed himself. That would have been impossible without him taking legal advice of a kind that could not have been contemplated by the requirements of the death benefit clause. It might well be that if he had positively misdirected himself in law, his opinion would be unreasonable, but that was not the case. The investigation team had decided that suicide "was the most likely scenario". That was the ordinary language of probability and S's conclusion was based on it (paras 17-20). (2) It was not right to say that the investigation team did not take into account the fact that B might have had legitimate reasons for being on deck. They had investigated the whole history of the matter and were aware that work in the engine room was contemplated. Even if the team had failed to take that into account, that failure, in the absence of a mechanism explaining how he could accidentally fall overboard, could not make BP's opinion unreasonable (para.22). (3) The judge should have held that the respondent's attack on the investigation team's opinion failed. They had made an appropriate, detailed and careful inquiry, and their conclusion of suicide was a reasonable one in the circumstances. However, it was S's opinion that was relevant. He had to make up his own mind, but it was hardly surprising that he thought the team's opinion was reasonable (paras 24-34).

BRAGANZA v BP SHIPPING LTD; BRITSH UNITY,THE, [2013] EWCA Civ 230, [2013] 2 Lloyd's Rep. 351, Longmore, L.J., CA (Civ Div).

956. Contracts of employment–Implied terms–Fairness–Withdrawal from post for misconduct–Employee's right to fair treatment–Employer's failure to provide details of allegations

The claimant employee (Y) sought damages from the defendant employer (FCO) for breach of his contract of employment and of its duty of care in removing him from his position as HM High Commissioner to Belize. Y was appointed in 2007. Following a management review in May 2008, Y was given an informal warning based on allegations of bullying and harassment. He was not provided with any examples of the alleged behaviour. He left Belize a few days later on leave. In June 2008, a minister (C) in Belize made allegations of sexual misconduct against Y and stated that he was damaging United Kingdom relations. Y was again provided with no details on the basis that they were confidential. He disputed all the allegations. The FCO decided to withdraw Y from his post with immediate effect. A fact-finding inquiry by the FCO concluded that the allegation of sexual misconduct was unreliable but Y's position was untenable given comments by staff about bullying and harassment. A disciplinary hearing conducted by the same person (G) found that the allegations of bullying and harassment constituted serious misconduct and a penalty of a final written warning was imposed which would remain on Y's file for one year. Counselling for Y was arranged by the FCO. He was diagnosed with depression due to feeling badly treated by the FCO and was unable to return to work. Y submitted that (1) the FCO had unlawfully withdrawn him from his post; (2) G's approach had been unfair: he had not interviewed all relevant witnesses, Y had not been provided with information relating to the allegations and G had reached unreasonable conclusions; (3) financial loss and psychiatric injury flowed as a result of the FCO's breach. The FCO submitted that (1) there was a reasonable perception at the time the decision to withdraw Y was made that an urgent operational decision was needed as there was a risk of significant reputational damage to the UK; (2) G was following the FCO guidance; (3) the losses flowing from Y's depression were too remote.

Held: Judgment for claimant. (1) It was an express term of Y's contract that he was entitled to fair treatment and an implied term of mutual trust and confidence. Before the decision to withdraw Y from his post there should have been some basic analysis of C's allegations, including some discussion with Y. The failure to do that was a breach of the obligation of fair treatment and if the FCO had complied with its contractual obligations there would have been no basis for the withdrawal decision and an inquiry would not have proceeded in the way it did. Fair treatment trumped confidentiality which could not override the very important right of Y to know what was alleged against him and to have his responses fairly valued before a judgment was made. C's allegations lacked credibility, went against the FCO's own knowledge and C had motivation to make them. Elementary investigation would have demonstrated that some of the less serious allegations were untrue and some of the more serious could be discounted. The reputational damage to the UK was significantly overblown. An informal warning had been given to Y regarding the allegations of bullying and he had left Belize a few days later with no new complaints about his behaviour. The FCO acted in breach of contract in withdrawing him from his post without affording him fair treatment (see paras 80-82, 114, 117-119, 122-125, 147 of judgment). (2) G's fact-finding investigation was not methodologically flawed or unfair and he had not reached conclusions which were not open to him. However in the instant case fair treatment demanded that a different person should have conducted the disciplinary hearing. It was a breach of a basic principle of natural justice (paras 129, 131). (3) The withdrawal from post caused Y financial loss and the depression he began to suffer was also attributable to the decision to withdraw. Y's career would otherwise have followed its normal trajectory and he would have worked until retirement. It could be reasonably contemplated when Y was appointed as High Commissioner in 2007 that depression would be a not unlikely result of a knee-jerk withdrawal from post, *Gogay v Hertfordshire CC* [2000] I.R.L.R. 703, [2000] C.L.Y. 4890 followed (paras 132, 135-137). (4) The FCO was also in breach of its duty of care to Y in withdrawing him from post without informing him of the case against him. Y was only aware of the full details at his interview with G in July 2008. That was not the way an employer concerned with an employee's welfare would act. Following the withdrawal decision, the FCO fulfilled its duty in providing him with counselling (paras 143-144).

YAPP v FOREIGN AND COMMONWEALTH OFFICE, [2013] EWHC 1098 (QB), [2013] I.R.L.R. 616, Cranston, J., QBD.

957. Contracts of employment–Implied terms–Incapacity benefit–Employee dismissed after incapacitated from work–Entitlement to benefits under private health insurance policy–Entitlement to sum in lieu of holiday pay

The appellant employee (L) appealed against a decision of an employment tribunal dismissing his claims, including for unfair dismissal, against the respondent employer (B). L had been absent from work for several years because of ill-health before his dismissal. During his absence he had received benefits under a private health insurance policy provided by B. L's employment contract post-dated the policy and made no reference to the policy. His contract provided that B could terminate his employment by giving notice less than 28 days after the end of the 26th week in any period of 52 weeks in which L had not worked because of illness, and that in that event B would pay L a sum equal to six months' salary. L's contract also included a term that the contract superseded all previous agreements and arrangements relating to his employment. L argued that (1) the tribunal had failed to consider the fact that he was contractually entitled to a "golden handshake" payment of a sum equivalent to six months' salary; (2) there was an implied term that an employer would not terminate the contract of an employee who was in receipt of benefits under a health insurance policy while the employee was incapacitated where the effect would be to disqualify the employee from receiving the benefits; (3) he was entitled to a sum in lieu of holiday pay for the period in which he was unable to work because of incapacity.

Held: Appeal dismissed. (1) The tribunal had not granted L permission to introduce the golden handshake claim. It therefore had no valid claim before it, and even if it had done L's argument was doomed to fail: B had given notice well after the end of the 28-day period (see paras 35-37 of judgment). (2) L had received all of the benefits guaranteed under the policy and so had suffered no loss as a result of his termination. In any event, the term in L's contract which stated that the contract superseded all previous agreements constituted an express term which was inconsistent with the implied term contended by L, and it showed why there was no scope for implying L's term, especially as there was no evidence to show that L had a contractual right to benefits under the policy. The fact that the express term was contained in a contract which post-dated the introduction of the policy and that L's contract did not refer to his entitlement to health insurance cover showed that L had no contractual right to the continuation of his policy. There was nothing to suggest that B had a contractual obligation to keep the policy in place until L was 60-years-old. It was impermissible for L to seek to imply a term which negated an express contractual condition, *United Bank v Akhtar* [1989] I.R.L.R. 507, [1991] C.L.Y. 1612 applied. Further, the term in L's contract which permitted the termination of his contract by B giving notice showed that L could be dismissed in circumstances which differed from the implied term he contended for. Even if such a term were implied, it would have been subject to the exception suggested in *Briscoe v Lubrizol Ltd (No.2)* [2002] EWCA Civ 508, [2002] I.R.L.R. 607, [2003] C.L.Y. 1311, which said that such a term would only be implied where the dismissal was without reasonable and proper cause. L's dismissal was for good cause, namely because of his absence and the lack of any prospect of his return to work, and so his claim would have failed in any event, *Briscoe* considered (paras 41-42, 51-54, 57-58). (3) In relation to the holiday pay claim, the tribunal did not consider or reach conclusions on many critical issues, including: (i) during each period for which claims for holiday pay were made, whether L was unable or unwilling to take paid annual leave because of sickness; (ii) in respect of the days when the tribunal had concluded that L had actually taken holiday, whether the days fell in his working week or on weekends or public holidays; (iii) in respect of each period when L was entitled to holiday pay, the amount of holiday pay he should have received and the amount of sickness pay he had actually received; (iv) whether L had to make a request to carry forward an entitlement to annual leave which had accrued, *NHS Leeds v Larner* [2012] EWCA Civ 1034, [2012] 4 All E.R. 1006, [2012] C.L.Y. 1040 considered. The holiday pay issue was remitted to a different tribunal to consider those issues and others (paras 91-93).

LLOYD v BCQ LTD [2013] 1 C.M.L.R. 41, Silber, J., EAT.

958. Contracts of employment–Penalty clauses–Clause providing for termination of employment before expiry of fixed term–Whether requirement to pay unexpired balance constituted penalty clause–Whether managing director had implied authority to conclude contract of employment

[Civil Procedure Rules 1998 (SI 1998/3132) r.14.1 (5).]

The applicant football club (B) applied to withdraw an admission of liability to pay £2.25 million claimed by the respondent former club manager (H). H had negotiated a service agreement with B's managing director (S) to last for a fixed period of approximately three years. It was common ground that S was actually authorised to negotiate and conclude a contract with H, but B contended that the negotiations had been on the basis that the owners' approval was necessary before completion. A clause in H's service agreement stated that his employment was to continue subject to the remaining terms of the agreement. Subsequent clauses provided that B was entitled to terminate the agreement with immediate effect, provided that it paid the unexpired balance of the fixed period. B terminated the agreement six months after it began but did not pay the £2.25 million allegedly due. B filed a formal admission of liability to pay but then sought to withdraw it, invoking the court's discretion under CPR r.14.1 (5). It was B's case that H ought to have known the owners had to authorise the contract. Evidence was led that it was proper for a manager to accept that a managing director had authority to offer the terms they were offering. The issue was whether B would have a realistically arguable defence if it were allowed to withdraw its admission. B submitted that (1) the clause was arguably a penalty and was unenforceable beyond the sum representing H's actual loss; (2) S did not have authority to enter into a contract other than on the basis set by the owners, which was allegedly that it was terminable on 12 months' notice and that compensation for early termination was capped at 12 months' salary.

Held: Application refused. (1) It was not realistically arguable that the clause was a penalty. A sum of money payable under a contract on the occurrence of an event other than a breach of a contractual duty owed by the paying to the receiving party was not a penalty, *Bridge v Campbell Discount Co Ltd* [1961] 1 Q.B. 445, [1961] C.L.Y. 3908 and *Export Credits Guarantee Department v Universal Oil Products Co* [1983] 1 W.L.R. 399, [1983] C.L.Y. 434 considered. The clauses meant that termination of H's employment prior to the expiry of the fixed term did not constitute a breach of contract and so the law relating to penalty clauses was entirely immaterial. Given the effect of the express terms, it was not arguable that the clause should be construed as being a disguised or hidden penalty clause (see paras 33-34 of judgment). (2) There was no evidence that H was ever aware that S's authority was restricted in the manner suggested. By appointing S to be the managing director, he had been held out as having the usual authority of someone holding that office. It was unarguable to suggest that B's managing director did not have implied or usual authority to sign employment contracts (paras 37-39).

BERG v BLACKBURN ROVERS FOOTBALL CLUB & ATHLETIC PLC, [2013] EWHC 1070 (Ch), [2013] I.R.L.R. 537, Judge Pelling Q.C., Ch D (Manchester).

959. Contracts of employment–Personal contracts–Interpretation of "employment" in Employment Equality (Age) Regulations 2006 and Employment Equality (Religion or Belief) Regulations 2003–Correct approach to question of subordination

[Employment Equality (Age) Regulations 2006 (SI 2006/1031); Employment Equality (Religion or Belief) Regulations 2003 (SI 2003/1660).]

The appellant firm of solicitors (C) appealed against an employment judge's decision that the respondent solicitor (V) had been its employee for the purposes of his claims of age and religious discrimination. V had worked as a consultant for C. He brought claims under the Employment Equality (Age) Regulations 2006 and the Employment Equality (Religion or Belief) Regulations 2003. The employment judge found that V was integrated into the firm and thus under the control of its policies and procedures. She concluded that he was an employee, within the meaning of both Regulations. C submitted that (1) integration into an organisation was not sufficient to establish the subordination necessary to show that a person was an employee as defined in both Regulations, rather than an independent contractor; (2) the employment judge's finding that V was under its broad direction was unsupported by the factual findings she made and therefore perverse.

Held: Appeal dismissed. (1) The definition of employment contained in both Regulations included both a contract of service and a contract personally to do any work. It was the latter which was relevant in the instant case. An employee would perform services for and under the direction of another person in return for which he received remuneration, as opposed to being an independent provider of services who was not in a relationship of subordination with the person who received the services, *Allonby v Accrington and Rossendale College (C-256/01)* [2005] All E.R. (EC) 289, [2004] C.L.Y. 1258 and *Jivraj v Hashwani* [2009] EWHC 1364 (Comm), [2010] 1 All E.R. 302 applied. Whether a person was integrated into an organisation was relevant to the question of whether that person was in a position of subordination to the organisation. It had not been an error of law for the employment judge to concentrate on the question of subordination by considering the extent to which V was integrated into the firm, rather than considering the question of whether he was in a subordinate relationship to C as an independent issue. Contrary to the premise of C's submission, the employment judge would have erred in law if she had tried to decide whether V was in a subordinate relationship to C as an independent issue without taking into account all the circumstances, including whether he was integrated into the firm. The weight to be attached to integration was fact-sensitive (see paras 15, 26, 29, 33 of judgment). (2) The employment judge's finding that V was under C's broad direction was not entirely contrary to the evidence that she heard. In fact, C had previously contemplated starting legal proceedings against V, asserting breach of contract in failing to introduce new business to it and failing to ensure, as far as possible, continuity of existing clients. The employment judge had taken into account that view of the relationship which C had held (para.35).

CVS SOLICITORS LLP v VAN DER BORGH [2013] Eq. L.R. 934, Slade, J., EAT.

960. Contracts of employment–Repudiation–Duty of fidelity to employer–Withholding of contingent future interest in fund units–Application of penalty doctrine

The claimant (S) brought proceedings against the defendant (B), his former employer, for entitlement to unvested fund units following the termination of his employment. S was a senior employee of B, an asset management company. The terms of S's remuneration included the granting of fund units due to vest in 2012. In the event of S's employment terminating before the vesting date, his entitlement to the unvested fund units depended on the terms on which he had left. In July 2011, S formed the intention to leave B's employment and concluded a compromise agreement which provided for him to be on garden leave until December 31. Clause 2.2 of the compromise agreement provided that, subject to S's compliance with other terms of the agreement and with his employment contract, he would be treated as a "good leaver" and would not forfeit entitlement to the 2012 fund units. S's employment contract contained an express obligation to act in B's best interests and a covenant not to compete with B during his employment. The contract also stated that S remained bound by its terms during his notice period. From January 2012, S began working for a rival company (G). B refused to grant S entitlement to the 2012 fund units, alleging that he had assisted G in setting up its competing business.

Held: Judgment for defendant. (1) Not all preparation for future competitive activity undertaken by an employee would be regarded as a breach of his duty of loyalty to his employer, *Helmet Integrated Systems Ltd v Tunnard* [2006] EWCA Civ 1735, [2007] I.R.L.R. 126, [2007] C.L.Y. 1324 followed. The precise scope and content of the duty of fidelity, and whether it had been breached, was a question of fact which depended on the particular circumstances of each case, *Hivac Ltd v Park Royal Scientific Instruments Ltd* [1946] Ch. 169 followed. The duty of fidelity might also require an employee to report to his employer a competitive threat of which he became aware, irrespective of whether he was involved in that threat. Although S was relieved of the obligation to work while on garden leave, the negative obligations imposed on him by his employment contract remained part of his duties. Accordingly, S's employment contract and his implied duty of fidelity to B required him not to assist G in setting up and launching its business before December 31, save by negotiating the terms on which he would join G after that date and by co-operating in the arrangements necessary to enable him to do so. The duty of fidelity also required him to tell B that G intended to launch a competitive business and had the necessary resources to do so. There was evidence that S had been involved in substantial discussions with G while on garden leave concerning specific aspects of the structural and operational implementation of the proposed business. He had also failed to disclose the new business to B. It followed that S was in repudiatory breach of his employment contract and of the compromise agreement, with the result that cl.2.2 never came into effect (see paras 121, 126, 132-133, 144, 150-151, 157, 159, 183 of judgment). (2) The penalty doctrine rendered unenforceable a term in a contract by which a contract breaker was required to pay a sum which was regarded as a penalty. That doctrine extended to terms which provided that the contract breaker was to forfeit sums to which he was entitled, or would otherwise have been entitled, from the innocent party, *Gilbert Ash (Northern) Ltd v Modern Engineering (Bristol) Ltd* [1974] A.C. 689, [1973] C.L.Y. 262 followed. Where it applied, the doctrine rendered unconscionable a contract which enabled a party to recover more than the amount of the loss which he had suffered by way of the breach, although the fact that such a clause would have some coercive effect in encouraging performance of the contract was not sufficient to render it unenforceable. In the absence of commercial justification, a clause which was predominantly deterrent rather than compensatory would be unconscionable. It would be easier to justify a provision for payment of a single sum where the loss which might foreseeably be caused by breach might be difficult to quantify, was remote or where financial recompense could not fully compensate for the loss. In determining whether there was justification, the court had to take account of all the terms of the bargain and the circumstances of the contracting parties. In the instant case, the compromise agreement did not provide for forfeiture of S's interest in the 2012 fund units because its effect was that he never acquired any rights to them by reason of his breaches of that agreement. Contingent future interests were not equivalent to the payment of a money sum so as to come within the penalty doctrine, which therefore did not apply. Even if that doctrine had applied, the provisions of the compromise agreement were not so penal as to be unenforceable (paras 187, 189-190, 196-197, 199, 205-8, 210, 233).

IMAM-SADEQUE v BLUEBAY ASSET MANAGEMENT (SERVICES) LTD, [2012] EWHC 3511 (QB), [2013] I.R.L.R. 344, Popplewell, J., QBD.

961. Department of Health–Dismissal–Employers' powers and duties–NHS trusts

THE TRANSFER OF UNDERTAKINGS (PROTECTION OF EMPLOYMENT) (TRANSFERS OF PUBLIC HEALTH STAFF) REGULATIONS 2013, SI 2013/278; made under the Employment Relations Act 1999 s.38. In force: April 1, 2013; .

These Regulations are intended to effect the transfer of public health staff from NHS Trusts, Foundation Trusts and universities into the Department of Health. From April staff performing the functions in the organisations listed in the schedule to the Regulations will transfer into Public Health England, a new executive agency of the Department of Health. The purpose of the Regulations is to transfer the relevant staff contracts to the Secretary of State, and to provide protection of existing terms and conditions of employment for the staff affected, in line with the treatment of staff who will be transferring into Public Health England from other employers.

962. Disability–Assessment–Correct approach of tribunal for identifying substantial effect of disability on day to day activities

[Equality Act 2010 (c.15) s.212(1).]

The appellant employee (P) appealed against a decision of an employment tribunal dismissing his claims of unfair dismissal and disability discrimination against the respondent employer (L). P had been employed by L as a station attendant at London Bridge Station. P's role involved working in the station gate line as a first point of contact for customers and checking tickets. P had to be on his feet for substantial periods of the day during his nine-hour shifts. The prolonged standing appeared to have affected P's back, causing him lower back pain. P was dismissed for reasons of capability, after he claimed to have great difficulty performing the ordinary contractual duties of his post. P's case was that the dismissal amounted to discrimination under the Equality Act 2010 and was unfair. To establish unfairness under the Act, P had to satisfy the tribunal that he was disabled. The tribunal found that although he had a physical impairment which sometimes caused him severe pain, it did not have a substantial long-term effect on his ability to carry out day-to-day activities. P submitted that the tribunal erred in law by not addressing the activities which P could not do as a consequence of the condition, but concentrated instead on matters which he could do. P argued that the tribunal did not follow the approach in *Paterson v Commissioner of Police of the Metropolis* [2007] I.C.R. 1522, [2007] C.L.Y. 1332.

It was clear from the Act that the focus of a tribunal had to be upon what a claimant maintained he could not do as a result of his physical or mental impairment and not what he could do. Once a claimant had established an adverse effect on his ability to carry out day-to-day activities, a tribunal had to assess whether it was substantial. The tribunal then had to bear in mind the definition of substantial under s.212(1) which was more than minor or trivial. Unless a matter could be classified within the heading "trivial" or "insubstantial" it had to be treated as substantial. There was therefore little room for any form of sliding scale between one and the other. The tribunal did not, except briefly in one paragragh, deal with what P could not do. There had been no evaluation using the comparative approach in *Paterson* to look at what P could not do because of his alleged disability compared with what he could do without it, Paterson applied. The tribunal had taken the wrong approach in determining the question of disability and therefore the matter would be remitted (see paras 27-28 and 33 of judgment).

ADEREMI v LONDON AND SOUTH EASTERN RAILWAY LTD [2013] I.C.R. 591, Langstaff, J. (President), EAT.

963. Disability–Medical treatment–Physical impairment–Whether substantial adverse effect if medication disregarded–Immunodeficiency

[Equality Act 2010 (c.15) s.6, Sch.1 Pt 1 para.2(2), Sch.1 Pt 1 para.5(1).]

The appellant employer (S) appealed against an employment tribunal's conclusion that the respondent job applicant (N) was a disabled person within the meaning of the Equality Act 2010 s.6. N had brought a discrimination claim alleging that S had withdrawn a job offer because she was disabled. N had been diagnosed with an immunodeficiency, which S maintained did not amount to a disability. The tribunal first found that N's condition was a physical impairment which, although it did not have a substantial adverse effect on her ability to carry out normal day-to-day activities at the relevant time, was likely to have had such an effect were it not for her medication. Secondly, the tribunal found that whilst the substantial adverse effect of N's impairment, having only lasted three months a few years earlier, was not long-term in the sense of having lasted for at least 12 months, it was long-term in the sense of being likely to recur. The tribunal therefore concluded that the impairment had a substantial adverse and long-term effect on N's ability to carry out normal day-to-day activities, meaning she was disabled for the purposes of the Act. S submitted that the tribunal erred in law and was perverse in making those two findings.

Held: Appeal allowed. Under s.6, a person had a disability if he had a physical or mental impairment which had a substantial and long-term adverse effect on his ability to carry out normal day-to-day activities. Under Sch.1 para.5(1), an impairment would be treated as having a substantial adverse effect if that effect was likely without medical treatment. Under para.2(2), when assessing whether the effect was long-term, an impairment which had ceased to have a substantial adverse effect would be treated as continuing to have that effect if that effect was likely to recur (see para.6 of judgment). The medical evidence was that N's immunodeficiency did not itself have any effect on her ability to carry out normal day-to-day activities but it rendered her susceptible to recurrent infections. The medication which the tribunal disregarded for the purpose of considering the deduced effect of the impairment under para.5(1) was medication to help prevent her getting those infections. The expert medical evidence did not establish that increased susceptibility to infection would, or would necessarily, have a substantial adverse impact on N's ability to carry out day-to-day activities. On the basis that the deduced effect of N's impairment was that she would be likely to suffer more frequent infections, the material question for the tribunal had been whether increased frequency of infections would itself have a substantial adverse effect on her ability to carry out normal day-to-day activities. In deciding that infections which were more likely to occur would result in such an effect, the tribunal came to a conclusion which was not, or not adequately, supported by the medical evidence it relied on (paras 35-38, 42-43). In regard to para.2(2), the tribunal had concluded that the fact that N had a three-month period when her impairment had a substantial adverse effect on her ability to carry out normal day-to-day activities and the fact that her impairment was life-long were sufficient to support a conclusion that it could well happen that the substantial adverse effects of her impairment would recur. However, that conclusion was insufficiently supported by the expert medical evidence and it did not take into account the fact that N could give no examples of her impairment having caused a recurrence in the years following the three-month period (para.50). The issue of whether N was, at the material time, a disabled person within the meaning of the Act would be remitted for re-hearing before a differently constituted tribunal (para.54).

SUSSEX PARTNERSHIP NHS FOUNDATION TRUST v NORRIS [2012] Eq. L.R. 1068, Slade, J. DBE, EAT.

964. Disability–Obesity–Genuine symptoms diagnosed as functional overlay–Effect of impairment–Whether amounting to disability

[Disability Discrimination Act 1995 (c.50).]

The appellant employee (W) appealed against a decision of an employment judge that he was not disabled. W had suffered from functional overlay compounded by obesity; he weighed 137kg. The judge accepted that diagnosis, and that the conditions from which he suffered genuinely included asthma, dyslexia, knee problems, diabetes, high blood pressure, chronic fatigue syndrome, bowel and stomach problems, chemical sensitivity, hearing loss, anxiety and depression, persistent cough, recurrent fungal infections, carpel tunnel syndrome, eye problems and sacro-iliac joint pains. The symptoms arising from those conditions included pains in the head, knee, abdomen, lower back, left shoulder, arm, knee and leg, and the anal area, loss of control causing his leg to give way, bowel symptoms including constipation and diarrhoea, difficulty in swallowing, shortness of breath, constant fatigue, poor concentration and memory, and a bulging spinal disc. The judge accepted the opinion of an occupational physician that W suffered from a chronic permanent condition that affected his daily living. Another expert concluded that W's range of symptoms had a significant functional/behavioural component. There was no evidence of any pathological process or significant structural changes of a physical nature that would lead to significant impairment or disability. The judge held that, although W had difficulties in his life, in the absence of any mental condition there was no physical or organic cause for his conditions apart from his obesity, and that his symptoms were exacerbated by a functional overlay. The issues were whether someone suffering from functional overlay accented by obesity could claim to be disabled, and whether obesity was an impairment within the meaning of the Disability Discrimination Act 1995.

Held: Appeal allowed. "Impairment" should be given its natural meaning. The Guidance for the Code to the Act stated that it should be given its "ordinary" meaning, and went on to say at A8 that it was not necessary to consider how an impairment was caused, even if the cause was a consequence of an excluded condition; the important thing was the effect of an impairment. The absence of a cause could be significant for evidential, but not legal reasons. It was not necessary to categorise an impairment as physical or mental; they overlapped, and the effect on individuals might be widely different. Plainly, W had a physical or mental impairment, and some of his conditions mixed the two. He also suffered from significant cognitive difficulties. On any view he was substantially impaired and there could be no other conclusion on the evidence. The judge had erred in relying on authorities decided before the Act was changed in 2005 to remove the requirement that an impairment said to be mental could be ascribed to a well-recognised medical condition. Obesity itself did not render a person disabled, but on an evidential basis it might make it more likely that he was disabled and that he did suffer from an impairment, and might help decide how long that impairment might last. W was disabled for the purposes of the Act at the relevant time (see paras 7, 9-18, 21-22 of judgment).

WALKER v SITA INFORMATION NETWORKING COMPUTING LTD [2013] Eq. L.R. 476, Langstaff, J., EAT.

965. Disability–Stress–Whether employee suffering from disability–Right of employer to rely on advice from occupational health advisors–Admissibility of negotiations for compromise agreement

The appellant employee (G) appealed against the dismissal of his claim for disability discrimination against the respondent local authority employer. He also appealed against a reduction in his compensatory award following a finding that he had been unfairly dismissed. The local authority cross-appealed regarding an 11-week period in which G had been awarded both loss of earnings and pay in lieu of notice. G had complained of work-related stress. He was referred to the local authority occupational health advisors, who signed him off with a stress-related illness but said that he was not "disabled" because he was not suffering from a depressive illness. G's general practitioner diagnosed depression, and G informed the local authority of that in a grievance letter. During the following two years, the local authority asked the occupational health advisors whether the disability discrimination legislation was applicable to G and were repeatedly told that it was not. In the meantime, there were unsuccessful attempts between the parties to reach a compromise agreement. The local authority eventually summarily dismissed G for gross misconduct. In proceedings for unfair dismissal and disability discrimination, it was held that G was disabled, but his claim was dismissed on the ground that the local authority had not had constructive knowledge of that disability. Upholding the unfair dismissal claim, the tribunal asked about a document in the bundle which referred to "mutual termination" and G was cross-examined about the unsuccessful settlement negotiations. The tribunal found that, but for the dismissal, a compromise agreement would have been reached and it reduced the compensatory award by 50 per cent to reflect that likelihood. G submitted that knowledge by an employer of the constituent elements of an employee's medical condition and its effect upon him was sufficient for the purposes of a disability discrimination claim, and it was not necessary that the employer knew that the condition met the statutory definition of a disability. G also argued that it was manifestly unjust when assessing remedy for unfair dismissal to penalise him for not having entered into a compromise agreement. The local authority contended that in awarding loss of earnings from the effective date of termination in addition to 11 weeks' notice pay for the same period, there had been an element of double-counting.

Held: Appeal allowed in part. (1) The local authority had been entitled to rely on the advice of its occupational health advisors that despite G's medical condition, he was not disabled within the meaning of the legislation. The fact that the local authority had conceded, long after G's employment ended, that he was disabled, did not preclude it from raising the issue of knowledge at the substantive hearing. The tribunal's finding that the local authority did not have the necessary knowledge was a permissible finding (see paras 25-26 of judgment). (2) The tribunal had been wrong to make an assessment of the chances of a compromise agreement being reached and to reduce G's compensatory award accordingly. Employment tribunals should not enquire into negotiations between the parties where no agreement had been reached or where there had been no clear and unequivocal waiver of privilege, *Brennan v Sunderland City Council* [2009] I.C.R. 479, [2009] C.L.Y. 334 referred to. In the instant case, privilege had clearly not been waived (paras 16-17). (3) The 11-week period starting with the date of G's summary dismissal had been double-covered by awards for both loss of earnings and pay in lieu of notice, and needed to be varied. The total award for unfair dismissal was varied from £33,045 to £60,060.

GALLOP v NEWPORT CITY COUNCIL [2013] I.R.L.R. 23, Judge Peter Clark, EAT.

966. Disability discrimination–Amnesia–Non-disclosure of conviction in job application–Inability to remember conviction–Existence of disability and effect on ability to carry out day-to-day activities

[Disability Discrimination Act 1995 (c.50) s.1 (1), Sch.1 para.4(1) (g).]

The appellant police community support officer (S) appealed against an employment judge's decision that she was not disabled as a result of her dissociative amnesia. S had applied to the respondent commissioner to become a police constable. However, when the police discovered that S had a previous conviction, they refused her application and gave her a disciplinary reprimand for failing to disclose the conviction when she had applied for her current position and to become a constable. Subsequently, the police refused a second application by S to become a constable. S maintained that when she had originally applied, as a result of her condition, she had forgotten about her conviction and the facts to which it related. She brought a claim before an employment tribunal, alleging that the commissioner had discriminated against her on the ground of her disability. However, the employment judge found that S's dissociative amnesia was not one which had a substantial and long-term adverse effect on her ability to carry out normal day-to-day activities, within the meaning of the Disability Discrimination Act 1995 s.1 (1). He reached that conclusion having found that, on the evidence of a consultant neuropsychiatrist, S's condition did not affect the day-to-day functioning of her memory, for the purposes of Sch.1 para.4(1) (g).

Held: Appeal allowed. The sort of activity contemplated by s.1 was not using one's memory, but an activity for which one used one's memory. The particular activity which had been affected by S's amnesia was the application she made for the new position. Although her application was a one-off activity, day-to-day activities encompassed the activities which were relevant to participation in professional life. So the key issue was whether S's impairment was hindering her full and effective participation in professional life on an equal basis with other workers, *Chacon Navas v Eurest Colectividades SA (C-13/05)* [2007] All E.R. (EC) 59, [2007] C.L.Y. 1333, *HK Danmark v Dansk almennyttigt Boligselskab (C-335/11)* [2013] 3 C.M.L.R. 21 and *Paterson v Commissioner of Police of the Metropolis* [2007] I.C.R. 1522, [2007] C.L.Y. 1332 applied. Although S's loss of memory was limited to just one aspect of her past, in that respect it had an adverse and long-term effect on any activity of hers which required her to recall whether she had any previous convictions. One of those activities was applying to become a constable. That was an activity to which the definition of disability in s.1 (1) should be treated as applying (see paras 13-14, 17-19 of judgment).

SOBHI v COMMISSIONER OF POLICE OF THE METROPOLIS [2013] Eq. L.R. 785, Keith, J., EAT.

967. Disability discrimination–Continuing acts–Time limits–Allegations of discrimination on grounds of disability and nationality–Whether entries posted on Facebook by work colleagues over sustained period of time constituted one continuous act

[Disability Discrimination Act 1995 (c.50).]

The appellant employee (N) appealed against an employment tribunal judge's decision at a pre-hearing review that discrimination claims he had made against the respondent employer (P) had been made out of time. N, the manager of one of P's stores, had fallen down the stairs at work during February 2010, and had been absent from work since. He made claims under the Disability Discrimination Act 1995. P conceded that N had a physical impairment that included post-concussion syndrome. N was from the United States and claimed that he had been discriminated against by reason of his nationality and national origin. The first claim was commenced in September 2010 and the second in December 2011. The nature of the claims was criticism by N of his fellow employees for deriding his industrial accident, and against P for failing to take such steps as were required by statute to stop what he regarded as a discriminatory state of affairs. The background to the dispute was comments made by colleagues on Facebook. The primary Facebook owner (W), another employee, used the open public network. The first allegations related to entries made by W between March 31 and May 21, 2010 which remained on the site until July 9, 2010. A substantial group of employees contributed to the site and made comments to which N took exception. N became aware of that Facebook conversation in June 2010. The judge found that the comments were connected and constituted a continuing act throughout the period March 31 to May 21. However, although the entries were not taken down until July, the judge did not find that date was the end of the relevant period and refused to extend time in respect of the first claim. The second allegation related to the defacement of a safety sign at the workplace in April 2010 by another employee (T). The sign was made known to N in June 2010, but it was not taken down until August 2010. The judge refused to exercise his discretion to extend time. A third allegation related to Facebook entries between July 26 and July 28, 2010. The judge determined that the third allegation was not a continuing act linked to the first, but that the allegation was in time. A fourth allegation was that a photograph posted on Facebook by T on March 10,

2010 and taken down in November 2011, was the beginning of the humiliation which went on until the photograph was taken down.

Held: Appeal allowed. The first claim was in time in respect of the first and second sequences of Facebook entries and the April defacement. The judge had erred in not linking the two sets of Facebook entries into one continuous act. The individuals concerned in the second Facebook entry were the same as those who contributed to the earlier entry, and the subject matter, by implication N's fall down the stairs, was the same. There was a break of some seven weeks between the two sets of comments, with a total time span of 17 weeks. The gap did not mean that the treatment complained of was not continuing. In the circumstances, the defacement of the safety notice was part of the continuing act bracketed between the Facebook entries and, accordingly, the complaint in respect of the safety notice was in time. The photograph was the beginning of the events and was connected to the Facebook entries as the subject matter and the individuals were the same. The fact that the photograph predated the Facebook entry on March 31 did not mean that it was not connected and continuing. It was sufficient to resolve the instant appeal to find that N had a good arguable case that the events complained of were one continuous act until July 26, 2010 when the last posting occurred, and therefore the first claim was in time. Whether there was a further extension to July 28, 2010 or November 2011 was a matter which could be dealt with by the tribunal if a decision on that point was necessary (see paras 15-17, 19, 21, 23-24 of judgment).

NOVAK v PHONES 4U LTD [2013] Eq. L.R. 349, Judge McMullen Q.C., EAT.

968. Disability discrimination–Mental impairment–Failure to make reasonable adjustments–Timing of diagnosis where correct label to condition given later

[Disability Discrimination Act 1995 (c.50).]

The appellant employee (J) appealed against an employment tribunal's dismissal of his claims of unfair dismissal and disability discrimination against the respondent employer (B), who cross-appealed the tribunal's finding that it had imputed knowledge that J was disabled. J was dismissed in 2008 for poor attendance. He had been intermittently absent from work throughout his nine years of employment. Initially, the absences were short-term and mostly related to back problems. Then in 2006 he was absent for 49 days with back pain which he claimed, but the tribunal rejected, was due to a motorcycle accident. In early 2007 he was absent for 44 days following what transpired to be an incorrect diagnosis of angina. He was then absent for several days in July and in August owing to stress. He was off again with stress in September and did not return to work. B began disciplinary proceedings. J was seen several times by B's occupational health department who noted anxiety symptoms and indicated that he was suffering from post-traumatic stress disorder (PTSD), although that later turned out to be inaccurate. J was asked to identify the stress-causing aspects of his work, but did not do so. He did not attend any disciplinary hearings. In January 2008, B's health department indicated that J would be ready for a phased return to work by March, but no date was set. B concluded that J might not return and so dismissed him. B accepted that J suffered from a mental impairment, personality disorder and major depression which constituted a disability under the Disability Discrimination Act 1995. It did not accept a duty to make reasonable adjustments claiming that it did not have constructive knowledge of J's disability or of its comparative disadvantageous effect. The tribunal found that the disability discrimination claims consisted of complaints of failures to make reasonable adjustments and were not legally viable since *Malcolm v Lewisham LBC* [2008] UKHL 43, [2008] 1 A.C. 1399, [2008] C.L.Y. 2466. It also found that following *Project Management Institute v Latif* [2007] I.R.L.R. 579, J had to raise at least a prima facie case to show that B failed to comply with some identified reasonable adjustment.

Held: Appeal dismissed, cross-appeal dismissed. (1) The tribunal overstated the effect of *Malcolm*. Complaints of failures to make reasonable adjustments might be legally viable provided an appropriate comparator could be identified and less favourable treatment established. In the instant case, the tribunal's inaccurate statement of the position was immaterial because on the facts, no comparison could be made, *Malcolm* considered. A claimant only had to raise the reasonable adjustments he considered should have been made and do so with a sufficient degree of specificity so as to enable a respondent to address them evidentially and the tribunal to consider their reasonableness. The concept of shifting burdens was an unnecessary complication in what was essentially a straightforward factual analysis of the evidence presented, *Latif* considered. The case had not been determined on the basis of the tribunal's erroneous statement in relation to *Latif*. Although it was unclear from the judgment, the tribunal had adopted the approach in *Environment Agency v Rowan* [2008] I.C.R. 218, [2008] C.L.Y. 1134, *Rowan* considered. All aspects of what were considered to be the relevant provision, criteria or practice (PCP) and the only relevant adjustment to it were thoroughly investigated. The PCP was identified as the application to J's case of B's short-term absence policy. The generality of comparators was so obvious that no error arose from the tribunal's failure to state it, as was the disadvantage suffered by J. The tribunal assumed comparative disadvantage and considered the reasonableness of the suggestion that a bespoke policy was required for J's needs. There was no error in that. The judgment adequately explained the conclusion that a bespoke policy was unreasonable. It was a question of fact and there was no error of law (see paras 90-94, 96-98, 101 of judgment). (2) In relation to unfair dismissal, J's absence record was extremely poor justifying departures from procedure and B's refusal to allow any further period. The tribunal examined the facts carefully and there was no basis for interfering with its conclusion (para.103). (3) In relation to the cross-appeal, although PTSD was an erroneous diagnosis, it was a type of mental impairment. Subsequently applying the correct label to a condition was not diagnosing a mental impairment for the first time using the benefit of hindsight; it was giving the same mental impairment a different name. There was sufficient factual material for the conclusion that B, through its occupational health department, ought to have known that J was suffering from a mental impairment that amounted to a disability (paras 88-89).

JENNINGS v BARTS AND THE LONDON NHS TRUST [2013] Eq. L.R. 326, Judge Hand QC, EAT.

969. Disability discrimination–Mental impairment–Medical treatment–Failure of employment tribunal to consider effect of counselling in determining effect of employee's mental impairment–Whether necessary to remit matter to tribunal

[Disability Discrimination Act 1995 (c.50) Sch.1 para.6; Employment Tribunals (Constitution and Rules of Procedure) Regulations 2004 (SI 2004/1861) Sch.1 para.40(3), Sch.1 para.40(2).]

The appellant employee (S) appealed against decisions of the Employment Appeal Tribunal not to remit to the employment tribunal her claims for disability discrimination against the respondent employer local authority and not to set aside a costs order. S had been employed by the local authority since 1986. In July 2005, she sustained a shoulder injury during a fall at home and was absent from work for the rest of 2005. She returned in February 2006 but continued to have further periods of absence for work-related stress. She worked from home from February until September 2007. The local authority undertook a staffing review and decided to abolish S's position. She was dismissed and her attempts to secure redeployment were unsuccessful. It was accepted that S had a physical disability as a result of her injury, but there was an issue about whether she had mental disability by reason of her depression and anxiety disorder, which she claimed affected her concentration. S's expert (R) indicated that from February 2006, S had been receiving counselling and medication to help with sleep and insomnia, expressing the opinion that without them she would, on the balance of probabilities, have functioned even more poorly. The tribunal concluded that she was not disabled by reason of a mental impairment. S brought various claims for disability discrimination. The tribunal dismissed all of them except for a claim of disability discrimination by reason of the failure to make reasonable adjustment to accommodate her physical disability and enable her to work at home. It ordered her to pay 50 per cent of the local authority's reasonable costs. The EAT concluded that there had been an error of law because the tribunal had failed to appreciate that the evidence of R in respect of counselling was relevant to the deduced effect of S's illness under the Disability Discrimination Act 1995 Sch.1 para.6. However, it concluded that none of her claims for discrimination arising out of such disability would have succeeded. It therefore upheld the tribunal's decisions and the costs order. S submitted that (1) the EAT had failed to take account of the general principle that whenever it identified an error of law, it should remit the case for rehearing in the employment tribunal; (2) the costs order should be set aside because the approach of the tribunal was too "broad brush" and failed to engage in sufficient analysis.

Held: Appeal dismissed. (1) Given that S had claimed discrimination on the basis of mental disability during the substantive hearing before the tribunal, the case, if remitted would simply require consideration by the same tribunal as to the deduced effect in Sch.1 para.6 of the Act. If the tribunal resolved the issue in S's favour, it would then need to review the relevant evidence and its findings of fact on the basis of that additional element. There would be no justification for reopening the evidence in the case. Even if the tribunal had accepted that S was disabled on account of mental impairment, that would not have affected the overall conclusions that the local authority had not treated her less favourably than others for a reason that related to disability. The conclusion of the tribunal was plainly and unarguably right, irrespective of its failure to address the deduced effect of S's treatment. The EAT had not erred in deciding that the issue was an academic one and that the case should not be remitted, *Dobie v Burns International Security Services (UK) Ltd* [1985] 1 W.L.R. 43, [1984] C.L.Y. 1310 applied (see paras 56-66 of judgment). (2) An award of costs against a paying party in the employment tribunal was exceptional and the tribunal had to focus principally on the criteria in the Employment Tribunals (Constitution and Rules of Procedure) Regulations 2004 Sch.1 para.40(2) and para.40(3). In the instant case, the tribunal had identified separate heads of unreasonable conduct to justify awarding costs against S. First, it had found that the manner in which one claim was brought was unfocussed and extensive, resulting in substantial expenditure. Second, S had not justified her approach of obtaining R's report without leave and serving it extremely late, with the result that he had to be called to give evidence, lengthening the hearing and causing unnecessary expenditure. Third, unnecessary expense was caused by S serving a witness statement containing inadmissible material, requiring an admissibility hearing even though the witness concerned was unavailable. Fourth, it had been clear that S had not been prepared to accept any reasonable and appropriate sum in settlement of her claims and she responded to offers from the local authority by focussing on an exorbitant sum by way of suggested compensation, *Kopel v Safeway Stores Plc* [2003] I.R.L.R. 753, [2003] C.L.Y. 1263 applied. The tribunal had clearly specified the reasons for the order without attempting to identify a precise causal link between the unreasonable conduct and the specific costs that were awarded. It had exercised its broad discretion and had correctly avoided an over-analytical approach. The 50 per cent award could not be criticised as falling outside the parameters of a legitimate decision, *Lodwick v Southwark LBC* [2004] EWCA Civ 306, [2004] I.C.R. 884, *Yerrakalva v Barnsley MBC* [2011] EWCA Civ 1255, [2012] 2 All E.R. 215, [2012] C.L.Y. 1091 and *McPherson v BNP Paribas SA (London Branch)* [2004] EWCA Civ 569, [2004] 3 All E.R. 266, [2004] C.L.Y. 1314 applied (paras 67-85).

SUD v EALING LBC, [2013] EWCA Civ 949, [2013] 5 Costs L.R. 777, Maurice Kay, L.J. (VP, CA Civ), CA (Civ Div).

970. Disability discrimination–Reasonable adjustments–Accrual of cause of action–Employer's negligent continuing omission–Treating omission as occurring on given date for limitation purposes

The appellant (C) appealed against a decision of an employment tribunal dismissing his claim against the respondent, his former employer (B), for disability discrimination on the basis that it was out of time and that it was not just and equitable to extend time. C had been employed by B as a caretaker. He had deliberately misled B in his application form and with false references, thereby concealing the fact that he had had a knee replacement operation in the previous year and as a result had had significant sickness absence. After more than a year in post without problems, C began to have difficulty with his other knee and he was off work as a result. A specialist told him that it was incurable. B carried out a risk-assessment with C, but he did not tell B that he was disabled or give them the prognosis. B had asked all its employees to complete forms about their personal details. C stated on his form that he was registered as disabled, but B did not look at the form. C went off work and resigned about three weeks later, on the eve of a disciplinary hearing about his application process. C issued his claim within three months of the end of his employment. The tribunal found that C was disabled and that B should have made reasonable adjustments for his disability from the date when he had stated that he was disabled, and at the latest three months later. However, it found that his claim was out of time and that it was not just and equitable to extend time, in part because he had complained of discrimination for the first time when he resigned in order to forestall the disciplinary process. C submitted that (1) the tribunal should have found that B's negligent failure to make an adjustment for his disability continued until the end of his employment, so his claim was in time; (2) the tribunal's decision that it was not just and equitable to extend time was perverse.

Held: Appeal dismissed. (1) There was no express statutory provision relating to a negligent omission. A negligent omission was to be treated as a deliberate omission as of a given date, and that date was the date at which the tribunal found that the employer, had he been acting reasonably, would have made the reasonable adjustments. Once three months had passed from that date, the primary time limit had expired albeit that the negligent omission was continuing, *Kingston upon Hull City Council v Matuszowicz* [2009] EWCA Civ 22, [2009] 3 All E.R. 685, [2009] C.L.Y. 1179 followed. The tribunal had applied the correct test and correctly said that the answer to the application of that test was one of fact. Its factual conclusion was not said to be perverse and had to stand (see paras 17, 21-26, 28 of judgment). (2) C's arguments did not overwhelmingly demonstrate, as they needed to, that the tribunal had reached a conclusion, on the issue of whether it would be just and equitable to extend time, that no tribunal could have reached, *Crofton v Yeboah* [2002] EWCA Civ 794, [2002] I.R.L.R. 634, [2002] C.L.Y. 1398 and *Chief Constable of Lincolnshire v Caston* [2009] EWCA Civ 1298, [2010] I.R.L.R. 327, [2010] C.L.Y. 1076 followed. It was entitled to reach the conclusion it did, particularly in the light of what it had said about C's motives for complaining of a failure to make reasonable adjustments; those motives were clearly a material factor (paras 30-40).

CYPRIEN v BRADFORD GRAMMAR SCHOOL [2013] Eq. L.R. 596, Jeffrey Burke Q.C., EAT.

971. Disability discrimination–Reasonable adjustments–Disabled employee failing to return to former post after secondment and going on sick leave–Whether requirement to return to former post amounting to provision, criteria or practice putting her at substantial disadvantage–Failure to make reasonable adjustments by considering alternative roles

[Disability Discrimination Act 1995 (c.50) s.4A.]

The appellant employee (R) appealed against a decision of an employment tribunal dismissing her claims for unfair dismissal and disability discrimination against the respondent employer local authority. R was disabled as a result of asthma and spinal problems. She was employed as a nursery officer at a children's centre run by the local authority. She was seconded to another post at a different centre but, when that secondment ended, she was unable to return to her former post because of her disability and went on sick leave. The local authority initiated its management attendance policy, which related to sickness absence. The local authority repeatedly informed R that she was required to return to her former post. She never returned and was subsequently dismissed on capability grounds. The tribunal found that the local authority's requirement that she return to work amounted to a provision, criterion or practice (PCP) which placed her at a substantial disadvantage when compared with persons who were not disabled within the meaning of the Disability Discrimination Act 1995 s.4A, but it decided that the PCP had not been applied because R had never actually returned to work. The issue was whether the local authority had a duty to make reasonable adjustments for R under s.4A because (i) the requirement that she return to her former post amounted to the application of a PCP; (ii) the application of the local authority's sickness absence policy amounted to the application of a PCP.

Held: Appeal allowed. (1) The tribunal identified the PCP as being the requirement that R should return to her former post, and it accepted that R was at a substantial disadvantage as a disabled person in comparison with non-disabled persons who were forced to return to work. However, on the tribunal's findings, because the PCP was not in fact applied by the local authority, R could not demonstrate that she had suffered a substantial disadvantage. The tribunal took a very restricted view as to whether the PCP had been applied. The local authority had required R to return to her former post, it was clearly reluctant to accept ill-health retirement, and it had never looked at alternative roles or other adjustments that could be made. The local authority persisted in requiring R to return to her former post without considering alternatives, despite the fact that her return was potentially injurious to her health. The fact that R was not immediately able to return to her former post because of a disability-related sickness did not relieve the local authority of its obligation to make reasonable adjustments, *Commissioner of Police of the Metropolis v Hendricks* [2002] EWCA Civ 1686, [2003] 1 All E.R. 654, [2003] C.L.Y. 1298 applied. Since the local authority never offered R an alternative post or enquired to see if there was one, it had not made reasonable adjustments at the time that it was insisting that she should return to her former post. Informing an employee that she was bound to return to a particular post in due course was sufficient to amount to applying a PCP, and in the instant case the repeated requirement that R return to her former post amounted to the application of a PCP. The local authority's failure to consider or propose reasonable adjustments, notwithstanding that R was on sick leave, amounted to continued discrimination (see paras 68-70, 72, 74-75, 79, 82 of judgment). (2) Since the local authority's policy related only to sickness absence, the appropriate comparison for assessing whether R had suffered discrimination was to compare her with someone who was also subject to the policy by reason of an illness, but who was not disabled. R had not been placed at a substantial disadvantage compared to such comparators. Application of the local authority's policy did not amount to application of a PCP, and therefore no obligation to make reasonable adjustments arose (paras 87, 91-92). (3) The appeal was allowed only in respect of the local authority's requirement that R return to her former post without making reasonable adjustments. The matter was remitted to a fresh tribunal (paras 93-94).

RIDER v LEEDS CITY COUNCIL [2013] Eq. L.R. 98, Judge Serota Q.C., EAT.

972. Disability discrimination–Reasonable adjustments–Duty to make reasonable adjustments to provide one-to-one counselling–Failure to identify correct comparator

[Disability Discrimination Act 1995 (c.50) s.4A.]

The appellant local authority appealed against a decision that it had failed to make a reasonable adjustment under the Disability Discrimination Act 1995 s.4A by not providing the respondent employee (H) with one-to-one counselling. H had worked for the local authority as a family support worker. She was suspended pending investigations of allegations of misconduct. She was issued with a final written warning and was made the subject of a capability procedure. She returned to work on reduced hours under a reduced work load. She attended a return-to-work meeting with her line manager and was assessed by an occupational health advisor. H went on sick leave and did not return to work. She attended an appointment with a consultant psychiatrist and had regular occupational health assessments on a monthly basis for several months thereafter. H's appeal against her final written warning was dismissed. Two meetings were held under the local authority's managing attendance policy (MAP) but H was unable to attend either. H was offered access to the local authority's outsourced counselling programme but turned it down on the basis that she needed more in-depth counselling. H was then assessed as having a disability based on the long term nature of her illness, which was depression. Two contract review hearings were held and H was then dismissed with notice. H brought a claim on the basis that she had been discriminated against on grounds of disability, in particular that there had been a failure to make reasonable adjustments, and the tribunal found in her favour. The local authority submitted that the tribunal (1) erred in its choice of comparator by incorrectly identifying the relevant comparator group; (2) erred in failing to conclude that, by offering H access to its counselling course, it had discharged the duty said to arise under s.4A and, further or alternatively, erred in concluding that the counselling course provided group counselling only and did not provide one-to-one counselling.

Held: Appeal allowed. (1) The MAP applied to other persons who had an illness and so were absent from work but who did not fall within the definition of a disabled person within the meaning of the Act, *Rider v Leeds City Council* [2013] Eq. L.R. 98, [2013] 4 C.L. 89 applied. The tribunal had erred by incorrectly identifying the relevant comparator group. The relevant comparator group was other persons who by reason of illness were subject to application of the MAP but who were not disabled like H. If the tribunal had approached the matter in that way it was clear that H was not being treated any differently. She was not subject to any substantial disadvantage by comparison to the correct comparator group and the duty to make reasonable adjustments should not have arisen (see paras 21-26 of judgment). (2) There was no cross-examining of the evidence that the counselling course offered one-to-one counselling and there was no allegation that there had been any refusal by the local authority to provide one-to-one counselling as the tribunal concluded. In fact the counselling course involved face-to-face counselling and was not simply a counselling hotline. There was no suggestion in H's witness statement that one-to-one counselling had been sought or refused. Even if the tribunal was correct in its earlier finding that the duty to make reasonable adjustments arose, the only respect in which the tribunal found that there was a breach by the local authority of that duty was the assumed failure to provide one-to-one counselling to H. On a fair and proper reading of the evidence before the tribunal, it was simply not open to it to make that finding of fact. Accordingly, even if the duty had arisen, the only answer which could be given to the question as to whether that duty was reached was that there was no such breach (paras 27-37).

HILLINGDON LBC v BAILEY [2013] Eq. L.R. 729, Singh, J., EAT.

973. Disability discrimination–Reasonable adjustments–Employer's duty to make reasonable adjustments–Appropriateness of tribunal using person without relevant disability as comparator–Compatibility of approach with Directive 2000/78

[Directive 2000/78 on equal treatment in employment Art.5.]

The appellant lecturer (F) appealed against the employment tribunal's dismissal of her claim for disability discrimination brought against her respondent employer (C). F suffered from chronic fatigue syndrome. Academic duties were distributed between staff on a points-based system, where points were allocated for teaching activities based on how demanding they were. F had a number of periods off work due to her disability. C implemented temporary measures to manage F's workload. F became concerned about the allocation of work for the next academic year as C wanted to increase the target for each person to 350 points; for years F had been allocated fewer points than the average. F went off sick until October 2012. While F was off sick, the teaching allocation was distributed and F was allocated 331 points. Although an increase on what she had previously had, it was still below average and one of the lowest allocations received. Following a meeting after F's return to work, her allocation was reduced to 307 points. At a later meeting it was agreed that F would be allocated 120 points for supervising PhD students, which was subsequently reduced to 100 points. F went off sick and did not return to work. She issued a grievance which was rejected, with the appeal to be determined pending the outcome of the instant litigation in which F had brought claims for harassment, arising out of one of the meetings, and disability discrimination on the basis that reasonable adjustments had not been made. The tribunal dismissed F's claim for disability discrimination, holding that C was under a duty to take reasonable steps to remove the disadvantages that resulted from F's disability, but not to reduce her associated levels of anxiety. It also dismissed her harassment claim. F submitted that the employment tribunal erred in (1) its approach to what her disability was, in particular in that it did not take stress and anxiety into account; (2) considering that in a reasonable adjustment case the correct comparator with her was someone who did not have the relevant disability and in failing to interpret the domestic legislation compatibly with Directive 2000/78; (3) misunderstanding the uncontested material before it; (4) ignoring the evidence on the allocation of points for the supervision of PhD students which had been agreed at a meeting; (5) failing to find harassment had occurred at a meeting or to take into account a witness statement.

Held: Appeal dismissed. (1) The tribunal had not erred. It correctly directed itself that, in appropriate cases, anxiety and stress should be taken into account when they went to the nature of the disability itself. However F's was not such a case. Anxiety and stress acted as triggers for her condition and so went to its cause, but the law did not require a tribunal to investigate the causes of a disability, only its effects, *Chief Constable of West Midlands v Gardner* [2012] Eq. L.R. 20, [2012] C.L.Y. 1066 applied. The tribunal's judgment was consistent with authority and the relevant guidance (see paras 45, 49-51 of judgment). (2) There was no incompatibility between the way in which the domestic legislation had been interpreted and the Directive, particularly art.5. The duty to make "reasonable accommodation" in art.5 was laid down to give effect to the principle of equal treatment and to prevent a seemingly neutral provision criterion or practice placing a person with a relevant disability at a disadvantage. That necessarily involved a comparison between a person with a relevant disability and a person without the relevant disability. Domestic legislation required there to be not merely a substantial disadvantage but a substantial disadvantage in comparison with a person who did not have the relevant disability. That was consistent with the requirements of the Directive (paras 65-67). (3) F had misunderstood the tribunal's reasoning, which was sound. Despite C's wish to allocate F 350 points, she was allocated 307. The tribunal was aware that F was no longer permitted to use alternative teaching provision and referred to that fact in its judgment. Having regard to all the evidence before it, the tribunal was entitled to conclude that C was prepared to make reasonable adjustments (paras 70, 72-73). (4) It had been agreed at the meeting that F would be allocated 120 points for the supervision of PhD students but a proposal after the meeting reduced the number to 100. The tribunal's failure to deal expressly with the reduction in points for the supervision of PhD students was not an error of law as the explanation for the reduction was simply that a mistake had been made at the meeting, and F had been allocated more points than she should have been. The documentary evidence before the tribunal reflected that (paras 76-77). (5) The tribunal's failure to take into account the witness statement was not an error of law. The fact that not every piece of evidence was not expressly referred to did not mean that it had not been taken into account. In any event, the witness statement in question was from an individual who had not actually attended the meeting and was only able to give hearsay evidence as to what F had said to her about the meeting. The tribunal had heard live evidence from those present at the meeting, including F, and was entitled to conclude that hearsay evidence added nothing (paras 81-83).

FOSTER v CARDIFF UNIVERSITY [2013] Eq. L.R. 718, Singh, J., EAT.

974. Disability discrimination–Reasonable adjustments–Employer's failure to conduct reasonable investigation during disciplinary process–Employee suffering from depression–Existence of provision, criterion or practice through flawed application of disciplinary process

[Disability Discrimination Act 1995 (c.50) s.4A(1); Equality Act 2010 (c.15).]

The appellant company (N) appealed against a finding of disability discrimination, through failing to make a reasonable adjustment, made in favour of the respondent (H). H had been employed by N as a cleaner. He was being eased back into full-time work following a long period of absence caused by his disability of depression. Shortly after his return to work, H was called to a disciplinary meeting concerning alleged misconduct on three occasions, and was dismissed. All three occasions involved leaving work between seven and 19 minutes early, failing to clock off, and compiling timesheets to suggest that he had worked his full hours. H's behaviour had been caused by his perception that the staff car park barrier system was malfunctioning and anxiety over his ability to leave the car park late in the evening. H commenced proceedings for unfair dismissal and disability discrimination. The employment tribunal found that H had been unfairly dismissed because N had not held a reasonable investigation into his behaviour and whether his disability had had any effect on his conduct. The tribunal also found that N's failure to conduct a reasonable investigation had led to disability discrimination through a failure to make a reasonable adjustment. It determined that N's conduct of the disciplinary process had constituted the application of a provision, criterion or practice (PCP) that placed H as a disabled person at a substantial disadvantage, because it failed to address any of the issues that might have exonerated him and to give sufficient credence to any mitigating factors. N submitted that, contrary to the guidance in *Environment Agency v Rowan* [2008] I.C.R. 218, [2008] C.L.Y. 1134, no proper PCP had been identified, and that a one-off flawed disciplinary process did not constitute the application of a PCP as envisaged by the Disability Discrimination Act 1995.

Held: Appeal allowed. (1) In applying the words of the 1995 Act and the successor provisions contained in the Equality Act 2010, it was essential for the tribunal to have the statute's terms and requirements at the front of its mind, *Rowan* applied, *Smith v Churchills Stairlifts Plc* [2005] EWCA Civ 1220, [2006] I.C.R. 524, [2006] C.L.Y. 1299 and *Royal Bank of Scotland Plc v Ashton* [2011] I.C.R. 632, [2011] C.L.Y. 1058 considered. The starting point was that there had to be a PCP. It was not sufficient to merely identify that an employee had been disadvantaged, in the sense of badly treated, and to conclude that had he not been disabled, he would not have suffered. Pursuant to s.4A(1) of the 1995 Act, there had to be a causative link, in that the substantial disadvantage had to arise out of the PCP (see para.17 of judgment). (2) It was common ground that N had not applied any provision or criterion that could be called into question, and the issue was N's practice. As emphasised by the original wording of the 1995 Act, "practice" had the element of repetition about it, and if it related to a procedure, it had to be something that was applicable to people other than the person suffering from the disability. Given that there was no evidence of N's having made a practice of holding disciplinary hearings in a way that eliminated the consideration of mitigation or in which there was no reasonable investigation, there was insufficient evidence to show that the application of N's disciplinary process in H's case was a PCP. While it represented the unfair treatment of H, as the tribunal's finding of unfair dismissal had recognised, not all unfair treatment involved a failure to adjust a PCP. A one-off flawed application of N's disciplinary process could not in the circumstances reasonably be regarded as a practice. The tribunal had plainly erred in law by identifying the disciplinary process undergone by H as a PCP and as showing that because of his disability it had caused him a disadvantage over others who were not disabled, when it might seem obvious that a failure to consider mitigating circumstances and a failure to reasonably investigate was likely to cause misery whoever was the victim (paras 18-21). (3) The matter was remitted to the same tribunal for further consideration and to make findings in relation to other matters that had been raised by H as allegedly giving rise to a

PCP and consequently to disability discrimination through a failure to make a reasonable adjustment, *Sinclair Roche & Temperley v Heard* [2004] I.R.L.R. 763, [2005] C.L.Y. 1274 considered (paras 22-23, 25-26).

NOTTINGHAM CITY TRANSPORT LTD v HARVEY [2013] Eq. L.R. 4, Langstaff, J. (President), EAT.

975. Disability discrimination–Reasonable adjustments–Failure to vary redeployment policy in redundancy situation–Employee's loss of chance of obtaining alternative role

[Equality Act 2010 (c.15) s.15, s.20(3), s.39(2)(c).]

The appellant employer (R) appealed against a decision that it had failed to make reasonable adjustments for the respondent employee (L) and had unfairly dismissed her. L cross-appealed against a finding that her dismissal was not an act of disability discrimination. L had worked for R in a band 6 role. Her vision deteriorated and she was registered blind. R offered redeployment in a band 4 role which she accepted. Subsequently, L's new post disappeared as a result of restructuring. Under stage one of R's redeployment policy staff affected by the restructuring could apply for posts at one grade higher than their current post. At stage two staff could apply for vacant posts in competition with their colleagues. L wished to apply for a band 6 role but was prevented from doing so at stage one. R told her that she could apply for the role at stage two if it remained vacant. However, it was filled at stage one by another employee from a band 6 role. The tribunal concluded that R had failed to make a reasonable adjustment by permitting L to apply for the band 6 role in competition with the other candidate.

Held: Appeal dismissed, cross-appeal allowed. (1) Under the Equality Act 2010 s.20(3) where a provision, criterion or practice put a disabled person at a substantial disadvantage in relation to a relevant matter, in comparison with persons who were not disabled, an employer was required to take such steps as were reasonable to avoid the disadvantage. A like for like comparison with a non-disabled comparator was not appropriate on the facts of the instant case, *Environment Agency v Rowan* [2008] I.C.R. 218, [2008] C.L.Y. 1134 and *Fareham College Corp v Walters* [2009] I.R.L.R. 991, [2010] C.L.Y. 1046 applied. The substantial disadvantage suffered by L lay in the fact that, as a direct result of her visual impairment, she was redeployed from a band 6 to a band 4 post. That was why she was precluded from applying for the band 6 role at stage one of the policy. The redeployment was not "too remote" in relation to the discriminatory dismissal when considering the duty to make adjustments. Had L not become disabled, she would have remained in her original band 6 post and would then have been eligible to compete with the successful candidate for the new band 6 role. Instead, she was disadvantaged by not being able to apply for that alternative role. The tribunal had taken into account R's desire to treat all staff equally, but that overlooked the fact that sometimes disabled people had to be treated more favourably than those who were not disabled, *Archibald v Fife Council* [2004] UKHL 32, [2004] 4 All E.R. 303, [2004] C.L.Y. 4707 followed. In all the circumstances, it was not unreasonable to make an exception under the policy to allow for L's disability and its consequences. Accordingly, the tribunal was correct to find that there had been a failure to make a reasonable adjustment (see paras 16, 20-21 of judgment). (2) There was no definite answer to the question of whether L would have been successful had she applied for the band 6 role. However, it was enough that there was a real prospect of the adjustment removing the disadvantage suffered by L as a result of her disability. The loss of chance of successfully applying for that post could properly be reflected in the assessment of loss in the same way as loss of chance fell to be assessed under the Polkey principle when assessing compensatory awards for unfair dismissal (para.21). (3) In dismissing L's claim concerning the discriminatory dismissal, the tribunal appeared to be addressing the claim under s.15 whereas, having found a breach of the duty under s.20, the tribunal was bound to conclude that the dismissal was inextricably linked with the failure to make that adjustment. It was therefore an act of discrimination contrary to s.39(2)(c). L's cross-appeal was therefore allowed and R's appeal against unfair dismissal was dismissed. The case was remitted to the same tribunal for assessment of compensation (paras 22-24, 27).

REDCAR AND CLEVELAND PRIMARY CARE TRUST v LONSDALE [2013] Eq. L.R. 791, Judge Peter Clark, EAT.

976. Disability discrimination–Reasonable adjustments–Requirement to attend competitive interviews–Suitability for role

[Disability Discrimination Act 1995 (c.50) s.4A.]

The appellant employee (W) appealed against a decision that the respondent university (R) had not breached its duty to make a reasonable adjustment. W was disabled by an allergic condition. R had carried out a university-wide restructure following which W was put on gardening leave. She was later interviewed for a vacancy but failed to meet two essential criteria. Two years later the same job for which she had been rejected arose again. She was required by R to attend a competitive interview process despite her disability. The tribunal found that R's duty to make a reasonable adjustment under the Disability Discrimination Act 1995 s.4A was engaged as the requirement to attend a competitive interview was to her disadvantage, but that the duty was not breached as the adjustment which W sought, namely not to have to go through the interview process, was tantamount to requiring R to appoint her to a role for which she did not meet the requirements. W submitted that there should have been a different approach to the competitive interview process because there ought to have been a discussion about W's difficulties. R contended that the tribunal was correct when it said that the only adjustment that W had put forward was tantamount to being given a job by reason of her history, and that in itself was not an adjustment if the job involved criteria that W could not meet.

Held: Appeal dismissed. The tribunal recognised that W had been through the interview process twice and that twice she had failed to meet essential requirements for the role. W had failed to recognise that the job had evolved and changed, and when considering whether she was to be redeployed into it the tribunal held it was reasonable for R to consider the essential requirements. W had not narrowly missed being appointed to the role. W's sole contention, that she should not have been put through the interview process, was not an adjustment that the tribunal held to be reasonable, for it would mean giving her the job when she was not appointable by reason of being found wanting under the majority of the criteria. There was no error in the tribunal's judgment and it had not failed to grapple with the essential point that it was asked. The tribunal, correctly directing itself on the law, went on to make a permissible decision on reasonable adjustments, *Project Management Institute v Latif* [2007] I.R.L.R. 579 and *Jennings v Barts and the London NHS Trust* [2013] Eq. L.R. 326, [2013] 6 C.L. 117 applied (see paras 16-20 of judgment).

WADE v SHEFFIELD HALLAM UNIVERSITY [2013] Eq. L.R. 951, Judge McMullen Q.C., EAT.

977. Disability discrimination–Voluntary workers–Whether voluntary workers falling within scope disability discrimination protection afforded by Directive 2000/78

[Disability Discrimination Act 1995 (c.50); Directive 2000/78 on a general framework for equal treatment in employment and occupation Art.3(1)(c), Art.3(1).]

The appellant (X) appealed against a decision ([2011] EWCA Civ 28, [2011] 2 C.M.L.R. 18, [2011] C.L.Y. 1060) that she, as a volunteer advice-worker, fell outside the scope of the disability discrimination protection provided by the Disability Discrimination Act 1995 and Directive 2000/78. X had been a volunteer adviser for the respondent bureau. She had signed a "volunteer agreement" which was not a contract of employment and was not legally binding. She claimed that a year after taking up the position she was asked to cease acting as a volunteer, in circumstances amounting to disability discrimination. The bureau denied the claim, and there had been no adjudication on its substance. The employment tribunal, the EATand the Court of Appeal had all held that the employment tribunal had no jurisdiction to hear the claim because volunteers fell outside the scope of the disability discrimination protection afforded by the 1995 Act and the Directive. X submitted that her voluntary activities amounted to "an occupation" for the purposes of art.3(1) of the Directive.

Held: Appeal dismissed. (1) The Directive did not cover voluntary activity. Its scope was defined in art.3 and it sat within a complex of measures relating to discrimination. The scope of those measures was carefully defined and differed according to context. It was an important part of X's case that the concept of "occupation" in art.3(1)(a) had to be understood as operating at the same level as "employment" and "self-employment", and that it thus had to envisage voluntary work. However, the reference to "occupation" had to be viewed in context. It was part of a clause dealing with "conditions for access" to employment, self-employment or occupation. There were many areas in which either a professional qualification was required or a restrictive condition had to be satisfied if a worker was to undertake particular work or to advance in a particular sphere. The reference to "access... to occupation" contemplated access to a sector of the market, rather than to particular employment or self-employment. Once "occupation" was understood in that sense, there was no imperative to treat it as envisaging voluntary activity. That analysis was not undermined by consideration of the French, Dutch and German versions of the article. Moreover, had the Directive been intended to apply to voluntary activity, it might have been expected that the concept of "occupation" would have been carried through expressly into art.3(1)(c), which dealt with working conditions and dismissal. It had not, and that was a striking omission if voluntary workers were intended to be protected against dismissal on discriminatory grounds. Neither the European Commission's original proposal nor the impact assessment leading to the Directive considered or addressed voluntary activity, and a proposed amendment by the European Parliament to include in art.3(1)(a) a reference to voluntary work had been rejected. The European Commission had kept Member States' implementation of the Directive under review, but had never suggested that the United Kingdom, or any other Member State, had failed properly to implement it by failing to include voluntary activity. Finally, X did not suggest that all voluntary activity was covered by the Directive. If that was right, and the Directive was intended to cover some, but not all, voluntary activity, it would surely have given some indication as to where the line should be drawn (see paras 24, 27-34, 37-45 of judgment). (2) The conclusion that the Directive did not apply to volunteers was not open to reasonable doubt. The position, having regard to the English language material, was clear, and the other language versions to which the court had been referred reinforced that conclusion. There was thus no need to make a reference to the European Court of Justice. Rulings of the French equivalent of the Equality and Human Rights Commission which suggested otherwise could not be given greater weight than the submissions of that Commission. While both were entitled to serious consideration, neither demonstrated any scope for reasonable doubt about the Directive's true meaning and effect (paras 46-57). (3) It was unnecessary to go into the questions that would have arisen had it been concluded that art.3(1) did cover voluntary activity. Assuming that the principle in *Marleasing SA v La Comercial Internacional de Alimentacion SA (C-106/89)* [1990] E.C.R. I-4135 would not have assisted X, there would have been the question of whether the principle in *Mangold v Helm (C-144/04)* [2006] All E.R. (EC) 383 might have been extended to protect her. That might well have had to be referred to the ECJ, Marleasing and Mangold referred to (para. 58).

X v MID SUSSEX CITIZENS ADVICE BUREAU, [2012] UKSC 59, [2013] 1 All E.R. 1038, Lord Neuberger (President), SC.

978. Disciplinary procedures–Breach of contract–Investigation into relationship breakdown–Potential reason for dismissal–Applicability of Maintaining High Professional Standards framework

The claimant consultant obstetrician and gynaecologist (K) claimed declarations, injunctions and damages against the defendant trust for breach of her contract of employment. K's practice had been restricted as a result of concerns expressed about her competence by two other consultants. The then medical director conducted an investigation into clinical concerns and concluded that there was no justification for continuing to restrict her practice or taking any other action against her. He said that the issues he had been asked to investigate did not arise from any lack of competence on her part, but reflected inter-personal difficulties. K then made a formal complaint under the trust's grievance policy against the two consultants and the medical director. The complaint was rejected but the independent investigator questioned K's clinical competence. A new medical director (S) referred her case to the National Clinical Assessment Service (NCAS). The NCAS report was that K's clinical performance was satisfactory. The report raised a single issue for consideration by the trust, namely whether her reintegration into the department was feasible given the breakdown in K's relationship with her colleagues. S then initiated an investigation to identify whether the relationship had broken down beyond repair. S was informally excluded from work on the basis that termination of her employment might be the outcome if her working relationships had broken down and pending a formal hearing into that issue. K submitted that, since the matter involved conduct or capability, the trust was in breach of her contract of employment in not following the procedures for investigations and hearings set out in Maintaining High Professional Standards in the Modern NHS (MHPS); and that, whether the trust's procedure was regular or not, she had wrongly been informally excluded from work.

Held: Declaration granted. (1) The trust at all material times acted in good faith in its dealings with K (see para.108 of judgment). S and the trust did not act arbitrarily or unreasonably in taking the steps that were taken after receipt of the NCAS report (paras 111-121). (2) MHPS was intended to be a binding supervening scheme for dealing with all conduct, capability and ill-health concerns in respect of practitioners such as K. It replaced all that went before in terms of contractual arrangements, in particular the HC(90)9 framework (para.132). MHPS Parts I to IV were incorporated into the contract of employment in so far as they dealt with concerns over conduct and capability. By contrast, the terms of the trust's investigation policy were matters of guidance which were not apt for incorporation into the contract. In any event, on its proper construction, the investigation policy applied only to work-related issues involving the conduct or capability of individual employees and complaints by such employees raised as grievances. It was inappropriate for the policy to be applied to the investigation of a possible breakdown in relationships between employees where the suggested basis of the breakdown was a perception of lack of capability and the alleged lack of capability had already been formally investigated and found to have no substance. Whilst the involvement of NCAS was a necessary contractual step in a conduct and capability case before referral could be made to a capability panel, there was no other contractual requirement to follow any particular advice given by NCAS (para.151). (3) The trust was not the final arbiter of the procedure to be adopted. The question was whether the decision by the trust that the matter was not one of conduct and capability, and therefore that it should be dealt with other than by use of the MHPS procedure, was objectively correct. If it was not, it amounted to a breach of contract, *Skidmore v Dartford and Gravesham NHS Trust* [2003] UKHL 27, [2003] 3 All E.R. 292, [2003] C.L.Y. 1789 and *Mattu v University Hospitals of Coventry and Warwickshire NHS Trust* [2012] EWCA Civ 641, [2012] 4 All E.R. 359, [2012] C.L.Y. 1071 followed (paras 152-156). The issue to be investigated at the hearing was not one of conduct or capability or a hybrid of both so as to engage MHPS (paras 158-176). (4) The decision to undertake an investigation into relationship breakdown and the manner of the investigation did not breach the implied term of trust and confidence. Nor did the decision to convene a hearing to consider the possibility of terminating K's employment. The implied term of trust and confidence did not require any particular form of investigation into an issue between K and the trust if it was not one of conduct and capability, and the implied term could not be relied upon to require the same form of procedure to be employed by the trust as if it were a conduct and capability matter, *Kulkarni v Milton Keynes Hospital NHS Trust* [2009] EWCA Civ 789, [2010] I.C.R. 101, [2009] C.L.Y. 1739 and *Mattu* considered (paras 195-197). (5) The trust had acted in breach of K's contract of employment by excluding her from work without complying with the procedural requirements of MHPS and she was entitled to a declaration to that effect. The remainder of her claim failed (paras 221-228).

KERSLAKE v NORTH WEST LONDON HOSPITALS NHS TRUST, [2012] EWHC 1999 (QB), [2012] Med. L.R. 568, Judge Curran Q.C., QBD.

979. Disciplinary procedures–Res judicata–Disciplinary proceedings resulting in written warning–Second set of disciplinary proceedings based on same facts resulting in dismissal–Application of doctrines of res judicata and abuse of process

The appellant employees (C and W) appealed against a decision ([2012] I.R.L.R. 622, [2012] C.L.Y. 1171) that their dismissals by the respondent local authority were fair and did not constitute double jeopardy or abuse of process. W was a social worker responsible for the care of "baby P", who died as a result of chronic lack of care and abuse by his mother and two men while on the child protection register and subject to a local authority child protection plan. C was W's manager. After P's death, C and W were disciplined under the simplified disciplinary procedure and given written warnings, W for three procedural failures and C for three acts of misconduct. Following extensive media reporting, a fresh review of P's case was undertaken by a newly appointed Director of Children's Services. Further disciplinary proceedings were held, which involved reopening determinations made at the first disciplinary process, and which resulted in C and W being summarily dismissed for gross misconduct. Internal appeals were dismissed. C and W began proceedings for unfair dismissal on the basis that it had been unfair to subject them to a second disciplinary process. The employment tribunal rejected those claims. The Employment Appeal Tribunal, upholding the tribunal's decision, found that the simplified procedure did not constitute an adjudication so as to engage the *res judicata* doctrine, and that the doctrine of abuse of process did not apply. C and W submitted that (1) there was no public interest exception which could modify the strict application of the doctrine of *res judicata* so as to justify reopening disciplinary matters which had already been determined; (2) since the parties had expressly agreed to the use of the simplified procedure in circumstances where such consent was a prerequisite, it was an abuse of process to undermine that agreement; (3) even if a second bite at the cherry was legitimate in principle, both tribunals had failed to give cogent reasons why it had been fair to reopen the cases.

Held: Appeal dismissed. (1) The doctrine of *res judicata* was a rigorous rule with few exceptions. It operated so as to provide finality in litigation, and to prevent a party from being vexed by being twice subjected to the same litigation. It was, however, wrong to describe the exercise of disciplinary power by an employer as a form of adjudication. Disciplinary proceedings were not "a determination of any issue which establishes the existence of a legal right", nor could they properly be regarded as "determining a dispute", *Thrasyvoulou v Secretary of State for the Environment* [1990] 2 A.C. 273, [1990] C.L.Y. 4426 considered. Disciplinary power was conferred on an employer by the hierarchical nature of the relationship. Its purpose was to enable the employer to establish whether the employee had acted inappropriately and, if so, how that should affect relations between them. Even if the procedure invoked had been contractually agreed, as in the instant case, it was still far removed from the process of litigation or adjudication to which the doctrine of res judicata attached, *Mattu v University Hospitals of Coventry and Warwickshire NHS Trust*

[2012] EWCA Civ 641, [2012] 4 All E.R. 359, [2012] C.L.Y. 1071 applied. Res judicata might apply in an employment context, but generally not where the procedure was staffed by the employer's own personnel. The critical question was not the formality of the procedure, but whether it operated independently of the parties such that it was appropriate to describe its function as an adjudication, *Meyers v Casey* 17 C.L.R. 90 and *R. (on the application of Coke-Wallis) v Institute of Chartered Accountants in England and Wales* [2011] UKSC 1, [2011] 2 A.C. 146, [2011] C.L.Y. 1 considered. In any event, although the factual background was the same in both sets of disciplinary proceedings, the focus of complaint in the second set was on substantive errors of judgment and breaches of P's care plan, which was very different from the first set, which concerned procedural errors (see paras 39-42, 47-55 of judgment). (2) The doctrine of abuse of process was no more strictly applicable to a case of the instant type than res judicata, and not a great deal turned on its application. A tribunal considering whether dismissal was fair would have to ask itself whether it had been fair for the employer to institute the second proceedings, and that was the same as asking whether there had been an abuse of process (para.56). (3) On the evidence, there was a proper and sufficient basis for the tribunals' conclusion that the dismissals were fair notwithstanding that the principle of double jeopardy had been infringed (para.63).

CHRISTOU v HARINGEY LBC, [2013] EWCA Civ 178, [2014] Q.B. 131, Laws, L.J., CA (Civ Div).

980. Disclosure–Public interest

THE PUBLIC INTEREST DISCLOSURE (PRESCRIBED PERSONS) (AMENDMENT) ORDER 2013, SI 2013/2213; made under the Employment Rights Act 1996 s.43F, s.236. In force: October 1, 2013 except for art.4 on April 6, 2014.; .

This Order amends the list of prescribed persons in the Public Interest Disclosure (Prescribed Persons) Order 1999 (SI 1999/1549). Workers can benefit from employment protection if they make a disclosure to a prescribed person.

981. Discrimination–Compensation–Joint and several liability to pay compensation–Assessment of contribution

[Civil Liability (Contribution) Act 1978 (c.47) s.2; Race Relations Act 1976 (c.74); Sex Discrimination Act 1975 (c.65).]

The appellant local authority appealed against an award of compensation made against it on the basis that it was jointly and severally liable to pay £421,415 to the respondent (S) for victimisation. S had applied for two posts with a body (H) which had been set up by the local authority and the Commission for Racial Equality. The interview panels consisted of members of H's executive committee and an employee (W) of the local authority. S had previously been a member of H's executive committee and had successfully brought proceedings against it for racial discrimination. When she was not selected for either post, she brought victimisation claims against H's director and the panel members as primary discriminators, and against H, its executive committee and the local authority as being vicariously liable for the primary discriminators. The tribunal found that there had been victimisation contrary to both the Sex Discrimination Act 1975 and the Race Relations Act 1976. At a remedies hearing the tribunal assessed compensation payable by W as £1,905. At a second remedies hearing the tribunal found all of the respondents except W to be jointly and severally liable to pay £421,415 to S for victimisation. The local authority was not represented at the second remedy hearing because it had been debarred from taking part for failing to comply with a disclosure order. The local authority argued on appeal before the Employment Appeal Tribunal that the tribunal should have awarded different amounts of compensation according to the relative degrees of responsibility for the loss suffered by S. The EAT ruled that no question of apportionment arose as the damage suffered was indivisible. The issue on appeal was whether it was wrong in law for the tribunal to hold the local authority liable to S for the full amount of loss assessed in the second remedy decision.

Held: Appeal dismissed. Legal errors were made in the remedy process undertaken by the tribunal, however it was not fair in the circumstances to criticise the tribunal for those errors, which did not, in any case, affect the outcome of the appeal. By securing the exclusion of the local authority from the remedy hearing, S obtained the advantage of no opponent, but the tribunal lost the advantage of the professional legal assistance that it might otherwise have had from the local authority's legal team. Nor was the tribunal to blame for citing and relying on the guidance on apportionment in *Way v Crouch* [2005] I.C.R. 1362, [2005] C.L.Y. 1231, which had been followed by other tribunals. However the tribunal was wrong in its view based on Way, namely that it had the power to apportion the liability of the respondents to the claimant. In *Way* the EAT had derived the power to apportion from the Civil Liability (Contribution) Act 1978 s.2, but it was mistaken, because the 1978 Act was not about apportioning as between defendants/respondents, liability to the claimant; it was about proceedings between joint tortfeasors to recover contribution to the amount which a joint tortfeasor had been found liable to pay to the claimant: the claimant was not involved or affected by inter-tortfeasor claims for contribution. Way should be overruled on that point, Way overruled in part. However, the tribunal's mistaken but understandable reliance on *Way* had no impact on the local authority's appeal from the award against it. The tribunal's decision not to apportion was legally correct, though for the reason that it had no power in law to make an apportionment rather than because there was no case for apportionment on the facts. The tribunal did err in making the award against W. It purported to exercise a power to apportion W's liability to S, which it did not have. However, that error of law was irrelevant to the instant appeal, because no appeal had been brought against the award against W: the instant appeal was from the award against the local authority. The tribunal's error in making an apportionment as the regards the liability of W to S did not prevent S from pursuing her claims against other joint tortfeasors. The damage suffered by S in consequence of victimisation was indivisible. The indivisible character of the damage for which the local authority and other respondents were jointly liable was not altered by the tribunal's error of law in purporting to apportion the liability of W to S. There was no error of law in the tribunal's remedy decision awarding compensation, including aggravated damages, against the local authority in excess of the amount of compensation that it had awarded to S as against W as part of an erroneous apportionment exercise (see paras 81-84, 88-89, 101 of judgment).

HACKNEY LBC v SIVANANDAN; *sub nom.* SIVANANDAN v HACKNEY LBC, [2013] EWCA Civ 22, [2013] 2 All E.R. 940, Mummery, L.J., CA (Civ Div).

982. Discrimination–Employment tribunals–Interest

THE EMPLOYMENT TRIBUNALS (INTEREST ON AWARDS IN DISCRIMINATION CASES) (AMENDMENT) REGULATIONS 2013, SI 2013/1669; made under the Equality Act 2010 s.139, s.207. In force: July 29, 2013; .

These Regulations amend the Employment Tribunals (Interest on Awards in Discrimination Cases) Regulations 1996 (SI 1996/2803). They amend the legislative reference on interest in England and Wales, so that the rate is the same as that in Scotland (currently 8 per cent), and also correct the reference to Scottish legislation on interest.

983. Discrimination–Jurisdiction–Air Force claimant–Employment tribunal's jurisdiction to hear discrimination complaints following out-of-time appeal on service complaint

[Armed Forces Act 2006 (c.52) s.334; Equality Act 2010 (c.15) s.121 (1) (b); Armed Forces (Redress of Individual Grievances) Regulations 2007 (SI 2007/

3353); Directive 2006/54 on equal treatment of men and women in matters of employment; European Convention on Human Rights 1950 Art.6.]

The appellant employee (W) appealed against an employment tribunal's decision that it did not have jurisdiction to hear her complaints that the Ministry of Defence had discriminated against her contrary to the Equality Act 2010. W was a nurse in the Air Force, and therefore before she could bring a complaint before the tribunal, had to make a service complaint under the Armed Forces Act 2006 s.334. She had presented her complaint to her commanding officer. His decision was contained in an outcome letter which he sent to her. When she did not appeal internally against the decision, the MoD treated her complaint as having been withdrawn. However, W maintained she had not received the outcome letter. The tribunal found that even if she had not received the letter, she had subsequently read a copy but had not appealed within 30 days of doing so, that being the time limit imposed by the Armed Forces Redress of Individual Grievances Procedures and Time Limits Regulations 2007 reg.22(b). Therefore, her complaints were treated as withdrawn and, in accordance with s.121 (1)(b) of the 2010 Act, the tribunal held that it did not have jurisdiction to hear her claim. W submitted that (1) the Regulations were in breach of her right under the European Convention on Human Rights 1950 art.6 to have the out-of-time issue determined by an independent authority; (2) she had been denied an effective remedy, contrary to Directive 2006/54.

Held: Appeal dismissed. (1) The art.6 argument had not been put to the tribunal and the new point could not be taken on appeal, *Celtec Ltd v Astley* [2006] UKHL 29, [2006] 1 W.L.R. 2420, [2006] C.L.Y. 1379 and *Leicestershire CC v UNISON* [2005] I.R.L.R. 920 applied. In any event, the argument could not be sustained as Parliament had decided that the prescribed officer would make the decision and give reasons. It had also decided that the same officer would decide the out-of-time issue. That was not a breach of W's right to have her complaint dealt with in an independent way. After all, if the matter were to be wholly independent, then Parliament could have decided that there should be some internal procedure that did not involve the commanding officer of that particular unit. It decided not to do that, and the approach in reg.23 was fully consistent with art.6. Furthermore, if the commanding officer failed to abide by simple principles of justice in applying the Regulations, then the matter was amenable to judicial review, *Molaudi v Ministry of Defence* [2011] I.C.R. D19 and *Crompton v United Kingdom (42509/05)* (2010) 50 E.H.R.R. 36, [2010] C.L.Y. 1732 applied (see paras 26-28 of judgment). (2) Procedural matters, provided that an effective remedy was given, were for the Member States, *UNISON v Brennan* [2008] I.C.R. 955, [2008] C.L.Y. 1185 and *Preston v Wolverhampton Healthcare NHS Trust (C-78/98)* [2001] 2 A.C. 415, [2000] C.L.Y. 2162 applied. There was no argument over the UK's right to introduce measures as to time limits for the presentation of an equal pay claim, and W had not been barred from an effective judgment by the operation the time limit. She had, as a matter of fact, been given the opportunity under reg.23 to argue her case that it had not been reasonably practicable to appeal at an earlier date (para.31).

WILLIAMS v MINISTRY OF DEFENCE [2013] Eq. L.R. 27, Judge McMullen Q.C., EAT.

984. Discrimination–Jurisdiction–Allegations of discrimination and harassment–Alleged acts occurring before doctor's name struck from register and immediate suspension imposed–Whether tribunal's jurisdiction precluded by Equality Act 2010 s.120(7)

[Equality Act 2010 (c.15) s.120(7); Medical Act 1983 (c.54) s.35, s.38(1), s.38(8), s.40(7).]

The appellant doctor (D) appealed against an employment tribunal's decision that by reason of the Equality Act 2010 s.120(7) it did not have jurisdiction to determine his complaints of direct and indirect race discrimination and harassment related to race made against the respondent General Medical Council. Following an investigation into a complaint made against D, the Fitness to Practice Panel of the GMC concluded that his fitness to practice had been impaired. It struck his name from the register under the Medical Act 1983 s.35 and imposed an order for immediate suspension under s.38(1). D's appeal under s.40(7) of the 1983 Act was unsuccessful, and there had been no adjudication on his application under s.38(8) of the 1983 Act for termination of the order for his immediate suspension. D appealed to the employment tribunal. The employment judge determined that the 1983 Act and judicial review provided "an appeal or proceedings in the nature of an appeal" from such acts as those complained of by D within the meaning of s.120(7) of the 2010 Act, which prevented the tribunal from hearing claims based on those acts. However, the acts complained of were unparticularised in the judgment. D submitted that his claims arose from actions preceding the decision of the Panel to suspend him, and that, since steps in the disciplinary process preceding the Panel's decision were not subject to appeal under the 1983 Act, those acts did not fall within the exclusionary provisions of s.120(7).

Held: Appeal allowed. There was no right of appeal under s.40 or s.38 of the 1983 Act in respect of acts complained of by D which led up to but did not include the erasure of his name from the register and the imposition of immediate suspension. Unless the acts alleged to constitute harassment or discrimination falling within the 2010 Act were susceptible to judicial review and judicial review were "proceedings in the nature of an appeal" under an enactment within the meaning of s.120(7), those claims of harassment and discrimination would not be excluded from the jurisdiction of the tribunal by operation of that provision. In the absence of particularisation of the acts relied upon by D as constituting harassment or discrimination, it was not possible to determine whether they would have been susceptible to challenge in judicial review proceedings. The tribunal had erred in holding that it had no jurisdiction to hear D's claims because of the availability of an appeal under the 1983 Act. No appeal was provided by that Act in respect of events before the erasure of D's name from the register and the order for immediate suspension, *Khan v General Medical Council* [1996] I.C.R. 1032, [1995] C.L.Y. 2027 applied (see paras 30-32 of judgment). Moreover, the tribunal had erred in deciding that judicial review was available to challenge the matters complained of by D without considering and setting out in the judgment what those acts were. Furthermore, the tribunal had erred in relying on obiter remarks in *Tariquez-Zaman v General Medical Council* as holding that judicial review proceedings were proceedings in the nature of an appeal by virtue of an enactment within the meaning of s.120(7), *Tariquez* considered. The case was remitted to a different employment judge to consider whether the jurisdiction of an employment tribunal to hear D's claims was excluded by s.120(7), whether the claims were presented in time and whether D could pursue claims against individual members of the GMC (para. 34-37).

UDDIN v GENERAL MEDICAL COUNCIL [2013] I.C.R. 793, Slade, J., EAT.

985. Discrimination–Victimisation–Compensation for injury to feelings–Tribunal's reliance on statements in closing submissions–No material evidence produced

The appellants (X) appealed against an employment tribunal's award in respect of claims of wrongful dismissal and victimisation by a former employee (R). The tribunal made an award for injury to feelings based on what was said in a closing submission without receiving any evidence on the question. Thus, there had been no opportunity for cross-examination. X submitted that the tribunal could only make an award for injury to feelings upon evidence.

Held: Appeal allowed. A tribunal did not have to follow the strict rules of evidence, but it had to have some material evidence on the question of injury to feelings. Almost always the convenient course would be for the matter to be dealt with in witness statements and evidence under oath. Closing submissions were the parties' arguments and comments upon evidence already received: they were not material evidence. The tribunal was not entitled to make an award for injury to feelings in reliance on statements made in closing submissions. The matter was remitted to the same tribunal for evidence to be heard and the question of injury to feelings to be considered afresh (see paras 7-9 of judgment).

ESPORTA HEALTH CLUBS v ROGET [2013] Eq. L.R. 877, Judge David Richardson, EAT.

986. Discrimination–Victimisation–Whether Equality Act 2010 encompassed post-termination victimisation

[Equality Act 2010 (c.15) s.39, s.108(7), s.108; National Minimum Wage Regulations 1999 (SI 1999/584) reg.2(2)(a)(ii), reg.2(2).]

The appellant employers (X) appealed against a decision that they had discriminated against the respondent (Y) on the grounds of her race and failed to pay her the national minimum wage. Y cross-appealed against the dismissal of her claim for post-termination victimisation. Y, a Nigerian woman, had worked for X as a domestic worker in their home. X were also Nigerian. Y was required to clean, cook and look after X's daughter. She worked 84 hours per week and X retained her passport. She was paid £50 per month, rising to £150 per month by her third year of employment. She was badly treated and eventually walked out. She alleged that after bringing employment tribunal proceedings, X had made threatening telephone calls to her sister in Nigeria. X submitted that (1) Y fell within the "family exception" in the National Minimum Wage Regulations 1999 reg.2(2) and was not entitled to the national minimum wage; (2) when considering direct discrimination the proper enquiry should be into the "activating" cause of the detrimental treatment, and Y's status as a migrant worker was merely part of the background circumstances; (3) the Equality Act 2010 did not expressly provide for post-termination victimisation claims.

Held: Appeal dismissed in part, cross-appeal allowed in part. (1) In determining whether Y was treated as a member of the family under reg.2(2)(a)(ii) the test was whether the worker was integrated into the family, *Nambalat v Taher* [2012] EWCA Civ 1249, [2013] I.C.R. 1024, [2013] 1 C.L. 110 followed. The tribunal decided that Y was not treated as a member of the family. Its reasons related to accommodation, Y taking meals apart from the adults in the family, and matters such as X's abuse and their retention of her passport. None of those matters relied impermissibly upon Y having to do the work she was contracted to do as a domestic worker. The tribunal's findings were not perverse and should stand (see paras 25-32 of judgment). (2) The tribunal had applied *Mehmet (t/a Rose Hotel Group) v Aduma* in order to determine that the burden of proof should pass to X. Since it did not accept their explanation, it held that racial discrimination was made out. However, the decision in *Mehmet* was reached per incuriam. It did not apply the approach set out in *Madarassy v Nomura International Plc* [2007] EWCA Civ 33, [2007] I.C.R. 867, [2007] C.L.Y. 1401 and *Wong v Igen Ltd (formerly Leeds Careers Guidance)* [2005] EWCA Civ 142, [2005] 3 All E.R. 812, [2005] C.L.Y. 1221, *Mehmet* not followed, *Madarassy* and *Igen* referred to. A difference in race, namely migrant as opposed to non-migrant status, and less favourable treatment of the migrant compared with the non-migrant, would give rise to the possibility of discrimination but was not enough for the burden of proof to pass to the employers. What Y complained of consisted of treatment falling short of appropriate United Kingdom standards. No part of the treatment was inherently bound up with Y's race. It was strongly associated with Y's subordinate position, but her migrant-worker status was a background factor rather than an immediate cause of the discrimination. Accordingly, the tribunal's decision on direct discrimination could not stand (paras 41, 44-51). (3) The Equality Act 2010 s.108 specifically mentioned discrimination and harassment as claims which could be brought after the end of the employment relationship but did not include victimisation. Interpretation should be approached in two stages: first, to enquire what the meaning of the statute was if construed as a domestic statute; second, if that construction did not accord with the European obligations, to ask whether it might be possible to interpret it to do so, even if that involved writing words into or omitting them from the legislation (paras 60-61, 70). The purpose of s.108(7) was troubling. If the draftsman assumed that post-termination victimisation was provided for elsewhere in the statutes, then the effect of s.108(7) would be to prevent double-recovery for the same act. Otherwise the section made no legislative sense. The existence of s.108 did not colour the meaning of "employer" and related expressions in s.39 so as to limit them to current employment, *Rhys-Harper v Relaxion Group Plc* [2003] UKHL 33, [2003] 4 All E.R. 1113, [2003] C.L.Y. 1315 followed, *Rowstock Ltd v Jessemey* [2013] I.C.R. 807 and *Taiwo v Olaigbe* [2013] I.C.R. 770 not followed. Rather, subsections 108(1) and (2) had a function in closely defining the circumstances in which discrimination and harassment must occur if they were to give rise to a claim where there was no longer a subsisting employment relationship. Therefore, applying domestic canons of construction, the Employment Appeal Tribunal rejected X's argument that s.108(7) had the effect of excluding post-termination victimisation. The definition in s.39 encompassed victimisation whether employment under the contract of employment was continuing or it had ceased. Y's victimisation claim had been wrongly dismissed (paras 81, 86, 92, 96, 99, 112). (4) Even if that interpretation was wrong, there was sufficient ambiguity about the proper meaning of the statute to require resort to the "Marleasing" approach that the national courts should interpret domestic statutory provisions in a way that was compatible with applicable EU directives, *Marleasing SA v La Comercial Internacional de Alimentacion SA (C-106/89)* [1990] E.C.R. I-4135 considered. That was a powerful argument for an interpretation which provided a remedy for post-termination victimisation (para.105).

ONU v AKWIWU; AKWIWU v ONU [2013] I.C.R. 1039, Langstaff, J. (President), EAT.

987. Dismissal – Date of termination – Decision in internal appeal to change date of termination of employment – Effect of change on calculation of effective date of termination for purposes of s.97 Employment Rights Act 1996

[Employment Rights Act 1996 (c.18) s.97(1)(a), s.97.]

The appellant employer (H) appealed against a majority decision of the employment tribunal regarding the effective date of termination (EDT) of the employment of the respondent employees (X). X had been summarily dismissed by letter dated October 5, 2010 following "an act of stock loss" by one or more of the group. They appealed under the internal disciplinary procedure and were paid until notification of the appeal outcome contained in a letter dated November 4. The letter upheld their dismissals, stating that the EDT was the date of the letter. X started employment tribunal proceedings on January 27, 2011, citing the EDT as November 4. A fortnight before the hearing, H alleged that the EDT was October 5. Both lay members of the tribunal found that X had understood the November letter to supersede the earlier letter and that, as they had been paid until that date with no indication that it was notice pay or an ex gratia payment, both parties must had proceeded on the basis that November 4 was the relevant date. The employment judge disagreed, finding that the October letter contained clear words of dismissal terminating the contracts of employment and that the EDT could not be agreed or unilaterally adopted or extended. H submitted that the tribunal's majority decision was wrong because the EDT crystallised at the date when the summary dismissal was communicated and could not be varied by what occurred during the internal appeal.

Held: Appeal dismissed. The tribunal majority had not found that H had artificially labelled November 4 as the EDT, but that it had decided to keep X's contracts open until that date. Such a finding accorded with the contents of the November letter and with the manner in which X had been paid. The tribunal had been fully entitled to reach it. It could not be said that the EDT always crystallised on the date of summary dismissal. Although it was unusual for an employer to vary the date of a summary dismissal, the instant case was one such unusual case. The initial dismissals had been based on X being within a group suspected of misconduct. On the internal appeal, the summary dismissal had changed to a dismissal on notice because H had taken a decision which affected the duration of the employment. Therefore the Employment Rights Act 1996 s.97(1)(a) had become applicable, and the EDT became the date on which the termination took effect, *Gisda Cyf v Barratt* [2010] UKSC 41, [2010] 4 All E.R. 851, [2010] C.L.Y. 1142 applied and *Fitzgerald v University of Kent at Canterbury* [2004] EWCA Civ 143, [2004] I.C.R. 737, [2004] C.L.Y. 1207 considered. The EDT was a statutory construct whose application had to be guided principally by the protection of employees' rights. The provision of an internal appeal was integral to the protection of employment rights and it was to be expected that they would sometimes result in decisions that would change the date on which the termination actually took effect. In the rare instances where that happened, the decision to change the date on which the employment was terminated was to be taken into account in determining the EDT (see paras 26-34, 37-44, 47 of judgment).

HAWES & CURTIS LTD v ARFAN [2012] I.C.R. 1244, Judge David Richardson, EAT.

988. Employee consultation–Protective awards–Errors by employment tribunal–Correct application of s.188 Trade Union and Labour Relations (Consolidation) Act 1992

[Trade Union and Labour Relations (Consolidation) Act 1992 (c.52) s.188(2), s.189.]

The appellant employees (K and J) appealed against a decision of an employment tribunal dismissing their claim for a protective award in respect of failures in a consultation process by the respondent employer (H). In August 2010, H sought the agreement of 300 employees to proposed changes to their contracts. By November 2010, it became apparent that there was a possibility of job losses if proposals were not agreed. All but 32 of the employees accepted the varied terms. H proposed to terminate the contracts of the remaining 32 employees and offer re-engagement on the new terms. It was therefore obliged to consult them under the Trade Union and Labour Relations (Consolidation) Act 1992 s.188. In February 2011, H wrote to those employees to advise them that it would enter into collective consultation in relation to its proposal. There was no union recognised for the purpose of consultation and H chose to consult with the employee members of a joint consultative committee (the JCC). Representatives were co-opted onto the JCC and they included K and J. The constitution of the JCC excluded negotiation from its role. When K and J issued their claim for a protective award, the tribunal found it to be irrelevant that negotiation was excluded from the role of the JCC because negotiation was a separate concept from consultation. It found that the JCC met the requirements of s.188(1B)(b)(i). The tribunal also found that the representatives had authority to receive information and be consulted because it had heard no evidence from K or J to suggest that they did not have authority. K and J submitted that (1) H had been under a duty to consult by November 2010 when it contemplated the dismissal of employees who refused to sign up to the new contractual terms and the decision in *MSF v Refuge Assurance Plc* [2002] 2 C.M.L.R. 27, [2002] C.L.Y. 1402 should not be applied; (2) the "appropriate representatives" appointed under s.188(1) did not have authority from the affected employees to receive information and be consulted about the proposed dismissals on their behalf; (3) the tribunal had impermissibly placed the onus upon the employees to raise the matters upon which s.188(2) required consultation; (4) the tribunal had wrongly accepted H's case that its duty to supply the information required by s.188 to the appropriate representatives had been discharged by the letter it wrote to employees in February 2011.

Held: Appeal allowed. (1) The approach taken in *MSF v Refuge Assurance* had to be applied for the same reasons it had been applied in *UK Coal Mining Ltd v National Union of Mineworkers (Northumberland Area)* [2008] I.C.R. 163, [2008] C.L.Y. 1183. That ground of appeal failed, *MSF v Refuge Assurance* and *UK Coal Mining* applied (see paras 11-16 of judgment). (2) The tribunal had said nothing about the method and process of co-option of the representatives, which was of particular relevance when considering authority to speak for those for whom the representatives purported to act. In determining the question of authority, the tribunal had been entitled to take into account the fact that neither K nor J had said that they did not have authority. However, the tribunal had not asked them about that, whereas s.189 required an affirmative finding of such authority by the tribunal. The burden of proof had been misplaced. The tribunal was required, by s.188(1B)(b)(i), to consider what the purposes of the election were, with a view to considering whether there was authority not simply to receive information, but to consult with a view to reaching agreement. The tribunal had said nothing clearly to show it had done so. The constitution of the JCC expressly excluded negotiation: the tribunal should have considered whether that ruled out that the authority extended to attempting to reach agreement. It had not addressed the question of "negotiation" as compared to "consultation" in that context. It had not dealt appropriately with the significance of the non-negotiating role of the JCC: it could not be dismissed as irrelevant. Further, without any factual finding about what the affected employees knew of what the JCC did in practice, and hence the authority with which it might be supposed they clothed those who were elected or appointed to it on their behalf, it could not be clear whether they had the authority (paras 32-38). (3) H had been wrong to place the onus upon the employees to raise the matters. A close focus on the statute showed that it was not sufficient for the employer to offer an opportunity to employees to discuss matters of concern to them: it was for the employer to ensure that the matters set out in s.188(2) were raised, *Susie Radin Ltd v GMB* [2004] EWCA Civ 180, [2004] 2 All E.R. 279, [2004] C.L.Y. 1285 applied (paras 39-41). (4) The letter which H wrote to employees did not set out each of the six matters referred to at s.188(4). The requirement to do so was mandatory (paras 48-49). (5) Apart from the first ground of appeal, the appeal succeeded. The matter would be remitted for determination before the same tribunal (paras 52-53).

KELLY v HESLEY [2013] I.R.L.R. 514, Langstaff, J. (President), EAT.

989. Employees' rights–National Insurance Fund–Eligibility of former employees to claim arrears of pay where employer in liquidation after trading under company voluntary arrangement–Meaning of "date on which the employer became insolvent" in s.185 Employment Rights Act 1996–Appropriate construction of s.183(3)(c) of Employment Rights Act 1996

[Employment Rights Act 1996 (c.18) s.183(3)(c), s.185, s.185(a); Regulation 1346/2000 on insolvency proceedings.]

In conjoined appeals, the secretary of state appealed against decisions that the respondents (X and P), former employees of two companies that had been compulsorily wound up, were entitled to claim arrears of pay and unpaid holiday pay from the National Insurance Fund (the fund). The companies had gone into liquidation owing X and P pay arrears. The arrears related to a period during which, unbeknown to them, their employers had traded under a company voluntary arrangement. The secretary of state, relying on the Employment Rights Act 1996 s.183(3)(c), refused to reimburse X and P out of the fund. He asserted that, according to the definition of insolvency in Directive 2008/94 art.2(1), the point when the employers became insolvent was the date on which their respective CVAs were approved. He maintained that X and P had not been owed money on those dates, which meant that they could not claim the protection of the fund. The claims were upheld by separate employment tribunals, one of which found that a company became insolvent only when it entered into liquidation, and the other finding that the Act allowed for more than one form of insolvency.

Held: Appeals allowed. In P's case, the employment tribunal had applied a definition of insolvency which, although corresponding to a popular view of what insolvency amounted to, was not in the Act and was not legally correct. It had construed insolvency as being a situation which brought the business to an end. That construction imported an additional requirement which was not present in the statute and which was inconsistent with s.183(3)(c). Under the latter provision, "insolvency" occurred when a CVA was approved. A CVA hoped to resuscitate a company which was barely functional by allowing it to try and trade its way out of debt; "insolvency" could not therefore be construed as an event bringing the business to an end (see paras 22-25 of judgment). In X's case, the tribunal had construed the Act in accordance with the Directive, finding that the date of the insolvency was the date of the CVA. It held, however, that for the secretary of state to succeed, the word "first" had to be added to s.185(a) so that the appropriate date became the "date on which the employer first became insolvent". The tribunal found that there was no justification for reading the provision that way. It was permissible to read words into a statute, but only as long as it did not go against the grain of the legislation. The instant Act did not permit the notion of "serial insolvency"; a company became insolvent when the CVA was approved, and only then. It was a fixed date and there could never be more than one insolvency situation. The purpose of having a fixed date was to provide a reference point. If the reference point could change, the Act would be deprived of certainty and predictability, *Litster v Forth Dry Dock & Engineering Co Ltd* [1990] 1 A.C. 546, [1989] C.L.Y. 4304 applied (paras 26-31, 34-38, 52, 58). Furthermore, the European Commission had been aware, when adopting in the Directive the definition of "insolvency" from Regulation 1346/2000, that the approval of a CVA was an "insolvency proceeding", and that the term "insolvency" would not apply to liquidations preceded by a CVA. It left it open to individual Member States to fix a reference date, whilst acknowledging that claims relating to periods after that date would be unprotected. When the Directive was implemented, the Commission did not provide that claims falling after the reference date had to be covered. The United Kingdom fixed its reference date by implementing s.185 of the Act. The unfairness of the provision to X and P was evident, but the general purpose of the Directive was to extend protection by recognising circumstances other than liquidation as deserving of payments from the fund. That general protection could not be affected by adverse results in individual cases, especially where those results had been recognised by the Commission as potentially arising. The domestic implementation of the Directive was not inconsistent with the Directive's purpose and the secretary of state was not obliged to pay X's and P's claims (paras 45-50, 54, 63).

SECRETARY OF STATE FOR BUSINESS, INNOVATION AND SKILLS v McDONAGH; SECRETARY OF STATE FOR BUSINESS, INNOVATION AND SKILLS v PENGELLY [2013] I.C.R. 1177, Langstaff, J. (President), EAT.

990. Employment Appeal Tribunal–Extensions of time–Lodging documents one day out of time–Whether disability caused delay

The appellant (O) appealed against an Employment Appeal Tribunal's decision refusing his application for an extension of time for appealing. O had commenced a disability discrimination claim in an employment tribunal. The tribunal's decision was notified to the parties on December 16, 2009. O had until January 27, 2010, in which to appeal to the EAT on a question of law. On January 26 he lodged a notice of appeal form in person, mistakenly believing that it was the last day for doing so. He failed to lodge at the same time other documents required for the institution of an appeal, namely the judgment and reasons of the employment tribunal. O suffered a panic attack as a result of stress caused by those events and consequently he was ill on January 27. On January 27, he posted the written reasons by special delivery. On January 28, he scanned and emailed the remaining required documents to the judge. The appeal was rejected as out-of-time on the basis that there was no exceptional reason why it could not have been presented within the time limit. The judge took into account that O was depressed after the employment tribunal decision; he had mistakenly believed the deadline was January 26; and that his disability had inhibited him from working on his grounds of appeal for two weeks. However, the judge found that O had had ample opportunity to lodge the notice of appeal and had failed to do so in time because he had left it to the last minute to submit the required documents, not because of his disability. O contended that his disability, which was supported by medical evidence, explained why his appeal was out of time. It amounted to a good excuse and justified the exceptional step of granting a short extension of time to enable an appeal to be brought.

Held: Appeal dismissed. The fact that O had lodged his notice of appeal form in time was not, on its own, enough to institute the appeal. The EAT rules required that the specific additional documents be lodged within the same six-week time limit; that rule was as strictly enforced as the requirement to lodge the notice of appeal in time. The documents were lodged only one day out of time. The length of the delay was a material factor; however, the crucial issue was whether there was a good excuse for the delay, rather than whether it was long or short. O had not submitted all the documents on time because he had left lodging the appeal until the end of the period for appealing. That carried the obvious risk that things could go wrong without having enough time left to correct them. The effects of O's disability were relevant factors in deciding whether he had a good excuse for not complying with the time limit and whether there were exceptional circumstances justifying an extension. It was accepted that he had been unable to start work on his appeal for two weeks as a result of his disability, leaving him with four weeks to prepare for the appeal. The EAT found as fact that he was not disabled from lodging the appeal within the relevant period: he had produced long and complex grounds of appeal and submitted them in time. His disability did not explain or excuse his failure to attach the required documentation. O had demonstrated by his own conduct that his disability did not prevent him from meeting time limits. His disability was a contributory factor in his inability to travel on January 27, but the EAT had concluded that his delay in lodging the additional documents was not referable to and did not arise out of his disability. In particular, his disability did not mean that he was unable to lodge all the documents before January 27 in advance of the deadline. Additionally, the documents did not have to be lodged in person; other methods could have been used and were in fact used, but too late, because he had left taking the necessary steps until the very end of the six weeks. O had failed to demonstrate that the EAT's refusal to extend time was wrong, or that it had erred in principle, or that it was plainly wrong to refuse to extend time (see paras 25-29 of judgment).

O'CATHAIL v TRANSPORT FOR LONDON, [2012] EWCA Civ 1004, [2012] I.R.L.R. 1011, Mummery, L.J., CA (Civ Div).

991. Employment references–Victimisation–Post-employment victimisation–Statutory construction

[Employment Rights Act 1996 (c.18) s.98ZG; Equality Act 2010 (c.15) s.108; Directive 2000/78 on a general framework for equal treatment in employment and occupation.]

The appellant employer (R) appealed against a decision in favour of the respondent (J) on his claim for unfair dismissal and unlawful age discrimination. J cross-appealed against a decision to refuse his claim of post-employment victimisation. The Equality and Human Rights Commission (C) was granted permission to intervene. J had been employed by R from March 5, 2008 and reached 65 on January 17, 2010. On January 10, 2011, J was given two weeks' notice of termination and two weeks' pay in lieu of notice. He did not return to the workplace. In response to J's claim for unfair dismissal, R gave "retirement" as the principal reason for J's dismissal and also conceded that it had not complied with the statutory retirement procedures. Subsequently, R gave an employment agency a very poor reference for J. The employment tribunal (ET) found that J's dismissal had been manifestly and automatically unfair and contrary to the Employment Rights Act 1996 s.98ZG, and made an award to J for injury to feelings from unlawful age discrimination. The tribunal held that, although the poor reference had been given as a result of J's unfair dismissal claim, it had no jurisdiction to give a remedy by reason of the Equality Act 2010 s.108(7). J contended that s.108(7) could not have been intended by Parliament to remove post-employment victimisation, which was unlawful discrimination for the reasons set out by the House of Lords in *Rhys-Harper v Relaxion Group Plc* [2003] UKHL 33, [2003] 4 All E.R. 1113, [2003] C.L.Y. 1315. J and C argued that the wording of s.108(7) was a "legislative blunder" and Parliament could not have intended to create an enactment which was not compliant with Directive 2000/78. R submitted that the tribunal had failed to make any *Polkey* reduction for the fact that, if a fair procedure had been followed, J was likely to have been fairly dismissed a few months later.

Held: Appeal allowed, cross-appeal dismissed. (1) The function of s.108 was to extend the reach of the Equality Act into dealings between parties who had formerly been in employment or other relationships (see para.10 of judgment). However, s.108(7) expressly disapplied the concept of victimisation where a relationship had ended and thereby produced a lacuna in the statutory scheme of protection from discrimination, harassment, and victimisation, which the UK was required to enact (para.29). Unfortunately, the judicial role was not geared to amendment of primary statutes and the Tribunal could not interpret s.108(7) in a completely contrary way to that which Parliament had enacted, *Ghaidan v Godin-Mendoza* [2004] UKHL 30, [2004] 2 A.C. 557, [2004] C.L.Y. 2538 followed, *Rhys-Harper* and *EBR Attridge Law LLP (formerly Attridge Law) v Coleman* [2010] 1 C.M.L.R. 28, [2010] C.L.Y. 1049 distinguished (paras 34-40). (2) The ET had erred if it had concluded that *Polkey v AE Dayton Services Ltd* [1988] A.C. 344, [1988] C.L.Y. 1353 had no application in a case of automatic unfair dismissal, *Polkey* followed, *Compass Group Plc v Ayodele* [2011] I.R.L.R. 802, [2011] C.L.Y. 1031 and *Abbey National Plc v Chagger* [2009] EWCA Civ 1202, [2010] I.C.R. 397, [2010] C.L.Y. 1026 applied. The reasoning of the tribunal was unclear and its focus should have been on whether such a dismissal could, and would, have been likely to follow had the proper procedures been applied. The case was remitted for reassessment of compensation, and permission to appeal was granted (para.50).

ROWSTOCK LTD v JESSEMEY; JESSEMEY v ROWSTOCK LTD [2013] I.C.R. 807, Recorder Luba Q.C., EAT.

992. Employment status–Control–Absentee owner appointed caretaker/managers of farm–Importance of degree of right of control over worker–Employment status of caretaker/managers

The appellant workers (W) appealed a finding by an employment tribunal that they were not employees of the respondent (T). T owned a substantial farmhouse and small farm estate. A written agreement between the parties stated that T would "employ" W as caretaker/managers of the property. T was owned by a man who, along with his family, rarely visited the farm. Notice to terminate the agreement was given four years later, after which the parties fell into dispute. The tribunal found that T had deliberately divested day-to-day control of the farm to W, and that being absentee owners, the family wanted someone to be responsible for the maintenance and management of the farm and to make decisions themselves, but that that was not employment.

Held: Appeal allowed. (1) The question was whether there was, to a sufficient degree, a contractual right of control over the worker, not whether in practice the worker had day-to-day control of his own work. All aspects of control were relevant. Many workers had very substantial autonomy in their work, but were still employees. It did not follow that because an absentee property owner had entrusted day-to-day control over the property to another he had divested himself of the contractual right to give instructions to them. If the express terms of the employment contract did not expressly provide which party should have the right of control, then the question had to be answered by implication. In relation to that, a term did not have to have been enforced for it to be part of the agreement. The tribunal did not analyse the terms of the agreement between the parties in the instant case to see whether expressly or by implication T retained a right of control to a sufficient degree. It was not inconsistent with the concept of employment for an absentee owner to want someone to be responsible for maintaining and managing their property. It was a question of with whom and to what extent the ultimate right to control resided. Therefore the tribunal's approach was wrong in law. There were strong indications in the written agreement that T retained a sufficient right of control.

Unless T retained the right to give instructions concerning maintenance involving expenditure, the contractual provision requiring W to notify T of all such maintenance before work commenced would be superfluous. Also, being responsible for that expenditure, it would be surprising if T had not retained the right to give associated instructions. Therefore, clear words would be required before T could be found to have divested itself of a right to give instructions concerning such expenditure. It was relevant that although the family were rare visitors, the property was available for their use. It would be surprising if, when visiting, the family had no right to give W instructions concerning the upkeep of the house and estate. Clear words would be required to divest T of such rights. T also retained a right of control in relation to when W could take holiday and in other work that W could undertake. Looking at the agreement in the round, whilst substantial day-to-day responsibility was placed on W, T retained a sufficient right of control. W were manager/caretaker and housekeeper of a substantial asset belonging to T. It would be surprising if T had divested itself of the right to control and there was no reason to suppose that it had, *Ready Mixed Concrete (South East) Ltd v Minister of Pensions and National Insurance* [1968] 2 Q.B. 497, [1968] C.L.Y. 2550 and *Autoclenz Ltd v Belcher* [2011] UKSC 41, [2011] 4 All E.R. 745, [2011] C.L.Y. 1074 applied (see paras 32, 40-47, 50-51 of judgment). (2) It was plain that W agreed to be subject to a sufficient degree of control for T to be their employer. It was also plain that W were employed by T. The other provisions of the contract were consistent with that. Had there been any real doubt or ambiguity then the label so clearly placed by the parties upon the relationship would have been treated as decisive, *Massey v Crown Life Insurance Co* [1978] 1 W.L.R. 676, [1978] C.L.Y. 1116 considered (para.54).

WHITE v TROUTBECK SA; *sub nom.* TROUTBECK SA v WHITE [2013] I.R.L.R. 286, Judge David Richardson, EAT.

993. Employment status–Equity partners–Effect of s.4(4) Limited Liability Partnerships Act 2000–Whether member of LLP could be employee or worker

[Employment Rights Act 1996 (c.18) s.230(3); Limited Liability Partnerships Act 2000 (c.12) s.4(4); Partnership Act 1890 (c.39).]

The appellant limited liability partnership (P) appealed against a decision ([2012] I.R.L.R. 548, [2012] C.L.Y. 1181) that the respondent (V) was a "worker" for the purposes of the Employment Rights Act 1996 s.230. P was a British law firm. V was an equity member and had been seconded to Tanzania as part of a joint venture with a Tanzanian law firm. She worked in Tanzania for the majority of the time but worked in London several times a year, for approximately two weeks at a time. She paid tax in Tanzania and National Insurance in Britain. She was dismissed by the Tanzanian firm after alleging that it was involved in money laundering. P expelled her from the partnership. She brought a whistle blowing claim and a sex discrimination claim against P. Her claims could only succeed if she was found to be a "worker" within the meaning of s.230(3), and if the tribunal had jurisdiction to hear her claims. P submitted that V could not be a worker because of the effect of the Limited Liability Partnerships Act 2000 s.4(4). P also argued that when determining the question of jurisdiction the tribunal should have compared the factors pointing towards Britain with those pointing towards Tanzania.

Held: Appeal allowed in part. (1) The concept of a "worker" embraced employees, being persons employed under contracts of employment under s.230(3)(a), and those under s.230(3)(b) who personally undertook to provide work for another, but did not qualify as employees (see para.17 of judgment). (2) The meaning of s.4(4) of the 2000 Act had to be gleaned from the context in which it was passed. The intention was that whatever the employment status of the partners under the Partnership Act 1890, it should not alter when the partners were transformed into members of a limited liability partnership under the 2000 Act. It followed that the words "employed by the limited liability partnership" in s.4(4) meant employed as an employee or as a worker under s.230(3)(a) and (b). Therefore, in the instant case the first question was whether, if there had been a partnership under the 1890 Act, V would have been a partner. There was no doubt that she would have been a partner. She was plainly pursuing a business for profit in common with others. The next question was whether, as a partner of a partnership formed under the 1890 Act, she could be a worker under s.230(3)(b). There was clear authority for the proposition that a partner in an 1890 Act partnership could not be an employee, *Ellis v Joseph Ellis & Co* [1905] 1 K.B. 324, *Cowell v Quilter Goodison Co* [1989] I.R.L.R. 392, [1990] C.L.Y. 1972 and *Tiffin v Lester Aldridge LLP* [2012] EWCA Civ 35, [2012] 1 W.L.R. 1887, [2012] C.L.Y. 1081 followed. The partnership was not a separate legal entity. The parties were in a relationship with each other. To be an employee a partner would have to be both workman and employer, which was a legal impossibility. Further, the concept of employment presupposed the worker being subordinate to the employer, but where the relationship was one of partners in a joint venture, that characteristic was absent. The reasoning in *Ellis* and *Cowell* provided no rational basis for distinguishing between employees and workers under s.230(3)(b). A member of an LLP who would have been a partner in an 1890 Act partnership had it not been registered as an LLP could be neither an employee under s.230 nor a worker under s.230(3)(b). It followed that V could not pursue her whistle blowing claim, *Ellis* and *Cowell* followed (paras 42-50, 61-67). (3) When determining jurisdiction, the comparative exercise would be appropriate where the claimant was employed wholly abroad. In those circumstances it was necessary to identify factors which were sufficiently powerful to displace the territorial pull of the place of work. However, that was not necessary where the claimant lived and/or worked for at least part of the time in Britain, *Ravat v Halliburton Manufacturing & Services Ltd* [2012] UKSC 1, [2012] 2 All E.R. 905, [2012] C.L.Y. 1176 followed. In the latter situation all that was required was that the tribunal should satisfy itself that the connection with Britain was sufficiently strong to enable it to be said that Parliament would have regarded it as appropriate for the tribunal to deal with the claim. That aspect of P's appeal was therefore dismissed and it followed that V could pursue her discrimination claims (paras 98-100). (4) (Obiter) The court also considered the position in the absence of s.4(4) of the 2000 Act and tentatively concluded that members of an LLP would not, by virtue of that status alone, constitute either an employee or a worker (paras 70-74).

BATES VAN WINKELHOF v CLYDE & CO LLP; CLYDE & CO LLP v BATES VAN WINKELHOF, [2012] EWCA Civ 1207, [2013] 1 All E.R. 844, Lloyd, L.J., CA (Civ Div).

994. Employment status–Ministers of religion–Whether Methodist minister engaged under contract of employment

The President of the Methodist Conference appealed against a decision ([2011] EWCA Civ 1581, [2012] Q.B. 735, [2012] C.L.Y. 1082) that a former minister (P) who wished to bring a claim for unfair dismissal had been an employee of the Methodist Church for that purpose. Methodist ministers had no written contract of employment. Their relationship with the Church was governed by its constitution, which was contained in what was known as the Deed of Union, by the standing orders of the Methodist Conference (the Church's governing body) and by such specific arrangements (if any) as might be made with a particular minister.

Held: Appeal allowed. (Lady Hale dissenting) (1) Unless some special arrangement was made with a particular minister, the rights and duties of ministers of the Methodist Church arose entirely from their status in the constitution of the Church and not from any contract. Three points were cumulatively decisive. First, the manner in which a minister was engaged was incapable of being analysed in terms of contractual formation. Neither the admission of a minister to full "connexion" nor his or her ordination were themselves contracts. Thereafter, the minister's duties were not consensual. They depended on the unilateral decisions of the Conference. Second, the minister's stipend (pay) and manse (accommodation) were due by virtue only of his or her admission into full connexion and ordination. While he or she remained in full connexion and in active life, those benefits continued even in the event of sickness or injury, unless he or she was given leave of absence or retired. In addition to the stipend and the manse, the minister had certain procedural rights derived from the disciplinary scheme of the Deed of Union and the standing orders, which determined the manner in which he or she might be suspended or removed from ministerial duties. But the disciplinary scheme was the same for all members of the Church whether they were ministers or ordinary lay members. Third, the relationship between the minister and the Church was not terminable except by the decision of the Conference or its Stationing Committee or a disciplinary committee. There was no unilateral right to resign, even on notice. The ministry described in the relevant instruments was a vocation, by which candidates submitted themselves to the discipline of the Church for life. That was the position in P's case. In finding that she was an employee, the Employment Appeal Tribunal and the Court of Appeal had over-analysed the decision in *Percy v Church of Scotland Board of National Mission* [2005] UKHL 73, [2006] 2 A.C. 28, [2006] C.L.Y. 5318 and paid insufficient attention to the Deed of Union and the standing orders, which were the foundation of P's relationship with the Methodist Church. The correct approach was to examine the rules and practices of the particular church and any special arrangements made with the particular minister, *Percy* applied (see paras 20, 23, 26 of judgment). (2) (Per Lady Hale) Everything about the arrangement between the Methodist Church and its ministers looked contractual. It was a very specific arrangement for a particular post, at a particular time, with a particular manse and a particular stipend, and with a particular set of responsibilities. It was an arrangement negotiated at local level but made at national level (para.49).

MOORE v PRESIDENT OF THE METHODIST CONFERENCE; *sub nom.* PRESTON v PRESIDENT OF THE METHODIST CHURCH; PRESIDENT OF THE METHODIST CONFERENCE v PRESTON (FORMERLY MOORE), [2013] UKSC 29, [2013] 2 A.C.163, Lord Hope, J.S.C. (Deputy President), SC.

995. Employment status–Mutuality of obligation–GP working for out-of-hours service–Whether "employee" or "worker" within meaning of s.47B and s.230 Employment Rights Act 1996

[Employment Rights Act 1996 (c.18) s.47B, s.212(3)(b), s.230.]

The appellant general practitioner (S) appealed against an employment tribunal's decision that he was neither an "employee" nor a "worker" within the meaning of the Employment Rights Act 1996 s.47B and s.230 for the purposes of his claims against the respondent (H) for unfair dismissal or breach of contract. H provided out-of-hours GP services on behalf of the local primary care trust. S had worked as an out-of-hours GP for H and for similar service providers in London and Yorkshire. H regarded the GPs as self-employed and the Revenue also treated them as self-employed. A service level agreement (SLA) formed the basis of the agreement between S and H. S was required to provide his own medical equipment but transport was arranged by H. He was informed that he would not be required to work any further shifts and claimed unfair dismissal. The judge found that the SLA was unequivocal and made clear that the GPs were self-employed. She found that there was no guarantee or obligation on H to provide work, or for S to carry out work, and that S had the right to substitution, to arrange for someone else to attend in his place. S contended that the facts showed that he was an employee or a worker, as pension payments were deducted by H, he had a shift manager and had received training, albeit that it was minimal. He argued that the contract of employment was a fait accompli and the substitution clause a sham.

Held: Appeal dismissed. It was clear on the judge's findings that there could be no overarching contract of employment, nor could there be a joining up of individual sessions under s.212(3)(b), *Cotswold Developments Construction Ltd v Williams* [2006] I.R.L.R. 181, [2006] C.L.Y. 1313 considered. It was equally clear that during those individual sessions S was neither an employee nor a worker. The judge had material before her to justify the finding that there was no mutuality of obligation between S and H. The substitution clause was clearly intended to have effect and there was insufficient control of S's work. Such findings were nowhere near perverse. The crucial and conclusive finding by the judge that S was in business on his own account was fatal to the suggestion that he was either an employee or a worker. He was clearly marketing his services to whichever provider of medical services might wish to provide him with work, and was able to take work as a locum at any time he chose. The judge clearly found that the written agreement represented the parties' true intentions. The substitution clause was entirely reasonable, as H would wish to ensure proper medical cover was available and if S was unable to attend it was his responsibility to find a suitably qualified substitute. The clause was real and effective and even if S had not availed himself of it, other GPs had. The fact that H was employing doctors who would not expect to be, and were not expected to be, supervised and had complete clinical independence, pointed to the judge's conclusion that S was one of a number of GPs who worked for H and others in business on his own account. It was certainly not inconsistent with his being in business on his own account, *Morren v Swinton and Pendlebury BC* [1965] 1 W.L.R. 576, [1965] C.L.Y. 1440 considered. The judge had weighed the various factors as to whether S was an employee or worker before concluding that he was neither. That decision could not be faulted on the facts as found by the judge, *Autoclenz Ltd v Belcher* [2011] UKSC 41, [2011] 4 All E.R. 745, [2011] C.L.Y. 1074 followed (see paras 43-48 of judgment).

SUHAIL v HERTS URGENT CARE (2013) 130 B.M.L.R. 27, Judge Serota Q.C., EAT.

996. Employment status–Mutuality of obligation–Market research interviewer engaged on assignment basis only–Whether employee or worker–Mutuality of obligation sufficient to create contract of employment

The appellant market research interviewer (D) appealed against a decision of an employment judge that he was not an employee of the respondent market research company (M). D was engaged by M on an assignment basis only. He was not issued with a contract of employment or any statement of terms and conditions, although M had various guides and a handbook. M's handbook stated that there was no obligation on it to offer work to any individual interviewer, no interviewer was obligated to accept the work offered and acceptance of an assignment was considered to be a verbal contract. D brought a claim for unfair dismissal. The judge found that D was not an employee because there was no mutuality of obligation from one assignment to another or during the course of any individual assignment. D submitted that the employment judge's conclusion that there was no mutuality of obligation was perverse.

Held: Appeal allowed. There was no doubt that a contract was in place and the requisite mutuality when D was undertaking an assignment for M, *Stephenson v Delphi Diesel Systems Ltd* [2003] I.C.R. 471, [2003] C.L.Y. 1338 and *McMeechan v Secretary of State for Employment* [1997] I.C.R. 549, [1997] C.L.Y. 2195 applied. The fact that the assignment could be brought to an end did not mean that there was no contract in existence while the assignment was continuing. Plainly there was a contract while the assignment was continuing: there was an agreement to undertake work in return for payment. When M in its handbook described the acceptance of an assignment as a "contract" it was correct. The fact that either side might terminate the contract at will did not mean that there was no contract. Accordingly, the employment judge's decision could not stand. However, the instant tribunal would not be entitled to substitute its own decision on the question of whether D was employed under successive contracts of employment and findings would be required on the conditions set out in *Ready Mixed Concrete (South East) Ltd v Minister of Pensions and National Insurance* [1968] 2 Q.B. 497, [1968] C.L.Y. 2550, *Ready Mixed Concrete* applied. It seemed plain, but the employment judge would need to find, that under each contract D was obliged to work personally for M unless and until he returned or completed the assignment or M withdrew it. A fresh hearing was ordered (see paras 32, 46-50, 54 of judgment).

DRAKE v IPSOS MORI UK LTD [2012] I.R.L.R. 973, Judge David Richardson, EAT.

997. Employment status–Mutuality of obligation–Self-employed lap dancers–Examination of mutuality of obligation–Whether contract of employment between lap dancer and nightclub

The appellant nightclub owner (S) appealed against the findings of the Employment Appeal Tribunal that the respondent lap dancer (Q) was an employee and that she had the necessary continuity of employment for the purposes of an unfair dismissal claim. Q had danced at S's club on a rota basis for some 18 months. The employment tribunal found that there was a club agreement which Q had not received but in practice matters had been conducted consistently with those terms. Appended to the agreement were house rules, which Q had not received but she had received a booklet that contained similar material. The tribunal found that whilst Q had been obliged to follow those rules and had been subject to a degree of control by S, the level of control did not amount to mutual obligation. The tribunal held that S was under no contractual obligation to provide work for which Q would be paid; Q's earning came directly from S's customers who paid by vouchers bought from S's clubs; the vouchers had to cover the cost of a tip out fee, house fee fines and commission; and Q was not required to work a set number of nights per week. The tribunal also held that there was no mutuality of obligation in the periods when Q was not dancing at S's club. If Q put herself forward to go on the rota she could be fined for not turning up but she was not under an obligation to dance at the club. The EAT held that the tribunal had erroneously concluded that there was no contract of employment; that there was no obligation on S to provide work, that S was under no obligation to pay wages to Q. The EAT held that the fact that customers provided the source of pay was irrelevant and that Q was integrated into the business and S had not merely provided Q with premises. S submitted that the EAT misread the tribunal's conclusion when it concluded that it had found that there was no contract and that the finding that it was not obliged to pay any remuneration to Q for the work she did was entirely consistent with the evidence before the tribunal. S also submitted that the tribunal was entitled to find that S was under no duty to provide Q the opportunity to dance even when she was present at the club, and that there were no continuing obligations of the kind necessary to establish an umbrella contract, in existence between rotas.

Held: Appeal allowed. (1) The tribunal s decision confusingly used the concept of mutual obligations in two distinct senses: there were no obligations of any kind and no obligations of the kind necessary to establish a contract of employment. However the tribunal was not saying that there was never any contract in place at all. The critical question was whether the nature of those contractual obligations were such as to render it a contract of employment. The tribunal properly inferred from the evidence that S was under no obligation to pay Q anything at all: Q negotiated her own fees with the clients, took the risk that on any particular night she would be out of pocket and received back from S only monies received from clients after deductions, *Spearmint Rhino Ventures (UK) Ltd v Revenue and Customs Commissioners* [2007] EWHC 613 (Ch), [2007] S.T.C. 1252, [2007] C.L.Y. 4344 considered. S did not employ Q to dance; rather Q paid S for an opportunity to earn money by dancing for clients, *Cheng Yuen v Royal Hong Kong Golf Club* [1998] I.C.R. 131, [1998] C.L.Y. 2140 considered. The fact that S also derived profits from selling food and drink to clients did not alter that fact. The economic risk Q took was also a powerful pointer against there being a contract of employment and the lack of any obligation to pay precluded the establishment of such a contract, *O'Kelly v Trusthouse Forte Plc* [1984] Q.B. 90, [1983] C.L.Y. 1225 considered. The tribunal s conclusion was reinforced by the fact that the contract terms involved Q accepting that she was self-employed, and she conducted her affairs on that basis, paying her own tax, *Calder v H Kitson Vickers (Engineers)* [1988] I.C.R.

232, [1988] C.L.Y. 1952 applied. In addition, she did not receive sick pay or holiday pay. Whilst there were some mutual obligations in play when Q was at work; and indeed she had a duty, at least once on the rota, to work certain days, and S was under some obligation to allow Q to dance when she was at work, but there was no relationship of employer and employee constituted by that arrangement (see paras 42, 45-46, 48, 50-52, 54 of judgment). (2) Although it was not necessary to consider if each engagement had constituted a separate contract of employment, there was nonetheless sufficient continuity of employment between engagements to constitute the necessary qualification period for claiming unfair dismissal (para.58).

QUASHIE v STRINGFELLOW RESTAURANTS LTD; *sub nom.* STRINGFELLOW RESTAURANTS LTD v QUASHIE, [2012] EWCA Civ 1735, [2013] I.R.L.R. 99, Ward, L.J., CA (Civ Div).

998. Employment status–Recorders–Entitlement of recorders to protection under Part-time Workers (Prevention of Less Favourable Treatment) Regulations 2000

[Part-time Workers (Prevention of Less Favourable Treatment) Regulations 2000 (SI 2000/1551); Directive 97/81 on the Framework Agreement on part-time work concluded by UNICE, CEEP and the ETUC - Annex: Framework agreement on part-time work.]

The court reconvened, having referred certain questions to the European Court of Justice, to hear an appeal by the appellant (O) against a decision ([2008] EWCA Civ 1448, [2009] 2 C.M.L.R. 15, [2009] C.L.Y. 1223) that recorders were not "workers" within the meaning of the Part-time Workers (Prevention of Less Favourable Treatment) Regulations 2000 and were not entitled to the protection of part-time workers against discrimination. O had been a barrister who for a number of years had sat as a recorder. Recorders were part-time judges who were remunerated by way of a fee for each day they sat. They were not entitled to a pension. The instant court had referred two questions to the ECJ: the first was whether it was for national law to determine whether or not judges as a whole were "workers who [had] an employment contract or employment relationship" within the meaning of cl.2.1 of the Framework Agreement on part-time work; the second was whether, if judges were such workers, it was permissible for national law to discriminate between full-time and part-time judges in the provision of pensions. The ECJ had answered the first question in the affirmative. As the second question, it had held that the Framework Agreement precluded, for the purpose of access to the retirement pension scheme, national law from establishing a distinction between full-time judges and part-time judges remunerated on a daily fee-paid basis, unless such a difference in treatment was justified by objective reasons, which was a matter for the referring court to determine. The instant court proceeded to rule on those two issues.

Held: Appeal allowed. (1) As the ECJ had made clear, the spirit and purpose of the Framework Agreement required that a distinction be made between the category of "worker" and that of self-employed persons. The following factors were significant: the character of the work that a recorder did in the public service differed from that of a self-employed person; the rules for the appointment and removal of recorders, to which no self-employed person would subject himself; the way their work was organised for them, bearing in mind that recorders, in common with all other part-time judges, were expected to work during defined times and periods; their entitlement to the same benefits during service as full-time judges. The self-employed person had the comparative luxury of independence. He could make his own choices as to the work he did and when and where he did it. He worked for himself and was not subject to the direction or control of others. When referring questions to the ECJ, the instant court had held that judicial office partook of most of the characteristics of employment; nothing in the ECJ's judgment was inconsistent with that provisional view and much of the judgment supported it. Accordingly, recorders were in an employment relationship within the meaning of cl.2.1 of the Framework Agreement and, as the result to be achieved by Directive 97/81 was binding on the United Kingdom, they had to be treated as "workers" for the purposes of the 2000 Regulations (see paras 33, 37, 39, 42 of judgment). (2) The respondent Ministry of Justice had struggled to explain what it was seeking to achieve by denying a pension to part-timers while granting one to full-timers. In effect, the argument was that if recorders got a pension, the pensions payable to circuit judges would have to be reduced. That was a pure budgetary consideration. It depended on the assumption that the present sums available for judicial pensions were fixed for all time. Of course there was not a bottomless fund of public money available and of course we were currently living in very difficult times. But the fundamental principles of equal treatment could not depend on how much money happened to be available in the public coffers at any one time or on how the state chose to allocate the funds available between the various responsibilities it undertook. That argument would not avail a private employer and it should not avail the state in its capacity as an employer. No objective justification had been shown for departing from the basic principle of remunerating part-timers *pro rata temporis*. O was therefore entitled to a pension on terms equivalent to those applicable to a circuit judge (paras 71, 74-75).

DEPARTMENT OF CONSTITUTIONAL AFFAIRS v O'BRIEN; *sub nom.* O'BRIEN v DEPARTMENT OF CONSTITUTIONAL AFFAIRS; O'BRIEN v MINISTRY OF JUSTICE; MINISTRY OF JUSTICE v O'BRIEN, [2013] UKSC 6, [2013] 1 W.L.R. 522, Lord Hope, J.S.C., SC.

999. Employment tribunals–Adjournment–Ll health of claimant–Fairness of adjournment

[European Convention on Human Rights 1950 Protocol 1 Art.6.]

The appellant employer (T) appealed against a decision of an employment tribunal to allow an application by the employee (O) for an adjournment of the substantive hearing in O's disability discrimination claim against T. O had become T's employee in June 2007. In January 2008 he went on sick leave and never returned. He was dismissed in December 2010. O brought seven complaints against T. The hearing in relation to the second complaint was fixed for October 4, 2010. Late in September 2010 O made unsuccessful applications for an adjournment. An adjournment on the ground of medical unfitness was ultimately granted on October 4, 2010 and the hearing was refixed for February 21, 2011. On that day the tribunal received an application from O for an adjournment on the grounds that he was unfit to attend. That application was refused. O appealed and the Employment Appeal Tribunal allowed his appeal on the basis that the decision not to adjourn was unfair as it had denied O an opportunity to participate in the hearing.

Held: Appeal allowed. There was no error of law in the judgment of the tribunal in refusing to exercise its broad discretion to grant the adjournments requested by O. The tribunal's decision was scrupulous and careful. It was clear that the most anxious consideration was given to taking the exceptional step of refusing an adjournment applied for on unchallenged medical grounds. The judgment cited the guidance in the relevant decisions of the instant court on the established approach to adjournment applications to an employment tribunal. It was not contended that the tribunal took into account irrelevant factors for and against an adjournment. The decision was reached solely on the basis of relevant considerations. The tribunal correctly took the overarching fairness factor into account in assessing the effect of its decision on both sides. The position of the potentially absent claimant was highly relevant in all cases of adjournment refusal but it was not determinative in every case. The tribunal expressly stated that it was "a very rare case" in which it was more unfair in general for the matter not to proceed than it would be to adjourn. There was no error of law in failing to take the approach laid down in *Berezovsky v Russian Television and Radio Broadcasting Co* [2010] EWCA Civ 1345, which was distinguishable on the ground that it was not a decision on the wide powers of the tribunal or on the more limted appellate jurisdiction of the EAT, as compared with appeals under the Civil Procedure Rules 1998, *Terluk* distinguished. It would not be fair for T to be repeatedly denied a hearing on the ground of O's recurrent health problems. The crucial point of difference from *Terluk* was that decisions of the employment tribunal could only be appealed on questions of law, whereas under the CPR the appeal was normally by way of review. Overall fairness to both parties was always the overriding objective and the assessment of fairness had to be made in the round. The EAT's application of the *Terluk* approach led it into substituting its own decision on the exercise of the discretion for that of the tribunal. That was an error of law on its part. The European Convention on Human Rights 1950 Protocol 1 art.6 did not compel the tribunal to the conclusion that it was always unfair to refuse an application for an adjournment on medical grounds, if it would mean that the hearing would take place in the party's absence. There were two sides to a trial, which should be as fair as possible to both sides (see paras 40-46 of judgment).

O'CATHAIL v TRANSPORT FOR LONDON; *sub nom.* TRANSPORT FOR LONDON v O'CATHAIL, [2013] EWCA Civ 21, [2013] C.P. Rep. 21, Mummery, L.J., CA (Civ Div).

1000. Employment tribunals–Bias–Apparent bias–Findings on liability–Pre-judging question of costs

The appellant employee (X) appealed against an order of the employment tribunal that she pay the entire costs of proceedings she had brought against the respondent employer NHS trust. X, who was a nurse, claimed for constructive unfair dismissal, direct race discrimination and victimisation. The tribunal dismissed the claims and stated that it had serious concerns about the genuineness of her complaints. It found that she was not a reliable or satisfactory witness and criticised her conduct of the proceedings as unreasonable. It ordered costs against her and stated that X had the means to pay. The amount of costs was expected to be substantial. X submitted that (1) the tribunal should have recused itself on grounds of apparent bias as the remarks made in its liability reasons were so closely related to the question of costs, an application not then before it, that a fair-minded and informed observer would conclude that there was a real possibility that the tribunal was biased; (2) the tribunal was not justified in concluding that X had the means to pay costs without any enquiry.

Held: Appeal allowed. (1) It was in the interests of justice that the tribunal which dealt with liability should also deal with costs. The mere fact that the tribunal expressed itself in terms adverse to a claimant while giving reasons for the liability judgment was not a ground for recusal. The tribunal in the instant case had been entitled to make its observations to deal with its liability reasoning. It should not, however, have expressed itself in a way which suggested that it had already made up its mind, prior to hearing argument, on issues which only arose if an application for costs was made, *R. v Odewale (Ayodele Oluseye)* [2005] EWCA Crim 709, [2005] 2 Cr. App. R. (S.) 102, [2005] C.L.Y. 890 applied. The tribunal had made findings on the conduct of the proceedings which recalled the threshold tests for the grant of a costs order, and it expressed concluded views on the application of those tests. A fair-minded and informed observer would have concluded that there was a real possibility that the tribunal had pre-judged the question of costs in the instant case. A tribunal dealing with the question of liability could and should express itself fully and properly on that issue but it should not reach or express concluded views which anticipated arguments on the question of costs which had not yet been put before it. The tribunal should have recused itself from hearing the application for costs (see paras 26-34, 37 of judgment). (2) The tribunal's finding that X had the means to pay an award of costs could not stand. The tribunal had material before it that she only had a state pension and it did not state that it might make any contrary finding (para.43).

ONI v NHS LEICESTER CITY (FORMERLY LEICESTER CITY PRIMARY CARE TRUST) [2013] I.C.R. 91, Judge David Richardson, EAT.

1001. Employment tribunals–Expert evidence–Claimant's refusal to attend medical examination with respondent's expert–Appropriate test for stay or strike out

The appellant employer (G) appealed against an employment tribunal's refusal to strike out or stay a claim brought by the respondent employee (B). B had resigned and claimed constructive dismissal and disability discrimination. He claimed to suffer from acute anxiety and alleged that G had failed to make reasonable adjustments and had harassed him by reason of his disability. At a case management discussion G made it clear that it wished to adduce medical evidence on the question of disability and reasonable adjustments. B was ordered to choose one of three psychiatric experts proposed by G and attend an assessment. He objected to G's experts and refused to attend. He obtained his own medical evidence and sought to adduce it at the final hearing. G made applications for a stay and/or a strike-out of the claim. The tribunal rejected G's applications and concluded that it was able to determine whether B was a disabled person from the GP records and occupational health reports. It refused to allow B to adduce his report. G submitted that the tribunal had failed to consider whether G was unable to properly prepare its defence without a psychiatric examination and report.

Held: Appeal allowed. (1) In the instant case it was plain that both parties considered that expert medical evidence was required. Guidance had been given as to the procedure to be adopted for obtaining expert medical evidence in *De Keyser Ltd v Wilson* [2001] I.R.L.R. 324, [2001] C.L.Y. 2271. The preferred course was for a joint expert report. Alternatively, either side could instruct their own expert, *De Keyser* applied. In the instant case the tribunal permitted B to choose from one of three names put forward by G. That was a more favourable order than B was entitled to expect. Quite exceptional reasons would have been required before B could properly veto G's choice of expert, and no such reasons existed. The question was therefore what should be done in the light of B's refusal to co-operate with G's choice of expert (see paras 27-32 of judgment). (2) The tribunal could stay the claim or impose an unless order, requiring B to present himself for examination by a certain date with the consequence that his case would be struck out if he refused. The test laid down by *Lane v Willis* [1972] 1 W.L.R. 326, [1972] C.L.Y. 835 was apposite: the party applying for the order had to show that he was unable to properly prepare his defence without the medical examination. That was the critical question, *Lane* applied and *Abegaze v Shrewsbury College of Arts & Technology* [2009] EWCA Civ 96, [2010] I.R.L.R. 238, [2010] C.L.Y. 1116 considered. However, the question which the tribunal actually considered was whether it could decide the issue of disability on the basis of the existing evidence. Even if it could decide that issue on the existing evidence it did not follow that G should have been prevented from seeking other, better, evidence to call on the issue. The tribunal had left out of account the prejudice caused to G by the course which it took. It had been entirely legitimate for G to seek to instruct an expert. It was proportionate to the issues and reasonable to do so, given that the issues were far from straightforward and the losses claimed amounted to nearly £200,000. There were a range of issues which the existing documentation did not cover, and upon which medical evidence was potentially important (paras 34-37, 45-50). (3) The tribunal had erred in law in reaching its conclusion. The correct course was to impose an unless order upon B requiring him to present himself for examination by G's expert on a stated date, with the consequence that his case would be struck out for non-compliance if he did not do so (para.51).

GOVERNMENT COMMUNICATIONS HEADQUARTERS v BACCHUS [2012] Eq. L.R. 1002, Judge David Richardson, EAT.

1002. **Employment tribunals–Failure to attend–Claimant scared of attending tribunal hearing–Respondent admitting acts took place but denying sexual harassment–Finding of harassment based on claimant's written evidence**

[Employment Tribunals (Constitution and Rules of Procedure) Regulations 2004 (SI 2004/1861).]

The appellant (D) appealed against a decision of an Employment Appeal Tribunal ([2013] I.C.R. D5) upholding an employment tribunal's decision that he had sexually harassed the respondent colleague (G). G had brought sex discrimination claims against D after he had sent her text messages with sexual content and had presented her with a vibrator. She also complained of other events. He subsequently sent her a letter enclosing a copy of her horoscope with a comment implying that she had fabricated the allegations and would suffer for it. G was scared of attending the hearing and requested that the tribunal make an order that she was not required to attend. The tribunal refused, informing her that she was not required to attend but that her absence might affect the weight to be attached to her evidence. Written evidence was submitted on her behalf. In her absence, the tribunal upheld the two specific acts of harassment and dismissed the other claims: D had admitted that the two acts had taken place but denied that they amounted to sexual harassment because they were "part of the pattern of mutual banter" in which they had engaged; he had denied that the other alleged acts of harassment took place or that they amounted to sexual harassment. D appealed to the EAT on the basis that the tribunal had not been entitled to make adverse findings against him without G's attendance for cross-examination. The EAT held that there had been ample material on which the tribunal could reach the conclusion that D's conduct was unwanted.

Held: Appeal allowed. (1) There could be circumstances in which, with procedural adjustments to ensure that the hearing was a fair one, it was legally permissible for an employment tribunal to reach a decision against a party who had not had the opportunity to cross-examine the other party. If there was an error of law in the instant case, it was a procedural one. The tribunal had refused G's request not to attend, but then held a hearing at which it heard evidence from D, who had opposed G's application and made it clear that he had questions to put to her in cross-examination. The tribunal accepted his denial that some of the alleged acts had taken place and dismissed those claims, as G had not attended to give oral evidence. However, it had not accepted his evidence in support of the overall defence throughout that there was no harassment because of the banter between them and his evidence that "she gave as good as she got". That defence would apply to all the acts, whether or not he admitted them. In those circumstances, the tribunal had made a procedural error in not first holding a pre-trial review for directions to consider the options available under the Employment Tribunals (Constitution and Rules of Procedure) Regulations 2004 for the conduct of a fair and just substantive hearing in the light of G's resolve not to attend to give oral evidence. The tribunal needed to explore with the parties, either separately or together, the following procedural points and possibilities: (a) whether the tribunal was satisfied by evidence that the claimant had grounds for and was fearful of attending the inter partes hearing to be cross-examined by the defendant; (b) if so, whether it should dispense with an inter partes hearing; (c) if so, whether separate hearings should be held at which each party could give evidence in the absence of the other; (d) if so, whether the parties should be invited to submit to the tribunal advance questions to be put to the other party at the separate hearing. In the light of any representations made, the tribunal would be in a position to give directions about the conduct of the case in a manner which it considered would best achieve the overriding objective in accordance with the Regulations. The matter was to be remitted to a differently constituted tribunal for re-hearing in accordance with directions giving a pre-hearing review (see paras 37-44 of judgment).

DUFFY v GEORGE, [2013] EWCA Civ 908, [2013] I.C.R. 1229, Mummery, L.J., CA (Civ Div).

1003. Employment tribunals–Interest

THE EMPLOYMENT TRIBUNALS (INTEREST) ORDER (AMENDMENT) ORDER 2013, SI 2013/1671; made under the Employment Tribunals Act 1996 s.14, s.41; and the Equality Act 2010 s.139, s.207. In force: July 29, 2013; .

The order amends the way in which interest is charged on an Employment Tribunal award made in a non-discrimination case.

1004. Employment tribunals–Procedure

THE EMPLOYMENT TRIBUNALS (CONSTITUTION AND RULES OF PROCEDURE) (CONSEQUENTIAL AMENDMENTS) REGULATIONS 2013, SI 2013/1948; made under the Employment Tribunals Act 1996 s.7, s.41. In force: August 30, 2013; .

This Order amends various pieces of secondary legislation to reflect the coming into force of the Employment Tribunals (Constitution and Rules of Procedure) Regulations 2013 which revoked and replaced the Employment Tribunals (Constitution and Rules of Procedure) Regulations 2004 on July 29, 2013.

1005. Employment tribunals–Spent convictions–Admissibility–Admissibility of evidence of claimant employee's spent conviction

[Rehabilitation of Offenders Act 1974 (c.53) s.4(1), s.7(3).]

The appellant employee (X) appealed against an employment judge's ruling that the respondent employer (Y) could give evidence of his spent conviction when the employment tribunal heard his claims for unfair and wrongful dismissal as well as race discrimination, victimisation and harassment. X had been convicted of kerb-crawling, but as the conviction was more than five years old, it was spent under the Rehabilitation of Offenders Act 1974. When X was dismissed because of his alleged behaviour towards women, he claimed, among other things, he had suffered discrimination on the ground of his race. Y argued that if X had been treated differently, the tribunal would need to consider whether it was due to his race or to his managers' knowledge of his conviction, and therefore the evidence of the latter had to be admitted. The general rule, found in s.4(1), was that a spent conviction was inadmissible; the exception, found in s.7(3), was that it was admissible if justice could not otherwise be done in the case. The employment judge found that the evidence regarding the spent conviction was relevant to the claim of race discrimination and decided it was admissible. X submitted that (1) the employment judge failed to appreciate the need to balance the degree to which his conviction was relevant to the issues which the tribunal had to decide against the prejudicial effect of the conviction being admitted; (2) if she had been aware of that need, she had not actually carried out the balancing exercise as she had not referred to the tribunal being prejudiced by knowing of his conviction for a sexual offence.

Held: Appeal dismissed. (1) The employment judge had given an impeccable summary of the correct approach to the matter and had expressly stated that when deciding whether to admit evidence of a spent conviction, she had to balance the degree of relevance of that conviction against the prejudice that would be occasioned by its admission. She had concluded that the evidence was so important that Y could not have a fair trial without it (see para.15 of judgment). (2) The prejudice which X would suffer as a result of the risk that the tribunal might not consider his case fairly if its members knew that he had been convicted of kerb-crawling was never advanced to the employment judge as the nature of the prejudice which he might suffer if the evidence of his conviction was admitted. The argument which was advanced to her was that the conviction was not relevant, it did not go to his credibility as a witness or to his propensity to act in the way in which he was alleged to have behaved, and the argument that its admission would have a prejudicial effect was only that it would undermine his rehabilitation which the 1974 Act was designed to promote. No other argument relating to prejudice was advanced (para.17).

A v B [2013] I.R.L.R. 434, Keith, J., EAT.

1006. Employment tribunals–Time limits–Claim form drafted by litigant in person–Requirement on employment tribunal to properly construe complaint–Findings of fact

The appellant employee (C) appealed against a decision of the Employment Appeal Tribunal that his complaint of race discrimination against the respondent supermarket (T) had been presented outside the statutory time limit so that the employment tribunal lacked jurisdiction to hear it. C, who was black, had lodged a grievance against a colleague in June 2009. On June 4, 2010, the grievance was dismissed. It was upheld on appeal. A meeting to communicate the outcome of the appeal took place on August 17, 2010 and C was offered compensation. The offer was withdrawn after consultation with T's managers. C presented his complaint to the employment tribunal on October 29, 2010 alleging delay and disparate treatment in the handling of the grievance process. The tribunal concluded that the offer and withdrawal of compensation did not form part of C's complaint; that the last act of discrimination relied upon occurred on June 4, 2010, that being the point at which the statutory time limit began to run. The EAT dismissed C's appeal on the ground that it was against a finding of fact that the employment tribunal had been entitled to make. C submitted that time had not started to run until August 17, 2010 and that both tribunals had erred in ignoring, without explanation, a complaint in his ET1 about the offer and withdrawal of compensation on that date.

Held: Appeal allowed. C was acting in person and his complaint form was not easy to read. However, it was reasonably clear from a fair reading of the completed ET1 as a whole that his complaint did not stop at the events on June 4. He had ticked "Race" as the ground of discrimination. That could also include discrimination by way of victimisation, which was not in the list of printed headings as a separate item. In his written account of events, he had referred to the meeting on August 17, but it did not come across as a separate complaint of discrimination. In later sections of the ET1, he made complaints about the August meeting which fell short of discriminatory acts, but he also referred to the offer of compensation being rescinded because of his previous involvement in employment tribunal proceedings. That came across as a complaint of continuing discrimination, or even victimisation in the sense of detrimental treatment for asserting his employment rights. He had specifically referred to "continued victimisation and harassment, abuse, intimidation and discrimination in racism". Neither tribunal had fully appreciated the significance, for time limit purposes, of the full extent of C's complaints in the ET1. They had both erred in treating the identification of the complaint as a finding of primary fact. They ought instead to have construed the ET1 as a document and treated the time limit question as involving a determination of what complaints were actually being made. There were very many reasons why the tribunals might have gained the impression that C's main complaint was the delay in processing his grievance, but upon closer scrutiny, that was not the case: C was making a complaint of continued detrimental treatment at the August meeting, and his complaint had therefore been lodged in time (see paras 11-22 of judgment).

CHARLES v TESCO STORES LTD, [2012] EWCA Civ 1663, [2013] Eq. L.R. 260, Mummery, L.J., CA (Civ Div).

1007. Employment tribunals–Unless orders–Requirement to provide sufficient particulars of claims–Appropriate test for issue of "substantial compliance"

In two appeals heard together, the local authority appealed against a decision that the respondent employee (J) had complied with an unless order, and J appealed against the stay of her claim against the local authority. J had been employed as a solicitor by the local authority before she resigned after a lengthy period of sick leave. She claimed constructive dismissal, direct disability discrimination, a failure to make reasonable adjustments, victimisation, and detriment by reason of a public interest disclosure. Her lengthy grounds of claim were expressed in general terms. She failed to provide particulars to enable the local authority to know the case it had to meet, despite case management orders. Following a second unless order, J provided some, but not all, of the particulars required. The judge held that there had been substantial compliance. At a separate hearing, an employment judge stayed J's employment tribunal claim until the resolution of a High Court claim that she had issued on the same factual basis. The local authority submitted that the claim was automatically struck out because there had not been substantial compliance with the unless order. J submitted that in staying the proceedings the judge had failed to take account of her personal circumstances, particularly that she could not fund the High Court claim and had issued it as a protective measure.

Held: Local authority's appeal allowed, employee's appeal dismissed. (1) Where a claim or response led to uncertainty about what was being alleged, case management powers could be exercised to order particulars to be given. If they were not given, an unless order could be made. If such an order was not complied with by the date set out in the order, the claim or response would stand struck out without the need for any further order, *Marcan Shipping (London) Ltd v Kefalas* [2007] EWCA Civ 463, [2007] 1 W.L.R. 1864, [2008] C.L.Y. 285 followed. In the instant case the judge's understanding, based on *Royal Bank of Scotland v Abraham*, was that where there was non-compliance, the whole of the claim had to be struck out even if the matters required by the unless order did not relate to that part of the claim. However, the principles expounded in *Abraham* did not extend that far. That would amount to a penal rather than a facilitative approach, although it might be appropriate when considering one claim on its own, *Abraham* explained. Where an ET1 raised two or more separate causes of action, they were legally separate claims. Judges making an unless order should consider tailoring the order with care. The order could provide that any allegations not sufficiently particularised might be struck out. That would leave it open to a subsequent judge to conclude that there had been compliance in respect of some allegations, which were not automatically struck out, but there had been non-compliance in respect of others which were struck out. When considering whether the order had been complied with, compliance should be "material". What was material was whether the particulars given enabled the other party to know the case it had to meet. The use of the word "substantial" when considering compliance erroneously indicated a quantitative approach, when qualitative compliance was more important (see paras 2-7 of judgment). The judge did not indicate why, having demonstrated a number of ways in which she plainly had to conclude that the particulars required by the order had not been supplied, she nonetheless concluded that there was substantial compliance. The judge had approached the matter quantitatively rather than qualitatively. In a number of respects the local authority would not have been able to know what case it had to meet. The judge should have found that there had not been compliance with the order. J's claims of disability discrimination and detriment on the basis of public interest disclosure were struck out for non-compliance with the unless order. However, it was anticipated that J would apply for relief from sanction, to be considered by a fresh employment tribunal (paras 48-51, 79). (2) The judge had considered J's contention that the claim had been issued for protective purposes only. The claimed inability to fund a High Court claim was inconsistent with having brought one. Further, it was plainly relevant when considering that argument to consider whether there was any material which supported or denied that fact. As J relied on the protective nature of the claim, it was open to the judge to note that there had been no clear undertaking from J not to pursue the claim if she was able to pursue all the matters before the Employment Appeal Tribunal. That did not mean that the judge required such an undertaking as a precondition to proceeding; it was to appropriately evaluate whether J's conduct belied the reason she had given. J could not complain that it was an abuse of process for the local authority to initiate proceedings to argue that one set of proceedings should be permitted rather than the other. It was inevitable that one or the other sets of proceedings would be stayed. The stay was lifted to the extent necessary to allow J to make an application for relief from sanction but would otherwise remain in place (paras 68-69, 72, 76-77).

JOHNSON v OLDHAM MBC; OLDHAM MBC v JOHNSON [2013] Eq. L.R. 866, Langstaff, J. (President), EAT.

1008. Employment tribunals–Written submissions–Tribunal not received claimant's written submissions–Duty to enquire about submissions before reaching decision

The appellant employee (Q) appealed against an employment tribunal's decision that she had not been unfairly dismissed by the respondent employer (M). Q, an assistant in a care home, had been dismissed after a scuffle with a fellow employee. After an oral hearing, the tribunal stated that both parties should lodge written submissions. Q served her submissions on M; she claimed that she had also sent a copy to the tribunal, but due to a mishap they were never received. The case was delayed for various reasons and the tribunal did not realise that it had not received Q's submissions until five months later at a meeting in chambers. The tribunal did not seek to ascertain whether Q had ever sent her submissions, nor did it consider doing so. It concluded that she did not intend to lodge submissions and went on to decide the case having considered only M's written submissions. Q submitted that the tribunal had simply relied on the absence of submissions as being the only evidence that no submissions were intended. She further argued that the tribunal should have considered why there were no submissions and, at the very least, considered whether or not to telephone her representative to enquire.

Held: Appeal allowed. There was a fair analogy between the instant case, where there was the absence of an important document directed to be submitted by the tribunal, and the case of someone who had absented himself or had failed to attend a hearing. Although absence from a hearing was more prejudicial, denying a party the right to make submissions on the evidence and the law, especially if that opportunity had been furnished to the other party, was serious. The making of a telephone call was good practice. Failure to make such a call was "an extreme step" and there would need to be a very good reason why the course of making the call could not have been followed, *Southwark LBC v Bartholomew* [2004] I.C.R. 358, [2004] C.L.Y. 1245 and *Cooke v Glenrose Fish Co* [2004] I.C.R. 1188 considered. There was no burden on Q to prove that consideration of her submissions would definitely have made a difference to the decision, but having regard to the nature of the breach, there had to be a real possibility that consideration of the document might have led to a different result. It was impossible for the Employment Appeal Tribunal to say that the submissions would have made no difference. The tribunal had never enquired as to whether there was a response from Q. It had reached its conclusion without any evidence to support the finding that it was because Q did not intend to file written submissions. It never asked itself the right question, namely what was the reason for the absence of the submissions. That was unsafe and perverse in itself. Accordingly, the decision could not stand. There had been a serious procedural irregularity. The matter would be remitted for a fresh hearing before a different tribunal, *Mayo-Deman v Lewisham College* considered (see paras 28-31 of judgment).

QUASHIE v METHODIST HOMES HOUSING ASSOCIATION [2012] I.C.R. 1330, Judge Serota Q.C., EAT.

1009. Enterprise and Regulatory Reform Act 2013 (c.24)–Commencement No.2 Order

THE ENTERPRISE AND REGULATORY REFORM ACT 2013 (COMMENCEMENT NO.2) ORDER 2013, SI 2013/1648; made under the Enterprise and Regulatory Reform Act 2013 s.10. Commencement details: bringing into force various provisions of the 2013 Act on July 29, 2013.; .

This is the second Commencement Order made under the Enterprise and Regulatory Reform Act 2013. Certain provisions came into force on the passing of the Act. This Order commences certain provisions of Pt 2 of the Act, which concerns employment.

1010. Equal pay–Abuse of process–Second set of proceedings issued following withdrawal of original claim–Substantially similar causes of action

[Equal Pay Act 1970 (c.41) s.1(2)(b), s.1(2)(c); Employment Tribunals (Constitution and Rules of Procedure) Regulations 2004 (SI 2004/1861) Sch.1 para.25(4).]

The appellant employees (F) appealed against an employment judge's dismissal of their equal pay claims against the respondent local authority. F were employed by the local authority as housing needs officers and were all members of a trade union. They complained that they were not receiving equal pay in respect of emergency call-out rates when compared with male officers working in the environmental health and pest control departments. That grievance was not resolved in F's favour and they issued proceedings under the Equal Pay Act 1970 s.1 (2) (b) and (c). F subsequently notified the employment tribunal that they wished to withdraw their claims and bring a new equal pay claim in respect of call-out and stand-by payments to a "male-dominated comparator". The local authority applied for the first claim to be dismissed under the Employment Tribunals (Constitution and Rules of Procedure) Regulations 2004 Sch.1 para.25(4). F opposed that application on the basis that their new claim related to a different element of pay. They issued their second claim, with the comparators identified as pest control officers. The employment judge directed himself that the question was not only whether the second claim could have been raised in the original proceedings, but whether it should have been raised. He found that the late change of attack amounted to unjust harassment of the local authority. F's first claim was dismissed under para.25(4) and the second claim as an abuse of process. F argued that different causes of action were engaged as the second proceedings relied on a different comparator and pay element.

Held: Appeal dismissed. Where a claimant sought to terminate a first set of proceedings by withdrawal, with a view to bringing a second set of proceedings which raised the same, or substantially the same, cause of action, or otherwise in circumstances amounting to an abuse of process, a tribunal would be entitled to dismiss the first proceedings and bar the claimant from bringing the second proceedings, *Verdin v Harrods Ltd* [2006] I.C.R. 396, [2006] C.L.Y. 1318 and *Johnson v Gore Wood & Co (No.1)* [2002] 2 A.C. 1, [2001] C.L.Y. 410 applied. The issue in the instant case was whether it could properly be said, in accordance with para.25(4) and taking a broad merits-based approach, that the second proceedings raised the same or substantially the same cause of action. It was clear that the judge had placed the onus on the local authority to establish abuse of process, and his finding of such an abuse was not perverse. The facts favoured the local authority more than was the position before the judge, who found that there was no evidence that F had been advised by the union when raising the initial grievance, when in fact they had been advised not only by the branch but by the regional office. The complaint about call-out rates in comparison with the rates paid to the male pest control officers, the subject of the second proceedings, was therefore one which had been raised on the advice of the union regional office in the original grievance. In those circumstances, the judge was plainly entitled to find that not only could F have pursued the second set of claims in the original proceedings, but also that they should have done so. The judge had also fully explained his reasoning, which was *Meek*-compliant. There were no grounds for interfering with the order made, *Verdin* and *Johnson* applied (see paras 19, 21-27 of judgment).

FOX v BASSETLAW DC [2013] Eq. L.R. 219, Judge Peter Clark, EAT.

1011. Equal pay–Comparators–Meaning of "in the same employment" in s.1(6) Equal Pay Act 1970

[Equal Pay Act 1970 (c.41) s.1 (6); Treaty Establishing the European Community (Nice version) Art.141; Treaty on the Functioning of the European Union Art.157.]

The appellants (N), female support staff employed by the respondent local authority to work in schools and nurseries, appealed against a decision ([2011] CSIH 2, 2011 S.C. 372, [2011] C.L.Y. 4218) that they were not entitled, in their claims for equal pay, to select as their comparators males employed by the local authority as groundsmen, roadworkers, refuse collectors and a leisure attendant. N worked under a collective agreement known as the "Blue Book". They were based at a variety of schools, working less than 35 hours per week and only during school terms. They wished to compare themselves with males employed in the local authority's combined services under the "Green Book", who were based at specific depots, who worked full time, and who, unlike N, were entitled to substantial bonuses and supplements. The local authority applied for a pre-hearing review as to whether N were "in the same employment" as their chosen comparators within the meaning of the Equal Pay Act 1970 s.1 (6). The employment tribunal held that the correct test was whether, if the comparators were employed at N's establishments, they would be employed under broadly similar terms to those that they currently enjoyed. It found the test to be satisfied and ruled that N's choice of comparator was valid. That decision was reversed on appeal, the Court of Session finding that the evidence did not support the tribunal's factual findings. N submitted that the employment tribunal had adopted the correct test and that the Court of Session should not have interfered with it. The local authority argued that in order to use their chosen comparators, N did not need to demonstrate a "real possibility" that the comparators could be transferred to N's workplace, but they had to show, in accordance with the test in *British Coal Corp v Smith* [1996] 3 All E.R. 97, [1996] C.L.Y. 2549, that it was at least feasible that they might be.

Held: Appeal allowed. N's argument was preferred over that of the local authority for the following reasons: (a) *British Coal* did not introduce, or even hint at, a "real possibility" or "feasibility" test. Both terms added an unwarranted gloss to the wording of s.1 (6) as interpreted in that case, *British Coal* considered (see paras 10-14, 33 of judgment); (b) to adopt such a test would be to defeat the object of the exercise, which was to secure equality of treatment, not only for the same work but also for work rated as equivalent, or assessed by experts to be of equal value. It stood to reason, therefore, that some very different jobs which were not, and could not, be performed in the same workplace might nevertheless be rated as equivalent. The fact that necessity required jobs to be carried out in different places was no barrier to equalising the terms on which the work was done. Historically, jobs requiring physical strength were better rewarded than those requiring dexterity; one of the objects of the equality legislation was to iron out traditional inequalities of reward where the work involved was of genuinely equal value (para.34); (c) it was not the function of the "same employment" test to establish compatibility between the jobs done. Such compatibility was established by the "like work", "work rated as equivalent" and "work of equal value" tests. The "same employment" test was not to be used as a proxy for those tests, or as a means of avoiding the, often difficult and complex, issues which they raised; its function was to establish the terms and conditions with which the comparison was to be made (para.35); (d) the construction of s.1 (6) favoured by N was more consistent with EU law, currently enshrined in TFEU art.157, but formerly in the EC Treaty (Nice) art.141, *Defrenne v SA Belge de Navigation Aerienne (SABENA) (43/75)* [1981] 1 All E.R. 122, [1976] C.L.Y. 1164 and *Lawrence v Regent Office Care Ltd (C-320/00)* [2002] E.C.R. I-7325, [2002] C.L.Y. 1363 applied. For the principle of equal pay to have direct effect, the difference in treatment had to be attributable to a "single source" which was capable of putting it right. In the instant case, it was quite clear that the difference was attributable to the local authority employer, which could put the discrepancy right if required to do so, *Robertson v Department for the Environment, Food and Rural Affairs* [2005] EWCA Civ 138, [2005] I.C.R. 750, [2005] C.L.Y. 1258 considered (paras 36-42).

NORTH v DUMFRIES AND GALLOWAY COUNCIL, [2013] UKSC 45, [2013] 4 All E.R. 413, Lord Hope (Deputy President), SC.

1012. Equal pay–Indirect discrimination–Employer's application of pay protection scheme on re-structuring–Resultant pay disparity between male and female employees–Whether prima facie indirect discrimination and legitimate aim

[Equal Pay Act 1970 (c.41).]

The appellant female employees (H) appealed against a decision of the Employment Appeal Tribunal (EAT/0123/10/LA) that an employment tribunal had erred in allowing their equal pay claims. H had been employed in administrative support roles by the Commission. In October 2007, their posts were amalgamated with those of senior administrators, leading to a competitive assessment for 11 new roles. Before amalgamation, there were 11 administrators together with two full-time male and two part-time female senior administrators. Both roles were within the same pay scale, but the senior administrators were placed at a higher point within its range. Nine female administrators and two male administrators were appointed to the new roles. The Commission applied a pay protection policy which protected pre-amalgamation pay levels, resulting in a pay disparity between the former administrators and the two former senior administrators (the comparators). H brought proceedings under the Equal Pay Act 1970. The tribunal found that there was a prima facie case of indirect discrimination, which could not be objectively justified. The EAT overturned that decision, holding that there was no prima facie case of indirect discrimination because there was no reason to believe that pre-amalgamation remuneration levels were discriminatory. It also found that protecting the pay of employees affected by a re-structuring was plainly a legitimate aim, both as a matter of fairness to employees and because if their pay were reduced, it would be difficult to retain them. The issues were whether the employment tribunal had made errors of law in its findings that (i) H had established a prima facie case of indirect sex discrimination which the Commission had not rebutted; (ii) the pay discrimination was not objectively justified as being for a legitimate aim.

Held: Appeals allowed in part. (Mummery L.J. dissenting on the issue of remittal to the employment tribunal) (1) No question of law arose from the decision of the employment tribunal on the issue of indirect sex discrimination. There were no grounds for finding an error of law in the way that it had approached the matter of indirect discrimination, either on a "practice, criterion or policy" basis or an "Enderby" basis, *Enderby v Frenchay HA (C-127/92)* [1994] 1 All E.R. 495, [1994] C.L.Y. 4813 considered. Its unchallenged findings were based on relevant evidence and spoke for themselves. The employment tribunal's conclusion on indirect discrimination was not flawed by the fact that the Commission applied the pay protection policy equally to all employees: the true question, which was correctly appreciated by the employment tribunal, was whether its application had a disparate adverse impact on H, which the tribunal found it did. The fact that H benefited from the application of the pay protection policy was irrelevant when considering whether its application had a disproportionate adverse impact on them as compared with men. It was irrelevant that the make-up of the comparator group was not the result of indirect sex discrimination, but resulted from a non-discriminatory selection process. The tribunal had been entitled to find that the administrator role was "women's" work. The point was that H were disadvantaged by reason of having done lower paid women's work prior to the amalgamation. The lack of historic discrimination was irrelevant: the claim was only in respect of the period after October 2007. H relied on the combined effect of the amalgamation and the application of the pay protection policy after October 2007 and the fact that, after that date, H and the comparators were doing "like work", but with a significant difference in pay. There was, in those circumstances, a rebuttable presumption of discrimination, which the Commission had not rebutted. There had been no error of law in the employment tribunal's conclusion that the case was one of indirect sex discrimination (see paras 114-125 of judgment). (2) In relation to objective justification, the Commission had relied on two legitimate aims: to stop H and the comparators from suffering reductions in pay and to prevent the loss of skills and experience. The employment tribunal appeared to have accepted those as being aims, not as being legitimate. It seemed to have accepted H's submission that it could not be right to have a legitimate aim that was contrary to the equal pay legislation. However, as the EAT correctly pointed out, whether the aims were contrary to the equal pay legislation or the Commission's gender and diversity policy was the very question at issue. The tribunal had not asked itself the right question. The EAT had been correct that it had been wrong to reject the Commission's aims as legitimate ones and it had been entitled to overturn the decision of the tribunal on that point. However, there was an issue about whether it was entitled to substitute its own view, or whether it should have remitted the case to the employment tribunal. H had not suggested any further facts which needed to be found and the EAT had worked on the basis of the facts as found by the tribunal. The EAT was well equipped to assess whether any issue meriting remission arose and the EAT's decision to substitute conclusions was within its discretion. That appeal would therefore be dismissed without the need to remit the case (paras 142-144, 148-150, 153-158).

AUDIT COMMISSION v HAQ; *sub nom.* HAQ v AUDIT COMMISSION, [2012] EWCA Civ 1621, [2013] I.R.L.R. 206, Mummery, L.J., CA (Civ Div).

1013. Equal pay–Time limits–Entitlement to bring claim in High Court outside time limit applicable to employment tribunal claims

[Equal Pay Act 1970 (c.41) s.1 (1), s.2(4); Equality Act 2010 (c.15) s.128(1); Sex Discrimination Act 1975 (c.65) s.8(1).]

The appellant local authority appealed against a decision ([2011] EWCA Civ 1412, [2012] 2 All E.R. 591, [2012] 3 C.L. 81) upholding the dismissal of its application for a direction that the equal pay claims of the respondents (E) should be struck out. E had brought their claims in the High Court. The claims were founded on an alleged breach of the "equality clause" which, by the Equal Pay Act 1970 s.1 (1), as substituted by the Sex Discrimination Act 1975 s.8(1), was deemed to have been included in their contracts of employment. They issued their claims outside the time limit that would have applied had their claims been presented in the employment tribunal. The issue was the proper construction of s.2(3) of the 1970 Act, the first part of which provided that where it appeared to the court in which any proceedings were pending that a claim or counterclaim in respect of the operation of an equality clause could more conveniently be disposed of separately by an employment tribunal, it could direct that the claim or counterclaim should be struck out. The local authority argued that, except where they could provide a reasonable explanation for their failure to present their claims in time to the tribunal, E's claims should be struck out under s.2(3).

Held: Appeal dismissed. (Lords Sumption and Carnwath dissenting) (1) The adverb used in s.2(3) was "conveniently". That adverb qualified the type of disposal addressed in the subsection and mandated a straightforward practical inquiry into the forum more convenient for investigation of the merits. For the purpose both of the first part of the subsection and of its successor, namely the Equality Act 2010 s.128(1), a claim in respect of the operation of an equality clause could never more conveniently be disposed of by the tribunal if it would there be time-barred, *Restick v Crickmore* [1994] 1 W.L.R. 420, [1994] C.L.Y. 3785 approved (see paras 27-29 of judgment). (2) No doubt one aspect of the local authority's concern about the prospect that claims in respect of the operation of an equality clause could be brought against employers in court, rather than in the tribunal, related to the court's general rule, which did not apply in the tribunal, to make an order for costs against the unsuccessful party. But the court could make a different order and, in deciding what order, if any, to make in respect of costs, it had to have regard to all the circumstances, including the conduct of the parties. It was to that inquiry that the factor incorrectly urged as relevant to the instant appeal might well become relevant. The court's conclusion that, instead of bringing it in court, a claimant should, in all the circumstances, reasonably have presented her claim, in time, to the tribunal might well be relevant to its survey in relation to costs: insofar as, had she done so, she would not have obtained an order for costs, such might well be relevant to the court's decision as to the appropriate order (para.30). (3) E had invoked the principle of equivalence. However, the decision in *Preston v Wolverhampton Healthcare NHS Trust (No.2)* [2001] UKHL 5, [2001] 2 A.C. 455, [2001] C.L.Y. 2279, which some might now consider borderline but from which the court had not been invited to depart, was authority for the proposition that, in its application to what after 2003 was known as the standard case, the six-month rule in s.2(4) of the 1970 Act did not offend against the principle of equivalence, *Preston* considered (paras 33-34). (4) (Per Lord Sumption) According to the majority, the notion of "convenience" in s.2(3) was directed only to the efficient distribution of judicial business between the available forums. That was far too narrow a test, because it excluded the broader interests of justice, which should be decisive. "Convenient" was used in s.2(3) in a sense analogous to that which it had in the expression "forum non conveniens". The question was whether the disposal of the claim in an employment tribunal was appropriate in the interests of justice. The fact that the claim would be time-barred in the tribunal would be a highly relevant factor, albeit not conclusive (paras 46-47).

ABDULLA v BIRMINGHAM CITY COUNCIL; *sub nom.* BIRMINGHAM CITY COUNCIL v ABDULLA, [2012] UKSC 47, [2013] 1 All E.R. 649, Lady Hale, J.S.C., SC.

1014. Fixed-term contracts–Length of service–Successive fixed-term contracts–Some awarded under government training scheme, some not–Calculating period of continuous service for purposes of reg.8 Fixed-term Employees (Prevention of Less Favourable Treatment) Regulations 2002

[Fixed-term Employees (Prevention of Less Favourable Treatment) Regulations 2002 (SI 2002/2034) reg.8, reg.9(5), Pt 5, reg.18, reg.19; Directive 1999/70 on the framework agreement on fixed-term work concluded by ETUC, UNICE and CEEP.]

The appellant Department appealed against a decision of the Employment Appeal Tribunal ([2012] I.R.L.R. 900, [2012] C.L.Y. 1107) that the respondent (H) was entitled to a declaration under the Fixed-term Employees (Prevention of Less Favourable Treatment) Regulations 2002 reg.9(5) that she was a permanent employee. H had worked for the Department under a series of successive fixed-term contracts. The first, a one-year contract, ran from April 2006 and had been offered pursuant to a Government training scheme. That contract was extended twice, first in April 2007 and then again in April 2009. In October 2009, H applied for, and secured in open competition, another post within the Department on an 18-month fixed-term contract. In April 2010, when she had worked for the Department for four continuous years, she sought confirmation that, pursuant to reg.8 of the Regulations, she had become a permanent employee. The Department took the view that she remained a fixed-term employee, reasoning that her employment between April 2006 and October 2009 was pursuant to a training scheme and was therefore excluded by reg.18 and did not count for the purposes of reg.8. H applied to the employment tribunal for a declaration under reg.9(5) that she was a permanent employee. Her application was rejected on the basis that the scheme under which her original contract had been offered fell within reg.18 and that, therefore, time did not begin to run for the purposes of reg.8 until October 2009. The EAT allowed H's appeal against that decision, finding that the exclusions in the Regulations were to be construed narrowly. It found that reg.18 was only concerned with the contract under which the employee was currently employed, and did not apply to earlier fixed-term contracts. It found that, at the time of her application, H was not employed on a contract that fell within reg.18 and that nothing in reg.8 prevented her from relying on her 2006-2009 employment.

Held: Appeal allowed. (Dame Janet Smith dissenting) The Regulations had been enacted to implement Directive 1999/70, which had had the twin purposes of prohibiting discrimination against those working under fixed-term contracts and preventing the abusive use of such contracts. It was not suggested that the Regulations fell short of being a proper implementation of the Directive. The court was not in the territory of approaching the interpretation of the Regulations to ensure that domestic law reflected EU law, and nor was it concerned with any ambiguity leading to absurdity. While there were anomalies, there was nothing unusual about statutory provisions producing anomalies at the margins. The task of interpreting the Regulations was thus to be approached by considering the natural meaning of the words used in the context of the Regulations as a whole, keeping in mind their purposes. Had reg.8 stood alone, H would plainly have come within it. At the time of her application to the tribunal she could have said "I am an employee employed under a fixed-term contract and I was previously employed on a fixed-term contract before the start of the current one". However, reg.8 did not stand alone; Pt 5 provided for exclusions. The exclusion in reg.18 disapplied reg.8 in relation to a fixed-term contract under a training scheme, regardless of when that scheme began or ended. In reaching that conclusion, significance was attached to two matters. First, reg.19 contained an exclusion which resulted in the total disapplication of the Regulations, including reg.8, to agency workers, irrespective of whether the agency work was current or completed. The language of that exclusion was the same as that used in reg.18. It was not significant that in reg.18 the reference was to "a fixed-term employee", whereas reg.19 referred to "employment under a fixed-term contract". If reg.19 was a total disapplication of the Regulations, then so was reg.18. Second, it was important to keep in mind that the Directive and the Regulations treated fixed-term contracts as capable of being either detrimental or beneficial to employees. While they were detrimental when they were discriminatory or abusive, they had the potential to enhance employment opportunities, particularly within the context of Government-sponsored schemes. The construction contended for by H had the potential to disincentivise employers from participating in such schemes, and an employer was not to be placed in the position of having to await the decision of an employment tribunal before knowing whether or not time spent on a particular fixed-term contract counted for the purposes of reg.8 (see paras 8-17 of judgment). (2) (Per Dame Janet Smith) The EAT's interpretation of the Regulations was correct. Regulation 18(1) meant that anybody employed on a contract awarded pursuant to a Government training scheme fell outside the scope of the Regulations. However, at the time of her application, H was not employed on such a contract and was therefore not excluded. Regulation 18 excluded a person, not a period of time. It excluded a fixed-term employee who was currently employed on a contract pursuant to a Government training scheme. It did not refer to past contracts (paras 32-33, 37).

HUDSON v DEPARTMENT FOR WORK AND PENSIONS, [2012] EWCA Civ 1416, [2013] 1 All E.R. 1370, Sir Maurice Kay (VP CA Civ), CA (Civ Div).

1015. Gangmasters–Licensing–Exclusions

THE GANGMASTERS LICENSING (EXCLUSION) REGULATIONS 2013, SI 2013/2216; made under the Gangmasters (Licensing) Act 2004 s.6. In force: October 1, 2013; .

This instrument amends the Gangmasters Licensing (Exclusions) Regulations 2010 (SI 2010/649) which specify the circumstances where a person acting as a gangmaster, as defined by the Gangmasters (Licensing) Act 2004, is not required to obtain a gangmasters' licence.

1016. Grievance procedures–Amendments–Purported appeal meeting–Failure by employment tribunal to assess procedure–Balancing prejudice regarding amendments

[Employment Rights Act 1996 (c.18) Pt X, s.103A.]

The appellant (B) appealed against a decision of the employment tribunal refusing permission to amend his claim for unfair constructive dismissal and dismissing it. B had worked for the respondent supermarket (S) as an LGV driver. He expressed concerns about health and safety matters at the depot. He alleged that the management had rebuffed him, but the tribunal found that at the material time those incidents were in the past and S's depot had satisfactory health and safety audits. After an altercation with a manager B raised a grievance, citing, amongst other things, some health and safety issues. The managing director dealt with B's grievance, and to some extent acknowledged what B said about health and safety, but accepted the manager's version of the altercation. B wished to appeal and in a 20-minute meeting the managing director reiterated his previous decision. B resigned after the meeting, asserting that he had been effectively denied an appeal. His claim relied on making a public interest disclosure pursuant to the Employment Rights Act 1996 Pt X s.103A and ordinary unfair dismissal under s.98, relying on breach of the implied term of trust and confidence. He sought to amend his claim to say that the grievance procedure was, or might be, an express term of his contract. The tribunal gave no reasons for its refusal to allow an amendment. It scarcely mentioned the altercation and reached no findings about the appeal meeting. B submitted that the tribunal unduly restricted the scope of the implied term of trust and confidence, that denial of a grievance appeal was capable of being a breach of the implied term, and that the tribunal should have made findings as to what happened at the appeal meeting. B maintained that the amendment was a simple relabeling of facts already pleaded, and that the tribunal had not correctly balanced prejudice between the parties. S argued that, while the grievance procedure provided for an appeal, it was silent regarding who should hear it. S contended that the meeting on the date in question could be and was an appeal hearing, that there was a finding that should be taken as meaning there was no failure to hear an impartial appeal, and that therefore there was no repudiatory breach.

Held: Appeal allowed. (1) The grievance procedure was not to be read as if it were a statute. The ACAS Codes were a reliable indication of the employment context and stated that appeals should be impartial and where possible dealt with by a manager not previously involved, *Malik v Bank of Credit and Commerce International SA (In Liquidation)* [1998] A.C. 20, [1997] C.L.Y. 2192 applied. Failure to adhere to a grievance procedure was capable of amounting or contributing to a breach of the term of trust and confidence and whether it did so was a matter for the tribunal to determine against the *Malik* test. The right to an appeal was significant, and an organisation the size of S should have been able to provide for an appeal meeting that met that test. The tribunal should have assessed what happened at the meeting and considered whether there had been a breach of the implied term, but it did not do so although it was an important part of B's case, which was an error of law. (2) Applications for leave to amend should be approached according to the principles in *Selkent Bus Co Ltd v Moore* [1996] I.C.R. 836, [1996] C.L.Y. 2661 *Selkent* applied. They included taking into account all the circumstances and balancing the injustice and hardship of allowing the amendment against that of refusing it. The tribunal considered that S was prejudiced by the claim being made at the last minute, but that depended on whether there was difficulty in meeting the claim and the tribunal did not comment on that. It did not decide whether or not B would be prejudiced by refusal of the amendment, and its assessment was therefore flawed. While B's case on the purported appeal meeting had strength, precisely what had happened there remained to be resolved, so the matter was remitted to a different tribunal.

BLACKBURN v ALDI STORES LTD [2013] I.R.L.R. 846, Judge David Richardson, EAT.

1017. Grievance procedures–Right to be accompanied–Trade union representatives–Whether requirement of reasonableness in s.10(1)(b) Employment Relations Act 1999 extending to identity of proposed companion

[Employment Protection (Consolidation) Act 1978 (c.44) s.140; Employment Relations Act 1999 (c.26) s.10(3)(b), s.10, s.11(3); Employment Rights Act 1996 (c.18) s.203; Trade Union and Labour Relations (Consolidation) Act 1992 (c.52) s.199.]

The appellant employees (T and H) appealed and the employer (G) cross-appealed against a decision of an employment tribunal concerning T and H's right to be accompanied at grievance meetings. T and H had raised a grievance with G, and G had invited them to a grievance meeting. Each had made it clear to G that, pursuant to the Employment Relations Act 1999 s.10, he wished to be accompanied at the meeting by a particular individual (L), who was an elected trade union official appropriately certified under s.10(3)(b). G refused to allow T and H to be accompanied by L, and they therefore chose a different companion. When the outcome of the meetings was unsatisfactory from their point of view, they appealed. The central issue for the tribunal was whether an employee's choice of companion had to be "reasonable" within the meaning of s.10(1)(b). It held that it did not, and that the requirement of reasonableness related only to the request for accompaniment, not to the choice of companion. It found that if the proposed companion met the requirements of s.10(3) then the employer had to permit him to accompany the employee to grievance meetings. However, it went on to find that in choosing an alternative companion after G's rejection of L, T and H had waived any breach of statutory duty by G. G appealed on the reasonableness issue, while T and H appealed on the waiver issue. G submitted that the tribunal erred in concluding that the word "reasonably" in s.10(1)(b) had nothing to do with the identity of the proposed companion. It argued that, in construing s.10(1)(b), the tribunal was entitled to follow the guidance in an Acas Code of Practice issued in 2009 under the Trade Union and Labour Relations (Consolidation) Act 1992 s.199. T and H submitted that the tribunal's finding on waiver was not open to it as a matter of law.

Held: Appeal allowed, cross-appeal dismissed. (1) Under s.10(2)(a) of the 1999 Act, an employer had to grant a worker's request to be accompanied at a grievance hearing provided the companion met the requirements of s.10(3). The companion was to be chosen by the worker, not by the employer. The word "reasonably" applied only to the requirement to be accompanied. It did not apply to the choice of companion. An Acas Code of Practice was not an available aid to the construction of a statute. To say that it was contravened the basic constitutional principle that it was for Parliament to legislate for the ends it sought to accomplish, and that it was for the courts to interpret its legislation by applying established methods of construction. Moreover, s.10 worked perfectly well, read and understood in accordance with its straightforward language (see paras 13-22 of judgment). (2) The Employment Rights Act 1996 s.203 provided a statutory prohibition on waiver. The case of *Secretary of State for Employment v Deary* [1984] I.C.R. 413, [1984] C.L.Y. 1261, decided under the Employment Protection (Consolidation) Act 1978 s.140, an identically worded predecessor section, established that it was not open to employer and employee to agree, either expressly or by implication, to waive a statutory requirement. There was no reason to depart from that principle, *Deary* applied and *ICI Ltd v Shatwell* [1965] A.C. 656, [1964] C.L.Y. 2561 followed. The tribunal's finding that T and H had waived their right to be accompanied by the union official of their choice necessarily involved a finding that they had tacitly agreed to waive G's breach of its statutory obligation (paras 22-29). (3) Once a tribunal had found that a complaint under s.10 was well founded, s.11(3) of the same Act required it to order the employer to pay compensation in an amount not exceeding two weeks' pay. There was no requirement that the employer pay a minimum sum. The tribunal had to assess the loss or detriment suffered by the employee and fix compensation accordingly, subject to the statutory cap. It did not have the right to order that no compensation should be payable, so where it was satisfied that there had been no loss or detriment, it was to make a nominal award. The issue of compensation would be remitted to the tribunal (paras 30-34).

TOAL v GB OILS LTD [2013] I.R.L.R. 696, Mitting, J., EAT.

1018. Growth and Infrastructure Act 2013 9 (c.27)–Commencement No.3 and Savings Order

THE GROWTH AND INFRASTRUCTURE ACT 2013 (COMMENCEMENT NO.3 AND SAVINGS) ORDER 2013, SI 2013/SI 2013/1766 (C.72); made under the Growth and Infrastructure Act 2013 s.35. Commencement details: bringing into force various provisions of the 2013 Act on September 1, 2013 and October 1, 2013.; .

This Order brings into force on September 1, 2013 the Growth and Infrastructure Act 2013 s.31, which amends the Employment Rights Act 1996 in order to create the new employment status of employee shareholder.

1019. Immunities–Diplomatic immunity–Discrimination–Former diplomat claiming residual immunity from liability for discrimination and harassment claims by former domestic servant–Whether employment of domestic servant amounting to act in exercise of diplomatic function

[Diplomatic Privileges Act 1964 (c.81) s.2; Vienna Convention on Diplomatic Relations 1961 Art.39(2).]

The former diplomat first appellant (X) appealed against a finding that he was liable for acts of discrimination against the respondent employee (T). X had been employed in a diplomatic role as First Secretary to the Sudanese Embassy. His post ended in December 2007, but T had worked for him as a domestic servant until May 2008. She subsequently claimed against X and his wife alleging direct race discrimination and harassment, harassment on grounds of her religion and sexual harassment. The claim was undefended and the employment tribunal found T s allegations proved against X and his wife and ordered them to pay compensation. X submitted that he had diplomatic immunity in respect of the acts complained of, so that the tribunal had erred in law in hearing and determining the claim against him when it had no jurisdiction to do so, pursuant to the Diplomatic Privileges Act 1964 s.2. He contended that the residual diplomatic immunity conferred upon him by the Vienna Convention on Diplomatic Relations 1961 art.39(2) in respect of acts performed in the exercise of his functions, even after he had left the United Kingdom, should be extended to acts done in respect of domestic servants engaged to support a diplomat whilst in his post. T argued that the employment of a domestic servant in a diplomat's private household was not capable of being an exercise of a diplomat's functions.

Held: Appeal dismissed. The Convention drew a clear distinction between functions performed as a member of the mission and other functions performed by a diplomat whilst present in the receiving state. Since immunity was no longer necessary to respect the diplomatic purpose of the mission once the diplomat had retired from his post, but continued by way only of a residual protection, it should be construed no more widely than the words required. Whatever was a function had to be closely related to those matters specifically identified as functions within the Convention, which left little scope for the act of employing a domestic servant to be part of the function of the diplomat in his mission. However, some matters ancillary to the mission's central functions would be included in the protection such as entertaining nationals of the receiving state and employing staff to facilitate that. The employment by a diplomat of another to provide personal service to him whilst engaged in his mission might therefore attract protection as a function of the mission. There was a spectrum. The employment of a domestic worker who performed no task outside the diplomat's home was unlikely to be an act performed in the exercise of a diplomat's functions. There was a clear distinction between the acts of a domestic servant and someone working as a personal assistant, whose job was dealing with official and personal correspondence and managing a diplomat's diary and travel arrangements. The distinction was between acts allegedly committed which were performed in furtherance of the diplomatic functions, such that they were in law the acts of the sending state, and other acts: the former were official acts whereas all other acts were private acts for which residual immunity was not available. The question was whether the act of employment was official or private, *Wokuri v Kassam* [2012] EWHC 105 (Ch), [2013] Ch. 80, [2012] C.L.Y. 1076 applied. In the case of a claim made under the discrimination statutes the contract of employment was a necessary passport to the assertion of the rights relied on. In the instant case, the act complained of was centrally the act of discrimination alleged. It could not be sensibly argued that acts of that nature could be regarded as acts carried out in the exercise of the functions of the mission. Accordingly, residual diplomatic immunity did not extend to X (see paras 29-32, 35-36 of judgment).

ABUSABIB v TADDESE [2013] I.C.R. 603, Langstaff, J. (President), EAT.

1020. Immunities–Judicial proceedings immunity–Witnesses–Allegation that employer had breached implied contractual term not to damage relationship of trust and confidence by procuring false evidence from witness

The appellant headteacher (S) appealed against a decision ([2013] I.C.R. 738, [2013] 8 C.L. 125) refusing to allow her to amend her form ET1. S was a non-white British citizen of Indian origin. She had been appointed headteacher of a school maintained by the respondent local authority. During her first year, there were serious difficulties in her relationships with parents, staff and governors, although she had had a good working relationship with the school business manager and clerk to the governing body (H). In June 2010, she received a petition, expressed to constitute a vote of no confidence in her. The local authority appointed an independent investigator, who expressed serious concerns about the school and recommended that S be removed from her post pending the outcome of the review. S therefore took voluntary paid leave. The investigator's final report identified several serious problems concerning S's performance. In September 2010, S issued her ET1, complaining of race discrimination, harassment and victimisation. She telephoned H to ask if she would be a witness for her. H replied with a text message indicating that she had been instructed to have no contact with S. On January 31, 2012 the local authority served a witness statement from H. A few weeks later, S wrote to the chair of the governing body indicating that she felt she had no alternative but to resign. She sought to amend her ET1 to complain that the local authority had placed undue pressure on H to produce a witness statement containing false or otherwise inaccurate evidence and in doing so had breached the implied contractual term of mutual trust and confidence. The EAT refused to allow the amendment because judicial proceedings immunity covered all the local authority's activities in gathering evidence for the purpose of defeating S's discrimination claim. The issue was whether judicial proceedings immunity applied.

Held: Appeal allowed. It was well established that no action in defamation could be brought against a witness for anything he said in evidence before a court or tribunal. There had been several unsuccessful attempts to outflank that rule, but the instant court had not been shown any case in which a claim for breach of contract had been held to fall within the rule (see paras 21-22, 28-37 of judgment). The broad statement of principle of Auld J at para.17 of *Heath v Commissioner of Police of the Metropolis* [2004] EWCA Civ 943, [2005] I.C.R. 329, [2004] C.L.Y. 1221 could not be taken literally. For example, the immunity from liability in negligence given to advocates conducting and preparing for court proceedings had been abolished and an expert witness no longer enjoyed immunity from suit for negligence in relation to an expert report prepared for the purpose of litigation or in relation to evidence that he gave in litigation, *Saif Ali v Sydney Mitchell & Co* [1980] A.C. 198, [1978] C.L.Y. 2323, *Arthur JS Hall & Co v Simons* [2002] 1 A.C. 615, [2000] C.L.Y. 4269 and *Smart v Forensic Science Service Ltd* [2013] EWCA Civ 783, [2013] P.N.L.R. 32 followed. In those circumstances, it could no longer be said that immunity from civil suit attached to anything said or done by anybody in the course of judicial proceedings whatever the nature of the claim made in respect of such behaviour or statement, *Heath* not followed (paras 43-46). The core immunity related to the giving of evidence and its rationale was to ensure that persons who might be witnesses in future cases would not be deterred from giving evidence by fear of being sued for what they said in court. The core immunity also included statements of case and other documents placed before the court. It extended only to that which was necessary to prevent the core immunity from being outflanked. Whether something was necessary was to be decided by reference to what was practically necessary. Where the gist of the cause of action was not the allegedly false statement itself, but was based on things that would not form part of the evidence in a judicial enquiry, there was no necessity to extend the immunity. In such cases, the principle that a wrong should not be without a remedy prevailed. The key point was that an action would be allowed to proceed if it was not brought on or in respect of any evidence given, *Lincoln v Daniels* [1962] 1 Q.B. 237, [1961] C.L.Y. 4999, *Taylor v Director of the Serious Fraud Office* [1999] 2 A.C. 177, [1998] C.L.Y. 1768, *Darker v Chief Constable of West Midlands* [2001] 1 A.C. 435, [2000] C.L.Y. 4543 and *Roy v Prior* [1971] A.C. 470, [1970] C.L.Y. 1040 followed (paras 47-67). S's claim was not based on anything that H might or might not say to the employment tribunal. It was based on what happened outside the tribunal, particularly the means by which the local authority procured H to give the statement, which was a freestanding act. While alleged untruths in H's witness statement might help S to prove the allegation that undue pressure was applied, the complaint was not about the content of the statement but the means by which it was procured. Judicial proceedings immunity did not apply (paras 70-73).

SINGH v READING BC; *sub nom.* SINGH v MOORLANDS PRIMARY SCHOOL GOVERNING BODY, [2013] EWCA Civ 909, [2013] 1 W.L.R. 3052, Maurice Kay, L.J. (VP, CA Civ), CA (Civ Div).

1021. Jobseekers (Back to Work Schemes) Act 2013 (C.17)

This Act makes provision about the effect of certain provisions relating to participation in a scheme designed to assist persons to obtain employment and about notices relating to participation in such a scheme.

This Act received Royal Assent on March 26, 2013.

1022. National minimum wage–Domestic workers–Live-in housekeepers–Application of exemption in reg.2(2)(a)(ii) National Minimum Wage Regulations 1999–Determination of whether worker treated as family member–Meaning of "the sharing of tasks"

[National Minimum Wage Regulations 1999 (SI 1999/584) reg.2(2)(a)(ii).]

The appellant migrant workers (N and U) appealed against a decision of the Employment Appeal Tribunal ([2012] I.C.R. 487, [2012] C.L.Y. 1111) that they were not entitled to be paid the national minimum wage. The central issue in each case was whether N and U fell within the National Minimum Wage Regulations 1999 reg.2(2)(a)(ii) and whether the tribunal had correctly construed the phase "the sharing of tasks" in that provision. N had been employed by the first respondent family for nine years as a housekeeper and child minder. She lived in their home with no deductions from her pay for accommodation and did the bulk of the household work. The tribunal found that she was free to take meals and watch television with the family, that cooking and clearing up after meals was shared with them, that she spent time beyond the scope of her duties with the children, and that her work was therefore not defined as work for the purposes of the Regulations. U lived with the second respondent family. Cooking, washing up and laundry tasks were shared between the adults of the family, including U. She performed other household tasks and helped out on trips by looking after the smaller children. The tribunal found that because she was free to decline family leisure trips, the reason for inviting her was because she was seen as being part of the family, not because the family wished to make use of her services and that she was therefore exempted from receiving the national minimum wage. N and U submitted that the exclusionary provisions in reg.2(2) should be narrowly construed as applying to au pairs living with a family and sharing the household tasks in return for improving their language skills, and not as applying to domestic workers whose employment was specifically to relieve the family of most of its household tasks.

Held: Appeals dismissed. (1) For the exemption in reg.2(2) to apply, the work had to relate "to the employer's family household" and the work had to be done in the context of that household. The central requirement was that the worker had to be treated as a member of the family. That requirement involved looking at the provision of accommodation and meals. The test for accommodation was more about how it was allocated than a requirement that it be of a particular standard (see paras 36-37, 39-40 of judgment). The use in reg.2(2) of the word "task" instead of "work" was not significant; "task" was commonly used to describe domestic duties in the "family household" and its use did not lead to the conclusion that the provision could only be concerned with chores within the home falling outside the scope of the paid duties of a worker (para.41). There was no requirement for the worker and the family members to split the work equally between them. A person receiving free accommodation and meals might be expected to perform a larger share. What mattered was whether the work was done in a context in which the worker was treated as a family member rather than as a domestic servant. Therefore the way in which household tasks were shared and leisure activities organised was relevant (para.42). (2) In the instant cases, the respective tribunals had taken the correct approach and included the correct considerations in their reasoning. They had addressed the statutory test, looked at the manner in which tasks and leisure activities were shared and formed a judgement on whether N and U were treated as family members. However, they had been wrong to suggest that, in assessing whether a worker was treated as a family member, the extent of the work done under their contract of employment could be ignored. Onerous and extensive demands upon a worker would reach a point of being inconsistent with their being treated as family members. It would be an abuse to argue that the exemption was satisfied where only a handful of tasks were left outside the employment and shared within the family. Tribunals needed to be astute when assessing whether an exemption was being used as a device for obtaining cheap domestic labour (paras 45-48).

NAMBALAT v TAHER; UDIN v CHAMSI-PASHA, [2012] EWCA Civ 1249, [2013] I.C.R. 1024, Pill, L.J., CA (Civ Div).

1023. NHS employees–Remuneration–Part-time employee moving to lower-paid full-time training post–Extent of pay protection

The appellant doctor (V) appealed against a decision ([2011] EWCA Civ 1129) that, in moving from a part-time post in the NHS to a lower-paid full-time training post, she was entitled to pay protection only in respect of the hours worked in her previous post and not for the full hours worked in her new post. V had worked at hospital practitioner grade, a part-time position where she worked for two half-day sessions per week. Her pay was calculated by the number of sessions worked. She moved to a full-time, 40-hour per week training post with the respondent NHS trust which had significantly lower pay, calculated as an annual figure. The NHS Terms and Conditions of Service para.132 provided that where a practitioner took a training appointment in a lower grade, she would continue to be paid on the incremental point in the pay scale she had reached in her previous appointment. The trust considered that her pay should only be protected to the extent of the two sessions per week she had worked. The Employment Appeal Tribunal found that payment protection applied for the full time worked at the lower grade. The Court of Appeal held that payment protection only applied to five sessions per week, the maximum she could have worked as a hospital practitioner.

Held: Appeal allowed. (1) The issue had to be approached by applying ordinary principles of construction. The "incremental point" in para.132 was clearly a reference to the relevant point in the scale for the practitioner's grade. Since, for V's grade, that point was expressed in sessional rates some means had to be found to convert those rates into a form which could be applied to the different terms of her training post, in which her periods of work were measured in hours, not sessions. The most obvious way of doing that was by conversion of the sessional rates to hourly rates. Although it might be counter-intuitive that the rates should not be limited by reference to the number of sessions which were, or could have been, worked in the former post, there was nothing in the wording of para.132 which could be relied on to support such a limitation. Nor was there such a limitation in the relevant interpretation provision: para.135(a) simply confirmed that no distinction was to be made in the application of the rates between part-time and full-time practitioners. The order of the EAT would be restored; in accordance with that the case would be remitted to the employment tribunal (see paras 26-29 of judgment). (2) It was disturbing that a condition designed to confer important rights on employees should be so obscure. The differences of view between experienced judges in the Court of Appeal was testament enough that the condition was not well drafted and required reconsideration (para.21).

VERMA v BARTS AND THE LONDON NHS TRUST; *sub nom.* BARTS AND THE LONDON NHS TRUST v VERMA, [2013] UKSC 20, [2013] I.C.R. 727, Lord Hope (Deputy President), SC.

1024. Parental leave–Unpaid leave

THE PARENTAL LEAVE (EU DIRECTIVE) REGULATIONS 2013, SI 2013/283; made under the European Communities Act 1972 s.2. In force: March 8, 2013; .

These Regulations implement Directive 2010/18 on the revised framework agreement on parental leave. They amend provisions relating to parental leave in the Employment Rights Act 1996 and the Maternity and Parental Leave etc. Regulations 1999 to: increase the amount of unpaid parental leave available to parents under the Maternity and Parental Leave Regulations 1999 (as amended) from 13 weeks to 18 weeks; and extend the right to request flexible working to employed agency workers who are returning from parental leave.

1025. Protected disclosures–Detriment–Claim by general practitioner against health board under Employment Rights Act 1996–Causation–Meaning of "subjected to" and "failure to act" within s.47B

[Employment Rights Act 1996 (c.18) Pt IVA, s.43K, s.47B.]

The appellant health board appealed against an employment tribunal's refusal to strike out a claim by the respondent general practitioner (F) that she had been subjected to a detriment in respect of a protected disclosure. F had disclosed concerns that another partner in her practice had wrongly prescribed a particular drug. F claimed that her partners had caused her detriment as a result of the disclosure, and that the board had also acted, and failed to act, so as to subject her to a detriment. She brought a claim under the whistleblower provisions of the Employment Rights Act 1996 Pt IVA. The board's strike out application was refused as the tribunal considered that the matter could only be resolved by hearing evidence, including evidence on the issue of causation. The issue centred on the precise meaning of s.47B of the Act, which provided that a "worker has the right not to be subjected to any detriment by any act, or any deliberate failure to act, by his employer done on the ground that the worker has made a protected disclosure". F constituted a worker within s.43K for the purposes of her claim. The board contended that it was F's partners who had subjected her to the detriment and that the critical words within s.47B were "subjected to" and "failure to act". The board argued that Parliament had chosen not to adopt the more general word "caused" rather than "subjected to", which was specific and connoted wilfulness, a capacity to control events and to bestow on the person subject to them the consequences of the act or omission.

Held: Appeal dismissed. (1) The meaning of "subjected to" as advanced by the board, that it had to be shown that the board could control what had happened to F, was not accepted, *Advocate General for Scotland v MacDonald* [2003] UKHL 34, [2004] 1 All E.R. 339, [2003] C.L.Y. 1309 followed. That argument might be correct to the extent that the word "subjected" might have been deliberately chosen as a word of causation, equivalent in meaning to "cause", but not using that precise word because the statute had to deal not only with an "act", which would almost by definition be capable of "causing" a detriment, but also with a "deliberate failure to act". If a course of events harmful to a worker was ongoing, a failure to stop it could amount to a deliberate failure to act. However, it might be difficult to talk of the failure as having "caused" the ongoing detriment, as that was being caused by the ongoing course of events. Linguistically, "subjecting to" better conveyed the sense of what the legislature wished to achieve. The word "subjected" therefore had the force of causation and had been adopted by Parliament as a suitable alternative to cover positive acts and omissions to act. It did not have within it any connotation of wilfulness. A deliberate failure to act had to be seen in context. In the instant case, that context was the relationship between a doctor and the board. The first part of the relationship was contractual; the second part depended on the statutory provisions under which the board operated. If the board had a discretion to act within the contract, and if the statutory provisions permitted it to take actions ancillary to the discharge of its duties, then it had the power to do so within the broader sense argued by F, namely that it extended to the more general sense of being legally entitled to do what might have been done but was not. It did not necessarily extend to cover a failure to fulfil an expectation that the board would act in a particular way. On that basis, the board would have a choice as to how it behaved. If it chose not to take action when it could legitimately have done so, that was capable of being a deliberate failure to act. If it was established that it subjected F to any detriment, she would succeed in a claim if it was also shown that the board had deliberately decided not to act as it had on the ground that she had made a protected disclosure. The answers to the questions of causation and of the "reason why" were heavily dependent on the particular facts. The tribunal had to take F's allegations at their reasonable highest. It had correctly focused on the words of the statute and asked not whether it was likely that F would make out her case but whether, legally, the alleged facts taken at their highest in her favour might be such that she could make out her case. On that basis, the tribunal was right to reject the board's application (see paras 12-19, 25-32 of judgment). (2) (Obiter) Strike out applications might save time, expense and anxiety and might succeed in a proper case. However, in a case which was always likely to be fact-sensitive, such as one involving discrimination or the closely allied ground of public interest disclosure, the circumstances in which it would be possible to strike out a claim were likely to be rare. It was generally better to determine a case on the evidence in light of all the facts. At the conclusion of the evidence gathering it was likely to be much clearer whether there was truly a point of law in issue (para.33).

ABERTAWE BRO MORGANNWG UNIVERSITY HEALTH BOARD v FERGUSON [2013] I.C.R. 1108, Langstaff, J. (President), EAT.

1026. Protected disclosures–Detriment–Decision of Chief Adjudicator of Traffic Parking Tribunal not to allocate cases to particular adjudicator–Whether made in execution of judicial functions

[Crown Proceedings Act 1947 (c.44) s.2(5); Employment Rights Act 1996 (c.18) s.47B; Civil Procedure Rules 1998 (SI 1998/3132) r.2.5(1).]

The appellant parking adjudicator (E) appealed against a decision of the employment tribunal to strike out his claim that he had been subjected to a detriment under the Employment Rights Act 1996 s.47B by the respondent Joint Committee. The Joint Committee was a consortium of local authorities responsible for traffic enforcement. It had appointed E as a parking adjudicator to hear appeals in respect of penalty charges relating to road traffic contraventions. He determined appeals either at oral hearings or by considering written representations (postal cases). In June 2011, the Chief Adjudicator of the Traffic Penalty Tribunal ceased to allocate personal hearings to E because of concerns about his conduct of them. In August 2011, E complained about that in a protected disclosure to the Joint Committee, but the Chief Adjudicator's concerns were found to be justified. The Chief Adjudicator then asked E not to decide any further postal cases pending a meeting between them to address his "judicial performance and misconduct". E lodged his complaint that he had been subjected to a detriment under s.47B because of the protected disclosure which he had made. The tribunal struck out E's claim on the basis that it had no reasonable prospect of success. It held that the decisions of the Chief Adjudicator not to allocate personal and postal cases to E were taken in the exercise of judicial functions, in respect of which she was entitled to judicial immunity. E submitted that (1) a decision to allocate or not to allocate an appeal to an adjudicator was not a decision made in the exercise of judicial functions; (2) the decision not to allocate him any personal or postal cases was not a listing or allocation decision, but a decision to suspend him from work.

Held: Appeal dismissed. (1) It was long-established that a decision about whether to allocate an appeal to an adjudicator was, in principle, made in the exercise of judicial functions. The Crown Proceedings Act 1947 s.2(5) provided a defence to a claim brought by an aggrieved litigant as a result of listing errors. Decisions about listing and allocation could have a significant impact upon the judicial determination of a dispute. For example, a decision as to when a case might be heard and as to the time available for it to be heard might affect the evidence upon which the parties might be able to rely. The knowledge and experience of a judge or group of judges in particular classes of case might require such cases to be allocated to him or to them for their just and efficient determination. Many listing and allocation decisions were made by judges and clearly had to attract immunity. It would be surprising if such decisions did not attract immunity if made by a listing officer. Such decisions were not of a purely formal or administrative character and so were not authorised to be performed by a court officer under CPR r.2.5(1). Listing and allocation remained the prerogative of judges, even though the task was performed by listing officers in practice (see paras 15-16 of judgment). (2) It was accepted that taking disciplinary steps against an adjudicator would not be in the exercise of the Chief Adjudicator's judicial functions. It was clear that the Chief Adjudicator had made the decision not to allocate any further cases to E in the context of addressing issues of "performance and misconduct". A possible interpretation of those words was that the Chief Adjudicator took the decision in the context of disciplinary action which was not undertaken in the exercise of judicial functions. A decision not to allocate cases to a judge was sometimes taken pending consideration of a disciplinary complaint against him. In the case of a complaint which might call into question his suitability to remain in office or to continue to try cases of a particular class, the decision would normally be taken to maintain public confidence in the administration of justice and to avoid any litigant whose case was determined by that judge having cause to challenge his treatment on the ground that he had heard the case. Non-allocation would, in those circumstances, clearly be a decision taken in the exercise of judicial functions. If that was the Chief Adjudicator's purpose, judicial immunity applied to her decision. Even if her decision was taken as a free-standing disciplinary measure, and even if it was taken for the improper purpose of subjecting E to a detriment because of his protected disclosure, it would still be covered by judicial immunity. The principle of immunity for the exercise of judicial functions was ultimately a policy decision which had to be upheld, even in extreme circumstances, *Sirros v Moore* [1975] Q.B. 118, [1974] C.L.Y. 2974 applied. The judge had been correct to find that the Chief Adjudicator had taken her decision not to allocate further personal or postal cases to E in the exercise of judicial functions in her capacity as a judicial officer holder. For that reason, it was not open to an employment tribunal to determine that the Joint Committee had subjected E to a detriment contrary to s.47B (paras 17-19).

ENGEL v JOINT COMMITTEE FOR PARKING AND TRAFFIC REGULATION OUTSIDE LONDON (PATROL) [2013] I.C.R. 1086, Mitting, J., EAT.

1027. Protected disclosures–Detriment–Post-termination disclosures–Whether allowed if disclosures led to detrimental treatment–Meaning of s.47B Employment Rights Act 1996

[Employment Rights Act 1996 (c.18) s.43A, s.43C, s.47B, s.230.]

The appellant (O) appealed against a decision of the employment tribunal that he could not bring a complaint of detrimental treatment under the Employment Rights Act 1996 s.47B based on a protected disclosure he had made after he left his employment with the respondent solicitors (B). O had been employed by B for over a year. He sought to rely on a letter before claim to B and a report to the Legal Complaints Service as protected disclosures, which had led to allegations of forgery and dishonesty made by B against O, and in turn led to O being investigated by the Solicitors Regulatory Authority. The issue for the tribunal was whether O could bring a complaint of detrimental treatment under the Employment Rights Act 1996 s.47B on the ground that he made a protected disclosure after the termination of his employment with B. The tribunal held that he could not. O submitted that there was nothing in the statutory wording that limited it to protected disclosures made during the course of the relevant employment.

Held: Appeal allowed and case remitted to a different employment tribunal. A person making a s.47B complaint could rely on post-termination detriment to complete the statutory tort, *Rhys-Harper v Relaxion Group Plc* [2003] UKHL 33, [2003] 4 All E.R. 1113, [2003] C.L.Y. 1315 and *Woodward v Abbey National Plc (No.1)* [2006] EWCA Civ 822, [2006] 4 All E.R. 1209, [2006] C.L.Y. 1398 followed. The only question in the instant case was whether the protected disclosure itself might occur after termination of the relevant employment. The possibility was not excluded in *Woodward*, but the issue did not arise in that case. The words "worker" and "employer" were defined in s.230 as those who were, or had been, in a contractual relationship of service or core services. O and B were so related. As the detriment had to occur and be causatively linked to the protected disclosure, it followed that it had to come later in time, and as the detriment might arise post-termination, there was no reason for limiting the disclosure temporally to the duration of the employment. The fact that the present tense was used in s.43A to s.43C made no difference, as those provisions were concerned only with the quality of the disclosures when they were made. As a matter of pure interpretation of the statute, post-termination disclosures could be relied upon if they led to detrimental treatment. That accorded with the legislative purpose of protection for whistleblowers and was entirely consistent with recent authority, *Relaxion* and *Woodward* applied. The employment tribunal had been wrong to decline jurisdiction to consider the s.47B complaint for the reasons it gave (see paras 4-9 of judgment).

ONYANGO v BERKELEY (T/A BERKELEY SOLICITORS) [2013] I.R.L.R. 338, Judge Peter Clark, EAT.

1028. Race discrimination–Agency workers–Agency workers banned from working on principal's site–Whether limitation period ran from date of ban

[Race Relations Act 1976 (c.74) s.7, s.68(1).]

The appellants (O) appealed against a decision of the Employment Appeal Tribunal that their claims of racial discrimination on the part of the respondent companies had been brought out of time. The first respondent (T) was a construction company which employed temporary agency workers through the second and third respondent employment agencies (C and M). On April 6, 2008, O were engaged through C, but when they arrived at T's site, they were advised that no appropriate work was available. T claimed that there had been a mix-up in the bookings. T alleged that O responded to the supervisor who turned them away by behaving in an aggressive and intimidating manner. O returned to the site the following day and were told that they were banned. On April 18, O obtained another engagement at the site through M but, again, T told them that they were banned. After April 18, they made no further application for work on the site. O claimed that the ban was racially motivated. The EAT found that O were contract workers for the purposes of the Race Relations Act 1976 s.7, but held that the ban was a one-off decision and the last act complained of was on April 18, 2008, meaning that the complaint had been brought outside the three-month limitation period. O submitted that there was a distinction between one-off acts and continuing acts and that a ban was an ongoing state of affairs, even if there was no continuing relationship with the party imposing it. T argued that in the absence of any ongoing relationship or contract, to which any policy or rule could attach, the ban was "the act complained of", under s.68(1) of the Act.

Held: Appeal dismissed. T's submissions were substantially accepted. The "act complained of" was the ban imposed by T in April 2008. In the terms of s.7, it was a ban by a principal on contract workers. That was a one-off act and was equivalent, in that respect, to dismissal of an employee by an employer. It terminated the relationship between the principal and the contract workers and time ran from the date the ban was imposed, just as time began to run from the termination of the employment in *Barclays Bank Plc v Kapur* [1991] 2 A.C. 355, [1991] C.L.Y. 1652, *Calder v James Finlay Corp* [1989] I.C.R. 157 and *Tyagi v BBC World Service* [2001] EWCA Civ 549, [2001] I.R.L.R. 465, [2001] C.L.Y. 2299. In the absence of a continuing relationship between the parties, there was no continuing state of affairs on which a complaint could be based, *Kapur, Calder* and *Tyagi* applied (see paras 35-37 of judgment). Other decisions had considered the distinction between a one-off act and a continuing act, but in the instant case, there was no suggestion that there had been a reconsideration of the ban in the way that reconsideration of alleged acts of discrimination was contemplated in *Cast v Croydon College* [1998] I.C.R. 500, [1998] C.L.Y. 2200, *Cast* considered. The ban was imposed on April 7 and subsequent statements on April 8 and 18 were reiterations of that. There having been no further attempt by O to work on T's site and hence no need for a reaction to such an attempt, it was not necessary to consider what would have been the position if there had been. The latest date on which time could begin to run was April 18 and it had been necessary to make a claim within three months of that date (paras 38-40).

OKORO v TAYLOR WOODROW CONSTRUCTION LTD, [2012] EWCA Civ 1590, [2013] I.C.R. 580, Pill, L.J., CA (Civ Div).

1029. Race discrimination–Continuing acts–Claim against General Medical Council and Care Quality Commission–Test set out in Hendricks v Commissioner of Police of the Metropolis [2003] IRLR 96 inappropriate for claims against regulatory bodies

[Equality Act 2010 (c.15) s.53, s.120(7); Senior Courts Act 1981 (c.54) s.31; Employment Appeal Tribunal Rules 1993 (SI 1993/2854) r.3(10).]

The appellant doctor (J) appealed against the striking-out of his discrimination claims against the respondents. J ran a business providing medical services. The Care Quality Commission alleged that the business was not appropriately registered and J was invited to attend an interview. He declined and the General Medical Council made an interim order suspending him from practice. At a further review it decided to continue the suspension. The GMC also referred the matter to the police. J brought judicial review proceedings against the GMC but they were dismissed. He also brought claims of race and disability discrimination against the GMC, its 25 trustees, the Commission and the Secretary of State for Health. An employment tribunal struck out his claims, finding that it had no jurisdiction to hear them as they were out of time and J had an alternative remedy by way of judicial review. J's appeal to the Employment Appeal Tribunal was rejected at the sift stage, save for one issue concerning continuing acts of discrimination which was referred to a preliminary hearing. J sought a hearing under the Employment Appeal Tribunal Rules 1993 r.3(10).

Held: Rule 3(10) application dismissed, preliminary hearing determined in favour of respondents. (1) The question for the EAT on the r.3 application was whether there were any reasonable grounds in the appeal, *Haritaki v South East England Development Agency* [2008] I.R.L.R. 945, [2009] C.L.Y. 1192 considered. The employment judge had applied the correct test, and had regard to the relevant provisions of the Equality Act 2010, including s.53. He was also correct to strike out J's claim against the 25 trustees. J had misunderstood the nature of corporate liability. The judge was correct when he stated that the acts complained of were primarily acts of a body corporate. Liability could attach to individuals who had aided a corporation in its acts, but J had been unable to show that any of the named trustees had aided the particular acts of which he complained. J's claims therefore had no reasonable prospect of success (see paras 35-41 of judgment). (2) J's claims were subject to the exception in s.120(7) of the 2010 Act because he had the right to bring proceedings for judicial review. Although that had originally been a common law remedy, the right was now controlled by the Senior Courts Act 1981 s.31, which prescribed rules for running the proceedings and the remedies available. It was therefore aptly described as "arising under an enactment", *Tariquez-Zaman v General*

Medical Council considered and *Khan v General Medical Council* [1996] I.C.R. 1032, [1995] C.L.Y. 2027 applied (paras 41-44). (3) The question on the preliminary hearing was whether the GMC's decisions amounted to a continuing act. The rather liberal approach to continuing acts in cases such as *Commissioner of Police of the Metropolis v Hendricks* [2002] EWCA Civ 1686, [2003] 1 All E.R. 654, [2003] C.L.Y. 1298 was inappropriate for cases of continuing-act allegations against a regulatory body, *British Medical Association v Chaudhary (No.1)* [2003] EWCA Civ 645, [2003] I.C.R. 1510, [2003] C.L.Y. 1294 applied and *Hendricks* not applied. The GMC's decisions did not represent a continuing act. The removal of J's registration to practice had been appropriate. J's case against the GMC had therefore correctly been struck out as having no reasonable prospects of success, as had his case against the Commission. His claim against the secretary of state did not fall under s.53 of the 2010 Act and the tribunal therefore had no jurisdiction to hear it (paras 45-49).

JOOSTE v GENERAL MEDICAL COUNCIL [2012] Eq. L.R. 1048, Judge McMullen Q.C., EAT.

1030. **Race discrimination–Detriment–Allegations of discrimination by barrister against chambers–Detrimental treatment on grounds of race**

[Disability Discrimination Act 1995 (c.50); Race Relations Act 1976 (c.74).]

The appellant barrister (B) appealed against the decision of an employment tribunal dismissing her claim of race and disability discrimination against the respondents (S). S were the three successive heads of chambers and the senior clerk at chambers where B was a tenant. B considered that her practice had not flourished as she had been subjected to direct discrimination, victimisation and harassment contrary to the Race Relations Act 1976 and the Disability Discrimination Act 1995, and she brought claims consisting of 32 complaints. Complaint 8 concerned the alleged failure to prevent, abate or condemn the racist conduct of three clerks in chambers in 2000 and against one of the clerks in separate incidents in 2004 and 2006. The tribunal held in relation to that complaint, that for there to have been a detriment under the 1976 Act, there had to be some factor operating on the mind of the decision-maker, whether consciously or unconsciously, which related to the person alleging the detriment, or at least a specific defined group of which she was a member. That feature was absent in B's case and therefore, none of the decisions relating to the handling of those episodes constituted detrimental treatment of B. It held that the decision not to dismiss the clerks was not taken on grounds of race. Complaint 9 alleged a failure to provide equal opportunities training for the clerks from the outset of their employment onwards, to monitor their conduct and performance or to appoint an equal opportunities officer and or committee in chambers. The tribunal found that although management over the period in question fell short of best practice the explanation for the way in which those matters was handled overall was not in any sense targeted at B or black and ethnic minority members and did not include any element of detrimental treatment of B on grounds of race. Complaint 10 concerned the appointment of the three clerks as B's clerks. The tribunal held that that there was no basis to conclude that B was consciously or unconsciously, given any of those clerks as an act of detrimental treatment on grounds of race, related to a disability or by way of victimisation. The tribunal dismissed all the complaints. Permission to appeal was granted only in relation to complaints 8, 9 and10. B submitted that the tribunal had erred in its consideration as to whether S subjected B to a detriment. B argued that the tribunal erred in failing to find that the decision not to dismiss the clerks involved in the first incident in 2000 was taken on grounds of race.

Held: Appeal dismissed. (1) There was no basis on which to conclude that the decision not to dismiss the clerks was taken on the grounds of race. The tribunal did not err in concluding that S had not failed to act on grounds of race (see paras 98, 102 of judgment. (2) In relation to complaint 9, the tribunal made findings that positive efforts had been made, and, in so far as, by modern best standards, there were shortcomings in what was implemented and achieved, the explanations for that were not antipathy, but a lack of appreciation of the full extent of actions that such standards required, issues of resource and time, the fact that the matter was handled "in-house", and views taken about priority areas for action given the profile of that particular set of chambers. In the light of those findings of fact the tribunal had not erred in concluding that the explanation for the way in which equal opportunities matters were handled did not include any element of detrimental treatment on grounds of race. It rightly considered whether the reason that that state of affairs existed involved discriminatory grounds or other reasons, *Qureshi v Newham LBC* [1991] I.R.L.R. 264, [1991] C.L.Y. 1655 considered (para.103). (3) With regard to complaint 10, the tribunal's finding that there was no basis to conclude that B was given any of the clerks as a result of a decision taken whether consciously or unconsciously on grounds of race was not reached in error of law or perverse (para.104).

BIJLANI v STEWART [2013] Eq. L.R. 80, Slade, J. DBE, EAT.

1031. Race discrimination–Lists of issues–Employment tribunal's finding of race discrimination–Employer failing to reply to email–Whether matter properly defined as allegation for employment tribunal to consider

The appellant employer (T) appealed against a finding of the employment tribunal that a claim of direct race discrimination brought by the respondent (R) was well-founded in one respect, namely that in failing to reply to a specific email it had discriminated against R on the grounds of race. R, who was employed by T as a science teacher, had brought a claim of racial discrimination. As part of her complaint she made reference to writing an email to a member of staff (P) setting out her concerns and questions following a lesson observation where she had been marked as being unsatisfactory and she complained that she had not received a reply. P had forwarded the email to a senior member of staff who had advised him not to reply for fear that R would bring a complaint. The tribunal rejected all allegations of race discrimination except in respect of the failure to reply to the email finding that it was the fear of a race claim which prompted the failure to reply. T submitted that the tribunal's finding was procedurally unfair as the matter had not been identified by R as an alleged act of discrimination.

Held: Appeal allowed. The failure to reply to the email had never been properly or sufficiently raised by R as an allegation of race discrimination. R's further and better particulars had not alleged inconsistent treatment on the grounds of race and it had not been listed as an issue; it was important for tribunals to deal with complaints of less favourable treatment as defined by the applicant, *British Gas Services Ltd v McCaull* [2001] I.R.L.R. 60, [2001] C.L.Y. 2240 considered. If the question of replying to the email had truly been an issue and defined as such it would have been the subject of much more careful evidence and submissions. The issue was never properly before the tribunal and therefore the tribunal's finding of unlawful race discrimination would be set aside (see paras 29, 33-36 of judgment).

UNITED LEARINING TRUST v ROSE [2012] Eq. L.R. 1077, Judge David Richardson, EAT.

1032. Race discrimination–Migrant workers–Mistreatment of migrant domestic workers–Reason for mistreatment being worker's vulnerability–Whether vulnerability capable of amounting to race discrimination

In a lead case, the appellant (T), a migrant domestic worker, appealed against a decision that her mistreatment by the respondent employers (O), a wealthy married couple, did not amount to race discrimination. She also appealed against a refusal of a costs order in her favour. It was common ground that T, who was Nigerian, had been callously and systematically exploited by O. Mr O was also Nigerian, and his wife Ugandan. They had provided poor working and living conditions, subjected her to abuse, restricted her access to food, paid her less than the national minimum wage, imposed onerous working hours, failed to comply with statutory working time requirements, and failed to provide a written contract of employment. T put her case on the basis that she had been ill-treated on account of being Nigerian. Her hypothetical comparator was "a domestic worker of British national origin". The employment tribunal rejected the claim for both direct and indirect discrimination, finding that the correct comparator would be a migrant worker whose employment and residence in the United Kingdom was governed by immigration control and by the employment relationship itself. It found that there was no evidence or inference that O would have treated T differently had she not been Nigerian, and that the reason for the treatment was her status as a vulnerable migrant worker, reliant on O for continued employment and residence. Regarding costs, the tribunal had relied on *Walsall MBC v Sidhu* [1980] I.C.R. 519, [1980] C.L.Y. 903 as entitling it to refuse a costs order in T's favour on the ground that she had not personally incurred costs because her case had been funded by a publicly funded law centre. T submitted that the tribunal had departed from the authority of *Mehmet (t/a Rose Hotel Group) v Aduma* without any reasoned basis for doing so, and had erred in determining that immigration status was dissociable from nationality or origin.

Held: Appeal dismissed. (1) The *Mehmet* case did not have the same factual circumstances as those in the instant case and the tribunal below had, therefore, not been bound by it. In any event, *Mehmet* had been reached *per incuriam* because it had not properly applied the approach in *Wong v Igen Ltd (formerly Leeds Careers Guidance)* [2005] EWCA Civ 142, [2005] 3 All E.R. 812, [2005] C.L.Y. 1221 and *Madarassy v Nomura International Plc* [2007] EWCA Civ 33, [2007] I.C.R. 867, [2007] C.L.Y. 1401, *Mehmet* overruled, *Wong* and *Madarassy* considered (see paras 20-22 of judgment). (2) Where a tribunal identified a reason for treatment causing particular disadvantage, the focus of legal analysis had to be that reason. In the instant case, the tribunal had specifically found as a fact that which was not the reason, namely that T was Nigerian. If T's appeal was to succeed, she would have to satisfy the instant tribunal that that finding was plainly and obviously wrong. No part of T's exploitation had been inherently bound up with her race, but her race was strongly associated with her vulnerability. Vulnerability was not an attribute that was particular to any racial group. In the instant case, T had been vulnerable because of her poor socio-economic background, her lack of English, the absence of a support network, and the imbalance of power in her relationship with O. If the way she was treated arose from her vulnerability, the fact that she was subject to immigration control would be a mere contributing factor, rather than the reason for, her treatment. Vulnerability was not indissociably linked with migrant status, even though the latter contributed to the former. Therefore, the factual cause of T's unfavourable treatment was not indissociably linked to immigration status and the tribunal had not erred in concluding that there was no direct discrimination (paras 42-48, 57). (3) With regard to indirect discrimination, the tribunal had erred in its approach because it had gone straight to the question whether there was sufficient evidence to show relative disadvantage without identifying a "provision, criterion or practice" (PCP). A structured approach to assessing disadvantage had to be adopted: a PCP had to be identified and shown to have been applied. If it did not automatically demonstrate disadvantage to the claimant, the effect on the claimant as one member of a group had to be considered. That group had to be shown to be at a disadvantage by comparison with another group from different race or origin, and disadvantage had to be shown as real rather than statistical. In the instant case, although the tribunal had erred, its finding that there had been no indirect discrimination was valid. The PCP contended for by T, namely "mistreatment of migrant workers" was not acceptable. That was because, where the issue was whether mistreatment had been caused to a person because of the application of a PCP, it was pointless to argue that the PCP was the mistreatment. It would not be right to remit the case for the hearing of a PCP which had never, before the instant hearing, been part of T's case (paras 50-54, 57). (4) Properly interpreted, the Employment Tribunal Rules r.38(3) covered expense incurred by the law centre on T's behalf. *Sidhu*, although not overturned, was a case relating to historic statutory wording, and it could therefore only operate as persuasive authority, if at all. In the instant case, it was of no persuasive weight, *Sidhu* doubted (paras 58, 61-64, 67, 72-75).

TAIWO v OLAIGBE; ONU v AKWIWU [2013] I.C.R. 770, Langstaff, J. (President), EAT.

1033. Race discrimination–Sexual orientation discrimination–Police–Handling of complaints brought by gay officer of mixed race

The appellant commissioner appealed against a decision that the police were liable in respect of unlawful discrimination against the respondent police officer (M) on grounds of race and sexual orientation. M had been employed by the police as a detective constable. He was of mixed race and was gay. He made over 120 allegations of direct discrimination, harassment and victimisation on grounds of race and sexual orientation in relation to the police's handling of complaints he had made. Although some of the complaints had been brought to the tribunal out of time, the tribunal regarded most of them as relating to a continuing act by the police, and it extended time to bring claims. Two complaints relating to particular officers (X and Y) were brought out of time; the tribunal found that the claim regarding X was not part of an ongoing situation, meaning that it had no jurisdiction for that claim, but did extend time in relation to the claim regarding Y. M also alleged victimisation in respect of information regarding his claim obtained by a newspaper. The tribunal found that the information had been leaked by an employee of the police and that the police were vicariously liable for that. The commissioner argued that the tribunal had erred in (1) finding a prima facie case where the case was based solely on M's recollection, particularly as a psychiatrist had given evidence that M's perspective seemed exaggerated; (2) finding direct discrimination; (3) finding harassment; (4) finding victimisation; (5) extending time; (6) finding the police vicariously liable regarding the leak.

Held: Appeal dismissed. (1) The tribunal had had proper regard to the psychiatrist's evidence. There was nothing perverse about rejecting M's evidence on some allegations on the basis that the tribunal was not satisfied that he had an accurate reflection of certain events but accepting his evidence in respect of other allegations. The commissioner's submission was effectively that the tribunal should have ruled that it could not accept any evidence from M which was not corroborated; there was no foundation for that submission (see para.23 of judgment). (2) In relation to each allegation of direct discrimination, the tribunal had been entitled on the evidence to find that there was a prima facie case of discrimination in the police's approach to M's complaints, *Wong v Igen Ltd (formerly Leeds Careers Guidance)* [2005] EWCA Civ 142, [2005] 3 All E.R. 812, [2005] C.L.Y. 1221 considered. The exception to that was the tribunal's finding that an officer involved in M's complaint had been aggressive in tone to M because he was angry at criticism of himself in a letter sent by M; the tribunal had been entitled to find harassment and victimisation, but not direct discrimination (paras 24-48). (3) The tribunal had been aware of the test for harassment; it had been entitled to make all the findings of harassment that it had, having considered the evidence (para.53). (4) The tribunal had been aware of the test for victimisation and had been entitled to make its findings on the evidence (paras 54-68). (5) The case against Y, like that against X, was a stand-alone case not relating to M's day-to-day work. The tribunal's reasoning regarding the claim relating to X applied equally in Y's case, and the tribunal therefore also lacked jurisdiction to consider Y's claim (paras 70-71). In determining whether there had been a continuing act, although the tribunal had expressed itself when summarising continuing act by reference to the reporting wrongdoing policy and M had not complained that that policy had been applied in a discriminatory way, it was clear from its detailed examination of the individual complaints that it had had proper regard to all the evidence (para.73). M had set out in his witness statement the material facts of when he sought legal advice and his health and state of mind at the time. He had not been cross-examined on those matters. The tribunal had made findings of fact it was entitled to make on the evidence (para.74). (6) The commissioner's submission that the tribunal had failed to have regard to the obligation to prove at stage 1 of the two-stage *Igen* test the primary facts, in particular that the leaker was acting in the course of his employment, was rejected. The tribunal had been entirely satisfied on the evidence that on the balance of probabilities the information about M's case came from an officer working for the police. It had been entitled to find that the leak had come from an individual for whose actions the police were vicariously liable, given the detailed knowledge the journalist had had of the claim and of the police's potential defence (paras 81-83).

COMMISSIONER OF POLICE OF THE METROPOLIS v MAXWELL [2013] Eq. L.R. 680, Supperstone, J., EAT.

1034. Race discrimination–Time limits–Reasonableness of decision that claim presented out of time

The appellant (C) appealed against a decision of an employment judge that his claim of race discrimination against the first and second respondents (M and X) had been presented out of time and that it was not just and equitable to extend time. C, who was of Afro-Caribbean ethnicity, had been employed as a housing officer by M. X was his line manager. C issued his claim form on December 6, 2010. His allegations comprised a requirement in the form of a letter dated October 2, 2009 to attend a capability meeting, the holding of that meeting on January 21, 2010 and the issue of a warning on April 30, 2010 in respect of unsatisfactory performance. The employment judge identified the issues as whether any of the allegations of less favourable treatment had occurred after September 7, 2010 (which would lead to a finding that the claim had been brought in time), whether they comprised part of an act extending over a period that went beyond that date and, if the answers to those questions was no, whether it was just and equitable to extend time. C argued before the employment judge that he had been waiting for the outcome of his appeal against a decision dismissing a grievance that he had lodged with M, that that appeal had not been determined until November 2010 and that that matter formed part of an act extending over a period. The employment judge rejected that submission and found that C's allegations of less favourable treatment had all occurred before September 7, 2010. She also concluded that it would not be just and equitable to extend time. Among other things, she did not accept C's assertion that he had been advised by his trade union to postpone the filing of his claim. She also commented that, although medical reports indicated that he had been suffering from depression and anxiety, his state of health was not such as to prevent him from filing a claim within the time limit.

Held: Appeal dismissed. The employment judge had been entitled to reach the decision that she had. There was no need to specifically plead a continuing act; however, sufficient facts had to be pleaded from which it was clear that a continuing act was asserted. C's pleaded case was limited to the requirement to attend a capability meeting, the holding of that meeting on January 21, 2010 and the issue of a warning on April 30, 2010 in respect of his performance. There was no reference at all to C's grievance in the claim form. It was not for the employment tribunal to find a complaint that had not been pleaded. As to extending time, a very strong case was required to show that there had been a flawed exercise of discretion on its merits. In this case, the employment judge clearly exercised a discretion and weighed up various factors, including the balance of prejudice. It was impossible to say that her exercise of discretion was plainly wrong (see paras 48-50, 52, 57 of judgment).

CHIKWE v MOUCHEL GROUP PLC [2012] Eq. L.R. 1040, Judge Serota Q.C., EAT.

1035. Race discrimination–Victimisation–Dismissal following allegedly racist remark–Reason for dismissal

[Employment Equality (Religion or Belief) Regulations 2003 (SI 2003/1660) reg.3.]

The appellant employee (W) appealed against a decision ([2012] Eq. L.R. 392, [2012] C.L.Y. 1130) of the Employment Appeal Tribunal overturning a judgment by the employment tribunal which allowed her claim against the respondent employer (P) for unlawful discrimination by way of victimisation. W, who was a white Irish Muslim, worked as a trainee pharmacist for P. She became dissatisfied with her training and uncomfortable that her manager spoke in Punjabi which was not familiar to her. Complaints were made about her attitude and timekeeping. She was told at a meeting of the possibility of disciplinary action and W allegedly stated that P was "a little Sikh club which only looked after Sikhs". P's head of human resources (J) was told about the comment and she wrote to W to inform her that she was suspended due to her racist and offensive comments. W denied making the comments. She was dismissed for poor timekeeping and a failure to follow procedures. W brought proceedings in the tribunal for unlawful discrimination. W argued that if the remark was made then it was a complaint of direct discrimination contrary to the Employment Equality (Religion or Belief) Regulations 2003 reg.3 and was a protected act. The tribunal found that W had made the comment, that she felt that she was being treated less favourably on religious grounds, and that it was that comment which prompted J to dismiss her. The EAT found that the tribunal had erred in law by overlooking the finding that W had been dismissed for making the comment and then inferring a complaint by W of religious discrimination and imputing that inference to J. W submitted that the EAT was not entitled to reject the tribunal's finding of fact in relation to how J regarded the comment and substitute its own finding.

Held: Appeal dismissed. The difficulty with W's submission was that the continuing theme of the tribunal's judgment was that J thought that the comment was racist. J admitted that she would have dismissed W on that ground alone. There was no room for an assertion that a protected act played a part in W's dismissal. If there had been, there would have been an analysis of that issue in the tribunal's judgment. The EAT was correct in their analysis of the issue and it had not substituted its own finding of fact. There had been an inadequate analysis by the tribunal and the EAT was correct to find an error of law. J had not perceived the comment as an allegation of unfair treatment. The EAT had correctly found errors in the tribunal's reasoning in that it ignored the principles expounded in *Chief Constable of West Yorkshire v Khan* [2001] UKHL 48, [2001] 1 W.L.R. 1947, [2001] C.L.Y. 2302; attributed to J the tribunal's understanding of the nature of the comment; and made an unwarranted leap from that finding to a finding of discrimination, *Khan* followed, *Martin v Devonshires Solicitors* [2011] I.C.R. 352, [2011] C.L.Y. 1063 applied.

PASAB LTD (T/A JHOOTS PHARMACY) v WOODS; *sub nom.* WOODS v PASAB LTD (T/A JHOOTS PHARMACY), [2012] EWCA Civ 1578, [2013] I.R.L.R. 305, Hallett, L.J., CA (Civ Div).

1036. Race discrimination–Victimisation–Relocation–Misstatement of law on victimisation–Analysis of employer's reasons required

[Race Relations Act 1976 (c.74) s.2, s.54A.]

The appellant employer (M) appealed against findings by the employment tribunal that the respondent employee (B) had been victimised and had been the subject of direct discrimination. B appealed against the finding that he was fairly dismissed. In 2008 B was employed at M's branch in Fareham. B was the only black employee and there was banter between B and the other employees of a racial nature. B complained in September 2009 and in November 2009 told M's human resources manager (S). He made a grievance. His complaints were addressed by S who informed him that the area manager would tell all staff at Fareham to cease that type of conduct and the matter would be dealt with informally. B's appeal against S's determination was dismissed. On his return to work, M suggested that B relocate to the Micheldever branch. B refused and was subsequently dismissed. He brought a claim against M in the employment tribunal which found that no meeting with staff by the area manager took place. It found that B had been discriminated against and that he had been victimised because he had been dismissed after having raised a grievance, but that he was fairly dismissed. On the issue of victimisation, the tribunal found that as B was asked to move, but his colleagues were not, that was unfavourable treatment and M's motive was immaterial. M submitted that (1) the tribunal was not entitled to reach the conclusion that there was a failure by M to take firm and decisive action upon B's grievance without conducting a detailed analysis of the thought processes of all involved in the procedural failings; (2) the tribunal had misunderstood the law on victimisation. B submitted that he had not been fairly dismissed as the act of direct racial discrimination had set the chain of events which led to his dismissal.

Held: Appeal allowed in part. (1) The tribunal had correctly identified that M had not investigated B's serious complaints with the speed and diligence required and that they had not taken the steps recommended by S to ensure that they would not occur again. M did not call the person in charge of enforcing discipline at Fareham. In those circumstances it was hardly surprising that the tribunal concluded that M had not discharged the burden cast upon them by the Race Relations Act 1976 s.54A of proving that conduct which was on its face capable of being discriminatory was not. M's appeal against that finding was dismissed (see paras 22-23 of judgment). (2) The tribunal had misstated the law on B's victimisation claim. It was not sufficient simply to compare what had happened to someone who had undertaken a protected act with what had not happened to someone who had not. The tribunal had misstated the statutory test from s.2 of the Act. The critical phrase was "by reason that" which required an analysis of the reason for taking the step said to constitute victimisation, *Chief Constable of West Yorkshire v Khan* [2001] UKHL 48, [2001] 1 W.L.R. 1947, [2001] C.L.Y. 2302 followed. It was necessary for the tribunal to ask itself whether the less favourable treatment, the requirement to move to Micheldever, was by reason that B had undertaken a protected act, the raising of a grievance. On the clear findings of the tribunal, the decision to relocate B had nothing to do with his having raised a grievance. M's proposal was a reasonable one and a solution to the problem that had arisen after the grievance had been resolved. The tribunal made an error of law in reaching its conclusion. M's appeal against that finding was allowed (paras 25-28, 33-34). (3) The tribunal was entitled to conclude that it was reasonable for M to treat B's refusal to relocate as sufficient to justify his dismissal. It made no error of law in reaching its conclusion that B's dismissal was fair. B's appeal against that finding was dismissed (paras 35-36).

BURRELL v MICHELDEVER TYRE SERVICE LTD [2013] Eq. L.R. 695, Mitting, J., EAT.

1037. Race discrimination–Victimisation–Tribunal failing to explain connection between act of victimisation and protected act

The appellant (L) appealed against a decision of an employment tribunal to reject two of her complaints of racial harassment against the respondent (E). E appealed against the tribunal's decision to uphold L's complaint of victimisation. L, who was of Afro-Caribbean origin, worked for E, an institute of higher education, as an assistant chef manager. She asserted that the chef manager (M) at the hall of residence where she worked had referred in her presence to "gollywog" and "gollywog jam". She also complained that M had investigated a complaint made by two fellow employees against her while failing to investigate a complaint which she had made in relation to the same incident. As to L's victimisation complaint, she complained that E had suspended her for taking cakes without permission, even though she had left money for the cakes. The tribunal concluded that M's "gollywog" comments constituted an isolated act of harassment but that the effect on L was short-lived, that the complaint was presented out of time and that it would not be appropriate to extend time. As to the second incident, the tribunal made a distinction between L and her fellow employees in that they had put their complaints in writing whereas she had not done so, despite being asked. Upholding L's victimisation complaint, the tribunal made a link between the decision to suspend her and her lodging of a grievance some four months earlier.

Held: Appellant's appeal dismissed, respondent's appeal allowed. (1) As to M's "gollywog" comments, the tribunal had been entitled to give considerable weight to the fact that L had put the matter behind her. The decision to refuse the application to extend time was one which was open to the tribunal to make.

It directed itself correctly on the law and made appropriate findings, and its discretion would not be interfered with (see para.23 of judgment). (2) As to the second complaint, the tribunal had directed itself correctly on the law and made findings which explained the apparently separate treatment of the two employees and of L (para.27). (3) As to the victimisation complaint, the tribunal had erred by, among other things, failing to explain the connection between the decision to suspend L and her earlier grievance and by failing to identify which manager had taken the decision to suspend. The victimisation claim would be remitted to the tribunal (paras 37, 39).

LONDON SCHOOL OF ECONOMICS AND POLITICAL SCIENCE v LINDSAY; LINDSAY v LONDON SCHOOL OF ECONOMICS AND POLITICAL SCIENCE [2013] Eq. L.R. 10, Judge McMullen Q.C., EAT.

1038. Racial harassment–Injury to feelings–Damages for racist remark made to army chef by superior officer

[Race Relations Act 1976 (c.74) s.32(2).]

The appellant employer Ministry of Defence appealed against a decision that an individual, who had made a racist remark about the respondent employee (K), was the MoD's agent and appealed against the amount of compensation awarded to K. K was a black African employed as a chef by the MoD. Part of the catering was contracted out by the MoD to a contractor which sub-contracted out part of the operation to another company which employed a butcher (B). In two separate incidents, B and a senior non-commissioned officer (S) spoke to K in a way which K's commanding officer later found amounted to bullying and/or racial harassment. An employment tribunal found that B was the MoD's agent for the purposes of the Race Relations Act 1976 s.32(2) and so it was responsible for her racial remark. For injury to feelings, the MoD was ordered to pay £3,500 in relation to B's remark and £12,000 for S's remark. The instant tribunal considered (i) the agency point; (ii) the amount awarded for S's remark.

Held: Appeal allowed. (1) It was common ground that the common law principles of agency applied to the construction of s.32(2) of the Act. In those circumstances, the employment tribunal had applied the wrong legal test when directing itself that common law principles concerning agency were not necessarily applicable when dealing with s.32(2). However, the necessary causative link could not be made out on the evidence before, and the facts found by, the employment tribunal. There was no warrant for the employment tribunal's reasoning that the nature of the contract for the provision of services by the contractor to the MoD, or the fact that civilian employees of the sub-contractor were subject to day-to-day control by the military, gave rise to any relationship of agency at common law between the MoD and the sub-contractor and its employees. In those circumstances, the appeal on the agency point was allowed and the award made in respect of B's remark set aside (see paras 9, 14-15 of judgment). (2) A distinction had to be drawn between the case of S, K's superior officer, and that of B, an employee of a civilian contractor. However, placing S's remark in the middle band set out in *Vento v Chief Constable of West Yorkshire* [2002] EWCA Civ 1871, [2003] I.C.R. 318, [2003] C.L.Y. 1306 was wrong in principle and manifestly excessive. Such an award would be appropriate for a course of discriminatory conduct. In the instant case, the proper award, at the top of the lower band, was £6,000, *Vento* applied. It was therefore appropriate to substitute an award of £6,000 for that of £12,000 in relation to S's remark (paras 18-19).

MINISTRY OF DEFENCE v KEMEH; *sub nom.* KEMEH v MINISTRY OF DEFENCE [2013] Eq. L.R. 605, Judge Peter Clark, EAT.

1039. **Recruitment–Trade union membership–Employer party to collective agreement with union to support engagement of experienced shop stewards–Employer refusing to accept union recommendation–Whether breach of s.137(1) Trade Union and Labour Relations (Consolidation) Act 1992 and reg.5 Employment Relations Act 1999 (Blacklists) Regulations 2010**

[Trade Union and Labour Relations (Consolidation) Act 1992 (c.52) s.137(1); Employment Relations Act 1999 (Blacklists) Regulations 2010 (SI 2010/493) reg.5.]

The appellants (X), three trade union members, appealed against the dismissal of their claims that they had been refused employment by the respondent company (C) on grounds related to their union membership. C was party to a collective agreement with a union (U). The agreement provided that C would "assist in encouraging the selection of [accredited] shop stewards from amongst their workforce, including a senior steward...". U regarded that provision as entitling it to nominate members for recruitment with a view to their acting as shop stewards. X had a history of acting as shop stewards. An official of U gave their names to C's recruitment manager, firmly indicating that they should be engaged under the terms of the collective agreement. X were not engaged. Their case was that C's manager had made a mental note not to recruit them because of the manner in which they had been put forward, which refusal amounted to a breach of the Trade Union and Labour Relations (Consolidation) Act 1992 s.137(1) and the Employment Relations Act 1999 (Blacklists) Regulations 2010 reg.5. The employment tribunal found that the reason for non-engagement was not X's union membership or activities, but rather a resentment of U""'s interference and the bullying nature of U's official, and a desire to make objective recruitment decisions. X submitted that their trade union activities must, at least subconsciously, have been part of what operated in the mind of C's manager when he made his decision, and that the tribunal had made a meaningless distinction in distinguishing between his resentment at being bullied and the thing he was being bullied to do, namely to recruit particular union members who would act as shop stewards.

Held: Appeal dismissed. (1) The tribunal's distinction was admissible in principle. If C's manager had been motivated wholly by pique at what he regarded as unacceptable pressure from U, that was genuinely distinct from the issue of what he was being put under pressure about. There was a real difference between him deciding that he did not want to employ activist shop stewards, and him resolving not to give U's official what he wanted. The objection to recruiting X would not relate to their individual actions or characteristics, but only to the fact that they were the ones who U was trying to dictate should be chosen (see para.16 of judgment). Given that the distinction was acceptable in principle, the issue was one of fact as to whether the reasons were truly as C's manager claimed, or whether they were a cover for a wish not to employ X because of their trade union activities. On the evidence, the industry in which C operated was highly unionised. It was not plausible that C's manager would have been troubled by X's union membership. He might have found X unattractive by virtue of their previous union activities, but the tribunal had made no finding of fact that he knew about those activities. It had heard him give evidence and had been well-placed to judge his mental process. On the evidence, the reasons for non-engagement had nothing to do with X's trade union activities. It was unfortunate that they had been caught up in the crossfire between two individuals, but there was no law against unfair non-recruitment (paras 16-18). (2) (Obiter) it had been argued before the employment tribunal that a "mental" list, which was not reduced to any form of writing, did not fall within the terms of the Regulations. The tribunal rejected that argument and the point was not appealed, although it remained open for future argument (para.12).

MILLER v INTERSERVE INDUSTRIAL SERVICES LTD [2013] I.C.R. 445, Underhill, J., EAT.

1040. Redundancy–Disability discrimination–Employer's failure to consider employee for two alternative roles when making redundancies–Decision-maker's awareness of employee's absence history–Whether burden of proof shifted to employer

[Equality Act 2010 (c.15) s.13, s.15.]

The appellant employer (X) appealed against a decision of an employment tribunal that its dismissal of the respondent employee (M) was unlawful because it had discriminated against her owing to her disability. M had been employed by X an Assistant Editor and then a Features Editor until 2008 when, due to serious knee problems, she became a copy editor in order to work from home two days a week. In 2009 and 2010, M had a number of knee operations resulting in significant absences from work, and was due to have another in 2011. In 2011, two of X's magazines merged, which involved a redundancy exercise. M was told by the publishing director (F) that she would be dismissed unless an alternative role was found. M appealed against that decision, raising her health and age. At the appeal, F raised two alternative positions that M could apply for but stated that they had not been signed off yet. M received a letter the next day confirming her dismissal; it stated that her age and health had played no part in the redundancy decision and that no suitable alternative positions were available. M brought a claim for direct and indirect discrimination under Equality Act 2010 s.13 and s.15. F gave evidence that she knew that a copy editor role had been created for M in 2008, that she had discussed selection pools for redundancy with the person who had created M's copy editor role, that M had not been able to attend all of the scheduled meetings due to illness, that she had attended M's appeal hearing and that she was aware of another employee who had several periods of sick leave. The employment tribunal dismissed M's claim under s.13, but allowed her claim under s.15 in the absence of any persuasive evidence that X's failure to consider her for the alternative posts was not due to her past and anticipated future absences. X submitted that the tribunal's reasoning was flawed as (1) there was no evidence that F had any knowledge of the history of M's absences; (2) it was not entitled to find that there had been no persuasive explanation of the decision to defer advertising the two posts; (3) its finding of discrimination under s.15 was inconsistent with its rejection of the claim of direct discrimination under s.13.

Held: Appeal allowed. (1) The facts did not justify an inference that F knew about M's absences. It was entirely speculative whether F knew that M had become a copy editor because of her knee problems. Even if F had been told, it did not follow that she had been told that there were continuing problems leading to significant absences. The discussion of the selection pools would not have required any discussion of the characters of the individuals doing the jobs in question. The meeting that M had not attending through illness was not due to her knee problems. Whilst F had been present at M's appeal hearing during which M's health was raised, it was M that had raised her health and it was not discussed substantively. The fact that F was aware of another staff member's sickness absences bore no relevance to M. The tribunal made no explicit finding as to what F knew. Its reasoning was based on the burden of proof and was very short. In such cases, tribunals did not always give the same detailed attention to facts relied on to infer knowledge as they would if they had been relying on those facts to reach a definitive factual finding. However, it was important that they did so as even where the burden of proof provisions were deployed a finding of a discriminatory motivation was a real finding of fact, not a legal presumption (see paras 30-31 of judgment). (2) Had the burden of proof shifted, which it had not, F's explanation as to why M was not given an opportunity to apply for the positions would have been the decisive question in the case. In which case, the tribunal's reasoning would need to explicitly state why it had found F's explanation unpersuasive. The tribunal's reasoning had not been explicit and F was not directly challenged about deferring the advertising of the posts (para.35). (3) There was nothing inconsistent about the tribunal rejecting the direct disability claim but finding discrimination under s.15 (para.36).

IPC MEDIA LTD v MILLAR [2013] I.R.L.R. 707, Underhill, J., EAT.

1041. Redundancy–Redeployment–Appellant's refusal of alternative employment–Employment tribunal's erroneous application of test for determining whether refusal unreasonable–Employment Appeal Tribunal's reliance on band of reasonable responses test

[Employment Rights Act 1996 (c.18) s.141 (3) (b), s.141.]

The appellant primary care trust appealed against a decision of the Employment Appeal Tribunal allowing the appeal of the respondent (R) against a decision of the Employment Tribunal that R's refusal of alternative employment was unreasonable. R had commenced a career as a nurse in 1976. From 1985 onwards, she had worked as a community nurse, eventually being promoted to a community modern matron, a Band 8A role involving management duties. In 2007 she was advised that she was at risk of redundancy. R was offered three alternative positions, one of which was a band 8A modern matron role at a small community hospital. Ten per cent of the duties were management duties, 45 per cent were nurse team leader duties and the remaining 45 per cent were matron duties. R rejected the offer as she had spent her career working in the community and had no desire to work in a hospital. Instead, she accepted one of the band 7 offers, which was a lesser role, on a trial basis. In the interim, R was offered a community-based role in Canada and eventually moved there in 2009. In November 2008 she was made redundant. The ET held that the band 7 role was not suitable alternative employment within the meaning of the Employment Rights Act 1996 s.141 (3) (b), that R had wanted to emigrate to Canada, that the modern matron role was practically identical to R's previous role, that it was suitable alternative employment and that her rejection of it was unreasonable unders.141 (2). On appeal the EAT held that the ET had failed to address the core reason for R's refusal, that emigration to Canada was not the main reason for her refusal, and that the reason given for R's refusal was reasonable, sound and justifiable. The trust sought a review of the EAT's decision, upon which the EAT held that it was plain and obvious that R's refusal of the job offer was within the reasonable band of responses and that the contrary was unarguable. The EAT further held that it was bound to substitute its own findings on the law. The issues for consideration were whether (i) the ET had erred in considering that R had unreasonably refused the job offer; (ii) if so, should the EAT have remitted the case.

Held: Appeal allowed. (1) The ET had applied the right test when it stated that the reasonableness of a job refusal included factors personal to an employee, *Everest's Executors v Cox* [1980] I.C.R. 415, [1980] C.L.Y. 958 applied. However, the ET had failed to address the central point made by R. It had not been unreasonable for R to decline to work in the hospital when she had spent so many years working in the community. The relevance of R's emigration to Canada needed further analysis. If the ET had decided that that was the reason for R's refusal, it had not clearly stated so. R's intention to take advantage of the redundancy payment did not defeat the claim. The ET's analysis had been so inadequate that it amounted to an error of law. (2) Remittal to the ET as the fact finding tribunal was necessary. Whether or not a refusal was reasonable was a matter of fact for the ET, *Cambridge & District Cooperative Society v Ruse* [1993] I.R.L.R. 156, [1993] C.L.Y. 1730 applied. The EAT's reliance on the reasonable band of responses test was misplaced. It was not useful to import that test, which was the test for unfair dismissal, into a s.141 context, *Iceland Frozen Foods Ltd v Jones* [1983] I.C.R. 17, [1983] C.L.Y. 1325 considered. When dealing with s.141, a specific judgment had to be made concerning the employee in question; it was not a question of whether the refusal was within the reasonable band of responses. The test in *Everest's Executors* was clear and had been applied by the ET for many years. The ET had clearly stated the necessary test and there was no reason to cloud *Everest's Executors* by importing the reasonable band of responses test into s.141 territory.

READMAN v DEVON PRIMARY CARE TRUST; *sub nom.* DEVON PRIMARY CARE TRUST v READMAN, [2013] EWCA Civ 1110, [2013] I.R.L.R. 878, Pill, L.J., CA (Civ Div).

1042. **Redundancy payments–Contract terms–Enhanced severance terms set out in redundancy policy in employee handbook–Whether incorporated in contract of employment**

[Employment Rights Act 1996 (c.18) s.1.]

The appellant employees (K) appealed against a decision that the redundancy policy of the respondent employer (T) had not been incorporated and was not implied into their contracts of employment. The redundancy policy was contained in an employee handbook and contained enhanced severance terms. It had been formally agreed by an advisory council on which management and employees were represented. The employee handbook contained an express promise to implement the redundancy policy in the event of redundancies and T also made the same promises in subsequent correspondence, confirming that the policy would remain as it was until it was renegotiated in 2010. K's statement of terms and conditions of employment made reference to the employee handbook, but there was no general statement that terms and conditions were to be found there. Before the redundancy policy fell to be renegotiated, K were made redundant, but T did not honour the policy. The employment judge concluded that the enhanced terms were not contractual because the terms and conditions did not refer to the redundancy policy and there was no express term that was incorporated into the contracts of employment. He also found that there was no implied term that the policy would be applied on every occasion. K submitted that the tribunal had erred in concluding that the terms as to severance payments were not express terms of the contract and had ignored the employee handbook and the redundancy policy itself as a potential source of contractual obligation. They also argued that the tribunal had erred in concluding that there was no implied term of the contract by which employees were entitled to severance payments under the policy.

Held: Appeal allowed. The statement of main terms and conditions which an employer was obliged to provide under the Employment Rights Act 1996 s.1 was not required to cover all matters of contractual entitlement. The provision of enhanced severance payments was precisely the kind of matter which might be dealt with orally, by custom and practice, or by different documents, such as an employee handbook. Because redundancy policies contained that which was "apt for incorporation" along with that which was not, it was inherently unlikely that they would be found in a s.1 statement, *Keeley v Fosroc International Ltd* [2006] EWCA Civ 1277, [2006] I.R.L.R. 961, [2007] C.L.Y. 1396 considered. The question was whether an objective examination of the circumstances in which the enhanced redundancy package had become known supported the inference that T intended to become contractually bound by it, *Quinn v Calder Industrial Materials Ltd* [1996] I.R.L.R. 126 applied. The tribunal had to keep firmly in mind the consideration that provision for redundancy had become a widely accepted feature of employees' remuneration packages. Tribunals had to scrutinise with care arguments by employers that payments which were intended to be part of an employee's remuneration package were merely matters of policy and discretion (see paras 61, 70-71, 75 of judgment). In the instant case, the policy was prescriptive as to the amounts to be paid and appeared to allow no room for discretion. The tribunal should have considered whether the employee handbook was in that respect a source of contractual obligation. There was no indication that it had done so. In its reasons, the tribunal had made a bare reference to the handbook, but had not set out the promise made to employees to implement the policy in the event of redundancies. The employee handbook was capable of being a source of contractual obligation and the tribunal ought to have considered it. Its conclusion that there was no evidence of any inference that T intended to be contractually bound by the redundancy policy depended on whether the employee handbook was capable of being a source of contractual obligation. There was no basis for the conclusion that K could not have had a reasonable expectation that payment, having been agreed with the advisory council, would be made in accordance with the express promise in the employee handbook. The tribunal had also placed no weight on promises that the policy would stay as it was until renegotiated in 2010, *Albion*

Automotive Ltd v Walker [2002] EWCA Civ 946 considered. The tribunal had erred in law in considering whether T was contractually obliged to pay the enhanced severance terms set out in the redundancy policy. The matter would be remitted for reconsideration by a freshly constituted tribunal (paras 73-79, 81-82).

ALLEN vTRW SYSTEMS LTD [2013] I.C.R. D13, Judge David Richardson, EAT.

1043. Redundancy payments–Custom and practice–Finding that enhanced redundancy payments paid automatically–Lack of supporting factual findings–Considerations relevant to assessment of employees' understanding

The appellant employer (P) appealed against a decision of the Employment Appeal Tribunal that an employment tribunal had been wrong to find that enhanced redundancy payments had not been paid to their employees as a matter of custom and practice. The respondent employees (C) had worked at a factory that had been transferred to P's ownership in 2007. C were made redundant in 2009. They claimed to be contractually entitled to enhanced redundancy payments of twice the statutory amount, plus a lump sum of £600, under a formal redundancy scheme that had been operated for many years. P claimed that the payments had been made under a company policy rather than a contractual obligation, and that the policy had not been communicated to the employees. The ET held that such payments as had been made up to 2006 had not been made automatically and rejected C's claim. The EAT held that the ET should have found that the enhanced payments had been made without exception up to 2007, and remitted the claim for reconsideration. P argued that the EAT had not been entitled to interfere with the ET's decision because there had been sufficient evidence before the ET to support its finding that enhanced redundancy payments had not been automatic; the ET had made a clear finding that there had been no agreement or policy drawn to the employee's attention which indicated P's intention to pay the claimed benefit as a contractual obligation; and because uncertainty about the £600, which was a component part of the claimed benefits, undermined any argument that the claimed benefits had crystallised into a contractual term.

Held: Appeal dismissed. (1) The essential object was to ascertain what the parties must have, or must be taken to have, understood from each other's conduct and words, applying ordinary contractual principles: the terminology of "custom and practice" should not be allowed to obscure that enquiry, *Garratt v Mirror Group Newspapers Ltd* [2011] EWCA Civ 425, [2011] I.C.R. 880, [2011] C.L.Y. 1053 applied. The essential question had to be whether, by its conduct in making available a particular benefit to employees over a period, in the context of all the surrounding circumstances, the employer had evinced to the relevant employees an intention that they should enjoy that benefit as of right. The focus had to be on what the employer had communicated to the employees. What it might have personally understood or intended was irrelevant except to the extent that the employees were, or should reasonably have been, aware of it. The circumstances that might be relevant were: the number of occasions, and over how long a period, the benefits in question had been paid; whether the benefits were always the same; the extent to which the benefits were publicised generally; how the terms were described; what was said in the express contract; whether the employer's practice was equally explicable on the basis that it was pursued as a matter of discretion rather than legal obligation (see paras 34-36 of judgment). (2) Although the ET had made a finding that payments up to 2006 had not been made automatically, it had also and separately declined to find that the benefits had been paid on every occasion. That was plainly an error, as the majority had said that the evidence was all one way. It was not safe or appropriate to ignore that error on the basis that the ET could perhaps have reached the same conclusion by a different route. In addition, it was not clear that the ET had appreciated the distinction between what P believed internally and what was understood by the employees. Even if the ET had meant to reach a conclusion about the employees' understanding, the findings of primary fact and the expressed reasoning were inadequate to support such a conclusion (paras 47-48). (3) The fact that there had been no explicit publication of the policy underlying a practice of making payments was significant in deciding whether that practice had crystallised into an obligation, but it was not necessarily decisive, *Duke v Reliance Systems* [1982] I.C.R. 449, [1982] C.L.Y. 1114 applied. That being so, the ET's failure to find that the claimed benefits had been paid invariably prior to the transfer of ownership remained a material flaw in its reasoning (para.51). (4) The fact that C might have no entitlement to the £600 did not mean that they could have no entitlement to the other claimed benefits (para.53). (5) The EAT's decision was upheld and the matter remitted to the ET for reconsideration.

SHUMBA v PARK CAKES LTD; PARK CAKES LTD v SHUMBA, [2013] EWCA Civ 974, [2013] I.R.L.R. 800, Moore-Bick, L.J., CA (Civ Div).

1044. Redundancy payments–Short-time working–Calculation of payment–Determination of calculation date

[Employment Rights Act 1996 (c.18) s.147(2), s.148, s.148(1)(a), s.153(a), s.221(2), s.221(1), s.226(5), s.226(4).]

The appellant (D) appealed against the amount an employment judge had calculated as his redundancy payment arising from short-time working. D had worked five or five-and-a-half days per week for the respondent (J), earning £250 per week. He went onto short time, working one day a week, in June 2011. On October 4, 2011 D served a notice claiming a redundancy payment under the Employment Rights Act 1996 s.148. The judge considered that, applying s.226(4), the calculation date was four weeks before service of D's notice, namely September 6, 2011. Based on that, she calculated D's weekly pay for the purposes of his redundancy payment to be £48.

Held: Appeal allowed. (1) The employment judge had correctly referred to s.226(4) to ascertain whether D had been on short-time working. He obviously had been. However, the judge had failed to understand that the reference in s.226(4) to s.147(2) made s.226(4) relevant to whether there was short-time working; she had been concerned with not only that issue, but also the amount of any redundancy payment. For the latter she should have been considering the calculation date prescribed by s.226(5) and (6). The calculation date in the instant case was that specified in s.226(6), namely the date on which notice would have been given had the employer terminated the contract giving such notice as was required to terminate the contract, and had the notice expired on the effective date of termination or the relevant date. The relevant date for the purposes of short-time working and lay-off triggered by giving notice under s.148(1) was to be found in s.153(a). Accordingly, for the purpose of calculating a redundancy payment in a short-time working context, one started with the end of the last week of consecutive short-time working before the notice given under s.148(1)(a) claiming a redundancy payment, and worked back from that date to a date when the statutory notice necessary to terminate the employee's contract of employment would have been given, had it been given. In the instant case, that meant looking to the week before the notice claiming a redundancy payment was given on October 4, 2011; in practical terms that would be the previous Saturday, as there had been Saturday working. Going back from that date over the period of the notice that the employer would have had to give to terminate the employment on that date, which in J's case would have been 12 weeks, one arrived at July 9, 2011 as the calculation date. On that date the first issue under s.221(1) would have been whether there were normal working hours; if so, his week's pay would be calculated in accordance with s.221(2). That would have been the money he would have been paid had he been working his normal hours. In D's case, that would have been £250. However, both on the date arrived at by the judge and on that date, D had been on short-time working. It was implicit in the judgment that the judge had considered that the short-time hours had become D's normal working hours, presumably by some variation to the contract of employment. That was wrong. An employee who went on to short-time working was not to be regarded as having accepted a permanent variation in his terms involving a reduction to his normal working hours. Consequently, the contract of employment in force on the calculation date remained the original contract even if there was short-time working on that date. As J had not attended and had not had chance to make representations, the matter would be remitted to the employment judge for recalculation (see paras 14-15, 18-30 of judgment). (2) Even if the judge had been following the right route, September 6 would not have been the correct date. She must have interpreted "the first of the four" in s.226(4) as implying the first of the four weeks working back from the date an employee's notice was served, whereas "the first of the four" should be read as the first of the four or more consecutive weeks mentioned in s.148(2) (para.17).

DUTTON v JONES (T/A LLANDOW METALS) [2013] I.C.R. 559, Judge Hand Q.C., EAT.

1045. Religious discrimination–Harassment–Claimant overhearing Pope referred to in derogatory way–Relevance of respondent's purpose in making allegedly offensive remark

[Employment Equality (Religion or Belief) Regulations 2003 (SI 2003/1660) reg.5, reg.5(2).]

The applicant sub-editor (H) applied for a reconsideration of a decision that he had no reasonable grounds for bringing an appeal against the dismissal of his harassment claim against the respondent newspaper publisher (T). H was a Roman Catholic who worked for T when it was preparing a story about the Pope. Due to a delay in producing the story, an editor (W), while in the newsroom, shouted to his colleagues: "Can anyone tell what's happening to the fucking Pope?". When there was no response, he repeated the question more loudly. H was upset and offended, raised a complaint and subsequently brought a claim for harassment on the grounds of his religious belief pursuant to the Employment Equality (Religion or Belief) Regulations 2003 reg.5. An employment tribunal found that W had engaged in unwanted conduct but that to the extent that the conduct had the effect of violating H's dignity or creating an intimidating, hostile, degrading, humiliating or offensive environment for him, that was not a reasonable reaction under reg.5(2). It also found that it had not been proven that W's conduct was on the grounds of H's religion. H submitted that (1) in considering the question of reasonableness, the tribunal inadmissibly introduced the question of W's purpose in using those words; (2) in considering whether W's remark was made on the ground of H's religion, the tribunal erroneously considered W's motive, which was immaterial.

Held: Application refused. (1) It was plainly right that, to the extent that H felt his dignity was violated or that an adverse environment had been created, that was not a reasonable reaction. People were not perfect and sometimes used bad language thoughtlessly: a reasonable person would have understood that and made allowance for it. It had been said that dignity was not necessarily violated by things said or done which were trivial or transitory, particularly if it should have been clear that any offence was unintended, and that it was important not to encourage a culture of hypersensitivity or the imposition of legal liability in respect of every unfortunate phrase. Those observations were just as applicable to the question of reasonableness as to the question of whether a claimant's dignity had in fact been violated in the first place, *Richmond Pharmacology Ltd v Dhaliwal* [2009] I.C.R. 724, [2009] C.L.Y. 1229 applied. If the tribunal had committed itself to a general proposition that because W had been making an enquiry, then as a matter of law his conduct could not, or could not reasonably, have produced the proscribed consequences, that would have been wrong. However, the tribunal was simply saying that the context in which the phrase was used was relevant to its effect and that, in the instant case, it was such that it was not reasonable for H to feel that his dignity had been violated or that he had been subjected to an adverse environment. To have regard to the evident purpose of a remark in that way was entirely orthodox, *Dhaliwal* and *Land Registry v Grant* [2011] EWCA Civ 769, [2011] I.C.R. 1390, [2011] C.L.Y. 1095 considered (see paras 10, 12 of judgment). (2) Sometimes an act complained of could only be shown to have been done on the proscribed ground by showing that the person doing it was motivated by the fact that the claimant had the protected characteristic, *Martin v Devonshires Solicitors* [2011] I.C.R. 352, [2011] C.L.Y. 1063 considered. However, that was not always the case. If the inherent character of the act concerned meant that the protected characteristic was the ground of the action complained of, it would be unnecessary to consider the mental processes of the person in question at all. That might often be so in harassment cases, *Dhaliwal* considered. However, in the instant case it was unnecessary to consider the matter further (para.14).

HEAFIELD v TIMES NEWSPAPER LTD; *sub nom.* HEATHFIELD v TIMES NEWSPAPER LTD [2013] Eq. L.R. 345, Underhill, J., EAT.

1046. Religious discrimination–Sunday trading–Care worker required to work some Sundays despite religious beliefs–Whether objective justification in employer's requirement

The appellant (M) appealed an employment tribunal's decision that the respondent local authority had not discriminated against her on the grounds of religion and belief. M began working for the local authority at a children's care home. Despite a fixed rota that required staff to work certain weekends, M's managers had offered to take reasonable steps, at least in the short term, to accommodate M's wish not to work on Sundays because of her religious beliefs. Problems arose soon after M began work. After a grievance she raised concerning the local authority's approach was rejected, M was scheduled to work on Sundays in accordance with the normal rota. She refused to do so. After unsuccessfully appealing a final written warning, she resigned. The tribunal accepted that the local authority's provision, criterion or practice (PCP), which required M to work some Sundays each month, impacted her deeply held religious belief and observance. However, weighing all relevant factors, it found that the imposition of the PCP was proportionate. M submitted that the tribunal (1) was wrong to find that not working on Sundays was not a core component of the Christian faith; (2) failed to apply the proper test; (3) failed to place the onus upon the local authority to justify the proportionality test.

Held: Appeal dismissed. (1) The tribunal had not expressed itself well when it said that the belief that Sunday should be a day of rest was not a "core" component of the Christian religion. That could have placed the court in the position of judging the tenets of faith, which would have been a misdirection of law. However, by virtue of the context in which that statement was made and its reference to a summary of the relevant legal principles, it was clear that the tribunal was not adjudicating in evaluative terms upon religious beliefs. When assessing proportionality, the weight to be given to the degree of interference with religious belief of a certain kind inevitably differed depending upon the numbers of believers who would be affected by the particular PCP. The tribunal's reference to the Bishop accepting that Sunday as a day of rest was not a "core" component of Christianity was inelegant in its phraseology. However, read in context and bearing in mind that the tribunal was dealing with balancing the weight to be attached to the local authority's objectives against the discriminatory impact on Christians generally, the tribunal meant that the Bishop's statement was evidence that many Christians would work on the Sabbath and that it was appropriate for it to have regard to that evidence in weighing the impact of the PCP. Therefore there was no error of law (see paras 42-43, 46, 48 of judgment). (2) There was evidence from which the tribunal could reach the conclusions it had and there was nothing in the way it considered proportionality which suggested that it was any less than properly scrupulous about those conclusions. Although there was much to be said for an employer taking care that its PCPs did not disadvantage people who were protected in the characteristics they had, because it might be called upon to justify its approach, it was for the court to decide whether a PCP was justifiable. The employer had to justify the PCP to the court at the time when it was called into question. It was plain that the local authority had considered much of the case and the justification for the PCP at a stage before it was called upon to do so at the tribunal. The tribunal was not therefore obliged to regard the justification advanced to it as so recently configured that it lacked cogency. Therefore, concluding that applying the PCP was proportionate did not indicate that the tribunal must have taken a wrong approach (paras 36-39). (3) The tribunal's approach was that the local authority had to justify the PCP. There was no error in its conclusions. It was setting the standard too high to suggest that the employer had to make all possible efforts to accommodate an employee, though it was important to eliminate discrimination on the grounds of religion and belief. In the instant case and on its particular facts, the local authority had established a legitimate aim. The tribunal had not erred in concluding that the local authority had justified a PCP relevant to achieving that aim; and that although the effect was that M had then to surrender her job, that did not give rise to a proper claim by her of discrimination on the grounds of religion and belief (paras 50-53).

MBA v MERTON LBC [2013] I.C.R. 658, Langstaff, J. (President), EAT.

1047. **Restrictive covenants–Non-competition covenants–Employee's acceptance of new contract including restrictive covenants**

The court was required to determine a preliminary issue in a claim brought by the claimant (N) against its former employee, the first defendant (L). L had resigned from N to join a rival company. N alleged that, while it had employed L, he had collated confidential information belonging to it and passed it on to the rival. L had initially been employed by N on the basis of a contract signed in 2003 which contained no restrictive covenants. He was promoted in 2009 to a "Grade E" senior management position. He was sent a new contract including restrictive covenants preventing him from working for rival businesses, but did not sign or return it. He applied to move from the final salary pension scheme he had joined under the 2003 contract to the defined contribution scheme described in the 2009 contract, and applied for private medical insurance, which was available under the 2009 contract but not the 2003 contract. The issue for the court was whether L was bound by the terms of the 2009 contract, including the restrictive covenants. L submitted that his actions did not show that he had accepted the terms of the 2009 contract, as he had been required to move to the defined contribution scheme as a result of becoming a Grade E employee, and he had applied for medical insurance as that was a benefit available to Grade E employees rather than a benefit arising from the contract.

Held: Preliminary issue determined in favour of claimant. (1) The benefits necessarily had their source in the 2009 contract. The fact that the benefit was available to all Grade E employees and was associated with that grade did not assist in determining the legal source of the benefit. Grade E employees enjoyed the benefit because Grade E contracts provided for it; its source was necessarily contractual. Each employee's relationship with his employer was necessarily defined by contract; a term could be implied from custom and practice, but the source of benefits was contractual. L must have appreciated that. Upon a step change of grade, an employee's relationship with his employer obviously and materially changed. Such a change was ultimately defined in legal terms by a new contract. L had been provided with a new contract, and at least after being provided with the contract, and especially after he had read it, he must have appreciated that any new benefits would have their source in that contract. In any event, in proceeding, without any protest or reservation, voluntarily to apply for benefits not previously available to him, L had to be taken to have accepted the legal incidents of the new definition of the relationship. L's joinder of the pension scheme provided for by the 2009 contract had not been voluntary and was not clearly and uniquely referable to the contract. It was referable, at least in part, to a mandatory policy. By contrast, L's application for medical insurance in the form mandated by the 2009 contract, after he had read its terms and without expressing protest or reservation, had been an unequivocal act referable only to his having accepted all the terms of the 2009 contract from the date of that application, *Solectron Scotland Ltd v Roper* [2004] I.R.L.R. 4 applied and *Khatri v Cooperative Central Raiffeisen-*

Boerenleenbank BA [2010] EWCA Civ 397, [2010] I.R.L.R. 715, [2010] C.L.Y. 1039 followed (see paras 70-74 of judgment). (2) The preliminary issue had been determined at a separate trial before the trial of the overall dispute. That course was unusual, for good reason. Where the issue was not even properly characterised as a preliminary issue, was not determinative of the proceedings, and required cross-examination and documentary disclosure, it would seldom be wise to determine it at a separate mini-trial (para.80).

FW FARNSWORTH LTD v LACY, [2012] EWHC 2830 (Ch), [2013] I.R.L.R. 198, Hildyard, J., Ch D.

1048. Restrictive covenants–Non-competition covenants–Enforceability–Whether reasonable restraint of trade

The claimant employer (C) sought to enforce post-termination covenants against its former employee (H). C had been involved in a business providing financial planning advice to clients. Under the terms and conditions of employment H was prohibited from "directly or indirectly be[ing] engaged or concerned in" any business or activity of a direct competitor. H's position involved him having access to C's information about clients. He had been employed until the required six-months' notice for resignation had expired and started working for a company (F) whose business included the provision of retail financial advice, insurance broking and employee benefit services. Since joining F two of H's clients with C had moved to F, and C had learnt that at least four individuals who worked under H had also started working for F. C sought to enforce post-termination covenants against H and an order preventing him from working for F for a further six months. H denied that he had acted in breach of his duties to C and maintained that the non-competition covenant was unenforceable as a restraint of trade.

Held: Claim dismissed. To determine whether the restrictive covenant was enforceable (a) the court had to properly construe the meaning of the covenant; (b) the court had to consider whether the former employer had shown that it had legitimate business interests requiring protection; (c) the covenant must be shown to be no wider than reasonably necessary for the protection of those interests; (d) and even if reasonable the court had to decide whether as a matter of discretion the relief sought should in all the circumstances be granted, having regard, amongst other things, to its reasonableness as at the time of trial, *TFS Derivatives Ltd v Morgan* [2004] EWHC 3181 (QB), [2005] I.R.L.R. 246, [2005] C.L.Y. 700 applied. The clause prohibited H from "directly or indirectly be[ing] engaged or concerned in" any business or activity of a direct competitor. On a literal reading those words might be understood to prohibit H from being "concerned in" a competitor without working or having active involvement in the competitor's business activities, for example by "directly" holding shares or "indirectly" through a unit trust with a holding in a competitor. Such an interpretation would give it a wider application than anything reasonably necessary to protect C's legitimate interests including holding shares or investments. However, the covenant could have a narrower and more natural interpretation limiting it to prohibiting H from being engaged or concerned in the business or activities of competitors by working but not from holding investments in them or having a purely financial "engagement" or "concern" in them. The narrow interpretation was preferred (see para.39 of judgment). (ii) Business interests that employers could legitimately protect included the names of customers and the goods which they bought, *Lansing Linde Ltd v Kerr* [1991] 1 W.L.R. 251, [1991] C.L.Y. 446 considered. H not only had access to, but actually knew information of that kind about C's clients. Such information was clearly by way of a business interest of C that they could legitimately protect by restrictive covenants (para.41). (iii) The covenant not only covered H being directly involved in dealing with clients when working for a competitor or being indirectly so involved by way of business development; it covered being indirectly concerned in such activities by way of a management role, regulatory compliance, training, research into investment products and other fiscal planning for the competitor business. There was no obvious justification for preventing

H from working for a competing business in such roles. The potential scope of the covenant seemed wider than required to protect C's legitimate business. The additional restraints of the non-competition covenant would, if enforced, prohibit H from working in many parts of the financial services industry in ways in which it could not reasonably be said that C's legitimate interests would or might be compromised. If C's clients wished to change their advisers, they would need to contact C to request and authorise the release of their information to the new adviser. To that extent C would be alerted to possible misuse of information about their clients. Balancing those considerations, the non-competition covenant was in restraint of trade and not enforceable (paras 48, 50).

ASHCOURT ROWAN FINANCIAL PLANNING LTD v HALL, [2013] EWHC 1185 (QB), [2013] I.R.L.R. 637, Andrew Smith, J., QBD.

1049. Restrictive covenants–Non-competition covenants–Enforcement–Clause unenforceable at time of contract–Subsequent promotion to role where covenant reasonable–Enforceability without re-agreement

The claimant employer (C) claimed to enforce a non-competition covenant in its employment contract with the defendant employee (D). D had signed the contract when he was initially hired as an account manager. He was promoted several times in the subsequent years, and was ultimately appointed to an executive-level position that entailed substantial responsibility. He endorsed the promotion letter acknowledging that he agreed to certain variations in the terms of his employment as stated in the letter and agreed that all other terms in his original employment contract remained unchanged. The letter did not expressly address the non-competition covenant. After several years D resigned to take a job with one of C's competitors. The primary issue was whether the covenant was enforceable.

Held: Claim dismissed. It was common ground that the non-competition covenant was void when D was first engaged, given his status and responsibilities at that time. It could not be saved simply because a subsequent change of circumstances meant that it would have been reasonable at the time it fell to be enforced, *Gledhow Autoparts v Delaney* [1965] 1 W.L.R. 1366, [1965] C.L.Y. 1468 and *Commercial Plastics Ltd v Vincent* [1965] 1 Q.B. 623, [1964] C.L.Y. 1307 applied. It was therefore necessary for C to show that a fresh covenant had been entered into when D was promoted. If that had explicitly been done, the covenant's reasonableness could be judged as of that date. However, the general acknowledgement in the promotion letter that D's previous terms remained unchanged could not be construed as an agreement to reinstate a term that was a nullity. It did not convey an intention to make a fresh start in the relevant respect. If the non-competition covenant was void when initially entered into, it could not be revived, save where that was clearly and unequivocally the contractual intention. That approach was also right on grounds of policy and practicality. Contracts of employment were frequently varied over their lifetimes. It would be undesirable that every such change could in principle have the potential to revive a defunct non-competition covenant. That would introduce complexity and uncertainty into employment contracts. Employees were entitled to know their positions, and the occasions where a complex assessment was required should be as few and as well-marked as possible. It was undesirable that an employee should have to survey the whole of his employment history to consider whether an initially unreasonable contract could have changed its character. It ought to be necessary to look only at the most recent date at which such a covenant had been explicitly entered into. For those reasons a non-competition covenant that was unenforceable *ab initio* was to be disregarded until explicitly re-agreed (see paras 36-54 of judgment).

PATSYSTEMS HOLDINGS LTD v NEILLY; *sub nom.* PAT SYSTEMS v NEILLY, [2012] EWHC 2609 (QB), [2012] I.R.L.R. 979, Underhill, J., QBD.

1050. Restrictive covenants–Non-competition covenants–Good faith–New employee bringing discrete type of work to new employment and taking it away again when leaving–Distinction between fiduciary duty and duty to act in good faith

The claimant (T) claimed breach of contract against the first defendant (E), his former employer, and against the second defendant (W), who was E's managing director. E counterclaimed for breach of restrictive covenants in T's contract of employment and for breach of fiduciary duty. T was a journalist and business news broadcaster with a track record of having moderated high-profile events for corporate or public sector organisations. E was a small communications consultancy business looking to expand. T had been headhunted by W to join E as "Head of Media" on a generous financial package, which included a salary, a quarterly bonus payment, and an eight per cent equity stake in E. His employment contract included a six-month non-competition clause. Although event moderation did not form part of T's express duties for E, he continued to attract that work. He performed it, not as a private sideline, but in the course of his employment with E, the latter receiving the fee. After a couple of years, W informed T by email that he wished to increase his equity stake in E to 20 per cent. Three years later, T gave notice and moved to an entirely different job. His case against E and W was for specific performance of his employment contract. He sought an eight per cent share in E, increasing to 20 per cent from November 2003; payment of dividends; and a bonus payment for the final quarter of his employment, which W had refused to pay on the alleged ground of under-performance. E's case was that in the six months following T's termination of employment, he had undertaken moderation events for organisations which were E's clients and was therefore in breach of the non-competition clause and implied duties of good faith and fidelity.

Held: Judgment for claimant in part. (1) On the evidence, event moderation did not form part of E's activities before T joined or after he left. It was a niche market, the work coming to T because of his personal qualities and his background in broadcasting. The work was therefore defined by the person who carried it out. When T left E, the work followed him because of his personal reputation, not because he had left E to increase his involvement in that kind of work or with the intention of being in competition with E. Even if he had refused the work for six months in accordance with the non-competition clause, the work would still not have fallen to E. The non-competition clause was therefore not applicable because the work that T had engaged in was not "business relating to management and communications development", which was the description applied to E's work at the time the contract of employment was entered into. Before T left, however, he ought to have told W about the event he had already committed to at the time of giving notice, but which would not take place until after he had left. It was an existing contract for E to be paid for T's services, and T had thus diverted income away from E (see paras 32-33, 46-47, 52-53, 58, 92-93, 103-110 of judgment). (2) Regarding the equity stake, W's evidence that his email suggesting an increased equity stake was a proposal falling short of a firm agreement was not credible. On the evidence, there had been a concluded agreement amounting to a variation of T's contract of employment. E had wrongfully and in breach of contract failed to pay T a sum representing 20 per cent of its equity. It had also failed to pay dividends in respect of T's equity share (paras 67-68, 71-72, 77, 90, 95, 102). (3) Although T's bonuses had started off as an elaborate mathematical formula, W had unilaterally changed the basis upon which they were calculated, stating that they would be discretionary. Thereafter, T had received quarterly payments of at least £9,800. Provision had already been made for the payment of a similar bonus at the end of the final quarter of T's employment, therefore it could not be said that the true reason for non-payment was under-performance. On the evidence, W had felt aggrieved that T was diverting work away from E and, wishing to reduce his financial burden, had simply decided upon a nil bonus. That decision was not so irrational or perverse that no reasonable employer would have exercised its discretion that way. T's claim for a bonus payment was therefore dismissed, *Clark v Nomura International Plc* [2000] I.R.L.R. 766, [2000] C.L.Y. 2098 applied (paras 78-79, 81, 86-87, 97-102). (4) T had not been a director of E and did not owe any specific contractual obligations of a type giving rise to a fiduciary duty. He had been a senior employee but nevertheless under the close management of W. He had a contractual duty to act in good faith, but that was different from a fiduciary duty, *Helmet Integrated Systems Ltd v Tunnard* [2006] EWCA Civ 1735, [2007] I.R.L.R. 126, [2007] C.L.Y. 1324 and *Customer Systems Plc v Ranson* [2012] EWCA Civ 841, [2012] I.R.L.R. 769, [2012] C.L.Y. 1054 applied. Although T's conduct in arranging, while employed by E, to moderate an event after his employment had ended did not constitute a breach of the non-competition covenant, it did constitute a breach of the implied term of good faith. E was therefore entitled to judgment on that aspect of its counterclaim (paras 111-116, 118-126).

THRELFALL v ECD INSIGHT LTD, [2012] EWHC 3543 (QB), [2013] I.R.L.R. 185, Lang, J., QBD.

1051. Settlement agreements–Indemnity clauses–Newspaper agreeing to pay ex-editor's legal costs in proceedings arising from role–Whether indemnity extending to defence of criminal allegations

[Prevention of Corruption Act 1906 (c.34); Regulation of Investigatory Powers Act 2000 (c.23) s.79.]

The appellant (C) appealed against a decision ([2011] EWHC 3482 (QB), [2012] I.R.L.R. 385, [2012] C.L.Y. 1039) rejecting his claim for a declaration in relation to the meaning of a contract between him and the respondent newspaper group (N). The contract was entered into as part of the termination of C's employment by N as editor of one of its newspapers. Clause 4.6 provided that N would "pay any reasonable professional... costs and expenses properly incurred by C after [the termination of his employment] which [arose] from his having to defend, or appear in, any administrative, regulatory, judicial or quasi-judicial proceedings as a result of his having been the editor...". C was subsequently arrested on suspicion of conspiracy unlawfully to intercept communications, contrary to the Regulation of Investigatory Powers Act 2000 s.79, and making unlawful payments to police officers contrary to the Prevention of Corruption Act 1906. N told C that it would not pay costs incurred by him in defence of or appearance in any criminal or other proceedings relating to alleged conduct outside the scope of the terms of his employment contract, meaning it would not fund his defence of the criminal proceedings. The judge rejected C's claim that cl.4.6 meant that N should pay those costs, and decided in any event that "proceedings" for the purposes of cl.4.6 had not begun. Since the judge's decision C had been charged with five offences contrary to s.79 of the 2000 Act and further offences. C applied to admit fresh evidence, namely a statement from his solicitor including documents that indicated that N was financially supporting another former newspaper editor in respect of similar charges she faced. C submitted that N's obligation was to pay his reasonable legal costs properly incurred in all types of proceedings, including criminal proceedings, concerning his conduct as editor. N submitted that it was not obliged to pay the costs of criminal proceedings because they were not incurred as a result of his having been editor but because of his own personal misconduct outside an editor's lawful duties.

Held: Appeal allowed. (1) C's solicitor's evidence satisfied the *Ladd v Marshall* criteria for the admission of fresh evidence on appeals. It was obviously material to N's submission that an indemnity to cover costs of criminal proceedings made no sense in the circumstances of C's case. N did not deny that it was supporting the other former editor facing similar allegations; in the absence of such a denial the court would infer that such support was being given (see paras 28-31 of judgment). (2) There was nothing in the criminal nature of the proceedings to render it objectionable that the indemnity should apply. Once the costs of defence of some criminal charges were allowed within the indemnity, the scope of the indemnity could not be defined simply by the criminal nature of the proceedings in question. The limit had to be bounded by the question whether the criminal allegations arose out of how the employee performed his job or out of some act having nothing whatever to do with performing the job. The charges which C faced arose out of the allegedly criminal manner of his performance of his role as editor, in contrast to, for example, a criminal allegation that he had made a fraudulent claim for expenses, which would not. If the charges that C faced were made out, they would show a dishonest complicity in telephone hacking in a misguided attempt to fulfil his contractual duty as editor. Dishonest extortion of money, for illegitimate expenses, would not be an attempt to do the job at all. The judge was wrong in his view that because C's duties as editor comprised only lawful duties, it could not have been intended that activities outside his lawful responsibilities would be covered by the indemnity: that would surely deprive the indemnity of all practical use. It would not even cover the editor for the costs of defending proceedings arising out of the publication of alleged libels or publications said to be a contempt of court, the very occupational hazards of editorship referred to by N in argument (paras 44-48). (3) Given the factual background to the contract, including that the parties used wide words (in contrast to C's employment contract), that as a matter of language the clause covered criminal proceedings and that the agreement was made with C as an editor on whose watch interception of communications offences had been carried out, and for which two offenders had just a month earlier been imprisoned, it would be artificial to have expected the indemnity to be subject to a scrutiny of the nature or merits of the intended defence to the charges or subject to the outcome of the trial itself. The phrase costs "properly incurred" in cl.4.6 simply meant costs of a nature properly to be regarded as required in the defence of the particular proceedings in question, *Investors Compensation Scheme Ltd v West Bromwich Building Society (No.1)* [1998] 1 W.L.R. 896, [1997] C.L.Y. 2537 applied. Therefore cl.4.6 covered C's costs of defending the criminal allegations (paras 50-53). (4) The indemnity covered pre-charge costs incurred by C, even if no charges were ultimately preferred. Advice and representation in relation to proceedings at a police station where a person was suspected of a criminal offence were for the purpose of this agreement part and parcel of the criminal process, of defending and appearing in "judicial proceedings". Conduct at police interview and in seeking police bail were important steps in the process and could not be sensibly separated from events after charge, *R. (on the application of Hale) v North Sefton Justices* [2002] EWHC 257 (Admin), Times, January 29, 2002, [2002] C.L.Y. 863 considered (paras 54-60). (5) The doctrine of ex turpi causa was no answer to C's claim. There was nothing contrary to public policy in one person providing funds to another for that other to defend himself against a criminal charge. The Criminal Defence Service did it all the time, and there could be no objection to private persons agreeing to do so for consideration (para.61).

COULSON v NEWS GROUP NEWSPAPERS LTD, [2012] EWCA Civ 1547, [2013] 1 Costs L.O. 117, Laws, L.J., CA (Civ Div).

1052. Sex discrimination–Pregnancy discrimination–Maternity leave–General practitioner's claims for indirect discrimination, harassment and expulsion from partnership in relation to denial of nine months' maternity leave

[Sex Discrimination Act 1975 (c.65) s.1 (2) (b), s.4A.]

The appellant employee (M) appealed against a decision of an employment tribunal to dismiss her claims for indirect discrimination on the grounds of sex and maternity, harassment and expulsion against her respondent colleague and employer (D and P). M was employed as a general practitioner and was a partner in P's medical practice. The partnership agreement stated that partners could take maternity leave, provided that for half the six-month period there was locum cover. M went on maternity leave in January 2010 and indicated that she would return to work after nine months, in October 2010. At a partnership meeting in April 2010, the partners discussed an away-day to which M was not invited. M complained, and D initially refused to allow her to attend but subsequently relented. The partners refused to accede to M's written proposal that she return to work after between six and nine months' on a job-share arrangement and she resigned. M argued before the tribunal that there had been an oral agreement that she would have nine months' leave. The tribunal said that its unanimous decision was that her harassment and expulsion claims failed, but it set out the majority and minority judgments in relation to indirect discrimination. The majority said that M had not formally requested to return to work part-time, whether by job-share arrangement or otherwise, and even if she had she had not explained how such an arrangement would work. As to harassment and expulsion, the tribunal said that factors she relied on in support of harassment, including that she felt bullied by D, did not fall within the Sex Discrimination Act 1975 s.4A, and that M had not been expelled but had resigned. The issues were whether the tribunal had erred in relation to (i) indirect discrimination; (ii) harassment; (iii) expulsion from the partnership.

Held: Appeal allowed in part. (1) There was no requirement to make a formal application to return to work on a part-time basis, and therefore the tribunal's insistence that M's proposal lacked formality was misplaced. It was plain that M had requested to return by way of job-sharing. She had provided two options in her proposal as to how that arrangement might work, and the tribunal had erred in failing to recognise her proposal for what it said, namely that she was willing to return to work in a job-share position. The tribunal should have asked itself whether the partnership's failure to respond to her request for part-time working and its refusal to countenance it constituted a breach of s.1 (2)(b) (see paras 24-26, 30 of judgment). (2) The tribunal had failed to give proper reasons on M's case for harassment. It could not be said that the actions M relied on, including that she felt bullied by D, did not fall within s.4A. The contention that she had been bullied was in itself an allegation of unfavourable treatment and was capable of creating an effect in her mind of something humiliating or an offensive environment for her. The tribunal had to consider the wording of s.4A, whether the facts asserted by M were true, and if so whether they fell within the meaning of s.4A. The tribunal fell short of the standards required of it to explain why what had been alleged by M fell outside s.4A (paras 34-36). (3) The tribunal was justified in dismissing M's expulsion claim. The claim's success depended on M's case on the nine-month oral contractual term being accepted by the tribunal when it had not been: she relied on that oral agreement as being the reason why she resigned the partnership, but the tribunal had held that she was wrong in relying on an agreement which she had misunderstood. Further, there was no mention of any implied terms as to her right to nine months' maternity leave, and the tribunal was right not to determine matters about her constructive expulsion because the point was not properly put before it (paras 39-40). (4) M's indirect discrimination and harassment claims were remitted to a fresh tribunal for reconsideration. It was appropriate that a fresh tribunal consider the claims because the original tribunal was divided as to M's indirect discrimination claim and because, in light of the instant tribunal's decision that the tribunal was wrong to hold that bullying and other matters did not fall within s.4A, it would have been difficult for the tribunal to decide the same matters on a reconsideration of the statutory definition of harassment under s.4A (paras 42-43).

MATHER v DEVINE & PARTNERS BRAMHALL PARK MEDICAL CENTRE [2012] Eq. L.R. 1082, Judge McMullen Q.C., EAT.

1053. Sex discrimination–Striking out–Lawfulness of tribunal striking out discrimination claims part way through hearing–Importance of hearing and evaluating evidence from both sides

[Equality Act 2010 (c.15); Employment Tribunals (Constitution and Rules of Procedure) Regulations 2004 (SI 2004/1861) Sch.1 para.18.]

The appellant employee (T) appealed against the decision of an employment tribunal to dismiss her race and sex discrimination claims against the respondent employer (G) part way through the hearing. On the third day of the four-day hearing G applied to strike out T's claims. It argued that her claims were of dual discrimination and were bound to fail because the law prior to the Equality Act 2010 did not make provision for dual discrimination. It also argued that T's evidence could not be accepted on any significant issue and that there was no prospect of her establishing primary facts from which it could infer discrimination. The tribunal granted G's application, describing it as a submission of no case to answer. It found that several issues depended on T's credibility as a witness, but found that her credibility was flawed. T argued that it was not open to the tribunal to dismiss her claims as it did because they depended on disputed fact, and therefore it should have heard the evidence from both sides. G submitted that it was an exceptional case because the tribunal had found T's evidence so fundamentally flawed that it could place no reliance on it, and therefore it was entitled to strike out the claims.

Held: Appeal allowed. Although the tribunal described G's application as a submission of no case to answer, it was an application made expressly under the Employment Tribunals (Constitution and Rules of Procedure) Regulations 2004 Sch.1 para.18(7)(b) to strike out T's claims on the grounds that they were misconceived. In light of the approach in *Anyanwu v South Bank Students Union* [2001] UKHL 14, [2001] 1 W.L.R. 638, [2001] C.L.Y. 2300, G's argument before the tribunal on dual discrimination was hopeless: whether there was dual discrimination and whether the law prior to the 2010 Act allowed for such discrimination were matters to be determined after the evidence had been heard. It was highly undesirable that a striking-out application be made on a hypothetical basis when a difficult issue of discrimination law might be raised after the case was heard and findings made, *Anyanwu* followed. The tribunal correctly recognised that T's case depended to a significant extent on her credibility as a witness: it identified issues which it could not determine, but made a conclusive finding that it could never, in any circumstances, accept anything that T had said about them. It was inappropriate to make such a judgment on a striking-out application. Although the tribunal said that it was applying the guidance given in *Ezsias v North Glamorgan NHS Trust* [2007] EWCA Civ 330, [2007] 4 All E.R. 940, [2007] C.L.Y. 1428, it did not do so. There was a crucial core of disputed facts which was not susceptible to determination other than by hearing and evaluating the evidence. That being so, the tribunal should not have acceded to the application, but should have heard and evaluated all the evidence, *Ezsias* followed. It was one thing for a tribunal to reach a provisional view halfway through a hearing that a witness's evidence was unsatisfactory and was unlikely to be accepted if there was evidence to the contrary, but it was another to reach a concluded view that a witness's evidence inevitably had to be rejected in its entirety even if there was no evidence to contradict it. It was an error of law to reason in such a way on a striking-out application made before all the evidence had been heard, *Williams v Real Care Agency Ltd* [2012] I.C.R. D27 applied. T's claims could not be described as inherently frivolous or incredible without hearing the evidence on both sides, and accordingly they were remitted for reconsideration (see paras 31, 34, 46-49 of judgment).

TIMBO v GREENWICH COUNCIL FOR RACIAL EQUALITY [2012] Eq. L.R. 1010, Judge David Richardson, EAT.

1054. Sex discrimination–Voluntary redundancies–Exclusion from eligibility for voluntary severance scheme–Measure of compensation

The appellant employer (L) appealed against the quantum of compensation awarded to the respondent employee (M) following her successful claim for sex discrimination. In 2008 M began a career break which she could stay on until 2013, but from which she could return to work at any time upon reasonable notice. Later in 2008, L sought to reduce staff numbers and devised an early release scheme to encourage staff to volunteer for severance. M expressed interest. In 2009 L decided to exclude from consideration for the scheme those who were on a career break and were not due to return until after March 2010. The employment tribunal found that had M returned to work or indicated an intention to do so before March 2010, she would have been successful in the scheme. It therefore found that she had been indirectly discriminated against as those in the ineligible group were far more likely to be women. It awarded her £12,000 for injury to feelings, an aggravated award of £5,000, and a compensatory award of £71,710.95 based on the sum she would have received had she been able to apply for voluntary severance. L argued that (1) the injury to feelings award was too high; (2) no aggravated award should have been made; (3) since M had remained in work, the compensatory award should be assessed at nil.

Held: Appeal allowed in part. (1) As a matter of principle, awards made in respect of injury to feelings were not susceptible to close calculation. They would therefore not be interfered with unless they were manifestly excessive or wrong in principle. The making of an award had plainly not been wrong in principle. The effect of L's conduct had been to deny M the opportunity to obtain a very large benefit enabling her to obtain release from her employment; that was something which for her had been of particular importance. The Employment Appeal Tribunal had been shown a number of comparable cases, but a difficulty with being guided too tightly by such cases was the brevity of any report and the difficulty of knowing precisely how the discrimination set out in each report had actually affected the individual. They did not clearly demonstrate that the tribunal had adopted the wrong bracket. The EAT could not properly interfere with the award (see paras 25-29 of judgment). (2) The tribunal had not made an objective finding in respect of aggravated damages. It had had regard to the sense of aggravation caused to M. A tribunal examining whether there was a case for aggravated damages had to consider whether, objectively viewed, the conduct was capable of being aggravating, namely aggravating the sense of injustice which the individual felt and injuring their feelings still further. The distress could be made worse by (a) being done in an exceptionally upsetting way; (b) motive, as conduct based on prejudice, animosity, spite or vindictiveness was likely to cause more distress; (c) subsequent conduct, for example where a trial was conducted in an unnecessarily offensive manner. In each case the emphasis was one of degree. A tribunal should be cautious not to award damages for injury to feelings for the same conduct as it awarded aggravated damages. Aggravated damages were not punitive and did not depend on any sense of outrage by a tribunal as to the conduct. The tribunal had not found that L's conduct had been deliberate or that it had lied. There was insufficient to meet the hurdle for the award of aggravated damages. The award was wrong in principle (paras 30-40). (3) The victim of a wrong was to be placed financially in the position she would have been in had the wrong not been committed. Had the wrong not been committed, M would have been eligible for the early severance scheme, would have been selected and would have accepted the offer. She would therefore have been £71,000 better off. That was therefore the starting point. The argument that such a payment was intended for loss of a job was beside the point. It was not necessarily the case that M would have been without work and income had she accepted the offer. Had it been established before the tribunal that she would earn less in other work than she had with L, that difference would have been capable of being offset against the benefit she would have had by accepting the offer; however, the tribunal had made no findings of fact about that (paras 42-49).

LAND REGISTRY v McGLUE [2013] Eq. L.R. 701, Langstaff, J. (President), EAT.

1055. Sexual orientation discrimination–Harassment–Office banter–Use of abusive phrases referring to employee's sexual orientation–Effect of unwanted conduct on employee

[Employment Equality (Sexual Orientation) Regulations 2003 (SI 2003/1661) reg.5(1).]

The appellant employee (S) appealed against an employment tribunal's decision concerning his victimisation claim against the respondent (X). S was a gay man. He had been involved in an altercation with another employee, after which disciplinary proceedings were instigated against him. He sought an adjournment of the disciplinary hearing, stating that he would be raising a grievance about homophobic bullying and harassment by other members of staff. He was dismissed shortly afterwards, four days before the disciplinary hearing was due to take place. His grievance was dismissed. The tribunal found that although his dismissal amounted to victimisation, he would have been dismissed in any event at the conclusion of the disciplinary process. It also concluded that comments made by staff about S's sexual orientation, for example by referring to him as "Big Gay Wayne"and "Val's Bitch", were not homophobic where S used the some of the same terms when referring to himself. S submitted that the tribunal had (1) misdirected itself in relation to harassment; (2) erred in concluding that dismissal was inevitable, because he had not received a prior written warning, because dismissal was merely one option open to the disciplinary panel, and because when difficulties had arisen previously between him and his superior, he had been promoted.

Held: Appeal allowed. (1) The tribunal had misdirected itself in relation to harassment by failing to have regard to the definition of harassment in the Employment Equality (Sexual Orientation) Regulations 2003 reg.5(1), which referred to unwanted conduct which had the "purpose or effect" of violating a person's dignity. It had focused on "the purpose" of the unwanted conduct and failed to have regard to "the effect" of the conduct. That was a plain error of law. It also appeared to have treated the fact that S was openly gay, and promoted his sexuality, as meaning that it was unlikely or impossible for any remark about his sexual orientation to constitute harassment. A person who paraded their particular characteristic loudly might expect to receive from colleagues responses which made reference to that characteristic. That was quite distinct from the abusive use of references to sexual orientation or any other protected characteristic (see paras 23-25, 28-29 of judgment). (2) The tribunal was entitled to investigate the question of what loss followed from the wrongful act of unlawful victimisation, *Abbey National Plc v Chagger* [2009] EWCA Civ 1202, [2010] I.C.R. 397, [2010] C.L.Y. 1026 followed. If, given the factual background, the tribunal was saying that the only possible outcome of the proposed disciplinary hearing was that S would inevitably have been summarily dismissed, it needed to explain in very clear terms why that was so. Given that the sanction of dismissal was only one of a range of alternatives open to the disciplinary panel, and given the history of past dealings between X and S, the requisite explanation was not contained in the tribunal's judgment. In the absence of a satisfactory explanation, the tribunal's conclusion could not stand. A reduction of projected loss could have been made based on the prospects of dismissal, but the reasoning offered by the tribunal could not sustain its assessment that dismissal was 100 per cent likely. Accordingly, S's case was remitted to a fresh tribunal for redetermination of the questions of harassment and the loss flowing from S's dismissal (paras 30, 38-40).

SMITH v IDEAL SHOPPING DIRECT LTD [2013] Eq. L.R. 943, Recorder Luba Q.C., EAT.

1056. Termination of employment–Repudiation–Employer's wrongful repudiation of contract not accepted by employee–Whether contract terminated automatically

The appellant (G) appealed against a decision ([2011] EWCA Civ 307, [2011] I.R.L.R. 482, [2011] C.L.Y. 1122) that his contract of employment had been terminated when the respondent employer (S) had made a payment in lieu of notice (PILON) into his bank account. S cross-appealed against the decision that its earlier repudiation of the contract by summarily dismissing G had not automatically terminated the contract. G's contract provided for termination on the expiry of three months' written notice. S's staff handbook contained further terms of employment, including s.8.3, which provided that S could terminate G's employment at any time with immediate effect by making a PILON. On November 29, 2007, S told G that his employment was being terminated "with immediate effect", and he was escorted from the building. On December 18, S paid a substantial amount of money directly into G's bank account. On January 2, G's solicitors wrote to S stating that G had decided to affirm his contract. Two days later S sent G a letter confirming the details of the termination of his employment. It stated that the payment made to his bank account was a PILON. The Court of Appeal held that G's contract of employment had been terminated on December 18 when the PILON was made. It rejected S's argument that its repudiatory dismissal of G on November 29 had automatically terminated the contract. The instant court was required to determine, amongst other things, (i) whether a repudiation of a contract of employment by the employer which took the form of an express and immediate dismissal automatically terminated the contract, or whether the normal contractual rule that the repudiation had to be accepted by the other party applied equally to that situation; (ii) the date of termination of G's contract of employment.

Held: Appeal allowed, cross-appeal dismissed. (Lord Sumption dissenting on the issues of repudiation and date of termination) (1) A party's repudiation of a contract of employment did not automatically terminate the contract. The contract would only be terminated if and when the other party elected to accept the repudiation, *Sanders v Ernest A Neale Ltd* [1974] 3 All E.R. 327, [1974] C.L.Y. 1350 disapproved, *Gunton v Richmond upon Thames LBC* [1981] Ch. 448, [1980] C.L.Y. 895, *Vine v National Dock Labour Board* [1957] A.C. 488, [1957] C.L.Y. 1264 and *Francis v Municipal Councillors of Kuala Lumpur* [1962] 1 W.L.R. 1411, [1962] C.L.Y. 1131 considered. The overall effect of the automatic theory was to reward the wrongful repudiator of a contract of employment with a date of termination which he had chosen, no doubt as being most beneficial to him and most detrimental to the innocent party. The automatic theory also failed to explain cases where, following an unaccepted wrongful repudiation, provisions which did not survive the termination of the contract had been enforced against the repudiator, such as covenants against competition and clauses relating to disciplinary procedures, *Lumley v Wagner* 42 E.R. 687, *William Robinson & Co Ltd v Heuer* [1898] 2 Ch. 451, *Warner Bros Pictures Inc v Nelson* [1937] 1 K.B. 209, *Jones v Lee* [1980] I.C.R. 310, [1980] C.L.Y. 860 and *Robb v Hammersmith and Fulham LBC* [1991] I.C.R. 514, [1991] C.L.Y. 1610 considered. Difficult questions arose as to how far the automatic theory might extend, for example, whether dismissals or resignations should be treated differently according to whether they were express or implied, immediate or delayed, outright or something less than outright. Also, there was the question whether the automatic theory would extend to wrongful repudiations of contracts of services as well as of contracts of employment (see paras 15-19, 68-97 of judgment). (2) It was quite clear that s.8.3 did not dispense with the contractual requirement that the employee be notified of the termination of his employment. It was necessary that the employee not only receive his PILON, but that he receive notification from the employer, in clear and unambiguous terms, that such a payment had been made and that it had been made in the exercise of the contractual right to terminate the employment with immediate effect. An employee should not be required to check his bank account regularly in order to discover whether he was still employed. S could easily have given clear and unambiguous notice to G, but had failed to do so. It was only on January 6, when G received S's letter of January 4, that the contractual right to terminate under the PILON method was validly exercised and G's employment with S came to an end (paras 54-61). (3) (Per Lord Sumption) There was a general rule that the innocent party to a repudiated contract could not treat it as subsisting if performance on his part required the co-operation of the repudiating party, and the contract was incapable of specific performance, with the result that that co-operation could not be compelled. *Gunton* had been wrongly decided, and was contrary to the case law as it stood up until the 1970s, *Gunton* considered. In the instant case, although G had suffered no loss as a result of S's mistake, the operation of the elective theory rather than the automatic theory would result in a substantial windfall to him in terms of the calculation of his compensation payment (paras 108-140).

GEYS v SOCIETE GENERALE; *sub nom.* SOCIETE GENERALE (LONDON BRANCH) v GEYS, [2012] UKSC 63, [2013] 1 A.C. 523, Lord Hope, J.S.C. (Deputy President), SC.

1057. Trade unions–Trade union recognition–Admissibility of application for recognition–Interpretation of Sch.A1 para.35 Trade Union and Labour Relations (Consolidation) Act 1992 in light of rights under art.11 European Convention on Human Rights 1950–Meaning of "collective bargaining" within 1950 Convention

[Trade Union and Labour Relations (Consolidation) Act 1992 (c.52) Pt I, s.2, s.3, s.178(2)(f), s.178(1), Sch.A1 Pt I para.35, Sch.A1 Pt VI; European Convention on Human Rights 1950 Art.11.]

The applicant trade union (P) made an application to the Central Arbitration Committee for recognition for collective bargaining. P had sought recognition in relation to a bargaining unit comprising all registered pharmacists employed by the respondent (B) in the United Kingdom. P estimated that B employed 5500 such pharmacists. Of those, 2100 were members of P. B rejected P's recognition requests and suggested a stay of P's application to the CAC pending discussions. B then entered into an agreement with the Boots Pharmacists Association (BPA) on March 1, 2012, and argued that P's application was inadmissible because the BPA was already recognised for the same bargaining unit. Under the March agreement the BPA had collective bargaining rights only in relation to "facilities for its officials and the machinery for consultation", but not in relation to pay, hours or holiday. The BPA was a listed trade union but did not have a certificate of independence. The CAC was required to determine (i) whether the BPA was a trade union; (ii) whether the March agreement was a collective agreement; (iii) how the terms of the European Convention on Human Rights 1950 art.11 should affect the interpretation of the Trade Union and Labour Relations (Consolidation) Act 1992 Sch.A1 Pt I para.35. P submitted that the right to bargain collectively over facilities for officials and consultation machinery did not fulfil art.11.

Held: Judgment accordingly. (1) The admissibility of a union's application for statutory recognition where an employer had a relationship with another body was governed by the terms of Sch.A1 para.35, *R. (on the application of Kwik-Fit Ltd) v Central Arbitration Committee* [2002] EWCA Civ 512, [2002] I.C.R. 1212, [2002] C.L.Y. 1423 considered. Paragraph 35 stated that applications were not admissible if there was already in force a collective agreement under which a union was recognised as entitled to conduct collective bargaining. The BPA was a trade union within the meaning of s.1. It had the power to do more than consult with B, if it chose to do so. The March agreement was not a sham, meetings took place and the consultative process described in the agreement did not preclude negotiations as part of the procedure. Further, the BPA had been listed as a trade union by the Certification Officer under ss.2 and 3. That was a highly relevant factor to be taken into account (see paras 4, 35, 51-52 of judgment). (2) The March agreement was a collective agreement within the meaning of s.178(1) since it covered the matters listed in s.178(2)(f) and (g) and was made between B and the BPA. It was clear from the statutory wording that an agreement relating to just one of the matters listed in s.178(2) was sufficient to come within the definition of a collective agreement. P's proposed bargaining unit included workers within the March agreement. The scope of the agreement therefore overlapped with the bargaining unit proposed by P, potentially bringing Sch.A1 para.35 into play (paras 53-59). (3) Schedule A1 had to be construed to give proper effect to the art.11 right to bargain collectively with the employer, *Netjets Management Ltd v Central Arbitration Committee* [2012] EWHC 2685 (Admin), [2013] 1 All E.R. 288 applied. The purpose of para.35 was to prevent the CAC from being drawn into disputes between unions. However, P and the BPA were not competing with each other to negotiate on hours, pay and holiday as neither union had that facility, *R. (on the application of National Union of Journalists) v Central Arbitration Committee* [2005] EWCA Civ 1309, [2006] I.C.R. 1, [2006] C.L.Y. 1375 distinguished. The right to bargain collectively over facilities for trade union officials and consultation machinery did not, on the face of it, amount to collective bargaining within the meaning of the 1950 Convention, the International Labour Organisation Convention 98, and EU jurisprudence since it expressly excluded bargaining on matters to do with working conditions, terms of employment, hours, pay and holiday, *Demir v Turkey (34503/97)* [2009] I.R.L.R. 766, [2009] C.L.Y. 1938 applied. Under Pt VI of the 1992 Act, unions could be derecognised where they were not independent. However, the s.178 definition of "collective agreement" did not apply to Pt VI. The BPA's agreement could not therefore be dislodged by the members in the proposed bargaining unit to enable P to bring a Pt I claim, which left P in a "catch-22". B had deliberately misled P in order to buy time to conclude arrangements with the BPA and block P's request for recognition without conferring those rights on any other union. The workers in the proposed bargaining unit were therefore denied the opportunity for an independent trade union to bargain collectively on their behalf in relation to pay, hours and holiday under the statutory procedure. The prohibition on an independent union from seeking recognition under the statutory procedure where no other union, whether independent or otherwise, had collective bargaining rights concerning pay, hours and holidays was an infringement of art.11. Schedule A1 para.35 should be read as precluding an application for recognition where there was already in force an agreement under which a union was "recognised as entitled to conduct collective bargaining in respect of pay, hours and holidays on behalf of any workers falling within the relevant bargaining unit". Accordingly, P's application was admissible subject to a membership and support check (paras 27, 60-61, 67, 71-76, 82-85).

PHARMACISTS' DEFENCE ASSOCIATION UNION v BOOTS MANAGEMENT SERVICES LTD [2013] I.R.L.R. 262, Mary Stacey (Chairperson), CAC.

1058. Transfer of undertakings–Collective agreements–Whether transferee bound by collective agreements reached after date of transfer–European Union

[Charter of Fundamental Rights of the European Union Art.16; Directive 2001/23 on the safeguarding of employees' rights in the event of transfers of undertakings, businesses or parts of undertakings or businesses Art.3, Art.8; Directive 77/187 on the safeguarding of employees' rights in the event of transfers of undertakings, businesses or parts of businesses.]

The court was asked to give a preliminary ruling concerning the interpretation of Directive 2001/23 art.3. The dispute in the main proceedings involved a private-sector undertaking (P) which had taken on staff formerly employed by a local authority. The original contracts of employment of those employees had provided that, during their employment with the local authority, their terms and conditions of employment would accord with collective agreements negotiated from time to time by the National Joint Council for Local Government Services. The issue was whether P was bound by a new collective agreement which had been reached after the transfer of the undertaking to it. The question referred was whether Directive 2001/23 art.3 had to be construed as precluding a Member State from providing, in the event of a transfer of an undertaking such as that at issue, that dynamic clauses referring to collective agreements negotiated and agreed after the date of transfer were enforceable against the transferee.

Held: Preliminary ruling given. Directive 77/187, which Directive 2001/23 codified, did not aim solely to safeguard the interests of employees in the event of a transfer of an undertaking: it sought to ensure a fair balance between the interests of those employees and those of the transferee. More particularly, it made clear that the transferee had to be in a position to make the adjustments and changes necessary to carry on its operations. In that regard, it should be pointed out that the transfer of the undertaking at issue had taken place between a legal person governed by public law and a legal person governed by private law. As the transfer was of an undertaking from the public sector to the private sector, the continuation of the transferee's operations would require significant adjustments and changes, given the inevitable differences in working conditions that existed between those two sectors. However, a dynamic clause referring to collective agreements negotiated and agreed after the date of transfer of the undertaking concerned that were intended to regulate changes in working conditions in the public sector was liable to limit considerably the room for manoeuvre necessary for a private transferee to make such adjustments and changes. In such a situation, such a clause was liable to undermine the fair balance between the interests of the transferee in its capacity as employer and those of the employees. Further, it was settled case-law that the provisions of Directive 2001/23 had to be construed consistently with the fundamental rights as set out by the Charter of Fundamental Rights of the European Union. The interpretation of art.3 of the Directive had to comply with art.16 of the Charter, laying down the freedom to conduct a business. That fundamental right covered freedom of contract. In the light of art.3, it was apparent that, by reason of the freedom to conduct a business, the transferee had to be able to assert its interests effectively in a contractual process to which it was party and to negotiate the aspects determining changes in the working conditions of its employees with a view to its future economic activity. P was unable to participate in the collective bargaining body at issue. In those circumstances, it could neither assert its interests effectively in a contractual process nor negotiate the aspects determining changes in working conditions for its employees with a view to its future economic activity. Its contractual freedom was therefore seriously reduced to the point that such a limitation was liable to adversely affect the very essence of its freedom to conduct a business. Article 3, read in conjunction with art.8, could not be construed as entitling the Member States to take measures which, while being more favourable to employees, were liable to adversely affect the very essence of the transferee's freedom to conduct a business. Accordingly, art.3 had to be construed as precluding a Member State from providing, in the event of a transfer of an undertaking, that dynamic clauses referring to collective agreements negotiated and adopted after the date of transfer were enforceable against the transferee, where that transferee did not have the possibility of participating in the negotiation process of such collective agreements (see paras 25-37 of judgment).

ALEMO-HERRON v PARKWOOD LEISURE LTD (C-426/11) [2014] 1 C.M.L.R. 21, Judge Silva de Lapuerta (President), ECJ (3rd Chamber).

1059. Transfer of undertakings–Employee consultation–Breach of information and consultation obligations–Proposed transfer of two parts of business–Affected employees

[Transfer of Undertakings (Protection of Employment) Regulations 2006 (SI 2006/246) reg.13(1), reg.13(2), reg.15.]

The appellant employer (C) appealed against a decision of an employment tribunal that the respondent employees (R) were "affected" employees within the Transfer of Undertakings (Protection of Employment) Regulations 2006 reg.15. C provided services to the film and television industry and operated in both "rushes" work, and in post-production work. The two parts of the business operated in different premises and did different kinds of work at different hours. C had been facing insolvency and at one point considered transferring both parts of its undertaking. In fact the liquidator transferred only the rushes part of the undertaking and not the post-production part in which R was involved. The post-production part was then closed down, making R redundant. R brought a claim against C for breach of the information and consultation obligations under reg.13 and reg.15 of TUPE. The tribunal found that C had an obligation to inform and consult with R as "affected" employees. C submitted that the only transfer which occurred was the transfer of the rushes part of C's undertaking and that R were not affected by that transfer as they would not transfer under it and their jobs were not placed in jeopardy by it; so that they were not affected employees. R contended that the tribunal's reasoning, properly understood, was not based simply on their exclusion from the transfer and that what generated the obligation to inform and consult was not the transfer in its final form but the plan in its earlier form, which did not proceed.

Held: Appeal allowed. (1) If a single employer had two self-contained businesses, the sale of one business would not "affect" employees in the other. It could not make a difference if, at the same time that the employer sold one business, he closed the other. If the buyer might realistically have considered purchasing both businesses, one could perhaps say that one business was excluded from the sale; but that would not alter the basic fact that what had "affected" the employees was not the sale of the other business but the closure of their employing business. The phrase "affected by the transfer" within the meaning of reg.13(1) was not apt to cover that kind of indirect effect, where the transfer had no impact on the employees. In such a case the effect on them would be the result of the closure of the business employing them. The position was no different in principle in the case of two parts of the same undertaking. A transfer might well affect an employee of the transferor who was not transferred if they did some work in or for the undertaking whose transfer was proposed as the loss of part of their work might affect them. But that was different from saying that they were affected simply because the transfer had left the remaining part of the undertaking less viable (see para.16 of judgment). (2) The tribunal clearly attached some importance to the earlier but aborted transfer plan, but the outcome of the instant appeal should not depend on precisely how the case was analysed before the tribunal. Cases of the instant kind were notoriously difficult and it would not be surprising if either the advocates or even an experienced employment judge did not get the reasoning quite right. Where an envisaged transfer was aborted before it happened the employer would have had to start his consultation weeks previously and if he had not done so he should be regarded as in breach, even though the deal had fallen through at the last minute. However it was necessary to appreciate that the time at which an employer must comply with the obligations under reg.13(2) and reg.13(6) was not defined by reference to when he first envisaged that he would take relevant measures. The obligation was to take the necessary steps long enough before the transfer to allow consultation to take placeThat being so, it could not be said that an employer was in breach of that obligation until the transfer had occurred. The scheme of reg.13 through to reg.15 meant that there could be no complaint of a breach of the obligations under them unless there had indeed been a relevant transfer. Even if the tribunal was to be regarded as having based its decision, not on a failure to inform and consult the post-production employees about the transfer which actually occurred, but on a failure with regard to the earlier form of the proposal, which did not proceed, the decision could not be upheld on that basis and the claim under reg.15 was dismissed (paras17-21).

I LAB FACILITIES LTD v METCALFE [2013] I.R.L.R. 605, Underhill, J., EAT.

1060. Transfer of undertakings–Sale of business–Transferee's liability for dismissal of employees of football club

[Transfer of Undertakings (Protection of Employment) Regulations 2006 (SI 2006/246) reg.7.]

The appellants (K), who had been employed by the owners of Crystal Palace Football Club as administrative staff, appealed against a decision of an employment tribunal that liability for their dismissal did not pass to the third respondent company (C), which had taken over ownership of the club in 2010. The company which had owned the club had been put into administration in January 2010. The aim of the administrator (G) from the outset was to sell the club as a going concern. The only alternative was liquidation, which, because of the particular nature of the business of a football club, would leave few or no assets to be realised for the benefit of the creditors. As at May 2010, the club was in a parlous funding position in the absence of an imminent purchase. At that point, G decided to "mothball" the club over the close season, when no matches would be played, in the hope that it might be possible to sell the club at a future date, and to that end he asked for a list of employees who could be made redundant. K were made redundant. Shortly thereafter, the sale of the club to C was completed. The tribunal found that, for the purposes of the Transfer of Undertakings (Protection of Employment) Regulations 2006 reg.7, K's dismissal was for a reason connected with the transfer but that their dismissal was for an economic, technical or organisational reason, with the result that liability for their dismissal did not pass to C.

Held: Appeal allowed. In *Spaceright Europe Ltd v Baillavoine* [2011] EWCA Civ 1565, [2012] 2 All E.R. 812, [2012] C.L.Y. 1164, the Court of Appeal had posited two alternative positions: the first was where the reason for the dismissal was an intention to change the workforce and to continue to conduct the business; the second was where the dismissal was part and parcel of a process aimed at selling the business. In the former case, there could be a dismissal for an economic, technical or organisational reason, but in the latter case there could not. The tribunal had made very clear findings that G's intention from the outset had been to sell the club as a going concern, failing which there would have to be a liquidation, and that, at the time of K's dismissal, his purpose was to put the club in mothballs pending the possibility of a sale. Those findings pointed unambiguously to the fact that there had been no intention on G's part to continue to conduct the business; instead, the only possible conclusion the tribunal could draw was that K's dismissal was for the purpose of selling the business, albeit it was not at that stage certain that there would be a sale or who the buyer would be. The tribunal's conclusion would therefore be replaced with a finding that liability for K's claims did pass to C, *Spaceright* considered (see paras 26, 30-32 of judgment).

KAVANAGH v CRYSTAL PALACE FC 2000 LTD; *sub nom.* CRYSTAL PALACE FC LTD v KAVANAGH [2013] I.R.L.R. 291, Wilkie, J., EAT.

1061. Transfer of undertakings–Service provision change–Company in administration–In-house solicitor's work carried out by solicitors appointed by administrator–Whether solicitors acting on behalf of company or administrator

[Insolvency Act 1986 (c.45) Sch.B1 para.69; Transfer of Undertakings (Protection of Employment) Regulations 2006 (SI 2006/246) reg.3(1)(b).]

The employment appeal tribunal was required to determine questions concerning service provision changes under the Transfer of Undertakings (Protection of Employment) Regulations 2006 reg.3(1)(b). The first respondent (K) had worked as director of a legal department in the second respondent company. The company held contracts to provide facilities management services, but ran into financial difficulties. During the last few years of her employment, K spent most of her time disposing of the service contracts to outside purchasers. The company's finances did not improve and the appellant administrators (D) were appointed. D appointed a firm of solicitors to act on their behalf. K was made redundant but the task of disposing of the service contracts continued. That task was carried out by D's solicitors. K argued that a service provision change had taken place under reg.3(1)(b)(i) and her contract had transferred to the solicitors. The employment tribunal agreed. The EAT was required to consider whether: (i) the "activities" in reg.3(1)(b) were to be determined by the nature or the purpose of the activity; (ii) solicitors' activities were carried out on behalf of the company rather than the administrators; (iii) an administration expected to be completed within a year was a single event or a task of short-term duration within reg.3(3)(a).

Held: Appeal allowed. (1) It was for the tribunal to define the relevant activities. Providing that the legal approach was correct, and the conclusion was not perverse, its findings of fact had to be respected, *Metropolitan Resources Ltd v Churchill Dulwich Ltd (In Liquidation)* [2009] I.C.R. 1380, [2009] C.L.Y. 1251, *Kimberley Group Housing Ltd v Hambley* [2008] I.C.R. 1030, [2008] C.L.Y. 1199 and *Taurus Group Ltd v Crofts* applied. The word "activities" was commonly used to describe what was being done. If there was a distinction between the nature of the activities and their purpose, the statute looked to the nature of the activities. The tribunal's conclusion that the "the activities" were disposal of the company's service contracts was within the scope of permissible findings open to it (see paras 20-22 of judgment). (2) The wording of reg.3(1)(b)(i) looked to activities "that cease to be carried out by a client on his own behalf". The client was plainly one and the same person as that expression was used throughout reg.3, *Hunter v McCarrick* [2012] I.C.R. 533, [2012] C.L.Y. 1161 applied. The Insolvency Act 1986 Sch.B1 para.69 stated that in exercising functions under the Act the administrator acted as the company's agent; however, that agency was of a design peculiar to its purpose. A finding that solicitors engaged to act for the administrators were acting on behalf of the company could potentially bring those solicitors into a situation of conflict. Although the administrator and the company would often have a common purpose, the administrator owed his duty to the creditors of the company. On the facts of the instant case, the tribunal had erred in finding that merely because the administrator could act as agent for the company it meant that the solicitors retained by the administrators were themselves acting on behalf of the company when they acted in the administration, *Edenwest Ltd v CMS Cameron McKenna* [2012] EWHC 1258 (Ch), [2013] B.C.C. 152, [2013] 5 C.L. 198 applied and *Key2Law (Surrey) LLP v De'Antiquis* [2011] EWCA Civ 1567, [2012] B.C.C. 375, [2012] C.L.Y. 1157 considered (paras 23-25, 38-40). (3) It was not necessary to determine whether the draftsman of reg.3(3)(a) intended the words "a single specific event" to be qualified by "of short-term duration" as well as the word "task". However, the EAT tentatively concluded that "short-term duration" was intended to cover both events because the point was essentially one of time and permanence. The wording of reg.3(3)(a)(ii) began with the intention of the client. Therefore, the primary finding of fact required of the tribunal was as to the intention of the client, not the transferee. In the absence of any clear statement as to what term the tribunal had in mind, and what the company's intentions were, its judgment on the issue could not stand (paras 41-48).

SNR DENTON UK LLP v KIRWAN [2013] I.C.R. 101, Langstaff, J. (President), EAT.

1062. Transfer of undertakings–Service provision change–Interpretation of reg.3(1)(b) Transfer of Undertakings (Protection of Employment) Regulations 2006

[Transfer of Undertakings (Protection of Employment) Regulations 2006 (SI 2006/246) reg.3(1)(b).]

The appellant employee (M) appealed against a decision ([2012] I.C.R. 533, [2012] C.L.Y. 1161) that the transfer of his employment to the respondent individual (H) did not amount to a service provision change within the Transfer of Undertakings (Protection of Employment) Regulations 2006 reg.3(1)(b). M managed a property portfolio owned by a company of which H was the managing director. In February 2009, H sold his company, including the property portfolio, but the sale did not formally proceed. Nevertheless, it was agreed that some employees, including M, would still transfer to the new company (WCP). M therefore continued to manage the property portfolio, but was paid by WCP instead of by H's company. In August 2009, WCP ceased to perform the property management services because receivers appointed by the mortgagee of H's company assumed control of the properties. The receivers appointed a new property management company. However, H paid M out of his own pocket to assist the new company in the portfolio management. The employment tribunal considered that both the February and the August transfers constituted service provision changes within reg.3(1)(b). The Employment Appeal Tribunal disagreed, holding that, on a straightforward and common sense application of the statutory language, the August transfer could not be a service provision change because the portfolio activities before and after the transfer were not carried out for the same client. M submitted that, although, read literally, reg.3(1)(b) envisaged that the same service would be provided to the same client throughout, its clear purpose was to protect employees, and that objective could not be achieved unless a wider interpretation of the provision was adopted.

Held: Appeal dismissed. (1) There was no room for a purposive construction with respect to the scope of reg.3(1)(b). The provision gave protection beyond that circumscribed by EU law and was therefore not subject to the requirement for a purposive interpretation. Rather, a natural construction gave effect to the draftsman's purpose. The concept of a change of service provision was not complex and the ordinary language of reg.3(1)(b) accurately defined the range of situations that it was intended to protect. There was no basis on which to give a broader or expanded meaning, *Metropolitan Resources Ltd v Churchill Dulwich Ltd (In Liquidation)* [2009] I.C.R. 1380, [2009] C.L.Y. 1251 and *Eddie Stobart Ltd v Moreman* [2012] I.C.R. 919, [2012] C.L.Y. 1162 approved (see paras 19-23, 37-38 of judgment).

HUNTER v McCARRICK; *sub nom.* McCARRICK v HUNTER, [2012] EWCA Civ 1399, [2013] I.C.R. 235, Sir Maurice Kay (VP CA Civ), CA (Civ Div).

1063. Tribunals–Procedure

THE EMPLOYMENT TRIBUNALS (CONSTITUTION AND RULES OF PROCEDURE) REGULATIONS 2013, SI 2013/1237; made under the Health and Safety at Work etc. Act 1974 s.24; the Employment Tribunals Act 1996 s.1, s.4, s.7, s.7A, s.7B, s.9, s.10, s.10A, s.11, s.12, s.13, s.13A, s.19, s.41; the Scotland Act 1998 Sch.6 para.37; and the Government of Wales Act 2006 Sch.9 para.32. In force: July 29, 2013 except for reg.1, reg.3 and reg.11 on July 1, 2013.; .

These Regulations replace the Employment Tribunals (Constitution and Rules of Procedure) Regulations 2004. The rules of procedure in Schs 1 to 3 replace the existing rules of procedure in the Employment Tribunals set out in Schs 1 to 6 to the 2004 Regulations.

1064. Unfair dismissal–Band of reasonable responses–Nurse falsifying one patient's chart and failing to make proper observations in respect of another–Assessment of seriousness of misconduct

The appellant (T) appealed against a decision of the Employment Appeal Tribunal that her dismissal by the respondent (B) was not unfair. T was a registered nurse who had been employed in a care home run by B. She worked night shifts, in charge of the home's second floor. Her contract provided that in the event of gross misconduct she could be dismissed without notice, and B's employee handbook identified examples of the sort of things that would be deemed to be gross misconduct. Following disciplinary proceedings in which T admitted making a false entry on a patient's drip-feed record, and failing to make proper observations in respect of a patient who had fallen, she was summarily dismissed for gross misconduct. The employment tribunal found, in relation to both matters, that dismissal was not within the band of reasonable responses open to B. It found that the falsification of written records was not as serious as some of the examples of gross misconduct in the employee handbook; that because T had not been promptly suspended after that incident, her subsequent dismissal was an inconsistent response; and that B had failed to take into account mitigation available to T in respect of her failure to properly observe the patient who had fallen. It concluded that her dismissal was unfair. The EAT found that the tribunal had erred in law. It decided not to remit the case for rehearing, finding that T's actions amounted to gross misconduct for which B had been entitled to dismiss. It therefore substituted its own decision that T's dismissal was not unfair. T submitted that (1) deciding whether dismissal was within the band of reasonable responses open to an employer was exclusively the function of the employment tribunal, and there was no justification for the EAT's substitution of its own view on that issue for that of the tribunal; (2) had the tribunal fallen into error such that its decision could not stand, the EAT should have remitted the case rather than simply substituting its own decision that the dismissal was not unfair.

Held: Appeal dismissed. (1) The employment tribunal was responsible for making findings of fact and applying the law to the facts as found. Whether T's dismissal was within the band of reasonable responses open to B was a question of fact, and appeals to the EAT lay only on questions of law. A finding of fact could only be challenged if, as in the instant case, it was said to be vitiated by an error of law. A tribunal would err in law if it simply substituted its own views for those of the employer, or if it misdirected itself as to the applicable law. In the instant case, the tribunal had erred in considering that the falsification of the drip-feed record was less serious than some of the other examples of gross misconduct in B's employee handbook. That was an error of law. In principle, the falsification of written records was a serious matter capable of meriting dismissal. That was how it was regarded by B, and for the tribunal to overturn B's decision on the basis of its own mistaken assessment of seriousness was an error of approach. B operated care homes for elderly and vulnerable people, and it was obvious that the scrupulous maintenance of accurate and reliable records was of the greatest importance. B was entitled to regard T's infraction as serious. Moreover, the fact that B had not suspended T immediately upon discovering her falsification of the record did not mean that the incident did not merit dismissal. Whether the employee had been suspended was a material consideration, but in the instant case it did not make any difference: B had been entitled to regard the falsification of the record as being serious enough to warrant dismissal. The tribunal's error had been to substitute its own subjective view that the falsification of the record was not so serious as to warrant dismissal. In relation to the failure to carry out proper observations, there was no genuine mitigation, and the EAT was justified in concluding that the tribunal had misdirected itself in concluding otherwise (see paras 53-55, 59-68 of judgment). (2) The EAT had thus been right to conclude that the tribunal's decision could not stand. It was not bound to remit the matter for as fresh decision. The tribunal had found all the primary facts but had misdirected itself in relation to its secondary finding about whether the dismissal fell within the band of reasonable responses open to B. In those circumstances the EAT had been right to take the sensible view that once the errors were removed from consideration, there was only one conclusion, namely that B had been entitled to regard T's actions as amounting to gross misconduct meriting dismissal, and that dismissal was within the band of reasonable responses open to it (paras 69-70).

BARCHESTER HEALTHCARE LTD v TAYEH; *sub nom.* TAYEH v BARCHESTER HEALTHCARE LTD, [2013] EWCA Civ 29, [2013] I.R.L.R. 387, Pill, L.J., CA (Civ Div).

1065. Unfair dismissal–Band of reasonable responses–Whether band of reasonable responses test complied with requirements of art.8 European Convention on Human Rights 1950

[European Convention on Human Rights 1950 Art.8.]

The appellant employee (T) appealed against her dismissal by the respondent train operator (E). T had worked for E and its predecessors for 12 years as a train conductor. Conductors were issued with ticket machines. The machines sometimes produced faulty tickets which could not be sold to customers. Conductors were obliged to return such tickets at the end of their shift. Statistics showed that during a 36-week period T had issued 132 faulty tickets; other conductors had issued 20 or less. A large number of T's tickets were missing. E believed she had manipulated the ticket machine to produce faulty tickets and had fraudulently sold them to members of the public, and kept the proceeds. She was dismissed for misconduct. The tribunal concluded that the evidence before E was sufficient to justify its conclusions and it had therefore acted within the band of reasonable responses test set out in *British Home Stores Ltd v Burchell* [1980] I.C.R. 303, [1980] C.L.Y. 1004. T accepted that E's investigations were adequate by the standards of domestic unfair dismissal law, but submitted that the dismissal had damaged her reputation thereby engaging her rights under the European Convention on Human Rights 1950 art.8. She argued that the band of reasonable responses test did not meet the requirements of art.8.

Held: Appeal dismissed. (1) The band of reasonable responses test did not simply apply to the question of whether the sanction of dismissal was permissible: it applied to all aspects of the dismissal process, including whether the procedures adopted by the employer were adequate, *Burchell, Orr v Milton Keynes Council* [2011] EWCA Civ 62, [2011] 4 All E.R. 1256, [2011] C.L.Y. 1139, *Whitbread Plc (t/a Whitbread Medway Inns) v Hall* [2001] EWCA Civ 268,

[2001] I.C.R. 699, [2001] C.L.Y. 2344 and *Sainsbury's Supermarkets Ltd v Hitt* [2002] EWCA Civ 1588, [2003] I.C.R. 111, [2002] C.L.Y. 1440 applied. It was not a subjective test. It provided an objective assessment of the employer's behaviour whilst reminding the employment tribunal that the fact that it would have assessed the case differently from the employer did not necessarily mean that the employer had acted unfairly. It was not to be confused with the classic Wednesbury test adopted in administrative law cases. Further, when determining whether an employer had acted as the hypothetical reasonable employer would do, it was relevant to have regard to the nature and consequences of the allegations. If dismissal for misconduct damaged the employee's opportunity to take up further employment in the same field, or involved an allegation of immoral or criminal conduct, then a reasonable employer should have regard to the gravity of those matters when determining the nature and scope of the appropriate investigation, *A v B (Unfair Dismissal)* [2003] I.R.L.R. 405 and *Salford Royal NHS Foundation Trust v Roldan* [2010] EWCA Civ 522, [2010] I.C.R. 1457, [2010] C.L.Y. 1143 applied (see paras 17-20 of judgment). (2) It was very difficult to see how a procedure which could be considered objectively fair if adopted by a reasonable employer could nonetheless be described as unfair within the meaning of art.8. The court accepted that where art.8 interests were engaged, matters bearing on the culpability of the employee had to be investigated with a full appreciation of the potentially adverse consequences to the employee. However, the band of reasonable responses test allowed for a heightened standard to be adopted where those consequences were particularly grave, *X v Y (Employment: Sex Offender)* [2004] EWCA Civ 662, [2004] I.C.R. 1634, [2004] C.L.Y. 1312, *A v B* and *Roldan* applied. The assessment of the procedure was made by the tribunal, not by the employer, and in making it the tribunal was adopting an objective test of whether the employer had acted as a reasonable employer might do. Accordingly, there was no breach of art.8. That conclusion was strongly reinforced by the fact that in the employment sphere, the Strasbourg court had recognised that some leeway should be given to the employer in the discharge of his powers of dismissal, *Palomo Sanchez v Spain (28955/06)* [2011] I.R.L.R. 934 applied. The band of reasonable responses test provided a sufficiently robust, flexible and objective analysis of all aspects of the decision to dismiss to ensure compliance with art.8. It did not fall short of the procedural safeguards required by art.8 (paras 52-56). (3) Even if art.8 imposed higher procedural safeguards than were afforded by domestic law, nothing turned on that in the instant case as the decision reached would inevitably have been the same (paras 68-69).

TURNER v EAST MIDLANDS TRAINS LTD, [2012] EWCA Civ 1470, [2013] 3 All E.R. 375, Sir Maurice Kay (VP CA Civ), CA (Civ Div).

1066. Unfair dismissal–Compensatory awards–Contributory fault–Allegation that employee revealed confidential information–Proper approach to art.10 European Convention on Human Rights 1950

[European Convention on Human Rights 1950 Art.10.]

The appellant (H) appealed against the quantum of a compensatory award made in her favour after her unfair dismissal. H had worked for the respondent school as a dinner assistant. Her contract included a confidentiality clause. She witnessed an incident in which a seven-year-old girl (X) was tied to a fence and whipped with a skipping rope by two older boys, whilst two other boys acted as guards. The accident form given to X's parents did not accurately state what had happened. H told X's mother the details. The school suspended H for breaching confidentiality. H contacted the press about her suspension. International media coverage ensued, which was unfavourable to the school. H was dismissed for breaching confidentiality and bringing the school into disrepute. The tribunal found that the dismissal was procedurally unfair, but made a Polkey reduction on the basis that H would have been dismissed within two months in any event. It applied a reduction for contributory fault of 80 per cent. H submitted that (1) the tribunal had approached Polkey in the wrong way; (2) the tribunal had not properly considered her right to freedom of expression; (3) the school had no reputation to protect pursuant to *Derbyshire CC v Times Newspapers Ltd* [1993] A.C. 534, [1993] C.L.Y. 2581; (4) the finding on contributory fault was flawed because she had not revealed confidential information.

Held: Appeal allowed. (1) A Polkey reduction required the tribunal to consider whether the employer could have fairly dismissed the employee, and if so, the chances that they would have done so. In assessing that question the tribunal had to consider the employer who was before the tribunal, not a hypothetical employer. There was no sign that the tribunal understood that it was dealing with an assessment of chance relating to what the school, as the employer actually before it, might have done. The tribunal's use of the word "could" and the phrase "range of reasonable responses" suggested that it might have been asking whether if following a fair procedure the employer had decided to dismiss, such a decision would have been upheld by a tribunal. That was the wrong approach (see paras 22-24, 32-33 of judgment). (2) The tribunal should have asked whether what had occurred fell within the ambit of freedom of expression. If so, the school as a public body would be bound to respect the exercise of that right, unless it could be qualified by the European Convention on Human Rights 1950 art.10(2). In considering whether the restriction on free speech could be justified it had to: (a) identify the aim which the restriction sought to serve; (b) satisfy itself that the restriction imposed in the light of that aim was one prescribed by law. That did not mean that it had to be provided for by statute. A contractual term requiring respect for confidential communications would be sufficient, so too would a common law right to confidentiality; (c) consider if the restriction was "necessary in a democratic society". That involved considering whether the measure was appropriate to the legitimate aim, and whether the interference to the exercise of the right was proportionate to the importance of the particular aim it sought to serve. The tribunal had not adopted the proper test when considering art.10. Accordingly, its decision that H would have been dismissed after two months in any event had to be reconsidered (paras 35, 39, 44-45, 57, 88). (3) The decision in *Derbyshire* related to a local authority exercising governmental functions and was directed at bodies with a political composition, and a politically-driven administrative role, *Derbyshire* considered. The school lacked the features discussed in *Derbyshire*. Its reputation was a matter of importance in attracting staff and pupils. The disciplinary proceedings against H constituted a restriction upon her freedom of speech, but it was open to the school to seek to justify it by reference to the legitimate aims of protecting the reputation and rights of others, and preventing the disclosure of information received in confidence. It was open to the tribunal to conclude that the common law or contractual duties owed by H to the school was such that the restriction was prescribed by law, and then to carry out the appropriate balancing exercise (paras 60-63). (4) The tribunal had not clearly identified what was confidential about the information that H supplied, nor to whom it was confidential. Further, the tribunal's incorrect approach to art.10 meant that it might have placed more weight upon factors of blame than it would have done if it had carefully balanced H's right to free speech against her obligations to keep matters confidential. The decision on contributory fault could not stand. H's case was remitted for reconsideration on the issue of compensation (paras 79-81).

HILL v GREAT TEY PRIMARY SCHOOL GOVERNORS; *sub nom.* HILL v GOVERNING BODY OF GREAT TEY PRIMARY SCHOOL [2013] I.C.R. 691, Langstaff, J. (President), EAT.

1067. Unfair dismissal–Compensatory awards–Stigma loss–Alleged effect of successful employment tribunal proceedings on chances of future employment

The appellant (U) appealed against the quantum of a compensatory award made in his favour after his unfair dismissal by the respondent mosque (M). U had worked as an imam. M had dismissed him because they wanted an English-speaking imam and did not believe that U could improve his English within a reasonable timescale.

U then obtained work for 17 weeks before being employed by an educational trust. A trustee gave evidence that a member of M had spoken to the trust, stating that U had taken them to an employment tribunal "and was sure to repeat that trick" with the trust. U claimed that he was dismissed by the trust after refusing to withdraw his claim against M. He claimed stigma damages from M, but the tribunal concluded that there was no link between U's dismissal by the trust and M's conversation with the trustee. It also found that U would have been fairly dismissed by M within six months because he was not fluent in English. U submitted that stigma damages were available not just where an employer had acted in a disreputable manner but also where an employee was at a disadvantage because he had brought tribunal proceedings against a former employer.

Held: Appeal dismissed. (1) There had to be evidence to support a claim for loss consisting of difficulty in obtaining or keeping employment due to "stigma", particularly where the stigma consisted not of taking unjustified proceedings but taking successful ones against a former employer. The evidence had to address whether, in relation to finding new employment, stigma from the former employee's previous employment had a real and substantial effect, and if it did, how great that effect was. In answering that question it was appropriate to have regard to the entire history of the former employee's search for new employment, including the number of jobs applied for, how well-targeted and presented the applications were, the number of interviews obtained, and any reasons given for rejection, *Bank of Credit and Commerce International SA (In Liquidation) v Ali (No.3)* [2002] EWCA Civ 82, [2002] 3 All E.R. 750, [2002] C.L.Y. 1318 followed. If, taking the evidence as a whole, it was insufficient to conclude that stigma had an effect, then a tribunal could make no award (see paras 17, 20 of judgment). (2) The Employment Appeal Tribunal was in no position to second-guess the finding to which the tribunal came concerning U's dismissal by the trust. It heard the questioning and concluded that, whatever M said to the trust, it did not cause U's dismissal. On the limited material available that conclusion could not be said to be perverse. The central point at issue was whether or not there was a stigma affecting U's employability, caused by the fact that he had taken proceedings against M. The manner in which he came to leave the trust was only part of the overall picture which would inform that conclusion. U had plainly had little difficulty in obtaining employment within six months and none of the evidential questions raised in *Bank of Credit and Commerce* was answered in a way which suggested stigma. Accordingly, the allegation of stigma could not succeed (paras 21-31).

UR-REHMAN v AHMAD [2013] I.C.R. 28, Langstaff, J., EAT.

1068. Unfair dismissal–Covert surveillance–Employee's absence during working hours–Secret monitoring by employer–Whether violation of right to private life rendering dismissal unfair

[Data Protection Act 1998 (c.29); Employment Rights Act 1996 (c.18) s.98(4); European Convention on Human Rights 1950 Art.8.]

The appellant local authority employer appealed against an employment tribunal's decision that it had unfairly dismissed the respondent employee (G). On two occasions G had claimed to be at work when he had been spotted at a sports centre. The local authority then hired a private investigator who videoed G on five more occasions attending the gym during working hours. The tribunal found that although the local authority had had reasonable grounds which justified its dismissal of G, the dismissal was rendered unfair by the covert surveillance it had carried out on him because (i) it violated his right to a private life under the European Convention on Human Rights 1950 art.8 or (ii) the local authority had been ignorant of its obligations under the Data Protection Act 1998, as clarified in the Employment Practices Data Protection Code.

Held: Appeal allowed. (1) Generally, the taking of photographs or the making of observations of individuals in public places would not breach art.8(1) because such individuals would not in those places have a reasonable expectation of privacy. In the instant case, there was no breach of art.8(1) because the video was taken in a public place of G outside the sports centre; he was there when he should have been working for the local authority, which was entitled to know where he was; and he was defrauding his employer and therefore had no reasonable expectation that his conduct was entitled to privacy, *Rugby Football Union v Viagogo Ltd* [2012] UKSC 55, [2012] 1 W.L.R. 3333, [2013] 2 C.L. 54 and *McGowan v Scottish Water* [2005] I.R.L.R. 167, [2005] C.L.Y. 5219 applied (see paras 14-19, 23 of judgment). (2) It was not obvious why ignorance of a code to which the employer was not bound in law to have regard would render its investigation into the wrongdoing of an employee unreasonable when it would otherwise have been reasonable. It was not clear that it would lead the employer to do anything which made the investigation unreasonable within the meaning of the Employment Rights Act 1996 s.98(4) (para.29).

CITY AND COUNTY OF SWANSEA v GAYLE [2013] I.R.L.R. 768, Langstaff, J. (President), EAT.

1069. Unfair dismissal–Death benefits–Loss of death-in-service benefit–Death of employee following termination of employment–Estate claiming compensation entitlement

The appellant (B) appealed against a decision ([2013] I.C.R. 51, [2013] 3 C.L. 77) that a death-in-service benefit was payable to the respondent (F) following the death of his son (D), despite D's unfair dismissal from employment one month earlier. In June 2010, following a six-month period of sickness leave and having exhausted his sick pay entitlement, D was given notice of dismissal for medical incapacity. D died one month after his employment terminated. Prior to his dismissal, D had been contractually entitled to a death-in-service benefit. If D had been employed when he died, the benefit payable would have been £85,000. F brought proceedings claiming that B was liable for unfair dismissal and/or disability discrimination. The principal object was to obtain compensation for loss of the death-in-service benefit. B claimed that even if such liability was established, F would not as a matter of law be entitled to recover compensation for the lost benefit. The Employment Appeal Tribunal made a declaration to the effect that if liability were established, D's estate would be entitled to compensation in a sum equivalent to the full amount of the benefit that would have been payable under the scheme if F had remained in employment at the date of his death.

Held: Appeal dismissed. (1) In *Auty v National Coal Board* [1985] 1 W.L.R. 784, [1985] C.L.Y. 942, diminution in the value of widows' pensions following their spouses' move to less remunerative work was treated as a loss suffered by the claimants, notwithstanding that the sums in question would never have been payable to them, because it constituted a diminution in the value of benefits which the employer had agreed to procure as part of the terms of their employment. That reasoning appeared to apply squarely to the instant case, regardless of the fact that the value of the death-in-service benefit had been wholly extinguished. The lost benefit was part of the package of benefits under the pension scheme to which D was accorded access as part of his terms of employment and which was in part funded by his contributions, *Auty* applied. The starting point in considering the recoverability of compensation for loss of a death-in-service benefit was that the benefit formed part of the employee's remuneration. The law would be seriously defective if an employee were unable to claim compensation where such rights were adversely affected as a result of a wrong, merely because the subject matter of the right was a payment to be made to a third party. That was all the more so since the potential beneficiaries of such a payment would themselves have no claim. It reflected reality to treat the loss of the benefits in question as a pecuniary loss suffered by the claimants themselves. The law did not take the absolute position that the only pecuniary loss for which a claimant may recover was the loss of a payment that would have been made to him personally, *Lowe v Guise* [2002] EWCA Civ 197, [2002] Q.B. 1369, [2002] C.L.Y. 3411 considered. Accordingly, the loss of the chance of death-in-service benefit being paid was to be regarded as a pecuniary loss suffered by D for which he could have claimed in proceedings brought prior to his death (see paras 25-26, 28-29, 31 of judgment). (2) The facts of the instant case were unusual. It had been too late for D to seek alternative life insurance cover. In those circumstances it was necessary to go back to first principles. D's estate was entitled to be put in the position that he would have been in had he not been unfairly dismissed when he was. In that case, he would virtually certainly still have been in employment at the date of his death; the possibility that his employment would have been lawfully terminated for some other reason was too small to require any discount. His beneficiaries would at that point have become entitled to £85,000. Since that entitlement was to be regarded as a benefit to him, he, or his estate, could only be put in the position that he would have been in but for his dismissal if it was put in a position to enable an equivalent payment to be made; that could only be done by the award of compensation in the full amount. The right approach was not to make an artificial prospective valuation of the loss as at the date of the termination of the employment but to value it in the light of the events which actually happened. The outcome of the present case depended on the particular, and very unusual facts. In all ordinary cases, the cost of obtaining insurance which would provide equivalent benefits would be the appropriate measure (paras 35-38).

FOX v BRITISH AIRWAYS PLC; *sub nom.* FOX (DECEASED), RE; BRITISH AIRWAYS PLC v FOX, [2013] EWCA Civ 972, [2013] I.C.R. 1257, Moore-Bick, L.J., CA (Civ Div).

1070. Unfair dismissal–Fair reasons–Tribunal failing to identify reason for dismissal

[Employment Rights Act 1996 (c.18) s.98(1), s.98.]

The appellant (T) appealed against a decision of an employment tribunal to dismiss his claims against the respondent college (H) for unfair dismissal, automatically unfair dismissal and disability discrimination. T began working for H in 2007. He was employed under a succession of fixed-term contracts which expired at the end of each academic year. For the 2009/2010 academic year, his contract required him to work as a "sessional communication support worker". T, who was himself deaf, provided support services to hearing-impaired students such as interpreting, note-taking and lip-speaking. There were differences of view between him and H about the way in which support services for such students were being delivered. He was not re-engaged by H for the 2010/2011 academic year. He issued proceedings in the employment tribunal. In his claim form he alleged that he had been dismissed because he had raised protected disclosures regarding H's legal obligation not to discriminate against students. H, on the other hand, asserted that he had been dismissed by reason of redundancy. DismissingT's claims, the tribunal held that he had been dismissed by reason of the expiry of the fixed term of his contract. H argued that, to decide the unfair dismissal claim, the tribunal had to determine two basic questions, namely the "reason" for the dismissal and, if the dismissal was for a permissibly fair reason, whether in all the circumstances it had been fair; insofar as the tribunal had undertaken the task of asking what the reason for dismissal was, it had confined itself to stating that the reason was the expiry of the fixed term; if that was really its finding on the reason for dismissal, rather than being simply an acknowledgment of the fact of a dismissal, it was not a potentially fair reason because expiry of a fixed term was not included in the list of potentially fair reasons set out in the legislation.

Held: Appeal allowed. It was absolutely fundamental that a tribunal hearing a claim for unfair dismissal should set out clearly the terms of the Employment Rights Act 1996 s.98 or at least offer a distillation of the questions that the section required it to decide. It should then show that it had decided those questions, what answers it had given to them and the reasons for those answers. The structure of s.98(1) clearly provided that where the fact of dismissal was not in issue, as in this case, the burden was on the employer to show what the "reason" for the dismissal was. The question for the tribunal was then whether the employer had met that burden. Section 98(2) provided that the reason had to be one of those listed or some other substantial reason. The question for the tribunal was whether the reason proven by the employer was among those listed. A tribunal dismissing an unfair dismissal claim would not discharge its statutory responsibility to give reasons unless it stated, first, that it was satisfied that the employer had proved a reason for the dismissal, second, what that reason was and, third, that the reason was one of those provided for by the statute. In that respect, the tribunal had failed in its task in this case. It had elided the mode of dismissal, namely the termination of a fixed-term contract by expiry and without renewal, with the reason for that dismissal. It had not, in terms, stated what it found to be the reason, if any, for the dismissal. That failing affected all of T's claims. Those claims would be remitted to a differently consisted tribunal (see paras 26-28, 32-33 of judgment).

TANSELL v HENLEY COLLEGE COVENTRY [2013] I.R.L.R. 174, Recorder Luba Q.C., EAT.

1071. Unfair dismissal–Gross misconduct–Teacher allegedly assaulting pupil–Alleged confession–Claims of wrongful and unfair dismissal

The appellants (N) appealed against a decision of the Employment Appeal Tribunal that the respondent teacher (B) had been unfairly dismissed and remitting the case to a differently constituted tribunal for rehearing. B had been supervising a lunchtime detention of three boys with a classroom assistant (D). D alleged that B manhandled one of the boys (X), but B denied such treatment. Internal disciplinary proceedings found her to have been guilty of gross misconduct and she was summarily dismissed. The tribunal determined that D was a more credible witness than B, and that in any event B had confessed to assaulting X. The EAT concluded that the tribunal decision was founded upon misapprehension of what was and was not undisputed fact and contained a perverse finding, and it considered that there had been material errors of law which vitiated the rejection of her claims for unfair and wrongful dismissal. The grounds of appeal sought to challenge the findings of errors of law in relation to both claims, and further contended that the EAT also committed a legal error by remitting to a differently constituted rather than the same tribunal. N submitted that (1) in relation to unfair dismissal, the criticisms expressed by the EAT were criticisms not of N but of the tribunal, and went to the issue of why the tribunal had rejected important aspects of B's evidence; (2) in relation to wrongful dismissal, the EAT took an over-pedantic approach to the tribunal's language.

Held: Appeal allowed in part. (1) There was no reason to suppose that N's decision-makers in the disciplinary proceedings misunderstood the evidence or reached unsustainable conclusions about it in the way the EAT found the tribunal had. The tribunal permissibly found that N's decision-makers had a genuine belief in B's wrongdoing, and that they had had reasonable grounds upon which to sustain that belief, such grounds being based on their preference for D's evidence. The investigation had been a reasonable one having regard to the seriousness of the allegation. There was nothing to suggest that N's decision-makers had considered that B had confessed. Accordingly, the EAT had no proper grounds for interfering with the tribunal's decision that the dismissal was fair, *British Home Stores Ltd v Burchell* [1980] I.C.R. 303, [1980] C.L.Y. 1004 considered (see paras 16-18 of judgment). (2) The EAT resorted to the Oxford English Dictionary in order to fix on a definition of "manhandling" as being "to handle roughly by striking or pushing". That was the usual meaning, but it was not what the tribunal meant. Reading the tribunal's judgment as a whole, it was not using the word "manhandling" in accordance with the dictionary definition. However, the tribunal undoubtedly realised that the fundamental issue of fact was whether B had manhandled X in the dictionary sense. The findings were not in any way conditioned by an assumption that it was common ground that B had been guilty of rough handling. They knew she had disputed that. The tribunal simply used the wrong word, *Brent LBC v Fuller* [2011] EWCA Civ 267, [2011] I.C.R. 806, [2011] C.L.Y. 1133 considered (para.22). (3) N had not submitted that B had effectively confessed. Nor could it be fairly said that she had. From beginning to end she had denied wrongdoing. The tribunal did not see or hear her give evidence on that issue. Applying the high threshold for perversity set out in *Crofton v Yeboah* [2002] EWCA Civ 794, [2002] I.R.L.R. 634, [2002] C.L.Y. 1398, no sensible tribunal could properly find that B had confessed to wrongdoing, *Yeboah* applied. The case on wrongful dismissal turned overwhelmingly on the issue of the credibility of B and D. A flawed finding of confession on the part of B could not be ignored. In the circumstances, the EAT was right to allow B's appeal on wrongful dismissal (paras 26-27). (4) Since wrongful dismissal was the only remaining claim, a remittal to a differently constituted tribunal was of more limited potential. It could not be said that there was a legal error in terms of the remittal, *Sinclair Roche & Temperley v Heard* [2004] I.R.L.R. 763, [2005] C.L.Y. 1274 applied (paras 28-30).

BOARDMAN v NUGENT CARE SOCIETY; *sub nom.* CLARENCE HIGH SCHOOL GOVERNORS v BOARDMAN, [2013] EWCA Civ 198, [2013] I.C.R. 927, Maurice Kay, L.J. (VP, CA Civ), CA (Civ Div).

1072. Unfair dismissal–Gross misconduct–Working while certified sick–Whether gross misconduct automatically justified dismissal–Effect of mitigating circumstances

The appellant doctor (B) appealed against a decision of an employment tribunal dismissing her claim for unfair dismissal against the respondent employer (the trust). B was a consultant haematologist who had been employed by the trust under a contract that permitted her to have private patients. While on sick leave and certified as unfit to work and in receipt of her full contractual sick pay, B worked for her private patients. Disciplinary proceedings were brought against B. The disciplinary panel had regard to two previous letters given to B by the trust that stated that if certified sick she should not work in private practice. B was dismissed for gross misconduct. The tribunal held that B's dismissal fell within the range of reasonable responses. The trust was entitled to find that B's actions amounted to gross misconduct. Once gross misconduct was found, dismissal had to always fall within the range of reasonable responses and it was not its role to substitute any sanctions it might have imposed in the circumstances. It could not be said that the dismissal was outside the range of reasonable responses. B argued that the tribunal could not properly come to the conclusion that there was gross misconduct, but, if it did, that did not necessarily follow that the dismissal must fall within the range of reasonable responses. B argued that dismissal was not automatically fair just because of gross misconduct and mitigating circumstances, such as the length of exemplary service and the consequences of dismissal from the NHS had to be considered in deciding whether the dismissal was reasonable.

Held: Appeal allowed. The tribunal was entitled to conclude that it was reasonable for the trust to find B guilty of gross misconduct. First, B had twice specifically been given a lawful direction by the trust not to do what she did. Secondly B submitted certificates that purported to show that she was unwell. Although she had not signed the reverse saying that she had done the work, it was plain that submitting the certificates resulted in her being paid her full pay from the trust on the basis that she was unfit to work when on the facts the trust was entitled to conclude she was doing similar work, albeit not at the same intensity elsewhere. However, the logical jump from gross misconduct to the proposition that the dismissal must then inevitably fall within the range of reasonable responses gave no room for considering whether, though the misconduct was gross and dismissal almost inevitable, there were mitigating factors that might be such that dismissal was not reasonable. The tribunal's function was to look at the trust's conclusion. It was not sufficient to point to the fact that the trust considered the mitigation and rejected it, largely upon the basis that the failure to observe the verbal notice and the letter undermined it, because a tribunal could not abdicate its function to that of the employer. It was the tribunal's task to assess whether the employer's behaviour was reasonable having regard to the reason for dismissal. It had to consider the whole of the circumstances with regard to equity and the substantial merits of the case. But that general assessment necessarily included a consideration of those matters that might mitigate, such as long service, the consequences of dismissal and a previous unblemished record. For that reason, there had been an error of direction to itself by the tribunal. The case would be remitted to the same tribunal, which had to take a proper approach in asking whether the gross misconduct justified dismissal in the light of all the mitigation available personally to B (see paras 35, 38, 40, 42-43 of judgment)..

BRITO-BABAPULLE v EALING HOSPITAL NHS TRUST [2013] I.R.L.R. 854, Langstaff, J. (President), EAT.

1073. Unfair dismissal–Interim relief–Employee claiming unfair dismissal for trade union activities–Successful application for interim relief–Appropriateness of tribunal's approach to application

[Trade Union and Labour Relations (Consolidation) Act 1992 (c.52) s.161.]

The appellant employer (L) appealed against an employment tribunal's decision to grant interim relief in favour of the respondent employee (C) in unfair dismissal proceedings. C had claimed that he was unfairly dismissed for trade union activities, and applied for interim relief under the Trade Union and Labour Relations (Consolidation) Act 1992 s.161. The tribunal said that the sole issue was whether C was likely to succeed in his claim that the reason or principal reason for his dismissal was his trade union activities. It considered the expedition with which L had conducted the disciplinary procedures, compared with the relative slowness of its grievance process, and the fact that there had been serious allegations made against other employees who had not been disciplined, let alone dismissed. Weighing those factors in the balance, the tribunal ordered L to continue to remunerate C as though his terms and conditions of employment were still in place. L conceded that the tribunal had directed itself to the correct law, but argued that it had failed to apply the correct test in the right way. In particular, L submitted that the tribunal (1) failed adequately to consider its evidence in support of the fact that misconduct was the true reason for C's dismissal; (2) failed to specifically find any trade union connection between the dismissal and C's activities; (3) erred in placing the emphasis that it did on the identified factors.

Held: Appeal dismissed. (1) The tribunal did not fail to undertake the required balancing exercise. It clearly went into the documentation in some detail, and it was impossible to successfully assert that, having carefully considered the relevant documents and L's submissions about them, it forgot about L's evidence when making the ultimate decision as to whether the claim was likely to succeed. All C needed to show was that, whatever conduct or misconduct there might have been on his part, the principal or sole reason for his dismissal was his trade union activities. On an interim relief application, the tribunal was doing the best that it could with the untested evidence of each party, and it was enough for it to indicate the essential gist of its reasoning on such an application, *Taplin v C Shippam Ltd* [1978] I.C.R. 1068, [1978] C.L.Y. 1135 and *Dandpat v University of Bath* [2010] EWCA Civ 305 applied. That was what the tribunal had done, and there was no error of law (see para.28 of judgment). (2) It was impossible for L to assert that the tribunal had failed to identify the trade union activity flavour of the way in which C's claim was put. Not least, it had found that L was unequivocally against trade union recognition. The tribunal was entitled to weigh in the balance L's pronounced attitude to trade union recognition and other findings that it had made which were contrary to C's case. It was also obliged to have regard to the fact that C's application could only be granted if it was supported by a requisite certificate of the trade union concerned, which it was. Those matters went into the balance in weighing the question of whether there might be a trade union connection between the dismissal and C's activities, and it followed that there was material to sustain the tribunal's conclusion that the claim for unfair dismissal for trade union reasons was likely to succeed (paras 29-31). (3) Consideration of the relevant factors was supremely a matter for assessment by the tribunal, and it was doing the best that it could on the material before it (paras 35-36). (4) The tribunal's decision was not perverse: it had set out the relevant law and applied it to the factual material and submissions that it received (para.39).

LONDON CITY AIRPORT LTD v CHACKO [2013] I.R.L.R. 610, Recorder Luba Q.C., EAT.

1074. Unfair dismissal–Misconduct–Reliance on final written warning in unfair dismissal case–Final warning issued in good faith

[Employment Rights Act 1996 (c.18) s.98(4).]

The appellant teacher (D) appealed against the rejection of her unfair dismissal claim against the respondent local authority. D had been employed in February 2003 and was dismissed at the end of 2006 for alleged misconduct between November 2005 and February 2006. In reaching that decision the local authority had taken account of a prior final written warning issued by it on February 10, 2005, which had been given in respect of alleged misconduct by D on October 8, 2004 during a lesson. That warning was preceded by a period of suspension, investigation and a disciplinary hearing. The local authority notified D that the warning was to remain on her record for 24 months. D returned to work and lodged an internal appeal against the misconduct finding at the disciplinary hearing and against the issue of the final warning. D's appeal was never heard and the final warning remained on D's record at the time of her alleged subsequent misconduct and of her dismissal. The tribunal dismissed her unfair dismissal claim on the basis that the decision to dismiss was for a conduct reason; that it was within the range of reasonable responses; that the existence of the final written warning was essential to the decision and that the dismissal was fair. The local authority accepted that, absent the final warning, it would not have dismissed D. The issue on appeal was whether the final written warning on which the local authority relied should be treated as a nullity in circumstances where, although there was evidence to support the decision to issue the warning, the employer had deliberately chosen not to consider evidence which, objectively, might have caused it to believe that the misconduct alleged had not been committed and therefore not to issue the warning.

Held: Appeal dismissed. (1) It was legitimate for an employer to rely on a final warning, provided that it was issued in good faith, that there were at least prima facie grounds for imposing it and that it was not manifestly inappropriate to issue it. The guiding principle in determining whether a dismissal was fair in cases where there had been prior final warning did not originate in the cases, which were but instances of the application of Employment Rights Act 1996 s.98(4) to particular sets of facts, *Stein v Associated Dairies* [1982] I.R.L.R. 447, [1983] C.L.Y. 1313 and *Tower Hamlets HA v Anthony* [1988] I.C.R. 499, [1988] C.L.Y. 1333 considered. The broad test laid down in s.98(4) was whether, in the particular case, it was reasonable for the employer to treat the conduct reason, taken together with the circumstance of the final written warning, as sufficient to dismiss the claimant (see paras 20-22 of judgment). (2) In answering the question of whether a dismissal was fair, it was not the function of the employment tribunal to reopen the final warning and rule on an issue raised by the claimant as to whether it was a legally valid warning or a nullity. The function of the tribunal was to apply the objective statutory test of reasonableness to determine whether the final warning was a circumstance which a reasonable employer could reasonably take into account in the decision to dismiss the claimant for subsequent misconduct (para 23). (3) It was relevant for the tribunal to consider whether the final warning was issued in good faith, whether there were prima facie grounds for following the final warning procedure and whether it was manifestly inappropriate to issue the warning. They were material factors in assessing the reasonableness of the decision to dismiss by reference to, inter alia, the circumstance of the final warning. The instant tribunal made relevant findings of fact on those points and did not err in law in concluding that the final warning was properly taken into account by the local authority when it decided to dismiss D (paras 24-26).

DAVIES v SANDWELL MBC, [2013] EWCA Civ 135, [2013] I.R.L.R. 374, Mummery, L.J., CA (Civ Div).

1075. Unfair dismissal–Overseas employees–Claims of unfair dismissal and breach of right to be accompanied–Territorial scope of employment legislation–Effect of superseding case law on judge's conclusions

[Employment Relations Act 1999 (c.26) s.10; Employment Rights Act 1996 (c.18) s.94(1); Working Time Regulations 1998 (SI 1998/1833) reg.16(2).]

The appellant employee (H) appealed against a decision that the employment tribunal did not have territorial jurisdiction to hear his claims of unfair dismissal under the Employment Rights Act 1996 s.94(1) and of breach of the Employment Relations Act 1999 s.10 against the respondent employer (R). R cross-appealed against a decision that the tribunal did have jurisdiction to hear H's claim for accrued holiday pay under the Working Time Regulations 1998 reg.16(2). H had been employed by R in London but subsequently wanted a role based in the Middle East and Africa. As R was opening an office in Dubai, H moved there. The Dubai office was not successful and closed. H was asked to relocate to Singapore but did not do so and was dismissed. He brought his claims against R in the employment tribunal. In determining whether the tribunal had jurisdiction to hear the claims, the judge applied the approach in *Lawson v Serco Ltd* [2006] UKHL 3, [2006] 1 All E.R. 823, [2006] C.L.Y. 1390, particularly focussing on whether the Dubai branch was a representative branch of R. The parties agreed that the same territorial limitation applied to the claim for unfair dismissal and the s.10 right. The judge concluded that the tribunal did not have jurisdiction to hear H's claims of unfair dismissal and breach of s.10 as he was not an exception to the general rule that the right to claim unfair dismissal would only exceptionally cover employees who were working or based abroad. He found that the tribunal did have jurisdiction to hear H's claim for holiday pay.

Held: Appeal allowed, cross-appeal allowed. (1) The approach taken to exceptions to the general rule, and therefore the question of whether an individual fell within the territorial scope of s.94(1), had developed since the hearing before the judge, *Ravat v Halliburton Manufacturing & Services Ltd* [2012] UKSC 1, [2012] 2 All E.R. 905, [2012] C.L.Y. 1176, *Duncombe v Secretary of State for Children, Schools and Families* [2011] UKSC 36, [2011] 4 All E.R. 1020, [2011] C.L.Y. 1134, *Bates van Winkelhof v Clyde & Co LLP* [2012] EWCA Civ 1207, [2013] 1 All E.R. 844 and *Lawson v Serco Ltd* [2006] UKHL 3, [2006] 1 All E.R. 823, [2006] C.L.Y. 1390 considered. In cases in which an employee was employed wholly abroad and lived abroad, it might not be sufficient to establish in a comparative exercise that his employment had much stronger links with Great Britain and British employment law than with that of the jurisdiction in which he worked. It was also necessary to show that those links were sufficiently strong to enable it to be said that Parliament would have regarded it as appropriate for the tribunal to deal with the claim (see paras 42, 51 of judgment). (2) The overarching question was whether Parliament was to be presumed to have intended an employee in H's circumstances to be within the scope of s.94(1). As the main focus of the hearing had been on whether the Dubai operation where H worked was a branch or representative office of R, an example given in *Serco*, the judge understandably did not compare the strength of H's connections with Great Britain to the strength of his connections to Dubai to the extent required by the later cases, *Ravat*, *Duncombe* and *Bates Van Winkelhof* applied and *Serco* considered. Many of the facts found would have supported his conclusion, however, the question of the relative strength of connection of an expatriate employee with Great Britain and with the country in which he worked and, if the connection with Great Britain was the greater, whether it was sufficient to bring H within the territorial scope of s.94(1), was one of degree. The judge had viewed the facts in light of the guidance in *Serco*. It could therefore not be said with the degree of confidence required to uphold his decision that the outcome would have been the same notwithstanding the fact that the applicable test for determining whether H fell within the scope of s.94(1) required a different enquiry than that which he had undertaken. Further findings of fact might be necessary and a different emphasis might be given to the relevant facts (para.56). (3) The judge had erred in holding that the Regulations contained an implied territorial limitation. Regulation 1(2) contained a clear express territorial limitation that the Regulations extended to Great Britain only. They expressly did not apply to Dubai (para.59).

DHUNNA v CREDITSIGHTS LTD [2013] I.C.R. 909, Slade, J., EAT.

1076. Unfair dismissal–Right to representation–District probate registrar–Whether dismissal creating legal barrier to professional practice–Engagement of art.6 European Convention on Human Rights 1950

[European Convention on Human Rights 1950 Art.6.]

The appellant employer (E) appealed against an employment tribunal's decision that the respondent employee (P) had been unfairly and wrongfully dismissed. P had been employed as a district probate registrar. E found her guilty of gross misconduct for bullying and a final written warning was issued, to expire after 12 months. Within that 12-month period, she was again found guilty of bullying and was dismissed. Her dismissal meant that she was automatically removed from the list of district probate registrars. P appealed and asked if she could be represented by a solicitor at the appeal hearing. That request was declined, although E considered the solicitor's submissions during the appeal process. The tribunal held that the decision to dismiss was unfair primarily because P had been assured that she would not be dismissed at the disciplinary hearing, and also because the lack of legal representation breached her right to a fair trial under the European Convention on Human Rights 1950 art.6. The tribunal considered that if the procedure had been fair P would not have been dismissed and so made no Polkey reduction, but it assessed her contributory fault at 50 per cent. It also found that her actions could not be described as gross misconduct and so she had been wrongfully dismissed. The issues were whether (i) the primary reason for holding the dismissal unfair was correct; (ii) art.6 applied; (iii) the tribunal approached Polkey by applying the wrong burden of proof; (iv) the tribunal took an erroneous approach to identifying whether P had been in repudiatory breach so as to justify dismissal.

Held: Appeal allowed. (1) There was no evidential basis for the tribunal's conclusion that P had been assured that she would not be dismissed at the end of the disciplinary hearing. Accordingly, the primary reason for holding the dismissal unfair was illusory (see paras 12, 14 of judgment). (2) The guarantees provided by art.6 only arose where a civil right was adjudicated on in a manner that was dispositive of the right to practise one's chosen profession. That disposition could be in one set of proceedings, such as internal disciplinary proceedings, or in two sets of proceedings, the internal proceedings and an outside professional body's determination, provided there was a sufficient link between them, *Mattu v University Hospitals of Coventry and Warwickshire NHS Trust* [2012] EWCA Civ 641, [2012] 4 All E.R. 359, [2012] C.L.Y. 1071 applied. The tribunal had been in error to decide that art.6 was engaged, as, on the evidence, it could not have been satisfied that the disciplinary proceedings were dispositive not just of P's contract of employment but also of her entitlement to work again elsewhere as a probate registrar. There might be some exceptional cases where, although there had been a violation of art.6 at one point, the dismissal might be held fair. Accordingly, even if art. 6 was engaged, the tribunal still needed to consider whether that rendered the decision overall an unfair one. That had not been done (paras 29, 32-33, 37). (3) The tribunal appeared to have approached Polkey by applying the balance of probabilities rather than assessing the percentage chance of P being dismissed. It was very difficult to conceive, on the facts, that P would have been entirely free from any risk of dismissal, especially given the tribunal's assessment of her contributory fault at 50 per cent (paras 42-45). (4) Wrongful dismissal was a contractual concept to which conventional contractual principles applied. In the case of constructive dismissal, the "last straw" that led an employee to resign might not always be unreasonable provided that it was an act in a series, the cumulative effect of which was to amount to a breach of contract. There was no reason in principle why the same should not apply if it was the employer who sought to rely on repudiation by the employee. The employee's conduct should be seen as a whole. An employer would usually be justified in dismissing an employee who committed a further act of misconduct within the period of effect of a warning, even though the act on its own might not merit dismissal. The tribunal should have viewed the event that led to P's dismissal in context, and in expressly ruling out the necessary context it had erred, *Lewis v Motorworld Garages Ltd* [1986] I.C.R. 157, [1986] C.L.Y. 1261 applied (paras 51-53). (5) The case was remitted to a fresh tribunal for a complete rehearing.

MINISTRY OF JUSTICE v PARRY [2013] I.C.R. 311, Langstaff, J. (President), EAT.

1077. Unfair dismissal–Warnings–Dismissal for second incident of misconduct–Reasonableness of employer's reliance on earlier written warning

[Employment Rights Act 1996 (c.18) s.98(4).]

The appellant employer (W) appealed against a decision that its dismissal of the first and second respondents (R1 and R2) was unfair. A key factor in R1 and R2's dismissal was the "totting up" of a previous warning with a second disciplinary offence. R1 and R2 had refused to comply with a new policy requiring them to work from two depots instead of one, and were given first written warnings. R1 subsequently brought employment tribunal proceedings concerning the correct interpretation of his contract on that issue, and those proceedings were ongoing. He was dismissed after pulling out of a loading bay when the traffic light was on red, injuring a fellow employee. Another employee who had committed a similar offence had received a final written warning. However, because R1 already had a written warning, W took the view that he was guilty of repeated misconduct and dismissed him. R2 was dismissed after being disqualified from driving. W had told him that it would consider whether alternative work was available for him, but failed to do so.

Held: Appeal allowed in part. (1) The employment tribunal's focus should be upon the reasonableness or otherwise of the employer's act in treating conduct as a reason for dismissal under the Employment Rights Act 1996 s.98(4). If a tribunal was satisfied that the first warning was issued for an oblique motive, was manifestly inappropriate, was not issued in good faith or with prima facie grounds for making it, then the warning would not be valid and could not be subsequently relied upon. However, where the tribunal was not satisfied of any of those matters, the earlier warning would be valid and: (a) the tribunal should take into account the fact of that warning; (b) the tribunal should take into account any proceedings that could affect the validity of that warning, usually an internal appeal. Where an employer was aware of the fact that the validity of a warning was being challenged in other proceedings, it could be expected to take account of that fact too, and a tribunal was entitled to give that such weight as it felt was appropriate; (c) to find that a warning should not have been issued, or should have been downgraded to some lesser category of warning, would be to go behind the warning. A tribunal should not go behind the warning unless satisfied as to its invalidity; (d) it was not going behind a warning to take into account the factual circumstances giving rise to the warning. A degree of similarity between the circumstances giving rise to the first warning and those currently being considered would tend to favour a more severe penalty, whereas dissimilarity would tend the other way; (e) a tribunal could take account of the employer's treatment of similar matters relating to other employees prior to the instant dismissal; (f) a final written warning always implied that any further misconduct of whatever nature would usually be met with dismissal, subject only to the individual terms of a contract, and it would be an exception where that did not occur, *Stein v Associated Dairies* [1982] I.R.L.R. 447, [1983] C.L.Y. 1313, *Tower Hamlets HA v Anthony* [1989] I.C.R. 656, [1990] C.L.Y. 1960 and *Davies v Sandwell MBC* applied (see para.37 of judgment). (2) The tribunal had concluded that the earlier written warning given to R1 and R2 was valid. Accordingly, it could not look behind it and ask whether it was justified. The tribunal had taken into account an irrelevant consideration by looking at the justification for the earlier warning. It had also stated that the warning should have been held in abeyance until the contractual issue was resolved. That was contrary to the law. An employer was obliged to have regard to a warning. The weight that he placed upon it was another issue. A warning for conduct might have greater force if subsequent conduct was of the same type, but it could not be sensibly suggested that an employer would not be entitled to have regard to the totality of an employee's behaviour, even if the acts of misconduct were quite different from each other. In relation to R1 the only other incident of similar misconduct had not involved personal injury to a fellow worker, nor did it involve an employee who already had one warning. The tribunal therefore could place no reliance on it. W's appeal in relation to R1's case was well-founded (29-36, 38). (3) R2 had been encouraged by W to believe that it would consider reasonable opportunities for him elsewhere in its business. The tribunal found those assurances to be false. In those circumstances the tribunal was entitled to conclude that W had not acted reasonably. W's appeal in relation to R2's case therefore failed (paras 40-43).

WINCANTON GROUP PLC v STONE [2013] I.R.L.R. 178, Langstaff, J. (President), EAT.

1078. Unfair dismissal–Warnings–Misconduct identified in informal warning–Necessity of warning that repetition might lead to dismissal–Dismissal of over-authoritarian managers

[Employment Rights Act 1996 (c.18) s.98(4).]

The appellant employer (J) appealed against an employment tribunal decision that the respondent employee (K) had been unfairly dismissed. K had been employed by J for 14 years. He had been promoted to warehouse manager and then stock control manager. He had received an informal warning highlighting deficiencies in his management style. Several months later, following an investigation into a complaint by several employees, J dismissed K on the basis that he had abused his position to threaten employees' job security, which had created an intimidating environment for his subordinates, and had communicated in Turkish with employees who understood Turkish, putting other employees at a disadvantage. The employment tribunal accepted that K had been dismissed for the stated reason but found that his dismissal without having formally warned him that his management style had to change and, if it did not, he might be dismissed, especially since he had not been given any management training after the informal warning, was outside the range of reasonable responses. J contended that (1) in considering whether the decision to dismiss was fair, the tribunal had wrongly considered what it would have done, rather than asking objectively whether J's decision was fair in accordance with the Employment Rights Act 1996 s.98(4); J relied on the fact that the tribunal had described as the sole reason for K's dismissal the manner in which he had acted as a manager of staff, which downplayed the gravity of what had occurred; (2) the decision was perverse on the basis that the tribunal had downplayed the effect of the informal warning, which was a shot across the bows in circumstances where K, having managed for some years, must have known that his behaviour amounted to gross misconduct justifying dismissal.

Held: Appeal dismissed. (1) In order to see if a tribunal had gone outside the scope of its duty as set out in s.98(4), it was necessary to consider the tribunal's decision as a whole; what one was looking for was some indication that the tribunal had asked not whether the employer's decision was fair but what it would have done in light of the basic and underlying facts. On that approach, there was nothing in the tribunal's decision in the instant case which showed that it had substituted its own decision for J's. The passage relied on was an appropriate synopsis of the material which had gone before; the tribunal had already recognised that the reason for K's dismissal was the reason J had given at the time (see paras 18-20 of judgment). (2) It was accepted that there was no special magic about a written warning; however, the issue was whether K had sufficiently been told or should sufficiently have realised that his behaviour might lead to dismissal. The significant point on which the tribunal had focused was that it thought he had not been told, in the informal warning letter or otherwise, that a consequence of further such misconduct might be dismissal, and he had not received training which would have indicated the same to him. There was some force in the argument that an employee in K's position should have known that dismissal might be the consequence of further such misconduct. However, the tribunal was in a position to properly evaluate all the facts before it, and its decision could not be regarded as perverse, *McCall v Castleton Crafts* [1979] I.R.L.R. 218, [1979] C.L.Y. 996 considered. The over-authoritarian manager was not unknown in industry, and it would be unfortunate if such managers were not warned, where they might not clearly have understood, that a repeat of such conduct might lead to dismissal (paras 22-25).

JJ FOOD SERVICE LTD v KEFIL [2013] I.R.L.R. 850, Langstaff, J. (President), EAT.

1079. Unlawful deductions from wages–Expenses–Food and housing allowances–Included in or paid on top of salary–Correct amount of relocation benefit

[Employment Rights Act 1996 (c.18) s.27(2)(b), s.27(1).]

The appellant employer (Q) appealed against an employment tribunal's decision that it had made unauthorised deductions from the wages of the respondent employees (L), while they cross-appealed against its decision on the amount of the deductions. Q was a United Kingdom subsidiary in a group of companies. L had been seconded to it from an Australian subsidiary in the same group. Q gave them a contract which stated that their total salary would include food and housing allowances and that they would be paid relocation benefits of £5,000. A month later, they signed a second contract which stated that their basic salary would include food and housing allowances and that they would be paid relocation benefits of £14,500. After they were paid, L complained that their allowances should have been paid on top of their basic salary and the benefits should have been based on the higher rate. Q maintained that the relevant contract was the second one, but that the higher relocation benefit figures had clearly been an error. L brought their claim and the tribunal found that the relevant contract was the first one. On that basis, the tribunal found in favour of L on the food and housing allowances but against them on relocation benefits; it also found the higher rates for relocation had been an error.

Held: Appeal allowed, cross-appeal dismissed. (1) The second contract represented the true agreement between the parties. However, if that was wrong, the first contract's use of the term "included" indicated that the payments of food and housing allowances were not to be on top of salary. Furthermore, the first contract sought to promote tax efficiency and so, construed in that context, the relevant clauses meant that for the purposes of tax structuring, the whole of the payment forthcoming to L would be presented and a notional figure within it would be earmarked to the allowances and those figures would not attract tax. In other words, the clauses had the same meaning as the versions in the second contract (see paras 47, 55 of judgment). (2) (Obiter) L's claims did not relate to wages, within the meaning of the Employment Rights Act 1996 s.27(1), but to expenses, within the meaning of s.27(2)(b). Their salaries included an element of payment for the cost of living in London for a period of time. It followed from the fact that it was tax efficient and tax would not be levied upon it in Australia that it was in respect of expenses and not wages (para.56). (3) The higher figures for relocation in the second contract were a mistake: they appeared once correctly and once incorrectly in that contract. In the light of the first contract and the information subsequently given to L, they knew there was a mistake, and so as a matter of construction the higher figures were incorrect. Since the tribunal had held that the correct document was the first contract, L could not possibly mount an argument based upon the higher figures which occurred only in the second contract (paras 60-61).

QANTAS CABIN CREW (UK) LTD v LOPEZ [2013] I.R.L.R. 4, Judge McMullen Q.C., EAT.

1080. Unlawful deductions from wages–Industrial action–Trade union ban on members performing tasks as part of industrial action–Deduction from wages for individual's continued refusal to perform tasks–Employment tribunal's jurisdiction to hear claim

[Employment Rights Act 1996 (c.18) s.14(5).]

The appellant employee (N) appealed against an employment judge's dismissal, for lack of jurisdiction, of his claim that the respondent employer (L) had made unlawful deductions from his wages. L had required N to "act up" by taking on the responsibilities of a higher role. However, when a dispute about shift patterns led to official industrial action, N complied with his union's temporary ban on acting up. L made deductions from his wages, in accordance with the Employment Rights Act 1996 s.14(5). After the official action had finished, N continued to refuse to act up, and L made further deductions. N claimed the further deductions were unlawful, but the employment judge held that his refusal to act up was a continuation of the industrial action as it concerned the same dispute and therefore the deductions fell within s.14(5), meaning an employment tribunal lacked jurisdiction to hear his claims. N submitted that (1) he had personal reasons for not wishing to act up which pre-dated the industrial action and were independent of it; (2) his refusal could not constitute industrial action because no other employee was involved.

Held: Appeal allowed. (1) There was no definition in the Act of a strike or industrial action, for the purposes of s.14(5). However, where an employee refused to carry out a task which he believed he was under no obligation to perform, that did not, in the absence of any other element, constitute industrial action in the ordinary understanding of the term, *Power Packing Casemakers Ltd v Faust* [1983] Q.B. 471, [1983] C.L.Y. 1335 and *Tramp Shipping Corp v Greenwich Marine Inc (The New Horizon)* [1975] 1 W.L.R. 1042, [1975] C.L.Y. 3166 applied. Whilst the employment judge had found other elements, namely that N's dispute with L about acting up was the same as the collective dispute about shift patterns and he was trying to coerce L into improving his terms and conditions, that conclusion had not been open to her. N had wished to cease acting up before the dispute about shift patterns arose. The two issues were different: it would in principle have been entirely possible for N to accept the change in the shift patterns while still maintaining he was under no obligation to act up. Furthermore, N had not been refusing to act up in order to achieve some other object such as putting pressure on L, but had simply refused to do something which he did not believe that he was obliged to do (see paras 15, 19-23 of judgment). (2) Industrial action did not include action by one person alone, *Bowater Containers Ltd v Blake*applied and *Lewis and Britton v E Mason & Sons* [1994] I.R.L.R. 4, [1994] C.L.Y. 2020 not followed. As a matter of ordinary language, it was unnatural to refer to a single person taking part in action undertaken by no-one else (paras 25-26).

NORRIS v LONDON FIRE AND EMERGENCY PLANNING AUTHORITY [2013] I.C.R. 819, Underhill, J., EAT.

1081. Unlawful deductions from wages–Markets–Distribution of "porterage" payments between market porters–Whether only registered porters could take share

[Employment Rights Act 1996 (c.18) s.13.]

The appellants (H) appealed against a decision of the Employment Appeal Tribunal ([2012] I.C.R. 1171, [2012] C.L.Y. 1050) dismissing their claim that the respondent employers had made unauthorised deductions from their wages contrary to the Employment Rights Act 1996 s.13. H were porters at a wholesale fruit and vegetable market. The respondents were fruit and vegetable importers. H were all "registered porters", who had begun working as such during the existence of a collective agreement made in 1974 with the involvement of the union. The other porters employed by the respondents, who were not party to the proceedings, were "unregistered porters" who were employed after the termination of the 1974 agreement in 2009. Porterage was a charge made to customers by traders at the market for the movement of goods. Traditionally it would be pooled and shared between registered porters in accordance with the number of porters employed. Thus they received a basic wage plus their share of porterage. The unregistered porters were paid a higher wage but did not receive separate payment for porterage; their share of the porterage was held by the employers. H's case was that the porterage entitlement earned by both registered and unregistered porters was to be shared exclusively between the registered porters, in accordance with the 1974 agreement, which was incorporated into their employment contracts. The employment tribunal allowed their claim. The Employment Appeal Tribunal allowed the employers' appeal, holding that the intention and purpose of the 1974 agreement was to reward those actually performing the functions of porters in the market, not only those who satisfied the conditions of being registered and union members.

Held: Appeal dismissed. The EAT was correct in its interpretation. The 1974 agreement was no doubt about registered porters, and could fairly be read as directed to identifying their entitlement to porterage. The reason, however, that it focused on registered porters was because, at the time it was made registered porters were the only species of porter known to the market. It would be unreal to interpret the agreement as intended to prescribe that, in circumstances in which the qualifications to work as a porter in the market had changed, and unregistered porters could also lawfully work there, the porterage earned by all porters was nevertheless to be paid exclusively to registered porters. The architects of the agreement could not rationally have intended that, in circumstances in which both registered and unregistered porters could lawfully be employed in the market, the porterage earned by the efforts of the unregistered porters should be shared exclusively by the registered porters. That would not be sensible or fair. The sense of the 1974 agreement was that, insofar as it could be read as referring only to registered porters, it was simply using all references to registration as no more than descriptive of what was then a qualification for the job of porter. The description was, however, no more than that. It could not, in the changed circumstances that had come about, be elevated to the status of a qualifying condition of entitlement to porterage (see para.34 of judgment).

GILGROVE LTD v HAY; *sub nom.* HAY v GILGROVE LTD, [2013] EWCA Civ 412, [2013] I.C.R. 1139, Sir John Thomas (President QBD), CA (Civ Div).

1082. Unlawful deductions from wages–Statutory grievance procedures–Absence of tribunal's jurisdiction to consider claims for unlawful deductions from wages–Non-compliance with statutory grievance procedure–Effect of temporary variation of normal working hours on guarantee payment entitlement

[Employment Rights Act 1996 (c.18) s.28, s.28(1), s.30(5), s.31(6), s.34; Employment Act 2002 (Dispute Resolution) Regulations 2004 (SI 2004/752) reg.9(1)(b); Employment Act 2008 (Commencement No. 1, Transitional Provisions and Savings) Order 2008 (SI 2008/3232).]

The appellant employees (B) appealed against an employment tribunal's decision to dismiss two claims against the respondent employer (G) for unlawful deductions from wages, including non-payment of guarantee payments. After an agreement with G, B's trade union proposed a temporary reduction of working hours to B in order to avoid redundancies, which included no working on Fridays, and an equivalent reduction in pay from January to June 2009. After G refused to confirm that guarantee payments would be paid in respect of that period, the union lodged a formal grievance and in June 2009 B claimed for unlawful deductions from wages in respect of statutory guarantee payments under the Employment Rights Act 1996 s.28. The reduced working hours were extended by agreement until the end of 2009. In February 2010 B made a second claim. In June 2010, G alleged that the 2009 grievance had not complied with the relevant Statutory Grievance Procedure (SGP) or the Employment Act 2002 (Dispute Resolution) Regulations 2004 reg.9(1)(b) as it had failed to name any employees to whom it related. B accepted that there had been a failure to comply and sought leave to amend the 2009 claim to claim for guarantee payments under s.34 of the Act on the basis that such claims were not subject to the SGP. The employment judge refused that application and dismissed the two claims. The relevant SGP was repealed in April 2009 and an interim regime was put in place by the Employment Act 2008 (Commencement No. 1, Transitional Provisions and Savings) Order 2008. B submitted that (1) the temporary contractual variation did not change B's "normal working hours" for the purpose of guarantee payments; (2) it was wrong not to permit the amendment as it was the same claim brought under a different label which would not have prejudiced G; (3) G's failures to make guarantee payments from April 2009 had constituted separate actions which the interim regime did not apply to; (4) as G had not raised the issue before June 2010, it was estopped from disputing B's compliance with the SGP; (5) the 2010 claim should have been upheld under s.28 as valid.

Held: Appeal dismissed. (1) The wording of s.28(1) did not preclude an agreed temporary variation constituting a change to an employee's normal working hours so as to prevent the award of a guarantee payment, *Clemens v Peter Richards (t/a John Bryan)* [1977] I.R.L.R. 332, [1977] C.L.Y. 994.5 and *Daley v Strathclyde RC* [1977] I.R.L.R. 414, [1977] C.L.Y. 994.2 applied. The fact that an arrangement was not permanent was not conclusive. However, it was the intention of the legislature that s.30(5) and s.31(6), which concerned variations to employment contracts, would not apply to issues of entitlement to guarantee payments. The right to a guarantee payment required consideration, in respect of a day or part of a day when work was not provided, as to whether the employee concerned was normally required to work in accordance with his contract of employment. B no longer "normally" worked on Fridays following the variation of the contract and accordingly there were no normal working hours on that day for which guarantee payments were due. The judge had therefore been entitled to reject the claims (see paras 19, 21, 31, 33, 38 of judgment). (2) The 2009 claim had been a nullity in any event as B had not complied with the required SGP, *Highland Council v TGWU* [2008] I.C.R. 1150, [2008] C.L.Y. 4750 and *Hounslow LBC v Miller*applied. There had been no jurisdiction to hear those claims and therefore the amendment application had to be refused as the judge had no power to grant it, *Cocking v Sandhurst (Stationers) Ltd* [1974] I.C.R. 650, [1975] C.L.Y. 1119 applied, *British Newspaper Printing Corp (North) Ltd v Kelly* [1989] I.R.L.R. 222, [1990] C.L.Y. 1893 and *Transport and General Workers Union v Safeway Stores Ltd* (2007) 151 S.J.L.B. 806 considered. Even if he had had the power, he was entitled to refuse the application on the basis that it was made out of time and could have been made earlier (paras 48, 50-53). (3) Although the SGP had been repealed with effect from April 2009, the judge had not erred in dismissing the 2009 claim as the deductions had constituted a series of actions and not separate actions. The provisions in the Order meant that the SGP applied to G's failure to make payments from April 2009 and not just before the SGP's repeal (paras 61, 77). (4) G was not estopped from disputing that B had complied with the SGP. The requirements under the SGP could not be dispensed with by agreement or otherwise, including by estoppel by convention, in order to confer jurisdiction on the tribunal, *Keen v Holland* [1984] 1 W.L.R. 251, [1984] C.L.Y. 34 applied (paras 67-68). (5) The judge was correct to reject the 2010 claim as there was no basis for contending that it had not been reasonably practicable for B to present the claim within the statutory three-month period. The amendment application had come too late and in any event the claim could not have succeeded as B's "normal" working hours had changed with the variation and, as with the 2009 claims, s.28(1) did not apply (paras 75, 77).

ABERCROMBIE v AGA RANGEMASTER LTD [2013] I.C.R. 213, Silber, J., EAT.

1083. Working time–Rest periods–Right of lorry drivers to rest breaks–Effectiveness of enforcement under the Road Transport (Working Time) Regulations 2005

[Employment Rights Act 1996 (c.18); Road Transport (Working Time) Regulations 2005 (SI 2005/639); Working Time Regulations 1998 (SI 1998/

1833); Directive 2002/15 on the organisation of the working time of persons performing mobile road transport activities; Directive 2003/88 on certain aspects of the organisation of working time.]

The appellant trade union (U) appealed against a decision dismissing its claim for judicial review of the respondent secretary of state's refusal to amend legislation concerning road transport workers. U represented lorry drivers who, as mobile workers, were subject to the Road Transport (Working Time) Regulations 2005. Unlike the Working Time Regulations 1998 governing general workers, the 2005 Regulations did not provide a civil remedy for drivers to enforce provisions concerning rest breaks against their employer. The secretary of state maintained that those drivers could rely on the protected disclosure provisions of the Employment Rights Act 1996 in the event that they were dismissed or suffered a detriment for asserting a right to rest breaks. The judge held that the fact that the 1998 and 2005 Regulations differed in the provision of access to an employment tribunal, where a worker was required to work in breach, did not infringe the principle of equivalence. He also rejected the argument that the 2005 Regulations infringed the principle of effectiveness by being framed in such a way as to render impossible in practice the exercise of rights conferred by Community law. He considered that the Regulations did not give rights to mobile workers but imposed obligations upon them and if a worker was required to work in breach, then the current remedies, in the form of enforcement by VOSA and a system of penalties, were effective.

Held: Appeal dismissed. (1) The judge was correct in his reasoning that the principle of equivalence had no application in the instant case. The principle required comparing and contrasting an action based upon European law and an action based upon domestic law. The relevant rights under both Regulations derived from European law in the form of Directive 2002/15 and Directive 2003/88. There was no basis for allowing the principle to be applied to domestic remedies implementing different European obligations even where those obligations were sufficiently similar in respect of their purpose and essential characteristics, *Paquay v Societe d'Architectes Hoet -Minne SPRL (C-460/06)* [2007] E.C.R. I-8511, [2008] C.L.Y. 1139 considered. The judge was right to determine that *Paquay* provided no authoritative basis for a submission that comparison between two European rights was sufficient to trigger the principle of equivalence; the principle was not even mentioned in that case. In any event, the matter was settled by the binding authority of *Oyarce v Cheshire CC* [2008] EWCA Civ 434, [2008] 4 All E.R. 907, [2008] C.L.Y. 1182 which restated the principle in conventional form, *Oyarce* applied (see paras 37-42 of judgment). (2) With regard to the principle of effectiveness, the recitals to the 2002 Directive indicated that the safety and health of mobile workers was one of the aimed-for protections and the reference in the 2005 Regulations to improving working conditions was consistent with that. Therefore, the court considered that an element of "right" on the part of the mobile workers in question did exist even if the principal focus was on road safety and on obligations. Where an employed driver was required to work in breach but declined to do so, the enforcement provisions enshrined in the Regulations were not such as to render his rights practically impossible or effectively difficult to assert. Parliament had elected to provide for criminal penalties, potentially applicable to both drivers and employers, and had further bestowed on VOSA wide powers of enforcement in that regard. Any employee had access to VOSA to make a relevant complaint. If he was threatened with dismissal he could further rely on the protected disclosure provisions of the employment legislation. Also, if instructed to act in breach of the Regulations he would have a potential civil claim against his employer for breach of implied duty in the contract of employment. The fact that some might think that the enforcement regime was not ideal and could be improved upon by bringing it into line with the position in relation to general workers was, ultimately, nothing to the point and did not in itself mean that enforcement was practically impossible or effectively difficult (paras 45-54).

R. (ON THE APPLICATION OF UNITED ROAD TRANSPORT UNION) v SECRETARY OF STATE FOR TRANSPORT, [2013] EWCA Civ 962, [2014] R.T.R. 9, Jackson, L.J., CA (Civ Div).

ENERGY

1084. Administration–Electricity supply industry–Gas supply

THE ENERGY SUPPLY COMPANY ADMINISTRATION RULES 2013, SI 2013/1046; made under the Insolvency Act 1986 s.411; and the Energy Act 2004 s.159. In force: June 7, 2013; .

These Rules set out the procedure for the conduct of energy supply company administration proceedings in England and Wales. Energy supply company administration is a special insolvency regime specifically created for the companies that supply gas and electricity in Britain.

1085. Building regulations–Construction law–Energy performance certificates

THE BUILDING (AMENDMENT) REGULATIONS 2013, SI 2013/1105; made under the European Communities Act 1972 s.2; and the Building Act 1984 Sch.1 para.1, Sch.1 para.4, Sch.1 para.4A, Sch.1 para.7, Sch.1 para.8, Sch.1 para.10. In force: June 3, 2013; .

These Regulations amend the Building Regulations 2010 (SI 2010/2214), adding regulations that transpose Directive 2010/31 arts 2, 6, 7, 9 and 11 on the energy performance of buildings to the list of regulations that cannot be dispensed with or relaxed under sub-sections (1) to (5) of the Building Act 1984 s.8.

1086. Buildings–Energy performance certificates–England and Wales

THE ENERGY PERFORMANCE OF BUILDINGS (ENGLAND AND WALES) (AMENDMENT) (FEES) REGULATIONS 2013, SI 2013/603; made under the European Communities Act 1972 s.2. In force: April 6, 2013; .

These Regulations amend the Energy Performance of Buildings (England and Wales) Regulations 2012 to set revised fees for entering documents on the register.

1087. Codes of practice–Energy conservation–Energy efficiency–Registers

THE GREEN DEAL FRAMEWORK (DISCLOSURE, ACKNOWLEDGMENT, REDRESS ETC.) (AMENDMENT) REGULATIONS 2013, SI 2013/139; made under the Energy Act 2011 s.3, s.4, s.6, s.11, s.16, s.34, s.40. In force: January 28, 2013; .

These Regulations makes amendments to the Green Deal Framework (Disclosure, Acknowledgment, Redress etc.) Regulations 2012 inter alia to insert new definitions to those Regulations.

1088. Consent–Electricity generation–Power stations–Variation

THE ELECTRICITY GENERATING STATIONS (VARIATION OF CONSENTS) (ENGLAND AND WALES) REGULATIONS 2013, SI 2013/1570; made under the Electricity Act 1989 s.36C, s.60. In force: July 31, 2013; .

These Regulations make provision about the procedures for handling applications to vary consents for the construction, extension and operation of electricity generating stations that have been granted under the Electricity Act 1989 s.36.

1089. Decommissioning–Licences–Nuclear power

THE NUCLEAR INDUSTRIES SECURITY (AMENDMENT) REGULATIONS 2013, SI 2013/190; made under the Anti-terrorism, Crime and Security Act 2001 s.77. In force: February 28, 2013; .

These Regulations update legislation to nuclear sites from the point a nuclear site licence is issued for the period until nuclear material is removed from the site as part of the decommissioning of that site. These Regulations also extend the Principal Regulations to a nuclear construction site in prescribed circumstances.

1090. Decommissioning–Nuclear power–Power stations–Waste management

THE NUCLEAR DECOMMISSIONING AND WASTE HANDLING (FINANCE AND FEES) (AMENDMENT) REGULATIONS 2013, SI 2013/1875; made under the Energy Act 2008 s.50, s.104. In force: August 22, 2013; .

The purpose of this instrument is to amend the Nuclear Decommissioning and Waste Handling (Finance and Fees) Regulations 2013 (SI 2013/126) to correct an ambiguity identified by the Joint Committee on Statutory Instruments.

1091. Development consent–Electricity generation–Power stations–Northumberland

THE NORTH BLYTH BIOMASS POWER STATION ORDER 2013, SI 2013/1873; made under the Planning Act 2008 s.114, s.115, s.120, s.149A. In force: August 15, 2013; .

This Order authorises the construction and operation of a biomass fuelled electricity generating station and associated works to be situated at the Blyth Harbour Commission's Battleship Wharf, North Blyth, in the County of Northumberland.

1092. Electricity generation–Bedfordshire

THE ROOKERY SOUTH (RESOURCE RECOVERY FACILITY) ORDER 2011, SI 2013/680; made under the Planning Act 2008 s.114, s.115, s.120. In force: February 28, 2013; .

This Order is concerned with a proposal to develop an electricity generating station fuelled by waste and a post-combustion materials recovery facility to treat incinerator bottom ash at Rookery South Pit, Stewartby, Bedfordshire.

1093. Electricity generation–Electricity licences–Exemptions

THE ELECTRICITY (EXEMPTION FROM THE REQUIREMENT FOR A GENERATION LICENCE) (LOCHLUICHART) ORDER 2013, SI 2013/2473; made under the Electricity Act 1989 s.5. In force: October 28, 2013; .

This Order grants an exemption from the requirement to hold an electricity generation licence to LZN Ltd in respect of the Lochluichart onshore wind farm, a 69 MW plant, situated near Dingwall in the Highland region of Scotland.

1094. Electricity generation–Electricity licences–Exemptions

THE ELECTRICITY (EXEMPTION FROM THE REQUIREMENT FOR A GENERATION LICENCE) (MARKINCH) ORDER 2013, SI 2013/1031; made under the Electricity Act 1989 s.5. In force: June 1, 2013; .

This Order grants exemption from the requirements of the Electricity Act 1989 s.4 (which prohibits the generation of electricity for supply to any premises without a licence) to RWE Npower Renewables (Markinch) Ltd in relation to the Markinch Biomass CHP facility, a combined heat and power generating station situated approximately 1.5 km east of Glenrothes, Scotland.

1095. **Electricity generation–Exemptions–Licences–England and Wales**

THE ELECTRICITY (EXEMPTION FROM THE REQUIREMENT FOR A GENERATION LICENCE) (MIDDLEMOOR) (ENGLAND AND WALES) ORDER 2013, SI 2013/426; made under the Electricity Act 1989. In force: March 28, 2013; .

This Order gives an indefinite exemption, subject to certain conditions, from the requirement to hold an electricity generation licence to RWE Npower Renewables Ltd in respect of the Middlemoor onshore wind farm, a 54MW wind farm located close to Alnwick in Northumberland.

1096. **Electricity licences–Electricity supply industry–Extensions of time–OFGEM**

THE ELECTRICITY (EXTENSION OF TRANSITIONAL PERIOD FOR PROPERTY SCHEMES) ORDER 2013, SI 2013/968; made under the Electricity Act 1989 s.6E, Sch.2A para.5. In force: May 19, 2013; .

This Order extends the period in which an application can be made to the Gas and Electricity Markets Authority for a scheme to transfer property, rights and liabilities to the successful bidder for an offshore transmission licence.by a period of 12 years, until May 19, 2025.

1097. **Electricity licences–Exemptions–Wind farms**

THE ELECTRICITY (EXEMPTION FROM THE REQUIREMENT FOR A GENERATION LICENCE) (BAILLIE) ORDER 2013, SI 2013/1011; made under the Electricity Act 1989 s.5. In force: May 27, 2013; .

This Order grants an exemption from the requirement to hold an electricity generation licence to Baillie Windfarm Ltd in respect of the Baillie onshore wind farm, a 52.5 MW plant, situated east of the town of Thurso, in the Caithness region of North Scotland.

1098. **Electricity lines–Fees–Oral hearings–Orders**

THE ELECTRICITY (NECESSARY WAYLEAVES AND FELLING AND LOPPING OF TREES) (CHARGES) (ENGLAND AND WALES) REGULATIONS 2013, SI 2013/1986; made under the Energy Act 2004 s.188. In force: October 1, 2013; .

The Secretary of State has power to grant a necessary wayleave to enable an electricity company to install and keep installed an electric line on, under or over any land, and also has power to make an order to empower an electricity company to fell or lop trees close to electric lines. In both cases the Secretary of State must give the owner or occupier of the land the opportunity to be heard before making such a decision. This instrument introduces a full cost recovery charging regime that is applicable to electricity companies for the processing by Government of applications for necessary wayleave and tree lopping and tree felling orders, and services relating to hearings.

1099. **Electricity lines–Oral hearings–Orders–England and Wales**

THE ELECTRICITY (NECESSARY WAYLEAVES AND FELLING AND LOPPING OF TREES) (HEARING PROCEDURES) (ENGLAND AND WALES) RULES 2013, SI 2013/1987; made under the Tribunals and Inquiries Act 1992 s.9. In force: October 1, 2013; .

The Secretary of State has power to grant a necessary (compulsory) wayleave to enable an electricity company to install and keep installed an electric line on, under or over any third party land, and also has power to make an order to empower an electricity company to fell or lop trees close to electric lines to ensure compliance with statutory obligations that are placed upon them to safeguard public safety and ensure continuity of supply. In both cases the Secretary of State must give the owner or occupier of the land the opportunity to be heard before making a decision. This instrument sets out the hearing procedure to be followed in respect of an application for a necessary wayleave or a reference for an order for the felling or lopping of trees.

1100. **Electricity supply industry–Gas supply industry–Registers**

THE GAS AND ELECTRICITY (REGISTERS) (REVOCATION) ORDER 2013, SI 2013/1420; made under the Gas Act 1986 s.36; and the Electricity Act 1989 s.49. In force: July 12, 2013; .

This Order revokes the Gas (Register) Order 1988 and the Electricity (Register) Order 1990. The Gas (Register) Order 1988 prescribed the hours during which the register maintained by the Director General of Gas Supply (later the Gas and Electricity Markets Authority) under the Gas Act 1986 s.36 was to be kept open for public inspection and the fees payable to the Director for the supply of copies or extracts from that register.

1101. **Electricity transmission–Offshore installations–Tenders**

THE ELECTRICITY (COMPETITIVE TENDERS FOR OFFSHORE TRANSMISSION LICENCES) REGULATIONS 2013, SI 2013/175; made under the Electricity Act 1989 s.6C, s.6D, s.60. In force: February 22, 2013; .

These Regulations set out the process for competitive tenders that will apply to the grant of offshore transmission licences.

1102. **Emissions–Heating–Metering–Renewable energy**

THE RENEWABLE HEAT INCENTIVE SCHEME (AMENDMENT) (NO.2) REGULATIONS 2013, SI 2013/2410; made under the Energy Act 2008 s.100, s.104. In force: September 24, 2013; .

These Regulations, which extend to Great Britain, amend the Renewable Heat Incentive Scheme Regulations 2011 to introduce new requirements relating to emissions from plant generating heat from solid biomass, to introduce new metering provisions, and to make various incidental and miscellaneous amendments.

1103. **Energy–Market abuse–Penalties–Transparency**

THE ELECTRICITY AND GAS (MARKET INTEGRITY AND TRANSPARENCY) (ENFORCEMENT ETC.) REGULATIONS 2013, SI 2013/1389; made under the European Communities Act 1972 s.2. In force: June 29, 2013; .

These Regulations are intended to establish an investigatory, enforcement and penalty regime for breaches of the EU Regulation on wholesale energy market integrity and transparency (REMIT).

1104. **Energy Act 2011 (c.16)–Commencement No.2 Order**

THE ENERGY ACT 2011 (COMMENCEMENT NO.2) ORDER 2013, SI 2013/SI 2013/125 (C.7); made under the Energy Act 2011 s.121. In force: bringing into operation various provisions of the 2011 Act on January 28, 2013.; .

This Order brings into force for all remaining purposes certain provisions the Energy Act 2011 relating to green deal plans, disclosure of a green deal plan and related matters, and early repayment of green deal finance. It also makes amendments to the gas code and the electricity code (which are contained in the Gas Act 1986 and the Electricity Act 1989 respectively) and certain provisions of the Consumer Credit Act 1974.

1105. **Energy policy–Renewable energy**

THE PROMOTION OF THE USE OF ENERGY FROM RENEWABLE SOURCES (AMENDMENT) REGULATIONS 2013, SI 2013/829; made under the European Communities Act 1972 s.2. In force: June 1, 2013; .

These Regulations amend the Promotion of the Use of Energy from Renewable Sources Regulations 2011 (SI 2011/243) to correct drafting errors.

1106. **Environmental designs–Household appliances**

THE ECODESIGN FOR ENERGY-RELATED PRODUCTS AND ENERGY INFORMATION (AMENDMENT) REGULATIONS 2013, SI 2013/1232; made under the European Communities Act 1972 s.2. In force: September 1, 2013 except for reg.2(3) on November 1, 2013.; .

These Regulations amend the Ecodesign for Energy-Related Products Regulations 2010 (SI 2010/2617) (the 2010 Regulations) and the Energy Information Regulations 2011 (SI 2011/1524) to add three further products (motors, household tumble driers and directional lamp including LEDs) through amendments to the Schedule of the 2010 Regulations and amend the reference to electrical lamps and luminaires to the Schedule of products subject to the 2011 Energy Information Regulations. The effect of these changes is to extend the Market Surveillance Authority's enforcement powers to these products.

1107. **Feed-in tariffs**

THE FEED-IN TARIFFS (AMENDMENT) ORDER 2013, SI 2013/1099; made under the Energy Act 2008 s.43, s.104. In force: July 1, 2013; .

This Order amends the Feed-in Tariffs Order 2012 (SI 2012/2782) to provide for a set of administrative changes to the feed-in tariff Scheme, which impact on the operation and administration of the policy.

1108. **Fees–Gas storage–Licences–Petroleum licences**

THE GAS AND PETROLEUM (CONSENTS) CHARGES REGULATIONS 2013, SI 2013/1138; made under the Energy Act 2004 s.188. In force: June 17, 2013; .

These Regulations make provision for the Secretary of State to require a charge when a person seeks the consent, approval or authorisation of the Secretary of State to a matter under a carbon dioxide appraisal and storage licence, gas storage licence, or a petroleum licence.

1109. **Funded decommissioning programmes–Nuclear industry–Nuclear power**

THE NUCLEAR DECOMMISSIONING AND WASTE HANDLING (FINANCE AND FEES) REGULATIONS 2013, SI 2013/126; made under the Energy Act 2008 s.49, s.50, s.54, s.55, s.104. In force: March 4, 2013; .

These Regulations set out the legislative framework for funded decommissioning programmes. They contain a transitional provision for any funded decommissioning programme already submitted under the Nuclear Decommissioning and Waste Handling (Finance and Fees) Regulations 2011.

1110. **Gas licences–Oil–Sanctions–Iran**

THE HYDROCARBONS (TEMPORARY MANAGEMENT SCHEME) REGULATIONS 2013, SI 2013/1329; made under the European Communities Act 1972 s.2. In force: June 30, 2013; .

These Regulations establish a power for the Secretary of State to take a UK oil or gas licence into his control under a temporary management scheme, where the licence holder is designated under EU sanctions against Iran.

1111. Growth and Infrastructure Act 2013 (c.27)–Commencement No.2 and Transitional and Saving Provisions Order

THE GROWTH AND INFRASTRUCTURE ACT 2013 (COMMENCEMENT NO.2 AND TRANSITIONAL AND SAVING PROVISIONS) ORDER 2013, SI 2013/1488; made under the Growth and Infrastructure Act 2013 s.35. Commencement details: bringing into force various provisions of the 2013 Act on June 19, 2013, June 25, 2013, July 31, 2013, October 1, 2013 and December 1, 2013.; .

This Order brings into force on the day after the day on which this Order is made the Growth and Infrastructure Act 2013 s.20 for the purposes of enabling the Secretary of State or Scottish Ministers to make regulations about the procedure for varying consent in respect of electricity generating stations which have been granted under the Electricity Act 1989 Act s.36.

1112. Non-road mobile machinery–Renewable energy–Road fuel

THE RENEWABLE TRANSPORT FUEL OBLIGATIONS (AMENDMENT) ORDER 2013, SI 2013/816; made under the European Communities Act 1972 s.2; and the Energy Act 2004 s.124, s.125A, s.125B, s.127, s.129, s.132, s.192. In force: April 9, 2013 except for regs 3 to 11 on April 15, 2013.; .

This Order gives effect to aspects of Directive 98/70 as amended by Directive 2009/30, by amending the Renewable Transport Fuel Obligations Order 2007 (SI 2007/3072) so that suppliers of fuel for use in various forms of mobile machinery are subject to the Renewable Transport Fuel Obligation.

1113. Offshore installations–Planning permission–Suffolk–Wind farms

THE GALLOPER WIND FARM (CORRECTION) ORDER 2013, SI 2013/2086; made under the Planning Act 2008 s.119, Sch.4. In force: August 21, 2013; .

The Order corrects errors in the Galloper Wind Farm Order 2013 (SI 2013/1203), a development consent order under the Planning Act 2008, following a request under para.1 (6) (a) of Sch.4 to that Act.

1114. Offshore installations–Planning permission–Wind farms–Suffolk

THE GALLOPER WIND FARM ORDER 2013, SI 2013/1203; made under the Planning Act 2008 s.114, s.115, s.120, s.149A. In force: June 15, 2013; .

This Order grants development consent for, and authorises Galloper Wind Farm Limited to construct, operate and maintain, an offshore generating station in the sea approximately 30km off the coast of Suffolk and to erect and keep overhead lines near Sizewell Wents, Sizewell in Suffolk, together with all necessary and associated development. For the purposes of the development that it authorises, Galloper Wind Farm Limited is authorised by the Order compulsorily or by agreement to acquire land and rights in land and to use land, as well as to override easements and other rights. The Order imposes requirements in connection with the development for which it grants development consent.

1115. Offshore installations–Safety zones

THE OFFSHORE INSTALLATIONS (SAFETY ZONES) ORDER 2013, SI 2013/1758; made under the Petroleum Act 1987 s.22. In force: in accordance with art.1 (2).; .

This Order establishes, under the Petroleum Act 1987 s.22, safety zones having a radius of 500 metres from the specified point around the thirteen installations specified in the Schedule to this Order stationed, or to be stationed, in waters to which s.21 of that Act applies.

1116. Power stations–Accreditation–Lawfulness of refusing accreditation–Existence of extant qualifying arrangement for building of generating stations–Appropriate basis for award of just satisfaction for breach of human rights

[Electricity Act 1989 (c.29); Human Rights Act 1998 (c.42) s.8; Renewables Obligation Order 2006 (SI 2006/1004) Art.6(4); Renewables Obligation Order 2009 (SI 2009/785) Art.21; European Convention on Human Rights 1950 Protocol 1 Art.1.]

The appellant authority appealed against a decision ([2011] EWHC 1873 (Admin), [2011] A.C.D. 109) that its refusal of accreditation for a Renewables Obligation Certificate (ROC) for power stations owned and operated by the respondents (X) was unlawful. Under the Electricity Act 1989 and statutory instruments made under it, public electricity suppliers were required to enter into arrangements to secure electricity from non-fossil fuel sources and could thereafter obtain an ROC if those requirements were met, otherwise they would have to pay a charge. X had sought accreditation for two generating stations fuelled by landfill gas. The authority found that for each site, there was at the relevant time an arrangement, known under the Renewables Obligation Order 2009 art.21 as a Non-Fossil Fuel Order (NFFO) arrangement, and under the Renewables Obligation Order 2006 art.6(3) and art.6(4) as an extant qualifying arrangement, providing for the building of a generating station which had not yet been commissioned. The authority held that since such arrangements existed, X's stations were excluded generating stations and no ROC could be issued for the electricity generated at them, and that it could not, consequently, grant the stations accreditation. X applied for judicial review of that decision on the basis that, for either station, the Replacement Power Purchase Agreement (RPPA) entered into between its predecessors in title and the interested party, the Non-Fossil Purchasing Agency (NFPA), was of no force and effect by the time the authority made its decision, because the stations had not been built by a designated date, so that no NFFO arrangement then subsisted. They sought damages by way of just satisfaction under the Human Rights Act 1998 s.8 in respect of the violation of their rights under the European Convention on Human Rights 1950 Protocol 1 art.1. The judge accepted that by the time X had applied for accreditation, there was no longer an extant qualifying arrangement or an NFFO arrangement in existence for either of the two sites, so that the statutory exclusion under art.6(3) and art.6(4) of the 2006 Order and art.21 of the 2009 Order did not apply and the authority had been wrong to conclude that it did. He found that as a consequence of that unlawful decision, X had been deprived of a valuable economic benefit since the refusal to accredit their generating stations and grant ROCs meant that they had suffered a clear and calculable financial loss, and they were awarded damages by way of just satisfaction in respect of the monetary value of the ROCs which should have been issued earlier, based on the principle of restitutio in integrum. The authority contended that there remained an extant qualifying arrangement providing for the building of generating stations because those provisions of the RPPA which required X to use reasonable endeavours to procure the fulfilment of the commissioning of the facility continued to have force and effect. It submitted that that obligation necessarily encompassed an obligation to build the facility, since the facility could not be commissioned without first having been built. The authority asserted that, even if the decision to refuse accreditation was unlawful, there had been no breach of Protocol 1 art.1 because X's claim to be accredited was not sufficiently established to amount to a "possession", and that the judge had erred by failing to distinguish between the role that compensation played in human rights cases and cases of breach of statutory duty.

Held: Appeal dismissed. (1) The authority's submission on the obligation to commission the facility might have had some force if the RPPA had contained no other provision for the building of the facility, but they did, and those obligations were no longer in force. The generating facility could not be operated unless it had first been installed; commissioning would follow installation and operation. The RPPA contained two separate and distinct obligations: to use reasonable endeavours to (a) install a generating station; (b) commission it.

Since the first obligation had been of no force and effect after a certain date, there was simply no basis upon which its existence could be impliedly continued as part of the remaining obligation. Any clauses of the RPPA that remained in effect did not provide for the building of a generating station. That conclusion did not conflict with the purpose of the statutory scheme encouraging the generation of electricity from non-fossil fuel sources (see paras 11, 14-15, 22 of judgment). (2) X had a legitimate expectation of the right to accreditation under the statutory scheme. A legal provision or a legal act such a judicial decision sufficed in giving a party an entitlement to some pecuniary benefit. X had been wrongly deprived of a pecuniary benefit to which they were entitled by statute. Where the breach of a Convention right had clearly caused significant pecuniary loss, that would usually be assessed and awarded, *Anufrijeva v Southwark LBC* [2003] EWCA Civ 1406, [2004] Q.B. 1124, [2004] C.L.Y. 1986 applied. Since the amount of X's lost "benefit" was readily calculable, restitutio in integrum was manifestly appropriate and the judge had been entitled to assess X's damages on that basis (paras 25, 27).

R. (ON THE APPLICATION OF INFINIS PLC) v GAS AND ELECTRICITY MARKETS AUTHORITY; *sub nom.* GAS AND ELECTRICITY MARKETS AUTHORITY v INFINIS PLC, [2013] EWCA Civ 70, [2013] J.P.L. 1037, Sir James Munby (President, Fam), CA (Civ Div).

1117. Renewable energy–Renewables obligations

THE RENEWABLES OBLIGATION (AMENDMENT) ORDER 2013, SI 2013/768; made under the European Communities Act 1972 s.2; and the Electricity Act 1989 s.32, s.32A, s.32C, s.32D, s.32E, s.32J, s.32K. In force: April 1, 2013; .

The Order implements the outcome of the review of support levels for renewable electricity under the Renewables Obligation.

1118. Renewable heat incentive–Tariffs

THE RENEWABLE HEAT INCENTIVE SCHEME (AMENDMENT) REGULATIONS 2013, SI 2013/1033; made under the Energy Act 2008 s.100, s.104. In force: April 30, 2013; .

These Regulations amends the Renewable Heat Incentive Scheme Regulations 2011 (SI 2011/2860) to establish a long-term financial control mechanism for the non-domestic renewable heat incentive scheme (the RHI scheme) until the end of March 2015. This mechanism will replace the current mechanism of financial control under the RHI Regulations. Under the revised mechanism, tariffs will be reduced if the levels of renewable heat deployment exceed that needed to achieve the RHI scheme's renewables objectives.

ENVIRONMENT

1119. Air quality–Emissions–Failure to comply with art.13 Directive 2008/50–Whether requirement to seek extension of time for compliance–Interpretation of Directive 2008/50 art.22

[Treaty on the Functioning of the European Union Art.258; Directive 2008/50 on ambient air quality and cleaner air for Europe Art.13, Art.22, Art.23; Directive 96/62 on ambient air quality assessment and management.]

The appellant environment law organisation (C) appealed against a refusal ([2011] EWHC 3623 (Admin), [2012] 1 C.M.L.R. 47, [2012] 6 C.L. 151) to grant a mandatory order requiring the respondent secretary of state to issue a notification under Directive 2008/50 art.22. By February 2009, it had become clear that, for certain zones, the United Kingdom was unlikely to be able to comply with the requirement in art.13(1) of the Directive to ensure that emissions of nitrogen dioxide did not exceed certain limits by January 1, 2010. For those zones, rather than preparing time extension notifications under art.22, to demonstrate a plan for compliance by January 1, 2015, the secretary of state indicated an intention to submit plans to the European Commission under art.23, setting out actions to keep the exceedance periods as short as possible. The issue was whether the Directive required compliance by January 1, 2015. The judge found that the use of the word "may" in the English text of art.22(1) and "peut" in the French text conferred a discretion to postpone the deadline by a maximum of five years. It held that a state was not obliged to use the machinery provided by art.22(1) and could simply admit its breach, as the UK had done, and leave it to the Commission to take whatever action it thought right by way of enforcement under TFEU art.258. C submitted that art.23 of the Directive had to be read together with art.22, which provided for a maximum extension period of five years and meant that the UK could not avoid compliance by January 1, 2015. In particular, it argued that (1) rather than conferring a discretion to postpone the deadline, the word "may" was used in art.22(1) because the period of extension was or might be uncertain; (2) the rigour of art.22(3) tended to show that art.22(1) was intended as a compulsory regime; (3) article 22(4) applied even where no proposal for an extension was made under art.22(1).

Held: Appeal dismissed. (1) The judge had been right to hold that the words "may" and "peut" were unequivocal. Giving full weight to the more liberal approach to construction applicable to European measures, the legislature could not have intended to create a mandatory and absolute cut-off point for compliance with carbon dioxide limit values as at January 1, 2015. The word "may" was not used because the period of extension was or might be uncertain; that was catered for by the expression "a maximum of five years". The use of the term "shall" in art.22(2) did not throw any light on how the verb "may" was to be understood in art.22(1) because art.22(2) concerned a different pollutant (see para.15 of judgment). (2) Article 22(3) only applied where art.22(1) or art.22(2) was deployed. It was unsurprising that rigorous requirements were attached to art.22 extensions (para.16). (3) Article 22(4) only applied where the conditions in art.22(1) or art.22(2) were met and either or both of those paragraphs were engaged (para.19). (4) While art.22(1) cross-referred to art.23, the two articles were dealing with separate states of affairs. Article 23 recalled earlier provisions of Directive 96/62, which included a requirement that in the case of zones where the level of pollutant exceeded the limit value a Member State had to draw up a plan to secure compliance by the specified deadline. Article 22, however, was not prefigured at all in that Directive. The duty to comply with either paragraph of art.23(1) was not conditional on the Member States proposing a five-year extension under art.22. The first paragraph of art.23 applied where exceedances were found to have occurred before the deadline and the second where they occurred after that date, whether as originally provided or as extended by up to five years. That interpretation of the Directive did not render art.22 nugatory or undermine the purpose of the Directive. The machinery of art.22 allowed a Member State, with the Commission's approval, to extend the time for compliance in conformity with the Directive by up to five years. However, there might be occasions, as in the instant case, where even that extended period could not be met. In such a case, it seemed at least doubtful whether the art.22 procedure could be honestly or properly applied at all. In such a case, the Member State would be in breach once the deadline of January 1, 2010 had passed and the Commission could bring infraction proceedings under TFEU art.258. However, the policy of the legislation was not merely to condemn breaches of its provisions and seek imposition of heavy sanctions. It was to promote the reduction of pollutant levels in any event. Accordingly, the first sentence of art.23(1) was designed to support that process by requiring the production of air quality plans before the deadline expired. That was irrespective of a notification under art.22. The viability of the plans produced under art.23 might constitute a material factor in the Commission's decision about whether to take action under TFEU art.258 where there had been a violation of art.13. Approached in that way, the scheme of environmental protection which the Directive secured was fully effective (paras 17, 19-20).

R. (ON THE APPLICATION OF CLIENTEARTH) v SECRETARY OF STATE FOR THE ENVIRONMENT, FOOD AND RURAL AFFAIRS, [2012] EWCA Civ 897, [2013] Env. L.R. 4, Laws, L.J., CA (Civ Div).

1120. Air quality–Emissions–Time limits applying to UK's obligation not to exceed limit values in respect of nitrogen dioxide–Questions referred to European Court of Justice

[Directive 2008/50 on ambient air quality and cleaner air for Europe Art.13, Art.22, Art.23.]

The appellant environmental-law organisation (C) appealed against a decision ([2012] EWCA Civ 897, [2013] Env. L.R. 4) on the interpretation of Directive 2008/50 art.22. Article 13 of the Directive required Member States to ensure that limit values for nitrogen dioxide should not be exceeded from January 1, 2010. Article 22 provided as follows: "Where, in a given zone or agglomeration, conformity with the limit values for nitrogen dioxide... cannot be achieved by the deadlines specified..., a Member State may postpone those deadlines by a maximum of five years for that particular zone or agglomeration, on condition that an air quality plan is established in accordance with [art.23] for the zone or agglomeration to which the postponement would apply (para.1)... Member States shall notify the Commission where, in their view, paragraphs 1 or 2 are applicable, and shall communicate the air quality plan referred to in paragraph 1 including all relevant information necessary for the Commission to assess whether or not the relevant conditions are satisfied". Article 23 provided as follows: "Where, in given zones or agglomerations, the levels of pollutants in ambient air exceed any limit value or target value, plus any relevant margin of tolerance in each case, Member States shall ensure that air quality plans are established for those zones and agglomerations in order to achieve the related limit value... In the event of exceedances of those limit values for which the attainment deadline is already expired, the air quality plans shall set out appropriate measures, so that the exceedance period can be kept as short as possible". The respondent secretary of state accepted that the United Kingdom was in breach of art.13 in relation to certain zones and that for certain zones it had not produced plans showing conformity by 2015; it was asserted, however, that for those zones compliance within that timetable was not realistically possible, owing to circumstances beyond the UK's control and unforeseen in 2008. The parties disagreed about the effect of arts 22 and 23. The European Commission had stated as follows in a letter to C: "The Commission would have some considerable concerns if [art.23] were seen to be a way of allowing Member States to circumvent the requirements of [art.22]. Article 22... was introduced in order to afford Member States additional time for compliance for up to a maximum of 5 years, on condition that an air quality plan is established in accordance with [art.23] and communicated to the Commission for assessment. It is only under these conditions that Member States can be afforded additional time for compliance and [art.23] itself cannot be relied upon to further extend this clearly prescribed and limited time extension clause".

Held: Questions referred to ECJ. (1) It would be appropriate to grant a declaration that the UK was in breach of art.13. Such an order was appropriate both as a formal statement of the legal position and to make clear that, regardless of arguments about the effect of arts 22 and 23, the way was open to immediate enforcement action at national or European level (see para.37 of judgment). (2) The other issues raised difficult issues of European law, the determination of which required the guidance of the European Court of Justice in the form of a preliminary ruling. The following questions appeared appropriate: (a) where in a given zone or agglomeration conformity with the limit values for nitrogen dioxide could not be achieved by the deadline of January 1, 2010, whether a Member State was obliged to seek postponement of the deadline in accordance with art.22; (b) if so, in what circumstances (if any) might a Member State be relieved of that obligation; (c) if the answer to (a) was no, to what extent (if at all) were the obligations of a Member State which had failed to comply with art.13, and had not made an application under art.22, affected by art.23; (d) in the event of non-compliance with art.13, and in the absence of an application under art.22, what (if any) remedies should a national court provide as a matter of European law (paras 38-39).

R. (ON THE APPLICATION OF CLIENTEARTH) v SECRETARY OF STATE FOR THE ENVIRONMENT, FOOD AND RURAL AFFAIRS, [2013] UKSC 25, [2013] 2 All E.R. 928, Lord Hope, J.S.C., SC.

1121. Antarctic Act 2013 (C.15)

This Act makes provision consequential on Annex VI to the Protocol on Environmental Protection to the Antarctic Treaty; and amends the Antarctic Act 1994.

This Act received Royal Assent on March 26, 2013.

1122. Canals–Flood defences–Assessment of flood risk–Classsification of sluices as formal flood defence–Correctness of classification

The appellant agency (E) appealed against a decision [2012] EWHC 1643 (QB), [2013] J.P.L. 515, [2013] 7 C.L. 133that it had been irrational to conclude that sluices were formal flood defences and that it had failed to interpret, apply or have regard to its own policies. The respondents (M) had wished to develop land adjacent to the Manchester Ship Canal. The local planning authority had proposed 1,500 dwellings on the adjacent land, which it subsequently reduced to 800 following E's classification of that land as falling within Flood Zone 3 on its flood map. Under Planning Policy Statement 25 (PPS25), development was steered away from areas at the greatest risk of flooding. Preference was given to Flood Zone 1, with recourse to development in areas of a greater risk if land with a lesser flood risk was not available. The part of the canal affecting M contained sluices, which were a flood defence. When designating flood zones, E, in line with its policies, distinguished between only two types of flood defence: those whose primary purpose was flood prevention, a formal flood defence, which were ignored, and those whose secondary purpose was flood prevention, a de facto defence, which were presumed operational. When designating the land on which M wanted to develop a flood zone, E categorised the sluices as a formal flood defence. Had they been categorised as de facto defences, the land would not have been designated as Flood Zone 3 and its development potential inhibited. M successfully applied for judicial review of E's decision to classify the sluices as formal defences. E submitted that it was entitled to categorise the sluices as a formal flood defence as they had a dual primary purpose, namely flood defence and navigation, which were of equal significance, and nothing in its policies prevented it from identifying such a dual purpose.

Held: Appeal dismissed. E had erred in its categorisation of the sluices as formal flood defences. It had created and relied upon a category of formal flood defence which was nowhere to be found within its own policies and guidance. It would have been open to E to create more than two categories of flood defence to deal with situations like the instant one where it was impossible to say which of a structure's functions was of greater significance. However, it was not open to E to meet that difficulty by departing from its published policies, at least without telling the affected party that it was doing so and allowing argument, and by creating a third category of flood defence which it would ignore when preparing its flood map. E's categorisation of sluices as a formal flood defence, when on its own view its functions of enabling navigation and preventing flooding were of equal significance, was to misunderstand and misconstrue its policies. E's difficulty in deciding which of the sluices' functions was the most important underlined the second reason that it had erred. The operation of the canal itself was in opposition: it created and attenuated the risk of flooding. It made no sense to describe the canal as a formal flood defence; it operated to permit sea-going ships to be navigated inland. The operation of the sluices was integral to the function of the canal and enabled it to achieve its purpose. The canal and its associated structures could not operate unless it controlled the flow of water. It controlled the flow of that water whether it would flood or not. The mere fact that it controlled and regulated the flow of that water could not be a basis for categorising either the canal or its associated structures as a formal flood defence. The sluices were no more a formal flood defence than the canal was. Planning Policy Guidance 25 attested to that fact, as did the other relevant guidance. E's decision was outside the range of reasonable conclusions (see paras 24-29 of judgment).

R. (ON THE APPLICATION OF MANCHESTER SHIP CANAL CO LTD) v ENVIRONMENT AGENCY, [2013] EWCA Civ 542, [2013] J.P.L. 1406, Moses, L.J., CA (Civ Div).

1123. Capacity–Developing countries–Environmental protection–Sustainable development

THE GLOBAL GREEN GROWTH INSTITUTE (LEGAL CAPACITIES) ORDER 2013, SI 2013/785; made under the International Organisations Act 1968 s.1. In force: in accordance with art.1.; .

This Order confers the legal capacities of a body corporate on the Global Green Growth Institute, an international organisation established with the aim of promoting sustainable development of developing and emerging countries.

1124. Carbon capture and storage–Electricity generation–Development consent orders

THE CARBON CAPTURE READINESS (ELECTRICITY GENERATING STATIONS) REGULATIONS 2013, SI 2013/2696; made under the European Communities Act 1972 s.2. In force: November 25, 2013; .

These Regulations implement Directive 2010/75 art.36 of the European Parliament and of the Council on industrial emissions.

1125. Carbon dioxide emissions–Climate change agreements–Fees

THE CLIMATE CHANGE AGREEMENTS (ADMINISTRATION) (MISCELLANEOUS AMENDMENTS) REGULATIONS 2013, SI 2013/508; made under the Finance Act 2000 Sch.6 para.52D, Sch.6 para.52E, Sch.6 para.52F, Sch.6 para.146. In force: March 31, 2013; .

These Regulations amend the Climate Change Agreements (Administration) Regulations 2012. Amendments include changing terms to be included in an agreement in relation to the buy-out fee to provide that the buy-out fee is calculated by reference to emissions of tonnes of carbon dioxide equivalent.

1126. Climate change agreements–Energy conservation–Energy policy

THE CLIMATE CHANGE AGREEMENTS (ELIGIBLE FACILITIES) (MISCELLANEOUS AMENDMENTS) REGULATIONS 2013, SI 2013/505; made under the Finance Act 2000 Sch.6 para.50, Sch.6 para.146. In force: March 31, 2013; .

These Regulations amend the Climate Change Agreements (Eligible Facilities) Regulations 2012. The Regulations provides that until May 31 2014, if, at the time it falls to be determined whether a facility is eligible to be covered by a climate change agreement, the operator of the facility has insufficient data available on the supply or use of reckonable energy by the installation for the previous 12 month period in order to determine the intended supply or use of reckonable energy by the installation, the intended supply or use of reckonable energy by the installation must instead be estimated by the administrator.

1127. **Codes of practice–Noise–England**

THE CONTROL OF NOISE (CODE OF PRACTICE ON NOISE FROM ICE-CREAM VAN CHIMES ETC.) (ENGLAND) ORDER 2013, SI 2013/2036; made under the Control of Pollution Act 1974 s.71, s.104. In force: October 1, 2013; .

The instrument revokes and replaces the Control of Noise (Code of Practice on Noise from Ice-Cream Van Chimes Etc.) Order 1981.

1128. **CRC energy efficiency scheme**

THE CRC ENERGY EFFICIENCY SCHEME ORDER 2013, SI 2013/1119; made under the Climate Change Act 2008 s.44, s.46, s.49, s.90, Sch.2, Sch.3 para.9. In force: May 16, 2013; .

Order makes provision for the implementation of a simplified energy efficiency scheme called the CRC Energy Efficiency Scheme.

1129. **CRC energy efficiency scheme–Payments**

THE CRC ENERGY EFFICIENCY SCHEME (ALLOCATION OF ALLOWANCES FOR PAYMENT) (AMENDMENT) REGULATIONS 2013, SI 2013/1097; made under the Finance Act 2008 s.21. In force: June 1, 2013; .

These Regulations amend the CRC Energy Efficiency Scheme (Allocation of Allowances for Payment) Regulations 2012 (SI 2012/1386) to: replace the requirement to have primary and secondary allocation periods with a single allocation period; create separate application periods (when main allocations of allowances can be requested) and payment periods (when main allocations should be paid for); and require that, when payments are received after a payment period, they are repaid on request and the Secretary of State can deduct costs reasonably incurred in making the repayment.

1130. **Designation–Emissions–Industry–England and Wales**

THE POLLUTION PREVENTION AND CONTROL (DESIGNATION OF DIRECTIVES) (ENGLAND AND WALES) ORDER 2013, SI 2013/123; made under the Pollution Prevention and Control Act 1999 Sch.1 para.20. In force: February 10, 2013; .

This Order designates 22 Directives as relevant directives for the purposes of the Pollution Prevention and Control Act 1999 Sch.1 para.20(2) (c).The effect of this Order is that Regulations may be made under that Act making provision which corresponds or is similar to any provision made, or capable of being made, under s.2 of the European Communities Act 1972.

1131. **Emissions–Industry–Integrated pollution prevention and control**

THE POLLUTION PREVENTION AND CONTROL (DESIGNATION OF THE INDUSTRIAL EMISSIONS DIRECTIVE) (OFFSHORE) ORDER 2013, SI 2013/669; made under the Pollution Prevention and Control Act 1999 Sch.1 para.20. In force: March 15, 2013; .

This Order, which applies to the sea within the area of the continental shelf of the UK and to the territorial sea adjacent to Northern Ireland, designates Directive 2010/75 on industrial emissions for the purposes of the Pollution Prevention and Control Act 1999 para.20.

1132. **Emissions trading–EU law;**

THE GREENHOUSE GAS EMISSIONS TRADING SCHEME (AMENDMENT) REGULATIONS 2013, SI 2013/1037; made under the European Communities Act 1972 s.2; and the Pollution Prevention and Control Act 1999 s.2, Sch.1. In force: May 23, 2013; .

These Regulations transpose a Decision derogating temporarily from Directive 2003/87 establishing a scheme for greenhouse gas emission allowance trading within the Community.

1133. Environment–Environmental protection–Nitrate vulnerable zones–Water pollution

THE NITRATE POLLUTION PREVENTION (DESIGNATION AND MISCELLANEOUS AMENDMENTS) REGULATIONS 2013, SI 2013/2619; made under the European Communities Act 1972 s.2. In force: November 18, 2013; .

These Regulations amend the Nitrate Pollution Prevention Regulations 2008 (SI 2008/2349), which give effect in England to Directive 91/676. They give statutory effect to the revised designation of nitrate vulnerable zones in England, and make minor amendments to other provisions.

1134. Environment agency–Reservoirs–England

THE RESERVOIRS ACT 1975 (CAPACITY, REGISTRATION, PRESCRIBED FORMS, ETC.) (ENGLAND) REGULATIONS 2013, SI 2013/1677; made under the Reservoirs Act 1975 s.A1, s.2, s.3, s.5, s.11, s.20, s.21B. In force: July 30, 2013; .

For the purposes of the Reservoirs Act 1975 these Regulations provide for measures including: the calculation of the capacity of a large raised reservoir; registration of a large raised reservoir; notification of changes to, and the keeping and inspection of, the English register, and transitional arrangements in relation to the English register; and the making and content of reports by the Environment Agency to the Secretary of State.

1135. Environmental noise–Waste management

THE ENVIRONMENTAL NOISE, SITE WASTE MANAGEMENT PLANS AND SPREADABLE FATS ETC. (REVOCATIONS AND AMENDMENTS) REGULATIONS 2013, SI 2013/2854; made under the European Communities Act 1972 s.2; the Food Safety Act 1990 s.16, s.26; and the Clean Neighbourhoods and Environment Act 2005 s.54. In force: December 1, 2013; .

These Regulations: revoke the Environmental Noise (Identification of Noise Sources) (England) Regulations 2007 (SI 2007/415), the Environmental Noise (Identification of Noise Sources) (England) (Amendment) Regulations 2007 (SI 2007/2458) and the Site Waste Management Plans Regulations 2008 (SI 2008/314); and amend the Spreadable Fats (Marketing Standards) and the Milk and Milk Products (Protection of Designations) (England) Regulations 2008 (SI 2008/1287) to revoke regulation 4 (which prohibits the sale by retail of margarine unless it contains specified proportions of vitamins A and D) and make consequential amendments.

1136. Environmental protection–Nitrate vulnerable zones–Water pollution–Wales

THE NITRATE POLLUTION PREVENTION (WALES) REGULATIONS 2013, SI 2013/SI 2013/2506 (W.245); made under the European Communities Act 1972 s.2. In force: October 25, 2013; .

These Regulations revoke and replace the Nitrate Pollution Prevention (Wales) Regulations 2008 (SI 2008/3143), which controlled the application of nitrogen fertiliser in nitrate sensitive areas.

1137. Farmers–Nitrate vulnerable zones–Pollution control–England

THE NITRATE POLLUTION PREVENTION (AMENDMENT) AND WATER RESOURCES (CONTROL OF POLLUTION) (SILAGE, SLURRY AND AGRICULTURAL FUEL OIL) (ENGLAND) (AMENDMENT) REGULATIONS 2013, SI 2013/1001; made under the European Communities Act 1972 s.2. In force: in accordance with reg.1 (2).; .

These Regulations: amend the Nitrate Pollution Prevention Regulations 2008 (SI 2008/2349); give statutory effect to the revised designation of nitrate vulnerable zones in England, and amend the measures required to be undertaken by farmers within the nitrate vulnerable zones; and make provision exempting certain grassland farmers from aspects of the measures.

1138. Flood and Water Management Act 2010 (c.29)–Commencement No.2, Transitional and Savings Provisions (England) Order

THE FLOOD AND WATER MANAGEMENT ACT 2010 (COMMENCEMENT NO.2, TRANSITIONAL AND SAVINGS PROVISIONS) (ENGLAND) ORDER 2013, SI 2013/SI 2013/1590 (C.64); made under the Flood and Water Management Act 2010 s.48, s.49. Commencement details: bringing into force various provisions of the 2010 Act on July 30, 2013.; .

This Order brings into force in relation to England provisions of the Flood and Water Management Act 2010 and introduces, in England, a new legal framework relating to the safety of large raised reservoirs.

1139. Flood defences–Compensation–Effect of construction of new flood defence scheme on river trip provider–Determination of issues regarding completion of works and quantification of loss

[Water Resources Act 1991 (c.57) s.65.]

The claimant (P) applied for compensation for loss caused by works carried out by the defendant agency to construct a new flood defence scheme. P ran a business providing river trips and was the owner of the wharf where the boats were moored. The boats were reached by a flight of steps from the wharf. The agency was empowered under the Water Resources Act 1991 s.65 to prevent or alleviate flooding. It devised a scheme to improve flood defences, which prevented P's use of the wharf while the works were carried out. The agency acknowledged that it was liable to compensate P for the costs of removing and storing the boats. There was a dispute regarding when the works were completed. P had expressed concern since the works had been carried out that the steps to the wharf now "bounced" at the bottom, and that the new flood gate was so heavy that it was not reasonably practical to operate. The agency stated that P had said he would rectify the problem with the steps and had not informed it otherwise. It further argued that P had never seriously intended to restart the business. The issues to be determined were (i) when the works were completed so as to allow P to resume the trips; (ii) whether he would have carried on the business if the works had not interfered; (iii) if he would have done, whether the basis of a 2007 compensation payment made to P should be used; (iv) if not, what other evidence there was to prove and quantify his loss of earnings. The agency contended that there was no evidence that P would have provided trips during the relevant period, and that, even if he would have done, there was no evidence to quantify his loss. P argued that he should be compensated on the basis of the 2007 payment, which included an agreed element of loss of earnings.

Held: Judgment for defendant in part. (1) P was entitled to say that the works could not be taken as having been completed until everything had been done that was reasonably necessary for him to resume the business as near as possible as it had previously been run. The two potential obstacles to the resumption of business were the "bouncy" steps and the heavy floodgate. There was no evidence that the steps "bounced" before the work was carried out. However, they had been left in an unsatisfactory condition such as to prevent P from obtaining a licence to resume business, and the works could not be said to have been properly completed until the steps were fixed. However, given P's concession that he had said he would rectify the problem, it was difficult to see how the agency could be held responsible for non-completion of that work. The necessary work was not particularly difficult or costly and it was not unreasonable for the agency to accept P's assurance that he would do it. The failure to complete the work to the steps was not something for which the agency could be held responsible. With regard to the gate, P's account of the serious difficulties the heavy flood gate would present if he tried to run his business in the usual way was accepted. It would be quite impractical to expect passengers to operate it, and P was entitled to expect the provision of some method of access that passengers could negotiate for themselves, as they had before. The lightweight gate was the chosen option and the works could not be said to have been completed until that was provided (see paras 46-51 of judgment). (2) On the balance of probabilities, P had intended to recommence providing trips as soon as he could (paras 52-53). (3) No reliance could be placed on the 2007 payment as an acknowledgement of an appropriate level of trade loss (para.55). (4) There was no evidence to substantiate P's loss of profit. It was for P to prove his claim on the balance of probabilities, though the nature and degree of proof required changed according to the circumstances. What might be demanded of a large business was not expected of one man running river trips. However, there had to be something. Given some sort of credible substantiation, the view might have been formed that P would probably have made a profit. However, in the complete absence of any evidence substantiating his claim, it could not be concluded that he would have made a profit. P's claim therefore failed (paras 56-59).

PARKHILL v ENVIRONMENT AGENCY, [2012] UKUT 23 (LC), [2012] R.V.R. 272, Judge Mole Q.C., UT (Lands).

1140. Fuel–Smoke control areas–England

THE SMOKE CONTROL AREAS (AUTHORISED FUELS) (ENGLAND) REGULATIONS 2013, SI 2013/447; made under the Clean Air Act 1993 s.20. In force: April 6, 2013; .

These Regulations revoke and replace with amendments the Smoke Control Areas (Authorised Fuels) (England) (No.2) Regulations 2012 (SI 2012/2281), outline which fuels are authorised for the purposes of Part 3 of the Clean Air Act 1993, and adds three new fuels (Coalite Ovals, Zip 100 per cent Natural Firelog and ZIP 100 per cent Natural firelogs) to the list of authorised fuels.

1141. Fuel–Smoke control areas–Wales

THE SMOKE CONTROL AREAS (AUTHORISED FUELS) (WALES) (AMENDMENT) REGULATIONS 2013, SI 2013/SI 2013/562 (W.65); made under the Clean Air Act 1993 s.20. In force: April 3, 2013; .

These Regulations amend the list of authorised fuels in the Schedule to the Smoke Control Areas (Authorised Fuels) (Wales) Regulations 2008 (SI 2008/3100).

1142. Greenhouse gas emissions–Integrated pollution prevention and control–Offshore installations–Oil and gas industry

THE OFFSHORE COMBUSTION INSTALLATIONS (POLLUTION PREVENTION AND CONTROL) REGULATIONS 2013, SI 2013/971; made under the Pollution Prevention and Control Act 1999 s.2. In force: May 19, 2013; .

These Regulations transpose the appropriate provisions of Directive 2010/75 on industrial emissions (integrated pollution prevention and control) in respect to combustion installations on offshore platforms undertaking activities involving oil and gas production and gas and carbon dioxide unloading and storage.

1143. Hazardous substances–Landfill–Metals–England and Wales

THE ENVIRONMENTAL PERMITTING (ENGLAND AND WALES) (AMENDMENT) (NO.2) REGULATIONS 2013, SI 2013/766; made under the Pollution Prevention and Control Act 1999 s.2, s.7, Sch.1. In force: April 26, 2013; .

These Regulations implement Directive 2011/97, which amends Directive 1999/31 on the landfill of waste as regards specific criteria for the storage of metallic mercury considered as waste.

1144. **Natural England–Public rights of way–Rural areas–England**

THE COUNTRYSIDE AND RIGHTS OF WAY ACT 2000 (REVIEW OF MAPS) (ENGLAND) REGULATIONS 2013, SI 2013/514; made under the Countryside and Rights of Way Act 2000 s.10, s.45. In force: April 6, 2013; .

These Regulations amend s.10 of the Countryside and Rights of Way Act 2000. Section 10 prescribes the time limits by when Natural England (as the appropriate countryside body in relation to England) is required to review the conclusive maps prepared under the Act showing all registered common land and all open country in England (excluding inner London).

1145. **Natural Resources Wales–Transfer of functions–Wales**

THE NATURAL RESOURCES BODY FOR WALES (FUNCTIONS) ORDER 2013, SI 2013/SI 2013/755 (W.90); made under the Public Bodies Act 2011 s.13, s.14, s.15, s.35. In force: April 1, 2013; .

This Order makes further provision about the Natural Resources Body for Wales, including provision about the modification and transfer of environmental functions to the Body.

1146. **Natural Resources Wales–Wales**

THE NATURAL RESOURCES BODY FOR WALES (CONSEQUENTIAL PROVISION) ORDER 2013, SI 2013/1821; made under the European Communities Act 1972 s.2; and the Government of Wales Act 2006 s.150, s.157. In force: July 18, 2013; .

This instrument makes necessary provision in consequence of the creation of the Natural Resources Body for Wales (NRBW), and the transfer to the NRBW of the Welsh devolved functions of the Environment Agency and the Forestry Commissioners.

1147. **Noise–Suspension notices–Suspension notice prohibiting operation of metal recycling yard–Risk of serious pollution by noise–Notice specifying required steps to reduce risk**

[Environmental Permitting (England and Wales) Regulations 2010 (SI 2010/675) reg.37(4)(a)(ii), reg.37.]

The claimant company (C) applied for judicial review of the decision of the defendant Environment Agency (E) to serve it with a suspension notice under the Environmental Permitting (England and Wales) Regulations 2010 reg.37. C operated a metal waste disposal and reclamation yard pursuant to an environmental permit issued by E as the regulator. Following complaints from local residents about the noise generated by C on its site, E concluded that that C's activities involved a risk of serious pollution by noise and served it with a suspension notice under reg.37. The notice stated that C had to design and implement measures that eliminated the risk of serious pollution by noise by a certain date. Regulation 37(4)(a) provided that a suspension notice had to specify the risk of serious pollution, the steps that had to be taken to remove that risk, and the period within which the steps had to be taken. C argued that (1) there was no basis for E concluding that there was a risk of serious pollution by noise; (2) the wording of the notice did not comply with the requirements of reg.37(4)(a) because it failed to specify what steps C was required to take to remove risk, failed to provide defined threshold criteria for compliance with the notice and was otherwise vague and imprecise.

Held: Application granted. (1) It was for E to decide whether there was a risk of serious pollution and its decision could only be challenged as being irrational. E's decision was not irrational: the material available to it when it made its decision clearly entitled it to conclude that a risk of serious pollution was made out. The length of time that had elapsed between C commencing operations at the site and the service of the suspension notice was immaterial, and E's failure to identify the existence of a serious risk in the course of earlier formal assessments did not lead to the conclusion that there was no proper basis on which such a conclusion could be reached. C's challenge to there being a risk of serious pollution was misconceived (see paras 18-20 of judgment). (2) As a matter of language, the requirement under reg.37(4)(a)(ii) for E to state explicitly the steps required to eliminate an identified risk could not sensibly be said to be satisfied by a requirement to design and implement measures to eliminate that risk; what was required was the identification of either outcomes or criteria that had to be achieved by whatever means C chose to adopt and/or the identification of specific steps that were required to be taken, *R. v Falmouth and Truro Port HA, Ex p. South West Water Ltd* [2001] Q.B. 445, [2000] C.L.Y. 2304 considered. E had made no attempt to adopt an outcome-based specification or to identify what steps had to be taken to remove the risk of serious pollution as required by its own regulatory guidance. E was not entitled to require the elimination of a risk of serious pollution without identifying the steps by which that was to be achieved. Accordingly, C was entitled to an order quashing the suspension notice (paras 24-25, 27, 30, 35).

R. (ON THE APPLICATION OF EUROPEAN METAL RECYCLING LTD) v ENVIRONMENT AGENCY, [2012] EWHC 2361 (Admin), [2013] Env. L.R. 14, Judge Pelling Q.C., QBD (Admin).

1148. Packaging–Packaging waste

THE PACKAGING (ESSENTIAL REQUIREMENTS) (AMENDMENT) REGULATIONS 2013, SI 2013/2212; made under the European Communities Act 1972 s.2. In force: September 30, 2013; .

These Regulations implement Directive 2013/2, which amends Directive 94/62 on packaging and packaging waste. The 2013 Directive adds more examples to the illustrative list of items considered to be packaging.

1149. Packaging waste–Producer responsibility–Waste management

THE PRODUCER RESPONSIBILITY OBLIGATIONS (PACKAGING WASTE) (AMENDMENT) REGULATIONS 2013, SI 2013/1857; made under the European Communities Act 1972 s.2; and the Environment Act 1995 s.93, s.94, s.95. In force: July 24, 2013; .

These Regulations amend the Producer Responsibility Obligations (Packaging Waste) Regulations 2007 (SI 2007/871) which implement Art.6(1) of the European Parliament and Council Directive 94/62/EC on packaging and packaging waste. The 2007 Regulations, in particular provisions in Sch.2 to those Regulations, were amended by the Producer Responsibility Obligations (Packaging Waste) (Amendment) Regulations 2012.

1150. Referees–Appointment–Reservoirs–England

THE RESERVOIRS ACT 1975 (REFEREES) (APPOINTMENT, PROCEDURE AND COSTS) (ENGLAND) RULES 2013, SI 2013/1676; made under the Reservoirs Act 1975 s.19. In force: July 30, 2013; .

These Rules make provision, as to reservoirs in England, as to the time within which a referee may be appointed by agreement between the undertakers and the engineer for the purposes of the Reservoirs Act 1975 s.19; the manner in which any request to the Secretary of State to appoint a referee in default of agreement must be made; the procedure for appointing a referee and the payment of the referee's costs.

1151. Smoke control areas–England

THE SMOKE CONTROL AREAS (AUTHORISED FUELS) (ENGLAND) (NO.2) REGULATIONS 2013, SI 2013/2111; made under the Clean Air Act 1993 s.20. In force: October 1, 2013; .

This instrument revokes and replaces with amendments the Smoke Control Areas (Authorised Fuels) (England) Regulations 2013 (SI 2013/447). It sets out which fuels are authorised for the purposes of the Clean Air Act 1993 Pt 3 and adds one new fuel (ZIP 100 per cent Natural Stove Log) to the list of authorised fuels.

1152. Smoke control areas–England

THE SMOKE CONTROL AREAS (EXEMPTED FIREPLACES) (ENGLAND) (NO.2) ORDER 2013, SI 2013/2112; made under the Clean Air Act 1993 s.21. In force: October 1, 2013; .

This Order revokes and replaces with amendments the Smoke Control Areas (Exempted Fireplaces) (England) Order 2013 (SI 2013/462). It exempts the fireplaces listed in the Schedule from the provisions of the Clean Air Act 1993 s.20 (prohibition of smoke emissions in smoke control areas), subject to the conditions set out in the Schedule.

1153. Smoke control areas–Exempted fireplaces–England

THE SMOKE CONTROL AREAS (EXEMPTED FIREPLACES) (ENGLAND) ORDER 2013, SI 2013/462; made under the Clean Air Act 1993 s.21. In force: April 6, 2013; .

This Order revokes and replaces with amendments the Smoke Control Areas (Exempted Fireplaces) (England) Order 2012 (SI 2012/2282). It exempts the fireplaces listed in the Schedule from the provisions of section 20 of the Clean Air Act 1993 (prohibition of smoke emissions in smoke control areas), subject to the conditions set out in the Schedule. Several additional fireplaces have been exempted.

1154. Smoke control areas–Wales

THE SMOKE CONTROL AREAS (EXEMPTED FIREPLACES) (WALES) ORDER 2013, SI 2013/SI 2013/561 (W.64); made under the Clean Air Act 1993 s.21. In force: April 3, 2013; .

This Order revokes and replaces with amendments the Smoke Control Areas (Exempted Fireplaces) (Wales) Order 2012 (SI 2012/244).

1155. Waste–Trans-frontier waste shipments–Hazardous waste–Transporting defective electrical appliances to non-OECD country

[Transfrontier Shipment of Waste Regulations 2007 (SI 2007/1711) reg.23, reg.57; Regulation 1013/2006 Art.2, Art.36(1); Directive 2006/12 on waste Art.1 (1) (a), Art.3; Directive 2006/12 on waste Annex II B.]

The appellants (E) appealed against convictions for offences of transporting hazardous waste, as defined in Regulation 1013/2006 art.36(1), to a country that was not a member of the Organisation for Economic Co-operation and Development (OECD), contrary to the Transfrontier Shipment of Waste Regulations 2007 reg.23. E had transported to Nigeria, a non-OECD country, cathode ray tube televisions and fridge/freezers containing ozone-depleting substances. E had recovered the appliances from waste disposal sites; they could not economically be repaired in the United Kingdom. However, they were repaired and re-used at a market in Nigeria. E claimed that by their process of selection and testing before shipment, by the time the appliances were consigned to Nigeria, they were no longer waste as defined in Directive 2006/12 art.1 (1) (a). E argued that (1) "waste" in the Regulation should be read, in light of an OECD decision of 2001, with the definition in the Basel Convention on waste, and the appliances did not fulfil that definition; (2) the test applied by the jury in determining whether they had "intended to discard" the appliances was subjective, but the judge had directed the jury that E's intention was irrelevant; (3) the prosecution could not prove that the process to which the appliances were to be subjected in Nigeria was "recovery"; (4) the judge had wrongly ruled that the offence was one of strict liability.

Held: Appeals dismissed. (1) The 2007 Regulations were specific as to the meanings of terms also used in the 2006 Regulation, and the OECD decision had dealt only with the movement of waste within and between OECD countries. Further, the ECJ had adopted an autonomous meaning of "waste" which it had applied since 1991, under which re-use did not exclude material from the definition of waste, *ARCO Chemie Nederland Ltd v Minister van*

Volkshuisvesting, Ruimtelijke Ordening en Milieubeheer (C-418/97) [2002] Q.B. 646, [2002] C.L.Y. 1519 considered. Had the Community legislature intended to abandon that definition, it would have said so in art.2 of the Regulation (see para.49 of judgment). (2) There was a consistent line of authority holding that once a substance or object had been discarded, and had therefore become waste, whether it had changed its status was a question of objective fact, *OSS Group Ltd v Environment Agency* [2007] EWCA Civ 611, [2007] Bus. L.R. 1732, [2007] C.L.Y. 1518 applied. However, the fact of which the jury had to be sure was that the substance or object was one which the holder discarded or intended to discard. That could cause confusion for the jury. The trial judge had to adapt his directions so as to eliminate the apparent contradictions between the words used and their purposeful interpretation. What mattered was whether the holder of the objects took, or intended to take, some action which changed their status; whether the holder discarded or intended to discard the objects was judged by what he did with them, not by his subjective belief as to whether he was discarding them. There was little doubt that the appliances' original owners had discarded them; the jury had had to decide whether the process E claimed to have subjected the appliances to had had the effect of rendering them non-waste. The judge had rightly directed the jury to that question (paras 51-52, 56 of judgment). (3) "Recovery" meant any of the operations in Directive 2006/12 Annex II B. Article 3 showed that the Directive recognised re-use as a possible form of recovery of waste. The objective of art.36 of the Regulation was to protect non-OECD countries from dangers to health and the environment by prohibiting the export of hazardous waste to those countries for recovery. The majority of the appliances had not been suitable for re-use without undergoing repair or regeneration. The re-use had fallen within Annex II B, generously and properly construed (paras 57-59). (4) No state of mind by the defendant was required by the words used in reg.23 unless that was to be presumed. English law presumed that an offence required mens rea unless by necessary implication it was excluded. The scheme of the 2007 Regulations was to create a series of offences comprising breaches of the requirements of the 2006 Regulation. The offences were created for failure to take the procedural steps required by the Regulation or taking a step prohibited by it. That was the language of strict liability. There were exceptions, but there the draftsman explicitly defined the required mens rea. Further, reg.57 implied that a person could commit an offence, without fault on his own part, due to the actions of another person. That was consistent with at least some of the offences being of strict liability. The offence created by reg.23 was one of strict liability, *R. v V* [2011] EWCA Crim 2342, [2012] Eu. L.R. 302, [2012] C.L.Y. 1262 applied (paras 63, 69-74, 77).

R. v EZEEMO (GODWIN CHUKWNAENYA); R. v RELIANCE EXPORT LTD; R. v BJ ELECTRONICS LTD; R. v EZEEMO (CHIKA); R. v BENSON (JOSEPH); R. v ORIENT EXPORT LTD; R. v EZECHUKWU (NNAMDI CHINEDU), [2012] EWCA Crim 2064, [2013] 4 All E.R. 1016, Pitchford, L.J., CA (Crim Div).

1156. Waste disposal–Escape–Unintentional escape of sewerage–Whether conviction under s.33(1)(a) Environmental Protection Act 1990 required deliberate deposit of waste–Meaning of "deposit"

[Environmental Protection Act 1990 (c.43) s.33, s.33(7)(a), s.34.]

The claimant sewerage undertaker (T) sought judicial review of its conviction by the defendant court under the Environmental Protection Act 1990 s.33(1)(a). Between February and April 2003, sewage had escaped from T's network into surrounding gardens, allotments and highways. The issue was whether, on a true construction of s.33(1)(a), the unintended escape of sewage amounted to a "deposit" of the sewage by T on the surrounding land. Following a preliminary ruling in *R. (on the application of Thames Water Utilities Ltd) v Bromley Magistrates' Court (C-252/05)* [2007] 1 W.L.R. 1945, [2008] C.L.Y. 1266 that escaped sewage not covered by any other legislation was "waste" as a matter of Community law, and a finding in *R. (on the application of Thames Water Utilities Ltd) v Bromley Magistrates' Court* [2008] EWHC 1763 (Admin), [2009]

1 W.L.R. 1247, [2008] C.L.Y. 3981 that domestic legislation did not contain provisions for the management of waste after it had escaped, the case was remitted to the respondent court for determination on its merits. The district judge held that unintended and unwanted escape of waste amounted to a "deposit" within the meaning of s.33(1)(a) because it had been "put, place(d) or set down" within the ordinary linguistic meaning of the word. He also held that T could not establish a defence under s.33(7)(a). T submitted that as s.33(1)(a) imposed criminal liability, the words "shall not deposit controlled waste" referred to a deliberate act of depositing waste, not to an unintentional escape, and that such a construction permitted s.33 and s.34 of the Act to be read sensibly together.

Held: Application refused. The unintended escape of sewage amounted to a "deposit" within s.33(1)(a). As "deposit" was an ordinary English word, it had a range of meanings, and the question was whether an unintended escape fell within any of those meanings. That question could not be answered by considering the word in isolation (see paras 25-28 of judgment). The structure of s.33(1)(a) supported the district judge's conclusion, as did the existence of the due diligence defence in s.33(7). Importation into the first limb of s.33(1)(a) of a requirement that the deposit must be intentional would not emasculate the s.33(7) defence, but the "fit" of s.33(1)(a) with s.33(7) was certainly better without it because the strictness of the former provision would then be mitigated by the latter, as had been envisaged in *Shanks & McEwan (Teesside) Ltd v Environment Agency* [1999] Q.B. 333, [1997] C.L.Y. 2353, *Shanks, Remet Co Ltd v Newham LBC* [1981] R.T.R. 502, [1981] C.L.Y. 1280 and *Scott v Westminster City Council* [1995] R.T.R. 327, [1996] C.L.Y. 5145 considered (paras 21, 24, 33-34). Regarding the relationship between s.33 and s.34 of the Act, the latter was inapplicable on the facts because once the sewage had escaped, it was no longer in T's control. Although there might be an overlap between the two provisions in some situations, that was not so in the instant case (para.45). In the 2008 decision, Carnwath LJ indicated that he did not view unplanned escapes as falling outside a reasonable range of meanings for the word "deposit" in s.33. Although *obiter*, because the court had been concerned with the meaning of "controlled waste" rather than "deposit", those observations were nevertheless significantly persuasive (paras 28, 46). Statutory language creating a criminal offence was to be strictly construed; the presumption was that *mens rea* was an an essential ingredient of every offence unless there was some reason for it not being necessary, *Gammon (Hong Kong) Ltd v Attorney General of Hong Kong* [1985] A.C. 1, [1984] C.L.Y. 951 applied. The presumptions in that case, although plainly not statute, provided an authoritative framework of reference. The Act clearly displaced the usual and strong presumption of *mens rea* but, looking at the matter in the round, it was clear that the legislature had intended to impose strict liability under the first limb of s.33(1)(a) (paras 47-52).

R. (ON THE APPLICATION OF THAMES WATER UTILITIES LTD) v BROMLEY MAGISTRATES' COURT; *sub nom.* THAMES WATER UTILITIES LTD v BROMLEY MAGISTRATES' COURT, [2013] EWHC 472 (Admin), [2013] 1 W.L.R. 3641, Gross, L.J., QBD (Admin).

1157. Waste management–Groundwater–England and Wales

THE ENVIRONMENTAL PERMITTING (ENGLAND AND WALES) (AMENDMENT) REGULATIONS 2013, SI 2013/390; made under the Pollution Prevention and Control Act 1999 s.2, s.7, Sch.1. In force: in accordance with reg.1(1)(2)(3)(4).; .

The primary purpose of the instrument is to amend the Environmental Permitting (England and Wales) Regulations 2010 (SI 2010/675) so as to transpose Directive 2010/75 on industrial emissions (integrated pollution prevention and control). That Directive recasts seven current Directives into a single one about regulating emissions from various industrial activities, ranging from power generation to intensive pig farming and waste incineration to dry cleaning. Much of the material in the component Directives is substantively unchanged, but there are some tightened or clarified requirements.

1158. **Waste management–Protected species–Grant of planning permission for development of "energy from waste" recovery facility in Buckinghamshire–Compliance with Directive 92/43, Conservation legislation and national planning policy**

[Conservation of Habitats and Species Regulations 2010 (SI 2010/490) reg.9(5); Town and Country Planning (Development Management Procedure) (England) Order 2010 (SI 2010/2184) Art.31; Directive 92/43 on the conservation of natural habitats and of wild fauna and flora Art.16.]

The claimant (P), a local resident, applied for judicial review of the defendant local authority's grant of planning permission for an "energy from waste" recovery facility on land adjoining a landfill site. The local authority believed that there was an urgent need for the facility under its waste planning strategy. The site was intended to take all waste produced in Buckinghamshire to convert into energy, thus diverting it from landfill. The environmental statement addressed the likely ecological impact and the appropriate mitigation, including the fact that derogation licences would be required under the Conservation of Habitats and Species Regulations 2010 for the demolition of a building where protected species were roosting. Licensing conditions were considered met. After planning permission had been granted, derogation licences were obtained from Natural England, its initial objections having been mitigated. P's objections to the development were largely ecological. The issues were whether the local authority had failed to: (i) comply with Directive 92/43 and the Regulations; (ii) apply relevant national policy on nature conservation in the National Planning Policy Framework; (iii) provide adequate reasons for the grant of planning permission.

Held: Application refused. (1) Under reg 9(5) of the Regulations, a local authority had to have regard to the requirements of the Directive in so far as they might be affected by a planning permission decision. It was the function of Natural England, as an executive, non-departmental public body responsible to the secretary of state, to enforce compliance with the Directive by prosecuting those who committed offences contrary to its provisions. Regulation 9(5) did not require a planning authority to carry out the assessment that Natural England had to make, so the lawfulness of the local authority's acts was not to be tested by imposing upon it a duty that was not its own, *R. (on the application of Morge) v Hampshire CC* [2011] UKSC 2, [2011] 1 W.L.R. 268, [2011] C.L.Y. 1233 applied and *R. (on the application of Woolley) v Cheshire East BC* [2009] EWHC 1227 (Admin), [2010] Env. L.R. 5, [2010] C.L.Y. 2616 doubted. In the instant case, the local authority had discharged its duty under reg.9(5) in accordance with the approach indicated in *Morge*. It had, in fact, satisfied even the more burdensome remit envisaged by *R. (on the application of Morge) v Hampshire CC* [2010] EWCA Civ 608, [2010] P.T.S.R. 1882, [2010] C.L.Y. 2615 and *Woolley*, even though neither of those authorities was any longer good law, *Morge (CA)* not applied. The likely effect on protected species had been dealt with in detail and alternative routes for the access roads considered. The officers' reports were pragmatic and evidenced the right approach. P had relied heavily on guidance in the European Commission's guidance document that derogation was to be a "last resort" and that competent national authorities should select a development option that would ensure the best protection of species. However, that guidance was not the law. Article16 of the Directive did not provide that a licence had to be refused if there was an alternative mode of development with no foreseeable impact, or an impact less harmful, on protected species. Any such provision would produce very odd results. In any event, the Commission guidance made it clear that there were other considerations besides protected species. Judging what might be a satisfactory alternative in a particular case required a focus on what was sought to be achieved through the derogation, and on the likely effects of the works on the species in question. In light of the advice it had been given and the absence of ongoing objection from Natural England, the local authority had been entitled, if not bound, to conclude that the derogation tests were at least likely to be met (see paras 85-86, 93-105, 112-123). (2) Assessing the nature, extent and acceptability of the effects of a development on the environment was a task for the planning authorities, not for the court. The local authority had been entitled to rely on the ecological analysis presented to it, and to give significant weight to the views of Natural England. If the latter had been uneasy about the mitigation proposals, it would have persisted in its objection. The local authority's conclusions were entirely reasonable and congruent with national policy (paras130-131, 135-137, 144-157). (3) Under the Town and Country Planning (Development Management Procedure) (England) Order 2010 art.31, the local authority had to provide in its decision notice a summary of the relevant policies in the development plan. It did not have to list the provisions of the Directive, the Habitats Regulations or the national policy framework that it had considered. The summary reasons given were terse, but lawful (paras 164-165-168).

R. (ON THE APPLICATION OF PRIDEAUX) v BUCKINGHAMSHIRE CC, [2013] EWHC 1054 (Admin), [2013] Env. L.R. 32, Lindblom, J., QBD (Admin).

1159. Waste management–Recycling–Whether reg.13(4) Waste (England and Wales) Regulations 2011 properly transposed obligations in art.11(1) Directive 2008/98 into domestic law–Meaning of "where technically, environmentally and economically practicable" in reg.13(4)

[Waste (England and Wales) (Amendment) Regulations 2012 (SI 2012/1889) reg.2; Waste (England and Wales) Regulations 2011 (SI 2011/988) reg.13(4)(b), reg.13(4); Directive 2008/98 on waste Art.4(1), Art.10, Art.11, Art.13.]

The claimant waste recycling companies (X) issued proceedings against the first defendant secretary of state and the second defendant Welsh Ministers for their alleged failure properly to transpose the obligations in Directive 2008/98 art.11 (1) into domestic law. Article 11 (1) required Member States to organise a system for the separate collection of paper, metal, plastic and glass by 2015. That obligation had only one express limitation, namely that it was "subject to Article 10(2)". The defendants' case was that separate collection was only required if both a "necessity requirement" and a "practicability requirement" were met, namely that separate collection was (i) "necessary" to ensure that the waste underwent recovery operations in accordance with the waste hierarchy in art.4(1) of the Directive; and (ii) "technically, environmentally and economically practicable" within the meaning of the second paragraph of art.11 (1). X's case was that the reference to art.10(2) imported only a practicability requirement, not a necessity requirement, so that the only way to evade the requirement for separate collection was if such collection was not "technically, environmentally and economically practicable". They maintained that, by introducing the necessity requirement into the Waste (England and Wales) Regulations 2011 reg.13(4), as amended by the Waste (England and Wales) (Amendment) Regulations 2012 reg.2, the defendants had failed properly to transpose the Directive. The court was essentially required to determine whether the words "subject to Article 10(2)" imported the necessity requirement as well as the practicability requirement, and whether the Regulations properly transposed the requirements of art.11 of the Directive. X submitted that, as a matter of law, Parliament could not leave the decision as to whether separate collection was "technically, environmentally and economically practicable" to be determined by a local authority or an agency such as the Environment Agency, but that, in any event, evidence existed to support a finding that separate collection of the four streams of waste met the practicability requirement in all possible circumstances of collection throughout England and Wales.

Held: Judgment for defendant. (1) A Member State had a broad discretion as to the choice of form and methods of transposition. The Directive required Member States to "take measures" towards various aims and objectives, without qualification. It was open to the UK to fulfil its obligations by the system created by the 2011 Regulations, which allowed a local authority to determine within its area whether separate collection was practicable, and which created a system of enforcement operated by the Environment Agency. Whether separate collection met the practicability requirement depended upon a sophisticated and content-specific balancing exercise, and local authorities were uniquely placed to take into account local circumstances. It was an extremely bold assertion that separate collection of the four streams of waste was practicable throughout the UK. The court was not required to make a factual finding in respect of it, but the available evidence did not support X's contention (see paras 42-45, 47-51, 62 of judgment). (2) On a purposive approach to the wording of art.10 and art.11 of the Directive, art.10(2) imported both a practicability requirement and a necessity requirement. The European Commission publication issued on June 12, 2012 called "Guidance on the Interpretation of Key Provisions of Directive 2008/98" was very strong support for such an interpretationThe word "where" in the second paragraph of art.11(1) meant "if"; the phrase "where necessary" in art.10(2) governed both "to comply with paragraph 1" and "to facilitate or improve recovery". Therefore the opening words of art.10(2) meant what they said: that waste should be collected separately where such collection was necessary to comply with art.10(1), namely to ensure that the waste underwent recovery operations and to facilitate or improve recovery. The recovery operations had to be performed in accordance with art.4 and art.13. They required the correct priority to be given to recovery, subject to the Directive's overarching aim of delivering "the best environmental outcome". Therefore, on the words used in the Directive itself, the clear meaning was that in addition to the practicability requirement, before an obligation arose to collect the four streams of waste separately, the necessity requirement also had to be met. The primary aim of the Directive was not the separate collection of waste, but the protection of the environment and human health. Separate collection was, at most, a means to better recovery, which was, in turn, a means of achieving the Directive's primary aim. Prioritising recycling over disposal was a subsidiary aim and subservient to the higher objective of "the best environmental outcome" in art.4(2) of the Directive. Where, in particular circumstances, separate collection did not lead to a better environmental and human health outcome, it was not necessary for the objective of the Directive. There was an overlap between the necessity and practicability requirements, but the latter did not fully encompass the former; they were analytically distinct (paras 54-56, 60-61, 64, 66).

R. (ON THE APPLICATION OF UK RECYCLATE LTD) v SECRETARY OF STATE FOR THE ENVIRONMENT, FOOD AND RURAL AFFAIRS, [2013] EWHC 425 (Admin), [2013] 3 All E.R. 561, Hickinbottom, J., QBD (Admin).

EQUITY

1160. Marshalling–Creditors–Whether exception to common debtor rule in doctrine of marshalling

The claimants (H and C) sought a declaration that they were entitled to deploy the doctrine of marshalling to give them the benefit of a co-creditor's unused securities. H, C and the sixth defendant bank (B) were creditors of the first defendant (Z). B had loaned money to Z, secured by a charge over a property (no.31) owned by Z. B then loaned money to four of Z's affiliates, each loan being secured by a charge over each affiliate's property. As additional security, Z guaranteed the loans, that guarantee being secured by the charge over no.31. Z subsequently borrowed money from H and C, the loan being secured by second and third charges over no.31. Z and its affiliates defaulted on all the loans. B demanded repayment and no.31 was sold, part of the proceeds being used to discharge B's loan to Z. Rather than pursue the affiliates' properties, B applied the surplus from the sale of no.31 in part satisfaction of Z's liability under the guarantee. Had it not done so, the surplus would have wholly repaid the sums due to H and C under the second and third charges on no.31. As it was, H and C stood as unsecured creditors. In the meantime, a restraint order was made in respect of his assets of a consultant to a shareholder of Z. The Serious Fraud

Office regarded the assets held by Z and its affiliates, including no.31, as being covered by that order. H and C's case was that the doctrine of marshalling applied so as to give them the benefit of B's unused security over the affiliates' properties. The issues were whether the doctrine of marshalling permitted the marshalling of securities held over property that did not belong to the common debtor and, in particular, whether a creditor of a guarantor was entitled to marshal securities granted to another creditor of the guarantor by the primary debtor under the guaranteed debt; whether the answer depended on the rights the guarantor had as against the holder of the guarantee or as against the primary debtor; and whether such a claim to marshalling or subrogation took precedence over prohibitions in the restraint order.

Held: Application granted. (1) The doctrine of marshalling as explained in *Serious Organised Crime Agency v Szepietowski* [2011] EWCA Civ 856, [2011] 3 Costs L.O. 408, [2011] C.L.Y. 1249 was conditional upon two or more creditors being owed money by the same debtor, and only one of those creditors having a charge over more than one of the debtor's assets, *Szepietowski* considered. The question was whether there was an exception to those conditions where a common debtor owed money to two or more creditors and had a right, as between himself and a debtor who owed money to only one creditor, to ensure that the latter bore the ultimate liability. Authority for such an exception could be found in the dictum of Lord Eldon in *Kendall, Ex parte* 34 E.R. 199. While strictly obiter, Lord Eldon's summary of the law had long been accepted as a true summary and was authoritative, *Kendall* considered. B had a claim against Z as surety. It could look to either the charge over no.31 or to the charges over the affiliates' properties to satisfy Z's indebtedness. As regards H and C's claim to marshal, the charges over the affiliates' properties could be brought into account because, in equity, Z could call on the affiliates to bear the burden of the debt. Thus, the doctrine of marshalling and the exception to the "common debtor" rule applied. However, if H and C's ability to avoid the constraints of the common debtor rule was dependent upon the equities that existed as between Z and the affiliates, then those equities had to include not only the right to demand payment, but also the right to enforce any security. If those rights were restricted by the contract creating the principal-surety relationship, then that restriction had to be recognised in the marshalling of the security. If Z would not be subrogated to B's rights until the debt had been repaid, then H and C could not, by a process akin to subrogation, become entitled to any greater right. There would therefore be a declaration that H and C were entitled to participate in the security constituted by the charges over the affiliates' properties when all sums due to B, and secured by those charges, had been paid (see paras 16-18, 25, 41-42, 45, 48-52 of judgment). (2) (Obiter) Although the third question was no longer live, it had been fully argued, though not sufficiently to enable a determination of whether the application of the doctrine of marshalling could, of itself, create a property interest. However, doubts about that did not matter. The correct focus was H and C's interest in a legal charge that predated the restraint order. The essential matter was that, by a process akin to subrogation, H and C were entitled to enforce B's pre-existing interest in the affiliates' properties. B's actions had therefore not deprived H and C of the interest previously recognised by the restraint order (paras 53, 68-70).

HIGHBURY PENSION FUND MANAGEMENT CO v ZIRFIN INVESTMENTS LTD, [2013] EWHC 238 (Ch), [2013] 3 All E.R. 327, Norris, J., Ch D.

1161. Promissory estoppel–Reversionary leases–Contents of letter from residents' association concerning purchase of reversion–Effect of reference to "no ground rent to pay"–Whether letter making unequivocal promise estopping future recovery of ground rent from tenants

The appellants (K) appealed against a decision that the respondent management company (C) was not estopped from seeking to recover ground rent from them. K held the leasehold interest in a flat within a residential development. Under the lease, they covenanted to pay an annual ground rent of £100 and a service charge. The leaseholder subsequently indicated its intention to dispose of the reversion. In August 2006, the residents' association wrote to the tenants asking them to indicate whether they would like to participate in the acquisition of what was described, inaccurately, as the "freehold". The letter referred to the "benefits of owning the freehold" as including "no ground rent to pay". K indicated that they would like to participate. The residents' association set up C to acquire the reversion and act as managing agent. C acquired the reversion and informed the tenants that it had decided to continue to charge the £100 ground rent in order to build up a fund to cover accountancy and legal fees and other eventualities. K refused to pay the ground rent due. C issued proceedings to recover arrears of rent and service charges. K contended that they had a defence of promissory estoppel based on the representations in the letter of August 2006. The judge found that K had fundamentally misunderstood the effect on the existing lease of the acquisition of what was described as the freehold, and interpreted the letter as a statement of the effect of purchasing the reversion rather than as a statement of what C itself intended to do in respect of tenants' liabilities under the existing lease. He concluded that, because of their misunderstanding, K had not materially relied upon the representation in an unequivocal way so as to establish a promissory estoppel binding on C. It fell to be determined whether the August 2006 letter had made an unequivocal promise to abolish the ground rent or was simply a list of the potential benefits which would come from a purchase of the reversion. C contended that the contents of the August 2006 letter had to be read in the context of being sent by the residents' association in an attempt to gauge the level of support amongst tenants for a possible acquisition of the freehold (as it was described), where there was no certainty of any such bid succeeding or any certainty as to whether the acquisition would be affordable. C argued that the financial constraints it would face once it became the landlord were unpredictable, so that the letter had to be read as no more than a summary of the potential benefits which could flow from owning the reversion rather than an unqualified promise of what it would do if successful in the purchase, and that any reasonable reader of the letter would have regarded them as, at most, stated aims rather than promised outcomes. K submitted that the letter contained the clear inference that tenants who participated in the purchase would not continue to pay ground rent, and that the letter had been sent for the purpose of inducing tenants to support the purchase.

Held: Appeal dismissed. In order to found a promissory estoppel the representation or promise had to be clear and unambiguous, *Low v Bouverie* [1891] 3 Ch. 82 and *Woodhouse AC Israel Cocoa SA v Nigerian Produce Marketing Co Ltd* [1972] A.C. 741, [1972] C.L.Y. 495 followed. The August 2006 letter did not promise anything. Even putting aside its obvious conditionality on the successful completion of the purchase, the fact that it was written well in advance of any possible acquisition and without the benefit of detailed knowledge of the financial position that would obtain once a purchase had taken place pointed to it being little more than a list of possible potential benefits rather than a guarantee or promise of what would be done. The real purpose of acquiring the reversion was to enable the leases of the participating tenants to be replaced by new leases for significantly longer terms, which was something of real value to all the tenants. The residents' association was not promising that a participating tenant would have his existing ground rent waived; it was referring to what could be the terms of the new lease, which would have to be considered by C and the residents' association once they were in charge of the estate. It would not have been reasonable for K to have relied on the contents of the letter as promising them a new lease with no ground rent. The contents of the letter were incapable of forming a safe foundation for any kind of estoppel (see paras 23-26, 31-34 of judgment).

KIM v CHASEWOOD PARK RESIDENTS LTD, [2013] EWCA Civ 239, [2013] H.L.R. 24, Patten, L.J., CA (Civ Div).

1162. Proprietary estoppel–Promises–Deceased promising farm to his son contrary to terms of will–Existence of reliance, detriment and change of position–Proportionality of relief

The appellant daughter (C) appealed against a decision that her brother (J) was entitled to part of the estate of their deceased father (F), namely farmland and a farmhouse. F's estate included 400 acres of farmland, a farmhouse and two other properties. During F's lifetime, aside from a nine-month period, J had assisted F with jobs around the farm for no wage. F had provided J with accommodation, paid his living expenses, and given him a share of grain harvest and sheep sales as well as other opportunities and benefits. At times J had supplemented his income from other employment. J attended agricultural college at F's expense, but failed to complete the course. F decided that J was not fit to run the farm, and entered into successive farm-sharing agreements with other farming families. At the time of F's death, J was living in the farmhouse with his family, and C was living in another of F's properties with her child. In his will, F left his entire estate to C with the expressed wish, but without imposing a trust, that if at any time, in C's absolute opinion, J showed himself capable of managing the farmland, C was to transfer it to him. Following F's death, C did not effect a transfer, and J issued a proprietary estoppel claim. The judge determined that despite F's concerns about J's abilities, before his death he had given J a repeated unconditional promise that the farmland and, by implication, somewhere to live, would be his at some point after his death, and that J had acted in some measure to his detriment or changed his position in reliance on F's promises and in the expectation that he would inherit. The judge held that it would be unconscionable to deprive J of his reasonable expectations based on the assurances, and concluded that J was entitled to the farmland and the farmhouse. C submitted that (1) reliance and detriment had to be real in order to give rise to an estoppel claim, there was insufficient evidence of either, and therefore it was unreasonable for J to rely on F's promise; (2) there also had to have been a significant change of position; (3) relying on *Jennings v Rice* [2002] EWCA Civ 159, [2003] 1 F.C.R. 501, [2002] C.L.Y. 4319, the relief granted was disproportionate.

Held: Appeal dismissed. (1) C had not challenged the judge's finding that unconditional promises were made to J, and therefore reliance and detriment had to be considered on the basis that they had been made. There had undoubtedly been substantial benefits to J in living on the farm. However, it had been for the judge to determine as a matter of fact whether there was sufficient reliance and detriment. That decision could only be interfered with if it was perverse or clearly wrong. The judge was satisfied on the evidence that J had positioned his whole life on the basis of the assurances given to him, and which he reasonably believed. The instant court could not say that the judge had not been entitled to reach the conclusion he did, *Gillett v Holt* [2001] Ch. 210, [2000] C.L.Y. 2321 considered (see paras 28, 36-37, 39 of judgment). (2) Although there was no evidence that J would have pursued some other career that he expressly gave up, he had returned to the farm and was available for work when F asked him. Whilst J had obtained substantial benefits from F, for the same reason given above the court could not interfere with the judge's decision on the issue of change of position. He had had to evaluate whether there was a real change of position, and was so satisfied on the evidence. Nothing that C had put forward indicated that his finding was perverse (para.40). (3) The principle from *Jennings* did not mean that there had to be a relationship of proportionality between the level of detriment and the relief awarded, but rather that if the expectations were extravagant or out of all proportion to the detriment suffered, the court should recognise that the claimant's equity should be satisfied in another, generally more limited way, *Jennings* explained. The question was whether the relief granted to J was out of all proportion to the detriment suffered, which again was a question of evaluation and judgement. Since F had promised that J should have the farmland unconditionally, granting him the farmland could not be said to be out of all proportion. Furthermore, the judge clearly found that the assurances given included assurances of a place to live, and that F had given J the farmhouse by implication. That had been a question for the judge on the evidence about the assurance and its terms. It could not be said that his judgment on that point was perverse or such that the court should interfere. Although the farmland and the farmhouse were very valuable, the values only reflected the assurances made by F (paras 44, 47-50).

SUGGITT v SUGGITT; SUGGITT v ROBINSON, [2012] EWCA Civ 1140, [2012] W.T.L.R. 1607, Sir Nicholas Wall (President, Fam), CA (Civ Div).

EUROPEAN UNION

1163. Biocidal products–Fees and charges

THE BIOCIDAL PRODUCTS (FEES AND CHARGES) REGULATIONS 2013, SI 2013/1507; made under the European Communities Act 1972 s.2. In force: September 1, 2013; .

These Regulations provide the charging regime in relation to Regulation 528/2012 concerning the making available on the market and use of biocidal products.

1164. European Parliament–Members of the European Parliament

THE EUROPEAN PARLIAMENTARY (UNITED KINGDOM REPRESENTATIVES) PENSIONS (AMENDMENT) ORDER 2013, SI 2013/481; made under the European Parliament (Pay and Pensions) Act 1979 s.4. In force: March 29, 2013; .

This Order amends the European Parliamentary (United Kingdom Representatives) Pensions (Consolidation and Amendment) Order 1994 (SI 1994/1662) and sets out a pension scheme for UK representatives to the European Parliament.

1165. European Union (Approvals) Act 2013 (9)

This Act to makes provision approving for the purposes of the European Union Act 2011 s.8 certain draft decisions under art.352 of the Treaty on the functioning of the European Union; and makes provision approving for the purposes of s.7 of that Act a draft decision under art.17 of the Treaty on European Union about the number of members of the European Commission.

This Act received Royal Assent on February 28, 2013.

1166. European Union (Croatian Accession and Irish Protocol) Act 2013 (5)

This Act makes provision consequential on the treaty concerning the accession of the Republic of Croatia to the European Union, signed at Brussels on December 9, 2011, and provision consequential on the Protocol on the concerns of the Irish people on the Treaty of Lisbon, adopted at Brussels on May 16, 2012; and makes provision about the entitlement of nationals of the Republic of Croatia to enter or reside in the United Kingdom as workers.

This Act received Royal Assent on January 31, 2013.

1167. Freedom of movement for workers–Right to reside–Migrant workers–Temporary cessation of work due to pregnancy–Whether status as "worker" retained

[Social Security Contributions and Benefits Act 1992 (c.4) s.124(1)(b), s.124(1)(e); Income Support (General) Regulations 1987 (SI 1987/1967) reg.21AA, reg.21AA(2); Directive 2004/38 on the right of citizens of the Union and their family members to move and reside freely within the territory of the Member States amending Regulation (EEC) No 1612/68 and repealing

Directives 64/221/EEC, 68/360/EEC, 72/194/EEC, 73/148/EEC, 75/34/EEC, 75/35/EEC, 90/364/EEC, 90/365/ Art.7(3).]

The appellant (S), a French national, appealed against a decision ([2011] EWCA Civ 806, [2011] 3 C.M.L.R. 48, [2012] C.L.Y. 3117) upholding a refusal by the respondent secretary of state of her application for income support. S worked as a teaching assistant in the United Kingdom. She enrolled on a course of study but withdrew from it before the end because she became pregnant. She took agency work in nursery schools until she was nearly six months pregnant, when the demands of that work became too strenuous. S stopped that work and looked for lighter work, but none was available. Eleven weeks before her expected date of confinement, S applied for income support on the basis that she was not required to be available for, or actively to seek, work and therefore fell within "a prescribed category of person" for the purposes of the Social Security Contributions and Benefits Act 1992 s.124(1)(e). Her application was refused on the ground that she no longer held the status of "worker". It was common ground that S did not fall within any of the categories of person specified in Directive 2004/38 art.7(3) who were to retain the status of worker for the purpose of art.7(1)(a). S contended that, as a European Union citizen who had travelled to another Member State to work, and who had only ceased work temporarily owing to pregnancy, she remained a "worker" within the meaning ascribed to that term by the European Court of Justice. Further, S argued, it would be a substantial deterrent to the free movement of female workers if they were faced with the prospect of being left destitute and without the right to reside should they become pregnant and temporarily give up work. S also argued that her exclusion from art.7 constituted direct discrimination. The secretary of state contended that art.7 of the Directive was intended to codify the existing law and that art.7(3) exhaustively listed the people who fell outside that definition but were nevertheless to be treated as workers. The secretary of state also submitted that S's case left it uncertain how long a pregnant woman remained a "worker" if she did not have a continuing employment contract and was not self-employed.

Held: Questions referred to ECJ. A "person from abroad" was effectively excluded from entitlement to income support because the "applicable amount" prescribed for such a person pursuant to s.124(1)(b) of the 1992 Act was nil. According to the Income Support (General) Regulations 1987 reg.21AA, a "person from abroad" was a claimant not habitually resident in the UK. By reg.21AA(2), no claimant was to be treated as habitually resident in the UK unless he or she had a right to reside. By reg.21AA(4), a claimant was not classed as a person from abroad if he or she was a worker for the purposes of the Directive. In the instant case, the Supreme Court was not persuaded that the case of either party was clearly right. Although it was likely that the Directive codified the law as it stood at the time of enactment, that did not necessarily preclude further elaboration of the concept of "worker" in relation to situations not envisaged at that time. Since only women could become pregnant and bear children, they could not be compared to men in that respect. Pregnancy was not to be equated with illness or disability. However, unless special account was taken of pregnancy and childbirth, women would suffer comparative disadvantage in the workplace. There were also health and policy reasons for allowing women to take reasonable periods of maternity leave without losing the advantages attached to their status as worker. Equal treatment of men and women was one of the fundamental principles of EU law and it would be consistent with that principle for the ECJ to develop the concept of "worker" to meet the instant situation. Therefore, the ECJ was asked to determine (i) whether the right of residence conferred upon a worker in art.7 of the Directive applied only to those who were in an existing employment relationship, seeking work or covered by the extensions in art.7(3), or whether art.7 was capable of including persons outside those categories as "workers"; if the latter (ii) whether art.7 extended to a woman who gave up work or seeking work in late pregnancy and the aftermath of childbirth; and if so (iii) whether such a woman was entitled to the benefit of the national law's definition of when it was reasonable for her to do so (see paras 5, 21-22 of judgment).

ST PRIX v SECRETARY OF STATE FOR WORK AND PENSIONS, [2012] UKSC 49, [2013] 1 All E.R. 752, Lord Neuberger (President), SC.

1168. Ministers' powers and duties–Orders–Regulations–Schemes

THE EUROPEAN COMMUNITIES (DESIGNATION) ORDER 2013, SI 2013/1445; made under the European Communities Act 1972 s.2. In force: July 12, 2013; .

In England, Wales and Northern Ireland, only "designated" Ministers and departments can exercise the powers under the European Communities Act 1972 s.2 to make orders, rules, regulations and schemes. This is one of a series of Orders by which Ministers and departments are designated for the purposes of s.2 in relation to different subject areas.

1169. Mutual assistance–Armenia–Chile–Ukraine

THE CRIME (INTERNATIONAL CO-OPERATION) ACT 2003 (DESIGNATION OF PARTICIPATING COUNTRIES) (ENGLAND, WALES AND NORTHERN IRELAND) ORDER 2013, SI 2013/296; made under the Crime (International Co-operation) Act 2003 s.51. In force: February 15, 2013; .

By virtue of the power conferred by s.51 of the Crime (International Co-operation) Act 2003 (the 2003 Act), this Order designates Armenia, Chile and Ukraine as participating countries for the purposes of section 31, 47 and 48 of, and Part 2 of Schedule 2 to, the 2003 Act, following their ratification of the Second Additional Protocol to the 1959 European Convention on Mutual Assistance in Criminal Matters.

1170. Rights of entry and residence–Accession states–Nationals of states acceding to European Union after nationals' entry to other Member State–EU law basis for right of residence–European Union

[Income Support (General) Regulations 1987 (SI 1987/1967) reg.21AA; Regulation 1612/68 on freedom of movement for workers within the Community Art.12; Directive 2004/38 on the right of citizens of the Union and their family members to move and reside freely within the territory of the Member States amending Regulation (EEC) No 1612/68 and repealing Directives 64/221/EEC, 68/360/EEC, 72/194/EEC, 73/148/EEC, 75/34/EEC, 75/35/EEC, 90/364/EEC, 90/365/ Art.7(1), Art.16(1).]

The European Court of Justice was asked for a preliminary ruling on whether, under European Union law, nationals of states which had acceded to the EU after the nationals had moved to another Member State had a right of residence in the host Member State, where they had been self-employed and where their children were in education. The respondents (C and P) in the main proceedings were, respectively, Polish and Czech nationals who had arrived in the United Kingdom before their countries had acceded to the EU. Their claims for income support, made after their countries' accession, had been refused by the appellant secretary of state on the ground that they were persons from abroad, within the meaning of the Income Support (General) Regulations 1987 reg.21AA, because they did not have a right to reside in the UK. Both had been self-employed in the UK before their claims and both had three children who had been born in the UK. The First-tier Tribunal allowed their appeals, holding that they were not persons from abroad because they had a right to reside, and they were therefore entitled to income support. The Upper Tribunal referred the question to the ECJ.

Held: Preliminary ruling given. The right of access to education in Regulation 1612/68 art.12 implied that the child of a migrant worker had a right of residence in order to attend educational courses in the host Member State, and that the parent who was the child's primary carer had a corresponding right of residence, *Harrow LBC v Ibrahim (C-310/08)* [2010] P.T.S.R. 1913, [2010] C.L.Y. 1250 applied. Therefore, P, as the primary carer of a child in education while the child's father had been employed in the UK, had a right of residence under art.12.

However, C could not derive a right of residence from the sole fact that she was the primary carer of a child who entered the educational system when neither she nor the father had been employed in the UK. Article 12 concerned only employed persons and did not also apply to the self-employed. Nevertheless, C did have a right of permanent residence under Directive 2004/38 art.16(1) because at the time she claimed income support, she had resided in the UK for more than five years, in view of the fact that periods of residence in a Member State completed by a national of a non-Member State before the latter state's accession had to be taken into account and her residence had complied with the condition in art.7(1)(b), *Ziolkowski v Land Berlin (C-424/10)* [2014] All E.R. (EC) 314 applied (see paras 24-30, 33-38 of judgment).

SECRETARY OF STATE FOR WORK AND PENSIONS v CZOP (C-147/11); SECRETARY OF STATE FOR WORK AND PENSIONS v PUNAKOVA (C-148/11) [2013] P.T.S.R. 334, Judge Lenaerts (President), ECJ (3rd Chamber).

1171. Supply of goods–Liability to tax–Supplier selling mail order goods through agent on commission basis–Whether taxable value of goods capable of reduction by amount of commission paid

[Directive 67/228 on turnover taxes -Structure and procedures for application of the common system of value added tax Art.8(a); Directive 77/388 on turnover taxes -Common system of value added tax: uniform basis of assessment Art.11 (C) (1).]

On a reference for a preliminary ruling, the court was required to interpret Directive 67/228 art.8(a) and Annex A point 13. The claimant in the substantive proceedings (G) was a representative member of a group of mail order retailers who used agents as a means of widening their customer base. The agents distributed G's catalogues to potential consumers, placed orders on their behalf, received the goods for onward distribution, and collected payment for remittance. The agents received a commission of 10 per cent of the remittance amount. One of the ways in which they claimed their commission was a method known as "in cash", whereby they could claim it either as a cheque payment or offset it against the cost of their own purchases from G. G accounted for VAT on the full catalogue price of the goods, including the amount of commission paid to the agents. It claimed repayment from the respondent commissioners of the amounts paid by way of VAT corresponding to the amount of commission. It did so on the ground that the commission constituted a discount reducing the consideration for, or taxable amount of, supplies of goods to the agents. The commissioners repaid the VAT relating to the commission, except for the commission taken "in cash" in the period between 1973 and 1978. The question referred was whether art.8(a) had to be interpreted as conferring upon a taxable person the right to treat the basis of assessment of a supply of goods as retrospectively reduced where, after the time of that supply, the recipient received a credit from the supplier, which he elected to take as a payment of money or as a credit against amounts owed to the supplier in respect of supplies that had already taken place.

Held: Preliminary ruling given. (1) The expression "consideration" used in art.8(a) was defined in Annex A point 13 as covering "everything received in return for the supply of goods or the provision of services, including incidental expenses (packing, transport, insurance, etc) that is to say not only the cash amounts charged, but also, for example, the value of the goods received in exchange". It was therefore part of a provision of EU law which did not refer to the law of the Member States for the determination of its meaning and scope. It followed that interpretation of the expression could not be left to the discretion of individual Member States. Determining whether art.8(a) obliged Member States to permit consideration to be altered, thereby allowing the basis of assessment to be regularised after the chargeable event had taken place, involved examining the Directive's provisions governing the calculation, declaration and payment of VAT. Under art.5(5), a chargeable event occurred at the moment when delivery was effected. The term "chargeable event" was defined in Annex A point 8 as "the event giving rise to the tax". Nowhere did the Directive provide for occurrence of the chargeable event to be set at a subsequent time or for any other form of deferral. Therefore, a taxable person's tax debt arose in an amount derived from a basis of assessment which was to be determined at the time of delivery. Neither art.8(a) nor any other article could be interpreted as meaning that regularisation of the basis of assessment, or of the output tax, after delivery had to be permitted (see paras 21-27 of judgment). (2) A consequence of the principle of fiscal neutrality was that taxable persons had not to be treated differently in respect of similar supplies which were in competition with each other. The principle was not a rule of primary law which enabled, on its own, determination of the basis of assessment within the meaning of art.8(a); nor could it make up for the fact that the Directive did not include any provision comparable to Directive 77/388 art.11 (C)(1). The amount of VAT to be collected by a tax authority had to correspond exactly with the amount of VAT declared on the invoice and paid by the final consumer to the taxable person. In the instant case, customers purchasing goods through G's agents paid the catalogue price for the goods. Under the principle of fiscal neutrality, the consideration for the supply corresponded to that price rather than to the price as reduced by the commission. The basis for assessment was therefore the full catalogue price (paras 28-31).

GRATTAN PLC v REVENUE AND CUSTOMS COMMISSIONERS (C-310/11) [2013] S.T.C. 502, Judge Rosas (President), ECJ (2nd Chamber).

1172. Trade marks–Registrability–Interpretation of Directive 2008/95–Extent of clarity and precision required in describing relevant goods or services requiring trade mark protection–Guidance on use of Nice Classification

[Directive 2008/95 on trade marks Art.3(1)(b), Art.3; Nice Agreement concerning the International Classification of Goods and Services for the Purposes of the Registration of Marks 1957.]

In proceedings between the claimant Institute and the respondent Registrar concerning the latter's refusal to register a national trade mark, the court was required to give a preliminary ruling on the interpretation of Directive 2008/95. The Institute had identified the services covered by the registration as being within Class 41 of the classification system in the Nice Agreement concerning the International Classification of Goods and Services for the Purposes of the Registration of Marks 1957. The Registrar had refused the registration on the basis of national provisions corresponding to art.3(1)(b) and art.3(1)(c) of the Directive. He held that the registration covered not only the services identified by the Institute but also every other service falling within Class 41, including translation services, and that in respect of those additional services it lacked distinctive character and was descriptive in nature. The Institute appealed to the Appointed Person, who referred questions for a preliminary ruling. The issue was essentially whether the Directive had to be interpreted as meaning that it required that the goods and services for which protection by a trade mark was sought had to be identified with a certain degree of clarity and precision, and if so, whether an applicant for a national trade mark was precluded from identifying its goods and services by means of the class headings and general indications of the Nice Classification.

Held: Preliminary ruling given. The fact that there was no express provision in the Directive governing the question of the identification of goods and services was not sufficient to support a finding that the determination of goods and services for the purposes of registration was outside its ambit (see paras 38-39 of judgment). Determination of the nature and content of the goods and services eligible for protection was subject to substantive conditions, which were required to be identical in all Member States. The question whether any of the grounds for refusal in art.3 applied to the trade mark was to be assessed by reference to the description of the goods or services in respect of which registration was sought. The Directive required such descriptions to be of sufficient clarity and precision to enable the competent authorities and economic operators to determine the extent of the protection sought. Competent authorities needed to know the precise nature of the signs so that they could fulfil their obligations in relation to the prior examination of applications for registration and the publication and maintenance of an appropriate and precise register of trade marks; economic operators had to be able to acquaint themselves, with clarity and precision, with registrations or applications for registration from actual or potential competitors (paras 40-49). Use of the Nice Classification was obligatory, not under the Directive, but under the Nice Agreement art.2(3). The Directive did not therefore preclude identification using the Nice Classification, but such identification had to meet the Directive's own requirements of clarity and precision. Some of the general indications in the class headings of the Nice Classification were too general and covered goods or services which were too variable to be compatible with the trade mark's function as an indication of origin. The competent authorities therefore had to make an assessment on a case-by-case basis as to whether the Nice indications met the Directive's requirements of clarity and precision. In any event, an applicant using the general indications in the Nice Classification had to specify whether its application for registration was intended to cover all the goods and services included in the alphabetical list of the particular class concerned, or only some of them, and if so, which ones (paras 50-56, 61).

CHARTERED INSTITUTE OF PATENT ATTORNEYS v REGISTRAR OF TRADE MARKS (C-307/10) [2013] Bus. L.R. 740, Judge Skouris (President), ECJ (Grand Chamber).

1173. Books

Loos, Marco; Diaz, Odavia Bueno (eds)–Principles of European Law: Mandate Contracts. European Civil Code Series. Hardback: £95.00. ISBN 9780199568291. (Oxford University Press).

EXTRADITION

1174. Appeals–Extradition–Human rights–Jurisdiction

THE EXTRADITION APPEALS (ENGLAND AND WALES AND NORTHERN IRELAND) ORDER 2013, SI 2013/2384; made under the Crime and Courts Act 2013 s.58, s.59. In force: October 14, 2013; .

This Order makes consequential provision to modify the application of s.109(2) to(4) of the Extradition Act 2003 (court's powers on appeal under s.108 -appeal against extradition order). This is to clarify that the High Court has the power to allow or dismiss appeals brought on human rights grounds against a decision of the Secretary of State to order a person's extradition under the 2003 Act, as amended by the Crime and Courts Act 2013.

1175. Crime and Courts Act 2013 (c.22)–Commencement No.5 Order 2013

THE CRIME AND COURTS ACT 2013 (COMMENCEMENT NO.5) ORDER 2013, SI 2013/SI 2013/2349 (C.96); made under the Crime and Courts Act 2013 s.61. Commencement details: bringing into force various provisions of the 2013 Act on September 18, 2013 and October 14, 2013.; .

This Order commences a number of provisions of the Crime and Courts Act 2013 relating to extradition on September 18, 2013 and October 14, 2013.

1176. Dual criminality–Fraud by false representation–Provision to bank of cheque as security–Insufficient funds to meet cheque–Provision of cheque as false representation under s.2 Fraud Act 2006

[Extradition Act 2003 (c.41) s.138(2)(b); Fraud Act 2006 (c.35) s.2.]

The appellant requesting state appealed against a district judge's refusal of its application for the extradition of the respondent (J). J had taken a loan from a bank in Abu Dhabi in order to buy a property. J was to repay the loan in monthly instalments, and provided the bank with an undated cheque for a similar sum to the loan on the terms that, if she defaulted in her repayments, the bank was authorised to insert the date and present the cheque for payment. J subsequently defaulted. On presentation of the cheque, the bank learnt that there was no credit in J s account to meet the cheque. J returned to the United Kingdom, and in her absence was convicted in Abu Dhabi of an offence of issuing an uncovered cheque? as described in the extradition request. Her extradition was sought to serve the three years imprisonment imposed for that offence. The district judge refused the UAE's request for J's extradition, concluding that the conduct specified in the extradition request did not constitute an extradition offence under the Extradition Act 2003 s.138(2)(b) and that there was insufficient evidence to establish a prima facie case against J. The UAE submitted that J's conduct constituted an extradition offence because it equated to an offence of making a false representation under the Fraud Act 2006 s.2, namely because (1) by providing the cheque, J had represented that it would be met in the ordinary course if it was presented; (2) the representation became false when J depleted her account or failed to maintain it in credit so that the balance was insufficient to meet the cheque on its presentation.

Held: Appeal dismissed. (1) The intended method of repayment was monthly instalments through J's credit card account; the cheque was only to be presented upon a certain contingency, in the event of a default, and was required by the bank as a form of security. Any banker would know that over the 20-year term of the loan there were many reasons why a borrower might default other than a deliberate intention to do so, and any commercial lender would take those possibilities into account when deciding the terms on which it would lend. The provision of the loan was for the purpose of buying property, and therefore no banker could have supposed that J was suggesting that her financial circumstances when taking out the loan were such that she would be able to keep the amount of the loan in her bank account. The bank knew J's financial circumstances as she was required to disclose them as part of her application, and there was no evidence that she did not make full and frank disclosure. Accordingly, a reasonable bank would not have understood J, by agreeing to provide the cheque, to be representing impliedly that her current financial circumstances were such as to be able to say that, in the event of defaulting at any time during the 20-year term of the loan, the cheque would be met in the ordinary course, R v Hazleton (1874) LR 2 CCR 134, *Commissioner of Police of the Metropolis v Charles (Derek Michael)* [1977] A.C. 177, [1976] C.L.Y. 529 and *R. v Gilmartin (Anthony)* [1983] Q.B. 953, [1983] C.L.Y. 728 considered (see paras 35-36, 39 of judgment). (2) As a matter of common law, a representation had to be capable of being expressed as a statement of the past or present. A statement as to the future might have effect as a contractual promise, but would not come within the legal classification of a representation. Logically, any statement by a representor about his state of mind could only be about his present or past state of mind, and his state of mind as to the future could only be a current perception, *British Airways Board v Taylor* [1976] 1 W.L.R. 13, [1976] C.L.Y. 2471 and *Gilmartin* considered. Further, the alleged representation did not take effect as a continuing representation: after the loan account had been opened, J gave no undertaking to provide the bank with information about any change in her circumstances, and there was no principled basis for constructing a fictional, implied, continuing representation. The bank's requirement for an undated cheque was not rendered commercially pointless if its provision did not operate as a continuing representation: it provided the bank with a simple cause of action on the cheque with the reinforcement of criminal sanctions under Abu Dhabi law. Accordingly there was no false representation by J (paras 42, 49, 56-57, 59).

UNITED ARAB EMIRATES v ALLEN, [2012] EWHC 1712 (Admin), [2012] 1 W.L.R. 3419, Toulson, L.J., QBD (Admin).

1177. European arrest warrants–Bars to extradition–Nature of particulars required by s.2(6)(b) Extradition Act 2003–Lawfulness of mixed warrants in Category 1 territories–Effect of delay on extradition order

[Extradition Act 2003 (c.41) Pt1, s.2(6)(b), s.11(1)(c), s.14, Pt 2; Decision 2002/584.]

The appellant (P), who had been arrested pursuant to two European arrest warrants, appealed against an order extraditing him to Poland. The first arrest warrant concerned a number of convictions and accusations, the second only an accusation. When P first appealed against the extradition order, the Divisional Court held that his appeal was out of time (*Pomiechowski v Poland* [2011] EWHC 2060 (Admin), [2012] 1 W.L.R. 391, [2012] 5 C.L. 119), but the Supreme Court ruled in his favour (*Pomiechowski v Poland* [2012] UKSC 20, [2012] 1 W.L.R. 1604, [2012] C.L.Y. 1287) and remitted his case to the instant court for determination. P submitted that (1) the first arrest warrant was invalid because it failed to provide particulars as required by the Extradition Act 2003 s.2(6)(b) and because it sought extradition in respect of both convictions and an accusation, which the Act did not permit; (2) extradition was time-barred.

Held: Appeal dismissed. (1) Both the accusation and conviction parts of the arrest warrant fully satisfied the s.2 requirements. Even though the various sets of information were not linked up, place and dates of court judgments being separate from the case reference numbers and the details of the conduct alleged, the warrant, read as a whole, provided particulars of the four convictions to which it related and gave P all the necessary information to enable him to know precisely what he faced on return to Poland, *Sandi v Romania* [2009] EWHC 3079 (Admin) and *R. (on the application of Denis) v Poland* [2010] EWHC 3507 (Admin) considered (see paras 7-8, 12-13, 18 of judgment). Regarding mixed warrants, although Pt 2 of the Act appeared not to allow for them, there was no indication that Pt 1 of the Act made them unlawful. If the statute had created a scheme which anomalously might lead to the discharge of a requested person in limited circumstances, even where there was nothing wrong with the accusation part of the warrant, that provided no basis for extending the anomaly to all mixed warrant cases. Interpretation of Part 1 had to give effect to the intentions of Decision 2002/584. The Decision could be clearer about whether both accusation and conviction matters could be included within the same warrant, but nowhere did it state that the two had to be kept separate; there was no identified purpose for maintaining such separation, especially given that one of the main purposes of the Decision was to establish streamlined, quick, and simple procedures for the surrender between Member States of fugitives, *Ciesielski v Poland* [2011] EWHC 1503 (Admin), [2011] A.C.D. 93 and *Zacharski v Poland* [2011] EWHC 2386 (Admin) applied (paras 5, 9-10, 23-25). (2) The principles governing delay as a bar to extradition turned on whether it would be "unjust or oppressive" to extradite within the meaning of s.11(1)(c) and s.14 of the Act. "Unjust" was directed primarily to the risk of prejudice to the accused and the conduct of the trial itself; "oppressive" was directed towards hardship to the accused resulting from changes in circumstances during the relevant period. Between them, they covered all cases where returning the requested person would not be fair, *Gomes v Trinidad and Tobago* [2009] UKHL 21, [2009] 1 W.L.R. 1038, [2009] C.L.Y. 1474 and *Kakis v Cyprus* [1978] 1 W.L.R. 779, [1978] C.L.Y. 1451 followed. On the evidence, P was to be treated as a fugitive for the purposes of consideration of the passage of time and could not rely on any delay since leaving Poland in early 2001. If that was wrong, the passage of time did not, in the circumstances, amount to oppression for the purposes of s.14 of the Act (paras 26-32).

POMIECHOWSKI v POLAND, [2012] EWHC 3161 (Admin), [2013] 1 W.L.R. 2653, Burnett, J., QBD (Admin).

1178. **European arrest warrants–Extradition–Croatia**

THE EXTRADITION ACT 2003 (AMENDMENT TO DESIGNATIONS) ORDER 2013, SI 2013/1583; made under the Extradition Act 2003 s.1, s.69, s.71, s.84, s.86, s.223. In force: July 1, 2013; .

This Order amends the Extradition Act 2003 (Designation of Part 1 Territories) Order 2003 (SI 2003/3333) (the Part 1 Order) and the Extradition Act 2003 (Designation of Part 2 Territories) Order 2003 (the Part 2 Order) (SI 2003/3334) to designate Croatia as a Part 1 territory, enabling the UK to operate the European Arrest Warrant scheme with Croatia from July 1, 2013.

1179. **European arrest warrants–Judicial decision-making–Whether ministry of justice constituting judicial authority for purposes of s.2(2) Extradition Act 2003**

[Extradition Act 2003 (c.41) s.2(2); Decision 2002/584 Art.6.]

In three conjoined appeals, the court was required to consider the validity of European arrest warrants issued in the Republics of Lithuania and Estonia. The warrants related to two Lithuanian nationals (B and S) and one Estonian national (L) living in the United Kingdom. They had been signed, respectively, by the Lithuanian Minister of Justice and by an official of the Estonian Ministry of Justice, and each was a "conviction" warrant, requesting that the UK authorities surrender the individual concerned to complete a term of imprisonment imposed by the courts in his home country. It was accepted that each warrant was in the correct form and contained all the necessary information. The only question was whether the issuing bodies, the Ministries of Justice of Lithuania and Estonia, were judicial authorities within the meaning of the Extradition Act 2003 s.2(2). The issues were (i) whether, on the correct construction of s.2(7) and s.2(8) of the Act, certificates issued by the Serious Organised Crime Agency were conclusive of the status of warrant-issuing bodies as judicial authorities; (ii) if not, then how the term "judicial authority" in Decision 2002/584 art.6 was to be defined as a matter of EU law; (iii) whether the Lithuanian and Estonian Ministries of Justice were judicial authorities for the purposes of s.2(2) of the Act.

Held: Appeals allowed in part. (1) A SOCA certificate meant only that the body issuing a European arrest warrant had the function of doing so. It was not conclusive of the status of that body as a judicial authority for the purposes either of the Act or the Decision. The term "arrest warrants" in s.2(7) and s.2(8) referred only to European arrest warrants, and the words "has the function of issuing..." meant that SOCA had simply to believe that the issuing body had been given the function of issuing the warrants in the relevant territory pursuant to art.6(3) of the Decision. It was not certifying that it believed it to be a "judicial body" truly within the terms of art.6(1). Insofar as the High Court in *Enander v Brixton Prison Governor* [2005] EWHC 3036 (Admin), [2006] 1 C.M.L.R. 37, [2006] C.L.Y. 1599, *Harmatos v Belgium* [2011] EWHC 1598 (Admin) and *Howell v France* [2012] EWHC 150 (Admin) stated that a SOCA certificate was conclusive of status, or could not be challenged save by judicial review, the instant court disagreed, Enander, Harmatos and Howell not applied. Rather, the decisions in *Assange v Sweden* [2011] EWHC 2849 (Admin), (2011) 108(44) L.S.G. 17 and *Dhar v Netherlands*were preferred, Assange and Dhar considered (see paras 73-76, 84-86 of judgment). (2) The Court of Justice of the European Union would be likely to say that there could be no preconceived template of what constituted a judicial authority, so long as the designated authority accorded with certain autonomous, objective, norms. Nevertheless, it would find that a judicial authority had to be capable of making a "judicial decision", and whether that was so depended on the Member State's legal framework for issuing warrants, and how the process was actually done in practice. While the CJEU would countenance a ministry of justice being a judicial authority for the purposes of issuing conviction warrants in certain circumstances, it would emphasise the need for the decision-maker to be sufficiently independent of the executive. In respect of conviction warrants, there was much force in Lord Phillips' words in *Assange v Sweden* [2012] UKSC

22, [2012] 2 A.C. 471, [2012] C.L.Y. 1284 about the requisite safeguards being predominantly in the antecedent process forming the basis of the warrant. If the relevant national law provided that before a conviction warrant could be issued there had to be an enforceable judgment and sentence, and the sentencing court had to request that the warrant be issued, then the scope for executive interference was reduced. Thus, the CJEU would not be likely to say that a ministry of justice was incapable of being a judicial authority, at least in the case of conviction warrants, *Assange* considered. In that regard, the court disagreed with the Divisional Court in *Assange*, if that court's remarks were intended to apply to conviction warrants (paras 89, 97-100). (3) For the reasons given by the majority of the Supreme Court in *Assange*, the words "judicial authority" in s.2(2) had to be interpreted no less restrictively than those in art.6 of the Decision. In the cases of B and S, the warrant request was made by a court and based on an enforceable conviction and sentence. Thus, the antecedent process was judicial. The functions of the officials of the Lithuanian Ministry of Justice were tightly defined by national law, and the decision to issue a conviction warrant amounted to a judicial decision within art.1 of the Decision. There was much less material on the procedure in Estonia, where it was the Ministry of Justice which instigated the issue of a conviction warrant. There was no requirement that the sentencing court should prepare a draft warrant and there were no rules dictating what the Ministry officials had to do. In those circumstances, the decision to issue a conviction warrant could not be regarded as a judicial decision. The appeal by the Lithuanian Ministry of Justice in the case of B would be allowed; S's appeal would be dismissed; and L's appeal would be allowed (paras 101, 104-107, 109-111)

LITHUANIA v BUCNYS; LAVROV v ESTONIA; SAKALIS v LITHUANIA; *sub nom.* BUCNYS v LITHUANIA, [2012] EWHC 2771 (Admin), [2013] 1 All E.R. 1220, Aikens, L.J., DC.

1180. European arrest warrants–Particulars–Conviction warrant specifying number of individual convictions and sentences–Sentences subsequently aggregated–Whether warrant satisfying requirements of s.2(6)(e) Extradition Act 2003

[Extradition Act 2003 (c.41) s.2(6)(e), s.65; Decision 2002/584.]

The appellant requesting authority appealed against a decision ([2012] EWHC 173 (Admin), [2012] 1 W.L.R. 2248, [2012] C.L.Y. 1282) that a European arrest warrant issued in respect of the respondent (Z) was invalid. The warrant, a "conviction warrant", specified four separate sentences of imprisonment imposed on Z in Poland between 2003 and 2005. Z was arrested in the United Kingdom and extradition proceedings were begun and adjourned. During the adjournment, the Polish court aggregated Z's sentences, imposing a cumulative sentence of 22 months' imprisonment rather than the 45 months that Z would have served had each sentence run consecutively. In the resumed extradition proceedings, he argued that the only relevant sentence was the cumulative sentence, and that the warrant was invalid because it no longer gave the particulars required by the Extradition Act 2003 s.2(6)(e). The district judge rejected that argument and made the extradition order. His decision was overturned by the High Court, which held that the warrant had to relate to the "current operative sentence" and not to earlier sentences subsumed in an aggregated order.

Held: Appeal dismissed. (1) As a general rule, the scheme of the Act and Decision 2002/584 was that the executing court had to take the information in the warrant at face value. The validity of the warrant depended on whether it contained the prescribed particulars, not whether they were correct. A defendant could not challenge the warrant's validity by referring to extraneous evidence to show that the particulars were wrong. Validity was not a transient state. A warrant was either valid or not, and it could not change its status over time. If the prescribed particulars were, or became, incorrect, the remedy had to be found when the court was considering extradition. There were two safeguards against unjustified extradition in those circumstances. The first was the mutual trust between parties to the Decision. The requesting state had a right to forward additional information at any time, and the executing court could receive that information into evidence and, if necessary, request more. The Decision proceeded on the assumption that the requesting state could be trusted to ensure that the information in the warrant was true. The second safeguard was the English court's inherent right to ensure that its process was not abused. In that context it might, in some circumstances, be necessary for the court to question statements made in the warrant, *Caldarelli v Italy* [2008] UKHL 51, [2008] 1 W.L.R. 1724, [2008] C.L.Y. 1395 considered. As to the nature of the circumstances sufficient to trigger such questioning, it had to be borne in mind that the jurisdiction was exceptional. The statements in the warrant had to be wrong or incomplete in some respect that was misleading; the facts required to correct the error had to be clear and beyond legitimate dispute; and the court's power to prevent abuse of process was not to be used as a way of challenging the factual or evidential basis for the conduct alleged in the warrant. The error had also to be material to the operation of the statutory scheme. Materiality was of critical importance in the context of abuse of process. It would be inconsistent with the statutory scheme to refuse to act on a warrant which included the prescribed particulars, merely because those particulars contained immaterial errors, *Spain v Murua* [2010] EWHC 2609 (Admin) considered. In Z's case, the warrant was valid upon issue and was effective to authorise the commencement of extradition proceedings. It did not become invalid when the aggregation order was made. The only basis on which Z could object to his extradition was that the requesting authority's conduct in persisting with extradition proceedings after the aggregation order was an abuse of process. However, the requesting authority had supplied further information explaining that while the original sentences remained valid, the cumulative sentence under the aggregation order was to be treated as satisfying them. Thus, the particulars in the warrant, although no longer complete, were not wrong. The prosecution of extradition proceedings on a warrant containing incomplete particulars could be an abuse of process only if the information omitted was material to the operation of the statutory scheme. In Z's case, the omitted information was wholly immaterial. All the court needed to know was that the sentence was long enough to constitute an extradition offence under s.65 of the Act, which, in Z's case, it was. The warrant's failure to specify the "current operative sentence" was not fatal. The sentence of the court would rarely be the "current operative sentence" since the actual period to be served would be affected by a number of factors, including aspects of criminal procedure that would vary from one jurisdiction to another without undermining the purpose of the statutory scheme (see paras 8-16 of judgment). (2) Ordinarily, the appeal would have been allowed and the order of the District Judge restored. However, Z had voluntarily returned to Poland. He had been arrested and the warrant had been withdrawn. While that did not affect the issue for the court's decision, it meant that the appeal had, formally, to be dismissed (para.17).

ZAKRZEWSKI v POLAND, [2013] UKSC 2, [2013] 1 W.L.R. 324, Lord Neuberger (President), SC.

1181. Extradition–Prison conditions–Polish prison conditions constituting breach of art.3 European Convention on Human Rights 1950–Guidance on procedure for extradition appeals brought under art.3 relying on Polish prison conditions

[European Convention on Human Rights 1950 Art.3.]

The appellants (X) appealed against decisions that their extraditions to the respondent requesting state, Poland, would not be in breach of the European Convention on Human Rights art.3 by reason of Polish prison conditions. X's extradition was sought pursuant to accusation and conviction European Arrest Warrants. The first four appellants had raised the issue of Polish prison conditions before the district judge but the fifth and sixth appellants had not. In the instant appeals X relied on a report which identified several alleged failures in the

Polish prison service, the principal complaint being of overcrowding and relying on the case of *Orchowski v Poland (17885/04)* where the European Court of Human Rights had found that overcrowding in Polish prisons was a systemic problem. The report also raised concerns of categorising prisoners, lack of rehabilitation, cell space, poor health facilities and lack of independent monitoring. The Ministry of Justice provided the instant court with evidence on the conditions in Polish prisons by way of two letters, one of which concluded that there were no grounds for generalisations concerning systemic breaches of the rights of Polish prisoners.

Held: Appeals dismissed. (1) It was not in the interests of justice and the proper conduct of the business of the court that appeals raising the issue of Polish prison conditions in relation to art.3 were dealt with in the ordinary way. The court gave guidance that any appeal raising the issue in the future had to clearly identify any new factual issues that had not been considered in the instant appeal or in earlier cases which were said to give rise to a breach of art.3; set out a summary of the evidence relied on in support; explain how that evidence rebutted the presumption that Poland, as a Member State, would abide by the Convention and that other states could have confidence in that regard, N.S. v Secretary of State for the Home Department C-411/10 applied. Any such appeal would be listed within days of being lodged at the court, and if there were no new factual issues and the evidence was not capable of rebutting the presumption the court would consider whether to hear the appeal there and then and, if appropriate, dismiss it. District judges should require a requested person or their advocate who sought to raise an art.3 issue relying on Polish prison conditions to identify any new factual issues not considered in the instant appeal or earlier cases, and should consider whether the evidence adduced in support was of the necessary type. If the requested person or his advocate failed in either regard, the district judge would ordinarily be entitled to deal with the claim briefly by relying on decisions of the High Court (see paras 9-10 of judgment). (2) Notwithstanding the fact that a statement had to be served explaining the circumstances where there was an intention to rely on evidence on appeal which had not been adduced before a district judge, the court took the exceptional step in the overall interests of justice to admit the report in light of the numerous appeals on the issue and the desirability of making the position for the future clear, *Hungary v Fenyvesi* [2009] EWHC 231 (Admin), [2009] 4 All E.R. 324, [2010] C.L.Y. 1262 considered (para.15). (3) The evidence in the report did not self-evidently begin to establish the type of evidence necessary to rebut the presumption and to find a breach of art.3. In any event, the principal criticism made was of overcrowding, but it was clear from the Ministry of Justice's evidence that the requirement of three metres squared of space in Polish prison cells was met and that the concerns raised in *Orchowski* had been remedied, *Orchowski* considered. The information provided by the Ministry of Justice showed that other points made by X were also unfounded, such as categorisation, rehabilitation and health provision. Even if it was possible to consider the report as evidence of the type that was required, it was insufficient to rebut the presumption (paras 21-22).

KROLIK v POLAND; WALACHOWSKI v POLAND; SOLTAN v POLAND; LACHOWSKI v POLAND; ZWOLINSKI v POLAND; KAZMIERCZAK v POLAND, [2012] EWHC 2357 (Admin), [2013] 1 W.L.R. 490, Sir John Thomas (President), DC.

1182. Extradition–Prosecutors–England and Wales

THE EXTRADITION ACT 2003 (DESIGNATION OF PROSECUTORS) (ENGLAND AND WALES AND NORTHERN IRELAND) ORDER 2013, SI 2013/2388; made under the Extradition Act 2003 s.19F, s.83E, s.223. In force: October 14, 2013; .

This Order designates prosecutors and descriptions of prosecutors as "designated prosecutors" for the purposes of the Extradition Act 2003 s.19F and s.83E. The effect of this will be that the prosecutors and descriptions of prosecutors listed in the Order will be able to give a prosecutor's certificate in "forum proceedings" conducted pursuant to the amended 2003 Act.

1183. Extradition hearings–Adjournment–Extraditee suffering from severe post-traumatic stress disorder and depression–Whether extradition unjust and oppressive under s.91 Extradition Act 2003

[Extradition Act 2003 (c.41) s.91 (3) (b), s.91 (3) (a); Mental Health Act 1983 (c.20) s.3; European Convention on Human Rights 1950 Art.2, Art.3.]

The appellant (D) appealed against an order for his extradition to the respondent requesting state to face a murder charge. D's wife had been killed when they were on honeymoon in South Africa. On his return to the United Kingdom he exhibited symptoms of depression and post-traumatic stress disorder (PTSD). He was arrested under a provisional arrest warrant under the Extradition Act 2003. He took an overdose and developed psychotic symptoms. He was later admitted to a medium secure hospital under the Mental Health Act 1983 s.3. The requesting state sought his extradition and gave undertakings regarding his treatment if returned. Evidence was given at the extradition hearing by the Head of the Judicial Inspectorate of Correctional Services in South Africa (Z) and by psychiatrists for both parties. The psychiatrists agreed that D was suffering from severe PTSD and depression, that there was a real risk of suicide and that he was unfit to plead though they disagreed regarding prognosis. D argued that he should be discharged under s.91 (3) (a) of the 2003 Act or, alternatively, that the hearing should be adjourned under s.91 (3) (b). The district judge accepted Z's evidence regarding the suitability and appropriateness of the prisons referred to in the undertakings and dismissed D's objections. He found that the test under s.91 had not been met. The issues to be determined were whether (i) the prison conditions in South Africa were such that it would be a breach of the European Convention on Human Rights 1950 art.2 and art.3 if D was extradited; (ii) D's mental condition and the attendant risk of suicide were such that he should not be extradited. D contended that he should not be extradited given (1) the real risk of breach of art.2 and art.3 from the high risk of HIV/AIDS infection and attack, particularly sexual violence, by other inmates; (2) his mental illness and the attendant high risk of suicide.

Held: Appeal allowed in part. (1) There was no basis for differing from the judge's findings of fact and conclusions in relation to Z's evidence on the adequacy of the conditions under which D would be held in South Africa. There was no merit in calling into question Z's independence and impartiality, which was unaffected by the fact that he was a witness for the requesting state. There were plainly risks of violence, particularly sexual violence, to a prisoner held in a communal cell in South Africa. However, a clear undertaking had been given that D would be held in a single cell and the judge had been entitled to accept that undertaking. South Africa now had a material track record of respect for democracy and the rule of law. Further reassurance given by Z in the course of his evidence was also taken into account as evidence that those undertakings would be monitored and followed. It was therefore accepted that there would be no violation of art.2 and art.3 by reason of the risk of infection by HIV/AIDS or of attack by fellow-prisoners (see paras 31-35 of judgment). (2) In the light of the psychiatric evidence before the district judge, the instant case was not one where there was unlikely to be recovery within a reasonable time; in fact the evidence pointed to recovery within a reasonable time. The judge was therefore right not to order D's discharge under s.91 (3) (a). With regard to s.91 (3) (b), what was unjust or oppressive was fact-sensitive and the test was more difficult to apply where the quantification of the degree of risk to life and the prognosis were less certain. In such a case, the interests of justice in seeing that persons accused of crimes were brought to trial had to be taken into account and it was plainly in the interests of justice that D be tried in South Africa as soon as he was fit to be tried. The strength of the psychiatric evidence was a striking feature of the case and, given the unusual combination of PTSD and severe depression, and D's other conditions, it was clear that extradition would present a real and significant risk to his life. Considerable significance was to be attached to the evidence that extradition would worsen D's condition and make it more difficult to get him into a position where he was fit to plead. It had to be an exceptional case where the expert called on behalf of the requesting state was of the view that extradition at the present time would jeopardise the treatment and the prospects of recovery. Balancing D's unfitness to plead, the risk of deterioration in his condition, the increased prospects of a speedier recovery and, to a lesser degree, the risk of suicide and the lack of clear certainty regarding what would happen to him if he was returned in his present condition, it would be unjust and oppressive to order D's extradition. The district judge should have exercised his powers under s.91(3)(b) and ordered the extradition hearing to be adjourned (paras 66-84).

SOUTH AFRICA v DEWANI, [2012] EWHC 842 (Admin), [2013] 1 W.L.R. 82, Sir John Thomas (President), DC.

1184. Extradition orders–Inhuman or degrading treatment or punishment–Conditions of detention in US super-maximum security prison–Human rights violation by extreme sentences without parole

[European Convention on Human Rights 1950 Art.3.]

The applicants (X) opposed their extradition to the United States to face terrorism charges claiming a breach of the European Convention on Human Rights 1950 art.3. X had all been indicted in the US on various terrorism charges and the US Government had requested each applicant's extradition. The US issued Diplomatic Notes giving assurances that the US would not seek or carry out the death penalty against X nor designate them as enemy combatants and that, if they were acquitted, proceedings were discontinued, or sentence was served, they would be returned to the UK. X complained that if convicted in the US, they would be detained at ADX Florence (ADX) and would be subjected to special administrative measures. They submitted that (1) conditions of detention at ADX would violate art.3 of the Convention; (2) they would face sentences of life imprisonment without parole and extremely long determinate sentences in violation of art.3 of the Convention. The government submitted that, in the extradition context, a distinction had to be drawn between torture and other forms of ill-treatment. It conceded that a real risk of torture in the receiving state was an absolute bar on extradition but argued that for all other forms of ill-treatment, it was legitimate to consider the policy objectives of extradition in deciding whether the ill-treatment reached the minimum level of severity required by art.3.

Held: Complaints dismissed. (1) Although the conditions at ADX were highly restrictive, there was not complete sensory or social isolation. Consequently, if the first, third, fifth and sixth applicants were extradited to the US, there would be no violation of art.3 as a result of conditions at ADX nor from the imposition of special administrative measures post-trial. (2) Incarceration at ADX was not necessarily indefinite so there was no breach of art.3 from the length of their possible sentences. (3) The applications of the first, third, fourth, fifth and sixth applicants had a similar factual and legal background and were joined; that of the second applicant was adjourned. (4) The Court noted that the House of Lords in *R. (on the application of Wellington) v Secretary of State for the Home Department* [2008] UKHL 72, [2009] 1 A.C. 335, [2009] C.L.Y. 1473 had identified a tension between *Soering v United Kingdom (A/161)* (1989) 11 E.H.R.R. 439, [1989] C.L.Y. 1712 and *Chahal v United Kingdom (22414/93)* (1997) 23 E.H.R.R. 413, [1996] C.L.Y. 3130, which required clarification of the proper approach to art.3 in extradition cases, given the distinctions (a) between extradition cases and other cases of removal from the territory of a contracting state; (b) between torture and other forms of ill-treatment proscribed by art.3; and (c) between the assessment of the minimum level of severity required in the domestic context as opposed to the extra-territorial context, *Wellington* and *Soering* considered, and *Chahal* applied (see para.167 of judgment). (a) A real risk of treatment contrary to art.3 in another state did not depend on the legal basis for removal. In practice, there was little difference between extradition and other removals and it was not be appropriate for a different test to be applied to an extradition case (para.168); (b) No distinction should be made between torture and other forms of ill-treatment, *Chahal* applied and *Mamatkulov v Turkey (46827/99)* (2005) 41 E.H.R.R. 25, [2005] C.L.Y. 2076 and *Saadi v Italy (37201/06)* (2009) 49 E.H.R.R. 30, [2009] C.L.Y. 1984 considered (paras 169-171); (c) There was no room for balancing the risk of ill-treatment against the reasons for expulsion in determining whether a state's responsibility under art.3 was engaged, *Chahal* applied and *Saadi* considered. The correct approach to the assessment of whether the minimum level of severity had been met for the purposes of art.3 was to assess it independently of the reasons for removal or extradition. In the 22 years since *Soering* the Court had never undertaken an examination of the proportionality of a proposed extradition or other form of removal from a contracting state in an art.3 case and had now departed from the approach at paras [89] and [110] of *Soering* (paras 172-173).

AHMAD v UNITED KINGDOM (24027/07); AL-FAWWAZ v UNITED KINGDOM (67354/09); BARY v UNITED KINGDOM (66911/09); MUSTAFA (AKA ABU HAMZA) v UNITED KINGDOM (36742/08); AHSAN v UNITED KINGDOM (11949/08) (2013) 56 E.H.R.R. 1, Judge Garlicki (President), ECHR.

1185. Extradition orders–Mental illness–Risk of suicide if extradited to requesting state–Factors to be taken into account

[Extradition Act 2003 (c.41) s.25, s.91; European Convention on Human Rights 1950 Art.3.]

The appellant requested persons (W, B and R) appealed against orders for their extradition to the requesting states, Poland and Lithuania on the grounds that they might commit suicide by reason of their mental conditions. W and B were issued with European arrest warrants for offences in Poland. W raised the issue of his physical and mental health at his extradition hearing and there was conflicting evidence from psychiatrists as to whether he was at risk of suicide if extradited. The district judge preferred the evidence of one psychiatrist that W was not depressed and found that it would not be unjust or oppressive under the Extradition Act 2003 s.25, to extradite him. In B's case, the district judge, having heard psychiatric evidence as to the risk of suicide, held that his extradition was not barred by reason of his mental health on the basis that the Polish authorities could provide adequate treatment and protection for him. R was requested by Lithuania under a European arrest warrant. At her extradition hearing, a psychiatrist gave evidence on the risk of suicide if she were extradited. The judge received assurances from Lithuania as to the care R would receive there and ordered her extradition. W, B and R appealed on the basis that it was unjust or oppressive to return them to the requesting states under s.25 or it was in breach of the European Convention on Human Rights 1950 art.3. W submitted that the district judge's finding that he preferred the evidence of one psychiatrist was unsustainable. B submitted that there could be no doubt about his serious mental illness and the psychiatric evidence should have been accepted. R submitted that the judge was wrong to find that she did not pose a sufficiently high risk of suicide to amount to oppression.

Held: Appeals dismissed. (1) A useful summary of the approach a court should adopt to s.25 and s.91 was provided in *Turner v United States* [2012] EWHC 2426 (Admin), *Turner* applied. The key issue in almost every case was a consideration of the measures that were in place to prevent a successful attempt at suicide by a requested person with a mental illness. The court looked at the measures to prevent such an attempt in relation to while the requested person was in the United Kingdom, while he was being transferred to the requesting state and when he was received by the requesting state. It was only in a very rare case that a requested person would be likely to establish that measures to prevent a substantial risk of suicide would not be effective. In each case the instant court heard additional psychiatric evidence that was not before the district judge. That was in the interests of justice, in part because of the delay that had elapsed in the hearing of the appeals. The court would in future ordinarily aim to hear such appeals within two to three weeks of the notice of appeal being lodged and parties should be prepared for that (see paras 8, 10, 13-

15 of judgment). (2) In the case of W, the reasons given by the district judge for preferring the evidence of one psychiatrist were clear and fully supported by the evidence. There was nothing to suggest that effective steps could not be taken to mitigate any risk of suicide while he was in custody in the UK and during his removal to Poland. There was no evidence to impugn the ability of the Polish authorities to take similar steps (paras 36, 39-40). (3) It was accepted that B had a serious mental illness but his condition and the risks had been properly managed by the UK authorities and there was no evidence that they could not be properly managed while he was transferred to Poland and by the Polish authorities when he was held there (para.56). (4) It was clear that R was suffering from a mental illness and there was a significant risk of self harm and suicide so the real issue was whether the facilities for dealing with it were adequate during her removal to Lithuania and after her arrival. There was direct evidence of her treatment in Lithuania and it was impossible to contend that the judge was not entitled to reach her conclusion of fact. It was not unjust or oppressive to order her extradition (paras 72-74).

WOLKOWICZ v POLAND; BISKUP v POLAND; RIZLERIENE v LITHUANIA; *sub nom.* POLAND v WOLKOWICZ; POLAND v BISKUP; LITHUANIA v RIZLERIENE, [2013] EWHC 102 (Admin), [2013] 1 W.L.R. 2402, Sir John Thomas (President), QBD (Admin).

1186. Extradition orders–Mistake–Application of s.142 Magistrates' Courts Act 1980 to extradition proceedings

[Extradition Act 2003 (c.41) s.7(6), s.7, s.8A, s.9(1), s.77(1); Magistrates' Courts Act 1980 (c.43) s.142, s.150(5).]

The claimant offender (K) applied for judicial review of a judge's decision to quash, pursuant to the Magistrates' Courts Act 1980 s.142, his earlier order for K's extradition to Latvia. K had been arrested in the United Kingdom on fraud charges. It materialised that he was also wanted under a European arrest warrant issued in Latvia. On K's first appearance in the magistrates' court, the judge complied with the prescribed procedure in the Extradition Act 2003 and, K having given the necessary consent, ordered extradition to take place within 10 days. Unbeknown to the judge, K had been charged the previous day with a further offence committed in the UK. The advocate representing the Crown, who was an interested party in the instant action, had overlooked the charge in her file of papers and had not drawn it to the judge's attention. Had she done so, the judge would have had to adjourn the extradition proceedings under s.8A of the 2003 Act until the domestic criminal proceedings were disposed of. The Crown, relying upon s.7(6) of the 2003 Act, applied to the magistrates' court for K's extradition proceedings to be re-opened under s.142 of the 1980 Act so as to enable the court to adjourn extradition under s.8A. The issue was whether s.142 applied to extradition proceedings. The judge concluded that it did. K submitted that the powers in s.142 were neither directly applicable to extradition proceedings nor imported via s.7(6), s.9(1), or s.77(1) of the 2003 Act.

Held: Application granted. (1) Section 142 did not apply directly to extradition proceedings. It was concerned to provide separate but complementary powers to correct mistakes made, either when sentencing or otherwise dealing with an offender, or when a person was convicted after a trial or on his guilty plea. It would be necessary, to find in favour of the Crown, to construe the word "offender" in s.142(1) as including "alleged offender" because K had neither been convicted of, nor admitted to, the offences for which he was wanted in Latvia. The definition of "offence" in s.150(5) of the 1980 Act included "alleged offence", but that provision could not be read as suggesting that "offender" should include "alleged offender", first because it was not what the definition section actually said, and second, because to do so was inconsistent with other terms in the 1980 Act, where an alleged offender was consistently referred to as an "accused" (see paras 22-23 of judgment). (2) Neither s.9(1), nor s.77(1) of the 2003 Act could import the powers of s.142 into extradition proceedings because both of the former were concerned with the "extradition hearing" and, in the instant case, no extradition hearing had commenced. Section 7(6) was concerned only with the intial hearing relating to an arrested person; the "proceedings" with which the section was concerned were those envisaged within s.7 itself, and s.7(6) had no life once those matters had been completed. Its language was not broad enough to import its powers more generally into extradition proceedings as a whole. More importantly, the 2003 Act provided a self-contained code, with a strict timetable for the completion of each step and for appeals, and if s.142 were available and capable of being read broadly to enable a judge to undo whatever had gone before in the extradition proceedings, that strict timetable would be swept away,*R. (on the application of Mann) v Westminster Magistrates' Court* [2010] EWHC 48 (Admin) considered and *R. (on the application of Berners) v Westminster Magistrates' Court* [2010] EWHC 1010 (Admin), [2010] A.C.D. 58 explained (paras 17-18, 25-30).

R. (ON THE APPLICATION OF KLIMETO) v WESTMINSTER MAGISTRATES' COURT, [2012] EWHC 2051 (Admin), [2013] 1 W.L.R. 420, Hughes, L.J., DC.

1187. Extradition orders–Right to fair trial–Allegations of systematic judicial corruption in Albania–Closer examination of allegations necessary

[Criminal Procedure (Scotland) Act 1995 (c.46) s.34, s.288AA(4); Extradition Act 2003 (c.41); Scotland Act 2012 (c.11) s.36(4); Scotland Act 1998 (c.46) Sch.6 Pt I para.1 (d); European Convention on Human Rights 1950 Art.6.]

The appellant Albanian national (K) appealed against a decision ([2012] HCJAC 84, 2013 S.C.L. 471) that his extradition to Albania would not breach his right to a fair trial under the European Convention on Human Rights 1950 art.6. K was an illegal immigrant. He was suspected of the murder of another Albanian national in England but fled to Scotland and could not be found. The police handed their files of evidence to the Albanian authorities. K was convicted of murder in his absence by an Albanian court and sentenced to 22 years' imprisonment. Several years later K was traced to Glasgow. The Albanian authorities issued an extradition request which was granted by Scottish Ministers. K lodged a devolution minute alleging that he could not receive a fair trial in Albania because of systematic corruption in the judicial system. He relied upon a Foreign and Commonwealth Office Annual Report on Human Rights and other international reports. The Lord Advocate argued that there was nothing in the reports which addressed the issue of whether corruption would lead to a flagrant denial of justice in K's case.

Held: Appeal allowed. (1) The scope of K's appeal depended upon whether the issue was a compatibility issue under the Criminal Procedure (Scotland) Act 1995 s.34 or a devolution issue under the Scotland Act 2012 s.36(4). Extradition proceedings were not "criminal proceedings" for the purpose of s.288AA(4) of the 1995 Act. The roles given to the Scottish Ministers and the Lord Advocate under the Extradition Act 2003 in relation to extradition proceedings in Scotland were separate from those that they were required to perform under the 1995 Act. It followed from the nature of the statutory provisions, under which the Lord Advocate performed his functions in extradition cases, that the issue which gave rise to the instant appeal was a devolution issue as defined by the Scotland Act 1998 Sch.6 Pt I para.1 (d), *H v Lord Advocate* [2012] UKSC 24, [2013] 1 A.C. 413, [2012] C.L.Y. 1289 applied (see paras 16-23 of judgment). (2) Where allegations of corruption were widespread they had to be taken seriously. The threshold test required a flagrant breach of the relevant right, such as would completely deny or nullify the right in the destination country, *Mamatkulov v Turkey (46827/99)* (2005) 41 E.H.R.R. 25, [2005] C.L.Y. 2076, *Othman v United Kingdom (8139/09)* (2012) 55 E.H.R.R. 1, [2012] C.L.Y. 1664, Insanov v Azerbaijan (Application no.16133/08) considered, *Devaseelan v Secretary of State for the Home Department* [2002] UKIAT 702, [2003] Imm. A.R. 1, [2004] C.L.Y. 2013 applied. None of those cases was concerned with the way that the test was to be applied where the complaint was of systematic judicial corruption. The stark fact was that systematic corruption in a judicial system affected everyone who was subjected to it. No tribunal that operated within it could be relied upon to be independent and impartial. It was impossible to say that an individual who was returned to such a system would receive the right to a fair trial, the most fundamental of all the rights provided for by art.6 of the Convention. For those reasons, the allegations that K made were sufficiently serious for it to be necessary to have a closer look at the material in order to determine how systematic or widespread the problem was. The proper course was for the case to be returned to the appeal court so that it could be provided with up-to-date information and reach a properly informed decision as to whether the threshold test was satisfied. Further delay was regrettable but it was of the highest importance that due process be observed where a person's liberty and his right to a fair trial were at issue. Accordingly, the appeal court's interlocutor was recalled and the case was remitted to the High Court of Justiciary for further consideration (paras 28-35).

KAPRI v LORD ADVOCATE; *sub nom.* KAPRI v ALBANIA, [2013] UKSC 48, [2013] 1 W.L.R. 2324, Lord Hope, J.S.C. (Deputy President), SC.

1188. Surrender–Delay–Time limit for surrendering after end of appeals process–Reasonable grounds for delay in surrendering

[Extradition Act 2003 (c.41) s.91, s.118(7), s.118; Human Rights Act 1998 (c.42) s.6; Civil Procedure Rules 1998 (SI 1998/3132) r.52.17.]

The claimant (T) applied for judicial review of a decision of the first defendant magistrates' court to refuse his discharge from extradition proceedings under the Extradition Act 2003 s.118(7), sought to reopen under CPR r.52.17 his statutory appeal against extradition, and sought judicial review of the second defendant secretary of state's decision to extradite him to the United States. T was a former Iranian ambassador. The US had sought his extradition on charges relating to the export of defence articles. The court rejected his appeal under s.91 based on his medical condition; the High Court refused to certify a point of general public importance in May 2008. Before he could be surrendered, T was admitted to hospital; the secretary of state acknowledged that she should consider new medical information as part of her obligation under the Human Rights Act 1998 s.6 to act compatibly with T's human rights. By January 2009, she had concluded that T's medical condition was not such as to render his extradition unlawful under s.6. She asked the US to consider withdrawing its extradition request because of its diplomatic impact. Despite repeated requests, the US did not tell the secretary of state of its refusal to withdraw until September 2011. The secretary of state decided in November 2011 that she had no option but to surrender T. The secretary of state argued that since T had sought an extra-statutory decision as to his medical condition after the dismissal of his appeal, the extradition process had continued running, so the 28-day period to effect surrender under s.118 ran from her November 2011 decision; any further delay was attributable to the instant proceedings.

Held: Applications granted in part. (1) Section 118 stated that the 28 days was to run from the day on which the decision of the relevant court became final. It did not contemplate any extra-statutory decision necessary to fulfil human rights obligations. No exception for situations when the proposed extraditee instituted judicial review proceedings could be read into s.118. The statutory scheme had removed the secretary of state's discretion in that regard. Time had started to run when s.118 said it did, namely May 2008, when the High Court refused to certify a point of general importance (see paras 20-25 of judgment). There was, however, room for extra-statutory consideration by the secretary of state, but any such consideration was subject to the court's judgement as to whether reasonable cause had been shown for delay following conclusion of the appeal process. The court was required to look at all the circumstances to decide whether there had been reasonable cause. By January 2009 the secretary of state had been in a position to reach her decision as to T's health. The reason for delay thereafter was the decision to ask the US to withdraw its request. No explanation had been given for the US' failure to answer requests as to whether it would withdraw. The inference was inescapable that the US had not wished to decide between 2009 and August 2011, but chose to commit itself at a time it regarded as convenient. The request to ask the US to withdraw was justified and was reasonable cause for some further delay after January 2009, but thereafter, no explanation other than the US' failure to respond had been offered. It was not open to either the United Kingdom or the requesting country to extradite at a time of its own choosing without offering justification for delay. To allow the approach taken by the US would undermine the structure of the 2003 Act. No reasonable cause had been shown for the delay; the magistrates' court's decision would be quashed and T would be discharged (paras 26-32, 38-50). (2) In the light of the construction of s.118, it was unnecessary to reopen the statutory appeal in order to avoid real injustice. Consideration of s.118(7) required consideration of all the circumstances; those included a consideration of the justice of extradition in the light of the circumstances leading to delay. There was no need for further consideration of those questions (para.53). (3) (Obiter) If the only issue was T's physical and mental condition after the substantial delay, the secretary of state's consideration afforded him an effective remedy and there would be no need to re-open the appeal, *Taylor v Governor of Wandsworth Prison* [2009] EWHC 1020 (Admin), [2009] Extradition L.R. 287 considered. There had been full legal analysis and assessment of the evidence in the secretary of state's decision; it could not be impugned. The issue of whether, because of the passage of time, it would be oppressive to extradite T was not an issue within the secretary of state's consideration. However, it would not have been oppressive: T had been under no illusion that there was a serious likelihood that he would be surrendered and had not therefore had any false hope caused by the delay (paras 54-57, 63-76).

R. (ON THE APPLICATION OF TAJIK) v CITY OF WESTMINSTER MAGISTRATES' COURT; TAJIK v UNITED STATES; R. (ON THE APPLICATION OF TAJIK) v SECRETARY OF STATE FOR THE HOME DEPARTMENT, [2012] EWHC 3347 (Admin), [2013] 1 W.L.R. 2283, Moses, L.J., DC.

FAMILY LAW

1189. Adoption–Adoption orders–Mother's opposition to adoption order–Detrimental CAFCASS report not disclosed to mother–Effect of procedural irregularity on fairness of order

[Adoption and Children Act 2002 (c.38) s.47(5), s.47(7).]

The appellant mother (M) appealed against a decision making an adoption order in respect of her child (T) and dismissing her application for permission to oppose the grant of that order. M and T's father had served prison sentences for offences relating to T's older siblings. T was made subject to a care and placement order and placed with her prospective adopters. They applied for an adoption order, and T applied for permission to oppose the grant of that order under the Adoption and Children Act 2002 s.47(5). The judge adjourned those applications, and appointed a CAFCASS officer, the respondent, as T's guardian. The guardian produced a report of an interview with M, which alleged that her circumstances had deteriorated since the care and placement order had been made. M never had an opportunity to read that report. At the hearing, where M was unrepresented, the judge dismissed her application under s.47(7) on the basis that her circumstances had not changed for the better, but had actually worsened as alleged in the report. M submitted that, in accordance with principles in *D (Minors) (Adoption Reports: Confidentiality), Re* [1996] A.C. 593, [1996] C.L.Y. 474, the judge had erred in not allowing M an opportunity to read the report which prejudiced her application. The guardian contended that, while she accepted that there had been procedural deficiencies, the orders should not be set aside because M had no case on which she could hope to succeed, and accordingly remitting the case would waste time and money and subject T's adopters to unnecessary anxiety.

Held: Appeal allowed. There was no doubt that the procedural deficiency was too grave to uphold the result reached on the judge's exercise of discretion. The judge had been unaware that M had not read the report, but her lack of representation meant she could not draw the deficiency to the judge's attention. The proper approach was to set aside the orders and direct a retrial before a different judge.

T (A CHILD), *Re*, [2012] EWCA Civ 191, [2013] 1 F.L.R. 360, Thorpe, L.J., CA (Civ Div).

1190. Adoption–Adoption orders–Whether adoption order in respect of baby girl open to challenge

The appellant parents (M and F) appealed against a care order and a placement-for-adoption order which had been made in respect of their baby daughter (S). Care proceedings had previously been issued in respect of three older children of M. They were now aged seven, five and three. The judge concluded that it was not safe to return those three girls to the family and placement-for-adoption orders were made in respect of them shortly before S was born. A psychiatrist had formed the view that M suffered from an emotional and unstable personality disorder; it was stated that M acted in a way which was impulsive and, from a young child's point of view, on occasions harmful; while she might not wish to act in that way, her own self-motivation at those moments took over and prevented her from being a safe and good parent.

Held: Appeal dismissed. The judge who had made the challenged orders in respect of S had given a careful and thoughtful judgment. It was not a case that pointed all one way, factors in favour of the parents having been identified: among other things, both had made "considerable efforts" to engage in relevant treatment; they had remained together; further, they had been subject to significant pressure through the course of the proceedings. On the other hand, factors militating against their case existed. The judge had to evaluate their potential for care, not just on the basis of whether they were able to show progress, but with an eye on what had happened to the three older girls. Although that harm was in the past, it was significant harm; this had been bad and harmful parenting, albeit delivered in a way which was neither deliberate nor malevolent. Further, all the professional evidence pointed away from M and F. The judge had also concluded that neither M nor F could be trusted to be open and frank with the local authority should S live with them. M and F deserved enormous sympathy, and it was to be hoped that they would continue with their positive progress, but there was no basis on which it was possible to say that the judge had been plainly wrong in making the orders that he had (see paras 36-37, 39-41 of judgment).

W (A CHILD) (CARE PROCEEDINGS: CONSIDERATION OF PARENTS AS CARERS), *Re*, [2012] EWCA Civ 1828, [2013] 1 F.L.R. 1500, Pill, L.J., CA (Civ Div).

1191. Adoption–Costs between the parties–Protracted adoption proceedings owing to lack of support of placement by local authority–Adoptive parent not eligible for legal aid–Court's powers to make costs order against local authority in absence of unreasonable or reprehensible conduct

[Family Procedure Rules 2010 (SI 2010/2955).]

The applicant (Z), who had adopted her eight-year-old niece (C), applied for an order that the respondent local authority pay her costs for the latter part of the proceedings. C had been brought up by her parents in an environment involving a serious risk to life. A foster placement did not go well. In June 2010, Z volunteered herself as C's carer. The local authority was vehemently opposed to C living with any family member. However, the court made an interim care order in Z's favour on the basis that it was C's only chance of stability. That order involved C and Z moving to a secret address, and Z liaising with various local authority departments, the court, and C's school while holding down full-time employment in which she earned £29,000 gross per annum, narrowly above the legal aid threshold. The relationship between Z and social services was not harmonious and despite a recommendation by a psychiatrist for C's long term placement with Z, the local authority did not support the placement for around 18 months, by which time Z had incurred legal fees of around £23,000. She had asked the local authority for financial assistance, which they had repeatedly declined until two weeks before the final hearing, when they offered £2,000 after approving her as an adopter. The issue was whether it was appropriate for the court to make a costs order against the local authority in favour of a litigant who needed, but could not afford, legal representation. The local authority disputed an order for costs on the grounds that its conduct had not been reprehensible or unreasonable; there had been no need for Z to receive legal advice; there had been no displacement of the general proposition that there should be no order for costs; and it was inappropriate in principle for a local authority to be used as a secondary funding authority in cases where Parliament had decided that litigants were not entitled to public funding.

Held: Application granted. Z's position needed to be acknowledged. C had been placed with her in a highly charged situation where the placement had been largely opposed and Z had been overloaded with the demands of settling in and looking after a disturbed child, disclosing to her only part of what had happened within her family, and preserving the secrecy of the placement against both family members and outsiders. As well as holding down a full-time job and having to deal with a range of professionals whose support was uncertain, Z had been expected to participate in the instant proceedings without having the means to do so. She was the most important adult participant and the only one who was not publicly funded. She had plainly needed legal advice and representation at, and between, hearings, otherwise C's placement would have been jeopardised. The proceedings had been active for longer than they might have been because the local authority had been slow to recognise that the placement was worthy of their support. While it had not behaved unreasonably or reprehensibly, it could have acted differently to reduce the need for legal representation. The offer of £2,000, which would be appropriate for formal advice in a straightforward adoption, did not meet the needs of the instant case. One aspect of dealing with a case justly pursuant to the overriding objective in the Family Procedure Rules 2010 was by ensuring, as far as practicable, that the parties were on an equal footing. Z was also entitled to a right of effective access to the court. Therefore an order had to be made which was just in the circumstances and which reflected the conduct of the parties. It was unusual to order costs in children cases, but the circumstances in which that was possible were not limited to the exceptions established in *Sutton LBC v Davis (No.2)* [1994] 1 W.L.R. 1317, [1995] C.L.Y. 4005, *Sutton* considered. The fact that local authorities exercised their discretion to offer discretionary funding to candidates chosen as adopters amounted to a practical acceptance that they had to step in and bridge a funding gap occasionally. Their discretion with regard to the funding of adopters could not exclude the court's power to make wider provision for those who were chosen late or those who were never chosen, but who did succeed in becoming adopters. Whilst a local authority was not to be treated as a secondary funding authority for litigants who were not entitled to public funding, the court could make an order for costs where the individual circumstances made it just to do so. That would only be in exceptional cases, of which the instant case was one. The appropriate contribution was one half of Z's costs.

A LOCAL AUTHORITY v C, [2012] EWHC 1637 (Fam), [2012] 2 F.L.R. 1087, Peter Jackson, J., Fam Div.

1192. Adoption–Freeing orders–Local authority abandoning adoption plan and failing to revoke freeing orders–Breach of art.3, art.6 and art.8 European Convention on Human Rights 1950–Importance of local authority responding to failed placement orders and freeing orders

[Adoption and Children Act 2002 (c.38) s.24; Human Rights Act 1998 (c.42) s.8(1); European Convention on Human Rights 1950 Art.3, Art.6, Art.8.]

The claimant children (X) sought declarations pursuant to the Human Rights Act 1998 s.8(1) that the respondent local authority and an independent reviewing officer (IRO) had breached their rights under the European Convention on

Human Rights 1950 art.3, art.6 and art.8. X had been removed from their birth mother and placed into the local authority's care in their early infancy. The local authority obtained freeing orders which freed X for adoption and thereby ended their membership of their birth family. Three years later, having failed to find X an adoptive family, the local authority abandoned the adoption plan and its search for adopters in favour of long-term fostering, but it did not apply to revoke the freeing orders. X's IRO was subsequently appointed. The freeing orders remained in place for 10 years which meant that, over that period, there was no natural person with parental responsibility for X. X were regularly moved between placements over those 10 years, sometimes because they had suffered abuse at the hands of their foster parents, and they suffered from psychological difficulties as a result of their turbulent care history. The local authority and the IRO accepted that they had breached X's rights under art.3, art.6 and art.8.

Held: Declaration granted in favour of claimants. (1) The court made declarations that the local authority and the IRO had acted incompatibly with X's rights under art.3, art.6 and art.8. The local authority's failure to revoke the freeing orders meant that X's status was not returned to being children under care orders, and accordingly they lost their links with their birth family without gaining a new family of their own (see paras 12,124 of judgment). (2) (Obiter) Freeing orders had not been available for more than six years at the time of the instant hearing, and accordingly any child who remained "freed" had lacked a legal tie to any natural person for more than six years. If freeing orders were still in place in respect of any child, it was not a true reflection of their care plan. When children, such as X, were left with an incorrect legal status, it had significant welfare consequences for them. It was not the instant court's role to require local authorities who were not before it to disclose information about children in their care in order to ascertain whether any freeing orders were still in place. However, it did have a responsibility to bring the situation to wider attention, and sent a copy of the instant judgment to the Children's Commissioner, the President of the Family Division and to designated family judges. The instant case also highlighted the position of children who were living under failed placement orders: the Adoption and Children Act 2002 s.24 provided a means by which local authorities could apply to revoke failed placement orders, and the instant case illustrated how important it was for local authorities to follow that statutory route and bring changes of placement orders back to court where adoption orders were not pursued or where an adoption failed. Further, whilst respite care would continue to be an essential element in many foster placements, it was important that the impact on the looked-after child was considered alongside the benefits to the foster carers and the placement overall (paras 147-150, 163-165, 167). (3) (Obiter) In light of the fact that the IRO had not acted in X's interests by his failure to monitor, persuade, cajole, encourage or criticise his fellow professionals, the local authority needed to invigorate its independent reviewing system (paras 168, 170).

A v LANCASHIRE CC, [2012] EWHC 1689 (Fam), [2013] 2 F.L.R. 803, Peter Jackson, J., Fam Div.

1193. Adoption–Grandparents–Whether judge erred in declining to order further assessment of grandparents as carers

[Children Act 1989 (c.41).]

The appellant grandparents (G) appealed against a decision to place their infant grandson (M) for adoption rather than deferring that decision pending a further assessment of them as his potential carers. G had had four children, two of whom were raised in exemplary fashion and were thriving as adults, and two who had learning disabilities and had fared less well. When one of the latter children had M, she rejected the first respondent local authority's offer of a place with him in a secure setting, and M was taken into care. The local authority's care plan was to place M for adoption using a combination of care and placement orders. That was supported by the second respondent guardian. A joint expert report from a psychologist made it clear that M should not be placed with G and that any delay in determining M's future would be detrimental to him. G's suggestion that there should be further assessment of their ability to care for M was first raised at the hearing of the local authority's application for final orders. By the time of that hearing, M was seven months old. The judge noted that, as a result of his mother's decision, M had never lived with his family, and that any further delay would be prejudicial to M. He indicated that he understood G's argument as to their parenting ability, but that he did not think M's placement with them was realistic. The judge acknowledged that wherever possible it was always better for a child to grow up in his birth family, but found that the instant case was one of those where that was not a possibility. He therefore concluded that there was no real option other than to grant a final care order to place M for adoption. G contended that the judge was plainly wrong in having insufficiently considered the virtues and potential that they offered M, and that he had placed too much reliance on what were perceived by the local authority to be their failings and weaknesses. The guardian emphasised that it was difficult to see the purpose of directing further assessment of G, given that they had raised two of their children successfully.

Held: Appeal dismissed. (1) It was always tempting for an appellate court to wonder if it might not have decided an issue differently, but it had always to guard against substituting its discretion for that of the trial judge who alone had seen and heard the witnesses and been influenced by the impression they had made. That influence was a fundamental part of decision-making at first instance. It was exceptionally rare for the Court of Appeal to declare that a judge was plainly wrong, especially in respect of the weight he had given to different factors. The instant case was a very sad one. The judge's conclusion that he really had no option but to grant the local authority's applications was a product of a decision-making process in which he had recognised all of the difficulties G would face and the risk of their failure, and that all they sought was a period of further assessment. Given that that would lead to inevitable delay, which the expert had cautioned against, the judge had had no alternative but to make the order he had. His options had become very circumscribed. The tragic fact was that M's mother had cast the die in rejecting the offer of a placement with M. The judge was not, therefore, considering whether to remove M from G's care, only whether he should place M with them. In all the circumstances, the judge had been entitled to come to the conclusion he had. (2) (Per Lewison, L.J.) The judge had to choose the least worst outcome between further assessment or a final order for placement and adoption, in effect, between uncertainty and finality. Given the emphasis the Children Act 1989 placed on the detriment to a small child caused by delay, the decision to make final orders was one the judge was entitled to reach.

C (A CHILD) (ADOPTION: ASSESSMENT OF GRANDPARENTS), *Re*, [2012] EWCA Civ 1787, [2013] 2 F.L.R. 59, Thorpe, L.J., CA (Civ Div).

1194. Adoption–Intercountry adoption–Recognition of Indian private placement adoption

[Adoption and Children Act 2002 (c.38) s.49; Convention on Protection of Children and Co-operation in respect of Intercountry Adoption (Hague XXXIII) 1993.]

The applicant married couple (H and W) applied for recognition in the United Kingdom of their adoption in India of a child (R). W was a British citizen and H was born in India but had indefinite leave to remain in the UK. They had adopted R through a private placement, considered by the Indian authorities to be outside the scope of the Hague Convention on Protection of Children and Co-operation in respect of Intercountry Adoption 1993, so that it could not be automatically recognised in the United Kingdom. The Indian court had made an order for recognition of the adoption. That procedure included a home circumstances report, an investigation and the hearing of oral evidence. H contended that he had not lost his domicile of origin in India. R's admission to the UK to live with H and W depended on the court's recognition of the Indian adoption. The court was bound by *Valentine's Settlement, Re* [1965] Ch. 831, [1965] C.L.Y. 3556 which decided that questions of status were dependent on domicile and refused to recognise a South African adoption on the basis that the adoptive father was domiciled in Rhodesia. H and W submitted that changes in the law had occurred since *Valentine*, in particular the concept of a married woman's dependent domicile had been abolished and the qualifying conditions for adoption were since governed by the Adoption and Children Act 2002 s.49 which provided that only one of the couple needed to be domiciled in the UK.

Held: Application granted. The ratio of *Valentine* was that the court would recognise an order affecting status only where the conditions existed which permitted a domestic court to make such an order, *Valentine* followed. It was clear that H had retained his domicile of origin in India but W was domiciled in the UK, *Cyganik v Agulian* [2006] EWCA Civ 129, [2006] 1 F.C.R. 406, [2006] C.L.Y. 4082 followed. The requirement of *Valentine* was met in the instant case and accordingly the court had jurisdiction to recognise the Indian adoption. The Indian adoption, after full enquiry and recognition in India, was sufficiently similar to the concept of adoption in the UK and there were no public policy objections to recognition in the UK (see paras 16-22 of judgment).

R (A CHILD) (RECOGNITION OF INDIAN ADOPTION), *Re*, [2012] EWHC 2956 (Fam), [2013] 1 F.L.R. 1487, Hedley, J., Fam Div.

1195. Adoption–Intercountry adoption–Validity of Indian adoption order–Factors for consideration in granting declaration of validity

[Adoption and Children Act 2002 (c.38) s.1.]

The applicants (X), an Indian couple living in the United Kingdom, applied for a declaration recognising the validity of an Indian adoption order. X had offered to adopt the newborn baby of relatives (R) living in India. The agreement to do so had been reached before the baby was born. A couple of months after the birth X and R undertook a religious adoption ceremony in India. The adoption was registered by deed in the local court. The baby came to the UK with R on a visitor's visa. R returned to India shortly afterwards, and X made the instant application. R acknowledged service of the application and indicated that they had no intention of opposing the order sought. The baby was made a ward of court and the local authority safeguarding report recommended that she remain permanently with X. Expert evidence on Hindu adoptions confirmed that the adoption was valid and entitled to UK recognition. The UK Border Agency indicated that they had no wish to intervene in the case.

Held: Declaration granted. (1) A foreign adoption order could only be recognised if the adopting parents were domiciled in India at the relevant time. Both of X had given evidence that they considered themselves to be Indian domiciled. That evidence was accepted by the court. The court also accepted that the adoption order had been lawfully obtained in the Indian jurisdiction and that the concept of adoption in that jurisdiction substantially conformed to the English concept, the baby being deemed to be the child of the adoptive parents for all purposes with effect from the adoption date. There were no public policy considerations to militate against recognition as UKBA had no intention of intervening in the proceedings. The test in *T v OCC* [2010] EWHC 964 (Fam), [2011] 1 F.L.R. 1487 was therefore satisfied, *T v OCC* applied (see paras 10-15 of judgment). (2) Pursuant to the Adoption and Children Act 2002 s.1, the court was satisfied that recognition of the adoption would promote the baby's welfare throughout her life. She was thriving in the care of loving parents who had her best interests at the centre of their lives (para.16). (3) It was not necessary for CAFCASS to undertake standard welfare inquiries because they were undertaken by the relevant local authority. The role of CAFCASS in future such cases was to act as advocate to the court, not to perform an investigatory function (para.17).

J (RECOGNITION OF FOREIGN ADOPTION ORDER), *Re*, [2012] EWHC 3353 (Fam), [2013] 2 F.L.R. 298, Moor, J., Fam Div.

1196. Adoption–Parental consent–Guidance to social workers in relation to obtaining parent's consent to removal to local authority care under s.20 Children Act 1989

[Adoption and Children Act 2002 (c.38) s.52; Children Act 1989 (c.41) s.20; Human Rights Act 1998 (c.42) s.7; Mental Capacity Act 2005 (c.9) s.3.]

The applicant local authority applied for care and adoption orders in respect of a child (C). C's mother (M) sought her immediate return. C had been removed from M on the day of her birth, with M's consent having been obtained under the Children Act 1989 s.20. M had significant learning difficulties and had endured a disruptive childhood and adolescence which left her vulnerable and devoid of parenting instincts. Her three other children had been placed for adoption. C had been placed with prospective adopters. The local authority conceded M's claim under the Human Rights Act 1998 s.7. It acknowledged that a s.20 consent should not have been sought on the day of C's birth, and that C's removal had not been a proportionate response to the risks that existed at that time.

Held: Applications granted. (1) C's future welfare could only be promoted by her being in permanent substitute care. M was unable to provide for her needs, and would be unable to learn to do so in any appropriate timescale. It followed that, in the acknowledged absence of any other family member to care for C, the care order had to be made. C's future permanent care would be best secured by adoption and a placement order would be made. The court was satisfied, under the Adoption and Children Act 2002 s.52, that C's welfare required M's consent to be dispensed with (see paras 19-20 of judgment). (2) Although the court should be careful to avoid excessive prescription when offering guidance to social workers in respect of obtaining parental consent under s.20 to the removal of a child immediately or soon after birth, there were important aspects, namely that (a) every parent had a right, if capacitous, to exercise their parental responsibility to consent under s.20 to have their child accommodated by the local authority, and every local authority had the power under s.20(4) so to accommodate, provided that it was consistent with the child's welfare; (b) every social worker obtaining consent was under a personal duty to be satisfied that the person giving consent did not lack the required capacity; (c) the social worker had to actively address the issue of capacity, take into account all the prevailing circumstances and consider the questions raised by the Mental Capacity Act 2005 s.3, and in particular the mother's capacity to use and weigh all the relevant information; (d) if the social worker had doubts about capacity, no further attempt should be made to obtain consent on that occasion, and advice should be sought from the social work team leader or management; (e) if the social worker was satisfied that the person did not lack capacity, they had to be satisfied that the consent was fully informed. That involved questioning whether the parent fully understood the consequences of giving such a consent, whether they fully appreciated the range of choices available and the consequences of refusal, and whether the parent was in possession of all the facts and issues material to the giving of consent; (f) if not satisfied that the answers to those questions were all "yes", no further attempt should be made to obtain consent on that occasion, advice should be sought and the social work team should further consider taking legal advice if thought necessary; (g) if satisfied that the consent was fully informed, the social worker also had to be satisfied that the giving of such consent and the subsequent removal was both fair and proportionate; (h) in considering that, it might be necessary to ask what the current physical and psychological state of the parent was, whether they had a solicitor, whether they had been encouraged to seek legal advice and/or advice from family or friends, whether it was necessary for the safety of the child for them to be removed at that time, and whether it would be fairer for the matter to be the subject of a court order rather than an agreement; (i) if, having done all that and, if necessary, having taken further advice, including where necessary legal advice, the social worker considered that a fully informed consent had been received from a capacitous mother in circumstances where removal was necessary and proportionate, consent could be acted upon; (j) local authorities might want to approach with great care the obtaining of s.20

consent from mothers in the aftermath of birth, especially where there was no immediate danger to the child and where it was probable that no order would be made (paras 45-46). (3) The guidance was not intended to cast doubt on or discourage the use of s.20 consent from capacitous parents in circumstances where it was perfectly proper to seek agreement to immediate post-birth accommodation (paras 36, 47).

COVENTRY CITY COUNCIL v C, [2012] EWHC 2190 (Fam), [2013] 2 F.L.R. 987, Hedley, J., Fam Div.

1197. Adoption–Parental consent–Withholding of consent–Whether adoption "required"–Benefits of Scottish system

[Adoption and Children Act 2002 (c.38) s.52(1)(b); European Convention on Human Rights 1950.]

The applicant (X) applied for an adoption order in respect of a six-year-old child (Z). Z had been removed from the care of her mother (M) at the age of four months under a child protection order made in Glasgow. M and Z's father (F), a failed asylum-seeker from Africa, had separated shortly after Z's birth. Z was placed with a foster carer and remained with her until placed with X at her home in London in April 2011. A number of children's hearings had taken place in Scotland; the hearing which took place in March 2011 authorised Z's placement with X, and at a hearing in October 2011 the local authority's adoption plan, whereby Z would be adopted by X, was approved. The adoption application was strongly supported by the guardian. However, it was resisted by M and F, chiefly on the ground that their rights under the European Convention on Human Rights 1950 had been comprehensively violated by the process in Scotland.

Held: Application granted. (1) By virtue of the Adoption and Children Act 2002 s.52(1)(b), the court could not dispense with M and F's consent unless Z's welfare required their consent to be dispensed with. The question was whether adoption was "required". If a measure short of adoption would meet the welfare needs of the child, it could not be said that adoption was "required". The decision was crystal clear. M and F were total strangers to Z. Their only connection to her was biological. There was no psychological or emotional connection whatsoever. So far as nurture, as opposed to nature, was concerned, Z's upbringing had been entrusted to others. X, who was plainly an eminently suitable person to adopt Z, was her true parent in every sense of the word other than biological. And Z's welfare demanded that that simple truth should be formalised by adoption. Any measure short of adoption was likely to foster in Z's mind with her growing maturity the thought that the commitment of both the state and of X to the security of her future was questionable. Above all, she needed permanence and normality, which could only be achieved by adoption (see paras 52, 61, 63 of judgment). (2) The assault on the processes in Scotland which led to Z's placement in England was completely misguided. All comparisons were odious but it should be said that a system like the Scottish system that embraced informality and eschewed the black-letter formality of an adversarial expert-evidence based contest had much to recommend it. It was very clear that at all stages M and F's Convention rights had been faithfully observed by the judicial and other state authorities in Scotland (para.64).

Z (ADOPTION: SCOTTISH CHILD PLACED IN ENGLAND: CONVENTION COMPLIANCE), *Re*, [2012] EWHC 2404 (Fam), [2013] 1 F.L.R. 618, Mostyn, J., Fam Div.

1198. Adoption–Placement orders–Failure to engage prospective adopters in placement proceedings–Procedural impropriety

The appellant parents (P) appealed against a care order and placement order made in respect of one of their children on the application of the respondent local authority. The child (X) was almost four years old. Care proceedings had begun in 2009 in respect of all five minor children of the family. In relation to X there was evidence of a significant failure to thrive, and when he was aged about one he was taken into foster care, where he remained. After a judicial fact-finding process and a multi-disciplinary assessment, it was decided that the four older children could be in the home but subject to intensive support. It was decided that X should not return to live with P. By that time a couple (B), who were X's aunt and her husband, had expressed their willingness to provide a home for him. The local authority conducted an assessment of B, the result of which was essentially positive. The afternoon before the relevant hearing P's solicitors called B and told them that they should attend, but at short notice they could not, due to work commitments. At the hearing P applied for an adjournment so the court could clarify B's position. The local authority and guardian opposed that. The judge gave a short judgment in which he referred to the assessment of B, and the fact that B had not attended or intervened or sent a statement to court or applied to intervene. He said that as the proceedings had already been very lengthy, X could wait no longer for a final decision. He made a placement order. P appealed against that decision, and B attended the appeal at the court's invitation.

Held: Appeal allowed. The procedure had fallen short of what was sufficient, for B's interests and above all for X's. It was a watershed decision for X and a procedurally sound approach was needed. The judge had been factually entirely correct in what he said about B's lack of involvement before the hearing and their absence at court, but in order to place substantial weight on their absence it was necessary for the court or the local authority to have given a timely warning to B that they should engage with the hearing. That was not done. It would have been entirely possible at earlier hearings in the proceedings for the court to invite them to attend at the next one. Further, B had been entitled to think that the local authority was still considering X's placement with them and would be in contact with them. There had been no process at all to engage B. Although it seemed that the judge had considered whether to adjourn, he did not refer to that issue in his judgment. The issue was whether to press on or to allow a relatively short adjournment, of perhaps a month or two, to allow B to take part. That balancing exercise had not been at the forefront of the judge's mind. He was making a draconian order and the process needed to be fair and proper, so a comparatively short adjournment was both necessary and proportionate. The case would be remitted to a different judge. Although there were many advantages in a case being retained by a judge who had been steeped in it for a long time, in this case the judge had expressed in very strong terms his view that a placement order was required, so a new judge was needed.

P (CHILDREN) (CARE PROCEEDINGS), *Re*, [2012] EWCA Civ 401, [2012] 2 F.L.R. 1184, Ward, L.J., CA (Civ Div).

1199. Adoption–Placement orders–Revocation–Assessing parents' ability to provide good enough parenting within appropriate timescale–Difference between making findings of fact about past and predictions about future

[Adoption and Children Act 2002 (c.38) s.24.]

The appellant mother (M) appealed against the dismissal of her application to revoke placement orders made in respect of her two sons (X and Y) pursuant to the Adoption and Children Act 2002 s.24. X and Y were aged six and four-and-a-half respectively. They had been placed in foster care in April 2010, following concerns about their parents' long-standing alcohol abuse and consequent inability to look after them, and their father's violence towards M. Care and placement orders were made in September 2011, the judge finding that M had an alcohol problem about which she was in denial, and which impeded her ability to care for X and Y. In April 2012 an adoptive placement was identified. That August, M sought revocation of the placement orders. She had by then separated from the boys' father, acknowledged that she had a drink problem and arranged to undergo a course of psychotherapy. She claimed to be alcohol-free. The judge found that X and Y needed a permanent placement and there could be no delay. He indicated that before he could return them to M he would need a high degree of confidence that their return was achievable, and a high level of confidence that M's rehabilitation from alcohol dependency would be successful. However, he concluded that, on the balance of probabilities, he could not find either that M would remain alcohol free or that she would develop the necessary insight into the boys' needs in an appropriate timescale. M submitted that the judge had applied the wrong test, requiring her to cross too high a threshold.

Held: Appeal dismissed. The judge's decision was unimpeachable. M's argument was based on the proposition that the judge had to ask himself whether there was a good chance that she would be able to parent safely and adequately within an appropriate timeframe. In fact, what the judge had to ask himself was what arrangement was in the best interests of the children for the rest of their lives. In answering that, he had to exercise his judgment on a range of issues, including his findings of fact about the past, and his assessment of what might happen in the future. The question of whether M was able to provide "good enough" parenting was a major issue. The factors to be assessed were, principally, the likelihood of her rehabilitation from alcohol dependence, and her ability to develop insight into the boys' needs. When the judge heard the evidence, M had been alcohol-free for seven months but was still deeply preoccupied with her own difficulties. She had not begun to develop the requisite sensitivity to the children's needs, and the judge had therefore been right to consider the prospects of her rehabilitation separately from her ability to develop insight. In terms of her recovery from alcohol dependence, the prognosis was "good, but guarded" and the experts agreed that it was too early to be confident of a successful outcome. While there was thus some cause for optimism, the judge had been entitled to take the pessimistic view that he did. Rehabilitation aside, there remained the problem of M's lack of insight. In that respect, the experts were less able to assist. Psychotherapy had been suggested at a fairly late stage in the evidence, no work on insight had begun, and there was no assessment of the prospects of success. The forecast was that psychotherapy might not work, but that if it did, it would take between 6 and 12 months. It was thus not surprising that the judge was unable to find that M would develop the necessary insight within a timescale appropriate for the children. Both in that respect, and in relation to rehabilitation, it would have been better had he not used the phrase "balance of probabilities": he was not making a finding of fact, but was assessing future risk. In any event, though, anything other than a fairly pessimistic view would have been perverse. The uncertainties had brought the judge to the inevitable conclusion that it would be too risky for the children to lose the opportunity of an immediate adoption in favour of awaiting the uncertain outcome of M's therapy. In those circumstances, he was right to say that he needed a high degree of confidence that M would remain alcohol free (see paras 57-63 of judgment). (2) (Per Black L.J.) There was a difference between making findings of fact about the past and making predictions about the future. In dealing with the past, the court's task was to see what facts were established on the balance of probability. When it came to the future, the exercise was rather different. Where the child's history had been damaging and it was critical for him to be in a long-term, dependable placement without further delay, the judge was likely to look for a greater degree of certainty than he might otherwise in relation to the parent's ability to provide a safe and appropriate home. He might express his prediction in various ways, and there was nothing wrong with him looking, in an appropriate case, for a "very high level of confidence" (paras 80-83).

MA v CAMDEN LBC, [2012] EWCA Civ 1340, [2013] 2 F.L.R. 883, Longmore, L.J., CA (Civ Div).

1200. Adoption–Placement orders–Revocation–Guidance on management of applications to revoke placement orders

[Adoption Act 1976 (c.36) s.18(6), s.18(1), s.20(3)(b), s.20; Children Act 1989 (c.41) s.31; Legal Aid, Sentencing and Punishment of Offenders Act 2012 (c.10) s.10, Sch.1 Pt 1; European Convention on Human Rights 1950 Art.6, Art.8.]

The applicant local authority applied for the revocation of an order freeing the third respondent child (J) from adoption. J had been the subject of a care order made under the Children Act 1989 s.31 followed by an order under the Adoption Act 1976 s.18(1) declaring him free for adoption, upon which parental responsibility vested in the local authority and the first respondent mother (C) and the second respondent father (W) became "former parents". J's adoption placement broke down and was terminated in 2007, since when he had been in long-term foster care. J had had no contact with C or W since being placed for adoption in 2006. In 2012, the freeing order was revoked and an interim care order imposed. At that hearing, W indicated his wish to have contact with J, but failed to respond to subsequent attempts from J's social worker to contact him. The case was adjourned to determine the issue of the form of order which would be made after the revocation of the freeing order.

Held: Application granted. (1) The court had the power to revoke the freeing order, *J (A Child) (Freeing for Adoption), Re* [2000] 2 F.L.R. 58, [2000] C.L.Y. 2432 and *C (A Minor) (Adoption: Freeing Order), Re* [1999] Fam. 240, [1998] C.L.Y. 2366 applied. Further, s.20(3)(iia) of the 1976 Act was only capable of one interpretation; in the context of the instant case, the full care order made immediately before the freeing order would be restored, and thus the interim care order was discharged. Accordingly, the full care order would determine J's legal status following the court's exercise of its inherent jurisdiction to revoke the freeing order. Section 20(3)(iia) was unambiguous and did not provide the court with any residual discretion. Restoration of the full care order was not incompatible with the European Convention on Human Rights 1950 art.6 or art.8; s.20(3)(b) of the 1976 Act also reinstated parental responsibility to C and W, the former parents, who were entitled to apply for discharge of the care order or contact (see paras 18, 29, 30, 32, 43 of judgment). (2) Irrespective of the fact that former parents might have signed a s.18(6) declaration when the freeing order was made, all former parents, save in exceptional circumstances, should be served with an application to revoke a freeing order (para.37). (3) In relation to funding for reinstated parents, from April 2013 onwards, parents would not be eligible for public funding in respect of applications to revoke freeing or placement orders as they were not civil legal aid services described within the Legal Aid, Sentencing and Punishment of Offenders Act 2012 Sch.1 Pt 1. Subject to a means test and merits assessment, public funding would be available to parents seeking to discharge a care order or applying for contact to a child in care. Pursuant to s.10 of the 2012 Act, in exceptional cases public funding might be available where a local authority applied to the High Court for it to exercise its inherent jurisdiction to revoke a freeing order (para.38). (4) Owing to the not-so-insignificant number of children in J's position, the instant court indicated the approach that local authorities should take when making applications to revoke freeing orders, and the form of the first hearing and the type of directions that should be made (paras 42-43).

A CITY COUNCIL v DC, [2013] EWHC 8 (Fam), [2013] 1 W.L.R. 3009, Eleanor King, J., Fam Div.

1201. Adoption–Prospective adopters–Prospective adopter becoming visually impaired–Fairness of local authority decision to remove placed child–Appropriateness of injunction to prevent removal

[Adoption and Children Act 2002 (c.38) s.35(5), s.35(2); Equality Act 2010 (c.15) s.15; Human Rights Act 1998 (c.42) s.7; European Convention on Human Rights 1950 Art.6, Art.8.]

The applicant (R), a prospective adopter, applied for an injunction under the Human Rights Act 1998 s.7 to prevent the respondent local authority from removing the child in question (S) from her care. S was a year old and had been paced with R, a single woman, under a placement order in October 2012 when she was eight months old. By all accounts, the placement was extremely successful. However, in January 2013 R was diagnosed as having a benign brain tumour. By January 4, 2013, when it was open to R to make an application for adoption, she was in hospital undergoing an emergency operation to remove the tumour, having made arrangements for S to be cared for in her own home by friends with whom she was familiar. While the operation was successful in removing the tumour, it resulted in R losing her sight. It was unclear whether the sight loss was to be temporary or permanent. While R was still in hospital, the local authority held a planning meeting and discussed S either remaining with R or being placed with an alternative adopter. R was discharged on January 24 and, by January 30, after three social work visits, the local authority decided that S should be removed from R's care. It put its intention in writing on February 4, the letter reaching R on the afternoon of February 5. Meanwhile, on the morning of February 5, R had lodged with the court an application for an adoption order. When, two days later, the local authority set a date for S's removal, R made the instant application for urgent injunctive relief, which raised issues as to the interplay between the Adoption and Children Act 2002 s.35(2) and s.35(5). R submitted, essentially, that (1) she was entitled to the protection of s.35(5), which would prevent the local authority from removing S without a court order, because she had "made" an application to adopt before receiving notice of the intention to remove; (2) even if that was not the case, any removal under s.35(2) would infringe her rights under the European Convention on Human Rights 1950 art.8; (3) because she had neither been involved in the decision to remove S nor been given the opportunity to make representations, her rights under art.6 of the Convention had been violated; (4) S's removal contravened the Equality Act 2010 s.15.

Held: Application granted. While it was unclear whether R had "made" her application within the meaning of s.35(5) before receiving notice of the local authority's intention to remove S, there was a prima facie case that she had. While "making" an application might well refer to the point at which the application was lodged with, rather than formally issued by, the court, it was not necessary to determine the question. Had timing been the only issue, the court would have been minded to grant the injunction to allow the parties to establish whether R's application had been issued immediately upon lodging on the morning of February 5. However, there was a much more substantial basis for the grant of relief. A decision to remove a child from a prospective adopter was a momentous one. It had to be a solidly welfare-based decision, and it had to be reached fairly. It was difficult to identify on what material the local authority could truly contend that it had reached a proper welfare-based evaluation. By the time it made its decision there had been limited direct observation and assessment, no apparent discussions with R's friends and supporters, and little knowledge of her condition or its likely prognosis. R had not been invited to the meetings at which S's future placement had been discussed, and there was nothing to indicate that her views had been sought. The local authority failed to give her a full and informed opportunity to address its concerns, and in that respect it had breached the common law principle of fairness and R's rights under art.6 and art.8. The local authority's difficulties in defending its decision were compounded by its acknowledgement that it did not know whether R's visual impairment was temporary or permanent. R had made entirely appropriate arrangements, and S was receiving good physical care. It could not be said that R could not give an appropriate level of emotional care to S simply by virtue of her visual impairment. Visual impairment did not, of itself, disqualify an adult from being a capable, loving parent. R's ability to provide good emotional care for S, probably with support, had to be properly assessed, and that had not happened. The decision to remove S was based on an incomplete assessment of the situation and had been made in a manner which was unfair to R. The court stopped short of finding that the assumptions made by the local authority were discriminatory but, in ruling R out as a prospective carer so summarily, it had shown a worrying lack of enquiry into the potential for good care offered by a visually impaired parent (see paras 27-39 of judgment).

RCW v A LOCAL AUTHORITY, [2013] EWHC 235 (Fam), [2013] 2 F.L.R. 95, Cobb, J., Fam Div.

1202. **Adoption agencies**

THE ADOPTION AGENCIES (MISCELLANEOUS AMENDMENTS) REGULATIONS 2013, SI 2013/985; made under the Children Act 1989 s.22C, s.28, s.104, Sch.2 para.12F; the Adoption (Intercountry Aspects) Act 1999 s.1;

and the Adoption and Children Act 2002 s.4, s.9, s.11, s.12, s.45, s.54, s.83, s.94, s.140, s.142. In force: July 1, 2013; .

These Regulations amend the Adoption Agencies Regulations 2005 by substituting a new Part 4 (Duties of Adoption Agencies in Respect of a Prospective Adopter). Part 4 makes provision for the assessment of prospective adopters and is amended to introduce a new two-stage approval process.

1203. Adoption support–Aqdoption support agencies–Guardianship–Wales

THE ADOPTION SUPPORT SERVICES AND SPECIAL GUARDIANSHIP (WALES) (AMENDMENT) REGULATIONS 2013, SI 2013/SI 2013/2901 (W.206); made under the Children Act 1989 s.14F, s.104; and the Adoption and Children Act 2002 s.2, s.4, s.140, s.142. In force: October 1, 2013; .

These Regulations make amendments to the Adoption Support Services (Local Authorities) (Wales) Regulations 2005 and the Special Guardianship (Wales) Regulations 2005 as regards financial support.

1204. Ancillary relief–Beneficial interests–Shares and properties held by bankrupt–Vesting of bankrupt's estate in trustee in bankruptcy

[Insolvency Act 1986 (c.45) s.306.]

The court was required to consider the legal consequences flowing from a previous fact finding decision arising from ancillary relief where the husband (H) had been adjudged bankrupt. H had held shares in two companies (S and X) and had interests in various properties. Numerous issues arose including whether the beneficial interest in the shares in S vested in the official receiver; the ownership of the shares and the impact of any vesting of a beneficial interest in the shares in the official receiver and relevant tax issues; beneficial ownership of the shares in X and the impact of any vesting in the official receiver.

Held: Issues determined. (1) The court had found that H had transferred 99 shares in S to his sister to protect the business of the company from his creditors and on the basis that she would hold the shares for him. The remaining share held by another party was not held by him beneficially, but as a nominee. A transfer of that one share to the sister was at H's direction, and on the basis that she held it in the same way as the other 99 shares, she therefore held it for H. When H was adjudicated bankrupt, all the shares in S were held by the sister as a trustee for H and so his beneficial interest in them vested in his trustee in bankruptcy, the official receiver, pursuant to the Insolvency Act 1986 s.306. (2) The primary claim advanced by the official receiver was in respect of a property which had been bought in the name of H's wife with dividends declared by S. It was clear that those dividends were paid out to fund the purchase of the property, so the official receiver was beneficially entitled to the purchase price and could therefore claim the beneficial interest in the property on the basis of a proprietary tracing claim, or of a resulting trust. It followed that he was entitled to the proceeds from the property. The official receiver could follow his beneficial interest in all the issued shares in S into all the issued shares in X, because the ownership of the shares in X was based on, and so was a product of the shares in S. (3) The official receiver, in carrying out his statutory task as an officer of the court, should investigate the possibility that tax and penalties were due in respect of the dividends of S that were used to purchase the property, and to raise those matters with Revenue and Customs. In any event, the parties, and failing that the court, should disclose those issues because of the tax liabilities that needed to be identified.

KK v MA, [2012] EWHC 788 (Fam), [2012] B.P.I.R. 1137, Charles, J., Fam Div.

1205. **Ancillary relief–Disclosure–Wife's application to ascertain true extent of former husband's assets–Documents sought containing information received under Mutual Legal Assistance regime–Competing public interest considerations**

[Matrimonial Causes Act 1973 (c.18).]

The applicant former wife (W) applied for disclosure of documents arising out of criminal proceedings brought against the first respondent former husband (H) by the second respondent Crown Prosecution Service. W's application for ancillary relief had been determined by a consent order in 2004 following the breakdown of her marriage to H. The order recorded that she did not believe that H had provided full and frank disclosure. H had alleged that he had no assets and substantial debts. He was ordered to pay £270,000 to W. From 2007 H was convicted of, or pleaded guilty to, multiple offences of high value fraud and money laundering. The CPS applied for a confiscation order against H, alleging that he had realisable assets of around £35 million. W applied to set aside the consent order on the basis of material non-disclosure, fraud and misrepresentation and sought disclosure of the confiscation proceeding documents in order to ascertain the true extent of H's untainted assets. The CPS and the third respondent secretary of state opposed the application on the basis that the documents sought contained information received from foreign governments or other authorities under the Mutual Legal Assistance regime (the regime). The issues were whether the disclosure sought (i) was necessary for the fair disposal of W's substantive application; (ii) was likely to undermine or hinder the operation of the regime, at least to the extent that the public interest in supporting the regime outweighed the public interest in W's application being determined on all the relevant evidence. The CPS and secretary of state submitted that considering the potential harm to the regime and to effective co-operation between states in the fight against crime, the public interest against disclosure outweighed the public interest for it.

Held: Application granted. (1) The prospect of the court being able to effect justice, and discharge its obligations under the Matrimonial Causes Act 1973, was likely to be very considerably enhanced by the disclosure and could be very seriously impeded if the disclosure was not effected. Limited references in the evidence to H's resources provided justification alone for concluding that the information contained in the documents sought was clearly necessary for the fair disposal of W's application (see paras 70, 71, 73, 75 of judgment). (2) That conclusion had to be balanced against the undoubted public interest which underpinned the regime: the effective investigation and prosecution of international crimes. All the information sought by W was in the hands of H and it was difficult to conceive that the court would prevent him from deploying that information in the substantive proceedings. W should be in the same position. The fact that some of the information obtained under the regime had been deployed already in the substantive proceedings and that disclosure would be ordered only to the extent that it had already been disclosed to H militated against any detrimental effect that disclosure might have on the regime. Such potential damage was further diminished by the fact that the disclosure was sought by an alleged victim of H's alleged deceit during the course of confidential/private proceedings, and would be subject to an undertaking that W would not disclose the information beyond the proceedings. It was appreciated that if such orders were made too readily, the effectiveness of the regime could well be undermined. However, provided that such orders were made only on limited occasions and in closely confined circumstances, the regime was unlikely to be materially damaged. To order the disclosure sought in the instant case would not undermine the regime in any significant respect and not to the extent that the public interest in supporting the regime outweighed the public interest in the evidence being available for W and the court so that justice could be done in her application. The balance came down in favour of exercising the court's discretion to order the disclosure (paras 76, 79-80, 82-83).

P v P (FINANCIAL REMEDIES: DISCLOSURE), [2012] EWHC 1733 (Fam), [2013] 1 F.L.R. 1003, Moylan, J., Fam Div.

1206. Appeals–Applications without hearing–Family proceedings–High Court judges

THE FAMILY PROCEDURE (AMENDMENT) RULES 2013, SI 2013/SI 2013/530 (L.4); made under the Courts Act 2003 s.75, s.76. In force: April 1, 2013; .

These rules amend the Family Procedure Rules 2010 by: changing references to certain rules in the Civil Procedure Rules 1998 (1) to reflect re-numbering of some of those rules; and, in Part 30 (appeals), giving High Court Judges and Designated Family Judges power when refusing permission to appeal without a hearing, where the application is considered to be totally without merit, to make an order that the person seeking permission may not request the decision to be reconsidered at a hearing.

1207. Care orders–Adopted children–Breakdown of adoption placement–Child suffering from attachment disorder–Whether child beyond parental control

[Children Act 1989 (c.41) s.20, s.31, s.100(2)(b).]

The applicant local authority applied for a care order in respect of a fifteen-year old adopted girl (K). K, who had had a traumatic early childhood, was adopted when she was 6 years old. Her adoptive parents (M and F), who were Roman Catholics and had been married for 25 years, had two children who attended university. M was a school teacher and F was self-employed. Following the adoption, K's behaviour slowly deteriorated and K's parents had to deal with some profoundly difficult problems they had not anticipated; K suffered from a reactive attachment disorder. Although K's parents had sought assistance from the local authority on numerous occasions, they couldn't cope and agreed to K being placed in residential care when she was 13. K subsequently ran away and was sexually assaulted. She was also arrested for a serious assault on a member of staff at the care home and had a contraceptive implant fitted but her parents had not been consulted. The working relationship between K's parents and the local authority was very poor. The local authority's case for a care order was based upon the conviction of professionals that that was what K wanted. The local authority contended that the threshold for a care order under the Children Act 1989 s.31(2) had been met as K was likely to suffer significant harm and that harm was attributable to her being beyond parental control. K's parents contended that no care order should be made but that the local authority should provide accommodation under s.20.

Held: Application granted. (1) The court had to determine as a matter of fact whether K was beyond parental control; it was immaterial who, if anyone, was to blame. It was plain that K was beyond parental control and that was a manifestation of her attachment disorder; the shortcomings in the parenting provided by K's adoptive parents would not have either caused or exacerbated the problem. However, that argument could not be allowed to subvert the primary purpose of s.31(2) which was one of child protection. In the instant case, the facts set out in the local authority's threshold document justified a finding that K was beyond parental control. They also justified a finding that K was likely to suffer significant harm and that that likelihood was attributable to her being beyond parental control. The threshold under s.31(2)(b) was met (see paras 152-153, 166-167, 174 of judgment). (2) For accommodation under s.20 to work in K's best interests, there needed to be at least a basic level of communication and co-operation between K's parents and the local authority. In light of everything that had happened over the last two years, it was difficult to imagine that that level of co-operation could be achieved. It would be unhelpful and potentially damaging for K to find herself caught in the middle of a legal no-man's land. Therefore, accommodation under s.20 was not an option. A wardship would have more to offer than a care order as both the local authority and K's parents would be made accountable to the court. However, due to the obstacle of s.100(2)(b) the court lacked jurisdiction to use wardship in the circumstances of the case. The court had no alternative but to make a final care order. It was not the best outcome for K but it was a better outcome than making no order (paras 193, 204-206).

K (A CHILD) (POST ADOPTION PLACEMENT BREAKDOWN), *Re*, [2012] EWHC 4148 (Fam), [2013] 1 F.L.R. 1, Judge Clifford Bellamy, Fam Div (Coventry).

1208. Care orders–Interim orders–Whether to remove baby from mother serving custodial sentence–Baby's interim safety assured in mother and baby unit at prison

The appellant mother (M) appealed against an interim care order made in respect of her son (L), aged four months. The appeal of the local authority (X) against an earlier declaration that L had been unlawfully removed by X from M's care within days of his birth was adjourned. M had an extensive history of Class A drug misuse dating back to her early teens and continuing during her pregnancies. M had engaged in criminal activity, including theft, burglary and prostitution, in order to fund her drug habit. She also had a history of involvement with violent men, namely the father of her older two boys and L's father. M's eldest child had been accommodated on a voluntary basis by the local authority when he was just under four months old because of concerns about M's drug use and chaotic and risky behaviour. He now lived with the maternal grandmother under a residence order. The middle sibling had been removed and adopted when M refused to terminate her relationship with the father. M was imprisoned for three years for domestic burglary shortly after giving birth to L but had recently obtained a place in the mother and baby unit in prison. The judge recognised that L would be physically safe in prison but decided that his safety included his emotional safety which would be affected by his removal from foster care to be with his mother and a likely further move while M was assessed on release. The central issue was how the courts should approach an application for an interim care order where the safety of the child was not in question but for other reasons it might be in the child's interests not to be reunited with their parent. M submitted that the judge had failed to apply the correct "test" for an interim care order.

Held: Appeal allowed. The judge had been wrong to decide that the likely delay constituted a danger to L's "emotional safety" in the sense contemplated by the interim care order authorities, *K & H (Children), Re* [2006] EWCA Civ 1898, [2007] 1 F.L.R. 2043, [2007] C.L.Y. 1714, *A Local Authority v KAB* [2010] EWCA Civ 871, [2011] 1 F.L.R. 669, [2010] C.L.Y. 1303, and *H (A Child) (Interim Care Order), Re* [2002] EWCA Civ 1932, [2003] 1 F.C.R. 350, [2003] C.L.Y. 1515 applied and *M (Children) (Interim Care Order: Removal), Re* [2005] EWCA Civ 1594, [2006] 1 F.C.R. 303, [2006] C.L.Y. 1657, *B (A Child) (Care Proceedings: Interim Care Order), Re* [2009] EWCA Civ 1254, [2010] 1 F.L.R. 1211, [2010] C.L.Y. 1308 and *B (Children) (Interim Care Order), Re* [2010] EWCA Civ 324, [2010] 2 F.L.R. 283, [2010] C.L.Y. 1304 considered (see paras 33-38 of judgment). The interim care order regime was designed to ensure that a child was kept safe prior to the full hearing and should be focused on the likely result of the child being returned to live with his parents. It was not designed to evaluate the longer term future, especially if it afforded an advantage to the local authority, or prejudiced a parent's ability to put forward proposals for care, *G (Minors) (Interim Care Order), Re* [1993] 2 F.L.R. 839, [1994] C.L.Y. 3112 applied (para.53). The limits on an interim order were sensible given that evidence was likely to be incomplete. In the instant case, there was no danger to L's physical or emotional safety in the prison unit and it was inappropriate to class longer term issues as a danger to L's emotional safety. The relationship between L and M should be preserved pending a final hearing. Any concerns about delay should have been met by a prompt listing for the final hearing rather than by affecting the outcome with an interim care order which kept M and L apart (para.60).

L (A CHILD) (INTERIM CARE ORDER: PRISON MOTHER AND BABY UNIT), *Re*; *sub nom.* L (A CHILD) (INTERIM CARE ORDER: MOTHER'S IMPRISONMENT), *Re*, [2013] EWCA Civ 489, [2013] 3 F.C.R. 90, Lloyd, L.J., CA (Civ Div).

1209. **Care orders–Orders without notice–Immediate removal of child from grandparents pending inter partes hearing–Child's welfare**

[Children Act 1989 (c.41) s.7, s.37; Family Procedure Rules 2010 (SI 2010/2955).]

The appellant maternal grandparents (S) appealed against a without notice interim care order made under the Children Act 1989 s.37 sanctioning the immediate removal of a child (M) to the care of the respondent local authority, pending an inter partes hearing. M had been placed on the child protection register at birth because of her mother and father's drug misuse. By the time she was three months old, M had moved to live with S, who had obtained a special guardianship order, where she remained until she was nine. S consistently failed to co-operate with social services and to keep the court, M's guardian, and the local authority informed of M's residence and changes of school. Ultimately M was made a ward of court. The local authority prepared a s.7 welfare report recommending M's immediate removal, but, there was widespread concern that M might suffer additional emotional harm as a result of S's potential reaction if they became aware of it and the interim order was made at a without notice hearing just prior to the on notice hearing. S contended that (1) a without notice s.37 interim care order was impermissible and unfair where the local authority had already provided a s.7 welfare report and had determined to issue an application for a care order; (2) the judge had predetermined the outcome before the on notice hearing, which had immediately followed; and (3) the burden of proof had been reversed by requiring S to convince the judge as to why the interim order should be discharged.

Held: Appeal dismissed. (1) The judge had been justified in holding that M's safety required the protection of an immediate order for compulsory removal from her home and the course she had adopted of a s.37 order was not excluded by any provision in the Children Act 1989, the Family Procedure Rules 2010, or elsewhere (see para.74 of judgment). (2) It was plain from the transcripts of the two hearings that the s.37 order had been designed only to hold the situation and protect M pending consideration at the on notice hearing which had immediately followed (para.76). (3) Although S had been at a disadvantage by receiving the s.7 report at short notice, the judge had done all that she possibly could to ensure that S understood what was being proposed, and why, and to permit S to have their say (para.77).

L (A CHILD) (INTERIM CARE ORDER: EXTENDED FAMILY), *Re*, [2013] EWCA Civ 179, [2013] 2 F.L.R. 302, Thorpe, L.J., CA (Civ Div).

1210. **Care orders–Ordinary residence–Child spending time in two local authority areas–Whether provided with accommodation–Child's competence to form settled intention for ordinary residence**

[Children Act 1989 (c.41) s.22C, s.31 (8), s.105(6).]

The appellant local authority (S) appealed against a decision that it was the designated local authority in respect of a final care order regarding a child (C) rather than the respondent local authority (B). C had lived with his mother (M) in B's administrative area. Following a serious argument between them when C was 13 years old, M had agreed that C could stay overnight with an aunt (Z) in S's area. C indicated strongly his desire to remain permanently with Z. A report by B in April 2011 recorded M's agreement to C remaining with Z pending assessments being made. In June 2011 M agreed that C could be accommodated by B, and B obtained an interim care order. In January 2012 a judge decided under the Children Act 1989 s.105(6) that C was ordinarily resident in S's area because when living with Z he had not been "provided with accommodation" by B, and he therefore designated S as the local authority in the final care order. The issues were (i) the correct approach under the Act; (ii) whether C had been "provided with accommodation" by B between April and June 2011, with the result that under s.105(6) his residence with Z was to be disregarded for the purpose of determining his ordinary residence; (ii) whether C was ordinarily resident with Z between April and June 2011.

Held: Appeal dismissed. (1) The judge had erred in applying the approach under s.23 of the Act, which had been repealed shortly before C went to live with Z. The approach to s.23 in *H (A Child) (Care Order: Appropriate Local Authority), Re* [2003] EWCA Civ 1629, [2004] Fam. 89, [2004] C.L.Y. 1456 was no longer applicable, *Re H* disapproved. Under the new s.22C, arrangements made for a child to live with a relative were specifically a "placement", which had to amount to the provision of accommodation for the purposes of s.105(6) (see paras 19, 21 of judgment). (2) From April till June 2011, C had lived with Z with the agreement of M, so during that time C was not being "provided with accommodation" by B. Accordingly, the time he spent living with Z was to be considered when determining his ordinary residence (paras 28-29). (3) M had not agreed between April and June that C was to be ordinarily resident in S's area. However, the evidence revealed that from at least April C had been *Gillick* competent to form his own settled intention about his future. C's strong views about not returning to M's home were unwavering and indicated that C's accommodation with Z was sufficiently secure and settled. In the circumstances, a duration of two months was regarded as an appreciable period of time for acquiring ordinary residence, *Northamptonshire CC v Islington LBC* [2001] Fam. 364, [1999] C.L.Y. 2312 considered. It followed that C became ordinarily resident in S's area from April to June. The fact that s.105(6) provided for C's accommodation with Z after June to be disregarded did not alter that. Accordingly, under s.31(8) S had been the appropriate local authority to designate in the final care order (paras 31, 33-36).

SHEFFIELD CITY COUNCIL v BRADFORD MBC [2013] 1 F.L.R. 1027, Bodey, J., Fam Div.

1211. Care orders–Parental contact–Separated parents–Emotional harm to child–Need for care order after placement in foster care

The applicant local authority sought a care order for a 13-year-old child (C). The respondent mother (M) and father (F) had separated when C was about three years old. A year later M and C went to live with M's new partner (T), but in the following year a judge found she was suffering emotional harm and granted F a residence order. Over the ensuing years, and against the background of continuing litigation, C's emotional state became increasingly fragile so that when she was 11 she was placed in foster care. The local authority sought a final care order, which would allow M and F to each have supervised contact with C six or seven times a year. M and F opposed the making of a care order and suggested that the foster care should continue, although M sought the subsequent return of C to her care. The local authority also applied for an order preventing M and F from making further application to the court until C was 16.

Held: Application granted. (1) If, as M and F wanted, C was to continue in foster care, they could, as a matter of law, remove her from her accommodation in the absence of a care order. Not only would it be extremely damaging for C to be removed from her accommodation by M or F, but such a move would immediately spark conflict between them and with the local authority, which would cause C yet more damage. Neither parent was capable of providing exceptional parenting of the kind so desperately needed by C. The need for a care order was therefore plain (see paras 57-58, 60 of judgment). (2) There had to be a transition upon the making of that order into the permanence of long-term foster care, and M and F had to acknowledge that during the transition C should not be confused by substantial contact with them. M and F's suggestion that contact ought to take place either fortnightly or monthly with each of them would interfere with the foster carer family and their attempts to maintain a normal family life with C, and would send out the wrong message. Contact should remain supervised to avoid assertions by M that C was to return home or have overnight contact, and to prevent C's anxiety in F's presence. Contact should be six times per year for each parent and that would be reviewed after six months (paras 68-71, 74, 80). (3) In light of the profound impact of the private law proceedings on C's development, there should be no further application without the leave of the court until C was 16 (paras 84-86).

A CITY COUNCIL v M [2013] 1 F.L.R. 517, Judge Cleary, Fam Div.

1212. **Care orders–Reports–Previous positive reports on mother's parenting ability–Later assessment raising concerns–Entitlement of judge to exclude mother as future carer of children**

[Children Act 1989 (c.41) s.20, s.31, s.37.]

The appellant mother (M) appealed against a decision excluding her as a possible future carer for her two children (S). Reports on M's parenting had been compiled by the first respondent local authority in 2006 and 2008. They regarded her parenting capacity as excellent. A further report in 2009 recorded the emotional norm of M's interaction. In September 2010, however, S passed into local authority care by voluntary arrangements under the Children Act 1989 s.20 and the local authority sent M a letter explaining its high level of concerns for S arising from incidents of domestic violence and M's level of supervision over them. A report of November 2010 recommended that M would require support and information if she was to resume care of S. The court ordered an assessment under s.37 of the Act. The subsequent report referred to a number of concerns over M's care of S. Two weeks later, the local authority applied for care orders, with the ultimate intention of obtaining placement orders for S's adoption. At trial in November 2011, the question of whether the threshold for granting a care order under s.31 was crossed was no longer live, M having made certain concessions, and the essential matter before the judge was which of several future management options would best promote S's welfare. The author of the s.37 assessment was cross-examined and the judge recorded her acceptance that prior to the issue of proceedings, M had functioned well as a parent, but also her opinion that, since then, M had given her reason to understand that there was domestic violence in the relationship between M and S's father. The judge excluded M as a possible future carer, but left open the possibility of S's uncle caring for them. The uncle subsequently withdrew. M appealed against her exclusion from S's future care. In January 2012 the local authority was granted care orders but the placement order application was deferred pending M's appeal. M contended that ruling her out as a future carer was a disproportionate intervention and plainly wrong given the strong evidence of good-enough parenting before proceedings began, and that the judge had erred in failing to give sufficient weight to that evidence. The local authority served a respondent's notice expressing support for the judge's reasoning and conclusion. The guardian also served a respondent's notice, relying on the local authority's contentions.

Held: Appeal dismissed. (1) The judge had considered the earlier positive reports about M's parenting and had had regard to them when making his choice between the care options for S presented by M and those presented by the local authority. Those earlier reports did not, however, present the full picture. It was crucially relevant that the s.37 assessment concerned the facts and circumstances as they were immediately preceding the issue of proceedings. In reaching his conclusion that M should be excluded as future carer of S, the judge had explained himself comprehensively in a judgment which was a model of conscientious care. There was no real force in M's criticism of the judgment and her attack on it had no prospect of success (see paras 18, 21, 23-24 of judgment). (2) (Per curiam) Respondents' notices which simply asserted their support for the conclusion arrived at by a judge for the reasons he had given were entirely superfluous (paras 8-9).

S (CHILDREN) (CARE AND PLACEMENT ORDERS), *Re*, [2012] EWCA Civ 847, [2013] 1 F.L.R. 354, Thorpe, L.J., CA (Civ Div).

1213. **Care orders–Threshold criteria–Care plan involving permanent removal of child from parents on ground of anticipated future harm–Meaning of "significant harm" in s.31(2) Children Act 1989–Whether permanent removal proportionate**

[Children Act 1989 (c.41) s.31 (9); Human Rights Act 1998 (c.42) s.6; European Convention on Human Rights 1950 Art.8.]

The appellant parents (M and F) appealed against a decision ([2012] EWCA Civ 1475, [2013] 2 F.L.R. 388, [2013] 10 C.L.145) upholding the making of a care plan providing for the adoption of their three-year-old daughter (D). D had spent her life in foster care, having supervised contact with M and F. The local authority did not assert that she had suffered harm attributable to her parents' care, but based its case on anticipated future harm within the meaning of the Children Act 1989 s.31 (1) (a). It proposed that D be placed for adoption on the basis that M and F had psychological issues likely to impair their ability to provide good enough physical and emotional care for her. M had severe personality problems, multiple psychological problems, and had suffered from severe somatisation disorder, which had manifested itself in her frequently presenting for medical treatment. It was not clear whether that disorder would recur. In addition, she had a history of compulsive dishonesty, made frequent false complaints against professionals, and had failed to co-operate reasonably with the local authority. F used drugs, had a history of dishonesty, and did not accept that M was a risk to D. The expert evidence presented opposing views. The judge found that although M and F had a loving relationship with D and had behaved unimpeachably towards her during contact, the threshold criteria had been crossed, though "not perhaps in the most extreme way". He endorsed the local authority's care plan, expressing serious concerns about M and F's capacity to adequately promote D's emotional welfare and finding that neither had the capacity to engage with professionals in such a way that D would be safe from emotional or physical harm. His decision was upheld by the Court of Appeal. The case raised profound issues about the extent to which the law was to distinguish between emotional or psychological harm warranting state intervention and the natural tendency of children to grow up and behave like their parents; the scope of the court's powers to remove children from their birth families; and the function of the appellate court.

Held: Appeal dismissed. (Lady Hale dissenting in the result, and Lady Hale and Lord Kerr dissenting regarding the function of the appellate court) (1) The making of a care order required the court to be satisfied that the child was "likely" to suffer "significant harm". "Harm" was defined in s.31 (9), but there was no statutory definition of "significant". The court should avoid attempting to explain the word; it was already established that the concept of "significant harm" was fact-specific. However, a degree of consistency was important. There had to be something more than commonplace human failure or inadequacy, but conduct did not have to be intentional or deliberate; it was enough that the harm, or likelihood of harm, was attributable to the parents. There had to be a deficiency in parental care rather than in parental character, but character remained relevant to the extent that it might affect the quality of parenting. Added to the difficult question of identifying significant harm was the question of identifying the degree of likelihood that harm above the threshold would be suffered in the future. The threshold of likelihood, namely "a real possibility" of harm, was comparatively low. In the instant case, the judge had been right to make a care order with a view to adoption. There were features of the parents' personalities and M's psychiatric conditions which raised a real possibility that D would suffer impairment of her emotional development if she were placed in their care. Furthermore, the degree of their antagonism towards social workers was above the level commonly tolerated by the courts and precluded the success of any rehabilitative programme (see paras 24-27, 30, 48, 56, 64, 68-71, 177-193 of judgment). (2) (Lord Kerr and Lady Hale dissenting) In determining whether the threshold conditions for a care order were met, an appellate court was not to depart from its normal function of secondary review. The Human Rights Act 1998 s.6 did not mandate fresh appellate determination where arguments were made in reliance on the European Convention on Human

Rights 1950 (paras 35-47, 52-53, 57-61, 80-96,134-142). (Per Lord Kerr and Lady Hale) The appellate court, while giving due weight to the enormous benefit the trial judge had had in reading and hearing the evidence first-hand, was the "public authority" responsible for the invasion of Convention rights and had to decide for itself whether the judge's order was compatible with those rights (paras 108-127, 199-205). (3) Adoption could only occur if parents were unwilling, or were deemed by judicial process to be unable, to discharge their responsibilities towards the child. The assessment of the latter had to take account of support available from the authorities. Adoption of a child against her parents' wishes was, therefore, a last resort and potentially raised issues under art.8 of the Convention. There were stringent requirements of the proportionality doctrine where family ties had to be broken to allow adoption to take place. In the instant case, that threshold was crossed (paras 105-106, 128-133, 194-198). (Per Lady Hale) It had not been sufficiently demonstrated that it was necessary to bring the relationship between D and her parents to an end. The harm that was feared was subtle, long term, and might never happen. In the absence of a fresh, in depth enquiry, adoption was not proportionate to the risks identified (paras 223-224).

B (A CHILD) (CARE PROCEEDINGS: APPEAL), *Re*; *sub nom.* B (A CHILD) (CARE ORDER: PROPORTIONALITY: CRITERION FOR REVIEW), RE; B (A CHILD) (CARE PROCEEDINGS: THRESHOLD CRITERIA), *Re*, [2013] UKSC 33, [2013] 1 W.L.R. 1911, Lord Neuberger, J.S.C., SC.

1214. Care orders–Threshold criteria–Death of sibling from non-accidental injury–Effect on mother–Safety of remaining children

The applicant local authority applied for care and placement orders in relation to the three children of the first and second respondent mother and father (M and F). M and F had had three children, two of whom were twins (B and J). In February 2011, B suffered a violent death and a coroner's inquest found that an older brother (C), then aged four, was responsible for B's death. Shortly after B's death, M fell pregnant and M and F married. Contrary to the coroner's findings, later judicial proceedings determined that it was F and not C who was responsible for B's death. M was exonerated from playing any part in his death. M and F then separated, and the third child (Y) was born and immediately removed from M. The other children were also removed from M. In July 2012, care proceedings were adjourned in order to allow M to undertake therapy, while F subsequently exhausted his appeal rights in relation to the finding as to B's death. In considering what was in the best interests of each of the children, the issue was whether M had come to acknowledge that F could be dangerous and was willing to distance herself and the children from him, in order to ensure their safety and well-being. M's position until July 2012 had been that she did not believe that F was responsible, and during therapy she had expressed the opinion that she could not say for sure what had happened at the time of B's death as she had not been present, an opinion repeated to other medical professionals. M also asserted that her cultural and religious beliefs prevented her from divorcing F. During the instant hearing, M sought to distance herself from a letter written by a community leader which was critical of the judgment establishing F as responsible for B's death and suggesting that C was responsible as the coroner had found. M submitted that she had moved forward positively in therapy and that regardless of her beliefs she was determined to act in the way required of her, that she had disassociated herself from the community leader's views, that any risk of physical harm could be effectively mitigated through supervision, and that any risk of emotional harm was insufficient to deprive the children of an upbringing in their own family.

Held: Application granted. The court made care orders having approved of the local authority's plans for the children's future placements, and made placement orders in relation to Y and J. The children could not be returned to M: the nature of the risk was of the utmost gravity and there were no effective measures that could be taken to ensure the children's safety over time. M would not be able to reliably exclude F from her or her children's lives which would be necessary for their safety and well-being, and even if able to exclude F, emotional harm to the children would result from being brought up in an environment in which the prevailing belief was that F was innocent, with the consquence that C would learn that he was thought to have harmed B. M's views had not moved on in any meaningful way since she had undertaken therapy and it was her deep scepticism about F's responsibility for B's death, and not her cultural and religious views, that explained M's decision to remain married. Moreover, M had not involved her witnesses in planning with social services as their views did not coincide with her own and it remained the view of the family and significant community members that C was probably responsible for B's death. Making all allowances, the court rejected M's evidence in relation to her present beliefs and found that she had a quiet belief that F was probably innocent (see paras 57-62 of judgment).

A LONDON BOROUGH v A, [2013] EWHC 96 (Fam), [2013] 2 F.L.R. 139, Peter Jackson, J., Fam Div.

1215. Care orders–Threshold criteria–Order sought in respect of second child where first child removed from parents after suffering injury–Rehearing of findings of fact in relation to first child

[Children Act 1989 (c.41) s.31; Children and Young Persons Act 1933 (c.12) s.1; Offences against the Person Act 1861 (c.100) s.20.]

The applicant parents (M and F) applied for increased contact with their five-year-old daughter (X). The respondent local authority sought a care order in respect of M and F's three-year-old daughter (Y). When seven-weeks-old, X suffered a collapse with a triad of injuries while in F's care, raising the possibility of non-accidental injury. On a previous occasion she had suffered burns which F claimed were due to him placing her too close to an electric fire. A fact-finding hearing found F responsible for the collapse and the burns and that M had failed to protect X. Once she had made a full recovery, X was placed with her maternal grandparents under a special guardianship order. She had contact with M six times a year and F twice a year. F was convicted under the Offences against the Person Act 1861 s.20 and the Children and Young Persons Act 1933 s.1, and spent seven months in prison before the conviction was quashed by the Court of Appeal. While he was in prison, M gave birth to Y and, in an attempt to avoid local authority involvement, relocated to another part of the country. However, when Y was six-months-old the police traced them and Y was removed under a police protection order. The local authority initiated care proceedings, asserting that the threshold in the Children Act 1989 s.31 had been crossed in relation to Y on the basis of the findings of fact in relation to X. M and F sought a rehearing of the facts due to his conviction being overturned. They concealed the result of paternity tests, showing that F was Y's father, from the local authority in the belief that it could damage M's chances of caring for Y. Extensive medical evidence given during the hearing provided no common consensus as to the cause of X's injuries. A possibility had arisen that the collapse could have been caused by an airway obstruction.

Held: Judgment accordingly. (1) There was no evidence to indicate that the burn injuries were inflicted maliciously, deliberately or intentionally to cause injury. As an inexperienced parent, F's actions were inappropriate and potentially dangerous within the confines of new parent carelessness rather than recklessness, *B (Children) (Sexual Abuse: Standard of Proof), Re* [2008] UKHL 35, [2009] 1 A.C. 11, [2008] C.L.Y. 1501 applied (see paras 630-631 of judgment). (2) M had not failed to protect X by allowing her to stay with him following the burns injury. That was not an intentional or culpable event and M had no reason to believe that X was at risk. X had suffered an accident; M believed that F was a loving and caring parent who had taken time to learn how to care for his child (para.636). (3) On the medical evidence alone, there was no strong pointer that the injuries X had suffered were inflicted through a loss of control or temper by a perpetrator shortly before her collapse. There were too many pointers which questioned a conclusion of inflicted injury. There was a strong pointer indicating an innocent explanation for the collapse, being the airway obstruction accepted as possible by certain experts. On the medical evidence alone the local authority had failed to establish on the balance of probabilities that the injuries were non-accidental. There was too much strong evidence flowing the other way, *R (Care Proceedings: Causation), Re* [2011] EWHC 1715 (Fam), [2011] 2 F.L.R. 1384, [2012] C.L.Y. 1354 applied (paras 655-657). (4) In order to provide X and Y with as much clarity as possible, it was appropriate to take the matter further and completely exonerate F from culpability. All three generations had suffered as a result of the previous fact findings (paras 659-672). (5) M and F admitted that they had not been open and honest about the extent of their relationship and that they had concealed Y's birth and paternity. Now that they had been unburdened from the shadow of findings against them, they had felt able to unburden themselves, admitted concealment, secrecy and their determination to recover Y and avoid her adoption. M and F needed a fair and supportive assessment. Accordingly, the local authority had failed to demonstrate that the threshold had been met in relation to physical and emotional harm (paras 673-698).

SUTTON LBC v G, [2012] EWHC 2604 (Fam), [2013] 1 F.L.R. 833, Hogg, J., Fam Div.

1216. Care orders–Threshold criteria–Possibility that parent caring for child had harmed another child in past–Whether sufficient to establish child now being cared for likely to suffer harm in future

[Children Act 1989 (c.41) s.31 (2).]

The appellant local authority appealed against a judge's refusal ([2012] EWCA Civ 1511) to make care orders in respect of three children living with the respondent mother (JJ) and her partner (DJ). JJ had had three children with her former partner (SW). Their eldest child (TL) had died of non-accidental injuries in 2004. Care proceedings were commenced when their second child was born in 2005. The judge found that either JJ or SW had caused the injuries to TL and the other had colluded to hide the truth. JJ and SW eventually agreed to the second child being adopted. Their third child was born in 2009, by which time JJ and SW had separated. JJ moved in with DJ and his two children. The instant proceedings related to JJ and SW's third child and DJ's two children. The High Court held that the likelihood of significant harm could only be proved by reference to past facts, which had to be proved on the balance of probabilities. It concluded that the only facts available to the local authority had not been proved to that standard and dismissed the proceedings. The Court of Appeal upheld that decision. In 2011, JJ and DJ had a child together. The issue was whether a possibility that a parent caring for a child had harmed another child in the past was sufficient to establish that the child now being cared for was "likely to suffer" harm in the future for the purposes of the Children Act 1989 s.31 (2).

Held: Appeal dismissed. (1) The simple balance of probabilities was the test for the identification of a perpetrator. The threshold test came in two limbs. In the first, the court had to be satisfied that the child was suffering significant harm, and that harm was attributable to the care given to him not being what it would be reasonable to expect a parent to give him. In the second limb, the court had to be satisfied that the child was likely to suffer significant harm, and that likelihood was attributable to the care likely to be given to him if the order was not made. It would be odd if the first limb had to be proved to the satisfaction of the court but the basis for the prediction in the second limb did not. A correct statement of the law was set out in *S-B (Children) (Care Proceedings: Standard of Proof), Re* [2009] UKSC 17, [2010] 1 A.C. 678, [2010] C.L.Y. 1325 at para.49. That had to be followed in preference to the obiter dicta of Wall J in *B (Minors) (Care Proceedings: Practice), Re* [1999] 1 W.L.R. 238, [1998] C.L.Y. 2401. Reasonable suspicion was a sufficient basis for the authorities to investigate, and even take interim protective measures, but could not be a sufficient basis for the long-term intervention entailed in a care order. Since the firm establishment of the flexible test of likelihood in *H (Minors) (Sexual Abuse: Standard of Proof), Re* [1996] A.C. 563, [1996] C.L.Y. 632, it had become more important to require an objective factual basis from which to draw the inference that future harm was likely. Prediction was only possible where past facts were proved. A real possibility that something had happened in the past was not enough to predict that it would happen in the future. The decision in *S-B* was not authority for the proposition that if the past perpetrator could not be identified, future likelihood could not be established: there might be a multitude of established facts from which such likelihood could be established. However, *S-B* was authority for the proposition that a real possibility that a parent had harmed a child in the past was not, by itself, sufficient to establish the likelihood that she would cause harm to another child in the future, *S-B* followed, *H (Minors)* applied, *B (Minors)* considered (see paras 36, 43-44, 47-50, 54 of judgment). In the instant case, there were several findings which might have been relevant to assessing whether it was likely that JJ would harm children in the future. There was gross and substantial collusion, expressly designed to prevent the court identifying the perpetrator; failure to protect TL; and the deliberate act of keeping TL away from health professionals to avoid detection of injury. However, the local authority had chosen not to rely on those. JJ had been looking after the children and her new baby for some time without any cause for concern. In those circumstances, it would be unfair to the whole family for the proceedings to continue. If the local authority wished to make a case that any of the children was likely to suffer significant harm in the future, it would have to bring new proceedings (paras 56-57). (2) (Per Lord Wilson) Although the majority had been correct to dismiss the appeal, it was illogical of them to suggest that a parent's consignment to a pool of possible perpetrators could, if weighed together with other relevant facts, figure as part of the requisite factual foundation. If, for the purpose of the requisite foundation, that parent's consignment to a pool had a value of zero on its own, it could, for that purpose, have no greater value in company (paras 78-80).

J (CHILDREN) (CARE PROCEEDINGS: THRESHOLD CRITERIA), *Re; sub nom.* J (CHILDREN) (NON-ACCIDENTAL INJURY: PAST POSSIBLE PERPETRATOR IN NEW FAMILY), RE; J (CHILDREN) (CARE PROCEEDINGS: PAST POSSIBLE PERPETRATORS IN NEW FAMILY UNIT), *Re,* [2013] UKSC 9, [2013] 1 A.C. 680, Lord Hope, J.S.C. (Deputy President), SC.

1217. Care orders–Threshold criteria–Refusal of application for interim care orders–Whether reasonable grounds for thinking children at risk of significant harm–Whether children's immediate removal necessary and proportionate

[Children Act 1989 (c.41) s.31 (2), s.38(2).]

The appellant local authority appealed against a decision refusing its application for interim care orders in respect of two children (C and D), the daughters of the first and second respondent mothers (M1 and M2). M2 was M1's mother. M1 was the child of M2's marriage with a man who was accused of sexually abusing two of his daughters, which led to M1 being brought up in foster care. M2 subsequently married a man (B), who was D's father. D was eight years old. When M1 was 16, she returned to spend time living with M2. By the time she was 17, she had entered into a sexual relationship with B, despite his role to her as quasi-stepfather. M1 bore B a daughter, C, who was aged seven months. B subsequently died, and M1 and M2 lived together in one household with C and D. The family had been known to social services for many years. The local authority expressed an interest in C after her birth, and following investigation also became concerned about D. It applied for interim care orders in respect of both children, with a care plan that involved their immediate removal from M1 and M2. The local authority, supported by the children's guardian, contended that both C and D were at risk of significant harm. The recorder directed himself as to the conditions for making an interim care order under the Children Act 1989 s.38(2), that the threshold criteria under s.31 (2) were made out, and concluded that the local authority had not satisfied that test. He held that even if he was wrong about that, immediate removal of the children was neither necessary nor proportionate. The local authority, supported by the guardian, contended that the recorder was wrong to find that there were no reasonable grounds to believe that the threshold criteria were not satisfied. It submitted that there was a reasonable risk of significant harm to C and D arising from (i) the lack of sexual inhibition or proper sexual boundaries by M1 and M2, which gave rise to a sexual risk to the girls from which they would not be adequately protected; (ii) their chaotic lifestyle, neglect and lack of stimulation; (iii) the failure by M1 and M2 to cooperate sufficiently with relevant professionals, in particular their failure to adhere to an agreement with the local authority that they would provide details of every adult who visited the household.

Held: Appeal dismissed. (1) The position for determining a care order at the interim stage was set out in *A Local Authority v KAB* [2010] EWCA Civ 871, [2011] 1 F.L.R. 669, [2010] C.L.Y. 1303. The test for making an interim, as opposed to a final, care order was that there had to be reasonable grounds for believing that the s.31(2) criteria were satisfied: it was not necessary to prove that they were. If there were reasonable grounds for such belief, the court had then to consider whether an interim care order was called for. The test was the normal one of paramountcy of the child's welfare. An interim care order was not a substitute for a final order and at the interim stage a child's separation from her parent was justified if and only if her welfare and safety, including any risk of emotional harm, demanded it, *A Local Authority v KAB* followed (see paras 26-29 of judgment). (2) It was not possible to uphold the recorder's finding that there were no reasonable grounds for believing that the threshold criteria were met, in particular for D. There was the plainest possible case for saying that they were. The sharing of B between M2 and M1 at a time when M1 was a quasi-stepdaughter demonstrated lax and uninhibited sexual relationships and the absence of protective boundaries. The combination of neglect, lack of stimulus and sexual risk was sufficient to pass the s.38(2) test (para.31). (3) The recorder was, however, plainly right to have considered that the children's removal was not necessary or proportionate. Whilst there might be a risk to C and D in the future, that would be determined at the final hearing and did not justify immediate removal. There was no risk in the short term, and the interim care orders sought had rightly been refused on that basis (para.34).

B (CHILDREN) (REFUSAL TO GRANT INTERIM ORDER), *Re*, [2012] EWCA Civ 1275, [2013] 2 F.L.R. 153, Hughes, L.J., CA (Civ Div).

1218. Care proceedings–Case management–Care order and placement for adoption order made in issues resolution hearing–Whether judge acted justly and fairly

[Family Procedure Rules 2010 (SI 2010/2955); European Convention on Human Rights 1950 Art.6.]

The appellant parents (P) appealed against a care order made by a judge at an issues resolution hearing in care proceedings in respect of their child (T), and orders dispensing with their consent to a placement for adoption order and for T to be placed for adoption. T was 18 months old. At the date of the hearing the mother had recently given birth to another child (M), a daughter, and there were parallel proceedings relating to her. The mother had lost two older children to care orders on earlier occasions. The grounds of appeal were that at the hearing the judge effectively heard no submissions from P as to the merits of the case, made no provision for evidence to be filed by them after that hearing and conducted herself in a manner which was outside the scheme of the Family Procedure Rules 2010 and in breach of the European Convention on Human Rights 1950 art.6 in failing to provide a fair trial.

Held: Appeal allowed. The courts had the benefit of the decision in *B (Minors) (Contact), Re* [1994] 2 F.L.R. 1, [1995] C.L.Y. 3491, together with the benefit of the public law outline on the approach to managing care proceedings set out in Practice Direction 12A to the Rules, *Re B* applied. It was possible in an appropriate case for a family court to make final orders at an issues resolution hearing. Equally, there was a spectrum of procedure, and where on the spectrum a particular case sat on a particular day and what was permissible or impermissible in terms of a court's approach varied from case to case and must be proportionate to the issue. In the instant case the court considered making orders at the most draconian end of the spectrum of orders open to a family court, being the permanent removal by adoption of a child from not only the care of his parents but also legally from his family. The overriding objective in the

Rules was to discharge the determination of cases justly and fairly, and that was also the requirement of art.6. There was a line beyond which it was impermissible for the court to go: that line would vary from case to case, dependent on the facts and the proportionate approach to procedure. The judge's approach was plainly on the wrong side of the line and was impermissible. The care order and the placement for adoption order were set aside and the case was relisted for a fresh issues resolution hearing (see paras 7-8, 10-12 of judgment).

N (A CHILD) (CARE PROCEEDINGS: ADOPTION), *Re*, [2012] EWCA Civ 1563, [2013] 1 F.L.R. 1244, Hallett, L.J., CA (Civ Div).

1219. Care proceedings–Case management–Correct approach by court to drug testing of parents

The applicant local authority sought care and placement orders in respect of a one-year-old child (C). Shortly after C's birth, she developed a severe illness, which had resulted from the cocaine addiction of her mother (M). The local authority began care proceedings and C was placed with a foster carer. The local authority proposed to place her for adoption. C's father, who at 56 was 28 years older than M, wanted C to come and live with him. The proceedings were subject to significant delays, which primarily resulted from F's insistence on challenging hair-testing evidence which indicated that he, like M, had been using drugs.

Held: Application granted. (1) It would be appropriate to make the care and placement orders sought. F had shown himself to be selfish and dishonest, as well as unprepared to seek out and follow advice. The court had been left with glaring gaps in its knowledge of F and his family, and placing C with him would give rise to unacceptable risks (see paras 46-48 of judgment). (2) F's pursuit of his challenge to the hair-testing analysis, coupled with his adamant denial of cocaine use, had taken centre stage and had derailed the timely resolution of questions about C's future. The delay had inevitably been harmful. In this instance, the courts had been complicit in that delay. In cases like this, it was the court's duty to (a) set a timetable, (b) see that that timetable was adhered to, (c) look critically at the use and pursuit of experts and further expert investigation and (d) remain fully focused throughout on the principle of the likelihood of prejudice to the child's welfare by any delay (para.15). (3) Trichological drug tests had reached a level of maturity and sophistication over the past 20 years or so, and they were not essentially different from drug tests made on other human material. Methods of obtaining the samples for testing, procedures for the care and custody of the sample, contamination and control and the like were all well-established procedures in reputable and accredited laboratories, and the process of analysis had a reputable reliability; it was unlikely to make it prone to fail at the hurdle of the civil standard of proof at the very least. That said, if a test result was to be challenged, the challenge had to be made immediately, to enable the laboratory to reappraise the test result before the opportunity was lost. The responsibility for that rested squarely on the solicitor for the party pursuing the challenge (para.11).

T (CARE PROCEEDINGS: DRUG TESTING), *Re*, [2012] EWHC 4081 (Fam), [2013] 2 F.L.R. 467, Sir Andrew Kirkwood, Fam Div.

1220. Care proceedings–Case management–Court's power to discharge intervener

The appellant local authority appealed against an order that the first respondent intervener (D) in care proceedings be discharged and not be legally represented. The proceedings concerned the five children of the second respondent father (F) and mother (M), and a further child of M's by a different father. The five siblings were taken into care due to longstanding concerns regarding their physical and emotional neglect. The two oldest children made allegations that they had been abused by three of M's brothers, including D, who was 18 years old at the time of the instant proceedings. All three were joined as interveners in the proceedings. There was also an allegation against D by his younger sister, namely that he had sexually abused her when he was about eight or nine and she was five or six. In the past D had admitted to having sexually touched another boy in the same foster home when he was about 13; he said at that time by way of explanation that F had done the same to him. The local authority sought to prove those incidents in the care proceedings. The trial judge decided that D should be present as a witness and purported victim of abuse but not as a suspect, and that it would be unduly stressful and disproportionate to have him present and represented for the whole trial. Hence he discharged D as an intervener. The trial was adjourned part-heard. The local authority submitted that it would be impossible to use the evidence of D's behaviour if no findings were made against him.

Held: Appeal dismissed. As the local authority recognised, the case against D in relation to the oldest of M's children was not that strong. The judge was entitled to have regard to the prospects of its success. F wished to cross-examine D in relation to his credibility and character, while the local authority sought to prove the allegations against D by relying on written records and the evidence of his sister. If he was discharged the most that F could do was challenge D's credibility. F and the local authority would be bound by the answers D gave. Therefore, if he denied all the allegations against him, they could not go further than that. The judge had been entitled to treat the allegations against D as peripheral to the case, which was principally one of severe parental neglect. The main complaint of sexual abuse was against D's eldest brother, not D. Arguably it was not fair to charge an 18-year-old with inappropriate sexual behaviour from when he was much younger. But it was a matter for the judge. He had been right to find it disproportionate to raise three separate allegations, which added complication to an already complex case. The judge would deal with the issue of D's credibility during the trial. He would know full well how much weight to place on the different factors. The issue was one of case management and the judge was best placed to deal with it. He had not erred, *Oxfordshire CC v DP* [2005] EWHC 1593 (Fam), [2005] 2 F.L.R. 1031, [2006] C.L.Y. 1660 applied (see paras 17, 24-28 of judgment).

T (CHILDREN) (CASE MANAGEMENT: DISCHARGE OF PARTY), *Re*, [2011] EWCA Civ 1818, [2013] 2 F.L.R. 795, Ward, L.J., CA (Civ Div).

1221. Care proceedings–Case management–Father's challenge to care order and placement order for adoption–Failure of judge to carry out proper balancing exercise

[Children Act 1989 (c.41) s.31 (2).]

The appellant father (F) appealed against orders made in care proceedings brought by the respondent local authority in respect of a child (P). P's mother (M) and F had separated in 2010. Social services became involved and a child protection plan was implemented, as there were concerns regarding the standard of care P was receiving, domestic violence she was witnessing, and F's aggressive stance towards professionals involved. M moved to a different part of the country with P in 2011 and began a relationship with another man. P was aged one. She was subject to a new child protection plan but suffered non-accidental injuries caused by M's new partner, and was raped by him. An interim care order was imposed in August 2012 and a care order and placement order for adoption made in October 2012. F also challenged case management decisions from April 2012 made in preparation for those orders. F had maintained regular contact with P.

Held: Appeal allowed. (1) The judge's decisions to make a care order with a care plan for adoption and a placement order were wrong, *B (A Child) (Care Proceedings: Appeal), Re* [2013] UKSC 33, [2013] 1 W.L.R. 1911, [2013] 9 C.L. 182 followed. The judge had failed to carry out a proper balancing exercise in order to determine whether it was necessary to make the orders or, if she did, it was not apparent from her judgments. The first difficulty was that the basis on which the judge had approached the historical facts of the case was unclear. A fundamental feature of the case for care and adoption was F's aggressive and violent behaviour and there was some force in his submission that the judge might have proceeded on the basis that his conduct had been more violent or aggressive than had been established on the evidence. The local authority's assessors might have done the same. There needed to be active thought from the outset about the factual and evidential basis of a local authority's case. The President of the Family Division had emphasised the need rigorously to avoid all unnecessary detail in social work chronologies and statements and the threshold statement. Threshold statements which exposed the essential nature of the problems which had led the local authority to consider intervention into the family's life should be contemplated. That required social workers and lawyers to adjust their approach. There was a need to distinguish between fact and what fell into what might loosely be called the processing of those facts. The assessments and opinions of social workers and other professionals would only be valid if the facts on which they proceeded were properly identified. The way to proceed would depend very much on the circumstances of each case. The threshold statement would sometimes sufficiently convey the factual basis on which the court would determine whether the Children Act 1989 s.31 (2) was satisfied and what order was to follow. Where a parent did not accept what was asserted, the local authority would have to produce evidence to establish the allegations. There was also force in F's submission that the positive features of his care of P, when he was looking after her for three days a week unsupervised with the approval of social services, had not been sufficiently recognised. It had to be remembered that it was the conduct of M's boyfriend that precipitated local authority intervention. The original local authority involved had not actually begun care proceedings. The judge had also failed properly to consider the mitigating circumstances in relation to F's apparent aggression to the social workers. His aggression had to be set against the backdrop of what had subsequently happened to P, which was no fault of F's. He had attempted to get the local authority to check up on her and it had not done what it should. There was also little acknowledgement of the fact that adoption was a last resort. The lack of a transcript from the August 2012 hearing ruling F out as P's carer meant that it was not possible to see precisely how the judge's decision was put, and an appellate court had to be careful of placing an unrealistically high burden on the trial judge in relation to the giving of reasons, *B (A Child)* considered. However, what was required was an identification of the nature and risk of the harm it was thought P was at risk of suffering in F's care. It would be good practice for specific matters relied on by the judge to be spelled out. Removal from F's care depended on additional matters being established, including his aggression in other respects. Any remaining intractable risk would need to be weighed against the positive features of his care and the benefits to P of living with her own family. It was not apparent from the judge's available transcripts that she had gone through that process. The matter would be remitted for consideration by another judge (see paras 106-129 of judgment). (2) It was vital that the Court of Appeal had access to transcripts of the judgments which were material to an appeal and, where material, transcripts of the arguments and evidence. It was very important that systems were in place in all courts to ensure that the necessary steps were taken without delay to obtain them. Otherwise proceedings were delayed, which was not in the interests of the parties and, in particular, the children (para.6).

P (A CHILD) (CARE AND PLACEMENT: EVIDENTIAL BASIS OF LOCAL AUTHORITY CASE), *Re*; *sub nom.* P (A CHILD) (CARE PROCEEDINGS: BALANCING EXERCISE), *Re*, [2013] EWCA Civ 963, [2013] 3 F.C.R. 159, Lloyd, L.J., CA (Civ Div).

1222. Care proceedings–Child neglect–Death of two children whilst in sole care of mother–Whether evidence of non-accidental injury or child neglect

[Children Act 1989 (c.41) s.31.]

A local authority brought care proceedings concerning a child (Z). The mother (M) was a single mother with learning difficulties and a low IQ. Her first child (X) had been placed into the care of his grandmother when he was a year old. Her second child (Y) was born a year later, and Z was born the following year. Y died when aged two. M claimed to have found him unconscious in bed. He had been admitted to hospital twice in the week preceding his death and had been suffering from chickenpox. The cause of his death was unknown. Three months later X died, aged four. He had been in M's sole care at the time. M claimed that she had checked on him about an hour after putting him to bed and found he was not breathing. The cause of his death could not be ascertained. The local authority obtained an emergency protection order in respect of Z, who was placed into interim foster care. It then issued care proceedings, alleging that M had asphyxiated X and Y. The court was required to determine whether (i) M was responsible for X and Y's death; (ii) M had neglected the children.

Held: Judgment accordingly. (1) It was for the local authority to prove its allegations on the balance of probabilities based on the evidence, *B (Children) (Sexual Abuse: Standard of Proof), Re* [2008] UKHL 35, [2009] 1 A.C. 11, [2008] C.L.Y. 1501 followed. The court had to consider each piece of evidence in the context of all the other evidence, *T (Children) (Abuse: Standard of Proof), Re* [2004] EWCA Civ 558, [2004] 2 F.L.R. 838, [2004] C.L.Y. 1463 followed and *A Local Authority v K* [2005] EWHC 144 (Fam), [2005] 1 F.L.R. 851, [2005] C.L.Y. 1529 applied. It was also important to have regard to the principles arising from *R. v Cannings (Angela)* [2004] EWCA Crim 1, [2004] 1 W.L.R. 2607, [2004] C.L.Y. 714 and *U (A Child) (Serious Injury: Standard of Proof), Re* [2004] EWCA Civ 567, [2005] Fam. 134, [2004] C.L.Y. 1458. There were a number of features which undermined the local authority's case that X and Y were deliberately killed by M. First, it was significant that no mark was found on either child that might have been linked to an attempt to smother them. Second, it was notable that M had given a consistent account concerning the collapse of both children. The detail of her account, given her learning disability, was a significant pointer to the truth of her account. It was also instructive to consider Y's earlier hospital admissions. If M had attempted to harm him he might have been expected to display some apprehension towards her, but hospital staff reported good interaction between them. Fourth, M's reaction to the collapse of the children was exactly what one would expect if her account were true. Her emphatic denial that she had killed her children was credible. She had genuinely loved her sons. M had a variety of medical conditions which were likely to be genetic in origin. There was evidence that a variant found in one of X's genes might have lead to a risk of arrhythmia in the presence of other genetic or environmental factors. That could be associated with his death in some unknown way. The exclusion of currently known natural causes of infant death did not establish that the death resulted from the deliberate infliction of harm, *Cannings* applied and *U (A Child)* followed. The local authority had not proved on the balance of probabilities that M had killed X or Y (see paras 62-70, 73-76, 144-157 of judgment). (2) There was evidence that M struggled to cope with the children. As a result she did not always provide adequate attention, stimulation or boundaries for them. She failed to prioritise their physical and emotional needs, on occasion putting her own needs and interests first. She was sometimes emotionally neglectful towards them and the home conditions in which they lived were frequently poor. On a number of occasions she failed to protect and supervise the children, so that their safety was at risk. She struggled to keep them clean and provide appropriate food. She also found it difficult to manage their behaviour, sometimes resorting to harsh chastisement that was inappropriate for their age and generally excessive. Taken together, those findings amounted to serious and chronic neglect at a time when she was receiving considerable support through social services as well as from her mother and from friends and neighbours. On that basis the threshold conditions for the making of a care order under the Children Act 1989 s.31 were satisfied (paras 81-83, 162).

AA (A CHILD) (FACT-FINDING HEARING), *Re; sub nom.* A LOCAL AUTHORITY v A MOTHER, [2012] EWHC 2647 (Fam), [2013] 1 F.L.R. 534, Baker, J., Fam Div.

1223. Care proceedings–Disclosure–Police providing confidential information regarding child–Imposition of blanket non-disclosure order–Continuation of order

[European Convention on Human Rights 1950 Art.6, Art.8.]

The court was required to determine whether a blanket non-disclosure order should be continued in care proceedings brought by the applicant local authority in relation to a 16-year-old girl (H). H had been taken into police protective custody after it was alleged that her parents (P) had sexually and physically abused her. The local authority issued care proceedings and sought an interim care order, a no contact order and a non-disclosure order. The application was accompanied by a Form C2 which detailed information provided by the police. The local authority considered that the material met the threshold for the interim care order and justified the making of the further orders on the basis that it was confidential and should not be disclosed to P. The orders were granted and subsequently renewed, and the proceedings transferred to the High Court.

Held: Application granted. (1) The risk to H of significant harm resulting as a consequence of disclosure was a proper and appropriate consideration for the court in the context of an application to withhold relevant material from a party to the proceedings. That risk formed as much a part of the balancing exercise for the court in an application by the police for public interest immunity as it did in an application made by a local authority for the non-disclosure of confidential material, *D (Minors) (Adoption Reports: Confidentiality), Re* [1996] A.C. 593, [1996] C.L.Y. 474 and *M (Disclosure), Re* [1998] 2 F.L.R. 1028, [1999] C.L.Y. 2360 followed. In carrying out the balancing exercise, the serious and deleterious effect to P of non-disclosure was taken into account. The nature and substance of the confidential material at issue was such that a blanket ban was required (see paras 30-34 of judgment). (2) In cases where public interest immunity was in issue, it was the practice, where appropriate and fair to do so, for special advocates to be appointed to assist the court on the issue of whether the immunity claim should be upheld and, once appointed, to sift the evidence with a view to identifying summary material that could be disclosed. The police authority had been entirely open and provided the court with complete disclosure at the earliest possible stage. None of the confidential material was to be disclosed even in summary form. It followed that the court did not require the assistance of a special advocate, *T (Wardship: Impact of Police Intelligence), Re* [2009] EWHC 2440 (Fam), [2010] 1 F.L.R. 1048, [2010] C.L.Y. 1395 applied (paras 36-42). (3) In order to give P proper protection of their rights under the European Convention on Human Rights 1950 art.8 and art.6, it was essential that a special advocate be appointed to represent their interests in relation to continuing and future disclosure and, in the event that there was to be no disclosure going forward, in the testing of the evidence at any subsequent trial (para.49).

BCC v FZ, [2012] EWHC 1154 (Fam), [2013] 1 F.L.R. 974, Eleanor King, J., Fam Div.

1224. Care proceedings–Expert evidence–Baby sustaining personal injury–Admissibility of biomechanical evidence

[Family Procedure Rules 2010 (SI 2010/2955) r.25.1.]

The appellant father (F) appealed against a decision to refuse him permission to adduce expert evidence from a biomechanical engineer in care proceedings brought in respect of his children. F's son (T) had been found, aged 12 days, to have sustained numerous bone fractures and haemorrhages. The local authority instituted care proceedings in respect of T, his brother (M), who was 13 months older, and another older sibling. F gave an account of an incident which he said might have caused T's injuries. He said that he had heard a banging noise in another room, whereupon he discovered T's bouncy chair upside down, with M on top of T. F suggested that M had caused the chair to tip over with T in it. He sought to adduce evidence from an expert biomechanical engineer to show how the suggested incident could have caused T's injuries.

Held: Appeal dismissed. (1) The judge had directed himself correctly as to the principles he had to apply, had not misunderstood the law, had taken into account all relevant matters and had not considered irrelevant matters. He had exercised his discretion in an entirely reasonable way. Nor could any complaint be made about the judge's reasoning as set out in a judgment which more than adequately explained why he had reached his decision. There was no ground on which the court could properly interfere, *Piglowska v Piglowski* [1999] 1 W.L.R. 1360, [1999] C.L.Y. 2421 followed. A biomechanical engineer would be able to obtain values in relation to a variety of factual scenarios for the forces required to tip over the bouncy chair with T in it and the forces applied to T as his body and head hit the floor, but that information was of very limited value. It was unknown, even on F's case, what had really happened. The various possible scenarios were likely to provide a range of very different values for both the tipping forces and the impact forces. It was unknown whether M had been capable of exerting the required tipping forces. Even assuming that those problems could be overcome, there was only a very imperfect understanding of how a baby's body worked, and in particular of how much force was required to produce a particular form of injury, *R (Care Proceedings: Causation), Re* [2011] EWHC 1715 (Fam), [2011] 2 F.L.R. 1384, [2012] C.L.Y. 1354 considered. The prospect of the expert's work providing any useful evidence in the instant case was sufficiently slight as to fall well short of the "reasonably required" test in the Family Procedure Rules 2010 r.25.1. The fundamental problem was that there was no witnessed incident to reconstruct. The case was too far into the realm of speculation for biomechanical engineering to be capable of providing significant assistance (see paras 55-56, 65-67 of judgment). (2) Representation of litigants in family proceedings had to be funded out of the public purse if there was to be equality of arms, and the public purse was not limitless. Money spent on separate representation of litigants in family cases who did not need to be separately represented was money unavailable to pay for representation which was required. The court had been dismayed by what appeared to be the separate representation of parties who stood together in the same interest: the mother had stood behind F's appeal and the children's guardian had supported the local authority in resisting the appeal. There had been four counsel and four solicitors when two of each might have sufficed. Very often in such a case, all that would be needed was a skeleton argument, or even a letter, setting out the absent party's stance. The profession, and the relevant professional bodies, had to take heed of the adverse costs consequences that could follow where legal representation was unnecessarily duplicated, *Birmingham City Council v H* [1994] 2 A.C. 212, [1994] C.L.Y. 3180 and *J (A Child) (Adopted Child: Contact), Re* [2010] EWCA Civ 581, [2011] Fam. 31, [2010] C.L.Y. 1272 considered (paras 73-76).

TG (A CHILD) (CARE PROCEEDINGS: BIOMECHANICAL ENGINEERING EVIDENCE), *Re*; *sub nom.* TG (CHILDREN) (CARE PROCEEDINGS: CASE MANAGEMENT: EXPERT EVIDENCE), *Re*, [2013] EWCA Civ 5, [2013] 1 F.L.R. 1250, Sir James Munby (President, Fam), CA (Civ Div).

1225. Care proceedings–Expert witnesses–Guidance on instruction of publicly funded expert witnesses

[Community Legal Service (Funding) Order 2007 (SI 2007/2441) Sch.5, Sch.6 Pt 002 para.2; Family Procedure Rules 2010 (SI 2010/2955) r.25.1; FPR PD 25A (Experts and Assessors in Family Proceedings) 2010 para.4.3(h).]

The court was required to give guidance on the way in which publicly funded expert witnesses were to be instructed in care proceedings. Permission had been granted in contested care proceedings for the parties to jointly instruct a named independent social worker to undertake an assessment of the parents. It was ordered that the cost of that assessment was to be shared between the parties on the basis that the assessment was a "reasonable and necessary disbursement on the certificates of the publicly funded parties". The mother's application to the

Legal Services Commission for prior authority for a parenting and risk assessment, to be undertaken by the specified social worker, was refused. The mother maintained that the hourly rate charged by the social worker was within the LSC's funding limit for a risk assessment. The LSC eventually granted prior authority for the instruction of the social worker, but only at a capped rate below her hourly charging rate.

Held: Judgment accordingly. (1) The LSC had the power, given to it by Parliament, to refuse to fund the instruction of an expert, or to fund the instruction in part only. Moreover, the LSC had the power to cap the level of fees which might be expended by the expert at a given level. Under the Community Legal Service (Funding) Order 2007 Sch.5, payment by the LSC to an independent social worker was limited to £30 per hour; however, the LSC had a discretion under Sch.6 Pt 002 para.2 to pay in excess of that limit in exceptional circumstances (see paras 38-39 of judgment). (2) It was not appropriate to determine whether the social worker in the instant case should have been instructed, or on what terms. That question was reserved for the tribunal hearing the case. However, it was necessary to provide the following general guidance: (a) the words "the cost thereof is deemed to be a necessary and proper disbursement on [a named individual's] public funding certificate", or words to equivalent effect, were no longer to be used when the court ordered an expert report. Those words did not bind the LSC or anyone else. It was far better to follow the wording of the relevant Regulations, particularly if the court was being asked to approve rates in excess of those allowed under the Order. (b) The word "necessary" in the Family Procedure Rules 2010 r.25.1 was shortly to be substituted for "reasonably required", and the question that the court would need to ask was whether the expert report was necessary for the resolution of the case. (c) Good case management required the court to identify the issues on which it wanted the expert to report. (d) Where the court determined an expert report was necessary it should say so and give its reasons, which could be done by providing a preamble to the order or by a short judgment. (e) A decision by the LSC, and any order of the court, including a consent order, needed to be supported by reasons. (f) An application for prior authority was to be made at the earliest opportunity and had to be carefully drafted and supported by reasons. (g) It was necessary for the LSC to deal with applications promptly and to give reasons for its decision, particularly if the application was refused or granted only to a limited extent. (h) Any urgent case should be marked as such with reasons for its urgency. (i) Courts should be aware that FPR PD 25A para.4.3(h) provided that the person wishing to instruct an expert must explain why the expert evidence proposed could not be given by social services undertaking a core assessment or by the children's guardian (para.45). (3) The court provided a suggested form of order that could be used to direct the instruction of an expert. Such an order was to be buttressed by reasons as set out in the above guidance (paras 54-55).

A LOCAL AUTHORITY v DS, [2012] EWHC 1442 (Fam), [2012] 1 W.L.R. 3098, Sir Nicholas Wall (President, Fam), Fam Div.

1226. Care proceedings–Findings of fact–Entitlement of judge to find children exposed to explicit sexual conduct between visitors to family home

[Children Act 1989 (c.41) s.37.]

The appellant mother (M) appealed against a finding of fact made by the judge in ongoing care proceedings concerning her three daughters. In early 2008, when M and the girls' father (F) had separated, the children lived with M. Both M and F had indulged in excessive and uncontrolled drug and alcohol abuse, which M continued whilst she was the girls' sole carer between March and May 2008, when they were aged six, five and three. During that period, M encouraged and entertained a group of teenagers and other individuals in her home to socialise. The children were removed from M's care in May 2008 and went to live with F. In 2011, one of the children alleged that M might have had some direct sexual involvement with her. All three children were interviewed. In care proceedings brought by the respondent local authority, the judge was invited to make findings of fact against M, in accordance with a schedule of allegations, concerning her direct involvement in sexual conduct with her children. The judge held that there was insufficient evidence to find the allegations proved, but expressed his concerns over the children having described the commission of adult sexual acts and the acknowledged circumstances in M's home in 2008. He departed from the schedule and stated his conclusion that, on the balance of probabilities (i) whilst in M's care in March to May 2008 the children had been exposed to and had witnessed inappropriate sexual conduct including explicit sexual conduct between young persons and adults; (ii) M had not protected the children from witnessing that conduct. By her appeal, M sought to strike out the words "including explicit sexual conduct between young persons and adults" from that finding. The local authority accepted that the appeal should be allowed. Attempts to agree an alternative form of words that M, the local authority and F would all accept were thwarted by F's failure to engage in that process.

Held: Appeal allowed. (1) The judge had gone further than the strength of the evidence permitted; the children had not described the activity found by the judge. He had understandably been concerned about the children and the general adult behaviour they had been exposed to whilst in M's care, but it was not open to him on the available material to find that they had actually been exposed to sexual acts between young people and adults in their home. The words "including explicit sexual conduct between young persons and adults" would, accordingly, be struck out from the judge's findings of fact. The case would be returned to continue in the county court, before the same judge, since irrespective of the excision from his finding of the contested words, it was plain that the threshold criteria under the Children Act 1989 s.37 was nevertheless met. (2) It was regrettable that nobody had communicated with the Court of Appeal to indicate that the appeal was not contested. Had that happened, the Court of Appeal would have directed the other parties to respond to draw up an agreed order.

J-L (FINDINGS OF FACT: SCHEDULE OF ALLEGATIONS), *Re*, [2012] EWCA Civ 1832, [2013] 1 F.L.R. 1240, Longmore, L.J., CA (Civ Div).

1227. Care proceedings–Findings of fact–Injuries and murder of baby–Fact-finding hearing on mother and father's culpability–Necessary standard of proof

The court was required to make findings of fact in an application by the applicant local authority for care orders in respect of the third and fourth respondent children of the first and second respondent mother and father (M and F). M and F claimed that one morning M had found their baby son (S) lying face down in his cot whereupon she telephoned for an ambulance. Paramedics unsuccessfully attempted to resuscitate S. S's autopsy and post-mortem examination revealed multiple injuries, some extremely serious, including a torn upper lip fraenulum, a laceration and scabs on his feet, and bruising, most notably to his hands. Various witnesses gave oral evidence at the fact-finding hearing including M and F, lay witnesses, pathologists and paediatric consultants and workers. Photographic evidence of S's injuries, of his bedding and clothing on the morning he died and of family outings was also put before the court. Some of the pathologists suggested that the histological evidence indicated that S's injuries had been caused before his death and that his injuries were non-accidental. The local authority argued that the medical evidence was balanced, measured and compelling to such an extent that for the court to conclude that S's injuries were caused accidentally there would need to be a heavy investment in M and F's credibility, and such an investment was unjustified because their evidence was inconsistent, contradictory and implausible.

Held: Judgment for defendants. The court decided that it should not judge the histological evidence in isolation, but should weigh it against its assessment of M and F's credibility and the improbability, from a non-scientific stance, that they had caused S's injuries and death. M and F appeared to be straightforward, decent, fundamentally honest and loving and caring parents when giving their evidence. They had not been materially inconsistent in relation to circumstantial or peripheral matters. M's distress in the 999 call was obviously authentic. In judging M and F's truthfulness as to the events in question the court had to consider the implausibility of what the local authority sought to prove, and the sequence of events it advocated was very unlikely. Based on the court's survey of the lay and psychological evidence, it was extremely improbable, but still possible, that M and F had deliberately inflicted injury on S. The paediatric and photographic evidence did not alter the conclusion that it was improbable that M and F had caused the injuries: there were innocent explanations for blood being found on the S's bedding and clothes because he suffered from nose-bleeds, had an erupting tooth and had bleeding feet as a result of a foot infection. Whilst the histological evidence was powerful, it also did not displace that conclusion. The court was left with two improbable explanations: namely that S was brutalised and murdered by his parents, or that he suffered a sequence of pathologically unlikely events that gave rise to his injuries and overwhelmed him, *Rhesa Shipping Co SA v Edmunds (The Popi M)* [1985] 1 W.L.R. 948, [1985] C.L.Y. 3207 considered. The instant case was one of those very rare cases where the burden of proof came to the court's rescue as the local authority, with the burden of showing that what it alleged took place, had not satisfied the court that it did, *S-B (Children) (Care Proceedings: Standard of Proof), Re* [2009] UKSC 17, [2010] 1 A.C. 678, [2010] C.L.Y. 1325 and *B (Children) (Sexual Abuse: Standard of Proof), Re* [2008] UKHL 35, [2009] 1 A.C. 11, [2008] C.L.Y. 1501 followed. Accordingly, M and F were entitled to the return of a value of zero and the local authority's account, that they deliberately inflicted violence on their children, was to be treated in law as not having happened. That did not mean that there was not a real possibility that M and F had grossly mistreated their children, but a suspicion of risk was not enough at a fact-finding hearing. The court was not satisfied, on the balance of probabilities and having surveyed all of the evidence, that M and F had deliberately abused their children or that they had murdered and neglected S (see paras 232, 235-236, 238-239, 261-264 of judgment).

A COUNTY COUNCIL v MOTHER, [2011] EWHC 1804 (Fam), [2012] 2 F.L.R. 939, Mostyn, J., Fam Div.

1228. Care proceedings–Foreign states–Placement of child in another Member State–Requirement to consult responsible authority

[Regulation 2201/2003 Art.56(1), Art.56.]

The appellant (B) appealed against an order remitting the case from the High Court to the county court for a decision as to the future care of her four-year-old daughter (D). B was a Lithuanian national who lawfully resided in England by virtue of Lithuania's membership of the European Union. In response to a communication from the Lithuanian authority responsible for child welfare, the local authority obtained an emergency protection order and D had since been in foster care. Because it was believed that the Lithuanian authorities were going to seek D's return to Lithuania for placement there, the county court judge transferred the case to the High Court. The High Court judge found that the Lithuanian authorities were content for the English court to decide whether D could be returned to B or not, but if she was not they had made clear that they wanted to undertake her replacement in Lithuania. He therefore remitted the case to the county court to consider whether B was able to care for D, and in the event that she was not, the arrangements necessary to comply with the request of the Lithuanian authorities pursuant to Regulation 2201/2003 art.56 to undertake her placement in Lithuania.

Held: Appeal allowed in part. Regulation 2201/2003 art.56(1) and art.56(2) did not give a Member State an entitlement to call for the placement of a child within its jurisdiction. Nor therefore did they eliminate or constrict the domestic court's ordinary obligation to make its own judgment of where the child's best interests lay. The sole purpose and effect of art.56(1) and (2) was to require a court which was considering placing a child in institutional or foster care in another Member State to consult any authority responsible for child placements in that Member State and not to decide on any such placement without that authority's consent, *Health Service Executive v SC (C-92/12 PPU)* [2013] C.E.C. 235 followed. In short, it was to ensure that children at risk were not sent into a transnational void. Article 56(2) tended to mislead by the use of the terms "requesting" and "requested" state, when no request was involved. What was meant were, respectively, the consulting state and the state consulted. If D could not safely be returned to B, then return to Lithuania would be under consideration. In that connection art.56 would have a role, but it was a consultative role, not one which tied the hands of the English court or excluded or reduced its obligation to arrive at its own judgment as to the child's best interests. The judge had fallen into error and that part of his order for remission was deleted (see paras 5-10 of judgment).

AB (A CHILD) (BIIR: CARE PROCEEDINGS), *Re*, [2012] EWCA Civ 978, [2013] I.L.Pr. 4, Thorpe, L.J., CA (Civ Div).

1229. **Care proceedings–Genetic testing–Possibility that children susceptible to Huntington's disease–Appropriateness of predictive testing**

The court had to rule on the issue of whether two very young boys, who were subject to care proceedings in which the local authority was likely to propose adoption, should be tested for susceptibility to Huntington's disease. The boys' father had said at a child protection conference that his mother and brother suffered from the disease and that he suspected that he too suffered from it. The disease was a hereditary disorder of the central nervous system caused by a defective gene on chromosome IV. Anyone whose parent had the disease was born with a 50 per cent chance of inheriting the gene. Symptoms usually emerged when people were between 30 and 50. The local authority was in favour of testing, asserting that finding an adoptive placement would be much more difficult if testing was not done. A consultant clinical geneticist (P) gave evidence. He opposed testing. His view was that predictive testing would not produce any medical gain for the children; while there might be no medical harm as a result of the test, there could be adverse psycho-social consequences from having a diagnosis of an adult disorder in the future; he highlighted, in particular, the risk of discrimination, altered relationships with parents and siblings, and the removal of the children's autonomy in making their own decisions at a later and more relevant stage in their lives; further, whereas the likelihood of both children being free from the disease mutation was 25 per cent, the chances that one was affected and the other not was 50 per cent, which gave rise to a significant risk that testing might lead to the children being separated if an adoptive placement could be found for the child who did not carry the gene.

Held: Judgment accordingly. (1) There was a significant possibility that both boys carried the gene and a greater possibility that one boy carried it but not the other. There were factors in favour of testing and factors against it. Overall, however, it was not in the welfare interests of the boys for the court to order testing. The risk, identified in the consensus of opinion among professionals working in the field, including P, of emotional and psychological harm to the boys if one or both of them had the gene, including the risk of separation of the siblings and the damage to their personal autonomy by being deprived of the right, available to all other children, to decide for themselves when they reached adulthood whether or not to undergo the test, outweighed the risk of harm arising from the likelihood that it would be harder (though not impossible) to find an adoptive placement if testing was not carried out (see paras 43, 51 of judgment). (2) As to similar applications made in the future, while it was likely that, in most instances, a court would reach a similar conclusion, each case would turn on its own facts and in some cases the balancing exercise would lead to a different outcome. It was to be stressed that this decision involved an untreatable condition which was unlikely to develop until mid-adult life. Cases involving conditions that developed during childhood, or which were susceptible to treatment in childhood, would involve a very different balancing exercise and were likely to lead to a different conclusion (para.53).

Y (MINORS) (CARE PROCEEDINGS: GENETIC TESTING), *Re; sub nom.* X COUNTY COUNCIL v A MOTHER, [2013] EWHC 953 (Fam), [2013] 2 F.L.R. 249, Baker, J., Fam Div.

1230. Care proceedings–Grandparents–Order directing removal of baby from grandmother's care–Wrongful characterisation of risk on evidence–Grandmother's mental health

[Mental Health Act1983 (c.20) s.3; Care Planning, Placement and Case Review (England) Regulations 2010 (SI 2010/959).]

The appellant mother (M) appealed against an interim care order granted in respect of her nine-month-old child (C) which directed the immediate removal of C from her care and the care of the respondent maternal grandmother (G). M had become unwell shortly before C's birth and was admitted to hospital under the Mental Health Act1983 s.3 in November 2011. In February 2012 M was gradually discharged with C to G's home. The local authority obtained an interim care order supporting that arrangement and G subsequently became C's primary carer. Despite a previous positive report of G, interviews conducted in July 2012, during which G had reported her perception of M's previous mental health collapse in 2009, raised substantial concerns. G regarded M's behaviour at that time as demonic, but failed to involve medical professionals and instead sought help from the church before medical help was sought. The fostering panel requested psychological assessments of G, but they could not be obtained prior to the date by which, under the Care Planning, Placement and Case Review (England) Regulations 2010, the local authority had to end the placement in default of a successful assessment of G. The local authority applied to remove C from G's home pending the assessments. The judge acceded to that application and directed C's immediate removal irrespective of the Regulations as he concluded that C was in a "deeply unsafe place" and that G could hallucinate at any time, possibly hallucinating that C was possessed, and consequently C could be harmed. Those conclusions were based on the July interviews and G's own mental health history which included G suffering from hallucinations 30 years earlier. There had been no significant mental health events since that date. The issue was whether, on the evidence, the risks were so significant that C had to be removed to foster care whilst the assessment of G was undertaken. M and G submitted, with the father and guardian's support, that the judge had had no evidential basis to conclude that C would be at risk of harm from G as nothing of the sort predicted by him had occurred in the seven months that C had been in G's home.

Held: Appeal allowed. Despite the care that the judge had taken in the conduct of the proceedings and delivery of his judgment, the characterisation of the case that he made on the evidence had not been open to him and had been plainly wrong. In particular, the conclusion that C herself might act in a way that G might think she was possessed by demons had not been supported on the evidence. Although there had been some evidence that G had suffered from hallucinations previously, that had been 30 years ago and there had been no reported repeat of that behaviour. What seemed more concerning to the judge was what G had reportedly seen and heard during M's mental health collapse in 2009. However, those reports did not seem to justify the label "hallucinations". It had been G's perception and understanding of the physical actions and sounds experienced in 2009. There was no evidence that M was harmed by G's actions; help had been sought and that help had led to M's hospitalisation. Even if C had been present in 2009, it was unlikely that she would have been directly harmed or discomforted at her age. There had, therefore, been no grounds for the concern that C would be directly harmed by G. C was not going to exhibit any physical manifestations of poor mental health at her age that could possibly trigger a misinterpretation by G, who was otherwise described as a positive carer. Although the appeal would have been allowed without it, there was also the benefit of new information in the form of an initial psychological assessment of G which supported that nothing untoward was likely to happen to C in her care. Due to the Regulations it was not open to the court to make an interim care order in favour of G; however, on the material before the court there was clearly no pressing need from C's point of view for her to be removed from G's home, where she had remained throughout proceedings. Accordingly, a residence order in favour of G and a supervision order for the local authority were granted.

S (A CHILD) (INTERIM RESIDENCE), *Re*, [2012] EWCA Civ 1915, [2013] 2 F.L.R. 446, Ward, L.J., CA (Civ Div).

1231. **Care proceedings–Judgments and orders–Judge making oral decision in fact-finding hearing–Whether entitled to change mind before order sealed**

The appellant father (F) appealed against a decision ([2012] EWCA Civ 984, [2013] 1 F.L.R. 209, [2012] C.L.Y. 1357) that a judge who had announced her decision in family proceedings ought not to have subsequently changed her mind. On December 15, 2011 the judge had given an oral judgment following a fact-finding hearing in the course of care proceedings. The child concerned had sustained non-accidental injuries and F and the child's mother (M) were the only possible perpetrators. The question was whether either could be identified as the sole perpetrator. The judgment, which was partially transcribed, was not sealed until February 28, 2012. In it, the judge identified F as the sole perpetrator. On February 15, 2012, shortly before the final hearing, she delivered a "perfected judgment" in which she changed her mind, finding that either parent could have inflicted the injuries. M appealed, asking that the matter be remitted to the judge for amplification and clarification. The Court of Appeal allowed her appeal, quashing the February 15 judgment and ordering that the December 15 judgment should stand. The issue was whether and in what circumstances a judge who had announced her decision in family or civil proceedings was entitled to change her mind.

Held: Appeal allowed. (1) A judge was entitled to reverse his decision at any time before his order was drawn up and perfected. Under the Civil Procedure Rules r.40.2(2)(b), the order was perfected by being sealed by the court. Once that had been done, the judge had no jurisdiction to change his mind unless he had an express power to vary the previous order. In the instant case, the judge had clearly had jurisdiction to change her mind, her original judgment not having been sealed. The question was whether she was right to have exercised it. The instant court was not bound by *Barrell Enterprises, Re* [1973] 1 W.L.R. 19 or by any previous authority to hold that a judge could revisit his own unperfected decision only in exceptional circumstances. The judge's overriding objective was to deal with the case justly, *Stewart v Engel (Permission to Amend)* [2000] 1 W.L.R. 2268, [2000] C.L.Y. 585 considered, and a relevant factor had to be whether any party had acted on the original decision to his detriment. In *Blenheim Leisure (Restaurants) Ltd (No.3), Re* Times, November 9, 1999, [1999] C.L.Y. 453, Neuberger J gave some examples of cases where it might be just to revisit the earlier decision. Those were only examples. Every case depended on its facts, and a carefully considered change of mind could be sufficient to make it just to revisit the earlier decision, *Blenheim Leisure* considered. In allowing M's appeal, the Court of Appeal had applied the exceptionality test, which was not the correct approach, *Barrell* disapproved. None of the parties had irretrievably changed their position as a result of the December 15 judgment; the child had remained where she was; her future placement had yet to be decided; and the final decision on the care order had yet to be taken. No judge was to be required to decide the future placement of a child upon what he believed to be a false basis. When it came to the final decision, the child's welfare was the paramount consideration. The judge's discretion had to be exercised judicially and not capriciously. While that might entail offering the parties the opportunity of making submissions on the proposed change, it was difficult to see what that would have done in the instant case other than to reiterate what had already been said. In the circumstances, the judge was entitled to exercise her power to change her mind (see paras 16-19, 21-27, 29-30 of judgment). (2) (Obiter) The considerations would have been similar had the original order been sealed before the change of mind. In care proceedings, the fact-finding hearing was merely part of the process of trying the case, and even when it was completed, the case was part-heard until the final hearing. The judge was entitled to revisit an identification of the perpetrator made in a fact-finding hearing if subsequent evidence warranted it, *S-B (Children) (Care Proceedings: Standard of Proof), Re* [2009] UKSC 17, [2010] 1 A.C. 678, [2010] C.L.Y. 1325 considered. He had to be able to keep an open mind until the final decision, at least if fresh evidence or further developments indicated that an earlier decision was wrong. Moreover, the court's case management powers included the power to vary or revoke previous case management orders. Where there was such a power, there was no magic in the sealing of the order. The question was whether it was proper to vary it. The power to vary had to be exercised judicially rather than capriciously, and it had to be exercised in accordance with the overriding objective of dealing with cases justly. It would be inconsistent with that objective if the court could not revisit factual findings in the light of later developments. However, if the later development was simply a judicial change of mind, the arguments were finely balanced and cases involving children might be different from other civil proceedings. As the point did not arise in the instant case, the court declined to express any view on it (paras 32-45). (3) The best safeguard against a judge having to change his mind was for him to give a fully and properly reasoned judgment from which a dissatisfied party could appeal (para.46).

L-B (CHILDREN) (CARE PROCEEDINGS: POWER TO REVISE JUDGMENT), *Re*; *sub nom.* L-B (CHILDREN) (REVERSAL OF JUDGMENT), RE; L (CHILDREN) (PRELIMINARY FINDING: POWER TO REVERSE), *Re*, [2013] UKSC 8, [2013] 1 W.L.R. 634, Lord Neuberger (President), SC.

1232. Care proceedings–Judgments and orders–Parents exonerated from culpability in relation to injuries to first child–Dismissal of care proceedings and revocation of special guardianship order

The applicant parents (M and F) sought the dismissal of care proceedings in relation to their daughters (X and Y) and the revocation of a special guardianship order in relation to X. Following the judgment of the court in *Sutton LBC v G* [2012] EWHC 2604 (Fam), [2013] 1 F.L.R. 833, [2013] 8 C.L. 152, in which F was exonerated from injuring X and M was exonerated from any culpability in respect of her, the respondent local authority had withdrawn all allegations against M and F and assessments had taken place to plan the placement of Y with them.

Held: Judgment accordingly. (1) The care proceedings in relation to both X and Y were dismissed (see para.6 of judgment). (2) Directions were given in relation to M and F's application to revoke the special guardianship order. The maternal grandparents had successfully cared for X for the last five-and-a-half years but, due to their mature years and periods of ill health combined with the realisation of what would be best for her, agreed for her to be returned to the care of her parents (paras 14-17).

SUTTON LBC v G [2013] 1 F.L.R. 914, Hogg, J., Fam Div.

1233. Care proceedings–Right of access to court–Appointment of Official Solicitor for benefit of mother in care proceedings–Whether violation of art.6(1) European Convention on Human Rights 1950

[European Convention on Human Rights 1950 Art.6(1).]

The complainant (R) complained that the respondent state had violated her rights under the European Convention on Human Rights 1950 art.6(1) by appointing the Official Solicitor to act on her behalf. R, who had learning difficulties, had given birth to a baby (K) prematurely. K suffered from a number of significant medical conditions and required constant care. The local authority, having doubts about R's ability to care for K, initiated care proceedings. R instructed a solicitor, who doubted her ability to understand the advice she was being given. A clinical psychologist assessed R and reported that she would find it difficult to understand the advice given by her solicitor, would not be able to make informed decisions on the basis of that advice, and did not have the capacity to give informed consent to a placement order. The Official Solicitor consented to act for R's benefit. The court granted the local authority's application for a placement order. R submitted that the question of whether she had litigation capacity had not been fully tested by a court and she had not been told the implications of the Official Solicitor being instructed; she not had a full opportunity to challenge the appointment; she had not been advised to seek independent legal advice; she had not been told that she could challenge the report; and that the Official Solicitor had acted in K's interests rather than hers.

Held: Complaint dismissed. There had been no violation of art.(6)(1). The right was not an absolute one and the article gave the state a free choice about the means by which it was to be guaranteed. While the state was allowed a certain margin of appreciation, any limitation on the rights guaranteed by art.6 had to be proportionate and pursue a legitimate aim, and the right was not to be restricted in such a way that its very essence was impaired. In cases involving people with disabilities, the European Court of Human Rights had permitted the domestic courts a certain margin of appreciation for the making of procedural arrangements to secure the good administration of justice and protect the health of the person concerned. Again, such arrangements were not to affect the essence of the art.6(1) right. In the instant case, the proceedings were of the utmost importance to R. While the issue before the domestic court had been relatively straightforward, the evidence was not: there were a significant number of expert reports which an applicant with a learning disability would have obvious difficulty in understanding, in terms of both their content and their implications. It had been not only appropriate but also necessary for the state to take measures to ensure that R's best interests were represented in the proceedings. A failure to do so might in itself have amounted to a violation of art.6(1). The decision to appoint the Official Solicitor had not been taken lightly. It was imperative that there was some means whereby R could challenge the Official Solicitor's appointment or the continuing need for his services. While there was no formal review procedure, further assessments had been made of R's litigation capacity in the course of the proceedings, and she had been told that she could make a complaint or apply to have the Official Solicitor discharged. That afforded her an appropriate and effective means by which to challenge either his appointment or the continuing need for his services. It would not have been appropriate for the court to have carried out periodic reviews of R's litigation capacity because that would have caused unnecessary delay and been prejudicial to K's welfare. Nor would it have been appropriate for R to have been encouraged to seek separate legal advice. Given that she had been found to lack the capacity to instruct a solicitor, that would not have been an effective means by which to protect her interests. Any means of challenging the Official Solicitor's appointment would only satisfy the requirements of art.6(1) if the fact and implications of his appointment, and the way in which it could be challenged, were clearly explained to the protected person in language appropriate to her level of understanding. That had been done and adequate safeguards had thus been in place to ensure that the nature of the proceedings were fully explained and that, had R sought to challenge the Official Solicitor's appointment, procedures were in place to enable her to do so. The Official Solicitor's role was to act for R's benefit. Nevertheless, K's interests were the touchstone by which the domestic court would assess the case, and the Official Solicitor had therefore had to consider what was in K's best interests. The fact that he had borne K's interests in mind did not amount to a violation of R's art.6(1) rights. Nor did acting in R's best interests require him to advance any argument R wished, so long as her views about K's future were made known to the domestic court. It was clear that that had happened and that the essence of R's art.6(1) right had not been impaired (see paras 61-78 of judgment).

RP v UNITED KINGDOM (38245/08) [2013] 1 F.L.R. 744, Judge Garlicki (President), ECHR.

1234. **Care proceedings–Transfer of proceedings–Baby born in Ireland to English mother–Mother returning to England–Transfer of Irish care proceedings to England**

[Children Act 1989 (c.41) Pt IV, s.31 (8); Family Procedure Rules 2010 (SI 2010/2955) r.12.66; Regulation 2201/2003 Art.15, Art.56.]

The court considered a request from the High Court of the Republic of Ireland under Regulation 2201/2003 art.15(1)(b) to accept jurisdiction over care proceedings begun in Ireland in respect of a baby girl (L). The older children of L's mother (M) had been the subject of public law proceedings brought by her local authority (X) in England. M gave birth to L in Ireland to avoid X bringing proceedings in respect of her. However, the Health Service Executive of Ireland immediately brought care proceedings and L was placed in foster care. M returned to England, to the area of another local authority. She sought, and all parties agreed, that the care proceedings should be transferred to England. The instant court considered (i) whether to accept jurisdiction; (ii) the practicalities of a transfer; (iii) which local authority should be the applicant in any public law proceedings in England.

Held: Judgment accordingly. (1) The Irish courts had the sole habitual residence-based jurisdiction. However, England was the place of L's nationality. M was habitually resident in England, which was another basis upon which L could have a particular connection with England. The English court was prima facie better placed to hear the case: M had returned to England and it would be preferable for her to have the opportunity to oppose any order in respect of L in the courts of the country where she lived; further, the evidence justifying public intervention in the family's life had originated in England, in X's area. Article 15(1) and art.15(5) of the Regulation indicated that the court's function in determining a transfer request was limited to a "best interests" determination, rather than a wider review of all the criteria for transfer. In all the circumstances, particularly the facts that L was British and had no family in Ireland, M was in England, and the history of L's siblings originated entirely in X's area, it was in L's best interests that the proceedings should be transferred (see paras 31-38 of judgment). (2) Although no formal request under art.56 had yet been made, a competent English authority, namely either X or Y, would consent to the placement of L as art.56 required, *Health Service Executive v SC (C-92/12 PPU)* [2013] C.E.C. 235 applied. The Irish court would exercise a residual jurisdiction to achieve the transition of L and the proceedings to England, after which its jurisdiction would cease. The Family Procedure Rules 2010 r.12.66 essentially provided that the court should proceed as if a public law order had been made in respect of L under the Children Act 1989 Pt IV; it followed that the provisions of Pt IV in their entirety applied to the future management of the case once English jurisdiction was engaged. Rule 12.66(2) contemplated that the court would take preparatory steps to give effect to the imminent receipt of the proceedings. That was an exception to the principle that the courts would not generally exercise jurisdiction in relation to a child who was neither physically present nor habitually resident in England, but it was a legitimate approach, *W v W (A Minor) (Mirror Order)* [2011] EWCA Civ 703, [2011] 3 F.C.R. 151, [2011] C.L.Y. 1393 followed. The case would be allocated to the Family Division of the High Court and reserved to the instant judge (paras 42-47). (3) The identified applicant authority should be the one which was likely to be the designated authority under s.31 (8) of the 1989 Act. "Ordinary residence", for the purposes of s.31 (8) (a), was broadly synonymous with "habitual residence". A child's habitual residence was generally that of her parents, but where a child had been born abroad, and had never set foot in England, she could not be said to be habitually resident in England, *A v A (Children) (Habitual Residence)* [2012] EWCA Civ 1396, [2013] Fam. 232 applied. Accordingly, L was not ordinarily resident in any authority in England. Regarding s.31 (8) (b), the circumstances in consequence of which the application before the court was to be considered could not be said to have arisen in Y's area. The circumstances of M's older children formed the essential factual foundation of public authority intervention in Ireland, and that would be relied on by the applicant authority to establish the threshold criteria under s.31. Accordingly, X would be designated for the purpose of a care order in the instant case; it was therefore the appropriate applicant authority, and would be the competent authority under art.56 (paras 48, 62-67). (4) Where an art.15 request was made, it would be helpful for the requesting state to communicate such a request at once through the International Judicial Network; further or alternatively, the court in the requesting state should invite one of the parties to drive along the request in the requested state (para.39).

M (A CHILD) (FOREIGN CARE PROCEEDINGS: TRANSFER), RE; *sub nom.* LM (A CHILD) (TRANSFER OF IRISH PROCEEDINGS), *Re,* [2013] EWHC 646 (Fam), [2013] Fam. 308, Cobb, J., Fam Div.

1235. **Chief Inspector of Education Children's Services and Skills–Local safeguarding children boards–Reviews**

THE LOCAL SAFEGUARDING CHILDREN BOARDS (REVIEW) REGULATIONS 2013, SI 2013/2299; made under the Children Act 2004 s.14, s.15A, s.66. In force: October 9, 2013; .

These Regulations make provision for the review of local safeguarding children boards by Her Majesty's Chief Inspector of Education, Children's Services and Skills.

1236. **Child benefit–Child support**

THE CHILD SUPPORT (MISCELLANEOUS AMENDMENTS) REGULATIONS 2013, SI 2013/1517; made under the Child Support Act 1991 s.28G, s.42, s.51, s.52, s.54, s.55, Sch.1 para.10, Sch.1 para.10C; and the Child Maintenance and Other Payments Act 2008 s.55, s.57. In force: in accordance with art.1 (2) (3) (4).; .

These Regulations contain provisions amending various sets of Child Support Regulations. Some of the provisions in these Regulations make amendments to child support provisions following changes to legislation which allow a person to make an election for payments of child benefit not to be made in cases where the person or their partner has income of over £50,000 per year.

1237. **Child Maintenance and Other Payments Act 2008 (c.6)–Commencement No.11 and Transitional Provisions Order**

THE CHILD MAINTENANCE AND OTHER PAYMENTS ACT 2008 (COMMENCEMENT NO.11 AND TRANSITIONAL PROVISIONS) ORDER 2013, SI 2013/SI 2013/1860 (C.79); made under the Child Maintenance and Other Payments Act 2008 s.62. Commencement details: bringing into force various provisions of the 2008 Act on July 29, 2013.; .

This Order brings into force provisions of the Child Maintenance and Other Payments Act 2008 for the purpose of applying new rules for calculating child support maintenance to certain applications made on or after July 29 2013 and certain cases linked to those applications.

1238. **Child protection–Reporting restrictions–Local authority's public report concerning child abuse–Appropriate extent of redaction–Balancing rights under art.8 and art.10 European Convention on Human Rights 1950**

[Children Act 2004 (c.31); Local Safeguarding Children Boards (Wales) Regulations 2006 (SI 2006/1705); European Convention on Human Rights 1950 Art.8, Art.10.]

The appellant children's guardian appealed against a decision concerning the extent to which a document produced by the respondent local authority which referred to two children (X and Y) should be redacted. A parent had been convicted in the Crown Court of a serious offence relating to X. The local authority gave an undertaking in accordance with the Children Act 2004 and the Local Safeguarding Children Boards (Wales) Regulations 2006 which required it to produce an overview report and an anonymised summary of the overview report. Guidance published by the Welsh Assembly Government also provided that the local authority should arrange for an anonymised executive summary to be prepared, which was to be made available publicly at the local authority's offices. The local authority prepared an executive summary which referred to the Crown Court proceedings in such a way as to enable many readers to recognise immediately which family was being referred to. It also referred to the fact that Y, another child in the family, had also been a victim of parental abuse, which was a fact that had not emerged during the criminal proceedings and was not in the public domain. A reporting restrictions order was granted preventing publication of the executive summary. The local authority applied for a variation of the reporting restrictions order to permit publication of the executive summary, but with the redaction of the number, gender and ages of the children. The judge referred to the fact that he had to balance the rights protected by the European Convention on Human Rights 1950 art.8 and art.10, but decided to allow the local authority to present the executive summary with the proposed redactions. The judge inserted into the reporting restriction order a proviso permitting publication of the executive summary in its redacted form.

Held: Appeal allowed. (1) Although the judge had summarised the relevant law correctly, the way in which he struck the balance between art.8 and art.10 was wrong. Publication of the references to the proceedings in the Crown Court and to Y suffering abuse needed to be balanced against the children's fragile situation and the real concerns about their welfare. The judge had correctly identified that the executive summary required redaction, but the redactions he required were confined solely to the number, gender and ages of the children. That did not address the difficulty presented by the references to the Crown Court proceedings and to Y also being a victim of parental abuse, given that what was said about the proceedings in the Crown Court would enable many readers to recognise immediately which family was being referred to and would enable anyone else to obtain that information by way of a simple internet search. The judge did not seem to have grappled with that fundamental problem, and had certainly not identified how the redactions would adequately achieve the desired objective. If the executive summary was published in the form authorised by the judge, the children would suffer from inevitable media reporting, which was likely to be upsetting. The children, Y in particular, would have to live with the realisation that a painful part of their intensely private family history had been exposed to the world. A more drastic form of redaction than approved by the judge was necessary (see paras 51-56 of judgment). (2) (Obiter) The form of the reporting restrictions order was thoroughly objectionable and left it wholly unclear precisely what document might be published and what the intended ambit of the injunction was. It was intolerable that a layman who risked imprisonment from publishing a document which he believed to be of public interest and importance should be left to decipher a court order in such a way (paras 60, 64). (3) (Per curiam) As a consequence of the devolution settlement, family law in Wales differed increasingly from family law in England. The court expressed the view that it would be of great assistance if, in such cases and as a matter of practice, advocates brought to the court's attention the fact that there was such a difference and were able to both identify the corresponding provisions applicable in the other country and, at least in summary, to indicate the nature of the differences between the two regimes (paras 66-67).

X (CHILDREN) (SERIOUS CASE REVIEW: PUBLICATION), *Re*; *sub nom.* X (CHILDREN) (EXECUTIVE SUMMARY OF SERIOUS CASE REVIEW: REPORTING RESTRICTIONS), *Re*, [2012] EWCA Civ 1500, [2013] 2 F.L.R. 628, Pill, L.J., CA (Civ Div).

1239. Child support–Committal orders–Wilful refusal or culpable neglect in making child maintenance payments–Practice and procedure under s.39A Child Support Act 1991–Compliance with art.6 European Convention on Human Rights 1950

[Child Support Act 1991 (c.48) s.36, s.39A; European Convention on Human Rights 1950 Art.6.]

In conjoined appeals, the non-resident parent appellants (K and G) appealed against suspended committal orders imposed under the Child Support Act 1991 s.39A in respect of their wilful refusal or culpable neglect concerning child support payments. As insufficient evidence had been provided by K and G to enable the respondent Commission to make a "full maintenance assessment", it had made a default maintenance decision in respect of each of them. Before committal summonses were issued, liability and charging orders were obtained in respect of K, and a liability order in respect of G. K and G contended that the committal proceedings under s.39A did not comply with their right to a fair trial under the European Convention on Human Rights 1950 art.6

Held: Appeals allowed. (1) The issue was whether the pre-condition set by s.39A(1) that the Commission "has sought (a)... to levy an amount by distress... or (b) to recover an amount by virtue of s.36" required the Commission to have attempted enforcement in one of those ways or merely to have given consideration to such enforcement. The statutory scheme set out a hierarchy of steps to be taken to enforce payment. It was not inconsistent with such a scheme that all steps had to be taken before resorting to imprisonment or disqualification from driving. That the distress might be wasted could be the price to pay before depriving the defendant of his liberty. As no distress had been sought to be levied against G, and no attempt made to recover an amount by third-party debt order or charging order, the necessary pre-condition had not been satisfied and his appeal would be allowed. The pre-condition was satisfied in K's case as a charging order had been obtained. However, the judge had not considered whether imprisonment was more appropriate than disqualification. No reference was made to the mandatory requirement to enquire into the need for a driving licence and nothing to indicate that the possibility of disqualification had been considered. That was an error and the committal order in respect of K would also be set aside (see paras 11-20, 31 of judgment). (2) (Per Ward L.J.) A procedure properly applying s.39A would be fully compliant with art.6 obligations. A practical problem arose in the need for the Commission to obtain and then provide evidence of the defendant's means and his neglect or default. The defendant could not be required to incriminate himself, yet the effect of a means inquiry as part and parcel of the committal hearing was just that, and compelled him to prove the case against himself. The procedures adopted did not therefore comply with the rights to a fair trial and were flawed. However, the position was capable enough of easy remedy. The regulations needed to distinguish between a means enquiry and the committal proceedings. Rules analogous to the Practice Direction for committal in the High Court and County Court could remove the other anomalies (paras 47-49). (Per Richards L.J. and Patten L.J.) The statutory scheme was capable of being operated in compliance with art.6. Although s.39A(3) provided for the court to "inquire" as to the defendant's means and whether there had been wilful refusal or culpable neglect on his part, and s.40(1) required the court to be of the "opinion" that there had been wilful refusal or culpable neglect, the burden lay on the Commission to prove to the criminal standard that there had been wilful refusal or culpable neglect. That necessarily included proving that the defendant had, or had had, the means to pay the unpaid amount. It followed that, in practice, the Commission had to adduce sufficient evidence to establish at least a case to answer. In the generality of cases, that exercise might not need to be a particularly elaborate one, as there would be a history of default from which inferences could properly be drawn. However, it was an essential exercise. The defendant was not required to give evidence or to incriminate himself, and in the absence of a case to answer, he would be entitled to have the application against him dismissed. If the Commission established a case to answer, there would be an evidential burden on the defendant to answer it, but that was unobjectionable in art.6 terms. There was also no requirement under art.6 for the Commission to serve evidence in advance of the hearing, but the court had to ensure that the defendant was not taken by surprise and that the hearing could proceed without unfairness to him. Provided that the burden and standard of proof and the need for procedural fairness were borne clearly in mind, there was no inherent objection to considering the defendant's means and the issue of wilful default or culpable neglect in a single hearing. They were closely related matters and the statute contemplated that they would be inquired into at one and the same time, *Mubarak v Mubarak (No.1)* [2001] 1 F.L.R. 698, [2001] C.L.Y. 2637 and *Benham v United Kingdom (19380/92)* (1996) 22 E.H.R.R. 293, [1996] C.L.Y. 3155 considered. Although the Commission had not been giving sufficient thought in practice to the implications of the burden of proof upon it, and the practice and procedure in that area needed to be urgently improved, the changes required in order to bring the practice and procedure into line with art.6 were relatively limited (paras 56-61).

KAROONIAN v CHILD MAINTENANCE AND ENFORCEMENT COMMISSION (CMEC); GIBBONS v CHILD MAINTENANCE AND ENFORCEMENT COMMISSION (CMEC), [2012] EWCA Civ 1379, [2013] P.T.S.R. 635, Ward, L.J., CA (Civ Div).

1240. Child support–Maintenance–Treaties

THE LEGAL AID (FINANCIAL RESOURCES AND PAYMENT FOR SERVICES) (LEGAL PERSONS) (AMENDMENT) REGULATIONS 2013, SI 2013/754; made under the Legal Aid, Sentencing and Punishment of Offenders Act 2012 s.21, s.41, Sch.3 para.6. In force: April 1, 2013; .

These Regulations amend the Legal Aid (Financial Resources and Payment for Services) (Legal Persons) Regulations 2013 (SI 2013/512) to give effect to the Hague Convention on the International Recovery of Child Support and Other Forms of Family Maintenance 2007.

1241. Child support–Maintenance assessments–Self-employed workers–Whether child support decision maker required to accept income declared in tax returns or make own assessment

[Income Tax (Trading and Other Income) Act 2005 (c.5) Pt 2; Child Support (Maintenance Assessments and Special Cases) Regulations 1992 (SI 1992/1815) Sch.1 Pt I para.2A.]

The appellant father (F) appealed against a decision of the Upper Tribunal upholding the First-tier Tribunal's evaluation of his earnings from self-employment for the purposes of calculating his liability to pay child maintenance. A maintenance assessment had been made on the basis of F's evidence as to his income as shown on income and expenditure accounts prepared for submission to Revenue and Customs. The children's mother appealed to the First-tier Tribunal on the grounds that F had misstated his income. The tribunal made its own findings as to his true income. The issues for determination were (i) whether a child support decision maker was bound by the Child Support (Maintenance Assessments and Special Cases) Regulations 1992 Sch.1 Pt I para.2A to accept that a liable parent's gross income was as stated in the information provided by him to Revenue and Customs, or whether the decision maker was entitled to make his own findings of fact as to the parent's actual income; (ii) where the child support decision maker made his own conclusion about the level of the liable parent's taxable profits, whether the tax to be deducted under Sch.1 para.2A(2) was the notional tax due on the child support figure for earnings or the actual tax payable on the Revenue's calculation of profits.

Held: Appeal allowed in part. (1) The ascertainment of taxable profits required a calculation to be made; that was to proceed in accordance with the Income Tax (Trading and Other Income) Act 2005 Pt 2; the calculation had to be done by whomsoever had to make the decision, namely the secretary of state or the First-tier Tribunal. Nothing in the language constituted a deeming provision, nor did it require blind adherence to any calculation carried out by the Revenue. The words had a natural and ordinary meaning; the contrary position, that the decision maker was bound to accept the information placed before or supplied by the Revenue, was far from conclusive. The decision maker was entitled to rely on an evaluation of F's actual profits from self-employment in the relevant period rather than the figures submitted in his tax return, *KB v Child Maintenance and Enforcement Commission* [2010] UKUT 434 (AAC) and *DB v Child Maintenance and Enforcement Commission* [2011] UKUT 202 (AAC) approved. In construing the legislation, one had to pay attention to the purpose it was intended to serve. The intention had been to simplify the maintenance calculation process so as to eliminate delays and to remove the antagonism frequently generated by parents' separation. Although the aspiration of the Regulations was to reflect the policy intention so that self-employed earnings were the same as earnings for child support, they did not go so far as to state that a father's earnings were to be treated as his earnings for child support purposes. Statutory construction also required the court to have regard to the consequence of the construction. In the vast majority of cases a trader would be liable to have his accounts scrutinised whenever there was credible evidence that he had under-declared income or over-declared expenses, meaning that two arms of government could reach different answers for tax purposes and child support purposes, and that more and more of such enquiries could be undertaken, causing complications and delay. There was therefore force in the argument that if the child support authorities were unhappy with the tax liability notice, they should seek a variation on lifestyle grounds or refer the matter back to the Revenue (see paras 21-28 of judgment). (2) If the child support officer increased the profit above the level accepted by the Revenue, his responsibility was to deduct the tax which would be payable on that level of profit. The case would be remitted to the secretary of state to recalculate the child support assessment to allow for a deduction of the income tax and national insurance on the notional surplus between the earnings found by the First-tier Tribunal and the earnings accepted by the Revenue (para.30).

GRAY v SECRETARY OF STATE FOR WORK AND PENSIONS, [2012] EWCA Civ 1412, [2013] P.T.S.R. 520, Ward, L.J., CA (Civ Div).

1242. Children–Consent to treatment–Child with malignant brain tumour–Mother refusing consent to orthodox treatment–Whether court should give consent

The applicant NHS trust applied for a declaration that a medical procedure proposed for the respondent child (N) was lawful. N, aged seven, had a malignant brain tumour, which was removed surgically at a hospital recognised as a centre of excellence. The orthodox treatment to follow such surgery was radiotherapy and chemotherapy, which had a success rate of about 80 per cent, sometimes put at 86 per cent. N's father (F) agreed to the post-operative treatment proposal, but his mother (M) did not, believing that there were alternative methods which would avoid or reduce the undoubtedly detrimental long-term side effects involved. Doctors explained the treatment in detail to M, including the need to start radiotherapy 28-49 days after surgery to combat the spread of any residual cancer cells. M failed to take N to three necessary appointments and when the trust applied for declarations regarding N's treatment she disappeared, taking N with her. A judge asked the media to help find them, and when they were located an interim care order was made in favour of F with visiting rights for M. An MRI scan showed that N had more cancer cells at the site and judgment was postponed while he had more surgery, authorised by the court, during which another tumour was removed. The trust applied to the court for consent to the radio-and chemotherapy. The trust and M each called expert witnesses, and M produced papers that she claimed supported her position. F and N's guardian agreed with the trust. The trust submitted that all reputable research, trials and clinical experience showed that the outcome for children of N's age with his condition was best where radiotherapy and chemotherapy were used following surgery. It argued that without such treatment N would die. The trust contended that that while there were side-effects, including some intellectual detriment, possibly minimal, N's personality would not change and he would still be able to go to school, play sports and do normal things. M submitted that she wanted complementary therapies for N and that there were Chinese, Russian and other reports telling of thousands of children surviving cancers without mainstream treatment, including radiotherapy, although she did not wish to pass the papers over to the NHS, despite its request, for fear that they would think she was seeking support from "quacks". She argued that the orthodox view was the product of indoctrination, and that there would be intellectual and other detriments to N from having the treatment.

Held: Declaration granted. The package of treatment proposed by the NHS trust was lawful. The balance of advantage and disadvantage was well in favour of radiotherapy and chemotherapy, notwithstanding the detrimental side-effects. People could not enjoy even a diminished quality of life if they were not alive. Regarding complementary therapies, it was not just a question of demonstrating that there was research and experimentation going on, or that there were ideas and possibilities being entertained, or even that there were success stories of cures occurring without radio-and chemotherapy. What M needed to show was a clinician experienced in treating children aged about seven years having N's kind of cancer, with access to the necessary equipment and infrastructure to put the suggested treatment into effect and able and willing to take over the medical care of and responsibility for N, *AVS v An NHS Foundation Trust* [2011] EWCA Civ 7, [2011] 2 F.L.R. 1, [2011] C.L.Y. 2240 applied. Such a treatment should have been properly studied, tested, reported on and peer-reviewed, and in order to be selected by the court for a child, would have to have a prognosis as to probable survival rate of not much less than, and preferably equal to, the rate achievable through the orthodox treatment universally applied at present by oncologists in the United Kingdom. It might well be that some of the complementary therapies, for example as to diet and lifestyle or oxygen therapy, could be beneficial in conjunction with the orthodox treatment. M's views were obviously important in the balancing exercise, but there was a concern that her judgment had gone awry as to the extent of the seriousness of the threat that N faced. The instant decision was final. M had been fully aware for over six weeks that treating clinicians believed that N required radio-and chemotherapy. She had had sufficient opportunities to assemble and put forward her evidence and she had been represented by leading counsel and solicitors for the second half of that time (see paras 14-15, 18-26 of judgment).

AN NHS TRUST v SR, [2012] EWHC 3842 (Fam), [2013] 1 F.L.R. 1297, Bodey, J., Fam Div.

1243. Children–Habitual residence–Child born in Spain after parents fled English jurisdiction–Local authority instigating care proceedings–Whether child habitually resident in Spain or England

[Regulation 2201/2003 Art.13; Hague Convention on the Civil Aspects of International Child Abduction 1980.]

The applicant local authority applied for a care order in respect of a six-month-old child (S). The respondent mother (M) opposed the application. M had another child who had been taken into care following concerns about M's mental health and drug and alcohol abuse. Thereafter, she formed a relationship with S's father (F) and fell pregnant. Following concerns about their volatile relationship, the local authority became involved. F had threatened to kill a social worker, and M was sectioned twice and continued to abuse drugs throughout her pregnancy. The local authority informed them that they would instigate care proceedings in respect of S. M and F fled to Spain, where S was born. They removed S from the hospital against medical advice. A Spanish court order required her return to hospital. S was found to have cannabis in her system. Spanish social services and M and F entered into a "plan of intervention" allowing S to be monitored and access to their home. Meanwhile, the English local authority was granted an emergency protection order and an application was made for S's removal from Spain. The High Court expressed a summary assessment that S was habitually resident in England and Wales and invited the Spanish authorities, should they remove S, to place her in the care of the English local authority. F returned to England following the breakdown of his relationship with M. S was located and removed by the English local authority pursuant to a Spanish court order. The issue was whether the court had jurisdiction to determine S's future care.

Held: Application granted. (1) M had not established habitual residence in Spain. Her move there was not considered: it was a desperate flight to attempt to avoid S being taken into care. She made no preparations prior to leaving, such as obtaining a job or studying the language. She had abandoned her home there as soon as she had felt threatened by social services. It was clear that she was hiding in Spain rather than being there to establish a permanent life. She had continued to claim income support in the United Kingdom until she was caught. The court would not make a finding of fact that M was habitually resident in England and Wales; it did not need to do so given that it was satisfied that she was not habitually resident in Spain (see paras 34-37 of judgment). (2) A child's habitual residence normally followed that of those with parental responsibility for it. F did not have parental responsibility. Given that M was not habitually resident in Spain, S was never habitually resident in Spain either. She had been there because M was there. If M had moved to France to avoid the local authority, S would not have become habitually resident in France. S's birth was not registered in Spain. M and F had deliberately fled from the address at which they had agreed to reside. They were on the run, and therefore so was S (para.39). (3) As no finding of fact had been made that M was habitually resident in England and Wales, it was impossible to see how S could have been. At the time of S's removal from Spain she had never been physically present in the UK. It would be for others to conclude whether a baby could be habitually resident in a jurisdiction, even if it had never lived there. As S was not habitually resident in Spain, the Hague Convention on the Civil Aspects of International Child Abduction 1980 did not apply and therefore it would not be possible to institute proceedings under that Convention to secure her return to Spain. The Spanish court had exercised its jurisdiction pursuant to Regulation 2201/2003 art.13; however, they no longer had jurisdiction as S was no longer present there. Conversely, the instant court did have jurisdiction under art.13 because she was present in England. The circumstances of S's removal did not make a difference. If there was a wrongful removal in a child abduction case, but the child was not habitually resident in the requesting state, there was no automatic return, as the Hague Convention did not apply. There could be no requirement for an automatic return in the instant case. Since her arrival into the jurisdiction, S had been physically present in England. As she was not habitually resident in Spain, art.13 provided that jurisdiction was based on physical presence. Accordingly, the court had jurisdiction (paras 40-43). (4) The current proceedings were flawed on the basis that they had been issued one day before S arrived in England. The proceedings were dismissed and the local authority ordered to issue fresh proceedings (para.45). (4) It was likely that S would suffer significant harm if removed from the local authority's care. An injunction preventing her removal from such care would be granted until fresh proceedings were issued (para.46).

BRIDGEND CBC v GM, [2012] EWHC 3118 (Fam), [2013] 1 F.L.R. 987, Moor, J., Fam Div.

1244. Children–Habitual residence–Child living in England with relatives for five years–Removal of child by parents–Court's jurisdiction to determine habitual residence

[Regulation 2201/2003 Art.8.]

The court considered whether it had jurisdiction to determine applications of the applicant aunt and uncle (X) in relation to their seven-year-old nephew (M). The respondents were M's parents (P). P, who were Nigerian, had placed M in X's care in England when he was two-years-old. From that time, X had been responsible for M's upbringing. P possessed sole parental responsibility, but they had not exercised it to any real extent for many years and had delegated it almost entirely to X. When M was seven-years-old, the mother visited M and took him to Nigeria without X's permission. X obtained a residence order and an order requiring P to return M. The issue was whether M was habitually resident in England at the time that the proceedings were issued such that the court had jurisdiction to entertain proceedings concerning him in accordance with Regulation 2201/2003 art.8.

Held: Judgment accordingly. The determination of habitual residence was a question of fact. When considering the issue of jurisdiction, it was not a case in which P had any right to change M's habitual residence simply by an exercise of will. They were not his physical carers and his habitual residence had not automatically followed theirs. For the past five of his seven years M had been habitually resident in England while P had been habitually resident in Nigeria. His family life revolved around X, his primary carers, under day-to-day authority delegated by P. During that period, M had not returned to Nigeria. Considerable weight was attached to the length of time that M had lived a settled life in England and to his ties to X. P's intentions and actions in removing him did not deprive M of his ties to England, which created a proximity that entitled him to a proper consideration of his best interests, *J (A Minor) (Abduction: Custody Rights), Re* [1990] 2 A.C. 562, [1990] C.L.Y. 3151 and *Mercredi v Chaffe (C-497/10 PPU)* [2012] Fam. 22, [2011] C.L.Y. 1429 considered, *M (Minors) (Residence Order: Jurisdiction), Re* [1993] 1 F.L.R. 495, [1993] C.L.Y. 2866 distinguished. M was habitually resident in England at the time that the proceedings were issued and the court had jurisdiction (see paras 22-25, 28, 33, 35-37 of judgment).

I (A CHILD) (HABITUAL RESIDENCE), *Re*; *sub nom.* A v I, [2012] EWHC 3363 (Fam), [2013] 1 F.L.R. 1452, Peter Jackson, J., Fam Div.

1245. Children–Habitual residence–Emigration of family to Canada–Separation of parents–Whether children habitually resident in England and Wales or Canada

The applicant mother (M) applied for the summary return of her two children (X and Y) to Canada. X and Y were aged two and four. Their parents (M and F) were British nationals who had acquired permanent residency in Canada. The family relocated permanently to Canada in 2012. M and F separated a few months later. F took the children's passports but reassured M that he would not take the children out of the country without her permission. During a period of agreed contact F took the children back to the United Kingdom and refused to return them to Canada. F submitted that before moving to Canada, he and M had agreed that if one of them was unsettled or did not feel it was working they would return to the UK with the children. He argued that because they had retained a property in the UK and had separated less than three months after the move to Canada, the children remained habitually resident in England and Wales.

Held: Application granted. (1) Habitual residence was a question of fact to be determined by the trial judge standing back from the evidence and taking a general view, rather than conducting a microscopic search. An appreciable period of time and a settled intention would be necessary to enable a person to become habitually resident in a country. The requisite period of time was not fixed and depended upon the facts of each case. Factors to be taken into account included bringing possessions, establishing residence before coming, having a right of abode, seeking to bring family, and durable ties with the country of residence or intended residence. Habitual residence could be acquired despite the fact that the move might only have been temporary or on a trial basis. In relation to "settled intention", there had to be a degree of settled purpose. The habitual residence of young children of married parents all living together as a family was the same as the habitual residence of the parents themselves. Neither parent could change it without the express or tacit consent of the other, or order of the court (see paras 2-6 of judgment). (2) It was indisputable that the children had acquired habitual residence in Canada by the time of F's unilateral and clandestine decision to remove them to the UK. On any objective analysis of the events and the documentary evidence, any other result would be perverse. Over a period of several years the parents had successfully engaged in the process of applying for permanent residency in Canada. Emigration was their agreed long-term plan. M's motivation, at least in part, was for the children to have dual nationality and be raised and educated in Canada. It was fair to assume that F shared those ambitions at the time they relocated to Canada. M and F had resigned from their jobs, sold their car, and shipped all of their possession to Canada. The family home was put up for sale six months before the move. M obtained a job in Canada and F had been in the process of establishing a construction business there. F had been attending a school in Canada and N had been attending nursery. There was no evidence of the agreement alleged by F and the children were to be returned to Canada (paras 20-29).

FT (CHILDREN) (ABDUCTION: HABITUAL RESIDENCE), *Re*, [2013] EWHC 850 (Fam), [2013] 2 F.L.R. 690, Pauffley, J., Fam Div.

1246. Children–Habitual residence–Wrongful removal–Applying test of habitual residence for purpose of court's jurisdiction–Whether habitual residence lost as a result of covert removal

[Regulation 2201/2003 Art.8, Art.8(2).]

The court was required to determine whether it had jurisdiction to make orders in favour of the applicant father (B) regarding his child (X). X was a seven-year-old child who resided with her maternal grandparents (E) in England. Her mother (J) had given birth to her in England. When X was one J moved to the United States and did not return to England, or meet with X, for six years. X was brought up by E and J's only involvement was through video contact. Initially B did not know he was the biological father of X, but when that was confirmed by DNA testing he undertook a significant role in her life. He had regular contact, including staying contact. E flew to the United States with X, with the intention of emigrating, without B's knowledge or consent. B issued an application for parental responsibility which was granted at a without notice hearing and obtained orders declaring him to be X's father and ordering that E return X to England. E and J challenged the jurisdictional basis of the orders. The issue was whether the courts of England and Wales had jurisdiction to entertain proceedings concerning X. The question of jurisdiction depended on whether X was habitually resident in England and Wales for the purposes of the test in Regulation 2201/2003 art.8(2). E submitted that although X had not become habitually resident in the United States at the relevant date, she also had no habitual residence in England and Wales for the purposes of granting the instant court jurisdiction.

Held: Judgment accordingly. X had not lost her habitual residence status during her 13-day absence in the US. The unusual aspects of X's family situation called for particular respect to be paid to her individuality as opposed to treating her as an adjunct to any of the contending adults. X's parental figures at the time of removal were E but, while they might have been the most important figures in her life, it could not be said that E could simply choose where X was habitually resident, even if J agreed with that choice, *Mercredi v Chaffe (C-497/10 PPU)* [2012] Fam. 22, [2011] C.L.Y. 1429 applied. E were granted parental responsibility by the court, subject to a clear restriction in relation to permanent removal. The position of B and X had to be considered when assessing habitual residence (see paras 42-43). Considerable weight had to be attached to the reality of X's situation and less weight given to the legal technicalities. The reality was that she was an English child who had spent all her life as a habitual resident of England and she did not lose that status as a result of a contrived absence of 13 days. Her roots in England were deep and her habitual residence did not change as a result of a legally insecure removal. X was habitually resident in England and Wales at the time the proceedings were issued and the court had jurisdiction to make the orders that it did (see para.45).

J (A CHILD) (HABITUAL RESIDENCE), *Re*; *sub nom.* J v B, [2012] EWHC 3364 (Fam), [2013] 1 F.L.R. 1460, Peter Jackson, J., Fam Div.

1247. **Children–Oral evidence–Children's right to be heard in care proceedings–Purpose of meeting between judge and child–No right to give evidence**

[Children Act 1989 (c.41) s.1 (3), s.96; Family Procedure Rules 2010 (SI 2010/2955) Pt 22; Convention on the Rights of the Child (United Nations) 1989; European Convention on Human Rights 1950 Art.6.]

The appellant 15-year-old child (X) appealed against the dismissal of his application for leave to attend court to give evidence in support of his case to return to the care of his mother (M), and against a care order. X had travelled from Romania to Ireland with M at a young age and had later moved to Wales with M and his younger half-brother. Both children were taken into care following incidents of neglect. X was joined as a party to the care proceedings. He made the instant application because he did not feel that "the strength of his feelings" had been sufficiently understood and he wanted an opportunity to express himself in person before the judge. He stated that he wished to return to M's care and would be extremely distressed if forced to remain in foster care. The judge held that, if he were allowed to give evidence in person or by video link, there was a risk of an extreme emotional outburst from M which would be detrimental to X, and that there was nothing to be gained from assessing his demeanour that would enable her to determine the relevant issues. In relation to the care application, the judge accepted the evidence she heard concerning the inadequate standard of M's parenting, which led her to conclude that M prioritised her own needs above those of her children. Accordingly, a risk of harm to X was overwhelmingly likely in the event of a return to M's care.

Held: Appeals dismissed. (1) Under the Children Act 1989 s.96, a child's evidence might be heard by the court if, in its opinion, he understood that he had a duty to speak the truth and had sufficient understanding to justify his evidence being heard. Guidelines for judges meeting children who were subject to family proceedings were given by the Family Justice Council in April 2010. The purpose of those guidelines was to encourage judges to enable children to feel more involved in proceedings in which important decisions were made in their lives, and to give them an opportunity to satisfy themselves that the judge had understood their wishes and feelings. It was noteworthy that the purpose of the guidelines was not to satisfy the judge that, if he saw the children, he would be better able to understand what their wishes were. Thus, such meetings were not for the purpose of gathering evidence. Although the Convention on the Rights of the Child 1989 (United Nations) had not been made part of English law, the court was obliged to have regard to it when considering matters to which it related. The Convention recognised that the voice of the child might be conveyed either directly or through a representative or appropriate body. Accordingly, although children had a right to be heard in proceedings, that right did not specify how they were to be heard. It did not seem to be essential that it had to be the judge who heard directly from the child. It followed that a child had no right to give evidence (see paras 28, 32, 35-36 of judgment). (2) As a party to care proceedings, a child was entitled to a fair and public hearing in accordance with the European Convention on Human Rights 1950 art.6. However, no one had a right to give evidence. A trial might nonetheless be fair if the court exercised fair and reasonable powers to control the evidence, as provided for by Family Procedure Rules 2010 Pt 22. Once there was undisputed evidence of a fact which might, for example, be a fact admitted on the pleadings, there was no need for further oral evidence to prove that fact. In the instant case, X's wishes were well known. The relevant fact under the checklist set out in s.1 (3) of the 1989 Act was clearly established and undisputed. There was abundant evidence before the judge to assess the strength of X's wishes; his demeanour was of no assistance in carrying out an assessment of his welfare. When exercising the welfare discretion, the judge had struck a balance between the benefits and burdens. She had arrived at a conclusion which was plainly and obviously correct; namely that, having explained the procedure to X, she did not need to see him again and certainly did not require him to give evidence. That judgment was unassailable (paras 38-41). (3) There was no rebuttable presumption that a mature child's wishes should prevail. The weight to be given to the wishes and feelings of the child under s.1 (3) of the 1989 Act would vary from case to case and might be a very weighty factor; however, that provision should not be construed so as to read into it some hierarchy of weight or presumptions of precedence over other factors. Each case was fact-sensitive. In the instant case, the judge had had no alternative but to make the care order (paras 43, 46).

P-S (CHILDREN) (FAMILY PROCEEDINGS: EVIDENCE), *Re*; *sub nom.* P-S (CHILDREN) (CHILD AS WITNESS), RE; P-S (CHILDREN) (CARE PROCEEDINGS: RIGHT TO GIVE EVIDENCE), *Re*, [2013] EWCA Civ 223, [2013] 1 W.L.R. 3831, Elias, L.J., CA (Civ Div).

1248. Children–Removal from jurisdiction–Children's welfare–Application of Payne v Payne [2001] EWCA Civ 166 in cases where applicant not primary carer

The appellant father (F) appealed against a county court order granting the respondent mother (M) permission permanently to remove their son (P) from the United Kingdom. P's parents were both Spanish. They came to the UK in 2009 when F took up a two-year posting by his employer. In May 2011 that period was extended to at least 2013. M, P's primary carer, returned to Spain in August 2011 following a breakdown of the relationship. P was left with F who became P's primary carer. M wished to continue living in Spain. F intended to remain in the UK for the time being. Both parties began proceedings for a residence order. The judge made a shared residence order but granted M permission permanently to remove P from the jurisdiction, allowing for certain arrangements for holidays to be spent with F in the UK. The case was very finely balanced. P, aged eight at the time of the instant hearing, would have been happy in either country, although he regarded himself as Spanish, and apart from F, all of P's family lived in Spain. The judge focused on the decisions in *Payne v Payne* [2001] EWCA Civ 166, [2001] Fam. 473, [2001] C.L.Y. 2596 and *K v K (Children: Permanent Removal from Jurisdiction)* [2011] EWCA Civ 793, [2012] Fam. 134, [2011] C.L.Y. 1382, asking himself whether the instant case was one to which *Payne* applied. He decided that he was entitled to "look at" the *Payne* guidelines, being the "discipline" set out by Thorpe LJ. Having done that, he then turned to an investigation and evaluation of P's best interests, having regard to the "welfare checklist", before reaching his conclusion. F claimed that the judge erred in his application of *Payne* and *K v K* and in his evaluation of the facts.

Held: Appeal dismissed. The four stage process set out in the "discipline" was highly relevant where the applicant was a primary carer, but it was not relevant only to such cases. The issues raised could arise in many relocation cases where the application was being made by someone other than a primary carer. Therefore, the guidance in *Payne* could be utilised in other kinds of relocation cases if the judge considered it helpful and appropriate to do so, *K v K* applied. Although the instant case was not a case where the primary carer was making the application, the judge was entitled to have regard to the "discipline" as set out in *Payne*. He correctly appreciated that the case had to be decided by reference to P's best interests and that was what he did, *Payne* applied. The judge carefully took into account P's current circumstances in the UK, the quality of F's care and F's own plans, wishes and feelings. There was nothing to suggest that there was any presumption in favour of M's claim. He also took into account and gave appropriate weight to each of the factors to which F had drawn attention. He acknowledged that F was the primary carer and recognised the importance F attached to the argument based upon the status quo. He gave appropriate weight to both those points, whilst correctly appreciating that neither could be decisive. There was no sustainable basis for any complaint that the judge either took into account irrelevant factors or failed to take into account any relevant factors, or that he erred in either the weight he chose to attach to the various factors he had to take into account or in his evaluative decision as to where the ultimate balance fell. Therefore, there was no proper basis upon which the instant court could intervene (see paras 45, 49-52 of judgment).

F (A CHILD) (PERMISSION TO RELOCATE), *Re; sub nom.* F (RELOCATION), *Re*, [2012] EWCA Civ 1364, [2013] 1 F.L.R. 645, Pill, L.J., CA (Civ Div).

1249. Children–Removal from jurisdiction–Judge departing from CAFCASS officer's recommendation to refuse permission–Sufficiency of reasons for decision

The appellant father (F) appealed against a decision granting the respondent mother (M) permission to remove their two children from the jurisdiction to live in the United States. Following the parties' separation in 2008, the children lived with M. She was granted a residence order, F having acknowledged that M could not be faulted as a mother. His contact with them on alternate weekends was formalised. M had developed a relationship with a US citizen she had met through the internet. She visited the US and met him for the first time in 2009.They subsequently decided to marry, and in early 2012 M applied for permission to remove the children, by then aged 11 and five, permanently from the jurisdiction to enable them to relocate with her in the US. M proposals for the children's contact with F post-relocation included the offer to bring them to the United Kingdom for three months every summer, and to spend alternate Christmas holidays in the UK. F opposed the application. The judge heard oral evidence from M, F and the appointed CAFCASS officer, whose report indicated that she felt unable to recommend the children's removal to the US because of the significant impact that relocation would have on F's contact with the children. In an extempore judgment given at the conclusion of the one-day hearing, the judge stated that the CAFCASS officer did not seem to have taken into account the quality of M's proposals for contact. Having considered *Payne v Payne* [2001] EWCA Civ 166, [2001] Fam. 473, [2001] C.L.Y. 2596, he indicated that those proposals, by M as the primary carer, were reasonable and that the effect on her and her new family of refusing the application was very important. The judge concluded that M's ability to care for the children in the way she had done hitherto would be adversely affected if permission was refused. He therefore granted M's application on condition that she obtain from the equivalent first instance court in the US a mirror order containing the proposed contact regime. F contended that the judge had failed to give cogent reasons for rejecting the CAFCASS officer's recommendation, and had erred in the exercise of his discretion in the weight given to the various relevant factors.

Held: Appeal dismissed. (1) The judge had directed himself in law in accordance with *Payne*, in particular as to the summary of factors to be considered by trial judges dealing with relocation applications. By his consideration of the reasonableness of proposals by the parent with primary care, he had referred directly to President's judgment in *Payne*. In his judgment, the CAFCASS officer's report had not been a balanced one. He was absolutely entitled to have reached that conclusion, *Payne* followed. Whilst the report had correctly brought into the balance the significant impact that relocation would have on the children's relationship with F, it was silent as to the effect of refusal upon M. At no point had the CAFCASS office investigated or evaluated that important factor. Her report was incomplete, one-sided and liable to be rejected by a judge who had to look at cases in the round. (2) Submissions going to the weight given by a judge to various factors were rarely made good in the Court of Appeal. The assessment of the weight to be given to any relevant factor was one for the judge, not the instant court. Accordingly, F's appeal had to stand or fall on the submission that the judge's departure from the CAFCASS's officer's recommendation was impermissible, and it failed.

E (CHILDREN) (RELOCATION: REMOVAL FROM JURISDICTION), *Re; sub nom.* E (CHILDREN) (LOCATION: REMOVAL FROM JURISDICTION), *Re* [2012] EWCA Civ 1893, Thorpe, L.J., CA (Civ Div).

1250. Children–Removal from jurisdiction–Jurisdiction to order sending to UK of small child born and remaining overseas

[Family Law Act 1986 (c.55) s.1 (1) (a), s.1 (1) (d), s.2; Regulation 2201/2003 Art.8, Art.14; Hague Convention on the Civil Aspects of International Child Abduction 1980.]

The appellant mother (M) appealed against a decision of the Court of Appeal ([2012] EWCA Civ 1396, [2013] Fam. 232, [2013] 1 C.L.139) that the judge at first instance had been wrong to order the sending of her youngest child (H) to England and Wales. M and the respondent father (F) were of Pakistani origin. F was born in England and had dual British and Pakistani nationality. F and M married in Pakistan in 1999. M came here in 2000. Between 2001 and 2005, they had three children. The marriage began to break down in 2006. In 2008, M moved with the three children into a refuge following complaints of physical abuse by F. F had begun to spend time in Pakistan. In 2009, M went to Pakistan with the children to visit her father. While there, she was coerced into reuniting with F. She became pregnant with H. She managed to leave the country but had to leave the children behind. On her application, the judge made all four children wards of court and ordered that they be returned to England and Wales forthwith. Those orders were confirmed by Parker J., who held that all four children were habitually resident in England and Wales. The Court of Appeal allowed F's appeal but only in relation to H; the court held that the acquisition of habitual residence in any country required the child to be physically present there.

Held: Appeal allowed. (1) The order made by the judge and repeated by Parker J. did not fall within the Family Law Act 1986 s.1 (1) (a) or s.1 (1) (d) and was therefore not covered by the jurisdictional prohibitions in s.2 of that Act. The order was one that related to parental responsibility within the scope of Regulation 2201/2003, which embraced cases where there was a rival jurisdiction in a non-Member State. Article 14 of the Regulation provided that, where no court of a Member State had jurisdiction under arts 8 to 13, jurisdiction should be determined, in each Member State, by the laws of that state. In that respect, the inherent jurisdiction of the High Court could be exercised if the child was a British national. The case would be remitted to Parker J. for her to consider whether to exercise jurisdiction on that basis. As Thorpe L.J. had said in *Al-H (Rashid) v F (Sara)* [2001] EWCA Civ 186, [2001] 1 F.L.R. 951, [2001] C.L.Y. 2676, the court should be "extremely circumspect" when deciding to exercise that jurisdiction. But all would depend on the circumstances of the case. Here, for example, the circumstances in which the children came to be in Pakistan, and the coercion to which M was subject, would be highly relevant, *Al-H* considered (see paras 23, 28-30, 59-60, 65, 68 of judgment). (2) Should Parker J. decide not to exercise jurisdiction on the basis of H's nationality, it would be necessary to decide whether he was habitually resident here for the purposes of art.8 of the Regulation. The parties should have liberty to apply to the instant court for a reference to be made to the European Court of Justice on that issue, since the matter was not *acte claire*. The court would be asked to decide which approach accorded most closely with the factual situation here: an approach which held that presence was a necessary precursor to residence and thus to habitual residence or an approach which focused on the relationship between the child and his primary carer. The instant court inclined to the view that the former approach was correct but could not say so with confidence; among other things, there was judicial, expert and academic opinion in favour of the child acquiring his mother's habitual residence in circumstances such as these. Principal among those judicial opinions was the conclusion reached by Lord Hughes in this very case today (paras 55-57, 67). (3) As to habitual residence, all were agreed that it was a question of fact and not a legal concept such as domicile. The test adopted by the ECJ was "the place which reflects some degree of integration by the child in a social and family environment" in the country concerned. That depended on numerous factors, including the reasons for the family's stay in the country in question. It was now unlikely that that test would produce any different results from that hitherto adopted in the English courts under the 1986 Act and the Hague Convention on the Civil Aspects of

International Child Abduction 1980. The test adopted by the ECJ was preferable to that earlier adopted by the English courts, the ECJ's test being focused on the situation of the child, with the parents' purposes and intentions being merely one of the relevant factors. The test derived from *R. v Barnet LBC, Ex p. Shah* [1983] 2 A.C. 309, [1983] C.L.Y. 1157 should be abandoned when deciding the habitual residence of a child, *Ex p. Shah* considered. Further, the essentially factual and individual nature of the inquiry should not be glossed with legal concepts which would produce a different result from that which the factual inquiry would produce (para.54).

A v A (CHILDREN) (HABITUAL RESIDENCE); *sub nom.* A (CHILDREN) (JURISDICTION: RETURN OF CHILD), RE; ZA v NA (ABDUCTION: HABITUAL RESIDENCE), [2013] UKSC 60, [2014] 1 A.C. 1, Lady Hale, J.S.C., SC.

1251. Children–Removal from jurisdiction–Mother seeking to move to Australia with children–Factors for consideration by court in permitting removal of children from jurisdiction

[Hague Convention on the Civil Aspects of International Child Abduction 1980.]

The applicant mother (M) sought an order allowing her to relocate her two children (C) to Australia. M was Australian, while the respondent father (F) was British. They married in Australia and lived there until 2010, when they came to the United Kingdom. M became unhappy and the marriage began to break down. In May 2011, F told M that he wanted a divorce. Three days later, M took C, who were then aged three and two, and flew with them back to Australia. Proceedings under the Hague Convention on the Civil Aspects of International Child Abduction 1980 were issued, and in August 2012 C returned to the UK with F. The parties had agreed that, whatever decision the court reached as to which country C should reside in, they would both reside in that country and look after C under a shared-care arrangement. An expert had commented that F would be entitled to return to reside and work in Australia. As to M's immigration position here, it appeared that an application for leave to enter or remain would take between 40 and 48 weeks to be resolved; she stated that, if she had to stay in the UK, she would be prevented from working and have to live at subsistence level, without family and friends.

Held: Application granted. (1) In Kacem v Bashir [2010] NZSC 112, [2011] N.Z.L.R. 1, the Supreme Court of New Zealand had made some highly acute observations demonstrating the fallacy of the suggestion that there was some kind of presumption in favour of an application to relocate. There was no presumption in favour of the mother in a case like this; the court's determination would involve a factual evaluation and a value judgment, *Kacem* considered (see paras 14-18 of judgment). (2) The instant decision should be based from first to last on the interests of C; the court had to shut out its strong feelings of sympathy for F in relation to what had been M's high-handed, selfish and autocratic conduct, just as it should eschew any temptation to punish her for that conduct. C were not at risk of harm on either choice of country, and their physical, emotional and educational needs would be much the same in both countries. This was a knife-edge decision. The decisive factor was the impact the court's decision would have on M and F. An adverse decision would bear far more heavily on M than it would on F. F was highly competent and self-sufficient; there would be no obstacles to his obtaining employment in Australia and to his finding a home suitable to share the care of the children in. M, on the other hand, was a fragile character. Her account of the misery she had suffered when residing in the UK had not been challenged. Even apart from the financial pressures she would endure here, she was less well equipped to face the relevant challenges were C to stay here than F would be were C to return to Australia. This was a case where F was the victim of his own virtues. An order would be made that, once in Australia, C would spend equal amounts of time with M and F (paras 47-48, 50-54).

TC (CHILDREN) (RELOCATION), *Re*, [2013] EWHC 292 (Fam), [2013] 2 F.L.R. 484, Mostyn, J., Fam Div.

1252. Children–Removal from jurisdiction–Mother's application for sole residence and permission to relocate–Whether relocation in child's paramount welfare interests–Consideration of shared residence

[Children Act 1989 (c.41) s.1(3); Hague Convention on the Civil Aspects of International Child Abduction 1980.]

The applicant mother (M) sought sole residence of the three-year-old child (X) of her marriage to the respondent father (F), and leave to remove him permanently from the jurisdiction to live in the USA, her country of origin. M and F had met while she was a student in London. They married in New York but decided to settle in England. When X was a year old, M took him to the USA. She eventually returned, but expressed a wish to permanently relocate to the USA. M and F agreed that she and X could visit the USA for a temporary period of four months, but that she would return him to the United Kingdom thereafter. While in the USA, M petitioned for divorce and sought sole residence of X. F issued proceedings under the Hague Convention on the Civil Aspects of International Child Abduction 1980, and after a return order was made issued an application for sole residence. M refused to return X and Hague Convention proceedings took place before the Federal Court. A judgment from the High Court declared X's place of habitual residence to be England and Wales and that he had been unlawfully retained in the USA in flagrant breach of the agreement with F. The Federal Court dismissed M's objections and made a return order.

Held: Judgment accordingly. A child's welfare was paramount in relocation cases, as it was in relation to applications for residence orders, *Payne v Payne* [2001] EWCA Civ 166, [2001] Fam. 473, [2001] C.L.Y. 2596 applied. In assessing a child's welfare regard had to be paid to the statutory list of matters in the Children Act 1989 s.1(3), but different weight and importance would be attracted to those matters depending on the individual circumstances of each case. Regard had also to be paid to the guidance given in *Payne* as to how the court should approach certain aspects which were peculiar to relocation cases, such as the impact of refusal on the child's welfare, the genuineness of the motive to relocate and the well thought out, realistic and practical proposals associated with it and the genuineness of the opposition to relocate. In applying the guidance in *Payne* to the instant case, there was no doubt that M's application to relocate was genuine, to enable her to be with her family in her homeland. However, her proposals for contact had not been honestly and accurately thought through. Her proposals changed during the hearing and were characterised by a lack of commitment to contact, and her impaired insight into the importance of F's relationship with X, a need to control it and the obstacles she had placed in the path of contact in the past. While F and X had a good relationship, it was uncertain whether it had the strength to withstand X's relocation to the USA at such a young age. F's concerns had substance and were genuine. His relationship with X was unlikely to be sustained and supported by M's contact proposals. Their relationship should be on an upward trajectory that would be better provided if X was living in the United Kingdom. X's welfare required a shared residence order which would serve as a reminder to M and F that neither had greater entitlement or rights than the other and that each had much to contribute to X's welfare (see paras 8-9, 59, 62, 66, 68-69 of judgment).

L (RELOCATION: SHARED RESIDENCE), *Re*, [2012] EWHC 3069 (Fam), [2013] 1 F.L.R. 777, Stephen Bellamy Q.C., Fam Div.

1253. Children–Removal from jurisdiction–Proposed adoptive parents going to United States for employment reasons–Permission sought to remove four-year-old child

[Adoption and Children Act 2002 (c.38) s.28(2), s.28(2)(b); Convention on Protection of Children and Co-operation in respect of Intercountry Adoption (Hague XXXIII) 1993.]

The applicant local authority applied for permission to remove a four-year-old child (C) from the United Kingdom so that she could go to live in the United States with a married couple (H and W). H and W had been approved as foster carers. They had adopted C's half-sister in 2003. They were living in the United States largely as a result of H's employment. They were British citizens and remained domiciled in England and Wales. They intended to apply for an adoption order in respect of C under the Hague Convention 1993. Leave to remove C was required under the Adoption and Children Act 2002 s.28(2)(b) because she had been made the subject of a placement order, because her mother had not given her written consent and because the proposal was for removal for more than one month.

Held: Application granted. It would be appropriate to give the local authority permission to remove C from the UK and to place her with H and W for a time-limited visit which, in the first instance, was envisaged to be of one year in length. C would be able to live with and grow up alongside her half-sister, whom she already referred to as "my sister". H and W were very impressive individuals who would be able to offer C a safe, secure and nurturing home where all of her physical and emotional needs could be met. C was ready and able to move now. She had met and begun to engage very favourably with H and W. Any delay could frustrate her development. Her mother was, by reason of her very sad history and mental-health difficulties, excluded as a potential carer, and it was difficult to conceive of any reasonable objection she might have. Further, it had been established that, for the purposes of art.2 of the Convention, C would remain habitually resident in England, such being the intention of the local authority, of the court and of H and W (see paras 5, 28-29 of judgment).

A (A CHILD) (ADOPTION: PLACEMENT OUTSIDE JURISDICTION), *Re; sub nom.* KENT CC v A-K, [2013] EWHC 578 (Fam), [2014] Fam. 1, Pauffley, J., Fam Div.

1254. Children–Removal from jurisdiction–Transnational parenting–Assumption that parties foreseeing consequences of ending of relationship

The applicant mother (M) sought permission to relocate with her one-year-old son (S) to Russia. The respondent father (F) was from England, while M was a Russian national. They met while on holiday in Portugal in 2010 and married in the United Kingdom in August 2011. S was born in December 2011. F and M separated in May 2012. M had remained with F's mother in the former matrimonial home, while F went to stay in his mother's home. He enjoyed regular visiting contact and once-fortnightly staying contact. M wished to relocate to a township outside Moscow, where she proposed to return to work and where her family was based. She had a degree in logistics and was fluent in English. As to contact, she proposed to return to the UK four times a year and stated that F was free to come to Russia to see S. F wished S to remain in the UK under a shared-care arrangement. As to M's proposals, he objected, among other things, to the surroundings of the tower block in which M proposed to live; he also believed that there would be hostility to foreigners in the township in question.

Held: Application granted. Both parties were essentially genuine in their motivations: M's fundamental motivation was to go home, while F's fundamental motivation was child-centred, with S's interests as his chief consideration. His objections were not groundless. Both parties would be devastated by a decision adverse to them, and the choices they had made would undoubtedly bring some disadvantages to S whatever the court decided. On balance, it would be appropriate to accede to M's application. S was always going to have his home essentially with M, although time with F and his family would undoubtedly have increased. Further, when parties entered into transnational parenting, they were taken to be doing so with their eyes wide open and with an understanding that, if their relationship broke down, the possibility of a move abroad would be a major issue. Moreover, if breakdown took place while the child was very young, the child was likely to follow the one with whom he spent most of his time. If, of course, the breakdown took place much later in the child's life, it was far less likely that his or her position would be disrupted. The pain of separation was part of the price of a choice to enter into this kind of relationship, and there was simply nothing anyone could do to spare parties that pain in the event that the relationship went wrong. The fact was that M's plans were no more and no less than would have been obvious to the parties had they considered, at the time they agreed to be parents, what would happen if there was an early breakdown in their relationship. On balance, it had been shown that M was motivated to sustain contact; she had persuaded the court that she believed that S needed a proper paternal relationship and that she saw advantages for him in maintaining contact with all things English (see paras 11-12, 14-15, 20-21, 23 of judgment).

S v T (PERMISSION TO RELOCATE TO RUSSIA); *sub nom.* S v T (CHILDREN: RELOCATION), [2012] EWHC 4023 (Fam), [2013] 2 F.L.R. 457, Hedley, J., Fam Div.

1255. Children–Wrongful removal or retention–15-year-old in agreement with consent order to return her to Canada–Subsequent change of mind–Remittal to Family Division

[Hague Convention on the Civil Aspects of International Child Abduction 1980.]

The appellant 15-year-old child (C) appealed against a decision made by consent to return her to Canada. C's father (F), the first respondent, was Canadian and lived in Canada. Her mother (M), the second respondent, was British. They had all been living in Canada until M took C, along with other siblings, from Canada to England on holiday and decided not to go back. F applied under the Hague Convention on the Civil Aspects of International Child Abduction for C's return. C was initially opposed to returning to Canada, but by the time of the hearing she wanted to return, so the judge made a consensual return order without investigating the issues. Shortly afterwards, C began to state clearly and firmly that she had changed her mind and would not go back to Canada. The matter returned to the judge, who gave C permission to appeal because he did not have the power to set aside his order. C submitted that her case was so plain that the court should not only allow her appeal but should dismiss F's originating application. M supported C's appeal, as did the third respondent guardian, who submitted that ordering C's return to Canada would be pointless as it would lead to a successful application for relocation. The guardian further submitted that C was a fragile child who had had troubles in Canada, including a lifestyle of drinking and drug taking, and she would suffer if put through further litigation or returned to Canada without M's support. F submitted that the case was not at all cut and dried and it should be remitted for what would be its first full hearing.

Held: Appeal allowed. The order that C sought was not just a strong order; it was a very rare one for the Court of Appeal to make. It could only make it if it could demonstrate that the outcome on any remission was so plain that it would be almost abusive to put the parties and the trial judge through the process and therefore would be a futile and sterile direction. The pursuit of further litigation was likely to be at the expense of C's wellbeing. It was not for the Court of Appeal to judge the prospects of a successful outcome for F. In practical terms it was extremely unlikely that an order for C's return would be enforceable if she remained in her current emotional state. The prospect for her future was on any evaluation fragile unless both her parents combined to work together to help her through the next three or four years of adolescent vulnerability. If they only litigated, and drew her into the arena of litigation, her prospect of fulfilling her ambition of graduating from school would be diminished. The Court of Appeal could order mediation, but it would have to be child-inclusive. Already F had refused it when it was offered. Therefore, mediation would probably prolong the case. Further, mediation would be considerably impeded if F was on the other side of the world. Unless mediation could get F, M and C under one roof and with no time pressure its prospects were not sufficient to justify the inevitably delay it would cause. Reluctantly, the court concluded that F had demonstrated that there were issues that would make it impossible to declare that the outcome was so obvious that remission was rendered pointless. It would be wrong to deny F the process of trial as there had not been one. However, the court urged the parents to seize what could be the last opportunity to talk to each other about the near crisis C was in. The case would be remitted to the Family Division with a request that it be heard at the earliest possible date (see paras 5, 9-14 of judgment).

C (A CHILD) (ABDUCTION: SETTING ASIDE RETURN ORDER: REMISSION), *Re*, [2012] EWCA Civ 1144, [2013] 1 F.L.R. 403, Thorpe, L.J., CA (Civ Div).

1256. Children and Families (Wales) Measure 2010 (nawm 1)–Commencement No.6 Order

THE CHILDREN AND FAMILIES (WALES) MEASURE 2010 (COMMENCEMENT NO.6) ORDER 2013, SI 2013/SI 2013/18 (W.9) (C.2); made under the Children and Families (Wales) Measure 2010 s.74, s.75. Commencement details: bringing into force various provisions of the 2010 Act on February 1, 2013.; .

This Order brings into effect provisions in Part 3 of the Children and Families (Wales) Measure 2010 in Neath Port Talbot, Bridgend and Swansea on February 1, 2013.

1257. Children's welfare–Occupation orders–Appropriatness of occupation order–Absence of violence

[Family Law Act 1996 (c.27) s.33.]

The appellant father (F) appealed against orders made in family proceedings. F and his wife, the respondent mother (M), were the parents of eight-year old twins (C). Relations between F and M had deteriorated and F had recorded audio and video exchanges between them. The judge found that the children were adversely affected by the heated arguments between the parents and were likely to suffer significant emotional harm attributable to the presence of both parents in the house. He made an occupation order under the Family Law Act 1996 s.33 requiring F to vacate the matrimonial home for three months, and a shared residence order for C to live with M and to spend frequent time with F. F submitted that the judge was wrong (1) to make the occupation order as there was no proof of violence, it was too draconian a response to the situation in the home, and he should have considered an alternative order; (2) to decide that the children should reside permanently with M.

Held: Appeal dismissed. (1) The judge had first considered s.33(7) which required him to make the order if there was evidence that any child would suffer significant harm. He had then considered s.33(6) which gave him a broader discretion. There was nothing in s.33(6) that limited the making of the order to cases where there had been violence or reprehensible conduct. The provision was broadly drafted and required the court to weigh up at all the circumstances. The order could be granted if there were exceptional circumstances, which did not just mean violence, *Chalmers v Johns* [1999] 1 F.L.R. 392, [1999] C.L.Y. 2439 and *Dolan v Corby* [2011] EWCA Civ 1664, [2012] 2 F.L.R. 1031, [2012] C.L.Y. 1447 applied. F's argument had to proceed on the basis that the judge had wrongly exercised his discretion. The preliminary question was whether the judge proceeded on the basis of the correct facts. Many allegations had been made by F and M and it was clear that the situation between them was untenable, and the children were exposed to it. It was not incumbent on the judge to comment on every allegation that was made and he had to make findings that were relevant to the exercise of his discretion. He was entitled to make a decision on the facts as he found them. He considered each of the headings under s.33(6)(a) to 33(6)(d) as required. The judge was an experienced family judge and well able to take the view that he did. He found that C were suffering significant harm, which was the threshold for intervention by a local authority. It was clear that he considered that the conduct of both parents contributed to the situation and that they could not live together without damage being caused to the children. Given the finding that the children would be adversely affected he had to intervene (see paras 17-19, 21-29 of judgment). (2) The decision that M should be the primary carer was reasonable. M had given up her career and F was required to go abroad frequently during the duration of the order (para.29). (3) It was true that the courts should not intervene in property rights and impose such a draconian order other than in exceptional circumstances. However, the judge had formed a view of the harmful situation in the home. After seeing the parties and listening to the recordings he concluded that there was a risk of significant harm to C, and he made the order for a short period. He did not err in the exercise of his discretion. The appeal would be dismissed, but that was not a prejudgment of any future order, and the matter would have to be considered in the circumstances at the relevant time (paras 29-30, 32).

L (CHILDREN), *Re*, [2012] EWCA Civ 721, [2012] 2 F.L.R. 1417, Thorpe, L.J., CA (Civ Div).

1258. Children's welfare–Religious education–Parental preferences–Best interests of children from ultra-orthodox Jewish family

The appellant father (F) appealed against a decision relating to the education of his children (C). F and the respondent mother (M) were from families which had for many generations been part of the Hasidic or Chareidi community of ultra-orthodox Jews. Their marriage broke down. F wanted C to attend ultra-orthodox schools whilst M wanted them to attend orthodox but not ultra-orthodox schools, where they could pursue higher education and wider career opportunities. M accepted that the change of schools she had proposed would involve a change of lifestyle. A CAFCASS report was produced which concluded that it was in C's best interest to reside with M and move to schools of her choosing. The judge accepted the CAFCASS report and held that notwithstanding the change of lifestyle, it was in the best interests of C to have the much fuller, rounded and more extensive education which was available to them at the schools proposed by M. F submitted that the judge was plainly wrong in his decision about C's schooling. F argued that the judge failed to consider the law in relation to change of lifestyle, save for a fleeting reference to *T (Minors) (Custody: Religious Upbringing), Re* (1981) 2 F.L.R. 239 and failed to consider various criticisms that had been made of the CAFCASS assessment and should have departed from its recommendations and reasoning.

Held: Appeal dismissed. The judge had not misunderstood or misapplied the law. He referred appropriately to *Re T (Minors)*, correctly summarised the key principle and proceeded faithfully to apply it, *Re T (Minors)* considered. There could be no criticism of the CAFCASS report; it was carefully reasoned and sensitive and a powerful analysis which the judge was entitled to accept. The dispute which the judge had to resolve was whether, on balance, M's argument based on education should prevail over F's, based on way of life. It was quite clear that the judge understood the significance of the issue and that it extended far beyond the narrowly educational. He recognised that M's proposals involved "a change of lifestyle". The judge's reasoning was based on four strands. The first focussed on educational opportunity; he was plainly entitled to conclude that the schools to which M wished to send C would provide superior opportunities for them to gain much fuller and wider education and thereafter much greater job opportunities. The second and third strand was his acceptance of the analysis by the report of the emotional impact on C and that although they might have difficulty making a decision to embrace M's lifestyle when they were older, they would be able to return to their religious roots within the sort of community that their mother had proposed. The judge was plainly entitled to proceed on that basis. Finally, the judge was plainly entitled to conclude that in his view, as shared with the CAFCASS report, on balance C's interests were best served by M's proposals. The court could only interfere if it could be shown that the judge was plainly wrong. Far from being plainly wrong, he was in all probability right in the decision to which he came (see paras 72, 76, 84-88 of judgment).

G (CHILDREN) (RELIGIOUS UPBRINGING: EDUCATION), *Re*, [2012] EWCA Civ 1233, [2013] 1 F.L.R. 677, Maurice Kay, L.J., CA (Civ Div).

1259. Children's welfare–Secure accommodation–Detention of Irish child in English treatment unit pending registration of Irish order–Urgent order under art.20 Regulation 2201/2003

[Regulation 2201/2003 Art.20.]

The applicant Health Service Executive of Ireland (HSE) applied for an urgent order under Regulation 2201/2003 art.20 that the respondent 17-year-old girl (S) should reside at an English treatment unit. S was born and lived in Ireland. She had severe psychological and behavioural problems and had been in care since she was three. Her behaviour had worsened, and she was very seriously self-harming, such that staff at the high support unit where she lived considered that they could no longer keep her safe and the HSE obtained an order permitting her to be detained at a special care unit. However, those responsible for her care concluded that there were no facilities appropriate to her needs in Ireland and a unit in England was found. S consented to being transferred to the English unit. Once the necessary consent under Regulation 2201/2003 was obtained, a court order was made in Ireland for S's detention and treatment at the English unit.

Held: Application granted. (1) On the evidence the court was satisfied on an interim basis that it was in S's interests to reside and be treated at the English unit, whether or not she continued to consent to remaining there. It was urgent that an interim order be made to allow for staff at the English unit to detain and treat her. For the purposes of art.20 the proposed protective measures were provisional measures that would cease to have effect upon the completion of the registration of the Irish order. There was no cause to question the validity of the Irish order, or the process by which consent had been obtained from the relevant authority in England to the placement at the English unit. S's circumstances, including the deprivation of her liberty to which she would be subject upon her transfer to and placement in the English unit, were to be the subject of regular reviews by the High Court in Ireland. Accordingly, it was appropriate in S's best interests to make the interim orders sought under art.20 pending the registration and enforcement of the Irish order, *Health Service Executive v SC (C-92/12 PPU)* [2013] C.E.C. 235, *Proceedings Brought by A (C-523/07)* [2010] Fam. 42, [2009] C.L.Y. 1552, *Deticek v Sgueglia (C-403/09 PPU)* [2010] Fam. 104 and *C (A Minor) (Medical Treatment: Court's Jurisdiction), Re* [1997] 2 F.L.R. 180, [1997] C.L.Y. 428 considered (see paras 14-23 of judgment). (2) The court felt able to make the order under art.20 with limited scrutiny of the evidence. Other cases might necessitate a far more detailed analysis of the situation, including the separate representation of the child in the proceedings in England (para.25). (3) Judicial cooperation was not only encouraged but essential to facilitate the making and enforcement of orders for the welfare of children. Manifestly it was appropriate that there be judicial communication between the High Court in Ireland and the High Court in England so as to ensure that S's circumstances were reviewed on a regular basis (para.26).

HSE IRELAND v SF (A CHILD), [2012] EWHC 1640 (Fam), [2012] 2 F.L.R. 1131, Baker, J., Fam Div.

1260. Children, Schools and Families Act 2010 (c.26)–Commencement No.3 Order

THE CHILDREN, SCHOOLS AND FAMILIES ACT 2010 (COMMENCEMENT NO.3) ORDER 2013, SI 2013/SI 2013/668 C.27); made under the Children, Schools and Families Act 2010 s.29. Commencement details: bringing into force various provisions of the 2010 Act on April 15, 2013.; .

This Order is the third Commencement Order made by the Secretary of State for Education under the Children, Schools and Families Act 2010 and brings into force s.8 of the Act on April 15, 2013, giving Local Safeguarding Children Boards in England the power to request any person or body to supply such information as is specified in the request either to the Local Safeguarding Children Board or to another person or body.

1261. **Children, Schools and Families Act 2010 (c.26)–Commencement No.4 Order**

THE CHILDREN, SCHOOLS AND FAMILIES ACT 2010 (COMMENCEMENT NO.4) ORDER 2013, SI 2013/SI 2013/1573 (C.63); made under the Children, Schools and Families Act 2010 s.29. Commencement details: bringing into force a provision of the 2010 Act on July 3, 2013.; .

This Order brings into force the Children, Schools and Families Act 2010 s.10. Section 10 of the Act inserts s.15A into the Children Act 2004. Section 15A gives the Secretary of State the power to make regulations to make provision for the Chief Inspector to conduct a review of the performance of Local Safeguarding Children Boards.

1262. **Civil partnerships–Premises–Hotels–United Reformed Church**

THE MARRIAGES AND CIVIL PARTNERSHIPS (APPROVED PREMISES) (AMENDMENT) REGULATIONS 2013, SI 2013/2294; made under the Marriage Act 1949 s.46A; and the Civil Partnership Act 2004 s.6A, s.258. In force: October 7, 2013; .

These Regulations make two amendments to the Marriages and Civil Partnerships (Approved Premises) Regulations 2005 (SI 2005/3168). These amendments are: the correction of a drafting error (use of the word "fully" instead of "finally"); and the addition of the United Reformed Church to the table of persons who must consent to an application for religious premises to be approved as places where civil partnerships may take place.

1263. **Contact orders–Parental contact–Divergent CAFCASS reports on supervised contact–Need for oral evidence from CAFCASS officers**

The appellant mother (M) appealed against a contact order for the respondent father (F) in relation to their child (C). C had been living with M. F had had very little contact with C and was virtually unknown to her. The judge found that F had been violent towards M and her older child and that F was neglectful towards C, and ordered a CAFCASS report. The report stated that professionally supervised contact could be a way of re-introducing contact whilst reassuring M about her fears with regard to contact. The judge made a supervised contact order which M did not object to. F was referred to a centre for supervised contact. A different CAFCASS officer was asked to submit another report, and she expressed concerns about contact. She stated that contact should be indirect until F had engaged in therapeutic sessions to deal with his issues. A meeting was held because of the divergence of opinions but no agreement was reached. M maintained that supervised contact should not proceed until the court had heard the oral evidence of both CAFCASS officers. The judge rejected that argument and held that it was in C's interest for supervised contact to begin, and that such contact would provide valuable information for the court.

Held: Appeal allowed. The judge was making a welfare decision that contact would continue despite the second CAFCASS report and M's opposition to contact. The court was not persuaded by the argument that contact had been decided at the first hearing and that nothing had happened since then to change that view. M had received the views of a second CAFCASS officer, which was a change of circumstance and M had also changed her stance. The court did not wish to tie the hands of judges so that decisions could not be made without oral evidence. However, in the instant case, the legal representatives of both parties should have had the chance to make submissions if the matter was going to be resolved without the attendance of the CAFCASS officers. It was inappropriate for the judge to determine the issue without hearing the two officers. He was faced with two professionals who were adhering to their opposing views. The judge was in a difficult position, as he did not want to delay the start of the contact and waste the time of the court and the CAFCASS officers. However, he should not have made his decision without their attendance (see paras 29-32, 34 of judgment).

S (A CHILD) (CONTACT ORDER), *Re*, [2012] EWCA Civ 617, [2013] 1 F.L.R. 825, Sir John Thomas (President), CA (Civ Div).

1264. Contact orders–Parental contact–Father applying for contact shortly before child's 16th birthday–Fairness of making costs order against him–Proportionality of granting permission to appeal

[Family Procedure Rules 2010 (SI 2010/2955) r.30.3(7)(a).]

The applicant father (F), who had applied for contact with his 15-year-old daughter (C), sought permission to appeal against a costs order made in favour of the mother (M) at the conclusion of a first hearing dispute resolution appointment. The parents had separated when C was five years old. F had regular contact with her until shortly before C's 15th birthday, when M announced its end. Six months later, F indicated an intention to apply for a contact order which, M maintained, was a form of harassment and an abuse of the court process given C's age. She said that if an application was made, she would seek a costs order against him. At the first hearing appointment, both parties were represented. C was around three months short of her 16th birthday. She said, through a CAFCASS officer, that she found F controlling and did not want contact. F accepted the information and agreed that no contact order should be made against her wishes. The district judge exercised his discretion to order costs against F, summarily assessing them at almost £2,500. He held that the court was not a meeting house to be used to establish a child's wishes and feelings and that, before issuing his application, F should have "stood back and asked himself whether... there was any chance at all... of the court being willing to make an order". The judge characterised the application as "entirely misconceived" and the conclusion as "absolutely foregone", given that C was only a few months short of the cut-off point for making such orders. F sought permission to appeal against the costs order on the basis that, the judge having unfairly criticised him and used inappropriate language, his appeal had a real prospect of success as required by the Family Procedure Rules 2010 r.30.3(7)(a).

Held: Permission refused. The judge had been wrong to characterise F's contact application in the manner that he did; it had been a perfectly reasonable and justifiable application and F's indignation at the costs order was understandable. The express purpose of the first hearing dispute resolution appointment under the revised private law programme was precisely to provide "a forum" as a means "to reach understanding of issues" and for their resolution. There was no practical distinction between a "meeting house" and a "forum". Without issuing an application, there was no mechanism whereby a parent in F's position could engage the services of CAFCASS so as to ascertain the wishes and feelings of a child with whom he was denied contact. C had been almost 16 years old at the date of the hearing, but at the outset of the proceedings she had still been six months short of that age. Courts frequently used the opportunity in the run-up to a chronological cut-off point to make age-appropriate orders, and it might have been possible, in this case, to have explored whether contact could somehow be re-established (see paras 15-19 of judgment). However, although there was undoubtedly a real prospect that F's appeal would succeed, the exercise of the discretion to grant permission to appeal depended on consideration of other matters, including the overriding objective. Proportionality was an issue. F's legal team, moved by the injustice of the situation, had offered to act in the appeal free of charge, which meant that F's costs would be limited to the issue fee and the transcribing fee. That might be a proportionate amount to spend when appealing an allegedly unfair order for the payment of some £2,500, but there were also M's costs to take into account, which would be a minimum of £2,000. The Family Division's desperately hard-pressed resources also had to be considered. A further relevant factor was the financial position of each party. The amount of the costs order was very small when compared to F's salary and general wealth. The appeal was really about F's sense of grievance that he had been unfairly criticised. He had been able to ventilate his grievance and had had the satisfaction of a more senior judge agreeing with him, but the appeal lacked any proportionality to the amount at stake and permission to appeal would not be granted (paras 22-36).

HH v BLW (APPEAL: COSTS: PROPORTIONALITY), [2012] EWHC 2199 (Fam), [2013] 1 F.L.R. 420, Holman, J., Fam Div.

1265. Contact orders–Parental contact–Father in prison for sexual abuse of daughter–Adequacy of reasons for order providing father with annual photograph

The appellant local authority appealed against a recorder's order that a passport-sized photograph of a child (C) be sent to the respondent father (F), who was in prison, once a year. C had been abused by F. The recorder ordered that there be indirect contact between C and F which would include a small photograph of C to be sent once a year. The recorder had not given reasons for making that decision and later provided an addendum judgment which stated his reasons as being that C had retained a close relationship with F's family, F was a living presence in C's mind and, in reliance on the expert psychological evidence, that indirect contact would assist C's therapy. The local authority submitted that the recorder's decision went against the evidence of the social worker, the guardian and the expert psychological evidence which had been that any indirect contact should have been in consultation with C's therapist, and not to assist C's therapy.

Held: Appeal allowed. The background to the case suggested that the seemingly innocuous provision ordered by the recorder paid scant regard to the interests and rights of C whose welfare was paramount, and ignored the preponderance of evidence which went against that request. The recorder had not correctly understood the expert evidence and accordingly his conclusion rested on the shakiest of foundations. There had been an inadequate consideration of C's position. It might amount to a violation of her rights that, without any benefit to her or need in her, she was the participant in a process which might be impossible for her to understand in years to come as she acquired an understanding of her past and of the sort of father that she had. The recorder's order was insufficiently or erroneously reasoned and was set aside (see paras 3, 6-7 of judgment).

C (A CHILD) (INDIRECT CONTACT), *Re*, [2012] EWCA Civ 1281, [2013] 2 F.L.R. 272, Thorpe, L.J., CA (Civ Div).

1266. Contact orders–Parental contact–Father seeking contact with daughter–Appropriateness of ordering disclosure of allegations of child sexual abuse made against him by vulnerable third party

[Human Rights Act 1998 (c.42); European Convention on Human Rights 1950 Art.3, Art.6, Art.8.]

The appellant (X) appealed against a decision ([2012] EWCA Civ 1204, [2013] 1 F.L.R. 919, [2013] 1 C.L. 131) that allegations of sexual abuse made by her should be disclosed in contact proceedings involving a 10-year-old girl (C). X was a vulnerable young woman who had made an allegation in confidence to the authorities that while she was a child she had been seriously sexually abused by C's father (F). She was adamant that she did not want any action to be taken on her allegations or her identity revealed. F, who was seeking contact with C, denied sexually abusing anyone and wished X's allegations to be disclosed, as did C's mother and her guardian. A consultant psychiatrist who had been treating X had produced a report stating that her physical health had deteriorated, at times to the point of being life-threatening, and that disclosure would be potentially detrimental to her health.

Held: Appeal dismissed. (1) If the case were decided on common-law principles alone, the answer would be clear. X's allegations had to be properly investigated and tested so that C could either be protected from any risk of harm which F might present to her or resume her normal relationship with him; that simply could not be done without disclosing to the parents and to the guardian X's identity and the detail and history of her allegations (see paras 29-30 of judgment). (2) The answer was the same under the Human Rights Act 1998. In play were the right of C and her parents to have a fair trial in the determination of their civil rights under the European Convention on Human Rights 1950 art.6 and their right to respect for their private and family lives under art.8. X had a right to respect for her private life under art.8. However, she relied principally on her art.3 right not to be subjected to inhuman or degrading treatment; in that respect, she relied on the views of the consultant psychiatrist. When considering what treatment was sufficiently severe to reach the high threshold required for a violation of art.3, the European Court of Human Rights had consistently said that that "[depended] on all the circumstances of the case, such as the nature and context of the treatment, the manner and method of its execution, its duration, its physical or mental effects and, in some instances, the sex, age and state of health of the victim". The context here was not only that the state was acting in support of some important public interests; it was also that X was currently under the specialist care of a consultant physician and a consultant psychiatrist, who would no doubt do their utmost to mitigate any further suffering which disclosure might cause her. Accordingly, disclosure would not violate her rights under art.3. As to art.8, the family life and fair trial rights of all three parties to the proceedings were a sufficient justification for the interference with X's privacy rights; put the other way round, her privacy rights were not a sufficient justification for the grave compromise of the fair trial and family life rights of the parties which non-disclosure would entail. A closed material procedure had been suggested but, even if it were theoretically possible to devise such a procedure, it would not meet the minimum requirements of a fair hearing in this case (paras 25-26, 32, 34-35). (3) It did not follow from requiring disclosure that X would have to give evidence in person. Disclosure might be enough to resolve matters. If any party wished to call her to give oral evidence, up-to-date medical evidence could be obtained to discover whether she was fit to do so. Further, there were many ways in which her evidence could be received without recourse to the normal method of courtroom confrontation. The court had the power to receive and act on hearsay evidence. It was commonplace for children to give their accounts in videotaped conversations with specially trained police officers or social workers; such arrangements might be extended to other vulnerable witnesses such as X (para.36).

A (A CHILD) (DISCLOSURE OF THIRD PARTY INFORMATION), *Re*; *sub nom.* X, RE; J (A CHILD: DISCLOSURE), RE; A (A CHILD) (SEXUAL ABUSE: DISCLOSURE), RE; A (A CHILD) (FAMILY PROCEEDINGS: DISCLOSURE OF INFORMATION), *Re*, [2012] UKSC 60, [2013] 2 A.C. 66, Lord Neuberger, J.S.C., SC.

1267. Contact orders–Parental contact–Father's denial of sending Facebook request to daughter in breach of injunction–Judge's finding of breach–Appropriateness of sentence imposed

The appellant father (F) appealed against a judge's finding of fact that he had breached injunctions and the consequent imposition of a suspended sentence of imprisonment. F's daughter (B) had been subject to a care order and a care plan which endorsed her placement in a foster home. F objected to the validity of the process that the court and the local authority had engaged in. The court determined that it was not in B's interests to have unauthorised or unrestricted contact with F and that F was to be restrained from interfering with B's placement. Accordingly, a non-harassment injunction and an injunction restricting the publicity of B's placement were imposed upon F by consent. The local authority initiated committal proceedings owing to F's alleged breaches of the injunctions. F admitted some breaches, which included writing a letter to the school which the foster carers' child was to attend making allegations of criminality and domestic violence. However, F denied sending a Facebook friend request to B, and requested that B give oral evidence. The judge refused that request. In reaching his final decision, the judge took into account the severity of the breaches, the most serious being the letter to the school; the fact that it was F's first breach of the injunctions; the aggravating features of the breaches; and F's mitigation. The judge concluded that F had sent the request on Facebook and imposed concurrent sentences of three months' imprisonment for the breaches suspended until B reached her eighteenth birthday. F submitted that (1) B's needs were not being met or understood, that an investigation into the Facebook request should have been conducted, and that robust scrutiny of B's hearsay evidence was required; (2) the judge should not have imposed a penalty upon him as although he breached the orders, he had done so to protect B.

Held: Appeal dismissed. (1) The judge was entitled to refuse F's request to call B as a witness concerning the Facebook request. B was merely the recipient of the request; calling her as witness would shed no light on its origin, which was what F disputed. The judge's finding of fact that the Facebook message came from F could not be called into question. It could only be interfered with if it had been made in an erroneous way or in a way that was unsupported by the evidence, which was not the case. (2) That was not a view that the judge or anyone else could have accepted. There was no doubt that F wanted B out of the foster home. The judge had been sure that F had wanted to embarrass and undermine the foster carers; F's motives had not been benign. That was the only conclusion that could have been drawn from the letter to the school. The penalty imposed by the judge had been merciful and proportionate.

B (A CHILD) (FOSTER PLACEMENT: RESTRAINING ORDERS), *Re*, [2013] EWCA Civ 166, [2013] 2 F.L.R. 265, Thorpe, L.J., CA (Civ Div).

1268. Contact orders–Parental contact–Jurisdiction to hear application to vary consent contact order–Determination of habitual residence–Meaning of "relevant date" pursuant to s.7(c) Family Law Act 1986

[Children Act 1989 (c.41) s.8; Family Law Act 1986 (c.55) s.2(1), s.3, s.7(c), s.7.]

The appellant mother (M) appealed against a decision that the court had jurisdiction to hear an application made by the respondent father (F) to vary contact with his daughter (X). M and F had separated in 2005 when X was a year old. F's contact with X ended in March 2006 when M unilaterally removed her from the south of England to Scotland without F's knowledge or consent. F immediately applied to his local county court in England for residence and contact orders, and an order to trace X and M in Scotland. They were located in August 2006. A residence order was made in favour of M cementing X's residence with her in Scotland in April 2008. In March 2009, the county court made a detailed contact order governing supervised contact between F and X. There was no return date for review of contact, and X's guardian was discharged. Over a year later, F made a fresh application in the English county court seeking to vary the March 2009 order to provide for unsupervised contact. The parties reached agreement and a consent order was made in February 2011. Four months later, F applied to vary the consent order. At the hearing, M queried the English county court's jurisdiction to determine the application. The judge took account of the Family Law Act 1986 and indicated that the court's jurisdiction depended on whether X was habitually resident in England at the "relevant date". He concluded that the relevant date was the beginning of the whole process, namely F's applications in March 2006, and that since X was not then habitually resident in Scotland, it was appropriate to hear F's application in the English, rather than Scottish, county court. M contended that, on the proper construction of the Act, the judge's conclusion on jurisdiction was unsustainable.

Held: Appeal allowed. (1) The Act was designed to clarify and fix issues of jurisdiction between constituent parts of the United Kingdom. Section 2(1), which was in imperative terms, provided that the court lacked jurisdiction unless, inter alia, the condition under s.3, that of habitual residence in England or Wales, was satisfied. Section 7(c) concerned the relevant date at which habitual residence was to be considered. Although the Act had been criticised by commentators and the Court of Appeal as lacking clarity in a number of respects, the structure established by s.7 went a long way to providing a statutory scheme for clarifying and fixing which of the constituent parts of the UK had jurisdiction over private law children cases. Whilst the judge had correctly identified the issue as being the relevant date, his conclusion was unsustainable. The proceedings commenced in 2006 had run their course by the time of F's application and concluded in March 2009. The order made at that time was to all intents and purposes a final order. By the time of F's application to vary the consent order, which was the relevant date under s.7(c), X was habitually resident in Scotland. Any proceedings before the county court after

March 2009 were made without jurisdiction. The fact that M had engaged in those proceedings was irrelevant. The Act was strictly worded and she was not able to attribute jurisdiction to the English county court. Accordingly, the English courts lacked jurisdiction and any further applications concerning X would need to be made in Scotland (see paras 13, 14, 16, 20-24 of judgment). (2) (Per Thorpe, L.J.) The principal aim of the Act was to resolve conflicts of jurisdiction in the UK; it had not been successful in that objective. Its provisions were difficult and had not prevented conflicting decisions in different jurisdictions of the UK in respect of the same child. However, the essential focus for the instant court was upon s.7(c), and that provision was free from the complications that bedevilled other sections. It was simple in its terms and simple to apply: the relevant date was the date of the order sought or application made. Whilst the judge had adopted the correct approach in looking at the relevant date, he had made the wrong choice. That decision was not explained in his judgment, but reflected his sympathy with F's application and his desire to see effective delivery of contact between F and X (paras 29-31).

W-B (A CHILD), *Re*, [2012] EWCA Civ 592, [2013] 1 F.L.R. 394, Thorpe, L.J., CA (Civ Div).

1269. Contact orders–Parental contact–Parents suspected of sexually abusing baby daughter–Appropriateness of judge refusing parental contact at interm stage

[Children Act 1989 (c.41) s.34(4).]

The appellant mother and father (M and F) appealed against a judge's decision to continue a direction made under the Children Act 1989 s.34(4) which permitted the respondent local authority to withhold contact to their four children. M and F's relationship was characterised by a history of domestic violence. M and F's one-year-old daughter (K) had been admitted to hospital due to bleeding in her genital area. A consultant paediatrician had found various injuries to K's genital area, including a laceration to her hymen and perineal tears, which she indicated were consistent with penetrative vaginal and anal injury. K and her two siblings were removed from M and F's care and care proceedings were initiated. M and F attended two supervised contact sessions, and notes of those sessions indicated that they had gone positively. M later gave birth to a fourth child (X). In June 2012 a judge made an order under s.34(4) giving the local authority permission to refuse M and F contact to their four children until a hearing two weeks' later. He also ordered the instruction of a psychologist to help in assessing the issue of future contact. At that later hearing in July 2012 the same judge extended the s.34(4) direction in relation to all four children; he said that K had suffered trauma at the hands of one or both of her parents, that it was difficult to see how contact could be in her interests and that similar considerations applied in relation to the children's domestic circumstances. The judge had considered X separately to the other three children, but had still decided that a s.34(4) direction was appropriate. A fact-finding hearing in respect of K's injuries was due to take place in November 2012. M and F submitted that the judge had acted prematurely in determining the case as he did and that he had effectively determined the issue of contact for all four children solely on the basis of K's injuries. They argued that he had been wrong to look to the outcome of the proceedings and predict the facts that would be found at the final hearing, and was wrong to have ruled out the prospect of reunification. They also contended that the judge was wrong to have extended the s.34(4) direction in a blanket, open-ended way which envisaged it continuing until the fact-finding hearing without review.

Held: Appeal allowed. (1) Whilst the s.34(4) direction had no formal limit, the psychologist was instructed in order to furnish the court with information on the issue of contact. The judge had expressly entertained the prospect of reviewing the s.34(4) direction in his judgment, and therefore he had not intended for it to be open-ended (see para.14 of judgment). (2) When the judge said that K had suffered trauma at the hands of one or both of her parents and that it was difficult to see how contact could be in her interests, he was basing his view on contact on his own concluded view of the facts. At the fact-finding hearing there would be further investigation into K's injuries and more was likely to be known about the circumstances surrounding her injuries. The judge had not analysed matters for and against some form of interim contact; he had simply decided that there should be no contact without considering the various ways in which contact could be arranged. He had not considered the possible benefit of contact for the children, whether any risk to them could have been contained by supervised or less regular contact, or the positive accounts from the contact sessions. Further, when he said that similar considerations applied in respect of the children's domestic circumstances, the judge had wrongly equated K's injuries with the family's history of domestic violence. The judge was correct to say that the children needed to be protected, but he should have analysed whether that protection could have been provided through contact, which he had not done. Accordingly, the judge had erroneously determined the issue of contact on the basis of K's apparent abuse and had conflated the seriousness of her injuries with the history of domestic violence. Whilst the judge was correct to approach the question of X's contact on a different basis, considering her very young age and the fact that there was no risk of retraumatisation to her since she had not been born when K suffered the injuries, he had similarly determined the outcome of the contact issue on the basis of K's injuries. The judge's view on contact had been coloured by K's serious injuries with the effect that he had fallen into the trap of pre-determining issues which should have been left for the final fact-finding hearing; he should merely have decided whether there should be some form of interim contact, *A v M and Walsall MBC* [1993] 2 F.L.R. 244, [1994] C.L.Y. 3115 considered. It was appropriate to discharge the s.34(4) direction and to remit the case to the county court for further consideration by the same judge (paras 29-31, 34-35, 38-42).

H-T (CHILDREN) (CONTACT: SEXUAL ABUSE), *Re*; T-H (CHILDREN), *Re*, [2012] EWCA Civ 1215, [2013] 1 F.L.R. 705, Richards, L.J., CA (Civ Div).

1270. Contact orders–Procedural irregularity–No procedural irregularity in judge's decision based on submissions alone

[Children Act 1989 (c.41) s.1 (3).]

The appellant father (F) appealed against a decision to vary a contact order in respect of his seven-year-old son (S). For some time the contact arrangement had been that on every other weekend S went to F after school on Friday and stayed until F dropped him at school on Monday morning. An application was made to vary that arrangement. The hearing of that and other issues was listed for one day. On the morning of the hearing, the parties were attempting to settle. At around 11.45am counsel for F, and for the mother and for S indicated to the judge that they needed more time to negotiate. They met with the judge in chambers, without the parties. All counsel agreed that the two remaining issues could be dealt with without the need for oral evidence but by way of submissions only. On that basis the judge allowed the parties more time to negotiate. She decided the two unsettled issues: one in favour of F, the other, namely the duration of F's alternate weekend contact with S, she decided against F, reducing the duration so that S would go to F on a Saturday morning. F obtained permission to appeal. On the basis of a direction given by the judge granting permission, a note of the meeting was prepared and agreed by the judge and the three counsel. F submitted that (1) the judge's discussion with counsel, and the making of her decision on the issues without hearing oral evidence, were an impermissible way to proceed; (2) the judge in deciding to reduce his contact with S had focused impermissibly on just one aspect of the welfare checklist in the Children Act 1989 s.1 (3).

Held: Appeal dismissed. (1) In light of the agreed note of the meeting held between the judge and counsel, it was clear that everything the judge did on the day of the hearing was not only permissible but sensible and in line with the general approach of judges to case management when the parties were in lengthy negotiation which threatened to prevent the trial of contested issues in the time permitted (see para.4 of judgment). (2) The judge had the clear report of S's guardian before her and quite rightly it played a large part in her determination. The guardian had reported that S was uncomfortable with the existing contact arrangement because he did not like not seeing his mother from Friday morning when he arrived at school until Monday evening after school. That was a clear representation of S's wishes and feelings. However, it was implicit from the judge's conclusion that she had borne in mind the other welfare criteria. There could be no legitimate basis for criticism of the judge, who had heard submissions from all three counsel at some length (paras 6-8).

H (A CHILD) (CONTACT ORDER: PERMISSIBILITY OF JUDGE'S ACTIONS), *Re*, [2012] EWCA Civ 714, [2012] 2 F.L.R. 1114, Thorpe, L.J., CA (Civ Div).

1271. **Contact orders–Sperm donors–Children conceived by artificial insemination to lesbian couple–Application for leave to apply for contact orders by biological fathers**

[Children Act 1989 (c.41) s.1, s.8, s.10(9); Human Fertilisation and Embryology Act 2008 (c.22); European Convention on Human Rights 1950 Art.8.]

The applicant men (S and T) applied for leave to apply for contact orders under the Children Act 1989 s.8 for children conceived using their sperm by women in a civil partnership. S agreed to provide sperm to his friends (D and E) who were a lesbian couple wishing to have children. D and E stated that they made it clear to S that he would have no parental title, no parental responsibility and no financial commitment. In March 2008 E became pregnant. D and E entered into a civil partnership in September 2008 and a daughter (F) was born in December 2008. S visited them in hospital and thereafter there was regular contact. In August 2008, S's partner, T, provided sperm to a lesbian couple (X and Y) who were in a civil partnership and who were friends of D and E, and X gave birth to a son (Z). X and Y stated that they wanted to have the same arrangement as D and E had with S and they wanted T to be a role model for Z. In September 2009 S and T entered a civil partnership. D, E and F were seated at the top table at the reception. D, E, S and T then discussed a sibling for F and S again agreed to provide sperm and a son was born (G) in September 2010. Following the Human Fertilisation and Embryology Act 2008, D's name was included on the birth certificate. S and T continued to see F and G frequently. Disagreements then began as to the amount of contact S and T could have. Neither S in the case of G nor T in the case of Z was entitled to apply for a contact order as they were not legal parents following the 2008 Act so they needed the court's leave to make the application. S was F's legal father. D, E, X and Y contended that it was the intention of Parliament to protect same sex families who had conceived with sperm donors and their status as parents should be exclusive and absolute. S and T argued that the 2008 Act did not eradicate their status as genetic parents who might be allowed by the court to play a role in the life of the child.

Held: Applications granted. When deciding an application by a biological father for leave to apply for an order under s.8 in respect of a child conceived using his sperm by a woman who, at the time of the artificial insemination, was party to a civil partnership, the court could take all relevant matters into account, including the reforms implemented in the 2008 Act, the policy underpinning those reforms and the factors identified in s.10(9) of the 1989 Act and the prospects of success were not decisive, *B (A Child) (Paternal Grandmother: Joinder as Party), Re* [2012] EWCA Civ 737, [2012] 2 F.L.R. 1358, [2012] C.L.Y. 1344 followed. The policy of the 2008 Act put lesbian couples and their children in exactly the same legal position as other types of parent and children. The relationship between a same sex couple constituted family life for the purposes of the European Convention on Human Rights 1950 art.8 which was entitled to respect, Schalk and Kopf v Austria [2010] ECHR 995 considered. Each case was fact specific. S and T were not strangers to G and Z. As a result of choices made by D, E, X and Y both S and T had regular and frequent contact with G and Z. D and E chose S, an old friend, to provide sperm to enable them to have a child. They wanted their second child to have the same genetic background. They involved S in the preparations before the birth and allowed him contact. Equally X and Y selected T to provide sperm to enable them to conceive a child and allowed him frequent contact. It was also significant that they expressly wanted T to be a role model for Z. D, E, X and Y had exercised their parental responsibility to facilitate some sort of relationship between the children and their biological fathers. It was arguable that they had allowed S and T to establish a family life with the children under art.8. Disputes between the parties about the frequency of past conduct could only be resolved by a substantive fact-finding hearing. On the facts of the instant case, the most important factor was the connection that S and T were allowed by D, E, X and Y to form with each child. S and T had a good arguable case for contact orders and they were granted leave to make applications for contact orders in respect of G and Z. S was refused leave to apply for a residence order. It did not follow that any substantive order for contact would be made. Decisions on contact would be made applying s.1 of the 1989 Act (see paras 63-65, 113-118, 120, 126, 129, 132-137 of judgment).

G (CHILDREN) (CHILDREN: SPERM DONORS: LEAVE TO APPLY FOR CHILDREN ACT ORDERS), *Re*; Z (A CHILD), *Re*; *sub nom.* T v X; S v D, [2013] EWHC 134 (Fam), [2013] 1 F.L.R. 1334, Baker, J., Fam Div.

1272. County courts–Family hearing centres–Transfer of proceedings–Wiltshire

THE ALLOCATION AND TRANSFER OF PROCEEDINGS (AMENDMENT) ORDER 2013, SI 2013/421; made under the Children Act 1989 s.92, Sch.11 Pt.1. In force: March 25, 2013; .

This Order amends the Allocation and Transfer of Proceedings Order 2008. On March 25, 2013, Trowbridge County Court will cease to be family hearing centre and Chippenham and Trowbridge County Court will become a family hearing centre.

1273. Divorce–Decrees absolute–Appropriateness of setting aside order for decree nisi to be made absolute

The court had to decide whether to set aside the order for a decree nisi to be made absolute on the basis that fresh evidence had been made available. The appellant wife (W) petitioned for divorce from the respondent husband (H) and obtained a decree nisi. Her ancillary relief claims were made subject to trial at the conclusion of which H made an oral application for the grant of decree absolute. H's application was not dealt with in the judgment that was handed down but was renewed by him as part of a request to the judge on other issues. The judge subsequently ordered that the decree nisi be made absolute. W appealed against the judgment in the ancillary relief proceedings and obtained a stay of the order for the grant of decree absolute. W then received from her legal team in America a letter expressing the opinion that if the decree was made absolute in advance of W's ancillary relief appeal, she would be severely prejudiced because she would lose the prospects of enforcing whatever order might be made in relation to a transfer of shares between her and H. W submitted that had the letter been available, the judge would not have expressed himself as he did in his judgment and he would have or might have made a different order. H contended that W had been aware for some time that he sought the grant of decree absolute and that as she had not made the point at the substantive hearing, it was hardly fair that she take it now.

Held: Appeal allowed. W made a powerful point and the appropriate course was to accept that the judge might have made a different order had the letter been available. That possibility had been supported by H's proposal to transfer a portion of his shares to W pending her completion of confidentiality and non-competition documents. It was a matter of principle to allow the appeal and to set aside the terms for the making of a decree absolute (see paras 5, 7-8 of judgment).

EVANS v EVANS, [2012] EWCA Civ 1293, [2013] 2 F.L.R. 295, Thorpe, L.J., CA (Civ Div).

1274. Divorce–Forum non conveniens–Parallel proceedings in England and India–Indian petition first in time–Whether English court retaining discretion to stay English petition

[Domicile and Matrimonial Proceedings Act 1973 (c.45) Sch.1 para.9; Matrimonial Causes Act 1973 (c.18) s.22, s.27; Regulation 2201/2003; Regulation 4/2009.]

The court was required to determine a series of applications arising out of parallel sets of divorce proceedings in England and India. The husband (H) and wife (W) were Indian nationals. They had married in India and their daughter (D) had been born there. In 2006 they had moved to the United Kingdom for the purposes of H's employment. In June 2009 the family returned to India for a holiday, but H came back to the UK alone. In August 2009 he began divorce proceedings in India. W and D returned to the UK, but went back to India in August 2010 when W's application for leave to remain was rejected. In the meantime, however, she had issued an application under the Matrimonial Causes Act 1973 s.27 and H had been ordered to pay interim maintenance. Upon W's return to India, H's payments became sporadic, significant arrears accrued, and W applied under s.22 for maintenance pending suit. In November 2011, W's s.27 application was stayed. The following month she petitioned for divorce in England, the petition being stayed in January 2012. Three months later, H resigned his employment and returned to India. The issues were (i) whether the English court retained a discretion to stay properly constituted English divorce proceedings in favour of proceedings in a foreign jurisdiction; (ii) forum non conveniens; (iii) whether, by virtue of Regulation 2/2009 or otherwise, W's s.22 application would survive a stay of the English divorce proceedings; (iv) what was to happen to W's s.27 application in the event of a stay.

Held: Judgment accordingly. (1) The court's discretion under the Domicile and Matrimonial Proceedings Act 1973 Sch.1 para.9 to stay the English divorce proceedings in favour of the Indian proceedings had not been displaced by the decision in *Owusu v Jackson (t/a Villa Holidays Bal Inn Villas) (C-281/02)* [2005] Q.B. 801, [2005] C.L.Y. 604. The decision in *JKN v JCN (Divorce: Forum)* [2010] EWHC 843 (Fam), [2011] 1 F.L.R. 826, [2011] C.L.Y. 1402, that it was neither necessary nor desirable to extend the *Owusu* principle to cases where there were parallel proceedings in a non-European Union member state, was correct, *JKN* applied, *Ferrexpo AG v Gilson Investments Ltd* [2012] EWHC 721 (Comm), [2012] 1 Lloyd's Rep. 588, [2012] C.L.Y. 557 and *Owusu* considered. It would be an oddity if, while under Regulation 2201/2003 (Brussels II Revised) the court seised second had to stay its proceedings until the jurisdiction of the court first seised was established, there was no equivalent mechanism where the competing jurisdiction was not an EU member state. Without such a mechanism there would be a lacuna, with both sets of proceedings continuing competitively, creating duplication, uncertainty, unnecessary expense and the risk of irreconcilable decisions. Had the intention been to abolish the Sch.1 para.9 discretion when the competing jurisdiction was a non-EU member state, primary legislation would have said so in terms (see paras 15-22 of judgment). (2) India was the more appropriate forum: both parties were Indian nationals living in India, both were Hindu, the Indian divorce proceedings were first in time, and proceedings for guardianship and contact were underway in India. Neither party had assets in, or any continuing connection with, the UK. All the evidence, some of which was in Hindi, was in India, and the issues to be resolved included questions concerning Indian culture and the cost of living in India. All considerations of closest connection, expense, convenience and the practicalities of litigation called for the divorce and financial proceedings to take place in India. Even though H had not behaved fairly towards W and there was evidence that maintenance proceedings in India could be cumbersome and fraught with delay, it was clear that India was the preferable jurisdiction, *De Dampierre v De Dampierre* [1988] A.C. 92, [1987] C.L.Y. 399 followed. The English divorce proceedings would therefore be stayed. If the Indian proceedings did not proceed at a reasonable pace, W could apply to release the stay (paras 23-31). (3) Financial applications ancillary to a divorce depended on the continuation of the petition and had no independent life. If a petition was dismissed, maintenance pending suit under s.22 came to an end. If a petition was stayed, any application for maintenance pending suit was stayed with it. Regulation 4/2009 did not create a free-standing substantive right and remedy (para.32). (4) W's s.27 application was, however, a free-standing application. It was independent of the divorce, it was not subject to the forum non conveniens discretion, and there was no parallel application in India. However, while it was theoretically possible for a s.27 application to stand alongside a s.22 application, it would almost never happen. Given that W's s.22 application would be stayed with the staying of the divorce petition, it would not be logical to perpetuate the s.27 application without good reason. To so would give rise to the difficulty of litigating from England what was, essentially, an Indian case. There was no completely satisfactory answer. The court could not remit the arrears without up to date financial information, and H had no assets or income in the UK against which to enforce. In those circumstances, the s.27 application would remain stayed on the basis that it would be dismissed when decree absolute was pronounced in India. Were the Indian court to delay unreasonably in dealing with such financial applications as W might make, she could, theoretically, apply for the stay to be lifted (paras 33-37).

AB v CB (DIVORCE AND MAINTENANCE: DISCRETION TO STAY); *sub nom.* M v M; AB v CB (DIVORCE: JURISDICTION), [2012] EWHC 3841 (Fam), [2013] 2 F.L.R. 29, Bodey, J., Fam Div.

1275. Documentary evidence–Intercountry adoption–Recognition–Savings provisions

THE ADOPTION (RECOGNITION OF OVERSEAS ADOPTIONS) ORDER 2013, SI 2013/1801; made under the Adoption and Children Act 2002 s.87, s.140, s.142. In force: January 3, 2014; .

This Order prescribes the countries and territories whose adoption orders are prescribed as "overseas adoptions" for the purposes of the Adoption and Children Act 2002 s.37 and therefore recognised as adoptions under s.66 of the Act.

1276. Family proceedings–Allocation of jurisdiction–Divorce proceedings issued in England and Switzerland–Stay of English proceedings under art.27 or art.28 Lugano Convention 1988–Balance of fairness under Domicile and Matrimonial Proceedings Act 1973

[Domicile and Matrimonial Proceedings Act 1973 (c.45); Lugano Convention on Jurisdiction and the Enforcement of Judgments in Civil and Commercial Matters 1988 Art.2, Art.27, Art.28.]

The applicant husband (H) sought a stay under the Lugano Convention 1988 art.27 or art.28, or under the Domicile and Matrimonial Proceedings Act 1973, of divorce proceedings issued by the respondent wife (W). H was Greek and W was Italian. They married in Italy and lived in various other countries, including the United States, Argentina and England. Their two sons attended private schools in England. Upon separation, W remained in the matrimonial home in England, and H lived and worked in Switzerland. He issued divorce proceedings in Switzerland in July 2011. They were served on W in November 2011. By then, she had issued the instant proceedings in England, which were served on H in October 2011. She also applied for maintenance. A case management hearing took place in the English proceedings in February 2013, at which it was determined that issues concerning the Convention and the 1973 Act would need to be addressed. The first substantive hearing in the Swiss proceedings was listed for June 2013. H wanted the English proceedings, particularly the maintenance application, to be stayed until the Swiss courts had decided whether they were seised. W had largely ignored the Swiss proceedings and wanted the English divorce to be expedited.

Held: Petition stayed. (1) Although H had not expressly raised a cause of action upon which art.27 or art.28 of the Convention could bite, there was a real possibility that the Swiss courts would consider that the wording of H's petition raised claims in relation to child support. Therefore, on the facts, England could be the appropriate forum under art.2(a) of the Convention, and both countries could each be the appropriate forum under art.2(b). As there was an imminent hearing in Switzerland, where issues of seisin were not likely to be complex, it would be futile for English judges to hear arguments concerning the relevant Swiss law, *Bentinck v Bentinck* [2007] EWCA Civ 175, [2007] I.L.Pr. 32, [2007] C.L.Y. 661 applied. Seisin was unquestionably a matter for the Swiss courts (see paras 17, 25-29 of judgment). (2) Spousal maintenance and child maintenance constituted the same cause of action between the same parties and fell within art.27 of the convention. The English proceedings therefore had to be stayed until Switzerland had determined seisin (para.34). (3) If art.27 had not been applicable, the court would have exercised its art.28 discretion to stay the English proceedings because, without a stay, there was a real risk of there being mutually irreconcilable judgments in the two states, *Owens Bank Ltd v Bracco (C-129/92)* [1994] Q.B. 509, [1994] C.L.Y. 4801 applied. The actions were related actions as defined by art.28(3) (paras 35-43). (4) In considering the balance of fairness under the 1973 Act, it was relevant that H lived and worked in Switzerland, and that the family's income was generated from there; W had attempted to avoid the Swiss court's exercise of its powers by taking no steps to make claims in those proceedings, choosing instead to pursue claims in England at huge expense; the family was truly to be regarded as an international family, having considerable assets in countries other than Switzerland and England; litigation costs in Switzerland were lower than in England and while the family was wealthy, there was considerable dispute as to the value of the assets. For all of those reasons, a stay of W's suit was fair (paras 44-53).

T v P (JURISDICTION: LUGANO CONVENTION AND FORUM CONVENIENS), [2012] EWHC1627 (Fam), [2013] 1 F.L.R. 478, Roderic Wood, J., Fam Div. [*Ex rel.* NO.TEXT].

1277. Family proceedings–Case management–Judge holding truncated hearing as matter of urgency–Making findings of fact on limited evidence–Safety of findings

[Family Procedure Rules 2010 (SI 2010/2955) Pt 22.]

The appellant mother (M) appealed against an interim residence order made in respect of her five-year-old daughter (S) in favour of the respondent father (F). Following M and F's separation, S had lived with M and her new partner (C). When the local authority expressed concerns that C posed a risk to children, F applied for a residence order. M purported to separate from C, which narrowed the issues to whether there should be a shared residence order, or a residence order in M's favour. The matter was listed for a two-day hearing. However, shortly before the hearing, certain matters came to light which suggested that M and C had not separated. Amongst them was the report of a private investigator (P) who claimed to have seen C at M's house. The judge decided to use the hearing to make findings about what the position in relation to C really was. He regulated the proceedings to ensure that they did not exceed the two-day listing, refusing to hear evidence from C or to admit documents suggesting that his credit card had been used at a location far from M's house at the time P claimed to have seen him there. He accepted P's evidence and considered that of M to be untruthful and unreliable. He found that M and C were living together and, on the basis of that finding, he made an immediate residence order in favour of F. He made it clear that he saw that order as an interim one, and he listed the matter for review and directions. M submitted that the judge's rigorous management of the hearing resulted in unfairness to her, that he had deprived himself of relevant and potentially significant evidence, and that his finding was unsafe.

Held: Appeal allowed. While it was an uphill task to appeal against case management decisions, those made by the judge in the instant case not only deprived M of the opportunity to answer the case against her, but also deprived the court of the evidence necessary to enable it to make reliable findings of fact. The judge apparently considered that he could determine the truth or otherwise of the allegations about C's presence in the house simply by choosing between M's evidence and P's evidence. However, he did not have to make the decision in a vacuum. First, other evidence was available, as was demonstrated by the position in relation to C's credit card. The fact that the card might have been used at a location far from M's house at the relevant time did not necessarily mean that C had been at that location himself, but evidence supporting such use could not be dismissed as robustly as the judge had dismissed it. Second, C was a central witness and the judge's refusal to hear from him could not be supported. Nor was it any answer to say that the transfer of residence was an interim solution. Although the order was finite, the findings were not. Once findings of fact had been made by a judge who had heard evidence, it would take powerful evidence before a party might be permitted to reopen them. The judge might have had the impression that he faced the stark choice of either holding an immediate truncated hearing or risking S's safety by leaving her in M's care. His anxiety about that might have led him to give too much weight to the urgency of the situation. However, he should have considered whether he could safeguard S's welfare in any other way. He could, for example, have ordered that she stay with F under an extended contact order or a short-term residence order until a fuller hearing could be arranged. In summary, it was clear that the judge had erred in the way that he regulated the evidence that M could produce, and therefore his finding of fact could not be supported. A fresh hearing before another judge was required. It was to be noted, however, that the instant case turned very much on its own facts. The Family Procedure Rules 2010 Pt 22 entitled the court to control the evidence in a case by giving directions. That was a wide power which could be used to exclude evidence that would otherwise be admissible. Robust case management very much had a place in family proceedings, but it also had its limits (see paras 35-48 of judgment).

B (A CHILD) (RESIDENCE ORDER: CASE MANAGEMENT), *Re*; *sub nom.* B (A CHILD) (CASE MANAGEMENT), *Re*, [2012] EWCA Civ 1742, [2013] 1 F.L.R. 963, Moore-Bick, L.J., CA (Civ Div).

1278. Family proceedings–Cross-examination–Judge's restriction of cross-examination–Factual investigation–Right to fair trial

The appellant father (F) appealed against a recorder's decision to make a residence order concerning their son (J) in favour of the respondent mother (M). F and M had been litigating issues of contact and residence for approximately eight years. M had frequently prevented contact, but at court hearings had conceded that contact should take place. Several contact orders had been made by consent before arrangements broke down. A joint residence order was made by consent after a CAFCASS report had recommended it as a means of removing M's ability to withhold contact. M later applied for sole residence and contact was again disrupted. The recorder decided to ignore all of the past hearings and to take the current level of contact as his starting point. He refused to allow F's counsel to cross-examine M upon the reasons she had changed her mind and sought to reduce contact. The recorder ordered that J reside with M, and that F have contact on alternate weekends. F submitted that the recorder had erred by restricting his counsel's cross-examination of M.

Held: Appeal allowed. The recorder was right to say that one had to look to the future; his task was to determine J's future living arrangements. However, he had erred in refusing F's counsel's entirely justified desire to cross-examine M on a number of issues. The investigation that F's counsel wished to undertake was why M's attitude had changed, and why the arrangements previously agreed between the parties had not worked out. Those matters cried out for investigation. Whilst a judge should stop irrelevant or time-wasting cross-examination, he should always bear in mind that however carefully he had read the papers beforehand, counsel was likely to have a better grasp of the inner forensic realities of the case. A judge would do well to think twice if, as in the instant case, his intervention was met by counsel standing her ground and carefully explaining why she wished to cross-examine in a particular way, especially if counsel's reasons had obviously been carefully considered. The effect of the recorder's intervention was to deny F, and J, a fair hearing. It was therefore necessary for a re-trial to take place before a different judge (see paras 32, 35-37 of judgment).

J (A CHILD) (RESIDENCE AND CONTACT DISPUTE), *Re*, [2012] EWCA Civ 1231, [2013] 1 F.L.R. 716, Maurice Kay, L.J., CA (Civ Div).

1279. Family proceedings–Financial orders–Legal services

THE FAMILY PROCEDURE (AMENDMENT NO.2) RULES 2013, SI 2013/1472; made under the Courts Act 2003 s.75, s.76. In force: July 8, 2013; .

These rules amends the Family Procedure Rules 2010 by amending the definition of a "financial order" in rule 2.3(1) so that it includes an order for payment in respect of legal services under s.22ZA of the Matrimonial Causes Act 1973 or Pt.8 of Sch.5 to the Civil Partnership Act 2004, in consequence of the commencement of ss.49 to 54 of the Legal Aid, Sentencing and Punishment of Offenders Act 2012. These rules also make consequential amendments to other rules so that they cover orders for payment in respect of legal services appropriately.

1280. Family proceedings–Findings of fact–Finding of assault by mother at supervised contact session–Whether judge gave adequate reasons for decision

The appellant mother (M) appealed against a finding by a judge that she had assaulted two workers during a supervised contact session with her children. An incident had occurred during a supervised contact session between M and her two children. Two workers employed by the first respondent local authority to supervise the contact sesssion alleged that M had assaulted them. At a hearing to determine the issue of contact, a judge found that M had assaulted the workers following their attempt to intercept the passing of documents from M to her children without their prior approval. M submitted that the judge's decision was inadequately reasoned and that it was impossible to understand why he preferred the workers' evidence over hers, given that there were discrepancies in their accounts of the incident and that neither of them had sustained any visible injuries. The local authority accepted that the judge's reasoning was sparse but contended that it was sufficient when taken in context. The second respondent guardian submitted that M's appeal should be dismissed, but that the judge should be invited to give reasons to enable the children to understand how he had reached his decision.

Held: Appeal dismissed. (1) It was not appropriate to dismiss the appeal and invite the judge to give reasons for his decision. It was only appropriate to consider inviting a trial judge to provide further reasons for his decision where that might have a bearing on whether to allow the appeal. Further, it was not necessary to invite the trial judge to give reasons for his decision on the basis that it would benefit the children. What was likely to matter to the children was what the judge had found to have occurred at the contact session, rather than why he had made those findings (see para.38 of judgment). (2) The court was conscious of the practicalities of giving first-instance decisions. It was well established that judges had to explain sufficiently what they had found, and their process of reasoning. However, a judgment should be read on the assumption that, unless the contrary was demonstrated, the judge knew how to perform his functions. An appellate court had to resist the temptation to subject a judgment to a narrow analysis, and had to recognise the limitations of language when seeking to explain the complexities of issues that arose during a hearing, *English v Emery Reimbold & Strick Ltd* [2002] EWCA Civ 605, [2002] 1 W.L.R. 2409, [2002] C.L.Y. 301, *Piglowska v Piglowski* [1999] 1 W.L.R. 1360, [1999] C.L.Y. 2421, and *A (Children) (Fact-finding Hearing: Extempore Judgment), Re* [2011] EWCA Civ 1611, [2012] 1 F.L.R. 1243, [2012] C.L.Y. 1346 considered. The trial judge had had the advantage of watching the witnesses as they gave evidence, and had formed a view on their credibility. It was sometimes difficult to explain, on the basis of the impression that the witnesses created, why one witness was preferred over another. In the instant case, it was open to the judge to make his findings on the evidence, and he was entitled to accept the workers' accounts of the incident. His acceptance that they were genuinely distressed when recounting the incident was a sound foundation on which to conclude that they were telling the truth. It was to be expected that there would be some discrepancies in the evidence in such a case, and the presence or absence of visible injuries was not always a reliable way of assessing whether there had been an assault. In the circumstances, the judgment was explained sufficiently, albeit briefly (paras 40-42, 45-46).

F (CHILDREN) (SUPERVISED CONTACT: DISPUTED EVIDENCE), *Re*, [2012] EWCA Civ 828, [2013] 1 F.L.R. 665, Ward, L.J., CA (Civ Div).

1281. Family proceedings–Judicial decision-making–Private family proceedings–Judge's power to make repeated directions to local authority under s.37 Children Act 1989

[Children Act 1989 (c.41) s.37, Sch.14 Pt 4.]

In an appeal by a mother (M) and her husband (H) the court was required to determine whether the court had jurisdiction to make sequential directions to a local authority under the Children Act 1989 s.37. M and her former partner (F) had two children (X and Y). The children lived with F. Private law proceedings concerning M's contact with them had been ongoing since 2006. In 2010, F had a breakdown. X was removed from his care and placed with his grandparents, whilst Y resided with M and H. H was accused of bullying Y and causing him emotional harm. A judge made a s.37 direction to two local authorities concerning the children, coupled with interim care orders in the local authorities' favour. X was subsequently placed permanently with his grandparents. The local authority concluded that Y could return to live with M and H, but the judge was dissatisfied with its report and made a second s.37 direction and interim care order. The local authority opposed any further interim care orders, but the judge made a third s.37 direction and interim order concerning Y. This resulted in M and H withdrawing their co-operation from the local authority, and it subsequently issued care proceedings. A special guardianship order was eventually granted in favour of Y's grandparents. The guardian submitted that the judge had exceeded his powers by making repeated s.37 directions and associated interim care orders, causing impermissible pressure upon the local authority to initiate care proceedings. M and H adopted his submissions.

Held: Appeal dismissed. (1) Section 37 provided a jurisdictional bridge between private law proceedings, in which a local authority normally played no part, and the public law provisions in Pt.4. The legal context in which s.37 operated was that Parliament had entrusted to the local authority, not the court, the role of determining whether public law proceedings should be issued. In an appropriate case the jurisdiction in private law proceedings for the court to make a s.37 direction was an important and useful facility under which a local authority was required to investigate a child's circumstances and consider issuing care proceedings. A private law case could last for a significant time and the circumstances of the child could change. It would be wholly artificial to limit the court's ability to utilise the s.37 jurisdiction to "one shot" in each case. Nothing in the statutory language suggested that there was such a limitation. Circumstances sufficient to justify a direction could occur for a variety of reasons and at different stages during a single set of proceedings. Where a judge was satisfied that the local authority had either not complied with an initial s.37 direction, or had conducted an investigation which failed to engage with the court's concerns, the court had jurisdiction to extend or renew its s.37 direction, *M (Intractable Contact Dispute: Interim Care Order), Re* [2003] EWHC 1024 (Fam), [2003] 2 F.L.R. 636, [2003] C.L.Y. 1550 considered (see paras 22-23, 31-32, 45 of judgment). (2) There was no unfairness or material error in the judge's approach to the first s.37 direction. He had ample expert evidence to be satisfied that a direction was necessary. His second s.37 direction concerning Y was also justified. The judge had identified specific deficiencies in the local authority's report, and the local authority had accepted that it was appropriate for an addendum report to be provided. By the time of the third direction the local authority had plainly discharged its duty under s.37 to investigate Y's circumstances. It had provided a comprehensive report and described the reasons for its considered opinion that a care or supervision order was not justified. The judge had failed to appreciate the limitation of his powers in making the third direction. However, M and H had not appealed against the order at the time. Their unilateral action in withdrawing from co-operation with the local authority and the court had also contributed to the way in which their claim to have Y in their care became progressively less tenable. Despite the judge exceeding his jurisdiction, the proceedings as a whole were sound and free from judicial bias and it was not appropriate to consider the matter afresh (paras 38, 41, 46-48, 60-61).

K (CHILDREN) (DIRECTION TO INVESTIGATE: JURISDICTION), *Re; sub nom.* K (CHILDREN) (PRIVATE LAW PROCEEDINGS: DIRECTION TO INVESTIGATE CHILD'S CIRCUMSTANCES), *Re*, [2012] EWCA Civ 1549, [2013] 1 W.L.R. 1538, Lord Dyson (M.R.), CA (Civ Div).

1282. Family proceedings–Jurisdiction–Principles to be applied when considering making transfer of jurisdiction request under art.15 Regulation 2201/2003 (Brussels II Revised)

[Regulation 2201/2003 Art.12, Art.15(3), Art.15.]

In care proceedings issued by the applicant local authority in relation to a 10-month-old boy (T), the court was required to determine whether it should issue a request to the Slovakian courts to assume jurisdiction under Regulation 2201/2003 art.15 (Brussels II Revised). T's mother (M) and father were both Slovakian citizens of Roma descent. When M had become pregnant, the Slovakian court had placed her in a children's home for underage mothers. M then fled to the UK where T was born. M and T were placed in a mother and baby unit but M left the unit leaving T behind. The local authority sought an adoption order. The Slovakian authorities sought transfer of jurisdiction in respect of proceedings relating to T to the Slovakian courts so that ultimately M and T could be returned to the children's home in Slovakia. M agreed to that plan. The court determined the principles to be applied when it was considering making a transfer of jurisdiction request under art.15.

Held: Judgment accordingly. (1) Article 15 should be interpreted conformably with the principles derived from domestic law, as succinctly summarised in *M v M (Stay of Proceedings: Return of Children)* [2005] EWHC 1159 (Fam), [2006] 1 F.L.R. 138, in relation to jurisdiction in child proceedings, whether that jurisdiction was statutory or inherent. Those principles were statements of the obvious and it was inconceivable that the framers of the Regulation would not have had them in mind when drafting art.15 (see paras 14-18 of judgment). Further, the scope of any enquiry under art.15 as to the best interests of the child should be the same as that required when determining jurisdiction under art.12 of the Regulation, as set out by the Supreme Court in *I (A Child) (Contact Application: Jurisdiction), Re* [2009] UKSC 10, [2010] 1 A.C. 319, [2010] C.L.Y. 1413. It should not involve a profound investigation of the child's situation and upbringing but upon the sort of considerations which came into play when deciding upon the most appropriate forum (paras 19-21). Accordingly, when considering whether to make a request under art.15 the applicable principles could be summarised as follows: (a) art.15 applied to public law as well as private law proceedings; (b) as a precondition, the court must be satisfied within the meaning of art.15(3) that the child had a "particular connection" with the relevant other Member State; (c) in assessing the appropriateness of each forum, the court must discern the forum with which the case had the more real and substantive connection in terms of convenience, expense and availability of witnesses; (d) if the court were to conclude that the other forum was clearly more appropriate, it should issue a transfer request and grant a stay unless other more potent factors were to drive the opposite result; (e) in the exercise to be conducted at (a)-(d), the best interests of the child was an important, but not paramount, consideration; (f) in making the best interests analysis at (e), the court would not embark on a profound investigation of the child's situation and upbringing but would dwell in an attenuated inquiry upon the sort of considerations which came into play when deciding upon the most appropriate forum, *B v B (Brussels II Revised: Article 15)* [2008] EWHC 2965 (Fam), [2009] 1 F.L.R. 517, [2009] C.L.Y. 1600 considered, *M* and *I (A Child)* followed (para.24). (2) Applying the above principles to the instant case, the court determined that a transfer request should be issued. M's habitual residence was Slovakia and it was argued that T's habitual residence was also Slovakia. T's parents only spoke Slovakian. M had agreed to return to Slovakia and to the children's home. T had not been put in a permanent placement in the UK. The plan outlined by the Slovakian authorities for M and T were they to return to their native country best promoted the possibility of preserving T's Slovakian and Roma heritage, which the court considered to be a matter of great importance. For the local authority to argue that the Slovakian plan was inflexible and not in T's best interests came very close to the profound best interests enquiry concerning a child's future care, which was emphatically rejected in *I (A Child)*. The analysis of best interests only went to inform the question of forum and should not descend into a divisive value judgment about the laws and procedures of another European state (paras 25-38).

T (A CHILD) (CARE PROCEEDINGS: REQUEST TO ASSUME JURISDICTION), *Re; sub nom.* A LOCAL AUTHORITY v A MOTHER; T (A CHILD: ARTICLE 15 OF BRUSSELS II REVISED), RE; K (A CHILD) (BRUSSELS II REVISED: ART.15), *Re*, [2013] EWHC 521 (Fam), [2013] Fam. 253, Mostyn, J., Fam Div.

1283. Family proceedings–McKenzie friends–Challenge to refusal to allow father assistance by McKenzie friend

The appellant father (F) appealed against a case management decision in family proceedings between F and the respondent mother (M) concerning their children. F had appeared at the proceedings in person accompanied by a McKenzie friend (Y). The judge referred to the *Practice Note (Sen Cts: McKenzie Friends: Civil and Family Courts)* [2010] 1 W.L.R. 1881, [2010] C.L.Y. 396 and rejected Fs application for Y to be granted rights of audience and refused to allow Y to act as a McKenzie friend on the basis that Y was intimidating towards M.

Held: Appeal dismissed. The judge had heard evidence from F and Y and from the children s representative and was anxious to achieve equality of arms. Even though the judge dismissed the application to allow Y to act as a McKenzie friend she did not oppose F using a different McKenzie friend. The judge made a swift, rough and ready case management decision and the court would not interfere with it. The reasons that she gave were perfunctory but they did not have to be elaborate. The judge had referred to the Practice Guidance on McKenzie friends which made it clear that McKenzie friends should not manage a litigant's case outside court. The judge was entitled to decide as she did.

H (CHILDREN) (APPEAL: CASE MANAGEMENT DECISIONS), *Re*, [2012] EWCA Civ 1797, [2013] 1 F.L.R. 1234, Sir Nicholas Wall (President, Fam), CA (Civ Div).

1284. Family proceedings–Recognition of judgments–Portuguese order concerning parental responsibilities for child–Scope of exception to recognition and enforcement of foreign judgments in family proceedings–Jurisdiction of English court to determine application for residence order

[Regulation 2201/2003 Art.21, Art.23(a), Art.41.]

The appellant Portuguese father (F) appealed against a decision ([2012] EWHC 983 (Fam), [2013] 1 F.L.R. 796, [2013] 7 C.L. 149) refusing his application for recognition and enforcement of a Portuguese judgment providing for shared-care arrangements for his child (L) with the English respondent mother (M). After L's birth in England in April 2011, M and F had moved to Portugal. After a failed attempt by M to remove L to England in November 2011, M and F had entered into an "Agreement on the Exercise of Parental Responsibilities" that provided for equal shared care on a rotating two-monthly basis in England and Portugal until L's third birthday. A Portuguese judge homologated the agreement, ordering M and F to abide by its terms. M then returned to England with L to begin her first two-month rotation. She then applied to the English courts for a residence order. That application was stayed and F sought to recognise and enforce the Portuguese judgment under Regulation 2201/2003 art.41 or art.21. M, relying on art.23(a) of the Regulation as a basis for resisting recognition of the Portuguese order, contended that the agreed arrangements for L were so contrary to his welfare that recognition of the homologated order would be manifestly contrary to public policy taking into account L's best interests. The judge found that F's application should be determined under art.21 rather than art.41. She rejected M's case that the arrangements for L qualified as an exceptional case justifying non-recognition of the Portuguese order, but found that M's mental health at the time of the agreement raised concerns about her ostensible consent and her ability to make any dissent known so that, pursuant to art.23(a), it would be manifestly contrary to public policy to recognise the judgment. The judge went on to consider whether the English courts had jurisdiction to hear M's application for a residence order. She considered that L had been habitually resident in Portugal when the Portuguese order was made, but that the agreement between M and F had the effect of changing L's habitual residence every two months, and that M's application for a residence order had been made when the English courts were endowed with jurisdiction. The stay on that application was, accordingly, lifted. F contended that (1) the judge had erred in finding that an exception to recognition of the Portuguese order existed under art.23(a) on the basis of M's emotional and mental health; (2) the English court lacked jurisdiction since L's habitual residence remained in Portugal.

Held: Appeal allowed. (1) The exception to recognition of the judgment of another Member State under art.23(a) of the Regulation was a very narrow one and, consistently with the entire scheme and underlying philosophy of the Regulation, set the bar very high. The proper approach where art.23(a) was relied on was to consider whether recognition was manifestly contrary to English public policy, *S (Brussels II: Recognition: Best Interests of Child) (No.1), Re* [2003] EWHC 2115 (Fam), [2004] 1 F.L.R. 571, [2004] C.L.Y. 1486 approved. A high onus rested on a parent who sought to reopen welfare issues and a foreign judgment would not be subverted save in the most exceptional of circumstances; the use of the word "manifestly" in art.23(a) indicated that a high degree of disparity was required between the effects of the order if enforced and the child's welfare interests, *W v W (Foreign Custody Order: Enforcement)* [2005] EWHC 1811 (Fam) and *LAB v KB (Abduction: Brussels II Revised)* [2009] EWHC 2243 (Fam), [2010] 2 F.L.R. 1664, [2011] C.L.Y. 1359 approved. The judge had, accordingly, been right to find that the arguments based on L's welfare did not suffice to bring the case within art.23(a). However, having done so, she was wrong to have found that the test in art.23(a) was met by virtue of M's mental or emotional state. It was not possible to see how those circumstances could render it manifestly contrary to public policy to recognise the Portuguese order. M's complaints about the effect of the process in Portugal on her emotional and mental health fell far short of what was required to bring art.23(e) into play (see paras 46, 49-54, 56 of judgment). (2) The judge was wrong to have held that L was habitually resident in England when M applied for a residence order; he was still habitually resident in Portugal. At any given time, a person could have only one habitual residence for the purpose of the Regulation. L's arrival in England pursuant to the agreement for the purpose of living with M for two months did not have the effect of changing his habitual residence, *Proceedings Brought by A (C-523/07)* [2010] Fam. 42, [2009] C.L.Y. 1552 and *Mercredi v Chaffe (C-497/10 PPU)* [2012] Fam. 22, [2011] C.L.Y. 1429 followed. L's presence in England on a two-month basis lacked the necessary degree of permanence to change his habitual residence; the cycle, whilst regular, nonetheless provided for presence in England which on each occasion was only temporary and intermittent. L's perpetual oscillation between Portugal and England was simply inconsistent with his acquisition of habitual residence in the latter (paras 64, 75, 78-80). (3) It followed that the Portuguese order would be recognised under art.21 of the Regulation. L remained habitually resident in Portugal and the Portuguese court alone had jurisdiction (para.82).

L (A CHILD) (RECOGNITION OF FOREIGN ORDER), *Re; sub nom.* L (A CHILD) (BRUSSELS II REVISED), *Re*, [2012] EWCA Civ 1157, [2013] Fam. 94, Thorpe, L.J., CA (Civ Div).

1285. Family proceedings courts–Reporting restrictions–Untoward events occurring while child in foster care–Extent of matters subject to publication

[European Convention on Human Rights 1950 Art.8, Art.10.]

The applicant local authority sought a reporting restriction order arising out of care proceedings conducted before a family proceedings court. Before the hearing, the child in question (C), a five-year-old girl, had been placed with foster parents. Also present in the foster home were another foster child (S) and two other members of the household (R and T). During the hearing, the following information was revealed: on May 14, 2012, the local authority had received information from the police suggesting that someone living at the foster home had had access to child pornography; at a contact visit that afternoon, C told her parents that R had grabbed her around the throat; a red mark on her neck was seen by her father and the contact supervisor; when the foster mother arrived to collect C, the contact supervisor informed her of what C had said but she denied the allegation and C returned to the foster home; later that evening, C's father contacted the police and told them of the marks around her neck; the police immediately passed that information to the social services emergency duty team; the next morning, C's social worker met C, who stated that the assault had occurred at 2am, that T had been cuddling S at the time and that the assault had been witnessed by both T and S; on May 28, police and social services visited the foster carers, told them of the concerns about pornography and moved C to another foster home; on the following day, the foster father was found dead, having apparently committed suicide. The magistrates described the events as "extremely concerning" and stated that the local authority had failed to follow child-protection procedures: among other things, as soon as C disclosed the assault, the contact worker should have informed C's social worker or the emergency duty team; the contact worker should not have disclosed the allegation to the foster mother until C had been interviewed; C should not have been allowed to return to the foster home while the allegation was unresolved; she should have been referred to a doctor; further, the local authority had failed to remove C for a period of 14 days. A temporary reporting restriction order was made but notice of the hearing was not given to the media.

Held: Judgment accordingly. (1) The parties had agreed that a reporting restriction order should be made to protect C's identification (see para.16 of judgment). (2) Where, as here, a family proceedings court identified matters of general concern about the way in which a local authority had performed its statutory child-protection duties, it was manifestly in the public interest for there to be wider dissemination of the court's concerns (para.21). (3) It was in the public interest for the fourth respondent newspaper-publisher to be entitled to publish its account of the failure to give proper notice of the application for a reporting restriction order. There was a danger that those who practised in the family-justice system failed to give proper consideration to the rights of the media under the European Convention on Human Rights 1950 art.10. This was not the first time that an ex parte order had been made without notice to the media in circumstances which could not be described as exceptional. That had now to cease (para.24). (4) It was in the public interest for published reports of the magistrates' facts and reasons to include the alleged assault and the alleged cuddle but those involved should be described as persons present in the foster household, without reference to their name, age, status or relationship; identifying their status or relationship would breach their art.8 rights, and any breach would be compounded by the fact that those involved had been given no opportunity to respond to the allegations made against them (paras 34, 36). (5) Publication of the name of the key social worker and her team manager would be allowed: there was a clear public interest in facilitating an open discussion of the issues relating to child protection and fostering which had arisen (para.39). (6) Publication would also be allowed of the fact or allegation that the foster father had committed suicide. The local authority had produced no evidence to support the assertion that publication in reports of the care proceedings of the fact or allegation that he had taken his own life would increase the risk of identifying C when subsequent reports of the inquest were published (para.42).

BRISTOL CITY COUNCIL v NGN LTD; *sub nom.* BRISTOL CITY COUNCIL v C (CARE PROCEEDINGS: REPORTING RESTRICTIONS), [2012] EWHC 3748 (Fam), [2013] 1 F.L.R. 1205, Baker, J., Fam Div.

1286. Financial dispute resolution appointments–Practice Notes–Guidance for preparation, conduct and aftermath of financial dispute resolution appointments

The Money and Property Committee of the Family Justice Council produced a Best Practice Guidance Note for financial dispute resolution appointments covering: the information that should be explained to clients prior to the FDR; preparation before the FDR, including instructing counsel and arrangements for attendance by representatives of the solicitor's firm; the documentation required; the conduct of the FDR; the role of the judge; reaching agreement, including heads of agreement and consent orders; the actions to be taken if no agreement was reached, including possible directions; and costs.

PRACTICE GUIDANCE (FAM DIV: FINANCIAL DISPUTE RESOLUTION APPOINTMENTS: BEST PRACTICE GUIDANCE) [2013] 1 F.L.R. 1109, Thorpe, L.J., Fam Div.

1287. Financial orders–Bankruptcy proceedings–Issues relevant to Chancery Division and Family Division proceedings–Appropriate case management

[Law of Property Act 1925 (c.20) s.53(1) (c).]

The court was required to consider how issues relevant to both ancillary relief proceedings between a husband and wife (H and W) in the Family Division, and to H's bankruptcy proceedings in the Chancery Division, might sensibly be managed. W had petitioned for divorce. Shortly afterwards, H was made bankrupt on his own petition. The only asset in the bankruptcy estate was the former matrimonial home. W had previously executed a declaration of trust under which H was declared to be the absolute beneficial owner of the property. H contended that the property had needed refurbishment and that his son by another marriage (S) had invested £500,000 in exchange for becoming an equal joint beneficial owner. H also claimed to be indebted to a business associate (D) in the sum of £500,000. W could not force an effective examination of S and D's claims in H's bankruptcy as she had no real standing in the bankruptcy. The nature of the assets in the estate meant that there were no monies out of which the costs of any detailed investigation or litigation could be paid, and so the trustees in bankruptcy had not settled upon the commencement of proceedings. The judge in the Family Division proceedings gave directions for a preliminary oral hearing to determine the consequences on H's financial resources of the effects of the transactions, and the extent of any personal debts between W, H, S and D. At issue was whether certain issues were to be determined by the Family Division or the Chancery Division.

Held: Judgment accordingly. (1) There would be a hearing of a preliminary issue to determine whether S was the beneficial owner of a 50 percent share in the property, or entitled to some other interest, or a creditor of H in respect of all or some of the alleged payments (see para.24 of judgment). The trustees in bankruptcy would be joined for that purpose. Although the determination of the beneficial interest issue was to be in the Family Division, the Chancery Division was where control of the bankruptcy proceedings was. H was to be joined not because he had any subsisting interest in the property, but because the outcome might affect any order that might be made against him in the ancillary relief proceedings, since he was to be discharged from bankruptcy (para.25). S was to be the claimant in the issue because the burden was on him. It was common ground that there was a deed declaring that the entire beneficial interest was vested in H. S could only have acquired a beneficial interest if H had disposed of part of his interest, which had to have been in writing under the Law of Property Act 1925 s.53(1)(c). The best evidence of S and H did not include a written disposition. The lack of information on the refurbishment costs meant that it was necessary for S to plead all of the facts that he relied on as establishing the constructive trust which he asserted (paras 26-27). (2) There was to be a hearing of a preliminary issue to determine whether S had repaid sums of money borrowed from H, W and others. S was to be the claimant in that matter as it was clear on the documents that borrowings were made and applied for his benefit, and it was for him to show that he had repaid those borrowings and was no longer liable to indemnify his trustees, H and W (paras 30-31). (3) It was not right to direct the joinder of D and the formulation of a preliminary issue in relation to the sums due to him. The relationship between D and his group on the one hand and H and his company on the other was plainly not simply that of client and accountant/financial adviser, and there might have been inquiries that the trustees might want to make. That was pre-eminently a matter for them and there was no reason to bring debt questions into the Family Division. Family relationships undoubtedly influenced the dealings of H and S but they did not appear to influence the commercial dealings of H and D (para.46). (4) It was not right to conduct in the Family Division an inquiry into whether S had collected monies due to H's company. It did not have anything to do with what debts were provable in H's estate in bankruptcy, or consequently with whether there was a surplus available for W. It might have gone to the credit of S, but disclosure going to credit was a wholly exceptional thing to order or pursue (para.47). (5) There was no reason to examine in the Family Division claims made by H's friends for repayments of loans. It was for the trustees to decide whether to admit those to proof and they could require S to demonstrate repayment to the relevant creditors and, if that was established, payment by the relevant creditors to H in the first place (para.48).

ARIF v ANWAR, [2013] EWHC 624 (Fam), [2013] B.P.I.R. 389, Norris, J., Fam Div.

1288. Financial orders–Charging orders–Application by former wife for financial relief–Judgment creditor obtaining interim charging order–Balancing interests of judgment creditor and wife

The appellant (C) appealed against a decision ([2012] EWHC 45 (Fam), [2012] 2 F.L.R. 414, [2012] C.L.Y. 1310) dismissing his application for an interim charging order to be made final. The respondent (W) had brought proceedings for financial orders against her former husband (H). He was the beneficial owner of a property which was registered in the name of a company. H agreed to transfer the sole share in the company to a friend (K) who in turn agreed to sell it to C. The court held that the disposition by H to K was a sham and that the agreement with C was to be treated as having been made by H with the intention of defeating W's claim to financial relief. The transfer to C was therefore set aside, but the judge ordered H to indemnify C against all the expenses and costs he had incurred in connection with the transaction itself and the subsequent litigation. C sued H under the indemnity and obtained judgment in default and an interim charging order over the property. C's application for a final charging order was heard at the same time as W's claim for financial relief. The judge awarded W £12.5 million. The only assets of H within the jurisdiction available to satisfy that award were a sum of about £600,000 in court and the equity in the property thought to be about £400,000. The judge declined to make C's charging order final.

Held: Appeal dismissed. (1) When striking a balance between the interests of a judgment creditor and those of a wife, the interests of the judgment creditor should be respected, save to the extent that it was necessary to override them in order to make appropriate provision for the wife and any minor children, *Harman v Glencross* [1986] Fam. 81, [1986] C.L.Y. 1662 considered. Each case depended on its own facts. There could never be automatic predominance for any claim; each case depended upon striking a fair balance between the normal expectations of the judgment creditor and the hardship to the wife and children if a charging order was made, *Austin-Fell v Austin-Fell* [1990] Fam. 172, [1990] C.L.Y. 2319 considered. In some cases justice to the creditor would demand that the wife accept a degree of provision that in other circumstances would have been regarded as inadequate (see para.13 of judgment). (2) C as a bona fide judgment creditor was entitled to have his interests as such taken fully into account and the judge had erred to the extent that he had not done so (para.14). (3) The court was not concerned only with the need for reasonable accommodation. It had to have regard to all the circumstances including the wider financial needs of W and her two minor children, *Harman* considered (paras 15-16). (4) The equity in the property and the money in court amounted to about £1 million. If some allowance was made for living expenses, in addition to providing adequate accommodation, it was clear that a substantial part would be required for W's purposes and would be used up fairly quickly. There was little prospect of her recovering any other amount from H. She and her children were likely to suffer a degree of hardship if the charging order was made final. On the other hand, C was a wealthy man and was the author of his own misfortune in the sense that he had proceeded with the transaction to purchase the company, and thereby the property, when he knew that there was at least a risk that it would be challenged and be held to be ineffective. It was not in the interests of justice to make a final charging order (paras 20-21).

KREMEN v AGREST, [2013] EWCA Civ 41, [2013] 2 F.L.R. 187, Sir Terence Etherton (Chancellor), CA (Civ Div).

1289. Financial orders–Committal for debt–Proceedings under Debtors Act 1869 to enforce maintenance order–Admissibility of evidence obtained in separate proceedings

[Administration of Justice Act 1970 (c.31) s.11; Debtors Act 1869 (c.62) s.5; Human Rights Act 1998 (c.42); Family Procedure Rules 2010 (SI 2010/2955) r.33.14(1)(a); European Convention on Human Rights 1950 Art.6.]

The appellant wife (W) appealed against a judge's decision to exclude evidence given by the respondent husband (H) in proceedings for enforcement of a financial order. W and H were divorced. H had agreed to pay W 31 per cent of the proceeds of sale of the former matrimonial home. He paid two-thirds of that sum leaving a balance of £667,066 outstanding. He was ordered to pay £100,000 within 28 days and the balance within another specified period. He paid a further £50,000 after which no other payments were made. W issued a general application for enforcement and on June 22, 2011 H was ordered to serve a fully completed Form E with a sworn statement providing all relevant information and exhibiting documents. He duly did so, serving annotated bank statements and three files of documents. W then issued a request for a judgment summons under the Debtors Act 1869. A judge applied *R. v K* [2009] EWCA Crim 1640, [2010] Q.B. 343, [2009] C.L.Y. 764 and excluded all information and documentation disclosed/produced by H under the order of June 22, 2011 because it had been given under compulsion. The advocate to the court submitted that at the hearing of a judgment summons under the 1869 Act it was not permissible to rely upon any statements made by the debtor in response to orders made in prior general enforcement proceedings.

Held: Appeal allowed. (1) Under s.5 of the 1869 Act the court could commit to prison a person who defaulted in payment of any debt due under any order, where it was proved that the debtor had the means to pay and had refused or neglected to pay the sum ordered. The scope of s.5 was curtailed by the Administration of Justice Act 1970 s.11 which, in the family context, limited its application to maintenance orders. Following the introduction of the Human Rights Act 1998 the old procedure under which the debtor was effectively compelled to give evidence to avoid imprisonment was no longer tenable, *Mubarak v Mubarak (No.1)* [2001] 1 F.L.R. 698, [2001] C.L.Y. 2637 referred to. A general application simplified the enforcement of maintenance orders. Under the general application one or more orders from a menu of five enforcement mechanisms could be made. A judgment summons was not included in that menu, as the menu was confined to orders that did not carry the risk of penal sanction. Accordingly, the respondent to a general application was compellable and could be subjected to examination as to means in advance of the hearing, before the creditor elected which of the orders to seek (see paras 30-34 of judgment). (2) H was an international entrepreneur with no assets within the jurisdiction. It was obvious that none of the five remedies open to the court on a general application would be effective. However, the strategic prior issue of the general application could not be used as a device to achieve disclosure and examination for deployment in subsequent proceedings under the 1869 Act. W's advisors might have concluded that given H's mobility and absence of assets in the jurisdiction, the only effective remedy was the immediate issue of a summons under the 1869 Act. Very little evidence would have been necessary from W in support. The reality was that if H attended, although not compellable, he would have been obliged to proffer explanation and excuse. If he failed to attend then he would liable to sentence under the Family Procedure Rules 2010 r.33.14(1)(a). However, the judge was wrong to conclude that *R v K* could not be distinguished. That case raised the very different question of whether the state was entitled in prosecuting a husband for tax evasion to rely upon his evidence in prior ancillary relief proceedings. It did not concern enforcement or the balance of the creditor and debtor's rights under the European Convention on Human Rights 1950 art.6, *R v K* distinguished. The embargo rested upon the protection of the debtor from the compulsion to testify with the risk of self-incrimination. The judge was therefore right to exclude the statements filed by H but wrong to exclude the documents themselves (paras 40-51).

MOHAN v MOHAN, [2013] EWCA Civ 586, [2013] C.P. Rep. 36, Thorpe, L.J., CA (Civ Div).

1290. Financial orders–Confiscation orders–Husband bringing wealth to family through criminal activity–Tainted and untainted funds heavily intermingled within family's finances–Extent to which wife entitled to joint assets

[Matrimonial Causes Act 1973 (c.18).]

The applicant wife (W) applied for financial relief against the respondent husband (H) whilst he was serving a prison sentence for fraud and money laundering offences. H and W married in 1994. Their two children were aged 17 and 15. The younger child had special medical needs. H was jailed in 2010 following his guilty plea to fraudulent activity relating to two investment policies in his name. One of the policies had been funded primarily by a remortgage over the former matrimonial home. A confiscation order was made against him in a sum of more than £4.8 million. H accepted that he held assets greater than that sum. W was a nurse with a projected annual income of £17,000 once the children were no longer dependent on her. She asserted a 50 per cent beneficial interest in the former matrimonial home and sought a lump sum to enable her to pay off the mortgage and start a bed and breakfast business. She also claimed a half interest in a second home which, she maintained, was a pre-criminal untainted joint investment, and half of the sale proceeds of a French property in joint names on the basis that it had been purchased with funds from an earlier untainted French property. The Crown disputed her entitlement, conceding only that some of the surplus over the amount required to meet the confiscation order against H could be transferred to her. The nature and extent of the tainted assets was in dispute.

Held: Application granted. (1) W was a credible and reliable witness of her own lack of financial sophistication and her entire and unquestioning reliance on H in such matters. It was patently obvious from her evidence that she had not known of H's fraud at the time he perpetrated it, and that her knowledge of financial matters was superficial. H's investment activity had been consistent throughout their relationship and, together with his well-paid employment, had always produced high levels of income and a good standard of living for the family. Whilst W's contribution to the marriage was equal to his, she had taken a detached view to their finances because she trusted H in what had always turned out well. For those reasons, she had not questioned the remortgage of the former matrimonial home. She had not inspected the documents, and even if she had, she was unlikely to have recognised that a fraud was being perpetrated. H had subsequently reduced the mortgage using tainted money. It was not clear from the evidence that the remortgage had necessarily been part of the criminal conduct. A balancing payment into the mortgage account, even if made with tainted funds, did not deprive the Crown because it still had access to the full value of the funds in the policy which the remortgage loan had been used to purchase, and those funds included untainted money reflecting part of W's beneficial entitlement. That was a broad brush approach, but it was consistent with the court's task where tainted and untainted funds were intermingled. A detailed tracing exercise would not be appropriate (see paras 19-23, 30 of judgment). As both the former matrimonial home and the French property were in joint names, there was no statutory provision or public policy jurisdiction which could be invoked to deprive W of her half share, *Gibson v Revenue and Customs Prosecution Office* [2008] EWCA Civ 645, [2009] Q.B. 348, [2008] C.L.Y. 782 applied. Even if that were not so, it could not be said that H's payment of the mortgage and regular outgoings, which W benefited from, were gifts to be brought into account for the purposes of the confiscation order: W had provided consideration by bringing up the children and looking after the home. She was, however, obliged to give credit for maintenance costs to the French property, which had been funded by the proceeds of H's criminality (paras 33-37). (2) Taking into account the principles in *Stodgell v Stodgell* [2009] EWCA Civ 243, [2009] 2 F.L.R. 244, [2009] C.L.Y. 1491, and performing the discretionary exercise under the Matrimonial Causes Act 1973, W needed to be housed with the children. It was appropriate for her to remain in the former matrimonial home rather than downsizing because the potential for a bed and breakfast business provided her with extra earning capacity. It was untainted property and there was no argument to reduce her interest in it. There were sufficient untainted assets to enable a lump sum payment to discharge the mortgage. She was also entitled to a lump sum representing her interest in the family's other properties, *Stodgell* considered (paras 40-47).

W v W (FINANCIAL REMEDIES: CONFISCATION ORDER), [2012] EWHC 2469 (Fam), [2013] 2 F.L.R. 359, Ryder, J., Fam Div.

1291. Financial orders–Failure to disclose–Re-opening of financial order made by consent

The appellant wife (W) sought to re-open an order for financial provision made by consent. W and the respondent (H) were married in 1994 and had two children. Following the breakdown of the marriage in August 2009, H and W began to discuss financial arrangements and there was a short exchange of correspondence between their solicitors on the subject. W asked for a valuation of H's shareholding in certain companies but received no response. In October 2009, the parties reached agreement. F produced a Form M1 disclosing an annual net income of £126,000 and a 20 per cent shareholding in a non-trading company (P). He claimed that the value of his shareholding in P was nil, and he failed to mention that he had a 100 per cent shareholding in another company (M). At that stage, W was unaware of M's existence and had no reason to doubt what H said about his interest in P. A consent order, expressed to be on a clean break basis, was approved in December 2009. Under the order, W gave up her claim for periodical payments. She received the former matrimonial home and a lump sum, together worth some £1.8 million. Three years later she discovered documents revealing that between 2004 and 2009 H had received income of £1.4 million from M. She also discovered that P had been trading since 2004, that it had an annual gross turnover of about £50 million, and that H's shareholding was worth at least £500,000. W submitted that H had been guilty of serious non-disclosure. H argued that it had not been necessary for him to disclose his interest in M because by the time of the divorce it was in the final stages of being discontinued and its income stream had subsequently dried up. He argued that the nil valuation of his shareholding in P was accurate given that he had taken out a loan equivalent to the value of his shareholding. Finally he argued that even if his disclosure had been inadequate, it was not material since the settlement was very favourable to W.

Held: Appeal allowed. (1) Non-disclosure cases such as the instant one had to clear a high bar if they were to be re-opened. There had to have been material non-disclosure in the sense that but for the non-disclosure there was a strong possibility that the court would have made a substantially different order. Different considerations applied when negotiations took place directly between the parties without proper disclosure: some claimants were happy to proceed without disclosure provided that what was offered was fair and adequate; others, like W, wanted to know the basic financial picture but would accept the respondent's word on the detail. In any event, regardless of whether the application was contested or resolved by consent, the parties had a duty to give full, frank and clear disclosure, not only to each other, but also to the court. That was the purpose of the form M1, particularly where, as in the instant case, no form Es had been completed (see paras 2, 28-29 of judgment). (2) W was an honest witness who was to be believed when she said that it was not until after the consent order that she had learned of the existence of M and the true extent of H's involvement with P. H, on the other hand, was disingenuous in the extreme and was a master of the half-truth. Where their evidence conflicted, that of W was to be preferred. H's disclosure in relation to M was completely inadequate. The actions surrounding M's shutting down had been taken to ensure that the company had disappeared by the time of the financial negotiations. Its existence ought to have been disclosed. To ascribe a nil value to H's interest in P was a disingenuous half-truth, and W had been entitled to know the extent of his investment in it. She had plainly cared about disclosure, and H's non-disclosures were designed to make further inquiry less likely. In any event, whatever W's knowledge, H had kept the court completely in the dark before it approved the consent order. The fact that W had proceeded with the agreement without her solicitor's blessing did not afford H any sort of protection. He had presented W with a deliberately false picture. Both his non-disclosures were material, and at the very least they had prevented W and the court from properly considering the true value of his offer. W was thus entitled to ask the court to set aside the consent order and reconsider her claim. (3) (Per curiam) In an era when parties were often having to litigate without proper legal advice or representation, it was more important than ever that financial details were presented to the other side and to the court, especially on the form M1 or its current equivalent, in a simple, clear, concise and accurate way (para.38).

W v C (FINANCIAL REMEDIES: APPEAL: NON-DISCLOSURE); *sub nom.* C v C (FINANCIAL REMEDIES: NON-DISCLOSURE: SET-ASIDE), [2012] EWHC 3788 (Fam), [2013] 2 F.L.R. 115, Coleridge, J., Fam Div.

1292. Financial orders–Family property–Appropriateness of lump sum awarded to wife in ancillary relief proceedings–Availability of husband's inherited hotel business for division

The appellant husband (H) appealed against a decision to award the respondent wife (W) a lump sum of £2.2 million in addition to the matrimonial home in ancillary relief proceedings. H had inherited sole control of a hotel business from his father, who had in turn inherited the business from his father. When H and W had entered into their relationship, H owned the hotel property jointly with his two sisters. He subsequently bought out his sisters to become the sole owner of the properties as well as the business. The judge found that at the beginning of H's and W's relationship, the net assets in the business apart from the hotel properties themselves were effectively nil. He concluded that W had made a high contribution to the hotel's success and that it would be impossible to identify H's and W's differing fractions of contribution, and accepted W's argument that one-third of the available assets should be attributed to H and excluded from the sharing principle, and the remaining two-thirds should be divided between her and H. H submitted that the judge had denied him relief from the general sharing principle to reflect the fact that a substantial part of the available assets had derived from family inheritance and inter-generational transfer. He argued that the judge should have identified the value of the inherited assets, ring-fenced them, and removed them from the tally of assets properly available for division by the court, and following that course he should have awarded W a lump sum of £1.5 million instead of £2.2 million.

Held: Appeal dismissed. The judge erred in accepting that the business itself was of effectively no value at the date H acquired it from his father, but the result he ultimately ordered was not infected by that error. In light of the financial information available, the business would have had some value at the date of transfer to H. However, valuation experts were not pressed to provide a valuation of the business at that time, and such a valuation would have been a difficult exercise, *Whiteman Smith Motor Co Ltd v Chaplin* [1934] 2 K.B. 35 considered. It was unlikely that the value of the business was as significant as H had suggested, and in any event W's commitment had played an important role in maintaining such value as it had. Further, W had conceded that one-third of the total net assets should be extracted and protected from her claim, and had demonstrated that the judge had acted on that concession, without which the award might have exceeded £2.2 million. The effect of the order was to give W approximately one-third and H two-thirds of the total available assets, and that reflected the derivation of the hotel and its trade. Accordingly, it was inappropriate to interfere with the judge's assessment of the appropriate split of assets (see paras 16-17, 27-28, 33-34, 36 of judgment).

D v D, [2012] EWCA Civ 1641, [2013] 1 F.C.R. 459, Thorpe, L.J., CA (Civ Div).

1293. Financial orders–Freezing injunctions–Debt claim–Width of order–Omission of words from CPR 25A para 11 (2) standard form

[Armed Forces Act 2006 (c.52) s.356; Crown Proceedings Act 1947 (c.44); Limitation Act 1980 (c.58); Matrimonial Causes Act 1973 (c.18) s.32; Civil Procedure Rules 1998 (SI 1998/3132) r.25.3(3), r.25.3(2), r.66.7; CPR PD 25A (Interim Injunctions) 1999.]

The court was required to determine a number of issues between a husband (H) and his wife (W) relating to the enforcement of two judgments made in divorce proceedings in Germany. H and W had been married and cohabited in Germany, but later separated. H had been in the British Army. By order of two German judgments in 2003, H was ordered to make maintenance payments to W. The judgments were registered in the English High Court in 2009, and served on H via the army. No payments were made in the three years preceding the issue of the proceedings. W's request to the Service Veterans Personnel Agency (SVPA) for payments to be made from H's salary was declined, as H was soon to be discharged. On becoming aware of a lump sum to be paid on discharge, W successfully applied, without notice, for a freezing injunction. The order was continued at a later hearing. H informed W that the injunction prevented him from withdrawing his weekly allowance and sought £7,500 for legal expenses; W agreed to £3,000. A third party debt order for the judgment amounts was made against the army which was disputed on the basis of the Armed Forces Act 2006 s.356. H sought further funds for legal expenses, which W refused. W eventually conceded that she could only claim maintenance payments due in respect of the three years preceding the enforcement proceedings, reducing the claim from approximately £84,000 to approximately £40,000. H applied for the freezing injunction to be discharged or varied. The issues for consideration were whether (i) the High Court orders were valid and enforceable; (ii) a third party debt order could be made against the army, and if so whether it could be made in respect of monies referred to in s.356 of the 2006 Act; (iii) the claims under the German judgments were barred by the Limitation Act 1980; (iv) the orders of the German court as registered in the High Court could be enforced in respect of money that became due more than 12 months before the proceedings began without leave being obtained under the Matrimonial Causes Act 1973 s.32; (v) the freezing injunction should be discharged or varied on a number of different grounds.

Held: Judgment accordingly. An order of the High Court against which appeal rights had not been exercised or exhausted could not be a nullity (see para.31 of judgment). (2) The third party debt order identified the Armed Forces -British Army SVPA, which was part of the Crown for the purposes of the

Crown Proceedings Act 1947, as the third party. CPR r.66.7 precluded such orders against the Crown and, therefore, it had to be discharged (paras 36-37). (3) Under German law judgment for a lump sum was subject to a 30-year limitation period. That was the appropriate limitation period and the claims were not time-barred (para.51). (4) The sum enforceable by W was limited to the arrears which became due no more than 12 months before the proceedings to enforce payment began. For the purposes of a freezing injunction, W had an arguable case that leave should be granted under s.32 of the 1973 Act such that if an injunction was appropriate, one would have to be granted to restrain dissipation of the sum for which W might apply under s.32, subject to an undertaking (paras 58-59). (5) There was no basis for making the application without notice. No good reason had been given and the evidential requirements of CPR r.25.3(2) and CPR r.25.3(3) had not been fulfilled. There was no suggestion that H would receive the discharge payment earlier than suggested; therefore, advance notice did not create a risk of dissipation. Irrespective of the criticisms that could be made of the evidence initially put before the judge, there was reason for finding a risk of dissipation at the second hearing when the order was continued, and the risk still existed, despite the new evidence tendered by H at the instant hearing. The order had been drawn too widely. Given that it was a debt claim, it should have included words from CPR PD 25A para 11 (2) of the standard form. W went too far in refusing to allow H to spend the sums for which agreement was sought for legal expenses. Only if W could claim a right in property, or a right akin to it, would she have had a right to refuse H from disposing of that money. W should have agreed to a relaxation of the injunction once she had made the concession regarding maintenance payments. The application should have been made for the total amount now pursued, which, in any event, would not have been necessary after making the third party debt order. A freezing order would be made for the sum of the German judgments subject to a suitable undertaking from W to make and pursue the application expeditiously (paras 68-69, 74-75, 81-83, 86-90).

O'FARRELL v O'FARRELL, [2012] EWHC 123 (QB), [2013] 1 F.L.R. 77, Tugendhat, J., QBD.

1294. Financial orders–Lump sum orders–Failure to pay by lump sum instalments by dates specified in consent order–Whether judge entitled to vary lump sum provision in consent order

[Matrimonial Causes Act 1973 (c.18) s.23(1)(c), s.31.]

The appellant husband (H) appealed against the variation of provision for the payment of capital by the respondent wife (W) in a consent order made in ancillary relief proceedings. W had remained in the former matrimonial home with the two young children of the family. At the time of the original order she was a successful businesswoman, while H was in receipt of benefits. The relevant provisions of the original order were that W was to pay to H a lump sum in five instalments. W paid the first instalment and £90,000 of the second instalment, but there remained £60,000 of the latter and £150,000 in respect of the final three instalments. She had been unable to pay due to a decline in her business, which went into administration. W issued proceedings under the Matrimonial Causes Act 1973 s.31 seeking a variation of the order in respect of the remaining capital owing, arguing that it was an order for a lump sum payable by instalments. H submitted that the original order could not be varied as it was, in reality, an order for a series of individual lump sums. A judge in the High Court found that the provisions of the original order constituted an order for the payment of a lump sum by instalments within s.23(3)(c), and accordingly varied the terms. The issue which fell to be determined was whether the judge was entitled to vary the provision for payment of capital given the terms of the consent order. H submitted that where a consent order was drafted in the form of a series of lump sums under s.23(1)(c), that was an end to the matter because a court could not ever interfere or seek to discover or interpret whether the order, as drafted, accurately reflected the underlying agreement that was approved by the judge.

Held: Appeal dismissed. (1) Section 23(1)(c) gave the court the power to order a lump sum or sums at one time, and, save for a limited exception as to timing, orders made under s.23 were not variable. That accorded with the provision of the Act which did not include orders made under s.23 within the terms of s.31. There had to be a mechanism whereby parties could agree or the court could effect a clean break. Accordingly, the judge was wrong to conclude that "any" order for the payment of a lump sum over time was an order for a lump sum by instalments (see para.39 of judgment). (2) Where there was disagreement as to whether the terms of the order were, in reality, correct, then the court retained jurisdiction and must assess what the parties agreed against the factual matrix of what occurred during the relevant period. In the event of a dispute as to the nature of the agreement, the court was entitled to look at the surrounding facts and circumstances which bore upon the terms as drafted. The test was objective as the court was not looking to assess the subjective beliefs of the parties, rather it was looking at the objective factual matrix to interpret what was agreed in the light of the words used and communications that passed. In the circumstances, there was sufficient evidence upon which the judge was able to conclude that H and W had agreed a lump sum payable by instalments over time. That finding was open to her despite the wording of the order. Accordingly, although she had misdirected herself on the meaning of s.23(1)(c), she was entitled to hold that, objectively, the case did not fall within that section but rather within s.23(3). Her analysis of the facts could not be faulted (paras 41-42). (3) The judge did not vary the amount of the lump sum, she simply adjusted the period for payment. However, s.23 was widely drafted, and as it gave the court the power to vary a lump sum it stood to reason that that power had to extend to quantum as well as timing (para.43). (4) The judge's exercise of variation under s.31 was a matter of discretion. There was no misdirection in law and her order was within the broad range of orders that could be made. Her decision was just in the circumstances (para.44).

HAMILTON v HAMILTON, [2013] EWCA Civ 13, [2013] Fam. 292, Thorpe, L.J., CA (Civ Div).

1295. Financial orders–Lump sum orders–Procedure for compensating party for wasted costs at conclusion of ancillary relief proceedings

[Matrimonial Causes Act 1973 (c.18) s.25; Family Procedure Rules 2010 (SI 2010/2955) r.28.3.]

The appellant husband (H) appealed against the final order in ancillary relief proceedings brought by the respondent wife (W). H and W had been married for over 30 years. H was a successful businessman, involved mainly in property investment and management. When the marriage broke down, W applied for ancillary relief. The case was unusual in that the parties' expert forensic accountants had agreed the value of their assets. The business assets, held by companies or trusts under H's direction, were valued at £2.637 million. The family assets outside corporate ownership, mainly property owned equally by H and W, were valued at £2.04 million. The parties had agreed that they should share the net worth of those assets equally. The judge's sole task was therefore to decide how to redistribute the assets to achieve an equal share for each party. H contended that the privately owned assets should be sold and the proceeds divided, and that 50 per cent of the shares in the business assets should be transferred to W. W submitted that she should receive all the privately owned properties together with a lump sum of £322,000 to equalise the assets. She also complained that H's conduct, albeit as a litigant in person, had inflated her legal costs way above what it otherwise would have been. The judge, having found that H had forged W's signature on a remortgage application, concluded that H could not be trusted to act fairly towards W in the future so that it would be dangerous for W's financial security to rest in substantial part on her equal ownership of company shares. He therefore awarded W the whole beneficial interest in the family assets. The judge acknowledged that the lump sum required to provide equality was £322,000 but stated that, in order to reflect other matters and H's misconduct in relation to the proceedings, H should pay W a lump sum of £500,000. H contended that (1) the judge had erred in awarding W all the "copper-bottomed" and liquid assets, leaving him with only the risk-laden and illiquid assets; (2) the uplift of £178,000 had not been explained.

Held: Appeals allowed in part. (1) H's first ground of appeal failed simply because the view the judge had taken on the division of assets was justified on the agreed evidence of the two experts as to the value of the business assets (see para.17 of judgment). (2) The judge had, however, fallen into error in quantifying the lump sum as he had. He had undoubtedly been fully entitled to have had regard to W's strong submissions that H's conduct in the case had inflated her legal costs. It was open to the judge, under the Family Procedure Rules 2010 r.28.3, to have concluded that the instant case was not one that fitted comfortably within the general rule that there should be no order for costs at the conclusion of an ancillary relief trial and to have penalised H by making an order for costs so as to compensate W for that element of wasted costs. It was, however, unorthodox simply to inflate a lump sum in the way that he had. That produced the mathematical consequence that the sum for wasted costs was £178,000, but that was not a considered or reasoned quantification. The safe and orthodox procedure was to assess the lump sum in accordance with the criteria under the Matrimonial Causes Act 1973 s.25 and then to make a distinct costs order. The lump sum ordered by the judge was impossible to support as a matter of principle and for want of reasons. The order would, accordingly, be rewritten to award W a lump sum of £322,000, together with an order that H pay W the costs she had unnecessarily incurred in consequence of his misconduct. That matter would be remitted to the trial judge, asking him to have regard to the fact that H had been a litigant in person in complex ancillary relief proceedings and that at various interlocutory hearings he had been condemned to pay the costs incurred by W. That latter step was necessary to ensure that there was no double penalty in combining the interlocutory and final orders. The trial judge was also to have regard to the fact that W's legal bill had not been subject to any summary or detailed assessment by a costs judge, and it was therefore likely that the full extent of her claimed costs bill would shrink when subjected to a process of assessment (see paras 18-22 of judgment).

EZAIR v EZAIR, [2012] EWCA Civ 893, [2013] 1 F.L.R. 281, Thorpe, L.J., CA (Civ Div).

1296. Financial orders–Maintenance–Maintenance pending suit–Appropriateness of orders being made without sufficient information

[Family Procedure Rules 2010 (SI 2010/2955) r.33.1.]

The appellant husband (H) appealed against an order requiring him to pay maintenance pending suit to his respondent wife (W) and against an the imposition of a freezing injunction. H and W were both from affluent families who provided them individually with financial support. H suffered from high-functioning Asperger's syndrome and depression. H and W were married in 2007 but separated the following year when W moved out of H's family home into a property owned by the company of H's father (F). H was convicted of making fraudulent VAT claims and was fined £1.5 million that was paid by F. In 2012, F served on W a notice to quit the property. W applied for maintenance pending suit and the parties disputed the level of support. The application had a 30-minute time estimate. H was ordered to pay W to meet the costs of her accommodation, general living expenses, and her costs. H failed to comply with the order and W applied to enforce it under the Family Procedure Rules 2010 r.33.1. During that hearing, which also had a 30-minute time estimate, W successfully applied *ex parte* for a freezing order in relation to a series of bank accounts holding a total of £5,000. H was granted leave to appeal both orders. Further evidence had been filed including Forms E for H and W, a statement from F stating that he would not be providing H with financial support, and confirmation that the notice to quit proceedings had been transferred and incorporated into the ancillary relief matters.

Held: Appeals allowed. (1) The instant case was a graphic illustration of the very real pressures that faced the family court. Time estimates for both hearings had been ridiculously short; in these types of family money cases, it was necessary for the courts to be able establish as clearly as possible what the true historical position had been, in particular, the extent to which there had been an established payment stream or other regular financial provision. They were not matters that could be dealt with in a 30-minute hearing. At neither hearing had a judgment been given, and there was no real information as to how the judges had exercised their discretion. The process that had been taken and the lack of proper court time lay at the root of the problems that had arisen (see paras 35, 40-41, 52 of judgment). (2) The maintenance order was plainly wrong. The judge had failed properly to consider H's resources and to carry out any balancing exercise of his resources against the parties' individual needs. There had been a gulf in evidence about the level of support to H and from H to W. Financial history was crucial to the finding where a dispute as to the level of support existed. Matters had since progressed and the instant court had significantly more information to evaluate H's position, crucially F's statement. There was a very real possibility that W would get nothing or next to nothing in the end. The facts did not easily lead to the assumption that H would be expected to provide significant financial support to W either by way of capital or income. Additionally, W was no longer in imminent danger of being removed from the property. Historically, both H and W had been very heavily dependent on their respective families and H had provided almost no support to W. F's support was limited to paying H's debts to avoid prison or bankruptcy and there had not been a pattern of regular support. There was a strong possibility that H would not provide financial support to W either by way of capital or income, and W was getting very real and valuable interim provision by staying in the property rent-free and with utilities paid for by F. The same reasoning applied to the order for costs; H did not have the ability to meet it, and he never did (paras 29-30, 37, 44-46, 48-49). (3) There had never been any evidence that H had an intention to dissipate his assets, and H should have been given proper time to prepare his case. Freezing £5,000 had no practical purpose. Given that the maintenance pending suit order should not have been made, it could not be enforced and the freezing injunction had to be discharged (para.51).

S v M (MAINTENANCE PENDING SUIT), [2012] EWHC 4109 (Fam), [2013] 1 F.L.R. 1173, Coleridge, J., Fam Div.

1297. Financial orders–Non-payment–Appropriateness of committal for non-payment–Appropriateness of continuing writ ne exeat regno

[Debtors Act 1869 (c.62) s.5.]

The applicant wife (W) applied for the committal of the respondent husband (H) under the Debtors Act 1869 s.5 for failing to satisfy an award made in divorce proceedings. H and W had owned a jewellery shop in the United States. In December 2010 W left the family home. H and his father disabled the CCTV in the shop and stripped it bare of all jewellery stock. A US judge ordered H to pay W a lump sum of $2 million, and to pay her $4,000 per month pending payment of that lump sum. The parties returned to the United Kingdom and the US order was registered in the UK. H did not pay the lump sum or the monthly payments. W successfully applied for a writ ne exeat regno against H. H, who owned a 25 per cent interest in a UK property, gave evidence at the instant hearing that he had sold all of the jewellery stock for little in exchange but had kept no receipts. The issues were whether it was appropriate to (i) commit H for non-payment of the sums; (ii) continue the writ made against him.

Held: Application granted. (1) The evidence demonstrated that in December 2010 there was inventory in the shop with a retail value of approximately $5 million. Immediately following the breakdown of the marriage, H selfishly took steps to appropriate all of that value for himself, and sought to cover his trail by disabling the CCTV and pretending that there was no documentation as to its alleged disposal. The instant court was satisfied that the shop items themselves or money representing their value were retained by H either directly or by his family members. H had the means to pay at all times but had refused. The scale of default was extremely high, and the situation was seriously aggravated by the completely false evidence that H had given before the instant court. H was sentenced to the maximum imprisonment term that s.5 allowed, namely six weeks, suspended for three months (see paras 48-50 of judgment). (2) After judgment, an injunction restraining movement out of the jurisdiction could not be made as a free-standing enforcement measure: it had to be linked to another measure and be time-limited, *B v B (Injunction: Restraint on Leaving Jurisdiction)* [1998] 1 W.L.R. 329, [1997] C.L.Y. 639 applied. Accordingly, it was appropriate to discharge the existing writ and make a fresh injunction restraining H's movement out of the jurisdiction (para.51). (3) A final charging order was made in relation to H's property interest (para.52).

BHURA v BHURA, [2012] EWHC 3633 (Fam), [2013] 2 F.L.R. 44, Mostyn, J., Fam Div.

1298. Financial orders–Shares–Shares held by couple to be sold after separation–Fair division of shares

The applicant wife (W) applied for a financial order in connection with her divorce from the respondent husband (H). H had founded a company early in the marriage. The couple's shares in the company were estimated to be worth £32 million, but they could not be sold for two to three years. The couple had loaned money to the company and were receiving repayments from it. H continued to work for the company following the parties' separation. The court had to determine how the parties' resources should be divided, including whether property should be added back in W's favour on the basis that H had been wantonly spending money; whether H had made a special contribution to the marriage such as to justify dividing the shares in his favour; and whether his post-separation endeavour justified dividing the shares in his favour. The court also had to determine whether H should pay W maintenance for herself and whether trusts held on behalf of the parties' children should be used for their maintenance.

Held: Judgment accordingly. (1) The parties' total assets, apart from the shares, were worth £8.7 million. H's net earned annual income was taken as £280,000; he would also receive half the loan interest of £110,000 net and rental and utilities payments from the company until at least 2014. H's current wife's income was also taken into account. W's only income in the near future would be what she received from her capital resources: her income from the loan would provide her with £105,000 net annually. The level and nature of housing which the parties could obtain in the immediate future was limited by the resources available until the sale of the shares. However, if the resources were available, it would be reasonable for each party to purchase accommodation costing around £3 million. Given the family's standard of living, the parties would be able to justify an income needs schedule of £300,000, although the level at which they could meet those needs was also limited by the resources available until the share sale (see paras 83-89, 100-101 of judgment). (2) The question of add-back depended on what both parties had been spending: it was insufficient merely to point to certain aspects of H's expenditure. Both parties' expenditure had been, to a large extent, funded from capital. There had to be clear evidence of wanton dissipation which it would be inequitable to disregard, *Vaughan v Vaughan* [2007] EWCA Civ 1085, [2008] 1 F.L.R. 1108, [2007] C.L.Y. 1692 followed. H's level of expenditure had been very high. There was no clear picture of W's expenditure; however, the evidence suggested that she had also been spending at a significant rate. W had only partly established the evidential foundation for a notional reattribution. It was not possible to carry out a proper comparison to determine whether H's expenditure had been wanton. Further, the notional reattribution involved around 1-2 per cent of the total wealth: that degree of adjustment was not necessary in order to achieve a fair result (paras 105-114). (3) The question of a special contribution did not depend on any detailed analysis of contributions. It required a striking evidential foundation which so clearly stood out that the question almost answered itself. H had accepted in his evidence that he considered that an equal division of the shares would have been fair up until the end of the marriage: in that case, it was difficult for the court to conclude that there had been such disparity in the parties' contributions that it would be inequitable to disregard it, *Lambert v Lambert* [2002] EWCA Civ 1685, [2003] Fam. 103, [2002] C.L.Y. 1690 applied (paras 132-134). (4) The issue of post-separation endeavour involved considering what was meant by marital property and then addressing the manner in which the sharing principle was applied. The shares had been generated during the marriage, but their value could not be realised until some years after its end. That value would in part be the product of H's endeavours, not the parties' joint endeavours and would therefore, in part, not be marital property. The weight to give H's post-separation endeavour was part of the court's discretion. The overall division which effected a fair outcome was an award that gave H 55 per cent of the capital wealth and W 45 per cent. There was no justification for dividing the non-share assets other than broadly equally, although the manner in which that was effected had to take into account their current needs (paras 138-143, 150-151). (5) An immediate clean break would not be fair. It would not allow W to meet her current income needs. H was able to pay maintenance as a result of his earned income. On the basis of his net income, he should pay W maintenance for herself of £100,000 annually. It was reasonable for the children's trusts to be used for the payment of both school fees and maintenance, given the parties' current financial position and the level of resources in the trusts (paras 160-162, 167).

E v E, [2013] EWHC 506 (Fam), [2013] 2 F.L.R. 999, Moylan, J., Fam Div.

1299. Financial orders–Talaq divorce–Application for financial relief following foreign divorce–Marriage not recognised under English law

[Marriage Act 1949 (c.76); Matrimonial and Family Proceedings Act 1984 (c.42) Pt III, s.12(1).]

The appellant husband (H) appealed against an order that an application by the respondent wife (W) for financial relief under the Matrimonial and Family Proceedings Act 1984 Pt III was well-founded and that H's jurisdictional challenge failed. H and W were Saudi nationals. In 1994, H, although already married, went through a ceremony at a London hotel which purported to be an Islamic marriage to W. It was not a valid marriage in England and Wales as it did not comply with the Marriage Act 1949. The marriage broke down in 2001 and W petitioned for divorce, which was amended to a nullity petition. A financial settlement was reached. It was agreed by way of security for future performance of the periodical payments that, after H had obtained a Talaq divorce in Saudi, W could issue an application under Pt III which would be adjourned generally and activated if H fell into substantial breach. In 2012, W sought to activate her Pt III claim. At the hearing H argued that there had been no marriage as recognised by English law so, according to s.12(1) of the 1984 Act, there was no jurisdiction to hear a Pt III claim. The judge found in favour of W and a trial of the merits of her claim was listed. H submitted that it was as much incumbent on an applicant to prove that a marriage was valid or void according to the *lex loci celebrationis* as it was to establish that the overseas divorce was entitled to be recognised as valid in England and Wales. He argued that there was plainly not a marriage which was void or valid according to English law but a non-marriage. W submitted that the requirement on the applicant was to prove that the divorce was entitled to recognition as valid in the jurisdiction and the requirements of s.12(1)(a) were met because the marriage was valid under Saudi law which flowed from the fact that the marriage had been dissolved according to Saudi law.

Held: Appeal allowed. Fundamental to the right of spouses to apply for the equitable redistribution of family assets was the existence of a marriage recognised as valid or void by the *lex loci celebrationis*, *Dukali v Lamrani* [2012] EWHC 1748 (Fam), [2012] 2 F.L.R. 1099, [2012] C.L.Y. 1443 approved. It would be fanciful and contrary to policy to suggest that a person without that foundation could acquire a right of application by virtue of a Talaq divorce in another jurisdiction. In an application under Pt III, there had to be not only a foreign divorce but such divorce had to be based upon a marriage which was, or under English law was recognised as, a valid or at least a void marriage. The ceremony of marriage in the instant case could not even have achieved the status of a void marriage in English law (see paras 33-35, 40 of judgment).

SHAGROON v SHARBATLY; *sub nom.* SHARBATLY v SHAGROON, [2012] EWCA Civ 1507, [2013] Fam. 267, Thorpe, L.J., CA (Civ Div).

1300. Financial orders–Transfer of property orders–Order for transfer to wife of property held by company operated and controlled by husband–Lifting corporate veil

[Matrimonial Causes Act 1973 (c.18) s.24(1).]

In proceedings for ancillary relief, the appellant wife (W) appealed against a decision ([2012] EWCA Civ 1395, [2013] 2 W.L.R. 557, [2013] 2 C.L. 157) that an order transferring to her certain properties held by the respondent group of companies (X), which were operated and controlled by her former husband (H), could not be made since there were no legitimate grounds for piercing the corporate veil. X was the legal owner of seven residential properties. The trial judge concluded that H was entitled to possession or reversion of those properties within the Matrimonial Causes Act 1973 s.24(1), thereby entitling the court to pierce the corporate veil, and ordered him to transfer them to W. The question on the instant appeal was whether the court had power to order the transfer of those properties to W given that they legally belonged not to H but to his companies. Consideration was given to three possible legal bases on which the assets of X could be available to satisfy the lump sum order against H: this was a case where, exceptionally, the Court could disregard the corporate veil in order to give effective relief; s.24(1)(a) confered a distinct power to disregard the corporate veil in matrimonial cases; or X held the properties on trust for H, not by virtue of his status as sole shareholder and controller, but in the particular circumstances of the case.

Held: Appeal allowed. (1) The principle of English law which enabled a court in very limited circumstances to pierce the corporate veil applied when a person was under an existing legal obligation or liability or subject to an existing legal restriction which he deliberately evaded or the enforcement of which he deliberately frustrated by imposing a company under his control. In such a case, the court could pierce the corporate veil for the purpose only of depriving the company or its controller of the advantage that they would otherwise have obtained by the company's separate legal personality. Although H had acted improperly in many ways, his actions had not evaded or frustrated any legal obligation to W, nor had he concealed or evaded the law in relation to the distribution of assets of the marriage upon its dissolution, and accordingly the piercing of the corporate veil could not be justified by reference to the general principle of law, *Salomon v Salomon & Co Ltd* [1897] A.C. 22, *Lazarus Estates Ltd v Beasley* [1956] 1 Q.B. 702, [1956] C.L.Y. 7545, *Ben Hashem v Ali Shayif* [2008] EWHC 2380 (Fam), [2009] 1 F.L.R. 115, [2009] C.L.Y. 1489, *VTB Capital Plc v Nutritek International Corp* [2012] EWCA Civ 808, [2012] 2 Lloyd's Rep. 313, [2012] C.L.Y. 474 applied (see paras 16, 18, 25-26, 35-36 of judgment). (2) It was not correct to state that a broader principle applied in matrimonial proceedings by virtue of s. 24(1)(a). That section invoked concepts with an established legal meaning and recognised legal incidents under the general law, which could not be suspended or taken to mean something different in matrimonial proceedings. The judge's reasoning cut across the statutory schemes of company and insolvency law, which were essential for the protection of those dealing with companies (paras 37, 40-41). (3) The only basis on which X could be ordered to convey the disputed properties to W was if they belonged beneficially to H by virtue of the particular circumstances in which they came to be vested in X (para.43). The trial judge found that the husband had deliberately sought to conceal facts, and H and X had failed to comply with court orders for the disclosure of evidence; adverse influences could therefore be drawn. It was a fair inference, from all the facts, taken cumulatively, that the main, if not the only, reason for X's failure to co-operate was to protect the properties. That in turn suggested that proper disclosure would have revealed the properties to have been held beneficially by H. The Court of Appeal inferred that the reason for X's failure to co-operate was to protect the properties, which suggested that proper disclosure would have revealed them to be beneficially owned by H. It was determined that the most plausible inference from the known facts was that each of the properties was held on a resulting trust by X for H (paras 45, 47). There was no reliable evidence to rebut that inference, and accordingly the seven disputed properties were required to be transfered to W (paras 49-51, 55).

PETRODEL RESOURCES LTD v PREST; *sub nom.* PREST v PREST; P RESOURCES LTD v PREST; PREST v PETRODEL RESOURCES LTD, [2013] UKSC 34, [2013] 2 A.C. 415, Lord Neuberger, J.S.C., SC.

1301. Financial orders–Unmarried couples–Lump sum payment for provision of housing fund for benefit of child

[Children Act 1989 (c.41) Sch.1.]

The appellant father (F) appealed against a financial provision order made pursuant to the Children Act 1989 Sch.1 requiring him to pay £335,000 to the respondent mother (M) for the benefit of their son (C). F and M were in a relationship for a short period but never married. After C's birth F contributed towards nanny costs and nursery school fees, and made periodical payments in accordance with a child support assessment. Although F was unemployed, the district judge assessed his earning capacity as being £100,000 and noted that his house was worth £1.2 million. He ordered that F should sell his house, which had a net equity of £358,000. Out of that F was to pay a lump sum of £85,000 in order that M could reduce her outstanding debts and provide a trust fund of £250,000 to assist with C's housing until he attained majority and ceased full-time education, at which point the money would revert to F. By the time of the instant hearing F had paid £40,000 to M. F argued that the award was excessive and that he would be left "effectively with nothing".

Held: Appeal allowed in part. Given the net equity remaining after the sale of his house, the district judge had been absolutely justified in ordering F to contribute £250,000 towards a housing fund. In reality it was a long-term loan which would be recovered in time and which would provide C with a secure house (see para.42 of judgment). The district judge's analysis of the additional £85,000 had been plainly wrong and the court was free to exercise its discretion to amend that part of the award, *Cordle v Cordle* [2001] EWCA Civ 1791, [2002] 1 W.L.R. 1441, [2001] C.L.Y. 2630 applied. The impact on F, who would have been left with effectively little or no capital after the very significant contribution towards housing for C, was unfair. F had already paid £40,000, which M had used to repay some of her debts. Assuming that he made no further payment and that she sold her house, she would at least be in a position where she could cover smaller debts over time. Moreover, the trust fund meant that she would have sufficient monies to enable her to purchase a home with a manageable mortgage until C grew up (paras 43-44).

DE v AB (FINANCIAL PROVISION FOR CHILD), [2010] EWHC 3792 (Fam), [2012] 2 F.L.R. 1396, Baron, J., Fam Div.

1302. Financial orders–Variation–Appeal against changes to financial provision for child–Costs of parties

[Children Act 1989 (c.41) Sch.1; Civil Procedure Rules 1998 (SI 1998/3132) r.44.3(4)(c); Family Procedure Rules 2010 (SI 2010/2955) r.28.2(1), r.28.3; Rules of the Supreme Court (Revision) 1965 (SI 1965/1776) Ord.62 r.3.]

The appellant mother (M) appealed against the variation of a financial order made under the Children Act 1989 Sch.1. Under the original 2005 order the respondent father (F) had been ordered to pay a £40,000 lump sum, general child support for their child (C) of £21,600 annually, all C's secondary education school fees, and M's costs. In 2012, the index-linked general support figure had risen to £28,000. C was 17. F semi-retired later that year but still received a net salary of £102,000 and a potential bonus. He also had a private pension fund, from which he had initially taken an annuity but no longer did. M earned £42,000 net annually. Both parties had significant debts. M sought a further lump sum and an increase in the general support figure; F sought a decrease. It was ordered that general support be reduced to £18,000, but be paid to the conclusion of C's tertiary education; F was to pay £24,000 of C's £31,500 annual school fees and was to pay M 20 per cent of any bonus. There was no further lump sum award and no order regarding costs. The judge did not consider F's net income to include the bonus or pension annuity. M was granted permission to appeal against the school fees award and the costs decision. F sought an order for his costs of the instant appeal. M contended that the judge's findings in relation to F's bonus and pension were untenable. M further contended that she should have been awarded her costs as she was the effective winner, F was guilty of litigation misconduct and because of the economic impact on her.

Held: Appeal dismissed. (1) The judge's findings in relation to F's bonus and pension were factual determinations and were not merely tenable but correct. F had been ordered to pay £42,000 of his £102,000 basic income, together with 20 per cent of his bonus. That was a very high proportion and could only seriously be criticised if it could be convincingly shown that M genuinely could not meet her reasonable budget and pay the school fees shortfall from her resources as augmented by the child maintenance. The judge was not explicit regarding how M was to meet the shortfall. However, inferences could be drawn. The judge had allowed M a cushion of £6,000 a year to meet her expenses which, combined with the 20 per cent of F's bonus, exceeded the school fees shortfall (see paras 9-13 of judgment). (2) The parties' costs completely dwarfed the sums argued about. Time and again judges pointed out the madness of litigating in that way and their admonitions fell on deaf ears. If such concerns were ignored, the parties had to live with, and take responsibility for, the consequences of their decisions. Since April 6, 2011, by virtue of the Family Procedure Rules 2010 r.28.3, Sch.1 proceedings had been excepted from the general rule of no order as to costs introduced for almost all family financial proceedings from April 3, 2006. The position before April 3, 2006 had been that the general rule in RSC Ord.62 r.3(5), that costs should follow the event, was formally disapplied. Following the decision in *Gojkovic v Gojkovic (No.2)* [1992] Fam. 40, [1992] C.L.Y. 2090, an equivalent but more flexible principle prima facie applied, at least to financial provision proceedings between husband and wife. However, in Sch.1 proceedings, where the mother's application was made as representative for the child, the court should start with a "clean sheet", *Baker v Rowe* [2009] EWCA Civ 1162, [2010] 2 Costs L.R. 175, [2010] C.L.Y. 1284 and *Gojkovic* considered. Even if the rule in *Gojkovic* did apply in the instant case, it was by no means clear that M could be said to have "won" the case. In fact, objective analysis would suggest that, overall, F had been more successful. A consequence of r.28.2(1) of the 2010 Rules, and its incorporation of CPR r.44.3(4)(c), was that, in relation to those proceedings excepted from r.28.3, protection in respect of costs could be achieved by making a *Calderbank* offer. However, no such offer had been made in the instant case; only open offers were made and the result was much closer to F's position than M's. Under r.44.3(4), the court had to also consider the parties' conduct; whether a party had been successful in whole or in part; and any admissible offers made. Although F's conduct prior to the issue of proceedings did not directly relate to costs, it was relied on by M as raising her suspicions to the extent that a trial had been inevitable because she was unable to accept F's representations regarding his means without having them tested by a judge. However, F's pre-proceedings conduct was not relevant to the issue of costs. It could only be relevant where it had a direct causal connection to the later generation of costs. M's argument on economic impact also had no merit as the parties were in a comparably disastrous position (paras 15-28). (3) On any financial remedy appeal, including an appeal in Sch.1 proceedings, costs should prima facie follow the event. Even if F had not made an offer he would prima facie be entitled to his costs, but the existence of his offer strengthened his case considerably.

There was no good reason why he should not have his costs of the instant appeal (paras 29-36).

KS v ND (SCHEDULE I: APPEAL: COSTS), [2013] EWHC 464 (Fam), [2013] 2 F.L.R. 698, Mostyn, J., Fam Div.

1303. Financial orders–Variation of settlement orders–Discretionary Jersey trust owning various companies–Application for transfer of assets owned by companies–Principles applicable to joinder of parties

[Family Procedure Rules 2010 (SI 2010/2955) r.9.26B, Pt 18.]

The applicant wife (W) applied for a variation of a settlement order in settlement of monies owed to her by the first respondent husband (H) following divorce proceedings. The third to sixth respondents (X) applied to be disjoined from the proceedings. Over half of the total assets were held in a post-nuptial settlement. That settlement was the second respondent discretionary Jersey trust (T). T owned the third respondent company which in turn owned the fourth respondent company which owned the fifth and sixth respondent companies which owned two retirement villages and other assets. W wished to receive an outright transfer of one of the retirement villages. Over the course of the proceedings T's trustees and X were joined as parties. No application for joinder was made and neither H nor X nor the trustees had any notice of any application to join; W's counsel had simply turned up with a draft order providing for joinder. The issues for the court were whether (i) the interposition of the companies between the trust at the top of the tree and the assets at the bottom impeded the making of a variation disposing of the assets at the bottom; (ii) X could be disjoined from the proceedings.

Held: Judgment accordingly. (1) A nuptial settlement was "any arrangement which makes some form of continuing provision for both or either parties of the marriage", *Brooks v Brooks* [1996] A.C. 375, [1995] C.L.Y. 2354 considered. A family company which, under an arrangement, made some form of continuing provision for both or either spouses was capable of itself of amounting to a variable nuptial settlement whether or not the company was owned by a trust of which the spouses were formal beneficiaries. If under an arrangement "some form of continuing provision for both or either of the parties to a marriage" had been made from assets held by a group of family companies then the entire set-up, when viewed as a whole, was capable of amounting to a variable nuptial settlement. If the top company was owned by a trust of which the spouses were formal beneficiaries then the position was a fortiori. Accordingly, the entire structure comprised a variable post-nuptial settlement and the court was entitled to deal directly with, and to make orders in respect of, the trust assets owned by X, *BJ v MJ (Financial Order: Overseas Trust)* [2011] EWHC 2708 (Fam), [2012] 1 F.L.R. 667, [2012] C.L.Y. 1440 applied (see paras 8, 15-16, 18, 47 of judgment). (2) The following principles were applicable on the question of joinder: (a) the joinder of trustees or underlying companies was not an essential precondition for the validity of a variation of settlement order; (b) beneficiaries under 18 had to be joined unless the court could say that the proposed variation would not adversely affect their rights or interests. That requirement could be modified but the court should be very sparing in doing so. Failure to comply with the rule would not nullify any order later made. The application to join minor beneficiaries was to be made at the first appointment following the issue of the application; (c) the applicant, respondent, trustees and/or companies could apply for joinder. In each instance both the substantive terms of, and the procedure prescribed in, the Family Procedure Rules 2010 r.9.26B had to be carefully complied with; (d) under r.9.26B, the applicant for joinder had to show that there was an existing matter in dispute requiring the joinder of the new party for its resolution and that the issue could not be effectually and validly resolved without the joinder; (e) alternatively, under r.9.26B, it had to be shown that there was a separate matter in dispute between a party and the proposed new party which was connected to the main matters in dispute between the parties and that it was desirable to resolve all the issues together; (f) if better enforcement of an order in a foreign jurisdiction was relied on under an application under (d) or (e) there had to be evidence that joinder would actually make a difference; mere assertions of belief would not suffice; (g) an application for joinder had to be made on notice under Pt 18 of the Rules, which required seven days' notice, and be supported by clear evidence. It would be preferable if the application were served on the proposed new party (paras 21-35). Applying those principles to the instant case there was no good reason why either the trustees or the companies had been joined. Apart from the failure to comply with the prescribed procedure it did not appear that either limb of r.9.26B was engaged. The substantive application for joinder did not require the joinder of the proposed new parties in order that it could be effectually resolved. There was no separate dispute between W and either the trustees or X which it would be desirable to determine alongside the variation application. There was no evidence that enforcement of any variation order would be better achieved if the trustees or X were joined. There was a mere assertion to that effect but that was belied by the decision in *IMK Family Trust, Re* [2009] 1 F.L.R. 664, *IMK* applied. Accordingly, X succeeded on their application to be disjoined (paras 36-37).

DR v GR (FINANCIAL REMEDY: VARIATION OF OVERSEAS TRUST), [2013] EWHC 1196 (Fam), [2013] 2 F.L.R. 1534, Mostyn, J., Fam Div.

1304. Financial orders–Variation of settlement orders–Trust property–Non-payment by husband–Need for impropriety

The applicant wife (W) applied for a variation of a nuptial settlement and of a family trust so that funds could be pulled out of the trust for her in settlement of monies owed to her by the respondent husband (H) following divorce proceedings. She also sought a non-statutory civil restraint order against H preventing him from embarking on any kind of satellite litigation against her. H had been ordered to pay W a lump sum of £268,000 and a contribution to her costs. H had not paid anything to W. The family trust included within it two properties, a motorcycle and two cars. The trust owned a company (C) which in turn owned another company (D). D owned the trust properties. H ran C and D and his extravagant lifestyle was funded by C. W argued that the properties and cars should be vested in her as part of the settlement monies.

Held: Application granted in part. (1) Nothing that the instant court had heard had caused it to doubt that H had undisclosed assets. In relation to H's financial affairs and those of C and D nothing was transparent. The mere fact that a husband had run his company from behind a corporate veil did not of itself demonstrate impropriety. When seeking a telescoping order in the specific factual context almost invariably encountered in financial remedy proceedings *Nicholas v Nicholas* [1984] F.L.R. 285, [1984] C.L.Y. 1121 was binding authority and nothing said in *VTB Capital Plc v Nutritek International Corp* [2012] EWCA Civ 808, [2012] 2 Lloyd's Rep. 313, [2012] C.L.Y. 474 altered that, *Nicholas* applied and *VTB* considered. The fact that H used the trust structure to conduct all of his financial affairs did not of itself mean that there was an independent wrong that involved fraud or dishonest misuse. However, even if C or D were in H's direct ownership there would be no need to find impropriety to make a telescoping order in relation to D's assets. The properties and the cars were the only positive equity assets within the court's jurisdiction. If they were pulled out and vested in W then around £283,000 of the award would still remain unsatisfied. The trust should therefore be varied in order to appoint the properties and the cars in W's name absolutely and in addition any remaining sums owed to W under the settlement following the sale of the properties and the cars would be provided to W from the trust (see paras 14-35 of judgment). (2) W was in effect seeking a limited civil restraint order under PD 4B para.3. The threshold requirement for making such an order was, per para.3.1, that a party had "persistently made applications which were totally without merit". H had made one such application without merit, and so far H had not therefore crossed the threshold for a limited restraint order under PD 4B para.2 which required two such findings. It would be quite wrong to deploy the court's inherent powers to outflank the statutory scheme (paras 36-45).

HOPE v KREJCI, [2012] EWHC1780 (Fam), [2013] 1 F.L.R.182, Mostyn, J., Fam Div.

1305. Financial remedies–Avoidance of disposition orders–Setting aside transaction under s.37(2) Matrimonial Causes Act 1973–Interpretation of s.37–Whether orders operating retrospectively

[Insolvency Act 1986 (c.45) s.423; Law of Property Act 1925 (c.20) s.172; Matrimonial Causes Act 1973 (c.18) s.37.]

The applicant wife (W) applied under the Matrimonial Causes Act 1973 s.37(2) to set aside a transaction made by the first respondent husband (H) of his majority shareholding in a company (DH) to the ninth respondent company. DH was the holding company of the second respondent company and was valued at between £75 million and £100 million. H and W's marriage broke down and H was subsequently diagnosed with frontal lobe dementia. After W had petitioned for divorce, H transferred his shares in DH to the ninth respondent in its capacity as the sole trustee of second respondent's Limited Employee Benefit Trust. The shares were then appointed under a sub-fund for the benefit of H, W, and other members of his family. Under the terms of the trust, a decree absolute of divorce removed W as a beneficiary and limited her right to make any applications in the administration of the trust. The third to the eighth respondents later entered into sale and purchase agreements by which they acquired the shares. W applied to set aside H's initial transfer of the shares on the ground that it had compromised her future claims for a financial remedy.

Held: Application granted. (1) From inception, s.37 was intended as a bespoke statutory alternative to the equitable right to seek rescission or avoidance of a transaction procured by misrepresentation and to the general statutory anti-avoidance measure within the Law of Property Act 1925 s.172 that was replaced by the Insolvency Act 1986 s.423. "Avoidance" in s.37 and the language in s.37(2)(c) was the language of nullity, not of repayment or re-vesting, and so by reference to the literal words of the Act, an order under s.37 operated retrospectively to void the transaction from the beginning, *Kemmis v Kemmis (Welland intervening)* [1988] 1 W.L.R. 1307, [1989] C.L.Y. 1757 applied. H had failed to demonstrate that he had effected the transaction without the intention to defeat W's claims, and the transaction had the effect of defeating them as it either prevented relief from being granted, or it had the result that lesser relief would be granted, *Kremen v Agrest* [2010] EWHC 2571 (Fam), [2011] 2 F.L.R. 478, [2011] C.L.Y. 1291 applied. Third parties that subsequently acquired in good faith the property in issue were not prejudiced by an order under s.37. An order made under s.37 operated in exactly the same way as the equitable remedy of rescission so as not to disturb bona fide concluded third party transactions, *Ansari v Ansari* [2008] EWCA Civ 1456, [2010] Fam. 1, [2009] C.L.Y. 3178, *Lonrho Plc v Al-Fayed (No.2)* [1992] 1 W.L.R. 1, [1991] C.L.Y. 2967, *Bristol & West Building Society v Mothew (t/a Stapley & Co)* [1998] Ch. 1, [1996] C.L.Y. 4503] and *Shalson v Russo* [2003] EWHC 1637 (Ch), [2005] Ch. 281, [2003] C.L.Y. 3611 considered. It followed that it was fair and just to set aside the transaction (see paras 12, 16-19, 23, 28-30 of judgment). (2) Unless a taxing statute said to the contrary, the right of the state to charge tax in relation to a given transaction was subject to the effect of that transaction as defined by the general law. Therefore, the tax effects of a transaction subsequently declared void would be annulled retrospectively, IRC v Spence (1941) 24 TC 312 considered. If tax liabilities survived the setting aside of a transaction, the purpose of s.37, to preserve family assets, would likely be frustrated in part as they would frequently attach to the disponor or the assets disposed of so as to diminish their resources and the court's ability to restore the same state as before. There was no public policy reason why a third party, such as tax authorities, should benefit from the brief life of transactions that had for all other purposes been set aside, particularly when that benefit was at the cost of the family's assets (paras 31, 40-41).

AC v DC (FINANCIAL REMEDY: EFFECT OF S.37 AVOIDANCE ORDERS), [2012] EWHC 2032 (Fam), [2013] 2 F.L.R. 1483, Mostyn, J., Fam Div.

1306. Financial remedies–Delay–Wife seeking ancillary relief 19 years after divorce–Appropriateness of order for husband to fund wife's litigation–Whether appropriate to strike out ancillary relief claim

[Matrimonial Causes Act 1973 (c.18); Civil Procedure Rules 1998 (SI 1998/3132) r.3.4(2), r.24.2; Family Procedure Rules 2010 (SI 2010/2955) r.4.4(1)(a), r.4.4.]

The appellant husband (H) appealed against a decision dismissing his application to strike out the claim of the respondent wife (W) for financial remedy and granting W's application for an order to finance the claim in the sum of £125,000 pursuant to the principle in [2001] 1 W.L.R. 605, [2000] C.L.Y. 2528. The couple had married in 1981. They separated in 1986 and divorced in 1992. Neither H nor W had assets or income, and there was no evidence that any substantive order for ancillary relief was made. W entered into a long relationship with a partner (C) which eventually ended. H subsequently created a successful and valuable business generating electricity from wind power. In 2011, W applied for ancillary relief from H. He applied to strike out the application under the Family Procedure Rules 2010 r.4.4(1)(a) and r.4.4(1)(b). The judge found that W's delay in bringing her claims was potentially explained and excusable and would be a matter for the judge hearing the case, and that whilst W had a steep hill to climb, that was not enough in itself for taking the draconian step of striking out. Having accepted W's case that she could not take the matter to a final hearing without funding, he made an order under *A v A* so that she could continue the proceedings. H contended that in the circumstances r.4.4 was directly engaged. He referred to the 19-year delay and consequential prejudice to him of W's application, and the fact that her relationship with C was tantamount to marriage and during its currency a claim against him would have carried little credibility. At any time when her claim for financial remedy was live and should have been advanced an order would not have resulted simply because of his and W's joint impecuniosity. He submitted that whatever his present fortune, it was all achieved years after the breakdown of the relationship, years after the divorce and years after the breakdown of W's relationship with C.

Held: Appeal allowed. (1) The introduction of r.4.4 was intended to ensure that the power to strike out in financial remedy proceedings mirrored the court's power to strike out in civil proceedings. As in civil proceedings the rule was complementary to the court's inherent powers of case management. The judge had erred in his construction of r.4.4 and approached his essential task too narrowly. It was not apt simply to ask whether there was inordinate delay and, if so, whether the prejudice to H was greater than the prejudice to W. He had to have regard to all relevant considerations within the history and exercise his case management powers not just to protect against the greater prejudice but also to look after the court's resources. The facts of the instant case were extreme. Impecuniosity had been the experience of all W's adult life. Both the men with whom she had entered into family life were seemingly equally impecunious. H was the most improbable candidate for affluence. W could no doubt appeal to his sense of charity but he was not to be compelled to boost W's income by the exercise of the jurisdiction under the Matrimonial Causes Act 1973. H was not W's insurer against life's eventualities (see paras 32-33, 35 of judgment). (2) H's appeal against the *A v A* order accordingly fell away, but would have been successful. In deciding whether to exercise the *A v A* jurisdiction to enable a wife to fund litigation, the judge had to have regard to all the factors that bore on his discretionary decision to allow the case to go forward. The instant case was not the conventional one where an impecunious wife faced an affluent husband and was unable to achieve equality of arms without an *A v A* order. On the exceptional facts, the *A v A* order should not have been made (paras 36, 42-43). (3) (Per Jackson, L.J.) It was unfortunate that the 2010 Rules contained no rule which was equivalent to CPR r.24.2. That omission prompted the question whether the court had to allow a claim for financial relief which had no real prospect of success to proceed to trial. It was hard to believe that that was the intention of the rule-makers. The solution to that problem lay in r.4.4(1)(b) whose wording was identical to that of CPR r.3.4(2). The interpretation and operation of those two rules should be essentially the same. Although there was no statutory bar to bringing a claim for financial relief long after the divorce, the court should not allow either party to a former marriage to be harassed by claims for financial relief which were issued many years later and had no real prospect of success. An application to strike out under r.4.4(1)(b) would only succeed in rare and exceptional cases, but the instant case fell into that category (paras 56, 58-60, 62).

VINCE v WYATT; *sub nom.* WYATT v VINCE, [2013] EWCA Civ 495, [2013] 1 W.L.R. 3525, Thorpe, L.J., CA (Civ Div).

1307. Financial remedies–Disclosure–Use in family proceedings of evidence given in criminal proceedings and obtained pursuant to letters of request–Need for consent of appropriate overseas authority

[Crime (International Co-operation) Act 2003 (c.32) s.7, s.9(2); Criminal Justice (International Co-operation) Act 1990 (c.5) s.3(7).]

The appellant CPS and secretary of state appealed against a decision requiring the CPS to disclose to the first respondent (W) various documents which it had obtained from foreign states pursuant to letters of request. W had divorced the second respondent (H) and applied for financial remedy. A consent order was made for H to pay a lump sum. W believed that H had concealed his assets and commenced proceedings in the Family Division to set aside the consent order. H had been convicted of money-laundering and conspiracy to defraud and sentenced to 10 years' imprisonment. The evidence given in the criminal proceedings against H included evidence which had been obtained by the CPS pursuant to requests under the Crime (International Co-operation) Act 2003 s.7. W applied to the Family Division for disclosure by the CPS of the papers in the criminal proceedings. Section 9(2) of the Act provided that evidence obtained pursuant to a request for assistance under s.7 could not, without the consent of the appropriate overseas authority, be used for any purpose other than that specified in the request. The judge held that he was bound by the decision in *BOC Ltd v Instrument Technology Ltd* [2001] EWCA Civ 854, [2002] Q.B. 537, [2001] C.L.Y. 390 that the predecessor of s.9(2), the Criminal Justice (International Co-operation) Act 1990 s.3(7), implicitly prohibited the use of evidence obtained under a letter of request in criminal proceedings, other than the criminal proceedings specified in the letter of request, but did not prohibit its use in civil proceedings. He therefore had a discretion whether or not to order disclosure, which he exercised in favour of W on the grounds that the material was necessary for the fair disposal of her application. The appellants submitted that the *BOC* decision was plainly wrong and given per incuriam.

Held: Appeal allowed. (1) The decision in *BOC* was plainly wrong as a matter of ordinary statutory interpretation. Section 3(7) of the 1990 Act, which was in materially the same terms as s.9(2) of the 2003 Act, was subject to a single express exception, namely that it did not apply if the requested authority consented to the wider use of the evidence. There was no justification for interpreting the prohibition as not extending to civil proceedings or for the implication of a different restriction (see paras 25-28 of judgment). (2) The decision in *BOC* was reached per incuriam and was therefore not binding, *BOC* not followed, *Young v Bristol Aeroplane Co Ltd* [1944] K.B. 718 applied, *Morelle v Wakeling* [1955] 2 Q.B. 379, [1955] C.L.Y. 351 and *Davis v Johnson* [1979] A.C. 264, [1978] C.L.Y. 1590 considered. The court had failed to have regard to the well-established principle that Parliament was presumed to legislate in conformity with the United Kingdom's international obligations, *R. v Lyons (Isidore Jack) (No.3)* [2002] UKHL 44, [2003] 1 A.C. 976, [2002] C.L.Y. 844 and *Assange v Sweden* [2012] UKSC 22, [2012] 2 A.C. 471, [2012] C.L.Y. 1284 applied. The relevant legislation should have been interpreted by the court in conformity with the UK's international undertakings that, absent the consent of the requested state, material obtained for the purpose of specified criminal investigations and proceedings would be used only for that purpose. No reference was made by the court to that principle of statutory interpretation (paras 29-35). (3) The effect of s.9(2) was that there was a statutory prohibition on the use of evidence for any purpose other than that specified in the request without the consent of the requested authority. The prohibition applied in other criminal investigations and proceedings and in civil proceedings of any description (para.36). (4) Section 9(2) prohibited the use of documents obtained as a result of the letters of request, even where they had been adduced in evidence in open court, *R. v Gooch (Malcolm George) (No.2)* [1999] 1 Cr. App. R. (S.) 283, [1998] C.L.Y. 1178 applied. Although W could not adduce the documents, she could use the evidence adduced in open court as a springboard for conducting her own enquiries, with a view to obtaining other evidence on which she could rely without contravening s.9(2) (paras 40-41).

CROWN PROSECUTION SERVICE v GOHIL; *sub nom.* GOHIL v GOHIL, [2012] EWCA Civ 1550, [2013] Fam. 276, Lord Dyson (M.R.), CA (Civ Div).

1308. Financial remedies–Lump sum payments–Mother seeking lump sum under Sch.1 Children Act 1989 following clean break

[Children Act 1989 (c.41) Sch.1.]

The applicant mother (M) brought an application against the respondent father (F) under the Children Act 1989 Sch.1. The parties had separated in 2007 after a seven-year marriage. They had one child (C), who was now eight years old. In 2007, a consent order was made in ancillary-relief proceedings; M received the net proceeds of sale of the former matrimonial home, in the sum of £950,000, on a clean-break basis, and F agreed to pay periodical payments for C's benefit of £15,000 per year together with her school fees. Owing to a change in his employment and a resulting drop in his income, F approached the Child Support Agency in 2009. Assessments were made, the latest of which required him to pay the sum of £8,468 per year for C's benefit. M's statement revealed that had bought a two-bedroom flat, which was worth £572,500 mortgage-free, that she had cash of £30,000 and that she had paid legal fees of £177,160.

Held: Application refused. It was now accepted that the court did not have jurisdiction to make a periodical payments order in favour of C, given that that aspect was now exclusively dealt with by the Child Support Agency. However, M was also claiming a lump sum, both in relation to housing provision and to provide a car for C. Any provision for cars would have been either encompassed in the lump sum of £950,000 which M accepted on a clean-break basis or incorporated in the maintenance provision ordered in C's favour. It followed either that the car was covered by the clean break, in which case there could be no further order, or that it was encompassed by the periodical payments, in which case it was barred by the Child Support Agency's jurisdiction. The court had jurisdiction to consider awarding a further lump sum payment under Sch.1 even where there had been a clean break in divorce proceedings, *MB v KB* [2007] EWHC 789 (Fam), [2007] 2 F.L.R. 586, [2007] C.L.Y. 1685 applied. However, the circumstances would have to be exceptional. When two parties entered into an ancillary-relief clean-break order, they were putting behind them their financial disputes. A mother would have to overcome a very high hurdle to bring a further application for financial provision by way of housing. If it was to occur, it would of course be for a settlement of property order; she could not claim an outright lump sum, given the authorities. So what M would be asking would be for F to provide capital on a trust basis that would return to him once C had completed her full-time education or attained majority. It was impossible to see how a mother who had a mortgage-free property worth £572,500 could bring a claim against a father for capital provision for housing when there had been a clean break which provided her with a capital sum for housing for herself and C. Her application was misconceived and would be dismissed (see paras 11-15 of judgment).

PK v BC (FINANCIAL REMEDIES: SCHEDULE I), [2012] EWHC 1382 (Fam), [2012] 2 F.L.R. 1426, Moor, J., Fam Div.

1309. Financial remedies–Matrimonial property–Allegations of placing matrimonial assets beyond powers of court–Claim based on doctrine of add-back–Withdrawal of claim not giving rise to estoppel

[Matrimonial Causes Act 1973 (c.18) s.37.]

The court had to determine preliminary issues in relation to res judicata and the doctrine of add-back for the purposes of financial remedy proceedings between the petitioner wife (W) and the respondent husband (H). H owned a successful investment management company (X). In 2006, an investigation began into X's affairs following allegations of market abuse. H entered into an agreement with a friend (N) under which N agreed to buy shares in a fund for £7,766,959. Under that agreement, H was to guarantee any losses arising from a decrease in the value of the fund apart from £100,000. According to N and H, the agreement was signed in March 2008. Later that month, H received notice that the investigation was complete and a complaint would be filed against X. Litigation ensued and the complaint was found partly proved. In 2012, X went into administration. The value of N's funds collapsed and he sued H under the agreement. H did not defend the claim and judgment was entered in default in the sum of £6,540,767. H's position was that that judgment debt had to be satisfied out of the family assets. W alleged that the agreement had not been entered into in 2008, but in 2010, after the breakdown of the marriage. She also alleged that the agreement was a sham designed to remove the great majority of their assets from the powers of the court. W applied to set aside the default judgment. That application was still pending at the time of the instant hearing. In October 2012, N had some of his shares compulsorily redeemed, giving him £2,326,910. Under a compromise agreement between H, W and N, N agreed to receive £3,826,640 in respect of his judgment debt and sell his remaining shares to H, who would put them in the joint names of himself and W. As a result, the loss to H and W was reduced from £7,302,005 to somewhere between £2,258,931 and £3,826,640, depending on the true value of N's unredeemed shares. W contended that the loss should be attributed to H under the "add-back" doctrine at the final hearing. H contended that W should be debarred from arguing that the agreement was formed after the breakdown of the marriage on the basis of res judicata, and also because of an order that would be entered as a term of the compromise dismissing her application to set the default judgment aside.

Held: Preliminary issues determined. (1) The asserted fact that the agreement was formed in 2008 was not a cardinal fact without which the judgment in default could not stand. The contract was equally valid whether it was executed in 2008 or 2010. N's rights under it were equally valid on either date, and the impact of H's failure to comply with his obligations was the same whenever it was formed. The withdrawal by W of her claim to set aside N's default judgment, by means of a consent order not yet made, did not give rise to estoppel in proceedings for a financial remedy between her and H. It could not seriously be argued that H would suffer abusive harassment if W were allowed to pursue her contention in the financial remedy proceedings as to the date of formation of the agreement because the overall compromise that had been reached provided for a dismissal by consent of W's claim for a set-aside against N. Moreover, H had been a party to that compromise agreement and the consent order embodying it had specifically recorded W's contentions. On a merits-based view, the compromise was hugely beneficial to H as well as W, *Johnson v Gore Wood & Co (No.1)* [2002] 2 A.C. 1, [2001] C.L.Y. 410 followed. It followed that W was not estopped from seeking a finding as to the date on which the agreement was formed at the final trial in support of her add-back argument (see paras 25, 27, 29-30 of judgment). (2) When considering the doctrine of add-back pursuant to the Matrimonial Causes Act 1973 s.37, the first key function of the court was to establish with more or less precision the size of the pool in respect of which the sharing principle would be applied, *White*

(Pamela) v White (Martin) [2001] 1 A.C. 596, [2000] C.L.Y. 2530 and *Miller v Miller* [2006] UKHL 24, [2006] 2 A.C. 618, [2006] C.L.Y. 1629 followed, *Scallon v Scallon* [1990] 1 F.L.R. 194, [1990] C.L.Y. 2296 considered. It was likely that H had entered into the agreement with N wantonly and that H would dispute that allegation; however, those arguments would have to be tested at trial. The court would not decide on a proleptic basis that W's arguments of financial misconduct had no realistic prospect of success. Moreover, when entering into the compromise W never intended to abandon the issue of when the agreement was made, *Spicer v Tuli* [2012] EWCA Civ 845, [2012] 1 W.L.R. 3088 and *Ako v Rothschild Asset Management Ltd* [2002] EWCA Civ 236, [2002] 2 All E.R. 693, [2002] C.L.Y. 1309 followed (paras 32-33, 36-40).

BP v KP (FINANCIAL REMEDY PROCEEDINGS: RES JUDICATA), [2012] EWHC 2995 (Fam), [2013] 1 F.L.R. 1310, Mostyn, J., Fam Div.

1310. Financial remedies–Matrimonial property–Matrimonial assets–Wife's contribution to family business

[Matrimonial Causes Act 1973 (c.18) s.25(2).]

The applicant wife (W) applied for financial remedy orders on dissolution of marriage and the respondent husband (H) resisted the application in terms of quantum and form sought. W and H had separated when H's relationship with another woman came to light. They had two grown up children. W was subject to an individual voluntary arrangement and had significant debt attributable to the closure of her solicitor's practice. She lived in the heavily mortgaged former matrimonial home and was dependent on maintenance. She had minimal personal assets but hoped to recover a not insubstantial sum in ongoing contentious litigation. H's financial position was secure. He was the majority shareholder in a company (Z) from which he was able to draw significant earnings. Z had been incorporated shortly after H and W married and both H and W had been heavily involved in its inception and subsequent growth. There was no real dispute as to valuation of assets and the notional pot amounted to approximately £7.65million net. W sought the transfer of all real property forming or associated with the former matrimonial home, ultimately free of mortgage, a lump sum payment of £1.3million within 28 days, the transfer of shares to the value of £3million within 28 days, the assignment of H's interest in the joint life endowment policy and ongoing periodical payments thereafter in a sum equivalent to £8,333 per month less any dividends and net salary that she might from time to time receive from Z during their joint lives subject to further review, mortgage repayments and costs. H argued that the court should depart from the principle of equality when making its financial orders and that whatever quantum the court determined to be fair and appropriate should not include any shareholding in Z. H sought the transfer of all real property forming or associated with the former matrimonial home, ultimately free of mortgage, a lump sum payment of £1million within 3 months, loan notes to secure further payment of £800,000 within 4 years, the assignment of his interest in a joint life endowment policy and periodical payments in the interim to include mortgage repayments and a sum equivalent to £24,000 per annum less any income generated by interest payable on the loan notes for a limited term.

Held: Application granted. (1) The exercise of judicial discretion had to seek to achieve a fair outcome in the particular circumstances of the case paying due regard to the Matrimonial Causes Act 1973 s.25(2) as interpreted in *Miller v Miller* [2006] UKHL 24, [2006] 2 A.C. 618, [2006] C.L.Y. 1629 and *Charman v Charman* [2007] EWCA Civ 503, [2007] 1 F.L.R. 1246, [2007] C.L.Y. 1691, *Miller* and *Charman* applied. Where there was an issue of fact the court preferred W's evidence. W's debts were not due to her negligence, recklessness or misfeasance and she had had little option but to apply for an IVA. Z was a matrimonial asset. H would be unlikely to have succeeded in the same or in any degree without W's positive contribution as legal and business adviser, bank guarantor and provider of the family bankroll during the early years of their marriage and business formation. It was W's property that was sold and traded up into the matrimonial home. W was far more than a sleeping partner in H's business ventures and her early contributions outmatched those of H. Z was the sole source of financial provision for the family and W had been an equal driving force in Z with H. After the breakdown of the marriage Z had merely achieved its latent potential accrued during the course of the marriage. However, save as a last resort, parity should not be achieved by transfer of shares in Z to W (see paras 14,19, 29, 41,44, 50 of judgment). (2) H would transfer to W his legal and beneficial interest in the former matrimonial home, accompanying land and endowment policy. H would pay to W a lump sum of £4million, £1.25million of which should be paid within 28 days. The remainder would be deferred in payment on set dates as set by the court, with £1.25million to be paid by December 31, 2013 or on sale of H's shares whichever was the sooner from which W would redeem the mortgage on the former home. The remaining £1.5million would be paid on or before December 31, 2015 or on the sale of H's shares whichever was soonest. In the interim H would pay periodical payments of £12,000 per month until payment of the first £1.25million and thereafter £7,500 per month until further order together with a sum equal to the mortgage interest repayments in relation to the former matrimonial home until the mortgage was redeemed from the second lump payment. W would give credit for any interest on the loan notes to which she would otherwise be entitled and one half of any net monies she recovered as the result of outstanding litigation. There was a clean break as to capital (para.56).

R v R (FINANCIAL REMEDIES); *sub nom.* R v R (FINANCIAL ORDERS: CONTRIBUTIONS), [2012] EWHC 2390 (Fam), [2013] 1 F.L.R. 106, Macur, J., Fam Div.

1311. Foster care–Mothers–Judge adjourning care proceedings and ordering interim mother and baby foster placement–Whether judge entitled to make orders

The appellant local authority appealed against a judge's orders by which he adjourned care proceedings in respect of a child (H) and made an interim placement order placing H and his mother (M) with foster carers. The local authority had instituted care proceedings within days of H's birth given M's parenting history. It arranged for M and H to be put in a mother and baby foster placement with foster carers (F). M made good progress during the placement, but the local authority's assessment concluded that M's parenting had not improved enough such that H should be put in her independent care. M and H were moved to another mother and baby foster placement. M did not flourish at the placement and was required to leave, and H remained in the placement alone. M's relationship with F was very positive, which the judge took into account when considering the appropriate course. The judge rejected the local authority's argument that care and placement orders should be made, but instead adjourned the care proceedings for three months and made an interim supervision order stipulating that M and H be placed with F. The judge said that he contemplated that M and H would move into F's home for at least three months, and if after that time M was not assessed to be a serious carer, she would be summarily ruled out. The local authority submitted that the judge had failed to take full account of the limited prospects of success of M and H's placement with F and the impact that the delay in deciding on H's permanent placement would have on H's welfare.

Held: Appeal dismissed. There was no doubt that the judge had exposed H to a degree of risk in making his orders, but the appropriate question was whether the judge's actions were justified and within the limits of the discretion afforded to him. The judge's chosen approach was opposed by most of the professional evidence. If the judge had adopted the local authority's preferred approach and granted care and placement orders, H would have lost the prospect of living with his biological family but would have gained the opportunity of a permanent placement with an adoptive family. When making the orders the judge had envisaged that H would have further opportunity to stay with M, and F's offer to provide a network of safety and support allowed M the chance to further develop her parenting skills for H's welfare. The judge had it in mind that the placement with F could go wrong, as was evidenced by his warning that M would be ruled out as a serious carer if the placement did not succeed. He also had in mind that in directing H's move to F's home from his current foster carers, he was definitely imposing one move on H and potentially more if the placement did not succeed. However, the judge had immense experience and had decided with his eyes wide open to do something that was out of the ordinary. It would have been wrong if the law meant that he was not able to deal with individual cases on an individual basis. He was aware of the orders' potential adverse consequences for H, but in the context of the options open to him, the judge's approach was one that he was entitled to take in advancing H's welfare. Although the order was unusual, it was logical, humane and carefully considered, and it was based on the personal qualities of those in whom he reposed his trust, namely F and M.

H (A CHILD) (CARE PROCEEDINGS: FOSTER CARE PLACEMENT FOR MOTHER AND BABY), *Re*, [2012] EWCA Civ 1700, [2013] 1 F.L.R. 1445, Thorpe, L.J., CA (Civ Div).

1312. International child abduction–Habitual residence–Application for return of child from Lebanon–Child not habitually resident in UK–Court's refusal to exercise inherent jurisdiction

[Family Law Act 1986 (c.55); Regulation 2201/2003.]

The appellant mother (M) appealed against a decision of the High Court refusing to exercise its inherent jurisdiction to order the return of her daughter (T) from Lebanon. The respondent father (F) was born in Lebanon but had British citizenship and longstanding ties with the United Kingdom. M was Thai. T was born overseas in 2007. In 2009 M, F and T settled in the United Kingdom. T was then habitually resident in the UK. She had Thai and British nationality. In December 2009 F and M married and both had parental responsibility for T. A few months later F abducted T to Lebanon. M applied to the High Court to act under its inherent jurisdiction to order T's return from Lebanon and further to accept jurisdiction to make welfare decisions. The judge declined to order T's return, finding that at the date of issue of M's proceedings T was habitually resident in Lebanon, and he further declined to exercise the inherent jurisdiction over T on welfare grounds, on the basis that any disputes should be resolved in the courts in Lebanon. M appealed against the judge's refusal to exercise the court's inherent jurisdiction but not against the finding on habitual residence. M, relying on the decision in *B (A Child) (Forced Marriage: Wardship: Jurisdiction), Re* [2008] EWHC 1436 (Fam), [2008] 2 F.L.R. 1624, [2009] C.L.Y. 1569, submitted that the court should exercise its inherent jurisdiction to protect T.

Held: Appeal dismissed. It was well settled that the court's jurisdiction under either Regulation 2201/2003 or the Family Law Act 1986 was limited to cases where the child was habitually resident or physically present in England and Wales. The instant case was very far removed from the dire circumstances of the child in *B (A Child)*, *B (A Child)* distinguished. The situation could well be difficult for M, but it was not outside the circumstances that might be expected in an international family situation. Moreover, the problems were M's, not T's; if T were facing great difficulties that could take the case to the extreme needed for the court to exercise its inherent jurisdiction. It would be good for T to have contact with both her parents. On ordinary welfare grounds, it was to T's detriment that she was not seeing M. But the inherent jurisdiction did not come into the equation. Therefore it was not necessary to look afresh at the matters before the judge (see paras 17, 29-32 of judgment).

N (A CHILD) (ABDUCTION: APPEAL), *Re*, [2012] EWCA Civ 1086, [2013] 1 F.L.R. 457, Thorpe, L.J., CA (Civ Div).

1313. International child abduction–Habitual residence–Wrongful removal or retention–Whether children habitually resident in Latvia or England–Whether parental consent to removal by other parent

[Hague Convention on the Civil Aspects of International Child Abduction 1980.]

The applicant father (F) applied pursuant to the Hague Convention on the Civil Aspects of International Child Abduction 1980 for the return of his two children (S and K) to Latvia from whence they had been taken by their mother (M) to the United Kingdom. M and F were Latvian nationals. S, aged five, and K, aged four, were born there while their parents were cohabiting. M and F came to the United Kingdom to work, leaving S and K with grandparents. M brought them to the UK where they lived with their parents. Six months later M and F returned to Latvia and bought a property in M's name. On other visits they refurbished it, and M registered the children for kindergarten. The parents' relationship broke down, they took the children to Latvia to live with F's aunt, in whose favour M executed a power of attorney to last one year, and F obtained an order from the Orphans' Court for the placement. M and F returned to the UK separately to work. The children were registered with a general practitioner in Latvia and went to school. Months later F returned to Latvia and two days later so did M, who wanted to take the children back to England. The Orphans' Court said it would make an order for residence and custody if the parents could not agree. In a handwritten agreement signed by each the parents agreed that M would take K and F would take S, and in six month's time, if F had not bought a flat in Latvia, then S would go to England with M. F gave M K's birth certificate and passport. M took K to England, though F's case was that he did not consent to the removal, but he took no further action. He returned to England and worked. S stayed with the aunt. After six months M went to Latvia with K, revoked the power of attorney, and removed S with the help of the police. F objected. He went to Latvia, took a job and lived with the aunt. He applied for custody of the children and a hearing was pending. F applied under the Hague Convention for the children's return. M's case was that placement with the aunt was temporary and that F, by failing to get a flat in Latvia had consented to her bringing them to England. The issues were whether (i) the children were habitually resident in Latvia when they were removed; (ii) F consented to their moving from Latvia to England.

Held: Application granted in part. (1) The existence of habitual residence was a matter of fact. The words carried their natural and ordinary meaning, *J (A Minor) (Abduction: Custody Rights), Re* [1990] 2 A.C. 562, [1990] C.L.Y. 3151. It could mean being resident for a settled purpose that might be of short duration or conditional on future events, *P-J (Children) (Abduction: Habitual Residence: Consent), Re* [2009] EWCA Civ 588, [2010] 1 W.L.R. 1237, [2009] C.L.Y. 1541 applied. Obiter remarks in *Al-H (Rashid) v F (Sara)* [2001] EWCA Civ 186, [2001] 1 F.L.R. 951, [2001] C.L.Y. 2676 were correct: habitual residence could be acquired, even if the purpose of the move was intended to be fulfilled within a comparatively short time, or if the move was on a trial basis, *Al-H* considered. The parents came to England to work, intending to stay for a few years only. They became habitually resident as they stayed for settled purposes as part of regular life for the time being, *H-K (Children) (Habitual Residence), Re* [2011] EWCA Civ 1100, [2012] 1 F.L.R. 436, [2012] C.L.Y. 1371 applied. When the children were brought over, their habitual residence moved from Latvia to England. The habitual residence of young children living as a family was the same as that of their parents. However, the parents' intention was to educate them in Latvia, so they bought a flat there in M's name and registered the children in a local kindergarten. When their relationship broke down and they separated, if only on a trial basis, they returned the children to Latvia to stay with the aunt. The children then became habitually resident in Latvia, as evidenced by the arrangement with the aunt; the power of attorney, which declared that M was resident in Latvia; the Orphans' Court decisions; the registration with a general practitioner and a school (see paras 20-21, 26-28, 32 of judgment). (2) The parents' manuscript agreement was clear and unequivocal. F agreed freely and stuck to it for the six months. M's defence of consent in regard to K succeeded. However, it did not in regard to S. Although F had not acquired accommodation as agreed, M knew that he had withdrawn his consent by the time S was removed, *P-J* applied. M's behaviour was clandestine. She did not have the court's permission to remove S to Latvia, and it had told her earlier that she needed F's permission or a court order. F had rights of custody for which he applied while M was still in Latvia, and he applied pursuant to the Convention immediately after S's removal. Therefore, S's removal was wrongful (paras 22-23, 33, 35-37).

VK v JV (ABDUCTION: CONSENT), [2012] EWHC 4033 (Fam), [2013] 2 F.L.R. 237, Moor, J., Fam Div.

1314. International child abduction–Registration of foreign judgments–Registration of foreign judgments–Order for residence or other parental responsibility made by court of another Member State–Appropriate procedure for seeking child's return

[Senior Courts Act 1981 (c.54) s.49(2); Family Procedure Rules 2010 (SI 2010/2955) r.1.1 (2)(e), r.1.1 (2)(d), r.31.8; Regulation 2201/2003 Art.28; Hague Convention on the Civil Aspects of International Child Abduction 1980.]

The applicant father (F) applied for an order under the Hague Convention 1980 requiring the respondent mother (M) to return three children of the family to France. F's application was issued on May 8, 2012; he alleged that the children had been wrongfully retained in this country from April 23, M having agreed that they would be returned to France following a two-week holiday here. On April 12, a French court had made an order that the children should reside with F and have contact with M. F did not apply for the registration of the French court's order under Regulation 2201/2003. In her defence to F's application, M asserted that: the children had never become habitually resident in France; F had consented to their removal, having accepted that the older children would return to live in England when school places became available; the oldest child objected to returning to France; she had been the children's primary carer for most of their lives.

Held: Application adjourned. It would be appropriate to decline to adjudicate on F's application and to adjourn it, given: the primacy of the French court in making the welfare adjudication; the precedence of Regulation 2201/2003 over the 1980 Convention; the clear route laid down in the Regulation for recognition and enforcement of the French court's order, which would only be withheld in the most exceptional circumstances; the probability that, were the court to find M's defences proved, that decision would soon be overturned under Regulation 2201/2003; the terms of the overriding objective in the Family Procedure Rules 2010 r.1.1 (2)(d) and r.1.1 (2)(e); the terms of the Senior Courts Act 1981 s.49(2). The following steps should be taken: F should apply, as soon as legal aid could be arranged, for registration of the French court's order under art.28(1) of Regulation 2201/2003 and r.31.8 of the 2010 Rules; the court would invite the Senior District Judge to deal with the application personally as soon as it was lodged; a booking should be made for an apprehended appeal by M against registration. Where a residence or other relevant parental responsibility order had been made in a fellow Member State, the route of registration/appeal in Regulation 2201/2003 should normally be adopted. The cost to the taxpayer and the demands on court time caused by applications under the 1980 Convention were heavy indeed. The time and money expended on an application like this one was likely to be completely wasted (see paras 16-17 of judgment).

JRG v EB (ABDUCTION: BRUSSELS II REVISED), [2012] EWHC 1863 (Fam), [2013] 1 F.L.R. 203, Mostyn, J., Fam Div.

1315. International child abduction–Return orders–Children removed from Sweden to England by mother–Mother relying on defence of consent

[Hague Convention on the Civil Aspects of International Child Abduction 1980.]

The applicant father (F) applied for an order under the Hague Convention on the Civil Aspects of International Child Abduction 1980 that his two children, who were aged four and two, should be returned to Sweden, where they had been habitually resident. F was Swedish, while the respondent mother (M) was English. They moved to Sweden before the children were born. M became unhappy living there and suffered bouts of depression together with anxiety attacks. In December 2006, M and F executed an agreement setting out the terms of the living arrangements of any children that they might have should M decide to leave Sweden. It was stated that she did not anticipate living there on a permanent basis. Under the agreement, F gave "all permissions necessary to enable [M] and the offspring to leave Sweden whether temporarily or permanently at any time and for any reason whatsoever". It was M's case that in many subsequent conversations F reiterated his agreement that he would allow her and the children to leave Sweden to go to England whenever she wanted to do so. In February 2011, F signed a document whereby he consented to the children travelling with M "to anywhere in the world indefinitely without limitation either in place or time whatsoever". In March 2011, he signed a document whereby he consented to the children travelling with M "to anywhere in the world whether on a temporary or permanent basis without limitation either in place or time whatsoever". In June 2011, M travelled with the children to England, intending to return to Sweden at the end of the summer. However, in July she decided to stay in England with the children, and she began divorce proceedings against F. She and the children had remained in England ever since. The issues were (i) whether F had given his consent to the permanent removal of the children from Sweden; (ii) if he had not given such consent, whether he had subsequently acquiesced in the retention of the children in England; (iii) if the answer to either of those questions was yes, how the court should exercise its discretion.

Held: Application refused. (1) The authorities showed, among other things, that consent to the removal of a child had to be clear and unequivocal, that consent was not to be viewed in the context of or governed by the law of contract and that it could therefore be withdrawn at any time before actual removal, *P-J (Children) (Abduction: Habitual Residence: Consent), Re* [2009] EWCA Civ 588, [2010] 1 W.L.R. 1237, [2009] C.L.Y. 1541, *K (Abduction: Consent), Re* [1997] 2 F.L.R. 212, [1997] C.L.Y. 389 and *L (Abduction: Future Consent), Re* [2007] EWHC 2181 (Fam), [2008] 1 F.L.R. 914, [2008] C.L.Y. 1466 applied. The terms of the 2006 agreement were clear and unequivocal. Further, F had never withdrawn his consent; on the contrary, he reaffirmed it on a number of occasions, both in oral conversations and in the documents signed by him in February and March 2011. Moreover, the circumstances of M's trip to England in June 2011 could not be interpreted as suspending or modifying that clear and unequivocal consent in any way. Accordingly, F had given his consent to the children's removal (see paras 31-32, 35 of judgment). (2) It was strictly unnecessary to consider the alternative defence of acquiescence. However, it was appropriate to point out that there was no evidence from which the court could conclude either that F's subjective intention was to acquiesce in the children's removal or that there was any behaviour of the type which would lead M to conclude that he was not asserting his rights. Accordingly, had the consent defence not been made out, the defence of acquiescence would not have succeeded (para.36). (3) The court had to have regard to the importance of observing agreements entered into by parties to a marriage. In this case, it was a fundamental feature of the marriage, agreed to before the children were born, and fully understood by both these intelligent adults, that if M decided to leave Sweden at any point she would be able to take the children with her. The court should therefore exercise its discretion by refusing to order the return of the children to Sweden (para.40).

A v T (ABDUCTION: CONSENT); *sub nom.* A v T (RELOCATION: CONSENT), [2011] EWHC 3882 (Fam), [2012] 2 F.L.R. 1333, Baker, J., Fam Div.

1316. International child abduction–Return orders–Lawful removal from country of habitual residence–Setting aside of return order

[Hague Convention on the Civil Aspects of International Child Abduction 1980 Art.3, Art.18.]

The appellant father (F) appealed against a decision that he was not entitled to a return order in relation to his child (K) who had been brought to the United Kingdom from the United States by the respondent mother (M). F and M had married in the US and had K in 2006. In 2008 F petitioned for divorce and in July 2008 M brought K to the UK where she remained until March 2010. A final order in March 2010 in the US divorce and custody proceedings granted F custody of K and the exclusive right to designate his place of residence. M issued an application for a return order under the Hague Convention on the Civil Aspects of International Child Abduction 1980 on the basis that K was habitually resident in the UK by March 2010 and F had wrongfully retained K in the US. The resulting order required F to deliver K to M immediately. F appealed and M sought the dismissal of F's appeal on the basis that it was academic, as she had established K's residence in the UK even before the appeal was launched. The US Court of Appeal allowed F's appeal but M refused to return K. M's failure in the US Supreme Court and F's failure to obtain a return order from the UK court left the orders of the US and UK courts in conflict. F submitted that (1) the judge was wrong in law as K's US habitual residence was not lost during the appeal process; (2) M's removal of K to the UK was clearly wrongful once the appellate decision removed its lawfulness and F held rights of custody pursuant to the orders of the US court and was merely exercising those rights; (3) the judge failed to give proper weight to the US court orders and proceeded on the basis of K's return in the abstract whilst F had offered a range of protective undertakings that would have allowed M to return with K to create a regime of shared care in the US, at least during the currency of any proceedings then issued by M.

Held: Appeal dismissed. (1) There was no distinction to be drawn between the test according to domestic law, the test expounded by the Court of Justice of the European Union in *Proceedings Brought by A (C-523/07)* [2010] Fam. 42, [2009] C.L.Y. 1552 and *Mercredi v Chaffe (C-497/10 PPU)* [2012] Fam. 22, [2011] C.L.Y. 1429 and the autonomous law of the Convention. The application of the law to the facts did not necessitate a finding that K did not lose his habitual residence in the US. K's departure from the US was a lawful removal pursuant to the order of the Court of Competent Jurisdiction and, albeit acting under compulsion, F had co-operated in K's departure. K had been obviously resident in UK jurisdiction for an extended period and in all probability had acquired habitual residence by the date of the filing of F's appeal. It was artificial, indeed almost fanciful, to label his residence in the UK as conditional upon the outcome of F's appeal and therefore transient (see paras 48-51 of judgment). (2) It was artificial to assert that the effect of the appellate decision was to render a lawful removal wrongful and that F was exercising rights of custody prior to the issue of his Convention application and/or at the date of trial. The language of art.3 of the Convention did not support that interpretation. The Convention was never foreseen or intended to be used in the instant circumstances. Once there had been a lawful departure, annulled 12 months later by a successful appeal, only art.18 provided a remedy for the successful appellant (para.52). (3) Ideally the judge would have referred to the protective undertakings and the extent to which they would have resulted in M and K returning together. However it must be doubted whether any protective undertakings would have cleared the obvious impediments. There was insufficient evidence to allow any welfare conclusion to be drawn. Whether a case required further investigation, further evidence or more expertise was essentially one for the discretion of the trial judge who bore the responsibility for the outcome of a welfare based judgment (paras 54-55).

DL v EL (HAGUE ABDUCTION CONVENTION: EFFECT OF REVERSAL OF RETURN ORDER ON APPEAL); *sub nom.* L (A CHILD) (CUSTODY: HABITUAL RESIDENCE), RE; KL (A CHILD) (ABDUCTION: HABITUAL RESIDENCE: INHERENT JURISDICTION), *Re*, [2013] EWCA Civ 865, [2013] 3 F.C.R. 69, Thorpe, L.J., CA (Civ Div).

1317. International child abduction–Return orders–Return orders–Father abducting children from Australia–Reliance on risk arising from employment as undercover police officer

[Hague Convention on the Civil Aspects of International Child Abduction 1980.]

The applicant mother (M) sought the summary return to Australia of her three children, who were aged between 7 and 13. M and the first respondent father (F) were British nationals who had relocated to Australia. The marriage having run into difficulties, F abducted the children and took them to the United Kingdom. M, too, had now returned to the UK. F put forward two defences to M's application. First, a summary return would place the children at grave risk of harm, or otherwise put them in an intolerable situation, because he had been employed as an undercover police officer for many years and, after being relocated in Australia a few years previously, circumstances had arisen which rendered it unsafe for him or his family to return to Australia, at least until extensive further work had been carried out by the UK police force which had employed him and its Australian counterpart, including a detailed and thorough risk assessment. The family had moved to Australia with the assistance of the F's police-force employer. Before they left, the police force, F and M signed a memorandum of understanding covering detailed arrangements about the relocation placement. After they left, the officer (O) responsible for managing F continued to liaise with them. His view was that, as a result of the conduct of both M and F, the family's safety in Australia had been compromised. F's second defence was that the oldest child (X) objected to being returned to Australia; in the light of that objection, the court should exercise its discretion not to return him; further, to return the two younger children without their older brother would place them in an intolerable situation, so that the court should refuse to order their return. M accepted that the children should not be separated.

Held: Application refused. (1) F's first defence was made out. It had the strong support of the UK police force which had employed him. O's evidence should be accepted. He had said that F was at a particularly high risk as a result of his work as an undercover officer, given the extent of that work and his successful involvement in a number of serious operations against organised crime. Before the family could safely return to Australia, the agreement of the Australian Government was needed and it was by no means clear that such agreement would be forthcoming. A careful reappraisal of the risk was necessary by the UK police force and its Australian counterpart, and there would be a period of several months when the Australian court and authorities would not be able to put in place safety measures, even on an interim basis. To return the children to Australia would put them in an intolerable situation where the risk of harm could not be safely or effectively understood or managed (see paras 24, 31, 33, 35 of judgment). (2) F's second defence was also established. He had behaved in a highly manipulative way in an attempt to influence both M and the children. Further, he had arranged the abduction in a blatant and disgraceful way. There was also the very important matter of the policy considerations underpinning the Hague Convention on the Civil Aspects of International Child Abduction 1980, namely to protect children from the harmful effects of a wrongful removal by ensuring their proper return to the state of their habitual residence. On the other hand, X was a mature and articulate child who had expressed a clear and unequivocal objection to returning to Australia. He was also of an age and a degree of maturity at which it was appropriate to take account of his views. Further, there were welfare considerations which militated in favour of the court's exercising its discretion not to order the children's return. Among other things, the children had been in the UK for six months and had to an extent settled down in a pattern of shared care established by M and F. X had started at school in England and had settled there. Moreover, it might take as long as a year before a safe return could be effected to Australia, if indeed it could be effected at all (paras 48-49, 51, 54-56).

A (MINORS), *Re*; *sub nom.* X v Y, [2012] EWHC 2838 (Fam), [2013] 1 F.L.R. 1277, Baker, J., Fam Div.

1318. International child abduction–Undertakings–Undertakings given as protective measures for returning abductor and child–Whether undertakings capable of recognition under art.23 Hague Convention on Parental Responsibility and Child Protection 1996

[Regulation 2201/2003 Art.11 (4); Convention on Jurisdiction, Applicable Law, Recognition, Enforcement and Co-operation in Respect of Parental Responsibility and Measures for the Protection of Children (Hague XXXIV) 1996 Art.23, Art.24, Art.26, Art.28; Hague Convention on the Civil Aspects of International Child Abduction 1980 Art.13(b).]

The appellant mother (M) appealed against a decision that undertakings given by the respondent father (F) in child abduction proceedings amounted to "protective measures" pursuant to Regulation 2201/2003 art.11 (4). M and F were Cypriot and the parents of a four-year-old girl (X). When M removed her from Cyprus to England, F applied for a return order under the Hague Convention on the Civil Aspects of International Child Abduction 1980. M advanced a defence under art.13(b) of the Convention asserting that, if returned, she and X were at risk from domestic violence or abuse by F. The judge considered those allegations highly contentious and held that they should be investigated by a Cypriot court. She ordered X's return subject to protective measures under art.11 (4) of the Regulation. A raft of protective measures were expressed in an undertaking given by F. An issue arose between the parties as to the form of the order. F drafted an order on the basis that undertakings would effectively be as valid in Cyprus as in the United Kingdom, pursuant to the Hague Convention on Parental Responsibility and Child Protection 1996 art.23, which had come into force in the UK in November 2012, shortly before the hearing. The judge made an order in that form. M submitted that protection by way of undertaking was ineffective. She contended that the useful machinery of the 1996 Convention, by which measures taken in one contracting state were to be recognised and enforced in all contracting states, was only effective if the protective measures were expressed by the state ordering a child's return in the form of a concrete order.

Held: Appeal dismissed. (1) The terms of art.23, art.24, art.26 and art.28 of the 1996 Convention identically referred to "the measures". That term was to be construed broadly, not narrowly, for the common law jurisdiction of the UK. To say that undertakings could not be classed as "measures" was erroneous and devoid of practical sense. Those who had negotiated the 1996 Convention would, by the date of its arrival, have been fully familiar with undertakings. (2) The whole purpose of the 1996 Convention was to support and supplement the effective operation of its parent, the 1980 Convention. Undertakings had been used widely for protective measures since the early years of the 1980 Convention. It was simply unthinkable that the 1996 Convention should intend or expect to diminish and not fortify the effect of undertakings and their use as one of a number of mechanisms available to provide protection to a returning abductor and child.

Y (A CHILD) (ABDUCTION: UNDERTAKINGS GIVEN FOR RETURN OF CHILD), *Re*, [2013] EWCA Civ 129, [2013] 2 F.L.R. 649, Thorpe, L.J., CA (Civ Div).

1319. International child abduction–Writs ne exeat regno–Writs ne exeat regno–Grant of without notice Tipstaff orders–Wasted costs orders

[Child Abduction and Custody Act 1985 (c.60); Hague Convention on the Civil Aspects of International Child Abduction 1980.]

In proceedings in relation to the abduction of their child by the respondent mother (M), the applicant father (F) applied for and was granted without notice location and disclosure orders. M applied for costs against F and wasted costs against his solicitors. M and F were born and married in Pakistan, then lived in the United States where they later divorced. M initially obtained custody of their child and F had contact, together with an order mutually prohibiting removal of the child without notice to the other party. M's sister took the child to live in Pakistan and M followed. F was aware of M's address in Pakistan. He subsequently obtained custody in the US, where M was indicted for "felony parental abstraction". On the basis of information on Facebook that M was in England, F applied without notice for location and disclosure orders. These were granted and then renewed despite the failure of service on M and a lack of further evidence of the presence of M or the child in the UK. F's application was adjourned indefinitely with liberty to restore if the location order was executed. The location order was continued on an open-ended basis, without further evidence, and without consideration of the habitual residence of mother and child, or of jurisdiction. When M subsequently visited the UK, alone, her passport was removed on a £25,000 surety. It showed that neither she nor the child had been in the UK at the time F had sought the orders. When F discovered that the US was not seeking M's extradition, he offered to withdraw his application with no order for costs but M refused. F then pursued his application contending that the UK court had jurisdiction under the Hague Convention on the Civil Aspects of International Child Abduction 1980 and the Child Abduction and Custody Act 1985.

Held: Applications granted in part. Guidance had been given in *KY v DD (Without Notice Applications)* [2011] EWHC 1277 (Fam), [2012] 2 F.L.R. 200, [2012] C.L.Y. 1410 confirming the need for caution, care, rigour and close scrutiny in respect of applications for the grant of Tipstaff orders on a without notice basis and it was to be applied by every applicant and every judge in applications for without notice relief in the Family Division, particularly if that relief involved the grant of a Tipstaff order, *KY* applied (see para.8 of judgment). In this case there had been a flagrant and serious breach of the principles and procedures which was to be deprecated (para.34). The case revealed a number of serious and inexcusable failures by (a) F and his legal advisers, and (b) the court. There had been a failure to provide proper reasons for the asserted beliefs, to update information to the court, and to address the issue of jurisdiction, which meant the court did not have a candid and fair account of the position or of the strengths and weaknesses of F's case (para.79). The court had no jurisdiction where the child was habitually resident in Pakistan. With regard to the costs applications, in addition to the general policy that there should be no order for costs in children cases, F appeared to have a strong case that M had abducted the child as a baby and had refused F contact for four years. He was not liable for M's costs, *EC-L v DM (Child Abduction: Costs)* [2005] EWHC 588 (Fam), [2005] 4 Costs L.R. 576, [2005] C.L.Y. 1540 applied. However, the serious failures of F's solicitors to comply with the principles and practices were negligent and could not be justified or excused by endemic failures to apply them by practitioners and judges in the Family Division. A wasted costs order in the sum of £18,000 was granted, *Ridehalgh v Horsefield* [1994] Ch. 205, [1994] C.L.Y. 3623 applied (para.107).

B v A (WASTED COSTS ORDER), [2012] EWHC 3127 (Fam), [2013] 2 F.L.R. 958, Charles, J., Fam Div.

1320. Legal Aid, Sentencing and Punishment of Offenders Act 2012 (c.10)–Commencement No.7 Order

THE LEGAL AID, SENTENCING AND PUNISHMENT OF OFFENDERS ACT 2012 (COMMENCEMENT NO.7) ORDER 2013, SI 2013/SI 2013/773 (C.36); made under the Legal Aid, Sentencing and Punishment of Offenders Act 2012 s.151. Commencement details: bringing into force various provisions of the 2012 Act on April 1, 2013.; .

This Order commences, on April 1, 2013, sections of the Legal Aid, Sentencing and Punishment of Offenders Act 2012 making provision for a general power, not limited to maintenance pending suit, for a court in divorce, nullity of marriage or judicial separation proceedings to order payment by one party to the other for the purpose of securing legal services; and making corresponding provision in relation to proceedings for a dissolution, nullity or separation order in respect of a civil partnership.

1321. Marriage–Forced marriages–Circumstances justifying protection order under Pt IVA Family Law Act 1996

[Family Law Act 1996 (c.27) Pt IVA, s.63A.]

The applicant (Z), a 20-year-old woman of Muslim faith who had been born and raised in England, applied under the Family Law Act 1996 Pt IVA for forced marriage protection orders against the respondents (P), her parents, in respect of herself and her six younger siblings. The family had gone to Bangladesh on holiday. Z's case was that P had lied about there being a return flight, telling her upon arrival that she would be getting married and would stay there forever. She escaped with the help of the Forced Marriage Unit at the British High Commission. A few weeks later, while still in Bangladesh, Z's sister (B) was married against her will. Z obtained interim forced marriage protection orders, and an order that all her siblings be immediately returned to the United Kingdom and made wards of court. At a hearing three weeks later, B and P denied the forced marriage allegations. Those denials were repeated in witness statements. Before the final hearing, B was witnessed being dragged into a car by P. It materialised that she was being taken to an unknown address. B was removed to a secret location where she disclosed that she had been pressurised by P to marry, that she hadn't realised until afterwards that the ceremony in Bangladesh was the actual marriage because it had been conducted in Arabic not Bengali, and that she had been forced to consummate the marriage. The issues were whether P had intended to force Z to marry, and/or had forced B to marry in the sense explained in s.63A of the Act.

Held: Application granted. The evidence of Z and B was accepted over the evidence of P. What had happened was an example of exactly the type of conduct which the forced marriage protection order had been created to prevent. B was a particularly compelling witness, who had lied in her first witness statement under pressure from her father. He had had the statement prepared and had directed her to sign it without reading it. She had married because she had become worn down by the constant pressure from P. She had kept quiet about it upon return to the UK because she had believed P's threats that if she did not, her siblings would be taken into care. Z, who had a strong and independent personality, had been genuinely fearful that she would be forced into marriage at the time of contacting the British High Commission in Bangladesh. The subsequent events concerning B confirmed that her fears had been justified. Forced marriage was a serious problem in certain communities in the UK and, where young applicants could prove that they had been forced into marriage, or were at risk of being so forced, the court would protect them. In the instant case, the interim forced marriage protection orders were renewed and would remain in force without limit of time. The five children under the age of 18 would remain wards of court until further order. All passports and travel documents were to be retained and there should be a further urgent hearing to determine whether interim care orders should be made in respect of the five younger children (see paras 16, 24-28 of judgment).

A v SM (FORCED MARRIAGE PROTECTION ORDERS), [2012] EWHC 435 (Fam), [2012] 2 F.L.R. 1077, Baker, J., Fam Div.

1322. Marriage–Validity–Marriage ceremony–Failure to give notice or register marriage

[Marriage Act 1949 (c.76).]

The applicant (H) and the respondent (W) sought a declaration that their marriage ceremony had resulted in a valid marriage. The Attorney General intervened to oppose the application. In 2002 H and W took part in a marriage ceremony conducted by an Imam under Sharia law at a mosque. They were asked whether they freely consented to marriage and whether there was any reason why they could not marry. After the ceremony H was told by the Imam that they were married and there were no further formalities. However, unknown to H and W, they had failed to give notice of the marriage to the superintendent registrar and the marriage was not formally registered so there was no certificate. The Attorney General submitted that the ceremony was of no effect under English law as it failed to comply with the requirements of the Marriage Act 1949 and was a non-marriage or void marriage. H and W relied on the presumption of marriage and also submitted that the marriage ceremony was in its character of the kind contemplated by the Act. They argued that they had lived together as a married couple since the ceremony; accepted the assurances of the chairman of the mosque and the Imam that they had done everything they needed to do; the ceremony purported to be a lawful marriage, it bore enough of the hallmarks of marriage and the parties intended it to be a valid marriage; the mosque was a registered building and the ceremony took place in the presence of an authorised person.

Held: Declaration granted. The central issue was whether what took place was sufficiently within the 1949 Act for the marriage to be capable of being a valid marriage under English law. The evidence clearly established that some of the requirements of the Act were not fulfilled and the presumption of marriage could not be relied upon to establish that the relevant missing statutory requirements were fulfilled. However it was in the public interest that the rights and obligations consequent on marriage were provided to and imposed on those who "married" in the jurisdiction. It was not in the public interest that such obligations could be too readily avoided. It was clear that the parties intended to contract a marriage which was valid under English law but intention alone was unlikely to be sufficient to make a marriage potentially valid under English law, *Hudson v Leigh* [2009] EWHC 1306 (Fam), [2013] Fam. 77, [2009] C.L.Y. 1617 applied. In addition to the parties' intention, the ceremony which took place was sufficient as a ceremony to constitute a valid marriage. It was clearly a ceremony of marriage and it was solemnised in a registered building and in the presence of an authorised person, *Collett (otherwise Sakazova) v Collett* [1968] P. 482, [1967] C.L.Y. 1876 applied. There was no statutory provision which resulted in a marriage being void because it was solemnised without notice or certificate, but was otherwise within the scope of the Act, unless the parties knowingly and wilfully married without having complied with those requirements. The ceremony of marriage that had taken place was of the kind permitted by English law and in a form capable of producing a valid marriage, *Hudson* applied (see paras 82-85, 89, 95-103 of judgment).

A v A; *sub nom.* MA v JA, [2012] EWHC 2219 (Fam), [2013] Fam. 51, Moylan, J., Fam Div.

1323. Marriage (Same Sex Couples) Act 2013 (30)

This Act makes provision for the marriage of same sex couples in England and Wales, about gender change by married persons and civil partners, about consular functions in relation to marriage, for the marriage of armed forces personnel overseas, for permitting marriages according to the usages of belief organisations to be solemnized on the authority of certificates of a superintendent registrar, for the review of civil partnership, for the review of survivor benefits under occupational pension schemes.

This Act received Royal Assent on July 17, 2013.

1324. Marriage (Same Sex Couples) Act 2013 (c.30)–Commencement No.1 Order

THE MARRIAGE (SAME SEX COUPLES) ACT 2013 (COMMENCEMENT NO.1) ORDER 2013, SI 2013/SI 2013/2789 (C.110); made under the Marriage (Same Sex Couples) Act 2013 s.21. Commencement details: bringing into force various provisions of the 2013 Act on October 31, 2013; .

This Order brings into force certain provisions of the Marriage (Same Sex Couples) Act 2013 for the purpose of making subordinate legislation. These are powers of the Secretary of State in Sch 1 (to make regulations concerning the registration of places of worship and shared places of worship for the solemnization of marriages of same sex couples, and the appointment of authorised persons); and in Sch 4 para.14 (to make regulations concerning graduated retirement benefit). The power to make regulations at Sch 4 para.5 and para.8 is for the Lord Chancellor (concerning the jurisdiction of the courts in

England and Wales regarding marriages of same sex couples). The Order also brings into force s.14, s.17, s.18, s.19, s.20, Sch 2 para.1 and para.2; and Sch 4 para.27.

1325. Matrimonial proceedings–Arbitration–Reference of matrimonial proceedings to arbitration by rabbinical authorities

[Children Act 1989 (c.41); Family Procedure Rules 2010 (SI 2010/2955); European Convention on Human Rights 1950 Art.8; Hague Convention on the Civil Aspects of International Child Abduction 1980.]

The court issued a judgment to explain its approach to making a consent order in matrimonial proceedings after the parties (H and W) had reached agreement as a result of arbitration carried out by rabbinical authorities. H was Canadian and W was British. They were both observant orthodox Jews. The parties had difficulties in their marriage while living in Canada. W went to England and, against H's wishes, did not return to Canada with the children. H made an application in Canada under the Hague Convention on the Civil Aspects of International Child Abduction 1980. Before the final hearing was due to be held in England, the parties agreed to refer the matter to arbitration by the New York Beth Din. The issues between the parties included the children's welfare, financial matters, and the obtaining of a get, or religious divorce. The court, having obtained information as to the approach of the Beth Din and the effects of its rulings, stayed its proceedings to allow a non-binding arbitration to take place. The Beth Din issued its ruling 18 months later. The court subsequently considered and approved the order.

Held: Judgment accordingly. (1) There were several legal principles particularly relevant to referring the dispute to arbitration. Insofar as the court had jurisdiction to determine issues arising out of the marriage, or concerning the children's welfare and upbringing, that jurisdiction could not be ousted by agreement, *Hyman v Hyman* [1929] A.C. 601 applied. Save where statute provided otherwise, regarding issues concerning the upbringing of children, the child's welfare was the paramount consideration. Statute provided otherwise in respect of summary return applications under the Convention, but summary return applications under the inherent jurisdiction were to be determined by reference to the child's welfare, *J (A Child) (Custody Rights: Jurisdiction), Re* [2005] UKHL 40, [2006] 1 A.C. 80, [2005] C.L.Y. 1569 followed. The court gave appropriate respect to the practice and beliefs of all cultures and faiths, but that did not oblige it to depart from the welfare principle, because that principle was sufficiently broad and flexible to accommodate many cultural and religious practices. It was always in parties' interests to try to resolve disputes by agreement wherever possible, including disputes concerning the future of children and ancillary relief. The rule in *Hyman* prevented arbitration awards in matrimonial cases from being binding, but it had been suggested that an award should be a "magnetic factor" in the court's subsequent analysis of the issue. In arbitration, the parties could select the arbitrator, unlike in litigation. In that respect, arbitration was in line with the principle underpinning the Children Act 1989 that primary responsibility rested with parents, who were entitled to raise their children without interference from the state save where the children would suffer significant harm. That principle was in line with the European Convention on Human Rights 1950 art.8 (see paras 26-32 of judgment). (2) Further features of the process warranted further comment. It was an integral aspect of the arbitration that it had taken place under the auspices of the Beth Din. The parties' profound belief had been that a marriage solemnised within the tenets of their faith should be dissolved within those tenets. Having been reassured as to the principles which would be applied by the rabbinical authorities, the court was content to respect the parents' wishes, subject to the proviso that the outcome could not be binding without the court's endorsement. It did not necessarily follow that a court would be content in other cases to endorse a proposal that a dispute concerning children should be referred for determination by another religious authority. Each case would turn on its own facts. It was notable that the court was able not only to accommodate the parties' wish to resolve their dispute by reference to religious authorities, but also to buttress the process at crucial stages, by adjourning the case for arbitration, by using wardship as a protective mechanism for the children pending the outcome of the arbitration, by making "safe harbour" orders that enabled W to travel to New York with the children to take part in the process, by holding an emergency interim contact hearing, and by giving provisional approval of the draft final order to facilitate the granting of the get. The resolution of the issues by arbitration had largely been in accordance with the overriding objective of the Family Procedure Rules 2010. The court had some concern about the delays in the process, raising questions about whether the case could be said to have been dealt with expeditiously, and it had no information as to costs. However, the outcome had been in the interests of the children's welfare, and the terms of the financial settlement had been unobjectionable (paras 33-37).

AI v MT (ALTERNATE DISPUTE RESOLUTION); *sub nom.* RAI (CHILDREN), *Re*, [2013] EWHC100 (Fam), [2013] 2 F.L.R. 371, Baker, J., Fam Div.

1326. Non-accidental injury–Burden of proof–Applicable burden of proof–Proper approach to determining perpetrator of fatal injuries to baby

The appellant father (F) appealed against a decision in care proceedings that he was responsible for inflicting fatal injuries on his young baby (B). In his judgment following a fact-finding hearing, the judge had considered who had caused B's injuries by referring to B's mother (M), his four-year-old brother (C) and F in turn. He stated that the burden of proving a fact was on the party alleging it. He first eliminated M as being responsible for B's injuries, and went on to conclude that there was no real possibility that C had caused B's injuries. He found that F was responsible for causing B's injuries, and said that he had reached that conclusion by eliminating the only possible alternatives and by rejecting F's account. Since the trial, C had been involved in an incident where he had kicked a carer on the shoulder and caused her severe bruising. F submitted that, as a matter of law, the judge had misdirected himself as to his approach, and that if he had correctly and fully applied the principles in *S-B (Children) (Care Proceedings: Standard of Proof), Re* [2009] UKSC 17, [2010] 1 A.C. 678, [2010] C.L.Y. 1325, he would not have expressed himself in the way that he did when concluding that F was responsible for B's injuries. In particular, F argued that the judge had (1) implicitly reversed the applicable burden of proof, requiring F to prove that he was not responsible for the injuries; (2) decided that F was responsible for B's injuries by conducting a process of elimination: it was only by eliminating M and C that F was left as the only remaining possible perpetrator.

Held: Appeal dismissed. (1) The judge's reference to the burden of proof had to be taken in the context of the surrounding passages of the judgment in which he considered who was responsible for B's injuries. In the words that he had used, the judge was saying that he had to consider whether F's explanation was a real possibility or plausible. That was a permissible and sensible approach. Accordingly, the judge had not reversed the burden of proof by requiring F to prove anything, *S-B* considered (see para.10 of judgment). (2) It was likely that it would be the same judge who would conduct the second stage of the trial. There was no doubt that the incident involving C kicking the carer was a subsequent event which the judge would be entitled and bound to consider. It would be open to the judge to reconsider the findings of fact that he had already made if that subsequent event was sufficiently material (para.14). (3) (Per Black, L.J.) It was open to F to criticise the judge for conducting a process of elimination, given that he had said that he reached his conclusion by eliminating the only possible alternatives. However, the judge had to reach a realistic conclusion and be as specific as the evidence permitted him to be. Overall, the judge's conclusion was supported by the evidence and was acceptably reasonable (para.22).

A (CHILDREN) (FACT-FINDING HEARING: APPEAL), *Re*, [2012] EWCA Civ 1278, [2013] 1 F.L.R. 771, Thorpe, L.J., CA (Civ Div).

1327. Non-accidental injury–Burden of proof–Baby sustaining unusual bruising–Whether lack of explanation enough to support conclusion that injury non-accidental

[Children Act 1989 (c.41) s.31.]

The appellant mother (M) and father (F) appealed against a decision that their baby (B) had suffered non-accidental injuries, that both parents were possible perpetrators and that there had been a failure to protect by the parent who had not inflicted the injuries. B was only a few weeks old when the injuries were suffered. He had been bathed and put to bed in the evening. At that time there were no marks visible. The following day at about midday it was noticed that he had visible bruising. M accused F and took photographs of the injuries. At a later hospital examination eight separate instances of bruising were noted on the left forearm, right arm and left thigh. The parents could not explain the injuries and the local authority was concerned that they were non-accidental. It commenced care proceedings and there was a fact finding inquiry to see whether the threshold in the Children Act 1989 s.31 had been crossed. The local authority's case was that the injuries were non-accidental, had been inflicted by one parent in circumstances in which the other had failed to protect B and were not sustained in the course of ordinary everyday care of B because he would have been in pain and the parent not inflicting the injury could not have failed to notice. The judge considered all the explanations put forward by the parents and rejected them. She considered the medical evidence that the injuries were unexplained, and were unusual for accidental injuries but also for non-accidental injuries. She found the parents' evidence not wholly credible. She was satisfied that the parents were not telling the entire truth and that the injuries were non-accidental.

Held: Appeal allowed. The s.31 threshold consisted of two elements: first, significant harm, and it was not suggested that that had not been demonstrated even if the injuries were at the lower end of the scale, and secondly, causation, in that the harm was attributable to care which was not reasonable care. The local authority relied on the "constellation" of injuries, the different sites, the nature of the injuries and the timescale to raise the inference that they were not accidental and to justify the inference that the threshold had been crossed. However, the judge was not considering a general failure to take reasonable care. The judge found that the injuries had been deliberately inflicted. The medical evidence was that the marks were imprints or pressure marks from an object, but it was not possible to say what object or even what kind of object or how the pressure was exerted. Nor was it possible to say whether there was a momentary infliction of pain or a sustained pressure. The instant case was not one of a broken limb, or a cigarette burn or finger pressure. The court simply did not know what had happened or how. The judge had accepted the evidence of one of the doctors that in the absence of a benign explanation from the parents it could be concluded that the injuries were not accidental, but that conclusion did not follow, unless the burden of proof, which lay on the local authority on the balance of probabilities, was wrongly reversed and the parents were required to satisfy the court that the injuries were non-accidental. The judge had erred in finding that the parents had deliberately caused the injuries. Her decision on lack of protection was not supported by the local authority, was inadequately reasoned and could not be upheld.

M (A CHILD) (FACT-FINDING HEARING: BURDEN OF PROOF), *Re*, [2012] EWCA Civ 1580, [2013] 2 F.L.R. 874, Ward, L.J., CA (Civ Div).

1328. Non-accidental injury–Findings of fact–Child suffering from congenital rickets–Determination of cause of death–Whether parents caused non-accidental injury

The court was required to determine the cause of death of the first and second respondents' child (J). J had been taken to hospital where he appeared to be having fits. He later died. His parents were charged with J's murder and their second child was taken into the local authority's care. It was later discovered that J had suffered from congenital rickets due to vitamin D deficiency. The post-mortem revealed that

J had sustained fractures, including a skull fracture and fissure, brain injury and retinal haemorrhages. The parents were subsequently acquitted of J's murder following the judge's conclusion that the case should not be put to the jury. The local authority, while accepting that J's rickets had caused some of his fractures, maintained that J had died as a result of non-accidental injury caused by one or both of his parents.

Held: Judgment accordingly. (1) It was not possible to conclude, on the balance of probabilities, that any of the fractures or traumatised fissure were the result of inflicted deliberate harm by either of J's parents. The fractures could have been caused by the day-to-day handling of J due to the particular fragility of his bones caused by the severity of his undetected rickets. The hospital treatment was sub-optimal: the evidence suggested that J's fitting was not adequately controlled at the hospital, and that there was not proper management of J's blood gas which was likely to have contributed to his deteriorating condition. It was more likely than not that the retinal haemorrhages were not caused by inflicted trauma. While the brain haemorrhage was more likely to have been caused by trauma, it was necessary to assess that evidence in the context of all the other evidence which pointed the other way (see paras 213, 218-219, 224-225, 232-233 of judgment). (2) (Obiter) The court endorsed the view that there was a need for further research, particularly in relation to the different aspects of the non-accidental head injury triad and the impact of vitamin D deficiency and rickets in respect on babies under six months old (para.235). (3) (Obiter) The Children's Guardian took no part in the instant hearing. The role of the children's guardian could include drawing the court's attention to all relevant matters to assist in the fact-finding exercise. Given the complexity of the instant case, and with the benefit of hindsight, the guardian's role should perhaps have been given more robust encouragement at a case management hearing (para.238).

ISLINGTON LBC v AL-ALAS, [2012] EWHC 865 (Fam), [2012] 2 F.L.R. 1239, Theis, J., Fam Div.

1329. Non-accidental injury–Findings of fact–Death from unknown causes

In care proceedings concerning a four-year-old child (X), a fact-finding hearing took place to determine the cause of death of X's sister (Y), at the age of four months. X and Y's mother (M) had a troubled history. She had experienced an abusive childhood, suffered from an emotionally unstable personality disorder, had had significant involvement with social care and had been convicted of child neglect after leaving X alone one day. At the time of Y's death, she, M and X had been in the house. All the experts agreed that Y had died either from an unknown cause or because she had been smothered or suffocated, and that, if the latter applied, only M or X could have been the perpetrator.

Held: Judgment accordingly. On the totality of the evidence, it had not been established on the balance of probabilities that either M or X had been the perpetrator of a fatal act of smothering. Due regard should be had to the agreed expert position that the likely cause of death was asphyxia. However, as the oral evidence had unfolded, two of the experts had shown themselves to be uncomfortable with that categorical position, feeling that the alternative of death from an unknown cause was a real candidate. Nor had it been established on the balance of probabilities that M and X constituted membership of a pool of possible perpetrators that inflicted a fatal act of smothering on Y. It was possible that one or the other did so, but the probability of either occurrence was very low. As to M, various factors were significant. Among other things, for all her faults, she was a loving and, in her own deficient way, caring mother. Further, the evidence showed that she had been on the telephone for 38 minutes immediately before she dialled 999; the expert evidence was to the effect that there would have to have been seven to 12 minutes of continuous occlusion of Y's airway to produce death by smothering. As to X, the expert evidence was to the effect that he was unlikely to have had the patience or concentration to lie or sit on Y's face for seven to 12 minutes. This was one of those rare cases where the burden of proof came to the court's rescue, so that both M and X would be treated in law as if they did not fatally smother Y. The result was that Y joined the small, sad constituency of infants whose deaths were recorded as resulting from unknown causes (see paras 53-58 of judgment).

BRADFORD MDC v F, [2012] EWHC 557 (Fam), [2012] 2 F.L.R. 1374, Mostyn, J., Fam Div.

1330. Non-accidental injury–Findings of fact–Judge's finding inconsistent with expert evidence–Failure to properly address inexplicable nature of injuries

The appellant parents (P) appealed against a judge's findings of fact in relation to care proceedings brought by the respondent local authority in respect of P's child (M). M had been five months old when she was admitted to hospital with multiple fractures to her ribs and skull. P denied deliberately causing any injuries and referred to M having hit her head on a table when dropped and her chest having been squeezed on another occasion to avoid dropping her. Although the skull fractures were described by the four expert paediatricians as "spectacular", she had not suffered the very serious brain injuries normally associated with such severe fractures. The experts stated that "conventional" medical opinion was that such fractures would be expected to be accompanied by extensive brain damage, whereas N had no significant brain injury. Their opinion was that M's case was unique; none of them had seen such a case before or could identify one from the relevant medical literature. They could not provide an explanation beyond speculation. One expert referred to the possibility that M might have abnormal bone fragility, but that was ruled out by another expert (B), a bone specialist. The judge accepted B's evidence. The judge described M's clinical presentation as "not just unusual but inexplicable". However, she found that, on the balance of probabilities, P had not provided a truthful account of what had happened, and that that supported a finding that the injuries, to M's skull and ribs, were non-accidental. P contended that the judge had erred in not properly addressing the fact that the experts found M's presentation to be inexplicable and, therefore, that there was good reason to conclude that M had some unknown and undiagnosed bone disorder.

Held: Appeal allowed. The judgment could not stand. There was no difficulty with the judge's finding that P's evidence was not so compelling or reliable that she was persuaded to accept what they said and reject well-founded medical evidence. However, the judge had erred. Her acceptance of B's evidence did not resolve the case but made it more difficult. She had not explained how, in the light of the expert evidence, she was able to conclude that it was not a case where the court should find that there was something unexplained beyond current medical knowledge. That omission was fatal and necessarily vitiated her findings, *U (A Child) (Serious Injury: Standard of Proof), Re* [2004] EWCA Civ 567, [2005] Fam. 134, [2004] C.L.Y. 1458 and *R (Care Proceedings: Causation), Re* [2011] EWHC 1715 (Fam), [2011] 2 F.L.R. 1384, [2012] C.L.Y. 1354 applied. It might be that given the collection of M's injuries, arising in circumstances where there was no suggestion that anyone other than P could have been responsible, and where P's accounts and explanations had appropriately been rejected, it would be open to a judge to find as the instant judge had. It would have been if the case had fallen to be determined in accordance with a conventional medical frame of reference. However, so far as the skull fractures were concerned, M's presentation was inexplicable if assessed by reference to conventional medical opinion and experience. It had to follow from the inability of conventional learning to explain the skull fractures that the judge's findings in relation to the rib fractures were also vulnerable. There was therefore no scope for drawing a distinction and upholding the judge's findings in relation to one while upsetting her judgment on the other (see paras 50-58 of judgment). (2) The matter would be retried before a judge of the Family Division. An appropriately extensive search of the medical literature should be undertaken, and thought needed to be given as to how the expert evidence could be condensed or summarised for the retrial so as to avoid covering the same ground (paras 60-62).

M (FACT FINDING HEARING: INJURIES TO SKULL), *Re*, [2012] EWCA Civ 1710, [2013] 2 F.L.R. 322, Munby, L.J., CA (Civ Div).

1331. Non-accidental injury–Findings of fact–Thoroughness of approach in family court

The applicant parents (P), whose child (C) had been made the subject of a care order, sought permission to appeal against the dismissal of their application to reopen the fact-finding process. When C was four weeks old, it was discovered that he had sustained 12 fractures to different parts of his body. Further, a week earlier worrying signs in his genital area had indicated either some form of infection or inflicted trauma. At a fact-finding hearing, the judge concluded that C had been injured in the period between birth and final presentation at the hospital and that P were the only possible perpetrators. P sought to reopen the fact-finding process, relying on 26 factors which, it was argued, fell to be reconsidered in the light of suggested developments in medical understanding or which had not been given sufficient prominence. The judge rejected each point, noting that at the previous hearing the court had allowed the instruction of every expert/test requested by P. In seeking permission to appeal, P relied on the case of *Islington LBC v Al-Alas* [2012] EWHC 865 (Fam), [2012] 2 F.L.R. 1239, [2013] 2 C.L. 159 and argued that the development of medical understanding in relation to vitamin D deficiency, rickets and brittle bones justified considering whether the judge had been correct in refusing to permit the reopening of the fact-finding exercise. P were given permission to instruct an endocrinologist (N). He prepared a report stating that, while it was likely that C had been born with vitamin D deficiency, it was clear that he had been bottle-fed with vitamin D and iron-supplemented feed, rendering it unlikely that vitamin D deficiency played a significant role in bone fragility predisposing the fractures. He concluded that a medical condition did not account for C's injuries. Those representing C had instructed the barrister who had appeared for the parents in *Al-Alas*; she was asked to advise whether the case warranted further examination in the light of the science explored, and the expert evidence given, in *Al-Alas*; she expressed confidence in the safety of the judge's findings and sought to identify why this case was not one which fell to be reconsidered in the light of *Al-Alas*. P argued that N had made the crucial finding that C was vitamin D deficient at birth; that was at odds with the understanding of the experts at the fact-finding process, so that those experts should be instructed to review their conclusions; a paediatric radiologist should also be instructed; further, there were signs that C had congenital rickets.

Held: Application refused. (1) The matters raised by P had been given anxious consideration: it was important that the court should keep an open mind to the clarification of medical knowledge as it progressed over time; there was also the draconian nature of the orders made and the fact that they were entirely reliant on the opinion of medical experts. Nevertheless, it would not be appropriate to grant permission to appeal. N's conclusion that C was likely to have been vitamin D deficient at birth did not support the string of consequences that P sought to extrapolate from it. Among other things, no evidence had been adduced to suggest, let alone establish, that C's bone formation was adversely affected by a lack of vitamin D before birth. The matter had been thoroughly canvassed by the experts at the fact-finding hearing, including an expert of international renown, and the conclusion was that that was not a factor. The signs of congenital rickets to which P had drawn attention were all known at the fact-finding hearing and were not considered diagnostic, or even indicative, of rickets by the experts. It was also impossible to ignore the reasoned and entirely neutral opinion of N; he had expressed the clear conclusion that, despite C's vitamin D deficiency at birth, there was no medical condition identifying a cause for the fractures. There was no basis for now taking time to canvass the opinion of the fact-finding experts or that of a new expert (see paras 39-40, 42, 45, 47-48 of judgment). (2) There had been sustained press comment to the effect that child-abuse allegations which turned primarily on medical evaluation were conducted with superficial examination by the courts, which relied on experts chosen and paid for by the local authority; the evidence, it was said, was not disclosed to the parents, who were not themselves permitted to instruct experts of their choosing. So that those who were interested in such matters could form their own view of the thoroughness and fairness of the process adopted by the family court, an anonymised copy of the two key judgments in this case would be released for publication. Those judgments revealed that at every stage the judge permitted P's legal team to instruct experts on any aspect of the case that P considered relevant and that P's choice of expert was accepted by the court. Further, the court had agreed to the testing of C whenever such was sought on P's behalf, even when that testing was contrary to medical advice, *Al-Alas* cited (paras 49-51).

A (A CHILD) (PERMISSION TO APPEAL FACT-FINDING JUDGMENT), *Re*, [2012] EWCA Civ 1477, [2013] 1 F.L.R. 1187, McFarlane, L.J., CA (Civ Div).

1332. Parental contact–Children's welfare–Order for cessation of direct contact with father–Mother's anxiety about contact transferred to child–Need for mother to address problem

The applicant father (F) applied for permission to appeal against a ruling upholding a decision of a district judge that direct contact with his four-year-old son (S) should cease. F had been enjoying supervised contact. The district judge found that nothing that he was doing in the contact sessions with S presented any reason for stopping contact. However, he also found that S's mother (M) was very anxious that S was spending time with F and that such anxiety was having an adverse effect on, and causing emotional harm to, S. He decided to stop contact because of S's reaction to being in the middle of two adults who were unable to relate to each other in a way that allowed him to enjoy an ordinary relationship with both of them. Although the district judge did not place an embargo on further applications, he indicated that a gap of two years was necessary to give the family time out from almost continuous litigation and allow the dust to settle before the issue of contact could be considered again.

Held: Application refused. (1) The district judge had given a careful judgment which was unassailable. It followed that there was no mileage in F's understandable attempt, in human terms, to appeal against that judgment. There were no important matters of practice or principle raised and no other compelling reason as a matter of law for the case to come before the Court of Appeal (see para.30 of judgment). (2) It had been the very clear expectation of the district judge that M would seek to engage in therapy to put herself in a better position to cope with matters if and when contact resumed. The court had just handed down judgment in the case of *W (Children) (Direct Contact), Re* [2012] EWCA Civ 999, [2013] 1 F.L.R. 494, [2012] C.L.Y. 1450. The court stressed the responsibility on parents who had primary care of a child to do what they had to do to meet the child's need to have an ordinary and meaningful relationship with the other parent even if they themselves did not want to. The needs of S would include having a settled relationship with F just as he had one with M, unless there was a very good reason to the contrary. Parents were engaged in the task not just of looking after a child but of bringing up an adult, and part of bringing up an adult was for that individual to feel comfortable about himself, his identity and the relationships he had with his parents, grandparents and other relatives on both sides of the family. The ball was in M's court during the two-year gap mentioned by the district judge, and it was anticipated that the court would look to see what she had done and how she had best used that time to improve S's life in this most important regard, *Re W* considered (paras 32-35).

W (A CHILD) (CONTACT: PERMISSION TO APPEAL), *Re*, [2012] EWCA Civ 1214, [2013] 1 F.L.R. 609, McFarlane, L.J., CA (Civ Div).

1333. Parental orders–Setting aside–Appropriate test

[Adoption and Children Act 2002 (c.38); Children Act 1989 (c.41); Human Fertilisation and Embryology Act 2008 (c.22) s.54; Family Procedure Rules 2010 (SI 2010/2955) r.13.9.]

The applicant (G) applied to set aside a parental order made under the Human Fertilisation and Embryology Act 2008 s.54. G and the respondent (X) had entered into a surrogacy agreement with a surrogate (K) which resulted in the birth of a child (D) in January 2011. G and X separated in September 2011, since which time D had been in the primary care of X; G had contact with him. G and X applied for a parental order in respect of D in November 2010. Such an order was made at a directions hearing in May 2011. Numerous procedural defects occurred: a final order was made at the directions hearing; the judge had no parental reporter's report; there was no analysis of the requirements of s.54(8), although it appeared that at least £10,000 had changed hands; there was no consideration of welfare issues so far as D was concerned; although the application was made under the correct Act, the order as drawn referred to the repealed statute of 1990; a CAFCASS report was filed in June 2011 but there was no evidence that it was ever considered by the judge; the report contained no consideration of the matters required under s.54(8) other than an acknowledgment of the sum of money that had changed hands and an assertion that it constituted reasonable expenses; further, the report considered the checklist in the Children Act 1989, whereas the proper statutory checklist was in the Adoption and Children Act 2002. The Family Procedure Rules 2010 r.13.9 specified what was to be done at the first directions hearing but none of the steps mentioned had been taken. G argued that the order should be set aside, first, because of the procedural defects which had occurred and, second, because X had concealed her true intentions from the court: she had had an affair and intended to live separate from him.

Held: Application refused. (1) There appeared to be no known case of an attempt to set aside a parental order. However, the authorities on the setting aside of adoption orders indicated that the court had jurisdiction to set aside the parental order on the two grounds relied on by G, *B (Adoption Order: Jurisdiction to Set Aside), Re* [1995] Fam. 239, [1995] C.L.Y. 3376, *K (A Minor) (Adoption: Foreign Child), Re* [1997] 2 F.L.R. 221, [1996] C.L.Y. 465 and *M (Minors) (Adoption), Re* [1991] 1 F.L.R. 458, [1991] C.L.Y. 2498 applied (see paras 33-38 of judgment). (2) It would not be appropriate to set aside the parental order. First, given that such an order was like an adoption order, an order conferring status, there should, so far as possible, be certainty and clarity and therefore the court in considering such an application should be guided by the authorities on setting aside adoption orders, where the bar was set very high. Second, although the court, G and K had undoubtedly been misled by X in her silence, both as to her affair and as to her pessimistic perception of the marriage, that came nowhere near the circumstances that existed in *Re M* or *Re K*. Third, revoking the order would not be consistent with D's welfare; G was the only mother that he had known and his welfare would be undermined were she to be deposed from that role. Fourth, the court would have reached the same decision as it had, even if all the matters revealed in the CAFCASS report had been considered properly by the judge; it was more likely than not that an order would have been made had all the information been disclosed, provided, of course, that K's consent and G's application had continued. As to whether the order should be set aside for the purposes of protecting the integrity of the court process, the third and fourth reasons mentioned above meant that it would not be appropriate to do so (paras 43-44). (3) (Obiter) An application for a parental order should be treated with the same care and caution that attended every application for an adoption order. Both s.54 of the 2008 Act and Pt 13 of the 2010 Rules were in mandatory form; they had to be observed and care had to be taken (para.45).

G v G, [2012] EWHC 1979 (Fam), [2013] 1 F.L.R. 286, Hedley, J., Fam Div.

1334. Parental orders–Surrogacy–Proper approach when court asked to dispense with surrogate mother's consent on ground she could not be found

[Human Fertilisation and Embryology Act 2008 (c.22) s.54(7), s.54.]

The applicants (X) sought a parental order under the Human Fertilisation and Embryology Act 2008 s.54 in respect of twin boys (D). X were a male couple living in England who, having undergone a marriage ceremony in Belgium, were to be treated as civil partners. They wanted to start a family and entered into a surrogacy arrangement with a clinic in India. The relevant agreement, to which the director of the clinic and the woman chosen as the surrogate mother (B) were parties, provided, among other things, that B would "surrender sole and exclusive custody, parental responsibility, decision making, care and control of the child to the intended parents immediately upon the child's birth, acknowledging that it [was] in the best interests of all concerned to do so". X paid roughly £17,000 to the clinic. Aware of the requirement in s.54 that a parental order required the consent of the surrogate mother, to be given not less than six weeks after the birth, X asked the clinic to supply such consent. It was not forthcoming. Some seven weeks after making their request, X received a package, purportedly from the director of the clinic, containing a sheet of paper on which was printed an obscene gesture. An enquiry agent was instructed to attempt to locate B, whom X had never met, but he was unable to do so. The main issues were (i) whether the court should dispense with B's consent under s.54(7) on the ground that she could not be found; (ii) whether the court should retrospectively authorise the payment made by X in respect of the surrogacy.

Held: Application granted. (1) Where the court was asked to dispense with the surrogate mother's consent under s.54(7) on the ground that she could not be found, the following points should be noted. First, the court had to carefully scrutinise the evidence as to the efforts which had been taken to find her. It would only be when all reasonable steps had been taken to locate her without success that a court would be likely to dispense with the need for valid consent. Further, it would normally be prudent for the applicants to lay the ground for satisfying those requirements at an early stage. Even where they did not meet the surrogate, they should establish clear lines of communication with her, preferably not simply through one person or agency, and ensure that she was made aware during the pregnancy that she would be required to give consent six weeks after the birth. Second, although a consent given before the expiry of six weeks after birth was not valid for the purposes of s.54, the court was entitled to take into account evidence that the woman did give consent at earlier times to giving up the baby. The weight attached to such earlier consent was, however, likely to be limited. The courts had to be careful not to use such evidence to undermine the legal requirement that a consent would only be valid if given after six weeks. Third, the child's welfare was now the paramount consideration when the court was "coming to a decision" in relation to the making of a parental order. That included decisions about whether to make an order without the consent of the woman who gave birth in circumstances in which she could not be found or was incapable of giving consent. It would, however, be wrong to use that provision as a means of avoiding the need to take all reasonable steps to attain the woman's consent. In this case, it would be appropriate to dispense with B's consent. Among other things, it was not X's fault that they found themselves in the position in which they were in. B appeared to have given informal consent earlier. Any further delay in reaching a decision was likely to be prejudicial to D's welfare. Moreover, there was realistically no likelihood that they would have any relationship with B (see paras 27-34 of judgment). (2) Although X had accepted that the sum that they had paid exceeded a level that could be described as "reasonable expenses" for the purposes of s.54(8), it would be appropriate to retrospectively authorise the payment made. D's welfare would unquestionably be enhanced by the making of a parental order. Further, X had acted in good faith and had been entirely candid in all of their dealings with the court and the other authorities, *X (Children) (Parental Order: Foreign Surrogacy), Re* [2008] EWHC 3030 (Fam), [2009] Fam. 71, [2009] C.L.Y. 1646, *S (Parental Order), Re* [2009] EWHC 2977

(Fam), [2010] 1 F.L.R. 1156, [2010] C.L.Y. 1442, *L (A Child) (Parental Order: Foreign Surrogacy), Re* [2010] EWHC 3146 (Fam), [2011] Fam. 106, [2011] C.L.Y. 1457, *IJ (A Child) (Foreign Surrogacy Agreement: Parental Order), Re* [2011] EWHC 921 (Fam), [2011] 2 F.L.R. 646, [2011] C.L.Y. 1456 and *X (Children) (Parental Order: Retrospective Authorisation of Payments), Re* [2011] EWHC 3147 (Fam), [2012] 1 F.L.R. 1347, [2012] C.L.Y. 1454 applied (paras 36-39).

D (CHILDREN) (SURROGACY: PARENTAL ORDER), *Re*; *sub nom.* D v L (SURROGACY); D (CHILDREN) (PARENTAL ORDER: FOREIGN SURROGACY), [2012] EWHC 2631 (Fam), [2013] 1 W.L.R. 3135, Baker, J., Fam Div.

1335. Parental responsibility–Allocation of jurisdiction–Child's habitual residence determining jurisdiction–Exception under Regulation 2201/2003 art.12(1)(b)–Best interests of child

[Regulation 2201/2003 Art.8, Art.12.]

The applicant father resident in France (F) applied for a stay of an application by the mother (M) for a residence order in respect of their daughter (S). F, a French national, had met and married M in France where they settled, and where S was born. After eight years M returned to the United Kingdom to care for her ill mother and took S with her. They visited F in France, but M refused to return to live there and F moved to the UK. The marriage broke down the next year and while F and S were visiting France, F applied there for a divorce and for custody of S. He brought S back to the UK as agreed, but returned to France. By then, S had lived in the UK for 22 months, all with F's agreement. M and S lived on a housing estate with M's mother, which F believed was an unsuitable place for S to live. M applied via her legal advisors for an adjournment of the French proceedings and obtained an interim residence order in the UK. Since S's school year was about to begin the French court fixed S's residence with F on an interim basis. It noted the family circle around her in France and suggested visiting rights for M, adding that parental authority should be exercised jointly. M appealed unsuccessfully; the French High Court noting that S had been born and had spent her early years in France. F submitted that (1) although S was habitually resident in England the court should apply the exception under Brussels II Revised, namely Regulation 2201/2003 art.12(1)(b) and stay the proceedings to allow S's future to be decided by a French court, which was already seised of the matter; (2) the estate on which M and S lived had an endemic drugs problem and was a rough environment unsuitable for S's upbringing.

Held: Application refused. (1) Under art.8 of Brussels II jurisdiction lay with the Member State of the child's habitual residence. As an exception, art.12(1)(b) allowed another Member State to have jurisdiction under three conditions: the holders of parental responsibility had accepted its jurisdiction expressly or otherwise in an unequivocal manner, its court was seised of the matter at the time, and if it was in the superior interests of the child. The acceptance of jurisdiction did not have to be in writing and subsequent acts and contact could illuminate the quality of the acceptance at the time the court was seised. However, the acceptance had to be unequivocal and, even putting F's case at its highest, M did not unequivocally accept French jurisdiction, but had appealed against the French order, instituted and pursued proceedings in the UK, and sought a residence order to ensure that S was returned to her. S had never been away from M, who under the French order would have only visiting rights until a final hearing at a distant and unknown time. Even if that conclusion were wrong, S's best interests were served by having any welfare hearing or consideration by a court of the exercise of parental responsibility conducted in the UK where she had lived for more than the two previous years. It was her home, where she attended school and lived within the maternal extended family (see paras 16, 19, 29-35 of judgment). (2) The issues raised about the suitability of the estate were potentially serious and could best be investigated by the English courts with the assistance of CAFCASS, rather than long-distance from France (para.33). *Bush v Bush* [2008] EWCA Civ 865, [2008] 2 F.L.R. 1437, [2008] C.L.Y. 1557 and *I (A Child) (Contact Application:*

Jurisdiction), Re [2009] UKSC 10, [2010] 1 A.C. 319, [2010] C.L.Y. 1413 followed.

VC v GC (JURISDICTION: BRUSSELS II REVISED ART.12), [2012] EWHC 1246 (Fam), [2013] 1 F.L.R. 244, Eleanor King, J, Fam Div.

1336. Parental responsibility–Allocation of jurisdiction–Family law proceedings commenced in English court–Application to enforce Belgian court order–Jurisdiction of English court

[Children Act 1989 (c.41); Regulation 2201/2003 Art.8(1), Art.11 (7), Art.12; Hague Convention on the Civil Aspects of International Child Abduction 1980.]

The applicant father (F) applied to enforce a Belgian court order granting him custody of his child (B) and ordering her immediate return from the United Kingdom to Belgium. B had been a habitual resident of Belgium until March 2011 when she left with the respondent mother (M) to live in England. In October 2011, F contended that B's move constituted a wrongful removal. His application for her summary return under the Hague Convention on the Civil Aspects of International Child Abduction was dismissed and the court declared that F had consented to B's removal in March 2011 and that she was now habitually resident in England. F applied under the Children Act 1989 for a residence order and the court gave directions in respect of the application in December 2011. Although the Belgian court had been sent a copy of the judgment declaring B a habitual resident of England, in March 2011 it awarded F custody of B pursuant to Regulation 2201/2003 art.11 (7). The issues were (1) whether the court had jurisdiction to determine matters relating to parental responsibility, pursuant to the Regulation; (2) the point at which the court had been seised. The respondent local authority, supported by M and B, submitted that the English court had jurisdiction as B had been declared habitually resident and each person having rights of custody had acquiesced to B's removal or retention from at least November 2011. They contended that the Belgian judgment should not be enforced as F had expressly and unequivocally accepted the English court's jurisdiction by applying for a residence order. Alternatively, even if the Belgian court had jurisdiction, they argued that the English proceedings relating to parental responsibility preceded the invoking of that jurisdiction so that the Belgian court was the second court seised.

Held: Application refused. (1) The court had or appeared to have had jurisdiction, pursuant to the Regulation, from at least November 2011 when it was declared that B was habitually resident in England and Wales. F had not appealed against that decision and it would be wrong to go behind the declaration. Having regard to F's commencement of a residence order application in England and the content of that application, he had expressly accepted, in an unequivocal manner, the English court's jurisdiction and accordingly, it had jurisdiction pursuant to art.12(3) of the Regulation (see paras 68-69 of judgment). (2) There were pending proceedings relating to parental responsibility in England, under the provisions of the Regulation, which were brought earlier than the proceedings in the Belgian courts. The court was therefore seised by at least December 2011 when it gave directions in F's application. That preceded the Belgian court becoming seised in January 2012 when F filed documents with the Belgian court. When a court first seised concluded that it had jurisdiction under the Regulation, judgments given by a court second seised did not have to be recognised or enforced nor did they have any effect on a judgment delivered by the court first seised, *Mercredi v Chaffe (C-497/10 PPU)* [2012] Fam. 22, [2011] C.L.Y. 1429 applied. Given that the court had jurisdiction from at least November 2011 pursuant to art.8(1) of the Regulation, or alternatively at least December 2011, pursuant to art.12(3), and given that the child was located in England and was the subject of continuing proceedings in the jurisdiction, the Belgian court order was not enforced (paras 70-72, 90-92).

C (A CHILD) (JURISDICTION AND ENFORCEMENT OF ORDERS RELATING TO CHILD), *Re*, [2012] EWHC 907 (Fam), [2012] 2 F.L.R. 1191, Moylan, J., Fam Div (Newcastle).

1337. Parental responsibility–Termination–Father's conviction for sexual abuse

[Children Act 1989 (c.41) s.1 (3), s.4(2A), s.91 (14); European Convention on Human Rights 1950 Art.8, Art.14.]

The applicant mother (M) applied for the termination under the Children Act 1989 s.4(2A) of the parental responsibility of the respondent father (F) in respect of their eight-year-old son (D). F applied for a specific issue order requiring M to supply annual reports on D's progress. F had pleaded guilty to sexually abusing M's daughters while he lived with the family, although he subsequently claimed to have made a false confession to spare the girls from giving evidence. F wrote from prison stating that he wanted contact with D. Shortly after F's release from prison, M made her application. F argued that *P (Terminating Parental Responsibility), Re* [1995] 1 F.L.R. 1048, [1996] C.L.Y. 591, the only reported case found which concerned an application to terminate parental responsibility, should not be applied because of the factual differences between the cases and because s.4 had since been amended; further, s.4(2A) breached the European Convention on Human Rights 1950 art.8 and art.14 since it discriminated against unmarried fathers in a way that infringed their right to family life.

Held: Applications granted in part. (1) *Re P* outlined the correct approach to be adopted on an application to terminate parental responsibility under s.4(2A). The statutory changes had not narrowed the court's powers under s.4(2A): Parliament had expressly extended the court's power to terminate parental responsibility. Further, *Smallwood v United Kingdom (29779/96)* (1999) 27 E.H.R.R. CD155, finding that the termination of an unmarried father's parental responsibility was permissible, remained good law: its conclusions remained firmly in line with the legal and social context of unmarried fathers. Section 4(2A) was compatible with art.8 and art.14, *Re P* and *Smallwood* applied (see paras 22-23 of judgment). (2) Save in exceptional circumstances, a court in family proceedings would proceed on the basis that a criminal conviction was correct. F's account of having made a false confession was wholly unconvincing. The court therefore proceeded on the basis that F's convictions were genuine and that, in his persistent denial of the allegations, he had lied. F's statement that he did not wish to pursue further applications regarding D was rejected. He wished to extend his involvement to include ultimately direct contact. As he continued to deny his culpability, it was highly unlikely that he appreciated the damage he had caused to the family, or the danger of further damage should he have further involvement with them. The court considered the s.1 (3) welfare checklist: it was duty-bound to have regard to that when considering the specific issue order application, and it was helpful in the welfare evaluation for the application to terminate parental responsibility. The main factors in the instant case were D's emotional needs, the harm he had suffered, and the risk of future harm. D had suffered emotional harm as a result of the harm inflicted on other members of his family. Because of his parentage, D's position in the family was difficult and there was a risk of his suffering further stigma. The court also took into account D's expressed wish to have no involvement with F, and M's capacity to meet D's needs. Were F to retain parental responsibility, M would be placed under great strain, given the probability that F would subsequently apply for contact. Equally, requiring M to send F a regular report concerning D would impinge on D's emotional security. In certain circumstances a child's need to have a relationship with each biological parent had to give way to more important considerations, in particular, the need for emotional security. D's emotional security would be imperilled were F to have further involvement in his life. Although, as an aspect of their art.8 rights, D and F had a family life together, that was outweighed by D's overriding need for security within his family. The court considered to what extent the factors for making parental responsibility orders would be satisfied in the instant case. The commitment F had shown to D while living in the household had been wholly undermined by his sexually abusing the girls; that was compounded by his subsequent denials. There had been some attachment between D and F, but there had been no contact for several years. If F had not already had parental responsibility, it was inconceivable that it would be granted to him; that was a factor to be taken into account in considering the application to terminate parental responsibility. Further, there was no element of parental responsibility that F could foreseeably exercise in a way beneficial for D, Re P applied. F's parental responsibility for D would therefore be terminated. F's application would be refused (paras 47-61). (3) F would be permitted to write a letter to D to be given to him if he made any enquiry about F. The court's prima facie view was that it would be appropriate for F to be joined as a party to any application to adopt D. No order would be made under s.91 (14) preventing F from making further applications without permission: such orders were to be made sparingly (paras 64-67).

DW (A CHILD) (TERMINATION OF PARENTAL RESPONSIBILITY), *Re; sub nom.* CW v SG, [2013] EWHC 854 (Fam), [2013] 2 F.L.R. 655, Baker, J., Fam Div.

1338. Parental wishes–Capacity–Life-sustaining treatment of child in foster care–Wishes and feelings of parents lacking litigation capacity

The applicant NHS trust sought declarations in relation to the best interests of a three-year-old child (H), and sought approval of an advanced care plan. H had suffered devastating and widespread brain destruction when he was five weeks old. He had made no developmental progress and functioned below the level of a newborn baby. He had major physical disabilities including twisting of the spine, deformity of the rib cage, gastric reflux, severe visual impairment and inability to communicate. His life expectancy was short, as his condition had a progressive, deteriorating course. His parents lacked capacity to make decisions about his medical treatment or to conduct the instant proceedings on their own behalf. H lived with long-term foster carers, but his parents took an interest in his welfare and had monthly supervised contact. The overall purpose of the care plan, which had been prepared by H's consultant paediatric neurologist (S), was to continue to give H the fullest treatment while he remained in his present state, and to treat minor medical issues as they arose, but not to give aggressive treatment if he were to deteriorate seriously, on the basis that it would be unkind and contrary to his best interests to do so. The care plan was agreed between the trust, H's father and his foster mother (B), and it was not opposed by the local authority and the children's guardian. H's mother agreed with the general approach of the care plan, but did not agree to three particular matters: she wished H to have a blood test if he got an infection such as pneumonia; she wished H to be given a short period of mouth-to-mouth resuscitation if he were to stop breathing; and she wished for two attempts to be made to restart H's heart if it stopped beating. The trust submitted that regard should be had to H's parents' wishes to the extent that they related to H's best interests, but referred to the statement made in *An NHS Trust v MB* [2006] EWHC 507 (Fam), [2006] 2 F.L.R. 319, [2006] C.L.Y. 1847 to the effect that those wishes, "however understandable in human terms, [were] wholly irrelevant to consideration of the objective best interests of the child save to the extent in any given case that they may illuminate the quality and value to the child of the child/parent relationship". The trust argued that that caveat had to apply more forcefully to the views or wishes of parents without capacity who were not themselves looking after the child in question.

Held: Declaration granted. (1) Although an involved parent who had capacity might be better placed to express views that assisted in assessing the child's best interests than one who was less involved or capacitous, that was a matter of evidence and not one of principle. Parents who lacked capacity might still make telling points about welfare, and it would be wrong to discount the weight to be attached to their views simply because of incapacity (see para.16 of judgment). (2) Treatment of H in the event of the inevitable deterioration that he would experience might prolong his life, but would improve neither his quality of life nor his potential, and might be futile. It was clear that if he were to reach the point of requiring ventilation or CPR, his overall condition would have deteriorated so markedly that he would be likely to be facing a life of pain, if he could experience pain, with no possibility of pleasure in the face of such serious deterioration. In such circumstances, aggressive treatment would amount to preserving life for its own sake and would not be in H's best interests, *An NHS Trust v MB* applied (paras 30-32). (3) S was not in favour of H having a blood test if he got an infection such as pneumonia because of the admission to hospital that that would require: an important goal was to allow H to remain at home with B, where he was best cared for, as far as possible. In relation to mouth-to-mouth resuscitation, S considered that H's condition would have deteriorated to such an extent that it would not be right to start resuscitation if he had stopped breathing. In relation to cardiac arrest, it was S's view that if H suffered such an event it would probably be the result of interruption in his breathing and would mean that he was in a terrible predicament from which it would not be possible to restore him. Intervention to attempt to reverse the situation would only prolong his suffering. Although H's mother was acutely and understandably anxious to do everything possible for him, the medical view was to be preferred. It was not in his best interests to do more than S advised (paras 35-36). (4) Any declarations made should only extend to matters where the factual basis was known. It would be unwise to endorse aspects of care plans that might change in their details, *Portsmouth NHS Trust v Wyatt* [2005] EWCA Civ 1181, [2005] 1 W.L.R. 3995, [2005] C.L.Y. 1794 considered. As H was relatively well at the present time, the medical situation had not crystallised, as it would by definition have done in a crisis situation (paras 39-43). (5) The court made various declarations as to H's best interests in relation to medical treatment (para.44).

AN NHS TRUST v H; *sub nom.* KH (MEDICAL TREATMENT: ADVANCED CARE PLAN), RE; AN NHS TRUST v KH [2013] 1 F.L.R. 1471, Peter Jackson, J., Fam Div (Liverpool).

1339. Parents–Assessment–Refusal of father's application for further assessment as potential carer for child

The appellant father (F) appealed against a decision refusing his application for further assessment as a potential parent for his daughter (T), who was almost two years old. The second respondent mother (M) had limited capacity and the first respondent local authority had commenced an assessment of T's maternal aunt as a potential carer for T. F's paternity was subsequently established by DNA testing and, following an initial assessment, he applied for party status and a further assessment. The local authority opposed the application on the basis that an assessment would take up to 14 weeks and throw out the timetable it had mapped for the proceedings, including referral to an adoption panel, and that T was already in suspense and her limbo would be unnecessarily and unreasonably extended. It was common ground that F would be part of T's life in her future, if only as a contact parent. The judge balanced the local authority's pleas for expedition and warning against losing the timetable against F's argument that, as a parent, he should not be discarded without further assessment. She held that the scale came down in favour of the arguments adduced by the local authority, and refused F's application. A neighbouring local authority subsequently provided the local authority with reports on F containing material which was more against him than for him. F contended that, notwithstanding the fresh evidence, T deserved the fullest assessment and he, as a parent, had an obvious right to be fully assessed since, without that, his potential for T would never be brought into the scales of justice. The local authority submitted that the judge's decision was within the permissible margin of appreciation given to her, and that if she had had sight of the new material that would only have fortified her refusal. M, who had adopted a neutral position below, opposed the appeal, having raised assertions that she had been assaulted, victimised and threatened by F during their relationship.

Held: Appeal allowed. (1) The court expressed misgivings in interfering with the case management decision of a circuit judge who had the greatest experience and ability in managing difficult cases. However, the situation before the instant court was distinctly different to that before the judge. The legal requirements for the procedural steps to be taken before the issue of any placement application were being relaxed or removed by the government, and the time pressure created by the need to refer T's case to the best interests panel was in the process of disappearing. Further, it had emerged that an independent social worker would be able to complete a further assessment of F within three months. If the assessment of the maternal aunt proved negative, it was highly likely that F would be assessed further before any placement order could be deployed. Even if the assessment of the maternal aunt was positive, T was entitled to a judicial declaration as between two potential positive assessments. Accordingly, whichever way the assessment of the maternal aunt went, there seemed to be a foreseeable need to carry out a further assessment of F, and there was an obvious advantage in commencing such an assessment as soon as possible. That was the surest safeguard against future delay. The judge's decision refusing F's application was, accordingly, substituted by a direction for further assessment of F by the identified independent social worker (see paras 10-14 of judgment). (2) (Per Black, L.J.) It was rare for the instant court to interfere with case management decisions, *TL v Hammersmith and Fulham LBC* [2011] EWCA Civ 812, [2012] 2 F.L.R. 308, [2012] C.L.Y. 1329 considered. The judge in the instant case had had a difficult decision to make and the landscape was no longer the same, given the pending changes to the regulations concerning the involvement of the local authority's panel and the identification of an independent social worker willing to undertake the assessment. The circumstances were now right to provide for F to be assessed as a carer of T as he sought (paras 15-18).

N (A CHILD) (PARENTING ASSESSMENT), *Re*, [2012] EWCA Civ 1141, [2013] 1 F.L.R. 1159, Thorpe, L.J., CA (Civ Div).

1340. Presumption of Death Act 2013 ()

This Act makes provision in relation to the presumed death of missing persons. This Act received Royal Assent on March 26, 2013.

1341. Residence orders–Burden of proof–Discretion of judge–Welfare of children

The appellant father (F) appealed against a decision of a judge in the county court relating to residence of his children (C). C had been living with their mother (M) in accordance with a residence order made by a court, which granted F contact rights. A district judge temporarily suspended contact and at the hearing F maintained that C's day-to-day care was deficient. On appeal the county court judge made an order for future contact and F withdrew his appeal, however, the position was reviewed within a short time. At the renewed hearing F suggested that a fact-finding investigation was needed to address his concerns about C's care. The judge ordered an investigation and for F to file a response. F listed allegations of missed medical appointments, non-accidental injuries, verbal abuse and blocked contact. M provided detailed responses to the allegations. Although the matter was listed for two days, after F had given evidence for 1 hour and 15 minutes, the judge stopped the proceedings and gave judgment and explained why he was doing so. In relation to the missed medical appointments he stated that there was no real evidence of neglect and that F did not have specific evidence of non-accidental injury. The judge said that the other allegations did not justify an order that C should be moved and that F had failed to show that the residence order should be changed. F submitted that the judge erred by stopping the proceedings after he had given evidence for a short time and in not requiring M to give evidence. F argued that the test applied by the judge, namely that F had to show on the balance of probabilities that there were compelling reasons for the children to be moved, was set too high and that he would have been able to prove many of the allegations if he had had the opportunity to cross-examine M.

Held: Appeal dismissed. It was important to recognise that the proceedings before the judge were family proceedings and the judge was not required to act as an umpire as in civil litigation. In civil litigation a judge's ability to stop a case was limited. In family proceedings a judge had an inquisitorial role and his duty was to further the welfare of the children, which was the paramount consideration. For that reason a judge exercised a far broader jurisdiction than in a civil jurisdiction to determine how an application should be pursued. He could summarily dismiss it as groundless or determine it as one to be dealt with by written or oral evidence or he could hear the evidence and take stock of where the matter stood after that. The judge would always be concerned to ask if there was a reason in the interests of the children as to why to continue a matter raised by a parent. If the judge was satisfied that the children would gain no advantage, it was within his discretion to decide that the proceedings should go no further. The reality was that the residence order was in place and that was the starting point. Given that the judge had heard F's evidence in chief, it was entirely appropriate for him to direct himself as he did, namely that F had to establish on the balance of probabilities that there were compelling reasons why the children should be moved. It was the correct exercise of his discretion for the judge to say F had failed to meet that test. There was no error of law or approach either in his determining the standard by which F s evidence was to be evaluated or to say he was satisfied that F had failed to prove any of the matters to satisfy the court that the residence order should be changed. The judge's view was robust, but he did not exceed the ambit of his discretion (see paras 14-19 of judgment).

C (FAMILY PROCEEDINGS: CASE MANAGEMENT), *Re,* [2012] EWCA Civ 1489, [2013] 1 F.L.R. 1089, Thorpe, L.J., CA (Civ Div).

1342. **Residence orders–Grandparents–Mother opposed to contact between child and paternal family–Propriety of transferring residence from mother to paternal grandmother without making findings about mother's allegations of violence and abuse**

The appellant mother (M) appealed against a residence order granted in respect of her four-year-old daughter (K) in favour of the paternal grandmother (G). Following the separation of M and the father (F), K had lived with M. M regarded the paternal family as abusive and dangerous and opposed contact between them and K. Contact orders were made in favour of F and G during a hearing in 2010 when M was in hospital and was not represented. M disobeyed the orders. An expert assessed M's capacity to litigate and concluded that she had capacity, but needed the support of a community practice nurse at hearings. A fact-finding hearing was listed on August 11, 2011 in relation to M's allegations of violence and abuse. M applied to adjourn it because neither her counsel nor her community practice nurse were available, but the judge refused and the hearing went ahead. M was represented by a barrister whom she had only just met. She made compromises in respect of the allegations and agreed a contact order. M disobeyed the contact order and G applied for residence. The local authority undertook a risk assessment and recommended that K should remain with M because the emotional harm involved in moving her to G for the purposes of keeping contact with both sides of the family seemed too extreme. The judge refused to allow M's counsel to investigate her accusations against F and G because those issues had been compromised on August 11. He departed from the recommendation of the local authority on the basis that M's hostility towards G was unreasonable and must be causing emotional harm to K. He concluded that it was better for K to live with G and have contact with M than to live with M and have no contact with any member of the paternal family. M argued that procedural unfairness had resulted from the judge's refusal to permit her counsel to investigate any of the history so vital to justifying her allegations; the judge had been wrong to treat her as implacably hostile without making clear findings; and the judge had been plainly wrong in failing sufficiently to explain why he had rejected the clear recommendation of the experts.

Held: Appeal allowed. The security of the outcome of the hearing on August 11 seemed to be impaired by the very difficult circumstances confronting M on that day. The expert opinion as to her capacity made it plain that she was vulnerable and required protection, but the protection that she needed had not been there. The compromise of August 11 had been in the context of contact applications. Once a graver case had been presented to the court, namely a case for transfer of care from M to G, an issue had arisen about whether it was safe to conclude that the past had been sufficiently investigated to the extent that the parties had compromised the fact-finding hearing. The judge had expressed a different conclusion to the social work team but had not perhaps sufficiently explained why. The transfer of contact from an obdurate parent to an alternatively available parent was a weapon of last resort. The court knew of no case where such a dire sanction had been exercised against an obdurate parent to transfer the primary care to a grandmother. Grandparents were manifestly not on equal footing with parents. Inevitably, there were disadvantages to a child in being brought up by an adult of a different generation to either of her parents. Ultimately, the judge could not make his negative findings against M or his positive findings about F without looking into the history in the context of an application for the transfer of primary care of K from M to G. A more extensive re-trial would be directed to allow the judge a better opportunity to make a balanced assessment of the respective merits of both G and her family and M and her family (see paras 12-15 of judgment).

B (TRANSFER OF RESIDENCE TO GRANDMOTHER), *Re,* [2012] EWCA Civ 858, [2013] 1 F.L.R. 275, Thorpe, L.J., CA (Civ Div).

1343. Residence orders–Jurisdiction–Final residence order amounting to judgment on custody under art.10(B)(IV) Regulation 2201/2003–Retention of jurisdiction pending compliance with art.10(b)

[Regulation 2201/2003 Art.10.]

The court was required to decide whether a final residence order ought to be made in relation to a child (C). C's father (F) was from Kazakhstan and his mother (M) from Poland. Following a three week holiday to Poland, M failed to return C to England in breach of an undertaking. F then obtained a declaration that C was habitually resident in England and Wales. Meanwhile, in Polish proceedings, M had been successful in overturning a first instance decision ordering that C be returned to England. In earlier proceedings, the court examined the source of its jurisdiction to make orders in relation to C, and had found that it had been seised before the Polish proceedings, and that the English court therefore retained jurisdiction until the requirements of Regulation 2201/2003 art.10 or art.10(b) (Brussels II Revised) had been satisfied. The court held that the requirements of art.10(b) had in fact been satisfied, save for the fourth requirement as there had not been "a judgment on custody that did not entail the return of the child within the meaning of art.10(b)(iv)". The court also refused F's application for an order returning C to England. The court was required to determine whether a final residence order in relation to C ought to be made. F submitted that rather than a final residence order, there should be a further period of contact between F and C in England to be observed by the guardian, followed by a further hearing. M submitted that a final residence order, that is, a "judgment on custody" should be made incorporating orders for contact between C, his parents and C's paternal grandparents.

Held: Judgment accordingly. The time had come for the court to make a residence order amounting to a judgment on custody within the meaning of art.10(b)(iv) as M had shown that she had been committed to taking all necessary steps to ensure that C had had contact with F; an adjournment simply to permit one further occasion for contact over a few days in England was neither a necessary nor an appropriate procedure given the policy of art.10(b)(iv); there was some evidence that the fact that there had been no final order for residence had been creating uncertainty in circumstances where F and his parents needed to accept that C would be staying with M in Poland, and it was manifestly obvious that any future contact issues would be best dealt with by the Polish courts. Accordingly, a final residence order was made with a detailed contact order providing for contact both in England and Poland (see paras 26-29 of judgment).

AJ (A CHILD) (CONTACT: BRUSSELS II REVISED), *Re*; *sub nom.* SJ v JJ, [2012] EWHC 931 (Fam), [2012] 2 F.L.R. 1065, Baker, J., Fam Div.

1344. Residence orders–Shared residence orders–Children of same sex couple–Litigants in person–Guardian's duty to ensure procedural fairness

The court was required to determine issues concerning child contact in a case between the appellant (W) and the first respondent (G). W and G had been in a same sex relationship. During their relationship G had conceived two children from anonymous donor insemination. W and G separated and a shared residence order was made. G, in breach of the order, had relocated with the children from the Midlands to Cornwall. Several years of litigation followed (see *G (Children) (Residence: Same Sex Partner), Re* [2006] UKHL 43, [2006] 1 W.L.R. 2305, [2006] C.L.Y. 1694). G sought to terminate W's contact with the children and W issued a fresh application for contact. The parties could no longer afford legal representation. An expert (X) recommended the immediate resumption of contact and a therapeutic programme for the children. Contact was resumed by consent and W's application was adjourned for a year. During that time a new guardian was appointed. Contact again broke down and W complained to the new guardian. He had met the children twice, and they told him that they did not wish to have contact with W. He recommended that the shared residence order be replaced with a sole residence order in G's favour. The judge accepted his recommendation. The Court of Appeal was required to determine whether the judge was right to vary the shared residence order, thereby depriving W of parental responsibility and terminating contact.

Held: Appeal allowed. (1) The judge's variation of the shared residence order should be set aside on the basis of procedural unfairness. There had been no application before him for a variation of the shared residence order. The notion of a variation had come from the guardian, not the parties, and it emerged only three days before trial. It was not endorsed by any legal submissions. Neither he nor the judge seemed to consider W's need for advice and protection as a litigant in person. Had she been represented, her counsel would have opposed the variation not only on grounds of substance but also on grounds of procedural unfairness (see paras 36-37 of judgment). (2) W's application had been adjourned on the basis of a shared endeavour between the parents, the old guardian, X and the court. If all went according to plan the parties were to re-assemble after 12 months to decide the future. If it did not go to plan, it was extremely important for the court to be informed. G had no incentive to return to court, and W had failed to do so. In those circumstances the new guardian had a clear duty to take the initiative. He knew that W had no representation and she was appealing to him to act. The maintenance of the relationship between the children and W had been declared by X and by the courts to be of the first importance (paras 41-43). (3) The children's wishes were an important factor, but there was a danger in taking them too literally. Their criticisms of W had no objective foundation. She had always been a warm and loving parent who had never failed them. There was also a clear mismatch between what they said and how they behaved: the new guardian had himself noted the warmth of the interaction between the children and W which froze as soon as he made himself known. The children were aware of G's antipathy to W and to contact. The judge had to have regard to the assessments of all of those previously involved with the case, and to G's intention to estrange W from the children. He had failed to sufficiently take account of the importance of the relationship between the children and W, and the damage that would be caused to them by its loss. X was an internationally renowned expert but had been given no opportunity to assess the breakdown or advise on the prospects of reparation. He had declared himself ready to return to the challenges that the case presented and had access to charity funding for that purpose. The judge's order was therefore premature and was set aside. W's application was remitted for retrial. A direction was made for the immediate re-engagement of X (paras 47-50). (4) (Obiter) The instant case illustrated the difficulties that courts faced when the parties were unrepresented, particularly in complex cases. The children's guardian, as the only party with the benefit of legal advice and representation, should be vigilant to avoid procedural or other unfairness to one or other of the unrepresented parties (para.32).

G (CHILDREN) (RESIDENCE AND CONTACT), *Re; sub nom.* G (CHILDREN) (SHARED RESIDENCE), *Re,* [2012] EWCA Civ 1434, [2013] 1 F.L.R. 1323, Thorpe, L.J., CA (Civ Div).

1345. Special guardians–Payments–Lawfulness of local authority's policy on payment of allowances to special guardians

[Local Authority Social Services Act 1970 (c.42) s.7.]

The claimant (T), the special guardian of a four-year-old boy, applied for judicial review of the policy of the defendant local authority in relation to the financial assistance that was payable to special guardians. The Special Guardianship Guidance, which had been issued under the Local Authority Social Services Act 1970 s.7, provided, at para.65, that in determining the amount of any ongoing financial support, a local authority should have regard to the amount of fostering allowance which would have been payable had the child been fostered. However, the local authority's policy provided as follows: "Children who are the subject of Special Guardianship Orders are not looked after children, they have become part of the family unit. The additional costs for a looked after child are therefore not applicable to a child in a Special Guardianship arrangement. The Local Authority therefore adjusts the figures given by the Fostering Network and takes two-thirds of this as the figure which will be required to look after a child of that age. This deducts the additional 50 per cent which is allowed for by the Fostering Network". The Department for Education and Skills had developed a standardised means-test model for use in assessing the financial support for carers in adoption and special guardianship cases, but the local authority decided not to use it, having identified four aspects of it with which it disagreed. T argued that (1) the local authority's policy failed to set a level of allowance for special guardians that was comparable to the minimum core rate for foster carers recommended by the National Fostering Network, as para.65 of the Guidance required; (2) the means test adopted by the local authority was so heavily slanted against the special guardian by comparison with the model suggested that it would act as a deterrent to prospective special guardians; it was therefore contrary to the statutory purpose of the allowance.

Held: Application granted in part. (1) Where a local authority proposed to have a policy in which the allowance to be paid to special guardians was set, it was required, in order to comply with the Guidance and unless there were cogent reasons for departing from it, to consider the Fostering Network's minimum recommended allowances and make such adjustments to those allowances to reflect the (lower) costs to a special guardian as it considered appropriate, *R. (on the application of B) v Lewisham LBC* [2008] EWHC 738 (Admin), [2008] 2 F.L.R. 523, [2008] C.L.Y. 1518 applied. Any such adjustment would inevitably be somewhat arbitrary, but that was what the Guidance required. Compliance was not achieved by ignoring the additional costs of caring for a child not born into the family, as the local authority's policy did, or by assessing them at nil. The local authority had not complied with para.65 of the Guidance and had produced no reasons, cogent or otherwise, for not doing so. In those circumstances, the decision to adopt a level of allowance for special guardians of two-thirds of the Fostering Network's minimum allowances was unlawful and had to be quashed (see paras 64, 67-68 of judgment). (2) The reasons given by the local authority for departing from the model were perfectly rational. Further, local authorities had a wide margin of appreciation in matters such as the allocation of resources, which was effectively what this amounted to, and a court should not intervene on an application for judicial review save in the clearest of cases (paras 72-73).

R. (ON THE APPLICATION OF T) v MERTON LBC, [2012] EWHC 2055 (Admin), [2013] P.T.S.R. 710, Edwards-Stuart, J., QBD (Admin).

1346. **Special guardianship orders–Local authorities' powers and duties–Out-of-area placements–Judicial guidance concerning correct approach to execution and funding of statutory duties where more than one local authority involved**

[Children Act 1989 (c.41) s.14A, s.14F, s.20(1)(c), s.22(1); Special Guardianship Regulations 2005 (SI 2005/1109) reg.5.]

The appellant local authority (S) appealed against a special guardianship order declaring that it was responsible for the financial assistance and other services to be provided to two boys (B1 and B2) who were the subjects of an out-of area placement from the respondent local authority (N). The boys' parents had become unable to care for them. With their consent, B1 became a looked-after child within the Children Act 1989 s.20(1)(c) and was placed in foster care; B2 remained with his mother, who was the only parent with parental responsibility. She agreed, a couple of months later, that he should join B1. The parents lived within N's area and the foster parents lived within S's area. By the time B2 joined his brother, there was a general recognition that the foster carers would provide long-term care for both boys under a special guardianship order, although no application for such an order had ever been made. The foster carers acquired parental responsibility for both boys and cared for them under an interim residence order. A dispute developed between the two local authorities as to who was responsible for exercising the duties and powers under the special guardianship provisions. N provided an assessment pursuant to s.14F and provided a plan for services and financial support. Its case was that the plan ought to be implemented by S. The dispute was complicated by the fact that S remained unconvinced that, under its own criteria, the foster parents would qualify for financial support. A judge held that she was bound by *C v D* [2009] EWHC 1942 (Fam), [2010] 1 F.L.R. 583, [2010] C.L.Y. 1306 and declared S responsible. She found that N had been statutorily entitled to perform its own assessments and plans. S denied that it was responsible for implementation of N's plan, but maintained that if it was so responsible, then it was entitled to prepare its own plan.

Held: Appeal allowed. (1) The law in the area of special guardianship was quite settled despite the powerful criticisms that could be made of it, *C v D* and *D (A Child) (Care Proceedings: Designated Local Authority), Re* [2012] EWCA Civ 627, [2013] Fam. 34, [2012] C.L.Y. 1356 applied. The key question in determining which local authority was responsible was whether a child was "looked after" by one of the local authorities within the meaning of s.22(1); if so, then that authority was responsible. If the child was not a looked-after child, the responsible authority was the one in whose area the child was living. Crucially, a child ceased to be a looked-after child as soon as parental responsibility became vested in another by, for example, the making of a residence order or a special guardianship order. In such a situation, local authorities were bound by the Special Guardianship Regulations 2005 reg.5 to co-operate with each other in the discharge of functions. Every authority would be both a sender and a receiver over time and there ought to be self-regulation of financial consequences. Any site-specific hardship might be addressed in the national allocation of funds to local authorities in the light of actual experience (see paras 17-20 of judgment). (2) In the instant case, N had been the responsible authority for B1 while he was a looked-after child, but its responsibility ceased when parental responsibility passed to the foster carers, at which point S inherited the responsibility. B2 had never been a looked-after child so N had been the responsible authority while he lived with his mother, the responsibilities passing to S when he went to live with B1. N ought, however, to have involved S in the assessments and plans at a much earlier stage. S was entitled to perform its own assessment and devise its own plan, and the judge below had erred in her understanding of the statutory procedure. There was a risk that S's assessments might be less generous to the foster parents than N's plan but both local authorities had to work together to sustain placements conducive to the children's welfare (paras 21-25, 27). (3) Out-of-area placements in prospective special guardianship cases were likely to become much more common. It was of critical importance, when a child was placed, to have regard to whether they would, or should, remain looked after under an interim care order, or whether they should cease to be looked after by the making of a residence order. It was also crucial that the local authorities involved co-operated from the earliest stage about who would execute and fund the statutory duties. Although the court could make a valuable contribution, its powers to regulate were quite limited (paras 28-31).

SUFFOLK CC v NOTTINGHAMSHIRE CC; *sub nom.* NOTTINGHAMSHIRE CC v SUFFOLK CC, [2012] EWCA Civ 1640, [2013] P.T.S.R. 619, Thorpe, L.J., CA (Civ Div).

1347. Wardship–Looked-after children–Whether s.100(2)(b) Children Act 1989 preventing child in local authority accommodation from being made ward of court

[Children Act 1989 (c.41) s.20, s.100(2), s.100(2)(a); FPR PD 12D Inherent Jurisdiction (including Wardship) proceedings 2010.]

The court was required to determine whether it was prevented by the Children Act 1989 s.100 from making a child (E) a ward of court where E was accommodated under s.20. E had been voluntarily accommodated by the local authority under s.20. The judge in the hearing below had to choose between making E the subject of a care order, as sought by the first respondent local authority, no order at all, or a wardship order. In making that decision the judge noted that s.100(3) prevented the local authority from making an application for wardship without the leave of the court, and that if E's parents, the appellants, wished to issue wardship proceedings they would face the obstacle of s.100(2). The judge concluded that for the same reasons in *K (Children with Disabilities: Wardship), Re* [2011] EWHC 4031 (Fam), [2012] 2 F.L.R. 745, [2012] C.L.Y. 1360, a wardship order offered more than a care order, but that were it not for s.100(2) he would have made E a ward of the court. He also stated that notwithstanding *Re K* and *F (A Child) (Mental Health Act: Guardianship), Re* [2000] 1 F.L.R. 192, [1999] C.L.Y. 3934, he did not have jurisdiction to make E a ward of court given that she was accommodated pursuant to s.20. The judge therefore made a care order, having ruled that no order at all would have been an even worse outcome. The appellants submitted, in reliance on Re K and the FPR PD 12D, that it could not be the case that s.100(2)(b) rendered it impossible for a wardship order to co-exist with the accommodation of a child pursuant to s.20. The local authority contended that *Re K* was of little assistance as it could not be stated authoritatively that the accommodation of the children considered therein was voluntary accommodation; they might have been accommodated under another statutory provision. It further argued, in reliance on footnote 3A-1930 in a handbook on the operation of the Act, that FPR PD 12D was erroneous in law.

Held: Appeal allowed. The local authority's submissions were not as persuasive as those of the appellants. In respect of Re K, it was more likely that the accommodation of the children therein had been made under s.20, *Re K* considered. It was very unlikely that the court had not had proper regard to the statutory limitations clearly spelt out within s.100. The suggestion that FPR PD 12D had been written in error was a bold submission given the care and expertise that went into the drafting of those guides. The footnote referenced did not support the local authority's argument, not least because it was directed at s.100(2)(a) and not s.100(2)(b). The intention and effect of s.100 was to prevent a court from making any order which had the effect of requiring a child to be placed into care or under local authority supervision. That end could only be achieved by going through the proper route of threshold finding opening the court's discretionary jurisdiction to make either a care or a supervision order. The same result could not be achieved under the court's inherent jurisdiction. There was nothing in s.100 that either explicitly or implicitly precluded the court from making a wardship order where a child was not required to be accommodated but was voluntarily accommodated. If agreement for accommodation ceased, the court would not be in a position to require the local authority to accommodate or supervise a child, but so long as the s.20

placement remained, the judge had not been prevented from making the order which he had clearly found to be the one most likely to promote the child's welfare. Accordingly, the care order was set aside and replaced with the wardship order that the judge had wished to make but felt himself prevented from making by express statutory provision (see paras 13-14, 16-18 of judgment).

E (A CHILD) (WARDSHIP ORDER: CHILD IN VOLUNTARY ACCOMMODATION), *Re*, [2012] EWCA Civ 1773, [2013] 2 F.L.R. 63, Thorpe, L.J., CA (Civ Div).

1348. Books

Norrie, Professor Kenneth McK–Law Relating to Parent & Child in Scotland. £235.00. ISBN 9780414018105. (Sweet & Maxwell).

FINANCIAL REGULATION

1349. Approved persons–Misconduct–Failure to take reasonable steps to ensure compliance with requirements and standards of regulatory system

The applicant (P) referred to the tribunal a decision of the respondent authority (F) that, as an approved person, he was guilty of misconduct by failing to take reasonable steps to ensure that a business complied with the requirements and standards of the regulatory system. P was the chief executive of the wealth management business of a financial services company (U), where F had found there were serious flaws in the operation, structure and terms of reference of the executive committees, in the management information available to P and other members of the senior management team, in the operational risk framework, and in compliance monitoring. It concluded that P had failed to take reasonable steps in relation to those flaws: he had not carried out an adequate initial assessment and, in particular, had not effectively questioned the assurances he received that there were no fundamental deficiencies with the design and operational effectiveness of the governance and risk-management frameworks; he should also have carried out continuous monitoring and, in particular, adequately considered the wider implications for the governance and risk-management frameworks of the warning signals; and he should have recognised that there were such fundamental deficiencies, and implemented the systematic overhaul sooner than he did.

Held: Reference allowed. (1) There were serious flaws within aspects of the business. The operational risk framework, as designed, was not inherently flawed. The problems arose at the ground level of implementation. They arose because appropriate operational controls to ensure correct transaction procedures were not being performed properly or were non-existent. The issue, however, was whether the design and operational effectiveness of the governance and risk management frameworks in place in the business were seriously flawed. The evidence demonstrated that there were flaws in the operational effectiveness of U's risk management system. They were serious because they were at the centre of the means by which U looked after and managed transactions in clients' assets and money (see paras 81, 84 of judgment). There were also deficiencies in compliance monitoring. U had failed to have an effective independent monitoring function in place over the ground-level activities of operations. The problems that arose, particularly those relating to client money, reconciliations and unauthorised transactions and transfers of funds, were arising because of non-compliance at ground level (paras 103-104). However, the evidence did not establish that the structure and operation of the executive committees was properly to be regarded as a serious flaw (para.124). The management information had been deficient. There would, in principle, be a deficiency if the information was incorrect or insufficient. It would be incorrect where the sources from which it was captured were inaccurate or misleading. It would be insufficient if the system failed to provide access to the required data.

It was not in dispute that a number of events happened that caused errors and insufficiencies in the quality and quantity of management information relating to U's core activities. The question of whether there was a serious deficiency in management information could not be determined without examining the integrity of the risk-management framework adopted by the firm in question and the standard of its compliance monitoring. There were deficiencies in both those areas at U. It almost inevitably followed that those deficiencies would cause knock-on deficiencies in the quality and quantity of the management information. Seen in the context of a wealth-management business such as that of U, they had to be classed as serious flaws (paras 135, 138). (2) Although F had established there were three serious flaws, it had not established that P had failed to take reasonable steps. There had been insufficient evidence apparent to him during the period of the initial assessment that there were flaws such that he needed to dig deeper in challenging his team's assurances that there were no fundamental deficiencies in the design and operational effectiveness of the governance and risk-management frameworks. Nor had there been sufficient evidence apparent to him that should have called for the initiation of a major systematic overhaul. As for the allegation that he failed to perform a continuous process of monitoring, the circumstances and events that should have been construed as warning signals had not been so serious in themselves as to have demanded a systematic overhaul earlier than P actually did so. The fact remained that every specific control failure identified in the business had been fully investigated and had been remedied or was being dealt with in accordance with a defined plan. Thus, the evidence as a whole did not establish that P was guilty of misconduct. In fact, the actions he took to deal with the operational and compliance issues as they arose were reasonable steps (paras 140, 187, 203, 207, 212, 218, 226-227).

POTTAGE v FINANCIAL SERVICES AUTHORITY [2013] Lloyd's Rep. F.C. 16, Sir Stephen Oliver Q.C., UT (Tax).

1350. **Bank administration–Bank of England–Consequential amendments–Financial markets**

THE FINANCIAL SERVICES ACT 2012 (CONSEQUENTIAL AMENDMENTS AND TRANSITIONAL PROVISIONS) (NO.3) ORDER 2013, SI 2013/1765; made under the Financial Services Act 2012 s.115, s.118, s.119. In force: September 1, 2013; .

This Order makes transitional provision and amendments to subordinate legislation in connection with the Financial Services Act 2012.

1351. **Bank of England–Financial Conduct Authority–Financial instruments–Prudential Regulation Authority**

THE FINANCIAL SERVICES ACT 2012 (TRANSITIONAL PROVISIONS) (RULES AND MISCELLANEOUS PROVISIONS) ORDER 2013, SI 2013/161; made under the Financial Services Act 2012 s.115, s.119. In force: February 20, 2013; .

This Order, which comes into force on February 20, 2013, provides that the Financial Conduct Authority the Prudential Regulation Authority and the Bank of England may designate various instruments made by the Authority.

1352. **Bank of England–Financial Conduct Authority–Financial Services Authority–Fines**

THE PAYMENT TO TREASURY OF PENALTIES (ENFORCEMENT COSTS) ORDER 2013, SI 2013/418; made under the Financial Services and Markets Act 2000 s.109, s.110, s.115, Sch.1ZA para.20, Sch.1ZB para.28. In force: April 1, 2013; .

This Order relates to new arrangements to require revenue from fines received by regulators of financial services to be passed to theTreasury net of enforcement case costs for the year. The Order specifies the functions of prosecuting any criminal offence under the law of any part of the United Kingdom (other than those already specified in section 109 of the Financial Services Act 2012), the functions of the Financial Services Authority (FSA) and the Financial Conduct Authority (FCA) in relation to insolvency proceedings where there has been a breach of the regulatory perimeter. The Order also allows the FSA, FCA and Bank of England to net off against FSMA penalties those enforcement costs incurred under the various "stand alone" regulatory regimes which those regulators operate -such as the Money Laundering Regulations 2007.

1353. Benchmarking–Financial regulation–Financial services

THE FINANCIAL SERVICES AND MARKETS ACT 2000 (REGULATED ACTIVITIES) (AMENDMENT) ORDER 2013, SI 2013/655; made under the Financial Services and Markets Act 2000 s.22, s.428, Sch.2 para.25. In force: April 2, 2013; .

This Regulation amends the the Financial Services and Markets Act (Regulated Activities) Order 2001 to create new regulated activities related to the setting of specified benchmarks, the first of which will be LIBOR (the London Inter-Bank Offered Rate).

1354. Consultation–Financial Conduct Authority–Prudential Regulation Authority

THE FINANCIAL SERVICES AND MARKETS ACT 2000 (EXERCISE OF POWERS UNDER PART 4A) (CONSULTATION WITH HOME STATE REGULATORS) REGULATIONS 2013, SI 2013/431; made under the Financial Services and Markets Act 2000 s.55R. In force: April 1, 2013; .

Financial Services and Markets Act 2000 requires the Financial Conduct Authority or the Prudential Regulation Authority when it is giving permission under Pt 4A of the Act in response to an application made by a person who is connected with certain EEA firms to consult with the home state regulator of the EEA firm in prescribed circumstances. The appropriate regulator must also consult the home state regulator when cancelling or varying such a permission, in prescribed circumstances. These regulations prescribe two circumstances in which consultation with the home state regulator must take place.

1355. Consumer credit–Consumer credit agreements–Credit brokers–Debt collection

THE FINANCIAL SERVICES AND MARKETS ACT 2000 (REGULATED ACTIVITIES) (AMENDMENT) (NO.2) ORDER 2013, SI 2013/1881; made under the European Communities Act 1972 s.2; and the Financial Services and Markets Act 2000 s.22, s.428, Sch.2 para.25. In force: in accordance with art.1.; .

This Order specifies additional activities which are to be treated as "regulated activities" for the purposes of the Financial Services and Markets Act 2000. The effect of this is that a person who carries on such an activity in the UK must be authorised under the Act to carry out the activities or an exempt person. The new regulated activities include credit broking, operating an electronic system in relation to lending, debt adjusting, debt-counselling, debt-collecting, debt administration, entering into etc. a regulated credit agreement, entering into etc. a regulated consumer hire agreement, providing credit information services and providing credit references.

1356. Data sharing–Financial Conduct Authority–Prudential Regulation Authority

THE FINANCIAL CONGLOMERATES AND OTHER FINANCIAL GROUPS (AMENDMENT) REGULATIONS 2013, SI 2013/1162; made under the European Communities Act 1972 s.2. In force: June 10, 2013; .

These Regulations implement, in part, Directive 2011/89 as regards the supplementary supervision of financial entities in a financial conglomerate. The Prudential Regulation Authority (PRA) and the Financial Conduct Authority (FCA) are responsible for implementing the majority of the provisions of this Directive. The Regulations make a limited number of technical and definitional amendments to existing secondary legislation which imposes obligations on the PRA and FCA with regard to their supervisory functions, in particular concerning information sharing and consultation requirements.

1357. **Enforcement–Financial Conduct Authority**

THE ENTERPRISE ACT 2002 (PART 8) (DESIGNATION OF THE FINANCIAL CONDUCT AUTHORITY AS A DESIGNATED ENFORCER) ORDER 2013, SI 2013/478; made under the Enterprise Act 2002 s.213, s.277. In force: April 1, 2013; .

This Order provides for the designation of the Financial Conduct Authority as a designated enforcer under Part 8 of the Enterprise Act 2002 and the revocation of the Enterprise Act 2002 (Part 8) (Designation of the Financial Services Authority as a Designated Enforcer) Order 2004 (SI 2004/935) as of April 1, 2013. As a result the Financial Conduct Authority will be able to obtain enforcement orders under Part 8 of the Enterprise Act 2002 to protect the collective interests of consumers.

1358. **Financial Conduct Authority–Financial services–Prudential Regulation Authority**

THE FINANCIAL SERVICES AND MARKETS ACT 2000 (THRESHOLD CONDITIONS) ORDER 2013, SI 2013/555; made under the Financial Services and Markets Act 2000 s.55C, s.428. In force: April 1, 2013; .

This Order amends the threshold conditions set out in Sch.6 to the Financial Services and Markets Act 2000.

1359. **Financial Conduct Authority–Financial services–Prudential Regulation Authority–Regulated activities**

THE FINANCIAL SERVICES AND MARKETS ACT 2000 (PRA-REGULATED ACTIVITIES) ORDER 2013, SI 2013/556; made under the Financial Services and Markets Act 2000 s.22A, s.428. In force: in accordance with art.1.; .

This Order specifies, for the purposes of the Financial Services and Markets Act 2000, which regulated activities are "PRA-regulated activities" and so are the regulated activities which are subject to prudential regulation by the Prudential Regulation Authority (PRA), rather than the Financial Conduct Authority.

1360. **Financial Conduct Authority–Financial Services Authority–Mutual societies–Prudential Regulation Authority**

THE FINANCIAL SERVICES ACT 2012 (MUTUAL SOCIETIES) ORDER 2013, SI 2013/496; made under the Financial Services Act 2012 s.50, s.51, s.52, s.115, s.118. In force: April 1, 2013; .

This instrument allocates the Financial Services Authority's existing responsibilities for the regulation of mutual societies between the two new regulatory bodies, the Prudential Regulation Authority and the Financial Conduct Authority.

1361. **Financial Conduct Authority–Prudential Regulation Authority–Rules**

THE FINANCIAL SERVICES AND MARKETS ACT 2000 (FINANCIAL SERVICES COMPENSATION SCHEME) ORDER 2013, SI 2013/598; made under the Financial Services and Markets Act 2000 s.213. In force: April 1, 2013; .

This Order specifies what the Prudential Regulation Authority (PRA) may make rules for and what the Financial Conduct Authority (FCA) may make rules for under the Financial Services and Markets Act 2000.

1362. Financial markets–Financial services–Penalties–Treasury

THE PAYMENT TO TREASURY OF PENALTIES REGULATIONS 2013, SI 2013/429; made under the European Communities Act 1972 s.2. In force: April 1, 2013;.

These Regulations amend specified regulations to provide that the amounts received by the regulator by way of penalties imposed under the regulations is to be paid by the regulator to the Treasury.

1363. Market abuse–Derivatives–Whether "layering" constituting market abuse contrary to s.118 Financial Services and Markets Act 2000

[Financial Services and Markets Act 2000 (c.8) s.118, s.118(1), s.123(2).]

The applicant company (C) referred to the tribunal a decision of the respondent FSA that it had committed market abuse in breach of the Financial Services and Markets Act 2000 s.118. C had formerly carried on business as Swift Trade (S), a non-FSA-authorised Canadian company dissolved in 2010. The FSA's case was that, for about a year, S had systematically and deliberately engaged in a manipulative trading activity known as "layering" in relation to shares traded on the London Stock Exchange. Essentially, it had attempted to move particular share prices up so it could sell at a high price, then to move them down so it could buy at a lower price. Dealers based in various countries had placed orders for "contracts for differences" (CFDs) using S's facilities with two direct market access providers (M and P) regulated in the United Kingdom. The CFDs were placed in relation to shares quoted on the LSE. As the orders were placed, M and P's computers automatically hedged them by placing orders to buy or sell an equivalent quantity of the shares. Once the price had moved and a profit made on an actual trade, the CFD orders would be cancelled, usually within seconds of being placed, and M and P would cancel the hedging orders. C submitted that (1) the FSA had no jurisdiction, S having been dissolved before the issue of the decision notice; (2) because the CFDs were in derivatives, they were not "qualifying investments" for the purposes of s.118(5); or, alternatively, the trades had been undertaken by M and P rather than by S; (3) in any event, its activity was neither manipulative nor abusive; independent dealers were simply using its direct market access platform; or it could rely on the defence in s.123(2) of the Act; (4) the FSA's actions were inappropriate given that S's conduct had been investigated in Canada by the Ontario Securities Commission (OSC) and a negotiated settlement had been reached.

Held: Judgment in favour of FSA. (1) The FSA and the tribunal had jurisdiction. Canadian law provided that S had a continuing existence for the purpose of the instant proceedings (see paras 21-25, 144 of judgment). (2) S's conduct fell within s.118. The CFD orders had been placed with the intention that M and P would immediately hedge them. Even though it was M and P that had placed the orders on the LSE, they had done so in response to S's orders for CFDs. In interpreting the phrase "behaviour... which occurs... in relation to qualifying investments" in s.118(5), it was not necessary for there to be trading directly in a qualifying investment. Moreover, s.118(1) showed that it was not necessarily the conduct of one person alone that was relevant. Derivatives trading could fall within the scope of s.118(5). For the same reasons, the argument that it was M and P, and not S which had placed the orders was unsustainable (paras 37-41, 144). (3) The FSA had to adduce cogent evidence to support its allegations, but did not have to establish them beyond the balance of probabilities. The burden of establishing the s.123 defence rested with S. S's trading had been deliberate, manipulative, profit-driven, and designed to deceive other market users. There was nothing to support its contention that it had merely acted as a subsidiary direct market access provider. Rather, the dealers had been acting in accordance with a strategy that S had devised and encouraged, and S had concealed what it was doing from the regulators. S was thus guilty of market abuse within the meaning of s.118(5)(a) and s.118(5)(b). Section 123(2) did not help it. While it was unnecessary to examine the FSA's alternative argument that, if s.118(5) was not offended, s.118(8) was, it would have been open to the tribunal to deal with the argument had the need arisen, even though it had not been referred to in the decision notice. The tribunal had to reach its own conclusions. While it could not embark on a wide-ranging enquiry into unrelated topics, it could consider material other than that available to the FSA. The only limitation was that it had to confine itself to the trading conduct that was the subject of the reference. It followed that if the tribunal concluded that the appropriate action was to make a determination in accordance with s.118(8) rather than s.118(5), it could do so (paras 42-49, 125-133, 144). (4) There was no overlap between the OSC's investigation and that of the FSA, and there was nothing in the OSC's settlement to preclude the FSA from examining S's activities on the UK markets (paras 134-138, 144). (5) Determination of the appropriate penalty would not be approached by reference to the profits made by S or its ability to pay, the evidence on those issues being somewhat vague. What was clear, however, was that S's conduct amounted to a cynical, year-long, intensive manipulation of the LSE that showed a wholesale disregard of regulatory requirements and was not in accordance with recognised market practice. S had tried to conceal its conduct and had done everything possible to escape the consequences. While the £8 million penalty imposed by the FSA seemed insufficient, it would stand (paras 139-143, 144).

7722656 CANADA INC (FORMERLY SWIFT TRADE INC) v FINANCIAL SERVICES AUTHORITY [2013] Lloyd's Rep. F.C. 381, Judge Colin Bishopp, UT (Tax).

1364. Payment protection insurance–Stay of proceedings–Misselling claims–FSA scheme for handling PPI complaints–Guidance on staying proceedings for consideration under scheme

The defendant bank (B) applied to stay claims alleging the misselling of payment protection insurance (PPI). B sought to stay the claims of the five claimants for eight weeks so that their claims could be processed as complaints in accordance with the scheme established by the Financial Services Authority, which provided for an eight-week resolution period. Two claimants (C) agreed to a stay pending a Supreme Court decision in another PPI case, but would have objected to a shorter eight-week scheme stay. They argued that in the light of the history B's application for the shorter stay would not have succeeded and accordingly they should have their costs of the stay application or there should be no order for costs. The other claimants (G) would not consent to any wider stay than the eight-week scheme stay. B contended that the court should direct that, if the scheme stay was not productive, the stay should continue on the wider basis.

Held: Application granted. (1) A person with a PPI claim who failed to engage with the FSA scheme but instead proceeded straight to litigation would be at risk of an adverse costs order even if the claim succeeded, *Halsey v Milton Keynes General NHS Trust* [2004] EWCA Civ 576, [2004] 1 W.L.R. 3002, [2004] C.L.Y. 291 considered. The fact that the scheme was one which the FSA required B to undertake, as compared with mediation which both parties had to agree to, did not take PPI cases in the scheme outside the ambit of the principles laid down in *Halsey*. The CPR made clear that claimants did not have the unfettered right to litigate any claim without regard to the overriding objective and the desirability of alternative dispute resolution. Cases involving limitation issues might have to be dealt with differently (see paras 27-28, 31 of judgment). (2) Where a claimant brought a claim without having engaged in the scheme, it was likely that the court would order a stay at an early stage in order to facilitate ADR via the scheme. An eight-week stay was both modest and proportionate. A claimant who resisted such a stay was likely to be ordered to pay the costs of such an application if it succeeded (para.38). (3) The court would have ordered a scheme stay of C's claims. Letters before claim had been sent to B and not responded to. But what had happened in the past was not necessarily an indication of what would happen in the future and the whole basis of the stay application was that B would deal with the claim within the eight-week period. The stay would not cause any real prejudice. There should be no order as to costs (paras 40-43). (4) Of G's claims, two should be stayed and one should not, since it did not raise any issues of unfair relationship or extortionate credit bargain, which were likely to be considered by the Supreme

Court. The two claims should be subject to an eight-week scheme stay and thereafter, if not settled, stayed pending the decision of the Supreme Court. There should be no order as to costs (paras 45-52).

ANDREW v BARCLAYS BANK PLC; CARROLL v EGG BANKING PLC [2012] C.T.L.C. 115, Judge Waksman Q.C., QBD (Manchester).

1365. Regulated activities–Deposits–Acceptance of deposits–Carrying on unauthorised regulated activity–Whether activity carried on by way of business

[Financial Services and Markets Act 2000 (c.8) s.19, s.23; Financial Services and Markets Act 2000 (Carrying on Regulated Activities by Way of Business) Order 2001 (SI 2001/1177) Art.2(1).]

The appellant (N) appealed against his conviction for carrying on unauthorised regulated activity, contrary to the Financial Services and Markets Act 2000 s.19 and s.23. N had been the chairman of a company which had received a deposit of £1 million and a deposit of £625,000. N accepted that he had carried on a regulated activity of accepting deposits, or purported to do so, when not authorised or exempt from such authorisation, but denied that he had done so by way of business. N maintained that he had not held himself out as accepting deposits on a day-to-day basis and had only accepted deposits on particular occasions, namely two occasions which were separated by about 18 months. N relied on the Financial Services and Markets Act 2000 (Carrying on Regulated Activities by Way of Business) Order 2001 art.2(1), which provided that a person who did not hold himself out as accepting deposits on a day-to-day basis and who only accepted deposits on particular occasions was not to be regarded as accepting deposits by way of business, and maintained that there was no evidence from which a jury properly directed could conclude that the Order did not apply in his case. N submitted that the judge had been wrong to have rejected his submission of no case to answer.

Held: Appeal dismissed. (1) The first question was whether or not there was evidence from which a jury properly directed could conclude that N had, during the relevant period, accepted the deposits, or purported to do so, by way of business. There clearly was such evidence in the instant case: the deposits were of very large sums of money, and were made to the company of which N was the chairman; the deposits were made pursuant to detailed contracts; the deposits were paid into corporate bank accounts; the deposits were made in anticipation of substantial returns both to the company receiving the deposits and the depositors; N had plainly purported to accept deposits by way of business by offering depositors an investment opportunity and representing that that he was able and willing to accept deposits of £10 million; and N had described his financial activities, in his curriculum vitae and when interviewed by police, in terms of a business. Those features of the evidence alone would have entitled a jury to conclude that N had accepted deposits, or purported to do so, by way of business, *Financial Services Authority v Anderson* [2010] EWHC 599 (Ch), [2011] Bus. L.R. D22 applied. In addition, the recovery of draft documents, apparently prepared in contemplation of the receipt of deposits, provided further support for the conclusion that deposits received by N during the relevant period were received by way of business (see para.29 of judgment). (2) The second question was whether there was evidence from which a jury properly directed could have concluded that art.2(1) of the Order did not avail N. That question gave rise to two subsidiary questions: first, whether there was evidence that N had held himself out as accepting deposits on a day-to-day basis; and secondly, whether there was evidence that during the relevant period N did not accept deposits only on particular occasions. On the evidence, it would have been open to the jury to conclude that N had held himself out as accepting deposits on a day-to-day basis, and that he did not accept deposits only on particular occasions (paras 30-32).

R. v NAPOLI (JOHN FRANCIS), [2012] EWCA Crim 1129, [2012] Lloyd's Rep. F.C. 599, Rafferty, L.J., CA (Crim Div).

1366. Regulated activities–Fit and proper persons–Upper Tribunal failing to consider whether trader fit and proper person–Error of law

[Financial Services and Markets Act 2000 (c.8) s.56, s.57, s.389.]

The appellant authority appealed against a decision that it had failed to make out its case that the respondent trader (H) was not a fit and proper person to perform functions in relation to a regulated activity. H traded in coffee futures and associated derivatives on the London International Financial Futures and Options Exchange. The authority found him guilty of market abuse and imposed a prohibition order under the Financial Services and Markets Act 2000 s.56 and s.57 on the ground that he was not a fit and proper person. On referral, the Upper Tribunal found that H's trading was carried out for legitimate reasons and in conformity with accepted market practices, and that although H's assertions about his dealings with another broker were false, he had not engaged in market abuse. It found that the authority had not made out its case that H was not a fit and proper person. The authority published that result on its website and stated that it was discontinuing its action against H. That was based upon a mistaken assumption that a decision had been made not to appeal. Once it was realised that an appeal might be pursued that statement was removed. The authority did apply for permission to appeal and that was refused upon the basis that the press release showed that it had decided to discontinue its action against H even though the appropriate notice of discontinuance had not been issued under s.389 of the Act. Permission to appeal was subsequently granted. The issues were (i) whether the authority had discontinued its proceedings against H; (ii) if proceedings had not been discontinued, whether the tribunal had considered whether H had been shown not to be a fit and proper person; (iii) if the tribunal had not so considered, whether it had erred in law.

Held: Appeal allowed. (1) The communication of a decision to take no further action or to discontinue under the Act was an intrinsic part of the process. Parliament had specified in s.389 to whom and how notice was to be given. A statement on the authority's website, not addressed in any way to the person to whom the decision notice was addressed, was not a sufficient notice of a decision to take no further action for the purposes of the Act so as to render it irrevocable (see para.15 of judgment). Further, on the evidence before the court, there was no decision to take no further action made by anyone on behalf of the authority with the requisite authority. The authority could be criticised for its failure to document and to enforce its internal procedures for making discontinuance decisions with the appropriate authority, but those failures did not amount to a decision to discontinue which could be said to be binding upon it (paras 25-28). (2) The tribunal's reasons had not addressed whether H had been shown not to be a fit and proper person to carry out trading by reason of his false assertions (para.29). (3) The authority"s case against H, reflected in both its decision notice and its statement of case before the tribunal, was that by his conduct H had sought to mislead it and that he therefore lacked honesty and integrity. It was important for the tribunal to consider all the facts and evidence put before it on a reference under s.57. First, its consideration of a reference was not ordinary civil litigation; there was a public interest in ensuring that those who were not fit and proper persons to perform functions in relation to a regulated activity were precluded from doing so. A narrowing of the inquiry by a tribunal that excluded relevant material from its assessment of an applicant was to be avoided, provided that the applicant was given a fair opportunity to address the authority's case. In H's case, it was not suggested that he did not have a fair opportunity to address the allegations that he had been guilty of persistent and repeated lying. Second, if the tribunal incorrectly restricted its determination, it might be difficult for the authority to rely on the excluded facts in future in assessing, for example, whether the applicant was a fit and proper person, or should be granted an authorisation he sought to engage in a regulated activity. For those reasons, it was incumbent on the tribunal to address whether, even if H was not guilty of market abuse, his lying, which it found as a fact, demonstrated that he was not a fit and proper person. By not doing so, it had erred in law. The matter was remitted to the tribunal to consider whether a prohibition order was appropriate in the circumstances (paras 31-39).

FINANCIAL CONDUCT AUTHORITY v HOBBS; *sub nom.* HOBBS v FINANCIAL SERVICES AUTHORITY; HOBBS v FINANCIAL CONDUCT AUTHORITY, [2013] EWCA Civ 918, [2013] Bus. L.R. 1290, Rimer, L.J., CA (Civ Div).

1367. **Regulated activities–Insurance contracts–Extended warranties for replacement or repair–Contracts for benefits in kind–Member States not prevented from regulating insurance business falling outside standard classes in Directive 73/239**

[Financial Services and Markets Act 2000 (Regulated Activities) Order 2001 (SI 2001/544) Sch.1 para.16(c); Directive 73/239 on the taking-up and pursuit of the business of direct insurance other than life assurance; Directive 84/641 on the taking-up and pursuit of the business of direct insurance other than life assurance.]

The first appellant company and the second appellant partnership (D) appealed against a decision of the Court of Appeal ([2011] EWCA Civ 1413, [2012] 2 All E.R. (Comm) 38, [2012] C.L.Y. 1469) dismissing their appeal against decisions to make winding-up orders against them following public interest petitions brought by the respondent FSA. D sold and performed extended warranty contracts under which they contracted to repair or replace satellite television dishes, digital boxes and associated equipment in return for a period payment. There was no contractual obligation to pay money under the contracts. The FSA alleged that the contracts which D entered into were contracts of general insurance within the meaning of the Financial Services and Markets Act 2000 (Regulated Activities) Order 2001 and that D neither had authorisation to carry on such regulated activities, nor were exempt from such authorisation. The 2001 Order implemented Directive 73/239. Classes 1 to 17 listed in the Annex to the Directive set out the types of business for which the Member States had to make regulatory provision. The Directive was later amended by Directive 84/641 to introduce Class 18, which provided that benefits in kind insurance could be regulated in relation to assistance for persons travelling. D maintained that, even if they were making and performing insurance contracts, the contracts were not of a kind which required authorisation. The High Court rejected that argument and made a winding-up order. D's appeal was dismissed. The main issue was whether, in specifying certain categories of direct non-life insurance business which Member States had to regulate in accordance with EU law, the Directive precluded Member States from regulating further or wider categories under their national law. D accepted that Member States were entitled to regulate additional categories of direct non-life business besides those specified in classes 1 to 17 in the Directive, but submitted that they could not do so in the same legislative provisions which transposed the Directive into national law, and not by redefining classes of business specified in the Directive more broadly than the Directive itself.

Held: Appeal dismissed. (1) The Directive was concerned only to prescribe what kinds of business had to be regulated by national law and not what other kinds of business might be regulated by it. Still less was it concerned with the legislative technique that Member States might employ to regulate other kinds of business to which the Directive did not apply. There was therefore nothing to prevent the United Kingdom from legislating to regulate the provision of insurance for benefits either in cash or in kind, or both. The Directive, whether in its original or amended form, was not intended to impose a comprehensive scheme of authorisation. The 18 standard classes of insurance business listed in the Annex could not have been intended to limit the freedom of Member States to regulate other categories of business. Indeed, the recitals to the Directive showed an appreciation that there would continue to be significant differences between national schemes of authorisation which would present partial barriers to the freedom of establishment. It was clear from the scheme of the Directive as a whole that its object was to impose certain uniform principles of authorisation and regulation on insurance business in the standard classes. It was impossible to discern any rational reason why the EU legislature would have wished to prevent Member States from imposing their own authorisation regime on insurance business outside the standard classes (see paras 4, 12-13, 15 of judgment). (2) As to whether the Order did in fact apply to D's business, there was no reason to depart from the analysis given by Warren J in the High Court that a contract for repair or replacement only in the event of breakdown or malfunction, which did not oblige the insurer to indemnify the insured for costs incurred by the insured himself, fell within Sch.1 para.16(b) or para.16(c) to the Order. A contract which brought about a result which the insured would otherwise have to achieve by payment, namely having functioning equipment, could properly be categorised as a contract which protected him from financial loss. The only contrary argument was that the schedule to the Order should be read subject to an implied exclusion of insurance providing for benefits in kind. That was not the position at common law. However, given that the Directive did not prevent Member States from regulating any insurance business falling outside the 18 classes, the common law position that an insurance contract was a contract for the payment of a sum of money or for some corresponding benefit was not displaced by any requirement to construe domestic legislation in conformity with mandatory requirements of EU law (paras 18-19).

DIGITAL SATELLITE WARRANTY COVER LTD, *Re*; NATIONWIDE DIGITAL SATELLITE WARRANTY SERVICES LTD, RE; FREEMAN (T/A SATELLITE SERVICES), *Re*; *sub nom.* DIGITAL SATELLITE WARRANTY COVER LTD v FINANCIAL SERVICES AUTHORITY; FREEMAN (T/A SATELLITE SERVICES) v FINANCIAL SERVICES AUTHORITY, [2013] UKSC 7, [2013] 1 W.L.R. 605, Lord Neuberger (President), SC.

FISHERIES

1368. Aquaculture–Fishery products–Labelling

THE FISH LABELLING REGULATIONS 2013, SI 2013/1768; made under the European Communities Act 1972 Sch.2 para.1A; and the Food Safety Act 1990 s.6, s.16, s.17, s.26, s.48. In force: September 9, 2013; .

These Regulations designate the Secretary of State to draw up and publish the list of commercial designations of fish species accepted in the UK pursuant to Regulation 104/2000 art.4(2) on the common organisation of the markets in fishery and aquaculture products.

1369. Fisheries–Oyster fishery–Wales

THE MUMBLES OYSTER FISHERY ORDER 2013, SI 2013/SI 2013/2020 (W.198); made under the Sea Fisheries (Shellfish) Act 1967 s.1. In force: September 10, 2013; .

This Order confers on the Mumbles Oyster Company Ltd (Company Number: 08181012) (the Grantee) a right of several fishery for native oysters (Ostrea edulis) over an area of approximately 35 hectares in Swansea Bay which is in the vicinity of the Mumbles for a period of 15 years starting on September 10, 2013.

1370. Fishing rights–Shellfish–Essex–Kent

THE RIVER ROACH OYSTER FISHERY ORDER 2013, SI 2013/1979; made under the Sea Fisheries (Shellfish) Act 1967 s.1. In force: August 31, 2013; .

This Order confers on the Kent and Essex Inshore Fisheries and Conservation Authority a right of several fishery for oysters (Ostrea edulis and Crassostrea gigas) for a period of 10 years commencing on August 13, 2013.

FOOD

1371. Additives–Flavouring

THE FOOD ADDITIVES, FLAVOURINGS, ENZYMES AND EXTRACTION SOLVENTS (WALES) REGULATIONS 2013, SI 2013/SI 2013/2591 (W.255); made under the Food Safety Act 1990 s.16, s.17, s.26, s.48. In force: October 31, 2013; .

These Regulations, which apply to Wales, provide for the execution and enforcement of the EU Regulations on food.

1372. Additives–Flavouring–Solvents–England

THE FOOD ADDITIVES, FLAVOURINGS, ENZYMES AND EXTRACTION SOLVENTS (ENGLAND) REGULATIONS 2013, SI 2013/2210; made under the Food Safety Act 1990 s.16, s.17, s.26, s.48. In force: October 31, 2013; .

The proposed Regulation revokes the current statutory instruments on food additives, flavourings, food enzymes, smoke flavourings and extraction solvents and replaces them with a single statutory instrument.

1373. Animal products–Food–Pesticide residues

THE ANIMALS AND ANIMAL PRODUCTS (EXAMINATION FOR RESIDUES AND MAXIMUM RESIDUE LIMITS) (AMENDMENT) REGULATIONS 2013, SI 2013/804; made under the European Communities Act 1972 s.2, Sch.2 para.1A; and the Food Safety Act 1990 s.16, s.17, s.26, s.48, Sch.1 para.7. In force: May 6, 2013; .

These Regulations amend the Animals and Animal Products (Examination for Residues and Maximum Residue Limits) Regulations 1997 (SI 1997/1729) to provide for the enforcement of Regulation 470/2009 and Regulation 37/2010.

1374. Beverages–Maintained schools–Nutrition–Wales

THE HEALTHY EATING IN SCHOOLS (NUTRITIONAL STANDARDS AND REQUIREMENTS) (WALES) REGULATIONS 2013, SI 2013/SI 2013/1984 (W.194); made under the Healthy Eating in Schools (Wales) Measure 2009 s.4, s.10. In force: September 2, 2013; .

These Regulations set out the types of food and drink that can, and cannot, be provided during the school day and define the nutrient content of school lunches.

1375. Contamination–Food safety–Product contamination–England

THE CONTAMINANTS IN FOOD (ENGLAND) REGULATIONS 2013, SI 2013/2196; made under the Food Safety Act 1990 s.16, s.17, s.26, s.48. In force: October 31, 2013; .

This instrument will revoke the Contaminants in Food (England) Regulations 2010 (Contaminants in Food (England) Regulations 2010 (SI 2010/2228) and remake them, with necessary amendments in order to provide for the execution and enforcement of certain amended EU requirements. This instrument will also revoke and remake the provisions currently contained in the Erucic Acid in Food Regulations 1977 as amended.

1376. Contamination–Food safety–Wales

THE CONTAMINANTS IN FOOD (WALES) REGULATIONS 2013, SI 2013/SI 2013/2493 (W.242); made under the Food Safety Act 1990 s.16, s.17, s.26, s.48. In force: October 31, 2013; .

These Regulations, which apply in relation to Wales, revoke and re-enact with changes the Contaminants in Food (Wales) Regulations 2010 (SI 2010/2394) to make provision for: the continuing implementation of Directives 76/621 and 80/89 relating to the fixing of the maximum level of erucic acid in oils and fats intended as such for human consumption and in foodstuffs containing added oils or fats; and the continuing execution and enforcement of Regulation 1881/2006 setting maximum levels for certain contaminants in foodstuffs.

1377. Food hygiene–Food safety–Labelling–England

THE FOOD (MISCELLANEOUS AMENDMENT AND REVOCATION) (ENGLAND) REGULATIONS 2013, SI 2013/466; made under the Food Safety Act 1990 s.16, s.17, s.26, s.48. In force: April 6, 2013; .

These Regulations will revoke the Arsenic in Food Regulations 1959 and its amendments, the Chloroform in Food Regulations 1980 and the Ungraded Eggs (Hygiene) Regulations 1990, and also make an amendment to the Food Labelling Regulations 1996.

1378. Food hygiene–Food safety–Qualifications–Wales

THE FOOD SAFETY (SAMPLING AND QUALIFICATIONS) (WALES) REGULATIONS 2013, SI 2013/SI 2013/479 (W.55); made under the Food Safety Act 1990 s.27, s.30, s.31, s.48, s.49. In force: April 6, 2013; .

These Regulations: specify the qualifications necessary to be a public analyst or food analyst or food examiner for the purposes of the Food Safety Act 1990; prohibit specified persons from carrying out analyses or examinations; specify the procedures to be followed when a sample has been procured under that Act for analysis or examination and exclude from these procedures samples taken under Regulations which have their own procedures (regulation 3 and Schedule 1); and prescribe the form of certificate to be used by analysts and examiners in making their reports (regulation 10 and Schedule 3).

1379. Food hygiene–Food safety–Wales

THE FOOD (MISCELLANEOUS AMENDMENT AND REVOCATION) (WALES) REGULATIONS 2013, SI 2013/SI 2013/545 (W.58); made under the Food Safety Act 1990 s.16, s.17, s.26, s.48. In force: April 6, 2013; .

These Regulations make a further amendment to the Food Labelling Regulations 1996 (SI 1996/1499) reg.50, in so far as they apply in relation to Wales, in order to correct an error in a previous amending instrument (SI 2011/465). These Regulations also revoke five other Regulations on food safety.

1380. Food Hygiene Rating (Wales) Act 2013 (anaw 2)

This Act makes provision for the production of food hygiene ratings of food business establishments; displays of information about food hygiene ratings; and the enforcement of requirements to display information.

This Act received Royal Assent on March 4, 2013.

1381. Food safety–Beverages–Fruit

THE FRUIT JUICES AND FRUIT NECTARS (ENGLAND) REGULATIONS 2013, SI 2013/2775; made under the European Communities Act 1972 Sch.2 para.1A; the Food Safety Act 1990 s.6, s.16, s.17, s.48; and the School Standards and Framework Act 1998 s.114A, s.138. In force: November 20, 2013; .

These Regulations implement Council Directive 2001/112 relating to fruit juices and certain similar products intended for human consumption [2001] OJ L10/58.

1382. Food safety–Public analysts–Qualifications–England

THE FOOD SAFETY (SAMPLING AND QUALIFICATIONS) (ENGLAND) REGULATIONS 2013, SI 2013/264; made under the Food Safety Act 1990 s.27, s.30, s.31, s.48, s.49. In force: April 6, 2013; .

These Regulations specify: the qualifications necessary to be a public analyst, a food analyst or a food examiner for the purposes of the Food Safety Act 1990, prohibiting specified persons from carrying out analyses or examination under the Act; and the procedures to be followed when a sample has been procured under that Act for analysis or examination, and exclude from these procedures samples taken under Regulations which have their own procedures.

1383. Food safety offences–Food storage–Selling food after date shown on "use by" label–Requirements for successful prosecution

[Food Labelling Regulations 1996 (SI 1996/1499) reg.44(1)(d).]

The appellant local authority appealed against a decision of the Divisional Court ([2012] EWHC 296 (Admin), [2012] 3 All E.R. 489, [2012] C.L.Y. 1489) that under the Food Labelling Regulations 1996 reg.44(1)(d) the prosecution did not have to show that the food was in a highly perishable state at the date of the alleged offence, but that it did have to show that the food had at some stage been in a state which required it to have been labelled with a "use by" date, which had passed. Charges were brought against D following a visit by inspectors from the local authority's trading standards department on D's premises, where they found a number of packages of frozen meat labelled with "use by" dates which had passed. The charges were dismissed by magistrates who accepted D's arguments and concluded that, at the time of the relevant inspection, the food items were in a frozen state and therefore not highly perishable so that they did not require a "use by" date. The local authority appealed by way of case stated. The Divisional Court certified that the case involved the following point of law of general public importance: whether an offence under reg.44(1)(d) required the prosecution to prove that the label or marking bearing the "use by" date, after which the food was sold, was applied at a time when the food was ready for delivery to the ultimate consumer or a catering establishment, and when it was highly perishable and in consequence likely after a short period to constitute an immediate danger to human health. The local authority submitted that the prosecution had to show only that D was selling food which was the subject of a "use by" label displaying a date which had passed.

Held: Appeal allowed. The Divisional Court was right to reject D's argument that the prosecution had to prove that the food was in a highly perishable state at the time of the alleged offences under reg.44(1)(d). On the wording of the paragraph, the prosecution had only to prove that the food was in D's possession for sale, that the food had a "use by" mark or label "relating to it", and that that date had passed. To read into the paragraph an additional requirement that the food was in a highly perishable state at the time of the alleged offence would have seriously weakened the regulatory system and the protection provided to customers. It would have enabled a retailer of perishable food, which had passed its "use by" date, to freeze it and then sell it without consumers knowing how long it had been unfrozen (see paras 21-22 of judgment). The phrase "relating to" in the phrase "sells any food after the date shown in a "use by" date relating to it" was synonymous with "referring to" and denoted a factual connection rather than a legal requirement: it simply meant that the food sold was the subject of a mark or label with a "use by" date (para.24). Once food had been labelled with a "use by" date the Regulations protected the customer by prohibiting the removal or alteration of that label without the written authority of the original labeller, and by prohibiting the sale of the food after the "use by" date had passed (paras 25-27). On the Divisional Court's construction, questions would have arisen as to when the marking had been done and what state the food was in at the time of the marking, which matters would have been unknown to the inspectors and potentially would have complicated the practical problems of enforcement (para.28). Thus, under reg.44(1)(d) it was sufficient for the prosecution to prove that a defendant had food in its possession for the purpose of sale which was the subject of a mark or label showing a "use by" date which had passed. The answer to the question certified by the Divisional Court, was no. The matter was remitted to a different panel of justices for rehearing (para.30).

TORFAEN CBC v DOUGLAS WILLIS LTD, [2013] UKSC 59, [2013] 4 All E.R. 1, Lady Hale (Deputy President), SC.

1384. Groceries Code Adjudicator Act 2013 (c.19)–Commencement Order

THE GROCERIES CODE ADJUDICATOR ACT 2013 (COMMENCEMENT) ORDER 2013, SI 2013/SI 2013/1236 (C.53); made under the Groceries Code Adjudicator Act 2013 s.25. Commencement details: bringing into force various provisions of the 2013 Act on June 25, 2013.; .

This Order brings into force on June 25th 2013 those provisions of the Groceries Code Adjudicator Act 2013 which are not already in force.

1385. Healthy Eating in Schools Measure 2009 (nawm 3)–Commencement Order–Wales

THE HEALTHY EATING IN SCHOOLS (WALES) MEASURE 2009 (COMMENCEMENT) ORDER 2013, SI 2013/SI 2013/1985 (W.195) (C.84); made under the Healthy Eating in Schools (Wales) Measure 2009 s.12. Commencement details: bringing into force various provisions of the 2009 Measure on August 8, 2013 and September 2, 2013.; .

This Order brings into force the Healthy Eating in Schools (Wales) Measure 2009.

FORESTRY

1386. Due diligence–Timber

THE TIMBER AND TIMBER PRODUCTS (PLACING ON THE MARKET) REGULATIONS 2013, SI 2013/233; made under the European Communities Act 1972 s.2, Sch.2 para.1A. In force: March 3, 2013; .

These Regulations set out the obligations of operators who place timber and timber products on the market. They also explain detailed rules concerning the due diligence system and the frequency and nature of the checks on monitoring organisations as provided for under EU timber regulations.

GOVERNMENT ADMINISTRATION

1387. Accounts–Designation–Executive agencies–Non-departmental public bodies

THE WHOLE OF GOVERNMENT ACCOUNTS (DESIGNATION OF BODIES) ORDER 2013, SI 2013/1796; made under the Government Resources and Accounts Act 2000 s.10. In force: August 9, 2013; .

This Order designates the bodies listed in the Schedule in relation to the financial year ending on March 31, 2013 for the purposes of the Government Resources and Accounts Act 2000. The effect of designation is that these bodies are required to prepare and present to the Treasury such financial information in relation to that financial year as the Treasury require to enable them to prepare Whole of Government Accounts.

1388. **Animal health–Department for Environment Food and Rural Affairs–Fees**

THE ANIMAL HEALTH (MISCELLANEOUS FEES) REGULATIONS 2013, SI 2013/1240; made under the European Communities Act 1972 s.2. In force: June 24, 2013; .

These Regulations provide for increases in the fees payable in relation to services delivered by the Animal Health Veterinary Laboratories Agency, an executive agency of the Department for Environment, Food and Rural Affairs, as part of a move towards full cost recovery of such fees.

1389. **British Library–Public lending right–Register of public lending right–Transfer of functions**

THE PUBLIC BODIES (ABOLITION OF THE REGISTRAR OF PUBLIC LENDING RIGHT) ORDER 2013, SI 2013/2352; made under the Public Bodies Act 2011 s.1, s.6, s.23, s.24, s.35. In force: October 1, 2013 except for Sch.1 para.15 on October 2, 2013.; .

This Order abolishes the Registrar of Public Lending Right, transferring its functions, property, rights and liabilities to the British Library Board.

1390. **Complaints–Independent Police Complaints Commission–Misconduct–National Crime Agency**

THE NATIONAL CRIME AGENCY (COMPLAINTS AND MISCONDUCT) REGULATIONS 2013, SI 2013/2325; made under the Police Reform Act 2002 s.26C, s.105. In force: October 7, 2013; .

These Regulations make provision for the Independent Police Complaints Commission to exercise independent oversight of complaints and other matters (including an incident in which a death or serious injury has occurred) relating to the conduct of a National Crime Agency (NCA) officer (including the Director General of the NCA), in a similar way to the oversight exercised by the Commission in respect of the police.

1391. **Fire services–Government trading funds**

THE FIRE SERVICE COLLEGE TRADING FUND (REVOCATION) ORDER 2013, SI 2013/490; made under the Government Trading Funds Act 1973 s.1, s.6. In force: April 1, 2013; .

This Order revokes the Fire Service College Trading Fund Order 1992. As a result, the trading fund established by the 1992 Order ceases to exist.

1392. **Habeas corpus–Prisoners of war–Unlawful detention by US of Pakistan national captured by UK forces in Iraq–Extent of UK's control over detainee–Whether sufficient response by UK Government to writ of habeas corpus**

The appellant secretaries of state appealed against a decision ([2011] EWCA Civ 1540, [2012] 1 W.L.R. 1462, [2012] C.L.Y. 1292) to issue a writ of habeas corpus in respect of the respondent detainee (R). R cross-appealed against a decision (*Rahmatullah v Secretary of State for Foreign and Commonwealth Affairs* [2012] EWCA Civ 182, [2012] 1 W.L.R. 1462, [2012] C.L.Y. 1506) that the secretaries of state had made a sufficient return to the writ. R, a Pakistani national, had been captured by United Kingdom forces in a United States controlled area of Iraq. He was transferred to Afghanistan in US custody and detained. A Memorandum of Understanding (MoU) provided for the return of prisoners of war on request between the UK and US. It was to be implemented in accordance with the Geneva Conventions, including the Geneva Convention Relative to the Protection of Civilian Persons in Time of War (GC4). R applied for a writ of habeas corpus on the grounds that his detention was unlawful, and that the UK had sufficient control over him to justify his release in accordance with the MoU. The Divisional Court refused R's application, but the Court of Appeal allowed his appeal on the basis that it was arguable that the UK enjoyed a sufficient degree of control over him. The US considered that R should be transferred to Pakistan and refused the UK's request for his release.

Held: Appeal dismissed, cross-appeal dismissed. (Lord Carnwath and Lady Hale dissenting on the cross-appeal) (1) There was prima facie evidence that R was unlawfully detained and that the UK was under an obligation to seek his return unless it could bring about effective measures to correct the breaches of GC4 that his continued detention constituted. Habeas corpus was not a discretionary remedy; entitlement to the issue of a writ was a matter of right. That reflected the fundamental importance of the right to liberty. The effectiveness of the remedy would be substantially reduced if it was not available to require someone who had the means of securing a detained person's release to do so, because they did not have physical custody of the detainee, *Secretary of State for Home Affairs v O'Brien* [1923] 2 K.B. 361 applied. Alternatively, it would not be proper to issue a writ if the respondent did not have custody of the person detained or the means of procuring their release. The real issue therefore concerned the UK's control over R's custody. The Court of Appeal's decision did not amount to an "instruction" to the UK Government to demand R's return. It merely reflected the court's conclusion that there were sufficient grounds for believing that the UK had the means of obtaining control over his custody. It might be that the only means of establishing whether the UK could obtain control was to ask for his return, but that remained a matter for the secretaries of state. The Court of Appeal's judgment did not require the secretaries of state to act in any particular way in order to demonstrate whether they could exert control; it required that they show, by whatever efficacious means they could, whether or not control in fact existed. The decision did not require the UK to engage in a process of persuasion or involve an attempt to "dictate to the executive government steps that it should take in the course of executing Government foreign policy". Rather, it required the Government to test whether it had the control that it appeared to have over R's custody, and to demonstrate, if it was the case, that it did not have sufficient control. There had been ample reason to believe that the UK's request for R's return would be granted (see paras 40-45, 59-60, 63-64 of judgment). (2) (Per Lord Phillips) The issue regarding whether the UK's hand over of R to the US was unlawful in itself, therefore allowing R to invoke domestic proceedings under the Geneva Conventions, had not been considered and remained unresolved (paras 100-107). (3) (Per Lord Reed) The appeal would be dismissed on the narrower ground that the Court of Appeal's conclusion that there was sufficient uncertainty regarding the UK's control over R's custody to justify the issuing of the writ was a reasonable one (paras 109-113). (4) The US authorities had been provided with the Court of Appeal's judgment and had been afforded ample opportunity to consider it. It could not have been lost on them that their response would be closely examined. They were fully aware of the basis on which the court considered the UK to have retained control of R, but the US was explicit in its assertion that it was legally entitled to hold R and that, if he was to be released, it would be to Pakistan. In those circumstances, the Court of Appeal was entitled to hold that a sufficient return to the writ had been made (paras 83-84). (5) (Per Lord Carnwath and Lady Hale) The governing consideration for the court should be that R remained in detention, many years after the conflict in Iraq had ceased. He had been assessed by the US as suitable for release but there was no clear indication as to when a transfer to Pakistan was likely to happen. In those circumstances, an inconclusive response was insufficient and the re-submission of the request to the US, in terms specifically relying on the UK's continuing responsibility under GC4 and its continuing rights under the MoU, was required (paras 124-131).

RAHMATULLAH v SECRETARY OF STATE FOR FOREIGN AND COMMONWEALTH AFFAIRS; *sub nom.* RAHMATULLAH v SECRETARY OF STATE FOR DEFENCE; SECRETARY OF STATE FOR FOREIGN AND COMMONWEALTH AFFAIRS v RAHMATULLAH, [2012] UKSC 48, [2013] 1 A.C. 614, Lord Phillips, J.S.C. (President), SC.

1393. Marriage registration–Religious premises–Refused registration of Scientology Chapel as place of worship–Scientology not involving acts of worship within the meaning of s.2 Places of Worship Registration Act 1855–Whether significant changes in practices of Scientology since R v Registrar General ex parte Segerdal [1970] 2 QB 697

[Equality Act 2010 (c.15) s.191, Sch.22 para.1; Human Rights Act 1998 (c.42) s.3; Places of Worship Registration Act 1855 (c.81) s.2.]

The claimants (H and S) applied for judicial review of a decision of the defendant Registrar General of Births, Deaths and Marriages refusing to register a chapel owned by S as a place of meeting for religious worship under the Places of Worship Registration Act 1855. H, a Scientologist, had wanted to marry her fiance, also a Scientologist, at a chapel owned by S. S applied to the registrar for the chapel to be registered as a place of meeting for religious worship under s.2 of the 1855 Act. The registrar, following the Court of Appeal decision in *R. v Registrar General, Ex p. Segerdal* [1970] 2 Q.B. 697, [1970] C.L.Y. 838 which stated that Scientology did not involve acts of worship, refused the application on the ground that the chapel was not a place of "religious worship". The claimant sought to challenge that decision and presented evidence detailing the changes in Scientology since *Segerdal*, including changes to the main congregational services, which they claimed were services of worship, prayers and a new form of wedding ceremony. The registrar submitted that she was bound to refuse the registration by the decision in *Segerdal*. The claimants contended that even if *Segerdal* was binding, it did not preclude a finding that the chapel was a place of worship. They further contended that the Human Rights Act 1998 and the Equality Act 2010 meant that the distinction drawn by the Court of Appeal in *Segerdal* between Buddhism, a non-theistic religion, and Scientology, also a non-theistic religion, could not be upheld to the disadvantage of Scientology, and that the registration of Buddhist temples but not Scientology chapels as places of worship discriminated against Scientologists.

Held: Application refused. (1) *Segerdal* did not decide whether Scientology was a religion or not; it decided that Scientology services did not involve acts of worship, *Segerdal* followed. It also decided that a place for religious worship could cover a place for non-theistic religious worship, *Church of the New Faith v Commissioner of Pay-Roll Tax (Victoria)* 154 C.L.R. 120, [1986] C.L.Y. 2862 doubted. The registrar's approach could not be criticised. She had not misunderstood the decision in *Segerdal*. She had refused to register the chapel on the basis that Scientologists did not worship, not on the basis that Scientology if a religion was not a theistic one, although it could be said that Scientology was a religion for the purposes of the 1855 Act. The thinking in Scientology appeared to have more in common with a non-theistic path to enlightenment. Further, the registrar had not rejected the application on the basis that the further evidence submitted was irrelevant because of the decision in *Segerdal*; she rejected the application because the evidence had failed to show any material change in the fundamental nature of Scientology since *Segerdal*. On the evidence there had been no significant change in the beliefs of Scientologists or in their services since *Segerdal*. What had changed was the greater acceptance of Scientology as a religion, not the nature of Scientology itself. Although the definition of "worship" in *Segerdal* was undoubtedly inadequate for non-theistic and similar beliefs, it still applied to them. Absent a significant change in the way Scientologists "worshipped", *Segerdal* remained binding, *Segerdal* followed (see paras 33, 38, 41, 67, 101-102 of judgment). (2) Section 3 of the 1998 Act did not provide a basis on which the 1855 Act could be read differently: the 1855 Act was not incompatible with H's human rights; there was no interference with the right to marry according to national laws or the right of Scientologists to practise their religion, if it could be classified as such; and there was no discrimination on the ground of religion. The 1855 Act drew a distinction between places of religious worship and other places. That discriminated between those places where religion which involved worship undertook that worship and other places. It did not discriminate on the grounds of religion or the enjoyment of the right to freedom of worship, practice and observance. Similarly, the 2010 Act did not relieve the court from the binding nature of *Segerdal*. Any discrimination that there might have been was required by the 1855 Act and therefore could not contravene the 2010 Act by virtue of s.191 and Sch.22 para.1 of the 2010 Act (paras 91, 93, 96).

R. (ON THE APPLICATION OF HODKIN) v REGISTRAR GENERAL OF BIRTHS, DEATHS AND MARRIAGES, [2012] EWHC 3635 (Admin), [2013] P.T.S.R. 875, Ouseley, J., QBD (Admin).

1394. National Crime Agency

THE NATIONAL CRIME AGENCY (LIMITATION OF EXTENSION TO NORTHERN IRELAND) ORDER 2013, SI 2013/2326; made under the Crime and Courts Act 2013 Sch.24 para.2, Sch.24 para.3. In force: October 7, 2013; .

This Order makes provision in relation to the application of the functions of the National Crime Agency under the Proceeds of Crime Act 2002 to Northern Ireland.

1395. National Crime Agency–National Policing Improvement Agency–Serious Organised Crime Agency

THE CRIME AND COURTS ACT 2013 (CONSEQUENTIAL AMENDMENTS AND SAVING PROVISION) ORDER 2013, SI 2013/2318; made under the Crime and Courts Act 2013 s.59, s.60. In force: October 7, 2013; .

This Order makes amendments to secondary legislation in consequence of the Crime and Courts Act 2013 Pt 1 on the establishment of the National Crime Agency and the abolition of the Serious Organised Crime Agency and the National Policing Improvement Agency.

1396. National Crime Agency–Remuneration

THE NATIONAL CRIME AGENCY (REMUNERATION REVIEW BODY) REGULATIONS 2013, SI 2013/1958; made under the Crime and Courts Act 2013 s.14, s.58. In force: August 29, 2013; .

These Regulations: provide for the Secretary of State to determine, from time to time, the rates of pay and allowances to be paid to officers of the National Crime Agency, of a lower grade than Deputy Director, who have been designated under the Crime and Courts Act 2013 s.10; establish a National Crime Agency Remuneration Review Body; and outline how the Review Body will operate and how members will be appointed.

1397. Police Service of Scotland–Scottish Fire and Rescue Service–Scottish Police Authority

THE POLICE AND FIRE REFORM (SCOTLAND) ACT 2012 (CONSEQUENTIAL PROVISIONS AND MODIFICATIONS) ORDER 2013, SI 2013/602; made under the Scotland Act 1998 s.104, s.112, s.113, s.114. In force: April 1, 2013; .

This Order contains provision will amend references in existing UK legislation to refer to the newly created Police Service of Scotland, Scottish Police Authority and Scottish Fire and Rescue Service. The Order will also make provision for mutual aid and collaboration agreements between Scotland and the other parts of the UK.

1398. Public Audit Wales Act 2013 ()

This Act strengthens and improve the accountability and governance arrangements relating to the Auditor General for Wales (AGW) and the Wales Audit Office (WAO) whilst protecting the AGW's independence and objectivity.

1399. Statistics–Statistics Board

THE OFFICIAL STATISTICS ORDER 2013, SI 2013/1163; made under the Statistics and Registration Service Act 2007 s.6. In force: May 10, 2013; .

This Order designates the statistics produced, or to be produced, by certain bodies as "official statistics" under the Statistics and Registration Service Act 2007, making them subject to the monitoring of the Statistics Board.

1400. Statistics–Statistics Board–Wales

THE OFFICIAL STATISTICS (WALES) ORDER 2013, SI 2013/SI 2013/649 (W.73); made under the Statistics and Registration Service Act 2007 s.6. In force: April 1, 2013; .

The Statistics and Registration Service Act 2007 provides that statistics produced by the Statistics Board, a government department, the Scottish Administration, a Welsh Ministerial authority (the Welsh Ministers, the First Minister for Wales, or the Counsel General to the Welsh Assembly Government), a Northern Ireland department, or any other person acting on behalf of the Crown are official statistics. This Order designates the statistics produced, or to be produced, by the persons listed in the Schedule as official statistics.

HEALTH

1401. Ambulance trusts–Dissolution

THE GREAT WESTERN AMBULANCE SERVICE NATIONAL HEALTH SERVICE TRUST (DISSOLUTION) ORDER 2013, SI 2013/4; made under the National Health Service Act 2006 s.25, s.272, s.273, Sch.4 para.28. In force: February 1, 2013; .

This Order provides for the dissolution on February 1, 2013 of the Great Western Ambulance Service National Health Service Trust established on April 1, 2006 and revokes the Great Western Ambulance National Health Service Trust (Establishment) and the Avon Ambulance Service National Health Service Trust, the Gloucestershire Ambulance Service National Health Service Trust and the Wiltshire Ambulance Service National Health Service Trust (Dissolution) Order 2006 that established the trust.

1402. Animal health–Infectious disease control–Slaughter–England

THE TRANSMISSIBLE SPONGIFORM ENCEPHALOPATHIES (ENGLAND) (AMENDMENT) REGULATIONS 2013, SI 2013/336; made under the European Communities Act 1972 s.2, Sch.2 para.1A. In force: April 6, 2013; .

These Regulations amend the Transmissible Spongiform Encephalopathies (England) Regulations 2010 (SI 2010/801) (the Principle Regulations) inter alia to ensure that the compensation payable to the keeper of animals killed under the principal Regulations is based upon sale price data for animal categories as identified in the table in paragraph 9(6).

1403. Animal tissue–Electronic communications–Medical equipment

THE MEDICAL DEVICES (AMENDMENT) REGULATIONS 2013, SI 2013/2327; made under the European Communities Act 1972 s.2; the Finance Act 1973 s.56; and the Consumer Protection Act 1987 s.11. In force: October 21, 2013; .

This instrument implements two EU Regulations on the use of animal tissues and the provision of instructions for use in electronic form in connection with medical devices. It does so by making the provisions of the EU Regulations enforceable in the UK.

1404. Anti-competitive practices–NHS Commissioning Board–Patients' rights–Regulatory bodies

THE NATIONAL HEALTH SERVICE (PROCUREMENT, PATIENT CHOICE AND COMPETITION) REGULATIONS 2013, SI 2013/257; made under the Health and Social Care Act 2012 s.75, s.76, s.77, s.304. In force: April 1, 2013; .

These Regulations impose requirements on the NHS Commissioning Board and clinical commissioning groups to ensure good practice when procuring health care services for the purposes of the NHS, to protect patients' rights to make choices and to prevent anti-competitive behaviour. The Regulations provide scope for complaints to, and enforcement by Monitor, an independent health regulator, as an alternative to challenging decisions in the courts.

1405. Appointments–NHS trusts–Primary care trusts–Strategic health authorities

THE NATIONAL HEALTH SERVICE TRUST DEVELOPMENT AUTHORITY (ESTABLISHMENT AND CONSTITUTION) AMENDMENT ORDER 2013, SI 2013/260; made under the National Health Service Act 2006 s.28, s.272, s.273. In force: April 1, 2013; .

This Order amends the National Health Service Trust Development Authority (Establishment and Constitution) Order 2012 (the Establishment Order), inter alia to: amend the Establishment Order to provide for the transfer of property and liabilities from the Secretary of State to the Authority; and provide for the transfer of staff from the Secretary of State for Health, Strategic Health Authorities, Primary Care Trusts and the National Institute for Improvement and Innovation, to the Authority, and gives some post transfer employment protection to those staff in the event the Authority proposes to dismiss any of them between April 1, 2013 and March 31, 2015.

1406. Bodily samples–Corpses–Tests for communicable diseases for benefit of doctor helping deceased–Lack of available qualifying relatives to consent

[Human Tissue Act 2004 (c.30) s.3(6)(c), s.27(8), s.27(4)(h).]

The applicant doctor (M) applied for declarations that samples could lawfully be taken from the body of a deceased person (J) and tested for communicable diseases. While off duty, M had attempted to save J's life after she had fallen from a building. In the course of her efforts, her hands were covered in J's blood. She later noticed that she had abrasions to her hands. Anxious about the risk of being infected with a blood-borne disease, M began a course of antiretroviral medication, which had severe side effects. M sought to obtain samples from J's body to determine whether she had been infected with such a disease. The coroner with custody of the body gave consent subject to M having appropriate authorisation. The police traced a family member, J's mother's cousin (P), who stated that J's parents lived abroad and did not yet know of her death; he gave permission for samples to be taken. The application was brought and determined as a matter of urgency on the day of the post-mortem examination: samples had been taken, and the longer the delay in testing the material, the greater the risk of deterioration of the samples, with consequent impact on the reliability of the results.

Held: Declarations granted. (1) The issue of consent had underpinning importance in the relevant legislation. It was not reasonably practicable, for the purposes of the Human Tissue Act 2004 s.27(8), to seek the consent of J's parents. They were unaware of her death, and time was of the essence. There was no indication that J had other qualifying relatives available from whom consent could be taken. That said, P was a person in a qualifying relationship within the definition of s.3(6)(c) and s.27(4)(h): as a reasonably close relative, he could properly be regarded as falling within the definition of a "friend of longstanding". P had given relevant consent for the purposes of the Act. Further, the coroner had indicated his agreement to the removal and testing of the material. That opened the gateway to the exercise of the court's discretion under the inherent jurisdiction to authorise the removal, storage and use of the samples as sought. High regard was paid to the importance of respecting the integrity of the body prior to burial or cremation; however, it was borne in mind that it had inevitably been subject to post-mortem examination, necessarily involving dissection and inspection. There was a need to be vigilant to the ethical considerations relevant to permitting the removal of body tissue, particularly on behalf of a third party who was not known to the deceased. The constrictions of the statutory regime and the code of practice made under it were borne firmly in mind. However, M's request only arose because she had undertaken an act of great humanity in attempting to save J's life. While conscious that J herself could not express a view on the issue, the court considered P's appreciation of M for taking steps to attempt to save J's life, and his consent. Further, if the testing were not undertaken, M would live for the foreseeable future in uncertainty as to whether she had contracted a serious illness. That would affect her personal well-being and her ability to treat other patients; further, M was suffering the harmful side-effects of the antiretroviral medication (see paras 19-25 of judgment). (2) The court declared that it would be lawful for (a) blood, bodily fluid and/or tissue to be removed from J's body for the purposes of testing for blood-borne diseases on behalf of M; (b) tests on the samples to be performed to establish whether J had been infected with any communicable blood-borne diseases; (c) M to be informed of the results of the testing; (d) M to destroy the samples; (e) the coroner and M to discuss what samples had been or were to be taken for the purposes of the coroner's investigations (para.26).

CM v EJ'S EXECUTOR, [2013] EWHC 1680 (Fam), [2013] 2 F.L.R. 1410, Cobb, J., Fam Div.

1407. Capital–NHS trusts

THE NATIONAL HEALTH SERVICE TRUSTS (ORIGINATING CAPITAL) ORDER 2013, SI 2013/569; made under the National Health Service Act 2006 s.272, Sch.5 para.1. In force: March 31, 2013; .

This Order determines the amount of the originating capital, in accordance with paragraph 1 (1) of Schedule 5 to the National Health Service Act 2006, of National Health Service trusts established under that Act on April 1, 2012.

1408. Care Quality Commission–Members

THE CARE QUALITY COMMISSION (MEMBERSHIP) (AMENDMENT) REGULATIONS 2013, SI 2013/2157; made under the Health and Social Care Act 2008 Sch.1 para.3. In force: October 1, 2013; .

These Regulations amend the Care Quality Commission (Membership) Regulations 2008 (SI 2008/2252) to make provision for the Care Quality Commission to be able to have a larger board to accommodate the appointment of three new chief inspectors, for hospitals, social care, and general practice.

1409. Certificates–Fees–Licences–Marketing authorisation

THE MEDICINES (PRODUCTS FOR HUMAN USE) (FEES) REGULATIONS 2013, SI 2013/532; made under the Medicines Act 1971 s.1. In force: in accordance with reg.1.; .

These Regulations make provision for the fees payable under the Medicines Act 1971 and other fees payable in respect of EU obligations relating to marketing authorisations, licences and certificates and registrations in respect of medicinal products for human use.

1410. Change of name–NHS trusts–London

THE LEWISHAM HEALTHCARE NATIONAL HEALTH SERVICE TRUST (CHANGE OF NAME) (ESTABLISHMENT) AMENDMENT ORDER 2013, SI

2013/2376; made under the National Health Service Act 2006 s.25, s.272, s.273. In force: October 1, 2013; .

This Order amends the Lewisham Hospital National Health Service Trust (Establishment) Order 1993 (SI 1993/694) to change the name of the trust from the Lewisham Healthcare National Health Service Trust to the Lewisham and Greenwich National Health Service Trust, and increases the number of non-executive directors (excluding the chair) of the trust from five to seven.

1411. Clinical commissioning groups–Dissolution–Public Health England–Special health authorities

THE NATIONAL TREATMENT AGENCY (ABOLITION) AND THE HEALTH AND SOCIAL CARE ACT 2012 (CONSEQUENTIAL, TRANSITIONAL AND SAVING PROVISIONS) ORDER 2013, SI 2013/235; made under the National Health Service Act 2006 s.28, s.272, s.273; and the Health and Social Care Act 2012 s.303, s.304. In force: April 1, 2013; .

This Order: abolishes the National Treatment Agency, a Special Health Authority, the functions functions are planned to be transferred to Public Health England, a new executive agency of the Department of Health; and amends and revokes secondary legislation in consequence of the Health and Social Care Act 2012, with effect from April 1, 2013. The amendments take account of the abolition of various bodies by the Act and of the assumption of new responsibilities by other bodies (including the NHS Commissioning Board, clinical commissioning groups, local authorities and Public Health England.

1412. Clinical commissioning groups–NHS

THE NATIONAL HEALTH SERVICE (GENERAL DUTIES OF THE NATIONAL HEALTH SERVICE COMMISSIONING BOARD IN RELATION TO CLINICAL COMMISSIONING GROUPS -SPECIFICATION OF DATE) ORDER 2013, SI 2013/124; made under the National Health Service Act 2006 s.14A. In force: March 31, 2013; .

This Order, inter alia: imposes a duty on the National Health Service Commissioning Board to ensure that at any time after a day specified by order of the Secretary of State each provider of primary medical services is a member of a clinical commissioning group (CCG); and imposes a duty on the Board to ensure that at any time after a day specified by order of the Secretary of State the areas that are specified in the constitutions of CCGs taken together cover the whole of England and do not coincide or overlap.

1413. Clinical commissioning groups–NHS–Public health

THE NATIONAL HEALTH SERVICE AND PUBLIC HEALTH (FUNCTIONS AND MISCELLANEOUS PROVISIONS) REGULATIONS 2013, SI 2013/261; made under the Mental Health Act 1983 s.130A; the European Communities Act 1972 s.2; the National Health Service Act 2006 s.3B, s.6D, s.7, s.8, s.14Z4, s.14, s.19, s.73A, s.73B, s.75, s.236, s.269, s.272, s.273; and the Health and Social Care Act 2012 s.300, Sch.23. In force: April 1, 2013; .

These Regulations make provision for a range of matters relating to the functions of the National Health Service Commissioning Board and clinical commissioning groups. The provisions, inter alia, are for: responsibilities for the NHS Commissioning Board with respect to certain EU functions; and arrangements about how information relating to births and deaths will be notified to local authorities, the Board and Clinical Commissioning Groups.

1414. Clinical commissioning groups–Payments–Quality

THE NATIONAL HEALTH SERVICE (CLINICAL COMMISSIONING GROUPS - PAYMENTS IN RESPECT OF QUALITY) REGULATIONS 2013, SI 2013/474;

made under the National Health Service Act 2006 s.223K, s.272. In force: April 1, 2013; .

These regulations make provision in relation to payments to Clinical Commissioning Groups in respect of quality.

1415. Compensation–Fees–Medical treatment–Personal injury

THE PERSONAL INJURIES (NHS CHARGES) (AMOUNTS) AMENDMENT REGULATIONS 2013, SI 2013/SI 282; made under the Health and Social Care (Community Health and Standards) Act 2003 s.153, s.195. In force: April 1, 2013; .

These Regulations are intended to increase the charges recoverable from persons who pay compensation to a person for an injury in cases where that injured person receives National Health Service hospital treatment or ambulance services. The increase in charges reflects the uplift to Hospital and Community Health Services (HCHS) annual inflation.

1416. Contact lenses–Eye tests–NHS–Optical appliance

THE NATIONAL HEALTH SERVICE (OPTICAL CHARGES AND PAYMENTS) REGULATIONS 2013, SI 2013/461; made under the National Health Service Act 2006 s.179, s.180, s.181, s.182, s.272, s.274. In force: April 1, 2013 except for reg.8(3)(j)(4)(e) on April 29, 2013.; .

These Regulations consolidate with amendments the National Health Service (Optical Charges and Payments) Regulations 1997 (the 1997 Regulations), and provide a scheme for payments to be made in respect of costs incurred by certain categories of persons in connection with sight tests and the supply, replacement and repair of optical appliances (glasses and contact lenses).

1417. Controlled drugs–Medical use–Misuse of drugs

THE MISUSE OF DRUGS (DESIGNATION) (AMENDMENT) (ENGLAND,WALES AND SCOTLAND) ORDER 2013, SI 2013/177; made under the Misuse of Drugs Act 1971 s.7. In force: February 26, 2013; .

This Order amends the Misuse of Drugs (Designation) Order 2001 by inserting into Pt 1 of the Schedule to that Order 2-((dimethylamino)methyl)-1-(3-hydroxyphenyl)cyclohexanol, commonly known as O-desmethyltramadol; new categories of synthetic cannabinoids; and 2-(ethylamino)-2-(3-methoxyphenyl)cyclohexanone, commonly known as methoxetamine, and other compounds related to ketamine and phencyclidine.

1418. Controlled drugs–Supervision

THE CONTROLLED DRUGS (SUPERVISION OF MANAGEMENT AND USE) REGULATIONS 2013, SI 2013/373; made under the Health Act 2006 s.17, s.18, s.20, s.79. In force: April 1, 2013; .

These Regulations replace the Controlled Drugs (Supervision of Management and Use) Regulations 2006 (SI 2006/3148) as the Regulations which underpin the arrangements, in England and Scotland, for securing the safe management and use of controlled drugs, such as opiates, in hospitals and in the wider community. Certain NHS and independent sector healthcare bodies are required to appoint controlled drugs accountable officers (CDAOs), and these Regulations describe CDAOs' responsibilities. They also require specified bodies to co-operate with each other in local intelligence networks, and deal with ancillary matters such as powers of entry.

1419. Dental charges–NHS–Wales

THE NATIONAL HEALTH SERVICE (DENTAL CHARGES) (WALES) (AMENDMENT) REGULATIONS 2013, SI 2013/SI 2013/544 (W.57); made under the National Health Service (Wales) Act 2006 s.125, s.203. In force: April 1, 2013; .

These Regulations amend the National Health Service (Dental Charges) (Wales) Regulations 2006 (SI 2006/491). Among the amendments is an increase in the applicable charge payable for a Band 1 and a Band 2 course of treatment.

1420. Dentistry–Fees

THE NATIONAL HEALTH SERVICE (PRIMARY DENTAL SERVICES) (MISCELLANEOUS AMENDMENTS TO CHARGES) REGULATIONS 2013, SI 2013/711; made under the National Health Service Act 2006 s.176, s.272. In force: March 31, 2013 except for reg.4 on April 1, 2013.; .

These Regulations make miscellaneous amendment to dental charges.

1421. Dentistry–Fees–NHS

THE NATIONAL HEALTH SERVICE (PRIMARY DENTAL SERVICES) (MISCELLANEOUS AMENDMENTS AND TRANSITIONAL PROVISIONS) REGULATIONS 2013, SI 2013/364; made under the National Health Service Act 2006 s.102, s.104, s.105, s.108, s.109, s.176, s.177, s.272. In force: April 1, 2013; .

These Regulations amend the National Health Service (General Dental Services Contracts) Regulations 2005, the National Health Service (Personal Dental Services Agreements) Regulations 2005, and the National Health Service (Dental Charges) Regulations 2005, inter alia to: implement relevant changes introduced in the Health and Social Care Act 2012; implement the Capitation and Quality Scheme 2; and introduce a new dental charge (the Band 1A charge) which will apply to persons receiving additional treatment from contractors participating in the Capitation and Quality Scheme 2.

1422. Dentistry–NHS Business Services Authority–NHS Commissioning Board–England

THE FUNCTIONS OF THE NATIONAL HEALTH SERVICE COMMISSIONING BOARD AND THE NHS BUSINESS SERVICES AUTHORITY (AWDURDOD GWASANAETHAU BUSNES Y GIG) (PRIMARY DENTAL SERVICES) (ENGLAND) REGULATIONS 2013, SI 2013/469; made under the National Health Service Act 2006 s.7, s.272, s.273. In force: April 1, 2013; .

These Regulations, relating to the provision of dental services in England, provide for functions of the National Health Service Commissioning Board established by section 1H of the National Health Service Act 2006, to be exercised by the NHS Business Services Authority.

1423. Department of Health–NHS–Transfer of assets–England

THE HEALTH EDUCATION ENGLAND (ESTABLISHMENT AND CONSTITUTION) AMENDMENT (NO.2) ORDER 2013, SI 2013/1197; made under the National Health Service Act 2006 s.28, s.272, s.273. In force: July 1, 2013; .

This Order amends the Health Education England (Establishment and Constitution) Order 2012 to make provision for: the transfer of property and liabilities, from the Department of Health (specifically a contract related to websites development for the NHS careers service) and the small team of staff, employed by the NHS Confederation (Employers) Company Ltd, who deliver the service; and the transfer of specified properties and liabilities, namely electronic records from the University of Nottingham.

1424. Direct payments–Health care–NHS

THE NATIONAL HEALTH SERVICE (DIRECT PAYMENTS) (AMENDMENT) REGULATIONS 2013, SI 2013/2354; made under the National Health Service Act 2006 s.12A, s.12B, s.272. In force: October 14, 2013; .

This instrument amends the National Health Service (Direct Payments) Regulations 2013 (SI 2013/1617), which govern the rules for the making of direct payments for health care to secure the provision of certain health services under the National Health Service Act 2006. The amendments: allow an individual living in the same household, a family member or a friend to be paid to provide care using part of a patient's direct payment in exceptional circumstances and which were omitted in error; and insert review provisions for applicants who have had their original application for a direct payment refused, for those whose direct payments have been reduced and for those who have had a particular service within their care plan refused.

1425. Direct payments–NHS–Pilot schemes–Primary care trusts

THE NATIONAL HEALTH SERVICE (DIRECT PAYMENTS) REGULATIONS 2013, SI 2013/1617; made under the National Health Service Act 2006 s.12A, s.12B, s.75, s.272. In force: August 1, 2013; .

In the light of the positive evidence from the personal health budget pilot programme (which included direct payments for healthcare), the Government now wishes to enable direct payments for healthcare to be made available across England, not just in pilot schemes. These Regulations revise and replace the current negative instrument which governs the rules for the making of direct payments: The National Health Service (Direct Payments) Regulations 2010 (SI 2010/1000).

1426. Direct payments–NHS–Pilot schemes–Primary care trusts

THE NATIONAL HEALTH SERVICE (DIRECT PAYMENTS) (REPEAL OF PILOT SCHEMES LIMITATION) ORDER 2013, SI 2013/1563; made under the National Health Service Act 2006 s.12C. In force: August 1, 2013; .

This Order repeals ss.12A and 12C(1) to (4) of the National Health Service Act 2006.

1427. Dissolution–NHS trusts

THE SOUTH LONDON HEALTHCARE NATIONAL HEALTH SERVICE TRUST (DISSOLUTION) ORDER 2013, SI 2013/2378; made under the National Health Service Act 2006 s.25, s.272, s.273, Sch.4 para.28. In force: October 1, 2013; .

This Order provides for the dissolution on October 1, 2013 of the South London Healthcare National Health Service Trust established on April 1, 2009 and revokes the South London Healthcare National Health Service Trust (Establishment) and the Bromley Hospitals National Health Service Trust, the Queen Elizabeth Hospital National Health Service Trust and the Queen Mary's Sidcup National Health Service Trust (Dissolution) Order 2006 that established the trust.

1428. Doctors–Registration–Application to revoke interim conditional registration order–Requirement to register with Care Quality Commission–Power to impose restrictions of up to 18 months

[Medical Act 1983 (c.54) s.41A(10), s.41A(2).]

The applicant medical practitioner (W) applied under the Medical Act 1983 s.41A(10) to revoke an order made by the respondent Council's interim orders panel for interim conditional registration. The Care Quality Commission had carried out an unannounced inspection and allegedly found W performing a liposuction in unhygienic conditions and in unregistered premises. The Commission referred W to the GMC and the panel determined that it was necessary for the protection of the public, in the public interest, and in W's own interests to make an interim order imposing conditions on his registration. W was subsequently convicted in criminal proceedings of carrying on an independent hospital without being registered in respect of it. Since the original order in May 2010, it had been reviewed and extended several times. A week before the instant hearing, the GMC had applied to extend the order and W had himself invited the court to extend the order for a further 12 months, which the court did. At the instant hearing, W sought the court's permission to refer two questions to the European Court of Justice, namely whether the statutory requirement that medical practitioners register with the Commission and the power to impose restrictions of up to 18 months on practitioners' registrations were contrary to European law.

Held: Application refused. Although W claimed that he had consented to the most recent extension so that the order remained in place for the instant application, he could not complain if the evidence that he invited an extension was taken at face-value. If he wished to argue that the extension was excessive, he should not have invited an extension at the previous hearing. The panel was entitled to rely on W's criminal conviction as conclusive evidence of the offence committed for the purpose of making an interim order. W's argument that the requirement that practitioners register with Commission was contrary to European law was based on a fundamental misunderstanding of the judgment in *Waghorn v Care Quality Commission* [2012] EWHC 1816 (Admin), [2013] Med. L.R. 80, [2013] 2 C.L. 170. In that case the judge had held that W was required to be registered in respect of the relevant hospital; she had not ruled that every medical practitioner was required to register with the Commission every time he performed a procedure in a registered hospital, *Waghorn* considered. Accordingly, it was not necessary to refer W's first question to the ECJ. Further, there was nothing to justify a reference in respect of the power to impose restrictions of up to 18 months: the panel's procedure was designed to protect the public, and the position of practitioners was protected by the fact that the panel was required to carry out periodic reviews of an interim conditional registration order under s.41A(1) and s.41A(2) of the 1983 Act, and by the fact that a practitioner could apply to vary or revoke any conditions imposed under s.41A(10). W's application was dismissed as totally without merit.

WAGHORN v GENERAL MEDICAL COUNCIL, [2012] EWHC 3427 (Admin), [2013] 1 C.M.L.R. 45, Stuart-Smith, J., QBD (Admin).

1429. Doctors–Registration–Doctor obtaining Primary Medical Qualification overseas–General Medical Council's refusal to accept qualification–Legitimate expectation

[Medical Act 1983 (c.54) s.21B(1), s.21C(2); European Convention on Human Rights 1950 Protocol 1 Art.2.]

P appealed against a decision ([2012] EWHC 2120 (Admin), (2012) 128 B.M.L.R. 146, [2013] 2 C.L. 165) dismissing his application for judicial review of the refusal of the General Medical Council (GMC) to accept his Primary Medical Qualification (PMQ) from a Caribbean university (U) as an acceptable overseas qualification. P contacted the GMC to establish if his proposed course of study was acceptable and received replies confirming that it would be. He performed his pre-clinical studies by distance learning at U and then completed his supervised clinical rotations at United Kingdom hospitals. He estimated his expenditure at $40,000 over six years of study. Registration of his PMQ was subsequently refused because the registration criteria had been changed. P submitted that (1) the court below had erred in finding that the GMC had not unlawfully fettered its discretion by defining the acceptable overseas qualification by reference to criteria that did not allow exceptions, whereas the wording of the Medical Act 1983 s.21B(1) and s.21C(2) conferred a general discretion to consider exceptional cases such as his; (2) the judge had erred in holding that the retrospective change in the requirement was not irrational or arbitrary even though it imposed blanket criteria, which excluded high quality candidates with the requisite knowledge and skill; (3) the refusal to recognise P's qualification was contrary to the European Convention on Human Rights 1950 Protocol 1 art.2; (4) the refusal to recognise P's PMQ after confirming by email that it would, was a breach of his legitimate expectation.

Held: Appeal allowed. (1) The judge had been correct to decide that neither s.21B(1) nor s.21C(2) of the 1983 Act gave the GMC a discretion to allow registration where the criteria had not been satisfied, rather they provided a discretion to refuse registration even where the criteria had been satisfied. Parliament's intention was that the GMC, as an expert body, should set minimum criteria for registration. Although the exercise of that judgement had to be reasonable, the boundaries were wide enough to include the criteria that any PMQ had to satisfy and there was no unlawful fettering of discretion by G, *R. v Specialist Training Authority of the Medical Royal Colleges, Ex p. British Medical Association* [1999] Ed. C.R. 661, [1999] C.L.Y. 2660 considered (see paras 31-34 of judgment). (2) The retrospective change was not irrational when examined in its context, which included the absence of universally recognised standards for PMQs, Parliament's intention that G had to provide criteria for accepting PMQs, and the impracticability of verifying the many PMQs issued around the world. Nor was the lack of transitional provision irrational, as G was entitled to change the criteria with immediate effect if necessary (paras 36-37). (3) Article 2 of Protocol 1 was not engaged and, therefore, resort to principles of proportionality was not appropriate, *Belgian Linguistic Case (A/6)* (1979-80) 1 E.H.R.R. 252, [1981] C.L.Y. 1088, *R. (on the application of Sivills) v General Social Care Council* [2007] EWHC 2576 (Admin)and *R. v Secretary of State for the Home Department, Ex p. Brind* [1991] 1 A.C. 696, [1991] C.L.Y. 71 considered (para.38). (4) P had received a clear, unequivocal, and unqualified assurance from G that if he completed the proposed course in a reasonable time his qualification would be recognised. The Medical Act 1983 did not exclude the principle of legitimate expectation and the statutory duty had to be exercised in accordance with established principles of substantive fairness. It had not been open to G to change its policy without adopting some transitional provision for P. There was no public interest which outweighed the unfairness of refusing to honour the assurance given and to recognise P's qualification (para.85). The relief granted was specific to P and compelled G to recognise his PMQ (para.93).

R. (ON THE APPLICATION OF PATEL) v GENERAL MEDICAL COUNCIL, [2013] EWCA Civ 327, [2013] 1 W.L.R. 2801, Lord Dyson (M.R.), CA (Civ Div).

1430. Drugs–Misuse of drugs–Pharmaceuticals

THE MISUSE OF DRUGS ACT 1971 (AMENDMENT) ORDER 2013, SI 2013/239; made under the Misuse of Drugs Act 1971 s.2. In force: February 13, 2013; .

This Order controls the following as Class B drugs under Part 2 of Schedule 2 of the Misuse of Drugs Act 1971: (i) Synthetic cannabinoid receptor agonists (synthetic cannabinoids); (ii) 2-(ethylamino)-2-(3-methoxyphenyl)cyclohexanone (commonly known asmethoxetamine) and other compounds related to ketamine (Class C) and phencyclidine (Class A); and (iii) 2-((dimethylamino)methyl)-1-(3-hydroxyphenyl)cyclohexanol (commonlyknown as "O-desmethyltramadol", a metabolite of the prescription only medicine, tramadol).

1431. Executive directors–NHS trusts–Non-executive directors

THE WIRRAL COMMUNITY NATIONAL HEALTH SERVICE TRUST (ESTABLISHMENT) AMENDMENT ORDER 2013, SI 2013/1698; made under the National Health Service Act 2006 s.25, s.272, s.273. In force: July 24, 2013; .

This Order amends the Wirral Community National Health Service Trust (Establishment) Order 2011 (SI 2011/805) to increase the number of executive directors of the trust from two to four and the number of non-executive directors of the trust from two to four.

1432. **Exemptions–NHS–Student loans–Travelling expenses**

THE NATIONAL HEALTH SERVICE (TRAVEL EXPENSES AND REMISSION OF CHARGES) (AMENDMENT) REGULATIONS 2013, SI 2013/1600; made under the National Health Service Act 2006 s.182, s.183, s.184, s.272. In force: August 1, 2013 except for reg.3 on September 1, 2013 and reg.4 on November 1, 2013.; .

These Regulations amend the National Health Service (Travel Expenses and Remission of Charges) Regulations 2003 (SI 2003/2382), to update the provisions of those Regulations that refer to the student funding arrangements that apply in Scotland and Wales, and to extend the existing arrangements for providing exemption from NHS charges, and assistance with travel costs, to people in receipt of Universal Credit to the period beginning on November 1, 2013 and ending on April 5, 2014.

1433. **Fees–Medical equipment**

THE MEDICAL DEVICES (FEES AMENDMENT) REGULATIONS 2013, SI 2013/525; made under the European Communities Act 1972 s.2; and the Finance Act 1973 s.56. In force: April 1, 2013; .

These Regulations amend the the Regulations which set out fees payable by the medical devices industry in relation to services provided by, and regulatory functions carried out by the MHRA in relation to medical devices on the UK market. They increases only some of the fees payable (ie fees for Clinical Investigation Notifications); the overall effect is to increase fees by about £52,000 overall per annum.

1434. **Fees–Osteopaths–Registration**

THE GENERAL OSTEOPATHIC COUNCIL (APPLICATION FOR REGISTRATION AND FEES) (AMENDMENT) RULES ORDER OF COUNCIL 2013, SI 2013/1026; made under the Osteopaths Act 1993 s.6, s.35. In force: May 1, 2013; .

This Order amends the General Osteopathic Council (Application for Registration and Fees) Rules Order of Council 2000 (SI 2000/1038) by reducing, in certain circumstances, the "entry fee" payable by an osteopath when first entered on to the register, by reducing the "retention fee" payable by an osteopath in order to remain on the register subsequently, and by reducing the "restoration fee" payable by an osteopath in order to have an entry restored to the register.

1435. **Fitness to practise–Doctors–Interim orders panel's suspension of general practitioner–Wrongdoing unrelated to clinical matters–Proportionality of suspension**

[Medical Act 1983 (c.54) s.41A.]

The applicant general practitioner (P) applied to terminate an 18-month interim suspension order imposed upon him by an interim orders panel of the respondent GMC. P had been a member of the Board of Governors at a school and was Chairman of the Finance Committee. He was arrested in connection with the discharge of his duties as a governor and the authorisation of substantial payments to staff to which they were allegedly not entitled. P was charged with a conspiracy to defraud and with committing fraud by abuse of his position, which was said to have occurred over six years and involved £1.8 million. The panel made an 18-month suspension order in accordance with the Medical Act 1983 s.41A, noting that suspension was necessary to maintain public confidence in the profession, because of the substantial sum involved, and that whilst suspension removed P's ability to practise, in view of the probity concerns and seriousness of the charges, no conditions could be imposed to adequately protect the public interest whilst resolving matters. P submitted that the interim order was neither necessary nor proportionate, nor in the public interest given that the allegations were not related to clinical matters.

Held: Application granted. Although a large sum of money was involved in the conspiracy charge, it was the nature of the wrongdoing that was critical, not the sum involved. No complaint had hitherto been made about P's clinical competence or his honesty; he denied the conspiracy charge and was thus innocent until proven guilty; the prosecution were not alleging that he had made any personal gain; the charges arose from a scheme whereby teachers were eligible in certain circumstances for incentive payments or bonuses, which P could authorise in his capacity as chairman; and the scheme required examination to determine whether the payments P authorised were in fact dishonest. Applying the test in the Guidance for Interim Orders Panels para.33 as to what a reasonable onlooker would think of P being allowed to continue to practise if convicted of the conspiracy, it was clear that no reasonable onlooker would be offended to learn that P had been allowed to continue to practise in the interim. There was no evidence of a threat to the public's welfare. Such a decision would not undermine the public confidence in the profession, and it could not be said that the public interest required P's suspension (see paras 27-30 of judgment).

PATEL v GENERAL MEDICAL COUNCIL, [2012] EWHC 3688 (Admin), [2013] 1 W.L.R. 2694, Eady, J., QBD (Admin).

1436. Fitness to practise–Doctors–Suspended doctor seeing patient for post-operative review–Failure to inform patient of suspension–Meaning of "clinical care and treatment"

[Medical Act 1983 (c.54) s.35E(3), s.41A(11), s.41C(2), s.41C(1), Pt VI.]

The appellant doctor (D) appealed against a decision of the respondent GMC's Fitness to Practise Panel ordering his suspension from the medical register for 12 months. D operated a cosmetic surgery business, but he was suspended for 18 months on an interim basis after he was charged with misconduct. Shortly before the suspension, D first met with a patient (S) to discuss breast augmentation surgery. He failed to inform her that he had been suspended at subsequent appointments, including a joint consultation with her surgeon. D was listed on S's consent form as her responsible health professional, and he saw her for post-operative reviews and when she was suffering from post-operative problems. S subsequently complained to the GMC and D was charged with disciplinary offences, including providing "clinical care and treatment" whilst he was suspended. The panel found that D had breached his interim order because clinical care and treatment? included having appointments with S and changing her dressings, and suspended him for 12 months. D submitted that whilst he did provide clinical care and treatment to S, he had not done any activity that necessitated medical registration.

Held: Appeal dismissed. (1) The Medical Act 1983 identified categories of clinical care and treatment that were made the exclusive preserve of registered medical practitioners. One of the privileges of being registered was being entitled to hold oneself out as a duly registered and licensed medical practitioner, and Part VI of the Act was clearly aimed at ensuring that only registered medical practitioners could provide clinical care and treatment to patients in that capacity. It followed that it was not open to a doctor who was suspended from the register to provide clinical care and treatment to a patient in his capacity as a registered practitioner. In accordance with s.35E(3) and s.41A(11) of the Act, the legal effect of D's interim suspension was that he was treated as not being registered, and pursuant to s.41C(1) and s.41C(2), his licence to practise was withdrawn. D had treated S whilst giving the impression that he was still registered and licensed to practise and there was no suggestion that he had informed her of his suspension. It followed that the panel was right to find that D had breached his interim suspension order by doing the one thing he was not permitted to do under the Act. The GMC had explained to D the effect of his suspension, and that it was his responsibility to check the appropriateness and legality of any activity he undertook whilst suspended (see paras 26, 34, 36-39, 41-42 of judgment). (2) The panel had correctly approached the question of whether it was in S's best interests for her to continue to be treated by D whilst he was suspended. It could not be suggested that there was no other doctor to whom S could have been referred (paras 47-48).

DUTTA v GENERAL MEDICAL COUNCIL, [2013] EWHC 132 (Admin), (2013) 132 B.M.L.R. 212, Haddon-Cave, J., QBD (Admin).

1437. Fitness to practise–General Medical Council

THE GENERAL MEDICAL COUNCIL (FITNESS TO PRACTISE AND CONSTITUTION OF PANELS AND INVESTIGATION COMMITTEE) (AMENDMENT) RULES ORDER OF COUNCIL 2013, SI 2013/815; made under the Medical Act 1983 s.35CC, Sch.1 para.19A, Sch.1 para.19B, Sch.1 para.19C, Sch.1 para.19D, Sch.1 para.19E, Sch.1 para.23B, Sch.4 para.1. In force: May 8, 2013; .

The General Medical Council (GMC) is the regulator for doctors in the UK, ensuring that registrants adhere to standards and requirements for the safe and effective practice of medicine. This Order approves rules made by the GMC, which amend the General Medical Council (Fitness to Practise) Rules 2004 (SI 2004/2608) and General Medical Council (Constitution of Panels and Investigation Committee) Rules 2004 (SI 2004/2611).

1438. Fitness to practise–General Osteopathic Council–Opticians

THE GENERAL OPTICAL COUNCIL (FITNESS TO PRACTISE) RULES ORDER OF COUNCIL 2013, SI 2013/2537; made under the Opticians Act 1989 s.13E, s.23C, s.23D, s.23E, s.31A. In force: April 1, 2014; .

The Rules scheduled to this Order make provision for revised procedures to be followed in relation to fitness to practise proceedings brought under the Opticians Act 1989 against a registered optometrist, a registered dispensing optician or a business registrant of the General Optical Council.

1439. Fitness to practise–Locum doctors–Conduct amounting to dishonesty–Likelihood of deletion of declaration of truth on timesheet on part of someone intending to commit fraud

The appellant (F) appealed against a decision of the respondent GMC's Fitness to Practise Panel finding one specific allegation of dishonesty established. F was a consultant anaesthetist who had undertaken various locum posts. Allegations of misleading and dishonest conduct were made against him by the locum agency: (i) that he had not paid for accommodation provided by the agency; (ii) that he had wrongly recorded his hours worked and claimed payment for time during which he had not worked; (iii) that he had deliberately deleted a declaration on the agency's timesheets that the information given on the form was correct and complete. F denied that he had removed the declarations from the timesheets and alleged that the agency had fabricated the documents. The panel dismissed the first allegation, having found that there was no contractual obligation on F to pay for accommodation, and found that the second allegation could not be proved, since it was likely that F had rounded up the time he had worked to the nearest hour, as he was permitted to do. In respect of the "declaration allegation", however, the panel found that the timesheets submitted by F were different to those submitted by other doctors and that it was evident that F had altered the timesheet by removing the declarations. It concluded that that was deceitful and had led the agency to assume that the content of the forms F submitted was as required by its locums. The panel was satisfied that that conduct could be regarded as dishonest, and that F had to have realised that what he was doing was dishonest by the ordinary standards of reasonable and honest people. It therefore found the third allegation proved, and imposed a penalty of one year's suspension from the register. It fell to be determined whether the panel was entitled to reach that conclusion.

Held: Appeal allowed. In finding the third allegation proved, the panel had not ascribed a motive to F for having deliberately excised the declaration from the time sheet. It had concluded that that was deceitful and led the agency to assume the content of the forms was as required, but that was all it had said. The logic of that proposition could not be understood. Removing a statement of truth could not possibly lead the recipient of the form to believe that its content was "as required" by the maker of the form. If the declaration was standard and appeared in every other form submitted to the agency, the forms returned by F had to have contained a gaping hole which was obvious to anyone receiving it, which raised the question why that was not noticed until later when other issues were raised by the agency. One fairly obvious answer to that was that such a declaration did not appear in every timesheet required to be completed by a locum of the agency. If that was so, greater credence ought to have been given to F's evidence that he was never supplied with a form which contained the declaration. If, on the other hand, it was a standard provision which had been deleted, the fact that it went unnoticed suggested that little, if any, attention was ever paid by the agency to the declaration. The panel had not considered what possible reason a fraudster who was overstating the hours he had worked, which was what the GMC was alleging against F, could have had for drawing attention to his fraud by deleting the declaration of truth. Having found the allegation that F had overstated his hours unproved, the panel had not been entitled to draw the inference that he had deliberately deleted the declarations and that he had done so for some dishonest motive. When the question of why anyone should have done that was addressed, any evidential balance that tipped in favour of a conclusion that there was such a deletion swung back decidedly the other way, given that there was no firm evidence to the contrary. In those circumstances, the panel had not been right to conclude that F had deliberately deleted the declaration from the time sheets. Deliberate deletion of a declaration of truth on the part of someone out to commit fraud was so unlikely that it could not be proved even on the balance of probabilities. The panel should not have found F guilty of acting dishonestly in that fashion. That finding and the consequent sanction imposed had both to be set aside (see paras 73-75, 78-80, 84, 89-90 of judgment).

FISH v GENERAL MEDICAL COUNCIL, [2012] EWHC 1269 (Admin), [2012] Med. L.R. 512, Foskett, J., QBD (Admin).

1440. Fitness to practise–Nurses–Failure to cooperate in investigation of colleague–Impairment of fitness–Interpretation of para.56 Nursing and Midwifery Council Code of Practice 2008

The appellant nurse (H) appealed against the decision of a panel of the conduct and competence committee of the respondent council that her fitness to practise was impaired by reason of misconduct and the imposition of a condition of practice order for a period of six months. F had been employed as a practice nurse at a doctors' surgery. An investigation began after H raised concerns about a colleague's fitness to practise after receiving adverse comments and complaints from patients about the colleague. H was asked by letter on two occasions to provide a list of patients who had complained but she did not reply. It was alleged that H had failed to cooperate in the investigation by failing to provide a list of the relevant patients. H maintained that her refusal did not amount to misconduct and that her fitness to practise was not impaired. The panel applied the definition of misconduct in *Roylance v General Medical Council (No.2)* [2000] 1 A.C. 311, [1999] C.L.Y. 2663. It concluded that as a registered nurse H had a duty to cooperate with internal and external investigations as set out in the Nursing and Midwifery Council Code (May 2008): Standards of conduct, performance and ethics for nurses and midwives para.56. The panel concluded that H's failure to cooperate potentially caused harm to patients as their complaints could not be dealt with and potentially jeopardised their trust and confidence in the nursing profession. H submitted that (1) the panel applied the wrong test in determining whether misconduct had been proved and that para.56 of the Code imposed an obligation to cooperate with internal and external investigations only insofar as they related to a registrant; (2) the panel was wrong to conclude that her fitness to practise was impaired and failed to have proper regard to H's explanation as to why she had not provided a list of patients' names and to her evidence to the effect that if similar circumstances were to be repeated she would disclose the names of patients because she had come to recognise that patients' safety was paramount.

Held: Appeal dismissed. (1) The panel had not misdirected itself on the appropriate test. It was very unlikely that an expert and experienced panel did not apply the correct legal test particularly when it made express reference to the leading authority, *Roylance* considered. The panel was fully aware of the correct approach and applied it. There was no good reason why para.56 should be interpreted narrowly as circumstances could arise where it would be wholly unprofessional if a registrant failed to cooperate with internal and external investigations which related to persons other than the registrant. It was clear that H had failed to comply with an important provision within her professional code of practice. The panel expressly acknowledged that that did not necessarily mean that misconduct had been proved; it went on to consider whether the breach of the Code constituted misconduct in the particular circumstances of the case. The panel was not wrong in reaching its conclusion. H had received two detailed letters asking for a list of patients who had complained. The letters clearly explained why that information was wanted. H did not reply and gave no reason why she was unwilling to provide the list. H made it more difficult for it to be ascertained whether or not the colleague was performing her work properly and professionally. The panel's decision on misconduct was well within the reasonable range of decisions which was open to it (see paras 31-36 of judgment). (2) The decision letter did not say, in terms, that H's evidence as to her future conduct had been rejected by the panel. That did not mean, however, that the panel was wrong in its conclusion about impairment. The task for the panel was to make an assessment of the whole of H's evidence and to make a judgment about H. The panel had the advantage of seeing and hearing H and it provided sufficient cogent reasoning to justify its conclusion that H s fitness to practise was impaired. In particular, it concluded that H had limited insight into the potential harm to patients which would be caused by a repeat of her misconduct and the potential her actions had for undermining the trust and confidence of the public in the nursing profession. It said it was "not confident" that H truly understood the relationship and potential tension between confidentiality on the one hand and protection of patients on the other. Although a differently constituted panel might have viewed the evidence given by H as to her future conduct in a more favourable light it could not be said that the instant panel had been wrong in holding that H's fitness to practise was impaired. H enjoyed a very high reputation within the profession, as made clear by her testimonials, and her clinical skills had never been called into question. The panel took full account of those matters yet felt itself compelled to reach its conclusion on impairment, *Council for Healthcare Regulatory Excellence v Nursing and Midwifery Council* [2011] EWHC 927 (Admin), [2011] A.C.D. 72, [2011] C.L.Y. 1540 applied.

HARFORD v NURSING AND MIDWIFERY COUNCIL, [2013] EWHC 696 (Admin), [2013] Med. L.R. 179, Wyn Williams, J., QBD (Admin).

1441. Fitness to practise–Nurses–Interim suspension of nurse–Nursing and Midwifery Council's refusal to hear evidence on substance of allegations–Fairness of proceedings

[Nursing and Midwifery Council (Fitness to Practise) Rules Order of Council 2004 (SI 2004/1761); European Convention on Human Rights 1950 Art.6, Art.8.]

The appellant nurse (P) appealed against the rejection of his claim that an interim orders hearing before the Investigating Committee of the respondent Nursing and Midwifery Council (NMC) and an 18-month order of suspension infringed his rights under the European Convention on Human Rights 1950 art.6 and art.8. P had worked as part of a youth offending service. He was summarily dismissed after a client made allegations that he had had an inappropriate and sexualised relationship with her. The NMC notified P that it had received an allegation that his fitness to practise was impaired and that pending a decision as to whether there was a case to answer, an interim orders hearing would be held where conditions or suspension could be imposed. At the hearing, the committee allowed P to give evidence on what he admitted and denied, and indicated that it would hear evidence that suggested that the allegations were clearly unfounded or malicious, but prevented P's legal representative from exploring the allegations with him in evidence. The committee referenced the NMC guidance and stated that its function was not to weigh-up the evidence but to be satisfied that there was a prima facie case for imposing an interim order. The committee suspended P from the register. P submitted that fairness dictated that he was given an opportunity to give evidence to address the substance of the allegations against him, and that the committee had, in preventing him from doing so, breached his rights under art.6 and art.8, and that the hearing failed to comply with the common law requirements of fairness.

The committee had a duty to determine whether to make an interim order, and P had a right under the Nursing and Midwifery Council (Fitness to Practise) Rules Order of Council art.26 to give any evidence relevant to that question. The committee had to decide whether, on the basis of the allegation and evidence against P, it was satisfied that an order was necessary for protection of the public or otherwise in the public interest. In exercising that duty it had to permit both parties to make submissions on the need for an interim order, which involved considering the nature of the evidence on which the allegation was based. It was entitled to discount evidence that was inconsistent with objective or undisputed evidence or which was unreliable. It could also receive evidence on the effect of an order on a registrant, and a registrant was entitled to give evidence on that. A registrant could also give evidence to establish that the allegation was unfounded or exaggerated, but the committee was not required to hear evidence as to whether a substantive allegation was well-founded. It could not decide the credibility or merit of a disputed allegation; that was a matter for the panel at the substantive hearing. The matters taken into account on a court application for the continuation of a suspension order were the same as those relevant to the making of an order by the committee, which was to ascertain whether allegations made against a medical practitioner, rather than their veracity, justified the prolongation of a suspension, and that in general there was no need to look beyond the allegations, *General Medical Council v Hiew* [2006] EWHC 2699 (Admin) applied. Fairness did not require that a registrant to an allegation of unfitness to practise be given an opportunity to give evidence on the substance of that allegation before the committee considered whether to make an interim suspension order, *R. (on the application of Wright) v Secretary of State for Health* [2009] UKHL 3, [2009] 1 A.C. 739, [2009] C.L.Y. 3682 considered. If a registrant was given an opportunity to give evidence to the committee on the substance of the allegations made against him, with a view to the committee rejecting those allegations, fairness would require that the NMC should be able to call the complainant to give evidence in support of its allegations. That would result in a trial before the trial, which was not what the statutory scheme envisaged or what fairness required at the interim stage. If that was the case, the court would have to reconsider the procedure applicable to granting interim relief, in particular the grant of injunctions in all civil cases, and the guidance in *American Cyanamid* would be liable to be set aside. The current procedure employed by the committee satisfied the requirements of fairness. The NMC guidance was compatible with the common law and the Convention rights of registrants. The hearing before the committee had been fair and had not infringed P's rights under art.6 or art.8 (see paras 13-14 16-20, 27, 31-36 of judgment).

PERRY v NURSING AND MIDWIFERY COUNCIL, [2013] EWCA Civ 145, [2013] 1 W.L.R. 3423, Hughes, L.J., CA (Civ Div).

1442. **Fitness to practise–Psychiatrists–Fitness to Practise Panel relying on own expertise and reaching conclusions without giving parties opportunity to address issues–Failure to assess expert evidence**

[General Medical Council (Fitness to Practise) Rules Order of Council 2004 (SI 2004/2608).]

The appellant psychiatrist (L) appealed against certain procedural decisions and factual findings of the Fitness to Practise Panel of the respondent General Medical Council. The Panel had made findings of misconduct by L, in respect of a patient (B). B had experienced erotic transference and alleged that L had acted inappropriately in several ways, including continuing to treat her after becoming emotionally involved with her; telling her she was attractive; and revealing sexual fantasies about her. He claimed that one aspect of B's erotic transference was an inaccurate fantasy that he reciprocated her feelings. The Panel did not accept that and reasoned that from its own expertise, a woman with low self-esteem was unlikely to fantasise that she was attractive to another without encouragement. It also found that erotic transference alone would be unlikely to cause B to believe that L reciprocated her feelings. B had moved to Australia and the Panel allowed her to give evidence by video link, finding that she was a vulnerable witness under the General Medical Council (Fitness to Practise) Rules Order of Council 2004 r.36(1)(b) and r.36(1)(e). L argued that (1) B should not have been allowed to give evidence by video link; (2) the issue of whether a woman with low self-esteem was likely to fantasise that she was attractive to another without encouragement had not been raised at the hearing and the Panel had relied on expertise which it did not have; (3) the conclusion that erotic transference alone was unlikely to cause B to believe that L reciprocated her feelings was unsupported by expert evidence; (4) the Panel had plainly been wrong to find the allegations against L proved.

Held: Appeal allowed in part. (1) It had not been wrong or irrational to find that there would be no unfair prejudice to L if B gave her evidence by video link. The conditions in both r.36(1)(b) and r.36(1)(e) were satisfied. There was compelling psychiatric evidence that B had a major depressive episode in partial remission, but that if she gave evidence at the hearing, there was a real prospect of a relapse, which would affect the quality of her evidence. It would defeat the purpose of r.36 if the Panel did not have power to allow a witness to give testimony by video link in such circumstances. The Panel had also been properly satisfied that it would be able to make observations on body language and demeanour, *Polanski v Conde Nast Publications Ltd* [2005] UKHL 10, [2005] 1 W.L.R. 637, [2005] C.L.Y. 303 followed (see paras 90-92, 98, 102-106 of judgment). (2) It had not been open to the Panel to conclude that a woman with low self-esteem would be unlikely to fantasise that she was attractive to another without giving L notice of the issue and an opportunity to adduce evidence or make submissions on it. Its failure to do so was a material procedural irregularity (paras 201, 209-210, 213). That error was compounded by the fact that although the Panel considered that it had relevant expertise, it did not. Its conclusion purported to derive from the expertise of the psychiatrist chairman, who was not a psychotherapy expert. In the absence of evidence, the conclusion was not one which any lay tribunal would have been entitled to reach. The rules of natural justice precluded members of specialist tribunals, including experts, from giving evidence to themselves which the parties had no opportunity to challenge, *Watson v General Medical Council* [2005] EWHC 1896 (Admin), [2006] I.C.R. 113, [2005] C.L.Y. 1800, *White v Ealing LBC* [1999] 1 F.C.R. 356, [1998] C.L.Y. 1977, *Southall v General Medical Council* [2010] EWCA Civ 407, [2010] 2 F.L.R. 1550, [2010] C.L.Y. 1547 and *M v Worcestershire CC* [2002] EWHC 1292 (Admin), [2003] E.L.R. 31 applied (paras 202, 217-230, 235-6). (3) The only legitimate basis for the statement that erotic transference alone was unlikely to cause B to believe that L reciprocated her feelings would have been expert evidence, which the Panel had been under a duty to assess. However, in critical respects, it was not clear what findings the Panel had made or why it had made them. The degree of detail needed to satisfy the requirement to give reasons was fact-sensitive, but particular rigour was likely to be necessary when dealing with expert evidence, *English v Emery Reimbold & Strick Ltd* [2002] EWCA Civ 605, [2002] 1 W.L.R. 2409, [2002] C.L.Y. 301 and *Phipps v General Medical Council (Application for Permission to Appeal)* [2006] EWCA Civ 397, [2006] Lloyd's Rep. Med. 345, [2006} C.L.Y. 1817 followed. The interests of justice required that the findings of misconduct be quashed (paras 185-200, 246, 251, 255-256, 271-273, 283-285, 290-291). (4) Aside from the above errors, the evidence, as a whole, did not justify a conclusion that the Panel's findings of misconduct were plainly wrong. However, the Panel had made insufficient reference to various issues and given inadequate reasons. Those flaws contributed to the conclusion that its findings of misconduct should be quashed (paras 300-514).

LAWRENCE v GENERAL MEDICAL COUNCIL; *sub nom.* R. (ON THE APPLICATION OF LAWRENCE) v GENERAL MEDICAL COUNCIL, [2012] EWHC 464 (Admin), [2012] Med. L.R. 608, Stadlen, J., QBD (Admin).

1443. Health Act 2006 (c.28)–Commencement No.3 Order–Wales

THE HEALTH ACT 2006 (COMMENCEMENT NO.3) (WALES) ORDER 2013, SI 2013/SI 2013/1112 (W.118) (C.48); made under the Health Act 2006 s.83. Commencement details: bringing into force various provisions of the 2006 Act on May 9, 2013.; .

This Order is the third commencement order made by the Welsh ministers under the Health Act 2006. It brings into force a section containing a power enabling charges to be made for applications for inclusion in or amendment to a pharmaceutical list.

1444. Health and safety at work–Employers–Health care–Hospitals

THE HEALTH AND SAFETY (SHARP INSTRUMENTS IN HEALTHCARE) REGULATIONS 2013, SI 2013/645; made under the Health and Safety at Work etc. Act 1974 s.15, s.82, Sch.3 para.1, Sch.3 para.8, Sch.3 para.14, Sch.3 para.15, Sch.3 para.16, Sch.3 para.20. In force: May 11, 2013; .

These Regulations impose duties on employers in the healthcare sector to protect employees from injuries caused by medical sharps, implementing Council Directive 2010/32/EU of May 10 2010 implementing the Framework Agreement on prevention from sharp injuries in the hospital and healthcare sector.

1445. Health and Social Care Act 2012 (c.7)–Commencement No.4, Transitional, Savings and Transitory Provisions Order

THE HEALTH AND SOCIAL CARE ACT 2012 (COMMENCEMENT NO.4, TRANSITIONAL, SAVINGS AND TRANSITORY PROVISIONS) ORDER 2013, SI 2013/SI 2013/160 (C.9); made under the Health and Social Care Act 2012 s.304, s.306. Commencement details: bringing into force various provisions of the 2012 Act on April 1, 2013.; .

This Order brings into force specified provisions of the Health and Social Care Act 2012.

1446. Health and Social Care Act 2012 (c.7)–Commencement No.5, Transitional, Savings and Transitory Provisions Order

THE HEALTH AND SOCIAL CARE ACT 2012 (COMMENCEMENT NO.5, TRANSITIONAL, SAVINGS AND TRANSITORY PROVISIONS) ORDER 2013, SI 2013/SI 2013/671 (C.28); made under the Health and Social Care Act 2012 s.304, s.306. Commencement details: bringing into force various provisions of the 2012 Act on April 1, 2013, July 1, 2013 and September 1, 2013.; .

This Order brings into force provisions of the Health and Social Care Act 2012, including those that: prescribe which Monitor is to have regard to in the exercise of its functions; and impose obligations on Monitor in relation to managing conflicts between its general duties and between certain of its functions, reviewing regulatory burdens and carrying out impact assessments.

1447. Health and wellbeing boards–Local authorities' powers and duties

THE LOCAL AUTHORITY (PUBLIC HEALTH, HEALTH AND WELLBEING BOARDS AND HEALTH SCRUTINY) REGULATIONS 2013, SI 2013/218; made under the Local Government Act 2000 s.9DA, s.9J, s.9JA, s.105; the National Health Service Act 2006 s.244, s.245, s.247, s.272, Sch.1 para.7B; the Localism Act 2011 s.81, s.235; and the Health and Social Care Act 2012 s.194, s.304. In force: in accordance with art.1 (2) (3) (4).; .

These Regulations make provision in relation to Health and Wellbeing Boards established under s.194 of the Health and Social Care Act 2012 (Pt 2), local authority public health functions (Pt 3) and review and scrutiny of the local health service by local authorities (Pt 4).

1448. Health authorities–NHS–NHS trusts

THE NATIONAL HEALTH SERVICE TRUSTS (ESTABLISHMENT) AMENDMENT ORDER 2013, SI 2013/593; made under the National Health Service Act 2006 s.25, s.272, s.273, Sch.4 para.5. In force: April 1, 2013; .

This Order amends the definition of "community health services" in the establishment Orders of the National Health Service trusts listed in the Schedules to the Order.

1449. Health care–Medical treatment–NHS–Patients' rights

THE NATIONAL HEALTH SERVICE (PROCUREMENT, PATIENT CHOICE AND COMPETITION) (NO.2) REGULATIONS 2013, SI 2013/500; made under the Health and Social Care Act 2012 s.75, s.76, s.77, s.304. In force: April 1, 2013; .

These Regulations impose requirements on the National Health Service Commissioning Board and clinical commissioning groups in order to ensure good practice in relation to the procurement of health care services for the purposes of the NHS, to ensure the protection of patients' rights to make choices regarding their NHS treatment and to prevent anti-competitive behaviour by commissioners with regard to such services.

1450. Health care–NHS–Licences

THE NATIONAL HEALTH SERVICE (LICENCE EXEMPTIONS, ETC.) REGULATIONS 2013, SI 2013/2677; made under the Health and Social Care Act 2012 s.81, s.83, s.150, s.304. In force: April 1, 2014; .

This instrument: provides exemptions to the requirement for a provider of NHS services to hold a licence with Monitor; and defines, for the purposes of licensing, the person who provides health care services.

1451. Health care–Patients' rights–Social security

THE NATIONAL HEALTH SERVICE (CROSS-BORDER HEALTHCARE) REGULATIONS 2013, SI 2013/2269; made under the European Communities Act 1972 s.2. In force: October 25, 2013; .

These Regulations implement in England and Wales provisions of Directive 2011/24 on the application of patients' rights in cross-border healthcare.

1452. Health Education England–Transfer of assets

THE HEALTH EDUCATION ENGLAND (ESTABLISHMENT AND CONSTITUTION) AMENDMENT ORDER 2013, SI 2013/647; made under the National Health Service Act 2006 s.28, s.272, s.273. In force: May 1, 2013; .

This Order amends the Health Education England (HEE) (Establishment and Constitution) Order 2012, which established Health Education England. It also amends the Establishment Order to provide for the transfer to HEE of specified property and liabilities from the Derby Hospitals NHS Foundation Trust on May 1 2013.

1453. **Hospitals–Consultation–Determination of relief after finding consultation process unlawful–Whether court should dictate future steps to be taken by defendant**

The court had to determine what relief to grant the claimant (S) following its decision that the defendant committee (J) had conducted a consultation process unlawfully. The consultation process, which was found to be unfair, related to a proposed reduction in paediatric cardiac surgery centres. S submitted that J's decision based on the consultation should be quashed. J contended that S did not have standing to seek relief and that there was no need to grant declaratory relief because it was a public body and the judgement therefore spoke for itself. Alternatively, it contended that a quashing order was not appropriate as that would lead to further delay in the process which was not in the public interest. The interested party submitted that the court should make the decision afresh.

Held: Judgment for claimant. (1) It was undisputed that there was a compelling and urgent clinical case for reform of congenital paediatric cardiac services but the court's finding that the consultation process was flawed went beyond the technical. S had been successful and a good reason was needed to refuse to quash the resulting decision. The fact that the judgment was made against a public body was not of itself a good enough reason to refuse relief. Further, J's contention that S lacked standing to obtain relief gave no proper recognition of who the individuals were that supported it; those individuals included clinicians from the affected hospitals and parents of children who had been in need of cardiac services or who could be in need. Although all parties recognised the need for change and it was imperative that further delay was avoided or at least limited, J's decision to accept the recommendation which agreed the implementation and designation of children's congenital cardiac services to the identified surgery centres had to be quashed. (2) The court was not in a position to dictate the steps that consequently should be taken as it did not have the knowledge or the evidence to do so. The quashing order was limited to the particular decision that had been found to be unfair and no part of the judgment should be taken to be advocating a need for J to return to the start of the reconfiguration process.

R. (ON THE APPLICATION OF SAVE OUR SURGERY LTD) v JOINT COMMITTEE OF PRIMARY CARE TRUSTS, [2013] EWHC 1011 (Admin), [2013] Med. L.R. 172, Nicola Davies, J., QBD (Admin).

1454. **Hospitals–Consultation–Proposed reduction in paediatric cardiac surgery centres–Centres receiving sub-scores for relevant criteria–Whether sub-scores material consideration**

The claimant (S) applied for judicial review to quash a decision of the defendant committee (J) which identified seven specialist centres in England for the future performance of paediatric cardiac surgery. Reports by groups of experts had recommended reorganisation of the centres providing paediatric cardiac surgery services. The consensus was that in order to achieve better and safer results surgical expertise needed to be concentrated in fewer, larger centres. A review was initiated and J was responsible for the conduct of the consultation for the review and for taking decisions on issues which were the subject of the consultation. The existing centres were sent a self-assessment template. The self-assessments were evaluated by members of an independent assessment panel who visited the centres and then produced sub-scores for each criterion. The sub-scores were weighted and fed into a final consensus score that was the result of the panel's discussions. J published a consultation document which proposed a number of reconfigurations which involved reducing the number of centres. Following the consultation J decided that an option excluding Leeds General Infirmary but including the Freeman Hospital in Newcastle would provide the best quality care. S was a company created for the purposes of the litigation. Its case was that the consultation was procedurally unfair because failure to disclose the sub-scores deprived consultees of the ability to make informed responses; and that there had been a failure by J to take into account material considerations by failing to inquire into and have regard to the sub-scores. J challenged S's standing to bring the proceedings.

Held: Application granted. (1) The issue for the court was whether the consultation process was so unfair that it was unlawful, *Devon CC v Secretary of State for Communities and Local Government* [2010] EWHC 1456 (Admin), [2011] B.L.G.R. 64, [2011] C.L.Y. 52 applied. Lawful consultation had to include sufficient reasons for particular proposals to allow those consulted to give intelligent consideration and an intelligent response, and the product of the consultation had to be conscientiously taken into account when the ultimate decision was taken. Disclosure of every submission or all of the advice received was not required. If the person making the decision had access to information but chose not to consider it, that of itself did not justify non-disclosure; it would be for the court to consider the reason for non-disclosure. Even where a consultation process demonstrated a high degree of disclosure and transparency, non-disclosure could limit the ability of a consultee to make an intelligent response to something that was central to the appraisal process (see para. 27 of judgment). (2) S had a sufficient interest in the proceedings. It represented many individuals who had contributed financially in order to bring the proceedings. It included individuals who could be directly affected by the closure of the Leeds unit and clinicians who worked within the unit. Incorporation was a proper means of allowing the interests of a substantial number of such persons to pursue the litigation (para.102). (3) Fairness did require disclosure of the sub-scores to enable Leeds to provide a properly focussed and meaningful response to the consultation. J's refusal of a specific request by Leeds for disclosure was ill-judged. J was on notice of the importance of the criterion of "quality" and within it the use being made of the sub-scores. With those considerations in mind, even if J chose not to look at the sub-scores, consultees should have been given such an opportunity (paras 112-117). (4) The sub-scores provided the basis for the consensus score which was ultimately one of the most significant tools in the assessment of "quality" of the respective centres. That criterion became more significant as the process developed. Commensurate with its duty properly to scrutinise and assess all relevant evidence, J should have considered the sub-scores, which provided the basis of what ultimately was the difference of one point in the critical quality scoring as between Leeds and Newcastle. The sub-scores were a material consideration (para.120).

R. (ON THE APPLICATION OF SAVE OUR SURGERY LTD) v JOINT COMMITTEE OF PRIMARY CARE TRUSTS, [2013] EWHC 439 (Admin), [2013] Med. L.R.150, Nicola Davies, J., QBD (Admin).

1455. Independent hospitals–Registration–Single medical practitioner performing cosmetic surgery in single basement room–Need for registration as independent hospital under Care Standards Act 2000

[Care Standards Act 2000 (c.14) s.11 (1).]

The appellant medical practitioner (W) appealed by way of case stated against a decision of a district judge that he carried on an independent hospital without being registered in respect of an offence under the Care Standards Act 2000 s.11 (1). Two Care Quality Commission authorised inspectors made an unannounced visit to a private clinic on the basis that they had reasonable cause to believe the premises were being used to provide services that required persons carrying on or managing an establishment to register with the CQC under s.11 (1). In the basement of the building, they discovered W performing liposuction on a female patient (P). During an interview, W admitted that he had met P a week earlier; was carrying out the procedure as a favour and was not being paid for it; did not know P's name; was working as an individual practitioner; was not employed by anyone; no company was involved in P's treatment that day; had provided his own medical equipment, and had undertaken to collect and dispose of the medical waste himself. W was found guilty of an offence under s.11 (1). The issues were whether (i) a medical practitioner who undertook a cosmetic surgical procedure at an independent hospital deemed to have "carried on" that independent hospital and whether W enjoyed practising privileges that exempted him from registration; (ii) it necessary for a medical practitioner to have an interest in the independent hospital in order to be deemed to have "carried on" that independent hospital; (iii) the term "carrying on an establishment" was deemed to encompass only those persons who were regarded as manager and/or owner of the particular establishment; (iv) whether the evidence as a whole supported a finding that on the relevant date W was "carrying on" an independent hospital. W submitted that in order to be convicted of an offence under s.11 (1), a practitioner had to be carrying on an independent hospital as the owner or proprietor, or managing it on a day-to-day basis and that he was neither an owner, nor a manager carrying on an independent hospital.

Held: Appeal dismissed. The two expressions in the phrase "carries on or manages" in s.11 (1) were used in the alternative and were not interchangeable; the former was capable of encompassing a broad range of personal involvement and control, extending beyond that involved in "manages an establishment". As such, "carry on" was plainly broader than the term "manages". As the primary purpose of the Act was the proper regulation of independent hospitals to ensure the safety and welfare of those who sought medical advice and treatment, many of whom would be vulnerable, the restrictive definition of "carrying on an establishment" which W argued for ran contrary to the Act's fundamental purpose in requiring compulsory registration. Another purpose was the importance of having a person accountable for the delivery of services in a relevant establishment; that much was clear from regulations published by the secretary of state under s.23(1) of the Act. On the facts of the instant case, it could not have been Parliament s intention to permit an unregistered surgeon, working entirely on his own, to perform an invasive, surgical procedure on a patient on an ad hoc basis, in a one room hospital owned and managed by another or other persons unknown, and yet escape the reach of s.11 (1). The only sensible conclusion was that W was carrying on the hospital as defined by the Act. However, even if a narrower interpretation of "carries on" was correct, requiring activity closer, or equivalent to, management or control of a hospital, on the facts W was still correctly held to be carrying on an independent hospital on the relevant date. Although the answer to question 1 was not inevitably yes if it could be shown that a practitioner held practising privileges, there was no evidence that W held any such privileges (see paras 36, 38-39, 42, 44-46 of judgment). (2) It was not necessary for a practitioner to have any interest, proprietary or non-proprietary, in a hospital to be found to be carrying on that hospital. To hold otherwise would defeat the whole purpose of the legislation (paras 49-50). (3) Although there would be many cases where the person carrying on the establishment was in fact the owner and/or manager of the establishment, that was not a prerequisite to liability under s.11 (para.51). (4) The evidence clearly supported the findings of the district judge. W had, as a registered medical practitioner, performed a listed service in a room which was an independent hospital under the Act when he had not been registered to do so and he had not enjoyed relevant practising privileges. Other relevant considerations included the fact that W had no contract with the clinic and did not pay for the room's use, nor did he receive payment for the surgery; W organised the venue and provided his own equipment; W performed all the necessary medical procedures, gained consent, and had undertaken to remove and dispose of all medical waste himself (para.56).

WAGHORN v CARE QUALITY COMMISSION, [2012] EWHC 1816 (Admin), [2013] Med. L.R. 80, Cox, J., QBD (Admin).

1456. Liabilities–Medical treatment–NHS–Third parties

THE NATIONAL HEALTH SERVICE (CLINICAL NEGLIGENCE SCHEME) AMENDMENT REGULATIONS 2013, SI 2013/497; made under the National Health Service Act 2006 s.71, s.272. In force: April 1, 2013; .

These Regulations amend the National Health Service (Clinical Negligence Scheme) Regulations 1996 which established a Scheme whereby certain NHS bodies and other bodies providing NHS services may make provision for meeting liabilities to third parties in connection with personal injury arising out of negligence in the carrying out of their functions.

1457. Licensing–NHS–National tariff–Pricing

THE NATIONAL HEALTH SERVICE (LICENSING AND PRICING) REGULATIONS 2013, SI 2013/2214; made under the Health and Social Care Act 2012 s.100, s.105, s.118, s.120, s.150, s.304. In force: September 5, 2013; .

This instrument provides for the levels of objections that would require further consideration of any proposals by Monitor for: modifications to the standard conditions included in licences, which all providers of NHS services will have to hold, unless exempt under separate regulations made under the Health and Social Care Act 2012 s.83; and its proposed methodology for calculating national prices to be paid for NHS services as set out in the national tariff.

1458. Local authorities' powers and duties–Local healthwatch organisations–Public health

THE LOCAL AUTHORITIES (PUBLIC HEALTH FUNCTIONS AND ENTRY TO PREMISES BY LOCAL HEALTHWATCH REPRESENTATIVES) REGULATIONS 2013, SI 2013/351; made under the National Health Service Act 2006 s.6C, s.186A, s.272; and the Local Government and Public Involvement in Health Act 2007 s.225, s.229, s.240. In force: in accordance with reg.1 (2).; .

These Regulations make provision for the steps to be taken by local authorities in exercising certain public health functions, for the exercise by local authorities of the Secretary of State's public health functions and the making and recovering of charges by local authorities in respect of their public health activities. It also makes provision in relation to Local Healthwatch organisations.

1459. Local authorities' powers and duties–Monitor–NHS foundation trusts

THE MID STAFFORDSHIRE NHS FOUNDATION TRUST (TRUST SPECIAL ADMINISTRATORS EXTENSION OF TIME) (NO.2) ORDER 2013, SI 2013/2671; made under the National Health Service Act 2006 s.65J. In force: October 22, 2013; .

This Order extends the period of time within which the trust special administrators of Mid Staffordshire NHS Foundation Trust must provide a final report to Monitor. The final report must state the action which the trust special administrators recommend that Monitor should take in relation to Mid Staffordshire NHS Foundation Trust. The statutory period of 15 working days for the provision of the final report is extended to 55 working days.

1460. Marketing authorisation–Pharmaceuticals

THE HUMAN MEDICINES (AMENDMENT) (NO.2) REGULATIONS 2013, SI 2013/2593; made under the European Communities Act 1972 s.2. In force: November 11, 2013; .

These Regulations amend the Human Medicines Regulations 2012 (SI 2012/1916) to implement Directive 2012/26 and Regulation 1027/2012, both as regards pharmacovigilance. The Regulations also allow general sale list medicines to be sold on trains and aircraft.

1461. Medical treatment–Life-sustaining treatment–Withdrawal of treatment–Best interests of patient–Futility of treatment

[Mental Capacity Act 2005 (c.9) s.1 (5).]

The appellant hospital trust appealed against a judge's refusal to make a declaration that it would be lawful for treatment for the first respondent patient (J) to be withheld in the event of a clinical deterioration. J had fought colon cancer and was left with a stoma. He was admitted to the hospital in May 2012 due to a complication with his stoma and then acquired an infection that was complicated by the presence of chronic obstructive pulmonary disease and the development of an acute kidney injury and persistent low blood pressure. He suffered multi-organ failure, with respiratory failure, cardiovascular failure and renal failure and remained in hospital on ventilator support in the critical care unit. His condition continued to deteriorate and over a period of time he suffered necrosis, pneumonia, septic shock, acute myocardial infarction and a stroke. He remained in a minimally conscious state, although his family gave evidence of his responding to their visits. The hospital wished to place a "Do Not Attempt Resuscitation" instruction on his medical records but his family disagreed. He lacked the capacity to litigate. The medical evidence was not optimistic and he was assessed at having a less than one per cent chance of ever being discharged from the unit. His medical team gave evidence that attempts at cardiopulmonary resuscitation (CPR) and invasive support would be painful for him and would put him at risk of further complications. The judge decided not to grant the hospital's application as he was not persuaded that treatment would be futile or overly burdensome and he decided that it would not be in J's best interests to withhold treatment. He went on to say that, though it was not necessary to decide, it was unlikely that further CPR would be in J's best interests. The hospital submitted that the judge had erred in finding that further CPR would not be in J's best interests but failing to grant a declaration to that effect; in applying a test which required the quality of life to be "truly awful or non-existent"; in eliding the test of best interests being futile, overly burdensome and/or there being no prospect of recovery and failing to find that that was the case for J; in placing decisive weight on J's family's evidence of his likely views; and in finding the pre-condition of there being "a significant clinical deterioration" too uncertain to justify declarations being made.

Held: Appeal allowed. (1) The test under the Mental Capacity Act 2005 s.1(5) was simply what was in the best interests of the patient. The judge had not allowed his decisions on futility to govern his decision but he had erred in adopting too narrow a view of futility. To decide whether the proposed treatment was futile one had to ask what result the treatment sought to produce. The crucial question was to determine the proper goal for the life-sustaining treatment. The futility of treatment had to be judged in the light of whether the patient would secure any therapeutic benefit which had the real prospect of curing or at least palliating the life-threatening disease from which he suffered. The judge was wrong to look at the past successful effect of such treatment on J without also having regard to the lack of improvement that such treatment would bring to his general health (see paras 33, 35-39 of judgment). (2) Having found that all the treatments, including CPR, could not be said to be futile, the judge erred in finding that in another crisis it was unlikely that CPR would be in J's best interests. That was precisely what he had been asked to consider in the hospital's application and conflicted with his previous conclusion (para.39). (3) The evidence was overwhelming that the forms of treatment were very discomforting and extremely painful. They could not be said to be not overly burdensome (paras 40-41). (4) The judge applied the wrong test when considering the guidance in the Mental Capacity Act Code of Practice in deciding that a prospect of recovery meant a resumption of a quality of life that J would regard as worthwhile. The focus was on the medical interests of the patient when treatment was considered to sustain life. In the context of life ebbing away, "no prospect of recovery" meant no prospect of recovering such a state of good health as would avert the looming prospect of death if the life-sustaining treatment was given. There was no prospect of J ever overcoming the multiple organ failure (para.44). (5) The court had to try to ascertain J's wishes which would, if they were the product of full informed thought, have to recognise the futility of treatment, that treatment would be extremely burdensome to endure and that he would never recover enough to go home. It was in his best interests that it would be lawful to withhold treatment and the declarations should be granted to that effect (paras 47, 50).

AINTREE UNIVERSITY HOSPITALS NHS FOUNDATION TRUST v JAMES; *sub nom.* JAMES v AINTREE UNIVERSITY HOSPITALS NHS FOUNDATION TRUST, [2013] EWCA Civ 65, [2013] 4 All E.R. 67, Laws, L.J., CA (Civ Div).

1462. Misconduct–Midwives–Striking off for misconduct–Admissibility of fresh evidence

The appellant midwife (M) appealed against the decision of a panel of the Conduct Competence Committee of the respondent council striking her name off the register of midwives and nurses and ordering an 18-month suspension until the final order came into effect. M had been employed as a midwife at a hospital. Allegations of misconduct spanning a three-and-a-half year period including breach of confidentiality, dishonesty, unprofessional and aggressive behaviour and the sending of aggressive and inappropriate correspondence. M's case was that all the allegations were false and raised against her as a result of a conspiracy by managers in the NHS to victimise her as a whistleblower. At a preliminary meeting M raised an issue concerning one of the panel members whom she said was inappropriate because he was an acquaintance of an individual who had allegedly falsified allegations against her. M was given due notice of the date of the substantive hearing but failed to attend. The panel proceeded with the hearing in her absence. The panel concluded that apart from one allegation all the remaining 12 allegations of misconduct had been proved; that her fitness to practise was impaired by reason of such misconduct; that her misconduct was fundamentally incompatible with her continued registration as a midwife and that the only appropriate and proportionate sanction was a striking-off order. On appeal M sought to introduce a copy of a letter dated March 18, 2009 from the hospital where she worked which had been signed by the head of employment and addressed to M and was said to be crucial in relation to charge two. M submitted that the fact that the letter was not before the panel undermined its decision in relation to charge two and that its conclusions on that charge potentially infected its conclusions on the other charges thereby vitiating the overall conclusion of the panel to strike M off. M argued that the panel member should have recused himself; the hearing should not have proceeded in her absence; the hearing was conducted unfairly; the 12 allegations which the panel upheld against M could be explained and without the benefit of that explanation the finding of the panel was unsafe and should be overturned.

Held: Appeal allowed. (1) In the ordinary course of a hearing, any attempt to introduce new evidence should be made by a proper application on notice to the opposing party supported by an affidavit or witness statement explaining the basis of such application and why such new evidence was not previously provided. The fact that this was not done in the instant case was most regrettable, although it could be explained in part by the fact that M had not, until recently, been legally represented. There was no doubt however that the March 18 letter was a crucial document and potentially threw a completely new light on the charges against M. Although the issue was not raised in the grounds of appeal, M would exceptionally be given leave to rely upon it. The panel's decision had to be quashed and the matter remitted to the committee. It was best to remit to a new panel as the previous panel had reached certain conclusions without considering the entirety of the evidence because it was not shown the letter. A new panel would be able to address the issues in the light of all the evidence with a fresh mind. That was the better course in the interests of justice (see paras17, 51, 57 of judgment). (2) All the other points of challenge of the panel's decision were rejected.

McDAID v NURSING AND MIDWIFERY COUNCIL, [2013] EWHC 586 (Admin), (2013) 132 B.M.L.R. 190, Eder, J., QBD (Admin).

1463. Misconduct–Nurses–Unreasonable delay in conduct of disciplinary proceedings–Sufficiency of evidence to find misconduct by manager and deputy manager of nursing home–Whether allegations capable of amounting to misconduct even if proved

[European Convention on Human Rights 1950 Art.6.]

The claimants (J and M) applied for judicial review of the defendant NMC's professional conduct committee's finding that they were guilty of misconduct. J and M were registered nurses who had been the manager and deputy manager of a nursing home. In 2003, the NMC notified them that they were the subject of allegations of misconduct. The NMC's subsequent investigation took over two years. A hearing before the professional conduct committee started in July 2007 and finally concluded in December 2011. The committee found both J and M guilty of failing to ensure that adequate nursing records were maintained because no risk assessment or care plan in relation to residents' falls had been kept on four occasions. J was found guilty of failing to ensure a safe system for the administration of medicines by failing to ensure that medication was consumed by residents after it was dispensed, and failing to report to M that medication had been found in residents' rooms which should have been consumed. Despite the findings of misconduct, the committee took no further action. J and M contended that in finding them guilty of misconduct, the NMC's committee had made several errors of law, including failing to understand the correct test for misconduct. They submitted that the committee's findings of misconduct were not justified by its findings of fact and/or that the reasons for its findings were inadequate. J and M argued further that the findings of fact on which the findings of misconduct were based were perverse and contrary to the evidence. They made a subsidiary complaint that the delays in the proceedings made them unfair.

Held: Application granted. (1) The disciplinary hearing had lasted 86 days spread over two years and nine months. By the time the committee made its decision, the events that were subject of the charges were between 9 and 13 years old. The total time which elapsed from when J and M were notified of the allegations until the disciplinary proceedings' conclusion was over eight years. The length of time the proceedings took was disgraceful and the delays violated the rights of J and M to a hearing within a reasonable time contrary to the European Convention on Human Rights 1950 art.6 (see paras 8-11 of judgment). (2) The committee had not failed to understand the relevant law. It had expressly noted that misconduct had to be "serious" and as such would be seen as "deplorable" by fellow practitioners. J and M's complaint that the committee had misunderstood the law was merely another way of asserting that it came to a wrong decision when applying the law to the facts of their case: such an argument was not a permissible ground of judicial review (paras 32-33, 35). (3) In a disputed case where a person was charged with professional misconduct, procedural fairness required reasons to be given for any adverse finding. It was not necessary for such reasons to be elaborate, but they had to be sufficient to enable the person affected to understand what the tribunal had concluded on the principal important controversial issues in the case and why it had reached that decision. The committee's reasons met the purposes for which they were required (paras 36, 38). (4) A court would only intervene with factual findings if the evidence or tribunal's reasoning was not reasonably and rationally capable of supporting its findings. It was difficult to see how the evidence could support a finding that it was negligent for a nurse responsible for a resident's care not to have compiled a separate falls risk assessment for the resident. It was, therefore, difficult to see how the committee could reasonably have found the charges against J and M proved. Simple negligence was not sufficient: "gross professional negligence" or "deplorable" conduct was required. The finding against J suffered from an additional flaw in that the allegations found proved against her in respect of inadequate nursing records were never put to her before she had given evidence. Accordingly, the first set of misconduct findings made against M and J were unreasonable, unfair and unlawful (paras 40, 51, 87-90). (5) In respect of the findings that J had failed to administer medicines safely, there was no evidence on which the committee could have fairly found that J had failed to pass on to M that medication had been found in residents' rooms. Even if there was such evidence, it was not capable of proving the charge of misconduct. The committee had, at that point, lost a sense of perspective. Its finding of misconduct against J was so far out of proportion to the nature of the failure found that it was not one that the committee could reasonably reach. Accordingly, the findings of misconduct made against J and M were unlawful and had to be quashed. Their names were clear (paras 99, 102, 104-107).

JOHNSON v NURSING AND MIDWIFERY COUNCIL, [2013] EWHC 2140 (Admin), (2013) 133 B.M.L.R. 151, Leggatt, J., QBD (Admin).

1464. Monitor–NHS foundation trusts–Reports

THE MID STAFFORDSHIRE NHS FOUNDATION TRUST (TRUST SPECIAL ADMINISTRATORS EXTENSION OF TIME) ORDER 2013, SI 2013/1483; made under the National Health Service Act 2006 s.65. In force: June 19, 2013; .

This Order extends the period of time within which the trust special administrators of Mid Staffordshire NHS Foundation Trust must provide a draft report to Monitor.

1465. National Institute for Health and Care Excellence–Non-departmental public bodies–Special health authorities

THE NATIONAL INSTITUTE FOR HEALTH AND CARE EXCELLENCE (CONSTITUTION AND FUNCTIONS) AND THE HEALTH AND SOCIAL CARE INFORMATION CENTRE (FUNCTIONS) REGULATIONS 2013, SI 2013/259; made under the Health and Social Care Act 2012 s.235, s.237, s.238, s.239, s.240, s.242, s.268, s.274, s.304, Sch.16 para.8. In force: April 1, 2013; .

These Regulations confer a number of functions on the National Institute for Health and Care Excellence (NICE) and the Health and Social Care Information Centre (the Information Centre) which are to be established as executive non-departmental public bodies under the Health and Social Care Act 2012. The Regulations will enable NICE and the Information Centre to carry out similar functions to those that the predecessor bodies currently perform as Special Health Authorities.

1466. NHS–Clinical commissioning groups–Disapplication

THE NATIONAL HEALTH SERVICE (CLINICAL COMMISSIONING GROUPS-DISAPPLICATION OF RESPONSIBILITY) REGULATIONS 2013, SI 2013/350; made under the National Health Service Act 2006 s.3, s.272. In force: April 1, 2013; .

Section 3(1A) of the National Health Service Act 2006 provides for a clinical commissioning group (CCG) to have the duty to commission health services for persons who are provided with primary medical services by a member of the CCG, and persons who usually reside in the CCG's area and who are not provided with primary medical services by a member of any CCG. However, by virtue of section 3(1D) of the 2006 Act, inserted by the same provision of the 2012 Act, regulations may provide for certain exceptions to this. These Regulations provide, by way of exception, that a CCG does not have the duty to commission services for certain groups of people or persons in specified circumstances, even if they would otherwise be the responsibility of the CCG.

1467. NHS–Contracts–Prescriptions–Wales

THE NATIONAL HEALTH SERVICE (GENERAL MEDICAL SERVICES CONTRACTS) (PRESCRIPTION OF DRUGS ETC.) (WALES) (AMENDMENT) REGULATIONS 2013, SI 2013/SI 2013/683 (W.81); made under the National Health Service (Wales) Act 2006 s.46, s.203. In force: April 12, 2013; .

These Regulations amend the National Health Service (General Medical Services Contracts) (Prescription of Drugs Etc.) (Wales) Regulations 2004 (SI

2004/1022), which make provision as to the drugs, medicines or other substances that may be ordered for patients in the provision of medical services under a general medical services contract within the meaning of the National Health Service (Wales) Act 2006 s.42.

1468. NHS–Dental charges–Prescription charges–Travelling expenses

THE NATIONAL HEALTH SERVICE (CHARGES FOR DRUGS AND APPLIANCES), (DENTAL CHARGES) AND (TRAVEL EXPENSES AND REMISSION OF CHARGES) (AMENDMENT) REGULATIONS 2013, SI 2013/475; made under the National Health Service Act 2006 s.172, s.176, s.182, s.183, s.184, s.188, s.272. In force: in accordance with reg.1 (2).; .

These Regulations amend the National Health Service (Charges for Drugs and Appliances) Regulations 2000 (SI 2000/620), the National Health Service (Dental Charges) Regulations 2005 (SI 2005/3477) and the National Health Service (Travel Expenses and Remission of Charges) Regulations 2003 (SI 2003/282). Among the changes is an increase in prescription and other charges payable under the Charges Regulations.

1469. NHS–Doctors–English language–Training

THE MEDICAL PROFESSION (RESPONSIBLE OFFICERS) (AMENDMENT) REGULATIONS 2013, SI 2013/391; made under the Medical Act 1983 s.45A. In force: April 1, 2013; .

These Regulations amends the Medical Profession (Responsible Officer) Regulations 2010, to to makes consequential changes to take account of the new NHS architecture, as set out in the Health and Social Care Act 2012, and to enable more doctors to be evaluated with regard to their fitness to practise and, for doctors practising in England, to ensure that those doctors have sufficient knowledge of English language to perform their work when they are appointed to an organisation.

1470. NHS–Eye tests–Universal credit

THE NATIONAL HEALTH SERVICE (PRIMARY OPHTHALMIC SERVICES) (MISCELLANEOUS AMENDMENTS) REGULATIONS 2013, SI 2013/2555; made under the National Health Service Act 2006 s.115, s.116, s.272. In force: November 1, 2013; .

This instrument amends the Primary Ophthalmic Services Regulations 2008 (SI 2008/1186) and the Optical Charges and Payments Regulations 2013 (SI 2013/461) to revise entitlement to NHS sight tests and optical vouchers in relation to recipients of universal credit.

1471. NHS–NHS Commissioning Board–Primary care trusts–Social care

THE HEALTH AND SOCIAL CARE ACT 2012 (CONSEQUENTIAL AMENDMENTS) ORDER 2013, SI 2013/594; made under the Health and Social Care Act 2012 s.303. In force: April 1, 2013; .

This Order amends seven Acts of Parliament in consequence of the Health and Social Care Act 2012.

1472. NHS–NHS Litigation Authority–National Clinical Assessment Service–National Institute for Health and Care Excellence

THE NATIONAL HEALTH SERVICE LITIGATION AUTHORITY (ESTABLISHMENT AND CONSTITUTION) AMENDMENT ORDER 2013, SI 2013/295; made under the National Health Service Act 2006 s.28, s.272, s.273; and the National Health Service (Consequential Provisions) Act 2006 s.4, Sch.2 para.8. In force: April 1, 2013; .

This Order makes the necessary provisions to transfer staff, property and liabilities of the National Clinical Assessment Service (NCAS), currently part of the National Institute for Health and Clinical Excellence (NICE), to the National Health Service Litigation Authority (NHS LA) on April 1, 2013. It also amends one of the specific functions of the NHSLA. It will now carry out the Secretary of State's appellate and other functions in relation to decisions and functions of the National Health Service Commissioning Board, instead of the decisions and functions of Primary Care Trusts which are being abolished. It also makes changes to the NHSLA's constitution.

1473. **NHS–Opticians**

THE NATIONAL HEALTH SERVICE (PRIMARY OPHTHALMIC SERVICES) (MISCELLANEOUS AMENDMENTS AND TRANSITIONAL PROVISIONS) REGULATIONS 2013, SI 2013/365; made under the National Health Service Act 2006 s.115, s.116, s.119, s.121, s.122, s.185, s.186, s.272. In force: April 1, 2013 except for reg.23(2) (d) (e) on April 29, 2013.; .

These Regulations amend the General Ophthalmic Services Contracts Regulations 2008 (SI 2008/1185), the Primary Ophthalmic Services Regulations 2008 (SI 2008/1186) and the National Health Service (Charges for Appliances) Regulations 1974 (SI 1974/284). Most of these amendments are as a consequence of the transfer of functions relating to primary ophthalmic services to the National Health Service Commissioning Board from Primary Care Trusts, and the abolition of Strategic Health Authorities and Primary Care Trusts.

1474. **NHS–Opticians–Vouchers–Wales**

THE NATIONAL HEALTH SERVICE (OPTICAL CHARGES AND PAYMENTS) (AMENDMENT) (WALES) REGULATIONS 2013, SI 2013/SI 2013/543 (W.56); made under the National Health Service (Wales) Act 2006 s.71, s.128, s.129, s.130, s.203. In force: April 1, 2013; .

These Regulations, which amend the National Health Service (Optical Charges and Payments) Regulations 1997 (SI 1997/818) increase the NHS sight test fee and increase the redemption value of specified vouchers.

1475. **NHS–Performers lists–England**

THE NATIONAL HEALTH SERVICE (PERFORMERS LISTS) (ENGLAND) REGULATIONS 2013, SI 2013/335; made under the National Health Service Act 2006 s.91, s.106, s.123, s.272. In force: April 1, 2013; .

These Regulations are intended to ensure that the performers list system set out in the National Health Service (Performers Lists) Regulations 2004 continues to operate in the light of changes to the NHS arising from the Health and Social Care Act 2012. The Regulations also implement recommendations for improvements to the system.

1476. **NHS–Pharmaceuticals**

THE NATIONAL HEALTH SERVICE (GENERAL MEDICAL SERVICES CONTRACTS) (PRESCRIPTION OF DRUGS ETC) (AMENDMENT) REGULATIONS 2013, SI 2013/2194; made under the National Health Service Act 2006 s.88, s.272. In force: October 1, 2013; .

These Regulations amend the National Health Service (General Medical Service Contracts) (Prescriptions of Drugs etc) Regulations 2004 (SI 2004/629), which make provision in respect of the drugs, medicines and substances that may be ordered for patients in the provision of services under a general medical services contract within the meaning of the National Health Service Act 2006 s.84.

1477. **NHS–Pharmacy**

THE NATIONAL HEALTH SERVICE (PHARMACEUTICAL AND LOCAL PHARMACEUTICAL SERVICES) REGULATIONS 2013, SI 2013/349; made under the National Health Service Act 2006 s.7, s.8, s.126, s.128A, s.129, s.130, s.132, s.136, s.139, s.140, s.142(b), s.143, s.145, s.148, s.150A, s.151, s.154, s159, s.160, s.161, s.162, s.163, s.164, s.169, s.272, Sch.11 para.1, Sch.12 para.2, Sch.12 para.3. In force: April 1, 2013; .

These Regulations replace, from April 1, 2013, the National Health Service (Pharmaceutical Services) Regulations 2012 (SI 2012/1909, as amended) as the Regulations which govern the arrangements, in England, for the provision of pharmaceutical services, making provisions for contractors and dispensing doctors to provide, between them, a range of NHS community pharmaceutical services to patients. These Regulations also replace the Local Pharmaceutical Regulations 2006 (SI 2006/552) to take account of the new NHS structure.

1478. NHS–Pharmacy–Wales

THE NATIONAL HEALTH SERVICE (PHARMACEUTICAL SERVICES) (WALES) REGULATIONS 2013, SI 2013/SI 2013/898 (W.102); made under the National Health Service (Wales) Act 2006 s.15, s.80, s.83, s.84, s.86, s.88, s.104, s.107, s.110, s.115, s.116, s.118, s.203, s.205. In force: May 10, 2013; .

These Regulations revoke and replace the National Health Service (Pharmaceutical Services) Regulations 1992 (SI 1992/662) (as amended) as the Regulations which, in Wales, govern the provision of pharmaceutical services as part of the National Health Service under the National Health Service (Wales) Act 2006 Pt 7.

1479. NHS–Primary care trusts–Primary medical services providers–Transitional provisions

THE NATIONAL HEALTH SERVICE (PRIMARY MEDICAL SERVICES) (MISCELLANEOUS AMENDMENTS AND TRANSITIONAL PROVISIONS) REGULATIONS 2013, SI 2013/363; made under the National Health Service Act 2006 s.83, s.85, s.86, s.88, s.89, s.90, s.91, s.93, s.94, s.97, s.259, s.272. In force: April 1, 2013; .

These Regulations amend the National Health Service (General Medical Services Contracts) Regulations 2004, the National Health Service (Personal Medical Services Agreements) Regulations 2004, the National Health Service (General Medical Services Contracts) (Prescription of Drugs etc.) Regulations 2004, and the Primary Medical Services (Sales of Goodwill and Restrictions on Sub-contracting) Regulations 2004. Inter alia these Regulations contain the mandatory contractual terms that must be contained in primary medical services contracts and agreements made between primary care trusts and primary medical services contractors.

1480. NHS–Transfer of assets

THE NHS BODIES (TRANSFER OF TRUST PROPERTY) ORDER 2013, SI 2013/132; made under the National Health Service Act 2006 s.213, s.217, s.272. In force: March 8, 2013; .

This Order transfers property held on trust (in these cases charitable property) between NHS bodies, in particular from the bodies listed as relevant old Trusts in column 1 of the Schedule to the bodies listed as relevant new Trusts in column 2 of the Schedule.

1481. NHS Commissioning Board–Optical charges

THE NATIONAL HEALTH SERVICE (OPTICAL CHARGES AND PAYMENTS) (AMENDMENT) REGULATIONS 2013, SI 2013/1856; made under the National Health Service Act 2006 s.180, s.272, s.274. In force: November 1, 2013; .

This instrument amends the National Health Service (Optical Charges and Payments) Regulations 2013 (SI 2013/461) to make a consequential amendment as a result of the abolition of certain bodies and the creation of the NHS Commissioning Board by the Health and Social Care Act 2012. This consequential amendment was omitted from the 2013 Regulations and this instrument corrects that omission.

1482. **NHS constitution**

THE NATIONAL HEALTH SERVICE (REVISION OF NHS CONSTITUTION-PRINCIPLES) REGULATIONS 2013, SI 2013/317; made under the Health Act 2009 s.4. In force: April 1, 2013; .

The NHS Constitution is due to be revised and republished for April 1, 2013 to take account of proposals to amend the Constitution. Those proposals have been subject to public consultation. Some of the proposed changes involve amendments to the principles of the Constitution, which can be revised only by regulations made by the Secretary of State. Accordingly, this instrument revises the guiding principles of the NHS Constitution, to have effect at the same time as republication of the NHS Constitution.

1483. **NHS foundation trusts–Appointments–Staffordshire–Trust special administrators**

THE MID STAFFORDSHIRE NHS FOUNDATION TRUST (APPOINTMENT OF TRUST SPECIAL ADMINISTRATORS) ORDER 2013, SI 2013/838; made under the National Health Service Act 2006 s.65D. In force: April 16, 2013; .

This Order authorises the appointment of three trust special administrators to exercise the functions of the chair, directors and governors of Mid Staffordshire NHS Foundation Trust. It also makes provision for the date on which the appointment of the trust special administrators is to take effect.

1484. **NHS trusts–Appointment of trustees**

THE NATIONAL HEALTH SERVICE TRUSTS (TRUST FUNDS: APPOINTMENT OF TRUSTEES) (AMENDMENT) ORDER 2013, SI 2013/679; made under the National Health Service Act 2006 s.272, s.273, Sch.4 para.10. In force: April 1, 2013; .

This Order amends the National Health Service Trusts (Trust Funds: Appointment of Trustees) Order 2000, to replace references to the Barts and The London National Health Service Trust, which has been dissolved, with references to the Barts Health National Health Service Trust. The staff, property and liabilities of the Barts and The London National Health Service Trust have been transferred to the Barts Health National Health Service Trust and the effect of this Order is that the Secretary of State must appoint trustees to Barts Health NHS Trust and the trustees so appointed may be a company.

1485. **NHS trusts–Change of name–West Midlands**

THE WALSALL HOSPITALS NATIONAL HEALTH SERVICE TRUST (ESTABLISHMENT) AMENDMENT ORDER 2013, SI 2013/59; made under the National Health Service Act 2006 s.25, s.272, s.273. In force: February 11, 2013; .

This Order amends the Walsall Hospitals National Health Service Trust (Establishment) Order 1990, which established the Walsall Hospitals National Health Service Trust, the name of which was subsequently changed to the Walsall Healthcare National Health Service Trust. Article 2 increases the number of non-executive directors of the trust from 5 to 6.

1486. **NHS trusts–Disciplinary procedures–Admitted breach of patient confidentiality by doctor–Entitlement of NHS trust to hold disciplinary hearing–Limitations of "fair blame" procedure**

The appellant NHS trust appealed against an injunction preventing it from referring to a disciplinary hearing alleged breaches of confidentiality by the respondent employee (C), a consultant psychiatrist. There had been a complaint about C reading notes and discussing patients whilst on public transport. C largely admitted the patient confidentiality breaches, apologised, and promised that there would be no repeats in future. Under the disciplinary procedure relating to conduct, an investigating officer was appointed, who upheld the confidentiality breaches. A case manager decided to refer charges of gross misconduct to a disciplinary panel, and notified C of that decision, indicating that unrelated capability concerns would be referred to the National Clinical Assessment Service. C argued for implementation of the "fair blame" procedure, which was an alternative method of discipline for situations where mistakes had been openly acknowledged by the perpetrator. She also alleged, in legal action commenced by her, that it was inappropriate to undergo a disciplinary hearing while the NCAS inquiry was ongoing. The court held that the trust had erred in classifying the confidentiality breaches as gross misconduct, that it ought to have activated the fair blame procedure, and that it had breached C's contract of employment in making disciplinary charges against her. The trust submitted that it had been entitled to regard the confidentiality breaches as sufficiently serious to require a determination by a disciplinary panel, that it would be unfair to both parties to proceed to a capability assessment while the conduct issue remained unresolved, and that there was no contractual term, either express or implied, preventing it from classifying the admitted misconduct as gross misconduct.

Held: Appeal allowed. The court was entitled to intervene in cases where it was alleged that a trust was adopting the wrong procedure, *Edwards v Chesterfield Royal Hospital NHS Foundation Trust* [2011] UKSC 58, [2012] 2 A.C. 22, [2012] C.L.Y. 1167 and *Skidmore v Dartford and Gravesham NHS Trust* [2003] UKHL 27, [2003] 3 All E.R. 292, [2003] C.L.Y. 1789 applied, *Hussain v Surrey and Sussex Healthcare NHS Trust* [2011] EWHC 1670 (QB), [2012] Med. L.R. 163, [2012] C.L.Y. 1528 considered. The trust's disciplinary policy, and its policy document on handling concerns about a doctor's performance, which was made pursuant to the Department of Health document issued in 2005 and entitled "Maintaining High Professional Standards in the Modern NHS", had to be read together. Contractual force had to be given to the applicable rules and procedures. Although the role of the case investigator appointed at the beginning of the disciplinary procedure was to establish the facts and report the findings, it was ultimately for an independent disciplinary panel, not the investigating officer, to resolve factual issues. The investigating officer had to provide sufficient information to enable a case manager to decide whether there was a case of misconduct to put to a conduct panel. The reference to a case investigator "establishing the facts" did not disqualify a case manager from taking action on a complaint; the trust's policies clearly contemplated a quasi-judicial procedure before a panel and the panel was not confined to considering findings of fact already made by the case investigator. There was a threshold to be crossed, in terms of seriousness, before a decision to refer to a panel could properly be taken, *Makhdum v Norfolk and Suffolk NHS Foundation Trust* [2012] EWHC 4015 (QB) applied. While the fair blame procedure was undoubtedly encouraged, the documents repeatedly reserved a power to refer disciplinary matters to a conduct panel. The 2005 Department of Health document expressly provided that the fair blame procedure was "not intended to weaken accountability or avoid disciplinary action where there was genuinely serious misconduct". The trust's policy document envisaged occasions when issues of capability and conduct might have to be separately pursued. Reference was made to an employee's right to use the grievance procedure if a matter had been incorrectly classified. That right had been exercised by C, though the result had been unfavourable to her. The case manager's decision to refer C's case to a disciplinary hearing had been justified. Patient confidentiality was fundamental in the health service and had to be respected. The case manager had been entitled to regard a breach in a public place as a potentially serious offence (see paras 60-81 of judgment).

CHHABRA v WEST LONDON MENTAL HEALTH NHS TRUST; *sub nom.* WEST LONDON MENTAL HEALTH NHS TRUST v CHHABRA, [2013] EWCA Civ 11, [2013] I.R.L.R. 398, Pill, L.J., CA (Civ Div).

1487. NHS trusts–Gloucestershire

THE GLOUCESTERSHIRE CARE SERVICES NATIONAL HEALTH SERVICE TRUST (ESTABLISHMENT) ORDER 2013, SI 2013/531; made under the National Health Service Act 2006 s.25, s.272, Sch.4 para.5, Sch.4 para.7. In force: March 22, 2013; .

This Order establishes on March 22 2013 a National Health Service trust called the Gloucestershire Care Services National Health Service Trust.

1488. NHS trusts–Kent

THE DARTFORD AND GRAVESHAM NATIONAL HEALTH SERVICE TRUST (ESTABLISHMENT) AMENDMENT ORDER 2013, SI 2013/2375; made under the National Health Service Act 2006 s.25, s.272, s.273. In force: September 30, 2013; .

This Order amends the Dartford and Gravesham National Health Service Trust (Establishment) Order 1993 (the Establishment Order), which established the Dartford and Gravesham National Health Service Trust. The amendments change the nature and functions of the trust, to provide hospital accommodation and services and community health services for the purposes of the health service.

1489. NHS trusts–Trust property–Trustees

THE BARTS HEALTH NATIONAL HEALTH SERVICE TRUST (TRANSFER OF TRUST PROPERTY) ORDER 2013, SI 2013/1441; made under the National Health Service Act 2006 s.272, Sch.4 para.10. In force: June 17, 2013; .

This Order transfers trust property held by the Barts Health National Health Service Trust to the trustee appointed for that Trust pursuant to the National Health Service Trusts (Trust Funds: Appointment of Trustees) Order 2000 (as amended) made under para.10 of Sch.4 to the National Health Service Act 2006 and makes related provision.

1490. Nursing and Midwifery Council–Appeals–Time limit for appeal to High Court against Council's decision–Extension of time limit

[Human Rights Act 1998 (c.42) s.3; Nursing and Midwifery Order (2001) 2002 (SI 2002/253) Art.29(10); European Convention on Human Rights 1950 Art.6.]

The appellants (B) appealed against a decision ([2012] EWHC 2615 (Admin)) that their appeals against decisions of the respondent Nursing and Midwifery Council to remove them from its register were brought out of time. B were found to have brought their appeals outside the 28-day time limit provided for in the Nursing and Midwifery Order (2001) 2002 art.29(10). On the basis that the time limit was absolute, the court found that no extension of time was possible. B argued that the absolute approach exemplified by cases such as *Mitchell v Nursing and Midwifery Council* [2009] EWHC 1045 (Admin) and *Reddy v General Medical Council* [2012] EWCA Civ 310, [2012] C.P. Rep. 27, [2012] C.L.Y. 317 had to be revisited in the light of the decision, relating to extradition, in *Pomiechowski v Poland* [2012] UKSC 20, [2012] 1 W.L.R. 1604, [2012] C.L.Y. 1287: the Human Rights Act 1998 s.3 required that an ostensibly non-extendable time limit should be read down so as to comply with the European Convention on Human Rights 1950 art.6.

Held: Appeals dismissed. (1) There were obvious differences between extradition appeals and appeals in disciplinary or regulatory cases: the consequences of removal from the register, while serious, were not as grave as the prospect of loss of liberty and removal to another country; the time limits in extradition were significantly shorter than the 28 days in the instant case; the putative extradition appellant would have to cope with the shorter time limits in the more difficult position of custody; and there was widespread recognition of the problems created by short time limits in extradition, but there was no such evidence in relation to disciplinary appeals. Those differences, however, were not enough to leave the *Mitchell* and *Reddy* line of authority untouched by *Pomiechowski*, *Mitchell* overruled, *Reddy* not followed. Exclusion from a profession was still of great importance to an appellant. There was good reason for time limits with a high degree of strictness, but without some margin for discretion, circumstances could cause absolute time limits to impair the very essence of the right of appeal conferred by statute. The real difficulty was where to draw the line. Parliament's omission of any general discretion to extend time was no doubt deliberate. If art.6 of the Convention and s.3 of the Act required art.29(10) of the Order to be read down, that had to be to the minimum extent necessary to secure Convention compliance. That required the same approach as in *Pomiechowski*: a discretion could only arise in exceptional circumstances and where the appellant personally had done all he could to bring the appeal timeously, *Pomiechowski* applied (see paras 13-15 of judgment). (2) The scope for departure from the 28-day time limit was extremely narrow and did not extend to B's cases. Their circumstances were not exceptional: they had simply left it too late (paras 16-18).

ADESINA v NURSING AND MIDWIFERY COUNCIL; BAINES v NURSING AND MIDWIFERY COUNCIL; *sub nom.* R. (ON THE APPLICATION OF ADESINA) v NURSING AND MIDWIFERY COUNCIL, [2013] EWCA Civ 818, [2013] 1 W.L.R. 3156, Maurice Kay, L.J., CA (Civ Div).

1491. Pharmaceuticals–Physiotherapists–Prescribed substances

THE HUMAN MEDICINES (AMENDMENT) REGULATIONS 2013, SI 2013/1855; made under the Medicines Act 1968 s.58; the Medicines Act 1971 s.1; and the European Communities Act 1972 s.2. In force: in accordance with reg.1 (2).; .

The instrument: introduces measures designed to strengthen the medicines supply chain from the threat of counterfeit medicine; and introduces two offences in relation to pharmacovigilance obligations and introduces independent prescribing for registered physiotherapists and podiatrists.

1492. Professional conduct–Osteopaths–Meaning of "unacceptable professional conduct" in s.20(1)(a) and s.20(2) Osteopaths Act 1993

[Medical Act 1983 (c.54); Osteopaths Act 1993 (c.21) s.19(4), s.20(1)(a), s.20(2).]

The appellant (S), a registered osteopath, appealed against a finding of the respondent Council's Professional Conduct Committee that he was guilty of unacceptable professional conduct within the meaning of the Osteopaths Act 1993 s.20(1)(a) and s.20(2). S had treated a patient for pain and discomfort in the right shoulder and the left sacro-iliac joint. The committee found that on two occasions he had failed to make adequate notes of his consultations with the patient. It found that he had failed to adequately record the onset and progression of twinges in the sacro-iliac joint; the signs, symptoms, and aggravating and relieving factors associated with those twinges; the progression of the twinges; and the result of his examination of the patient's hip joints. S accepted the committee's findings of fact, but asserted that they did not justify a finding of unacceptable professional misconduct. S submitted that the threshold for a finding of unacceptable professional misconduct was the same as that for misconduct in the Medical Act 1983 and was governed by the caselaw relating to serious professional misconduct. The Council argued that the differences between the regulatory regimes governing doctors and osteopaths meant that S's analogy could not be made out. It argued that because it could impose no sanction in cases where an osteopath had breached his professional code of practice but was not guilty of unacceptable professional conduct, the threshold for unacceptable professional misconduct had to be lower than that for misconduct in the 1983 Act.

Held: Appeal allowed. The starting point for interpreting the 1993 Act had to be the language of the Act itself. While s.20(2) defined "unacceptable professional conduct" as conduct falling short of the standard required of a registered osteopath, there was an unhelpful circularity to that definition. The critical term was "conduct", whose dictionary definition was "behaviour" or "the manner of conducting oneself". A finding of misconduct or unacceptable professional conduct implied at least a degree of moral blameworthiness and opprobrium. That starting point was supported by s.19(4) of the 1993 Act, which provided that a breach of the code of practice did not, of itself, constitute unacceptable professional conduct. A breach of the code could thus be relevant to a finding of professional incompetence, as opposed to unacceptable professional conduct, and no single instance of negligence or unacceptable care would be sufficient to found a conclusion of professional incompetence. Hence, for both purposes, a breach of the code could not be definitive. Nor could it raise a presumption that either professional incompetence or unacceptable professional conduct was made out. While the Council's submission had some force, the purposive interpretation it argued for could not prevail over the language of the statute. Had Parliament intended to give the Council formal powers of warning or admonition in respect of osteopaths who had breached the code without being guilty of unacceptable professional conduct, it would have been very simple for it to have done so. The 1993 Act stipulated that if unacceptable professional conduct was made out, there had to be at least a formal admonition and publicity. Those were considerable sanctions which were bound to affect the osteopath's professional reputation. That pointed to the threshold for a finding of unacceptable professional conduct being indistinguishable from that applicable to misconduct in the medical and dental legislation. In S's case, the committee had sought, quite rightly, to apply the principles set out in *Calhaem v General Medical Council* [2007] EWHC 2606 (Admin), [2008] LS Law Medical 96, [2008] C.L.Y. 1800. However, it had not applied those principles correctly, *Calhaem* considered. While note-taking was very important for osteopaths, it was no more important than it was for doctors. S had not taken proper notes, but he had properly assessed the patient, devised a treatment plan and given proper treatment. That was not "incompetence or negligence of a high degree" and it was hard to construe S's failures as being worthy of the moral opprobrium and the publicity that flowed from a finding of unacceptable professional conduct. The committee's finding of unacceptable professional conduct would therefore be quashed (see paras 23-29 of judgment).

SPENCER v GENERAL OSTEOPATHIC COUNCIL, [2012] EWHC 3147 (Admin), [2013] 1 W.L.R. 1307, Irwin, J., QBD (Admin).

1493. Books

Ward, Adrian–Adult Incapacity-2nd edn. Hardback: £95.00. ISBN 9780414018525. (Sweet & Maxwell).

HEALTH AND SAFETY AT WORK

1494. Accidents–Diseases and disorders–Hazardous substances–Industrial diseases

THE REPORTING OF INJURIES, DISEASES AND DANGEROUS OCCURRENCES REGULATIONS 2013, SI 2013/1471; made under the Health and Safety at Work etc. Act 1974 s.15, s.52, Sch.3 para.15, Sch.3 para.16, Sch.3 para.20. In force: October 1, 2013; .

These Regulations revoke and replace, with amendments, the Reporting of Injuries, Diseases and Dangerous Occurrences Regulations 1995 and the Reporting of Injuries, Diseases and Dangerous Occurrences (Amendment) Regulations 2012. They maintain requirements that the responsible person must notify, and subsequently send a report to, the relevant enforcing authority by an approved means in relation to fatal and certain non-fatal work-related accidents, specified diseases contracted by persons at work and certain specified dangerous occurrences.

1495. Bereavement–Fatal accidents–England and Wales

THE DAMAGES FOR BEREAVEMENT (VARIATION OF SUM) (ENGLAND AND WALES) ORDER 2013, SI 2013/510; made under the Fatal Accidents Act 1976 s.1A. In force: April 1, 2013; .

This Order, which applies only to causes of action accruing on or after April 1st 2013, amends s.1A of the Fatal Accidents Act 1976 by increasing the sum which may be awarded as damages for bereavement in England and Wales from £11,800 to £12,980.

1496. Breach of statutory duty–Civil proceedings–Health and safety at work–Liabilities

THE ENTERPRISE AND REGULATORY REFORM ACT 2013 (HEALTH AND SAFETY) (CONSEQUENTIAL AMENDMENTS) ORDER 2013, SI 2013/SI 1666; made under the Enterprise and Regulatory Reform Act 2013 s.99. In force: October 1, 2013; .

Section 69 of the Enterprise and Regulatory Reform Act 2013 made amendments to s.47 of the Health and Safety at Work etc. Act 1974. As a consequence some references to s.47 in other legislation are redundant and this Order deletes them.

1497. Breach of statutory duty–Health and safety at work–Liabilities–Mothers

THE HEALTH AND SAFETY AT WORK ETC. ACT 1974 (CIVIL LIABILITY) (EXCEPTIONS) REGULATIONS 2013, SI 2013/SI 1667; made under the European Communities Act 1972 s.2; and the Health and Safety at Work etc. Act 1974 s.15, s.47, s., s.50. In force: October 1, 2013; .

These Regulations create some exceptions to s.47 of the Health and Safety at Work etc. Act 1974 which provides that a breach of a duty in certain health and safety legislation is not actionable except to the extent provided for in regulations. They create exceptions from the exclusion of civil liability for breach of statutory duty for pregnant workers and workers who have recently given birth or are breastfeeding in relation to certain rights derived from Directive 92/85 [1992] OJ L348/1 and Directive 2008/104 [2008] OJ L327/9).

1498. Children's homes–Fire precautions–Residential property

THE DOMESTIC FIRE SAFETY (DEFINITION OF RESIDENCE) (WALES) ORDER 2013, SI 2013/SI 2013/2727 (W.262) (C.109); made under the Domestic Fire Safety (Wales) Measure 2011 s.6, s.8. In force: April 30, 2014; .

This Order amends the description of classes of residential premises contained in the definition of "residence" in s.6(1) of the Domestic Fire Safety (Wales) Measure 2011. It adds children's homes as a class of residential premises.

1499. Docks–First aid–Health and safety at work

THE HEALTH AND SAFETY (MISCELLANEOUS REVOCATIONS AND AMENDMENTS) REGULATIONS 2013, SI 2013/1512; made under the Health and Safety at Work etc. Act 1974 s.15, s.43, Sch.3 para.1 Sch.3 para.8, Sch.3 para.9, Sch.3 para.10, Sch.3 para.14. In force: October 1, 2013 except for reg.3 and reg.5 on April 6, 2014.; .

This Regulation amends the Health and Safety (First-Aid) Regulations 1981 (SI 1981/917) by removing the requirement for the Health and Safety Executive to approve training and qualifications for the purposes of first aid at work. This instrument also revokes the Docks Regulations 1988 (SI 1988/1655), which impose duties for the management of workers' health, safety and welfare in relation to specific docks-related activities, because they have been superseded by more recent legislation. Consequential amendments are made within the instrument in light of both the amendment and revocation.

1500. Explosives–Identification–Traceability

THE IDENTIFICATION AND TRACEABILITY OF EXPLOSIVES REGULATIONS 2013, SI 2013/449; made under the Health and Safety at Work etc. Act 1974 s.15, s.82, Sch.3 para.1, Sch.3 para.3, Sch.3 para.6, Sch.3 para.15, Sch.3 para.16. In force: in accordance with reg.1.; .

This instrument implements Directive 2008/43 setting up a system for the identification and traceability of explosives for civil uses, as amended by Directive 2012/4. The instrument consolidates the Identification and Traceability of Explosives Regulations 2010 (SI 2010/1004) and the Identification and Traceability of Explosives (Amendment) Regulations 2012 (SI 2012/638).

1501. Factories–Hazardous substances

THE HEALTH AND SAFETY (MISCELLANEOUS REPEALS, REVOCATIONS AND AMENDMENTS) REGULATIONS 2013, SI 2013/448; made under the Health and Safety at Work etc. Act 1974 s.15, s.49. In force: April 6, 2013; .

These Regulations repeal one Act and revoke twelve instruments plus a related provision in the Factories Act 1961 relating to health and safety provisions. They are being revoked because they have either been overtaken by more up to date Regulations, are redundant or do not deliver the intended benefits.

1502. Health and safety at work–Application outside Great Britain

THE HEALTH AND SAFETY AT WORK ETC. ACT 1974 (APPLICATION OUTSIDE GREAT BRITAIN) ORDER 2013, SI 2013/240; made under the Health and Safety at Work etc. Act 1974 s.84. In force: April 6, 2013; .

This Order revokes and re-enacts with amendments the Health and Safety at Work etc. Act 1974 (Application outside Great Britain) Order 2001, which applied sections 1 to 59 and 80 to 82 of the Health and Safety at Work etc. Act 1974 to certain premises and activities in the territorial sea adjacent to Great Britain and to areas designated under the Continental Shelf Act 1964.

1503. Personal protective equipment–Breach of statutory duty–Police officer dismantling cannabis factory–Failure to provide thick gloves–Whether breach of duty under Personal Protective Equipment at Work Regulations 1992

[Control of Substances Hazardous to Health Regulations 2002 (SI 2002/2677); Personal Protective Equipment at Work Regulations 1992 (SI 1992/2966).]

The appellant chief constable (C) appealed against a decision that he had breached his duty to the respondent police officer (T) under the Personal Protective Equipment at Work Regulations 1992. T and other officers had been tasked with removing cannabis plants and related equipment from a cannabis factory. Whilst removing the plants, T felt nauseous and decided to open a window, but failed to notice that it had been sealed. She pushed at the window causing the glass to break, and consequently cut her right thumb. T claimed damages from C under the 1992 Regulations for not providing thick gloves, and under the Control of Substances Hazardous to Health Regulations 2002 for not preventing or reducing her exposure to cannabis. The judge dismissed T's claim under the 2002 Regulations, but concluded that C had breached his duty under the 1992 Regulations by failing to provide T with thick gloves to protect against sharp edges, and held that had she been wearing them, the injury probably would not have occurred. The judge ordered C to pay all of T's costs. C argued that (1) the judge was wrong to find that the 1992 Regulations were engaged; (2) even if they were engaged, they did not require gloves to be provided when T was dealing with the cannabis plants since at that point there was no risk from sharp edges; (3) T should have shown that she would have worn the gloves if they had been available, and there was no evidence to demonstrate that she would have done; (4) the judge was wrong to award T all of her costs because she had been unsuccessful under the 2002 Regulations.

Held: Appeal dismissed. (1) Once a risk was proved to be more than de minimis, an employer had to provide suitable equipment unless working methods could provide equal or more effective protection, *Threlfall v Hull City Council* [2010] EWCA Civ 1147, [2011] I.C.R. 209, [2011] C.L.Y. 1634 considered. In the instant case, the judge found that there was a low but not de minimis level of risk in the cannabis factory generally. That was a conclusion that was plainly open to him; he had explained that he was unsatisfied by the evidence that the risks could be eliminated by working methods. It followed that C had a duty under the 1992 Regulations to provide T with thick gloves to prevent against those risks (see paras 11, 14 of judgment). (2) In his findings the judge inferred that T might have been required to do work at the cannabis factory other than actually removing the plants, and that that other work could have involved contact with sharp edges. That was a perfectly proper inference. T had not been told specifically to limit her work to removing the plants; on the contrary, she was tasked with dismantling the factory which could involve her carrying out a whole range of tasks. It would have been wholly unrealistic for the judge to seek to distinguish between those duties which placed T at risk from sharp edges and those which did not, and it would have undermined the protection which the 1992 Regulations were designed to provide (para.17). (3) Once an employer was shown to be in breach of duty to provide equipment, the assumption was that the equipment would have been used, because a reasonable employee would use it, unless the employer proved otherwise, *McWilliams v Sir William Arrol & Co Ltd* [1962] 1 W.L.R. 295, [1962] C.L.Y. 1267.a applied. Accordingly, the judge's analysis was correct (para.19). (4) The costs award was not outside the generous ambit given to judges in relation to costs, and it was inappropriate to interfere with it (para.22).

CHIEF CONSTABLE OF HAMPSHIRE v TAYLOR; *sub nom.* TAYLOR v CHIEF CONSTABLE OF HAMPSHIRE, [2013] EWCA Civ 496, [2013] I.C.R. 1150, Elias, L.J., CA (Civ Div).

1504. Plant and machinery–Ergonomics–Whether position of crane controls contributing to operators' back pain–Proper application of reg.17(2) Provision and Use of Work Equipment Regulations 1998

[Provision and Use of Work Equipment Regulations 1998 (SI 1998/2306) reg.17(2); Directive 2009/104 on the minimum safety and health requirements for the use of work equipment by workers at work; Directive 89/391 on the introduction of measures to encourage improvements in the safety and health of workers at work; Directive 89/655 on the minimum safety and health requirements for the use of work equipment by workers at work.]

The appellants (W) appealed against the dismissal of their claim against the respondent (C) for damages for personal injuries sustained at work. C was a large-scale steel manufacturer which employed W as overhead crane drivers. Each crane had a sling that could be raised, lowered and moved sideways, and a "grab" that could be opened and closed. All the movements were controlled by the driver from the overhead cab, and there was a separate control for each movement. Although the cabs had seats, W claimed that they had to stand for much of the time. In particular, they claimed that for long periods they had to lean forward and look down in order to watch the sling's movements while at the same time reaching back to operate the controls. They claimed that that had resulted in their suffering back pain or discomfort. Over the years, C had received a number of complaints from the crane drivers about back pain. In 2003 it had proposed replacing the controls with joysticks. However, that proposal had been rejected by the drivers during consultation and had not been proceeded with. The appeal centred on the correct application of the Provision and Use of Work Equipment Regulations 1998 reg.17(2). W's case was that C had failed to ensure that the controls were not in a position which exposed the driver to a risk to his health or safety. The judge found against W, finding that the problem could have been remedied by the rejected modification. He did not decide whether there had been a breach of the Regulations. Rather, he found that even if there had been, it had not caused any injury. The issues were whether (i) the judge's conclusion on causation was right; (ii) the Regulations applied only to dangers arising from the operator or others coming into contact with dangerous machinery or equipment, and not to dangers arising from inadequate ergonomics in the positioning of controls; (iii) the judge's findings on the primary facts led to the conclusion that there had been a breach.

Held: Appeal allowed. (1) Had it been clear that causation could not be established, then the judge could not be criticised for not considering whether there had been a breach of the Regulations. However, that was not the case. W's argument was that the position of the controls contributed to their back pain because it was part of the reason that they had adopted the postures that had produced that pain. If the location of the controls involved a breach of the Regulations because it exposed the drivers to the risk of injury, there was no break in the chain of causation. The judge had not held that the position of the controls made no difference either to the posture or the back pain. Rather, he held that the chain of causation had been broken by the drivers' refusal to agree to a change to joystick controls. However, that could not, by itself, break the chain. The drivers had no veto over the proposed modification, and C had been in a position to override their rejection of it. In those circumstances, the drivers' rejection of the proposal could not be described as a novus actus interveniens. Nor could it be said that the drivers were the sole cause of the breach, and nor had contributory negligence been asserted. Thus, the judge's conclusion on causation could not stand (see para.15 of judgment). (2) The Regulations applied to the instant case, and reg.17(2) could apply to a risk of injury by back pain if it arose from the positioning of controls. While Directive 89/655 and Directive 2009/104, which were issued in accordance with Directive 89/391, sought to avert the danger of people coming into harmful contact with machinery or equipment, they did not confine themselves only to that danger. Paragraph 2.1 of the Annex to the 2009 Directive referred to "any additional hazard", and that was wide enough to refer to a risk such as that posed in the instant case. There was no reason why reg.17(2) should be limited to avoiding contact with dangerous machinery. Moreover, the fact that separate sets of Regulations existed for workstations and computers did not shed any light on the extent of the instant Regulations (paras 20-23). (3) It was not clear whether the judge had addressed the critical issue in relation to reg.17(2), namely whether the location of the controls, aside from the principal problem of the drivers' having to maintain a leaning-forward position, was a contributory factor in causing the back pain of which they complained. W's appeal had to be allowed because of the judge's causation error, and the case had to be remitted to him to decide whether they had established that the location of the controls contributed to their back pain. If it did, there had been breach of reg.17(2) and judgment for W had to follow (paras 25-27).

WILLOCK v CORUS UK LTD, [2013] EWCA Civ 519, [2013] P.I.Q.R. P21, Lord Hughes of Ombersley, CA (Civ Div).

1505. Work equipment–Directors' powers and duties–Failure of sole director to comply with health and safety regulations–Bringing of personal injury claim by director in breach of statutory obligations

[Companies Act 2006 (c.46) s.174(2)(a); Provision and Use of Work Equipment Regulations 1998 (SI 1998/2306) reg.5(1).]

The appellant director and shareholder (P) of the first respondent company (M) appealed against the dismissal of his claim for damages for personal injuries sustained by him whilst working for M. P was the sole director and shareholder in M, which specialised in servicing motor vehicles. The second respondent (X) was M's insurer. P had severed a finger while he was trying to climb down to ground level from a raised hydraulic ramp in M's workshop after the compressor in the ramp mechanism failed. There had also been a problem with the ramp in 2006. The judge found that M was in breach of its obligation under the Provision and Use of Work Equipment Regulations 1998 reg.5(1) to ensure that work equipment was maintained in an efficient state, in efficient working order and in good repair; that the defect in the compressor was causative of the accident and therefore there was primary liability on P's part; and that P had not given any consideration to health and safety matters in the workshop, including the need to comply with the 1998 regulations, was responsible for the breach and 100 per cent contributorily negligent. P submitted that the finding of 100 per cent contributory negligence was wrong on the facts and the judge was not entitled to conclude that the accident would not have occurred had appropriate health and safety measures, in particular an assessment of the risk and routine inspection of the equipment, been undertaken. The respondents submitted that M's breach of statutory duty in not carrying out a risk assessment or servicing and inspecting the compressor was wholly caused by and co-extensive with P's own failings and that therefore the judge was wrong to find M primarily responsible for breach of reg.5(1).

Held: Appeal dismissed. (1) The instant case fell within the principle and defence identified in *Ginty v Belmont Building Supplies Ltd* [1959] 1 All E.R. 414, [1959] C.L.Y. 1291 and *Boyle v Kodak* [1969] 1 W.L.R. 661, [1969] C.L.Y. 316. Both *Ginty* and *Boyle v Kodak* concerned an employee claimant, and not a claimant who was the employer company's director, and its sole director and shareholder. In the instant case it was P's acts and omissions that constituted M's breach of its duty under the 1998 Regulations. Where, as was P's position, a director/claimant had paid no attention whatsoever to health and safety issues and had abrogated his responsibilities for them as owner and director of the company for them, he was in breach of his duty as a director under the Companies Act 2006 s.174(2)(a). P was therefore a wrongdoer in this context and fell within the common law principle that a person could not derive advantage from his own wrongdoing. It did not lie in the mouth of a claimant who was the defendant's sole director and shareholder, and through whom the company must act, to assert that the company had not proved that it had done all it could to ensure compliance when it was only through the claimant director's acts that the company could act. P, as a director, should have been but was not aware of his duties and responsibilities in relation to health and safety matters, and the need to comply with the 1998 Regulations. The onus was on the employer to prove that he did all he could to ensure compliance with the duty. Only if the employer did that would he have a defence against the injured employee whose act or omission put the employer in breach of the 1998 Regulations. M was entitled to rely on the *Ginty* and *Boyle v Kodak* defence and there was therefore no need to consider fault and the question of apportionment, *Ginty* and *Boyle v Kodak* applied (see paras 19, 47-56 of judgment).

BRUMDER v MOTORNET SERVICE AND REPAIRS LTD, [2013] EWCA Civ 195, [2013] 1 W.L.R. 2783, Ward, L.J., CA (Civ Div).

1506. Work equipment–Foreseeability–Jockey sustaining injuries during horse race–Judge importing reasonable foreseeability test into reg.4 Provision and Use of Work Equipment Regulations 1998–Whether perimeter rail suitable work equipment

[Provision and Use of Work Equipment Regulations 1998 (SI 1998/2306) reg.4(4), reg.4; Directive 89/391 on the introduction of measures to encourage improvements in the safety and health of workers at work Art.5(4); Directive 89/655 on the minimum safety and health requirements for the use of work equipment by workers at work Art.3.]

The appellant jockey (H) appealed against a decision that the respondents (S) were not liable for personal injuries he had sustained during a horse race. H had sustained his injuries when jumping over the first hurdle at a racecourse. After clearing the hurdle, H's horse stumbled and fell, which caused H to fall, hit the ground and move at speed into a post on the rail running around the outside of the track. H claimed under the Provision and Use of Work Equipment Regulations 1998 reg.4, which had been enacted into English law pursuant to the United Kingdom's obligations under Directive 89/391 and Directive 89/655. He argued that the hurdle was placed too close to the perimeter rail, which was too unyielding and/or insufficiently padded. The judge held that the concept of "reasonable foreseeability" was imported into reg.4. He decided that the way in which H was injured was very unusual, S had complied with the requirements laid down by the British Horseracing Authority, and that both the hurdle and rail were suitable equipment under reg.4. The issue was whether the judge was correct to import the concept of "reasonable foreseeability" into reg.4.

Held: Appeal allowed. (1) Whilst both art.3.1 of Directive 89/655 and reg.4 of the Regulations imposed a requirement that work equipment had to be suitable for the purpose for which it was used, and, expressly or by necessary implication, that the equipment could be used without impairment to health and safety, neither Directive 89/391 nor Directive 89/655 defined "suitable". Conversely, reg.4(4) of the Regulations stated that "suitable" meant "suitable in any respect which it is reasonably foreseeable will affect the health or safety of any person". The concept of reasonable foresight was thus introduced into the Regulations but was absent from the Directives, which raised the question of whether the Regulations had correctly implemented the Directives (see para.19 of judgment). (2) Under art.5(4) of Directive 89/391, there were two categories of occurrences in respect of which a defendant might seek to excuse his liability, namely (a) occurrences due to unforeseeable circumstances beyond his control; and (b) occurrences due to exceptional events, the consequences of which were unavoidable despite the exercise of all due care, *Robb v Salamis (M&I) Ltd* [2006] UKHL 56, [2007] 2 All E.R. 97, [2007] C.L.Y. 5269 applied. Both of those categories recognised the concept of foreseeability. In those circumstances, it was difficult to say that the introduction of the concept of reasonable foreseeability in reg.4(4) meant that the Directives had not been appropriately or accurately transposed into English law. However, the words "reasonably foreseeable" fell to be construed in a way which was consistent with the limited concept of foreseeability envisaged by art.5(4) of Directive 89/391. It was for a defendant to prove that the accident was attributable to either category of occurrence envisaged in art.5(4). Accordingly, the fact that an injury occurred in an unexpected way would not excuse a defendant, unless he could show further that the circumstances were "unforeseeable" or "exceptional" in the sense given to those words by art.5(4). So construed, the Regulations were consistent with the Directives (paras 22-23, 25). (3) It followed that the judge in the instant case was incorrect to import into reg.4 the classic common law phrase of reasonable foreseeability, and then to dismiss the claim on the basis that the way in which H was injured was very unusual and that S had abided by all requirements of the British Horseracing Authority. As the judge had said, an accident of H's kind, while not likely, was possible and in that sense foreseeable. S could not show that the accident was due to unforeseeable circumstances beyond its control or to exceptional events, the consequences of which were unavoidable (paras 26-27).

HIDE v STEEPLECHASE CO (CHELTENHAM) LTD, [2013] EWCA Civ 545, [2014] 1 All E.R. 405, Longmore, L.J., CA (Civ Div).

1507. Workers' compensation–Payment of claims

THE PNEUMOCONIOSIS ETC. (WORKERS' COMPENSATION) (PAYMENT OF CLAIMS) (AMENDMENT) REGULATIONS 2013, SI 2013/690; made under the Pneumoconiosis etc. (Workers' Compensation) Act 1979 s.1, s.7. In force: April 1, 2013; .

These Regulations increase the amounts of compensation paid to sufferers or certain dust-related diseases, or their dependants, under the Pneumoconiosis etc. (Workers' Compensation) Act 1979 Act by 2.2 per cent from April 1, 2013.

HERITABLE PROPERTY

1508. Warrandice–Title to land–Title to subjects of person making threat of eviction

The appellant (M) appealed against a decision ([2011] CSIH 30, 2011 S.C. 654, [2011] C.L.Y. 4351) that its action against the respondent seller (R) for breach of a warrandice obligation was irrelevant owing to the fact that no breach of warrandice had arisen. In 2004, R had sold land to a company (C) and given an express grant of absolute warrandice, namely a contractual warranty against all defects in title in the event of an eviction from the land. It subsequently materialised that the land was, in fact, owned by a company (J), and that R had never had title to it. J threatened to evict C from the land; C paid J to avoid eviction. Later, it came to light that J had, in 1991, inadvertently transferred title to the land to an individual (L). J procured the grant of a disposition of the land by L to C in 2006 and C's title was finally registered. In 2007, C went into liquidation and assigned its rights in the land to M, who started proceedings for breach of warrandice against R. R's defence was that a challenge by J, being a party whose ownership of the land was not registered or otherwise established at the time of the eviction threat, was not sufficient to engage a remedy in warrandice. A judge allowed M's action to proceed, but the Extra Division dismissed the action as irrelevant, finding that no breach of warrandice had arisen because at the time when C submitted to the threat of eviction, J had not had an unquestionable title to the land. The issue was whether, as a matter of principle, a seller's liability under the warrandice could be triggered where the person making the threat of eviction had title to the property at the time when the threat was made, but whose ownership was only subsequently registered.

Held: Appeal allowed. Previous authorities did not impose a rigid requirement that the person making the threat of eviction had to have an unquestionable title to the land at the time when the threat was made. Some of the dicta in *Clark v Lindale Homes Ltd* 1994 S.C. 210, [1994] C.L.Y. 5897 might be construed as such, but they could properly be regarded as obiter, *Clark* considered, *Abram Steamship Co Ltd (In Liquidation) v Westville Shipping Co Ltd (In Liquidation)* [1923] A.C. 773 applied and *Doughty Shipping Co Ltd v North British Railway Co (The Mountfields)* 1909 1 S.L.T. 267 and *Tayplan Ltd v D&A Contracts* 2005 S.L.T. 195, [2005] C.L.Y. 5451 considered. The key point was that in order to trigger the warrandice obligation, there had to be an eviction, or a threat of eviction, by a person who was in a position to make good his challenge to the purchaser's title. There was no good reason why the manner in which that challenge was made good, could not vary on a case by case basis. Although warrandice was a contractual remedy, and depended on what the parties had agreed to, not what the court considered to be just and equitable, there was force in the idea that the law had to seek practical solutions in working out a contractual remedy. It was settled law that a challenge had to be made by a party with a competing title to the land, but it would be wrong in principle, and would deprive the remedy of utility, to insist that such title had to be formally vested. All that a grantee needed to show in order to establish that the threatened demand amounted to an eviction, was that he had transacted with the right person; the party making the threat had to be in a position to make it good if the dispute were to proceed to an actual eviction. An incomplete title would be good enough if he was undoubtedly in a position to compel the party in whom the real right was vested to transfer the title to him (see paras 2, 24-27, 51-55 of judgment). In the instant case, M was entitled to warrandice if he could prove that when C yielded to the threat of eviction, J would have been immediately able to secure title to the land by calling upon L to transfer the title without the need for legal proceedings. That was consistent with the principles stated in James, Viscount of Stair, Lord President of the Session, The Institutions of the Law of Scotland, edited by David M. Walker (Edinburgh and Glasgow: The University Presses 1981) and R.J. Pothier, Treatise on the Contract of Sale (translated from the French by L.S.Cushing 1839). The Extra Division's interlocutor was recalled, the judge's interlocutor was restored and the case was remitted to the Outer House for the hearing of a proof before answer (paras 32, 50).

MORRIS v RAE, [2012] UKSC 50, 2013 S.C. (U.K.S.C.) 106, Lord Hope, J.S.C. (Deputy President), SC.

HOSPITALITY AND LEISURE

1509. Bookmakers–Betting exchanges–Whether customers of betting exchanges liable for horserace betting levy–Meaning of "bookmaker" within s.55 Betting, Gaming and Lotteries Act 1963

[Betting and Gaming Act 1960 (c.60); Betting and Gaming Duties Act 1981 (c.63); Betting and Lotteries Act 1934 (c.58); Betting, Gaming and Lotteries Act 1963 (c.2) s.27, s.55; Finance Act 1926 (c.22); Finance Act 2003 (c.14).]

The appellant bookmakers (W) appealed against a decision ([2012] EWHC 2039 (Admin), [2012] 1 W.L.R. 3504, [2013] 2 C.L. 175) that customers using betting exchanges were not "bookmakers" within the meaning of the Betting, Gaming and Lotteries Act 1963. W also appealed against an order that it should pay 25 per cent of the costs of the second interested party bookmakers (B). W had applied for judicial review of a decision of the first respondent board that customers of internet betting exchanges did not have to pay a horserace betting levy under s.27 of the 1963 Act. Customers of a betting exchange would fall within the statutory definition of a "bookmaker" if they carried on the business of "receiving or negotiating bets". The appeal turned on the construction of s.55 of the Act.

Held: Appeals dismissed. (1) The traditional distinction between bookmaker and punter had been adopted throughout the legislative history which led to the 1963 Act. The definition of bookmaker in s.55 was to be found in the Finance Act 1926 s.18, which introduced betting duty on bets made with a bookmaker. Section 18, in its definition of betting premises, drew a distinction between making and receiving a bet. The Betting and Lotteries Act 1934 and Betting and Gaming Act 1960 adopted materially identical definitions of "bookmaker". All those legislative provisions preserved the difference between bookmakers and their customers by drawing a distinction between those who received or negotiated bets and those who made bets (see paras 12-19 of judgment). The question in the instant appeal was whether the statutory definition of bookmaker was broad enough to encompass those who entered into a bet on a betting exchange. It was not difficult to identify a statutory purpose; Parliament intended to permit the board to impose a levy on bookmakers and not on their customers. Under a statutory scheme which distinguished between bookmakers and customers, it was not possible to do away with that distinction and say that customers were also bookmakers. To limit the scope of the statutory definition to those who operated the exchange preserved the distinction. There was also no sufficient distinction between the operation of a betting exchange and a traditional bookmaker to justify distinguishing between customers who made bets on an exchange and those who made bets with a traditional bookmaker. Once the statutory distinction was recognised, the size and organisation of those customers who made bets on an exchange was irrelevant (paras 20-22, 33-34). It was impossible to regard those who used the facilities of a betting exchange as bookmakers when Parliament had distinguished, in the Betting and Gaming Duties Act 1981, as amended by the Finance Act 2003, between bookmakers, betting exchanges and those who made bets with each other using facilities provided by a third party. W's arguments flew in the face of statutory distinctions which had persisted up to the advent of the betting exchange and its recognition by Parliament. The answer to the question of construction lay in the persistence with which the legislation had maintained the difference between those who made bets and those who received them, between the customer and the bookmaker. In the light of that distinction, those who used a betting exchange did not receive or negotiate bets within the meaning of s.55 of the 1963 Act (paras 40, 44). (2) The instant case was, in reality, a commercial dispute between parties. W thought it was being unfairly treated in comparison with its competitors, particularly B. However, B had every reason to actively participate to protect its own commercial interests, and its helpful participation was properly reflected in the costs order made, an order which flouted no principle (paras 45-46).

R. (ON THE APPLICATION OF WILLIAM HILL ORGANISATION LTD) v HORSERACE BETTING LEVY BOARD; *sub nom.* R. (ON THE APPLICATION OF WILLIAM HILL ORGANIZATION LTD) v HORSERACE BETTING LEVY BOARD, [2013] EWCA Civ 487, [2013] 1 W.L.R. 3656, Maurice Kay, L.J., CA (Civ Div).

1510. Disability discrimination–Service providers–Restaurant's refusal to serve disabled child outside official seating area–Reasonable adjustments–Whether restaurant required to adjust nature of service

[Disability Discrimination Act 1995 (c.50) s.19, s.21.]

The appellant (E) appealed against a county court's decision that the respondent (F) had not discriminated against her on the grounds of her disability. F operated a large theme park which included a restaurant and bar area. E had Down's syndrome and autism. Whilst at the theme park E and her family decided to go for a meal. They sat at a picnic bench adjacent to the restaurant's outside seating area. E's parents were told that they could not be served in the picnic area. Her parents offered to carry the food outside, but were prevented from doing so by the manager. They attempted to explain that, because of E's disabilities, it would upset her if she had to move. At trial they further explained that E often lashed out when upset. The manager returned E's parents' money and asked them to leave. E's claim succeeded before the district judge but was overturned on appeal, where it was found that E's parents had failed to explain adequately at the time why she could not move to the appropriate seating area. The judge did not go on to consider the supplementary ground of appeal that F was running a restaurant rather than a takeaway service.

Held: Appeal dismissed. (1) Under the Disability Discrimination Act 1995 s.19 and s.21, it was unlawful for providers of services to discriminate against a disabled person in failing to comply with a duty to make reasonable adjustments. The first question was what services F was providing. The district judge thought that F was "providing meals" and that it "had a policy that these should not be consumed in the picnic area". However, that was too broad an approach. An owner of a restaurant was not a mere meal provider; he provided a service which could be best described as "serving meals and drinks at tables prepared with chairs and eating equipment such as glasses and cutlery". That might be outside or inside but was usually within the area operated by the restaurant. It was different from the service of a takeaway establishment which provided food and drink to be consumed away from the premises without any accompanying services. The Code of Practice published by the Disability Rights Commission made it clear that the duty to make reasonable adjustments did not require a service provider to take any steps that would fundamentally alter the nature of its service, trade or business. F was providing a restaurant service and there was therefore no policy which required adaptation. E's appeal therefore failed on that ground (see paras 10-17 of judgment). (2) Before a service provider was required to adapt a policy, common sense required some form of reason or explanation to be given. What was sufficient in any particular case depended on the facts. In the instant case, the judge, having heard the evidence, concluded that an explanation was not given. The Court of Appeal could not have gone behind that finding in any event (para.20).

EDWARDS v FLAMINGO LAND LTD, [2013] EWCA Civ 801, [2013] Eq. L.R. 888, Longmore, L.J., CA (Civ Div).

1511. **Dissolution–Olympic lottery distribution fund**

THE OLYMPIC LOTTERY DISTRIBUTOR (DISSOLUTION) ORDER 2013, SI 2013/207; made under the Horserace Betting and Olympic Lottery Act 2004 s.32. In force: April 1, 2013; .

This Order dissolves the Olympic Lottery Distributor.

1512. **Gambling Commission–Mergers–National Lottery Commission–Transfer of functions**

THE PUBLIC BODIES (MERGER OF THE GAMBLING COMMISSION AND THE NATIONAL LOTTERY COMMISSION) ORDER 2013, SI 2013/2329; made under the Public Bodies Act 2011 s.2, s.6, s.23, s.24, s.35. In force: October 1, 2013 except for art.9 on October 2, 2013.; .

This Order Order abolishes the National Lottery Commission; transfers the National Lottery Commission's functions to the Gambling Commission; transfers the property, rights and liabilities of the National Lottery Commission to the Gambling Commission; and imposes duties on the Gambling Commission in respect of reporting and accounting obligations in relation to the National Lottery Commission which have not been discharged in respect of any financial year at the time of its abolition.

1513. **Heritage Lottery Fund–National Heritage Memorial Fund–Parks–England**

THE NEW PARKS FOR PEOPLE (ENGLAND) JOINT SCHEME (AUTHORISATION) ORDER 2013, SI 2013/1098; made under the National Lottery etc. Act 1993 Sch.3A para.2, Sch.3A para.3. In force: June 1, 2013; .

This Order authorises a New Parks for People (England) joint scheme pursuant to an application by the participating bodies, the Big Lottery Fund and the National Heritage Memorial Fund (operating under the name of the Heritage Lottery Fund).

1514. **Holidays–Disability discrimination–Lack of assistance to arthritis-sufferer while waiting to check in at airport–Whether tour operator's duty under s.29 Equality Act 2010 displaced by Regulation 1107/2006**

[Equality Act 2010 (c.15) s.29; Regulation 1107/2006 Art.1, Art.3, Art.4, Art.10.]

The claimant (C) claimed damages for unlawful discrimination from the defendant tour operator (T). C had booked a 49-day holiday in Tunisia through T. When she booked her holiday, she made known her need for wheelchair assistance at the airports in England and Tunisia. She suffered from arthritis and had difficulty in walking and standing. She was also prone to migraines. Owing to civil unrest in Tunisia occurring shortly after C's arrival, T offered to repatriate holiday-makers. C was taken to the airport but, after a four-hour wait there, was taken back to her hotel. She was taken back to the airport the following day, when she caught a flight home. Her case was that nothing effective had been done to try to alleviate her pain and discomfort arising from standing in queues while at the airport on the two days in question.

Held: Judgment for claimant. T was a service provider within the Equality Act 2010 s.29 and as such was under a duty not to discriminate against C in the provision of the service of providing her holiday. T was under a duty to make reasonable adjustments in respect of C by the provision of auxiliary aids such as some form of seating or seeking to facilitate her check-in procedure or both. It had failed to provide such auxiliary aids and thus had discriminated against C. She had suffered substantial physical pain and discomfort directly related to her disabilities which T had done nothing to attempt to relieve. An award of damages of £7,500 would be appropriate, provided that s.29 was not displaced by Regulation 1107/2006. Article 1 (2) of the Regulation did not apply as the only airports covered by that provision were those located in Member States. Article 1 (3) of the Regulation provided that art.3, art.4 and art.10 would apply to passengers departing from an airport situated in a third country to an airport situated in the territory of a Member State, if the operating carrier was a Community air carrier. Article 1 (3) therefore was applicable. However, arts 3 and

4 did not relate to airport services, being directed to the issue of ensuring that a person who was disabled or who had reduced mobility was permitted to board an aircraft. As to art.10, it required the air carrier to provide, without additional charge, the assistance specified in Annex II to the Regulation: such assistance was limited to matters connected with the flight itself and items of luggage which had to be carried. Nothing within art.10 or Annex II covered the provision, within the airport, of items such as wheelchairs or any chairs while queuing to check-in. Nor did they cover the provision of check-in assistance. Accordingly, T's duties under s.29 were not displaced by the Regulation (see paras 30-31, 35, 39, 49, 51-57 of judgment).

CAMPBELL v THOMAS COOK TOUR OPERATIONS LTD [2013] Eq. L.R. 658, Judge Robinson, CC (Sheffield).

1515. National Lottery–Community interest companies–Delay in bringing judicial review application–Running Health Lottery for private gain–External lottery managers

[Gambling Act 2005 (c.19) s.19(1), s.19, s.98, s.99(3), s.99, s.254, s.260.]

The claimant (C) applied for permission to apply for judicial review of a decision of the gambling commission refusing to review the grant of a licence to the first interested party (T) to act as an external lottery manager and to the remaining interested parties, which were community interest companies, (CICs) to conduct lotteries. In February 2011 T announced the launch of the Health Lottery stating that it would incorporate CICs. Each week at least one CIC would promote the scheme with additional CICs joining as more tickets were sold in order to prevent any CIC from exceeding the £4 million threshold for a single lottery under the Gambling Act 2005 s.99. The CICs outsourced the management and day-to-day conduct of their lotteries to T for agreed fees. Each CIC also agreed to donate 20.34 per cent of the lottery proceeds to a registered health charity. The Health Lottery was formally launched seven months later. C asked the commission to consider the legality of the Health Lottery and contended that the purpose for which the CICs had been established was to generate profits for T and that none of the CICs were operated for a non-commercial purpose within the meaning of s.19. C alleged that the Health Lottery was one single lottery and in breach of the Act. The commission stated that the lottery schemes were legal and complied with the Act and refused a review. C issued proceedings in 2012. The commission contended that permission to apply for judicial review should be refused as C had not filed its claim promptly and had not advanced any compelling grounds for its delay

Held: Application refused. (1) The relevant facts about the Health Lottery were available and known to C in February 2011. Whilst judicial review proceedings should not be instituted precipitately, there was considerable undue delay on the part of C in bringing the proceedings. C's contentions as to the effect of s.98 and s.19 went to the legality of the Health Lottery and could and should have been asserted to the commission shortly after the announcement and, if the commission did not accept that the scheme was unlawful, should immediately have been the subject of legal proceedings (see paras 63-64 of judgment). (2) The commission had correctly construed s.98 and s.19. Section 19 focussed on the non-commercial society and not on those who were contracted by it to provide services of any kind. Accordingly, it could pay its officers and employees, and their private gain was not a private gain for the purposes of s.19(1). It was clear that the Act did not require an external lottery manager to be non-profit making and it followed that the fact that such manager would make profits that would involve private gain on the part of its shareholders, officers or staff did not of itself result in an infringement of s.19(1) on the part of a non-commercial society that contracted with it. Parliament had enacted a control on the profits of an external lottery manager under s.254. If a non-commercial society paid an external manager an excessive sum in respect of the manager's services it would contravene s.260. Even if the Health Lottery scheme was initially proposed with a view in part for private gain on the part of T, provided the charges for its services were reasonable, the CICs were not ineligible for the grant of operating lottery licences. Equally, the fact that T might profit was not a bar to the CICs retaining their licences (paras 68, 70-71). (3) Whilst the CICs were under common control, they were separate legal entities. The fact they had common directors did not of itself justify their being treated as if they were a single corporate entity. Unless the sales of lottery tickets in any week exceeded the sum specified by T and the CICs, each week's lottery was a separate lottery and if each week's lottery was that of a different CIC there was no legal basis for aggregating the proceeds of each of them. The fact that all of the CICs employed T did not of itself allow their separate proceeds to be amalgamated for the purpose of ascertaining whether there had been a breach of the £10 million limitation in annual proceeds imposed by s.99(3) (paras 72-74).

R. (ON THE APPLICATION OF CAMELOT UK LOTTERIES LTD) v GAMBLING COMMISSION, [2012] EWHC 2391 (Admin), [2013] P.T.S.R. 729, Stanley Burnton, L.J., DC.

HOUSING

1516. Assured tenancies–Students–England

THE ASSURED AND PROTECTED TENANCIES (LETTINGS TO STUDENTS) (AMENDMENT) (ENGLAND) REGULATIONS 2013, SI 2013/38; made under the Housing Act 1988 Sch.1 para.8. In force: February 11, 2013; .

This instrument amends Schedule 2 to the Assured and Protected Tenancies (Letting to Students) Regulations 1998. The reference to "University of Leicester Students' Union" is being replaced with "Student Union Lettings Limited". This is to reflect the fact that lettings services previously provided by University of Leicester Students Union are now being provided by Student Union Lettings Limited, a joint venture between University of Leicester Students' Union and University of De Montfort Students' Union.

1517. Caravan sites–Gypsies–Mobile homes–Wales

THE HOUSING AND REGENERATION ACT 2008 (CONSEQUENTIAL AMENDMENTS TO THE MOBILE HOMES ACT 1983) (WALES) ORDER 2013, SI 2013/SI 2013/1722 (W.166); made under the Housing and Regeneration Act 2008 s.320, s.321. In force: July 10, 2013; .

Section 318 of the Housing and Regeneration Act 2008 (the 2008 Act) amends the Mobile Homes Act 1983 s.5 (the 1983 Act) to bring land occupied by a local authority as a caravan site providing accommodation for gypsies and travellers within the definition of protected sites for the purposes of the 1983 Act. The purpose of this Order is to make amendments to the 1983 Act which are consequential on the coming into force of s.318 of the 2008 Act in relation to Wales and on the making of related transitional provisions made under section 322 of that Act.

1518. Educational institutions–Houses in multiple occupation

THE HOUSES IN MULTIPLE OCCUPATION (SPECIFIED EDUCATIONAL ESTABLISHMENTS) (ENGLAND) REGULATIONS 2013, SI 2013/1601; made under the Housing Act 2004 Sch.14 para.4. In force: August 1, 2013; .

These Regulations specify educational establishments for the purposes of the Housing Act 2004 so that any building managed or controlled by such an establishment and occupied solely or principally by its students will not be a house in multiple occupation for the purposes of the Act (except Pt 1, which deals with housing conditions), whilst the establishment is a member of one of the specified codes of practice.

1519. Fees–Mobile homes–Mobile homes agreements

THE MOBILE HOMES (PITCH FEES) (PRESCRIBED FORM) (ENGLAND) REGULATIONS 2013, SI 2013/1505; made under the Mobile Homes Act 1983 s.25A, Sch.1 Part 1 Chapter 2. In force: July 26, 2013; .

These Regulations prescribe the form of the document that must accompany a mobile home pitch fee review notice, which proposes an increase in the pitch fee.

1520. Foreign nationals–Homelessness–Housing allocation–England

THE ALLOCATION OF HOUSING AND HOMELESSNESS (ELIGIBILITY) (ENGLAND) (AMENDMENT) REGULATIONS 2013, SI 2013/1467; made under the Housing Act 1996 s.160ZA, s.172, s.185, s.215. In force: July 1, 2013; .

These Regulations amend the provisions of the Allocation of Housing and Homelessness (Eligibility) (England) Regulations 2006 which determine which persons from abroad, other than persons subject to immigration control, are ineligible for an allocation of housing accommodation under the Housing Act 1996 Pt.6 or for housing assistance under Pt.7 of that Act.

1521. Gifts–Mobile homes–England

THE MOBILE HOMES (SELLING AND GIFTING) (ENGLAND) REGULATIONS 2013, SI 2013/981; made under the Mobile Homes Act 1983 s.2C, Sch.1 Part 1 para.7A, Sch.1 Part 1 para.7B, Sch.1 Part 1 para.7C, Sch.1 Part 1 para.8A, Sch.1 Part 1 para.8B, Sch.1 Part 1 para.8C, Sch.1 Part 3 para.A1. In force: May 26, 2013; .

These Regulations set out the detail of new procedures for the selling and gifting of mobile homes. These procedures are designed to make it easier for mobile home owners to sell or gift (give away) their homes without interference from the site owner, and also to help potential purchasers of a mobile home to ensure they have all the information they need in order to make an informed decision regarding the purchase.

1522. Gifts–Mobile homes–Mobile homes agreements–England

THE MOBILE HOMES ACT 2013 (SAVING PROVISIONS) (ENGLAND) ORDER 2013, SI 2013/1168; made under the Mobile Homes Act 2013 s.15. In force: May 26, 2013; .

This Order makes saving provisions in relation to the Mobile Homes Act 1983 Sch.1 Pt 2 Ch.2 so that where, prior to May 26, 2103, an occupier of a mobile home has served a request on a site owner for the approval of the person to whom the occupier proposes to sell or gift the mobile home, the transaction may proceed (if the occupier so wishes) under the existing statutory provisions.

1523. Homelessness–Housing assistance–Subsequent application for housing assistance–Re-arguing same points as abuse of process

[Housing Act 1996 (c.52) Pt VII, s.185(2); Immigration (European Economic Area) Regulations 2006 (SI 2006/1003) reg.6.]

The appellant Polish national (K) appealed against a decision affirming the decision of the respondent local authority's housing review officer that she was not eligible for housing assistance because she was subject to immigration control. The local authority had determined that K was ineligible for housing assistance under the Housing Act 1996 Pt VII because she was subject to immigration control pursuant to s.185(2) of the Act. K challenged that decision on the grounds that she had been a migrant worker at a hotel and thereafter self-employed while her son was attending school, and that she was not therefore subject to immigration control. K had made an earlier application to the local authority for homelessness assistance under Part VII of the Act, but had been found to be ineligible. That decision was upheld on review and K had appealed to the Court of Appeal where she sought to rely on different grounds. In the circumstances, her appeal was found to have been abandoned and was accordingly dismissed. K thereafter obtained privately rented accommodation and when required to leave, made the instant application for accommodation. On review, the housing review officer found that whereas K had been in registered employment following which she was self-employed for a period of time, she did not enjoy ongoing rights of residence in the United Kingdom and was thus ineligible for housing assistance. He also found that, although K was ill, she did not enjoy retained worker status because she could not show temporary illness. K submitted that she should not have been prevented from reasserting her initial claim because she had made a new housing application as a result of a fresh incident of homelessness, and in any event her claim to have retained her worker status or to have self-employment status had never been adjudicated on. She argued that doctrines of res judicata and issue estoppel did not apply in public law; to the extent that the court could control abuse of its process, there was no abuse in seeking to re-argue points on successive applications.

Held: Appeal dismissed. (1) It was clearly abusive for K to seek to argue the same point which she had expressly abandoned in the face of the Court of Appeal. There could be no doubt that in public law, as much as in private law, the court had to be able to stop abuse of its own process, *O'Reilly v Mackman* [1983] 2 A.C. 237, [1982] C.L.Y. 2603 considered. One of the most obvious forms of abuse was to attempt to re-litigate matters which had already been disposed of by a final judgment which was unappealed. On any application for housing assistance a local authority, if satisfied that the applicant was or might be homeless or threatened with homelessness, was obliged to make enquiries as to the applicant's eligibility; if no new facts were revealed since the last application, the local authority could reject the application, *Begum (Rikha) v Tower Hamlets LBC* [2005] EWCA Civ 340, [2005] 1 W.L.R. 2103, [2005] C.L.Y. 1986 and *Baumbast v Secretary of State for the Home Department (C-413/99)* [2002] E.C.R. I-7091, [2002] C.L.Y. 2628 considered (see paras 12-14 of judgment). (2) There was no reason why the general approach in modern private law should not apply as much in public as in private law, with the possible qualification that a public body with statutory obligations to provide, for example, housing assistance should not be over-protected from addressing points which were truly new, even if they arose on facts which had already been subject to a determination, *Johnson v Gore Wood & Co (No.1)* [2002] 2 A.C. 1, [2001] C.L.Y. 410 applied. The housing review officer had dealt with the new points and, on the broad approach adopted by Lord Bingham in *Johnson*, it would be right for the Court of Appeal to do so also (paras 16-17). (3) The question whether K had retained her worker status or acquired a self-employed status depended on whether she was at the time of the decision on eligibility "temporarily unable to work as the result of an illness or accident" pursuant to the provisions of the Immigration (European Economic Area) Regulations 2006 reg.6. In holding that K was "unlikely to work in the foreseeable future", the housing review officer had not erred in law and had applied the correct test, *FMB (Uganda) v Secretary of State for the Home Department* [2010] UKUT 447 (IAC), [2011] Imm. A.R. 236, [2011] C.L.Y. 1769 applied. The question whether K was unable to work was a question of fact; the housing review officer had considered the evidence and there was no legal flaw in his reasoning. It was also important that decisions of housing review officers were not combed over to find errors of law when the same legal concept could be expressed in varying ways (paras 18, 20-23).

KONODYBA v KENSINGTON AND CHELSEA RLBC, [2012] EWCA Civ 982, [2013] P.T.S.R. 13, Lord Neuberger (M.R.), CA (Civ Div).

1524. Homelessness–Housing provision–Offer of accommodation for person together with family members–Accommodation comprising two adjoining flats–Meaning of "together with" in s.176 Housing Act 1996

[Housing Act 1996 (c.52) s.176.]

The appellant local authority appealed against a decision ([2011] EWCA Civ 463, [2011] P.T.S.R. 1695) that its provision of two adjoining flats to the respondent (S) and her family did not constitute accommodation enabling the family to live together for the purposes of the Housing Act 1996 s.176. S had lived with her father, for whom she acted as a carer, and her younger sister, who was a minor. The local authority had secured temporary accommodation for all three of them in a private sector three bedroom house. The authority then offered S by way of further temporary accommodation two separate flats some yards apart on the same floor of a hostel. The intention was that one flat would be occupied by S and her sister, and the other by her father. S refused the offer. The local authority argued that a family could live together even if their accommodation was not in a single unit.

Held: Appeal allowed. (Lord Kerr J.S.C. dissenting) (1) The word "accommodation" was not in its ordinary sense to be equated with "unit of accommodation". It was no abuse of language to speak of a family being accommodated in two adjoining flats. The limitation, if any, therefore had to be found in the words "available for occupation... together with" the other members of the family. The statutory test would be satisfied by a single unit of accommodation in which a family could live together, but it could also be satisfied by two units of accommodation if they were so located that they enabled the family to live together in practical terms. That came down to an issue of factual judgement for the local authority; short of irrationality it was unlikely to raise any issue of law for the court. Any qualification that "accommodation" had to enable the family to carry on the operations of daily life there had been rejected in *R. v Hillingdon LBC, Ex p. Puhlhofer* [1986] A.C. 484, [1986] C.L.Y. 1619 and that remained the position, *Puhlhofer* applied. Further, S's interpretation would produce surprising results: a local authority would be unable to improve the position of a family living within a single overcrowded unit by offering it an additional unit next door. It would also be odd and potentially onerous if, while considering the merits, the local authority could not house the family in two adjoining units even temporarily. Moreover, if separate rooms in the same hotel or hostel would discharge the duty, as observed in *R. v Ealing LBC, Ex p. Surdonja* [1999] 1 All E.R. 566, [1998] C.L.Y. 3027, it was hard to see why two adjacent flats would not, *Surdonja* considered (see paras 17-20 of judgment). (2) The narrowness of the instant decision was emphasised. It did not give local authorities a free hand. It was still a fundamental objective of the Act to ensure that families could "live together" in the true sense. Accommodation, whether in one unit or two, was not suitable unless it enabled that objective to be achieved (para.21). (3) (Per Lord Kerr J.S.C.) If living together as a family was to mean anything, it had to mean living as a distinct entity in a single unit of accommodation. If the opportunity was available to house families in different living units, there was every reason to suppose that local authorities would, understandably, seek to exploit that opportunity to the fullest extent. There was therefore a real risk that one of the principal purposes of the legislation, that of keeping families together, would be put under considerable strain (paras 31-39).

SHARIF v CAMDEN LBC, [2013] UKSC 10, [2013] 2 All E.R. 309, Lord Hope, J.S.C. (Deputy President), SC.

1525. Homelessness–Intentional homelessness–Transfer of property rights to former partner–Causation–Failure to properly consider individual's financial ability to remain in property alone

[Housing Act 1996 (c.52) s.191, s.202.]

The appellant (C) appealed against a decision dismissing her appeal against a homelessness review completed by the respondent local authority pursuant to the Housing Act 1996 s.202. C and her partner (P) had bought a property which was conveyed into their joint names. They later separated and came to an agreement in 2008 that P would purchase C's share in the property. P paid C £15,000 for her share. C continued to live in the property paying P rent, but P paid all of the outgoings, including the mortgage repayments. C and P reconciled in 2010 and P moved back into the property. The property was formally transferred into P's name. Their relationship broke down again and C left the property. She made a homelessness application to the local authority which was refused on the basis that she had made herself intentionally homeless within the meaning of s.191 by transferring her property rights to P when she knew that that would put her at risk of homelessness. C requested a review of that refusal but the local authority upheld its decision on review. It decided that the breakdown of C and P's relationship did not break the chain of causation for C becoming homeless because the up-and-down nature of their relationship meant that a breakdown was foreseeable. It found that the causal link was C's deliberate transfer of her property rights to P and not the breakdown in the relationship. C's appeal against that review decision was dismissed. C submitted that: it was the breakdown of her relationship that had caused her homelessness; the local authority had improperly imported an ingredient of foreseeability into its assessment of whether C had intentionally become homeless; the local authority had failed to consider whether it would have been financially possible for C to remain in the property alone in 2008, discharging the outgoings as a sole proprietor; after P had paid the £15,000, a proprietory estoppel arose in his favour which entitled him to a right to claim the entire beneficial interest in the property.

Held: Appeal allowed. It was clear that in light of the facts provided in the decision letter and the review letter, the local authority was entitled to find that C and P's relationship was turbulent. The reviewing officer was entitled to take into account the fact that the relationship had broken down in 2008 and that the relationship had once again broken down within months of their reconciliation. It was not wrong for the local authority to assess whether C was intentionally homeless by reference to the likelihood that her relationship would or might break down, thereby leaving her at risk of homelessness. However, it was clear that both the decision and review letter referred to the situation before C and P's break-up in 2008, evidenced by the fact that they referred to C and P's joint incomes rather than C's ability to meet any outgoings as a sole proprietor. Therefore, there was no finding in either letter that after the agreement for sale was made in 2008 C could afford the outgoings, including mortgage repayments. The absence of such a finding by the local authority that C could have taken over the outgoings on the property in 2008 was a significant and critical defect. C's proprietory estoppel point was unsustainable because the 2008 agreement for sale was not in writing and was therefore unenforceable. In any event, it was impossible to say without more facts how the equity would have been satisfied even if proprietory estoppel could be established. Accordingly, the review decision could be impugned on a public law basis because the local authority had failed to conclude on whether C could have afforded to remain in the property in 2008 as a sole proprietor, which was a critical to deciding whether someone had become homeless intentionally within the meaning of s.191. It was appropriate to quash the review decision, leaving it open to the local authority to conduct a fresh review, with particular regard to the issue of affordability.

CARTHEW v EXETER CITY COUNCIL, [2012] EWCA Civ 1913, [2013] H.L.R. 19, Thorpe, L.J., CA (Civ Div).

1526. Homelessness–Migrant workers–Eligibilty for housing assistance–Incapacity for work–Temporary or permanent inability to work

[Housing Act 1996 (c.52); Immigration (European Economic Area) Regulations 2006 (SI 2006/1003) reg.6; Directive 2004/38 on the right of citizens of the Union and their family members to move and reside freely within the territory of the Member States amending Regulation (EEC) No 1612/68 and repealing Directives 64/221/EEC, 68/360/EEC, 72/194/EEC, 73/148/EEC, 75/34/EEC, 75/35/EEC, 90/364/EEC, 90/365/ Art.7(3)(a).]

The appellant Austrian citizen (S) appealed against a decision affirming the decision of the respondent local authority's housing review officer that he was not eligible for housing provision. Since his arrival in the United Kingdom in 2005 he had worked for a period of approximately 10 months, but lost that job in 2006 and had not worked since. He was in poor health, his principal illness being clinical depression which was chronic and had originated over 20 years earlier. The prognosis of the treating psychologist was that complete recovery was unlikely, and that S would "continue to have a significant degree of dysfunction". He sought housing assistance under the homeless provisions in the Housing Act 1996. The question for the instant court was whether the reviewer had made an error of law in determining that S was not "temporarily unable to work as a result of an illness or accident" and accordingly had not met the test of eligibility for housing assistance as provided by the Immigration (European Economic Area) Regulations 2006 reg.6(2)(a).

Held: Appeal dismissed. The purpose of the relevant Directive, Directive 2004/38, was to confirm and enhance the free movement of workers between Member States. It was an underlying principle of European law that the self-sufficient were entitled to move freely, with their families, between Member States, but that was not an unqualified principle. The qualification was that Member States were not obliged to make their separate and disparate social benefits schemes available to those who came from other Member States unless it was incidental to their right to free movement for the purpose of supporting themselves and their families by work or otherwise, *Ziolkowski v Land Berlin (C-424/10)* [2014] All E.R. (EC) 314 and *Orfanopoulos v Land Baden-Wurttemberg (C-482/01)* [2004] E.C.R. I-5257, [2005] C.L.Y. 1456 considered. Article 7(3)(a) of the Directive together with reg.6(2)(a) contained a specific test, namely whether the interruption was a temporary one. Temporary was to be contrasted with permanent. The question was one of fact in every case. It would generally be helpful to ask whether there was a realistic prospect of a return to work. That approach to the legislation was entirely consistent with the objectives of the Directive, *de Brito v Secretary of State for the Home Department* [2012] EWCA Civ 709, [2012] 3 C.M.L.R. 24, [2012] C.L.Y. 1781 and *Konodyba v Kensington and Chelsea RLBC* [2012] EWCA Civ 982, [2013] P.T.S.R. 13 applied. The reviewer did not specifically ask herself whether S's inability to work was permanent, nor did she expressly pose the question whether there was a realistic prospect of him returning to work. That was because the decisions in *de Brito* and *Konodyba* were not then available to her. She asked herself the statutory question, whether his inability to work was temporary. That was the right question. The judge was right to find that, in the context of the instant case, her decision that it was not temporary was also a decision that it was permanent. Her decision would undoubtedly have been the same if she had posed the question in terms of a realistic prospect of return to work. S had scarcely worked at all in the time he had been in the UK. His principal disabling illness was of very long standing and the prospect of it changing sufficiently to get him into work could only be regarded as unrealistic. It was wholly unrealistic and therefore legally wrong to characterise S as a worker who was continuing to exercise his occupation but temporarily interrupted by illness (see paras 11, 18-19, 21, 31, 34 of judgment).

SAMIN v WESTMINSTER CITY COUNCIL, [2012] EWCA Civ 1468, [2013] 2 C.M.L.R. 6, Hughes, L.J., CA (Civ Div).

1527. Homelessness–Priority needs–Heroin addict and persistent offender–Existence of vulnerability under s.189(1)(c) Housing Act 1996 or art.5(3) Homelessness (Priority Need for Accommodation) (England) Order 2002

[Housing Act 1996 (c.52) s.189(1)(c); Homelessness (Priority Need for Accommodation) (England) Order 2002 (SI 2002/2051) Art.5.]

The appellant (J) appealed against a decision dismissing his appeal against a review decision made by the respondent local authority that he was not in priority need for housing under the Housing Act 1996 s.189(1)(c). J was 37 years old. He was a heroin addict and prescribed methadone for his addiction. He suffered from depression. He had been a persistent criminal offender since he was 13 or 14 and had spent many periods in custody. For several years he had not had his own home, and would either stay with friends or family or sleep rough. He applied to the local authority for accommodation on the basis that he was homeless and in priority need because he was vulnerable under s.189(1)(c) of the 1996 Act. The reviewing officer decided, applying the test in *R. v Camden LBC, Ex p. Pereira* (1999) 31 H.L.R. 317, [1999] C.L.Y. 3062, that J was not less able to fend for himself if street homeless than an ordinary homeless person. The county court upheld the reviewing officer's decision. J submitted that (1) the reviewing officer had wrongly applied the test of vulnerability, as she had used as the comparator a homeless person affected by drug use rather than a homeless person who did not have such issues; (2) the composite assessment approach required of the reviewing officer when she considered "other special reason" under s.189(1)(c) meant that she should consider the individual factors and how they related to each other; (3) the judge had been wrong to limit to long-term prisoners the application of the Homelessness (Priority Need for Accommodation) England Order 2002 art.5(3), which provided that a person who was vulnerable as a result of having served a custodial sentence had a priority housing need.

Held: Appeal dismissed. (1) The concept of an ordinary homeless person was necessarily imprecise, *Osmani v Camden LBC* [2004] EWCA Civ 1706, [2005] H.L.R. 22, [2005] C.L.Y. 1989 and *Pereira* followed. It was a real-world question for the housing authority in each case. It was not surprising that many homeless people had drug issues. It had been open to the reviewing officer, when determining who was the ordinary homeless person, to refer to and make use of a report containing statistics about the proportion of homeless people with mental illness and/or drug problems. (2) It was correct that the reviewing officer had to consider all the factors together and could arrive at a different result by their combination. However, the reviewing officer had adopted that approach and had not misdirected herself. (3) The judge had suggested in his judgment that only long-term prisoners would fall under art.5(3). However, the relevant point was that the real basis of the reviewing officer's decision regarding J's release from prison was that he had not become institutionalised and hence less able to cope with homelessness than an ordinary homeless person. It would not always be the case that a person released from prison would not cope. The reviewing officer had referred to other evidence showing that J's release did not lead to his being vulnerable. That was a holistic assessment and her conclusion was not irrational.

JOHNSON v SOLIHULL MBC, [2013] EWCA Civ 752, [2013] H.L.R. 39, Arden, L.J., CA (Civ Div).

1528. Houses–Right to buy–London

THE HOUSING (RIGHT TO BUY) (LIMIT ON DISCOUNT) (ENGLAND) ORDER 2013, SI 2013/677; made under the Housing Act 1985 s.131. In force: March 25, 2013; .

A person exercising the right to buy a dwelling-house under Part V of the Housing Act 1985 may be entitled, under sections 129 to 131 of and Schedule 4 to the Act, to a discount equal to a percentage of the price before discount. The discount may not reduce the price by more than such sum as the Secretary of State may by order prescribe nor may it reduce the price below an amount representing the costs incurred by the landlord over a specified period of time in respect of the dwelling-house in accordance with a determination by the Secretary of State. This Order prescribes the maximum discount as £100,000 in respect of dwelling-houses situated within the areas of London authorities.

1529. Houses in multiple occupation–Rent repayment orders–Guidance on amount payable under rent repayment orders

[Housing Act 2004 (c.34) s.74(5), s.74(6)(d).]

The appellant (P), the owner of a house in multiple occupation (HMO), appealed against a rent repayment order (RRO) made by a residential property tribunal in favour of the six respondents (W). W occupied rooms in the house in question. They sought an RRO on the basis that the house was not licensed as a HMO. The tribunal made an order in their favour for the repayment of 100 per cent of the rent that each of them had paid in the 12 months preceding the application.

Held: Appeal allowed. (1) Any consideration of the exercise of the tribunal's power to make an RRO in favour of an occupier had to start from an identification of the purpose for which the power was given. The occupier RRO provisions had a number of purposes: to enable a penalty in the form of a civil sanction to be imposed in addition to the fine payable for the criminal offence of operating an unlicensed HMO; to help prevent a landlord from profiting from renting properties illegally; and to resolve the problems arising from the withholding of rent by tenants. Under the Housing Act 2004 s.74(5), the amount required to be paid by virtue of an RRO was to be such amount as the tribunal considered "reasonable in the circumstances". That amount had to be considered in the context of the identified purposes. The following points were among those that should be borne in mind. A tribunal should have regard to the total amount that the landlord would have to pay by way of a fine and under an RRO. There was no presumption that the RRO should be for the total amount received by the landlord during the relevant period; the tribunal had to take an overall view of the circumstances in determining what amount would be reasonable. An RRO was limited to the period of 12 months ending with the date of the occupier's application, but the tribunal ought also to have regard to the total length of time during which the offence was being committed. The fact that the tenant would have had the benefit of occupying the premises during the relevant period was not a material consideration or, if it was, one to which significant weight should be attached. Payments made as part of the rent for utility services counted as part of the periodical payments in respect of which an RRO could be made, but as the landlord would not himself have benefited from them, it would only be in the most serious case that they should be included in the RRO. Section 74(6)(d) required the tribunal to take account of the landlord's conduct and financial circumstances. The circumstances in which the offence was committed were always likely to be material. A deliberate flouting of the requirement to register would obviously merit a larger RRO than instances of inadvertence. A landlord who was engaged professionally in letting was likely to be more harshly dealt with than the non-professional (see paras 20, 26 of judgment). (2) In the instant case, the tribunal had erred in that part of the RRO related to a period which post-dated P's application for a licence. It had also erred in treating the 2004 Act as providing that an RRO should require the repayment of the maximum amount that could be ordered to be repaid unless there were good reasons to order less. Further, the tribunal had been wrong to treat as immaterial the amounts included in respect of utility costs and council tax in the rents paid by W. It would not be appropriate to impose on P an RRO of an amount that exceeded his profit in the relevant period. In view of his culpability as a professional engaged in the letting of residential property, he should under the RRO pay 75 per cent of his profit less the amount of the fine imposed on him (paras 27-28, 32, 35, 42-43).

PARKER v WALLER, [2012] UKUT 301 (LC), [2013] J.P.L. 568, George Bartlett Q.C. (President), UT (Lands).

1530. Houses in multiple occupation–Student accommodation–Number of storeys–Meaning of art.3 Licensing of Houses in Multiple Occupation (Prescribed Descriptions) (England) Order 2006

[Housing Act 2004 (c.34) Pt 2; Licensing of Houses in Multiple Occupation (Prescribed Descriptions) (England) Order 2006 (SI 2006/371) Art.3.]

The claimant local authority sought declaratory relief in respect of a property owned by the defendant (U) for student accommodation. The property comprised a five-storey block of purpose built self-contained flats. The ground floor consisted of a shop and the four upper floors were residential accommodation. Most such accommodation was in the form of cluster flats with four to six bedrooms with en-suite bathrooms and a communal living room and kitchen. Each flat was on one storey. The cluster flats were each a house in multiple occupation (HMO) within the meaning of the Housing Act 2004 Pt 2 as a self-contained flat. The issue was whether the HMOs at the property were HMOs for which a licence from the local authority was required. U submitted that each HMO in the property was the individual cluster flat and not the whole building so that, under the Licensing of Houses in Multiple Occupation (Prescribed Descriptions) (England) Order 2006 art.3, none of the HMOs were subject to the duty to apply for a licence because none comprised three storeys or more. U argued that licensing was intended to be restricted to vulnerable properties where there were risks to health and safety and self-contained flats were not considered a health risk. The local authority contended that under art.3(2)(a) business premises situated below living accommodation counted towards the qualifying number of storeys and that, under art.3(3)(f), all four of the residential storeys in the building were used wholly or partly as living accommodation or in connection with an integral part of the HMO and that the legislator had intended that any HMO should be licensed if it was occupied by five or more persons and was situated in a building containing three storeys or more.

Held: Judgment for defendant. The consultation document "Licensing in the Private Sector" published by the Deputy Prime Minister's Office as part of its regulatory assessment of Pt 2 referred to a survey of housing conditions and health risks. That report was not concerned with blocks of purpose built flats. It was the size of the HMO that was the focus of concern rather than the size of the building in which an HMO was found. In the final regulatory impact assessment the point was repeated that not all HMOs were to be licensed. Article 3(3) did not substitute art.3(2) and deprive it of its natural meaning, but set out special rules for the limited purpose of bringing business premises and certain uses associated with the HMO into the equation. It was the HMO that had to comprise three storeys and not the building in which the HMO happened to be found. The Order was not intended to apply to purpose built flats in tower blocks. Article 3(3)(f) did not bring each cluster flat in the property into the licensing regime because each flat was on one storey and was self-contained. The living accommodation in the HMO did not comprise more than one storey so when the ground-floor business premises were added, the three-storey threshold was not reached. U was granted a declaration (see paras 20-21, 24, 29-34 of judgment).

ISLINGTON LBC v UNITE GROUP PLC, [2013] EWHC 508 (Admin), [2013] P.T.S.R. 1078, Blake, J., QBD (Admin).

1531. Housing allocation–Suitability–Offer of sixteenth-floor flat–Medical evidence of fear of heights–Rationality of conclusion that mere dislike of heights

The appellant (E) appealed against the dismissal of his appeal against a review decision of the respondent local authority that he had refused an offer of suitable accommodation. E and his wife (W) had been accommodated by the local authority in a ninth-floor flat. It was not obvious when looking out of the windows how high the flat was. Six months later E completed a medical assessment form indicating that the accommodation affected W's health because she had a fear of heights, but there was no evidence that an assessment had been carried out. In 2009, due to overcrowding, E was offered a larger flat on the sixteenth floor of another block. The windowsills of that flat were low and the view showed the street below. When viewing the flat W had a panic attack and collapsed, and was taken to hospital. E refused the accommodation. The local authority considered that it was suitable and that, as he had refused the offer, its duty to accommodate him had ended. On a review of that decision the review officer had two letters from W's general practitioner which said that W should be offered accommodation on a lower floor to avoid any further health problems in the form of panic attacks and anxiety and that W had a long-standing fear of heights. In response to a request for clarification, the GP said that W had suffered episodes of panic and anxiety when she had moved to the ninth-floor flat. The review officer concluded that although W did not like heights, she had been able to live on the ninth floor despite her condition and that she would settle into the property on the sixteenth floor in time. E's appeal was dismissed. E argued that (1) the review officer had failed to make sufficient enquiries as to whether W had suffered from an irrational fear, or a general dislike, of heights; (2) the conclusion that W suffered from a general dislike of heights was irrational.

Held: Appeal allowed. (1) Those acting for E had made no specific request for the review officer to undertake further enquiries. Bearing in mind that the review officer had sought clarification from the GP, it could not be said that no reasonable local authority could have failed to regard it as necessary to seek an independent further medical report, *Cramp v Hastings BC* [2005] EWCA Civ 1005, [2005] 4 All E.R. 1014, [2006] C.L.Y. 2022 applied (see para.21 of judgment). (2) The conclusion that W would have settled in to the property in time failed to give proper weight to the medical evidence. Her GP had twice referred to a long-standing fear of heights, and had given her medical opinion that W should be accommodated on a lower floor to avoid further heath problems in the form of panic attacks and anxiety. There was no countervailing evidence from a medical expert to refute the GP's opinion, and the review officer was simply not entitled to disregard it. On the basis of that medical evidence, it could not be rationally concluded that W simply had a general dislike of heights. The review officer had ignored the central point that from E's current flat the road could not be seen, but that from the flat offered it could be seen. Within six months of moving into the ninth-floor flat E had sought a medical assessment because of W's fear of heights, and throughout W's occupation of that flat she had suffered with the effects of anxiety caused by living at that height. The finding that the flat was suitable was outside the band of decisions available to the review officer and was perverse (paras 23-26).

EL-DINNAOUI v WESTMINSTER CITY COUNCIL, [2013] EWCA Civ 231, [2013] H.L.R. 23, Hughes, L.J., CA (Civ Div).

1532. Housing and Regeneration Act 2008 (c.17)–Commencement No.3 and Transitional, Transitory and Saving Provisions Order–Wales

THE HOUSING AND REGENERATION ACT 2008 (COMMENCEMENT NO.3 AND TRANSITIONAL, TRANSITORY AND SAVING PROVISIONS) (WALES) ORDER 2013, SI 2013/SI 2013/1469 (W.140) (C.57); made under the Housing and Regeneration Act 2008 s.322, s.325. Commencement details: bringing into force various provisions of the 2008 Act on July 10, 2013.; .

This Order appoints July 10, 2013 as the day on which the Housing and Regeneration Act 2008 s.318 (on protected mobile home sites to include sites for gypsies and travellers) and related repeals in Sch.16 to that Act are brought into force in relation to Wales.

1533. Housing assistance–Immigrants–Child with British citizenship cared for in UK solely by parent of non-EU nationality with no domestic leave to remain or right to work–Entitlement to housing assistance–Application of Ruiz Zambrano v Office National de l'Emploi (ONEm) (C-34/09) [2012] Q.B. 265

[Asylum and Immigration Act 1996 (c.49); European Communities Act 1972 (c.68) s.2(1); Housing Act 1996 (c.52) s.185(2); Immigration Act 1988 (c.14) s.7(1); Immigration (European Economic Area) Regulations 2006 (SI 2006/1003); Treaty on the Functioning of the European Union Art.20.]

The appellant (P), a Jamaican national, appealed against the upholding of a decision of the respondent local authority that she was not eligible for housing assistance under the Housing Act 1996 s.185(2) because she was a "person subject to immigration control" within the meaning of the Asylum and Immigration Act 1996. P's children had been born in the United Kingdom and their father was a British citizen. P's case was that although she was, under domestic law, unlawfully present in the United Kingdom, she had an EU right to residence under the Immigration Act 1988 s.7(1) in conjunction with the Immigration (European Economic Area) Regulations 2006 because she was the sole carer of children who were British citizens. She maintained that such a right derived from TFEU art.20 and from *Ruiz Zambrano v Office National de l'Emploi (ONEm) (C-34/09)* [2012] Q.B. 265, and that she was therefore not subject to immigration control. The local authority conceded her appeal but the secretary of state, as intervener, expressed disagreement with the agreed position. The case was thought to raise a significant point of law and was put before the court for treatment analogous to that of a test case. The issue was whether TFEU art.20 conferred an automatic substantive right of residence on its beneficiaries which precluded national measures which interfered with the exercise of that right, or whether it was limited merely to conferring a right to be granted, upon application, domestic permission to work and reside in the relevant Member State.

Held: Appeal allowed. (1) Having regard to the significance of the point involved and its likely application to many cases, it was in the public interest for there to be a public hearing and for a judgment to be made available to housing authorities and applicants for housing assistance, *R. v Secretary of State for the Home Department, Ex p. Salem* [1999] 1 A.C. 450, [1999] C.L.Y. 8 considered (see paras 11-12 of judgment). (2) P's children were nationals of an EU Member State and held an additional status as EU citizens. Article 20 contained treaty rights which were directly applicable in the UK national legal order by virtue of the European Communities Act 1972 s.2(1) without the need for transposition into national law. A person who could rely on art.20 to refute a refusal of a right of residence was not a "person subject to immigration control" for the purposes of the Housing Act 1996 s.185 or the Immigration Act 1988 s.7. *Zambrano* established that where an EU citizen child was within his EU Member State of nationality, his EU citizenship might have consequential effects for a parent who was not a national of any EU Member State and who lacked domestic leave to remain and/or permission to work in that state. The emerging concept of the "Zambrano carer" encompassed third-party national carers of UK national children; the local authority had determined that P met the Zambrano criteria. It followed therefore, that she derived a right of residence from EU law and was eligible for homelessness assistance, *Zambrano* explained. It was important to remember, when reading the instant judgment, that the local authority had made concessions, prior to the implementation of an amendment to the 2006 Regulations, to give full effect to the *Zambrano* decision; the court had not heard contrary submissions on the effect of *Zambrano*. Also, its application was fact-sensitive, and its principles were likely to be subject to further analysis (paras 19-20, 27, 30, 32).

PRYCE v SOUTHWARK LBC, [2012] EWCA Civ 1572, [2013] 1 W.L.R. 996, Pill, L.J., CA (Civ Div).

1534. Intentional homelessness–Effective cause–Use of counterfeit passport in application for housing assistance–Likelihood of homelessness at time of act–Whether reasonable to continue occupancy

[Housing Act 1996 (c.52) s.191, s.193(6)(a), s.193.]

The appellant (C) appealed against the refusal of housing assistance by the respondent local authority. C was assessed as being a person of priority need who was not homeless intentionally, and was granted a non-secured tenancy of a flat under the Housing Act 1996 s.193. The United Kingdom Border Agency subsequently discovered that C had been using a counterfeit British passport and that her leave to remain in the UK was due to expire. The local authority gave C notice to quit on the basis that, as she was an overstayer, she was ineligible for housing under s.193(6)(a). An order for possession was made. C was subsequently granted leave to remain in the UK for a further three years, thereby becoming eligible for welfare benefits and homelessness assistance. Her renewed application for housing was refused on the basis that, by using the counterfeit passport in her previous application, she had deliberately done something which led her to ceasing to occupy accommodation that was available and reasonable for her to occupy, thereby becoming homeless intentionally within the meaning of s.191. The issue for the court was whether C had become homeless intentionally within the meaning of s.191.

(1) It was sufficient for the purpose of the s.191 that a deliberate act or omission led to homelessness; it was not necessary that it was done with the intention of causing homelessness, Devenport v Salford CC *R. v Salford City Council, Ex p. Devenport* (1983) 8 H.L.R. 54, [1984] C.L.Y. 1642 considered. What mattered was the objective likelihood of homelessness at the time of the act or omission, which was a question of fact for the local authority, *Stewart v Lambeth LBC* [2002] EWCA Civ 753, [2002] H.L.R. 40, [2002] C.L.Y. 2340 considered. (2) The local authority erred when considering that acts or omissions that occurred

before the accommodation had been granted were the same as those that occurred afterwards. C had never had a lawful right to the housing assistance. The immediate and proximate cause C becoming homeless was the discovery of the fraud. Her non-entitlement was the effective cause of her no longer being able to occupy the property. (3) The local authority erred in failing to consider whether it would have been reasonable for C to continue to occupy the property. C should not have been granted housing assistance in the first place. Once the deception arose, there was no possible justification for continued occupancy, *R. v Exeter City Council, Ex p. Gliddon* [1985] 1 All E.R. 493, [1985] C.L.Y. 1618 considered.

CHISHIMBA v KENSINGTON AND CHELSEA RLBC, [2013] EWCA Civ 786, [2014] P.T.S.R. 49, Richards, L.J., CA (Civ Div).

1535. Intentional homelessness–Reviews–Review decision missing error of law in original decision–Application of procedure under reg.8(2) Allocation of Housing and Homelessness (Review Procedures) Regulations 1999

[Housing Act 1996 (c.52) s.190(2), s.204(3), s.204; Allocation of Housing and Homelessness (Review Procedures) Regulations 1999 (SI 1999/71) reg.8(2).]

The appellant (F) appealed against a decision that the defendant local authority had been entitled on a homelessness review not to engage the procedure under the Allocation of Housing and Homelessness (Review Procedures) Regulations 1999 reg.8(2) where there had been an error of law in the original decision. The local authority had informed F that it considered her to be in priority need of housing but that she was intentionally homeless. The decision letter erroneously stated that the local authority's duty was limited to providing advice and assistance to find alternative accommodation, but in fact it had a duty under the Housing Act 1996 s.190(2) to secure interim accommodation. Nevertheless, the local authority provided F with interim accommodation. F sought a review, but did not draw attention to the failure to mention the duty to provide interim accommodation. The reviewer failed to notice the error. She confirmed the decision that F was intentionally homeless, and correctly set out the duty to provide interim accommodation. On appeal to the County Court under s.204, the judge held that, where F was being provided with interim accommodation, the reviewer's failure to notice the error had not been of sufficient importance to justify engaging the procedure under reg.8(2) that required a reviewer to give notice if "minded to" make a decision against the interests of an applicant where there was a deficiency or irregularity in the original decision. The local authority argued that reg.8(2) did not apply unless the reviewer considered that a deficiency or irregularity affected the fairness of the procedure.

Held: Appeal dismissed. (1) It was first necessary to consider whether the deficiency or irregularity relied on as a falling within reg.8(2) was one that related to a relevant decision, which was a decision adverse to the applicant and which she wished to challenge by way of review. If there was such a deficiency or irregularity, the reviewer was obliged to consider whether it was of sufficient importance to engage the duty to notify the applicant under reg.8(2). If the reviewer failed to do that, or decided that the deficiency or irregularity was of insufficient importance to engage that duty, then that failure or decision was only challengeable by way of appeal under s.204 on judicial review principles. In the instant case, the original decision was not a relevant decision for the purposes of reg.8(2) since it was not the subject of any complaint by F, it was not a decision that the reviewer upheld, and the reviewer did not make any decision on the same matter against F's interests, but had stated the local authority's duty correctly. Even if the reviewer had identified the deficiency, she would have been bound to conclude that there was no requirement to serve a "minded to" notice under reg.8(2), and there would have been no scope for challenging the review letter under s.204 (see paras 36-38 of judgment). (2) (Per Stephen Sedley L.J. concurring in the result for different reasons) Although the error in the original decision was irrelevant to the outcome, because F had been provided with interim accommodation in any event, the error was a deficiency because it went to the heart of the local authority's obligations and

F's entitlements. A statutory appeal contained principles of causation and the court was able, by reason of the power to make such order confirming, quashing or varying the decision as it thought fit under s.204(3), to give those principles practical effect, *Holmes-Moorhouse v Richmond upon Thames LBC* [2009] UKHL 7, [2009] 1 W.L.R. 413, [2009] C.L.Y. 1900 considered. The failure of the reviewer to identify and address the deficiency was, in the event, irrelevant to the review's outcome, since that outcome corresponded with the local authority's true statutory duties (paras 23, 26, 28-29).

IBRAHIM v WANDSWORTH LBC, [2013] EWCA Civ 20, [2013] P.T.S.R. 898, Mummery, L.J., CA (Civ Div).

1536. Local authority housing–Occupation–Possession sought under Sch.2 ground 16 Housing Act 1985–Alleged under-occupation of property–Whether genuine occupation by family members of successor to secure tenancy

[Housing Act 1985 (c.68) s.89, Sch.2.]

The appellant local authority appealed against the refusal of its application under the Housing Act 1985 Sch.2 ground 16 for possession of a property occupied by the respondent (T). T's mother had had a secure tenancy of the six-bedroom property until her death in March 2009. T applied to succeed to the tenancy under s.89 of the Act. She named four members of her family as living with her: her disabled brother, another brother (C) and his two children. The local authority considered the property to be under-occupied and sought possession in March 2010 on the basis that the property was "more extensive than [was] reasonably required by [T]". It alleged that C actually lived at another address with his partner and children. The court had to decide which family members were living at the premises and which of them T reasonably required to be accommodated. The judge found that four of the six bedrooms of the property were reasonably required to accommodate T and her family and that it was not under-occupied. The principal ground of appeal was that the judge was wrong to find that the reasonable requirement included two bedrooms for C and his children. Further grounds were that the manner in which the judge had requested and admitted evidence regarding C's alternative address was procedurally unfair, and that he had failed to give reasons for accepting some parts of C's evidence but not others, and for rejecting evidence contradicting C's claim to have lived at the property since 2007. The local authority contended that no reasonable court could have accepted C's account of having lived at the property since 2007 given the inconsistencies in the evidence to that effect.

Held: Appeal dismissed. (1) In his extempore judgment the judge had correctly identified the legal test to be whether there was genuine occupation of the property by C and his children at the date of the hearing. However, the judgment was not clearly structured; the reasons were not set out in an ordered manner and did not deal with the implications of his rejection of important parts of C's evidence in a way that was understandable without extensive recourse to the underlying documentary material and the transcript of the proceedings. It had, however, been open to the judge to reach the conclusion he did on the evidence before him in respect of the first ground. He acknowledged that there was evidence which undermined C's evidence that his occupation of the property commenced in 2007 and had continued since then, but there was no witness of fact with knowledge of the occupancy of the property who contradicted T's factual case. The judge's doubts regarding C's credibility and the documents which appeared to contradict his account led him to examine other documentary evidence, which supported C's assertion that he had "migrated" to the property after his marriage breakdown. It was apparent from the judge's overall conclusion that, despite the weaknesses in C's evidence, he accepted and preferred the key parts of it as putting him and his children in the property. The evidence about the alternative address was not obtained in a procedurally unfair way. There was no finding in the judgment to the effect that the local authority had not been given any proper opportunity to investigate the evidence, or that that property could not accommodate C, his former partner and their three children without difficulty. It was therefore difficult to see how that issue adversely affected the local authority. It was clearly desirable for judges to give reasons. However, it was also clearly established that there was no duty on a judge to deal with every submission presented by counsel, *Eagil Trust Co v Pigott-Brown* [1985] 3 All E.R. 119, [1985] C.L.Y. 2728 applied. What was important was for the parties to know why one had lost and the other had won. *English v Emery Reimbold & Strick Ltd* [2002] EWCA Civ 605, [2002] 1 W.L.R. 2409, [2002] C.L.Y. 301 considered. After an examination of the material before the judge, it was apparent that the local authority had lost because, notwithstanding his reservations, the judge preferred the documentary evidence putting C in the property with his children at the material time (see paras 29-37 of judgment). (2) The approved transcript of the judgment contained a number of passages marked "inaudible". The judge had stated that counsel should be able to deal with at least some of those passages from their notes. They had done their best but there remained passages marked "inaudible" and "no note". In most cases, a judge would have sufficient notes from the hearing to resolve gaps in a transcript without leaving the matter to counsel. A judge could also refresh his memory by asking for the case papers to be returned to him to approve the transcript. Counsel's note of a judgment was generally only used in the instant court where there was no official recording. It was important to keep in mind that a defective transcript could lead to a party not being able to establish their case on appeal. For that reason, judges should assist the appeal process by completing gaps in transcripts themselves so far as reasonably possible (para.12).

BRENT LBC v TUDOR, [2013] EWCA Civ 157, [2013] H.L.R. 20, Arden, L.J., CA (Civ Div).

1537. Localism Act 2011 (c.20)–Commencement No.2 and Transitional Provisions Order

THE LOCALISM ACT 2011 (COMMENCEMENT NO.2 AND TRANSITIONAL PROVISIONS) ORDER 2013, SI 2013/SI 2013/722 (C.33); made under the Localism Act 2011 s.240. Commencement details: bringing into force various provisions of the 2011 Act on April 1, 2013.; .

This Order brings into force, in relation to England provisions of the Localism Act 2011 (matters relating to the housing ombudsman).

1538. Mobile homes–Traveller sites–Travellers–Wales

THE MOBILE HOMES ACT 1983 (AMENDMENT OF SCHEDULE 1 AND CONSEQUENTIAL AMENDMENTS) (WALES) ORDER 2013, SI 2013/SI 2013/1723 (W.167); made under the Mobile Homes Act 1983 s.2A; and the Housing Act 2004 s.229, s.250. In force: July 10, 2013; .

This Order is made amends the Mobile Homes Act 1983 Sch.1 and makes a number of consequential amendments. The implied terms for permanent pitches provided by virtue of the Order are similar to those for occupiers of mobile homes on park home sites. One of the main differences are the provisions relating to assignment. Occupiers of permanent pitches on local authority Gypsy and Traveller sites may, with the agreement of the local authority, assign their agreement to a member of their family or exchange their agreement with another occupier.

1539. Mobile Homes Act 2013 (C.14)

This Act amends the law relating to mobile homes.

This Act received Royal Assent on March 26, 2013.

1540. Suitable alternative accommodation–Possession orders–Sole occupier of three-bedroom council house–Relevant factors in assessment of reasonableness of moving to one-bedroom property–Appropriateness of possession order being conditional upon offer of suitable alternative accommodation

[Housing Act 1985 (c.68) s.84(2), s.84(2)(b), Sch.2 Pt IV.]

The appellant tenant (H) appealed against an order requiring her to deliver possession of her home to the respondent local authority. H, aged 59, had lived in the property with her parents all her life. It was a three-bedroom detached house with front and rear gardens. Her father died in 1977 and her mother in 2010. For the last 20 years of her mother's life, she had suffered debilitating illness, and H had been her sole, round-the-clock, carer. In 2011, the local authority determined that H was an "under-occupier" and asked her to apply for a one-bedroom property. It helped her to complete an application form and allocated her a high level of priority because of huge demand on its small stock of three-bedroom houses. H viewed several properties, but refused to bid for them because of her deep attachment to her home. In determining the possession proceedings, the recorder found that the support given by H to her mother was a very significant factor, but that H's attachment was borne of familiarity rather than of specific engagement with neighbours or the local community, and that a move would not prejudice her health. She accepted that H would be profoundly upset to leave, but that the needs of others outweighed her personal circumstances, and that the balance lay in favour of her vacating the property. She made the possession order conditional upon an offer of suitable alternative accommodation being made. She specified the essential characteristics that the alternative accommodation should include. H submitted that (1) the shortfall in availability of local authority housing should not be the decisive consideration in the assessment of reasonableness, and the recorder had not given sufficient weight to the support given by H to her mother; (2) the recorder had failed to satisfy herself, as required by the Housing Act 1985 s.84(2) that the alternative accommodation would be suitable and available when the order took effect.

Held: Appeal dismissed. (1) The recorder had considered, carefully and in detail, the effect that a move would have on H. She had taken account of the length of time H had lived in the house, and its lifetime of belongings and memories; she accepted that H had been her mother's sole carer for many years without respite. She had properly recognised those as highly material factors and had addressed the real risk that H might not settle elsewhere. However, she had also found that H was reasonably fit and able to cycle, that it was two years since her mother's death and she should no longer feel constrained to remain at the property, and that she had had no substantive objection to other properties. It would be wrong to treat H's circumstances as imposing a fetter on the assessment of reasonableness. The pressure on local authority housing stock was a powerful, but not overriding, consideration. Also, reasonableness had to be decided on a case-by-case basis and it was not appropriate to draw comparisons with the conclusions in other cases (see paras 37-45 of judgment). (2) The Act did not require that an offer of accommodation had to be made before the date of the hearing of the application for possession; the words of s.84(2) expressly contemplated that it might not be, *Wandsworth LBC v Randall* [2007] EWCA Civ 1126, [2008] 1 W.L.R. 359, [2008] C.L.Y. 2478 followed. Nor did the Act specify that reasonable suitability had to be fulfilled by reference to a particular property. If the court was satisfied that accommodation having particular characteristics would be reasonably suitable to meet a tenant's needs, and that such accommodation would become available, it had jurisdiction to make a possession order which would not take effect until the accommodation had, in fact, become available. A local authority could not be expected to hold properties vacant pending the hearing of a possession claim where it was confident that other suitable properties would become available within a reasonable time (paras 51-57). (3) It would not always be appropriate for the court to make possession conditional on an offer of suitable alternative accommodation being made. Where a conditional order was made, it should include liberty to apply; it was important that the court retained the power to scrutinise the suitability of any particular property and to vary its orders at any time, *Manchester City Council v Finn* [2002] EWCA Civ 1998, [2003] H.L.R. 41, [2003] C.L.Y. 2769 applied. A conditional order should also include a time limit for suitable alternative accommodation to be made available, and a provision that the order would lapse if the time limit was exceeded. If tenants were particularly vulnerable, a direction that a warrant of possession should not be issued without the court's permission might also be desirable (paras 58-61).

HOLT v READING BC; *sub nom.* READING BC v HOLT, [2013] EWCA Civ 641, [2013] H.L.R. 40, Arden, L.J., CA (Civ Div).

1541. Unintentional homelessness–Local housing authorities' powers and duties–Offer of permanent accommodation withdrawn where property found to be unsuitable on review–Legitimacy of replacing offer of permanent accommodation with offer of temporary accommodation

[Housing Act 1996 (c.52) Pt VII, s.193, s.204; Allocation of Housing and Homelessness (Review Procedures) Regulations 1999 (SI 1999/71) reg.8(2).]

The appellant (O) who had lodged an appeal under the Housing Act 1996 s.204 against a review decision of the respondent local housing authority, appealed against the dismissal of that appeal. It was common ground that the local authority had a duty under s.193 of the Act to secure accommodation for O. In May 2004, it offered her permanent accommodation, but later agreed that the property was not suitable and withdrew the offer. It accepted that she needed a property in the Lee Green area. However the same property was re-offered to her as permanent accommodation three more times in 2006 and 2007 before the offer was withdrawn. The local authority said it would make her "one management offer" of permanent accommodation after six months. A year later, towards the end of 2008, it offered permanent accommodation at a different location. O did not reply. The local authority therefore purported to end its s.193 duty. By that time, O had lodged a formal complaint, asserting that she had been assured that after about two years, she would receive an offer of permanent accommodation in the Lee Green area. An independent adjudicator rejected that complaint. In December 2009, the local authority reviewed its offer relating to the second property. After hearing O's representations, it decided that the second property was unsuitable and that O should be nominated for accommodation in Lee Green. However, the local authority no longer had property there. In April 2011, it made a final offer of permanent accommodation in a third property elsewhere, which O rejected. In June 2011, it made an offer of temporary accommodation in a fourth property. O believed she was entitled to an offer of permanent accommodation, but the offer was upheld on review. The reviewing officer said that if O had accepted the offer on the fourth property, it might subsequently have become permanent. County court proceedings concluded in the local authority's favour, the judge finding that O had had no legitimate expectation of an offer of permanent accommodation and that there had been no unfairness. O submitted that (1) the local authority's allocation policy document stated under the heading "Offer Guarantees" that if an offer of accommodation was accepted as not meeting the applicant's accepted requirements, "the offer will be withdrawn and another one made when a suitable property becomes available" and that there was a legitimate expectation that such an offer would be a permanent one; (2) the local authority was in breach of the Allocation of Housing and Homelessness (Review Procedures) Regulations 1999 reg.8(2) which rendered the review process unfair and unlawful; (3) it was unfair of the reviewing officer to have told her only after she had rejected the offer of temporary accommodation in the fourth property that it might have been offered to her on a permanent basis if she had accepted.

Held: Appeal dismissed. (1) The local authority's statutory allocation scheme committed the local authority, at best, to the making of a further offer in circumstances where an offer of permanent accommodation had been withdrawn as unsuitable. There was nothing to indicate that once an offer of permanent accommodation had been made, no offers of temporary housing would or could be made. There was also nothing to suggest that the local authority's position under Part VII of the Act had been restricted by what had happened; at no stage after 2009 had it in any way represented that a permanent dwelling would be offered within a set timeframe, or that it was giving up its right to offer alternative temporary accommodation in discharge of its statutory obligations to O. She might have misunderstood her entitlement, but that misunderstanding had not been caused or encouraged by the local authority (see paras 27-32 of judgment). (2) A pre-condition of the obligation to notify under reg.8(2) was that the reviewer considered that there was a deficiency or irregularity in the original decision. The original decision in the instant case was the decision to offer the fourth property as temporary accommodation. There was no evidence, either that the reviewer considered there to be such a deficiency or irregularity, or that there actually was one. Therefore, the reg.8(2) obligation had never arisen (paras 33-35). (3) It might have been kind to inform O of the possibility of the fourth property becoming permanently available, but the local authority had not been under any obligation, statutory or otherwise, to do so and had therefore not acted unfairly (paras 37-38).

OBIORAH v LEWISHAM LBC, [2013] EWCA Civ 325, [2013] H.L.R. 35, Kitchin, L.J., CA (Civ Div).

1542. Unintentional homelessness–Priority needs–Assessment of whether applicant vulnerable under s.189(1)(c) Housing Act 1996–Relevance of availability of personal support

[Housing Act 1996 (c.52) s.189(1)(c).]

The appellant (H) appealed against a decision that he was not in priority need within the meaning of the Housing Act 1996 s.189(1)(c). H was a 23-year-old foreign national who had leave to remain in the United Kingdom until 2016. While in the UK he had been living with his brother (E). In 2011 they became homeless and applied to the local authority for accommodation. The application was made in H's name, E not at that time having leave to remain. It was common ground that H had learning difficulties, suffered from depression and post-traumatic stress disorder, and relied on E for daily personal support. It was also common ground that, but for E's support, H would probably be treated as "vulnerable" for the purposes of determining whether he was in priority need under s.189(1)(c). The local authority decided that although H was eligible for assistance and was unintentionally homeless, he was not in priority need. It found that he was not "vulnerable" within the meaning of s.189(1)(c): because he received, and would continue to receive, assistance from E, he would not suffer injury or detriment or be less able to fend for himself than would an ordinary street-homeless person. The county court upheld the local authority's decision and dismissed H's appeal. The issue for the instant court was whether a local authority, when assessing whether an applicant was in priority need by reason of vulnerability, was entitled to have regard to assistance he had been receiving, and would continue to receive, from the family member with whom he was currently living, were they to become homeless.

Held: Appeal dismissed. The question to be considered under s.189(1)(c) was whether the applicant would suffer greater harm from homelessness than would an ordinary homeless person, *R. v Camden LBC, Ex p. Pereira* (1999) 31 H.L.R. 317, [1999] C.L.Y. 3062 followed. That was a matter of judgement. The circumstances of the instant case were unusual: H was young and physically fit, and at a disadvantage only to the extent that he needed regular reminders to fulfil the requirements of his daily living. E was committed to providing the support necessary to ensure that he would not come to harm or suffer disadvantage by reason of homelessness. Hitherto, the courts had not unequivocally addressed the question of whether all an applicant's circumstances, including any assistance available to him, could be considered when evaluating his vulnerability. In *Osmani v Camden LBC* [2004] EWCA Civ 1706, [2005] H.L.R. 22, [2005] C.L.Y. 1989, the court had treated the existence of support systems maintaining the applicant's capacity to function normally as material to the application of the *Pereira* test. The applicant in Osmani was supported by his wife and would continue to receive that support were he to become homeless, and the court clearly regarded that as material to whether he could fend for himself when homeless. It regarded as axiomatic the proposition that support was relevant to whether the applicant would, whether, by reason of his mental disorder, be less able to fend for himself than would homeless person without his disorder, so that injury or detriment would result, *Osmani* considered. While the Homelessness Code of Guidance 2006 could not assist in interpreting s.189(1)(c), its repeated references to the need to consider all the circumstances of an applicant who might be vulnerable accorded with common sense. Moreover, wording of s.189(1)(c) imported a requirement of cause and effect between the qualifying condition and the vulnerability. The assessment process was fact-sensitive and practical, and involved a judgement as to the harm or detriment that might befall the applicant once he became homeless. All and any of the applicant's personal circumstances might be relevant to the statutory assessment. If the evidence was that by reason of the support willingly given by the family member, the applicant would be no less able to fend for himself than would a man without a qualifying disability, he would not have demonstrated vulnerability "as a result of mental...handicap...or other special reason". The local authority was not required to make an assessment of vulnerability in isolation from the applicant's known personal circumstances, whether they served to emphasise his vulnerability or to demonstrate that, despite the existence of a qualifying reason, he was not vulnerable. The weight to be given to the evidence was, however, a separate and important consideration. The local authority had to assess the applicant's vulnerability as it would be when he became homeless. The effect of support in his existing home was unlikely to be the same as that of similar support when he was homeless. Even if the local authority was satisfied that the support would remain in place, it might not be sufficient to enable the applicant to fend for himself to the same degree as the average homeless person. A fair evaluation of all the evidence was critical to the sustainability of the decision. In the instant case, however, H had not sought to argue that local authority had not had material upon which it could base its conclusion that E's continuing support was decisive. The judge made no error of law (see paras 33-44 of judgment).

HOTAK v SOUTHWARK LBC, [2013] EWCA Civ 515, [2013] P.T.S.R. 1338, Moore-Bick, L.J., CA (Civ Div).

HUMAN RIGHTS

1543. Duty to undertake effective investigation–Forced labour–Lack of specific offence of domestic servitude–Adequacy of investigations

[Asylum and Immigration (Treatment of Claimants, etc.) Act 2004 (c.19) s.4; European Convention on Human Rights 1950 Art.4.]

The complainant (C) complained that the respondent state had breached its obligation under the European Convention on Human Rights 1950 art.4 to have in place criminal laws penalising forced labour and servitude. C had travelled from Uganda to the United Kingdom on a false passport, aided by a relative (S), who warned her not to speak to anyone and told her that she might easily come to harm. C claimed that she had been forced to work as a carer and security guard in circumstances where she was on-call 24 hours a day with only a couple of hours' leave once a month. Her wages were paid to S and not passed on to her. After approximately four years, C went to the police but collapsed and was taken to hospital, where she was diagnosed as HIV-positive and suffering from psychosis. C applied for asylum, claiming that she had fled Uganda to escape sexual and physical abuse. Her application was unsuccessful and her appeal dismissed. Following an investigation, it was concluded that there was no evidence that C had been trafficked to the UK. C was assessed by a project providing housing and support for victims of trafficking, which concluded that she had been subjected to five of the six recognised indicators of forced labour. The police conducted further investigations but again concluded that the evidence did not support exploitation of any kind, and that there was no offence in English law to cover the facts of the case. C was informed that the circumstances of her case did not constitute an offence of trafficking people for the purposes of exploitation contrary to the Asylum and Immigration (Treatment of Claimants, etc.) Act 2004, and no other applicable offence of forced labour or servitude existed. C contended that the UK government was under a positive obligation to enact domestic law provisions specifically criminalising the conduct prohibited by art.4 of the Convention, and had failed to do so. The UK government contended that the reason no action was taken following investigation of C's complaints was not the absence of appropriate legislation but the absence of evidence supporting the credibility of her account.

Held: Complaint upheld. (1) Article 4 of the Convention entailed a specific positive obligation on Member States to penalise and prosecute effectively any act aimed at maintaining a person in a situation of slavery, servitude or forced or compulsory labour, *Siliadin v France (73316/01)* (2006) 43 E.H.R.R. 16 considered. Article 4 might require a state to take operational measures to protect victims or potential victims of treatment in breach of that article if the state authorities were aware, or ought to have been aware, that an identified individual had been or was at real and immediate risk of being subject to such treatment, *Rantsev v Cyprus (25965/04)* (2010) 51 E.H.R.R. 1 and *Osman v United Kingdom (23452/94)* [1999] 1 F.L.R. 193, [1998] C.L.Y. 3102 applied. Article 4 also entailed a procedural obligation on the authorities to investigate where there was a credible suspicion that an individual's rights under that article had been violated. In the instant case, the fact that the domestic authorities conducted an investigation into C's complaints strongly indicated that, at least on their face, they were not inherently implausible. Consequently, those complaints gave rise to a credible suspicion that C had been held in conditions of domestic servitude. That placed the domestic authorities under an obligation to investigate her complaints. In view of the Court's findings in *Siliadin*, the facts of which were very similar to the instant case, it had to be found that the criminal law in force in the UK at the relevant time was inadequate to afford practical and effective protection against treatment falling within the scope of art.4 of the Convention. Consequently, there had been a breach of that provision (see paras 66-69, 72, 76-77 of judgment). (2) The investigation had focused mainly on the offence of trafficking for exploitation as set out in s.4 of the 2004 Act and had referred only occasionally to slavery, forced labour and domestic servitude. However, domestic servitude was distinct from trafficking and exploitation; a thorough investigation into complaints of such conduct required an understanding of the many subtle ways an individual could fall under the control of another. Due to the absence of a specific offence of domestic servitude, the domestic authorities were unable to give due weight to those factors. In particular, it was a matter of concern that no attempt appeared to have been made to interview S, despite the gravity of the offence he was alleged to have committed. Consequently, the investigation into C's complaint of domestic servitude was ineffective due to the absence of specific legislation criminalising such treatment (paras 80-81).

CN v UNITED KINGDOM (4239/08) (2013) 56 E.H.R.R. 24, Judge Garlicki (President), ECHR.

1544. Freedom of assembly and association–Freedom of expression–Restrictions on erecting and using tents in Parliament Square in s.143 and s.145 Police Reform and Social Responsibility Act 2011–Compatibility with art.6, art.10 and art.11 European Convention on Human Rights 1950

[Police Reform and Social Responsibility Act 2011 (c.13) s.143, s.145; European Convention on Human Rights 1950 Art.6, Art.10, Art.11.]

The appellant (G) appealed against a decision ([2012] EWHC 1123 (Admin), [2012] 4 All E.R. 401) that the Police Reform and Social Responsibility Act 2011 s.143 and s.145 were compatible with the European Convention on Human Rights 1950. G was a campaigner who had been camping in Parliament Square, London in pursuance of a round-the clock protest until she was given a direction to move on under s.143 of the Act. That section conferred powers on the police and authorised officers of the local authority to stop protesters erecting and keeping tents in Parliament Square. G submitted that s.143 and s.145 of the 2011 Act were incompatible with art.6, art.10, and art.11 of the Convention because (1) s.143 did not contain any element of discretion; (2) s.143 interfered with the exercise of art.10 and art.11 rights where the use of a tent was essential to the protest; (3) the interference was not prescribed by law because the circumstances in which it was unlawful to use a tent were not sufficiently clear; (4) the sections did not pursue a legitimate aim; (5) even if they did, they amounted to a blanket ban on tents and were not proportionate; (6) in any event, they did not satisfy the state's positive obligation to facilitate the exercise of art.10 and art.11 rights; (7) there was no access to courts as required by art.6.

Held: Appeal dismissed. (1) Section 143(1) conferred a power, but not a duty, to make a direction. *Padfield v Minister of Agriculture, Fisheries and Food* [1968] A.C. 997, [1968] C.L.Y. 1667 did not support G's arguments that "may" in s.143(1) meant "shall", and that s.143(1) conferred no discretion. Rather, it supported the proposition that there was a discretion which had to be exercised so as to promote the policy and objectives of the Act, *Padfield* explained. The aim of the Act was to stop the use of tents in Parliament Square, but Parliament intended that it might be appropriate in certain circumstances for the power not to be exercised. The nature and extent of the discretion was not spelled out, but since the aim of the legislation was clear, Parliament must have intended that the discretion was only to be exercised in exceptional circumstances. While it was not possible to define "exceptional circumstances", it would be wholly wrong for there to be any weighing of the importance or validity of the protest in deciding whether circumstances were exceptional (see paras 18-23 of judgment). (2) Section 143 and s.145 were capable of interfering with the art.10 and art.11 rights, even though the general right to protest in Parliament Square would remain substantially unimpaired by a direction to remove a tent. There could be interference where the manner of the protest (the use of a tent) was part and parcel of the protest. The supposed distinction between the essence of a protest and the manner of its exercise had to be treated with considerable care. Depending on the facts, the manner of a protest might constitute its actual nature and message *Tabernacle v Secretary of State for Defence* [2009] EWCA Civ 23, Times, February 25, 2009, [2009] C.L.Y. 1941 followed. For some protesters, the ability to maintain a round-the-clock presence in Parliament Square was essential to the nature of the protest. However, in considering compatibility, the limited nature of the interference was not to be overlooked (paras 24-27). (3) Section 143 and s.145 were prescribed by law. It could not be said that protesters were unable to discern the boundaries of legality, *De Freitas v Permanent Secretary of Ministry of Agriculture, Fisheries, Lands and Housing* [1999] 1 A.C. 69, [1998] C.L.Y. 3084 considered. While the erection of a tent in Parliament Square was not unlawful, a refusal to comply with a removal direction without reasonable excuse was. The giving of the direction introduced the necessary certainty into the statutory scheme. The aim of the Act was to ban long-term camping in Parliament Square, and so protesters knew that the power to require removal would normally be exercised (paras 28-30). (4) Section 143 and s.145 conferred powers for the protection of the rights and freedoms of others, aiming to preserve the amenity and availability of the square, to prevent crime and to prevent risks to health and safety arising from encampments. Those were legitimate aims which went much further than protecting aesthetic values (para.31). (5) Section 143 and s.145 did not amount to a blanket ban on tents. Even if they did, they were not disproportionate. Member States were allowed a margin of appreciation, and considerable weight would be given to the fact that Parliament had conducted the proportionality balancing exercise before concluding in favour of a blanket ban, *Hirst v United Kingdom (74025/01)* (2006) 42 E.H.R.R. 41, [2006] C.L.Y. 2150 distinguished and *TV Vest AS v Norway (21132/05)* (2009) 48 E.H.R.R. 51, [2009] C.L.Y. 1940 considered. The nature and extent of the blanket ban was relevant; each case turned on its own facts and a line had to be drawn somewhere (paras 40-47). (6) There was no positive obligation on the state to take further steps to preserve G's art.10 and art.11 rights (paras 48-50). (7) A removal direction was not a determination of civil rights for the purposes of art.6. A protester could issue proceedings to restrain the making of a direction, or could refuse to comply and raise a defence under s.143(8). Both courses amounted to effective access to a court, *R. (on the application of Wright) v Secretary of State for Health* [2009] UKHL 3, [2009] 1 A.C. 739, [2009] C.L.Y. 3682 distinguished (paras 54-59).

R. (ON THE APPLICATION OF GALLASTEGUI) v WESTMINSTER CITY COUNCIL, [2013] EWCA Civ 28, [2013] 1 W.L.R. 2377, Lord Dyson (M.R.), CA (Civ Div).

1545. Freedom of association–Positive obligations–Obligation to protect employees from dismissal on grounds of political opinion or affiliation–Protection to be extended to employees with less than one year's service

[Employment Rights Act 1996 (c.18); European Convention on Human Rights 1950 Art.11.]

The complainant (R) complained that the respondent state had breached his right to freedom of assembly and association enshrined in the European Convention on Human Rights 1950 art.11. R, who was white British, complained that he had been dismissed from his employment because of his affiliation with the British National Party, a political party which extended membership only to white nationals and was opposed to integration between British and "non-European" peoples. R had worked as a driver. His employer (E), a private company, provided transport services for a local authority. R's passengers were children and adults with physical and mental disabilities, and the majority were of Asian origin. There had been no complaints about R's work or his conduct, and he had been nominated for a "first-class employee" award. He was summarily dismissed following his election as a local councillor for the BNP because, E claimed, his continued employment could cause anxiety among his passengers and their carers, jeopardise its reputation, and possibly lead to the loss of its contract with the local authority. Lacking the necessary length of service to bring a complaint of unfair dismissal under the Employment Rights Act 1996, R claimed race discrimination. The Court of Appeal dismissed his claim, finding that it amounted to a claim of discrimination on political grounds, which fell outside domestic anti-discrimination laws. R submitted that the state had a positive obligation under art.11 to enact legislation affording him protection from dismissal on the ground of his involvement with the BNP, regardless of the length of his employment.

Held: Complaint upheld. (Judges Bratza, Hirvela and Nicolaou dissenting in part) Although art.11 aimed to protect individuals against arbitrary interference by public authorities, the state could, in certain circumstances, be obliged to intervene in relationships between private individuals by taking reasonable and appropriate measures to secure the effective enjoyment of art.11 rights. It had a positive obligation either to provide protection against dismissals motivated solely by the employee's membership of a particular political party, or to at least to provide the means whereby the proportionality of such dismissals could be independently evaluated. Employers could lawfully restrict employees' art.11 rights in certain circumstances, for example where necessary to protect the rights of others or to maintain the political neutrality of civil servants. Given the BNP's policies, E might have found itself in a difficult position when R's candidature became public knowledge. Even without specific complaints from service users, R's membership of the BNP could have affected E's contract with the local authority, especially as the majority of its service users were vulnerable persons of Asian origin. However, although R had an exemplary work record, he had been summarily dismissed without any apparent consideration being given to the possibility of transferring him to a non-customer facing role, *Stedman v United Kingdom (Admissibility) (29107/95)* (1997) 23 E.H.R.R. CD168 considered. Moreover, given his age, he was likely to have considerable difficulty finding alternative employment. The consequences of his dismissal were serious and capable of striking at the very substance of his art.11 rights. The court had to determine whether a fair balance had been struck between his art.11 rights and the risks posed by his continued employment. Contracting states could not guarantee the effective enjoyment of art.11 rights absolutely and had a wide margin of appreciation where sensitive social and political issues were involved. A claim for unfair dismissal under the 1996 Act was an appropriate domestic remedy for a person dismissed on account of his political beliefs or affiliations. However, R could not avail himself of that remedy, and the race discrimination legislation did not offer him any protection. He had clearly suffered a detriment as a consequence of the one-year qualifying period under the 1996 Act, as it deprived him of the only means by which he could effectively challenge his dismissal at the domestic level. Given the margin of appreciation afforded to contracting states in formulating and implementing social and economic policies, it was reasonable for the state to bolster the domestic labour market by preventing employees from bringing unfair dismissal claims until they had been employed for one year. However, while employees dismissed on certain prohibited grounds, such as race, sex and religion, were exempted from the one-year qualifying period, no protection was afforded to those dismissed on account of their political opinion or affiliation. Political parties were essential to the proper functioning of democracy and, in the absence of judicial safeguards, a legal system that allowed dismissal from employment solely on account of membership of a political party carried with it the potential for abuse. Article 11 applied not only to those whose views were inoffensive, but also those whose views offended, shocked or disturbed. What was decisive was that the domestic courts should be allowed to pronounce on whether the employer's interests should prevail over the art.11 rights asserted by the employee, regardless of the length of the employee's period of employment. Consequently, it was incumbent on the state to take reasonable and appropriate measures to protect employees, including those with less than one year's service, from dismissal on grounds of political opinion or affiliation, either through the creation of an exception to the one-year qualifying period or through a free-standing claim for unlawful discrimination on grounds of political opinion or affiliation. As the United Kingdom legislation was deficient in that respect, there had been a violation of art.11 (see paras 32, 42-57 of judgment).

REDFEARN v UNITED KINGDOM (47335/06) [2013] 3 Costs L.O. 402, Judge Garlicki (President), ECHR.

1546. Freedom of expression–Advertisements–Transport for London refusing to carry advertisement–Restrictions in advertising policy–Whether refusal justified and proportionate

[Equality Act 2010 (c.15) s.149; European Convention on Human Rights 1950 Art.8, Art.10, Art.10(2), Art.14.]

The claimant (C) applied for judicial review of a decision made by the defendant (T) not to allow an advertisement placed on behalf of C to appear on the outside of T's buses. T had an advertising policy under which it would not approve advertisements likely to cause widespread or serious offence to members of the public, or which related to matters of public controversy and sensitivity. As a public body, T had also to exercise its powers in accordance with the public sector equality duty in the Equality Act 2010 s.149. C's advertisement was designed and intended as a response to an earlier advertisement which had appeared on the outside of T's buses, placed by a campaigning organisation which sought to promote equality and justice for lesbians, gay men, bisexual and transgender individuals. T's advertising was managed by external contractors which entered into arrangements with bus operators. T had previously permitted controversial and potentially offensive advertisements on its transport system. C's advertisement was submitted to the advertising contractor which cleared it with the Committee of Advertising Practice. The contractor then informed T of the intention to run the advertisement. Later that day T decided that the advertisement should not run on London's buses. T did not consult C before that decision was taken. T contended that the advertisement was likely to cause offence and related to matters of public controversy or sensitivity under its advertising policy. C submitted that T had abused its powers for an improper purpose, that its decision-making process demonstrated procedural unfairness and a lack of proper consideration of relevant issues, and that its decision was contrary to C's rights under the European Convention on Human Rights 1950 art.10.

Held: Application refused. (1) T acted in its own interests to avoid causing offence to a section of the public and to avoid criticism and controversy. Its interests coincided with those of the Mayor of London, who also wished to avoid causing offence and avoid criticism which might damage his election campaign. The overlap in interests did not render the decision unlawful (see para.58 of judgment). (2) T's decision-making process was procedurally unfair, in breach of its own procedures, and demonstrated a failure to consider the relevant issues. The decision was taken too quickly without analysis of its own policy and its past practice. It did not consider a possible breach of C's human rights. It did not notify C or give reasons for its decision as soon as reasonably practicable. However, the legality of the decision was not challenged on free-standing procedural grounds (paras 59-67). (3) Article 10 was engaged in the instant case, *R. (on the application of ProLife Alliance) v BBC* [2003] UKHL 23, [2004] 1 A.C. 185, [2003] C.L.Y. 2934 distinguished (paras 72-82). T's advertising policy met the requirement of legal certainty and was prescribed by law for the purposes of art.10(2) (paras 83-89). The application of the policy pursued a legitimate aim, namely to protect the rights of those who might be affected by the promotion of an anti-gay message (paras 90-91). The restrictions in T's policy on advertisements likely to cause widespread or serious offence or which related to matters of public controversy or sensitivity were necessary in order to meet the legitimate aims under art.10(2). In reaching that conclusion, the court accorded due weight to the judgment of T, as an experienced operator in the field (para.128). Advertisements on the side of London buses were highly intrusive (para.129). T had applied its policy in a partial and inconsistent manner, but the advertisement would cause serious offence to a significant section of the large number of people who would view it; for those who were gay, it was liable to interfere with the right to respect for their private and family life under art.8 (paras 137-138). The advertisement was a confrontational assertion, not a reasoned, informed contribution to a debate. It was liable to encourage homophobic views. T would be acting in breach of its public sector equality duty if it allowed the advertisement to appear on its buses (paras 142, 144). T's refusal to display the advertisement was justified and proportionate, in furtherance of the legitimate aim of protecting the rights of others. Therefore it was not in breach of art.10 (para.148). (4) There was no breach of art.14 and C was not protected under the 2010 Act (paras 19-158). (5) Article 9 was not engaged (paras 159-166). (6) T's decision was not irrational (para.172).

R. (ON THE APPLICATION OF CORE ISSUES TRUST) v TRANSPORT FOR LONDON; *sub nom.* CORE ISSUES TRUST v TRANSPORT FOR LONDON, [2013] EWHC 651 (Admin), [2013] P.T.S.R. 1161, Lang, J., QBD (Admin).

1547. Freedom of information–Requests for information–Information sought on NHS trusts' compromise agreements with doctors–Existence of gagging clauses

[Data Protection Act 1998 (c.29) Sch.2; Employment Rights Act 1996 (c.18) s.43J; Freedom of Information Act 2000 (c.36) s.40; Public Interest Disclosure Act 1998 (c.23).]

The appellant (B) appealed against decisions of the first respondent commissioner (C) to uphold the refusals of the respondent NHS trusts (T) to supply him with information or to confirm or deny that they held the information. He had asked for copies of all the compromise agreements T had entered into with doctors over the past 10 years and the reasons why they had entered into those agreements. B believed that the agreements contained gagging clauses preventing individuals from raising concerns they might have about patient safety. T refused, relying principally on the Freedom of Information Act 2000 s.40. C found that personal data was involved and that compromise agreements would constitute such data of the employee to whom the agreement might relate. He also found that any relevant data subjects would have had a reasonable expectation of privacy and would not expect T to confirm or deny the information was held. He went on to say that although the public had a legitimate interest in knowing whether T had entered into any agreement, confirming or denying whether the requested information was held would breach the first data protection principle under the Data Protection Act 1998 Sch.2 and therefore any response provided would have contravened the fairness element within that first principle.

Held: Appeal dismissed. (1) It was not uncommon in compromise agreements for there to be a confidentiality clause to the effect that the parties agreed that the details of the agreement in the circumstances leading to a termination of employment would remain confidential. That would weigh in the balance when considering to what extent, if any, an individual would have a reasonable expectation of privacy. Furthermore, as there were likely to be only a few instances of compromise agreements against the backdrop of T's total workforce, there was always the chance that other members of staff would be able to identify the individual or the individuals involved should even limited disclosure of the information sought be made. In cases where very few compromise agreements had been entered into, then even the revelation of that mere fact might be enough for someone with sufficient relevant knowledge to be able to speculate with some degree of assurance about the identity of the individuals concerned. Therefore, even redaction of an individual's name might in certain circumstances cause there to be such a risk. Once an identity was known or at least speculated upon, then there could be unsolicited approaches from the media and others who could have an interest in ascertaining the recent circumstances behind a particular agreement or set of agreements that had been entered into and the circumstances leading to such agreements. Accordingly, C's position was to be endorsed (see paras 28-29, 73 of judgment). (2) The First-tier Tribunal had no jurisdiction to decide whether any of the provisions in any compromise agreement that might be entered into by any NHS trust was or could be void under the Employment Rights Act 1996 s.43J, as inserted by the Public Interest Disclosure Act 1998 (para.23).

BOUSFIELD v INFORMATION COMMISSIONER (2012) 128 B.M.L.R. 184, Judge David Marks Q.C., FTT (GRC).

1548. Freedom to manifest one's religious belief–Employees' rights–Lawfulness of action taken against employees seeking to exercise religious beliefs

[European Convention on Human Rights 1950 Art.9, Art.14.]

The complainants (E, C, L and M) complained that the domestic law of the United Kingdom failed adequately to protect their right to manifest their religion. E, C and M invoked the European Convention on Human Rights 1950 art.9 in conjunction with art.14, while L complained under art.14 taken in conjunction with art.9. E had been employed by British Airways, a private company. She wanted to wear a cross as a sign of her commitment to the Christian faith. Between September 2006 and February 2007, she was not allowed to remain in her post while visibly wearing the cross. C was a Christian who had worn a cross since 1971. She had been employed as a nurse by an NHS trust. Her employer's uniform policy prohibited the wearing of necklaces "to reduce the risk of injury when handling patients". When C refused to remove the cross and chain she was wearing, she was moved to a non-nursing post which shortly thereafter ceased to exist. L had been employed by a local authority as a registrar of births, deaths and marriages. She was a Christian and believed that same-sex civil partnerships were contrary to God's law. She refused to be designated as a registrar of civil partnerships, which resulted in disciplinary proceedings and the loss of her job. M, a Christian, had been employed by Relate, a private company with a policy of requiring employees to provide services equally to heterosexual and homosexual couples. M had refused to commit himself to providing psycho-sexual counselling to same-sex couples, which resulted in disciplinary proceedings being brought against him.

Held: Complaints upheld in part. (1) In E's case, the necessary fair balance had not been struck. On one side of the scales was her desire to manifest her religious belief. On the other was the employer's wish to project a certain corporate image. While that aim was undoubtedly legitimate, the domestic courts had accorded it too much weight. E's cross was discreet and could not have detracted from her professional appearance, and there was no evidence that the wearing of other, previously authorised, items of religious clothing by other employees had had any negative impact on British Airways' brand or image. The domestic authorities had failed sufficiently to protect E's right to manifest her religion, in breach of the positive obligation under art.9 (see paras 94-95 of judgment). (2) In C's case, the reason for asking her to remove her cross, namely the protection of health and safety on a hospital ward, was inherently of a greater magnitude than that which applied in respect of E. Moreover, this was a field where the domestic authorities had to be allowed a wide margin of appreciation. The hospital managers were better placed to make decisions about clinical safety than a court, particularly an international court which had heard no direct evidence. The measures of which C had complained were not disproportionate. It followed that the relevant interference with her freedom to manifest her religion was necessary in a democratic society and that there had been no breach of art.9 (paras 99-100). (3) Given the strength of L's religious conviction, she considered that she had no choice but to face disciplinary action rather than be designated a civil partnership registrar and ultimately she lost her job. On the other hand, the local authority's policy aimed to secure the rights of others, which were also protected under the Convention. The court generally allowed the national authorities a wide margin of appreciation when it came to striking a balance between competing Convention rights. Accordingly, the local authority which brought the disciplinary proceedings and the domestic courts which rejected L's discrimination claim had not exceeded the margin of appreciation available to them. It could not therefore be said that there had been a breach of art.14 taken in conjunction with art.9 (para.106). (4) The loss of M's job was a severe sanction with grave consequences for him. However, the most important factor was that the employer's action was intended to secure the implementation of its policy of providing a service without discrimination. The state authorities therefore benefited from a wide margin of appreciation in deciding where to strike the balance between M's right to manifest his religious belief and the employer's interest in securing the rights of others. That margin of appreciation had not been exceeded. The refusal by the domestic courts to uphold his complaints therefore did not give rise to a breach of art.9, taken alone or in conjunction with art.14 (paras 109-110).

EWEIDA v UNITED KINGDOM (48420/10); McFARLANE v UNITED KINGDOM (36516/10); LADELE v UNITED KINGDOM (51671/10); CHAPLIN v UNITED KINGDOM (59842/10) [2013] I.R.L.R. 231, Judge Bjorgvinsson (President), ECHR.

1549. Inhuman or degrading treatment or punishment–Extradition–Whether extradition of mentally disordered offender would give rise to breach of art.3 European Convention on Human Rights 1950

[European Convention on Human Rights 1950 Art.3.]

The complainant (X) complained that his extradition from the United Kingdom to the United States would give rise to a breach of the European Convention on Human Rights 1950 art.3. X had been indicted in the United States in respect of a conspiracy to establish a jihad training camp in Oregon. He was arrested in the UK and made subject to an extradition order. He was currently detained in Broadmoor High Security Psychiatric Hospital. The medical evidence indicated that he was suffering from paranoid schizophrenia. The last psychiatric report submitted to the court indicated that his condition was well controlled on anti-psychotic medication and that participation in occupational and vocational activities at Broadmoor, including attendance at a mosque, had helped prevent any significant deterioration in his mood; however, X had only limited insight into his illness and would be likely to relapse if he ceased taking his medication. In giving evidence to the First-tier Tribunal, a consultant psychiatrist stated that if he were to be returned to prison, his compliance with medication would be uncertain, particularly in the medium to long term, and that would be likely to lead to a relapse. The tribunal concluded that detention and treatment in a medical hospital were necessary for X's own health and safety. X argued that, if extradited and convicted, he would be at real risk of ill-treatment either as a result of conditions at ADX Florence, a maximum-security facility, or because of the length of his sentence.

Held: Complaint upheld. Whether X's extradition would breach art.3 very much depended on the conditions in which he would be detained and the medical services that would be made available to him. Any assessment of those detention conditions was hindered by the fact that it could not be said with any certainty in which detention facility he would be housed, either before or after trial. That was particularly the case with respect to the pre-trial period, about which very little information had been provided. The US Department of Justice had given no indication of where X would or could be held, although it had advised that if he consented to his medical records being provided to the US authorities on extradition, they would be able to take his mental-health concerns into account in deciding where to house him while on remand. It was also unclear how long he might expect to remain on remand pending trial. If extradited, his representatives would be entitled to argue that he was not fit to stand trial on account of his mental disorder. A district judge would then have to assess his competency and, if found competent, he could appeal to the Court of Appeals. There was no information concerning the potential length of a competency assessment or any subsequent appeals procedure, but it was reasonable to assume that the length of pre-trial detention might be prolonged if X were to assert those rights. There was a complete absence of information about the consequences for X if it were found that he was not fit to stand trial. Moreover, there was no guarantee that, if tried and convicted, he would not be detained in ADX Florence, where he would be exposed to a highly restrictive regime with long periods of social isolation. There was no evidence to indicate the length of time that he would spend in ADX Florence. X was facing extradition to a country where he had no ties and where he would not have the support of family and friends. Given the current medical evidence, there was a real risk that his extradition to a different country and to a different, and potentially more hostile, prison environment would result in a significant deterioration in his mental and physical health; such a deterioration would be capable of reaching the art.3 threshold. In the circumstances, his extradition would give rise to a breach of art.3. Although the evidence suggested that X could be sentenced to anything up to 35 years' imprisonment, he had not shown that any sentence imposed would be grossly disproportionate (see paras 52, 56-58, 62 of judgment).

ASWAT v UNITED KINGDOM (17299/12) (2014) 58 E.H.R.R. 1, Judge Bjorgvinsson (President), ECHR.

1550. Inhuman or degrading treatment or punishment–Prisoners' rights–Lawfulness of whole-life orders

[Crime (Sentences) Act 1997 (c.43) s.30(1); European Convention on Human Rights 1950 Art.3.]

The complainants (V) alleged that the whole-life orders which had been imposed on them following their conviction for murder amounted to ill-treatment contrary to the European Convention on Human Rights 1950 art.3. The effect of a whole-life order was that the prisoner could not be released other than at the discretion of the secretary of state. The secretary of state's power to release a prisoner was provided for in the Crime (Sentences) Act 1997 s.30(1). In accordance with Prison Service Order 4700, she would only exercise her discretion on compassionate grounds when the prisoner was terminally ill or seriously incapacitated.

Held: Complaints upheld. There were a number of reasons why, for a life sentence to remain compatible with art.3, there had to be both a prospect of release and a possibility of review. It was axiomatic that a prisoner could not be detained unless there were legitimate penological grounds for that detention.

Those grounds would include punishment, deterrence, public protection and rehabilitation. Many of those grounds would be present at the time when a life sentence was imposed. However, the balance between those justifications for detention was not necessarily static and might shift in the course of the sentence. It was only by carrying out a review of the justification for continued detention at an appropriate point in the sentence that those factors or shifts could be properly evaluated. Moreover, if a prisoner was incarcerated without any prospect of release and without the possibility of having his life sentence reviewed, there was the risk that he could never atone for his offence: whatever he did in prison, however exceptional his progress towards rehabilitation, his punishment would remain fixed and unreviewable. If anything, the punishment became greater with time: the longer the prisoner lived, the longer his sentence. Thus, even when a whole-life sentence was condign punishment at the time of its imposition, with the passage of time it would become a poor guarantee of just and proportionate punishment. Further, as the German Federal Constitutional Court had recognised in a life-imprisonment case, it would be incompatible with the provision on human dignity in the Basic Law for the State forcefully to deprive a person of his freedom without at least providing him with the chance to some day regain it. It was that conclusion which led the Constitutional Court to find that the prison authorities had a duty to strive towards a life prisoner's rehabilitation and that rehabilitation was constitutionally required in any community that established human dignity as its centrepiece. Indeed, the court went on to make clear in a subsequent case that that applied to all life prisoners, whatever the nature of their crimes, and that release only for those who were infirm or close to death was not sufficient. Similar considerations had to apply under the Convention system, the very essence of which was respect for human dignity. Indeed, there was also now clear support in European and international law for the principle that all prisoners, including those serving life sentences, be offered the possibility of rehabilitation and the prospect of release if rehabilitation was achieved. The instant court had already had occasion to note that, while punishment remained one of the aims of imprisonment, the emphasis in European penal policy was now on the rehabilitative aim of imprisonment, particularly towards the end of a long sentence. In the context of a life sentence, art.3 had to be construed as requiring reducibility of the sentence, in the sense of a review which allowed the domestic authorities to consider whether any changes in the prisoner were so significant, and such progress towards rehabilitation had been made in the course of the sentence, as to mean that continued detention could no longer be justified on legitimate penological grounds. Given the contrast between the broad wording of s.30 and the restrictive and exhaustive conditions in the Prison Service Order, as well as the absence in the United Kingdom of any dedicated review mechanism for whole-life orders, V's life sentences could not be regarded as reducible for the purposes of art.3; there had therefore been a breach of that article (see paras 110-115, 119, 130 of judgment).

VINTER v UNITED KINGDOM (66069/09); BAMBER v UNITED KINGDOM (130/10); MOORE v UNITED KINGDOM (3896/10) 34 B.H.R.C. 605, Judge Spielmann (President), ECHR.

1551. Inhuman or degrading treatment or punishment–Removal–Removal of failed asylum seeker with disabilities–Difficulties faced by disabled people in Afghanistan caused by lack of resources not intentional acts or omissions by state

[European Convention on Human Rights 1950 Art.3.]

The complainant failed asylum seeker (H) complained that if he was removed from the United Kingdom to Afghanistan he would face a real risk of ill-treatment contrary to the European Convention on Human Rights 1950 art.3. H was an Afghan national who had entered the UK and claimed asylum on the basis that if returned he would be arrested and killed by the Afghan authorities because of his role as a military commander for Hizb-i-Islami. He also claimed that Hizb-i-Islami would force him to become a suicide bomber. Finally, he claimed that he had been seriously injured during a rocket launch in Afghanistan four years earlier and had been left disabled. He relied on the fact that his lower right leg and penis had both been amputated and he had a false limb, that his left leg and right hand had been seriously injured, and that he suffered from depression. His asylum claim was refused, his account of his activities with Hizb-i-Islami having been rejected, and he appealed, asserting that his removal to Afghanistan would breach his rights under art.3 of the Convention. The First-tier Tribunal dismissed the appeal, having found that H could return without fear from the authorities and that there were 80,000 amputees and 400,000 individuals rendered disabled by the effects of war who continued to live in Afghanistan. The Upper Tribunal refused H permission to appeal against that decision on the basis that it contained no error of law. H contended that his return would breach art.3 because disabled persons were at particular risk of violence in the armed conflict in Afghanistan, because they would be unable to remove themselves from dangerous situations swiftly and would be at greater risk of homelessness and thus more prone to being affected by the indiscriminate violence which occurred on the streets of Afghanistan. He submitted that whilst the difficulties faced by persons with disabilities in Afghanistan might not engage art.3 if they had family support, a person, like him, without close family connections would suffer the full consequences of the discrimination against, and ignorance surrounding, persons with disabilities. The respondent state argued that there was no evidence in any country guidance case to suggest that disabled persons in Afghanistan were at an enhanced risk of ill-treatment from indiscriminate violence, and that H had managed with his disability in Afghanistan for three to four years before he came to the UK.

Held: Complaint dismissed. The ill-treatment a failed asylum seeker alleged that he would face if returned had to attain a minimum level of severity if it was to fall within the scope of art.3. The instant court had to examine the foreseeable consequences of sending H to Afghanistan, bearing in mind the general situation there and his personal circumstances. Socio-economic and humanitarian conditions in a country of return did not necessarily have a bearing, and certainly not a decisive bearing, on the question of whether the persons concerned would face a real risk of ill-treatment within the meaning of art.3, *Sheekh v Netherlands (1948/04)* (2007) 45 E.H.R.R. 50, [2008] C.L.Y. 1911 applied. It was significant that H had failed to adduce any additional substantive evidence to support his claim that disabled persons were per se at greater risk of violence, as opposed to other difficulties such as discrimination and poor humanitarian conditions, than the general Afghan population. Independent reports on Afghanistan made no reference to disabled persons being at greater risk of violence, ill-treatment or attacks. H had failed to demonstrate that, as a result of his disabilities, he would be subjected to an enhanced risk of indiscriminate violence in Afghanistan such as to engage art.3. Any future harm he faced would emanate from a lack of sufficient resources to provide either medical treatment or welfare rather than the intentional acts or omissions of the authorities of the receiving state, *N v United Kingdom (26565/05)* (2008) 47 E.H.R.R. 39, [2008] C.L.Y. 1909 applied, *MSS v Belgium (30696/09)* (2011) 53 E.H.R.R. 2 distinguished. The Convention did not purport to be a means of requiring contracting states to impose Convention standards on other states, *Al-Skeini v United Kingdom (55721/07)* (2011) 53 E.H.R.R. 18, [2011] C.L.Y. 1696 applied. There were no very exceptional circumstances in H's case amounting to compelling reasons to prevent his removal on humanitarian grounds. The decision to remove him to Afghanistan would not give rise to a violation of art.3 (see paras 70, 72, 74, 86-92, 95 of judgment).

SHH v UNITED KINGDOM (60367/10) (2013) 57 E.H.R.R. 18, Judge Ziemele (President), ECHR.

1552. Protection of Freedoms Act 2012 (c.9)–Commencement No.2 Order–Wales

THE PROTECTION OF FREEDOMS ACT 2012 (COMMENCEMENT NO.2) (WALES) ORDER 2013, SI 2013/SI 2013/1566 (W.143) (C.62); made under the

Protection of Freedoms Act 2012 s.120. Commencement details: bringing into force various provisions of the 2012 Act on September 1, 2013.; .

This Order brings into force on September 1, 2013 the Protection of Freedoms Act 2012 ss.26 to 28 to regulate the biometric information of children and young persons in schools in Wales and further education institutions in Wales.

1553. **Protection of Freedoms Act 2012 (c.9)–Commencement No.9 Order**

THE PROTECTION OF FREEDOMS ACT 2012 (COMMENCEMENT NO.9) ORDER 2013, SI 2013/SI 2013/2104 (C.88); made under the Protection of Freedoms Act 2012 s.120. Commencement details: bringing into force various provisions of the 2012 Act on September 1, 2013 and October 31, 2013.; .

This Order brings into force the Protection of Freedoms Act 2012 ss.26, 27 and 28 of the Act on September 1, 2013. These sections concern a requirement on schools, 16-19 academies and further education institutions to notify parents and obtain parental consent before processing a child's biometric information.

1554. **Reporting restrictions–Children–Local councillor guilty of being drunk in public place while in charge of child under age of seven–Whether reporting restrictions justified**

[Children and Young Persons Act 1933 (c.12) s.39; Licensing Act 1902 (c.28) s.2(1); European Convention on Human Rights 1950 Art.6, Art.8, Art.10.]

The claimant (X) applied for judicial review of a decision of the defendant magistrates' court refusing to make an order under the Children and Young Persons Act 193 s.39 to prohibit the reporting of her conviction. X had been in a supermarket with her child (B) who was two-and-a-half years old. The manager of the store believed she was drunk and called the police. After a breath screening test X was found to be four times over the legal limit for driving. X pleaded guilty to a charge of being drunk in a public place, while in charge of a child under the age of seven contrary to the Licensing Act 1902 s.2(1). The magistrates refused X's application for reporting restrictions under s.39. X was a local councillor and was likely to be well-known in her community. The issues were (i) whether for the purposes of s.39, B was a child "concerned" in the relevant criminal proceedings against X, on the footing that she was a child "in respect of whom" the relevant proceedings were taken; (ii) if so, the nature of the relevant considerations that the magistrates had to take into account in deciding whether to make an order under s.39, and in deciding if any, restrictions should be imposed; (iii) whether on the material before them and in the light of relevant considerations, the magistrates reached a decision which was reasonably open to them. X submitted that the magistrates erred in law in refusing to make an order under s.39.

Held: Application refused. (1) In a strictly formal sense, it could be argued that the only two parties to criminal proceedings were the prosecution and the defendant, and that criminal proceedings are not taken "in respect of" any other person. However, it was plain that in enacting s.39 the legislature sought to capture, in wide language, at least the central participants in proceedings, whether civil or criminal, who would be likely to be the focus of any report of the proceedings; and a narrow interpretation of s.39 tended to defeat the main objective of protecting, where appropriate, the identity of a child or young person in that position. It was unnecessary to show under s.2(1) of the 1902 Act that a defendant had positively inflicted physical or psychological harm on the young child, or even that the defendant in the particular circumstances was likely to do so. In that strict sense the child might not be considered a victim as in the case of a violent or sexual assault, or of child cruelty. However, whatever the original intent of s.2(1), it could be interpreted as promoting the welfare of small children who could be at risk of physical or psychological harm, because the person responsible for their welfare was intoxicated. Accordingly, the child that was specifically referred to in any charge under s.2(1) was in a real sense a subject of the criminal proceedings, and those proceedings on any sensible construction of s.39 were taken "in respect of", and thus "concerned", that child (see paras 8-9 of judgment). (2) The application of s.39 engaged important, and competing, principles, namely the private and family life of a child, and the best interests of that child on one hand, and, the freedom of the media to publish, and of the public to receive, information or comment, and the requirements of open justice on the other hand. Those principles were enshrined on one side in the European Convention on Human Rights 1950 art.8, and in the jurisprudence recognising the best interests of the child as a primary consideration, and on the other in art.6 and art.10 (para.10). (3) The magistrates had a reasonable basis for concluding that no order under s.39 was justified in the instant case. The balance of the relevant competing principles came down firmly in favour of art.10 and open justice, given the immediate, direct and considerable extent of the interference with those rights, and taking due account of the much weaker, remote and uncertain impact on B's rights under art.8 and on her best interests. The magistrate's decision was correct (para.27).

R. (ON THE APPLICATION OF A) v LOWESTOFT MAGISTRATES' COURT, [2013] EWHC 659 (Admin), (2013) 177 J.P. 377, Pitchford, L.J., QBD (Admin).

1555. Right to effective remedy–Right to life–Death of schizophrenic son–Non-availability of civil proceedings for mother to determine liability and compensation

[Fatal Accidents Act 1976 (c.30); Human Rights Act 1998 (c.42); Law Reform (Miscellaneous Provisions) Act 1934 (c.41); European Convention on Human Rights 1950 Art.2, Art.3, Art.8, Art.13.]

The complainant mother (R) complained that there had been no effective domestic mechanism whereby issues of civil liability could be determined in respect of the alleged negligent care of her deceased son (S), and through which she could have obtained compensation for the non-pecuniary loss sustained, such as grief, loss and distress. S, who suffered from schizophrenia, had been hearing voices ordering him to kill himself. As there was no bed available at the local hospital, he was given a bed at a unit run by the local authority. Although he had been assessed earlier at the hospital as being a low suicide risk, he died a few hours later after breaking a window and falling from his sixth-floor room at the unit. A coroner recorded an open verdict because there was insufficient evidence that S had intended to kill himself. R brought an action for damages, arguing that the hospital and the local authority had failed to adequately discharge their duties to S in breach of the European Convention on Human Rights 1950 art.2, art.3 and art.8. The county court struck out her case because the test laid down in *Savage v South Essex Partnership NHS Foundation Trust* [2006] EWHC 3562 (QB), [2007] LS Law Medical 291, [2007] C.L.Y. 2238, namely that the negligence had to be of a kind sufficient to sustain a charge of manslaughter, had not been met. R submitted that the lack of a mechanism for establishing any liability and compensation violated art.13, taken in conjunction with art.2.

Held: Complaint upheld. There was an arguable claim for the purposes of art.2 as it could be argued that S's position was such that an operational duty had arisen to take reasonable steps to protect him from a real and immediate risk of suicide, and that that duty was not fulfilled. R's case had not been rejected in the county court as failing to disclose negligence but rather as not disclosing a cause of action under the Human Rights Act 1998, *Savage* considered. She continued to not have an action for damages under that Act for her non-pecuniary loss until the judgment in *Rabone v Pennine Care NHS Foundation Trust* [2012] UKSC 2, [2012] 2 A.C. 72, [2012] C.L.Y. 1671, *Rabone* considered. Furthermore, as the mother of a non-dependant adult child, she would have been unable to claim damages under the Fatal Accidents Act 1976 on her own behalf. Moreover, a negligence action on behalf of S's estate was not available to R even assuming she could have applied to be an executor of that estate, and no such award to his estate could constitute compensation for her bereavement. The survival of any such action on behalf of S and in favour of his estate was governed by the Law Reform (Miscellaneous Provisions) Act 1934. Given the circumstances of S's instantaneous death, there was no evidence that he inflicted physical injury on himself before the moment of his death. While it was likely that he had suffered significant anguish and fear, there was no evidence that it would be regarded as psychiatric injury in the sense recognised by domestic law. The most that could therefore be recovered under the 1934 Act on behalf of S's estate would have been the funeral expenses, *Keenan v United Kingdom (27229/95)* (2001) 33 E.H.R.R. 38, [2001] C.L.Y. 3572 and *Bubbins v United Kingdom (50196/99)* (2005) 41 E.H.R.R. 24, [2006] C.L.Y. 2166 considered. Therefore, R had no prospect of obtaining adequate compensation for the non-pecuniary damage suffered by her as a result of S's death, either directly or as a beneficiary of his estate. That lack of compensation would itself reduce access to the civil remedy. The lack of compensation for non-pecuniary damage would almost certainly have had a negative bearing on any application by R for legal aid to take civil proceedings. Accordingly, there had been a violation of art.13 in conjunction with art.2 (see paras 61, 63, 65-68 of judgment).

REYNOLDS v UNITED KINGDOM (2694/08) (2012) 55 E.H.R.R. 35, Judge Garlicki (President), ECHR.

1556. Right to fair trial–Criminal appeals–Conduct of parties–Delay–Failure of judicial authorities to progress matters of own motion

[Criminal Procedure (Scotland) Act 1995 (c.46) s.107(8); European Convention on Human Rights 1950 Art.5, Art.6(1), Art.13.]

The complainant (B), who had been convicted of murder, complained that the length of his appeal proceedings breached the "reasonable time" requirement under the European Convention on Human Rights 1950 art.6(1), and that the failure of the domestic courts to expedite the proceedings or provide interim relief breached his right to an effective remedy under art.13. Following his conviction in October 2001, B lodged his intention to appeal but did not lodge a formal note of appeal until July 2, 2002, after six extensions of time. The trial judge's report on the note of appeal was issued on November 28, 2002. The "single sift" judge restricted leave to appeal against conviction and sentence to a limited number of the grounds specified in the note of appeal. On January 17, 2003 B notified his intention to have the partial refusal reviewed. On August 20, 2003 the second sift judges refused B's appeal and on June 14, 2004 B lodged a petition to the nobile officium to challenge their decision. On December 8, 2004 the petition was granted and the High Court set aside the decision of the second sift judges. On April 25, 2005 B applied for leave to argue the refused grounds under the Criminal Procedure (Scotland) Act 1995 s.107(8) and on November 25, 2005 the Appeal Court granted leave to appeal on all grounds set out in the note of appeal. In November 2006, B applied unsuccessfully for interim release. The appeal against conviction was heard between September 29 and October 9, 2009 and on March 9, 2010 the Appeal Court refused all grounds of appeal. On December 16, 2010, the Supreme Court refused B's application for leave to appeal against conviction.

Held: Complaint upheld in part. (1) Given that there had been issues relating to the competency of the indictment, extradition proceedings and pre-trial publicity, it was clear that the proceedings were particularly complex. The importance of what was at stake for B, namely a conviction for a serious criminal offence and a sentence of life imprisonment, was not in doubt. In assessing whether the length of the appeal proceedings was reasonable, it therefore remained to assess the conduct of the parties. B's delay in lodging the note of appeal could not be attributed to the authorities. In seeking six extensions of time and making late requests, the delay encountered at that stage of the proceedings was wholly attributable to B's conduct and that of his legal team. In view of the length and complexity of the trial proceedings, the trial judge could not be criticised for the length of time it had taken to lodge his report. B's application to the second sift and the resulting petition to the nobile officium had been made on an erroneous interpretation of the law and had resulted in a delay of almost two years, for which the authorities were not responsible. However, there was unreasonable delay by the judicial authorities by their apparent inactivity during the seven-month period taken for the examination of B's application under s.107(8) of the 1995 Act. The authorities were also responsible for the delay of over four years and three months in handing down judgment in the appeal against conviction once leave to appeal on all grounds had been granted. Further delays had been incurred through no fault of either party as a result of clarifications of the law regarding the correct procedure for appealing a decision of the single-sift judge. Therefore, although a substantial proportion of the delay was attributable to B's own conduct, the failure of the judicial authorities to progress matters of their own motion had resulted in a breach of art.6(1) (see paras 235-240, 246-250, 252, 254, 260-261, 272-273 of judgment). (2) It was doubtful whether the availability of interim release in post-conviction cases, where detention was justified under art.5(1)(a) of the Convention, was required under art.13 in order to establish the existence of effective remedies for a complaint regarding the length of proceedings. In any event, B had been able to make an application for interim release. The fact that, due to the gravity of the crime, his history of violence and the risk to the public, the court had declined to grant interim release in his case did not render the procedure ineffective. Accordingly, B's complaint under art.13 was ill-founded (paras 276-277).

BEGGS v UNITED KINGDOM (25133/06) (2013) 56 E.H.R.R. 26, Judge Garlicki (President), ECHR.

1557. Right to fair trial–Mentally disordered persons–Divesting mentally ill persons of legal capacity–Conduct of proceedings

[European Convention on Human Rights 1950 Art.8, Art.6.]

The first applicant (X), an elderly lady with dementia, complained to the European Court of Human Rights that the manner in which legal proceedings divesting her of legal capacity had been conducted in the respondent state violated the European Convention on Human Rights 1950 art.6. The second applicant (Y), who was X's daughter, complained that legal proceedings started by the state with a view to divesting her of legal capacity violated art.8 of the Convention. X and Y had lived together until 2006 when, at the instigation of the local social welfare centre (the centre), X was moved into a care home. It was stated that Y could not adequately care for her because of her own ill-health. Y visited X every day and, for more than two years, bombarded the care home with constant queries, demands and criticisms. In April 2008, the centre began proceedings to divest X of legal capacity in reliance on medical evidence that she was incapable of independent life. It appointed X's niece as guardian. Despite Y's objections to both decisions, X was divested of legal capacity. The centre also began proceedings to divest Y of legal capacity on the ground that she had suffered a recurrence of historic mental health problems when X moved to the care home, such that she was displaying strange and aggressive behaviour and neglecting her physical health. It appointed a guardian for Y. Y's appeal against the proceedings and the appointment of the guardian was still ongoing at the date of the instant hearing. X submitted that her proceedings were unfair because she had not participated in them, because submissions made by Y on her behalf had been ignored, and because the decision had not been served on her or Y. Y contended that her proceedings and the appointment of a guardian had been unnecessary because there was no evidence that she was incapable of looking after herself or fulfilling her obligations.

Held: Complaints upheld. (1) In cases involving a mentally ill person, domestic courts enjoyed a margin of appreciation, but measures taken should not affect the very essence of a person's right to a fair hearing. Furthermore, court judgments had to adequately state their reasoning, although they did not have to give a detailed answer to every argument. Judges adopting decisions having serious consequences for a person's private life ought to have personal contact with those persons. Decisions had to be supported by expert medical evidence, but it was ultimately for a judge, not a physician, to assess the facts and the person's circumstances. Any risk of arbitrariness had to be kept to a minimum, *Shtukaturov v Russia (44009/05)* (2012) 54 E.H.R.R. 27, [2009] C.L.Y. 2024 considered. In X's case, it would have been preferable for the judge to have verified the medical evidence (see paras 79-86 of judgment). It was legitimate for a state to provide care for the sick, elderly, or persons with diminished capacity, but it was an entirely different thing to deprive someone of their legal capacity, because it deprived them of independence in all legal spheres and was a measure which was to be saved for exceptional circumstances. The court had to assess the proceedings as a whole, including any decisions of the appeal courts. The judge at first instance had completely ignored Y's arguments in his assessment of X's condition, and his decision had not been served on X even though she still had legal capacity at the time. That failure had deprived her of remedying any possible defects in his decision at further instance. There had been a violation of art.6 (paras 90-94). (2) The mere act of instituting proceedings to divest a person of legal capacity was a serious interference with that person's private life because they became subject to various intrusive assessments and to the wide range of powers exercised by their appointed guardian. In Y's case, the issues of the legality of the interference, the legitimate aim pursued and its necessity were closely interconnected. In order to be able to institute such proceedings, a social welfare centre needed to present convincing evidence comprising specific facts rather than general statements. The court had to be satisfied that divesting the person of legal capacity was an adequate answer to the situation at issue. The centre had produced no specific facts. While it was true that she had twice been hospitalised in a psychiatric unit, the discharge letters indicated a complete recovery and an optimistic prognosis. There was no indication of any specific damage that Y had committed against her own interests or those of others. The medical report, which was not favourable, had been drawn up by a psychiatrist who had never treated Y and who had only had a telephone conversation with her. It was doubtful that a person's mental capacity could be accurately assessed in that way. In the circumstances, the relevant proceedings had not observed the prescribed procedure and requirements, did not pursue a legitimate aim and were not necessary in a democratic society and therefore contravened art.8 (paras 102-117).

X v CROATIA (5193/09) [2012] M.H.L.R. 1, Judge Kovler (President), ECHR.

1558. Right to liberty and security–Imprisonment for public protection–Continued detention beyond minimum term–No access to rehabilitative courses

[Crime (Sentences) Act 1997 (c.43) s.28; Criminal Justice Act 2003 (c.44) Pt 12 s.225; Criminal Justice and Immigration Act 2008 (c.4); European Convention on Human Rights 1950 Art.5(4), Art.5(1).]

The complainant prisoner (J) complained that his continued detention beyond the expiry of the minimum term of his sentence of imprisonment for public protection without access to rehabilitative courses violated the European Convention on Human Rights 1950 art.5(1) and art.5(4). Imprisonment for public protection sentences were first introduced in April 2005, by virtue of the Criminal Justice Act 2003 Pt 12 s.225. They were indeterminate sentences which required the Parole Board's direction before the prisoner could be released. They were mandatory in all cases where an individual was convicted of a serious offence and was deemed by the sentencing judge to be at risk of committing a further specified offence. Risk was to be assumed in cases where the individual had previously been convicted of a relevant offence. The scheme was amended by the Criminal Justice and Immigration Act 2008, when the sentence ceased to be mandatory and only applied to cases where, if imposed, the minimum sentence would be more than two years subject to certain limited exceptions. In September 2005, J had pleaded guilty to unlawful wounding with intent. He had previous convictions for, among other things, battery, common assault, affray, disorderly behaviour, racially abusive behaviour and assault occasioning actual bodily harm. J was sentenced to imprisonment for public protection with a minimum term of two years. He took all courses that he was able to take at his local prison, but some courses which the Parole Board had recommended were unavailable there. He was unable to move to a first-stage lifer prison to complete the rest of the courses needed for release because all the places at the first-stage lifer prisons were full. J applied for judicial review of the secretary of state's management and treatment of prisoners in light of the failure to provide him with the relevant courses to address his offending behaviour. Meanwhile, his minimum term had expired. A High Court judge found his detention unlawful and ordered his release but the Court of Appeal held it was not unlawful in light of the express terms of s.225 of the 2003 Act and the Crime (Sentences) Act 1997 s.28, which rendered detention lawful until the Parole Board was satisfied that he was no longer dangerous. The House of Lords dismissed his appeal, having found that there had been no violation of art.5(1) or art.5(4). In the meantime, J had been transferred to a first-stage prison and three months later the Parole Board had directed his release on licence. J submitted that (1) his detention following the expiry of his minimum term was unlawful and arbitrary; (2) there had been no meaningful review of the legality of his detention beyond his minimum term.

Held: Complaints upheld in part. (1) The object and purpose of art.5(1) was to ensure that no-one was dispossessed of his liberty in an arbitrary fashion. Any deprivation of liberty had to fall within one of the exceptions set out in art.5(1)(a) to art.5(1)(f) and had to also be lawful. The relevant exception in the instant case was that contained in art.5(1)(a) as J had been detained after conviction by a competent court. In the context of art.5(1)(a), a concern might arise in the case of persons who, having served the punishment element of their sentences, were in detention solely because of the risk they posed to the public, if there were no special measures, instruments or institutions in place aimed at reducing the danger they presented and at limiting the duration of their detention to what was strictly necessary in order to prevent them from committing further offences, *M v Germany (19359/04)* (2010) 51 E.H.R.R. 41 and *Grosskopf v Germany (24478/03)* (2011) 53 E.H.R.R. 7 applied. However, in assessing whether the place and conditions of detention were appropriate, it would be unrealistic to expect the authorities to ensure that relevant treatment or facilities be available immediately, in view of the need for efficient management of public funds, *Brand v Netherlands (49902/99)* 17 B.H.R.C. 398, [2005] C.L.Y. 2108 applied. Accordingly, a reasonable balance had to be struck between the competing interests involved. Furthermore, a real opportunity for rehabilitation was a necessary element of any part of the detention which was to be justified solely by reference to public protection. Following the expiry of J's minimum term and until steps were taken to progress him through the prison system with a view to providing him with access to appropriate rehabilitative courses, his detention was arbitrary and therefore unlawful within the meaning of art.5(1) (see paras 187-188, 194, 209, 221 of judgment). (2) (Judge Kalaydjieva dissenting) The complaint under art.5(4) gave rise to no separate issue (para.226).

JAMES v UNITED KINGDOM (25119/09); LEE v UNITED KINGDOM (57877/09); WELLS v UNITED KINGDOM (57715/09) (2013) 56 E.H.R.R. 12, Judge Garlicki (President), ECHR.

1559. Right to life–Positive obligations–Duty of police to protect witnesses in criminal proceedings–Perception of real and immediate risk to life

[European Convention on Human Rights 1950 Art.2.]

The complainants (V), the parents of a murder victim (G), complained that the police authorities of the respondent state had failed to fulfil their positive obligation to protect G's life, in breach of the European Convention on Human Rights 1950 art.2. G, an optometrist, had hired an assistant (B) who turned out to be concealing convictions for common assault and disorderly behaviour under a false identity. B was arrested for theft and items belonging to G were found at his home. G made a witness statement confirming that the items were his. B later attempted to bribe a witness (P) not to give evidence. That incident was reported to one of the police officers dealing with the investigation (R). On the same day, B made threats to G over the telephone. G reported that incident to R. During the investigation, cars belonging to G and to P's wife were set on fire. There was also a fire at P's business premises. Those incidents were thought to be accidental at the time but were later attributed to arson. B made a further threatening call to G and the matter was reported to R, who arranged to take a statement the next day. On the same day,

G was shot dead by B. V brought proceedings for breach of art.2. The High Court identified the legal principles from *Osman v United Kingdom (23452/94)* [1999] 1 F.L.R. 193, [1998] C.L.Y. 3102 and held that the police had failed to fulfil their positive obligation to protect G's life. That decision was overturned by the House of Lords, which held that the High Court had misdirected itself on the *Osman* test. The United Kingdom government contended that, insofar as V complained on their own behalf, they were not victims, although it was accepted that they could complain on G's behalf as his executors. V argued that the *Osman* test should be adapted by lowering the threshold for state responsibility when the state created the relevant risk for the deceased, such as by calling him as a witness in criminal proceedings.

Held: Complaint dismissed. (1) Close family members, such as parents, of a person whose death was alleged to engage the responsibility of the state could themselves claim to be indirect victims of a violation of art.2. The question of whether they were legal heirs of the deceased was not relevant (see para.86 of judgment). (2) Article 2(1) entailed an obligation on a state to safeguard the lives of those within its jurisdiction. That might imply a positive obligation on the authorities to take preventive operational measures to protect an individual whose life was at risk from the criminal acts of another. However, for the Court to find a violation of that positive obligation, it had to be established that the authorities knew or ought to have known at the time of the existence of a real and immediate risk to the life of an identified individual from the criminal acts of a third party, and that they had failed to take measures within the scope of their powers which, judged reasonably, might have been expected to avoid that risk, *Osman* applied. In cases concerning prior threats by third parties later ending in the killing of another individual, the fact that the deceased might have been particularly vulnerable was only one of the relevant circumstances to be assessed in answering the first of the two questions which made up the *Osman* test (paras 88, 91). (3) In determining whether R ought to have considered the need to protect G's life, it was relevant to note that B was a petty offender charged with minor theft offences at low risk of a custodial sentence. G was not the only or even the main witness in the proceedings. B's record did not indicate a propensity to serious violence and there was nothing to suggest he had used weapons before. Accordingly, the fact that G was a witness in B's prosecution did not in itself give reason to fear for his life. Even if R had carried out further inquiries after the fires so as to reveal B's involvement with them, that additional knowledge should not necessarily have led R to perceive B's activities as life-threatening. The risk factors in the instant case were no greater than those in *Osman*, in which no violation of art.2 was found. Accordingly, while it ought to have been known to R that there was an escalating situation of intimidation of a number of witnesses, including G, by B, it could not be said that there was a decisive stage in the sequence of events leading up to the shooting of G when R knew or ought to have known of a real and immediate risk to G's life (paras 95-97, 99, 102-103).

VAN COLLE v UNITED KINGDOM (7678/09) (2013) 56 E.H.R.R. 23, Judge Garlicki (President), ECHR.

1560. Right to respect for home–Gypsies–Lack of domestic procedure for challenging possession order–Adequacy of s.4 Caravan Sites Act 1968 to meet procedural guarantees under art.8 European Convention on Human Rights 1950

[Caravan Sites Act 1968 (c.52) s.4; European Convention on Human Rights 1950 Art.8.]

The applicant (B), a gypsy, complained that the upholding of a possession order made against her constituted an unjustified breach of her right to respect for her home and family life. B lived on a caravan site under a licence agreement. The agreement, terminable on 28 days' notice, specified that the licensee and those living with her had not to create a nuisance or contravene site rules. B was served with notice of termination after nine months. Her parents, who occupied a different pitch, were given notice to quit. Seven months later possession proceedings were issued on the ground that B and her extended family had caused very substantial nuisance. B's parents consented to the order and agreed a date to move. B challenged the proceedings, but said that she would leave on the same date. A judge, following *Kay v United Kingdom (37341/06)* (2012) 54 E.H.R.R. 30, [2011] C.L.Y. 1699, held that the only possible challenges to the making of the possession order were to the domestic law itself, or on conventional judicial review grounds. He found that B was not guilty of any offensive behaviour apart from a minor failure to pay water charges, but that her son, who lived part-time with her, had been part of the behaviour complained of. Under amendments to the Caravan Sites Act 1968 s.4, which introduced a power for courts to suspend possession orders for up to 12 months, the judge formally extended the order until the date on which B had agreed to leave. B did not leave. Her appeal was dismissed, the court finding that the order was justified and that the procedural safeguards introduced by the amendment to s.4 of the Act were within the wide margin of appreciation available to national authorities. B submitted that the absence of any domestic measures for challenging the possession order provided insufficient procedural protection for the purposes of the European Convention on Human Rights 1950 art.8 and that, in light of her own conduct and the state's positive obligation to facilitate her traditional way of life, the grant of a possession order had been wholly disproportionate. The Government argued that the domestic courts' power of suspension was adequate protection and gave B control over when the possession order was to take effect. It considered the possession order to be proportionate given her son's misconduct, the absence of reasons which would make her case "exceptional" and her plans to leave the site in any event.

Held: Complaint upheld. (1) The loss of one's home was the most extreme form of interference with the right to respect for the home. Any person at risk of an interference of such magnitude should, in principle, be able to have the proportionality of the measure determined by an independent tribunal in light of the relevant principles under art.8, notwithstanding that, under domestic law, their right of occupation had come to an end. B had been unable to challenge the possession order, her rights being limited to seeking a suspension. The availability of suspension, while being welcome protection to individuals faced with eviction, was inadequate, on its own, to provide the necessary procedural guarantees under art.8. Suspension merely delayed possession; it did not remove the threat of eviction. The fact that individuals might remain in their homes long-term by making repeated applications to extend suspension of a possession order did not remove any incompatibility of the procedure with art.8. Therefore, the procedural safeguards required by art.8 for the assessment of the proportionality of interference had not been observed, *Kay* and *Connors v United Kingdom (66746/01)* (2005) 40 E.H.R.R. 9, [2004] C.L.Y. 1992 considered. B was awarded EUR 4,000 for non-pecuniary damage, and reimbursement of her costs (see paras 65-70, 77, 80 of judgment).

BUCKLAND v UNITED KINGDOM (40060/08) (2013) 56 E.H.R.R. 16, Judge Garlicki (President), ECHR.

1561. Right to respect for home–Peaceful enjoyment of possessions–Entitlement of joint tenant to remain in property after other joint tenant unilaterally giving notice to quit tenancy–Compatibility of common law with art.8 and art.1 European Convention on Human Rights 1950 and Human Rights Act 1998–Appropriateness of granting permission to appeal to Supreme Court

[Human Rights Act 1998 (c.42); European Convention on Human Rights 1950 Art.8, Protocol 1 Art.1.]

The appellant (S) appealed against a decision that he had no right to remain in a property as a sole tenant after his wife (W), who was a joint tenant, had given notice to the respondent local authority landlord quitting the joint tenancy. S and W had occupied the property under a joint secure weekly tenancy granted by the local authority. W subsequently left the property and gave the local authority notice purporting to terminate the tenancy. The local authority refused to transfer the tenancy into S's sole name so as to allow him to remain in the property, and issued possession proceedings. By his defence, S contended that the decision in *Hammersmith and Fulham LBC v Monk* [1992] 1 A.C. 478, [1992] C.L.Y. 2684, that at common law a periodic joint residential tenancy was terminated automatically if one joint tenant unilaterally served a notice to quit on the landlord, was incompatible with his rights under the European Convention on Human Rights 1950 art.8 and that the court should construe the common law to make it compatible. The plea failed and a possession order was made. S's appeal against that decision was transferred to the Court of Appeal without any intervening substantive judgment. S subsequently accepted that, given binding authority, the instant court had to dismiss his appeal. The issue was whether S should be granted permission to appeal to the Supreme Court and stay the possession order, so that S could challenge, under the Human Rights Act 1998, the compatibility with the Convention of the current state of the law on the termination of periodic joint tenancies of residential property. S contended that the effect of *Monk* was irreconcilable with the trend of authority from the European Court of Human Rights on art.8 and Protocol 1 art.1 of the Convention, and that the common law should evolve as a living and developing entity to achieve the result that was most compliant with the Convention.

Held: Appeal dismissed, permission to appeal to Supreme Court refused. (1) S's challenge was solely about the compatibility of the rule in *Monk* with art.8 and Protocol 1 art.1, not about the engagement of those articles by the local authority's possession proceedings against S, nor whether such proceedings were justifiable by the local authority (see para.33 of judgment). (2) It was not the object of the appeal to secure respect for the home lived in by S as a joint tenant or even to protect from interference or deprivation the property and contract rights that he had acquired (with his wife) from the local authority as joint tenants. The sole aim was to enhance property rights conferred by contract by securing for him a sole tenancy of the property without the concurrence of the local authority as owner of the property. If S was right, he would acquire, by force of Convention law and in the absence of any agreement with the owner of the property, greater and different property and contract rights binding on the local authority than he and his wife had originally acquired from the local authority by agreement. The instant case seemed to be more one of interference with the local authority's enjoyment of its possessions than of an interference by the local authority with S's possessions (para.34). (3) Article 8 was not engaged. *Monk* laid down a substantive rule of property and contract law under which one joint tenant had the right to serve notice unilaterally terminating a periodic joint tenancy. W had that right, as did S: its defeasibility by an act of one of them was inherent in the legal nature of the joint tenancy granted to them. W had exercised her right. There was nothing in the legal rule per se or in its exercise by W that was an interference by her or by the local authority with respect for S's home, *Monk* followed (para.35). (4) Article 1 of the First Protocol was not engaged because the rule in *Monk* was a proprietary and contractual legal right inherent in the joint tenancy granted by the local authority to S and W, and W's notice to the local authority was in exercise of her rights as a joint tenant. There was no "interference" by her or the local authority in S's enjoyment of his possessions. His relevant possession was an interest in a joint tenancy that was, in its very nature, terminable unilaterally by W or by him. The local authority's role regarding the rule in *Monk* was simply as recipient of the notice given to it by W terminating the joint tenancy. The local authority itself had done nothing in relation to the termination of the joint tenancy that could possibly be described as interference with S's peaceable enjoyment of property (para.36). (5) The proposed appeal to the Supreme Court was unarguable. There was no incompatibility between the rules of English property and contract law relating to the termination of a joint tenancy by one joint tenant and the Convention. No sensible purpose would be served by the expenditure of yet more public funds, on both sides, on a repeat of the debate before the Supreme Court (para.37).

SIMS v DACORUM BC; *sub nom.* DACORUM BC v SIMS, [2013] EWCA Civ 12, [2013] C.P. Rep. 19, Mummery, L.J., CA (Civ Div).

1562. Right to respect for home–Possession orders–Trespasser relying on right to respect for home as defence to possession claim–Entitlement of trespasser to invoke art.8 of European Convention on Human Rights 1950 only in exceptional circumstances–Circumstances justifying possession order

[European Convention on Human Rights 1950 Art.8.]

The appellant local authority appealed against a decision dismissing its claim for possession of a property occupied by the respondent (L) as a trespasser. The local authority had granted L's brother (G) a secure tenancy of a flat. L was a tenant of another local authority property with a history of rent arrears. When G died, L moved into his flat without the knowledge or consent of G's estate or the local authority. He was warned by the local authority that he remained liable for the rent on his own flat unless its tenancy was determined. The local authority subsequently informed L that it was not prepared to grant him a new tenancy of G's flat and that he should return to his own flat. L served notice on the local authority determining the tenancy of his own property. Despite the dismissal of his appeal against the refusal to grant him a tenancy of G's flat, he remained in the property and the local authority issued possession proceedings. The district judge allocated the case to the multi-track and it was heard by a recorder who refused to grant the local authority possession on the basis that, even though L was a trespasser, eviction would amount to a disproportionate interference with his rights under the European Convention on Human Rights art.8. In reaching that conclusion, the recorder took account of L's history of depression, his financial circumstances and previous history of rent arrears which would make it difficult for him to find other accommodation, the fact that he had secured a start-up business loan which would be wasted if he was evicted, confusion over the circumstances in which L gave up the tenancy of his own property and the fact that L was not guilty of nuisance, criminal conduct or anti-social behaviour and got on well with neighbours. The local authority contended that the recorder had been wrong in refusing to grant it a possession order.

Held: Appeal allowed. (1) A person who had no right to remain in a property under domestic law could invoke art.8 to defend a claim for possession, but only in very highly exceptional circumstances, *Manchester City Council v Pinnock* [2010] UKSC 45, [2011] 2 A.C. 104, [2011] C.L.Y. 2066, *Hounslow LBC v Powell* [2011] UKSC 8, [2011] 2 A.C. 186, [2011] C.L.Y. 2069 and *Corby BC v Scott* [2012] EWCA Civ 276, [2013] P.T.S.R. 141, [2012] C.L.Y. 2055 followed. A striking feature of the instant case was that L was not merely a trespasser in the property but that he had never had any right to occupy the premises. He had entered as a trespasser and remained one. Public authorities were entitled to preserve property for a public purpose and bring unlawful occupation to an end, *Kay v Lambeth LBC* [2006] UKHL 10, [2006] 2 A.C. 465, [2006] C.L.Y. 2173 followed. Article 8 could not be invoked so as to require a contracting state to allow unauthorised use of public property, Chapman v United Kingdom (27238/95) and Yordanova v Bulgaria (25446/06) applied. The effect of the recorder's decision in the instant case was to usurp the local authority's role in allocating housing. The administration of housing was allocated to local authorities, *Pinnock* followed. It was in the whole community's interest that such decisions were taken by a local authority and the court was not equipped to take decisions of housing management, *Powell* followed. Accordingly, whilst it was not appropriate to say that it was never right to permit a person who was a trespasser to invoke art.8 as a defence against a possession claim, a trespasser seeking to raise that argument faced an uphill task of establishing most exceptional circumstances (see paras 12-18 of judgment). (2) In the instant case, even if L had been an ex-tenant rather than a trespasser, the circumstances were not strong enough to justify refusing a possession order. The fact of L's depression was not supported by evidence and it was apparent that that condition was in abeyance. The difficulty with the financial reasons relied on by the recorder was that they missed the point of art.8, which concerned respect for a person's current home and not a duty to ensure that he had a home. Business concerns were also marginal to art.8. In respect of the alleged confusion over L surrendering his own tenancy, the highest that L's expectation of securing the tenancy of G's flat could be put was that he might have been able to succeed to it. Finally, the point that L was not a nuisance and got on well with neighbours was not a reason which assisted in establishing an art.8 argument (paras 19-22, 24). (3) When an art.8 defence was raised in possession proceedings, the district judge should ensure that it had a real prospect of succeeding before allowing the matter to go to trial, *Pinnock* followed. That course had not been taken in the instant case. The district judge should have decided that L's art.8 defence was not maintainable and not let it proceed to trial. The recorder had consequently determined that the art.8 defence was made out, but he was wrong to have done so. The local authority was, accordingly, granted a possession order (paras 26-28).

BIRMINGHAM CITY COUNCIL v LLOYD, [2012] EWCA Civ 969, [2012] H.L.R. 44, Lord Neuberger (M.R.), CA (Civ Div).

1563. Right to respect for private and family life–Children–Publication of articles and photograph of child alleged to be result of politician's extramarital affair

[European Convention on Human Rights 1950 Art.8, Art.10.]

The claimant child (C) claimed for damages for breach of privacy against the defendant newspaper publisher (X) and for an injunction restraining it from further publication of her photograph or personal details. It was claimed that C had been born as a result of an extramarital affair between her mother (M) and an elected politician (P). M alleged that journalists and photographers had "laid siege" to her home. X published a series of articles containing speculation as to C's paternity, three of which included a photograph of C taken in public without M's knowledge when C was less than a year old. Evidence was given on X's behalf stating that the story for the first article and the photograph had been supplied by a freelance agency. C sought (1) damages in respect of the behaviour of the journalists and photographers, acting as X's agents, who had "laid siege"; (2) damages in respect of the publication of the articles and her photograph; (3) an injunction to restrain X from further publishing her photograph or any particulars likely to lead to her identification in conjunction with information concerning her paternity.

Held: Judgment for claimant in part. (1) There was no evidence that X had taken, or instructed anyone to take, the photograph which it subsequently published. There was no evidence of a siege by X's employees or agents. Nor could C allege "targeting" of her by X as discussed in *Murray v Express Newspapers Plc* [2008] EWCA Civ 446, [2009] Ch. 481, [2008] C.L.Y. 1984. C had not sued the freelance agency that had taken the photographs. The highest C's case could be put was that the agency would have known that X was likely to be interested in the obtaining of photographs; there was no evidence of instructions by X to take photographs or target C. Further, other media organisations had been interested in the story prior to the first article. Such targeting as might have taken place had already begun; X could not be held solely responsible. In relation to the period following the first article, given the prior interest of other newspapers, it would be unfair to attribute the presence of unidentified photographers or reporters to the publication of one article by X. C's allegation of a siege for which X was responsible was not made out on the facts, *Murray* considered (see paras 40-49 of judgment). (2) C's paternity was a matter engaging her rights under the European Convention on Human Rights art.8. C had a reasonable expectation of privacy such as would allow M time to decide when to tell her who her father was. However, M had compromised that by discussing C in conversations and in a magazine article. C had been less than a year old at the time of the first newspaper article and the final article had been published seven months later; M had time to consider when and how to deal with the matter of her paternity. X's art.10 rights had to be recognised. The test of "exceptional public interest" required to justify publication was a high one. There was a public interest in P's professional and private life. Of itself, the fact of an extramarital affair did not render inevitable the publishing of information that a child had been conceived. However, C was alleged to be the second such child conceived as a result of an extramarital affair of P. It was said that such information went to the issue of recklessness on P's part, relevant to both his private and professional character. Balancing C's expectation of privacy against the public interest in P, the publication of the fact of C's birth had been justified. Further, the matter had been in the public domain at the time the subsequent articles were published, and those articles had added little to the first or followed up articles in other newspapers. However, even allowing for the margin of journalistic appreciation, the publication of the photographs was not reasonable, nor did X's claim that the photographs were published to enable readers to see any family resemblance between C and P justify publication. The articles had provided sufficient information (paras 113-122). Damages were assessed on the basis that on three occasions X had published unpixelated pictures of C. On the third occasion X had been aware that the family had been given an assurance regarding the publication of photographs. It would have been a simple step to seek M's consent to publication of that photograph. Any award should reflect the fact that C's rights had been breached and serve as notice as to how seriously the court regarded infringement of a child's rights, particularly where there was such interest in the public persona of the alleged father. The total award would be £15,000 (paras 123-127). (3) So much information was in the public domain that an injunction would serve no real purpose. However, an undertaking by X not to publish further photographs of C would be accepted and included in an order (para.131).

AAA v ASSOCIATED NEWSPAPERS LTD, [2012] EWHC 2103 (QB), [2013] E.M.L.R. 2, Nicola Davies, J., QBD.

1564. Right to respect for private and family life–Criminal record certificates–Disclosure of cautions held on police national computer–Proportionality of statutory scheme

[Police Act 1997 (c.50) s.115(7); Rehabilitation of Offenders Act 1974 (c.53); Rehabilitation of Offenders Act 1974 (Exceptions) Order 1975 (SI 1975/1023); European Convention on Human Rights 1950 Art.8.]

The first appellant (T) and the second appellant (B) appealed against decisions ([2012] EWHC 147 (Admin), [2012] 2 Cr. App. R. 3, [2012] C.L.Y. 1678) and ([[2011] EWHC 2197 (Admin)) respectively refusing their claims for judicial review of the statutory scheme for issuing criminal records certificates and requiring the disclosure of spent warnings to potential employers. The applicant (W) renewed her application for permission to appeal against a decision ([2011] EWHC 2161 (Admin)) that any interference with her rights under the European Convention on Human Rights 1950 art.8 resulting from that scheme had been proportionate and therefore justified. At the age of 11, T had received two warnings from the police in connection with stolen bicycles. At the age of 17, those warnings were revealed by an enhanced criminal record certificate (ECRC) when he applied for a job and again two years later when he applied for a university course. In his application for judicial review, T claimed that the statutory scheme provided for by the Rehabilitation of Offenders Act 1974, the Rehabilitation of Offenders Act 1974 (Exceptions) Order 1975 and the Police Act 1997 was incompatible with art.8 of the Convention. His claim was dismissed on the basis of the decision in *R. (on the application of L) v Commissioner of Police of the Metropolis* [2009] UKSC 3, [2010] 1 A.C. 410, [2010] C.L.Y. 2633, in which it was held that s.115(7) of the 1997 Act could be read down so as not to be incompatible with art.8. B, who was in her forties, had accepted a police caution for leaving a shop with an item she had forgotten to pay for and was later refused employment as a carer when the caution was revealed by an ECRC. At the age of 16, W had received concurrent sentences of five years and four years' detention respectively for offences of manslaughter and robbery. As she wanted to serve in the army, she sought judicial review of the statutory scheme on the basis that it prevented her convictions from ever being regarded as spent and was therefore incompatible with art.8.

Held: Appeal allowed, application refused. (1) The administering of a caution was part of an individual's private life, since it took place in private. Also, the disclosure of historic information about cautions might lead to a person's exclusion from employment and therefore adversely affect his ability to develop relations with others: that too involved an interference with the right to respect for private life. Excluding a person from employment in his chosen field was liable to affect his ability to develop relationships with others and to earn a living, which also had serious repercussions on the enjoyment of private life (see para.31 of judgment). (2) In T's case, the disclosure of the warning on an ECRC interfered with his art.8(1) rights because it involved the disclosure of sensitive personal information which was an aspect of his private life and because that disclosure was liable to affect his ability to obtain employment and to form relationships with others. The statutory regime requiring the disclosure of all convictions and cautions relating to recordable offences was disproportionate to the legitimate aims of (a) protecting employers and vulnerable individuals in their care; and (b) enabling employers to assess the suitability of a candidate for a particular kind of work. Although disclosable offences did not include those which were so insignificant that they were not recorded on the Police National Computer (PNC), that was not a proportionate filtering scheme in the context of art.8 considerations. The blanket nature of the disclosure regime went beyond what was necessary to achieve its protective purpose and could not be justified by the view that it was a "bright-line" rule which had the merit of simplicity and ease of administration, *R. (on the application of F) v Secretary of State for the Home Department* [2010] UKSC 17, [2011] 1 A.C. 331, [2010] C.L.Y. 2970 and *MM v United Kingdom (24029/07)* Times, January 16, 2013 considered. *L v Commissioner* was not concerned with the scheme for disclosure of convictions or cautions held on the PNC and did not preclude the conclusion that that statutory scheme was inconsistent with art.8, *L v Commissioner* considered. It followed that neither the disclosure provisions of the 1997 Act nor the 1975 Order were compatible with art.8. T was entitled to a declaration of incompatibility in relation to the 1997 Act and a declaration that the Order was ultra vires the 1974 Act because that Act did not permit the making of regulations in breach of art.8 (paras 32, 37, 39-41, 53-54, 56, 62, 69). (3) Save for B's age at the time of the caution, the same arguments deployed on behalf of T in relation to the disclosure provisions of the 1997 Act applied with equal force to her case. It followed that she was also entitled to a declaration of incompatibility in relation to the 1997 Act (para.70). (4) Parliament was entitled to take the view that some offences were so serious that they should never be regarded as "spent". That was not a blanket policy: it discriminated between offences which were very serious and those which were not. On that basis, W's application was refused (para.73).

R. (ON THE APPLICATION OF T) v CHIEF CONSTABLE OF GREATER MANCHESTER; R. (ON THE APPLICATION OF AW) v SECRETARY OF STATE FOR THE HOME DEPARTMENT; R. (ON THE APPLICATION OF JB) v SECRETARY OF STATE FOR THE HOME DEPARTMENT, [2013] EWCA Civ 25, [2013] 1 W.L.R. 2515, Lord Dyson (M.R.), CA (Civ Div).

1565. Right to respect for private and family life–Data retention–Lawfulness of collection and retention by police of personal information–Whether retention of data justified and proportionate

[European Convention on Human Rights 1950 Art.8, Art.8(2).]

The court was required to determine two appeals relating to the power of police to collect and retain personal information about members of the public. In the first appeal, the appellant (C) had attended public demonstrations organised by a group (S) campaigning against the operations of a weapons manufacturer. Some of S's core supporters were prone to violence and criminal behaviour, but C had never been convicted of any criminal conduct. Reports of S's activities were held on the "National Domestic Extremism Database". They included written and photographic reports on C. He challenged the police's decision not to remove those references to him from the database, contending that it amounted to an interference with his rights under the European Convention on Human Rights 1950 art.8. The Divisional Court accepted the need for the police to obtain intelligence material generally and that there was intelligence value in knowing the identities of those who attended protests organised by S and similar groups, even if they had not themselves been convicted of any offence. It regarded C's suggestion that police should be required to trawl through reports in order to consider each person named in them in isolation with a view to weeding out information no longer of value as unworkable. The court concluded that continued retention of C's information on the database was in accordance with the law and justified as proportionate to a legitimate aim pursuant to art.8(2) of the Convention. C appealed. In the second appeal, the appellant (T) had been served with a warning letter following an allegation made to the police that she had directed a single homophobic insult towards a neighbour. The letter informed her that an allegation of harassment had been made against her and that a repetition of her behaviour could involve the commission of the criminal offence of harassment. She denied the allegation and sought an order, based on her art.8 rights, that the police destroy their copy of the letter and remove all references to it from their records. The court held that the mere retention of information of the kind involved in T's case was potentially justifiable because it served a useful social purpose, and that although the police's expressed need to retain such information for up to 12 years was surprising, the court should be slow to interfere with that decision. It concluded that there was no illegality in the continued retention of the information. T appealed and the police subsequently agreed to expunge the record of her letter, but given the importance of the issues raised, the court agreed to determine the appeal in the usual way.

Held: Appeals allowed. (1) Although C was not the specific object of any of the reports, the inclusion of his personal information on the database involved an interference with his right to respect for his private life which required justification. The importance to modern policing of detailed intelligence gathering was accepted, as was the need for caution before overriding the judgment of the police about what information was likely to assist them in their task. That task was to obtain a better understanding of how S was organised, to be in a position to forecast the place and nature of its next protest and to anticipate the number of people likely to attend and the tactics they were likely to adopt. It was not easy to understand how the information currently held on C could provide any assistance in relation to any of those matters. The systematic collection, processing and retention on a searchable database of personal information, even of a relatively routine kind, involved a significant interference with the right to respect for private life. It could be justified by showing that it served the public interest in a sufficiently important way, but the police had not shown that the value of C's information was sufficient to justify its continued retention. There was no evidence to support the Divisional Court's conclusion that it was not practically possible to weed out information held on particular individuals and the instant court was not satisfied that that conclusion was correct. The interference with C's art.8 rights was disproportionate and unjustified (see paras 31, 44-46 of judgment). (2) The current policy was to retain police information letters and criminal reporting information system (CRIS) reports relating to single allegations of conduct of a kind which, if repeated, could constitute harassment, for a 12-year period. The blanket policy of retaining CRIS reports did not discriminate between serious offences, minor offences and conduct that did not amount to an offence at all. There was an obvious justification for retaining a copy of the letter for a limited period, because it might help to identify a course of conduct amounting to harassment, but since harassment required a course of conduct, it was difficult to see how the retention of the letter or the CRIS report for a period of more than a year could possibly be of any assistance in connection with a prosecution for that offence. The police's indication that they were content for T's record to be expunged made clear that the continued retention of her information was unnecessary, disproportionate and unjustifiable (para.61).

R. (ON THE APPLICATION OF CATT) v ASSOCIATION OF CHIEF POLICE OFFICERS OF ENGLAND, WALES AND NORTHERN IRELAND; R. (ON THE APPLICATION OF T) v COMMISSIONER OF POLICE OF THE METROPOLIS, [2013] EWCA Civ 192, [2013] 1 W.L.R. 3305, Lord Dyson (M.R.), CA (Civ Div).

1566. **Right to respect for private and family life–Deportation–Return of offender to country of origin after drugs offences**

[European Convention on Human Rights 1950 Art.8, Art.3.]

The complainant (B), a Nigerian national, complained that his deportation by the respondent state to Nigeria would breach the European Convention on Human Rights 1950 art.3 and art.8. B had lived in the United Kingdom since he was a child and had been granted indefinite leave to remain when he was 17. However, he had several drug-related convictions and when he was 20 he was sentenced to three years' imprisonment for two counts of possession of Class A drugs with intent to supply. The secretary of state decided to deport him. The Asylum and Immigration Tribunal dismissed his appeal because he did not have any protected family life in the UK and his ties with the country were not sufficiently strong to render his deportation an interference with his private life. B was taken into immigration detention and attempted suicide. B submitted that his deportation would, (1) in view of his suicide risk, breach art.3; (2) in view of his family life in the UK with his half-brother, aunt and girlfriend and his private life due to his length of residence, breach art.8, especially as his offending was not sufficiently grave.

Held: Complaints dismissed. (1) Expulsion by a contracting state could give rise to an issue under art.3 where substantial grounds had been shown for believing that the person concerned, if deported, faced a real risk of being subjected to treatment contrary to art.3. There could be a violation of art.3 even where the treatment arose not from the intentional acts of public authorities or non-state actors in the receiving state, but from the complainant's own physical or mental health, *Bensaid v United Kingdom (44599/98)* (2001) 33 E.H.R.R. 10, [2002] C.L.Y. 2514 applied. Nevertheless, appropriate and adequate steps taken by the relevant authorities to mitigate a risk of suicide would weigh against a conclusion that the high threshold of art.3 had been reached, *Nikovic v Sweden (28285/95)*applied. Whatever concerns there might be as to the previous handling of B's case, the Government was now fully aware of the risk posed by B to himself and could be relied upon to take the necessary steps to prevent his committing suicide. In the light of the precautions to be taken by the Government and the existence of adequate psychiatric care in Nigeria, should B require it, his deportation would not result in a real and imminent risk of treatment of such a severity as to reach the necessary threshold. It therefore followed that B's complaint under art.3 was manifestly ill-founded and thus inadmissible (see paras 30-31, 34 of judgment). (2) (Judges Garlicki and Bjorgvinsson dissenting) The totality of social ties between settled migrants such as B and the community in which they were living constituted part of the concept of private life, within the meaning of art.8. Indeed it would be a rare case where a settled migrant was unable to demonstrate that his deportation would interfere with his private life, *Miah v United Kingdom (37401/97)* (1998) 26 E.H.R.R. CD199 applied. Not all settled migrants would have equally strong family or social ties in the contracting state where they resided but the comparative strength or weakness of those ties was, in the majority of cases, more appropriately considered in assessing the proportionality of the complainant's deportation under art.8(2). It would depend on the circumstances of the particular case whether it was appropriate to focus on family life rather than private life, *Maslov v Austria (1638/03)* [2009] I.N.L.R. 47, [2009] C.L.Y. 2070 applied. However, there would be no family life between parents and adult children or between adult siblings unless they could demonstrate additional elements of dependence, *Slivenko v Latvia (48321/99)* [2004] 2 F.C.R. 28 applied. An interference with a person's private or family life would breach art.8 unless it could be justified under art.8(2) as being in accordance with the law, as pursuing one or more of the legitimate aims listed therein, and as being necessary in a democratic society to achieve the aim or aims concerned. In the instant case, B's relationships with his girlfriend and relatives in the UK did not amount to family life. However, it was clear that he enjoyed private life in the UK and that his various relationships formed part of, and strengthened, that private life. Nevertheless, B's deportation would be in accordance with the law and pursued a legitimate aim, namely the prevention of crime. It would also be necessary in a democratic society, in pursuit of that aim, because in light of the seriousness of his offending and the nature of his ties with the UK and Nigeria, his deportation would not be disproportionate (paras 43-44, 47-49, 53).

BALOGUN v UNITED KINGDOM (60286/09) (2013) 56 E.H.R.R. 3, Judge Garlicki (President), ECHR.

1567. Right to respect for private and family life–Refugees–Analogous situation to students and workers–Difference in treatment–Time of marriage

[European Convention on Human Rights 1950 Art.8, Art.14.]

The complainants (C1 and C2), a married couple, complained that they had been treated differently in respect of their rights under the European Convention on Human Rights 1950 art.8, read alone and in conjunction with art.14, than other persons and their spouses who had been granted temporary leave to remain in the United Kingdom. C1 had arrived in the UK as a refugee and was granted asylum and five years' leave to remain. During that period, he married C2 in Djibouti. C2 was refused leave to enter the UK on the ground that "family reunion" under the Immigration Rules at that time only applied to spouses who were part of a refugee's family unit before he left the country of permanent residence. C2 was also refused leave to enter the UK as the spouse of a person present and settled in the UK on the ground that C1 did not have indefinite leave to remain. The Immigration Rules were subsequently amended to allow refugees to be joined in the UK by post-flight spouses during their initial period of leave to remain, subject to certain conditions. C1 and C2 contended that other persons and their spouses, such as students and workers who had been granted temporary leave to remain, were treated differently from refugees, regardless of whether the marriage took place before or after the grant of leave to remain. They also contended that they had been treated differently from refugees and their spouses who were married at the date of flight. The UK government contended that refugees were not in an analogous situation to students and workers because the UK sought to encourage applications from those categories of person by offering incentives, whereas no such policy decision had been made in favour of refugees and asylum seekers.

Held: Complaint upheld. (1) Only differences in treatment based on an identifiable characteristic or "status" were capable of amounting to discrimination within the meaning of art.14. Moreover, in order for an issue to arise under art.14 there had to be a difference in the treatment of persons in analogous, or relevantly similar, situations. Such a difference of treatment was discriminatory if it had no objective and reasonable justification. In the instant case, the treatment of which C1 and C2 complained did not fall within one of the specific grounds listed in art.14. Therefore, in order for their complaint to succeed, they had to demonstrate that they enjoyed some "other status". The fact that immigration status was a status conferred by law, not one which was inherent to the individual, did not preclude it from amounting to an "other status" for the purposes of art.14. C1 and C2 therefore fell within that category (see paras 44-48 of judgment). (2) The requirement to demonstrate an "analogous situation" did not require that the comparator groups be identical. Refugees who married before leaving their country of permanent residence were in an analogous position to C1 and C2 as they were also in receipt of a grant of refugee status and a limited period of leave to remain in the UK. The only relevant difference was the time at which the marriage took place. As students and workers, whose spouses were entitled to join them, were usually granted a limited period of leave to remain in the UK, they too were in an analogous situation to C1 and C2 for the purposes of art.14. (para.50). (3) Contracting states enjoyed a wide margin of discretion in assessing the extent to which differences in otherwise similar situations justified a difference in treatment. Because of their direct knowledge of their society and its needs, the national authorities were usually better placed than the international judge to appreciate what was in the public or economic interest. However, the offering of incentives to certain groups of immigrants had not been advanced as justification in recent domestic cases; indeed, the secretary of state had been called upon to give urgent attention to amending the Immigration Rules so as to extend them to the spouses of those with limited leave to remain as refugees, *A (Afghanistan) v Secretary of State for the Home Department* [2009] EWCA Civ 825 and *FH (Iran) v Entry Clearance Officer, Tehran* [2010] UKUT 275 (IAC), [2011] Imm. A.R. 29, [2011] C.L.Y. 1787 considered. It followed that the difference in treatment between C1 and C2 on the one hand, and students and workers on the other, was not objectively and reasonably justified. Moreover, there was no justification for treating refugees who married post-flight differently from those who married pre-flight. There had therefore been a breach of art.14 read together with art.8 (paras 52-56).

HODE v UNITED KINGDOM (22341/09) (2013) 56 E.H.R.R. 27, Judge Garlicki (President), ECHR.

1568. Sexual orientation discrimination–Bed and breakfast accommodation–Refusal of double bed to homosexual couple–Direct or indirect discrimination

[Equality Act (Sexual Orientation) Regulations 2007 (SI 2007/1263) reg.3(1), reg.4, reg.6; European Convention on Human Rights 1950 Art.8, Art.9.]

The appellant bed and breakfast owner (W) appealed against a decision ([2013] EWCA Civ 820, [2013] 1 W.L.R. 2490, [2013] 10 C.L. 183) that she had unlawfully discriminated against the respondent homosexual couple (B) on the grounds of their sexual orientation contrary to the Equality Act (Sexual Orientation) Regulations 2007. As a result of her Christian beliefs, W restricted the sharing of her double rooms to heterosexual, preferably married couples. She refused to accommodate B in the double room they had booked when she realised that they were a homosexual couple. The judge followed *Hall v Bull* [2012] EWCA Civ 83, [2012] 1 W.L.R. 2514, [2012] C.L.Y. 1682 and found that there was unlawful direct discrimination on the ground of sexual orientation contrary to reg.3 and reg.4. W submitted that (1) her bed and breakfast accommodation was not a boarding house or similar establishment within the meaning of reg.4(2)(b); (2) the exception in reg.6(1)(a) applied to her provision of accommodation as she provided a special degree of care and attention to her guests so that reg.4 did not apply; (3) she objected to sexual relations outside marriage which was not a protected characteristic and was different from sexual orientation so that it was not direct discrimination; (4) any indirect discrimination was justified by reference to her right to manifest her Christian beliefs under European Convention on Human Rights 1950 art.9 and her rights to enjoyment of her home under art.8.

Held: Appeal dismissed. (1) The judge was correct to find that W offered accommodation in a boarding house or similar establishment within the meaning of reg.4(2)(b), *Otter v Norman* [1989] A.C. 129, [1988] C.L.Y. 2062 followed (see para.11 of judgment). (2) The judge was correct to reject W's interpretation of reg.6(1). The exception only applied to anything done by a person who took into his home and treated as if they were members of his family people requiring a special degree of care and attention. B were not persons requiring a special degree of care and attention (para.15). (3) In the court's view, *Hall* was not a case of direct discrimination against a homosexual couple on the ground of their sexual orientation, since there were other unmarried couples who would also be denied accommodation on the ground that they too were unmarried. It was a case of indirect discrimination because the defendants' policy in that case put homosexual couples at a disadvantage as compared to heterosexual couples on the ground of their sexual orientation. The former could not marry, whereas the latter could. The policy under scrutiny in *Hall* and in the instant case was to exclude unmarried couples. However there were no grounds for distinguishing *Hall* in the instant case so the judge was right to follow *Hall* and to hold that there was unlawful direct discrimination on the ground of sexual orientation, *Hall* followed (paras 21-23). (4) Although not necessary to the outcome of the appeal, in the court's view, it was indirect discrimination. The court was required to have regard to the effect on a person of an interference with her right to manifest religious belief, *Eweida v United Kingdom (48420/10)* [2013] I.R.L.R.

231 followed. The judge was right to hold that the balance came down in favour of B. The judge had correctly given weight to the balance struck by the Regulations themselves and had considered the impact on W of holding that her policy was contrary to the Regulations. The Convention and Parliament attached importance to protecting persons against discrimination on the grounds of sexual orientation and W had failed to show that she would suffer serious damage if she was not permitted to refuse her double rooms to homosexual couples so her defence of justification would fail (paras 26, 54-58, 60).

BLACK v WILKINSON, [2013] EWCA Civ 820, [2013] 1 W.L.R. 2490, Lord Dyson (M.R.), CA (Civ Div).

IMMIGRATION

1569. Accession–Freedom of movement–Treaties–Croatia

THE ACCESSION OF CROATIA (IMMIGRATION AND WORKER AUTHORISATION) REGULATIONS 2013, SI 2013/1460; made under the European Union (Croatian Accession and Irish Protocol) Act 2013 s.4. In force: July 1, 2013; .

These Regulations make provision in relation to the entitlement of nationals of the Republic of Croatia to reside and work in the United Kingdom on the accession of that State to the European Union on July 1 2013. They give effect to Annex V to the treaty concerning the accession of the Republic of Croatia to the European Union, signed at Brussels on December 9, 2011. That Annex permits member States to derogate from various provisions of freedom of movement of persons provisions under EU law relating to access to their labour markets by Croatian nationals for a transitional period.

1570. Accession state workers–Habitual residence–Migrant workers–Croatia

THE SOCIAL SECURITY (CROATIA) AMENDMENT REGULATIONS 2013, SI 2013/1474; made under the Social Security Contributions and Benefits Act 1992 s.123, s.135, s.137, s.175; the Jobseekers Act 1995 s.4, s.35, s.36; the Immigration and Asylum Act 1999 s.115; the State Pension Credit Act 2002 s.1, s.17; and the Welfare Reform Act 2007 s.4, s.24, s.25. In force: July 1, 2013; .

These Regulations insert a new category of persons who are exempt from the habitual residence test, namely nationals of Croatia who are subject to the worker authorisation scheme established by the Accession of Croatia (Immigration and Worker Authorisation) Regulations 2013 and who are treated as workers pursuant to those Regulations.

1571. Applications–Citizenship–English language–Naturalisation

THE BRITISH NATIONALITY (GENERAL) (AMENDMENT) REGULATIONS 2013, SI 2013/2541; made under the British Nationality Act 1981 s.41. In force: October 28, 2013; .

These Regulations amend provisions in the British Nationality (General) Regulations 2003 (SI 2003/548) for determining whether a person has sufficient knowledge of language and of life in the UK for the purpose of an application for naturalisation as a British citizen under the British Nationality Act 1981 s.6.

1572. Applications–Fees

THE IMMIGRATION AND NATIONALITY (FEES) (AMENDMENT) ORDER 2013, SI 2013/249; made under the Immigration, Asylum and Nationality Act 2006 s.51, s.52. In force: February 8, 2013; .

This Order amends the Immigration and Nationality (Fees) Order 2011, which enables the Secretary of State to charge fees for any applications, services and processes listed in the Order.

1573. Applications–Fees–Immigration–Nationality

THE IMMIGRATION AND NATIONALITY (COST RECOVERY FEES) REGULATIONS 2013, SI 2013/617; made under the Immigration, Asylum and Nationality Act 2006 s.51, s.52. In force: April 6, 2013; .

These Regulations specify fees for applications, services and processes relating to immigration and nationality where those fees are at or below the administrative cost of dealing with the application or providing the process or service. They replace the Immigration and Nationality (Cost Recovery Fees) Regulations 2012 and are to come into force on April 6, 2013.

1574. Applications–Fees–Nationality

THE IMMIGRATION AND NATIONALITY (FEES) REGULATIONS 2013, SI 2013/749; made under the Immigration, Asylum and Nationality Act 2006 s.51, s.52. In force: March 27, 2013; .

These Regulations specify fees relating to immigration and nationality. They are made for the purposes of the Immigration and Nationality (Fees) Order 2011, which sets out the applications, services and processes related to immigration and nationality for which fees may be specified in regulations.

1575. Asylum seekers–Age assessments–Local authority undertaking age assessment under Children Act 1989–Whether bound by assessments undertaken by secretary of state in discharge of immigration functions

[Children Act 1989 (c.41) s.20; Directive 2003/9 on minimum standards for the reception of asylum seekers Art.21; Directive 2004/83 on minimum standards for the qualification and status of third country nationals or stateless persons as refugees or as persons who otherwise need international protection and the content of the protection granted; Directive 2005/85 on and withdrawing refugee status; Directive 2005/85 on granting and withdrawing refugee status Art.39(1)(e), Art.39(1)(a).]

The court had to determine issues relating to age assessments carried out by local authorities for the purposes of the Children Act 1989 and by the Secretary of State for the Home Department in discharging her immigration functions. The various appeals had been brought in relation to a number of asylum seekers (K), and arose from situations where a local authority and the secretary of state had made different age assessments, one determining an individual to be a child and the other an adult. To support a co-operative approach to age assessment, a joint working protocol had been agreed, in 2005, between the Association of Directors of Social Services for the United Kingdom Local Government and Statutory Childcare Agencies and the former Immigration and Nationality Directorate of the Home Office. The issues were whether (i) the local authority had failed to apply the protocol by not attempting a reconciliation of its age assessments with the secretary of state's or agreeing to refer the disputed assessments to the binding adjudication of a nominated third party; (ii) under EU law, a local authority was bound to accept and apply the decision of the secretary of state as to the age of an individual, or decisions made by the First-tier Tribunal (Immigration and Asylum Chamber) on appeal. K argued that (1) the local authority's decision not to follow the protocol was unlawful and even if the protocol was not its policy, the decision was unconscionable and unreasonable; (2) the secretary of state was the UK's designated authority responsible for examining and determining asylum applications and to permit a local authority to have an independent power to refuse welfare and support to a person whom she had determined to be a child was incompatible with the rights and protections to children guaranteed under Directive 2003/9, Directive 2004/83 and Directive 2005/85.

Held: Judgment accordingly. (1) The local authority had not accepted the protocol as part of its policy, it had not followed it in practice, and it was not a legally binding document. It was not unconscionable or unreasonable for the local authority not to apply the protocol because there was no freestanding public law principle of unconscionability. Although it was desirable for local authorities and the secretary of state to attempt to agree age assessments, it was quite another matter to insist on differences being referred to the binding decision of a third party, particularly since the adjudication process envisaged by the protocol was vague and unworkable. In any event, an adjudicator's decision which was binding between the local authority and the secretary of state could not be determinative of an age issue for the purposes of the 1989 Act because the question of whether a person was a child for the purposes of s.20 was one of jurisdictional fact (see paras 21-32 of judgment). (2) If the local authority disagreed with the secretary of state's assessment of an applicant's age, that had no necessary effect on the secretary of state's asylum decision and the local authority would plainly not be taking a decision on the asylum application, or a decision which only the secretary of state was competent to take, *Samba Diouf v Ministre du Travail, de l'Emploi et de l'Immigration (C-69/10)* [2012] 1 C.M.L.R. 8 applied. For the same reason, the local authority would not be denying the applicant a right of appeal to a tribunal to which he was entitled under Directive 2005/85 art.39(1)(a) or art.39(1)(e). It was true that a remedy limited to judicial review of the local authority's decision to refuse accommodation under s.20 of the 1989 Act would unfairly place the burden on the child of requiring him to prove his minority for a second time, and to a higher standard than in an asylum application. However, that was the very procedure envisaged by Directive 2003/9 art.21, namely access to the national law procedures for an appeal against a negative decision concerning the grant of benefits under the Directive. Such a decision was different from the refusal of an asylum claim or the revocation of refugee status and EU law did not require the standard of proof to be the same for both. A Member State had a significant margin of appreciation in the methods by which it implemented a Directive. It was undesirable that a person's age should be subject to successive examination, but that did not mean that the principle of effectiveness had been breached. EU law did not require a local authority to be bound by an age assessment of the secretary of state. Further, as a matter of domestic law, a local authority was not bound by a tribunal's decision on an appeal against a decision of the secretary of state as to an applicant's age, *R. (on the application of PM) v Hertfordshire CC* [2010] EWHC 2056 (Admin), [2011] P.T.S.R. 269, [2011] C.L.Y. 2165 applied (paras 33-49, 54).

R. (ON THE APPLICATION OF K) v BIRMINGHAM CITY COUNCIL; R. (ON THE APPLICATION OF YK (AFGHANISTAN)) v BIRMINGHAM CITY COUNCIL; R. (ON THE APPLICATION OF JS (AFGHANISTAN)) v BIRMINGHAM CITY COUNCIL; R. (ON THE APPLICATION OF MWA) v BIRMINGHAM CITY COUNCIL, [2012] EWCA Civ 1432, [2013] 1 W.L.R. 1755, Lord Dyson (M.R.), CA (Civ Div).

1576. Asylum seekers–Credibility–Extent to which First-tier Tribunal entitled to reject medical evidence in determining entitlement to asylum

[Tribunal Procedure (Upper Tribunal) Rules 2008 (SI 2008/2698) r.15(2A)(b).]

The appellant (Y), a Turkish national of Alevi Kurd ethnicity, appealed against a refusal of asylum. At his screening interview upon arrival in the United Kingdom, Y indicated that he was in good health and fit to be interviewed. He described having been tortured and beaten by the police in Turkey because of his political activities. The respondent secretary of state rejected his claim and recommended his removal. Y appealed to an immigration judge and served a psychiatric report, prepared five months after his arrival in the UK and diagnosing post traumatic stress disorder said to have resulted from his traumatic experiences in Turkey. The report detailed why its author believed that Y's symptoms were genuine. The expert did not attend to give oral evidence. The immigration judge found that Y had fabricated his entire story, that he was fit and well, as he had said in his initial interview, and that the medical expert had been "hoodwinked" by him. Y appealed to the Upper Tribunal on the basis that the immigration judge had made a material error of law in rejecting the findings in the psychiatric report. His application to adduce as fresh evidence a supplementary letter from the expert psychiatrist, which commented on the findings of the immigration judge, was summarily refused. Having reviewed the background and evidence in detail, the tribunal concluded that the judge's decision did not constitute an error of law, and that while a judge had to be cautious in reaching such a conclusion, he was not obliged to blindly accept any medical evidence before him. The issues on the instant appeal were (i) whether the tribunal should have permitted Y to adduce the supplementary medical report; (ii) the extent to which the immigration judge had been entitled to reject the written report of an expert witness, which had not been tested in cross-examination.

Held: Appeal dismissed. (1) The tribunal had, pursuant to the Tribunal Procedure (Upper Tribunal) Rules 2008 r.15(2A)(b), properly refused to adduce the supplementary medical report. The statutory scheme, in an asylum context, did not generally permit an entire rehearing on the facts by the Upper Tribunal unless a point of law was identified; the efficiency of the whole appeal system would be seriously undermined if parties conceived that they could readily adduce on appeal evidence not placed before the tribunal below. In construing r.15(2A)(b), it was generally appropriate for the tribunal to have regard to the three criteria identified in *Ladd v Marshall* [1954] 1 W.L.R. 1489, [1954] C.L.Y. 2507. In the instant case, the first limb of that case, which concerned reasonable diligence in obtaining the report, was not satisfied, and there was, therefore, no reason to interfere with the tribunal's discretion not to accept it. The supplementary report was partly an acceptance that some matters had not been covered in the first report, and partly a running critique of the reasoning of the immigration judge, which was not the proper province of an expert (see paras 32-39 of judgment). (2) A material error of law was capable of arising where a tribunal made adverse findings on credibility before considering relevant expert evidence. That was not the situation in the instant case, where the first medical report had been appraised as part of the totality of evidence bearing on Y's account of events. In order to reject medical evidence, a tribunal had to have, and articulate, justifiable reasons, *SS (Sri Lanka) v Secretary of State for the Home Department* [2012] EWCA Civ 155 followed, *R. (on the application of M) v Immigration Appellate Authority* [2004] EWHC 582 (Admin) and *Y (Sri Lanka) v Secretary of State for the Home Department* [2009] EWCA Civ 362, [2009] H.R.L.R. 22, [2009] C.L.Y. 2082 considered. The question of whether an appellant's account was credible or plausible was ultimately a question of legal appraisal for the tribunal judge. Doctors had to assess symptoms and would therefore clinically assess an appellant's account of events; a judge had to look at the totality of the evidence, which might involve finding that the account given to the doctor was, in fact, falsified. In the instant case, the immigration judge had given rational and justifiable reasons for rejecting the medical report as corroborating the veracity of Y's account. That account had been found not plausible or credible in several respects and Y's mental health could not readily be relied upon as an explanation for such implausibility. That another judge might have reached a different conclusion on the evidence was not to the point (paras 41, 43-47, 49, 52-53).

IY (TURKEY) v SECRETARY OF STATE FOR THE HOME DEPARTMENT, [2012] EWCA Civ 1560, [2013] Imm. A.R. 391, Longmore, L.J., CA (Civ Div).

1577. Asylum seekers–Removal–Return of asylum seeker to state in which asylum claim first made–Allegations of mistreatment in receiving state–Absence of systematic deficiency in asylum procedure in receiving state

[Asylum and Immigration (Treatment of Claimants, etc.) Act 2004 (c.19) Sch.3 Pt 2 para.3, Pt 2 para.6; Regulation 343/2003.]

The appellant asylum seeker (T) appealed against a decision upholding the respondent secretary of state's decision to remove him to Romania to have his asylum claim determined there pursuant to Regulation 343/2003. T was a Sri-Lankan national who claimed to have experienced persecution there. He used an agent to leave Sri Lanka and entered Romania in 2010. T was arrested there and fingerprinted, and then claimed asylum. He returned to Sri Lanka but, having secured the services of another agent, left and entered the United Kingdom in 2011. T claimed asylum and in interview said that he had not claimed asylum or been fingerprinted in any other country outside Sri Lanka. Fingerprints taken in the UK revealed his presence and asylum claim in Romania. Following a formal request by the secretary of state, the Romanian authorities accepted responsibility for considering T's asylum application under the Regulation. The secretary of state informed T that by virtue of the Asylum and Immigration (Treatment of Claimants, etc.) Act 2004 Sch.3 Pt 2 para.3, Romania was to be treated as a safe country and that he would be removed there as an illegal immigrant. T was removed to Romania in May 2011 and detained. Once outside the UK, he appealed to the First-tier Tribunal against the removal decision on the basis that the Romanian authorities had not fairly processed his earlier asylum claim. The tribunal held that T had been properly returned to Romania and that T's out of country appeal was not valid. T contended that the tribunal had erred in finding that there was no valid appeal. He submitted that he was currently experiencing racially-motivated ill-treatment at the hands of the Romanian authorities and non-state agents in the shape of fellow detainees, and that such mistreatment meant that the Romanian authorities did not comply with EU minimum standards for asylum seekers' reception conditions. T argued that the irrebuttable presumption in Sch.3 Pt 2 para.6 of the Act that Romania, as a safe state, would not act in a way contrary to EU law was qualified by *R. (on the application of NS) v Secretary of State for the Home Department (C-411/10)* [2013] Q.B. 102, [2012] C.L.Y. 1698 in that if there were substantial grounds for believing that there were systemic flaws in the asylum procedure and reception conditions for asylum applicants in the receiving Member State responsible, resulting in inhuman or degrading treatment, transfer to that country by the removing state would be incompatible with his rights as a refugee.

Held: Appeal dismissed. (1) The tribunal had erred in law in holding that there was no valid appeal before it. A person in T's position was not precluded from appealing, once outside the UK, an immigration decision to remove him. The tribunal's determination was set aside and the decision in T's appeal fell to be re-made by the instant tribunal (see paras 35-36 of judgment). (2) An individual applicant might experience less than satisfactory treatment in the processing of his asylum, and that might be the case with T. It would however, undermine the Regulation and the legislation underpinning it if an individual who had been returned to the state tasked with processing his asylum claim were able to have the returning state adjudicate upon (a) the receiving state's treatment of that person as an asylum seeker; (b) whether that person had a well-founded fear of persecution if returned to a non-Member State. In such a scenario, judicial fact-finders in the UK would face the obvious problem that, unlike their counterparts in the receiving state, they would be unable to receive oral evidence from the appellant and were likely to be in a worse position to make sustainable findings of fact, compared with the court in the receiving state. There were manifest problems in accepting T's allegations regarding his treatment in Romania. Schedule 3 Pt.2 para.6 fell to be qualified or read down only where there was shown, on the basis of the kinds of evidence identified in *R. (on the application of NS)*, to be in the receiving state a "systemic deficiency in the asylum procedure and in the reception conditions of asylum seekers" in that state; where such evidence was lacking, the tribunal had to apply para.6, without any qualification, *R. (on the application of NS)* considered. It was not permissible to read down that provision on the basis only of evidence concerning the individual appellant. It followed that T was precluded from bringing the grounds he sought to advance by reason of Sch.3 Pt 2 para.6 (paras 58, 61, 63, 65, 69).

VT (DUBLIN REGULATION: POST-REMOVAL APPEAL: SRI LANKA), *Re; sub nom.* VT (SRI LANKA) v SECRETARY OF STATE FOR THE HOME

DEPARTMENT, [2012] UKUT 308 (IAC), [2013] Imm. A.R. 45, Judge Lane, UT (IAC).

1578. Asylum seekers–Responsible Member State–Second asylum application made in United Kingdom–Whether Italy guilty of systematic failures in its treatment of aslyum seekers

[Nationality, Immigration and Asylum Act 2002 (c.41) s.92(4)(a), Sch.3; Regulation 343/2003 on asylum applications lodged in a Member State by a third-country national Art.3(2); European Convention on Human Rights 1950 Art.8.]

In four joined cases the court was required to determine whether the appellant asylum seekers (W, X, Y and Z) should be returned to Italy. The appellants had applied for asylum in Italy before eventually making their way to the United Kingdom. X, Y, Z, and her two children, had lived on the streets in Italy, without food or assistance. Y and Z alleged that during that time they had been raped. The home secretary had certified their claims for asylum as unfounded by virtue of Regulation 343/2003 and the Nationality, Immigration and Asylum Act 2002 s.92(4)(a) and Sch.3, and ordered their removal to Italy, where they had first claimed asylum. A report by the United Nations High Commissioner for Refugees (UNHCR) in July 2012 set out a number of concerns about Italy's inability to cope with sudden influxes of asylum seekers and the uneven quality of provision. The appellants argued that they would be at real risk of inhuman or degrading treatment if returned to Italy. Z also relied upon the European Convention on Human Rights 1950 art.8 and argued that it was in the best interests of her two children to remain in the UK. The secretary of state submitted that there was a presumption of law that Italy's treatment of asylum seekers was compliant with its international obligations and, in order to rebut the presumption, the appellants had to show that Italy was in systematic breach of its obligations.

Held: Appeals dismissed. (1) The assessment of risk on return depended on a combination of personal experience and systematic shortcomings which, in total, could suffice to rebut the presumption of compliance. The judgement of the UNHCR remained pre-eminent and possibly decisive in that exercise, *KRS v United Kingdom (Admissibility) (32733/08)* (2009) 48 E.H.R.R. SE8 and *MSS v Belgium (30696/09)* (2011) 53 E.H.R.R. 2 applied. In *R. (on the application of NS) v Secretary of State for the Home Department (C-411/10)* [2013] Q.B. 102, [2012] C.L.Y. 1698, the European Court of Justice had consciously elevated the finding of the European Court of Human Rights in *MSS* that there was a systematic deficiency in the Greek system of refugee protection, into a condition of intervention. Without it, proof of individual risk, however grave, and whether or not arising from operational problems in the state's systems, could not prevent a return under the 2003 Regulation. The court had no choice but to approach the instant cases on the same footing, *NS* followed (see paras 39-41, 47-48 of judgment). (2) The UNHCR's report had made a series of recommendations, but, in contrast to reports on Greece, it had not suggested that the Italian asylum system was systematically deficient. However, support from the UNHCR was not a legal necessity. The question was whether the appellants' evidence, including various reports from non-governmental organisations and a report from the Council of Europe's Commissioner for Human Rights, could fill the gap. The evidence supported the accounts given by X, Y and Z of their experiences of seeking asylum in Italy. If the question was whether each appellant faced a real risk of inhuman or degrading treatment if returned to Italy, their claims would plainly be arguable. However, that was not the law. The decision in NS had set a threshold in return cases which existed nowhere else in refugee law. The sole ground on which a second state was required to exercise its power under art.3(2) of the Regulation to entertain a re-application for asylum, and to refrain from returning the applicant to the state of first arrival, was that the source of risk to the applicant was a systematic deficiency, known to the second state, in the first state's asylum and reception procedures. Short of that, even powerful evidence of individual risk was of no avail. The totality of the evidence about Italy, although extremely troubling, did not come up to that mark. Therefore W, X, Y and Z's claims were incapable of succeeding under art.3 of the 1950 Convention and the secretary of state was justified in certifying them as unfounded (paras 51-52, 61-64). (3) In gauging the proportionality of an interference with private life under art.8 the interests of children were a paramount consideration, but not a trump card, *ZH (Tanzania) v Secretary of State for the Home Department* [2011] UKSC 4, [2011] 2 A.C. 166, [2011] C.L.Y. 1790 followed. There was no real possibility of Z's art.8 claim being upheld on an in-country appeal to an immigration judge. Her daughter was an adult and could not legitimately have her interests aggregated with Z's. Her son, aged 14, was only in the UK because his mother had been able to resist removal for four years. The court was required to deem conditions for refugees in Italy to be compliant with international obligations. The case against Z's removal was too exiguous to stand up when set against the history of her entry and the legal/policy imperatives for returning her to Italy (para.71).

R. (ON THE APPLICATION OF EM (ERITREA)) v SECRETARY OF STATE FOR THE HOME DEPARTMENT; R. (ON THE APPLICATION OF EH (IRAN)) v SECRETARY OF STATE FOR THE HOME DEPARTMENT; R. (ON THE APPLICATION OF AE (ERITREA)) v SECRETARY OF STATE FOR THE HOME DEPARTMENT; R. (ON THE APPLICATION OF MA (ERITREA)) v SECRETARY OF STATE FOR THE HOME DEPARTMENT; *sub nom.* EM (ERITREA) v SECRETARY OF STATE FOR THE HOME DEPARTMENT; MA (ERITREA) v SECRETARY OF STATE FOR THE HOME DEPARTMENT, [2012] EWCA Civ 1336, [2013] 1 W.L.R. 576, Richards, L.J., CA (Civ Div).

1579. Asylum seekers–Unaccompanied minors–Secretary of State's duty to endeavour to trace asylum seeker's family–Correct approach to appeals where statutory duty breached

[Borders, Citizenship and Immigration Act 2009 (c.11) s.55; Asylum Seekers (Reception Conditions) Regulations 2005 (SI 2005/7) reg.6.]

The court was required to determine the correct approach to applications by unaccompanied minors for asylum. The appellants (K) were eight young men from Afghanistan who had arrived in the United Kingdom aged 15 or 16 and unsuccessfully claimed asylum. They were granted discretionary leave to remain until they were aged seventeen-and-a-half. At age 17 they made applications for asylum or humanitarian protection, which were refused. Their appeals to the First-tier Tribunal were refused before they reached age 18. Their appeals to the Upper Tribunal were heard and dismissed after they had reached 18. The issue was whether in those circumstances they should retain the advantages, in immigration terms, of their minority when their appeals were heard.

Held: Judgment accordingly. (1) The general rule was that the specialist tribunals dealing with asylum appeals considered them on the basis of the facts and circumstances prevailing at the time of the hearing. If the facts changed between the determination in the First-tier Tribunal and the hearing in the Upper Tribunal, it was the changed facts and circumstances which had to be addressed, *R. v Secretary of State for the Home Department, Ex p. Ravichandran (No.1)* [1996] Imm. A.R. 97, [1996] C.L.Y. 3216 applied. The question was whether there was something about the instant cases which took them outside the *Ravichandran* principle. In determining that question it was important to consider whether the secretary of state had failed to discharge the duty to endeavour to trace K's families under the Asylum Seekers (Reception Conditions) Regulations 2005 reg.6. A failure to discharge that duty might be relevant to judicial consideration of an asylum or humanitarian protection claim, and might also be relevant to a consideration of the duty under the Borders, Citizenship and Immigration Act 2009 s.55, *DS (Afghanistan) v Secretary of State for the Home Department* [2011] EWCA Civ 305, [2011] I.N.L.R. 389, [2011] C.L.Y. 1711 and *HK (Afghanistan) v Secretary of State for the Home Department* [2012] EWCA Civ 315 followed. The reg.6 duty was not discharged by simply informing the minor of the tracing facilities of the Red Cross. The court drew an inference that the secretary of state had failed to discharge that duty in relation to unaccompanied minors from Afghanistan because she adopted the policy of granting them leave to remain until they reached the age of seventeen-and-a-half. By that time, the duty was close to expiration because of the imminence of them reaching the age of majority. That amounted to a systematic breach of the duty. It was therefore necessary to consider whether that triggered the principles set out in *R. (on the application of Rashid) v Secretary of State for the Home Department* [2005] EWCA Civ 744, [2005] Imm. A.R. 608, [2005] C.L.Y. 2154 and *R. (on the application of S) v Secretary of State for the Home Department* [2007] EWCA Civ 546, [2007] Imm. A.R. 781, [2008] C.L.Y. 2019 (see paras 2, 12-17, 24 of judgment). (2) In summary, the *Rashid/R(S)* principles were that when serious administrative errors caused conspicuous unfairness, and illegality, the court should give such relief as it properly could. However, the court had no power to grant indefinite leave to remain, nor could it direct the secretary of state to do so. Nevertheless, it was open to the court to determine that a legally material factor in the secretary of state's exercise of discretion was the correction of injustice, *Rashid/R(S)* applied. When those principles were applicable, they modified the strict application of the *Ravichandran* principle. Further, although the duty to trace did not endure beyond the age of 18, it could not be the case that the assessment of risk on return was subject to such a bright line rule. The risks of the forced recruitment or sexual exploitation of vulnerable young males still existed after the age of 18, *DS (Afghanistan)* applied (paras 12, 17-18). (3) Much would turn on the specific facts of each case. At one end of the spectrum was an applicant who gave a credible and cooperative account of having no surviving family in Afghanistan or of having lost touch with surviving family members. Even if he had reached the age of 18 by the time his appeal was considered by the tribunal, he might have the basis of a successful appeal by availing himself of the *Rashid/R(S)* principle and/or s.55 by reference to the secretary of state's failure to discharge the duty to endeavour to trace. In such a case *Ravichandran* would not be an insurmountable obstacle. At the other end of the spectrum was an applicant whose claim to have no surviving family members was disbelieved, and who was uncooperative and frustrated any attempt to trace his family. He might put himself beyond the bite of the protective and corrective principle, not as punishment for his mendacity, but because he had failed to prove the risk on return, and because there was no causative link between the secretary of state's breach of duty and his claim to protection (para.25). (4) All of K's appeals, save one, which was granted, were to be determined at a further hearing using the principles outlined above (para.29).

KA (AFGHANISTAN) v SECRETARY OF STATE FOR THE HOME DEPARTMENT; *sub nom.* AR (AFGHANISTAN) v SECRETARY OF STATE FOR THE HOME DEPARTMENT; EU (AFGHANISTAN) v SECRETARY OF STATE FOR THE HOME DEPARTMENT; AK (AFGHANISTAN) v SECRETARY OF STATE FOR THE HOME DEPARTMENT; QA (AFGHANISTAN) v SECRETARY OF STATE FOR THE HOME DEPARTMENT; FU (AFGHANISTAN) v SECRETARY OF STATE FOR THE HOME DEPARTMENT; SU (AFGHANISTAN) v SECRETARY OF STATE FOR THE HOME DEPARTMENT; SA (AFGHANISTAN) v SECRETARY OF STATE FOR THE HOME DEPARTMENT, [2012] EWCA Civ 1014, [2013] 1 W.L.R. 615, Maurice Kay, L.J., CA (Civ Div).

1580. Asylum seekers–Unaccompanied minors–Secretary of state's duty to endeavour to trace families of unaccompanied minors seeking asylum–Application of correct approach where statutory duty breached

[Asylum Seekers (Reception Conditions) Regulations 2005 (SI 2005/7) reg.6; European Convention on Human Rights 1950 Art.8.]

The appellants (EU, FU, SU, AR, QA and AK) appealed against decisions of the Upper Tribunal, upholding the refusal of the respondent secretary of state to grant them indefinite leave to remain in the United Kingdom. The appellants were all young Afghan men who had arrived in the UK as unaccompanied minors and claimed asylum. In each case, the secretary of state had refused the asylum application, but granted discretionary leave to remain until the age of seventeen-and-a-half, in accordance with her policy on unaccompanied minors. Shortly before reaching that age, each applied for asylum or humanitarian protection, which was refused. The court had already considered the generic legal issues and had established the principles which were applicable, in the associated case of *KA (Afghanistan) v Secretary of State for the Home Department* [2012] EWCA Civ 1014, [2013] 1 W.L.R. 615, [2013] 3 C.L. 119 in which Maurice Kay L.J. had given the lead judgment. The appellants submitted that they were entitled to indefinite leave to remain by reason of the secretary of state's breach of her duty to endeavour to trace their respective families under the Asylum Seekers (Reception Conditions) Regulations 2005 reg.6, which gave rise to their right to benefit from the "protective principle" established in *R. (on the application of Rashid) v Secretary of State for the Home Department* [2005] EWCA Civ 744, [2005] Imm. A.R. 608, [2005] C.L.Y. 2154.

Held: Appeals dismissed. (1) Like the Court of Appeal in *R. (on the application of S) v Secretary of State for the Home Department* [2007] EWCA Civ 546, [2007] Imm. A.R. 781, [2008] C.L.Y. 2019, the instant court had great difficulties with the judgments in *Rashid*. In cases concerned with asylum claims, the purpose of the grant of leave to remain was to grant protection to someone who would be at risk, or whose rights under the European Convention on Human Rights 1950 would be infringed if he were returned to his country of nationality. Of course, breaches of the secretary of state's duties in addressing a claim might lead to an independent justification for leave to remain, of which the paradigm was the art.8 claim of an asylum seeker whose claim had not been expeditiously determined, with the result that he established private and family life in the country. However, to grant leave to remain to someone who had no risk on return, whose Convention rights would not be infringed by his return and who had no other independent claim to remain there was to use the power to grant leave to remain for a purpose other than that for which it had been conferred. The court should not require or encourage the secretary of state to grant leave in such circumstances, either to mark its displeasure at her conduct, or as a sanction for her misconduct, *KA* followed, *S* applied, *Rashid* doubted (see para.6 of judgment). It was necessary to take into account the reason for the secretary of state's policy to grant children limited leave to remain, irrespective of their asylum claim. In cases such as the instant, it would be inhumane to return an unaccompanied child to Afghanistan, at least where there would be no family to take care of him or her. However, that rationale applied with less force with increasing age. It was also necessary to bear in mind that the birthday which had been ascribed to a claimant was often arbitrary, which was a further reason why the achievement of adulthood could not of itself necessarily change the assessment of risk on return. Another point which was of substance was that unaccompanied children who arrived in the UK from Afghanistan had done so as a result of someone, presumably their families, incurring considerable costs and they were unlikely to be happy to co-operate in their child's return (paras 8-10). (2) All of the appellants' appeals were dismissed. AK and QA had failed to give any sensible information about their addresses. They would not be at risk on return, and although QA's 18th birthday had inappropriately been treated as a bright line, there was no suggestion that he would be regarded as vulnerable in Kabul. There was no basis upon which it could be said that if the secretary of state had failed to perform her duty to endeavour to trace, her decision had been materially in error (paras 12-16, 31-35). AR's appeal was dismissed because he had returned to Afghanistan (paras 17-18). The claims of EU and SU to have lost touch with their families had been rejected (paras 19-26). FU had been treated as being over 18 when both his asylum claim and art.8 claim were heard, meaning that there was no duty to endeavour to trace. He would not be at risk upon return and his removal would not be disproportionate (paras 27-30). (3) Maurice Kay, L.J. stated that although the lead judgment was more overtly critical of the previous jurisprudence than he had been in his judgment in *KA*, he did not disagree with it (para.38).

EU (AFGHANISTAN) v SECRETARY OF STATE FOR THE HOME DEPARTMENT; FU (AFGHANISTAN) v SECRETARY OF STATE FOR THE HOME DEPARTMENT; SU (AFGHANISTAN) v SECRETARY OF STATE FOR THE HOME DEPARTMENT; AR

(AFGHANISTAN) v SECRETARY OF STATE FOR THE HOME DEPARTMENT; QA (AFGHANISTAN) v SECRETARY OF STATE FOR THE HOME DEPARTMENT; AK (AFGHANISTAN) v SECRETARY OF STATE FOR THE HOME DEPARTMENT, [2013] EWCA Civ 32, [2013] Imm. A.R. 496, Maurice Kay, L.J. (VP, CA Civ), CA (Civ Div).

1581. Asylum seekers–Work permits–Incorrect interpretation of effect of Directive 2003/9 art.11–Entitlement to damages

[Directive 2003/9 on minimum standards for the reception of asylum seekers Art.11, Art.11.2; European Convention on Human Rights 1950 Art.8.]

The appellant asylum seekers (N and L) appealed against separate decisions ([2011] EWHC 386 (Admin), [2011] 2 C.M.L.R. 36, [2011] C.L.Y. 1717and [2011] EWHC 2042 (Admin), [2011] A.C.D. 118 respectively) refusing their applications for judicial review of the respondent secretary of state's decisions not to allow them permission to work (PTW) in the United Kingdom. N arrived in the UK in 2005. Following refusal of his asylum application, further representations purporting to be a fresh claim were made in 2007 to which there was no response. N's application for PTW in late 2008 was rejected. A further application citing Directive 2003/9 art.11 was made in 2009. L overstayed his six-month visa in 2004. He applied for asylum in 2009 and was eventually successful in 2012. His application in 2010 for PTW was rejected within four weeks and then again two months later. The issue in relation to N's claim concerned the acknowledged failure to recognise that art.11.2 extended to fresh claims. In L's claim, the issue concerned the construction of art.11. Both cases raised the question whether the refusal of PTW violated their rights under the European Convention on Human Rights 1950 art.8.

Held: Appeals dismissed. (1) Although in some cases failure to transpose a specific provision by a required date could amount to a sufficiently serious breach of EC law, a bona fide attempt at transposition attracted a more nuanced approach, *Haim v Kassenzahnarztliche Vereinigung Nordrhein (C-424/97)* [2000] E.C.R. I-5123, [2002] C.L.Y. 1571 considered. The breach of EC law in the instant case did not entitle N to automatic reparation: the UK's breach was unintentional, arising from a genuine misapprehension of the true legal position (see paras 12-13 of judgment). (2) The evaluation of the seriousness of the breach was quite finely balanced. The history of the Directive and the transposition instrument coupled with the litigation history of *R. (on the application of ZO (Somalia)) v Secretary of State for the Home Department* [2010] UKSC 36, [2010] 1 W.L.R. 1948, [2010] C.L.Y. 1760 afforded the secretary of state some mitigation when considering the seriousness of the breach, *Cooper v Attorney General* [2010] EWCA Civ 464, [2011] Q.B. 976, [2010] C.L.Y. 1255 considered. Notwithstanding the points in N's favour, the most significant being the total exclusion of the subset of applicants for asylum of which he was one, the breach was not of sufficient seriousness to satisfy the test, being the result of a misunderstanding of new provisions. The misunderstanding was not deliberate, cynical or egregious and was not confined to the secretary of state. Although the position was clarified by *ZO (Somalia),* it was not self-evidently clear before that case, *ZO (Somalia)* considered*, Francovich v Italy (C-6/90)* [1991] E.C.R. I-5357, [1992] C.L.Y. 4815 applied (paras 15-20). (3) Alternatively, if the breach of EC law was sufficient then it was necessary to consider causation. Although art.11.2 imposed the duty to decide conditions for granting access to the labour market, the conditions were matters of subsidiarity. Once aware that art.11.2 extended to fresh claims, the secretary of state prescribed conditions. It was permissible to conclude that had she appreciated the full meaning of art.11.2 earlier, similarly restrictive conditions would have been set at that time. The effectiveness of a remedy required by EC law had to be measured by reference to the breach in question. When the breach was of an obligation to prescribe conditions, it was pertinent to consider what conditions would have been imposed but for the breach. The obligation under art.11.2 when read in conjunction with art.11.4 was a relatively soft obligation (paras 21-24). (4) L's case focused on whether art.11.1 required the secretary of state to prescribe a specific period of time, at the end of which any applicant for asylum whose claim had not been finally determined was entitled to access the labour market subject to any restrictions imposed pursuant to art.11.4. The conclusion that there was no basis for adopting such a purposive construction of art.11.1 was correct. It was too broad a proposition to propose that applicants for asylum were entitled to do anything which they were not expressly prohibited from doing. L was granted admission on the express condition that he did not undertake employment. No infraction of EC law or any other international obligation impacted upon that (paras 28-32). (5) It could not be said in either case that the secretary of state interfered with the respect for private life required by art.8 by refusing PTW. Although the threshold for interference was not especially high, it was meaningful, *AG (Eritrea) v Secretary of State for the Home Department* [2007] EWCA Civ 801, [2008] 2 All E.R. 28, [2008] C.L.Y. 2036 applied. Where it was common ground that art.8 did not embrace a general right to work, the protected right to respect for private life did not embrace the right of a foreign national, with no Treaty, statutory or permitted right of access to the domestic labour market, to an entitlement to work. The facts of *R. (on the application of Tekle) v Secretary of State for the Home Department* [2008] EWHC 3064 (Admin), [2009] 2 All E.R. 193 went way beyond those in the instant case, *Tekle* considered.

R. (ON THE APPLICATION OF NEGASSI) v SECRETARY OF STATE FOR THE HOME DEPARTMENT, [2013] EWCA Civ 151, [2013] 2 C.M.L.R. 45, Maurice Kay, L.J. (VP, CA Civ), CA (Civ Div).

1582. Asylum support–Adult dependants–Qualification as dependant of person receiving asylum support–Requirement for two-year cohabitation period–Whether requirement discriminatory and contrary to right to family life

[Human Rights Act 1998 (c.42) s.3; Immigration and Asylum Act 1999 (c.33) s.95; Asylum Support Regulations 2000 (SI 2000/704) reg.2(4)(f); European Convention on Human Rights 1950 Art.3, Art.8, Art.14.]

The claimant Chinese national (C) applied for judicial review of the second defendant tribunal's decision upholding the first defendant secretary of state's refusal to treat another Chinese national (W) as her dependant for the purposes of the law on asylum support. C's claim for asylum in the United Kingdom had been refused but she continued to receive support and subsistence, including accommodation, from the National Asylum Support Service (NASS) under the Immigration and Asylum Act 1999 s.95 because she had a dependent child, born in 2009. C was in an "off/on" relationship with W, who was the child's father. His application for asylum had been refused. C applied for additional support and permission for W to reside with her at the accommodation provided by NASS on the basis that he was to treated as her dependant under the Asylum Support Regulations 2000 reg.2(4)(f) as a person who had been living with her as a member of an unmarried couple for at least two of the previous three years. The secretary of state refused that application, having found that the criteria in reg.2(4)(f) were not met. C appealed to the tribunal, which upheld the secretary of state's decision. It was common ground that W did not qualify as C's dependant on any ordinary reading of the Regulations. It fell to be determined whether the ordinary, common law interpretation of reg.2(4)(f) complied with the requirements of the European Convention on Human Rights 1950 art.8 and art.14 and, if not, whether the court was required, under the Human Rights Act 1998 s.3, to construe reg.2(4)(f) so as to make it comply with the Convention. C contended that if W could not be treated as her dependant, the family would not be able to maintain their rights to family life under art.8.

Held: Application refused. (1) Article 8 did not in itself guarantee a right to be provided with accommodation or other welfare assistance, *R. (on the application of Q) v Secretary of State for the Home Department* [2003] EWCA Civ 364, [2004] Q.B. 36, [2003] C.L.Y. 4070 followed and *Chapman v United Kingdom (27238/95)* (2001) 33 E.H.R.R. 18, [2001] C.L.Y. 4744 applied. The special circumstances in which art.8 might impose such an obligation were generally ones in which the impact was so severe that art.3 of the Convention was engaged, *Anufrijeva v Southwark LBC* [2003] EWCA Civ 1406, [2004] Q.B. 1124, [2004] C.L.Y. 1986 followed. Where children's welfare was involved, an obligation pursuant to art.8 to provide accommodation or other welfare assistance might be easier to establish, but the test remained whether, absent an art.8 obligation, family life could continue. There was no evidence that the effect of the refusal to regard W as C's dependant and to allow him to share her accommodation would have effectively ruptured their family life, that W had no resources for travelling to see them, or that he was unable to obtain accommodation in a location near C and their child. Even if art.8 was engaged, the refusal to accept W as C's dependant and to accommodate him with her was justifiable under art.8(2) as proportionate in the interests of immigration control and as preventing abuse of the asylum support system. It was open to W to visit the accommodation to enjoy aspects of family life with C and his child, or for the three of them to meet elsewhere and to enjoy family life while so doing (see paras 28-30, 32 of judgment). (2) The different treatment under reg.2(4)(f) of persons who had lived with an unmarried partner for the two-year period and those who had not did was not based on a person's "status" within the meaning of art.14. The Regulations did not impose a ban on a cohabitee, as opposed to a spouse, being treated as a dependant; the difference in treatment was based not on cohabitation itself, rather than marriage, but on the length of cohabitation. It was legitimate for the Regulations to have a threshold for the qualifying period of cohabitation, otherwise any cohabitation, however short, would be considered analogous to the positions of a married couple and a couple who had cohabited for two out of the past three years, *Swift v Secretary of State for Justice* [2012] EWHC 2000 (QB), [2012] P.I.Q.R. P21, [2012] C.L.Y. 1675 applied. The qualifying period in reg.2(4)(f) was neither irrational nor unjustified. The length of a relationship was a relevant and sensible factor to use as a workable objective indicator of the nature and permanence of a relationship. It balanced the need to avoid abuse of the asylum support system by applications in respect of those with whom the person in receipt of s.95 support was no longer in a relationship with, and the need to recognise recent relationships which met a threshold of constancy (paras 45, 51, 55, 58).

R. (ON THE APPLICATION OF CHEN) v SECRETARY OF STATE FOR THE HOME DEPARTMENT, [2012] EWHC 2531 (Admin), [2012] H.R.L.R. 33, Beatson, J., QBD (Admin).

1583. Citizenship–Fraud–Deprivation of citizenship

[British Nationality Act 1981 (c.61) s.40.]

The first appellant secretary of state appealed against a determination of the First-tier Tribunal that she should not have deprived the first respondent (X) of his British citizenship on the basis that it was obtained by fraud. The second appellant (Y) appealed against the tribunal's decision that the second respondent entry clearance officer (Z) had been entitled to refuse her entry clearance as X's fiancee. X, who claimed to be a Kosovan national, had been granted British citizenship by naturalisation after being given leave to remain in the United Kingdom on human rights grounds. When Y, an Albanian national, applied for entry clearance as his fiancee, investigations indicated to the secretary of state that X was an Albanian citizen. She therefore deprived him of his British citizenship under the British Nationality Act 1981 s.40 on the basis that it had been obtained fraudulently. Z then refused Y's application, not being satisfied that her relationship with X was genuine or, in the light of the decision to deprive X of his citizenship, that she was engaged to a person who could properly be regarded as present and settled in the UK. X and Y appealed to the tribunal, which allowed X's appeal, finding that the secretary of state had not discharged the onus of proving that he had obtained his citizenship by fraud. It dismissed Y's appeal on the basis that she had not established that she was seeking leave to enter the UK for the purpose of marriage or that the parties intended to live permanently together as spouses after any marriage. The secretary of state submitted that the tribunal had not placed sufficient weight on evidence from the British Embassy, the Ministry of Internal Affairs in Kosovo and the Albanian authorities indicating that X was Albanian rather than Kosovan. Y argued that the tribunal had failed to put to X a number of relevant matters on which it had drawn adverse inferences as to their intentions, and that its credibility findings were unsafe because of the long delay between its hearing the appeals and promulgating its determination.

Held: Appeals dismissed. (1) The tribunal had been entitled to find that the evidence from Kosovo and Albania was unconvincing: the information from the British Embassy lacked detail; that from the Kosovan ministry was unreliable as most of the records had been destroyed or taken during the Kosovo War; and whilst the Albanian authorities' records showed that someone with X's name had been born in Albania, the name of the mother was different. In substance, the secretary of state's challenge was to a question of fact, and the tribunal had reached a decision that was neither unreasonable nor irrational, and was properly open to it (see paras 22-27 of judgment). (2) There was no obligation on the tribunal, particularly in appeals where the parties were represented by competent counsel, to raise each and every matter on which it had concerns. Whether a failure to raise a particular matter amounted to a procedural irregularity or lack of fairness depended upon the circumstances of the case, *R. (on the application of Maheshwaran) v Secretary of State for the Home Department* [2002] EWCA Civ 173, [2004] Imm. A.R. 176 applied. In the instant case, the tribunal had not erred in law by not raising certain issues. It had heard X's evidence about the extent of the contact between him and Y, and what inferences could properly be drawn from that evidence was a question of fact. The onus was on Y to show that she could meet the requirements for entry clearance. X had given oral evidence about his contact by telephone, and the tribunal could not be faulted for not pursuing for itself the specific issues which Y raised (paras 32-33). In an asylum appeal where credibility was in issue, the decision should be reached within a reasonable period of time, with no more than three months from the date of hearing to the date the determination was handed in for typing, *Sambasivam v Secretary of State for the Home Department* [2000] Imm. A.R. 85, [1999] C.L.Y. 3152 considered. However, if excessive delay was to be relied upon in attacking a judgment, a fair case had to be shown for believing that the judgment contained errors that were probably, or even possibly, attributable to that delay. In order to show that delay had led to an error of law it had to be shown that the judgment was not safe and was therefore unlawful, *RK (Algeria) v Secretary of State for the Home Department* [2007] EWCA Civ 868 applied and *Cobham v Frett* [2001] 1 W.L.R. 1775, [2001] C.L.Y. 49 considered. In the instant case, it had not been shown that the decision was unsafe or that there had been any error of law (paras 34-38, 42).

ARUSHA (DEPRIVATION OF CITIZENSHIP: DELAY: KOSOVO), *Re*; DEMUSHI (DEPRIVATION OF CITIZENSHIP: DELAY: ALBANIA), *Re*; *sub nom.* DEMUSHI v ENTRY CLEARANCE OFFICER, TIRANA; SECRETARY OF STATE FOR THE HOME DEPARTMENT v ARUSHA, [2012] UKUT 80 (IAC), [2012] Imm. A.R. 645, Judge Latter, UT (IAC).

1584. Citizenship–Statelessness–Effect of order depriving person of British citizenship where person could have acquired another nationality–Statelessness test in s.40(4) British Nationality Act 1981–Meaning of "if he is satisfied that the order would make a person stateless"

[British Nationality Act 1981 (c.61) s.40(4).]

The secretary of state appealed against a decision ([2012] EWCA Civ 358) quashing her order purporting to deprive the respondent (J) of his British citizenship. J had been born in Iraq, but had settled in the United Kingdom after seeking asylum. Under Iraqi law, he automatically lost his Iraqi nationality upon being granted British citizenship in 2000. In 2004, while visiting Iraq, he was arrested on suspicion of being a member of a terrorist group and detained by the British forces for three years without charge. The secretary of state made her order in December 2007, shortly before J was released, on the ground that deprivation of his British citizenship was conducive to the public good within the meaning of the British Nationality Act 1981 s.40(2). After his release, J brought a number of claims relating to his internment, including claims for judicial review and habeas corpus.

One of his grounds was that the secretary of state's order had made him stateless and was therefore void under s.40(4) of the Act. On that issue, the Special Immigration Appeals Commission held that between 2004 and 2006 J had automatically regained Iraqi nationality owing to changes in Iraqi law. The Court of Appeal set aside that decision as wrong in law and rejected the secretary of state's assertion that if J had not automatically become an Iraqi national by December 2007, it had been open to him to regain such nationality by application, and that his statelessness had been caused by his failure to do so rather than by her order. The court accepted that any such application by J would have been bound to succeed, but made its decision on the basis that s.40(4) demanded consideration of the "effect" of the order, and its effect had been to make J stateless irrespective of whether he could previously have acquired another nationality had he chosen to do so. The secretary of state invited the court to determine the instant appeal on a premise that, under Iraqi law, J, as a former Iraqi citizen, would have had a right to the immediate restoration of his former nationality had he so applied. She submitted that, upon release from his internment, J had applied for an Iraqi passport using a certificate of Iraqi nationality issued on the same date, which incontrovertibly demonstrated the validity of her premise. She also submitted that the word "satisfied" in s.40(4) conferred latitude upon her to look beyond the ostensible effect of the order to the active cause of any statelessness. J maintained that the Iraqi passport referred to by the secretary of state had been acquired on the black market and was a fake.

Held: Appeal dismissed. (1) It was clear from express provisions of Iraqi law that an Iraqi who had renounced his Iraqi nationality and who wished to regain it would have to return to Iraq legally, stay there for at least one year, and apply for restoration during the course of that year. If he fulfilled those requirements, his Iraqi nationality "may" be restored with retrospective effect; there was discretion to refuse the application. Therefore, although it was somewhat indulgent to adopt the secretary of state's premise, the court was prepared to do so given the time, effort and expense which had been devoted to the case. However, the validity of J's Iraqi passport was not for the instant court to determine. Its existence could not be used to support the validity of the secretary of state's premise (see paras 25-26, 29 of judgment). (2) Section 40(4) did not permit, let alone require, analysis of the relative potency of causative factors relating to a person's statelessness. The secretary of state was inviting the court to place a substantial and unwarranted gloss upon the provision. The inquiry was a straightforward exercise as to whether the person held another nationality at the date of the order. That conclusion was supported by the "Guidelines on Statelessness No.1" issued by the United Nations High Commissioner for Refugees on February 20, 2012 (paras 30-34).

AL-JEDDA v SECRETARY OF STATE FOR THE HOME DEPARTMENT; *sub nom.* SECRETARY OF STATE FOR THE HOME DEPARTMENT v AL-JEDDA, [2013] UKSC 62, [2013] 3 W.L.R. 1006, Lord Neuberger (President), SC.

1585. Civil partnerships–Immigrants–Immigration policy–Register offices

THE IMMIGRATION (PROCEDURE FOR FORMATION OF CIVIL PARTNERSHIPS) (AMENDMENT) REGULATIONS 2013, SI 2013/227; made under the Civil Partnership Act 2004 Sch.23 para.4. In force: March 7, 2013; .

These Regulations update the lists of specified registration districts in England and Wales and the registration authorities in England and Wales that appear in Schedule 1 of the Immigration (Procedure for Marriage) Regulations 2011 and Schedule 2 of the Immigration (Procedure for Formation of Civil Partnerships) Regulations 2011. The lists have been updated to reflect a change made by Ceredigion local authority to the organisation of their registration service. The revised information enables persons who are subject to immigration control within the UK to continue to give notice of marriage and civil partnership within Ceredigion local authority following the organisational change.

1586. Country guidance–Failed asylum seekers–Well-founded fear of persecution by reason of imputed political opinion–Hangers-on–Lawfulness of country guidance in TL (Burma) v Secretary of State for the Home Department [2009] UKAIT 17

[Directive 2004/83 on minimum standards for the qualification and status of third country nationals or stateless persons as refugees or as persons who otherwise need international protection and the content of the protection granted.]

The appellant failed asylum seekers (K and N) appealed against Upper Tribunal and First-tier Tribunal decisions upholding the respondent secretary of state's refusal of their asylum claims. K and N were Burmese nationals who had claimed asylum following, or just before, expiry of their student visas but were otherwise unconnected. They had both claimed asylum as political dissidents and, in both cases, the First-tier Tribunal found that their involvement in demonstrations against the Burmese government while in the United Kingdom had been undertaken in bad faith, namely to enhance subsequent asylum claims. The Upper Tribunal upheld the First-tier Tribunal decisions. K and N's cases were therefore based on sur place activities which were not genuine manifestations of political protest but were cynical and opportunistic attempts to fabricate asylum claims, although it was accepted that there might be cases in which such circumstances gave rise to a well-founded fear of persecution on the ground of imputed political opinion. In *TL (Burma) v Secretary of State for the Home Department* [2009] UKAIT 17, where country guidance was given in respect of Burma, such persons were characterised as "hangers-on". K and N challenged the lawfulness of the guidance given in *TL*.

Held: Appeals allowed, remitted to Upper Tribunal for redetermination. (1) The country guidance system was anomalous. However, it was well-established and it was plain that, were it not for such a system, the overburdened tribunal system would become overwhelmed. The system was not productive of injustice, provided that the guidance was not legally flawed. It was important that, when there was a legal challenge to guidance, it was subject to rigorous scrutiny. The court would need to satisfy itself that the particular part of the guidance called into question was the subject of evidence that was properly evaluated by the Upper Tribunal after full argument, regardless of whether it applied strictly to the appellant before it (see paras 16-20 of judgment). (2) The First-tier Tribunal and Upper Tribunal were specialist tribunals whose assessment of evidence was entitled to respect. Also, "activities other than bona fide political protest [could] create refugee status sur place", *YB (Eritrea) v Secretary of State for the Home Department* [2008] EWCA Civ 360 considered. The Upper Tribunal was correct when it stated in *TL* that each case had to be decided on its facts. Nothing in Directive 2004/83 or the Immigration Rules detracted from those propositions. However, the Upper Tribunal's reasoning in *TL* was flawed. First, in its attempt to draw an analogy between hangers-on in the instant sense and failed asylum seekers, as that was a false analogy. While it was true that the failed asylum seeker might have made false allegations of persecution in relation to their time in Burma and would have been critical of the Burmese authorities in advancing his claim, that would all have been done in communications with the secretary of state or her officials, and in the course of tribunal hearings. Although such hearings took place in public, there was no evidence or suggestion that the apparatus of the Burmese state authority was so ubiquitous that it routinely obtained information from individual asylum cases. When the failed asylum seeker was returned to Burma, there was no evidence that the authorities would generally be in a position to know about the details of his failed claim or to hold it against him. The position was quite different in relation to hangers-on. The Upper Tribunal accepted the evidence of routine photography and video recording of demonstrations outside the embassy and of efficient identification processes which resulted in the relaying of information to Burma. Second, there was an underlying assumption that the Burmese authorities operated a rational decision-making process which could reliably be trusted to distinguish between a genuine political opponent and a hanger-on. There was no evidence of how the authorities, faced with a person identified and photographed participating in an anti-government demonstration outside the London embassy, might go about satisfying themselves that the person in question was simply an opportunistic hanger-on. The general evidence about the behaviour of the authorities did not support a tendency to rational, careful assessment. The accepted evidence was of a repressive, arbitrary regime, and a presumption of rational assessment was counter-intuitive in the context of the rest of the accepted evidence. The Upper Tribunal's reasoning in *TL* could not be supported, *TL* overruled in part. The fact was that the assessment of risk in relation to a hanger-on who had probably been photographed, filmed and identified was inherently difficult. It was unpalatable that someone could become entitled to refugee status as a result of their cynical manipulation but if, objectively, they had a well-founded fear of persecution by reason of imputed political opinion, that might be the reality, *YB* considered. Country guidance was required to assist decision-makers in deciding individual cases on their own facts. The guidance in relation to Burma might usefully benefit from a more structured approach, *BA (Demonstrators in Britain -risk on return) Iran CG, Re* [2011] UKUT 36 (IAC) considered (paras 29-33).

KS (BURMA) v SECRETARY OF STATE FOR THE HOME DEPARTMENT; NL (BURMA) v SECRETARY OF STATE FOR THE HOME DEPARTMENT, [2013] EWCA Civ 67, [2013] Imm. A.R. 525, Maurice Kay, L.J. (VP, CA Civ), CA (Civ Div).

1587. Criminal investigations–Immigration officers–Powers of arrest–Revenue and Customs offences

THE POLICE AND CRIMINAL EVIDENCE ACT 1984 (APPLICATION TO IMMIGRATION OFFICERS AND DESIGNATED CUSTOMS OFFICIALS IN ENGLAND AND WALES) ORDER 2013, SI 2013/1542; made under the Borders, Citizenship and Immigration Act 2009 s.23, s.37. In force: June 25, 2013; .

This Order applies certain provisions of the Police and Criminal Evidence Act 1984 to criminal investigations conducted by immigration officers, and designated customs officials and to persons detained by designated customs officials. This includes powers of arrest, search of premises and seizure of evidence as well as obligations in respect of persons detained on suspicion of having committed customs offences.

1588. Decisions–Removal–Permissibility of simultaneous notification of removal decision and refusal to vary leave to remain

[Immigration Act 1971 (c.77) s.3C(2)(b), s.3C(1)(c), s.3D(2)(a), s.4(1); Immigration, Asylum and Nationality Act 2006 (c.13) s.47; Nationality, Immigration and Asylum Act 2002 (c.41) s.82(1), s.82; Immigration (Continuation of Leave) (Notices) Regulations 2006 (SI 2006/2170) reg.2.]

The appellant secretary of state appealed against the Upper Tribunal's decision ([2012] UKUT 147 (IAC), [2012] Imm. A.R. 875, [2013] 2 C.L. 190) that her decision to remove the respondent (J) had been invalid. The secretary of state had decided not only to refuse J's application for variation of his leave to remain in the United Kingdom but also that he would be removed by way of directions under the Immigration, Asylum and Nationality Act 2006 s.47. The decision notice which she sent J contained both decisions. The First-tier Tribunal and the Upper Tribunal each dismissed J's appeals. However, the Upper Tribunal found that the removal decision was invalid because it should have only been made after the variation decision had been given to J. That was because a s.47 decision could be taken only after the person's leave to enter or remain had been extended by the Immigration Act 1971 s.3C(2)(b), and leave was extended by s.3C(2)(b) when an appeal under the Nationality, Immigration and Asylum Act 2002 s.82 could be brought against the decision on the application for variation. But, under s.3C(6) and the Immigration (Continuation of Leave) (Notices) Regulations 2006 reg.2, such a decision was reached when notice had been given. The secretary of state submitted that the Upper Tribunal had erred (1) in construing s.47 in the light of the 2006 Regulations, which had been enacted for the different purpose of determining when an application was decided for the purpose of s.3C(1)(c) and s.3C(2)(a) of the 1971 Act, and so had no application to s.3C(2)(b); (2) by adopting an interpretation which meant that Parliament, in enacting s.47, had legislated in vain in view of the practical obstacles to the exercise of the s.47(1) power; (3) in not referring to Hansard, under the rule in *Pepper (Inspector of Taxes) v Hart* [1993] A.C. 593, [1993] C.L.Y. 459, in order to establish Parliament's intention that s.47 would allow an enforcement decision to be made at the same time as the decision to revoke, curtail or refuse to vary leave.

Held: Appeal dismissed. (1) The 2006 Regulations determined when an application for variation of leave was decided for the purposes of s.3C as a whole, not just s.3C(1)(c) and s.3C(2)(a). There had to be a consistent approach throughout the section to the question of when an application was decided. Section 3C(2)(b) extended leave during any period when an appeal could be brought under s.82(1) of the 2002 Act against the decision on the application for variation. Before an appeal could be brought under s.82 there had to be a decision on the application for variation against which the person could appeal. Section 3C(6) and the 2006 Regulations made it clear that there was no decision on the application for variation for the purpose of s.3C(2)(b) until notice of the decision had been given. Furthermore, the notice did not follow the exercise of the power, but was the manner in which the power was exercised (see paras 24-25 of judgment). (2) Where the statutory language was capable of more than one meaning, the interpretation which led to a reasonably practicable result should be adopted, and an interpretation which led to absurdity or unworkability should be rejected. However, the Upper Tribunal had correctly concluded that the statutory language was clear and did not admit of more than one interpretation (para.28). (3) Although Hansard made clear the intention behind the enactment of s.47, whether that intention was carried into effect depended not upon the wording of s.47 itself but on when leave was extended by s.3C(2)(b) or s.3D(2)(a) of the 1971 Act. And the answer to that question was to be found in s.3C(6), the 2006 Regulations made thereunder, and s.4(1) of the 1971 Act, which were not mentioned in the government's statement of intention recorded in Hansard. Moreover, while Hansard might in certain limited circumstances be an aid to interpretation if there was ambiguity in an enactment, there was no ambiguity in s.3C(6) of the 1971 Act and reg.2 of the 2006 Regulations: there was no decision on an application for variation of leave against which an appeal could be brought under s.82(1) until notice of the decision had been given (para.31). (4) Having concluded that the removal decision was invalid but the variation decision was valid, the Upper Tribunal should not have dismissed J's appeal against the First-tier Tribunal's determination, it should have dismissed his appeal against the variation decision and allowed his appeal against the removal decision (paras 4, 32).

AHMADI (S.47 DECISION: VALIDITY: SAPKOTA: AFGHANISTAN), *Re; sub nom.* AHMADI v SECRETARY OF STATE FOR THE HOME DEPARTMENT; SECRETARY OF STATE FOR THE HOME DEPARTMENT v AHMADI, [2013] EWCA Civ 512, [2014] 1 W.L.R. 401, Sullivan, L.J., CA (Civ Div).

1589. Deportation–Bail conditions–Power to grant bail pending deportation–Imposing conditions on basis of undisclosed national security case–Disclosure to appellant of case against him

[European Convention on Human Rights 1950 Art.6, Art.8.]

The appellant (B) appealed against a decision ([2011] EWHC 2129 (Admin), [2012] 1 All E.R. 229, [2011] C.L.Y. 1726) that the Special Immigration Appeals Commission was not obliged by the European Convention on Human Rights 1950 art.6 to disclose the gist of the allegations relied on against him when imposing bail conditions. The Secretary of State for the Home Department had decided to deport B, an Algerian national, in the interests of national security. B was arrested and detained. He was initially refused bail on the basis of undisclosed national security material. He was subsequently granted bail by the commission subject to strict curfew conditions on the basis of the undisclosed national security case. He sought disclosure of the case against him on the basis that art.6 applied. The

Divisional Court held that it did not. B submitted that he was entitled to art.6(1) procedural protection and, therefore, had a right to be told the gist of the case against him in justification of the bail conditions that were imposed by the commission; he also submitted that he was entitled to the same procedural protection by virtue of art.8.

Held: Appeal dismissed. (1) Decisions of the state regarding the entry, stay and deportation of aliens did not involve the determination of an applicant's civil rights within the meaning of art.6, *Maaouia v France (39652/98)* (2001) 33 E.H.R.R. 42, [2001] C.L.Y. 3526 applied (see paras 8-17 of judgment). Just as the power to deport was exercised by the state in the public interest, so too was the power to detain pending deportation. There was a close relationship between the decision to detain and the deportation order which it was intended to facilitate. On that basis the detention of an individual pending deportation did not involve the determination of civil rights within art.6, *Maaouia, Ferrazzini v Italy (44759/98)* [2001] S.T.C. 1314, [2001] C.L.Y. 5298 and *R. (on the application of Khaled) v Secretary of State for Foreign and Commonwealth Affairs* [2011] EWCA Civ 350, [2012] Q.B. 477, [2011] C.L.Y. 1689 considered (paras 18-25). It would be surprising if art.6(1) did not apply to detention but did apply to bail conditions. Bail was granted as an alternative to detention in order to facilitate a deportation. It made no sense to afford greater procedural protection to an individual who was challenging the conditions of bail than to one who was challenging a notice of detention. Cases on the validity of employment contracts were of no relevance in the context of deportation, *Coorplan-Jenni GmbH v Austria (10523/02)* (2008) 46 E.H.R.R. 26 considered. Nor was the jurisprudence relating to control orders, *R. (on the application of Secretary of State for the Home Department) v BC* [2009] EWHC 2927 (Admin), [2010] 1 W.L.R. 1542, [2010] C.L.Y. 1728 considered (paras 26-31). Even if deportation involved the determination of a civil right, art.6(1) would not apply to the bail proceedings in any event since they were interlocutory proceedings relating to interim measures, *Micallef v Malta (17056/06)* (2010) 50 E.H.R.R. 37 considered (paras 33-34). (2) The bail conditions interfered with B's art.8 rights, but were justified under art.8(2) as being in accordance with the law and necessary in the interests of national security. Even where national security was at stake, measures affecting fundamental human rights had to be subject to some form of adversarial proceedings before an independent body, and the individual had to be able to challenge the executive's assertion that national security was at stake, *Al-Nashif v Bulgaria (50963/99)* (2003) 36 E.H.R.R. 37, [2003] C.L.Y. 2116. The Court of Appeal had held that those requirements were satisfied by the commission's proceedings, *IR (Sri Lanka) v Secretary of State for the Home Department* [2011] EWCA Civ 704, [2012] 1 W.L.R. 232, [2011] C.L.Y. 1798 followed. 49. The court should only decline to follow *IR (Sri Lanka)* if satisfied that there had been a subsequent clear line of Strasbourg jurisprudence which showed that it was wrongly decided, and there was no such clear line of authority, *Liu v Russia (No 2)* (application no 29157/09, 26 July 2011) considered (paras 35-52).

R. (ON THE APPLICATION OF BB (ALGERIA)) v SPECIAL IMMIGRATION APPEALS COMMISSION, [2012] EWCA Civ 1499, [2013] 1 W.L.R. 1568, Lord Dyson (M.R.), CA (Civ Div).

1590. Deportation–EU nationals–Effect of period of imprisonment on permanent right of residence–Method of calculating continuity of residence–European Union

[Immigration (European Economic Area) Regulations 2006 (SI 2006/1003) reg.21; Directive 2004/38 on the right of citizens of the Union and their family members to move and reside freely within the territory of the Member States amending Regulation (EEC) No 1612/68 and repealing Directives 64/221/EEC, 68/360/EEC, 72/194/EEC, 73/148/EEC, 75/34/EEC, 75/35/EEC, 90/364/EEC, 90/365/ Art.27(1), Art.28(3), Art.28.]

The Upper Tribunal considered issues arising from an appeal by an EU national (M) against a deportation decision by the respondent secretary of state. M and her husband (J), Portuguese citizens, moved to the United Kingdom in 1998. M was employed in the UK for approximately 10 months before giving up work to have her first child. The couple had two further children in October 2001 and March 2004. J supported M until the breakdown of their relationship in 2006. Although separated, M and J remained married. In August 2009, M was convicted of cruelty and assault against her children and sentenced to 21 months' imprisonment. In May 2010, M applied for permanent residence in the UK. That application was refused and a deportation order was made on grounds of public policy and public security pursuant to the Immigration (European Economic Area) Regulations 2006 reg.21. Although M had been in the UK for over 10 years, the secretary of state took the view that the continuity of her residence had been broken by her period of imprisonment. According to her decision, M was not entitled to the highest level of protection under Directive 2004/38 art.28(3) and reg.21 because she did not meet the requirement based on the degree of integration into the UK on account of her imprisonment. Nor, in the view of the secretary of state, could she benefit from the second-highest level of protection provided for by art.28(2) because she had not acquired permanent residence; in any event there were serious grounds of public policy and security for deporting her, so that the basic level of protection under art.27(1) and art.28(1) did not apply either. The secretary of state later accepted that M had qualified for permanent residence in May 2003 by virtue of a combination of her own employment and her status as a family member of her husband, being an EU national exercising his Treaty rights.

Held: Questions referred to ECJ. As a result of the secretary of state's concession that M had acquired permanent residence by May 2003, she had to be entitled either to the highest-level or to the second-highest level of EU protection against expulsion. The appeal could not be resolved by reference to the basic level of protection because the secretary of state had established that there were grounds of public policy and public security on which to order M's deportation. However, the law on whether imprisonment broke continuity of residence for art.28(2) or art.28(3) purposes was in a state of uncertainty. M's case was different from one in which a person could only show 10 years' continuous residence if, for art.28(3)(a) purposes, the period in prison was counted towards assessment of that period of residence. Further, it was arguable that, in deciding whether a claimant had 10 years' continuous residence so as to be able to benefit from art.28(2) or art.28(3), it was appropriate to count forward from the commencement of the claimant's residence in the host Member State instead of counting back from the decision to deport, as had been done in the instant case. Clearly, the approach taken made a significant difference in M's case because, counting forward from the date on which she first exercised her Treaty rights, she acquired permanent residence in May 2003; whereas, counting back from the deportation decision in July 2010, she could only benefit from the highest level of protection if her period of imprisonment did not breach the continuity of her residence between July 2000 and July 2010. Accordingly, questions were referred to the European Court of Justice as to whether (i) a period of imprisonment such as that at issue broke the residence period required in order to benefit from art.28(3)(a); (ii) the reference to "previous ten years" in art.28(3)(a) meant that the residence had to be continuous in order to benefit from that protection; (iii) the period of 10 years' residence had to be calculated by (a) counting back from the expulsion decision or (b) counting forward from the commencement of residence in the host Member State; and if (a) was correct, whether it made a difference if the person had accrued 10 years' residence prior to imprisonment (see paras 17, 23, 29, 35-36, 40, 44 of judgment).

MG (EU DEPORTATION: ARTICLE 28(3): IMPRISONMENT: PORTUGAL), *Re*; *sub nom.* SECRETARY OF STATE FOR THE HOME DEPARTMENT v MG (PORTUGAL), [2012] UKUT 268 (IAC), [2013] 1 C.M.L.R. 20, Judge Storey, UT (IAC).

1591. Deportation–Family proceedings–Automatic deportation in context of ongoing family proceedings–Correct approach to relationship between proceedings

[UK Borders Act 2007 (c.30) s.32(5); European Convention on Human Rights 1950 Art.6, Art.8.]

The appellant (M) appealed against the dismissal of his appeal against a decision that he was liable to automatic deportation pursuant to the UK Borders Act 2007 s.32(5). M was a Jamaican national who had been in the United Kingdom illegally since 2000. He had a daughter (T) with his ex-wife (C) in 2001. M commenced a new relationship in 2005 and had another daughter. In 2006, he was removed as an overstayer. He returned three months later and was promptly imprisoned for driving offences and illegal entry. In May 2008, M and his partner had another daughter. In July 2009, he was convicted of a drug offence, and sentenced to imprisonment. He became liable to automatic deportation. In June 2008, M had applied for a residence order in respect of T. The family proceedings remained extant when he was arrested for the drug offence, and were subsequently adjourned. The Upper Tribunal concluded that M had only "belatedly" taken steps to revive the family proceedings, with the intention of delaying or preventing his removal, and held that deportation would not infringe his rights under either the European Convention on Human Rights 1950 art.6 or art.8. M argued that the tribunal had misdirected itself in its approach to the inter-relationship between the family proceedings and the immigration proceedings, and had misapplied the law to the facts of the case. He submitted that the tribunal had impermissibly pre-empted and pre-judged the family proceedings. The secretary of state argued that the tribunal found, and was entitled to find, that whatever conclusion might eventuate in the family proceedings, the immigration appeal would inevitably be dismissed.

Held: Appeal allowed. (1) The analysis in *Nimako-Boateng (Residence Orders: Anton Considered: Ghana), Re* [2012] UKUT 216 (IAC) of the different tests applicable in the two jurisdictions was undoubtedly correct. It was that analysis which lay behind the guidance subsequently given in *RS (Immigration and family court proceedings) India* [2012] UKUT 218 (IAC). The general approach of the tribunal in *RS* and *Nimako* represented the correct reconciliation of the conflicting concepts of automatic deportation and art.8 in immigration and family proceedings, *RS* and *Nimako* approved (see paras 16-21 of judgment). (2) There was a lack of evidence to support the tribunal's finding that M had revived the family proceedings belatedly and with the intention of delaying or preventing his removal. He had instituted the residence application long before he was arrested for the drug offence. Although little progress had been made during the following year, there was evidence that M had attempted to move things forward, but that C was being uncooperative. It could not be said that the inception of the application was a cynical ploy or an attempt to thwart removal by reference to a crime that M had not yet committed. From June 2009 until October 2011, M had been in custody, so it was hardly surprising that he had been advised by his solicitors that he could not pursue the residence proceedings at that time (paras 24-28). (3) The tribunal had erred in its approach to the relationship between the deportation appeal and the family proceedings. There was sufficient material before the tribunal to compel the conclusion that the family court could conclude that it was contrary to T's best interests to reside with C, and emphatically in accordance with those interests for her to reside with M and his new partner. The family court was best placed to make the necessary evaluation. In *Nimako,* there was material before the tribunal to justify the conclusion that to delay determination of the deportation appeal in order to await the judgment of the family court was not necessary, because the material in favour of the appellant lacked substance and the public interest in deportation was overwhelming. That was not the situation in the instant case. The judgment of the family court, with all the tools at its disposal, including the assistance of CAFCASS and the opportunity to assess all the adults, including C, could and should inform the decision-making of the tribunal on the issue of the proportionality of deportation, in relation to the best interests of T (paras 29-31).

MOHAN v SECRETARY OF STATE FOR THE HOME DEPARTMENT, [2012] EWCA Civ 1363, [2013] 1 W.L.R. 922, Sir Maurice Kay (VP CA Civ), CA (Civ Div).

1592. Deportation–Foreign criminals–Automatic deportation of foreign criminals under s.32 UK Borders Act 2007–Proportionality of deportation

[UK Borders Act 2007 (c.30) s.32, s.33; European Convention on Human Rights 1950 Art.8.]

The secretary of state appealed against a decision that the deportation of the respondent (R) would be a disproportionate interference with his family life. R was Nepalese. His father had served in the Gurkhas and had been granted indefinite leave to remain in the United Kingdom at the end of his service. His immediate family were permitted to join him. Three years after R came to the UK he was convicted of manslaughter and sentenced to three years' imprisonment. He had been involved in a group attack on a man, and the unconscious victim was thrown into the river Thames where he drowned. R was approximately 20 years old at the time of the offence and had been drunk. Under the UK Borders Act 2007 s.32 he was subject to automatic deportation. However, the Upper Tribunal found that automatic deportation would breach the European Convention on Human Rights 1950 art.8. It took into account the fact that no judicial recommendation had been made for R's deportation, he was unlikely to reoffend and all of his immediate family were in the UK. It also found that the nature of his offence was not such as to justify interference with his family life.

Held: Appeal allowed. (1) There was no longer any requirement for the Home Secretary to form her own view of where the public interest lay when deciding on the need to deport a foreign criminal falling within the 2007 Act. She, like the tribunals and the courts, was bound by the legislative policy spelt out in s.32 and s.33 of the Act which stated that where a person fell within the definition of a "foreign criminal" his deportation was conducive to the public good, *RU (Bangladesh) v Secretary of State for the Home Department* [2011] EWCA Civ 651, [2011] Imm. A.R. 662, [2012] C.L.Y. 1705 followed. However, in considering the proportionality of deportation, the public interest was not only to be treated as served by deporting foreign criminals, it was also among the factors capable of affecting proportionality. That meant that while the public interest in deportation had already been established by legislation, its content and extent in the particular case had to be separately evaluated, initially by the Home Secretary, and thereafter, if necessary, by the tribunal. The tribunal should accordingly entertain both sides' submissions on the public interest, along with such elements as the nature and gravity of the offence. The Home Secretary's estimation of the public interest commanded no additional weight. To let it do so would be to upset the equal footing on which the Crown and the individual came before the tribunals and courts, not least where Parliament had already decided where, other things being equal, the public interest lay (see paras 9-12 of judgment). (2) Much of the tribunal's decision had the appearance of a search for reasons not to deport R, rather than an inquiry into whether, despite the statutory policy of automatic deportation, art.8 would be violated by its implementation. That required recognition, among other things, of the fact that R had helped push an unconscious victim into the river. The absence of a judicial recommendation for deportation did not carry the weight accorded to it by the tribunal, and the absence of a risk of reoffending was not the ultimate aim of the deportation regime. The court was also troubled by the proposition that the nature and seriousness of R's offence did not, by themselves, justify interference with family and private life without prospective regard to the public interest. Section 32 of the 2007 Act decided that the nature and seriousness of the offence, as measured by the sentence imposed, justified deportation unless an exception recognised by the Act applied. For those reasons there had been an error of approach on the part of the tribunal and R's case was remitted for redetermination (paras 15, 21-26).

RG (NEPAL) v SECRETARY OF STATE FOR THE HOME DEPARTMENT; *sub nom.* RG (AUTOMATIC DEPORT: SECTION 33(2)(A) EXCEPTION: NEPAL), RE; GURUNG v SECRETARY OF STATE FOR THE HOME DEPARTMENT, [2012] EWCA Civ 62, [2012] I.N.L.R. 401, Rix, L.J., CA (Civ Div).

1593. Deportation–Inhuman or degrading treatment or punishment–Irreversible chronic advanced kidney disease–Difficulty accessing treatment available in receiving country–Inevitablity of death without treatment–Whether circumstances were "exceptional"

[European Convention on Human Rights 1950 Art.3.]

The Upper Tribunal was required to redetermine appeals made by the appellants (G and E) against the respondent secretary of state's decision that their deportation would not interfere with their rights under the European Convention on Human Rights 1950 art.3. G, an Indian, and E, a Ghanaian, were overstayers in the United Kingdom. Both suffered from irreversible chronic advanced kidney disease requiring dialysis three times a week. Without dialysis, they would die within weeks. Dialysis was available in their respective countries but it would be unavailable to them due to the cost and practical difficulty of accessing it. The secretary of state refused their applications for leave to remain under art.3 and art.8 of the Convention. The First-tier Tribunal allowed their appeals on the basis that each case fell within the "exceptional" category recognised in *D v United Kingdom (30240/96)* (1997) 24 E.H.R.R. 423, [1997] C.L.Y. 2763 and *N v Secretary of State for the Home Department* [2005] UKHL 31, [2005] 2 A.C. 296, [2005] C.L.Y. 2160. The UT upheld the secretary of state's appeal that the FTT had erred in law in finding as such; the UT remade the decisions, dismissing both appeals. G and E appealed to the Court of Appeal. The Court of Appeal remitted G's case to the UT for redetermination. E's case was remitted to the UT, which again found that the FTT had erred in law in allowing the appeal and adjourned the hearing in order for the decision to be remade. The issues were whether (i) the FTT erred in law in allowing G's appeal; (ii) G and E's deportation would constitute an interference with their art.3 rights.

Held: Appeals dismissed. (1) The certainty and immediacy of death did not in itself bring G's circumstances within the "exceptional" case contemplated in *D v UK* and *N v UK*. That assessment required a dispassionate consideration of all the circumstances facing him on his return to India. That included a consideration of the circumstances in which he would die, including any care and support available to him from family and others. In itself the shortening of an individual's life expectancy to one to two weeks because of the absence of medical treatment did not bring a case within art.3. The FTT, in considering that it did, had erred in law and its decision could not stand. It fell to the instant tribunal to remake the decision, *BC (India) v Secretary of State for the Home Department* [2007] EWCA Civ 1438 applied (see paras 80, 85, 92 of judgment). (2) Inevitable death was not determinative in leading inevitably to a breach of art.3. The "exceptional" category was not restricted to those cases where the individual had already reached a critical stage in the dying process in the UK. A dispassionate judgement based on all the circumstances which G and E would face on returning to their respective countries had to be made. Inevitable death was one factor. There was no suggestion that during the period leading up to death either would not have the support and comfort of his family. There was no evidence of the impact that dying and death would have on their families beyond what would ordinarily be expected. Equally, there was nothing to suggest that either would be unable to obtain at least palliative care to alleviate any suffering. Those facts differed from *D v UK* where the appellant would have had no family or social support or medical care upon his return. Both G and E would return to their families. They would have time to prepare and removal would be done in carefully controlled circumstances where it was appropriate and safe to do having regard to their medical condition. There was no evidence to establish any such aggravation as seen in Soering. They would return to their families. They would have time to prepare and removal would be in accordance with the secretary of state's guidelines and would be in carefully controlled circumstances where it was appropriate and safe to do so having regard to their medical condition. Neither case reached even the level of concern identified in *Soering v United Kingdom (A/161)* (1989) 11 E.H.R.R. 439, [1989] C.L.Y. 1712, *Soering* considered. Neither G nor E's circumstances fell within the "exceptional category". They did not reach the high threshold to establish a real risk of "inhuman or degrading treatment" as a result of suffering an undignified death, *D v UK* and *N v UK* followed (paras 89-101).

GS (ARTICLE 3: HEALTH CASES: INDIA), *Re*; *sub nom*. SECRETARY OF STATE FOR THE HOME DEPARTMENT v GS; SECRETARY OF STATE FOR THE HOME DEPARTMENT v EO, [2012] UKUT 397 (IAC), [2013] Imm. A.R. 223, Blake, J. (President), UT (IAC).

1594. **Deportation–National security–Lawfulness of Ethiopian national's deportation for reasons of national security**

[European Convention on Human Rights 1950 Art.3, Art.6.]

The appellant (X) appealed against a decision upholding the respondent secretary of state's decision to deport him to Ethiopia for reasons of national security. X, an Ethiopian national, had been granted indefinite leave to remain in the United Kingdom. During a visit to Ethiopia in 2005, he learned that family members had been arrested and detained in connection with the failed bombing attacks in London on July 21, 2005. Upon his return to the UK, he was detained and refused leave to enter, the decision having been taken to exclude him from the UK. The secretary of state later decided to deport him. X appealed. The Special Immigration Appeals Commission found that X had been closely connected with individuals who had gone on to carry out terrorist acts in and against the UK, that he shared and supported their views, and that he posed a continued threat to the UK's national security. It found that X would not face ill-treatment contrary to European Convention on Human Rights 1950 art.3 if returned to Ethiopia, that there was no real risk that he would be prosecuted if removed, and that the Ethiopian government had, in a memorandum of understanding (MoU), given assurances that it would comply with its human rights obligations under international law if X was to be detained. The appeal was therefore dismissed. X contended that (1) the commission had erred in law in failing to exclude evidence obtained by UK security service officers from individuals held in secret detention; (2) in the light of fresh evidence of later proceedings concerning another individual (J) facing deportation to Ethiopia, in which the commission had found it very likely that J would be detained and interrogated by the Ethiopian authorities and faced a real risk of ill-treatment, the commission had erred in finding that there was no real risk he would be prosecuted or be subjected to an unfair trial contrary to art.6 of the Convention; (3) the secretary of state had failed to follow guidance as to mandatory prerequisites to be satisfied before deportation pursuant to government assurances could be lawful, in particular as to verification of compliance with assurances under the MoU.

Held: Appeal dismissed. (1) The evidence X sought to exclude concerned the conditions experienced during detention and the nature of treatment received by detainees rather than evidence obtained as a result of secret detention, such as confessions. It would not threaten basic human rights, be an affront to the rule of law or compromise the integrity of the judicial process for such evidence to be given, or cause public confidence in the legal system to be undermined, *R. v Horseferry Road Magistrates Court, Ex p. Bennett (No.1)* [1994] 1 A.C. 42, [1993] C.L.Y. 1867 considered. There was no general rule that evidence obtained by unlawful means was inadmissible in legal proceedings, albeit its admission was subject to controls. The debate concerning the admissibility of evidence obtained by torture highlighted the exceptional nature of any exclusionary rule, *A v Secretary of State for the Home Department* [2005] UKHL 71, [2006] 2 A.C. 221, [2006] C.L.Y. 2200 considered. The exceptional step of exclusion would not be justified in the instant case and the commission had been entitled to take the security officers' evidence into account (see paras

39-43 of judgment). (2) On the evidence before it, the commission had been entitled to find that there was no real risk that X would be prosecuted on his return. The fresh evidence created difficulty for X since an appeal from the commission lay only on a point of law, and the instant case was not one in which a mistake of fact might amount to a mistake of law, *E v Secretary of State for the Home Department* [2004] EWCA Civ 49, [2004] Q.B. 1044, [2004] C.L.Y. 2030 considered. Since the fresh evidence was not capable of showing an error of law, permission to adduce it was refused. In light of the finding that X would not be prosecuted if returned, the remainder of X's case under art.6 fell away (paras 50, 56, 58-59, 65). (3) If effective verification was an essential ingredient for there to be a sufficient guarantee against ill-treatment of which a person was otherwise at risk, there was a problem with the commission's acceptance of the MoU as providing a sufficient safeguard. However, it was strongly arguable that the decisions in *RB (Algeria) v Secretary of State for the Home Department* [2009] UKHL 10, [2010] 2 A.C. 110, [2009] C.L.Y. 2101 and *MS (Algeria) v Secretary of State for the Home Department* [2011] EWCA Civ 306 did not constitute binding authority for the point that effective verification was an essential ingredient, since in neither case was that point directly in issue, *RB (Algeria)* and *MS (Algeria)* considered. The overall conclusion the commission had reached on the reliability of the assurances given was sustainable. None of the points raised by X disclosed an error of law by the commission (paras 73-75, 78).

XX (ETHIOPIA) v SECRETARY OF STATE FOR THE HOME DEPARTMENT, [2012] EWCA Civ 742, [2013] Q.B. 656, Lord Neuberger (M.R.), CA (Civ Div).

1595. Deportation–Residence–Protection from deportation of Community nationals with 10 years' continuous residence–Whether imprisonment affecting residence period–Whether deportation necessary on imperative grounds of public security

[Immigration (European Economic Area) Regulations 2006 (SI 2006/1003) reg.21.]

The appellant secretary of state appealed against a decision of the Asylum and Immigration Tribunal allowing an appeal by the respondent (F) against deportation. F was an Italian national who had arrived in the United Kingdom in 1985. He married and had five children. In 2001, he was convicted of the manslaughter of his then flatmate and sentenced to eight years' imprisonment. He remained in prison between May 2002 and July 2006. In 2007, the secretary of state served him with notice of intention to issue a deportation order. F appealed, complaining that the decision to deport was unlawful and inconsistent with the high threshold set under the Immigration (European Economic Area) Regulations 2006 reg.21 (4) (a). He submitted that, as a national of the European Economic Area who had been resident in the UK for a continuous period of over 10 years, a deportation decision might not be taken except on imperative grounds of public security. The tribunal found that reg.21 (4) (a) was satisfied because there was a medium risk of F killing again, which amounted to imperative grounds of public security justifying deportation. F appealed against that decision and reconsideration was ordered. The second tribunal allowed F's appeal against deportation, having found that there was no risk of him randomly killing members of the public so that his circumstances did not fall within the true ambit of imperative grounds for deportation. The issues for determination included whether F had protection under reg.21 (4) on the basis that he had resided in the UK for a continuous period of at least 10 years prior to the decision to deport, notwithstanding his imprisonment for over four years during that period, and if so, whether there were imperative grounds of public security justifying his deportation.

Held: Appeal dismissed. (1) On the correct interpretation of reg.21 (4) (a), the fact that F had been imprisoned did not affect his residence in the UK for a continuous 10-year period immediately prior to the deportation decision. (Per Pill, L.J.) The question whether the requirement of a continuous 10-year period of residence was established at the date of the decision to deport turned on the degree of integration established at that time, which was a question of fact for the tribunal. Periods of absence within the 10 years immediately preceding the decision did not of themselves disqualify and neither did a period of imprisonment. The period of imprisonment was, however, relevant as a factor to be considered when deciding upon integration at the date of decision. Time spent in prison would not normally establish integration save that it might have limited relevance by contributing to the severance of links with the country of origin. If integration had been established prior to the custodial term, it would not necessarily be lost by that term. The decision would turn on an overall qualitative assessment having regard to all relevant factors, including the length of residence, family connections and any interruptions in integration, *Land Baden-Wurttemberg v Tsakouridis (C-145/09)* [2013] All E.R. (EC) 183 and *PI v Oberburgermeisterin der Stadt Remscheid (C-348/09)* [2012] Q.B. 799 followed, *LG (Italy) v Secretary of State for the Home Department* [2009] UKAIT 24, [2009] Imm. A.R. 691, [2010] C.L.Y. 1775, *HR (Portugal) v Secretary of State for the Home Department* [2009] EWCA Civ 371, [2010] 1 W.L.R. 158, [2009] C.L.Y. 2104 and *C v Secretary of State for the Home Department* [2010] EWCA Civ 1406, Times, March 11, 2011 considered (see paras 83-86 of judgment). (Per Aikens, L.J. and Rafferty, L.J.) The key questions for a tribunal to ask when considering whether there had been a period of 10 years' residence prior to the decision to deport were whether imprisonment involved either the transfer to another state of the centre of the personal, family or occupational interests of the person concerned and/or whether "integrating links" previously forged with the host Member State had been broken, *Tsakouridis* followed. Decisions of the Court of Appeal to the effect that the period of permanent residence had to start again after time in prison were confined to particular factual situations, *HR (Portugal)* and *C* distinguished. F's imprisonment for four years could not lead to a conclusion that his existing "integrating links" with the UK had thereby been broken or that his "centre of interest" had thereby become transferred to another Member State (paras 118, 121, 124-128). (2) The test for deportation on imperative grounds of public security was whether the person concerned represented a "genuine and present threat to the fundamental interests of society or of the Member State concerned". Previous criminal convictions were not, in themselves, enough to satisfy the test, nor could a Member State rely on general justifications isolated from the facts of the case or on "considerations of general prevention". The facts of the particular case had to be closely examined to see if the only way that those fundamental interests could be protected was by expulsion, *Tsakouridis* and *PI* followed. In those circumstances, the first tribunal had plainly erred in its approach to the expression "imperative grounds of public security" and the second tribunal had reached the correct conclusion on that issue (paras 95-96, 99, 129, 134).

SECRETARY OF STATE FOR THE HOME DEPARTMENT v FV (ITALY); *sub nom.* FV (ITALY) v SECRETARY OF STATE FOR THE HOME DEPARTMENT, [2012] EWCA Civ 1199, [2013] 1 W.L.R. 3339, Pill, L.J., CA (Civ Div).

1596. Deportation–Right to respect for private and family life–Conflict with Immigration Rules–Proportionality of deportation to legitimate aim–Meaning of "no ties" pursuant to para.399A Immigration Rules

[Borders, Citizenship and Immigration Act 2009 (c.11); Human Rights Act 1998 (c.42) s.6; Nationality, Immigration and Asylum Act 2002 (c.41); Convention on the Rights of the Child (United Nations) 1989 Art.3; European Convention on Human Rights 1950 Art.8.]

The appellant (O), a Nigerian national, appealed against a decision of the First-tier Tribunal upholding the respondent secretary of state's decision to deport him. O lawfully entered the United Kingdom aged six and was granted indefinite leave to remain. He had been resident in the UK ever since and was aged 28 at the date of the instant hearing. He had had a relationship with a woman (T) with whom he had a son (S), who was a British citizen. O moved out of the family home when S was aged three or four, but continued to have contact with him. He had a subsequent relationship with another woman (X), who already had a daughter (Y) and was pregnant with O's child. Both as a juvenile and as an adult O was convicted of numerous offences, including possessing drugs, the use of drugs, including class A drugs, and one involving the supply of class C drugs. The secretary of state imposed a deportation order on O as a persistent offender. O appealed unsuccessfully against that decision, relying on his long residence and that he was the father of, and maintained contact with, a British citizen. He was granted permission to appeal out of time against the decision of the First-tier Tribunal. O submitted that his deportation constituted a breach of his rights pursuant to the European Convention on Human Rights 1950 art.8.

Held: Appeal allowed. (1) The First-tier Tribunal had failed to direct itself in accordance with *Maslov v Austria (1638/03)* [2009] I.N.L.R. 47, [2009] C.L.Y. 2070; failed to recognise the strength of the private life claim by reason of long residence alone; failed to identify the need for very serious reasons to justify the expulsion and, accordingly, failed to determine the human rights appeal lawfully. As a consequence, the decision could not stand, *Maslov* applied (para.36 of judgment). (2) O's deportation was conducive to the public good as a persistent offender pursuant to the Immigration Rules (HC194) para.398(c). However, consideration had to be given to whether he was entitled to the benefit of paragraphs 399(a), 399(b) or 399A and, if not, whether he had established that there were exceptional circumstances that entitled him to remain. O could not satisfy para.399(a) as T was able to care for S. However, since the terms of paragraph 399(a) did not provide for a consideration of where the best interests of a child lay, little weight would be given to that aspect when assessing the proportionality of the interference with the family life of the remaining family under art.8, as its terms conflicted with the secretary of state's duty under the Convention on the Rights of the Child 1989 (United Nations) art.3 to make the child's welfare and best interests a primary consideration: that duty had been imported into art.8 considerations. It was not in a child's best interests to lose contact and support with a caring and devoted parent because someone else could be found to care for them (paras 93-96). O satisfied all the requirements of para.399(b). It was unreasonable to expect X or Y to relocate to Nigeria (paras 113-114). Under para.399A, the natural and ordinary meaning of the word "ties" involved a continued connection to life in the country of proposed deportation. Circumstances relevant to assessing whether a person had ties to the country to which they would go included, but were not limited to, the length of time he had spent there, the age he was when he left, the exposure he had had to the cultural norms there, whether he spoke the language, the extent of the family and friends he had there, and the quality of his relationships with those friends and family members. O had no ties with Nigeria (paras 123-125). (3) The severity of the interference with O's private and family life as a consequence of his deportation was such that Article 8 was engaged. O's deportation would likely result in him being separated from his family for a considerable time. Under the Borders, Citizenship and Immigration Act 2009, the instant tribunal had to treat the best interests of X and Y as a primary consideration. It was in the best interests of X that O remained in the UK. Y had lived in the same household as O for over half her life and O apparently had a positive relationship with her and played an active role in her care. Deportation was not proportionate to the legitimate aim. O was not persistently offending and the addiction that led him to commit a previous serious offence had been addressed. Deportation was unlawful under the Human Rights Act 1998 s.6 and not in accordance with the law within the meaning of the Nationality, Immigration and Asylum Act 2002 (paras 128, 134-140). (4) (Obiter) It was only in exceptional cases that permission to appeal to the Upper Tribunal should be granted where the lodging of the application for permission was more than 28 days out of time. Where, in such a case, a judge was minded to grant permission, the preferable course was to provide an opportunity to the respondent to make representations. That might be achieved by listing the permission application for oral hearing (paras 20-21).

OGUNDIMU (ARTICLE 8: NEW RULES: NIGERIA), *Re; sub nom.* OGUNDIMU v SECRETARY OF STATE FOR THE HOME DEPARTMENT, [2013] UKUT 60 (IAC), [2013] Imm. A.R. 422, Blake, J. (President), UT (IAC).

1597. Deportation–Third country nationals–Non-EU national guilty of criminal offences–Effect of deportation on EU national spouse's right to reside–Whether principle in Ruiz Zambrano v Office National de l'Emploi (ONEm) (C-34/09) [2012] Q.B. 265 engaged

[European Convention on Human Rights 1950 Art.8.]

The Court of Appeal was required to determine whether decisions concerning the deportation of the respondents (B and H) should be overturned. B was a Moroccan citizen, and H was a Jamaican citizen. Both men had come to the United Kingdom, married a British national and been granted indefinite leave to remain. H had three children with another partner, whom he did not marry. He was imprisoned for conspiracy to supply a Class A drug and possession of a weapon. An order was made for his deportation. B was convicted of a serious sexual assault upon a 61-year-old woman. After serving four years in prison he was deported. His marriage was dissolved. However, he returned to the UK and married an Irish citizen. They had two children together. He was arrested following a domestic dispute and a second order was made for his deportation. He claimed residence as the spouse of an EU national, but his claim was rejected. The court was required to determine whether B and H fell within the scope of the European Court of Justice's decision in *Ruiz Zambrano v Office National de l'Emploi (ONEm) (C-34/09)* [2012] Q.B. 265.

Held: Appeals dismissed. (1) The application of the *Zambrano* test required a court to focus on whether, as a matter of reality, the European Union citizen would be obliged to give up residence in the EU if the non-EU national were removed from the EU. There was no de facto compulsion in B or H's case. The question was therefore whether the *Zambrano* principle could apply where an EU citizen was not forced to follow the non-EU national out of the EU, but where their continuing residence in the EU was affected in some way, for example, their quality of life was diminished (see para.55 of judgment). (2) If the EU citizen, whether child or wife, would not in practice be compelled to leave the country if the non-EU family member were refused residence, there was nothing in the authorities to suggest that EU law was engaged, *McCarthy v Secretary of State for the Home Department (C-434/09)* [2011] All E.R. (EC) 729, [2011] C.L.Y. 1263, *Dereci v Bundesministerium fur Inneres (C-256/11)* [2012] All E.R. (EC) 373 and *Iida v Stadt Ulm (C-40/11)* [2013] Fam. 121 considered. Rights under the European Convention on Human Rights 1950 art.8 might then come into play to protect family life, but that was an entirely distinct area of protection. The right of residence was a right to reside in the territory of the EU. It was not a right to any particular quality of life or to any particular standard of living. Accordingly, there was no impediment to exercising the right to reside if residence remained possible as a matter of substance, albeit that the quality of life was diminished. If the quality or standard of life would be seriously impaired by excluding the non-EU national such that it was likely, in practice, to compel the EU citizen to give up residence and travel with the non-EU national, the *Zambrano* doctrine would apply, and the EU citizen's rights would have to be protected, *Zambrano* considered. It was also highly pertinent that the ECJ had confirmed in *Dereci* that the fact that the right to family life was adversely affected, or that the presence of the non-EU national was desirable for economic reasons, was not capable of triggering the Zambrano principle, *Dereci* considered. The position was *acte clair* and B and H were seeking to extend the *Zambrano* doctrine beyond its legitimate limits (paras 63, 67-70). (3) Given that B was at all times an illegal entrant and had committed a serious criminal offence, there was every justification for the conclusion reached by all judges who considered his case, namely that his deportation would not infringe his art.8 rights or those of his family (paras 72-77). (4) H had obtained indefinite leave to remain by deception since he had been in another relationship at the same time as the marriage on which he had based his application for leave to remain. Moreover, the relationship with his partner had been formed when his precarious immigration status was known to her. The Upper Tribunal had recognised that H's children were the innocent victims of his conduct and would suffer if he was deported. The approach of the courts below was appropriate and the balancing exercise was conducted fully and fairly. It was difficult to see how the courts could have come to any other conclusion in B and H's cases (paras 78-80).

HARRISON v SECRETARY OF STATE FOR THE HOME DEPARTMENT; AB (MOROCCO) v SECRETARY OF STATE FOR THE HOME DEPARTMENT; *sub nom.* DH (JAMAICA) v SECRETARY OF STATE FOR THE HOME DEPARTMENT, [2012] EWCA Civ 1736, [2013] 2 C.M.L.R. 23, Ward, L.J., CA (Civ Div).

1598. Deportation orders–In-country right of appeal–Exercise of court's discretion to return deportee pending reconsideration of deportation decision

[Nationality, Immigration and Asylum Act 2002 (c.41) s.96(2).]

The appellant Chinese national (Z), who had been deported, appealed against a refusal of a High Court judge to exercise his discretion to return him to the United Kingdom pending reconsideration of the deportation order. Z, who had been granted indefinite leave to remain in the UK, had been recommended for deportation following his conviction for drugs offences. The deportation order was served in February 2011 after two periods of imprisonment. Z applied for its revocation on the ground that he had been in a relationship for approximately four years and had recently fathered a child. The application was refused because the information contradicted previous information given by him and was thought to be a deliberate attempt to frustrate his removal. The judge certified the case under the Nationality, Immigration and Asylum Act 2002 s.96(2). Permission to apply for judicial review of the certification and the refusal to revoke the deportation order was refused on February 24, the judge stating that renewal of the permission application was not to operate as a bar to Z's removal. Z was therefore removed in March 2011. His renewed permission application was successful. A week before the case was to be heard, the secretary of state offered to withdraw the s.96(2) certificate and undertook to reconsider the application to revoke the deportation order. She denied that her original decision was flawed, maintaining that her change of mind was for purely pragmatic reasons, and refused to return Z to the UK pending the reconsideration. When Z challenged that decision in the High Court, the judge refused to rule upon the validity of the s.96(2) certificate, indicating that he would assume it had been withdrawn because it had been unlawfully granted. He found that, had certification not occurred, Z could have remained in the UK to pursue his appeal. He concluded, however, that the deportation had been lawful because the February 24 order had stipulated that renewal of the permission application was not to be a bar to removal, and that although the lawfulness of removal was not determinative, it was a highly material factor against the exercise of discretion. He also found that Z had provided insufficient evidence of family life or paternity in his initial revocation application and that, balancing all the competing considerations, it was not appropriate for him to exercise his discretion. The issue was whether he had adopted the right approach towards the exercise of discretion.

Held: Appeal dismissed. Where a person in Z's position was removed from the UK on the strength of an unlawful s.96(2) certificate, the effect was to deprive him unlawfully of an in-country appeal to which he was statutorily entitled. That was to be the court's starting point in considering whether to order a person's return and was a strong factor in favour of return. The judge below had taken a sensible course in declining to rule on the lawfulness of the s.96(2) certificate, and in making an assumption in Z's favour. That assumption carried as much weight as a ruling would have done. It was, however, unhelpful and undesirable to see it as a "presumption" in favour of return, and to assume that good reasons were needed to rebut that "presumption"; the court's discretion was wide and all relevant factors had to be put in the balance (see paras 47-49 of judgment). In the instant case, the judge had adopted a correct approach and his decision was not flawed. He had recognised that the assumed illegality of the certificate was the strongest thing in Z's favour and had taken that as his starting point. He had recognised that removal had been lawful, had assumed that Z was the father of the relevant child and had considered both the child's and the mother's interests. He had pointed out that the mother would be able to give oral evidence in the UK and that there could be no serious objections to Z giving video link evidence. Although an in-country appeal was of very real importance, and although there were undoubted disadvantages of an out of country appeal, context remained important: in appeals relating to family life, where the other members of the family were situated in the UK, it could not be said that an out of country appeal would always be ineffective, *R. (on the application of CM (Jamaica)) v Secretary of State for the Home Department* [2010] EWCA Civ 160 applied, *Lewis v Secretary of State for the Home Department* [2010] EWHC 1749 (Admin) approved, and *R. (on the application of E (Russia)) v Secretary of State for the Home Department* [2012] EWCA Civ 357, [2012] 1 W.L.R. 3198, [2013] 2 C.L. 187 considered (paras 28-34, 50-57).

R. (ON THE APPLICATION OF Z) v SECRETARY OF STATE FOR THE HOME DEPARTMENT; *sub nom.* R. (ON THE APPLICATION OF YZ(CHINA)) v SECRETARY OF STATE FOR THE HOME DEPARTMENT, [2012] EWCA Civ 1022, [2013] I.N.L.R. 60, Lloyd, L.J., CA (Civ Div).

1599. Deportation orders–Revocation–Application to revoke deportation order based on new evidence–Meaning of "matter" within s.96(1)(b) Nationality, Immigration and Asylum Act 2002–Whether evidence included or limited to issues

[Nationality, Immigration and Asylum Act 2002 (c.41) s.96(1)(b).]

The claimant (K) applied for judicial review of the defendant secretary of state's refusal to revoke a deportation order made against him. K, a Pakistani national, had come to the United Kingdom as the spouse of a UK national and was granted indefinite leave to remain. He was sentenced to 14 months' imprisonment for dangerous driving and perverting the course of justice. A deportation order was made, and K's appeal against it was dismissed. The secretary of state received further submissions from K, as well as an independent social worker's report concerning his children. K argued that if the report had been before the immigration judge in his earlier appeal, he would not have upheld the deportation order. The secretary of state treated K's new submissions as an application to revoke the deportation order. Under the Nationality, Immigration and Asylum Act 2002 s.96(1)(b), she certified that K's application relied on a matter that could have been raised in his earlier appeal, and therefore refused his application. The issue was whether K was correct that "matter" under s.96(1)(b) was limited to an "issue", or whether the secretary of state was correct that it was a broad term which included evidence as well as issues.

Held: Application refused. The case of *R. (on the application of ZA (Nigeria)) v Secretary of State for the Home Department* [2010] EWCA Civ 926, [2011] Q.B. 722 was persuasive in showing that s.96 was not limited to issues but included evidence within its scope, *ZA* applied, *R. (on the application of J) v Secretary of State for the Home Department* [2009] EWHC 705 (Admin) and *Lamichhane v Secretary of State for the Home Department* [2012] EWCA Civ 260, [2012] 1 W.L.R. 3064, [2012] C.L.Y. 1730 considered. If "matter" had any special meaning, one would have expected to see a specific definition either in the glossary or in a free-standing provision in the Act. It was to have its ordinary, unadorned meaning: "matter" was a noun that was apt to include as broad a section of relevant material as possible, and should be given a broad interpretation within the scope of s.96(1)(b). Accordingly, the deportation order was upheld (see paras 6-10 of judgment).

R. (ON THE APPLICATION OF KHAN) v SECRETARY OF STATE FOR THE HOME DEPARTMENT; KHAN v SECRETARY OF STATE FOR THE HOME DEPARTMENT, [2013] EWHC 601 (Admin), [2013] 3 All E.R. 499, Turner, J., QBD (Admin).

1600. Designation–Immigration–Travel bans

THE IMMIGRATION (DESIGNATION OF TRAVEL BANS) (AMENDMENT NO.2) ORDER 2013, SI 2013/1745; made under the Immigration Act 1971 s.8B. In force: July 17, 2013; .

This Order amends the Immigration (Designation of Travel Bans) Order 2000 (the 2000 Order) by adding a Resolution to the list of Resolutions of the Security Council of the United Nations and by adding several Decisions to the list of European Union Council Decisions listed in the Schedule to the 2000 Order. The Schedule lists United Nations' Security Council Resolutions and European Union Council Decisions or Common Positions which impose restrictive travel measures against named individuals.

1601. Detention–Children–Lawfulness of detention of child mistakenly believed to be adult under Sch.2 Pt I para.16(2) Immigration Act 1971–Interpretation of s.55 Borders, Citizenship and Immigration Act 2009

[Borders, Citizenship and Immigration Act 2009 (c.11) s.55; Children Act 1989 (c.41) s.20; Immigration Act 1971 (c.77) Sch.2 Pt I para.16; Convention on the Rights of the Child (United Nations) 1989 Art.3; European Convention on Human Rights 1950 Art.5.]

The appellant (X) appealed against a decision ([2012] EWCA Civ 1383) that the respondent secretary of state's decision to detain him under the Immigration Act 1971 Sch.2 Pt I para.16(2) was not unlawful. X, born in Afghanistan, had claimed asylum on his arrival in the United Kingdom. He stated that he was 14. An age assessment carried out by the local authority concluded that he was over 19. He was granted temporary admission. However, his asylum claim was unsuccessful and a decision made to remove him. The First-tier Tribunal was satisfied that he was over 18 and dismissed his appeal. X was later detained under para.16(2) and removal directions issued. He sought judicial review of the decision. The secretary of state accepted a further age assessment which confirmed that X was 17. It was agreed that he would be treated as a child under the Children Act 1989 and provided with accommodation and support. X's judicial review claim in respect of the original decision to detain him was dismissed. The Court of Appeal found that the secretary of state's power of detention under para.16(2) was wide enough to permit the detention of a person with a view to removing them on the mistaken belief that the person was an adult. The issue was regarding the effect of the Borders, Citizenship and Immigration Act 2009 s.55 on the lawfulness of X's detention. X submitted that s.55 should be read in a similar fashion to s.20 of the 1989 Act. He argued that his welfare had not been taken into account and that there had therefore been a breach of s.55.

Held: Appeal dismissed. (1) A material breach of s.55 would make the decision unlawful, *R. (on the application of Lumba) v Secretary of State for the Home Department* [2011] UKSC 12, [2012] 1 A.C. 245, [2011] C.L.Y. 1727 followed. Section 55 and s.20 contained the same definition of children, but their structure and language were very different. Under s.55(1), the secretary of state had a direct responsibility for making arrangements for the specific purpose of ensuring that immigration functions were discharged in a way which safeguarded and promoted the welfare of children. She also had a vicarious responsibility, under s.55(3), for any failure by any person exercising the secretary of state's functions, including immigration officers, to have regard to the guidance for safeguarding and promoting the welfare of children, applicable to public bodies generally, and specifically to the UK Border Agency, or to the welfare principle. Proper systems had to be established for arriving at a reliable assessment of a person's age. That was not an easy matter. However, guidance in relation to the policy and procedures to be followed was detailed and careful, and complied with the obligations under s.55(1). There was no basis for finding that there had been a failure by any official to follow that guidance. It followed that there had been no breach of s.55 and that the exercise of the secretary of state's detention power had not been unlawful, *AAM (A Child) v Secretary of State for the Home Department* [2012] EWHC 2567 (QB) overruled in part (see paras 44-48, 50-51 of judgment). (2) On its natural construction, s.55 was not inconsistent with the European Convention on Human Rights 1950 art.5 or the Convention on the Rights of the Child 1989 (United Nations) art.3. The risk of an erroneous assessment could never be entirely eliminated, but could be minimised by a careful process. There were appropriate safeguards. In addition to the process for making the initial assessment, which included a requirement for the benefit of any doubt to be given to the claimant, the secretary of state was under a continuing obligation to consider any fresh evidence. A local authority's age assessment could be challenged on judicial review and the secretary of state would be bound to give proper respect to the outcome of such proceedings (para.49). (3) (Obiter) The court had the power to develop its habeas corpus jurisdiction where necessary to achieve effective justice in matters of personal liberty. In the instant type of situation that jurisdiction should not be confined to determining whether the secretary of state had acted lawfully, but should extend to enable the court to make a fresh determination of the claimant's age, which would necessarily impact on the lawfulness of his continued detention. The effect of a finding in the claimant's favour would not take him outside the scope of para.16, but would impact on the operation thereafter of the secretary of state's policies introduced to implement s.55. In practical terms it would mean that the court was able to reach a final determination of the claimant's age not only when his Children Act rights depended on it but, more fundamentally, when his liberty depended on it (para.53). (4) (Per Carnwath L) Given the constitutional importance of the "Great Writ" of habeas corpus, there should be a full exploration of all the legal and practical implications before accepting it as a suitable procedure for the narrow, factual inquiries likely to be required in a case of the instant type (paras 56-59).

R. (ON THE APPLICATION OF AA (AFGHANISTAN)) v SECRETARY OF STATE FOR THE HOME DEPARTMENT, [2013] UKSC 49, [2013] 1 W.L.R. 2224, Lord Neuberger (President), SC.

1602. Detention–Lawfulness of detention–Indication made under r.39 Rules of Court (ECHR)–Reasonable prospect of removal

[Rules of Court (ECHR) 2011 r.39.]

The appellant Somali national (M) appealed against a decision ([2011] EWHC 2707 (Admin)) dismissing his claim for judicial review of his detention by the respondent secretary of state. M had been detained from February 2008 pending deportation. Removal directions were cancelled in June 2009 following receipt of an indication from the European Court of Human Rights under the Rules of Court (ECHR) r.39 that M should not be deported until it had determined the lead case of *Sufi v United Kingdom (8319/07)* (2012) 54 E.H.R.R. 9, [2012] C.L.Y. 1659. Judgment in *Sufi* was given on June 28, 2011. M was bailed on July 13. M argued that (1) his detention breached the principles in *R. v Governor of Durham Prison, Ex p. Singh* [1984] 1 W.L.R. 704, [1984] C.L.Y. 1726: he should have been released on receipt of the r.39 indication; the judge had been wrong to distinguish his case from *R. (on the application of Abdi) v Secretary of State for the Home Department* [2011] EWCA Civ 242, Times, March 11, 2011, where there had been no realistic prospect of removal because of the detainee's having to go to an area of Somalia other than Mogadishu; and he should have been released, at the latest, one week after the *Sufi* judgment, as had been considered sufficient time in *Abdi*; (2) his detention had been vitiated by public law errors, namely the secretary of state's failure to ascertain when the r.39 indication might be lifted and the maintenance of detention on the basis that M could reduce his detention time by voluntarily returning to Somalia.

Held: Appeal dismissed. (1) At the time of receipt of the r.39 indication there had been a realistic prospect of the ECtHR proceedings being resolved within a reasonable period. It had been possible but not apparent that they would drag on. Nor had it been apparent that the ECtHR's decision would prevent M's removal. "Apparent" was stressed because that was the word used in *Singh*; it was important not to water that down so as to cover situations where removal within a reasonable period was merely uncertain. It was unnecessary for the secretary of state to identify the timescale within which removal could be effected for continued detention to be lawful, *R. (on the application of MH) v Secretary of State for the Home Department* [2010] EWCA Civ 1112 followed (see paras 36-38 of judgment). The judge's distinction in respect of *Abdi* had been valid. There was a reasonable prospect of it being established that M could lawfully be removed to Mogadishu, *Abdi* considered. Generally, comparison with particular outcomes in other cases was unlikely to be useful in a highly fact-sensitive area (para.41). The secretary of state had been entitled to take the time she had at least to consider what to do after the issue of *Sufi*. The week allowed in *Abdi* was not intended to have wider application, but was based on the particular circumstances of that case, *Abdi* considered. The secretary of state would have had numerous cases to reassess in the light of *Sufi*; there could not be a limit of one week on a reasonable time for such assessments. There was force in the argument that it had been reasonable to wait until M's next detention review, since one of the reviews' purposes was to reassess justification for detention in the light of up-to-date information. The judge had properly concluded that M's release before that review, two weeks after the Sufi judgment, had been within the time the secretary of state had been entitled to take, *Singh* considered and *Sufi* referred to (para.45). The instant court would rarely interfere with a first instance judge's application of the *Singh* principles; that approach was preferred to the statement in *AS (Sudan) v Secretary of State for the Home Department* [2009] EWCA Civ 1518 that the Court of Appeal was in as good a position as the first instance judge, *Abdi, MH* and *AS* considered (paras 46-48). (2) If M were able to show that the decisions to maintain his detention were vitiated by public law errors, he would succeed in establishing that the detention was unlawful, *R. (on the application of Lumba) v Secretary of State for the Home Department* [2011] UKSC 12, [2012] 1 A.C. 245, [2011] C.L.Y. 1727 and *R. (on the application of Kambadzi) v Secretary of State for the Home Department* [2011] UKSC 23, [2011] 1 W.L.R. 1299, [2011] C.L.Y. 1733 followed. However, the secretary of state had been aware at all times of the position regarding the ECtHR proceedings. Appropriate inquiries had been made; it was unrealistic to suggest that any better indication of the timescale could have been obtained. Nor did the references to the possibility of voluntary return give rise to an error of law. Pursuit of that question did not mean that M had been pressured to withdraw his ECtHR application or his tribunal appeal. As long as his detention did not exceed a reasonable period, it could properly be pointed out to him that voluntary return would reduce the length of detention, *Lumba* considered (paras 57-64, 67-72).

R. (ON THE APPLICATION OF MUQTAAR) v SECRETARY OF STATE FOR THE HOME DEPARTMENT; *sub nom.* MUQTAAR v SECRETARY OF STATE FOR THE HOME DEPARTMENT, [2012] EWCA Civ 1270, [2013] 1 W.L.R. 649, Lloyd, L.J., CA (Civ Div).

1603. Detention pending deportation–Third country nationals–Lawfulness of detention of third country national pending deportation–Compatibility of art.27 Directive 2004/38 with reg.24 Immigration (European Economic Area) Regulations 2006–Whether detention regime under reg.24 discriminatory

[Immigration Act 1971 (c.77) Sch.3; Immigration (European Economic Area) Regulations 2006 (SI 2006/1003) reg.19(3)(b), reg.21, reg.24(1), reg.24; Directive 2004/38 on the right of citizens of the Union and their family members to move and reside freely within the territory of the Member States amending Regulation (EEC) No 1612/68 and repealing Directives 64/221/EEC, 68/360/EEC, 72/194/EEC, 73/148/EEC, 75/34/EEC, 75/35/EEC, 90/364/EEC, 90/365/ Art.27; Directive 2008/115 on common standards and procedures for returning illegally staying third-country nationals Art.15.]

The claimant (N) applied for judicial review of the defendant secretary of state's decision to detain him pending deportation. N, an Algerian national, had arrived in the United Kingdom in 1996. He married a French citizen, and was granted a right of residence as a family member of a national of the European Economic Area (EEA). N was convicted of theft and imprisoned. Around his release date, N was served with notice of a decision to deport him. The notice said that the secretary of state had considered his conduct in accordance with the Immigration (European Economic Area) Regulations 2006 reg.21, and that she had decided under reg.19(3)(b) that he should be removed and a removal order made in accordance with reg.24(3). N was held in immigration detention before being released on bail. He was subsequently notified of a new decision to remove him and was re-detained in immigration detention. The issues were whether (i) Directive 2004/38 art.27 expressly or impliedly prohibited any detention prior to a decision to remove, and if not whether reg.24(1) of the Regulations was inconsistent with art.27; (ii) N's detention under reg.24 was unlawful under EU law because the exercise of that power discriminated against him on the grounds of nationality when compared to the detention of an alien under the Immigration Act 1971 Sch.3.

Held: Application refused. (1) The words "may restrict freedom of movement" in art.27 of the 2004 Directive were, as a matter of ordinary language, wide enough to include any detention of any kind, subject to the requirements listed in art.27. It was relatively plain that the object of Directive 2008/115 was to establish common rules concerning the return, removal, use of coercive measures, detention and entry bans in stipulated circumstances. On that basis, the harmonisation regime set out in art.15 of the 2008 Directive did not necessarily say anything about the scope of art.27 of the 2004 Directive. Accordingly, art.27 did not restrict, but on the contrary expressly permitted, a Member State to restrict freedom of movement of any family member of an EEA national, subject to the conditions under art.27. There was no reason in principle why, even though a decision to remove had not yet been made on grounds of public policy or safety, a decision to detain pending such a decision should not be made on those grounds. Whilst that might constitute a very significant restriction on an individual's rights of liberty and freedom of movement, there was no necessary incompatibility between reg.24(1) and art.27, provided that the conditions in art.27(1) and art.27(2) were satisfied. It therefore followed that the immigration detention of a family member of an EEA national pending removal and following a conviction in a Member State was not prohibited by EU law, that such detention complied with EU law, and that reg.24(1) was compatible with EU law (see paras 33-35, 38-39, 41 of judgment). (2) The respective regimes which existed to detain non-British citizens under Sch.3 of the 1971 Act and EEA nationals and their family members under the Regulations were different: unlike the regime under the Regulations, there was no power to remove or deport in the regime under the Act. However, that did not necessarily mean that there was any relevant disadvantage to EEA nationals or their family, or other discrimination in any relevant sense. The starting point was to recognise that under the 2004 Directive and the Regulations, EEA nationals and their family members benefitted from extended rights which non-EEA nationals did not. Further, it was also significant to take into account the different tests for deportation under the Act and the Regulations: the test under the Act was of a lower threshold than that which existed with regard to the secretary of state's power to remove under reg.19(3)(b). Given those differences, there was no proper basis for comparing the different circumstances which existed to deport/remove under each applicable regime. It followed that neither reg.24(1) nor reg.24(3) gave rise to any relevant discrimination of a kind which offended EU law (paras 52-54). (3) Accordingly, N's detention in custody was not unlawful (para.56).

R. (ON THE APPLICATION OF NOUAZLI) v SECRETARY OF STATE FOR THE HOME DEPARTMENT, [2013] EWHC 567 (Admin), [2013] 2 C.M.L.R. 54, Eder, J., QBD (Admin).

1604. Entry clearances–Appeals–Reasonableness of First-tier Tribunal's decision

[Nationality, Immigration and Asylum Act 2002 (c.41) s.86(3)(b).]

The appellant entry clearance officer appealed against a decision of the First-tier Tribunal to allow the appeal of the respondent (U) against a refusal to grant him entry clearance to the United Kingdom as a spouse. The entry clearance officer had relied on the Immigration Rules para.320(18), which provided that entry clearance would normally be refused where the person concerned had been convicted of an offence which was punishable with at least 12 months' imprisonment, save where admission would be justified for strong compassionate reasons. The officer considered whether U and his wife were involved in a serious relationship in which they maintained regular contact. He found that they were not and was not therefore satisfied that they intended to live permanently with each other in a subsisting marriage. The officer also found that U had made a false representation and had failed to declare material facts, thereby undermining his credibility in relation to the purpose and duration of his stay. He noted that U had a relevant conviction. On U's appeal, the First-tier Tribunal concluded that there were strong compassionate circumstances which the entry clearance officer had failed to take into account sufficient for the discretion contained in para.320(18) to have been exercised differently. The tribunal found that the marriage was a subsisting one, that U's wife had given unchallenged evidence that he was permitted to reside with her in accommodation she rented and that his wife's earnings were substantially in excess of the minimum income support level so that there was nothing to show that she would not be able to support both of them without recourse to public funds. The entry clearance officer argued that the tribunal, having concluded that he had failed to reach a decision in accordance with the law, should have remitted the matter for reconsideration instead of granting U entry clearance.

Held: Appeal dismissed. The entry clearance officer's submission was misconceived, as he had not failed to reach a decision in accordance with the law. Instead, this was a classic example of the lawful exercise of a discretion. The officer recognised the part of the Immigration Rules that he was applying, acknowledged that that involved him in the exercise of a discretion, identified the factors that he was required to take into account in reaching his decision and balanced those factors, reaching a conclusion that they were not sufficiently compelling for the exercise of discretion in U's favour. In the circumstances, it was open to the tribunal, under the Nationality, Immigration and Asylum Act 2002 s.86(3)(b), to determine that the discretion should have been exercised differently. There were four possible situations where the tribunal would be considering an appeal arising from the exercise of a discretionary power: (a) the decision-maker had failed to make a lawful decision in the purported exercise of the discretionary power vested in him and a lawful decision was required; (b) the decision-maker had lawfully exercised his discretion and the tribunal had no jurisdiction to intervene; (c) the decision-maker had lawfully exercised his discretion and the tribunal upheld the exercise of his discretion; (d) the decision-maker had lawfully exercised his discretion and the tribunal reached its decision exercising its discretion differently. It would only be if (a) applied that the tribunal would be required to allow the appeal to the extent of deciding that a fresh decision had to be made. In this case, the entry clearance officer had made a lawful decision and the tribunal was, on appeal, permitted to make its own decision by the exercise of its discretion and to reach a conclusion different from that of the officer (see paras 12-14, 22-23 of judgment).

UKUS (DISCRETION: WHEN REVIEWABLE: NIGERIA), *Re; sub nom.* UKUS v ENTRY CLEARANCE OFFICER (LAGOS), [2012] UKUT 307 (IAC), [2013] Imm. A.R. 37, CMG Ockelton (Vice President), UT (IAC).

1605. Entry clearances–Children–Father in polygamous marriage granted right of settlement in United Kingdom but not mother–Child not meeting requirements of Immigration Rules–Whether refusing entry breached art.8 European Convention on Human Rights 1950

[European Convention on Human Rights 1950 Art.8.]

The Upper Tribunal was required to determine whether it was a breach of the European Convention on Human Rights 1950 art.8 to refuse the child of a polygamous marriage (S) entry to the United Kingdom where the father (F) had a right to live but the mother did not. S, who was nine years old, had been refused entry clearance to the UK from Nepal. F had served in the Brigade of Ghurkhas and as a result had a right to settlement in the UK. His application for entry clearance had been granted, along with his second wife and son. S's mother was F's third wife and it was accepted that she was not eligible for settlement in the UK and would continue to reside in Nepal. S was refused entry clearance on the basis that F did not have sole responsibility for her. S's appeal was allowed because the judge found that S was entirely dependent on F, who made all decisions about her welfare. On appeal by the entry clearance officer, the Upper Tribunal considered that responsibility was shared and ordered the instant hearing to consider the impact of art.8. S's mother agreed that S should live in the UK, where her education and employment opportunities would be better. S submitted that (1) even where a non-sponsoring mother was caring for her child there could be exceptional circumstances justifying the conclusion that responsibility for the child's welfare was the father's sole prerogative; (2) there were compelling reasons why her exclusion from the UK was undesirable within the meaning of the Immigration Rules; (3) the decision amounted to discrimination on the grounds of social status because she was the child of a polygamous marriage, and was a disproportionate and unjustified interference with the right to respect for that family's life and therefore contrary to art.8.

Held: Judgment accordingly. (1) Where a child's natural parent had cared for and continued to care for the child, responsibility had to be considered joint between the parties (see para.10 of judgment). (2) Economic and educational betterment of the child in the UK was not the kind of factor that made exclusion undesirable. The wishes of S and her parents were a factor in the assessment but would rarely be decisive in the immigration context. S's best interests did not required her to be separated from her biological mother who was well able to care for her. Accordingly, S had not made out a case of admission under the Rules, nor under the supplemental policies regarding Ghurkha soldiers (paras 11, 13). (3) (a) It was doubtful that r.296, which denied a child entry whose parents were a party to a polygamous marriage and where the parent did not have a right of settlement, could be used to refuse admission to a child where the father had sole responsibility or whose exclusion was considered undesirable, let alone cases where the art.8 balance favoured the admission of the child. Use of the rule to deny admission to a child whose welfare and best interests suggested should otherwise be admitted would be directly contrary to the principle that the welfare of the child was the primary consideration, *ZH (Tanzania) v Secretary of State for the Home Department* [2011] UKSC 4, [2011] 2 A.C. 166, [2011] C.L.Y. 1790 considered. However, that did not assist S. Her position was akin to a child of a divorcee who was not admissible because the sponsor did not intend to live with his former spouse and the child was excluded because neither the sole responsibility nor exclusion undesirable test could be satisfied. Furthermore, the difference in treatment between S and the child of a polygamous marriage who was a British citizen by descent was not an illogical and unjustified difference, but simply a consequence of the principle that entry by a British national to the UK was not subject to immigration control (paras 28, 30, 35-38). (b) Denying S entry clearance had an impact on the family life she enjoyed but the degree of impact was not such as could be said to interfere with it or to impose a positive obligation on the state to admit her. F was not being required to make an invidious choice between continued residence in the UK with a spouse and family who had grown up there and leaving another child of the family behind in the country of origin. Furthermore, there was a legitimate aim being pursued in denying admission to a child who did not comply with the rules on admission (paras 42, 44-45). (c) The interference was justified, proportionate and represented a fair balance of the competing interests. Admission would take S out of continuity of the daily care of her mother who had cared for her and whose care was satisfactory and appropriate. The separation of F and S was a consequence of F's choice of place of residence rather than the imposition on him of an intolerable choice. Furthermore, although parents were entitled to make decisions for their children, parental wishes could not outweigh the best interests of the child objectively construed. They could not themselves impose a positive obligation on the state to admit a child because the father wanted the child to be brought up there. Accordingly, the art.8 case failed (paras 48-49, 52).

SG (CHILD OF POLYGAMOUS MARRIAGE: NEPAL), *Re; sub nom.* ENTRY CLEARANCE OFFICER, NEW DELHI v SG (NEPAL), [2012] UKUT 265 (IAC), [2012] Imm. A.R. 939, Blake, J., UT (IAC).

1606. Entry clearances–Deportation orders–Process for obtaining entry clearance where applicant subject to deportation order

[Nationality, Immigration and Asylum Act 2002 (c.41) s.84(1), s.85(2), s.85(4), s.85A, s.120; European Convention on Human Rights 1950 Art.8.]

The appellant Pakistani national (L) appealed against a decision of the respondent entry clearance officer to refuse him entry clearance into the United Kingdom. L had arrived in 1993 on a spouse visa. He remained as an overstayer after the breakdown of his marriage despite a deportation order made against him in 1996. In 2003 he started a relationship and had a daughter with a woman who was still married to somebody else. They had an Islamic ceremony with the intention that they would later marry. In 2005 he applied for leave to remain as a prospective spouse. The application was refused because of the existence of the deportation order, which there were no grounds for revoking. The family went to Pakistan voluntarily for a short time. Mother and daughter returned but L's application to return as a fiance was refused because he was still subject to the deportation order. L appealed to the First-tier Tribunal, alleging that the officer ought to have treated his application for entry as a request to revoke the deportation order. The immigration judge held that the application had been correctly rejected. He also found, in relation to submissions made under the European Convention on Human Rights 1950 art.8, that family life was currently enjoyed by telephone and there was no reason why that should not continue. L submitted that, under both the Immigration Rules and the Nationality, Immigration and Asylum Act 2002 s.120, the application for entry clearance automatically fell to be treated as an application for revocation of the deportation order, since entry clearance could not be granted without revocation.

Held: Appeal dismissed. (1) An application for revocation of a deportation order had to be made under the Immigration Rules (HC 395) para.390. People in L's situation had to apply for the deportation order to be revoked, and achieve revocation, before applying for entry clearance. It was a two-stage procedure: there was no obvious link between the two rules which obliged the tribunal to consider both at the same time. L was the author of his own misfortune; he had failed to apply under the correct rule and his application for settlement was bound to attract a mandatory refusal. The entry clearance officer had made the only decision which was open to him (see paras 24-30, 34 of judgment). (2) Under s.85(2) of the Act, the tribunal had to consider any matter raised by an appellant in a s.120 statement which constituted a ground of appeal of a kind listed in s.84(1). Under s.85(4), the tribunal had a discretion to consider evidence about any matter which it thought relevant to the substance of the decision, including matters arising after the date of the decision being appealed. That power was subject to the exceptions in s.85A, the effect of which was to restrict the tribunal's consideration in entry clearance cases to circumstances appertaining at the time of the decision. At the time of the decision to refuse L entry clearance, he was subject to a deportation order, and therefore the fact that he mentioned revocation in his grounds of appeal against that refusal could not assist him. *AS (Afghanistan) v Secretary of State for the Home Department* [2009] EWCA Civ 1076, [2011] 1 W.L.R. 385, [2010] C.L.Y. 1791 was not authority for the proposition that any issues raised under s.120 were to be treated as a fresh application to the tribunal. The principle in that case was not a mechanism which permitted an appellant to make an entirely new application; it only permitted expansion of the existing grounds of appeal, *AS (Afghanistan)* not applied. To allow L to raise a fresh application in his grounds for entry clearance would negate the purpose of s.85A (paras 36-47). (3) The conclusion of the immigration judge that family life could continue by telephone contact was not consistent with the holistic view of family life as developed by recent case law. Family life could not reasonably be conducted via telephone calls, emails and an occasional visit. The decision to refuse entry clearance was also an interference with L's intention to marry. Nevertheless the refusal was lawful and necessary. Where there was a clear procedure to be followed and an appellant chose not to follow it, it would rarely be proportionate to allow the Immigration Rules to be circumvented by reliance on art.8 (paras 57-64).

LATIF (S.120: REVOCATION OF DEPORTATION ORDER: PAKISTAN), *Re; sub nom.* LATIF v ENTRY CLEARANCE OFFICER, [2012] UKUT 78 (IAC), [2012] Imm. A.R. 659, Judge DE Taylor, UT (IAC).

1607. Entry clearances–Right of appeal–Refusal of entry because of previous breaches of immigration policy–Fairness of restricted appeal rights in s.84(1)(b) and s.84(1)(c) Nationality, Immigration and Asylum Act 2002

[Immigration, Asylum and Nationality Act 2006 (c.13) s.4(1); Nationality, Immigration and Asylum Act 2002 (c.41) s.82(1), s.88A(3), s.88A; Immigration, Asylum and Nationality Act 2006 (Commencement No. 8 and Transitional and Saving Provisions) Order 2008 (SI 2008/310) Art.4.]

The appellant (X), a Nigerian citizen, appealed against a decision of the respondent entry clearance officer to refuse him entry clearance into the United Kingdom. X had applied for entry as a Tier-2 migrant in order to take up a job with an NHS trust. Entry had been refused under the Immigration Rules para.245ZD(a), para.320(7A) and para.320(7B) because, on two previous occasions, X had breached immigration policy by entering the UK on a visitor's visa when his true intention had been to take a study placement following refusal of a student visa. The officer also found that X's instant application failed to disclose, in response to specific questions, his previous breaches and the fact that he had been refused a visa in South Africa. The notice of appeal accompanying the officer's refusal indicated that his application did not attract the full right of appeal described in the Nationality, Immigration and Asylum Act 2002 s.82(1), but that it was limited to race discrimination and human rights grounds. The immigration judge hearing the appeal stated that since X had only a limited right of appeal, it was not necessary for him to determine whether the officer's reasons for refusing entry were valid. Nevertheless, he stated that he had seen evidence which supported the officer's reasons. X submitted that his right of appeal was not limited in the manner described in the notice of appeal, that it was in the interests of justice for there to be a full appeal and that the relevant legislation was unclear.

Held: Appeal dismissed. (1) The limitation on entry clearance appeals under s.88A of the Act was confined to applications under the points-based system. Section 88A was an amendment to the 2002 Act introduced by the Immigration, Asylum and Nationality Act 2006 s.4(1). It was brought into force by the Immigration, Asylum and Nationality Act 2006 (Commencement No. 8 and Transitional and Saving Provisions) Order 2008. Article 4 of the Order expressly stipulated that s.88A was so confined. Section 88A(3) of the 2002 Act, however, retained rights of appeal for applicants under the points-based system if they related to race discrimination or human rights issues. X's arguments were therefore irrelevant to any exercisable right of appeal because they were directly caught by art.4 of the Order. It was not unfair for X's appeal rights to be so restricted; the "administrative review" referred to in Home Office guidance was the correct forum for him to raise issues in respect of paras 320(7A) and (7B) of the Immigration Rules (see paras 9-14 of judgment). (2) There were no race discrimination issues and the immigration judge had given sustainable reasons for concluding that human rights grounds were not engaged. The fact that the refusal of entry clearance had caused "misery and untold hardship" to X and that he had reduced opportunities in Nigeria to develop his career did not mean that it interfered with, or showed a lack of respect for, his private life (paras 15-16).

ABISOYE (ENTRY CLEARANCE APPEAL: TIER 2: NIGERIA), *Re; sub nom.* ABISOYE v ENTRY CLEARANCE OFFICER, PORT LOUIS, [2012] UKUT 82 (IAC), [2012] Imm. A.R. 712, Judge Kopieczek, UT (IAC).

1608. EU nationals–Dependants–Dependant of spouse of EEA national seeking to reside in UK–Meaning of "extended family member" in reg.8 Immigration (European Economic Area) Regulations 2006

[Immigration (European Economic Area) Regulations 2006 (SI 2006/1003) reg.8(2)(c), reg.8(2)(a); Directive 2004/38 on the right of citizens of the Union and their family members to move and reside freely within the territory of the Member States amending Regulation (EEC) No 1612/68 and repealing Directives 64/221/EEC, 68/360/EEC, 72/194/EEC, 73/148/EEC, 75/34/EEC, 75/35/EEC, 90/364/EEC, 90/365/.]

The appellant Brazilian national (S) appealed against a decision upholding a decision of the respondent secretary of state to refuse his application for a residence card. S had been born in 1993 and had lived in Brazil with his mother and his aunt (O); O had been the breadwinner of the household. O married a man (F) with dual Brazilian and Italian nationality. F did not join the household in Brazil. F came to reside in the United Kingdom, which he was entitled to do as a European Union citizen. O joined him and was given a residence card as a spouse of a European Economic Area national. S came to the UK in 2009 as a visitor, residing with O and F, and overstayed. In 2011 he applied for a residence card. The secretary of state refused S's application on the ground that he did not meet the criteria to be an extended family member in the Immigration (European Economic Area) Regulations 2006 reg.8 because he had not established that he had been residing with or dependent on F, the EEA national, before his arrival in the UK. The Upper Tribunal upheld that decision. S argued that reg.8(2) should be construed so as to extend not only to dependence on, or household membership of, an EEA national, but also to dependence on, or household membership of, a spouse or partner of an EEA national; that would allow him to rely on his having been dependent on and a member of the household of O in Brazil.

Held: Appeal dismissed. Regulation 8(2)(a) was specific in requiring that a person was residing in a country other than the UK and was dependent upon the EEA national or was a member of his household. The requirements of reg.8(2)(a) were expressly incorporated into reg.8(2)(c). On the facts, S could not meet such a requirement. He had not been, before coming to the UK, either dependent upon or a member of the household of F. He had been both dependent on and a member of the household of O, but she was not herself an EEA national. S's construction argument could not be accepted. Directive 2004/38, which the Regulations implemented, had not included, with regard to "other family members", the spouse or partner of the EEA national to whom dependence or household membership could relate. The Regulations followed that approach. Regulation 8(2)(a) and (c) did not extend to dependence on or household membership of a spouse or partner of the EEA national. There was no obligation on the UK to extend the qualifying categories wider than required by the Directive. Accordingly, the Upper Tribunal had reached the correct conclusion, having regard to the facts (see paras 22-24, 27 of judgment).

SOARES v SECRETARY OF STATE FOR THE HOME DEPARTMENT, [2013] EWCA Civ 575, [2013] 3 C.M.L.R. 31, Longmore, L.J., CA (Civ Div).

1609. European Economic Area–Immigration

THE IMMIGRATION (EUROPEAN ECONOMIC AREA) (AMENDMENT) REGULATIONS 2013, SI 2013/1391; made under the European Communities Act 1972 s.2. In force: July 1, 2013; .

These Regulations amend the Immigration (European Economic Area) Regulations 2006 (SI 2006/1003), removing the requirement that certain documents issued under the 2006 Regulations be issued free of charge.

1610. Failed asylum seekers–Appeals–Proper interpretation of s.83 Nationality, Immigration and Asylum Act 2002

[Nationality, Immigration and Asylum Act 2002 (c.41) s.83.]

The appellant (W) appealed against a decision of the First-tier Tribunal that she had no right of appeal under the Nationality, Immigration and Asylum Act 2002 s.83 against a decision of the respondent secretary of state to reject her asylum claim. W, a national of Myanmar, had been granted leave to enter the United Kingdom as a student in 2010; such leave was valid until July 2012. She claimed asylum in November 2011 but her claim was refused the following month. She appealed to the First-tier Tribunal under s.83, but the tribunal held that she had no right of appeal under that section. Section 83(2) provided for a right of appeal to the tribunal against the rejection of an asylum claim. Section 83(1) stated that the section applied where a person had made an asylum claim and "(a) his claim [had] been rejected by the Secretary of State, but (b) he [had] been granted leave to enter or remain in the United Kingdom for a period exceeding one year".

Held: Appeal dismissed. In concluding that W had no right of appeal, the First-tier Tribunal had been correct to apply the decision in *R. (on the application of O (Kenya)) v Secretary of State for the Home Department* [2009] EWHC 827 (Admin), (2009) 159 N.L.J. 631 to the effect that, for s.83 to apply, the grant of leave to enter or remain had to post-date the refusal of asylum. Contrary to W's assertion, the decision in *O (Kenya)* had not been disapproved by Beatson J. in *R. (on the application of S) v First-tier Tribunal (IAC)* [2011] EWHC 627 (Admin), [2011] A.C.D. 49 or overruled by the Court of Appeal in *R. (on the application of S) v First-tier Tribunal (IAC)* [2011] EWCA Civ 1319, [2012] Imm. A.R. 217, [2012] C.L.Y. 1688. The requirement in *O (Kenya)* that the refusal of asylum had to precede the grant of leave was, on the contrary, assumed to be correct by both Beatson J. and the Court of Appeal, *O (Kenya)* followed and *R. (on the application of S) v First-tier Tribunal* considered (see paras 26, 31 of judgment).

WIN (S.83: ORDER OF EVENTS: MYANMAR), *Re; sub nom.* WIN v SECRETARY OF STATE FOR THE HOME DEPARTMENT, [2012] UKUT 365 (IAC), [2013] Imm. A.R. 154, CMG Ockelton (Vice President), UT (IAC).

1611. Fees–Passports–Visas

THE CONSULAR FEES (AMENDMENT) REGULATIONS 2013, SI 2013/762; made under the Consular Fees Act 1980 s.1. In force: April 6, 2013; .

These Regulations amend the Consular Fees Regulations 1981 (SI 1981/476) to allow for consular fees to be paid in Sterling by debit or credit card at the discretion of a consular officer. Payment can still be made in currency circulating at the place of payment.

1612. First-tier Tribunal–Jurisdiction–Failure to make human rights claim before notice of appeal–Jurisdiction of tribunal to hear claim where no in-country right of appeal

[Nationality, Immigration and Asylum Act 2002 (c.41) s.92(4), s.113; European Convention on Human Rights 1950 Art.8.]

The appellant (N) appealed against a decision ([2011] EWHC 3336 (Admin)) refusing his application for judicial review of a decision of the respondent First-tier Tribunal that he had no in-country right of appeal against the decision to remove him as an illegal entrant. N, a Nepalese national, had entered the United Kingdom with entry clearance as a work permit holder. He was granted indefinite leave to remain. His application for citizenship was refused, as he admitted that he had entered the UK using false identification and was therefore an illegal entrant. The secretary of state notified N of the decision to remove him and informed him of his right to appeal outside the UK. N filed an in-country notice of appeal to the tribunal relying upon the Nationality, Immigration and Asylum Act 2002 s.92(4), claiming that the decision was incompatible with his rights under the European Convention on Human Rights

1950 art.8. N had not previously invoked art.8 to justify remaining in the UK. The tribunal concluded that the right to an in-country appeal under s.92(4) required any human rights claim to be made before the notice of appeal, and it therefore had no jurisdiction to determine N's appeal whilst he was in the UK. The court refused N's application for judicial review. The issues were whether (i) a human rights claim under s.92(4) had to be made before a notice of appeal to the tribunal was served; (ii) if the claim was not so made, the tribunal could raise the question of its jurisdiction to hear the appeal of its own motion or could only decide the question if the secretary of state specifically raised the point.

Held: Appeal dismissed. (1) Under s.92(4), the use of the auxiliary perfect tense in the phrase "has made a human rights claim" strongly implied that the claim must precede any appeal and that must mean before the institution of an appeal rather than the date of hearing of the appeal. The reason why those words were chosen was presumably to give the secretary of state the opportunity to give a decision on any human rights claim before the appeal was determined so that her decision on that question could become part of any appeal. That orderly process would be disrupted if, without any prior notification to the secretary of state, an appellant could simply put a human rights claim in his notice of appeal. That was reinforced by the definition of a human rights claim in s.113 as "a claim made by a person to the secretary of state". A notice of appeal seeking to appeal a decision for removal was not addressed to the secretary of state but to the tribunal, *SS (Turkey) v Secretary of State for the Home Department* [2006] UKAIT 74, [2007] Imm. A.R. 193, [2007] C.L.Y. 2282 and *R. (on the application of Rainford) v Secretary of State for the Home Department* [2008] EWHC 2474 (Admin) approved (see paras 17-25 of judgment). (2) The tribunal was clearly entitled to take a point on its own jurisdiction of its own motion and it was not the case that only the secretary of state could take the jurisdictional point. Any tribunal was entitled, and indeed well-advised, to air any doubts it had about its own jurisdiction, invite submissions on that question, and then decide it. Further, in cases such as the instant one, there was an air of unreality in any suggestion that, if the tribunal took the jurisdictional point, the secretary of state did not. The secretary of state might not be represented before the tribunal and in that event it would border on the absurd to say that the tribunal could not take the point of its own motion. If the secretary of state was represented, as it was in the instant case, the representative would naturally permit the tribunal to make the running. If an appellant failed to persuade the tribunal that it had jurisdiction, it would again border on the absurd for the tribunal to have specifically to ask the representative if he wanted to object to its jurisdiction to hear the appeal and to wait for an affirmative answer, *Anwar v Secretary of State for the Home Department* [2010] EWCA Civ 1275, [2011] 1 W.L.R. 2552, [2011] C.L.Y. 1755 considered (paras 30-34).

R. (ON THE APPLICATION OF NIRULA) v FIRST-TIER TRIBUNAL, [2012] EWCA Civ 1436, [2013] 1 W.L.R. 1090, Longmore, L.J., CA (Civ Div).

1613. Immigrants–Immigration policy–Marriage–Register offices

THE IMMIGRATION (PROCEDURE FOR MARRIAGE) (AMENDMENT) REGULATIONS 2013, SI 2013/226; made under the Asylum and Immigration (Treatment of Claimants, etc.) Act 2004 s.20. In force: March 7, 2013; .

These Regulations update the lists of specified registration districts in England and Wales and the registration authorities in England and Wales that appear in Schedule 1 of the Immigration (Procedure for Marriage) Regulations 2011 (SI 2011/2678) and Schedule 2 of the Immigration (Procedure for Formation of Civil Partnerships) Regulations 2011 (SI 2011/2679). The lists have been updated to reflect a change made by Ceredigion local authority to the organisation of their registration service. The revised information enables persons who are subject to immigration control within the UK to continue to give notice of marriage and civil partnership within Ceredigion local authority following the organisational change.

1614. Immigration–Notices

THE IMMIGRATION (NOTICES) (AMENDMENT) REGULATIONS 2013, SI 2013/793; made under the Nationality, Immigration and Asylum Act 2002 s.105, s.112. In force: April 28, 2013; .

These Regulations amend the Immigration (Notices) Regulations 2003 to ensure that notices can be served to file in accordance with reg.7 electronically and without the need for a signed document.

1615. Immigration–Travel bans–Travel restriction orders

THE IMMIGRATION (DESIGNATION OF TRAVEL BANS) (AMENDMENT) ORDER 2013, SI 2013/678; made under the Immigration Act 1971 s.8B. In force: March 27, 2013; .

This Order amends the Immigration (Designation of Travel Bans) Order 2000 (SI 2000/2724) by updating the list of EU Council Decisions in the existing Schedule to the 2000 Order. The Schedule lists UN Security Council Resolutions and EU Council Decisions or Common Positions which impose restrictive travel measures against named individuals.

1616. Immigration decisions–Appeals–Deemed abandonment of appeal in case of departure from UK–Meaning of "leaves" in s.104(4) Nationality, Immigration and Asylum Act 2002

[Nationality, Immigration and Asylum Act 2002 (c.41) s.104(4).]

The applicant (M) applied to set aside an order that he was to be treated, under the Nationality, Immigration and Asylum Act 2002 s.104(4), as having abandoned an application for permission to appeal against a decision of the Upper Tribunal upholding a deportation order made against him; alternatively, he sought to challenge the tribunal's decision by way of judicial review. M had filed a notice seeking permission to appeal against the Upper Tribunal's decision. His solicitors then wrote to the respondent secretary of state stating that he intended to leave the United Kingdom temporarily while the appeal was ongoing and to return in the event that his appeal was allowed. He duly departed to his native Ghana, knowing that he would not be allowed back into the UK with a deportation order outstanding against him. The UK Border Agency had written to his solicitors stating that it would consider his appeal as having been abandoned should he leave the country. The issues were (i) whether, on a proper construction of s.104(4), M had left the UK so that his appeal was to be treated as abandoned; (ii) if so, whether the court had jurisdiction to treat the application for permission to appeal as an application for permission to apply for judicial review of the Upper Tribunal's decision.

Held: Application refused. (1) The first issue depended on the meaning of the word "leaves" in s.104(4). Chadwick L.J. had been correct to suggest in *Dupovac v Secretary of State for the Home Department* [2000] Imm. A.R. 265, [2000] C.L.Y. 3284 that the purpose of the provision appeared to be that the tribunal should be required to treat an appeal or application for permission to appeal as abandoned upon the applicant "leaving" the UK, without any further enquiry into the facts of the particular case, and that included without further enquiry into the intentions of the departing person as to his return. In some cases, the result might seem draconian, but not in this case, where M was aware before he flew to Ghana that the secretary of state would treat his departure as an abandonment of his appeal. The word "leaves" bore a purely physical meaning, the question being whether the applicant had by his voluntary action physically left the UK, whether for a short or a long term. There remained the territorial question raised by Waller L.J. in *Dupovac* about how far a person had to travel by sea or by air from the land mass of the UK before he was considered to have left: a person who landed or attempted to land in another country had clearly "left" the UK. As to the status of one who left the UK shoreline on a sea outing which began and ended on UK soil and involved no visit to any other country, a decision should be left for another case. M's application for permission to appeal was to be treated as abandoned, *Dupovac* and *Shirazi v*

Secretary of State for the Home Department [2003] EWCA Civ 1562, [2004] 2 All E.R. 602, [2004] C.L.Y. 2087 considered (see paras 30-34, 43 of judgment). (2) To entertain an application to treat M's abandoned appeal as an application for judicial review would be wrong: that would undermine the legitimate purpose of s.104(4) and add yet another tier to the already complex tiers of adjudication in immigration and asylum claims (para.41).

R. (ON THE APPLICATION OF MM (GHANA)) v SECRETARY OF STATE FOR THE HOME DEPARTMENT, [2012] EWCA Civ 827, [2012] Imm. A.R. 928, Toulson, L.J., CA (Civ Div).

1617. Immigration decisions–Appeals–Secretary of state seeking consent to withdraw appeal to Upper Tribunal–Respondent seeking to use respondent's notice to challenge adverse First-tier Tribunal findings

[Nationality, Immigration and Asylum Act 2002 (c.41) s.82(1), s.82, s.84(1), s.104(2); Tribunals, Courts and Enforcement Act 2007 (c.15) s.11 (1); Asylum and Immigration Tribunal (Procedure) Rules 2005 (SI 2005/230) r.17; Tribunal Procedure (Upper Tribunal) Rules 2008 (SI 2008/2698) r.17, r.24, r.24(3)(e); European Convention on Human Rights 1950 Art.3.]

The appellant secretary of state sought the Upper Tribunal's consent to her withdrawing her appeal against the First-tier Tribunal's decision that the respondent Ethiopian nationals (G) should not be removed from the United Kingdom. G sought to challenge aspects of the FTT's decision, relying on a notice under the Tribunal Procedure (Upper Tribunal) Rules 2008 r.24. G had committed offences in the UK. The secretary of state considered their removal conducive to the public good. They appealed under the Nationality, Immigration and Asylum Act 2002 s.82. The FTT found against them on several grounds, but found a real risk of their rights under the European Convention on Human Rights 1950 art.3 being breached and so allowed their appeals. The secretary of state sought and obtained permission to appeal to the UT against that ground of the decision under the Tribunals, Courts and Enforcement Act 2007 s.11 (1). She subsequently sought to withdraw her appeal under r.17 of the 2008 Rules, accepting that the FTT's decision had been correct, but intending to seek assurances from the Ethiopian authorities to address its concerns and then make fresh decisions to remove G. G issued a r.24 notice challenging those decisions of the FTT adverse to them. The UT considered (i) the effect of consenting to withdrawal; (ii) whether consent should be given when there were points that G wanted to argue.

Held: Judgment accordingly. (1) If the UT consented to the secretary of state's case being withdrawn, the proceedings would end. In other UT chambers, an appeal ended if it was withdrawn. The difference between the reference to an "appeal" being withdrawn in the Asylum and Immigration Tribunal (Procedure) Rules 2005 r.17 and the reference in r.17 of the 2008 Rules to "a case or part of it" being withdrawn did not demonstrate a distinction to be drawn between the effects of withdrawal in each tribunal. Rule 17 of the 2008 Rules had to accommodate the UT dealing with cases that were not appeals: that could explain the difference in wording. When an appeal under s.82(1) was withdrawn, it was no longer pending; neither was the appeal under s.11 of the 2007 Act, because s.11 appeals did not exist independently of the s.82(1) appeals from which they arose. The secretary of state had no s.82(1) appeal to abandon, but, although s.104(2) of the 2002 Act identified circumstances in which an appeal was not finally determined, it did not define the circumstances in which an appeal was finally determined. An appeal that had been withdrawn was not awaiting determination for the purpose of s.104. Withdrawing an appeal with consent when consent was needed was a final disposal for the purposes of s.104(1)(b) (see paras 19-28 of judgment). (2) The UT could not create a right of appeal not requiring permission. G could not appeal against the FTT's decision because they did not have permission to appeal. The UT could not give permission to appeal unless the FTT had refused permission. Parties could not rely on r.24 notices as an alternative to seeking permission (paras 34-35). The secretary of state could not rely on the grounds of appeal to the FTT given in s.84(1) of the 2002 Act, which were all grounds of appeal against immigration decisions. Accordingly, "grounds" in r.24 had to have a wider meaning and include any reason relied on by the parties to support the decision. It did not follow that a respondent could raise a point in a response that should have been raised in the respondent's own appeal. The words "in the proceedings which are the subject of the appeal" in r.24(3)(e) were not limited to the grounds on which permission to appeal had been given. The proceedings that were the subject of the appeal were those that had come before the FTT; those proceedings were the subject of the further appeal. However, G's contention that r.24 was meaningless unless it permitted raising any points that had failed before the FTT was wrong. Although s.11 of the 2007 Act extended the right of appeal to an appeal "on any point of law", a party would not normally be given permission to appeal a point that would not make a material difference to the outcome. However, that party could still have reasons to respond to an appeal by arguing that the FTT should have determined the appeal on grounds which had been unsuccessful in the proceedings that were the subject of the appeal. Rule 24 therefore did have a meaning that did not depend on G's premise, and their construction of it was rejected (paras 40-46). (3) G could have challenged the findings they did not like by notice of appeal. They had chosen to wait until they knew what the secretary of state was saying in order to consider how they should respond. Consequently, they were too late to appeal the decision. The secretary of state wished to withdraw her appeal. There was no purpose in the expense of a further appeal. The UT consented to the withdrawing of the appeal and made no findings on the r.24 notice (paras 48-51).

EG (UT RULE 17: WITHDRAWAL: RULE 24: SCOPE: ETHIOPIA), *Re; sub nom.* SECRETARY OF STATE FOR THE HOME DEPARTMENT v EG; EG v SECRETARY OF STATE FOR THE HOME DEPARTMENT, [2013] UKUT 143 (IAC), [2013] Imm. A.R. 670, Judge Eshun, UT (IAC).

1618. Immigration policy–Leave to enter–Right to respect for private and family life–Status of new Immigration Rules

[Human Rights Act 1998 (c.42); European Convention on Human Rights 1950 Art.8.]

The appellant secretary of state appealed against the overturning of her refusal of leave for the respondent (X) to enter as the spouse of a British citizen (Y). X was a Nigerian citizen who had visited the United Kingdom on several occasions. She had overstayed twice and had been convicted of using false identity papers to work. She returned to Nigeria where she married Y, and applied for entry clearance which was refused. Y had dual British/Nigerian citizenship and had lived in the UK for 23 years. The judge allowed the appeal on human rights grounds, finding that X had established a strong family life in the UK over the previous three years and that it was not reasonable to expect Y to move to Nigeria to continue it. The secretary of state submitted that the judge had erred in failing to follow the new Immigration Rules (HC 194), which had restored the "exceptional circumstances" and the "insurmountable obstacles" test for cases under the European Convention on Human Rights 1950 art.8. X argued that the new Rules were merely statements of executive policy not having the force of law and could not reverse, or repeal, binding judicial decisions made pursuant to the Human Rights Act 1998 as primary law.

Held: Appeal allowed. Neither submission could be accepted in full. The Rules applied to any decision made after July 9, 2012 unless they were struck down as unlawful or irrational, *MF (Article 8: New Rules: Nigeria), Re* [2012] UKUT 393 (IAC), [2013] Imm. A.R. 256 applied. Appropriate weight was to be given to them as a statement of policy, *Huang v Secretary of State for the Home Department* [2007] UKHL 11, [2007] 2 A.C. 167, [2007] C.L.Y. 2340 followed (see paras 30-38 of judgment). Judges making decisions in art.8 cases to which the new Rules applied should first consider whether a claimant was able to benefit under them. If so, the appeal would be allowed because the decision had not been made in accordance with the Rules. Otherwise, a judge had to make an art.8 assessment to decide whether the interference with the right to family and/or private life was a justified and proportionate means of achieving a legitimate aim (paras 41-42). The secretary of state had overstated the significance of the Rules, which had been brought in under the negative resolution procedure, a weak form of parliamentary scrutiny. The requirement for "exceptional circumstances" or "insurmountable obstacles" had been declared wrong in the art.8 immigration context by the House of Lords and by the Court of Appeal, *Huang, EB (Kosovo) v Secretary of State for the Home Department* [2008] UKHL 41, [2009] 1 A.C. 1159, [2008] C.L.Y. 2037, *LM (Democratic Republic of Congo) v Secretary of State for the Home Department* [2008] EWCA Civ 325, [2008] I.N.L.R. 254, [2008] C.L.Y. 2030, *VW (Uganda) v Secretary of State for the Home Department* [2009] EWCA Civ 5, [2009] Imm. A.R. 436, [2009] C.L.Y. 2163, and *JO (Uganda) v Secretary of State for the Home Department* [2010] EWCA Civ 10, [2010] 1 W.L.R. 1607, [2010] C.L.Y. 1773 followed. It was open to Parliament to change the law by primary legislation but unless and until it did, those decisions were binding on the Upper Tribunal and would be followed by it (paras 54-59). In the instant case, the judge had failed to consider whether X had complied with HC 194 and Appendix FM and it was common ground that she did not. However, the error of law was immaterial if she had good art.8 grounds. The judge had failed to remind himself that the family life had been established in precarious circumstances, and overall he reached a conclusion in X's favour that he was not entitled to reach. There was a material error of law and the decision allowing the appeal was set aside. Although the judge had not erred in finding that it was unreasonable for Y to live in Nigeria, the court was entitled to revisit the matter afresh. In the circumstances, it was not unreasonable for Y to have to decide between retaining his residence in the UK and following his wife to Nigeria. The secretary of state's decision was in accordance with the Rules and the applicable policy and was not unlawful (paras 72, 80, 82). It had been taken in support of a legitimate aim of protecting public order and the rights and freedoms of others, was a proportionate and fair balance in all the circumstances and was thus a justified interference with art.8 rights.

IZUAZU (ARTICLE 8: NEW RULES: NIGERIA), *Re*; *sub nom.* SECRETARY OF STATE FOR THE HOME DEPARTMENT v IZUAZU, [2013] UKUT 45 (IAC), [2013] Imm. A.R. 453, Blake, J. (President), UT (IAC).

1619. Immigration policy–Points-based system–Admissibility of fresh evidence–Effect of s.85A Nationality, Immigration and Asylum Act 2002

[Nationality, Immigration and Asylum Act 2002 (c.41) s.84(1)(a), s.85A, s.85A(4)(c), s.120; UK Borders Act 2007 (Commencement No. 7 and Transitional Provisions) Order 2011 (SI 2011/1293) Art.2.]

The appellants (C1, C2 and C3) in conjoined appeals appealed against the dismissal by the Upper Tribunal of their appeals against the refusal of applications for leave to remain in the United Kingdom as Tier 4 students under the points-based system in the Immigration Rules. The applications had been refused by the respondent secretary of state because the appellants had failed to submit with their application a document specified as necessary under the points-based system. At the time of the applications the First-tier Tribunal had a wide discretion to admit new evidence on appeal. By the time of the appeal hearings the discretion had been removed by the Nationality, Immigration and Asylum Act 2002 s.85A, brought into force on May 23, 2011 by the UK Borders Act 2007 (Commencement No.7 and Transitional Provisions) Order 2011 art.2, but the tribunal accepted the new evidence. The Upper Tribunal overturned those decisions on appeal by the secretary of state. It was submitted that (1) properly construed s.85A did not apply to an appeal against an application refused before May 23, 2011, or to an appeal refused before that date; (2) s.85A only applied to appeals to the First-tier Tribunal, not to appeals from that tribunal to the Upper Tribunal; (3) the "application" referred to in s.85A included "the additional grounds for the application" submitted by an appellant in response to a s.120 notice requiring additional grounds; (4) the common law duty of fairness imposed on the secretary of state a duty to contact an applicant when specified documents were missing from his application and give him an opportunity to rectify the omission; (5) the Upper Tribunal had erred in dismissing C1's case because it had failed to recognise that his was not a "near miss" case, but a "no miss" case under the Rules; (6) C2 was entitled to rely on the missing document under s.85A(4)(c) because it was adduced in order to prove that his confirmation of acceptance for studies was valid; (7) the secretary of state had been under a duty to C2 to inform him that documents were missing because C2 had been told by letter that he would be informed if there were any defects in his application; (8) C3's appeal rights had been unfairly and retrospectively altered because her hearing date had been postponed until after May 23, 2011 with the effect that her trial bundle of documents on which she intended to rely, including the missing document, could no longer be considered by the tribunal.

Held: Appeals dismissed. (1) The consequences of applying art.2 of the Order to all appeals as from May 23, 2011 were not "so unfair" that art.2 had to be interpreted as having effect only where the points-based system application had been made on or after May 23, 2011, *L'Office Cherifien des Phosphates Unitramp SA v Yamashita-Shinnihon Steamship Co Ltd (The Boucraa)* [1994] 1 A.C. 486, [1994] C.L.Y. 221 applied, Shahzad (s.85A: commencement) (2012) UKUT 81 (IAC) overruled in part. Bringing s.85A into force had deprived applicants under the points-based system of a "second bite at the cherry" in respect of earlier decisions to refuse applications, but it did not retrospectively alter the basis on which those applications were to be allowed or refused under the Rules and it was not unlawful. The Rules, the Policy Guidance and the application form all made it clear that submission of the specified documents with the application was mandatory (see paras 34, 55 of judgment). (2) Section 85A applied when the decision was re-made by a judge of the Upper Tribunal, *LB (Jamaica) v Secretary of State for the Home Department* [2011] EWCA Civ 1420, [2012] Imm. A.R. 637, [2012] C.L.Y. 1734 applied (para.40). (3) If and insofar as the "additional" grounds raised in response to a s.120 notice were merely a repetition of the grounds of appeal under s.84(1)(a) they fell within s.85A (para.42). (4) The price of securing consistency and predictability in dealing with applications under the points-based system was a lack of flexibility that might result in "hard" decisions in individual cases, but that was not a justification for imposing an obligation on the secretary of state to conduct a preliminary check of all applications for the specified documents and giving applicants an opportunity to supply the missing documents (para.45). (5) C1's "no miss" argument ignored the fact that prior to May 23, 2011 a failure to submit the specified documents with the application could be corrected at the appeal stage, but after that date it was no longer possible (para.47). (6) There had been no suggestion that C2's certificate of acceptance for studies was invalid; the missing document was a qualification document used to assign the certificate to him and was not admissible under s.85A(4)(c) to prove that the certificate was valid (para.48). (7) There was a distinction between an invalid application that would not be considered unless the defect was cured, and a valid application that was rejected because on examination the documents required to obtain the necessary points had not been submitted. The letter could not, and did not, lead C2 to believe that he would be notified of a failure to supply the specified documents (para.51). (8) The admissibility of documents in C3's trial bundle would be determined not by the notice of hearing date, but by the provisions of the Act in force at the hearing date (para.54).

ALAM v SECRETARY OF STATE FOR THE HOME DEPARTMENT; ANWAR v SECRETARY OF STATE FOR THE HOME DEPARTMENT; EGHAN v SECRETARY OF STATE FOR THE HOME DEPARTMENT, [2012] EWCA Civ 960, [2012] Imm. A.R. 974, Maurice Kay, L.J., CA (Civ Div).

1620. Immigration policy–Right to respect for private and family life–Effect of new Immigration Rules on consideration of art.8 claims–Whether two-stage assessment required

[UK Borders Act 2007 (c.30) s.32(5); European Convention on Human Rights 1950 Art.3, Art.8.]

The appellant (F) appealed against the First-tier Tribunal's dismissal of his appeal against the respondent secretary of state's decision to make a deportation order against him pursuant to the UK Borders Act 2007 s.32(5). F had arrived in the United Kingdom from Nigeria in 1998 as an illegal entrant, and only claimed asylum in 2006. In 2008 he commenced a relationship with a British citizen (W), whom he married in 2009. A few months later he was convicted of handling stolen goods and possessing or using a false instrument, and was sentenced to 18 months' imprisonment. W's daughter, aged 16, regarded F as her de facto father. The First-tier Tribunal dismissed F's appeal on asylum and humanitarian protection grounds as well as grounds based on the European Convention on Human Rights 1950 art.8 and art.3. The instant appeal was based solely on art.8 grounds. The secretary of state, citing para.A362 of the Immigration Rules, argued that F's appeal fell to be considered under the new rules, which came into effect on July 9, 2012, notwithstanding that the deportation order had been made in 2010. F's primary case was that the new rules did not apply to his appeal, but he argued that if they did, the Upper Tribunal should find that his claim involved exceptional circumstances under the art.8-related provisions of the rules dealing with deportation and removal.

Held: Appeal allowed. (1) Prior to July 2012, the rules made no specific references to art.8. Cases involving art.8 ordinarily required a two-stage assessment; firstly to assess whether the decision appealed against was in accordance with the rules, and secondly to assess whether the decision was contrary to the appellant's art.8 rights. There appeared to be tensions within the new rules between an approach which saw them as a complete code for dealing with art.8 claims, and an approach which saw them as requiring decision-makers sometimes to go beyond the rules. The rules could not be construed as providing a complete code for art.8 claims. Judges and tribunals would still be obliged by primary legislation to continue, ordinarily, to use a two-stage approach. That was because the new rules did not fully reflect Strasbourg jurisprudence as interpreted by the higher courts in the United Kingdom, and, in particular, they did not encapsulate the criteria in *Maslov v Austria (1638/03)* [2009] I.N.L.R. 47, [2009] C.L.Y. 2070, *Maslov* considered (see paras 3-41 of judgment). (2) The new rules gave greater specificity as to what circumstances were seen to attract the greatest weight in respect of the public interest side of the art.8 balancing exercise. That had to inform any judicial consideration of art.8 outside of the rules (paras 42-48). (3) Two features of the new rules dealing with deportation were of signal importance. Firstly, they started from the presumption that the secretary of state's view was that the person's deportation was deemed to be conducive to the public good, before proceeding to identify certain limited categories of person who might nevertheless be entitled to limited leave subject to their meeting stringent requirements, and then stating that for the rest, they could only succeed if they could show exceptional circumstances. Secondly, beyond stipulating that someone in F's situation must establish exceptional circumstances, the new rules disclosed very little else about the factors the secretary of state considered should inform the balancing exercise governed by that criterion. Those two factors tilted the scales very heavily against a person such as F who sought to resist a deportation order on art.8 grounds within the new rules (para.62). (4) The tribunal was not persuaded that the new rules applied to F's appeal. However, had it been so persuaded, it would have found that F had failed to show exceptional circumstances. It remained for the tribunal, applying Strasbourg jurisprudence as interpreted by the higher courts, to decide whether F's deportation was a proportionate measure such that his removal would not breach his Convention rights. Very significant weight had to be attached to the serious view taken by the secretary of state of F's criminality and poor immigration history. However, it had been conceded that it would not be reasonable to expect W and her daughter to accompany F to Nigeria to live as a family there. W's daughter's best interests were to have a de facto father present as she grew up. Weighing all the evidence in the balance, it would not be proportionate to deport F (paras 59-81).

MF (ARTICLE 8: NEW RULES: NIGERIA), *Re*; *sub nom.* MF (NIGERIA) v SECRETARY OF STATE FOR THE HOME DEPARTMENT, [2012] UKUT 393 (IAC), [2013] Imm. A.R. 256, Judge Storey, UT (IAC).

1621. Immigration policy–Veterans–Discretionary policy for Gurkha veterans–Position of adult dependants–Weighing historic injustice as relevant factor

[European Convention on Human Rights 1950 Art.8(1).]

The appellants appealed against decisions refusing them leave to remain in the UK as the dependent adult children of Gurkha veterans who had settled in the United Kingdom. The respondent secretary of state had a discretionary policy set out in Immigration Directorates' Instructions dealing with applications from both Gurkhas and foreign and Commonwealth nationals who were seeking settlement in the United Kingdom on discharge from the armed forces. It also provided in section 13.2 in relation to dependants that in exceptional circumstances discretion might be exercised in favour of a dependant over the age of 18. Annex A set out discretionary arrangements for former Gurkhas discharged before July 1, 1997 and made provision in respect of dependants similar to that in section 13.2. A number of Gurkhas challenged the policy as unlawful so far as it concerned dependent children over the age of 18, on the grounds that it was uncertain and irrationally frustrated the purpose of the policy. The judge rejected that challenge. A second group of cases from the Upper Tribunal raised two issues: the weight to be given, when considering proportionality under the European Convention on Human Rights 1950 art.8(2), to the "historic injustice" that before 2004 Gurkha veterans were treated less favourably than other comparable non-British Commonwealth veterans and were not entitled to settle in the UK; and whether family life within art.8(1) existed between adult children and their parents.

Held: Judgment accordingly. (1) The appellants argued that a policy which permitted departure from a general rule in exceptional circumstances was lawful only where the general rule itself was clearly defined. However, the general rule was clearly stated in Annex A: it was that dependent adult children would not normally qualify for the exercise of discretion in line with the main applicant and were expected to apply for leave to enter or remain under the relevant provisions of the Immigration Rules or under art.8. There was nothing ambiguous or unclear about that. It was inherent in any policy which permitted a departure from a general rule in exceptional circumstances that there might legitimately be scope for different views as to whether there were exceptional circumstances on the facts of a particular case. The range of reasonable responses might be wide, but that did not mean that a discretionary rule or policy was unlawful on grounds of uncertainty. The decision in *R. (on the application of Limbu) v Secretary of State for the Home Department* [2008] EWHC 2261 (Admin), [2008] H.R.L.R. 48, [2008] C.L.Y. 2065 did not compel a different conclusion on the issue of certainty, *Limbu* considered. That case was concerned with a policy relating to the settlement in the UK of Gurkha veterans where the purpose of the policy was stated by the secretary of state to be to remedy the historic denial to Gurkhas of a right to settle in the UK. By contrast, the instant appeals were concerned not with veterans but with their adult children who would normally not be given the right to settle. The purpose of the policy was not to facilitate the settlement in the UK of adult dependent children and thus it could not be said that the purposes of the policy were frustrated (see paras 17-26 of judgment). (2) The historic injustice was only one of the factors to be weighed against the need to maintain a firm and fair immigration policy. It was not necessarily determinative. The weight to be given to the historic injustice in Gurkha cases was not as strong as the weight to be given to the injustice caused to British Overseas Citizens who had been denied the right to settle in the UK by legislation and policies that were racially and sexually discriminatory, but it was not substantially less. If a Gurkha could show that, but for the historic injustice, he would have settled in the UK when his child would have been able to accompany him as a dependent child under the age of 18, that was a strong reason for holding that it was proportionate to permit the adult child to join his family. To that extent the Gurkha and British Overseas Citizens cases were similar, *Entry Clearance Officer v NH (India)* [2007] EWCA Civ 1330, [2008] I.N.L.R. 154 and *Patel v Entry Clearance Officer, Mumbai* [2010] EWCA Civ 17 applied (paras 38-43). (3) Whether an individual enjoyed family life depended on all the facts. The Upper Tribunal had adopted the correct approach (paras 45-46). (4) In two cases the decision that the appellants did not enjoy family life with their parents was correct and their appeals were dismissed. If it was not possible to resolve the remaining appeals by agreement in light of the court's decision, it would consider further submissions (paras 50, 53).

R. (ON THE APPLICATION OF GURUNG) v SECRETARY OF STATE FOR THE HOME DEPARTMENT; GHSING v SECRETARY OF STATE FOR THE HOME DEPARTMENT; GR (NEPAL) v SECRETARY OF STATE FOR THE HOME DEPARTMENT; NL (NEPAL) v ENTRY CLEARANCE OFFICER; SG (NEPAL) v SECRETARY OF STATE FOR THE HOME DEPARTMENT; KR (NEPAL) v ENTRY CLEARANCE OFFICER, DELHI; RG (NEPAL) v SECRETARY OF STATE FOR THE HOME DEPARTMENT; NR (NEPAL) v SECRETARY OF STATE FOR THE HOME DEPARTMENT, [2013] EWCA Civ 8, [2013] 1 W.L.R. 2546, Lord Dyson (M.R.), CA (Civ Div).

1622. **Indefinite leave to remain–Deportation orders–Home Secretary's refusal to grant or reinstate indefinite leave to remain following revocation of deportation order–Whether original leave to remain revived on revocation of order–Construction of s.5 Immigration Act 1971 and s.76 Nationality, Immigration and Asylum Act 2002**

[Immigration Act 1971 (c.77) s.5; Nationality, Immigration and Asylum Act 2002 (c.41) s.76; European Convention on Human Rights 1950 Art.8.]

The appellant (G) appealed against the dismissal ([2011] EWHC 3247 (Admin)) of his claim for judicial review of the respondent secretary of state's refusal to grant or reinstate his indefinite leave to remain (ILR). G was a citizen of Grenada but had lived in the United Kingdom since 1995, when he was aged 11. He was granted ILR when he was 16, but had since been involved in serious criminal conduct resulting in imprisonment. The secretary of state had ordered his deportation. However, an Asylum and Immigration tribunal upheld G's appeal against the secretary of state's refusal to revoke the deportation order, on the basis that deportation would breach his rights under the European Convention on Human Rights 1950 art.8. The AIT did not direct that his ILR should be reinstated. The secretary of state refused to further grant ILR or to reinstate the previous grant, but made successive grants of six months' leave to remain. G sought judicial review of the refusal to reinstate his ILR. He claimed that revocation of his deportation order automatically revived the original grant of ILR. The judge held that the wording of the Immigration Act 1971 s.5 was clear and there was no reason to imply that the effect of a successful appeal against deportation was to revive a claimant's ILR. G contended that the 1971 Act and the Nationality, Immigration and Asylum Act 2002 should be construed consistently with each other, and that "revocation" of a deportation order involved setting it aside, with the consequence that its effect on a deportee's ILR was similarly set aside.

Held: Appeal allowed. (Stanley Burnton L.J. dissenting) (1) Section 5(1) spelt out the prospective effect of the making of a deportation order on the deportee's existing leave to remain: the leave ceased to be valid. Section 5(2) provided for revocation of a deportation order, but did not say what was to happen to the individual's leave to remain. Section 76 of the 2002 Act provided the answer. Where a foreign criminal could not be deported for legal reasons, as in the instant case, the secretary of state had the power to revoke any ILR previously granted. That provision had two unspoken but inescapable premises. First, unless the secretary of state decided to use the s.76(1) power, the foreign national's leave to enter or remain continued, as otherwise there would be no need for the provision at all, save for the limited extent to which it also covered people who could be but had not been made subject to a deportation order. Second, the existence of legal reasons for withholding deportation need not require a tribunal determination, as in clear cases the secretary of state could decide on human rights grounds that an order should not be made. Section 76 also had the important consequence that an appealable immigration decision came into being. That was orderly and respected the rule of law. The automatic collapse of leave to remain for which the secretary of state contended left the individual without any status whatever; he could neither lawfully stay, nor lawfully be deported. Therefore, while under s.5(1) the deportation order automatically invalidated G's ILR, revocation of the order logically meant that it could no longer have that effect. However, it was still open to the secretary of state, under s.76(1), to revoke G's ILR, giving him a right of appeal against that decision. Section 5(1), s.5(2) and s.76(1) provided a simple and intelligible logic which gave the last word to the secretary of state, but ensured that her decision was subject to independent adjudication (see paras 30-36 of judgment). (2) (Per Stanley Burnton L.J.) Although the 1971 and 2002 Acts should so far as possible be construed consistently with each other, s.5(1) could not be construed as providing that revocation of a deportation order returned the person in question and the secretary of state to the situation they were in regarding leave to remain immediately before the order was made. Revocation caused the order to cease to exist, but the effect of the making of a deportation order was to cancel the leave to remain (paras 19-28).

R. (ON THE APPLICATION OF GEORGE) v SECRETARY OF STATE FOR THE HOME DEPARTMENT; *sub nom.* GEORGE v SECRETARY OF STATE FOR THE HOME DEPARTMENT, [2012] EWCA Civ 1362, [2013] 1 W.L.R. 1319, Maurice Kay, L.J., CA (Civ Div).

1623. Indefinite leave to remain–In-country right of appeal–Notice revoking indefinite leave to remain erroneously asserting no in-country right of appeal

[Immigration (Notices) Regulations 2003 (SI 2003/658).]

The appellant Russian national (E) appealed against a decision ([2011] EWHC 1047 (Admin)) dismissing his claim for judicial review of a decision of the respondent secretary of state cancelling his indefinite leave to remain. Whilst E was abroad, the secretary of state directed that he should be excluded from the United Kingdom on the grounds that his presence was not conducive to public good for reasons of national security. As a result she cancelled his indefinite leave to remain. The decision notice informed E of his out of country right of appeal to the Special Immigration Appeals Commission (SIAC) within 28 days and indicated that he should not seek to return to the UK as he would be refused entry. It was common ground that when a person situated abroad was given notice of the secretary of state's intention to deprive him of his leave to remain he had 10 days to return to the UK and make an in-country appeal. E applied for judicial review and sought the quashing of the notice. The claim was dismissed and the judge held that the notice should not be treated as totally invalid as the assertion that he had no in-country right of appeal he was not entirely deprive of an effective right of appeal.

Held: Appeal allowed. Whilst it was true that the fact E did not have an in-country right of appeal did not entirely deprive him of an effective right of appeal, it did deprive him of a valuable right, namely, the right to pursue his appeal in-country, *R. (on the application of MK (Tunisia)) v Secretary of State for the Home Department* [2011] EWCA Civ 333, [2012] 1 W.L.R. 700, [2012] C.L.Y. 1692 applied. The Immigration (Notices) Regulations 2003 provided that a notice of decision must state that there was a right to appeal but also how that right might be exercised. Parliament intended that a failure to comply with the requirement to advise E that he was entitled to an in-country right of appeal rendered the notice invalid, *R. v Soneji (Kamlesh Kumar)* [2005] UKHL 49, [2006] 1 A.C. 340, [2005] C.L.Y. 842 applied. An appellant who had to pursue an appeal while he was out of the country faced considerable disadvantages, particularly in the context of an appeal to SIAC as the procedure deprived them of a fundamental right to see the whole of the case against them. The court should be vigilant to ensure that appellants in SIAC cases were not further disadvantaged by a failure on the secretary of state's part to comply with the Regulations. The Regulations were made because it was recognised that people needed clear advice about their rights of appeal. It was the statutory responsibility of the secretary of state to provide that information. If it was discovered that the advice in the notice was erroneous, as happened in the instant case as a result of the decision in *MK*, the secretary of state would normally be required to take steps to remedy the error. If she refused or failed to take steps to rectify the error it was difficult to see how the court could properly decline to quash the defective notice (see paras 39,41, 43, 45 of judgment).

R. (ON THE APPLICATION OF E (RUSSIA)) v SECRETARY OF STATE FOR THE HOME DEPARTMENT; *sub nom.* E1 (OS RUSSIA) v SECRETARY OF STATE FOR THE HOME DEPARTMENT, [2012] EWCA Civ 357, [2012] 1 W.L.R. 3198, Pill, L.J., CA (Civ Div).

1624. Leave to enter–Leave to remain–Notices–Service

IMMIGRATION (LEAVE TO ENTER AND REMAIN) (AMENDMENT) ORDER 2013, SI 2013/1749; made under the Immigration Act 1971 s.3A, s.3B. In force: ; .

This Order amends the Immigration (Leave to Enter and Remain) Order 2000 2000 (SI 2000/1161) to set out the procedures that the Home Office may follow for the giving, refusing or varying of leave by notice in writing in accordance with the Immigration Act 1971 s.4.

1625. Leave to enter–Spouses–Amendment to r.281 Immigration Rules introducing pre-entry language skills requirement–Compatibility with European Convention on Human Rights 1950

[European Convention on Human Rights 1950 Art.8(1), Art.12, Art.14.]

The appellants (B) appealed against the refusal ([2011] EWHC 3370 (Admin), [2012] 2 All E.R. 653, [2012] C.L.Y. 1746) of their application for judicial review of amendments to the Immigration Rules r.281. The amendments required the foreign spouse or partner of a British citizen or person settled in the United Kingdom to produce a test certificate of knowledge of the English language to a prescribed standard before entering the UK. That requirement applied unless the applicant could bring himself within one of a number of exemptions set out in the rule. Nationals of countries designated as "majority English-speaking" were not required to take the test, nor were those who had certain academic qualifications. Before the amendments, applicants had to demonstrate a knowledge of the English language two years after entering the UK, but the standard of knowledge required by the amended rule was lower. In the court below, B had argued that the amended rule breached the European Convention on Human Rights 1950 art.8, art.12 and art.14. The judge dismissed the challenge on all grounds. The issues on appeal were (i) whether the amended rule amounted to an interference with family life within the meaning of art.8(1); (ii) if so, whether that interference was in accordance with the law, pursued a legitimate aim and was proportionate in accordance with art.8(2); (iii) whether the amended rule was discriminatory within the meaning of art.14 read in conjunction with art.8; (iv) whether the amended rule violated art.12.

Held: Appeals dismissed. (Sir David Keene dissenting) (1) The amended rule interfered with the right to respect for family life within the meaning of art.8(1), and that interference was sufficient to call for justification, *Abdulaziz v United Kingdom (A/94)* (1985) 7 E.H.R.R. 471 considered and *R. (on the application of Aguilar Quila) v Secretary of State for the Home Department* [2011] UKSC 45, [2012] 1 A.C. 621, [2011] C.L.Y. 1762 followed (see paras 11-15 of judgment). (2) The interference was justified. It was in accordance with the law, pursued a legitimate aim, and was proportionate. In terms of proportionality, the central questions were whether the amended rule was no more intrusive than was than necessary to meet its legitimate aim, and whether it struck a fair balance between the rights of the individual and the interests of the community. In determining those questions, the judge had taken the correct, heightened-scrutiny approach and had addressed the question of whether a pre-entry test was more intrusive than a post-entry one. There was no doubt that the amended rule would create anomalies, but it was not possible to estimate precisely how many. B's principal complaint was that the justification offered by the secretary of state was short on empirical proof that the amended rule would not operate in a disproportionate manner. However, that submission misunderstood the scope for judicial intervention in a case such as the instant one. The pre-entry test had been conceived as a benign measure designed to facilitate the integration of non-English-speaking spouses, and it would be regrettable if, in justifying such a measure, the secretary of state faced a burden that could only be discharged by irrefutable empirical evidence. It was appropriate for the state to be accorded a margin of appreciation in the formulation of its social policy, and that margin had, in some situations, to be pitched at a level that allowed for change, even if there was a risk that some individuals would be adversely affected by it, *Stec v United Kingdom (65731/01)* (2006) 43 E.H.R.R. 47, [2006] C.L.Y. 2089 applied. In the instant case, the secretary of state identified a social problem, considered an ameliorating solution, assessed the implications of introducing it, and provided for exceptional cases. The judge was right to conclude that the shift to a pre-entry requirement, pitched at a rudimentary level, was proportionate (paras 17-33). (3) The underlying concern in the instant case was not one of an immutable characteristic such as ethnicity, but was, rather, the ability to speak rudimentary English as a qualification for long-term residence. Nationality was being used as a proxy for familiarity with the English language. That embraced the question of whether it was justifiable to have a "bright line" rule that inevitably produced anomalies. The judge was right to conclude that exemptions based on nationality and academic qualifications were not direct discrimination based on nationality, because those who were exempt were not in a "relevantly similar situation" to those who were not. In terms of indirect discrimination, any difference in treatment between the exempt and the non-exempt nationalities had an objective, reasonable and proportionate justification (paras 41-46). (3) For the reasons given by the judge below, art.12 did not avail B of a free-standing right (para.37). (4) (Per Sir David Keene) The amended rule was a clear interference with the right to respect for family life under art.8. While it was in accordance with law and pursued, to a modest degree, a legitimate aim, it was not proportionate. The secretary of state had to produce some empirical evidence to demonstrate the extent of the problem that the measure was designed to overcome, and she had failed to demonstrate by any substantial empirical evidence that the amended rule was no more than was necessary to achieve the legitimate aim (paras 53-59).

R. (ON THE APPLICATION OF BIBI) v SECRETARY OF STATE FOR THE HOME DEPARTMENT, [2013] EWCA Civ 322, [2014] 1 W.L.R. 208, Maurice Kay, L.J., CA (Civ Div).

1626. Leave to remain–Administrative decisions–Turkish national applying for leave to remain as self-employed business person under Ankara Agreement–Working in breach of condition–Home Office contemporaneous policy and exercise of discretion

The appellant (K) appealed against a decision of the Asylum and Immigration Tribunal to uphold the respondent secretary of state's refusal to grant him leave to remain as a self-employed business person. K, a Turkish national, who originally had been granted leave to remain in the United Kingdom as a visitor, had applied for leave to remain as a self-employed business person under the standstill clause of the EC-Turkey Association Agreement, known as the Ankara Agreement. After making his application, K had commenced self-employment on the advice of his solicitors and then a short time later ceased trading. His application was refused on two occasions on the basis that he had commenced his business in breach of the conditions of his previous leave to remain which prohibited economic activity. The second refusal identified the wrong-doing as an abuse of rights. K's appeal to the

AIT was dismissed as the judge considered that there was no basis on which he was entitled to interfere with the secretary of state's exercise of her discretion under the rules. K submitted that (1) the immigration judge had failed to consider for himself the discretion contained in the rules and had approached the decision of the secretary of state as if it were a decision subject only to judicial review rather than appeal; (2) in the light of the Home Office's pragmatic approach that operated at the time of K's application whereby working in breach of condition would not form the sole basis of a refusal, it was unfair of the secretary of state to hold against him the fact that, in reliance on appropriate legal advice, he had first commenced and then ceased trading shortly afterwards.

Held: Appeal allowed. (1) The immigration judge had erred in law in not considering for himself the original statutory discretion which was his. There was no sign that the judge had considered the facts or the exercise of discretion for himself, other than in his expression of some sympathy for K who had taken appropriate legal advice throughout the process. The determination was flawed (see para.88 of judgment). (2) It was a matter of common law fairness that K's case should have been treated in the same manner as others of that period. Even in a true case of fraud or abuse of rights, the standstill clause would still apply, *Oguz v Secretary of State for the Home Department (C-186/10)* [2012] 1 W.L.R. 709, [2012] C.L.Y. 1752 applied. K's case was on all fours with the case of Karaaslan v Secretary of State (C5/2009/0886), Karaaslan considered. It had not been shown that K had taken any advantage of commencing trading in order to leverage his position. K's short period of working in breach was used as the sole basis of refusal and no other reason had been given. The secretary of state was entitled to change her policy on due notice. However, K's case should have been weighed in the context of the policy or practice contemporaneous to his application and breach of condition. The process was conspicuously unfair to K. The second refusal decision was not in accordance with the law. Leave to remain under the standstill clause would be granted for the standard initial period of 12 months (paras 51, 92-93, 95).

KA (TURKEY) v SECRETARY OF STATE FOR THE HOME DEPARTMENT, [2012] EWCA Civ 1183, [2013] 1 C.M.L.R. 2, Rix, L.J., CA (Civ Div).

1627. Leave to remain–Appeals–Senior immigration judge's jurisdiction to deal with argument not considered by immigration judge

[European Convention on Human Rights 1950 Art.8.]

The appellant (K) appealed against a decision of the Upper Tribunal upholding the respondent secretary of state's decision to refuse him further leave to remain. K, a student from India, had enrolled on a course in the United Kingdom. K's college was later removed from the register of Tier 4 student sponsors, as a result of which the secretary of state refused to grant him further leave to remain. An immigration judge in the First-tier Tribunal allowed K's appeal against the refusal to extend his leave to remain on the mistaken basis that the secretary of state's policy guidance entitled him to an extended period of leave to remain. On appeal by the secretary of state, the Upper Tribunal found that the immigration judge had erred by misconstruing the effect of the secretary of state's policy guidance. K accepted that the immigration judge had erred in his consideration of the policy guidance, but maintained that the senior immigration judge should consider his right to private life under the European Convention on Human Rights 1950 art.8. The senior immigration judge refused to consider the application of art.8 on the ground that the immigration judge had not erred in failing to consider that issue.

Held: Appeal allowed. The senior immigration judge was wrong to have looked for an error of law in the immigration judge's decision in relation to the art.8 issue. There was no need for any further error of law in order to give the senior immigration judge jurisdiction to deal with K's appeal anew. There was already the common ground error of law in relation to the proper interpretation of the secretary of state's policy guidance. Therefore, the senior immigration judge was in a position to either remake the decision himself, or remit it back to the First-tier Tribunal. The senior immigration judge had a discretion to consider the art.8 point, and he had erred in rejecting any possibility of considering the art.8 issue on the mistaken ground that he could not do so unless the immigration judge had erred by not considering it. It was appropriate to set aside the senior immigration judge's decision and remit it to another judge of the Upper Tribunal to decide the outcome of K's appeal (see paras 28, 30, 33 of judgment).

KIZHAKUDAN v SECRETARY OF STATE FOR THE HOME DEPARTMENT, [2012] EWCA Civ 566, [2012] Imm. A.R. 886, Rix, L.J., CA (Civ Div).

1628. Leave to remain–Applications–Difference in treatment between postal and personal applications for extension of leave to remain–Recommendations for measures to address difference

[Immigration and Nationality (Fees) Regulations 2011 (SI 2011/1055) reg.37.]

The appellant (B), a Nepalese national, appealed against a determination of the First-tier Tribunal. B had made a postal application for an extension of his leave to remain in the United Kingdom. His leave was valid until May 28. On May 17, he received an acknowledgement of receipt. On June 21, he received notice that his application was invalid because the specified fee had not been paid. The letter was silent as to the specific reason for non-payment. He reapplied on June 22, but that application was refused on the basis that it was made when he no longer had valid leave to remain in the UK; the letter stated that there was no right of appeal against the decision. It was not disputed that at all material times B had funds available in his bank account such that an "in time" application would have succeeded. B unsuccessfully appealed to the First-tier Tribunal against the decision. The judge's findings, issued in the form of a determination, stated that the case must fail "for want of jurisdiction". B submitted that (1) it was competent for the Upper Tribunal to consider the matter, on the authority of *Abiyat (Rights of Appeal: Iran), Re* [2011] UKUT 314 (IAC), [2011] Imm. A.R. 822, [2012] C.L.Y. 1737; (2) the First-tier Tribunal was wrong to conclude it did not have jurisdiction.

Held: Appeal allowed. (1) The case was on all fours with *Abiyat* and the appeal was validly before the Upper Tribunal: the First-tier Tribunal had reached its decision following full consideration of the matter at a hearing, and expressed its conclusion in the form of a determination, *Abiyat* applied (see para.16 of judgment). (2) The First-tier Tribunal's jurisdiction turned on whether a valid application had been made prior to the expiry of leave. The Immigration and Nationality (Fees) Regulations 2011 reg.37 provided that an application was not validly made unless it was accompanied by the specified fee. The validity of the first application therefore depended not on whether payment was successfully processed, but on whether it was accompanied by the fee. B's application was accompanied by valid authorisation to obtain the entire fee that was available in the relevant bank account and was therefore validly made, *BE (Application Fee: Effect of Non-Payment), Re* [2008] UKAIT 89 considered. The First-tier Tribunal's decision was set aside and remade (paras 17-20). (3) The May 17 letter could not act as an acknowledgement of a valid application because the fee was not processed at that stage. There were no instructions to process an application before the expiry of an applicant's leave. When an application was subsequently processed and the fee could not be collected, for whatever reason, a standard letter was sent to the applicant with the original application except the page providing for payment of the fee, which was shredded for security reasons. Consequently, an applicant was not (a) given the opportunity to check the accuracy of billing data and resubmit his application before his leave expired; (b) given the opportunity to check whether the billing data was accurate after the processing had failed; (c) given any evidence-based specific reason why the processing had failed. Further, no record was kept of what went wrong with the payment. However, an application made in person at an office was processed immediately with the applicant being advised immediately of any failed payment. B was an intelligent man and was well aware of the importance of accurately completing the application form, and demonstrated efficiency in the timing of his application, and in replying to all correspondence. It was accepted that he had had the funds in his account at all material times and he made a statement that he was certain that he had provided the correct financial data. Against that was merely the fact of failure to collect the money. It was more probable than not that B was accurate in his assertion that he provided the correct data; the secretary of state had not given sufficient information to conclude to the contrary (paras 22-30). (4) (Obiter) The marked difference in treatment between postal and personal applications indicated substantive unfairness. The postal application process required immediate review. One or more of the following measures were to be adopted to prevent similar disputes in the future: (a) the fee was to be processed immediately on receipt of the application and before an acknowledgement letter was distributed; (b) the standard letter was to be amended so that it constituted an acknowledgement that a valid application had been made; (c) in cases of failure to collect the fee in an application made in time, there should be prompt communication with the applicant to afford an opportunity to check or correct the billing data; (d) the application should be securely retained along with the processing report (para.32).

BASNET (VALIDITY OF APPLICATION: RESPONDENT: NEPAL), *Re; sub nom.* BASNET v SECRETARY OF STATE FOR THE HOME DEPARTMENT, [2012] UKUT 113 (IAC), [2012] Imm. A.R. 673, Blake, J. (President), UT (IAC).

1629. Leave to remain–Fees–Refusal to accept application for extension of discretionary leave without payment of fee–Application on human rights grounds–Lawfulness of refusal

[Human Rights Act 1998 (c.42) s.3; Immigration and Nationality (Fees) Regulations 2010 (SI 2010/778) reg.6, reg.30; European Convention on Human Rights 1950 Art.8.]

The claimant immigrant (O) applied for judicial review of the decision of the defendant secretary of state refusing to consider his application for leave to remain for non-payment of the required fee. O, a Cameroon national, had entered the United Kingdom unlawfully and was later served with a deportation notice following a conviction for a criminal offence. An appeal against deportation was allowed on the grounds that O had strong family ties in the UK and was in a poor health. O applied for immigration status documents and the secretary of state granted him six months' discretionary leave. O applied for further discretionary leave to remain without including the relevant fee. O claimed that he was housed and supported by The National Asylum Support Service (NASS) and had insufficient funds to pay the fee and that although no fee was enclosed his application was valid and that failure to consider his application breached his rights under the European Convention on Human Rights 1950 art.8. In a letter dated 12 July 2010 the secretary of state stated that the Immigration and Nationality (Fees) Regulations 2010 reg.6 did not provide an exemption for payment of a fee for art.8 claims. The combined effect of Rule 34C of the Immigration Rules and reg.30 of the Regulations was that an application not accompanied by the specified fee, was "not validly made" and the application would not be considered. It was implicit in the secretary of state's letter that her position was that she could not waive the fee in the light of the Regulations. The issue was whether the secretary of state had acted unlawfully in refusing to accept O's application for an extension of discretionary leave without a fee where there it was not possible for the secretary of state to waive the fee in the case of an applicant who was seeking leave on human rights grounds but could not afford the fee because he was either destitute or in receipt only of NASS support.

Held: Application granted. The secretary of state, as a public official, was under a duty to make and interpret rules in the light of the Human Rights Act 1998 s.3. The requirement in reg.6 and reg.30 that a fee had to be paid and an application without a fee "was not validly made" and where there was no provision to waive the fee had to read, in the light of s.3, subject to a qualification that the specified fee was not due where to require it to be paid would be incompatible with a person's Convention rights. Implying qualifying words with that effect did not contradict the essential principles or scope of the Regulations, *Ghaidan v Godin-Mendoza* [2004] UKHL 30, [2004] 2 A.C. 557,

[2004] C.L.Y. 2538 applied. Accordingly, the decision made by the Secretary of State on 12 July 2010 was unlawful.

R. (ON THE APPLICATION OF OMAR) v SECRETARY OF STATE FOR THE HOME DEPARTMENT, [2012] EWHC 3448 (Admin), [2013] Imm. A.R. 601, Beatson, J., QBD (Admin).

1630. Leave to remain–Points-based system–Appeals–Appellant relying on evidence post-dating initial application–Whether dismissal of appeal justified

[Nationality, Immigration and Asylum Act 2002 (c.41) s.85A(4)(a).]

The appellant (M) appealed against a decision of the First-tier Tribunal upholding a decision of the respondent secretary of state refusing to vary his leave to remain. M had applied for leave to remain as a Tier 1 (General) Migrant under the points-based system. His application was refused because, among other things, the MBA issued by the university at which he had attended was not included in the list of MBA eligible programmes; further, the evidence provided did not show that he had been awarded the qualification at the date of the application. On appeal, M asserted that he also qualified for leave to remain as a Tier 1 (Post-study work) Migrant. He relied on the fact that, six days before the secretary of state made her decision, he had been awarded a qualifying degree. Dismissing the appeal, the tribunal concluded that, M's application having been made under the points-based system, the position had to be considered as at the date of his application, not at the date of the secretary of state's decision.

Held: Appeal dismissed. M was unable to surmount the limitation in the Nationality, Immigration and Asylum Act 2002 s.85A(4)(a), which, in this case, precluded reliance on the evidence on which he sought to rely. There was a clear statutory framework which specifically precluded the consideration of post-application evidence adduced by the appellant in particular categories of case, of which this was one. The fact that the case involved a claim that M satisfied a different requirement of the points-based system, rather than an attempt to rely on further evidence in support of an application that had already been made, was a distinction without substance. Both situations came within the exception set out in s.85A(4)(a). In cases governed by s.85A, it was clear that, in respect of evidence adduced, the material date was the date of the application, not the date of the decision (see para.20 of judgment).

ALI (S.120: POINTS-BASED SYSTEM: PAKISTAN), *Re*; *sub nom.* ALI v SECRETARY OF STATE FOR THE HOME DEPARTMENT, [2012] UKUT 368 (IAC), [2013] Imm. A.R. 165, Judge Allen, UT (IAC).

1631. Leave to remain–Points-based system–Applicant failing to meet "level of funds" requirement–Effect of secretary of state's failure to apply own policy

The appellant foreign student (R) appealed against a decision of the First-tier Tribunal upholding the refusal of the respondent secretary of state to grant her extended leave to remain under the points-based system. To secure extended leave to remain, R had to show that she had been in possession of £1,200 during a period of 28 days from December 28, 2011 to January 24, 2012. Upon receiving the relevant application form, R received a letter stating that "a case worker would write... as soon as possible if there was any problem with the validity of the application, such as missing documentation". It was decided that R failed to meet the relevant requirement: the bank statements supplied by her spanned a period of only 17 days, and the balance in her account fell below £1,200 during a four-day period. Evidence submitted by R later showed that she in fact satisfied the "level of funds" requirement during the 28-day period in question. The secretary of state's policy at the time was referred to in a letter of the UK Border Agency dated May 19, 2011. The letter stated as follows: "UK Border Agency Case Workers employ a measure of flexibility when considering PBS applications. For example, case owners [sic] operate a system which allows them to contact applicants to request further documentation or clarification where appropriate. In addition a validation stage is being trialled [sic] whereby applicants are contacted where mandatory evidence is missing and given the opportunity to provide it before their application is rejected".

Held: Appeal allowed. The passage from the UK Border Agency's letter was of unmistakable importance and unambiguously clear import. It did not merely notify certain interested agencies of the advent of a new "flexibility policy"; it also heralded unequivocally the introduction of a new practice whereby all applicants would be notified of the absence of mandatory evidence from their applications and be given the opportunity to rectify the relevant shortcoming before rejection. That had not been done in R's case. As an elementary principle of public law, public authorities were required to give effect to the policies which they promulgated from time to time. This case was simplicity itself: a relevant policy was adopted and promulgated by the secretary of state, who, in determining R's application, manifestly failed to give effect to it. In consequence, two errors of public law occurred. The first was that in determining the application the secretary of state disregarded a plainly material consideration, namely her own policy. The second was that the decision-making process was procedurally unfair, as the policy conferred on R a procedural right to be afforded the opportunity of correction, rectification and expansion; she was denied that right. The secretary of state's decision was not in accordance with the law and the decision of the First-tier Tribunal, which espoused that error of law, was unsustainable in consequence. The secretary of state was under a public-law duty to remake the decision lawfully, in accordance with this judgment (see paras 12, 14, 26, 28 of judgment).

RODRIGUEZ (FLEXIBILITY POLICY), *Re*; *sub nom.* RODRIGUEZ v SECRETARY OF STATE FOR THE HOME DEPARTMENT, [2013] UKUT 42 (IAC), [2013] Imm. A.R. 509, McCloskey, J., UT (IAC).

1632. Leave to remain–Removal directions–Appellant challenging refusal of leave to remain and concurrent removal decision–Tribunal's duty to determine lawfulness of both decisions

[Immigration, Asylum and Nationality Act 2006 (c.13) s.47; Nationality, Immigration and Asylum Act 2002 (c.41) s.86(2), s.86(3).]

The appellant secretary of state appealed against decisions of the First-tier Tribunal allowing the appeals of the first and second respondents (X and J) against earlier decisions affecting their right to remain in the United Kingdom. X, a Sri Lankan national, had come to the UK with entry clearance as a dependent spouse of a Tier 4 student, valid from October 28, 2008 to October 28, 2011. On October 19, 2011, she applied for leave to remain. Her application was refused and at the same time the secretary of state purported to make a decision under the Immigration, Asylum and Nationality Act 2006 s.47 that she should be removed. She appealed. Following *Ahmadi (S.47 Decision: Validity: Sapkota: Afghanistan), Re* [2012] UKUT 147 (IAC), [2012] Imm. A.R. 875, [2013] 2 C.L. 190, in which it was held that a decision under s.47 would not be lawful if it was in the same document as or accompanied by the decision refusing further leave, the First-tier Tribunal judge decided that the removal decision was unlawful. He purported to determine the whole appeal by "remitting" the case to the secretary of state and made no enquiry into, or decision on, the merits of the refusal to vary leave. J, a national of Pakistan, had entered the UK as a student. His final period of leave expired on March 27, 2011. On March 16, 2011, he applied for indefinite leave to remain. His application was refused and at the same time the secretary of state purported to decide that he should be removed by way of directions under s.47. He appealed. The First-tier Tribunal judge also followed *Ahmadi* and decided that the decision under s.47 could not stand. She made no enquiry into the merits of the decision refusing leave and again "remitted" the decision to the secretary of state. X argued that there had been a single appeal before the tribunal; that in cases such as this because the appeal against the s.47 decision fell to be allowed, the appeal as a whole had to be allowed; that the immigration judge need not concern himself with the merits of the decision refusing leave; and that it was necessary for the secretary of state to start the whole process again and make anew whatever decisions were appropriate.

Held: Appeals allowed. There was indeed one appeal before the tribunal but the wording of the Nationality, Immigration and Asylum Act 2002 s.86(3) and s.86(5) made it clear that it was open to the tribunal to allow an appeal in part and to dismiss it in part. Indeed, that might well happen when there was only one decision under consideration but different grounds were relied on, all of which had to be considered in accordance with s.86(2). In cases such as this, there was nothing in the wording of s.86 which prevented a judge from disposing of the appeal by allowing it in relation to a decision made purportedly under s.47 but dismissing it in relation to a decision refusing a variation of leave. At the end of the day, the result should be that the tribunal determined in substance the appeal brought against the lawful decision and declared the other decision unlawful. Both First-tier Tribunal judges had erred in law by failing to appreciate the need to determine the appeals insofar as they related to each of the included decisions. They correctly decided that the decisions under s.47 were not in accordance with the law but their decisions on the merits of the refusal to vary X and J's leave were still awaited. The cases would be remitted to the tribunal with the following directions. The judges were to allow the appeals insofar as they related to the decisions under s.47. They were to determine the grounds of appeal raised in relation to the refusal to vary leave and decide whether the appeals fell to be allowed or dismissed insofar as they related to those decisions, *Ahmadi* followed (see paras 23, 25-26, 28 of judgment).

ADAMALLY (SECTION 47 REMOVAL DECISIONS: TRIBUNAL PROCEDURES), *Re; sub nom.* SECRETARY OF STATE FOR THE HOME DEPARTMENT v ADAMALLY, [2012] UKUT 414 (IAC), [2013] Imm. A.R. 306, CMG Ockelton (Vice President), UT (IAC).

1633. Leave to remain–Right to respect for private and family life–Dismissal of art.8 claim on purely procedural basis–Application of C (Zimbabwe) v Secretary of State for the Home Department [2008] UKHL 40

[European Convention on Human Rights 1950 Art.8.]

In the first case, the appellant secretary of state appealed against a decision of the Upper Tribunal upholding an application by the respondent (H) for leave to remain in the United Kingdom based on a claim under the European Convention on Human Rights art.8. In the second case, the appellant (T) appealed against a decision of the Upper Tribunal which upheld a finding that T had no right to remain on art.8 grounds. H, a citizen of Pakistan, had entered the UK lawfully as a student. He applied for further leave to remain on the ground that his wife, who was also a student, could not continue her studies if required to live independently of him. She had no other relatives in the UK. An immigration judge held that H and his wife were only in the UK on a temporary basis and could have had no expectation of a right to remain in order to further their family life; therefore, refusal of leave to remain did not breach H's rights under art.8. The Upper Tribunal held that the immigration judge had failed to apply *C (Zimbabwe) v Secretary of State for the Home Department* [2008] UKHL 40, [2008] 1 W.L.R. 1420, [2008] C.L.Y. 2052 on the basis that H was not seeking to remain in the UK as a spouse, and had taken insufficient account of the practical and emotional support supplied by H to his wife. T, a citizen of Mauritius, had entered the UK with valid entry clearance as a student and was granted further leave to remain as a spouse of a student dependent. The marriage broke down and T's wife returned to Mauritius. T's application for further leave to remain was refused. The First-tier Tribunal rejected the contention that T had any residual family life following the separation from his wife and the Upper Tribunal upheld that finding. T submitted that the requirement for him to return to Mauritius to apply for entry clearance achieved no legitimate objective and was inconsistent with the principle in *C (Zimbabwe).*

Held: Appeals allowed in part. (1) The effect of *C (Zimbabwe)* and subsequent Court of Appeal cases in which it had been considered was that (a) where an applicant lacked lawful entry clearance, the dismissal of his art.8 claim on the procedural ground that he should, as a matter of policy, have made the application from his own state, might constitute a disruption of family or private life sufficient to engage art.8; (b) where art.8 was engaged, it was a disproportionate interference with family or private life to enforce such a policy unless there was a sensible reason for doing so; (c) whether it was sensible to enforce that policy was fact-sensitive; potentially relevant factors included the prospective length and degree of disruption of family life and whether other family members were settled in the UK; (d) where art.8 was engaged and there was no sensible reason for enforcing the policy, the decision-maker should determine the art.8 claim on its substantive merits, notwithstanding that the applicant had no lawful entry clearance; (e) it would be a very rare case where it was appropriate for the Court of Appeal, having concluded that a lower tribunal had disproportionately interfered with art.8 rights in enforcing the policy, to make the substantive art.8 decision for itself; (f) nothing in *C (Zimbabwe)* was intended to alter the way the courts should approach substantive art.8 issues; (g) if the secretary of state had no sensible reason for requiring the application to be made from the home state, her failure to do so should not thereafter carry any weight in the substantive art.8 balancing exercise (see para.30 of judgment). (2) In H's case, the immigration judge had not dismissed the art.8 application simply on the formalistic basis that it should be renewed from Pakistan because rules should be obeyed. On the contrary, he had taken into account that neither H nor his wife had a legitimate expectation of a right to remain; that their family life could continue in Pakistan, although the wife would obviously not wish to return there before the end of her course; and that any period of separation would be short. Those were all proper considerations to weigh in the balance when considering the merits of the art.8 claim. Accordingly, there were cogent factors justifying the conclusion that art.8 was not infringed by requiring H to return to that country. There was no error in the approach of the immigration judge, and the Upper Tribunal had erred in holding to the contrary. It followed that it was not open to the Upper Tribunal to re-assess the relevant considerations and reach its own decision on art.8 (paras 49-53). (3) IN T's case, the first-tier immigration judge had not made his decision on a procedural basis at all; rather, he had considered the merits of the art.8 claim and rejected it after a full proportionality assessment. Although he had added that any subsequent application could be lodged from Mauritius, the application had not been dismissed on that basis. Accordingly, *C (Zimbabwe)* was irrelevant to T's case, *C (Zimbabwe)* considered (para. 81)

HAYAT v SECRETARY OF STATE FOR THE HOME DEPARTMENT; TREEBHOWAN v SECRETARY OF STATE FOR THE HOME DEPARTMENT; *sub nom.* SECRETARY OF STATE FOR THE HOME DEPARTMENT v HAYAT, [2012] EWCA Civ 1054, [2013] Imm. A.R. 15, Sir Maurice Kay (VP CA Civ), CA (Civ Div).

1634. Leave to remain–Students–College not on list of approved sponsors–Student's failure to meet requirements of Immigration Rules–Fairness

The appellant (C) appealed against the respondent secretary of state's decision to refuse his application for leave to remain in the United Kingdom as a Tier 4 student. C's existing leave to remain in the UK as a student expired on May 31, 2012, and on that day he applied for leave to undertake a diploma computing course at a particular college. His application relied on a confirmation of acceptance for studies (CAS) assigned by the college on the same day as his leave expired. Accordingly, C had made his application on the last day. On June 23 the secretary of state refused the application on the basis that the college was not an A-rated or highly trusted sponsor. In fact, it held a B-rated sponsor licence. Further, C's course was below degree level and he had failed to achieve the required level B1 in each of the four areas of an English language test. C appealed to the First-Tier tribunal which upheld the secretary of state's decision. In the grounds of appeal, C suggested that the secretary of state had acted unfairly in failing to give C sufficient warning of two changes in the Immigration Rules introduced in April 2011, namely para.116(da) which stipulated that a new course had to be at an A-rated college, and para.118(c)(iii) which required an applicant starting a new course at below degree level to achieve level B1 in all four components of an English language test.

Held: Appeal dismissed. There could be no doubt that the secretary of state was entitled to refuse C's original application for leave to remain. First, the college was not A-rated and was not a highly trusted sponsor. Thus, because C had applied to study a new course his CAS failed to meet the requirements of para.116(da) and (e). Secondly, C's application failed to comply with para.118(c)(iii) in that he had failed to achieve level B1 in two of the four components. His application was bound to be refused and the tribunal was correct to uphold the secretary of state's refusal (see paras 8-9 of judgment). On the issue of fairness, the fact that the UK Border Agency announced the proposed changes to the Rules in March 2011 and that such changes did not come into force for a further four weeks meant that those who stood to be affected by the changes had adequate time to take appropriate action. Both C and the college would have been aware of the proposed changes at least a month in advance. It was noted that C did nothing until the very last day of his existing leave, when he applied to extend it. C had failed the necessary English language test, and that was nobody's fault but his own. In the circumstances, having been given reasonable notice of the changes, C was not treated unfairly: the reasons for the refusal came down to the particular facts of his case, *Patel v Secretary of State for the Home Department* [2011] UKUT 211 (IAC), [2011] Imm. A.R. 647, [2012] C.L.Y. 1761 considered.

CONTRACTOR (CAS: TIER 4), *Re; sub nom.* CONTRACTOR v SECRETARY OF STATE FOR THE HOME DEPARTMENT, [2012] UKUT 168 (IAC), [2012] Imm. A.R. 823, Coulson, J., UT (IAC).

1635. Migrant workers–Points-based system–Status of accountancy qualification

[Education Reform Act 1988 (c.40) s.214(2)(c).]

The appellant (M) appealed against a ruling of the First-tier Tribunal upholding a decision of the respondent secretary of state that he had not been awarded a United Kingdom-recognised degree at Bachelor's level for the purposes of the points-based system applying to those, like him, who had sought leave to remain as a tier 1 (post-study work) migrant. M had attained the Association of Chartered Certified Accountants (ACCA) fundamental level qualification. He relied on a letter from the National Recognition Information Centre for the United Kingdom in which it was said that such a qualification was "considered comparable to British Bachelor (honours) degree standard". M argued that he was entitled to rely on a qualification of equivalent or comparable level to a degree.

Held: Appeal dismissed. Neither the Immigration Rules nor the guidance issued by the secretary of state provided that the required qualification could be either equivalent or comparable to a UK-recognised degree. The relevant requirement under the Rules was clear and unambiguous. The requisite points could only be given if an applicant had been awarded a "UK recognised degree" at Bachelor's level or above. The guidance itself provided that professional and vocational qualifications could not be used to obtain the award of points unless they fell within the qualifications listed in para.53. The qualifications listed in para.53 of the guidance merely reflected those set out in Table 10 to the Immigration Rules. The ACCA fundamental level qualification was not a relevant qualification for the purposes of Table 10 to Appendix A, nor was it of a type referred to in the guidance. It was not a UK-recognised degree or a postgraduate certificate or professional graduate diploma in education. In order to come within the definition of "a UK Bachelor's degree" contained within para.6 of the Immigration Rules, a qualification designated as being at Bachelor's degree level must have been awarded by a body authorised (a) by Royal Charter or (b) by, or under, an Act of Parliament to grant degrees; alternatively, it had to be a qualification designated as being at Bachelor's degree level and be "a recognised award for the purposes of Section 214(2)(c) of the Education Reform Act 1988". There was no evidence that ACCA was a body authorised by Royal Charter or by an Act of Parliament to grant degrees. Under the Education

Reform Act 1988 s.214(2)(c), the secretary of state was given the power to designate as a "recognised award" a specified award; however, on the evidence neither M's qualification nor any other qualification awarded by ACCA had been designated pursuant to that section (see paras 34-38 of judgment).

MIRZA (ACCA FUNDAMENTAL LEVEL QUALIFICATION: NOT A RECOGNISED DEGREE), *Re; sub nom.* MIRZA v SECRETARY OF STATE FOR THE HOME DEPARTMENT, [2013] UKUT 41 (IAC), [2013] Imm. A.R. 412, Judge Craig, UT (IAC).

1636. Migrant workers–Rights of entry and residence–Italian national living in United Kingdom–Working for only 80 hours during 11-year residence–Whether "employed" for purposes of art.12 Regulation 1612/68

[Immigration (European Economic Area) Regulations 2006 (SI 2006/1003) reg.14, reg.15; Regulation 1612/68 on freedom of movement for workers within the Community Art.12; Directive 2004/38 on the right of citizens of the Union and their family members to move and reside freely within the territory of the Member States amending Regulation (EEC) No 1612/68 and repealing Directives 64/221/EEC, 68/360/EEC, 72/194/EEC, 73/148/EEC, 75/34/EEC, 75/35/EEC, 90/364/EEC, 90/365/; European Convention on Human Rights 1950 Art.8.]

The appellants, a mother and her two sons (M, S1 and S2) appealed against a decision of the Upper Tribunal ([2010] UKUT 161 (IAC), [2010] Imm. A.R. 628, [2011] C.L.Y. 1794) upholding the respondent secretary of state's refusal to certify their status as permanent residents in the United Kingdom under the Immigration (European Economic Area) Regulations 2006 reg.15. M, an Argentinian national, had come to the UK in 2001 and had married an Italian national (F), who had been living in the UK since 1999. M and F had then lived together in the UK, S1 being born in November 2001 and S2 being born in December 2004. The marriage broke down in 2006. Although S1 and S2 were Italian nationals, they had lived nowhere but the UK. For most of his time in the UK, F had been unemployed. Between 2002 and 2003 he had sought employment and, for a 10-week period in 2007 he had worked as a cleaner, working eight hours per week. That was his only period of employment during his 11 years in the UK. It was agreed that if, after S1 and S2's birth, F had been employed in the UK within the meaning of Regulation 1612/68 art.12, then S1 and S2 were entitled to the benefits of that article, together with a right of residence in the UK. It was also agreed that if S1 and S2 were entitled to reside in the UK, then M had a right of residence as their carer. The immigration judge and the tribunal concluded that F had not been "employed" in the UK for the purposes of art.12, and that S1 and S2 were therefore not entitled to the benefits of that article. The issues were (i) whether S1 and S2 were entitled to the benefits of art.12; (ii) the relationship between the rights under art.12 and the rights to acquire extended or permanent resident status under reg.14 and reg.15 of the 2006 Regulations; (iii) the impact of the decision in *Ruiz Zambrano v Office National de l'Emploi (ONEm) (C-34/09)* [2012] Q.B. 265; and (iv) the application of European Convention on Human Rights art.8.

Held: Appeal allowed in part. (1) As to the period when F was looking for work in the UK: a child did not obtain art.12 rights simply because his parent was a national of another Member State looking for work in the host state. A person looking for work could not be described as "employed" within the meaning of art.12 (see para.22 of judgment). The next question was whether F's 80 hours of employment in 11 years meant that he had been "employed" within the meaning of art.12. The secretary of state had conceded that if a person was a "worker" within the meaning of Directive 2004/38, then he was "employed" for the purposes of art.12. Although the court wondered whether that concession should in fact have been made, considering it arguable that the test in art.12 was more stringent than the test to be applied under the Directive, it proceeded on the basis that it had rightly been made. For the purposes of the Directive, there had to be a real link between the person claiming to be a worker and the labour market, and in deciding whether a person was actively pursuing, or seriously wished to pursue, activities as an employed person, the court was entitled to examine his motives. The immigration judge's findings of fact showed that F had not been exercising his right to work: he had not actively sought work during his time in the UK, had not been self-sufficient, and he had apparently undertaken the 80 hours' work in 2007 in order to maintain his claim for benefits. In those circumstances, the tribunal had been entitled to conclude that F was not a "worker" for the purposes of the Directive and had therefore not been "employed" for the purposes of art.12, *Ninni-Orasche v Bundesminister fur Wissenschaft, Verkehr und Kunst (C-413/01)* [2004] All E.R. (EC) 765, [2004] C.L.Y. 1263 and *Barry v Southwark LBC* [2008] EWCA Civ 1440, [2009] P.T.S.R. 952, [2009] C.L.Y. 1241 considered (paras 25-26, 29, 61-69). (2) Given the court's conclusion on the first issue, the second fell away (para.69). (3) Although the secretary of state had not, in her decision letter, required S1 and S2 to leave the UK, the immigration judge had found that they should remain in their mother's care and return with her to Argentina. The tribunal upheld that decision. The secretary of state conceded, however, that in the light of *Zambrano*, a decision which post-dated the tribunal's decision, S1 and S2 could not be required to leave the European Union, *Zambrano* referred to. Given that the secretary of state had not, in her decision letter, required S1 and S2 to leave the UK, it was difficult to see how the apparent decision to remove M to Argentina could have been lawful. However, the secretary of state accepted that she had made no decision to remove M from the UK, and that concession could be reflected in the court order if necessary. Finally, it was clear that M and S had no right to a permanent or extended right of residence under the 2006 Regulations (paras74-77). (4) Pursuant to an agreement between the parties, the art.8 issue would be remitted to the tribunal. M and S's appeal therefore succeeded only to that extent (paras 6, 78).

MDB (ITALY) v SECRETARY OF STATE FOR THE HOME DEPARTMENT; *sub nom.* MDB (ARTICLE 12, 1612/68: ITALY), *Re*, [2012] EWCA Civ 1015, [2012] 3 C.M.L.R. 43, Maurice Kay, L.J. (VP, CA Crim), CA (Civ Div).

1637. Passports–Identity documents–EEA national's non-EEA family members–Application by family members for permanent residence card–Lawfulness of requirement to produce EEA national's passport

[Immigration (European Economic Area) Regulations 2006 (SI 2006/1003) reg.15(1)(b), reg.17(1)(a), reg.17(1), reg.18.]

The appellant secretary of state appealed against a First-tier Tribunal decision that the respondents (B) qualified for a permanent residence card as the family members of a national of the European Economic Area. B were a mother and two children from Jamaica. They applied for a permanent residence card pursuant to the Immigration (European Economic Area) Regulations 2006 reg.17(1) on the basis that, in accordance with reg.15(1)(b), they were the family members of a Polish citizen (X) with whom they had resided in the United Kingdom for a continuous period of five years after he married the mother. The secretary of state requested them to submit a valid passport or national identity card for X. They submitted X's Polish identity card but the secretary of state refused their application because the UK Border Agency no longer accepted that type of national identity card as a valid form of identification. The First-tier Tribunal allowed B's appeal against that decision, finding that there was no reason why the secretary of state had accepted EEA nationals' identity cards in the past as a valid form of identification but would not accept them now. The secretary of state brought the instant appeal, arguing that reg.17(1) had required B to submit X's passport, not his identity card.

Held: Appeal dismissed. Under reg.17(1), the secretary of state had to issue a residence card to a non-EEA national who was the family member of an EEA national with a permanent right of residence under reg.15 on production of a valid passport and proof that the non-EEA national was such a family member. The passport which was required was that of the family member, not that of the EEA national. Therefore, the secretary of state and the First-tier Tribunal had been wrong in thinking that it was X's passport which had to be produced. However, reg.17(1) did not apply in the instant case: the person who had to have the permanent right of residence under reg.15 was the EEA national, not the non-EEA national. The secretary of state should have determined B's applications by reference to reg.18, but had wrongly determined them by reference to reg.17(1)(a). Under reg.18(2), B would be required to provide proof of their permanent right of residence under reg.15, which might entail proving the identity of the EEA national. However, in order to grant a permanent residence card under reg.18, the secretary of state generally could not lawfully insist on an applicant's producing the EEA national's passport or other identity document, unless it was genuinely required in order to prove the right which the applicant was asserting. As the secretary of state had accepted that B met the reg.15 requirements, it was wholly unnecessary for her to require any identification document relating to X to demonstrate that they were still related to him. Given that they had lived for over five years with X, it was irrelevant whether the mother thereafter remained married to him. She had already acquired a permanent right of residence. In any event, the secretary of state had taken no issue with whether they were still married (see paras 18-26 of judgment).

BARNETT (EEA REGULATIONS: RIGHTS AND DOCUMENTATION: JAMAICA), *Re*; *sub nom.* SECRETARY OF STATE FOR THE HOME DEPARTMENT v BARNETT, [2012] UKUT 142 (IAC), [2012] Imm. A.R. 828, Judge Lane, UT (IAC).

1638. Refugees–Grounds for refusal–Art.1F(c) Convention relating to the Status of Refugees 1951 (United Nations)–Applicant allegedly guilty of acts contrary to purposes of United Nations–Definitions and burden of proof

In appeals heard together, two asylum seekers (S and D) appealed against decisions ([2009] EWCA Civ 222, [2009] Imm. A.R. 624, [2010] C.L.Y. 1753 and [2010] EWCA Civ 1407) denying them refugee status. S, an Egyptian national, and D, an Afghan national, had claimed asylum in the United Kingdom. S had written contributions for books linked to proscribed terrorist organisations, had been found in possession of Al-Qaeda videos and had transferred large sums of money to foreign countries. He had also been charged with conspiring to murder the leader of the Northern Alliance in Afghanistan. Those charges were eventually dismissed as the evidence was as consistent with his innocence as with his guilt. D had allegedly fought against the Afghan government and against the international security assistance force (ISAF), a United Nations-mandated force. Their asylum claims were refused on the basis of the Convention relating to the Status of Refugees 1951 (United Nations) art.1F(c) because there were "serious reasons" for considering that they were guilty of acts contrary to the purposes and principles of the United Nations. The court was required to determine (i) whether all activities defined as terrorism by UK domestic law were acts contrary to the purposes and principles of the UN; (ii) whether armed insurrection was contrary to the purposes and principles of the UN if directed against the incumbent government and against the UN-mandated force supporting that government; (iii) the appropriate standard of proof.

Held: Appeals dismissed. (1) It was clear that the phrase "acts contrary to the purposes and principles of the UN" had to have an autonomous meaning. Member States were not free to adopt their own definition. There was no internationally agreed definition of terrorism. However, the principal purpose of the UN was to maintain international peace and security, to remove threats to that peace and to develop friendly relations among nations. In those circumstances, the appropriately cautious and restrictive approach was to adopt the United Nations High Commissioner for Refugees (UNHCR) Guidelines para.17, *Germany v B (C-57/09)* [2012] 1 W.L.R. 1076 considered. That guidance stated that art.1F(c) was only triggered by attacking the very basis of the international community's coexistence; such activity had to have an international dimension; crimes capable of affecting relations between states and serious and sustained violations of human rights also fell under that category. It was very likely that inducing terror in the civilian population or putting such extreme pressures upon a government would also have the international repercussions referred to by the UNHCR. Whether a person plotting in one country to destabilise conditions in another was enough to meet the test depended on the circumstances of the case. It would clearly be enough if the government of one state offered a safe haven to terrorists to plot their terrorist operations against another state, as that would have clear implications for inter-state relations. The test was whether the resulting acts had the requisite serious effect upon international security and peaceful relations between states (see paras 16, 36-40 of judgment). (2) An attack on the ISAF was, in principle, capable of being an act contrary to the purposes and principles of the UN. The fundamental aims and objectives of the ISAF accorded with art.1 of the UN Charter. By attacking the ISAF, D was seeking to frustrate that purpose, *AB v Refugee Appeals Tribunal* [2011] IEHC 198 considered (paras 65-68). (3) Article 1F(c) required "serious reasons" for considering that a person was guilty of the relevant acts. The exclusion clauses in the Convention had to be restrictively interpreted and cautiously applied. The court drew the following conclusions: (a) "serious reasons" was stronger than "reasonable grounds"; (b) the evidence from which those reasons were derived had to be clear and credible or strong; (c) "considering" was stronger than suspecting or believing, *Germany v B* and *R. (on the application of JS (Sri Lanka)) v Secretary of State for the Home Department* [2010] UKSC 15, [2011] 1 A.C. 184, [2010] C.L.Y. 1816 considered. It required the considered judgement of the decision-maker; (d) the decision-maker need not be satisfied beyond reasonable doubt or to the standard required in criminal law; (e) it was unnecessary to import UK domestic standards of proof into the question. However, if the decision-maker was satisfied that it was more likely than not that the applicant had not committed the acts in question, it was difficult to see how there could be serious reasons for considering that he had done so. In reality, there were unlikely to be sufficiently serious reasons for considering the applicant to be guilty unless the decision-maker could be satisfied of his guilt on the balance of probabilities (para.75). (4) S and D's appeals were dismissed but the Court of Appeal's orders remitting their cases to the relevant tribunal remained unchanged (paras 76-77).

AL-SIRRI v SECRETARY OF STATE FOR THE HOME DEPARTMENT; DD (AFGHANISTAN) v SECRETARY OF STATE FOR THE HOME DEPARTMENT, [2012] UKSC 54, [2013] 1 A.C. 745, Lord Phillips, J.S.C. (President), SC.

1639. Refugees–Grounds for refusal–Correct approach to art.1F(b) and (c) Convention relating to the Staus of Refugees 1951 (United Nations)–European Union

[Immigration, Asylum and Nationality Act 2006 (c.13) s.54(1); Directive 2004/83 on minimum standards for the qualification and status of third country nationals or stateless persons as refugees or as persons who otherwise need international protection and the content of the protection granted Art.12; Convention relating to the Status of Refugees 1951 Art.1F.]

The appellant asylum seeker (X) appealed against the Asylum and Immigration Tribunal's determination, confirming the respondent secretary of state's decision, that he was excluded from the Convention relating to the Status of Refugees 1951 (United Nations) under art.1F. X was a stateless person, formerly of Algerian nationality. In 1993 he was convicted in Algeria of being involved in a bombing, and in his absence was sentenced to death. At the time of trial he was in France. In 1999 X was convicted in France of being a member of an association formed with a view to the preparation of acts of terrorism, sentenced to two years' imprisonment and made subject to an exclusion order. He arrived in the United Kingdom in 2001 and claimed asylum. X submitted that (1) in respect of art.1F(c), the tribunal had misdirected itself by applying the approach in *Gurung v Secretary of State for the Home Department* [2002] UKIAT 4870, [2003] Imm. A.R. 115, [2003] C.L.Y. 2259, which had subsequently been disapproved; (2) the offence of which he had been convicted and sentenced to two years' imprisonment was not sufficiently serious to be a serious non-political crime within the context of art.1F(b).

Held: Appeal allowed. (1) The fact of a conviction by a court might well make the task of assessing whether a person fell within art.1F much easier, but it would do so only if the nature of the offence of which the person had been convicted and/or the findings made by the court were sufficient to enable the tribunal to reach a conclusion as to the individual's "own personal involvement and role in the organisation", or the "true role" played by the individual in the acts perpetrated by the organisation, *R. (on the application of JS (Sri Lanka)) v Secretary of State for the Home Department* [2010] UKSC 15, [2011] 1 A.C. 184, [2010] C.L.Y. 1816 applied. Although *JS* was concerned with art.1F(a), the same criteria applied when art.1F(c) was under consideration, *Secretary of State for the Home Department v DD (Afghanistan)* [2010] EWCA Civ 1407 applied. *JS* made it clear that the nature of the organisation itself was only one of the relevant factors to be considered. Further, the mere fact of membership of a terrorist organisation could not automatically exclude a person from refugee status under Directive 2004/83 art.12, *Germany v B (C-57/09)* [2012] 1 W.L.R. 1076 applied. The tribunal had erred in relying on the decision in *Gurung,* which was the relevant authority at the date of its determination but which had subsequently been disapproved of in *JS.* The facts found by the French appeal court were so sparse that they did not enable the tribunal to determine X's personal involvement or true role in the grouping. The bare fact that X was knowingly part of a criminal conspiracy or grouping formed with a view to committing terrorist acts could not, unless the presumption in *Gurung* was applied, have justified the tribunal's conclusion that X fell within the definition in the Immigration, Asylum and Nationality Act 2006 s.54(1). There was simply no evidence of instigation, encouragement or inducement. It was clear that that was a misdirection and the tribunal had erred in that respect, *Gurung* not applied (see paras 10, 13-14, 16-17, 22-25 of judgment). (2) Each signatory state was not free to adopt its own definition of what constituted serious crime for the purpose of art.1F(b), and the proposition that the states did not have an unfettered discretion in that regard was supported by academic authority. While the Convention left it to the domestic courts to decide whether, in any particular case, a non-political crime was serious, that determination had to be founded on a common starting point as to the level of seriousness that must be demonstrated. There had been no discussion in the tribunal's determination of either the seriousness of the particular terrorist offence, or the appropriate threshold of seriousness. Even if the tribunal had considered the seriousness of X's offence in the context of the appropriate threshold of seriousness, it would have done so in the context of its conclusions in respect of art.1F(c), and those conclusions could only have been reached by the application of the discredited *Gurung* presumption. Being an international Convention, it must be given an autonomous meaning. The words "serious crime" were ordinary words and should be given their ordinary universal meaning. However, "serious" had shades of meaning and the appropriate colour was given by the context in which the word was used. The case was remitted for reconsideration (paras 30-32, 39, 42-43, 49-52).

AH (ALGERIA) v SECRETARY OF STATE FOR THE HOME DEPARTMENT, [2012] EWCA Civ 395, [2012] 1 W.L.R. 3469, Ward, L.J., CA (Civ Div).

1640. Removal–Illegal entrants–Leave to remain obtained by deception–Children aged over 18 by time of removal directions–Meaning of "family" in s.10(1)(c) Immigration and Asylum Act 1999

[Immigration Act 1971 (c.77) s.3(5)(aa), s.3(5)(a), s.5(4), Sch.2 Pt I para.9, Sch.2 para.10A; Immigration and Asylum Act 1999 (c.33) s.10(1)(c), s.10(1)(b); Nationality, Immigration and Asylum Act 2002 (c.41) s.86(3).]

In an appeal against a decision upholding decisions to remove illegal entrants, the tribunal was required to determine as a preliminary issue whether there was power in law to remove children who were aged over 18 under the Immigration and Asylum Act 1999 s.10(1)(c) as family members of an adult being removed under s.10(1)(b).

The appellant families had entered the United Kingdom and claimed asylum on false bases. The families included children who were dependent on their parents' asylum claims and were granted derivative refugee status and indefinite leave to remain. After the parents engaged in fraudulent activities, the grants of refugee status and indefinite leave to remain were rescinded. The secretary of state made decisions to remove the family members. Some of the children (X) were by that time aged over 18. X argued that they could not be removed as they did not belong to their parents' family within s.10(1)(c); "family" should be limited to those specified in the Immigration Act 1971 s.5(4), as had been understood by the draftsman of the Immigration Rules para.395B, in force at the time of the secretary of state's decisions.

Held: Preliminary issue determined in favour of appellants. (1) Parliament had not made clear whether the limitation to the meaning of "family" contained in s.5(4) of the 1971 Act was to be transferred to the 1999 Act. "Family" was a word which could be used in a number of senses, but it had to take its meaning from its context, *Joram Developments v Sharratt* [1979] 1 W.L.R. 928, [1979] C.L.Y. 1642 and *Fitzpatrick v Sterling Housing Association Ltd* [2001] 1 A.C. 27, [1999] C.L.Y. 3715 applied. There could be no doubt that sons and daughters over 18 could properly be regarded as continuing to be members of their parents' family. However, the meaning of family in context had to have some limitation. Section 10(5A) recognised that family members could cease to be such. All the appellants had entered by deception, whether or not they were personally aware of that deception, but their removal was not necessarily to be based on s.10(1)(c). If an adult over the age of 18 had established an independent life and was not aware of the deception, it was difficult to see how his removal would necessarily be desirable; if he had been complicit in the deception, he could be removed under s.10(1)(b) or on another basis. If the secretary of state were correct, a son or daughter who before the day the 1999 Act had come into force was over 18, and so could not be deported as a family member, would suddenly become on that day liable to removal. The purpose behind s.10 was to make those within s.3(5)(a) and s.3(5)(aa) of the 1971 Act who could be deported thereafter subject to administrative removal. No-one could be subject to penal consequences upon an ambiguous or unclear provision, *R. v Secretary of State for the Home Department, Ex p. Khawaja* [1984] A.C. 74, [1983] C.L.Y. 1908 applied. It would be extraordinary if Parliament was to be taken as having, without making clear that it was intending to do so, made a person who had been irremovable because he had not been liable to deportation suddenly liable to administrative removal when the deportation powers had been transferred. The limitations on who should be regarded as family members were as set out in s.5(4) of the 1971 Act (see paras 23-25, 29-30, 39 of judgment). (2) The Immigration Rules para.395B was consistent with X's submissions, and the tribunal was entitled to have regard to it. Moreover, the secretary of state's decision had not been in accordance with para.395B, and whether the tribunal was right or wrong in finding in X's favour on the construction of s.10(1)(c), it was therefore required under the Nationality, Immigration and Asylum Act 2002 s.86(3) to allow the appeals of those over 18. Reliance on Sch.2 para.9 of the 1971 Act could not change that result: para.9(2) required leave to enter to be disregarded if obtained by deception, but did not require leave to remain to be disregarded even if obtained by deception. Section 10(1)(b) of the 1999 Act dealt with that situation, but only where the person to be removed had himself been involved in the deception (paras 32-36). (3) (Obiter) The tribunal was strongly inclined to the view that, in context and having regard to the legislative history, the limitations in s.5(4) should apply to Sch.2 para.10A of the 1971 Act; the failure to apply the definition to that paragraph was a drafting error (para.39).

AHMAD (REMOVAL OF CHILDREN OVER 18: PAKISTAN), *Re; sub nom.* AHMAD (AKA MOHAMMED) v SECRETARY OF STATE FOR THE HOME DEPARTMENT, [2012] UKUT 267 (IAC), [2013] Imm. A.R. 1, Collins, J., UT (IAC).

1641. **Removal–Pending appeals–Country guidance case being appealed–Appropriateness of stay of removal in other cases pending outcome–Guidance**

The appellant asylum seeker (G) appealed against a refusal ([2011] EWHC 2428 (Admin)) of permission to seek judicial review of a decision of the respondent secretary of state to remove him to Iraq and to refuse to grant G a stay of removal. G was an Iraqi Kurd who had twice applied for asylum in the UK. Both applications were refused, his appeals against both decisions were dismissed, and removal directions were set. In September 2010, the Upper Tribunal gave its country guidance in *HM (Iraq) v Secretary of State for the Home Department* [2010] UKUT 331 (IAC), deciding that Iraqi nationals could generally be safely returned to Iraq. Permission to appeal to the Court of Appeal was subsequently granted in *HM*. G sought permission to seek judicial review of the decision to remove him and a stay of removal until the conclusion of his judicial review claim. The judge found that on the basis of the determination in *HM*, G had no prospect of succeeding in his challenge to the decision to remove him and he thus refused permission. The judge further refused to grant a stay pending the determination of the appeal in *HM*, although he recognised that there was uncertainty and divergent practice between judges as to whether stays should be granted in such circumstances. The issue on appeal was therefore whether the courts should grant a stay of proceedings in circumstances where relevant country guidance decisions were the subject of a pending appeal.

Held: Appeals dismissed. (1) It was necessary to consider the purpose of country guidance determinations. They enabled appropriate resources, in terms of the representations of the parties to the country guidance appeal, expert and factual evidence and the personnel and time of the tribunal, to be applied to the determination of conditions in, and therefore the risks of return to, the country in question. The procedure was aimed at arriving at a reliable and accurate determination. It was for those reasons, as well as the desirability of consistency, that decision makers were required to take such determinations into account and to follow them unless very strong grounds supported by cogent evidence were adduced, justifying their not doing so (see paras 43-50 of judgment). (2) A country guidance determination of the Upper Tribunal remained authoritative unless and until it was set aside on appeal or replaced by a subsequent country guidance determination, *R. (on the application of Qader) v Secretary of State for the Home Department* [2011] EWHC 1765 (Admin) applied. The filing of an application for permission to appeal a country guidance determination could not of itself justify the court granting an injunction staying the removal of anyone whose removal was justified by that determination. In circumstances where permission had been granted to appeal a country guidance determination, whether such a stay was justified would depend on the facts and evidence relied upon by the claimant. Those facts would include the content of the country guidance determination and the reasons given for the grant of permission to appeal. If the evidence relied upon had been considered by the Upper Tribunal giving the country guidance determination, it was unlikely a stay would be appropriate unless the reasons given for the grant of permission to appeal cast doubt on the findings of the Tribunal. If the evidence had not been considered by the Tribunal, in particular evidence of subsequent events, the court should not stay removal pending the Court of Appeal decision unless the claimant had adduced a clear and coherent body of evidence that the findings of the Tribunal were in error, *HM* considered (paras 67-71). (3) On the facts, the judge had been entitled to refuse G permission to apply for judicial review and to refuse a stay (paras 61-66).

R. (ON THE APPLICATION OF SG (IRAQ)) v SECRETARY OF STATE FOR THE HOME DEPARTMENT; R. (ON THE APPLICATION OF OR (IRAQ)) v SECRETARY OF STATE FOR THE HOME DEPARTMENT; *sub nom.* SG (IRAQ) v SECRETARY OF STATE FOR THE HOME DEPARTMENT; OR (IRAQ) v SECRETARY OF STATE FOR THE HOME DEPARTMENT, [2012] EWCA Civ 940, [2013] 1 W.L.R. 41, Maurice Kay, L.J., CA (Civ Div).

1642. Removal directions–Dependants–Lawfulness of making removal decisions or directions concerning principal subject and dependants at same time

[Immigration and Asylum Act 1999 (c.33) s.10, s.10(1)(a).]

The appellant Indian citizen (J) appealed against a decision of the Upper Tribunal dismissing his appeal against the respondent secretary of state's decision to remove him, his wife and two daughters from the United Kingdom. J, his wife and one daughter had continued staying in the UK after their visa ran out in 2005. Their second daughter was born in the UK in 2007. The secretary of state served notice on J and his wife to have them removed from the UK, pursuant to the Immigration and Asylum Act 1999 s.10(1)(a). On the same day, notice was served on his two daughters under s.10(1)(c) and s.10(3). J submitted that the removal decision in respect of him, as principal subject, and his wife could not be taken at the same time as the decision to remove his dependants. He contended that the reference in s.10(1)(c) to "have been given" showed that the decision to remove him had to precede the decision to remove his daughters.

Held: Appeal dismissed. The tribunal had been correct to make the critical distinction between removal decisions and removal directions. However, it was wrong to say that removal directions could only be given sequentially, *MS (Palestinian Territories) v Secretary of State for the Home Department* [2010] UKSC 25, [2010] 1 W.L.R. 1639, [2010] C.L.Y. 1792 considered. Section 10 was about the power to remove. Section10(1)(c) meant that removal of dependants from the UK under the Act could only take place after the decision to remove the principal had been made, but there was nothing to stop the secretary of state giving directions or a decision to issue directions under s.10(1)(a) and s.10(1)(c) at the same time (see paras 7, 9 of judgment).

RJ (INDIA) v SECRETARY OF STATE FOR THE HOME DEPARTMENT, [2012] EWCA Civ 1865, [2013] Imm. A.R. 407, Laws, L.J., CA (Civ Div).

1643. Removal directions–Local housing authorities' powers and duties–Illegal entrant intending to exercise right of appeal against removal directions–Whether local authority entitled to withdraw accommodation and support

[Children Act 1989 (c.41); Nationality, Immigration and Asylum Act 2002 (c.41); European Convention on Human Rights 1950 Art.8.]

The claimant (K) applied for judicial review of the defendant local authority's refusal to provide accommodation and support to her and her family pursuant to the Children Act 1989. K, a Nigerian citizen, and her husband had entered the United Kingdom illegally in 2002. They had three children, all of whom were born in the UK. K made five unsuccessful applications for leave to remain. She applied for reconsideration of the Border Agency's refusal of her application in reliance on the European Convention on Human Rights 1950 art.8 and sought an immigration decision in the alternative. K wrote to the local authority concerning its failure to assess and provide accommodation under the 1989 Act and issued proceedings for judicial review. The local authority provided accommodation and support, and the judicial review proceedings were settled by consent. The local authority conducted a needs and human rights assessment of K and her family, and concluded there would be no breach of art.8 if the support provided was withdrawn and the family returned to Nigeria. The local authority notified K that it would be terminating its support. K wrote to the local authority challenging its decision, notifying it of her right of appeal against an immigration decision, her efforts to persuade the Border Agency to make an immigration decision, and her refusal to return voluntarily to Nigeria. K wrote another letter indicating her intention to make another application for leave to remain if an immigration decision was not made. The local authority agreed to extend its support to a specified date. In its response to her letter, it stated that there was no application or outstanding appeal and that it was unable to comment on the strength of any proposed case, and it denied both its obligation to provide support and breaching art.8. K issued proceedings for judicial review. She made the further application for leave to remain, which was undetermined at the time of the instant hearing. The issue was whether in principle or on the facts K's putative right of appeal against the issue of removal directions would preclude the local authority from withdrawing support based on its own assessment of the effect on her art.8 rights, at least in the absence of a finding that the prospective appeal was obviously hopeless or abusive.

Held: Application granted. Save where a case was obviously hopeless or abusive, a local authority could not generally deny support under the 1989 Act if the effect would be to negate the procedural right for protection of convention rights, *R. (on the application of Clue) v Birmingham City Council* [2010] EWCA Civ 460, [2011] 1 W.L.R. 99, [2010] C.L.Y. 2203, R (on the application of AW) v Croydon London Borough Council [2005] 9 CCLR 2540 and *Binomugisha v Southwark LBC* [2006] EWHC 2254 (Admin), [2007] 1 F.L.R. 916, [2007] C.L.Y. 2313 applied. The Nationality, Immigration and Asylum Act 2002 secured the procedural safeguard required in Convention cases by the statutory right to appeal to the immigration tribunal, where there was an appealable immigration decision. Where a claimant had refused to leave the country voluntarily, as K had, and had a substantive Convention right claim, Parliament had determined that the decision to issue removal directions would be subject to appeal to the tribunal to enable the reconsideration of Convention rights. Depriving a person of that protection would breach their Convention rights. The existence of judicial review would not be a complete answer to the denial of that right, *R. (on the application of Daley-Murdock) v Secretary of State for the Home Department* [2011] EWCA Civ 161, [2011] Imm. A.R. 500, [2011] C.L.Y. 1775 applied. The right to appeal against removal directions if and when made would be a significant right to which K and her family would be entitled in protection of their art.8 rights. It was clear that there would have been arguable grounds of appeal with a reasonable prospect that a different immigration decision might be made. The local authority knew at the time of its decision that K and her family would not voluntarily return to Nigeria, and that they were seeking an immigration decision to enable an appeal and were in any event seeking a further application for leave to remain. Therefore, there was clearly a substantive Convention procedural right comprised in the statutory right to appeal against the immigration decision. It was equally plain that the decision to remove support was made knowing that the consequence would be the return of K and her family to Nigeria, which would effectively deprive them of their procedural right of appeal under the 2002 Act against the immigration decision when made. Notwithstanding the link between the decision to withdraw support and the procedural right, the local authority had failed to consider properly, if at all, the implications of its decision. It had not suggested that K's potential appeal would be hopeless or abusive; instead it had stated that it was unable to assess the strength of the proposed appeal. The correct approach would have been to provide support so far as necessary to preserve the procedural right to protect K's and her family's art.8 rights, unless it concluded that it was hopeless or abusive (see paras 50-59 of judgment).

R. (ON THE APPLICATION OF KA (NIGERIA)) v ESSEX CC, [2013] EWHC 43 (Admin), [2013] 1 W.L.R. 1163, Robin Purchas Q.C., QBD (Admin).

1644. Removal directions–Urgent applications–Guidance regarding consequences for solicitors' firms and legal representatives of non-compliance with procedural requirements

When considering an application for judicial review by the claimant overstayer (H) of a decision by the defendant secretary of state to order his removal from the United Kingdom, the court gave guidance regarding the consequences for solicitors' firms and legal representatives of non-compliance with procedural requirements. H, a Bangladeshi national, had been served with removal directions. His representations through immigration advisors were rejected. Further representations made by a solicitors' firm the day before he was to be removed were rejected. At 16.00 on the day before his removal, an application was made to the Administrative Court for removal to be deferred. Because of the substantial number of such applications, the court had revised the relevant form to be completed. The revised form required the reasons for urgency and the timetable for the matter to be heard to be stated, and the justification for immediate consideration of the application. In particular, the form required the date and time when it was first appreciated that an immediate application might be necessary and, if there had been any delay, the reasons for that delay. The form also required any efforts to put the secretary of state and any interested party on notice to be set out. H's application did not meet any of those requirements. The application was refused as being totally without merit.

Held: Judgment accordingly. Many such applications were filed towards the end of the working day, often on the day of removal or the evening before. Frequently, the person concerned had known for some time, at least a matter of days, of their removal. Many of the cases were totally without merit, the inference being that such applications were left to the last minute in the hope that it would result in deferral. There were circumstances in which professional misconduct could arise if an application was made with the view to postponing the implementation of a decision where there were no proper grounds for so doing, *Madan v Secretary of State for the Home Department* [2007] EWCA Civ 770, [2007] 1 W.L.R. 2891, [2007] C.L.Y. 56 applied. With regard to future applications, failure to provide the information required on the form, and in particular an explanation of the reasons for urgency, the time at which the need for immediate consideration was first appreciated and the efforts made to notify the secretary of state, would result in the requirement for the attendance in open court of the solicitor from the firm responsible, together with their senior partner. The court would list the name of the case and the firm concerned. Non-compliance could not be allowed to continue. Further consequences of failing to complete the requirements set out in the form could be that, if the form was not completed, or if the reasons were not properly set out, did not explain why there had been delay or were otherwise inadequate, the court might simply refuse to consider the application. That applied equally to the forms soon to be introduced for out of hours applications and for renewals when an application had been refused on the papers. Late, meritless applications by people who faced removal or deportation were an intolerable waste of public money, a great strain on the court's resources and an abuse of a service offered by the court. The most vigorous action would be taken against any legal representatives who failed to comply with the rules. The court would not hesitate to refer persistent failure to follow the procedural requirements to the Solicitors Regulation Authority.

R. (ON THE APPLICATION OF HAMID) v SECRETARY OF STATE FOR THE HOME DEPARTMENT, [2012] EWHC 3070 (Admin), [2013] C.P. Rep. 6, Sir John Thomas (President QBD), QBD (Admin).

1645. Residence–Student support–Eligibility for student grant and requirement for ordinary residence–Whether ordinary residence requiring lawful residence

[Immigration Act 1971 (c.77) s.24(1)(b); Education (Student Support) Regulations 2009 (SI 2009/1555) Sch.1 Pt 2 para.5.]

The claimant (T) applied for judicial review of a decision of the defendant secretary of state that she had not met the ordinary residence qualification for a student grant under the Education (Student Support) Regulations 2009. T had entered the United Kingdom from Nigeria in 2003 and since January 2004 was an overstayer in breach of the Immigration Act 1971 s.24(1)(b). In 2006, she sustained serious brain injury in a domestic accident and her application for discretionary leave was not made until 2007 after she was released from hospital. Discretionary leave to remain was granted in 2009. In 2010, T enrolled on a degree course and applied for a student loan with the student loans company but her status as an overstayer led to cancellation of her student grant payments on the ground that she had not met the ordinary residence requirement of three years. T's appeal was unsuccessful. The secretary of state recovered jurisdiction over the claim and confirmed that it was appropriate to withdraw the grant since unlawful residence could not constitute ordinary residence under the Regulations. The main issue on judicial review was whether ordinary residence for the purpose of the Regulations required residence which was lawful within the meaning of the Act.

Held: Application refused. The fundamental requirement for ordinary residence over a period of three years was to demonstrate an established connection with the UK as a precondition to eligibility for a student grant from public funds. The basis for the conclusion of Lord Scarman in *R. v Barnet LBC, Ex p. Shah* [1983] 2 A.C. 309, [1983] C.L.Y. 1157 that a person should not be able to rely on his own unlawful act to secure an advantage, was not undermined through the passage of time, *Shah* considered. Ordinary residence for the purposes of Sch.1 Pt 2 para.5(1)(c) of the Regulations required lawful residence and would not include residence in breach of the immigration rules. In the instant case, T had remained in the UK illegally as an overstayer only applying for leave to remain in 2007, which was granted in 2009 (see paras 56-58, 67-68 of judgment).

R. (ON THE APPLICATION OF AROGUNDADE) v SECRETARY OF STATE FOR BUSINESS, INNOVATION AND SKILLS, [2012] EWHC 2502 (Admin), [2012] E.L.R. 520, Robin Purchas Q.C., QBD (Admin).

1646. Rights of entry and residence–Family reunification–Third-country family members of EU citizens–Dependency requirement under art.3(2) Directive 2004/38–European Union

[Directive 2004/38 on the right of citizens of the Union and their family members to move and reside freely within the territory of the Member States amending Regulation (EEC) No 1612/68 and repealing Directives 64/221/EEC, 68/360/EEC, 72/194/EEC, 73/148/EEC, 75/34/EEC, 75/35/EEC, 90/364/EEC, 90/365/ Art.2(2), Art.3(2), Art.10.]

The Upper Tribunal (Immigration and Asylum Chamber) asked the European Court of Justice for a preliminary ruling on the interpretation of Directive 2004/38 art.3(2) in relation to third country family members of an EU citizen seeking entry and residence on the basis of dependency. A Bangladeshi national (R) married an Irish national working in the United Kingdom. R's brother, half-brother and nephew (X) obtained EEA family permits, pursuant to art.3(2), in order to acquire the right to reside in the UK as dependants of R and his wife. After their arrival in the UK, X applied for residence cards to confirm their right of residence. Those applications were refused because X had not shown that they had resided with R's wife, the relevant EU citizen, in the same EEA Member State before she came to the UK, or that they continued to be dependent on her or were members of her household in the UK. The ECJ was asked to determine a number of questions on the application of the art.3(2) requirements, the ability of Member States to impose particular conditions as to the nature or duration of dependence, and conditions applicable to the issue of a residence card under art.10 of the Directive.

Held: Preliminary ruling given. (1) Although Member States were under no obligation to accord rights of entry and residence to family members who were dependent on EU citizens, the term "shall facilitate" in art.3(2) did impose a duty on them to confer a certain advantage, compared with applications from third country nationals, on applications submitted by persons who had a relationship of particular dependence with an EU citizen. In order to meet that obligation, Member States had to make it possible for persons envisaged in the first subparagraph of art.3(2) to obtain a decision based on an extensive examination of their personal circumstances, and had to justify any refusal with reasons. The extent of economic or physical dependence and the degree of relationship between the family member and the EU citizen were relevant factors to be taken into account when making that assessment. Member States had to ensure that their legislation contained criteria which were consistent with the normal meaning of the term "facilitate" and of the words relating to dependence used in art.3(2). Even though the wording used in that provision was not sufficiently precise to enable an applicant to rely directly on it in order to invoke criteria to be applied when assessing his application, an applicant for entry or residence was entitled to a judicial review of whether the national legislation remained within the limits of the discretion set by the Directive (see paras 21-25 of judgment).

(2) On reading art.3(2) and art.10(2)(e) together it was clear that the country referred to was, in the case of a third country national who declared that he was a "dependant" of an EU national, the state in which he was resident on the date when he applied to accompany or join the EU citizen. The objective of art.3(2) was to maintain the unity in the former sense by facilitating entry and residence for persons who were not included in the definition set out in art.2(2) but who nevertheless retained close and stable family ties with an EU citizen. It was for the national court to establish whether X were dependent on R's wife in Bangladesh at the time when they applied to join her in the UK (paras 31-32, 34). (3) Although Member States were entitled to impose particular requirements relating to the nature and duration of dependence, those requirements had to be consistent with the normal meaning of the words relating to the dependence referred to in art.3(2)(a) and were not to deprive that provision of its effectiveness (para.40). (4) The question of whether issue of the residence card referred to in art.10 might be conditional on the requirement that the situation of dependence for the purposes of art.3(2)(a) had endured in the host Member State did not fall within the scope of the Directive, since that provision confined itself to listing the documents to be presented in order to obtain such a card and did not settle the issue of a requirement for dependence (paras 42-45).

SECRETARY OF STATE FOR THE HOME DEPARTMENT v RAHMAN (C-83/11) [2013] Q.B. 249, Judge Skouris (President), ECJ (Grand Chamber).

1647. Rights of entry and residence–Qualifying periods–Qualifying residence periods–Effect of imprisonment upon acquisition of right to permanent residence

[Immigration (European Economic Area) Regulations 2006 (SI 2006/1003) reg.15, reg.21(5).]

The appellant Lithuanian national (J) appealed against the respondent secretary of state's decision to deport him to Lithuania. J claimed to have arrived in the United Kingdom in 2004, but had produced no evidence to that effect. He was convicted of driving with excess alcohol in 2007 and received a community order. He was convicted of breaching that order in 2008 and received a curfew for one month. In 2010 he was convicted of conspiracy to handle stolen goods following his participation in a sophisticated car-cloning operation. He was detained on remand for a period prior to conviction, before being released on bail. The secretary of state concluded that J had not acquired permanent rights of residence under the Immigration (European Economic Area) Regulations 2006 reg.15 as he could not demonstrate five years' continuous residence in the UK before his imprisonment, and periods of imprisonment could not count towards the five-year period. She further concluded that even if he could meet the five-year requirement, his deportation was justified on public policy grounds. Her decision was upheld by the First-tier Tribunal.

Held: Appeal dismissed. (1) The First-tier Tribunal had found reliable evidence that J was working from March 2005. He had been remanded in custody nine months before he would have acquired a right of permanent residence by employment or self-employment. He was then on bail for six months before sentencing. Even if that period were added to the period he had already achieved, he would not have acquired five years' residence unless the period on remand counted in his favour. However, the tribunal was bound by *C v Secretary of State for the Home Department* [2010] EWCA Civ 1406, Times, March 11, 2011 to conclude that periods spent in detention did not count towards the accrual of the five years' continuous lawful residence, *C v Secretary of State* followed. Accordingly, J had no right of permanent residence (see paras 54-57 of judgment). (2) The cases cited by the parties drew a distinction between acquisition of the right to reside permanently and the loss of that right. The European Court of Justice suggested that: (a) once a right of permanent residence had accrued, it was not lost by a remand in custody or a short sentence of imprisonment, or a sequence of them, *Nazli v Stadt Nurnberg (C-340/97)* [2000] E.C.R. I-957 and *Dogan v Sicherheitsdirektion fur das*

Bundesland Vorarlberg (C-383/03) [2005] E.C.R. I-6237, [2006] C.L.Y. 1521 considered; (b) time in prison was not to be equated to voluntary unemployment that could lead to the loss of worker status and the loss of continuity of lawful residence for the purpose of acquiring the right of permanent residence, *Orfanopoulos v Land Baden-Wurttemberg (C-482/01)* [2004] E.C.R. I-5257, [2005] C.L.Y. 1456 considered; (c) continuity of residence for 10 years for the purpose of reg.21(4)(e) was not broken by a period of imprisonment, *Land Baden-Wurttemberg v Tsakouridis (C-145/09)* [2013] All E.R. (EC) 183 considered. That could mean that the conclusions of the Asylum and Immigration tribunal in *LG (Italy) v Secretary of State for the Home Department* [2009] UKAIT 24, [2009] Imm. A.R. 691, [2010] C.L.Y. 1775 and of the Upper Tribunal in *Ogunyemi (Imprisonment Breaks Continuity of Residence: Nigeria), Re* [2011] UKUT 164 (IAC) might have to be re-examined, *LG* and *Ogunyemi* doubted (paras 59-60). (3) The tribunal had not erred in concluding that J's continued residence was contrary to public policy within the meaning of reg.21(5) because: (a) J had been convicted of a conspiracy to handle stolen goods, it was not a case of a single offence of handling but an agreement to play a significant part in organised criminality for financial gain over a period of time. Gang-related crime was more serious than single acts of dishonesty; (b) J was not of previous good character: his previous convictions showed evidence of an unwillingness to abide by the laws of the UK; (c) J had denied his guilt and minimised his actions. He showed little or no remorse and lacked insight into the seriousness of his activities (paras 62-63). (4) Even if J had acquired a right of permanent residence, the tribunal was entitled to conclude that his conviction amounted to serious grounds of public policy justifying his removal. The UK Borders Agency Criminal Casework Directorate Instructions did not set out an exhaustive list of which convictions would lead to an assessment of serious grounds of public policy or public security. J's offence, like serious sexual and violent offences, carried a maximum penalty of more than 10 years' imprisonment and was a serious crime (paras 64-67).

JARUSEVICIUS (EEA REG.21: EFFECT OF IMPRISONMENT: LITHUANIA), *Re; sub nom.* JARUSEVICIUS v SECRETARY OF STATE FOR THE HOME DEPARTMENT, [2012] UKUT 120 (IAC), [2012] Imm. A.R. 760, Blake, J. (President), UT (IAC).

1648. Sponsor licences–Ministerial guidance–Licence decisions made under ministerial guidance–Requirement to lay guidance before Parliament

[Immigration Act 1971 (c.77) s.1(4), s.3(2).]

The first appellant further education college (N) appealed against a decision ([2012] EWCA Civ 51, [2012] Imm. A.R. 563, [2012] C.L.Y. 1764) upholding the respondent secretary of state's decision to revoke its Tier 4 sponsor licence. The second appellant college (W) appealed against a decision ([2013] EWHC 31 (Admin)) upholding the secretary of state's decision not to grant it Highly Trusted Sponsor status. The secretary of state's decisions had been made in accordance with her Tier 4 Sponsor Guidance. The Immigration Rules required Tier 4 migrants to be sponsored by an institution with a sponsor licence, but the system for licensing sponsors was wholly governed by the guidance. N and W argued that the guidance contained mandatory requirements for obtaining and retaining a sponsor licence which were "rules" within the Immigration Act 1971 s.1(4) and therefore, under s.3(2), had had to be laid before Parliament; the secretary of state's failure to do so meant she was not entitled to have regard to those requirements in determining the status of sponsors. The intervener Migrants' Rights Network argued that the guidance did not fall within s.3(2), but, on the basis that there was no power to control immigration otherwise than by rules falling within s.3(2), there was no power to operate a system of sponsor licensing at all.

Held: Appeals dismissed. (1) The mandatory criteria in the guidance for the award and retention of a sponsor licence were rules. However, subject to one reservation, they were not rules requiring compliance by the migrant as a condition of his obtaining leave to enter or remain. The guidance was wholly concerned with the position of the sponsor. The criteria for sponsor licensing were not part of the criteria for granting leave to enter or remain which the migrant had to satisfy and which determined the fate of his application, *R. (on the application of Alvi) v Secretary of State for the Home Department* [2012] UKSC 33, [2012] 1 W.L.R. 2208, [2012] C.L.Y. 1755 applied. The reservation arose out of the cross-references to the guidance in the Immigration Rules. Since the guidance was liable to be changed without Parliamentary scrutiny at the discretion of the secretary of state, the Rules could not lawfully incorporate by reference from the guidance anything which constituted a rule that if not satisfied would lead to the migrant being refused leave to enter or remain. The cross-referenced requirements concerned documentation. They required the sponsor to enter on the migrant's electronic file information which the migrant had to produce to obtain the offer of a place on the sponsor's course. The Rules required migrants to produce the same material in support of their applications for leave to enter or remain; accordingly, none of the guidance incorporated by reference in the Rules raised the bar against migrants any higher than the Rules themselves did. Accordingly, the criteria for sponsor licensing in the guidance did not fall within s.1(4) or s.3(2) and did not therefore fall to be laid before Parliament (see paras 24-26 of judgment). (2) Neither *R. (on the application of Abbassi) v Secretary of State for the Home Department* [2012] UKSC 32, [2012] 1 W.L.R. 2192, [2012] C.L.Y. 1735 nor *Alvi* went as far as to say that s.3(2) excluded the possibility of exercising prerogative powers to control immigration in ways not disclosed by the Rules, *Abbassi* and *Alvi* considered. The intervener's submission was therefore unsupported by authority. It was also wrong in principle. The secretary of state's statutory power to administer the immigration control system necessarily extended to a range of ancillary powers not expressly spelt out in the Act, including the vetting of sponsors. Since the secretary of state was entitled to prescribe and lay before Parliament rules for the grant of leave to enter or remain which depended on the migrant having a suitable sponsor, she also had to be entitled to take administrative measures for identifying sponsors who were suitable, even if those measures did not themselves fall within s.3(2). That right was not unlimited: the secretary of state could not adopt measures which were inconsistent with the Act or the Rules; and without specific statutory authority, she could not adopt measures which were coercive or infringed the legal rights of others, or which were irrational or unfair. However, she had not transgressed any of those limitations in the system of approved sponsors (paras 27-29).

R. (ON THE APPLICATION OF NEW LONDON COLLEGE LTD) v SECRETARY OF STATE FOR THE HOME DEPARTMENT; *sub nom.* R. (ON THE APPLICATION OF WEST LONDON VOCATIONAL TRAINING COLLEGE) v SECRETARY OF STATE FOR THE HOME DEPARTMENT, [2013] UKSC 51, [2013] 1 W.L.R. 2358, Lord Hope, J.S.C. (Deputy President), SC.

1649. Sponsored migrants–Third parties–Maintenance without recourse to public funds–Relevance of financial support from third party

The appellant (X) appealed against a decision of the Upper Tribunal upholding a refusal of the respondent entry clearance officer to grant her leave to enter as she did not satisfy the requirement under the Immigration Rules r.317(iva) that she could be maintained adequately without recourse to public funds. X was a citizen of Somalia whose son (M) had settled in the United Kingdom. X applied for entry into the UK, relying on M as her sponsor and, for additional financial support, a third party who was a British citizen and settled in the UK. M stated that X was to live with him and his family. The third-party stated that he was willing to provide financial support to be used to maintain X so that there would be no recourse to public funds. An entry clearance officer refused X's application. On appeal an immigration judge directed herself that the proper test of adequacy was by reference to the income support rates. She considered M's salary, did not accept his evidence that he had a further income from a second job, and found that his income fell short of the income support levels and that there would be a shortfall, even after taking into account the third-party's contribution. That decision was upheld by the Upper Tribunal. X submitted that (1) the judges had been wrong to assess the requirements of r.317(iva) by reference to the cumulative income of the family unit as a whole; (2) alternatively, she could be adequately maintained without recourse to public funds.

Held: Appeal dismissed. (1) The language of r.317(iva) pointed to a global approach in assessing whether an applicant's presence in the UK would result in recourse to additional public funds. In assessing adequacy in relation to other provisions under the Rules, the courts had previously had regard to the joint resources available to the applicant and sponsor; it was not expected that there would be a different approach for r.317(iva), *MK (Somalia) v Secretary of State for the Home Department* [2007] EWCA Civ 1521, [2008] Imm. A.R. 412, [2009] C.L.Y. 2167 and *Mahad (Ethiopia) v Entry Clearance Officer* [2008] EWCA Civ 1082, [2009] Imm. A.R. 254, [2009] C.L.Y. 2166 applied. The practical reality in such cases was that the third-party support would be routed, or accrued, if not directly then indirectly to the sponsor; the reality was that there was one family unit and one family financial pot. Moreover, that overall approach as to the realities fitted better with what was contemplated in r.317(iii) and r.317(iv) relating to financial dependence and accommodation for an applicant. In cases of third-party support proffered to assist an applicant seeking entry, there was no ring-fencing that support in the applicant's favour and separating the third party from the financial position of the family unit as a whole (see paras 33-36 of judgment). (2) X had not raised the adequacy point before the immigration judge, and the Upper Tribunal did not have any primary findings of fact on that point before it. Further, M's case at the hearing before the immigration judge had been that he had two incomes which overtopped the income support level. That evidence had been rejected by the immigration judge who had, rightly, focused on what his actual income was at the relevant date. On the immigration judge's findings, even if the third-party support was included, the family income would still have been below the benchmark level of income support and so not adequate. X could not be adequately maintained without recourse to public funds, *French v Entry Clearance Officer, Kingston* [2011] EWCA Civ 35, [2011] Imm. A.R. 387, [2011] C.L.Y. 1744 followed, KA (Pakistan) v Secretary of State for the Home Department [2006] UKAIT 65, [2007] Imm. A.R. 155 applied (paras 40-41).

ABUBAKAR v ENTRY CLEARANCE OFFICER, SANNA'A, [2012] EWCA Civ 377, [2012] Imm. A.R. 801, Carnwath, L.J., CA (Civ Div).

1650. Third country nationals–Rights of entry and residence–EEA spouse not exercising Treaty rights in UK when divorced from third-country national–Child beginning education after EEA national parent stopped exercising treaty rights–Third-country national parent's entitlement to residence in host state

[Immigration (European Economic Area) Regulations 2006 (SI 2006/1003); Regulation 1612/68 on freedom of movement for workers within the Community Art.12; Regulation 492/2011 on freedom of movement for workers within the Union; Directive 2004/38 on the right of citizens of the Union and their family members to move and reside freely within the territory of the Member States amending Regulation (EEC) No 1612/68 and repealing Directives 64/221/EEC, 68/360/EEC, 72/194/EEC, 73/148/EEC, 75/34/EEC, 75/35/EEC, 90/364/EEC, 90/365/ Art.13; European Convention on Human Rights 1950 Art.8.]

The appellant third-country national (N) appealed against the First-tier Tribunal's dismissal of her appeal against the respondent secretary of state's refusal to grant her a permanent residence card. N's husband (H) obtained German nationality and the couple moved to the United Kingdom. In 2005, N was given a residence card valid until 2009. She was domestically abused by H, and in 2006 he left the marital home. H purported to divorce N in 2007, and in 2009 a decree absolute was issued. N and H had had two children born in the UK in 2005 and 2007 but who were German nationals. N's eldest child was in full-time education. The secretary of state refused N's application for a permanent residence card on the basis that H was not exercising treaty rights in the UK at the date of divorce. The First-tier Tribunal dismissed her appeal against that decision on the same basis, and also dismissed her claim under the European Convention on Human Rights 1950 art.8. The issues were whether (i) N had a retained a right of residence given that at the date of divorce H was not resident in the UK; (ii) N had a Zambrano C-34-/09 [2011] ECR 1-0000 derived right of residence based on the status of her EEA national children, despite them not being nationals of the host member state; (iii) N had a derived right of residence under the new Immigration (European Economic Areas) Regulations 2006 art.15A or under Regulation 1612/68 art.12 based on her eldest child having commenced full-time education; (iv) N's right under art.8 of the Convention had been breached by reason of refusing to grant her a permanent residence card even though her children were EEA nationals.

Held: Appeal allowed. (1) In order for a spouse to retain a right of residence, their former spouse had to be resident in the UK exercising Treaty rights at the time of divorce, *Amos v Secretary of State for the Home Department* [2011] EWCA Civ 552, [2011] 1 W.L.R. 2952, [2011] C.L.Y. 1766 followed. Amos had been applied and followed in later cases and had regarded Regulation 492/2011 art.10 as a faithful transposition of Directive 2004/38 art.13, and the tribunal was not minded to depart from that line of cases, *Samsam v Secretary of State for the Home Department* [2011] UKUT 165 (IAC), [2011] Imm. A.R. 563, [2011] C.L.Y. 1796 and Idezuna (EEA permanent residence) Nigeria [2011] UKUT 00474 (IAC) considered. The structure of art.13 left no room for doubt as to the construction of art.13(2) of the Directive. To qualify for a retained right, that right had to have existed up until the event giving rise to its possible retention. Article 13(2)(a)-(d) did not set out conditions which were in themselves sufficient to give rise to a retained right of residence. Further, art.13(2)(c) was not, as N had suggested, sui generis and could not create a free-standing right of residence outwith the conditions set out in art.13(1) and art.13(2). N's proposed approach to art.13(2) and art.13(1) of the Directive, namely that divorce had to be taken to be de facto and not de jure, was not consistent with the existing Court of Justice jurisprudence or a literal, teleological or contextual approach. A spouse continued to enjoy a right of residence as the spouse of an EEA national notwithstanding that they might be living apart from each other, *Diatta v Land Berlin (C-267/83)* [1985] E.C.R. 567, [1986] C.L.Y. 1411 and OE (EEA retained of residence) Nigeria (Rev 1. [2010] UKAIT 00003 applied (see paras 51-57, 59, 61 of judgment). (2) Nothing said by the Court of Justice in any of the Treaty of the Functioning of the European Union art.20 cases excluded the application of Zambrano principles to third-country nationals if the practical effect of a refusal decision was that the children would have to leave the territory of the Union as a whole, notwithstanding that the children in the instant case were not citizens of the host Member State. The test was whether the adverse decision required the child to leave the territory of the Union. N had no immigration status in Germany nor could she rely in Germany on an EU right of residence, and it was not realistic for N to live in Germany with her children, nor was there a suggestion that they could live with H. Accordingly, N could rely on her children's art.20 right of Union citizenship under the Treaty (para.68). (3) Although N did fulfil the criteria of art.15(3)(c) of the 2006 Regulations as her child had not been in full-time education when her former spouse was exercising his treaty rights, the position was not the same under art.12 of Regulation 1612/68. It was not necessary for the EEA national parent to exercise Treaty rights in the host Member State at a time when their child was in education, Teixeira (European citizenship) [2009] EUECJ C-480/08.O and *GBC Echternach v Minister van Onderwijs en Wetenschappen (389/87)* [1989] E.C.R. 723, [1991] C.L.Y. 3999 applied. The Department of Work of Pensions had also made that concession. Accordingly, N had derived a right of residence based solely on art.12 of Regulation 1612/68 (paras 72-73, 76-78). (4) Although N did not satisfy all of the requirements under the 2006 Regulations, she satisfied all of the relevant material requirements and would have been successful under them. However the new rules were not applicable as N's application was made prior to their implementation. Notwithstanding that, it would not be proportionate for N to face the threat of removal posed by the refusal decision, as N had been lawfully present in the UK for eight years up until her application for permanent residence. Further, she had been self-employed for four years, suffered domestic violence, and her children were Union citizens 5 (paras 79-83, 86-86).

AHMED (AMOS: ZAMBRANO: REG. 15A(3)(C) 2006 EEA REGS), *Re; sub nom.* AHMED v SECRETARY OF STATE FOR THE HOME DEPARTMENT, [2013] UKUT 89 (IAC), [2013] Imm. A.R. 540, Lang, J., UT (IAC).

1651. Travel documents–Entry clearances–Refusal of visa application under Immigration Rules para.320–Whether answers on visa application form honest and sufficient

The appellant Indian citizen (S) appealed against a decision of the respondent entry clearance officer refusing him entry clearance into the United Kingdom as a domestic worker. S had entered the UK in September 2006 on a working holidaymaker visa which expired in August 2008. During that period, his application as a Tier 1 (General) Migrant was refused and his appeal was dismissed in November 2008. He remained in the UK as an overstayer until April 2009 when he returned to India. Whilst flight-side at the airport, he was encountered by immigration officers by chance, who served him with form IS151A. In December 2010, S applied for a domestic worker visa, stating, in answer to question 6.6 on the application form, that he had never been deported, removed or otherwise required to leave any country in the last 10 years, and in answer to question 6.7 that he had made an application to the Home Office previously, at which point he provided the reference number and date of his in-country application. His application was refused under the Immigration Rules para.320(7A) on the basis that he had failed to disclose material facts. On appeal, the immigration judge upheld refusal under para.320(7A), having found that, whilst S had left the UK voluntarily in 2009, he had been served papers indicating that he was an overstayer and was required to leave the UK, to which S should have made some reference in his reply to question 6.6. He also found that question 6.7 required S to provide details and that provision of the Home Office reference number alone was insufficient, since that did not include the fact that his in-country application was unsuccessful and that he had overstayed in the UK. The immigration judge therefore concluded that S's answers had contained false representations and omissions for the purpose of deception. The issue was whether that decision was correct.

Held: Appeal allowed. (1) It was unclear why the immigration judge should have regarded S's answer to question 6.7 as a false representation or omission. S had correctly answered the question and given his Home Office reference number and the application date. The judge had regarded that information as insufficient, because S had not stated that it had been unsuccessful. However, the form only stated that an applicant should "provide details"; it did not say what those details should be and did not require S to indicate whether or not any application had been unsuccessful. The provision of the reference number should have been enough to have enabled the ECO to access the necessary details. Accordingly, insofar as the immigration judge might have found that S's answer to question 6.7 constituted deception, he had erred by applying an excessively harsh test (see para.10 of judgment). (2) The appeal therefore turned upon the answer S gave to question 6.6. It was accepted that he had never been deported or removed from the UK. The issue was whether he had been "otherwise required to leave". All that was known was that S had been served with a Form IS151A at the airport. That form notified a recipient that he was a person liable to be detained; it did not require a person to leave the UK. It was Form IS151B which made such a demand, and there was no evidence that S had been served with that form. As S had been served with Form IS151A only, which did not require him to leave the UK, he had not given a false answer when he had stated that he had not been required to leave any country in the last 10 years. Accordingly the judge had erred in dismissing the appeal and his determination was set aside (paras 13, 15, 20). (3) Although S had breached the UK's immigration laws by overstaying before, his application for entry clearance should not be thwarted by para.320(7B) because he fell within that category of applicant that had left the UK voluntarily over 12 months ago, and not at the Home Secretary's expense (para.21).

SINGH (PARAGRAPH 320 (7A): IS151A FORMS: PROOF: INDIA), *Re; sub nom.* SINGH v ENTRY CLEARANCE OFFICER, NEW DELHI, [2012] UKUT 162 (IAC), [2012] Imm. A.R. 838, Judge Lane, UT (IAC).

1652. **Travel documents–Visas–Guidance on assessing whether applicant genuinely seeking entry as visitor–Meaning of "visitor" under para.41 Immigration Rules–Effect of successive visits to family in United Kingdom**

The appellant (S), a Mauritian citizen, appealed against a refusal to allow her entry clearance as a family visitor into the United Kingdom. S, who was retired, had family in the UK and in Canada. Between November 2001 and October 2010 S made 10 visits to the UK with her last visit, shortly after her husband's death in 2010, lasting substantially longer. Her application for entry as a family visitor was refused in May 2011. On appeal there were statements from S's family which detailed that she intended to continue her regular visits, that the UK was a convenient travel route for Canada and that it was more cost effective to visit her family rather than have them visit her. S claimed that she had no intention to settle in the UK. The immigration judge refused her appeal noting that as she was now a widow she had few family members left in Mauritius, that she was not an "ordinary visitor" and would probably use such visits as a preliminary to settlement in the UK. The issue was whether S should have been granted entry as a visitor under the Immigration Rules para.41.

Held: Appeal allowed. (1) The judge's reasoning was wrong in law; he had not been required to determine the issue of S's future intentions as he had done. In doing so he had apparently accepted that S was a visitor, albeit for a purpose not permitted under the Rules. The sole issue for him had been whether S intended to visit, which necessitated her also establishing that she would leave at the end of the period permitted for a single visit, and not whether she was an "ordinary visitor". There was no evidentiary reason to dismiss S's claims about being a visitor; the death of her husband was a reasonable explanation for her wishing to spend more time with her children (see paras 12-14, 16 of judgment). (2) The following considerations were material to the assessment of whether an applicant was genuinely seeking entry as a visitor under the Immigration Rules: the periods of time spent in the UK and the country of residence; the expressed purpose of the visit and what the applicant had done in the past, intended to do and the length of time that had elapsed since previous visits; and the links retained with the country of residence such as access to accommodation and the presence of other family members. The number of visits a person could make to the UK was not restricted and there was not a specified time lapse that was required between successive visits. The provision of care to a family member whilst on a visit did not take the individual outside the definition of a genuine visitor. The tribunal was required to ascertain the reality of an arrangement between an applicant and a host. That could be approached by considering whether the reality was that the applicant was no more than a visitor to their country of residence because the purpose of return was confined to gaining readmission to the UK. That did not, however, preclude them from remaining in that country for the least amount of time sufficient to maintain the status of a genuine visitor. Family emergencies requiring longer visits than the established pattern should not be regarded as taking up residence without adequate supporting evidence to that effect (para.17).

SAWMYNADEN (FAMILY VISITORS: CONSIDERATIONS: MAURITIUS), *Re; sub nom.* SAWMYNADEN v ENTRY CLEARANCE OFFICER, [2012] UKUT 161 (IAC), [2012] Imm. A.R. 815, Lang, J., UT (IAC).

INDUSTRY

1653. Alcohol–Revenue and Customs–Solvents

THE DENATURED ALCOHOL (AMENDMENT) REGULATIONS 2013, SI 2013/1195; made under the Finance Act 1995 s.5; and the Alcoholic Liquor Duties Act 1979 s.77. In force: July 1, 2013; .

These Regulations amend the Denatured Alcohol Regulations 2005 (SI 2005/1524) to: allow educational establishments to receive (and use) small amounts of industrial denatured alcohol (IDA) and trade-specific denatured alcohol (TSDA) without prior written authorisation from HM Revenue and Customs; allow the supply of free samples of IDA and TSDA without prior written authorisation; and alter the prescribed formulation for completely denatured alcohol.

1654. Buying scrap metal for cash–Scrap metal dealing–Verification

THE SCRAP METAL DEALERS ACT 2013 (PRESCRIBED DOCUMENTS AND INFORMATION FOR VERIFICATION OF NAME AND ADDRESS) REGULATIONS 2013, SI 2013/2276; made under the Scrap Metal Dealers Act 2013 s.11, s.20. In force: October 2, 2013; .

Under the Scrap Metal Dealers Act 2013, a scrap metal dealer must not receive scrap metal from a person without verifying their full name and address by using documents, data or other information from a reliable and independent source. These Regulations prescribe what documents or information is sufficient to do this.

1655. Cosmetics–Product safety–Regulations

THE COSMETIC PRODUCTS ENFORCEMENT REGULATIONS 2013, SI 2013/1478; made under the European Communities Act 1972 s.2, Sch.2 para.1A. In force: July 11, 2013; .

These Regulations provide for the enforcement of Reg.(EC) No.1223/2009 of the European Parliament of the Council of November 20 2009 on cosmetic products. The Regulations include identifying the Secretary of State and the enforcement authority as the competent authorities for the purposes of the EU Cosmetics Regulation.

1656. Defence industry–Export controls

THE EXPORT CONTROL (AMENDMENT) ORDER 2013, SI 2013/428; made under the Export Control Act 2002 s.1, s.2, s.4, s.5, s.7. In force: March 20, 2013; .

This Order implements Directive 2012/47/EU amending Directive 2009/43/EC of the European Parliament and of the Council as regards the list of defence related products.

1657. Scrap Metal Dealers Act 2013 (10)

This Bill amends the law relating to scrap metal dealers.

This Act received Royal Assent on February 28, 2013.

1658. Scrap Metal Dealers Act 2013 (c.10)–Commencement and Transitional Provisions Order

THE SCRAP METAL DEALERS ACT 2013 (COMMENCEMENT AND TRANSITIONAL PROVISIONS) ORDER 2013, SI 2013/SI 2013/1966 (C.83); made under the Scrap Metal Dealers Act 2013 s.20, s.23. Commencement details: bringing into force various provisions of the 2013 Act on September 1, 2013, October 1, 2013 and December 1, 2013.; .

This Order brings into force the Scrap Metal Dealers Act 2013 and the system of registration contained therein, and replaces it with a new system of licensing to be administered by local authorities.

INFORMATION TECHNOLOGY

1659. **Data protection–Damages–Breach of data protection provisions–Compensation for distress**

[Data Protection Act 1998 (c.29) s.13(2); Directive 95/46 on the processing of personal data and on the free movement of such data Art.24.]

The appellant (H) appealed against the dismissal of his claim for substantial damages having obtained default judgment against the respondent (C). H had purchased a television under a credit agreement with C. The credit agreement was discharged by a consent order and it was ordered that C pay H £1000 plus £500 costs. C agreed to delete all data it held on H and by any third party to whom it had released such data. C tried to credit H's bank account with the sum but the account was closed so it paid the money directly to H. The bank refused to return C's payment. C began proceedings against the bank and H. H then discovered that C had forwarded his data to a credit rating agency which, for a four-month period, showed H owed C £1500. H brought a Part 20 counterclaim against C alleging breach of the court order. Judgment in default was entered for H with damages to be assessed. The judge awarded H nominal damages but did not fix the amount. He found that there was not sufficient evidence of damage to reputation or credit to award substantial damages and declined to consider H's claim for distress. H appealed against the dismissal of his claim for substantial damages. H submitted that (1) his nominal damages should be assessed; (2) the remedy of nominal damages was not an effective remedy so that it did not comply with the Directive 95/46; (3) the court should impose a sanction under art.24 of the Directive for infringement; (4) the Court of Appeal should assess an award of damages for distress.

Held: Appeal allowed. (1) Nominal damages were assessed at £1. (2) The violation of the data protection principles and of the Data Protection Act 1998 led to a claim for nominal and other damages so national law had provided an effective remedy. However H's proof fell short in relation to the damage to his reputation and credit. (3) Art.24 was about adoption of legislative measures which the United Kingdom had done by enacting the 1998 Act which contained provisions to implement the Directive. An individual could not directly enforce the provision in private proceedings. It was not the function of the civil court to impose sanctions. (4) There was evidence from H that he had been caused distress by C's non-compliance with the data protection provisions which fell within s.13(2) of the 1998 Act. There had been a wrongful processing of H's data but it had not led to a loss of credit or reputation. There had been no malicious or fraudulent intent by C, it had been a technical error and was a single episode. There was no contemporaneous evidence of injury to his feelings or distress apart from frustration but it was important to mark that frustration at C's non-compliance with some kind of remedy, *Franchet v Commission of the European Communities (T-48/05)* [2008] E.C.R. II-1585 considered. H's compensation for distress was assessed at £750.

HALLIDAY v CREATION CONSUMER FINANCE LTD, [2013] EWCA Civ 333, [2013] 3 C.M.L.R. 4, Arden, L.J., CA (Civ Div).

1660. Data protection principles–Credit reference agencies–Statutory duty to take reasonable steps to ensure accuracy of data–Existence of co-extensive duty of care in tort

[Data Protection Act 1998 (c.29) s.13; Insolvency Rules 1986 (SI 1986/1925).]

The appellant credit reference agency (E) appealed against a decision ([2012] EWHC 2322 (QB), [2012] 4 All E.R. 460, [2012] C.L.Y. 1784) that it had breached the Data Protection Act 1998 in failing to take reasonable steps to ensure the accuracy of its data, and had breached the duty of care in tort which it owed to the respondent (S). Between May 2002 and July 2006, E's credit file relating to S stated that he was subject to a bankruptcy order. However, the bankruptcy order had been rescinded in May 2002. In 2006, S approached a bank and applied for a business account and a loan. The applications were rejected due to "adverse data" on S's credit file. S brought a claim against E for compensation under s.13 of the Act, and sought damages for breach of duty at common law. It was his case that E's breaches of duty caused him to be unable to raise finance for his company, resulting in a loss of forecast profits and his descent into homelessness. The judge held that, by deciding to operate as a credit reference agency (CRA), E had assumed a responsibility to the consumers whose personal data it held, and had to act with reasonable skill and care. He concluded that E's breaches of its statutory duties and the co-extensive duty of care in tort had caused S loss, in that they prevented his company from obtaining a loan in and after mid-2006.

Held: Appeal allowed. (1) The judge's conclusion that S's applications for credit had been refused on the sole ground of the bankruptcy entry on his credit file was unsustainable: the file showed numerous items of adverse data apart from the bankruptcy order. The judge's finding that E's alleged breaches of duty caused S loss was also unsustainable. The consequences which it was claimed arose from the alleged breaches of duty were far too remote to give rise to liability under either the Act or at common law (see paras 34-39 of judgment). (2) Up until 2008, E obtained its data relating to bankruptcy orders from the London Gazette. The Official Receiver was required to advertise all bankruptcy orders in the Gazette. Prior to 1986, annulments and rescissions of bankruptcy orders were also required to be advertised in the Gazette; however, the Insolvency Rules 1986 introduced a change whereby the former bankrupt was given the option of requiring the secretary of state to advertise the annulment or rescission, upon payment of an appropriate fee. CRAs would only learn of a rescinded bankruptcy order if the debtor chose to advertise the rescission or contacted the CRA directly. Upon being notified of an order annulling or rescinding a bankruptcy order, the secretary of state was not under any duty to advertise the fact of the annulment or rescission in the Gazette or anywhere else. The judge had erred in law in holding that courts were subject to an implied obligation to notify the secretary of state when a bankruptcy order had been rescinded (paras 46-51). (3) The judge had effectively concluded that E had breached its duty to take reasonable steps to ensure the accuracy of its data because it failed to attempt to persuade the secretary of state and the Insolvency Service to initiate modifications to the legislative and regulatory framework, and in particular failed to secure the reversal of the legislative choice made in 1986 no longer to require the automatic advertisement of annulments and rescissions. That was not a realistic conclusion. It was not reasonable either to expect CRAs to have identified the alleged "blind spot" in the scheme, or to lobby for a change to the legislative framework. The judge had erred in concluding that E had failed to take reasonable steps to ensure the accuracy of its data (paras 65-71). (4) The judge had erred in concluding that there was a duty of care in tort which was co-extensive with the duties under the Act, *Customs and Excise Commissioners v Barclays Bank Plc* [2006] UKHL 28, [2007] 1 A.C. 181, [2006] C.L.Y. 2880 considered. It would not be fair, just or reasonable to impose such a duty. The judge had erred in concluding that a CRA assumed a responsibility to every member of the public simply by choosing to operate that type of business. Imposing a duty owed to members of the public generally would potentially give rise to an indeterminate liability to an indeterminate class. A co-extensive duty of care in tort would also be otiose, given that the Act provided a detailed code for determining the civil liability of credit reference agencies and other data controllers arising out of the improper processing of data (paras 73-76).

SMEATON v EQUIFAX PLC; *sub nom.* EQUIFAX PLC v SMEATON, [2013] EWCA Civ 108, [2013] 2 All E.R. 959, Tomlinson, L.J., CA (Civ Div).

INSOLVENCY

1661. Administration–Disposition of property–Transactions made after presentation of winding-up petition–Appropriateness of administration order

[Insolvency Act 1986 (c.45) s.127.]

The court was required to determine an application for an administration order in respect of a company (U). The Revenue and Customs had presented a winding-up petition against U. Knowing that U's bank account was about to be frozen, U's director had arranged for an employee's company to receive payment from a customer so that U could continue trading. It was proposed that U's business would be sold to the employee's company.

Held: Application refused. The arrangement for switching U's funds to the employee's company was at best a disposition of U's assets that was potentially void under the Insolvency Act 1986 s.127 if U were wound up. Alternatively, the arrangement could be seen as pre-empting the court's decision. The court had the power to make an administration order as U was, on the evidence, insolvent. Further, there was evidence that the result of an administration would be better than a liquidation. However, as a matter of discretion, an administration order would not be made. It was appropriate to put U into liquidation so that the post-petition transactions could be considered against the background of s.127. Accordingly, a winding-up order was made.

UK STEELFIXERS LTD, *Re*, [2012] EWHC 2409 (Ch), [2012] B.C.C. 751, Judge Purle Q.C., Ch D (Birmingham).

1662. Administration–Expenses–Solicitors applying for fees and disbursements relating to winding-up petition–Whether fees and disbursements expenses of administration, company voluntary arrangement or liquidation

[Insolvency Act 1986 (c.45) Sch.B1 Pt 6 para.40(1)(b), Sch.B1 para.79; Senior Courts Act 1981 (c.54) s.51; Insolvency Rules 1986 (SI 1986/1925) r.1.23(2), r.2.67, r.4.218(3)(h), r.4.218(3).]

The applicant solicitors firm (N) applied for a determination that certain fees and disbursements said to be payable by the insolvent company were an expense of the administration. Alternatively, N applied for determinations that those sums were expenses of the liquidation or of a company voluntary arrangement (CVA). The company had instructed N in connection with a winding-up petition. N ceased to act less than two months later when their instructions were withdrawn. Administrators were appointed with the effect that the winding-up petition was automatically suspended under the Insolvency Act 1986 Sch.B1 Pt 6 para.40(1)(b). The administrators' proposals for a CVA were approved and they acted as the supervisors of the CVA. The administration was subsequently brought to an end on the administrators' application under Sch.B1 para.79. Liquidators were appointed. N sought alleged unpaid fees and disbursements from the company. The issues were whether the fees and disbursements should be determined to be an expense of the (i) administration; (ii) CVA; (iii) liquidation. N submitted that under the Senior Courts Act 1981 s.51, the court could order that the company's costs in relation to the winding-up petition, including its unpaid fees and disbursements, should be paid by the administrators, and that if the court made such an order, the payment of the fees would be "necessary disbursements" within the Insolvency Rules 1986 r.2.67(1)(f) and so would be expenses of the administration.

Held: Application granted in part. (1) The court proceeded on the assumption that it had jurisdiction to consider N's application under s.51 when the company had declined to apply for such an order in its own favour. An order that the company or the administrators should pay the fees would not make any such payment a disbursement within r.2.67(1)(f), and certainly not a disbursement in N's favour. N had not incurred any costs and it was not open to the court under s.51 to order that the company or the administrators pay N's fees. In substance, N were seeking an order that the company's costs in relation to the fees and disbursements be added to the permissible list of administration expenses, but s.51 did not confer power to make such an order. Accordingly, it was not open to the court to hold that it had power to make an order under s.51 which indirectly turned the costs into an administration expense, *Gosscott (Groundworks) Ltd, Re* (1988) 4 B.C.C. 372, [1988] C.L.Y. 296, *Irish Reel Productions Ltd v Capitol Films Ltd* [2010] EWHC 180 (Ch), [2010] Bus. L.R. 854, [2010] C.L.Y. 1838 and *Bickland Ltd, Re* [2012] EWHC 706 (Ch), [2013] Bus. L.R. 361, [2013] 2 C.L. 44 considered. Further, the fees were not to be treated as if they were within r.2.67 under the *Lundy Granite* principle, Lundy Granite Co, Re (1870-71) L.R. 6 Ch. App. 462 applied and *Toshoku Finance UK Plc (In Liquidation), Re* [2002] UKHL 6, [2002] 1 W.L.R. 671, [2002] C.L.Y. 2718 considered (see paras 66, 84, 110 of judgment) (2) Before the CVA, the company was in administration and so r.1.23(2) of the 1986 Rules applied. In view of the court's conclusions on administration expenses, N's fees were not expenses properly incurred and payable under the 1986 Act or Rules. It followed that there was no relevant sum due to the administrators which the supervisors of the CVA were obliged to discharge under r.1.23(2) (para.112). (3) It was appropriate to adopt the same general approach in principle to the costs of a company unsuccessfully applying to strike out a petition as to the costs of a company unsuccessfully opposing a petition, *Bathampton Properties, Re* [1976] 1 W.L.R. 168, [1976] C.L.Y. 272 and *Company (No.004055 of 1991), Ex p. Record Tennis Centres, Re* [1991] 1 W.L.R. 1003, [1992] C.L.Y. 2570 considered. In view of the fact that the administrators did not oppose a determination that the company's costs should be allowed as an expense of the liquidation, and that the liquidators had stated that they did not oppose that result, it was appropriate to allow the company's costs of appearing on the petition, represented by whatever their liability was to pay N's fees for their work in that respect, as an expense pursuant to r.4.218(3)(h) of the 1986 Rules (paras 126, 128).

PORTSMOUTH CITY FOOTBALL CLUB LTD (IN LIQUIDATION), *Re; sub nom.* NEUMANS LLP v ANDRONIKOU, [2012] EWHC 3088 (Ch), [2013] 1 All E.R. 975, Morgan, J., Ch D (Companies Ct).

1663. Administration–Investment banks–Appointment of administrators pursuant to Investment Bank Special Administration Regulations 2011–Whether event of default under repurchase agreement–Act of insolvency

[Investment Bank Special Administration Regulations 2011 (SI 2011/245); Securities Investor Protection Act (United States).]

The applicant administrators of a United Kingdom investment bank (M) sought directions on an issue arising under the terms of a repurchase agreement (GMRA) made between M and the respondent United States company (X). M and X were in the same group of companies. The group had a policy of investing in European sovereign debt. M purchased the securities in the market, and entered into repurchase transactions with X. The repurchase transactions were governed by the GMRA. Paragraph 10 of the GMRA defined "events of default", all but one of which required the occurrence of an event and the service by the non-defaulting party of a default notice on the defaulting party. The only exception was the occurrence of an "act of insolvency" comprising "the presentation of a petition for winding-up or any analogous proceeding or the appointment of a liquidator or analogous officer of the defaulting party". On October 31, 2011, the group's parent company filed for bankruptcy protection under US law. A few hours later, on the application of M's directors, a judge in the instant court appointed the administrators pursuant to the regime for special administration created by the Investment Bank Special Administration Regulations 2011. Later the same day, the US District Court appointed a trustee under the Securities Investor Protection Act (United States) 1970 (SIPA). The issue was whether the appointment of the administrators constituted an immediate and complete event of default under the GMRA, without the need for service of a notice by X declaring it an event of default. X conceded that the appointment of the SIPA trustee was an appointment of an officer "analogous" to a liquidator, so that, unless there was a prior event of default, that appointment constituted an event of default in which M was the non-defaulting party. X submitted that the earlier appointment of the administrators under the Regulations also constituted the appointment of officers analogous to a liquidator, with the result that an event of default occurred at that time, with X as the non-defaulting party. X argued that it would only rarely, if at all, be possible to rescue an investment bank which had gone into special administration, so the appointment of administrators to an investment bank should be treated as analogous to the appointment of a liquidator.

Held: Directions given. (1) The administrators were not officers analogous to a liquidator for the purposes of the GMRA, and their appointment on October 31 did not constitute an event of default under the GMRA (see para.67 of judgment). (2) The essential characteristic of a liquidation and the appointment of a liquidator, which distinguished them from other insolvency proceedings and the appointment of other officers, was that the sole purpose of a liquidation was the realisation of assets and the distribution of assets amongst creditors. Save in limited circumstances and then only for a limited time, the business of the company would cease upon the appointment of a liquidator. An administration and other insolvency proceedings might result in the realisation of a company's assets and a distribution of the proceeds amongst creditors, but the alternative of a rescue of the company as a going concern was at least one of the purposes or objectives of those proceedings (paras 48-52). (3) X's approach would undermine the need for the maximum level of certainty in the definition of "acts of insolvency" and the occurrence of events of default. The consequences of an event of default were profound for both parties, and there must be certainty so far as possible, in the interests of both parties, as to whether an automatic event of default had occurred (paras 54-57).

MF GLOBAL UK LTD (IN ADMINISTRATION), *Re; sub nom.* HEIS v MF GLOBAL INC, [2012] EWHC 3068 (Ch), [2013] 1 W.L.R. 903, David Richards, J., Ch D (Companies Ct).

1664. Administration–Investment banks–Client money trust–Procedure for determining claims to client money and making distributions–Court's inherent jurisdiction in relation to trusts

[Investment Bank Special Administration Regulations 2011 (SI 2011/245).]

The applicant administrators (H) applied for directions as regards the administration of a client money trust and the distribution of its assets. H had been appointed as administrators of a company (M) under the Investment Bank Special Administration Regulations 2011. M was part of a group of companies carrying on business as broker-dealers in financial markets throughout the world. As an investment bank authorised to carry on business by the Financial Services Authority M was required by the relevant rules to hold client money on the terms of a client money trust. However, there were no provisions in the rules setting out a procedure whereby claims to client money could be made and adjudicated or a process whereby client money could be distributed among those entitled to it. H had issued statements to clients reflecting what they believed to be each client's entitlement to share in a distribution of the client money trust, and had also received client money claims from other claimants. Many claims had been agreed but others remained disputed. H had made an interim distribution of client money. They asked the court to sanction a procedure for the making of claims to, and distribution of, client money. The order which H sought provided for distribution to those who had lodged a claim by the last date for making claims specified in the notice of distribution and that any claim which had been rejected was not to be treated as a claim to client money, unless the claimant had applied to the court to vary or reverse the rejection; and neither M nor H would have any liability with respect to that distribution to any client who subsequently established its claim. The order did not purport to vary the beneficial interests of any clients and provided that the exclusion of any claimant from such a distribution was without prejudice to their right to participate in any subsequent distribution from the client money trust, if they duly established their claim.

Held: Application granted. (1) Assuming that the court had jurisdiction to make the order sought, it was in the best interests of the proper administration of the client money trust and in the best interests of the clients that the order should be made and the client money distribution procedure proposed by H adopted. It was highly unlikely that clients with a claim were unaware of the situation. The overriding interest of all clients was to participate in distributions of the client money as soon as that was practicable. The procedures proposed by H gave claimants a full opportunity of lodging and pursuing their claims if they had not already done so. In the circumstances it was reasonable that the onus of pursuing a rejected claim should lie on the claimant (see para.24 of judgment). (2) There was no relevant statutory jurisdiction but the court did have an inherent jurisdiction in relation to trusts, *Schmidt v Rosewood Trust Ltd* [2003] UKPC 26, [2003] 2 A.C. 709, [2003] C.L.Y. 4485, *Finers v Miro* [1991] 1 W.L.R. 35, [1991] C.L.Y. 3379 and *Benjamin, Re* [1902] 1 Ch. 723 considered. The inherent jurisdiction did not enable the court to vary beneficial interests but enabled trust property to be distributed according to the practical probabilities; it protected the trustees but equally it preserved the right of any person who established a beneficial interest to pursue such remedies as might be available to them. That part of the proposed order which would permit H to distribute the client money without providing for those claims which were rejected in whole or in part but in respect of which no appeal to the court was made would not simply be an application of the decision in *Re Benjamin* and subsequent similar cases. But that did not mean that it fell outside the proper scope of the inherent jurisdiction. In context there was no difference in principle between third party claims to trust property and rejected claims to a beneficial interest, *Finers v Miro* considered. The purpose of the client money trust established by the rules was to protect the position of clients and to facilitate the timely return of client money in the event of the failure of the firm. That purpose was not well served by long delays while claims which had been made but not pursued were determined through court proceedings. If persons who had made claims were seriously concerned to pursue them, it would be open to them under H's proposals to lodge an application with the court, in which event full provision would be made for their claims while they were litigated. H's proposals properly balanced both the interests of established clients to a timely return of their money and the interests of persons with serious but unresolved claims to be treated as clients. Accordingly the court made the order sought (paras 25-33).

MF GLOBAL UK LTD (IN SPECIAL ADMINISTRATION), *Re*, [2013] EWHC 1655 (Ch), [2013] 1 W.L.R. 3874, David Richards, J., Ch D (Companies Ct).

1665. Administration–Judicial co-operation–Jurisdiction to grant application for administration order–Interpretation of and approach to application of s.426(4) Insolvency Act 1986

[Insolvency Act 1986 (c.45) s.426.]

The appellant bank (H) appealed against an English court's decision that it had no power to appoint administrators in respect of the respondent Jersey-registered company (T) at the request of the Royal Court of Jersey. T's sole business was to invest in and develop residential properties in England. In 2007 T was granted substantial borrowing by H to fund a particular development, and legal charges over various properties and other securities were granted to H. The development proved a disaster and H demanded repayment of its loan and interest, then totalling in excess of £8 million. The demands were not met. It was considered that liquidation proceedings in England or "desastre" proceedings in Jersey were inappropriate and would not be advantageous to T or its creditors. The parties obtained a letter of request from the Royal Court of Jersey asking the High Court of Justice of England and Wales, pursuant to the Insolvency Act 1986 s.426, to assist it by appointing administrators. The judge found that the court did not have jurisdiction to make the order sought, although he stated that, were it not for the jurisdictional point, the case was an appropriate one for the appointment of administrators; he considered that the decision turned on the meaning and effect of the word "assist" in s.426(4). H submitted that the judge had misunderstood the purpose of s.426(4) and misconstrued its provisions.

Held: Appeal allowed. The judge had erred in his interpretation of s.426(4) and in his approach to its application, both of which were unduly and unnecessarily restrictive. Section 426(4) was not by its actual wording applicable to courts exercising jurisdiction in relation to insolvency law: it was by its wording applicable to courts having jurisdiction in insolvency law. Courts should be astute to equate "having" jurisdiction with "exercising" jurisdiction, in the sense of connoting a requirement for the existence of some formal insolvency proceedings in the requesting state. The words of s.426(4) were amply sufficient, broadly read, to enable the English court to "assist" the Jersey court in the way requested in the instant case. There was neither linguistic necessity nor purposive compulsion to adopt a narrow and restrictive approach. The approach of the judge seemed to require the maintenance of separate formal insolvency procedings in the requesting state, even where such proceedings were not desired, would serve no purpose and would run up needless costs. The instant court did not accept the judge's proposition that the English court was not being asked to assist the Jersey court in an "endeavour": it was demonstrable that the Jersey court was involved in an endeavour, which was to further the interests of T and its creditors and to facilitate the most efficient collection and administration of its assets. In that regard T had itself resolved that it should seek to be placed in administration in England: the Royal Court had itself considered its jurisdiction to issue a letter of request and the desirability, in the interests of the creditors, to do so. Accordingly, the judge did have jurisdiction to grant an application for an administration order (see paras 35-38, 40-42, 45 of judgment).

TAMBROOK JERSEY LTD, *Re; sub nom.* HSBC BANK PLC v TAMBROOK JERSEY LTD, [2013] EWCA Civ 576, [2014] 2 W.L.R. 71, Longmore, L.J., CA (Civ Div).

1666. Administration–Jurisdiction–Failure to secure permission to bring proceedings against company in administration–Court's jurisdiction to grant retrospective permission where company no longer in administration

[Insolvency Act 1986 (c.45) s.130(2), Sch.B1 Pt 6 para.43(6).]

The applicant professional footballer (G) applied for permission to continue proceedings alleging negligence and breach of contract against the respondent insurance broker (O). When G suffered an injury which brought his career to an end, he was insured through O, which provided specialist financial services and insurance advice for professional sportsmen. The risk of G incurring the injury that he had suffered, however, had not been covered by the policy. G initiated proceedings alleging O's negligence and breach of contract. Before proceedings were issued, G's solicitors did a search at Companies House, which failed to reveal that O had, in fact, entered administration. G's advisers subsequently discovered that fact. Correspondence ensued between the parties, and the time for service of G's claim form was extended, without prejudice to O's rights to challenge the claim form and to raise a limitation defence. The claim form was duly served. O did not serve a defence, but issued an application seeking a declaration that the court did not have jurisdiction over the claim, and an order that the claim form, or the service of the claim form, be set aside on the ground that O was in administration prior to its issue so that either the administrator's, or the court's, permission was required under the Insolvency Act 1986 Sch.B1 Pt 6 para.43(6) and that G had failed to seek that permission. Those proceedings were due to be heard at a future date.

G issued an application seeking the court's retrospective permission under para.43(6) to continue the substantive proceedings against O as a company in administration. Unknown to G and prior to the hearing of that application, O entered into creditors' voluntary liquidation. G then issued an application to proceed with the original proceedings under s.130(2) of the Act. O submitted that (1) the proceedings were a nullity as G had failed to obtain the required permission prior to service of the claim form as required by para.43(6); (2) alternatively, the court's jurisdiction to give permission was exhausted once administration had come to an end as para.43(6) only applied to companies that were in administration; (3) alternatively, the court should refuse relief on the basis of G's delay in taking action to rectify the lack of permission in bringing the substantive proceedings.

Held: Judgment accordingly. (1) Although no permission had been sought to commence proceedings, that did not mean that the proceedings were necessarily a nullity, as the proceedings were existing and capable of redemption by the late giving of leave, *Saunders (A Bankrupt), Re* [1997] Ch. 60, [1996] C.L.Y. 3444 and *Carr v British International Helicopters Ltd* [1993] B.C.C. 855, [1994] C.L.Y. 2019 applied. Although *Saunders* was not a case about administration, it applied not just to bankruptcy proceedings but to insolvency proceedings generally; there was no meaningful distinction between the bankruptcy requirement of leave to "commence" proceedings and the administration requirement of permission to "institute" them. Additionally, there was no question that if proceedings were commenced before the start of administration those proceedings were valid. Although it was possible for the court to give retrospective permission for the continuation of the proceedings, that was unnecessary in the instant case. The proceedings had not been a nullity when they were commenced and had had an existence which was suspended during O's administration. Once O's administration had been replaced by a creditors' voluntary liquidation, a regime under which there was no bar to bringing an action against O, the previous procedural inhibition came to an end and there was nothing to prevent the continuation of G's substantive proceedings (see paras 12, 16, 19-20 of judgment). (2) There was no time limit under para.43(1), which also set out the ambit of the court's power. Additionally, para.43(6) did not give guidance on whether permission ought to be granted. Accordingly, although it would be rare to give permission once administration had ended, the court possessed the jurisdiction to grant permission in an appropriate case. In the instant case, if the court was wrong on its primary conclusion, it should exercise its jurisdiction to grant retrospective permission to G (paras 21-22). (3) G's delay was explicable by a misunderstanding regarding what was required in the relevant area of law and could not be blamed for having issued the claim form in ignorance of O's administration. There was no evidence that O had suffered any prejudice. Although it had not been referred to in the evidence, the fact that other creditors might suffer could be dealt with by O's liquidators, and any serious concerns held could be addressed by an application for a stay of G's action. However, that was insufficient to prevent C's claim progressing (paras 22-23). (4) G's application to proceed with the proceedings under s.130(2) was misplaced; the provision did not apply to a voluntary winding up (para.9).

GAARDSOE v OPTIMAL WEALTH MANAGEMENT LTD (IN LIQUIDATION), [2012] EWHC 3266 (Ch), [2013] Ch. 298, John Martin Q.C., Ch D.

1667. Administration–Loans–Bank applying for administration order in respect of company–Whether bank creditor

[Insolvency Act 1986 (c.45) Sch.B1 Pt 3 para.14, Pt 5 para.35(2)(b), Pt 5 para.35.]

The applicant bank (G) applied under the Insolvency Act 1986 Sch.B1 Pt 5 para.35 as the holder of a floating charge for an administration order in respect of the respondent company (J). G had granted J a facility in exchange for J providing security in the form of a debenture over its assets. G had subsequently granted various additional facilities by way of supplementary facility letters. G's general conditions provided that repayments would be made without set-off or counterclaim. Disputes arose over the basis on which G had originally agreed to make the facilities available: J asserted that G had reassured it that it would be able to provide the facilities on a "risk funding basis", whereas G denied that it had ever made such representations. J subsequently entered into a company voluntary arrangement (CVA). G made a formal demand for repayment when J had not repaid the facilities upon the expiry of their terms. G subsequently applied to the court under Sch.B1 Pt 5 para.35 for administrators to be appointed. Under Sch.B1 Pt 5 para.35(2)(b), the court could make an administration order under Sch.B1 Pt 5 para.35 only if it was satisfied that G, as the applicant, could appoint an administrator under Sch.B1 Pt 3 para.14. J argued that (1) G could not make an appointment under Sch.B1 Pt 3 para.14 because it was not a current creditor of J: it argued that G had released its debt by way of a supplementary facility letter in exchange for a contingent liability, or alternatively that the relevant facility letter should be rectified so as to have that effect; (2) its indebtedness to G was discharged by the CVA; (3) G's application should be refused because it had substantial cross-claims against G for negligent misrepresentation and breach of contract and it should be allowed to litigate them.

Held: Application granted. (1) There was nothing in the letter to release the debt owed to G; on the contrary, it was plain from the letter, which included provisions to extend the terms of the loans and repayment, that the debt was maintained. There was nothing to convert the loans into a contingent liability and there was no full and final settlement of the debt. As to rectification, there was no evidence that G had formed the requisite intention that the debt was to be released in order to show that the letter should be rectified. It followed that J's primary case that G was not a creditor failed (see paras 29-31 of judgment). (2) J's indebtedness to G was not discharged by the CVA and it could not have been given the statutory limitation inherent in a CVA in relation to secured creditors (para.32). (3) J's claim based on negligent misrepresentation was extremely weak: the basis upon which it was alleged that G owed J a duty of care was unclear, and evidence of the misrepresentations was lacking. It was unclear why the alleged misrepresentations were negligent, and there was no explanation as to how such misrepresentations caused the loss alleged. Further, J had failed to establish any breach of contract by G. Even if J's claims of negligent misrepresentation and breach of contract had been stronger, the no-set off clause meant that they would not prevent G from being a creditor who was entitled to appoint an administrator under Sch.B1 Pt 3 para.14: J was precluded from bringing its cross-claims as a set-off against the debts due to G so as to enable it to claim that G was not entitled to appoint an administrator under Sch.B1 Pt 3 para.14, *Deutsche Investitions und Entwicklungsgesellschaft mbH (DEG) v Koshy* [2000] B.C.C. 1127, [2000] C.L.Y. 3956 applied (paras 35-37). (4) Accordingly, G could appoint an administrator under Sch.B1 Pt 3 para.14 and the precondition under Sch.B1 Pt 5 para.35 was satisfied. The court decided it was appropriate to exercise its discretion to grant the administration order sought (paras 38-41).

ST JOHN SPENCER ESTATES AND DEVELOPMENT LTD, *Re; sub nom.* AIB GROUP (UK) PLC v ST JOHN SPENCER ESTATES AND DEVELOPMENT LTD, [2012] EWHC 2317 (Ch), [2013] 1 B.C.L.C. 718, Robert Ham Q.C., Ch D (Companies Ct).

1668. Administration–Notices–Creditors' voluntary liquidation–Whether filing conversion notice converted administration into creditors' voluntary liquidation–Necessity for registration of conversion notice by registrar

[Insolvency Act 1986 (c.45) Sch.B1 para.76(1), Sch.B1 para.83.]

The appellant registrar appealed against a decision of a judge that conversion of a company from administration into a creditors' voluntary liquidation (CVL) took effect on the date of filing a notice of conversion. A company had been placed in administration from December 17, 2009. No extension to the administration had been sought and it was therefore due to end on December 16, 2010. On December 13, 2010, the company's administrators, the respondents, signed a conversion notice in the form prescribed for by the Insolvency Act 1986 Sch.B1 para.83, which was received by the registrar on December 14, 2010. The registration of a notice in the prescribed form under para.83 provided that a company could be moved directly from administration to a CVL. The notice required the proposed liquidators' names and addresses to be inserted but only their names had been included, and the Registrar rejected the notice as incomplete. The rejection letter was received on December 29, 2010. An amended notice was mistakenly also rejected by the registrar. A third notice was registered on February 4, 2011, and the records purported to show that the company's administration had ended and CVL had commenced on that date. The judge, applying a purposive interpretation of para.83, held that the date of commencement of the CVL was December 14, 2010. The registrar submitted that on both an ordinary and purposive interpretation of para.83, a conversion notice did not take effect until a registrar had registered it. The respondents contended that para.83 should be construed as extending an administrator s term of office, where he had served a conversion notice, until the conversion date.

Held: Appeal allowed. (1) A conversion notice took effect when it was registered by the registrar, which was the natural meaning of para.83(4). Second, "register" had to bear the same meaning in para.83(4) as in para.83(6). Third, para.83 should be interpreted with a view to achieving its statutory objectives where the wording permitted it, which included achieving a streamlined conversion from administration to a CVL. Fourth, the ordinary interpretation of para.83(4) avoided a gap between a liquidator's appointment and publication of that appointment on a company's file. Fifth, the date of registration would almost certainly always be subsequent to the date of receipt and that underscored the need to interpret para.83 in a way that treated those dates differently. Sixth, prior to the registration of a conversion notice, a registrar would check the information in some way, and the court should prefer an interpretation that allowed that checking to happen prior to conversion. Seventh, registration normally only took around three days and there was no practical difficulty which warranted giving the words in para.83(6) a different meaning from their natural meaning. Registration of the third notice was not a valid conversion of the first notice as the administrator's term of office had been terminated by the date it was filed and executed. However, since the registrar had a statutory obligation to register the valid first conversion notice, the court should, in order to give effect to Parliament's intention, treat his registration of the third notice as amounting to effective registration of the first notice. Accordingly, registration occurred on February 4, 2011 (see paras 41-52 of judgment). (2) An administrator's term of office was by implication from the words in para.83(6) extended by filing a conversion notice from the date on which it would otherwise expire by effluxion of time until para.83(6) came into effect upon registration of the conversion notice. Like para.76(1), that automatic extension was subject to paras 87 to 89. Thus, the term of office would end if an administrator resigned, died, was removed from office by court or ceased to be qualified before the conversion date occurred (paras 58-64).

GLOBESPAN AIRWAYS LTD (IN LIQUIDATION), *Re; sub nom.* CARTWRIGHT v REGISTRAR OF COMPANIES, [2012] EWCA Civ 1159, [2013] 1 W.L.R. 1122, Lord Neuberger (M.R.), CA (Civ Div).

1669. Administration–Occupational pensions–Event triggering application of s.75 Pensions Act 1995–Reduction in proof of debt owing to principle of "double dipping"–Status of deposit in trust fund

[Pensions Act 1995 (c.26) s.75; Insolvency Rules 1986 (SI 1986/1925) r.2.78; Occupational Pension Schemes (Employer Debt) Regulations 2005 (SI 2005/678).]

The applicant pension scheme trustee (B) applied under the Insolvency Rules 1986 r.2.78 to reverse a decision of the administrators of the respondent company (K) to reduce B's proof of debt by £2 million. K had traded as a bank and was the sponsoring employer of the occupational pension scheme of which B was trustee. The scheme held a bank account with K. In October 2008, K was in financial difficulties. Upon instructions from the Financial Services Authority, it opened a trust account in October 2008 and credited it with amounts specified by the FSA. On the same day, the scheme paid £2 million into its account with K, which was credited to the trust account. A week later, K went into administration. The scheme had a funding deficit as at that date, which was quantified by B as being the debt owed to the scheme by K under the Pensions Act 1995 s.75. That quantification process did not complete until July 2012, when the s.75 debt was assessed at almost £75 million. No value was attributed to the £2 million deposited by the scheme with K in October 2008 because B was unsure whether it could be recovered from the scheme's bank account, the court having held in July 2009 that the money in the trust account was held on trust for certain specified beneficiaries. In August 2012, K's administrators informed B that the £2 million reduction in its proof of debt was appropriate because the accounts used to calculate the s.75 valuation report did not acknowledge the £2 million held in the trust account, and that the rule against "double dipping" prevented recovery of what was, in substance, the same claim against two estates. The administrators also relied on the principle of unjust enrichment.

Held: Application granted. There were two insurmountable problems for the administrators in the stance they had taken: first, they did not challenge the certified amount of the s.75 debt, nor did they challenge the nil value attributed to the £2 million deposit into the trust account. Therefore, they accepted that, as at the date of the valuation, the £2 million deposit into the trust account had no value because of the uncertainty about recovery. The Occupational Pension Schemes (Employer Debt) Regulations 2005 required assets and liabilities of a pension scheme to be valued, for the purposes of ascertaining the s.75 debt, in a notional exercise immediately before the trigger event which, in the instant case, was K going into administration in October 2008. Changes in the value of assets after that time were irrelevant. Just as the value of the £2 million deposit increased after K went into administration, as the rights of the beneficiaries entitled to make a claim on the trust fund were clarified, so too did the scheme's "buy out" liabilities, in other words, the notional cost of going into the market to purchase the annuities which would match the scheme's liabilities to its pensioners and members. There were no grounds for reviewing the nil value placed in the audited accounts on the £2 million deposit because no challenge had been made to it (see paras 33-36 of judgment). The second insurmountable problem for the administrators was that the £2 million held in the trust account for the scheme had been held on a bare trust for B since the date of the deposit. It had always been B's property. Therefore, the relationship between B and K in relation to that deposit had been one of trustee and beneficial owner; it had never been one of creditor and debtor. The money could not, therefore, be used to discharge any part of the s.75 debt because it had never been part of that debt, neither in form nor substance. For the same reasons, the rule limiting double dipping had no relevance (paras 37-39). (2) The claim in unjust enrichment for over-recovery failed on many counts. There had not been an over-recovery by B, nor would there be one. Even if the £2 million was taken into account, there would still be a substantial shortfall (para.40).

BESTRUSTEES PLC v KAUPTHING SINGER & FRIEDLANDER (IN ADMINISTRATION); *sub nom.* KAUPTHING SINGER & FRIEDLANDER (IN ADMINISTRATION), *Re,* [2013] EWHC 2407 (Ch), [2013] Pens. L.R. 339, Sir Terence Etherton (Chancellor), Ch D (Companies Ct).

1670. Administration–Permission to issue legal proceedings against company in administration–Whether court having jurisdiction to grant retrospective permission

[Criminal Justice Act 2003 (c.44) s.329; Insolvency Act 1986 (c.45) s.130(2), s.285(3), Sch.B1 Pt 6 para.43(6); Mental Health Act 1983 (c.20) s.139(2).]

The applicants (B) applied under the Insolvency Act 1986 Sch.B1 Pt 6 para.43(6) for retrospective permission to institute legal proceedings against the first respondent, a company in administration (C). C was a firm of property valuation surveyors. In 2006 it had, upon B's instructions, valued care homes let to and operated by a group of companies (S). B had lent money to S on the strength of those valuations. In 2011, companies in the S group went into administration. Valuations obtained by B indicated much reduced values for the care homes, and they started to investigate whether C had been negligent in its valuations. C went into administration in March 2012. In May, B notified C's administrators of its potential claims and entered into a series of standstill agreements to prevent time running. Upon the expiry of the last of those agreements in September 2012, B issued claims in negligence against C and made the instant application, which was not opposed by C's administrators. The issue was whether the court had jurisdiction under Sch.B1 para.43(6) to grant retrospective permission to issue proceedings.

Held: Application granted. Jurisdiction had been considered in a number of authorities, and two contrasting views had emerged. On the one hand, there was a practice, endorsed in *Saunders (A Bankrupt), Re* [1997] Ch. 60, [1996] C.L.Y. 3444, of not treating proceedings commenced without permission as a nullity, but of giving leave for their continuation where appropriate. On the other hand, *Wilson v Banner Scaffolding Ltd* Times, June 22, 1982, [1982] C.L.Y. 1853 held that proceedings commenced against a company in compulsory liquidation without prior permission were a nullity and could not be continued. That decision relied on the "absolute and unqualified" nature of the legislative requirement that permission should be obtained before the issue of proceedings. Similarly, in *Davenham Trust Plc v CV Distribution (UK) Ltd* [2006] EWHC 3029 (Ch), [2007] Ch. 150, [2007] C.L.Y. 374, the High Court relied on the unqualified language of the legislative requirement for prior permission and concluded that *Saunders* had been wrongly decided. *Saunders* was, however, preferred in a series of subsequent decisions (see paras 9-13 of judgment). Although a statutory requirement for prior permission appeared in a number of different contexts, none of the relevant provisions indicated whether a failure to obtain such permission could be cured retrospectively. In *Seal v Chief Constable of South Wales* [2007] UKHL 31, [2007] 1 W.L.R. 1910, [2007] C.L.Y. 2908, the House of Lords concluded that proceedings brought without the permission required by the Mental Health Act 1983 s.139(2) were a nullity. However, that decision was based on factors peculiar to the mental health legislation and did not suggest that *Saunders* had been wrongly decided, quite the reverse (paras 14-19). The general approach to provisions requiring prior permission was restated in *Adorian v Commissioner of Police of the Metropolis* [2009] EWCA Civ 18, [2009] 1 W.L.R. 1859, [2009] C.L.Y. 436, which concerned the Criminal Justice Act 2003 s.329. There, the Court of Appeal identified a number of reasons why a failure to obtain prior permission under s.329 did not involve the "drastic step" of nullifying proceedings. Although the court was not referred to *Davenham Trust*, it clearly considered that *Saunders* had been correctly decided. The approach it took and the factors on which it relied were equally applicable to the 1986 Act and were strongly supportive of the decision in *Saunders*. Equally, there were no special factors applicable to the 1986 Act that were analogous to those identified in *Seal* as applying to the mental health legislation. Following *Seal* and *Adorian*, the "absolute and unqualified" language of a legislative requirement for prior permission was an insufficient basis for concluding that proceedings begun without such permission were a nullity. Those decisions required the court to look beyond the language of the requirement and to consider its context, purpose, and any consequences of a decision as to its effect, with a general pre-disposition that the lack of prior permission should not render the proceedings a nullity. There was little to support a conclusion that proceedings brought without the permission required by the 1986 Act were a nullity, and much to support the contrary conclusion. The relevant considerations were precisely those relied on in *Adorian* and *Saunders*. In an insolvency context the purpose of the requirement for prior permission was to ensure that when a winding-up order had been made by the court, any proceedings having any bearing on the winding up remained under that court's supervision and control. Given that purpose, it was hard to see why the court should not be permitted to grant retrospective permission, where appropriate. Furthermore, there was no convincing reason why an administrator should not be permitted to grant retrospective consent. *Saunders* had been correctly decided and retrospective permission could be given for the commencement of proceedings, whether under s.130(2), s.285(3) or Sch.B1 para.43(6) of the 1986 Act, *Saunders* and *Adorian* applied, *Seal* considered, and *Wilson* and *Davenham Trust* not followed. Jurisdiction having been established, the instant case was clearly one in which permission should be granted (paras 8, 20-24, 30-35).

BANK OF IRELAND v COLLIERS INTERNATIONAL UK PLC (IN ADMINISTRATION); *sub nom.* COLLIERS INTERNATIONAL UK PLC (IN ADMINISTRATION), *Re*, [2012] EWHC 2942 (Ch), [2013] Ch. 422, David Richards, J., Ch D (Companies Ct).

1671. Administration orders–Sufficiency of evidence–Deficiencies in applicants' evidence–Whether compulsory winding-up more appropriate

[Insolvency Act 1986 (c.45) Sch.B1 Pt 2 para.13.]

The applicant directors of a travel company (B) sought an administration order in respect of the company. The application was made on the basis that it was urgent. Such urgency was said to have been caused by, among other things, the recent presentation by a major creditor (T) of a winding-up petition and the freezing of B's bank account.

Held: Compulsory winding-up order made. When the court was asked to exercise its powers under the Insolvency Act 1986 Sch.B1 Pt 2 para.13 by making an administration order, it was essential that the evidence presented to the court was reliable. Implicit in the noun "reliable" in this context was not only that it was accurate evidence and true insofar as it was factual but also that (i) a clear account was given of all potentially relevant facts and circumstances (ii) where explanations were given or judgments, estimates or opinions stated, they should be supported by the underlying material, and not contradicted by it; they should also be credible in the sense of being realistically likely to be true. Such a requirement should be neither onerous nor unreasonable. It required no more than that an applicant, who, as a director, should know what had been going on at the company, told the court the informed truth and did not attempt to mislead, including by omission. Here, the evidence appeared to be contradicted by underlying documents in material respects. Where, as also occurred in this case, important matters were not addressed in the evidence, one likely consequence would be a want of confidence in the evidence; that, in turn, was likely to cast a shadow over reliance on the applicants' witness evidence as the basis for determining the outcome of the application. By way of example, a sudden and catastrophic decline in intra-group indebtedness had not been explained or even addressed in the applicants' evidence. Further, T had expressed concern over recent transactions which were said to involve land and vehicles being transferred, in part by B, at suspected undervalues to or for the benefit of one of B's directors. The appropriate course was to make a compulsory winding-up order. For years, B's solvency had been propped up by the existence of intra-group debtors which did not appear to have been subjected to anything approaching adequate scrutiny by those responsible for the accounts. Liquidation was inevitable, and this was a case in which the sooner the voice of the creditors was heard the better. A particular advantage of a compulsory winding-up was that the Official Receiver had a statutory duty to investigate B's failure and its business, dealings and affairs; he could make such report to the court as he thought fit. In an appropriate case, an investigation might provide a very important service to the creditors, and a report to the court might benefit the creditors and the wider public interest; this was such a case (see paras 14, 19, 21-22, 31, 37, 39 of judgment).

BOWEN TRAVEL LTD, *Re*, [2012] EWHC 3405 (Ch), [2013] B.C.C. 182, Judge Simon Barker Q.C., Ch D (Birmingham).

1672. **Administrators–Appointments–Appointment of administrators more than 10 business days after filing notice of intention to appoint–Whether appointment automatically invalid**

[Insolvency Act 1986 (c.45) Sch.B1 Pt 4 para.22(2), Pt 4 para.28(2); Insolvency Rules 1986 (SI 1986/1925) r.7.55.]

The court was required to determine whether the appointment of administrators in respect of the applicant company (E) was valid. E's directors had decided to appoint administrators and gave the holders of qualifying floating charges written notice of their intention to appoint in accordance with the Insolvency Act 1986 Sch.B1 Pt 4 para.22(2), which required giving at least five business days' notice. E's directors filed a copy of the notice of intention to appoint with the court, and 11 business days later they filed a notice of appointment of two administrators. The Insolvency Act 1986 Sch.B1 Pt 4 para.28(2) provided that directors may not appoint administrators more than 10 business days after filing the notice of intention to appoint. The issue was whether an appointment of administrators in breach of the 10-day expiry period provided in Sch.B1 Pt 4 para.28(2) had no legal effect because it was a nullity, or whether it had some conditional effect because it was defective or irregular and that irregularity could be regarded as curable.

Held: Judgment accordingly. The correct approach was to focus on the consequences of non-compliance with the 10-day expiry period and, taking into account those consequences, consider whether Parliament intended the outcome of non-compliance to be that the appointment was totally invalid, *Hill v Stokes Plc* [2010] EWHC 3726 (Ch), [2011] B.C.C. 473, [2011] C.L.Y. 1826 and *Assured Logistics Solutions Ltd, Re* [2011] EWHC 3029 (Ch), [2012] B.C.C. 541, [2012] C.L.Y. 1800 applied. If a company or its directors noticed the 10-day expiry period and had not made an appointment within that timeframe, they could immediately serve a fresh notice of intention to appoint and thereby open a new 10-day window. If, as in E's case, a company or its directors did not notice the expiry of the 10-day period and had made an appointment outside that timeframe, the consequence was that the administration commenced five business days earlier than it would have done had the expiry been noticed and a fresh notice of intention given, because the appointers had overlooked giving the qualifying chargeholders fresh notice of intention with its minimum notice period of five business days. Parliament could not have intended that an inadvertent appointment outside the 10-day window incurably invalidated the appointment. The instant court was disinclined to treat non-compliance as leading to nullity as, on a fair reading of the language of para.28(2) and following the approach set out in *R. v Soneji (Kamlesh Kumar)* [2005] UKHL 49, [2006] 1 A.C. 340, [2005] C.L.Y. 842, it could be treated as an irregularity, *Soneji* followed. Considerable weight had to be given to the fact that the object of out-of-court appointments was to streamline the process of business rescue, and so it was highly undesirable to have a multiplicity of circumstances in which the appointment of an administrator could be automatically invalidated, *Virtualpurple Professional Services Ltd, Re* [2011] EWHC 3487 (Ch), [2012] B.C.C. 254, [2012] C.L.Y. 1809 applied. Further, the structure of Sch.B1 suggested that non-compliance with para.28(2) should be treated as an irregularity rather than a nullity. The fact that the non-compliance related to a time limit did not compel the conclusion that the defect was fundamental and the purported act a nullity. Accordingly, the appointment was irregular and not a nullity, which meant that the Insolvency Rules 1986 r.7.55 was engaged. The court made a declaration that the administrators were in office, that they would remain so and that no prior act of theirs in the administration was invalidated by reason of the defect in their appointment (see paras 17, 22-26, 28-29, 32-33, 42 of judgment).

EUROMASTER LTD, *Re*; *sub nom.* DANTE v EUROMASTER LTD, [2012] EWHC 2356 (Ch), [2013] Bus. L.R. 466, Norris, J., Ch D.

1673. Administrators–Appointments–Creditors proposing administrators–Rival candidates–Value of creditors' debts as deciding factor in determining appointment of administrators

The applicant creditor (H) applied for an administration order in respect of an insolvent company of which it was creditor, and the court was also required to determine whether to appoint the administrators nominated by H or by another creditor (J). H and J had been the creditors of an insolvent company. Both proposed nominees to be appointed as administrators of the company, to which the other took exception. J submitted that, all else being equal, its nominees should be selected as it was the creditor with the larger value of debt.

Held: Application granted. (1) The court was satisfied that the company was unable to pay its debts and an administration order was reasonably likely to achieve the purpose of administration. There was no reason not to make the order sought (see paras 4-5 of judgment). (2) There was nothing to choose between the rival candidates. They were persons of competence, experience and integrity who would perform the office of administrator in an entirely satisfactory way. However, there appeared to be a principle identified in the authorities that where there was a difference of view between creditors, the views of the majority were to be given greater weight. If there was nothing else to put against that weight, then that was the weight which would prevail, *Stanley International Betting Ltd v Stanleybet UK Investments Ltd* [2011] EWHC 1732 (Ch), [2011] B.C.C. 691, [2012] C.L.Y. 1801 and *Fielding v Seery* [2004] B.C.C. 315, [2004] C.L.Y. 2176 applied. However, the instant decision should not be regarded as a kind of encouragement to dispute the choice of the nominated person put forward by the applicant for an administration order. In other cases, the views of the majority creditor might not prevail, as there might be something to put alongside and perhaps counter-balance the weight to be given to their views. In the instant case there was no point that could be given particular weight. In those circumstances, since the parties had failed to agree, the relative value of the debts owed to the creditors would be used as a tie-breaker. On the balance of probabilities, J was owed a greater debt than H, and therefore J's proposed nominees were appointed as administrators (paras 8, 16, 28-29).

HEALTHCARE MANAGEMENT SERVICES LTD v CAREMARK PROPERTIES LTD, [2012] EWHC 1693 (Ch), [2013] B.C.C. 484, Morgan, J., Ch D (Companies Ct).

1674. Administrators–Appointments–Qualifying chargeholder appointing administrator–Defects in appointment process–Whether appointment rendered nullity

[Insolvency Act 1986 (c.45) Sch.B1 Pt 3 para.14(1), Pt 3 para.15, Pt 3 para.16; Insolvency Rules 1986 (SI 1986/1925) r.7.55.]

The court was required to determine whether an individual had been validly appointed as administrator of a company. One of the company's creditors, a qualifying chargeholder, had made a written demand requiring repayment by the company within two days. The next day it exercised its power under the Insolvency Act 1986 Sch.B1 Pt 3 para.14(1) to file a notice of appointment. The company argued that certain formal defects and irregularities, including that it was not given the full two-day period required under Sch.B1 Pt 3 para.15 to deal with the demand, were incurable and meant that the administrator's appointment was a nullity.

Held: Judgment accordingly. Even if the court ignored the reference in the demand to two days, at least enough time had to elapse to allow for the demand to be met, assuming that the company could meet it. That had not happened in the instant case. The probability, therefore, was that the appointment was not properly made and was irregular. However, despite that defect, it was impossible to ignore the fact that the company was not in a position to meet the demand, within two days or at all. In those circumstances, what had occurred at worst was a premature appointment. That premature appointment was properly characterised as a defective exercise of an undoubted power of appointment, which was procedural in nature but not fundamental to the existence of the power. The requirement under Sch.B1 Pt 3 para.16 of the Act that an administrator could not be appointed while a floating charge on which the appointment relied was not enforceable was not of such fundamental importance as to render the appointment a nullity, *Euromaster Ltd, Re* [2012] EWHC 2356 (Ch), [2013] Bus. L.R. 466, [2013] 4 C.L. 180 applied. However, it was undoubtedly a factor for the court to have in mind when deciding whether to set aside the appointment, as was the consideration of whether there had been substantial irremediable injustice to the company under the Insolvency Rules 1986 r.7.55. Since an appointment would have followed at most two days later in any event, the prejudice to the company was very limited and there was no substantial injustice. There was, however, room for real prejudice to creditors if an undoubtedly insolvent company was taken out of administration. Accordingly, as the company had suffered no substantial injustice, the appointment was declared valid, notwithstanding the defect (see paras 13-16 of judgment).

CARE PEOPLE LTD (IN ADMINISTRATION), *Re*, [2013] EWHC 1734 (Ch), [2013] B.C.C. 466, Judge Purle Q.C., Ch D (Birmingham).

1675. Administrators–Appointments–Validity of appointment by floating charge holder–Importance of notice requirement in Sch.B1 Pt 3 para.15 Insolvency Act 1986–Comparison with s.362A Financial Services and Markets Act 2000

[Financial Services and Markets Act 2000 (c.8) s.362A; Insolvency Act 1986 (c.45) s.84(2A), Sch.B1 Pt 3 para.15.]

The applicant liquidators of a company in creditors' voluntary liquidation sought a declaration that the purported appointment of administrators was invalid. The company had given written notice, as required by the Insolvency Act 1986 s.84(2A), to its two floating charge holders (C1 and C2) of the resolution for voluntary liquidation. C1, which held the first floating charge, agreed with the resolution; C2, which held a second-ranking charge, and which was based overseas, did not reply. Later that same morning, C2 telephoned to say that it had appointed administrators 20 minutes before the start of the meeting for the passing of the resolution. The liquidators' case was that C2's appointment of administrators was invalid, first because it had not given notice to C1 as required by Sch.B1 para.15, and second because the form of appointment filed at court was defective on the grounds that it contained a statutory declaration that Sch.B1 para.15 notice had been given when it had not, and it misidentified the qualifying floating charge document. The liquidators submitted that Sch.1B para.15 disqualified a person from making an appointment if the notice condition was not satisfied. The administrators argued that there was a close similarity between the language of Sch.B1 para.15 and that of the Financial Services and Markets Act 2000 s.362A, which had been held in *Ceart Risk Services Ltd, Re* [2012] EWHC 1178 (Ch), [2013] Bus. L.R. 116, [2012] C.L.Y. 1803 not to imply incurable invalidity if it was not complied with.

Held: Declaration granted. (1) The difference between the provisions in the 1986 Act and the 2000 Act was that the former indicated that an administrator could not be appointed unless "he has given at least two business days' written notice", whereas the latter merely stated that an administrator may not be appointed without the consent of the Authority. The judge in *Ceart* had been able to construe s.362A as not necessarily requiring the consent to be given before the appointment, but such a construction was not available in relation to Sch.B1 para.15 because the language used the past tense. That was for the obvious purpose of enabling the holder of the prior floating charge to make his own appointment, if he wished to, before the second floating charge holder was able to act. C1 would be potentially prejudiced if the provision was to be construed as being one that permitted C2 to act first and seek consent later. Parliament could not be taken to have intended such a consequence. That being so, the purported appointment of administrators was invalid, *Ceart* considered (see paras 15, 17-19, 20, 24, 26-29 of judgment). (2) (Obiter) Misidentification of the qualifying floating charge document was unlikely to have been intended by Parliament to render an appointment of administrators invalid. It was not appropriate to express an opinion whether the incorrectness of the statutory declaration in itself would have rendered the appointment invalid (paras 31-32).

ECO LINK RESOURCES LTD, *Re* [2012] B.C.C. 731, Judge David Cooke, Ch D (Birmingham).

1676. Administrators–Liabilities–Personal liability for judgment debt–Effect of being sued "as administrator"

The appellant firm of solicitors (W) appealed against an order ([2012] EWHC 188 (Ch), [2012] B.C.C. 624, [2012] 9 C.L. 5) that the respondent administrator (M) was not personally liable for fees owed by two companies of which he was the administrator. W had been instructed to act for the companies under conditional fee agreements, which were signed by M. W began proceedings to recover its fees against M "as administrator" and obtained judgment. W received no payment, so it applied within the insolvency proceedings for directions regarding payment. The judge considered that naming the defendant "as administrator" recognised that he was sued as agent rather than in his personal capacity, and that the claim and order did not by necessary implication indicate personal liability. He ordered that M was not personally liable under the judgment.

Held: Appeal allowed. The trial judge could only have given judgment against a party to the action before him, and the companies were not parties to the action. Accordingly, the order in the insolvency action that liability had been imposed on the companies and not on M personally could not stand. The rest of the order could not stand either; judgment had been given based on the terms of a contract against the person who had signed it and who was before the court as the sole party, and there had been no appeal against that order. There was no authority that limited the liability of a defendant sued in representative form so that he was not personally liable on a judgment against him. There was also no authority that naming a defendant as an individual "as administrator" recognised that he was sued as an agent rather than in a personal capacity. There was no requirement to specifically plead that personal liability was alleged. The judge had been wrong to use those matters as a basis for finding that the judgment was against the companies rather than M personally. Further, the companies could only have been parties with the consent of the administrator or the court, and if they were defendants they should have been described in the pleadings by their name followed by "(in Administration)" (see paras 42-44, 46-47 of judgment).

WRIGHT HASSALL LLP v MORRIS, [2012] EWCA Civ 1472, [2013] B.C.C. 192, Mummery, L.J., CA (Civ Div).

1677. Bankruptcy–Annulment–Bankruptcy debt founded on unpaid legal fees–Fresh evidence of serious misconduct against retained solicitor–Whether bankruptcy should be annulled on basis of fresh evidence

[Civil Procedure Rules 1998 (SI 1998/3132) r.52.11 (2) (b).]

The appellants (O) appealed against an order of a deputy registrar refusing to annul their bankruptcies. A dispute had arisen between O and the first respondent solicitors' firm (D) and a solicitor (M), who worked for D, in relation to fees. On a summary judgment application before a deputy district judge to recover those fees, D was awarded damages to be assessed and an interim payment, and ordered to file and serve a fully itemised bill of costs. D failed to comply with that order and refused to accept payment from O unless they withdrew a complaint to the Law Society, D petitioned for O's bankruptcy as they had failed to comply with the order for an interim payment and adverse costs orders. O were adjudicated bankrupt. O's application to set aside the orders of the deputy district judge was dismissed. An application for annulment by O, founded on pending proceedings for M's professional misconduct, was also dismissed by a deputy registrar as premature. Meanwhile the Solicitors Disciplinary Tribunal made many findings of serious misconduct against M and he was struck off the roll. The issues were whether (i) the fresh evidence of the SDT's findings against M ought to be admitted; (ii) permission to appeal out of time ought to be granted; (iii) O's bankruptcies ought to be annulled.

Held: Application granted. (1) The power to admit fresh evidence was governed by CPR r.52.11 (2) (b) and had to be exercised in accordance with the overriding objective; it was not fettered by case law considerations, *Ladd v Marshall* [1954] 1 W.L.R. 1489, [1954] C.L.Y. 2507 considered. In the instant case, where O could have made a renewed annulment application, the overriding objective required the admission of the fresh evidence that was clearly relevant (see para.6 of judgment). (2) Permission to appeal out of time was granted as there had been serious irregularities in relation to the district judge's order. In particular, an order for damages to be assessed was not appropriate on a claim by solicitors in unpaid fees; that was a claim in debt, not damages. D had also failed to provide a properly itemised bill, and there was no power under CPR PD 5.1 to order an interim payment. It was appropriate to reconsider those matters in the light of the fresh evidence (para.9). (3) Given the decision of the SDT, it was appropriate to reconsider the dismissal of O's annulment application afresh. There had been a miscarriage of justice in the instant case; the authorities indicated that a bankruptcy court could go behind a judgment where there was some fraud, collusion or miscarriage of justice, *Dawodu v American Express Bank* [2001] B.P.I.R. 983, [2002] C.L.Y. 2673 applied. As D had held M out to be a duly qualified solicitor, that entitled O to rescind the retainer on the basis of misrepresentation. However, in exercising its residual discretion as to whether to grant an annulment, the courts provisional view was that annulment be granted subject to two conditions: firstly, that a sum equal to the amount of the proofs accepted by the trustee in bankruptcy be paid into court, and that O undertook not to defend a creditor's claim on the ground that the limitation period had expired during the bankruptcy. Leave was given to the parties to address the court on the terms of the conditions if any that ought to be attached to the annulment, and notice was given to other creditors that they had 42 days to apply for additional conditions (paras 11-12, 15).

ORAKI v DEAN & DEAN, [2012] EWHC 2885 (Ch), [2013] B.P.I.R. 88, Robert Ham, Q.C., Ch D (Bankruptcy Ct).

1678. Bankruptcy–Bankrupt's estate–Receipt of compensation for mis-sold payment protection insurance by discharged bankrupt–Whether compensation "property" for purposes of s.436 Insolvency Act 1986

[Insolvency Act 1986 (c.45) s.303, s.436.]

The applicant (W), a discharged bankrupt, applied under the Insolvency Act 1986 s.303 for an order requiring the Official Receiver to release to him payments received from his bank in respect of mis-sold payment protection insurance (PPI). W had taken out three bank loans. By 2007, he had repaid two, but the third was still outstanding when he petitioned for bankruptcy in February 2009. The Official Receiver was appointed as his trustee. W obtained his automatic discharge from bankruptcy in September 2009. When the mis-selling of PPI policies came into the public eye in 2011, W made a complaint to the Financial Ombudsman, which resulted in a payment by the bank of £16,000 in respect of PPI policies attached to all three loans. That payment was made direct to the Official Receiver. W accepted that the Official Receiver was entitled to keep the payment relating to the loan which had been unpaid at the time of the bankruptcy order, but claimed an entitlement to the payments relating to the two loans which he had repaid. The issue was whether the PPI payments fell within the definition of "property" in s.436 of the Act.

Held: Application refused. The payment formed part of W's "property" for the purposes of s.436 and therefore became part of his bankruptcy estate. The right to complain about the mis-selling of the PPI and to receive payment in respect of that arose from the policy itself. That policy had been paid for by W prior to his bankruptcy and was therefore an interest incidental to property within the meaning of s.436. W was not entitled to reclaim payment from the Official Receiver (see paras 12-13 of judgment). Alternatively, the payment was a thing in action: the essential basis of the PPI mis-selling claim was misrepresentation. A right to make a claim for misrepresentation arose when the misrepresentation was made, which was when the loans were taken out. Since that time pre-dated W's bankruptcy, the ensuing payment formed part of his estate (para.14). The fact that W only found out about his entitlement to make a claim after the discharge of bankruptcy did not prevent the right or the thing in action from falling within the estate (para.15).

WARD v OFFICIAL RECEIVER [2012] B.P.I.R. 1073, District Judge Khan, CC (Manchester).

1679. Bankruptcy–Bankruptcy orders–Annulment–Re-litigation of points already disposed of in bankruptcy proceedings–Limitations of s.282 and s.375 Insolvency Act 1986

[Insolvency Act 1986 (c.45) s.282(1)(a), s.282(1), s.375(1), s.375; European Convention on Human Rights 1950 Art.6.]

The applicant (C) applied for permission to appeal against the dismissal of his application under the Insolvency Act 1986 s.282(1) to annul or rescind a bankruptcy order made against him. The bankruptcy order was the result of C defaulting on his mortgage of £423,500. The creditor, a building society, obtained possession, sold the property for some £120,000, and approved an individual voluntary arrangement. It later recovered £300,000 in damages in an action against surveyors, which it credited to C's mortgage account. An issue arose as to how the damages had been appropriated as between the principal and the interest. Almost four years later, the creditor served a statutory demand on C for £417,000. It was initially set aside, but the creditor successfully appealed. C's argument that the damages ought to have been appropriated so as to extinguish the capital element of the loan failed, the judge finding that the creditor had been entitled to appropriate them against interest. At the hearing of the bankruptcy petition, other issues concerning limitation and whether the creditor was still bound by the terms of the IVA were determined unfavourably to C, a bankruptcy order was made, and permission to appeal refused. In his application under s.282(1), C relied on various grounds including the binding effect of the IVA, wrongful apportionment of the damages against interest instead of capital, judicial error in the exercise of discretion and violation of the European Convention on Human Rights 1950 art.6. The judge held that C was attempting to re-litigate points already disposed of in the bankruptcy proceedings. In the instant application, C sought leave to appeal against that decision.

Held: Permission refused. (1) The reality of the instant application was that all the points of substance had already been considered and disposed of in the bankruptcy proceedings; permission to appeal had been refused and C's attempt to attack the exercise of the judges' discretion lacked proper basis and was bound to fail. Section 282(1)(a) of the Act did not enable the court to annul a bankruptcy order on points which had been raised in response to the statutory demand or at the hearing of the petition and had been rejected. The court would only allow such points to be re-litigated in exceptional circumstances. If a bankrupt had grounds which had not been adjudicated upon, and which would have been an effective answer to the petition, he could raise them on an annulment application even though he might have raised them earlier. The court had to review the bankruptcy order in the light of the new material and might exercise its discretion to annul it if there was a bona fide dispute as to the existence of the petition debt. That discretion would not be exercised if the creditor had acted reasonably and the debtor had failed to raise defences which had been open to him earlier. The court also had power to review, rescind, or vary a bankruptcy order under s.375(1) of the Act, but would not normally do so where the bankrupt was seeking to re-argue points already decided at the original bankruptcy hearing. In principle, that section was limited to new material and/or a material change of circumstances (see paras 4-7, 25 of judgment). (2) Refusals to set aside a statutory demand or a bankruptcy order were both subject to a right of appeal, so any challenge under art.6 of the

Convention to the principles on which the court exercised its discretion under s.282 and s.375 would fail (para.8).

CRAMMER v WEST BROMWICH BUILDING SOCIETY, [2012] EWCA Civ 517, [2012] B.P.I.R. 963, Rimer, L.J., CA (Civ Div).

1680. Bankruptcy–Centre of main interests–Annulment of bankruptcy order for non-disclosure of Germany as centre of main intrests–Exercise of discretion to annul bankruptcy order

[Insolvency Act 1986 (c.45) s.282(1)(a); Regulation 1346/2000 on insolvency proceedings Art.3(1).]

The appellant (B) appealed against a decision of the deputy registrar annulling B's bankruptcy. B had petitioned for his own bankruptcy and obtained a bankruptcy order. He was automatically discharged a year later. The respondent German bank (D) was a secured creditor of B. Six months after B's discharge, it applied under the Insolvency Act 1986 s.282(1)(a) for the court to annul the bankruptcy order. The deputy registrar annulled the bankruptcy on grounds that B's centre of main interests under Regulation 1346/2000 art.3(1) was Germany and not England and that there had been material non-disclosure. B contended that his centre of main interests was England at the relevant time where he had been living and working and that the deputy registrar had not properly exercised her discretion; D was fully secured and therefore had no legitimate ground for applying to annul and the delay before applying to annul was prejudicial. D argued that the bankruptcy order had been made without jurisdiction since B's centre of main interests was in Germany and not England, and was therefore rightly annulled; the deputy registrar had in any event come to the right conclusion in the exercise of her discretion.

Held: Appeal dismissed. (1) There was no express restriction in the legislation on who could apply to annul. A secured creditor had a sufficient interest. That interest was not a matter of jurisdiction but a matter to be taken into account as part of the exercise of discretion. It was not necessary to decide whether D was right in its jurisdictional arguments based on the wording of the Regulation. It was common sense that D was pursuing the proceedings in England and pursuing proceedings in Germany because it was not fully secured and there was a shortfall. (2) The usual case for an application to annul after discharge was by the debtor where all the debts had been paid. The court would be slow to annul where many years had passed after the discharge. B said that the delay was prejudicial but he admitted hiding his English address from his creditors. Delay had not been relied on at the hearing before the registrar and the registrar had been aware of the discharge. (3) The registrar had exercised her discretion, even if she had thought that it was a plain case for exercise of the jurisdiction to annul if D's case was made out. The centre of main interests had to be ascertainable by third parties and had to have an element of permanence, *Shierson v Vlieland-Boddy* [2005] EWCA Civ 974, [2005] 1 W.L.R. 3966, [2005] C.L.Y. 2293 followed. The centre of main interests was not immutable and the debtor could relocate his home and business but the court would scrutinise a self-serving change to see that it was based on substance and not illusion. The registrar found that B was working in England but his income was not enough to maintain him; he received payments from his wife in Germany and was involved with real property in Germany. In the circumstances the employment was to create an illusion of permanence. He retained significant economic and emotional ties with Germany. His German creditors corresponded with his German address. As a matter of fact the registrar was entitled to conclude that B's centre of main interests was in Germany. She had not erred in law. (4) The grounds of appeal did not deal with the non-disclosure. B had failed to disclose the income from his wife and the real property in Germany. It was said that that did not matter because he was plainly insolvent. That was contrary to the important principle of disclosure on ex parte applications, *Official Receiver v Mitterfellner* [2009] B.P.I.R. 1075, [2010] C.L.Y. 1859 and *Irish Bank Resolution Corp Ltd v Quinn* [2012] NICh 1, [2012] B.C.C. 608, [2012] C.L.Y. 3599 applied. The non-disclosure was of the very matters which had led to the finding that B's centre of main interests was in Germany. The bankruptcy order would probably not have been made if the court had been alerted to the centre of main interests issue.

SPARKASSE BREMEN AG v ARMUTCU, [2012] EWHC 4026 (Ch), [2013] B.P.I.R. 210, Proudman, J., Ch D.

1681. Bankruptcy–Centre of main interests–Irish national petitioning for own bankruptcy–Place of "centre of main interests"

The court had to consider whether it had jurisdiction to make a bankruptcy order and open main insolvency proceedings against the debtor (O). O was an Irish national. He had been a property developer in Ireland and had many enterprises there. His businesses suffered significantly as a result of the property crash. In 2009, he separated from his wife, who continued to look after their two children, and in 2010 he came to England in search of work. In January 2011, he began work for a construction company (C). He maintained that he had a full-time and permanent post. However, he continued to spend a considerable amount of time in Ireland; in 2011, he spent 165 days there. He maintained that his main reason for returning regularly to Ireland was to see his children. He also asserted that, because of his qualities as an employee and the success he had had in securing work for C, C paid for his return trips to Ireland. A business plan produced in 2011 indicated that O was helping the National Asset Management Agency to obtain the best possible outcome from the assets accumulated in Ireland by the enterprises in which he had an interest. The property crash in Ireland had left him with significant personal debts.

Held: Judgment accordingly. O had established on the balance of probabilities that his "centre of main interests" was in England as at the date of his petition, namely February 2012, with the result that the court had jurisdiction. The objective test to be applied was whether he was carrying on his commercial, domestic and economic activities in a new centre of main interests. As at the date of the petition, his economic activities were carried out in London. His bank statements showed spending in England, he paid council tax here and his work, pay and income tax were all in England; by contrast, there was no evidence of economic activities in Ireland at the time. O no longer had any ascertainable interests in the Irish companies and partnerships with which he had been associated. Although the "root of insolvency" was clearly in Ireland, that was just one of many factors to be taken into account, as was the fact that he retained emotional interests in Ireland. O's habitual residence was in London, as was shown by his bills, his tenancy agreement, his bank statements and the fact that he was registered with a dentist and a doctor there. Further, his base in London was ascertainable by third parties (see paras 25, 35, 96, 99-100, 103, 105, 107-109, 112 of judgment).

O'MAHONY v NATIONAL IRISH BANK [2012] B.P.I.R. 1174, Deputy Registrar Nicholas Briggs, Ch D.

1682. Bankruptcy–Debtors' bankruptcy petitions–Jurisdiction–Meaning of "ordinarily resident" in s.265(1)(c) Insolvency Act 1986

[Insolvency Act 1986 (c.45) s.265(1)(c); Regulation 1346/2000 on insolvency proceedings.]

The court had to consider four debtors' petitions where a jurisdictional issue arose. Two of the debtors had taken up permanent residence in Turkey and two in New Zealand. Because Regulation 1346/2000 did not apply, the only jurisdictional requirement that had to be met was one of those set out in the Insolvency Act 1986 s.265(1)(c). Each of the debtors had lived abroad for over a year before their petition was presented. Each petition contained a statement that the debtor had, for a period within the three years immediately preceding presentation of the petition, ordinarily resided within England and Wales. The issue was whether, for the purposes of s.265(1)(c), a debtor could say that he had been ordinarily resident in England and Wales in circumstances where he had moved abroad, apparently permanently; was now ordinarily resident abroad; and had not resided in the jurisdiction for some time. The debtors submitted that it was sufficient for the petitioning debtor at any time in the period of three years preceding presentation of the petition to have had a period in which it could be said that he had been ordinarily resident in the jurisdiction. They argued that to interpret the section as requiring persistence of residence during the whole of the three-year period was at the least to ignore the words "at any time" and at worst to replace them with the word "throughout" which was the opposite of the words enacted.

Held: Bankruptcy orders made. The debtors' interpretation of s.265(1)(c) had to be right. It was puzzling that Parliament had provided an alternative in s.265(1)(c) that would more obviously fit the bill, namely having had a place of residence in England and Wales, but the two were independent tests that must have been designed to contemplate different circumstances. The court had no alternative but to accept that there had been a period within the relevant three-year period in which each debtor could be said to have been ordinarily resident in England and Wales. That was sufficient to found jurisdiction. Bankruptcy orders could therefore be made.

AKAYDIN, *Re* [2013] B.P.I.R. 539, Registrar Baister, Ch D.

1683. Bankruptcy–Insolvency

THE INSOLVENCY (AMENDMENT) RULES 2013, SI 2013/2135; made under the Insolvency Act 1986 s.412. In force: October 1, 2013; .

These Rules make amendments to the Insolvency Rules in order that the Rules reflect the repeal of early discharge from bankruptcy provisions made by the Enterprise and Regulatory Reform Act 2013 s.73 and Sch.21 Pt 3, which will be brought into force on October 1, 2013.

1684. Bankruptcy–Jurisdiction–Debt evidenced in judgment of Hong Kong court–Entitlement of creditor to present bankruptcy petition

[Insolvency Act 1986 (c.45) s.267.]

The applicant (H) sought an order dismissing a bankruptcy petition which had been presented against her by the respondent company (S). H resided in England. S had obtained a judgment against her in Hong Kong for a substantial sum. After a statutory demand had been served on H, her solicitors stated that a bankruptcy petition would not be resisted. However, H changed her stance, asserting now that a creditor was not entitled to present a bankruptcy petition based on a sum alleged to be due under a judgment of the Hong Kong courts until that judgment was recognised in England.

Held: Application refused. The issue was whether, for the purposes of the Insolvency Act 1986, S was a creditor and whether it had a debt within the meaning of s.267. The answer was yes. English law could refuse to recognise that the requisite state of indebtedness existed if the alleged liability was based on a foreign judgment which was unable to command recognition under the relevant rules of English private international law; as to that, a court of a foreign country had jurisdiction to give a judgment in personam capable of enforcement or recognition if the person against whom the judgment was given had submitted to the jurisdiction of that court by voluntarily appearing in the proceedings. H had done that. Further, it was clear that she had acknowledged her liability to S. S had a cause of action and was in exactly the same position as any other creditor who sought to pursue bankruptcy without holding an English judgment. S would therefore be permitted to proceed with its petition (see paras 20, 23-25, 28, 30 of judgment).

SUN LEGEND INVESTMENTS LTD v HO [2013] B.P.I.R. 533, District Judge Musgrave, CC (Birmingham).

1685. Bankruptcy–Remedies–Whether creditor prevented from entering judgment by s.285(3) Insolvency Act 1986

[Insolvency Act 1986 (c.45) s.285(3); Civil Procedure Rules 1998 (SI 1998/3132) r.19.8(2)(b)(ii).]

The applicants, being a company in liquidation (H) and its liquidator (W), sought an order for the repayment of certain sums paid to H's sole director (R) out of H's funds. In the latter part of 2009, H was faced with a substantial claim in the employment tribunal by a former employee (S). In December 2009, H paid £48,920 to a third party in connection with the purchase of a car by R. In February 2010, payments totalling £80,000 were paid by H into R's personal bank account. Shortly thereafter, R told W that he wanted to put H into liquidation to defeat S's claim. The following month, H went into creditors' voluntary liquidation. In October 2010, R died. He left a will in which he named as executors three individuals, including the second and third respondents (L and H). W took the view that he should try to recover from R's estate the payments made by H in December 2009 and February 2010. He convened a creditors' meeting and was given the necessary authority. L had attended the meeting and had opposed the sanctioning of proceedings against R's estate. In correspondence, L accused W of acting unprofessionally and of being "of very low integrity". The applicants issued the instant claim in December 2011, asking that L and H be appointed under the CPR r.19.8(2)(b)(ii) to represent R's estate. They were so appointed on May 11, 2012. In September 2012, probate was obtained and an order for administration in bankruptcy made.

Held: Judgment accordingly. (1) Whether on the basis of misfeasance, or preference, or both, an order for the repayment of the monies paid by H in December 2009 and February 2010 had inevitably to be made. There was no doubt that H had been insolvent at the time. R had acted in a thoroughly dishonest manner, fully intending to defeat H's creditors while retaining the core business for his own benefit. It was necessary, however, to have regard to the Insolvency Act 1986 s.285(3), which placed a restriction on the pursuit of remedies by a creditor after the making of a bankruptcy order. The applicants had been correct to argue that, while s.285(3)(a) barred the enforcement of a judgment, it did not prevent the mere entry of a judgment. The key to the issue lay in s.285(1), which gave the court the power to stay proceedings where proceedings on a bankruptcy petition were pending or an individual had been adjudged bankrupt. The corollary was that, if the power to stay was not exercised, the proceedings could continue to their normal conclusion. The object of s.285(3)(a) had to be to prevent one creditor from getting his hands on part of the bankrupt's estate to the actual or potential detriment of the general body of creditors. Allowing proceedings to run their normal course up to judgment did not undermine that object and was consistent with s.285(1), which envisaged that a claim already commenced against the bankrupt would, unless stayed, remain on foot against him. There would therefore be judgment against R's estate for the amount claimed (see paras 35, 38-40 of judgment). (2) It was necessary to decide whether costs should be awarded against L and H. L had argued that his position was not analogous to that of an ordinary defendant and that his presence on the record was attributable to the requirement that the action be duly constituted, so that he was a mere "technical" defendant. That argument could not be accepted. There were strong reasons for making an order for costs against him. Among other things, he had presented himself from the outset as a person who was going to resist any unravelling of the impugned payments, and he had done everything in his power to delay and frustrate the claim. H would also be ordered to pay costs but only from the date when he was appointed to represent R's estate (paras 44-45, 48-49).

HEATING ELECTRICAL LIGHTING AND PIPING LTD (IN LIQUIDATION) v ROSS, [2012] EWHC 3764 (Ch), [2012] B.P.I.R. 1122, Judge Peter Langan, Q.C., Ch D.

1686. **Bankruptcy orders–Annulment–Challenge to decision refusing to annul bankruptcy order**

[Consumer Credit Act 1974 (c.39) s.82A(1).]

The appellant (S) appealed against a decision of a district judge refusing to annul a bankruptcy order made against her. The bankruptcy order had been made on the petition of the first respondent finance company (F), claiming as assignee of a Halifax credit card debt of £4,262.33. At the hearing, doubt was cast on the affidavit evidence of the process server (W) that he had served the statutory demand and petition in May and August 2009 respectively. It was stated in the affidavit of service that it had been sworn at a firm called SJ Vickers & Co before a Steven Pearle. In fact, SJ Vickers & Co had changed its name to Stapletons in October 2007 and there was no person named Steven Pearle working for Stapletons in 2009. The district judge found that, whatever may have been the explanation for the incorrect affidavit of service, W's oral evidence, supported by his contemporary notes, that he had indeed effected service was true. S argued that (1) the district judge had been wrong to accept the evidence of W, who must have been lying; (2) F was not a creditor of hers, as no notice of assignment of the debt due to the Halifax had been given to her; the Consumer Credit Act 1974 s.82A(1) required the assignee to "arrange for notice of the assignment to be given to the debtor", which required the assignee to ensure that notice of the assignment was given to the borrower by the assignor, not by itself; that had not been done.

Held: Appeal dismissed. (1) There was no basis for reversing the district judge's findings on the issue of service (see para.7 of judgment). (2) There was clear evidence which the district judge had rightly accepted as proof of service of notice of the assignment. The evidence indicated that notice had been given both by F and by the Halifax. In any event, s.82A should not be construed as requiring that notice should be given by the assignor; the assignee could arrange for notice to be given by itself or by the assignor (paras 9-10, 12).

SMITH v 1ST CREDIT (FINANCE) LTD, [2012] EWHC 2600 (Ch), [2013] B.P.I.R. 129, Nicholas Strauss Q.C., Ch D.

1687. **Bankruptcy orders–Annulment–Whether German nationals having centre of main interests in UK**

[Regulation 1346/2000 on insolvency proceedings.]

The Official Receiver applied to annul bankruptcy orders made in respect of five German nationals (B) on their own petitions. The Official Receiver's case was that B had petitioned for bankruptcy in the United Kingdom to take advantage of the more favourable bankruptcy regime which applied here. The issue was whether, at the time they presented their petitions, B had their centre of main interests in the UK for the purposes of Regulation 1346/2000.

Held: Application granted. The five cases had common features. For example, each man had been assisted by a company which had advertised in the German press that it was able to assist German nationals wishing to petition for bankruptcy in the UK. Each man had opened an account with a particular bank in the UK; the use of those accounts was very limited and did not evidence day-to-day living. There was also a marked absence of documentary evidence to show that B in fact had their base in the UK at the relevant times. The arrangements made were transitory and illusory, being designed to create an impression of a centre of main interests in this country which did not exist. In the circumstances, it would be appropriate to annul the bankruptcy orders made.

OFFICIAL RECEIVER v BECKER [2013] B.P.I.R. 352, District Judge Dancey, CC (Bournemouth).

1688. **Bankruptcy orders–Centre of main interests–German resident practising as notary–Suspension of practice–Alleged change of COMI to England**

[Regulation 1346/2000 on insolvency proceedings Art.3(1).]

The applicant bank (S) applied for the annulment of a bankruptcy order made in respect of the first respondent (B). B was formerly a German resident practising as a notary and his centre of main interests (COMI) was then in Germany. He claimed that he had moved from Germany to England and established his COMI in England when he had been suspended from his notarial position in Germany, and thereby prevented from carrying on his economic activities there, and he no longer had any management or control of his real property interests in Germany since they were the subject of enforcement proceedings by S. He claimed that he was working in England as a sports photographer, had rented a flat, owned and insured a car, had obtained a national insurance number and undertook normal day-to-day life in England. S was one of B's creditors, owed more than EUR 3 million. Its case was that B's COMI was and remained in Germany when he presented his bankruptcy petition and the order was made; therefore the order was not properly made under Regulation 1346/2000 art.3(1) and should be annulled; B's presence and activities in England were both temporary and contrived, so as to allow him to take advantage of the more favourable insolvency regime in England.

Held: Application granted. B's COMI was at all material times in Germany. He was a professional notary in Germany. When he was suspended an administrator was installed to carry on his notarial practice. He appealed, unsuccessfully, against his preliminary suspension and against his final suspension. There remained an outstanding challenge to his suspension to the European Court of Human Rights. Though his appeals were unsuccessful, they indicated that B's real purpose might have been to opt for an English bankruptcy and resume his activities as a notary in Germany once that bankruptcy had been discharged. He appeared to have relied on his English discharge, potential or actual, in pursuing his appeals. B had no viable means of support in England other than a dependence on his partner. His activities as a sports photographer were loss-making and offered no long-term prospect of economic survival. His best option was to resume his notarial practice, if he could. B had also brought proceedings in Germany attempting unsuccessfully to prevent S from enforcing its rights against his real estate and pension fund. In so doing, he had relied on his English bankruptcy. He was pursuing his own economic interests in Germany. The activities in England were window-dressing. B had lived with his partner in England and had been financially dependent on her. It was appropriate to consider her circumstances when deciding where B's COMI was. Her habitual residence and COMI had been in Germany throughout. She had funded their life in England through use of German credit cards and bank accounts and had retained her residential address in Germany. She returned to Germany soon after his automatic discharge. B followed her in due course and lived for most of the time in Germany. That was where they were habitually resident as a couple and they were only temporary residents in England. Most of B's creditors were in Germany, but he appeared to have taken no formal steps to notify them of his change of COMI to England. He remained on the register of notaries in Germany, although he could not practice as a notary after his suspension. The bankruptcy order was based on a false assertion of an English COMI and was annulled (see paras 25-31 of judgment).

SPARKASSE HILDEN RATINGEN VELBERT v BENK, [2012] EWHC 2432 (Ch), [2012] B.P.I.R. 1258, Judge Purle Q.C., Ch D (Birmingham).

1689. Bankruptcy petitions–Individual voluntary arrangements–Discretion to adjourn bankruptcy petition in order to allow relevant property to be auctioned–Best interests of creditors

[Insolvency Act 1986 (c.45) s.252, s.276, s.376; Insolvency Rules 1986 (SI 1986/1925) Pt 5 r.5.24.]

The petitioner supervisors (P) applied for a bankruptcy order against the debtor (M) on the basis that his applications for individual voluntary arrangements would not succeed. M sought an adjournment of that order. M had sought an individual voluntary arrangement but had been prevented from doing so by his former wife's claims within divorce proceedings. In particular he had been prevented from selling a property thought to be valued at nearly £3 million. The papers revealed that an IVA would be accepted and successful if M's equity in the property could be realised. M's first IVA proposal (the first arrangement) had been approved, but a meeting of creditors determined that P should petition for M's bankruptcy by reason of its failure. M applied for an interim order pursuant to the Insolvency Act 1986 s.252 whilst he sought approval of a proposal for a second IVA (the second proposal). That led to an order being made based on a payment in full of debts totalling just under £3.4 million within 8 months by the sale of assets including the property. M sought an adjournment to allow an auction of the property to take place and to make proposals for the payment of his creditors. The issues were whether (i) the court should consider a late objection to the petition relying on s.276 of the Act and if so whether it should conclude that the petition should be dismissed because it was not satisfied either that M failed to comply with the terms of the first arrangement or that he failed to do all such things reasonably required of him for its purposes; (ii) the second proposal had been deemed rejected after a final adjournment of the meeting of creditors or, if not, whether a further adjourned meeting should be held with the court extending time for that purpose retrospectively pursuant to s.376 of the Act and the interim order should be extended; (iii) in accordance with the court's discretion under s.276 the petition should be adjourned because the creditors could be paid whether through a continuation of the first arrangement or under the terms of the second proposal.

Held: Judgment accordingly. (1) As at the relevant date there was no financial settlement, the property could not be sold and there was a failure of the first arrangement. P were entitled to report to the creditors to seek a variation. The creditors voted that a petition should be presented because of failure of the arrangement. In those circumstances the arrangement came to an end prematurely and the prohibition in s.276 of the Act did not apply (see paras 13-14 of judgment). (2) The Insolvency Rules 1986 Pt 5 r.5.24 should be construed on the basis that there was to be one meeting to achieve finality over the proposal. Whilst that meeting could be adjourned, it should still be concluded quickly. The purpose was to conclude one meeting in order to approve or reject the proposal and not to give time for payment whilst that was occurring. The decision to adjourn should only arise if approval could not be given but there was a reasonable prospect of it being given in the near future. It was right for the court to take into account the wishes of the creditors when exercising its discretion. On the evidence M's proposal would not obtain the approval of the majority of creditors required. Whilst it was true that r.5.24 required that there might be adjournments in order to persuade creditors, it also required finality. In circumstances where the evidence led to the conclusion that there would be a deemed rejection, it would not be a judicious exercise of the court's discretion to extend time in the hope that matters might change. The fundamental problem for the s.376 applications was that there was no adjournment and M was seeking approval in order that he would then be able to adjourn the meeting. Rule 5.24(5) applied. Even if there had been an adjournment it would be wrong in principle to adjourn in the hope that something might induce a change of mind and the s.376 applications were dismissed. (3) However it was in the best interests of all the creditors to allow the auction to take place without a bankruptcy order being made and to provide further time to allow M to resolve his financial position. An adjournment was therefore granted until the hearing of the validation application (paras 54-59).

BONNEY v MIRPURI; *sub nom.* MIRPURI, *Re* [2013] B.P.I.R. 412, Registrar Jones, Ch D.

1690. Bankruptcy petitions–Liquidated sums–Whether guarantee giving rise to conditional payment obligation–Effect of eight-month delay between statutory demand and petition

[Insolvency Act 1986 (c.45) s.267(2)(b), s.267, s.271.]

The petitioning creditor bank (B) petitioned for a bankruptcy order against the respondent guarantor (F). F had been a property developer who gave three guarantees to B to support the borrowings of various businesses. B served a statutory demand on F, but did not present the petition until eight months later. During that time, the receiver allegedly told F that B had decided to review all options and for time being not to sell the properties on which the borrowings were secured. The guarantee that F signed contained two clauses, the first guaranteed discharge of the principal debtor's liability on demand, and the second contained an obligation to indemnify B against losses arising out of a failure by the principal debtor to perform its obligations. The issues were whether (i) the petition debt was a liquidated sum as required by the Insolvency Act 1986 s.267(2)(b) or was, due to the obligation to indemnify in the second clause, a liability in damages; (ii) B had unreasonably refused offers to secure or compound for the debt within the meaning of s.271 of the Act; (iii) F had a counterclaim against B giving rise to losses resulting from B's intermeddling in the activities of the receiver; (iv) B had misled the court about the reason for the delay in presenting its petition.

Held: Petition granted. (1) To determine the nature of a guarantee one had to ask who paid, and what did he pay for? If the answers were "the guarantor pays" and "he pays the principal debtor's debt", the guarantee gave rise to a conditional payment agreement, *McGuinness v Norwich and Peterborough Building Society* [2011] EWCA Civ 1286, [2012] 2 All E.R. (Comm) 265, [2012] C.L.Y. 1819 applied. The first clause gave rise to a plain conditional payment obligation on F. That was a liquidated debt within the meaning of s.267(2)(b) of the Act. The two clauses were separate but cumulative, F was simply bound by both promises (see paras 9, 13, 18 of judgment). (2) The test for whether an offer to secure a debt had been unreasonably refused was that no reasonable hypothetical creditor would have refused the offer, and that the refusal of the offer was beyond the range of possible reasonable actions in the context, *Debtor (No.32 of 1993), Re* [1994] 1 W.L.R. 899, [1994] C.L.Y. 284 applied. F's offer would have required B to settle for no more than the market value of the properties and to abandon any claim under the personal guarantees, which would have meant giving up something valuable for nothing. It could not be said that no reasonable hypothetical creditor could refuse that offer (see paras 23-25). (3) There was no evidence of loss flowing from any decision that had been taken in relation to the properties under the receiver's control. A creditor with both personal security from a guarantor and fixed charged security over the principal debtor's property was under no obligation to realise the principal debtor's property before enforcing the guarantee (paras 27-28). (4) It was not possible to reach any conclusion on the accuracy of the reasons for the delay. However, if the purpose of the requirement for an explanation of a delay of over four months was to prevent a petitioner from relying on a stale statutory demand, as contended in John Briggs and Chris Brougham, Muir Hunter on Personal Insolvency (London: Sweet & Maxwell), para. 7-267, it could not be said to be a mischief requiring dismissal in the instant case. F had not suffered any prejudice as a result of the passage of a further four months. Much of the time was taken up by settlement negotiations, so F must have contemplated the possibility of a petition being presented throughout the whole of the period. The statutory demand could not be said to be "stale" in the sense that F was lulled into any false sense of security about his position as a result of the delay in presenting it (para.36).

DUNBAR ASSETS PLC v FOWLER; *sub nom.* FOWLER, *Re* [2013] B.P.I.R. 46, Registrar Baister, Ch D (Bankruptcy Ct).

1691. Bankrupts–Locus standi–Attempt to reargue merits of decision relating to charge over property as a costs-only appeal–Appeal challenging substance of decision rather than costs–Whether bankrupt had standing to appeal

[Insolvency Act 1986 (c.45) s.303(1).]

The appellant (D), a bankrupt, appealed against a decision relating to a charge held by the respondent (C) over his property. The Official Receiver had taken no position in the litigation below, which was resolved in C's favour. D was ordered to pay costs on an indemnity basis. His grounds of appeal challenged not the costs order but the substance of the ruling. C argued that D did not have locus standi to bring the appeal.

Held: Appeal dismissed. (1) Following D's bankruptcy, his interest in the property became vested in the Official Receiver, who was tasked with dealing with any indebtedness within the bankruptcy. D had no right to appeal in his own name from a judgment against his estate vested in his trustee in bankruptcy, *Heath v Tang* [1993] 1 W.L.R. 1421, [1993] C.L.Y. 222 and *James v Rutherford-Hodge* [2005] EWCA Civ 1580, [2006] B.P.I.R. 973 followed. His interest in a potential surplus was protected by the Insolvency Act 1986 s.303(1), which allowed him to challenge the trustee's decisions. As the only grounds for appeal were points of substance, the appeal fell squarely within the bar of *Heath* and *James, Heath and James* followed (see paras 10-12, 14 of judgment). (2) D could not get around that by rearguing the merits as a costs-only appeal, *Heath* and *James* followed. There had been no grounds put forward against the costs order itself: the only grounds for setting aside the costs order were predicated on the rest of the order being set aside. In those circumstances there was no freestanding costs appeal (paras 14, 17).

COWEY v INSOL FUNDING LTD, [2012] EWHC 2421 (Ch), [2012] B.P.I.R. 958, Judge Purle Q.C., Ch D.

1692. Bankrupts–Oral trusts–Vesting property interest in non-bankrupt spouse

[Insolvency Act 1986 (c.45) s.339.]

The applicant (T), trustee in bankruptcy for the first respondent (H), applied for declaratory relief and an order for the possession and sale of the residential property occupied by H and his wife, the second respondent (W). The property had always been registered jointly in H and W's names. In late 2007 or early 2008 solicitors had advised W that she could protect the property from H's creditors if they executed a trust deed. The deed, signed in February 2008, purported to record that as of July 2007 W was beneficially entitled to the whole of the net equity in the property, leaving H with no interest in it. H and W claimed that the deed was evidence of an oral declaration of trust made in July 2007, but there was no contemporaneous evidence of that agreement. T argued that (1) no declaration of trust had been made in July 2007; (2) if there were a trust, it was a transaction at an undervalue within the meaning of the Insolvency Act 1986 s.339; (3) there had not been an implied trust in favour of W.

Held: Application granted. (1) There was little to no evidence to support a July 2007 agreement between H and W for a declaration of trust. In particular, there had been no real change in H and W's financial arrangements in July 2007: both before and after that date H had been responsible for the mortgage payments. Additionally, it was not until late 2007 that W had sought advice from solicitors regarding protecting the property from creditors. There had therefore been no declaration of trust created in July 2007 (see paras 19-20 Of judgment). (2) Even if there were a trust, it lacked consideration and would have been a transaction at an undervalue under s.339 (para.22). (3) There had not been an implied trust in W's favour. There had been no express discussions between H and W regarding an agreement for a beneficial interest, and there had been no detrimental reliance by W, *Lloyds Bank Plc v Rosset* [1991] 1 A.C. 107, [1990] C.L.Y. 706 followed (paras 23-24).

GARWOOD v AMBROSE; *sub nom.* AMBROSE, *Re,* [2012] EWHC 1494 (Ch), [2012] B.P.I.R. 996, Peter Leaver Q.C., Ch D.

1693. Centre of main interests–Bankruptcy petitions–Irish property investment business with assets in Europe and America–Residence move of directors shortly before petition presentation–Establishing COMI

The court had to determine whether the centre of main interest for the petitioners (D) was within the court's jurisdiction. D, both Irish citizens, were husband and wife and had presented petitions for their bankruptcy in the United Kingdom in March 2012. The husband qualified as an Irish solicitor in 1976 and ran his own practice in Dublin until around February 2012. D began to invest in Irish properties during the 1980s. From 2005 to 2008 they invested in properties in the UK, Sweden and America using various companies of which they were directors. Two of the companies were incorporated in the UK; others were registered outside the UK and Ireland. In 2008 D registered "Vico Capital" in Ireland as a business name, and they were known by this trading name in the real estate market. D had a family home near Dublin, where three of their four children, who were all over the age of 18, were still living at the time of the instant hearing. In 2007 D acquired a large house in London. Both houses were vested in a "Vico" company; one was an Isle of Man company and the other was incorporated in Jersey. The respondent bank, which was D's main creditor, issued proceedings in Ireland against D in 2010. A settlement agreement was reached, but D failed to make the payments due and in December 2011 judgment was entered in the bank's favour. Shortly afterwards D began living in the London house. In January 2012, D's solicitors wrote to the bank asserting that D's centre of main interest (COMI) was in London. D initially contended that their COMI moved to the UK between 2005 and 2007, when the London property was acquired.

Held: Petition dismissed. A debtor's COMI fell to be determined at the date of presentation of a bankruptcy petition rather than the date, if different, on which the petition was heard. Further, the COMI should be ascertainable by third parties. It appeared that until 2011, D's economic activities were centred in Ireland and that was how creditors would have perceived matters. D spent considerable time in England on business, but their office premises were in Ireland and there were no permanent staff in England. D used the London property for business use as well as a home. That address was given in various agreements and materials, but Irish addresses were also used in such documents and also in transactional documents. D had investments outside the UK and Ireland. They conducted their business dealings from wherever they were at the time, and as many of the properties were vested in companies, their work essentially involved administration of the company's interests, rather than the directors'. Even after the London property was acquired, D's main home was in Dublin. They were on the electoral roll there, they submitted tax returns there and their cars were registered there. The husband changed his position by claiming in his third witness statement that his COMI was in London from "the end of 2011/ beginning of 2012". D were going to stay in London, which was understandable given the extent of press interest in them in Ireland. However, that did not mean that a change of COMI would have been apparent to third parties. Certainly, it was only after March 2012 that the Irish Companies Registration Office and Companies House in the UK showed D's resignation as directors of a number of Irish companies and of UK companies respectively. D's country of residence was still shown at Companies House to be Ireland and the Dublin property was given as D's address in an annual return. Although D were entered on the electoral roll in the UK by March 2012, they remained on the roll in Ireland. Not all of D's creditors had been informed of their move to the UK. In all the circumstances, the COMI for which D contended, namely the UK, was not sufficiently ascertainable by third parties. An objective observer would have taken D's COMI to be in Ireland at March 2012. Accordingly D's COMI was in Ireland rather than the UK and the bankruptcy petitions had to be dismissed, *Eurofood IFSC Ltd, Re (C-341/04)* [2006] Ch. 508, [2007] C.L.Y. 2428, *Interedil Srl (In Liquidation) v Fallimento Interedil Srl (C-396/09)* [2012] Bus. L.R. 1582, *Shierson v Vlieland-Boddy* [2005] EWCA Civ 974, [2005] 1 W.L.R. 3966, [2005] C.L.Y. 2293, *Irish Bank Resolution Corp Ltd v Quinn* [2012] NICh 1, [2012] B.C.C. 608, [2012] C.L.Y. 3599, *Proceedings Brought by Staubitz-Schreiber (C-1/04)* [2006] E.C.R. I-701, [2006] C.L.Y. 2338 considered (see paras 28, 35-36, 43-47, 51-53, 55-56 of judgment).

O'DONNELL v BANK OF IRELAND, [2012] EWHC 3749 (Ch), [2013] I.L.Pr. 16, Newey, J., Ch D.

1694. Creditors' bankruptcy petitions–Dates–Purpose of r.6.5(6) Insolvency Rules 1986–Appropriateness of dismissing debtor's cross-claims

[Insolvency Rules 1986 (SI 1986/1925) r.6.5.]

The appellant debtor (D) appealed against the bankruptcy order made against him in favour of the respondent petitioners (P). D's application to set aside a petition for a statutory demand had been dismissed. It was not specified at that hearing the date that P could present the bankruptcy petition, as required by the Insolvency

Rules 1986 r.6.5(6). In any event, the petition was presented the following day, and D was subsequently adjudged bankrupt by the district judge. D was not present. At that hearing, the judge did not deal with the alleged procedural defect in the petition pursuant to r.6.5(6). She referred to the fact that D was not present, and that he had not filed a statement of truth. She summarily dismissed D's assertion that he had cross-claims which could extinguish the debt, and rejected his request for an adjournment. D submitted that (1) there was a procedural defect in the petition pursuant to r.6.5(6) and accordingly the petition was flawed and should not have been made; (2) the judge had been wrong to proceed to the subsequent determination of the petition at that hearing without making a finding of evidence on the cross-claims; (3) D should have been granted an adjournment in order to allow him to pay the debt.

Held: Appeal allowed. (1) The purpose of r.6.5(6) was to allow D to ask for time to pay the debt before the petition was presented, or to reach a compromise. The default position in the absence of any request by a debtor for more time was to authorise the petition forthwith. Rule 6.5(6) did not prohibit the petitioner from presenting a petition forthwith if there was no date for the presentation of the bankruptcy petition specified in the order, *Bezier Acquisitions Ltd, Re* [2011] EWHC 3299 (Ch), [2012] 2 All E.R. (Comm) 322, [2012] C.L.Y. 1806 considered. (2) The judge had to consider whether there was any prospect of success of D establishing the cross-claims. They were matters which required evidence. The judge appeared to have been influenced by the fact that D was not present, which was not a material consideration, and that he had not signed a statement of truth, when he was under no obligation to do so. (3) D had not shown any way he could have paid back the debt, and accordingly the judge was right to reject his request for an adjournment. (4) The matter was to be remitted to the County Court where directions were to be made for the filing of evidence.

DARBYSHIRE v TURPIN, [2013] EWHC 954 (Ch), [2013] B.P.I.R. 558, Arnold, J., Ch D.

1695. Creditors' bankruptcy petitions–Guarantees–Presentation of bankruptcy petition–Whether good arguable case person carried on business in England or Wales under s.265(1)(c)(ii) Insolvency Act 1986

[Insolvency Act 1986 (c.45) s.265(1)(c).]

The appellant bank (B) appealed against a decision of the chief registrar refusing to allow its bankruptcy petition to be presented against the respondent (F) on the basis that F had not carried on business in England or Wales, a requirement under the Insolvency Act 1986 s.265(1)(c)(ii). B had granted loan facilities between 2000-2004 to a group of seven companies registered in England (P) that had been special vehicle companies created to invest in real estate. F, who was resident in Andorra, was the guarantor of each of the facilities. P defaulted under the loan facilities and B sought repayment from P as guarantor. B presented a bankruptcy petition against F when no payment was received pursuant to a statutory demand. Before the registrar, B failed to satisfy s.265(1)(c)(ii). The registrar held that the only facts that he could be sure about in relation to F were that he was an Irish national resident in Andorra; that he had some connections with P in that he had once held shares in P; that he was guarantor of P's debts under the facilities, and had no involvement in P's management save for the renegotiation of a facility fee. It was common ground that F's sister (E) had been the sole director of each of the companies in P. F gave evidence that he had never participated in P's management, and that while he had once been the ultimate beneficial owner of shares in P, that interest had ceased in 2003, and the shares were thereafter held in discretionary trusts for the benefit of F's children. F contended that he was not a trustee, nominee or beneficiary of any interest in P. B relied on three documents in attempting to establish that there was a good arguable case that F was carrying on a business in England and Wales: (i) a creditor committee application which showed that F dealt with B as a non-director, and illustrated the importance B attributed to F's involvement with the application; (ii) a bank memorandum which noted that B was happy to dispense with credit references given F's personal introduction to B and that B considered F to be the ultimate beneficial owner of shares in P; (iii) various correspondence between E and F.

Held: Appeal dismissed. (1) The credit committee application did not take B's argument very far: the fact that it showed that F was a guarantor on its own could be explained in more than one way and it was not an obvious inference that that specific company was to be used as part of a business that was carried on independently by F. Furthermore, the fact that B hoped to obtain further business from F did not add anything of importance. Similarly, the bank memorandum did not take matters very far. Although there was documentation which showed that B understood F to be the ultimate beneficial owner of shares in P, that evidence was not inconsistent with F's own evidence that he had at an earlier stage been the ultimate beneficial owner of P. Although the correspondence between E and F confirmed the importance E attached to F's role as guarantor, it did not provide any real evidence that F had a role in P's management. (2) A significant point was that there was nothing to gainsay F's claim made in evidence, and supported by contemporaneous documents, that he ceased to have any interest in P in 2003 and that from that point P was ultimately owned for F's children. As there was nothing of any weight to contradict that, it was very hard to sustain a contention that F was himself carrying on business in connection with P during the relevant period. Even if there were substantially more evidence of F's involvement with P and the entities behind P, it was hard to see how it could be maintained that F himself was carrying on business. There was no basis for saying that the registrar had erred; the evidence amply supported his conclusion. Moreover, the instant court would have arrived at the same conclusion on the basis of evidence before it.

ANGLO IRISH BANK CORP LTD v FLANNERY, [2012] EWHC 4090 (Ch), [2013] B.P.I.R. 165, Newey, J, Ch D.

1696. Cross-border insolvency–Foreign judgments–Enforceability of foreign judgments in avoidance proceedings in insolvency–Applicability of Dicey rule

[Foreign Judgments (Reciprocal Enforcement) Act 1933 (c.13); Insolvency Act 1986 (c.45) s.426(4), s.426; Cross-Border Insolvency Regulations 2006 (SI 2006/1030).]

In conjoined appeals brought by the appellants (E and G) against decisions of the Court of Appeal ([2010] EWCA Civ 895, [2011] Ch. 133, [2010] C.L.Y. 1872 and [2011] EWCA Civ 971, [2012] Ch. 538, [2012] C.L.Y. 1849) the court was required to determine whether and in what circumstances an order of a foreign court in avoidance proceedings in insolvency would be recognised and enforced in England. In *Rubin*, a judgment of a United States court in respect of fraudulent conveyances and transfers had been enforced against E in England at common law. In *New Cap*, an Australian judgment in respect of unfair preferences had been enforced against G under the Foreign Judgments (Reciprocal Enforcement) Act 1933, and the Insolvency Act 1986 s.426. At common law and under the 1933 Act a foreign court had jurisdiction to give a judgment in personam capable of enforcement if the person against whom it was given was present in that country when the proceedings were instituted; claimed or counterclaimed in the proceedings; submitted to the jurisdiction of the court by voluntarily appearing in the proceedings; or had agreed to submit to the jurisdiction of the court. Those principles were known as the "Dicey rule". Neither E nor G had been present or resident in the US or Australia, though there was an issue as to whether G had submitted to the jurisdiction of the US court. Relying on *Cambridge Gas Transport Corp v Official Committee of Unsecured Creditors of Navigator Holdings Plc* [2006] UKPC 26, [2007] 1 A.C. 508, [2006] C.L.Y. 2360 and *HIH Casualty & General Insurance Ltd, Re* [2008] UKHL 21, [2008] 1 W.L.R. 852, [2008] C.L.Y. 2158, the Court of Appeal decided in *Rubin* that the Dicey rule did not apply to foreign judgments in avoidance proceedings, and that the US judgment was enforceable at common law. That decision was followed in *New Cap*, where it was decided that the judgment was enforceable under the 1986 Act and at common law. The issues were whether (i) the Dicey rule applied to foreign judgments in avoidance proceedings; (ii) in *Rubin*, enforcement could be effected through the assistance provisions in the Cross-Border Insolvency Regulations 2006, which implemented UNCITRAL's Model Law on cross-border insolvency; (iii) the judgments were enforceable by reason of E or G's submission to the jurisdiction of the foreign courts (iv) in *New Cap*, enforcement could be effected through s.426 of the 1986 Act, the common law or under the 1933 Act.

Held: Appeals allowed in part. (Lord Clarke dissenting on E's appeal in Rubin) (1) The judgments were in personam and the Dicey rule applied. There was no reason why, as a matter of policy, there should be a more liberal rule for avoidance judgments in insolvency proceedings. Such a rule would represent a radical departure from substantially settled law, and a change of that nature was a matter for the legislature. The limited scope of the Dicey Rule was because there was no expectation of reciprocity on the part of foreign countries. The dicta in *Cambridge Gas* and *HIH* did not justify the result reached by the Court of Appeal in *Rubin*. Moreover, *Cambridge Gas* was wrongly decided, *Cambridge Gas* and *HIH* considered (paras 106, 115-117, 128-132). (2) The Model Law was not designed to provide for the reciprocal enforcement of judgments. Neither it nor the Regulations said anything about the enforcement of foreign judgments against third parties, and it would be surprising if it was intended to deal with insolvency judgments by implication. There was nothing to suggest that it applied to the recognition and enforcement of foreign judgments against third parties (paras 142-144). (3) G had submitted to New Cap's Australian insolvency proceedings and was thus to be regarded as having submitted to the jurisdiction of the Australian court responsible for supervising those proceedings. It could not to be allowed to benefit from the proceedings without taking the burden of complying with orders made therein. The position was different in *Rubin*. While it would have been arguable that E had submitted to the jurisdiction of the US court, they had not appeared in the adversary proceedings. Since it had not been argued that they had submitted to the jurisdiction of the US court in any other way, it was not necessary to explore the matter further (paras 166-169). (4) In view of the conclusion that G had submitted to the Australian court's jurisdiction, the issues on s.426 of the 1986 Act did not arise. However, since the matter had been fully argued a view would be expressed: s.426(4) and s.426(5) were not concerned with the enforcement of judgments. Section 426(1) dealt with the intra-UK enforcement of orders, and s.426(4) dealt with intra-UK assistance, and assistance for foreign designated countries. If s.426(4) applied to intra-UK enforcement, then s.426(1) would be largely redundant. The history of the 1933 Act showed that insolvency proceedings were included in the definition of "civil and commercial matters". The Act therefore applied to the *New Cap* judgment and enforcement should be by way of registration under it (paras 145, 152, 170-176). (5) E's appeal in *Rubin* would be allowed, but G's appeal in *New Cap* would be dismissed on the ground that G had submitted to the jurisdiction of the Australian court (para.177). (6) (Per Lord Mance) While *Cambridge Gas* was distinguishable, it had not necessarily been wrongly decided (para.178).

RUBIN v EUROFINANCE SA; NEW CAP REINSURANCE CORP LTD (IN LIQUIDATION) v GRANT, [2012] UKSC 46, [2013] 1 A.C. 236, Lord Walker, J.S.C., SC.

1697. **Cross-border insolvency–Jurisdiction–Secondary insolvency proceedings involving Greek airline company–Jurisdiction of English courts–Meaning of "establishment" within art.2(h) Regulation 1346/2000**

[Pensions Act 2004 (c.35) s.127; Regulation 1346/2000 on insolvency proceedings Art.2(h).]

The appellant airline company (O) appealed against a decision ([2012] EWHC 1413 (Ch), [2012] B.C.C. 841, [2012] C.L.Y. 1853) that the English courts had jurisdiction to issue a winding-up order, on an application by the respondent pension scheme trustees (T), on the basis that O had an establishment in England for the purposes of Regulation 1346/2000 art.2(h). O, a company incorporated in Greece, had commenced operations as a state-owned airline in 2003, providing flights to European destinations, including London Heathrow. Its head office in England was in London, with further premises in Manchester and a ticket office at Heathrow. The majority of its employees in England were members of the company pension scheme. O was placed in liquidation by the Court of Appeal in Greece in October 2009. The Heathrow office was closed in November 2009 and the Manchester office in May 2010. O's bank in England was instructed to cancel all standing orders and direct debits on June 29, 2010. On July 2, 2010, the Greek liquidator terminated the employment of O's employees in England. Two employees were retained at the London office on short-term contracts. There was a £15 million deficit in the pension scheme and T presented its petition in England on July 20, 2010. Responsibility for the scheme would only be assumed by the Pension Protection Fund, under the Pensions Act 2004 s.127, if a secondary winding-up of O could be constituted in England. The High Court found that the fact that O had 27 employees until the week before T's petition was presented, and kept a skeleton staff and a fully equipped office for a further several months, constituted economic activity. The court rejected the need for that economic activity to be market-facing. O contended that the Regulation's definition of "establishment" required external and market-facing economic activity which was more than transitory. It argued that the desultory running down of a business such as might have been indicated by the court's finding did not count.

Held: Appeal allowed. The court had erred in overlooking the 1996 Virgos-Schmit report on the European Convention on Insolvency Proceedings as an authoritative commentary on the Regulation, and in failing to take into account the fact that the Regulation was concerned with all insolvency proceedings. The definition of establishment applied to any secondary insolvency proceedings, including forms of insolvency proceedings under which the debtor company might well seek to trade out of its difficulties. The question was not so much what the debtor company did in the period after the commencement of proceedings, but in the period immediately leading up to commencement, as the issue of whether or not the company had an establishment for the purposes of the Regulation had to be answered as at the point at which the jurisdiction of the insolvency court was invoked. There was therefore no difficulty in giving the definition of establishment within the Regulation a meaning which required more economic activity than the mere process of winding-up. On the contrary, at the point of entering insolvency proceedings it was likely that the debtor company would be trading and would continue to trade to some extent. The question was whether at that point it had an establishment in a country other than the country of its "main interests", which depended on whether it had in that other country a "place of operations", where non-transitory economic activity was carried on with human and physical resources. The definition was clearly intended to lay down a rule that the mere presence of an office or branch at which the debtor was located was not sufficient. It had to be a place "of operations". Applying the Virgos-Schmit report to the facts of the instant case, there was therefore no possible alternative to concluding that the definition of establishment required by the Regulation had not been fulfilled. By the critical date of July 20, 2010, O had already been in liquidation for 10 months, had ceased all commercial operations for a similar length of time and, more recently, had dismissed and paid off its remaining employees with money acquired from the liquidator in Greece. Thereafter, only a skeleton, ad-hoc, staff was maintained, for the purposes of the winding-up. The London office had no assets of any real value. Nothing that took place at or beyond July 20, 2010 seemed to have any external economic function other than as part of a desultory liquidation. O did not have an "establishment" within the meaning of the Regulation as at July 20, 2010, and its subsequent winding-up in England, even if relevant at all, did not amount to "economic activity" within the definition, *Interedil Srl (In Liquidation) v Fallimento Interedil Srl (C-396/09)* [2012] Bus. L.R. 1582 and *Trillium (Nelson) Properties Ltd v Office Metro Ltd* [2012] EWHC 1191 (Ch), [2012] B.C.C. 829, [2012] C.L.Y. 1852 considered. There had therefore been no jurisdiction on that date for T to commence secondary insolvency proceedings in England (see paras 30-38 of judgment).

OLYMPIC AIRLINES SA, *Re*; *sub nom.* TRUSTEES OF OLYMPIC AIRLINES SA PENSION AND LIFE ASSURANCE SCHEME v OLYMPIC AIRLINES SA, [2013] EWCA Civ 643, [2013] B.C.C. 728, Moore-Bick, L.J., CA (Civ Div).

1698. Discharge from bankruptcy–Compliance–Order suspending automatic discharge from bankruptcy–Defendant granted certificate of discharge–Whether defendant had complied with order

[Insolvency Act 1986 (c.45) s.375(1).]

The applicant receiver applied pursuant to the Insolvency Act 1986 s.375(1) to vary an order to delete a direction that a certificate of discharge be granted to the bankrupt respondent (B). B had been adjudged bankrupt in 2007. In March 2008, the trustee in bankruptcy obtained an order suspending B's automatic discharge from bankruptcy after it was alleged that he had failed to cooperate with the trustee's enquiries. In September 2008 an income payment agreement dated August 5, 2008 was put in place. The trustee wrote a letter to the receiver explaining that B was cooperating, but did not inform the court. Following that, B applied for a certificate of discharge to be effective from August 14, 2008, contending that he had complied with the conditions set out in the March 2008 order and had fully cooperated within the required time. The certificate was granted and dated May 15, 2008. The trustee sought to challenge the discharge on the basis that there were questions regarding B's role in a company for which he was being prosecuted. The issue was whether B had complied with the conditions set out in the March 2008 order giving rise to the discharge.

Held: Application refused. The issue was whether full cooperation had been given, not whether B had been guilty of any criminal offence. The receiver had to demonstrate a material difference to what was before the judge when she made the original order granting the discharge, *Papanicola v Humphreys* [2005] EWHC 335 (Ch), [2005] 2 All E.R. 418, [2005] C.L.Y. 2277 applied. The trustee had written to the receiver in September 2008 following the income payment agreement and said that he believed that B had cooperated. At that stage the receiver was aware of B's application for a certificate of discharge yet he did nothing, and did not attend the hearing. He only became proactive after the event when the prosecution team met to discuss the implication of that order upon charges that were before the crown court. B had fully cooperated with the trustee and was entitled to his certificate. The trustee was satisfied in September 2008 that cooperation had taken place. It was not a situation where B simply had one meeting and gave no information; there had been ongoing and lengthy correspondence and B had done all that he could to assist. There were no other conditions that B had to fulfil under the terms of the March 2008 order. Accordingly, the order would stand. Under the Insolvency Rules 1986 r.6.193A(1), an income payments agreement could only be entered into prior to the discharge of a bankrupt. So as not to render the payments agreement void, it was necessary to vary the date of the discharge order, which pre-dated the income payments agreement, to August 15, 2008 (see paras 9-11, 13-15 of judgment).

OFFICIAL RECEIVER v COOKSEY [2013] B.P.I.R. 526, District Judge Stewart, CC (Kingston on Thames).

1699. Discharge from bankruptcy–Matrimonial orders–Ambit of discretion conferred on court by s.281(5) Insolvency Act 1986 to release discharged bankrupt from order made in family proceedings–Jurisdiction to vary amount of debt

[Insolvency Act 1986 (c.45) s.281(5)(b).]

The applicant husband (H), a discharged bankrupt, applied for an order under the Insolvency Act 1986 s.281(5) releasing him from a debt owed to his former wife (W) by way of financial provision ancillary to their divorce. In 2003, H had been required to pay W a lump sum by monthly instalments due to end in 2009. He defaulted on the payments, was made bankrupt in 2006 and discharged from bankruptcy in 2007. By virtue of s.281 (5) (b), the default position was that H's obligation to pay W was not released by his discharge from bankruptcy. The issue was the ambit of the discretion conferred on the court by s.281 (5) to release discharged bankrupts from a debt falling within s.281 (5) (b). H submitted that the relief granted to W had been wrongly expressed in the 2003 order as a lump sum payable by instalments, rather than as regular monthly maintenance payments, which would have been capable of variation under the matrimonial jurisdiction. That being so, he maintained that the instant court, its discretion being unfettered, could review, release, or modify the debt in the same way as the matrimonial courts, according to its perception of what would be fair and just in the circumstances.

Held: Application refused. The court had to balance the prejudice to the party who was owed the money, if there was any prospect of repayment, with the potential prejudice to the debtor's realistic chances of building a viable future if the obligation remained. In striking that balance, the burden was on the applicant to defeat the rationale of excluding s.281 (5) (b) debts from automatic discharge. The discretion conferred by the provision was unfettered and could be exercised at any time after discharge, but it had to be exercised for the proper purposes for which it was conferred. The approach taken in *Hayes v Hayes* [2012] EWHC 1240 (Ch), [2012] B.P.I.R. 739, [2012] C.L.Y. 1821 and the factors identified in that case were sound, *Hayes* applied. The purpose of the discretion was to enable the court to release an obligation where its continuance served no substantial purpose, either because it was unlikely ever to be satisfied, or where release was necessary to allow the debtor to re-establish himself. The provision was not to be deployed by the instant court as a means of reviewing the debt, even where the parties' circumstances had changed and modification appeared to be necessary. Review ought to be reserved to the matrimonial courts. In the instant case, taking into consideration all the circumstances and the *Hayes* factors, the balance remained in favour of keeping in place the obligation. There was no sufficient reason to override the default provision (see paras 21-27, 47-50, 53 of judgment).

McROBERTS v McROBERTS, [2012] EWHC 2966 (Ch), [2013] 1 W.L.R. 1601, Hildyard, J, Ch D.

1700. Discharge from bankruptcy–Suspension–Power to suspend discharge from bankruptcy under s.279 Insolvency Act 1986–Purpose of suspension from discharge

[Insolvency Act 1986 (c.45) s.252, s.256, s.278(b), s.279, s.303.]

The appellant trustee in bankruptcy (T) appealed against a decision ([2012] EWHC 1279 (Ch), [2012] B.P.I.R. 672, [2012] C.L.Y. 1820) suspending the respondent bankrupt's discharge from bankruptcy, and ordering T to personally pay his costs. The respondent bankrupt (B) had made a proposal for an individual voluntary arrangement (IVA) shortly before the automatic discharge of his bankruptcy. It was supported by the majority of B's creditors, but T did not support it, as he believed that B had hidden assets. T refused to apply for an order suspending B's discharge from bankruptcy. B therefore made an application under the Insolvency Act 1986 s.279 and s.303. The judge concluded that it would be in the creditors' interests for B's discharge to be suspended, and he granted a suspension from discharge for six weeks, thus enabling B to seek the creditors' agreement to the IVA with a view to applying to annul his bankruptcy. T applied to have the suspension set aside. He believed that the proposed IVA was designed to thwart his efforts to carry out a thorough investigation of B's affairs, and that B had misled the creditors. The application was refused and the judge concluded that T had acted unreasonably in objecting to the suspension of B's discharge. He was ordered to personally pay B's costs. T submitted that (1) ss.279 and 303 did not provide a proper jurisdictional basis for an order suspending B's discharge for the purpose of an IVA; (2) the judge had erred in concluding that T had acted unreasonably; (3) the judge had erred in exercising his discretion as to costs.

Held: Appeal allowed. (1) A purpose of the power conferred by s.279 was to extend the period of the bankruptcy and to ensure that the bankrupt continued to suffer the disabilities arising from his undischarged bankruptcy until he complied with his obligations under the Act, *Shierson v Rastogi (A Bankrupt)* [2007] EWHC 1266 (Ch), [2007] B.P.I.R. 891, [2008] C.L.Y. 2125 considered. The power was intended to be penal and used for purposes connected with the functions of the trustee to realise and distribute the bankrupt's estate. It was clear that the order made in B's case was not linked to his failure to comply with his obligations, but was made to give him time to put an IVA proposal before the creditors, and thereafter secure the annulment of his bankruptcy order. That was impermissible and outside the scope of the jurisdiction conferred by s.279(3) (see paras 47, 50-52, 65 of judgment). The proper gateway for B to have made an application for the suspension of his bankruptcy lay in ss.252 to 256. Section 252 conferred jurisdiction upon the court to make an order which had the effect that, during the period for which it was in force, the bankruptcy petition could not proceed. The court could stay proceedings or modify s.278(b) which provided that the bankruptcy continued until the individual was discharged under the provision of Chapter 1. Therefore, in an appropriate case, the court could make an order under s.252 suspending the automatic discharge of the bankrupt for a specified period (paras 57-64). (2) The judge had fallen into error in concluding that T's actions were unreasonable because: (a) he had adopted the *Wednesbury* unreasonableness test when he ought to have asked himself whether T had acted perversely; (b) it was wholly impossible to say that T had acted perversely in refusing to allow B to make an application on his behalf under s.279(3) to put the IVA before the creditors when that subsection provided no jurisdictional basis for such an application; (c) it was not the duty of a trustee to respond affirmatively to a bankrupt's request that he co-operate in the promotion of an IVA proposal. T had believed that B was in continuing default of his obligations and that the proposed IVA was defective and prejudicial to the interests of the creditors with whom he had no personal connection. In those circumstances, T had not acted perversely or as no other reasonable trustee would have acted, *Osborn v Cole* [1999] B.P.I.R. 251, [1999] C.L.Y. 382 applied (paras 71-74). (3) In the light of the findings above, the judge's order for costs could not stand. He had no proper basis for ordering T to pay B's costs (para.77).

BRAMSTON v HAUT, [2012] EWCA Civ 1637, [2013] 1 W.L.R. 1720, Rix, L.J., CA (Civ Div).

1701. Individual voluntary arrangements–Creditors' meetings–Admission of creditor into voting–Amount of indebtedness–Valuation of security held by creditor

[Insolvency Rules 1986 (SI 1986/1925) Pt 5 r.5.22(4).]

The appellant (M) appealed against a district judge's decision to adjudge him bankrupt and to uphold a decision of the first respondent chairman of an individual voluntary arrangement creditors' meeting to admit the second respondent bank (B) to voting in the sum of £2.9 million. B was a secured creditor of M, owed £3.4 million. In June 2011 it served a statutory demand, valuing its security, a property owned by M, at £350,000; the statutory demand related to the balance. B also valued its security at £350,000 on a bankruptcy petition it presented in August 2011, petitioning for the balance. That figure coincided with an earlier settlement agreement between M and B, which provided that upon payment of £350,000 B would release its security; that sum was never paid. B had obtained a valuation in November 2010 valuing the property at £650,000 to £700,000. B held a first charge for £350,000; another secured creditor had priority for the next £250,000 under a deed of priority; B's charge then secured the remainder of its debt. B considered that, after the costs of realisation, it would recover no more than £350,000. Following the chairman's decision, B voted against the IVA, thus defeating it. M argued that the district judge had been wrong to summarily dismiss his challenge to B's debt, because there was a real issue to be tried as to the level of unsecured indebtedness, as calculated by the valuation of the property and the inclusion of a number of expenses M alleged were merely contingent.

Held: Appeal dismissed. (1) The chairman had marked the unsecured part of B's claim as objected to, but allowed the votes to be cast in the amount claimed by B, as provided by the Insolvency Rules 1986 Pt 5 r.5.22(4). That was appropriate as the chairman had been in no position to value the property himself. The fact that the claim had been marked as objected to did not of itself demonstrate that there was a real issue to be tried requiring directions for expert evidence. The position fell to be decided before the district judge, who had to decide himself whether there was a real issue to be tried. M's submission that in admitting B's vote in the amount claimed, the chairman had treated B as having abandoned its security over £350,000 was incorrect. B had never abandoned its security but had valued it as having no greater value than £350,000. If, in the event, the security had realised more, B would have been entitled to priority after discharge of the £250,000 charge. The real issue had therefore been whether B had established that its security was correctly valued at no more than £350,000. As M had put in no valuation evidence, he faced an uphill struggle unless his comments on B's valuation were so compelling as to show that there was a real issue to be tried. His comments had not been of that order. The facts that the valuation had been made in November 2010 and had been based on a single inspection, that there was a lack of comparables and that the property was difficult to value accurately did not demonstrate that the value was wrong. Further, it was an open market, not forced sale, valuation. The property's value was to be ascertained on a forced sale basis. Moreover, there was no evidence that prices had risen in the area between November 2010 and February 2012, which was the relevant date for valuing the unsecured element of B's claim for the IVA. Accordingly, B had been entitled to continue to rely on the valuation it had. As the same figure had been agreed by the parties in the settlement agreement, there had been an onus on M to disturb that valuation by proper evidence (see paras 23-27 of judgment). (2) M's point regarding the correct figure to take into account for expenses did not matter. If the disputed costs and continuing interest were taken into account, the position was comfortably in B's favour. B's evidence demonstrated that there were substantial historical costs, which had been charged against the property and fell to be recouped from the proceeds of sale. Those costs had to be taken into account in valuing the security. Further, it would not be appropriate to ignore even future anticipated costs on the ground that they were not provable. To the extent that costs were bound to be incurred, they had to be taken into account in valuing the security. The court should not proceed on the basis that exceptional or unusual costs would be incurred, but where receivers were in place, the ongoing costs associated with their appointment were inevitable and could not be ignored, *Owo-Samson v Barclays Bank Plc (No.1)* [2003] EWCA Civ 714, [2003] B.P.I.R. 1373, [2003] C.L.Y. 2367 considered. Costs which inevitably had to be incurred before or in realisation of the security had to be taken into account in ascertaining the unsecured balance, as the value of the security was necessarily reduced by the amount of those future costs (paras 30-33).

McNALLY, *Re*; *sub nom.* McNALLY v DYMOND, [2013] EWHC 1685 (Ch), [2013] B.P.I.R. 604, Judge Purle Q.C., Ch D.

1702. Individual voluntary arrangements–Suspension–Suspension of IVA approval pending creditor's challenge to debt valuation–Whether final IVA binding upon those who became creditors after suspension

[Insolvency Act 1986 (c.45) s.252, s.262(4), s.262; Insolvency Rules 1986 (SI 1986/1925) Pt 5 r.5.21 (2).]

The appellant creditors (P) appealed against orders setting aside statutory demands served upon the respondent debtors (D). P had provided funds to D for investment and later issued proceedings to recover the money when the investment failed. D obtained interim orders under the Insolvency Act 1986 s.252 to enable them to put forward proposals for Individual Voluntary

Arrangements. P lodged a proof of debt but their claim was treated as a contingent liability and valued at £1, and the IVAs were approved. P issued an application under s.262 challenging that valuation. The district judge suspended the approval of the IVAs and found that P's claim should be admitted to voting in the sum of approximately £35,000. He ordered D to pay P's costs of £7,010.52. At a further creditors' meeting the IVAs were approved. P issued statutory demands to recover their costs. P submitted that because the IVAs had been suspended rather than revoked, they did not encompass claims which had arisen since the date of the first creditors' meeting.

Held: Appeal dismissed. (1) An IVA bound every creditor who was entitled to vote at the meeting at which the IVA was approved. For those purposes, neither the 1986 Act nor the Insolvency Rules 1986 distinguished between the original meeting at which the IVA was considered and any subsequent meeting held pursuant to a direction of the court made under s.262(4). Every creditor who had notice of the meeting was entitled to vote at it, and the calculation of a creditor's entitlement to vote was undertaken in accordance with r.5.21(2). Again, no distinction was drawn between an original meeting and a subsequent meeting. There was no provision in the Act or the Rules that a revised proposal put to a further meeting of creditors was restricted in its effect to those who were creditors at the date of the original meeting. Nor was there any provision to the effect that notice of the further meeting was only to be given to those who were entitled to vote at the first meeting (see para.27 of judgment). (2) The distinction between the suspension and revocation of an IVA's approval did not have the effect of determining the creditors to be bound by the IVA to be considered at the further meeting. If the Act provided that directions for a further meeting could be given in the case of the suspension of approval, but not in the case of revocation of approval, it would be clear that in the case of revocation the debtor was required to start again from scratch. It would be more of a basis for suggesting that it was implicit in the concept of suspension that the IVA, once approved by a further meeting, bound only the original creditors. However, s.262(4) empowered the court to give a direction for a further meeting whether the approval given by the first meeting was revoked or suspended. As a matter of principle there was no strong reason why, where a debtor was putting a proposal for an IVA to a further meeting of creditors, it should not include those who had become creditors since the last meeting. Accordingly, D's liability for the costs was a debt subject to the terms of the IVAs approved at the further meetings. P were therefore not entitled to serve statutory demands in respect of the costs (paras 29-34).

DAVIS v PRICE; *sub nom.* PRICE v DAVIS, [2013] EWHC 323 (Ch), [2013] B.P.I.R. 200, David Richards, J., Ch D.

1703. Individual voluntary arrangements–Variation–Entitlement of secured creditors to vote at creditors' meeting–Basis of challenge to supervisor's decision

[Insolvency Act 1986 (c.45) s.263, s.263(3), s.303(1); Insolvency Rules 1986 (SI 1986/1925) Pt 2 (6) r.2.38, r.2.39.]

The applicant (L), whose application to vary the terms of his individual voluntary arrangement had been refused at a creditors' meeting, applied under the Insolvency Act 1986 s.263 and under condition 64 of the R3 Standard Conditions for IVAs to challenge decisions of the first respondent supervisor (S) concerning the voting rights of two secured creditors (B1 and B2). The IVA incorporated the R3 Standard Conditions for IVAs. L's application to vary the arrangement had been made after S served a default notice on him alleging various breaches of his obligations. Initially, S had refused to convene the necessary creditors' meeting to consider variation, but he had eventually been summoned to do so by the court. S had chaired the meeting. B1 had a first charge over a substantial country house owned by L, and was owed around £4.5 million. B2 had a second charge over a development site, and was owed just short of £1 million. Votes to the value of £6.5 million were cast in favour of the variation as compared to £4.8 million against. However, both B1 and B2 voted against. B1 voted in the sum of £2.5 million, and B2 in the sum of

£500,000. Accordingly, the variation was rejected by 42.07 per cent of the creditors voting. L's case was that B1 and B2 should not have been permitted to vote, or alternatively that their votes should have been admitted in the sum of £1. B1 and B2 relied on condition 39 of the IVA Standard Conditions, which, they submitted, set out the procedure in relation to the valuation of a secured creditor's security. They also relied upon conditions 63 and 64. There was also an issue as to the scope of the court's powers to determine the instant application, and as to whether there was an analogy between s.263(3) and s.303(1) of the Act.

Held: Application refused. (1) While s.303 had no application to IVAs, the construction of that section was helpful in the construction of s.263(3). The rationale behind the restrictive construction of s.303 was set out in *Osborn v Cole* [1999] B.P.I.R. 251, [1999] C.L.Y. 382 and the same considerations applied to the exercise of the supervisor's powers and discretions in an IVA. Furthermore, the approach to deciding, in company administrations, on the votes to be accorded to a creditor of a company under the Insolvency Rules 1986 Pt 2 (6) r.2.38 and r.2.39 and the process for dealing with appeals against the chairman's decision were identical in all material respects to the provisions in condition 64, *Osborn, National Westminster Bank Plc v Yadgaroff* [2011] EWHC 3711 (Ch), [2012] B.P.I.R. 371, [2012] C.L.Y. 1860, *Revenue and Customs Commissioners v Maxwell* [2010] EWCA Civ 1379, [2011] Bus. L.R. 707, [2011] C.L.Y. 1817, and *Power v Petrus Estates Ltd* [2008] EWHC 2607 (Ch), [2010] B.C.C. 11, [2009] C.L.Y. 2242 applied. It was therefore clear that whether the instant application was treated as one under condition 64 of the Standard Conditions or one under s.263(3) of the Act, the court was confined to events as at the date of the meeting and was not entitled to look at subsequent events (see paras 56-64 of judgment). (2) Condition 39 of the Standard Conditions was of central importance in determining L's application. It was for the secured creditor to value its security. B1 had valued the property to which its charge related, supported by a professional valuation. Under condition 39(4), S had a right to obtain a professional valuation, but had accepted that of B1. He could not be criticised for adopting B1's valuation. The crucial question was whether he had been *Wednesbury* unreasonable in doing so without adjourning the meeting to investigate it further, especially in light of an offer for the property, which had been made a week earlier. There were good grounds for scepticism about the offer, which was shared by both S and B1: it came from an unidentified source where proof of funding had not been provided; it was for an unusual sum, and a figure more than double the valuation; and it had been made subject to contract. There was no suggestion that S's decision had been made in bad faith. It could not be characterised as perverse or absurd and L's challenge in respect of it was therefore dismissed. The same conclusion would have been reached applying the more generous test under condition 64 (paras 65-70). (3) (Obiter) The court had concerns about S's actions in relation to B2. The latter's valuation demonstrated an error of law: it had been required to value its security as at the date of the meeting, and had been wrong to profess to do so by taking the average of two very different valuations obtained over the preceding six months. S had also been unreasonably suspicious of an offer received shortly before the meeting from an identified purchaser. Such factors would have been sufficient for a successful challenge, even on the strict test to be applied under s.263(2) of the Act. However, in light of the findings on B1's claim, the court's views on B2's claim were academic (paras 71-73).

LINFOOT v ADAMSON [2012] B.P.I.R. 1033, Judge Behrens, CC (Leeds).

1704. Liabilities–Loan notes–Criteria for balance-sheet insolvency–Effect of post-enforcement call options on liability in default

[Insolvency Act 1986 (c.45) s.123(2).]

The appellant trustee for investors (B) appealed against a decision ([2011] EWCA Civ 227, [2011] 1 W.L.R. 2524, [2011] C.L.Y. 216) that the respondent company (E) was not balance-sheet insolvent for the purposes of the Insolvency Act 1986 s.123(2) until it reached "a point of no return". E cross appealed on whether a Post-Enforcement Call Option (PECO) was effective to limit its liability. E acquired a portfolio of sub-prime mortgage loans, secured on residential property in the United Kingdom, funded by the issue of loan notes in several classes. The conditions of issue defined events of default incorporating, inter alia, Insolvency Act 1986 s.123(1) and s.123(2). Following the collapse of the Lehman Brothers group, with which E had currency and interest-rate hedging arrangements, and the detrimental changes in both interest and currency rates together with the poor performance of the domestic mortgage market, E's audited accounts showed liabilities substantially higher than assets. Although sterling had depreciated against both the euro and the dollar, the low level of interest rates had resulted in a surplus which had enabled E to pay in full the interest on all the outstanding notes. Accounting rules required the use of current spot exchange rates despite the fact that the redemption date was not until 2045. A certain class of noteholders relied on the liabilities in the audited accounts to assert that E was deemed unable to pay its debts within the meaning of s.123(2) in order to obtain priority.

Held: Appeal dismissed, cross-appeal dismissed. (1) It was unclear how s.123(1)(e) and s.123(2) of the 1986 Act interacted, but their introduction should be seen as making little significant change in the law beyond underlining that the "cash flow test" was also concerned with debts falling due in the future; how far ahead would depend on the nature of the business and other circumstances, *A Company, Re* [1986] B.C.L.C. 261 and *Byblos Bank SAL v Rushingdale Ltd SA* (1986) 2 B.C.C. 99509, [1986] C.L.Y. 323 considered and *Cheyne Finance Plc (In Receivership), Re* [2007] EWHC 2402 (Ch), [2008] 2 All E.R. 987, [2008] C.L.Y. 2152 approved (see para.37 of judgment). The express reference to assets and liabilities was a practical recognition that beyond the reasonably near future any attempt to apply a cash-flow test was completely speculative, and a comparison of present assets with present and future liabilities (discounted for contingencies and deferment) became the only sensible test. However it was far from an exact test, and the burden of proof remained on the party asserting balance-sheet insolvency (para.37). E was a special purpose vehicle and its current assets were a better guide to solvency than for a normal trading company, but currency movements, interest rate fluctuations, and the success of the UK property market were outside its control so its liabilities were speculative. The "point of no return" test was incorrect and should not pass into common usage as a paraphrase of the effect of section 123(2). The correct test was the need to satisfy the court, on the balance of probabilities, that a company had insufficient assets to be able to meet all its liabilities, including prospective and contingent liabilities (para.48). The effect was that E's ability to pay its debts could not be determined until much closer to 2045 (para.49). (2) Given the result of the appeal, the cross-appeal did not need to be answered, but in the light of the widespread use of PECOs in securitisation transactions, Lord Hope agreed with the Chancellor and the Master of the Rolls below in holding that the PECO would have had no effect on E's liability to the noteholders (para.51).

BNY CORPORATE TRUSTEE SERVICES LTD v EUROSAIL-UK 2007-3BL PLC; BNY CORPORATE TRUSTEE SERVICES LTD vV NEUBERGER BERMAN EUROPE LTD, [2013] UKSC 28, [2013] 1 W.L.R. 1408, Lord Hope, J.S.C., SC.

1705. Liquidation–Contingent liabilities–Deferment of steps in liquidation pending crystallisation of contingent claims

[Insolvency Act 1986 (c.45) s.112; Insolvency Rules 1986 (SI 1986/1925) r.4.84, r.4.86, r.4.182A.]

The appellant creditors (R) appealed against a decision ([2012] EWHC 579 (Ch)) that the respondent liquidators of a company (D) had been entitled to make a distribution in D's voluntary liquidation. D had indemnified R in respect of the tax liabilities of companies R had acquired. When the liquidation commenced, R had contingent claims under the indemnities, comprising their potential tax liabilities. The liquidators issued a notice under the Insolvency Rules 1986 r.4.182A requiring creditors to prove their debts. R set out their tax liabilities, but requested the liquidators to defer any further steps in the liquidation until all their claims could be quantified. R considered that the liquidators should ring-fence a reserve out of which the contingent claims could be paid once crystallised. The liquidators considered it unnecessary to wait until all the liabilities became crystallised or to create a reserve, and that they were obliged to value contingent claims under r.4.86.

Held: Appeal dismissed. (1) The judge had correctly regarded R's application as limited to the correctness of the valuation and the liquidators' power to make a retention against distribution. The liquidators had come under a statutory duty to proceed with the liquidation. The first step had been to ascertain the extent of D's liabilities, which was achieved by a r.4.182A notice. R had engaged with the process by proving for their contingent claims and then negotiating on the valuation issue. The court was not therefore concerned with a direct challenge to the decision to admit the claims to proof and value them. R's challenge had to operate within the statutory process that had begun. The first issue was therefore whether the judge had been right to conclude that once the contingent claims had been admitted, the liquidators had had no alternative but to value them. If the liquidators were able to make a retention of the kind R claimed then the correctness of the valuations was not in issue; however, if no such discretion existed, R could only guarantee the possibility of a full indemnity by challenging the valuations (see paras 16-17 of judgment). (2) The instant case concerned how liquidators should process existing, known contingent claims which had been admitted to proof and which had been valued by the liquidator. The existence of a right to challenge under the Insolvency Act 1986 s.112 might be thought to be a strong factor against the existence of a further overriding discretion to make a retention to await the contingency rather than proceeding to distribute any surplus on the basis of the valuation. A liquidator was under an obligation to complete the liquidation even though the effect of the winding-up could be to defeat the contingent claims of its creditors, *House Property and Investment Co Ltd, Re* [1954] Ch. 576, [1953] C.L.Y. 536 applied and *R-R Realisations, Re* [1980] 1 W.L.R. 805, [1980] C.L.Y. 292 considered. Consequently, the liquidator was not obliged to set aside a fund to meet those contingent claims in full and the contingent creditors' claims fell to be satisfied through the valuation of their claims under r.4.86, *Stanhope Pension Trust Ltd v Registrar of Companies* [1994] B.C.C. 84, [1994] C.L.Y. 425 applied. It was clear from the wording of r.4.86 that there had to be a valuation of contingent claims in order for them to be admitted to proof. There might be cases where the contingency was so imminent that the liquidator could wait for the event to occur. Even where such a degree of imminency did not exist, the valuation of contingent claims remained open to valuation in the light of subsequent events under r.4.84 until the completion of the liquidation. However, there were real difficulties in seeing how a liquidator who had already valued the contingent claims came under a legal duty to provide for the contingency in full by making a reserve. The effect of the Rules was to allow the liquidator to distribute the assets free from any further claims by creditors. The liquidators were entitled to proceed to a distribution to members on the basis of debts admitted to proof (paras 29, 32, 36-38). (3) There had been no error by the liquidators in the valuation of the claims. Any valuation of a contingent liability had to be based on a genuine assessment of the chances of the liability occurring. Although the contractual liability of a party offering an indemnity operated as insurance against prospective loss, nothing in r.4.86 required the liquidator to guarantee a 100 per cent return on the indemnity by assuming a worst case scenario in favour of the creditors. That would produce a valuation unfair to the company and its other creditors and members (para.43).

DANKA BUSINESS SYSTEMS PLC (IN LIQUIDATION), *Re; sub nom.* RICOH EUROPE HOLDINGS BV v SPRATT, [2013] EWCA Civ 92, [2013] Ch. 506, Mummery, L.J., CA (Civ Div).

1706. **Liquidation–Leases–Claim for unpaid rent–Applicability of principle in Lundy Granite Co, Re (1870-71) L.R. 6 Ch. App. 462 to provisional liquidations**

[Insolvency Act 1986 (c.45).]

The joint administrators of the applicant company (M) asked the court to determine certain issues in respect of M's claim for unpaid rent against an aviation company in liquidation (X). In 2007, M and X, M's parent company, had entered into a sale and leaseback agreement whereby X sold its main operating premises to M for roughly £8.3 million, M paid X £5.5 million, leaving roughly £2.8 million outstanding, and M leased the premises back to X for 15 years at an annual rent of £520,000, which was payable on the usual quarter days. The payment of £5.5 million was financed by a bank, which had a legal charge over the property; that charge included an assignment of the rent payable under the lease. X went into administration in June 2008. It was in provisional liquidation from June to October 2010, when it was ordered to be wound up. The respondent liquidators of X disclaimed the lease in March 2011. M claimed rent arrears due from X, the bank having reassigned the rent claim. The issues were (i) whether there had been a binding agreement to reduce the rent in December 2008; (ii) whether the rent due during the provisional liquidation period was to be treated as an expense of the liquidation and payable in priority to most other liquidation expenses, on the basis of the principle set out in *Lundy Granite Co, Re* (1870-71) L.R. 6 Ch. App. 462, which applied where the liquidator retained property for the benefit of the liquidation and "when he continues to use it"; (iii) whether the disclaimer was valid; (iv) whether X was entitled to set off the sum of £2.8 million due under the sale and leaseback agreement against the rent due; alternatively, whether the rule in *Cherry v Boultbee* 41 E.R. 171 entitled it to require M to meet its claim for rent out of that amount.

Held: Judgment accordingly. (1) As there was uncertainty over whether consideration had been given for the reduction in rent and whether the bank had consented to the reduction, it would not be appropriate to reach a conclusion on the first issue (see para.26 of judgment). (2) Contrary to the liquidators' submission, the *Lundy Granite* principle applied to provisional liquidations. However, merely retaining and securing property situated on the leased premises did not constitute a use which was sufficient to engage the principle. That was the case in respect of the first quarterly rent period falling within the provisional liquidation period, *ABC Coupler and Engineering Co (No.3), Re* [1970] 1 W.L.R. 702, [1970] C.L.Y. 311 considered. However, by the time rent fell due on September 29, 2010, the provisional liquidators' purpose in retaining the premises was to benefit the provisional liquidation; the principle therefore applied to that period, *Lundy Granite* applied (paras 35, 39, 41-42). (3) M had argued that the disclaimer was invalid, because there was a conflict between the stated intention of the notice of disclaimer and the actual intention, which was to hang on to the property for some time. That could not be accepted: there was nothing in the Insolvency Act 1986 which required a company, when disclaiming, to intend to vacate the property immediately. The liquidators had continued to store aircraft assets in the property after trying unsuccessfully to sell them but they had not acted perversely in disclaiming the lease. Their decision made perfectly good financial sense: X's liability to trespass was not at the time seen as likely to be as great as its liability for unpaid rent, in circumstances where the liquidators hoped to sell the aircraft assets within a few weeks. The disclaimer was therefore valid (paras 56-57, 59, 61, 63). (4) Any right of set-off or right under the rule in *Cherry v Boultbee* was excluded by the terms of the lease, which M continued to be entitled to rely on despite the disclaimer, *Cherry v Boultbee* considered (para.67).

MK AIRLINES LTD (IN LIQUIDATION), *Re*; *sub nom.* MK AIRLINES PROPERTY LTD (IN ADMINISTRATION) v KATZ, [2012] EWHC 2764 (Ch), [2013] Bus. L.R. 243, Nicholas Strauss Q.C., Ch D (Companies Ct).

1707. **Liquidation–Transactions at an undervalue–Payments made from accountant's client account–Monies removed pursuant to accountant's fee agreement**

[Insolvency Act 1986 (c.45) s.238, s.238(4)(a).]

The first respondent insolvency practitioner (H) applied for summary judgment or for an order striking out the claim brought by the applicant liquidator (L). L sought an order that H pay to him, as liquidator of a company (O), the sum of £224,951.11, on the basis that payments made to H from the client account of a firm of accountants (S) on behalf of O were transactions at an undervalue pursuant to the Insolvency Act 1986 s.238(4)(a). S had been engaged by O to provide accountancy services. S's fees were to be paid on a basis of time spent on affairs. O also entered into a separate fee agreement with S's sole proprietor (T), under which T would be entitled to a fee in respect of a distribution that was payable to S's client account. That was a sum which was going to be paid to O by a company in liquidation (C) in satisfaction of claims that O had intimated against C. At the time of the fee agreement, H was one of the joint liquidators of C and would therefore be making the payment that O was to receive. T's agreed fee was 25 per cent of any distribution in excess of £250,000. O wrote to H giving him authority to remit any funds due to O to S's client account. T was given authority to transfer his agreed fees out of the client account and into his office account. The fee agreement was subsequently varied to the effect that, if the distributions from C in favour of O exceeded £916,667, then T would be entitled to retain fees of the difference between the sum received and £750,000. Payments were made out of S's client account to H or for his benefit. H claimed that the payments were repayment of private loans that he had made to T. O received total dividend payments from C of £1.267 million. Accordingly, T was apparently entitled to £517,000. L argued that the fee agreement provided a limited authority to T to transfer the agreed fees: T had to transfer the monies to his office account and then transfer them out to H. L submitted that, because the monies did not route through T's office account, T was not entitled to them. H argued that, for there to be an invocation of s.238, there had to be a transaction made by O which the liquidator or administrator wished to challenge, and, secondly, there had to be mutuality. H submitted that there was no transaction to which O was a party, and there was no mutuality as between it and H.

Held: First respondent's application granted. The monies, whilst they were in S's client account, belonged beneficially to O. Once they were removed by T in discharge of his fees, they became his money unless the fee agreement was challenged in the sense that it was set aside. The fact that T did not use the stated destination, namely the office account, did not affect his entitlement to remove the fees. H clearly gave T "consideration" because the monies were used to discharge his indebtedness. If T were called upon to repay those monies he could simply set his fees off to reduce the payment by the same amount. It was impossible to see how O effected the transactions of the payments to H. The payments made by T were either disbursements of his fees to which he was entitled, or they were unauthorised payments away. T had no actual authority to make payments using O's money for the benefit of H. There was no basis for suggesting that O authorised or held T out as being authorised to make any disbursements from the fund, save in accordance with the terms of the fee agreement. O had not entered into a transaction which L could review. The only transaction it had entered into was the fee agreement, and that was not under challenge. If the payments were unauthorised, there was no transaction by O, *Manson v Smith (Liquidator of Thomas Christy Ltd)* [1997] 2 B.C.L.C. 161, [1998] C.L.Y. 3341, *Knights v Seymour Pierce Ellis Ltd (formerly Ellis & Partners Ltd)* [2001] 2 B.C.L.C. 176, [2002] C.L.Y. 2690 and *Brabon, Re* [2000] B.C.C. 1171, [2000] C.L.Y. 3450 applied. There needed to be a transaction to which O was a party and that involved mutuality: it did not extend to unilateral actions taken by somebody who had no authority to do what he was doing. The instant proceedings were not appropriate because there was no transaction upon which s.238 could bite. L's claim as presently formulated was bound to fail, and/or had no prospect of success.

OVENDEN COLBERT PRINTERS LTD (IN LIQUIDATION), *Re; sub nom.* HUNT (LIQUIDATOR) v HOSKING, [2013] EWHC 311 (Ch), [2013] 2 B.C.L.C. 388, Peter Smith, J., Ch D (Companies Ct).

1708. Liquidators–Fraudulent evasion of VAT–Appointment of provisional liquidators pending hearing of winding-up petition–Likelihood of obtaining winding-up order–Factors relevant to appointment or maintenance of provisional liquidators

[Insolvency Act 1986 (c.45) s.127.]

The applicant company (S) applied to discharge an order appointing provisional liquidators. The respondent commissioners had presented a petition for S's compulsory winding-up. The petition was founded on S's alleged indebtedness of over £3 million arising from VAT assessments, the commissioners having denied S's claims to recover input tax in respect of purchases made from six suppliers on the basis that they were connected with the fraudulent evasion of VAT by missing trader fraud. On the commissioners' application, the judge made a without notice order appointing provisional liquidators, but giving S the opportunity to apply to discharge that order by a specified date, which it took.

Held: Application refused. (1) A judge dealing with an application for the appointment or maintenance of provisional liquidators had to consider whether the petitioner and applicant had demonstrated that it was likely to obtain a winding-up order on the hearing of the petition and, if so, whether it was right that a provisional liquidator should be appointed or maintained in office pending the hearing of the petition. The factors to consider in deciding whether to appoint or maintain provisional liquidators included (a) questions as to the integrity of the company's management and/or accounting and record keeping function; (b) whether there was any real risk of dissipation of the company's assets and/or any real need to take steps to preserve them; (c) whether there was any real risk that the company's books and records would be destroyed and/or any real need for steps to be taken to ensure that they were properly preserved and maintained; (d) whether there was any real need for steps to be taken to facilitate immediate inquiries into the conduct of the company's management and affairs and/or to investigate possible claims against directors for fraudulent or wrongful trading; (e) whether or not the company had a realistic prospect of obtaining a validation order under the Insolvency Act 1986 s.127, because if not, it might not be able to trade in any event; (f) generally, which course seemed likely to cause the least irremediable prejudice to one party or the other, *Revenue and Customs Commissioners v Rochdale Drinks Distributors Ltd* [2011] EWCA Civ 1116, [2012] S.T.C. 186, [2012] C.L.Y. 1875 followed (see paras 11, 16 of judgment). (2) The commissioners had to demonstrate that it was likely that they would be able to satisfy the court at the hearing of the petition both that S's purchases were connected with the fraudulent evasion of VAT and that S, in the person of its sole director, either knew that its purchases were so connected or should have known that the only reasonable explanation for the circumstances in which they took place was that they were so connected, or had ignored obvious inferences to that effect from the facts and circumstances in which it had been trading. On the evidence, the commissioners were able to meet those requirements. S and its suppliers' pattern of trading raised a powerful inference that fraudulent evasion of VAT had occurred in actual or purported supplies, which S's director had been aware of. There was no realistic prospect that S might succeed in explaining away all the indications of likely VAT fraud as a series of unfortunate coincidences (paras 14, 34, 37, 40, 50). (3) The provisional liquidators held £139,000 in cash and there were real grounds for doubt as to whether that sum would remain available for S and its creditors if a winding-up order was made, but control of S and its assets had been returned to its own management in the meantime. There were also real grounds for doubt as to whether any renewed trading would be accurately and reliably documented. The court was unlikely to accede to an application for a s.127 order prospectively validating trading transactions entered into before the hearing of the petition. Returning S to the control of its own management for the next few weeks would not be safe or sensible, and the court therefore exercised its discretion so as to maintain the provisional liquidators in office (paras 59-61, 64-65).

REVENUE AND CUSTOMS COMMISSIONERS v SED ESSEX LTD; *sub nom.* SED ESSEX LTD, *Re*, [2013] EWHC 1583 (Ch), [2013] B.V.C. 314, John Randall QC, Ch D.

1709. Liquidators' powers and duties–Appeals–Power to assign conduct of liquidated company's appeal against tax assessment–Whether right to appeal a property right

[Insolvency Act 1986 (c.45) s.436, Sch.4 Pt III para.6.]

The applicant liquidator sought directions concerning the assignment of conduct of tax appeals by the company in liquidation (C). The liquidator had begun misfeasance proceedings against the respondent former directors (D). Revenue and Customs later raised discovery assessments against C for corporation tax. At D's request, the liquidator caused C to appeal against the assessments. The liquidator informed D that unless the appeals succeeded he would allege in the misfeasance proceedings that they were liable to account to C for the debts created by the assessments. D requested the liquidator to assign the appeals to them. The liquidator could have power to assign the appeals only if the right to appeal was property capable of being sold within the meaning of the Insolvency Act 1986 Sch.4 Pt III para.6.

Held: Directions given. (1) *Heath v Tang* [1993] 1 W.L.R. 1421, [1993] C.L.Y. 222 suggested by implication that a right to appeal was not to be treated as property; *Royal Bank of Scotland Plc v Farley* [1996] B.P.I.R. 638, [1997] C.L.Y. 3009 was apparently consistent with that approach, *Heath* and *Farley* considered. There was also a Court of Appeal decision on an application for permission to appeal that on one reading was consistent with a right of appeal being a thing in action, and two Upper Tribunal decisions containing obiter observations supporting that approach, *Wordsworth v Dixon* [1997] B.P.I.R. 337, [1995] C.L.Y. 419, *R. (on the application of Singh) v Revenue and Customs Commissioners* [2010] UKUT 174 (TCC), [2010] S.T.C. 2020, [2010] C.L.Y. 74 and *McNulty v Revenue and Customs Commissioners* [2012] UKUT 174 (TCC), [2012] S.T.C. 2110, [2012] C.L.Y. 3331 considered. Further, *Cummings v Claremont Petroleum NL* [1998] B.P.I.R. 187, [1998] C.L.Y. 3293 had concluded that a bare right of appeal was not property, but that decision was not binding on the instant court and it had not been necessary on the facts of *Cummings* to decide the point, *Cummings* considered. It was therefore necessary to approach the issue as a novel point that had not been decided by binding authority, but from a starting point that the definition of property in s.436 of the Act was cast in the widest terms and that the court in *Heath* could have proceeded, but had chosen not to proceed, on the basis that a right of appeal was a property right. Firstly, a bare right to appeal against what would otherwise be a liability did not satisfy the classical definition of a chose in action: it was not a right that could be claimed by action, but a right unconditionally conferred on C; nor was it a property right that could only be enforced by action, *Torkington v Magee* [1903] 1 K.B. 644 applied. Secondly, there was a distinction between a chose and the remedies available for its enforcement. The right to a remedy was an incident of the ownership of the chose; the remedy was not something capable of being sold or assigned separately from the right to which it related, *Investors Compensation Scheme Ltd v West Bromwich Building Society (No.1)* [1998] 1 W.L.R. 896, [1997] C.L.Y. 2537 applied. The right of appeal was conferred on C by reason of it having been assessed to tax; the tax liability to which the right of appeal was appurtenant could not be assigned, *Linden Gardens Trust Ltd v Lenesta Sludge Disposal Ltd* [1994] 1 A.C. 85, [1993] C.L.Y. 303 applied. Accordingly, all that could be assigned in the instant case would be the right to appeal; such a right was no more capable of assignment than was a remedy independently of the chose to which it related.

Thirdly, that was consistent with the orthodox approach to whether a bankrupt had locus to appeal, *Heath* considered. Accordingly, a bare right of appeal of the sort under consideration was not property within the meaning of s.436. A right of appeal available to a bankrupt was one the bankrupt lost locus to bring or maintain once he was adjudicated bankrupt, because the only assets out of which the underlying liability could be met vested in the trustee, not because the right was a chose that vested in the trustee. The trustee had a statutory right, but not the obligation, to exercise any right of appeal that the bankrupt might have had from the moment the bankrupt was made subject to a bankruptcy order. Similarly, a right to appeal available to a company in liquidation could only be exercised by the office holder once appointed because he then became the only agent of the company entitled to do so, not because the right of appeal was treated as a property interest (see paras 24-31 of judgment). (2) (Obiter) Absent the agreement of the office holder, the court would not have sanctioned the assignment of the right of appeal to D. The assignment of the right to appeal without being able to assign the liability would place the office holder in a potentially invidious position. That was not a risk the court should sanction given the potential implications for creditors (para.32).

GP AVIATION GROUP INTERNATIONAL LTD, *Re; sub nom.* WILLIAMS v GLOVER, [2013] EWHC 1447 (Ch), [2014] 1 W.L.R. 166, Judge Pelling Q.C., Ch D.

1710. Liquidators' powers and duties–Data controllers–Company in liquidation receiving data subject access requests–Whether liquidators' status as data controllers also applicable to data processed in their capacity as agents for company

[Data Protection Act 1998 (c.29) s.1 (1), s.7.]

The applicant liquidators (L), who had been appointed in the voluntary winding up of a company (C), applied for the determination of questions concerning their duties under the Data Protection Act 1998 to data retained by C. C's business comprised the provision of personal loans. It was a member of the Lehman group. Whilst trading, it had collected and retained "personal data" relating to its borrowers. It was therefore a data controller within the meaning of s.1 (1) of the Act. The data was stored with a loan servicing company, which was also a member of the Lehman group. Even though the data was no longer required for the purpose of administering the loans, C continued to receive data subject access requests under s.7 of the Act, and other requests for information or copy documents. The statutory fee for making a request was £10, but the cost of complying with it was over £450. Since the date of its liquidation, C had been receiving around 88 data requests per month, resulting in an average monthly cost of over £40,000. L were concerned that a continuation of costs at that level would materially impact the distribution of available funds to C's creditors. They posed questions for the court, namely (i) whether they were "data controllers" for the purposes of the Act; (ii) if they were, whether they could dispose of all personal data in their control in their capacity as C's liquidators.

Held: Application granted. (1) It was important to differentiate between activities that liquidators performed by virtue of their office as liquidator, and activities that they performed as agents of the company in respect of which they were liquidator. Many activities in the former category, such as receiving and adjudicating upon proofs of debts, involved processing personal data, so that liquidators were commonly required to register as data controllers. Registration covered all data activities, irrespective of the capacity in which the liquidator undertook them. The issue in the instant case was whether L's status as data controllers was also applicable to data processed in their capacity as agents for the company. For that to be so, the relevant decisions as regards the processing of such data had to have been taken by L as principal in their capacity as office holders, not in their capacity as agents of the company, *Anglo-Moravian Hungarian Junction Railway Co, Ex p. Watkin, Re* (1875) 1 Ch. D. 130, [*Farrow's Bank Ltd, Re* [1921] 2 Ch. 164 and *Stead Hazel & Co v Cooper* [1933] 1 K.B. 840 considered. It could not be deduced from a liquidator's duty to call in a company's assets, or from the court's power to order delivery of property to a liquidator, that the liquidator held the company's assets as principal or as co-principal with the company. In a voluntary liquidation, title to the company's assets remained with the company. In taking control of the company's property, liquidators acted, not as principal by virtue of their office, but as agents for the company; they replaced the control formerly exercised by the board of directors, albeit to protect creditors and to give effect to the statutory scheme rather than to pursue the best interests of the company and its members. Accordingly, the relevant data in the instant case had been under C's control when it went into voluntary liquidation. The intellectual property rights remained vested in C. In exercising any rights in respect of that data, L would be acting as C's agents and would not be data controllers within the meaning of the Act. L were not, therefore, personally liable for compliance with the Act in respect of the data processed by C, including but not limited to responding to requests made under s.7. The position would be no different for liquidators in a compulsory winding up. C, however, remained under a statutory obligation to deal with such requests provided that they were properly made. The court commented upon the manner in which such requests should be dealt with (see paras 17-20, 24-28, 32-35, 37-38, 44-49). (2) L could dispose of all personal data in respect of which C was the data controller so long as disposal complied with the Act. There were two qualifications, namely that sufficient data to enable responses to s.7 applications had to be retained, as well as sufficient data to enable L to deal with any claims arising in the liquidation, such as personal protection insurance mis-selling claims. L was advised to advertise for such claims, inviting prospective claimants to submit proofs within a specified period (paras 39-41).

SOUTHERN PACIFIC PERSONAL LOANS LTD, *Re; sub nom.* SMITH v INFORMATION OFFICER, [2013] EWHC 2485 (Ch), [2014] 1 All E.R. 98, David Richards, J., Ch D (Companies Ct).

1711. Statutory demands–Guarantors–Guarantor's liability to pay solicitors' invoices–Nature of guarantee agreement–Whether statutory demand justified

The appellant (F) appealed against a decision of a district judge refusing to set aside a statutory demand served on him by the respondent firm of solicitors (S). S had entered into a deed of guarantee with F in December 2010 in which it agreed to continue to provide legal services to a group of clients (X) and agreed to defer demanding immediate payment of their guaranteed liabilities. In return, F personally agreed to repay the guaranteed liabilities by February 2011, which included all present and future monies X owed to S. A schedule of invoices up to that point was attached to the guarantee. In December 2011, S issued a statutory demand claiming the unpaid balance of sums invoiced under the schedule and in a subsequent invoice. F applied to set aside the statutory demand disputing the extent of liability and claiming that S had breached a condition precedent which had induced him to enter into the personal guarantee, namely, that S would continue to provide legal services to X and would take a flexible approach to the February payment date. The judge refused F's application. F submitted that the judge had erred in refusing to set aside the statutory demand as (1) there was an agreed collateral warranty that S would be flexible in respect of the payment deadline; (2) the fees claimed were unliquidated sums which could not be the subject of a bankruptcy petition.

Held: Appeal dismissed. (1) Even if on F's case that there was a collateral warranty whereby S had agreed that the February repayment date was wholly flexible provided that the indebtedness was reduced prior to that date, he had failed to comply with his obligations under it as evidenced by a document F produced which showed that there was no reduction in indebtedness between the date of the guarantee and the February deadline. There was no triable issue in relation to an alleged collateral warranty (see paras 17-18 of judgment). (2) Where an agreement to pay a fixed sum was made at the outset, or where further work was only undertaken on condition that a client agreed to pay outstanding invoices, there was consideration for the agreement and the client could not resile from it, *Truex v Toll* [2009] EWHC 396 (Ch), [2009] 1 W.L.R. 2121, [2009] C.L.Y. 2221 applied. In the instant case, the guarantee was clearly an agreement to pay the sums set out in the schedule by February 2011 under which S only agreed to undertake further work on the condition that F agreed to pay the outstanding invoices set out in the schedule, *Truex* applied. F was correct in that the guarantee did refer to moneys owed in the future which were unliquidated debts, but that did not make the sums in the detailed invoices unliquidated. The debt was a liquidated debt in so far as it had not been paid and F could not resile from his agreement. The instant argument did not provide a triable issue. Accordingly, a stay on the petition was lifted (paras.21-22, 25).

FRANCIS v SOLOMON TAYLOR & SHAW (A FIRM), [2013] EWHC 9 (Ch), [2013] B.P.I.R. 314, Roger Wyand Q.C., Ch D (Bankruptcy Ct).

1712. Transactions defrauding creditors–Intention–Purpose of property transfer–Judge's entitlement to set aside transfer

[Insolvency Act 1986 (c.45) s.423(3).]

The appellant trustee in bankruptcy (W) appealed against the dismissal of his application to set aside a property disposition made by the respondent bankrupt (T) as a transaction to defraud his creditors. T had been a director of a family company. In 2002 he had invested £120,000 that was lent by his wife (R) in the company. In April 2003 the company was placed in creditors' voluntary liquidation. T transferred a property into the joint names of himself and R to be held as tenants in common in equal shares. The transfer expressed no consideration. They later made a declaration of trust that recited that R had paid £120,000 towards improvement works to the property, £120,000 as a loan to his company, that T was able to pay his debts, and that a mortgage on the property, which had been obtained to discharge T's prior liabilities, was to be discharged first from his interest in the property. The property was later sold and half the proceeds were used to discharge the mortgage. The remainder was used to buy a property free of charge in R's sole name. In 2009 T was made bankrupt and W was appointed as his trustee. W applied to set aside the transfer into joint names and sought to recover the new property bought by R. The judge held that the real and substantial purpose of the transfer was to give effect to an earlier agreement that T had made with R and that escaping his liabilities had not been part of T's purpose. He held that W had failed to prove the statutory purpose under the Insolvency Act 1986 s.423(3) for the court to make a setting aside order.

Held: Appeal dismissed. Objectively the transaction was at an undervalue for the purposes of s.423(1) of the Act because what R was entitled to, in terms of the loan and the value of the improvement works, did not amount to 50 per cent of the value of the property. That left the question under s.423(3) of whether the judge had been right to find that it had been no part of T's intention to put assets beyond the reach of his creditors. The judge had been entitled to accept the evidence of T and R, and he had had well in mind the inconsistencies between their evidence and the declaration of trust. It had been legitimate for him to take the view that the recitals to the declaration of trust had stated the pre-existing position as understood by the parties and that the transfer only brought the position in line with their agreement. There was no error in the judge's approach. The objective factors pointing towards a transaction intended to defraud creditors were not so powerful that the judge could not possibly believe the evidence of T and R. His conclusion could not be challenged (see paras 18, 24-25, 30, 32 of judgment).

WILLIAMS v TAYLOR, [2012] EWCA Civ 1443, [2013] B.P.I.R. 133, Ward, L.J., CA (Civ Div).

1713. **Transactions defrauding creditors–Subsidiary companies–Letter of support from parent to subsidiary's board–Alleged creation of binding obligation to support subsidiary–Alleged agreement within s.423 Insolvency Act 1986 not to enforce obligation**

[Insolvency Act 1986 (c.45) s.423(1), s.424(1)(a).]

The applicant creditor (C) applied for leave under the Insolvency Act 1986 s.424(1)(a) to make an application for relief under s.423 against the second respondent company in liquidation (S) and its ultimate parent (P). C had been given an arbitration award against S in June 2011. Shortly afterwards, S was put into administration and its business and assets were sold to a new company within P's group. In May 2008, May 2009 and March 2010, P had sent S's board of directors letters of support. In each year, S had recorded a loss and considerable debts. P's letters stated that it would provide the necessary support to ensure that S continued as a going concern. P withdrew financial support on the day S was put into administration. C argued that (1) each letter created binding obligations on P to put S in sufficient funds to enable it to make payment of all its liabilities falling due during the period in question; (2) there had been an agreement between P and S that in anticipation of the sale of its business and assets to the new group company, S would not enforce its rights against P under the letter, and that that agreement constituted a transaction within s.423(1) made with the purpose described in s.423(3).

Held: Application refused. (1) The fact that the letters had been addressed to the board and not simply to S was deliberate, and it was significant that they had been provided during the preparation of S's year-end financial statements. The obvious purpose of each letter was to enable S's directors and auditors to consider whether it was appropriate for the financial statements for that year to be prepared on a going concern basis. The letters did not purport to be a contract with S, and there was no indication in the letters of what consideration was passing from S in return for P's financial support. The fact that S, as opposed to the directors, might have relied on the letters to continue trading did not constitute consideration. Further, it was extravagant to read the letters as committing P to ensuring that S should, on demand, be provided with funds to meet all its liabilities then due or falling due in the following 12 months. It was unlikely that P was undertaking in a contractually binding way to ensure the discharge of S's huge current debts or committing itself to discharge any other liabilities S should incur and which might fall due within the ensuing 12 months. It was improbable that P would have undertaken so extensive and open-ended an obligation in so summary a manner. The letters did not subject P to any enforceable obligation and C had demonstrated no realistic prospect of establishing that they did (see paras 34-37 of judgment). (2) Even if that conclusion was wrong, C had demonstrated no real prospect of establishing the existence of a transaction falling within s.423(1) or, therefore, of establishing that such a transaction had been entered into by S for the statutory purpose. The evidence did not support the assertion that S and P had viewed the letters as binding, and so did not support the assertion that they had agreed that the letters would not be enforced. The administrators had been closely involved in the attempts to sell S's assets; having failed to interest any third party, the decision had been made to sell them to a specially established company in P's group. If there had been an arrangement as C alleged, the administrators would have been privy to it, which seemed exceedingly unlikely. It would amount to the administrators being party to an arrangement contrary to the interests of S's creditors and instead assisting a course intended to benefit P's commercial interests. The existence of the transaction relied upon was based entirely on speculation (paras 38-43).

SIMON CARVES LTD, *Re; sub nom.* CARILLION CONSTRUCTION LTD v HUSSAIN, [2013] EWHC 685 (Ch), [2013] 2 B.C.L.C. 100, Sir William Blackburne, Ch D.

1714. **Trustees in bankruptcy–Recovery of expenses–Entitlement of trustee in bankruptcy to expenses where bankruptcy order set aside–Identity of party liable to pay expenses**

[Insolvency Act 1986 (c.45) s.375(1); Civil Procedure Rules 1998 (SI 1998/3132); Insolvency Rules 1986 (SI 1986/1925).]

The applicant trustee in bankruptcy (P) applied for directions for the payment of his expenses incurred in relation to the respondent (W). W had been made bankrupt on a petition. After the refusal of her application for permission to appeal against the bankruptcy order, P was appointed as her trustee in bankruptcy. W made a renewed application for permission to appeal. P was not informed of the date of that hearing in December 2011. The judge made no reference to W's application for permission but said that her appeal was allowed and that the bankruptcy order was set aside. He made no provision for the payment of P's expenses. P did not attend the hearing and only learnt that the bankruptcy order had been set aside in January 2012. The parties were agreed that P should be released from office, but the court was required, if it had jurisdiction, to decide whether W should pay P's unpaid expenses of over £6,500.

Held: Application granted. (1) The court had inherent jurisdiction to deal with the instant application and was not conducting a review of the December 2011 order under the Insolvency Act 1986 s.375(1). The December 2011 order had made no provision for P's expenses, and it could not be construed as containing an implied decision that P should not recover his expenses. The correct analysis was that dealing with P's expenses was a necessary consequence of the judge's order, and that the court had inherent jurisdiction to do so. There was no reason in principle why P's expenses should not be paid, at least to the extent that they were incurred prior to January 2012 when P was notified of the setting aside of the bankruptcy order. Until then he was simply doing his duty as trustee to identify the bankrupt estate and the number and size of creditors' claims on the understanding that W had been refused permission to appeal. A trustee who acted properly and innocently of any wrongdoing could expect to obtain payment of his reasonable expenses and was not to be expected to act gratuitously or to discharge expenses out of his own pocket, *Butterworth v Soutter* [2000] B.P.I.R. 582, [2001] C.L.Y. 3717, *Thornhill (Trustee in Bankruptcy) v Atherton* [2004] EWCA Civ 1858, [2005] B.P.I.R. 437, [2005] C.L.Y. 2270 and *Redbridge LBC v Mustafa* [2010] EWHC 1105 (Ch), [2010] B.P.I.R. 893, [2010] C.L.Y. 1860 considered. P's remedy was not limited to the exercise of a lien or equitable charge over assets in his name or under his control, *Mellor v Mellor* [1992] 1 W.L.R. 517, [1992] C.L.Y. 408 considered. As to who should pay his expenses, had P been notified of the December 2011 hearing he could have attended, armed if necessary with information about the amount of his expenses and the relevant authorities to ensure that provision was made for payment of his expenses. Whilst it could be argued that W was to blame for not notifying P of the impending hearing date, P had been unable to indicate any provision in the Act, the Insolvency Rules 1986 or in the CPR which required W to notify P of an appeal against the bankruptcy order, and it could not be said that she was procedurally in default by not doing so. However, the combined effect of the authorities was that P's right to recover his expenses, having acted properly and innocently until January 2012, prevailed over W's right to fully enjoy her estate upon its re-vesting in her, *Thornhill* and *Butterworth* applied. That was so even though the petitioner was largely to blame for those expenses being incurred. W should bear the burden of compensating P for his reasonable expenses incurred until January 2012, and the court directed that her property should stand charged with payment of P's expenses up until that date. The court made no such direction in relation to P's expenses incurred after January 2012 (see paras 17-18, 21-22, 30-34 of judgment). (2) (Per curiam) The court expressed the view that to the extent that the 1986 Rules failed to make it clear that a trustee in bankruptcy's expenses were as important a matter to be dealt with on an appeal against a bankruptcy order as they were in any application for rescission or annulment, consideration should be given to their amendment or to the issue of an appropriate practice direction (para.37).

APPLEYARD v WEWELWALA, [2012] EWHC 3302 (Ch), [2013] 1 W.L.R. 752, Briggs, J., Ch D.

1715. **Winding-up–Compulsory winding-up–Rejection of administrator's proposals at creditors' meeting–Administrator's duty to apply to court for directions–Power of court to make winding-up petition**

[Insolvency Act 1986 (c.45) Sch.B1 para.55(2), Sch.B1 para.55, Sch.B1 para.68(1), Sch.B1 para.68.]

The applicant unsecured creditors (X) applied for an order compelling the respondent administrator (S) to seek a compulsory winding-up order of the debtor company (B). B, which was insolvent, had been made subject to an administration order. X maintained that some of B's assets might have been fraudulently transferred under the administration. S's proposals, which envisaged that there would be insufficient funds to pay the unsecured creditors, were rejected by over 50 per cent of B's creditors, who voted for a resolution requiring S to petition for the compulsory winding-up of B. X maintained that a compulsory winding-up order was necessary so that a liquidator could carry out a proper investigation into the transfer of B's assets. S declined to apply for a compulsory winding-up order, and he declined to apply to the court for directions under the Insolvency Act 1986 Sch.B1 para.55. S maintained that he was not obliged to apply for directions. It was his case that he did not have sufficient funds to petition for a compulsory winding up, and that an immediate application for a compulsory winding-up order would prejudice B's preferential creditors. X submitted that an administrator was bound to apply to the court for directions under *Sch.B1 para.55* where an administrator's proposals were rejected. S submitted that an administrator had a discretion as to whether to make such an application.

Held: Application granted. (1) While *Sch.B1 para.55* did not expressly require S to bring the matter before the court where an initial creditors' meeting had failed to approve an administrators proposals, the language of Sch.B1 para.55(2) implied that there must be a hearing. There could only be a hearing if an application was made, and such an application was ordinarily to be made by an administrator. If, as in the instant case, an administrator did not make an application, there was no reason why an application should not be made by a creditor, *Platinum Developers Ltd v Assignees Ltd (unreported October 5, 2009)* and *Stanleybet UK Investments Ltd, Re* [2011] EWHC 2820 (Ch), [2012] B.C.C. 550, [2012] C.L.Y. 1811 considered. Under Sch.B1 para.68(1), an administrator was required to manage the company's affairs in accordance with the proposals approved under Sch.B1 para.53. If the proposals were rejected by the creditors it was difficult to see how the administrator could manage the companys affairs under Sch.B1 para.68 without making an application to the court for directions. While an administrator could manage a companys affairs without making an application for directions where his revised proposals were accepted, he would be required to make an application where his original proposals were rejected (see paras 62-66, 68-69 of judgment). (2) The court had a power to make a winding-up order of its own motion under Sch.B1 para.55(2)(e) but that power was to be exercised cautiously and in an exceptional case, *Lancefield v Lancefield* [2002] B.P.I.R. 1108, [2003] C.L.Y. 2445 applied. S had acknowledged that legitimate concerns had been raised regarding the transfer of assets under the administration which required investigation but he had not taken any steps to investigate them. It was also unclear whether there would have ever been sufficient funds for the preferential creditors. In those circumstances, it was appropriate that the court exercise its exceptional jurisdiction to make a winding-up order. Such an order would plainly be made if a winding-up petition was issued by a creditor and, in the particular circumstances of the instant case, it was expedient that the creditors were not put to the expense of making that application. Accordingly, S's appointment as an administrator was terminated and a compulsory winding-up order was made (paras 74-75, 77-78, 80, 83-84).

BTR (UK) LTD, *Re; sub nom.* LAVIN v SWINDELL, [2012] EWHC 2398 (Ch), [2012] B.C.C. 864, Judge Behrens, Ch D (Leeds).

1716. Winding-up petitions–Costs–Exceptions to principle that costs of failed petition ordinarily borne by petitioner save in exceptional circumstances–Exceptional circumstances

[Civil Procedure Rules 1998 (SI 1998/3132) Pt 7.]

The applicant company (C) applied for an order for costs arising from a dismissed petition that had been presented by the respondent petitioner (P), together with the costs of an application to restrain advertisement and to strike out. T had presented a petition on the basis of a relatively small undisputed debt. That debt was paid two days after the presentation of the petition, but before an application by C to restrain advertisement and to strike out. The petition was subsequently dismissed as the remaining debt under the petition had given rise to a genuine and substantial dispute. It was C's case that it had raised a dispute with P over the petition debt prior to presentation; P had contended that despite sending its final account, it had not received any notice of dispute; a subsequent letter from C had wrongly denied having received the final account, and that late disclosure of valuations exhibited to C's evidence in reply had been referred to in a misleading manner. P submitted that had C made its case known and produced the valuations earlier in a satisfactory manner, P could have had an opportunity to take the view that there was a dispute that could not be resolved in winding up proceedings. P further submitted C should pay its costs to reflect the late production of its defence. C submitted that although the costs of the petition up to the date of the payment of the undisputed debt should be borne by C, costs should otherwise follow the event.

Held: Judgment accordingly. There was considerable merit in adhering to the principle that save in exceptional circumstances, a petitioner whose petition failed on the basis that the debt was genuinely disputed on substantial grounds should pay the costs of that failure. However, in determining whether there were exceptional circumstances to justify departure from the general rule, the court was entitled to take into account the parties' communications prior to the presentation of the petition, *Fernforest Ltd, Re* [1991] B.C.C. 680, [1991] C.L.Y. 2162 and *GlaxoSmithKline Export Ltd v UK (Aid) Ltd (Costs)* [2003] EWHC 1383 (Ch), [2004] B.P.I.R. 528, [2004] C.L.Y. 2200 considered. In the instant case, notwithstanding that P gave C every reasonable opportunity to do so, C did not set out the basis for its dispute in relation to the final account in any, or any meaningful, way prior to the presentation of the petition. In fact, C had denied having received a final account from P, and it had only been when evidence in reply had been served that there had been any proper exposition of C's case and the production of valuation documents; it was that production that tipped the application against P. The fact that C had not given any meaningful account of its defence prior to the presentation of the petition, and belatedly produced documents which could, if authentic, support its case, amounted to exceptional circumstances to justify departure from the general rule, *Re Fernforest* and *Re UK (Aid) Ltd* applied. However, the most appropriate course to ensure that justice was achieved between the parties was to adjourn the question of costs until the outcome of other proceedings in which disclosure and cross-examination could take place, and the authenticity of the valuations could be addressed. In the event, C was ordered to pay P's costs up until the date C paid the undisputed debt, with the costs of the application and of the petition after that date adjourned (see paras 22-23, 26-27, 29-31, 39-41 of judgment).

SYKES & SONS LTD, *Re; sub nom.* TEAMFORCE LABOUR LTD v SYKES & SON LTD; SYKES & SON LTD v TEAMFORCE LABOUR LTD, [2012] EWHC 1005 (Ch), [2013] Bus. L.R. 106, Richard Snowden QC, Ch D.

1717. **Winding-up petitions–Defences–Striking out of petition where debt genuinely disputed on substantial grounds–Jurisdiction of Companies Court to determine existence of genuinely disputed debt**

[Unfair Contract Terms Act 1977 (c.50) s.12(1).]

The appellant company (T), and its controlling director (M), appealed against an order striking out a winding-up petition issued against the respondent leisure company (X). T's case was that X had supplied a defective yacht in respect of which it sought to recover the cost of work incurred to remedy the faults and significant lost charter income. T relied upon an alleged admission of liability in correspondence. A High Court judge struck out the petition on the ground that the debt was genuinely disputed on substantial grounds, namely that X was entitled to rely on its terms and conditions of business which excluded liability where the customer was not a consumer, and that the defects were disputed in any event. He found that winding-up proceedings were not the place to determine whether T could properly be regarded as a consumer. He also found that there were substantial grounds for saying that no admissions had been made by X. T challenged the judge's conclusions and argued that, even if the standard terms and conditions applied, there was no genuine dispute on substantial grounds as regards its claims.

Held: Appeal dismissed. (1) It was clear from the Unfair Contract Terms Act 1977 s.12(1) that a company, as well as an individual, could be a consumer. There was conflicting evidence about whether the boat had been purchased for commercial or personal purposes. M said that the boat had been purchased by T for the private leisure use of himself and his family, although it formed part of T's assets, yet the amount claimed by way of lost charter hire was arguably consistent with a purchase of a boat in the course of a business. The judge had been right to conclude that there was a genuine dispute on substantial grounds in that regard. There was also a significant dispute as to the content of emails between the parties and the possibility of doctoring (see paras 20-24, 27 of judgment). (2) X's standard terms and conditions included a 12-month warranty of satisfactory quality, but there were conditions attached. It was clear that, if the terms and conditions applied, there was a substantial dispute as to whether X's liability for some of the defects might have ceased because of T's non-compliance with the conditions (paras 29-30, 35). (3) The judge had been right to strike out T's petition. The case should never have been the subject of a winding-up petition. The Companies Court was not the right court to engage in a detailed examination of a claim and counterclaim, *Company (No.006685 of 1996), Re* [1997] B.C.C. 830, [1997] C.L.Y. 3101 and *Claybridge Shipping Co SA, Re* [1997] 1 B.C.L.C. 572, [1981] C.L.Y. 261 considered. The extent to which the court should go to determine whether there was a genuine dispute on substantial grounds was not intended to be lengthy or detailed; a long and elaborate hearing was neither practical nor appropriate and was likely to result in a wasteful duplication of court time. Petitioning creditors had to take a realistic view about whether the company was likely to establish a genuine and substantial dispute. In the instant case, proceedings in the county court would have been preferable (paras 38-42).

TALLINGTON LAKES LTD v ANCASTA INTERNATIONAL BOAT SALES LTD, [2012] EWCA Civ 1712, [2013] C.P. Rep. 18, Thorpe, L.J., CA (Civ Div).

1718. **Winding-up petitions–Injunctions–Whether claim for outstanding gas and electricity charges disputed on substantial grounds**

The claimant company (X) applied for an injunction restraining the defendant, British Gas (BG), from proceeding with a winding-up petition. X provided accommodation to asylum seekers, housing them in some 2,000 properties; X was responsible for the gas and electricity consumed at those properties, such gas and electricity being supplied by BG. X also ran a private-tenant letting operation; here a change in occupation might result in successive tenants becoming liable for energy consumed at the premises, with X only being liable in respect of any void periods. In its winding-up petition, BG claimed that the sum of

£619,733.60 was due under its running account with X. X argued, among other things, that no part of the sum claimed was indisputably due. It asserted that BG had: billed on the basis of estimates when it had no entitlement to do so; failed to take account of changes in the occupation of various properties; billed for amounts that had already been paid; applied incorrect VAT rates; billed at rates other than the agreed tariff; and applied standing charges when there had been no agreement that it would pay such charges.

Held: Application refused. It would not be appropriate to grant the injunction sought. If the question was asked whether a debt exceeding £750 was owed by X to BG which was not bona fide disputed on substantial grounds, the answer would clearly be yes, even allowing for all the points taken by X. There was a dispute as to the precise amount owed, but on the evidence it seemed plainly to exceed £750 and to be of the order of £100,000 (see paras 42-43 of judgment).

ANGEL GROUP LTD v BRITISH GAS TRADING LTD, [2012] EWHC 2702 (Ch), [2013] B.C.C. 265, Norris, J., Ch D.

1719. **Winding-up petitions–Jurisdiction–Proper forum for enforcement of adjudicator's decision–Existence of substantial defence to adjudication claim–Whether appropriate to issue winding-up petition**

[Housing Grants, Construction and Regeneration Act 1996 (c.53) s.108(3); Insolvency Act 1986 (c.45) s.122(1), s.122(1) (f).]

The petitioners (T) sought the compulsory winding-up of the respondent company (H) on the basis that it was indebted to them under an adjudicator's award. H was the parent of a group of companies engaged in developing and selling houses. T had been engaged to carry out plastering work at one of H's developments. It was T's case that they had contracted with H, but H claimed that the contract was made with one of its subsidiaries (S). T were not paid for some of the work they had carried out and referred a claim against H to adjudication. By that time, S and another subsidiary had entered creditors' voluntary liquidation. H defended T's claim on the basis that, since it was not the contracting party, the adjudicator lacked jurisdiction. The adjudicator gave what he described as a non-binding decision on the question of jurisdiction, finding in favour of T and against H. He then issued his substantive decision that H should pay T £17,322 by a certain date, together with 75 per cent of his fees and expenses. The sums were not paid, and T issued their petition. T contended that the adjudicator has determined what was owed and by whom, that his decision was binding, and that H was insolvent in that it had not paid the debts claimed in the petition as and when they fell due pursuant to the Insolvency Act 1986 s.122(1) (f). H submitted that the winding-up process was not appropriate for resolution of what remained an outstanding dispute, and that the proper forum for determining whether an adjudicator's decision should be enforced was the Technology and Construction Court (TCC). It argued that although an adjudicator's decision would generally be enforced even if it was wrong, that principle was not immutable and the court might decline to enforce an adjudicator's decision in certain circumstances, such as where there was no contract between the parties. It fell to be determined whether H had raised a dispute in relation to the underlying debts that was founded on substantial grounds and, even if it had, whether it was bound by the adjudicator's decisions so that the instant court could not go behind them.

Held: Petition dismissed. (1) The evidence raised considerable uncertainty about the contracting parties. Oral evidence would have to be heard before the parties to the contract could be established. The instant court could not be sure that H was the company which owed money to T and, but for the existence of the adjudicator's decision, there could be no question of it making a winding-up order in those circumstances (see paras 11-12, 18-19 of judgment). (2) Under the Housing Grants, Construction and Regeneration Act 1996 s.108(3) an adjudicator's decision, even if it was wrong, would generally be temporarily final and binding and had to be complied with until the dispute was finally determined as prescribed, *Macob Civil Engineering Ltd v Morrison Construction*

Ltd [1999] C.L.C. 739, [1999] C.L.Y. 794 applied, *Carillion Construction Ltd v Devonport Royal Dockyard Ltd* [2005] EWCA Civ 1358, [2006] B.L.R. 15, [2006] C.L.Y. 670 followed. The usual means of enforcing an adjudicator's decision was the process akin to an application for summary judgment developed by the TCC, *Harlow & Milner Ltd v Teasdale* [2006] EWHC 54 (TCC) considered. The power to wind up a company involved the exercise of a discretion, as s.122(1) of the 1986 Act made clear. The discretion to wind up would not generally be exercised where the petition debt was disputed on bona fide or substantial grounds, *Alipour v Ary* [1997] 1 W.L.R. 534, [1997] C.L.Y. 3088 followed. It was not, however, appropriate or necessary in the instant case to seek to reach a definitive view as to the status of an adjudicator's decision as a matter of general proposition. The adjudicator's decision on jurisdiction was expressed by him to be non-binding, and it followed that his substantive decision could not be regarded as binding either, since it necessarily took its force from his non-binding decision as to jurisdiction. The existence of the TCC procedure for the enforcement of an adjudicator's decision appeared to constitute a filtering process so that such a decision was subject to review before being turned into an enforceable judgment or order. Since there had been no enforcement proceedings in the TCC, the instant court had to apply the filter that otherwise would be applied by the TCC. The winding-up jurisdiction was not and never had been the proper forum for the determination of disputed claims. In the instant case, there was a bona fide defence of substance as to jurisdiction in relation to a debt that was not a judgment debt and, accordingly, it would not be just and equitable to make a winding-up order (paras 21, 28, 36-42, 47).

TOWSEY (T/A TOWSEY PLASTERING CONTRACTORS) v HIGHGROVE HOMES LTD; *sub nom.* HIGHGROVE HOMES LTD, *Re* [2013] B.L.R. 45, Registrar Baister, Ch D (Companies Ct).

1720. Winding-up petitions–Striking out–Whether serious and genuine counterclaim exceeding petition debt

[Housing Grants, Construction and Regeneration Act 1996 (c.53) s.111.]

The applicant (R) applied to strike out a creditor's winding-up petition that had been presented by the respondent (F). R was a specialist in fire suppression which had engaged F as a sub-contractor to install sprinkler systems. F made three successive applications for payment by R, and following non-payment of the third application after the service of a statutory demand, F presented a petition to wind up R. Under the Housing Grants, Construction and Regeneration Act 1996, a contractor could give a default notice where it considered contractual sums were due from an employer, in response to which an employer could issue a pay less notice if it considered that an amount less than that claimed was due. F alleged that it had a serious and genuine counterclaim in excess of the amount of the petition debt. F contended that the approach under the Act was for a debtor to pay now and litigate later, and that the Act advocated a fast-track system of adjudication that was temporarily binding until any dispute had been finally determined by legal proceedings, and that R was liable to pay F the debt owed under the third application. F submitted that the alleged counterclaim assumed that R had validly terminated the contract, in relation to which there was a dispute as to whether disputed terms had been incorporated, and whether a condition contained in an email, according to which F agreed not to suspend performance for seven days, and R agreed not to terminate the agreement, was contractually incorporated.

Held: Judgment accordingly. (1) The third application notice was to be considered as a default notice in circumstances where R had failed to issue a pay less notice; R was required to pay any amount under the third application to the extent that it was unpaid. R did not challenge the third application for interim payment and was therefore obliged to pay regardless of whether issue had been taken with previous applications. The absence of a witholding notice with specific content to say that the sums claimed are not due did not alter the position under s.111 that the employer was obliged to pay the sums claimed forthwith, the underpinning rational for which was to pay now and litigate later. Furthermore, s.111 obliged R to pay the sums owed without any deduction regardless of any defence based on defective workmanship it might have. As the relevant debt was due and payable, F was a creditor with locus standi to present the winding-up petition. (2) A court would not order the winding-up of a company where there was a serious and genuine counterclaim, save in exceptional circumstances, *Bayoil SA, Re* [1999] 1 W.L.R. 147, [1998] C.L.Y. 3324 followed. The question for the court was thus whether R had a genuine and serious counterclaim for an amount in excess of the petition debt. On the figures presented in the evidence, R had a counterclaim that far exceeded the petition debt. R had complained to F about its work when it made its second application for an interim payment, which was neither the first nor the last time that it complained about F's work. Furthermore, there was a strong case that the alleged term had been contractually incorporated, *Tekdata Interconnections Ltd v Amphenol Ltd* [2009] EWCA Civ 1209, [2010] 2 All E.R. (Comm) 302, [2010] C.L.Y. 2832 considered. However, whether the email condition had been contractually incorporated was a more difficult question. With a degree of hesitation, the court held that R's counterclaim possessed sufficient merit that it ought not be dismissed out of hand; it was inappropriate to determine that claim in winding-up proceedings. R had a genuine and serious counterclaim in an amount that exceeded the amount of the petition debt.

R&S FIRE AND SECURITY SERVICES LTD v FIRE DEFENCE PLC, [2013] EWHC 4222 (Ch), [2013] 2 B.C.L.C. 92, Newey, J, Ch D.

INSURANCE

1721. After the event insurance–Clinical negligence–Insurance premiums

THE RECOVERY OF COSTS INSURANCE PREMIUMS IN CLINICAL NEGLIGENCE PROCEEDINGS (NO.2) REGULATIONS 2013, SI 2013/739; made under the Courts and Legal Services Act 1990 s.58C. In force: April 1, 2013; .

These Regulations revoke and replace the Recovery of Costs Insurance Premiums in Clinical Negligence Proceedings Regulations 2013 (SI 2013/92) and have been made in consequence of defects in them. They make provision to enable successful parties to recover, by way of costs, after the event insurance premiums for expert reports in clinical negligence cases from losing parties, and limit recoverability of those premiums to the costs of insuring against the risk of incurring liability to pay for reports which relate to liability or causation in those cases.

1722. After the event insurance–Insurance premiums

THE RECOVERY OF COSTS INSURANCE PREMIUMS IN CLINICAL NEGLIGENCE PROCEEDINGS REGULATIONS 2013, SI 2013/92; made under the Courts and Legal Services Act 1990 s.58C. In force: April 1, 2013; .

These Regulations make provision for the recovery, by way of costs, of after the event insurance premiums for expert reports in clinical negligence cases and limits recoverability to reports which concern liability or causation in those cases.

1723. Business transfer schemes–Notification–Proposed transfer scheme of insurance businesses–Notification requirements–Whether appropriate to direct transferor and transferees to notify former policyholders individually

[Financial Services and Markets Act 2000 (c.8) s.108; Financial Services and Markets Act 2000 (Control of Business Transfers) (Requirements on Applicants) Regulations 2001 (SI 2001/3625) reg.3.]

The court was required to determine whether, in relation to a proposed transfer scheme of insurance business pursuant to the Financial Services and Markets Act 2000, to direct that certain former policyholders ought to be individually notified.

The transferor insurance company had agreed to transfer the whole of its general and long-term insurance businesses in its United Kingdom branch (C) to the transferee insurance companies. The transferor and transferees (X) sought directions in relation to notification of the proposed transfer scheme. The directions sought involved full compliance with the requirements of the Financial Services and Markets Act 2000 (Control of Business Transfers) (Requirements on Applicants) Regulations 2001 reg.3 in relation to press advertising in the UK and notification to outwards reinsurers, but relaxations of the Regulations in relation to press advertising in the European Economic Area, notification to policyholders remaining with the transferor, notification to current policyholders transferring from C, and notification to the transferees' policyholders. The Financial Services Authority did not oppose those applications but invited X to agree to give notice also to former policyholders of C, who might be affected by the outcome of a past business review (PBR). C had agreed for the PBR to be conducted by an independent expert to identify any customer detriment arising from the effecting or carrying out of the relevant insurance contracts and to calculate and provide appropriate redress to any customers who suffered loss as a result of C's failings from mis-selling insurance or failing properly to deal with customer complaints. C estimated that, in addition to many of its current policyholders, the PBR would be relevant to approximately 292,930 former policyholders. The scale of redress that might be required as a result of the PBR was presently unknown, but might be large. The PBR was not expected to be completed by the time the court was required to sanction the proposed transfer scheme. X declined the FSA's request to notify C's former policyholders of the proposed transfer scheme, and the FSA applied to the court to give such a direction.

Held: Directions given. Neither the Act nor the Regulations made under s.108 of the Act required X to give the direction the FSA sought. The court could, however, impose such a direction with a view to giving information to the former policyholders who were potentially entitled to be heard at a later hearing when the court would be asked to sanction the scheme. The Regulations imposed requirements as to general notification, by advertisement, of the proposed transfer. Such general notification theoretically provided the same benefit to former policyholders as it did to current policyholders. However, if all that happened in relation to former policyholders was that there was a general notification by advertisement, it was highly unlikely that many, if any, former policyholders would consider that the proposed transfer had anything to do with them. That would probably also be the case even if the advertisement mentioned the PBR, because the former policyholders were not thought to be financially sophisticated, would probably not find the advertisement to read it in the first place, and even if they read it would still not see that it had anything to do with them. If individual notification was to be given to former policyholders, the notice would have to explain something about the PBR to show the former policyholders why the proposed transfer might be relevant to their position. However, notice to former policyholders at the current stage of the PBR could be less than helpful to them since there was no certainty about the PBR's outcome. If former policyholders showed an interest in the notification to them, it was highly likely that they would show a greater interest in the possible result of the PBR and show little or no interest in the possible impact of the proposed transfer. In the absence of the proposed transfer, it would not be suggested that all former policyholders would be notified of the PBR at the current stage. Thus the result of notification as suggested by the FSA would result in notice being given which would otherwise not be thought to be necessary or appropriate. The court had to assess the real benefit of the suggested direction and compare it with any disadvantage from making that direction. The benefit to former policyholders of receiving individual notification and the resulting benefit to the independent expert, the FSA and the court had to be regarded as insubstantial. The disadvantages of individual notification to former policyholders at the current stage were that it could cause them confusion and might generate inappropriate false hope. It was also likely to give rise to enquiries of X which were not directed to the proposed transfer but the possible outcome of the PBR. Those enquiries could be time consuming and costly to X, whilst the benefit to the former policyholders of being given information would be very limited. On balance, it was not appropriate to impose on X a direction to notify C's former policyholders individually. Accordingly, the only directions given by the court concerned the agreed relaxation of the Regulations (see paras 43-44, 49, 50-51, 55-60 of judgment).

COMBINED INSURANCE CO OF AMERICA, *Re*, [2012] EWHC 632 (Ch), [2012] Lloyd's Rep. I.R. 714, Morgan, J., Ch D (Companies Ct).

1724. Compulsory insurance–Indemnities–Insured permitting uninsured to drive–Right of insurer to recover compensation from insured–Compatibility with EU law

[Road Traffic Act 1988 (c.52) s.151 (8); Directive 2009/103 on insurance against civil liability in respect of the use of motor vehicles Art.13(1).]

In conjoined appeals, the court was required to determine whether two insurers (C and E) had a right of recovery against the insured (W and X) after they were compensated for injuries in separate road traffic accidents in which they had been passengers of an uninsured driver. W and X had each allowed uninsured drivers to drive while they were passengers and each had been injured in road traffic accidents. In W's case, W's insurers (C) had not been entitled to reclaim compensation under the Road Traffic Act 1988 s.151 (8), however, in X's case, the opposite conclusion had been reached. C had argued below that s.151 (8) obliged the passenger, as the insured who had caused or permitted the tortfeasor to drive, to reimburse the insurers. W and X had argued that s.151 (8) conflicted with Directive 2009/103 art.13(1), wherein insurers could not exclude from insurance, vehicles driven by persons not authorised by the insurers. Two questions were referred to the European Court of Justice on the compatibility of an insurer's right of recovery under s.151 (8) with European Union law. The ECJ found that the Directives had to be interpreted as precluding national rules whose effect was to omit automatically the requirement that the insurer should compensate a passenger victim if that accident was caused by an uninsured driver when the passenger victim was insured and had given permission to the uninsured driver. It was common ground that s.151 (8) could be interpreted compatibly with the European Directives by the notional addition of some wording, but the parties disagreed over that wording. W and X submitted that the statutory right of recovery was absolute and not dependent upon proof of fault on the part of the insured. They argued that any interpretation of s.151 (8) which introduced a "fault-based" system was impermissible as contrary to a cardinal feature of the legislation, which was a right of indemnity that did not depend on fault. C and E contended that s.151 (8) was to be interpreted so that the right of recovery was not automatic but could only be exercised when it was proportionate to do so. They asserted that such a proposal was consistent with *Candolin v Vahinkovakuutusosakeyhtio Pohjola (C-537/03)* [2005] E.C.R. I-5745, [2006] C.L.Y. 2425, *Ambrosio Lavrador v Companhia de Seguros Fidelidade-Mundial SA (C-409/09)* [2012] R.T.R. 4 and the remarks of the ECJ in the instant case.

Held: Appeals allowed. It followed from the ECJ's analysis in *Candolin* and *Lavrador* that there were two key questions to ask about any national law dealing with whether the victim of a road accident could recover damages as a result of the civil liability of a driver of a vehicle, *Candolin* and *Lavrador* applied. The first question was whether the particular national law provision fell within what the ECJ in Lavrador called national "civil liability rules", which were in contrast to national law provisions defining or limiting the scope of insurance cover against civil liability of a vehicle driver in respect of a passenger victim of a road accident (see para.44 of judgment). Depending on the answer, the second question was whether those rules infringed the objectives and terms of the Directives. As a general rule, if the relevant national provision was a rule governing "civil liability", then the only limitation was that it should not deprive the Directives of their effectiveness. But if the national provision concerned the extent to which a passenger could benefit from civil liability insurance, then that directly concerned the Directives and the national law was not to conflict with their objectives (para.45). Considering, as "Case 1", an insured who had caused or permitted an uninsured driver to use the vehicle but had not been injured, the right of the insurer to recover its payment for injured passengers from the insured under s.151 (8) did not impinge on the ability of an injured party to obtain compensation through compulsory motor insurance against civil liability, and therefore it did not infringe the principles of the EU motor insurance Directives. "Case 2" was where the insured was an injured passenger. Any interpretation of s.151 (8) had to deal with both Case 1 and Case 2, but the interpretation proposed by W and X only preserved the insurer's right under Case 1, and excluded it altogether in Case 2 (para.65). According to the ECJ, the right to recover had to be based on the insured passenger victim's "contribution" to the "occurrence of the loss". Therefore, s.151 (8) was to be interpreted to both retain the insurer's right to obtain an indemnity from an insured when he was not a passenger victim, (Case 1), so not affecting the latter's right to compensation through compulsory motor insurance, but also to ensure that in the case of the insured passenger victim, (Case 2), it complied with the restrictions envisaged in the ECJ's judgment. The proposed wording of the insurers was preferred (paras 73-76).

CHURCHILL INSURANCE CO LTD v FITZGERALD; EVANS v COCKAYNE; *sub nom.* WILKINSON v CHURCHILL INSURANCE CO LTD; EVANS v EQUITY CLAIMS LTD; WILKINSON v FITZGERALD, [2012] EWCA Civ 1166, [2013] 1 W.L.R. 1776, Sir Maurice Kay (VP CA Civ), CA (Civ Div).

1725. Consumer Insurance (Disclosure and Representations) Act 2012 (c.6)–Commencement Order

THE CONSUMER INSURANCE (DISCLOSURE AND REPRESENTATIONS) ACT 2012 (COMMENCEMENT) ORDER 2013, SI 2013/SI 2013/450 (C.18); made under the Consumer Insurance (Disclosure and Representations) Act 2012 s.12. Commencement details: bringing into force various provisions of the 2012 Act on April 6, 2013.; .

This Order brings into force on April 6, 2013 those provisions of the Consumer Insurance (Disclosure and Representations) Act 2012 that are not already in force by virtue of section 12 of the Act. For consumers the Act replaces the duty to volunteer information material to the insurer's decision, as set out in the Marine Insurance Act 1906, with a duty on consumers to take reasonable care not to make a misrepresentation during pre-contractual negotiations. It also provides for the consequences of a misrepresentation. Further, it provides specific rules in relation to misrepresentations in group insurance and insurance taken out by a consumer on the life of an individual who is not party to the contract, and sets out a framework for determining the status of agents through whom consumer contracts are effected.

1726. Employers' liability insurance–Mesothelioma–Liability for mesothelioma caused by wrongful exposure to asbestos–Necessary causal link–Employer's entitlement to full indemnity from insurer which covered only part of period of exposure

The appellant company (X) appealed against a decision ([2012] EWHC 69 (Comm), [2012] Lloyd's Rep. I.R. 594, [2013] 1 C.L. 195) that it was not entitled to a full indemnity from the respondent insurer (Z) in respect of personal injury damages paid to a former employee (C) who had died of mesothelioma, and Z cross-appealed. C had worked for X's predecessor (G) for 27 years. He then worked for another employer for 20 years before retiring. Soon afterwards he was diagnosed as suffering from mesothelioma and he died a year or so later. Before his death he issued proceedings against G in the Royal Court of Guernsey. The claim was settled on the basis that during the whole period of his employment with G he had been exposed to asbestos dust and fibres without adequate protection in breach of G's duty of care to him. Z was G's employers' liability insurer for six of the 27 years. X sought an indemnity from Z in respect of C's claim. The judge held that X was entitled to a full indemnity in respect of its costs of defending C's claim, but that otherwise its right of indemnity was limited to the proportion representing the period of C's employment by G for which it was insured by Z. X appealed and Z cross-appealed arguing that it should be entitled as a matter of equity to a contribution from X in respect of the period for which G exposed C to asbestos and was not insured by Z.

Held: Appeal allowed. (1) The judge had erred in holding that the House of Lords had created a new basis of liability in tort in mesothelioma cases, the essence of which was not the causing of mesothelioma but the wrongful creation of a risk of suffering mesothelioma, and that on that basis the liability of G, and hence of Z, in each policy year was for the amount of the risk which it created in that year, calculated by reference to the total period of employment, *Barker v Corus UK Ltd* [2006] UKHL 20, [2006] 2 A.C. 572, [2006] C.L.Y. 2867 considered (see paras 9, 31 of judgment). (2) The position was governed by Supreme Court authority which post-dated the judge's decision, *Durham v BAI (Run Off) Ltd* [2012] UKSC 14, [2012] 1 W.L.R. 867, [2012] C.L.Y. 1884 followed. In *Durham* the court had reviewed *Barker* and *Fairchild v Glenhaven Funeral Services Ltd (t/a GH Dovener & Son)* [2002] UKHL 22, [2003] 1 A.C. 32, [2002] C.L.Y. 2225, and held that *Fairchild* had not recognised a new form of liability in tort consisting of increasing the risk of mesothelioma by exposing someone to asbestos; rather, it had decided that, as a matter of causation, wrongful exposure to asbestos in the course of employment met the necessary causal requirement for the victim to be entitled to hold the employer responsible in law for his illness, *Fairchild* considered. For the purpose of employer's liability insurance, liability for mesothelioma following upon exposure to asbestos created during an insurance period involved a sufficient causal link for the disease to be regarded as caused within the insurance period. The combined effect of the decisions in *Fairchild* and *Durham* was that there was a sufficient causal link between C's exposure to asbestos during the years when G was insured by Z and his contraction of mesothelioma for G to be liable for causing his disease; and G had a contractual right of indemnity under the policy against that liability. The fact that, by the same reasoning, C's exposure to asbestos during the rest of his employment was also an effective cause of the disease was irrelevant to G's right to indemnity on the wording of the policy and on ordinary principles of insurance law (paras 23-30, 38). (3) There was no room for the operation of any equitable principles that could counteract or mitigate the effects of the application of ordinary insurance contract law principles. The court had no equitable power to override the effect of the policies on their true construction. Once it was accepted that exposure during any policy period met the causal requirement for the employer's liability to the victim, for which the employer was potentially entitled to indemnity from the insurer under the terms of the relevant policies, to withhold part of that indemnity from the employer on account of its conduct in other years would be to deprive the employer of insurance coverage for which it had paid. To regard an employer as self-insuring in respect of any period for which it was unable to find details of any coverage which might have been issued could itself produce injustice (paras 37-42).

INTERNATIONAL ENERGY GROUP LTD v ZURICH INSURANCE PLC UK, [2013] EWCA Civ 39, [2013] 3 All E.R. 395, Maurice Kay, L.J. (VP, CA Civ), CA (Civ Div).

1727. Fire insurance–Avoidance–Misrepresentation–Non-disclosure–Breach of insurer's statutory duties

[Financial Services and Markets Act 2000 (c.8) s.138D, s.150.]

The claimant householder (B) claimed against the defendant insurers (X) for an indemnity and damages arising from an accidental fire at his property. B worked as a property consultant and loss assessor so was familiar with insurance. He had obtained a new home insurance policy from X for two residential properties on the same site. B had been, and was still, involved in significant reconstruction work to the main house and the surrounding buildings although they were not on the same title. B's previous insurers (Z) had refused to indemnify B for fire damage caused to the house by construction work to neighbouring properties on the basis that Z had excluded cover for the outbuildings and for damage caused by contractors. B disclosed that claim to X, but failed to disclose either that it referred to the current site, or that it had been repudiated. B also failed to disclose ongoing development work or business use of the property by him and by a development company that he ran. Another fire occurred and X asserted that it was entitled to avoid the policy for B's failure to disclose material facts, for his misrepresentation and for breach of a condition precedent. B rebuilt the main house and claimed from X under the Financial Services and Markets Act 2000 s.150 (now s.138D) the costs of rebuilding and consequential losses, including the costs of borrowing and damages for distress. B contended that (1) he was a retail customer for the purposes of the Financial Services and Markets Act 2000 s.150 (now s.138D); (2) Z had breached its statutory duties and that its obligations under the Insurance Conduct of Business Sourcebook (ICOB) were implied terms of the policies.

Held: Judgment for defendant. (1) The property had been B's home for a significant time and whatever development was going on around it, he was still a retail customer (see para.31 of judgment). (2) However, whether or not ICOB were implied terms of the policy, an insurer could not reject an insurance claim otherwise than in accordance with ICOB standards, *Parker v National Farmers Union Mutual Insurance Society Ltd* [2012] EWHC 2156 (Comm), [2013] Lloyd's Rep. I.R. 253, [2013] 7 C.L. 185 applied (para.33). B was an insurance professional and had been fully aware of making misleading statements about his previous claim against Z. He knew that he should have disclosed substantial building work to the adjoining buildings and that he was conducting business there as an assessor. He had also been actively dishonest in presenting his claim. Consequently, X's rejection of his claim was reasonable and there had been no breach of ICOB 7.3.6 (para.134).

BATE v AVIVA INSURANCE UK LTD, [2013] EWHC 1687 (Comm), [2013] Lloyd's Rep. I.R. 492, Judge Mackie, Q.C., QBD (Comm).

1728. Fraudulent claims–Road traffic accidents–Findings of fraudulent complicity in staged collision–Whether sufficient to justify inference of fraudulent complicity

The appellant (H) appealed against a decision dismissing his claim for damages arising out of a road traffic accident against the first respondent (Y) and ordering him to pay the costs of the second respondent insurance company (X) on an indemnity basis. Y had an insurance contract with X which offered seven days' free insurance under a specified scheme. The accident happened two days after Y took out the policy. H consulted a doctor three months after the accident to assist him to pursue his claim. The doctor's report stated that H had consulted his GP about ten days after the accident and had returned a couple of weeks later. H's medical notes showed that he had visited his GP, but no mention was made of H having been involved in an accident. X's defence was that the purported accident was a staged collision, designed to set up a dishonest insurance claim and that H had knowingly been complicit in that. Y did not participate in the trial and was found to have been engaged in a fraudulent campaign of insurance claims and to have collided with H's car shortly after he had obtained the free insurance for his car. In para.21 of his judgment, the judge concluded that H had been party to attempted fraud on the basis that (i) the rule "follow the money" applied, which made economic sense only if the two drivers were in concert (ii) H's credibility was seriously damaged by the absence of reference to the collision in his medical records and by what he had told the doctor about his visits to his GP.

Held: Appeal allowed. The judge was wrong to draw the inference that H had been a party to the attempted fraud in the way that he did. The judge's reasoning for that conclusion rested on the two propositions in para.21 of his judgment. His statement that it only made economic sense if the two drivers were in concert went too far. The judge clearly attached significant weight to those matters, describing them as giving rise to powerful inferences. While the question of likely or unlikely coincidence was properly to be considered, that overstated the position and was suspect if taken as a starting point. The judge had not duly balanced the various points against H being fraudulent and made no reference to them. The point about the medical records could not have the conclusive weight that the judge ascribed to them in support, in effect, of a total adverse credibility finding and a conclusion of fraud by H. The two matters identified in para.21 of the judgment, which were the sole identified bases for the finding of fraudulent involvement on H's part, were not sufficiently cogent to justify an inference of fraudulent complicity on H's part in a staged collision (see paras 31, 33-34, 41 of judgment).

HUSSAIN v HUSSAIN, [2012] EWCA Civ 1367, [2013] R.T.R. 11, Lord Dyson (M.R.), CA (Civ Div).

1729. Insurance claims–Fraudulent claims–Damage to property by fire–Whether fire set at direction of policyholder–Whether claim barred by breach of policy condition

[Unfair Terms in Consumer Contracts Regulations 1999 (SI 1999/2083).]

The claimant husband and wife (H and W) sought an indemnity from the defendant insurer (N) in respect of damage to a property by fire, loss of the contents and loss of rent. The property belonged to W. H and W lived in another property owned by H. The property belonging to W was damaged by fire which was an insured peril. H was named as an additional assured in the policy insuring the property. The cause of the fire was arson. H had been to the property on the evening of the fire. N purported to avoid the policy on account of the failure to disclose two earlier allegedly fraudulent claims, one by H in 2002 in respect of the alleged theft of an expensive watch and the other by H and W in respect of the alleged theft of two expensive watches from their luggage whilst in the custody of an airline. N alleged that the fire was deliberately set by H or by persons acting under his direction; H and W had relied on fraudulent means in support of their claim, namely false documents relating to the alleged lease of the property and false statements in response to N's investigation of the claim; they had also failed, in breach of a condition precedent in the policy, to provide documents requested by N in respect of the claim. N counterclaimed for what it had paid in respect of the 2002 and 2007 claims and its costs of investigating the claim arising out of the fire.

Held: Claim dismissed. (1) Bearing in mind the serious nature of the allegation being made against H, namely that he had made a fraudulent claim, N failed to discharge the burden of proving that a watch was not stolen in 2002 (see paras 60-65 of judgment). (2) N had proved that no watches were stolen from H's luggage in 2007. H's failure to include the suggested loss in his letter of complaint to the airline at a time when, if his evidence were true, he knew of the theft, and his admitted errors as to which watches had been stolen were only realistically explicable by there having been no theft of watches (para.80). (3) There was no credible explanation for the fire on the evidence other than that it was set by persons directed by H. The evidence which enabled that inference to be drawn was his presence at the property and the irrationality of his explanation for being there; the presence of the key in the outside lock of the conservatory door throughout the fire; and the fact that H had requested a supplier of equipment, said to have been lost in the fire, to give untrue evidence to support H's explanation for his presence at the property (paras 155-158). (4) The lease agreement was not a sham because there was no common intention that the lease was not intended to create the legal rights and obligations which it gave the appearance of creating (para.162). (5) H and W had different interests, and the policy was a composite policy (paras 165-167). (5) N was entitled to avoid the policy as against H for non-disclosure of the fraudulent 2007 claim. He could not in any event recover in respect of the fire because it had been caused by his own wilful misconduct (paras 168-170). (6) N was not entitled to avoid as against W because she was not aware that H had made a fraudulent claim in 2007. Nor was she a party to a conspiracy to set fire to the property and her right to claim was not affected by H's misconduct (paras 171-172). (7) W had failed to comply with the general condition of the policy requiring her to provide documents, namely bank statements, asked for by N following the claim in order to evidence the availability of funds to rebuild the house. The condition requiring the provision of details and documents was not unfair under the Unfair

Terms in Consumer Contracts Regulations 1999. The insured, rather than the insurer, would be in possession of the relevant documents. The discretion to ask for written details or documents had to be exercised reasonably; a request for documents had to be relevant to the claim being made (paras 176-192). N's rejection of the claim on the ground of W's breach of the condition was reasonable under the Insurance Conduct of Business Sourcebook r.8.1.1. The breach of condition was connected to the circumstances of the claim within r.8.1.2(3). N considered that there was evidence that the fire was deliberate and that H was involved in it. The bank statements requested by N were relevant to the question of motive (paras 193-201). W's claim was dismissed and N's counterclaim succeeded in respect of the sums paid out in 2007 and the costs of investigating the fire (paras 202-205).

PARKER v NATIONAL FARMERS UNION MUTUAL INSURANCE SOCIETY LTD, [2012] EWHC 2156 (Comm), [2013] Lloyd's Rep. I.R. 253, Teare, J., QBD (Comm).

1730. Insurance claims–Notification–"Claims made" policy–Extent of particularity necessary for valid notification

[Civil Procedure Rules 1998 (SI 1998/3132) r.40.20.]

The claimant solicitors (M) applied for a declaration that they had made a valid notification to the defendant (E), their professional indemnity insurer. M were partners in a firm of solicitors (MSR). E covered their risks from October 1, 2011 under a "claims made" policy, under which the event that had to occur within the insured period so as to fix liability on the insurer was the making of the claim, not the misconduct or negligence giving rise to it. MSR had been formed after a string of take-overs and it was common ground that it was, for insurance purposes, the successor practice to another firm (S). In November 2011, MSR received a claim from a former client of S, alleging negligence, breach of contract and breaches of fiduciary duty on S's part. A letter of claim was notified to E in December 2011. By May 2012, 17 claims had been directed to MSR as S's successor practice. All related to conveyancing conducted by S before its take-over. MSR investigated S's files and identified 32 that contained specific circumstances that might give rise to a claim. On September 21, 2012 it sent to E a letter headed "blanket notification of circumstances which may give rise to claims". It referred to the 32 files it had identified, but also indicated that all of S's estimated 5,000 files were likely to contain examples of malpractice, negligence or breach of contract. It went on "each and every file...should properly be notified to you as individually containing shortcomings on which claimants will rely for the purposes of bringing claims". E rejected the notification. It accepted that the 32 specific files revealed circumstances that might give rise to a claim, but it asserted that there had been no valid notification in respect of the other files.

Held: Judgment accordingly. (1) In both *J Rothschild Assurance Plc v Collyear* [1998] C.L.C. 1697, [1998] C.L.Y. 3397 and *HLB Kidsons (A Firm) v Lloyd's Underwriters* [2008] EWCA Civ 1206, [2009] 2 All E.R. (Comm) 81, [2009] C.L.Y. 2293, notifications were held to be valid in relation to subsequent claims even though they neither referred to the transactions from which the claims arose nor identified any defects in the handling of the clients connected with the claims. In *Rothschild*, the court rejected the suggestion that the insured could only make a notification when it had identified a possible defect in a specific case. In *Kidsons*, the assumption was that provided there were circumstances that might give rise to a claim, and provided those circumstances were notified to the insurer, the insurer had to pay out on any future claim arising out of those circumstances, *Rothschild* and *Kidsons* followed. Thus, E's stance was clearly wrong. E had purported to rule out the possibility that claims arising from S's other files could be laid at its door unless and until MSR had identified a specific incident, occurrence, fact, matter, act or omission on each file. Its contention that its liability was limited to identified files was misconceived and at odds with the authorities (see paras 38-45 of judgment). (2) It was common ground that the power to grant a declaration pursuant to CPR r.40.20 was not limited to cases in which the claimant had a subsisting cause of action. In exercising its discretion, the court had to take account of justice to the parties, whether the declaration would serve a useful purpose and whether there was any special reason why it should or should not be granted, *Financial Services Authority v Rourke (t/a JE Rourke & Co)* [2002] C.P. Rep. 14, [2001] C.L.Y. 543 considered. In the instant case, any declaratory relief would almost inevitably be too narrow or too broad and would risk creating more problems than it solved. A declaration would not serve any useful purpose, *Guaranty Trust Co of New York v Hannay & Co* [1915] 2 K.B. 536 considered. The best course was to follow the approach taken by the Court of Appeal in *Rolls-Royce Plc v Unite the Union* [2009] EWCA Civ 387, [2010] 1 W.L.R. 318, [2009] C.L.Y. 1162, which was for the court to set out its conclusions on the issues raised, as it had done, but to decline to make a declaration, *Rolls Royce* considered (paras 49, 53-54, 61-63).

McMANUS v EUROPEAN RISK INSURANCE CO HF; *sub nom.* EUROPEAN RISK INSURANCE CO HF v McMANUS, [2013] EWHC 18 (Ch), [2013] Lloyd's Rep. I.R. 533, Vivien Rose, Ch D.

1731. Insurance policies–Carriage by road–Fatigue cracking damage to boiler tubing–Carriage by road and sea–Whether damage caused during transit

The appellant insurer (C) appealed against a decision ([2012] EWHC 1245 (QB)) that the damage suffered by the insured (L) was covered by the marine policy issued by C. L was engaged in the construction of an energy-from-waste facility. The respondent insurers (E) provided cover under an erection "all risks" public liability and delay in start up insurance policy. C provided marine cargo insurance under a policy which covered loss in transit. The waste facility incorporated two boilers, which each housed an economiser or heat exchanger. The economisers consisted of blocks containing banks of vertical tubes through which water flowed. The tubes were welded at the top and bottom of each row to headers. The economisers were manufactured in Romania and transported to L's facility by a combination of road and sea. The economisers were installed while construction of the facility was ongoing. During commissioning cracks were discovered in weld joints where the tubes met the headers. Ultimately the weld joints were all replaced. The experts agreed that the cause of the damage in the relevant weld joints was fatigue failure due to cyclic stress loading caused by resonant vibration. The judge held that the damage had not been caused by the wind when the economisers were on site, but occurred during the road transport as a result of inadequate packing, and the loss thus fell within the marine policy. C submitted that the photographic record showed that the packing was satisfactory, and that the judge was wrong to have found that the damage occurred during the road transit.

Held: Appeal dismissed. (1) C failed to prove which photograph was of which block, let alone that the gaps between the relevant rows were adequately packed. Furthermore, C's case based on tying particular photographs to particular gaps between tubes in particular blocks was never put to E's expert witness. It was not right to say that unprovenanced photographs could speak for themselves and that the appeal court could examine them in the same way as the judge could. If a case was to be made that particular photographs showed particular blocks, that should have been placed before E's expert with time to assess it. It was not right for such a case to be mounted in written closing submissions for the first time, let alone in the appeal court. There was other evidence on which the judge had been entitled to rely in finding that the packing was inadequate (see paras 25-27 of judgment). (2) The judge had been entitled to make the findings he did on the roughness of the road and the journey times, which would have resulted in vibration if there had not been adequate packing (paras 28-32). (3) The judge had been entitled to reject the evidence of C's expert that for the damage to have occurred the frequency would have to have been a narrowband resonant response and it had not been shown how such a narrowband response could have been achieved (paras 33-34). (4) It was open to the judge on the evidence to conclude that it was more likely than not that the damage occurred during the road transportation (para.35).

ACE EUROPEAN GROUP LTD v CHARTIS INSURANCE UK LTD (FORMERLY AIG (UK) LTD AND AIG EUROPE (UK) LTD), [2013] EWCA Civ 224, [2013] Lloyd's Rep. I.R. 485, Longmore, L.J., CA (Civ Div).

1732. Insurance policies–Excesses–Programme of insurance cover containing different layers of excess insurance and top and drop policy–Whether each loss had to be met in order it occurred

The appellant insurer (T) appealed against a decision ([2011] EWCA Civ 1570, [2012] 1 All E.R. (Comm) 969, [2012] C.L.Y. 1889) in relation to the construction of a programme of insurance. T provided insurance to an engineering company (B). B had a professional liability insurance programme which provided for a self-insured retention and a deductible. Above those, the programme contained various layers. The primary layer was with an insurance company (L). L's policy required B to have "paid" the amount of the deductible and self-insured retention prior to L indemnifying the insured under the terms and conditions of the policy. Above the primary layer was an insurance "tower", three successive layers insured by T, which reinsured its risks with various reinsurers. The top layer was a "top and drop" policy, also with T. Unlike the layers beneath it, which provided worldwide cover, the top and drop policy excluded claims from the United States and Canada. Each excess layer policy, including the top and drop policy, was subject to the same terms as the primary policy with L. The top and drop insurance, and each of the lower excess layers, contained a clause making clear that no liability could arise under them unless and until underlying insurers had paid or had admitted liability or had been held liable to pay the full amount of their indemnity inclusive of costs and expenses. B had notified various claims to its insurers, some from the US and Canada and others not. The issue was whether B and T were entitled to choose which claims to meet from the primary and excess layers so as to ensure that those remaining were not US or Canadian claims and could be met from the top layer. T submitted that it was only when a claim was met by an insurer that the policy cover was pro tanto exhausted. It argued that until then, it was possible, if a second notified claim was made and ascertained against B as insured, to speak of a second cause of action or claim existing under the policy. It maintained that B was free to claim and the insurer was liable to make payment in respect of the later, rather than the earlier, ascertained claim.

Held: Appeal dismissed. T's submissions could not be accepted. Where an insurance had a limit, it made no sense to speak of the insured having causes of action or recoverable claims which together would exceed that limit. The ascertainment, by agreement, judgment or award, of the insured's liability gave rise to the claim under the insurance, which exhausted the insurance either entirely or pro tanto. The policy thus served the purpose of meeting each ascertained loss when and in the order in which it occurred. An insurer could forbear from notifying, or could withdraw or abandon, a claim under a policy. The insurance would not then be exhausted by that claim and the next claim would be recoverable in the ordinary course. What was proposed in the instant case, however, was not the withholding or withdrawal of a claim, but its continued pursuit, coupled with adjustment of its priority as against the insurance or programme of insurances (see paras 17-19 of judgment). The requirement under L's policy for B to have "paid" the amount of the deductible and self-insured retention prior to L indemnifying the insured under the terms and conditions of the policy did not mean that B had to have made a monetary disbursement. Instead, the word "paid" should probably be understood as being used only as a measure of liability incurred. Otherwise, the liability insurance would not meet the aim of providing the insured with an indemnity to avoid the insolvency which third party claims might otherwise threaten. Even if the word "paid" meant "disbursed", that did not give its insurer a right to say that it would only provide indemnity in respect of later ascertained expenses or liability, so promoting the claim in respect of such expenses or liability ahead of claims in respect of the earlier ascertained expenses or liability (paras 20-22). It followed that as and when expenses or third party liabilities were incurred and ascertained, they had to be taken into account against L's policy. First, the self-insured retention and deductible had to be used up and then the primary policy would respond up to its limit. Once that limit was used up, the next layer was engaged and so on until the top and drop policy was engaged (paras 24-28). That approach also made commercial common sense. The freedom of choice which T advocated could not readily be reconciled with the basic philosophy that insurance covered risks lying outside an insured's own deliberate control (paras 29-31).

TEAL ASSURANCE CO LTD v WR BERKLEY INSURANCE (EUROPE) LTD, [2013] UKSC 57, [2013] 4 All E.R. 643, Lord Neuberger (President), SC.

1733. Insurance policies–Indemnities–Claim against insured for pure economic loss–Insurer's liability under public liability or contractors' all risks sections

The applicant (X) sought summary judgment of its application for a declaration that it was under no liability to indemnify the respondent (T) under a commercial combined policy of insurance. T was a defendant in Irish proceedings for its alleged involvement in a construction project in Ireland. The main contractor (G) claimed that it had sub-contracted T to design, supply and install some basements at the development. When G discovered the work was defective, it claimed damages from T for breach of contract and warranty and for negligence. T denied it had been sub-contracted. Its policy with X included public liability and contractors' all risks sections, but as T took the view that it did not have any claim under the policy, it did not notify X of the proceedings. G, however, took a different view. Having commenced the proceedings and having subsequently learnt that T had gone into liquidation, G wrote to X stating that unless it confirmed cover for T in respect of the claims, it would seek to join X to the proceedings and enforce any judgment which it obtained against T directly against X. Although G had not yet applied to join X to those proceedings in the Irish High Court, X commenced the instant proceedings in the English High Court for negative declaratory relief. X submitted that (1) a public liability policy provided cover only for accidental damage to property of third parties, but G's claim was for damage to the very thing which T was alleged to have designed and installed and not for damage to any other property; (2) the contractors' all risks section contained an exclusion which would defeat a claim in respect of any damage to the contract works; (3) there could be no claim under any section because there had been a breach of the notification requirements applicable under the policy, which were conditions precedent to its liability.

Held: Application granted. (1) Public liability arose in tort and, as a general rule, a claim in tort could not be founded upon pure economic loss, *Tesco Stores Ltd v Constable* [2008] EWCA Civ 362, [2008] 1 C.L.C. 727, [2008] C.L.Y. 2218 applied. In the Irish proceedings, G's case was that T owed it duties in contract and tort. It was not alleged that T's breaches of its duties caused accidental loss or damage to any other property: G's case was purely that the basements themselves were defective and required remedial work. Therefore, if G's case succeeded, the only liability T could have was a liability for pure economic loss. However, on a true construction of the indemnity clause in the public liability section of the policy, X was liable to indemnify T against all sums that T was liable in tort to pay as damages for accidental injury to third parties or accidental physical damage to property other than property being constructed by T. The indemnity did not extend to liability for economic loss. Therefore, any claim for an indemnity under the public liability section would be bound to fail. In any event, the indemnity clause of the public liability section of the policy only provided cover in respect of accidental loss or damage to property occurring within the territorial limits as defined, which did not include Ireland. Furthermore, there were three separate exclusions that were fatal for any potential claim under the policy (see paras 59-65, 67, 70 of judgment). (2) The exclusion in the contractors' all risks section provided that X had no liability to T in respect of the costs necessary to replace, repair or rectify any insured property which was in a defective condition owing to any fault in design or workmanship on the part of T. It did not apply to property which was free of such defective condition but was damaged as a consequence of such defect. As it was not G's case that any other property was damaged as a result of the defective condition of the basements, any potential claim under the policy would be excluded (paras 71-73). (3) Even if X were liable to indemnify T under either the public liability or the contractors' all risks section of the policy, it had a complete defence because T had failed to notify it of any claim. There was a notification provision in the general conditions, and such general provisions in insurance contracts were effective to create conditions precedent, *Pilkington UK Ltd v CGU Insurance Plc* [2004] EWCA Civ 23, [2005] 1 All E.R. (Comm) 283, [2005] C.L.Y. 2378 applied (paras 74-75).

AXA INSURANCE UK PLC v THERMONEX LTD [2013] T.C.L.R. 3, Judge Simon Brown Q.C., QBD (Merc).

1734. Insurance policies–Service out of jurisdiction–Asbestos-related personal injury claims giving rise to US proceedings against insurers–Liability of London market excess insurers–Utility of insurer's English proceedings for declaratory relief

The appellant United States company (H) appealed against a decision refusing to set aside an order granting permission to the respondent excess insurers (R) to serve their claim form and particulars of claim on H out of the jurisdiction. H was part of a group and was the subject of asbestos-related personal injury claims in the US. It had claimed against its primary layer insurers and proceedings in Pennsylvania had been settled. It had also notified claims to insurers on the excess layers of its insurance programme and those notifications had given rise to further proceedings in Pennsylvania to which R were defendants. R were insurers under a number of excess layer policies covering the years 1995 to 1999 which did not contain any proper law or jurisdiction provisions. English law and Pennsylvanian law were not the same in respect of the extent of cover under such policies and the extent of cover was likely to be greater under Pennsylvanian law. R brought English proceedings for declarations that the policies were governed by English law and as to the effect of English law on liability under the policies. One of the Pennsylvanian actions had reached a fairly advanced stage and a hearing was scheduled to determine the applicable law. In both Pennsylvanian actions the judge had dismissed challenges by R to the jurisdiction on forum non conveniens grounds. The judge held that there was sufficient utility in respect of the declarations for the English court to exercise its jurisdiction over those claims: there was a real prospect that English law would be held to be the governing law, in which event it was reasonable to assume that the Pennsylvanian court would find the English judgment of assistance; the declarations sought would be useful in resisting enforcement in England of a judgment that ignored the express or implied choice of law of the parties. In another case, *Faraday Reinsurance Co Ltd v Howden North America Inc* [2012] EWCA Civ 980, [2012] 2 C.L.C. 956, [2013] 1 C.L. 197, an excess layer reinsurer had obtained permission to serve the claim for declaratory relief on H out of the jurisdiction and that judgment had been upheld by the Court of Appeal on the ground that they would have "utility". H submitted that the judge had erred in concluding that there was any utility in the proceedings on either of the bases of his decision.

Held: Appeal allowed. (1) Where permission to serve proceedings out of the jurisdiction was sought when a negative declaration was claimed the court had to consider both the question whether there was justification for that relief and the separate question of whether England was the appropriate forum, *New Hampshire Insurance Co Ltd v Philips Electronics North America Corp (No.1)* [1998] C.L.C. 1062, [1997] C.L.Y. 890 applied. That principle applied in the instant case where the claim was for positive rather than negative declarations. The requirement that there had to be "utility" in the proposed claim for declaratory relief was adopted on appeal in *Faraday* and that principle should be applied in the instant case (see paras 23-24 of judgment). (2) However, the situation in the instant case was different from that in *Faraday*. In that case the insurers had started the English proceedings before they became parties to the Pennsylvanian proceedings and argued that an English judgment would have "preclusive effect" in the Pennsylvanian proceedings. Also the judge's decision in Faraday was taken before the judge in Pennsylvania dismissed R's challenge to the jurisdiction on forum grounds. Since then the Pennsylvanian court had timetabled the resolution of the applicable law issue. It followed that the instant court was not bound to approach the issue of utility in the same way as the court in *Faraday*, because the question of utility could only be judged against all the facts, *Faraday* distinguished. The judge had erred in concluding that the English court's judgment would be of considerable assistance. The Pennsylvania court had provisionally decided that it was unlikely that English law would apply, and, if it did, that court was capable of applying it. Most importantly the judge in Pennsylvania had not asked for and did not need to be told by the English court what was, in its view and applying English conflict of laws rules, the applicable law of the policies, *CGU International Insurance Plc v Szabo* [2002] 1 All E.R. (Comm) 83, [2002] C.L.Y. 2736 considered. The judge was also wrong on the second ground of enforcement. The Pennsylvania court had ruled on its own jurisdiction. Its judgment on the merits would be that of a competent court applying its own law including its conflict rules. To obtain an English court's judgment on certain limited declarations for no other reason than to lay the ground for a defence to enforcement of a foreign judgment was a pre-emptive strike that could not properly be described as a useful exercise of the court's jurisdiction. Therefore R's permission to serve the claim on H out of the jurisdiction should be set aside (paras 31-40).

ACE EUROPEAN LTD v HOWDEN GROUP LTD; *sub nom.* HOWDEN NORTH AMERICA INC v ACE EUROPEAN GROUP LTD, [2012] EWCA Civ 1624, [2012] 2 C.L.C. 969, Sir Maurice Kay (VP CA Civ), CA (Civ Div).

1735. Insurance policies–Theft–Claims in respect of employee theft–Interpretation of policy wording–Evidence of market practice and admissible factual matrix

The court was required to determine coverage and certain related issues in relation to claims made by the claimants (T) against the defendant insurers (D) for the years 2004-2008 in respect of employee theft. T was a clothing retailer. As part of its stock take, it noticed losses at its warehouse in London. It was discovered that an employee at the warehouse who was in charge of processing returns of stock, along with two accomplice van drivers, was stealing stock. He was arrested and pleaded guilty to conspiracy to steal. T claimed for the loss of stock and consequential or business interruption loss. D's primary case was that the insurance wording did not, as a matter of construction, cover theft by or in collusion with an employee. In particular, D asserted that if such cover was going to be provided, then it would only be provided via a discrete form of cover known as "fidelity insurance" and, as that cover was not provided, employee theft was not covered. Alternatively, D advanced a claim for rectification and raised other defences based upon estoppel and non-disclosure.

Held: Judgment accordingly. (1) The literal effect of the theft extension endorsement in the policy wording was that direct losses by non-forcible and violent theft by employees were covered by the policy. That construction was not contrary to business commonsense nor was it plain that something had gone wrong with the wording. The terms of the policy were not open to more than one interpretation. It was not permissible to take into account as an aid to construction the fact that T had not selected the theft by employees section of the policy, *Mopani Copper Mines Plc v Millennium Underwriting Ltd* [2008] EWHC 1331 (Comm), [2008] 2 All E.R. (Comm) 976, [2008] C.L.Y. 2224 applied. In any event, the mere fact of non-selection of the theft by employees section did not necessarily lead to the conclusion that the theft extension endorsement was not objectively intended to provide cover for employee theft. As a matter of construction of the wording of the policy there was cover for employee theft under the theft section (see paras 77-85 of judgment). (2) Evidence of market practice did not displace the ordinary meaning of the words used. Separate cover, referred to as "fidelity insurance", was available and a key element of such cover was theft of property by employees. It would have been open to the parties to agree such fidelity insurance, but it was equally open to the parties to agree an extension to the standard cover in respect of non-forcible and violent theft (para.93). (3) D relied as part of the admissible factual matrix on matters which were said to have "crossed the line" between the parties, in particular the fact that the policy was intended to replicate the previous cover which it replaced. That evidence was part of the negotiations and could not override or affect the terms agreed by the parties in the policy. Even if it was admissible, it did not assist D (paras 97-104). (4) As a matter of the policy wording, business interruption losses arising from non-forcible and violent theft by employees were covered under the policy. There was an exclusion for consequential loss arising from theft or attempted theft but that had been deleted, and that deletion indicated an intention to bring within the cover consequential loss arising from theft. Also, an exclusion for consequential loss caused by fraud or dishonesty was not concerned with theft at all, but with fraud or dishonesty other than theft (paras 108-115). (5) The estoppel claim failed. There was no relevant shared assumption and it would be unconscionable for D to assert that there was no cover for employee theft (para.118). (6) The rectification claim failed. There was no shared intention and no outward expression of accord (paras 120-124). (7) There was no material misrepresentation or non-disclosure by T's brokers to co-insurers who participated in the cover in some of the relevant years (paras 125-127).

TED BAKER PLC v AXA INSURANCE UK PLC, [2012] EWHC 1406 (Comm), [2013] 1 All E.R. (Comm) 129, Eder, J., QBD (Comm).

1736. Insurance policies–Warranties–Claim under insurance cover in relation to construction contract–Breach of warranties contained in insurance proposal form–Whether proposal formed basis of insurance contract

The claimant housing association (G) sought to claim under an insurance policy with the defendant underwriter (L). L underwrote insurance policies administered by a broker (M). G had engaged a property development company (B) to carry out extensive alterations to a number of properties. B sought cover from M. A proposal form was completed by M and signed by G but contained errors. The contract cost was initially correctly identified as £4.6m but that had been scored out and £3.7m substituted. The "Builder" was also wrongly identified as another company (C). A declaration that the information in the proposal was correct and formed the basis of the insurance contract between them was signed by both parties. B subcontracted the construction work to another company and paid the insurance premium. The subcontractor became insolvent and B terminated the subcontract. B subsequently went into administration. G argued that the proposal was not incorporated into the contract and that, even if it was, the terms of the policy, which included cover in the event of B's insolvency, prevailed. L argued that the proposal form was effectively part of the contract between the parties and that breach of warranties in the proposal had rendered the contract void.

Held: Judgment for defendant. (1) It was well-established that, in principle, "basis of contract" clauses and warranties in relation to insurance were enforceable in law, *Dawsons Ltd v Bonnin* [1922] 2 A.C. 413 followed. Enforceability would generally arise by incorporation within the contract or as a stand-alone warranty by the insured given to the insurer through the proposal form or other document in which the "basis of contract" expression or declaration was given. If the insured had innocently or otherwise signed a document, usually the proposal, as the basis of the insurance contract to be entered into, which confirmed, to the best of the insured's knowledge or belief or absolutely, the contents of that document as true, the contract would be void or unenforceable if the contents were untrue, *Rozanes v Bowen* (1928) 32 Ll. L. Rep. 98 applied. The contract, whether contained in the policy itself or in any other documents such as the quotation or a certificate of insurance, could, as a matter of construction, modify, amend or even render of no or limited effect the "basis of contract" declaration or warranty. The ordinary principles of contractual interpretation applied to that exercise, *Investors Compensation Scheme Ltd v West Bromwich Building Society (No.1)* [1998] 1 W.L.R. 896,

[1997] C.L.Y. 2537 considered. Declarations said to be true or correct to the best knowledge or belief of the declarer would often be, in the case of an individual, reviewable by reference to the honesty of that person in making the declaration, *Economides v Commercial Union Assurance Co Plc* [1998] Q.B. 587, [1997] C.L.Y. 3137 applied, *Zeller v British Caymanian Insurance Co Ltd* [2008] UKPC 4, [2008] Lloyd's Rep. I.R. 545 considered. However, in determining whether a corporate organisation making a declaration as to various statements being true to the best of its knowledge and belief was wrongful, the Court had to determine what was likely to have been known corporately when it made the declaration. There did not have to be dishonesty as such on the part of the organisation but, if it actually knew that something said to be true on the declaration was in fact wrong, then it was making a statement which was not true to the best of its knowledge or belief, *Kumar v AGF Insurance Ltd* [1999] 1 W.L.R. 1747, [1999] C.L.Y. 3420 considered (see paras 28-38 of judgment). (2) It was not disputed that B had acted as agent for G in securing the insurance cover. It did not therefore matter that G had not seen, corrected, and signed the proposal form at that time. There were clearly errors in the form. The insurance quotation and certificate identified the sum insured as £4.6m and the inference was that the proposal form when signed by G also referred to that sum, and that M had later amended it. However, there was no escape from the error in the identification of the builder as C. There was no reliable evidence to suggest that C was to be the builder when the proposal was signed, and that error was material because C had a reasonable credit rating and had been in business for a number of years, whereas B was a new, special purpose vehicle company with no established credit rating. The error was repeated in the quotation and could well have impacted on the level of premium. G had no right of claim under the insurance cover, as it was, albeit innocently, in breach of warranty in that the statement it made in the proposal form to the effect that the builder was C was, within its knowledge and belief, incorrect, and because such warranty was not displaced or modified materially or at all by any other terms of the contract (paras 39-49).

GENESIS HOUSING ASSOCIATION LTD v LIBERTY SYNDICATE MANAGEMENT LTD, [2012] EWHC 3105 (TCC), [2012] 2 C.L.C. 837, Akenhead, J., QBD (TCC).

1737. Insurers' liabilities–Service out of jurisdiction–US proceedings against insurers relating to exposure to asbestos–Liability of English excess insurer–Usefulness of insurer's English proceedings for declaratory relief

The appellant United States insured (H) appealed against a decision ([2011] EWHC 2837 (Comm), [2011] 2 C.L.C. 897, [2012] C.L.Y. 1890) refusing to set aside proceedings instituted in England by H's insurers (F) claiming that they were not liable in respect of asbestos-related claims. The relevant policy was an excess layer policy covered H in respect of liability for asbestos claims. The period of insurance was July 1998 to May 1999. H had been engaged in litigation in Pennsylvania against its insurers in respect of asbestos claims since 2003, and related tort proceedings by victims of asbestos had been in progress since 1999. F had received a letter on behalf of H giving notice of occurrences which it was said might entitle H to claim on the policy. F brought English proceedings seeking declarations that the policy was governed by English law and subject to the jurisdiction of the English courts and that, as a matter of English law, effect had to be given to the period of cover under the policy. The court granted permission for service out of the jurisdiction which H applied to set aside on grounds that it was not arguable that the policy was governed by English law, that the English proceedings did not serve any useful purpose, because a judgment by the English court granting the relief sought would not establish "issue preclusion" in the Pennsylvanian court, and that Pennsylvania was the appropriate forum because of the longstanding proceedings in Pennsylvania between H and its many historical insurers. The judge held that the policy was, in the light of its London connection, governed by English law, that the proceedings did serve a useful purpose and that England was the convenient forum. After service of the English proceedings H applied to join F as an additional defendant to the Pennsylvanian proceedings. H submitted that the proceedings had no useful purpose since the Pennsylvanian court would not regard any decision by the English court either to the effect that the policy was governed by English law or to the effect that F was not liable thereunder as precluding it from coming to its own conclusions on those matters by reference to the law which the Pennsylvanian court found should be applied.

Held: Appeal dismissed. The judge was clearly aware of the need to ensure that the proceedings would serve a useful purpose and he directed himself accordingly. It had to be accepted that the courts of England and the United States had different rules to determine the proper law of the insurance and did not see eye to eye on the question of the liability of insurers to respond to asbestos claims. It was in those circumstances that the judge decided that it was inappropriate to resolve issues of preclusion under Pennsylvanian law and to exercise his discretion to allow F to continue its proceedings. The appeal court should be slow to interfere with that exercise of discretion or exercise of judgment, *New Hampshire Insurance Co Ltd v Philips Electronics North America Corp (No.1)* [1998] C.L.C. 1062, [1997] C.L.Y. 890 considered. H's argument that the judge should have resolved the conflict of evidence as to issue preclusion in Pennsylvania was misplaced. It was inappropriate to have battles about foreign law resolved at an interim stage of the proceedings. It only increased unnecessary expense and delay. The judge was entitled to take a broad view of the suitability of the proceedings for determination by the English court. He concluded that F had shown that the proceedings had utility. The judge had in mind the point that it might assist a Pennsylvanian court to know what the English law was, even if his judgment did not specifically mention the point that, on any view, an English judgment about liability in English law could be useful if a judgment was sought to be enforced outside Pennsylvania (see paras 30-35 of judgment).

FARADAY REINSURANCE CO LTD v HOWDEN NORTH AMERICA INC, [2012] EWCA Civ 980, [2012] 2 C.L.C. 956, Ward, L.J., CA (Civ Div).

1738. Legal expenses insurance–Solicitors–Insurance policy fettering insured's right to choose legal representation–Solicitors' remuneration restricted to non-panel rate

[Civil Procedure Rules 1998 (SI 1998/3132) Pt 48; Insurance Companies (Legal Expenses Insurance) Regulations 1990 (SI 1990/1159) reg.6; Directive 2009/138 on the taking-up and pursuit of the business of Insurance and Reinsurance Art.201.]

The appellant insurers (E) appealed against a decision ([2011] EWHC 2661 (Comm), [2012] 1 All E.R. 778, [2012] C.L.Y. 1892) making declarations in relation to provisions in before the event insurance policies restricting the insureds' choice of solicitors and their remuneration. The respondent firm of solicitors (W) acted for three claimant insureds, also respondents to the instant appeal, who had before the event insurance issued by E and wished to pursue employment and discrimination claims. E had retained a panel of solicitors to act for its insureds. W were not on the panel. E would not agree to W acting for the claimants unless they agreed not to charge more than the fixed hourly rate (the non-panel rate) prescribed under E's terms. W and the claimants brought proceedings for a declaration that E's position involved a fetter upon the right of the client to choose his solicitor in breach of the Insurance Companies (Legal Expenses Insurance) Regulations 1990 reg.6, implementing Directive 2009/138 art.201. E conceded at trial that the insureds were not restricted to recovering the non-panel rate. The judge declared that E were not entitled to decline to accept the insureds' choice of solicitors on the basis that their rates of remuneration were higher than the non-panel rate, and that those solicitors' fees were to be assessed pursuant to CPR Pt 48 and were not to be restricted to the non-panel rate. On appeal E sought to withdraw their concession that the insureds were not restricted to recovering the non-panel rate. E accepted that their pre-trial argument that they were entitled to refuse to accept the appointment of W unless W and the insureds agreed to the non-panel rates was wrong, but submitted that they were only bound to pay the rates set out in the standard terms of appointment.

Held: Appeal allowed in part. (1) E could withdraw the concession they had made before the judge, *Pittalis v Grant* [1989] Q.B. 605, [1989] C.L.Y. 2890 applied (see para.15 of judgment). To the extent that E had argued in pre-trial correspondence that they were entitled to refuse to accept the appointment of W unless W and the insureds agreed to the non-panel rates, that was wrong. They were right to concede on the appeal that that argument was inconsistent with the right of the insured to instruct a lawyer of his or her choice. A refusal to accept the appointment of an insured's lawyer of choice on the basis that he would only be accepted if he charged no more than the non-panel rates would be a serious inhibition of freedom of choice and thus contrary to the Regulations (para.21). The judge's conclusion that the non-panel rate could be a comparator when assessing the lawyers' remuneration was understandable in light of E's concession before him. Given the withdrawal of that concession, the question of whether the insured were restricted to recovering the non-panel rate had to be decided by the terms of the policy. Having regard solely to its terms, the insureds were entitled to recover the non-panel rate set out in the standard terms and conditions and no more; they were, however, entitled to recover at least at those rates. If that meant they would have to pay more to their chosen solicitors and arrange some other way to make such payment, that would then be their decision (paras 22-23). Neither the Regulations nor the Directive made any reference to charging rates. The fact that some potential insureds might be unable to pay extra to secure the solicitor of their choice could hardly mean that all insureds could always choose any solicitor however expensive and expect the insurers to pay (para.24). Insurers could limit the costs for which they were liable to the insured provided that the freedom of choice guaranteed by the Directive was not rendered meaningless. A court determining whether the remuneration offered by an insurance policy was so insufficient as to render the insured's freedom of choice meaningless would have to have evidence of such insufficiency before it could avoid or strike down any provision in an insurance contract relating to the level of costs and expenses payable in respect of a solicitor's services, *Stark v DAS Osterreichische Allgemeine Rechtsschutzversicherung AG (C-293/10)* applied. In the absence of such evidence in the instant case, it was not possible to say that E could not rely on the term restricting the insured's indemnity to the non-panel rate (paras 28-29). Therefore E were obliged to pay the appropriate non-panel rates to their insureds but no more (para.31). (2) The condition in the insurance contract which provided that E could choose not to accept the insured's choice of representative was in breach of the Regulations. So too was the condition which provided that if the insured's appointed representative refused to continue to act or if the insured dismissed an appointed representative, the cover would end at once unless E agreed to appoint another representative. Those conditions had to be deleted or comprehensively redrafted (paras 8-9, 33).

BROWN-QUINN v EQUITY SYNDICATE MANAGEMENT LTD; WEBSTER DIXON LLP v EQUITY SYNDICATE MANGEMENT LTD; BAXTER v EQUITY SYNDICATE MANAGEMENT LTD, [2012] EWCA Civ 1633, [2013] 1 W.L.R. 1740, Longmore, L.J., CA (Civ Div).

1739. Liability insurance–Standard forms of contract–Bermuda Form contracts of insurance–Insured's entitlement to indemnity following settlement of third party claims–Whether insured needing to demonstrate actual legal liability

The court was required to determine preliminary issues in proceedings brought by the claimant insurer (C) against the defendant reinsurers (X and B). C provided liability cover for a group of pharmaceutical companies (AZ) on a form based on XL004, a so-called Bermuda Form liability insurance. X and B had agreed to reinsure C in respect of that cover. AZ settled a number of personal injury actions brought against it in relation to one of its drugs. In turn, C settled claims presented by AZ for the moneys paid under the settlements and for legal costs incurred in defending the claims. C claimed that it was entitled to be indemnified by X and B pursuant to the reinsurance contracts. Although disputes arising under Bermuda Form policies were usually governed by New York law and resolved by London arbitration, the parties had waived the arbitration clause, and the contract was expressed to be subject to English law. C did not assert that AZ would, on a balance of probabilities, have been liable for the claims in question. Rather, its case was that the policy provided an indemnity not only where the insured had an actual legal liability, but also where it had settled an arguable liability. X and B refused to pay on the basis that the policy, and hence the reinsurance, only responded where there was actual legal liability. The issues were whether (i) in construing the policy, the court had to consider, as part of the background, the fact that Bermuda Forms were conventionally governed by New York law; (ii) the insured's entitlement to indemnity under the policy depended on there being an actual legal liability; (iii) the insured's entitlement to indemnity under the policy in respect of defence costs depended on there being an actual legal liability.

Held: Preliminary issues determined in favour of defendants. (1) The parties had chosen to amend the Bermuda Form contract to provide that it was to be governed by English law. What New York law might decide in terms of construction was irrelevant. There was no evidence of any settled understanding that the Bermuda Form did not require that actual liability be established; that was a matter of substantive New York law and did not arise from the construction of the contract. There was a consistent and well-established line of English authorities that the insured under a liability policy had to establish actual legal liability to a third party claimant before it could recover from the insurer, unless the language used in the policy clearly provided to the contrary. Ascertainment of loss by a judgment or settlement did not automatically establish actual legal liability. Thus, the determination of the first preliminary issue turned on whether, on the true construction of the amended Bermuda Form policy, that general principle of English law was displaced. Construction was to be determined on the basis of English law principles and was not to be influenced by the fact that, had the parties not amended the contract, it would have been governed by New York law (see paras 18-19, 29, 37-39, 96 of judgment). (2) The insured was only entitled to an indemnity if it could demonstrate that it was under an actual legal liability. Where it had settled the claim it had to show, on the balance of probabilities, that it would have been liable for it. The contract made it clear that the indemnity was in respect of what the insured paid by reason of "liability imposed by law". There had to be a causal link between what was paid and an actual legal liability, and it was quite clear that the ascertainment of liability by judgment or settlement was not conclusive. Such ascertainment was a necessary, but not a sufficient, condition to the insurer being liable to provide an indemnity, in the sense that the insured still had to demonstrate that it was under an actual legal liability covered by the policy (paras 97-136, 146). (3) The insured was only entitled to an indemnity for defence costs where it established that it was, or would have been, liable for the claim in the sense of an actual legal liability. As a matter of English law, in non-marine liability insurance there was no concept of "sue and labour", so that, if the insured acted to defend a claim and thereby avoided the insurer being under any liability, there was no entitlement to an indemnity in respect of the defence costs in the absence of some express provision. Under the instant contract, there was no duty on the insurer to defend or take over the defence of a claim which might give rise to an implied right for the insured to recover legal costs of defending a claim, if the insurer failed to do so. Any entitlement to recover defence costs depended on some free-standing entitlement as a matter of the construction of the contract. In the instant policy, the words "and shall include defence costs" were an adjunct to the definition of damages: the parties had expressed the intention that defence costs should only be recoverable where "traditional" damages were recoverable, not that there should be free-standing coverage for such. Since traditional damages were only recoverable where there was actual legal liability, it was difficult to see how defence costs could be recoverable where no actual legal liability was established (paras 137-146).

ASTRAZENECA INSURANCE CO LTD v XL INSURANCE (BERMUDA) LTD, [2013] EWHC 349 (Comm), [2013] 2 All E.R. (Comm) 97, Flaux, J., QBD (Comm).

1740. Marine insurance–Fraudulent claims–Validity of claim under marine policy–Whether damage caused by "perils of the seas"–Whether fraudulent device supporting claim rendering otherwise valid claim forfeit

[Marine Insurance Act 1906 (c.41) s.39(5).]

The claimant shipowners (V) claimed under a marine insurance policy for which the defendants (H) were the hull and machinery underwriters. Before embarking on a voyage, the crew of V's vessel had used the emergency fire hose but failed to empty it properly. Seawater remaining in the emergency fire pump and its filter then froze and expanded, causing a crack in the pump's casing and distorting the filter's lid so that it no longer formed a seal. After the vessel sailed, the ice melted and seawater leaked from the crack and distorted filter lid which eventually flooded the engine room and incapacitated the vessel, whose main engine was damaged beyond repair. V's claim under the policy for the resultant loss was resisted by H. H contended that (1) the loss was not insured since it had not been caused by a peril of the seas; (2) the loss was caused by the vessel's unseaworthiness to which V were privy, so that no liability attached pursuant to the Marine Insurance Act 1906 s.39(5), as there were blockages in the pipes in the ship's bilge systems; (3) the claim was forfeit because its presentation was supported by a fraudulent statement, namely a letter in which a crew member (K) deliberately or recklessly gave a false narrative of the casualty in explaining the quantity of water reaching the engine room, by wrongly claiming that the bilge alarms had gone off but been ignored because that was attributed to the vessel rolling in heavy weather.

Held: Judgment for defendants. (1) Whether or not a loss was covered by a marine policy depended on its proximate cause, *Global Process Systems Inc v Syarikat Takaful Malaysia Bhd (The Cendor Mopu)* [2011] UKSC 5, [2011] 1 All E.R. 869, [2011] C.L.Y. 1915 followed. There were two elements constituting a peril of the seas. Firstly, it had to be a "peril" in that it was a fortuity and not something which was bound to happen. Secondly, the peril giving rise to the marine casualty had to be "of the seas"; it was not sufficient merely to have happened on board a vessel. An ingress of seawater caused by crew negligence was a fortuitous accident which normally constituted a peril of the sea, as was an accidental incursion of seawater into part of a vessel and in a manner where seawater was not expected to enter, *Davidson v Burnand* (1868-69) L.R. 4 C.P. 117 and *Canada Rice Mills Ltd v Union Marine & General Insurance Co Ltd* [1941] A.C. 55 applied. In the instant case, the casualty was a loss proximately caused by a peril of the seas, namely the fortuitous entry of seawater during the voyage, albeit caused by crew negligence at the loading port (see paras 30-31, 34, 36, 38-40 of judgment). (2) Under s.39(5) of the Act, where, with the privity of the assured, the ship was sent to sea in an unworthy state, the insurer was not liable for any loss attributable to unseaworthiness. On the evidence, neither V nor the vessel's crew had been aware of the blockages in the bilge lines. In any event, H had failed to show that had the bilge systems been working properly the ingress of seawater would have been controlled and the casualty averted (paras 110, 131, 135). (3) An insured who had made a fraudulent claim forfeited any lesser claim which he could properly have made. A fraudulent device was used if the insured believed that he had suffered the loss claimed, but sought to improve or embellish the facts surrounding the claim by some lie, *Agapitos v Agnew (The Aegeon) (No.1)* [2002] EWCA Civ 247, [2003] Q.B. 556, [2002] C.L.Y. 2732 followed. The threshold for the materiality of the fraudulent part of the claim was not high, *Galloway v Guardian Royal Exchange (UK) Ltd* [1999] Lloyd's Rep. I.R. 209, [1999] C.L.Y. 3391 applied. There was no requirement that the insurer should have been deceived by the lie, or that the lie should have played any part in its consideration of whether or when to pay the claim; it was the assured's attempt to deceive which was sufficient to attract the penalty of forfeiture of the valid claim, *Agapitos* followed. K had no grounds to believe the account he had given in his letter was true. It was an untruth told recklessly to promote the claim in the hope of a prompt settlement. It followed that H's defence of fraudulent device succeeded, and V's claim, which was otherwise valid, was forfeit (paras 145-146, 150, 156-157, 166, 221-224). (4) (Obiter) That conclusion, whilst inevitable, was regrettable. In a scale of culpability which might attach to fraudulent conduct relating to the making of claims, K's conduct was at the low end. It was a reckless untruth, not a carefully planned deceit, told on only one occasion and not persisted in at trial. For V to be deprived of a substantial valid claim as a result of such reckless untruth was a disproportionately harsh sanction. The law should require a sufficiently close connection between the fraudulent device and the valid claim to make it just and proportionate that the valid claim should be forfeit. What would be just and proportionate would depend on the circumstances of each case (paras 177, 225).

VERSLOOT DREDGING BV v HDI GERLING INDUSTRIE VERSICHERUNG AG; DC MERWESTONE,THE, [2013] EWHC1666 (Comm), [2013] 2 All E.R. (Comm) 465, Popplewell, J., QBD (Comm).

1741. Marine insurance–Machinery breakdowns–Loss of hire policy–Successive machinery breakdowns–Whether breaking chain of causation

The appellant insurers (V) appealed against a decision ([2012] EWHC 50 (Comm), [2012] 1 Lloyd's Rep. 252, [2012] 6 C.L. 238) that the respondents (X), who were the owners and managers of a specialist well-drilling vessel, were entitled to an indemnity under a loss of hire policy of marine insurance. The vessel was propelled by two azimuth thrusters, driven by electric motors, which enabled the vessel's position to be precisely controlled. While the vessel was on long-term charter to a Mexican oil company the port motor broke down. The vessel put into port for repairs. The starboard motor had previously been replaced by a motor which could operate on either side of the vessel. X intended to move that motor to the port side and reinstall the original starboard side motor. While that work was being undertaken, maintenance work was done for which there would not otherwise have been easy access. In the course of that work there was a failure of the starboard azimuth hydraulic system which resulted in the consequential failure of the starboard azimuth thruster. That incident necessitated dry-docking. While the vessel was in dry-dock X used the occasion to carry out an intermediate general survey and other owners' work. A few days after leaving dry-dock the starboard motor failed and the vessel had to put into port. The port motor was moved back to the starboard side and the original port motor, which had by then been repaired, was reinstalled on the port side. The vessel then returned to service 82 days after the initial breakdown. The sum insured under the policy was $70,000 per day with a limit of 30 days and a 21 day excess in respect of a machinery claim. The judge held that the claim succeeded in full on the basis that there was nothing X could reasonably have done additionally or differently to get the vessel back on hire after the first breakdown. V submitted that (1) the initial breakdown of the port motor had been overtaken by the second breakdown resulting from the hydraulics failure, which was a separate causative occurrence breaking the chain of causation and could not be described as an unsuccessful attempt to mitigate on X's part; (2) the fact that there had been three breakdowns called for the application of three excess periods of 21 days each; (3) so far as the claim hinged on the hydraulics failure, no hire had been lost as a result, given that X undertook their own work and the survey at the same time thus saving time and earning capacity later.

Held: Appeal dismissed. (1) There was no basis for overturning the judge's conclusion on causation which was essentially factual. Whether the chain of causation had been broken was a fact-sensitive question, *Borealis AB v Geogas Trading SA* [2010] EWHC 2789 (Comm), [2011] 1 Lloyd's Rep. 482, [2011] C.L.Y. 529 considered. The hydraulics failure did not break the chain of causation. It was plain that the work which led to the hydraulics failure was closely and reasonably related to X's efforts to mitigate. It was entirely reasonable for X to utilise the opportunity and advantage of access to undertake the work they did.

The hydraulics failure was no more than a vicissitude, incidental to the failed attempt to mitigate by swapping the engines. The correct analysis was that from the time of the second breakdown there were two operative causes for X's loss of hire: the breakdown of the port motor and the hydraulics failure (see paras 24-25 of judgment). (2) The initial breakdown of machinery had prevented the vessel from earning hire for a period in excess of 21 days. Allowing for the excess of 21 days and confining the claim to the policy maximum of 30 days, X were entitled to the indemnity awarded by the judge. X had satisfied the contractual threshold in respect of the first occurrence and were entitled to be indemnified, subject to the policy excess and limits. As a matter of construction, the policy wording did not permit or oblige account to be taken of the excess which would have been applicable to the second and third occurrences, had X's claims hinged on those occurrences. Circumstances could not be ruled out where the factual relationship between occurrences was such that multiple excesses might come into play; that would be a matter of fact or, perhaps, causation, not of construction (para.28). (3) X would have been entitled to succeed on the third issue had it not become academic. There was a liability under the policy if X were prevented from earning hire for the period in question. The clause looked at simple chronology; there was no provision for exploring ultimate net loss. For V to succeed it would be necessary to read into the policy a requirement for X to give credit for time saved later. There was no warrant for reading any such term into the policy and very good reasons for not doing so, *Ruabon Steamship Co Ltd v London Assurance (The Ruabon)* [1900] A.C. 6, *Ferdinand Retzlaff, The* [1972] 2 Lloyd's Rep. 120, [1972] C.L.Y. 3212 and *Elpidoforos Shipping Corp v Furness Withy (Australia) Pty Ltd (The Oinoussian Friendship)* [1987] 1 Lloyd's Rep. 258, [1986] C.L.Y. 3114 considered (para.32).

SEALION SHIPPING LTD v VALIANT INSURANCE CO; TOISA PISCES, THE; *sub nom.* VALIANT INSURANCE CO v SEALION SHIPPING LTD, [2012] EWCA Civ 1625, [2013] 1 All E.R. (Comm) 1179, Pill, L.J., CA (Civ Div).

1742. Motor insurance–Damage to property–Property damage caused deliberately by driver–Motor insurance policy excluding damage deliberately caused–Whether motor insurer obliged to satisfy judgment obtained by property insurer against driver

[Road Traffic Act 1988 (c.52) s.145(4)(d), s.151(2)(a).]

The appellant motor insurer (E) appealed against a decision ([2011] EWHC 1657 (QB), [2011] 2 All E.R. (Comm) 1113, [2012] C.L.Y. 1899) that the insurer of the respondent property owner (B) was entitled to recover from E in respect of property damage deliberately caused by a driver (W). W deliberately crashed his car into a shop owned by B causing substantial damage. B's property insurer brought a subrogated claim against W and obtained judgment against him. W had motor insurance but his policy issued by E excluded damage caused by his deliberate act. B's insurer contended that on the proper construction of the policy, the Road Traffic Act 1988 s.145 and s.151, and the European Directives on motor insurance, E had to cover damage to property whether deliberately caused or not. E contended that because the policy expressly excluded damage deliberately caused it was not obliged to indemnify the property owner on the correct interpretation of s.151. The judge decided as a preliminary issue that B's insurer was entitled to recover from E. E submitted that because the policy excluded liability for deliberate acts, the judgment did not relate to a liability "covered by the terms of the policy" within s.151(2)(a) so as to impose a duty on it to satisfy the judgment.

Held: Appeal allowed. Under the 1988 Act not all damage to property had to be covered. Under s.145(4)(b) the policy was not required to provide for insurance of more than £1 million in respect of damage to property arising out of any one accident, and under s.145(4)(d) it was not required to cover liability in respect of damage to goods carried for hire or reward in the vehicle. The list was not exclusive and other forms of liability could be excluded by agreement between insurer and insured. There were time-honoured limitations on use for social, domestic or pleasure purposes and the validity of such limitations had never been doubted. If there was such a limitation then use for hire or business would be uninsured. Liability for the damage caused by W to the shop was not "covered by the terms of the policy" within s.151 (2) (a) because the terms of the policy expressly excluded damage caused by the deliberate act of the driver. It could not be right that the only requirement of s.151 was that the liability was of the kind which ought to have been covered by a policy complying with s.145 even if the actual policy did not cover that particular liability. The scheme of the Act coupled with the Motor Insurers' Bureau arrangements satisfied the aim and spirit of the European motor insurance directives to enable third party victims of accidents caused by vehicles to be compensated for all damage to property and personal injuries sustained by them, *Criminal Proceedings against Bernaldez (C-129/94)* [1996] All E.R. (EC) 741, [1996] C.L.Y. 3614 considered. There was no justification for reading *Bernaldez* in such a way as to preclude E relying on the exclusion clause. The exclusion of liability meant that W was uninsured, but the directives allowed for such uninsured losses to be paid under the Motor Insurers' Bureau scheme even if that was a measure of last resort. Section 151 gave no right of recovery against E with the result that ordinarily a claim would be made against the Motor Insurers' Bureau. However, the Motor Insurers' Bureau scheme did not extended to compensating those who suffered property damage where such damage was insured by the victim's own insurer which brought a subrogated claim for recovery (see paras 34, 40, 42, 46-48, 63-64, 66 of judgment).

BRISTOL ALLIANCE LTD PARTNERSHIP v WILLIAMS; *sub nom.* EUI LTD v BRISTOL ALLIANCE LTD PARTNERSHIP; BRISTOL ALLIANCE LTD PARTNERSHIP v EUI LTD, [2012] EWCA Civ 1267, [2013] Q.B. 806, Ward, L.J., CA (Civ Div).

1743. Motor insurance–Exclusion of liability–Liability of motor insurer for default judgment obtained against uninsured driver–Whether passenger knowing or suspecting vehicle was stolen or unlawfully taken

[Road Traffic Act 1988 (c.52) s.151 (2) (b); Directive 2009/103 on insurance against civil liability in respect of the use of motor vehicles.]

The court was required to determine as a preliminary issue whether, at the time of a road traffic accident in which the claimant (S) was injured, S had known or had had reason to believe that the car in which he was a passenger had been stolen or was unlawfully taken within the meaning of the Road Traffic Act 1988 s.151 (4). S had been given a lift home from the garage at which the first defendant (D) worked in a car belonging to a customer. An accident occurred in which S sustained a spinal injury leading to tetraplegia. S claimed damages from D. D did not enter a defence and judgment in default was entered against him. S also sued the second defendant, who was the vehicle's insurer (T), for damages and a declaration that it was liable to meet the judgment obtained against D pursuant to s.151 (2) (b) of the Act. Since D had not been authorised to use the car, he was not covered by the customer's insurance policy. However, provided that D's liability to S was not an excluded liability for the purpose of s.151 (2) (b), it would be covered by T's all persons insurance. The question whether T was liable to pay S the sums recovered under his default judgment against D depended on whether S's judgment against D related to an excluded liability as defined by s.151 (4). That was tried as a preliminary issue. S contended that he had assumed that D had been permitted to drive customer cars. D submitted that S had known that he had taken the customer's car without permission and with the intention of taking it for a joy ride the next morning.

Held: Preliminary issue determined in favour of claimant. (1) In order to discharge the burden of proving that the liability which the default judgment relied on was an excluded liability, T had to prove that S had known or had reason to believe that the car had been stolen or unlawfully taken. The Act had been enacted to implement Directive 84/85, which was subsequently consolidated in Directive 2009/103. Section 151 (4) had to be construed as far as possible so as to fulfil the United Kingdom's obligations under the Directive, in which the requirement of knowledge to exclude liability was a requirement of actual knowledge or "blind eye" knowledge, consisting of suspicion accompanied by a deliberate refraining from asking questions, *White v White* [2001] UKHL 9, [2001] 1 W.L.R. 481, [2001] C.L.Y. 3828 and *Churchill Insurance Co Ltd v Wilkinson* [2010] EWCA Civ 556, [2010] Lloyd's Rep. I.R. 591, [2010] C.L.Y. 1928 followed (see paras 18-20, 35-36 of judgment). (2) The central issue in the instant case turned on whether S was telling the truth about what happened or whether he was lying and D's evidence was correct. S was a very impressive witness who was honest and credible, whereas D was an unsatisfactory witness and not reliable. Where their testimony was in conflict, S's evidence was to be preferred. D was known by S to have driven cars belonging to customers, both in the garage and for short distances out on the road. If the purpose of the lift S had taken was simply to go the short distance home, rather than to take the car for a joy ride as D alleged, it was plausible that it had not occurred to him that, if asked, the owner of the car would not have permitted D to drive him home. Accordingly, S had not known when he allowed himself to be driven by D that the car had been taken without permission and driven unlawfully. Nor had S suspected that to be the case and deliberately refrained from asking questions lest his suspicions should be confirmed. It followed that D's liability to S was not an excluded liability within s.151 (4) (paras 237-238, 241, 251, 264-265).

STYCH v DIBBLE, [2012] EWHC 1606 (QB), [2013] Lloyd's Rep. I.R. 80, Stadlen, J., QBD (Birmingham).

1744. Motor insurance–Sexual assault–Sexual assaults by taxi driver–Claims by victims against driver's motor insurer–Meaning of "arising out of the use of the vehicle" in s.145(3)(a) Road Traffic Act 1988

[Road Traffic Act 1988 (c.52) s.145(3)(a), s.151.]

The court was required to determine preliminary issues in a claim against the motor insurer of a taxi driver (W) who had been convicted of a number of offences against women. W committed his offences after finishing his legitimate work as a taxi driver. He targeted women who were alone at night and who needed transport home. During their journeys home, W persuaded them with lies to accept alcoholic drinks, which he had previously laced with sedatives. He then carried out sexual assaults on his sedated victims. W's victims had brought claims against W for damages alleging assault by poisoning, sexual assault and false imprisonment. The preliminary issues were concerned with whether, and to what extent, the claimants (C) had, in addition to their claims against W, valid causes of action against the defendant insurer (D) as the provider of the compulsory motor insurance required by the Road Traffic Act 1988. W's insurance policy provided cover for "social, domestic and pleasure purposes and for use for public hire". The preliminary issues were whether (i) the bodily injuries suffered by C "arose out of the use of W's vehicle on a road or other public place" within the meaning of s.145(3)(a) of the Act; (ii) liability in respect of W's acts of poisoning and sexual assault was required by s.145(3)(a) to be covered by a policy of insurance, and was covered by the policy issued by D; (iii) W's use of the vehicle at the material times was a use insured by the policy; (iv) D was liable pursuant to s.151 to pay to C any sum payable pursuant to a judgment obtained against W.

Held: Preliminary issues determined in favour of defendant. (1) The concept of "arising out of" was wider than "caused by" and contemplated more remote consequences. It was necessary to consider whether the injuries of the claimant were matters "arising out of the use of the car" and to analyze the activities of the driver to see what he was doing at the time when the injuries were suffered in order to ascertain if they were "arising out of the use of the car", *Dunthorne v Bentley* [1996] R.T.R. 428, [1996] C.L.Y. 5652 followed, *Beazley Underwriting Ltd v Travelers Companies Inc* [2011] EWHC 1520 (Comm), [2012] 1 All E.R. (Comm) 1241, [2012] C.L.Y. 1904 considered. Following *Dunthorne*, C's injuries were caused by the criminal acts of W in administering sedatives and then in attempting to or actually assaulting C, and did not arise out of the use of the taxi on a road (see paras 58-65 of judgment). (2) The injuries sustained by C did not arise out of W's use of a vehicle on a road and so they were not required by s.145(3)(a) to be covered by insurance, *Charlton v Fisher* [2001] EWCA Civ 112, [2002] Q.B. 578, [2001] C.L.Y. 3843 considered. The decision in *Charlton* assumed that the provisions of s.145(3)(a) related solely to injuries caused by or in relation to criminal driving and not extraneous conduct such as poisoning and carrying out or attempting to carry out sexual assaults. The wording in W's insurance policy covered "accidents involving your vehicle" and that could not be interpreted as covering deliberate poisoning and sexual assaults. Those words showed that there was a requirement for W's taxi to be involved in an accident, and the deliberate acts of poisoning and of committing sexual assaults could not be regarded as satisfying that requirement even if they occurred in the taxi (paras 79-84). (3) To determine if a use was permitted under a policy, the court had to ask what was the primary purpose or essential character of the journey in the course of which the particular incident occurred, *Seddon v Binions* [1978] 1 Lloyd's Rep. 381, [1978] C.L.Y. 2592 and *Caple v Sewell* [2001] EWCA Civ 1848, [2002] Lloyd's Rep. I.R. 627 followed. The purpose had to be determined at the time when the incident occurred and not at the start of the journey, *Keeley v Pashen* [2004] EWCA Civ 1491, [2005] 1 W.L.R. 1226, [2005] C.L.Y. 2376 followed. The critical factor was the driver's intention, *Caple* followed. If the essential character of the journey consisted of use for a criminal purpose then the vehicle would not be covered, *Keeley* followed. By the time that C were sedated and assaulted or the subject of attempted assaults, the essential character or purpose of the journey was criminal and the use was not covered by the insurance (paras 105-108). (4) Having regard to the answers to the first three issues, D was not liable, pursuant to s.151, to pay C any sum payable pursuant to a judgment obtained against W (para.109).

AXN v WORBOYS, [2012] EWHC 1730 (QB), [2013] Lloyd's Rep. I.R. 207, Silber, J., QBD.

1745. Professional indemnity insurance–Apportionment–Mitigation costs incurred for insured reason and uninsured reason–Whether apportionment applied under policy wording or general principle

The appellant insurers (D) appealed against a decision ([2012] EWHC 104 (Comm), [2012] Lloyd's Rep. I.R. 655, [2013] 2 C.L. 200) that the respondent (S) was entitled to recover the full amount of its claim under a professional indemnity insurance policy, without apportionment. The policy indemnified S against civil liability for third party claims arising out of the provision of financial services, including costs incurred in mitigating such claims. S had re-valued asset backed securities held by a pension fund, resulting in a significant drop in its value. It then faced substantial claims by investors who had been misled by S into believing that the fund's assets were in cash or the equivalent of putting money on deposit. In order to avoid and reduce the potential claims against it, and to avoid or reduce further damage to its brand, S paid a lump sum into the fund to restore its value and sought to claim an indemnity in respect of that payment under the policy. D denied liability and S began proceedings. The judge held that the cash payment fell within the definition of mitigation costs and was recoverable. He also held that another equally efficacious objective of making the payment had been to avoid brand damage, but rejected D's argument that the mitigation costs should be apportioned between the insured mitigation costs and the uninsured brand damage. D argued that, unless the policy provided otherwise, there was a rule of law that required apportionment of the mitigation costs by reference to the insured and uninsured interests. D argued that a provision under a liability policy to recover mitigation costs was analogous to a sue and labour provision traditionally found in marine policies on ship and goods, in respect of which the default position was that apportionment applied where both the insured and the insurer benefitted from the expenditure in question.

Held: Appeal dismissed. (1) As a matter of construction of the policy, any apportionment would involve D failing to honour its promise to indemnify S for mitigation costs. The whole payment was incurred for the insured purpose and there was no basis for saying that because the payment also achieved, and had been intended to achieve, another incidental objective that it was in some part irrecoverable as mitigation costs, which would be inconsistent with the plain words of the policy, (see para.22 of judgment). (2) There was no default position applicable outside the field of marine property insurance. The approach in that field derived from the practice of adjusting marine losses of ship and cargo on the assumption that the subject matter assured was fully covered by insurance. That assumption was inapposite, and in any event unworkable, in the field of liability insurance. The rationale of the apportionment principle was underinsurance of the property insured, and the concept had not been extended to liability insurance, *Royal Boskalis Westminster Nv & ors v Trevor Rex Mountain & ors, Joyce v Kennard* (1871-72) L.R. 7 Q.B. 78 and *Cunard Steamship Co Ltd v Marten* [1902] 2 K.B. 624 considered. The concept of underinsurance made no sense in the context of liability insurance where the extent of the liabilities to be incurred was unknown when the policy was agreed (paras 37, 41-42, 45).

STANDARD LIFE ASSURANCE LTD v ACE EUROPEAN GROUP; *sub nom.* ACE EUROPEAN GROUP v STANDARD LIFE ASSURANCE LTD, [2012] EWCA Civ 1713, [2013] 1 All E.R. (Comm) 1371, Longmore, L.J., CA (Civ Div).

1746. Professional indemnity insurance–Exclusion clauses–Scope of insurance coverage–Claim not arising from neglect, omission or error of solicitor–Claim excluded under trade debts exclusion clause

On a trial of preliminary issues, it fell to be determined whether the defendant and Part 20 claimant firm of solicitors (B) was entitled to an indemnity under its professional indemnity insurance policies in respect of a claim brought against it by the claimant finance company (S). B had acted under conditional fee agreements for clients pursuing claims for damages for personal injuries, and after-the-event legal expenses insurance (ATE) was taken out in each case. As the ATE policy did not address the problem of interim funding, B entered into an agreement with S whereby S provided loan finance to B's clients to cover interim costs such as fees for medical reports and the premium payable for the ATE policy. Many claims were unsuccessful or remained unresolved after 18 months when the loan from S was due for repayment. In many cases, the manner in which the second defendant solicitor (C) conducted the claims was such as to permit ATE insurers to refuse to provide an indemnity to the client. S invoked its rights under the agreement with B. In Part 20 proceedings, B claimed an indemnity under its two professional indemnity insurance policies in respect of S's claim. Each policy contained a trade debts exclusion clause. The main issues for consideration were whether (i) the claim made by S against B fell within the insuring provisions of the professional indemnity insurance policies; (ii) the claim fell within the trade debts exclusion in each policy.

Held: Preliminary issues determined. (1) B had chosen the particular method of funding litigation on behalf of its clients in order to secure a benefit for itself. S's claim had not arisen from any neglect, omission or error by C in his professional capacity as a solicitor. The claim therefore did not fall within the insuring clause of B's professional indemnity insurance policies (see para.99 of judgment). (2) The liability of B to S under the agreement was one which arose from a "trading or personal debt" which was excluded from cover under the minimum terms and conditions, as incorporated in each of the two policies. B's obligations under the agreement amounted to a guarantee or indemnity given by the firm in connection with the provision of finance directly to the firm and in connection with the provision of other benefits or advantages indirectly to the firm. Consequently, B would not be entitled to an indemnity even if the claim would otherwise have come within the scope of the insuring provisions of the policies (paras 151, 165-166).

SUTHERLAND PROFESSIONAL FUNDING LTD v BAKEWELLS (A FIRM), [2011] EWHC 2658 (QB), [2013] Lloyd's Rep. I.R. 93, Judge Hegarty Q.C., QBD (Manchester).

1747. Reinsurance–Loss–Losses arising out of 9/11 terrorist attacks–Whether losses arising out of one event–Application of unities test

The appellant reinsurers (C) appealed against an arbitrators' award deciding that losses sustained by the respondent reinsurers (D) arising out of the 9/11 attacks on the Twin Towers of the World Trade Center In New York City were caused by two separate occurrences arising out of separate events. Four aircraft had been hijacked by terrorists on September 11, 2001. One had been flown into each of the Twin Towers, one into the Pentagon and one had crashed in Pennsylvania en route to Washington DC. A large number of actions were started in the United States against the two airlines involved and the companies which had carried out security screening at the airports. Personal injury and wrongful death claims and property and business interruption claims were settled. Claims on "inward" reinsurances contracts issued by D were settled on the basis that the attacks on each of the Twin Towers were separate events. C had written retrocession excess of loss reinsurance in favour of D. That "outward" reinsurance was subject to London Standard Wording 351 which provided in art.4 that the term "each and every loss" meant "each and every loss or accident or occurrence or series thereof arising out of one event". C contended that for the purpose of applying the policy limits and deductibles in the outward reinsurance the losses sustained by D on the inward reinsurance contracts were caused by one or more occurrences or series of occurrences "arising out of one event". That contention led to an arbitration. With the parties' agreement, the arbitrators relied for their findings of primary fact on the relevant findings in the Final Report of the National Commission on Terrorist Attacks upon the United States. They concluded that the losses arising on the inward reinsurances caused by the attacks on the World Trade Center arose out of two events and not one.

Held: Appeal dismissed. (1) An occurrence or an event was not the same as a loss, for one occurrence could embrace a plurality of losses; the losses' circumstances had to scrutinised to see whether they involved such a degree of unity as to justify their being described as, or arising out of, one occurrence; in assessing the degree of unity regard should be had to such factors as cause, locality and time, and the intentions of the human agents, *Kuwait Airways Corp v Kuwait Insurance Co SAK (No.1)* [1996] 1 Lloyd's Rep. 664, [1996] C.L.Y. 3570 considered. The utility of the unities analysis had been affirmed by the Court of Appeal, *Mann v Lexington Insurance Co* [2001] 1 All E.R. (Comm) 28, [2001] C.L.Y. 3837 and *Scott v Copenhagen Reinsurance Co (UK) Ltd* [2003] EWCA Civ 688, [2003] 2 All E.R. (Comm) 190, [2003] C.L.Y. 2452 considered (see paras 9-12 of judgment). (2) The arbitrators did not ignore the underlying terrorist plot, but the plot could not itself be an occurrence. The arbitrators accurately summarised the law relating to the unities and proceeded fairly and properly to undertake the exercise in judgment that that analysis involved. They were entitled to find that there were two separate causes for the insured losses because there were two successful hijackings of two aircraft, and that there was no factor amounting to an event of sufficient causative relevance to override the conclusion that two separate hijackings caused separate loss and damage. They were entitled to find that there was no sufficient unity of time or location for the losses to have arisen out of one event, notwithstanding that the Twin Towers were part of an overall complex and notwithstanding the relative closeness in time between the commencement of each flight and the subsequent crashes. The Towers were separate buildings; they did not stand or fall together. The timing of the personal injuries or deaths on board the two aircraft were independent of each other, and the timing of the collision into the North Tower, with subsequent fatalities and collapse, was likewise independent of the timing of the collision into the South Tower and its subsequent fatalities and collapse. The arbitrators made no error of law in reaching their conclusion that the insured losses caused by the attacks on the World Trade Center arose out of two events and not one (paras 36-40).

AIOI NISSAY DOWA INSURANCE CO LTD (FORMERLY CHIYODA FIRE AND MARINE INSURANCE CO LTD) v HERALDGLEN LTD, [2013] EWHC 154 (Comm), [2013] 2 All E.R. (Comm) 231, Field, J., QBD (Comm).

1748. **Reinsurance–Stay of proceedings–Reinsurers bound to follow settlements of insured–Whether exception to rule that stay of proceedings only appropriate in rare and compelling circumstances**

The appellant insurer (O) appealed against a refusal to order a stay of proceedings brought by the respondent reinsurers (R) to establish that they were not liable under a contract of reinsurance. In 2008, a passenger cargo vessel had been lost after sailing into a typhoon off the coast of the Philippines. Over 500 people had died. The owners of cargoes carried on board made numerous claims in the Philippines against O, the vessel's cargo liability insurer. Under a reinsurance contract, R had agreed to indemnify O in respect of its insurance of the vessel. The reinsurance contract included a clause to follow all terms, conditions and settlements of the original insurance policy. Both the insurance and reinsurance contracts contained a typhoon warranty that the vessel would not sail out of sheltered port when there was a typhoon warning or when her destination or intended route might be within the typhoon's path. The reinsurance contract was also expressed to be subject to the exclusive jurisdiction of the courts of England and Wales. R issued an English claim for declarations that they were not liable to indemnify O because the typhoon warranty had been breached and that O was not liable under the original policy for the same reason. O sought a stay of that action pending the outcome of the Philippine claims. The judge refused, holding that such a stay should only be granted in rare and compelling circumstances, which were not present. R's case in the English proceedings was that the vessel had set sail following a typhoon warning when her intended route was in the typhoon's path. That was also O's case in the Philippine proceedings, but if the English claim proceeded, O would have to argue the opposite, namely that although a storm warning had been given, it did not apply and the route intended to avoid its path. O submitted that (1) in a normal reinsurance case, where reinsurers were bound to follow the settlements of the reinsured, the starting point had to be that the reinsurers should wait for the reinsured to settle a claim and only then address the question of their own liability; (2) the judge had given excessive weight to the exclusive English jurisdiction clause in the reinsurance contract; (3) there was a risk of inconsistent decisions in the English and Philippine courts and it was inherently unfair to place O in a position where it would have to assert the opposite of its real case in England, particularly because it was already subject to hostility and vilification because of the stance it had taken in the Philippines and was therefore unlikely to receive assistance in advancing the opposite case in England.

Held: Appeal dismissed. (1) Reinsurance did not constitute any general exception to the normal rule that a stay of proceedings could only be granted in rare and compelling circumstances, *Reichhold Norway ASA v Goldman Sachs International* [2000] 1 W.L.R. 173, [1999] C.L.Y. 546 applied. Otherwise, a stay would be normal in reinsurance cases and that could not be right (see para.21 of judgment). (2) The presence of an exclusive jurisdiction clause conferring jurisdiction on the English courts was just one of the relevant circumstances to bear in mind when a judge exercised his discretion. That was what the judge had done (para.22). (3) It was clear that the judge had the risk of different evidence and inconsistent decisions well in his mind and his assessment of the risk as modest was well within his discretion. The assertions of hostility and vilification had not been supported by any actual evidence before the court. The judge had, to some extent, been influenced by the long delays before judgment was expected in the Philippines, but there was no reason why he should not have taken that into account as part of the overall exercise of his discretion (paras 25-28).

AMLIN CORPORATE MEMBER LTD v ORIENTAL ASSURANCE CORP; PRINCESS OF THE STARS, THE, [2012] EWCA Civ 1341, [2013] 1 All E.R. (Comm) 495, Longmore, L.J., CA (Civ Div).